2002
The Complete
Directory for
People with Disabilities

A Comprehensive
Source Book for
Individuals and Professionals

A SEDGWICK PRESS Book

Grey House
Publishing

MILLERTON, NY 12546

PUBLISHER:	Leslie Mackenzie
EDITORIAL DIRECTOR:	Laura Mars-Proietti
EDITORIAL ASSISTANT:	Pamela Michaud
PRODUCTION MANAGER:	Karen Stevens
PRODUCTION COORDINATOR:	Jessica Jamieson
PRODUCTION ASSISTANTS:	Carrie Alexander, Linda Bartolomeo, Cecilia Fletcher, David Fletcher, Andrew Howard, Claudine Landry, Emily Marturana
MARKETING DIRECTOR:	Jessica Moody

A Sedgwick Press Book
Grey House Publishing, Inc.
185 Millerton Road
Millerton, NY 12546
518.789.8700
FAX 518.789.0545
www.greyhouse.com
e-mail: books @greyhouse.com

Table of Contents

The Complete Directory for People with Disabilities

Tenth Edition

Introduction

Welcome to the tenth and largest edition of *The Complete Directory for People with Disabilities*. Like its previous award-winning editions, this directory contains thousands of resources, products, and services for people with disabilities. Coverage extends from associations that provide important support for families, individuals, and professionals, to products that enable and enhance lifestyles, plus summer camps, independent living facilities, video tapes and so much more. Be sure to use the Table of Contents as your guide through the 26 chapters and nearly 100 subchapters contained in this rich, comprehensive resource.

This year, we have concentrated on funding resources, and have increased this chapter by over 500 records. You will find financial resources organized by state, as well as many helpful publications to further aid in your research. We have also substantially strengthened existing chapters on Living Centers, Facilities, and Vocational Programs. As a result, the total number of listings in this tenth edition of *The Complete Directory for People with Disabilities* has grown from 8,500 to 9,790. You will find listings that are more comprehensive, with brief descriptions, phone, fax, e-mail addresses, web sites, and key contacts. This edition includes nearly 7,000 fax numbers, 4,000 e-mail addresses and 4,200 web sites.

The careful research and compilation is a year-long effort and as the the directory's reputation in the disability, education, and library fields continues to grow, professionals and organizations across the country are in touch with us, providing valuable editorial support and comments. The strength of the directory today is due in large part to their cooperation and support.

We feel confident that this resource will save hours of research time, even if you search the Web. It can take hours to find the wide range of comparative healthcare resources on the Internet, and those resources are often scattered and unedited. *The Complete Directory for People with Disabilities* provides comprehensive, critical, and immediate information in just once source that can be accessed in minutes.

> *"This book is a great, quick reference source for those who are not sure where to start searching for information on disabilities... This comprehensive, easy-to-read and well-organized directory will be a welcome addition to any library's reference collection..."*
>
> – ARBA

Following this Introduction is a User's Guide that illustrates the kind of information that is or might be included in an entry. All entries include primary contact information, such as organization name, address, phone, and fax numbers. Most entries include e-mail and web site addresses, key executives, a brief description, and founding year. Media resources, such as books, periodicals, and videotapes, may all include number of pages or minutes, and frequency.

In addition, there are three indexes: Disability & Subject Index; Entry & Company Index; and Geographic Index.

We hope you find this tenth edition to be as informative and helpful as the previous editions. Your comments, suggestions, and additions to our database are always welcome so please don't hesitate to call or write.

We look forward to another year of expanding and renewing our information.

Other healthcare standards from Sedgwick Press, an imprint of Grey House Publishing, include: the fifth edition of *The Complete Directory for People with Chronic Illness*, just off the press; the ninth edition of *The Complete Learning Disabilities Directory*, due in September; and *The Complete Directory for People with Rare Disorders*. Other Sedgwick Press titles that are quickly becoming industry standards are *The Complete Mental Health Directory* and *The Complete Directory for Pediatric Disorders*, both of which will have new editions in the spring of 2002. Complete descriptions for all titles appear in the back of this directory.

User's Guide

Descriptive listings in *The Complete Directory for People with Disabilities (CDD)* are organized into 26 chapters, by resource type. You will find the following types of listings throughout the book:

- National Agencies & Associations
- State Agencies & Associations
- Camps & Exchange Programs
- Manufacturers of Assistive Devices, Clothing, Computer Equipment & Supplies
- Print & Electronic Media
- Living Centers & Facilities
- Libraries & Research Centers
- Conferences & Trade Shows

Below is a sample listing illustrating the kind of information that is or might be included in an Association entry. Each numbered item of information is described in the paragraphs on the following page.

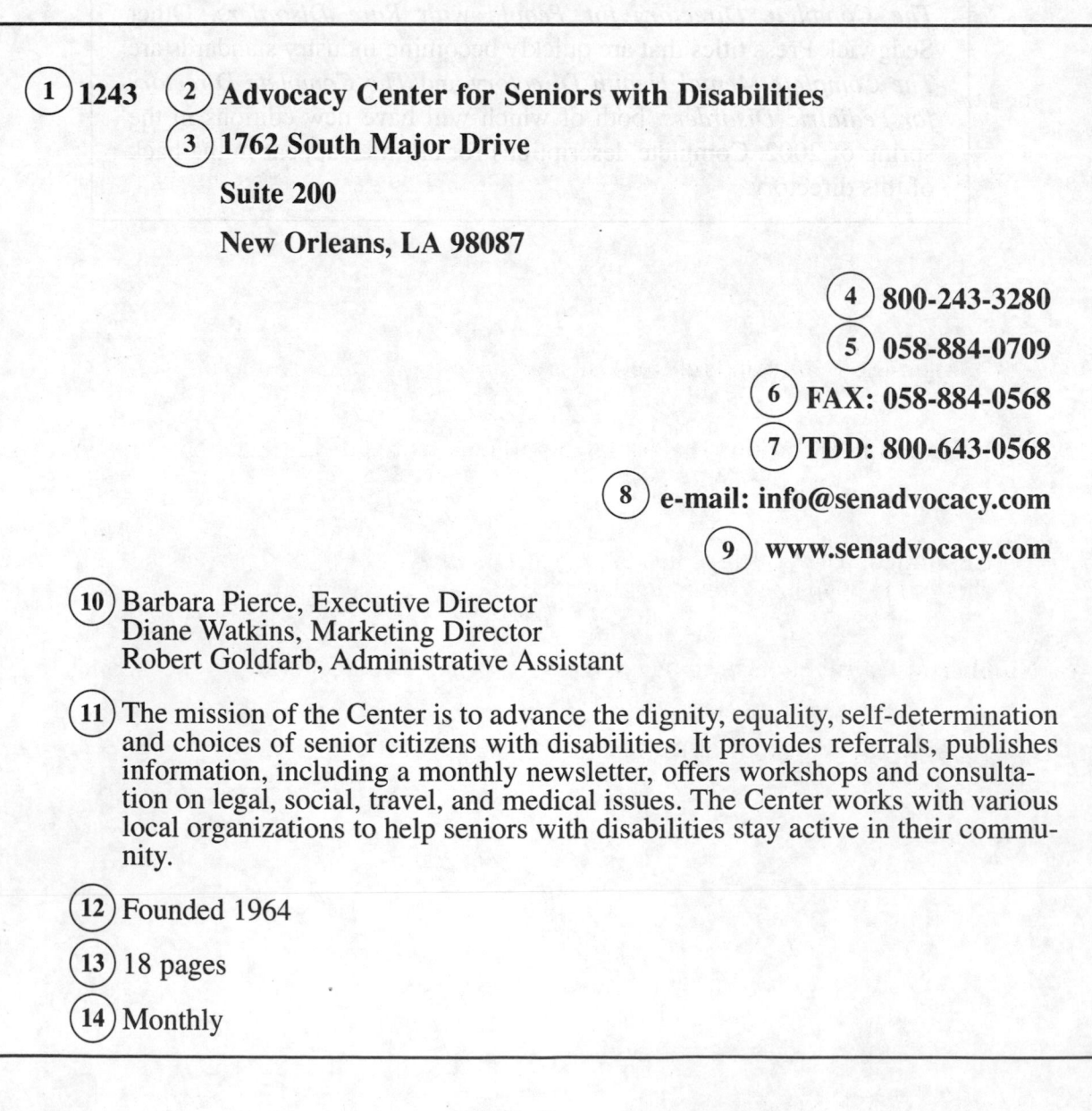

(1) 1243 (2) Advocacy Center for Seniors with Disabilities

(3) 1762 South Major Drive

Suite 200

New Orleans, LA 98087

(4) 800-243-3280

(5) 058-884-0709

(6) FAX: 058-884-0568

(7) TDD: 800-643-0568

(8) e-mail: info@senadvocacy.com

(9) www.senadvocacy.com

(10) Barbara Pierce, Executive Director
Diane Watkins, Marketing Director
Robert Goldfarb, Administrative Assistant

(11) The mission of the Center is to advance the dignity, equality, self-determination and choices of senior citizens with disabilities. It provides referrals, publishes information, including a monthly newsletter, offers workshops and consultation on legal, social, travel, and medical issues. The Center works with various local organizations to help seniors with disabilities stay active in their community.

(12) Founded 1964

(13) 18 pages

(14) Monthly

(1) Record Number: Entries are listed alphabetically within each category and numbered sequentially. The entry numbers, rather than page numbers, are used in the indexes to refer to listings.

(2) Organization Name: Formal name of company or organization. Where organization names are completely capitalized, the listing will appear at the beginning of the alphabetized section. In the case of publications, the title of the publication will appear first, followed by the publisher.

(3) Address: Location or permanent mailing address of the organization.

(4) Toll-Free Number: This is listed when provided by the organization.

(5) Phone Number: The listed phone number is usually for the main office of the organization, but may also be for the sales, marketing, or public relations office as provided by the organization.

(6) Fax Number: This is listed when provided by the organization.

(7) TDD Number: This is listed when provided by the organization. It refers to Telephone Device for the Deaf.

(8) E-Mail: This is listed when provided by the organization and is generally the main office e-mail.

(9) Web Site: This is listed when provided the organization and is also referred to as an URL address. These web sites are accessed through the Internet by typing *http://* before the URL address.

(10) Key Personnel: Names and titles of department heads of the organization.

(11) Organization Description: This paragraph contains a brief description of the organization and their services.

(12) Year Founded: The year in which the organization was established or founded. If the organization has changed its name, the founding date is usually for the earliest name under which it was known.

(13) Number of Pages: Number of pages if the listing is a publication.

(14) Frequency: The frequency of the listing if it is a publication.

General

1 Accentuate the Positive - Expressive Arts for Children with Disabilities

MMB Music
3526 Washington Avenue
Saint Louis, MO   63103   314-531-9635
                                 800-543-3771
                            FAX: 314-531-8384
                    e-mail: mmbmusic@mmbmusic.com
                                 www.mmbmusic.com

Designed to promote awareness of learning potential in creative abilities for young children who have moderate to severe disabilities. *$20.00*

2 American Art Therapy Association

1202 Allanson Road
Mundelein, IL   60060   847-837-1190
                          FAX: 847-566-4580
                               www.arttherapy.org

Organization of professional who believe the art process is a beneficial and healing process.

3 American Dance Therapy Association

2000 Century Plaza
Suite 930
Columbia, MD   21044   410-997-4040
                         FAX: 410-997-4048
                              www.adta.org

Dance-movement therapy is a pshyco theraputic use of movement as a process which furthers the emotional, cognitive and physical intagration of the individual.

4 American Music Therapy Association (AMTA)

8455 Colesville Road
Suite 1000
Silver Spring, MD   20910   301-589-3300
                              FAX: 301-589-5175
                      e-mail: info@musictherapy.org
                                  www.musictherapy.org

Andrea H Farbman, Executive Director
Judy Simpson, Gov't. & Public Relations Assoc.

Advances public awareness of music therapy benefits and increases accessibility to quality music therapy services. Establishes criteria for the education and clinical training of music therapists. Members of AMTA adhere to a Code of Ethics and Standards of Practice in their delivery of music therapy services.

5 Arena Stage

1101 Sixth Street SW
Washington, DC   20024   202-488-3300
                           FAX: 202-488-4056
                   e-mail: jbarasch@arenastage.org
                               www.arenastage.org

Jody Taylor Barasch, Access Ability Director
Wayne White, Operations Manager

A pioneer in providing access to theater for people with disabilities and the birthplace of Audio Description. Offers infrared assistive listening devices (both loop and headset), program books in braille, large print and wheelchair accessible seating with adjacent companion seating. Audio cassette format available upon request. Sign Interpretation and Audio Description are offered at selected performances. Cafe menus and shop lists in braille. Wheelchair-accessible with lifts and ramps.

6 Art and Disabilities

Brookline Books
PO Box 1046
Cambridge, MA   02238   617-868-0360
                               800-333-2665
                          FAX: 617-868-1772
                 e-mail: brooklinebks@delphi.com
                              www.brooklinebooks.com

Florence Ludins-Katz, Author
Elias Katz, Author

A step-by-step guide to establishing creative arts centers for people with disabilities. Includes philosophy and making creative arts centers happen.

7 Art for All the Children: Approaches to Art Therapy for Children with Disabilities

Charles C. Thomas
2600 South 1st Street
Springfield, IL   62704   217-789-8980
                                 800-258-8980
                            FAX: 217-789-9130
                      e-mail: books@ccthomas.com
Frances E. Anderson, author

This second edition is for art therapists in training and for in-service professionals in art therapy, art education and special education who have children with disabilities as a part of their case/class load. Cloth cover edition available for $72.95 (ISBN# 0-398-05797-4) *$50.95*

398 pages Paperback
ISBN 0-398060-60-7

8 Artificial Language Laboratory

405 Computer Center
Michigan State University
East Lansing, MI   48824   517-353-5399
                             FAX: 517-353-4766
                       e-mail: artlang@msu.edu
                               www.msu.edu/~artlang

Dr. John Eulenberg, Director
Katie Smith, Manager

Multidisciplinary research center in the Audiology & Speech Science department, Michigan State University. Its basic research program includes speech analysis and synthesis. Applied research is carried out on computer-based systems for persons who are blind and for persons with cerebral palsy and head injury. The labratory develops physical, cognitive and linguistic assessment technology.

9   Association for Theatre and Accessibility

300 Ucla Medical Plaza
Suite 3330
Los Angeles, CA   90095   323-960-3530

e-mail: oraynor@mednet.ucla.edu
www.nadc.ucla.edu

Dr. Olivia Raynor, Executive Director
Beth Sotffmacher, Technical Coordinator

A nonprofit with the purpose of fostering the full participation and involvement of individuals with all types of disabilities in drama and theater. Newsletters and annual conferences.

10   Deaf Artists of America

87 North Clinton Avenue
Suite 408
Rochester, NY   14604   716-244-3460
FAX: 716-325-2413
TDY:716-325-2400

11   Disability and Social Performance: Using Drama to Achieve Successful Acts

Brookline Books
PO Box 1046
Cambridge, MA   02238   617-868-0360
800-666-2665
FAX: 617-868-1772
e-mail: brooklinebks@delphi.com
www.brooklinebooks.com

Bernie Warren, author

This book makes a major contribution to the understanding of disability, people with disabilities and the creative power they possess which can be unleashed through performance. *$17.95*

12   Effective Teaching Methods for Autistic Children

Charles C. Thomas
2600 South 1st Street
Springfield, IL   62704   217-789-8980
800-258-8980
FAX: 217-789-9130
e-mail: books@ccthomas.com
www.ccthomas.com

Rosalind C. Oppenheim, author

Also avalable in cloth for $30.95 (ISBN# 0-398-02858-3) *$20.95*

124 pages Paper
ISBN 0-398063-09-5

13   Freedom to Create

National Institute of Art and Disabilities
551 23rd Street
Richmond, CA   94804

Florence Lundins-Katz, Author
Elias Katz, Author

Presents philosophy and practical experiences enabling teachers to stimulate creativity in the visual arts for students with and without disabilities.

14   Friends-In-Art

American Council of the Blind
1155 15th Street NW
Suite 1004
Washington, DC   20005   202-467-5081
800-424-8666
FAX: 202-467-5085

Aims to enlarge the art experience of blind people, encourages blind people to visit museums, galleries, concerts, the theater and other enjoyable public places, offers consultation to program planners in establishing accessible art and museum exhibits and presents Performing Arts Showcases at the American Council of the Blinds national convention.

15   Institute for Therapy Throughout the Arts

7 Happ Road
Suite A
Northfield, IL   60093   847-635-1654
FAX: 847-446-8458

Ted Rubenstein, Managing Director
Victoria Storm, Associate Director

In its twentieth year of service, ITA provides creative arts therapies for adults and children with special needs through the use of music, art, drama and or dance. Services include: assessment, treatment planning, one-to-one services and group therapy. ITA also offers adaptive lessons to students with special needs and workshops on topics related to the expressive arts therapies.

16   Manual of Sequential Art Activities for Classified Children and Adolescents

Charles C. Thomas
2600 South 1st Street
Springfield, IL   62704   217-789-8980
800-258-8980
e-mail: books@ccthomas.com

Rocco A.L. Fugaro, author

Offers information to the special education professional on art therapy and management. *$41.95*

246 pages Softcover
ISBN 0-39805 -85-6

17   National Arts and Disability Center (NADC)

300 UCLA Medical Plaza
Suite 3330
Los Angeles, CA   90095

e-mail: oraynor@npimain.medsch.ucla.edu
www.dcp.ucla.edu/nadc

Dr. Olivia Raynor, Executive Director

NADC has a database and website which deals with access and participation of the arts by people with disabilities.

18   National Association for Drama (NADC) Therapy

5505 Connecticut Avenue NW
280
Washington, DC   20015

FAX: 301-990-9771
e-mail: nadt@mgmtsol.com

19 **National Theatre Workshop of the Handicapped (NTWH)**
354 Broome Street
Loft 5F
New York, NY   10013   212-941-9511
                              FAX: 212-941-9486
                              e-mail: ntwhny@aol.com
                              www.ntwh.org

20 **Non-Traditional Casting Project**
1560 Broadway
1600
New York, NY   10036   212-730-4750
                              FAX: 212-730-4820
                              e-mail: info@ntcp.org
                              www.ntcp.org

Sharon Jensen, Executive Director

21 **VSA arts**
JFK Center for the Performing Arts
1300 Connecticut Avenue NW
Suite 700
Washington, DC   20036   202-628-2800
                              800-933-8721
                              FAX: 202-737-0725
                              TDY:202-737-0645
                              e-mail: info@vsarts.com
                              www.vsarts.org

Doris Dixon, CEO

International coordinating agency for quality arts programs for disabled individuals from 68 countries. Purpose is to assure that disabled individuals have year-round opportunities to participate in educational programs demonstrating the value of the arts and to provide experiences to help them become active participants in mainstream society.

Automobile

22   Adaptive Driving Conversions
156 East Commodore Boulevard
Jackson, NJ 08527

800-866-1529
FAX: 732-928-2449

Debra Jackrel, Office Manager
Vehicle modifications: automobile/vans/minibuses and driving aids for independent travel include: hand controls, left gas pedals, foot pedals, wheelchair lifts and more. Serves New Jersey, New York, Pennsylvania and Delaware.

23   Adaptive Vans for the Physically Challenged
Mobility Works
810 Moe Drive
Akron, OH 44310

800-638-8267
FAX: 330-633-0330
e-mail: bkoeblitz@mobility-works.com
www.mobility-works.com

Bill Koeblitz, President
Taylor F. Clark, V.P. & General Mgr.
Mobility Works builds adaptive vans for the disabled and their special needs. Adaptations include lowered floors, raised roofs, wheelchair lifts, custom interiors, custom exteriors, driving systems, power transfer seats, wheelchair tie downs, wheelchair ramps, remote entry systems and rooftop wheelchair carriers for cars.

24   Aeroquip Wheelchair Securement System
Aeroquip Corporation
300 S E Avenue
Jackson, MI 49203   517-789-4144

Wheelchair users can have adaptable, safe, easily attached securement during transportation.

25   Arcola Mobility
51 Kero Road
Carlstadt, NJ 07072   201-507-8500
800-ARC-OLA1
FAX: 201-507-5372
www.arcolasales.com

Arcola sells new and used accessible vehicles and adaptive driving equipment including hand controls, wheelchair lifts and securement systems. Daily, weekly and monthly vehicle rentals available. Stairway lift, porch elevators and ramps for the home sold and rented.

26   Automobile Lifts for Scooters, Wheelchairs and Powerchairs
Bruno Independent Living Aids
1780 Executive Drive
PO Box 84
Oconomowoc, WI 53066   414-567-4990
800-882-8183
FAX: 414-567-4341
e-mail: webmaster@bruno.com
www.bruno.com

Patrick Foy, National Sales Manager
Karla Branham Shaw, Marketing
Over 18 different styles of automobile lifts for scooters, wheelchairs and powerchairs for nearly any car, van, truck or sport utility vehicle that can raise most scooters or wheelchiars under 200 pounds and powerchairs up to 300 pounds. All Bruno lifts are eligible for reimbursement of up to $1000.00 from GM, Saturn, Ford, and Chrysler under the terms of their Mobility Programs.

27   Automotion Mobility Division of Handicapped Mobility
727 Ulster Avenue
Kingston, NY 12401   845-331-2003
800-626-4448
FAX: 845-331-5248

John Zadroga, President
Chet Hindman, Sales Manager
Mobility products for the physically challenged, Ricon/IMS dealer, lifts, ramps, hand controls and custom vehicle conversions; commercial, recreational, as well as mobility.

28   Ball Bearing Spinner
Kroepke Kontrols
104 Hawkins Street
Bronx, NY 10464   718-885-1100
FAX: 212-885-1110

One lever fingertip control which is custom designed for each car but does not interfere with normal operation of your car and ball joints for perfect alignment. *$44.00*

29   Blinker Buddy II Electronic Turn Signal
HARC Mercantile, Ltd.
PO Box 3055
Kalamazoo, MI 49003   616-324-1615
800-445-9968
FAX: 616-324-2387
e-mail: home@harcmercantile.com
www.harcmercantile.com

Ronald Slager, President
Sounds a loud tone and flashes a light when the turn signal is on. *$79.95*

30   Braun Corporation
631 West 11th Street
Winamac, IN 46996

800-843-5438
FAX: 219-946-4670
www.braunlift.com

Jeff Ruff, Executive Vice President Sales
Manufactures wheelchair lifts and lowered floor minivans as well as many other mobility products.

31 Care Concepts
3145 West Lewis Avenue
Phoenix, AZ 85009   602-942-9430
    800-322-1432
    FAX: 602-272-5949
e-mail: minivans@care_concepts.com
www.care_concepts.com

Cheri R. Sanchez, Sales Manager

Lowered floor, wheelchair accessible Chrysler or Ford Windstar minivans featuring in-floor or fold-down ramp system, cable operated power door, electro-mechanical kneel and a wide range of adaptive equipment.

32 Classic
Ricon
12450 Montague Street
Pacoima, CA 91331   818-899-7588
    800-322-2884
    FAX: 818-890-3354

Deluxe van conversion with equipment and accessories to offer freedom to the physically challenged.

33 Classic Coach Interiors
Classic Coach Interiors
Burlington Avenue
Industrial Park
Kewanee, IL 61443   309-852-4656
    800-209-7225
    FAX: 309-852-3463

George Giesenhagen, Manager

Offers van conversions with state-of-the-art equipment for the physically challenged.

34 DW Auto & Home Mobility Specialties
1208 North Garth Avenue
Columbia, MO 65203   573-449-3859
    800-568-2271
    FAX: 573-449-4187
e-mail: info@dwauto.com
www.dwauto.com

Sheila Lynch, Business Manager
Darrell Whitmarsh, President

Paratransit conversions and personalized conversions for the physically challenged. Home elevators and lifts.

35 Drive-Master Company
9 Spielman Road
Fairfield, NJ 07004   973-808-9709
    FAX: 973-808-9713
e-mail: drivemaster@drivemaster.net
www.drivemaster.net

Peter B. Ruprecht, President
Tina Ruprecht, Operations Manager
Shelby , Sales

Full service mobility center, raised tops/doors, drop floors, custom driving equipment, distributor of name brand devices and systems for full sized and mini vans. Sister company Van Master rents mobility equipped vans.

36 Dual Brake Control
Kroepke Kontrols
104 Hawkins Street
Bronx, NY 10464   718-885-1100
    FAX: 212-885-1110

One lever fingertip brake controls, precision machines of the finest quality steel, are inconspicuous and do not take up lots of leg room. *$105.00*

37 Escort II XL
Worldwide Engineering
3240 N Delaware Street
Chandler, AZ 85225   480-545-0033
    800-848-3433
    FAX: 480-545-0037

Automatically lifts and secures for transportation a fully assembled three wheel electric scooter.

38 Foot Steering
Drive Master Company
9 Spielman Road
Fairfield, NJ 07004   973-808-9709
    FAX: 973-808-9713
e-mail: drivemstr1@aol.com

Custom installed system to steer a vehicle with your foot.

39 Freedom Carrier
Freedom Carrier
3466 Great Neck Street
Port Charlotte, FL 33952

Ralph H. White, President

Allows a scooter to be loaded or unloaded in minutes behind the bumper of the car. *$949.00*

40 Genesis Mini-Van
Contact Technologies
11600 Western Avenue
Stanton, CA 90680   714-890-8262

e-mail: catalog.pueblo@gsa.gov

Offers rear or side entry designed with painstaking craftsmanship using steel and lead.

41 Gresham Driving Aids
30800 Wixon Road
PO Box 930334
Wixom, MI 48096   248-624-1533
    800-521-8930
    FAX: 248-624-6358

Ofers a full-service package to physically challenged individuals including lowered floors, raised roofs and doors and high-quad driver control systems. Dealer for Braun, Ricoh, Crow River and Bruno wheelchair lifts.

42 HD Hand Controls and Wheelchair Carriers
Hand Drive Company
211 Orchard Street
Golden, CO 80401   303-271-3868
    FAX: 303-271-3878
e-mail: info@handdrive.com
www.handdrive.com

Gage Fellows, President

Offering hand controls and wheelchair carriers: (1) HD portable push/pull hand control that can be installed in minutes, (2) Hand Drive a hand control that fits inside the steering wheel allowing driving with only one hand, (3) Easy Drive a hand control for drivers without good hand function, (4) Robot 2000 a trunk based wheelchair carrier that automatically retrieves a chair from the driver's side and places it into the trunk. $325.00 and up.

43   Hand Brake Control Only

Kroepke Kontrols
104 Hawkins Street
Bronx, NY   10464   718-885-1100
                           FAX: 212-885-1110

One lever fingertip brake controls that are custom designed to fit each car, completely adjustable and offers positioning operation at your fingertips. *$130.00*

44   Hand Control Systems

Wright-Way
PO Box 460907
Garland, TX   75046   972-240-8839
                           800-241-8839
                       FAX: 972-240-0412
       e-mail: mobility@wrightwayinc
             www.wrightwayinc.com

Various automobile control systems that use hand, foot and steering aids for the disabled, including complete vehicle modifications.

45   Hand Dimmer Switch

Gresham Driving Aids
PO Box 930334
Wixom, MI   48393   248-624-1533
                           800-521-8930
                       FAX: 248-624-6358

This switch is recommended for left leg handicaps or when a right leg handicap uses a left foot throttle. *$36.25*

46   Hand Dimmer Switch with Horn Button

Gresham Driving Aids
PO Box 930334
Wixom, MI   48393   248-624-1533
                           800-521-8930
                       FAX: 248-624-6358

Attaches to the handle of control with a chrome plated steel insulated switch box, giving an instant warning without removing your hand from the steering wheel. *$28.75*

47   Hand Drive

211 Orchard Street
Golden, CO   80401
                           800-224-8156
                       FAX: 303-271-3878
             e-mail: handdrive@aol.com
                 www.handdrive.com

Gage Fellows, President

An advancement beyond traditional hand controls that operates soley from the steering wheel, offering the driver the comfort and convenience of driving safely with one hand and the security of being able to drive with both hands on the steering wheel for greater control and quick reaction to road hazards.

48   Hand Gas & Brake Control

Kroepke Kontrols
104 Hawkins Street
Bronx, NY   10464   718-885-1100
                       FAX: 212-885-1110

Driving controls that are attached by a control level right on to the gas and brake pedals for easy maneuvering and convenience. *$220.00*

49   Hand Operated Parking Brake

Gresham Driving Aids
PO Box 930334
Wixom, MI   48393   248-624-1533
                           800-521-8930
                       FAX: 248-624-6358

Converts foot parking brake to a hand operation for easy access and maneuverability. *$30.20*

50   Hand Parking Brake

Kroepke Kontrols
104 Hawkins Street
Bronx, NY   10464   718-885-1100
                       FAX: 212-885-1110

One lever fingertip brake controls for your car that offer easy installment, complete adjustability, complete independence and more. *$25.00*

51   Handicapped Driving Aids

Handicapped Driving Aids of Michigan
4020 2nd Street
 # 30
Wayne, MI   48184   734-595-4400

Automobiles and vans customized, modified and equipped with industry approved handicapped equipment for ease of operation.

52   Headlight Dimmer Switch

Kroepke Kontrols
104 Hawkins Street
Bronx, NY   10464   718-885-1100
                       FAX: 212-885-1110

One lever fingertip controls for the disabled driver. *$23.00*

53   Health & Mobility Systems

9151 Hampton Overlook
Capitol Heights, MD   20743   301-499-1000
                           800-835-2002
                       FAX: 301-324-0121

Denise Terribile, Sales

Mobility needs, van conversions, ramps and lifts, retail products, healthcare equipment and medical supplies, orthodontics and prosthetics, seating systems, augmentative communications, assistive technology, rehab and technical support services.

54   Horizontal Steering
Drive Master Company
9 Spielman Road
Fairfield, NJ 07004   973-808-9709
                          FAX: 973-808-9713
          e-mail: drivemaster@drivemaster.net
                    www.drivemaster.net

Peter Ruprecht, President
Christina Ruprecht, Vice President
Shelby Wells, Sales Manager
Horizontal steering system is customized to meet the
needs of the high-level spinally injured and all others
who experience limited arm strength and range of
motion.

55   Horn Control Switch
Kroepke Kontrols
104 Hawkins Street
Bronx, NY 10464   718-885-1100
                          FAX: 212-885-1110
One lever fingertip controls that do not interfere
with the normal operation of your car. *$23.00*

56   Institute for Driver Rehabilitation
156 East Commodore Boulevard
Jackson, NJ 08527   609-734-8000
                                   800-866-1529
                          FAX: 732-928-2449

Debra Jackrel, President
Ted Jackrel, Program Director
Driver evaluation training for the physically/mentally
challenged offering state certified driving instructors.
Door-to-door pickup at home, work or rehab centers.

57   Joystick Driving Control
Ahnafield Corporation
3219 W Washington Street
Indianapolis, IN 46222   317-631-7272
                                   800-636-8060
                          FAX: 317-636-8098

Joe Grooms, Sales Manager
Electronic microprocessor controlled hydraulic system specifically designed for persons with disabilities. It allows one-handed individuals and persons
with impaired dexterity or limited and strength and
range of motion to drive.

58   Key Holders, Ignition & Door Keys
Gresham Driving Aids
PO Box 930334
Wixom, MI 48393   248-624-1533
                                   800-521-8930
                          FAX: 248-624-6358
Easy for arthritic hands to handle. Easily in-
stalled. *$18.70*

59   Kneelkar Mednet
Kneelkar Mednet
555 Industrial Park Drive
Battle Creek, MI 49015   616-964-7920
                          FAX: 616-962-8841
Offers the ultimate van conversions with equipment that is easily installed and accessible for the
physically challenged.

60   Lazy Days RV Center
Lazy Days R.V. Center
6130 Lazy Days Boulevard
Seffner, FL 33584   813-246-4777
                                   800-626-7800
                          FAX: 813-246-4408
                          www.lazydays.com

Jack Graham
Customized recreational vehicles for people with disabilities. Specializing in wheelchair accessible bathrooms.

61   Left Foot Accelerator
Gresham Driving Aids
PO Box 930334
Wixom, MI 48393   248-624-1533
                                   800-521-8930
                          FAX: 248-624-6358
A custom pedal designed for left-foot usage. Stain-
less steel cross bar attaches above the throttle
pedal and leaves right pedal free for right foot use.
$80.50

62   Left Foot Gas Pedal
Kroepke Kontrols
104 Hawkins Street
Bronx, NY 10464   718-885-1100
                          FAX: 212-885-1110
One lever fingertip controls that offer custom design, easy installment and complete freedom for
the disabled driver. *$90.00*

63   Left Hand Shift Lever
Gresham Driving Aids
PO Box 930334
Wixom, MI 48393   248-624-1533
                                   800-521-8930
                          FAX: 248-624-6358
Converts steering wheel lever or automatic trans-
mission selector lever to left hand usage for right
arm handicaps. *$34.50*

64   Low Effort and No Effort Steering
Drive-Master Company
9 Spielman Road
Fairfield, NJ 07004   973-808-9709
                          FAX: 973-808-9713
          e-mail: drivemstr1@aol.com

Peter B. Ruprecht, President
Christina M Ruprecht, General Manager
J. Shelby Wells, Sales Manager
Reduced effort steering modifications available for
nearly all vehicles. Additional products are pedal
extensions which are 1 inch to 4 inch clamp-on aluminum blocks and 6 inch to 12 inch adjustable fold-
down pedals.

65 Mini-Bus and Mini-Vans

Arcola Bus Sales
51 Kero Road
Carlstadt, NJ 07072   201-507-8500
                              800-ARC-OLA1

Offers a virtually unlimited choice of chassis size, body style, floor plan and optional features. We provide transporters for almost every use, including school buses, vans, mini-coaches, medium-duty buses and personalized vans for the disabled.

66 Mini-Rider

Ricon
12450 Montague Street
Pacoima, CA 91331   818-899-7588
                              800-322-2884
                         FAX: 818-890-3354

Deluxe van conversions.

67 Monarch Mark 1-A

Manufacturing & Product Services
7948 Ronson Road
San Diego, CA 92111   619-292-1423

A system of hand controls which incorporates a popular method of operation by pushing the control handles directly toward the brakes.

68 Monmouth Vans, Access and Mobility

5105 Routes 33/34
Farmingdale, NJ 07727   732-919-1444
                              800-221-0034
                         FAX: 732-919-0256
         e-mail: info@monmouthvans.com
                 www.monmouthvans.com

Eugene Morton, President
Raymond Morton, Vice President
Arthur Smith, Sales Manager

Full vehicle modifications for driving and for transport of people with disabilities. Access equipment for buildings, e.g. ramps, stair lifts, pool lifts, automatic door openers and patient transfer lifts, pride jazzy portable and modular wheelchairs and scooters. Large selection of modified vans in stock.

69 New Quad Grip

Gresham Driving Aids
PO Box 930334
Wixom, MI 48393   248-624-1533
                              800-521-8930
                         FAX: 248-624-6358

Automobile aids for the disabled. *$40.25*

70 Portable Vehicle Controls

Contact Technologies
1033 Business Center Court
Newbury Park, CA 91320   805-498-8157

The first fully portable integrated automotive hand control unit.

71 Power Seat Base (6-Way)

Ricon
12450 Montague Street
Pacoima, CA 91331   818-899-7588
                              800-322-2884
                         FAX: 818-890-3354

Facilitates a driver's self-transfer from a wheelchair to the driving seat and allows optimal driving positioning.

72 Quad Grip with Pin

Gresham Driving Aids
PO Box 930334
Wixom, MI 48393   248-624-1533
                              800-521-8930
                         FAX: 248-624-6358

Automobile aids for the disabled. *$40.25*

73 Rampvan

Independent Mobility Systems
4100 W Piedras Street
Farmington, NM 87401   505-326-4538

Accessible van offering automatic door and ramps.

74 Right Hand Turn Signal Switch Lever

Gresham Driving Aids
PO Box 930334
Wixom, MI 48393   248-624-1533
                              800-521-8930
                         FAX: 248-624-6358

Converts signal switch to right hand usage for left arm handicaps. *$34.50*

75 Scooter Lift/Carrier

RD Butler & Company
65 Ryan Drive
F-1
Raynham, MA 02767

Loading without lifting gives greater mobility for the physically challenged.

76 Single Hand Driving Control

Mobility Plus Corporation
10 Birch Street
Lisbon Falls, ME 04252   207-353-5977

A single hand control joy stick for steering, braking and acceleration.

77 Slim Line Brake Only

Gresham Driving Aids
PO Box 930334
Wixom, MI 48393   248-624-1533
                              800-521-8930
                         FAX: 248-624-6358

A chrome plated steel handle, contour shaped, with a left hand or right hand unit available. *$155.25*

78   Slim Line Control

Gresham Driving Aids
PO Box 930334
Wixom, MI   48393   248-624-1533
                                  800-521-8930
                            FAX: 248-624-6358

A plated, strong, compact unit designed to be easily transferred from car to car. Built of heavy steel tubing, welded and chrome plated and contour-shaped for maximum driving room. *$201.25*

79   Slim Line Control - Brake and Throttle

Gresham Driving Aids
PO Box 930334
Wixom, MI   48393   248-624-1533
                                  800-521-8930
                            FAX: 248-624-6358

Brake is actuated by pushing the control lever directly towards the brake. Throttle is actuated by moving the lever at right angles to the brake movement, toward the seat. The weight of the operator's hand is sufficient to hold the throttle at any designed speed. *$300.00*

80   Superarm Lift

Handicaps
4335 South Santa Fe Drive
Englewood, CO   80110

Made for vans and motorhomes. No platform is necessary and no doorways are blocked by lift that is simple and safe to use.

81   Tim's Trim

30 Bermar Park
Rochester, NY   14624   716-429-6270
                            FAX: 716-429-6355
                 e-mail: timstrim@aol.com

Offers vehicle modifications, drop floors, raised tops/doors, driving equipment, touch pads and lifts.

82   Transportation Equipment for People with Disabilities

Drive Master Company
9 Spielman Road
Fairfield, NJ   07004   973-808-9709
                                  877-282-8267
                            FAX: 973-808-9713
                 e-mail: drivemstr1@aol.com

Wheelchair lifts and ramps, hand and foot controls, steering and braking modifications, complete van conversions, home modifications, wheelchairs and scooters and wheelchair accessible van rentals.

83   Tri-Post Steering Wheel Spinner

Gresham Driving Aids
PO Box 930334
Wixom, MI   48393   248-624-1533
                                  800-521-8930
                            FAX: 248-624-6358

Three nylon posts, adjustable for proper fit to drivers hand, to control the wheel, for use by persons with weak or limp wrists. *$40.25*

84   Trunk Lift

Fortress
PO Box 489
Clovis, CA   93613   559-322-5437
                            FAX: 559-323-0299

Scooters trunk lifts.

85   Ultra-Lite XL Hand Control

Drive Master Company
9 Spielman Road
Fairfield, NJ   07004   973-808-9709
                            FAX: 973-808-9713
                 e-mail: drivemstr1@aol.com

Allows the driver to operate a gas and brake by hand - push for brake - pull for gas. Can be installed in nearly every vehicle.

86   Vantage Mini-Vans

Vantage Mini Vans
5202 South 28th Place
Tempe, AZ   85040   602-243-2700
                            FAX: 602-304-2804
                 www.vantagemobility.com

Personalized vehicles with lowered floors and swing-away ramps.

Bath

87   Adaptive Design Shop

12847 Point Pleasant Drive
Fairfax, VA   22033   703-631-1585
                                  800-351-2327
                            FAX: 703-631-1585
         e-mail: adaptivedesignshop@mail.com
                 www.adaptivedesignshop.com

Joe Rickerson, Marketing Director

Offers various adjustable models of bath and shower chairs, as well as adjustable toilet and commodes supports for toddlers through adults. Call for a free brochure. Prices range from $200 to $800.

88   Adjustable Bath Seat

Arista Surgical Supply Company
67 Lexington Avenue
New York, NY   10010   212-679-3694
                                  800-223-1984

Bath seat that fits easily in any size tub. Easily adjustable to any height for easier maneuverability. *$44.00*

89   Adjustable Raised Toilet Seat

Maxi Aids
42 Executive Boulevard
Number 3209
Farmingdale, NY   11735   516-752-0521
                                  800-522-6294
                            FAX: 516-752-0689
         e-mail: sales@maxiaids.com
                 www.maxiaids.com

Seat adjusts above the bowl. *$45.95*

90 **Adjustable Raised Toilet Seat & Guard**

Frohock-Stewart
39400 Taylor Parkway
N Ridgeville, OH 44035   440-329-6000

The seat features an exclusive pivot locking system so it won't slip or tip and the adjustable guard rail fits all toilets.

91 **BIT Talking Scale Bathroom Scale**

Sense-Sations
919 Walnut Street
Philadelphia, PA 19107   215-629-2990
                                 800-876-5456

Push the on button and the scale will invite you to jump on and discover how much weight you have lost or gained. *$91.50*

92 **Bath Lift**

Ted Hoyer and Company
2222 Minnesota Street
2744
Oshkosh, WI 54901

For anyone who can operate the lift alone. The seat swings over the tub, lowers the person into the bath water and locks in place. *$1099.00*

93 **Bath Products**

Snug Seat
PO Box 1739
Matthews, NC 28106   704-882-0668
                             800-336-7684
                             FAX: 704-882-0751
                             e-mail: sales@snugseat.com
                             www.snugseat.com

Steve Scribner, National Sales Manager
Kirk MacKenzie, President

Offers a wide range of products to meet the transportation, mobility, seating and bath aid needs for people of all ages. From car seats and standers for children with special needs to versatile wheelchairs that offer adults customized options and the freedom to go anywhere with confidence.

94 **Bath Shower & Commode Chair**

Clarke Health Care Products
1003 International Drive
Oakdale, PA 15071   724-695-2122
                           888-347-4537
                           FAX: 724-695-2922
                           e-mail: info@clarkehealthcare.com
                           www.clarkhealthcare.com

Posterior and anterior tilt, fits over most toilets. Includes soft seat, collection pan, adjustable footrest and headrest.

95 **BathEase**

3815 Darston Street
Palm Harbor, FL 34685   727-786-2606
                                888-747-7845
                                FAX: 727-786-2604
                                e-mail: bathease@aol.com

Tom FitzGerald, President
Terry Stickler, Director, R&D
Gerry Grondin, Production Manager

BathEase is the original standard size, residential style, acrylic bathtub with a door. Ideal for use in private homes by all who are ambulatory, the award winning design was specially created as an aid to daily living for the elderly and physically challenged. BathEase also features the first shower stall that may be converted to a bathtub with a door. *$1897.00*

96 **Bathtub Safety Rail**

Arista Surgical Supply Company
67 Lexington Avenue
New York, NY 10010   212-679-3694
                             800-223-1984

Made of stainless steel, this safety rail fits in any size bathtub and offers safety and independence at bathing time. *$55.00*

97 **Braun Corporation**

Braun Corporation
1014 South Monticello Street
Number 310
Winamac, IN 46996   219-946-6153
                            800-843-5438
                            FAX: 219-946-4670

Carolyn Watts, Public Affairs Contact

Offers a variety of assistive devices for the bath and surrounding environment.

98 **Columbia Medical Manufacturing Corporation**

PO Box 633
Pacific Palisades, CA 90272   310-454-6612
                                      800-454-6612
                                      FAX: 310-305-1718
                                      e-mail: cmedonline@aol.com
                                      www.columbiamedical.com

Offers a full line of toilet supports, positioning commodes, wrap-around bath supports, reclining chairs and car seats for children from 20 to 102 pounds.

99 **Commode**

Maxi Aids
42 Executive Boulevard
Number 3209
Farmingdale, NY 11735   516-752-0521
                                800-522-6294
                                FAX: 516-752-0689
                                e-mail: sales@maxiaids.com
                                www.maxiaids.com

Adjustable seat height for patient comfort. *$65.95*

100 **Crane Plumbing/Fiat Products**

1235 Hartrey Avenue
Evanston, IL 60202   847-864-7600
                             FAX: 847-864-7652
                             www.craneplumbing.com

Carla Lindsey, Marketing Administrator

Manufacturers plumbing fixtures for the disabled. Products include toilets, lavatories, showers and tub/shower units.

101   Deluxe Bath Bench with Adjustable Legs

Maxi Aids
42 Executive Boulevard
Number 3209
Farmingdale, NY   11735   516-752-0521
                                 800-522-6294
                          FAX: 516-752-0689
                 e-mail: sales@maxiaids.com
                          www.maxiaids.com

Bath bench with back support and adjustable legs.
$ 49.95

102   Driving Systems

16141 Runnymede Street
Van Nuys, CA   91406   818-782-6793
                          FAX: 818-782-6485
                 e-mail: info@wavegrip.com
                          www.wavegrip.com

Greg Paquin, Marketing Manager

Designer grab bars with ergonomic grip. Available in
colors and custom shapes. New fold down shower
seat. Support grips extend out form the wall 24 or 30.
Concealed fastener and modular components for
many design possibilities. Price ranges from $30.00
to $280.00.

103   Easy-Care Shower Chairs

Guardian Products
12800 Wentworth Street
 # C-4522
Arleta, CA   91331
                          FAX: 818-504-2833

Molded back and contoured, textured seat, with
hand holds for shower and bath.

**104   Electric Leg Bag Emptier and Tub Slide Shower
Chair**

RD Equipment
230 Percival Drive
West Barnstable, MA   02668   **508-362-7498**
                          FAX: 508-362-7498
                 e-mail: rdeuip@capecod.net
                          www.rdequipment.com

Richard J. Dagostino, Inventor/President
Diana M. Pontieri, Sales Manager

Designed for independence, this small, lightweight
battery-operated valve attaches to the bottom of the
leg bag. A simple flip of the switch empties the leg
bag, allowing the user to take in unlimited amounts
of fluids. Tub Slide Shower Chair is a complete bathroom care system, with no need of costly renovations.
Eliminates all transfers in the bathroom. *$200.00*

105   Great Big Safety Tub Mat

Maxi Aids
42 Executive Boulevard
Number 3209
Farmingdale, NY   11735   516-752-0521
                                 800-522-6294
                          FAX: 516-752-0689
                 e-mail: sales@maxiaids.com
                          www.maxiaids.com

Tub mat provides security against falls in the bath
and shower. *$16.95*

106   Hal Hen Bed Shaker

Assistive Devices Network
2241 S Triangle X Lane
Tucson, AZ   85713   866-674-3549

          www.assistivedevices.net/about.htm
$59.00

107   Long Handled Bath Sponges

Therapro
225 Arlington Street
Framingham, MA   01702   508-872-9494
                                 800-257-5376
                          FAX: 508-875-2062
                 e-mail: info@theraproducts.com
                          www.theraproducts.com

Plastic-handled, 18-inch bath sponge. Handle may
be heated and bent for easy reach. *$2.50*

108   Modular Wall Grab Bars

Frohock-Stewart
39400 Taylor Parkway
N Ridgeville, OH   44035   440-329-6000

Engineered for strength and beauty, these bars
can be assembled in various combinations to fit
any bath or shower.

109   Pik Stik

Mobilelectrics Company
4014 Bardstown Road
Louisville, KY   40218
                          800-URM-OVIN
                          FAX: 502-495-2476

Provides reaching and grasping power with accuracy and ease.

110   Portable Shampoo Bowl

Ambulatory Cosmetology Technicians
12762 Brookhurst
 # 532
Garden Grove, CA   92640   949-833-1432

Shirley D. Smith

A bowl designed to allow a person who is in a wheelchair or sitting on a regular chair to shampoo hair.

111   Suregrip Bathtub Rail

Frohock-Stewart
39400 Taylor Parkway
N Ridgeville, OH   44035   440-329-6000

Compact and versatile, the bars have a soft-touch,
contoured, white vinyl gripping area for added
safety.

112   Talking Bathroom Scale

Independent Living Aids
200 Robbins Lane
Jericho, NY   11753   516-937-1848
                                 800-537-2118
                          FAX: 516-937-3906
          e-mail: can-do@independentliving.com
                          www.independentliving.com

Marvin Sandler, President

Talking scale that will talk your weight. *$59.95*

113   Terry-Wash Mitt - Medium Size

Therapro
225 Arlington Street
Framingham, MA 01702   508-872-9494
                                                     800-257-5376
                                         FAX: 508-875-2062
                          e-mail: info@theraproducts.com
                                         www.theraproducts.com

Includes a thumb socket and a palm pocket to hold a bar of soap. *$8.00*

114   Toilet Guard Rail

Maxi Aids
42 Executive Boulevard
Number 3209
Farmingdale, NY 11735   516-752-0521
                                                     800-522-6294
                                         FAX: 516-752-0689
                             e-mail: sales@maxiaids.com
                                         www.maxiaids.com

Made of chrome-plated, heavy gauge steel. Fits securely to the toilet for maximum sturdiness. *$43.95*

115   Transfer Tub Bench

Arista Surgical Supply Company
67 Lexington Avenue
New York, NY 10010   212-679-3694
                                                  800-223-1984

Curved padded backrest for comfortable support. Backrest also assists patient during lateral transfer. *$64.00*

116   Tri-Grip Bathtub Rail

Maxi Aids
42 Executive Boulevard
Number 3209
Farmingdale, NY 11735   516-752-0521
                                                     800-522-6294
                                         FAX: 516-752-0689
                             e-mail: sales@maxiaids.com
                                         www.maxiaids.com

Two gripping heights for easy bathtub entrance or exit. *$36.95*

117   Tub Grab Bars

Guardian Products
12800 Wentworth Street
 # C-4522
Arleta, CA 91331
                                         FAX: 818-504-2833

Bi-level grab bar allows for proper grasp when entering or exiting the tub.

118   Tub Slide Shower Chair

RD Equipment
230 Percival Drive
West Barnstable, MA 02668   508-362-7498

                          e-mail: rdequip@capecod.net
                                         www.capecod.net/rdequip

Richard J. Dagostino, Proprietor/Inventor
Diana M. Pontieri, Sales Manager

The tub slide shower chair was designed for the elderly and disabled to make any bathroom (at home or when travelling) accessible with little or no renovations. Go from the bed, over the commode and over the bathtub for a shower using one product. No transfers in the bathroom what so ever. *$2000.00*

119   Tublift

Guardian Products
12800 Wentworth Street
 # C-4522
Arleta, CA 91331
                                         FAX: 818-504-2833

Water powered bath chair lift that can be easily operated by bather or attendant.

120   Wall Grab Bars

Guardian Products
12800 Wentworth Street
 # C-4522
Arleta, CA 91331
                                         FAX: 818-504-2833

Provides an extra measure of support and safety for bath, bedroom, kitchen and stairways.

Bed

121   Adjustable Bed

Golden Technologies
401 Bridge Street
Old Forge, PA 18518   570-451-7477
                                              800-624-6374
                                  FAX: 570-451-7974
                     e-mail: info@goldentech.com
                                  www.goldentech.com

Rich Golden, CEO
Fred Kiwax, V.P.
Bob Smith, V.P. of Sales

Trouble-free gear motor, safety features, dual massage variable speed timer and more, for the ultimate sleep experience.

122   Bed Shaker

Assistive Devices Network
2241 S Triangle X Lane
Tucson, AZ 85713   866-674-3549

                          e-mail: info@assistivedevices.net
                          www.assistivedevices.net/about.htm
$39.00

123   Blanket Support

Guardian Products
12800 Wentworth Street
 # C-4522
Arleta, CA 91331
                                         FAX: 818-504-2833

Sturdy wire support lifts bed linens off feet or legs for better air circulation and comfort.

124 Bye-Bye Decubiti Air Mattress Overlay
Ken McRight Supplies
7456 South Oswego Avenue
Tulsa, OK 74136   918-492-9657
                                 FAX: 918-492-9694

Ken McRight, President
Originally designed for hospital beds, converts any
bed into an exceptionally therapeutic flotation unit
when used between the conventional mattress and
pad. The complete overlay is comprised of five individually inflatable, 100 percent natural rubber, venti-
lated sections enclosed within separate pockets of a
soft fleece cover. This sectional conformation to any
configuration of electric or manual beds. *$731.50*

125 Cervical Support Pillow
Wise Enterprises
5017 El Don Drive
Rocklin, CA 95677   916-624-3848
                                      888-947-3368
                                 FAX: 916-624-3866
www.wisent.com/ordering_lifestyle_products
These hypoallergenic, antimicrobial fiber pillows
support the neck in a natural position. Standard,
midsize and petite pillows support the neck while
sleeping on the back or side. The compact travel
pillow offers support while sitting or lying down.
The cervical roll had a gentle center and firm ends
to ensure maximum comfort and proper support.
Position the roll under the neck, back or knees.
Standard and midsize fits adults, petite fits children and small adults.

126 Foam Decubitus Bed Pads
Profex/Professional
PO Box 16043
Saint Louis, MO 63105   314-727-2996

Convoluted foam provides extra back support and
comfort for wheelchair users.

127 Hard Manufacturing Company
230 Grider Street
Buffalo, NY 14215   716-893-1800
                                      800-873-4273
                                 FAX: 716-896-2579
                   e-mail: currier@hardmfg.com

Kevin Currier, Home Care Manager
Manufacturer of pediatric cribs and age appropriate
youth beds. Free catalog.

128 Helping Handle
Access with Ease
PO Box 1150
Chino Valley, AZ 86323   520-636-9469
                                      800-531-9479
                                 FAX: 520-636-0292
                   e-mail: KMJC@northlink.com
Gives you a hand getting out of bed. Fits any stand-
ard mattress and can be relocated up or down
alongside the bed. *$44.95*

129 Homecare Beds
Guardian Products
12800 Wentworth Street
C-4522
Arleta, CA 91331
                                 FAX: 818-504-2833
Manual and electric beds, with interchangeable
motors and accessories.

130 Jackson Cervipillo
Wise Enterprises
5017 El Don Drive
Rocklin, CA 95677   916-624-3848
                                      888-947-3368
                                 FAX: 916-624-3866
www.wisent.com/ordering_lifestyle_products
The Jackson Cervipillo confortably supports the
neck vertebre when sleeping on the side or on the
back. Pillow measures 7" in diameter and is 17"
long. A machine-washable cover is available
seperately.

131 Motivator
Global Assistive Devices
4950 North Dixie Highway
Fort Lauderdale, FL 33334   954-784-0035
                                 FAX: 954-784-0047
           e-mail: info@globalassistive.com
           www.catalog.globalassistive.com
This useful innovation shakes you awake without
disturbing others. It even wakes the heaviest
sleeper.

132 NeckEase
Wise Enterprises
5017 El Don Drive
Rocklin, CA 95677   916-624-3848
                                      888-947-3368
                                 FAX: 916-624-3866
www.wisent.com/ordering_lifestyle_products
Microwave NeckEase for penetrating heat that
sooths stiff necks and shoulders, easing tension.
NeckEase features a unique filling of organic, long
grain rice and aromatic herbs and spices. When
heated, this filling provides soothing, moist aromatherapy. Heat lasts about 30-45 minutes. Available in two sizes: small fits snugly around the
neck, applying gentle pressure at the base of the
skull; Large may be worn for a snug fit, or loosely
for application on the shoulder and upper back.

133 Permaflex Home Care Mattress
BG Industries
8550 Balboa Boulevard
Suite 214
Northridge, CA 91325   630-257-1077

Mattress with flame retardant upholstery material, water-repellant, anti-microbial and tear-re-
sistant cover, for extra comfort.

134   Priva
PO Box 448
Champlain, NY   12919   514-356-8881
                                         800-761-8881
                              FAX: 514-356-0055
                    e-mail: piv@priva-inc.com
                              www.priva-inc.com

David Horowitz, President
Reusable incontinence care products including briefs, liners, inserts and sheet protectors.

135   Sonic Alert Bed Shaker
Assistive Devices Network
2241 S Triangle X Lane
Tucson, AZ   85713   866-674-6549

             www.assistivedevices.net/about.htm
    $49.00

136   Vibes Bed Shaker
Assistive Devices Network
2241 S Triangle X Lane
Tucson, AZ   85713   866-674-3549

             e-mail: info@assistivedevices.net
             www.assistivedevices.net/about.htm

137   Waterproof Sheet-Topper Mattress and Chair Pad
Pillow Talk
348 Pond Road
Freehold, NJ   07728   732-780-9483
                              FAX: 732-708-0279

Jack Fajerman, President
This soft pad lies on the top sheet, absorbing accidents from incontinence, pregnancy or medical problems. Waterproof barrier locks out moisture, soiling and stains and eliminates midnight linen changes and the resulting laundry. Available in bed sizes W/4 Anchor; twin; full; queen; king; and crib.

Communication

138   ACS Wireless
10 Victor Square
Scotts Valley, CA   95066
                                         800-995-5500
                              FAX: 831-438-2745

This company makes a telephone headset.

139   ADA Hotel Built-In Alerting System
HARC Mercantile, Ltd.
PO Box 3055
Kalamazoo, MI   49003   616-324-1615
                                         800-445-9968
                              FAX: 616-324-2387
                e-mail: home@harcmercantile.com
                              www.harcmercantile.com

Ronald Slager, President
Ronald Damstra, Technical Sales Mgr.

Visual alerting system for ADA compliance for multi housing/rooms facilities, like hospitals, dorms, senior housing for persons who are hard of hearing or deaf. Alerts to five conditions: smoke, door bell, telephone ring, wake up and House central alarm.

140   APT Technology
APT Technology
236A North Main Street
Shreve, OH   44676   330-567-2001
                                         888-549-2001
                              FAX: 330-567-3073
                e-mail: info@apt-technology.com
                              www.apt-technology.com

Larry Shirer, President
Manufacturers of assistive technology products including environmental controls, computer access, adaptive switches, adaptive telephones and TV controls. *$490.00*

141   Able-Phone 100
DQP
14167 Meadow Drive
Grass Valley, CA   95945
                                         800-456-4979
                              FAX: 530-477-7122

Cordless headset telephone.

142   Able-Phone 110
DQP
14167 Meadow Drive
Grass Valley, CA   95945
                                         800-456-4979
                              FAX: 530-477-7122

Cordless headset telephone with keypad.

143   Able-Phone 1100
DQP
14167 Meadow Drive
Grass Valley, CA   95945
                                         800-456-4979
                              FAX: 530-477-7122

Amplified headset adapter.

144   Able-Phone 1900
DQP
14167 Meadow Drive
Grass Valley, CA   95945
                                         800-456-4979
                              FAX: 530-477-7122

Speakerphone with operation.

145   Able-Phone 2000
DQP
14167 Meadow Drive
Grass Valley, CA   95945
                                         800-456-4979
                              FAX: 530-477-7122

Adaptive speakerphone.

146 Able-Phone 2500
DQP
14167 Meadow Drive
Grass Valley, CA 95945

800-456-4979
FAX: 530-477-7122

Remote control emergency message telephone.

147 Able-Phone 900
DQP
14167 Meadow Drive
Grass Valley, CA 95945

800-456-4979
FAX: 530-477-7122

Cordless headset telephone with top button.

148 Able-Switch 300
DQP
14167 Meadow Drive
Grass Valley, CA 95945

800-456-4979
FAX: 530-477-7122

Wireless remote control.

149 Able-Switch 500
DQP
14167 Meadow Drive
Grass Valley, CA 95945

800-456-4979
FAX: 530-477-7122

Wireless remote receiver/controller.

150 Able-Switch SW-1
DQP
14167 Meadow Drive
Grass Valley, CA 95945

800-456-4979
FAX: 530-477-7122

Touch switch.

151 Adaptek Systems
2320 Brighton-Henrietta Town Line
Rochester, NY 14623

800-685-4566
FAX: 716-475-9889

Developers of a voice output module designed to work with the Kurzweil voice-recognition system. The device provides voice output of what the computer hears for persons with visual impairments.

152 Aiphone Corporation, Environment Control System/NHX Nurse Call System
1700 130th Avenue NE
Bellevue, WA 98005

800-692-0200
FAX: 425-455-0071
e-mail: info@aiphone.com
www.aiphone.com

Chuck Watkins, Eastern Regional Sales Manager
Nancy McAlister, Western Regional Sales Manager
Roy Paeth, Midwestern Regional Sales Mgr

AIPHONE manufactures audio and video intercom systems for home or business to help the physically disabled answer doors and communicate through physical barriers; also ADA-compliant emergency call intercom stations for use in public facilities and an Environmental Control System for persons with limited mobility.

153 Akron Resources
11606 Clark Street
Suite D
Arcadia, CA 91006

FAX: 626-303-6157

Lisa Avalos, Operations Manager
Manufacturers of infrared amplification systems for televisions or stereos. $29-$69.00.

154 Ameriphone
12082 Western Avenue
Garden Grove, CA 92841

800-874-3005
FAX: 714-897-4703
e-mail: ameriphone@ameriphone.com
www.ameriphone.com

Vivian Elliot, Sales Manager
George Cheung, President
Tom Hefner, Product Manager

The Ameriphone Dialogue RC is a remote controlled speakerphone that can be activated up to 40 feet away. It features up to 20 memory buttons that you scan and select by gently pressing the remote control or blowing in the optional Airswitch or squeezing the optional pillow switch. Features voice activated answering for complete independence and access to telephone company services such as call waiting. Phones $299.00-$399.00. Accessories $39-$99.

155 Ameriphone - Wireless Notification System
Budd Lake, NJ

e-mail: HEARYOUARE@aol.com

Larry Cagno, Vice President
System alerts to activators in the home, telephone ringing, knock at the door, sounding of an alarm, motion detection sensor. The table top receiver has a digital clock and connectors for your notification lamp and/or bed vibrator. *$209.95*

156 Ameriphone Hearing Assistance Telephone
Hear You Are
4 Musconetcong Avenue
Stanhope, NJ 07874

800-287-EARS
FAX: 973-347-7662

A communication enhanced telephone with a large button and contrasting graphics for optimum visibility and dialing ease. Amplifies incoming voice by 30 db gain and has a frequency screening feature that permits user to identify sound frequencies. *$119.95*

157 Amplified Handsets

HARC Mercantile, Ltd.
PO Box 3055
Kalamazoo, MI 49003   616-324-1615
    800-445-9968
    FAX: 616-324-2387
    e-mail: home@harcmercantile.com
    www.harcmercantile.com

Ronald Slager, President

Choices of touch activated electronic control, rotary (thumb wheel) volume control, that can directly replace old handset, stocked in round and square styles. This also includes an electric transmitter with variable settings. *$39.95*

158 Amplified Phones

HARC Mercantile, Ltd.
PO Box 3055
Kalamazoo, MI 49003   616-324-1615
    800-445-9968
    FAX: 616-324-2387
    e-mail: home@harcmercantile.com
    www.harcmercantile.com

Ronald Slager, President

Low frequency ringer, indicator light, enhances or amplifies sound, some that automatically returns to normal dial tone when phone receiver is hung up, lighted easy to read dial pad and volume control boosts incoming sound. *$95.00*

159 Amplified Portable Phone

HARC Mercantile, Ltd.
PO Box 3055
Kalamazoo, MI 49003   616-324-1615
    800-445-9968
    FAX: 616-324-2387
    e-mail: home@harcmercantile.com
    www.harcmercantile.com

Ronald Slager, President

Portable amplified phones. *$199.00*

160 Answerall 100

DQP
14167 Meadow Drive
Grass Valley, CA 95945
    800-456-4979
    FAX: 530-477-7122

Answering machine for TDD and voice.

161 Artificial Larynx

HARC Mercantile, Ltd.
PO Box 3055
Kalamazoo, MI 49003   616-324-1615
    800-445-9968
    FAX: 616-324-2387
    e-mail: home@harcmercantile.com
    www.harcmercantile.com

Ronald Slager, President

For people unable to use their larynx, a hand held speaking aid that simulates the natural vibrations on voice. *$220.00*

162 Assistive Technology

7 Wells Avenue
Newton, MA 02459   617-641-7000
    800-793-9227
    e-mail: customercare@assistivetech.com
    www.assistivetech.com

Jane Oles, Customer Service Manager
Roxanne Varteressian, Marketing Specialist

A premiere developer of innovative technology solutions for people with physical and learning disabilities. Breakthrough products enable people of all ages and abilities to live and learn independently. Supportive material for teachers, clinicians and those with disabilities.

163 BESTspeech

Berkeley Speech Technologies
2409 Telegraph Avenue
Berkeley, CA 94704   510-843-1852
    FAX: 415-841-5083

This text-to-speech facility is useful to persons who are blind or vision impaired and may be used by those with speech, hearing and learning difficulties.

164 Circline Illuminated Magnifer

Dazor Manufacturing Corporation
4483 Duncan Avenue
Saint Louis, MO 63110   314-652-2400
    800-345-9103
    FAX: 314-652-2069
    e-mail: info@dazor.com
    www.dazor.com

Mark Malott, Marketing Coordinator

Provides even, shadow free light under the magnifying lens with a 22-watt circline fluorescent. The magnifier is mounted on a floating arm that allows you to position the light source and lens with the touch of a finger.

165 Cornell Communications

1640 West Silver Spring Drive
Milwaukee, WI 53209
    800-558-8957
    FAX: 414-351-4657
    e-mail: sales@cornell.com
    www.cornell.com

David D. Thompson, Sales Manager
Bruce Glaub, Director of Sales
Pauline Haack, Customer Service

Cornell's Rescue Assistance Systems allow personnel to request emergency assistance. Applications include handicapped evacuations, parking garages and elevators. Voice, intercom and visual only signaling systems are available.

166 Davis Center for Hearing, Speech, Leraning and Well-Being

98 Rt 46 West
Budd Lake, NJ 07828   973-347-7662
    800-278-EARS
    FAX: 973-691-0611
    www.thedaviscenter.com

Dorinne S. Davis, MA, CCC-A, FAAA, President

sound-based therapies that help hearing learning, speech and well-being, complete hearing, speech and CAP testing. *$26.20*

167   DeltaTalker

Prentke Romich Company
1022 Heyl Road
Wooster, OH   44691   **330-262-1984**
                                        800-262-1984
                                    FAX: 330-263-4829
                                    www.prentrom.com

Cherie Weaver, Mktg Administrative Coordinator

A portable, electronic communication device that uses Minspeak so that symbols are used to represent words, sentences and phrases. The DT can be accessed by pressing keys scanning or optical pointing and can be configured with 8, 32 or 128 locations. It has both digitalized and synthesized speech. Optional infrared capabilities allow operation of remote controlled devices. *$4995.00*

168   Developmental Lever Control

Handicapped Children's Technological Services
PO Box 7
Foster, RI   02825

A switch device with two levers mounted on a speaker which can plug into the auxiliary port to control a tape recorder.

169   Door Flashing Announcment System

Hear You Are
4 Musconetcong Avenue
Stanhope, NJ   07874

                                        800-287-EARS
                                    FAX: 973-347-7662

System provides audible and visual signals of doorbell actuation. Bell rings as long as pushbutton is depressed. Light continues to flash at a 100 flashes per minute rate after audible signal stops. *$163.45*

170   Flashing Lamp Telephone Ring Alerter

Independent Living Aids
27 East Mall
Plainview, NY   11803   **516-752-8080**
                                        800-537-2118

Once your phone is plugged into the Telephone Ring Alerter, the lamp light will flash with each ring, alerting you that there is a phone call. *$62.00*

171   GABBI TALK Phone

Sense-Sations
919 Walnut Street
Philadelphia, PA   19107   **215-629-2990**
                                        800-876-5456

The talking telephone for mistake-free dialing lets the individual know what numbers they have dialed. *$28.50*

172   Headmaster Plus

Prentke Romich Company
1022 Heyl Road
Wooster, OH   44691   **330-262-1984**
                                        800-262-1984
                                    FAX: 330-263-4829
                                    www.prentrom.com

A headpointing system that takes the place of a mouse and allows individuals who cannot use their hands but have good head control access to the computer. A transmitting unit sits atop the monitor and sends signals to the user's headset. The user puffs into a tube connected to the headset to make selections. Typing can be done with optional on-screen keyboards. *$1195.00*

173   Hear-a-Clock

Ring-a-Lite
PO Box 9362
Kansas City, MO   64133
                                    FAX: 816-765-3301
                                e-mail: telus@tfs.net
                                    www.tfs.net/utelus

Ralph Taylor, Partner

Takes an existing alarm or clock radio and makes it a light signalling unit. Set next to your alarm clock or clock radio speaker, it will flash a lamp when the alarm sounds. This requires no wiring. *$ 39.95*

174   Ideal-Phone

IDEAMATICS
1364 Beverly Road
Suite 101
Mc Lean, VA   22101   **703-903-4972**
                                        800-247-IDEA
                                    FAX: 703-903-8949
                        e-mail: ideamatics@ideamatics.net
                                    www.ideamatics.org

David L. Danner, author
David L. Danner, President

Integrates the personal computer and the telephone into a single, efficient workstation. It is ideal for mobility-impaired persons and others who need a hands-free operation of the phone. The Ideal-Phone includes one PC Board, a Plantronics headset, software for access and logging and complete documentation. It can be integrated into programs or pops-up over any application. MS-DOS based, version 3.0 or higher are available. *$195.00*

175   LPB Communications

28 Bacton Hill Road
Frazer, PA   19355
                                    FAX: 610-644-8651
                            e-mail: lpbsales@lpbinc.com
                                    www.lpbinc.com

John Devecka, VP Sales

Limited area AM and FM broadcast systems for hearing assistance and language translation manufacturing since 1960. Systems for small conference halls, churches and Olympic stadiums. Components or complete system. *$400.00*

176 Language, Learning & Living

Prentke Romich Company
1022 Heyl Road
Wooster, OH   44691   330-262-1984
                                       800-262-1984
                                  FAX: 330-263-4829
                                  www.prentrom.com

A Minspeak application program designed for adolescent and adult individuals with developmental disabilities and associated learning difficulties. The software is used with Prentke Romich Company augmentative communication devices. $355.00

177 Large Button Speaker Phone

HARC Mercantile, Ltd.
PO Box 3055
Kalamazoo, MI   49003   616-324-1615
                                       800-445-9968
                                  FAX: 616-324-2387
                      e-mail: home@harcmercantile.com
                               www.harcmercantile.com

Ronald Slager, President
Speakerphone with or without remote control. $395.00

178 Large Print Telephone Dial

Maxi Aids
42 Executive Boulevard
Number 3209
Farmingdale, NY   11735   516-752-0521
                                       800-522-6294
                                  FAX: 516-752-0689
                          e-mail: sales@maxiaids.com
                                    www.maxiaids.com

Pressure sensitive dial with numbers that are easy to see for the disabled. $.69

179 Large Print Touch-Telephone Overlays

Maxi Aids
42 Executive Boulevard
Number 3209
Farmingdale, NY   11735   516-752-0521
                                       800-522-6294
                                  FAX: 516-752-0689
                          e-mail: sales@maxiaids.com
                                    www.maxiaids.com

Pressure-sensitive and easy to apply overlays that make everyday phones accessible. $.49

180 Large Print Typewriter

Typewriting Institute for the Handicapped
3102 West Augusta Avenue
Phoenix, AZ   85051   623-939-5344

A reconditioned, converted IBM Model D electric typewriter with upper/lower case keys.

181 Liberator

Prentke Romich Company
1022 Heyl Road
Wooster, OH   44691   330-262-1984
                                       800-262-1984
                                  FAX: 330-263-4829
                                  www.prentrom.com

A portable electronic communication device that used Minspeak so that symbols are used to represent words, sentences or phrases. Liberator can be accessed by pressing keys, optical headpointing and a wide variety of switch activated scans. It can be configured with 8, 32 or 128 locations. It offers a variety of unique features to permit the most effective communication possible. $7,345-$8,575.

182 Meroni Premiapri Press-Button Door Knob

Meroni Locks of America
8012 NW 75th Avenue
Tamarac, FL   33321
                                       800-749-5625
                                  FAX: 305-556-2405

Michael Knight, Director
P Carlo Cau, Vice President
Door lock used in environments where barrier free access is required.

183 Metropolitan Washington Ear

35 University Boulevard East
Silver Spring, MD   20901   301-588-1965
                                  FAX: 301-681-5227
                             e-mail: info@washear.org
                                      www.washear.org

Nancy Knauss, Administrative Director
Multi-media reading service for blind and visually impaired. Offering 24 hour audio radio reading, dial-in newspapers and web casting, as well as audio description at theaters, museums and films.

184 Mini Teleloop

HARC Mercantile, Ltd.
PO Box 3055
Kalamazoo, MI   49003   616-324-1615
                                       800-445-9968
                                  FAX: 616-324-2387
                      e-mail: home@harcmercantile.com
                               www.harcmercantile.com

Ronald Slager, President
Home induction loop amplifier for use with hearing aids equipped with T-Coil. $159.95

185 Multiple Phone/Device Switch

HARC Mercantile, Ltd.
PO Box 3055
Kalamazoo, MI   49003   616-324-1615
                                       800-445-9968
                                  FAX: 616-324-2387
                      e-mail: home@harcmercantile.com
                               www.harcmercantile.com

Ronald Slager, President
Used to switch phone lines between two devices. $34.95

186 Oticon Portable Telephone Amplifier

Hear You Are
4 Musconetcong Avenue
Stanhope, NJ 07874

800-287-EARS
FAX: 973-347-7662

Attaches to any sound source, picks up sound, amplifies it and induces it onto hearing aid tele-coils. *$93.00*

187 Outdoor Loud Bell

Hear You Are
4 Musconetcong Avenue
Stanhope, NJ 07874

800-287-EARS
FAX: 973-347-7662

This outdoor bell with a loud mechanical ringer features an easy plug-in installation to either a modular or hook-up. *$79.16*

188 Personal FM Systems

HARC Mercantile, Ltd.
PO Box 3055
Kalamazoo, MI 49003

616-324-1615
800-445-9968
FAX: 616-324-2387
e-mail: home@harcmercantile.com
www.harcmercantile.com

Ronald Slager, President

Wireless FM systems transmits sound via a radio carrier wave. *$599.95*

189 Personal Infrared Listening System

HARC Mercantile, Ltd.
PO Box 3055
Kalamazoo, MI 49003

616-324-1615
800-445-9968
FAX: 616-324-2387
e-mail: home@harcmercantile.com
www.harcmercantile.com

Ronald Slager, President

Wireless method if listening to TV and radio with individually controlled amplification. *$199.00*

190 Plantronics SP-04

DQP
14167 Meadow Drive
Grass Valley, CA 95945

800-456-4979
FAX: 530-477-7122

Headset telephone for people who have a hard time grasping the telephone.

191 Prentke Romich Company

1022 Heyl Road
Wooster, OH 44691

330-262-1984
800-262-1984
FAX: 330-263-4829
e-mail: info@prentrom.com
www.prentrom.com

Barry Romich, Chairman
Joe Durbin, President

The Prentke Romich Company is a full service company offering easy, yet powerful communication aids. The company believes in supporting customers before and after the sale by offering funding assistance, distance learning training, extended warranty, service assistance and much more. Visit our web-site to view our full-line catalogue, read about our success stories and to sign up for our on-line newsletter.

192 Push to Talk Amplified Handset

HARC Mercantile, Ltd.
PO Box 3055
Kalamazoo, MI 49003

616-324-1615
800-445-9968
FAX: 616-324-2387
e-mail: home@harcmercantile.com
www.harcmercantile.com

Ronald Slager, President

Replacement receiver which is hearing aid compatible and is designed for high noise conditions. *$79.95*

193 Remote Control Speakerphone

Ameriphone
12082 Western Avenue
Garden Grove, CA 92841

714-897-0808
800-874-3005
FAX: 714-897-4703

A multi-functional speaker phone specially designed to meet the needs of motion-impaired persons who are unable to use a conventional phone without assistance.

194 Ring-a-Lite

PO Box 9362
Kansas City, MO 64133

FAX: 816-765-3301
e-mail: telus@tfs.net
www.tfs.net/utelus

Ralph Taylor, Partner

Allows persons to see a telephone ringing, eliminating missing calls. This easy to use unit connects directly to existing telephone connections and also works to signal incoming TDD messages. *$39.95*

195 Scanning Director II

APT Technology
236A North Main Street
Shreve, OH 44676

330-567-2001
800-549-2001
FAX: 330-567-3073
e-mail: sales@apt-technology.com
www.apt-technology.com

Grace Miller, Office Manager

Controls all features of a TV, VCR, satellite system, etc. by means of scanning controlled by a single or dual switch. Operates also as an accessory to an ECU, also controls 16 lamps/appliances using X-10. *$795.00*

196 Silent Call - Portable Visual and/or Vibratory Alerting System

Hear You Are
4 Musconetcong Avenue
Stanhope, NJ   07874

800-278-EARS
FAX: 973-347-7662

Small portable alerting device strobe light and vibrator announcer. Alerts to doorbell, telephone, smoke detector or sound monitors activations. Each alert is identified by a different colored light indicator. *$249.95*

197 Silent Call Communications

PO Box 868
Clarkson, MI   48347

800-572-5227
FAX: 248-673-5442
e-mail: silentcall@ameritech.net
www.silentcall.com

Harris Boshak, Director Sales & Marketing
Suzie Wright, Office Manager
George Elwell, President

Alerting devices such as paging systems and smoke detectors for deaf and deaf-blind people.

198 Sonic Alert

Harris Communications
15159 Technology Drive
Eden Prairie, MN   55344

612-906-1180
800-825-6758
FAX: 612-906-1099
e-mail: mail@harriscomm.com
www.harriscomm.com

Bill Williams, National Sales Manager

Offers visual alerting devices that provides safety and convenience by turning vital sound into flashing light: telephone ring signalers, doorbell signalers, baby cry signalers and wake up alarms.

199 Sonic Alert - Visual and Vibratory Alarm Clock

Hear You Are
4 Musconetcong Avenue
Stanhope, NJ   07874

800-284-EARS
FAX: 973-347-7662

Clock features a large green led display with extremely loud pulsating alarm. The tone and volume is adjustable so users can select their individual needs. Outlets are provided for a table lamp and a bed shaker. *$52.45*

200 Sound Induction Receiver

HARC Mercantile, Ltd.
PO Box 3055
Kalamazoo, MI   49003

616-324-1615
800-445-9968
FAX: 616-324-2387
e-mail: home@harcmercantile.com
www.harcmercantile.com

Ronald Slager, President

Sound induction receiver to be used with any loop system. *$67.00*

201 SpeakEasy Communication Aid

AbleNet
1081 10th Avenue SE
Minneapolis, MN   55414

800-322-0956
FAX: 612-379-9143
e-mail: customerservice@ablenetinc.com
www.ablenetinc.com

SpeakEasy is a digitalized Voice Output Communication Aid that is ideal for anyone who is beginning to develop communication skills such as making choices and identifying symbols. It holds 12 messages totaling four minutes and 20 seconds of recording time. It measures 7 1/2 inch by 1 3/4 inch and weighs only one pound. Activate messages using the built in keyboard or via external switch. *$399.00*

202 Speakwriter 2000

HumanWare
6140 Horseshoe Bar Road
Suite P
Loomis, CA   95650

916-652-7253

Talking typewriter.

203 Speech Discrimination Unit

HARC Mercantile, Ltd.
PO Box 3055
Kalamazoo, MI   49003

616-324-1615
800-445-9968
FAX: 616-324-2387
e-mail: home@harcmercantile.com
www.harcmercantile.com

Ronald Slager, President

Speech Adjust-A-Tone improves speech discrimination for use with telephone and/or TV and radio. *$189.95*

204 Speechmaker-Personal Speech Amplifier

HARC Mercantile, Ltd.
PO Box 3055
Kalamazoo, MI   49003

616-324-1615
800-445-9968
FAX: 616-324-2387
e-mail: home@harcmercantile.com
www.harcmercantile.com

Ronald Slager, President

Portable, body worn personal speech amplifier for people with a weak voice. *$316.00*

205 Standard Touch Turner Sip & Puff Switch

443 View Ridge Drive
Everett, WA   98203

FAX: 425-259-4390

A page turning device. *$920.00*

206 **Stretch-View Wide-View Rectangular Illuminated Magnifier**

Dazor Manufacturing Corporation
4483 Duncan Avenue
Saint Louis, MO 63110   314-652-2400
                                800-345-9103
                          FAX: 314-652-2069
                     e-mail: info@dazor.com
                               www.dazor.com

Richard Kupferer, Marketing Coordinator

Provides shadow-free illumination or a highlighting effect under the magnifying lens with an 18-watt compact fluorescent light source. The magnifier is mounted on a floating arm that allows you to position the light source and lens with the touch of a finger.

207 **Strobe Light Signalers**

HARC Mercantile, Ltd.
PO Box 3055
Kalamazoo, MI 49003   616-324-1615
                              800-445-9968
                        FAX: 616-324-2387
               e-mail: home@harcmercantile.com
                       www.harcmercantile.com

Ronald Slager, President

Strobe alerts. Plugs into receivers for signaling systems. *$39.95*

208 **TALKBACK Wireless Doorbell Intercom**

Rice International Corporation
7952 Pines Boulevard
Pmbk Pines, FL 33024   954-983-6464
                        FAX: 305-895-7660

Donald Van Der Laan, General Manager
Suzanne Minnick, Advertising Manager

Wireless radio frequency combined with doorbell and intercom. Outside unit uses 9 volt battery and features hands free operation. This device automatically turns off after one minute. *$ 99.95*

209 **TTY's - Telephone Device for the Deaf**

HARC Mercantile, Ltd.
PO Box 3055
Kalamazoo, MI 49003   616-324-1615
                              800-445-9968
                        FAX: 616-324-2387
               e-mail: home@harcmercantile.com
                       www.harcmercantile.com

Ronald Slager, President
With or without printer. *$239.00*

210 **TalkTrac Wearable Communicator**

Ablenet
1081 10th Avenue SE
Minneapolis, MN 55414
                              800-322-0956
                        FAX: 612-379-9143
          e-mail: customerservice@ablenetinc.com
                       www.ablenetinc.com

The TalkTrac Wearable Communicator is a personal, portable communication aid that is wearable on the wrist. TalkTrac features: simple to user, 75 seconds of recording time, four 3/4" x 1/2" message locations, rechageable, water resistant, adjustable 9" band, Boardmaker compatible

211 **Talking Calculators**

Assistive Device Network
2241 S Triangle X Lane
Tucson, AZ 85713   866-674-3549

              e-mail: info@assistivedevices.net
              http://assistivedevice.net/about.htm

212 **Talking Clocks**

HARC Mercantile, Ltd.
PO Box 3055
Kalamazoo, MI 49003   616-324-1615
                              800-445-9968
                        FAX: 616-324-2387
               e-mail: home@harcmercantile.com
                       www.harcmercantile.com

Ronald Slager, President

Talking clocks with loud alarms, high and low volume control, choices of sound effects, hourly report options. Other languages are available. *$20.50*

213 **Talking Watches**

HARC Mercantile, Ltd.
PO Box 3055
Kalamazoo, MI 49003   616-324-1615
                              800-445-9968
                        FAX: 616-324-2387
               e-mail: home@harcmercantile.com
                       www.harcmercantile.com

Ronald Slager, President

Digital display, hourly reports, alarm with rooster crow, in English or Spanish. *$20.25*

214 **Telecaption Adapter**

HARC Mercantile, Ltd.
PO Box 3055
Kalamazoo, MI 49003   616-324-1615
                              800-445-9968
                        FAX: 616-324-2387
               e-mail: home@harcmercantile.com
                       www.harcmercantile.com

Ronald Slager, President

Caption opens up the world of television to hearing impaired people. Viewers can read on the screen what they may not be able to hear. Closed captions are the dialogue and sound effects of a TV program or home video printed on the screen, similar to subtitles. *$ 159.95*

215 **Touch Turner-Page Turning Devices**

Touch Turner Company
13621 103rd Avenue NE
Arlington, WA 98223   360-651-1962

Turns pages in either direction powered by flashlight batteries and holds the reading at the proper angle for sitting or reclining.

216 **Ultratec - Auto Answer TTY**

Hear You Are
4 Musconetcong Avenue
Stanhope, NJ 07874

800-278-EARS
FAX: 973-347-7662

Full featured primitive TTY with auto answering features for business or emergency services. Has direct connect or acoustic coupling with turbo communications mode, equipped with auto ID and erelay Voice Announcer. Large memory buffer supports storing of conversation, memory message and directories. *$549.00*

217 **Unity/128**

Prentke Romich Company
1022 Heyl Road
Wooster, OH 44691

330-262-1984
800-262-1984
FAX: 330-263-4829
www.prentrom.com

A Minspeak application program available for the Liberator and Delta Talker communication devices. Provides single word vocabulary to people of all ages at varying stages of language development, who may be either cognitively intact or challenged. *$355.00*

218 **Vantage**

Prentke Romich Company
1022 Heyl Road
Wooster, OH 44691

330-262-1984
800-262-1984
FAX: 330-263-4829
www.prentrom.com

Vantage is a portable communication aid that features the Unity Enhanced vocabulary software and a large high quality dynamic display. Vantage also employs the recently upgraded 4.0 operating system that makes system settings quick and easy. Vantage has synthesized speech powered by DEC-talk Software, Spelling and Word Protection software, built-in visor (flip-up protective cover), digitized speech capability and built-in computer access and ECU controls. 15 and 45 location key-guards are also av *$6295.00*

219 **Vibrotactile Personal Alerting System**

HARC Mercantile, Ltd.
PO Box 3055
Kalamazoo, MI 49003

616-324-1615
800-445-9968
FAX: 616-324-2387
e-mail: home@harcmercantile.com
www.harcmercantile.com

Ronald Slager, President

Composed of a small wireless personal device that receives coded signals and a group of transmitters that send them. *$195.95*

220 **Viewstar**

Viewstar
15303 Ventura Boulevard
Sherman Oaks, CA 91403

818-382-4104

Leonard Weinstein, Technical Director

A stand-alone CCTV system for single view reading, writing and examining small objects. *$1545.00*

221 **Visual Voice: Audio Description Service**

15466 Los Gatos Boulevard
Suite 109-117
Los Gatos, CA 95032

FAX: 406-275-1850

222 **Voice Amplified Handsets**

HARC Mercantile, Ltd.
PO Box 3055
Kalamazoo, MI 49003

616-324-1615
800-445-9968
FAX: 616-324-2387
e-mail: home@harcmercantile.com
www.harcmercantile.com

Ronald Slager, President

Designed for the person who has a weak speaking voice. Control increases the level of the user's voice and can increase as much as 30%. *$65.00*

223 **WalkerTalker**

Prentke Romich Company
1022 Heyl Road
Wooster, OH 44691

330-262-1984
800-262-1984
FAX: 330-263-4829
www.prentrom.com

A portable direct selection communication device for active persons. The 16 location keyboard and speakers are carried in a belt that straps comfortably around the waist. The keyboard can be removed from its pouch to use by activating keys. Two versions are available, standard memory and expanded memory. *$1195.00*

224 **Whisper 2000**

DQP
14167 Meadow Drive
Grass Valley, CA 95945

800-456-4979
FAX: 530-477-7122

Personal sound amplification system that features a transmitter, phone and relay system for the hard-of-hearing.

Chairs

225 **Adjustable Amputee Stool**

McBuddy
PO Box 541
Whitehall, MT 59759

406-287-3265
800-421-5152

Offers strong durable support.

226   **Adjustable Chair**

Bailey Manufacturing Company
118 Lee Street
PO Box 130
Lodi, OH 44254   330-948-1080
     800-321-8372
FAX: 330-948-4439
e-mail: baileymfg@baileymfg.com
www.baileymfg.com

Adelle McClendon, Customer Service
Sandy Mooney, Customer Service
Judie Butler, Dealer Contact

The seat and footboard of this versatile chair can be adjusted to accommodate children of various sizes.

227   **Adjustable Classroom Chair**

Bailey Manufacturing Company
118 Lee Street
130
Lodi, OH 44254   330-948-1080
     800-321-8372
FAX: 330-948-4439
e-mail: baileymfg@attmail.com
www.baileymfg.com

This adjustable classroom chair with accessory tray has a seat and footboard that can be adjusted to fit children of various sizes.

228   **Adjustable Clear Acrylic Tray**

Bailey Manufacturing Company
118 Lee Street
130
Lodi, OH 44254   330-948-1080
     800-321-8372
FAX: 330-948-4439
e-mail: baileymfg@attmail.com
www.baileymfg.com

Adjusts for height and depth and is equipped with a spill rim for easy to clean edges.

229   **Adjustable Rigid Chair**

Kuschall of America
3601 Rider Trail South
Earth City, MO 63045   314-512-7000
     800-654-4768
FAX: 800-542-3567

The Champion 3000 is a fully adjustable rigid frame chair weighing only 21 pounds with a new clamping system that adjusts seat height and angle without tools.

230   **Adjustable Tee Stool**

Bailey Manufacturing Company
118 Lee Street
130
Lodi, OH 44254   330-948-1080
     800-321-8372
FAX: 330-948-4439
e-mail: baileymfg@attmail.com
www.baileymfg.com

May be used to encourage balance as well as develop integrative and perceptual motor skills.

231   **BackSaver Posture Chair**

BackSaver Products Company
53 Jeffrey Avenue
Holliston, MA 01746   508-429-5940
     800-251-2225
FAX: 508-429-8698
www.backsaver.com

Eliminates slouching and extra pressure on your back and thighs which impairs circulation.

232   **Better Back**

Orthopedic Products Corporation
4100 1/2 Glencoe Avenue
Marina Del Rey, CA 90292   323-584-6977
     FAX: 310-306-0177

An orthopedic multi-purpose seat.

233   **Convert-Able Table**

Rehab and Educational Aids for Living
187 South Main Street
Dolgeville, NY 13329
     800-696-7041
FAX: 315-429-3071

Kris Wohnsen, Sales

This table has push button height adjustment and interchangeable tops so it can become a desk, art easel or a sensory stim bowl.

234   **Evac + Chair Emergency Wheelchair**

Evac + Chair Corporation
PO Box 2396
New York, NY 10021   212-369-4094
     FAX: 212-369-3710
e-mail: sales@evac-chair.com
www.evac-chair.com

Robert McLean, Sales Manager

Gravity driven evaluation chair allows one non-disabled person to smoothly glide a seated passenger down fire stairs and across landings to exit on a combination of wheels and track belts. Pivots in own width for tight landing turns. Aluminum; weight 18 pounds. Compactly stores on wall mount, 38 by 20 by 9 inches. Maximum capacity 300 pounds. Self braking features. No installation, works on all fire exit stairs. *$950.00*

235   **Golden Technologies**

401 Bridge Street
Old Forge, PA 18518
     800-624-6374
FAX: 800-628-5165

236   **Grandstand Standing Frame**

Prime Engineering
4838 West Jacquelyn Avenue
Suite 105
Fresno, CA 93722   559-276-0991

Designed to ease the strain of those who stand for long periods of time.

237 High-Low Chair

Rehab and Educational Aids for Living
187 S Main Street
Dolgeville, NY 13329

800-696-7041
FAX: 315-429-3071

Kris Wohnsen, Sales

A high chair and mobile floor sitter in one. The high-low chair comes with colorful upholstered wipe clean seat and height adjustable tray. The chair has a single lever adjustment to change the seat height. Lateral and head supports are available as options. *$1199.00*

238 Hygea-Chair

TRIAID
PO Box 1364
Cumberland, MD 21501

800-306-6777
FAX: 301-759-3525

Iain A. MacDonald, Sales Director

Available in four sizes, the Hygea-Chair is an all purpose hygiene chair for children. It is supplied complete with a range of accessories fitted as standard to enhance the flexibility of the system: braked wheels, harness, footrest and seat insert comfort cover. It can be used in the shower, over the toilet or as a commode. *$950.00*

239 Ladybug Corner Chair

Rehab and Educational Aids for Living
187 South Main Street
Dolgeville, NY 13329

800-696-7041
FAX: 315-429-3071

For children 0-3 years. This chair is adjustable for long leg for conventional sitting.

240 Lumex Recliner

Lumex
100 Spence Street
Bay Shore, NY 11706

800-645-5272
FAX: 800-L4L-UMEX

Combines therapeutic benefits of position change with attractive appearance.

241 Mulholland Positioning Systems

215 North Main Street
PO Box 391
Santa Paula, CA 93061

800-543-4769
FAX: 805-933-1082
e-mail: webmaster@mulhollandinc.com
www.mulhollandinc.com

Provides a full line of standing aids, seating systems, adaptive components and bath aids.

242 Multi-Use Classroom Chair

Bailey Manufacturing Company
118 Lee Street
130
Lodi, OH 44254

330-948-1080
800-321-8372
FAX: 330-948-4439
e-mail: baileymfg@attmail.com
www.baileymfg.com

This classroom chair can be customized to meet the individual needs of any physically challenged child with the addition of easily attached accessories.

243 Quality Lift Chair

Mobilelectrics Company
4014 Bardstown Road
Louisville, KY 40218

800-876-6846
FAX: 502-495-2476

Come and go as you please, sit and stand when you want, without help from anyone.

244 Roll Chair

Bailey Manufacturing Company
118 Lee Street
130
Lodi, OH 44254

330-948-1080
800-321-8372
FAX: 330-948-4439
e-mail: baileymfg@attmail.com
www.baileymfg.com

The padded roll helps maintain proper hip abduction and prevents scissoring of the legs.

245 Safari Tilt

Convaid Products
PO Box 4209
Palos Verdes, CA 90274

310-534-3529
FAX: 310-539-3670
e-mail: convaid@west.net
www.convaid.com

A semi-contour seat provides positioning with 5-45 degree tilt adjustment. One step design folds compactly into a lightweight chair.

246 Spatial Tilt Custom Chair

Redman Powerchair
3840 S Palo Verde Road
Suite 201
Tucson, AZ 85714

800-727-6684

Custom chair designed for comfort with a solid seat and back with modifications available for seat depth, height or width.

247 Special Needs 5

Baby Jogger Company
PO Box 2189
Yakima, WA 98907

509-457-0925
800-241-1848
FAX: 509-453-7732
e-mail: janhille@babyjogger.com
www.babyjogger.com

Jan Hille, Special Needs Representative

BabyJogger strollers give passengers smooth rides on all terrains- even sand and snow. The light weight aluminum frame supports up to 150 pounds. Modifications available.

248 Transfer Bench with Back

Frohock-Stewart
39400 Taylor Parkway
N Ridgeville, OH 44035   440-329-6000

This bench with air-cushioned seat sections has a full, reversible backrest for safety and comfort.

Cushions & Wedges

249 ACU Massage Cushion

Massage Relaxation Products
PO Box 7243
Alhambra, CA 91802
                           800-999-1089

Hundreds of tiny massaging beads which help relieve lower back pain through massaging your own acupressure points.

250 Accu-Back/Better Body

615 West 33rd
Ada, OK 74820
                           800-432-2225
                      FAX: 580-310-0787
              e-mail: support@jobri.com
                         www.jobri.com

Tracie Clark, Office Manager
Jona Han, CEO

251 Action Products

22 N Mulberry Street
Hagerstown, MD 21740   301-797-1414
                              800-228-7763
                         FAX: 301-733-2073
        e-mail: service@actionproducts.com
                    www.actionproducts.com

Nancy Eddington, Customer Service Manager
Fred Nelson, Seating & Positioning Specialist
Michael Bredal, VP Sales - North America

Wheelchair pads, mattress pads, positioning cushions and insoles that aids in the prevention and cure of pressure sores by reducing pressure. All products are made of Akton viscoelastic polymer that doesnot leak, flow or bottom out. Manufacturer of the Xact line of positioning cushions for patients with high risk of skin breakdown.

252 Adjustable Wedge

Bailey Manufacturing Company
118 Lee Street
130
Lodi, OH 44254   330-948-1080
                        800-321-8372
                   FAX: 330-948-4439
       e-mail: baileymfg@attmail.com
                  www.baileymfg.com

Orthopedically and neurologically disabled children can freely move arms and hands while lying on this adjustable wedge.

253 Back Machine

Kingstar International America
PO Box 10157
Chicago, IL 50610
                           800-336-6550
                      FAX: 312-943-1727

Robin Morgenstern, President

A nine position adjustable lumbar support that is compact and lightweight, portable and able to fit most chairs, adaptable for different body sizes and will not lose its shape. The inner spring design will give the spinal column over-all support to compensate for stress, fatigue and improper posture.

254 Back-Huggar Pillow

Bodyline Combort Systems
3730 Kori Road
Jacksonville, FL 32257   904-262-4068
                                800-874-7715
                           FAX: 904-262-2225
               e-mail: info@bodyline.com
                        www.bodyline.com

Don Dodds, Office Manager

Exclusive design makes almost any seat more comfortable by exerting soothing pressure against back muscles and discs.

255 BetaBed Pressure Pad

Huntleigh Technology
227 Route 33
Manalapan, NJ 07726   732-446-2500
                             800-223-1218

Alternating pressure pad system automatically relieves tissue damaging pressure every 2 minutes.

256 Bye-Bye Decubiti (BBD)

Ken McRight Supplies
7456 South Oswego Avenue
Tulsa, OK 74136   918-492-9657
                    FAX: 918-492-9694

Ken McRight, President

The BBD therapeutic wheelchair cushions have been market-proven since 1951 — in the prevention and cure of pressure sores (decubiti). These natural rubber inflatable products have recently been expanded to include pediatric, sports and double-valve models. Moderately priced, they offer a viable and cost-effective alternative in the market. $84.00-$112.00

257 Dynamic Systems

235 Sunlight Drive
Leicester, NC 28748   828-683-3523
                        FAX: 828-683-3511
                  e-mail: dsi@cheta.net
                      www.cheta.net/dsi

Pamela Price, Office Manager
Ellie Brown, Operations Manager
Cathy Ramsey, Special Projects Manager

SunMate orthopedic foam sheets and cushions, pudgee pads for pressure relief and skin breakdown prevention, laminar wheelchair cushions and Foam-in-Place Seating for custom molding seat inserts. Sample packs and literature available upon request.

258 ENHANCER Cushion

ROHO Group
100 North Florida Avenue
Belleville, IL 62221

800-851-3449
FAX: 618-277-9561
e-mail: mail@therohogroup.com
www.rohoinc.com

Julie Repp, Marketing Assistant

Uses AIR IN PLACE progressive positioning for enhanced midline channeling of the femurs, lateral stability and tissue protection.

259 Econo-Float Water Flotation Cushion

Jefferson Industries
1940 Rutgers University Boulevard
Lakewood, NJ 08701

732-905-9001
800-257-5145
FAX: 732-905-9899

Charles Landa, General Manager

An inexpensive, yet effective approach to the problem of pressure ulcers for patients confined to wheelchairs, geriatric chairs, etc. *$15.00*

260 Econo-Float Water Flotation Mattress

Jefferson Industries
1940 Rutgers University Boulevard
Lakewood, NJ 08701

732-905-9001
800-257-5145
FAX: 732-905-9899

Charles Landa, General Manager

Helps prevent and treat pressure ulcers by reducing and distributing pressure over the patient's bony prominences while supporting the body evenly over a greater surface area. *$39.00*

261 Flex-Air Pressure Relief System

Relax-A-Flex
211 River Street
Bennington, VT 05201

802-447-1166
800-782-8889

Solves mattress problems.

262 Functional Forms

Consumer Care Products
PO Box 684
Sheboygan, WI 53082

920-459-8353
FAX: 920-459-9070

Terry Grall, President
Alice Maffongelli, Customer Service

These blocks, wedges, rolls, cervical pillows, head and leg supports and barrel rolls in resilient high density foam covered with durable antibacterial, antistatic, flame resistant, non-absorbent vinyl are used to attain individualized support for the most difficult positioning needs for children and adults. Unique sizes allow fitting for almost any person. Use during exercise, feeding, therapy, recreation and rest at home, school and health care facilities. Packages available.

263 GT Wheelchair Cushion

Relax-A-Flex
211 River Street
Bennington, VT 05201

802-447-1166
800-782-8889

The specially designed gel pads in this cushion help relieve pressure on the back.

264 Gaymar Industries

Gaymar Industries
10 Centre Drive
Orchard Park, NY 14127

716-662-2551
800-828-7341
FAX: 716-662-6120
e-mail: pmatteliano@gaymar.com
www.gaymar.com

Steve Snyder, Vice President of Marketing
Peggy Matteliano, Communications Specialist

Gaymar offers a complete line of support surfaces, including low-air-loss mattresses, specialty foam mattresses, turning mattresses, air overlays and fluid therapy beds. These products economically prevent and treat bedsores. Clinical and reimbursement professionals are available to answer any question related to bedsores (decubitus ulcers). Also offers a complete line of temperature control devices, The T-Pump delivers warm therapy to effectively difate vessels and increase blood flow.

265 Geo-Matt for High Risk Patients

Span-America Medical Systems
PO Box 5231
Greenville, SC 29606

Helps prevent pressure sores in high risk patients.

266 HIGH PROFILE Single Compartment Cushion

ROHO
100 North Florida Avenue
Belleville, IL 62221

800-850-7646
FAX: 618-277-6518
e-mail: rohoinc@rohoinc.com
www.rohoinc.com

Julie Petry, Corporate Marketing

With 4 inch cells, the HIGH PROFILE is the cushion of choice for individuals who suffer from ischemic ulcers (pressure sores) or who have a history of tissue breakdown.

267 Inflatable Back Pillow

Medic-Air Corporation
16 North Chatsworth Avenue
Larchmont, NY 10538

914-834-2727

Folds flat to fit into its own carrying case, this inflatable back pillow ensures comfort while at home or traveling.

268   **LOW PROFILE Single Compartment Cushion**
ROHO
100 North Florida Avenue
Belleville, IL   62221
800-850-7646
FAX: 618-277-6518
e-mail: rohinc@rohoinc.com
www.rohoinc.com

Julie Petry, Corporate Marketing
Offers 2 inch cells for active users protection against skin breakdown.

269   **Lumbo-Posture Back Support**
Ken McRight Supplies
7456 South Oswego Avenue
Tulsa, OK   74136
918-492-9657
FAX: 918-492-9694

Ken McRight, President
Rubber inflatable back support that offers therapeutic relief to all who must sit for lengthy periods of time, whether used in a wheelchair, auto or bed. *$97.65*

270   **Lumex's Cushions and Mattresses**
Lumex
100 Spence Street
Bay Shore, NY   11706
800-645-5272
FAX: 800-L4L-UMEX

Line of cushions and pillows give comfort and independence to the physically challenged.

271   **Medpro Static Air Chair Cushion**
Medpro
1950 Rutgers University Boulevard
Lakewood, NJ   08701
800-257-5145
FAX: 732-905-9899

Jody Gorran, President
Provides a protective layer of air beneath the patient helping prevent and treat pressure ulcers. *$94.95*

272   **Medpro Static Air Mattress Overlay**
Medpro
1950 Rutgers University Boulevard
Lakewood, NJ   08701
800-257-5145
FAX: 732-905-9899

Jody Gorran, President
Supports the patient on a cushioned network of air designed to redistribute the patient's weight reducing tissue interface pressure. Medpro's design incorporates a series of 65 air-breather vents that maintain air circulation. Medpro effectively reduces pressure and helps prevent and treat pressure ulcers. *$164.95*

273   **Mini-Max Cushion**
ROHO
100 North Florida Avenue
Belleville, IL   62221
800-850-7646
FAX: 618-277-6518
e-mail: rohoinc@rohoinc.com
www.rohoinc.com

Julie Petry, Corporate Marketing

Designed for the active individual with low risk of skin breakdown. The unique air cells of the MINMAX provide significant shock and impact absorption, skin protection and stability.

274   **NEXUS Wheelchair Cushioning System**
ROHO
100 North Florida Avenue
Belleville, IL   62221
800-850-7646
FAX: 618-277-6518
e-mail: rohoinc@rohoinc.com
www.rohoinc.com

Julie Petry, Corporate Marketing
A unique modular cushion that mates a contoured polyurethane foam base with a DRY FLOTATION support pad. It is designed to give the user positioning and stability, while offering maximum protection to the ischia, sacrum and coccyx.

275   **Nek-Lo, Nek-Lo Hot and Cold Pillow-Perfect, Body Buddy**
Rinz-L-O Pillow Company
340 West Maplehurst Street
Ferndale, MI   48220
248-548-3993
800-594-9093
FAX: 248-548-0447
e-mail: rinzlo@aol.com

G. Rick Rinz, President
Nek-Lo a U-shaped cervical pillow; Nek-Lo Hot and Cold - U-shaped pillow with hot/cold pack; PillowPerfect - Uses your conventional pillow to insert cover that has cervical support form piece. MagneAid and Magne-Systems - Magnetic therapy braces. *$12.98*

276   **Pediatric Seating System**
ROHO
100 North Florida Avenue
Belleville, IL   62221
800-850-7646
FAX: 618-277-6518
e-mail: rohoinc@rohoinc.com
www.rohoinc.com

Julie Petry, Corporate Marketing
ROHO Cushions for kids use individual air cells, creating the most versatile and dynamic cushioning products available. These cushions are designed to specifically fit pediatric wheelchairs.

277   **Posture Comfort Cushion Company**
Posture Comfort Cushion Company
5929 174th Street
Fresh Meadows, NY   11365

Made with different densities of foam which help correct posture, eliminate hammocking and will not bottom-out. This also has two patents. The Insert Kit and the Pouch, both of which alleviate or eliminate pressure on the sitting area of the body for people confined in a wheelchair. $150-$200.

278 QUADTRO Cushion

ROHO
100 North Florida Avenue
Belleville, IL   62221

800-850-7646
FAX: 618-277-6518
e-mail: rohonic@rohoinc.com

Julie Petry, Corporate Marketing

For individuals who require special positioning of the pelvis or thighs and are at risk of skin breakdown, the QUADTRO, with 4 inch cell height and AIR IN PLACE, progressive positioning is the cushion of choice.

279 Silicone Padding

Spenco Medical Group
PO Box 2501
Waco, TX   76702

254-772-6000
800-433-3334

For the management of pressure sores, this padding provides a special support system which allows even distribution of pressure and cool, comfortable well-ventilated support.

280 Soft-Touch Convertible Flotation Mattress

Medpro
1950 Rutgers University Boulevard
Lakewood, NJ   08701

800-257-5145
FAX: 732-905-9899

Jody Gorran, President

Gives the patient the option to choose between water and gel flotation depending on the needs of the patient. The mattress helps prevent and treat pressure ulcers by spreading the patient's weight over a greater surface area. $164.95-$239.95.

281 Soft-Touch Gel Flotation Cushion

Medpro
1940 Rutgers University Boulevard
Lakewood, NJ   08701

732-905-9001
800-257-5145
FAX: 732-905-9899

Jody Gorran, President

Acts like an additional layer of fatty tissue beneath the patient to help prevent and treat pressure sores. $99.95

282 Spenco Medical Group

PO Box 2501
Waco, TX   76702

254-772-6000
800-433-3334
e-mail: spenco@spenco.com
www.spenco.com

Mark B. Connors, V P Sales & Marketing
Patty Smith, Controller
Steven B. Smith, CEO

Wheel chair cushions, Silicore mattress pads, wound dressings, second skin blister and burn pads, Polysorb insoles, elbow, knee, wrist supports, walking shoes.

283 Stop-Leak Gel Flotation Cushion

Jefferson Industries
1940 Rutgers University Boulevard
Lakewood, NJ   08701

732-905-9001
800-257-5145
FAX: 732-905-9899

Charles Landa, General Manager

Helps protect against pressure ulcers by functioning as an extra protective layer of fat which helps reduce and distribute pressure. $18.00

284 Stop-Leak Gel Flotation Mattress

Jefferson Industries
1940 Rutgers University Boulevard
Lakewood, NJ   08701

732-905-9001
800-257-5145
FAX: 732-905-9899

Charles Landa, General Manager

Protects persons from messy leaks while it protects from pressure ulcers. $54.00

285 Sun-Mate Seat Cushions

Dynamic Systems
235 Sunlight Drive
Leicester, NC   28748

828-683-3523
FAX: 828-683-3511
e-mail: dsi@cheta.net
www.cheta.net/dsi

Pamela Price, Office Manager
Ellie Brown, Operations Manager
Susan Kent, Customer Service

Line of cushions, pads and accessory items for personal comfort of the disabled. SunMate Orthopedic foam cushions and sheets that contours slowly to give uniform pressure distribution and soft spring back. Liquid SunMate for Foam-in-Place Seating (FIPS) to make custom molded seat inserts. $6.50

286 Synthetic Sheep-Skin Pads

Hallmark Orthopedic Company
20 La Porte Street
Arcadia, CA   91006

626-447-0995

Made of 100% Kodel polyester pile fabric these synthetic, sheepskin pads are autoclavable, retain resilience and act as an aid to prevent bed sores.

287 Twin-Rest Seat Cushion & Glamour Pillow

Better Sleep
57 Industrial Road
Berkeley Heights, NJ   07922

908-464-2200
FAX: 908-464-0058

Makes any seat more comfortable because it is ingeniously designed to soothe sensitive areas while at work, in the car or at home.

Dressing Aids

288 Button Aid

Maxi Aids
42 Executive Boulevard
3209
Farmingdale, NY 11735   516-752-0521
800-522-6294
FAX: 516-752-0689
e-mail: sales@maxiaids.com
www.maxiaids.com

Makes buttoning possible with the use of only one hand. *$9.95*

289 Clothing Identification Kit

Sense-Sations
919 Walnut Street
Philadelphia, PA 19107   215-629-2990
800-846-5456

This kit contains labels and tells you what is on the hanger. *$7.75*

290 Deluxe Sock and Stocking Aid

Therapro
225 Arlington Street
Framingham, MA 01702   508-872-9494
800-257-5376
FAX: 508-875-2062
e-mail: info@theraproducts.com
www.theraproducts.com

Flexible plastic, lined with blue nylon to reduce friction and outside with beige terry cloth to hold sock firmly until it is on the foot. *$12.95*

291 Dressing Stick

Maxi Aids
42 Executive Boulevard
3209
Farmingdale, NY 11735   516-752-0521
800-522-6294
FAX: 516-752-0689
e-mail: sales@maxiaids.com
www.maxiaids.com

Helps put on coats, sweaters and garments even when arm and shoulder movement is limited. *$7.95*

292 Elastic Shoelaces

Therapro
225 Arlington Street
Framingham, MA 01702   508-872-9494
800-257-5376
FAX: 508-875-2062
e-mail: info@theraproducts.com
www.theraproducts.com

The elastic laces allow the wearer to slip tied shoes on and off. *$4.25*

293 Featherweight Reachers

Therapro
225 Arlington Street
Framingham, MA 01702   508-872-9494
FAX: 508-875-2062
e-mail: info@theraproducts.com
www.theraproducts.com

Useful in dressing or retrieving objects. *$17.95*

294 Folding Dressing Stick

Access with Ease
PO Box 1150
Chino Valley, AZ 86323   520-636-9469
800-531-9479
FAX: 520-636-0292
e-mail: KMJC@northlink.com

Helps the physically-challenged user put on shirts, coats and jackets easily. The dressing sticks are available 12 to 28 inches long. Folds for easy storage. *$16.95*

295 Heavy Duty Sock Tuckers

Sense-Sations
919 Walnut Street
Philadelphia, PA 19107   215-629-2990
800-876-5456

This device keeps socks and hosiery paired throughout the laundering cycles. *$1.50*

296 Mirror Go Lightly

AbleNet
1081 10th Avenue SE
Minneapolis, MN 55414
800-322-0956
FAX: 612-379-9143
e-mail: customerservice@ablenetinc.com
www.ablenetinc.com

Framed in plastic, the mirror can be tilted to provide either a normal or magnified image or to direct its lights at, or away from, the user. *$22.00*

297 Molded Sock and Stocking Aid

Therapro
225 Arlington Street
Framingham, MA 01702   508-872-9494
800-257-5376
FAX: 508-875-2062
e-mail: info@theraproducts.com
www.theraproducts.com

Sock or stocking is pulled over the molded plastic and then can be put on more easily. *$13.25*

298 Say What

Maxi Aids
42 Executive Boulevard
3209
Farmingdale, NY 11735   516-752-0521
800-522-6294
FAX: 516-752-0689
e-mail: sales@maxiaids.com
www.maxiaids.com

Braille the tag with information that the wearer wants on the tag and place the tag on a hanger. The custom-identification program makes it easier for the user to remember and identify just the right clothes. *$4.95*

Health Aids

299   AMI

PO Box 808
Groton, CT   06340   860-536-3735
                                   800-248-4031
                          FAX: 860-536-4362
                   e-mail: amiaqua@aol.com
                          www.amiaqua.com

David Cote, President

The Aqua PT's 36 computer controlled water jets provide the effects of accupressure massage on three sides of the body in either two directions (pain management) or one direction (edema reduction). Concentrate on the full body, one area or one specific problem point. The client remains clothed and dry. Aqua PT has adjustable water pressure and pulsating frequency and an automatic frequency and travel speed control. Aqua PT is easy to operate. $20,000-$40,000.

300   Absorbent Dressing Powder

Baxter Healthcare Corporation
1 Baxter Parkway
851
Deerfield, IL   60015   847-948-2000
                          FAX: 847-948-2964

Powder dressing for the treatment of pressure sores and other skin ulcers.

301   American Medical Industries

330 E 3rd Street
Suite 2
Dell Rapids, SD   57022   605-987-4363
                          FAX: 605-428-5502
                   e-mail: amiusa@sd.value.net
                          www.ezhealthcare.com

Dan Anderson, Vice President

EZ-Swallow, EZ-Health, EZ-Home Care, Kleen-Handz, Kleen-Scent, EZ-Irrigator, EZ-VU, Pureshark, Gobot and AMI are all trademarks of American Medical Industries. Healthcare and Healthcare products made easy.

302   Aud-A-Mometer

Maxi Aids
42 Executive Boulevard
3209
Farmingdale, NY   11735   516-752-0521
                                   800-522-6294
                          FAX: 516-752-0689
                   e-mail: sales@maxiaids.com
                          www.maxiaids.com

Audible clinical thermometer. *$199.95*

303   BIPAP S/T Ventilatory Support System

Respironics
1001 Murry Ridge Drive
Murrysville, PA   15668   724-733-0200

Respiratory medical products for use in the home, hospitals and in emergency care situations. The company was recently awarded the American Association for Respirator Care's annual Zenith Award for quality of products and service for the third time in the past four years.

304   Drew Karol Industries

PO Box 1066
Greenville, MS   38702   601-378-2188
                          FAX: 601-378-3188
                   e-mail: dki@techinfo.com

Andrew Hoszowski, President

Orally operated toothbrush and dental care system for persons with limited or complete loss of hand or arm use - wheelchair accessible. *$600.00*

305   Duro-Med Industries

155 Polifly Road
Number 688
Hackensack, NJ   07601
                                   800-526-4753
                          FAX: 800-427-0664

Donald L. Mann, President
Albert Schmier, Vice President

Manufacturers of a complete line of Home Health Care products. Featured products are patient gowns, back and seat cushions, pillows and a complete line of aids for daily living.

306   Easy Ply

BioMedical Life Systems
2448 Cades Wayve
Vista, CA   92083   760-727-5600

This disposable electrode has a cloth backing of a super-breathable medical tape that allows for comfort and a longer life.

307   Electronic Stethoscopes

HARC Mercantile, Ltd.
PO Box 3055
Kalamazoo, MI   49003   616-324-1615
                                   800-445-9968
                          FAX: 616-324-2387
                   e-mail: home@harcmercantile.com
                          www.harcmercantile.com

Ronald Slager, President

High production fidelity with a number volume control wheel. *$454.95*

308   Emergency Medical Identification with Free Fax

Merion Station Mail Order Company
PO Box 11
Jenkintown, PA   19046   800-333-8247
                                   800-333-TAGS

Linda R. Katz, President
Alex Katz, Secretary/Treasurer

Emergency medical identification tags, pendants and bracelets. *$24.95*

309   Healing Dressing for Pressure Sores

Baxter Healthcare Corporation
1 Baxter Parkway
851
Deerfield, IL   60015   847-948-2000
                                   800-423-2311

A dressing specifically designed to promote healing of pressure sores and other dermal ulcers.

310 **Invacare Corporation**
One Invacare Way
Elyria, OH 44035   440-329-6000
                                800-333-6900
                    FAX: 440-329-6568
                e-mail: selder@invacare.com
                        www.invacare.com

Susan Elder, Director of Marketing

The world's leading manufacturer and distributor of medical products which promote recovery and active lifestyles through more than 25,000 providers worldwide.

311 **MADAMIST 50/50 PSI Air Compressor**
Mada Medical Products
60 Commerce Road
Carlstadt, NJ 07072   201-460-0454

The new compressor rated at 50 PSI is designed to drive humidifiers, nebulizers, mist tents and ideal to administer pentamidine aerosol therapy.

312 **MedDev Corporation**
2468 Embercadero Way
Palo Alto, CA 94303   650-494-1153
                                800-543-2789
                    FAX: 650-494-1464
                e-mail: info@meddev-corp.com
                        www.meddev-corp.com

Suzanne Grey, Marketing/Sales Manager

Aids to rehabilitate hands following injury or illness, including patented complementary FingerHelper, ThumbHelper and Iso HandHelper models. Med Dev also manufactures Soft Touch foam exercisers and the FiddlLink exerciser for digital dexterity. New for 2000, the Ultimate Hand Helper, an Ergonomically designed hand excerciser curved to confirm to the shape of the hand.

313 **Medi-Grip**
Therapro
225 Arlington Street
Framingham, MA 01702   508-872-9494
                                800-257-5376
                    FAX: 508-875-2062
                e-mail: info@theraproducts.com
                        www.theraproducts.com

Reasonably priced, non-skid material. This non-slip material is available in Marine Blue, Desert Sand and Burgundy, rolls 12 inches x 144 inches. *$11.95*

314 **Pocket Otoscope**
HARC Mercantile, Ltd.
PO Box 3055
Kalamazoo, MI 49003   616-324-1615
                                800-445-9968
                    FAX: 616-324-2387
                e-mail: home@harcmercantile.com
                        www.harcmercantile.com

Ronald Slager, President

Simple, durable and dependable pocket otoscope uses standard replaceable parts. *$24.00*

315 **Talking Thermometers**
Maxi Aids
42 Executive Boulevard
3209
Farmingdale, NY 11735   516-752-0521
                                800-522-6294
                    FAX: 516-752-0689
                e-mail: sales@maxiaids.com
                        www.maxiaids.com

Clearly announces temperature in Fahrenheit or Celcius. *$17.95*

Hearing Aids

316 **Battery Device Adapter**
AbleNet
1081 10th Avenue SE
Minneapolis, MN 55414
                                800-322-0956
                    FAX: 612-379-9143
                e-mail: customerservice@ablenetinc.com
                        www.ablenetinc.com

Mary Kay Walch

A cable which connects to and adapts battery-operated devices for external switch control. Two sizes are available to adapt devices with either AA or C and D size batteries. *$8.00*

317 **Custom Earmolds**
Lloyd Hearing Aid Corporation
128 Kishwaukee Street
PO Box 1645
Rockford, IL 61104   815-964-4191
                                800-323-4212
                    FAX: 815-964-8378
                e-mail: hearingaids@inwave.com

Andrew Palmquist, President

Hearing aid molds, custom built to the exact fit of the customer. *$29.95*

318 **Digital Hearing Aids**
Lloyd Hearing Aid Corporation
128 Kishwaukee Street
Rockford, IL 61104   815-964-4191
                                800-323-4212
                    FAX: 815-964-8378
                e-mail: hearingaids@inwave.com

Latest hearing technology. Most makes- huge discounts. *$7.50*

319 **Discounts on Hearing Aids**
Lloyd Hearing Aid Corporation
128 Kishwaukee Street
PO Box 1645
Rockford, IL 61104   815-964-4191
                                800-323-4212
                    FAX: 815-964-8378
                e-mail: hearingaids@inwave.com

Andrew Palmquist, President

Hearing aids at discounts of up to 60%. Most makes and models with service to/from anywhere in the U.S. with a 30-day home trial. Start at $300.

320 Doorbell Signalers

HARC Mercantile
PO Box 3055
Kalamazoo, MI   49003   616-324-1615
                               800-445-9968
                          FAX: 616-324-2387
          e-mail: home@harcmercantile.com
                 www.harcmercantile.com

Ronald Slager, President

Doorbell signalers to alert with either louder chime or flashing light. *$29.99*

321 Double Gong Indoor/Outdoor Ringer

HARC Mercantile
PO Box 3055
Kalamazoo, MI   49003   616-324-1615
                               800-445-9968
                          FAX: 616-324-2387
          e-mail: home@harcmercantile.com
                 www.harcmercantile.com

Ronald Slager, President

Loud outdoor ringer that attaches to the wall for outside applications. *$50.00*

322 Duracell & Rayovac Hearing Aid Batteries

Lloyd Hearing Aid Corporation
128 Kishwaukee Street
Rockford, IL   61104   815-964-4191
                               800-323-4212
                          FAX: 815-964-8378
          e-mail: hearingaids@inwave.com

Andrew Palmquist, President

Batteries for hearing aids at discounted prices. As low as 70 cents each.

323 Hearing Aid Batteries

HARC Mercantile, Ltd.
PO Box 3055
Kalamazoo, MI   49003   616-324-1615
                               800-445-9968
                          FAX: 616-324-2387
          e-mail: home@harcmercantile.com
                 www.harcmercantile.com

Ronald Slager, President

Hearing aid batteries in all popular sizes in mercury, zinc air, silver as well as Nicad and Varta and batteries for electrolarynx and infrared systems. $3.95-$25.00.

324 Hearing Aid Battery Testers

HARC Mercantile, Ltd.
PO Box 3055
Kalamazoo, MI   49003   616-324-1615
                               800-445-9968
                          FAX: 616-324-2387
          e-mail: home@harcmercantile.com
                 www.harcmercantile.com

Ronald Slager, President

From pocket size to professional type battery testers which test mercury, zinc air, silver, specialty and general usage batteries. *$11.95*

325 Hearing Aid Dehumidifier

HARC Mercantile, Ltd.
PO Box 3055
Kalamazoo, MI   49003   616-324-1615
                               800-445-9968
                          FAX: 616-324-2387
          e-mail: home@harcmercantile.com
                 www.harcmercantile.com

Ronald Slager, President

Removes moisture from hearing aids and valuables. Contains desiccant pack and humidity guide, all in a rugged, vinyl case which provides protection and is water resistant. *$6.00*

326 In the Ear Hearing Aid Battery Extractor

HARC Mercantile, Ltd.
PO Box 3055
Kalamazoo, MI   49003   616-324-1615
                               800-445-9968
                          FAX: 616-324-2387
          e-mail: home@harcmercantile.com
                 www.harcmercantile.com

Ronald Slager, President

Ideal tool to use when battery is stuck in battery compartment in ITE and canal hearing aids. *$3.00*

327 Micro Audiometrics Corporation

655 Keller Road
Murphy, NC   28906   828-644-0771
                               800-729-9509
                          FAX: 828-644-0772
          e-mail: sales@microaud.com
                 www.microaud.com

Jason Keller, President
Lance Ralph, Marketing

Manufacturer and distributor of hearing testing instruments, including the complete line of Earscan.

328 Model E-90W Hearing Aid

Rhodes Hearing
PO Box 358
Brookport, IL   62910   618-564-2026

This hearing aid slips directly into the ear. *$327.00*

329 Model F-188T Hearing Aid

Rhodes Hearing
PO Box 358
Brookport, IL   62910   618-564-2026

Designed to fit behind your ear at the most natural hearing level for detecting both distance and sound direction. *$329.00*

330 Mushroom Inserts

Lloyd Hearing Aid Corporation
128 Kishwaukee Street
PO Box 1645
Rockford, IL   61104   815-964-4191
                               800-323-4212
                          FAX: 815-964-8378
          e-mail: hearingaids@inwave.com

A universal earplug useful in wearing behind the ear type hearing instruments. *$2.50*

331 Oval Window Audio

33 Wildflower Court
Nederland, CO 80466   303-447-3607
                             FAX: 303-447-3607
e-mail: info@ovalwindowaudio.com
www.ovalwindowaudio.com

Norman Lederman, Director of R & D
Paula Hendricks, Educational Director

Manufacturer of induction loop hearing assistance
technologies compatible with hearing aids already
used by many hard of hearing people. Also multisensory sound systems for use in speech and music therapy and science classes.

Kitchen & Eating Aids

332 AIDS for Daily Living

ETAC USA
2325 Parklawn Drive
Suite J
Waukesha, WI 53186
                             800-678-3822
                        FAX: 414-796-4605
e-mail: etac1usa@execpc.com
www.execpc.com/~etac1usa

TAC offers an entire line of products for people
that have reduced or limited use of their hands.
Cutlery goblets, knives, cutting board, fix preparation boards, plates, grooming aids, and a contoured pen are available. $12.00 - $75.00.

333 Alternate Stoneware

Alternate Stoneware
PO Box 2071
Charleston, WV 25327

Unique, stable and safe dinnerware that is a pleasant alternative to institutional type dinnerware
for physically impaired individuals.

334 Bagel Holder

Maxi Aids
42 Executive Boulevard
3209
Farmingdale, NY 11735   516-752-0521
                                800-522-6294
                           FAX: 516-752-0689
e-mail: sales@maxiaids.com
www.maxiaids.com

Holds bagels in place for easy slicing. *$3.95*

335 Big Bold Timer Low Vision

Maxi Aids
42 Executive Boulevard
3209
Farmingdale, NY 11735   516-752-0521
                                800-522-6294
                           FAX: 516-752-0689
e-mail: sales@maxiaids.com
www.maxiaids.com

Sixty-minute mechanical timer with large, easy-to-read numbers for the vision impaired. *$9.95*

336 Box Top Opener

Sammons Preston/AbilityOne Company
4 Sammons Court
Bolingbrook, IL 60440   630-226-1300
                                800-323-5547
                           FAX: 800-547-4333
e-mail: sp@sammonspreston.com
www.sammonspreston.com

This handy device exerts the pressure on those
hard-to-open boxes of laundry/dishwasher soap,
rice and prepared dinners. *$2.95*

337 Capscrew

Access with Ease
PO Box 1150
Chino Valley, AZ 86323   520-636-9469
                                 800-531-9479
                            FAX: 520-636-0292
e-mail: KMJC@northlink.com

Remove lids and caps easily. Can be mounted on
walls or cupboards. Non-slip surface grips small
and large jars. *$7.95*

338 Cool Handle

Maxi Aids
42 Executive Boulevard
3209
Farmingdale, NY 11735   516-752-0521
                                800-522-6294
                           FAX: 516-752-0689
e-mail: sales@maxiaids.com
www.maxiaids.com

A specially designed, heat-resistant handle, available in three sizes which can be affixed to the
handles of most fry, sauce and saute pans. *$7.95*

339 Cordless Receiver

AbleNet
1081 10th Avenue SE
Minneapolis, MN 55414
                             800-322-0956
                        FAX: 612-379-9143
e-mail: customerservice@ablenetinc.com
www.ablenetinc.com

The Cordless Receiver in conjunction with the
Cordless Big Red Switch, can be used anywhere a
switch is currently used to control battery- or electrically - operated toys, games or appliances; augmentative communication systems; computers
(through a computer switch interface). *$79.00*

340 Deluxe Long Ring Low Vision Timer

Maxi Aids
42 Executive Boulevard
3209
Farmingdale, NY 11735   516-752-0521
                           FAX: 516-752-0689
e-mail: sales@maxiaids.com
www.maxiaids.com

Bold black numerals on white background allows
for easy reading at any distance. *$17.95*

341 Deluxe Roller Knife

Sammons Preston/AbilityOne Company
4 Sammons Court
Bolingbrook, IL   60440   630-226-1300
                                 800-323-5547
                          FAX: 800-547-4333
              e-mail: sp@sammonspreston.com
                     www.sammonspreston.com

Stainless steel blade rolls smoothly, cutting food
cleanly. *$10.95*

342 Dual Brush with Suction Base

Sammons Preston/AbilityOne Company
4 Sammons Court
Bolingbrook, IL   60440   630-226-1300
                                 800-323-5547
                          FAX: 800-547-4333
              e-mail: sp@sammonspreston.com
                     www.sammonspreston.com

Two brushes clean the inside and outside of bottles
and glasses at the same time using just one hand.
$14.50

343 Easy Pour Locking Lid Pot

Maxi Aids
42 Executive Boulevard
3209
Farmingdale, NY   11735   516-752-0521
                                 800-522-6294
                          FAX: 516-752-0689
                 e-mail: sales@maxiaids.com
                        www.maxiaids.com

Baked enamel and dishwasher safe, the pot comes
with an easy lid that locks in place for extra safety.
$24.95

344 Electric Can Opener & Knife Sharpener

Maxi Aids
42 Executive Boulevard
3209
Farmingdale, NY   11735   516-752-0521
                                 800-522-6294
                          FAX: 516-752-0689
                 e-mail: sales@maxiaids.com
                        www.maxiaids.com

Features include a powerful magnet lid holder, the
ability to open odd-shaped cans, and easy operation for the physically challenged. *$19.95*

345 Evio Plastics

310 Industrial Parkway
PO Box 2295
Sandysky, OH   44870   419-621-1105
                       FAX: 419-626-2183

Doug Didion, Admininstrator Director

Handi Holder is a plastic holder for 1/2 gallon paper
cartons of milk or juice. It is used to pour milk or juice
without spills by using the handle.

346 Food Markers/Rubberbands

Maxi Aids
42 Executive Boulevard
3209
Farmingdale, NY   11735
                                 800-522-6294
                          FAX: 516-752-0689
                 e-mail: sales@maxiaids.com
                        www.maxiaids.com

These are durable plastic markers, easily identified by touch, texture, shape and form which help
the visually impaired orient themselves to food
location on the plate. *$11.95*

347 Funnel

Sense-Sations
919 Walnut Street
Philadelphia, PA   19107   215-629-2990
                                  800-876-5456

Wide mouth funnel aids in pouring liquids or dry
goods from container to container. *$1.25*

348 Good Grips Cutlery

Therapro
225 Arlington Street
Framingham, MA   01702   508-872-9494
                                800-257-5376
                         FAX: 508-875-2062
              e-mail: info@theraproducts.com
                     www.theraproducts.com

Stainless steel utensils have a special twist built
into the metal to facilitate bending of a spoon or
fork at any angle for right or left handed people.
$7.50

349 Granberg Superior

1221 State Street
Suite 24
Santa Barbara, CA   93101   805-564-0850
                            FAX: 805-564-1340

Height adjustable cabinets for easy reach to food
and other necessities.

350 Guide A Knife

Maxi Aids
42 Executive Boulevard
3209
Farmingdale, NY   11735   516-752-0521
                                 800-522-6294
                          FAX: 516-752-0689
                 e-mail: sales@maxiaids.com
                        www.maxiaids.com

Adjustable food slicing system guides the knife for
even, uniform slices while protecting the user.
$11.95

351 Handy Caddy Basket

New Abilities Chapman Trimmers Company
PO Box 208
Excelsior, MN   55331

A unique, lightweight, utility basket designed for
the physically challenged individual who desires
more convenience and independence. *$119.00*

352 Handy-Helper Cutting Board

Maxi Aids
42 Executive Boulevard
3209
Farmingdale, NY 11735   516-752-0521
                              800-522-6294
                         FAX: 516-752-0689
              e-mail: sales@maxiaids.com
                       www.maxiaids.com

Laminated cutting board with unique features to hold food in place with corner ledge for cutting and spreading. *$19.95*

353 Innerlip Plates

Therapro
225 Arlington Street
Framingham, MA 01702   508-872-9494
                              800-257-5376
                         FAX: 508-875-2062
           e-mail: info@theraproducts.com
                    www.theraproducts.com

Food maybe pushed to the side of the plate, then scooped up with a fork and spoon. Available in beige or blue. *$5.00*

354 Jordan's Motility Solutions Adapt-Able Utensils

PO Box 132772
Tyler, TX 75713   903-526-2100
                         FAX: 903-526-2103
       e-mail: info@disabilityaccessories.com
               www.disabilityaccessories.com

Gene Howland, President

Adapt-Able eating utensils encourage independent eating for individuals with limited mobility. Angle and reach of utensils can be adjusted to reach specific needs.

355 Long Oven Mitts

Sammons Preston/AbilityOne Company
4 Sammons Court
Bolingbrook, IL 60440   630-226-1300
                              800-323-5547
                         FAX: 800-547-4333
          e-mail: sp@sammonspreston.com
                  www.sammonspreston.com

Protect hands and forearms from heat, flames and oven grates with these practical mitts that allow a longer reach and less bending. *$8.95*

356 Magnetic Card Reader

Maxi Aids
42 Executive Boulevard
3209
Farmingdale, NY 11735
                              800-522-6294
                         FAX: 516-752-0689
              e-mail: sales@maxiaids.com
                       www.maxiaids.com

Produces audible labels so a recorded card could be taped on cans of food or a box of cake mix; even adding instructions for baking. *$159.95*

357 Make-and-Shake Ice Tray

Sense-Sations
919 Walnut Street
Philadelphia, PA 19107   215-629-2990
                              800-876-5456

A covered ice tray that can be filled with water and then safely transported to the freezer without spilling. *$2.00*

358 Maxi Aid Braille Timer

Maxi Aids
42 Executive Boulevard
3209
Farmingdale, NY 11735   516-752-0521
                              800-522-6294
                         FAX: 516-752-0689
              e-mail: sales@maxiaids.com
                       www.maxiaids.com

Three raised dots at 15, 30 and 45, two raised dots at remaining five minute intervals and one raised dot at remaining two and a half minute intervals, offers ease of operation to make this a helpful aid for the visually impaired. *$12.95*

359 Nosey Cup

Therapro
225 Arlington Street
Framingham, MA 01702   508-872-9494
                              800-257-5376
                         FAX: 508-875-2062
           e-mail: info@theraproducts.com
                    www.theraproducts.com

For those with a stiff neck or persons who can't tip their head back while drinking. *$6.00*

360 Paring Boards

Therapro
225 Arlington Street
Framingham, MA 01702   508-872-9494
                              800-257-5376
                         FAX: 508-875-2062
           e-mail: info@theraproducts.com
                    www.theraproducts.com

Suction feet stabilize board and stainless steel prongs hold food in place for easy one-handed cutting. *$32.50*

361 PowerLink 2 Control Unit

AbleNet
1081 10th Avenue SE
Minneapolis, MN 55414
                              800-322-0956
                         FAX: 612-379-9143
         e-mail: customerservice@ablenetinc.com
                       www.ablenetinc.com

The PowerLink 2 Control Unit allows switch operation of electrical appliances. It can be used to activate 1 or 2 appliances (up to 1700 watts combined). If 2 appliances are used, they will activate simultaneously. There are four modes of control on the PowerLink 2; direct mode, timed (seconds) mode, timed (minutes) mode and latch mode. Meets safety standards from Underwriters Laboratory (UL) and Canadian Standards Association (CSA) for electrical appliances. *$159.00*

362 **Sammons Preston**
AbilityOne Company
4 Sammons Court
Bolingbrook, IL   60440   630-226-1300
                                                   800-323-5547
                               FAX: 800-547-4333
               e-mail: sp@sammonspreston.com
                   www.sammonspreston.com

Sammons Preston is a leading provider of rehabilitation and assistive devices to help those with disabilities meet daily physical challenges and achieve their greatest level of independence. With one of the industry's largest catalogs, Sammons Preston offers a wide range of products available.

Annualy

363 **Slicing Aid**
Snugseat
PO Box 1739
Matthews, NC   28106   704-882-0668
                                                   800-336-7684
                               FAX: 704-882-0751
                       e-mail: sales@snugseat.com
                           www.sungseat.com

Earlene Hucks, Marketing Coordinator

The design of these knives allows a better working posture and makes optimal use of strength in the arms and hands.

364 **Small Appliance Receiver**
AbleNet
1081 10th Avenue SE
Minneapolis, MN   55414
                                                   800-322-0956
                               FAX: 612-379-9143
           e-mail: customerservice@ablenetinc.com
                       www.ablenetinc.com

The Small Appliance Receiver, in conjunction with the Cordless Big Red Switch, allows you to control small electrical appliances in the environment without a cord. It should only be used with low-wattage appliances (under 500 watts) which have two prong plugs (ie, radios, fans, lamps, blenders, etc.). It should not be used with heat generating appliances. *$32.00*

365 **Steel Food Guard**
Maxi Aids
42 Executive Boulevard
 # 3209
Farmingdale, NY   11735   516-752-0521
                                                   800-522-6294
                               FAX: 516-752-0689
                       e-mail: sales@maxiaids.com
                           www.maxiaids.com

Provides stable area to push against while eating. *$ 10.95*

366 **Thick-n-Easy**
Therapro
225 Arlington Street
Framingham, MA 01702   508-872-9494
                                                   800-257-5376
                               FAX: 508-875-2062
               e-mail:info@theraproducts.com
                   www.theraproducts.com

Instant food thickener that sets in 30 seconds and will not become thicker even after refrigeration. *$6.50*

367 **Thumbs Up Cup**
Therapro
225 Arlington Street
Framingham, MA   01702   508-872-9494
                                                   800-257-5376
                               FAX: 508-875-2062
               e-mail: info@theraproducts.com
                   www.theraproducts.com

This cup is designed for those with limited strength or coordination or arthritis. The two backward-tilt handles and thumb rests allow finger joint to be used to their greatest mechanical advantage. *$9.50*

368 **UN-SKRU**
Multi-Marketing & Manufacturers
PO Box 1070
Littleton, CO   80160
                                                   800-506-0248
                       e-mail: penlane@xpert.net
                                   www.xpert.net

Janet Lane, President

This jar and bottle opener mounts permanently to the underside of a cabinet, shelf, table or counter so it is out of sight yet always ready to use. Opens all sizes of jar lids — easily and with little strength. *$7.95*

369 **Undercounter Lid Opener**
Sammons Preston/AbilityOne Company
4 Sammons Court
Bolingbrook, IL   60440   630-226-1300
                                                   800-323-5547
                               FAX: 800-547-4333
               e-mail: sp@sammonspreston.com
                   www.sammonspreston.com

The gripper of this unit which installs under the counter can help unscrew any cap. *$5.75*

370 **Uni-Turner**
Sammons Preston/AbilityOne Company
4 Sammons Court
Bolingbrook, IL   60440   630-226-1300
                                                   800-323-5547
                               FAX: 800-547-4333
               e-mail: sp@sammonspreston.com
                   www.sammonspreston.com

Odd-shaped handles can be turned easily with one-handed L-shaped Uni-Turner. *$16.50*

371 **Universal Hand Cuff**

Therapro
225 Arlington Street
Framingham, MA 01702   508-872-9494
                              800-257-5376
                      FAX: 508-875-2062
             e-mail: info@theraproducts.com
                  www.theraproducts.com

Comfortable cuff with Velcro strap holds utensils, toothbrushes, etc. *$9.95*

Lifts, Ramps & Elevators

372 **Accessibility Lift**

Inclinator Company of America
2200 Paxton Street
1557
Harrisburg, PA 17111   717-234-8065
                              800-343-9007
                      FAX: 717-234-0941
             e-mail: sales@inclinator.com
                  www.inclinator.com

Dotty Keith, Sales Manager

An economical lift for restricted usage that provides barrier-free access that can be used by churches, schools, lodging halls and meeting halls to meet compliance requirements, with the dignified convenience and freedom they deserve.

373 **Adjustable Base Lifter**

Ted Hoyer and Company
PO Box 2744
Oshkosh, WI 54903

Designed to safely and comfortably transfer someone from bed to wheelchair, car or commode, this lifter has a new release knob to gently lower the patient.

374 **Adjustable Incline Board**

Bailey Manufacturing Company
118 Lee Street
130
Lodi, OH 44254   330-948-1080
                        800-321-8372
                FAX: 330-948-4439
       e-mail: baileymfg@attmail.com
            www.baileymfg.com

Incline board for the physically challenged with a foot board with non-slip tread.

375 **AlumiRamp**

855 East Chicago Street
Quincy, MI 49082   517-639-8777
                          800-800-3864
                  FAX: 517-639-4314
         e-mail: ramps@alumiramp.com
              www.alumiramp.com

Linda Burke, President
Dave Jacobs, General Manager
Pam Kelley, Customer Service

Complete line of modular and portable ramps for both home and vehicle use. Welded construction and non-skid extended surfaces are featured on all our ramps.

376 **Area Access**

8117 Ransell Road
Falls Church, VA 22042   703-573-2111
                                800-333-2732
                        FAX: 703-207-0446
                        www.areaaccess.com

Cliff Wenn, Sales Manager
Dave Forman, Mobility Consultant
Danielle Dougherty, Sales Assistant

Serving the entire Mid-Atlantic with scooters, stairway lifts and elevators. Large inventory and fully stocked showrooms.

377 **Barrier Free Lifts**

9230 Prince William Street
Manassas, VA 20110   703-361-6531
                            800-582-8732
                    FAX: 703-361-7861
                    www.bflift.com

Deborah Hensley, V.P., Operations
Teresa Kirk, Administrative Asst.

Barrier Free ceiling and floor model lift systems are available in many models. Ceiling lifts can be portable, fully motorized and state-of-the-art to provide truly barrier-free equipment for lifting and transferring patients. Floor models include the premier LEXA with motorized spreader bar for patient positioning and the RAISA with motorized, adjustable knee pads for standing patients up and gait training. Ceiling lifts available with AIR TUBE controls for safe use around water.

378 **Bruno Independent Living Aids**

Bruno Independent Living Aids
1780 Executive Drive
PO Box 84
Oconomowoc, WI 53066   414-567-4990
                              800-882-8183
                      FAX: 414-567-4341
             e-mail: webmaster@bruno.com
                  www.bruno.com

Patrick Foy, National Sales Manager
Karla Branham Shaw, Marketing

An ISO 9001 Certified Manufacturer of automotive lifts for scooter, wheelchairs, and powerchairs, three and four wheel scooters, and straight and custom curve stairlifts.

379 **Butlers Wheelchair Lifts**

Flinchbaugh Company
390 Eberts Lane
York, PA 17403   717-848-2418
                        800-326-2418
                FAX: 717-843-7385

This wheelchair lift can be equipped with an end ramp and guard. Automatically retractable, it locks firmly into place when the lift is in operation.

380 **Cheney's Liberty II**

Handi-Lift
1051 Paulison Avenue
Clifton, NJ 07011   845-429-0368
                          800-503-2003
                  FAX: 914-947-4522

Economical lift for straight stairways.

381 Classique

Handi-Lift
1051 Paulison Avenue
Clifton, NJ 07011   845-429-0368
                          800-503-2003
                     FAX: 914-947-4522

The Classique elevator answers access problems in churches, schools and small offices.

382 Columbus McKinnon Corporation

140 John James Audubon Parkway
Amherst, NY 14228   716-639-4224
                          800-888-0985
                     FAX: 716-696-3220

Larry Smith, Manager

Columbus McKinnon supplies various lift and transfer systems for independent or attended applications including ceiling mounted or freestanding overhead track lifts and mobile floorbase units for homes, schools and healthcare facilities. Lift Systems for transferring between bed, chair, commode or bath are available with a variety of slings, scales and accessories.

383 Cub, SuperCub and Special Edition Scooters

Bruno Independent Living Aids
1780 Executive Drive
PO Box 84
Oconomowoc, WI 53066   414-567-4990
                          800-882-8183
                     FAX: 414-953-5501
      e-mail: webmaster@bruno.com
              www.bruno.com

Patrick Foy, National Sales Manager
Karla Branham Shaw, Marketing

Bruno Independent Living Aids, Inc. has over 12 different scooter models. Bruno Cub and SuperCub scooters, has front-or-rear wheel drive, in both 3-and-4 wheel versions and comes in four different colors plus a pediatric version. Each scooter can handle up to 300 pounds. Bruno Special Edition scooters resemble a fire engine, police car, Humvee and motorcycle. $2,000-$5,000

384 Custom Lift Residential Elevators

Waupaca Elevator Company
1050 South Grider Street
Appleton, WI 54914   920-991-9082
                          800-238-8739
                     FAX: 920-991-9087
      e-mail: upndown@famuid.com
           www.waupacaelevator.com

Custom-Lift home elevator is easy to install and delivers a smooth, quiet, safe ride.

385 Deluxe Convertible Exercise Staircase

Sammons Preston
PO Box 5071
Bowling Brook, IL 60440
                          800-631-7277
                     FAX: 800-547-4333
      e-mail: sp@sammonspreston.com

Here's an exercise staircase to fit any department configuration. Just reposition a few nuts and bolts to change from a straight to a corner type staircase.

386 Easy Pivot Transfer Machine

Rand-Scot
401 Linden Center Drive
Fort Collins, CO 80524
                          800-467-7967
                     FAX: 970-467-7967
      e-mail: randscot@webaccess.net
              www.easypivot.com

The Easy Pivot Patient Lifting System allows for strain-free, one-caregiver transfers of the disabled individual.

387 Easy Stand

Altimate Medical
PO Box 180
Morton, MN 56270   507-697-6393
                          800-342-8969
                     FAX: 507-637-3024

Designed to make standing fast and simple. The easy to operate hydraulic lift system provides a controlled lifting and lowering. With the convenience of simply transferring to the chair and reaching a standing position in seconds with no straps to hassle with.

388 EcoTrack Traction Tiles & Modular Accessible Path System

Bike Track
Box 235
Woodstock, VT 05091
                          888-663-8537
                     FAX: 802-457-3704
      e-mail: info@biketrack.com
              www.biketrack.com

Carol Weingeist, Director
Nancy Hoblin, Office Manager

EcoTrack tiles improve the surface quality of access ramps, steps, docks, gangways and boardwalks, protecting the surfaces and improving traction. EcoTrack structural panels are used to construct modular ramps and accessible paths. GSA Federal Supply Service listed.

389 Econol Elevator Lift Corporation

2513 Center Street
854
Cedar Falls, IA 50613
                          800-328-2560
                     FAX: 319-277-4778

Sharon R. Martin, President
Adrian L. Martin, Sales

Offers a full line of lifts, dumbwaiters, stair riders and elevators for persons with disabilities.

390 Econol Stairway Chair Ride

Econol Stairway Lift Corporation
2513 Center Street
Cedar Falls, IA 50613

This chair ride unit is of sturdy steel construction and rides sideways, not backwards.

391   Economical Liberty

Handi-Lift
1051 Paulison Avenue
Clifton, NJ 07011   845-429-0368
                                      800-503-2003
                              FAX: 914-947-4522

Installs quickly and easily on most straight stairways. It uses regular household current and mounts over the carpet or directly to the stairs without marring.

392   Electronic Scale Attachment

Ted Hoyer and Company
PO Box 2744
Oshkosh, WI 54903

Designed for use with all patient lifters, the digital electronic scale attachment can provide precise digital weight readouts up to 400 pounds or 182 kilograms.

393   Excel Stairway Lift

Access Industries
4001 East 138th Street
Grandview, MO 64030   816-763-3100
                                  800-925-3100
                              FAX: 816-763-4467
              e-mail: marketing@accessind.com
                           www.accessind.com

Evelyn Johnson, Marketing Supervisor
Installs easily on either side of a straight stairway for independent, step-free living. The lift fastens securely to the stairs without marring walls and is adjustable to match any stairway slope with an incline angle up to 45 degrees. Available with battery back up.

394   Freedom Wheelchair Lifts

1084 Katy Road
Keller, TX 76248   817-431-9437
                                  800-870-0629
                              FAX: 817-431-2292
                     e-mail: fwl@airmail.net
                           www.vansrus.com

Sandy Patterson
Complete vehicle modifications for the physically challenged.

395   Golden-Glide Stairway Lift

Access Industries
4001 East 138th Street
Grandview, MO 64030
                                  800-925-3100
                              FAX: 816-763-4467

Evelyn Johnson, Marketing Supervisor
Model 95 monorail track design can be custom-made to fit virtually any stairway. The unit can carry a side rider around stairway curves and corners with 90 to 180 degree turns and one or more landings. The lift can carry a maximum of 300 pounds up to 6 feet on its roomy 17-1/2 inch seat. Call and send controls are available at top or bottom landings. A four point safety sensor is a standard security feature.

396   Handi Home Lift

Handi-Lift
1051 Paulison Avenue
Clifton, NJ 07011   845-429-0368
                                      800-503-2003
                              FAX: 914-947-4522

An outdoor lift designed to provide access over porch stairs or other steps that impede movement.

397   Handi Prolift

Handi-Lift
1051 Paulison Avenue
Clifton, NJ 07011   845-429-0368
                                      800-503-2003
                              FAX: 914-947-4522

Provides dependable vertical transportation for multi-level buildings.

398   Handi-Ramp

Handi-Ramp
1414 Armour Boulevard
Mundelein, IL 60060   847-816-7525
                                      800-876-7267
                              FAX: 847-816-7689
              e-mail: deickhoff@handiramp.com
                           www.handiramp.com

Thom Disch, CEO
Doug Eickhoff, Production Manager
T.J. Brown, Sales Manager

Provides a complete line of economical, ADA Compliant access ramping products. Line includes Van attachable and Wheelchair Tie Dows; Aluminum or Expanded Meal Folding Portables; aluminum channels; Portable, Sectional Ramp Systems; Semi-Permanent Ramps, Platforms and Systems. All ramp series are available in varied lengths and widths in combination with platforms and optional hand railing, single or double bar construction with return ends. Special Order ramps and ramp systems. $575 and up.

399   Homecare Products EZ-Access Portable Ramps

15824 SE 296th Street
Kent, WA 98042
                                      800-451-1903
                              FAX: 800-630-2350
          e-mail: ezaccess@homecareproducts.com
                        www.homecareproducts.com

Don Everard, VP Marketing
Deanne Sandvold, VP Sales

EZ-ACCESS Ramps bridge gaps over curbs and steps, allowing scooters and wheelchairs to continue on a smooth, safe course. Available in several different styles and sizes, ranging from a two-foot curb ramp to a 10-foot multi-purpose ramp. All ramps are made of anodized aluminum.

400 Homewaiter

Inclinator Company of America
2200 Paxton Street
1557
Harrisburg, PA 17111   717-234-8065
                        FAX: 717-234-0941

With its roller truck riding in a specially formed monorail, it is easy to install and highly adaptable to existing conditions. It can travel up to 35 feet, opening on any or all three sides at different stations, whether at counter level or floor level.

401 Inclinette

Inclinator Company of America
2200 Paxton Street
1557
Harrisburg, PA 17111   717-234-8065
                        FAX: 717-234-0941

Inclinette provides comfort and convenience in providing multi-floor access to persons who have difficulty climbing stairs.

402 Independent Transport System

ITEC
5482 Business Drive
C
Huntington Beach, CA 92649
                        800-662-ITEC

Dressing, bathing, rising from bed and transferring to a wheelchair can be accomplished without any assistance.

403 Kartop Lift 1 & 2

Ted Hoyer and Company
2222 Minnesota Street
2744
Oshkosh, WI 54901

The Kartop Lift for wheelchairs attaches securely to the top of the car roof without drilling any holes, making traveling easy and enjoyable. *$1249.00*

404 LIFESTAND

Independence Providers
PO Box 232171
Encinitas, CA 92023
                        800-782-6324
                   FAX: 610-586-0847
              e-mail: Dallery@msn.com
                   www.lifestandusa.com

Jacques A. Dallery, President
Lifestand offers a full line of standing wheelchairs for manual, power assisted are fully motorized. *$7000.00*

405 Lectra-Lift

La-Z-Boy
1284 North Telegraph Road
Monroe, MI 48162

This power recliner has a single motor drive that operates three distinct cycles: lifting, leg elevation and full power recline.

406 Liberty LT

Handi-Lift
1051 Paulison Avenue
Clifton, NJ 07011   845-429-0368
                        800-503-2003
                   FAX: 914-947-4522

Stair lift with dual armrests that lock into position. The comfortable, contoured seat is designed to swivel and move forward at the bottom or top landings to facilitate transfer.

407 Lift-Aid Patient Lifts

Guardian Products
12800 Wentworth Street
C-4255
Arleta, CA 91331
                   FAX: 818-504-2833

Constructed of heavy tubular steel with welded joints and a curved lifting arm. Easily lifts patient from floor or into auto with minimum action.

408 LiftUp

Richard C. Peterson, P.E.
15 Highland Road
Eastham, MA 02642

Richard C Peterson, Prop

Plans for electric transfer device, especially suitable for bathroom use, lifts user erect with unique upper-body sling. Developed by an engineer to help cope with his multiple sclerosis quadriplegia, there are many now in use. Low-cost and simple make-it-yourself. *$19.00*

409 Lifts for Swimming Pools and Spas

Aquatic Access
417 Dorsey Way
Louisville, KY 40223   502-425-5817
                        800-325-5438
                   FAX: 502-425-9607
          e-mail: info@aquatic-access.com
                   www.aquatic-access.com

A variety of pool lifts transfer a person to/from inground and above ground swimming pools. Spa Lift Model SLE36 or SLE48 lift a person from a seated position up and over a spa wall and down into the water. Independent or assisted use, depending on capabilities. All lifts powered by water pressure from a garden hose. Mounts to deck or floor and lifts up to three-hundred pounds. *$2310.00*

410 Lizzie Lift

Handicap Helpers
604 West Main Street
Appalachia, VA 24216   540-565-1889
                   FAX: 540-565-3623
          e-mail: MEBLEVJ@ME.CC.VA.US
                   www.banda.mounet.com/LizzieLift

James W. Blevins, President

A stable patient lift that provides independence for the disabled by allowing one caregiver to move them from bed to upright position more easily and effectively. The Lizzie Lift which can be used as a gurney bed, lounge chair or wheelchair, not only decreases back injury for caregivers but also alleviates the fear of being moved. Can be used in hospitals, nursing homes, and homes. FDA listing, Patent pending. $7,000-$8,000.

411   Mecalift Sling Lifter

Arjo
8130 Lehigh Avenue
Morton Grove, IL   60053   847-967-0360

Marianne McGinn, Marketing Manager

Takes all the effort out of lifting while protecting the caregiver from the risk of backstrain.

412   Minivator Residential Elevator

Access Industries
4001 East 138th Street
Grandview, MO   64030   816-763-3100
                                   800-925-3100
                         FAX: 816-763-4467

Evelyn Johnson, Marketing Supervisor

The perfect choice for a person who is contemplating moving from their multi-storied home because they cannot get up and down the stairs. The low cost, compact Minivator elevator can help these people live independently. The Minivator can be installed in the corner of a room without a shaft or hoistway, so the elevator doesn't have to disfigure the structure. The Minivator elevator can take a person or persons between floors in less than a minute and can accommodate a standard size wheelchair.

413   One for All Lift All

Amigo Mobility International
6693 Dixie Highway
Bridgeport, MI   48722   517-777-0910
                                   800-248-9130

The Lift-All transports your wheelchair easily into the trunk of an automobile and neatly stores it for easy access.

414   One-Touch Power Lifter

Ted Hoyer and Company
2222 Minnesota Street
 # 2744
Oshkosh, WI   54901

An optional remote control allows a person who is physically able to raise or lower himself. Lifter boom can also be manually lowered by opening hydraulic and pressing down gently on boom. *$1899.00*

415   Ortho Kinetics

W220N507 Springdale Road
Waukesha, WI   53186
                                   800-824-1068
                         FAX: 414-542-4258

Anne Tyler, Director of Marketing

Products to enhance people's lives through mobility. These electric three and four wheel vehicles are designed to surpass consumer expectations by providing total comfort, convenience and performance features found nowhere else. Ortho-Kinetics has a full line of vehicles for any application.

416   Pool Lifts

Aquatic Access
417 Dorsey Way
Louisville, KY   40223   502-425-5817
                                   800-325-5438
                         FAX: 502-425-9607
         e-mail: info@AquaticAccess.com
              www.AquaticAccess.com

Aquatic Access manufacturers and sells water-powered lifts providing access to in-ground and above-ground swimming pools, spas, boats and docks. *$2310.00*

417   Pool Lifts for In-Ground Pools

Aquatic Access
417 Dorsey Way
Louisville, KY   40223   502-425-3361
                                   800-325-5438
                         FAX: 502-425-9607
         e-mail: info@aquatic-access.com
              www.aquatic-access.com

Provide independent or assisted access to in-ground pools. Lifts are powered with water pressure from a garden hose, and are portable. Some lifts have a three-hundred pound lift capacity and others have a four-hundred pound capacity, perfect for commercial installations or home use. ADA compliant *$3245.00*

418   Porch-Lift Vertical Platform Lift

Access Industries
4001 East 138th Street
Grandview, MO   64030   816-763-3100
                                   800-925-3100
                         FAX: 816-763-4467

Evelyn Johnson, Marketing Supervisor

Provide stairway access indoor and out for people who use wheelchairs. Lifting heights range from 1 to 144 feet and are available for both commercial and residential applications. Easy to install and operate, the units are space and cost efficient solutions to ADA compliance.

419   Porta Ramps

Porta Ramps
5592 E La Palma Avenue
Anaheim, CA   92807
                                   800-654-7267
                         FAX: 714-970-6875

Lightweight, portable, and fiberglass ramps for wheelchair users.

420   Power Door

11240 Gemini Lane
Dallas, TX   75229
                                   800-688-1758
                         FAX: 972-620-9875
              e-mail: info@powerdoor.com
                   www.powerdoor.com

Jim Goldthwaite, National Sales Manager

Power door, low energy door operators.

421 Ramplette Telescoping Ramp

Lumex
100 Spence Street
Bay Shore, NY   11706

800-645-5272
FAX: 800-L4L-UMEX

A multi-functional, easily moved economical ramp weighing 25 pounds.

422 Ricon Corporation

12450 Montague Street
Pacoima, CA   91331

818-899-7588
800-322-2884
FAX: 818-890-3354
www.riconcorp.com

Ricon corporation is a world leader in the manufacture of lifts and other mobility products for people with disabilities. The Ricon product line features the Activan(R) a lowered floor minivan conversion, wheelchair lifts power seat base and automatic door openers.

423 Silver Glide Stairway Lift

Access Industries
4001 East 138th Street
Grandview, MO   64030

816-763-3100
800-925-3100
FAX: 816-763-4467

Evelyn Johnson, Marketing Supervisor

The economical Silver-Glide easily installs on either side of a straight stairway. The seat, armrest and footrest can be folded to save stairway space when the unit is not in use. The unit plugs into an outlet at the top or bottom of the stairs and uses regular household current. Also available with battery operated system. Heavy duty steel cable drive system permits the rider to travel up to 20 feet.

424 Slide Board

Innovator of Disability Equipment and Adaptations
1393 Meadowcreek Drive
Apartment 2
Pewaukee, WI   53072

Solid oak slide board has the hand hole in the center for easier grasping, handling and transfers.

425 Smart Leg

Invacare Corporation
899 Cleveland Street
Elyria, OH   44035

440-329-6426

e-mail: info@invacare.com

An ingenious elevating leg rest that automatically extends to correctly fit every outstretched leg.

426 Smooth Mover

Dixie U.S.A.
PO Box 55549
Houston, TX   77255

713-688-4993
800-347-3494
e-mail: info@dixieusa.com

Patient mover is a board designed to transfer patients from bed to stretcher or table with one or two people. *$199.95*

427 SpectraLift

Inclinator Company of America
2200 Paxton Street
1557
Harrisburg, PA   17111

717-234-8065
800-343-9007
FAX: 717-234-0941
e-mail: sales@inclinator.com
www.inclinator.com

Dotty Keith, Sales Manager

A newly designed hydraulic wheelchair lift made of fiberglass construction suitable for commercial and residential use.

428 Spectrum Aquatics

7100 Spectrum Lane
Missoula, MT   59808

406-543-5309
800-776-5309
FAX: 406-728-7143
e-mail: info@spectrumproducts.com
www.specturmproducts.com

Keith Krumbeck, President
David Murray, VP Operations
Aaron Erickson, Sales Manager

Manufacturers of swimming pool disabled access products such as lifts, ramps, railings, ladders, and stainless steel hydrotherapy tanks for the swimming pool and medical therapy markets.

429 Stair & Glide Stairway Lift

Access Industries
4001 East 138th Street
Grandview, MO   64030

816-763-3100
800-925-3100
FAX: 816-763-4467

Evelyn Johnson, Marketing Supervisor

Solves many multi-level accessibility problems in home. Lifts easily to install on straight or curved stairways. The rail attaches directly to steps without disturbing walls or staircase. The heavy duty drive mechanism means reliable, trouble-free operation. Public building and outdoor packages available.

430 StairLIFT SC & SL

Inclinator Company of America
2200 Paxton Street
1557
Harrisburg, PA   17111

717-234-8065
FAX: 717-234-0941

Simple, self-contained and efficient stair units.

431 Stairway Elevators

Bruno Independent Living Aids
1780 Executive Drive
 # 84
Oconomowoc, WI   53066   414-567-4990
                                    800-882-8183
                                    FAX: 414-567-4341
                       e-mail: webmaster@bruno.com

Bruno offers a full line of stairway elevators, including the Electra-Ride II featuring access during power interruptions, convenient installation, comfort and a powerful drive system. The Electra-Ride which features battery-powered technology, a rail width of 25 inches and seat rotation for easy transfers. The Comfort-Ride AC stair lift which is battery operated, has a rail width of 7.25 inches and folded width of less than 14.5 inches.

432 Stand Aid

Stand Aid of Iowa
PO Box 386
Sheldon, IA   51201

                                    800-831-8580
                                    FAX: 712-324-5210
                       e-mail: standaid@connect.com
                                    www.standaid.com

Stand Aid can help you achieve independence and mobility safely and easily. Lifts you from a chair or bed with the flick of a switch, securing the user in an upright standing position.

433 Straight and Custom Curved Stairlifts

Bruno Independent Living Aids
1780 Executive Drive
PO Box 84
Oconomowoc, WI   53066   414-567-4990
                                    800-882-8183
                                    FAX: 414-953-5501
                       e-mail: webmaster@bruno.com
                                    www.bruno.com

Patrick Foy, National Sales Manager
Karla Branham Shaw, Marketing

Bruno stairlifts can fit almost any curve or straight rail application and requires little or no structural modification to the stairway. Normal rail position for a Bruno inside turn is 7 to 8 inches from the wall or obstruction which is the tightest radius of any stairlift manufacturing company in the world. The Bruno inside turn is ideal for bi-level homes or staircases with mid-level doors. Bruno's unique battery power allows for uninterrupted operation even during a power outage.

434 SureHands Lift & Care Systems

982 Route 1
Pine Island, NY   10969   845-258-6500
                                     800-724-5305
                                     FAX: 845-258-6634
                        e-mail: info@surehands.com
                                     www.surehands.com

Thomas Herceg, President
Joyce Moraczewski, Marketing Coordinator

SureHands Lift & Care Systems offer a unique, patented and exlusive range of lift and transfer systems to meet private and institutional needs of individuals with motor disabilties. Includes permanent and portable models for homes, workplaces and recreation. The SureHands Body Support offers safe, easy and secure transfers for user and the opportunity for independent transfers for some. They are a back-saver for caregivers. All lifts are easily maintained and operated with mininum assistance.

435 Swimming Pool Lifter

Ted Hoyer and Company
2222 Minnesota Street
 # 2744
Oshkosh, WI   54901

Makes recreational and therapeutic swimming safer and more enjoyable for both the patient and the attendant. *$991.00*

436 Swing-A-Way

Braun Corporation
1014 S Monticello Street
 # 310
Winamac, IN   46996   219-946-6157
                                 800-THE-LIFT
                                 FAX: 219-946-4670

A swing lift for transporting patients from bed to bath and more. It features a gravity-down operation made possible by a newly designed pump module package. The new, quieter module features a built-in hand pump and a plastic reservoir for easy fluid checking. This is a vehicle lift not bath lift.

437 Travel Lifter

Ted Hoyer and Company
2222 Minnesota Street
 # 2744
Oshkosh, WI   54901

The portable, lightweight Travel Lifter is the perfect solution for transfers from chair to car or bed to chair. Available in light gray painted finish. *$977.00*

438 VPL Series Vertical Wheelchair Lift

Access Industries
4001 East 138th Street
Grandview, MO   64030

                                 800-925-3100
                                 FAX: 816-763-4467

Evelyn Johnson, Marketing Supervisor

Provide stairway access indoors and out for people who use wheelchairs. Lifting heights from 1 to 144 feet for loads up to 750 pounds are available for both commercial and residential applications. Easy to install and operate, the units are space and cost efficient solutions to ADA access compliance. Attendant operation, toe-guard enclosure and restricted access hoistway enclosure options are available.

439 Vangater, Vangater II, Mini-Vangater

Braun Crow River
13805 First Avenue North
Plymouth, MN 55441
612-852-5040
800-488-7688
FAX: 612-745-0250
www.braunlift.com

Jerry Sirjord, General Manager

Tri-fold and fold-in-half lifts represent a major innovation in the field of adapted van transportation.

440 Vertical Home Lift Sales

2715 Seaboard Lane
Long Beach, CA 90805
800-795-6227
FAX: 562-634-4120

Rick Pierce, Vertical Home Lift Sales
Betty Haskings, Office Manager
Jerry MacDonald, President

Sales and service of van and truck lifts. Sales and service of wheel chair lifts for vans and automobiles. Sales, installation and service of vertical home lifts, scooter lifts and pool lifts. Sales of scooters.

441 Vertical Wheelchair Lift

Econol Stairway Lift Corporation
2513 Center Street
Cedar Falls, IA 50613
FAX: 319-277-4778

Adrian L. Martin, Sales
Sharon R. Martin, President

Provides easy access for those where stairways of architectural barriers pose a problem.

442 Vestibular Board

Bailey Manufacturing Company
118 Lee Street
130
Lodi, OH 44254
330-948-1080
800-321-8372
FAX: 330-948-4439
e-mail: baileymfg@attmail.com
www.baileymfg.com

Creates tilting in a rolling motion for reclining patients who need help developing balance.

443 Wecolator Stairway Lift

Access Industries
4001 East 138th Street
Grandview, MO 64030
800-925-3100
FAX: 816-763-4467

Evelyn Johnson, Marketing Supervisor

Solves many multi-level accessibility problems in home. Lifts easily to install on straight or curved stairways. The rail attaches directly to steps without disturbing walls or staircase. The heavy duty drive mechanism means reliable, trouble-free operation. Public building and outdoor packages available.

444 Wheelchair Carrier

726 Farnsworth Road
Waterville, OH 43566
419-878-8511
800-541-3213
FAX: 419-878-9438
www.wheelchaircarrier.com

Bob Dunlap, President
Tom Canham, Operations Manager

Wheelchair carriers for hitch mount on vehicles, portable steel ramps, the Rider Roaming Chair, a lightweight, foldable electric mobility aid. Carriers $199-$999, ramps $225-490, the Roamer $1,995.

445 Ziggy Medi-Chair

Laszlo Corporation
PO Box 1182
Florissant, MO 63031
314-830-3222
FAX: 314-830-3222
e-mail: suhayda@juno.com

Les Suhayda, President
Dale Bibko, Secretary

A lift and transfer system that maximizes time and safety for disabled and bedridden patients. A multifunctional product that benefits patients with disabilities and caregivers in a home or institutional government. A motorized system that lifts patients and saves caregivers from injury and workman's compensation claims.

Major Catalogs

446 AMI - Accessories for Mobile Independence

5235 Mission Oaks Boulevard
381
Camarillo, CA 93012
FAX: 805-987-8653

Gay Dawson, Owner

Ponchos, tote bags, gloves, and sweat pants for wheelchair-using consumers.

447 AbleNet

1081 10th Avenue East
Minneapolis, MN 55414
612-379-0956
800-322-0956
FAX: 612-379-9143
e-mail: customerservice@ablenetinc.com
www.ablenetinc.com

Allison Locey, Administrative Assistant
Kara Hans O'Brien, Marketing Coordinator

Creates and markets simple technology and educational services that enhance the quality of life for people with disabilities. By developing, and supporting easy-to-use, affordable and durable assistive technology to an individual's needs, capabilities, and interests, AbleNet's products foster independence, participation, inclusion and fun throughout a lifetime.

448   Access Store Products for Barrier Free Environments

Access Store.Com
820 West Seventh Street
Chico, CA   95928   530-879-5600
                                800-497-2003
                          FAX: 530-893-1560
    e-mail: moberholtz@accessstore.com
              www.accessstore.com

Matt Oberholtz, Operations Specialist

One of the largest ADA Complience Catalogs available. Offers everything from innovative barrier removal products to survey equipment, to unique specialty products.

449   Achievement Products

PO Box 9033
Canton, OH   44711   330-453-2122
                                800-373-4699
                          FAX: 330-453-0222
              e-mail: achievepro@aol.com

Teresa Cardon
Kyle Hall, Customer Service Manager

Offer a wide range of pediatric rehabilitation equipment and special education products including foam and adult weights, weighted vests, positioning equipment, sensory integration products, and ADL. Call for your free catalog.

450   Adaptive Clothing - Adults

Special Clothes
PO Box 333
East Harwich, MA   02645   508-896-7939
                          FAX: 508-896-7939
                          TDY:508-896-7939
        e-mail: SPECIALCLO@aol.com
              www.special-clothes.com

Judith Sweeney, President

Special Clothes produces a catalogue of garments for adults with disabilities and/or incontinence. Offerings include: undergarments, snap-crotch tee shirts, sleepwear, jumpsuits, bibs, and some footwear. The catalogue is available without charge. Comparable to department store prices. Special Clothes produces a catalog of adaptive clothing for children in sizes from toddler through young adults. A full line of clothing is included from undergarments through wheelchair jackets and ponchos.

451   Adrian's Closet

PO Box 9506
Rancho Santa Fe, CA   92067
                                800-831-2577
                          FAX: 619-759-0578
        e-mail: adrians@electriciti.com

Fashions for the physically challenged child. Clothing offers Velcro closures, front pockets, concealed back openings and fashions for seated posture.

452   Adult Long Jumpsuit with Feet

Special Clothes
PO Box 333
East Harwich, MA   02645   508-896-7939
                          FAX: 508-896-7939
                          TDY:508-896-7939
        e-mail: specialclo@aol.com
              www.special-clothes.com

Judith Sweeney, President

Line of clothing for people with disabilities. Child and adult catalog available.

$52 - $61

453   Adult Short Jumpsuit

Special Clothes
PO Box 333
East Harwich, MA   02645   508-896-7939
                          FAX: 508-896-7939
                          TDY:508-896-7939
        e-mail: specialclo@aol.com
              www.special-clothes.com

This pull-on jumpsuit provides comfort and full coverage without bulk. Wide leg ribbing ends at mid-thigh, with snaps at the crotch. We use fine quality, comfortable cotton knit. 100% cotton knit. Made in USA. Option: long sleeves - add $3.00. Colors: white, navy, teal, light blue, light pink, red, burgundy, royal blue, and black. Sm & Med: $36.50/3 for $104.00; L & XL: $39.00/3 for $111.25; and XXL: $42.00/3 for $119.25.

454   American Discount Medical

3412 Clark Road
Sarasota, FL   34231   941-927-1610
                                800-877-9100

Deeply discounts every major brand medical product available.

455   Apria Healthcare

3560 Hyland Avenue
Costa Mesa, CA   92626   714-427-2997
                          FAX: 714-885-6047
              www.apriahealthcare.com

Ronald J. Pion, MD

Lifts, chairs, bathroom aids, bedroom aids, eating utensils and independent living aids for the physically challenged.

19 pages

456   Armstrong Medical

575 Knightsbridge Parkway
Lincolnshire, IL   60069   847-803-4000
                                800-323-4220
                          FAX: 847-913-0138
              www.armstrongmedical.com

Training aids, anatomical models, medical equipment, pediatrics equipment and rehabilitation equipment.

457 Assistive Technology Sourcebook

Special Needs Project
3463 State Street
282
Santa Barbara, CA 93105
800-333-6867

Alexandra Enders, Editor
Marian Hall, Editor

Provides you with 18 chapters of practical information on all aspects of assistive technology for individuals with functional limitations. *$60.00*

576 pages

458 At Home with Medical Equipment Distributors

3223 South Loop 289
Suite 150
Lubbock, TX 79423
800-253-4134

Beds, wheelchairs, accessories, respiratory aids, oxygen, daily living aids and more.

30 pages

459 Bailey

118 Lee Street
PO Box 130
Lodi, OH 44254
330-948-1080
800-321-8372
FAX: 330-948-4439
e-mail: baileymfg@attmail.com
www.baileymfg.com

Ambulation aids, balance aids, benches, chairs, exercise devices, tables, stools, rehabilitation and physical therapy equipment for the physically challenged.

70 pages

460 Best 25 Catalog Resources for Making Life Easier

Meeting Life's Challenges, LLC
9042 Aspen Grove Lane
Madison, WI 53717
608-824-0402
FAX: 608-824-0403
e-mail: help@MeetingLifesChallenges.com
www.MeetingLifesChallenges.com

Shelley Peterman Schwarz, author

Unique reference guide to locate thousands of useful and hard-to-find adaptive devices to make dressing, eating, cooking, grooming, communicating, playing, exercising, etc. easier, safer and less frustrating for people of all ages and disabilities. A comprehensive, up-do-date reference for people with disabilities, caregivers and healthcare professionals. *$8.95*

36 pages
ISBN 1-891854-03-8

461 Bibs

Special Clothes
PO Box 333
East Harwich, MA 02645
508-896-7939
FAX: 508-896-7939
TDY:508-896-7939
e-mail: specialclo@aol.com
www.special-clothes.com

Judith Sweeney, Owner

A variety of bib styles are available to protect clothing inconspicuously.

$13 - $16.50

462 Body Suits

Special Clothes
PO Box 333
East Harwich, MA 02645
508-896-7939
FAX: 508-896-7939
TDY:508-896-7939
e-mail: specialclo@aol.com
www.special-clothes.com

Judith Sweeney, Owner

These are one piece garments that can be used to protect skin under braces, to add warmth and to shield incisions. Prices range from $18.25-22.50.

463 Carolyn's Low Vision Products

1415 57th Avenue West
Bradenton, FL 34207
800-648-2266
FAX: 941-739-5503
e-mail: carolynscatalog@aol.com
www.carolynscatalog.com

Carolyn Tojek, President

Free mail-order catalog of items for visually impaired people. We also have a retail store.

464 Communication Aids for Children and Adults

Crestwood Company
6625 North Sidney Place
Milwaukee, WI 53209
414-352-5679
FAX: 414-352-5679
e-mail: crestcomm@aol.com
www.communicationaids.com

Ruth B. Leff, M.S., CCC, Speech-Language Pathologist

A free catalog of communication aids for children and adults with disabilities. Over 300 light and high tech switches and aids, and a large selection of adapted and voice-activated toys. Talking Pictures and Passports communication boards, easy to use and moderately priced talking aids.

32 pages Yearly

465 Danmar Products

221 Jackson Industrial Drive
Ann Arbor, MI 48103
734-761-1990
800-783-1998
FAX: 734-761-8977
e-mail: danmarpro@aol.com
www.danmarproducts.com

Dan Russo, Sales/Marketing
Suzanne Gubachy, Sales Manager

Manufactures adaptive equipment for persons with physical and mental disabilities, from seating and positioning equipment, flotation devices, toileting aids to hard and soft shell helmets.

466   Dayspring Associates
2111 Foley Road
Havre De Grace, MD   21078   410-939-1768

This publisher provides a directory of 1,000 rehabilitation aids.

467   Engineering & Technology Support
219 Kewanee Drive
Byron, GA   31008   912-453-5130
                            FAX: 912-956-1783

David W. Felker, Senior Program
A service engineering firm that is structured to provide a wide range of support services on an as needed basis. Mobility aids such as modified wheelchairs, cars and recreational vehicles; job aids such as hand tools, desks and work tables; specialty electronics and control circuitry; modified personal computers and software; and customized exercise rehabilitation equipment.

468   Enrichments Catalog
Sammons Preston/AbilityOne Company
4 Sammons Court
Bowling Brook, IL   60440   630-226-1300
                            800-323-5547
                            FAX: 800-547-4333
                    e-mail: sp@sammonspreston.com
                    www.sammonspreston.com

Melinda Newtson, Director of Marketing Services
Provides people with physical challenges with the products they need to help live their lives to the fullest. Includes items for everyday tasks and personal care; assistive products for home use; toileting and bathing aids; grooming and dressing devices; kitchen and dining aids. Also items for range of motion, mobility and exercise such as weights, therapy putty and exercise equipment; ergonomic gloves and supports; canes, crutches, walkers and wheelchair accessories. 36-page catalog.

469   Equipment Shop
PO Box 33
Bedford, MA   01730   781-275-7681
                            800-525-7681
                            FAX: 781-275-4094
                    e-mail: info@equipmentshop.com
                    www.equipmentshop.com

Kenneth D. Larson, Owner
Pediatric therapy equipment including pezzi Gymnastik balls, Tripp Trapp chair, airex mats, tricycle accessories, sensory integration equipment and adaptive devices.

470   Everest & Jennings
Division of Graham Fields
3601 Rider Trail South
Earth City, MO   63045   314-937-3677
                            800-235-4661
                            FAX: 314-512-7123

Manufactures more than 200 items for persons with physical disabilities, including wheelchairs, seat cushions, shower chairs, grab bars, and more.

471   Express Medical Supply
200 Seebold Spur
Fenton, MO   63026
                            800-633-2139
                            FAX: 800-633-9188
                    e-mail: sales@exmed.net
                    www.exmed.net

Chris Winston, Manager
Offers a full line of medical and ostomy supplies.

472   Flaghouse Rehab Catalog
601 Flaghouse Drive
Hasbrouck Heights, NJ   07604   201-288-7600
                            800-793-7900
                            FAX: 800-793-7922
                    www.flaghouse.com

Contains over 2,000 products of interest to the health care professional.

473   Gem Wheelchair Scooter and Service
14467 Northern Boulevard
Flushing, NY   11354   718-463-3800
                            800-943-3578
                            FAX: 718-461-2621
                    e-mail: wheelsu@aol.com
                    www.wheelchairsusa.com

Jeff Bochner, President
GEM repairs and sells all makes and models of manual and motorized wheelchairs, power scooters, ramps and stairway lifts. Clients are in all five New York City Boroughs and Nassau County. Medicare and Medicaid accepted, pick-up and delivery and loaner equipment services available. Gem also buys and sells used equipment.

474   HAC Hearing Aid Centers of America HARC Mercantile Ltd.
Hearing Aid Center of Kalamazoo
1111 West Centre Avenue
PO Box 3055
Portaqe, MI   49029
                            800-445-9968
                            FAX: 800-413-5248
                            TDY:800-445-9968
                    e-mail: home@harcmercantile.com
                    www.harcmercantile.com

Ronald Slager, President
Specializes in products for the hard of hearing and deaf as required under ADA including visual alerting products for fire, phone, door, wake up, phone amplification, TTY, FM and infrared listening systems.

475   Harris Communications
15155 Technology Drive
Eden Prairie, MN   55344   952-906-1180
                                 800-825-6758
                          FAX: 952-906-1099
                          TDY: 952-906-1198
                   e-mail: mail@harriscomm.com
                             harriscomm.com

A national distributor of assistive devices for the deaf and hard-of-hearing with many manufacturers represented. Catalog includes a wide range of assistive devices as well as a variety of books and videotapes related to deaf and hard-of-hearing issues. Products available for children, teachers, hearing professionals, interpreters, and anyone interested in deaf culture, coping with hearing loss and sign language.

100 pages Catalog

476   Health and Rehabilitation Products
Luminaud
8688 Tyler Boulevard
Mentor, OH   44060   440-255-9082
                                800-255-3408
                          FAX: 440-255-2250
                    e-mail: info@luminaud.com
                             www.luminaud.com

Thomas Lennox, President
Dorothy Lennox, Vice President

Switches for limited capability, stoma and trach covers, shower protectors and thermo-stim oral motor stimulator. Personal voice amplifiers for people with weak voices. Artificial larynges for people with no voices. Small electronic communication boards. Books for laryngectomies and speech pathologists.

477   Hear You Are
125 Main Street
Netcong, NJ   07857   973-691-1156
                                800-278-EARS
                          FAX: 973-691-0611
                          TDY: 973-691-0663
                     e-mail: hearyoua@aol.com

Dorinne S. Davis, MA, CCC-A, President
Larry Cagno, Vice President

A large catalog of various assistive and communication devices for people who are hearing impaired.
$3.00

42 pages

478   Hig's Aluminum Products
10625 Maple Lane
Rogers, MN   55374   763-795-9478
                          FAX: 612-783-1788

Factory direct, lightweight aluminum, portable, 2 & 4-way folding, telescoping tracks, threshold, van, scooter and approach ramps.

479   Huntleigh Healthcare
40 Christopher Way
Eatontown, NJ   07724   732-578-9898
                                800-223-1218
                          FAX: 732-578-9889
                   www.huntleigh-healthcare.com

Doreen Faulkner, Graphic Artist

Offers quality products including support surfaces, seating surfaces, and intermittent pneumatic compression devices.

480   Hygienics Direct Company
3968 194th Trail
Miami, FL   33160   305-937-0824
                                800-463-7337
                          FAX: 305-937-0825
                     e-mail: hygienics.com
                             www.hygienics.com

Michael Brier, President

Offers a complete line of incontinence products and skin care products consisting of disposables and reuseables.

16 pages BiAnnual

481   Jesana Ltd. A Very Special Catalogue
979 Saw Mill River Road
Yonkers, NY   10710   914-376-2894
                                800-433-4728
                          FAX: 914-376-0021

Nana McIntosh, President

Offers a full range of products for children with physical and/or developmental disabilities. Selection includes a variety of capability switches, adapted toys and devices, positioning equipment, therapy balls and rolls, sensory manipulation items, recreation equipment, special tricycles, walkers, crawlers and augmentative communication devices. In addition, Jesana Ltd. is the exclusive distributor of the Universal TV Remote with plate switch activation for ease of use.

48 pages Yearly

482   LS & S Group
PO Box 673
Northbrook, IL   60065   847-498-9777
                                800-468-4789
                          FAX: 847-498-1482
                          TDY: 800-317-8533
                     e-mail: LSSGRP@aol.com
                             www.lssgroup.com

Specializes in products for the blind, visually impaired, hearing impaired, and physically disabled. Free catalog upon request.

148 pages

483   Lighthouse Low Vision Products
Lighthouse International
111 East 59th Street
New York, NY   10022   212-821-9707
                          FAX: 212-821-9702

This supplier provides vision-related products.

484   Luminaud
8688 Tyler Boulevard
Mentor, OH   44060   440-255-9082
                                800-255-3408
                          FAX: 440-255-2250
                    e-mail: info@luminaud.com
                             www.luminaud.com

Thomas Lennox, President
Dorothy Lennox, Vice President

Offers a line of artificial larynx, personal voice amplifiers, special switches, stoma covers and other communication, health and safety items.

50 pages
ISBN 0-96452-90-1

485   Maxi Aids

42 Executive Boulevard
Farmingdale, NY   11735   516-752-0521
                                     800-522-6294
                           FAX: 516-752-0689
                 e-mail: sales@maxiaids.com
                            www.maxiaids.com

Aids and appliances for the arthritic, visually impaired, hearing impaired, physically challenged, mature adult and for the needs of home health care.

131 pages

486   Med-Sell

PO Box 249
Rough and Ready, CA   95975   530-272-2071
                           FAX: 530-273-6788
                 e-mail: medsell@nccn.net
                            www.medsell.com

James Beeson, President
Maria Ternosky, Director

Non-profit organization that helps private parties buy, sell and trade their used medical equipment through the internet. All areas and countries served. Offers sponsorships for businesses to advertise their goods and services and offers low cost scooter and wheelchair carriers at wholesale prices to out customers.

487   New Breakthroughs

89911 Greenwood Drive
Leaburg, OR   97489
                           FAX: 505-896-0123

Offers catalogs of communication products for the disabled.

488   New Visions Store

919 Walnut Street
Philadelphia, PA   19107   215-629-2990
                                      800-876-5456
            e-mail: webmaster@thenewvisionstore.com
                    www.thenewvisionstore.com

Catalog for individuals with visual impairments, listing visual aids, magnifiers, large print books and more.

30 pages

489   Nightingale Medical Equipment Services

Rehabilitation Department
6161 Stewart Avenue
Cincinnati, OH   45227   513-271-5115
                           FAX: 513-527-3686

L.K. Barker, Director
Kim Fischer, Admin. Asst.

Quality rehabilitation equipment sales and rental. Available equipment includes manual and powered mobility, positioning/seating equipment, vehicle modification, environmental controls, augmentative and alternative communication devices, adaptive computer access, ambulance aids and aids for daily living. Equipment provision is carried out through a total team approach.

490   Nurion-Raycal

Station Square
Building 2
Paoli, PA   19301   610-647-2435
                           FAX: 610-647-2216

Nazir A. Ali, President

Electronic travel aids for the blind, deaf-blind, visually impaired persons, and those with Hemispatial neglect. Devices detect obstacles, finds clear path, landmarks. Lase Cane incorporates lasers to detect drop-ff, obstacles at different heights and distances. Polaron, a hand-held of chest-mounted unit, utilizes ultrasound to detect obstacles at various distances. Wheelchair Pathfinders incorporate ultrasound and lasers to detect drop-off and obstacles on the sides and forward.

491   Potomac Technology

1 Church Street
Suite 101
Rockville, MD   20850   301-762-4005
                                      800-433-2838
                           FAX: 301-762-1892
                 e-mail: info@potomactech.com
                            www.potomactech.com

Pat Relidan, Vice President

This catalog offers a variety of products for the deaf and hard of hearing, such as: wake-up devices, alarm clocks, alerting systems, assistive listening devices, signalers, smoke detectors, TTY, telephones and telephone amplifiers. We also carry novelties, and educational books and videos.

24 pages

492   Prentke Romich Company Product Catalog

1022 Heyl Road
Wooster, OH   44691   330-262-1984
                                      800-262-1984
                           FAX: 330-263-4829
                            www.prentrom.com

Larry Gigax

A full-line product catalog containing information on speech-output communication devices, environmental controls and computer access products.

493   Products for People with Disabilities

LS&S Group
PO Box 673
Northbrook, IL   60065   847-498-9777
                                      800-468-4789
                         TDY:800-317-8533
                 e-mail: LSSGRP@aol.com
                            www.lssgroup.com

Paul Lloyd
Pete Livas, Vice President

LS & S Group has a free catalog of products for the blind, deaf, visually and hearing impaired including: TTY's; computer adaptive devices; CCTV's; talking blood pressure, blood glucose and talking scales.

494   Rehabilitation Engineering and Assistive Technology Society of North America (RESNA)

1700 North Moore Street
Suite 1540
Arlington, VA   22209   703-524-6686
                                FAX: 703-524-6630
                         e-mail: info@resna.org
                                www.resna.org

Larry Pencak, Executive Director
Nell Bailey, Dir/Tech Asstistance Project

Association of rehabilitation professionals and people interested in advancing technology for people with disabilities.

495   Reid London House

9701 West Higgins Road
Rosemont, IL   60018   847-292-1900
                                    800-221-8378
                                FAX: 847-292-3400
                         www.reidlondonhouse.com

Amy Scott McLain, Group Product Marketing Manager

Publishes human resource assessment instruments for employment settings. The instruments include job analysis procedures to identify important characteristics for job success and objective assessment procedures to evaluate applicants and employees on these characteristics.

496   Sammons Preston Enrichments Catalog

Sammons Preston
4 Sammons Court
Bolingbrook, IL   60440   630-226-1300
                                    800-323-5547
                                FAX: 630-226-1388
                    e-mail: sp@sammonspreston.com
                         www.sammonspreston.com

Tony Napolitano, Director of Marketing Services

The complete source for rehabilitation professionals. Our Enrichnments Catalog offers products that make the tasks and challenges of living at home - bathing, getting dressed, getting around - a little easier. Choose from personal care items to kitchen and dining aids, household helpers to mobility devices, plus a complete selection of pain-reducing products, exercise items, health monitoring equipment and more.

40 pages Yearly

497   Science Products

1043 Lancaster Avenue
Berwyn, PA   19312   610-296-2111
                                     800-888-7400

Mary Ann Case, Marketing Director

Offers a full line of better vision products for better living: low vision aids, magnifiers, large print, and items that talk, conversation products.

498   Special Edition for Disabled People

Lawrence Research Group
PO Box 31039
San Francisco, CA   94131   415-468-3805
                                     800-242-2823
                                FAX: 415-468-3912
                         e-mail: info@xandria.com
                                www.xandria.com

Marcia Jackson, Marketing Director

Sexual aids for the handicapped. A catalog of product and informational resources and quotes from the top professionals in this field. *$4.00*

32 pages

499   Sportaid

78 Bay Creek Road
Loganville, GA   30052   770-979-0945
                                     800-743-7203
                                FAX: 770-554-5944
                         e-mail: stuffosportaid.com
                                www.sportaid.com

Jimmy Green

Offers an assortment of wheelchairs (everyday and racing), wheelchair sports equipment, replacement tires, hubs, spokes, pushrims, cushions and more. Call for free catalog.

68 pages Yearly

500   Synapse Adaptive Adaptive Technology Catalog

3095 Kerner Boulevard
Suite S
San Rafael, CA   94901   415-455-9700
                                FAX: 415-455-8901
                    e-mail: info@synapseadaptive.com
                         www.synapseadaptive.com

Speech regognition and adaptive technology for individuals with disabilities.

501   Therapy Products

CARD-ZINE Communications
8912 Ewing Avenue
Evanston, IL   60203

A catalog listing physical, occupational and rehabilitation products.

502   Ultratec

450 Science Drive
Madison, WI   53711   608-238-5400
                                     800-482-2424
                                FAX: 608-238-3008
                            TDY:800-482-2424
                      e-mail: service@ultratec.com
                                www.ultratec.com

Jackie Morgan, Director of Marketing

The world's largest manufacturer of text telephones and amplified telephones. Products include desktop TTYs with built-in printer, memory capabilities, as well as compact portable units for cellular and cordless use. Ultratec also manufactures public TTYs for pay phone accessibility.

503   WCI/Weitbrecht Communications
2716 Ocean Park Boulevard
Suite 1007
Santa Monica, CA   90405   310-452-8613
                                           800-233-9130
                                    FAX: 310-450-9918
                      e-mail: sales@weitrecht.com
                              www.weitrecht.com

Andie Squires, Sales Manager
Catalog featuring a wide range of assistive devices
for communication needs including telephones, amplifiers, signalers and more.

24 pages

504   Walgreens Home Medical Center
7173 Cermak Road
Berwyn, IL   60402   708-795-1295
                                           800-323-2828
                                    FAX: 708-795-1308

Paul Pankros, R. Ph., Director
Hospital supplies and home medical equipment with
nationwide direct mail delivery.

505   Walton Way Medical
1225 Walton Way
Augusta, GA   30901   706-722-0276
                                    FAX: 706-722-0279

Offers medical, therapeutic, urological, hygiene
and skin care products for disabled persons.

506   Wheelchair Batteries
Accent Books & Products
PO Box 700
Bloomington, IL   61702   309-378-2961
                                           800-787-8444
                                    FAX: 309-378-4420
                      e-mail: acmtlvng@aol.com

Raymond C. Cheever, Publisher
Betty Garee, Editor
Offers valuable tips for trouble-free travel at minimum cost: selecting the right battery the first time and
how to use and re-charge your battery to make it last
longer. *$3.50*

32 pages Paperback
ISBN 0-91570 -22-1

Miscellaneous

507   BeOK Key Lever
Sammons Preston/AbilityOne Company
4 Sammons Court
Bolingbrook, IL   60440   630-226-1300
                                           800-323-5547
                                    FAX: 800-547-4333
                      e-mail: sp@sammonspreston.com
                              www.sammonspreston.com

Handy accessory helps position key to provide
maximum leverage enabling the user to work the
most stubborn lock. *$11.50*

508   Big Lamp Switch
Maxi Aids
42 Executive Boulevard
3209
Farmingdale, NY   11735   516-752-0521
                                           800-522-6294
                                    FAX: 516-752-0689
                      e-mail: sales@maxiaids.com
                              www.maxiaids.com

This big, three-spoked knob replaces small rotating knobs which are a problem for those with
arthritis or other limitations of the fingers. *$6.75*

509   Big Red Switch
AbleNet
1081 10th Avenue SE
Minneapolis, MN   55414
                                           800-322-0956
                                    FAX: 612-379-9143
          e-mail: customerservice@ablenetinc.com
                              www.ablenetinc.com

Mary Kay Walch
Five inches across the top and activates no matter
where on its surface it is touched. It is made of
shatterproof plastic and contains a cord storage compartment. Also available in green, yellow and blue.
$42.00

510   Book Holder
Access with Ease
PO Box 1150
Chino Valley, AZ   86323   520-636-9469
                                           800-531-9479
                                    FAX: 520-636-0292
                      e-mail: KMJC@northlink.com

This hands free reading book holder enables the
user to read hands free. Moveable pegs prevent
legggs from slipping, yet allows easy turning.
Folds flat and has built in handle for easy carrying. *$ 16.95*

511   Bookholder: Roberts
Therapro
225 Arlington Street
Framingham, MA   01702   508-872-9494
                                           800-257-5376
                                    FAX: 508-875-2062
                      e-mail: info@theraproducts.com

Gray plastic, ideal for hand free reading, adjusts
to all sizes of books and prevents pages from flip-
ping for the physically challenged. *$27.50*

512   Brandt Industries
4461 Bronx Boulevard
Bronx, NY   10470   718-994-0800
                                           800-221-8031
                                    FAX: 718-325-7995
                      e-mail: brandtindinc@aol.com

Neil Brandt, President
Cathy Rice, Order Expediter

513 Bus and Taxi Sign

Maxi Aids
42 Executive Boulevard
3209
Farmingdale, NY   11735   516-752-0521
                                 800-522-6294
                            FAX: 516-752-0689
                      e-mail: sales@maxiaids.com
                            www.maxiaids.com

Signs that the individual with a disability can use to attract the attention of bus or taxi drivers. *$3.75*

514 Call Alarm/Switch Delay Unit

Words+
40015 Sierra Highway B-145
Palmdale, CA   93550
                                 800-869-8521
                            FAX: 805-266-8969

Ginger Woltosz, Vice President
Tim Ross, Manager

For use with any single system. Provides loud audible attention-getting alarm that can be either a steady or pulsating tone. Once activated, the alarm must be turned off by pressing a reset button. *$299.00*

515 Care Electronics

4700 Sterling Drive
Boulder, CO   80301   303-444-2273
                        FAX: 303-447-3502
             e-mail: tmoody@dnvr.uswest.net
                  www.careelectronics.com

Dawn Potts, Sales Manager
Tom Moody, President

Care Electronics manufactures safety monitoring systems for caregivers, home-health care, and nursing homes. WanderCARE monitors loved ones who tend to wander away from home. Care Deluxe Occupancy systems monitor patients in bed and in wheelchairs to help prevent falls. WetSENSE provides incontinence monitors.

516 Child Convertible Balance Beam Set

Bailey Manufacturing Company
118 Lee Street
130
Lodi, OH   44254   330-948-1080
                            800-321-8372
                       FAX: 330-948-4439
             e-mail: baileymfg@attmail.com
                  www.baileymfg.com

This convertible set is used to develop balance in two stages.

517 Child Variable Balance Beam

Bailey Manufacturing Company
135 South Mount Zion Road
Lebanon, IN   46052   330-948-1080
                            800-321-8372
                       FAX: 330-948-4439
             e-mail: baileymfg@attmail.com
                  www.baileymfg.com

The four walking beams can be arranged in several different ways for variable balance training.

518 Child's Mobility Crawler

Bailey Manufacturing Company
118 Lee Street
130
Lodi, OH   44254   330-948-1080
                            800-321-8372
                       FAX: 330-948-4439
             e-mail: baileymfg@attmail.com
                  www.baileymfg.com

Neurologically delayed or orthopedically involved small children can perform crawling and coordination exercises while being comfortably supported by the crawler.

519 Choice Switch Latch and Timer

AbleNet
1081 10th Avenue SE
Minneapolis, MN   55414
                                 800-322-0956
                            FAX: 612-379-9143
            e-mail: customerservice@ablenetinc.com
                  www.ablenetinc.com

A Choice Switch Latch and Timer allows one user to learn to make choices. It has two switch inputs and can control two devices. Once one device has been activated, the other will not function until the first one is turned off or completes its timed cycle. *$83.00*

520 Cordless Big Red Switch

AbleNet
1081 10th Avenue SE
Minneapolis, MN   55414
                                 800-322-0956
                            FAX: 612-379-9143
            e-mail: customerservice@ablenetinc.com
                  www.ablenetinc.com

The Cordless Big Red Switch, when used in conjunction with either the Cordless Receiver or the Small Appliance Receiver, gives you cordless control of toys, games, and appliances in your environment. *$89.00*

521 DEUCE Environmental Control Unit

APT Technology
236A North Main Street
Shreve, OH   44676   330-567-2001
                            888-549-2001
                       FAX: 330-567-3073
          e-mail: sales@apt-technology.com
               www.apt-technology.com

Grace Miller, Office Manager

Allows a severely disabled person to control a variety of useful devices via a dual switch. DEUCE controls phone, 4 AC powered devices such as a radio, 4 switch controlled devices such as a page turner and up to 16 lights and or appliances distributed around the environment. Starts at $1,500.

522 Dazor Manufacturing Corporation

4483 Duncan Avenue
St. Louis, MO   63110   314-652-2400
                               800-345-9103
                          FAX: 314-652-2069
                   e-mail: info@dazor.com
                        www.dazor.com

Richard Kupferer, Marketion Coordinator
Morris Zuckerman, Inside Accounts Manager

Dazor is a U.S. manufacturer of quality task lightning. Products include fluorescent, incandescent and halogen lighting fixtures to include illuminated magnifiers combine light and magnification to greatly enhance vision making activities such as reading as hobbies more enjoyable. All lamps come in a variety of mounting options to include desk bases, clamp on, floor stands and wall tracks. $95 - $450

523 Digi-Flex

Therapro
225 Arlington Street
Framingham, MA   01702   508-872-9494
                                800-257-5376
                          FAX: 508-875-2062
              e-mail: info@theraproducts.com
                    www.theraproducts.com

This is a unique hand and finger exercise unit. Recommended for use of individuation of fingers, web space and general strengthening of work hands. Available in a variety of resistances. *$17.50*

524 Dorma Group North America

Dorma Drive
Drawer AC
Reamstown, PA   17567
                                800-523-8483
                          FAX: 717-336-2106
              e-mail: archdw@dorma-usa.com
                    www.dorma-usa.com

Paul Kosakowski, President, CEO
John Bergstrom, Director of Sales

DORMA provides a complete line of door controls, including barrier-free units that comply with the Americans with Disabilities Act. A wide variety of surface applied and concealed closers, low energy operators, exit devices and electronic access control systems are available to address these equipments.

525 Dual Switch Latch and Timer

AbleNet
1081 10th Avenue SE
Minneapolis, MN   55414
                                800-322-0956
                          FAX: 612-379-9143
          e-mail: customerservice@ablenetinc.com
                    www.ablenetinc.com

A Dual Switch Latch and Timer allows two user's to activate two devices at a time in the latch, timed seconds or timed minutes mode of control. *$88.00*

526 Folding Reacher

Accent Books & Products
PO Box 700
Bloomington, IL   61702   309-378-2961
                                800-787-8444
                          FAX: 309-378-4420
              e-mail: acmtlvng@aol.com

Lightweight, adjustable, foldable reachers allowing one-handed operation. *$13.95*

527 Foot Inversion Tread

Bailey Manufacturing Company
118 Lee Street
130
Lodi, OH   44254   330-948-1080
                                800-321-8372
                          FAX: 330-948-4439
              e-mail: baileymfg@attmail.com
                    www.baileymfg.com

Effective for correcting flat feet. These angled boards require the patient to walk on the outside of the foot instead of the arch.

528 Foot Placement Ladder

Bailey Manufacturing Company
118 Lee Street
130
Lodi, OH   44254   330-948-1080
                                800-321-8372
                          FAX: 330-948-4439
              e-mail: baileymfg@attmail.com
                    www.baileymfg.com

Adjustable cross bars for different length steps. Reinforced metal crosses for easier climbing for the physically-disabled.

529 Handy Reacher

Access with Ease
PO Box 1150
Chino Valley, AZ   86323   520-636-9469
                                800-531-9479
                          FAX: 520-636-0292
              e-mail: KMJC@northlink.com

Long handled reacher works for retrieving items off shelves, picking fruit in the garden, dusting high places, getting objects behind the couch and lots of uses. Rubber jaws that opens 5 inches wide with a magnet on one tip, wooden arm that extends the reach 30 inches to a metal handle. Other model reachers are available. *$7.95*

530 Handy-Gadget

William Connection International
32802 Valle Road Spc 32
San Juan Capistrano, CA   92675   949-661-5068

Self-help appliance device for people with little or no hand action.

531 Hospital Environmental Control System

Prentke Romich Company
1022 Heyl Road
Wooster, OH   44691   330-262-1984
                                800-262-1984
                          FAX: 330-263-4829
                    www.prentrom.com

Permits the non-ambulatory patient to operate a variety of electrical items in a single room. A large liquid crystal display is mounted in front of the user and they scan through the menu of operations and make a selection using a sip-puff switch. Options include nurse call, standard telephone functions, electric bed control, hospital television operation and electrical appliance on and off. *$3860.00*

532 Knock Light

HARC Mercantile, Ltd.
PO Box 3055
Kalamazoo, MI   49003   616-324-1615
                               800-445-9968
                          FAX: 616-324-2387
        e-mail: home@harcmercantile.com
                www.harcmercantile.com

Ronald Slager, President

Easily attaches to a door with velcro, portable. *$29.95*

533 Leg Elevation Board

Bailey Manufacturing Company
118 Lee Street
130
Lodi, OH   44254   330-948-1080
                               800-321-8372
                          FAX: 330-948-4439
        e-mail: baileymfg@attmail.com
                www.baileymfg.com

Includes seven positions to a 30 degree incline, three pillows with Velcro, easy carry hand slot and a natural finish.

534 Leveron

Lindustries
21 Shady Hill Road
Weston, MA   02493   781-235-5452

Durable door opener features a patented split-ring which opens and rejoins around the neck of the knob. The invisible fastening system and resilient construction minimizes theft or damage from vandalism. *$12.95*

535 Lindustries

21 Shady Hill Road
Weston, MA   02493   781-237-8177

Willard H. Lind, President
Louise T. Lind, VP

Leveron is a doorknob lever handle for ease of operation. Leveron converts standard doorknobs to lever action without removing existing hardware. No gripping, twisting or pinching when hands are wet, arthritic or arms are full. Leveron provides convenience. Available in five colors: almond, satin brass, silver metallic, dark bronze and Hi-Glow (glows in the dark) at low cost to comply with ADA access requirements in public and private places. *$16.95*

536 Location Finder

Maxi Aids
42 Executive Boulevard
3209
Farmingdale, NY   11735   516-752-0521
                               800-522-6294
                          FAX: 516-752-0689
        e-mail: sales@maxiaids.com
                www.maxiaids.com

Helps find house, apartment, car or office. Just press the transmitter and sound will be emitted indicating the location. *$99.95*

537 Longreach Reacher

Therapro
225 Arlington Street
Framingham, MA   01702   508-872-9494
                               800-257-5376
                          FAX: 508-875-2062
        e-mail: info@theraproducts.com
                www.theraproducts.com

Reacher is useful when reaching, sitting or when standing. *$18.95*

538 Loop Scissors

Therapro
225 Arlington Street
Framingham, MA   01702   508-872-9494
                               800-257-5376
                          FAX: 508-875-2062
        e-mail: info@theraproducts.com
                www.theraproducts.com

Pliable, plastic handles that allow for easy and controlled cutting. *$14.25*

539 Magni-Cam

Innovations
5921 S Middlefield Road
Suite 102
Littleton, CO   80123   800-854-6554
                          FAX: 303-727-4940
        e-mail: magnicam@magnicam.com
                www.magnicam.com/magnicam

Tom Winter, Vice President, Marketing
Ed Bettinardi, President
Mollie Buchanan, Office Manager

Magni-Cam is a hand-held, light weight, inexpensive, auto-focus electronic magnification system designed to meet the reading and writing needs of those with low vision. The system presents the image in black and white or in color with three different view modes. Connects to any TV monitor in minutes. System reads any surfact with no distortion. Two battery powered systems are availabe providing total portability and flexibility.

540 Med Covers

Med Covers
1103 Transport Drive
Raleigh, NC   27603   919-779-3555
                               800-948-8917
                          FAX: 919-779-3540
        e-mail: medteam@medcovers.com
                www.medcovers.com

Ben Habets, Medical Sales Manager

Manufactures cases and covers for the medical and data capture industries. Specializing in oxygen cylinder, scooter and wheelchairs covers, and accessories.

541 Plastic Card Holder

Therapro
225 Arlington Street
Framingham, MA   01702   508-872-9494
                               800-257-5376
                          FAX: 508-875-2062
        e-mail: info@theraproducts.com
                www.theraproducts.com

For those with reduced finger control. *$4.00*

542   PortaPower Plus

Words+
1220 West Avenue J
Lancaster, CA   93534   805-266-8500
                                800-869-8521
                          FAX: 805-266-8969

Phil Lawrence, Vice President
Rachel Nielsen, Customer Support

Rechargeable battery pack designed to give longer life and remote usage time to laptop computers and other portable battery-operated devices and accessories. Requires a 12 volt auto adapter. *$149.00*

543   ProtectaCap, ProtectaCap+PLUS, ProtectaChin Guard and ProtectaHip

Plum Enterprises
500 Freedom View Lane
PO Box 85
Valley Forge, PA   19481   610-783-7377
                                800-321-PLUM
                          FAX: 610-783-7577
                   e-mail: lynn@plument.com
                          www.plument.com

Janice Carrington, President

Exquisite, Ergonomic ProtectiveWear, ProtectaCap custom-fitting headgear has earned an unparalleled reputation for quality, safety and comfort. Protecta-Cap+Plus technologically-advanced protective headgear closes the gap between hard and soft helmets. It comes with optional ProtectaChin Guard and new sporty design. ProtectaHip protective undergarment is the intelligent, innovative solution to the problem of hip injuries for both men and women.

544   Reacher

Guardian Products
12800 Wentworth Street
Arleta, CA   91331   818-768-1114
                          FAX: 818-504-2833

Allows users to reach items when needed.

545   Rocker Balance Square

Bailey Manufacturing Company
118 Lee Street
130
Lodi, OH   44254   330-948-1080
                                800-321-8372
                          FAX: 330-948-4439
              e-mail: baileymfg@attmail.com
                          www.baileymfg.com

The rocker is used in developing activity, balance control and coordination.

546   Room Valet Visual-Tactile Alerting System

HARC Mercantile, Ltd.
PO Box 3055
Kalamazoo, MI   49003   616-324-1615
                                800-445-9968
                          FAX: 616-324-2387
            e-mail: home@harcmercantile.com
                        www.harcmercantile.com

Ronald Slager, President

ADA compliant built-in visual-tactile alerting system. The Room Valet is fully supervised and has power failure back up. Alerts to in-room smoke, building alarm, door, phone and alarm clock. Designed for permanent installation.

547   Safe-T-Pole

Guardian Products
12800 Wentworth Street
C-4522
Arleta, CA   91331
                          FAX: 818-504-2833

Floor to ceiling pole mounts anywhere to safely assist standing, sitting, climbing stairs or transferring.

548   Scott Sign Systems

PO Box 1047
Tallevast, FL   34270   941-355-5171
                                800-237-9447
                          FAX: 941-351-1787
           e-mail: scottsigns@mindspring.com
                          www.scottsigns.com

Call for a brochure.

549   Series Adapter

AbleNet
1081 10th Avenue SE
Minneapolis, MN   55414
                                800-322-0956
                          FAX: 612-379-9143
          e-mail: customerservice@ablenetinc.com
                          www.ablenetinc.com

Allows two-switch operation of any battery-operated device or electrical devices. *$13.00*

550   Sharp Calculator with Illuminated Numbers

Independent Living Aids
27 East Mall
Plainview, NY   11803   516-752-8080
                                800-537-2118

A trim desktop calculator with large illuminated numbers that can be carried anywhere. *$34.95*

551   Signaling Wake-Up Devices

HARC Mercantile, Ltd.
PO Box 3055
Kalamazoo, MI   49003   616-324-1615
                                800-445-9968
                          FAX: 616-324-2387
            e-mail: home@harcmercantile.com
                        www.harcmercantile.com

Ronald Slager, President

Wake up devices. Vibrating alarm clocks, available with flashing lights, louder alarm noises and more. *$29.50*

552   Smoke Detector with Strobe

HARC Mercantile, Ltd.
PO Box 3055
Kalamazoo, MI   49003   616-324-1615
                                800-445-9968
                          FAX: 616-324-2387
            e-mail: home@harcmercantile.com
                        www.harcmercantile.com

Ronald Slager, President

Most of the smoke alarms are twice as loud, and have a 120+ candela strobe that will wake a person from a sound sleep. Mounting hardware for ceiling or wall. *$165.95*

553 SteeleVest

26112 Iowa Avenue NE
PO Box 7304
Kingston, WA 98346

FAX: 360-267-2816

Vest developed by N.A.S.A. provides an external cooling system.

554 Step-by-Step Communicator

AbleNet
1081 10th Avenue SE
Minneapolis, MN 55414

800-322-0956
FAX: 612-379-9143
e-mail: customerservice@ablenetinc.com
www.ablenetinc.com

The Step-by-Step Communicator allows you to record a series of messages (as many as you want up to the 75 second limit). It has a 2 1/2 inches diameter switch surface and is 3 inches at its tallest point. Angled switch surface makes it easy to see and access. *$129.00*

555 TV & VCR Remote

AbleNet
1081 10th Avenue SE
Minneapolis, MN 55414

800-322-0956
FAX: 612-379-9143
e-mail: customerservice@ablenetinc.com
www.ablenetinc.com

Controls a TV, a VCR or a TV that is connected through a VCR tuner. It may be programmed to control functions such as on and off, channel up, preprogrammed TV channels and if desired, other TV functions such as mute and pause. *$82.00*

556 Tactile Thermostat

Sense-Sations
919 Walnut Street
Philadelphia, PA 19107

215-629-2990
800-876-5456

Large embossed numbers on cover ring and raised temperature setting knob. *$31.50*

557 Talking Desktop Calculators

Maxi Aids
42 Executive Boulevard
3209
Farmingdale, NY 11735

516-752-0521
800-522-6294
FAX: 516-752-0689
e-mail: sales@maxiaids.com
www.maxiaids.com

Unique voice synthesizers call out numerals and functions as they are keyed in or read out data stored in memory. *$467.95*

558 Therapy Putty

Therapro
225 Arlington Street
Framingham, MA 01702

508-872-9494
800-257-5376
FAX: 508-875-2062
e-mail: info@theraproducts.com
www.theraproducts.com

Designed to exercise and strengthen hands, ranging from soft to firm for developing a stronger grasp. Available in two, four and six ounce sizes. Three ounce putty in unique clear fist shaped container.

$3.75 - $8.95

559 Transcription Services

Access-USA
PO Box 160
Clayton, NY 13624

800-263-2750
e-mail: info@access-usa.com
www.access-usa.com

Deborah Haight, EOA

Access-USA provides all types of alternate media for people with visual and/or hearing impairments. Documents (of all sizes) for transcription can be accepted as hard copy, disk copy and email. Formats available include braille, large-type, braille and print, audio recordings and electronic format.

560 Window-Ease

A-Solution
1332 Cobo Place NE
Albequeque, NM 87106

505-256-0115
FAX: 505-256-3756
www.windowease.com

Robert Gorrell, President
Jeff Dodd, Sales

Device adapts horizontally and vertically sliding windows to ANSI A117.1 standards. 10:1 mechanical advantage at the crank arm opens a 50lb window with 5lbs force. Price ranges from $350.00-$450.00.

Office Devices & Workstations

561 Auditech - Audioport Personal Amplifier

PO Box 821105
Vicksburg, MS 39182

800-229-8293
FAX: 800-221-8639
e-mail: info@auditechusa.com
www.auditechusa.com

Make everyday conversations more comfortable and easy to hear with the Audioport. This all-in-one unit has a powerful built-in microphone and amplifer, so no wires or separate transmitters are needed. Designed for one-on-one or small group conversations, it amplies up to eight feet away. It automatically adjusts for sharp sudden noises and allows user's voice to sound natural. All in one small, durable unit. *$189.00*

562 Auditech - Classroom Amplification Sy Focus CFM802

PO Box 821105
Vicksburg, MS 39182

800-229-8293
FAX: 800-221-8639
e-mail: info@auditechusa.com
www.auditechusa.com

The SOUNDFOCUS FM System is designed to cover background noise and compensate for distance. Students find it easier to focus their attention and not strain to be heard. Two speaker system. *$1052.00*

563 Auditech - DirectEar Transmitter and H

PO Box 821105
Vicksburg, MS 39182

800-229-8293
FAX: 800-221-8639
e-mail: info@auditechusa.com
www.auditechusa.com

Turn up the volume when watching TV. The headset can also be used separately in public theaters and cinemas, that have infrared transmission. Additional headset receivers can be purchased. A neckloop can also be added to the headset. *$219.00*

564 Auditech - Personal FM Educational System

PO Box 821105
Vicksburg, MS 39182

800-229-8293
FAX: 800-221-8639
e-mail: info@auditechusa.com
www.auditechusa.com

Personal FM Educational System is a portable system for classroom use. The teacher wears a microphone. Students use a portable receiver which works clearly and easily. For users who have a hearing problem, a switch, a necklooop telecoil coupler is available. *$679.00*

565 Auditech - Personal PA Value Pack System

PO Box 821105
Vicksburg, MS 39182

800-229-8293
FAX: 800-221-8639
e-mail: info@auditechusa.com
www.auditechusa.com

Reliable hearing assistance. This wireless FM system broadcasts to listeners with a hearing assistance system, helping them overcome background noise at a distance from the sound source. *$899.00*

566 Auditech - Pocketalker Pro

PO Box 821105
Vicksburg, MS 39182

800-229-8293
FAX: 800-221-8639
e-mail: info@auditechusa.com
www.auditechusa.com

Pocketalker Pro can help you hear virtually anywhere whether in a car, crowded restaurant or at a noisy gathering. It can work to reduce background noise and easily converts to the Telelink. *$ 140.00*

567 Combination File/Reference Carousel

Center for Rehabilitation Technology
490 10th Street NW
118
Atlanta, GA 30318

404-265-1650
800-457-9555
FAX: 404-875-9409
e-mail: rerc-br@scsn.net

T.W. Gannaway, Executive V.P.

Offers two reading platforms and file holders joined on one easily rotated carousel. The carousel is easily rotated by head, mouth or handstick. Page retainer adjusts to hold open a variety of books and magazines. *$299.00*

568 Extensions for Independence

555 Saturn Boulevard
B-368
San Diego, CA 92154

619-423-7709
FAX: 619-423-7709
e-mail: info@mouthstick.net
www.mouthstick.net

Arthur Heyer, President

Develops, manufactures and markets special vocational equipment for the physically handicapped. Products: mouthsticks, computer mechanical aids: key locks and diskette loaders. Also, turntable desks, wheelchair portable desks, filing trays with slanted sides, telephone adapters, and motorized artist easel. All these products have been designed to solve the functional limitations of people with little or no use of hands and/or arms.

569 Infogrip AdjustaCart

1794 East Main Street
Ventura, CA 93001

805-652-0770
800-397-0921
FAX: 805-652-0880
e-mail: sales@infogrip.com

Sit or stand while working with this easily adjustable desk. With a simple squeeze of a paddle the front surface travel range of 12 3/4. The front surface tilts 9 degrees toward and 15 degrees away from you Anthro carts are made of 1" thick industrial grade particleboard shelves with high-pressure laminated 16 gauge steel tube legs that safely hold 150 pounds. Spring assisted mechanism. There are holes in 1: increment in the legs so that you can put the shelves and accessories where needed. *$629.00*

570 Infogrip - BAT Personal Keyboard

1794 East Main Street
Ventura, CA 93001

805-652-0770
800-397-0921
FAX: 805-652-0880
e-mail: sales@infogrip.com

One handed, compact input device that replicates all the functions of a full size keyboard, but with greater efficiency and convenience. Bat is easy to learn and use. Letters, numbers, commands and macros are simple key combinations, "chords,"" that you can master in no time. BAT's unique ergonomic design reduces hand strain and fatigue for greater comfort and productivity. *$200.00*

571   Infogrip - ErgoPOD Model 500

1794 East Main Street
Ventura, CA   93001   805-652-0770
                            800-397-0921
                   FAX: 805-652-0880
            e-mail: sales@infogrip.com

ErgoPOD Model 500 provides a workstation solution to computer users who work from a reclining position. Model 500 straddles a bed or recliner and can hold up to 21" monitors anywhere on it's surface, and will securely position the monitor at angles up to 60 degrees. The adjustable keyboard mechanism and motorized height adjustment make ergonomic configuration easy - even for the most demanding cases. *$ 1895.00*

572   Infogrip - King Keyboard

1794 East Main Street
Ventura, CA   93001   805-652-0770
                            800-397-0921
                   FAX: 805-652-0880
            e-mail: sales@infogrip.com

Giant, 2.5" x 11" x 2.25", alternative keyboard that plugs directly into a computer - no special interface is required. The keys are 1.25 inches in diameter, slightly recessed, and provide both tactile and auditory feedback. The King has a built-in keyboard so that you can rest on its surface without activating keys. This keyboard allows you to control both keyboard and mouse functions, so it's great for people who have difficulty maneuvering a standard mouse. *$130.00*

573   Infogrip - Large Print Keyboard

1794 East Main Street
Ventura, CA   93001   805-652-0770
                            800-397-0921
                   FAX: 805-652-0880
            e-mail: sales@infogrip.com

Standard Windows keyboard with large print keys. The keyboard and its keys are the same size as a standard keyboard; however, the print has been enhanced. The characters measure .5" by .25", about 3 times larger than standard keyboard characters. *$130.00*

574   Infogrip - Large Print/Braille Keyboard Labels

1794 East Main Street
Ventura, CA   93001   805-652-0770
                            800-397-0921
                   FAX: 805-652-0880
            e-mail: sales@infogrip.com

Makes a standard keyboard more accessible for visually impaired individuals with large print or Braille keyboard labels. Characters on the large print labels are .5" by .25", about 3 times larger than standard keyboard characters. Braille labels are available as clear labels with Braille dots or large print with Braille. Each set includes all the keys used on a standard Windows keyboard. *$29.00*

575   Infogrip - OnScreen

1794 East Main Street
Ventura, CA   93001   805-652-0770
                            800-397-0921
                   FAX: 805-652-0880
            e-mail: sales@infogrip.com

OnScreen features word prediction/completion (with an editable distionary), Key Dwell Timer (a timer that selects a key under the cursor), integrated Verbal Keys Feedback, "Show and Hide Keys" (turns on/off keys to prevent access and minimize confusion) a Smart Window (automatically re-positions the keyboard or panels off of the area in use). On Screen also offers edit, numeric, macro, calculator and Windows enhancement capabilities. *$200.00*

576   Infogrip - OnScreen with CrossScanner

1794 East Main Street
Ventura, CA   93001   805-652-0770
                            800-397-0921
                   FAX: 805-652-0880
            e-mail: sales@infogrip.com

OnScreen features word prediction/completion (with an editable distionary), Key Dwell Timer (a timer that selects a key under the cursor), integrated Verbal Keys Feedback, "Show and Hide Keys" (turns on/off keys to prevent access and minimize confusion) a Smart Window (automatically re-positions the keyboard or panels off of the area in use). On Screen also offers edit, numeric, macro, calculator and Windows enhancement cabilities. CrossScanner launches, runs and controls Windows functions. *$200.00*

577   Liaison Computer Work Station

APT Technology
236A North Main Street
Shreve, OH   44676   330-567-2001
                            888-549-2001
                   FAX: 330-567-3073
      e-mail: sales@apt-technology.com
               www.apt-technology.com

Grace Miller, Office Manager

A full function computer work station for high level (C-2 to C-5) spinal cord injured users. It transparently emulates both keyboard and mouse, using rapid direct selection which commonly yields letter by letter typing rates of 15 to 20 words per minute. The user controls it via proportional IR remote control from the DU-IT controlled power wheelchair and chin or tongue/lip controller or via a desk-mounted proportional controller as a stand alone device. Full ECU features included. *$ 4685.00*

578   M.O.M.S. Mail Order Medical Supply

                            800-232-7443

Amplified cordless phone, the Dialogue CL-30 not only makes incoming sounds much louder, clearer, and easier to understand, it also offers you the mobility and convenience you want in a cordless phone. Now you can hear every word anywhere in your home. The powerful amplifier increases incoming sound up to 30 times louder, while the adjustable Tone Control lets you customize the amplifer for clarity so you can easily distinguish similar sounding words. Even blocks out background noise. *$159.99*

579 PhoneMax Amplified Telephone

Assistive Devices Network
2241 S Triangle X Lane
Tucson, AZ   85713   866-674-3549

580 Talking Electronic Organizers

Independent Living Aids
27 East Mall
Plainview, NY   11803   516-752-8080
                                      800-537-2118
                                 FAX: 516-752-3135
           e-mail: can-do@independentliving.com
                     www.independentliving.com

Marvin Sandler, President

Electronic, portable, personal organizers that talk the
user through all the functions and are totally voice
interactive. $199.95 and up.

581 Television Remote Controls with Large Numbers

Independent Living Aids
27 East Mall
Plainview, NY   11803   516-752-8080
                                      800-537-2118
                                 FAX: 516-752-3135
           e-mail: can-do@independentliving.com
                    · www.independentliving.com

Marvin Sandler, President

Large 5 1/2 inch x 8 1/2 inch unit that has easy to see
and use buttons. Can be used on nearly every TV,
VCR and cable boxes. $ 39.95

582 U-Shaped Computer Table

Craner Cabinetry
3190 South 4140 West
West Valley City, UT   84120

This computer workstation provides the user with
a U shaped table which can be folded up and
locked into a horizontal position.

Scooters

583 Alante

Golden Technologies
401 Bridge Street
Old Forge, PA   18518   570-451-7477
                                      800-624-6374
                                 FAX: 570-451-7494
              e-mail: info@goldentech.com
                      www.goldentech.com

Rich Golden, CEO
Fred Kiwak, V.P.
Bob Smith, V.P. of Sales

Rear-wheel-drive vehicle that represents the best in
powered mobility.

584 American Printing House for the Blind

American Printing House for the Blind
1839 Frankfort Avenue
PO Box 6085
Louisville, KY   40206   502-895-2405
                                      800-223-1839
                                 FAX: 502-899-2274
                     e-mail: info@aph.org
                            www.aph.org

The American Printing House for the blind promotes independence of blind and visually impaired persons by providing special media, tools
and materials needed for educatio and life.

585 Amigo Centra

Amigo Mobility International
6693 Dixie Highway
Bridgeport, MI   48722   517-777-0910

Features an adjustable handle that bends, making
steering comfortable and enjoyable. The rugged
construction and variable speed make it the perfect choice for indoor/outdoor mobility. *$2495.00*

586 Amphibious ATV Distributors

Amphibious ATV Distributors
2760 Greendale Drive
Sarasota, FL   34232   941-379-6186
                                      800-843-2811
                                 FAX: 941-377-8979
              e-mail: CBeach1419@aol.com
                     www.maxsixwheel.com

Clay Beach, Owner

A two and four passenger, all-terrain vehicle that can
provide you with year round activities the whole
family can enjoy. Accessible and drivable for the
physically disabled. Used in hunting, fishing and outdoor activities on land and in the water. Many options
and accessories available. Delivery anywhere in the
U.S. and worldwide. $5,000-$9,000.

587 Avant Walker

ETAC USA
2325 Parklawn Drive
Suite J
Waukesha, WI   53186

                                      800-678-3822
                                 FAX: 414-796-4605
              e-mail: etac1usa@execpc.com
                    www.execpc.com/~etac1usa

Elegant styling makes the Avant an attractive
companion. The adjustable height seat and backrest offer comfort and security whenever or wherever you choose to stop and rest. Pressure sensitive
brakes require little strength to operate. Folds
easily with one hand. Lifetime warranty on frame
and brake straps for original owner. $395-$50.

588 Bravo! + Three-Wheel Scooter

Ortho-Kinetics
PO Box 1647
Waukesha, WI   53187   414-542-6060
                                      800-824-1068
                                 FAX: 414-542-3990

Anne Tyler, Marketing Director

Designed to increase your mobility indoors. The Bravo! plus has extendible rear wheels for outdoor use and comes with easy to use finger tip controls and a maintenance free gel-cell battery. Available in red, blue, green or light sand gray with an optional power seat lift. Call for complete line of 3 and 4-wheel electronic vehicles.

589 Comb-O-Cycle

American Walker
900 Market Street
Oregon, WI 53575   **608-274-5274**

Combines 16 inch front wheels for stability outdoors, with swiveling rear wheels for maneuverability, even in the most confined spaces. The Comb-O-Cycle is a combination indoor-outdoor walking aid. The burgundy tubular steel frame is powder coated for a durable finish. The padded seat provides a comfortable resting place. Comb-O-Cycle folds flat and is made in U.S.A.

590 Cruiser Bus Buggy 4MB

Convaid Products
PO Box 2458
Pls Vrds Pnsl, CA 90274   **310-534-3529**

In sizes from infant through young adult, this positioning buggy is crash-tested.

591 Electric Scooter Covers

Employee Developmental Service
Midland, MI 48874   **517-636-6681**

Personalized mobility vehicle covers are designed for three and four wheeled electric scooters.

592 Explorer+ 4-Wheel Scooter

Ortho-Kinetics
PO Box 1647
Waukesha, WI 53187   **414-542-6060**
                                800-824-1068
                            FAX: 414-542-4258
                        www.orthokinetics.com

Anne Tyler, Director of Marketing

A tough and rugged 4-wheel, rear-wheel drive, transaxle scooter designed to take you just about anywhere you want to go. Easy to use finger-tip controls and maintenance free gel-cell batteries and an extendible, take-apart frame, make the Explorer+ a perfect fit for people seeking greater mobility. Available in red, blue, green and gray, with an optional power seat lift. $3,499-$3,999.

593 Gopher II

Gopher Research and Development
PO Box 2199
Fullerton, CA 92837

Specifically designed for quadriplegics and paraplegics, but everyone can ride it.

594 Invacare Fulfillment Center

Invacare Corporation
One Invacare Way
Elyria, OH 44036   **440-329-6426**
                                800-336-6900
                            FAX: 440-329-6568
                    e-mail: info@invacare.com
                            www.invacare.com

Invacare Corporation is the world's leading manufacturer and distributor of non-acute medical products which promote recovery and active lifestyles for people requiring home and other non-acute health care.

595 MVP+ 3-Wheel Scooter

Ortho-Kinetics
PO Box 1647
Waukesha, WI 53187   **414-547-1600**
                                800-824-1068
                            FAX: 414-542-3990

The MVP+ is the rugged 3-wheel rear-wheel drive, tranaxle scooter with finger tip controls, and featuring an extendible, take-apart frame for a perfect fit. The MVP+ comes with maintenance free gel-cell batteries and is available in red, blue, green or light sand gray, with an optional power seat lift. $2,599-$3,099.

596 Minova Walker

ETAC USA
2325 Parklawn Drive
Suite J
Waukesha, WI 53186
                                800-678-3822
                            FAX: 414-796-4605
                e-mail: etac1usa@execpc.com
                        www.execpc.com/~etac1usa

Childrens Walker shares the same basic principles as Adult Nova. The handles are adjustable for both width and height. The walker is easy to fold with a remarkable safety braking system. $498-$525.

597 Mitsubishi Truck: FE434

Mitsubishi Fuso Truck of America
PO Box 464
Bridgeport, NJ 08014   **609-467-4500**

A cab-over, turbo-charged diesel with optional four-speed automatic transmission, has wide angle front and side windows for improved visibility.

598 Motorized Stander

Advanced Technology Corporation
1601 Charlotte Street
Kansas City, MO 64108   **816-421-6688**
                            FAX: 816-221-8371
                e-mail: advancedtech@prodigy.net

Joel Poindexter

Occupant-operated motorized vehicle that offers independence, increased mobility and ease of movement to disabled people.

599 Motovator Three-Wheel Scooter

Motovator
22626 Normandie Avenue
Suite E
Torrance, CA 90502   310-320-5941

This three-wheel electric wheelchair is a very maneuverable scooter with a turning radius that will get you around furniture, around a corner, through a doorway and more.

600 New E & J Scooter

Everest & Jennings Avenue
3233 Mission Oaks Boulevard
Camarillo, CA 93012   805-389-7450

A rear-wheel drive scooter with a contoured seat for comfort and enough power to charge up to a 20 degree incline.

601 Nova Rollators

ETAC USA
2325 Parklawn Drive
Suite J
Waukesha, WI 53186
    800-678-3822
    FAX: 414-796-4605
    e-mail: etac1usa@execpc.com

Light and easy to handle, fully adjustable for individual needs. Large cushioned tires allow the Nova to roll outdoors and indoors. $498-$637.

$498 - $637

602 Outdoor Independence

Palmer Industries
PO Box 707
Endicott, NY 13760   607-754-1954

The futuristic electric three-wheeler designed to take you almost anywhere.

603 Pace Saver Plus II

Leisure-Lift
1800 Merriam Lane
Kansas City, KS 66106

The scooter combines outdoor ruggedness with indoor maneuverability at a low price.

604 Palmer Independence

Palmer Industries
PO Box 707
Endicott, NY 13760   607-748-8227
    800-847-1304

Futuristic electric three wheeler designed to take the rider almost anywhere.

605 Palmer Twosome

Palmer Industries
Box 707
Endicott, NY 13760   607-754-1954

All electric two seat vehicle for those who can't pedal.

606 Plus Three Wheeler

Burke
1800 Merriam Lane
Kansas City, KS 66106
    800-255-4147

Be free to be as active as you like with this three wheel scooter. *$2695.00*

607 Polaris Trail Blazer

Polaris Industries
1225 Highway 169 North
Minneapolis, MN 55441   612-542-0500

A four-wheeler that has many engineered innovations, features such as: full floorboards for full comfort, single lever breaking with auxiliary foot brake, electronic throttle control, parking brake and adjustable handlebars.

608 Quickie 2

Sunrise Medical/Quickie Designs
2842 N Business Park Avenue
Fresno, CA 93727   559-292-2171

This custom, ultralight, folding, everyday scooter offers portability and performance plus modular flexibility.

609 Rascal 3-Wheeler

Electric Mobility
1 Mobility Plaza
Sewell, NJ 08080   609-468-0270
    800-662-4548
    www.emobility.com

Tom Ehrmanh, National Sales Manager

For primarily outdoor use, this three wheeler provides extra strength, durability and reliability.

610 Rascal ConvertAble

Electric Mobility
1 Mobility Plaza
Sewell, NJ 08080   609-468-0270
    800-662-4548
    www.emobility.com

Tom Ehrmann, National Sales Manager.

An electric vehicle that's a compact mobile chair one minute and a rugged outdoor scooter the next. Use both indoors and outdoors. Also available with joystick controls.

611 Regal Scooters

Bruno Independent Living Aids
1780 Executive Drive
84
Oconomowoc, WI 53066   414-567-4990
    800-882-8183
    FAX: 414-567-4341
    e-mail: webmaster@bruno.com

This line includes the Regal Standard, the regal large Adult, the Regal Small Adult, the Regal Pediatric, The Regal Ten models 65 and 75, and The Regal Four. These scooters offer adjustable flip-up armrests, pneumatic tires front and rear, and more.

612 Regent

Golden Technologies
401 Bridge Street
Old Forge, PA   18518   570-451-747
                                 800-624-6324
                            FAX: 570-451-7974
                   e-mail: info@goldentech.com
                          www.goldentech.com

Top-rated performance scooter, with extra features and economically priced.

613 Safari Scooter

Ranger All Seasons Corporation
PO Box 132
George, IA   51237   712-475-2811
                                800-225-3811
                           FAX: 712-475-3320
                  e-mail: ranger@rconnect.com
                        www.rangerallseason.com

Aaron Stegeman, Sales Manager
Randy Riecks, Sales

Safari is Ranger's most popular scooter. Available in either a 40 inch or 43 inch frame length with an ultra-quiet, totally enclosed transacle drive. The Safari has some of the same features as the SOLO, the user-friendly take-apart and tiller adjustment, color impregnated - not painted- ABS plastic body. The most versatile Ranger Scooter, the Safari is an excellent choice for indoor use, and can take the place of most front wheel drive scooters. It is also an excellent outdoor scooter.

614 Scoota Bug

Golden Technologies
401 Bridge Street
Old Forge, PA   18518   570-451-7477
                                 800-624-6324
                            FAX: 570-451-7974
                   e-mail: info@goldentech.com
                          www.goldentech.com

A lightweight, completely modular scooter, that disassembles and fits into most auto trunks.

615 Scooter Discounters

1945 Winterhaven Drive
Virginia Beach, VA   23456   757-430-4322
                                800-229-1317
                           FAX: 757-430-2698
                  e-mail: info@scooterone.com
                         www.scooterone.com

Offers electric scooters, scooter lifts, ramps, batteries, and more at excellent value without sacrificing quality or service.

616 Shuttle

Mobilelectrics Company
4014 Bardstown Road
Louisville,]Y   40218
                                 800-876-6846
                            FAX: 502-495-2476

A three wheel scooter with safety features for ease of handling, comfort and maximum pleasure.

617 Sidekick Scooter

Mobilelectrics Company
4014 Bardstown Road
Louisville, KY   40218
                                 800-876-6846
                            FAX: 502-495-2476

The seat and foot space provides ample comfort for the average person and the length of the scooter gives it indoor maneuverability.

618 Sierra 3000/4000

Ortho-Kinetics
PO Box 1647
Waukesha, WI   53187   414-542-6060
                                800-824-1068
                           FAX: 414-542-3990

Look to the Sierra 3000/4000 series vehicles for comfort, convenience and performance. Increased leg and foot room, adjustable seat height and arm width, as well as adjustable tiller angle provide maximum comfort. For convenience, the Sierra is equipped with integrated cargo and cup holders and thumb/finger controls with built in wrist rest. Advanced safety features such as stall and freewheeling situation identification and correction, anti roll-back sensory device and audio/visual feedback.

619 Solo Scooter

Ranger All Seasons Corporation
PO Box 132
George, IA   51237   712-475-2811
                                800-225-3811
                           FAX: 712-475-3320
                  e-mail: ranger@rconnect.com
                        www.rangerallseason.com

Aaron Stegeman, Sales Manager
Randy Riecks, Sales

The SOLO is Ranger's ''flagship''model. Introduction of the SOLO 1991 set the standard for easy disassembly of a scooter. The SOLO has a long list of user friendly features including patented take-apart and tiller adjustment mechanisms, non-rusting aluminum frame, extra long, extra tall seats as standard, color impregnated-not painted-ABS plastic bodies, charger plug conveniently located on the Accelerator box and many more. Available in ultra-quiet and four wheel models.

620 SoloRider Industries

7060 South Tuscon Way
Englewood, CO   80112   303-858-0505
                                800-898-3353
                           FAX: 303-858-0707
                  e-mail: rpretekin@solorider.com
                         www.solorider.com

Roger Pretekin, President
Fred Wucher P. Fennig, Vice President of Operations

Manufactures and distributes the AteeA- the revolutionary single rider specifically designed to meet the needs of individuals with disabilities.

621 Surry Tricycloped

National Manufacturing Company
PO Box 3268
Boise, ID 83703   208-343-3639

The Surry has a sleek, aerodynamic design with canted side rails and simple hand controls for gas and brakes.

622 Systems 2000

BioMedical Life Systems
2448 Cades Way
Vista, CA 92083   760-727-5600

This five-mode TENS device has four adjustable modulations, plus conventional settings and comes with a five-year warranty.

623 TERRA-JET: Utility Vehicle

TERRA-JET U.S.A.
PO Box 918
Innis, LA 70747   225-492-2249
                         800-864-5000
              FAX: 225-492-2249
        e-mail: 207767@mcimail.com
           www.members.tripod.com

Larry Rabalais, President
Dora Rabalais, Secretary/Treasurer

TERRA-JET utility vehicles are unique in its ability to traverse many different types of terrain in remote areas otherwise inaccessible. It has a multitude of uses for industry, sportsmen or the whole family. Uniquely designed, industrial duty construction of low maintenance and low fuel consumption. $7,000-$9,000.

624 Terrier Tricycle

TRIAID
PO Box 1364
Cumberland, MD 21501
                         800-306-6777
              FAX: 301-759-3525

Iain A. MacDonald, Sales Director

Provides fun therapy and actively encourages participation, awareness, and the building of self confidence. Designed for children from about five years it features ATB styling, 16 inch wheels, adjustable steering stop and a supportive saddle. Handlebar and seat adjustments combine with a broad wheelbase to ensure the rider is in the optimum position to pedal and the tricycle gives good stability and confident handling. Support accessories are available.

625 Tri-Lo's

TRIAID
PO Box 1364
Cumberland, MD 21501
                         800-306-6777
              FAX: 301-759-3525

Iain A. MacDonald, Sales Director

Available in three sizes these Tricycles provide fun therapy for children from 2-15 years. Propelled by hand cranks the Tri-Lo's are highly recommended by therapists for Spina Bifida children and any other child where the use of the lower limbs is restricted. The Tri-Lo's feature a robust frame with allowance for growth, low foot platform for ease of transfer, padded seat and back cushion, padded armrests, two forms of braking and an anti-tipping device. *$740.00*

626 Tri-Wheelers

Braun Corporation
1014 South Monticello Street
310
Winamac, IN 46996   219-946-6157
                           800-843-5438
                FAX: 219-946-4670

Provides convenience features, producing a high efficiency performance with ultra-smooth operation.

627 Triumph 3000/4000

Ortho-Kinetics
PO Box 1647
Waukesha, WI 53187   414-542-6060
                            800-824-1068
                 FAX: 414-542-3990

The Triumph 3000/4000 series vehicles provide unique comfort and convenience features found nowhere else. Digital Dash with soft touch keypad, deluxe seat with suspension and integral cargo and cup holders are just a few of these features. Equipped with TOPS 24 (Total Ortho Power System) ensures maximum power, performance and reliability. Luxurious options such as velour or allante seat fabrics, stylized wheels, metallic or pearl color options and digital controls are all standard. $2,899-$3,399

628 Triumph Scooter

Ortho-Kinetics
PO Box 1647
Waukesha, WI 53187   414-547-1600
                            800-824-1068
                 FAX: 414-542-3990

The sleek rugged three-wheel, rear-wheel drive, transaxle scooter with up-top controls, designed to help increase mobility and become more active. The Triumph is designed for both indoor and outdoor use. Available in red, blue, green or gray, with an optional power seat lift. $2,899-$3,399.

629 Uno Walker

ETAC USA
2325 Parklawn Drive
Suite J
Waukesha, WI 53186
                         800-678-3822
              FAX: 414-796-4605
        e-mail: etac1usa@execpc.com
           www.execpc.com/~etac1usa

A number one in any language. Elegantly designed with height adjustable handles, seat mudguards, and adjustable wheel locks are standard. Accessories include tray assemble, basket, crutch/cane holder, backrest and oxygen holder. $299-$400.

630   X10 Powerhouse

Words+
40015 Sierra Highway B-145
Palmdale, CA   93550   805-266-8500
                                    800-869-8521
                               FAX: 805-266-8969

Ginger Woltosz, Vice President
Tim Ross, Manager

Controls AC-powered appliances with a control unit
and appliance modules. Plug the appliance modules
into the outlets, then plug the appliances into the
modules. *$199.00*

Stationery

631   Address Book

Sense-Sations
919 Walnut Street
Philadelphia, PA   19107   215-629-2990
                                    800-876-5456

The big print address book is the first personal
book to provide enlarged writing spaces, making
it easier to write down and retrieve information.
$12.50

632   Audio Recordings

Access-USA
PO Box 160
Clayton, NY   13624
                                    800-263-2750
                       e-mail: info@access-usa.com
                            www.access-usa.com

Deborah Haight, EOA

Access-USA produces autio recordings for businesses, organizations and entrepreneurs. Information
such as brochures, reports, documents and others can
be made accessible. Other formats available include
braille, large print, braille business cards and video
services.

633   Big Print Address Book

Access with Ease
PO Box 1150
Chino Valley, AZ   86323   520-636-9469
                                    800-531-9479
                               FAX: 520-636-0292
                       e-mail: KMJC@northlink.com

Karen Clymer, President

Oversized organizer makes locating information easier for those with limited vision. The 7 1/2 inch by 9
1/2 inch plastic coil bound book has more than 500
listings with laminated alphabet tabs. *$16.95*

634   Bold Line Paper

Sense-Sations
919 Walnut Street
Philadelphia, PA   19107   215-629-2990
                                    800-876-5456

This pad consists of 100 sheets of paper with bold
lines to help guide the writing of an individual with
limited vision. *$2.50*

635   Braille Notebook

Maxi Aids
42 Executive Boulevard
3209
Farmingdale, NY   11735   516-752-0521
                                    800-522-6294
                               FAX: 516-752-0689
                       e-mail: sales@maxiaids.com
                            www.maxiaids.com

Made of heavy-duty board, covered with waterproof imitation leather and three rings for binding, including braille paper and titles. *$12.95*

636   Braille: Greeting Cards

Sense-Sations
919 Walnut Street
Philadelphia, PA   19107   215-629-2990
                                    800-876-5456

Birthday, anniversary, get well, sympathy and
Christmas cards offering braille print for the
blind. *$.95*

637   Brailled Desk Calendar

Maxi Aids
42 Executive Boulevard
3209
Farmingdale, NY   11735   516-752-0521
                                    800-522-6294
                               FAX: 516-752-0689
                       e-mail: sales@maxiaids.com
                            www.maxiaids.com

Schedule appointments, remember birthdays or
write messages for a particular day. *$39.95*

638   Clip Board Notebook

Sense-Sations
919 Walnut Street
Philadelphia, PA   19107   215-629-2990
                                    800-876-5456

Kit includes a pack of Bold Line paper and black
ink pen. *$5.95*

639   Deluxe Signature Guide

Maxi Aids
42 Executive Boulevard
3209
Farmingdale, NY   11735   516-752-0521
                                    800-522-6294
                               FAX: 516-752-0689
                       e-mail: sales@maxiaids.com
                            www.maxiaids.com

Rods supported by two rubber blocks facilitate
writing. *$1.25*

640   Highlighter and Note Tape

Therapro
225 Arlington Street
Framingham, MA   01702   508-872-9494
                                    800-257-5376
                               FAX: 508-875-2062
                       e-mail: info@theraproducts.com
                            www.theraproducts.com

A great way to highlight and draw attention to
words without damaging original. Price ranges
from $4.00-$7.00.

641 Letter Writing Guide
Independent Living Aids
27 East Mall
Plainview, NY   11803   516-752-8080
                               800-537-2118
                          FAX: 516-752-3135
     e-mail: can-do@independentliving.com
              www.independentliving.com

Marvin Sandler, President
Sturdy plastic sheet with 13 apertures corresponding
to standard line spacing. *$3.49*

642 Lettering Guide Value Pack
Independent Living Aids
27 East Mall
Plainview, NY   11803   516-752-8080
                               800-537-2118

Included in this useful pack are four durable plastic lettering and number guides for tracing letters
when the individual is unable to write letters unassisted. *$6.29*

643 Maxi Marks
Maxi Aids
42 Executive Boulevard
3209
Farmingdale, NY   11735   516-752-0521
                               800-522-6294
                          FAX: 516-752-0689
           e-mail: sales@maxiaids.com
                   www.maxiaids.com

Braille writing and identification products. *$2.50*

644 Pencil/Pen Weighted Holders
Therapro
225 Arlington Street
Framingham, MA   01702   508-872-9494
                               800-257-5376
                          FAX: 508-875-2062
        e-mail: info@theraproducts.com
                www.theraproducts.com

Securely hold any pencil or pen, these weighted
holders allow for more control along with proprio-
ceptive feedback to encourage better writing
skills.

           $13.25 - $17.50

645 Raised Line Drawing Kit
Maxi Aids
42 Executive Boulevard
3209
Farmingdale, NY   11735   516-752-0521
                               800-522-6294
                          FAX: 516-752-0689
           e-mail: sales@maxiaids.com
                   www.maxiaids.com

For writing script or drawing graphs by the use of
special plastic paper. *$24.45*

646 Signature and Address Self-Inking Stamps
Independent Living Aids
27 East Mall
Plainview, NY   11803   516-752-8080
                               800-537-2118

Gives thousands of impressions before requiring
re-inking. *$11.95*

647 Steady Write
Maxi Aids
42 Executive Boulevard
3209
Farmingdale, NY   11735   516-752-0521
                               800-522-6294
                          FAX: 516-752-0689
           e-mail: sales@maxiaids.com
                   www.maxiaids.com

Furnishes the writer with increased holding capacity and stabilizes the hand. *$6.95*

648 Wings & Wheels Greeting Cards
Wings & Wheels
5 Cleveland Avenue
Dover, NJ   07801
                               800-422-5309
                          FAX: 973-989-9072
        e-mail: flyingspiritedmsn.com
                www.wings-wheels.com

Nanette Courtine, Owner
Offer inclusive greeting cards. Depicts people with
disabilities on the cards.

Visual Aids

649 Abacuses
American Printing House for the Blind
1839 Frankfort Avenue
6085
Louisville, KY   40206   502-895-2405
                               800-223-1839
                          FAX: 502-899-2274
              e-mail: info@aph.org
                      www.aph.org

American Printing House for the Blind, Inc. offers
three abacuses, including the Beginner's Abacus
for reinforcing beginning mathematical concepts,
the Cranmer Abacus used for such functions as
addition, subtraction, multiplication, division,
and calculating square and cube roots. And the
last one is the Large Abacus Description which is
similar to the regular Cranmer Abacus; however
the beads are beveled on top and bottom for easier
gripping.

650 Aluminum Adjustable Support Canes for the Blind
Maxi Aids
42 Executive Boulevard
3209
Farmingdale, NY   11735   516-752-0521
                               800-522-6294
                          FAX: 516-752-0689
           e-mail: sales@maxiaids.com
                   www.maxiaids.com

Adjustable canes for the visually impaired.
$17.95

651 Analog Clock Model

American Printing House for the Blind
1839 Frankfort Avenue
6085
Louisville, KY 40206 502-895-2405
800-223-1839
FAX: 502-899-2274
e-mail: info@aph.org
www.aph.org

The Analog Clock Model has hour and minute hands which are geared together and minute hands which are geared together and synchronized just like the hands on a functional clock. The hour hand is textured, while the minute hand is smooth and thin.

652 Audio Book Contractors

PO Box 40115
Washington, DC 20016 202-363-3429
FAX: 202-363-3429
e-mail: flogibsonABC@aol.com

Flo Gibson, President
Over 900 titles of unabridged classic books on audio cassettes in sturdy vinyl covers with picture and spine windows. *$ 101.95*

ISSN 1556-857

653 Beyond Sight

5650 South Windermere
Littleton, CO 80120 303-795-6455
FAX: 303-795-6425
e-mail: bsistore@beyondsite.com
www.beyondsight.com

Jim Misener, President
Donna Chatham, Administrative Assistant
Products for the blind and visually impaired including talking clocks, watches, and calculators. They also carry a large selection of Braille products, magnifiers, reading machines, and computer equipment. New products include: Accucheck Voicemate and PureFocus vision spray, and GPS Talk, the first talking GPS system for the blind.

654 Big Number Pocket Sized Calculator

Independent Living Aids
27 East Mall
Plainview, NY 11803 516-752-8080
800-537-2118

A handy pocket size calculator with big numbers that fits easily into purse or pocket. *$14.95*

655 Braille 'Touch-Time' Watches

Independent Living Aids
27 East Mall
Plainview, NY 11803 516-752-8080
FAX: 516-752-3135
e-mail: can-do@independentliving.com
www.independentliving.com

Marvin Sandler, President
White dial with black numerals and hands makes telling time possible quickly and easily for the visually impaired. *$44.95*

656 Braille Business Cards & More

Access-USA
PO Box 160
Clayton, NY 13624 800-263-2750
e-mail: info@access-usa.com
www.access-usa.com

Deborah Haight, EOA
Braille on business cards, greeting cards, invitations, folders, plastic credit/ATM cards, advertising inserts, specialties and more. Other formats include audio recordings, braille transcriptions and video formats.

657 Braille Compass

Maxi Aids
42 Executive Boulevard
3209
Farmingdale, NY 11735 516-752-0521
800-522-6294
FAX: 516-752-0689
e-mail: sales@maxiaids.com
www.maxiaids.com

The visually impaired can tell the direction by using this compass. *$42.95*

658 Braille Plates for Elevator

Maxi Aids
42 Executive Boulevard
3209
Farmingdale, NY 11735 516-752-0521
800-522-6294
FAX: 516-752-0689
e-mail: sales@maxiaids.com
www.maxiaids.com

The plates have curing type pressure sensitive material applied for metal to metal bonding. *$79.95*

659 Braille/Print Protractor

American Printing House for the Blind
1839 Frankfort Avenue
6085
Louisville, KY 40206 502-895-2405
800-223-1839
FAX: 502-899-2274
e-mail: info@aph.org
www.aph.org

This cleverly designed Braille/Print Protractor allows visually impaired users to measure angles up to 180 degrees. Bold large type numbers and braille dots mark the degrees along the half circle of the protractor. Two braille dots mark 10 degree increments, while a single braille dot marks the 5 degree increments.

660 Calendars

American Printing House for the Blind
1839 Frankfort Avenue
6085
Louisville, KY 40206 502-895-2405
800-223-1839
FAX: 502-899-2274
e-mail: info@aph.org
www.aph.org

The American Printing House for the Blind offers three different styles of large type/braille calendars for learning and daily living. The Classroom Calendar Kit, The Individual Calendar Kit and the APH InSights Art Calendar.

661   **Card Chart**

American Printing House for the Blind
1839 Frankfort Avenue
6085
Louisville, KY   40206   502-895-2405
                                   800-223-1839
                              FAX: 502-899-2274
                           e-mail: info@aph.org
                                      www.aph.org

The Card Chart is a handy device designed to hold
the 3 1/2 x 2 inch braille/print cards sold by APH
in a variety of products, such as the Expanded
Dolch Word Cards.

662   **Extra Loud Alarm with Lighter Plug**

HARC Mercantile
PO Box 3055
Kalamazoo, MI   49003   616-324-1615
                                   800-445-9968
                              FAX: 616-324-2387
                   e-mail: home@harcmercantile.com
                             www.harcmercantile.com

Ronald Slager, President

Battery operated, easy to read, digital clock with
extra loud alarm. *$45.00*

663   **Low Vision Telephones**

Assistive Devices Network
2241 S Triangle X Lane
Tucson, AZ   85713   866-674-3549

                   e-mail: info@assistivedevices.net
                 http://assistivedevices.net/about.htm

664   **Man's Low-Vision Quartz Watches**

Independent Living Aids
27 East Mall
Plainview, NY   11803   516-752-8080
                                   800-537-2118
                              FAX: 516-752-3135
                 e-mail: can-do@independentliving.com
                             www.independentliving.com

Marvin Sandler, President

An inexpensive, easy-to-read watch with chrome
case. *$ 27.95*

665   **Men's/Women's Low Vision Watches & Clocks**

Maxi Aids
42 Executive Boulevard
3209
Farmingdale, NY   11735   516-752-0521
                                   800-522-6294
                              FAX: 516-752-0689
                      e-mail: sales@maxiaids.com
                                  www.maxiaids.com

Choose from a wide range of watches from braille
automatic to quartz pocket watches.

666   **Rigid Aluminum Cane with Golf Grip**

Maxi Aids
42 Executive Boulevard
3209
Farmingdale, NY   11735   516-752-0521
                                   800-522-6294
                              FAX: 516-752-0689
                      e-mail: sales@maxiaids.com
                                  www.maxiaids.com

A straight, tubular, heavy gauge aluminum rigid
cane for blind and visually impaired persons.
$12.95

667   **TAJ Braille Typewriter**

Maxi Aids
42 Executive Boulevard
3209
Farmingdale, NY   11735   516-752-0521
                                   800-522-6294
                              FAX: 516-752-0689
                      e-mail: sales@maxiaids.com
                                  www.maxiaids.com

Smooth edged, simple and sturdy construction.
Creates braille on 8 1/2 x 11 paper. *$495.00*

668   **Three M Brailler**

Maxi Aids
42 Executive Boulevard
3209
Farmingdale, NY   11735   516-752-0521
                                   800-522-6294
                              FAX: 516-752-0689
                      e-mail: sales@maxiaids.com
                                  www.maxiaids.com

For visually impaired, blind and sighted persons,
produces braille on 3/8 and 1/2 inch vinyl tape.
The dial has braille and regular characters.
$47.95

669   **Three M Large Printed Labeler**

Maxi Aids
42 Executive Boulevard
3209
Farmingdale, NY   11735   516-752-0521
                                   800-522-6294
                              FAX: 516-752-0689
                      e-mail: sales@maxiaids.com
                                  www.maxiaids.com

Ideal for persons with low vision. Can also be read
tactually by blind persons with a knowledge of the
print alphabet. *$ 133.95*

670   **Timex Easy Reader**

Independent Living Aids
27 East Mall
Plainview, NY   11803   516-752-8080
                                   800-537-2118

An easy-to-read large face watch that's water resistant. *$29.95*

671 Unisex Low Vision Watch

Independent Living Aids
27 East Mall
Plainview, NY 11803   516-752-8080
                             800-537-2118
                             FAX: 516-752-3135
e-mail: can-do@independentliving.com
www.independentliving.com

Marvin Sandler, President

Unisex watch with large numbers and wide hands. Gold-toned case with either expansion or leather band. *$31.95*

672 Visual Alerting Guest Room Kit

HARC Mercantile, Ltd.
PO Box 3055
Kalamazoo, MI 49003   616-324-1615
                             800-445-9968
                             FAX: 616-324-2387
e-mail: home@harcmercantile.com
www.harcmercantile.com

Ronald Slager, President

ADA compliant visual alerting guest room kit for the hard of hearing and deaf. Includes visual smoke detector, phone alert, door knock sensor, tactile alarm clock and telephone amplifier. Variations include TTY.

Walking Aids: Canes, Crutches & Walkers

673 Air Lift Oxygen Carriers

Air Lift Unlimited
1212 Kerr Gulch Road
Evergreen, CO 80439   303-526-4700
                             800-776-6771
                             FAX: 303-526-4774
e-mail: info@airlift.com
www.airlift.com

Lori Fortier, Office Manager

Air Lift offers a full line of carriers for portable liquid and cylinder oxygen systems. These versatile carriers meet the needs of oxygen-dependent individuals and parents with oxygen-dependent children seeking more comfortable and convenient ways to transport oxygen. Carriers include backpacks, fanny packs, shoulder/hand bags and carriers for wheelchairs, scooters and walkers. All carriers feature non-flammable, washable fabric and adjustable straps; liquid carriers feature mesh pouches.

674 Aluminum Crutches

Arista Surgical Supply Company
67 Lexington Avenue
New York, NY 10010   212-679-3694
                             800-223-1984

Lightweight aluminum crutches with wood under-arms and handgrips. *$25.00*

675 Aluminum Walking Canes

Maxi Aids
42 Executive Boulevard
3209
Farmingdale, NY 11735   516-752-0521
                               800-522-6294
                               FAX: 516-752-0689
e-mail: sales@maxiaids.com
www.maxiaids.com

Lightweight but strong, these walking canes are made of a heavy gauge aluminum tube with safety locknuts and heavy-duty rubber tips. *$10.75*

676 Arrow Walker

TRIAID
PO Box 1364
Cumberland, MD 21501
                             800-306-6777
                             FAX: 301-759-3525

Iain A. MacDonald, Sales Director

A weight supportive walker designed for children with cerebral palsy or other neuromuscular handicaps. Its comprehensive range of accessories and adjustments allow The Arrow Walker to be tailored to each individual user's needs. The innovative design allows these alterations to be made quickly and easily enabling multiple daily therapy sessions to take place. The low profile shape allows easier access through doorways and around obstacles. *$957.00*

677 Deluxe Nova Wheeled Walker & Avant Wheeled Walker

Fred Sammons
PO Box 32
Brookfield, IL 60513   708-387-7272
                              800-323-5547
                              FAX: 800-547-4333

Lightweight and simple to handle with an easy-to-operate braking system. *$425.40*

678 Deluxe Standard Wood Cane

Arista Surgical Supply Company
67 Lexington Avenue
New York, NY 10010   212-679-3694
                            800-223-1984

A standard old-fashioned wooden cane for the physically challenged. *$10.00*

679 Maxi Superior Cane

Maxi Aids
42 Executive Boulevard
3209
Farmingdale, NY 11735   516-752-0521
                               800-522-6294
                               FAX: 516-752-0689
e-mail: sales@maxiaids.com
www.maxiaids.com

Convenient folding cane designed for optimum balance. Tapered joints provide rigidity when open, and are made of heavy gauge aluminum. *$17.50*

680 **Micro IntroVoice I**

Voice Connection
2324 North Batavia Street
Suite 105
Orange, CA 92865   714-685-1066
                           FAX: 714-685-1070
                           e-mail: voicecnx@aol.com
                           www.voicecnx.com

Shirlee Dworak

Complete voice input/output unit which provides voice recognition of 1,000 words and unlimited synthesized text-to-speech. Its small size is ideal for allowing handheld or forklift terminals to directly attach or cabling to the serial port of these systems. *$ 999.00*

681 **Micro IntroVoice II**

Voice Connection
2324 North Batavia Street
Orange, CA 92865   714-685-1066
                           FAX: 714-685-1070
                           e-mail: voicecnx@aol.com
                           www.voicecnx.com

This battery powered, stand-alone voice system provides 1,000-word recognition, recorded playback, and unlimited text-to-speech synthesis. *$1295.00*

682 **Micro IntroVoice III**

Voice Connection
2324 North Batavia Street
Orange, CA 92865   714-685-1066
                           FAX: 714-685-1070
                           e-mail: voicecnx@aol.com
                           www.voicecnx.com

Voice actuated interface unit that can be installed on most existing and all new wheel wheelchair occupant to speak commands to control the motion of the chair. *$2295.00*

683 **MicroTalker B**

Voice Connection
2324 North Batavia Street
Orange, CA 92865   714-685-1066
                           FAX: 714-685-1070
                           e-mail: voicecnx@aol.com
                           www.voicecnx.com

The MicroTalker B announces recorded voice messages in response to ASCII text received via its serial port. *$395.00*

684 **Nova Walker**

ETAC USA
2325 Parklawn Drive
Suite J
Waukesha, WI 53186
                           800-678-3822
                           FAX: 414-796-4605
                           e-mail: etac1usa@execpc.com
                           www.execpc.com/~etac1usa

Elegant design that provides a comfortable, natural walking style. The seat offers security and stability wherever you go. Folds easily with one hand. Offers lifetime warranty on frame and brake straps for original user.

685 **Out-N-About American Walker**

900 Market Street
Oregon, WI 53575   608-274-5274
                           FAX: 608-835-5234

Luann Smith, President

The lightweight Out-N-About is easy to handle. The four wheel design provides greater support and stability than any other walking aids. Its large rubber tires move effortlessly over most surfaces, indoors and out. The small turning radius makes it ideal or getting through confined spaces and narrow doorways. The attractive, burgundy colored, tubular steel frame is extremely durable. The Out-N-About folds flat and stands alone for easy storage. Made in U.S.A.

686 **Prone Support Walker**

Consumer Care Products
PO Box 684
Sheboygan, WI 53082   920-459-8353
                           FAX: 920-459-9070

Terry Grall, President
Alice Maffongelli, Customer Service

This walker, in five sizes for children to adults, facilitates semi-prone to full upright mobility and dynamic weight bearing. The walker requires the user to push off the floor teaching the user to work with the floor and achieving a more efficient gait. Options such as tray, back support, and hip pads allow adaptation to most needs. $750-$1,300.

687 **Push-Button Quad Cane**

Arista Surgical Supply Company
67 Lexington Avenue
New York, NY 10010   212-679-3694
                           800-223-1984

A reliable walking cane offering independence to the physically challenged user. *$25.00*

688 **Rand-Scot**

401 Linden Center Drive
Fort Collins, CO 80524   970-484-7967
                           800-467-7967
                           FAX: 970-484-3800
                           TDY:800-467-7967
                           e-mail: info@randscop.com
                           www.easypivot.com

Joel Lerich, President
Joellen Sarmast, Business Manager

Manufactures the Easy Pirot patient life live and the BBD wheelchair cushion line and Saratoga Exercise products for the disabled. Offers a line of patient lifts and standers for the disabled. Manufactures the EasyPivot patient lift for 1 person transfers. A video is available plus, no charge for potential users. $800.-$3,000.

689 **Reclining Power Wheelchairs**

LaBac Systems
3535 South Kipling Street
Denver, CO 80235   303-914-9914
                           800-445-4402

Power recline seating systems for wheelchairs, offering more comfort and dependability for the physically challenged.

690 Roleez Wheel System

5717 Sellger Drive
Norfolk, VA 23502   757-461-1122
                                     800-369-1390
                                     FAX: 757-461-0383

William E. Tuggle, President

Two all-terrain carts for transporting the disabled with ease over soft, sandy beaches, nature trails, and generally uneven terrain; use specifically-patented, soft pneumatic wheels invented specifically for soft sand and uneven terrain. The two carts, the Sport Wheeler for adults and the Fun Wheeler for children, will go all those wonderful places where a wheelchair cannot go. No longer manufactures beach wheelchairs for the disabled, but are the suppliers of the soft pneumatic wheels.

691 Scooter & Wheelchair Battery Fuel Gauges and Motor Speed Controllers

Curtis Instruments
200 Kisco Avenue
Mount Kisco, NY 10549   914-666-2971
                                    FAX: 914-666-2188
                                    e-mail: curtis1@cloud9.net
                                    www.curtisinst.com

Steve Waite, Vice President Sales

Provides a readable, accurate indication of battery, in easy to read type of display. Innovative, efficient motor speed controllers for single or dual PM motor vehicles.

692 Skyway

Skyway Machine
4451 Caterpillar Road
Redding, CA 96003

                                    800-332-3357
                                    FAX: 530-243-5104
                                    e-mail: sales@skywaywheels.com
                                    www.skywaytuffwheels.com

Parrey Cremeans, Sales Manager
Bart Weens, Sales/Customer Service

For over 20 years Skyway has been the world leader in composite wheels. Supplying over 650 different wheel combinations for wheelchairs, lawn and garden products, bicycles, and a large assortment of wheeled devices. Wheel sizes range from 4 inch to 24 inch diameter.

693 StairClimber

Martin Technology
29 North Main Street
Gloversville, NY 12078

                                    800-800-1410
                                    FAX: 518-725-9522

A walker-capable person can climb and descend stairs with this walker-designed StairClimber.

694 Standing Aid Frame with Rear Entry

Consumer Care Products
PO Box 684
Sheboygan, WI 53082   920-459-8353
                                    FAX: 920-459-9070

Terry Grall, President
Alice Maffongelli, Customer Service

This rugged stander, made of natural hardwood in sizes for one to twelve year olds, allows weight bearing in an upright position. Table, upper trunk and/or head support, hip pads and casters allow individualized fitting. The new hinged rear entry option makes entry into this stander easy and quick for parents, teachers and therapists. $572-$1,800.

695 Thomas Hardware, Parts & Fasteners

1001 Rockland Street
Reading, PA 19604
                                    800-634-4293
                                    FAX: 800-634-3099

Bob Ruhe, Marketing Manager
Wheelchair restraint kits.

696 Tilt-N-Table

Osterguard Enterprises c/o Jim's Shop
3228 West Olive Avenue
Fresno, CA 93722   559-275-4695

These are lightweight tables for wheelchairs that are angle and height adjustable to your changing needs.

697 Torso Support

Grandmar
5675-C Landregan Street
Emeryville, CA 94608

An aid for people who are unable to maintain an upright position in an automobile or a wheelchair.

698 Ventura Enterprises

35 Lawton Avenue
Danville, IN 46122   817-705-2589
                                    FAX: 317-745-3179
                                    www.venturaenterprises.com

Linda Plunkett, President

Manufacturer of everyday living mobility aids. Products include carrying aids for walkers and wheelchairs and also wheelchair cushions.

699 WCIB Heavy-Duty Folding Cane

Maxi Aids
42 Executive Boulevard
3209
Farmingdale, NY 11735   516-752-0521
                                    800-522-6294
                                    FAX: 516-752-0689
                                    e-mail: sales@maxiaids.com
                                    www.maxiaids.com

A four section aluminum folding cane with a golf-type grip handle and flexible wrist loop. #1749015, 34-60 *$17.95*

700 Walker Leg Support

Fred Sammons
PO Box 32
Brookfield, IL 60513   708-387-7272
                                    800-323-5547
                                    FAX: 800-547-4333

For lower externity trauma. An alternative to crutches that allows safe, stable ambulation and frees hands and arms for daily tasks. *$11.50*

701 Wheelchair Aide

Graham-Field
400 Rabro Drive
Hauppauge, NY 11788   516-582-5900

This is a heavy-duty wheelchair comfort tray which surrounds the wheelchair user and provides a large, smooth surface for dining, writing, hobbies or work. The heavy gauge plastic tray is easy to clean and attaches with two Velcro straps.

702 Wheelchair Back Pack and Tote Bag

Med Covers
1639 Green Street
Suite D
Raleigh, NC 27603   919-829-5777

Accessories are specifically designed with the wheelchair user in mind. The Back Pack has a main roomy pouch for larger items and has a full length zipper with four sliders for convenient access.

703 Wheelchair Work Table

Bailey Manufacturing Company
118 Lee Street
Lodi, OH 44254   330-948-1080
                        800-321-8372
          FAX: 330-948-4439
e-mail: baileymfg@attmail.com
          www.baileymfg.com

An adjustable height, functional, individual cut-out work table featuring a wood-grain laminate, scratch resistant top with chrome plated steel legs.

Wheelchairs: Accessories

704 Advantage Wheelchair & Walker Bags

Laurel Designs
5 Laurel Avenue
Belvedere, CA 94920
          FAX: 415-435-1451
e-mail: laureld@ncal.verio.com

Janet Sawyer, Co-Owner
Lynn Montoya, Co-Owner

Wheelchair sport packs include: long, short, neon, multi-color and blowin' in the wind socks. Prices range from $20.00 to $60.00.

705 Battery Operated Cushion

DA Schulman
7701 Newton Avenue North
Brooklyn Park, MN 55444   612-561-2908

Battery-operated, dynamic cushion for wheelchairs.

706 Dual-Mode Charger

Lester Electrical
625 W A Street
Lincoln, NE 68522   402-477-8988
          FAX: 402-474-1769
e-mail: sales@lesterelectrical.com
          www.lestereletrical.com

Edith Earnest, Sales Service Coord.
Paul Schmidt, Sales Engineer

Fully automatic battery charger.

707 EZBACK Recline Control

APT Technology
236A North Main Street
Shreve, OH 44676   330-567-2001
                        888-549-2001
          FAX: 330-567-3073
e-mail: sales@apt-technology.com
          www.apt-technology.com

Helen L. Thompson, Marketing Manager
David M. Bayer, Rehab Engineer

A versatile, easy to install and operate motor controller intended to control power recline and similar machinery on a power wheelchair. Optional EDMA permits control of 2 motors via a single or dual switch. Accommodates limit switches, various configurations and is rugged and reliable. *$685.00*

708 Featherspring

712 North 34th Street
Seattle, WA 98103   206-545-8585
          FAX: 206-547-8589
www.featherspring.com

Peter Rothschild, President

Foot supports for wheelchair users to prevent and treat cold feet, sore heels, swollen feet and weak ankles. *$199.95*

709 George H. Snyder Enterprises

5809 NE 21st Avenue
Fort Lauderdale, FL 33308
          FAX: 954-491-2886

George Snyder, President

Attachments for wheelchairs.

710 Latchloc Automatic Wheelchair Tiedown

Ahnafield Corporation
3219 West Washington Street
Indianapolis, IN 46222   317-631-7272
                        800-636-8060
          FAX: 317-636-8098

Is an independent wheelchair tiedown system utilized primarily by individuals who drive from their wheelchairs.

711 Mat Factory

760 West 16th Street
Building E
Costa Mesa, CA 92627   949-645-3122
                        800-628-7626
          FAX: 949-645-0966
e-mail: MATFACTORY@pop3.concentric.net
          www.matfactoryinc.com

Roger Maloney, President

The Safety Deck II is an interlocking grid system made from recycled rubber tires and recycled PVC. The tiles are set directly on top of the ground and permits grass to grow through the holes and cover the surface. The system provides safe, non-barrier access for wheelchairs over grass. Once the grass has covered the tiles the only maintenance required is watering and mowing. Safety Deck II also allows for beach and sand access.

712 Pac-All Wheelchair Carrier

Pac-All Carriers
2321 Carolton Road
Maitland, FL 32751   407-830-6604
                                 800-628-6672
                                 FAX: 407-339-2847

L.E. Angel

No more lifting and no more pain wheelchair carrier. VA approved. Made in USA.

$158 - $226.40

713 Wheel Life News

University of Virginia, Rehab Engineering Centers
3363 University Station
Charlottesville, VA 22903   804-924-0311

Features tie downs and other adaptive technology for persons with disabilities.

714 Wheelchair Accessories

Diestco Manufacturing Company
PO Box 6504
Chico, CA 95927   530-893-3136
                              800-795-2392
                              FAX: 530-893-2635
                              e-mail: info@diestco.com
                              www.diestco.com

John Onnen, VP Sales/Marketing

Diestco makes innovative accessories for wheelchairs, scooters, and walkers. Products include canopies, backpacks, cupholders, pouches, threshhold ramps, laptrays, and others. *$157.00*

Wheelchairs: General

715 Act Wheelchair

Etac USA
2325 Parklawn Drive
Suite J
Waukesha, WI 53186
                              800-678-3822
                              FAX: 414-796-4605
                              e-mail: etac1usa@execpc.com
                              www.execpc.com/~etac1usa

A carefully designed Swedish wheelchair made of lightweight titanium for active users. Seat frame and upholstery are adjustable to fit each individual. Available in Frame widths from 15.5 to 18 inches. The colors available are: black, red plum teal, blue and silver. Lifetime warranty on frame for original user.

716 Bariatric Wheelchairs Regency FL,TLC

Gendron
Lugbill Road
Archbold, OH 43502
                              800-537-2521
                              www.gendroninc.com

Steven Cotter, V.P. Sales

Bariatric wheelchairs, for users weighing up to seven hundred pounds. Manual and power styles built to order for specific needs.

717 Basic Wheelchair

ETAC USA
2325 Parklawn Drive
Suite J
Waukesha, WI 53186
                              800-678-3822
                              FAX: 414-796-4605
                              e-mail: etac1usa@execpc.com
                              www.execpc.com/~etac1usa

A carefully designed crossfolding wheelchair made from extruded aluminum, the Basic is designed with the caregiver in mind and easily folds for transportation or storage. Available in widths of 14 to 20 inches, has incontinence upholstery which is easily washable with mild soap and water. Swing away, detachable legrests and footrests are standard with fixed hub rear wheels. $1,000 - $2,000

718 Big Bounder Power Wheelchair

21st Century Scientific
4915 Industrial Way
Coeur D Alene, ID 83815   208-667-8800
                                      800-448-3680
                                      FAX: 208-667-6600
                                      e-mail: 21st@wheelchairs.com
                                      wheelchairs.com

R.D. Davidson, Sales & Mktg. Dir.

Manufactured for the obese in virtually any dimension. Its powerful motors and rugged frame can accommodate users up to 1000 lb. 21st Century Scientific, Inc.'s unique SWOW option can reduce the overall width of the chair by as much as 3 inches. This may make the difference between using normal doorways or remodeling a home. $10,495

719 Breezy

Sunrise Medical/Quickie Designs
2842 N Business Park Avenue
Fresno, CA 93727   559-292-2171

This lightweight chair is durable, comfortable and flexible enough to meet the needs of a wide range of wheelchair users.

720 Champion 1000

Kuschall of America
3601 Rider Trail South
Earth City, MO 63045   314-512-7000
                                   800-654-4768
                                   FAX: 800-542-3567

Ultralight wheelchair designed to improve mobility. $1,689

721 Champion 2000

Kuschall of America
3601 Rider Trail South
Earth City, MO 63045 314-512-7000
800-654-4768
FAX: 800-542-3567

Rigid chair that folds side-to-side. $1,765

722 Champion 3000

Kuschall of America
3601 Rider Trail South
Earth City, MO 63045 314-512-7000
800-654-4768
FAX: 800-542-3567

The high-performance chair built for perfectionists. $1,695

723 Convaid Products

PO Box 4209
Palos Verdes, CA 90274 310-539-6814
800-266-8243
FAX: 310-539-3670
e-mail: convaid@convaid.com
www.convaid.com

Five different styles of wheelchairs.

724 Cross Wheelchair

ETAC USA
2325 Parklawn Drive
Suite J
Waukesha, WI 53186
800-678-3822
FAX: 414-796-4605
e-mail: etac1usa@execpc.com
www.execpc.com/~etac1usa

A carefully designed crossfolding Swedish wheelchair made of aluminum. The cross has a contouring back rest upholstery that can be adjusted as the user needs to change. Frame widths available in 14 -20 inches. Seat frame and upholstery are adjustable to fit each individual. Lifetime warranty on frame for original user. $1,295 -$2,500

725 Custom

Fortress
PO Box 489
Clovis, CA 93613 559-322-5437
FAX: 559-323-0299

Ultralight aluminum wheelchair that can be customized to customer's requests. Fifteen frame colors, eight seat widths and depths, along with thirteen rear wheel combinations are just a few of the features offered at the standard package price.

726 Custom Durable

21279 Protecta Drive
Elkhart, IN 46516 219-266-1005
800-933-0256
FAX: 219-293-0202

Wheelchairs; accessories.

727 Custom Lite

Fortress
PO Box 489
Clovis, CA 93612 FAX: 559-323-0299

Offering a wide range of options, features and modifications all at a reasonable package price, this wheelchair is fully adjustable and excellent for the extremely active.

728 ETAC USA, F3 Wheelchair

2325 Parklawn Drive
Suite J
Waukesha, WI 53186
800-678-3822
FAX: 414-796-4605
e-mail: etac1usa@execpc.com
www.execpc.com/~etac1usa

A swedish wheelchair designed to provide function, comfort and flexibility. Seat frame and upholstery are adjustable to fit each individual. Swing away, detachable footrests are standard. Available in frame widths from 14, 18 and 20 inch. Numerous accessories are available in order to individualize each chair. Lifetime warranty on frame for original user.

729 ETAC USA, Sting Wheelchair

2325 Parklawn Drive
Suite J
Waukesha, WI 53186
800-678-3822
FAX: 414-796-4605
e-mail: etac1usa@execpc.com
www.execpc.com/~etac1usa

A swedish wheelchair designed to adjust to meet the growing child's every need. Both the seat and the backrest are width, height, and angle adjustable. Footrest, adjustable in height, depth and angle and swings back under the seat. Numerous accessories available. Lifetime warranty on frame for the original user.

730 Edge

Fortress
PO Box 489
Clovis, CA 93613 559-322-5437
FAX: 559-323-0299

An ultra lightweight aircraft aluminum wheelchair that is suitable for sports, school or the workplace.

731 Evacu-Trac

Garaventa Canada Ltd.
PO Box L-1
Blaine, WA 98230 360-332-2231
800-663-6556

This emergency evacuation chair is designed for safety and fast operation.

732 Folding Chair with a Rigid Feel

Kuschall of America
3601 Rider Trail South
Earth City, MO   63045   314-512-7000
                                             800-654-4768
                              FAX: 800-542-3567

The Champion 1000 is a new concept in folding chairs. Even though it's ultra light, it has the feel and performance of a rigid chair.

733 Formula Series Active Mobility Wheelchairs

Everest & Jennings Avenue
3233 Mission Oaks Boulevard
Camarillo, CA   93012   805-389-7450

This is a new series of lightweight wheelchairs designed for the active user.

734 Freestyle II

Fortress
PO Box 489
Clovis, CA   93613   559-322-5437
                              FAX: 559-323-0299

Effort-sparing, ultra-lightweight aircraft aluminum construction and design allow for easy propelling over various rolling surfaces.

735 Gadabout Wheelchairs

Gadabout Wheelchairs
1165 Portland Avenue
Rochester, NY   14621   716-338-1000
                                             800-828-4242

Enjoy independence with the wheelchair that is lightweight, portable, convenient, comfortable and sturdy.

736 Gendron

Lugbill Road
Archbold, OH   43502
                                             800-537-2521
                              FAX: 419-446-2631

Steven Cotter, V.P. Sales

Manufacturer of wheelchairs for a variety of other applications, specializing in bariatric mobility products.

737 HiRider

Gaymar Industries
10 Centre Drive
Orchard Park, NY   14127   716-662-2551
                                             800-828-7341

A wheelchair that provides mobility in both sitting and standing positions.

738 Innovative Products Ltd.

4351 West College Avenue
Appleton, WI   54914   616-684-5050
                                             800-424-3369
                              FAX: 414-738-9050

Wheelchairs; accessories.

739 Liberty

Fortress
PO Box 489
Clovis, CA   93613   559-322-5437
                              FAX: 559-323-0299

Ultra lightweight wheelchair provides a comfortable fit and leaves people able to function as normally as possible in daily activities.

740 Lightweight Breezy

Motion Design
2842 N Business Park Avenue
Fresno, CA   93727   559-292-2171

A lightweight wheelchair. *$750.00*

741 Majors Medical Supply

Corporate Headquarters
211 Rock Hill Road
Bala Cynwyd, PA   19004
                                             800-625-6770
                              FAX: 800-783-5825
             e-mail: majorsmedical@majorsmedical.com
                              www.majorsmedical.com

America's largest selection of wheelchairs and homecare equipment.

742 National Mobility Equipment Dealers Association

11211 North Nebraska Avenue
Suite A5
Tampa, FL   33612   813-977-6603
                              FAX: 813-977-6402
                              e-mail: nmeda@aol.com
                                       www.nmeda.org

Becky Plank, Executive Director

Trade association that will benefit anyone that manufactures, buys, sells, installs, prescribes or needs a working knowledge of adaptive equipment for transportation for the disabled.

743 Natural Access

PO Box 5729
Santa Monica, CA   90409   609-588-9830
                                             800-411-7789
                              FAX: 609-588-9836
                  e-mail: national@superlink.net
                                       www.landecz.com

John Egan, OWASC

Provides the Landecz all-terrain wheelchair, that can roll easily on sand, gravel and snow for outdoor fun. The entire chair can fit inside a travel bag!

744 One Thousand FS

Fortress
PO Box 489
Clovis, CA   93613   559-322-5437
                              FAX: 559-323-0299

Add-on power system installs in minutes, enabling the driver to relax and drive anywhere with smooth, silent electric power.

745 Posture-Glide Lounger
Lumex
100 Spence Street
Bay Shore, NY 11706

800-645-5272
FAX: 800-L4L-UMEX

Provides all day comfort and safe, independent mobilization with feet or hands. The ergonomically engineered seat back provides correct support.

746 Redman Apache
Redman Powerchair
3840 South Palo Verde Road
Tucson, AZ 85714

800-727-6684

These ultralight, active use wheelchairs offer quick release rear wheels, adjustable arm height and detachable arm swing-away.

747 Redman Crow Line
Redman Powerchair
3840 South Palo Verde Road
Tucson, AZ 85714

800-727-6684

Reclining wheelchair that reclines a full 90 degrees to flat and can be stopped anywhere on the axis.

748 Rolls 2000 Series
Invacare Corporation
899 Cleveland Street
Elyria, OH 44035

440-329-6426
800-333-6900
e-mail: info@invacare.com

These wheelchairs are the first light-weight wheelchairs designed for rental use.

749 Side-to-Side Folding Chair
Kuschall of America
3601 Rider Trail South
Earth City, MO 63045

314-512-7000
800-654-4768
FAX: 800-542-3567

The Champion 2000 is a folding chair with the ride and feel of a rigid chair.

750 Stand-Up Wheelchairs
Lifestand
PO Box 232171
Encinitas, CA 92023

800-782-6324
FAX: 610-586-0847
e-mail: dallery@msn.com

Jacques A. Dallery, President

Offers a complete line of manual, electric and stand-up wheelchairs for the disabled.

751 Surf Chair
2052 South Peninsula Drive
Daytona Beach, FL 32118

904-253-0986
800-841-6610
FAX: 904-253-7600

Wheelchairs; accessories.

752 Swede Elite
ETAC USA
2325 Parklawn Drive
Suite J
Waukesha, WI 53186

800-678-3822
FAX: 414-796-4605
e-mail: etac1usa@execpc.com

A carefully designed Swedish wheelchair made of lightweight titanium for the active user. Available in frame widths from 14-18 inches and colors available are: black, red, plus, teal-blue, and Silver. Custom colors available at additional cost and there is a lifetime warranty on the frame for original user. $1,740-$2,500

753 Swede Sting
ETAC USA
2325 Parklawn Drive
Suite J
Waukesha, WI 53186

800-678-3822
FAX: 414-796-4605
e-mail: etac1usa@execpc.com

A carefully designed Swedish wheelchair combining durability with individual adjustments to meet the changing needs of the growing child. Available in three widths 11, 12, and 13, and five colors: black, red, blue, teal and plum. $1595-$2,500

754 Vista Wheelchair
Arista Surgical Supply Company
67 Lexington Avenue
New York, NY 10010

212-679-3694
800-223-1984

Vista has a rugged cold-rolled steel frame, durable vinyl upholstery and steel bearings to assure a smooth ride. *$220.00*

755 Wheelchair Rocker
Artec
PO Box 25103-A
Greenville, SC 29616

864-288-2111

Randy Crew, President

The Carolina Rocker turns a wheelchair into a rocking chair for fun, relaxation and therapy for children and adults. $499

756 Wheelchair with Shock Absorbers
Iron Horse Productions
2624 Conner Street
Port Huron, MI 48060

810-987-6700
800-426-0354

The Iron Horse is a revolutionary concept in wheelchair design that offers comfort, indoors and outdoors. *$2375.00*

757 Wizz-ard

Wheelchairs of Kansas
PO Box 320
Ellis, KS   67637   785-726-4950
                                        800-537-6454
                               FAX: 800-337-2447
        e-mail: bigwheelchairs@hotmail.com
           www.wheelchairsofkansas.com

A large-frame wheelchair constructed of high quality, stress tested stainless steel to insure durability and peak performance.

758 YM 9000 Ride-Lite Series

Invacare Corporation
899 Cleveland Street
Elyria, OH   44035   440-329-6426

              e-mail: info@invacare.com

This wheelchair has adjustable toggle wheel locks with brackets that bolt through the frame, composite pneumatic wheels and casters, and foam-padded back upholstery.

Wheelchairs: Pediatric

759 Commuter & Kid's Commuter

Fortress
PO Box 489
Clovis, CA   93613   559-322-5437
                               FAX: 559-323-0299

The first of a new generation of power wheelchairs. These chairs feature direct drive power yet are foldable, transportable and affordable.

760 Convaid

2830 California Street
Torrance, CA   90503
                                        888-266-8243
                               FAX: 310-539-3670
           e-mail: convaid@earthlink.net
                    www.convaid.com

Merv Watkins, President
Rodolfo Restelli, Controller
Nathan Watkins, Exec. Vice President

Convaid manufactures Mobile Positioning Systems for children. The Expedition, Safari Tilt, Cruiser, EZ Rider and Metro offer a non-institutional styling and are lightweight and compact-folding. The steel/aluminum structure is engineered for maximum comfort and durability. The mobile positioning lines come with more than 20 positioning features and a full range of positioning adaptations. All chairs have been successfully crash-tested and offer a limited lifetime warranty (except the Metro).

761 Imp Tricycle

TRIAID
PO Box 1364
Cumberland, MD   21501
                                        800-306-6777
                               FAX: 301-759-3525

Iain A. MacDonald, Sales Director

Provides fun therapy and actively encourages participation, awareness and the building of self confidence. Designed for children from about 3 years it features ATB styling, 12 inch wheels, adjustable steering stop and a supportive saddle. handlebar and seat adjustments combine with a broad wheelbase to ensure the rider is in the optimum position to pedal and the tricycle gives good stability and confident handling. Support accessories are available. *$590.00*

762 Kid's Custom

Fortress
PO Box 489
Clovis, CA   93613   559-322-5437
                               FAX: 559-323-0299

Custom pediatric mobility needs. This ultra lightweight chair is tailor fit to each child, to make wheeling fun and encourages kids to be active because they feel free, safe and secure.

763 Kid's Edge

Fortress
PO Box 489
Clovis, CA   93613   559-322-5437
                               FAX: 559-323-0299

This wheelchair offers multiple options, features and modifications at no upcharge.

764 Kid's Liberty

Fortress
PO Box 489
Clovis, CA   93613   559-322-5437
                               FAX: 559-323-0299

Offers a broad range of seat heights, widths and depths, back heights and numerous other modifications to accommodate the specific and unique requirements of children.

765 Kid-Friendly Chairs

Vector Mobility
5030 East Jensen Avenue
Fresno, CA   93725
                                        800-441-0358
                               FAX: 559-441-0359

Manual base offers the lowest available floor to seat height, growth capability, one-third the parts of a conventional chair and no welds to break. The power unit features standard shapes and personality designs from elephants to inch worms and autos to rainbows, lowest seat height, and smallest turning radius on the market.

766 Pediatric Wheelchair

Wheel Ring
199 Forest Street
Manchester, CT   06040   860-647-8596

This wheelchair is designed to grow with the child.

767 Seven Fifty-Five FS

Fortress
PO Box 489
Clovis, CA   93613   559-322-5437
                               FAX: 559-323-0299

Unharness the curiosity of childhood with the modular power/base seating system that sets kids free. This device is engineered and built especially for children.

768 **TMX Tricycle**
TRIAID
PO Box1364
Cumberland, MD 21501

800-306-6777
FAX: 301-759-3525

Iain A. MacDonald, Sales Director

Provides fun therapy and actively encourages participation, awareness and the building of self confidence. Designed for children from about eight years it features ATB styling, 20 inch wheels, adjustable steering stop and a supportive saddle. Handlebar and seat adjustments combine with a broad wheelbase to ensure the rider is in the optimum position to pedal and the tricycle gives good stability and confident handling. Support accessories are available. *$795.00*

Wheelchairs: Powered

769 **Bounder Plus Power Wheelchair**
21st Century Scientific
4915 Industrial Way
Coeur D Alene, ID 83815

208-667-8800
800-448-3680
FAX: 208-667-6600
e-mail: 21st@wheelchairs.com
www.wheelchairs.com

R.D. Davidson, Sales & Mktg. Dir.

Available in widths of 16 to 20 inches for users up to 500 pounds with a 2 year warranty on the entire chair. It offers all the standard features of a BOUNDER, plus reinforced rear wheel mounts, reinforced caster barrels, and super duty upholstery (with double liner and web straps under every screw). The BOUNDER Plus also features tandem cross struts, middle vertical support strut, seat rails supported at five points, and back upholstery attached with machine screws. *$9795.00*

770 **Bounder Power Wheelchair**
21st Century Scientific
4915 Industrial Way
Coeur D Alene, ID 83815

208-667-8800
800-448-3680
FAX: 208-667-6600
e-mail: 21st@wheelchairs.com
www.wheelchairs.com

R.D. Davidson, Sales & Mktg. Dir.

Available in a variety of widths from 16 to 18 inches for users up to 250 pounds. Its powerful motors can achieve top speeds of over 120 mph. The rugged frame is constructed with steel tubing. The standard 12 position Adjustable Front Forks, made of 1/4 inch thick steel, provides impact dampening and seat tilt adjustment. A Dual Group 27 Sliding Battery Box provides extended range and easy battery maintenance. *$8695.00*

771 **Damaco D90**
Damaco
20542 Plummer Street
Chatsworth, CA 91311

800-432-2434
FAX: 818-709-5282

Portable power unit that fits manual wheelchairs with large rear wheels. Weighing just 22 pounds, the power system can be removed and stored in a matter of seconds. *$2495.00*

772 **Eagle Sportschairs**
2351 Parkwood Road
Snellville, GA 30039

770-972-0763
800-932-9380
FAX: 770-985-4885
e-mail: bewing@bellsouth.net
www.eaglesportschairs.com

Barry Ewing, Owner
Alice Kirk, Customer Service

The Eagle line of custom lightweight performance chairs includes a range of options to fit all racing and sport needs including; track, baseball, quad-rugby, tennis, field events and waterski. Also popular for daily use. We are able to customize any chair to accommodate size and disability, and all frames have a full five year warranty.

773 **Fortress**
PO Box 489
Clovis, CA 93613

559-322-5437
FAX: 559-323-0299

The pediatric rear wheel drive scooter is shorter and more compact, has smaller diameter wheels, and a shortened seat post and tiller.

774 **Geronimo**
Redman Powerchair
3840 South Palo Verde Road
Suite 202
Tucson, AZ 85714

800-727-6684

Wheelchair offering direct drive, two year electronic guarantee and micro controls.

775 **Lancer**
Everest & Jennings Avenue
3233 Mission Oaks Boulevard
Camarillo, CA 93012

805-389-7450

Modular power base wheelchair.

776 **Marathon LE Power Wheelchair**
Everest & Jennings Avenue
3233 Mission Oaks Boulevard
Camarillo, CA 93012

805-389-7450

The latest advancements have been incorporated into the new design. Includes streamlined belt covers and protective wheel covers.

777 **Penny & Giles Pilot**

Voice Connection
2324 North Batavia Street
Orange, CA   92865   714-685-1066
FAX: 714-685-1070
e-mail: voicecnx@aol.com
www.voicecnx.com

Motorized wheelchair that requires no special
mounting or installation.

778 **Permobil Max 90**

Permobil
30 Ray Avenue
Burlington, MA   01803   781-272-7410
FAX: 781-229-9841

The power wheelchair for those needing an easily
maneuverable and quiet indoor chair but who also
need to use their chair outdoors.

779 **Permobil Super 90**

Permobil
30 Ray Avenue
Burlington, MA   01803   781-272-7410
FAX: 781-229-9841

The power wheelchair is designed for travel over
uneven and hilly terrain outdoors and indoors.

780 **Power for Off-Pavement**

Redman Powerchair
3840 South Palo Verde Road
Suite 202
Tucson, AZ   85714
800-727-6684

Power-drive wheelchair has a solid seat and can
handle safely and securely knolls and off-pavement terrain.

781 **Pride Remote Plus**

Voice Connection
2324 North Batavia Street
Orange, CA   92865   714-685-1066
FAX: 714-685-1070
e-mail: voicecnx@aol.com
www.voicecnx.com

Motorized wheelchair that requires no special
mounting or installation.

782 **Quickie Qtronix**

Voice Connection
2324 North Batavia Street
Orange, CA   92865   714-685-1066
FAX: 714-685-1070
e-mail: voicecnx@aol.com
www.voicecnx.com

Motorized wheelchair that requires no special
mounting or installation.

783 **Roll-Aid**

Stand Aid of Iowa
PO Box 386
Sheldon, IA   51201
800-831-8580
FAX: 712-324-5210
e-mail: standaid@connect.com

Adapts to fit all standard collapsible wheelchairs.
It is convenient, portable and provides electric
rollator mobility instantly. *$1748.00*

784 **Steven Motor Chair**

Steven Motor Chair Company
20580 Placer Hills Road
Colfax, CA   95713   530-637-5919

Wesley Stephens, Managing Partner
Brian Stephens, Managing Partner
Completely self-powered, easy to operate, attractive
and rugged.

Wheelchairs: Racing

785 **Aeroedge**

Fortress
PO Box 489
Clovis, CA   93613   559-322-5437
FAX: 559-323-0299

The ultimate in racing wheelchair design. Two
innovative and exclusive Fortress features make
this the fastest machine on three wheels.

786 **East Penn Manufacturing Company**

East Penn Manufacturing Company
PO Box 147
Lyon Station, PA   19536   610-682-6361
FAX: 610-682-4781
e-mail: eastpenn@eastpenn-delu.com

Harold Eberly, V.P. Sales
Specially engineered for demanding deep-cycle applications Gelled electrolyte Deka Dominator Batteries provides maintenance-free operation, longer
battery life and hours of reliable performance. Their
excellent recharge characteristics provide quick turn-
a-round time.

787 **Invacare Top End**

Div. of Invacare Corporation
4501 63rd Circle
Pinellas Park, FL   33781   727-522-8677
800-532-8677
FAX: 727-522-1007
www.invacare.com

Mary Carol Peterson, Marketing
Manufacturers of light weight, rigid, sport-specific
wheelchairs such as the Eliminator line of racing
chairs, T-3 tennis and softball chairs, and the Termi-
nator for quad rugby and basketball. The Excelerator,
XLT three-wheel hand cycle for adults and juniors.
Check out our full line of wheelchairs to fit every
need. $1,895-$2,495

788 **Rigid Sports Wheelchair**

Magic In Motion
239 West Stewart Avenue
Puyallup, WA   98371   253-845-2152

This light-weight chair is designed for those who
prefer a rigid chair or do not require a folding
chair.

Aging

789 Aging in America

1500 Pelham Parkway South
Bronx, NY   10461   413-584-1460
FAX: 413-586-1121
e-mail: cemoylan@aol.com

Ralph Hall, President

Research and services organization for professionals in gerontology. Objectives are: to produce, implement and share effective and affordable programs and services that improve the quality of life for the elderly community; to better prepare professionals and students interested in or currently involved with, aging and the aged. Conducts research projects, educational and training seminars, and in-service curricula for long-term and acute care facilities.

790 Alabama Association of Homes and Services for the Aging

4401 Narrow Lane Road
Montgomery, AL   36116   205-281-6336
FAX: 205-281-6339

791 American Association of Homes and Services for the Aging

2519 Connecticut Avenue NW
Washington, DC   20008   202-783-2242
FAX: 202-783-2255
e-mail: info@aahsa.org
www.aahsa.org

The American Association of Homes and Services for the Aging (AAHS) represents not-for-profit organizations dedicated to providing high-quality health care, housing and services to the nation's elderly. AAHSA organizations serve more than one million older persons af all icome levels, creed and races.

792 Arizona Association of Homes and Housing for the Aging

3839 N 3rd Street
Suite 201
Phoenix, AZ   85012   602-230-0026
FAX: 602-230-0563

793 Association of Massachusetts Homes and Services for the Aging

45 Bromfield Street
Boston, MA   02108   617-423-0718
FAX: 617-423-2109

794 Association of Ohio Philanthropic Homes and Housing for Aging

855 South Wall Street
Columbus, OH   43206   614-444-2882
FAX: 614-444-2974

795 California Association of Homes and Services for the Aging

7311 Greenhaven Drive
Suite 175
Sacramento, CA   95831   916-392-5111
FAX: 916-428-4250
e-mail: lbloxham@aging.org
www.aging.org

796 Center for Understanding Aging

200 Executive Boulevard
Suite 201
Southington, CT   06489   718-824-4004
FAX: 718-824-4242
e-mail: couper.natla@snet.net

Donna Couper, Director

Seeks to dispel myths about aging and old age, encourages communication among generations and works to create a social environment where people of all ages can live together. Also serves as a clearinghouse of information on issues of aging and intergenerational programs. Provides professional speakers and workshop leaders.

797 Children of Aging Parents

1609 Woodbourne Road
Suite 302A
Levittown, PA   19057   610-293-6960
800-227-7294
FAX: 215-945-8720
e-mail: caps4caregivers@aol.com
www.caps4caregivers.org

Lorraine Sailot, Coordinator

A national clearinghouse for caregivers of the elderly. It provides information and referral, educational programs and materials and caregiver support groups. CAPS also produces a bi-monthly newsletter which is available through the organization. Individuals: $20.00. Organizational/Professional: $100.00.

798 Colorado Association of Homes and Services for the Aging

Colorado State Bank Building
1600 Broadway, Suite 1680
Denver, CO   80202   303-837-8834
FAX: 303-837-8836
e-mail: info@aahsa.org
www.aahsa.org

The American Association of Homes and Services for the Aging (AAHS) represents not-for-profit organizations dedicated to providing high-quality health care, housing and services to the nation's elderly. AAHSA organizations serve more than one million older persons af all icome levels, creed and races.

799 Colorado Association of Homes and Services for the Aging

Colorado State Building
1600 Broadway, Suite 1680
Denver, CO   80202   303-837-8834
FAX: 303-837-8836

800 Connecticut Association of Not-for-Profit Providers for the Aging

300 Piesearch Parkway
Meriden, CT   06450   203-237-4556
FAX: 203-237-4908
www.canpfa.org

801 Delaware Association of Nonprofit Homes for the Aging

c/o Westminister Village
1175 McKee Road
Dover, DE   19901   302-674-8030
FAX: 302-674-8650

802   District of Columbia Association Nonprofit Services for the Aging

c/o Bapt. Sr. Adult Ministries
1330 Massachusetts Avenue, NW
Washington, DC   20005   202-628-2092
                                FAX: 202-638-0649

803   Florida Association of Homes for the Aging

1812 Riggins Road
Tallahassee, FL   32308   904-671-3700
                                 FAX: 904-671-3790
                                 www.faha.org

804   Georgia Association of Homes and Services for the Aging

1678 Tullie Circle, NE
Suite 120
Atlanta, GA   30329   404-728-0223
                             FAX: 404-636-6753

805   Health and Housing Association Mid- Atlantic Non-Profit

10280 Old Columbia Road
Suite 250
Columbia, MD   21046   410-381-1176
                              FAX: 410-381-0240
                              www.manpha.org

806   Indiana Association of Homes for the Aging

9011 North Meridian Street
Suite 208
Indianapolis, IN   46260   317-581-1115
                                  FAX: 317-581-1297

807   Iowa Association of Homes and Services for the Aging

100 East Grand
Suite 140
Des Moines, IA   50309   515-283-9380
                                FAX: 515-283-9382

808   Kansas Association of Homes for the Aging

700 SW Harrison Street
Suite 1106
Topeka, KS   66603   785-233-7443
                            FAX: 785-233-9471
                            www.kahsa.org

809   Kemtucky Association of Not-for-Profit Homes and Services for the Aging

1244 South Fourth Street
Louisville, KY   40203   502-635-6468
                                FAX: 502-635-9286
                                www.kahsanet.org

810   Life Service Network of Illinois- Springfield

2 Lawrence Square
Springfield, IL   62704   217-789-1677
                                 FAX: 217-789-1778
                                 e-mail: info@aahsa.org
                                 www.aahsa.org

The American Association of Homes and Services for the Aging (AAHS) represents not-for-profit organizations dedicated to providing high-quality health care, housing and services to the nation's elderly. AAHSA organizations serve more than one million older persons af all icome levels, creed and races.

811   Life Services Network of Illinois

911 North Elm Street
Suite 228
Hinsdale, IL   60521   630-325-6170
                              FAX: 630-325-0749

812   Life Services Network of Illinois- Springfield

2 Lawrence Square
Springfield, IL   62704   217-789-1677
                                 FAX: 217-789-1778

813   Luisiana Association of Homes and Services for the Aging

5630 Bankers Avenue
PO Box 14615
Baton Rouge, LA   70808   504-928-1114
                                 FAX: 504-928-1319

814   Michigan Association of Homes and Services for the Aging

6215 West St. Joseph Highway
Lansing, MI   48917   517-886-1302
                             FAX: 517-886-1670

815   Minnesota Health and Housing Alliance

2550 University Avenue West
Suite 3505
St Paul, MN   55114   651-645-4545
                             FAX: 651-645-0002

816   Mississippi Association of Homes and Services for the Aging

c/o Naval Home
1800 Beach Drive
Gulfport, MS   39507   601-896-3110
                              FAX: 601-897-4013

817   Missouri Association of Homes for the Aging

308A Monroe
Jefferson City, MO   65101   573-635-6244
                                    FAX: 573-635-6618

818   National Center for Vision and Aging

Lighthouse
800 Second Avenue
New York, NY   10017   212-808-0077
                              800-334-5497

819   National Voluntary Organizations for Independent Living for the Aging

409 3rd Street SW
Washington, DC   20024   202-205-6770
                                FAX: 202-479-0735
                                www.ncoa.org

Stephanie Trapp, Program Manager

Emphasizes the needs for in-home and community-based health care and social services designed to help older persons remain in or return to their homes and live independently, works to educate and assist voluntary organizations to help develop such services. Encourages cooperation between voluntary organizations and the public, provides forum for organizations, agencies and consumer groups to share ideas and develop a network of services for the aged.

820   Nebraska Association of Homes for the Aging

625 South 14th Street
Suite 203, The Mayfair
Lincoln, NE   68508   402-434-5681
                                   FAX: 402-434-5685

821   New Jersey Association of Non-Profit Homes for the Aging

13 Roszel Road
Suite B113
Princeton, NJ   08540   609-452-1161
                                   FAX: 609-452-2907
                                   e-mail: info@aahsa.org
                                   www.aahsa.org

The American Association of Homes and Services for the Aging (AAHS) represents not-for-profit organizations dedicated to providing high-quality health care, housing and services to the nation's elderly. AAHSA organizations serve more than one million older persons af all icome levels, creed and races.

822   New York Association of Homes and Services for the Aging

194 Washibgton Avenue
4th Floor
Albany, NY   12210   518-449-2707
                                   FAX: 518-455-8908
                                   www.nyahsa.org

823   North Carolina Association of Nonprofit for the Aging

3301 Woman's Club Drive
Suite 145
Raleigh, NC   27612   919-571-8333
                                   FAX: 919-571-1297

824   Northern New England Association of Homes and Services for the Aging

345 Edward J. Roy Drive
Suite 201
Manchester, NH   03104   603-626-3479
                                   FAX: 603-626-3763

825   Oklahoma Association of Homes and Services for the Aging

c/o OK Christian Home
906 North Boulevard
Edmondton, OK   73034   405-341-0810

The American Association of Homes and Services for the Aging (AAHS) represents not-for-profit organizations dedicated to providing high-quality health care, housing and services to the nation's elderly. AAHSA organizations serve more than one million older persons af all icome levels, creed and races.

826   Oregon Association of Homes for the Aging

7360 South West Hunziker Street
Suite 207
Tigard, OR   97223   503-684-3788
                                   FAX: 503-624-0870

The American Association of Homes and Services for the Aging (AAHS) represents not-for-profit organizations dedicated to providing high-quality health care, housing and services to the nation's elderly. AAHSA organizations serve more than one million older persons af all icome levels, creed and races.

827   Pennsylvania Association of Non-Profit Homes for the Aging

Executive Park West, Suite 409
4720 Old Gettysbury Road
Mechanicsburg, PA   17055   717-763-5724
                                   FAX: 717-763-1057
                                   www.panpha.org

The American Association of Homes and Services for the Aging (AAHS) represents not-for-profit organizations dedicated to providing high-quality health care, housing and services to the nation's elderly. AAHSA organizations serve more than one million older persons af all icome levels, creed and races.

828   Quality Health Care Foundation of Wyoming

PO Box 3050
Cheyenne, WY   82003   307-637-7575
                                   FAX: 307-637-7575

The American Association of Homes and Services for the Aging (AAHS) represents not-for-profit organizations dedicated to providing high-quality health care, housing and services to the nation's elderly. AAHSA organizations serve more than one million older persons af all icome levels, creed and races.

829   Rhode Island Association of Facilities for the Aging

210 Cahir Street
Providence, RI   02903   401-453-0040
                                   FAX: 401-453-1160

The American Association of Homes and Services for the Aging (AAHS) represents not-for-profit organizations dedicated to providing high-quality health care, housing and services to the nation's elderly. AAHSA organizations serve more than one million older persons af all icome levels, creed and races.

830   South Carolina Association of Nonprofit Homes for the Aging

Greenwood Methodist Home
1110 Marshall Road
Greenwood, SC   29646   803-227-7231
                                   FAX: 803-227-7161

The American Association of Homes and Services for the Aging (AAHS) represents not-for-profit organizations dedicated to providing high-quality health care, housing and services to the nation's elderly. AAHSA organizations serve more than one million older persons af all icome levels, creed and races.

831   South Dakota Association of Homes and Services for the Aging

1116 South Minnesota Avenue
Sioux Falls, SD   57105   605-331-2927
                                   FAX: 605-331-2043

The American Association of Homes and Services for the Aging (AAHS) represents not-for-profit organizations dedicated to providing high-quality health care, housing and services to the nation's elderly. AAHSA organizations serve more than one million older persons af all icome levels, creed and races.

832 Tennessee Association of Homes for the Aging

4343 Lebanon Road
Hermitage, TN 37076   615-871-8162
                              FAX: 615-871-8164

The American Association of Homes and Services for the Aging (AAHS) represents not-for-profit organizations dedicated to providing high-quality health care, housing and services to the nation's elderly. AAHSA organizations serve more than one million older persons af all icome levels, creed and races.

833 Texas Association of Homes and Services for the Aging

2205 Hancock Drive
Austin, TX 78756   512-467-2242
                             FAX: 512-467-2275
                             www.tahsa.org

The American Association of Homes and Services for the Aging (AAHS) represents not-for-profit organizations dedicated to providing high-quality health care, housing and services to the nation's elderly. AAHSA organizations serve more than one million older persons af all icome levels, creed and races.

834 Virginia Association of Non-Profit Homes for the Aging

Innslake Place Building
4401 Dominion Boulevard, Suite 200
Glen Allen, VA 23060   804-965-5500
                              FAX: 804-965-9089
                              www.tahsa.org

The American Association of Homes and Services for the Aging (AAHS) represents not-for-profit organizations dedicated to providing high-quality health care, housing and services to the nation's elderly. AAHSA organizations serve more than one million older persons af all icome levels, creed and races.

835 Washington Association of Homes for the Aging

16000 Christensen Road
Suite 303
Seattle, WA 98188   206-248-7434
                              FAX: 206-241-2595
                              www.waha.org

The American Association of Homes and Services for the Aging (AAHS) represents not-for-profit organizations dedicated to providing high-quality health care, housing and services to the nation's elderly. AAHSA organizations serve more than one million older persons af all icome levels, creed and races.

836 West Virginia Hospital Association

100 Association Drive
Charleston, WV 25311   304-344-9744

www.wvha.com

The American Association of Homes and Services for the Aging (AAHS) represents not-for-profit organizations dedicated to providing high-quality health care, housing and services to the nation's elderly. AAHSA organizations serve more than one million older persons af all icome levels, creed and races.

837 Wisconsin Association of Homes & Services for the Aging

204 South Hamilton Street
Madison, WI 53703   608-255-7060
                              FAX: 608-255-7064
                              www.wahsa.org

The American Association of Homes and Services for the Aging (AAHS) represents not-for-profit organizations dedicated to providing high-quality health care, housing and services to the nation's elderly. AAHSA organizations serve more than one million older persons af all icome levels, creed and races.

Business Support

838 Council of Better Business Bureaus' Foundation

4200 Wilson Boulevard
Suite 800
Arlington, VA 22203   703-276-0100
                              FAX: 703-525-8277
                              e-mail: @cbbb.bbb.org
                              www.bbb.org

Candy McIlhenny, Executive Director

Seven Title III compliance guides are available for: car sales and service; restaurants and bars; recreation and fitness centers; grocery stores; retail stores; professional offices; and travel and tour agents. *$2.50*

839 Disability Community Small Business Development Center

2568 Packard Road
Ann Arbor, MI 48104   734-971-0277
                              800-433-5255
                              FAX: 734-971-0826
                              e-mail: cilstaff@aacil.org
                              www.comnet.org/local/orgs/dcsbdc

Edward Wollmann, Coordinator

Provides business counsel and services to entrepreneurs with disabilities in the state of Michigan. Our organization conducts feasibility studies, assists business plans and works with vocational rehabilitation organizations in helpinh entrepreneurs start and run small businesses.

840 Fedcap Rehabilitation Services

211 West 14th Street
New York, NY 10011   212-727-4200
                              FAX: 212-727-4374
                              e-mail: info@fedcap.org
                              www.fedcap.org

Susan Joual, Manager Communication

A private nonprofit organization providing vocational rehabilitation and job placement for people with disabilities and barriers to employment.

841 Independent Visually Impaired Enterprisers

c/o American Council of the Blind
1155 15th Street North West
Suite 1004
Washington, DC 20005   202-467-5081
    800-424-8666
    FAX: 202-467-5085

Strives to broaden vocational opportunities in business for the visually impaired. Works to improve rehabilitation facilities for all types of business enterprises and publicizes the capabilities of blind and visually impaired business persons.

842 Industry-Labor Council

National Center for Disability Services
201 I U Willets Road
Albertson, NY 11507   516-897-2527
    FAX: 516-747-2046
    www.business-disability.com

Gary Kishanuk, Manager

Helps the business community develop effective, low-cost corporate policies and practices for integrating people with disabilities in the workplace.

843 International Association of Machinists

3830 South Meridian Avenue
Wichita, KS 67217   316-522-1591
    FAX: 316-522-7989

Ron Eldridge, President

Placement programs for persons with disabilities.

844 Job Accommodation Network

PO Box 6080
Morgantown, WV 26505   304-293-7186
    800-526-7234
    FAX: 304-293-5407
    e-mail: jan@jan.icdi.wvu.edu
    www.jan.wvu.edu

Barbara Judy, Director
D. J. Hendricks, Assistant Director

JAN provides a service of the US Department of Labor's Office on Disability Employment Policy, information on practical accommodations that can be successfully utilized in business and industry. It enables businesses to communicate with others to find ways to manage and lower disability costs. JAN also collects job accommodation information and makes it available to those seeking ways to enable persons having functional limitations caused by disabilities to be productive in the work environment.

845 Learning How

Opportunity Plus
PO Box 35481
Charlotte, NC 28235   704-376-4735
    FAX: 704-376-4738
    e-mail: info@opportunity-plus.org
    www.opportunity-plus.org

Cheryl Shore, Managing Director

Strives to build self-esteem and confidence among disabled persons and encourages volunteer involvement. Seeks to train the disabled for leadership positions and to serve as a support group for disabled persons. Works to prepare members for participation in the job market and acts as a referral service.

846 Life Development Institute

1720 East Monte Vista Road
Phoenix, AZ 85006   602-261-7911
    FAX: 602-253-6878

Robert Crawford, President

Serves older adolescents and adults with learning disabilities, ADD and related disorders. The purpose of the training is to enable program participants to pursue responsible independent living, enhance academic/workplace literacy skills and facilitate placement in educational/employment opportunities, commensurate with individual capabilities. Includes a stand alone, regionally accredited 2-year college.

847 William D. Nee - Advocate for People with Disabilities

106 Packard Street
Apartment 109
Ann Arbor, MI 48104   734-930-0343

Consultant for the disabled.

General

848 AIDS Alternative Health Project

3223 North Sheffield Avenue
Chicago, IL 60657   312-327-6437

Chiropractic, acupuncture, bodywork, nutritional and herbal counseling, and massage therapy to HIV positive patients.

849 ARC

500 East Border Street
S-300
Arlington, TX 76010   817-261-6003
    800-433-5255
    FAX: 817-277-3491
    e-mail: thearc@metronet.com
    www.thearc.org

Nancy L. Bolding

Disseminates information regarding ADA as it applies to individuals with mental retardation. A national information center to develop and disseminate educational brochures to restaurants, hotels and motels, retail stores, and places of public assembly on how to provide cognitively accessible, integrated services.

850 Academy of Dentistry for Persons with Disabilities

211 East Chicago Avenue
5th Floor
Chicago, IL 60611   312-440-2661
    FAX: 312-440-2824
    e-mail: fosccdzz@worldnet.att.net
    www.specialdentistry.org

James Balija, CAE

A professional organization of individuals concerned with the oral health care of persons with special needs. Association publishes a bi-monthly journal entitled 'Special Care in Dentistry' and a newsletter interface.

851 **Access Unlimited**

570 Hance Road
Binghamton, NY   13903

800-849-2143
FAX: 607-669-4595
www.accessunlimited.com

Sherry Sinai, Admin. Coordinator
Sherry Lowry, Director

Assists educators, health care providers and parents in discovering how personal computers help children and adults with disabilities compensate for some of the barriers imposed by their conditions. Access Unlimited markets and offers technical support for over 500 special computer products and acts as a free information center and provides free telephone consultation to special educators, health care providers and other professionals.

852 **Accu-Chem Laboratories**

990 North Bowser Road
Suite 800
Richardson, TX   75081

214-234-5412
800-451-0116

853 **Acupressure Institute**

1533 Shattuck Avenue
Berkeley, CA   94709

510-845-1059

Information, career training and mail order catalog.

854 **Acupuncture/Traditional Chinese Medicine**

4101 Lake Boone Trail
Suite 201
Raleigh, NC   27607

919-787-5181

Trade organization of acupuncturists. Names and locations of local members arer available and referrals by written request.

855 **Advocacy Center for Persons with Disabilities**

2671 West Executive Center
Suite 100
Tallahassee, FL   32301

850-488-9070
800-342-0823
FAX: 850-488-8640
TDY:800-346-4127
e-mail: info@advocacycenter.org
www.advocacycenter.org

The mission of the Center is to advance the dignity, equality, self-determination and expressed choices of individuals with disabilities. The Center promotes, expands, protects and seeks to assure the human and legal rights of people through the provision of information and advocacy. The Center administers five federally-mandated programs in the State of Florida. It is completely independent of all state agencies providing services to persons with disabilities.

856 **After We're Gone - A Program for the Lifetime Care of Persons with Disabilities**

Life Services for the Handicapped
352 Park Avenue South
Suite 703
New York, NY   10010

212-532-6740
800-995-0066
FAX: 212-532-6740
e-mail: disabledandalone@aol.com
www.disabledandalone.com

A national non-profit humanitarian organization whose primary concern is the well-being of handicapped persons, particularly when their families can no longer care for them.

857 **Alliance for Alternative Medicine**

PO Box 59
Liberty Lake, WA   99019

509-255-9246

Provides information about alternative treatment centers and support groups that deal with the freedom of choice in medicine.

858 **Alliance for Technology Access**

2175 East Francisco Boulevard
Suite L
San Rafael, CA   94901

415-455-4575
800-455-7970
FAX: 415-455-0654
TDY:415-455-0491
e-mail: atainfo@ataccess.org
www.ataccess.org

Mary Lester, Associate Director
Libbie Butler, Administrative Assistant

Not-for-profit organization dedicated to providing technology information to people with disabilities. Consists of 39 resource centers nationwide that provide direct services to help people with disabilities explore computer hardware systems, adaptive devices, telecommunication services, and software.

859 **American Academy of Neural Therapy**

1468 South Saint Francis Drive
Sante Fe, NM   87501

505-988-3086

860 **American Academy of Pediatrics**

141 NW Point Boulevard
Elk Grove Village, IL   60007

847-228-5005
FAX: 847-228-5097
www.aap.org

Michelle Esquivel, Project Manager

Offers policy information, referrals and treatment information for children and adolescents.

861 **American Assoc. of University Affiliated Programs for Persons with Developmental Disability**

AAUAP
8630 Fenton Street
Suite 410
Silver Spring, MD   20910

301-588-8252
FAX: 301-588-2842
TDY:301-588-3319
e-mail: info@aauap.org
www.aauap.org

Roland Loudenburg, M.P.H., Technical Assistance

The central office for the 61 University Affiliated programs and 14 Mental Retardation and Developmental Disabilities Research Centers and is their representative to the federal government. UAPs are located at major universities and teaching hospitals in all 50 states, the District of Columbia, and many U.S. territories. UAPs target their activities to support the independence, productivity and integration into the community of individuals with developmental disabilities.

862   American Association for Rehabilitation Therapy

PO Box 93
North Little Rock, AR   72116

Offers information, referrals, programs and services for rehabilitation professionals and the disabled individual.

863   American Association for the Advancement of Science

Project on Science, Technology and Disability
1200 New York Avenue NW
Washington, DC   20005   202-483-2101
FAX: 202-371-9849
e-mail: vstern@aaas.org
www.aaas.org

Virginia Stern, Director

The Project on Science, Technology and Disability was founded in 1975, by the American Association for the Advancement of Science. Primarily an information center, the Project links people with disabilities, their families, professors, teachers and counselors with scientists and engineers with disabilities, who can share their education and career coping strategies in technical fields. Maintains a database of scientists and engineers with disabilities. Manages a summer internship program.

864   American Association of Music Therapy

PO Box 80012
Valley Forge, PA   19484   215-265-4006

865   American Board of Chelation Therapy

70 West Huron Street
Chicago, IL   60610   312-266-7246

866   American Botanical Council

PO Box 144345
Austin, TX   78714   512-926-4900
FAX: 512-926-2345
e-mail: tbennett@herbalgram.org
www.herbalgram.org

Offers information and HerbalGram magazine.

867   American Camping Association Project on Science, Technology and Disability

1333 H Street NW
Washington, DC   20005   301-218-6468
800-653-1409
www.acacamps.org

868   American Chiropractic Association

1701 Clarendon Boulevard
Arlington, VA   22209   703-276-8800
FAX: 703-243-2593
www.acatoday.com

Major source for chiropractic information.

869   American College of Hyperbaric Medicine Ocean Medical Center

4001 Ocean Drive
Suite 105
Lauderdale-by-the-sea, FL   33308   305-771-4000

870   American Counseling Association

5999 Stevenson Avenue
Alexandria, VA   22304   703-823-9800
800-347-6647
www.counseling.org

Richard Yep, Executive Director
Janice MacDonald, Director Professional Services

Provides a variety of programs and services that support the personal, professional and program development goals of its members. ACA works together with 17 divisions to provide quality services to the variety of clients who use their services in college, community agencies, substance abuse, and rehabilitation.

871   American Foundation for Pain Research

120 South Spalding Drive
Suite 210
Beverly Hills, CA   90212

Provides information on cystitis, endometriosis, and other conditions. Offers information on diet, self-help, and a free video called You Don't Have to Live With Pelvic Pain.

872   American Foundation for Urologic Disease

1128 North Charles Street
Baltimore, MD   21201
800-242-2383

873   American Foundation of Traditional Chineses Medicine

505 Beach Street
San Fransisco, CA   94133   415-776-0502

874   American Herbalists Guild

PO Box 1683
Sequel, CA   95073

Information on herbal therapies and a directory of schools and teachers.

875   American Institute of Hypnotherapy

1805 East Garry Avenue
Suite 100
Santa Ana, CA   92705   714-261-6400

Provides a large variety of media resources.

876 American Massage Therapy Association

820 Davis Street
Suite 100
Evanston, IL 60201   312-761-2682

Offers comprehensive information on massage and bodywork.

877 American Oriental Bodywork Association

6801 Jericho Turnpike
Syosset, NY 11791   516-364-5533

Information, professional membership, practitioner directory and referrals.

878 American Red Cross, National Headquarters

8111 Gatehouse Road
Falls Church, VA 22042   202-737-8300
                                  FAX: 703-248-4222
                          e-mail: info@usa.redcross.org
                              www.redcross.org/dc/ncc

Offers counseling, emergency relief for disaster victims, information and referrals and emergency assistance for members of the military and their families.

879 American Self-Help Clearinghouse

Saint Clare's Hospital
Denville, NJ 07834   908-813-9603
                                  800-367-6274
                              FAX: 973-625-8848
                          www.cmhc.com/selfhelp

Edward Madara, Director

A clearinghouse that makes referrals to self-help groups and self-help clearinghouses throughout the nation. Publishes a variety of materials that are helpful to professionals and consumers who would like to start self-help groups. The Self-Help Sourcebook has listings of over 800 national, international, and model groups. Helps individuals to start needed new groups.

880 American Social Health Association

PO Box 13827
Research Triangle Park, NC 27709 919-361-8400
                                  FAX: 919-361-8425
                              www.ashastd.org

Voluntary health agency working against STD's.

881 American Society of Teachers of the Alexander Technique

PO Box 60008
Florence, MA 01062   413-584-2359
                                  800-473-0620
                          www.alexandertech.com

Information, referrals and training.

882 Aromatherapy Seminars

3379 S Robertson Boulevard
Los Angeles, CA 90034   310-838-6122
                                  800-677-2368

Provides programs to become a certified aromatherapist.

883 Association for Applied Psychophysiology and Biofeedback

10200 West Avenue
Suite 304
Wheat Ridge, CO 80033   303-422-8436

Provides names and phone numbers of local chapters.

884 Association for Network Chiropractic Spinal Analysis

444 North Main Street
Longmont, CO 80501   303-678-8101

www.networkchiropractic.com

885 Association for Persons in Supported Employment

1627 Monument Avenue
Richmond, VA 23220   804-278-9187
                                  FAX: 804-278-9377
                              e-mail: apse@apse.org
                                  www.apse.org

Supported employment enables people with disabilities who have not been successfully employed to work and contribute to society. Focuses on a person's abiliities and provide the supports the individual needs to be successful on a long-term basis.

886 Association of Birth Defect Children

827 Irma Avenue
Orlando, FL 32803   407-245-7035
                                  800-313-2232
                              www.birthdefects.org

Beth Mekdeci, President

National not-for-profit organization that functinos as a clearinghouse, proving parents and professionals with information about birth defects and services for children with disabilities. Studies the links between drugs, radiation, alcohol, chemicals, lead, mercury, dioxin, and birth defects. Publishes newsletters and publications for parents, professionals, and interested organizations.

887 Association of Children's Prosthetic/Orthotic Clinics

6300 North River Road
Suite 727
Rosemont, IL 60018   847-698-1637
                                  FAX: 847-823-0536
                              e-mail: king@aaos.org
                                  www.acpoc.org

Sheril King, Executive Director

Established for the purpose of supporting clinical teams that treat children with prosthetic or orthotic devices. Goals are achieved through programs of professional education and clinical research.

888 Association on Higher Education and Disability

PO Box 21192
Columbus, OH 43221   614-488-4972
                                  FAX: 614-488-1174
                  e-mail: ahead@postbox.asc.ohio-state.edu
                                  www.ahead.org

Ed Suddath, Executive Vice President

This is a national association of professionals working on college campuses with disabled students.

889   Bastyr University Natural Health Clinic

1307 North 45th Street, Suite 200
Seattle, WA   98103   206-632-0354

890   Bazelton Center for Mental Health Law

1101 15th Street NW
Suite 1212
Washington, DC   20005   202-265-6363
                                FAX: 202-223-0409
                        e-mail: hn1660@handsnet.org
                                www.bazelon.org

Robert Bernstein, Executive Director
Lee Carty, Communications Dir.

A national nonprofit public interest organization, advocates for public policies that can enable people with mental disabilities to live in freedom and dignity.

891   Beach Center on Families and Disability

University of Kansas
311 Haworth Hall
1200 Sunnyside Avenue
Lawrence, KS   66045   785-864-7600
                             FAX: 785-864-7605
                             www.beachcenter.org

A federally funded center that conducts research and training in the factors that contribute to the successful functioning of families with members who have disabilities.

892   Bio-Electro-Magnetics Institute

2490 West Moana Lane
Reno, NV   89509   702-827-9099

893   Birth Defect Research for Children

930 Woodcock Road
Suite 225
Orlando, FL   32803   407-245-7035
                             800-313-ABDC
                        FAX: 407-895-8024
                        www.birthdefects.org

A nonprofit organization that provides information about birth defects of all kinds to parents and professionals. Offers a library of medical books and files of information on less common categories of birth defects and is involved in research to discover possible links between environmental exposures and birth defects.

894   Bonnie Pruden Pain Erasure

3661 North Campbell
Suite 102
Tucson, AZ   85719

                             800-221-4634

Provides a list of certified myotherapists and clinics where myotherapy is offered.

895   British Institute of Homepathy and College of Homepathy

520 Washington Boulevard, Suite 423
Marina Del Rey, CA   90292   310-306-5408

896   CAPP National Parent Resource Center

95 Berkeley Street
Suite 104
Boston, MA   02116   617-482-2915

A parent-run resource system designed to further the needs and goals of family-centered, community-based coordinated care for children with special health needs and their families. Offers written materials, training packages, workshops and presentations for parents and professionals on special education, health care financing and other topics.

897   CARF The Rehabilitation Accrediation Commission

4891 East Grant Road
Tucson, AZ   85712   520-325-1044
                            FAX: 520-318-1129
                            www.carf.org

Don Galvin, President/CEO

CARF serves as the standards-setting and accrediting body for rehabilitation and life enhancement programs and services. The independent, not-for-profit commission promotes quality, value, and optimal outcomes of services through a consultative accreditation process that centers on enhancing the lives of the persons served. At present, CARDhas accredited more than 19,000 programs and services in the US, Canada, and Sweden in the areas of adult day services, behavioral health, and medical rehab.

898   Canine Companions for Independence

National Offices
2965 Dutton Avenue
PO Box 446
Santa Rosa, CA   95402   707-577-1700
                                800-572-2275
                           FAX: 707-577-1711
                   e-mail: info@caninecompanions.org
                           www.caninecompanions.org

Corey Hudson, Executive Director
Petey Rapalus, Public Relations Manager

A nonprofit organization that provides highly trained assistance dogs for people with disabilities, helping them to achieve greater independence.

899   Canine Helpers for the Disabled

5699-5705 Ridge Road
Lockport, NY   14094   716-433-4035

A non-profit organization devoted to training dogs to assist people with disabilities to lead more independent, secure lives.

900   Center Academy & Center Family

6710 86th Avenue North
Pinellas Park, FL   33782   727-822-6914
                                 FAX: 727-544-8186
                        e-mail: centacadpp@aol.com
                                www.centeracademy.com

Lisa Steller, Intake Coordinator
Andrew P. Hicks, Ph.D., Director of Boarding
Robert Detweiler, J.D., Principal

Provides day and residential programs for students, grades 4-12, who have learning disabilities or who need motivation. Please call for more information.

901   Center for Accessible Housing

North Carolina State University
Box 8613
Raleigh, NC   27695   919-737-3082

e-mail: cahd@ncsu.edu

A federally funded research and training center that works toward improving housing for people with disabilities. Provides technical assistance, training and publications.

902   Center for Assistive Technology

University at Buffalo
515 Kimball Tower
Buffalo, NY   14214   716-829-3141
                             800-628-2281
                        FAX: 716-829-3217
                        TDY:800-628-2281
                e-mail: jweir@acsu.buffalo.edu
                www.wings.buffalo.edu/ot/cat

Jennifer Murphy, Coordinator

Nonprofit organization that conducts research and provides educational and services programs to increase consumer knowledge related to assistive technology for those with disabilities. Five specific areas of work: research on assistive devices used for all aspects of dailing living, education for students and clinical professionals, assistive device service provision, development and evaluation of new innovative technology ideas, and public policy analysis.

903   Center for Children with Chronic Illness and Disability

University of Minnesota School of Public Health
420 Delaware
Suite SE # 197
Minneapolis, MN   55455   612-625-5177

www.naric.com/naric/comp94

Dr. Joan Patterson, Director

904   Center for Developmental Disabilities

University of South Carolina
8301 Farrow Road
School of Medicine, Education Bldg.
Columbia, SC   29208   803-935-5231
                         FAX: 803-935-5059
                e-mail: scsis@dccisc.edu
                www.scsis.org

Denise Rivers, Project Coordinator
Information on early intervention and the elderly.

905   Center for Mind/Body Studies

5225 Connecticut Avenue
NW Suite 414
Washington, DC   20015   202-966-7338
                           FAX: 202-966-2589

906   Center for Universal Design

North Carolina State University, School of Design and School of Architecture
PO Box 8613
Raleigh, NC   27695   919-515-3082
                             800-647-6777
                        FAX: 919-515-3023
                e-mail: cud@ncsu.edu
                www.design.ncsu.edu/cud

A federally funded resource center that works toward improving housing for people with disabilities. Provides technical assistance, training and publications on accessible housing and universal design.

907   Children's Alliance

420 Capitol Avenue
Frankfort, KY   40601   502-875-3399
                          FAX: 502-233-4200
                e-mail: kyvoice@aol.com

An association of individual's and human services organizations committed to being a voice for at-risk children and families. Interacts with the legislative and executive branches of government and assists members in developing services that most effectively meet the needs of at-risk children and families.

908   Children's National Medical Center

111 Michigan Avenue NW
Washington, DC   20010   202-884-2160
                           FAX: 202-884-4492
                    e-mail: cnmc.org
                    www.cnmc.org

Donald Brown, President

Offers diagnosis, treatment, follow-up services, outpatient services and medical services to children.

909   Citizens Alliance for Venereal Disease Awareness

PO Box 1073
Chicago, IL   60648

Offers information on symptoms, treatment, and prevention of STD's.

910   Clearinghouse on Disability Information Office of Special Education

US Department of Education
Switzer Building
Room 3132
Washington, DC   20202

800-USA-LEAR

Provides information on federal disability legislation, funding for programs serving individuals with disabilities, and programs and services for people with disabilities on the national, state and local levels.

911   College of Maharishi Ayur-Veda Health Center

PO Box 282
Fairfield, IA   52556   515-472-8477

Provides referrals to health centers.

912 Disabled Children's Relief Fund

PO Box 7420
Freeport, NY   11520   516-377-1605
                            FAX: 516-377-3978
                            e-mail: dc1605@aol.com
                            www.dcrf.com

Jerome H. Blue, PhD, President

National not-for-profit organization that provides
modest grants for disabled children with preference
given to those with no health insurance. Grants are
provided for assistive devices, equipment and rehabilitative services.

**913 Disabled and Alone/Life Services for the
Handicapped**

352 Park Avenue South
11th Floor
New York, NY   10010   212-532-6740
                            800-995-0066
                            FAX: 212-532-3588
                            e-mail: disabledandalone@aol.com
                            www.disabledandalone.org

Roslyn Brilliant, Executive Director
Leslie D. Park, Chairman

National nonprofit organization providing life planning and direct services to persons with disabilities,
their families and organizations serving them by:
helping parents plan for when they will no longer able
to care for their disabled loved ones; and taking care
of disabled individuals whose families have provided
for their care.

Free literature

914 Distance Education and Training Council

1601 18th Street NW
Washington, DC   20009   202-234-5100
                             FAX: 202-332-1386
                             e-mail: detc@detc.org
                             www.detc.org

Michael Lambert, Executive Director

Advocates quality correspondence education in
America. Serves as a clearinghouse of information
about the field and sponsors a nationally recognized
accrediting agency distance education.

915 Division for Physical and Health Disabilities

1920 Association Drive
Reston, VA   20191   703-620-3660
                             FAX: 703-624-9494
                             www.cec.sped.org

Advocates for quality education for individuals
with physical disabilities, multiple disabilities, and
special health care needs served in schools, hospitals, or home settings. DPHD's members include
classroom teachers, administrators, related service personnel, hospital/homebound teachers, and
parents.

**916 Division on Mental Retardation and
Developmental Disabilities**

1920 Association Drive
Reston, VA   20191   703-620-3660
                             FAX: 703-264-9494
                             www.cec.sped.org

Promotes the education and general welfare of
indivduals with mental retardation, developmental disabilities, and intellectual challenges, and
those who serve them. MRDD's members include
professionals and paraprofessionals interested in
individuals who are mentally retarded, developmentally disabled, or have related learning problems.

917 Doctor's Data

PO Box 111
West Chicago, IL   60185   800-323-2784

Mineral and allergy testing.

918 Dynamic Learning Center

PO Box 1112
Ben Lomond, CA   95005   408-336-3457
                             FAX: 408-336-5854

919 Easter Seals

PO Box 1036
Solvang, CA   93464   805-543-4122
                             800-221-6827
                             FAX: 805-688-1603

Linda Lee Harry, Executive Director

A nonprofit referral agency, that maintains listings of
more than 12,000 organizations and community-
based resource centers for all ages and disabilities to
access. Also offers a quarterly newsletter, Direct
Connect.

920 Eden Acres Organic Network

12100 Lima Center Road
Clinton, MI   49236   517-456-4288

921 Educational Accessibility Services

Wayne State University
583 Student Center Building
5221 Gullen Mall
Detroit, MI   48202   313-577-1851
                             FAX: 313-577-4898
                             TDY:313-577-3365
                             e-mail: danders@teadmin.sa.wayne.edu
                             www.ed.accessibility.edu

Donald Anderson, Director
Jane DePriester-Morandini, Learning Specialist

A powerful advocating force for students with disabilities at the university. Our purpose is to provide
students with the resources they need to succeed and
to support their participation in all University programs and activities with dignity and independence.

922 Electro Medical

18433 Armistad
Fountain Valley, CA   92708   714-964-6776
                              800-422-8726

923 **Ellon USA**
644 Merrick Road
Lynbrook, NY   11563   516-593-2206

Largest flower remedy resource, for alternative
therapies.

924 **Employment Resource Program**
426 West Jefferson
Springfield, IL   62702   217-523-2587
                                 800-442-4221
                          FAX: 217-523-0427
                   e-mail: erp@springnet1.com
                                 www.scil.com

Ceceilia Harris, Program Manager

An employment, college, financial aid, pharmaceuti-
cal resource program which also includes an information and referral service that uses computer listings
and a large file system to answer requests related to
disabilities.

925 **Enviro-Tech Products**
17171 Southeast 29th Street
Choctaw, OK   73020   405-390-3499

Provides information for both the public and physicians.

926 **Environmental Health Center**
8345 Walnut Hill Land
Suite 205
Dallas, TX   75231   214-368-4132

Offers help for malnutrition and chemical exposure.

927 **Environmental Health and Light Research Istitute**
16057 Tampa Palms Boulevard
Suite 227
Tampa, FL   33647
                                 800-544-4878
Information for full spectrum lighting, and light
therapies.

928 **Esalen Institute**
Big Sur, CA   93920   408-667-3000

Offers weekend and extensive programs in holistic
health.

929 **Estate Planning for the Disabled**
3100 Arapahoe Avenue
112
Boulder, CO   30303
                                 800-683-4607
Counsels and assists parents of children with special needs to develop viable estate plans, letters of
intent, wills and special needs trusts. EPD will
work with the appropriate professionals and agencies to help put together an effective comprehensive plan.

930 **Family Resource Center on Disabilities**
20 East Jackson
Room 300
Chicago, IL   60604   312-939-3513
                                 800-952-4199
                          FAX: 312-939-7297
                          TDY:312-939-3519
www.ameritech.net/users/fredptiil/index.

Mary Mostissy, President
Charlotte Des Jardins, Executive Director

Not-for-profit advocacy organization dedicated to
improving services for all children with disabilities
by providing support and services to affected families, informing parents of their rights, and helping
parents become advocates for their children. Offers
family support services, training, seminars and information and referral services. Publishes monthly
newsletter.

931 **Family Voices**
3411 Candelaria NE
Suite M
Albuquerque, NM   87107   505-867-2368
                                 888-835-5669
                          FAX: 505-867-6517
           e-mail: kidshealth@familyvoices.org
                          www.familyvoices.org

Trish Thomas, National Outreach Coordinator

Not-for-profit voluntary organization dedicated to
ensuring that children's health issues are addressed
as public and private healthcare systems undero
change in communities, states and the nation. National grassroots clearinghouse for information and
education ways to assure and improve health care for
children with disabilities and chronic conditions. Provides materials including pamphlets, a newsletter,
and one-page papers on important topics.

932 **Favarh**
10 Tower Lane
Avon, CT   06001   860-678-0313
                          FAX: 860-676-0275
              e-mail: favarh@connix.com
              www.connix.com/~favarh/index.htm

Tom Thompson, Executive Director
Lyn Fierri, President

Provides a variety of programs and services to adults
with developmental, physical or mental disabilities
and their families, throughout the Farmington Valley
communities of Avon, Burlington and more. Favarh's
programs are designed to enhance the personal, social, emotional, vocational and living capabilities of
persons with disabilities.

933 **Federation for Children with Special Needs**
PO Box 992
Westfield, MA   01086   617-236-7210

A center for parents and parent organizations to
work together on behalf of children with special
needs.

934 Feldenkrais Guild of North America
3611 SW Hood Avenue
Suite 100
Portland, OR 97201   503-221-6612
                           800-775-2118
                      FAX: 503-221-6616
         e-mail: media@feldenkrais.com
                    www.feldenkrais.com

Information, practitioner training and certification.

935 Friends of Disabled Adults and Children
4900 Lewis Road
Stone Mountain, GA 30083   770-491-9014
                        FAX: 770-491-0026
              e-mail: fodac@fodac.org
                        www.fodac.org

Ed Butchart, President

Not-for-profit organization dedicated to providing necessary services and support to physically and mobility impaired people of all ages. Provides free mobility impairment, rehabilitative, and home healthcare equipment, clothing and household essentials. Also provides individual group counseling, employment opportunities, entry-level job skills trianing, and on-the-job mentoring. Provides variety of brochures and pamphlets.

936 Goodwill Industries International
9200 Wisconsin Avenue
Bethesda, MD 20814   301-530-6500
                      FAX: 301-530-1516
                        www.goodwill.org

Strives to achieve the full participation in society of disabled persons and other individuals with special needs by expanding their opportunities and occupational capabilities through a network of 179 autonomous, nonprofit, community-based organizations providing services throughout the world in response to local needs.

937 Great Lakes Association of Clinical Medicine
70 West Huron Street
Chicago, IL 60610   312-266-7246

Members practice chelation therapy.

938 HEAL
16 East 16th Street
New York, NY 10003   212-674-HOPE

Information on an alternative approach to health that includes physical, emotional, psychological, and spiritual efforts to strengthen the immune system. Referrals to hypnotherapists trained to deal with HIV patients.

939 HEATH Resource Center
One Dupont Circle NW
Suite 800
Washington, DC 20036   202-939-9320
                           800-544-3284
                      FAX: 202-833-5696

Vickie Barr, Director

National clearinghouse for information about education after high school for people with disabilities. Also serves as an information exchange about educational support services, policies, procedures, adaptations and opportunities on American campuses, vocational-technical schools, adult education programs, independent living centers and other training entities after high school.

940 Health Action
243 Pebble Beach
Santa Barbara, CA 93117   805-682-3230

941 Health Associates
PO Box 220
Big Sur, CA 93920
                      FAX: 408-667-0248

Workshops and training in alternative applications of healing.

942 Health Resource Center for Women with Disabilities
Rehabilitation Institute of Chicago
345 East Superior Street
Chicago, IL 60611   312-908-7997
                      FAX: 312-908-1087
                      TDY:312-908-8523

Judy Panko Reis, President

National, not-for-profit, general health and service center providing accessible medical services for women with disabilities. Conducts research into health issues concerning disabled women and offers educational resources for ehalthcare professionals and women with disabilities. Provides mateials and educational opportunities through its library and resource center, newsletter, information sheets, brochures, videos and free seminars for women and their healthcare providers.

943 Herpes Resource Center
PO Box 13827
Research Triangle Park, NC 27709919-361-8400
                      FAX: 919-361-8425
                    www.ashastd.org/hrc/

Support and information for those with recurring genital herpes infections.

944 Homeopathic Educational Services
2124 Kittredge Street
Berkley, CA 94704   510-649-0294
                           800-359-9051

945 Huggins Diagnostic Center
5080 List Drive
Colorado Springs, CO 80919 719-548-1600
                      FAX: 719-522-0563

Information on removal of mercury fillings.

946 Human Ecology Action League
PO Box 49126
Atlanta, GA 30359   404-248-1898

Support with and information on enviromental illness.

947 **ICBR North American Information Office**

PO Box 509
Florissant, MI   63032   314-921-3997
                               800-826-5366

948 **Il Center: Cape Organization for Rights of the Disabled**

1019 Iyannough Road #4
Hyannis, MA   02601   508-775-8300
                               800-541-0282
                          FAX: 508-775-7022
                   e-mail: bhcord@cape.com
                   www.vse.cape.com/~bhcord

Bill Henning, Executive Director

949 **Informed Birth and Parenting**

PO Box 3675
Ann Arbor, MI   48106   313-662-6857

Resources on pregnancy, childbirth, and parenting; refers midwives; certifies educators and assistants.

950 **Institute for Health and Disability**

University of Minnesota
420 Delaware Street SE
Box 721
Minneapolis, MN   55455   612-624-3939
                          FAX: 612-626-2134
                          TDY: 612-624-3939
                   e-mail: instihd@tc.umn.edu
                   www.peds.umn.edu/centers/ihd

Marty Smith, MA, Executive Director

951 **Institute for Music, Health, and Education**

PO Box 4179
Boulder, CO   80306   303-443-8484

952 **Institute for Scientific Research**

33 Bedford Street
Suite 19A
Lexington, MA   02420   781-862-6455
                          FAX: 781-861-7517

Steve Guberman, Director

Conducts research on the sociological aspects of disabilities and rehabilitation. Conducts evaluations of programs designed to train professionals and to rehabilitate individuals with disabilities.

953 **Institute of Transpersonal Psychology**

PO Box 4437
Stanford, CA   94305   415-327-2066

954 **International Academy of Oral Medicine and Toxicology**

PO Box 608531
Orlando, FL   32860

Professional organization of dentists, physicians and research scientists.

955 **International Association of Professional Natural Hygientists**

Regency Health Resorts & Spas
2000 South Ocean Drive
Hallandale, FL   33009   305-454-2220

Members are physicians who specialize in theraputic fasting.

956 **International Chiropractors Association**

1110 North Glebe Road
Suite 1000
Arlington, VA   22201   703-528-5000

957 **International College of Applied Kinesiology**

6405 Metcalf Avenue
Suite 503
Shawnee Mission, KS   66202   913-384-5336

Referall service for applied kinesiologists.

958 **International Institute of Reflexology**

PO Box 12462
St. Petersburg, FL   33733   813-343-4811

Information, seminars, publications and referrals.

959 **International Medical and Dental Hypnotherapy Association**

4110 Edgeland
Suite 800
Royal Oak, MI   48073   313-549-5594
                               800-257-5467

960 **International Ozone Association**

31 Strawberry Hill Avenue
Stamford, CT   06902   203-348-3542

961 **International Women's Health Coalition**

24 East 21st Street
New York, NY   10010   212-979-8500
                          FAX: 212-979-9009
                               www.iwhc.org

Information and pamphlets on sexually transmitted diseases and other health concerns.

962 **Invincible Athletics**

PO Box 541
Lancaster, MA   01523   508-368-1818

Teaches how to incorproate Ayurvedic training principles into athletic conditioning.

963 **Kessler Institute for Rehabilitation**

1199 Pleasant Valley Way
West Orange, NJ   07052   973-414-4700
                               888-537-7537
                               888-537-7537
                          FAX: 973-243-6861
                   www.kessler-rehab.com

Kathy Lewis, Vice-President of Marketing
Maura Bergen, Public Relations Coordinator

Kessler Institute for Rehabilitation is world renowned for treating individuals with physical disabilities, resulting from spinal cord and brain injuries, stroke and amputee, sports and work-related, and other illnesses and injuries. Kessler offers comprehensive programs designed to meet each person's individual needs.

964 Learning Disabilities Association of NYS

90 South Swan Street
Albany, NY 12210   518-436-4633

e-mail: LDA@associationresources.org

Michael Helman, President

965 Learning Disabilities Association of TX

1011 West 31st Street
Austin, TX   512-458-8234
                         800-604-7500
e-mail: lDAT@compuserve.com

966 Lifecycles for Women

101 First Street
Suite 301
Seattle, WA 98102   206-324-8230

Clearinghouse for books and nutritional supplements for various women's health issues; call for catalog.

967 Lighthouse International

Hudson Valley Region
170 Hamilton Avenue
White Plains, NY 10601   914-683-7500
                          888-222-9320
FAX: 914-686-5866
e-mail: visionrehab@lighthouse.org
www.lighthouse.org

Barbara Silverstone, DSW, President & CEO
Judith Millman, ACSW, MBA, VP, Hudson Valley Region
James P O'Toole, Chair, Regional Advisory Board

Lighthouse International is a leading resource worldwide on vision impairment and rehabilitation. Through its pioneering work in vision rehabilitation services, education, research and advocacy, Lighthouse International enables people of all ages who are blind or partially sighted to lead independent and productive lives. Founded in 1905 and headquartered in New York, Lighthouse International is a not-for-profit organization, depending on the support of individuals,foundations and corporations.

968 Lotus Light

PO Box 1008
Wilmot, WI 53170   262-889-8501
FAX: 800-905-6887
e-mail: lotuslight@lotuspress.com
www.internatural.com

Mail order distribution of aromatherapy videotapes, books and videotapes.

969 Mainstream

6930 Carroll Avenue
Suite 240
Takoma Park, MD 20912   301-891-8777
FAX: 301-891-8778
e-mail: info@mainstream.org
www.mainstreaminc.org

David A. Pichette, Executive Director
Karen Morgret, National Program Director
Janet Cassidy, Dallas, TX Regional Manager

Non-profit organization that works with employers and service providers around the country to increase employment opportunities for persons with disabilities.

970 MedEscort International

PO Box 8766
Allentown, PA 18105   610-791-3111
                           800-255-7182
FAX: 610-791-9189
e-mail: medescort@fast.net
www.medescort.com

Offers specially trained escorts for individuals who cannot travel alone due to age or disability.

971 Medizone International

123 East Street
New York, NY 10022   212-421-0303

972 Mental Health Association in Texas

8401 Shoal Creek Boulevard
Austin, TX 78757   512-454-3706

e-mail: scmullins@mhatexas.org
www.mhatexas.org

Stella C. Mullins, President/CEO

973 Mental Health Association of NY State

194 Washington Avenue
Suite 415
Albany, NY 12210   518-434-0439
                           800-766-6177
e-mail: mhanys@mhanys.org
www.mhanys.org

Joseph A. Glazer, President/CEO

974 Meridan Valley Clinical Laboratory

24030 132nd Avenue Southeast
Kent, WA 98042
                           800-234-6825

Variety of specialized testing.

975 MetaMatrix Medical Laboratory

5000 Peachtree Street
Industrial Boulevard
Norcross, GA 30071   404-446-5483

976 Mind-Body Clinic Harvard Medical School

185 Pilgrim Road
Cambridge, MA 02215   617-632-9530

977   Mind/Body Health Services

393 Dixon Road
Boulder, CO   80302   303-440-8460

978   Mobility International USA

PO Box 10767
Eugene, OR   97440   541-343-1284
                                 FAX: 541-343-6812
                                 TDY:541-343-1284
                                 e-mail: info@miusa.org
                                 www.miusa.org

Susan Sygall, Executive Director
Pamela Houston, Public Relations Coordinator
Tracy Scharn, Information Specialist

A US-based national non-profit organization dedicated to empowering people with disabilities around the world through leadership development, training, and international exchange to ensure inclusion of people with disabilities in international exchange and development programs. The National Clearinghouse on Disability & Exchange, a joint project, provides free information and referrals. Membership dues: $35 Individual membership, $50 Local or state organization, $150 National organization.

979   NIH Osteoporosis and Related Bone Diseases National Resource Center

1232 22nd Street NW
Washington, DC   20037   202-223-0344
                                 800-624-BONE
                                 FAX: 202-293-2356
                                 e-mail: orbdnrc@nof.org
                                 www.osteo.org

Distributes information to patients, health professionals, and the public on osteoporosis, Paget's disease of bone, osteogenesis imperfecta, and other metabolic bone diseases. Information on prevention, early detection, and treatment of these diseases is available.

980   NLP Comprehensive

2897 Valmont Road
Boulder, CO   80301   303-442-1102

981   National Association for Holistic Aromatherapy

PO Box 17622
Boulder, CO   80308   303-258-3791

Offers aromatherapy courses and acts as a referral service.

982   National Association of Developmental Disabilities Councils

1234 Mass Avenue NW
Suite 103
Washington, DC   20005   202-347-1234
                                 FAX: 202-347-4023
                                 e-mail: naddc@naddc.org
                                 www.naddc.org

Donna Heuneman, Executive Director

Represents Developmental Disabilities Councils in areas of public policy. Provides training and technical assistance to Councils.

983   National Association of Music Therapy

8455 Colesville Road
Suite 930
Silver Springs, MD   20910   301-589-3300

984   National Association of Retired Volunteer Program Directors

703 Main Street
Paterson, NJ   07503   973-754-2675

Maureen Mulligan, President

Seeks to provide national visibility and advocacy to facilitate communications among membership and to act as representative for those served by RSVP before national governmental bodies. Bestows grants and awards, compiles statistics and conducts workshops.

985   National Association of the Physically Handicapped

440 Lafayette Avenue
GA4
Cincinnati, OH   45220   330-724-1994

www.trumanjm@aol.com

Dedicated to the advancement of the social, economic, and physical welfare of the physically handicapped; promote public awareness of the needs of handicapped people and to push for government and leislation to meet those needs; adjustment of buildings for handicapped people; the implementation of programs to benefit the handicapped. Program activities include physcial fitness sessions, sports, and other programs; government and legislative concerns; and networking.

986   National Association to Aid Fat Americans

PO Box 188620
Sacramento, CA   95818   916-443-0303

Support and education for overweight people.

987   National Center for Education in Maternal and Child Health

2000 15th Street North
Suite 701
Arlington, VA   22201   703-524-7802
                                 FAX: 703-524-9335
                                 e-mail: info@ncemch.org
                                 www.ncemch.org

Dr. Rochelle Mayer, Director

Provides information on children with special health needs, child health and development, adolescent health, nutrition, violence and injury prevention and other issues of maternal and child health for health professionals and the public.

988   National Center for Family-Centered Care

7910 Woodmont Avenue
Suite 300
Bethesda, MD   20814   301-670-6331
                                 FAX: 562-986-4553

Karen Lawrence, Project Coordinator
Gail Johnson, Parent Network Dir.

The goals are to promote implementation of family-centered approaches to care for children with special needs in all settings and foster parent/professional collection at all levels of care.

989 National Chronic Pain Outreach Association

7979 Old Georgetown Road
Suite 100
Bethesda, MD 20814   301-670-6331
                           FAX: 301-907-0745

A nonprofit organization whose purpose is to lessen the suffering of people with chronic pain. NCPOA helps people with chronic pain regain control of their pain and their lives.

990 National Clearinghouse on Women and Girls with Disabilities

Educational Equity Concepts
114 East 32nd Street
Room 701
New York, NY 10016
                           FAX: 212-725-0947
                           TDY:212-725-1803
            e-mail: information@edequity.org
                           www.edequity.org

Ellen Rubin, Coord. of Individuality Program

Provides information, resources and referrals. Publishes Bridging the Gap, a national directory which lists organizations that serve women and girls with disabilities and gives resource information. Also publishes curriculum on of children with disabilities and programs in science for children with disabilties.

991 National College of Naturepathic Medicine

11231 Southeast Market Street
Portland, OR 97216   503-255-4860

992 National Council on Disability

1331 F Street
Suite 1050
Washington, DC 22004   202-546-8000
                           FAX: 202-272-2022
                           www.ncd.gov

Mark Quigley, Public Affairs Specialist

Federal agency led by 15 members appointed by the President of the United States and confirmed by the United States Senate. The overall purpose of the National Council is to promote policies, programs, practices and procedures that guarantee equal opportunities to persons with disabilities.

993 National Council on Independent Living

1916 Wilson Boulevard
Suite 209
Arlington, VA 22201   703-525-3406
                           888-525-3400
                           FAX: 703-525-3409
                       e-mail: ncil@ncil.org
                           www.ncil.org

Anne Marie Hughey, Executive Director

Offers information, referrals, advocacy and guides for the disabled regarding living independently.

994 National Early Childhood Technical Assistance System

500 Nation Bank Plaza
137 East Franklin Street
Chapel Hill, NC 27514   919-962-2001
                           FAX: 919-966-7463
                           www.nectas.unc.edu

Assists states and other designated governing jurisdictions as they develop multidisciplinary, coordinated and comprehensive services for children with special needs.

995 National Easter Seal Society

230 West Monroe Street
Chicago, IL 60606   312-422-0600
                           FAX: 312-726-8628
                           www.seal.com

Jaent D. Jamieson, Communications Mgr.

The mission of the Society is to help people with disabilities achieve independence. Easter Seals provides quality rehabilitation services; technological assistance; and disability prevention, advocacy and public education programs. A nationwide network of affiliate societies serving each of the 50 United States, the District of Columbia and Puerto Rico, all of which work together to serve more than 1 million people each year. There are 160 chapters offering more than 400 programs nationwide.

996 National Endowment for the Arts, Office for AccessAbility

1100 Pennsylvania Avenue NW
Suite 528
Washington, DC 20506   202-682-5532
                           FAX: 202-682-5715
                       www.arts.endow.gov/partner

Suzanne Richard, Accessibility Specialist

Offers technical assistance on making programs accessible to older adults and individuals with various disabilities.

997 National Guild of Hypnotists

PO Box 308
Merrimack, NH 03054   603-429-9438

998 National Information Center for Children and Youth with Disabilities (NICHCY)

PO Box 1492
Washington, DC 20013   202-884-8200
                           800-695-0285
                           FAX: 202-884-8441
                       e-mail: nichcy@aed.org
                           www.nichcy.org

Provides free information to assist parents, educators, caregivers, advocates and others in helping children and youth with disabilities become participating members of the community. In addition to a wealth of printed materials, the Center disseminates materia0000n cassette, computer disc, and in Spanish. The Center can also provide personal responses to specific questions.

999 National Information Clearinghouse

Association for the Care of Children's Health
7910 Woodmont Avenue
Suite 300
Bethesda, MD   20814   301-654-6549
                             800-922-9224
                             FAX: 301-986-4553

A national information and referral system providing assistance to meet the information needs of caregivers and to protect the rights of infants with disabilities and life-threatening conditions.

1000 National Institute on Disability and Rehabilitation Research

400 Maryland Avenue, SW
Washington, DC   20202   202-205-8134
                             FAX: 202-205-8515
                   www.ed.gov/offices/OSERS/NIDRR

Conducts comprehensive and coordinated programs of extramural research and related activities to maximize the full inclusion, social integration, employment, and independent living of disabled individuals of all ages. Provides funding for programs to assist ADA compliance, including Regional Disability and Business Technical Assistance Centers, Materials Development Projects, and Peer Training Projects.

1001 National Maternal and Child Health Clearinghouse

2070 Chain Bridge Road
Suite 450
Vienna, VA   22182   703-730-5200
                          FAX: 703-821-2098
                   e-mail: nmchc@circsol.com
                          www.nmchc.org

Linda Cramer, Director

Offers information, books and pamphlets to professionals, parents and children facing health issues or disabilities.

1002 National Mental Health Assocation

1021 Prince Street
Alexandria, VA   22314   703-684-7722
                             800-969-6642
                             FAX: 703-684-5968
                   e-mail: infoctr@nmha.org
                          www.nmha.org

Patrick Cody, Dir. Media Relations

The nation's oldest and largest non-profit organization addressing all issues related to mental health and mental illness. NMHA and its grassroots network of over 340 affiliated Mental Health Associations work to provide public education, direct services and advocacy for mental health and mental illness concerns in communities across the country.

1003 National Organization on Disability

910 16th Street NW
Suite 600
Washington, DC   20006   202-963-5960
                             FAX: 202-293-7999
                             TDY:202-293-5968
                   e-mail: ability@nod.org
                          www.nod.org

Alan Reich, President

A nationwide network concerned with all disabilities, all age groups, and all disability issues. The mission of the National Organization on Disability is to promote the full participation of America's men, women and children with physical, sensory, or mental disabilities, in all aspects of life, and thus expand their contribution to society.

1004 National Parent Network on Disabilities

1130 17th Street NW
Suite 400
Washington, DC   20036   202-463-2299
                             FAX: 202-463-9405
                   e-mail: npnd@mindspring.com
                          www.npnd.org

Linda Shpeherd, Executive Director

Established to provide a presence and national voice for parents of children, youth and adults with special needs. The organization shares information and resources in order to promote parents influence on policy issues concerning the needs of people with disabilities.

1005 National Parent to Parent Support and Information Systems

PO Box 907
Blue Ridge, GA   30513   706-374-3822
                             800-651-1151
                             FAX: 706-394-3826
                             TDY:706-632-8822
                   e-mail: nppsis@elligay.com
                          www.nppsis.org

Dedicated to strengthening, supporting, and empowering families by establishing one to one parent to parent contacts. Enhances the ability of parents to access services and resources for children with special needs by providing information, resources, and referrals to appropriate services; supports and empowers families to participate in parent programs and disability issues. Educational materials consist of a quarterly newsletter and a fact sheet containing managed care information.

1006 National Rehabilitation Association (NRA)

633 South Washington Street
Alexandria, VA   22314   703-836-0850
                             FAX: 703-836-0848
                             TDY:703-836-0849
                   e-mail: info@nationalrehab.org
                          www.nationalrehab.org

Dedicated to advocating, supporting, and enhancing the lives of individuals with disabilities and their families. disseminates up-to-date information, conducts educational seminars, and provides opportunities through knowledge and diversity for professionals int he field of rehabilitation. Produces educational materials and sponsors an annual training conference with exhibits displaying the latest in rehabilitation technologies, awards, and provides access to a nationwide employment network.

1007 National Rehabilitation Information Center

8455 Colesville Road
Suite 935
Silver Spring, MD 20910   301-588-9284
    800-322-0956

A library and information center on disability and rehabilitation to collect and disseminate information on disability and rehabilitation.

1008 National Respite Locator Service

800 Eastowne Drive
Suite 105
Chapel Hill, NC 27514   919-490-5577
    800-773-5433
FAX: 919-490-4905
e-mail: ylayden@intrex.net
www.respitelocator.org

Dedicated to assisting parents, caregivers, and professionals find temporary relief services in their state and local area. Provides appropriate referrals for further assistance and has a leaflet describing the organization.

1009 National Vaccine Information Center

512 West Maple Avenue
Suite 206
Vienna, VA 22180   703-938-0342
FAX: 703-938-5768
www.909shot.com

Kathi Williams, Director

A national, nonprofit, educational organization dedicated to preventing, through public education, vaccine injuries and deaths. NVIC represents vaccine consumers and health care providers, including parents whose children suffered illness or died following vaccination. NVIC supports the right of vaccine consumers to have access to the safest and most effective vaccine as well as the right to make informed, independent vaccination decisions.

1010 National Women's Health Network

514 10th Street
Suite 400
Washington, DC 20004   202-347-1140
FAX: 202-347-1168
www.womenshealthnetwork.org

Publications and information packets on all women's health issues.

1011 Native American Protection and Advocacy Project

DNA-Peoples Legal Services
PO Box 392
Shiprock, NM 87420   505-368-3216
FAX: 505-368-3220
e-mail: napa@cyberport.com

Therese Yanan, Project Director

1012 North America Riding for the Handicapped Association

PO Box 33150
Denver, CO 80233   303-452-1212
    800-369-7433
FAX: 303-252-4610
e-mail: narha@frii.com
www.narha.org

William Scebbi, Executive Director

National nonprofit equestrian organization dedicated to serving individuals with disability by giving disabled individuals the opportunity to ride horses. Establishes safety standards, provides continuing educatin, and offers networking opportunities for both its individuals and operating center members. Produces educational materials including fact sheets, brochures, booklets, newletter called NARHA, audio-visual tapes, and a directory.

1013 North Carolina Bio-Oxidative Health Center

4505 Fair Meadow Lane
Suite 111
Raleigh, NC 27607   407-967-6466
    800-473-9812

1014 Northwest Naturopathic Clinic

2606 Northwest Vaughn
Portland, OR 97210   503-224-8083

1015 Nurse Healers - Professional Associates

175 Fifth Avenue
Suite 2755
New York, NY 10010   212-886-3776

Cooperative among health professionals interested in healing.

1016 Occupational and Enviromental Unit Tri-Cities Hospital

7525 Scyene Road
Dallas, TX 75227   214-275-1430

1017 Orcas Island Foundation

Box 86, Route 1
East Sound, WA 98245   206-376-4526

Summers workshops on Therapeutic Touch.

1018 Overeaters Anonymous World Services Office

6075 Zenith Court Northeast
Rio Rancho, NM 87124   505-891-2664
FAX: 505-891-2664
e-mail: info@overeatersanonymous.org
www.overeatersanonymous.org

Support groups and a twelve-step method of healing for compulsive eaters.

1019 PHP - Parents Helping Parents

3041 Olcott Street
Santa Clara, CA 95054   408-727-5775
FAX: 408-727-0182
e-mail: info@php.com
www.php.com

Dedicated to assisting children with any type of special need: mental, physical, emotional, or learning disability. Their mission is to help children with special nees receive love, hope, respect, and services needed to achieve their full potential by strengthening their families and the professionals who serve them. Developed and implemented numerous programs; produce a variety of educational and support materials, including information packets, brochures, database, and a quarterly newletter.

1020 Pacific Institute of Aromatherapy

PO Box 6842
San Rafael, CA   94903   415-479-9121
                                FAX: 415-479-0614
                    pacificinstituteofaromatherapy.com

Offers courses in the practice of aromatherapy.

1021 Pacific Toxicology

1545 Pontius Avenue
Los Angeles, CA   90025   310-479-4911

1022 Parent Professional Advocacy League

95 Berkeley Street
Suite 104
Boston, MA   02116   617-482-2915
                                800-331-0688
                           FAX: 617-227-1765
                                www.ppal.net

An organization of families of children with mental, emotional or behavioral needs and concerned professionals. PALS support groups are run in many areas across the country.

1023 People First International

PO Box 12642
Salem, OR   97309

Margaret Whipple, Executive Officer

Seeks to provide mentally retarded and developmentally disabled persons with training in leadership skills and advocacy. Offers consultation and workshops in prospective skills and advocacy.

1024 People-to-People Committee for the Handicapped

PO Box 18131
Washington, DC   20036   202-333-1811
                           FAX: 202-342-6055
                    e-mail: ngvb096@prodigy.com

David Brigham, Chairman

Individuals concerned about the circumstances of handicapped people throughout the world. Disseminates information, acts as a consultant in promoting exchange activities, coordinates special assistance projects in developing countries and more.

1025 People-to-People International, Committee for the Handicapped

501 E Armour Boulevard
Kansas City, MO   64109

                                800-676-7874
                           FAX: 816-561-7502
                    e-mail: drdwaugh@aol.com

Dr. David Waugh, Chairman

Goals of this committee include: betterment of the handicapped through international unity; educating those with and without handicaps through technical assistance; opening access doors through sensory aids, prosthetic devices and travel tips; and coordination of major international cultural exchanges.

1026 Physicians for Social Responsibility

1000 16th Street Northwest
Suite 810
Washington, DC   20036   202-667-4260
                           FAX: 202-667-4201

1027 Polarity Wellness Center

10 Leonard Street
Suite A
New York, NY   10013   212-334-8392

Information, publications and referral directory.

1028 Portland Naturopathic Clinic NCNM National Health Centers Eastside Clinic

National College of Naturopathic Medicine
11231 Southeast Market Street
Portland, OR   97216   503-255-7355

                    www.ncnm.edu/clinic.htm

Outpatient clinic in naturopathic medicine with diagnostic services, naturopathic treatments and a natural pharmacy.

1029 Presbyterian Health, Education and Welfare Association

100 Witherspoon Street
3041
Louisville, KY   40202   502-569-5794
                                888-728-7228
                           FAX: 502-569-8034
                    e-mail: ntroy@ctr.pcusa.org

Rev. Nancy K Troy, Executive Director

Presbyterians for Disability Concerns welcomes those sharing ministry with, by and for people with disabilities. Advocacy group within the church providing material and events.

1030 Pumpkin Hollow Farm

Box 135, RR1
Craryville, NY   12521   518-325-3583

Site of Frequent Touch workshops.

1031 Quan Yin Healing Arts Center

1748 Market Street
San Francisco, CA   94102   415-861-4964
                           FAX: 415-861-0579
                    e-mail: qyhac@aol.com

Acupuncture, herbal medicine, yoga, and massage therapy; lectures, discussion groups and nutritional information.

1032 Quest International

1984 Coffman Road
PO Box 4850
Newark, OH   43058

                                800-446-2700
                           FAX: 740-522-6580
                    e-mail: questnet@alink.com
                                www.quest.edu

Alan Williams, Vice President

Independent, international, educational organizatins dedicated to equipping adults with the skills, tools, and strategies essential to nurturing responsibility and caring in young people. With its global network of partners, Quest works to impart the skills and ways of thinking about young people that help enhance their capacity to flourish in an often turbulent world. Mission is to empower and support adults throughout the world to nurture responsiblity and caring in young people.

1033 Rehabilitation International

25 East 21st Street
New York, NY 10010   212-420-1500
FAX: 212-505-0871
www.rehab-international.org

A federation of 120 disability organizations in 80 countries working together to promote the prevention of disability, the rehabilitation of disabled people, and the equalization of opportunities within society on behalf of disabled people and their families throughout the world.

1034 Rehabilitation Services Administration of the District of Columbia

810 First Street NW
Washington, DC 20002   202-442-8663
FAX: 202-442-8742
e-mail: elizabeth.parker@dc.gov

Elixabeth B. Parker, Administrator

Offers vocational rehabilatation services to people with disabilities.

1035 Research and Training Center on Independent Living

University of Kansas
4089 Dole
Lawrence, KS 66045   785-864-4154
FAX: 785-864-5063
e-mail: beach@dole.lsi.ukans.edu
www.lsi.ukans.edu/rtcil/rtcil.htm

James Budde, Director
Glen White, Co-Director

Reports all issues related to independent living for people with disabilities, such as technology, programs, philosophies, new publications and research. Also, the RTC/IL received a NIDRR grant concerning undeserved populations and independent living centers. The RTC/IL and consumers will develop and test the best ways for ILC's to assist underserved populations (e.g., people with TBI, psychiatric, and cognitive disabilities; and people with disabilities who are minorities, adolescents, etc.).

1036 Rocky Mountain Resource & Training Institute (RMRTI)

6355 Ward Road
Number 310
Arvada, CO 80004   303-420-2942
FAX: 303-420-8675
TDY:303-420-2942

Serves people with disabilties and provides training to the agencies that assist them. Daxilitating disabled individuals' transition from school to adult life; providing information and resources concerning assistive technology, devices, and services; promoting and ensuring compliance with the federal American with disabilities act (ADA) and other legislation promoting the rights and inclusion of people with disabilities; promoting supported employment, strategic planning, and development.

1037 Ronald McDonald House

Kroc Drive
Oak Brook, IL 60521   630-575-3329

Ann Fox
Henry Lienau

A home-away-from-home, a temporary lodging facility for the families of seriously ill children being treated at nearby hospitals. There are 150 Ronald McDonald houses in nine countries. All totaled more than 2,200 bedrooms are available for families, serving some 4,000 family members each night. Each house is run by a local nonprofit agency comprised of members of the medical community, McDonald's owners, businesses and civic organizations and parent volunteers.

1038 Safe Water Coalition

West 5615 Lyons Center
Spokane, WA 99208   509-328-6704

Educates legislators and the public on the hazards of fluoridation.

1039 Sharp Institute for Human Potential and Mind/Body Medicine

8010 Frost Street
Suite 300
San Diego, CA 92123
    800-827-4277
FAX: 858-551-7811
e-mail: info@chopra.com
www.sharp.com

1040 Sitike Counseling Center

1211 Old Mission Road
South San Francisco, CA 94080   415-589-9305

Treats addiction through dietary and nutritional intervention using Biochamical Restoration Program, acupuncture and counseling.

1041 Society for Light Treatment and Biological Rythems

PO Box 478
Wilsonville, OR 97070   503-694-2404

1042 Special Parents Project

5954 Van Keppel Road
Forestville, CA   95436   707-887-1011
                              FAX: 707-887-2154
                      e-mail: brucer@monitor.net

Lorna Catford, Executive Director

Voluntary not-for-profit organization dedicated to providing caring outreach, training, advocacy, and support for families who are adjusting to the distress of having an infant or young child with disabilities. Objective to give parents tools to enhance their family's quality of life and their ability to be effective advocates for their children. Coordinates support groups, encourages networking, supports research, promotes education, and provides appropriate referrals.

1043 Special Technologies Alternative Resources (STAR)

210 McMorran Boulevard
Port Huron, MI   48068

                              800-272-8570
                         FAX: 810-987-6768
                         TDY:877-472-7840
                    e-mail: star@sccl.lib.mi.us
                    www.sccl.lib.mi.us/star.html

Mary JoKoch, Coordinator

Serving St. Clair, Huron, Sanilac, and Tuscola Counties; provides library service to those who are legally blind and visually disabled, and for those who are physically and reading disabled.

1044 St. John Valley Associates

10C 11th Avenue
Madawaska, ME   04756   207-728-7197
                              FAX: 207-728-7550
                        e-mail: sjva@nci1.net

Michael St. John, Executive Director
Andrew McQuarrie, Board President

A nonprofit association with the mission of empowering adult citizens with mental retardation to dignify themselves. Three broad based programs and services (Independence Plus, Job Involvements, People Now) are designed to allow each individual to upgrade learning skills, assert rights, increase independence and accept new responsibilities. *$75.00*

1045 Standard Search: Oral Health Care for People with Developmental Disabilities

National Oral Health Information Clearing House
1 NOHIC Way
Bethesda, MD   20892   301-402-7364
                              FAX: 301-907-8830
                        e-mail: nidr@aerie.com
                        www.aerie.com/nchic.web

Giovonna Miller, Information Specialist

The National Oral Health Information Clearing House (NOHIC), a service of the National Institute of Dental and Cranofacial Research is ready to help meet the information needs of special care patients and health care providers. NOHIC staff provides the custom or standardized services or special care topicsin oral health, including developmental disabilities. Each record in the search contains a bibliographic citation and abstract including info for the user on how to obtain materials directly.

1046 Stress Reduction Clinic University of Massachusetts Medical Center

55 Lake Avenue, North
Worcester, MA   01655   508-856-2656

1047 TEACCH

University of North Carolina at Chapel Hill
CB # 7180 310 Medical School
Wing E
Chapel Hill, NC   27599   919-966-2173
                              FAX: 919-966-4127

This organization is the division for the treatment and education of Autistic and related communication handicapped children.

1048 Teacher Preperation and Special Education

21 G Street NW
Suite 416
Washington, DC   20052   202-994-6170
                              FAX: 202-994-3365
                    www.ed.gov/offices/OSERS/OSEP

Madeline Will, Asst. Secretary

Administers the Education of the Handicapped Act and related programs for the education of handicapped children, including grants to institutions of higher learning and fellowships to train educational personnel. Grants to states for the education of handicapped children, research and demonstration.

1049 Technology and Media Division

1920 Association Drive
Reston, VA   20191   703-620-3660
                         FAX: 703-264-9494
                         www.cec.sped.org

Promotes the availability and effective use of technolgy and media for individuals with disabilities and/or who are gifted. TAM's members include special education teachers, speech and language therapists, rehabilitation therapists, counselors, researchers, teacher educators, and others.

1050 Thresholds Psychiatric Rehabilitation Centers

4101 North Ravenswood Avenue
Chicago, IL   60613   773-477-7505
                              888-997-3422
                         FAX: 773-880-6279
                    e-mail: jerry@thresholds.org
                         www.thresholds.org

Dr Jerry Dincin, Executive Director
Jay Forman, Associate Director

A nationally-recognized psychosocial rehabilitation agency serving persons with severe and persistent mental illness. The agency offers its programming at 17 service locations and more than 30 residential facilities throughout Chicago and Northern Illinois. In addition to its primary care program, Thresholds offers specialized programming for older adults, young adults, parents, the homeless and the hearing impaired and mentally ill.

Sliding scale

1051 Trager Institute
33 Millwood
Mill Valley, CA 94941   415-388-2688

Practitioner directory, information, training and certification.

1052 United Cerebral Palsy Association of Greater Indiana
615 N Alabama Street
Indianapolis, IN 46204   317-632-3561
                                      800-723-7620
e-mail: ucpaindy@ucpaindy.org

Donna Roberts, Executive Director

1053 Upledger Institute
11211 Prosperity Farms Road
Palm Beach Gardens, FL 33410   407-622-4706

Offers informations to physicians and the public.

1054 Vocational Rehabilitation Center
1062 East Lancaster Avenue
Rosemont, PA 19010   610-525-1810
                                    800-221-1042
FAX: 610-520-0935
www.dll.state.pa.us/our

OVR is the Pennsylvania Office of Vocational Rehabilitation, a state agency that helps persons with disabilities help themselves to prepare for, start, and maintain a career. OVR has fifteen offices located around the State with over 400 professional vocational rehabilitation counselors. These counselors work every year with thousands of persons who have physical, mental and emotional disabilities.

1055 Western States Training Associates
2290 East 4500 South
Suite 120
Salt Lake City, UT 84117   801-278-1022
FAX: 801-278-1088

1056 Wheelchair Access
RD
PO Box 12
Glenmore, PA 19343   610-942-3266
FAX: 610-942-0282
e-mail: wanews@chesco.com
www.inet-usa.com/wca

Dedicated to providing comprehensive information to individuals with disabilities concerning wheelchair accessible homes for sale or rent, vans, wheelchairs, and any other equipment they require. Produces a variety of educational matierials including a regualr newsletter. Wheelchair Access maintains a web site.

1057 Women to Women
3 Marina Road
Yarmouth, ME 04096   207-846-6163
FAX: 207-846-6167
e-mail: thank_you@womentowomen.com
www.womentowomen.com

Focuses on creating wellness while enhancing the natural healing processes of the body. Publishes the Creating Health Guide, a quarterly collection of articles written by the health care professionals at Women to Women.

1058 World Institute on Disability
510 16th Street
Suite 100
Oakland, CA 94612   510-763-4100
FAX: 510-763-4109
e-mail: wid@wid.org
www.wid.org

Judy Heumann

A public policy center that is run by persons with disabilities. Research, public education, training and model program development as means to create a more accessible and supportive society for all people - disabled and nondisabled alike.

Hearing Impaired

1059 Academy of Dispensing Audiologists
3008 Millwood Avenue
Columbia, SC 29205   803-256-7181
FAX: 803-765-0860
e-mail: info@audiologist.org
www.audiologist.org

Carol Davis, Executive Director

Encourages audiology training programs to include pertinent aspects of hearing aid dispensing in their curriculum.

1060 Academy of Rehabilitative Audiology
307 Ronan
Mount Pleasant, MI 48859   517-463-2983

Dr. Robert McLaughlin, Executive Director

Provides professional education, research, and interest in programs for hearing handicapped persons.

1061 Advocates for Hearing Impaired Youth
PO Box 75949
Washington, DC 20013   301-589-8444
FAX: 202-651-5817
e-mail: spnolts@juno.com

Information on deafness, hearing impairments, child welfare and advocacy.

1062 Alexander Graham Bell Association for the Deaf
3417 Volta Place NW
Washington, DC 20007   202-337-5220
                               FAX: 202-337-8314
                               TDY:202-337-5220
                         e-mail: agbell2@aol.com
                               www.agbell.org

Stephen Epstein, M.D., President

Nonprofit membership organization that exists to: encourage children with hearing loss to communicate by developing maximum use of residual hearing, speech-reading and speech and language skills; promotes better understanding of hearing loss in children and adults; promotes detection of hearing loss in early infancy; informs, encourages and helps adults who are deaf or hard of hearing; collaborates on research; works for better educational opportunities; and provides in-service training.

1063 American Academy of Environmental Medicine
7701 East Kellogg
Suite 625
Wichita, KS 67207   316-684-5709
                              FAX: 316-684-5500
                       e-mail: administrator@aaem.com
                              www.aaem.com

Training for physicians in environmental medicine.

1064 American Academy of Otolaryngology-Head and Neck Surgery
1 Prince Street
Alexandria, VA 22314   703-739-1316
                              FAX: 703-683-5100
                              www.entnet.org

Charles Krause, President

Promotes the art and science of medicine related to otolaryngology-head and neck surgery, including providing continuing medical education courses and publications.

1065 American Association of Acupuncture and Oriental Medicine
4101 Lake Boone Trail
Suite 201
Raleigh, NC 27607   919-787-5181

National organization of acupuncturists.

1066 American Association of the Deaf-Blind
814 Thayer Avenue
Suite 302
Silver Spring, MD 20910   301-588-8705
                              FAX: 301-588-8705
                              TDY:3015886545
                         e-mail: aadb@erols.com

Harry Anderson, President

Promotes better opportunities and services for deaf-blind people. The mission is to assure that a comprehensive, coordinated system of services is accessible to all deaf-blind adults. *$15.00*

Membership dues

1067 American Hearing Research Foundation
55 East Washington Street
Suite 2022
Chicago, IL 60602   312-726-9670
                              FAX: 312-726-9695
                    e-mail: blederer@american-hearing.org
                          www.american-hearing.org

William L. Lederer, Executive Director
Lorraine L. Koch, Assistant Director

The purposes of the Foundation are to promote, conduct and furnish financial assistance for medical research into the cause, prevention and cure of deafness, impaired hearing and balance disorders; encourage the collaboration of clinical and laboratory research; encourage and improve teaching in the medical aspects of hearing problems; and disseminate the most reliable scientific knowledge to physicians, hearing professionals and the public.

1068 American Society for Deaf Children
1820 Tribute Road
Suite A
Sacramento, CA 95815   916-641-6084
                              800-942-2732
                              FAX: 916-641-6085
                              TDY:916-641-6084
                         e-mail: asdcl@aol.com
                              www.deafchildren.org

Elaine Ocuto, President

Formerly the International Association of Parents of the Deaf, this organization offers educational materials and counseling for deaf children and parents of deaf children. The 18,000 members include parents, families, and friends of deaf children, and offers 96 local chapters.

1069 American Society of Deaf Social Workers
11300 US Highway 19 North
Horizon Hospital
Clearwater, FL 33764   727-541-2646
                              FAX: 301-570-6665

1070 American Speech-Language-Hearing Association
10801 Rockville Pike
Rockville, MD 20852
                              800-638-8255
                              FAX: 301-897-7348
                     e-mail: actioncenter@asha.org
                              www.asha.org

John E. Bernthal, President
Frederick T, Spahr, Ph.D., Executive Director
Joanne Jessen, Editor

Provides information for both the general public and medical physicians in an easy-to-access manner, on speech, hearing and language disorders.

1071 American Tinnitus Association
PO Box 5
Portland, OR 97207
                              800-634-8978
                              FAX: 503-248-0024
                              www.ata.org

Cherly McGinnis, MBA, Executive Director

Information about tinnitus and referrals to local hearing professionals and suppot groups nationwide. Publishes the magazine Tinnitus Today.

1072 American Tinnitus Association/ Tinnitus Today

PO Box 5
Portland, OR 97207   503-248-9985
                          800-634-8978
                   FAX: 503-248-0024
                   e-mail: tinnitus@ata.org
                          www.ata.org

Gloria E Reich, Ph.D. Executive Director, author
Barbara Tabachnick Sanders, Client Services
Steve Laubacher, PhD, Executive Director

Membership organization that carries out and supports research and education on tinnitus. Provides resources to both professionals and patients about seeking help and information. Publishes quarterly journal, Tinnitus Today. $25 annual membership includes subscription to Tinnitus Today.

1073 Arkansas Rehabilitation Research and Training Center for the Deaf and Hard of Hearing

University of Arkansas
4601 West Markham Street
Little Rock, AR 72205   501-686-9691
                       FAX: 501-686-9698
                       TDY:501-686-9691
               e-mail: rehabres@cavern.uark.edu
                       www.uark.edu/deafrtc

Douglas Watson, Director

Focuses on issues affecting the employability of deaf and hard of hearing rehabilitation clients—career assessment, career mobility, and advancement. Provides information and/or databases related to the rehabilitation of deaf and hard of hearing people served by the Federal/State Vocational Rehabilitation Program.

1074 Association of Late-Deafened Adults

1145 Westgate Street
Suite 206
Oak Park, IL 60301
                          877-348-7537
                     FAX: 877-348-7537
               e-mail: president@alda.org
                          www.aldra.org

Candis Shannon, Editor of ALDA News

Provides resources, information, and advocacy of the needs of deafened adults. Publishes ALDA News.

1075 Auditory Learning Center

304 East Jones Street
Raleigh, NC 27601   919-828-1218
                       FAX: 919-828-1862
                       TDY:919-828-1218
               e-mail: nccue@sprynet.com

Mary E.E. Burch, E.D., Executive Director

Provides instruction, support services and information pertaining to deafness and the application of Cued Speech, a system of communication. The center provides classes and workshops in Cued Speech, maintains a speakers bureau and provides counseling and support for hearing-impaired people and their families.

1076 Auditory-Verbal International

2121 Eisenhower Avenue
Suite 402
Alexandria, VA 22314   703-739-1049
                       FAX: 703-739-0395
                       TDY:703-739-0874
               e-mail: audiverb@aol.com
                       www.auditory-verbal.org

Sara Blair Lahe, Executive Director
Tom Lucches, President

To provide the choice of listening and speaking as the way of life for children and adults who are deaf or hard of hearing.

1077 Better Hearing Institute

515 King Street
Suite 420
Alexandria, VA 22314   703-684-3391
                          800-EAR-WELL
                       FAX: 703-684-6048
               e-mail: mail@betterhearing.org
                       www.betterhearing.org

Implements national public information programs on hearing loss and medical, surgical, hearing aid, and rehabilitation assistance.

1078 Boys Town National Research Hospital

555 North 30th Street
Omaha, NE 68131   402-498-6511
                       FAX: 402-498-6638
               e-mail: peb@boystown.org
                       www.boystown.org

Patrick E. Brookhouser, M.D., Director

State-of-the-art research, diagnosis and treatment of individuals with ear diseases, hearing and balance disorders, cleft lip and palate, and speech/language problems.

1079 Caption Center

125 Western Avenue
Boston, MA 68131   617-300-3400
                       FAX: 617-300-1035
               e-mail: caption@wgbh.org
                       www.wgbh.org/caption

Lori Kay, Director

Produces captions for the television and video industries; services including off-line captions, real-time captions, dual-field, dual-language captions, subtitling, and open captions. Publishes Caption Center News, Consumer Information Series, and Tech Facts.

1080 Captioned Media Program

National Association of the Deaf
1447 East Main Street
Spartanburg, SC 29307
                          800-237-6213
                       FAX: 800-237-6819
               e-mail: info@cfv.org
                          www.cfv.org

Bill Stark, Project Director

Produce educational and general interest videos.

1081 Cochlear Implant Club International
PO Box 464
Buffalo, NY 14223 716-838-4662
FAX: 716-838-4662
TDY:716-838-4662
e-mail: 76207.3114@compuserve.com

Bev Fish, President
Craig G. Carpenter, Executive Director

Not-for-profit voluntary organization dedicated to serving implant users, candidates, their families and professional supporters. Purposes are to promote opportunities afforded by the use of cochlear implants through mutual sharing of ideas and personal experiences; enhance community awareness of hearing impairment and to promote better understanding of implants; and to promote improved financial support. Publishes educational materials including a newsletter, brochures, and audiovisual aids.

1082 Community Services for the Deaf
102 North Krohn Place
Sioux Falls, SD 57103 605-367-5760
800-642-6410
FAX: 605-367-5958
TDY:608-367-5760
www.c-s-d.org

Benjamin J. Soukup, CEO

Offers peer counseling, information and referrals and advocacy services.

1083 Conference of Educational Administrators Serving the Deaf
PO Box 1778
St. Augustine, FL 32086 904-810-5200

Joe Finnegan, Jr., President

Focuses on improvements in the education of deaf and hard of hearing people through research, personnel development, advocacy and training.

1084 Convention of American Instructors of the Deaf
CAID Membership Office
PO Box 377
Bedford, TX 76095 817-354-8414

e-mail: caid@swbell.net
www.caid.org

Carl J. Kirchner, President

Promotes professional development, communication, and information; publishes American Annals of the Deaf, News 'n Notes; hosts biennial convention.

1085 Davis Center for Hearing, Speech and Learning: Hearing Therapy
98 Route 46 West
Budd Lake, NJ 07828 973-347-7662
FAX: 973-691-0611
e-mail: info@daviscenter.net
www.daviscenter.net

Dorinne S. Davis, Director

This center offers hearing therapy to people with hypersensitive hearing, ADD, and Central Auditory Processing Problems. Therapies include: Auditory Integration Training, Tomatis Method, Fast Forward, and Earobics.

1086 Deaf Artists of America
302 Goodman Street North
Suite 205
Rochester, NY 14607 716-244-3460
800-421-1220
FAX: 716-244-3690

Tom Willard, Executive Director

Organized to bring support and recognition to deaf and hard of hearing artists. Goals are to publish information about deaf artists, provide cultural and educational opportunities, exhibit and market deaf artists' work, and collect and disseminate information about deaf artists.

1087 Deaf Entertainment Foundation (DEF)
Deaf Entertainment Guild (DEG)
8306 Wilshire Boulevard
Suite 906
Beverly Hills, CA 90211 323-782-1344
FAX: 323-782-1344
e-mail: deafent@aol.com
www.deo.org

Mark Brudney, Marketing & Public Relations
Eldon Greenfield, DEOnline Webmaster
Dan McClintock, DEOnline Editor

Provides information to promote and accelerate the presence of deaf and hard of hearing talents in motion pictures, television, theater, and the performing arts.

1088 Deaf REACH
3521 12th Street NE
Washington, DC 20017 202-832-6681
FAX: 202-832-8454
www.deafreach.org

Sarah Brown, Executive Director

Offers referral, education, advocacy, counseling, and housing services for deaf mentally ill, multihandicapped and/or low income deaf people in the metro District of Columbia area.

1089 Deaf and Hard of Hearing Entrepreneurs Council
814 Thayer Avenue
Suite 303
Silver Spring, MD 20910
FAX: 301-588-0390
e-mail: jmcfadden@macf.com

Jim McFadden, President

Encourages, recognizes, and promotes entrepreneurship by people who are deaf and hard of hearing. Publishes Deaf and Hard of Hearing Entrepreneurs Council (newsletter).

1090 Deafness Research Foundation

575 Fifth Avenue
Floor 11
New York, NY   10017   212-599-0027
                                        800-535-3323
                                FAX: 212-599-0039
                                        www.drf.org

John Wheeler, President

Nation's largest voluntary health organization for research, treatment, and prevention of all ear disorders. Provides information and referral services; publishes The Receiver.

1091 Deafness and Communicative Disorders Branch of Rehab Services Administration Office

Special Education and Rehab Services
Department of Education
330 C Street SW, Room 3228
Washington, DC   20202   202-205-9152
                                FAX: 202-205-9340

Annette Reichman, MS, CRC, Branch Chief

Promotes improved rehabilitation services for deaf and hard of hearing people and individuals with speech or language impairments. Provides technical assistance to public and private agencies and individuals.

1092 Dogs for the Deaf

10175 Wheeler Road
Central Point, OR   97502   541-826-9220
                                FAX: 541-826-6696
                        e-mail: info@dogsforthedeaf.org
                                www.dogsforthedeaf.org

Robin Dickson, CEO/President

Trains hearing dogs to alert deaf persons to certain sounds. Dogs are chosen from pet adoption shelters and assigned on the basis of a prioritized waiting list. Five to six months of training teaches them to alert their masters to the sounds of alarm clocks, smoke alarms, doorbells, oven timers, telephones, etc.

1093 EAR Foundation

1817 Patterson Street
Nashville, TN   37203   615-320-0816
                                    800-545-HEAR
                                FAX: 615-329-7935
                    e-mail: ear@earfoundation.org
                                www.theearfoundation.org

Amy G. Nielsen, Director of Educational Programs

A national, nonprofit organization dedicated to integrating the hearing and balance impaired person into the mainstream of society through public awareness and special education. Programs include the Meniere's Network, the Minnie Pearl Scholarship Fund and Young EARS Program, newsletter.

1094 Ear Foundation

1817 Patterson Street
Nashville, TN   37203   615-329-7809
                                    800-545-4327
                                FAX: 615-329-7935
                                www.earfoundation.org

C. Gary Jackson, M.D., President

National, nonprofit organization commited to integrating the hearing and balance impaired into the mainstream of society throuhgh public awareness and medical education. Also administers The Meniere's Network, a national network of patient support groups providing people with the opportunity to share experiences and coping strategies.

1095 Episcopal Conference of the Deaf

PO Box 27685
Philadelphia, PA   19118   215-247-1059
                                FAX: 315-449-1602

Reverend Virginia Nagel, President
Reverend Jay Croft, Deaf Episcopalian Editor

promotes ministry for deaf people throughout the Episcopal Church. Affiliated with approximately 65 congregations in the United States. Publishes The Deaf Episcopalian.

1096 Exploring the Bible: Bible Studies for the DEAF

LifeWay Church Resources
127 Ninth Avenue North
Nashville, TN   37234
                                    800-458-2772
                                FAX: 615-251-5933
                        e-mail: ofernan@lifeway.com
                                www.lifeway.com
Daniel C. Johnson, author
Oscar J. Fernandez, Editor in Chief

Bible study lessons for every three months written by and for persons who are deaf. Based on the Family Bible Series (International Sunday School Lessons).

1097 Gallaudet University

800 Florida Avenue NE
Washington, DC   20002   202-651-5000

                    e-mail: public.relations@gallaudet.edu
                                www.gallaudet.edu

I. King Jordan, Ph.D., President

The world's only four year liberal arts university for students who are deaf or hard of hearing. Established in 1864 by an act of Congress, Gallaudet offers more than 50 undergraduate and graduate degree programs and numerous continuing education and summer courses.

1098 Gallaudet University Alumni Association

Gallaudet University
800 Florida Avenue NE
Washington, DC   20002   202-651-5060
                                FAX: 202-651-5062
                    e-mail: alumni.relations@gallaudet.edu
                                www.alumni.gallaudet.edu

Mary Anne Pugin, Executive Director
Gerald Burstein, President
Mercy Coogan, Editor of Gallaudet Today

Represents more than 14,000 alumni of Gallaudet University across the United States and around the world. Publishes Gallaudet Today.

1099 HEAR Center

301 East Del Mar Boulevard
Pasadena, CA 91101   626-796-2016
                              FAX: 626-796-2320
                    e-mail: auditory@mindspring.com
                              www.hearcenter.org

Josephine Wilson, Executive Director

Auditory and verbal program designed to help hearing impaired children, infants and adults lead normal and productive lives. Seeks to develop auditory techniques to aid people who have communication problems due to deafness. Offers diagnostic evaluations for speech and hearing. Individual auditory, verbal training and speech-language therapy.

1100 Hands Organization

2501 West 103rd Street
Chicago, IL 60655   773-239-6662
                              FAX: 773-239-2565
                     e-mail: handsorg@aol.com
                              www.handsdeaf.org

Kate Kubey, Executive Director

A nonprofit organization of both deaf and hearing persons working together to address the needs and concerns of the deaf community. The organization is working to raise the consciousness of the hearing world to the realities of deafness, and to bridge the gap between services already in place for the deaf and the large number of deaf people who have never been reached by those services. Offers a monthly publication.

1101 Health Resource Center

National Council on Education
One Dupont Circle
Washington, DC 20036   202-939-9320
                                 800-544-3284
                              FAX: 202-833-4760
                    e-mail: health@ace.nche.edu
                              www.acenet.edu

Vickie M. Barr, Director

Offers publications and a telephone service of use to administrators, service providers, teacherxs, instructors, rehabilitation counselors, health professionals, and individuals with disabilities and the families.

1102 Hear Now

9745 East Hampden Avenue
300
Denver, CO 80231   303-695-7797
                                 800-648-4327
                              FAX: 303-695-7789
                     e-mail: jostelter@aol.com

Elaine Hansen, M.A.A., CCCA, Program Director
M. Bernice Dinner, Ph.D., President

Committed to making technology accessible to deaf and hard of hearing individuals throughout the United States. Provides hearing aids and cochlear implants for very low income, hard of hearing and deaf individuals.

1103 Hearing Education and Awareness for Rockers

PO Box 460847
San Francisco, CA   94146   415-431-3277
                              FAX: 415-552-4296
                     e-mail: hear@hearnet.com
                              www.hearnet.com

Kathy Peck, Executive Director

Dedicated to educating the public about the real dangers of hearing loss resulting from repeated exposure to excessive noise levels. Operates a 24-hour hotline (415-773-9590) to provide information on hearing loss and hearing protection, assistance and scientific research. Other programs include national public service announcements campaigns, outreach to schools, HEAR affiliates, hearing protection and Can't Hear You Knocking! video.

1104 Hearing Industries Association

515 King Street
Suite 420
Alexandria, VA   22314   703-684-5744
                              FAX: 703-684-6048
                    e-mail: crogin@clarionmr.com

Carole M. Rogin, President

For hearing aid manufacturers and suppliers of component parts.

1105 House Ear Institute

2100 West Third Street
5th Floor
Los Angeles, CA   90057   213-483-4431
                              FAX: 213-483-8789
                                 www.hei.org

John W. House, M.D., President

Offers pediatric hearing tests, otologic and audiologic evaluation and treatment, rehabilitation, hearing aid dispensing, and cochlear implant services. Outreach programs focus on families with hearing impaired children.

1106 International Catholic Deaf Association

United States Section
8002 South Sawyer Road
Darien, IL   60561   630-887-9472
                              FAX: 630-887-8850
                     e-mail: icdaus@cs.com

Kathleen Kush, Director

Responds to spiritual-related requests worldwide from deaf or hard of hearing catholics.

1107 International Hearing Dog

5901 East 89th Avenue
Henderson, CO   80640   303-287-3277
                              FAX: 303-287-3425
                     e-mail: ihdi@aol.com
                              www.ihdi.org

Martha A. Foss, Director

Trains dogs to assist for deaf persons by responding to - telephones, doorbells, babies, etc.

1108   International Hearing Society

16880 Middlebelt Road
Number 4
Livonia, MI   48154   734-522-7200
                                           800-521-5247
                                      FAX: 734-522-0200
                                      www.hearingihs.org

Robin L. Clowers, Executive Director
Cindy J. Helms, Director of Marketing/Communica.
Pyllis V. Wilson, Associate Director

Professional association of specialists who test hearing and select, fit and dispense hearing instruments. The society conducts programs of competence qualifications, education and training.

1109   International Lutheran Deaf Association

1333 South Kirkwood Road
St. Louis, MO   63122   314-965-9917
                                           800-433-3954
                                      FAX: 314-965-0959

James Swalley, President
Promotes ministry for deaf people throughout the Lutheran Church.

1110   Jewish Deaf Congress

9420 Reseda Boulevard
Suite 422
Northridge, CA   91324
                                      FAX: 818-993-2695

Barbara Boyd, President
Advocates for religious, educational, and cultural ideals and fellowship for jewish deaf people. Conducts workshops for rabbis, parents of deaf children, and interpreters. Works with 20 affiliates and maintains a Hall of Fame.

1111   John Tracy Clinic

806 West Adams Boulevard
Los Angeles, CA   90007   213-748-5481
                                           800-522-4582
                                      FAX: 213-749-1651
                                      www.johntracyclinic.org

James H. Garrity, Ed.D., President
Educational facility for preschool-aged children who have hearing losses and their families. In addition to on-site services, worldwide correspondence courses in English and Spanish are offered to parents whose children are preschool age and are hard of hearing, deaf, or deaf-blind. All services of JTC are free of charge to the families.

1112   Junior National Association of the Deaf

814 Thayer Avenue
Silver Spring, MD   20910   301-587-1788
                                      FAX: 301-587-1791
                                      e-mail: nadyouth@nad.org

Nancy B. Rarus, Executive Director
Developes and promotes citizenship, scholarship, and leadership skills in deaf and hard of hearing students of grades 7 through 12.

1113   League for the Hard of Hearing

71 West 23rd Street
New York, NY   10010   917-305-7700
                                      FAX: 917-305-7888
                                      e-mail: postmaster@lhh.org
                                      www.lhh.org

Keith D. Muller, Executive Director
National diagnostic rehabilitation, human services agency founded in 1910. Offers comprehensive services for infants, children and adults with hearing loss regardless of age or mode of communication. Clinical programs iclude Tinnitus Center and Cochlear Implant evaluation, consultation, auditory training. LHH also affers extensive public adeucation programs, advocacy, support and publications.

1114   Lexington School for the Deaf/Center for the Deaf

30th Avenue and 75th Street
Jackson Heights, NY   11370   718-899-8800
                                      FAX: 718-899-9846
                                      www.lexnyc.org

Oscar Cohen, Superintendent/Director

Offers a comprehensive range of services to deaf, hard of hearing and speech impaired persons from infancy to elderly through its affiliate agencies: The Center for Mental Health Services; The Lexington Hearing and Speech Center, Lexington Vocational Services, and the Lexington School for the Deaf. The Lexington Center also provides services through its research division which houses the only federally funded Rehabilitation Engineering Center.

1115   Michigan Association for Deaf, Hearing and Speech Services

2929 Covington Court
Suite 200
Lansing, MI   48912   517-487-0066
                                           800-968-7327
                                      FAX: 517-487-2586
                                      TDY:517-487-0202
                                      e-mail: yourear@pilot.msu.edu
                                      www.madhs.org

Jody Smith, Executive Director
Jennifer Mora, Associate Director

Substance Abuse Prevention for the deaf and hard of hearing students (alcohol, marijuana, inhalants) acted in sign language, voicing, and captioning. HIV/AIDS Prevention and Information for the deaf and hard of hearing. Lending Library books, videos and audio tapes. Accessibility in Courts video and information. TTY distribution Program. TRACK-MAN-Youth Substance Abuse Video and Education Series.

1116   Mount Vernon Center for Community Mental Health, Deaf Services

8119 Holland Road
Alexandria, VA   22306   703-768-1975
                                      FAX: 703-360-0899

Ken Disselkoen
Offers deaf persons in the Mt. Vernon area counseling, education and advocacy.

1117 National Association of the Deaf

814 Thayer Avenue
Suite 250
Silver Spring, MD 20910   301-587-1788
    FAX: 301-587-1791
    TDY:301-587-1789
    e-mail: nadinfo@nad.org
    www.nad.org

Dawn Bradley, author
Nancy J Bloch, Executive Director

Nation's largest organization safeguarding the accessability and civil rights of 28 million deaf and hard
of hearing Americans in eduaction, employment,
health care, and telecommunications. Focuses on
grassroots advocate and empowermet, captioned media deafness-related information and publications, legal assistance, and policy development.

1118 National Black Deaf Advocates

1 Lomb Memorial Drive
Rochester, NY 14623   716-475-2411
    800-421-1220
    FAX: 716-475-6500

Promotes leadership, deaf awareness and active
participation in the political, educational and economic processes that affect the lives of black deaf
citizens.

1119 National Captioning Institute

1900 Gallows Road
Vienna, VA 22182   703-917-7600
    FAX:703-917-9878
    TDY:703-917-7600
    e-mail: mail@ncicap.org
    www.ncicap.org

Jack Gates, President & CEO
Karen O'Connor, National Director of Sales

Formed in 1979, the nonprofit National Captioning
Institute is the global captioning leader, supplying the
highest quality closed-captioning services to the television, cable, and home video industries.

1120 National Catholic Office of the Deaf

7202 Buchanan Street
Landover Hills, MD 20784   301-577-1684
    FAX: 301-577-1690
    e-mail: ncod@erols.com
    www.ncod.org

Arvilla Rank, Executive Director

Helps coordinate efforts of deaf or hard of hearing
people who are involved in the ministry, acts as a
resource center, assists bishops and pastors become
available to the deaf and hard of hearing.

1121 National Center for Accessible Media

WGBH Educational Foundation
125 Western Avenue
Boston, MA 02134   617-300-3400
    FAX: 617-300-1035
    e-mail: ncam@wgbh.org
    www.wgbh.org/ncam

Larry Goldberg, Director

Aims to increase access to public mass media (television, radio, print, movies, multimedia) for unserved
customers, such as disables people or speakers of
other languages.

1122 National Center on Employment for the Deaf

National Technical Institute for the Deaf
52 Lomb Memorial Drive
Rochester, NY 14623   716-475-6219
    FAX: 716-475-6500
    www.rit.edu/ntid/co/ce

Operated by the National Technical Institute for
the Deaf at Rochester Institute of Technology, the
National Center was established to promote successful employment of RIT's deaf graduates.
NCED offers training and consultations to employers and professionals working with deaf persons.

1123 National Cued Speech Association

Information Service
23970 Hermitage Road
Shaker Heights, OH 44122
    FAX: 800-459-3529

Cathy Quenin, Ph.D., Editor

Membership organization that provides advocacy and
support regarding use of Cued Speech. Information
available.

1124 National Deaf Education Network and Clearinghouse

Gallaudet University
KDES PAS-6
800 Florida Avenue NE
Washington, DC 20002   202-651-5051
    FAX: 202-651-5054
    e-mail: infotogo@gallaudet.edu
    clerccenter.gallaudet.edu

Responds to inquiries about a diverse range of
topics related to deaf and hard of hearing children
in the age group of 0 to 21.

1125 National Family Association for Deaf-Blind

111 Middle Neck Road
Sands Point, NY 11050   516-944-8900
    800-225-0411
    FAX: 516-944-7302
    e-mail: NFADB@aol.com
    www.NFADB.org

Nancy O'Donnell, author
Ralph Warner, President

A membership organization which provide resources,
education, advocacy, referrals, and support for families with children who are deaf-blind; professionals
in the field; and individuals who are deaf-blind.

1126 National Fraternal Society of the Deaf

1118 South 6th Street
Springfiel, IL 62703   217-789-7429
    FAX: 217-789-7489
    e-mail: thefrat@nfsd.com
    www.nfsd.com

Al Van Nevel, Grand President
Ronald L. Delvislo, Treasure

Work in the area of life insurance and advocacy for
deaf people. Has 75 divisions across the country.

1127 National Information Clearinghouse for Children and Youth with Disabilities

PO Box 1492
Washington, DC 20013
202-884-8200
800-695-0285
FAX: 202-884-8441
e-mail: nichcy@aed.org
www.nichy.org

Suzanne Ripley, Director

Provides fact sheets, state resource sheets, and general information to assist parents, educators, caregivers, advocates, and others in helping children and youth with disabilities participate fully as possible in their community.

1128 National Information Clearinghouse on Children Who Are Deaf-Blind

Teaching Research
345 Monmouth Avenue
Monmouth, OR 97361
800-438-9376
FAX: 503-838-8150
e-mail: dblink@tr.wou.edu
www.tr.wou.edu/dblink

John Reiman, Ph.D., Director

Collects, organizes, and disseminates information related to children and youth of ages 0 to 21 who are deaf-blind and connects consumers of deaf-blind information to the appropriate information.

1129 National Institute on Deafness and Other Communication Disorders (NIDCD)

1 Communication Avenue
Bethesda, MD 20892
800-241-1044
FAX: 301-907-8830
TDY:800-241-1055
e-mail: nidcdinfo@nidcd.nih.gov
www.nih.gov/nidcd

Marin Allen, Project Officer
Mia Esserman, Project Manager

The NIDCD Information Clearinghouse is a national resource center for health information about hearing, balance, smell, taste, voice, speech, and language for health professionals, patients, industry, and the public.

1130 National Rehabilitation Information Center

1010 Wayne Avenue
Suite 800
Silver Spring, MD 20910
301-562-2400
800-346-2742
FAX: 301-562-2401
e-mail: naricinfo@kra.com
www.naric.com

Mark Odum, Director

Provides information and referral services on disability and rehabilitation, including quick information and referral, database searches of the bibliographic database REHABDATA, and document delivery.

1131 National Technical Institute for the Deaf

52 Lomb Memorial Drive
Rochester, NY 14623
716-424-3480
FAX: 716-475-6500
TDY:716-475-6906
e-mail: ntidmc@rit.edu
www.rit.edu/ntid

Admissions Department

Provides technological postsecondary education to deaf and hard-of-hearing students. One of seven colleges of Rochester Institute of Technology.

1132 National Theatre of the Deaf

5 West Main Street
PO Box 659
Chester, CT 06412
860-526-4971
FAX: 860-526-0066
e-mail: bookntd@aol.com
www.ntd.org

Camille L. Jeter, Director

Professional development of deaf actors.

1133 Okada Specialty Guide Dogs

7509 East Saviors Path
Floral City, FL 34436
352-344-2212
FAX: 352-344-0210
e-mail: okada@hitter.net
www.okadadogs.com

Pat Putnam, Director

Trains dogs to aid deaf, hearing-impaired, Alzheimer's, seizure, amnesia and residential companion guide dogs.

Price varies

1134 Rainbow Allaince of the Deaf

3209 Rainmaker Street
Las Vegas, NV 89129
FAX: 702-804-7832
e-mail: president@rad.org
www.rad.org

Scot A. Pott, President

National organization serving gay, lesbian, and bisexual people who are deaf and hard of hearing.

1135 Registry of Interpreters for the Deaf

8630 Fenton Street
Suite 324
Silver Spring, MD 20910
301-608-0050
FAX: 301-608-0508
e-mail: 72620.3143@compuserve.com
www.rid.org

Clay Nettles, Director

A membership organization with over 7,000 members, including professional interpreters and translators, individuals who are deaf or hard of hearing, and professionals in related fields.

1136 Rehabilitation Engineering Research Center on Hearing Enhancement and Assistive Devices

Lexington School for the Deaf/Center for the Deaf
30th Avenue and 75th Street
Jackson Heights, NY 11370   718-899-8800
FAX: 718-800-3433
e-mail: info@hearingresearch.org
www.hearingresearch.org

Harry Levitt, Ph.D., Project Director

Promotes and develops technological solutions to problems confronting individuals with hearing loss.

1137 Rehabilitation Research & Training Center for Persons Who Are Hard of Hearing or Deafened

California School of Professional Psychology
6160 Cornerstone Court East
San Diego, CA 92121   858-623-2777
800-432-7619
FAX: 858-642-0266
e-mail: rrtc@cspp.edu
www.hearinghealth.org

Raymond J. Trybus, Ph.D., Director

Focuses on conducting research and developing training programs related to employment and personal adjustment of individuals who are hard of hearing or late deafened.

1138 SEE Center for the Advancement of Deaf Children

PO Box 1181
Los Alamitos, CA 90720   562-430-1467
FAX: 562-795-6614
e-mail: seectr@aol.com
www.seecenter.com

Esther Zawolkow, Director

Information and referral for parents and educators of deafness-related topics and Signing Exact English (SEE).

1139 Scottish Rite Center for Childhood Language Disorders

Children's Hospital
1630 Columbia Road NW
Washington, DC 20009   202-939-4703
FAX: 202-939-4717
e-mail: trobinso@cnmc.org

Dr. Tommie L. Robinson, Jr., Director

Offers speech-language evaluations and treatment, hearing screening and consultations to children ages birth through adolescents. Bilingual services are also available.

1140 Self Help for Hard of Hearing People

7910 Woodmont Avenue
Suite 1200
Bethesda, MD 20814
FAX: 301-913-9413
TDY:301-657-2249
e-mail: national@shhh.org
www.shhh.org

Nancy Nizankiewicz, Director of Development
Bonnie Sporre, Business Manager

A nonprofit, educational organization that is dedicated to the well-being of people of all ages and communication styles who do not hear well. SHHH is the largest international consumer organization of its kind.

1141 Sound, Listening, and Learning Center

301 East Bethany Home Road
Suite A107
Phoenix, AZ 85012   602-381-0086
FAX: 602-957-6741
www.soundlistening.com

Provides education, workshops, consulting, therapeutic sessions, and information on the Tomatis method.

1142 Tele-Consumer Hotline

901 Fifteenth Street NW
Suite 230
Washington, DC 20005
800-332-1124
FAX: 800-332-1124

Sylvia Rosenthal, Executive Director

Impartial consumer information service about residential telecommunication concerns.

1143 Telecommunications for the Deaf (TDI)

8630 Fenton Street
Suite 604
Silver Spring, MD 20910   301-589-3006
FAX: 301-589-3797
TDY:301-589-3006
e-mail: info@tdi-online.org
www.tdi-online.org

Dedicated to promoting full visual access to information and telecommunications through consumer educaiton and involvement; technical assistance and consulting; application of existing and emerging technologies; networking and collaboration; uniformity of standards; and national policy development and advocacy. The organization serves people who are deaf, hear of hearing, deaf/blind and/or speech impaired. Provides a comprehensive overview of deafness and deaf culture.

1144 Tripod

1727 West Burbank Boulevard
Burbank, CA 91506   818-972-2080
FAX: 818-972-2090
e-mail: tripodschool@earthlink.net

Barbara Muntan, VP, Board of Directors

An educational program for deaf and hard-of-hearing students in conjunction with Burbank Unified School District. The program offers educational services from birth through 12th grade. This partnership features co-enrollment and co-teaching models.

1145 USA Deaf Sports Federation

3607 Washington Boulevard
4
Ogden, UT 84403
FAX: 801-393-7916
e-mail: homeoffice@usadsf.org
www.usadsf.org

Valerie G. Kinney, Administrative Assistant

Governing body for all deaf sports and recreation in the United States.

1146 Vestibular Disorders Association

PO Box 4467
Portland, OR 97208   503-229-7705
                                 800-837-8428
                        FAX: 503-229-8064
                e-mail: veda@vestibular.org
                        www.vestibular.org

Jerry Underwood, Executive Director

Provides information and support for people with inner-ear vestibular disorders and develops awareness of the issues surrounding these disorders.

1147 Windmoor Healthcare of Clearwater

Windmoor Healthcare
11300 US Highway 19 North
Clearwater, FL 33764   727-541-2646
                                 800-288-4673
                        FAX: 727-544-5825
            e-mail: windmoor01@aol.com
                www.windmoor-healthcare.com

E. Gay Hawk, Director of Admissions

Full-service inpatient psychiatric facilities are available 24-hours a day and are especially designed to provide help to people experiencing emotional problems in their lives. Also serves those with alcohol and other drug abuse issues.

1148 Windmoor Healthcare of Miami

Windmoor Healthcare
1681 NW South River Drive
Miami, FL 33125   305-642-3555
                                 800-444-4673
                        FAX: 305-642-6829
                www.windmoor-healthcare.com

Full-service inpatient psychiatric facilities are available 24-hours a day and are especially designed to provide help to people experiencing emotional problems in their lives.

1149 World Recreation Association of the Deaf

PO Box 3211
Quartz Hill, CA 93586
                        FAX: 805-943-6112
                        TDY:805-943-8879
                e-mail: Brucegross@aol.com

Bruce Gross, President

Established to foster the development of innovation in recreational and cultural activities for the deaf and hard of hearing community. Quarterly newsletter.

Professional

1150 ACB Government Employees

American Council of the Blind
1155 15th Street NW
Suite 1004
Washington, DC 20005   202-467-5081
                                 800-424-8666
                        FAX: 202-467-5085
                    e-mail: info@acb.org
                            www.acb.org

Members are present, former and retired employees of federal, state and local government agencies. Concerns of the organization include recruitment, placement and advancement of blind and visually impaired employees.

1151 ACB Social Service Providers

American Council of the Blind
1155 15th Street NW
Suite 1004
Washington, DC 20005   202-467-5081
                                 800-424-8666
                        FAX: 202-467-5085

Blind and visually impaired social workers, social service professionals, students pursuing careers in social work, and other interested persons are members of this organization. ACBSSP works to promote full participation by visually impaired social services professionals in the field of social welfare.

1152 AHEAD Association

PO Box 21192
Columbus, OH 43221   513-861-5819
                        FAX: 614-488-1174
        e-mail: ahead@postbox.asc.ohio-state.edu
                            www.ahead.org

This is a national association of professionals working on college campuses with disabled students.

1153 Academy of Learning and Developmental Disorders

1350 Beverly Road
Suite 115-327
McLean, VA 22101   703-790-8644

Taras Cerkevitch, Executive Director
Mark Long, Board of Directors

Certifies psychologists, counselors, educators, optometrists, neurologists, pediatricians and psychiatrists as specialists in learning and developmental disorders.

1154 American Academy of Biological Dentistry

PO Box 856
Carmel Valley, CA 93924   831-659-5385
                        FAX: 831-659-2417
        e-mail: mail@biologicaldentistry.org
                www.biologicaldentistry.org

Promotes non-toxic diagnostic and therapeutic approaches in dentistry; hosts seminars on biological diagnosis and therapy.

1155 American Academy of Environmental Medicine

PO Box 16106
Denver, CO 80216   303-622-9755

Training for physicians in environmental medicine.

1156 American Academy of Orthomolecular Medicine

Huxley Institute for Biosocial Research
900 North Federal Highway
Baca Raton, FL 33432
                                800-847-3802

Provides information and referrals to orthomolecular physicians.

1157 American Academy of Osteopathy

3500 DePauw Boulevard
Suite 1080
Indianapolis, IN 46268   317-879-1881
                          FAX: 317-879-0563
                    www.academyofosteopathy.com

Represents osteopathic practitioners.

1158 American Academy of Physical Medicine and Rehabilitation

1 IBM Plaza
Suite 2500
Chicago, IL 60611   312-464-9700
                          FAX: 312-464-0227
                      e-mail: info@aapmr.org
                              www.aapmr.org

John M. Wilson, Marketing & Communications

This national medical specialty society represents more than 6,500 physical medicine and rehabilitation physicians, whose patients include people with physical disabilities and chronic, disabling illnesses. The academy's mission is to maximize quality of life, minimize the incidence and prevalence of impairments and disability, promote societal health and enhance the understanding and development of the specialty. The organization offers information, referrals, and patient materials.

1159 American Association of Acupuncture and Oriental Medicine

4101 Lake Boone Trail
Suite 201
Raleigh, NC 27607   919-787-5181

National organization of acupuncturists.

1160 American Association of Children's Residential Centers

51 Monroe Place
Suite 1603
Rockville, MD 20850   301-738-6460
                          FAX: 301-738-6461
                      e-mail: aacrc@dc.net
                          www.aacrc-dc.org

Richard Biolsi, ACSW, President
Elissa Malter Schwartz, Association Director

Brings professionals together to advance the frontiers of knowledge pertaining to the spectrum of therapeutic living environments for children and adolescents with behavioral health disorders.

1161 American Association of Naturopathic Physicians

601 Valley Street
Suite 105
Seattle, WA 98109   206-298-0126
                          FAX: 206-298-0129
                          www.health.gov/nhic

Licensed naturopathic physicians.

1162 American College of Advancement in Medicine

23121 Verdugo Drive
Suite 204
Laguna Hills, CA 92653   714-583-7666
                          FAX: 949-455-9679
                              www.acam.org

Provides training and education to physicians and scientists. Also provides referrals and informational material.

1163 American College of Nurse Midwives

818 Connecticut Avenue NW
Suite 900
Washington, DC 20006   202-728-9860
                          FAX: 202-728-9897
                      e-mail: info@acnm.org
                              www.acnm.org

Refers local midwives.

1164 American Counseling Association

5999 Stevenson Avenue
Alexandria, VA 22304   703-823-9800
                              800-347-6647
                          FAX: 703-823-0252
                          TDY:703-823-6862
                          www.counseling.org

Richard Yep, Interim Executive Director
Cheryl Haas, Manager of Public Communications

Provides a variety of programs and services that support the personal, professional and program development goals of its members. ACA works together to provide quality services to the variety of clients who use their services in college, community agencies, in mental health, rehabilitation and related settings. Offers a large catalog of books, manuals and programs for the professional counselor.

1165 American Group Psychotherapy Association

25 East 21st Street
6th Floor
New York, NY 10010   212-477-2677
                              877-668-2472
                          FAX: 212-979-6627
                      e-mail: groupsinc@aol.com
                              www.agpa.org

Marsha S. Block, CAE, CEO
Jan I. Vadell, Associate Executive Officer
Angela Stephens, Communations & Ed. Director

AGPA serves as the national voice specific to the interests of group psychotherapy. Its 4,100 members and 31 affiliate societies provide a wealth of professional, educational and social support for group psychotherapists in the United States and around the world.

1166 American Holistic Medical Association

4101 Lake Boone Trail
Suite 201
Raleigh, NC 27607 919-787-5181

Professional organization for holistic practitioners.

1167 American Occupational Therapy Association

4720 Montgomery Lane
Bethesda, MD 20814 301-654-7655
800-789-2682
FAX: 301-652-7711
TDY:800-377-8555
e-mail: praota@aota.org
www.aota.org

Fred Whiting, P.R. Director
Anne Morris, PhD, Gerontology Manager

A national professional society representing the interests and concerns of occupational therapy practitioners, and to improve the quality of occupational therapy services. The ADA Consultants Network is a listing of occupational therapists who are available to help employers comply with the provisions of the Americans with Disabilities Act.

1168 American Psychiatric Association

Psychiatric Services
1400 K Street NW
Washington, DC 20005 202-682-6000
FAX: 202-682-6870
e-mail: psjournal@psych.org
www.psych.org

Connie Gartner, Managing Editor
John Blamphin, Director, Public Affairs

Works to promote the best interest of patients and those actually or potentially making use of psychiatric services.

$64 a year

1169 American School of Ayurvedic Sciences

10025 NW 4th Street
Bellevue, WA 98004 206-453-8022

Medical training for physicians and health care practitioners, as well as for people. Dr. Virender Sodhi's ayurvedic, naturopathic medical clinic is also located at this address.

1170 American Society of Bariatric Physicians

5600 South Quebec Street
Suite 109-A
Englewood, CO 80111 303-770-2526
FAX: 303-779-4834
e-mail: bariatric@asbp.org
www.asbp.org

Provides referrals for bariatric physicians.

1171 American Society of Clinical Hypnosis

130 East Elm Court
Suite 201
Roselle, IL 60172 630-980-4740
FAX: 630-351-8490
e-mail: info@asch.net
www.asch.net

Physicians and dentists trained in hypnosis for treating health conditions.

1172 American Venereal Disease Association

J.B. Lippincott
PO Box 1073
Baltimore, MD 21203 301-955-3150

Professionals and lay people interested in understanding and controlling STD's.

1173 Arlin J. Brown Information Center

PO Box 251
Fort Belvoir, VA 22060 703-752-9511

A clearinghouse for information regarding alternative cancer therapies. Information available upon requaest.

1174 Association for the Care of Children's Health

19 Mantua Road
Mount Royal, NJ 08061 609-423-3610
FAX: 301-986-4553
e-mail: acch@clark.net
www.look.net

Heather Bennett-McCabe,Phd., Executive Director

An international multidisciplinary organization which promotes the emotional, developmental, and psychosocial well-being of children and families in all health care settings.

1175 Behavior Therapy and Research Society

Temple University Medical School
Philadelphia, PA 19129 352-344-2212
FAX: 215-707-4086

This organization promotes behavior therapy by conducting and facilitating research in behavioral interventions and providing information through consultations, conferences and publications, about the use of these methods.

1176 College of Optometrists in Vision Development

353 H Street
Suite C
Chula Vista, CA 92010 619-425-6191
FAX: 619-420-3010

Certifies optometrists who specialize in vision therapy.

1177 Community Enterprises

41 Mechanic Street
PO Box 176
Windsor, CT 06095 860-688-7918
FAX: 860-688-5599
e-mail: cehftd@aol.com
www.communityenterprises.com

Susan Cauley, Vice President, CT Operation

Provide supported education services in a community college setting; supported employment including job training, placement and follow-up; transitional services from group homes and other settings to supported living within the community.

1178   Environmental Dental Association

9974 Scripps Ranch Boulevard
Suite 36
San Diego, CA   92131   619-586-1208
                              800-388-8124

Organization of alternative dentists concerned about the potential toxic effects of dental procedures.

1179   Feldenkrais Guild

PO Box 489
Albany, OR   97321   503-926-0981

Offers information, practitioner directory, training, and certification.

1180   Gallaudet University

800 Florida Avenue NE
Washington, DC   20002   202-651-5050
                              FAX: 202-651-5704
e-mail: public.relations@gallaudet.edu
www.gallaudet.edu

1181   International Association of Yoga Therapists

PO Box 2418
Sebastopol, CA   95473   707-928-9898

e-mail: mail@iayt.org
www.iayt.org

A nonprofit organization emphasizing education and research for yoga and yoga therapy; Journal of the International Association of Yoga Therapists.

1182   Job Accommodation Network

PO Box 6080
Morgantown, WV   26506   304-293-7186
                              800-526-7234
                         FAX: 304-293-5407
e-mail: jan@jan.icdi.wvu.edu
www.jan.wvu.edu

The JAN is an international information service for people with disabilities and their employers. They have information about implementation of workplace accommodations, as well as resources to promote an awareness of functional limitations associated with disability.

1183   Maharishi Ayur-Veda Medical Center

PO Box 282
Fairfield, IA   52556   515-472-5866

Provides referrals to health centers, also training and information to the lay public.

1184   National Association of Blind Educators

National Federation of the Blind
1800 Johnson Street
Baltimore, MD   21230   410-659-9314
                         FAX: 410-685-5653
                    e-mail: nfb@nfb.org
                         www.nfb.org

Mary Willows, President

Membership organization of blind teachers, professors and instructors in all levels of education. Provides support and information regarding professional responsibilities, classroom techniques, national testing methods and career obstacles. Publishes The Blind Educator, national magazine specifically for blind educators.

1185   National Association of Blind Lawyers

National Federation of the Blind
1800 Johnson Street
Baltimore, MD   21230   410-659-9314
                         FAX: 410-685-5653
                    e-mail: nfb@nfb.org
                         www.nfb.org

Scott LaBarre, President

Membership organization of blind attorneys, law students, judges and others in the law field. Provides support and information regarding employment, techniques used by the blind, advocacy, laws affecting the blind, current information about the American Bar Association and other issues for blind lawyers.

1186   National Association of Blind Secretaries and Transcribers

National Federation of the Blind
1800 Johnson Street
Baltimore, MD   21230   410-659-9314
                         FAX: 410-685-5653
                e-mail: nfb@iamdigex.net
                         www.nfb.org

Membership organization of blind secretaries and transcribers at all levels, including medical and paralegal transcription, office workers, customer-service personnel and many other similar fields. Addresses issues such as technology, accomodation, career planning and job training.

1187   National Association of Blind Teachers

American Council of the Blind
1155 15th Street NW
Suite 1004
Washington, DC   20005   202-467-5081
                              800-424-8666
                         FAX: 202-467-5085

Works to advance the teaching profession for blind and visually impaired people, protects the interest of teachers, presents discussions and solutions for special problems encountered by blind teachers and publishes a directory of blind teachers in the U.S.

1188 **National Association of Protection and Advocacy Systems**

900 2nd Street NE
Suite 211
Washington, DC 20002   202-408-9514
                              FAX: 202-408-9520
                  e-mail: napas@earthlink.net
                  www.protectionandadvocacy.com

Curtis Decker, Executive Director
Eugeria Wheeler, Receptionist
Barbara Spoor, Deputy Director

The membership association of the directors of three federally funded programs: the Protection & Advocacy Systems for persons with developmental disabilities and the P&A's for persons with mental illness, which provide legal advocacy for clients; and the Client Assistance Program, which assists clients of vocational rehabilitation services with eligibility and legal problems.

1189 **National Association of State Directors of Developmental Disabilities Services (NASDDDS)**

113 Oronoco Street
Alexandria, VA 22314   703-683-4202
                              FAX: 703-684-1395
                  e-mail: rgettings@nasddds.com
                  www.nasddds.com

Robert Gettings, Executive Director
Karol Snyder, Manager of Membership Services

A nonprofit organization devoted to improving and expanding services to persons with developmental disabilities. The primary aims of the association are to: facilitate an exchange of information regarding the most advanced and efficacious methods of providing care and training to this population and represent the interests of state programs for persons with mental retardation/developmental disabilities in the development and implementation of federal programs.

1190 **National Clearinghouse of Rehabilitation Training Materials**

Oklahoma State University
5202 North Richmond Hill Road
Stillwater, OK 74078   405-624-7650
                              800-223-5219
                              FAX: 405-624-0695
                  www.nchrtm.okstate.edu

David Brooks, Director

Offers reference materials on vocational rehabilitation for professionals and the disabled.

1191 **National Deaf Education Network and Clearinghouse**

KDES PAS-6
800 Florida Avenue NE
Washington, DC 20002   202-651-5051
                              FAX: 202-651-5054
      e-mail: clearinghouse.infotogo@gallaudet.edu
                  clercenter.gallaudet.edu

1192 **National Federation of the Blind -Blind Industrial Workers of America**

National Federation of the Blind
1800 Johnson Street
Baltimore, MD 21230

                  e-mail: nfb@iamdigex.net
                  www.nfb.org

Membership organization of blind persons employed in industrial and manufacturing work or in government job programs for the blind. Dedicated to protecting the rights of blind workers in salary, job stability, advancement, and labor issues.

1193 **National Federation of the Blind - Public Employees Division**

National Federation of the Blind
1800 Johnson Street
Baltimore, MD 21230   410-659-9314
                              FAX: 410-685-5653
                  e-mail: nfb@iamdigex.net
                  www.nfb.org

Organization of blind persons holding local, state or federal jobs. Focuses on issues such as changes in governmental hiring and retention practices, new job skills needed for the future, government employment downsizing, new electronic means of finding public sector jobs, self-advocacy and career planning strategies.

1194 **National Federation of the Blind - Science and Engineering Division**

National Federation of the Blind
1800 Johnson Street
Baltimore, MD 21230   410-659-9314
                              FAX: 410-685-5653
                  e-mail: nfb@iamdigex.net
                  www.nfb.org

Blind persons with expertise and experience in fields such as genetics, telecommunications, biology, chemistry, physics and nuclear physics or mechanical, electronic and chemical engineering. This is a strong support group to encourage blind persons in pursuit of these careers, many of which have been considered not possible for the blind in the past.

1195 **National Federation of the Blind - Writers Division**

National Federation of the Blind
1800 Johnson Street
Baltimore, MD 21230   410-659-9314
                              FAX: 410-685-5653
                  e-mail: nfb@iamdigex.net
                  www.nfb.org

Blind writers in all styles, including poetry, short story, fiction, non-fiction, magazine writing and theatrical work offer encouragement and support to blind writers and authors. Issues cover various aspects of this business, including selling your work, publishing, technology, motivation and discovering writing and publishing resources.

1196 National Federation of the Blind in Computer Science

National Federation of the Blind
1800 Johnson Street
Baltimore, MD   21230   410-659-9314
FAX: 410-685-5653
e-mail: nfb@iamdigex.net
www.nfb.org

Curtis Chong, Director of Technology

National organization of blind persons knowledgeable in the computer science and technology fields. Works to develop new technologies, to secure access to current technology and to develop new ways of using current or new technologies by the blind.

1197 National Federation of the Blind- Merchants Division

National Federation of the Blind
1800 Johnson Street
Baltimore, MD   21230   410-659-9314
FAX: 410-685-5653
e-mail: nfb@iamdigex.net
www.nfb.org

Membership organization of blind persons employed in either self-employment work or the Randolph-Sheppard vending program. Provides information regarding rehabilitation, social security, tax and other issues which directly affect blind merchants. Serves as advocacy and support group.

1198 North American Society of Teachers of the Alexander Technique

PO Box 3992
Champagne, IL   61826   217-359-3529

For information, referrals, and training

1199 Opportunities Unlimited and Brain Injury Services of Village Northwest

3407 Glen Oaks Boulevard
Sioux City, IA   51104   712-252-7135
FAX: 712-277-8602

We provide eight transitional rehabilitation services to individuals with brain injury, spinal cord injury and physical disabilities. Community inclusion is the cornerstone of both agencies. Therapies include: physical, occupational, speech, cognitive as well as vocational, recreational and nursing services.

1200 Project RSVP

5201 Leesburg Pike
Suite 600
Falls Church, VA   22041
888-606-7787
FAX: 304-292-2278

Project RSVP supports the SSA's initiative to expand operations vocational rehabilitation services through a national network of private providers. Rehabilitation companies interested in gaining access to a new clinet base, acquiring a new funding stream, and developing creative service delivery and entrepreneurial partnerships, may benefit from such a program.

1201 Quality Living

6409 North 70th Plaza
Omaha, NE   68104   402-573-3770
FAX: 402-573-3792

Survivors of traumatic brain injuries and severe physical disabilities MS & MD are the populations Quality Living serves. Using a functional approach, QLI offers a complete -based living and home health options.

1202 Res-Care Premier

4201 NE 56th Street
Altoona, IA   50009   515-967-0100
FAX: 515-967-0101

Res-Care Premier is a quality provider of rehabilitation, residential and community-based treatment programs for persons with acquired brain injury. Services are offered to a broad range of ages, acquities, and funding resources. Res-Care Premier currently operates programs in Illinois, Missouri, Iowa, Texas and Florida, with plans for program development across the United States.

1203 Rolf Institute

205 Canyon Boulevard
Boulder, CO   80302   303-449-5903
800-530-8875
FAX: 303-449-5978
e-mail: info@rolf.org
www.rolf.org

Offers information, practitioner directory, training, and certification.

1204 Teacher Education Division

1920 Association Drive
Reston, VA   20191   703-620-3660
FAX: 703-264-9494
www.cec.sped.org

Promotes the preparation and continuing professional development of effective professionals in special education and related fields. TED's members include person involved in the education and continuing development of professionals in special education and related fields, such as general education, allied health, speech and language pathology, rehabilitation, legal services, and more.

1205 United Educational Services

PO Box 1099
Buffalo, NY   14224
800-458-7900
FAX: 716-668-7875

David L. Slosson, Vice President
Cathy A. Rajca, Customer Service

Publisher and distributor of Curricular Materials, Tests, Developmental Resource and Collaborative Materials for Speech-Language Pathologists, special educators, and classroom teachers. United also sponsors professional workshops for special educators, classroom teachers, counselors, administrators and parents.

1206 Universal Institute , Rebah & Fitness Center

15-17 Microlab Road
Suite 101
Livingston, NJ   07039   973-992-8181
                                FAX: 973-992-9797

Universal institute is a 15,000 square foot, state of the art rehabilitation facility that specializes in neurological disorders such as brain injuries, spinal cord injury, strokes, etc. We offer PT, OT, Speech patholgy, Cognitive Remediation, Auqa Therapy and EMG Biofeedback.

1207 Universal Pediatric Services

475 S 50th Street
Suite 700
West Des Moines, IA   515-224-1122
                                FAX: 515-224-0630

Universal Pediatric Services, provides high tech care to medically fragile children and adults in the home setting. Emphasis is placed on the provision of services in the rural areas, the ability to service high tech needs and the promotion of primary nurse concept.

1208 Visually Impaired Data Processors

American Council of the Blind
1155 15th Street North West
Suite 1004
Washington, DC   20005   202-467-5081
                                  800-424-8666
                                FAX: 202-467-5085

Advocates for higher standards in the training of qualified blind students, creates a healthy environment for more employment opportunities in government, provides for the exchange of work technique ideas and works with agencies to increase the availability of braille and recorded materials.

1209 World Chiropractic Alliance

2950 North Dobson Road
Suite 1
Chandler, AZ   85224
                                  800-347-1011

Association that promotes the chiropractic profession.

Specific Disabilities

1210 ARRISE

9238 Parklane Avenue
Franklin Park, IL   60131   847-451-2740
                                FAX: 847-451-4008

Provides information about autism.

1211 Acid Maltase Deficiency Association-AMDA

PO Box 700248
San Antonia, TX   78270   210-494-6144
                                FAX: 210-490-7161
                        e-mail: tianrama@aol.com
                             www.amda-pompe.org

Marylyn House

Offers a newletter, informational materials, networking, referrals to local resources, national advocacy efforts, and also maintain a research registry.

1212 Alzheimer's Disease Education and Referral (ADEAR) Center

ADEAR Center
PO Box 8250
Silver Spring, MD   20907   301-495-3311
                                  800-438-4380
                                FAX: 301-495-3334
                    e-mail: adear@alzheimers.org
                             www.alzheimers.org

The Alzheimer's Disease Education and Referral (ADEAR) center provides information about Alzheimer's disease and related disorders to health professionals, patients and their families and the public. Most of the publications are provided at no charge as a service of the National Institute on Aging (NIA), one of the Federal Government's National Institutes of Health.

1213 American Academy for Cerebral Palsy and Developmental Medicine

6300 North River Road
Suite 727
Rosemont, IL   60018   847-698-1635
                                FAX: 847-823-0536
                        e-mail: king@aaos.org
                             www.aacpdm.org

Sheril King, Executive Director

Educational organization for professionals only.

1214 American Academy of Allergy, Asthma and Immunology

611 East Wells Street
Milwaukee, WI   53202   414-272-6071
                                  800-822-2762
                                FAX: 414-272-6070
                                  www.aaaai.org

The largest nonprofit association representing allergists, clinical immunologists, asthma specialists, allied health professionals, and others with a special interest in allergy and asthma. The AAAAI's mission is to advance the knowledge, education and practice of allergy, asthma and immunology.

1215 American Academy of Child and Adolescent Psychiatry

3615 Wisconsin Avenue NW
Washington, DC   20016   202-628-1816
                                FAX: 202-966-2891
                    e-mail: webmaster@aacap.org
                             www.aacap.org

Virginia Q. Anthony, Executive Director
Mary Crosby, Deputy Director
LaVurne Williams

Provides information to the public about different psychiatric and behavioral disorders in children and adolescents and represents over 6,500 child and adolescent psychiatrists

1216 American Amputee Foundation

PO Box 250218
Little Rock, AR   72225   501-666-2523
                                FAX: 501-666-8367

Amanda Erickson, Information Specialist
C.J. Walden, Executive Director
Kim McIntyre, Office Manager

Serves primarily as a national information clearinghouse and referral center assisting mainly amputees and their families. AAF researches and gathers information on prosthetic product information, services, self-help publications and reviews articles written within the field. AAF has helped claims, justification letters to payers, testimony and life care planning. Free information packet for phone or letter inquiries.

1217 American Association of Naturopathic Physicians

2366 Eastlake Avenue
Suite 322
Seattle, WA 98102   206-323-7610

Licensed naturopathic physicians.

1218 American Association of Spinal Cord Injury Nurses

75-20 Astoria Boulevard
Jackson Heights, NY 11370   718-803-3782
FAX: 718-803-0414
www.aascin.org

Sara Lerman MPH, Program Manager

A non-profit organization dedicated to promoting quality care for individuals with spinal cord impairmant. The AASCIN, founded in 1983, is a membership organization of registered and licensed practical nurses in the US and Canada who practice in diverse SCI settings. The AASCIN Nursing Research Program funds research in the area of spinal cord impairment and nursing practice. There is an annual educational conference sponsored by AASCIN. In addition, 'SCI Nursing' is published by AASCIN.

1219 American Association of Spinal Cord Injury Psychologists & Social Workers

7520 Astoria Boulevard
Flushing, NY 11370   718-803-3782
FAX: 718-803-0414
e-mail: ssofer@epua.org
www.aascipsw.org

Vivian Beyda, Dr PH, Associate Executive Director
Stephen Sofer, PhD, Program Manager

Organized and operated for scientific and educational purposes to advance and improve the psychosocial care of persons with spinal cord impairment, develop and promote education and research related to the psychosocial care of persons with spinal cord injury, recognize psychologists and social workers whose careers are devoted to the problems of spinal cord impairment.

1220 American Back Society Advanced Diagnosis and Treatment for Neck and Back

Pain 2001
International Boulevard, #401
Suite 401
Oakland, CA 94601   510-536-9929
FAX: 510-536-1812
e-mail: info@americanbacksoc.org
www.americanbacksoc.org

Aubrey A. Swartz, M.D.
Candy Lau, Office Manager

A membership organization dedicated to relieving the pain and impairment caused by back problems. Sponsors symposia for presenting research findings.

1221 American Board for Certification in Orthotics & Prosthetics

1650 King Street
Suite 500
Alexandria, VA 22314   703-836-7114
FAX: 703-836-0838
e-mail: opcertmail@aol.com
www.opoffice.org/agc

Lance O. Hoxie, Executive Director

The organization for the orthotic and prosthetic profession. ABC accredits facilities and certifies practitioners in accordance with established professional standards to help ensure quality care for the physically challenged.

1222 American Cancer Society

1599 Clifton Road NE
Atlanta, GA 30329   404-320-2424
800-ACS-2345
FAX: 404-325-2217
e-mail: bjubb@cancer.org
www.cancer.org

Cynthia Currence, Marketing Director

Offers counseling, seminars, conferences, support groups and transportation, providing 58 divisions and approximately 3,100 chapters.

1223 American Chemical Society Committee on Chemists with Disabilities

1155 16th Street NW
Washington, DC 20036   202-872-4600
800-227-5558
FAX: 202-872-6067
TDY:202-872-6355
e-mail: cwd@acs.org
membership.acs.org/C/CWD

Kathleen Thompson, Staff Liaison

Promotes the full involvement of individuals with physical and learning disabilities in educational and career opportunities in the chemical and allied sciences. CWD members lead the American Chemical Society's efforts to help: individuals with disabilities who seek education or employment in chemical and allied sciences; employers and educators of persons with disabilities; other committees, offices, and members of ACS who are interested in the full involvement of persons with disabilities.

1224 American Cleft Palate/Craniofacial Association

104 South Estes Drive
Suite 204
Chapel Hill, NC 27514   919-933-9044
FAX: 919-933-9604
e-mail: cleftline@aol.com
www.cleftline.org

Nancy Smythe, Executive Director

Professional society for healthcare specialists working with patients with cleft and craniofacial birth defects. Publishes Cleft Palate-Craniofacial Journal. Affiliated with Cleft Palate Foundation.

1225 American College of Addictionality and Compulsive Disorders

3303 Flaming Drive
Miami, FL 33140   305-534-3635

Board certifies doctors in acupuncture treatment of addition and compulsive disorders.

1226 American Heart Association: National Center

7272 Greenville Avenue
Dallas, TX 75231   972-735-8501
                         800-242-8721
                         FAX: 214-696-5211
                         www.americanheart.org

Barbra Jackson, Director

Fifty-five state affiliates monitoring local chapters offering educational materials, seminars, conferences and transportation for members nationwide. Maintains a listing of over 1,000 stroke support groups across the nation for referral to stroke survivors, their families, caregivers and interested professionals.

1227 American Juvenile Arthritis Organization (AJAO)

Arthritis Foundation
1330 West Peachtree Street
Atlanta, GA 30309   404-872-7100
                          800-283-7800
                          FAX: 404-872-9559
                          www.arthritis.org

A council established by the Arthritis Foundation which serves the special needs of young people with arthritis and their families. Provides information, inspiration and advocacy by identifying the needs of children with arthritis, and speaks out on their behalf.

1228 American Lung Association

1740 Broadway
New York, NY 10019   212-765-7036
                           800-LUN-GUSA
                           FAX: 212-315-8872
                           e-mail: info@lungusa.org
                           www.lungusa.org

Elaine Chapnick, Director

Offers information and computer networks providing 105 affiliates and constituents.

1229 American Network of Community Options and Resources

4200 Evergreen Lane
Suite 315
Annandale, VA 22003   703-642-6614
                            FAX: 703-642-0497
                            e-mail: ancor@ancor.org
                            www.ancor.org

Renee Pietrangelo, CEO
Suellen R. Galbraith, Director for Public Policy
Jerri McCandless, Communication & Member Services

The American Network of Community Options and Resources (ANCOR) is a trade association for agencies that provide support and services for people with disabilities. ANCOR successfully represents the needs and interests of private providers before Congress, federal agencies and national advocacy organizations. ANCOR also provides educational and technical assistance to its members.

1230 American Orthotic and Prosthetic Association

300 John Carlyle Street
Suite 200
Alexandria, VA 22314   703-836-7116
                             FAX: 703-836-0838
                             www.aopanet.org

Susan Tengesdal, Director of Communications

A national trade association representing patient care facilities and manufacturers of prosthetic and orthotic devices. A major focus is to provide industry companies with information about reimbursement, insurance and government regulations and other bussiness management issues.

1231 American Osteopathic Association

142 East Ontario Street
Chicago, IL 60611   312-280-5800

1232 American Paraplegia Society

Journal of Spinal Cord Medicine
75-20 Astoria Boulevard
Flushing, NY 11370   718-397-4181
                           FAX: 718-803-0414
                           www.epva.org/apshtml

Joel A. Delisa, M.D., author
Vivian Beyda, DrPH, Assocaite Executive Director
Stephen Sofer, PhD, Program Manager

Organized and operated for scientific and educational purposes to advance and improve health care of persons with spinal cord impairment, develop and promote education and research related to spinal cord impairment, recognize physicians and doctoral level researchers whose careers are devoted to the problems of spinal cord impairment.

Quarterly

1233 American Sleep Disorders Association

1610 14th Street NW
Suite 300
Rochester, MN 55901   507-287-6006

                            www.asda.org

Referrals to a local sleep disorders center.

1234 American Spinal Injury Association

345 East Superior Street, Room 1430
Rehpe Institute of Chicago
Chicago, IL 60011   313-238-1242
                          FAX: 312-238-0869
                          www.asia-spinalinjury.org

Lesley M Hudson, M.A., Meeting Coordinator

Professional association for physicans and other health professionals working in all aspects of spinal cord injury. Conducts annual scientific meeting to survey latest advancements in the field. See website for full details.

1235 American Stroke Association

PO Box 841750
Dallas, TX 75284

800-553-6321
FAX: 214-706-5231
e-mail: strokeconnection@heart.org
www.americanheart.org/stroke/index.html

Barbra Jackson, Director

Fifty-five state affiliates monitoring local chapters
offering educational materials, seminars, conferences
and transportation for members nationwide. Maintains a listing of over 1,000 stroke support groups
across the nation for referral to stroke survivors, their
families, caregivers and interested professionals.

1236 Amytrophic Lateral Sclerosis Association

27001 Agoura Road
Suite 150
Calabasas Hills, CA 91301

818-880-9007
800-782-4747
FAX: 818-880-9006
e-mail: alsinfo@alsa-national.org
www.alsa.org

Mary Lyon, Vice President

The only national health organization dedicated
solely to the fight against ALS. Purpose is to encourage, identify and fund quality research into the cause,
means of prevention and possible cures of ALS and
improve living with ALS.

1237 Arthritis Consulting Services

2787 East Oakland Park Boulevard
Suite 204
Ft. Lauderdale, FL 33306

954-739-3202
800-327-3027
FAX: 661-749-7712
e-mail: info@stoparthritis.com
www.stoparthritis.com

Provides information on holistic approaches to the
treatment of arthritis.

1238 Arthritis Foundation

1330 West Peachtree Street NW
Atlanta, GA 30309

404-872-7100
800-283-7800
FAX: 404-872-0457
e-mail: help@arthritis.org
www.arthritis.org

Eileen M. Rose, Administrative Asst.

Offers information and referrals regarding educational materials and programs, fund-raising, support
groups, seminars and conferences offered by 55 local
chapters across the United States.

1239 Association for Children with Down Syndrome

4 Fern Place
Plainview, NY 11803

516-933-4700
FAX: 516-933-9524
e-mail: smuzio@optonline.net
www.acds.org

Sebastian J. Muzio, Executive Director

Offers a preschool, toddler and infant program (birth
- 5 years), home-based and center-based educational,
therapeutic, health related services, parent education,
support and training and bilingual services for children with Down Syndrome and their families, prena-
tal support is available. ACDS 5 plus program
provides recreational and socialization programs for
ages five and up. After school, evenings and Saturday. A free publications list is available.

1240 Asthma and Allergy Foundation of America

1233 20th Street NW
Suite 402
Washington, DC 20036

202-466-7643
800-727-8462
FAX: 202-466-8940
e-mail: info@aafa.org
www.aafa.org

The Foundation was formed to alleviate suffering
and loss from asthma and allergy disorders. The
Foundation offers a nationwide network of chapters and support groups, and provides education
and emotional support for persons with allergies
and asthma. Also funds research for improved
treatments and ultimately a cure.

1241 Ataxia-Telangiectasia Children's Project

1 West Camin Road
Suite 212
Boca Raton, FL 33432

561-395-2621
800-543-5728
FAX: 561-395-2640
e-mail: bradmargus@delphi.com
www.atcp.org

Brad A. Margus, President
Rosa M. Frenandez, Executive Director

National not-for-profit organization. The purpose of
the project is to raise runds to accelerate scientific
research aimed at finding a cure or a therapy that
would improve the lives of children affected by
Ataxia-Telangiectasia. Specific goals including finding a cure or therapy, increawing awareness of the
disorder to help accurately diagnose affected individuals, and encouraging and funding scientific research directed specific treatments for AT.

1242 Attention Deficit Disorder Association

1788 Second Street
Suite 200
Highland Park, IL 60035

847-432-2332
800-487-2282

Mary Jane Johnson, President

The primary focus of this organization is to provide
a national network for all ADDA support groups,
individuals with ADD, their families and the professionals who work with them.

**1243 Attention Deficit Disorder Association- Southern
Region**

12345 Jones Road
Suite 287-7
Houston, TX 77070

281-897-0982

e-mail: addaoffice@pdq.net
www.adda-sr.org

1244 Attention Deficit Information Network

475 Hillside Avenue
Needham, MA 02494   781-455-9895
                                 FAX: 781-444-5466
                            e-mail: adin@gis.net
                          www.addinfonetwork.org

Libby Ostrofoky, President

A non-profit volunteer organization that offers support and information to families of children and adults with ADD, and to professionals.

1245 Autism Services Center

605 9th Street
PO Box 507
Huntington, WV 25710   304-525-8014
                                 FAX: 304-525-8026

Ruth C. Sullivan, PhD, Executive Director
Sue McClelland, Director of Office Administratio

Service agency for individuals with autism and other developmental disabilities and their families. Assists families and agencies attempting to meet the unique needs of individuals with autism and other developmental disabilities: makes available technical assistance in designing programs. Provides supervised apartments, groups homes, respite services, independent living programs and job-coached employment. Provides case management services for a four-county area in West Virginia.

1246 Autism Society of America

8601 Georgia Avenue
Suite 503
Silver Springs, MD 20910   301-565-0433
                                 FAX: 301-565-0834

List of 160 chapters throughout the United States; answers to questions on autism; quarterly newsletter with supportive information and research news; books on dealing with autism.

1247 Batten Disease Support and Research Association

2600 Parsons Avenue
Columbus, OH 43207   614-445-4161
                                 800-448-4570
                                 www.bdsra.org

Larry Killen, President
Lance W. Johnston, Executive Director

Voluntary not-for-profit organization dedicated to promoting the civil and human rights of people with Batten Disease. Provides referral services to help affected families secure benefits available by law and maintains a database of individuals with Batten Disease on state, national and international levels. Functions as a nation registry throughout the world who are studying Batten Disease. Variety of educational and support materials, including a quarterly newsletter, Illuminator.

1248 Bazelon Center for Mental Health Law

1101 15th Street NW
Suite 1212
Washington, DC 20005   202-467-5730
                                 FAX: 202-223-0409
                        e-mail: HN1660@HANDSNET.org
                                 www.bazelon.org

Robert Bernstein, Executive Director
Lee Carty, Communications Dir.

A national nonprofit public interest organization, advocates for public policies that can enable people with mental disabilities to live in freedom and dignity. Website offers resources on health care, fair housing, special education and enforcement of Americans with Disabilities Act. Publications list available.

1249 Brachia Plexus Injury Erb's Palsy Support & Information Network

PO Box 23
Larsen, WI 54947   920-836-9955

                    e-mail: nationalbpi@powernetonline.com
                          www.delphi.com/nationalbpi

Brenda Moore, President/Chairperson

Voluntary not-for-profit self-help orgnization dedicated to providing information and support to affected families, health care professionals, and social services agencies; increasing public awarness of Brachial Plexus Injury and Erb's Palsy; and discovering new ways to improve function for affected individuals. Engages in patient advocacy, provides appropriate referrals and enables affected families to exchange information, support, and resources. Produces educational and support materials.

1250 Brain Injury Association of New York State

10 Colvin Avenue
Albany, NY 12206   518-459-7911
                                 800-228-8201
                           e-mail: info@bianys.org
                                 www.bianys.org

1251 Brain Injury Association of Texas

Plaza 290 Office Building
Suite 306, 6633 East Highway 290
Austin, TX 78723   512-467-6872
                                 800-392-0040

Chip Howe, Representative

1252 Breast Cancer Action

55 New Montgomery Street
Suite 323
San Francisco, CA 94105   415-243-9301
                                 877-278-6722
                                 FAX: 415-243-3996
                           e-mail: info@bcaction.org
                                 www.bcaction.org

Holds monthly meetings and publishes a bimonthly newsletter on topics related to breast cancer. Works closely with California Breast Cancer Organization and the National Cancer Coalition.

1253 California Colon Hygienists Society

PO Box 588
Graton, CA 95444

Provides information and education on cellular detoxification and cleansing.

1254 Cancer Care National Office

275 Seventh Avenue
New York, NY 10001   212-221-3300
800-813-HOPE
FAX: 212-719-0263
e-mail: cancercareinc.org
www.cancercare.org

Diane Blum, Executive Director
Priscilla Hartung, Director Of Social Services

Cancer Care is a national nonprofit agency that offers support, information, and practical help to people with cancer and their loved ones. Services are provided by oncology social workers and are available through our toll-free line, over the internet, and from our offices in New York, Long Island, New Jersey, and Connecticut. Cancer Care's reach also extends to professionals providing education and valuable resources.

1255 Cancer Control Society

2043 North Berendo Street
Los Angeles, CA 90027   323-663-7801

e-mail: cfwintner@aol.com
www.cancercontrolsociety.com

Information on alternative cancer treatment centers and patients who have recovered from various cancers using them; emphasis on metabolic therapies; sponsors an annual convention.

1256 Cherub - Association of Families and Friends of Children with Limb Disorders

936 Delaware Avenue
Buffalo, NY 14209

Thomas Hauser, President
Sandra Richenberg, Executive Director

Voluntary not-for-profit organization dedicated to providing infomration and support to children with limb disorders, affected families, and friends through organized activities, phone suports, correspondence and visits. Conducts an annual summer camp for affected children ages eight to 18. Provides educational and support materials including a newsletter and brochures.

1257 Child Neurology Service

INOVA Hospital for Children
3300 Gallows Road
Fallschruch, VA 22042   202-298-7800
FAX: 703-204-6588

Offers infants and children to age 21 with neurological problems diagnosis, consultation, recommendations for therapy and more services. We also care for adults with cerebral palsy.

1258 Children and Adults with Attention Deficit Disorders (CHADD)

8181 Professional Plaza
Suite 201
Landover, MD 20765   301-306-7070

Offers general information to parents and professionals regarding ADHD.

1259 Christopher Reeve Paralysis Foundation

500 Morris Avenue
Springfield, NJ 07081   973-379-6299
800-225-0292
FAX: 973-912-9433
e-mail: info@crpf.org
www.paralysis.org

Mitchell R. Stoller, President & CEO

Dedicated to finding a cure for paralysis caused by spinal cord injury, head injury and stroke.

1260 Cleft Palate Foundation

104 South Estes Drive
Suite 204
Chapel Hill, NC 27514   919-933-9044
800-242-5338
FAX: 919-933-9604
e-mail: cleftline@aol.com
www.cleftline.org

Nancy C. Smythe, Executive Director
Amy Mackin, Deputy Director

The Foundation's major activities include the operation of the CLEFTLINE and the distribution of information. The CLEFTLINE is an 800-toll free service providing information and referral to parents of newborns with clefts and other craniofacial anomalies and to older children and adults with these conditions. Affiliated with American Cleft Palate-Craniofacial Association.

1261 College of Syntonic Optometry

1200 Robeson Street
Fall River, MA 02720   508-673-1251

1262 Community Services for Autitistic Adults and Children

751 Twinbrook Parkway
Rockville, MD 20851   301-762-1650
FAX: 301-762-5230
TDY:800-735-2258
e-mail: csaac@csaac.com
www.casaac.org

Patricia D. Juhrs, Executive Director

1263 Cranial Academy

3500 Depaw Boulevard
Indianapolis, IN 46268   317-879-0713

1264 Cure Cancer Now

PO Box 16327
Panama City, FL 32406   213-660-7563

e-mail: echo17@altavista.com
curecancernow.bizland.com/

Education on positive healing alternatives, including psychological and spiritual attitudes surrounding AIDS and HIV.

1265 DB-LINK

Teaching Research
345 North Monmouth Avenue
Monmouth, OR 97361

800-438-9376
FAX: 503-838-8150
TDY:800-854-7013
e-mail: eblink@tr.wou.edu
www.tr.wou.edu/dblink

John Reiman, Executive Director

National not-for-profit service organization that serves as a clearinghouse for information concerning children and youth who are deaf and blind. Publishes educational materials for affected individuals, their families, physicians, communities and the public. Offers referrals to appropriate regional services.

1266 Dental Amalgam Syndrome (DAMS)

725-9 Tramway Lane NE
Albuquerque, NM 87122

505-291-8239
FAX: 505-294-3339

Support and educational organization to help those suffering from mercury amalgam toxicity.

1267 Epilepsy Foundation

4351 Garden City Drive
Suite 500
Landover, MD 20785

301-459-3700
800-332-4050
FAX: 301-577-2684
e-mail: postmaster@efa.com
www.epilepsyfoundation.org

Eric Hargis, President & CEO

The nation's leading source of information about seizure disorders. The Foundation offers a toll-free information and referral service, legal advocacy, a national epilepsy library, and a catalog of epilepsy-related materials including books, videos and pamphlets.

1268 Exceptional Cancer Patients

1302 Chapel Street
New Haven, CT 06511

203-865-8392

Answers and assistance on various concerns and an extensive library of books and tapes.

1269 Facilitated Learning at Syracuse University

307 Huntington Hall
Syracuse, NY 13244

315-443-1870

College offering facilitated learning research into communication with persons who have autism or severe disabilities. Offers books, videos and public awareness information on the research projects.

1270 Families of Spinal Muscular Dystrophy

PO Box 196
Libertyville, IL 60048

847-367-7620
800-886-1762
FAX: 847-367-7623
e-mail: sma@fsma.org
www.fsma.org

Audrey Lewis, Executive Director
Colleen McCarthy

Voluntary not-for-profit organization dedicated to promoting a funding research, offering support to families affected by Spinal Muscular Atrophy Diseases, and promoting public awareness. Enables families to share information through support and networking. Publishes a quarterly newsletter.

1271 Federation of Families for Children's Mental Health

1021 Prince Street
Alexandria, VA 22314

703-684-7722
FAX: 703-836-1040
e-mail: ffcmh@ffcmh.org
www.nmha.org

Barbara Huff, Executive Director
Elaine Scaton, Technical Assistance Coordinator

A national parent-run organization focused on the needs of children with emotional, behavioral or mental disorders and their families. Call national office for local chapter referral. Sliding scale membership.

1272 Feingold Association of the U.S.

PO Box 6550
Alexandria, VA 22306

703-768-3287

www.feingold.org

Helps families of children with learning and behavior problems, including attention deficit disorder. Also helps chemically-sensitive and salicylate-sensitive adults. Program is based upon a diet which primarily eliminates certain synthetic food additives.

1273 Gazette International Networking Institute

4207 Lindell Boulevard
110
Saint Louis, MO 63108

314-534-0475
FAX: 314-534-5070
e-mail: gini_intl@msn.com
www.post-polio.org

Joan L. Headley, Executive Director

Holds periodic international conference concentrating on polio survivors, education of long-term effects, and ventilator users. Also concentration is on independent living practices and issues for all disabilities. Publishes Polio Network News, Rehabilitation Gazette, IVUN News, Rehabilitation into Independent Living, Handbook on the Late Effects of Poliomyelitis for Physicians and Survivors, IVUN Resource Directory, and Post-Polio Directory.

1274 Georgiana Organization

PO Box 2607
Westport, CT 06880

203-454-1221
FAX: 203-454-3788

Provides education, workshops, consulting, and information on the Berard method.

1275 Immuno Labs

1620 West Oakland
Park Boulevard
Fort Lauderdale, FL 33311

800-231-9197

Allergy and immunological testing.

1276 Information on Incontinence

National Association for Continence (NAFC)
PO Box 8310
Spartanburg, SC 29305

800-252-3337
www.nafc.org

1277 International Association for Cancer Victors and Friends

7740 West Manchester Avenue
Suite 203
Playa del Rey, CA 90293 310-822-5032
FAX: 310-822-4193
e-mail: iacrf@inetworld.net

Provides information and listings on alternative cancer treatment center and patients who have recovered from cancer using them.

1278 International Association for Colon Therapy

2051 Hilltop Drive
Suite A-11
Redding, CA 96002 916-222-1498

1279 International Dyslexia Association

8600 LaSalle Road
Suite 382
Baltimore, MD 21286 410-296-0232
800-ABC-D123
FAX: 410-321-5069
e-mail: info@interdys.org
www.interdys.org

Provides free information and referral services for diagnosis and tutoring for parents, educators, physicians, and individuals with dyslexia. The voice of our membership is heard in 48 countries. Membership includes yearly journal and quarterly newsletter. Call for conference dates and locations.

1280 International Polio Network

Polio Network News
4207 Lindell Boulevard
110
Saint Louis, MO 63108 314-534-0475
FAX: 314-534-5070
TDY:800-735-2966
e-mail: gini_intl@msn.com
www.post-polio.org

Joan Headly, author
Joan L. Headley, Executive Director

Not-for-profit voluntary organization dedicated to supporting the independent living, self direction, and personal achivement of people with disabilities worldwide. Committed to ongoing educational and advocacy efforts related to poliomyelitis and its late effects. Promotes patient and professional education, has a network of support groups, conducts workshops and conferecnes, and offers a networking program. Also provides mateials including directories, newsletters, booklets and brochures.

1281 International Rett Syndrome Association

9121 Piscataway Road
Suite 2-B
Clinton, MD 20735 301-856-3334
800-818-7388
FAX: 301-856-3336
e-mail: irsa@rettsyndrome.org
www.rettsyndrome.org

Kathy Hunter, President

Non-for-profit voluntary organization dedicated to serving as an information and referral center for physicians and families of children with Rett Syndrome. The Association's mission includes supporting and promoting research into the prevention, control, and cure of the disorder; increasing public awareness; and providing emotional support for affected families. Engages in patient advocacy; promotes family and professional education; and provides referrals to support groups.

1282 Joni and Friends

PO Box 3333
Agoura, CA 91376 818-707-5664
FAX: 818-707-2391
TDY:818-707-9709
e-mail: jafmin@joniandfriends.org
www.joniandfriends.org

N Douglas Mazza, Executive Vice President
John Wern, Director-Wheels for the World
Brad Stenberg, Director-Family Retreats

A nonprofit organization seeking to accelerate Christian ministry with people affected by disabilties. JAF educates churches and the community worldwide concerning the needs of the disabled and how those needs can be met. We sponsor family retreats for families with disabled members. Wheels for the World, a division of JAF Ministries, collects, restores and distributes used wheelchairs to disadvantaged populations around the world.

1283 Juvenile Diabetes Foundation International

120 Wall Street
New York, NY 10005 212-789-9500
800-533-2873
FAX: 212-785-9595
e-mail: info@jdfcom
www.jdf.org

Shira Kandel, Manager Public Information

The world's leading nonprofit, nogovernmental funder of diabetes research. It was founded in 1970 by parents of children with diabetes. JDF's mission is to find a cure for diabetes and its complications through the support of research. JDF also sponsors international workshops and conferences for biomedical researchers, individual chapters offer support groups and other activities for families affected by diabetes. JDF has more than 110 chapters and affiliates worldwide. Quarterly newsletter.

1284 Leukemia & Lymphoma Society

1311 Mamaroneck Avenue
White Plains, NY 10605 914-949-0084

www.leukemia.org

Rochelle Kaufman, Executive Director
Hildy Dillan, Contact

Dedicated to finding cures for leukemia and related cancers. Strives to improve the quality of life for patients and thier families.

1285   Little People of America

PO Box 745
Lubbock, TX   79048

888-572-2001
e-mail: lpadatabase@juno.com
www.lpaonline.org

Monica Pratt, Database Administrator

LPA assists dwarfs with their physical and developmental concerns resulting from short stature. LPA offers information on employment, education, disability rights, adoption of short statured children, medical issues, clothing, adaptive devices and parenting tips. LPA also provides opportunities for social interaction at chapter, district, regional meetings, national conferences, and participation in athletic events. LPA, Inc. provides educational scholarships and medical assistance grants. *$30.00*

1286   March of Dimes Birth Defects Foundation

1275 Mamaroneck Avenue
White Plains, NY   10605

914-428-7100
888-MOD-IMES
FAX: 914-997-4763
www.modimes.org

The mission of the March of Dimes is to improve the health of babies by preventing birth defects and infant morality. The Mod Resource Center provides information and referral services to the public from 9:00 am to 8:00 pm est.

1287   Moving Forward

2934 Glenmore Avenue
Kettering, OH   45409

937-293-0409

Dedicated to disseminating information and resources concerning families. A networking group that promotes awareness of Myoclonus and its many different forms; engages in patient and professional education; promotes and supports research. Offers brochures as well as a resource list of books, articles, and videos. Provides a listing of movement disorder clinics throughout the country as well as several organizationsthat can offer further information, assistance, networking services, and support.

1288   Multiple Sclerosis Foundation

6350 North Andrews Avenue
Fort Lauderdale, FL   33309

954-776-6805
888-673-6287
FAX: 954-351-0630
e-mail: support@msfocus.org
www.msfocus.org

Tammi Robinson, Director Program Services
Tea Barbaris, Special Event Coordinator

Contemporary national, nonprofit organization that provides free support services and public education for persons with Multiple Sclerosis, newsletters, toll-free phone support, grants for research, information and referrals.

1289   Muscular Dystrophy Association

3300 East Sunrise Drive
Tucson, AZ   85718

520-529-2000
800-572-1717
FAX: 520-529-5300
e-mail: mda@mdausa.org
www.mdausa.org

Bob Muckle, Director of Public Information

MDA provides comprehensive medical services to tens of thousands of people with neuromuscular diseases at some 230 hospital-affiliated clinics across the country. The Association's worldwide research program, which funds over 400 individual scientific investigations annually, represents the largest single effort to advance knowledge of neuromuscular diseases and to find cures and treatments for them. In addition, MDA conducts far-reaching educational programs for the public and professionals.

1290   NY State Speech-Language-Hearing Association

146 Washington Avenue
Albany, NY   12210

518-463-5272
800-697-7542
e-mail: nysslha@aol.com
www.healthcareresource.com/nysslha

Joan Arvedson, President

1291   National AIDS Fund

1400 I Street NW
Suite 1220
Washington, DC   20005

202-628-1558
FAX: 202-408-1818

Colleen Young, Program Mgr, Workplace Resources

Provides information on AIDS and HIV infection, and assists with identifying accommodations in the workplace. We are currently engaged in a project aimed at assisting people with AIDS who want and are able to return to work.

1292   National Academy of Certified Clinical Mental Health Counselors

5999 Stevenson Avenue
Alexandria, VA   22304

703-823-9800
FAX: 703-823-0252
e-mail: counseling.org
www.counseling.org

Provides standards for the independent practice of mental health counseling. The academy is a corporate affiliate of the American Association for Counseling and Development.

1293   National Allergy and Asthma Network/ Mothers of Asthmatics

3554 Chain Bridge Road
Suite 200
Fairfax, VA   22030

708-385-4403
800-878-4403

Jennifer M. Miller, Executive Director

A nonprofit health association dedicated to assisting 50 million allergy and asthma patients. The organization was founded in 1985 and maintains goals to facilitate communication of accurate allergy and asthma information among patients, parents and the industry, provides important communication links among the home, school and physicians in an effort to help families learn to overcome the struggles of living with children who have allergies and provides accurate resources and information.

1294 National Amputation Foundation

38-40 Church Street
 # 40
Malverne, NY   11565　　　**516-887-3600**
　　　　　　　　　　　　　　FAX: 516-887-3667
　　　　　　　　　e-mail: amps76@aol.com
　　　　　　　　www.nationalamputation.org

Donald Sioss, Editor
Michael Foutanetta, Executive Secretary

Helps people who have had amputations to adjust to society. Members are military veterans with service connected amputations, as well as civilian amputees, who help show new amputees how to cope. It provides legal, vocational and psychological services and facilitates self help groups. 2,000 members. Publishes a bi-monthly newsletter.

1295 National Arthritis and Musculoskeletal and Skin Diseases Info. Clearinghouse

1 AMS Circle
Bethesda, MD   20892　　　**301-495-4484**
　　　　　　　　　　　　　　FAX: 301-587-4352
　　　　　　　　　　　　　　www.nih.gov/niams

Supports and provides clinical and public information and research to increase understanding of the many rheumatic diseases and related disorders. Also provides lists and order forms for their resources and materials.

1296 National Association for Down Syndrome

PO Box 4542
Oak Brook, IL   60522　　　**630-325-9112**
　　　　　　　　　　　　　　FAX: 630-325-8842
　　　　　　　　　　　　　　www.nads.org
Ann Jonaitis, author
Kim Xidas, Family Support Coordinator

Works for a strong network of support systems within their own organization and with medical, educational and school service professionals who work with children and adults with Down Syndrome. NADS serves the Chicago Metropolitan area. $20.00/family, $25.00/professional. Published bi-monthly.

1297 National Ataxia Foundation

2600 Fernbrook Lane North
Suite 119
Minneapolis, MN   55447　　　**612-525-2282**
　　　　　　　　　　　　　　FAX: 612-553-0167
　　　　　　　　　　　e-mail: naf@mr.net
　　　　　　　　　　　　　　www.ataxia.org

Donna Gruetzmacher, Executive Director
Karla Brown, Administrative Assistant

Combats all types of hereditary Ataxia through education, service and research programs.

1298 National Center for Learning Disabilities

381 Park Avenue South
Suite 1401
New York, NY   10016　　　**212-545-7510**
　　　　　　　　　　　　　　888-575-7373
　　　　　　　　　　FAX: 212-545-9665
　　　　　　　　　　　　　　www.ld.org

Anne Ford, Chair
James H. Wendorf, Executive Director

National, nonprofit organziation dedicated to improving the lives of those affecting by learning disabilities. Services include national information and referral, public outreach and communicaitons, and legislative advocacy and public policy. Its mission is to promote public awareness and understanding of learning disabilities and to provide national leadership on behalf of children and adults with LD so they may achieve their potential and enjoy full participation in society.

1299 National Council for Community Behavioral Healthcare

12300 Twinbrook Parkway
Suite 320
Rockville, MD   20852　　　**301-670-6331**

　　　　　　　　　　　　　　www.nccbh.org

Charles Ray, CEO

Represents community behavioral health centers, works on Capitol Hill to ensure funding for community behavioral health services. Offers technical support and guidance and serves as a liaison with state organizations and other behavioral health related organizations.

1300 National Council on Spinal Cord Injury

151 Tremont Street
Boston, MA   02111　　　**617-451-5757**
　　　　　　　　　　　　　　FAX: 617-338-4266
　　　　　　　　　　e-mail: neuro@jiac.net

Arthur D. Vllian, President

A membership organization for agencies and individuals. Fosters communication among members of the spinal cord injury community and the general public. Supports research and works for the integration of individuals with spinal cord injury into the general community.

1301 National Diabetes Information Clearinghouse

1 Information Way
Bethesda, MD   20892　　　**301-654-3327**
　　　　　　　　　　　　　　800-860-8747
　　　　　　　　　　FAX: 301-907-8906
　　e-mail: ndic@info.niddk.nih.gov
　　　　　　　　　　www.niddk.nih.gov

Barbara Gordon, Co-Project Manager
Ruth Ann Spier, Co-Project Manager

An information and referral service of the National Institute of Diabetes and Digestive and Kidney Diseases, one of the National Institutes of Health. The clearinghouse responds to written inquiries, develops and distributes publications about diabetes, and provides referrals to diabetes organizations, including support groups. The NDIC maintains a database of patient and professional education materials, from which literature searches are generated.

1302 National Digestive Diseases Information Clearinghouse

2 Information Way
Bethesda, MD 20892
301-654-3810
800-891-5389
FAX: 301-907-8906
e-mail: nddic@info.niddk.nih.gov
www.niddk.nih.gov

Barbara Gordon, Project Manager

Information and referral service of the National Institute of Diabetes and Digestive and Kidney Diseases, one of the National Institutes of Health. A central information resource on the prevention and management of digestive diseases, the clearinghouse responds to written inquiries, develops and distributes publications about digestive diseases, provides referrals to digestive disease organizations and support groups, and maintains a database of patient and professional education materials.

1303 National Down Syndrome Society

666 Broadway
New York, NY 10012
202-460-9330
800-221-4602
FAX: 212-979-2873
e-mail: info@ndss.org
www.ndss.org

Myra E. Madnick, Executive Director

Provides information about Down Syndrome and referral to local, state and national resources; disseminates booklets, fact sheets, posters and videotapes; assists local parent support groups; sponsors national and international conferences; and supports research about Down Syndrome.

1304 National Hemophilia Foundation

The Soho Building
110 Greene Street
New York, NY 10012
212-756-5064
800-424-2634
FAX: 212-328-3777
e-mail: nhfofnyc@aol.com
www.hemophilia.org

Stephen Bajardi, Director

Offers counseling, educational materials, fundraising, loans, seminars and support groups with over 40 local chapters.

1305 National Hydrocephalus Foundation

12413 Centralia
Lakewood, CA 90715
562-402-3523
888-260-1789
FAX: 562-924-6666
e-mail: hydrobrat@earthlink.net
www.nhfonline.org

Debbi Fields, Executive Director

Provides educational assistance and information, along with peer support for individuals of all ages, their families and/or caregivers. Members have access to the various films on a rental basis, library of reference information, journal publications and more. Quarterly newsletter. Membership: $30 per year (U.S.).

1306 National Institute of Arthritis and Musculoskeletal and Skin Diseases

Information Office Bldg 31-Rm 4C-05
31 Center Drive - MSC2350
Bethesda, MD 20892
301-496-8188

Handles inquiries on the following - arthritis, bone diseases and skin diseases. Consumer and professional education materials are available.

1307 National Institute of Neurological Disorders and Stroke

PO Box 5801
Bethesda, MD 20824
301-496-5751
800-352-9424
FAX: 301-402-2186
www.ninds.nih.gov

America's focal point for support of research on brain and nervous system disorders. Its active public information program provides physicians, patients and the public with educational materials and research highlights. Materials provided by the public information program include brochures, fact sheets, information packets and special reports. All publications are FREE of charge.

1308 National Kidney and Urologic Diseases Information Clearinghouse

3 Information Way
Bethesda, MD 20892
301-654-4415
FAX: 301-907-8906
e-mail: nkudic@info.niddk.nih.gov
www.niddk.nih.gov

Barbara Gordon, Project Manager

Information and referral service of the National Institute of Diabetes and Digestive and Kidney Diseases, one of the National Institutes of Health. Responds to written inquiries, develops and distributes publications about kidney and urologic diseases, and provides referrals to kidney and urologic organizations, including support groups. Maintains a database of patient and professional education materials, from which literature searches are generated. Provides bulk orders at a minimal cost.

1309 National Mental Health Association

1021 Prince Street
Alexandria, VA 22314
703-684-7722
800-969-NMHA
FAX: 703-684-5968
e-mail: jspnmha@cais.com
www.nmha.org

Patrick Cody, Dir. Media Relations

The nation's oldest and largest non-profit organization addressing all issues related to mental health and mental illness. NMHA and its grassroots network of over 330 affiliated Mental Health Associations work to provide public education, direct services and advocacy for mental health and mental illness concerns in communities across the nation. NMHA sponsors the National Mental Health Month and runs the Mental Health Information Center which distributes information on mental health topics.

1310 National Mental Health Consumer's Self-Help Clearinghouse

311 South Juniper Street
Suite 1000
Philadelphia, PA 19107 215-751-1810
800-553-4539
FAX: 215-636-6312
e-mail: thekey@delphi.com
www.liberty.net.org/~mha/cl_house.html

Alex Morrsey, Information/Referral

Funded by the National Institute of Mental Health Community Support Program, the purpose of the Clearinghouse is to encourage the development and growth of consumer self-help groups.

1311 National Multiple Sclerosis Society

733 3rd Avenue
New York, NY 10017

800-344-4867
FAX: 212-986-7981
e-mail: nat@nmss.org
www.nationalmssociety.org

Michael Dugan, President General

Provides professional and public education; information and referral; and supports research. 140 local chapters and branches offer counseling services, advocacy, discount prescription and health care products program, and assistance in obtaining adaptive equipment.

1312 National Organization for Rare Disorders

NORD
100 Route 37
PO Box 8293
New Fairfield, CT 06812 203-746-6518
800-999-NORD
FAX: 203-746-6481
e-mail: orphan@rarediseases.org
www.rarediseases.org

Abbey S. Meyers, President
Marie Hardin, Vice President Patient Services
Mary Dunkle, Senior Director Communications

A nonprofit, voluntary agency composed of national health organizations and individuals dedicated to the interests of people concerned about rare debilitating disorders. Offers a Rare Disease Database on the Internet with hard copies of all information available through the mail. A federation of voluntary health organizations dedicated to helping people with rare orphan diseases and assisting the organizations that serve them.

1313 National Organization on Disability

910 16th Street NW
Suite 600
Washington, DC 20006 202-965-9850
FAX: 202-293-7999
TDY:202-293-5968
e-mail: ability@nod.org
www.nod.org

Alan A. Reich, President

Composed of individuals with and without disabilities as well as officials in government, professional associations and organized labor. It works to achieve the full participation of persons with disabilities in society by promoting access to buildings, and providing educational and vocational opportunities.

1314 National Parkinson Foundation

1501 NW 9th Avenue Bob Hope Road
Miami, FL 33136 305-243-6666
800-327-4545
FAX: 305-243-4403
e-mail: mailbox@npf.parkinson.org
www.parkinson.org

Lilliana Fong, Controller
Julian Pearson, Administrator

The purpose of this Foundation is to find the cause and cure for Parkinson's Disease and allied neurological disorders through research, to provide diagnostic training and therapeutic services and to educate the general medical practitioners on how to detect the early warning signs of Parkinson's Disease. Provides current information to patients, caregivers and families. Publishes quarterly newsletter.

1315 National Stroke Association

96 Inverness Drive East
Suite I
Englewood, CO 80112 303-649-9299
800-787-6537
FAX: 303-771-1886
e-mail: info@stroke.org
www.stroke.org

Thelma Edwards, RN, Director of Exhibits

The only national health organization solely committed to stroke prevention, treatment, rehabilitation and community reintegration. Provides packaged training programs, on-site assistance, physician, patient and family education materials to acute and rehab hospitals. Develops workshops; operates the Stroke Information & Referral Center and produces professional publications such as Stroke: Clinical Updates and the Journal of Stroke and Cerebrovascular Diseases.

1316 PACER Center

4826 Chicago Avenue
Minneapolis, MN 55417 612-827-2966
FAX: 612-827-3065
TDY:612-827-7770
e-mail: pacer@pacer.org
www.pacer.org

Paula F. Goldberg, Executive Director

An organization that serves families of children and adults with disabilities. PACER carries out the philosophy of parents helping parents through workshops, individual assistance and written information. PACER also provides programs and materials that assist multicultural families, programs for students, schools and professionals with disability awareness puppet and child abuse prevention programs. A Computer Resource Center and Software Lending Library are also available.

1317 Paralyzed Veterans of America

801 18th Street NW
Washinton, DC 20006   202-872-1300
                             800-424-8200
                       e-mail: info@ova.org
                            www.pva.org

Dedicated to serving the needs of its members, all of whom have catastrophic paralysis caused by spinal cord injury or disease. Has been in the forerun of improving health care, rehailitation, and access to society for paralyzed veterans and all citizens with a disabilty. Has funded a wide range of educational materials and videotapes for people with disabilities, their families, the general public and professionals in the field of spinal cord dysfunction.

1318 Parents of Down Syndrome Children

11600 Nebel Street
Rockville, MD 20852   301-984-5781
                        FAX: 301-816-2429

Joyce Glenner, President

Activities include formal and informal meetings; parent-to-parent counseling; contacting new parents of Down Syndrome children to offer support and information on community resources; providing information on doctors, hospitals and professionals.

1319 People Against Cancer

PO Box 10
Otho, IA 50569   515-972-4444
                        FAX: 515-972-4415
        e-mail: info@PeopleAgainstCancer.com
             www.peopleagainstcancer.com
Frank D. Wiewel, author

A nonprofit, grassroots membership organization dedicated to cancer prevention and medical freedom of choice; offers counseling and information on alternative cancer treatments.

1320 Polio Connection of America

PO Box 182
Howards Beach, NY 11414   718-835-5536
                        FAX: 718-738-1509
                     e-mail: w1066@msn.com
                  www.geocities.com/w1066w

George Cook, Executive Director

This is a voluntary not-for-profit organization dedicated to locating polio survivors and providing them with information concerning Post-Polio Syndrome. Committed to locating, informing and supporting polio survivors affected with Post-Polio Syndrome to help them receive appropriate treatment. Provides appropriate referrals, as well as educational materials including a newsletter, brochures and booklets. Also an advocate for Post-Polio Syndrome research.

1321 Polio Society

4200 Wisconsin Avenue
Suite 106273
Washington, DC 20016   301-897-8180
                        FAX: 202-466-1911
                           www.polio.org/

Ed Grebenstein, President
Jessica Scheer, PhD, Executive Director

National not-for-profit voluntary organziation created to provide education resources and support group services to people who had polio and arenow experiencing the late effects of polio. Activities include maintenance of a natinoal membership database of polio survivors and health care professionals; sponsorship of major national UPDATE conferences about post-polio issues; and publication of Options, quarterly newsletter.

1322 Prader Willi Foundation

223 Main Street
Port Washington, NY 11050   516-767-3100
                             800-253-7993
                        FAX: 516-944-3173
              e-mail: PWSyndrome@aol.com
                     www.prader-willi.org

Sheldon L. Tarakan, President

The Prader-Willi Foundation is a national, non profit public charity that works for the benefit of individuals with Prader-Willi syndrome and their families.

1323 Rasmussen's Syndrom and Hemispherectomy Support Network

8235 Lethbridge Road
Millersville, MD 21108   410-987-5221
                        FAX: 410-987-521
                  e-mail: rssnlynn@aol.com

Al & Lynn Miller, Founders

National not-for-profit organization dedicated to providing infomration and support to individuals affected by Rasmussen's Syndrome and Hemispherectomy. Publishes a periodic newsletter and disseminates reprints of medical jouranl articles concerning Rasmussen's Syndrome and its treatments. Maintains a support network that provides encouragement and information to individuals affected by Rasmussen's Syndrome and their families.

1324 SCI Psychosocial Process

7520 Astoria Boulevard
Flushing, NY 11370   718-803-3782
                        FAX: 718-803-0414
                    e-mail: ssofer@epua.org
                         www.aascipsw.org

E. Jason Mask, LCSW, Editor

Publishes a quarterly newsletter.

1325 Services for the Visually Impaired

8720 Georgia Avenue
Suite 210
Silver Spring, MD 20910   301-589-0894
                        FAX: 301-589-7281
                   e-mail: vvh@tidalwave.net
                          www.servicesvi.org

Judy Rasmussen, Executive Director

Offers services for the totally blind, legally blind, visually impaired, and more with counseling, educational, recreational, rehabilitation and computer training services. Braille transcription services for businesses. Audio cassette and quarterly newsletter. Provides volunteer readers/shoppers.

1326 Shake-A-Leg

76 Dorrance Street
Suite 300
Providence, RI   02903   401-421-1111
                                     FAX: 401-454-0351
                          e-mail: shake@shakealeg.org
                                    www.shakealeg.org

Paul Callahan, CEO
Eileen Callahan, Bookkeeper
Sarah Everhart, Program Director

A second-stage rehab facility offering a variety of therapy, life skills and adaptive sports programs to individuals with spinal cord injury and related nervous system disorders. Group and individual components encourage the development of human potential and the achievement of goals above and beyond what was thought possible. Newsletter, video cassette.

1327 Simonton Cancer Center

PO Box 890
Pacific Palisades, CA   90272   310-459-4434

Introduces medical professionals to new methods of healing various cancers.

1328 Society for Progressive Supranuclear Palsy (SPSP)

601 North Caroline Street
Suite 5065
Baltimore, MD   21287   410-955-2954
                                     800-457-4777
                               FAX: 410-614-9260
e-mail: epkatz@erols.com -or- spsp@erols.com
                                     www.psp.org

Dedicated to providing ingormation to families, health care professionals, and others interested or affected by Progressive Supranuclear Palsy (PSP). An advocate for affected individuals and acts as a self-help organization for people with this disorder. Promotes and supports research into the causes, treatment, and potential cure for PSP. Publishes a quarterly newletter. Reports finding in the area of PSP and includes editorials, updates, and comprehesnsive strategies for managing the disorder.

1329 Spina Bifida Association of America

4590 Macarthur Boulevard NW
Suite 250
Washington, DC   20007   202-944-3285
                                     800-621-3141
                               FAX: 202-944-3295
                          e-mail: sbaa@sbaa.org
                                    www.sbaa.org

Cindy Brownstein, CEO
Marsha Thomas, Coordinator, National Resource

SBAA was founded in 1973 to address the specific needs of the spina bifida community and serves as the national representative of almost 70 chapters nationwide. The mission of SBAA is to promote the prevention of spina bifida and to enhance the lives of all affected. The SBAA is a 501(c)(3) non-profit organization.

1330 Spinal Cord Society (SCS)

Wendell Road
Fergus Falls, MN   56537   218-739-5252
                                     FAX: 218-739-5262
                          www.members.aol.com/scsweb

Memberss include individuals with spinal cord injuries, their families, friends, and scientists and physicians who are dedicated to finding a cure for spinal cord paralysis through improved treatment and research. Instrumental in establishing civilian research conferences and cure research/treatment centers for spinal cord injury.

1331 Support Group for Brachial Plexus Injury

18 Staci Lane
Webster, NY   14580   716-787-0197
                                     FAX: 716-872-6158
                          e-mail: jdebryne@aol.com

Jeff DeBryne, President

The Support Group for Brachial Plexus Injury was established to provide resources and emotional support to families impacted by Erb's Palsy andother brachial plexus injuries by advising on how best to receive and obtain insurance and treatment for this disorder.

1332 Swank Multiple Sclerosis Clinic School of Medicine

Oregon Health Sciences University
3181 Sam Jackson Park Road
Portland, OR   97201   503-494-8370

                                    www.ohsu.edu

Publishes Swank Multiple Sclerosis Newsletter.

1333 TX Speech-Lenguage-Hearing Association

PO Box 140647
Austin, TX   78714   512-452-4636

                          e-mail: tsha@assnmgmt.com
                                    www.txsha.org

Roy K. Bohrer, Executive Director

1334 Tourette Syndrome Association

42-40 Bell Boulevard
Bayside, NY   11361   718-224-2999
                                     800-237-0717
                               FAX: 718-279-9596
                          e-mail: ts@tsa-usa.org
                                    tsa-usa.org

Mark Levine, Director Of Development

A growing number of local chapters nationwide provide educational materials, seminars, conferences and support groups for over 35,000 members.

1335 United Cerebral Palsy Association

1660 L Street NW
Suite 700
Washingron, DC   20036   202-776-0406
                                     800-872-5827
                               FAX: 202-776-0414
                               TDY:202-973-7197
                          e-mail: ucpanatl@ucpa.org
                                    www.ucpa.org

Charles H. Moses III, President

National not-for-profit self-help organization dedicated to providing information and support to individuals with Cerebral Palsy and other disabilities, and their families. Supports more than 160 local affiliates; these affiliates provide a variety of programs and services for affected families, including support groups. Offers several educational and support materials, including a quarterly magazine, regular newsletters, and research reports.

1336 United Cerebral Palsy Association of New York State

330 West 34th Street
New York, NY 10001 212-947-5770

e-mail: metroucpa@aol.com
www.ucpa-nys.org

Michael Parker, Executive Director

1337 Vermont Back Research Center

1 South Prospect Street
Burlington, VT 05401 802-656-0015
800-527-7320
FAX: 802-660-9243
e-mail: backtalk@salus.med.uvm.edu
salus.med.uvm.edu/~backtalk

Martin Krag, MD, Director

Conducts research aimed at reducing back-related disability following injury or acute pain episodes. Current research includes studies of posture, seating, vibration, materials handling, and exercise. The Center develops and tests assistive devices, and promotes employment of people with back disorders and rapid return to work after injury. The staff provides a variety of information services, including bibliographic searches and fact finding.

1338 Wood Hygienic Institute

PO Box 420580
Kissimmee, FL 34742 407-933-0009

1339 World's Best Books from the Diabetes Experts, Publications Catalog

American Diabetes Association
1701 North Beauregard Street
Alexandria, VA 22311 703-549-1500
800-232-6733
FAX: 770-442-9742
e-mail: bookorders@diabetes.org
www.diabetes.org

John Fedor, Associate Director
Janel Chrobot, Marketing Specialist

A 24 page, full-color catalog of more than 80 books and products for people with diabetes. Titles of categories of books include: cookbooks, meal planning and nutrition, new books and self-care.

1340 YAI - National Institute for People with Disabilities

460 West 34th Street
11th Floor
New York, NY 10001 212-563-7474
FAX: 212-947-7524
www.yai.org

Joel Levy, DSW, CEO
Phil Levy, COO
Jennifer Shoul, Coordinator of Link Department

A not-for-profit professional organization serving developmentally disabled children and adults in many programs throughout the New York metropolitan area. Provides over 200 program sites for thousands of participants. Services include residential, day, outpatient, clinical, early childhood, respite and family support, camping, employment training, case management and recreation opportunities.

Visually Impaired

1341 ACB Radio Amateurs

American Council of the Blind
1155 15th Street NW
Suite 1004
Washington, DC 20005 202-467-5081
800-424-8666
FAX: 202-467-5085

A radio amateur network of blind, visually impaired and sighted members who gather and share common problems and solutions to help members improve radio amateurs in getting started, provides access to educational materials in special media and publishes a directory for the visually impaired.

1342 Achromatopsia Network

PO Box 214
Berkeley, CA 94701 510-540-4700
FAX: 510-540-4767
e-mail: futterman@achromat.org
www.achromat.org

Frances Futterman, Facilitator

The Achromatopsia Network is a nonprofit organization for individuals concerned with achromatopsia. It is committed to sharing informaiton about achromatopsia and providing resources to meet the special needs of those affected by this eye condition; helping individuals and families concerned with achromatopsia to connect with one another; and promoting awareness and educating with a special emphasis on accomplishing this goal among those who provides services to the visually impaired.

1343 American Academy of Ophthalmology

Public Education Program
655 Beach Street
PO Box 7424
San Francisco, CA 94109 415-561-8500

Sponsors National Eye Care Project that gives free eye care to the elderly.

1344   American Action Fund for Blind Children and Adults

18440 Oxnard Street
Tarzana, CA   91356   818-343-2022

Jean Dyon Norris, Director Of Operations

Offers charitable and educational fund, braille assistive devices and a library for the visually impaired.

1345   American Association of the Deaf-Blind

814 Thayer Avenue
Room 302
Silver Spring, MD   20910
                          FAX: 301-588-8705
                          e-mail: aadb@erols.com

Joy Larson, Program Manager

The American Association of the Deaf-Blind is a nonprofit, beneficial society of persons with deaf-blindness and other concerned individuals. It was organized for the purpose of advancing the economic, educational, and social welfare of individuals with deaf-blindness and improving moral among persons with deaf-blindness.

1346   American Council of Blind Lions

American Council of the Blind
1155 15th Street NW
Suite 1004
Washington, DC   20005   202-467-5081
                                    800-424-8666
                          FAX: 202-467-5085

Educates Lions Club members about the needs and capabilities of blind people, exchanges information concerning Club activities in the field of work for the blind and encourages blind people to join Lions Clubs and other civic activities.

1347   American Council of the Blind

1155 15th Street NW
Suite 720
Washington, DC   20005   202-347-2693
                                    800-424-8666
                          FAX: 202-467-5085
                e-mail: ncrabb@access.digex.net
                          www.acb.org

Paul Edwards, President

A national membership organization whose members are visually impaired and fully sighted individuals who are concerned about the dignity and well-being of blind people throughout America. Formed in 1961, the Council has become the largest organization of blind people in the U.S. with over 70 state affiliates and special interest chapters.

1348   American Foundation for the Blind

11 Penn Plaza
Suite 300
New York, NY   10001   212-502-7600
                                    800-232-5463
                          e-mail: afbinfo@afb.net
                          www.afb.org

Carl R. Augusto, President & CEO

The American Foundation for the Blind, the organization to which Helen Keller devoted over 40 years of her life, is a national, nonprofit organization whose mission is to enable people who are blind or visually impaired to achieve quality of access and opportunity that will ensure freedom of choice in their lives. AFB is headquartered in New York City and maintains offices in Atlanta, Chicago, Dallas, San Francisco, and Washington, DC.

1349   American Optometric Association

243 North Lindbergh Boulevard
St. Louis, MO   63141   314-991-4100
                          FAX: 314-991-4101
                          www.aoanet.org

1350   American Printing House for the Blind

1839 Frankfort Avenue
PO Box 6085
Louisville, KY   40206   502-895-2405
                                    800-223-1839
                          FAX: 502-899-2274
                          e-mail: info@aph.org
                          www.aph.org

Fred Gissoni, Customer Support

The world's largest company devoted solely to producing products for people who are visually impaired. We manufacture books and magazines in braille, large type, recorded and computer disk form. We also make a wide range of educational and daily living aids, such as braille paper and styluses, talking book equipment, and synthetic speech computer products. APH also offers CARL ET AL, an electronic database that lists accessible books in all formats.

1351   Associated Blind

135 West 23rd Street
New York, NY   10011   212-766-6800
                          FAX: 212-766-6809
                          e-mail: hq@tabinc.org
                          www.tabinc.org

Ruth-Ellen Simmonds, Executive Director

Organization dedicated to fostering economic and social independence among individuals who are blind or visually impaired. Services include adaptive computer education, information and referral and life enrichment programs.

1352   Associated Services for the Blind

919 Walnut Street
4th Floor
Philadelphia, PA   19107   215-629-2990

Limited funding is available to assist aspiring, visually impaired users in the purchase of helpful high-tech equipment.

1353   Association for Education & Rehabilitation of the Blind & Visually Impaired

206 North Washington Street
Suite 320
Alexandria, VA   22314   703-548-1884
                          FAX: 703-683-2926

The only professional membership organization dedicated to the advancement of education and rehabilitation of blind and visually impaired children and adults.

1354 Association for Macular Diseases
210 East 64th Street
New York, NY   10021   212-605-3719
FAX: 212-605-3795
e-mail: macula@macula.org
www.macula.org

Nikolai Stevenson, President
Walter Ross, Editor in Chief
Joan Daly, Treasurer

Offers hotline, educational materials, quarterly newsletter, support groups, referrals and seminars for persons and families affected by macular disease.

1355 Association of Radio Reading Services
PO Box 3663
Pittsburgh, PA   15230   412-434-6023

Over 100 services in the United States, available in
most states, provides access to printed material for
the visually impaired on closed circuit radio. Daily
papers, magazines, books and local information
are provided.

1356 Association of Visual Science Librarians
Berkeley, CA   94720

Bette Anton, President

Promotes information services in ophthalmology and
optometry. Conducts institutes, workshops, and training courses for professional personnel and provides
legislative consultation.

1357 Blind Children's Center
4120 Marathon Street
Los Angeles, CA   90029   323-664-2153
800-222-3566
FAX: 323-665-3828
e-mail: info@blindchildrenscenter.org
blindchildrenscenter.org

Midge Horton, Executive Director

A nonprofit organization offering a program of diversified services which meet the special needs of blind,
visually impaired or multi-handicapped children,
birth through five years of age, their parents and
siblings. Services include an infant stimulation program; parent participation groups, educational preschool; family support services; research program
and an interdisciplinary assessment program. A toll
free national phoneline and educational correspondence program outside the LA area.

1358 Blinded Veterans Association
477 H Street NW
Washington, DC   20001   202-371-8880
800-669-7079
FAX: 202-371-8258
e-mail: bva@bva.org
www.bva.org

Thomas H. Miller, Executive Director
John K. Williams, Administrative Director
George E. Brummell, Nat'l Dir, Field Service
Program

Offers two main service programs without cost to
blinded veterans. Field service program provides
counseling to veterans and families, and information
on benefits and rehabilitation.

**1359 Books for Blind and Physically Handicapped
Individuals**
Library of Congress
1291 Taylor Street NW
Washington, DC   20542   202-707-5100
FAX: 202-707-0712
TDY:202-707-0744
e-mail: nls@loc.gov
www.loc.gov/nls

Frank Kurt Cylke, Director

Administers a national library service that provides
braille and recorded books and magazines on free
loan to anyone who cannot read standard print because of visual or physical disabilities who are eligible residents of the United States or American
citizens living abroad. Computerized version available online at www.loc.gov/nls/reference/facts.html.

1360 Braille Institute of America
741 North Vermont Avenue
Los Angeles, CA   90029   323-663-1111
800-272-4553
FAX: 323-666-5881
e-mail: media@brailleinstitute.org
www.brailleinstitute.org

Fortune Zuckerman, Director of Special Projects

Over 200 educational classes are offered in independent living skills, mobility, reading and writing
Braille, art and music. Also offered are adult counseling, career services, access technology training
and subsidies, child developement and youth services, low vision services, braille press, braille publications, talking book library services, retail store for
adaptive items, tours, speakers, and educational materials. Programs and services are offered at five regional centers, and all are free

1361 Braille Revival League
American Council of the Blind
1155 15th Street NW
Suite 1004
Washington, DC   20005   202-467-5081
800-424-8666
FAX: 202-467-5085

Encourages blind people to read and write in
braille, advocates for mandatory braille instruction in educational facilities for the blind, strives
to make available a supply of braille materials
from libraries and printing houses and more.

1362 Canine Helpers for the Handicapped
5699 Ridge Road
5705
Lockport, NY   14094   716-433-4035
FAX: 716-439-0822
e-mail: chhdogs@aol.com

Beverly Underwood, Executive Director
Rich Godfrey, Training Director

A non-profit organization devoted to training assistance dogs to assist people with disabilities to lead more independent, secure lives. We train hearing dogs, service dogs, multi-service dogs, seizure alert dogs and therapy dogs. All dogs in the program are rescued or donated, so the program has the double mission of savind dogs' lives and helping people. The program operates through the generous financial support of many caring people, organizations, and businesses. Application Fee $150.00.

1363   Caption Center

125 Western Avenue
Boston, MA   01234

FAX: 617-300-1020
e-mail: caption@wgbh.org
www.wgbh.org/caption

Mary Watkins, Communications Mgr.

A nonprofit, self-supporting division of the WGBH Educational Foundation. The Center pioneered captioning in 1972 and is the most experienced and versatile agency in the field today. A Consumer Information Series shares our experience on a wide range of topics from getting local newscasts captioned to nonbroadcast captioning methods for meetings.

1364   Chicago Lighthouse for People who are Blind or Visually Impaired

1850 West Roosevelt Road
Chicago, IL   60608

312-666-1331
FAX: 312-243-8539
www.chicagolighthouse.org

James Kesteloot, Executive Director
Terrence Longo, Assistant Director
Colleen Wunderlich, Intake & Referral

An organization offering progressive programs for the blind, visually impaired, deaf-blind and multi-disabled children and adults, including vocational programs, computer and office skills training, job placement, independent living skills, orientation and mobility training, counseling, and a low vision clinic.

1365   Christian Record Services

4444 South 52nd Street
Lincoln, NE   68516

402-488-0981
FAX: 402-488-7582
e-mail: info@christianrecord.org
www.christianrecord.org

Jerry Stevens, Editor

Organization that provides interdenominational services to the sight impaired.

1366   Collier County Public Library

392 Goodlette Road South
Naples, FL   34102

941-649-1122

Bill Bailey, President

A nonprofit organization dedicated to providing independent-living education; computer, Braille and mobility programs; peer support and fellowship; recreation and entertainment; and personal enrichment opportunities for individuals in Collier County who are visually impaired or blind.

1367   Columbia Lighthouse for the Blind

1120 20th Street NW
Suite 750
Washington, DC   20005

202-454-6400
877-324-5252
FAX: 202-454-6401
e-mail: info@clb.org
www.clb.org

Dale Otto, President
Tammy Koger, Vice President

Offers persons who are blind and visually impaired training in assistive technology, career development and rehabilitation and offers services such as speakers bureau, visionaries store, volunteer assistance, low-vision clinics and Columbia Extension recreational activities.

1368   Council of Families with Visual Impairments

American Council of the Blind
1155 15th Street NW
Suite 1004
Washington, DC   20005

202-467-5081
800-424-8666
FAX: 202-467-5085

A network of parents with blind or visually impaired children that offers support and outreach, shares experiences in parent/child relationships, exchanges educational, cultural and medical information about child development and more.

1369   Council of Families with Visual Impairment

6212 West Franklin Street
Richmond, VA   23226

804-288-0395

Roy Ward, Treasurer

National not-for-profit organization dedicated to providing advocacy services on behalf of children with visual impairments or blindness to ensure that they receive appropriate public education. Provides information and referrals to affected families. Publishes educational materials including a newsletter, audiovisual aids and brochures.

1370   Dallas Lighthouse for the Blind

4245 Office Parkway
Dallas, TX   75204

214-821-2375
800-735-2989
FAX: 214-824-4612
www.dallaslighthouse.org

Mike Orfinik, President
Ann Arnott, Business Mgr. Rehab Services
Steven Vandepre, VP Community Relations

Serves adults and senior citizens with vision disabilities. Programs include vocational rehabilitation, independent living rehabilitation and employment. Services include orientation and mobility skills training, information and referral, case work services, personal and social adjustment counseling, employment readiness training, on-the-job training, job placement assistance, technology training, adult basic education, Braille instruction, English as a second language classes and more.

1371 Deaf-Blind Division of the National Federation of the Blind

National Federation of the Blind
1800 Johnson Street
Baltimore, MD 21230 410-659-9314
FAX: 410-685-5653
e-mail: nfb@iamdigex.net
www.nfb.org

Membership organization of blind persons employed in industrial and manufacturing work or in government job programs for the blind. Dedicated to protecting the rights of blind workers in salary, job stability, advancement and labor issues.

1372 Extensions for Independence

555 Saturn Boulevard
San Diego, CA 92154 619-423-7709

Arthur Heyer, President

Develops, manufactures and markets vocational equipment for the visually handicapped. Promotes improvements in design, materials, production and quality of products while maintaining affordable prices.

1373 Eye Associates

5701 Greenbelt Road
Berwyn Heights, MD 20740 301-345-2053
FAX: 301-441-1752

Dr. Beverly Miller, Optometrist

Dr. Miller is an optometrist fluent in sign language. Since 1975, she has been providing eye care for the hearing impaired and deaf. Dr. Miller also is a low vision specialist providing special visual aids and magnification devices for the visually impaired.

1374 Eye Bank Association of America

1011 Connecticut Avenue NW
Suite 601
Washington, DC 20036 202-775-4999
FAX: 202-429-6036
e-mail: sightebaa@aol.com
www.restoresight.org

Patricia Acken-O'Neil, President

Not-for-profit organization dedicated to the restoration of sight through the promortion and advancement of eye blanking. Promotes research and professional education with a newsletter, brochures and pamphlets.

1375 Fidelco Guide Dog Foundation

PO Box 142
Bloomfield, CT 06002 860-243-5200
FAX: 860-243-7215
e-mail: info@fidelco.org
www.fidelco.org

George J. Salpietro, Executive Director

Purpose is to breed, train and place Fidelco German shepherd guide dogs with blind persons throughout the Northeast. Provides training services to blind persons, reviews performance of the guide dog teams to see that satisfactory level of achievement is maintained, utilizes genetic processes and clinical methods to improve and refine the breed and maintains an ongoing program for development and improvement of training methods.

1376 Fight for Sight

381 Park Avenue South
Suite 809
New York, NY 10013 212-679-6060
FAX: 212-679-4466

Voluntary health organization that works to conquer defective sight and blindness. Provides grants to accredited medical colleges and institutions to help supply equipment, technical assistance and materials for research projects and a limited number of clinical service projects.

1377 Guide Dog Users

American Council of the Blind
1155 15th Street NW
Suite 1004
Washington, DC 20005 202-467-5081
800-424-8666
FAX: 202-467-5085

Promotes the acceptance of blind people and their dogs, works for enforcement and expansion of laws admitting guide dogs into public places, advocates for quality training and follow-up services.

1378 Guide Dogs for the Blind

P0 Box 151200
San Rafael, CA 94915 415-499-4000
800-295-4050
FAX: 415-499-4035
e-mail: information@guidedogs.com
www.guidedogs.com

Joanne Ritter, Editor, author
Sue Sullivan, Admissions Manager

Offers dog guides for qualified visually impaired people in the United States and Canada. No charge for dog or training.

1379 Guiding Eyes for the Blind

611 Granite Springs Road
Yorktown Heights, NY 10598 914-245-4024
800-942-0149
FAX: 914-245-1609
e-mail: info@guidingeyes.org
www.guidingeyes.org

William D. Badger, President and CEO
Bev Klapman, Manager of Admissions Services

Provides the means for blind and visually impaired individuals to achieve mobility, independence and companionship through the use of our professionally bred and trained guide dogs. Each month Guiding Eyes graduates approximately 12 guide dog/student teams from all over the U.S., Canada, and internationally. The guide dogs, 26 day residential training program, special needs program and lifetime follow-up services are offered at no cost to the students. Also provides at home training at no cost.

1380 Helen Keller National Center

111 Middle Neck Road
Sands Point, NY 11050   516-944-8900
800-255-0411
FAX: 716-944-7302
e-mail: hkncdir@aol.com
www.helenkeller.org/national

Joseph J. McNutty, Director

Provides diagnostic evaluation, short term comprehensive vocational rehabilitation training, assistance with job and residential placement. Local services through 10 regional offices, some 44 affiliates, national training team, older adults program and more.

1381 Horizons for the Blind

2 North Williams Street
Crystal Lake, IL 60014   815-444-8800
FAX: 815-444-8830
e-mail: mail@horizons-blind.org
www.horizons-blind.org

Braille and large-print books offered at museums, zoos and theaters; also provides tactile pictures.

1382 Information Access Project: National Federation of the Blind

1800 Johnson Street
Baltimore, MD 21230   410-665-7881
FAX: 410-685-5653
e-mail: nfb@access.digex
www.nfb.org

Marc Maurer, President

Assists entities covered by the ADA in finding methods for converting visually displayed information, such as flyers, brochures and pamphlets, to formats accessible to individuals who are visually impaired.

1383 Institute for Families of Blind Children

Mailstop #111
PO Box 54700
Los Angeles, CA 90054   213-669-4649

Nancy Mansfield, MA, Executive Director

Not-for-profit voluntary organization dedicated to providing support, information and understanding to families affected by blindness. All services are provided at no cost. Provides consultation and therapy for parents, siblings and extended family members. Educational materials include journal articles, booklets, a newsletter, and videotapes with practical suggestions and coping strategies for individuals who are blind.

1384 International Agency for the Prevention of Blindness

National Eye Institute
Room 6AO3
Building 31
Bethesda, MD 20892   301-893-2311

Carl Kupfer, President

Ophthalmic societies and committees for the prevention of blindness whose members include ophthalmologists, public health officers, nutritionists, geneticists and other health workers. Coordinates international research into the causes of impaired vision or blindness; promotes measures calculated to eliminate such causes; disseminates information worldwide on preventing blindness and on matters pertaining to care of the eyes.

1385 Jewish Braille Institute of America

110 East 30th Street
New York, NY 10016   212-889-2525
800-433-1531
FAX: 212-689-3692
e-mail: admin@jbilibrary.org
www.jbilibrary.org

Dr. Ellen Isler, Executive Vice Pres.
Diane Rosenbaum, Program Director

Supplies books and reading material of Jewish interest in braille, on audio cassette and in large print. Provides various services to those in more than 50 countries.

1386 John Milton Society for the Blind

475 Riverside Drive
Suite 455
New York, NY 10115   212-870-3335
FAX: 212-870-3229
e-mail: order@jmsblind.org
www.jmsblind.org

Darcy Quigley, author
Darcy Quigley, Executive Director

Publishes free magazines and Bible studies in Braille, cassette and large print for blind and visually impaired youth and adults.

1387 Library Users of America

American Council of the Blind
1155 15th Street NW
Suite 1004
Washington, DC 20005   202-467-5081
800-424-8666
FAX: 202-467-5085

Provides for chapters in states through the U.S. to encourage the development, acquisition and use of technology which enables blind and visually impaired persons to use printed material independently in library settings and elsewhere.

1388 Lighthouse International

111 East 59th Street
New York, NY 10022   212-821-9200
800-829-0500
FAX: 212-821-9707
e-mail: info@lighthouse.org
www.lighthouse.org

Dr. Barbara Silverstone, President/CEO

The world's leading resource on vision impairment and vision rehabilitation. National programs include continuing education for eye care professionals; consumer and professional products and publications; and social and vision research.

1389 Lighthouse National Center for Vision and Child Development

111 East 59th Street
New York, NY   10022   212-821-9200
                                        800-821-9713
                                FAX: 212-821-9705
                        e-mail: info@lighthouse.com
                                www.lighthouse.com

Michelle Vusola

Provides for the needs of children who are visually impaired and their families through professional training, technical assisance, and research. Yearly newsletter.

1390 Lions World Services for the Blind

Lion's Clubs International
300 22nd Street
Oak Brook, IL   60521   312-571-5466

1391 Mobile Association for the Blind

2440 Gordon Smith Drive
Mobile, AL   36617   334-473-3585
                         FAX: 334-470-8622

Mahlon McCracken, Executive Director

Offers work adjustment training, job placement, activities of daily living, mobility, communication skills and sheltered employment for adults who are visually impaired and for persons with other disabilities.

1392 National Alliance of Blind Students NABS Liaison

American Council of the Blind
1155 15th Street NW
Suite 1004
Washington, DC   20005   202-467-5081
                                 800-424-8666
                         FAX: 202-467-5085
                    e-mail: info@nabs.cjb.net
                                nabs.cjb.net

Works to facilitate progress toward full accessibility of college programs and facilities, provides opportunities for discussion of issues important to students and assists with National Student Seminars.

1393 National Association for Parents of Children with Visual Impairments (NAPVI)

National Office
PO Box 317
Watertown, MA   02472   617-972-7441
                                 800-562-6265
                         FAX: 781-972-7444

Susan LaVenture, Executive Director
Mary Zabelski, President
Lars Anderson, Vice President

A partnership organization with the National Eye Health Education Program and the National Agenda for the Education of Children and Youths with Visual Impairments including those with multiple disabilities. Information and support network for parents of children with visual impairments.

1394 National Association for Visually Handicapped

22 West 21st Street
6th Floor
New York, NY   10010   212-255-4224
                         FAX: 212-727-2931
                        e-mail: staff@navh.org
                                www.navh.org

Lorraine Marchi, Executive Director

Serves the partially seeing (not the totally blind), providing visual aid counseling and distribution, large print - including a free by mail loan library, informational literature, a quarterly newsletter, educational outreach, referrals, emotional support, and advocacy. Works with eye care professionals and the business community regarding low vision resources and accommodations.

1395 National Association of Blind Students

National Federation of the Blind
1800 Johnson Street
Baltimore, MD   21230   410-659-9314
                         FAX: 410-685-5653
                    e-mail: nfb@iamdigex.net
                                www.nfb.org

For over 30 years, this national organization of blind students has provided support, information and encouragement to blind college and university students. Leads the way in offering resources in isues such as national testing, accessible textbooks and materials, overcoming negative attitudes about blindness from school personnels. Offers strong advocacy and motivational support.

1396 National Association of Guide Dog Users

National Federation of the Blind
1800 Johnson Street
Baltimore, MD   21230   410-659-9314
                         FAX: 410-685-5653
                    e-mail: nfb@iamdigex.net
                                www.nfb.org

Provides information and support for guide dog users and works to secure high standards in guide dog training. Addresses issues of discrimination of guide dog users and offers public education about guide dog use.

1397 National Association to Promote the Use of Braille

National Federation of the Blind
1800 Johnson Street
Baltimore, MD   21230   410-659-9314
                         FAX: 410-685-5653
                    e-mail: nfb@iamdigex.net
                                www.nfb.org

Dedicated to securing improved Braille instruction, increasing the number of Braille materials available to the blind and providing information about the importance of Braille in securing independence, education and employment for the blind.

1398 National Braille Association

3 Townline Circle
Rochester, NY   14623   716-427-8260
                         FAX: 716-427-0263
                        www.nationalbraille.org

Angela Coffaro, Executive Director

Providing continuing education to those who prepare braille, and provides braille materials to persons who are visually impaired. Maintains collection of braille textbooks, music, technical tables, and general interest items. Catalogs of the braille collection in print or braille are free on request.

1399   National Braille Press

88 St. Stephen Street
Boston, MA   02115   617-266-6160
                                       FAX: 617-437-0456
                                       e-mail: agrima@nbp.org
                                       www.nbp.org

Tony Grima, Marketing Manager

1400   National Center for Vision and Child Development

Lighthouse
800 Second Avenue
New York, NY   10017   212-808-0077

1401   National Diabetes Action Network for the Blind

National Federation of the Blind
1800 Johnson Street
Baltimore, MD   21230   410-659-9314
                                       FAX: 410-685-5653
                                       e-mail: nfb@iamdigex.net
                                       www.nfb.org

Leading support and information organization of persons losing vision due to diabetes. Provides personal contact and resource information with other blind diabetics about non-visual techniques of independently managing diabetes, monitoring glucose levels, measuring insulin and other matters concerning diabetes. Publishes Voice of the Diabetic, the leading publication about diabetes and blindness.

1402   National Eye Institute

National Institutes of Health
Building 31
Room 6A32
Bethesda, MD   20892   301-496-5248
                                       800-869-2020
                                       www.nei.nih.gov

Mission is to discover safe and effective methods to prevent, diagnose and treat diseases and disorders of the visual system. In this way the Institute helps to prevent, reduce and possibly eliminate blindness and visual impairment.

1403   National Federation of the Blind

1800 Johnson Street
Baltimore, MD   21230   410-837-6763
                                       FAX: 410-685-5653
                                       e-mail: nfb@access.digex.net
                                       www.nfb.org

Marc Maurer, President

The largest membership organization of blind people in the nation, with chapters in every state and approximately 50,000 individual members. It seeks to integrate the blind into society on the basis of equality with the sighted so that the blind are seen as normal, participating citizens. 50,000 members and 700 local chapters.

1404   National Federation of the Blind - Human Services Division

National Federation of the Blind
1800 Johnson Street
Baltimore, MD   21230   410-659-9314
                                       FAX: 410-685-5653
                                       e-mail: nfb@iamdigex.net
                                       www.nfb.org

Membership organization of blind persons working in counseling, personnel, psychology, social work, psychiatry, rehabilitation and other social science and human resource fields. Dedicated to improving employment opportunities and advancement for blind persons and provides resources regarding blindness-related techniques and methods used in these fields.

1405   National Federation of the Blind - Masonic Square Club

National Federation of the Blind
1800 Johnson Street
Baltimore, MD   21230   410-659-9314
                                       FAX: 410-685-5653
                                       e-mail: nfb@iamdigex.net
                                       www.nfb.org

Blind individuals committed to sharing of Masonic experiences, goals and history.

1406   National Federation of the Blind - Music Division

National Federation of the Blind
1800 Johnson Street
Baltimore, MD   21230   410-659-9314
                                       FAX: 410-685-5653
                                       e-mail: nfb@iamdigex.net
                                       www.nfb.org

Blind persons dedicated to advancing employment and entertainment opportunities in various music fields. Offers support and information regarding copyright, publishing, promotion and other career details.

1407   National Industries for the Blind

524 Hamburg Turnpike CN 969
Wayne, NJ   07474   973-595-9200
                                       FAX: 973-595-9122

A nonprofit organization that represents over 100 associated industries serving people who are blind in thirty-six states. These agencies serve prople who are blind or visually impaired and help them to reach their full potential. Services include job and family counseling, job skills training, instruction in Braille and other communication skills, children's programs and more.

1408   National Organization of Parents of Blind Children

National Federation of the Blind
1800 Johnson Street
Baltimore, MD   21230   410-659-9314
                                       FAX: 410-685-5653
                                       e-mail: nfb@iamdigex.net
                                       www.nfb.org

Barbara Cheadle

Support, information and advocacy organization of parents of blind or visually impaired children. Addresses issues ranging from help to parents of a newborn blind infant, mobility and Braille instruction, education, social and community participation, development of self-confidence and other vital factors involved in the growth of a blind child. Strong national network of contacts with other parents offers encouragement and positive philosophical support. Publishes Future Reflections.

1409   National Organization of the Senior Blind

National Federation of the Blind
1800 Johnson Street
Baltimore, MD   21230   410-659-9314
                           FAX: 410-685-5653
                        e-mail: nfb@iamdigex.net
                              www.nfb.org

Membership organization of elderly blind persons providing support and information to other blind seniors. Issues include concerns such as remaining active in community and social life, maintaining private homes or living in retirement communities or nursing homes, learning the techniques used by the blind, independently caring for oneself and maintaining a positive approach to vision loss.

1410   New Eyes for the Needy

549 Milburn Avenue
PO Box 332
Short Hills, NJ   07078   973-376-4903
                           FAX: 973-376-3807

Carl DeBell, Executive Director
Susan Rodbart, Office Manager

Provides new glasses for those with low vision who may not be able to afford them.

1411   Prevent Blindness America

500 East Remington Road
Schaumberg, IL   60173   708-843-2020
                              800-331-2020
                           FAX: 847-843-8458
                     e-mail: info@preventblindness.org
                           www.preventblindness.org

Dedicated to fighting blindness and saving sight. Nationwide affiliates, divisions, and chapters serves millions of people each year through public and professional education, community and patient service programs, and research. The organization produces educational materials including brochures. Also produces videos, posters, and brochures in Spanish, Portuguese, and Chinese. Program activities include support groups, patient advocacy, referrals, and a toll-free help line.

1412   Recording for the Blind & Dyslexic

20 Rosel Road
Princeton, NJ   08540   609-452-0606
                              800-221-4792
                           FAX: 609-987-8116
                        e-mail: info@rfbd.org
                              www.rfbd.org

Susan Garber, Consumer Publications Admin.

Provides recorded and computerized textbooks, library services and other educational resources to people who cannot effectively read standard print because of a visual impairment, learning disability or other physical disability. RFB&D also provides bibliographic reference services and acts as a recording service for additional titles. RFB&D has two membership programs—individual and institutional (school).

1413   Schepens Eye Research Institute

20 Staniford Street
Boston, MA   02114   617-742-3140
                           FAX: 617-523-3463
                  e-mail: geninfo@@vision.eri.harvard.edu

Prominent center for research on eye, vision, and blinding diseases; dedicated to reserach that improves the understanding, management, and prevention of eye diseases and visual deficiencies; fosters collaboration among its faculty members; trains young scientists and clinicians from around the world; promotes communication with scientists in allied fields; leader in the worldwide dispersion of basic scientific knowledge of vision.

1414   Seeing Eye

Washington Valley Road
PO Box 375
Morristown, NJ   07963   973-539-4425
                           FAX: 973-539-0922
                        e-mail: info@seeingeye.org
                              www.seeingeye.org

Judy Deuschle, Director Of Student Services

The Seeing Eye breeds, raises and trains dogs to guide blind and visually impaired people and instructs qualified individuals in the use and care of their Seeing Eye dogs.

1415   Taping for the Blind

3935 Essex Lane
Houston, TX   77027   713-622-2767
                           FAX: 713-622-2772

Cynthia Franzetti, Executive Director

Broadcasts on HTBR, Housting taping for the Blind radio, a free 24-hour radio reading service and records reading material on audiotape, copied onto cassettes, for use by blind and physically handicapped persons. Promotes increased interest in and use of, free audio materials.

1416   United States Association for Blind Athletes

33 North Institute Brown Hall
Colorado Springs, CO   80903   719-333-4195
                           FAX: 719-630-0616
                        e-mail: media@usaba.org
                              www.usaba.org

Mark Lucas, Acting Executive Director
Doris Fumai, Office Manager

Athletic association for blind athletes, this association is the national governing body for the United States visually impaired athletes. Quarterly newsletter.

1417 Vermont Association for the Blind and Visually Impaired

37 Elmwood Avenue
Burlington, VT 05401   802-863-1358
                             800-639-5861
                       FAX: 802-863-1481
                   e-mail: vabvi@aol.com
                             www.vabvi.org

Stephen Poyhiot, Executive Director

Information and referral services.

1418 Vision Foundation

818 Mount Auburn Street
Watertown, MA 02472   617-926-4232
                             800-852-3029
                       FAX: 781-926-1412

Barbara Kibler, Executive Director

Offers peer counseling, support groups, seminars, information and referral and services for persons with vision loss, AIDS project, rehabilitation services for elders with vision loss.

1419 Vision World Wide

5707 Brockton Drive
302
Indianaplis, IN 46220   317-254-1332
                             800-431-1739
                       FAX: 317-251-6588
                   e-mail: info@visionww.org
                             www.visionww.org

Patricia L. Price, author
Patricia L. Price, President/Managing Editor

Believing there is hope when vision fails, Vision World Wide provides relevant information on a variety of topics through its Information and referral Helpline, Website, E-Mail Announce List, Information Packets, and Journal, "Vision Enhancement"-all designed to encourage and support individuals with vision loss, family members, and professionals who serve them. Journal available in large print, audiocassette, computer disc and enhanced letter format. Also provides consumer protection services.

72-78 pages Quarterly

1420 Visions/Services for the Blind & Visually Impaired

500 Greenwich Street
Third Floor
New York, NY 10013   212-625-1616
                       FAX: 212-219-4078
                   e-mail: info@visionsvcb.org
                             www.visionsvcb.org

David Longmire, author
Albert Widman, Assoc. Exec. Dir.
Anisio Correia, Exec. Dir./Programs
Nancy D. Miller, Executive Director

Offers rehabilitation services for older blind persons in New York City; self study kits on audio cassette for blind and visually impaired persons in the areas of personal management, mobility training, and sensory development.

1421 Visually Impaired Veterans of America

American Council of the Blind
1155 15th Street NW
Suite 1004
Washington, DC 20005   202-467-5081
                             800-424-8666
                       FAX: 202-467-5085

Directs members to resources, promotes the rights of visually impaired veterans to receive all benefits, encourages research and development of new products for blind people.

1422 Washington Ear

35 University Boulevard East
Silver Spring, MD 20901   301-460-3617
                       FAX: 301-681-5227
                   e-mail: information@washear.org
                             www.washear.org

Nancy Knauss, Executive Director

A nonprofit organization providing reading and information services for the blind, visually impaired and physically disabled persons who cannot effectively read print, see plays, watch television programs or view museum exhibits. This organization provides radio reading services, dial-in telephone newspaper service, National Symphony Orchestra program notes on audio cassette and raised line and large print atlases and books.

Alabama

1423 Adventure Program
Lakeshore Foundation
3800 Ridgeway Drive
Birmingham, AL   35209   205-868-2065

1424 Basketball School
Alabama School for the Deaf
AL   205-761-3222

1425 Camp ASCCA
PO Box 21
Jackson's Gap, AL   36861
                                800-843-2267

1426 Camp ASCCA/Easter Seals
PO Box 21
Jackson's Gap, AL   36861   256-825-9226
                             800-THE-CAMP
                          FAX: 256-825-8332
                  e-mail: ascca@webshoppe.net
                          www.campascca.org

Tom Collier, Camp Director
Camp for children and adults with disabilities, ages 6+.

1427 Camp Alamisco
1771 Camp Alamisco Road
Dadeville, AL   36853   334-272-7493

1428 Camp Candlelight
Eplilepsy Foundation of North & Central Alabama
1801 Oxmoor Road
Suite 101
Birmingham, AL   35209   205-870-1146

1429 Camp M-A-S-H
300 Vestavia Parkway
Suite 3500
Birmingham, AL   35216   205-979-5700
                                800-879-7896

1430 Camp Newsong
PO Box 660833
Birmingham, AL   35266   205-877-2225

1431 Camp Smile-A-Mile
Brookwoods Diabetes Center
PO Box 550155
Birmingham, AL   205-323-8427

1432 Camp Sugar Falls
Brookwood Diabetes Center
539 Brookwood Boulevard
Birmingham, AL   35209   205-877-2035

1433 Chill Out '98
Low Vision Center
50 Medical Park East Drive
Birmingham, AL   35235   205-838-3162

1434 Summer Camp for Children with Muscular Dystrophy
400 Vestavia Parkways
Birmingham, AL   35216   205-823-8191

Alaska

1435 American Diabetes Summer Camp
2217 E Tudor Road
Suite 1
Anchorage, AK   99507   907-562-7372
                               800-DIA-BETE
                           FAX: 907-562-0545
                           TDY:907-563-8284
                                www.sesa.org

1436 Camp Alpine
Skaggs Foundation
2217 E Tudor Road
Suite 1
Anchorage, AK   99507   907-562-7372
                           FAX: 907-562-0545
                           TDY:907-563-8284
                                www.sesa.org

1437 Camp Wheeze Away
American Lung Association
2217 E Tudor Road
Suite 1
Anchorage, AK   99507   907-562-7372
                           FAX: 907-562-0545
                           TDY:907-563-8284
                                www.sesa.org

1438 Champ Camp
American Lung Association
2217 E Tudor Road
Suite 1
Anchorage, AK   99507   907-562-7372
                           FAX: 907-562-8284
                           TDY:907-563-8284
                                www.sesa.org

1439 Muscular Dystrophy Assocation Free Camp
Muscular Dystrophy Assocation
2217 E Tudor Road
Suite 1
Anchorage, AK   99507   907-562-7372
                                800-478-5683
                           FAX: 907-562-0545
                           TDY:907-563-8284
                                www.sesa.org

1440 Outdoor Recreation and Community Accesss
2217 E Tudor Road
Suite 1
Anchorage, AK   99507   907-790-2218
                           FAX: 907-562-0545
                           TDY:907-563-8284
                                www.sesa.org

Arizona

1441 **Camp Civitan**
Civitan Foundation of Arizona/Souther Nevada
444 West Camelback
Suite 307
Phoenix, AZ   85013   602-264-0435
                              FAX: 602-264-0628
                e-mail: info@campcivitan.com
                          www.campcivitan.com

1442 **Easter Seals Arizona**
903 N Second Street
Phoenix, AZ   85004   602-252-6061
                                      800-626-6061
                              FAX: 602-252-6065
                              www.azseals.org

Arkansas

1443 **Camp Aldersgate**
Med Camps Coordinator
2000 Aldersgate Road
Little Rock, AR   72205   501-225-1444

Ruth M. Eyres, Coordinator
A private nonprofit social service agency allied with
the United Methodist Church which co-sponsors a
series of summer medical camps with Med Camps of
Arkansas, Inc., and thirteen various health agencies.
The camps allow children and youth, ages 6-16, who
have various medical conditions and physical disabilities to enjoy traditional camping experiences
adapted to their abilities. The Camp also offers respite care, senior citizens programs, west side clinic
and the children's center.

California

1444 **Ability First**
2555 East Colorado Boulevard
Pasadena, CA   91107   626-396-1010
                              FAX: 626-396-1021
                e-mail: abilityfirst@earthlink.net
                          www.abilityfirst.org

Radawn Alcoin, Social Service Coordinator
Services include residential camping programs,
aquatics and infant through adult recreational programs and housing. *$110.00*

>   *Per day*

1445 **Ability First, Camp Paivika**
PO Box 3367
Crestline, CA   92325   909-338-1102
                              FAX: 909-338-2502
                e-mail: kkunsek@abilityfirst.org
                          www.abilityfirst.com

Kelly Kunsek, Camp Director

A nonprofit camp owned and operated by Ability
First to provide outdoor, recreational camping services for children and adults with physical and/or developmental disabilities. Located in the San
Bernadino mountains, the camp has a dining lodge
and rec room, four cabins, infirmary, program building and pool that are all fully accessible. Camp is
available to rent during winter/spring for up to 80
people.

1446 **All Nations Camp**
PO Box 1958
Wrightwood, CA   92397   760-249-3822
                              FAX: 760-249-6702

Ismael Nieto
Camp for children with disabilities, ages 8 to 18.

1447 **Bloomfield**
5300 Angeles Vista Boulevard
Los Angeles, CA   90043

This camp is dedicated to serving blind and developmentally disabled children and adults.

1448 **Camp Alex A. Krem**
Camping Unlimited
102 Brook Lane
Boulder Creek, CA   95006   510-222-6662

Gary Breland, Executive Director
Leon Wong, Program Director
Camp serves people of all ages and all handicaps.
Summer Program: five two-week sessions of residen-
tial or travel camp. Year-round: weekend outings
throughout the year. Vendorized by the California
Regional Centers; camperships are available. Mem-
ber of the American Camping Association.

1449 **Camp Esperanza-Arthritis Foundation**
YMCA Camp Whittle
PO Box 70
Fawnskin, CA   92333   909-866-3000
                              FAX: 909-866-5065
                          www2.kidscamps.com

1450 **Camp Joan Mier**
Ability First
11677 East Pacific Coast Highway
Malibu, CA   90265   310-457-9863
                              FAX: 310-457-6374
                          www2.kidscamps.com

1451 **Camp Ronald McDonald At Eagle Lake**
PO Box 172
Susanville, CA   96130   530-825-3158
                              FAX: 530-825-3158
                          www2.kidscamps.com

1452 Camp de los Ninos - Diabetes Society
1165 Lincoln Avenue
Suite 300
San Jose, CA   95125   408-287-3785
                                800-989-1165
                          FAX: 408-287-2701
                    e-mail: camp@diabetesscv.org
                          www.diabetesscv.org

Sharon Ogbor, Executive Director
Since 1974, the Diabetes Society of Santa Clara Valley has sponsored Camp de los Ninos, a resident camp for children 6 through 14. This camp provides an opportunity for children with diabetes to go to camp, meet other children and gain a better understanding on their diabetes. The total experience can help campers develop mroe confidence in their abilities to control their diabetes effectively while enjoying the traditional camp experience.

1453 Camp-A-Lot
5384 Linda Vista Road
Suite 100
San Diego, CA   92110
                                800-748-5575
                          FAX: 619-574-0317

Jaculin Taylor
Residential camping program for children and adults, ages 7 and up. San Diego locals offered transportation. *$600.00*

1454 Costanoan
13851 Stevens Canyon Road
Cupertino, CA   95014   408-867-1115
                          FAX: 408-867-4817
                          www.ccostanoan.org

Julie Duncan
Serves a wide range of disabilities.

1455 Easter Seal Summer Camp Programs
2645 Pleasant Hill Road
Pleasant Hill, CA   94523   925-689-1777

Beverly Mayhall
Offers education, adventure and the experience and enjoyment of living-out-of-doors in a striking and challenging wilderness environment. Serves ages 6 to 60, male and female.

1456 Enchanted Hills Camp
Lighthouse
214 Van Ness Avenue
San Francisco, CA   94102   415-431-1481
                          FAX: 415-863-7568

Paul Reid
For blind, deaf/blind children and adults, ages 5 and up. This program offers a basic camping experience. Activities include music, art, dance, hiking and riding. Camperships are available to California residents. Tuition: $50 per day for 1-2 weeks.

1457 Erutan
2700 Los Osos Valley Road
Los Osos, CA   93402

Lisa Tanzman
Serves disabled campers.

1458 Gloriana Opera Company
721 N Franklin Street
Fort Bragg, CA   95437   707-964-7469
                          FAX: 707-964-9653

Since 1977 superlative music theater productions all year long, plus concert, childrens workshops and classes.

1459 Junior Wheelchair Sports Camp
Santa Barbara Parks and Recreation Department
PO Box 1990
Santa Barbara, CA   93102   805-564-5324
                          FAX: 805-965-0500

This five-day camp is for children 5-19 years old that are physically disabled. Sports instruction in aquatics, tennis, track and field, basketball, archery and new sports activities introduced each year. The camp counselors and instructors are also physically disabled to provide the children with a role model. Fee based on fundraising efforts.

1460 Krem Camps
1302 Albina Avenue
Berkeley, CA   94706   831-338-7664

Gary Breland
Camp Krem offers an unstructured camping program for the mentally retarded, encouraging choice and decision-making. Activities include swimming, hiking, backpacking, independent living, and joint programs with camps for normal campers. A travel camp that enables campers to experience adventure and self-sufficiency is also available. Tuition $550 for 2 weeks.

1461 Quickie Sports Camps
Quickie Designs
2842 N Business Park Avenue
Fresno, CA   93727   559-292-2171
                                800-456-8168

Tennis and basketball camps for the wheelchair bound.

Colorado

1462 Breckenridge Outdoor Education Center
PO Box 697
Breckenridge, CO   80424   970-453-6422
                          FAX: 970-453-4676
                    e-mail: boec@boec.org
                          www.boec.com

Rich Cook, Executive Director

Provides year-round adventure based wilderness and adaptive ski programs for people with disabilities. The Center excels in offering challenging, rewarding outdoor experiences individually designed to the abilities and needs of participants.

1463 Challenge Aspen

PO Box M
Aspen, CO   81612   970-923-0578
                          800-530-3907
                    FAX: 970-923-7338
e-mail: possibilities@challengeaspen.com
            www.challengeaspen.com

Amanda Boxtel, Director Special Projects
Houston Cowan, Executive Director
Stacey Degen, Program Coordinator

1464 Colorado Lions Camp

Lions of Colorado
PO Box 9043
Woodland Park, CO   80866   719-687-2087

Jeanine Werner, Executive Director
Glenn Scofield, Program Supervisor

Outdoor recreational camping for the handicapped. All normal camp activities offered. 1 to 4 staff supervision with a nurse or doctor in attendance. One week: $300.00.

1465 Magic of Music and Dance

PO Box M
Aspen, CO   81612   970-923-0578
                          800-530-3901
                    FAX: 970-923-7338
                    www2.kidscamps.com

1466 Rocky Mountain Village

Easter Seals Colorado
PO Box 115
Empire, CO   80438   313-569-2333
                    FAX: 303-569-3857
          e-mail: campinfo@cess.org
              www.eastersealsco.org

Roman Kratczyk, Director

Sessions are conducted for both developmentally and physically disabled children and adults. Activities include swimming, horseback riding, outdoor education, zigline challenge course elements. Tuition: $580 for 5 days. Scholarships available.

1467 Sky Ranch Lutheran Camp

307 E Stuart Street
Fort Collins, CO   80525   970-493-5258
                    FAX: 970-493-7960

Pastor Ron Letnes
Daily Bible study and worship for disabled campers.

Connecticut

1468 Camp Harkness

301 Great Neck Road
Waterford, CT   06385   860-236-6201

1469 Hemlocks Easter Seals Recreation

PO Box 198
Hebron, CT   06248
                              800-221-6827

Carl Larson

Accepts campers, ages 6 and under, whose major disability is orthopedic. First preference is given to Connecticut residents. A computer camp is also available. Tuition: $260-655 for 1-2 weeks.

1470 Isola Bella

American School for the Deaf
139 N Main Street
W Hartford, CT   06107   860-527-2681

Hearing-impaired children, ages 6-19, blend educational instruction in communications with recreational activities. Qualified deaf and hearing staff members with experience in education, child care and counseling are employed at the camp. Tuition: $165-178 week.

1471 Mansfield's Holiday Hill

41 Chaffeeville Road
Mansfield Center, CT   06250   860-423-1375
                              FAX: 860-456-2444

Dudley Hamlin

A home not far from home where beautiful fields, forests, facilities and a caring staff support the activities and relationships of our camp families. The camp offers many programs such as: Outdoor Adventure; Tumbling; Dance; Adventure Ropes Course; Swimming; Arts & Crafts; Archery; Tennis and more to thirty boys and girls.

1472 Marvelwood Summer

Marvelwood School
476 Skiff Mountain Road
Kent, CT   06757

The emphasis in this summer program is on diagnosis and remediation of individual reading, spelling, writing, mathematics and study problems. Offered to ages 12-16. Tuition: $3,500; Day $3,000 for 6 weeks.

1473 Shadybrook Learning Center

PO Box 365
Moodus, CT   06469   860-873-8800
                          800-666-4752
                    FAX: 860-873-1849

Les Kershnar

Up to seven week summer residential, individualized program incorporating educational, recreational and vocational programs. This disguised learning environment promotes independence, friendships, and social appropriateness where learning is fun and fun is learning. Fee: $4,875 - $4,990.

1474 The Hole in the Wall Gang Camp

565 Ashford Center Road
PO Box 156
Ashford, CT   06278   860-429-3444
                    FAX: 860-429-7295
                    www2.kidscamps.com

1475 **Tourette Syndrome Association of CT Camp**
Sunrise Resort
Moodus, CT   06469   860-873-8681

www2.kidscamps.com

Delaware

1476 **Children's Beach House**
100 W 10th Street
Suite 411
Wilmington, DE   19801   302-655-4288
FAX: 302-655-4216
e-mail: childrens.beach.house@dol.net
www.cbhinc.org

Diane B. O'Hara, Summer Program Director
Summer camp for children from Delaware of normal mental level, with speech, language and hearing disorders are accepted, ages 6-13. Activities include aquatics, art, music, nature and dramatics. Speech and language therapy are provided. Also school-year environmental education for Delaware students of all exceptionalities.

District of Columbia

1477 **Lab School of Washington**
4759 Reservoir Road NW
Washington, DC   20007   202-965-6600
FAX: 202-965-5106
www.labschool.org

Sally Smith, Founder
Susan Ferley, Admissions Director

The Lab School six week summer session includes individualized reading, spelling, writing, study skills, and math programs. A multisensory approach addresses the needs of bright learning disabled children. Related services such as speech/language therapy and occupational therapy are integrated into the curriculum. Elementary/Intermediate; Junior High/High School.

Florida

1478 **Camp Thunderbird**
909 East Welch Road
Apopka, FL   32712   407-889-8088
FAX: 407-889-8072
e-mail: campthun@aol.com
www.questinc.com

Dr. Shirley O'Brien, Camp Director
Residential summer camping program for children and adults with a developmental disability. Campers enjoy swimming, sports, nature hikes, canoeing, etc.

1479 **Developmental Center**
6710 86th Avenue North
Pinellas Park, FL   33780

Dr. Eric Larson

Specifically designed for the learning disabled child and other children with difficulties in concentration, strategy, social skills, impulsivity, distractibility and study strategies. Programs offered include: attention training, visual-motor remediation, socialization skills training, relaxation training, horseback riding and more. The day camp meets weekdays from 9-3 for 3,4 or 5 week sessions. Tuition: 3 weeks $475; 4 weeks, $585; and 5 weeks, $685. Psychological services.

1480 **Easter Seals Camp Challenge**
31600 Camp Challenge Road
Sorrento, FL   32776   352-383-4711
FAX: 352-383-0744
e-mail: camp@fl.easter-seals.org
www2.kidscamps.com

Micheal Currence, Director of Camping/Recreation
Jennifer Hargroves, Summer Camp Director
Melissa Guinta, Assistant Director

1481 **Florida Camp for Children and Youth**
PO Box 14136
Gainesville, FL   32604   352-334-1323

Rhonda Rogers
An adventure camp for children and youth with diabetes.

1482 **Florida School-Deaf and Blind**
207 San Marco Avenue
St. Augustine, FL   32084
800-344-3732
www2.kidscamps.com

1483 **VACC camp**
Miami Children's Hospital
3200 Southwest 60th Center
Suite 203
Miami, FL   33155   305-662-8222

Georgia

1484 **Bunker-Hill Military Summer Camp**
Route 1 Box 1336
Clarksville, GA   30523

1485 **Camp Independence**
1655 Tullie Circle
Suite 111
Atlanta, GA   30329   404-248-1315

1486 **Camp Lookout**
RR 2
Rising Fawn, GA   30738

Randall Pasqua
Emphasis on outdoor Christian education.

1487 Squirrel Hollow

2619 Dodson Drive
East Point, GA   30344   404-669-2083
                               FAX: 404-669-4037
                        e-mail: bedfordschool@aol.com
                            www.thebedfordschool.org

Betsy E. Box, Director
Jeff James, Assistant Director
Bonnie Sides, Administrative Secretary

For ages 7-16, held on the campus of Atlanta Christian College. This camp provides remediation of reading, math and learning disabilities. A one-week camping trip to Unicoi State Park in the North Georgia Mountains supplements the academic program with field trips, hikes, swimming and other recreational activities. Tuition: 5-day boarding: $3,215.00, 7-day boarding: $3,615.00. Dates of camp are from June 17 to July 20.

Hawaii

1488   Camp Erdman YMCA

69-385 Farrington Highway
Waialua, HI   96791   808-637-4615
                               FAX: 808-637-8874
                               www.camperdman.net

Josh Hermowitz, Executive Director

A specialized youth camp serving the needs of the disabled.

Illinois

1489   Easter Seal-Timber Pointe Outdoor Center

Rural Route 2 Box 39
Hudson, IL   61748   309-365-8021
                               FAX: 309-365-8934
                        www2.kidscamps.com

1490   Easter Seals Camp-Illinois

11285A Fox Road
Yorkville, IL   60560   630-553-7361
                               FAX: 630-896-6257
                        www2.kidscamps.com

1491   Jewish Council for Youth Services

JCYS Camp Red Leaf
PO Box 297
Ingleside, IL   60041   847-740-5010
                               FAX: 847-740-5014
                        e-mail: cmiller@jcys.org
                        www.campredleaf.bunkl.com

Carissa Miller, CTRS, Director
Diane Gould, LCSW, Director of Special Services

Overnight summer camp for youth and adults with developmental disabilites. Family Camps, respite weekends, trips, and other special events are offered throughout the year.

1492   Olympia

Southern Illinois University
Mail Code 6519
Southern Illinois University
Carbondale, IL   62901   618-453-1423
                                FAX: 618-453-1445

Craig Dittmar

Located on 6,500 acres of forests and meadows on the shores of Little Grassy Lake, Olympia Camp is for mentally and physically handicapped children and adults. Among the activities offered are arts and crafts, hay wagon rides, canoeing and swimming. Tuition: $375 for 2 weeks.

1493   Parent Group for the Retarded

PO Box 764
Mattoon, IL   61938   217-895-2341
                               FAX: 217-895-3658

Don H. McDowell, Camp Director
Terri Taylor, Director's Assistant

Offers advocacy services, social and recreational services and a summer camp for the disabled.

1494   Peacock Camp

38685 N Deep Lake Road
Lake Villa, IL   60046   847-356-3931

David Bogenschutz, Camp Director

A residential summer camp for individuals ages 7-17 with a physical disability. Activities include swimming, arts and crafts, recreational game, nature activities and large group activities (such as campfires, carnivals, talent shows, etc.). There are four 12-day sessions per summer.

1495   Rimland Services for Autistic Citizens

Hoover Outdoor Education Center
11285A Fox Road
Yorkville, IL   60560

Tom Ewan, Director
Alan Kromanaker, Outdoor Education

An accessible camp facility that can be utilized by groups for day use or overnight camping experiences. Six winterized cabins, a meeting facility, indoor pool, full food service, and an excellent staff are available. Educational programs can be arranged or you can utilize the facility to manage your own programs. Prices starting at $10 per person for a single day trip.

1496   Shady Oaks

16300 Parker Road
Lockport, IL   60441   708-301-0816
                               FAX: 208-730-4127
                        e-mail: sor16300@aol.com
                            www.shadyoakscamp.org

Scott Steele, Executive Director

1497   Summer Wheelchair Sports Camp

University of Illinois/Division of Rehab Education
1207 South Oak Street
Champaign, IL   61860   217-333-4606

www2.kidscamps.com

1498 Touch of Nature Environmental Center

Southern Illinois University
6888
Carbondale, IL 62901   618-453-1121
FAX: 618-453-1188
www.pso.siu.edu

Randy Osborn, Camp Director
Chilang Lawless, Camp Registrant

Providing a traditional camping experience for non-traditional campers, including recreational and outdoor programs for adults and children with various developmental, mental and physical disabilities as well as learning and behavioral disorders.

1499 Tourette Syndrome Association of IL Camp

5102 Oakton Street
Suite 115
Skokie, IL 60077   847-675-2121
FAX: 847-675-2147
www.tsa-illinios.org

Indiana

1500 Bradford Woods Outdoor Education Center

5040 Street 67 North
Martinsville, IN 46151   765-342-2915
FAX: 765-349-1086
www.indiana.edu/~bradwood

Gary Robb

Set in a 2300 acre site, camp offers growth development for persons with disabilities and persons without disabilities.

1501 Camp Isanogel

7601 W Isanogel Road
Muncie, IN 47304   765-288-1073
FAX: 765-288-3103
e-mail: isanogel@iquest.net
www.isanogelcenter.og

Karen Kovacn, Executive Director
Monica Sauter, Recreation Director

Thirty-two years of programs for special needs of children through adults.Fee: 6 day session ($400); 12 day session ($675).

1502 Camp Millhouse

25600 Kelly Road
South Bend, IN 46614   219-287-9833
FAX: 812-358-4381
www2.kidscamps.com

1503 Easter Seal Society

4251 South 600 East
Columbus, IN 47203   812-342-0134

www2.kidscamps.com

1504 Happiness Bag Incorporated

3833 Union Road
Terre Haute, IN 47802   812-234-8867
FAX: 812-234-8867

Jodi Moan, Program Director
Patricia Porter, Executive Director

Serves developmentally disabled age 5-adult; day and residential camp program; after school program; scouting; Special Olympic anticipation (basketball, athletics, bowling, softball and aquatics); and a bowling league.

1505 Happy Hollow Children's Camp

3049 Happy Hollow Road
Nashville, IN 47448   812-988-4900
FAX: 812-988-7505
e-mail: hhcdir@aol.com

Bernard Schrader
Accepts disabled campers.

1506 John Warvel

American Diabetes Association
7363 E 21st Street
Indianapolis, IN 46219   317-352-9226
800-228-2897
e-mail: bookorders@diabetes.org

Carol Helming, Executive Director

Provides an enjoyable, safe and educational out-of-doors experience for children with insulin-dependent diabetes. A unique learning atmosphere for children to acquire new skills in caring for their disease. The camp experience instills confidence for the child's self-management of diabetes. Offers one-week sessions and can accommodate 200 campers.

1507 Kiwanis Twin Lakes Camp

15543 12th Road
Plymouth, IN 46563   219-941-2750

Serving the orthopedically handicapped children and young adults.

1508 Lake Luther Bible Camp

5215 N 450 West
Angola, IN 46703   219-833-2383

Richard Peterson
Year-round family camp.

1509 Worthmore Academy

5220 E Fall Creek Parkway N Drive
Indianapolis, IN 46220   317-253-5367

Brenda J. Jackson, Director
Diana Buser, Assistant

A center for learning disabilities providing educational assessments, alternative educational programs, academic guidance and public awareness services available as follows: full-time day school, K-8th, 1 to 1 teacher student ratio; six week summer school, K-12th, 1 to 1 teacher student ratio; after school tutoring; adult tutoring, educational assessments, counseling and educational seminars. Tutoring: $20.00/hour. Full-time day school: $5,500.00/year. Six week summer program: $1,500.00.

Iowa

1510   ADA Camp Hertko Hollow

YMCA Camps
Route 4
Box 182
Boone, IA   50036   515-432-7558
                                FAX: 515-432-5414

John Schmitz, Director

Diabetes education, recreation and fun.

1511   Camp Courageous of Iowa

12007 190th Street
Monticello, IA   52310   319-465-5916
                                FAX: 319-465-5919
                   e-mail: camp@campcourageous.org
                          www.campcourageous.com

Jeanne Muellerleile, Camp Director

A year round residential and respite care facility for
individuals with special needs. Campers range in age
from 3-80 years old. Activities include traditional
activities like canoeing, hiking, swimming, nature
and crafts plus adventure activities like caving, rock
climbing, etc. Campers with disabilities have opportunities to succeed at challenging activities. This feel-
ing of self-worth can transfer to home, work or school
environments. Price: $275.00 per week.

1512   Camp Tanager

1614 W Mount Vernon Road
Mount Vernon, IA   52314   319-363-0681
                                FAX: 319-365-6411

Robin Butler

Offers camp experiences for children 7 to 12 whose
special social, economic or medical needs might not
otherwise allow them to enjoy a summer camp experience. This private, non-profit camp serves over 600
children each summer with the staff-camper ratio being 1:6.

1513   Des Moines YMCA Camp

1192 166th Drive
Boone, IA   50036   515-432-7558

Dan Breitbach, Executive Director

For Boys and girls with cancer, diabetes, asthma,
cystic fibrosis, hearing impaired and other disabilities. *$255.00*

1514   Easter Seals Camp Sunnyside

Easter Seals Iowa
PO Box 4002
Des Moines, IA   50333   515-289-1933
                                FAX: 515-289-1281
                        e-mail: essia@netins.net
                          www.easterseals.org

Martha Wittkowski, President/CEO
Paul Thorne, Director, Camping and Recreation

Each summer from June through August, campers
with disabilities ages five and up, take part in one
week camping sessions, gaining skills and independence by participating in activities like swimming, horseback riding, canoeing, fishing, camping
and more. Financial assistance available.

1515   Riverside Lutheran Bible Camp

3001 Riverside Road
Story City, IA   50248   515-733-5271
                                FAX: 515-733-5096
                                www.riversidebc.org

James Cherry

Helps disabled people to develop, renew and nurture
their relationship with Jesus Christ in a unique Christian environment.

**1516   University of Iowa - Wendell Johnson Speech and
Hearing Clinic**

Iowa City, IA   52242   319-335-1845
                                FAX: 319-335-8851

Richard Hurtig, Professor & Chair
Ann L. Michael, Clinic Director

The clinic offers assessment and remediation for disordered communication in adults and children. The
clinic also offers a Intensive Summer Residential
Clinic for school age children needing intervention
services because of speech, language, hearing and/or
reading problems.

Kansas

**1517   Camp Discovery American Diabetes Association -
Kansas Area Office**

837 S Hillside
Wichita, KS   67208   316-684-6091
                                    800-362-1355
                                FAX: 316-684-5675
                        e-mail: lgiles@diabetes.org
                                www.diabetes.org

Lindsay Giles, District Manager

Offers young people with diabetes a week of fun at
rock springs 4-H Center. Special attention to diabetes
makes Camp Discovery a safe environment for active
youth while providing valuable diabetes managment
education. Call the American Diabetes Association-
Kansas area office for more information.

1518   Kansas Jaycees' Cerebral Palsy Ranch

6411 SW 50th Street
El Dorado, KS   67042   316-775-2421
                                FAX: 316-775-2421
                                www2.kidscamps.com

Kentucky

1519   Bethel Mennonite Camp

2952 Bethel Church Road
Clayhole, KY   41317   606-666-4911
                                FAX: 606-666-4911
                                www2.kidscamps.com

1520 Easter Seal Kysoc
1902 Easterday Road
Carrollton, KY 41008   502-732-5333
                             800-888-5377
                        FAX: 502-732-0783
                e-mail: ek1@cardinalhill.org
                        www.cardinalhill.org

Heide Miller, CCD, CTRS, Director
Designed for the fullest camping experience for children or adults with physical disabilities, blind, deaf, behavior disorders, mental retardation, diabetes and multiple handicaps, ages 7 and up. Tuition: $500 for 2 weeks.

1521 Hendon at Kysoc
1902 Easterday Road
Carrollton, KY 41008   502-732-5333
                             800-888-5377
                        FAX: 502-732-0783
                e-mail: ek1@cardinalhill.org
                        www.cardinalhill.org

C. Heideman Miller
Specializes in the needs of disabled campers.

1522 Life Adventure Camp
1122 Oak Hill Drive
Lexington, KY 40505   859-252-4733
                        FAX: 859-225-5115
                www.lifeadventurecamp.org

Wilderness camp for children, male and female, ages 9-18, with emotional and behavioral problems. Fees: $300 for 3-day camp sessions; $410 for 5-day sessions; $15 registration fee.

Louisiana

1523 Camp Bon Coeur
PO Box 53765
Lafeyette, LA 70505   337-233-8437
                        FAX: 337-233-4160
                        www2.kidscamps.com

1524 LA Lions Camp Pelican
PO Box 171
Leesville, LA 71496   337-239-0782
                        FAX: 318-239-9975
                e-mail: lalions@lionscamp.org

Troy Ricard
Provides residential camp for children with lung disorders.

1525 Louisiana Lions Camp for Crippled Children
PO Box 171
Leesville, LA 71496   337-239-0782
                        FAX: 318-239-9975
                e-mail: lalions@lionscamp.org

Raymond Cecil III
Camp for disabled children.

1526 Med-Camps of Louisiana
102 Thomas Road
Suite 615
West Monroe, LA 71291   337-329-8405
                          FAX: 337-329-8407
                          www2.kidscamps.com

Maine

1527 Bancroft Camp
Lighthouse Road
Owls Head, ME 04854
                          FAX: 207-729-1603
                          www.bancroft.org

Joseph Kuhn, Director
Has served as a summer camp for children and adults enrolled in Bancroft programs. The camp recognizes the need for individuals with developmental disabilities to vacation with their families. The camp offers a resort program for people wishing to explore the fascinating coast of Maine or to relax in the clean New England air. Accommodations include accessible rustic cabins and bayfront cottages.

1528 Camp Carpe Diem
Bear River Ranch
16795 Highway E
Rolla, ME 65401   573-458-2125

                          www.bearriverranch.com

1529 Camp Waban
5 Dunaway Drive
Sanford, ME 04073   207-324-7955
                      FAX: 207-324-6050
                      www2.kidscamps.com

1530 Capella
103 Texas Avenue
Bangor, ME 04401   207-941-2885
                      FAX: 207-941-2884
                      www2.kidscamps.com

1531 Pine Tree Camp Children - Adults
114 Pine Tree Camp Road
Rome, ME 04963   207-397-2141
                      FAX: 207-397-5324
            e-mail: ptcamp@pinetreesociety.org
                    www.pinetreesociety.org

Peter D. Phair, Director of Services
Harvey Chesley, Director of Operations

Maryland

1532 Camp Greentop
League: Serving People with Disabilities
1111 E Cold Spring Lane
Baltimore, MD 21239   410-323-0500
                        FAX: 410-323-3298
                        www.campgreetop.org

Alex Gieser, Camp Director
Janice Frey-Angel, CEO

Summer residential camp located in the Catoctin Mountain National Park. Since 1937, Greentop has been serving children and adults with physical and multiple disabilities in a completely accessible camp setting. Campers enjoy a traditional camping program. Medical facilities, staffed with registered nurses 24 hours a day. ACA/MD Youth Camp. Youth 1.5 wk $925; Leadership 5 days $525; Adventure 5 days $525; Mini Camp 4 days $375; Adult Camp 1 week $750

1533 Easter Seals Camp Fairlee Manor

22242 Bay Shore Road
Chestertown, MD   21620   410-778-0566
                                 FAX: 410-778-0567
                                 www2.kidscamps.com

1534 Kamp-A-Kom-Plish

9035 Ironsides Road
Nanjemoy, MD   20662   301-870-3226
                                 FAX: 310-870-2620
                                 www2.kidscamps.com

1535 Lions Camp for the Deaf

7202 Buchanan Street
Landover Hills, MD   20784   301-577-8057

Rev. Edward Helm, Executive Director

This recreational camp for deaf children offers a complete waterfront program including swimming, canoeing and fishing, for ages 6-14. Tuition $125 per week. Registration Fee: $25.00.

1536 Maryland National Capital Park and Planning Commission

Special Populations Division
6611 Kenilworth Avenue
 # 205
Riverdale, MD   20737

Offers year round and seasonal activities and programs for individuals with disabilities and families including day camps, horseback riding, beep ball, aquatics, special events and much more.

1537 Raven Rock Lutheran Camp

17912 Harbaugh Valley Road
Sabillasville, MD   21780   717-794-2667

Lee Sodowsky

Christ-centered program for youth and mentally retarded adults.

1538 Youth Leadership Camp

National Association of the Deaf
814 Thayer Avenue
Silver Spring, MD   20910   301-587-5940

Sponsored by the National Association of the Deaf, this camp emphasizes leadership training for deaf teenagers and young adults. In addition to many recreational activities and sports, there are academic offerings and camp projects.

Massachusetts

1539 Camp Joslin

1 Joslin Plaza
Boston, MA   02215   617-735-1925
                                 FAX: 617-732-2455
              e-mail: sarah.gorman@joslin.harvard.edu
                                 www.joslin.org

Michael Kasparian, Camp Director
Sarah Gorman, Camp Coordinator

For boys, ages 7-16, with diabetes. This program offers active summer sports and activities, supplemented by medical treatment and diabetes education. Coed Winter Camp and Coed Weekend Retreats are offered during the school year. Tuition: $625/wk-scholarships available.

1540 Camp Paul for Exceptional Children

PO Box 53
Chelmsford, MA   01824

Stephen Gannon

Speech and occupational therapy.

1541 Camp Ramah in New England (Summer)

39 Bennett Street
Palmer, MA   01069   413-283-9771
                                 FAX: 413-283-6661
                                 www.campramahane.org

Howard Blas, Director

8 week sleep-away camp for Jewish adolescents with developmental disabilities. Full camping program includes swimming, Hebrew singing and dancing, sports, arts and crafts, daily services, Kosher food, and Jewish studies classes.

1542 Camp Ramah in New England (Winter)

35 Highland Circle
Needham Heights, MA   02494   701-449-7090
                                 FAX: 413-283-6661
                                 www.campramahane.org

Howard Blas, Director

8 week sleep-away camp for Jewish adolescents with developmental disabilities. Full camping program includes swimming, Hebrew singing and dancing, sports, arts and crafts, daily services, Kosher food, and Jewish studies classes.

1543 Carroll School Summer Programs

25 Baker Bridge Road
Lincoln, MA   01773   781-259-8342
                                 FAX: 781-259-8852
                                 www.carrollschool.org

Academic and recreational programs designed to improve learning skills and build self-confidence. The school is a tutorial program for students not achieving their potential due to poor skills in reading, writing and math. The summer camp complements the summer school offering outdoor activities in a supportive, non-competitive environment.

1544 **Clara Barton Camp**
PO Box 356
North Oxford, MA 01537 508-987-2056
FAX: 508-987-2002
e-mail: bcdecamp@aol.com
www.bartoncenter.org

Kerry Packard, author
Brooke Beverly, Resident Camp Director
Kerry Packard, Day Camp Director
Beth Sayers, Adventure Camp Director

Girls, ages 6-17, with diabetes participate in a well-rounded camp program with special education in diabetes, health and safety. Activities include swimming, boating, sports, dance, music and arts and crafts. Tuition: $1600 for 2 weeks. Two week adventure camp for high school girls offering camping, hiking, canoeing, etc. Also a minicamp (one week) for girls 6-12. Tuition $800. Day camps are offered in Worcester, Boston, and New York City.

1545 **Eagle Hill School - Summer Program**
242 Old Petersham Road
Hardwick, MA 01037 413-477-6000
FAX: 413-477-6000
e-mail: admission@eaglehillschool.com
www.eaglehillschool.com

Erin E Wynne, Dean of Admission

For the child, age 9-19, with a specific learning disability or Attention Deficit Disorder, this summer program offers a structured curriculum designed to build a basic foundation of academic competence. Extracurricular and outdoor activities complement the educational program. Tuition: $4,900 for 6 weeks.

1546 **Easter Seals Society-Agassiz Village**
484 Main Street
6th Floor
Worcester, MA 01603 508-757-2756
FAX: 508-831-9780
www2.kidscamps.com

1547 **Handi-Kids/King Solomon Foundation**
470 Pine Street
Bridgewater, MA 02324 508-697-7557
FAX: 508-697-1529

Mary L. Gallant, Program Director

A therapeutic recreational facility in Bridgewater, Massachusetts offering after-school programs, special events, school vacation full-week and summer day camp programs. Every individual is welcome.

Sliding Scale

1548 **Kolburne School Camp**
Southfield Road
New Marlborough, MA 02130 413-229-8787
FAX: 413-229-7708

Jean Weinstein

Kolburne offers an academic program for those with learning, emotional and social problems.

1549 **Massachusetts Easter Seals Camping Program**
Various, MA 508-751-6343
800-922-8290
FAX: 508-831-9768
www2.kidscamps.com

1550 **New England Experience**
22 Addington Road
3
Brookline, MA 02445 617-244-1200

Clark Adams

Held at Avon Old Farms School, campers may attend for 2, 4, 6 or 8 weeks. Highlights are circus training, computers, electronic music, sports and courses in creative writing and desktop publishing. Tutoring and SAT preparation are available. Tuition: $995 for 2 weeks.

1551 **Tower Program at Regis College**
Regis College
235 Wellesley Street
Weston, MA 02493 781-894-6735

S. Marilyn MacGregor

Helps average and above average college-bound students, ages 16-17, having a diagnosed dyslexic learning disability, to adjust to a college setting. Emphasis is on instruction and academic reinforcement, affective support, awareness of support services available on most college campuses and strategy training. Tuition: $4,200, Day $3,500 for 6 weeks.

Michigan

1552 **Anchor Point Camp**
RBM Ministries
PO Box 128
Plainwell, MI 49080 616-342-9879

Accepts mentally and physically handicapped children ages 13 and up.

1553 **Big Crystal Camp**
8533 Williams Road
DeWitt, MI 48820 517-669-9367

Florence Curtis

One week residential camp sponsored by Lansing Area Chapter of Michigan Association for Children with Learning Disabilities.

1554 **Camp Barakel**
PO Box 159
Fairview, MI 48621 517-848-2279
FAX: 517-848-2280

Lee Brown, Program Director

Five-day Christian camp experience in mid-August for campers ages 13-55 who are physically disabled, visually impaired, upper trainable mentally impaired or educable mentally impaired, bus transportation provided from locations in Lansing, Flint, Bay City, and Marshall, Michigan.

1555 Camp Catch-A-Rainbow
American Cancer Society
1205 E Saginaw Street
Lansing, MI 48906   517-371-2920
                        800-ACS-2345

Open to any child who has, or has had, cancer.

1556 Camp Fish Tales
2177 Erickson Road
Pinconning, MI 48650   517-879-5199

                        www2.kidscamps.com

1557 Camp Niobe
4580 South Mill Road
Dryden, MI 48428   810-796-2480

Joanne Mandel, Director
A six week summer resident camp program for boys
and girls whose learning and behavior styles have
made successful participation in the traditional camp
program difficult. All camp activities have a special
emphasis on building self-esteem and peer relationships. Strong in waterfront, nature, campcrafts and a
special arts program. 2 weeks ($560.00); 4 weeks
($1075.00); Canoe Trip ($275).

1558 Central Michigan University Summer Clinics
444 Moore
Mount Pleasant, MI 48859   517-774-3803
                            FAX: 517-779-2799
Designed for children, ages 6 and up, with speech,
language and hearing disorders who can benefit
from intensive clinical work. A wide range of recreational and social activities form part of the
clinical program and promote the social use of
skills learned in class. Tuition: $1,800 for 6 weeks.

1559 Discovery Center of Michigan
1450 E Brown Road
Mayville, MI 48744

Alan Zsolzai, Executive Director
Accepts learning disabled campers ages 8-18.

1560 Eagle Village
4507 170th Avenue
Hersey, MI 49639   231-832-2234
                            800-748-0061
                        FAX: 231-832-1468
                    e-mail: alc@eaglevillage.org

Mendy Pate, Camp Director
This program accepts youth, ages 5-17, who are high
risk or special needs - behavioral problems, emotionally unstable or Attention Deficit. The camping experience includes canoeing, hiking, swimming and high
adventure activities. Tuition fee.

1561 Fowler Center
2315 Harmon Lake Road
Mayville, MI 48744   517-673-2050
                        FAX: 517-673-6355
                e-mail: info@thefowlercenter.org
                    www.thefowlercenter.org

Patricia Jordan, Office Registar

1562 Indian Trails Camp
0-1859 Lake Michigan Drive NW
Grand Rapids, MI 49544   616-677-5251
                        FAX: 616-677-2955
                    www.indiantrails-camp.org

Lynn Gust, Executive Director
Year round residential camping program for children
and adults with physical disabilities.

1563 Midicha
4205 Hollenbeck Road
Columbiaville, MI 48421   313-882-0658

Judy Boelstler
Disabled campers.

1564 O'Fair Winds Camp
Fair Winds Girl Scout Council
2029 Elms Road
Suite C
Swartz Creek, MI 48473   810-230-0244
                            800-482-6734
                        FAX: 810-230-0955

Accepts diabetic, and learning disabled girls ages
6-12.

1565 Roger
8356 Belding Road Northeast
Rockford, MI 49341   616-874-7286
                        FAX: 616-874-5734
                e-mail: camproger@juno.com
                    www.camproger.org

Robert Heetderks
Disabled campers.

Minnesota

1566 Camp Buckskin
8700 W 36th Street
Suite 6W
Saint Louis Park, MN 55426   612-930-3544
                        FAX: 612-938-6996
            e-mail: buckskin@spacestar.net
            www.spacestar.net/users/buckskin

Thomas R. Bauer, CCD, Camp Director

LD and ADD/ADHD youth have often experienced frustration and a lack of success. Buckskin assists these individuals to realize and develop the potentials and abilities which they possess. Teaches a combination of academic and camp activities, so the campers experience success in many areas. By necessity fairly structured, the 1:3 staff ratio ensures the program is individualized to meet each camper's needs. Parents report that their children benefit from the experience in many ways.

1567   Camp Courage

8046 83rd Street NW
Maple Lake, MN   55358   320-963-3132
                                   FAX: 320-963-3698
                          e-mail: camping@courage.org
                              www.couragecamps.org

Bob Pollond, Director

1568   Camp Friendship

Friendship Ventures
10509 108th Street NW
Annandale, MN   55302   952-852-0101
                                         800-450-8376
                                   FAX: 952-852-0123
                   e-mail: fv@friendshipventures.org
                           www.friendshipventures.org

Georgann Rumsey, President & CEO
Laurie Tschetter, Program Director
Margaret Schuster, Program Director

Camp Friendship offers resident camp programs for children, teenagers, and adults with developmental, physical or multiple disabilities, special medical conditions, Down Syndrome, Williams Syndrome, autism or other conditions. Summer camp offers archery, sailing, horseback riding, biking, fishing, creative arts, adventure challenge programs and other activities are available. Weekend camps and longer available. Other services available throughout the year.

1569   Camp New Hope

53035 Lake Avenue
McGregor, MN   55760   218-426-3560
                                   FAX: 218-426-3560
                           e-mail: newhope@ecp2.net
                              www.campnewhope.org

Lori Bittner, Director

CNH is a private, non-profit organization which provides quality educational, recreational and leisure opportunities to individuals with mental, physical and other developmental disabilities. Stimulating programs and quality care.

1570   Camp Winnebago

19708 Camp Winnebago Road
Caledonia, MN   55921   507-495-3265
                                   FAX: 507-724-3786
                          e-mail: campwinn@means.net

Cathy Greeley, Executive Director
Karen Reeve, Assitant Director

We offer one week summer sessions for children and adults with developmental disabilities. We also do integrated youth sessions to allow friends and siblings to attend with our traditional campers. Respite week-ends are offered monthly throughout the year. Travel vacations are also offered as an option. We also publish a newsletter and have a video available. *$350.00*

    8-12 pages

1571   Courage Camps

Courage Center
3915 Golden Valley Road
Golden Valley, MN   55422   612-588-0811
                                         888-846-8253
                                   FAX: 612-520-0577
                          e-mail: camping@mtn.org
                                  www.courage.org

Eric Stevens, Executive Director

Summer resident camp serving children and adults who have physical or sensory disabilities. Also for children who need the help of a speech clinician. Special sessions include those for children who have been burned, children who have cancer and their siblings, and children who have hemophilia or sickle cell anemia. Offers Special outdoor education or leadership sessions for deaf, or physically disabled teens and a sports camp for physically disabled and blind teens.

1572   Courage North

PO Box 1626
Lake George, MN   56458   218-266-3658
                                   FAX: 218-266-3458
                              www2.kidscamps.com

1573   Eden Wood Center

Friendship Ventures
6350 Indian Chief Road
Eden Prairie, MN   55346   952-852-0101
                                   FAX: 952-852-0123
                   e-mail: fv@friendshipventures.org
                           www.friendshipventures.org

Georgann Rumsey, President & CEO
Laurie Tschetter, Program Director
Margaret Schuster, Program Director

Offers resident camp programs for children, teenagers and adults with developmental, physical or multiple disabilities, Down Syndrome, special medical conditions, Williams Syndrome, autism and/or other conditions. Fishing, creative arts, golf, sports and other activities are available. Creative Options Respite Care offers weekend camps year round for children, teenagers and adults. Ventures Travel offers guided vacations for teens and adults with developmental disabilities or other unique needs.

1574   Groves Learning Center

3200 Highway 100 S
Saint Louis Park, MN   55416

Sue Kirchhoff, Head Of School

A nonprofit day school in Minnesota designed especially for children with learning differences. The Center has a full day academic program from September through June, as well as an 8 week summer program. Groves also offers community services such as: psychoeducational testing for children and adults, consulting services, workshops on learning disabilities and other special learning needs, and afternoon/evening tutorial services for children and adults.

1575 Knutson

523 N 3rd Street
4th Floor
Brainerd, MN 56401   218-828-7610

Robert Larson

Provides a camping program for mentally and physically disabled and emotionally disturbed children and adults. Campers must come with an established group that brings its own counselors. Swimming, sailing, archery, nature study and hiking are among the noncompetitive activities. Tuition: $180 per week.

1576 PDP Products

14524 61st Street
PO Box 2009
Stillwater, MN 55082   651-439-8865
                            FAX: 651-439-0421
                               www.pdppro.com

PDP Products acquires books and therapy materials recommended or developed by therapists and makes those materials available at PDP courses and through mail order.

1577 Professional Development Programs

14524 61st Street N
Stillwater, MN 55082   651-439-8865
                            FAX: 651-439-0421
                     e-mail: programs@pdppro.com
                               www.pdppro.com

PDP sponsors cutting edge and popular continuing education workshops and symposia of interest to professionals who provide services to children and adults with special needs.

1578 Search Beyond Adventures

400 South Cedar Lake Road
Miineapolis, MN 55405   612-374-4845
                                  800-800-9979
                              www2.kidscamps.com

1579 St. Paul Academy and Summit School

1712 Randolph Avenue
Saint Paul, MN 55105   651-698-2451
                            FAX: 651-698-6787
                                    www.spa.edu

Marlene Odahlen-Hinz, Assistant Director

Individualized instruction in basic skills, reading, math, composition, and study skills.

Mississippi

1580 Tik-A-Witha

PO Box 126
Van Vleet, MS 38877   601-447-3250

                              www2.kidscamps.com

Missouri

1581 Camp Black Hawk

16795 Highway E
Rolla, MO 65401   573-458-2125

                      e-mail: bugbite@mail.usmo.com
                           www.bearriverranch.com

1582 Camp Wee-Y

RR 2
Potosi, MO 63664   573-438-2724
                                  800-323-7300

Jean Jencks

The YMCA day camp for children ages 6-8. Children are under the direction and supervision of their counselors and engage in small group and camp-wide activities and work on developing their skills and self-confidence.

1583 Council for Extended Care of Mentally Retarded Citizens

1600 South Hanley Road
Suite 100a
Saint Louis, MO 63144   314-781-4950
                            FAX: 314-781-3850
                       e-mail: cecmrc@aol.com

Cynthia Compton, Executive Director
Marge Lindhorst, Supported Living Director
Angela Jackson, Development Director Camp

Services are provided to adults and children with developmental disabilities. Supported living arrangements are located in St. Louis city and St. Charles County. Group home and camp services are located in Dittmer, MO. Travel program also available.

1584 EDI

1460 Pepperhill Drive
Florissant, MO 63033

Fred Schaljo

Youngsters with diabetes learn how to care for themselves while participating in a wide variety of outdoor activities and trips. The camp, managed and financed by the American Diabetes Association Greater St. Louis Affiliate, offers camperships to children from the Greater St. Louis area, ages 7-16, but nonresidents may also apply. Tuition $300-500 for 2 weeks.

1585 Hickory Hill

PO Box 1942
Columbia, MO 65205   573-698-2510

William Mees

Educates diabetic children concerning diabetes and its care. In addition to daily educational sessions on some aspects of diabetes, campers participate in swimming, sailing, arts and crafts and overnight camping. Tuition: $200 for 2 weeks.

1586 Lions Den Outdoor Learning Center

1816 Lackland Hill Parkway
Suite 200
Saint Louis, MO 63146

Cris Rodriguez

Varied programs for mentally retarded children, ages 6 and up, includes daily living, socialization and language skills. Sports, tent camping, crafts, and nature study are also offered. Sliding scale tuition for 2 weeks.

1587 Sidney R. Baer Day Camp

2 Millstone Drive
St. Louis, MO 63146

Astrid Balzer, Special Needs
Andy Brown, Camp Director

Co-ed day camp serving campers ages 5-12 years old.

1588 Sunnyhill

PO Box 246
Dittmer, MO 63023   314-274-9044

Donald Dinnella

A special camp for the mentally retarded.

Nebraska

1589 Camp Easter Seals

609 North 60th Road
Nebraska City, NE 68410   402-578-3992
800-650-9880
www2.kidscamps.com

1590 Eastern Nebraska 4-H Center

21520 West Highway 31
Gretna, NE 68028   402-332-4496
FAX: 402-332-2580
e-mail: 4hcampea@unl.edu
www.ianr.unl.edu/ianr/4h

Kelly Krambeck, Camp Director

Beautiful modern facilities overlooking Platte River for the disabled campers.

1591 Floyd Rogers

PO Box 31536
Omaha, NE 68131   402-341-0866

Sherman Poska

A camp for diabetic children.

1592 National Camps for Blind Children

Christian Record
4444 S 52nd Street
Lincoln, NE 68506   402-488-0981
FAX: 402-488-7582
e-mail: info@christianrecord.org
www.christianrecord.org

Arturo Grayman, Director, National

Over 50 camps throughout the US and Canada are offered at no cost to legally blind children, ages 9-19. Activities include archery, beeper basketball, water sports, hiking and rock climbing and horseback riding. No fee for 1 week.

New Hampshire

1593 Camp Allen

56 Camp Allen Road
Bedford, NH 03110   603-622-8471
FAX: 603-626-4295

Bob Lane, Director
Debbie Schalte, Office Manager

A residential summer camp for individuals with disabilities. All of the activities are conducted by individual coordinators under the supervision of Program Director. Some of the activities include, aquatics, arts, crafts, games and nature programs. All camp events, special events, evening programs, and field trips are scheduled throughout the summer and are structured to meet the individual abilities and needs of each camper.

1594 Camp Dartmouth-Hitchcock

Dartmouth-Hitchcock Medical Center Pediatrics
1 Medical Center Drive
Lebanon, NH 03756   603-650-7708

www2.kidscamps.com

1595 Camp Sno-Mo

Rural Route 1 Box 623
Gilmanton, NH 03837   603-364-5818
FAX: 603-364-0230
e-mail: dgordon@eseals.org
www.eseals.org/services/camping

Douglas Gordon, Director of Camping/Recreation

1596 Crotched Mountain School and Rehabilitation Center

1 Verney Drive
Greenfield, NH 03047   603-547-3311
800-966-2672
FAX: 603-547-3232
e-mail: info@cmf.org
www.cmf.org

Rita Phinney, Director, Admissions
John Young, Registrar

Currently serves children ages 6-22 with multiple-handicaps including: Cerebral Palsy, Spina Bifida, visual and hearing impairments and neurological disabilities, developmental disorders, mental retardation, autism, behavioral and emotional disorders, seizure disorders, spinal cord and head injuries. The School is a member of the National Association of Independent Schools and accredited with the NE Association of Schools and Colleges, Independent Schools of Northern NE.

yearly

1597 Easter Seal Camp-New Hampshire

RFD 1, Box 623
Gilmanton Iron Works, NH 03857 603-364-5818
FAX: 603-364-0230
e-mail: dgordon@eseals.org
www.easeals.org/services/camping

Douglas Gordon, Director of Camping/Recreation

New Jersey

1598 Bancroft NeuroHealth

Hopkins Lane
PO Box 20
Haddonfield, NJ 08033 856-429-0010
800-774-5516
FAX: 856-429-4755
www.bancroftneurohealth.org

George Niemann, Ph.D., Chief Executive
Joseph Hess, Jr., President

Founded in 1883, Bancroft NeuroHealth, a New Jersey non-profit corporation, serves more than 900 children and adults with developmental disabilities, brain injuries and other neurological impairments. Based in Haddonfield, N.J., Bancroft NeuroHealth also has sites in Maine, Louisiana, and Delaware, and serves families throughout the U.S. and abroad. Programs include education, rehabilitation, vocational, residential, evaluation and treatment services, as well as behavioral crisis intervention.

1599 Camp Chatterbox

Hackettstown, NJ

www2.kidscamps.com

1600 Camp Merry Heart/Easter Seals Easter Seal Society

RD 21 O'Brian Road
Hackettstown, NJ 07840 908-852-3896
FAX: 908-852-9263

Mary Ellen Ross, Camping Director

An organized program of swimming, arts and crafts, boating, nature study and travel offered to the physically disabled, developmentally disabled, cerebral palsied, brain damaged and head injured children, ages 5-18, adults 19-75+. Fall and spring travel programs for adults. $75 per day. Call for rates..

1601 Camp Oakhurst

111 Monmouth Road
Oakhurst, NJ 07755 908-531-0215

www2.kidscamps.com

1602 Camp Sun 'N Fun

Routes 322 & 555
Williamstown, NJ 08094 856-629-4502
FAX: 856-875-1499
www2.kidscamps.com

1603 Camp Vacamas

256 Macopin Road
West Milford, NJ 07480 973-838-1394
FAX: 973-838-7534
e-mail: info@vacamas.org
www.vacamas.org

Michael Friedman, Executive Director
Philip Smith, Camp Director

Disadvantaged children with asthma or sickle cell anemia, ages 8-16, are offered special programs in canoeing, backpacking, camping, music and leadership training. Sliding scale tuition. Year round programs for groups.

1604 Cerebral Palsy Center Summer Program

7 Sanford Avenue
Belleville, NJ 07109 201-751-0200

www2.kidscamps.com

1605 Cross Roads Outdoor Ministries

29 Pleasant Grove Road
Port Murray, NJ 07865 908-832-7264
FAX: 908-832-6593
e-mail: crossroadsom@mindspring.com
www.crossroadoutdoorministries.org

Todd Garmer, Special Education Director
Peggy Mellors, Executive Director

Program for ages 6-15 offers Bible study, worship, swimming, crafts, hiking, canoeing and campfires. Special education program for those with developmental disabilities. Tuition: $345.00 weekly fee.

1606 Easter Seals Camp Merry Heart

21 O'Brian Road
Hackettstown, NJ 07840 908-852-3896
FAX: 908-852-9263

Mary Ellen Ross, Director of Camping

An organized program of swimming, arts and crafts, boating, nature study and travel offered to the physically disabled, developmentally disabled, cerebral palsied, brain damaged and head injured children, ages 5-18, adults 19-75+. Fall and spring travel programs for adults, Respite Weekends, call for rates.

1607 Handi-Camp-NJ

Newfield, NJ 610-352-7177
FAX: 610-352-5561
www2.kidscamps.com

1608 Nejeda

PO Box 156
Stillwater, NJ 07875 973-383-2611
FAX: 973-383-9891
e-mail: nejeda@nac.net

Cheryl Lyding, Executive Director
James Daschbach, Camp Director

For children with diabetes, ages 5-15, provides an active and safe camping experience which enables the children to learn about and understand diabetes. Activities include boating, swimming, fishing, archery, as well as camping skills. Tuition: $850 for 2 weeks.

1609   New Jersey Camp Jaycee
33 Lake Drive
Hightstown, NJ   08520   609-443-1200
                                 FAX: 609-443-1202

Jim Worrall, Executive Director
This camp is children and adults with mental retardation and is sponsored jointly by the New Jersey Jaycees and the ARC of New Jersey. Activities at the 185-acre Pocono Mountain camp include arts and crafts, games and sports, music, nature, swimming, boating, horseback riding and self-help skills. Tuition: $345 per week.

1610   Round Lake Camp
21 Plymouth Street
Fairfield, NJ   07004   973-575-3333
                                 FAX: 973-575-4188
                                 e-mail: rlc@njycamps.org
                                 www.njycamps.org

Sheira Director, Asst. Director
For ages 7-18, this camp provides individualized academics in reading, language development and math for children with mild learning disabilities, Round Lake also offers therapeutic recreation and Jewish cultural values to its participants. Tuition: $745 for 7 weeks.

New Mexico

1611   Dyslexia Centers
New Mexico State University
755 S Telshor Boulevard
Suite C102
Las Cruces, NM   88011   505-524-6450

Janice Kolosseus
Participants must enroll at the Audiology Center for a minimum of two weeks. Children and adults who are learning disabled or speech handicapped receive speech therapy and psychotherapy in addition to tutoring, academic instruction and remedial reading. Tuition: $500 per week.

1612   Easter Seal Camping Center Kamp Kiwanis
Easter Seal Camp Program General
Vanderwagen, NM   87326

Karen Elise Wright
Travel camp and traditional programs for persons with disabilities.

1613   Santa Fe Mountain Center
PO Box 449
Tesuque, NM   87574   505-983-6158
                              FAX: 505-983-0460

Skye Gray, Director

Camp sessions offered to disabled campers from the ages of 1-20.

New York

1614   Advocacy Center
277 Alexander Street
Suite 500
Rochester, NY   14607   716-546-1700
                                800-650-4967
                                e-mail: advocacycenter.com
                                www.advocacycenter.com

Paul Shew, Executive Director

1615   Advocates for Children of New York
151 Wets 30th Street
5th Floor
New York, NY   10001   212-947-9779

                                e-mail: info@advocatesforchildren.org
                                www.advocatesforchildren.org

Jill Chaifetz, Executive Director

1616   American Diabetes Association
149 Madison Avenue
Suite 701
New York, NY   10016   212-725-4925
                                888-DIA-BETE
                                FAX: 212-725-8916
                                www.diabetes.org

Lynne Perry
The American Diabetes Association provides research, and provides information and advocacy for people with diabets and their families. The Asssociation also provides seminars for health care professionals.

1617   Association for Neurologically Impaired Brain Injured Children
212-12 26th Avenue
Bayside, NY   11360   718-423-9550
                              FAX: 718-423-9838
                              e-mail: info@anibic.org

Jeanne Parisi, Executive Director
Lisa Eisenberg, Dir. of Family Support Services
ANIBIc is a voluntary, multi-service organization that is dedicated to serving individuals with severe learning disabilities, neurological impairments and other developmental disabilities. Services include: residential, vocational, family support services, recreation (children and adults), respite (adult), summer day camp, counseling, and tramatic brain injury services (adults).

1618   Autistic Adults at Bittersweet Farms
Haworth Press
Binghampton, NY   604-722-5857
                          800-429-6784
                          FAX: 607-722-6362
          e-mail: getinfo@haworthpressinc.com
                 www.haworthpressinc.com
Norman S. Giddan, PhD and Jane J. Giddan, MA, author

A detailed view of Bittersweet Farms, an eighty-acre residential program for autistic adults and adolescents in northwestern Ohio. The Bittersweet program is based upon the premise that autistic adults need specil care and training throughout their lives, which can be satisfying and productive.

1991

1619 Camp Huntington

56 Brunesville Street
High Falls, NY   12440   914-687-7840
                               FAX: 914-687-7211
                      e-mail: camphtgtn@aol.com

Bruria K. Falik, PhD

A co-ed residential camp for the learning disabled, ADD, neurologically impaired and mild-moderate mental retardation.

1620 Camp Venture

100 Convent Road
PO Box 402
Nanuet, NY   10954   845-624-3860
                          FAX: 845-624-7064
                          www.campventure.org

Rhys Ann Lukens
Alice Kayser

In more than a dozen Rockland neighborhoods, residential, employment, habilitation or recreation programs have arisen to help people with disabilities contribute to the life of the community. There are, for instance, more than a dozen Community Residential Facilities, Venture Industries, Venture Day Treatment, Day Habilitation, Venture Chorus, after school programs, and more.

1621 Client Assistance Program

401 State Street
Schenectady, NY   12305   518-381-7098

                e-mail: michaelp@cqc.state.ny.us
                        www.cqc.state.ny.us

Michael Peluso, CAP Director

1622 Families Together in NY State

15 Elk Street
Albany, NY   12207   518-432-0333
                               888-326-8644
                      e-mail: info@ftnys.org
                               www.ftnys.org

Paige MacDonald, Executive Director

1623 Freedom Camp

PO Box 2134
Auburn, NY   13021

Mary Ellen Perry, Executive Director

A summer day camp for youths with disabilities sponsored by Freedom Recreational Services. Freedom Camp is offered in two-week sessions at Casey Park in Auburn, New York.

1624 Gow School Summer Programs

Emery Road
South Wales, NY   14139   716-655-2900
                          FAX: 716-652-3457
                    e-mail: gowsummer@aol.com
                               www.gow.org

Bekah D Atkinson, Director

Co-ed summer programs for ages 8-19, offer a balance blend of morning academics, afternoon/evening traditional camp activities and weekend overnight trips (teen-tours). The primary purpose of these programs is to provide a positive experience while balancing these three elements. Committed to the creation of a positive and enjoyable experience for each participant, by defining and merging the goals of the camp and the school, with those of camper students, their families and educators.

1625 Henry Kaufmann Campgrounds Staten Island

667 Blauvelt Road
Pearl River, NY   10965   845-735-2718
                          FAX: 845-735-3544

Jeffrey Alan Coopersmith, Director
Disabled campers.

1626 Huntington

56 Bruceville Road
High Falls, NY   12440
                          FAX: 914-687-7211

Dr. Bruria Falik, Director

Summer activities include recreational, academic and vocational programs for the learning disabled, neurologically impaired and mildly ADA to mild/moderately retarded. An Olympic pool, horse riding and a special work training program are featured. Programs are tailored to meet individual needs, ages 6-21, and campers may enroll for 4 to 8 weeks.

1627 Maplebrook School

5142 Route 22
Amenia, NY   12501   845-373-8191
                          FAX: 845-373-7029
                      e-mail: mbsecho@aol.com

Donna M. Konkolios, Head of School
Jennifer Scully, Director of Admissions

A coeductional boarding school for students with learning differences and ADD. A New York State registered high school servicing ages 11-18. Post secondary options offered to 18-21.

1628 Marist Brothers Mid-Hudson Valley Camp

PO Box 197
Esopus, NY   12429   845-384-6620
                          FAX: 845-384-6479

Bro. Don Nugent, Administrator

Serves special people: deaf, retarded and children with cancer; HIV positive children.

1629 Oakhurst

853 Broadway
New York, NY   10003   212-253-8680

Marvin Raps

Accepts children and young adults who are physically handicapped, ages 8-18. The program includes physical therapy, recreational activities and a work program for teenagers. Tuition: $900 for 3 weeks.

1630 Presbyterian Center at Holmes

60 Dantan Lake Road
Holmes, NY   12531   845-878-6383
                                  FAX: 845-878-7824
                        www.presbyteriancenter.org

Peter Surgerior, Executive Director
Diane Ball, Administration Assistant

Disabled campers.

1631 Program for Children and Youth Who are Deaf or Hard of Hearing

One Commerce Plaza
Room 1601
Albany, NY   12234   518-474-5652

                        e-mail: dsteele@mail.nysed.gov
                                  www.nysed.gov

Dirothy Steel, Coordinator Deaf Services

1632 Programs for Children with Disabilities: Ages 3 through 5

1 Commerce Plaza
Room 1607
Albany, NY   12234   518-473-6108

                        e-mail: mpltzke@mail.nysed.gov

Michael C. Noyes, Ph.D., Director

1633 Programs for Children with Special Health Care Needs

Tower Building
Room 208
Albany, NY   12237   518-474-2084

                        e-mail: cx104@health.state.ny.us

Claudia Lee, Acting Director

1634 Programs for Infants and Toddlers with Disabilities: Ages Birth Through 2

Empire State Plaza
Corning Tower Building, Room 208
Albany, NY   12237   518-473-7016

                        e-mail: dmn02@health.state.ny.us

Donna M. Noyes, Ph.D., Director

1635 Radalbek

RR 1 Box 28K
Hancock, NY   13783   607-467-2159
                                  FAX: 607-467-2159

Grace Kinzer

A year-round residential program, for ages 14-18, to educate and train the mentally retarded, emotionally disturbed and learning disabled in self-help skills. The program curriculum is educational, vocational and recreational, with special workshops and programs for all ages. Tuition: $250 per week.

1636 Ramapo Anchorage Camp

PO Box 266
Rhinebeck, NY   12572   845-876-8403
                                  FAX: 845-876-8414

Bernie Kosberg, Executive Director
Michael Kunin, Associate Director

Residential program which serves children, ages 4-16, with a wide range of emotional, behavoral, and learning problems. A one-to-one ratio of counselors-to-campers enables children to build healthy relationships, increase self-esteem and improve learning skills. Character values such as honesty, concern for others, responsibility, and the courage to do one's best are encouraged. Campers demonstrate significant gains in their ability to maintain relationships, control impulses and adjust.

1637 Triangle

9 Camp Road
Rexford, NY   12148

Shirley Schofield

For learning disabled children, ages 7-18, with the emphasis on recreation and socialization skills. Vocational training, academics and speech therapy are available.

1638 VISIONS' Vacation Camp for the Blind

111 Summit Park Road
Spring Valley, NY   10977   914-354-3003
                                  FAX: 914-354-3003

Pamela Schneider, Camp Director

Respite services offered to 18 years or older visually impaired persons.

1639 Wagon Road

Children's Aid Society
431 Quaker Road
47
Chappaqua, NY   10514   914-238-4761
                                  FAX: 914-238-0714

Provides residential respite services to developmentally disabled children ages 7-18. At its 50 acre campus which is entirely wheelchair accessible, 24 hour RN and MD services are provided.

North Carolina

1640 Camp Sky Ranch

634 Sky Ranch Road
Blowing Rock, NC   28605   828-264-8600
                                  FAX: 828-265-2339
                        e-mail: jsharp1@triad.rr.com
                                  www.campskyranch.com

Jack Sharp, Director

A private, residential camp for the handicapped. This season is the camp's 53th year of providing a real camping experience for the handicapped. Camp Sky Ranch was the first private camp for the handicapped in the Southeast. Activities include: swimming, boating, horseback riding, and more. Campers must be able to walk, dress and feed themselves, and take care of their toilet needs. Tuition: $725.00 per two weeks.

1641 Camp Winding Gap

RR 1 Box 56
Lake Toxaway, NC 28747 828-966-4520
FAX: 828-883-8720
www.campwindinggap.com

Ann Hertzberg, Director

For boys and girls ages 8-16, with facilities for up to 75 campers. A high staff-camper ratio (less than 1 to 3) of carefully selected counselors provides a nurturing family atmosphere. A few children with disabilities are mainstreamed each session. Must be able to handle horseback riding and rugged terrain, this is a ranch type camp in a farm setting with many animals. Program includes regular camp activities.

1642 Cullowhee Experience

Western Carolina University
Culowhee, NC 28723 704-227-7249

1643 SOAR Summer Adventures

PO Box 388
Balsam, NC 28707 828-456-3435
FAX: 708-456-3449

John Willson, Dir. of LD/ADD Prg.
Jonathan Jones, Executive Director

A nonprofit adventure program working with disadvantaged youth diagnosed with learning disabilities in an outdoor, challenge based environment. Focuses on esteem building and social skills development through rock climbing, backpacking, whitewater rafting, mountaineering, sailing, snorkeling, and much more. Offers two week, one month, and semester programs available. SOAR programs utilize North Carolina, Florida, Colorado, American Southwest, Alaska, and Jamaica as program areas. $950-$1,950.

1644 Stone Mountain School at Camp Elliott

Talisman Schools
601 Camp Elliott Road
Black Mountain, NC 28711 828-669-8639
FAX: 828-669-2521
e-mail: talismansc@aol.com
www.stonemountainschool.org

Catherine Jennings, Director
Linda Tatsapaugh, Assistant Director

Year round therapeutic wilderness school for emotionally disturbed boys grades 6-12. Certified mental health program, licensed by the department of facility services and certified special education school. Tuition: $3,500 a month.

1645 Talisman Summer Programs

601 Camp Elliott Road
Black Mountain, NC 28711 828-669-8639
FAX: 828-669-2521
e-mail: talismansc@aol.com
www.stonemountainschool.org

Catherine Jennings, Administrative Director
Robiyn Mims, Program Director

Offers a program of hiking, rafting, climbing, and caving for learning disabled ADD/ADHD co-ed young people, ages 9-18. Tuition: $4,200 for 3 weeks, $4,400 for 6 weeks.

Ohio

1646 Beech Brook

3737 Lander Road
Cleveland, OH 44124 216-831-2255
FAX: 216-831-0436

Don Harris, Director

A year-round residential and day treatment center, accepts summer residents when there are openings in the regular enrollment. The program is designed for emotionally disturbed, learning disabled and autistic children, providing therapeutically oriented teaching and programming techniques in a camp setting.

1647 Camp Allyn

1414 Lake Allyn Road
Batavia, OH 45103 513-732-0240
FAX: 513-735-1461
e-mail: ssc@one.net
www.steppingstonecenter.org

Dennis Carter, Associated Director

A camp for children and adults with disabilities.

1648 Camp Nuhop

404 Hillcrest Drive
Ashland, OH 44805 419-289-2227
FAX: 419-289-2227
e-mail: cnuhop@bright.net
www.campnuhop.org

Jerry Dunlap, Director

A summer residential program for any youngster from 6 to 18 with a learning disability, behavior disorder or Attention Deficit Disorder. Sixty two campers and 35 staff members live on site in groups of to 7 campers to every 3 counselors. Activities focus on positive self-concept and behaviors and teaches children to learn how to find their strengths, abilities and talents from a positive, yet realistic viewpoint.

1649 Emanuel-Day

Emanuel-Day and Resident
331 Marlay Road
Dayton, OH 45405

Nan Crawford, Camp Director

Camp for hearing impaired and normal hearing youth.

1650 Happiness at St. Augustine Academy

14808 Lake Avenue
Lakewood, OH 44107

William Tighe

Serves mentally retarded campers with multiple handicaps.

1651 Highbrook Lodge Camp
12944 Aquilla Road
Chardon, OH 44024   216-791-8118
FAX: 216-791-1101
e-mail: mmullin@clevelandsightcenter.org
www.clevelandsightcenter.org

Mike Mullin, Director
A summer residential camp for blind and disabled children, adults and families. Weekly rate: $100-$260 per week.

1652 Stepping Stone
5650 Given Road
Cincinnati, OH 45243

Lucy Smith
Non-profit United Way affiliated camp serving all disabilities and charges on a sliding scale.

Oklahoma

1653 Easter Seals Oklahoma
2100 NW 63rd Street
Oklahoma City, OK 73116   405-848-2525
FAX: 405-842-9704
e-mail: easok@ilinkusa.net

Providing services such as adult day services, child development center, OTIPT, speech therapy, reading/tutoring, vision and hearing screening.

Oregon

1654 Easter Seals Oregon Camping Program
5757 Southwest Macadam Avenue
Portland, OR 97201   503-228-5108
800-556-6020
FAX: 503-228-1352
e-mail: camp@oregonseals.org
www2.kidscamps.com

1655 Meadowood Springs Speech and Hearing Camp
PO Box 1025
Pendleton, OR 97801   541-276-2752
FAX: 541-276-7227
e-mail: meadowood@oregontrail.net
www.meadowoodsprings.org

Rhonda Hack, Executive Administrator
On 143 acres in the Blue Mountains of Eastern Oregon, this camp is designed to help young people who have diagnosed clinical disorders of speech, hearing or language. A full range of activities in recreational and clinical areas is available. $925.00 for a 10-day session

1656 Mt Hood Kiwanis Camp
PO Box 206
Rhododendron, OR 97049   503-272-3288

www2.kidscamps.com

Pennsylvania

1657 ARC Allegheny Camping Program
711 Bingham Street
Pittsburgh, PA 15203   412-995-5000
FAX: 412-995-5001
www.arcalleghenycamping.com

Marsha Blanco, C.E.O
Camping program for the mentally and physically disabled.

1658 Briarwood Day Camp
1380 Creek Road
Wycombe, PA 18925   215-598-7143
FAX: 215-602-1060

Ted Levin
A comprehensive day camp providing lunch and transportation for children with disabilities.

1659 Camp AIM
51 McMurray Road
Pittsburgh, PA 15241   412-833-5600

Martin Brocco, Director
Disabled campers.

1660 Camp Joy
3325 Swamp Creek Road
Schweaksville, PA 19473   610-754-6878
FAX: 610-754-7880
www.campjoy.com

Shannon Durante, Camp Director
A year round residential camping program for children and adults with mental retardation and physical disabilities. Brochure, video, and application available upon request. Fee: $128/day, $256/weekend. Shorter and longer camping periods available.

1661 Camp Lee Mar
450 Route 590
Lackawaxen, PA 18435   215-658-1708
FAX: 215-658-1710
e-mail: gtour400@aol.com
www.leemar.com

Lee Morrone, Director
Ariel J. Segal, Assistant Director
A camp for childern with divelopmental challenges, ages 5-21. Offers a program of academics, speech therapy, vocational training and recreation. The academic program is designed to help each child develop skills in the areas of communication, reading and math. Activities include swimming, boating, team sports, tennis and perceptual motor training. Tuition: $5,500 for 7 weeks.

1662 Crestfield
RR 2 Box 71
Slippery Rock, PA 16057

Peter Surgenor
Disabled campers.

1663 Elling Camps

RR 1 Box 54
Thompson, PA 18465

FAX: 717-756-3306

Lloyd E. Elling, Director

For youth ages 6-21 with learning disabilities and accompanying difficulties. This camp allows them to learn to adjust socially in a community atmosphere. The structured camp program includes land and water sports, nature and forestry, industrial arts, construction and work programs, and arts and crafts. Tuition: $2,310 for 3 weeks.

1664 Helping Hands

415 Hoffmansville Road
Bechtelsville, PA 19505   610-754-6491
FAX: 610-754-7157
e-mail: handsinc@aol.com

Bruce McWaters, Director

Provides vocational and recreational programs for individuals with developmental disabilities. Offers support and information to parents, caregivers, and individuals impacted by disabilities.

1665 Ken-Crest Camp

1 Plymouth Meeting
Suite 200
Plymouth Meeting, PA 19462   610-825-9360
FAX: 610-825-4127

William Nolan, Director

Located on a 152-acre site in Pennsylvania, Ken-Crest provides traditional camping experiences to mentally retarded children, ages 7 and up. Among activities are swimming, biking, arts and crafts, music, and nature study. Tuition: $550 for 2 weeks.

1666 Keystone Community Resources

406 N Washington Avenue
Scranton, PA 18503   570-346-7561
FAX: 570-342-3461
e-mail: LCunningham@keycommres.com
www.keycommres.com

Robert Fleese, President
Lisa Cunningham, Director of Admissions

Keystone serves both children and adults in developmental disabilities in a variety of resdiential settings. Support services include 24 hour supervision, on site nursing services, spcoail and therapeutic recreation programs and psychological and psychiatric services.

1667 Make-a-Friend

3975 Conshohocken Avenue
Philadelphia, PA 19131   215-879-1000

Specialized day camp.

1668 Phelps School Summer School

Paoli Pike & Sugartown Roads
Malvern, PA 19355   610-644-1754
FAX: 610-644-6679
e-mail: adms@phelpsschool.org
www.phelpsschool.org

Jim Spiro

Open for grades 7-11 to make up academic deficiencies or complete studies in English, math and reading. Sports include riding, tennis and swimming. A program is also available to a limited number of international students in English as a Second Language. Tuition: $2,800, Day $2,800 for 5 weeks.

1669 Samuel Thompson Scout Camp

Elwyn Institutes
Elwyn, PA 19063

Jon Thompson

Camp is a one part program offered to our disabled residents.

1670 Souderton Special Needs Day Camp

149 Cherry Lane
Souderton, PA 18964   215-723-8555

Donna Huff

Field trips and special events for disabled campers.

1671 Summer Experience

Vanguard School
PO Box 730
Paoli, PA 19301   610-296-6700

Susan Snyder, Admissions Director
John D. Wilson, Education Director

For students who are experiencing learning difficulties due to neurological impairment, social/emotional disturbance and/or autism/pervasive developmental disorder.

1672 Variety Club Camp & Development Center

Variety Club
PO Box 609
Valley Forge and Potshop Roads
Worcester, PA 19490   610-584-4366
FAX: 610-584-5586
e-mail: djfindley@msn.com
www.varietyphila.org

Daniel Findley, Executive Director

Year-round camping and recreation facility for children with special needs and their families. Includes summer camping, aquatics, weekend retreats and other specialty programs.

1673 Wesley Woods

1 Fiddlegreen Road
Grand Valley, PA 16420   814-430-7802

Herb West

Exceptional children's camp for children with emotional and intellectual handicaps.

1674 Yomeca
75 Hill School Road
Douglassville, PA 19518

The YMCA day camp for children ages 9-13. Small group and camp-wide activities are offered. Streams, woods and trails to explore. Children ages 10-12 also have several overnights offered to them during the summer. Children continue to build upon established skills from earlier years, take on more leadership, challenge and responsibility and strengthen past friendships.

South Carolina

1675 Burnt Gin Camp
SC Department of Health and Environmental Control
Box 101106
Columbia, SC 29211   803-898-0455
FAX: 803-898-0613
e-mail: aimonemi@columb60.dhec.state.sc.us
www.state.sc.us

Marie I. Aimone, Camp Director
A residental camp for children who have physical disabilities and/or chronic illnesses. Camper/staff ratio is 2:1. Five seven-day sessions for 7-15 year olds and one six-day sesssion for 16-19 year olds. Limited to residents of South Carolina.

1676 Camp Gravatt
1006 Camp Gravatt Road
Aiken, SC 29805   803-648-1817
FAX: 803-648-7453
e-mail: gravatt@groupz.net

Project adventure includes swimming, fishing, music and art and more in which disabled campers participate. Enjoy the fun and adventure of exploring a river in a canoe in the new canoe program.

Tennessee

1677 Camp Discovery
400 Camp Discovery Lane
Gainesboro, TN 38562   865-558-8271
FAX: 865-450-9560
www2.kidscamps.com

1678 Camp Easter Seal
PO Box nders Ferry Road
Mount Juliet, TN 37122   615-444-2829
FAX: 615-444-8576
www2.kidscamps.com

Texas

1679 Client Assistance Program
7800 Shoal Creek Boulevard
Suite 171-E
Austin, TX 78757   512-454-4816
e-mail: info@advocacyinc.org
www.advocayinc.org

Judith Sokolow, CAP Coordinator

1680 Dallas Academy
950 Tiffany Way
Dallas, TX 75218   214-324-1481
FAX: 214-327-8537
e-mail: mail@dallas-academy.com
www.dallas-academy.com

Jim Richardson, Director
7-week summer session for students who are having difficulty in regular school classes.

1681 Gilmont Program Center
PO Box 254
Route 6
Gilmer, TX 75644   903-797-3639
FAX: 903-797-6400
e-mail: cgilmonttpc@aol.com

Tom Truitt, Director
Outdoor adventures for disabled campers which makes use of the center's twin lakes.

1682 Hill School of Fort Worth
4817 Odessa Avenue
Fort Worth, TX 76133   817-923-9482
FAX: 817-923-4894
e-mail: admission@hillschool.org
www.hillschool.org

Lucille H. Helton, Principal
Cathy Allen, Admissions Director
Grey Owens, Principal

Provides an alternative learning environment for students having average or above-average intelligence with learning differences. Hill school is an established leader in North Texas with a 25 year history of effectively serving LD children. Beginning in 1961 as a tutorial service, Hill became a formal school in 1973. Our mission is to help those who learn differently develop skills and strategies to succeed. We do this by developing academic/study skills, and self-discipline Tuition: $6600-6900.

1683 Hughen Center
2849 9th Avenue
Port Arthur, TX 77642   409-983-6659
FAX: 409-983-6408

Jeff Kuchar, Executive Director
The Center provides a therapeutic, educational, and recreational program for children with physical disabilities. Physical and occupational therapy are featured. Day and residential.

1684 Sweeney

PO Box 918
Gainesville, TX   76241   940-665-9502
                                 FAX: 940-665-2833
                        e-mail: info@campsweeney.org
                              www.campsweeney.org

Marlene E. Gray, Foundation Development Director

Teaches self-care and self-reliance to children with diabetes. Campers participate in such activities such as swimming, fishing, horseback riding, arts and crafts while learning about diabetes and how to cope with it. Tuition: $450 for 1 week; $1,400 for 3 weeks.

1685 Texas 4-H Center

RR 1 Box 527
Brownwood, TX   76801   915-784-5482

E.L. Copeland

Leadership activities and personal growth.

1686 Texas Lions Camp

Lions Clubs of Texas
PO Box 290247
Kerrville, TX   78029   830-896-8500
                               FAX: 830-896-3666
                           e-mail: tlc@ktc.com
                              www.lionscamp.com

Stephen Mabry, Executive Director
Amber Schrank, Program Director

The primary purpose of the League shall be to provide, without charge, a camp for physically disabled, hearing/vision impaired and diabetic children from the State of Texas, regardless of race, religion, or national origin. Our goal is to create an atmosphere wherein campers will learn the can do philosophy and be allowed to achieve maximum personal growth and self-esteem. The camp welcomes boys and girls ages 7-16.

Utah

1687 Camp Kostopulos

2500 Emigration Canyon
Salt Lake City, UT   84108   801-582-0700
                                    FAX: 801-583-5176
                                    www.campk.org

Gary Ethington, Director

One of only a few camps in the Intermountain region that provides recreational opportunities for individuals of all ages with mental or physical disabilities. Activities include fifteen days of swimming, fishing, fieldtrips, nature study, arts and crafts and traditional outdoor adventure games. Five year-round programs offered.

1688 Utada Camp

American Diabetes Association
250 East Third South
Suite 110
Salt Lake City, UT   84111   801-363-3024
                                    FAX: 801-363-3031
                          e-mail: gburns@diabetes.org
                                www.diabetes.org

Gayle Burns, Field Services Associate
Campers with diabetes aged 6-17.

Vermont

1689 Bennington School

992 Fairview Street
Bennington, VT   05201   802-447-1557
                                800-639-3156
                           FAX: 802-447-3234

Patrick Ramsay, Admissions Director
Jeff LaBonte, Executive Director

A 115 bed residential treatment center serving emotionally and behaviorally disordered adolescent male and female students. Offer a fully accredited on-grounds educational program in addition to comprehensive clinical and residential components. The beautiful rural setting provides many recreational opportunities as well as cultural experiences.

1690 Farm and Wilderness Camps

HCR 70 Box 27
Plymouth, VT   05056   802-422-3761

                       www2.kidscamps.com

1691 Silver Towers Camp

Goshen Road
Ripton, VT   05766   802-442-0979
                            FAX: 802-442-4675
                     e-mail: graymgt@sover.net
                          www.silvertowers.com

Dr. Valeri Allen, Camp Director
Brenda Metcalf, Office Manager

1692 Thorpe Camp

Rural Route 3 Box 3314
Goshen, VT   05733   802-247-6611

                       www2.kidscamps.com

Virginia

1693 Camp Baker Services

7600 Beach Road
Chesterfield, VA   23838   804-748-4789
                                  FAX: 804-796-6880

Melissa Wahers, Director
Jolene Loving, Assistant Director
Heather Elliot, Administrative Assistant

Year round support services for children and adults with disabilities. Operated by the Richmond Area ARC, programs include: an 8-week summer camp program; weekend congregate respite services; summer day camp (8 wks); spring fling (spring break).

1694 Camp Easter Seal - East,Camp Easter Seal- West
201 East Main Street
Salem, VA 24153 540-362-1656
800-365-1656
FAX: 540-563-8928
www.campeasterseal-va.org

Deborah Duerk, Director
Devin Brown, Director

Six and 12 day summer camp sessions for children and adults ages 5 and older with physical disabilities, cognitive disabilities, sensory impairments. Therapeutic recreation activities including swimming, fishing, sports, horseback riding, rock climbing, and more. 26 speech therapy camp children with disabilities ages 8-16. 12 day Spina Bifida Self Help Skills Camp.

1695 Camp Holiday Trails
PO Box 5806
Charlottesville, VA 22905 804-977-3781
FAX: 804-977-8814
e-mail: Cht@firstva.com

Mark D. Andersen, Executive Director

Private, nonprofit camp for children with special health needs, various chronic illnesses. Residential, 2 week sessions are open July 1 - August 10, $500 per 2 weeks; camperships are available. Coed 7-17, nationwide and international. Canoeing, swimming, horseback riding, arts and crafts, drama, ropes course, etc. 24-hr. medical supervision by doctor and nursing staff. Air conditioned cabins. $500/2w session.

1696 Loudoun County Parks & Recreation and Community Services Special Recreation Programs
PO Box 7000
Leesburg, VA 20177 703-777-0343

e-mail: pers@co.loudoun.va.us
www.co.loudoun.va.us

Kate Trask, Special Recreation
Jen Montgomery, Special Recreation

Offers and promotes integration opportunities for individuals with disabilities. Coordinates ADA issues and Very Special Arts and Special Olympics for Loudoun County. Summer camps, sports, socials and community trips.

1697 Makemie Woods Camp Conference Retreat
PO Box 39
Barhamsville, VA 23011
800-566-1496
FAX: 757-566-8003
www.makemiewoods.org

Michelle Burcher, Director

Counselors serve as teachers, friends and activity leaders. The individual is important within the small group. No camper is lost in the crowd, but is an integral partner in the group process. Residential Christian Camp and conference center. Summer camp for children 8-18 special camp for children with diabetes. $60-$280.

1698 Oakland School & Camp
Boyd Tavern
Keswick, VA 22947 804-293-9059
FAX: 804-296-8930
e-mail: www.oaklandschool.net
oaklandschool@earthlink.net

Joanne Dondero, President
Carol Smieciuch, Director

A highly individualized program stresses improving reading ability. Subjects taught are reading, English composition, math and word analysis. Recreational activities include horseback riding, sports, swimming, tennis, crafts, archery and camping. For girls and boys, ages 8-14. Tuition: boarding; $5275.00 day; $2765.00 for 7 weeks.

1699 Overlook
RR 1 Box 203
Keezletown, VA 22832 540-269-2267

Ronald Robey

A Christian life experience for youth and children, located at the base of the scenic Massanutten Mountains.

1700 Wingaroo
2600 Danieltown Road
Goochland, VA 23063 804-457-4798

Jean Wootton
Disabled campers.

Washington

1701 Camp Easter Seal West
PO Box 289
17809 Souith Vaughn Road KPN
Vaughn, WA 98394 253-884-2722
FAX: 253-884-0200
e-mail: campd@seals.org

West Virginia

1702 Mountain Milestones Stepping Stones
15 Cottage Street
Morgantown, WV 26501 304-296-0150
800-982-8799
FAX: 304-296-0194
e-mail: stepping@westco.net
www2.kidscamps.com

Missy Weimex, Recreation Coordinator

Non-profit organization that serves individuals with disabilities. Programs include recreation, summer camps, technology and speech therapy.

1703 Mountaineer Spina Bifida Camp
350 Capital Street
Room 427
Charleston, WV   25301   304-558-7098
                                 800-642-9704
                          FAX: 304-558-2866
                          www2.kidscamps.com

1704 Oak Leaf Camp
Jackson's Mill
Weston, WV   26452

Ray Beam
Program geared to the physically disabled.

Wisconsin

1705 Easter Seal Camp Wawbeek
N9888 Highway 13 N
Wisconsin Dells, WI   53965   608-277-8288
                                 800-422-2324
                          FAX: 608-277-8333
            e-mail: wawbeek@wi-easterseals.org
                    www.wi-easterseals.org

Kenneth Saville, VP Camp and Respite Services
Karen Sullivan, Respite Coordinator
Chris Hollan, Director Of camp And Respite

Disabled campers. Offers adventure programs, camp sessions for other health agencies, family camp opportunities and year round respite sessions.

1706 Timbertop Nature Adventure Camp
7290 County MM
Amherst Junction, WI   54407

For children who can benefit from an individualized program of learning in a non-competitive outdoor setting under the skilled leadership of people who understand the environment and the unique potential of these children.

1707 Triangle D Camp for Children
1724 W Main Street
Lake Geneva, WI   53147   414-248-1330

Marilyn Caras
Disabled campers.

1708 Wisconsin Badger Camp
PO Box 240
Platteville, WI   53818   608-348-9689
                          FAX: 608-348-9737
                          e-mail: wbc@pcii.net

Todd Holman, Executive Director

Mission is to provide a positive natural environment where developmentally challenged individuals can learn about their surroundings and realize their full potential. All developmentally disabled individuals, regardless of the severity of their disability or inability to pay are welcome. One week: $265.

1709 Wisconsin Lions Camp
3834 County Road A
Rosholt, WI   54473   715-677-4761

             e-mail: lioncamp@wi-net.com

Russell Link, Camp Director
Serves children who have either a visual, hearing or mild cognitive disability. Many of the children also have multiple disabilities or medical conditions. Program activities include sailing, ropes course, bike and canoe trips, environmental education, swimming, camping, canoeing, outdoor living skills and handicrafts. ACA accredited, located in central Wisconsin, near Stevens Point.

Dresses & Skirts

1710 Budget Cotton/Poly Open Back Gown

Buck & Buck
3111 27th Avenue South
Seattle, WA 98144

800-458-0600

Short raglan sleeves, lace at neck and bodice.
$11.00

1711 Budget Flannel Open Back Gown

Buck & Buck
3111 27th Avenue South
Seattle, WA 98144

800-458-0600

3/4 raglan sleeve, lace at neck and bodice. *$13.00*

1712 Cotton/Poly Nancy Frocks

Buck & Buck
3111 27th Avenue South
Seattle, WA 98144

800-458-0600

Comes in short and long sleeves, assorted florals
and plaids. *$35.00*

1713 Dusters

Buck & Buck
3111 27th Avenue South
Seattle, WA 98144

800-458-0600

Three types: Floral, Budget Better. Snap front
styles and gathered yokes, flannel $16.00-$24.00.

1714 Flannel Gowns

Buck & Buck
3111 27th Avenue South
Seattle, WA 98144

800-458-0600

Comes in long or short with a deep button-front
opening for ease of slipping on. Shorter long
length. *$16.50*

1715 Fleece Cape/Poncho

Laurel Designs
5 Laurel Avenue
Belvedere, CA 94920

FAX: 415-435-1451
e-mail: laureld@ncal.verio.com

Janet Sawyer, Co-Owner
Lynn Montoya, Co-Owner

Warm and cozy high insulated cape with hood for
wheelchair users, zip front, velcro side closure, self
belt. All sizes and a variety of colors. *$53.00*

1716 Float Dress

Buck & Buck
3111 27th Avenue South
Seattle, WA 98144

800-458-0600

A safe bet for everyone from a size medium to a
6X. Gathered yoke front and back and literally
yards of fabric for fullness. Come in cotton or
polyester. *$34.00*

1717 Muu Muu

Buck & Buck
3111 27th Avenue South
Seattle, WA 98144

800-458-0600

Comes in long and short styles, assorted bright
floral prints. $20.00-$22.00.

1718 Polyester Nancy Frocks

Buck & Buck
3111 27th Avenue South
Seattle, WA 98144

800-458-0600

Comes in short and long sleeves, assorted florals.
$ 35.00

Footwear

1719 Acrylic Leg Warmers

Buck & Buck
3111 27th Avenue South
Seattle, WA 98144

800-458-0600

Recommended for large or swollen legs where
knee socks are too restrictive. *$7.00*

1720 Adult Acorn Polartec Socks

Special Clothes
PO Box 333
East Harwich, MA 02645

508-896-7939
FAX: 508-896-7939
TDY:508-896-7939
e-mail: specialclo@aol.com
www.special-clothes.com

These plush socks are made of Polartec fleece for
unparalleled softness and comfort. The mid-calf
length keeps feet and lower legs warmer than any
conventional sock, and the fabric has 2 way
stretch to minimize binding. Polartec fleece is a
remarkable light-weight fabric which breathes
and insulates. Machine washable, of course. 100%
Polartec fleece. Made in USA. Colors: solid black
or charcoal print. *$18.00*

Per pair

1721 Adult Acorn Slippers

Special Clothes
PO Box 333
East Harwich, MA   02645   508-896-7939
                                  FAX: 508-896-7939
                                  TDY:508-896-7939
                    e-mail: specialclo@aol.com
                    www.special-clothes.com

These great looking, beautifully made slipper shoes keep chilly feet warm and comfortable. The sole is cut of fine suede leather, and the uppers and insoles are soft, plush Polartec fleece. The knit cuff at the ankle opens wide to slip on easily, yet is snug enough to keep the slippers in place. Machine washable. Polartec fleece, suede sole, acrylic cuff. Made in USA. Colors: burgundy with navy cuff or dark green with navy cuff. *$30.00*

Per pair

1722 Booties with Non-Skid Soles

Buck & Buck
3111 27th Avenue South
Seattle, WA   98144
                              800-458-0600

Acrylic knit or quilted cotton/poly and shearling inner. *$17.00*

1723 Foot Snugglers

Buck & Buck
3111 27th Avenue South
Seattle, WA   98144
                              800-458-0600

Quilted poly/cotton outers lined with plush shearling pile, provide a thick comfortable cushion which helps minimize the pressure points on tender areas. *$23.00*

1724 Lok-Tie Shoe Laces

Laurel Designs
5 Laurel Avenue
Belvedere, CA   94920
                    FAX: 415-435-1451
                    e-mail: laureld@ncal.verio.com

Janet Sawyer, Co-Owner
Lynn Montoya, Co-Owner

Specially designed slide locks laces in place. Can be used with one hand. Stretch laces allow maximum comfort. *$4.00*

1725 TRV-Mold Shoes

49 Lasalle Avenue
Buffalo, NY   14214
                              716-837-6663
                              800-843-6653
                    FAX: 716-837-3867

Paul Ross, Marketing Director
Husain Syed, Production Manager

Custom made fully molded shoes, relieve pressure in sensitive areas by taking all of the weight off the painful areas. *$ 350.00*

1726 Terrycloth Slippers

Buck & Buck
3111 27th Avenue South
Seattle, WA   98144
                              800-458-0600

Lines cotton/poly terrycloth upper with sewn-on, non-skid sole. *$18.00*

1727 Velcro Booties

Buck & Buck
3111 27th Avenue South
Seattle, WA   98144
                              800-458-0600

The high-domed toe, and extra-wide, non-skid sole design accommodates virtually every foot related problem. *$18.00*

1728 Velcro Sneaker

Buck & Buck
3111 27th Avenue South
Seattle, WA   98144
                              800-458-0600

Two velcro straps, nylon upper, rubber sole. *$22.00*

1729 Washable Shoes

Buck & Buck
3111 27th Avenue South
Seattle, WA   98144
                              800-458-0600

Vinyl upper with velcro closure, Non skid sole. *$18.00*

Jackets

1730 Fleece Bed Jacket

Buck & Buck
3111 27th Avenue South
Seattle, WA   98144
                              800-458-0600

Full snap front opening and collar. Assorted bright colors and pastel prints. *$22.00*

1731 Jackets

Special Clothes
PO Box 333
East Harwich, MA   02645   508-896-7939
                                  FAX: 508-896-7939
                                  TDY:508-896-7939
                    e-mail: specialclo@aol.com
                    www.special-clothes.com

Judith Sweeney, Owner

Available styles include a unique back opening jacket designed to fit easily over contractures and for wheelchair comfort. Prices range from $72.00-$89.00.

1732 Rain Poncho
Laurel Designs
5 Laurel Avenue
Belvedere, CA 94920
FAX: 415-435-1451
e-mail: laureld@ncal.verio.com

Janet Sawyer, Co-Owner
Lynn Montoya, Co-Owner
A favorite, this rain poncho slips on in a hurry to keep you dry. All sizes and a variety of colors. *$39.00*

1733 Wheelchair Ponchos
Special Clothes
PO Box 333
East Harwich, MA 02645   508-896-7939
FAX: 508-896-7939
TDY:508-896-7939
e-mail: specialclo@aol.com
www.special-clothes.com

Judith Sweeney, Owner
These ponchos are cut shorter in the back for wheelchair comfort. Prices range from $76.00-$95.00.

Miscellaneous & Catalogs

1734 AMI - Accessories for Mobile Independence
5235 Mission Oaks Boulevard
381
Camarillo, CA 93012
FAX: 805-987-8653

Gay Dawson, Owner
Ponchos, tote bags, gloves, and sweat pants for wheelchair-using consumers.

1735 Adaptive Clothing - Adults
Special Clothes
PO Box 333
East Harwich, MA 02645   508-896-7939
FAX: 508-896-7939
TDY:508-896-7939
e-mail: specialslo@aol.com
www.special-clothes.com

Judith Sweeney, President
Special Clothes produces a catalogue of garments for adults with disabilities and/or incontinence. Offerings include: undergarments, snap-crotch tee shirts, sleepwear, jumpsuits, bibs, and some footwear. The catalogue is available without charge. Comparable to department store prices. Special Clothes produces a catalog of adaptive clothing for children in sizes from toddler through young adults. A full line of clothing is included from undergarments through wheelchair jackets and ponchos.

1736 Adrian's Closet
PO Box 9506
Rancho Santa Fe, CA 92067
800-831-2577
FAX: 619-759-0578
e-mail: adrians@electriciti.com
Fashions for the physically challenged child. Clothing offers Velcro closures, front pockets, concealed back openings and fashions for seated posture.

1737 Adult Long Jumpsuit with Feet
Special Clothes
PO Box 333
East Harwich, MA 02645   508-896-7939
FAX: 508-896-7939
TDY:508-896-7939
e-mail: specialclo@aol.com
www.special-clothes.com

A full snap crotch for full access. For safety, feet have non-skid bottoms. 100% cotton knit. Made in USA. Also, identical in style, but are made of fleece for extra warmth. Fleece fabric is soft 100% cotton, and is available in Medium Blue only. Made in USA. Options on fleece jumpsuits available for additional charge. Long knit jumpsuit with feet: #A2051; Long fleece jumpsuit: #A2032; Long fleece jumpsuit with feet: #A2052.

$52 - $61

1738 Adult Short Jumpsuit
Special Clothes
PO Box 333
East Harwich, MA 02645   508-896-7939
FAX: 508-896-7939
TDY:508-896-7939
e-mail: specialclo@aol.com
www.special-clothes.com

This pull-on jumpsuit provides comfort and full coverage without bulk. Wide leg ribbing ends at mid-thigh, with snaps at the crotch. We use fine quality, comfortable cotton knit. 100% cotton knit. Made in USA. Option: long sleeves - add $3.00. Colors: white, navy, teal, light blue, light pink, red, burgundy, royal blue, and black. Sm & Med: $36.50/3 for $104.00; L & XL: $39.00/3 for $111.25; and XXL: $42.00/3 for $119.25.

1739 Bibs
Special Clothes
PO Box 333
East Harwich, MA 02645   508-896-7939
FAX: 508-896-7939
TDY:508-896-7939
e-mail: specialclo@aol.com
www.special-clothes.com

Judith Sweeney, Owner
A variety of bib styles are available to protect clothing inconspicuously.

$13 - $16.50

169

1740 Body Suits

Special Clothes
PO Box 333
East Harwich, MA   02645   508-896-7939
                                 FAX: 508-896-7939
                                 TDY:508-896-7939
                      e-mail: specialclo@aol.com
                      www.special-clothes.com

Judith Sweeney, Owner

These are one piece garments that can be used to protect skin under braces, to add warmth and to shield incisions. Prices range from $18.25-22.50.

1741 Buck and Buck Clothing

3111 27th Avenue South
Seattle, WA   98144   206-722-4196
                             800-458-0600
                      FAX: 206-722-1144
                      e-mail: julie@buckandbuck.com
                      www.buckandbuck.com

Julie & Bill Buck, Co-Owners

Clothing for the disabled and elderly.

45 pages

1742 Carolyn's

PO Box 14577
Bradenton, FL   34280   941-739-0433
                               800-648-2266
                      FAX: 941-761-8306

Carolyn Tojek, President

Free mail-order catalog of items for visually impaired people.

1743 Carryall Pocket Smock

Laurel Designs
5 Laurel Avenue
Belvedere, CA   94920
                      FAX: 415-435-1451
                      e-mail: laureld@ncal.verio.com

Janet Sawyer, Co-Owner
Lynn Montoya, Co-Owner

Carry your things with ease. Five various sized pockets keep things at hand. One size fits all. *$25.00*

1744 Cotton Stockings

Buck & Buck
3111 27th Avenue South
Seattle, WA   98144
                             800-458-0600

Come in regular and snug-fit, cover leg to mid-thigh and work well for swollen legs. *$7.00*

1745 Dressing Tips and Clothing Resources for Making Life Easier

Making Life Esier
933 Chapel Hill Road
Madison, WI   53711
                      FAX: 608-274-6993
                      e-mail: help@makinglifeeasier.com
                      www.makinglifeeasier.com

Shelley Peterman Schwarz

Learn hundreds of tips and techniques to making dressing easier. Learn how to adapt/modify ready-to-wear garments to make dressing easier. And, find out where to locate more than 100 resources offering specially designed or adapted clothing for men, women and children. *$ 22.95*

1746 Easy Dressing Fashions: J.C. Penney

6501 Legacy Drive
Plano, TX   75024   972-431-8676
                           FAX: 972-431-9103

Natalie Torre, Marketing Manager

This is an entire collection of women's and men's fashions that are designed for easy wear, easy care and complete comfort. Plus, a selection of women's apparel with velcro brand wavelock fasteners.

1747 Exquisite Egronomic Protective Wear

Plum Enterprises
PO Box 85
Valley Forge, PA   19481   610-783-7377
                                  FAX: 610-783-7577
                      e-mail: lynn@plument.com
                      www.plument.com

Janice Carrington, President

Egronomic Protective Wear; ProtectaCap custom-fitting headgear has earned an unparalleled reputation for quality, safety, and comfort. ProtectaCap+Plus technologically-advanced protective headgear closes the gap between hard and soft helmets. Comes with optional ProtectaChin Guard and new sporty design. Protecthip protective undergarment is the intelligent, innovative solution to the problem of hip injuries for both men and women. Laies' styles are covered with attractive stretch lace.

1748 Fashion Ease Division of MRR Health Care Apparel Company

1541 60th Street
Brooklyn, NY   11219
                                  800-221-8929
                      FAX: 718-436-2067
                      e-mail: fashionease.com@aol
                      www.fashionease.com

Helen Bencie, Buyer

Adaptive apparel and footwear for people who require ease in dressing.

28 pages

1749 Forde's Functional Fashions

225 S Meramec Avenue
Suite 925
Saint Louis, MO   63105   314-721-7705
                                 800-531-7705
                      FAX: 314-721-7705
                      e-mail: fashions@fordes.com
                      www.fordes.com

Patricia Forde, President

A fashion forward line of easy to wear clothing and accessories for men, women and children. Items include, sportswear, outerwear, ponchos, robes, sleepwear. Dresses, wheelchair bags, walker bags and more. Hard to find specialty items for many special needs. Designs for people who use wheelchairs. Velcro closures if buttons are a problem. Fun clothing protectors too. Choose from our terrific assortment of fabrics and colors to suit all your fashion needs in simply functional style.

1750 HEADLINER

Designs for Comfort
PO Box 671044
Marietta, GA   30066   **770-565-8246**
                                 800-443-9226
                          FAX: 877-350-0501
          e-mail: headliner@mindspring.com

Curt Maurer, President
Lynne Davis, VP Marketing

A patented cap and hairpiece combination, the Headliner is both a quick, stylish coverup and an upbeat wig alternative for women experiencing hair care problems or hair loss. Ideal for social gatherings and outdoor activities as well as for sleeping and hospital stays. *$ 25.00*

1751 Hidden Assets

530 E 76th Street
Apartment 18H
New York, NY   10021
                          FAX: 212-439-0694

Ellen Pekarsky, President

Offers lingerie and undergarments for the physically challenged, giving comfort and security.

1752 JC Distributors

6442 NW 64th Avenue
Ocala, FL   34482
                          FAX: 351-620-9362

Cara Lam, President/ CEO

We carry stylish 100% cotton knit and terry cloth turbans. Our turbans come in a wide variety of colors and different styles. We also customize and make special orders. Bulk orders are welcome call for pricing.

1753 Just for You Fashions

796 Busch Center
Columbus, OH   43229   **614-846-6133**
                                 800-445-8474
                          FAX: 614-846-0373

LeAnn Horn, President

Specialize in clothing for people that are confined to a wheel chair or have difficulty dressing.

1754 Knee Socks

Buck & Buck
3111 27th Avenue South
Seattle, WA   98144
                                 800-458-0600

Comes in regular and large size. *$3.50*

1755 Laurel Designs Catalog

Laurel Designs
5 Laurel Avenue
Belvedere, CA   94920   **415-435-1891**
                          FAX: 415-435-1451
          e-mail: laureld@ncal.verio.com

Janet Sawyer, Owner
Lynn Montoya, Owner

Clothing for wheelchair users including rain wear, panchos and fleece capes. Other items include quality carrying bags for wheelchairs, walkers, crutches, accessories, and cookbooks of four ingredients only recipes. Home remodeling video 'Building & Remodeling for Accessibility', reacher and large print dictionary.

8 pages BiAnnual

1756 M&M Health Care Apparel Company

Fashion Collection
1541 60th Street
Brooklyn, NY   11219   **718-871-8188**
                                 800-221-8929
                          FAX: 718-436-2067
          e-mail: fashionese.com

Abraham Klein, President

Specialized clothing for disabled people.

Yearly

1757 No-Run Nylon Stockings

Buck & Buck
3111 27th Avenue South
Seattle, WA   98144
                                 800-458-0600

A full-length, heavy-weight stocking. *$2.25*

1758 Professional Fit Clothing

831 North Lake Street
 # 1
Burbank, CA   91502   **818-563-1975**
                                 800-422-2348
                          FAX: 818-563-1834
          e-mail: kurt@professionalfit.com
                 www.professionalfit.com

Tom Pirruccello, President
Kurt Rieback, CFO

Professional fit clothing caters to homes that care for people with developmental disabilities and individuals who are physically challenged. Our clothing is fashionable, affordable and can be adapted to each persons special need. There is a free catalog.

20 pages

1759 Quilted Waterproof Bib

Buck & Buck
3111 27th Avenue South
Seattle, WA   98144
                                 800-458-0600

Made with a nylon backing, these attractive bibs will not soak through like most others, protecting clothing from stains. *$15.00*

1760 Rolli Moden

12225 World Trade Drive
Suite T
San Diego, CA   92128

800-707-2395
e-mail: rm@rolli-moden.com
www.rolli-moden.com

A line of fashionable clothing for adult wheelchair users availablee.

1761 Special Clothes Adult Catalogue

Special Clothes
PO Box 333
E Harwich, MA   02645

508-896-7939
FAX: 508-896-7939
TDY:508-896-7939
e-mail: specialclo@aol.com
www.special-clothes.com

Judith Sweeney, President

Produces a catalogue of adaptive clothing for adults with disabilities. Offers include undergarments, casual bottoms, jumpsuits, sleepwear, swimwear, footwear, and bibs. Prices are comparable to deparment store prices. The catalogue is free.

1-14 pages

1762 Special Clothes for Special Children

PO Box 333
East Harwich, MA   02645

508-432-8014
FAX: 508-896-7939
TDY:508-896-7939
e-mail: specialclo@aol.com
www.special-clothes.com

Judith Sweeney, Owner

Offers a variety of clothes for disabled children ranging from casual unisex clothes to undergarments. Clothing offers velcro closures, adjustable waistbands, drop-front briefs, wheelchair ponchos and more.

1763 Specialty Care Shoppe

16126 East 161st Street S
Bixby, OK   74008

918-366-1208
FAX: 918-366-1208
e-mail: deb@specialtycareshoppe.com
www.specialtycareshoppe.com

Deb Marshall, Ownder

Catalog of attractive, affordable clothing and accessories for adults with special needs. Includes items for edema, incontinence, Alzheimers, limited mobility, and hand impairment.

1764 Super Stretch Socks

Buck & Buck
3111 27th Avenue South
Seattle, WA   98144

800-458-0600

This sock has been improved to stretch laterally throughout the foot area as well as at the top. *$3.75*

1765 Swimwear

Special Clothes
PO Box 333
East Harwich, MA   02645

508-896-7939
FAX: 508-896-7939
TDY:508-896-7939
e-mail: specialclo@aol.com
www.special-clothes.com

Judith Sweeney, Owner

Cotton lycra swimsuits are available in boys and girls styles from size toddler - teen. One piece, designed to completely cover a diaper.

1766 Trisha's of Acton

PO Box 599
Acton, MA   01720

978-263-9318
877-955-5551
FAX: 978-263-4555
e-mail: trishas@tiac.net
www.trishasofacton.com

K. Julie McCarthy, President

Clothing and accessories that provide dignity, freedom of movement and independence for the physically challenged. Terrific gift ideas!

1767 White River Industries

PO Box 40
Cotter, AR   72626

870-435-6000
800-643-5656
FAX: 870-435-2062

Lorene Langley, Customer Service

Primarily easy-on, easy-off durable and fashionable clothing designed for people with physical challenges due to age, disability or cognitive limitations. *$25.00*

1768 Wishing Wells Clothing Collection

11684 Ventura Boulevard
965
Studio City, CA   91604

818-840-6919
FAX: 818-760-3878
e-mail: FABC@dawnwells.com
DawnWells.com

Dawn Wells, Owner
Lorraine Parker, General Manager

Features designs full of back overlap construction and all velcro closures clothing.

Robes & Sleepwear

1769   Adult Snap Front Sleeper

Special Clothes
PO Box 333
East Harwich, MA   02645   508-896-7939
FAX: 508-896-7939
TDY:508-896-7939
e-mail: specialclo@aol.com
www.special-clothes.com

This soft, comfortable, one piece garment is designed for easy dressing and full access. The top fastens down the front with snaps. The bottom section folds up from the back, and snaps to the waist. 100% cotton knit. Made in USA. Option, short sleeves - add $1.00. Colors: white, navy, teal, light blue, light pink, red, burgudy, royal blue, and black. Sm & Med: $36.50/ 3 for $104.00; L & XL: $39.00/ 3 for $111.25; XXL: $42.00/3 for $119.75.

1770   Chamois Shower Robe

Buck & Buck
3111 27th Avenue South
Seattle, WA   98144

800-458-0600

Totally covers a man or woman being wheeled to and from the shower or bath. Having test washed several fabrics, the chamois beat terry cloth for comfort, durability and faster drying time in the laundry. $34.00

1771   Creative Designs

Barbara Arnold
3704 Carlisle Court
Modesto, CA   95356   209-523-3166
800-335-4852
FAX: 209-523-5893
e-mail: robes4you@aol.com
www.robes4you.com

Barbara Arnold, Owner

Designer of the original Change-A-Robe and the new Handi-Robe, which allows the wearer to put it on without having to stand up. Robes are designed especially for physically challenged, disabled individuals, and wheelchair users.

1772   Flannel Pajamas

Buck & Buck
3111 27th Avenue South
Seattle, WA   98144

800-458-0600

$18.00

1773   Fleece Robe

Buck & Buck
3111 27th Avenue South
Seattle, WA   98144

800-458-0600

All with full-length, snap-front opening, patch pockets, short and long. Short: $39.00.

1774   His & Hers

Wishing Wells Collection
11684 Ventura Boulevard
Suite 965
Studio City, CA   91604   818-840-6919
FAX: 818-760-3878
www.dawnwishingwells

This sleep shirt is designed for him or her.

1775   Nightshirts

Buck & Buck
3111 27th Avenue South
Seattle, WA   98144

800-458-0600

Come in flannel or cotton patterns and prints in sizes S-XL, of men. *$16.00*

1776   Open Back Nightshirts

Buck & Buck
3111 27th Avenue South
Seattle, WA   98144

800-458-0600

Come in cotton or flannel (sizes S-XL). *$18.00*

1777   Terrycloth Robes

Buck & Buck
3111 27th Avenue South
Seattle, WA   98144

800-458-0600

Two pockets, sash belts, assorted colors. *$36.00*

Shirts & Tops

1778   Adult Pull-On Feeding Bib

Special Clothes
PO Box 333
East Harwich, MA   02645   508-896-7939
FAX: 508-896-7939
TDY:508-896-7939
e-mail: specialclo@aol.com
www.special-clothes.com

This basic bib does a great job of protecting clothing from messy food and drink spills. It is constructed of sturdy, rib knit neckband which slips on comfortably. The front pocket catches food particles, and is fastened at both sides with Velcro for easy cleaning. 100% nylon with nechband of 100% cotton rib. Made in USA. Colors: white or light blue. One size: 17 inches wide, & 23 inches from shoulder to bottom. *$15.00*

1779   Avoid Eye Strain, Feel it T-Shirt

Sense-Sations
919 Walnut Street
Philadelphia, PA   19107   215-629-2990
800-876-5456

This slogan is printed in raised writing boldly across the front of our T-shirt. *$5.95*

1780 Basic Rear Closure Sweat Top

Buck & Buck
3111 27th Avenue South
Seattle, WA 98144

800-458-0600

Top opens completely down the back for ease of dressing with velcro tab closures. *$20.50*

1781 Cotton Full-Back Vest

Buck & Buck
3111 27th Avenue South
Seattle, WA 98144

800-458-0600

Wide shoulder straps that don't slide off shoulders. *$ 4.50*

1782 Dutch Neck T-Shirt

Buck & Buck
3111 27th Avenue South
Seattle, WA 98144

800-458-0600

Stretchy neck makes it easy to get over the head. *$5.50*

1783 Open Back T-Shirts

Buck & Buck
3111 27th Avenue South
Seattle, WA 98144

800-458-0600

Velcro tabs down the back. *$8.00*

1784 Printed Rear Closure Sweat Top

Buck & Buck
3111 27th Avenue South
Seattle, WA 98144

800-458-0600

Comes in assorted colors, plain or with animal motifs. *$33.00*

1785 Rear Closure Shirts

Buck & Buck
3111 27th Avenue South
Seattle, WA 98144

800-458-0600

Velcro tabs down the back on T-shirts and Dress shirts. *$24.00*

1786 Rear Closure T-Shirt

Buck & Buck
3111 27th Avenue South
Seattle, WA 98144

800-458-0600

Closes down the back with velcro tabs. *$8.50*

1787 Serape

Laurel Designs
5 Laurel Avenue
Belvedere, CA 94920

FAX: 415-435-1451
e-mail: laureld@ncal.verio.com

Janet Sawyer, Co-Owner
Lynn Montoyo, Co-Owner

This unique sleeveless thermal vest is designed for active wheelchair persons. Multi-colored, one size fits all. *$30.00*

1788 T Shirt is Done in Braille: Read Gently

Sense-Sations
919 Walnut Street
Philadelphia, PA 19107

215-629-2990
800-876-5456

This slogan is printed in raised writing and braille dots. *$5.95*

Slacks & Pants

1789 Comanche Pants

Wheelies Bentwear
PO Box 455
Roseburg, OR 97470

541-673-8291
FAX: 541-673-8719

Alice King, Store Manager
Leslie Bozovich, Customer Service

An innovative answer to dressing a person who cannot stand. These pants are sculptured to provide total coverage. A new freedom in dressing; easy for attendant or for self-dressing. They can be put on a seated person right in the chair with no lifting or standing. *$35.00*

1790 Jumpsuits

Special Clothes
PO Box 333
East Harwich, MA 02645

508-896-7939
FAX: 508-896-7939
TDY:508-896-7939
e-mail: specialclo@aol.com
www.special-clothes.com

Judith Sweeney, Owner

Several styles of one-piece garments are available for dressing ease. Front opening styles are designed for easy access. Prices range from $32.20-$44.00.

1791 Knit Pants

Special Clothes
PO Box 333
East Harwich, MA 02645

508-896-7939
FAX: 508-896-7939
TDY:508-896-7939
e-mail: specialclo@aol.com
www.special-clothes.com

Offers the best in comfort and convience. Designed with a longer crotch and wider seat for a great fit. The elasticized waistband contains a hidden drawstring for size adjustments, and pockets are placed low for easy access while sitting. Order a full Snap Crotch (Option #1), for full access. Available in soft, 100% cotton knit. Made in USA. Colors: Light blue, teal, light pink, burgundy, navy, and black. Sm & Med: $41.00; L & XL $45.00; XXL $48.00. Add full snap crotch.

1792 Pants & Slacks
Special Clothes
PO Box 333
East Harwich, MA 02645   508-896-7939
                             FAX: 508-896-7939
                             TDY:508-896-7939
                e-mail: specialclo@aol.com
                www.special-clothes.com

Judith Sweeney, Owner
A variety of pant and skirt styles is available in sizes 2 toddler - 18 teen. These include straight leg and baggy jeans, drop front pleated dress pants, knit pants, shorts and skirted leggings. Prices range from $16.50-$44.00.

1793 Side Velcro Slacks
Buck & Buck
3111 27th Avenue South
Seattle, WA 98144
                             800-458-0600

Slacks open down both sides from waist to hip with velcro tab closures at sides. *$25.00*

1794 Side-Zip Sweat Pants
Buck & Buck
3111 27th Avenue South
Seattle, WA 98144
                             800-458-0600

Out-seam zippers un-zip 3/4 of the way down the sides to enable dressing a resident with severe leg contractures. *$32.00*

1795 Trunks
Buck & Buck
3111 27th Avenue South
Seattle, WA 98144
                             800-458-0600

Come in cotton or nylon, flare leg, full cut. *$4.00*

Undergarments

1796 Adult Absorbent Briefs
Special Clothes
PO Box 333
E Harwich, MA 02645   508-896-7939
                          FAX: 508-893-7939
                          TDY:508-896-7939
                e-mail: specialclo@aol.com
                www.special-clothes.com

Soft, comfortable, 100% cotton knit brief is seven layers thick at the crotch. Sides of the brief are a non-bulky single layer. The waistband elastic is encloed in a soft cotton knit casing, and does not touch the skin. Comfortable cotton rib knit bands circle the leg. This brief will not replace a diaper, but provides absorbency for light incontinence. Pure White: S/M $17/3 for $48.50; L/XL $18.50/3 for $52.75; XXL $19.50/3 for $55.75; Mixed Colors: S/M 3 for $50; L/XL 3 for $54; XXL 3/$57

1797 Adult Lap Shoulder Bodysuit
Special Clothes
PO Box 333
East Harwich, MA 02645   508-896-7939
                             FAX: 508-893-7939
                             TDY:508-896-7939
                e-mail: specialclo@aol.com
                www.special-clothes.com

Bodysuit styles fasten at the crotch with sturdy snaps to stay neatly tucked. All are made of soft, absorbent 100% cotton knit for maximum comfort. They are cut wide at the hip and seat for full coverage, and will accomodate a diaper if necessary. Soft knit rib circles the neck and leg. This cool tank style slips on easily. Deep armholes are banded with rib knit. all styles: Small/Medium $33.00/3 for $94.00; Large/X Large $38.00/3 for $108.00; XX Large $41.00/3 for $116.00. A chioce of 9 colors.

1798 Adult Sleeveless Bodysuit
Special Clothes
PO Box 333
East Harwich, MA 02645   508-896-7939
                             FAX: 508-896-7939
                             TDY:508-896-7939
                e-mail: specialclo@aol.com
                www.special-clothes.com

Bodysuit styles fasten at the crotch with sturdy snaps to stay neatly tucked. All are made of soft, absorbent 100% cotton knit for maximum comfort. They are cut wide at the hip and seat for full coverage, and will accomodate a diaper if necessary. Soft knit rib circles the neck and leg. This cool tank style slips on easily. Deep armholes are banded with rib knit. All styles: Small/Medium $33.00/3 for $94.00; Large/X-Large $38.00/3 for $108.00; XX Large $41.00/3 for $116.00. A choice of 9 colors.

1799 Adult Swim Diaper
Special Clothes
PO Box 333
East Harwich, MA 02645   508-896-7939
                             FAX: 508-896-7939
                             TDY:508-896-7939
                e-mail: specialclo@aol.com
                www.special-clothes.com

This pant is made of soft, silent, light-weight, impermeable fabric- waterproof and secure. It is a containment brief, designed to be used in the pool in place of cloth or disposable diapers, which can become waterlogged or disintegrate in the water. Waist and legbands should be snug for proper fit, so please consult sizing chart before ordering. Darlex with lining of 100% cotton knit. Lycra waist and legbands. Made in USA.

1800 **Adult Tee Shoulder Bodysuit**

Special Clothes
PO Box 333
East Harwich, MA   02645   508-896-7939
FAX: 508-893-7939
TDY:508-896-7939
e-mail: specialclo@aol.com
www.special-clothes.com

Styles fasten at the crotch with sturdy snaps to stay neatly tucked. All are made of soft, absorbent 100% cotton knit for maximum comfot. They are cut wide at the hip and seat for full coverage, and will accommodate a diaper if necessary. Soft knit rib circles the neck and leg. This bodysuit looks like a regular tee shirt, but snaps at the crotch for a neat appearance. Small/Medium $33.00/3 for $94.00; Large/X Large $38.00/3 fpr $108.00; XX Large $41.00/3 for $116.00. Choice of 9 colors.

1801 **Adult Waterproof Overpant**

Special Clothes
PO Box 333
E. Harwich, MA   02645   508-896-7939
FAX: 508-896-7939
TDY:508-896-7939
e-mail: specialclo@aol.com
www.special-clothes.com

Overpants are made of a soft, silent, lightweight fabric which is waterproof and very secure. It is designed to be used over our Adult Absorbent Brief, or cloth diapers. It is completely latex-free, and is an excellent non-allergenic substitute for rubber or vinyl pants. Waist and legbands should be snug to minimize leakage, so please consult the sizing chart before ordering. Darlex with lining of 100% cotton. Lycra waist and legbands. Made in USA.

1802 **Adult Wet Wrap Swim Vest**

Special Clothes
PO Box 333
East Harwich, MA   02645   508-896-7939
FAX: 508-896-7939
TDY:508-896-7939
e-mail: specialclo@aol.com
www.special-clothes.com

This vest is made of neoprene - the same material used in wet suits - and it effectively insulates the torso to retain body heat. Muscles relax, enhancing the quality of recreational swimming or water therapy. The wrap design allows full freedom of movement. Made of Neoprene in the USA. Note: Vest provides warmth ony. It is not a flotation device. Wet wrap sizes: Adult small(110-150lbs, 5'-5'7 inches)$70.00; Adult Medium(150-200lbs,5'5 inches-6'2 inches)$78.00; Adult Large(220-250lbs,5'6 inches-

1803 **Briefs**

Special Clothes
PO Box 333
East Harwich, MA   02645   508-896-7939
FAX: 508-896-7939
TDY:508-896-7939
e-mail: specialclo@aol.com
www.special-clothes.com

Judith Sweeney, Owner
A variety of unique brief styles available for easy access and practicality.

1804 **Cloth Diapers**

Angel Fluff Diaper Company
PO Box 1131
Lewisburg, TN   37091   931-359-9604

e-mail: afdc@angelfluff.com
www.angelfluff.com

Top quality cloth diapers.

1805 **Nylon Snip Slip**

Buck & Buck
3111 27th Avenue South
Seattle, WA   98144

800-458-0600

Just snip with scissors at the appropriate hem length and it's ready to wear. *$12.00*

1806 **Nylon Stretch Bra**

Buck & Buck
3111 27th Avenue South
Seattle, WA   98144

800-458-0600

Front hook closure with built-up shoulder straps. *$ 16.00*

1807 **Panties**

Buck & Buck
3111 27th Avenue South
Seattle, WA   98144

800-458-0600

Come in nylon or cotton, band leg for comfort. *$4.00*

1808 **Safe and Dry - Feel and Sure - Toddler Dry**

Hygenics Direct Company
114 Lemonton Way
Wayne, PA   19087   610-397-0788
888-463-7337
FAX: 610-397-0790
e-mail: mbrier1930@aol.com

Michael Brier, President

A variety of stress incontinence disposable liners which absorb 8-10 oz. of fluid packaged in 20 and 40 counts. Also available are patented knit nylon panties in medium, large and extra large sizes. All products are priced for the mass market.

1809 **Support Plus**

99 W Street
500
Medfield, MA   02052   508-359-2910
800-229-2910
FAX: 508-359-0139
www.supportplus.com

Offers a selection of support undergarments, braces and shoes for the physically challenged and medical professionals.

60 pages

Assistive Devices

1810   Ability Research

PO Box 721
Minnetonka, MN   55345   612-935-9459
FAX: 612-890-8393
e-mail: ability@skypoint.com
www.skypoint.com/~ability

Manufacturers and marketers of assistive technology equipment.

1811   Able Ergonomics Corporation

11305 Rancho Bernardo Road
Suite 116
San Diego, CA   92127
FAX: 619-675-0047

Manufacturers of keyboard wrist supports, rotating desk organizers, and computer monitor stands.

1812   Accu-u-trol

Ahnafield Corporation
3219 W Washington Street
Indianapolis, IN   46222   317-636-8061
800-636-8060
FAX: 317-636-8098

Computer-controlled device that operates all secondary accessory functions. These functions may include ignition, lift and door operation, windows, wipers, lights and flashers.

1813   Adaptivation

224 SE 16th Street
Suite 2
Ames, IA   50010
800-723-2783
FAX: 515-233-9815

Manufacturers of environmental control switches, auditory paging systems, a mouse emulator program, and communication devices.

1814   Adaptive Device Locator System

Academic Software
331 W 2nd Street
Lexington, KY   40507   606-233-2332
800-842-2357
FAX: 606-231-0725

Warren E. Lacefield, PhD, President
Penelope Ellis, Marketing Director

Employs a unique, goal-oriented approach to aid individuals in identifying adaptive devices with potential to support various physical limitations. Devices are categorized in seven database: Existence, Travel, In-situ Motion, Environmental Adaptation, Communication, and Sports & recreation. ADLS provides its users with device descriptions, pictures and lists of sources for locating products and product information. *$ 200.00*

1815   Analog Switch Pad

Academic Software
331 W 2nd Street
Lexington, KY   40507   606-233-2332
800-842-2357
FAX: 606-231-0725

Warren E. Lacefield, PhD, President
Penelope Ellis, Marketing Director

A touch-activated, force-adjustable, low-voltage DC, electronic switch designed to control battery-operated toys, environmental controls, and computer access interfaces. This device features a large activation area that is soft and compliant to the touch. Force sensitivity is adjusted by a small dial from approximately 1 ounce to 32 ounces activation pressure, applied over an area ranging from the size of a fingertip to the size of the entire switch surface. *$149.00*

1816   Arkenstone

1185-D Bordeaux Drive
Sunnyvale, CA   94089
800-444-4443
FAX: 408-745-6739

Offers various models of personal ready-to-read personal computers for the disabled.

1817   Assistive Software Products

Innovation Management Group
22311 Ventura Boulevard
Suite 104
Woodland Hills, CA   91364   818-346-3581
800-889-0987
FAX: 818-346-3973
e-mail: cs@imgpresents.com
www.imgpresents.com

Jerry Hussong, VP Sales / Marketing

IMG is the producer of My-T-Mouse, My-T-Mouse for Kids, and MY-T-Soft AT, Onscreen Keyboards, programmable Macro Buttons/Panels, and Word Prediction/Completion software. It also produces The Magnifier, magnification software; JAMBox, a multi-switch input box for joysticks; and Joystick-To Mouse, the only software that allows any joystick or gamepad to run Windows just like a mouse. UMG's products are recommended, by leading pointing device and systems manufacturers worldwide. $49.95-$199.95.

1818   Augmentative Communiation Systems (AAC)

ZYGO Industries
PO Box 1008
Portland, OR   97207   503-684-6006
800-234-6006
FAX: 503-684-6011
e-mail: zygo@zygo-usa.com
www.zygo-usa.com

Lawrence Weiss, President

Full range of AAC systems and assistive technology including computer-based systems and computer access programs and devices.

1819 BIGmack Communication Aid

AbleNet
1081 10th Avenue SE
Minneapolis, MN 55414

800-322-0956
FAX: 612-379-9143
e-mail: customerservice@ablenetinc.com
www.ablenetinc.com

A single message communication aid, BIGmack has 20 seconds of memory and has a 5 inches in diameter switch surface. *$86.00*

1820 Barrel Switch

Handicapped Children's Technological Services
PO Box 7
Foster, RI 02825

A cylinder mounted horizontally on a wooden base.

1821 C2ILMAX

Image Systems Corp.
6103 Blue Circle Drive
Minnetonka, MN 55343   612-935-1171

Laura Sorensen, Marketing

21 or 24 inch ultra-high resolution color or mono-chrome/grey scale monitors designed for applications requiring a larger viewing area and high to ultrahigh resolution.

1822 CLOSE-UP 6.5

Norton-Lambert Corporation
PO Box 4085
Santa Barbara, CA 93140   805-964-6767
FAX: 805-683-5679
e-mail: sales@norton-lambert.com
www.norton-lambert.com

Jeannie Vesely, Marketing Coordinator

Two-time winner of PC magazine Editor's Choice, Close-Up remotely controls PC's via modem. Tele-commute from your home or laptop PC to your office PC, or give remote support with unmatched speed. Run applications, update spreadsheets, print docu-ments remotely and access networks on remote PCs just as if you were there! Features: fastest screen and file transfers, synchronize files, unattended transfers, multi-level security, transaction logs, automated in-stallation. *$199.00*

1823 Center for Hi-Tech Training for Individuals with Disabilities

Valencia Community College
701 North Econolockhatchee Trail
Mail Code 3-12
Orlando, FL 32825   407-299-5000

A program for individuals with some hand func-tion.

1824 Computer Switch Interface

AbleNet
1081 10th Avenue SE
Minneapolis, MN 55414

800-322-0956
FAX: 612-379-9143
e-mail: customerservice@ablenetinc.com

Allows single switch access to an Apple computer. *$36.00*

1825 Darci Too

WesTest Engineering Corporation
810 Shepard Lane
Farmington, UT 84025   801-451-9191
FAX: 801-298-7102

Mary L. Lynds, Manager

A universal device which allows people with physical disabilities to replace the keyboard and mouse on a personal computer with a device that matches their physical capabilities. DARCI TOO works with al-most any personal computer and provides access to all computer functions. *$995.00*

1826 Don Johnston

26799 West Commerce Drive
Volo, IL 60073   847-740-0749
800-999-4660
FAX: 847-740-7326
e-mail: info@donjohnston.com
www.donjohnston.com

A provider of quality products and services that enable people with special needs to discover their potential and experience success. Products are de-veloped for the areas of Physical Access, Augmen-tative Communication and for those who struggle with reading and writing.

1827 EZ Touch Panel

Words+
40015 Sierra Highway B-145
Palmdale, CA 93550

800-869-8521
FAX: 805-266-8969

Ginger Woltosz, Vice President
Tim Ross, Manager

Touch screen input is the most direct and intuitive method for picture-based communication for those with the required motor skills. *$399.00*

1828 Expanded Keyboard Emulator

Words+
40015 Sierra Highway B-145
Palmdale, CA 93550

800-869-8521
FAX: 805-266-8969

Ginger Woltosz, Vice President
Tim Ross, Manager

Provides DUAl word prediction, abbreviation expan-sion (macrocapability), five different methods of voice output, keyboard control, RAM-resident and the ability to run in graphics mode and access to commercial software applications.

1829 Eyegaze Computer System

LC Technologies
4415 Glen Rose Street
Fairfax, VA 22032

800-733-5284
FAX: 703-425-7677

Nancy Cleveland, Medical Coordinator

Enables people with physical disabilities to do many things with their eyes that they would otherwise do with their hands.

1830 FingerFoniks

Words+
40015 Sierra Highway B-145
Palmdale, CA 93550

800-869-8521
FAX: 805-266-8969

Ginger Woltosz, Vice President
Tim Ross, Manager

One-pound, hand-held, communicator incorporating synthesized and recorded speech. The user makes words and sentences by pressing sound (phoneme) keys on a membrane keyboard. *$995.00*

1831 Florida New Concepts Marketing

Florida New Concepts Marketing
PO Box 261
Port Richey, FL 34673

727-842-3231
800-456-7097
FAX: 727-845-7544
e-mail: compulnz@ate.net
www.gulfside.com/compulenz

Alan Lezark, Market Representative

Compu-Lenz, a combination fresnel magnifier and glass glare filter in an adjustable hood. When placed on the front of a PC monitor it magnifies the character size, reduces glare and enhances contrast. *$ 204.95*

1832 GW Micro

310 Racquet Drive
Fort Wayne, IN 46825

FAX: 219-484-2510

Dan Weirich, Vice President
Doug Geoffray, Vice President

Computer hardware and software products for people with disabilities.

1833 Goals and Objectives

JE Stewart Teaching Tools
PO Box 15308
Seattle, WA 98115

FAX: 475-486-4510

J E Stewart, Owner

Goals and Objectives software helps teachers make student plans including IEP's, IPP's and IHP's. The system provides curricula for all students and programs to develop and evaluate plans, print reports and make data forms. Systems are available for IBM's and compatibles, Macintosh and for networks. $19.00/disk.

1834 Jelly Bean Switch

AbleNet
1081 10th Avenue SE
Minneapolis, MN 55414

800-322-0956
FAX: 612-379-9143
e-mail: customerservice@ablenetinc.com
www.ablenetinc.com

A momentary touch switch made of shatterproof plastic, small and sensitive to 2-3 ounces of pressure, this switch is provided audible feedback when activated and is a compact version of the Big Red Switch. *$42.00*

1835 KeyWiz

Words+
1220 W Avenue J
Lancaster, CA 93534

800-869-8521
FAX: 805-266-8969

Phil Lawrence, Vice President
Rachel Nielsen, Customer Support

A software and hardware product designed to operate on an IBM compatible PC. The software provides word prediction, abbreviation expansion and access to commercial software applications. *$695.00*

1836 Lift Mechanism

Van Norman/Design
202 E Cheyenne Mountain Boulevard
Colorado Springs, CO 80906   719-630-2140

Allows computer tables and other tables to be raised or lowered three inches with the push or pull of a lever.

1837 LinkPower 50

Words+
40015 Sierra Highway B-145
Palmdale, CA 93550

800-869-8521
FAX: 805-266-8969

Ginger Woltosz, Vice President
Tim Ross, Manager

DC-to-DC switching power converter provides a continuous, independent multi-output, multi-voltage power supply to any augcom device, laptop computer, pointing device, voice synthesizer, cellular phone, or other battery-operated device directly from a wheelchair. *$449.00*

1838 MessageMate

Words+
1220 W Avenue J
Lancaster, CA 93534

800-869-8521
FAX: 805-266-8969

Rachel Nielsen, Customer Support

Lightweight, hand-held communicator providing high-quality analog recording capability using either direct select keyboards or 1 to 2 switch access. Price ranges from $549.00 to $999.00.

1839 Morse Code Equalizer

Words+
40015 Sierra Highway B-145
Palmdale, CA 93550

800-869-8521
FAX: 805-266-8969

Ginger Woltosz, Vice President
Tim Ross, Manager

Provides complete word processing and voice output communications with single or dual switch Morse code inputs. Originally designed for a blind user with only eyelid movement. The system can be used by both sighted and visually impaired persons. *$1395.00*

1840 Mouthsticks

Fred Sammons
PO Box 32
Brookfield, IL 60513

708-387-7272
800-323-5547
FAX: 800-547-4333

Wide offering of mouthsticks featuring various functions (BK 5380, 5381, 5383, 5385, 6002, or BK 5370 series).

1841 Multi-Scan Single Switch Activity Center

Academic Software
331 W 2nd Street
Lexington, KY 40507

606-233-2332
800-842-2357
FAX: 606-231-0725

Warren E. Lacefield, PhD, President
Penelope Ellis, Marketing Director

A single switch activity center containing four educational games: Match, Maze, Dot-to-Dot, and Concentration, along with six graphics libraries; Dinosaurs, Sports, Animals, Independent Living, Vocations, and Cosmetology. MULTI-SCAN allows you to select a graphic library, choose games for each user, and adjust the difficulty level and other settings for each game. Other features allow you to save the game setups under each user's name and print out individual performance reports after sessions. *$154.00*

1842 Perfect Solutions

15950 Schweizer Court
W. Palm Beach, FL 33414

561-790-1070
800-726-7086
FAX: 561-790-0108
e-mail: perfect@gate.net
www.perfectsolutions.com

Andrew Kramer, President

A computer for every student and it speaks! Wireless laptop computers starting at $290.00 are ideal for students to carry with them all day. Text-to-speech and web browsing are available. *$290.00*

1843 Phillip Roy

PO Box 130
Indian Rocks Beach, FL 33785

727-593-2700
800-255-9085
e-mail: phillip@gte.net
www.philliproy.com

Ruth Bralman PhD, President

Offers multimedia materials appropriate for use with individuals with disabilities. Programs range from preschool through the adult level. Many of the programs are high interest topics/low vocabulary, ideal for transition and employability skills. Materials are also available which focus on social and personal development. Call for a free catalog.

1844 Phone-TTY

1246 US Highway 46 W
Parsippany, NJ 07054

973-299-6627
888-332-3889
FAX: 973-299-7768
e-mail: phonetty@aol.com
www.phone-tty.com

Anna M. Terrazzino, Executive Director

Develops and promotes better communications for the deaf using ordinary telephone equipment and current technology. Installs computerized phone-television equipment in the homes of individuals who are deaf, enabling these individuals to communicate with local police, hospitals, answering services and news services.

1845 SS-ACCESS Single Switch Interface for PC's with MS-DOS

Academic Software
331 West 2nd Street
Lexington, KY 40507

606-233-2332
800-842-2357
FAX: 606-231-0725

Warren E. Lacefield, PhD, President
Penelope Ellis, Marketing Director

A general purpose single switch hardware and software interface for DOS and the IBM and compatible PC family. It is designed to be easy to install, simple to use, and compatible with the widest possible range of computers and application software programs. SS-ACCESS! connects to one of the PC serial ports and provides a jack to connect an external switch. The DOS version of the software works by sending a user defined keystroke to the PC keyboard buffer whenever the switch is pressed. *$ 90.00*

1846 Simplicity

Words+
1220 W Avenue J
Lancaster, CA 93534

805-266-8500
800-869-8521
FAX: 805-266-8969

Phil Lawrence, Vice President
Rachel Nielsen, Customer Support

Swing-down mount for portable computers and other devices is made from high-quality aircraft aluminum. Simplicity contains very few moving parts and installs in minutes, providing a positive, secure support for computer/device in both the stored and overlap position. *$595.00*

1847   Slim Armstrong Mounting System

AbleNet
1081 10th Avenue SE
Minneapolis, MN   55414

800-322-0956
FAX: 612-379-9143
e-mail: customerservice@ablenetinc.com
www.ablenetinc.com

Slim Armstrong is a mounting system strong enough to hold up to five pounds in any position. Mix and match parts to create the system length you desire. *$188.00*

1848   Smart Modem

HARC Mercantile, Ltd.
PO Box 3055
Kalamazoo, MI   49003   616-324-1615
                               800-445-9968
                          FAX: 616-324-2387
e-mail: home@harcmercantile.com
www.harcmercantile.com

Ronald Slager, President

Smart modem makes your computer accessible to a TTY. *$ 349.00*

1849   String Switch

AbleNet
1081 10th Avenue SE
Minneapolis, MN   55414

800-322-0956
FAX: 612-379-9143
e-mail: customerservice@ablenetinc.com
www.ablenetinc.com

An activated switch beneficial for users with limited active movement or minimal strength. *$28.00*

1850   Symbi-Key Computer Switch Interface

AbleNet
1081 10th Avenue SE
Minneapolis, MN   55414

800-322-0956
FAX: 612-379-9143
e-mail: customerservice@ablenetinc.com
www.ablenetinc.com

The Symbi-Key can be programmed to simulate any key stroke or a series of keystrokes (up to 5 per key) for single switch access to software programs whether or not it was designed for switch access. Works well in DOS and all versions of Windows providing access to any IBM program. *$299.00*

1851   U-Control II

Words+
1220 W Avenue J
Lancaster, CA   93534

800-869-8521
FAX: 805-266-8969

Phil Lawrence, Vice President
Rachel Nielsen, Customer Support

Works with the Words+ system (EX Keys, Morse WSKE, Scanning WSKE, Talking Screen) to provide wireless, portable control of items which are already infrared-controlled such as a TV, VCR, CD player, etc. *$ 395.00*

1852   Universal Switch Mounting System

AbleNet
1081 10th Avenue SE
Minneapolis, MN   55414

800-322-0956
FAX: 612-379-9143
e-mail: customerservice@ablenetinc.com
www.ablenetinc.com

Mounting system that allows switch placement in any position. A single lever locks all joints securely in place. Extends to 20 1/2 inches and holds up to five pounds. A mounting system for quick and easy positioning. *$189.00*

1853   VISION

Artic Technologies
55 Park Drive
Troy, MI   48083   248-588-7370
                           FAX: 313-588-2650

The premier access system for blind users of IBM personal computers.

1854   WinSCAN - The Single Switch Interface for PC's with Windows

Academic Software
331 W 2nd Street
Lexington, KY   40507   606-233-2332
                               800-842-2357
                          FAX: 606-231-0725

Warren E. Lacefield, PhD, President
Penelope Ellis, Marketing Director

A general purpose single-switch control interface for Windows. It provides single-switch users independent control access to educational and productivity software, multimedia programs, and recreational activities that run under Windows 3.1 and higher versions on IBM and compatible PC's. The user can navigate through Windows; choose program icons and run programs, games, and CD's; even surf the Internet with WinSCAN and his or her adaptive switch. *$349.00*

1855   Words+ Equalizer

Words+
40015 Sierra Highway B-145
Palmdale, CA   93550

800-869-8521
FAX: 805-266-8969

Ginger Woltosz, Vice President
Tim Ross, Manager

A hardware/software product designed to operate on an IBM compatible PC. The software provides an intelligent word prediction scheme, a calculator, music, plus ability to draw and play games. Equalizer is a dedicated augmentative communication system designed for use by individuals with severe motor disability. *$1395.00*

1856   Words+ IST (Infrared, Sound, Touch)

Words+
1220 W Avenue J
Lancaster, CA   93534   805-266-8500
                               800-869-8521
                          FAX: 805-266-8969

Phil Lawrence, Vice President
Rachel Nielsen, Customer Support

A unique switch that is activated by slight movement or faint sound. The switch provides user control when connected to a device driven by a single switch. Individuals are currently accessing a wide variety of communication and computer systems with movement using the IST switch. Price ranges from $295.00 to $495.00.

Braille Products

1857 Access Systems International Ltd.

415 English Avenue
Monterey, CA 93940   831-373-6291
                               FAX: 831-375-5313

Developers of Braille printers.

1858 Braille Blazer

Blazie Engineering
11800 31st Court North
St. Petersburg, FL 33716

                               800-444-4443
                               FAX: 727-803-8001

Braille printer.

1859 Braille N' Speak

Blazie Engineering
11800 31st Court North
St. Petersburg, FL 33716

                               800-444-4443
                               FAX: 727-803-8001

A compact, portable talking device with a seven-key Braille keyboard, may be used as a talking computer terminal, a braille to print transcriber and a word processor.

1860 Braillemaster

Howtek
21 Park Avenue
Hudson, NH 03051   603-882-5200

A modified version of Howtek's Pixelmaster color ink jet printer, retains the functionality of Pixelmaster - a color printer capable of merging color graphics and images with crisp text on any standard paper at five to ten cents per page.

1861 Brailon Thermoform Duplicator

American Thermoform Corporation
2311 Travers Avenue
City Of Commerce, CA 90040   323-723-9021

This copy machine, for producing tactile images copies any Brailled or embossed original by a vacuum forming process. This model is for the reproduction of teaching aids and mobility maps.

1862 Computer Paper for Brailling

Maxi Aids
42 Executive Boulevard
3209
Farmingdale, NY   11735   516-752-0521
                               800-522-6294
                               FAX: 516-752-0689
                               e-mail: sales@maxiaids.com
                               www.maxiaids.com

Specially made paper for braille printing. 1,000 sheets/case *$69.95*

1863 Duxbury Braille Translator

Duxbury Systems
270 Littleton Road Unit
6
Westford, MA 01886   978-692-3000
                               FAX: 978-692-7912
                               e-mail: info@duxsys.com
                               www.duxburysystems.com

Neal Kuniansky

A complete line of braille easy to use word processing and translation software available for Windows (including NT), Macintosh, DOS, and UNIX. Applications for anyone wanting to produce or communicate with braille; signs, note cards, textbooks, business communications and forms, telephone bills, etc. Simple to use, FREE technical support. Free one year upgrades. DBT is for producing braille in English, Spanish, French, Portuguese, Italian, Latin, Greek, German, and other languages. *$ 600.00*

1864 Enabling Technologies Company

1601 NE Braille Place
Jensen Beach, FL 34957   561-225-3687
                               800-777-3687
                               FAX: 561-225-3299
                               e-mail: enabling@brailler.com
                               www.brailler.com

Chris Kraft, Marketing Department
Charlie Kiefer

Manufactures the most complete line of American made braille embossers, including desk top or portable models capable of producing high quality single sided or interpoint braille. Also carry a complete line of adaptive technology aids for the blind community at affordable prices.

1865 Eye Relief Word Processing Software

SkiSoft Publishing Corporation
PO Box 278
Lexington, MA 02420   781-863-1876
                               FAX: 781-861-0086
                               e-mail: info@skisoft.com
                               www.skisoft.com

Ken Skier, President
Cynthia Skier, CFO

Large-type word processing program for visually-impaired PC users. *$295.00*

1866 **Freedom Scientific Blind/ Low Vision Group**
11800 31st Court North
St Petersberg, FL   33716   727-803-8000
                                   800-444-4443
                              FAX: 727-803-8001
                         e-mail: info@hj.com
                       www.freedomscientific.com

Brian J. Blazie, Vice President

Developer and manufacturer of assistive technology products for blind and visually impaired individuals. Software: JANS for Windows, ScreenReader, Magic Screen Magnifier, Open Book Scanning and Reading Software. Hardware: Braille wireless, personal note takers: Braille 'n Speak, BrailleLite, Type 'n Speak, Type Lite, Braille Embossers, Computer Braille Displays. Training and tutorials availible. *$16.95*

1867 **MegaDots**
Raised Dot Computing
408 S Baldwin Street
Madison, WI   53703   608-257-9595
                                 800-347-9594
                            FAX: 608-257-4143
                       e-mail: info@rdcbraille.com
                         www.rdcbraille.com

Theresa Wantuch, Sales Manager
Caryn Navy, Vice Pres/ Technical Support
David Holladay, President

A revolutionary new braille translator for the PC that lets you finish projects quickly and easily. Intelligent document importation recognizes what word processor your text is from, and guesses that appropriate format for each paragraph, yielding high quality braille. *$540.00*

1868 **Raised Dot Computing**
408 South Baldwin Street
Madison, WI   53703   978-692-3000
                                 800-347-9594

Software for the visually impaired.

Information Centers & Databases

1869 **ABLEDATA**
8630 Fenton Street
Suite 930
Silver Spring, MD   20910   301-608-8998
                                       800-227-0216
                                  FAX: 301-608-8958
                                  TDY:301-608-8912
                         e-mail: ABLEDATA@macroint.com
                              www.abledata.com

Katherine Belknap, Director
Susan Carey, Information Specialist
Anjanette Daigle, Research Assistant

ABLEDATA is an electronic database of assistive technology and rehabilitation equipment products for children and adults with physical, cognitive, and sensory disabilities. ABLEDATA staff can perform database searches or the database can be searched on the ABLEDATA website database printouts, informer consumer guides, and fact website sheets are available at cost from the office or free from the website.

1870 **Academic Advisory Service**
1538 Woodland Road
Rydal, PA   19046   215-884-0656

                  e-mail: scottaas@aol.com

Suzanne F. Scott, Psychologist/Educational Consult

Offers a comprehensive approach to educational planning, assessment, and school selection. Personal knowledge of schools, colleges, summer and special programs throughout the country are provided. Works with families and students on an individual basis, helping them objectively assess student needs and set appropriate goals. Complete psychological and educational testing are also available.

1871 **Aloha Special Technology Access Center**
710 Green Street
Honolulu, HI   96813   808-523-5547
                         FAX: 800-523-5548
                    e-mail: stachi@aol.com
                      www.aloha.net.~stachi

Computer technology center.

1872 **Assistive Technology Through Action in Indiana (ATTAIN)**
Division of Disability, Aging & Rehab. Services
2346 South Lynhurst Drive
Suite 507
Indianapolis, IN   46241   317-486-8808
                                 FAX: 317-486-8809
                       e-mail: attain@attaininc.org

Cris Fulford, Director

Non-for-profit organization that creates system change by expanding the availability of community-based technology-related activities, outreach services, empowerment and advocacy activities through the development of a comprehensive, consumer-responsive, statewide program to serve individuals with disabilities, of all ages and all disabilities, their families, caregivers, educators, and service providers. Provides trainings, information and referral, and system change.

1873 **Audiogram/Clinical Records Manager**
Hear You Are
4 Musconetcong Avenue
Stanhope, NJ   07874
                                       800-287-EARS
                                  FAX: 973-347-7662

Keeps track of client audiogram history and can print or view client with audiogram. *$414.75*

1874 **Birmingham Alliance for Technology Access Center**
Birmingham Independent Living Center
206 13th Street South
Birmingham, AL   35804   256-722-0122
                                  TDY:205-251-2223
                       e-mail: tasc@travellers.com

Computer technology center.

1875 Bluegrass Technology Center

169 N Limestone Street
Lexington, KY 40507   606-255-9951
                            800-209-7767
                    FAX: 606-255-0059
                    TDY:606-491-8700
        e-mail: office@bluegrass-tech.org
               www.bluegrass-tech.org

Bob Glass, Executive Director

Provides assistive technology information, consulting and training for education, health professionals, consumers and parents of consumers. Maintains extensive lending library of assistive devices and adapted toys. Statewide training such as; AAC, how to obtain funding for assistive technology, augmentative and alternate communication, equipment implementation strategies, specific to hardware and software, etc.

1876 CARA

Southern Micro Systems
3335 S Church Street
Burlington, NC 27215   336-584-1661

Dick Swank, President

Provides psychologists with computer generated reports for WISC III; WAIS and other test reports.

1877 CHID Combined Health Information Database

National Institute of Health
Box CHID 9000 Rockville Pike
Rockville, MD 20892   301-402-8714
                    FAX: 301-770-5164

Richard Pike

A computerized bibliographic database, developed and managed by health-related agencies of the federal government.

1878 Carolina Computer Access Center

Metro School
700 East Second Street
Charlotte, NC 28202   704-342-3004
                    FAX: 701-342-1513
            e-mail: ccacnc@aol.com
                    ccac.utaccess.org

Judy Timms, Executive Director

Non-profit community-based technology resource center for people with disabilities, providing information about and demonstration of the technology tools that enable individuals with disabilities to control and direct their own lives. Services and programs include: assessments, demonstrations, resource information, lending library, workshops and outreach.

1879 Center for Accessible Technology

2547 8th Street
Suite 12-A
Berkeley, CA 94710   510-841-3224
                    FAX: 510-841-7956
            e-mail: info@cforat.org
                    www.cforat.org

Damitri Belser, Executive Director
Eric Smith, Administrative Director

The Center is a grassroots consumer-based agency with programs that connect people with all types of disabilities, family members, educators, therapists, and others with computer-based tools. Services include assessment, on-going training, curriculum adaption, classes, demonstrations, and a newsletter.

1880 Center for Applied Special Technology

39 Cross Street
Peabody, MA 01960   978-531-8555
                    FAX: 978-531-0192
                    www.cast.org

Bart Pisha, Director of Research
Chuck Hitchcock, Dir of Product Development

Expands opportunities for individuals with special needs through innovative use of computers and related technology. We pursue this mission through research and product development that further universal design for learning.

1881 Center for Enabling Technology

622 Route 10
Suite 22B
Whippany, NJ 07981   973-428-1455
                    FAX: 973-560-9751

Carmela Balacco, Office Manager

Computer technology center offering resource time, workshops, technology, training and evaluations.

1882 Center on Evaluation of Assistive Technology

National Rehabilitation Hospital
102 Irving Street NW
Washington, DC 20010   202-783-7971

The center develops ways of collecting, producing and distributing information to help users, prescribers and third-party payers make intelligent selections of devices.

1883 Compuserve - Handicapped Users' Database

5000 Arlington Centre Boulevard
Columbus, OH 43220   614-457-8600
                    FAX: 614-538-4023
                    www.compuserve.com

Audrey Weil, General Manager

This nationwide database with bulletin boards provides information for persons with disabilities and the issues and technologies that are of interest to them.

1884 Computer Access Center

5901 Green Valley Circle
Suite 320
Culver City, CA 90230   310-216-0818

                    e-mail: cac@cac.org
                    www.cac.org

Computer technology center.

1885 Computer CITE

215 East New Hampshire Street
Orlando, FL 32804   407-896-3177
FAX: 407-895-5255
e-mail: comcite@aol.com

Lee Nasehi, Interim Director
Computer technology center.

1886 Computer Center for Viasually Impaired People: Division of Continuing Studies

17 Lexington Avenue
PO Box H-648
New York, NY 10010   212-802-2140
FAX: 212-802-2103
e-mail: spkbb@cunyvm.cuny.edu
www.baruch.cuny.edu/ccvip

Offers courses, tutors, equipment and assistance.

1887 Computer-Enabling Drafting for People with Physical Disabilities

County College of Morris
Route 10 & Center Grove Road
Randolph, NJ 07869
888-226-8001

Joe Robinson
Computer service.

1888 Computers to Help People

825 East Johnson Street
Madison, WI 53703   608-257-5917
FAX: 608-257-3480
e-mail: techbri@chpi.org
www.chpi.org

Carl Durocher, Director
Johnny R. Lee, Operations Manager
John J. Boyer, Executive Director

A center for assistive technology, assessment, consulting and training, specializing in computer access products for persons with sensory or mobility impairments. Also provides a print-to-braille service with a specialty in technical writing.

1889 DIRLINE

National Library of Medicine
8600 Rockville Pike
Bethesda, MD 20894   301-496-6193
888-346-3656
e-mail: custserv@nml.nih.gov
www.nlm.nih.gov/

18,000 listings of organizations that serve as information resources, including libraries, professional associations and government agencies.

1890 Developmental Disabilities Council

200 Lafayette Street
PO Box 3455
Baton Rouge, LA 70821   225-342-6804
FAX: 225-342-1970
www.laddc.org

Sandee Winchell, Director
Computer technology center.

1891 Employment Resources Program

426 W Jefferson Street
Springfield, IL 62702   217-523-2587
800-447-4221
FAX: 217-523-0427

Ceceilia Haasis, Program Manager

An information and referral service that encourages inquiries from professionals, individuals with disabilities, family members, organizations or anyone requesting information pertaining to disabilities. The staff at DRN uses both computer listings and in-house library files to provide the programs services. The DRN program is funded by a grant from the Illinois Department of Rehabilitation Services.

1892 Functional Skills Screening Inventory

Functional Resources Enterprises
3905 Huntington Drive
Amarillo, TX 79104   806-354-5403

e-mail: ehammer@cortex.ama.ttnhsc.edu

Ed Hammer
Heather Becker

Assesses the individuals and level of functional skills and identifies supports needed by educational, rehabilitation and residential programs serving moderately and severely disabled persons. Includes enviromental assessments as well as profiles of jobs and training sites.

1893 High Tech Center

Cal State University
6000 J Street
Sacramento, CA 95819   916-278-6011
FAX: 916-278-7825

The Center offers Augumentative Communication Training modules: videotapes featuring clients participating in assessment and training to demonstrate procedures for selecting and using augmentative communication systems.

1894 IBM National Support Center

Special Needs Systems
PO Box 2150
Atlanta, GA 30301   404-238-3000
800-228-0752
FAX: 561-982-6059

Serves to help health care leaders, agency directors, policy makers, employers, educators, public officials and individuals learn how computers can enhance the quality of life for the disabled person in the school, home and workplace. Also provide information and resource guides on disabilities affecting hearing, learning, speech and language, mobility and vision.

1895 Increasing Capabilities Access Network

2201 Brookwood Drive
Suite 117
Little Rock, AR 72202   501-666-8868
800-828-2799
FAX: 501-666-5319
www.arkansas-ican.org

Sue Gaskin, Project Director

A consumer responsive statewide systems change program promoting assistive technology for persons of all ages with disabilities. The program provides information on new and existing technology and maintains an equipment exchange free of charge. Training on assistive technology is also provided.

1896 International Center for the Disabled

340 E 24th Street
New York, NY   10010   212-585-6000
                                        FAX: 212-585-6161
                                        www.icdrehab.org

Dan Rosen, CEO

This center trains and places persons with disabilities in jobs, especially those using computers.

1897 Kentucky Assistive Technology Service Network

8412 Westport Road
Louisville, KY   40242   502-327-0022
                                        800-327-5287
                                        FAX: 502-327-9974
                                        e-mail: katsnet@iglow.com
                                        www.katsnet.org

Ronji Dearborn, Info. & Referral Specialist

Statewide network of four regional assistive technology centers with a central coordinating office in Louisville and two regional centers in eastern Kentucky. Network services include but are not limited to assistive technology of services, loan of assistive devices, funding information and referral, assessment and evaluations, consultations on appropriate technologies, training, and technical assistance.

1898 Learning Independence Through Computers

1001 Eastern Avenue
Baltimore, MD   21202   410-659-5462
                                        FAX: 410-659-5472
                                        e-mail: lincmd@aol.com
                                        www.linc.org

Susan Pompa, Associate Director

Computer technology center.

1899 MEDLINE

Dialog Corporation
2440 West El Camino Real
Mountain View, CA   94040
                                        800-334-2564
                                        FAX: 650-254-7070
                                        www.dialog.com

Bibliographic citations to biomedical literature.

1900 Maine CITE

University of Maine at Augusta
University Heights
Augusta, ME   04330   207-621-3000

Computer technology center.

1901 Maryland Technology Assistance Program

Governor's Off. for Individuals with Disabilities
2301 Argonne Drive
Room T-17
Baltimore, MD   21218
                                        800-832-4827
                                        FAX: 410-554-9237
                                        e-mail: mdtap@clark.net
                                        www.mdtap.org

Paul Rasinski, Executive Director
Louise Calderan, Assistant Director

Assistive technology center.

1902 Massachusetts Special Technology Access Center

12 Mudge Way
1-6
Bedford, MA   01730   508-481-1100

Computer technology center.

1903 Minnesota STAR Program Governor's Advisory Council on Disabled Technology

685 Cedar Street
St. Paul, MN   55155   651-291-2512

Computer technology center.

1904 Mississippi Project START

PO Box 1698
Jackson, MS   39215   601-987-4872
                                        800-852-8328
                                        FAX: 601-364-2349
                                        e-mail: spower@mdrs.state.ms.us

Stephen Power, Project Director

Project START is a Tech Act project established to bring about systems change in the field of assistive technology in the state of Mississippi. Activities include providing training opportunities for consumers and service providers on subjects such as state-of-the-art AT devices, their application, and funding resources; referral information on AT evaluation centers; technical assistance to AT users; and establishment of an AT equipment loan program and an Information and Referral Service.

1905 National Lekotek Center

2100 Ridge Avenue
Evanston, IL   60201   847-328-0001
                                        800-366-PLAY
                                        FAX: 847-328-5514
                                        TDY:800-573-4446
                                        e-mail: lekotek@lekotek.org
                                        www.lekotek.org

Madelyn Jamesto, Director of Programs & Training

Maximizes the development of children with special needs through play. Supports families through nationwide family play centers, toy lending libraries and computer play programs. Publishes six-page newsletter three times per year.

1906 National Technology Database

American Foundation for the Blind/AFB Press
PO Box 1020
Sewickley, PA   15143   412-741-1142
                              800-232-3044
                        FAX: 412-741-0609
                e-mail: afborders@abdintl.com
                              www.afb.org

This database includes resources for visually impaired persons. *$99.00*

1907 New Jersey Department of Labor

Office of the Commissioner
110 Labarre Avenue Building Center
Trenton, NJ   08618   609-984-4248

Raymond Bramucci, Commissioner
Computer technology center.

1908 New Mexico Technology-Related Assistance Program

Department of Education
435 St Michael Drive
Building D
Santa Fe, NM   87505   505-827-3370

Computer technology center.

1909 Northern Illinois Center for Adaptive Technology

3615 Louisiana Road
Rockford, IL   61108   815-229-2881

Computer technology center.

1910 Occupational Center of Central Kansas

1710 West Schilling Road
Salina, KS   67402   785-827-9383
                      FAX: 785-823-2015
                e-mail: occk@occk.com
                          www.occk.com

Phyllis Anderson, Director, Community Resource Dev
Computer technology center; training center for employment and independent living for people with disabilities; family support center.

1911 Ohio Rehabilitative Services Commission

Division of Public Affairs, SW 4
400 E Campus View Boulevard
Columbus, OH   43235   614-438-1255
                              800-282-4536
                        FAX: 614-438-1257
                        TDY:614-438-1210

Robert Lake, Administrator
Computer technology center.

1912 Oklahoma Department of Human Services, Rehabilitation Services Division

PO Box 25352
Oklahoma City, OK   73125   405-521-4358
                            FAX: 405-521-2086

Computer technology center.

1913 PAM Assistance Center

Physically Impaired Association of Michigan
601 W Maple Street
Lansing, MI   48906
                              800-274-7426
                        FAX: 517-371-5898

Arselia S. Ensign, Director, PAM Centre
Barbara Warren, Administrative Asst.

One of three state-supported technology and media information centers in Michigan, all under the Physically Impaired Association of Michigan. Offers resources, booklets and pamphlets listing information on devices and resources helpful in addressing basic needs of persons with disabilities.

1914 Parents, Let's Unite for Kids

1500 N 30th Street
Billings, MT   59101
                              800-222-7585
                        FAX: 406-657-2061
                        TDY:406-657-2055
                e-mail: plukmt@aol.com

Computer technology center. Parents, Let's Unite for Kids offers an assistive technology lab that is open to people of all ages. The lab is a computer and assistive technology demonstration site. There is no charge for services.

1915 Pathfinder Parent Training and Information Center

1600 2nd Avenue SW
Minot, ND   58701   701-837-7500
                              800-245-5840
                        FAX: 701-837-7548
              e-mail: ndpath01@minot.ndek.net
                    www.pathfinder.minot.com

Katherine Erickson, Executive Director

A member of the National Parent Training and Information Program which helps parents to better understand their child's disability and to obtain information about the programs, services and resources available. The center provides referrals through their program, support for educational programs for children with disabilities and helps parents learn to communicate more effectively with those involved in their child's program.

1916 Pennsylvania's Initiative on Assistive Technology

Temple University Institute on Disabilities/UAP
13th Street & Cecil B Moore Avenue
Philadelphia, PA   19122   215-925-7379
                              800-204-7428
                        TDY:800-750-7428
              e-mail: tiat@astro.ocis.temple.edu

Amy Goldman, Project Director
Jo Watson, Info. & Referral

Assistive technology-related information and advocacy for Pennsylvanians with disabilities; assistance with funding; short-term equipment loan and used equipment exchange programs.

1917 Pre-Injury/Post-Injury Analysis

CAPCO, The Capability Corporation
1522 N Washington Street
Suite 200
Spokane, WA   99201
                           FAX: 509-535-1011

Used by vocational experts and attorneys in liti-
gated cases including personal injury, product liability, medical malpractice and workers
compensation.

**1918 Quick Reading Test, Phonics Based Reading,
Reading S.O.S. (Strategies for Older Students)**

Lexia Learning Systems
PO Box 466
Lincoln, MA   01773   781-259-8752
                            800-435-3942
                        FAX: 781-259-1349
        e-mail: info@lexialearning.com
             www.lexialearning.com

Jon Bower, President
Bob Baker, Sales Representative

Lexia's software helps children and adults with learning disabilities master their core reading skills. Based
on the Orton Gillingham method, Phonics Based
Reading and S.O.S. (Strategies for the Older Student)
apply phonics principles to help students learn essential sound-symbol correspondence and decoding
skills. The Quick Reading Tests generate detailed
phonemic skills reports in only 5-8 minutes per student to provide teachers with accurate data to focus
their instruction. Price: $67-$500.

1919 RESNA

1700 North Moore Street
Suite 1540
Arlington, VA   22209
                        FAX: 703-524-6630
        e-mail: nationaloffice@resna.org
                 www.resna.org

James R. Geletka, Executive Director
Jody Benford, Credentialing Program Manager
jerry reamer, Membership Coordinator

An information center to address research, development, dissemination, integration, and utilization of
knowledge in rehabilitation and assistive technology.

1920 SACC Assistive Technoloy Center

Simi Valley Hospital N Campus
PO Box 1325
Simi Valley, CA   93062   805-582-1881
                        FAX: 805-582-2855
             e-mail: dssaccca@aol.com

Debi Schultze, Chief Executive Officer

SACC connects children, adults and seniors with special needs to computers, technologies and resources.
We provide information and referral, assessments,
tutoring, presentations and outreach awareness.

1921 STAR Center

60 Lynoak Cove
Jackson, TN   38305   901-668-3888
                            800-464-5619
                        FAX: 901-668-1666
        e-mail: sallison@starcenter.tn.org
             www.starcenter.tn.org

Judy Duke, Outreach Coordinator

Nation's largest assistive technology center dedicated to helping children and adults with disabilities
achieve their goals for competitive employment, effective learning, returning to or starting school, and
independent living. Programs include: high-tech
training, music therapy, art therapy, low vision evalu-
taiton, orientation and mobility evaluation and training, augmentative communication evaluation,
vocational evaluations, assistive technology, job
placement services and job skills training

**1922 South Dakota Department of Human Services,
Division of Rehabilitation Services**

E Highway 34 500, Hillsview Plaza
c/o 500 East Capital
Pierre, SD   57501   605-773-5990
                            800-265-9684
                        FAX: 605-773-5483
                        TDY:605-773-3195
        e-mail: davem@dhs.state.sd.us

David Miller, Division Director
Computer technology center.

1923 Students with Disabilities Office

University of Texas at Austin
100-B West Dean Keeton Street
Austin, TX   78712   512-471-6259
                        FAX: 512-223-3963
             www.utexas/edu/depts/dos/ssd

Sherry Sanders, Associate Dean of Students

1924 TASK Team of Advocates for Special Kids

100 W Cerritos Avenue
Anaheim, CA   92805   714-533-8275
                        FAX: 714-533-2533
             e-mail: taskca@aol.com

Computer technology center.

1925 Target Teach

Evans Newton
15876 North 76th Street
Scottsdale, AZ   85260   480-998-2777

Aligns and monitors Special Education Instructional Materials to tests that are used to measure
the effectiveness of Special Education Instructional Programs.

1926 Tech Connection

35 Haddon Avenue
Shrewsbury, NJ   07702   732-747-5310
                        FAX: 732-747-1896
             e-mail: tecconn@aol.com
             www.techconnection.org

Joanne Castellano, Center Director

Offers a noncommercial center to examine and try computers, adapted equipment, alternative input devices, and a variety of software. Program of Family Resource Associates and a member of the Alliance for Technology Access (ATA), a growing national coalition of computer resource centers, professionals, technology developers and vendors, interacting with new technology to enrich the lives of people with disabilities. Tech Connection offers evaluations, training and computer technology.

1927 Tech-Able

1114 Brett Drive
Suite 100
Conyers, GA 30094   770-922-6768
                             FAX: 770-922-6769
                   e-mail: techable@bellsouth.net
                             www.techable.org

Carolyn McGonagill, Director
Pat Hanus, Executive Assistant

Provide assistive technology to individuals with disabilities, toy-lending and software libraries, product demonstration, access to technology devices and fabrication of keyguards for keyboards.

1928 Technical Aids & Assistance for the Disabled Center

1950 W Roosevelt Road
Chicago, IL 60608   708-867-6060
                             800-346-2939
                        FAX: 312-421-3464
                        TDY:312-421-3373

Andres Hernandez, Executive Director
Robert Kaige, Technologist

Provides consultation and technical advice on adaptive aids, software and hardware.

1929 Technology Access Center of Tucson

4710 E 29th Street
Tuscon, AZ 85732   520-323-2358

                     e-mail: tactaz@aol.com

Linda Bishop, Director Of Services
Sonia Rameriez, Service Coordinator

A resource center that provides assistive technology services for people with disabilities. Center personnel develop, provide and coordinate those services in communities throughout Middle Tennessee. Services are designed to assist people with disabilities to learn about, choose, acquire and use assistive technology devices. Services are offered to any child or adult with sensory, motor or cognitive disabilities, their family members, and professionals who serve them and employ them.

1930 Technology Assistance for Special Consumers

PO Box 443
915 Monroe Street
Huntsville, AL 35804   256-532-5336
                          FAX: 256-532-2355
                     e-mail: tasc@hiwaay.net
                             www.ataccess.org

Linda Rags, Executive Director

T.A.S.C. is a computer resource center with 10 computers, which are equipped with special adaptations for those who are blind, visually impaired, or severely physically disabled. Our staff demonstrates and trains individuals on this equipment so that they can become more independent at home, school, and work. Over 2,500 pieces of educational software are available for individuals who are learning disabled, mentally retarded or who have developmental delays.

1931 Techspress

Resource Center for Independent Living
401-409 Columbia Street
409
Utica, NY 13502   315-797-4642
                          FAX: 315-797-4247
                 e-mail: lana.gossin@rcil.com

Lana Gossin, Director

Services include consultation and training in computer based technology for consumers, family members, and service providers as a means of fostering personal, recreational, educational and vocational independence and integration.

1932 Tenessee Technology Access Project Department of Mental Health

706 Church Street
Suite 300
Nashville, TN 37203

Computer technology center.

1933 Tidewater Center for Technology Access Special Education Annex

960 Windsor Oaks Boulevard
Virginia Beach, VA 23462   757-474-8455
                               FAX: 757-474-8648
                               TDY:757-474-8650
                        e-mail: tcta@aol.com

Marlayne Castelluzzo, Speech/Lang Pathologist
Jane Quenneville, OT/Registered
Victoria Wilson, Speech/Lang Pathologist

Nonprofit organization providing persons with disabilities access, support, and knowledge—re: technology; organization contracts for consultations, workshops and training, or conventional and assistive technologies including computers, augmented communication devices and software; resources: extensive lending library of educational software; books and videotape library; yearly individual membership and corporate membership fees; working/presentation and evaluation fees available upon request.

1934 University of Idaho Center on Disabilities and Human Development

Idaho Assistive Technology Project
129 W 3rd Street
Moscow, ID 83843   208-885-3573
                          800-IDA-TECH
                 e-mail: seile861@uidaho.edu

Michelle Doty, Training Coordinator
Ron Seiler, Project Coordinator

A University affiliated project (UAP) dedicated to the implementation of a comprehensive system for the delivery of assistive technology devices and services to Idaho citizens with disabilities, their families, or representatives in a timely cost efficient manner. Our goals are to: provide training and technical assistance; to promote public awareness of assistive technology and to increase the capacity of public agencies and private entities to serve people with disabilities.

**1935 Vermont Assistive Technology Project
Department of Aging & Disabilities**

Agency of Human Services
103 S Main Street
Weeks Building
Waterbury, VT 05671   802-241-2620
                           FAX: 802-241-2174
                  e-mail: gailpk@dad.statevt.us
                         www.statevt.us/atp

Gail Koehler, Information and Referral
Betsy Ross, Administration
Dan Gilman, AT Access Specialist
Computer technology center.

1936 Washington Technology Access Center

8705 232nd Place SW
Edmonds, WA 98026   425-883-4141
                           FAX: 425-776-3663

Grant Lord, Founder

The center was formed as a nonprofit organization to demonstrate how computer technology can transform limitations into opportunities for those with special needs. WTAC's mission is to increase the awareness, understanding and implementation of computer technology for persons with special needs, their friends, families, educators, rehabilitation and health professionals, public officials and employees.

1937 WisTech Department of Health & Social Services

Division of Vocational Rehabilitation
1 W Wilson Street
 # 7852
Madison, WI 53702   608-262-1156

Laura Bublitz, Office Manager

1938 Xerox Imaging Systems/Adaptive Products Department

Personal Reader Department
9 Centennial Drive
Peabody, MA 01960   978-977-2000
                           800-248-6550

Offers information on new services, assistive devices and technology for blind, visually impaired, learning disabled and other print disabled individuals.

1939 Your Voice Village

171 River Drive
Hadley, MA 01035
                           800-637-8720
                      FAX: 413-585-1137

Michael Oestreicher, Director

A politically and socially interactive full-service computer on line service serving 43,000,000 people with disabilities. Make a difference. Be involved. Take part in polls. Let Washington know how you feel. The database also allows participants to make air line reservations, car rentals and more. *$19.95*

Keyboards, Mouses & Joysticks

1940 A4 Tech (USA) Corporation

20256 Paseo Robles
Walnut, CA 91789   909-468-0071
                            FAX: 909-468-2231

Manufacturers of a cordless mouse, trackballs and joysticks that emulate mouse controls, flatbed scanners, modified keyboards, and other specialty mouses.

1941 AJ Weiner, Graphics Unlimited

160 N Main Street
Randolph, MA 02368
                               800-634-6692
                          FAX: 781-932-2844

Develops keyboard macro creation with storage programs.

1942 Abacus

5370 52nd Street SE
Grand Rapids, MI 49512
                               800-451-4319
                          FAX: 616-698-0325

Designs a mouse software program that permits programs written for one computer to be run on another computer.

1943 Ability Center of Greater Toledo

5605 Monroe Street
Sylvania, OH 43560
                          FAX: 416-882-4813

Manufactures keyboard wrist supports to help prevent repetitive motion disorders.

1944 Step on It! Computer Control Pedals

BILBO Innovations
1290 Carmead Parkway
 # 118
Sunnyvale, CA 94086   408-736-6086
                               800-203-0092
                          FAX: 408-736-6083
                               www.bilbo.com

Sergei Burkov, President
Katie Sheinin, Manager

BILBO Innovations, Inc. manufactures and sells Step On It keyboard control pedals. Ergonomic foot switches to emulate keystrokes and mouse clicks. Designed for victims of Repetitive Strain Injury (RSI), Carpal Tunnel Syndrome (CTS), handicapped and disabled. *$99.00*

Scanners

1945 HelpWare Series

World Communications
245 Tonopah Drive
Fremont, CA 94539   510-656-0911

Help U Type, Help U Key and Freedom Writer.
Makes computer access easier for people with disabilities.

$295 - $595

1946 Scanmaster

Howtek
21 Park Avenue
Hudson, NH 03051   603-882-5200

A digital color scanner for desktop scanning. It
allows the user to digitalize, modify, enhance and
store images in color or black and white.

1947 Scanning WSKE

Words+
40015 Sierra Highway B-145
Palmdale, CA 93550
                          800-869-8521
                     FAX: 805-266-8969

Ginger Woltosz, Vice President
Tim Ross, Manager

A software and a hardware product designed to operate on an IBM compatible PC. The software provides
dual word prediction, abbreviation expansion, five
different methods of voice output, and access to commercial software applications.

1948 System 2000/Versa

Words+
40015 Sierra Highway B-145
Palmdale, CA 93550
                          800-869-8521
                     FAX: 805-266-8969

Ginger Woltosz, Vice President
Tim Ross, Manager

Provides all of the strategies currently being used in
AAC, from dynamic display color pictographic language, to dual-word prediction text language, in a
single system.

1949 Zygo Industries

ZYGO Industries
PO Box 1008
Portland, OR 97207   503-684-6006
                       FAX: 503-684-6011
              e-mail: zygo@aygo-usa.com

Lawrence Weiss, President

Screen Enhancement

1950 Beamscope II

Florida New Concepts Marketing
PO Box 261
Port Richey, FL 34673   727-842-3231
                               800-456-7097
                          FAX: 727-845-7544
                   e-mail: compulnz@gte.net

Alan Lezark, President

Meets the needs of low vision individuals in the
recreational area. All models utilize a diamond cut
freznel lens that can double the size of a TV screen.

$25 - $74

1951 Boxlight LCD Projector

Boxlight Corporation
19332 Powder Hill Place
Poulsbo, WA 98370   360-697-4008
                           800-762-5757
                      FAX: 888-353-4242
                      www.boxlight.com

Jill Miller, Sales Manager

Boxlight.com is a unique source for visual display
systems and creative services. Presenters access
quality hardware consultation either online or toll-
free and choose from top rated manufacturers and
award winning systems. In addition , boxlight.com
provides rentals, an authorized service center, 35mm
slide creation, presentation development, and professional meeting essentials.

1952 Compu-Lenz

Florida New Concepts Marketing
PO Box 261
Port Richey, FL 34673   727-842-3231
                               800-456-7097
                          FAX: 727-845-7544
                   e-mail: compulnz@gte.net
                www.gulfside.com/compulenz

Alan Lezark, President

A fresnel lens, doubles the size of computer screen
characters without distortion or light refraction and
reduces glare. For use on 9-15 monitors. *$204.95*

1953 FDR Series of Low Vision Reading Aids

Optelec U.S.
6 Lyberty Way
Westford, MA 01886
                           800-828-1056
                      FAX: 978-692-6073
               e-mail: chrish@optelec.com
                      www.optelec.com

Chris Harris, Customer Service

The Low Vision Reading Aids features; high resolution, positive and negative display, a high-quality
zoom lens, versatile swivel and a 12 inch or 19 inch
high-resolution monitor, color or black and white,
computer compatible, or portable.

1954 IBM Independence Series - Screen Reader

IBM Corporation Special Needs Systems
PO Box 1328
Boca Raton, FL 33429

800-426-2133

A screen to text speech conversion tool.

1955 InFocus

AI Squared
PO Box 669
Manchester Center, VT 05255 802-362-3612
FAX: 802-362-1670
e-mail: zoomtext@alsquared.com

A memory-resident program that magnifies text and graphics - the entire screen, a single line or a portion of the screen.

1956 Magic/Magic Lite

Microsystems Software
600 Worcester Road
Framingham, MA 01702 508-626-8511
800-828-2600
FAX: 508-879-1069
e-mail: info@microsys.com
www.handiware.com

Terri McGrath, Sales & Marketing
Bill Kilroy, Product Manager

This software will enlarge any DOS based text or graphics 2-20X and Windows program screens, 2-8X - instantly! MAGIC requires no hardware in order to enlarge DOS and Windows applications and provides such additional viewing options as: smooth fonts, cursor and mouse tracking, screen location indicator, eight direction smooth panning, reverse and high intensity video modes and the ability to set and move up to ten bookmarks per application program. Magic Lite provides 2x magnification. *$79.00*

1957 Megatrend/2

Intercolor Corporation
2150 Boggs Road
Duluth, GA 30096 770-232-5300
800-623-9145

A color monitor with a pixel resolution up to 1280 x 1024. Anti-glare screens and tilt/swivel bases are available.

1958 Portable Large Print Computer

HumanWare
6140 Horseshoe Bar Road
Loomis, CA 95650 916-652-0933

A portable large print computer which magnifies up to 64 times. It is linked to a PC and has a hand-held camera.

1959 ZoomText

AI Squared
PO Box 669
Manchester Center, VT 05255 802-362-3612
FAX: 802-362-1670
e-mail: zoomtext@alsquared.com
www.aisquared.com

Scott Moore, Product Manager

A RAM-resident program that enlarges screen characters up to eight times. It runs on IBM PC, XT, AT and PS/2.

1960 Zoomer

Kinetic Designs
14231 Anatevka Lane SE
Olalla, WA 98359

A resident monitor enlargement program which must be used with EGA/VGA videocard hardware and a high quality monitor.

Speech Synthesizers

1961 Aicom Corporation

2318 Zanker Road
Suite 160
San Jose, CA 95131 408-557-0370
FAX: 408-238-9397

Developers of speech synthesizers for computers to accommodate persons with limited vision.

1962 AniVox Computer Speech Systems

Animated Voice Corporation
222 7th Street
Seal Beach, CA 90740

Hardware and software voice input/output packages that enhance speech communication skills and understanding - including pitch, rate, intensity, resonance, and auditory training.

1963 Artic Business Vision (for DOS) and Artic WinVision (for Windows 95)

Artic Technologies
55 Park Drive
Troy, MI 48083 248-588-7370

Dale McDaniel, V.P. Marketing
Kathy Gargagliano, V.P. Operations

A speech processor for blind computer users featuring true interactive speech with spread sheets, word processors, database managers, etc. Now available with both Windows 3.1 and Windows 95 access. *$495.00*

1964 Audapter Speech System

Personal Data Systems
100 W Rincon Avenue
Campbell, CA 95008 408-364-2030

A speech synthesizer. Its features include: intelligibility over 93 percent on the industry standard MRT test, fast response, 700-word-per-minute speech rate, speech halt control, compact unit with built-in speaker and serial interface.

1965 Digital Voice for Talking Database

Hy-Tek Manufacturing Company
1980 Route 30
Sugar Grove, IL   60554   708-466-7664

This product adds speech to PC files. Uses include personnel identification and security, multilingual training, assembly instructions and reminders.

1966 DynaVox Devices & Software

DynaVox Systems
2100 Wharton Street
Pittsburgh, PA   15203   412-381-4883
                                            888-697-7332
                                         FAX: 412-381-5241

Allow non-speaking individuals to communicate their thoughts, ideas and feelings easily. The devices' built-in infrared technology also provides users with more independence, allowing them to access TVs, VCRs, and computers. DynaVox software helps turn Macintosh and Windows and computers into communication devices so clinicians can use their computers to conduct training and assessments.

1967 Electronic Speech Assistance Devices

Luminaud
8688 Tyler Boulevard
Mentor, OH   44060   440-255-9082
                                            800-255-3408
                                         FAX: 440-255-2250

Thomas Lennox, President

Offers a full line of speech aids, voice amplifiers, mini-vox amplifiers, laryngectomec products.

1968 Hawk Communication Device

Wayne County Regional Educational Service Agency
33500 Van Born Road
Wayne, MI   48184   734-334-1300
                                         FAX: 734-334-1432

Kimberly Kaminski, Internal Operations

The Hawk employs digital voice technology for high quality, natural voice output. The touch panel is divided into a three by three matrix for a total of nine selection areas. A bulletin microphone allows the recording of up to five seconds worth of digital speech into each of the nine selection areas. *$250.00*

1969 IN CUBE PRO Voice Command

Command Corporation
3761 Venture Drive
Duluth, GA   30096   770-418-1001
                                         FAX: 770-813-0113
                                  e-mail: in3@commandcorp.com
                                       www.commandcorp.com

Judy Copeland

Continuous speech recognition system which can be used by people with disabilities. IN CUBE provides greatly increased capability, enhanced computer control and access. Blind and low-vision users gain voice access to the graphic user interface. Mobility-impaired people, including quadriplegics, benefit from voice window navigation and voice macro command input. Victims of various repetitive strain injuries RSI use IN CUBE to replace and eliminate repetitive keyboard and mouse operations. *$395.00*

1970 KEYTALK

PEAL Software
PO Box 8188
Calabasas, CA   91372   818-883-7849

Beginning literacy activity for children from three years. Computer talks each letter, word and sentence as the child types. *$ 99.00*

1971 Keywi

Consultants for Communication Technology
508 Bellevue Terrace
Pittsburgh, PA   15202
                                         FAX: 412-761-7336
                                  e-mail: cct@concommtech.com
                                       www.concommtech.com

Kathleen H. Miller Ph.D, Partner

Keywi enables a laptop computer to become a complete communication device. Create entire conversations, call a friend on the telephone, manage your business or personal affairs. Requires minimal training. Multiple access methods-switch, mouse, joystick, keyboard. Custom vocabulary. Powerful word prediction abilities. *$495.00*

1972 Keywiz

Consultants for Communication Technology
508 Bellevue Terrace
Pittsburgh, PA   15202
                                         FAX: 412-761-7336
                                  e-mail: 70272.1034@compuserve.com

Kathleen H. Miller Ph.D, Partner

Keywiz enables a laptop computer to become a complete communication device without the need for an external speech synthesizer. Your choice of 9 DecTalk, high quality voices already built into the software. Create entire conversations, call a friend on the telephone, manage your business or personal affairs. Requires minimal training. Access with any switch, mouse, head mouse, joystick or directly from the keyboard. *$995.00*

1973 Laptalker

Automated Functions
7700 Irberge Pike
Suite 420
Falls Church, VA   22043   703-818-2731

A portable talking computer that gives visually impaired people complete desk top PC compatibility.

1974 MEGA WOLF Communication Device

Wayne County Regional Educational Service Agency
33500 Van Born Road
Wayne, MI   48184   734-334-1300
                                         FAX: 734-334-1432

Kimberly Kaminski, Internal Operations

A low cost voice output communication device which is primarily intended to provide the power of speech to those individuals who are most severely challenged mentally and/or physically. The WOLF device is User programmable and uses the Texas Instruments' Touch and Tell case and touch panel; ADAM-LAB electronics with synthesized (robotic) voice. For users able to point with approximately 6 ounces of pressure. *$400.00*

1975 One-Step Communicator

AbleNet
1081 10th Avenue SE
Minneapolis, MN 55414
800-322-0956
FAX: 612-379-9143
e-mail: customerservice@ablenetinc.com
www.ablenetinc.com

The One-Step Communicator has 20 seconds of memory and has an angled switch surface making it easy to see and access. The switch surface is 2 1/2 inches in diameter. Detachable mounting base makes it easy to position a single unit in a variety of locations. *$129.00*

1976 Phone Manager

Consultants for Communication Technology
508 Bellevue Terrace
Pittsburgh, PA 15202

e-mail: 70272.1034@compuserve.com
www.concommtech.com

Kathleen Miller, Partner
Jaime Olivia, Partner

Software that allows the user to dial an out-going call directly from the computer, even with a single switch. Synthesized speech is sent through the phone line. The synthesizer then turns into a speaker phone enabling hands free, two way conversations. *$300.00*

1977 Porta-Voice Speech System

Compeer
1409 Graywood Drive
San Jose, CA 95129
408-255-3950

An augumentative communication speech system that includes battery-operated computer, speech synthesizer and software.

1978 Representation Play

REAL Software
PO Box 8188
Calabasas, CA 91372
818-883-7849

Language intervention play activities using real toys and ECHO speech synthesizer. *$150.00*

1979 SKERF-Pad

Love Electronics
395 Vosberg Lane
Goldendale, WA 98620

The touch pad is a screen reading device for blind persons. It uses a touch pad to represent the computer screen - allowing the user to point to any area of the touch pad for corresponding synthetic speech reading of the screen.

1980 Talking Screen

Words+
1220 W Avenue J
Lancaster, CA 93534
800-869-8521
FAX: 805-266-8969

Phil Lawrence, Vice President
Rachel Nielsen, Customer Support

An augmentative communication program that allows the user to select graphic symbols on the display to produce speech output. Symbols can be used either singly or in sequence as picture abbreviations. *$1395.00*

1981 Turnkey Computer Systems for the Visually, Physically, and Hearing Impaired

EVAS
PO Box 371
Westerly, RI 02891
401-596-3155
FAX: 401-596-3979
e-mail: contact@evas.com
www.evas.com

Sara Swerdlick, Customer Service Manager

Offers clear speech with pleasant inflection and tonal quality as well as variable pitch, intonation and voices.

1982 Voice-It

Voice-It
1001 Snowden Farm Road
Collierville, TN 38017
901-853-4456

Adds voice to popular spreadsheet and word processing applications on IBM PCs and compatibles, turning spreadsheets and word processing documents into talking documents.

1983 Window-Eyes

GW Micro
725 Airport North Office Park
Fort Wayne, IN 46825
219-489-3671
FAX: 219-489-2608
e-mail: sales@gwmicro.com
www.gwmicro.com

Provides access to available software automatically reading information important to the user while ignoring the rest. A screen reader for the windows operative system.

Software: Math

1984 AIMS Multimedia

9710 Desoto Avenue
Chatsworth, CA 91311
818-773-4300
800-367-2467
FAX: 818-341-6700
e-mail: info@multimedia.com
www.aimsmultimedia.com

Wynn Sherman, President
Don Lukenbill, Communications Director

AIMS Multimedia is a leader in the production and distribution of trinaing and educational programs for the business and K-12 communities via YHS, interactive CD-ROM, DVD and Internet streaming video.

1985 Academic Skill Builders in Math

DLM Teaching Resources
3578 Powder Mill Road
Beltsville, MD 20705   301-937-3884

Part arcade and part academic, incorporates meteors, lasers, spaceships, alligators and green slime to drill and reinforce basic math.

1986 Access to Math

Don Johnston Incorporated
26799 North Commerce Drive
Volo, IL 60073   847-740-0749
    800-999-4660
FAX: 847-740-7326
e-mail: info@donjohnston.com
www.donjohnston.com

This macintosh math worksheet program is tow products in one. For teachers, it makes customized worksheets in a snap. For students who struggle, it provides individualized on-screen lessons that contribute to success. *$79.00*

1987 Basic Math Competency Skill Building

Educational Activities Software
PO Box 754
Baldwin, NY 11510   516-867-7878
    800-645-2796
FAX: 516-379-7429
e-mail: learn@edact.com

Alan Stern, Sales Director

Comprehensive MATH SKILLS software tutorials teach concepts ranging from rounding and tables to measuring area. Available for Macintosh, Windows and DOS. *$369.00*

Per Unit

1988 Basic Math: Detecting Special Needs

Allyn & Bacon
160 Gould Street
Needham Heights, MA 02194
    800-852-8024

Brian E. Enright, author

Describes special mathematics needs of special learners.

180 pages 1989
ISBN 0-205116-35-3

1989 Campaign Math

Mindplay
3130 N Dodge Boulevard
Tucson, AZ 85716   520-323-1303
    800-221-7911
FAX: 520-322-0363

A complete program on the electoral process as well as a math package which teaches ratios, fractions and percentages.

1990 Elements of Mathematics

Electronic Courseware Systems
1713 South State Street
Champaign, IL 61820   217-359-7099
    800-832-4965
FAX: 217-359-6578
e-mail: sales@ecsmedia.com
www.ecsmedia.com

Jodie Varner, Manager
David Peters, President

Includes two lessons and a test in addition of simple and complex fractions. The first lesson deals with the reduction and addition of fractions and mixed numbers having common denominators, using graphics (pie slices) for illustration. The second lesson moves to problems having unlike denominators. Test results are stored in a file which is accessible to both the student and the instructor. Computer/software.

1991 First Math

Dataflo Computer Services
PO Box 1
Enfield, NH 03748   603-448-2223

Teaches number concepts, addition and subtraction.

1992 Fraction Factory

Queue
338 Commerce Drive
Fairfield, CT 06432   203-579-4171

Children learn how to work with fractions.

1993 Hide and Find

Dataflo Computer Services
PO Box 1
Enfield, NH 03748   603-448-2223

Teaches the alphabetic and numeric characters and the basic math symbols encourages the user to focus and concentrate.

1994 King's Rule

WINGS for Learning
1600 Green Hills Road
Scotts Valley, CA 95066   831-464-3600
FAX: 831-464-3600

A software mathematical problem solving game. Students discover mathematical rules as they work their way through a castle and generate and test a working hypothesis by asking questions.

1995 Learning About Numbers Volume 1

C&C Software
5713 Kentford Circle
Wichita, KS 67220   316-683-6056
    800-752-2086

Carol Clark, President

Three programs use the power of computer graphics to provide young children with a variety of experiences in working with numbers. *$50.00*

1996 Learning and Practicing with Money

Resource Software International
330 New Brunswick Avenue
Fords, NJ   08863   732-747-4477

Math questions involving money and calculations with money are the core of this drill and practice program with multiple choice answers.

1997 Math Blaster 5th Grade

Davidson & Associates
PO Box 2961
Torrance, CA   90509   310-793-0600

Helps pre-algebra and algebra students develop an understanding of the algebraic process and learn the basic steps in solving algebraic problems.

1998 Math Rabbit

Learning Company
6493 Kaiser Drive
Fremont, CA   94555   510-490-7311

Teaches early math concepts by matching objects to numbers, then adding and subtracting up to 18.

1999 Math for Everyday Living

Educational Activities
PO Box 392
Freeport, NY   11520   516-223-4666
                                800-645-3739
                  e-mail: learn@edact.com

Al Harris, President
Alan Stern, Vice President

Real-life math skills are taught with this tutorial and practice software program. Examples include Paying for a Meal (addition & subtraction), Working with Sales Slips (multiplication), Unit Pricing (division), Sales Tax (percent), Earning with Overtime (fractions) plus more. Software: CD-Rom, Windows, MAC, and DOS. *$159.00*

2000 Math for Successful Living

Siboney Learning Group
PO Box 220520
St. Louis, MO   63122   314-909-1760
                                800-351-1404
                           FAX: 314-984-8063
                  e-mail: kculleton@siboneylg.com
                                www.gamco.com

Kim Culleton, Sales

These programs include managing a checking account, budgeting, shopping strategies and buying on credit.

2001 New Math Blaster Plus!

DLM Teaching Resources
3578 Powder Mill Road
Beltsville, MD   20705   301-937-3884

A six game program that features color graphics and musical tones.

2002 Optimum Resource Educational Software

Optimum Resource
18 Hunter Road
Hilton Head Island, SC   29926   843-689-8000
                                 888-784-2592
                            FAX: 843-689-8008
                  e-mail: sticky@stickybear.com
                                www.stickybear.com

Chris Gintz, Vice President/ Marketing

A complete topical curriculum of reading, math, keyboard skills and science programs that are age and skill specific. *$59.95*

2003 Piece of Cake Math

Queue
338 Commerce Drive
Fairfield, CT   06432   203-579-4171

Color, sound and animation combine forces in a program of five games focusing on basic mathematical operations.

2004 Puzzle Tanks

WINGS for Learning
1600 Green Hills Road
Scotts Valley, CA   95066   831-464-3600
                           FAX: 831-464-3600

A mathematical problem solving game that involves multi-step problems.

2005 Right Turn

WINGS for Learning
1600 Green Hills Road
Scotts Valley, CA   95066   831-464-3600
                           FAX: 831-464-3600

Requires students to predict, experiment and learn about the mathematical concepts of rotation and transformation.

2006 RoboMath

Mindplay
3130 N Dodge Boulevard
Tucson, AZ   85716   520-323-1303
                                800-221-7911
                           FAX: 520-322-0363

Players learn multiplication and division using a game paddle.

2007 Stickybear Math

Optimum Resource
18 Hunter Road
Hilton Head Island, SC   29926   843-689-8000
                                 888-784-2592
                            FAX: 843-689-8008
                  e-mail: sticky@stickybear.com
                                www.stickybear.com

Chris Gintz, VP Marketing Director

Sharpen basic addition and subtraction skills with this captivating, versatile series of math exercises. *$59.95*

2008 Stickybear Numbers

Optimum Resource
18 Hunter Road
Hilton Head Island, SC   29926   843-689-8000
888-784-2592
FAX: 843-689-8008
e-mail: sticky@stickybear.com
www.stickybear.com

Counting and number recognition are as easy as
1-2-3 with this award-winning program. *$59.95*

2009 Stickybear Word Problems

Optimum Resource
18 Hunter Road
Hilton Head Island, SC   29926   843-689-8000
888-784-2592
FAX: 843-689-8008
e-mail: sticky@stickybear.com
www.stickybear.com

Hundreds of different word problems make it easy
for students to practice basic math skills. *$59.95*

2010 Stickybear's Math Splash

Optimum Resource
18 Hunter Road
Hilton Head Island, SC   29926   843-689-8000
888-784-2592
FAX: 843-689-8008
e-mail: sticky@stickybear.com
www.stickybear.com

Chris Gintz, Vice President/ Marketing

Unique multiple activities keep the learning level
high while children acquire skills in addition, subtraction, multiplication, and division. *$59.95*

2011 Stickybear's Math Town

Optimum Resource
18 Hunter Road
Hilton Head Island, SC   29926   843-689-8000
888-784-2592
FAX: 843-689-8008
e-mail: sticky@stickybear.com
www.stickybear.com

Chris Gintz, Vice President/ Marketing

Children ages 5-10 gain proficiency in addition, subtraction, multiplication a and division, as well as life
skills and word problems. In english and spanish,
children sharpen skills both vertically and horizontally, clear crisp graphics and sound enable teachers
to monitor and access skills and development.
$59.95

2012 Tomorrow's Promise: Mathematics

Jostens Learning/Hartley
9920 Pacific Heights Boulevard
San Diego, CA   92121   858-587-0087
800-247-1380
FAX: 619-622-7873
www.compasslearning.com

Steve Allen, Accts. Mgr, Alternate Channels

By integrating interdisciplinary content and real-
world application of skills, this product emphasizes
the practical value of fundamental math skills. It
helps your students develop a problem-solving aptitude for ongoing mathematics achievement. *$279.95*

Software: Miscellaneous

2013 ARTN (Advanced Rehabilitation Technology Network)

25825 Eshelman Avenue
Lomita, CA   90717

This database supplies information pertinent to
rehabilitation and employment.

2014 Academic Software

331 W 2nd Street
Lexington, KY   40507   859-233-2332
800-842-2357
FAX: 859-231-0725
e-mail: ASISTAFF@acsw.com
www.acsw.com

Warren E. Lacefield, President
Penny D. Ellis, Marketing Director

Developers of academic programs and early childhood programs. Also developes switches and switch
interfaces for operating computers.

2015 Adaptive Computer Systems

1835 Hafor Drive
Iowa City, IA   52246   319-338-1449
FAX: 319-338-3320

Designers of web page creation software and on-
screen keyboard programs.

2016 Adventures in Musicland

Electronic Courseware Systems
1713 South State Street
Champaign, IL   61820   217-352-5510
800-832-4965
FAX: 217-359-6578
e-mail: sales@ecsmedia.com
www.ecsmedia.com

Litterst, Touchstone & Romeo, author
G. David Peters, President
Jodie Varner, Marketing Manager

This unique set of music games features characters
from Lewis Carroll's, Alice in Wonderland. Players
learn through pictures, sounds, and animation which
help develop understanding of musical tones, com-
posers, and musical symbols. Games include Mu-
sicMatch, Melody Mixup, Picture Perfect and Sound
Concentration. *$49.95*

2017 Ai Squared

PO Box 669
Manchester Center, VT   05255   802-362-3612
FAX: 802-362-1670
e-mail: zoomtext@aisquared.com
www.aisquared.com

Developers of software for the visually impaired.

2018 All About You - Appropriate Special Interactions and Self-Esteem

PCI Educational Publishing
PO Box 34270
San Antonio, TX   78212

800-594-4263
FAX: 888-259-8284
www.pcicatalog.com

This game offers parents and game players a new line of communication when discussing various issues such as learning to be thoughtful, respecting the rights and feelings of others, how to make and keep friends and more. *$49.95*

2019 All Star Review

Tom Snyder Productions
108A Clematis Avenue
Waltham, MA   02453

617-926-6000
800-342-0236
www.tomsnyder.com

This package turns group review into a baseball game for small and large groups.

2020 At Home with Stickybear

Optimum Resource
18 Hunter Road
Hilton Head Island, SC   29926

843-689-8000
888-784-2592
FAX: 843-689-8008
e-mail: sticky@stickybear.com
www.stickybear.com

Chris Gintz, Vice President/Marketing

This dynamic new multifaceted program covers a wide range of preschoolskills that go far beyone the stricktly academic! At Stickybear's house, children discover the alphabet, numbers, shapes, colors, plus social skills, important safety messages, and delightful off-screen activities that foster creativity. *$59.95*

2021 Attainment Company/IEP Resources

504 Commerce Parkway
PO Box 930160
Verona, WI   53593

608-845-7880
800-327-4269
FAX: 800-942-3865
e-mail: info@attainment.inc.com
www.attainment.inc.com

Brent Denu, Marketing Coordinator
Julie Denu, Technical Support
Theresa O'Connor, Office Manager

Software, videos, print and hands-on materials for developmental and cognitive disabilities.

2022 Automatic Test Author

Resource Software International
330 New Brunswick Avenue
Fords, NJ   08863

732-747-4477

This program, designed for the novice, has highlighted menus to guide the user through completion of tests, drills and exercises.

2023 Away We Ride

Soft Touch
4182 Pinewood Lake Drive
Bakersfield, CA   93309

Software for children. For Macintosh only.

2024 Bailey's Book House

Edmark Corporation
PO Box 97021
Redmond, WA   98073

425-556-8400
800-691-2986
www.edmark.com

Software for children.

2025 Battenberg & Associates

11135 Rolling Springs Drive
Carmel, IN   46033

317-843-2208

Offers various software programs that develop the user's visual memory, sequencing skills, word recognition, hand-eye coordination and more.

2026 Behavior Skills - Learning How People Should Act

Programming Concepts
PO Box 12428
San Antonio, TX   78212

800-594-4263
FAX: 218-248-055

Janie Haugen, Program Director
Jeff McLane, President/CEO

Helps players learn what behavior is acceptable and what behavior is not acceptable in the real world. *$49.95*

2027 Blocks in Motion

Don Johnston Incorporated
26799 North Commerce Drive
Volo, IL   60073

847-740-0749
800-999-4660
FAX: 847-740-7326
e-mail: info@donjohnston.com
www.donjohnston.com

This unique art and motion program makes drawing, creating and animating fun and educational for all users. Based on the Piagetian Theory for motor-sensory development, this program promotes the concept that the process is as educational and as much fun as the end result. *$79.00*

2028 Brain Train

Rehabilitation Psychology Associates
PO Box 1510
Beaverton, OR   97075

503-682-2275

A set of 55 programs to assist in remediating a wide range of cognitive and behavioral deficits which commonly follow brain injury.

2029 CINTEX2 - Speak to Your Appliances

NanoPac
4823 South Sheridan Road
Suite 302
Tulsa, OK 74145

FAX: 918-665-0361
e-mail: info@nanopac.com
www.nanopac.com

Silvio V. Cianfrone, CCSP, President

CINTEX2, with a voice recognition program, will control up to 256 off/on appliances, dial and answer the phone, flash for call waiting, dial from a directory, control TV's, VCR's, stereos and more — all with your voice. CINTEX2 includes the necessary hardware and voice macros which you can use to immediately control your environment. You can tailor these macros to your personal needs and add new macros. Pops-up over current application allowing instant access. $695-$1,390.

2030 Car Builder

Optimum Resource
18 Hunter Road
Hilton Head Island, SC 29926

843-689-8000
888-784-2592
FAX: 843-689-8008
e-mail: sticky@stickybear.com
www.stickybear.com

Chris Gintz, Vice President/ Marketing

As design engineers, users build cars on screen, specifying chassis length, wheelbase, engine type, transmission, fuel tank size, suspension, steering, tires and brakes. All functional choices are interrelated and will affect the performance of the final design. $ 59.99

2031 Cave Girl Clair

Rhiannon Software
3717 Titan Drive
Richmond, VA 23225

This program portrays believable children in realistic stories, rewards integrated and creative thinking.

2032 Center for Best Practices in Early Childhood

27 Horrabin Hall
Macomb, IL 61455

309-298-1634
FAX: 309-298-2305
e-mail: l-robinson1@wiu.edu
www.mprojects.wiu.edu

Linda Robinson, Assistant Director

A group of early childhood projects which focus on children ages birth to 8 with disabilities and their families. Services include technology training, curricula, books, software and other products.

2033 Clock

Jostens Learning/Hartley
9920 Pacific Heights Boulevard
San Diego, CA 92121

858-587-0087
800-247-1380
FAX: 619-622-7873
www.compasslearning.com

Steve Allen, Accts. Mgr, Alternate Channels

An extremely simple, easy-to-use program for children who are learning how to read the time of day from clocks and digital displays. Apple and MS-DOS and Mac available. $39.95

2034 Co:Writer

Don Johnston Incorporated
26799 North Commerce Drive
Volo, IL 60073

847-740-0749
800-999-4660
FAX: 847-740-7326
e-mail: info@donjohnston.com
www.donjohnston.com

A writing description program that helps construct sentences. This is an easy-to-use intelligent word prediction program that works in conjunction with any word processor or text application program to reduce the number of keystrokes necessary to complete an intended word or sentence. This invaluable program can help make the writing process easier, faster and even better for writers of all ages and ability levels. $290.00

2035 Community Skills - Learning to Function in Your Neighborhood

Programming Concepts
PO Box 12428
San Antonio, TX 78212

800-594-4263
FAX: 218-248-055

Janie Haugen, Program Director
Jeff McLane, President/CEO

Offers parents and educators a functional way to teach community life skills. $49.95

2036 Computerized Speech Lab

Kay Elemetrics Corporation
12 Maple Avenue
Pine Brook, NJ 07058

973-628-6200

Hardware/software for the acquisition, analysis/display, playback and storage of speech signals.

2037 Cooking Class - Learning About Food Preparation

Programming Concepts
PO Box 12428
San Antonio, TX 78212

800-594-4263
FAX: 218-248-055

Janie Haugen, Program Director
Jeff McLane, President/CEO

This game offers parents and educators a new way to teach basic preparation skills. Kitchen safety and sanitation are stressed throughout the game. $49.95

2038 Dilemma

Educational Activities Software
PO Box 754
Baldwin, NY 11510

516-867-7878
800-645-2796
FAX: 516-379-7429
e-mail: learn@edact.com

Alan Stern, Sales Director

Realistic stories with a choice of different gripping endings, color graphics, a built-in dictionary, and a user controlled reading rate make these computer programs compelling enough to interest all students. Comprehension and vocabulary questions follow each story. *$159.00*

2039 Dino-Games

Academic Software
331 W 2nd Street
Lexington, KY   40507   606-233-2332
                                                 800-842-2357
                                                 FAX: 606-231-0725

Warren E. Lacefield, PhD, President
Penelope Ellis, Marketing Director

Dino-Games are single switch software programs for early switch practice. Dinosaur games provide practice in pattern recognition, cause and effect demonstration, directionality training, number concepts and problem solving. They are compatible with most popular switch interfaces and alternate keyboards. For Macintosh, IBM and compatibles. DINO-LINK is a matching game; DINO-MAZE is a series of maze games; DINO-FIND is a game of concentration; and DINO-DOT is a collection of dot-to-dot games.

$39.95 per game

2040 Directions: Technology in Special Education

DREAMMS for Kids
273 Ringwood Road
Freeville, NY   13068   607-539-3027
                                                 FAX: 607-539-9930
                                                 www.dreamms.org

A CD containing all of 'Directions' past articles and information gathered from their newsletter which lists resources for assistive and adaptive computer tehnologies in the home, school and community. *$24.95*

2041 Director II/ Scanning Director II

Prentke Romich Company
1022 Heyl Road
Wooster, OH   44691   330-262-1984
                                                 800-262-1984
                                                 FAX: 330-263-4829
                                                 www.prentrom.com

Infrared controls which permit someone with a disability to operate TV's, VCR's, stereos, CD Players and anything that can be operated with an infrared remote control. The Scanning Director can be operated by either a single or dual switch. The Director allows you to store commands into your communication device and then transmit them using the keys of your device. *$495.00*

2042 ESI Master Resource Guide

Educational Software Institute
4213 South 94th Street
Omaha, NE   68127   402-592-3300
                                                 800-955-5570
                                                 FAX: 402-592-2017
                                                 e-mail: info@edsoft.com
                                                 www.edsoft.com

Lee Myers, President
Kathy Cavanaugh, Catalog Manager

Educational Software Institute (ESI) provides a one-stop shop to purchase software titles by all of the best publishers. The ESI Master Gold Book catalog and CD-ROM represents more than 400 software publishers, with information on more than 8,000 software titles. Take the confusion out of software selection by calling ESI for all of your software needs - including competitive prices, software previews, knowledgeable assistance, and the largest selection available all in one place.

Yearly

2043 EZ Keys

Words+
40015 Sierra Highway B-145
Palmdale, CA   93550   805-266-5800
                                                 800-869-8521
                                                 FAX: 805-266-8969

Ginger Woltosz, Vice President
Tim Ross, Manager

A software and hardware product designed to operate on an IBM compatible PC. The software provides dual word prediction, abbreviation expansion, five different methods of voice output and access to commercial software applications. *$1395.00*

2044 Early Games for Young Children

Queue
338 Commerce Drive
Fairfield, CT   06432   203-579-4171

Software that includes nine activities that entertain preschoolers in honing basic math and language skills.

2045 Early Music Skills

Electronic Courseware Systems
1713 South State Street
Champaign, IL   61820   217-352-5510
                                                 800-832-4965
                                                 FAX: 217-359-6578
                                                 e-mail: sales@ecsmedia.com
                                                 www.ecsmedia.com

Lolita Walker Gilkes, author
G. David Peters, President
Jodie Varner, Marketing Manager

A tutorial and drill program designed for the beginning music student. It covers four basic music reading skills: recognition of line and space notes; comprehension of the numbering system for the musical staff; visual and aural identification of notes moving up and down; and recognition of notes stepping and skipping up and down. *$ 39.95*

2046 Eating Skills - Learning Basic Table Manners

Programming Concepts
PO Box 12428
San Antonio, TX   78212
                                                 800-594-4263
                                                 FAX: 218-248-055

Janie Haugen, Program Director
Jeff McLane, President/CEO

Offers parents and educators a functional way to teach and reinforce basic table manners. *$49.95*

2047 EduCale

Houghton Mifflin
1 Beacon Street
Boston, MA   02108   617-371-9500

Teachers walk students through basic spreadsheet functions, providing a practice template for reinforcement and offering a step-by-step approach to help students become proficient in spreadsheet use.

2048 Electronic Courseware Systems

1210 Lancaster Drive
Champaign, IL   61821   217-352-5510
                               800-832-4965
e-mail: sales@ecsmedia.com
www.ecsmedia.com

Jodie Varner, Manager
David Peters, President
Offers a complete library of instructional software for music, math, science and social studies.

2049 European Nations and Locations

Britannica Software
345 4th Street
San Francisco, CA   94107   415-777-9876

Uses graphics and a game format to teach map skills and geographical, historical and economic facts.

2050 Freddy's Puzzling Adventure

DLM Teaching Resources
3078 Powder Mill Road
Beltsville, MD   20705   301-937-3884

Freddy the friendly turtle helps children acquire problem solving and logical thinking skills with three fun activities.

2051 Funzeez

Resource Software International
330 New Brunswick Avenue
Fords, NJ   08863   732-747-4477

This arithmetic and language package builds basic skills and provides elementary students four different programs: flashing numbers, arithmetic drills, unscrambling words and word guessing.

2052 GoalView Performance Information System for Special Education

Learning Tools International
2391 Circadian Way
Santa Rosa, CA   95407   707-521-3530
                               800-333-9954
FAX: 707-521-3535
e-mail: info@ltools.com
www.goalview.com

Cathy Zier, Vice President

An Internet information system for students, educators and parents that enables accountability and achievement tracking; prepares IDEA compliant IEP's in minutes; provides voer 250,000 Education Standards and Special Education goals and objectives in English and Spanish; generates Federal compliance reports; and creates IDEA GoalCard progress reports for students, schools and districts for every reporting period.

2053 HELP

VORT Corporation
PO Box 60132
Palo Alto, CA   94306   650-322-8282
                        FAX: 650-327-0747
www.vort.com

A software version of HELP, covers over 650 skills in 6 developmental areas; cognitive, motor skills, language, gross motor, social and self-help.

2054 Handbook of Adaptive Switches and Augmentative Communication Devices

Academic Software
331 W 2nd Street
Lexington, KY   40507   606-233-2332
                               800-842-2357
                        FAX: 606-231-0725
Cindy L. George and Warren E. Lacefield, author
Warren E. Lacefield, PhD, President, Author
Penelope Ellis, Marketing Director
Cindy L. George, Author
This second edition contains physical descriptions and laboratory test data for a variety of commercially available pressure switches and augmentative communication devices and chapters on physical interaction, seating and positioning, and control access. It is an essential tool for assistive technology professionals and therapists who make decisions concerning physical access. *$60.00*

300 pages Hardcover

2055 HandiWARE

Microsystems Software
600 Worcester Road
Framingham, MA   01702   508-626-8511
                                800-828-2600
                         FAX: 508-879-1069
e-mail: infor@microsys.com
www.handiware.com

Terri McGrath, Sales & Marketing
Bill Kilroy, Product Manager
Adapted access software, assists persons with physical, hearing and visual impairments in accessing computers running DOS and Windows. HandiWARE is a suite of 8 software programs which provide users with screen magnification, alternate keyboard access, word prediction, augmentative communication, hands free telephone access, a visual beep. $20.00-$595.00.

2056 How to Write for Everyday Living

Educational Activities
PO Box 392
Freeport, NY   11520   516-223-4666
                              800-645-3739
                       FAX: 516-623-9282
e-mail: learn@edact.com

Alan Stern, Vice President

An individualized Life Skills WRITING Software program emphasizing the reading, writing, communication, and reference skills needed for real-life tasks: preparing a resume, an employment form, a business letter and envelope, a learner's permit, a social security application, and banking forms. *$159.00*

2057 IntelliKeys Keyboard

IntelliTools
55 Leveroni Center
Suite 9
Novato, CA 94949

800-899-6687
e-mail: info@intellitools.com

Software for children. Includes one cable, eight standard overlays that work with most software programs. *$395.00*

2058 Intellipics

Intellipics
55 Leveroni Center
Suite 9
Novato, CA 94949

e-mail: intellitoo@aol.com

Software for children. For Macintosh only.

2059 Jenny of the Prairie

Rhiannon Software
3717 Titan Drive
Richmond, VA 23225

The child using this program enhances his or her problem solving skills with learning about the environment.

2060 KIDS (Keyboard Introductory Development Series)

Electronic Courseware Systems
1713 South State Street
Champaign, IL 61820

217-352-5510
800-832-4965
FAX: 217-359-6578
e-mail: sales@ecsmedia.com
www.ecsmedia.com

Brenna Bailey, author
G. David Peters, President
Jodie Varner, Marketing Manager

A four disk series for the very young. Zoo Puppet Theater reinforces learning correct finger numbers for piano playing; Race Car Keys teaches keyboard geography by recognizing syllables or note names; Dinosaurs Lunch teaches placement of the notes on the treble staff; and Follow Me asks the student to play notes that have been presented aurally. *$49.95*

2061 Katie's Farm

McGee Software, Lawrence Productions
1800 S 53th Street
Galesburg, MI 49053

800-421-4157

Software for children. For Macintosh of PC.

2062 Keyboard Tutor, Music Software

Electronic Courseware Systems
1713 South State Street
Champaign, IL 61820

217-352-5510
800-832-4965
FAX: 217-359-6578
e-mail: sales@ecsmedia.com
www.ecsmedia.com

Vincent Oddo, author
G. David Peters, President
Jodie Varner, Marketing Manager

Presents exercises for learning elementary keyboard skills including knowledge of names of the keys, piano keys matched to notes, notes matched to piano keys, whole steps and half steps. Each lesson allows unlimited practice of the skills. The program may be used with or without a midi keyboard attached to the computer. *$39.95*

2063 Keyboarding for Individual Achievement Learning Disabled and Dyslexic Edition

Teachers' Institute for Special Education
4 Gablin Center
Huntington, NY 11746

516-781-2020
FAX: 516-781-4070
e-mail: jackheller@aol.com
www.users.aol.com/jackheller

Jack Heller, Director

Allows the learning diabled or dyslexic student to acquire keyboarding skills through visually cued alphabetical approach designed and tested to meet the pecific learning style needs of this unique population at every grade level. Package contains: IBM software, a set of lesson plans and instructional goals; supplamental graded Data input exercises. *$148.95*

2064 Keyboarding for the Physically Handicapped

Teachers' Institute for Special Education
4 Gabalin Center
Huntington Station, NY 11763

631-549-1715
FAX: 516-549-1715
e-mail: jackheller@aol.com
www.users.aol.com/jackheller

Jack Heller, Director

Customed designed touch typing programs for any student. A person needs order by the number of usable fingers on each hand (not counting the thumb), and whether or not a one finger or a head-pointer edition is wanted. Package includes IBM software; a complete set of lesson plans and instructional goals. *$149.95*

2065 Keyboarding with One Hand

Teachers' Institute for Special Education
PO Box 2300
Wantagh, NY 11793

FAX: 516-781-4070
e-mail: jackheller@aol.com
www.users.aol.com/jackheller

Jack Heller, Director

This 22 lesson tutorial developed through 25 years of research, testing and teaching allows a student with one hand to aqure employable keyboarding skills using a touch system designed for the standard IBM PC keyboard. *$79.95*

2066 Kidsview Software
PO Box 98
Warner, NH 03278 603-927-4428
800-542-7501
FAX: 603-927-4428
e-mail: kidsview@conknet.com

Julie Griffiths

Large character software for students and adults with visual difficulties and the learning disabled. Including KIDSWORD, a full function word processor and the SCHOOLCRAFT series (Math 1, Word 1, Games 1). Students may work on-screen or print large character worksheets. All manuals are Large Print. Call for free brochure.

2067 LPDOS Deluxe
Optelec U.S.
6 Lyberty Way
Westford, MA 01886
800-828-1056
FAX: 978-692-6073
e-mail: chrish@optelec.com
www.optelec@optelec.com

Large print software programs. *$595.00*

2068 Large Print DOS
Optelec U.S.
PO Box 796
Westford, MA 01886 978-692-9496
800-828-1056
FAX: 978-692-6073
e-mail: chrish@optelec.com
www.optelec@optelec.com

2069 Laureate Learning Systems
110 E Spring Street
Winooski, VT 05404 802-655-4755
800-562-6801
FAX: 802-655-4757
e-mail: info@llsys.com
www.laureatelearning.com

Michelle L. Woodbury, Admin. Assistant
Kathy Hollandsworth, Office Manager

Laureate publishes award-winning talking software for children and adults with disabilities. Programs cover cause and effect, language development, cognitive processing, and reading. High-quality speech, colorful graphics and amusing animation make learning fun. Accessible with TouchWindow, single switch, keyboard and mouse. No reading required. Available for Apple II, IIGS, IBM, Windows '95 and Macintosh computers. Call for a free catalog.

2070 Learning Company
1 Martha's Way
Hiawatha, IA 52233 319-395-9626
800-752-3777
FAX: 319-378-7392
e-mail: Linda.Talcott@learningco.com
www.learningco.com

Linda Talcott, Asst Credit & Collections

Software for children. For Macintosh or Windows (3.1 DOS or Windows 95, Windows 98 required).

2071 Little Red Hen
Jostens Learning/Hartley
9920 Pacific Heights Boulevard
San Diego, CA 92121 858-587-0087
800-247-1380
FAX: 619-622-7873
www.compasslearning.com

Steve Allen, Accts. Mgr, Alternate Channels

Children learn about the rewards of hard work when they discover hwo the Little Red Hen's friends miss out on freshly baked bread. Puzzles, rhymes, story writing, and other interactive exercises enhance the creative learning process. *$34.95*

2072 Looking Good - Learning to Improve Your Appearance
Programming Concepts
PO Box 12428
San Antonio, TX 78212
800-594-4263
FAX: 218-248-055

Janie Haugen, Program Director
Jeff McLane, President/CEO

This game offers a creative way to discuss all areas of grooming. *$49.95*

2073 Magic Crayon
C&C Software
5713 Kentford Circle
Wichita, KS 67220 316-683-6056
800-752-2086

Carol Clark, author
Carol Clarke, President

Children can use Magic Crayon to draw pictures and designs on the computer's low-resolution graphics screen. Drawing, color selection and other options are controlled with simple keystroke commands. *$ 45.00*

2074 Mask Parade
Queue
338 Commerce Drive
Fairfield, CT 06432 203-579-4171

Allows children to use the computer to design their own masks, hats, glasses, jewelry, badges, accessories and more and then print them out and wear them.

2075 Morse Code WSKE
Words+
40015 Sierra Highway B-145
Palmdale, CA 93550
800-869-8521
FAX: 805-266-8969

Ginger Woltosz, Vice President
Tim Ross, Manager

A software and hardware product designed to operate on an IBM compatible PC.

2076 Muppet Learning Keys

WINGS for Learning
1600 Green Hills Road
Scotts Valley, CA 95066   831-464-3600
       FAX: 831-464-3600

Designed to introduce children to the world of the computer as they become familiar with letters, numbers and colors.

2077 Please Understand Me Software Program and Books

Cambridge Educational
PO Box 931
Monmouth Junction, NJ 08852
       800-468-4227
       FAX: 800-329-6687
       e-mail: lisa.schmuclei@films.com
       www.cambridgeeducational.com

Lisa Schmuclei, Marketing

Promotes self understanding while helping each student understand they are different from others. *$69.00*

     209 pages BiAnnual
     ISBN 0-927368-56-x

2078 Pond

WINGS for Learning
1600 Green Hills Road
Scotts Valley, CA 95066   831-464-3600
       FAX: 831-464-3600

Software game that teaches pattern recognition and encourages observation, trial and error and the interpretation of data.

2079 Productivity Plus (Basic Education)

Productivity Software International
211 East 43rd Street
Room 2202
New York, NY 10017   212-818-1144
       FAX: 212-618-1197
       e-mail: admin@sunflowersoft.com

Works together with other software programs under DOS or WINDOWS. Enables users to type abbreviations instead of words, phrases or commands. As abbreviation is followed with space, punctuation or Enter key, it expands into whatever it represents. Users save time and keystrokes and can avoid using awkward commands which require CTRL, ALT and other special key combinations.

2080 Public Domain Software

Colorado Easter Seal Society
5755 W Alameda Avenue
Lakewood, CO 80226   303-233-1666

Cathy Bodine, Director
Kitty Jones, Software Coordinator
Software through the Colorado Easter Seal Society.

2081 Stickybear Town Builder

Optimum Resource
18 Hunter Road
Hilton Head Island, SC 29926   843-689-8000
       888-784-2592
       FAX: 843-689-8008
       e-mail: sticky@stickybear.com

Chris Gintz, VP Marketing

Children learn to read maps, build towns, take trips and use a compass in this simulation program. *$59.95*

2082 Stickybear Typing

Optimum Resource
18 Hunter Road
Hilton Head Island, SC 29926   843-689-8000
       888-784-2592
       FAX: 843-689-8008
       e-mail: sticky@stickybear.com

Chris Gintz, VP Marketing

Sharpen typing skills with three challenging activities: Stickybear Keypress, Stickybear Thump and Stickybear Stories. *$59.95*

2083 Stickybear's Early Learning Activities

Optimum Resource
18 Hunter Road
Hilton Head Island, SC 29926   843-689-8000
       888-784-2592
       FAX: 843-689-8008
       e-mail: sticky@stickybear.com
       www.stickybear.com

Chris Gintz, Vice President/ Marketing

Two modes of play, structure and non-structured, allow youngsters to learn through prompted direction or by the discovery method. Lively animation and sound keep attention levels high and Stickybear's Early Learning Activities is bilingual, so youngsters can build skills in both English, and Spanish. *$59.95*

2084 Stickybear's Kindergarden Activities

Optimum Resource
18 Hunter Road
Hilton Head Island, SC 29926   843-689-8000
       888-784-2592
       FAX: 843-689-8008
       e-mail: sticky@stickybear.com
       www.stickybear.com

Chris Gintz, Vice President/ Marketing

This dynamic new multifaceted program covers a wide range of preschool skills that go far beyond the strictly academic! At Stickybear's house, children discover the alphabet, numbers, shapes, colors, plus - social skills, important safety messages, and delightful off-screen activities that foster creativity. Over three hours of original music can be compose by a chid and saved for future use. *$59.95*

2085 Stickybear's Science Fair: Light

Optimum Resource
18 Hunter Road
Hilton Head Island, SC 29926   843-689-8000
888-784-2592
FAX: 843-689-8008
e-mail: sticky@stickybear.com
www.stickybear.com

Chris Gintz, Vice President/ Marketing

The first in the new series of science-based programs Stickybear Science Fair: Light presents a content rich environment which allows students, ages 7-12 to explore, experiment with, and understand light and it's properties. The program presents experiments, both structured and free-form, which allow users to work with prisms, lenses, color mixing, optical illusions, and more. *$59.95*

2086 Storybook Maker Deluxe

Jostens Learning/Hartley
9920 Pacific Heights Boulevard
San Diego, CA 92121   858-587-0087
800-247-1380
FAX: 619-622-7873
www.compasslearning.com

Steve Allen, Accts. Mgr, Alternate Channels

Using Storybook Maker Deluxe and their imaginations, students can create and publish stories filled with exciting graphics. Students can write stories and watch as the text appears in the setting they've chosen. Engaging sounds and music, plus lively animations, provide positive learning reinforcement throughout the program. *$44.95*

2087 Super Challenger

Electronic Courseware Systems
1713 S State Street
Champaign, IL 61820   217-352-5510
800-832-4965
FAX: 217-359-6587
e-mail: sales@ecsmedia.com
www.ecsmedia.com

Jodie Varner, Manager
David Peters, President

An aural-visual musical game that increases the player's ability to remember a series of pitches as they are played by the computer. The game is based on a 12-note chromatic scale, a major scale, and a minor scale. Each pitch is reinforced visually with a color representation of a keyboard on the display screen. Computer/software. *$39.95*

2088 There are Tyrannosaurs Trying on Pants in My Bedroom

Jostens Learning/Hartley
9920 Pacific Heights Boulevard
San Diego, CA 92121   858-587-0087
800-247-1380
FAX: 619-622-7873
www.compasslearning.com

Steve Allen, Accts. Mgr, Alternate Channels

In this popular story, Saturday chores turn into fun-filled frolicking when dinosaurs come for a visit. Sounds, music, and animation make learning about phonics and vocabulary dyno-mite. *$34.95*

2089 Three Billy Goats Gruff

Jostens Learning/Hartley
9920 Pacific Heights Boulevard
San Diego, CA 92121   858-587-0087
800-247-1380
FAX: 619-622-7873
www.compasslearning.com

Steve Allen, Accts. Mgr, Alterante Channels

Motivating exercises and creative activities provide hours of learning fun while young students follow the adventure of The Three Billy Goats Gruff in this animated version of the timeless tale. *$ 34.95*

2090 Three Little Pigs

Jostens Learning/Hartley
9920 Pacific Heights Boulevard
San Diego, CA 92121   858-587-0087
800-247-1380
FAX: 619-622-7873
www.compasslearning.com

Steve Allen, Accts. Mgr, Alternate Channels

Help young students build reading comprehension and writing skills with this interactive version of the children's classic, The Three Little Pigs. Animated storytelling and creative activities inspire children to read, write, and rhyme. *$34.95*

2091 TouchWindow touch screen

Edmark Corporation
PO Box 97021
Redmond, WA 98073   425-556-8400
FAX: 425-556-8430
e-mail: edmarkteam@edmark.com
www.edmark.com

Software for children. *$335.00*

2092 Volcanoes

Earthware Computer Services
2386 Spring Boulevard
Eugene, OR 97403
FAX: 541-342-3416

Simulation of volcano in which children play the role of the scientists. *$49.50*

2093 What Was That!

Jostens Learning/Hartley
9920 Pacific Heights Boulevard
San Diego, CA 92121   858-587-0087
800-247-1380
FAX: 619-622-7873
www.compasslearning.com

Steve Allen, Accts. Mgr, Alternate Channels

In this bedtime story, noises in the night send three brother bears scurrying out of bed. Thoughtful questions test young readers' comprehension, while games, voice recording, writing practice, and other playful activities stimulate their creativity.

2094 You Tell Me - Learning Basic Information

Programming Concepts
PO Box 12428
San Antonio, TX 78212

800-594-4263
FAX: 218-248-055

Janie Haugen, Program Director
Jeff McLane, President/CEO

This game teaches and reinforces basic information all individuals need to know. Questions asked in this game help prepare people to communicate personal identification information important to community survival. *$49.95*

Software: Professional

2095 Acrontech International

625 Delaware Avenue
Suite 450
Buffalo, NY 14202

716-881-1500
800-245-2020
FAX: 716-854-4014
e-mail: info@acrontech.com
www.acrontech.com

This company supplies software, audio mixers, and closed-caption televisions.

2096 All of the Above

C&C Software
5713 Kentford Circle
Wichita, KS 67220

316-683-6056
800-752-2086

Carol Clark, President

A complete system for creating quizzes and electronic study guides. *$90.00*

2097 Compuscore

DLM Teaching Resources
3578 Powder Mill Road
Beltsville, MD 20705

301-937-3884

A psycho-educational assessment program for computerized scoring of standardized tests.

2098 DME VI

Dezine Associates
758 State Route 18
Suite 110
East Brunswick, NJ 08816

732-390-2120
FAX: 732-390-1729

This full-featured software package specific to the health care industry includes accounts receivable, order entry, inventory control and sale management in an easy-to-use format.

2099 DPS with BCP

VORT Corporation
PO Box 60132
Palo Alto, CA 94306

650-322-8282
FAX: 650-327-0747
www.vort.com

This program uses unique DPS branching techniques to access goals and objectives.

2100 Diagnostic Report Writer

Parrot Software
190 Sandy Ridge Road
State College, PA 16803

800-727-7681
FAX: 814-237-7282

Fred Weiner, Owner

Creates a three page single-spaced diagnostic report for a child with a communication disorder from a list of questions; sections of the report include developmental and background history, oral peripheral exam, speech and language analysis, summary and recommendations.

2101 Discriptive Language Arts Development

Educational Activities
PO Box 392
Freeport, NY 11520

516-223-4666
800-645-3739
e-mail: learn@edact.com

Al Harris, President
Alan Stern, Vice President

This software program includes six diagnostic tests and 36 progressive programs for a flexible and individualized series for students having difficulty with language arts. Software: CD-Rom, Windows, MAC, and DOS. *$395.00*

2102 EZ Dot

CAPCO, The Capability Corporation
1522 North Washington Street
Suite 200
Spokane, WA 99201

FAX: 509-535-1011

A critical software tool used in vocational counseling, job restructuring, recruitment and placement, better utilization of workers, and safety issues. This software offers occupational data by title, code, industry, GEO, DPT, or OGA. *$295.00*

2103 EZ Keys for Windows

Words+
1220 West Avenue J
Lancaster, CA 93534

800-869-8521
FAX: 805-266-8969

Phil Lawrence, Vice President
Rachel Nielsen, Customer Support

A software and hardware product designed to operate on an IBM compatible PC. The software provides dual word prediction, abbreviation expansion, five different methods of voice output and access to commercial software applications. *$1395.00*

2104 Goals and Objectives IEP Program

Curriculum Associates
PO Box 2001
North Billerica, MA 01862   978-667-8000
    800-225-0248
FAX: 800-366-1158
e-mail: info@curriculumassociates.com
www.curriculumassociates.com

BRIGANCE CIBS-R standardized scoring conversion software, is a teacher's tool that prints goal and objective pages of the IEP. In less than two minutes per student, a teacher types student data into the computer.

2105 IEP Generator

EBSCO Curriculum Materials
PO Box 1943
Birmingham, AL 35201   205-991-6600
    800-633-8623

This utility program for special education teachers allows the teacher to enter previously written goals and objectives which are selected and printed out for individual students.

2106 M MAC

Psychological Corporation
PO Box 9954
San Antonio, TX 78204   210-532-0971
    800-233-5682

A comprehensive microcomputer system that integrates data from psychological evaluations in order to assess the psychological and educational functioning of children ages 2-8.

2107 Math-A-Matic

EBSCO Curriculum Materials
PO Box 1943
Birmingham, AL 35201   205-991-6600
    800-633-8623

A teacher utility program that generates diagnostic tests, prescriptive worksheets and classroom management charts.

2108 Nasometer

Kay Elemetrics Corporation
12 Maple Avenue
Pine Brook, NJ 07058   973-628-6200

Measures the ratio of acoustic energy for the nasal and oral cavities. It is useful in evaluating clients and in therapy sessions by providing biofeedback.

2109 PEPPER

Lawrence Erlbaum Associates
365 Broadway
Hillsdale, NJ 07642   201-722-8500
    800-926-6579

A speech analysis program designed to examine phonetic, phonologic and prosodic aspects of normal and disordered speech.

2110 PSS CogRehab software

Psychological Software Services
6555 Carrollton Avenue
Indianapolis, IN 46220   317-257-9672
FAX: 317-257-9674
e-mail: obracy@inctdirect.net
www.neuroscience.cnter.com

Nancy Bracy, Sales/Production

PSS CogRehab Software is a comprehensive and easy-to-use multimedia cognitive rehabilitation software available, for clinical and educational use with head injury, stroke LD/ADD and other brain compromises. The packages include 64 computerized therapy tasks which contain modifiable parameters that will accomodate most requirements. Exercises include attention and executive skills, multiple modalities of visuopatial and memory skills, simple, complex, proble-solving skills.

$260 - $2500

2111 Parrot Easy Language Simple Anaylsis

Parrot Software
190 Sandy Ridge Road
State College, PA 16803
    800-727-7681
FAX: 814-237-7103

Fred Weiner, Owner

Designed for grammatical analysis of language samples. The user types and translates language samples of up to 100 utterances.

2112 TOVA

Universal Attention Disorders
4281 Katella Avenue
Suite 215
Los Alamitos, CA 90720   714-229-8770
    800-PAY-ATTN
FAX: 714-229-8782

Dr. Lawrence Greenberg, Developer

A computerized assessment which, in conjunction with classroom behavior ratings, is a highly effective screening tool for ADD. TOVA includes software, complete instructions, and supporting data including norms.

2113 TTAP Outreach: Technology Team Assessment Process

27 Horrabin Hall
Macomb, IL 61455
FAX: 309-298-2305
e-mail: L_Robinsonl@wiu.edu
www.mprojects.wiu.edu

Linda Robinson, Coordinator

Provides training to early childhood personnel and families on a team-based model for technology assessment. TTAP's procedures are designed to assess children's ability to use technology as a tool for achieving IEP/IFSP goals. Training and written materials are available.

2114 Visi-Pitch

Kay Elemetrics Corporation
12 Maple Avenue
Pine Brook, NJ   07058   973-628-6200

Family of products provides speech/language pathologists, educators, and researchers with the tools to analyze speech and voice characteristics and interface to an IBM PC or PS/2.

Software: Reading & Language Arts

2115 An Open Book

Arkenstone
PO Box 215
Moffett Field, CA   94035
                                800-444-4443
                                FAX: 408-745-6739

Complete reading machine. Users need learn only two buttons to learn all of their reading. *$4995.00*

2116 Bank Street Writer III

Scholastic
PO Box 7502
Jefferson City, MO   65102   573-636-5271
                                800-724-6527

Designed to teach word processing, writing and revision. *$79.95*

2117 CORE-Reading and Vocabulary Development

Educational Activities
PO Box 392
Freeport, NY   11520   516-223-4666
                                800-645-3739
                     e-mail: learn@edact.com

Al Harris, President
Alan Stern, Vice President

For older students who are beginning readers, CORE provides extensively guided drill and practice in core vocabularies used by so many major reading textbooks. CORE exercises a variety of modalities and integrates reading, writing, memory training and visual perception for more intensive learning. Software: CD-Rom, Windows, MAC, and DOS. *$ 675.00*

Full Program

2118 Choices, Choices

Tom Snyder Productions
108A Clematis Avenue
Waltham, MA   02453   617-926-6000
                                800-342-0236
                        www.tomsnyder.com

Based on Decisions, Decisions, these programs provide a structured concept that teaches critical thinking skills.

2119 Circletime Tales Deluxe

Don Johnston Incorporated
26799 North Commerce Drive
Volo, IL   60073   847-740-0749
                                800-999-4660
                           FAX: 847-740-7326
                e-mail: info@donjohnston.com
                        www.donjohnston.com

This interactive CD-ROM introduces and reinforces pre-literacy concepts using nursery rhymes and songs familiar to many children. This English/Spanish program emphasizes listening to and learning basic concepts such as opposites, directionality, colors and counting. *$59.00*

2120 Community Exploration

Jostens Learning/Hartley
9920 Pacific Heights Boulevard
San Diego, CA   92121   858-587-0087
                                800-247-1380
                           FAX: 619-622-7873
                     www.compasslearning.com

Steve Allen, Alternate Channels Accts. Mrg.

An award-winning learning adventure takes students who are learning English as a second language on a field trip to the make-believe town of Cornerstone. More than 50 community locations come to life with sound and animation. While exploring places in this typical American community where people live, work, and play, students also enhance important English language skills. Offers an exciting approach for any age student who needs to improve their English language proficiency. 4-12. *$19.95*

2121 Computer Assisted Writing

Educational Activities
PO Box 392
Freeport, NY   11520   516-223-4666
                                800-645-3739
                     e-mail: learn@edact.com

Al Harris, President
Alan Stern, Vice President

Provides individualized instruction and help with three forms of writing; the business letter of complaint, the report and the persuasive composition; software. *$159.00*

2122 Conversations

Educational Activities
PO Box 392
Freeport, NY   11520   516-223-4666
                                800-645-3739
                           FAX: 516-623-9282
                     e-mail: learn@edact.com
                            www.edact.com

Alan Stern, Vice President

Using American digitalized voices, CONVERSATIONS provides 14 different dialogues in which the student can participate. The topics offer learners important information about American culture and the workplace. Available for DOS. *$195.00*

2123 DISCOVERY

Orbit Computer Systems
PO Box 631
Elkhorn, NE 68022

A text editor for persons with dyslexia. It corrects misspelled words without any intervention.

2124 Day at Play A UKanDu Little Book

Don Johnston Incorporated
26799 North Commerce Drive
Volo, IL 60073 847-740-0749
800-999-4660
FAX: 847-740-7326
e-mail: info@donjohnston.com
www.donjohnston.com

One of the products in the UKanDu Little Book Series. This early literacy program consists of several four-page animated stories that help build language experience for emergent and early readers. Children fill-in-the-blank to complete a sentence on each page and then watch the page come alive with animation and sound. After completion, it can be printed to make a book. All children can be successful as there are no wrong answers. *$45.00*

2125 Detecting and Correcting Special Needs

Allyn & Bacon
160 Gould Street
Needham Heights, MA 02194
800-852-8024

Joyce S. Choate, author

Describes special reading needs of special learners.

180 pages 1989
ISBN 0-205116-38-8

2126 Easy as ABC

Queue
338 Commerce Drive
Fairfield, CT 06432 203-579-4171

Software with five games that introduce the alphabet. Children learn letter recognition, alphabetical sequence and upper and lower case.

2127 English Basics

Educational Activities
PO Box 392
Freeport, NY 11520 516-223-4666
800-645-3739
e-mail: learn@edact.com

Al Harris, President
Alan Stern, Vice President

Software that reviews and reinforces English skills, text material is displayed and highlighted in examples. Concepts in Language Arts: homonyms, synonyms, antonyms, contractions. *$199.00*

Per Unit

2128 Essential Roots

Educational Tutorial Consortium
4400 South 44th Street
Lincoln, NE 68516 402-473-0238

C. Wilson Anderson, T. Elli Cross & Joan M. Stoner, author

This computer program helps students internalize the pronunciations, spellings and meanings of the most commonly occurring roots. For Apple II, IBM 5.25 and 3.5 and MacIntosh. *$40.00*

Grades 7-12
ISBN 0-83887 -12-

2129 Essential Suffixes

Educational Tutorial Consortium
4400 South 44th Street
Lincoln, NE 68516 402-473-0238

C. Wilson Anderson, Elli Cross & Joan Stoner, author

In this program, students learn that changing a suffix changes the part of speech, and suffixes as a group do not alter the general meaning of a word. Examples provided for IBM 5.35, IBM 3.5 and MacIntosh.

$35 - $45

2130 Fancy Font

Softcraft
2701 University Avenue
 # 475
Madison, WI 53705
800-351-0500

Provides magnification of printing. Characters up to one inch square can be created from ASCII files.

2131 Friday Afternoon

Jostens Learning/Hartley
9920 Pacific Heights Boulevard
San Diego, CA 92121 858-587-0087
800-247-1380
FAX: 619-622-7873
www.compasslearning.com

Steve Allen, Accts. Mgr, Alternate Channels

Save hours of preparation time and dazzle your students with interesting new activities to supplement their classroom learning. With Friday afternoon, you'll produce flash cards, word puzzles, even customized bingo cards, and more, all at the click of a mouse. MacIntosh diskette. *$99.95*

2132 Grammar Examiner

Britannica Software
345 4th Street
San Francisco, CA 94107 415-777-9876

Software that uses a game format to teach basic grammar skills such as punctuation, capitalization, subject-verb agreement, verb tenses and so on.

2133 Grammar for the Real World

Davidson & Associates
PO Box 2961
Torrance, CA 90509 310-793-0600

Software that presents the basic rules of grammar, including abbreviations, agreement, capitalization, contractions, punctuation and sentence structure.

2134 How to Read for Everyday Living

Educational Activities
PO Box 392
Freeport, NY 11520 516-223-4666
800-645-3739
e-mail: learn@edact.com

Al Harris, President
Alan Stern, Vice President

Software that focuses on survival reading skills and teaches want ads, job ads, labels, forms and applications and other critical items. This interactive program constantly challenges students to think and reply. Software: CD-Rom, Windows, MAC, and DOS. *$159.00*

2135 Intermediate Prefixes, Roots, Suffixes

Educational Tutorial Consortium
4400 S 44th Street
Lincoln, NE 68516 402-473-0238

Joan Menke Stoner, Elli Cross & C. Wilson Anderson, author

The Word Book, Teacher's Manual and Practice Cards are designed for those middle-school students who need some extra help in written language skills related to reading, spelling, vocabulary and comprehension. For IBM 5.25 and Apple computers. *$35.00*

ISBN 0-83887-78-

2136 Juggles' Rainbow

Learning Company
6493 Kaiser Drive
Fremont, CA 94555 510-490-7311

Teaches spatial concepts at a beginning reading level using a game format.

2137 KEYTALK

PEAL Software
PO Box 8188
Calabasas, CA 91372 818-883-7849

A beginning literacy activity for children beginning to read and write.

2138 Learning English: Primary

Jostens Learning/Hartley
9920 Pacific Heights Boulevard
San Diego, CA 92121 858-587-0087
800-247-1380
FAX: 619-622-7873
www.compasslearning.com

Steve Allen, Alternate Channels Accts. Mgr.

Four stories and rhymes help students familiarize themselves with essential English language concepts, recognize patterns in language, and associate words with objects. *$49.95*

2139 Learning English: Rhyme Time

Jostens Learning/Hartley
9920 Pacific Heights Boulevard
San Diego, CA 92121 858-587-0087
800-247-1380
FAX: 619-622-7873
www.compasslearning.com

Steve Allen, Accts. Mgr, Alternate Channels

Using classic children's rhymes in an animated multimedia program, students work on language skills, vocabulary, and comprehension.

2140 Lelps

Dataflo Computer Services
PO Box 1
Enfield, NH 03748 603-448-2223

A spelling and vocabulary program with a utility to help the user modify existing word categories or create new ones.

2141 Letters and First Words

C&C Software
5713 Kentford Circle
Wichita, KS 67220 316-683-6056
800-752-2086

Carol Clark, President

Three programs provide a logical progression of activities to help children learn to identify letters, recognize their associated sounds and begin to spell simple words. *$60.00*

2142 Lexia I, II and III Reading Series

Lexia Learning Systems
PO Box 466
Lincoln, MA 01773 781-259-8752
800-435-3942
FAX: 781-259-1349
e-mail: info@lexialearning.com
www.lexialearning.com

Jon Bower, President
Heidi Brown, Marketing Director

Lexia's software helps children and adults with learning disabilities master their core reading skills. Based on the Orton Gillingham method, Lexia Early Reading, Phonics Based Reading and SOS (Strategies for Older Students) apply phonics principles to help students learn essential sound-symbol correspondence and decoding skills. The Quick Reading Tests generate detailed skill reports in only 5-8 minutes per student to provide data for further instruction. Price: $40-400 per workstation.

2143 Magic Spells

Learning Company
6493 Kaiser Drive
Fremont, CA 94555 510-490-7311

Utilizes an adventure game format to teach spelling skills.

2144   Memory Castle

WINGS for Learning
1600 Green Hills Road
Scotts Valley, CA   95066   831-464-3600
                          FAX: 831-464-3600

Introduces a strategy to increase memory skills via an adventure game. Set in a castle, the game requires memory, reading, spelling skills and more to win.

2145   On a Green Bus A UKanDu Little Book

Don Johnston Incorporated
26799 North Commerce Drive
Volo, IL   60073   847-740-0749
                                 800-999-4660
                          FAX: 847-740-7326
          e-mail: info@donjohnston.com
                  www.donjohnston.com

This early literacy program that consists of several create-your-own 4-page animated stories that help build language experience on each page and then watch the page come alive with animation and sound. After completing the story, students can print it out to make a book which can be read over and over again. Because there are no wrong answers, all children can have a successful literacy experience. *$ 45.00*

2146   Optimum Resource

Stickybear, Middleware, High School Curriculum
18 Hunter Road
Hilton Head, SC   29926   843-689-8000
                                  800-327-1473
                          FAX: 843-689-8008
          e-mail: stickyb@stickybear.com
                  www.optimumlearning.com

Rod Stangroom, Sales Director
Chris Gintz, Vice President Marketing

Optimum Resource publishes over 100 K-12 education curriculum software titles under its varietal brands, StickyBear, MiddleWare, High School and Tools for Teachers.

2147   Out and About A UKanDu Little Book

Don Johnston Incorporated
26799 North Commerce Drive
Volo, IL   60073   847-740-0749
                                 800-999-4660
                          FAX: 847-740-7326
          e-mail: info@donjohnston.com
                  www.donjohnston.com

One of the products in the UKanDu Little Book Series. This early literacy program consists of several four-page animated stories that help build language experience for emergent and early readers. Children fill-in-the-blank to complete a sentence on each page and then watch the page come alive with animation and sound. After completion, it can be printed to make a book. *$45.00*

2148   Please Help Me Software

Focus Media
839 Stewart Avenue
Garden City, NY   11530   516-222-0550
                                  800-645-8989

Software uses five activities to teach spelling on a variety of levels. Activities include drills, visualizing the shape of the word and games.

2149   Programs for Aphasia and Cognitive Disorders

Parrot Software
190 Sandy Ridge Road
State College, PA   16803
                                  800-727-7681
                          FAX: 814-237-7103

Fred Weiner, Owner

Over 50 different computer programs that facilitate language, memory and attention training. Programs are available for MS DOS, WINDOWS and Apple II.

2150   Punctuation Rules

Optimum Resource
18 Hunter Road
Hilton Head Island, SC   29926   843-689-8000
                                  888-784-2592
                          FAX: 843-689-8008
          e-mail: sticky@stickybear.com
                  www.stickybear.com

Chris Gintz, Vice President/ Marketing

Punctuation Rules is designed to help students improve their punctuation skills. Students work with appropriate level sentences which follow common rules of punctuation. The program covers material ranging from categories of sentences to forming possessives and allows students to gain strength in their ability to correctly use periods, commas, apostrophes, question makes, colons, hyphens, quotation marks, exclamation points, and more. *$59.95*

2151   Quick Talk

Educational Activities
PO Box 392
Freeport, NY   11520   516-223-4666
                                  800-645-3739
                          FAX: 516-623-9282
          e-mail: learn@edact.com
                  www.edact.com

Al Harris, President
Alan Stern, Vice President

Students will learn and use new vocabulary immediately: high-frequency, everyday vocabulary words are introduced and used contextually using human speech, graphics and text. Voice-interactive program (MS-DOS). *$65.00*

2152   Quickpad IR

K-12 Micro Media Publishing
16 McKee Drive
Mahwah, NJ   07430   201-529-4500
                                  800-292-1997
                          FAX: 201-529-5282
          e-mail: sales@k12mmp.com
                  www.k12mmp.com

Amanda Panfile, Sales

Assistive keyboard for writing. Wireless transfer of text may be downloaded into any computer application (Word, Excel, Powerpoint). Also can be used as a real-time wireless keyboard. Includes batteries, receiver and cables. *$1.99*

2153 Quiet Duck Learning Series

Computer Talk
1420 E Cypress Street
Covina, CA 91724 909-396-7100

A package of reading and spelling programs for the learning disabled student.

2154 Race the Clock

Mindplay
3130 N Dodge Boulevard
Tucson, AZ 85716 520-323-1303
800-221-7911
FAX: 520-322-0363

A matching game, uses the animation capabilities to teach verbs. The player chooses a matching game from a menu.

2155 Reader Rabbit

Learning Company
6493 Kaiser Drive
Fremont, CA 94555 510-490-7311

A fast-paced electronic word factory for children to have fun as they learn vital early reading and vocabulary skills.

2156 Reading Comprehension Series

Optimum Resource
18 Hunter Road
Hilton Head Island, SC 29926 843-689-8000
888-784-2592
FAX: 843-689-8008
e-mail: sticky@stickybear.com
www.stickybear.com

Chris Gintz, Vice President/ Marketing

The Reading Comprehension Series, includes six volumes for Windows, MacIntosh, DOS or Apple II computers. Packed with intriguing multi-level stories, each volume will capture the interest of children ages 8-14 while teaching them crucial reading comprehension skills. These open-ended programs are versatile and easy to use. *$59.95*

2157 Reading Strategy Series

Pearson Education
One Lake Street
Upper Saddle River, NJ 07632 201-236-7000

Consists of two authoring systems; one for the teacher and one for students.

2158 Realtime Writer

L&L Products
2700 Connecticut Avenue NW
Washington, DC 20008 202-986-4841
800-832-2472

Ronald L. Shapiro

A program that allows for social interactive writing and permits collaborative learning in which students build on their cognitive and social strength in a sharing environment. *$795.00*

2159 Roots

Educational Tutorial Consortium
4400 S 44th Street
Lincoln, NE 68516 402-473-0238

C. Wilson Anderson, Joan Menke Stoner & Elli Cross, author

Computer software for Apple II, IBM 5.35 & 3.5 for grades 5 and up. It teaches 100 common roots and comes with a manual and list of roots. *$40.00*

ISBN 0-83887 -00-

2160 SPELLIST

Castle Special Computer Services
9801 San Gabriel Road NE
Albuquerque, NM 87111

Talking software presenting words for spelling with the style of presentation adaptable to the student, practicing from dictation.

2161 Simon Sounds it Out

Don Johnston Incorporated
26799 North Commerce Drive
Volo, IL 60073 847-740-0749
800-999-4660
FAX: 847-740-7326
e-mail: info@donjohnston.com
www.donjohnston.com

This interactive phonics program enables students to learn and practice letter sounds with an instructional and nonthreatening on-screen tutor. This phonics program was designed by leading learning authorities and extensively tested in classrooms. Colorful graphics, digitalized sound and amusing animations reward students and motivate them to continue learning. *$59.00*

1998

2162 Simon Spells

Don Johnston Incorporated
26799 North Commerce Drive
Volo, IL 60073 847-740-0749
800-999-4660
FAX: 847-740-7326
e-mail: info@donjohnston.com
www.donjohnston.com

This innovative spelling program guides students through individualized instruction presented in a way that enables them to work at their own pace. Words are phonemically presented, as well as placed in the context of sentences so as to help increase vocabulary comprehension and spelling skills. Student progress is tracked and results are stored. *$59.00*

2163 Sound Sentences

Educational Activities
PO Box 392
Freeport, NY 11520 516-223-4666
800-645-3739
FAX: 516-623-9282
e-mail: learn@edact.com

Al Harris, President
Alan Stern, Vice President

This sound-interactive program breaks away from traditional language instruction. Instead of formal concentration on verb and basic vocabulary, students meet everyday English with colloquialisms they will hear in real life situations. They reinforce their knowledge of sentence structure while acquiring the ability to communicate in daily settings. (For MAC, MS-DOS and Windows). *$65.00*

2164   Special Needs Collection

**Humanities Software
PO Box 950
Hood River, OR   97031   541-386-6737
800-245-6737**

*Charlotte Arnold, Marketing Director
Paula Keran, Business Development*

Recommended for special needs students and those for whom English is a second language, these programs provide structured practice with basic language skills and offer opportunities for self-expression through open-ended writing. K-12 reading and writing software solutions for IBM, Macintosh and Apple II.

2165   Spell-A-Vision

**Cross Educational Software
508 E Kentucky Avenue
Ruston, LA   71270   318-255-8921
800-768-1969**

An independent software study program for students who need to improve their spelling and vocabulary.

2166   Spelling Rules

**Optimum Resource
18 Hunter Road
Hilton Head Island, SC   29926   843-689-8000
888-784-2592
FAX: 843-689-8008
e-mail: sticky@stickybear.com**

Chris Gintz, VP Marketing

A curriculum based, easy-to-use program, that provides students with the practice they need to build strong spelling skills. *$59.95*

2167   Spelling Test Generator

**Optimum Resource
18 Hunter Road
Hilton Head Island, SC   29926   843-689-8000
888-784-2592
FAX: 843-689-8008
e-mail: sticky@stickybear.com
www.stickybear.com**

Chris Gintz, Vice President/ Marketing

Using more than 3000 of the most commonly encountered words in the English language, the Spelling Test Generator prepares spelling lists on the basis of difficulty, grade level, vowels, diphthongs, word origins, and starting/ending letters or sounds. *$59.95*

2168   Stickbear Spelling

**Optimum Resource
18 Hunter Road
Hilton Head Island, SC   29926   843-689-8000
888-784-2592
FAX: 843-689-8008
e-mail: sticky@stickybear.com
www.stickybear.com**

Chris Gintz, Vice President/ Marketing

Children ages 6 and up discover and practice critical spelling skills as they work with three unique action-packed activities, each with four graded levels of difficulty. The program is open-ended and teachers may add, change, and modify the word lists for each individual. Stickybear Spelling contains more than 2000 recorded words. Levels may be set to allow students of different ages or abilities to compete effectively. *$59.95*

2169   Stickybear Parts of Speech

**Optimum Resource
18 Hunter Road
Hilton Head Island, SC   29926   843-689-8000
888-784-2592
FAX: 843-689-8008
e-mail: sticky@stickybear.com**

Chris Gintz

Children learn parts of speech with this exciting new program. *$59.95*

2170   Stickybear Reading

**Optimum Resource
18 Hunter Road
Hilton Head Island, SC   29926   843-689-8000
888-784-2592
FAX: 843-689-8008
e-mail: sticky@stickybear.com
www.stickybear.com**

Chris Gintz, VP Marketing

Children build vocabulary and reading comprehension skills using hundreds of word/picture sets and thousands of put-together sentence parts. *$49.95*

2171   Stickybear Reading Comprehension

**Optimum Resource
18 Hunter Road
Hilton Head Island, SC   29926   843-689-8000
888-784-2592
FAX: 843-689-8008
e-mail: sticky@stickybear.com**

Chris Gintz, VP Marketing Director

This multi-level reading comprehension program helps children improve reading skills with 30 high-interest stories and question sets created by the Weekly Reader editors. *$59.95*

2172   Stickybear Spellgrabber

**Optimum Resource
18 Hunter Road
Hilton Head Island, SC   29926   843-689-8000
888-784-2592
FAX: 843-689-8008
e-mail: sticky@stickybear.com**

Chris Gintz, VP Marketing

Build spelling and vocabulary skills with three different activities: Picture Spell, Word Spell and Bear Dunk. *$59.95*

2173 Stickybear Spelling Rules

Optimum Resource
18 Hunter Road
Hilton Head Island, SC   29926   843-689-8000
888-784-2592
FAX: 843-689-8008
e-mail: sticky@stickybear.com
www.stickbear.com

Chris Gintz, Vice President/ Marketing

Spelling Rules is designed to help students improve spelling accuracy and master the fundamentals - forming plurals (adding s, adding es, f, fe, to ves) and compound words I before E rule, capitalization, and many others.. *$59.95*

2174 Stickybear's Reading Fun Park

Optimum Resource
18 Hunter Road
Hilton Head Island, SC   29926   843-689-8000
888-784-2592
FAX: 843-689-8008
e-mail: sticky@stickybear.com
www.stickybear.com

Chris Gintz, Vice President/ Marketing

Children ages 4-8 discover and practice critical reading skills as the famous stickybear family guides users through unique, action-packed activities, each with multiple levels of difficulty and skills that address both the auditory and visual needs of budding readers. *$59.95*

2175 Stickybear's Reading Room Optmum Resource

18 Hunter Road
Hilton Head Island, SC   29926
FAX: 843-689-8008
e-mail: stickyb@stickybear
www.stickybear.com

Chris Gintz, Vice President/ Marketing

The perfect combination of learning and fun, our award winning Stickybear's Reading Room provides colorful motivating thinking skills practice for children ages 4-8 with four unique bilingual learning activities. *$59.95*

2176 Successful Inclusive Teaching: Proven Ways to Detect and Correct Special Needs, 2nd Edition

Allyn & Bacon
160 Gould Street
Needham Heights, MA   02494   781-455-1200
800-852-8024
Joyce S. Choate, author
Describes special reading needs of special learners.

478 pages
ISBN 0-20526 -78-7

2177 Talking Text Writer

Scholastic
PO Box 7502
Jefferson City, MO   65102   573-636-5271
800-724-6527

As users type words and phrases, the computer reads back what is on the screen. Users select whether they want the program to speak each letter after it is typed, each word or the whole screen. *$49.95*

2178 Tomorrow's Promise: Language Arts

Jostens Learning/Hartley
9920 Pacific Heights Boulevard
San Diego, CA   92121   858-587-0087
800-247-1380
FAX: 619-622-7873
www.compasslearning.com

Steve Allen, Accts. Mgr, Alternate Channels

You'll strengthen students' grammar, usage, and vocabulary skills promote higher order thinking skills with this comprehensive Language Arts curriculum. It utilizes cross-curricular, thematic instruction engaging multimedia learning exercises that encourage writing, speaking, and listening proficiency. Promotes higher order thinking skills. *$279.95*

2179 Tomorrow's Promise: Reading

Jostens Learning/Hartley
9920 Pacific Heights Boulevard
San Diego, CA   92121   858-587-0087
800-247-1380
FAX: 619-622-7873
www.compasslearning.com

Steve Allen, Accts. Mgr, Alternate Channels

This multimedia curriculum balances thematic, interactive exploration with core skills development, increasing your students' early reading proficiency, building a solid literacy foundation, and fostering a lifelong love for reading. *$279.95*

2180 Tomorrow's Promise: Spelling

Jostens Learning/Hartley
9920 Pacific Heights Boulevard
San Diego, CA   92121   858-587-0087
800-247-1380
FAX: 619-622-7873
www.compasslearning.com

Steve Allen, Accts. Mgr, Alternate Channels

Lovable characters and engaging multimedia effects put young students on a fast-track to early spelling proficiency with fourteen activities and three games. A full year's instruction on each CD includes 30 world lists, per grade, in story context, or create word lists to suit your needs. This program addresses students' multiple learning styles and rewards students as they progress through each stage of spelling skill acquisition. *$99.95*

2181 Vocabulary Development

Optimum Resource
18 Hunter Road
Hilton Head Island, SC 29926   843-689-8000
888-784-2592
FAX: 843-689-8008
e-mail: sticky@stickybear.com
www.stickybear.com

Chris Gintz, Vice President/ Marketing

A featured program in the middle school series. Vocabulary Development is designed to help students increase vocabulary as they strengthen reading skills. Students relate their current knowledge of vocabulary to the context in which they discover an unfamiliar word. Utilizing a variety of contextual aids, this program illustrates synonyms , antonyms, prefixes, suffixes, homophones, multiple meanings and context clues, allowing students to apply experience and context. *$59.95*

2182 Whoops

Cornucopia Software
626 San Carlos Avenue
Albany, CA 94706
FAX: 510-528-7000
e-mail: support@practicemagic.com
www.practicemagic.com

Phillip Manfield

Checks spelling three ways. It checks words as they are typed, it checks an entire screen and highlights the errors and it reads ASCII text files from a disk and lists errors.

Software: Vocational

2183 COMPASS Evaluation and Screening Assessment

Valpar International
PO Box 5767
Tucson, AZ 85703   520-293-1510
800-528-7070
FAX: 520-292-9755
e-mail: valpar@valparint.com
www.valparint.com

This program evaluates all factors of The Worker Qualification Profile of The Dictionary of Occupational Titles. It writes reports and presents scores and dot factor scores evaluating reading, spelling, math and language.

2184 Learning Activity Packets

Conover Company
1050 Witzel Avenue
Oshkosh, WI 54902   920-231-4667
800-933-1933
FAX: 920-231-4809
e-mail: conover@execpc.com
www.conovercompany.com

Terry Schmitz, President

Demonstrates how basic academic skills relate to 20 major career areas. LAPs provide valuable diagnostic in applied vocational applications, and demonstrate to users the importance of academics as they relate to the workplace; software. *$99.00*

2185 Microcomputer Evaluation of Careers & Academics (MECA)

Conover Company
1050 Witzel Avenue
Oshkosh, WI 54902   920-231-4667
800-933-1933
FAX: 920-231-4809
e-mail: conover@execpc.com
www.conovercompany.com

Terry Schmitz, President
Sharon Diedrich, Consultant

A cost-effective, technology-based career development system which provides users with opportunities to get their hands dirty. The MECA system utilizes work simulations and is built around common occupational clusters. Each cluster, or career area, consists of hands-on WORK SAMPLES which provide a variety of career exploration and assessment experiences, linked to LEARNING ACTIVITY PACKETS, which integrate basic academic skills into the career planning and placement process.

$580 - $1,070

2186 OASYS

Vertek
11811 NE 1st Street
Suite 306
Bellevue, WA 98005   425-455-9921
800-220-4409
FAX: 425-454-7264

Sue Squire, Marketing Director

A software system that matches a person's skills and abilities to occupations and employers.

2187 Placement Problem Solver

CAPCO, The Capability Corporation
1522 N Washington Street
Suite 200
Spokane, WA 99201
FAX: 509-535-1011

A complete vocational planning and job placement solutions software program for vocational planners.

2188 Reading in the Workplace

Educational Activities
PO Box 392
Freeport, NY 11520   516-223-4666
800-645-3739
FAX: 516-623-9282
e-mail: learn@edact.com

Al Harris, President
Alan Stern, Vice President

A job-based reading software program using real-life problems and solutions to capture students' attention and improve their vocabulary and comprehension skills. Units include: automotive, clerical, health care, and construction. *$295.00*

2189 SAVAS

Southern Micro Systems
3335 S Church Street
Burlington, NC 27215   336-584-1661

A complete vocational guidance system that matches client interest patterns with information about occupations listed in the Occupational Outlook Handbook.

2190 Stickybear Typing

Optimum Resource
18 Hunter Road
Hilton Head Island, SC 29926   843-689-8000
                                 888-784-2592
                            FAX: 843-689-8008
                     e-mail: sticky@stickybear.com
                            www.stickybear.com

Chris Gintz, Vice President/ Marketing
The award winning Stickybear Typing program allows users to sharpen typing skills and achieve keyboard mastery with three engaging and amusing multi-level activities. *$59.95*

2191 Vocational Interest Profile Report

Cambridge Educational
90 Maccorkle Avenue SW
South Charleston, WV 25303   304-744-2055
                                 800-468-4227
                            FAX: 800-329-6687
                    e-mail: melindab@citynet.net
                            www.cambridgeol.com

Melinda Ball, Marketing Director
Software that is designed to allow students to systematically define broad work categories that are of most interest. *$64.86*

ISBN 0-927368-59-5

2192 Workplace Skills - Learning How to Function on the Job

Programming Concepts
PO Box 12428
San Antonio, TX 78212
                                 800-594-4263
                            FAX: 218-248-055

Janie Haugen, Program Director
Jeff McLane, President/CEO
Offers parents and educators a functional means by which to discuss all aspects of finding and keeping a job. *$49.95*

Word Processors

2193 DARCI

WesTest Engineering
810 Shepard Lane
Farmington, UT 84025   801-451-9191
                            FAX: 801-292-7379

Provides transparent access to all computer functions by replacing the computer's keyboard with a smart joystick. *$975.00*

2194 Dreamer

TS Micro Tech
1209 John Reed Court
City of Industry, CA 91745   626-330-0086
                            FAX: 626-330-8896
                     e-mail: sales@fanca.com

An intelligent, add-on function keyboard providing single-keystroke access to multiple-keystroke functions.

2195 EasyKey Visual Keyboard

Inkwell Systems
PO Box 1318
Talent, OR 97540   541-535-1210

An on-screen keyboard that floats ontop of the program in any Windows application and allows the user to type via alternative input device. *$99.00*

2196 FlexShield Keyboard Protectors

Hooleon Corporation
411 S 6th Street
Cottonwood, AZ 86326   928-634-7515
                                 800-937-1337
                            FAX: 928-634-4620
                     e-mail: sales@hooleon.com
                            www.hooleon.com

Transparent keyboard protectors allowing instant recognition of keytop legends. They have a matte finish to reduce the glare. *$12.95*

2197 Freedom Writer

World Communications
245 Tonopah Drive
Fremont, CA 94539   510-656-0911

A word processor specifically designed for individuals with disabilities.

2198 Help U Key

World Communications
245 Tonopah Drive
Fremont, CA 94539   510-656-0911

For people who have difficulty using the computer keyboard, for those who hate repetitive commands, words and phrases and for people who want to increase productivity and reduce spelling mistakes.

2199 Hooleon Corporation

411 S 6th Street
Cottonwood, AZ 86326   928-634-7515
                                 800-937-1337
                            FAX: 928-634-4620
                     e-mail: sales@hooleon.com
                            www.hooleon.com

Joan Crozier, President
Large print and combination braille adhesive keytop labels for computer keyboards. Helps visually impaired computer users access correct key strokes either by sight or by touch. Raised braille meets ADA specifications and large print fills key top surface. *$21.95*

2200 IntelliKeys

IntelliTools
55 Leveroni Center
Suite 9
Novato, CA 94949

800-899-6687
FAX: 415-382-5950
e-mail: info@intellitools.com
www.intellitools.com

Paula Weinberger, Director Of Marketing

Alternative, touch-sensitive keyboards; plugs into any Mac, Apple II or IBM/compatible computer. *$395.00*

2201 IntelliKeys IIe (Smalle)

IntelliTools
55 Leveroni Center
Suite 9
Novato, CA 94949

800-899-6687
FAX: 415-382-5950
e-mail: info@intellitools.com
www.intellitools.com

Paula Weinberger, Director Of Marketing

Card and cable to create keyboard port on Apple IIe computer to allow use of IntelliKeys alternative keyboard. *$129.95*

2202 IntelliKeys Overlay Maker

IntelliTools
55 Leveroni Center
Suite 9
Novato, CA 94949

800-899-6687
FAX: 415-382-5950
e-mail: info@intellitools.com
www.intellitools.com

Paula Weinberger, Director Of Marketing

Software for creating custom overlays to use on IntelliKeys. *$69.95*

2203 IntelliTalk

IntelliTools
55 Leveroni Center
Suite 9
Novato, CA 94949

800-899-6687
FAX: 415-382-5950
e-mail: info@intellitools.com
www.intellitools.com

Paula Weinberger, Director Of Marketing

Talking word-processing program available for MacIntosh, Apple IIe, IBM compatible, and Windows computers. *$39.95*

2204 Internal I/O Port Adapter

AbleNet
1081 10th Avenue SE
Minneapolis, MN 55414

800-322-0956
FAX: 612-379-9143
e-mail: customerservice@ablenetinc.com

Mary Kay Walch

A converting cable designed to provide a 9-pin joystick port for Apple II+ and older model computers. *$18.00*

2205 Jouse

Prentke Romich Company
1022 Heyl Road
Wooster, OH 44691

330-262-1984
800-262-1984
FAX: 330-263-4829
www.prentrom.com

A joystick-operated mouse that is controlled with the mouth. Moving the joystick moves the cursor. Mouse button activations can be made with the sip and puff switch that is built into the joystick. Typing can be achieved through an on-screen keyboard. Nothing is attached to the operator. The adjustable Jouse arm mounts on a table or desktop and swings away when bumped. *$995.00*

2206 Key Tronic KB 5153 Touch Pad Keyboard

KeyTronic
PO Box 14687
Spokane, WA 99214

800-262-6006

Integrates a regular full-function keyboard, a numeric keypad with a cursor key capability and a touch pad into one unit.

2207 KeySpell

HumanWare
6140 Horseshoe Bar Road
Loomis, CA 95650

916-652-0933

A spell checker for use with KeyNote PC, it comes with a 50,000-word dictionary and allows user additions.

2208 Keyguards for IntelliKeys

IntelliTools
1720 Corporate Circle
Petaluna, CA 94954

800-899-6687
FAX: 707-773-2001
e-mail: info@intellitools.com
www.intellitools.com

Beth Davis, Inside Sales Manager

Acrylic keyguards for each of IntelliKeys six standard overlays. *$250.00*

2209 Large Print Labels, Braille Labels Large Print Computer Keyboards

Hooleon Corporation
411 S 6th Street
Building B
Cottonwood, AZ 86326

928-634-7515
800-937-1337
FAX: 928-634-4620
e-mail: sales@hooleon.com
www.hooleon.com

Barry Greene, General Manager

Large print and braille adhesive keytop labels for computer keyboards. Helps visually impaired computer users access correct key strokes either by sight or by touch. *$19.95*

2210 Large Type

National Institute for Rehab Engineering
PO Box T
Hewitt, NJ   07421   201-327-5550
                                          800-736-2216

Donald Selwyn, Director

Display enlargement programs for visually impaired users consist of a variety of programs for different needs, ranging from basic to full-featured.

2211 Magic Keyboard

Woodsmith Software
1810 W Lancaster Drive
Bloomington, IN   47404

A translation program using graphics to create large character sets and sixteen type styles for people with low vision.

2212 Magic Wand Keyboard

In Touch Systems
11 Westview Road
Spring Valley, NY   10977   845-354-7431
                                          800-332-6244
                                          www.magicwandkeyboard.com

Susan Crouch, Vice President

The magic wand keyboard allows your child to use a keyboard and mouse easily-no light beams, microphones, or sensors to wear of position. This miniature computer keyboard has zero-force keys that work with the slightest touch of a wand (hand-held of mouthstick). No strength required.

2213 McKey Mouse

In Touch Systems
11 Westview Road
Spring Valley, NY   10977   845-354-7431
                                          800-332-6244

Susan Crouch, Vice President

Microsoft compatible mouse for persons with little or no hand/arm movement; it's an option for the Magic Wand Keyboard and adds full mouse function without adding any extra devices.

2214 Morse Code Drills

Personally Developed Software
PO Box 3266
Wallingford, CT   06492   203-269-4222
                                          800-426-7279

A drill and practice program that teaches the dot and dash patterns for each letter of Morse Code.

2215 Morsek

Kinetic Designs
14231 Anatevka Lane SE
Olalla, WA   98359

A Morse code keyboard emulator program allowing all keyboards keys to be entered via Morse code using any input device connected to any I/O port including the standard keyboard.

2216 Pegasus LITE

Words+
1220 West Avenue J
Lancaster, CA   93534
                                          800-869-8521
                                          FAX: 805-266-8969

Phil Lawrence, Vice President
Rachel Nielsen, Customer Support

Provides all of the strategies currently being used in AAC, from dynamic display color pictographic language, to dual-word prediction text language, in a single system. *$6995.00*

2217 SuperKey

Corland International
1800 Green Hills Road
Scotts Valley, CA   95066   831-430-0455

A keyboard enhancement program that allows the user to store frequently-used commands and retrieve them with two keystrokes and to cut and paste text between applications programs and create single-page help screens for each set of macros created.

2218 Touchdown Keytop/Keyfront Kits

Hooleon Corporation
411 S 6th Street
Cottonwood, AZ   86326   928-634-9578
                                          800-937-1337
                                          FAX: 928-634-4620
                                          e-mail: sales@hooleon.com
                                          www.hooleon.com

These kits enlarge the key legends of a computer and include braille for easy recognition.

2219 Unicorn Keyboards

IntelliTools
1720 Corporate Circle
Petaluma, CA   94954
                                          800-899-6687
                                          FAX: 707-773-2001
                                          e-mail: info@intellitools.com
                                          www.intellitools.com

Paula Weinberger, Director

Alternative keyboards with membrane surface and large, user-defined keys. Large and small sizes are available. *$250.00*

2220 Up and Running

IntelliTools
5221 Central Avenue
Suite 205
Richmond, CA   94804
                                          800-899-6687
                                          FAX: 510-528-2225
                                          e-mail: info@intellitools.com

Instantly use hundreds of popular commercial software programs with this custom collection of setups and overlays. *$69.95*

2221   **Write This Way**

Jostens Learning/Hartley
9920 Pacific Heights Boulevard
San Diego, CA   92121   **858-587-0087**
                                    800-247-1380
                          FAX: 619-622-7873
                          www.compasslearning.com

Steve Allen, Accts. Mgr, Alternate Channels

An easy-to-use, versatile word processor designed with learning disabled or hearing-impaired individuals in mind category score fewer points. Apple or Mac available. *$99.95*

2222   **Write: OutLoud**

Don Johnston Incorporated
26799 North Commerce Drive
Volo, IL   60073   **847-740-0749**
                                  800-999-4660
                        FAX: 847-740-7326
            e-mail: info@donjohnston.com
                  www.donjohnston.com

The award-winning feasible and user friendly talking word processor with talking spell checker. Text-to-speech technology provides multi-sensory learning and positive reinforcements for writers of all ages and ability levels. *$99.00*

General

2223 ABDA/ABMPP Workshop: The Art of Courtroom Testifying

American Board of Disability Analysts
342 24th Avenue North
Suite 200
Nashville, TN 37203   615-327-2984
                              FAX: 615-327-9235
                         e-mail: americanbd@aol.com

February 17-18, 2001 Hawaii at Hilton Hawaiian Village, Honolulu, Hawaii $160 per night, reservations: 800-HILTONS or 808-949-4321, 2005 Kalia Road, Honolulu, Hawaii 96815; Workshop leader: Dr. William Tsushima.

2224 APSE Conference - Revitalizing Supported Employment, Climbing to the Future

Association for Persons in Supported Employment
1627 Monument Avenue
Richmond, VA 23220   804-278-9187
                            FAX: 804-278-9377
                       e-mail: apse@apse.com
                            www.apse.org

Mary Callender, Conference Planner

A major conference on Supported Employment. The conference includes 130 sessions presented by nationally recognized leaders in the field. Conference attendees come from all 50 states, Canada and several foreign countries and include professionals in supported employment, occupational therapy, rehabilitation technology and other related fields.

July

2225 Abilities Expo

Advanstar Communications
440 Wheelers Farm Road
Suite 101
Milford, CT 06460   203-882-1300
                             FAX: 203-882-1800
                         www.abilitiesexpo.com

Diane Waltersdorf, Show Director

Abilities Expo is the leading show of assisted and independent living products and services in the United States.

2226 Alexander Graham Bell Association for the Deaf Annual Conference

3417 Volta Place NW
Washington, DC 20007   202-337-5220

                        e-mail: agbell2@aol.com
                             www.agbell.org

Susan Coffman, Meeting Coordinator

Over 60 booths offering information on resources and technology for the deaf and hard of hearing.

June

2227 American Academy of Cerebral Palsy

1910 Byrd Avenue
Suite 118
Richmond, VA 23230   804-282-6060

Holds annual conference in October, with instructional courses such as: the fundamentals of normal walking, management of drooling in the developmentally disabled, technology dependent children, evaluation and treatment of feeding, nutritional and growth problems in the child with disabilities, Spina Bifida care, spasticity, measurement, sexual behavior and problems of the young disabled adult, grant seeking programs that care for the special needs child, etc.

2228 American Association on Mental Retardation AAMR Annual Meeting

444 N Capitol Street NW
Washington, DC 20001   202-783-1535
                             800-424-3688
                        FAX: 202-387-2193
                       e-mail: anam@aamr.org
                            www.aamr.org

Paula A Hirt, Director of Programs & Services
Malene S Ward, Meetings Coordinator

At The Crossroads: Ethics, Genetics, Leadership and Self-Determination, the 124th annual meeting offers a full compliment of workshops, symposia, and multiperspective sessions that fill four days including social events. *$245.00*

May/June

2229 American Board of Disability Analysts

Disability Analyst
345 24th Avenue North
Suite 200
Nashville, TN 37203   615-327-2984
                             FAX: 615-327-9235
                         e-mail: americanbd@aol.com

Alexander E. Horwitz, MD, Executive Officer
Kenneth N. Anchor, PhD, Administrative Officer/Editor
Gabriel Sella, MD, Continuing Education Coor.

2230 American Council of the Blind Annual Convention

1155 15th Street NW
Suite 1004
Washington, DC 20005   202-467-5081
                             FAX: 202-467-5085
                        e-mail: info@acb.org
                             www.acb.org

Charles Crawford, Executive Director
Offers 50-75 booths of information for the blind.

June/July

2231 American Diabetes Association Annual Conference

1660 Duke Street
Alexandria, VA 22314   703-379-7755

Christina Pappas, Marketing Planner

Trade show featuring exhibits of equipment and supplies used by professionals involved in the treatment of diabetes.

2232 **American Physical Therapy Association**
1111 N Fairfax Street
Alexandria, VA 22314   703-684-2782
FAX: 703-706-8519

Jane Mathews, President
National Physical Therapy Week in October hosts a variety of activities promoting healthy living. The theme for the week is Pro-Active Health Care. The Association celebration will feature fitness clinics, fun runs, athletic competitions, open houses and seminars on health and fitness topics. The APTA is a national professional organization representing more than 50,000 physical therapists, physical therapist assistants, and students. Goals are the improvement of physical therapy.

2233 **American Rehabilitation Counseling Association**
5999 Stevenson Avenue
Alexandria, VA 22304   703-823-9800
FAX: 800-473-2329
www.counseling.org

Steve Brooke, Marketing Director

     March/April

2234 **American Speech-Language-Hearing Association**
10801 Rockville Pike
Rockville, MD 20852   301-897-5700
800-638-8255
FAX: 301-897-7348
e-mail: actioncenter@asha.org
www.asha.org

John E. Bernthal, President
Frederick T. Spahr, Ph.D., Executive Director
Joanne Jessen, Editor
Exhibits by companies specializing in augmentative communication products, publishers, software and hardware companies, and hearing aid testing equipment manufacturers.

     November

2235 **Annual Santa Barbara Sports Festival**
Santa Barbara, CA 93102

Offers information on sports and events for the disabled.

2236 **Assistive Technology**
John B. Hynes Veterans Memorial Center
Boston, MA

Ashley Hunt
Information and demonstrations of products and services for home, work, education and recreation.

2237 **Children and Adolescents with Emotional and Behavioral Disorders**
Virginia Commonwealth University, Medical College
PO Box 980489
Richmond, VA 23298   804-741-7057
FAX: 804-828-2645

Cynthia R. Eillis, M.D., Program Chair

     October

2238 **Closing the Gap's Annual Conference**
PO Box 68
Henderson, MN 56044   507-248-3294
FAX: 507-248-3810
e-mail: info@closingthegap.com
www.closingthegap.com

International conference held annually on adaptive technology for people with disabilities.

     October

2239 **Contemporary Issues in Behavioral Health Care**
American Assn. of Children's Residential Centers
440 1st Street NW
3rd Floor
Washington, DC 20001   202-628-1816
FAX: 202-638-4004
e-mail: aacrc@dc.net
www.aacrc-dc.org

Richard Biolsi, ACSW, President
Elissa Malter Schwartz, Association Director
One-day program will address accreditation as it relates to current behavioral health care challenges. Four Points Sheraton Hotel in San Diego, California.

     July

2240 **Council for Exceptional Children Annual Convention and Expo**
1920 Association Drive
Reston, VA 20191   703-620-3660
888-232-7733
FAX: 703-264-9494
TDY:703-264-9446
e-mail: service@cec.sped.org
www.cec.sped.org

Nancy Safer, Executive Director
Meet leaders and innovators in special education, their products works and services for the exceptional and gifted child.

     April

2241 **Handicapped Student Program Postsecondary Education Association**
PO Box 21192
Columbus, OH 43221   614-488-4972
FAX: 614-488-1774
e-mail: ahead@postbox.acs.ohio-state.edu
www.ahead.org

Ed Suddeth, Executive Director

     July

2242 **Hospital Case Management Summit CMSA & American Health Consultants**
Sheraton Harbor Island Hotel
San Diego, CA

www.cmsa.org

Focusing on key issues and strategies for hospital-based case management systems. Sponsored by CMSA and American Health Consultants.

2243 Joint Conference with ABMPP Annual Conference

American Board of Disability Analysts
345 24th Avenue North
Suite 200
Nashville, TN 37203   615-327-2984
                                FAX: 615-327-9235
                    e-mail: americanbd@aol.com

Joint Conference with ABMPP Annual Conference Charleston, South Carolina.

May

2244 Joint Conference: The American Board of Medical Psychotherapists and Psychodiagnosticians

American Board of Disability Analysts
345 24th Avenue North
Suite 200
Nashville, TN 37203   615-327-2984
                                FAX: 617-327-9325
                    e-mail: americanbd@aol.com

Hilton Washington on Embassy Row, 2015 Massachusetts Avenue NW, Washington, DC 20036 (202)265-1600 Fax: (202)332-4870. Room rate $145.

May

2245 Journal of Rehabilitation and Annual Conference

National Rehabilitation Association
633 S Washington Street
Alexandria, VA 22314   703-836-0850
                                FAX: 703-836-0848
                    e-mail: info@nationalrehab.org
                        www.nationalrehab.org
Paul Alson, PhD, author
Carol Jaafar, Director of Program Services
Michelle Vaughan, Executive Director

The annual conference exhibits of companies that provide services and products to rehab professionals and persons with disabilities. Journal of Rehabilitation: Articles are written by professionals in the fields of rehabilitation and are peer reviewed. Editorial content reflects the broad perspectives of the association's memberhsip.

2246 Lowe's Syndrome Association

Lowe Syndrome Association
222 Lincoln Street
West Lafayette, IN 47906   765-743-3634

                    e-mail: info@lowesyndrome.org
                        www.lowesyndrome.org

Candy Smith, President
Kaye McSpadden, Director of Public Affairs

Conference held every 2 years. Provides information, newsletter, publications, parent directory, medical research and more. Annual membership fee of $15.00.

2247 MedTrade/Comtrade, FutureShow

SEMCO Productions
1130 Hightower Trail
Atlanta, GA 30350

                                FAX: 770-642-4715

Mark Simmering, Executive Vice President & COO
Beth Lange

A showplace for more than 250,000 healthcare products and services, including respiratory, rehab, home healthcare, long-term care/alternate site, wound care/skin care, med/surg, sports medicine, IV therapy, computer and automation technology, and telecommunications. Attendees include hospitals, physicians, RNs, HMOs, insurance companies, long-term care providers, medical device manufacturers, pharmacists, therapists and more.

October

2248 National Council on the Aging Conference

Conference Department
409 3rd Street SW
Washington, DC 20024   202-205-6770
                                    800-424-9046
                                FAX: 202-479-0735
                                    www.ncoa.com

Offers ideas and programs to increase your program and administrative skills through NCOA's professional development tracks and the offering of continuing education units.

May

2249 National Managed Health Care Congress

70 Blanchard Road
Suite 4000
Burlington, MA 01803   978-250-3977
                                FAX: 781-487-6709

Sue Deveaux, Sales Director

Attracts nearly 7,000 delegates, thereby reinforcing its status as the nation's largest conferences for all managed care constituencies.

2250 Network Conference

Learning Disabilities Network
72 Sharp Street
Suite A-2
Hingham, MA 02043   781-340-5605
                                FAX: 781-340-5603
                    e-mail: ldntwk@aol.com
                        www.ldnetwork.org

Carolyn Cowen, Executive Director

Largest conference in New England targeting individuals, parents and professionals.

April

2251 North Carolina Assistive Technology Project

1110 Navaho Drive
Suite 101
Raleigh, NC 27609   919-850-2787
                                FAX: 919-850-2792

Ricki Cook, Contact

Exists to create a statewide, consumer-responsive system of assistive technology services for all North Carolinians with disabilities. The project's activities impact children and adults with disabilities across all aspects of their lives.

2252 Orton Dyslexia Society Annual Conference

Chester Building
Suite 382
Baltimore, MD   21286

800-ABC-D123
FAX: 410-296-0232

Rose Mary Bowler, Executive Director

November

2253 PVA Sports and Recreation Program

National Veterans Wheelchair Games
801 18th Street NW
Washington, DC   20006   202-872-1300

Andy Fleming, Director

Holds annual conference in the summer.

2254 RESNA Annual Conference

1700 North Moore Street
Suite 1540
Arlington, VA   22209   703-524-6686
FAX: 703-524-6630
e-mail: national@resna.org

Susan Leone
Jim Geletka

A multidisciplinary association for the advancement of rehabilitation and assistive technologies, holds an annual conference in June. The conference brings together a large number of rehabilitation professionals, products and services from around the world, and has something to offer for both professionals and consumers. The conference provides an informative and thought provoking forum for anyone with interests in rehabilitation technology.

June

2255 Rehabilitation Technology Association

PO Box 1004
Institute, WV   25112   304-766-4602
800-624-8284
FAX: 304-766-2689
e-mail: wvrrtc@rtc2.icdi.wvu.edu

Betty Jo Tyler, RTA Coordinator
Dave Whipp, Information Manager

Holds annual conference in the spring. Publishes a quarterly newsletter and houses the Project Enable computerized bulletin board system.

2256 Santa Barbara Wheelchair Sports

Santa Barbara Parks and Recreation Department
PO Box 1990
Santa Barbara, CA   93102   805-564-5324
FAX: 564-548-0

Mariana de Sena, RT, CTRS, Recreation Spvr.
Richard Johns

Offers a yearly conference, offers programs and services for individuals with a physically disabling condition, head injured individuals that may be visually and hearing impaired. Offers excursions, outings, competition, recreation, etc.

2257 SubAcute Care: American SubAcute Care Association Annual Convention/Expo

PO Box 17413
Washington, DC   20041
FAX: 703-318-7568

Sherlyn Remley, Exhibit Sales
Jim Wasson, Exhibit Sales

Totally dedicated to servicing the subacute arena and its major entities. Features 100+ booths and over 75 exhibitors.

March

2258 Subacute Rehabilitation Conference

Barrow Neurological Institute
350 W Thomas Road
Phoenix, AZ   85013   602-406-3000

Beverly Pennington, Coordinator

This conference addresses the current growth and changes affecting subacute rehabilitation health care. Subacute rehabilitation meets the needs of patients who are too ill to go home, but too well for acute care units. Subacute rehabilitation fills the gap between the rehabilitation programs and discharging the patient home.

May

2259 TASH

29 West Susquehanna Avenue
Suite 210
Baltimore, MD   21204   410-828-8274
FAX: 410-828-6706
e-mail: info@tash.org
www.tash.org

International association of/for people with disabilities. Civil rights organization for, and of, people with mental retardation, autism, cerebral palsy, physical disabilities and other conditions.

November

2260 Tampa A New Horizon for the 21st Century

CMSA's Annual Case Management Conference
Tampa Convention Center
Tampa, FL

e-mail: annllew@gate.net

Pre-conference workshop at the Annual Disease Management Association of America Conference. The conference will offficially begin Sunday evening with an opening reception followed by two full days of leading edge informaation in the field of disease management.

November

2261 UM/CM Best Practices Conference

American Accrediation HeatlhCare Commission
Sheraton Harbor Island Hotel
San Diego, CA

www.cmsa.org

Sheraton Harbor Island Hotel, San Diego, California sponsored by URAC/American Accreditation HealthCare Commission and CMSA.

November

2262 Winter Conference

American Board of Disability Analysts
345 24th Avenue North
Suite 200
Nashville, TN 37203   615-327-2984
                              FAX: 615-327-9235
                         e-mail: americanbd@aol.com

Joint Conference: American Board of Disability,
Miami Beach, FL (305)538-1938, call for hotel reservations. Room rate $159. Provides ready access
to beaches and by shuttle to world-class shopping
and exciting tourist venues.

February

Organizations

2263 Adaptive Environments Center
374 Congress Street
Suite 301
Boston, MA 02210   617-695-1225
FAX: 617-482-8099
e-mail: adaptive@adaptenv.org
www.adaptenv.org

Valerie Fletcher, Executive Director
Lenie Kuit, Marketing Communications Coord.
Kathy Gips, Director of Training

Develops educational programs and materials on universal design, Americans with Disabilities Act, home adaptation, and more. Central Adaptive Environments publication list also available.

2264 American Institute of Architects (AIA)

Information Center
1735 New York Avenue NW
Washington, DC 20006   202-783-6500
FAX: 202-626-7887
e-mail: library@aiamail.aia.org
www.aia.org

Carole Twombly, Reference Librarian
Jenni Woolums, Reference Librarian

Research service in print and online information. Large collection of books and periodicals on the building/architectural environments.

2265 Building Owners and Managers Association International

1201 New York Avenue NW
Washington, DC 20005   202-216-9100
FAX: 202-371-0181
www.boma.org

Conducts seminars nationwide for building owners and managers on ADA requirements for commercial facilities and places of public accommodation.

2266 Carter and Company

10 Livermore Road
Wellesley, MA 02481
800-232-1990

Wendy Beck Von Peccoz, Sales & Marketing
Susan Carter, President

Provides barrier free office designs which comply with the Americans with Disabilities Act. Workplace accommodations for both large and small environments.

2267 Challenges Unlimited

171 River Drive
Hadley, MA 01035
800-637-8720
FAX: 413-585-1137

Michael Oestreicher, President

A multi-disciplined design firm founded in 1984 by concerned design professionals. The team includes architects, engineers, designers and landscape architects specializing in accessible corporate, municipal and private facilities.

2268 Committee for a Barrier Free Environment

419 West 16th Street
Traverse City, MI 49684

Offers architecturally accessible information.

2269 Do-Able Renewable Home

AARP Fulfillment
601 E Street NW
Washington, DC 20049   202-434-2277
800-424-3410
FAX: 202-434-3443
e-mail: member@aarp.org
www.aarp.org

Describes how individuals with disabilities can modify their homes for independent living. Room-by-room modifications are accompanied by illustrations.

2270 EPVA Action

Eastern Paralyzed Veterans Association
75-20 Astoria Boulevard
Flushing, NY 11370   718-397-4181
800-444-0120
FAX: 718-803-0414
e-mail: info@epva.org
www.epva.org

Association news and articles on architecture and barrier-free design, legislation and other current events affecting veterans.

Monthly

2271 Hanson Construction

410 Lake Avenue
Woodstock, IL 60098   815-338-1092

New constructions and modifications to make homes accessible to the handicapped.

2272 Mark Elmore Associates Architects

42 Eeast Street
Crystal Lake, IL 60014   815-455-7260
FAX: 815-455-2238
e-mail: mark@elmore-architects.com
www.elmore-architects.com

Mark Elmore, AIA

Architectural designs for accessible residential and commercial buildings. ADA compliance reviews.

2273 NHeLP

National Health Law Program
2639 S La Cienega Boulevard
Los Angeles, CA 90034   310-204-6010
FAX: 310-204-0891
e-mail: nhelp@healthlaw.org
www.healthlaw.org

NHeLP, author

Helps ensure equity and non-discrimination in federal, state, local and private health care programs by assisting local legal service attorneys, paralegal and non-LSC attorneys representing LSC-eligible clients. NHeLP provides advice, co-counsel and other litigation assistance and trainings. *$85.00*

30-32 pages Quarterly

2274 National Conference on Building Codes and Standards

505 Huntmar Park Drive
Suite 210
Herndon, VA 20170   703-437-1011
                           FAX: 703-481-3596

Barbara Divver, Director, Services & Membership

In conjunction with Paralyzed Veterans of America, this agency will promote the certification of State codes for equivalency with ADA standards, and encourage the development of alternative dispute resolution procedures within the existing State regulatory framework.

2275 National Legal Center for the Medically Dependent and Disabled

50 S Meridian Street
Suite 605
Indianapolis, IN 46204   317-638-1700
                            FAX: 812-232-0620
                   e-mail: nlcmdd@juno.com
                      www.tmarzon@aol.com

Litigation and support center for the disabled specializing in medical treatment lights/attendant care issues. *$49.00*

134 pages Quarterly

2276 Overcoming Mobility Barriers International

1022 S 41st Street
Omaha, NE 68105   402-342-5731
                        FAX: 402-342-5731

Kay Neil, Executive Director

Members are government officials, service consumers and providers, and other persons interested in removing mobility barriers for elderly, handicapped and disadvantaged persons. Advises and works in conjunction with other groups and government agencies to establish safety standards for special equipment used in retrofitting vehicles and works to retrain drivers in the use of nonconventional driving controls. Addresses such problems as possible allocation of fuel to social service agencies.

2277 Paradigm Design Group

801 18th Street NW
Washington, DC 20006   202-872-1300
                             FAX: 202-416-7647

Kim Beasley, Managing Principal
Thomas Davies, Jr., Principal

Specialized firm providing architectural consulting services related to accessible designs. Experience includes product design and building codes and standards.

2278 United States Access Board

1331 F Street NW
Suite 1000
Washington, DC 20004   202-331-1252
                             800-872-2253
                        FAX: 202-272-5447
               e-mail: info@access-board.gov
                      www.access-board.gov

Dave Yanchulis, Public Affairs Specialist

Offers information and referrals on architectural accessibility for architects, designers, government agencies, building owners and consumers. A list of free publications is available on request. The Access Board also enforces the Architectural Barriers Act, which covers buildings and facilities designed, built or altered since 1968 with certain federal funds or leased by federal agencies. Publications: Access Currents, bi-monthly newsletter.

Publications & Videos

2279 Access Equals Opportunity

Council of BBB's Foundation
4200 Wilson Boulevard
Suite 800
Arlington, VA 22203   703-247-9301
                            FAX: 703-525-8277
                              www.bbb.org

Barbara Bate, Vice President
Jennifer Ley, Special Assistant

These six Title III compliance guides for existing small businesses offer creative cheap and easy suggestions for complying with the public accommodations section of the ADA. Each guide is industry specific for: retail stores, car sales/service, restaurants/bars, medical offices and fun/fitness centers. They include suggestions for readily achievable removal of architectural barriers; effective communication; and guidance for nondiscriminatory policies or procedures. *$2.50*

2280 Access House

Northside Mental Health Center
1109 E 139th Avenue
Tampa, FL 33613   813-264-1811
                        FAX: 813-632-0933

Cecil Woodside, Director

Barrier free regulations for design and construction.

2281 Access for All: 2nd Edition

Hospital Audiences
220 West 42nd Street
New York, NY 10036   212-575-7678
                           FAX: 212-575-7669
                    www.hospitalaudiences.org

Tricia Hennessey, Access Director

Provides physical and program accessibility information for people with disabilities to New York City cultural institutions including theaters, museums, galleries, etc.

2282 Accessibility Standards Illustrated

401 S Spring Street
Springfield, IL 62706

Michael Jones
An illustrated guide to barrier-free design.

217 pages

2283 Adaptable Housing: A Technical Manual for Implementing Adaptable Dwelling

HUD USER (Distributor)
PO Box 6091
Rockville, MD 20849   301-251-5154
                             800-245-2691
                        FAX: 301-251-5767
                        www.huduser.org

An illustrated manual describing methods for implementing adaptability in housing. *$3.00*

2284 Adaptive Environments Center Home Assessment Form

Massachusetts College of Art
621 Huntington Avenue
Boston, MA 02115   617-232-1492

A handy checklist for evaluating a disabled person's abilities and his/her home limitations to determine what accessibility modifications will be most effective. *$5.00*

2285 An Accessible Home of Your Own

Accent Books & Products
PO Box 700
Bloomington, IL 61702   309-378-2961
                               800-787-8444
                          FAX: 309-378-4420
                 e-mail: acmtlvng@aol.com
                     www.accentonliving.com

Raymond C. Cheever, Publisher
Betty Garee, Editor

This guide includes 14 articles that have appeared in the magazine on the popular subject of how to make a disabled persons home more accessible. *$5.95*

52 pages Paperback
ISBN 0-91570 -29-9

2286 Arts and 504: A 504 Handbook for Accessible Arts Programming

Office for Special Constituencies (Distributor)
1100 Pennsylvania Avenue NW
Washington, DC 20004   202-208-7004

A handbook for compliance with Section 504 of the Rehabilitation Act of 1973, including technical assistance on making arts programs accessible to staff, performers, and audience.

2287 Consumer's Guide to Home Adaptation

Adaptive Environments Center
374 Congress Street
Suite 301
Boston, MA 02210   617-695-1225
                      FAX: 617-482-8099
              e-mail: adaptive@adaptenv.org
                     www.adaptenv.org

Valerie Fletcher, Executive Director
Gabriela Bonome-Simms, Director of Admissions
Mike DiLorenzo, Publications Coordinator

A workbook that enables people with disabilities to plan the modifications necessary to adapt their homes. Describes how to widen doorways, lower countertops, etc. *$12.00*

52 pages Paperback

2288 Directory of Accessible Building Products

NAHB Research Center
400 Prince Georges Boulevard
Upper Marlboro, MD 20774
                             800-638-8556
                        FAX: 301-249-0305
                     e-mail: nahbrc.org
                        www.nahbrc.org

Taria Singleton, Publication Department

Contains descriptions of over 190 commercially available products designed for use by people with disabilities and age-related limitations. Paperback. *$5.00*

94 pages Yearly

2289 ECHO Housing: Recommended Construction and Installation Standards

American Association of Retired Persons
601 East Street NW
Washington, DC 20049
                             800-424-3410
                        FAX: 202-434-6483
                        www.aarp.org

Illustrated design, construction, and installation standards for temporary dwelling units for elderly people on single family residential property.

2290 Electronic House: Enhanced Lifestyles with Electronics

Electronic House
526 Boston Post Road
Suite 150
Wayland, MA 01778   978-440-1000
                           800-375-8015
                      FAX: 978-358-5195
             e-mail: kmoyes@ehpub.com
                 www.electronichouse.com

Lisa Montgomery, author
Ken Moyes, Publisher

Electronic House is the only magazine dedicated to home automation. Featuring both extravagant and affordable smart homes that can be controlled with one touch. EH covers electronic systems that give homeowners more security, entertainment, convenience, and fun. Articles cover whole house control and subsystems like residential lighting, security, home theater, energy management and telecommunications. *$ 23.95*

84 pages BiMonthly
ISSN 0886-66 3

2291 Electronic House: Journal of Home Automation

Electronic House
302 Boston Post Road
Box 430
Waylandter, MA 01778   978-440-1000
                              800-375-8015
                         FAX: 978-358-5195
        e-mail: jacobson@ehpub.com
              www.electronichouse.com

Lisa Montgomery, author
Ken Moyes, Publisher

Electronic House is the only magazine dedicated to home automation. Featuring both extravagant and affordable smart homes that can be controlled with one touch. EH covers electronic systems that give homeowners more security, entertainment, convenience, and fun. Articles cover whole house control and subsystems like residential lighting, security, home theater, energy management and telecommunications. $ 23.95

        84 pages BiMonthly
        ISSN 0886-6643

2292 Fair Housing Design Guide for Accessibility

National Council on Multifamily Housing Industry
15th & M Street NW
Washington, DC 20005   202-862-1600
                         FAX: 202-822-0512
           e-mail: info@nahb.com
                www.nahb.com

Thomas D. Davies, Jr., Author/Editor

Specifically tailored to address the needs of architects and builders. The book includes a detailed technical analysis of the legislation's impact on multifamily design, highlights potential construction problems, and identifies possible solutions. $29.95

2293 Ideas for Making Your Home Accessible

Accent Books & Products
PO Box 700
Bloomington, IL 61702   309-378-2961
                               800-787-8444
                          FAX: 309-378-4420
           e-mail: acmtlvng@aol.com
                www.accentonliving.com

Raymond C. Cheever, Publisher
Betty Garee, Editor

Offers over 100 pages of tips and ideas to help build or remodel a home. Includes many special devices and where to get them. $7.50

        94 pages Paperback
        ISBN 0-91570 -08-6

2294 North Carolina State Building Code, Volume I-C

North Carolina Department of Insurance
PO Box 26387
Raleigh, NC 27611   919-733-3901
                      FAX: 919-733-9171
        e-mail: lwright@mail.doi.state.nc.us

Laurel W. Wright, Code Consultant

Making buildings and facilities accessible to and usable by the physically handicapped. $20.00

        269 pages

2295 Planner's Guide to Barrier Free Meetings

Barrier Free Environments
PO Box 30634
Raleigh, NC 27622   919-781-0959
                      FAX: 919-839-6380

An illustrated guide to both temporary and permanent modifications to hotel rooms and meeting spaces to accommodate disabled people. Also includes practical advice on including disabled people in all types of meeting activities. $22.95

2296 Removing the Barriers: Accessibility Guidelines and Specifications

APPA
1643 Prince Street
Alexandria, VA 22314   703-684-1446
                         FAX: 703-549-2772
          e-mail: webmaster@appa.org
                www.appa.org

Wayne Leroy, Exec. Vice President
Steve Glazner, Communications Dir.

Offers site accessibility, building entrances, doors, interior circulation, restrooms and bathing facilities, drinking fountains and additional resources. $45.00

        125 pages
        ISBN 0-91335 -59-9

2297 Smart Kitchen/How to Design a Comfortable, Safe & Friendly Workplace

Ceres Press
PO Box 87
Woodstock, NY 12498   845-679-5573
                             888-804-8848
                        FAX: 845-679-5573
          e-mail: cem620@aol.com
              www.healthiestdiet.com

David Goldbeck, author

This book provides information about designing kitchens that may be helpful to people with disabilities as well as safe and energy efficient. $16.95

        132 pages Paperback
        ISBN 0-96061 -87-0

2298 Universal Design

Office of Public Information
Washington, DC 20410

Describes a universal design concept which makes housing accessible to all individuals regardless of age, size or ability. No-cost and low-cost options are discussed.

General

2299 Able to Work National Business & Disability Council

201 I.U. Willets Road
Albertson, NY 11507   516-873-9607

e-mail: abletowork@ncds.org
www.abletowork.org/

Dedicated to increasing the employment of people with disabilities through a coordinated effort of North America's largest employers. Believing that people with disabilities bring value to the workplace, Consortium partners will provide the leadership necessary to infuse effective employment practices for workers with disabilities in our global economy.

2300 Accessibility Consultants

11 E Greenway Plaza
Suite 2218
Houston, TX 77046   713-728-0924
FAX: 409-826-7250

Robert McDonald, President
Joe Bontke, Vice President

A firm that focuses on the integration of people with disabilities into everyday life. Areas of concentration include adaptation of public facilities, preconstruction planning, corporate policies and training, job description seminars and workplace modifications.

2301 American Board of Professional Disability Consultants

1350 Beverly Road
Suite 115-327
Mc Lean, VA 22101   703-573-9313

Taras Cerkevitch, Operations Director
Mark Long, Development Director

Certifies physicians, psychologists, attorneys, and counselors as specialists in disability and personal injury.

2302 Augmentative Communication Consultants

280-B Moon Clinton Road
Moon Township, PA 15108

800-982-2248
FAX: 412-269-0923
e-mail: acci@usaor.net
www.acciinc.com

Millie Telega Horner, CCC,SLP, President

ACCI is owned by a mother of a multiple handicapped son who is non-verbal. ACCI specializes in communication devices, educational software, computer access, environmental controls, switches, resource books and in-service training. Offers a wide range of products, so that, ACCIcan help one make the right choice. Price Range $24 - $6,500.

2303 Behavior Service Consultants

16 Lakeside Drive
97
Greenbelt, MD 20770   301-474-2146

Leopold Walder

Offers consultative services regarding behavior modification techniques, neurological testing, therapy for individuals, families and groups.

2304 CM Carney and Associates

6600 SW 92nd Avenue
Portland, OR 97223   503-244-1956
800-289-2006

Bob Larson, Vice President
Coleen Carney, President

Vocational and medical case management services. Early return to work services, job site modification specialists, reasonable accommodation specialists (ADA). Vocational counseling for injured workers, veterans, career changers, etc.

2305 Community Alternatives Unlimited

8700 W Bryn Mawr Avenue
Suite 500
Chicago, IL 60631   773-778-0919
FAX: 773-714-8256

Joanell Voigt, Executive Director
Steve Zider, PhD, Associate Director

Provides freestanding case management to individuals with developmental disabilities and mental illness. Provides services throughout the North Side of Chicago, and additionally, the Northern Suburbs of Cook and Lake counties.

2306 Friedman, Domiano & Smith Company, L.P.A.

1370 Ontario Street 600
Standard Building
Cleveland, OH 44113

800-377-2415

Jeffrey Friedman, Esquire

Offers free consultation for the disabled individual.

2307 Immuno Labs

1620 West Oakland Park Boulevard
Suite 300
Fort Lauderdale, FL 33311

800-231-9197

Specialized allergy and immunology testing for physicians; referrals to physicians who do allergy testing.

2308 Rehab Assist

Case Management Company
6250 N River Road
Suite 3000
Rosemont, IL 60018   847-292-4444
FAX: 847-292-7424

Henry P. Brennan, MS, Director
Thomas J. Kleinhenz, RN, Director

Medical and catastrophic intervention consultants providing objective independent evaluations and recommendations. Services include assessments, on-site evaluations, life care planning, file and chart review, billing audits, medical and worker's compensation case management, and medical/legal consultations. *$65.00*

Per Hour

2309 RehabTech Associates

3640 Dry Creek Center
Ellicott City, MD   21043

FAX: 410-465-4072

Lynn Bryant, President

A disability consulting firm that conducts research and other projects related to disability. It also publishes and distributes publications on disability.

Classroom Aids

2310 AEPS Child Progress Record: For Children Ages Three to Six

Brookes Publishing
PO Box 10624
Baltimore, MD 21285   410-337-9580
                          800-638-3775
        FAX: 410-337-8539
e-mail: custserv@brookespublishing.com
        www.brookespublishing.com

This chart helps monitor change by visually displaying current abilities, intervention targets, and child progress. In packages of 30. *$21.00*

8 pages Gate-fold
ISBN 1-557662-51-7

2311 AEPS Curriculum for Three to Six Years

Brookes Publishing
PO Box 10624
Baltimore, MD 21285   410-337-9580
                          800-638-3775
        FAX: 410-337-8539
e-mail: custserv@brookespublishing.com
        www.brookespublishing.com

$49.00

304 pages Spiral-bound
ISBN 1-557661-88-X

2312 AEPS Data Recording Forms: For Children Ages Three to Six

Brookes Publishing
PO Box 10624
Baltimore, MD 21285   410-337-9580
                          800-638-3775
        FAX: 410-337-8539
e-mail: custserv@brookespublishing.com
        www.brookespublishing.com

These forms can be used by child development professionals on four separate occasions to pinpoint and then monitor a child's strengths and needs in the six key areas of skill development measured by the AEPS Test. Packages of 10. *$24.00*

36 pages Saddle-stiched
ISBN 1-557662-49-5

2313 AEPS Family Interest Survey

Brookes Publishing
PO Box 10624
Baltimore, MD 21285   410-337-9580
                          800-638-3775
        FAX: 410-337-8539
e-mail: custserv@brookespublishing.com
        www.brookespublishing.com

This is a 30-item checklist that helps families to identify interests and concerns to address in a child's IEP/IFSP. Comes in packages of 30. *$15.00*

8 pages Saddle-stiched
ISBN 1-557660-98-0

2314 AEPS Family Report: For Children Ages Birth to Three

Brookes Publishing
PO Box 10624
Baltimore, MD 21285   410-337-9580
                          800-638-3775
        FAX: 410-337-8539
e-mail: custserv@brookespublishing.com
        www.brookespublishing.com

This is a 64-item questionnaire that asks parents to rank their child's abilities on specific skills. In packages of 10. *$17.00*

20 pages Saddle-stiched
ISBN 1-557660-99-9

2315 Advanced Language Tool Kit

Educators Publishing Service
31 Smith Place
Cambridge, MA 02138   617-547-6706
                          800-225-5750
        FAX: 617-547-0412
        www.epsbooks.com

Paula D. Rome, Jean S. Osman, author

Provides an overview of the structure, organization, and sound units that are needed to develop skills for advanced reading and spelling. The kit contains a teacher's manual and threee packs of cards. *$60.00*

ISBN 0-838885-48-9

2316 Affix & Root Cards

Educators Publishing Service
31 Smith Place
Cambridge, MA 02138   617-367-2700
                          800-225-5750
        FAX: 617-547-0412
        www.epsbooks.com

Dorothy Bywaters, author

These cards are specially designed to reinforce the adolescent's knowledge of reading, spelling and vocabulary and should be used in conjunction with language-training materials found in the Alphabetic Phonics and Gillingham curricula. Color-coded cards present word parts, definitions, and example words. *$29.70*

140 Cards
ISBN 0-838803-24-5

2317 All Kinds of Minds

Educators Publishing Service
31 Smith Place
Cambridge, MA 02138   617-367-2700
                          800-225-5750
        FAX: 617-547-0412
        www.epsbooks.com

Dr. Mel Levine, author

A Young Student's Book about Learning Abilities and Learning Disorders is mainly a fictitious account of five appealing and realistic characters, each of whom has one or more learning disorders. Young readers will easily identify with the experiences of the characters as they appear in a variety of situations, and, at the level, there are suggestions for overcoming the effects of learning disorders. *$24.75*

296 pages
ISBN 0-838820-90-5

2318 American Sign Language Handshape Cards

TJ Publishers (Distributors)
817 Silver Spring Avenue
Suite 206
Silver Spring, MD   20910   301-585-4440
                                   800-999-1168
                              FAX: 301-585-5930
                        e-mail: TJPubinc@aol.com

Ben Bahan and Frank Allen Paul, author
Angela K Thames, President
Jerald A Murphy, Vice President

Durable flashcards illustrate basic handshapes, classifiers and the American manual alphabet. An instructional booklet describes games for differing skill levels to improve vocabulary, increase hand and eye coordination, sign recognition and usage. *$16.95*

ISBN 0-960080-91-5

2319 Auditory-Verbal Therapy for Parents and Professionals

3417 Volta Plaza NW
Washington, DC   20007   202-337-5220
                           FAX: 202-337-8314
                           TDY:202-337-5220

Warren Estabrooks, M.Ed, author
Elizabeth Quigley, Director Of Member Managment

To teach children to listen, process spoken language, and talk, auditory-verbal therapy develops language and speech through listening with effective use of hearing aids and partnership of parents, children, and professionals. *$39.95*

313 pages Paperback

2320 Basic Course in American Sign Language Package

TJ Publishers (Publisher & Distributor)
817 Silver Spring Avenue
Suite 206
Silver Spring, MD   20910   301-585-4440
                                   800-999-1168
                              FAX: 301-585-5930
                        e-mail: TJPubinc@aol.com

Angela K Thames, President
Jerald A Murphy, Vice President

Accompanying videotapes and textbooks will include voice translations. Hearing students can analyze sound for initial instruction, or opt to turn off the sound to sharpen visual acuity. Package includes the A Basic Course in American Sign Language text, Student Study Guide, the original four 1-hour videotapes plus the ABCASL Vocabulary Videotape. *$139.95*

280 pages Text & Videos

2321 Beginning Reasoning and Reading

Educators Publishing Service
31 Smith Place
Cambridge, MA   02138   617-547-6706
                               800-225-5750
                          FAX: 617-547-0412
                          www.epsbooks.com

Joanne Carlisle, author

This workbook develops basic language and thinkink skills that build the foundation for reading comprehension. Workbook exercises reingorce reading as a critical activity. *$10.45*

ISBN 0-838830-01-3

2322 Behavioral Objectives for Learning Disabilities

Psychological & Educational Publications
PO Box 520
Hydesville, CA   95547   707-768-1807
                                800-523-5775

A curriculum guide to help plan for your students with learning problems in pre-school to high-school.

2323 Board Games for Play and Say

Pro-Ed
8700 Shoal Creek Boulevard
Austin, TX   78757
                          FAX: 800-397-7633
                     e-mail: proed1@aol.com
                          www.priedine.com

Robert C. Warkomski, author

Designed to make therapy more fun and enhance simple words and the production of speech sounds in isolation, phrases and sentences. *$59.00*

8 Games

2324 Book of Possibilities: Elementary Edition

AbleNet
1081 10th Avenue SE
Minneapolis, MN   55414
                                  800-322-0956
                             FAX: 612-379-9143
          e-mail: customerservice@ablenetinc.com
                          www.ablenetinc.com

Helen Canfield, M.A. CCC/SLP, Author/Editor
Peggy Locke, Ph.D., Author/Editor

Activity ideas for all elementary age switch users to be included in a variety of math, science, language arts, social studies, spelling and reading activities. A valuable how to resource for every educator that serves students with severe disabilities. *$27.00*

2325 Book of Possibilities: Secondary Edition

AbleNet
1081 10th Avenue SE
Minneapolis, MN   55414
                                  800-322-0956
                             FAX: 612-379-9143
          e-mail: customerservice@ablenetinc.com
                          www.ablenetinc.com

Helen Canfield, M.A. CCC/SLP, Author/Editor
Peggy Locke, Ph.D., Author/Editor

Suggestions for including secondary age switch users in a variety of school experiences throughout the day. Includes sections on secondary academics, general classroom activities like giving tests or reports and non-curricular activities like school plays and sports events. A valuable how to resource for educators that serve students with severe disabilities. *$27.00*

2326 Buy!

JE Stewart Teaching Tools
PO Box 15308
Seattle, WA   98115   425-486-4510
                                     FAX: 425-486-4510

JE Stewart, author
J E Stewart, Owner

Teaches 50 words as they appear in commercial and community situations such as clinic, sale, receipt, price and cleaner. These words are functional at school, on the job and shopping. *$32.50*

116 pages
ISBN 1-877866-05-9

2327 Catalog for Teaching Life Skills to Persons with Development Disability

PCI Educational Publishing
PO Box 34270
San Antonio, TX   78264   210-377-1999
                                     800-594-4263
                                  FAX: 888-259-8284
                                  www.pcicatalog.com

Janie Haugen, Vice President
Jeff McLane, President
Leslie Boulet, Senior Marketing Manager

Over 200 educational products that help individuals learn and maintain the life skills they need to succeed in an inclusive society.

2328 Childs Spelling System: The Rules

Educators Publishing Service
31 Smith Place
Cambridge, MA   02138   617-367-2700
                                     800-225-5750
                                  FAX: 617-547-0412
                                  www.epsbooks.com

Sally & Ralph Childs, author

This book presents reasonable explanations of spelling rules, makes suggestions for more effective teaching and provides lists of examples and exceptions. Basic spelling rules are listed on inside front cover. *$7.15*

32 pages
ISBN 0-838801-12-9

2329 Classroom G.O.A.L.: Guide for Optimizing Auditory Learning Skills

2000 M Street
Washington, D.C.,   20007   202-337-5220
                                  FAX: 202-337-8314
                                  TDY:202-337-5220
                              e-mail: agbell2@aol.com

Jill B. Firszt And Ruth M. Reeder, author
Elizabeth Quigley, Director

This reader-friendly teacher's guide filled with tips, source materials, and sample charts and plans is designed for educators who have yearned for a resource that explains how to incorporate auditory goals into academic learning for students with different degrees of hearing loss. *$34.95*

Paperback

2330 Classroom Notetaker: How to Organize a Program Serving Students with Hearing Impairments

2000 M Street
Washington, DC   20007   202-337-5220
                                  FAX: 202-337-8314
                                  TDY:202-337-5220

Jimmie Joan Wilson, author
Elizabeth Quigley, Director Of Mem/Mht

This detailed manual for instructors, administrators, and staff notetakers promotes classroom notetaking within long-term educational programs as absolutely vital for students who are deaf and hard of hearing from elementary school to college. *$24.95*

127 pages Paperback

2331 Community Services for the Blind and Partially Sighted Store: Sight Connection

9709 3rd Avenue NE
Suite 100
Seattle, WA   98115   206-525-5556
                                     800-458-4888
                                  FAX: 206-525-0422
                              e-mail: csbstore@csbps.com
                              www.sightconnection.com

More than 200 practical products for living with vision loss selected by vision rehabilitation specialists from Community Services for the Blind and Partially Sighted. Easy-to-use online store features large pringt, large phontos, secure transactions, and links to other vision-related resources. Store catalog available by mail upon request in large print, Braille, audiotape or PC disk. Phone and mail orders welcom. Store open 9-5, M-F, Pacific Time.

2332 Community Signs

JE Stewart Teaching Tools
PO Box 15308
Seattle, WA   98115
                                  FAX: 475-486-4510
JE Stewart, author
J E Stewart, Owner

Teaches 50 words like go, fire, rest room, men, women, danger and walk needed to successfully navigate our environment. *$ 32.50*

2333 Comprehensive Assessment of Spoken Language (CASL)

AGS
Publishers Building
PO Box 99
Circle Pines, MN   827-1

                                     800-328-2560
                                  FAX: 612-786-9007
                                     www.agsnet.com

Robert Zaske, Market Manager

CASL is an individually and orally administered research-based, theory-drive oral language assessment battery for ages 3 through 21. Fifteen tests measure language processing skills - comprehension, expression, and retrieval - in four language structure categories: Lexical/Semantic, Syntactic, Supralinguistic and Pragmatic. *$299.95*

2334 Creative Arts Therapy and Catalog

MMB Music
3526 Washington Avenue
Saint Louis, MO 63103   314-531-9635
800-543-3771
FAX: 314-531-8384
e-mail: mmbmusic@mmbmusic.com
www.mmbmusic.com

Marcia Lee Goldberg, VP Sales & Marketing

Catalog of books, videos, recordingsfor the creative arts and wellness (music, art, dance, poetry, drama, therapies, photography).

2335 Cursive Writing Skills

Educators Publishing Service
31 Smith Place
Cambridge, MA 02138   617-367-2700
800-225-5750
FAX: 617-547-0412
www.epsbooks.com

Diana King, author

These two books, written by Diana King, for grades 7-Adult for right and left-handed students. Books include exercises to establish good posture; pencil grip and paper position for both lower case and upper case letters, students also practice joining letters and copying. $ 7.15

ISBN 0-83881 -05-

2336 Decisions for Health

Brown and Benchmark
25 Kessel Center
Madison, WI 53711

A classroom resource for the educator offering various parts of information. Choices and Decisions, Mental Health and Stress Choices, Consumer Choices, Nutrition, Chemical, and Aging.

2337 Don Johnston

26799 West Commerce Drive
Volo, IL 60073   847-740-0749
800-999-4660
FAX: 847-740-7326
e-mail: info@donjohnston.com
www.donjohnston.com

A provider of quality products and services that enable people with special needs to discover their potential and experience success. Products are developed for the areas of Physical Access, Augmentative Communication and for those who struggle with reading and writing.

2338 Dyslexia Training Program

Educators Publishing Service
31 Smith Place
Cambridge, MA 02138   617-367-2700
800-225-5750
FAX: 617-547-0412
www.epsbooks.com

Texas Scottish Rite Hospital, author

This program from the Texas Scottish Rite Hospital for grades 2-8 introduces reading and writing through a two-year, cumulative series of daily one-hour videotaped lessons and accompanying student's books and teacher's guides. It is presented in a structured multi-sensory sequence of alphabet, reading, spelling, cursive handwriting, listening, language history and review activities. Students are in a class of nor more than six who work with instructional tapes as teacher's guides are available.

$6.75 - $15

2339 Exceptional Teaching Aids

20102 Woodbine Avenue
Castro Valley, CA 94546   510-582-4859
800-549-6999
FAX: 510-582-5911
e-mail: exteaching@aol.com
www.exceptionalteaching.com

Phil Mangold, Owner/Manager
Susan Taylorolo, Order Information
Kelli Cooney, Order Information

Providing educational teaching aids for the blind and visually impaired via catalog. Price range $2-600.

2340 Explode the Code Books 1-8

Educators Publishing Service
31 Smith Place
Cambridge, MA 02138   617-367-2700
800-225-5750
FAX: 617-547-0412
www.epsbooks.com

Nancy Hall & Rena Price, author

A program of workbooks helps children learn to read by teaching them to use the sounds of letters. This carefully sequenced program provides experience recognizing and combining sounds in order to read words, phrases, sentences and stories, as well as to build vocabulary. A set of fifty-four illustrated cards to practice the sounds taught in books 1-3 is now available. *$6.20*

Grades K-4, 1-3
ISBN 0-83881 -60-

2341 First Course in Phonic Reading

Educators Publishing Service
31 Smith Place
Cambridge, MA 02138   617-367-2700
800-225-5750
FAX: 617-547-0412
www.epsbooks.com

Lida G. Helson, author

This book provides students with a basic foundation in phonics beginning with common consonants and short vowels, syllabication and spelling rules are also taught. There is a special emphasis on auditory and kinesthetic involvement. *$10.65*

Grades 2-3
ISBN 0-838801-24-2

2342 Food!

JE Stewart Teaching Tools
PO Box 15308
Seattle, WA 98115   425-486-4510
FAX: 425-486-4510

JE Stewart, author
J E Stewart, Owner

Teaches 50 words like salt, pepper, hamburger, fruit, milk and soup, seen commonly on menus, packages, and in directions used at home and at play. *$32.50*

2343 Fun for Everyone

AbleNet
1081 10th Avenue SE
Minneapolis, MN 55414
800-322-0956
FAX: 612-379-9143
e-mail: customerservice@ablenetinc.com
www.ablenetinc.com
Jackie Levin, author

Today, simple technology allows children and adults with disabilities to participate in leisure activities they were limited or excluded from in the past. *$20.00*

2344 Fundamentals of Autism

Slosson Educational Publications
PO Box 280
East Aurora, NY 14052
716-625-0930
888-756-7760
FAX: 800-655-3840
e-mail: slosson@slosson.com
www.slosson.com
Sue Larson, author

The Fundamentals of Autism handbook provides a quick, user friendly, effective and accurate approach to help in identifying and developing educationally related program objectives for children diagnosed as Autistic. These materials have been designed to be easily and functionally used by teachers, therapists, special education/learning disability resource specialists, psychologists and others who work with children diagnosed as Autistic. *$47.50*

Kits

2345 GO-MO Articulation Cards

Pro-Ed
8700 Shoal Creek Boulevard
Austin, TX 78757
FAX: 512-451-8542
e-mail: proed1@aol.com
www.proedinc.com

The most popular system used for remedying defective speech articulation in children and adults. This popular card set was the first and is still the best therapy tool of its kind, as it continues to produce results and maintains the interest of students of all ages. *$109.00*

Complete Set

2346 Get Ready/Get Set/Go for the Code

Educators Publishing Service
31 Smith Place
Cambridge, MA 02138
617-367-2700
800-225-5750
FAX: 617-547-0412
www.epsbooks.com
Nancy Hall, author

Primers for the Explode the Code series teaches consonants through engaging activities which includes: tracking, tracing, matching, copying, and following directions. The Activities progress is difficulty, and the three-book series for grades K-1 is cumulative. A set of picture letter cards are available.

80-96 pages $4.50 - $5.50
ISBN 0-83881 -80-

2347 Gillingham Manaual

Educators Publishing Service
31 Smith Place
Cambridge, MA 02138
617-547-6706
800-225-5750
FAX: 617-547-0412
www.epsbooks.com
Anna Gillingham & Bessie Stillman, author

Basic hardcover instructional manual for multisensory, phonetic technique of teaching reading to children with specific language disability. A classic. Many associated teaching materials, including drill cards, and stories.

352 pages $17.55 - $69
ISBN 0-83880 -00-

2348 Guide to Teaching Phonics

Educators Publishing Service
31 Smith Place
Cambridge, MA 02138
617-367-2700
800-225-5750
FAX: 617-547-0412
www.epsbooks.com
June Lyday Orton, author

This flexible teacher's guide presents multisensory procedures developed in association with the late Dr. Samuel Orton. They consist of 100 phonograms for teaching phonetic elements and their sequences in words for reading, writing and spelling. Also contains coordinated Phonics Cards. *$13.50*

96 pages
ISBN 0-838802-41-9

2349 Homemade Battery-Powered Toys

Special Needs Project
3463 Stat Street
 # 282
Santa Barbara, CA 93105
800-333-6867

Describes how to make simple switches and educational devices for severely handicapped children. *$7.50*

2350 How the Student with Hearing Loss Can Succeed in College, Second Edition

2000 M Street
Washington, DC 20007
202-337-5220
FAX: 202-337-8314
TDY:202-337-5220
Carol Flexer, Ph.D.; Denise Wray, Ph.D.,, author
Elizabeth Quigley, Director Of

This revised book informs student who are deaf and hard of hearing about the mutual and co-equal effort that students and professionals must exert together to achieve success for students to be successful. *$28.95*

278 pages Paperback

2351 If it is to Be, it is Up to Me

AVKO Educational Research Foundation
3084 W Willard Road
Clio, MI 48420   810-686-9283
          FAX: 810-686-1101
          e-mail: avkoemail@aol.com
          www.avko.org

Don McCabe, Research Director

This book is designed for parents to use. It will prove to the student that he isn't dumb. It builds self-confidence as the student learns he can learn without studying. *$9.95*

> *112 pages*
> *ISBN 1-56400 -42-1*

2352 Implementing Cognitive Strategy Instruction Across the School

Brookline Books
PO Box 1046
Cambridge, MA 02238   617-868-0360
          800-666-2665
          FAX: 617-868-1772
          e-mail: brooklinebks@delphi.com
          www.brooklinebooks.com

Irene Gaskins
Thorne Elliot

Describes basic classroom based programs planned and executed by teachers to focus and guide students with serious reading problems to be goal oriented, strategic and self-assessing. *$24.95*

> *Paperback*
> *ISBN 0-91479 -75-1*

2353 Inclusive Play People

Educational Equity Concepts
114 E 32nd Street
New York, NY 10016   212-686-2531
          FAX: 212-725-0947
          TDY:212-725-1803
          e-mail: information@edequity.org
          www.edequity.org

Six sturdy multiracial wooden figures that provide a unique variety of nonstereotyped work and family roles and are inclusive of disabled and nondisabled people of various ages. For block building and dramatic play. *$25.00*

2354 Instruction of Persons with Severe Handicaps

McGraw-Hill, School Publishing
220 East Danieldale Road
DeSoto, TX 75115   972-224-1111
          800-442-9685
          FAX: 972-228-1982
          mhschool.com

A complete introduction to the status of education as it pertains to people with severe handicaps.

2355 Integrating Transition Planning Into the IEP Process

Council for Exceptional Children
1920 Association Drive
Reston, VA 20191   703-620-3660
          888-232-7232
          FAX: 703-264-9494
          e-mail: service@cec.sped.org
          www.cec.sped.org

Lynda West, author
Cathy Mack, Production Manager

Helps students with disabilities make a smooth transition from school to adult life. *$15.70*

> *78 pages*
> *ISBN 0-88586 -22-2*

2356 International Journal of Arts Medicine

MMB Music
3526 Washington Avenue
Saint Louis, MO 63103   314-531-9635
          800-543-3771
          FAX: 314-531-8384
          e-mail: mmbmusic@mmbmusic.com
          www.mmbmusic.com

Marcia Lee Goldberg, VP Sales & Marketing

Exploration of the creative arts and healing. Presents peer-reviewed articles clearly written by educators in the creative arts, as well as internationally prominent physicians, therapists and health care professionals.

2357 Keeping Ahead in School

Educators Publishing Service
31 Smith Place
Cambridge, MA 02138   617-367-2700
          800-225-5750
          FAX: 617-547-0412
          www.epsbooks.com

Dr. Mel Levine, author

This book helps students not only understand their own strengths and weaknesses but also more fully appreciate their individuality. He suggests specific ways to approach work, bypass or overcome learning disorders, and manage other struggles that may beset students in school. *$24.75*

> *320 pages Paperback*
> *ISBN 0-838820-69-7*

2358 KeyMath Teach and Practice

AGS
Publishers Building
PO Box 99
Circle Pines, MN 55014
          800-328-2560
          FAX: 612-786-9007
          www.agsnet.com

Robert Zaske, Market Manager

This set of materials provides all the tools needed to assess students' math skills...and the strategies to deal with problem areas. Three sets are available: Basic Concepts Package; Operations Package; and Applications Package. $219.95 each or $599.95 for whole set.

2359 Kim Marshall Series in English

Educators Publishing Service
31 Smith Place
Cambridge, MA   02138   617-367-2700
                               800-225-5750
                               FAX: 617-547-0412
                               www.epsbooks.com

Kim Marshall, author

These two books for grades 4-8 contain a total of 36 cumulative units in grammar, writing skills and word analysis. English-Part A reviews writing skills and usage, while English-Part B reviews word analysis and parts of speech. There is a teacher's manual designed to accompany each book.

104 pages $8 - $8.95

2360 Kim Marshall Series in Math

Educators Publishing Service
31 Smith Place
Cambridge, MA   02138   617-367-2700
                               800-225-5750
                               FAX: 617-547-0412
                               www.epsbooks.com

Kim Marshall, author

These two books for grades 4-8 contain 35 units that cover basic computation skills, Roman numerals, English and metric measurements, graphing, fractions and basic geometry. There is a teacher's manual designed to accompany each book.

104 pages $10.45 - $11.60

2361 Kim Marshall Series in Reading

Educators Publishing Service
31 Smith Place
Cambridge, MA   02138   617-547-6706
                               800-225-5750
                               FAX: 617-547-0412
                               www.epsbooks.com

Kim Marshall, author

These two books for grades 4-6 contain 186 interesting stories with comprehension questions that encourage careful reading and stimulate thinking. Because of the wide appeal of the stories, these books can be used to meet the needs of a variety of students. $8.00

104 pages Grades 4-6

2362 Kim Marshall Series in Vocabulary

Educators Publishing Service
31 Smith Place
Cambridge, MA   02138   617-367-2700
                               800-225-5750
                               FAX: 617-547-0412
                               www.epsbooks.com

Kim Marshall, author

This approachable vocabulary program for grades 4-8 consists of 900 words chosen to be interesting and useful and to broaden vocabulary and improve spelling. The two books in the series each contain 18 units, and every one of these units introduces 25 words followed by 5 pages of exercises and a weekly test. A teacher's manual is available for each book. $9.75

128 pages

2363 Lakeshore Learning Materials

2695 E Dominguez Street
Carson, CA   90810   310-537-8600
                               800-421-5354
                               FAX: 310-537-5403
e-mail: lakeshore@lakeshorelearning.com
              www.lakeshorelearning.com

Offers books, resources, testing materials, assessment information and special education materials for the professional in the field of special education.

190 pages

2364 Language Parts Catalog

Educators Publishing Service
31 Smith Place
Cambridge, MA   02138   617-547-6706
                               800-225-5750
                               FAX: 617-547-0412
                               www.epsbooks.com

Dr. Mel Levine, author

Informatively and numorously explains the various aspects of language and how they operate, asking students to imagine that they are reading a catalog ffeaturing defferent parts to order that can help them improve their language abilities. $9.00

ISBN 0-838819-80-X

2365 Language Tool Kit

Educators Publishing Service
31 Smith Place
Cambridge, MA   02138   617-367-2700
                               800-225-5750
                               FAX: 617-547-0412
                               www.epsbooks.com

Paula Rome & Jean Osman, author

This kit teaches reading and spelling to students in grades 1-3 with specific language disability. It contains 163-426 cards and a comprehensive 32-page teacher's manual. Also available in Spanish. $ 30.00

32 pages English Edition
ISBN 0-838885-20-3

2366 Learning American Sign Language

Harris Communications
15159 Technology Drive
Eden Prairie, MN   55344   612-906-1180
                                800-825-6758
                                FAX: 612-906-1099
        e-mail: mail@harriscomm.com
                www.harriscomm.com

Tom Humphries & Carol Padden, author
Bill Williams, National Sales Manager

Offers ASL instruction book and videotape for teachers and instructors of the hearing impaired student. $78.95

350 pages Video & Book

2367 Learning to Listen

Educators Publishing Service
31 Smith Place
Cambridge, MA   02138   617-367-2700
                               800-225-5750
                               FAX: 617-547-0412
                               www.epsbooks.com

William McCart, author

A program to improve classroom listening skills in a variety of situations. Presents students, in grades 7-9 with instruction and 33 exercises on eight basic listening skills. After reading about a particular skill, students practice it by listening to a selection and then answering questions about the selection in writing. A teachers manual is available to accompany the student book. *$6.20*

48 pages
ISBN 0-838820-61-1

2368   Learning to Sign in My Neighborhood

TJ Publishers
817 Silver Spring Avenue
Suite 206
Silver Spring, MD   20910   **301-585-4440**
                                        800-999-1168
                            FAX: 301-585-5930
                  e-mail: TJPubinc@aol.com
Diane Schmidt and Karen Cameron, author
Angela K Thames, President
Jerald A Murphy, Vice President

Beautifully illustrated coloring book lets children learn signs from kids just like themselves! Recommended for ages 4 and up, let children have fun while they learn signs for words typically used in day-to-day activities. *$3.50*

32 pages Softcover
ISBN 0-93266 -36-1

2369   Learning to Use Cursive Handwriting

Educators Publishing Service
31 Smith Place
Cambridge, MA   02138   **617-367-2700**
                                    800-225-5750
                        FAX: 617-547-0412
                        www.epsbooks.com
Beth Slingerland & Marty Aho, author

This multisensory program with instructions for introducing, teaching, practicing and reviewing lower- and upper-case cursive letters; Masters, with letter forms and lined and patterned writing paper; and Wall Cards, for lower- and upper-case letters. *$ 10.60*

96 pages Manual
ISBN 0-838802-53-2

2370   Learning to Use Manuscript Handwriting

Educators Publishing Service
31 Smith Place
Cambridge, MA   02138   **617-367-2700**
                                    800-225-5750
                        FAX: 617-547-0412
                        www.epsbooks.com
Beth Slingerland & Marty Aho, author

This multisensory program contains a manual with instructions for introducing teaching, practicing and reviewing lower- and upper-case manuscript letters; masters with letter forms and lined and patterned writing paper; and wall cards for lower-. and upper-case letters. *$10.30*

76 pages Paperback
ISBN 0-838802-50-8

2371   Let's Read: A Linguistic Reading Program

Educators Publishing Service
31 Smith Place
Cambridge, MA   02138   **617-367-2700**
                                    800-225-5750
                        FAX: 617-547-0412
                        www.epsbooks.com
Leonard Bloomfield, Clarence & Robert Barnhart, author

This linguistic approach to teaching reading emphasizes the basic relationship of spelling to sound, presenting like concepts together, providing reading materials for practice, and building on previously mastered skills for grades 1-3. Word lists and Teacher's manuals are available for Let's Read books 1-4, and Let's Look workbooks accompany the texts.

$10.35 - $19.15

2372   Literacy Program

Educators Publishing Service
31 Smith Place
Cambridge, MA   02138   **617-367-2700**
                                    800-225-5750
                        FAX: 617-547-0412
                        www.epsbooks.com
Texas Scottish Rite Hospital, author

This one year course, developed by the Scottish Rite Hospital, consists of 160 one hour videotaped lessons accompanied by student workbooks, designed for high schoolers and adults who read below a sixth grade level. This program uses multisensory applications to teach alphabet, reading, cursive writing, spelling, math and listening comprehension with frequent new activities. This is an ideal series for a community adult reading program. Grades 1-4.

$2.25 -$18

2373   Literature Based Reading

Oryx Press
4041 N Central Avenue
 # 700
Phoenix, AZ   85012   **602-265-2651**
                                  800-279-6799
                        FAX: 800-279-4663

Series offering children's books and activities to enrich the K-5 curriculum.

2374   Living an Idea: Empowerment and the Evolution of an Alternative School

Brookline Books
PO Box 1046
Cambridge, MA   02238   **617-868-0360**
                                    800-666-2665
                        FAX: 617-868-1772
          e-mail: brooklinebks@delphi.com
                www.brooklinebooks.com

Edison Trickett

This book is about the creation and 14 year evolution of a public alternative inner-city high school. The school lived an idea - empowerment. Students were encouraged to participate in shaping many aspects of their education, teachers were responsible for running the school, and parents invited to help govern. *$27.95*

ISBN 0-91479 -68-9

2375 Low Tech Assistive Devices: A Handbook for the School Setting

Therapro
225 Arlington Street
Framingham, MA 01702   508-872-9494
                         800-257-5376
                    FAX: 508-875-2062
        e-mail: info@theraproducts.com
             www.theraproducts.com
Lynn Stoller, OTR/L, author

A how-to book with step by step directions and detailed illustrations for fabrication of frequently requested low-tech assistive devices. *$42.50*

312 pages Paperback

2376 MTA Readers

Educators Publishing Service
31 Smith Place
Cambridge, MA 02138   617-367-2700
                         800-225-5750
                    FAX: 617-547-0412
             www.epsbooks.com

Illustrated readers for grades 1-3 that accompany the MTA Reading and Spelling Program (Multisensory Teaching Approach). Phonetic elements in a structured, but entertaining context.

48+ pages $4.65 - $11.65
ISBN 0-83882 -33-3

2377 Making School Inclusion Work: A Guide to Everyday Practice

Brookline Books
PO Box 1047
Cambridge, MA 02238   617-868-0360
                         800-666-2665
                    FAX: 617-868-1772
        e-mail: brooklinebks@delphi.com
             www.brooklinebooks.com
Katie Blenk and Doris Fine, author

This book tells the reader how to conduct a truly inclusive program, regardless of ethnic or racial background, economic level, and physical or cognitive ability. *$24.95*

254 pages Paperback
ISBN 0-91479 -96-4

2378 Making the Writing Process Work: Strategie for Composition and Self-Regulation

Brookline Books
PO Box 1047
Cambridge, MA 02238   617-495-3682
                         800-666-2665
                    FAX: 617-868-0360
        e-mail: brooklinebks@delphi.com
             www.brooklinebooks.com
Karen Harris & Steve Graham, author

This book is geared toward students who have difficulty organizing their thoughts and developing their writing. The specific stategies teach students how to approach, organize, and produce a final written product.. *$24.95*

240 pages Paperback
ISBN 1-571290-10-9

2379 Manual Alphabet Poster

TJ Publishers (Distributors)
817 Silver Spring Avenue
Suite 206
Silver Spring, MD 20910   301-585-4440
                             800-999-1168
                        FAX: 301-585-5930
             e-mail: TJPubinc@aol.com
Frank Allen Paul, author
Angela K Thames, President
Jerald A Murphy, Vice President

Poster presents the manual alphabet. *$4.50*

2380 Many Faces of Dyslexia

Orton Dyslexia Society
Chester Building
Suite 382
Baltimore, MD 21286
                             800-ABC-D123
                        FAX: 410-296-0232
Margaret Byrd Rawson, author

Gives information on the teaching and rehabilitation techniques for people with dyslexia. *$16.50*

Paperback

2381 Match-Sort-Assemble JOB CARDS

Exceptional Education
PO Box 15308
Seattle, WA 98115   206-542-3971
                   FAX: 475-486-4510

J E Stewart, Owner

Teaches workers to use a series of symbolic cues to control their own production cycles. *$565.00*

Class Set

2382 Match-Sort-Assemble PICTURES

Exceptional Education
PO Box 15308
Seattle, WA 98115   206-542-3971
                   FAX: 475-486-4510

J E Stewart, Owner

People with profound, severe and moderate mental retardation have immediate access with MSA Pictures. Students work with pictures (and if necessary a template) to match, sort, assemble and disassemble parts that vary in shape, length and diameter. *$426.00*

Class Set

2383 Match-Sort-Assemble SCHEMATICS

Exceptional Education
PO Box 15308
Seattle, WA 98115   206-542-3971
                   FAX: 475-486-4510

J E Stewart, Owner

Students with moderate and mild mental retardation and those who have completed MSA Pictures are ready for MSA Schematics. It increases abstraction and displacement of instruction from the work clearly and simply. *$495.00*

Class Set

2384 Match-Sort-Assemble TOOLS

Exceptional Education
PO Box 15308
Seattle, WA 98115 206-542-3971
FAX: 475-486-4510

J E Stewart, Owner

Students and clients learn to use the tools required for many jobs in light industry. Mastery of the production cycle with independence, endurance and the ability to learn new tasks through pictures and schematics and basic hand functions will help clients acquire and maintain employment in a competitive field. *$595.00*

Class Set

2385 More Food!

JE Stewart Teaching Tools
PO Box 15308
Seattle, WA 98115 425-486-4510
FAX: 425-486-4510

JE Stewart, author

Teaches 50 more words found in restaurants, grocery stores, cookbooks such as pizza, carrot, tacos, oysters and pineapple. These words are functional at home, going shopping, and during leisure. *$32.50*

2386 More Work!

JE Stewart Teaching Tools
PO Box 15308
Seattle, WA 98115
FAX: 475-486-4510

JE Stewart, author

Teaches 50 words as they appear on parts, tools, job instructions, signs and labels, such as fill, grasp, release, lock, search, position and select. These words are functional in school and on-the-job. *$32.50*

2387 Multisensory Teaching Approach

Educators Publishing Service
31 Smith Place
Cambridge, MA 02138 617-367-2700
800-225-5750
FAX: 617-547-0412
www.epsbooks.com

Margaret Taylor Smith, author

Comprehensive multisensory program in reading, writing, spelling, alphabet and dictionary skills for remedial and regular instruction. Based on Orton-Gillingham and Alphabetic Phonics. A complete program organized in kits, with additional classroom materials, supplementary materials, and Handwriting Programs.

$110 - $140

ISBN 0-83888 -10-9

2388 Peabody Articulation Decks

AGS
Publishers Building
PO Box 99
Circle Pines, MN 55014
800-328-2560
FAX: 612-786-9007
www.agsnet.com

Robert Zaske, Market Manager

Complete kit of playing-card sized PAD decks let students focus on the 18 most commonly misarticulated English consonants and blends. *$115.95*

ISBN 0-88671 -75-4

2389 Phonemic Awareness in Young Children: A Classroom Curriculum

Brookes Publishing
PO Box 10624
Baltimore, MD 21285 410-337-9580
800-638-3775
FAX: 410-337-8539
e-mail: custserv@brookespublishing.com
www.brookespublishing.com

Marilyn Jager Adams, Ph.D., author

This is a supplemental, whole-class curriculum for improving pre-literacy listening skills. It contains activities that are fun, easy to use, and proven to work in any kindergarten classroom - general, bilingual, inclusive, or special education. This program takes only 15-20 minutes a day. *$24.95*

208 pages Spiral-bound 1997

ISBN 1-557663-21-1

2390 Phonics for Thought

Educators Publishing Service
31 Smith Place
Cambridge, MA 02138 617-367-2700
800-225-5750
FAX: 617-547-0412
www.epsbooks.com

Lorna Reed, author

This multisensory approach to phonics simultaneously teaches reading, writing and spelling to grades K-2. Two illustrated workbooks are accompanied by instructional manuals that provide procedures for each lesson; the pronunciation and formation of the letters, word lists and sentences for dictation, and games and activities for further enrichment. *$8.00*

Paperback

2391 Phonological Awareness Training for Reading

Pro-Ed
8700 Shoal Creek Boulevard
Austin, TX 78757
FAX: 512-451-8542
e-mail: proed1@aol.com

Joseph K. Torgesen & Brian R. Bryant, author

Designed to increase the level of phonological awareness in young children. Can be taught individually or in small groups and takes about 12 to 14 weeks to complete if children are taught in short sessions three or four times a week. *$129.00*

2392 Play and Say Cards, Second Edition

Pro-Ed
8700 Shoal Creek Boulevard
Austin, TX 78757 512-451-3246
FAX: 512-451-8542
e-mail: proed1@aol.com

16 decks of bright, full-color playing cards, each of which carriers a frequently, misarticulated speech sound. *$89.00*

2393 Play!
JE Stewart Teaching Tools
PO Box 15308
Seattle, WA 98115   425-486-4510
                          FAX: 425-486-4510
JE Stewart, author

Teaches 50 more words as they appear at recreation sites, on signs and labels, and in newspapers and magazines, such as movie, visitor, ticket, gallery and zoo. These words are functional in school and at leisure. *$32.50*

2394 Primary Phonics
Educators Publishing Service
31 Smith Place
Cambridge, MA 02138   617-367-2700
                            800-225-5750
                      FAX: 617-547-0412
                      www.epsbooks.com
Barbara Makar, author

A program of storybooks and coordinated workbooks that teach reading for grades K-2. A structured phonetic approach. Contains 8 student workbooks, with 8 sets of 10 coordinated storybooks; consonant workbooks; initial consonant blend workbooks; picture dictionary, and coloring book. *$3.65*

$3.65 - $26.35
ISSN 0838-83 0

2395 Programmed Phonics Books 1-2 & Cassettes
Educators Publishing Service
31 Smith Place
Cambridge, MA 02138   617-367-2700
                            800-225-5750
                      FAX: 617-547-0412
                      www.epsbooks.com
Lucy Carroll, author

This self-instructing program is for children who are having difficulty with the word-recognition phase of reading vocabulary that exceeds their reading vocabulary. The books review consonants and all consonant blends. A teacher's guide and Script includes dictation, which is also available on cassettes. *$7.70*

88 pages $7.50 - $45
ISSN 0838-83 0

2396 Programming Concepts
PO Box 12428
San Antonio, TX 78212

                          800-594-4263
                      FAX: 210-824-8055

2397 Reading for Content
Educators Publishing Service
31 Smith Place
Cambridge, MA 02138   617-367-2700
                            800-225-5750
                      FAX: 617-547-0412
                      www.epsbooks.com
Carol Einstein, author

This four book series for grades 3-6 has been completely revised and updated so that the reading passages are more current and interesting. Each book contains 43 one-page reading questions. A detachable answer sheet and progress graph are involved in each book.

96 pages $7.75 each

2398 Reading from Scratch
Educators Publishing Service
31 Smith Place
Cambridge, MA 02138   617-367-2700
                            800-225-5750
                      FAX: 617-547-0412
                      www.epsbooks.com
Dorothy van den Honert, author

Contains multisensory reading and spelling material and oral and written lessons and exercises in syntax, grammar, and precomposition topics. Complete set

$6.25 - $49.30
ISBN 0-83888 -75-5

2399 Reasoning and Reading Levels I and II
Educators Publishing Service
31 Smith Place
Cambridge, MA 02138   617-547-6706
                            800-225-5750
                      FAX: 617-547-5750
                      www.epsbooks.com
Joanne Carlisle, author

Three four-unit workbooks are based on the belief that reasoning, language, and reading comprehension go hand in hand. The four-units are word meaning, sentence menaing, paragraph meaning and reasoning skills. Completely revised.

$10.45 each

2400 Recipe for Reading
Educators Publishing Service
31 Smith Place
Cambridge, MA 02138   617-367-2700
                            800-225-5750
                      FAX: 617-547-0412
                      www.epsbooks.com
Nina Traub, author

A basic reading manual with 21 storybooks and 7 workbooks for grades K-3. For remedial work. Multisensory, phonetically structured. program also includes sequence chart, a record progress, and writing paper of assorted sizes.

$4.50 - $56.25
ISSN 0838-84 1

2401 Resourcing: Handbook for Special Education Resource Teachers
Council for Exceptional Children
1920 Association Drive
Reston, VA 20191   703-620-3660
                         888-232-7323
                    FAX: 703-264-9494
              e-mail: service@cec.sped.org
                      www.cec.sped.org
Mary Jackson, author
Cathy Mack, Production Manager

Everything you need to know to be a resource for other teachers and support personnel who work with special education students. *$12.00*

64 pages
ISBN 0-86586 -19-2

2402 Rewarding Speech

Speech Bin
1965 25th Avenue
Vero Beach, FL   32960   561-770-0007
                                     800-477-3324
                                     FAX: 561-770-0006
                                     www.speechbin.com

Julie A. Blonigan, author
Jan J. Binney, Senior Editor

Reproducible reward certificates for children. *$12.95*

32 pages

2403 Rule-ette

Educators Publishing Service
31 Smith Place
Cambridge, MA   02138   617-367-2700
                                     800-225-5750
                                     FAX: 617-547-0412
                                     www.epsbooks.com

Arlie Roffman, author

A spelling card game that teaches basic spelling rules. The game was developed for grades 3-Adult. *$14.65*

Ages 3-Adult
ISBN 0-838806-72-

2404 SAYdee Posters

Speech Bin
1965 25th Avenue
Vero Beach, FL   32960   561-770-0007
                                     800-477-3324
                                     FAX: 561-770-0006
                                     www.speechbin.com

Denise Grigas, author

Colorful speech and language posters. *$20.00*

24 pages
ISBN 0-93785 -47-5

2405 Second Course in Phonic Reading

Educators Publishing Service
31 Smith Place
Cambridge, MA   02138   617-367-2700
                                     800-225-5750
                                     FAX: 617-547-0412
                                     www.epsbooks.com

Lida G. Helson, author

Two structured phonetic workbooks to teach reading for grades 2-3 and 4-5. Book 1 focuses on sounds of the letters, phonogram combinations, word families, and spelling rules. Book 2 develops comprehension and vocabulary skills. *$10.65*

Per Book
ISSN 0838-81 6

2406 Sequential Spelling I - VII

AVKO Educational Research Foundation
3084 W Willard Road
Clio, MI   48420   810-686-9283
                                     FAX: 810-686-1101

Don McCabe, Research Director

Spelling books for individuals to classrooms. Builds from easier words of a word family to important power words that build self-confidence. Each of the seven levels contains 180 spelling lessons that teach phonics through the backdoor of spelling. Students learn the patterns without having to learn rules or studying. Teachers have no papers to correct.

72 pages $8.95 each
ISBN 1-56400 -11-6

2407 Signing Naturally Curriculum

Harris Communications
15159 Technology Drive
Eden Prairie, MN   55344   612-906-1180
                                        800-825-6758
                                        FAX: 612-906-1099
                                        e-mail: mail@harriscomm.com
                                        www.harriscomm.com

Bill Williams, National Sales Manager

A series based on the functional approach that is the most popular and widely used sign language curriculum designed for teaching American Sign Language. Book and videotape set for level 1 & 2. Teacher's curriculum is also available.

2408 Small Wonder

AGS
Publishers Building
PO Box 99
Circle Pines, MN   55014
                                     800-328-2560
                                     FAX: 612-786-9007
                                     www.agsnet.com

Robert Zaske, Market Manager

This infant through toddler program offers a delightful array of activities to teach babies about themselves, others, their surroundings and the world outside. Level One - zero to 18 months; Level Two 18-36 months. Discount price of $389.95 when both levels ordered. *$229.95*

ISBN 0-91347 -62-5

2409 Solving Language Difficulties: Remedial Routines

Educators Publishing Service
31 Smith Place
Cambridge, MA   02138   617-367-2700
                                     800-225-5750
                                     FAX: 617-547-0412
                                     www.epsbooks.com

Amey Steere, Caroline Peck & Linda Kahn, author

A basic workbook for children in grades 4-6 who have a specific language disability. It can be used in any corrective reading program. It deals extensively with syllables, syllable division, prefixes, suffixes, accent and other important topics. *$9.75*

176 pages
ISBN 0-838803-26-1

2410 Sound Workbook

Educators Publishing Service
31 Smith Place
Cambridge, MA   02138   617-367-2700
                                     800-225-5750
                                     FAX: 617-547-0412
                                     www.epsbooks.com

Mary Briggs, author

This workbook for grades 1-2 reinforces the teaching of specific vowel combinations. *$5.50*

44 pages
ISBN 0-838817-08-4

2411 Sound-Off 1-5

Educators Publishing Service
31 Smith Place
Cambridge, MA   02138   **617-367-2700**
                                   800-225-5750
                                   FAX: 617-547-0412
                                   www.epsbooks.com

Anne Welles & Eleanor Griffin, author

These five workbooks for grades K-2 cover the introduction of consonants and final consonant blends and consonant diagraphs, vowel-consonant-e combinations, and vowel + r combinations. There is a teacher's guide for each book. *$5.50*

32-48 pages Per Book
ISBN 0-83885 -34-

2412 Speech-Language Delights

Speech Bin
1965 25th Avenue
Vero Beach, FL   32960   **561-770-0007**
                                    800-477-3324
                                    FAX: 561-770-0006
                                    www.speechbin.com

Activities, worksheets and games to encourage practice of speech and language skills. *$25.00*

128 pages
ISBN 0-93785 -42-4

2413 Spell of Words

Educators Publishing Service
31 Smith Place
Cambridge, MA   02138   **617-367-2700**
                                   800-225-5750
                                   FAX: 617-547-0412
                                   www.epsbooks.com

Elsie Rak, author

This book can be used with any student, from grade 7-Adult, who needs help in spelling. It covers syllabication, word building with prefixes, word patterns, phonograms, suffixes, plurals and possessives. Chapters contain explanations of spelling rules, exercises and suggestions for short compositions. *$9.25*

128 pages Grades 7-Adult
ISBN 0-838801-55-2

2414 Spellbinding 2

Educators Publishing Service
31 Smith Place
Cambridge, MA   02138   **617-547-6706**
                                   800-225-5750
                                   FAX: 617-547-0412
                                   www.epsbooks.com

Elsie T. Rak, author

Spellbinding 2 adds practice exercises with more complicated spelling problems and introduces new areas of study. The manuals give answers to exercises and include a large number of new dictations. *$11.55*

96+ pages Each
ISBN 0-838814-75-1

2415 Spellbound

Educators Publishing Service
31 Smith Place
Cambridge, MA   02138   **617-367-2700**
                                   800-225-5750
                                   FAX: 617-547-0412
                                   www.epsbooks.com

Elsie T. Rak, author

This workbook begins with teaching simple, consistent rules and then moves on to those that are more difficult. By an inductive process, students use their own observations to confirm the spelling rules they learn. Each portion of the text is followed by exercises for drill and kinesthetic reinforcement. *$8.65*

144 pages Grades 7-Adult
ISBN 0-838801-65-X

2416 Spelling Dictionary

Educators Publishing Service
31 Smith Place
Cambridge, MA   02138   **617-367-2700**
                                   800-225-5750
                                   FAX: 617-547-0412
                                   www.epsbooks.com

Gregory Hurray, author

This handy reference is a dictionary/thesaurus of words most frequently used by student writers in the elementary grades. Words are listed without definitions, and synonyms are offered for commonly used words like said, big, good, etc. Children can add their own words at the bottom of each page. *$4.50*

52 pages
ISBN 0-838820-56-5

2417 Spelling Workbooks Emphasizing Rules and Generalization for Corrective Drill

Educators Publishing Service
31 Smith Place
Cambridge, MA   02138   **617-367-2700**
                                   800-225-5750
                                   FAX: 617-547-0412
                                   www.epsbooks.com

Mildred Plunkett, author

Includes exercises for children in grades 7-12 who have reading difficulties and closely associated spelling weaknesses. The material is divided into phonetic drills, spelling rules and generalizations, syllable concepts, and punctuation symbols. There are frequent review exercises. Similar programs are available for grades 4-6 ($11.70). *$12.25*

144 pages Grades 7-12
ISBN 0-838800-90-4

2418 Starting Over

Educators Publishing Service
31 Smith Place
Cambridge, MA   02138   **614-547-6706**
                                   800-225-5750
                                   FAX: 617-547-0412
                                   www.epsbooks.com

Joan Knight, author

This comprehensive program is for a student who is ready to try to learn to read again, or for those who are learning English as a second language. Employs multisensory phonics, whole words, and language experience techniques to teach the building of words, vocabulary, and sentences. *$24.00*

ISBN 0-838881-65-5

2419 Structure of Words

Educators Publishing Service
31 Smith Place
Cambridge, MA   02138   617-367-2700
                                   800-225-5750
                          FAX: 617-547-0412
                          www.epsbooks.com

Janet Rule, author

Designed to help students in grades 7-12 learn to spell by using logic as well as memorization and drill, and to help them pronounce and arrive at the meanings of unfamiliar words. The consistent theme throughout is that of spelling, gradually shifting into the analysis of word structure and the development of a rich vocabulary. *$21.15*

96 pages Grades 7-12
ISBN 0-838801-35-8

2420 Studio 49 Catalog

MMB Music
3526 Washington Avenue
Saint Louis, MO   63103   314-531-9635
                                     800-543-3771
                            FAX: 314-531-8384
                   e-mail: mmbmusic@mmbmusic.com
                          www.mmbmusic.com

Marcia Lee Goldberg, VP Sales & Marketing

Percussion instruments for school, therapy, church and family.

2421 Study Power: Study Skills to Improve Your Learning and Your Grades

Brookline Books
PO Box 1047
Cambridge, MA   02238   617-868-0360
                                   800-666-2665
                          FAX: 617-868-1772
                 e-mail: brooklinebks@delphi.com
                        www.brooklinebooks.com

William R. Luckie & Wood Smethurst, author

The techniques in the easy-to-use, self-teaching manual have yielded remarkable success for students from elementary to medical school, at all levels of intelligence and achievement. Key skills covered include: listening, note taking, concentration, summarizing, reading comprehension, memorization, test taking, preparing papers and reports, time management, and more. These abilities are vital to success throughout every stage of learning; the benefits will last a lifetime. *$15.95*

Paperback 1998
ISBN 1-57129-46-X

2422 Syracuse Community-Referenced Curriculum Guide for Students with Disabilties

Brookes Publishing
PO Box 10624
Baltimore, MD   21285   410-337-9580
                                   800-638-3775
                          FAX: 410-337-8539
            e-mail: custserv@brookespublishing.com
                    www.brookespublishing.com

Serving learners from kindergarten through age 21, this field-tested curriculum is a for professionals and parents devoted to directly preparing a student to function in the world. it examines the role of community living domains, functional academics, and embedded skills and includes practical implementation strategies and information for preparing students whose learning needs go beyond the scope of traditional academic programs. *$54.95*

416 pages Spiral-bound
ISBN 1-557660-27-1

2423 Teaching Individuals with Physical and Multiple Disabilities

McGraw-Hill, School Publishing
220 East Danieldale Road
DeSoto, TX   75115   972-224-1111
                                800-442-9685
                       FAX: 972-228-1982
                       mhschool.com

Focuses on the functional needs of the handicapped and the teaching skills of background teachers that they need to help them reach the highest possible level of self-sufficiency.

410 pages

2424 Teaching Students Ways to Remember

Brookline Books
PO Box 1046
Cambridge, MA   02238   617-868-0360
                                   800-666-2665
                          FAX: 617-868-1772
                 e-mail: brooklinebks@delphi.com
                        www.brooklinebooks.com

Dr. Thomas Scruggs
Dr. Margo Mastropieri

Teaches techniques for improving or strengthening memory. *$21.95*

Paperback
ISBN 0-91479-67-0

2425 Teaching Test-Taking Skills: Helping Students Show What They Know

Brookline Books
PO Box 1046
Cambridge, MA   02238   617-868-0360
                                   800-666-2665
                          FAX: 617-868-1772
                 e-mail: brooklinebks@delphi.com
                        www.brooklinebooks.com

Thomas Scruggs & Margo Mastropieri, author

Test-taking skills that, when used effectively, contribute to test-wise performance and help students work productively with test materials. *$21.95*

2426 **Tools for Transition**

AGS
Publishers Building
PO Box 99
Circle Pines, MN 55014

800-328-2560
FAX: 612-786-9007
www.agsnet.com

Robert Zaske, Market Manager

This program prepares students with learning disabilities for postsecondary education. *$129.95*

2427 **VAK Tasks**

Educational Tutorial Consortium
4400 S 44th Street
Lincoln, NE 68516   402-473-0238

C.W. Anderson, Jr., author

A workbook emphasizing the multisensory approach to teaching vocabulary and spelling. It is intended for middle-grade and older students working with prefixes, roots, suffixes, homonyms, and the spelling of easily confused endings. *$6.70*

96 pages Paperback

2428 **Volunteer Transcribing Services**

205 E 3rd Avenue
200
San Mateo, CA 94401   650-344-8664
FAX: 650-632-3510

Alanah Hoffman, Coordinator

VTS is a non-profit California corporation that produces large print school books for visually impaired students in grades K-12.

2429 **Word Attack Manual**

Educators Publishing Service
31 Smith Place
Cambridge, MA 02138   617-547-6706
800-225-5750
FAX: 617-547-0412
www.epsbooks.com

Josephine Rudd, author

This manual and test booklet are designed to develop word recognition and spelling skills for students in grades 6-10. Contents include lessons on syllables, syllabication and accent, consonants and consonant blends, diagraphs, diphthongs, prefixes, suffixes, and compound words, and using the dictionary. *$21.15*

176 pages Grades 6-10
ISBN 0-838881-00-5

2430 **Word Demons**

Educators Publishing Service
31 Smith Place
Cambridge, MA 02138   617-367-2700
800-225-5750
FAX: 617-547-0412
www.epsbooks.com

Caroline Peck, author

This spelling game helps students master the 86 nonphonetic words that are demons for the child in grades 2-4 with a language disability. *$14.40*

Grades 2-4
ISBN 0-838803-28-8

2431 **Word Elements-How They Work Together**

Educators Publishing Service
31 Smith Place
Cambridge, MA 02138   617-367-2700
800-225-5750
FAX: 617-547-0412
www.epsbooks.com

Alan Riese & Herbert LaSalle, author

This vocabulary workbook teaches common word elements - prefixes, suffixes, and roots and their meanings for grades 6-8. *$10.65*

112 pages Grades 6-8
ISBN 0-838815-50-2

2432 **Word Mastery**

Educators Publishing Service
31 Smith Place
Cambridge, MA 02138   617-367-2700
800-225-5750
FAX: 617-547-0412
www.epsbooks.com

Florence Akin, author

This phonics classic introduces over 3,500 words and supplements any reading program with its straightforward phonics instruction. It teaches students in grades 1-3 the letters of the alphabet with key words, and follows with vowels, consonants, vowel combinations, consonant diagraphs and blends, and phonetic rules. *$8.95*

124 pages Grades 1-3
ISBN 0-838820-00-X

2433 **Wordly Wise A,B,C**

Educators Publishing Service
31 Smith Place
Cambridge, MA 02138   617-367-2700
800-225-5750
FAX: 617-547-0412
www.epsbooks.com

K. Hodkinson, author

This series of three vocabulary books for grades 2-4 presents 8-12 words in each lesson with brief definitions, illustrations and sentences using each word in context. Exercises reinforce learning by teaching students to use words precisely in a variety of situations. Keys and tests are available for each book.

64 pages $5.50 each
ISSN 0838-84 8

2434 **Work!**

JE Stewart Teaching Tools
PO Box 15308
Seattle, WA 98115
FAX: 475-486-4510

JE Stewart, author

Teaches 50 words as they appear on parts, tools, job instructions, signs, labels such as: hard hat, assembly, clamp, cut, drill, package and schedule. These words are functional in school and on-the-job. *$32.50*

2435 Working Together & Taking Part

AGS
Publishers Building
PO Box 99
Circle Pines, MN 55014

800-328-2560
FAX: 612-786-9007
www.agsnet.com

Robert Zaske, Market Manager

Two programs to build children's social skills in grades 3-6 through folk literature. Has 31 activity-rich lessons, teaching skills like: following rules, accepting differences, speaking assertively and helping others. Discount price of $279.00 when ordering both. *$149.95*

2436 Writing Skills 1 and 2

Educators Publishing Service
31 Smith Place
Cambridge, MA 02138

617-367-2700
800-225-5750
FAX: 617-547-0412
www.epsbooks.com

Diana Hanbury King, author

Students practice writing sentences and developing paragraphs through writing about their ideas and personal experiences. A logical sequence takes students from individual sentences to basic paragraphs of 5 sentences, expanded paragraphs, and essays. *$7.50*

64 pages Grades 4-6, 7-9
ISBN 0-83882 -50-

2437 Writing Skills for the Adolescent

Educators Publishing Service
31 Smith Place
Cambridge, MA 02138

617-367-2700
800-225-5750
FAX: 617-547-0412
www.epsbooks.com

Diana Hanbury King, author

Teaches the writing process in a series of logical steps as students learn to write and improve sentences, they work on grammar; which is taught in terms of writing. Meanwhile, they learn to generate ideas to compose topic sentences and to use transitional words. They gradually progress from paragraph writing to essay writing. *$10.65*

96 pages Paperback
ISBN 0-838817-04-1

Associations & Organizations

2438 AVKO Dyslexia Research Foundation

3084 West Willard Road
Clio, MI 48420

810-686-9283
FAX: 810-686-1101
e-mail: avkoemail@aol.com
www.avko.org

Don McCabe, Research Director

Comprised of individuals interested in helping others learn to read and spell. Develops and sells materials for teaching dyslexics or others with learning disabilities using a method involving audio, visual, kinesthetic and oral (multi-sensory) techniques.

2439 Academy for Guided Imagery

PO Box 2070
Mill Valley, CA 94942

880-726-2070

Offers Interactive Guided Imagery, offering a 150-hour certification program; publishes a directory of imagery practitioners; supplies books and tapes for professionals and lay people, specifically relating to imagery in medicine and healing. Send for a free catalog.

2440 Alliance for Parental Involvement in Education

PO Box 59
East Chatham, NY 12060

A nonprofit organization to encourage and assist parental involvement in education, public, private and home.

2441 Alternative Work Concepts

PO Box 11452
Eugene, OR 97440

541-345-3043
FAX: 541-345-9669
e-mail: awc@teleport.com
www.teleport.com

To promote individualized, integrated, and meaningful employment opportunities in the community for adults with multiple disabilities; to improve the quality of life and provide continuous opportunities for personal growth for these individuals; and to assist businesses with workforce diversification.

2442 American College Testing Program

2201 North Dodge Street
PO Box 168
Iowa City, IA 52243

319-337-1000
FAX: 319-351-2450
www.act.org

Richard Ferguson, President

An independent, nonprofit organization that provides a variety of educational services to students and their parents, to high schools and colleges, and to professional associations and government agencies.

2443 American Council for Headache Education

875 Kings Highway
Suite 200
West Deptford, NJ 08096

800-255-ACHE

Referrals, support group, newsletter.

2444 American School Health Association, Journal of School Health

PO Box 708
Kent, OH 44240

330-678-1601
FAX: 330-678-4526
e-mail: asha@ashaweb.org
www.ashaweb.org

Susan Wooley, Executive Director

This is a monthly journal which offers information to professionals and parents on school health. Membership dues, $95.00.

Journal 1912

2445 Association for Individually Guided Education
Hutchinson United School District #308
PO Box 1908
Hutchinson, KS 67504 316-665-4400

Shirley Hutchinson, Executive Officer
Dedicated to the individual needs of all educable children and adults.

2446 Association on Higher Education and Disability
PO Box 21192
Columbus, OH 43221 614-488-4972

Lex Friedan, Executive Director
A multinational, nonprofit organization committed to promoting full participation of individuals with disabilities in postsecondary education. The Association's numerous training programs, workshops, conferences and publications are planned and developed by its elected officials and governing board and carried out by the full-time Executive Director and staff.

2447 Ayurvedic Institute
11311 Menaul Northeast
Suite A
Albuquerque, NM 87112 505-291-9698
FAX: 505-294-7572
e-mail: registrar@ayurveds.com
www.ayurveda.com
Directed by Dr. Vasant Lad, trains people in Ayurveda.

2448 CARF The Rehabilitation Accreditation Commission
4891 E Grant Road
Tucson, AZ 85712 520-325-1044
FAX: 520-318-1129
e-mail: postmaster@carf.org
www.carf.org

Donald E. Galvin Ph.D, President/CEO
The independent, not-for-profit commission promotes quality services for people with disabilities and others in need of rehabilitation. CARF establishes customer-focused standards to help organizations measure and improve the quality of their rehabilitation programs and services. When reviewing a rehabilitation program or service, CARF applies standards that have been developed and accepted by peers in the field.CARF has more than 16,000 programs in the US, Canada, & Sweden.

2449 CEC-Division for Early Childhood
Council of Exceptional Children
1920 Association Drive
Reston, VA 20191 703-620-3660
888-232-7733
FAX: 703-264-9494
e-mail: service@cec.sped.org
www.cec.sped.org

Helen Bogie, President
Cathy Mack, Production Manager

A division of The Council for Exceptional Children. Promotes education for young children and infants with special needs, initiates programs that cooperatively involve parents in their children's education, stimulates communication and joint activity among early childhood organizations, sponsors professional development, and disseminates research findings and information addressing issues of early childhood education and more.

2450 Chamber of Commerce for Individuals with Disabilities

www.chamber4us.org/
The Chamber is a national cross-disability consumer volunteer organization that uses business principles to improve the economic status of people with disabilities.

2451 Clearinghouse for Specialized Media and Technology
560 J Street
Suite 390
Sacramento, CA 95814 916-455-5103
FAX: 916-323-9732
e-mail: rbrawley@cde.ca.gov
www.cde.ca.gov
Free to Public Schools in California, author
Pamela Jackson, OA
Elizabeth Hoover, OA
Rebecca Escobar, AC

Assists schools and students in the identification and acquisition of textbooks, reference books and study materials, American Sign Language videos, aural media, braille, large print and electronic media access technology.

2452 Council for Exceptional Children
1920 Association Drive
Reston, VA 20191 703-620-3660
888-232-7733
FAX: 703-264-9494
TDY:703-264-9446
e-mail: service@cec.sped.org
www.cec.sped.org

Nancy D. Safer, Executive Director
Kathleen McLane, Director of Publications
Lynda Van Kuren, Public Relations Director

The largest international organization dedicated to improving educational success for indiviguals with exceptionalities. CEC sets professional standards, advocates for appropriate government policies, provides continual professional development and advocates for newly and historically underserved individuals with exceptionalities. Helps professionals obtain conditions and resources necessary for effective practice.

2453 East Brunswick Adult and Community Education Program, Adult Life Skills
380 Cranbury Road
East Brunswick, NJ 08816 732-613-6984
FAX: 732-613-6981

Philip Caccavale, Supervisor
Bernadette Methven LSW, Program Leader

Offers education, training, and social programs for adults with developmental disabilities in an integrated adult/evening school environment. Residents of Middlesex County, New Jersey, ages 18 and over are eligible to register. Limited transportation is also available. Annual enrollemnt fee $25.00.

2454   Educational Referral Service

Dr. Yvonne Jones and Associates
2222 Eastlake Avenue E
Seattle, WA   98102   206-325-2600
                                        FAX: 206-328-9172

Yvonne Jones

Specializes in matching children with the learning environments that are best for them and works with families to help them identify concerns and establish priorities about their child's education.

2455   Howard School-Central Campus

1246 Ponce De Leon Avenue NE
Atlanta, GA   30306   404-377-7436
                                        FAX: 404-377-0884

Sandra N Kleinman, Executive Director

Enrolls students whose language-learning disabilities and differences hinder their learning to their fullest potential. Goal is to help students simultaneously build basic academi skills, maximize academic progress, develop higher level thinking skills, gain self-advocacy strategies and become independent life-long learners. Average class size is less than 10 students.

2456   Howard School-North Campus

9415 Willeo Road
Roswell, GA   30075   770-642-9644
                                        FAX: 770-998-1398
www.howardschool.org

Sandra N Kleinman, Executive Director

Enrolls students whose language-learning disabilities and differences hinder their learning to their fullest potential. Goal is to help students simultaneously build basic academi skills, maximize academic progress, develop higher level thinking skills, gain self-advocacy strategies and become independent life-long learners. Average class size is less than 10 students.

2457   Institute on Disability/UAP

University of New Hampshire
312 Morrill Hall
Durham, NH   03824   603-862-2450
                                        FAX: 603-862-0555
e-mail: institutedisability@unh.edu

Sue Huber, Business Manager

This mission of the Institute is to improve the knowledge, policy and practice related to the economic and social participation of persons with disabilities. The Institute provides a blend of programs that address the needs of local schools, community services, and state and federal agencies. The Institute's goal is to increase the ability of the State of New Hampshire to foster inclusion of persons with disabilities into their communities.

2458   International Association of Parents and Professionals for Safe Alternatives in Childbirth

Route 4
PO Box 646
Marble Hill, MO   63764   573-238-2010

                        e-mail: napsac@clas.net
                              www.napsac.org

Educational organization that encourages natural childbirth in hospitals, and provides parental education.

2459   International Bio-Oxidative Medicine Foundation (IBOM)

PO Box 13205
Oklahoma City, OK   73113   312-761-2682

                        www.bio-proinc.com/index.html

Information on massage and bodywork, including review of scienctific research; publishes the Massage Therapy Journal.

2460   International Childbirth Education Association

PO Box 20048
Minneapolis, MN   55420   952-854-8660
                                        FAX: 952-854-8772
                                  e-mail: info@icea.org
                                        www.icea.org

Offer teaching certificates, seminars, continuing education workshops, and a mail order center.

2461   International Organization for the Education of the Hearing Impaired

2000 M Street
Washington, DC   20007   202-337-5220

                              e-mail: agbell2@aol.com
                                    www.agbell.org

Jill Bader, Education of The Hearing Impaire

Professional educators of the hearing impaired make up the members of this organization which promotes the excellence in teaching the hearing impaired child.

2462   Job Accommodation Network

West Virginia University
PO Box 6080
Morgantown, WV   26506
                                        800-526-7234
                                  e-mail: bloy@wvu.edu
                          http://.janweb.icdi.wvu.edu/

International toll-free consulting service that provides information about job accommodations and the employability of people with disabilities. Also provides information regarding the Americans with Disabilities Act (ADA).

2463   Mad Hatters: Theatre That Makes a World of Difference

PO Box 50002
Kalamazoo, MI   49005
                                        FAX: 616-385-5868

Bobbe A. Luce, Executive Director

A nationally-known theater which has presented effective and innovative programs to more than 175,000 people in over 1,150 performances in the past 15 years. Our presentations and training programs are a proven method of changing attitudes and behaviors. The Mad Hatters is a leader in the field of sensitivity-training to build community and foster the inclusion of all people in society. Fees: $500-$4000 per program, depending on topic and audience.

2464   Michigan Psychological Association

24350 Orchard Lake Road
Suite 105
Farmingtn Hills, MI   48336   248-324-0100

Marlene O'Neill, Director

Offers information to psychologists.

2465   National Association of Colleges and Employers

62 Highland Avenue
Bethlehem, PA   18017   610-868-1421
                                         800-544-5272
                              FAX: 610-868-0208
                              www.naceweb.org

Marilyn F. Mackes, Executive Director
Norita Rehrig, Assistant Executive Director
Sandra Dalious, Human Resources Manager

A national association with services for career planning, placement and recruitment professionals.

2466   National Center for Homeopathy

801 North Fairfax Street
Suite 306
Alexandria, VA   22314   703-548-7790
                                         877-624-0613
                              FAX: 703-548-7792
                   e-mail: info@homeopathic.org
                              www.homeopathic.org

Provides information, referral lists, and courses to professionals.

2467   National Clearinghouse for Professions in Special Education

Council for Exceptional Children
1920 Association Drive
Reston, VA   20191   703-620-3660
                                      800-641-7824
                           FAX: 703-264-9494
                   e-mail: service@cec.sped.org
                              www.cec.sped.org

Cathy Mack, Production Manager

Designed to encourage individuals to seek careers in the various fields related to the education of children and youth with disabilities.

2468   National Council on Rehabilitation Education

California State University - Fresno
School of Education and Human Dev.
5005 North Maple Avenue, M.S.3
Fresno, CA   93740   559-278-0325
                           FAX: 559-278-0016
                  e-mail: charlesa@csufresno.edu

Dr. Charles Arokiasamy, Administrative Sec.

Members include academic institutions and organizations, professional educators, researchers, and students. Assists in the documentation of the effect of education in improving services to persons with disabilities; determines the skills and training necessary for effective rehabilitation services; develops role models, standards and uniform licensure and certification requirements for rehabilitation personnel.

2469   National Education Association of the United States

1201 16th Street NW
Washington, DC   20036   202-833-4000

Don Cameron, Executive Director

Offers information to educational professionals.

2470   Presidents Committee on Mental Retardation Admin. for Children & Families

330 C Street SW
Room 3086
Washington, DC   20201   202-619-3482
                              FAX: 202-205-9519
                  e-mail: gblumenthal@acf.dhhs.gov
                  www.acf.dhhs.gov/programs/pcmr

Gary Blumenthal, Executive Director
Olivia Golden, Asst. Sec. for Children/Families

Administers the Education of the Handicapped Act and related programs for the education of handicapped children, including grants to institutions of higher learning and fellowships to train educational personnel. Grants to states for the education of handicapped children, research and demonstration.

2471   SSD (Services for Students with Disabilities)

College Board
45 Columbus Avenue
New York, NY   10023   212-713-8000
                              FAX: 212-713-8277
                              www.collegeboard.org

National, nonprofit membership association dedicated to preparing, inspiring and connecting students to college and opportunity. Founded in 1900, the association is composed of more than 3,800 schools, colleges, universities and other educational organizations. Services for Students with Disabilities (SSD) provides special arrangements to minimize the possible effects of disabilities on test performance through it's Admissions Testing Program (ATP).

2472   Services for Students with Disabilities The University of Michigan

G-625 Haven Hall 505 S State
Ann Arbor, MI   48109   734-763-3000
                              FAX: 734-936-3947
                      e-mail: sgoodin@umich.edu
                              www.umich.edu/~sswd/ssd

Sam Goodin, Director

Offers information to parents and students.

2473 **TASH: The Association for Persons with Severe Handicaps**
11201 Greenwood Avenue N
Seattle, WA 98133   206-362-1526

Liz Lindley, Executive Director

Over 8,000 members make up this organization of teachers, therapists, parents and administrators.

2474 **Typewriting Institute for the Handicapped**
3102 West August Avenue
Phoenix, AZ 85051   623-939-5344
                          FAX: 602-870-9371

Lynda Diamond, Co-Owner

A for-profit company which makes the Dvorak one-hand keyboard for typewriters and word processors that are re-arranged to accommodate one-handed typing. The Institute believes that any school or training facility can teach typing to a handicapped person using the Dvorak. It requires no special knowledge on the part of the teacher. A student using one of these keyboards can sit in a classroom along with two-handed typists and not require more supervision than others in the class. $1,150.00.

2475 **United Cerebral Palsy Research and Educational Foundation**
1660 L Street NW
Suite 700
Washington, DC 20036   202-269-1500
                              800-872-5827

Grants are awarded to institutions or organizations on behalf of a principal investigator in support of biomedical and bioengineering research in areas which have a significant relationship to cerebral palsy. While most research on central nervous system structure, function and disorder may be useful, the Foundation requires that research proposals address issues of relevance to cerebral palsy.

Directories

2476 **Complete Directory for People with Chronic Illness**
Sedgwick Press Imprint of Grey House Publishing
185 Millerton Road
PO Box 860
Millerton, NY 12546   518-789-8700
                             800-562-2139
                        FAX: 518-789-0545
              e-mail: books@greyhouse.com
                        www.greyhouse.com

Leslie Mackenzie, Publisher
Richard Gottlieb, Editor

Annual

2477 **Complete Learning Disabilities Directory**
Sedgwick Press Imprint of Grey House Publishing
185 Millerton Road
PO Box 860
Millerton, NY 12546   518-789-8700
                             800-562-2139
                        FAX: 518-789-0545
              e-mail: books@greyhouse.com
                        www.greyhouse.com

Leslie Mackenzie, Publisher

A comprehensive educational guide offering over 6,500 listings on associations and organizations, schools, government agencies, testing materials, camps, products, books, newsletters, legal information, classroom materials and more. *$145.00*

702 pages Annual
ISBN 1-891482-41-6

2478 **Diabetes: Caring for Your Emotions as Well as Your Health**
Harper Collins
10 East Third Street
New York, NY 10022   212-207-7000
                            800-242-7737
                       FAX: 212-207-7203

Jerry Edelwich, author

This book offers suggestions for adaptation, relationships with medical personnel, family strategies, employment questions, technology and support groups. *$15.00*

2479 **Dictionary of Special Education and Rehabilitation - 4th Edition**
Love Publishing Company
9101 E Kenyoun Avenue
Suite 2200
Denver, CO 80237
                            FAX: 303-221-7444
          e-mail: lovepublishing@compuserve.com
                       www.lovepublishing.com
Glenn A. Vergason, author

A valuable basic resource in the field. It incorporates hundreds of additions and changes. *$39.95*

Paperback
ISBN 0-891082-43-3

2480 **Directory for Exceptional Children 2001 - 2002**
Porter Sargent Publishers
11 Beacon Street
Suite 1400
Boston, MA 02108   617-523-1670
                          800-342-7470
                     FAX: 617-523-1021
         e-mail: orders@portersargent.com
                       portersargent.com

Daniel McKeever, Editor, author
John Yonce, General Manager
Daniel McKeever, Senior Editor
Leslie Weston, Production Editor

Now in its 14th edition, the Directory is a comprehensive, objective survey of 3000 schools, facilities and organizations across the country serving children and young adults with developmental, emotional, physical and mental disabilities. *$75.00*

1312 pages Hard Cover
ISBN 0-875581-41-2

2481 Directory of Mental Heatlh

Sedgwick Press Imprint of Grey House Publishing
185 Millerton Road
PO Box 860
Millerton, NY 12546   518-789-8700
                                  800-562-2139
                             FAX: 518-789-0545
                  e-mail: books@greyhouse.com
                          www.greyhouse.com

Leslie Mackenzie, Publisher
Richard Gottlieb, Editor

Annual

2482 Disability in the United States - A Portrait from National Data

Springer Publishing Company
536 Broadway
New York, NY 10012   212-431-4370
                                  877-687-7976
                             FAX: 212-941-7842
             e-mail: marketing@springerpub.com
Susan Thompson-Hoffman, Inez Fitgerald Storck, author
Annette Imperati, Marketing Director

Gives information and sources for places that will serve and help with the education of disabled children and youth. *$38.95*

260 pages
ISBN 0-826127-70-5

2483 Educators Resource Directory

Sedgwick Press Imprint of Grey House Publishing
185 Millerton Road
PO Box 860
Millerton, NY 12546   518-789-8700
                                  800-562-2139
                             FAX: 518-789-0545
                  e-mail: books@greyhouse.com
                          www.greyhouse.com

Leslie Mackenzie, Publisher
Richard Gottlieb, Editor

With the completely revised directory, education professionals have immediate access to the information that can help them grow professionally. It saves hours of time by providing immediate access to Associations and Organizations, Conferences and Trade Shows, Educational Research Centers, Employment Opportunities and Teaching Abroad, School Library Services, Scholarships, Financial Resources and much more. *$145.00*

591 pages Annual
ISBN 1-930956-48-7

2484 Enhancing Children's Communication: Research & Foundations

Paul H. Brookes Publishing Company
PO Box 10624
Baltimore, MD 21285   800-638-3775
                             FAX: 410-337-8539
          e-mail: custserv@brookespublishing.com
                        www.brookespublishing.com
Ann Kaiser, author

This groundbreaking book provides helpful insights, unique perspectives, and innovative strategies that are needed to intervene successfully with children whose developmental disabilities affect their use of communication and language. *$43.00*

448 pages 1992
ISBN 1-557660-76-X

2485 Exceptional Children: An Introductory Survey of Special Education

McGraw-Hill, School Publishing
220 East Danieldale Road
DeSoto, TX 75115   972-224-1111
                                 800-442-9685
                            FAX: 972-228-1982
                               mhschool.com
William Heward, author

The focus of this survey is on observable characteristics of exceptional persons, and the instructional practices which foster their fullest development.

704 pages

2486 Guide to Summer Camps and Schools

Porter Sargent Publishers
11 Beacon Street
Suite 1400
Boston, MA 02108   617-523-1670
                                 800-342-7470
                            FAX: 617-523-1021
                e-mail: info@portersargent.com
                        www.portersargent.com

Daniel McKeever, Senior Editor
Leslie Weston, Production Editor
John Yonce, General Manager

This 26th edition covers the broad spectrum of recreational and educational summer opportunities. Current facts from 1300 camps and schools, as well as specialized programs for those with special needs or learning disabilities, make the Guide a comprehensive and convenient resource. *$35.00*

560 pages Hardcover
ISBN 0-875581-33-1

2487 Increasing and Decreasing Behaviors of Persons with Severe Retardation

Research Press
PO Box 9177
Champaign, IL 61826   217-352-3273
                                  800-519-2707
                             FAX: 217-352-1221
                 e-mail: rp@researchpress.com
                          www.researchpress.com
Dr. Richard M. Foxx, author
Russell Pence, V P Marketing

These well-organized manuals are written for teachers, aides and persons responsible for designing or evaluating behavioral programs. Offers specific guidelines for arranging and managing the learning environment as well as standards for evaluating and maintaining success. In Volume two of this series, chapters address more restrictive procedures including physical restraint, punishment, time-out and overcorrection. Set of two volumes. *$32.95*

428 pages Item 2650
ISBN 0-878222-65-0

2488 Learning Disabilities: Basic Concepts, Assessment Practices & Strategies

Pro-Ed
8700 Shoal Creek Boulevard
Austin, TX 78757
FAX: 512-451-8542
e-mail: proed1@aol.com

Patricia I. Myers, Author
Donald D. Hammill, Author

A comprehensive book in the learning disability field, this textbook is now available in the fourth edition. The contents focus on the moderate-to-severe learning disabled student who requires special help. $43.00

593 pages Hardcover
ISBN 0-89079-25-9

2489 National Association of Private Special Education Center

1522 K Street NW
Suite 1032
Washington, DC 20005
202-408-3338
FAX: 202-408-3340
e-mail: napsec@aol.com
www.napsec.com

Sherry L. Kolbe, Executive Director and CEO

Membership directory offering information on NAPSEC member schools nationwide. $35.00

338 pages BiAnnual

2490 Special-Needs Reading List

Woodbine House
6510 Bells Mill Road
Bethesda, MD 20817
800-843-7323
www.woodbinehouse.com

Wilma Sweeney, author

In one easy-to-use volume, books, pamphlets, organizations, and other resources of interest to parents of children with disabilities are listed and described. $18.95

314 pages Paperback

2491 Teaching Special Students in Mainstream

Books on Special Children
PO Box 305
Congers, NY 10920
845-638-1236
FAX: 845-638-0847
e-mail: irene@boscbooks.com

Rena B. Lewis, author

Overview of mainstream, team of professionals managing classroom behavior, tips for teachers, social acceptance and handling of specific differences. $33.00

515 pages Softcover

2492 Young Children with Special Needs

McGraw-Hill, School Publishing
220 East Danieldale Road
DeSoto, TX 75115
972-224-1111
800-442-9685
FAX: 972-228-1982
mhschool.com

This text examines development in the critical areas of motor, self-help, cognitive, language, social, emotional and play skills.

526 pages

Educational Publishers

2493 American Association for Counseling and Development

5999 Stevenson Avenue
Alexandria, VA 22304
703-823-9800
800-347-6647
FAX: 800-473-2329

Offers tools and books for the professional.

2494 Brookline Books

PO Box 1047
Cambridge, MA 02238
617-868-0360
800-666-2665
FAX: 617-868-1772
e-mail: brooklinebks@delphi.com
www.brooklinebooks.com

Milt Budoff, PhD, Publisher

Offers books for teachers and parents on law and legislation, education, integration and mainstreaming for the disabled, their families, caregivers and teachers.

2495 Brooks/Cole Publishing Company

511 Forest Lodge Road
Pacific Grove, CA 93950
831-373-0728
FAX: 831-375-6414

Offers books in Special Education for those preparing to be special educators and for in-service professionals.

2496 Charles C. Thomas Publisher

Charles C. Thomas, Publisher
2600 S 1st Street
Springfield, IL 62704
217-789-8980
800-258-8980
e-mail: books@ccthomas.com

Offers books for the professional; educators, clinicians, paraprofessionals, psychologists, and more who work with the disabled.

2497 Gallaudet University Bookstore

Gallaudet University Press
11030 S Langley Avenue
Chicago, IL 60628
202-651-5488
800-621-2736
FAX: 202-651-5489
www.gallaudet.edu

Offers informational resources for the deaf, parents of the deaf, professionals, special educators and more. Produces a yearly catalog of materials on sign language and deafness.

2498 Greenwood Publishing Group
88 Post Road West
Westport, CT 06880   203-226-3571
                                   FAX: 203-222-1502
                                   www.greenwood.com

2499 McGraw-Hill Company
2460 Kerper Boulevard
Dubuque, IO 52001   319-589-4666
                                   800-553-4920
                                   FAX: 319-588-1451
                                   www.mcgraw-hill.com

Marc Bigelow, Director

Offers a catalog of testing resources and materials for the special educator.

2500 Merrill Publishing Company
4635 Hilton Corporate Drive
508
Columbus, OH 43232   800-848-1567
                                   FAX: 614-860-1877

2501 National Association of School Psychologists
4340 East West Highway
Suite 402
Bethesda, MD 20814   301-657-0270
                                   FAX: 301-657-0275
                                   e-mail: lnealis@naspweb.org
                                   www.nasponline.org

Libby Kuffner Nealis, Director of Public Policy

Represents over 22,500 school psychologists and related professionals. It serves its members and society by advancing the profession of school psychology and advocating for the rights, welfare, education and mental health of children, youth and their families.

2502 Oryx Press
4041 N Central Avenue
Suite 700
Phoenix, AZ 85012   602-265-2651
                                   800-279-6799
                                   FAX: 800-279-4663

2503 Paul H. Brookes Publishing Company
PO Box 10624
Baltimore, MD 21285   410-337-9580
                                   800-638-3775
                                   FAX: 410-337-8539

2504 Pro-Ed
8700 Shoal Creek Boulevard
Austin, TX 78757   512-451-3246
                                   800-897-3202
                                   FAX: 800-397-7633
                                   www.proedinc.com

Publishes, produces, and sells books, curricular therapy materials and journals dedicated to psychology, special education and speech, language, and hearing.

2505 Ragged Edge Magazine
Advocado Press
PO Box 145
Louisville, KY 40201   502-894-9492
                                   FAX: 502-899-9562
                                   e-mail: office@advocadopress.org
                                   www.raggededgemagazine.com

Mary Johnson, Editor

An anthology of writings from The Disablity Rag. *$17.50*

36 pages BiMonthly

2506 Research Press
PO Box 9177
Champaign, IL 61826   217-352-3273
                                   800-519-2707
                                   FAX: 217-352-1221
                                   e-mail: rp@researchpress.com
                                   www.researchpress.com

Dennis Wiziecki, Marketing Department

2507 Special Need Project
3463 Stat Street
282
Santa Barbara, CA 93105
                                   800-333-6867
                                   FAX: 805-969-4321

2508 Waterfront Books Publishing Company
85 Crescent Road
Burlington, VT 05401   802-658-7477

Government Agencies

2509 Alaska Department of Education
801 W 10th Street
Suite 200
Juneau, AK 99801   907-465-2800
                                   FAX: 907-465-3396
                                   www.eed.state.ak.us

Rick Cross, Commissioner

Administers special educational programs through the Division of Education Program Support to the disabled residing in the Alaska area.

2510 Arizona Department of Education
1535 West Jefferson Street
Phoenix, AZ 85007   602-542-5393
                                   FAX: 602-542-5440
                                   www.ade.state.az.us

Lisa Graham Keegan, Superintendent

A state agency providing consultation on educational services for visually handicapped students. Administers state funds available for blind children in public schools.

2511 Arkansas Department of Special Education

4 Capitol Mall
Room 105-C
Little Rock, AR   72201   501-682-4222
                                  FAX: 501-682-5159
                                  www.arkansas.com

Dr. Diane Sydoriak, Asoc. Dir. Spec. Ed.

Provides oversight of all educational programs for children and youth with disabilities, ages 3 to 21. Provides technical assistance to all public agencies providing educational services to this population.

2512 California Department of Education Special Education Division

721 Capitol Mall
Sacramento, CA   95814   916-654-5326

Shirley Thornton, Superintendent
Leo Sandoval, Dir. of Spec. Ed.

Through consultants, coordinates the establishment and operations of special public school programs for blind and partially sighted pupils. The staff includes two regionally based consultant specialists in the education of visually impaired children, and the eligible age for help is 3-21.

2513 Career and Technology Education

1701 North Congress Avenue
Austin, TX   78701   512-463-9446
                                  FAX: 512-475-3575
                      e-mail: wmccain@tmail.tea.state.tx.us
                              www.tea.state.tx.us/Cate

Ward N. McCain, Division Director

2514 Colorado Department of Education

201 East Colfax Avenue
Denver, CO   80203   303-866-6782
                                  FAX: 303-830-0793
                                  www.cde.state.co.us

Provides consultation on materials and educational services for visually handicapped children, supervises volunteer services, transcribes textbooks for visually handicapped students.

2515 Connecticut State Board of Education and Services for the Blind

184 Windsor Avenue
Windsor, CT   06095   860-602-4000
                                  800-842-4510
                                  FAX: 860-602-4030
                          e-mail: brian.sigman@po.state.ct.us

Brian Sigman, Director

Provides consultation for the education of visually disabled children, provide Braille instruction, independent living skills training, vocational rehabilitation services and community outreach and advocacy.

2516 Department of Public Health Human Services

Cogswell building, Room C-314
PO Box 202951
Helena, MT   59632   406-444-3622
                                  800-762-9891
                            FAX: 406-444-2750
                                  www.state.mt.us

Sharon Wagner, Section Manager

Provides consultation on educational services for local schools, offers psychological testing and evaluation, maintains resource rooms in district schools and more for the blind and handicapped throughout the state.

2517 Division for the Blind and Visually Impaired

State House Station
150
Augusta, ME   04333   207-624-5959
                                  FAX: 207-624-5980

Paul Cote, Program Manager

Provides consultation on educational services for local schools, assessment and instruction, maintains instructional material centers and more for the blind and handicapped throughout the state.

2518 Florida Department of Education/Bureau of Instructional Support and Community Services

325 West Gaines Street
614d Turlington Building
Tallahassee, FL   32399   850-488-1570
                                  FAX: 850-921-8246

Shan Goff, Chief
Carol Allman, Administrator
Lee Clark, Program Specialist

The Department of Education strives to improve educational services for students with special needs.

2519 Georgia State Department of Education

1970 Twin Towers East
Atlanta, GA   30334   404-656-2435

Joan Jordan, Director

Provides consultation on educational services for local schools, offers psychological testing and evaluation, maintains resource rooms in district schools and more for the blind and handicapped throughout the state.

2520 Hawaii Department of Education

4697 Kilauea Avenue
Honolulu, HI   96816   808-548-7487

Fay Ikei, District Specialist

Provides consultation on educational services for local schools, offers psychological testing and evaluation, maintains resource rooms in district schools and more for the blind and handicapped throughout the state.

2521 Illinois State Board of Education

100 North 1st Street
Springfield, IL   62702   217-782-4876

                          e-mail: pstadeke@spr6.isbe.il.us

Paula Stadeker, Vision Coordinator

Mission is to advance the human and civil rights of people with disabilities in Illinois. It is the only comprehensive statewide advocacy organization providing self-advocacy assistance, legal services, education and public policy initiatives. Designated by the Governor to implement the federal protection and advocacy system; has broad statutory power to enforce the rights of people with physical and mental disabilities, including developmental disabilities and mental illnesses.

2522   Kansas Division of Special Education

120 East Tenth Street
Topeka, KS 66612   785-291-3097
                                    FAX: 785-296-6715
                          e-mail: bpassman@ksde.org
                                    www.kansped.org

Bruce Passman, Director

Provides consultation on educational services for local schools, offers psychological testing and evaluation, maintains resource rooms in district schools and more for the blind and handicapped throughout the state.

2523   Kentucky Department of Education

Capital Plaza Tower
500 Mero Street
Frankfort, KY 40601   502-564-4970
                                    FAX: 502-564-6721
                    e-mail: marmstro@kde.state.ky.us
                                  www.kde.state.ky.us

Mike Armstrong, Director

Provides consultation on educational services for local schools, offers psychological testing and evaluation, maintains resource rooms in district schools and more for the blind and handicapped throughout the state.

2524   Maryland State Department of Education

200 West Baltimore Street
Baltimore, MD 21201   410-767-0100
                                    FAX: 410-333-6033
                                  www.msde.state.md.us

Nancy Grasmick, State Superintendent

Provides consultation on educational services for local schools, offers psychological testing and evaluation, maintains resource rooms in district schools and more for the blind and handicapped throughout the state.

2525   Michigan Department of Education

PO Box 30008
Lansing, MI 48909   517-373-3900
                                    FAX: 517-241-0514
                                  www.mde.state.mi.us

Dr. Philip Runkel, Superintendent

Provides consultation on educational services for local schools, offers psychological testing and evaluation, maintains resource rooms in district schools and more for the blind and handicapped throughout the state.

2526   Mississippi Department of Education

PO Box 771
Jackson, MS 39205   601-359-3513

Dr. Richard Boyd, Superintendent

Provides consultation on educational services for local schools, offers psychological testing and evaluation, maintains resource rooms in district schools and more for the blind and handicapped throughout the state.

2527   Missouri Department of Education

PO Box 480
Jefferson City, MO 65102   573-751-5739
                                    FAX: 573-526-4404
                          www.dese.state.mo.us/divspeced

Dr. Steven Barr, Assistant Commissioner

The Division of Special Education provides assistance to public school districts in the supervision, establishment, and improvement of programs of instruction for children with disabilities. The division operates the Missouri School for the Deaf, School for the Blind and State Schools for the Severely Handicapped. The division also supports a statewide system of sheltered workshops for adults with disabilities.

2528   National Clearinghouse on Family Support and Children's Mental Health

1 Dupont Circle NW
Suite 800
Washington, DC 20036   202-939-9320
                                          800-544-3284
                                    FAX: 202-833-4760
                          e-mail: heatah@ace.nche.edu

2529   Nebraska Department of Education Special Populations Office

301 Centennial Mall South
PO Box 94987
Lincoln, NE 68509   402-471-2471
                                    FAX: 402-471-5022
                          www.nde.state.ne.us/SPED/sped.html

Gary Sherman, Administrator
Don Anderson, Administrator

Assists school districts in establishing and maintaining effective special education programs for children with disabilities (date of diagnosis through the school year when a child reaches 21). Major function: provide technical assistance to school districts and to parents of children with disabilities, assist programs in meeting state and federal special education regulations. Also responsible for assuring that the rights of children with disabilities and their parents are protected.

2530   Nevada Department of Education

700 East Fifth Street
Suite 113
Carson City, NV 89701   775-687-9171
                                    FAX: 775-687-9123
                                  www.nsn.k12.nv.us/nvdoe

Gloria Dopf, Director, Educational Equity

The Educational Equity Team of the Nevada State Department of Education is responsible for management of state and federal programs providing educational opportunities for students with diverse learning needs. Included are such programs as: Special Education/disabled (IDEA); disadvantaged/at-risk programs (Title I/IASA); Early childhood programs (Title I/IASA); early childhood programs; Migrant education; English language learners; NRS 395 student placement program.

2531   New Hampshire Department of Education

101 Pleasant Street
Concord, NH   03301   603-271-3494

Robert Kennedy, Director

Provides consultation on educational services for local schools, offers psychological testing and evaluation, maintains resource rooms in district schools and more for the blind and handicapped throughout the state.

2532   New Mexico State Department of Education

300 Don Gaspar Avenue
Santa Fe, NM   87501   505-827-6606
                             FAX: 505-827-4473
                             www.sde.state.nm.us

James Newby, Director

Provides consultation on educational services for local schools, offers psychological testing and evaluation, maintains resource rooms in district schools and more for the blind and handicapped throughout the state.

2533   New York State Education Department

1 Commerce Plaza
Room 1606
Albany, NY   12234   518-474-2714
                           800-222-JOBS
                           FAX: 518-486-4154
                           TDY:518-486-3773
                           e-mail: nysed@mail.gov
                           www.nysed.gov

Lawrence Gloeckler, Deputy Commissioner

Provides vocational rehabilitation and educational services for eligible individuals with disabilities throughout New York State. Services include evaluation, counseling, job placement, and referral to other agencies.

2534   North Carolina Department of Public Instruction

301 N Wilmington Street
Raleigh, NC   27601   919-807-3969
                            FAX: 919-807-3243
                            e-mail: lharris@dpi.state.nc.us
                            www.publicschools.org

E. Lowell Harris, Director
Mary Watson, Chief, Policy Monitoring Audit.
David Mills, Chief, Areas of Exceptionality

Provides consultation on educational services for local schools, offers psychological testing and evaluation, maintains a continuum of educational sources in local schools for disabled children.

2535   North Dakota Department of Education Special Education

600 East Boulevard Avenue
Bismarck, ND   58505   701-223-6372
                             FAX: 701-328-4149
                             www.dpi.state.nd.us

Gary Gronberg, Director

Provides consultation on educational services for local schools, offers psychological testing and evaluation, maintains resource rooms in district schools and more for the blind and handicapped throughout the state.

2536   Ohio Department of Education/Division of Special Education

933 High Street
Worthington, OH   43085   614-846-4300
                                FAX: 614-728-1097

John Herner, Director

Provides technical assistance to educational agencies for the development and implementation of educational services to meet the needs of students with disabilities and/or those who are gifted. Provides information to parents. Administers state and federal funds allocated to educational agencies for the provision of services to students with disabilities and/or those who are gifted.

2537   Oklahoma State Department of Education

2500 North Lincoln Boulevard
Oklahoma City, OK   73105   405-521-4311
                                  FAX: 405-522-1520
                                  www.sde.state.ok.us

J.L. Prickett, Director

Provides consultation on educational services for local schools, offers psychological testing and evaluation, maintains resource rooms in district schools and more for the blind and handicapped throughout the state.

2538   Oregon Department of Education

700 Pringle Parkway
Salem, OR   97301   503-378-3569
                          FAX: 503-373-7968

Maurine Otos, State Coordinator

Provides consultation on educational services for local schools, offers psychological testing and evaluation, maintains resource rooms in district schools and more for the blind and handicapped throughout the state.

2539   Pennsylvania Bureau of Special Education

333 Market Street
Harrisburg, PA   17126   717-783-6913
                               FAX: 717-783-6139
                               e-mail: 00specialed@psupen.psu.edu
                               www.pde.state.pa.us

Fran James Warkomski, Ed.D, Director
John J. Tommasini, Assistant Director

Provides effective and efficient administration of the Commonwealth of Pennsylvania's resources dedicated to enabling school districts to maintain high standards in the delivery of special education services and programs for all exceptional students.

2540 Rhode Island Department of Education

555 Valley Street
Building 51, 3rd Floor
Providence, RI 02908   401-222-3731
FAX: 401-222-2873
www.ridoe.net

J,. Troy Earhart, Commissioner

Provides consultation on educational services for local schools, offers psychological testing and evaluation, maintains resource rooms in district schools and more for the blind and handicapped throughout the state.

2541 South Carolina Department of Education Office of Exceptional Children

808 Rutledge Building
1429 Senate Street
Columbia, SC 29201   803-734-8806
FAX: 803-734-4824
e-mail: sdurant@sde.state.sc.us

Susan DuRant, Director, Office Except.Children

Provides consultation on educational services for local schools, offers psychological testing and evaluation, maintains resource rooms in district schools and more for the blind and handicapped throughout the state.

2542 State of Indiana Department of Education

Room 229 State House
Indianapolis, IN 46204   317-232-0808

Harold Negley, Superintendent

Provides consultation on educational services for local schools, offers psychological testing and evaluation, maintains resource rooms in district schools and more for the blind and handicapped throughout the state.

2543 Tennessee Department of Education

132 Cordell Hull Building
Nashville, TN 37219   615-532-6176
FAX: 615-741-6126

Bob McElrath, Commissioner

Provides consultation on educational services for local schools, offers psychological testing and evaluation, maintains resource rooms in district schools and more for the blind and handicapped throughout the state.

2544 Texas Education Agency

1701 Congress Avenue
Austin, TX 78701   512-463-9734
FAX: 512-463-9838
www.tea.state.tx.us

Provides consultation on educational services for local schools, offers psychological testing and evaluation, maintains resource rooms in district schools and more for the blind and handicapped throughout the state.

2545 Texas School of the Deaf

1102 South Congress Avenue
PO Box 3538
Austin, TX 78764   512-462-5300

www.tsd.state.tx.us

Claire Bugen, Superintendent

2546 Utah State Office of Education

250 East 500th S
Salt Lake City, UT 84111   801-538-7500
FAX: 801-583-7500
www.usoe.k12.ut.us

Elwood Pace, Coordinator

Provides consultation on educational services for local schools, offers psychological testing and evaluation, maintains resource rooms in district schools and more for the blind and handicapped throughout the state.

2547 Vermont Special Education

120 State Street
Montpelier, VT 05602   802-244-5796

External Manager, Contact

Provides consultation on educational services for local schools, offers psychological testing and evaluation, maintains resource rooms in district schools and more for the blind and handicapped throughout the state.

2548 Virginia Department of Education

397 Azalea Avenue
Richmond, VA 23227   804-371-3145
FAX: 804-371-3351
www.cns.state.va.us/dvh

Glen Slonneger, Jr., Program Director

Provides consultation on educational services for local schools, offers psychological testing and evaluation, maintains resource rooms in district schools and more for the blind and handicapped throughout the state.

2549 West Virginia Department of Education

1900 Kanawha Boulevard E
Charleston, WV 25305   304-558-2681
FAX: 304-558-0048
wvde.state.wv.us

D. Bodkins, Director
Mary Nunn, Assistant Director

Provides consultation on educational services for local schools, offers psychological testing and evaluation, maintains resource rooms in district schools and more for the blind and handicapped throughout the state.

2550 Wyoming Department of Education

2300 Capitol Avenue
Cheyenne, WY 82001   307-777-5800

Lynn Simons, Superintendent

Provides consultation on educational services for local schools, offers psychological testing and evaluation, maintains resource rooms in district schools and more for the blind and handicapped throughout the state.

Journals

2551 Adapted Physical Activity Quarterly

Human Kinetics
PO Box 5076
Champaign, IL   61825

800-747-4457
FAX: 217-351-2674
e-mail: humank@hkusa.com
www.humankinetics.com
Claudine Sherrill, PhD., Editor, author
Linda Bump, Director of Journals

This quarterly journal contains information on current opinions, legislation, regulatory concerns, and trends. It also reports on research and investigations of case studies, programming, techniques, design of equipment and facilities. *$24.00*

Quarterly
ISSN 0736-58 9

2552 Advance for Providers of Post-Acute Care

Merion Publications
2900 Horizon Drive
Box 61556
King of Prussia, PA   19406

610-278-1400
800-355-1088
FAX: 610-278-1421
www.advanceforPAC.com

A free magazine for providers of post-acute care.

2553 Case Manager Magazine

Mosby
10809 Executive Center Drive
Suite 105
Little Rock, AR   72211

FAX: 501-227-8362

Tom Strickland, author
Tom Strickland, Editor In Chief
Nathania Sawyer, Editor

This national magazine is for medical case managers, social workers, counselors and home health professionals who work with people with serious injury or illness. It is a membership benefit of CMSA, the national association for case managers.

BiMonthly

2554 College and University

AACRAO
1 Dupont Circle NW
Suite 520
Washington, DC   20036

202-628-1816
FAX: 202-872-8857
e-mail: info@aacrao.com
www.aacrao.org

Scholarly research journal. American Association of Collegiate Registrars and Admissions Offers (AACRAO) is a nonprofit, voluntary, professional, educational association of degree-granting postsecondary institutions, government agencies, private educational organizations and education-oriented businesses in the United States and abroad. $50 per year US; $60 per year international.

30 pages Quarterly
ISSN 0010-0889

2555 Continuing Care

Stevens Publishing Corporation
5151 Beltline Road
10th Floor
Dallas, TX   75240

972-687-6700
FAX: 972-687-6769
e-mail: custserv@stevenspublishing.com

E. Kyle Steinhauser, Editor

A national magazine for case management and discharge planning professionals published monthly except for July/August. *$119.00*

34 pages Monthly

2556 Counseling Psychologist

American Psychological Association
2455 Teller Road
Thousand Oaks, CA   91320

805-499-9734
FAX: 805-499-0871
www.sagepub.com

Thematic issues in the theory, research and practice of counseling psychology. *$30.00*

2557 Focus on Autism and Other Developmental Disabilities

Pro-Ed
8700 Shoal Creek Boulevard
Austin, TX   78757

512-451-3246
800-897-3202
FAX: 512-451-8542
e-mail: proed1@aol.com
www.proedinc.com
Richard Simpson, John Kregel, EdD, author
Melissa Tullos, Senior Production Editor

Magazine providing practical elements of management, treatment, planning and education for persons with autism and pervasive developmental disorders. *$39.00*

64 pages Quarterly.

2558 **HomeCare Magazine**

Intertec Publishing Corporation
Stuart Ranch Road
Malibu, CA   90265   310-317-4522
                           800-543-4116
                      FAX: 310-317-9644
          e-mail: kcavallo@interec.com
                   www.homecaremag.com

Marie Blakey, Editor, author
Karen Cavallo, Publisher

The business magazine of the home medical equipment industry offering information on legislation and regulations affecting the homecare industry, monthly profiles of suppliers, operational tips, newest products in the industry, advice on sales, government regulations. *$ 65.00*

120 pages Monthly

2559 **Intervention in School and Clinic**

Pro-Ed
8700 Shoal Creek Boulevard
Austin, TX   78757   512-451-3246
                           800-897-3202
                      FAX: 512-302-9129
              e-mail: proed1@aol.com
                     www.proedinc.com

Brenda Smith Myles, author
Lisa Tippett, Managing Production Editor

One of the oldest and most widely read professional publications in special and remedial education. Professionals interested in the education of problem students will find it to be an innovative, readable periodical that provides educational information ready for immediate implementation. Published five times a year. *$35.00*

64 pages Magazine

2560 **JASH: The Journal of the Association for Persons with Severe Handicaps**

TASH
29 West Susquehanna Avenue
Suite 210
Baltimore, MD   21204   410-828-8274
                         FAX: 410-828-6706
                e-mail: info@tash.org
                       www.tash.org

Provides contemporary articles on specialized topics of interest to TASH members and others in the field of developmental disabilities.

2561 **Journal for Vocational Special Needs Education**

National Association of Vocational Education
University of Northern Texas
PO Box 13857
Denton, TX   76203   940-243-1211

Articles on vocational education for special needs population, including persons with physical and mental disabilities. *$7.00*

2562 **Journal of Autism and Developmental Disabilities**

Plenum Publishing Company
233 Spring Street
New York, NY   10013   212-229-2859
                           800-221-9369
                      FAX: 212-463-0742
              e-mail: info@plenum.com

Eric Shopler, Editor

This journal is devoted to all the severe psychopathologies in childhood, including autism and childhood schizophrenia. *$295.00*

BiMonthly
ISSN 0162-32 7

2563 **Journal of Counseling & Development**

American Counseling Association
5999 Stevenson Avenue
Alexandria, VA   22304   703-823-9800
                          FAX: 703-823-0252

Charles D. Claiborne, Editor
$65.00

BiMonthly

2564 **Journal of Developmental and Physical Disabilities**

Plenum Publishing Company
233 Spring Street
New York, NY   10013   212-229-2859
                           800-221-9369
                      FAX: 212-807-1047
              e-mail: info@plenum.com
                     www.plenum.com

Vincent B. Van Hasselt, Co-editor
Michel Hersen, Co-editor

This journal serves as a unified outlet for dissemination of work with all handicapped populations. research and clinical reports from a variety of services for multihandicapped individuals discuss such concerns as the deaf-blind, cerebral-palsied deaf, blind-mentally retarded, and emotionally disturbed retarded. Case studies originate from many professional fields including psychology, rehabilitation, special education, counseling, social work, psychiatry and rehabilitation medicine. *$46.00*

Quarterly
ISSN 1056-26 0

2565 **Journal of Emotional and Behavioral Disorders**

Pro-Ed
8700 Shoal Creek Boulevard
Austin, TX   78757   512-451-3246
                           800-897-3202
                      FAX: 512-302-9129
              e-mail: proed1@aol.com
                     www.proedinc.com

Douglas Cullinan, Michael Epstein, Authors, author
Lisa Tippet, Managing Production Editor

An international, multidisciplinary journal featuring articles on research, practice and theory related to individuals with emotional and behavioral disorders and to the professionals who serve them. *$39.00*

64 pages Quarterly

2566 **Journal of Learning Disabilities**

Pro-Ed
8700 Shoal Creek Boulevard
Austin, TX   78757
                           800-897-3202
                      FAX: 512-302-9129
              e-mail: proed1@aol.com
                     www.proedinc.com

Wayne Hresko, author
Judith K Voress, PhD, Periodicals Director

An international, multidisciplinary publication containing articles on practice, research and theory related to learning disabilities. Published bi-monthly. $49.00

Magazine

2567   Journal of Motor Behavior

Heldref Publications
1319 18th Street NW
Washington, DC   20036   202-296-6267
                                800-365-9753
                           FAX: 202-293-6130
                   e-mail: subcribe@heldref.org
                           www.heldref.org
Betty S, Adelman Managing Editor, author
Francine Hamme, Marketing Director

A professional journal aimed at psychologists, therapists and educators who work in the areas of motor behavior, psychology, neurophysiology, kinesiology, and biomechanics. Offers up-to-date information on the latest techniques, theories and developments concerning motor control. $71.00

115 pages

2568   Journal of Musculoskeletal Pain

Haworth Press
10 Alice Street
Binghamton, NY   13904   604-722-5857
                                800-429-6784
                           FAX: 607-722-6362
         e-mail: getinfo@haworthpressinc.com
                   www.haworthpressinc.com
I. Jon Russell, M.D., PhD, Editor, author
Jackie Blakeslee, Advertising
Barbara Runnells, Managing Editor

This journal serves as a central resource for the dissemination of information about musculoskeletal pain. $75.00

110 pages Quarterly

2569   Journal of Postsecondary Education & Disability

AHEAD
PO Box 21192
Columbus, OH   43221   614-488-4972
                         FAX: 614-488-1174
        e-mail: ahead@postbox.acs.ohio_state.edu
                         www.ahead.org

Provides in-depth examination of research, issues, policies and programs in postsecondary education.

2570   Journal of Prosthetics and Orthotics

Orthotics and Prosthetics National Office
1650 King Street
Suite 500
Alexandria, VA   22314   703-836-7114
                           FAX: 703-836-0838
                   e-mail: opjournal@aol.com
                           www.aopanet.org

Stacey L. Bell, Managing Editor

Provides the latest research and clinical thinking in orthotics and prosthetics, including information on new devices, fitting techniques and patient management experiences. Each issue contains research-based information and articles reviewed and approved by a highly qualified editorial board. $60.00

64 pages Quarterly
ISSN 1040-88 0

2571   Journal of Reading, Writing and Learning Disabled International

Hemisphere Publishing Corporation
1900 Frost Road
Suite 101
Bristol, PA   19007   215-785-5800

Articles on reading, writing and learning disabilities, including mainstreaming issues. $9.00

2572   Journal of Special Education

Pro-Ed
8700 Shoal Creek Boulevard
Austin, TX   78757
                                800-897-3202
                           FAX: 512-302-9129
                   e-mail: proed1@aol.com
                           www.proedinc.com
Lynn S. Fuchs, PhD, Douglas Fuchs, PhD, author
Judith K Voress, PhD, Periodicals Director

Internationally known as the prime research journal in special education. JSE provides research articles of special education for individuals with disabilities, ranging from mild to severe. Published quarterly. $39.00

Magazine

2573   Journal of Vocational Behavior

Academic Press, Journals Division
525 B Street
Suite 1900
San Diego, CA   92101   619-231-0926

Articles on validation of theoretical constructs, developments in information, program comparisons and research methodology as related to vocational behavior. $7.00

2574   Measurement and Evaluation in Counseling and Development

American Association for Counseling & Development
5999 Stevenson Avenue
Alexandria, VA   22304   703-823-9800

William D. Schafer, Editor

Journal with professional articles on testing and evaluation. $23.00

Quarterly

2575 **Pride Institute Journal of Long Term Home Health Care**

Pride Institute
St. Vincent's Hospital
153 West 11th Street
New York, NY 10011

Journal forum for discussion of home health care. $ 30.00

2576 **Psychiatric Staffing Crisis in Community Mental Health**

National Council of Community Mental Health Center
12300 Twinbrook Parkway
Suite 320
Rockville, MD 20852   301-670-6331

Find out some of the simple, low-cost ways you can increase workplace satisfaction among staff psychiatrists and compete successfully for their talents. $20.00

2577 **Readings: A Journal of Reviews and Commentary in Mental Health**

American Orthopsychiatric Association
330 7th Avenue
18th Floor
New York, NY 10001   212-268-1399
          FAX: 212-564-6180
          e-mail: amerortho@aol.com

Joan Adler, Managing Editor

Reviews of recent books in mental health and allied disciplines. Includes essay reviews and brief reviews. $25.00

32 pages Quarterly

2578 **Rehab Pro**

Int. Association of Rehabilitation Professionals
Framingham Office Park
1661 Worcester Road, Suite 203
Framingham, MA 01701   508-820-8889
          500-240-9059
          FAX: 508-820-4337
          e-mail: phawkes@ix.netcom.com
          www.rehabpro.org

Raph Crystal, Journal Editor
Leona Liberty, NASPPR Section Editor

The magazine is to promote the profession and to inform the public about the activities of the national organization, its state chapter affiliates, and the work of its special interest sections.

38 pages BiMonthly

2579 **Remedial and Special Education**

Pro-Ed
8700 Shoal Creek Boulevard
Austin, TX 78757   512-451-3246
          800-897-3202
          FAX: 512-302-9129
          e-mail: proed1@aol.com
          www.proedinc.com

Edward Polloway, PhD, author
Melissa Tullos, Senior Production Editor

A professional journal that bridges the gap between theory and practice. Emphasis is on topical reviews, syntheses of research, field evaluation studies and recommendations for the practice of remedial and special education. Published six times a year. $39.00

64 pages Magazine

2580 **Special Education Report**

Capitol Publications
1101 King Street
Suite 44
Alexandria, VA 22314   703-683-4100
          800-655-5597
          FAX: 703-793-6517

Xavier Briand, Editor
Claudia Moran, Marketing Manager

Current, pertinent information about federal legislation, regulations, programs and funding for educating children with disabilities. Covers federal and state litigation on the Individuals with Disabilities Education Act and other relevant laws. Looks at innovations and research in the field. $266.00

8 pages BiWeekly
ISSN 0194-22 5

2581 **Teaching Exceptional Children**

Council for Exceptional Children
1920 Association Drive
Reston, VA 20191   703-620-3660
          888-232-7323
          FAX: 703-264-9494
          e-mail: service@cec.sped.org
          www.cec.sped.org

Dave Edyburn, author
Cathy Mack, Production Manager

Journal designed for teachers of gifted students and students with disabilities, featuring practical methods and materials for classroom use. $58.00

96 pages Magazine 6 iss.

2582 **Topics in Early Childhood Special Education**

Pro-Ed
8700 Shoal Creek Boulevard
Austin, TX 78757

          e-mail: proed1@aol.com

Deals with timely and important issues in the growing field of special education. Articles present reports of original research, literature reviews, conceptual statements, position papers and program descriptions. $39.00

Quarterly

2583 **Topics in Language Disorders**

Aspen Publishers
200 Orchard Ridge Drive
Gaithersburg, MD 20878   301-698-7100
          800-234-1660
          FAX: 301-695-7931
          www.aspenpublishers.com

Jack Bruggeman, Publisher

Peer review journal for professionals in the field of language disorders. Published quarterly. $86.00

104 pages

Newsletters

2584 Academic Acceptance of ASL

Gallaudet University Bookstore
11030 S Langley Avenue
Chicago, IL   60628   202-651-5488
                                      800-621-2736
                                  FAX: 202-651-5489

Sherman Wilcox, author

This monograph presents a dozen articles that demonstrate clearly and convincingly that the study of ASL affords the same educational values and the same intellectual rewards as the study of any other foreign language. *$15.95*

196 pages

2585 Alert

Association on Handicapped Student Service Program
PO Box 21192
Columbus, OH   43221   614-365-5216
                                  FAX: 614-365-6718

Keeps members informed about Association activities, current legislative issues, innovative programs, and more. *$30.00*

2586 American School Counselor Association

801 N Fairfax Street
Suite 310
Alexandria, VA   22314   703-683-2722
                                      800-306-4722
                                  FAX: 703-683-1619
                      e-mail: asca@schoolcounselor.org
                             www.schoolcounselor.org

Kwok-Sze Wong, Executive Director

ASCA focuses on providing professional devleopment, enhancing school counseling programs, and research effective school counseling practices. Mission is to promote excellence in professional school counseling and the development of all students.

2587 CEC Catalog

Council for Exceptional Children
1920 Association Drive
Reston, VA   20191   703-620-3660
                                      888-232-7232
                                  FAX: 703-264-9494
                        e-mail: service@cec.sped.org
                                www.cec.sped.org

Cathy Mack, Production Manager

Semi-annual catalog from the Council for Exceptional Children offering books, guides, materials, products and services for the special educator.

18 pages

2588 Catalyst

Western Ctr. for Microcomputers In Special Ed.
1259 El Camino Real
275
Menlo Park, CA   94025   650-855-8064
                                  FAX: 650-324-1119
                  e-mail: thecatalyst@mail.earthlink.net
                          home.earthlink.net/nthecatalyst

Sue Swezey, Editor

Digest of news and information on the use of computers in special education. *$15.00*

20 pages Quarterly

2589 Clinical Connection

American Advertising Distibutors of Northern VA
708 Pendleton Street
Alexandria, VA   22314   703-549-5126

Georgina Ruley, Publisher

Covers speech language pathology.

2590 Counseling and Values

American Counseling Association
5999 Stevenson Avenue
Alexandria, VA   22304   703-823-9800

M. Harry Daniels, Editor

$12.00

TriAnnual

2591 Counselor Education and Supervision

American Counseling Association
5999 Stevenson Avenue
Alexandria, VA   22304   703-823-9800
                                  FAX: 703-823-0252
                                     www.counseling.org

Margaret L. Fong, Editor

$18.00

Quarterly

2592 Counterpoint

Nat'l Assoc. of State Directors of Special Educ.
10860 Hampton Road
Fairfax Station, VA   22039   703-239-1557

Newspaper designed for teachers of disabled and gifted students, featuring practical methods and materials for classroom use. *$36.00*

Quarterly

2593 Directions: Technology in Special Education

DREAMMS for Kids
273 Ringwood Road
Freeville, NY   13068   607-539-3027
                                  FAX: 607-539-9930
                                       www.dreamms.org

Janet P. Hosmer, Contact

Provides technology tips to ease home instruction and use; describes and reviews adaptive educational software and hardware; reviews pertinent literature and audio & videotapes; describes adaptive and assistive technology devices; provides on-line service information for the disabled; announces upcoming educational and technology conference; and reports on new Department of Education legislation. *$14.95*

Monthly

2594 Disability Compliance for Higher Education

LRP Publications
747 Dresher Road
980
Horsham, PA   19044   215-784-0941
                                  800-341-7874
                              FAX: 215-784-9639
                      e-mail: custserve@lrp.com
                                   www.lrp.com

Marsha Jaquays, author

The only newsletter that is dedicated to the exclusive coverage of disability issues that affect colleges and universities. *$190.00*

Monthly
ISSN 1086-1335

2595 Disability Resources Monthly

Disability Resources
4 Glatter Lane
Centereach, NY   11720   631-585-0290
                              FAX: 631-585-0290
          e-mail: jklauber@disabilityresources.org
                      www.disabilityresources.org

Julie Klauber, Managing Editor, author
Avery Klauber, Director

A newsletter that monitors, reviews and reports on resources for independent living. A monthly newsletter that features short topical articles, news items and reviews of books, pamphlets, periodicals, videotapes, on-line services, organizations and other resources for and about people with disabilities. It is intended primarily for librarians, social workers, educators, rehabilitation specialists, disability advocates, ADA coordinators and other health and social service professionals. *$30.00*

4 pages Monthly
ISSN 1070-72 0

2596 Disability Studies Quarterly

Department of Public Management
Suffolk University
Boston, MA   02108   617-725-8483
                              FAX: 617-573-8711
          e-mail: per00906@acad.suffolk.edu

David Pfeiffer, Editor
Monique Perrier, Administrative Asst.

Contains articles on aspects of disability, often focusing on one topic, such as gender and sexuality, communication technology and measurement in disability. Also includes information on books and resources available for persons with disabilities. *$35.00*

75 pages Quarterly

2597 Early Childhood Reporter

LRP Publications
747 Dresher Road
980
Horsham, PA   19044
                                  800-341-7874
                      e-mail: custserve@lrp.com
                                www.lrp.com/ed

Frank Diamond, Managing Editor

Monthly reports with information on federal, state, and local legislation affecting the implementation of early intervention and preschool programs for children with disabilities. *$145.00*

12-16 pages $10 shipping

2598 Early Intervention: Quarterly Newsletter

Illinois Early Childhood Intervention
830 South Spring Street
Springfield, IL   62704   217-544-5809
                                  800-852-4302
                              FAX: 217-524-5339
          e-mail: clearinghouse@eosinc.com

Chet Brandt, Project Director

Features articles, conference calendar, material reviews and news concerning early childhood intervention and disability.

8 pages Quarterly
ISSN 1058-83 6

2599 Equal Opportunities in the New Independent States (NIS)

Mobility International USA
PO Box 10767
Eugene, OR   97440   541-343-1284
                              FAX: 541-343-6812
                              TDY:541-343-1284
                      e-mail: info@miusa.org
                                   www.miusa.org

Josie Van Scholten, author
Susan Sygall, Executive Director
Rhonda Neuhaus, Public Relations Coordinator

Contains information for exchange advisors on how to include students with disabilities in NIS programs. Discusses cultural issues, offers accessibility information, describes differet types of disabilities and includes an extensive resource section. Available in alternative formats. *$40.00*

2600 Fact Sheets

Institution on Disability/UAP
7 Leavitt Lane
Suite 101
Durham, NH   03824   603-862-4320
                              FAX: 603-862-0555
                      e-mail: institute.disability@
                                   iod.unh.edu

Offers various journal articles touching on inclusion, and learning difference in the education system.

2601 Focus on Exceptional Children

Love Publishing Company
9101 East Kenyon Avenue
Suite 2200
Denver, CO   80237   303-221-7333
                              FAX: 303-221-7444
          e-mail: lovepublishing@compuserve.com

Scott Thomas, Manager

Contains research and theory-based articles on special education topics, with an emphasis on application and intervention, of interest to teachers, professors and administrators. *$30.00*

9x Year

2602 Forum

Ohio Coalition for the Education of Children with
165 West Center Street
Bank One Building, #302
Marion, OH   43302   740-382-5452
                                          800-374-2806
                                   FAX: 740-383-6421
                                   e-mail: oceed@gte.net

Margaret Burley, author

Forum is a newsletter reporting on legislative and other developments affecting persons with disabilities. Other books offered include (all prices include shipping and handling): How to Write an IEP ($12.95), Accessing the General Curriculum ($12.95), and It's My Turn: Board Game ($27.95).

8 pages BiMonthly

2603 Guidepost

American Association for Counseling & Development
5999 Stevenson Avenue
Alexandria, VA   22304   703-823-9800

Jennifer L. Sacks, Editor

Newspaper for guidance and counseling professionals. Diversified coverage of current news and issues, legislation at federal and state levels. *$30.00*

BiWeekly

2604 Healthline

CV Mosby Company
11830 Westline Industrial Drive
Saint Louis, MO   63146
                                   FAX: 314-432-1158
                                   e-mail: journal.service@mosby.com
                                   www.mosby.com

Paul Insel, Editor

Health and fitness information for healthcare professionals and the general public alike.

Monthly

2605 Help Newsletter

Learning Disabilities Assn. of Arkansas
7509 Camtrell # 1030
Little Rock, AR   72207   501-666-8777
                                   FAX: 501-666-4070
                                   e-mail: idaa@aristotle.net
                                   www.ldaarkansas.org

Janice Peters, author
Judy Powers, President
Dama K. Jackson, Director

Information on how to overcome obstacles and to achieve in spite of learning disabilities.

8 pages Newsletter

2606 Home Health Agency Gazette

American Federation of Home Health Agencies
1320 Fenwick Lane
Suite 500
Silver Spring, MD   20910   301-754-0400
                                   FAX: 301-588-4732
                                   e-mail: afhha@his.com
                                   www.his.com/afhha/usa.html

Joan Guberman, Editor

Focuses on regulatory and legislative issues of interest to the home health care industry.

2607 Horizons

Haras & Trebor
PO Box 985
Gambrills, MD   21054   301-621-9332
                                   FAX: 410-923-2120
                                   TDY:301-621-9332
                                   e-mail: storrsjh@aol.com

James Storrs, Publisher

Monthly newspaper for people with disabilities serving Maryland, Virginia, and Washington, D.C. *$17.00*

20 pages Monthly
ISSN 1064-64 4

2608 I Wonder Who Else Can Help

AARP Fulfillment
601 East Street NW
Washington, DC   20049   202-434-2277
                                          800-424-3410
                                   FAX: 202-434-3443
                                   e-mail: member@aarp.org
                                   www.aarp.org

Contains information about crisis counseling, needs and resources, written in lay terms.

2609 Information from HEATH Resource Center

National Clearinghouse on Postsecondary Education
1 Dupont Circle NW
Suite 800
Washington, DC   20036   202-939-9320
                                          800-544-3284
                                   FAX: 202-833-5696
                                   e-mail: heath@ace.nche.edu
                                   www.HEATH-resource-center.org

The HEATH Resource Center operates the national clearinghouse on postsecondary education for individuals with disabilities. Support from the US Department of Education enables the Center, a program of the America Council on Education, to serve as an information exchange on educational support services; adaptations; and opportunities at American campuses, vocational-technical schools, adult education programs, independent living centers, and other postsecondary training entities.

2610 Innovations

University of New Hampshire
Room 312 Morrill Hall
Durham, NH   03824   603-862-4320

                                   e-mail: institutedisability@unh.edu

Carol Tashie, Editor

For classroom teachers, integration facilities, consulting teachers, paraprofessionals and principals. Includes strategies and suggestions for inclusion of students with disabilities into neighborhood schools and typical education classrooms.

2611 **Inside the NIDCD Information Clearinghouse Newsletter**

NIDCD Information Clearinghouse
1 Communication Avenue
Bethesda, MD   20892

800-241-1044
FAX: 301-907-8830
e-mail: nidcdinfo@nidcd.nih.gov
www.nih.gov/nidcd

Biannual newsletter, resource directory, professional/consumer fact sheets, brochures, information packets, and reports.

192X

2612 **International Rehabilitation Review**

Rehabilitation International
25 E 21st Street
New York, NY   10010   212-505-8040
FAX: 212-505-0871
e-mail: rehabintal@aol.com

Barbara Duncan, Editor
Kathy Marchael, Editorial Assistant
International overview of activities and programs in vocational and medical rehabilitation, prosthesis and orthotics and special education. *$30.00*

TriAnnual

2613 **International Rolf Institute**

PO Box 1868
Boulder, CO   80306   303-449-5903

Information, practitioner training and certification.

2614 **Learning Disabilities Consultants Newsletter**

Learning Disabilities Consultants
PO Box 716
Bryn Mawr, PA   19010   610-668-2225
800-869-8336
FAX: 610-525-8337

Richard Cooper, Director
Newsletter providing information about learning disabilities and differences. It contains both local and national news items and includes in each issue articles about various aspects of learning problems encountered in both children and adults. *$10.00*

6 pages 5x Year

2615 **Lifespan**

Nat'l Council of Community Mental Health Center
12300 Twinbrook Parkway
Suite 320
Rockville, MD   20852   301-984-6200
FAX: 301-881-7159
www.nccbh.org

Information on tax tips, insurance, medical care, law and legislation for people with mental disabilities.

Monthly

2616 **Link**

21021 Ventura Boulevard
Suite 321
Woodland Hills, CA   91364   818-340-7500

e-mail: eajc27b@prodigy.com
www.alsa.org

Elliot Mancall, Director
Official newsletter updating the work and progress of the Amyotrophic Lateral Sclerosis Association.

2617 **MDA Newsmagazine**

Muscular Dystrophy Association
3300 E Sunrise Drive
Tucson, AZ   85718

Presents news related to muscular dystrophy and other neuromuscular diseases including research, personal profiles, fundraising activities and patient services.

2618 **NYALD News**

New York Association for the Learning Disabled
90 S Swan Street
Albany, NY   12210   518-432-5787
FAX: 518-432-5902

Kelly Jarrard, Executive Director
Newsletter offering information on the learning disabled in the New York area.

Monthly

2619 **Network Exchange**

Learning Disabilities Network
72 Sharp Street
Suite A-2
Hingham, MA   02043   781-340-5605

e-mail: ldntwk@aol.com

Cynthia Christopher, Director of Progress
Provides a forum for the exchange of ideas pertinent to learning disabilities for learning disabled individuals, their families and the professionals who work on their behalf. *$20.00*

BiAnnually

2620 **SAMHSA News**

US Department of Health and Human Services
5600 Fishers Lane
Room 13C-05
Rockville, MD   20857   301-443-8956
FAX: 301-443-9050
www.samhsa.gov

Mark Weber, Associate Administrator, Commun.
Deborah Goodmad, Public Affairs Specialist
This quarterly Agency newsletter reports on information on substance abuse, mental health treatment and prevention programs of the Substance Abuse and Mental Health Services Administration.

Quarterly

2621 SIBPAGE

AJ Pappanikou Center
249 Glenbrook Road
Unit U-64
Storrs Mansfield, CT   06269   860-486-3493

Lisa Glidden, Coordinator

Developed specifically for children containing games, recipes, pen pals, and articles written by siblings relating to developmental disabilities.

4 pages

2622 Sibling Information Network Newsletter

AJ Pappanikou Center
249 Glenbrook Road Unit U-64
Storrs Mansfield, CT   06269   860-486-3493

Lisa Glidden, Coordinator

Contains information aimed at the varying interested of our membership. Program descriptions, requests for assistance, conference announcements, literature summaries and research reports. *$8.50*

2623 Sower

Beatrice State Development Center
3000 Lincoln Boulevard
Beatrice, NE   68310   402-223-6002

Current programs, objectives and goals, needs and actual happenings at the institution.

12 pages

2624 Special Services in the Schools

Haworth Press
10 Alice Street
Binghamton, NY   13904   604-722-5857
                              800-429-6784
                       FAX: 607-722-6362
       e-mail: getinfo@haworthpressinc.com
              www.haworthpressinc.com

Charles A. Maher, PsyD, Editor, author
Jackie Blakeslee, Advertising

This journal disseminates the latest and the highest quality information to all professionals who provide special services in the schools and related educational settings. *$60.00*

BiAnnually

2625 Their World

National Center for Learning Disabilities
381 Park Avenue South
Room 1420
New York, NY   10016   212-532-0871
                       FAX: 212-545-9665

James H. Wendorf, Executive Director
Ruth O'Brien, Editor

Contains features, articles, human interest news and information and information, and other practical material to benefit the millions of children and adults with learning disabilities and their families, as well as educators and other helping professionals. Magazine

3x Year

2626 Treatment Review

AIDS Treatment Data Network
611 Broadway
Suite 613
New York, NY   10012   212-260-8868
                              800-734-7104
                       FAX: 212-260-8869
               e-mail: network@atdn.org
               www.aidsinfonyc.org/network

Ken Fernataro, Executive Director
Tracy Swan, Access Project Director

Individual members recieve treatment education, counseling, referrals and case management support. Services are available in both English and Spanish. The Treatment Review newsletter includes descriptions of approved, alternative and experimental treatments, as well as announcements of seminars and forums on treatments and clinical trials.

Quarterly

Professional Texts

2627 AEPS Curriculum for Birth to Three Years (Volume 2)

Brookes Publishing
PO Box 10624
Baltimore, MD   21285   410-337-9580
                              800-638-3775
                       FAX: 410-337-8539
       e-mail: custserv@brookespublishing.com
              www.brookespublishing.com

Julianne Cripe, PhD, author

Directly linked to IEP/IFSP goals developed for a child from the AEPS test measure, the AEPS curriculum provides a complete set of learning activities to facilitate children's acquisition of functional skills. *$59.95*

496 pages
ISBN 1-557660-96-4

2628 About the Tomatis Method

Listening Center Press

T. Gilmore, P. Madaule, and B. Thompson, author

Describes physicians research on the brain and communication.

2629 Academic Skill Builders in Language Arts

DLM Teaching Resources
One DLM Park
Allen, TX   75002

                              800-527-5030

This course offers six practice and drill programs for game control options. Speech, content, difficulty level, run time and sound on or off.

2630 Accepting Your Power to Heal: Personal Practice of Therapeutic Touch

Bear and Company

Dolores Krieger, author

In-depth details on the use of Therapeutic Touch.

1993

2631 Access to Health Care, Number 1 & 2

World Institute on Disability
510-16th Street
Suite 100
Oakland, CA   94612   510-763-4100
                             FAX: 510-763-4109
                             TDY:510-208-9493
                             e-mail: wid@wid.org
                             www.wid.org
Nora Groce, author

These health policy bulletins analyze health care needs. Volume 1 focuses on a wide range of information relevant to addressing the adequacy of the health care system for persons with disabilities or chronic illness. *$6.50*

63 pages Paperback

2632 Access to Health Care, Number 3 & 4

World Institute on Disability
510-16th Street
Suite 100
Oakland, CA   94612   510-763-4100
                             FAX: 510-763-4109
                             TDY:510-208-9493
                             e-mail: wid@wid.org
                             www.wid.org
Nora Groce, author

These policy bulletins focus on the capacity of the private and public health insurance systems to respond to the health care needs of persons with disabilities or chronic illness. *$6.50*

91 pages Paperback

2633 Adapting Early Childhood Curricula for Children with Special Needs

McGraw-Hill, School Publishing
220 East Danieldale Road
DeSoto, TX   75115   972-224-1111
                             800-442-9685
                             FAX: 972-228-1982
                             mhschool.com

Offers information on educating the disabled.

2634 Adaptive Education Strategies Building on Diversity

Paul H. Brookes Publishing Company
PO Box 10624
Baltimore, MD   21285
                             800-638-3775
                             FAX: 410-337-8539
Margaret Wang, author

Based on more than two decades of systematic research, this comprehensive manual provides a road map to the effective implementation of adaptive education. *$35.00*

304 pages Paperback 1992
ISBN 1-557880-84-0

2635 Advanced Sign Language Vocabulary: A Resource Text for Educators

Charles C. Thomas, Publisher
2600 S 1st Street
Springfield, IL   62704   217-789-8980
                                 800-258-8980
                             FAX: 217-789-9130
                             e-mail: books@ccthomas.com
Janet R. Coleman and Elizabeth E. Wolf, author

This book is a collection of advanced sign language vocabulary for use by educators, interpreters, parents or anyone wishing to enlarge their sign vocabulary. *$46.95*

202 pages Paperback
ISBN 0-398057-22-2

2636 Advances in Cardiac and Pulmonary Rehabilitation

Haworth Press
10 Alice Street
Binghamton, NY   13904   604-722-5857
                                800-429-6784
                             FAX: 607-722-6362
                   e-mail: getinfo@haworthpressinc.com
                             www.haworthpressinc.com
Mary Singleton, PhD, LPT, author
Jackie Blakeslee, Advertising

Enhance your rehabilitation program with this authoritative volume. *$29.95*

74 pages Hardcover
ISBN 0-866869-86-3

2637 Advances in Clinical Rehabilitation

Springer Publishing Company
536 Broadway
New York, NY   10012   212-431-4370
                              877-687-7476
                             FAX: 212-941-7842
                   e-mail: marketing@springer.com
                             www.springerpub.com
Myron G. Eisenberg, author
Annette Imperati, Marketing Director

Provides practical and current information about rehabilitation interventions from a multidisciplinary perspective. It addresses innovations in clinical assessment, rehabilitation, technology and research. *$48.95*

332 pages Hardcover
ISBN 0-82615 -62-4

2638 Aging Brain

Taylor & Francis
47 Runway Drive
G
Levittown, PA   19057   215-269-0400
                             FAX: 215-625-2940
H.K. Ulatowska, author

Elderly treatment.

225 pages Paperback
ISBN 0-85066 -78-0

2639 Aging and Rehabilitation II

Springer Publishing Company
536 Broadway
New York, NY   10012   212-431-4370
                             FAX: 212-941-7842
Stanley J. Brody, author

Current, multidisciplinary investigations of various practice issues. Leading experts in the field use a practical perspective to provide specific comments on interventions. The scope of this work encompasses the autonomy of elderly disabled, mobility, mental health and value issues, as well as basic aspects in rehabilitation of the elderly. *$41.95*

367 pages Hardcover
ISBN 0-82617 -80-3

2640   Alphabetic Phonics Curriculum

Educators Publishing Service
31 Smith Place
Cambridge, MA   02138   **617-367-2700**
                                  800-225-5750
                            FAX: 617-547-0412
                            www.epsbooks.com

Aylett Cox, author

Ungraded multisensory curriculum for teaching phonics and the structure of language. Uses Orton-Gillingham approach to teach handwriting, spelling, reading, reading comprehension, and oral and written expression. program includes basic manual, workbooks, tests, teachers' guides, drill cards and all cards. *$28.15*

ISSN 8388-42

2641   Alternative Educational Delivery Systems

National Association of School Psychologists
8455 Colesville Road
Suite 1000
Silver Spring, MD   20910   **301-681-3223**
                                  FAX: 301-495-8804

A book offering information to the professional on how to enhance educational options for all students.

2642   Alternative Teaching Strategies

Special Needs Project
3463 Stat Street
 # 282
Santa Barbara, CA   93105
                                  800-333-6867

Offers help for teachers who teach behaviorally troubled students achieve.

2643   Alzheimer's Disease Oryx Science Bibliographies Vol. 8

ORYX Press
4041 N Central
Phoenix, AZ   85012   **602-265-2651**
                                  800-279-ORYX
                            FAX: 800-279-4663
                            e-mail: info@oryxpress.com

$18.75

76 pages 1987
ISBN 0-897743-24-5

2644   An Activity-Based Approach to Early Intervention: Second Edition

Brookes Publishing
PO Box 10624
Baltimore, MD   21285   **410-337-9580**
                                  800-638-3775
                            FAX: 410-337-8539
            e-mail: custserv@brookespublishing.com
                      www.brookespublishing.com

Diane Bricker, author

Activity-based intervention shows how to use natural and relevant events to teach infants and young children, of all abilities, effectively and efficiently. *$24.00*

240 pages
ISBN 1-55766 -87-5

2645   An Independent Living Approach to Disability Policy Studies

World Institute on Disability
510 16th Street
Suite 100
Oakland, CA   94612   **510-763-4100**
                            FAX: 510-763-4109
                            TDY:510-208-9493
                            e-mail: wid@wid.org
                                  www.wid.org

Susan T. Brown, author

This collection of essays and bibliographies attempts to build a framework for understanding how the relationship between public policy, disability studies and disability policy studies will impact us in the future. *$17.50*

240 pages Paperback

2646   An Introduction to the Nature and Needs of Students with Mild Disabilities

Charles C. Thomas, Publisher
2600 South 1st Street
Springfield, IL   62704   **217-789-8980**
                                  800-258-8980
                            FAX: 217-789-9130
                      e-mail: books@ccthomas.com

Carroll J. Jones, author

Source of information for the special educator on the needs of students with mild disabilities. It has been designed as an introductory text for an undergraduate degree program in special education. The first chapter includes an overview of students who are at risk for academic failure. The remaining chapters are divided into three categorical units: students with mild mental retardation, behavior disorders, and learning disabilities. Also available in cloth for $66.95 (ISBN# 0-398-06711-2) *$50.95*

300 pages Paperback
ISBN 0-398067-12-0

2647   An Introduction to the Profession of Counseling

McGraw-Hill, School Publishing
220 East Danieldale Road
DeSoto, TX   75115   **972-224-1111**
                                  800-442-9685
                            FAX: 972-228-1982
                            mhschool.com

Frank Nugent, author

Offers information, theories and techniques for counseling numerous cases from drug addiction to special populations.

464 pages

2648 Andrew Taylor Still - 1828-1917

Thomas Jefferson University Press

Carol Trowbridge, author
Biography of the physician who changed modern medicine throughout the years.

2649 Antecedent Control: Innovative Approaches to Behavioral Support

Brookes Publishing
PO Box 10624
Baltimore, MD   21285   **410-337-9585**
                              800-638-3775
                         FAX: 410-337-8539
   e-mail: custserv@brookespublishing.com
        www.brookespublishing.com
This book explains the theory and methodology of antecedent control. The treatment techniques in this book are effective for both children and adults.

416 pages Paperback 1998
ISBN 1-55766 -34-3

2650 Applied Kinesiology: Muscle Response in Diagnosis, Therapy and Preventive Medicine

Inner Traditions
One Park Street
Rochester, VT   05767   **802-767-3174**
                              800-246-8648
                         FAX: 802-767-3726
        e-mail: orders@gotoit.com
                   www.gotoit.com

Tom & Carol Valentine, author
144 pages 1989
ISBN 0-892813-28-8

2651 Applied Rehabilitation Counseling

Springer Publishing Company
536 Broadway
New York, NY   10012   **212-431-4370**
                         FAX: 212-941-7842
T.F. Riggar, author
This comprehensive text describes current theories, techniques, and their applications to specific disabled populations. Perspectives on varying counseling approaches such as psychodynamic, existential, gestalt, behavioral and psychoeducational orientations are systematically outlined in an easy-to-follow format. Practical applications for counseling are emphasized with attention given to strategies, goal-setting and on-going evaluations. *$29.95*

400 pages Softcover
ISBN 0-82615 -70-4

2652 Art-Centered Education and Therapy for Children with Disabilities

Charles C. Thomas, Publisher
2600 South 1st Street
Springfield, IL   62704   **217-789-8980**
                              800-258-8980
                         FAX: 217-789-9130
        e-mail: books@ccthomas.com
Frances E. Anderson, author
This book has been written to help both the regular education, and art and special education teachers, both pre- and in-service, better understand some of the issues and realities of providing education and remediation to children with disabilities. The book is also offered as model concept that has govern the author's personal and professional career of over thirty years. Also available in cloth for $49.95 (ISBN# 0-398-05896-2) *$35.95*

284 pages Paperback
ISBN 0-398060-06-1

2653 Assessing Bilingual Exceptional Children

Los Amigos Research Associates
7035 Galewood Street
San Diego, CA   92120   **619-286-3162**

Donald R. Park, author
The immigration explosion in the past decade has resulted in significantly increased minority enrollment in our schools. *$100.00*

2654 Assessing the Handicaps/Needs of Children

Books on Special Children
PO Box 305
Congers, NY   10920   **845-638-1236**
                         FAX: 845-638-0847
        e-mail: irene@boscbooks.com
B. Cooper, author
Papers on treatment, rehab and social support in assessing the needs of mentally retarded children. *$66.00*

260 pages Hardcover
ISBN 0-12218 -02-0

2655 Assessment & Management of Mainstreamed Hearing-Impaired Children

Pro-Ed
8700 Shoal Creek Boulevard
Austin, TX   78757
                         FAX: 512-451-8542
        e-mail: proed1@aol.com

Mark Ross, Author
Diane Brackett, Author
Antonia Brancia Maxon, Author
The theoretical and practical considerations of developing appropriate programming for hearing-impaired children who are being educated in mainstream educational settings are presented in this book. *$41.00*

415 pages
ISBN 0-89079 -58-8

2656 Assessment Log & Developmental Progress Charts for the Carolina Curriculum-CCITSN & CCPSN

Brookes Publishing
PO Box 10624
Baltimore, MD   21285   410-337-9580
                                                  800-638-3775
                                   FAX: 410-337-8539
e-mail: custserv@brookespublishing.com
www.brookespublishing.com
Nancy M. Johnson-Martin, Ph.D., author

This 28-page booklet allows the progress of children with skills in the 12-36 month development range to be easily recorded. Available in packages of 10. $23.00

28 pages Saddle-stiched
ISBN 1-557662-21-5

2657 Assessment and Remediation of Articulatory and Phonological Disorders

McGraw-Hill, School Publishing
220 East Danieldale Road
DeSoto, TX   75115   972-224-1111
                                      800-442-9685
                          FAX: 972-228-1982
                               mhschool.com

Offers comprehensive coverage of articulation disorders.

2658 Assessment in Mental Handicap: A Guide to Assessment Practices & Tests

Brookline Books
PO Box 1046
Cambridge, MA   02238   617-868-0360
                                             800-666-2665
                               FAX: 617-868-1772
e-mail: brooklinebks@delphi.com
www.brooklinebooks.com
James Hogg, author

Helps professionals understand the rationale and uses for assessment practices, and provides details of appropriate instruments within each type: adaptive behavior scales, assessment of behavioral disturbances, early development and Plagetian tests. $20.00

Hardcover
ISBN 0-91479-31-X

2659 Assessment of Children and Youth

Longman Education/Addison Wesley
1185 Avenue of the Americas
New York, NY   10036   212-843-0352
                                            800-322-1377
                               FAX: 800-333-3328
www.longman.awl.com
Libby Cohen, Loraine Spenciner, author
Ginny Blanford, Editor

Introductory text for preservice and in-service special educators on assessment, based on the principle that every child is unique. Comprehensive coverage of both formal and informal assessment instruments. $50.00

640 pages Paperback
ISBN 0-80131-02-5

2660 Assessment of Individuals with Severe Disabilities

Paul H. Brookes Publishing Company
PO Box 10624
Baltimore, MD   21285   800-638-3775
                                   FAX: 410-337-8539
Diane M. Browder, author
Karen G. Radke, Marketing Director

This expanded text offers instructors guidelines to design a comprehensive educational assessment for individuals with severe disabilities. $34.00

432 pages Paperback 1991
ISBN 1-557660-67-0

2661 Assessment of the Technology Needs of Vending Facilitiy Managers In Tennessee

Rehab/Training Center on Blindness and Low-Vision
PO Box 6189
Mississippi State, MS   39762   662-325-2001
                                                   800-675-7782
                                       FAX: 662-325-8989
                                       TDY:601-325-8693
e-mail: rrtc@ra.msstate.edu
www.blind.msstate.edu/irr
Moore, Maxson, Cavenaugh, Johnson & Pearson, author
Kelly Schaefer, Publications Manager
John Maxson, Training Director

This report summarizes the results and recommendations of a survey conducted of vending facility managers throughout the state of Tennessee who participate in the Randolph-Sheppard program. $10.00

39 pages Paperback

2662 Assessment: The Special Educator's Role

Brooks/Cole Publishing Company
511 Forest Lodge Road
Pacific Grove, CA   93950   831-373-0728
                                       FAX: 831-375-6414
e-mail: bc-info@brookscole.com
Cheri Hoy & Noel Gregg, author

Aimed at students with little or no classroom experience in assessment, the book focuses on the integration of dynamic, curriculum-based and norm-referenced data for diagnostic decisions and program planning.

580 pages Casebound
ISBN 0-53421-32-1

2663 Aston Training Center

PO Box 3568
Incline Village, NV   89450   702-831-8228

Integrated system of movement education, 3-D soft tissue work, environmental modification and fitness training.

2664 Attention Deficit Disorder in Children and Adolescents

Charles C. Thomas, Publisher
2600 South 1st Street
Springfield, IL 62704   217-789-8980
                              800-258-8980
                              FAX: 217-789-9130
                    e-mail: books@ccthomas.com

Jack Fadely, Author
Virginia N. Hosler, Author

Presents an analysis of case studies of children and adolescents with attentional deficits and hyperactivity, demonstrating causal factors in these disorders and suggesting treatment strategies both in psychological and medical practice. Written as a review and summary of twenty years of private practice. Also available in cloth for $56.95 (ISBN# 0-398-05792-3) *$35.95*

292 pages Paperback
ISBN 0-39806-12-2

2665 Behavior Analysis in Education: Focus on Measurably Superior Instruction

Brooks/Cole Publishing Company
511 Forest Lodge Road
Pacific Grove, CA 93950   831-373-0728
                              FAX: 831-375-6414
                    e-mail: bc-info@brookscole.com
Ralph Gardner, III, author

Designed to disseminate measurably superior instructional strategies to those interested in advancing sound, pedagogically effective, field-tested educational practices, this book is intended for graduate-level courses and seminars in special education and/or psychology focusing on behavior analysis and instruction.

512 pages Casebound
ISBN 0-53422-60-9

2666 Behavior Modification

Sage Periodicals Press
2455 Teller Road
Thousand Oaks, CA 91320   805-499-9734
                              FAX: 805-499-0871
                    www.sagepublications.com

Describes in detail for replication purposes assessment and modification techniques for problems in psychiatric, clinical, educational and rehabilitation settings. *$53.00*

640 pages Quarterly

2667 Behavior Therapy for Developmentally Disabled

Books on Special Children
PO Box 305
Congers, NY 10920   845-638-1236
                          FAX: 845-638-0847
                e-mail: irene@boscbooks.com
J.L. Matson, author

Definitions, treatments, and behavioral approaches for language deficits, visually impaired, autistic children and adults. *$47.50*

416 pages Softcover

2668 Behavioral Disorders

Council for Exceptional Children
1920 Association Drive
Reston, VA 20191   703-620-3660
                          800-232-7733
                    FAX: 703-264-9494
            e-mail: service@cec.sped.org
                    www.cec.sped.org

Provides professionals with a means to exchange information and share ideas related to research, empirically tested educational innovations, and issues and concerns relevant to students with behavioral disorders. Individual, $20; Institution, $50.

Quarterly

2669 Behind Special Education

Love Publishing Company
4925 East Pacific Place
22353
Denver, CO 80222   303-221-7333
                          FAX: 303-221-7444
            e-mail: lovepublishing@compuserve.com
Thomas M. Skrtic, author

This new work is a critical analysis of the nature of disability, special education, school organization and reform progress. *$24.95*

ISBN 0-89108-17-4

2670 Beyond Drill & Practice: Expanding the Computer Mainstream

Council for Exceptional Children
1920 Association Drive
Reston, VA 20191   703-620-3660
                          888-232-7733
                    FAX: 703-264-9494
                    TDY: 703-264-9446
            e-mail: service@cec.sped.org
                    www.cec.sped.org

Susan Jo Russell, author
Nancy Safer, Executive Director

Explore the use of the computer for teaching and motivating children with disabilities and other problem learners. Let teachers use these programs and strategies that show you how it works. *$10.00*

120 pages
ISBN 0-86586-90-0

2671 Bilingual Exceptional Child

Los Amigos Research Associates
7035 Galewood Street
San Diego, CA 92120   619-286-3162

Donald Omark, author

This is the first book to examine clearly the many factors affecting children who are bilingual and disabled. *$31.00*

400 pages Illustrated

2672 Bilingualism and Learning Disabilities

Los Amigos Research Associates
7035 Galewood Street
San Diego, CA 92120   619-286-3162

Ann C. Willig, author

This volume examines policies and practices for teachers and administrators. *$36.00*

213 pages

2673 Biomedical Concerns in Persons with Down's Syndrome

Paul H. Brookes Publishing Company
PO Box 10624
Baltimore, MD   21285
800-638-3775
FAX: 410-337-8539
Siegfried Pueschel, author
Karen G. Radke, Marketing Director

Written by leading authorities and spanning many disciplines and specialties, this comprehensive resource provides vital information on biomedical issues concerning individuals with Down's Syndrome. *$45.00*

336 pages Hardcover 1992
ISBN 1-557660-89-1

2674 Breaking Barriers

AbleNet
1081 10th Avenue SE
Minneapolis, MN   55414
800-322-0956
FAX: 612-379-9143
e-mail: customerservice@ablenetinc.com
www.ablenetinc.com
Jackie Levin, author

A practical resource for parents, caregivers, teachers and therapists. *$15.00*

2675 Building and Evaluating Family Support Initiatives

Paul H. Brookes Publishing Company
PO Box 10624
Baltimore, MD   21285
800-638-3775
FAX: 410-337-8539
Carl Dunst, author
Karen G. Radke, Marketing Director

This essential sourcebook describes the conceptual framework, mythology and recent findings of a national study on the status of family support initiatives for persons with developmental disabilities. *$31.00*

336 pages Paperback 1993
ISBN 1-557661-22-7

2676 Building the Healing Partnership: Parents, Professionals and Children

Brookline Books
PO Box 1046
Cambridge, MA   02238
617-868-0360
800-666-2665
FAX: 617-868-1772
e-mail: brooklinebks@delphi.com
www.brooklinebooks.com
Patricia T. Leff & Elaine H. Walizer, author

Successful programs understand that the disabled child's needs must be considered in the context of a family. This book was specifically written for practitioner's who must work with families but who have insufficient training in family systems assessment and intervention. It is a valuable blend of theory and practice with pointers for applying the principles. *$24.95*

Paperback
ISBN 0-91479 -63-8

2677 Career Assessment Inventories Learning Disabled

CFKR Career Materials
11860 Kemper Road
Suite 7
Auburn, CA   95603
530-889-2357
800-525-5626
FAX: 530-889-0433

Janice Allen, Operations
Ariana Tyler, Customer Service

Takes personality, ability and interest into account in pointing learning disabled students of all ages toward intelligent and realistic career choices.   Contains binder with paperback teaching guide plus 50 interest inventories and 50 abilities inventories. *$50.00*

2678 Caring for Children with Chronic Illness

Springer Publishing Company
536 Broadway
New York, NY   10012
212-431-4370
FAX: 212-941-7842
Ruth E. Stein, author

A critical look at the current medical, social, and psychological framework for providing care to children with chronic illnesses. Emphasizing the need to create integrated, interdisciplinary approaches, it discusses issues such as the roles of families, professionals, and institutions in providing health care, the impact of a child's illness on various family structures, financing care, the special problems of chronically ill children as they become adolescents and more. *$36.95*

320 pages Hardcover
ISBN 0-82615 -00-1

2679 Carolina Curriculum for Infants and Toddlers with Special Needs, 2nd Edition

Brookes Publishing
PO Box 10624
Baltimore, MD   21285
410-337-9580
800-638-3775
FAX: 410-337-8539
e-mail: custserv@brookespublishing.com
www.brookespublishing.com
Nancy M. Johnson-Martin, Ph.D., author

This book includes detailed assessment and intervention sequences, daily routine integration strategies, sensorimotor adaptations, and a sample 24-page Assessment Log that shows readers how to chart a child's individual progress. *$40.00*

384 pages Spiral-bound
ISBN 1-55766 -74-3

2680 Carolina Curriculum for Preschoolers with Special Needs

Brookes Publishing
PO Box 10624
Baltimore, MD   21285   410-337-9580
                               800-638-3775
                          FAX: 410-337-8539
e-mail: custserv@brookespublishing.com
        www.brookespublishing.com

Nancy M. Johnson-Martin, Ph.D., author

This curriculum provides detailed teaching and assessment techniques, plus a sample 28-page Assessment Log that shows readers how to chart a child's individual progress. This guide is for children between 2 and 5 in their developmental stages who are considered at risk for developmental delay or who exhibit special needs. *$34.00*

352 pages Spiral-bound
ISBN 1-55766 -32-8

2681 Challenge of Educating Together Deaf and Hearing Youth: Making Manistreaming Work

Charles C. Thomas, Publisher
2600 South 1st Street
Springfield, IL   62704   217-789-8980
                                 800-258-8980
                            FAX: 217-789-9130
e-mail: books@ccthomas.com

Paul C. Higgins, author
Paul Higgins

Those who have this challenge of education: teachers, administrators, other professionals, parents, and concerned individuals will benefit from this book. Also available in cloth for $41.95 (ISBN# 0-398-05665-X) *$28.95*

198 pages Softcover
ISBN 0-398063-91-5

2682 Challenged Scientists: Disabilities and the Triumph of Excellence

Greenwood Publishing Group
88 Post Road West
5007
Westport, CT   06880   203-226-3571
                         FAX: 203-222-1502
                         www.greenwood.com

Robert A. Weisgerber, author

This volume points out how the increasing need for scientists in this country can be lessened by utilizing a long overlooked pool of scientific talent in those persons who are scientifically oriented but who happen to have physical or sensory disabilities. Hardcover. $49.95-$55.00.

208 pages
ISBN 0-275938-73-5

2683 Child with Disabling Illness

Lippincott, Williams & Wilkins
227 E Washington Square
Philadelphia, PA   19106   215-238-4200
                                  800-777-2295
                             FAX: 301-824-7390
                             www.lpub.com

John Downey, author
$108.50

700 pages

2684 Childhood Behavior Disorders: Applied Research & Educational Practice

Pro-Ed
8700 Shoal Creek Boulevard
Austin, TX   78757   FAX: 512-451-8542
                     e-mail: proed1@aol.com

Robert Algozzine, Rex Schmid & Cecil D. Mercer, author

The only comprehensive overview of childhood behavior disorders. This book gives you the how and why for helping children with behavior disorders. *$39.00*

399 pages
ISBN 0-89079 -19-6

2685 Children with ADD: A Shared Responsibility

Council for Exceptional Children
1920 Association Drive
Reston, VA   20191   703-620-3660
                            888-232-7323
                       FAX: 703-264-9494
e-mail: service@cec.sped.org
        www.cec.sped.org

Cathy Mack, Production Manager

Information on meeting the educational needs of children with ADD. *$8.90*

35 pages
ISBN 0-86586 -33-8

2686 Children with Disabilities: A Medical Primer, 4th Edition

Brookes Publishing
PO Box 10624
Baltimore, MD   21285   410-337-9580
                               800-638-3775
                          FAX: 410-337-8539
e-mail: custserv@brookespublishing.com
        www.brookespublishing.com

This revised and updated edition of a highly acclaimed reference provides in-depth descriptions of all the major types of disabilities in a style that can be understood by parents and professionals alike. *$29.00*

688 pages
ISBN 1-55766 -02-2

2687 Children's Needs Psychological Perspective

National Association of School Psychologists
8455 Colesville Road
Suite 1000
Silver Spring, MD   20910   301-681-3223
                              FAX: 301-608-2514

This very popular monograph was developed with the recognition that many factors beyond the classroom and the child's own personal characteristics influence school success.

637 pages

2688 Choices: A Guide to Sex Counseling for the Physically Disabled Adult

Krieger Publishing Company
PO Box 9542
Melbourne, FL 32902   407-724-9542
FAX: 407-951-3671
e-mail: info@Krieger.pub.com
www.com/krieger-publishing

Maureen E. Neistadt & Maureen Freda, author

Provides rehabilitation professionals with the basic information necessary for limited sexuality counseling of physically disabled adults. *$9.95*

132 pages
ISBN 0-89464 -01-4

2689 Choosing Options and Accommodations for Children

Brookes Publishing
PO Box 10624
Baltimore, MD 21285   410-337-9580
800-638-3775
FAX: 410-337-8539
e-mail: custserv@brookespublishing.com
www.brookespublishing.com

Michael Glangreco, author

Bridging the gap between the philosophy and practice of inclusive education, this important manual provides a practical assessment and planning process for the inclusion of students with disabilities in general education classrooms. *$29.00*

192 pages
ISBN 1-55766 -06-5

2690 Classroom Success for the LD and ADHD Child

John F. Blair, Publisher
1406 Plaza Drive
Winston Salem, NC 27103   336-768-1374
800-222-9796
FAX: 336-768-9194
e-mail: blairpub@aol.com
www.blairpub.com

Suzanne H. Stevens, author

This book offers suggestions on teaching techniques, adapting texts, recognition of children with disabilities and testing, grading and mainstreaming the learning disabled and ADHD child. *$13.95*

314 pages Paperback
ISBN 0-895871-59-9

2691 Clinical Management of Childhood Stuttering, Second Edition

Pro-Ed
8700 Shoal Creek Boulevard
Austin, TX 78757
FAX: 512-451-8542
e-mail: proed1@aol.com

Meryl J. Wall & Florence L. Myers, author

Updates and integrates recent findings in childhood stuttering into a broad range of therapeutic strategies for assessing and treating the young dysfluent child. *$38.00*

336 pages
ISBN 0-89079 -02-5

2692 Cognitive Approaches to Learning Disabilities, Third Edition

Pro-Ed
8700 Shoal Creek Boulevard
Austin, TX 78757
FAX: 512-451-8542
e-mail: proed1@aol.com

D. Kim Reid, Wayne P. Hresko & H. Lee Swanson, author

The first to bridge the gap between cognitive psychology and information processing theory in understanding learning disabilities. *$39.00*

495 pages Hardcover
ISBN 0-89079 -85-8

2693 Collaborating for Comprehensive Services for Young Children and Families

Paul H. Brookes Publishing Company
PO Box 10624
Baltimore, MD 21285
800-638-3775
FAX: 410-337-8539

William Swan, author
Karen G. Radke, Marketing Director

Taking collaboration a step beyond basic implementation, this useful book shows agency and school leaders how to coordinate their efforts to stretch human services dollars while still providing quality programs. Provides the building blocks needed to establish a local interagency coordinating council. *$37.00*

272 pages 1992
ISBN 1-557661-03-0

2694 Collaboration in Special Education

Fearon/Janus
500 Harbor Boulevard
Belmont, CA 94002   650-631-2525

Carol Downs-Taylor, author

How parents, classroom teachers, and special education teachers can work as a cooperative educational team. *$12.90*

2695 Collaboration with Parents of Exceptional Children

CPPC
605 3rd Avenue
New York, NY 10158   212-476-9000
800-433-8234

Marvin J. Fine, author

Intended for both students and practicing professionals who are concerned with parental involvements in the life of the exceptional individual. School and community mental health workers and special education personnel should find this book extremely useful. *$42.50*

352 pages

2696 **Collaborative Teams for Students with Severe Disabilities: Second Edition**

Brookes Publishing
PO Box 10624
Baltimore, MD 21285   410-337-9580
                                          800-638-3775
                            FAX: 410-337-8539
e-mail: custserv@brookespublishing.com
www.brookespublishing.com
Beverly Rainforth, author

How can educators, parents and therapists work together to ensure the best possible educational experience for students with severe disabilities? This resource describes how a collaborative team can successfully create exciting learning opportunities for students, while teaching them to participate fully at home, school, work and play. *$30.00*

304 pages
ISBN 1-55766 -88-3

2697 **Communicating with Parents of Exceptional Children**

Love Publishing Company
4925 East Pacific Place
22353
Denver, CO 80222   303-221-7333
                            FAX: 303-221-7444
e-mail: lovepublishing@compuserve.com
Roger L. Kroth, author

This book shows how teachers can facilitate parent involvement with children's education. It presents the mirror model of parent involvement, family, dynamics, how to listen actively to parents, values and perceptions, problem-solving, parent conferences and training groups. *$19.95*

ISBN 0-89108 -67-4

2698 **Communication & Language Acquisition: Discoveries from Atypical Development**

Brookes Publishing
PO Box 10624
Baltimore, MD 21285   410-337-9580
                                          800-638-3775
                            FAX: 410-337-8539
e-mail: custserv@brookespublishing.com
www.brookespublishing.com

This text demonstrates how the study of language acquisition in children with atypical development promotes advances in basic theory. *$44.00*

352 pages Hardcover 1997
ISBN 1-557662-79-7

2699 **Communication Skills for Working with Elders**

Springer Publishing Company
536 Broadway
New York, NY 10012   212-431-4370
                            FAX: 212-941-7842
Barbara Bender Dreher, author

How aging and illness affects communication. *$17.95*

160 pages Softcover
ISBN 0-82615 -20-7

2700 **Communication Skills in Children with Down Syndrome**

Woodbine House
6510 Bells Mill Road
Bethesda, MD 20817
                            800-843-7323
                   www.woodbinehouse.com
Libby Kumin, Ph. D., CCC-SLP, author

An expert shares her knowledge of speech and language development in children and adolescents with Down syndrome. A wealth of accessible information and advice, plus practical home activities. *$14.95*

256 pages Paperback
ISBN 0-933149-53-0

2701 **Communication Unbound**

Teachers College Press
Columbia University
New York, NY 10027
                            800-575-6566
                   FAX: 212-678-4149
             www.tc.columbia.edu/tcpress
Douglas Biklen, author

Complete title is 'Communication Unbound: How Facilitated Communication is Challenging the Traditional Views of Autism and Ability/Disablity'. Reveals the wonder of expression by people who have therefore between trapped in silence and diminished by presumptions of their incompetence. *$18.95*

240 pages Paperback
ISBN 0-087737-21-4

2702 **Comprehensive Assessment in Special Education**

Charles C. Thomas, Publisher
2600 S 1st Street
Springfield, IL 62704   217-789-8980
                                          800-258-8980
                            FAX: 217-789-9130
             e-mail: books@ccthomas.com
A Rotatori, Senior Author, author
J. Miller, Author
R. Fox, Author
D. Sexton, Author

The purpose of this book is to incorporate (1) detailed approaches to assessment, (2) assessment fundamentals, (3) traditional and emerging assessment, (4) today's special assessment concerns. *$104.95*

578 pages Hardcover
ISBN 0-398056-45-5

2703 **Computer Access/Computer Learning**

Special Needs Project
3463 Stat Street
282
Santa Barbara, CA 93105
                            800-333-6867

A resource manual in adaptive technology and computer training. *$22.50*

2704 Consulting Psychologists Press

3803 E Bayshore Road
PO Box 10096
Palo Alto, CA   94303   650-964-3722
                               800-624-1765
                               FAX: 650-969-8608
                               www.cpp-db.com

Catalog offering job assessment software, career development reports, educational assessment information and books for the professional.

2705 Counseling Persons with Communication Disorders and Their Families

Pro-Ed
8700 Shoal Creek Boulevard
Austin, TX   78757
                               FAX: 512-451-8542
                               e-mail: proed1@aol.com
David M. Luterman, author

A learning manual for speech-language pathologists and audiologists on how to deal with the emotional issues facing them in their work with clients with communication disorders and their families. $ 29.00

187 pages
ISBN 0-89079 -80-7

2706 Craniosacral Therapy and SomatoEmotional Release: The Self Healing Body

SLACK
Thorofare, NJ

Carol J. Maneheim, author

Reviews types of patients and the process of craniosacral therapy.

2707 Creating Positive Classroom Environments: Strategies for Behavior Management

Brooks/Cole Publishing Company
511 Forest Lodge Road
Pacific Grove, CA   93950   831-373-0728
                               FAX: 831-375-6414
                               e-mail: bc-info@brookscole.com
Betty Epanchin, author

A hands-on text that offers an approach to classroom management that encourages situation-specific decision making. Presenting research-based information on how to establish an effective behavior management system in both regular and special education settings, the book centers on ways to help students manage their own behavior, rather than on ways their behavior can be managed by teachers, peers, parents or other adults.

448 pages Paperbound
ISBN 0-53422 -54-4

2708 Critical Voices on Special Education

State University of New York Press
90 State Street
Albany, NY   12207   518-472-5000
                               800-666-2211
                               FAX: 800-688-2877
                               e-mail: info@sunypress.edu
                               www.sunypress.edu
Scott B. Sigmon, author

Problems and progress concerning the mildly handicapped. $21.95

265 pages Paperback
ISBN 0-79140 -20-3

2709 Cultural Diversity, Families and the Special Education System

Teachers College Press
Columbia University
New York, NY   10027
                               800-575-6566
                               FAX: 212-678-4149
Beth Harry, author

This timely and thought-provoking book explores the quadruple disadvantage faced by the parents of poor, minority, handicapped children whose first language is not that of the school they attend. $22.95

296 pages Paperback
ISBN 0-807731-19-6

2710 Curriculum Decision Making for Students with Severe Handicaps

Teachers College Press
Columbia University
New York, NY   10027
                               800-575-6566
                               FAX: 212-678-4149
Sianne Ferguson, author

The inclusion of severely handicapped students within the scope of public education has brought about many changes for teachers in special education, this book helps the professional to distinguish which avenues are the best to take. *$17.95*

192 pages Paperback
ISBN 0-807728-61-6

2711 Deciphering the System: A Guide for Families of Young Disabled Children

Brookline Books
PO Box 1046
Cambridge, MA   02238   617-868-0360
                               800-666-2665
                               FAX: 617-868-1772
                               e-mail: brooklinebks@delphi.com
                               www.brooklinebooks.com
Paula J. Beckman & Gayle Beckman Boyes, author

This book informs parents of disabled children (0-5) of their rights and the service system, e.g., ways to manage the cumulating information, tips on IEP and IFSP meetings and the educational assessment process, and how parents can work with multiple service providers. It includes contributions from both parents and professionals who have experience with the service system. *$21.95*

Paperback
ISBN 0-91479 -87-5

2712 Defining Rehabilitation Agency Types

Mississippi State University
PO Box 6189
Mississippi State, MS   39762 601-325-2001
                               800-675-7782
                               FAX: 662-325-8989
                               TDY:601-325-8693
                               e-mail: rrtc@ra.state.edu
                               www.blind.msstate.edu

Talor, Madson, Johnson, Robertson, author
Kelly Schaefer, Dissemination Specialist

Relationships of participant selection and cost factors of service delivery across rehabilitation agency types. A national survey of state agencies for the blind was conducted to examine factors that define the characteristics of different agencies; similar programs were grouped together. Classification criteria were developed to distinguish agencies into logical groups based on line of authority, funding, and operating procedures. *$10.00*

15 pages Paperback

2713 Designing and Using Assistive Technology: The Human Perspective

Brookes Publishing
PO Box 10624
Baltimore, MD   21285   410-337-9580
                                   800-638-3775
                        FAX: 410-337-8539
        e-mail: custserv@brookespublishing.com
                www.brookespublishing.com

Presented here is a holistic perspective on how and why people choose and use AT. Features personal insights and the latest research on design and development. *$31.00*

352 pages Paperback 1998
ISBN 1-55766 -14-9

2714 Developing Cross-Cultural Competence:Guide to Working with Young Children & Their Families

Brookes Publishing
PO Box 10624
Baltimore, MD   21285   410-337-9580
                                   800-638-3775
                        FAX: 410-337-8539
        e-mail: custserv@brookespublishing.com
                www.brookespublishing.com
Eleanor W Lynch, author

This enlightening book perceptively and sensitively explores cultural, ethnic, and language diversity in human services. For those who work with families whose infants and young children may have or be at risk for a disability or chronic illness. (Second Edition) *$ 32.00*

448 pages Paperback
ISBN 1-55766 -31-9

2715 Developing Individualized Family Support Plans: A Training Manual

Brookline Books
PO Box 1047
Cambridge, MA   02238   617-868-0360
                                   800-666-2665
                        FAX: 617-868-1772
        e-mail: brooklinebks@delphi.com
                www.brooklinebooks.com
Tess Bennett, Lingerfelt, and Nelson, author

This manual provides in-service training coordinators, administrators, supervisors, and university personnel with a compact package of functional and practical methods to train professionals about implementing family-centered individualized family support plans (IFSP'S). Also, case studies provide concrete examples to aid in learning to write IFSP's. Paperback. *$24.95*

ISBN 0-91479 -69-7

2716 Developing Staff Competencies for Supporting People with Disabilities

Brookes Publishing
PO Box 10624
Baltimore, MD   21285   410-337-9580
                                   800-638-3775
                        FAX: 410-337-8539
        e-mail: custserv@brookesopublishing.com
                www.brookespublishing.com
James Gardner, author

This timely second edition, now in a new easier to read format, gives service providers helpful strategies for increasing effectiveness and maintaining well-being while working in the rewarding yet challenging field of human services. *$34.00*

480 pages Paperback
ISBN 1-55766 -07-3

2717 Development Director's Letter

CD Publications
8204 Fenton Street
Silver Spring, MD   20910   301-588-6380
                                       800-666-6380
                            FAX: 301-588-6385
            e-mail: ddl@cdpublications.com
                    www.cdpublications.com
Editor: Phaedra Brotherton, author
Mark Bradshaw, Product Manager

Grantseeking tips and strategies for nonprofit, government administrators, plus proved fundraising ideas. Includes grant application critiques, ho-to advice, and private and public funding updates. *$ 199.00*

8 pages Monthly pub.

2718 Development of Language

McGraw-Hill, School Publishing
220 East Danieldale Road
DeSoto, TX   75115   972-224-1111
                                800-442-9685
                     FAX: 972-228-1982
                     mhschool.com

An organizational book based on the developmental stages of language.

464 pages

2719 Developmental Diagnosis, Treatment

Books on Special Children
PO Box 305
Congers, NY   10920   845-638-1236
                      FAX: 845-638-0847
            e-mail: irene@boscbooks.com
Shoji Nishimura, author

Account of diagnosis and treatment of severely handicapped people of Japan. *$30.50*

209 pages Hardcover

2720 Developmental Disabilities of Learning

Gallery Bookshop
PO Box 270
Mendocino, CA   95460   707-937-2665

George S. Baroff, author

Manual for professionals on developmental and learning disabilities in the growing child. *$25.00*

224 pages Illustrated

2721 Developmental Disabilities of Learning2

Gallery Bookshop
PO Box 270
Mendocino, CA   95460   707-937-2665

George S. Baroff, author

Manual for professionals on developmental and learning disabilities in the growing child. Illustrated. $25.00

224 pages

2722 Developmental Disabilities: A Handbook for Occupational Therapists

Haworth Press
10 Alice Street
Binghamton, NY   13904   604-722-5857
                                800-429-6784
                          FAX: 607-722-6362
          e-mail: getinfo@haworthpressinc.com
                   www.haworthpressinc.com

Jerry A. Johnson and David Ethridge, author
Jackie Blakeslee, Advertising

Provides broad coverage of the spectrum of problems confronted by patients with developmental disabilities and the many kinds of occupational therapy services these individuals need. Experts identify exemplary institutional and community service programs for treating patients with autism, cerebral palsy, epilepsy, and mental retardation. $69.95

268 pages Hardcover
ISBN 0-866569-59-6

2723 Developmental Disabilities: A Handbook for Interdisciplinary Practice

Brookline Books
PO Box 1047
Cambridge, MA   02238   617-868-0360
                                800-666-2665
                          FAX: 617-868-1772
          e-mail: brooklinebks@delphi.com
                   www.brooklinebooks.com
Bruce A Thyer & Nancy P. Kropf, author

Successful interdisciplinary team practice for persons with developmental disabilities that require each team member to understand and respect the contributions of the others. This handbook explains the professions most often represented on interdisciplinary teams: their natures, concerns, and roles in the interdisciplinary context. $29.95

256 pages Paperback
ISBN 1-57129 -03-6

2724 Developmental Disabilities:A Handbook for Occupational Therapists

Haworth Press
10 Alice Street
Binghamton, NY   13904   604-722-5857
                                800-429-6784
                          FAX: 607-722-6362
          e-mail: getinfo@haworthpressinc.com
                   www.haworthpressinc.com

Jerry A. Johnson, author
Jackie Blakeslee, Advertising

Provides broad coverage of the spectrum of problems confronted by patients with developmental disabilities and the many kinds of occupational therapy services these individuals need. Experts identify exemplary institutional and community service programs for treating patients with autism, cerebral palsy, epilepsy, and mental retardation. $69.95

268 pages Hardcover
ISBN 0-86656 -59-6

2725 Developmental Variation and Learning Disorders

Educators Publishing Service
31 Smith Pl
Cambridge, MA   02138   617-367-2700
                                800-225-5750
                          FAX: 617-547-0412
                   www.epsbooks.com

Dr. Mel Levine, author

Discusses seven major areas of development and four major areas of academic proficiency and then ties this information together by examining factors that predispose a child to dysfunction and disability, offering guidelines to assessment and management, and analyzing long-range outcomes and factors that promote resiliency for parents, educators and clinicians. $69.00

640 pages Cloth
ISBN 0-838819-92-3

2726 Diagnosis and Treatment of Old Age

S Karger Publishers
26 W Avon Road
529
Unionville, CT   06085

T.A. Ban, author

These papers furnish a concise update on the diagnosis and treatment of Alzheimer's disease. $57.75

112 pages Hardcover
ISBN 3-80554 -44-3

2727 Digest of Neurology and Psychiatry

Institute of Living
400 Washington Street
Hartford, CT   06106   860-545-5555

Abstracts of selected current literature in psychiatry, neurology and related fields.

2728 Directory of College Facilities and Services for People with Disabilities, 4th Ed.

ORYX Press
4041 N Central Avenue
Suite 700
Phoenix, AZ   85012   602-265-2651
                              800-279-6799
                        FAX: 800-279-4663
          e-mail: info@oryxpress.com
                   www.oryxpress.com

William E. Burgess, author

Each profile in this guide reveals a complete picture of each campus facility, including the accessibility of classrooms, labs studios, dorms, dining facilities, gyms, student unions, libraries, and other buildings. Clearly noted are the levels of degree(s) granted, the number of students with disabilities enrolled, and the disability category represented. *$125.00*

> *Paperback*
> *ISBN 0-89774 -94-8*

2729 Directory of Medical Rehabilitation Programs

ORYX Press
4041 N Central Avenue
Suite 700
Phoenix, AZ   85012   **602-265-2651**
800-279-6799
FAX: 800-279-4663
e-mail: info@oryxpress.com

Describes nearly 1,500 programs in hospital-sponsored departments, private hospitals and freestanding clinics. Indexes list facilities by name, by type and by diagnosis treated. *$95.00*

> *376 pages*
> *ISBN 0-89774 -30-2*

2730 Directory of Residential Centers for Adult with Mental Illness

ORYX Press
4041 N Central Avenue
Suite 700
Phoenix, AZ   85012   **602-265-2651**
800-279-6799
FAX: 800-279-4663
e-mail: info@oryxpress.com

The services and programs of over 900 group homes, supervised apartment programs, crisis shelters and outpatient/day treatment centers. *$68.50*

> *328 pages*
> *ISBN 0-89774 -63-9*

2731 Directory of Residential Facilities for Emotionally Handicapped Children

ORYX Press
4041 N Central Avenue
Suite 700
Phoenix, AZ   85012   **602-265-2651**
800-279-6799
FAX: 800-279-4663
e-mail: info@oryxpress.com

Barbara Smiley Sherman, author

For the family or professional seeking a residential treatment facility, this resource is invaluable. *$74.50*

> *304 pages*
> *ISBN 0-89774 -07-1*

2732 Disability and Rehabilitation

Taylor & Francis
47 Runway Drive
 # G
Levittown, PA   19057

800-821-8312
FAX: 215-785-5515

Mike Hunninghake, Journals Representative

An international, multidisciplinary journal seeking to encourage a better understanding of all aspects of disability, and to promote the rehabilitation process. *$395.00*

> *Monthly*
> *ISSN 0963-82 8*

2733 Divided Legacy: A History of the Schism in Medical Thought, Volume 4: The Bacteriological Era

North Atlantic Press
Berkeley, CA

Harris Coulter, author

Concluding volume of Coulter's history of medical philosophy, from ancient times to today. Covers the orgins of bacteriology and immunology in world medicine; describes the clash between orthodox and alternative medicine.

> *1993*

2734 Dual Relationships in Counseling

American Association for Counseling & Development
5999 Stevenson Avenue
Alexandria, VA   22304   **703-823-9800**
800-347-6647

Barbara Hearlihy & Geruld Corey, author

This new book helps you draw on the collective wisdom and perspectives of 15 respected colleagues and will help you decide whether to accept a client, whether to reveal information, whether to refer a case, whether to consider factors you might not otherwise consider and how to deal with gifts, invitations and social situations. *$23.95*

> *244 pages*

2735 Dyslexia

Fearon/Janus
500 Harbor Boulevard
Belmont, CA   94002   **650-631-2525**

Robert E. Valett, author

Practical applications of current knowledge in diagnosing and educating dyslexic students, with more than 40 sensory-motor, visual, auditory, and multisensory learning models. *$19.50*

2736 Early Intervention, Implementing Child & Family Services for At-Risk Infants

Pro-Ed
8700 Shoal Creek Boulevard
Austin, TX   78757
FAX: 512-451-8542
e-mail: proed1@aol.com

Marci J. Hanson & Eleanor W. Lynch, author

New directions and recent legislation have produced a need for this guide which is designed for professionals facing the challenge of program development for disabled and at-risk infants, toddlers, and their families. *$36.00*

> *394 pages*
> *ISBN 0-890796-21-1*

2737 Ecology of Troubled Children

Brookline Books
PO Box 1047
Cambridge, MA   02238   617-868-0360
                               800-666-2665
                          FAX: 617-868-1772
          e-mail: brooklinebks@delphi.com
                 www.brooklinebooks.com

Richard L. Munger, author

Designed for frontline mental health clinicians working with children with serious emotional disturbances; shows how to make childrens' worlds more supportive by changing the places, activities, and people in their lives. *$24.95*

256 pages Paperback
ISBN 1-57129-50-8

2738 Edades y Etapas:Un Cuestionario Completado por los Padres para Evaluar al los Ninos

Brookes Publishing
PO Box 10624
Baltimore, MD   21285   410-337-9580
                               800-638-3775
                          FAX: 410-337-8539
       e-mail: custserv@brookespublishing.com
                 www.brookespublishing.com

Diane Bricker PhD, Jane Squires PhD, author

This easy to use child-monitoring system is available in Spanish. Consists of a step-by-step User's Guide in English and a set of questionnaires for Spanish-speaking families to complete. Thirty questions covering five developmental domains: gross motor, fine motor, communication, personal-social, and problem solving. *$165.00*

ISBN 1-557663-69-6

2739 Educating Children with Multiple Disabilities: A Transdisciplinary Approach, 3rd Ed

Brookes Publishing
PO Box 10624
Baltimore, MD   21285   410-337-9580
                               800-638-3775
                          FAX: 410-337-8539
       e-mail: custserv@brookespublishing.com
                 www.brookespublishing.com

Fred P. Orelove, author

Emphasizing transdisciplinary cooperation between teachers, therapists, nurses and parents, this book describes a general model and specific techniques for effectively educating children with multiple disabilities. *$29.00*

496 pages Paperback
ISBN 1-557662-46-0

2740 Educating Students Who Have Visual Impairments with Other Disabilities

Brookes Publishing
PO Box 10624
Baltimore, MD   21285   410-337-9580
                               800-638-3775
                          FAX: 410-337-8539
       e-mail: custserv@brookespublishing.com
                 www.brookespublishing.com

This introductory text provides techniques for facilitating functional learning in students with a wide range of visual impairments and multiple disabilities. With a concentration on educational needs and learning styles, the authors of this multidisciplinary volume demonstrate functional assessment and teaching adaptations that will improve students' inclusive learning experiences. *$49.95*

552 pages Paperback
ISBN 1-557662-80-0

2741 Educating all Students in the Mainstream

Paul H. Brookes Publishing Company
PO Box 10624
Baltimore, MD   21285
                               800-638-3775
                          FAX: 410-337-8539

Susan Stainback, author

Incorporating the research and viewpoints of both regular and special educators, this textbook provides an effective approach for modifying, expanding, and adjusting regular education to meet the needs of all students. *$34.00*

304 pages 1989
ISBN 1-557660-22-0

2742 Education and Deafness

Longman Publishing Group
95 Church Street
White Plains, NY   10601   914-993-5000

This comprehensive introduction to educating students with hearing impairments provides extensive coverage of the interrelated issues that affect the teaching of these students. It concentrates on the severely to profoundly hearing impaired but includes an entire chapter devoted to students whose impairments are less severe (hard-of-hearing students).

320 pages Paperback 1990
ISBN 0-801300-26-6

2743 Education of Students with Phenylketonuria (PKU)

Nat'l Institute of Child Health/Human Development
Bethesda, MD   20892

Offers information for teachers, administrators and other school personnel.

2744 Educational Audiology for the Limited Hearing and Preschooler: Auditory-Verbal Program

Charles C. Thomas, Publisher
2600 South 1st Street
Springfield, IL 62704
217-789-8980
800-258-8980
e-mail: books@ccthomas.com

Doreen Pollack, Author
Donald Goldberg, Author
Nancy Coleffe, Author

Offers information to the special education professional regarding the management of the deaf infant or preschooler. Also available in cloth at $86.95 (ISBN# 0-398-06750-3) *$66.95*

410 pages Softcover
ISBN 0-39806 -28-1

2745 Educational Dimensions of Acquired Brain Injury

Pro-Ed
8700 Shoal Creek Boulevard
Austin, TX 78757
FAX: 512-451-8542
e-mail: proed1@aol.com

Ronald C. Savage, Author
Gary F. Wolcott, Author

This book is a compilation of the working experiences of the professionals concerned about the educational dimensions of acquired brain injury. *$43.00*

574 pages Hardcover
ISBN 0-89079 -98-3

2746 Educational Intervention for the Student with Multiple Disabilities

Charles C. Thomas, Publisher
2600 South 1st Street
Springfield, IL 62704
217-789-8980
800-258-8980
FAX: 217-789-9130
e-mail: books@ccthomas.com

Donna Irons-Reavis, Author

This text will assist those who want to teach severely, multiply disabled students by providing information on general principles of education and classroom organization and managing the behavior of students. Also available in cloth $34.95 (ISBN# 0-398-05793-1) *$24.95*

140 pages Softcover
ISBN 0-398061-73-4

2747 Educational Prescriptions

Educators Publishing Service
31 Smith Plaza
Cambridge, MA 02138
617-367-2700
800-225-5750
FAX: 617-547-0412
www.epsbooks.com

Lynne Meltzer, Author
Bethany Solomon, Author

This book provides specific recommendations for the classroom management of students who are experiencing subtle developmental and/or learning difficulties. Intended for regular classroom teachers, specific examples of accommodations teachers can make are provided for grades 1-3 and 4-6. *$13.50*

64 pages
ISBN 0-838819-90-7

2748 Effective Instruction for Special Education, Second Edition

Pro-Ed
8700 Shoal Creek Boulevard
Austin, TX 78757
FAX: 512-451-8542
e-mail: proed1@aol.com

Margo A. Mastropieri & Thomas E. Scruggs, author

This exciting and wide-ranging book provides special educators with effective methods for teaching students with mild and moderate learning and behavioral problems, as well as for teaching remedial students in general. *$37.00*

419 pages Paperback
ISBN 0-89079 -72-0

2749 Effectively Educating Handicapped Students

Longman Publishing Group
95 Church Street
White Plains, NY 10601
914-993-5000

Barbara Luetke-Stahlman, author

For teachers in training and practitioners who will work with deaf and hearing impaired students in preschool and elementary programs. A developmental approach provides the foundation for the proposed intervention methods: Preparing for instruction: Language, speech, audition and speechreading: Effective strategies for teaching academics to students with hearing impairments.

468 pages Paperback 1991
ISBN 0-801303-17-6

2750 Emotional Problems of Childhood and Adolescence

McGraw-Hill, School Publishing
220 East Danieldale Road
DeSoto, TX 75115
972-224-1111
800-442-9685
FAX: 972-228-1982
mhschool.com

For future special educators, psychologists and others who work with emotionally disturbed children and adolescents.

2751 Employment in the Mainstream

Mainstream
6930 Carroll Avenue
Suite 240
Takoma Park, MD 20912
301-891-8777
FAX: 301-891-8777
TDY:301-891-8777
e-mail: info@mainstreaminc.org
www.mainstreaminc.org

Fritz Rumpel, Editor, author

Reports on practical and legal issues affecting people with disabilities in the workplace. *$25.00*

32 pages Quarterly

2752 Enabling & Empowering Families: Principles & Guidelines for Practice

Brookline Books
PO Box 1047
Cambridge, MA 02238   617-868-0360
    800-666-2665
FAX: 617-868-1772
e-mail: brooklinebks@delphi.com
www.brooklinebooks.com

Carol Dunst, Carol Trivette, Angela Deal, author

This book was written for practioners who must work with families but who have insufficient training in family systems assessment and intervention. The authors' system enables professionals to help the family identify its needs, locate the formal and informal resources to meet these needs, and develop the abilities to effectively access these resources. *$24.95*

220 pages Paperback
ISBN 0-91479 -59-

2753 Enhancing Self-Concepts and Achievement of Mildly Handicapped Students

Charles C. Thomas, Publisher
2600 South 1st Street
Springfield, IL 62704   217-789-8980
    800-258-8980
FAX: 217-789-9130
e-mail: books@ccthomas.com

Carroll J. Jones, Author

This book is aimed towards students who are learning disabled, mildly mentally retarded, and who have behavior disorders. Individuals should be aware that unless they appreciate and understand themselves, it is difficult to relate to the world around them. This is no less true of exceptional than nonhandicapped learners. This book provides a wonderfully complete window of insight into the most tenuous of human aspects, the self-concept. Also available in cloth at $55.95 (ISBN# 0-398-05760-5) *$39.95*

294 pages Paperback
ISBN 0-398061-91-2

2754 Evaluation and Educational Programming of Deaf-Blind/Severly Multihandicapped Students

Charles C. Thomas, Publisher
2600 South 1st Street
Springfield, IL 62704   217-789-8980
    800-258-8980
e-mail: books@ccthomas.com

Carroll J. Jones, author

Offers information on the special education of deaf-blind students. Also available in cloth at $65.95 (ISBN# 0-398-05515-7) *$ 41.95*

314 pages Softcover
ISBN 0-398061-92-0

2755 Evaluation and Treatment of the Psychogeriatric Patient

Haworth Press
10 Alice Street
Binghamton, NY 13904   604-722-5857
    800-429-6784
FAX: 607-722-6362
e-mail: getinfo@haworthpressinc.com
www.haworthpressinc.com

Diane Gibson, MS, OTR, author
Jackie Blakeslee, Advertising

This pertinent book assists occupational therapists and other health care providers in developing up-to-date psychogeriatric programs and understands details of treating the cognitively impaired elderly. *$69.95*

111 pages Hardcover
ISBN 1-560240-52-0

2756 Exercise Activities for the Elderly

Springer Publishing Company
536 Broadway
New York, NY 10012   212-431-4370
FAX: 212-941-7842

Kay Flatten, author

A variety of exercises geared to clients with such conditions as arthritis, diabetes and Parkinson's disease, and others which are designed to build up muscular strength and maintain flexibility. *$23.95*

240 pages Softcover
ISBN 0-82615 -10-9

2757 Facilitating Self Care Practices in the Elderly

Haworth Press
10 Alice Street
Binghamton, NY 13904   604-722-5857
    800-429-6784
FAX: 607-722-6362
e-mail: getinfo@haworthpressinc.com
www.haworthpressinc.com

Barbara J. Horn, PhD, RN, author
Jackie Blakeslee, Advertising

This up-to-date book is a synthesis of current knowledge from published sources and expert consultants relating to three commonly occurring problems in home health care practice: self-administration of medications, family caregiving issues, and teaching the elderly. *$ 69.95*

185 pages Hardcover
ISBN 1-560240-13-X

2758 Family Assessment in Early Intervention

Books on Special Children
PO Box 305
Congers, NY 10920   845-638-1236
FAX: 845-638-0847
e-mail: irene@boscbooks.com

D.B. Bailey, Jr., author

Includes sources and measure used for assessment, strengths and weaknesses of families and comparisons between typical families and handicapped families. *$37.95*

280 pages Softcover

2759 Family-Centered Early Intervention with Infants and Toddlers

Paul H. Brookes Publishing Company
PO Box 10624
Baltimore, MD 21285   800-638-3775
FAX: 410-337-8539

Wesley Brown, author
Karen G. Radke, Marketing Director

This informative text provides professionals with insight and practical guidelines to help fulfill the federal requirements for provision of early intervention services. *$37.00*

> *368 pages Hardcover 1993*
> *ISBN 1-557661-24-3*

2760 Focal Group Psychotherapy

New Harbinger Publications
5674 Shattuck Avenue
Oakland, CA 94609
800-748-6273
www.newharbinger.com
Matthew McKay PhD and Kim Paley PhD, author
Lauren Dockett, Publicity Director

The definitive guide to leading brief, theme-based groups. This book offers an extensive week-by-week description of the basic concepts and interventions for 14 theme or focal groups. *$59.95*

> *544 pages Hardcover*
> *ISBN 1-879237-18-0*

2761 Free Hand: Enfranchising the Education of Deaf Children

TJ Publishers
817 Silver Spring Avenue
Suite 206
Silver Spring, MD 20910
301-585-4440
800-999-1168
FAX: 301-585-5930
e-mail: TJPubinc@aol.com
Margaret Walworth/Donald Moores/Terrence O'Rourke, author
Angela K Thames, President
Jerald A Murphy, Vice President

In August 1990, a select group of nationally prominent educators, linguists and researchers met at Hofstra University to consider the most vital and controversial question in education of the deaf: What role should ASl play in the classroom? Become part of that discussion with A Free Hand. *$16.95*

> *204 pages Softcover*
> *ISBN 0-93266 -40-X*

2762 Functional Assessment Inventory Manual

Stout Vocational Rehab Institute
University of Wisconsin-Stout
Menomonie, WI 54751
715-232-1342
FAX: 715-232-2356
e-mail: botterbuschd@uwstout.edu
Crewe, N. and Athelstan, G., author
Ronald R Fry, Manager
Darlene Botterbusch, Program Assistant

The Functional Assessment is a systematic enumeration of a client's vocationally relevant strengths and limitations. *$12.00*

> *96 pages Paperback*
> *ISBN 0-916671-53-4*

2763 Global Perspectives on Disability: A Curriculum

Mobility International USA
PO Box 10767
Eugene, OR 97440
541-343-1284
FAX: 541-343-6812
TDY:541-343-1284
e-mail: info@miusa.org
www.miusa.org
Susan Sygall, Executive Director
Rhonda Neuhaus, Public Relations Coordinator

Designed for secondary and higher education instructors. Includes five lesson plans covering disability awareness, disability rights and international perspectives on disability. Available in alternative formats. *$40.00*

2764 Glossary of Terminology for Vocational Assessment/Evaluation/Work

Rehabilitation Resource University
University of Wisconsin-Stout
Menomonie, WI 54751
715-232-1478
FAX: 715-232-2356
Ronald R. Fry, Manager
Darlene Botterbusch, Program Assistant

This glossary contains 254 terms and their definitions. Primary focus is on the terminology related to the practice and professionals of vocational assessment, vocational evaluation and work adjustment. *$9.50*

> *40 pages Softcover*

2765 HIV Infection and Developmental Disabilities

Paul H. Brookes Pulishing Company
PO Box 10624
Baltimore, MD 21285
800-638-3775
FAX: 410-337-8539
Karen G. Radke, Marketing Director

A resource for service providers pinpointing the most crucial medical, legal and educational issues to control HIV infection. *$47.00*

> *320 pages*
> *ISBN 1-557660-83-2*

2766 Handbook for Implementing Workshops for Siblings of Special Children

Special Needs Project
3463 Stat Street
 # 282
Santa Barbara, CA 93105
800-333-6867

Based on three years of professional experience, this handbook provides guidelines and techniques for those who wish to start and conduct workshops for siblings. *$40.00*

2767 Handbook for Speech Therapy

Psychological & Educational Publications
PO Box 520
Hydesville, CA 95547
707-768-1807
800-523-5775
Vee Medlin, author

This basic handbook for beginning speech teachers shows how speech sounds are made and how to correct any errors in their students.

2768 Handbook for the Special Education Administrator

Edwin Mellen Press
PO Box 450
Lewiston, NY 14092   716-754-2789
800-753-2788
FAX: 716-754-4056
e-mail: mellen@wzrd.com

Arthur R. Crowell, Jr., author

Organization and procedures for special education. *$49.95*

96 pages Hardcover
ISBN 0-88946 -22-9

2769 Handbook of Developmental Education

Greenwood Publishing Group
88 Post Road West
5007
Westport, CT 06880   203-226-3571
FAX: 203-222-1502
www.greenwood.com

Robert M. Hashway, author

This comprehensive handbook has brought together the leading practitioners and researchers in the field of developmental education to focus on the developmental learning agenda. Hardcover.

400 pages $65 - $75
ISBN 0-275932-97-4

2770 Handbook on Supported Education for People with Mental Illness

Brookes Publishing
PO Box 10624
Baltimore, MD 21285   410-337-9580
800-638-3775
FAX: 410-337-8539
e-mail: custserv@brookespublishing.com
www.brookespublishing.com

Karen V. Unger, Ed.D., M.S.W., author

Here you will find all necessary information that mental health professionals need in order to provide supported education services. There are specific suggestions on how to help people with mental illness return to or remain in college, trade school, or GED programs. Also addressed are funding and legal issues, accommodations, and specific interventions.

208 pages Paperback 1998
ISBN 1-55766-52-1

2771 Head Injury Rehabilitation: Children

Taylor & Francis
47 Runway Drive
G
Levittown, PA 19057
FAX: 215-785-5515

M. Ylvisaker, author

Rehabilitation guide for the help of children or adolescents that have suffered brain injury.

460 pages Cloth
ISBN 0-85066 -67-1

2772 Health Care Management in Physical Therapy

Charles C. Thomas, Publisher
2600 S 1st Street
Springfield, IL 62704   217-789-8980
800-258-8980
FAX: 217-789-9130
e-mail: books@ccthomas.com

Mark Brimer, Author

The focus of this book is on physical therapists as supervisors in health care settings of hospitals, nursing homes, home health agencies and in private practice. *$62.95*

328 pages Hardcover
ISBN 0-39805 -42-0

2773 Health Care Management in Physical Therapy

Charles C. Thomas, Publisher
2600 S 1st Street
Springfield, IL 62704   217-789-8980
800-258-8980
e-mail: books@ccthomas.com

Mark Brimer, author

The focus of this book is on physical therapists as supervisors in health care settings of hospitals, nursing homes, home health agencies and in private practice. Also in paper at $42.95 (ISBN# 0-398-06032-0) *$62.95*

328 pages Hardcover
ISBN 0-398056-42-0

2774 Health Care for Students with Disabilities

Paul H. Brookes Publishing Company
PO Box 10624
Baltimore, MD 21285   800-638-3775
FAX: 410-337-8539

J. Carolyn Graff, author
Karen G. Radke, Marketing Director

This practical guidebook provides detailed descriptions of the 16 health-related procedures most likely to be needed in the classroom by students with disabilities. *$25.00*

304 pages Paperback 1990
ISBN 1-557660-37-9

2775 Helping Learning Disabled Gifted Children Learn Through Compensatory Play

Charles C. Thomas, Publisher
2600 S 1st Street
Springfield, IL 62704   217-789-8980
800-258-8980
FAX: 217-789-9130
e-mail: books@ccthomas.com

James H. Humphrey, Author

About 3% of the school population is gifted and 5 to 8% of this number suffer from learning disabilities. These children experience a great deal more trauma than the normal child. Also available in cloth at $36.95 (ISBN# 0-398-05695-1) *$24.95*

164 pages Softcover
ISBN 0-398061-62-9

2776 Helping Students Grow

American College Testing Program
2201 Dodge
168
Iowa City, IA 52243   319-337-1000

James Humphrey, author

Designed to assist counselors in using the wealth of information generated by the ACT Assessment.

2777 Helping Students Succeed in the Regular Class

Jossey-Bass
350 Sansome Street
San Francisco, CA 94104   415-394-8677

Joseph E. Zins, author

The first book in a series from Jossey-Bass on psychoeducational interventions. Shows how to develop programs to help learning impaired, handicapped and other students within the regular classroom situation and avoid costly and often ineffective special education classes. Details the aspects and goals of intervention assistance programs - which use the collaborative consultation as an integral part of the educational system and presents both research and theory to show their benefits. *$26.95*

ISBN 1-55542 -96-6

2778 How to Teach Spelling/How to Spell

Educators Publishing Service
31 Smith Place
Cambridge, MA 02138   617-367-2700
                               800-225-5750
                          FAX: 617-547-0412
                          www.epsbooks.com

Laura Toby Rudginsky, Author
Elizabeth Haskell, Author

This is a comprehensive resource manual based on the Orton-Gillingham approach to reading and spelling. It recommends what and how much to teach at each grade level at the beginning of each lesson or section. There are four student manuals that accompany this. *$22.50*

Teachers Manual
ISBN 0-838818-47-1

2779 Human Exceptionality: Society, School, and Family, 6th Edition

Allyn & Bacon
160 Gould Street
Needham Heights, MA 02494   781-455-1200
                                    800-852-8024

Michael L. Hardman, author

This text is a comprehensive, well-balanced and objective presentation of the major topics and issues that make up an introductory course. After considering the foundations of the field of special education, the authors examine the definitions, classification, prevalence and characteristics of each category of exceptionality.

615 pages
ISBN 0-20528 -39-0

2780 I Heard That!

Alexander Graham Bell Association of the Deaf
3417 Volta Place NW
Washington, DC 20007   202-337-5220
                          FAX: 202-337-8314
                          TDY:202-337-5220
                     e-mail: lquigley@agbell.org
                          www.agbell.org

Winifred H. Northcott, Ph. D, author
Elizabeth Quigley, Director of Publications

Provides a framework for teachers, clinicians and parents when writing objectives and designing activities to develop listening skills in children with hearing loss from newborn to 3 years. *$7.95*

36 pages

2781 I Heard That!2

Alexander Graham Bell Association of the Deaf
3417 Volta Place NW
Washington, DC 20007   202-337-5220
                          FAX: 202-337-8314
                     e-mail: agbell2@aol.com
                          www.agbell.org

Winifred H. Northcott, Ph. D, author
Elizabeth Quigley, Director of Publications

Provides a framework for teachers, clinicians and parents when writing objectives and designing activities to develop listening skills in children who are deaf or hard of hearing. *$7.95*

36 pages

2782 Images of the Disabled, Disabling Images

Greenwood Publishing Group
88 Post Road West
5007
Westport, CT 06880   203-226-3571
                        FAX: 203-222-1502
                        www.greenwood.com

Alan Gartner and Tom Foe, author

Combines an examination of the presentation of persons with disabilities in literature, film and the media with an analysis of the ways in which these images are expressed in public policy concerning the disabled. *$55.00*

227 pages Hardcover
ISBN 0-275921-78-6

2783 Implementing Family-Centered Services in Early Intervention

Brookline Books
PO Box 1047
Cambridge, MA 02238   617-868-0360
                               800-666-2665
                          FAX: 617-868-1772
                 e-mail: brooklinebks@delphi.com
                     www.brooklinebooks.com

Donald B Bailey, McWilliams, Winton, Simeonson, author

This book describes a team-based decision-making workshop for implementing family-centered services in early interventions. Unlike a training curriculum, it focuses on the decisions that teams must make as they seek to become family-centered. *$19.95*

180 pages Paperback
ISBN 0-91479 -62-

2784 Including All of Us: An Early Childhood Curriculum About Disability

Educational Equity Concepts
114 East 32nd Street
New York, NY 10016   212-686-2531
FAX: 212-725-0947
TDY:212-725-1803
e-mail: information@equity.org
www.edequity.org

Merle Froschl, Linda Colon, Ellen Rubin, author
Barbara Sprung, Author

The first nonsexist, multicultural, mainstreamed curriculum. Step-by-step activities incorporate disability into three curriculum areas: Same/Different (hearing impairment), Body Parts (visual impairment), and Transportation (mobility impairment). $14.95

144 pages
ISBN 0-93162 -00-4

2785 Including Students with Severe and Multiple Disabilites in Typical Classrooms

Brookes Publishing
PO Box 10624
Baltimore, MD 21285   410-337-9580
800-638-3775
FAX: 410-337-8539
e-mail: custserv@brookespublishing.com
www.brookespublishing.com

June W. Downing, Ph.D., author

This straightforward and jargon gree resource gives instructors the guidance needed to educate learners who have one or more sensory impairments in addition to cognitive and physical disabilities. $32.95

224 pages Paperback
ISBN 1-55766 -39-8

2786 Including Students with Special Needs: A Practical Guide for Classroom Teachers, 2nd Ed.

Allyn & Bacon
160 Gould Street
Needham Heights, MA 02494   781-455-1200
800-852-8024

Marilyn Friend, William D. Bursuck, author

This book is designed for a mainstreaming/inclusion course taken by general education teacher trainees.

544 pages
ISBN 0-20528 -85-4

2787 Inclusive & Heterogeneous Schooling: Assessment, Curriculum, and Instruction

Brookes Publishing
PO Box 10624
Baltimore, MD 21285   410-337-9580
800-638-3775
FAX: 410-337-8539
e-mail: custserv@brookespublishing.com
www.brookespublishing.com

Presents methods for successfully restructuring classrooms to enable all students, particularly those with disabilities, to flourish. Provides specific strategies for assessment, collaboration, classroom management, and age-specific instruction. $34.95

448 pages Paperback
ISBN 1-55766 -02-9

2788 Information & Referral Center

Mississippi State University
PO Box 6189
Mississippi State, MS 39762   601-325-2001
800-675-7782
FAX: 662-325-8989
e-mail: rrtc@ra.msstate.edu
www.blind.msstate.edu

B.J. LeJune, Training Associate I
Kelly Schaefer, Editor

A comprehensive website that includes information about client assistance programs, vocational rehabilitation agencies, low vision clinics, and information about blindness and low vision. $25.00

150 pages

2789 Instructional Methods for Students

Allyn & Bacon
160 Gould Street
Needham Heights, MA 02194   800-852-8024

Patrick Joseph Schloss, author

Instructional methods for students with learning and behavior problems.

450 pages 1986

2790 Interactions: Collaboration Skills for School Professionals

Longman Education/Addison Wesley
95 Church Street
White Plains, NY 10601   914-328-2090
800-322-1377
FAX: 800-333-3328
www.longman.awl.com

Marilyn Friend, Lynne Cook, author

Shows school professionals how to develop and use the skills necessary for effective collaboration among teachers, school support staff, and parents of children with special needs. $35.00

270 pages Paperback
ISBN 0-80131 -21-2

2791 Interpreting Disability: A Qualitative Reader

Teachers College Press
Columbia University
New York, NY 10027   800-575-6566
FAX: 212-678-4149

Philip M. Ferguson, author

This book offers a collection of exemplary qualitative research affecting people with disabilities and their families. Instead of focusing upon methodological details, the chapters illustrate the variety of styles and formats that interpretive research can adopt in reporting its results. $24.95

328 pages Paperback
ISBN 0-807731-21-8

2792 Intervention Research in Learning Disabilities

Gallery Bookshop
PO Box 270
Mendocino, CA 95460   707-937-2665

Thomas E. Scruggs, author

Based on the Symposium on Intervention Research, this volume presents 12 papers addressing issues in intervention research, academic interventions, social and behavioral interventions. *$30.00*

347 pages

2793 Intervention Research in Learning 2 Disabilities

Gallery Bookshop
PO Box 270
Mendocino, CA 95460   707-937-2665

Thomas E. Scruggs, author

Based on the Symposium on Intervention Research, this volume presents 12 papers addressing issues in intervention research, academic interventions, social and behavioral interventions. *$30.00*

347 pages

2794 Introducing Students to Careers in Special Education and Related Services

Council for Exceptional Children
1920 Association Drive
Reston, VA 20191   703-620-3660
                          888-232-7232
                   FAX: 703-264-9494
         e-mail: service@cec.sped.org
                    www.cec.sped.org

Cathy Mack, Production Manager

Presents an array of activities appropriate for high school and college students to engage in to find out how it feels to be disabled. *$5.00*

25 pages
ISBN 0-86586-30-3

2795 Introduction to Learning Disabilities

Allyn & Bacon
160 Gould Street
Needham Heights, MA 02494   781-455-1200
                                   800-852-8024

Daniel P. Hallahan, Author
James M. Kauffman, Author
John W. Lloyd, Author

This is a thorough introduction to the area of learning disabilities. It covers the basic characteristics, causes, intervention approaches, theories and issues pertaining to the learning disabled.

608 pages
ISBN 0-20529-43-4

2796 Introduction to Mental Retardation

Allyn & Bacon
160 Gould Street
Needham Heights, MA 02194
                          800-852-8024

David L. Westling, author

A thorough overview of mental retardation with a level of knowledge suitable for an undergraduate or beginning graduate student.

350 pages Casebound 1986
ISBN 0-148792-79-

2797 Introduction to Special Education: Teaching in an Age of Challenge

Allyn & Bacon
160 Gould Street
Needham Heights, MA 02494   781-455-1200
                                   800-852-8024

Deborah Deutsch Smith, author

This intro text maintains all people first orientation with an emphasis on children with disabilities and their education. It also firmly believes that families must be involved in all aspects of their children's educational programs.

646 pages
ISBN 0-20526-94-4

2798 Issues and Practices in Special Education

Longman Publishing Group
95 Church Street
White Plains, NY 10601   914-993-5000

Donald S. Marozas, author

Utilizes current literature, classic articles and case histories to examine such topics as: withholding treatment from severely defective newborns, plastic surgery for Down Syndrome, handicapped offenders and AIDS.

290 pages Paperback 1988
ISBN 0-582286-39-5

2799 Issues and Research in Special Education

Teachers College Press
Columbia University
New York, NY 10027   800-575-6566
                            FAX: 212-678-4149

Robert Gaylord-Ross, author

Provides up-to-date research and discourse on a wide range of topics affecting professionals in the field of special education. *$38.00*

264 pages Hardcover
ISBN 0-807731-95-1

2800 Kendall Demonstration Elementary School Curriculum Guides

Gallaudet University Bookstore
800 Florida Avenue NE
Washington, DC 20002   202-651-5000
                              800-451-1073
                        FAX: 202-651-5489

These guides provide detailed information to help teachers organize curriculums and education programs. Pre-school: $15.95, Health: $8.95, Language Arts: $13.75, Social Studies: $14.95, Math: $11.95, Science: $17.95, Auditory & Speech: $10.95.

2801 Language Arts: Detecting Special Needs

Allyn & Bacon
160 Gould Street
Needham Heights, MA 02194
                          800-852-8024

Joyce S. Choate, author

Describes special language arts needs of special learners.

180 pages 1989
ISBN 0-205116-36-1

2802 Language Disabilities in Children and Adolescents

McGraw-Hill, School Publishing
220 East Danieldale Road
DeSoto, TX   75115   972-224-1111
                           800-442-9685
                      FAX: 972-228-1982
                           mhschool.com

A comprehensive review of research in language disabilities.

2803 Language Learning Practices with Deaf Children

Pro-Ed
8700 Shoal Creek Boulevard
Austin, TX   78757
                      FAX: 512-451-8542
                  e-mail: proed1@aol.com

Patricia L. McAnally, Susan Rose & Stephen Quigley, author

This new edition describes the variety of language-development theories and practices used with deaf children without advocating anyone. *$38.00*

> *321 pages Hardcover*
> *ISBN 0-89079-97-5*

2804 Language and Communication Disorders in Children

McGraw-Hill, School Publishing
220 East Danieldale Road
DeSoto, TX   75115   972-224-1111
                           800-442-9685
                      FAX: 972-228-1982
                           mhschool.com

Comprehensive coverage encompassing all aspects of children's language disorders.

> *512 pages*

2805 Learning Disabilities: Concepts and Characteristics

McGraw-Hill, School Publishing
220 East Danieldale Road
DeSoto, TX   75115   972-224-1111
                           800-442-9685
                      FAX: 972-228-1982
                           mhschool.com

Covers the conceptual basis of learning disabilities, identification, etiology and diagnosis.

> *448 pages*

2806 Learning Disability: Social Class and the Cons. of Inequality In American Ed.

Greenwood Publishing Group
88 Post Road West
5007
Westport, CT   06880   203-226-3571
                         FAX: 203-222-1502
                         www.greenwood.com

James Carrier, author

Presents a detailed historical description of the social and educational assumptions integral to the idea of learning disability.

> *167 pages $43.95 - $47.95*
> *ISBN 0-313253-96-X*

2807 Learning and Individual Differences

National Association of School Psychologists
8455 Colesville Road
Suite 1000
Silver Spring, MD   20910   301-681-3223
                              FAX: 301-608-2514

A multidisciplinary journal in education.

2808 Learning to See: American Sign Language as a Second Language

Gallaudet University Press
11030 S Langley Avenue
Chicago, IL   60628
                           800-621-2736
                      FAX: 800-621-8476
                      TDY:800-621-9347
                      gupress.gallaudet.edu

Sherman Wilcox, Co-Author
Phyliss Wilcox, Co-Author

This important book has been updated to help teachers teach American Sign Language as a second language, including information on Deaf culture, the history and structure of ASL, teaching methods and issues facing educators. *$19.95*

> *160 pages Softcover*

2809 Legal-Ethical Considerations, Restrictions and Obligations for Clinicians

Charles C. Thomas, Publisher
2600 S 1st Street
Springfield, IL   62704   217-789-8980
                             800-258-8980
                        FAX: 217-789-9130
                   e-mail: books@ccthomas.com

Franklin H. Silverman, author

Legal-Ethical Considerations, Restrictions and Obligations for Clinicians who Treat Communicative Disorders is a clinical functioning of speech-language pathologists and audiologists is determined not only by their clinical skills but by their awareness of the legal-ethical restrictions and obligations they are required by law to consider in their relationships with their clients and their families *$51.95*

> *258 pages Softcover*
> *ISBN 0-39806-29-6*

2810 Library Guide to Serving the Disabled

McFarland & Company
PO Box 611
Jefferson, NC   28640   336-246-4460
                           800-253-2187

Keith C. Wright and Judith F. Davie, author

Information for library staff on hiring and serving disabled persons. *$35.00*

> *171 pages Illustrated*
> *ISBN 0-89950-16-3*

2811 Life Beyond the Classroom: Transition Strategies for Young People: 2nd Edition

Brookes Publishing
PO Box 10624
Baltimore, MD   21285   410-337-9580
                            800-638-3775
                       FAX: 410-337-8539
          e-mail: custserv@brookespublishing.com
                       www.brookespublishing.com

Paul Wehman, author

This textbook is an essential guide to planning, designing, and implementing successful transition programs for students with disabilities. *$44.00*

496 pages
ISBN 1-55766 -05-7

2812 Life-Span Approach to Nursing Care for Individuals with Developmental Disabilities

Brookes Publishing
PO Box 10624
Baltimore, MD   21285   410-337-9580
                              800-638-3775
               FAX: 410-337-8539
e-mail: custserv@brookespublishing.com
www.brookespublishing.com

This reference book was written by and for nurses. This guide addresses fundamental nursing issues such as health promotion, infection control, seizure management, adaptive and assistive technology, and sexuality. Also offered are in-depth case studies, helpful charts and tables, and problem-solving strategies. *$49.95*

464 pages Hardcover
ISBN 1-557661-51-0

2813 Lipreading for Children

Health Publishing Company
PO Box 3805
San Francisco, CA   94119   415-282-8585
                    FAX: 415-750-6550
George S. Haspiel, Ph.D., author

Collection of games, activities and stories has been used for many years by teachers, educational therapists and language audiologists working with hearing impaired children. *$19.25*

2814 Look Now, Hear This: Combined Auditory Training and Speechreading Instruction

Charles C. Thomas, Publisher
2600 S 1st Street
Springfield, IL   62704   217-789-8980
                                800-258-8980
           e-mail: books@ccthomas.com
Janet Jeffers and Margaret Barley, author

A manual on combined auditory training and speech reading instruction. Also available in cloth at $42.95 (ISBN# 0-398-03830-9) *$30.95*

230 pages Softcover
ISBN 0-398061-81-5

2815 MA Report

National Allergy and Asthma Network
3554 Chain Bridge Road
Suite 200
Fairfax, VA   22030   703-385-4403
                    FAX: 703-352-4354

Offers information on medical breakthroughs, patient care, public awareness, activities and events focusing on the allergy and asthma patient. This newsletter is the only Monthly Asthma Report that a patient will need to keep fully informed with medical articles written by experts in the field.

Monthly

2816 Mainstreaming Deaf and Hard of Hearing Students: Questions and Answers

Gallaudet University Bookstore
800 Florida Avenue NE
Washington, DC   20002   202-651-5000
                                800-451-1073
               FAX: 202-651-5489
National Information Center on Deafness, author

This booklet presents mainstreaming as one educational option and suggests some considerations for parents, teachers and administrators. *$6.00*

40 pages

2817 Mainstreaming Exceptional Students: A Guide for Classroom Teachers

Allyn & Bacon
160 Gould Street
Needham Heights, MA   02494   781-455-1200
                                800-852-8024
Jane B. Schulz, C. Dale Carpenter, author

Provides a clear overview of mainstreaming and public law.

464 pages
ISBN 0-20515 -24-6

2818 Management of Autistic Behavior

Pro-Ed
8700 Shoal Creek Boulevard
Austin, TX   78757
                    FAX: 512-451-8542
               e-mail: proed1@aol.com
Richard L. Simpson & Madelyn Regan, author

This excellent reference is a comprehensive and practical book that tells what works best with specific problems. *$41.00*

450 pages
ISBN 0-89079 -96-1

2819 Managing Diagnostic Tool of Visual Perception

Gallery Bookshop
PO Box 270
Mendocino, CA   95460   707-937-2665

Manual Mangina, author

For diagnosing specific perceptual learning abilities and disabilities. *$14.00*

ISBN 0-80580 -83-4

2820 Medical Rehabilitation

Lippincott, Williams & Wilkins
227 E Washington Square
Philadelphia, PA   19106   215-238-4200
                                800-777-2295
               FAX: 301-824-7390
                    www.lpub.com
Lauro S Halstead, author

Information for the professional on new techniques and treatments in the medical rehabilitation fields. *$80.50*

368 pages Illustrated
ISBN 0-88167 -85-5

2821 Mental Health Concepts and Techniques for the Occupational Therapy Assistant

Lippincott, Williams & Wilkins
227 E Washington Square
Philadelphia, PA 19106

215-238-4200
800-777-2295
FAX: 301-824-7390
www.lpub.com

Mary Beth Early, author

This text offers clear and easily understood explanations of the various theoretical and practice health models. *$36.00*

344 pages
ISBN 0-88167 -53-X

2822 Mental Health and Mental Illness

Lippincott, Williams & Wilkins
227 E Washington Square
Philadelphia, PA 19106

215-238-4200
800-777-2295
FAX: 301-824-7390
www.lpub.com

Patricia D. Barry, author

Concise, comprehensive and completely up to date, this book presents the most current theory in mental health nursing for the student and the new practitioner. *$28.95*

480 pages
ISBN 0-39755 -73-7

2823 Mentally Ill Individuals

Mainstream
3 Bethesda Metro Center
Suite 830
Bethesda, MD 20814

301-951-6122
800-247-1380
e-mail: info@mainstreaminc.org

Mainstream, Inc., author

Mainstreaming mentally ill individuals into the workplace. *$2.50*

12 pages

2824 Mentally Retarded Individuals

Mainstream
3 Bethesda Metro Center
Suite 830
Bethesda, MD 20814

301-951-6122
800-247-1380
e-mail: info@mainstreaminc.org

Mainstream, Inc., author

Mainstreaming mentally retarded individuals into the workplace. *$2.50*

12 pages

2825 Midland Treatment Furniture

Sammons Preston/AbilityOne Company
4 Sammons Center
Bowling Brook, IL 60440

630-226-1300
800-323-5547
FAX: 800-547-4333
e-mail: sp@sammonspreston.com
www.sammonspreston.com

Edward Donnelly, President

This catalog has the biggest selection of OT/PT products anywhere. Whether you deal with larger or smaller caseloads, you need treatment furniture you can count on. Midland Treatment Furniture from Sammons Preston is designed and built to stand up to the heaviest use. From tilt tables and traction packages to mat platforms and parallel bars, you'll find the complete line of Midland Treatment Furniture inside this brochure. All products are assembled from premium materials and carefully crafted.

Free

2826 Multidisciplinary Assessment of Children

Gallery Bookshop
PO Box 270
Mendocino, CA 95460

707-937-2665

David L. Wodrich, author

Assessment of children with learning disabilities and mental retardation. *$24.00*

346 pages Illustrated
ISBN 0-93371 -62-1

2827 Multisensory Teaching of Basic Language Skills: Theory and Practice

Brookes Publishing
PO Box 10624
Baltimore, MD 21285

410-337-9580
800-638-3775
FAX: 410-337-8539
e-mail: custserv@brookespublishing.com
www.brookespublishing.com

This book presents specific multisensory methods for helping students who are having trouble learning to read due to dyslexia or other learning disabilities. Recommended techniques are offered for teaching alphabet skills, composition, comprehension, handwriting, math, organization and study skills, phonological awareness, reading and spelling. *$59.00*

608 pages Hardcover 1999
ISBN 1-557663-49-1

2828 National Benchbook on Psychiatric and Psychological Evidence and Testimony

ABA Commission on Mental & Physical Disability Law
740 15th Street NW
9th Floor
Washington, DC 20055

202-662-1581
800-285-2221
FAX: 202-662-1032

Focuses on three broad areas involving psychiatric and psychological evidence: civil and criminal competency; criminal responsibility; and dangerousness to self and others. It is divided into four parts: an executive summary; judges' checklists; nine substantive chapters; and appendices of references for each chapter. Key topics include civil competency, criminal responsibility, and dangerousness in commitment release and sentencing. Intended for judges, essential reading for lawyers. *$80.00*

2829 **No Longer Immune: A Counselor's Guide to AIDS**

American Association for Counseling & Development
5999 Stevenson Avenue
Alexandria, VA 22304   703-823-9800
     800-347-6647

Crai Kain, Editor

Covers a broad range of issues such as working with specific populations, handling pre and post testing situations, coping with fear, grief and survivor guilt, struggling with spiritual issues and dealing with counter transference. *$26.95*

     295 pages
     ISBN 1-55620-64-1

2830 **Occupational Therapy Across Cultural Boundaries**

Haworth Press
10 Alice Street
Binghamton, NY 13904   604-722-5857
     800-429-6784
     FAX: 607-722-6362
     e-mail: getinfo@haworthpressinc.com
     www.haworthpressinc.com
Susan Cook Merrill, MA, OTR/L, author
Jackie Blakeslee, Advertising

Examines the concept of culture from a unique perspective, that of individual occupational therapists who have worked in environments very different from those in which they were educated or had worked previously. *$39.95*

     107 pages Hardcover
     ISBN 1-560242-23-X

2831 **Occupational Therapy Approaches to Traumatic Brain Injury**

Haworth Press
10 Alice Street
Binghamton, NY 13904   604-722-5857
     800-429-6784
     FAX: 607-722-6362
     e-mail: getinfo@haworthpressinc.com
     www.haworthpressinc.com
Jerry Johnson, EdD, OTR, FAOTA, author
Jackie Blakeslee, Advertising

Focuses on the disabled individual, the family, and the societal responses to the injured, this comprehensive book covers the spectrum of available services from intensive care to transitional and community living. *$69.95*

     137 pages Hardcover
     ISBN 1-560240-64-4

2832 **Overcoming Dyslexia in Children, Adolescents and Adults**

Pro-Ed
8700 Shoal Creek Boulevard
Austin, TX 78757
     FAX: 512-451-8542
     e-mail: proed1@aol.com
Dale R. Jordan, author

This book describes some forms of dyslexia in detail and then relates those problems to the social, emotional and personal development of dyslexic individuals. *$34.00*

     350 pages Paperback
     ISBN 0-89079-42-4

2833 **Oxford Textbook of Geriatric Medicine**

Oxford University Press
198 Madison Avenue
New York, NY 10016   212-726-6000
     800-451-7556
     FAX: 919-677-1303
     www.oup-usa.org
J. Grimley Evans, author

This comprehensive text brings together extensive experience in clinical geriatrics with a strong scientific base in research. *$125.00*

     784 pages

2834 **PKU for Children: Learning to Measure**

University of Washington, PKU Clinic
CHDD
Box 537920
Seattle, WA 98195   206-685-1242
     FAX: 206-543-5771
     e-mail: vam@u.washington.edu
     www.depts.washington.edu/pku

Lesson format for parents and teachers.

2835 **Pain Centers: A Revolution in Health Care**

Lippincott, Williams & Wilkins
227 E Washington Square
Philadelphia, PA 19106   215-238-4200
     800-777-2295
     FAX: 301-824-7390
     www.lpub.com
Gerald Aronoff, author
$103.00

     280 pages

2836 **Parental Concerns in College Student Mental Health**

Haworth Press
10 Alice Street
Binghamton, NY 13904   604-722-5857
     800-429-6784
     FAX: 607-722-6362
     e-mail: getinfo@haworthpressinc.com
     www.haworthpressinc.com
Leighton C. Whitaker, PhD, author
Jackie Blakeslee, Advertising

An instructive guide for parents and mental health professionals regarding the most important issues about psychological development in college students. *$69.95*

     204 pages Hardcover
     ISBN 0-866567-20-8

2837 **Parents and Teachers**

Alexander Graham Bell Association of the Deaf
3417 Volta Place NW
Washington, DC 20007   202-337-5220
     FAX: 202-337-8314
     TDY:202-337-5220
     e-mail: lquigley@agbell.org
     www.agbell.org

Elizabeth Quigley, Director of Publications
Audrey Simmons Martin, Ph.D., Author
Karen Glover, M.A., Author

This excellent book offers in-depth guidance to parents and teachers whose partnership can foster language in school-aged children with hearing impairments. The first section examines roles of parents teachers professionals, and children in language acquisition, residual hearing and audiological management, language development stages and readying children for preschool. The second portion of the book presents specific objectives and teaching strategies to use at school and at home. *$27.95*

386 pages

2838 Patient and Family Education

Springer Publishing Company
536 Broadway
New York, NY 10012   212-431-4370
                            FAX: 212-941-7842
Marcia Hanak, author

This guide outlines the actual clinical content needed to develop, implement and maintain patient education programs. Conveniently arranged in one-hour long lesson plans, each disease or condition is organized in an easy-to-follow format. *$26.95*

272 pages Softcover
ISBN 0-82615-41-7

2839 Peer Tutoring: A Guide for School Psychologists

National Association of School Psychologists
8455 Colesville Road
Suite 1000
Silver Spring, MD 20910   301-681-3223
                                FAX: 301-608-2514

In recent years the term peer tutoring has received more attention as an alternative to the traditional academic arrangements in the classroom for at-risk students. Remedial instruction is often needed by at-risk students and peer tutoring is an attractive alternative due to its use of available resources.

36 pages

2840 Peer Tutoring: A Guide for School2 Psychologists

National Association of School Psychologists
8455 Colesville Road
Suite 1000
Silver Spring, MD 20910   301-681-3223
                                FAX: 301-608-2514

In recent years the term peer tutoring has received more attention as an alternative to the traditional academic arrangements in the classroom for at-risk students. Remedial instruction is often needed by at-risk students and peer tutoring is an attractive alternative due to its use of available resources.

36 pages

2841 Person to Person: Guide for Professionals Working with the Disabled, 2nd Ed.

Paul H. Brookes Publishing Company
PO Box 10624
Baltimore, MD 21285
                            800-638-3775
                            FAX: 410-337-8539
Lindsay Gethling, author
Karen G. Radke, Marketing Director

This second edition of an already-popular book helps professionals approach interactions with a people-first, disability second attitude. *$29.00*

288 pages Paperback 1992
ISBN 1-557661-00-6

2842 Personality and Emotional Disturbance

Taylor & Francis
47 Runway Drive
 # G
Levittown, PA 19057
                            FAX: 215-785-5515
Howard F. Jackson, author

The brain injured person has unique needs arising from unique aetiology. Recent findings have highlighted that it is the personality, behavioral and emotional problems which most prohibit a return to work, create the greatest burden for the long-term care and rehabilitation of physical and cognitive functions. *$72.00*

260 pages Cloth
ISBN 0-85066-71-3

2843 Peterson's Guide to Colleges with Programs for Learning Disabled Students

Special Needs Project
3463 Stat Street
 # 282
Santa Barbara, CA 93105
                            800-333-6867

The most complete and accurate guide to the more than 900 colleges with programs for the learning disabled. *$19.95*

406 pages

2844 Phenomenology of Depressive Illness

Human Sciences Press
233 Spring Street
New York, NY 10013   212-229-2859
                            800-221-9369
                            FAX: 212-463-0742
John J. Mann, author

Provides the reader with a detailed knowledge of the clinical characteristics of depressive disorders that will permit judgement of the general ability of the various theoretical models of depressive disorders. *$42.95*

263 pages Cloth
ISBN 0-89885-69-9

2845 Physical Disabilities and Health Impairments: An Introduction

McGraw-Hill, School Publishing
220 East Danieldale Road
DeSoto, TX 75115   972-224-1111
                         800-442-9685
                         FAX: 972-228-1982
                         mhschool.com

A comprehensive text which presents a wealth of up-to-date medical information for teachers.

2846 Physical Education and Sports for Exceptional Students

McGraw-Hill
2460 Kerper Boulevard
Dubuque, IA 52001

800-338-3987
www.mhhe.com/hper/physed

Physical education for exceptional students and teaching students with learning and behavior exceptionalities.

Cloth

2847 Physical Management of Multiple Handicaps: A Professional's Guide

Paul H. Brookes Publishing Company
PO Box 10624
Baltimore, MD 21285

800-638-3775
FAX: 410-337-8539

Beverly Fraser, author

Comprehensive guide, takes a transdisciplinary approach to therapeutic/technological management of persons with multiple handicaps. *$36.00*

352 pages Hardcover
ISBN 1-557660-47-6

2848 Physically Handicapped in Society

Ayer Company Publishers
RR 1 Box 85-1
N Stratford, NH 03590

603-669-9307
888-267-7323
FAX: 603-669-7945
e-mail: stg@ncia.net
www.scry.com/ayer

Kathy Train, Office Manager
Ellie Phipps, Customer Service

A group of 39 books. Biographies that offer studies on attitudes, sociological and psychological. Please write or call for catalog. *$965.00*

Hardcover
ISBN 0-40513-00-3

2849 Pitfalls & Pratfalls of Private Practice

Learning Disabilities Network
72 Sharp Street
Suite A-2
Hingham, MA 02043

781-340-5605

e-mail: ldntwk@aol.com

Carolyn Cowen, author
Cynthia Christopher, Director of Progress

Pitfalls provides practical information about the mechanics of starting a private practice with helpful guidelines for dealing with the related professional and ethical issues. *$40.00*

68 pages

2850 Practicing Rehabilitation with Geriatric Clients

Springer Publishing Company
536 Broadway
New York, NY 10012

212-431-4370
FAX: 212-941-7842

J. Dermot Frengley, author

Physical therapy in the geriatric client, psychological and psychiatric considerations in the rehabilitation of the elderly. *$32.95*

256 pages Hardcover
ISBN 0-82616-80-5

2851 Pragmatic Approach

Educators Publishing Service
31 Smith Plaza
Cambridge, MA 02138

617-547-6706
800-225-5750
FAX: 617-547-0412
www.epsbooks.com

Beth H. Slingerland, author

Monograph on evaluation of children's performances on Slingerland Pre-Reading Screening Procedures to Identify First Grade Academic Needs. *$6.00*

56 pages
ISBN 0-838816-85-1

2852 Preschoolers with Special Needs: Children At-Risk, Children with Disabilities

Allyn & Bacon
160 Gould Street
Needham Heights, MA 02494

781-455-1200
800-852-8024

Janet W. Lerner, Barbara Lowenthal, Rosemary Egan, author

This book explores ways of meeting the challenges of preschool children who have special needs by providing them with a learning environment that will help them develop and learn.

374 pages

2853 Preventing Academic Failure

Educators Publishing Service
31 Smith Place
Cambridge, MA 02138

617-367-2700
800-225-5750
FAX: 617-547-0412
www.epsbooks.com

Phyllis Bertin & Eileen Perlman, author

Ungraded multisensory curriculum coordinating Orton-Gillingham and Merrill Linguistic reading techniques for language disabled students. Teaches phonics, spelling and reading to reinforce the development of language skills. A separate handwriting program is available. *$42.00*

284 pages Paperback
ISBN 0-838852-71-8

2854 Preventing School Dropouts

Pro-Ed
8700 Shoal Creek Boulevard
Austin, TX 78757

FAX: 512-451-8542
e-mail: proed1@aol.com

Thomas C. Lovitt, author

For secondary teachers, special education and regular, who have difficulty teaching youth in their classes. Presented are 120 tactics, specific instructional techniques, for helping adolescents to stay in school. Each tactic is written in a format that includes five sections. *$38.00*

509 pages
ISBN 0-89079-54-5

2855 Prevocational Assessment

Exceptional Education
PO Box 15308
Seattle, WA 98115   206-542-3971
                           FAX: 475-486-4510

J E Stewart, Owner

Use the PACG to assess your students in nine areas (attendance and endurance, learning and behavior, communication skills, social skills, grooming and eating and toileting) covering 46 specific workshop experiences. *$12.00*

16 pages Complete Set
ISBN 1-87786 -23-7

2856 Progress Without Punishment: Approaches for Learners with Behavior Problems

Teachers College Press
Columbia University
New York, NY 10027
                           800-575-6566
                           FAX: 212-678-4149
Anne M. Donnellan, author

In this volume, the authors argue against the use of punishment, and instead advocate the use of alternative intervention procedures. *$17.95*

184 pages Paperback
ISBN 0-807729-11-6

2857 Promoting Postsecondary Education for Students with Learning Disabilities

Pro-Ed
8700 Shoal Creek Boulevard
Austin, TX 78757
                           FAX: 512-451-8542
                           e-mail: proed1@aol.com

Loring Brinkerhoff, Author
Stan F. Shaw, Author
Joan M. McGuire, Author

Primarily designed for postsecondary service providers who are responsible for serving college students with learning disabilities. *$41.00*

440 pages
ISBN 0-89079 -89-4

2858 Promoting Special Education Career Awareness

Council for Exceptional Children
1920 Association Drive
Reston, VA 20191   703-620-3660
                           888-232-7232
                           FAX: 703-264-9494
                           e-mail: service@cec.sped.org
                           www.cec.sped.org

Cathy Mack, Production Manager

Written for use by individuals or groups interested in promoting careers in special education. *$10.00*

57 pages
ISBN 0-86586 -29-0

2859 Psychiatric Mental Health Nursing

Lippincott, Williams & Wilkins
227 E Washington Square
Philadelphia, PA 19106   215-238-4200
                                 800-777-2295
                                 FAX: 301-824-7390
                                 www.lpub.com
Barbara Schoen Johnson, author

This text emphasizes and contrasts the roles of the generalist nurse and the psychiatric nurse specialist. *$52.00*

1120 pages Illustrated

2860 Psychoeducational Assessment of Hearing-Impaired Students

Pro-Ed
8700 Shoal Creek Boulevard
Austin, TX 78757
                           FAX: 512-451-8542
                           e-mail: proed1@aol.com

Sharon Bradley-Johnson, Author
Larry D. Evans, Author

This book includes a comprehensive presentation of issues and procedures related to the assessment of hearing-impaired students. *$29.00*

251 pages Paperback
ISBN 0-89079 -55-3

2861 Psychoeducational Assessment of Students Who Are Visually Impaired or Blind

Pro-Ed
8700 Shoal Creek Boulevard
Austin, TX 78757
                           FAX: 512-451-8542
                           e-mail: proed1@aol.com
Sharon Bradley-Johnson, author

Here is a professional reference book that addresses the problems specific to assessment of visually impaired and blind children. Of particular value to the practitioner are the extensive reviews of available tests, including ways to adapt those not designed for use with the visually handicapped. *$29.00*

253 pages
ISBN 0-89079 -99-1

2862 Rational-Emotive Therapy with Alcoholics

Pergamon Press
655 Avenue of the Americas
NY, NY 10010
                           800-257-5755
Albert Ellis, author

Therapy text on alcoholism and substance abusers. *$ 15.95*

176 pages Softcover
ISBN 0-08033 -74-3

2863 Reading and Deafness

Pro-Ed
8700 Shoal Creek Boulevard
Austin, TX 78757
                           FAX: 512-451-8542
                           e-mail: proed1@aol.com

Cynthia M. King, Author
Stephen P. Quigley, Author

Three areas are looked at in this book: deaf children's prereading development of real-world knowledge, cognitive abilities and linguistic skills. *$39.00*

> *422 pages*
> *ISBN 0-88744 -07-6*

2864 Reading and the Special Learner

Ablex Publishing Corporation
PO Box 811
Stamford, CT 06904
                                     FAX: 203-661-0792
Carolyn Hedley, author

Explores the needs of the special learner: compensatory methods and adaptive means. *$73.25*

> *272 pages*
> *ISBN 0-89391 -95-9*

2865 Readings on Research in Stuttering

Longman Publishing Group
95 Church Street
White Plains, NY 10601   **914-993-5000**

E. Charles Healey, author

This authoritative collection, comprised of the key journal articles published on stuttering over the past decade, sheds light on important trends in recent research in the field.

> *231 pages Paperback 1991*
> *ISBN 0-801304-10-5*

2866 Recreation Activities for the Elderly

Springer Publishing Company
536 Broadway
New York, NY 10012   **212-431-4370**
                                 FAX: 212-941-7842
Kay Flatten, author

Included in this volume are simple crafts that utilize easily obtainable, inexpensive materials, hobbies focusing on collections, nature, and the arts' and games emphasizing both mental and physical activity. *$23.95*

> *240 pages Softcover*
> *ISBN 0-82616 -30-1*

2867 Reference Manual for Communicative Sciences and Disorders

Pro-Ed
8700 Shoal Creek Boulevard
Austin, TX 78757
                           FAX: 512-451-8542
                     e-mail: proed1@aol.com
Raymond D. Kent, author

An indispensable guide to standards and values essential in the assessment of communication disorders. *$54.00*

> *393 pages*
> *ISBN 0-89079 -19-7*

2868 Rehabilitation Counseling and Services: Profession and Process

Charles C. Thomas, Publisher
2600 S 1st Street
Springfield, IL 62704   **217-789-8980**
                                    800-258-8980
                              FAX: 217-789-9130
                e-mail: books@ccthomas.com
Gerald Gandy, Edavis Martin, Richard E. Hardy, author

Gives information on the rehabilitation and counseling process, work evaluation, work adjustment and more. *$52.95*

> *376 pages Cloth*
> *ISBN 0-39052 -24-4*

2869 Rehabilitation Interventions for the Institutionalized Elderly

Haworth Press
10 Alice Street
Binghamton, NY 13904   **604-722-5857**
                                   800-429-6784
                             FAX: 607-722-6362
       e-mail: getinfo@haworthpressinc.com
                  www.haworthpressinc.com
Ellen Dunleavy Taira, Otr/L, Mph, author
Jackie Blakeslee, Advertising

Gerontology professionals offer suggestions to enrich the quality of rehabilitation services offered to the institutionalized elderly. This volume examines up to the minute ideas, some that would have been unlikely even a few years ago, that focus exclusively on rehabilitation services for the institutionalized elderly. *$39.95*

> *77 pages Hardcover*
> *ISBN 0-866568-33-6*

2870 Rehabilitation Nursing for the Neurological Patient

Springer Publishing Company
536 Broadway
New York, NY 10012   **212-431-4370**
                                 FAX: 212-941-7842
Marcia Hanak, author

A practical new reference written especially for practicing nurses who work with neurologically disabled persons. *$32.95*

> *240 pages*

2871 Rehabilitation Resource Manual: VISION

Resources for Rehabilitation
33 Bedford Street
Suite 19A
Lexington, MA 02420   **781-890-6371**
                                  FAX: 781-867-7517

Susan Greenblatt

A desk reference that enables service providers, librarians and others to make effective referrals. Includes guidelines on establishing self-help groups, information on research and service organizations, and chapters on assistive technology, for special population groups and by eye condition. *$44.95*

> *Biennial*

2872 Rehabilitation Technology

Haworth Press
10 Alice Street
Binghamton, NY 13904   604-722-5857
                              800-429-6784
                         FAX: 607-722-6362
e-mail: getinfo@haworthpressinc.com
www.haworthpressinc.com
Glenn Hedman, MEME, author
Jackie Blakeslee, Advertising

Learn how the use of technological devices can enhance the lives of disabled children. Informs physical therapists, occupational therapists, and rehabilitation technologists about the devices that are available today and provides important background information on these devices. *$49.95*

> *173 pages Hardcover*
> *ISBN 1-560240-33-4*

2873 Remediation of Learning Disabilities

Fearon/Janus
500 Harbor Boulevard
Belmont, CA 94002   650-631-2525

Robert E. Valett, author

A guide to describing disabilities and providing remedial activities. *$23.40*

2874 Report Writing in Assessment and Evaluation

Stout Vocational Rehab Institute
University of Wisconsin-Stout
Menomonie, WI 54751   715-232-1478
                        FAX: 715-232-2356
MDC, author
Ronald R. Fry, Manager
Darlene Botterbusch, Program Assistant

This examines questions of who are you writing for and what does the referral source want. Defines characteristics of good reports, common problems, writing in different settings, types of reports, getting ready to write, and writing prescriptive recommendations. *$17.75*

> *188 pages Softcover*

2875 Report on Disability Programs

Business Publishers
8737 Colesville Road
Suite 1100
Silver Spring, MD 20910
                              800-274-6737
                         FAX: 301-587-4530
e-mail: custserv@bpinews.com
www.bpinews.com
Bob Grupe, author
Leonard A. Eiserer, Publisher
Bob Grupe, Editor
Melissa Rao, Marketing Manager

Follows legislation, regulation, legal actions and funding in areas important to all persons with disabilities, including health care, employment, civil rights, housing and transportation. *$327.00*

> *25x Year*

2876 Resources for Rehabilitation

33 Bedford Street
Suite 19A
Lexington, MA 02420   781-862-6455
                         FAX: 781-861-7517

R. Frances Weisse, President

Provides training and information to professionals and the public about disabilities and resources available to help. Publishes resource guides, professional publications and patient/client educational materials. Conducts custom designed training programs and workshops.

2877 Restructuring High Schools for All Students: Taking Inclusion to the Next Level

Brookes Publishing
PO Box 10624
Baltimore, MD 21285   410-337-9580
                              800-638-3775
                         FAX: 410-337-8539
e-mail: custserv@brookespublishing.com
www.brookespublishing.com
Cheryl M. Jorgensen, Ph.D., author

Taking Inclusion to the Next Level. Details the process of creating an inclusive, collaborate community of learners and teachers at the secondary level. *$29.95*

> *304 pages Paperback 1998*
> *ISBN 1-557663-13-0*

2878 Restructuring for Caring and Effective Education: Administrative Guide, 2nd Edition

Brookes Publishing
PO Box 10624
Baltimore, MD 21285   410-337-9580
                              800-638-3775
                         FAX: 410-337-8539
e-mail: custserv@brookespublishing.com
www.brookespublishing.com
Richard Villa, author

In this empowering book, leading general and special education schools reform experts synthesize the major school restructuring initiatives and describe the processes and rationale for changing the organizational structure and instructional practices of schools. *$ 29.00*

> *384 pages Paperback*
> *ISBN 1-55766 -91-3*

2879 Screening in Chronic Disease

Oxford University Press
2001 Evans Road
Cary, NC 27513   212-726-6000
                         800-451-7556
                    FAX: 919-677-1303
www.oup-usa.org
Alan Morrison, author

Early detection, or screening, is a common strategy for controlling chronic disease, but little information has been available to help determine which screening procedures are worthwhile. *$42.50*

> *256 pages*

2880 Selective Nontreatment of Handicapped

Oxford University Press
2001 Evans Road
Cary, NC 27513   212-726-6000
                              800-451-7556
                      FAX: 919-677-1303
                          www.oup-usa.org

Robert F. Weir, author

Information on selective nontreatment of handicapped newborns, moral dilemmas in neonatal medicine. *$17.95*

304 pages Paperback

2881 Service Coordination for Early Intervention: Parents and Friends

Brookline Books
PO Box 1047
Cambridge, MA 02238   617-868-0360
                                800-666-2665
                         FAX: 617-868-1772
          e-mail: brooklinebks@delphi.com
                    www.brooklinebooks.com

Irene N. Zipper, Marie Weil, and Kathleen Rounds, author

This book helps administrators and professionals to structure early intervention and ongoing services so that professionals work collaboratively with parents to promote the health, well being and development of children with special needs. *$19.95*

110 pages Paperback
ISBN 0-91479-91-3

2882 Services for the Seriously Mentally Ill: A Survey of Mental Health Centers

National Council/Community Mental Health Centers
12300 Twinbrook Parkway
Suite 320
Rockville, MD 20852   301-670-6331

This ground-breaking report documents what administrators and practitioners have maintained for many years: community mental health organizations devote a significant percentage of the human and financial resources to serving the seriously mentally ill. *$30.00*

2883 Sharks Don't Get Cancer

Avery Publishing Group
Garden City Park, NY

I. William Lane, Ph.D. and Linda Comac, author

Describes new evidence concerning the cancer preventative properties of cartilage.

1992

2884 Shop Talk

Research Press
PO Box 9177
Champaign, IL 61826   217-352-3273
                                800-519-2707
                         FAX: 217-352-1221
          e-mail: rp@researchpress.com
                    www.researchpress.com

Eileen Shepman, author
Russell Pence, V P Marketing

A well-structured group training program that covers five crucial communication areas: social communication routines, identification information, basic language skills, language-related concepts and cognitive components. The authors emphasize direct cooperation between educators and parents by providing over 100 interesting activities that focus on the student's affective impact on others, unique identify as a person, self-care, grooming, leisure and ability to work independently. *$25.95*

236 pages Paperback
ISBN 0-878222-29-4

2885 Signed English Schoolbook

Gallaudet University Press
11030 S Langley Avenue
Chicago, IL 60628
                                800-621-2736
                         FAX: 800-621-8476
                         TDY:800-621-9347
                  gupress.gallaudet.edu

Harry Bornstein, Co-Author
Karen L. Saulnier, Co-Author

The Signed English Schoolbook provides vocabulary for teachers and others who serve school-age children and adolescents and covers the full range of school activities. *$13.95*

184 pages Softcover

2886 Social Studies: Detecting Special Needs

Allyn & Bacon
160 Gould Street
Needham Heights, MA 02194
                                800-852-8024

Lana J. Smith, author

Describes social studies and special needs for special learners.

180 pages 1990
ISBN 0-205121-51-9

2887 Social and Emotional Development of Exceptional Students: Handicapped

Charles C. Thomas, Publisher
2600 South 1st Street
Springfield, IL 62704   217-789-8980
                                800-258-8980
                         FAX: 217-789-9130
             e-mail: books@ccthomas.com

Carroll J. Jones, Author

Sixteen years after the passage of P.L. 94-142, the dream of special educators to educate the handicapped and nonhandicapped children and youth together resulting in increased academic gains and age-appropriate school skills for handicapped children and youth has not yet materialized. This book helps eliminate an existing void by providing teachers with understandable information regarding the social and emotional development of exceptional students. Also in cloth at $41.95 (ISBN# 0-398-05781-8) *$29.95*

218 pages Softcover
ISBN 0-398061-94-7

2888 Special Education Today

LifeWay Christian Resources Southern Baptist Conv.
127 9th Avenue N
Nashville, TN 37234   615-251-2000
                               800-458-2772
                 e-mail: specialed@lifeway.com
                               www.lifeway.com

Ellen Beene, Editor

This unique quarterly publications ministers to people with special education needs and to their families, the church, and other caregivers. It offers a variety of helps and encouragement, including: What's working in churches, Suggestions for adapting teaching techniques, inspirational stories about people who have disabilities, Parenting and family issues, Ideas for reaching, witnessing, worship, and recreation. *$4.25*

36 pages Quarterly

2889 Special Education Today2

LifeWay Christian Resources Southern Baptist Conv.
127 9th Avenue North
Nashville, TN 37234   615-251-2000
                               800-458-2772
                 e-mail: specialed@lifeway.com
                               www.lifeway.com

Ellen Beene, Editor

Quarterly magazine features articles about special needs from a Christian perspective. Focuses on both family issues and teaching persons with special needs in a church environment. Addresses a variety of disability areas. *$5.00*

32 pages Quarterly

2890 Special Education for Today

Allyn & Bacon
160 Gould Street
Needham Heights, MA 02194
                               800-852-8024
Rebecca Dailey Kneedler, author

An undergraduate introduction to special education covering all major areas of exceptionality. Contains pedagogical features designed to make the book accessible to the undergraduate.

576 pages 1984
ISBN 0-138264-53-8

2891 Speech and the Hearing-Impaired Child

Alexander Graham Bell Association of the Deaf
3417 Volta Place NW
Washington, DC 20007   202-337-5220
                         FAX: 202-337-8314
                         TDY: 202-337-5220
                 e-mail: lquigley@agbell.org
                               www.agbell.org
Daniel Ling, Ph. D, author
Elizabeth Quigley, Director of Publications

This textbook for professionals deals with basic theoretical issues in the acquisition of speech and the form of language (phonetics and phonology) in children with hearing losses. It provides a systematic framework to develop and evaluate speech target behaviors and their underlying subskills. *$29.95*

402 pages Paperback

2892 Speech-Language Pathology and Audiology: An Introduction

McGraw-Hill, School Publishing
220 East Danieldale Road
DeSoto, TX 75115   972-224-1111
                               800-442-9685
                         FAX: 972-228-1982
                               mhschool.com

Offers classroom-tested coverage of clinical objectives and functioning.

301 pages

2893 Spinal Cord Dysfunction

Oxford University Press
2001 Evans Road
Cary, NC 27513   212-726-6000
                               800-451-7556
                         FAX: 919-677-1303
                               www.oup-usa.org
L.S. Illis, author

Offers information on restoration of function after spinal cord damage as seen from the point of view of identification of impaired or absent function in the nerve cells and processes which survive after the initial insult, intact but with impaired functions. *$95.00*

368 pages

2894 Spotting Language Problems

Los Amigos Research Associates
7035 Galewood Street
San Diego, CA 92120   619-286-3162

Jack S. Damico, author

One of the major problems facing most teachers is deciding whether any child is experiencing difficulty in the areas of speech, language and hearing. *$30.00*

2895 Steps to Independence: Teaching Everyday Skills to Children with Special Needs, 3rd Edition

Brookes Publishing
PO Box 10624
Baltimore, MD 21285   410-337-9580
                               800-638-3775
                         FAX: 410-337-8539
         e-mail: custserv@brookespublishing.com
                       www.brookespublishing.com
Bruce L. Baker, Ph.D., and Alan J. Brightman, Ph.D, author

This step-by-step guide to teaching everyday skills to children with special needs is updated with even more practical teaching tips, & an expanded section on behavior problem management. Covers toilet training, play, self-help skills, information skills, advanced living skills, & more. Includes features such as sample activities, case examples, skills inventories, and cartoon illustrations, & a chapter devoted to computers & advice as to how using technology enhances children's learning. *$28.00*

392 pages Paperback 1997
ISBN 1-557662-68-1

2896 Strategies for Teaching Students with Learning & Behavior Problems

Allyn & Bacon
160 Gould Street
Needham Heights, MA 02494 781-455-1200
800-852-8024

Candace S. Bos, Sharon Vaughn, author

Prepares teachers and future teachers to work effectively with elementary and secondary students who have difficulty learning in effective and efficient manners.

544 pages
ISBN 0-20527-28-2

2897 Students with Acquired Brain Injury: The School's Response

Brookes Publishing
PO Box 10624
Baltimore, MD 21285 410-337-9580
800-638-3775
FAX: 410-337-8539
e-mail: custserv@brookespublishing.com
www.brookespublishing.com

This book is designed for school professionals and describes a range of issues that this population faces and presents proven means of addressing them in ways that benefit all students. Included topics are hospital-to-school transitions, effective assessment strategies, model programs in public schools, interventions to assist classroom teachers, and ways to involve family members in the educational program. *$29.95*

424 pages Paperback 1997
ISBN 1-55766-85-1

2898 Students with Mild Disabilities in the Secondary School

Longman Publishing Group
95 Church Street
White Plains, NY 10601 914-993-5000

Paul Retish, author

Comprehensive curriculum provides useful methods and strategies for its delivery to students with mild disabilities in the secondary school.

2313G pages Paperback 1991
ISBN 0-801301-66-1

2899 Support Groups for Practicing Special Education Professionals

Council for Exceptional Children
1920 Association Drive
Reston, VA 20191 703-620-3660
888-232-7232
FAX: 703-264-9494
e-mail: service@cec.sped.org
www.cec.sped.org

Lynne Cook, author
Cathy Mack, Production Manager

The demands and logistics of teaching make it difficult for teachers to form and maintain professional support networks as part of their working day. *$10.00*

56 pages
ISBN 0-86586-28-1

2900 Supporting and Strengthening Families

Brookline Books
PO Box 1047
Cambridge, MA 02238 617-868-0360
800-666-2665
FAX: 617-868-1772
e-mail: brooklinebks@delphi.com
www.brooklinebooks.com

Cail Dunst, Carol Trivette, And Angela Deal, author

A collection of papers addressing the theory, methods, strategies, and practices involved in adopting an empowerment and family-centered resources approach to supporting families and strengthening individual and family functioning. *$30.00*

252 pages Paperback
ISBN 0-91479-94-8

2901 Survival Guide for the First-Year Special Education Teacher

Council for Exceptional Children
1920 Association Drive
Reston, VA 20191 703-620-3660
888-232-7733
FAX: 703-264-9494
TDY:703-264-9446
e-mail: service@cec.sped.org
www.cec.sped.org

Mary Kemper Cohen, Maureen Gale, Joyce M. Meyer, author
Nancy Safer, Executive Director

Help for teachers. This survival guide was developed to help teachers be prepared for and enjoy the challenges of a new career. *$12.00*

47 pages
ISBN 0-86586-26-7

2902 TESTS

Slosson Educational Publications
PO Box 280
East Aurora, NY 14052 716-652-0930
800-828-4800
FAX: 800-665-3840
e-mail: slosson@slosson.com
www.slosson.com

Slosson Educational Publications, Inc. offers educators an extensive selection of testing products, along with books on Autism. ADED and other Special needs materials. Our catalog includes 30 pages of Speech-Language Testing and language Rehabilitation Products. The behavioral conduct. Special needs section includes checklist and scales on aberrant/disruptive behavior, Tapes on ADD, as well as products for dyslexia and Remediation of reversals.

2903 Teach Someone to Read

Fearon/Janus
500 Harbor Boulevard
Belmont, CA 94002 650-631-2525

Nadine Rosenthal, author

A step-by-step guide for adult literacy tutors. *$15.45*

2904 Teacher's Guide to Feeding Children with Special Needs

Nutrition Consultant for Crippled Children's Srvc.
Arizona Dept. of Health
Room 203
Phoenix, AZ 85007   602-759-9338

Resource book for families, teachers, and caregivers on nutrition, feeding skills development and positive mealtime experience targeting chidlren with special health care needsin child care centers. Available in English and Spanish. *$5.00*

2905 Teacher's Guide to Galatosemia

Nutrition Consultant for Crippled Children's Srvc.
Arizona Dept. of Health
Room 203
Phoenix, AZ 85007   602-759-9338

Resource book for preschool teachers and school staff on PKU basics, NutraSweet warning, and classroom activities. *$2.50*

13 pages

2906 Teacher's Guide to HCU

Nutrition Consultant for Crippled Children's Srvc.
Arizona Dept. of Health
Room 203
Phoenix, AZ 85007   602-759-9338

Resource book for preschool teachers and school staff on Homocysteinuria basics and classroom activities. *$2.50*

2907 Teacher's Guide to Including Students with Disabilities in Regular Physical Education

Brookes Publishing
PO Box 10624
Baltimore, MD 21285   410-337-9580
800-638-3775
FAX: 410-337-8539
e-mail: custserv@brookespublishing.com
www.brookespublishing.com
Martin E. Block, Ph.D., author

Provides simple and creative strategies for meaningfully including children with disabilities in regular physical education programs. *$39.00*

288 pages Paperback
ISBN 1-557661-56-1

2908 Teacher's Guide to Isovaleric Acidemia

Nutrition Consultant for Crippled Children's Srvc.
Arizona Dept. of Health
Room 203
Phoenix, AZ 85007   602-759-9338

Resource book for preschool teachers and school staff on Isovaleric Acidemia basics and classroom activities. *$2.50*

2909 Teacher's Guide to MSUD

Nutrition Consultant for Crippled Children's Srvc.
Arizona Dept. of Health
Room 203
Phoenix, AZ 85007   602-759-9338

Resource book for preschool teachers and school staff on MSUD basics and classroom activities. *$2.50*

2910 Teacher's Guide to Methylmalonic Acidemia

Nutrition Consultant for Crippled Children's Srvc.
Arizona Dept. of Health
Room 203
Phoenix, AZ 85007   602-759-9338

Resource book for preschool teachers and school staff on Methylmalonic Acidemia basics and classroom activities. *$2.50*

2911 Teacher's Guide to PKU

Nutrition Consultant for Crippled Children's Srvc.
Arizona Dept. of Health
Room 203
Phoenix, AZ 85007   602-759-9338

Resource book for preschool teachers and school staff on PKU basics, NutraSweet warning, and classroom activities. *$2.50*

13 pages

2912 Teacher's Guide to Propionic Acidemia

Nutrition Consultant for Crippled Children's Srvc.
Arizona Dept. of Health
Room 203
Phoenix, AZ 85007   602-759-9338

Resource book for preschool teachers and school staff on Propionic Acidemia basics and classroom activities. *$2.50*

2913 Teachers Working Together

Brookline Books
PO Box 1047
Cambridge, MA 02238   617-868-0360
800-666-2665
FAX: 617-868-1772
e-mail: brooklinebks@delphi.com
www.brooklinebooks.com

Hon Deshier, Author
Jean Schumaker, Author
Karen Harris, Author

This collection of papers describes collaboraborative efforts for such classroom settings as preschools, elementary, middle and high schools, for content area teaching and into the transition to work. Each chapter describes actual practice and analyzes what is required to accomplish this collaboration. *$19.95*

Paperback 1998
ISBN 1-57139-66-4

2914 Teaching Children with Autism: Strategies for Initiating Positive Interactions

Brookes Publishing
PO Box 10624
Baltimore, MD 21285   410-337-9580
                                         800-638-3775
                               FAX: 410-337-8539
e-mail: custserv@brookespublishing.com
www.brookespublishing.com

Stategies for initiating positive interactions and improving learning opportunities. This guide begins with an overview of characteristics and long-term strategies and proceeds through discussions that detail specific techniques for normalizing environments, reducing disruptive behavior, improving language and social skills, and enhancing generalization. *$32.95*

256 pages Paperback
ISBN 1-55766 -80-4

2915 Teaching Disturbed and Disturbing Students An Integrative Approach

Pro-Ed
8700 Shoal Creek Boulevard
Austin, TX 78757
                               FAX: 512-451-8542
                              e-mail: proed1@aol.com

Paul Zionts, author

Using an integrative approach, this text provides teachers with step-by-step details of how to implement and use the methods and theories discussed in each chapter. *$37.00*

465 pages
ISBN 0-89079 -23-8

2916 Teaching Every Child Every Day: Integrated Learning in Diverse Classrooms

Brookline Books
PO Box 1047
Cambridge, MA 02238   617-868-0360
                                        800-666-2665
                               FAX: 617-868-1772
e-mail: brooklinebks@delphi.com
www.brooklinebooks.com

Karen R Harris, Steve Graham, Don Deshler, author

Collection of articles addressing various issues in teaching to diverse classrooms—varied in need for special educational services, English proficiency, and socioeconomic and racial backgrounds. *$19.95*

224 pages Paperback
ISBN 0-57129 -40-0

2917 Teaching Infants and Preschoolers with Handicaps

McGraw-Hill, School Publishing
220 East Danieldale Road
DeSoto, TX 75115   972-224-1111
                                 800-442-9685
                          FAX: 972-228-1982
                               mhschool.com

Builds a solid background in early childhood special education.

380 pages

2918 Teaching Language-Disabled Children A Communication/Games Intervention

Brookline Books
PO Box 1046
Cambridge, MA 02238   617-868-0360
                                        800-666-2665
                               FAX: 617-868-1772
e-mail: brooklinebks@delphi.com
www.brooklinebooks.com

Susan Conant, Author
Milton Budoff, Author
Barbara Hecht, Author

Describes exactly how to play the communication games. It does not simply exhort practitioners to give topic-relevant responses and take advantage of opportunities. It provides specific teaching methods and not simply a new perspective on language remeditation. *$22.95*

Hardcover
ISBN 0-91479 -38-7

2919 Teaching Learners with Mild Disabilities: Integrating Research and Practice

Brooks/Cole Publishing Company
511 Forest Lodge Road
Pacific Grove, CA 93950   831-373-0728
                                       FAX: 831-375-6414
                            e-mail: bc-info@brookscole.com

Ruth Lyn Meese, author

The authors illustrate interactions among regular teachers, special education teachers and students with mild disabilities through the use of hypothetical case studies of students and teachers.

496 pages Paperbound
ISBN 0-53421 -02-0

2920 Teaching Mathematics to Students with Learning Disabilities

Pro-Ed
8700 Shoal Creek Boulevard
Austin, TX 78757
                               FAX: 512-451-8542
                               e-mail: proed1@aol.com

Nancy S. Bley, Author
Carl A. Thornton, Author

New trends in school mathematics have surfaced in the teaching world. Problem-solving, estimation and the use of computers are receiving considerably greater emphasis than in the past and these areas are included in the new text. *$38.00*

486 pages Paperback
ISBN 0-89079 -03-3

2921 Teaching Mildly and Moderately Handicapped

Allyn & Bacon
160 Gould Street
Needham Heights, MA 02194
                                       800-852-8024

Bill R. Gearhart, author

A cross-categorial text provides teaching ideas and techniques. The basic theme is that learning is a constructive process in which the learner interacts with the environment, constructing new systems of knowledge, however, behavioral techniques with recognized value are also presented.

1986

ISBN 0-138939-00-4

2922 Teaching Reading to Children with Down Syndrome

Woodbine House
6510 Bells Mill Road
Bethesda, MD 20817

800-843-7323
www.woodbinehouse.com

Patricia Logan Oelwein, author

Teach your child to read using the author's nationally recognized, proven method. From introducing the alphabet to writing and spelling, the lessons are easy to follow. The many pictures and flash cards included appeal to visual learners and are easy to photocopy. *$ 16.95*

392 pages Paperback

ISBN 0-933149-55-7

2923 Teaching Reading to Disabled and Handicapped Learners

Charles C. Thomas, Publisher
2600 S 1st Street
Springfield, IL 62704

217-789-8980
800-258-8980
FAX: 217-789-9130
e-mail: books@ccthomas.com

Harold D. Love, Author
Feddie W. Litton, Author

Designed as a text for undergraduate and graduate students, it's aim is to help the many children, adolescents, and adults who encounter difficulty with reading. It guides prospective and present special education teachers in assisting and teaching handicapped learners to read. The text integrates traditional methods with newer perspectives to provide and effective reading program in special education. Also available in cloth at $54.95 (ISBN# 0-398-05909-8) *$37.95*

260 pages Paperback

ISBN 0-398062-48-X

2924 Teaching Reading to Handicapped Children

Love Publishing Company
9101 East Kenyon Avenue
Denver, CO 80222

303-221-7333
FAX: 303-221-7444
e-mail: lovepublishing@compuserve.com

Charles Hargis, author

The author covers skills teaching through letter sound association, word identification, synthetic and analytic methods and others, plus testing and assessment. *$24.95*

ISBN 0-89108-13-5

2925 Teaching Self-Determination to Students with Disabilities

Brookes Publishing
PO Box 10624
Baltimore, MD 21285

410-337-9580
800-638-3775
FAX: 410-337-8539
e-mail: custserv@brookespublishing.com
www.brookespublishing.com

Michael L. Wehmeyer, Ph.D., Martin Agran, Ph.D., author

Basic skills for successful transition. This teacher-friendly source will help educators prepare students with disabilities with the specific skills they need for a satisfactory, self-directed life once they leave school. *$34.95*

384 pages Paperback 1997

ISBN 1-55766 -02-5

2926 Teaching Students with Learning and Behavior Problems

Pro-Ed
8700 Shoal Creek Boulevard
Austin, TX 78757

FAX: 512-451-8542
e-mail: proed1@aol.com

Donald D. Hammill, Author
Nettie Bartel, Author

Popular, classic text with a comprehensive overview of best practices in assessing and instructing students with mild-to-moderate learning and behavior problems. *$44.00*

520 pages Paperback

ISBN 0-89079 -10-6

2927 Teaching Students with Mild Learning Problems

Allyn & Bacon
160 Gould Street
Needham Heights, MA 02194

800-852-8024

John Langone, author

Provides teachers with skills for assisting students with mild to moderate handicaps in making successful transitions in school and community environments.

496 pages 1990

ISBN 0-205123-62-7

2928 Teaching Students with Moderate / Servere Disabilities, Including Autism

Charles C. Thomas, Publisher
2600 S 1st Street
Springfield, IL 62704

217-789-8980
800-258-8980
FAX: 217-789-9130
e-mail: books@ccthomas.com

Elva Duran, author

This resource and guide was written to help teachers, parents, and other caregivers provide the best educational opportunities for their students with moderate and severe disabilities. The author addresses functional language and other language intervention strategies, vocational training, community based instruction, transition and postsecondary programming, the adolescent student with autism, students with multiple disabilities, parent and family issues, and legal concerns. Cloth $79.95 *$58.95*

416 pages Paperback
ISBN 0-398067-01-5

2929   Teaching Students with Special Needs in Inclusive Settings, 2nd Edition

Allyn & Bacon
160 Gould Street
Needham Heights, MA   02494   781-455-1200
800-852-8024

Carol Dowdy, author
Tom Smith, Author
Ed Polloway, Author
James Patton, Author

This text is intended to be a survey text providing practical guidance to general education teachers. It will help them to meet the diverse needs of students with disabilities.

544 pages
ISBN 0-20527-16-6

2930   Teaching Young Children to Read Brookline Books

PO Box 1047
Cambridge, MA   02238   617-868-0360
800-666-2665
FAX: 617-868-1772
e-mail: brooklinebks@delphi.com
www.brooklinebooks.com

Wood Smethurst, author
Milt Budoff, Publisher

Detailed instructions on teaching reading to preschoolers. Gradually develops full fluency. *$16.95*

192 pages Paperback
ISBN 0-57129-48-6

2931   Teaching and Mainstreaming Autistic Children

Love Publishing Company
9101 East Kenyon Avenue
Denver, CO   80222   303-221-7333
FAX: 303-221-7444
e-mail: lovepublishing@compuserve.com
Peter Knoblock, author

Dr. Knoblock advocates a highly organized, structured environment for autistic children, with teachers and parents working together. His premise is that the learning and social needs of autistic children must be analyzed and a daily program designed with interventions that respond to this functional analysis of their behavior. *$24.95*

ISBN 0-89108-11-9

2932   Teaching the Bilingual Special Education Student

Ablex Publishing Corporation
PO Box 811
Stamford, CT   06904
FAX: 201-767-6717

Angela Carrasquillo, author

This book focuses on teaching those students who are bilingual, handicapped and in need of special instruction. It responds to the complex and practical issues of teaching these students in an effective way.

ISBN 0-89391-23-4

2933   Teaching the Learning Disabled Adolescent

Love Publishing Company
9101 East Kenyon Avenue
Denver, CO   80222   303-221-7333
FAX: 303-221-7444
e-mail: lovepublishing@compuserve.com
Gordon Alley, author

This book gives expert strategies and methods for teaching learning disabled adolescents how, rather than what, to learn. *$34.95*

ISBN 0-89108-94-5

2934   Teaching the Mentally Retarded Student

Allyn & Bacon
160 Gould Street
Needham Heights, MA   02194
800-852-8024

Richard L. Luftig, author

Represents a comprehensive approach to curriculum, methods and strategies for teaching the mildly mentally retarded student.

640 pages 1987

2935   Technology and Handicapped People

Springer Publishing Company
536 Broadway
New York, NY   10012   212-431-4370
FAX: 212-941-7842
Office Of Technology Assessment, author

Important information for concerned professionals about new rehabilitation techniques and treatments for handicapped people. *$29.95*

224 pages Hardcover
ISBN 0-82614-10-8

2936   Textbooks and the Student Who Can't Read Them: A Guide for Teaching Content

Brookline Books
PO Box 1046
Cambridge, MA   02238   617-868-0360
800-666-2665
FAX: 617-868-1772
e-mail: brooklinebks@delphi.com
www.brooklinebooks.com

Jean Ciborowski

Based on a careful analysis of 10 textbook programs, the author concisely and sensibly indicates the procedures that facilitate teachers' use of regular grade level textbooks with low-reading students. *$21.95*

Paperback
ISBN 0-91479-57-3

2937 There's a Hearing Impaired Child in My Class

Gallaudet University Bookstore
800 Florida Avenue NE
Washington, DC 20002   202-651-5000
    800-451-1073
    FAX: 202-651-5489

Debra Nussbaum, author

This complete package provides basic facts about deafness, practical strategies for teaching hearing impaired children, and the question-and-answer information for all students. *$16.95*

44 pages

2938 To Teach a Dyslexic

AVKO Educational Research Foundation
3084 W Willard Road
Clio, MI 48420   810-686-9283
    FAX: 810-686-1101

Don McCabe, Research Director

A dyslexic tells how luck enabled him to learn to read and how his blissful ignorance and stubbornness enabled him to discover how to teach other dyslexics to read and write. *$14.95*

288 pages Paperback

2939 Toward Effective Public School Program for Deaf Students

Teachers College Press
Columbia University
New York, NY 10027
    800-575-6566
    FAX: 212-678-4149

Thomas Kluwin, author

This book translates research and data into useable recommendations and possible courses of action for organizing effective public school programs for deaf students. *$22.95*

272 pages Paperback
ISBN 0-807731-59-5

2940 Traumatic Brain Injury: Mechanisms of Damage, Assessment & Internvention

Pro-Ed
8700 Shoal Creek Boulevard
Austin, TX 78757
    FAX: 512-451-8542
    e-mail: proed1@aol.com

Erin D. Bigler, author

Traumatic Brain Injury ranks as one of the most prevalent disorders with estimates ranging in hundreds of thousands of new cases each year. This book focuses on the mechanisms of acquired brain injury and the methods of assessment, along with treatment and outcome variables. *$41.00*

458 pages Hardcover
ISBN 0-89079 -01-1

2941 Treating Cerebral Palsy for Clinicians by Clinicians

Pro-Ed
8700 Shoal Creek Boulevard
Austin, TX 78757
    FAX: 512-451-8542
    e-mail: proed1@aol.com

Eugene T. McDonald, author

A clinical manual for professionals beginning to work with persons who have cerebral palsy. *$31.00*

312 pages
ISBN 0-89079 -41-4

2942 Treating Disordered Speech Motor Control

Pro-Ed
8700 Shoal Creek Boulevard
Austin, TX 78757
    FAX: 512-451-8542
    e-mail: proed1@aol.com

Deanie Vogel & Michael P. Cannito, author

This book about neuromotor disturbances of speech production is aimed at practicing professionals and advanced graduate students interested in the neuropathologies of communication. *$36.00*

410 pages
ISBN 0-89079 -99-2

2943 Treating Families of Brain Injury Survivors

Springer Publishing Company
536 Broadway
New York, NY 10012   212-431-4370
    FAX: 212-941-7842

Paul R. Sachs, author

Provides the mental health practitioner with a comprehensive program for helping families of head injury survivors cope with the change in their lives. Includes background on medical aspects of head injury, family structure functioning and special needs of various family members.

220 pages
ISBN 0-82616 -20-1

2944 Understanding and Teaching Emotionally Disturbed Children & Adolescents

Pro-Ed
8700 Shoal Creek Boulevard
Austin, TX 78757
    FAX: 512-451-8542
    e-mail: proed1@aol.com

Phyllis L. Newcomer, author

The teacher's handbook provides information that will change misconceptions about children who are frequently labeled as emotionally disturbed. It also gives information about a wide variety of intervention methods and approaches for use in educational settings. *$41.00*

620 pages Hardover
ISBN 0-89079 -75-4

2945 Using the Dictionary of Occupational Titles in Career Decision Making

Stout Vocational Rehab Institute
University of Wisconsin-Stout
Menomonie, WI 5413G
    FAX: 715-232-2356

Robert R. Fry, Manager
Darlene Botterbusch, Program Assistant

This is a self-study manual for learning how to use the 1991 U.S. Department of Labor's Dictionary of Occupational Titles. It gives the DOT user a tool to understand the DOT and then put its information to work. Shows how to quickly obtain information about the work performed in 12,741 occupations listed and described in the DOT and the worker requirements for those occupations. *$24.00*

142 pages Softcover

2946 VBS Special Education Teaching Guide

LifeWay Christian Resources Southern Baptist Conv.
127 9th Avenue N
Nashville, TN 37234   **615-251-2000**
                                      800-458-2772
                 e-mail: specialed@lifeway.com
                                www.lifeway.com

Ellen Beene, Editor

This book contains teaching plans for five bible study sessions with reproducible handouts for learners. The plans use multisensory, experiential-based learning activities designed for adults and older youth who have mental retardation. Suggestions for Bible learning, crafts, recreation, snacks and theme interpretation are included. Designed primarily for Vacation Bible School, but may be used in camp/retreat settings. *$9.95*

56 pages Yearly

2947 Vocational Evaluation in Private Sector Rehabiltitation

Stout Vocational Rehab Institute
University of Wisconsin-Stout
Menomonie, WI 54751   **715-232-1478**
                                 FAX: 715-232-2356

Ronald R. Fry, Manager
Darlene Botterbusch, Program Assistant

The purpose of this book is to present comprehensive information on vocational evaluation in private sector rehabilitation. Primarily designed to be used by individuals who are new to private rehabilitation or vocational evaluation (or both). *$24.00*

201 pages Softcover

2948 Vocational Rehabilitation and Employment

Books on Special Children
PO Box 305
Congers, NY 10920   **845-638-1236**
                                 FAX: 845-638-0847
                  e-mail: irene@boscbooks.com
M.S. Moon, author

Defines kinds of work, expectations, goals and programs. Contributions in general issues of supported employment, training and management and community based programs. *$47.00*

372 pages Hardcover

2949 We Can Speak for Ourselves/Self Advocacy by Mentally Handicapped People

Brookline Books
PO Box 1046
Cambridge, MA 02238   **617-495-3682**
                                    800-666-BOOK
                                 FAX: 617-868-1772
                e-mail: brooklinebks@delphi.com
Paul Williams & Bonnie Shoultz, author

The fundamental right of speaking for oneself has long been denied people with developmental disabilities. This book offers practical advice and support for parents, group home residence workers, day activity workers, citizens and professionals interested in developing self-advocacy for mentally handicapped people. *$17.95*

Paperback
ISBN 0-253363-65-9

2950 Wintergreen Orchard House

Wintergreen Orchard House
PO Box 15899
New Orleans, LA 70175   **504-866-8658**
                                    800-321-9479
                                 FAX: 504-866-8710

Allan B. Corderman, Publisher
$25.95

320 pages Annual

2951 Working Bibliography on Behavioral and Emotional Disorders

Natl. Clearinghouse for Alcohol & Drug Information
PO Box 2345
Rockville, MD 20847
                                    800-729-6686
                                 FAX: 301-468-6433
                      e-mail: info@health.org
                                www.health.org

Lizabeth J. Foster, Librarian/Info. Resource Mgr.

NCADI is a service of the U.S. Substance Abuse and Mental Health Services Administration. As the national focal point for information on alcohol and other drugs, NCADI collects, prepares, classifies, and distributes information about alcohol, tobacco and other drugs, prevention strategies and materials, research, treatment, etc.

40 pages

2952 Working Together with Children and Families: Case Studies

Paul H. Brookes Publishing Company
PO Box 10624
Baltimore, MD 21285
                                    800-638-3775
                                 FAX: 410-337-8539
P.J. McWilliam, author
Karen G. Radke, Marketing Director

Early interventionists will be able to bridge the gap between theory and practice with this edited collection of case studies. *$23.00*

336 pages 1993
ISBN 1-557661-23-5

2953 Working with Visually Impaired Young Students: A Curriculum Guide

Charles C. Thomas, Publisher
2600 S 1st Street
Springfield, IL 62704   **217-789-8980**
                                    800-258-8980
                                 FAX: 217-789-9130
                    e-mail: books@ccthomas.com

Ellen Trief, Author

The first step in the education process of a visually impaired child is the early identification and treatment by an eye care specialist. This book is geared to the age of birth through 3-years. Available in cloth, paperback and hardcover. *$36.95*

> *208 pages Paperback*
> *ISBN 0-398068-75-5*

2954 You Can Prevent or Correct Learning Disabilities

Gallery Bookshop
PO Box 270
Mendocino, CA   95460   707-937-2665

Hilde Mosse, author

The complete handbook of children's reading disorders. *$34.95*

> *732 pages Paperback*
> *ISBN 0-80772 -83-3*

Testing Resources

2955 AEPS Child Progress Report: For Children Ages Birth to Three

Brookes Publishing
PO Box 10624
Baltimore, MD   21285   410-337-9580
                                   800-638-3775
                               FAX: 410-337-8539
e-mail: custserv@brookespublishing.com
www.brookespublishing.com

This chart helps monitor change by visually displaying current abilities, intervention targets, and child progress. In packages of 30. *$18.00*

> *6 pages Gate-fold*
> *ISBN 1-55766 -65-0*

2956 AEPS Data Recording Forms: For Children Ages Birth to Three

Brookes Publishing
PO Box 10624
Baltimore, MD   21285   410-337-9580
                                   800-638-3775
                               FAX: 410-337-8539
e-mail: custserv@brookespublishing.com
www.brookespublishing.com

These forms can be used by child development professionals on four separate occasions to pinpoint and then monitor a child's strengths and needs in the six key areas of skill development measured by the AEPS Test. Packages of 10. *$23.00*

> *36 pages Saddle-stiched*
> *ISBN 1-55766 -97-2*

2957 AEPS Measurement for Birth to Three Years (Volume 1)

Brookes Publishing
PO Box 10624
Baltimore, MD   21285   410-337-9580
                                   800-638-3775
                               FAX: 410-337-8539
e-mail: custserv@brookespublishing.com
www.brookespublishing.com

Diane Bricker, PhD, author

This dynamic volume explains the Assessment, Evaluation and Programming System, provides the complete AEPS Test and parallel assessment/evaluation tools for families and includes the forms and plans needed for implementation. *$39.00*

> *352 pages*

2958 AEPS Measurement for Three to Six Years

Brookes Publishing
PO Box 10624
Baltimore, MD   21285   410-337-9580
                                   800-638-3775
                               FAX: 410-337-8539
e-mail: custserv@brookespublishing.com
www.brookespublishing.com

$57.00

> *400 pages Spiral-bound*
> *ISBN 1-55766 -87-1*

2959 AIR: Assessment of Interpersonal Relations

Pro-Ed
8700 Shoal Creek Boulevard
Austin, TX   78757
                               FAX: 512-451-8542
                         e-mail: proed1@aol.com

Bruce A. Bracken, author

A thoroughly researched and standardized clinical instrument assessing the quality of adolescents' interpersonal relationships in a hierarchical fashion, including global relationship quality and relationship quality with three domains: Family, Social and Academic. *$89.00*

2960 ALST: Adolescent Language Screening Test

Pro-Ed
8700 Shoal Creek Boulevard
Austin, TX   78757
                               FAX: 512-451-8542
                         e-mail: proed1@aol.com

Denise L. Morgan & Arthur M. Guilford, author

Provides speech/language pathologists and other interested professionals with a rapid thorough method for screening adolescents (ages 11-17). *$119.00*

2961 Academic Skills Problems

National Association of School Psychologists
8455 Colesville Road
Suite 100
Silver Spring, MD   20910   301-681-3223
                               FAX: 301-608-2514

Offers direct assessment and intervention information for professionals.

> *232 pages*

2962 Adaptive Mainstreaming

Longman Publishing Group
95 Church Street
White Plains, NY   10601

Maynard Reynolds, author

A practical introduction to education for handicapped and gifted students. It presents research-based rationales for teaching exceptional students in the least restrictive environment. It provides historical perspectives, offers realistic descriptions of prevailing practices in the field, and review trends and new directions.

366 pages Paperback 1988

ISBN 0-582285-04-6

2963 Ages & Stages Questionnaires: 2nd Edition

Brookes Publishing
PO Box 10624
Baltimore, MD 21285 **410-337-9580**
800-638-3775
FAX: 410-337-8539
e-mail: custserv@brookespublishing.com
www.brookespublishing.com
Diane Bricker, Ph.D., Jane Squires, Ph.D., author

ASQ is an economical & field-tested system for identifying whether infants & young children may require further developmental evaluation & offers a screening & tracking program that helps early intervention professionals, service coordinators, & administrators maximize financial resources while promoting the health & growth of the children they serve. Set includes 11 color-coded, reproducible questionnaires, 11 reproducible, age appropriate scoring sheets, 1 storage box, and the ASQ User's Guide *$135.00*

2964 Assessing Students with Special Needs

Longman Publishing Group
95 Church Street
White Plains, NY 10601 **914-993-5000**

Robert A. Gable, author

Step-by-step guide to informal, classroom assessment of students with special needs.

174 pages Paperback 1990

ISBN 0-801301-77-7

2965 Assessing Young Children

National Association of School Psychologists
8455 Colesville Road
Suite 1000
Silver Spring, MD 20910 **301-681-3223**
FAX: 301-608-2514

Assessment is the key topic in this manual which discusses why and how assessment is unique for the early childhood population.

63 pages

2966 Assessing and Screening Preschoolers

National Association of School Psychologists
8455 Colesville Road
Suite 1000
Silver Spring, MD 20910 **301-681-3223**
FAX: 301-608-2514

A comprehensive and practical source to help professionals in counseling, school, and clinical psychology, special education, and human development become more competent in assessing preschoolers with special needs.

484 pages

2967 Assessment Log & Developmental Progress Charts for the CCPSN

Brookes Publishing
PO Box 10624
Baltimore, MD 21285 **410-337-9580**
800-638-3775
FAX: 410-337-8539
e-mail: custserv@brookespublishing.com
www.brookespublishing.com

This 28-page booklet allows readers to actually chart the ongoing progress of each preschool child. Available in packages of 10. *$22.00*

28 pages Saddle-stiched

ISBN 1-55766 -39-5

2968 Assessment of Learners with Special Needs

Allyn & Bacon
160 Gould Street
Needham Heights, MA 02194
800-852-8024

Richard L. Luftig, author

The central goal of this book is to help teachers become sophisticated, informed test consumers in terms of choosing, using and interpreting commercially prepared tests for their special needs students.

508 pages Casebound 1989

ISBN 0-205227-33-3

2969 Benchmark Measures

Educators Publishing Service
31 Smith Place
Cambridge, MA 02138 **617-367-2700**
800-225-5750
FAX: 617-547-0412
www.epsbooks.com
Aylett Cox, author

Ungraded test containing three sequential levels that assess alphabet and dictionary skills, reading, handwriting and spelling, and correspond to the first three schedules of the Alphabetic Phonics curriculum. The tests can be used at any level to measure a student's general knowledge of phonics. *$64.40*

Kit

2970 CREVT: Comprehensive Receptive and Expressive Vocabulary Test

Pro-Ed
8700 Shoal Creek Boulevard
Austin, TX 78757
FAX: 512-451-8542
e-mail: proed1@aol.com
Gerald Wallace & Donald D. Hammill, author

A new, innovative, efficient measure of both receptive and expressive oral vocabulary. The CREVT has two subtests and is based on the most current theories of vocabulary development, suitable for ages 4 through 17. *$174.00*

Complete Kit

2971 DAYS: Depression and Anxiety in Youth Scale

Pro-Ed
8700 Shoal Creek Boulevard
Austin, TX 78757
FAX: 512-451-8542
e-mail: proed1@aol.com
Phyllis Newcomer/Edna Barenbaum & Brian R. Bryant, author

A unique battery of three norm-references scales useful in identifying major depressive disorder and over-anxious disorders in children and adolescents. *$129.00*

Complete Kit

2972   DOCS: Developmental Observation Checklist System

Pro-Ed
8700 Shoal Creek Boulevard
Austin, TX   78757
                    FAX: 512-451-8542
                    e-mail: proed1@aol.com

Wayne P. Hresko, Author
Shirley A. Miguel & Associates, Author

A three-part system for the assessment of very young children with respect to general development, adjustment behavior and parent stress and support. *$124.00*

2973   Daytime Development Center

Joseph Willard Health Center
3750 Old Lee Highway
Fairfax, VA   22030   703-246-7180
                    FAX: 703-246-7307

Susan Delauter, CU-SLP, Dir. of Health Services
Allan Phillips, Director of Early Intervention

Offers assessments, evaluations and educational/therapeutic infant programs for parents and their children.

Sliding Scale

2974   Developmental Services Center

Therapeutic Nursery Program
4525 Lee Street NE
Washington, DC   20019   202-388-3216
                    FAX: 202-576-8799

Alice Anderson

Offers assessment information and evaluation for developmentally delayed students.

2975   Dyslexia Screening Survey

Fearon/Janus
500 Harbor Boulevard
Belmont, CA   94002   650-631-2525

Robert E. Valett, author

Tests for possible dyslexia in reading-disabled students. *$9.60*

2976   Introduction to Special Education Assessment

Love Publishing Company
4925 East Pacific Place
22353
Denver, CO   80222   303-221-7333
                    FAX: 303-221-7444
          e-mail: lovepublishing@compuserve.com

Carol Gearhart, author

Includes informal assessment, preschool assessment and vocational assessment. It is not highly technical but readable and accurate. *$19.95*

ISBN 0-89108 -14-X

2977   K-BIT: Kaufman Brief Intelligence Test

AGS
Publishers Building
PO Box 99
Circle Pines, MN   55014
                    800-328-2560
                    FAX: 612-786-9007
                    www.agsnet.com

Robert Zaske, Market Manager

Quick and easy-to-use, KBIT assesses verbal and non-verbal abilities through two reliable subtests - vocabulary and matricies. *$ 124.95*

Ages 4-90

2978   K-FAST: Kaufman Functional Academic Skills Test

AGS
Publishers Building
PO Box 99
Circle Pines, MN   55014
                    800-328-2560
                    FAX: 612-786-9007
                    www.agsnet.com

Robert Zaske, Market Manager

Helps assess a person's capacity to function effectively in society regarding functional reading and math skills. *$99.95*

Ages 15-85+

2979   K-SEALS: Kaufman Survey of Early Academic and Language Skills

AGS
Publishers Building
PO Box 99
Circle Pines, MN   55014
                    800-328-2560
                    FAX: 612-786-9007
                    www.agsnet.com

Robert Zaske, Market Manager

An individually administered test of children's of both expressive and receptive skills, pre-academic skills and articulation. K-SEALS offers reliable scores usually in less than 25 minutes. *$ 179.95*

Ages 3-0; 6-11

2980   KLST-2: Kindergarten Language Screening Test Edition, 2nd Edition

Pro-Ed
8700 Shoal Creek Boulevard
Austin, TX   78757   512-451-3246
                    FAX: 512-451-8542
                    e-mail: proed1@aol.com

Sharon V. Gauthier & Charles L. Madison, author

Identifies children who need further diagnostic testing to determine whether or not they have language deficits that will accelerate academic failure. *$94.00*

2981 Kaufman Test of Educational Achievement (K-TEA)

AGS
Publishers Building
PO Box 99
Circle Pines, MN 55014

800-328-2560
FAX: 612-786-9007
www.agsnet.com

Robert Zaske, Market Manager

K-TEA is an individually administered diagnostic battery that measures reading, mathematics, and spelling skills. Setting the standards in achievement testing today, K-TEA Comprehensive provides the complete diagnostic information you need for educational assessment and program planning. The Brief Forum is indispensable for school and clinical psychologists, special education teachers when a quick a measure of achievement is needed. Now with a 1998 Normative Update. *$249.95*

2982 Life Centered Career Education: A Contemporary Based Approach 4th Ed.

Council for Exceptional Children
1920 Association Drive
Reston, VA 20191

703-620-3660
888-232-7232
FAX: 703-264-9494
e-mail: service@cec.sped.org
www.cec.sped.org

Donn Brolin, author
Cathy Mack, Production Manager

Provides a framework for building 97 functional skill competencies appropriate for preparing for adult life and special education students. *$28.00*

175 pages
ISBN 0-86586-41-9

2983 Managing Attention Disorders in Children

National Association of School Psychologists
8455 Colesville Road
Suite 1000
Silver Spring, MD 20910

301-681-3223
FAX: 301-608-2514

A guide for practitioners offering information on treating Attention Deficit Disorders.

2984 Measure of Cognitive-Linguistic Abilities (MCLA)

Speech Bin
1965 25th Avenue
Vero Beach, FL 32960

561-770-0007
800-477-3324
FAX: 561-770-0006
www.speechbin.com

Wendy Ellmo, et al, author

A diagnostic test of cognitive-linguistic abilities of adolescents and adults with traumatically induced brain injuries. High level. Normed. *$89.00*

100 pages
ISBN 0-93785-72-

2985 ONLINE

West Virginia Research and Training Center
PO Box 1004
Institute, WV 25112

304-766-4602
800-624-8284
FAX: 304-766-2689
e-mail: online @rtc2.icdi.wvu.edu
www.icdi.wvu.edu

On Line Editor

A quarterly newsletter offering information about hardware technology, software (commercial and home grown); applications that work and bonuses such as an exchange program for copyright-free software. *$25.00*

Quarterly

2986 OWLS: Oral and Written Language Scales LC/OE & WE

AGS
Publishers Building
PO Box 99
Circle Pines, MN 55014

800-328-2560
FAX: 612-786-9007
www.agsnet.com

Robert Zaske, Market Manager

One kit provides an assessment of listening comprehension while the other assesses oral expression tasks: semantic, syntactic, pragmatic, and supralinguistic aspects of language. Written Expression may be administered individually or in small groups. *$249.95*

2987 PAT-3: Photo Articulation Test, Third Edition

Pro-Ed
8700 Shoal Creek Boulevard
Austin, TX 78757

FAX: 512-451-8542
e-mail: proed1@aol.com

Stanley Dickey, Author
Anton Soder, Author
Barbara Lippke, Author

This test consists of 72 color photographs. The first 69 photos test consonants and all but one vowel and one diphthong. The remaining pictures test connected speech and the remaining vowel and diphthong. *$144.00*

Complete Kit

2988 Peabody Early Experiences Kit - PEEK

AGS
Publishers Building
PO Box 99
Circle Pines, MN 55014

800-328-2560
FAX: 612-786-9007
www.agsnet.com

Robert Zaske, Market Manager

1,000 activities and all the materials you need to build youngsters' cognitive, social and language skills. Manuals, puppets, manipulatives, picture card deck, picture mini decks and more to teach early development concepts. *$789.95*

2989 Peabody Individual Achievement Test-Revised Normative Update (PIAT-R-NU)

AGS
Publishers Building
PO Box 99
Circle Pines, MN 55014

800-328-2560
FAX: 612-786-9007
www.agsnet.com

Robert Zaske, Market Manager

PIAT-R-NU is an efficient individual measure of academic achievement. Reading, mathematics, and spelling are assessed in a simple, non-threatening format that requires only a pointing response for most items. This multiple choice format makes the PIAT-R ideal for assessing individuals who hesitate to give a spoken response, or have limited expressive abilities. *$289.98*

2990 Peabody Language Development Kits-PLDK

AGS
Publishers Building
PO Box 99
Circle Pines, MN 55014

800-328-2560
FAX: 612-786-9007
www.agsnet.com

Robert Zaske, Market Manager

The main goals of the Peabody Kit language program are to stimulate overall language skills in Standard English and, for each level of the program, advance children's cognitive skills about a year. *$ 649.95*

Level P
ISBN 0-88671-25-1

2991 Pediatric Early Elementary-PEEX II Examination

Educators Publishing Service
31 Smith Place
Cambridge, MA 02138

617-367-2700
800-225-5750
FAX: 617-547-0412
www.epsbooks.com

Dr. Mel Levine, author

Assesses the second-fourth grade child's performance on thirty-two tasks in six specific areas of development: fine-motor function, language, gross-motor function, memory, visual processing, and delayed recall. At three points during the exam, the child is rated on selective attention and behavior and effect.

$15.40 - $93
ISBN 0-83888-80-6

2992 Pediatric Exam of Educational-PEERAMID Readiness at Middle Childhood

Educators Publishing Service, Inc.
31 Smith Place
Cambridge, MA 02138

617-367-2700
800-225-5750
FAX: 617-547-0412
www.epsbooks.com

Dr. Mel Levine, author

Assesses the 4th-10th grade child's performance on thirty-one tasks in six specific areas: minor neurological indicators, fine-motor function, language, gross-motor function, temporal-sequential organization, and visual processing. Complete set.

$15.40 - $109
ISBN 0-83888-99-3

2993 Pediatric Examination of Educational Readiness

Educators Publishing Service
31 Smith Place
Cambridge, MA 02138

617-367-2700
800-225-5750
FAX: 617-547-0412
www.epsbooks.com

Dr. Mel Levine, author

Assesses the Pre-1st grade child's performance on twenty-nine tasks in six specific areas of development: orientation, gross-motor, visual-fine motor, sequential, linguistic and preacademic learning. The child is rated on ten dimensions of selective attention/activity processing efficiency and adaptation. Complete set.

$12.85 - $86.40
ISBN 0-83888-80-1

2994 Pediatric Extended Examination at-PEET Three

Educators Publishing Service
31 Smith Place
Cambridge, MA 02138

617-367-2700
800-225-5750
FAX: 617-547-0412
www.epsbooks.com

Dr. Mel Levine, author

Assesses the preschool-age child's performance on twenty-eight tasks in five basic areas of development: gross-motor, language, visual-fine motor, memory, and intersensory integration. Complete set.

$13.75 - $126
ISBN 0-83888-79-4

2995 Pre-Reading Screening Procedures

Educators Publishing Service
31 Smith Place
Cambridge, MA 02138

617-367-2700
800-225-5750
FAX: 617-547-0412
www.epsbooks.com

Beth Slingerland, author

This revised group test, for grades K-1, evaluates auditory, visual and kinesthetic strengths in order to identify children who may have some form of dyslexia or specific language disability. *$ 18.00*

Grades K-1
ISBN 0-83885-23-4

2996 Preparing for ACT Assessment

American College Testing Program
2201 Dodge
168
Iowa City, IA 52243   319-337-1000

Designed to help high school students ready themselves for the ACT Assessment's subject area tests, explains the purposes of the four tests, describes their content and format, provides tips and exercises to improve student's test-taking skills and includes a complete sample text with scoring key.

2997 Psycho-Educational Assessment of Preschool Children

National Association of School Psychologists
8455 Colesville Road
Suite 1000
Silver Spring, MD 20910   301-681-3223
                                 FAX: 301-608-2514

This is a contributed text on assessing specific skills of preschool children.

592 pages

2998 RULES: Revised

Speech Bin
1965 25th Avenue
Vero Beach, FL 32960   561-770-0007
                             800-477-3324
                             FAX: 561-770-0006
                             www.speechbin.com

Jane Webb, Author
Barbara Duckett, Author

Treatment program for young children who have phonological disorders. *$43.95*

280 pages
ISBN 0-93785 -51-3

2999 Receptive-Expressive Emergent-REEL-2 Language Test, Second Edition

Pro-Ed
8700 Shoal Creek Boulevard
Austin, TX 78757
                        FAX: 512-451-8542
                        e-mail: proed1@aol.com
Kenneth R. Bzoch & Richard League, author
Kenneth R. Bzoch, Author
Richard League, Author

A revision of the popular scale used for the multidimensional analysis of emergent language. The REEL-2 is specifically designed for use with a broad range of at risk infants and toddlers in the new multidisciplinary programs developing under P.L. 99-457. *$79.00*

3000 Slingerland High School/College Screening

Educators Publishing Service
31 Smith Place
Cambridge, MA 02138   617-367-2700
                             800-225-5750
                             FAX: 617-547-0412
                             www.epsbooks.com

Carol Murray, author

Assessments of high school and college level students to determine specific language disability and predict academic strengths as well as difficulties.

$17 - $23.95
ISBN 0-83882 -78-2

3001 Slingerland Screening Tests

Educators Publishing Service
31 Smith Place
Cambridge, MA 02138   617-367-2700
                             800-225-5750
                             FAX: 617-547-0412
                             www.epsbooks.com

Beth H. Slingerland, author

These tests, by Beth Slingerland, for individuals or groups of children, grades 1-6, identify children who show indications of having specific language disability in reading, handwriting, spelling or speaking. Form D evaluates personal orientation in time and space as well as the ability to express ideas in writing.

$14.80 - $27.45
ISBN 0-83882 -02-2

3002 Special Orientation and Sequencing Development Remedial Activities

Psychological & Educational Publications
PO Box 520
Hydesville, CA 95547   707-768-1807
                              800-523-5775

Designed to be used to remediate those children who perform poorly on any one or more activities of the Test of Pictures test. *$ 59.95*

3003 Specific Language Disability Test

Educators Publishing Service
31 Smith Place
Cambridge, MA 02138   617-367-2700
                             800-225-5750
                             FAX: 617-547-0412
                             www.epsbooks.com

Neva Malcomesius, author

Tests for individuals or groups to evaluate students in grades 6-8. Sub-tests I-V evaluate perception in visual discrimination, visual memory, visual motor-coordination. Sub-tests VI-X evaluate auditory discrimination, auditory-visual coordination, auditory-motor coordination and comprehension. Teacher's manual. test booklet, and charts and cards are also available.

$2.85 - $21.15
ISSN 0838-84 0

3004 Speech Bin

1965 25th Avenue
Vero Beach, FL 32960   561-770-0007
                             800-477-3324
                             FAX: 561-770-0006
                             www.speechbin.com

561-770-0006, author

Catalog offering test materials, assessment information, books and special education resources for speech-language pathologists, occupational and physical therapists, audiologists, and other rehabilitation professionals in schools, hospitals, clinics and private practices.

ISSN 4773-324

3005 Stocker Probe: Revised

Speech Bin
1965 25th Avenue
Vero Beach, FL   32960   561-770-0007
                                    800-477-3324
                             FAX: 561-770-0006
                             www.speechbin.com
Beatrice Stocker and Robert Goldfarb, author

Diagnostic and treatment program for stuttering and language impairment in children and adults. *$75.00*

144 pages
ISBN 0-93785 -58-0

3006 Stuttering Severity Instrument for Children and Adults

Psychological & Educational Publications
PO Box 520
Hydesville, CA   95547   707-768-1807
                                    800-523-5775

With this tool teachers can determine whether to schedule a child for therapy or to evaluate the effects of treatment.

3007 Survey of Educational Skills and the Survey of Problem-Solving Skills

Educators Publishing Service
31 Smith Place
Cambridge, MA   02138   617-367-2700
                                   800-225-5750
                             FAX: 617-547-0412
                             www.epsbooks.com
Lynn J. Meltzer, author

Both surveys are process measures designed to characterize the problem-solving and learning strategies of students in middle childhood. A detailed rating system enables educators and psychologists to observe each child's performance, to analyze error patterns and to guide the assessment procedure. *$10.00*

96 pages $10.65 - $37.90
ISBN 0-83881 -56-

3008 Taking Part: Introducing Social Skills to Young Children

AGS
Publishers Building
PO Box 99
Circle Pines, MN   55014
                                    800-328-2560
                             FAX: 612-786-9007
                             www.agsnet.com

Robert Zaske, Market Manager

The first social skills curriculum to be linked directly to an assessment tool. More than 30 lessons correlate with the skills assessed by the Social Skills Rating System, a multirater approach to assessing prosocial and problem behaviors. *$149.95*

3009 Teaching Resources & Assessment of Critical Skills

Becoming Independant
1425 Corporate Center Parkway
Santa Rosa, CA   95407   707-527-5904
                             FAX: 707-527-1206
                             becomingindependant.org
Marh Rice & Lauren Meiklejohn, author
John McCue, Chief Executive Officer
Tom Richardson, Chief Operating Officer

An independent living assessment tool consisting of four booklets and master forms and a cassette tape. The tool was developed by Becoming Independent/TRACE, incorporating over 15 years of experience in providing independent living services. *$129.00*

3010 Test Accommodations for Students with Disabilities

Charles C. Thomas, Publisher
2600 South 1st Street
Springfield, IL   62704   217-789-8980
                                     800-258-8980
                             FAX: 217-789-9130
                             e-mail: books@ccthomas.com
Edward Burns, author

Test Accommodations for Students with Disabilities considers legal questions, theoretical issues, and practical methods for meeting the assessment needs of students with diabilities. The book is comprised of ten chapters and includes test accommodations topics relating to federal and state regulations (including the IDEA Amendments Act of 1997), problems concerning reliability and validity, and practical strategies for planning test accomodations and adapting and modifying tests. Cloth $66.95 *$49.95*

340 pages Paperback 1998
ISBN 0-398068-45-3

3011 Test Critiques, Volumes I-X

Pro-Ed
8700 Shoal Creek Boulevard
Austin, TX   78757
                             FAX: 512-451-8542
                             e-mail: proed1@aol.com
Daniel J. Keyser & Richard C. Sweetland, author

Provides the professional and nonprofessional with in-depth, evaluative studies of more than 800 of the most widely used of these assessment instruments. *$649.00*

3012 Test of Early Reading Ability Deaf or Hard of Hearing

Pro-Ed
8700 Shoal Creek Boulevard
Austin, TX   78757
                             FAX: 512-451-8542
                             e-mail: proed1@aol.com

D. Kim Reid, Author
Wayne P. Hresko, Author
Donald D. Hammill, Author

This adaptation of the TERA-2 for simultaneous communication of American Sign Language is the ONLY individually administered test of reading designed for children with moderate to profound sensory hearing loss. *$169.00*

Complete Kit

3013 Test of Language Development- Primary, Third Edition

Pro-Ed
8700 Shoal Creek Boulevard
Austin, TX   78757   512-451-3246
                             FAX: 512-451-8542
                             e-mail: proed1@aol.com

Phyllis L. Newcomer, Author
Donald D. Hammill, Author

TOLD P:2 and TOLD 1:2 are the most popular tests of spoken language used by clinicians today. They are used to identify children who have language disorders and to isolate the particular types of disorders they have. Primary Edition for ages 1-4 to 8-11: Intermediate Edition for ages 8-6 to 12-11. *$218.00*

3014   Test of Mathematical Abilities Second Edition

Pro-Ed
8700 Shoal Creek Boulevard
Austin, TX   78757

FAX: 512-451-8542
e-mail: proed1@aol.com

Virginia Brown, Author
Mary Cronin, Author
Elizabeth McEntire, Author

The latest version was developed for use in grades 3 through 12. It measures math performance on the two traditional major skill areas in math as well as attitude, vocabulary and general application of math concepts in real life. *$84.00*

3015   Test of Nonverbal Intelligence Third Edition

Pro-Ed
8700 Shoal Creek Boulevard
Austin, TX   78757

FAX: 512-451-8542
e-mail: proed1@aol.com

Linda Brown, Author
Rita J. Sherbenou, Author
Susan K. Johnson, Author

A language-free measure of intelligence, aptitude and reasoning. The administration of the test requires no reading, writing, speaking or listening on the part of the test subject. The items included in this test are problem-solving tasks that increase in difficulty. Each item presents a set of figures in which one or more components is missing. The test items include one or more of the characteristics of shape, position, direction, rotation, contiguity, shading, size, movement, or pattern. *$229.00*

Complete Kit

3016   Test of Phonological Awareness

Pro-Ed
8700 Shoal Creek Boulevard
Austin, TX   78757

FAX: 512-451-8542
e-mail: proed1@aol.com
Joseph K. Torgesen & Brian R. Bryant, author

Measures young children's awareness of the individual sounds in words. Children who are sensitive to the phonological structure of words in oral language have a much easier time learning to read than children who are not. *$143.00*

3017   Test of Pictures/Forms/Letters/Numbers Spatial Orientation Skills

Psychological & Educational Publications
PO Box 520
Hydesville, CA   95547   707-768-1807
                                    800-523-5775

Developed to aid professionals in determining a child's ability to visually perceive forms and letters in the correct direction. *$35.00*

ISBN 0-93142 -09-8

3018   Test of Visual-Motor Skills: Upper Level

Psychological & Educational Publications
PO Box 520
Hydesville, CA   95547   707-768-1807
                                    800-523-5775

Measures accurately a child's, teenager's and an adult's eye-hand coordination. *$59.00*

ISBN 0-93142 -72-1

3019   Test of Written Spelling Third Edition

Pro-Ed
8700 Shoal Creek Boulevard
Austin, TX   78757

FAX: 512-451-8542
e-mail: proed1@aol.com
Stephen C. Larsen & Donald D. Hammill, author

This revised edition assesses the student's ability to spell words whose spellings are readily predictable in sound-letter patterns, words whose spellings are less predictable, and both types of words considered together. *$74.00*

3020   Welcoming Students who are Deaf-Blind into Typical Classrooms

Brookes Publishing
PO Box 10624
Baltimore, MD   21285   410-337-9580
                                   800-638-3775
                            FAX: 410-337-8539
e-mail: custserv@brookespublishing.com
www.brookespublishing.com

Facilitating School Participation, Learning, and Friendships. Examines successful inclusive educational practices that encourage the participation of students who are deaf-blind. *$37.00*

480 pages Paperback
ISBN 1-55766 -44-8

3021   Woodcock Reading Mastery Tests - Revised

AGS
Publishers Building
PO Box 99
Circle Pines, MN   55014
                            800-328-2560
                    FAX: 612-786-9007
                        www.agsnet.com

Robert Zaske, Market Manager

The Woodcock Reading Mastery Tests - Revised provides an interpretive system and age range to help you assess reading skills of children and adults. Two forms, G and II, make it easy to test and retest, or you can combine the results of both forms for a more comprehensive assessment. Now with a 1998 Normative Update. *$329.95*

3022   Young Children with Special Needs: A Developmentally Appropriate Approach

Allyn & Bacon
160 Gould Street
Needham Heights, MA   02494   781-455-1200
                                         800-852-8024
Michael Davis, Jen Kilgo, Michael Gamel-McCormick, author

This book is designed to prepare students in making curriculum decisions in order to care for and foster the development of young children with special needs in normal early childhood settings.

270 pages
ISBN 0-20518 -94-X

General

3023 Academic Year Abroad

International Education
809 United Nations Plaza
New York, NY 10017   212-949-1840

e-mail: publications@un.org

Howard Edrice, author

Describes over 18,000 study abroad programs, at both the undergraduate and graduate levels, conducted during the academic year by US colleges and universities in some 60 countries around the world. *$29.95*

3024 American Institute for Foreign Study

100 Greenwich Avenue
Greenwich, CT 06830   203-869-9617

Anthony Cook, Executive Director

Provides summer travel programs overseas and in the US ranging from one week to a full academic year.

3025 American Universities International Programs

305 West Magnolia Street
Suite 221
Fort Collins, CO 80521   970-495-0869
FAX: 970-484-6997
e-mail: auip@fru.com

Linda Tomson, Program Coordinator, AUIP
Mary Lowrey, Director For AUIP

Study abroad organization sending students to universities in Australia, New Zealand, and South Africa. Special spring semester program in Edinburg, Scotland. Special spring semester field study program in Belize, in conjunction with the University of Mississippi, offering hands-on experience and considerable travel. $5,495 and upper a semester, depending on program.

3026 American-Scandinavian Foundation

15 East 65th Street
New York, NY 10021   212-288-6400

e-mail: training@amscan.org
www.amscan.org

Jean Prahl, Director of Training

Offers young US citizens the opportunity to live in Scandinavia and train in their professional field.

3027 Antioch College

795 Livermore Street
Yellow Springs, OH 45387   937-767-7331
FAX: 937-754-5232
e-mail: aea@antioch-college.edu

Education abroad offers numerous programs which can be included in undergraduate and graduate study programs.

3028 Army and Air Force Exchange Services

PO Box 660202
Dallas, TX 75266   214-312-3333
FAX: 214-312-3429

Management Recruiter, Contact
HR-C3

A worldwide retail, food and service business. All careers include job training and education, on-the-job training and classroom instruction. The AAFES accepts responsibility for ensuring accessibility and making reasonable accommodations when needed. This program focuses on ability not disability.

3029 Association for International Practical Training

10400 Little Patuxent Parkway
Suite 250
Columbia, MD 21044   410-997-2200
FAX: 410-992-3924
e-mail: aipt@aipt.org
www.aipt.org

Molly Fritts, Communications Manager

Nonprofit organization dedicated to encouraging and facilitating the exchange of qualified individuals between the US and other countries so they may gain practical work experience and improve international understanding.

3030 Basic Facts on Study Abroad

International Education
809 United Nations Plaza
New York, NY 10017   212-949-1840
FAX: 212-963-3489
e-mail: publications@un.org

Barbara Cahn, author

Information book including foreign study planning, educational choices, finances and study abroad programs. *$35.00*

30 pages

3031 Beaver College

450 South Easton Road
Glenside, PA 19038   215-572-2901
888-232-8379
FAX: 215-572-2174
e-mail: cea@beaver.edu
www.beaver.edu/cea

Lorna Stern, Deputy Director

One of the largest college-based study abroad programs in the country. Prices from $8000.00 semester to $22000.00 a year.

3032 Davidson College, Office of Study Abroad

PO Box 1719
Davidson, NC 28036   704-892-2351
FAX: 704-892-2120
e-mail: caortmayer@davidson.edu
www.davidson.edu/administrative/study

Carolyn Ortmayer, Coordinator of Study Abroad

Recognizes the value of study abroad for both the development of world understanding and the development of the student as a broadminded, objective and mature individual. 1. Junior year abroad in Wurzburg, Germany. 2. Fall, Spring or full year in tours, France.

3033 High School Students Guide to Study, Travel, and Adventure Abroad

205 East 42nd Street
New York, NY 10017

888-COU-NCIL
FAX: 212-822-2649
www.councilexchanges.org

Priscilla Tovey, Info. Services
Cheryl Jeffries, Administrative Asst.

This guide provides high school students with all the information they need for a successful trip abroad. Included are sections to help students find out if they're ready for a trip abroad, make the necessary preparations and get the most from their experience. Over 200 programs are described including language study, summer camps, homestays, study tours and work camps. The program descriptions include information for people with disabilities. *$13.95*

308 pages Biennial
ISBN 0-31211-22-8

3034 Higher Education Consortium for Urban Affairs (HECUA)

2233 University Avenue West
Suite 210
St. Paul, MN 55114

651-646-8831
800-554-1089
FAX: 651-659-9421
e-mail: info@hecua.org
www.hecua.org

Michael Eaton, Director of Student Services

HECUA offers college-level off-campus study programs in Latin America, Asia, Europe and the U.S. Internships, field projects and other forms of experimental learning are combined with academic study. Programs focus on issues of inequality and ways to bring about positive social change. HECUA has thirty years of experience and a national reputation for the best in teaching and learning that engages students in meaningful study and action. Students with disabilities welcome to apply.

3035 Internatinal Partnership for Service-Learning

815 2nd Avenue
New York, NY 10017

212-986-0989
FAX: 212-986-5039
e-mail: lchisholm@dfms.org

Howard A. Barry, President

Academic (offering credits) programs for college students, Master Degree in International Service. There are 12 locations around the world.

3036 International Christian Youth Exchange

134 West 26th Street
New York, NY 10001

212-206-7307
FAX: 212-633-9085

Ed Gragert

Offers participants a unique experience to learn about another culture and make friends from different countries.

3037 International University Partnerships

University of Pennsylvania
1011 South Drive
Indiana, PA 15705

724-357-2295
FAX: 724-357-2514

Dr. Robert Morris

Offers a variety of international educational exchange programs to students who wish to study overseas.

3038 Lake Erie College

Academic Programs Abroad
Painesville, OH 44077

440-942-3872
FAX: 440-352-3533

Catherine Shaw

Sends students abroad for a term or longer to develop intellectual awareness and individual maturity.

3039 Lancaster University

North American Office
111 East 10th Street
New York, NY 10003

212-219-1000

e-mail: EthelSussman@compuserve.com
www.lancs.ac.uk/users/internat

Ethel Sussman, N. American Officer

Encourages North American students with physical and learning disabilities to participate in our long-established Study Abroad Program. All students completely integrated into the academic and social life of the University, and take regular University courses in humanities, social sciences, physical sciences and business studies. Summer, fall, spring, full year options. Fully accessible campus, excellent support services, video and alumni contacts available upon request.

3040 Lane Community College

4000 East 30th Avenue
Eugene, OR 97405

541-747-4501
FAX: 541-744-4171
www.lanecc.edu

Work Experience Program students work for credit and in some cases pay, in Europe, Asia, Mexico and Turkey.

3041 Lions Clubs International

300 22nd Street
Oak Brook, IL 60523

630-571-5466
FAX: 630-571-8890
e-mail: info@lionsclubs.org
www.lionsclubs.org

Deborah O'Malley, Health Research Coordinator

Over 44,500 individual clubs in over 186 countries and geographical areas which provide community service and promote better international relations. Clubs work with local communities to provide needed and useful programs for sight, diabetes and hearing.

3042 Lisle
900 County Road 269
Leander, TX 78641   512-259-7621
                                   FAX: 512-259-0392
                    e-mail: mkinney@utnet.utoledo.edu
                           www.lisle.utoledo.edu

Barbara Bratton, Executive Director

Educational organization which works toward world
peace and better quality of human life through increased understanding between persons of similar
and different cultures.

$750 - $3,500

3043 National 4-H Council
7100 Connecticut Avenue
Chevy Chase, MD 20815   301-961-2800
                                   FAX: 301-961-2894
                           www.fourhcouncil.edu

Edith Cowper

Offers two different types of international exchange
programs.

3044 National Society for Experiential Education
3509 Haworth Drive
Suite 207
Raleigh, NC 27609   919-772-0835

Gita Gulati, Program Associate

National nonprofit organization which advocates experiential learning and works with college administrators and high school and college internship
programs.

3045 New Directions for People with Disabilities
135 South Mount Zion Road
Suite 207
Lebanon, IN 46052
                                   FAX: 800-882-8583
                        e-mail: newdirec@sikom.com
                           www.silcom.com~newdirec/

Dee Duncan, Executive Director

Dedicated to providing local, national, and international travel and foreign exchange programs for people with disabilities. Promote understanding,
acceptance, and appreciation of people with disabilties as important and contributing members of our
society as well as to promote a sense of accomplish-
ment, belinging, and self-worth.

3046 People to People International
501 East Armour Boulevard
Kansas City, MO 64109   816-531-4701
                                     800-676-7874
                                   FAX: 816-561-7502
                        e-mail: internships@ptpi.org
                           www.ptpi.org/studyabroad

Jill Sigler, Adult Programs Coordinator

Nonpolitical, nonprofit organization working outside
the government to advance the cause of international
undestanding through international contact. We offer
overseas internships and volunteering opportunities.

3047 Rotary Youth Exchange
Rotary International
One Rotary Center
Evanston, IL 60201   847-866-3000
                                   FAX: 847-866-6116
                                     www.rotary.org

Exchanges for disabled youth are run by local
Rotary clubs and districts. The exchanges can
either be short term or long term exchanges. Contact your local Rotary Club for information.

3048 Scandinavian Seminar
24 Dickinson Street
Amherst, MA 01002   413-253-9736
                                     800-828-3343
                                   FAX: 413-253-5282
                           www.scandinavianseminar.com

Leslie Evans

Student exchange program founded in 1949.

3049 Sister Cities International
1424 K Street Northwest
Suite 600
Washington, DC 20005   202-347-8630
                                   FAX: 202-393-6524
                             www.sister-cities.org

Tim Honey, Executive Director

Committed to the goal of strengthening global understanding by encouraging and assisting sister city relationships between US and foreign communities.

3050 Southern Illinois University at Carbondale
Carbondale, IL 62901   618-453-2121

Study Abroad Programs

Main emphasis in international programs abroad are
school-to-school direct exchanges and exchanges
through organizations such as the International Student Exchange Program.

3051 State University of NY College at Buffalo
1300 Elmwood Avenue
Cleveland Hall 416
Buffalo, NY 14222   716-878-4620
                                   FAX: 716-878-3054
                        e-mail: intleduc@buffalostate.edu
                             www.buffalostate.edu

Dr. Lee Ann Grace, Director, Intl Education

Provides international educational exchange opportunities for students of university age and older
through its Office of International Education.

3052 State University of New York
1400 Washington Avenue
Albany, NY 12222   518-442-3300
                                   FAX: 518-442-3235
                                     www.albany.edu

Dr. Reynold Bloom

Offers over 150 international educational exchange
programs in 37 different countries.

3053 University of Minnesota at Crookston

2900 University Avenue
Crookston, MN   56716   218-281-8508
                               800-UMC-MINN
                               FAX: 218-281-8050
                 e-mail: mprada@mail.crk.umn.edu
                              www.crk.umn.edu

Mario Prada, Multicultural/Intenet Prog. Dir.

A four-year college with innovative educational programs for the acquisition of technical skills and a liberal arts education.

3054 University of Oregon International Service

330 Oregon Hall
Eugene, OR   97403   541-346-3508

Paul Primak

International programs offered through the University of Oregon offer participants the opportunity to gain academic, cultural, and personal experience.

3055 University of Portland

5000 North Willamette Boulevard
Portland, OR   97203   503-283-7337

Thompson Faller

Study/cultural experience is available in Tokyo and other Japanese cities as part of the Japan Studies Program at the University.

3056 Western Washington University

International Programs & Exchanges
Old Main 530E
Bellingham, WA   98225   360-650-3910
                               FAX: 360-650-9046
                 e-mail: ipewwu@cc.wwu.edu
            www.www.edu/~ipewwu   (not a typo)

Liz Partolan-Fray, Director, International Programs

Provides international educational exchange opportunities for students through various programs.

3057 World Experience

2440 South Hacienda Boulevard
Suite 116
Hacienda Heights, CA   91745   626-330-5719
                                     800-633-6653
                                  FAX: 626-333-4914
                         www.worldexperience.org

Nonprofit organization which sponsors, develops and carries out international student exchange programs for study and service abroad.

3058 You Can Study in the New Independent States

Mobility International USA
PO Box 10767
Eugene, OR   97440   541-343-1284
                         FAX: 541-343-6812
                         TDY:541-343-1284
                    e-mail: info@miusa.org
                         www.miusa.org

Susan Sygall, Executive Director
Rhonda Neuhaus, Public Relations Coordinator

A resource guide for students with disabilities. Assists US students with disabilities and sponsoring organizations in preparing for study in the NIS. Includes extensive resource section. Available in alternative formats. *$20.00*

3059 Youth for Understanding International Exchange

3501 Newark Street NW
Washington, DC   20016   202-966-6800
                               800-TEE-NAGE
                               FAX: 202-895-1104
                         e-mail: info@yfu.org
                  www.youthforunderstanding.org

Youth for Understanding (YFU) International Exchange, an educational, nonprofit organization, prepares young people for the opportunities and responsabilies in a changing, independent world. With YFU, students can choose a year, semenster, or summer program in one or more than 35 countries worldwide. More than 200,000 young people from more than 50 nations in Asia, Europe, North and South America, Africa and the Pacific have participated in YFU exchanges.

Alabama

3060 Alabama Power Foundation
600 18th Street N
17th Floor
Birmingham, AL   35203   205-250-1000

Giving is limited to Alabama. No support is given for religious or political organizations, individuals or for operating funds that duplicate the United Way support.

3061 Andalusia Health Services
PO Box 667
Andalusia, AL   36420   334-222-2030
                               FAX: 334-222-7844
                       e-mail: chamber@alaweb.com

George Proctor Sr., President
Only offers grants to the residents of Covington County in Alabama who are pursuing a degree in a medical field.

3062 Arc of Alabama
300 Hull Street
Montgomery, AL   36104   334-262-7688

                       e-mail: info@arcalabama.org

3063 Blount Foundation
4520 Executive Park Drive
Montgomery, AL   36116

D. Joseph McInnes
Established in 1970, the Foundation was created to serve as the voice with which the Blount Companies address the need to provide financial assistance to a variety of activities and programs concerned with the general welfare of our country and its citizens. The Foundation has a strong commitment to corporate citizenship and endorses the concept that companies, as well as individuals, must contribute to the well-being of society.

3064 William H. and Kate Stockham Foundation
Stockham Valves & Fitting
4000 10th Avenue North
10326
Birmingham, AL   35212   205-592-6361

Only supports projects that can directly or indirectly benefit employees of their company; also gives to the visually impaired, hard-of-hearing, physically disabled and education programs.

Alaska

3065 Arc of Alaska
2211-A Arca Drive
Anchorage, AK   99508   907-277-6677

3066 Rasmuson Foundation
National Bank of Alaska
PO Box 100600
Anchorage, AK   99510   907-265-2834

Mentally and physically disabled, accessibility projects, recreation and equipment grants for Alaska only.

Arizona

3067 Arc of Arizona
5610 S Central Avenue
Phoenix, AZ   85040   602-243-1787

                       e-mail: Arcofarizona@aol.com

3068 Arizona Commnity Foundation
2122 East Highland Avenue
Suite 4000
Phoenix, AZ   85016   602-381-1400
                             800-222-8221
                       FAX: 602-381-1575
           e-mail: rmayberry@azfoundation.com
                       www.azfoundation.org

Bennett Dorrance, Chairperson

3069 Frances Moynihan Huger Foundation
PO Box 34350
Phoenix, AZ   85067

Ray Huger, M.D., President

3070 Hermundslie Foundation
3762 North Harrison Road
Tucson, AZ   85749   520-749-8501

Funding for eye research.

3071 JW Kieckhefer Foundation
116 East Gurley Street
Prescott, AZ   86301

John Kieckhefer, Trustee

3072 Margaret T. Morris Foundation
PO Box 592
Prescott, AZ   86302   520-445-4010

Eugene P. Polk

3073 R. & M. Clark Family Foundation
c/o Marcella S. Clark
8249 Vista De Valle
Scottsdale, AZ   85255

Carole Lee Randall, Vice President

3074 Tucson Community Foundation

6842 East Tanque Verde Road
Tucson, AZ 85715   520-886-8433

Donna Grant

Learning disabled, physically and mentally disabled, mental health, visually impaired, recreation and equipment grants.

Arkansas

3075 Arc of Arkansas

2004 South Main Street
Little Rock, AR 72206   501-375-7770

3076 Charles M. and Joan R. Taylor Foundation

200 Louisiana
Little Rock, AR 72201

Judy Ledbetter, Reverend

3077 Roy and Christine Sturgis Charitable Trust

PO Box 92
Malvern, AR 72104   501-337-5109

Physically disabled, hospitals, child welfare and visually impaired are priorities of giving for this foundation.

3078 WalMart Foundation

702 SW 8th Street
Bentonville, AR 72716

800-530-9925
FAX: 501-273-6850
www.walmartfoundation.org

Major funding is its contributions to high school seniors who have a desire to further their education by attending colleges and universities. Annual scholarships in the amount of $1,000 are presented to students in each community where Wal-Mart stores are located. The Foundation also supports the endeavors of the United Way.

3079 Winthrop Rockefeller Foundation

308 East 8th Street
Little Rock, AR 72202   501-376-6854
FAX: 501-374-4797

Mahlon Martin

Their mission is to improve the quality of life in Arkansas. It focuses its grantmaking efforts in three areas: education, economic development and civic affairs. Education projects funded in the past have included grants to schools that are working to involve teachers and parents in making decisions about what happens at their schools, projects supported that work to remove prejudice from the educational process, and more. Major grants are made to support the development of new programs.

California

3080 Ahmanson Foundation

9215 Wilshire Boulevard
Beverly Hills, CA 90210   310-278-0770

Lee Walcott, Managing Director

The Foundation primarily gives in Southern California with major emphasis in Los Angeles County. The Foundation focuses on the arts and humanities, education, mental health and support for a broad range of social welfare programs.

3081 Alice Tweed Touhy Foundation

205 East Carrillo Street
Suite 219
Santa Barbara, CA 93101

Harris Seed, President
Eleanor Van Cott, Executive V.P.

Rehabilitation, recreation and building funds are given to organizations only within the Santa Barbara area.

3082 Amateur Athletic Foundation of Los Angeles

2141 West Adams Boulevard
Los Angeles, CA 90018   323-730-9600

Enables AAF to serve as an educational and research center for sport - a leading forum for the advancement of coaching, the exchange of ideas and exploration of important issues in sport.

3083 Annuziata Sanguinetti Foundation

420 Montgomery Street
5th Floor
San Francisco, CA 94104   415-477-1000

Eugene Ranghiasci

Hard-of-hearing, speech impaired and recreation. Serves only the San Francisco Bay area.

3084 Apple Computer

Worldwide Disability Solutions Group
2851 Park Avenue
Santa Clara, CA 95050   408-996-1010
800-692-7753
TDY:800-755-0601

Offers grants in the areas of education, health and in areas of company operations.

3085 Arc of California

1225 8th Street
Suite 590
Sacramento, CA 95814   916-552-6619

e-mail: arcca@quiknet.com

3086 Argyros Foundation
950 South Coast Drive
Suite 200
Costa Mesa, CA 92626

Physically disabled, Sheltered Workshop, speech impaired and hard-of-hearing.

3087 Atkinson Foundation
1100 Grundy Lane
140
San Bruno, CA 94066

FAX: 650-876-1252

Elizabeth Curtis, Administrator

The Foundation focuses and awards grants to community service and civic organizations serving the residents of San Mateo County, California through programs that benefit children, youth, seniors, the disadvantaged and those in need of rehabilitation. Grants are also made to local churches and schools, and overseas for sustainable development, health education and family planning. No grants to individuals or for research, travel, special events, annual campaigns, media and publications.

3088 Auen-Berger Foundation
PO Box 66178
Arcadia, CA 91066

Ronald M. Auen, Trustee

3089 Autry Foundation
5858 West Sunset Boulevard
710
Los Angeles, CA 90028

FAX: 213-460-5647

Karla Buhlman, Executive Assistant
Maxine Hansen, Secretary

Giving limited to the Los Angeles, CA, area and Riverside and Orange counties.

3090 Baker Commodities Corporate Giving Program
4020 Bandini Boulevard
Los Angeles, CA 90023

323-268-2801
FAX: 323-268-5166

Maxine Taylor, Executive Secretary

3091 Bank of Santa Clara Foundation
PO Box 243
Santa Clara, CA 95050

408-987-9426

Judith Reinartz, Executive Director

3092 BankAmerica Foundation
PO Box 37000
San Francisco, CA 94137

415-622-3456

Caroline Boitano

The Foundation will consider grants in four categories including: Health & Human Services, which provides support to health & human service organizations primarily through grants to the United Way campaigns; Education, with the focus on preparing people to become productive employees and participating citizens; Conservation & Environment, the improvement of California communities for the benefit of their citizens; and Culture & The Arts, supporting the leading performing and visual arts groups.

3093 Bergen Brunswig Corporation Contributions Program
4000 Metropolitan Drive
Orange, CA 92686

714-385-4000
FAX: 714-385-6948

Valerie Calleros, Chairperson

3094 Bertha Russ Foundation
PO Box 893
Ferndale, CA 95536

Grants are given to the Easter Seal Society, Association for Retarded Citizens, building and equipment funds.

3095 Bertha Russ Lytel Foundation
PO Box 893
Ferndale, CA 95536

George Hindley, Manager

3096 Bireley Foundation
144 North Brand Boulevard
Glendale, CA 91203

Sandra Franck, Assistant Secretary
Ernest Baldwin, Vice President

Specifically interested in adolescent medicine and research. Grants are given to tax exempt organizations only. No overhead is funded by grants.

3097 Blind Babies Foundation
1200 Gough Street
San Francisco, CA 94109

415-922-9185
FAX: 415-771-9026

Dennak Murphy, Executive Director

Founded in 1949, provides services and programs that enable and empower families, professionals and the broader community to meet the unique needs of infants and preschool children who are blind or visually impaired. *$5.00*

3098 Bothin Foundation
PO Box 29906
San Francisco, CA 94129

415-771-4300
FAX: 415-771-4064

Lyman J. Casey, Executive Director

The broad purpose of this foundation is to support public charities located in the five counties of San Francisco, Marin, Sonoma, San Mateo and Santa Barbara. Bothin elects to support charitable organizations that promote youth, elderly, disabled, health care, minorities, community social services and the environment. Grants for the arts are made mainly to those groups predominantly serving youth or with heavy emphasis on youth participation.

3099 Briggs Foundation

6106 La Flecha, Number 250
PO Box 1510
Rancho Santa Fe, CA   92067

Blaine A. Briggs

3100 Burns-Dunphy Foundation

Hearst Building
Suite 1200
San Francisco, CA   94103

Walter Gleason

Grants are given to promote wellness for the visually impaired, physically and mentally disabled and to promote research in these areas.

3101 CNF Transportation Corporate Giving Program

3240 Hillview Avenue
Palo Alto, CA   94304   650-494-2900

Henry A. Schmitt, Assistant Vice President

3102 California Community Foundation

3580 Wilshire Boulevard
Suite 1660
Los Angeles, CA   90010   323-583-6771

www.calfund.org

Jack Shakely

Areas of funding priority include grants for the disabled, child welfare, rehabilitation, developmentally disabled, employment projects, research and computer projects. Giving is limited to the greater Los Angeles area.

3103 California Endowment

21650 Oxnard Street
Suite 1200
Woodland Hills, CA   91367   818-703-3311
                                    800-449-4149
                              FAX: 818-703-4193
                   e-mail: bmartin@calendow.org
                           www.calendow.org

Rebecca Martin, Grants Manager

3104 Carrie Estelle Doheny Foundation

911 Wilshire Boulevard
Suite 1750
Los Angeles, CA   90017   213-488-1122
                              FAX: 413-488-1544
                   e-mail: doheny@earthlink.net

Robert A. Smith III, Presedent

3105 Charles Bloom Foundation

240 Eucalyptus Hill Drive
Santa Barbara, CA   93108   805-969-4174

Grants are given in the areas of health, education and community involvement projects.

3106 Clorox Company Foundation

1221 Broadway
Oakland, CA   94612   510-451-3300

e-mail: communityaffairs@clorox.com
www.clorox.com/community.html

Patricia Marino, President

Community Support Programs are offered to make the communities in which we live and work stronger, while providing measurable benefits to the Company and its shareholders. The Foundation's primary concern continues to be youth and K-12 education. The Foundation is helping our young people to improve their educational and job skills and develop their leadership potential.

3107 Community Foundation for Monterey County

99 Pacific Street
Suite 155A
Monterey, CA   93940   831-375-9712

Todd Lueders

Grants are given to projects that promote research and rehabilitation of physically disabled individuals.

3108 Community Foundation of Santa Clara County

111 West Saint John Street
Suite 230
San Jose, CA   95113   408-264-2437

Peter Hero

Visually impaired, mentally and physically disabled, hard-of-hearing, special education, mental health and employment projects are areas of priority. Giving is limited to Santa Clara and surrounding counties.

3109 Confidence Foundation

625 Fair Oaks Avenue
Suite 360
S Pasadena, CA   91030   626-445-0297

Linda Blinkenberg, Director

The Foundation prefers to initiate its grants in its areas of interest.

3110 Crescent Porter Hale Foundation

220 Bush Street
Suite 1069
San Francisco, CA   94104

FAX: 415-986-5197

Ulla Davis, Executive Director

Serves organizations in the San Francisco Bay Area who are involved in the following areas of concern: education in the fields of art and music; private elementary, high school and university education; capital funding; and other worthwhile programs which can be demonstrated as serving broad community purposes, leading toward the improvement of the quality of life.

3111 Darrow Foundation

1000 4th Street
Suite 375
San Rafael, CA 94901   415-453-0534

Grants are given in the areas of child welfare, visually impaired, projects involving independence, mentally and physically disabled.

3112 David and Lucile Packard Foundation

300 2nd Street
Suite 200
Los Altos Hills, CA 94022   650-948-7658

www.packfound.org

Colburn Wilbur, Executive Director

Supports and encourages organizations dependent upon private funding and volunteer leadership. The Board of Trustees have developed guidelines which reflect the interests and understanding of its members.

3113 Deutsch Foundation

2444 Wilshire Boulevard
Suite 600
Santa Monica, CA 90403

Learning disabled, visually impaired, mental health, eye research, child welfare, speech and hearing impaired, physically disabled and independence projects are funded through this Foundation. Giving is limited to California.

3114 Donald R. Barker Foundation

PO Box 936
Rancho Mirage, CA 92270   760-321-2345

It is an independent organization that gives its attention to organizations that are charitable or nonprofit under the laws of the state of Oregon or California.

3115 East Bay Community Foundation

200 Frank H Ogawa Plaza
Oakland, CA 94612   510-836-3223
                          FAX: 510-836-3287
              e-mail: admin@eastbaycp.org
                      www.eastbacf.org

David Pontecorvo, Program Director

A collection of funds created by many people, organizations and businesses, the Foundation helps those people and groups to support effective nonprofits organizaations to the East Bay and beyond.

3116 Elizabeth Firth Wade Endowment Fund

114 East De La Guerra Street
Suite 7
Santa Barbara, CA 93101   805-569-2482

A private, charitable foundation established in 1961. The Fund encourages, through its grants, greater support from the public, other foundations, or government agencies. Grants are made for broad general purposes including human service agencies, cultural institutions, the performing arts, youth activities and education.

3117 Evelyn and Walter Hans, Jr.

1 Lombard Street
Suite 305
San Francisco, CA 94111   415-398-4474

Ira Hirschfield, President

A private foundation interested in programs which assist people who are hungry, homeless, or at risk of homelessness; enable older adults to maintain independent lives in the community and support Hispanic community development in San Francisco's Mission District. The Foundation also encourages proposals for corporate social responsibility efforts within the business community.

3118 Fireman's Fund Foundation

777 San Marin Drive
Novato, CA 94998   415-899-2757
                          FAX: 415-899-2126

Barbara Friede, Director

Provides discretionary grants to the disabled only in Marin and Sonoma counties in the San Francisco Bay area.

3119 Florence Nelson Foundation

120 Montgomery Street
Suite 2425
San Francisco, CA 94104

Edwina Kump

Contribute only to organizations in the Santa Clara Valley area specializing in education, cultural and civic programs, health and the arts, specifically geared toward the physically disabled and child welfare.

3120 Foundation for Glaucoma Research

490 Post Street
Suite 830
San Francisco, CA 94102   650-986-3162

Tara L. Steele, Executive Director

A national organization dedicated to protecting the sight of people with glaucoma through research and education. The Foundation conducts and supports research that contributes to improved patient care and a better understanding of the disease process. Provides education, advocacy and emotional support to patients and their families.

3121 Foundation for New Options

2340 Sutter Street
Suite 210
San Francisco, CA 90212

Provides individuals with tools and knowledge of individual options that can be used to take a greater responsibility for personal actions and well-being.

3122 Foundation for the Advancement of the Blind

4058 Moore Street
Los Angeles, CA 90066   213-301-0344

Helps blind people attain and retain employment.

3123 Foundation for the Junior Blind

5300 Angeles Vista Boulevard
Los Angeles, CA 90043   323-295-4555
                               FAX: 323-296-0424
                               e-mail: info@fjb.org
                               www.fjb.org

Robert B. Ralls, President

The Foundation for the Junior Blind is a private, non-profit agency that provides a wide range of programs and services for the blind, visually impaired, and multiply disabled-blind children, youths, and adults and their families. Programs include: Infant-Family Program, Children's Special Education School, Children's Residential Program, Davidson Program for Independence (for adults), and a year-round recreation program that includes a summer residential camp-Camp Bloomfield.

3124 Foundation on Employment and Disability

3820 Del Amo Boulevard
246
Torrance, CA 90503   310-214-3430

Through multilingual toll-free information lines, pamphlets, articles in local publications, and presentations to community organizations, will provide written and oral information on the ADA that is understandable, linguistically and culturally.

3125 Frances Schermer Charitable Trust

PO Box 3189
Los Angeles, CA 90051

Funding for the physically disabled is the Trust's main priority.

3126 Fred Geldert Family Foundation

1 Embarcagero Center
Suite 2480
San Francisco, CA 94111   415-433-6174
                                 FAX: 415-433-7952

Peggy Lauer, Executive Director

3127 Fred Gellert Foundation

1 Embarcadero Center
Suite 2480
San Francisco, CA 94111
                          FAX: 415-433-7952

Fred Gellert, Jr., Chairman

Focuses on organizations and programs serving residents of San Mateo and San Francisco and Marin counties in California, with the exception of environmentally concerned organizations.

3128 Freeman E. Fairfield Foundation

3610 Long Beach Boulevard
PO Box 7798
Long Beach, CA 90807   562-427-7219

Edina E. Sellers

3129 Gallo Foundation

PO Box 1130
Modesto, CA 95353   209-341-3111

Physically and mentally disabled, child welfare, Special Olympics, United Cerebral Palsy and Easter Seal Society are among the grants provided by this foundation.

3130 Georges & Germaine Fusenot Charity Foundation

520 North Rossmore Avenue
Los Angeles, CA 90004

Richard Herlihy, Manager

Giving limited to the state of California. No political purposes and no religious organizations. Day care center, homeless shelter, etc. sponsored by religious organizations.

3131 Glaucoma Research Foundation

200 Pine Street
Suite 200
San Francisco, CA 94104   415-986-3162
                                 800-826-6693
                        e-mail: info@glaucoma.org
                        www.glaucoma.com

Committed to protecting the sight of people with glaucoma through m edical research and patient education.

3132 H.N. and Frances C. Berger Foundation

300 West Huntington Drive
Arcadia, CA 91007   626-445-4441

California area giving.

3133 Harden Foundation

PO Box 779
Salinas, CA 93902   831-442-3005
                           FAX: 831-443-1429

Joseph C. Grainger, Executive Director

3134 Harry and Grace Steele Foundation

441 Old Newport Boulevard
Suite 301
Newport Beach, CA 92663

Marie Kowert

Gives grants to qualified tax-exempt charitable organizations which are not private foundations. Tax-supported organizations of any kind, and applications are not accepted from individuals. Grants are made for altruistic purposes, charitable, benevolent or educational, primarily local giving.

3135 Henry J. Kaiser Family Foundation

2400 Samd Hill Road
Menlo Park, CA   94025 650-854-9400
800-656-4533
FAX: 650-854-4800
e-mail: rwells@kff.org
www.kff.org

Renee Wells, Grants and Contracts Manager

3136 Henry W. Bull Foundation

Santa Barbara Bank & Trust
PO Box 2340
Santa Barbara, CA   93120 805-884-7347
FAX: 805-884-1404

Janice Gibbons, VP & Senior Trust Officer
Sharon McGinness, Sr. Trust Admin. Assistant

Grant given to a wide range of organizations that include organizations which provide services for the hard-of-hearing, speech impaired, visually impaired and physically disabled; arts, education services for elderly and a quarterly newsletter. Grant size ranges from $500 to $5,000. Proposal deadlines Jan 1, May 1, Sept 1.

3137 Herbst Foundation

3 Embarcadero Center
Suite 21
San Francisco, CA   94111 415-252-1220

John Seigle, President

The foundation centers its principal support activities around providing capital funding (bricks and mortar) for facilities of various kinds within the city and county of San Francisco.

3138 International Foundation for Alternating Hemiplegia of Childhood

239 Nevada Street
Redwood City, CA   94062 650-365-5798
FAX: 650-365-5798
e-mail: laegan@aol.com
www.ahc.kids.org

Lynn Egan, President
Carol Presunka, Vice President

Voluntary not-for-profit organizatins dedicated to promoting professional and public awareness of Alternating Hemiplegia of Childhood (AHC) and providing current information on affected and individuals and their families. Supports ongoing medical research into the cause, treatment and potential cure of AHC. Disseminates information about this disorder to promote proper diagnosis and maintains a registry of families, affected chidren, and physicians who are familiar with AHC.

3139 Irvine Health Foundation

18301 Von Kraman Avenue
Irvine, CA   92612 949-253-2959
FAX: 949-253-2962
e-mail: ebk@ihf.org
www.ihf.org

Edward B. Kacic, President

3140 James S. Copley Foundation

7776 Ivanhoe Avenue
La Jolla, CA   92037 619-454-0411

Anita Baumgardner, Foundation Secretary

Welcomes the opportunity to support responsible & creative charitable and civic organizations within the immediate circulation areas of the Copley newspapers located in San Diego, Torrance, San Pedro and Santa Monica, California; Aurora, Elgin, Wheaton, Joliet, Springfield, Waukegan, Naperville and Lincoln, Illinois. Grants fall within these broad areas of concern: education, culture and the arts, medical and health, youth development, human services and urban/civic affairs.

3141 John & Geraldine Cusenza Family Foundaiton

578 West Portrero Road
Hidden Valley, CA   91361

Geraldine Cusenza, President

3142 Joseph Drown Foundation

1999 Avenue of the Stars
Suite 1930
Los Angeles, CA   90067 310-277-4488

Giving is focused primarily in California. No support for religious purposes or to individuals.

3143 Karl Kirchgessner Foundation

1900 Avenue of the Stars
Suite 2100
Los Angeles, CA   90067

Blind, eye research, vocational training, child welfare and scholarships for visually impaired students are among the priorities of the Foundation.

3144 Kenneth T. and Eileen L. Norris Foundation

11 Golden Shore
Suite 450
Long Beach, CA   90802 562-435-8444
FAX: 562-436-0584
e-mail: bover@ktn.org
www.norrisfoundation.org

Ronald Barnes, Executive Director
Nancy Boyer, Grants Manager
Savannah Gerringer, Grants Assistant

The Foundation is primarily focused on medicine and education. To a lesser extent the foundation contributes to community programs including visually impaired, autism, mentally and physically disabled, deaf and mental health in the southern California area. Average grant size in this area is $5,000-$10,000. Grants are also given in the area of culture and youth.

3145 Kings Daughter's Home Foundation

2501 Harrison Street
Oakland, CA 94612

Alice Smetts, President

3146 Koret Foundation

33 New Montgomery Street
Suite 1090
San Francisco, CA 94105   415-882-7740

Rosemary Peterson

3147 LJ Skaggs and Mary C. Skaggs Foundation

1221 Broadway
21st Floor
Oakland, CA 94612   510-451-3300

David Knight, Program Director

The Foundation presently makes grants under four
program categories: performing arts, social concerns,
projects of historic interests, and special projects.

3148 LK Whittier Foundation

625 Fair Oaks Avenue
Suite 360
S Pasadena, CA 91030

Linda Blinkenberg, Foundations Director

Giving is primarily offered to preselected organizations. No grants are given to individuals.

3149 Lauralie Irving Foundation

95 Robles Del Rio
Carmel Valley, CA 93924   831-659-4490

J.J. Irving, President

3150 Lawrence Welk Foundation

2700 Pennsylvania Avenue
Santa Monica, CA 90404   310-451-9077
                              FAX: 310-451-4268

Lisa Parker, Executive Director

Awards grants in the range of $500 to $10,000. They
are given to private, nonprofit organizations in Southern California whose focus is social services agencies
working in inner cities with families to alleviate the
effects of poverty. Fund is unable to allocate funds to
individuals, pass-through organizations, arts or environmental organizations, or to those requesting planning grants and prefers to fund capital improvements
and seed or special projects rather than operating
budgets.

3151 Legler Benbough Foundation

2550 5th Avenue
Suite 132
San Diego, CA 92103   619-235-8099
                              FAX: 619-235-8077

Peter K. Ellsworth, President

3152 Levi Strauss Foundation

1155 Battery Street
7th Floor
San Francisco, CA 94111   415-501-1361

Judy Belk, Executive Director

Has a funding initiative to support organizations
which provide services for people with AIDS, and/or
educational programs which help prevent the further
spread of the HIV virus. The Foundation will assist
in the development and enhancement of such services
only in those communities where Levi Strauss & Co.
has plants and distribution centers.

3153 Louis R. Lurie Foundation

555 California Street
Suite 5100
San Francisco, CA 94104

Robert Lurie

Visually impaired, hard-of-hearing and physically
disabled in the San Francisco Bay Area and Metropolitan Chicago areas only.

3154 Luke B. Hancock Foundation

360 Bryant Street
Palo Alto, CA 94301   650-321-5536
                              FAX: 650-321-0697

Joan Wylie

Concentrated on its resources over the past year on
programs which provide job training and employment
for at-risk youth. Consortium funding with other
foundations in areas where there is unmet need; emergency and transitional funding; and selected funding
for music education.

3155 Marin Community Foundation

17 East Sir Francis Drake Boulevard
Suite 200
Larkspur, CA 94939   415-461-3333
                              FAX: 415-464-2555
                              e-mail: www.marincf.org
                              mcf@marincf.org

Mark Koenig, Contact

3156 Mary A. Crocker Trust

233 Post Street
2nd Floor
San Francisco, CA 94108   415-392-2303

                              e-mail: mact95@aol.com

Barbaree Jernigan, Administrator

Established in 1889, the Foundation is interested in
Bay Area programs such as environment, education
and community relations.

3157 Maxx Factor Family Foundation

9777 Wilshire Boulevard
Suite 1015
Beverly Hills, CA

Barbara Factor, Trustee

3158 May and Stanley Smith Trust

720 Market Street
Suite 250
San Francisco, CA 94102   415-391-0292

Dale Matheny

3159 Morris Stulsaft Foundation

100 Bush Street
Suite 825
San Francisco, CA 94104   415-986-7117
    FAX: 415-986-2521
    e-mail: stulsaft@aol.com

Joseph W. Valentine, Executive Director
Katarina Memottl, Administrative Assistance

Grants are limited to projects located in the six counties of the San Francisco Bay Area serving children and youth with an emphasis on education, social services, health and the disabled, arts and recreation.

3160 National Foundation of Wheelchair Tennis

940 Calle Amanecer
Suite B
San Clemente, CA 92673   949-366-2410
    FAX: 949-361-6822

Bradley Parks, President

Founded in January of 1980, the intention of this foundation is to assist the newly physically disabled individual realize his full potential in society by enhancing his esteem, independence productivity and physical capabilities regardless of age, sex, creed or disability extent.

3161 Optometric Extension Program Foundation

1921 East Carnegie Avenue
Suite 3-L
Santa Ana, CA 92705   949-250-8070

    e-mail: smc.oep@worldnet.att.net
    www.healthy.net/oep/

Offers continuing education in behavioral optometry for consumers and optometrists.

3162 Parker Foundation

4365 Executive Drive
Suite 1600
San Diego, CA 92121   858-677-1431
    FAX: 858-677-1477

Robbin Powell, Asst. Secretary

The assets are directed to projects which will contribute to the betterment of any aspect of the people of San Diego County, California and solely to entities which, among other things, are organized exclusively for charitable purposes and are operating in San Diego County, California.

3163 Pasadena Foundation

16 North Marengo Avenue
Suite 300
Pasadena, CA 91101   626-796-2097
    FAX: 626-583-4738
    e-mail: pfstaff@pasadensfoundation.org
    www.pasadenafoundation.org

Virginia C. Krueger, Executive Director

The mission of the Pasadena Foundation is to improve the quality of life for citizens of the Pasadena area through support of nonprofit organizations that provide services beneficial to the community.

3164 Peninsula Community Foundation

1700 S El Camino Real
Suite 300
San Mateo, CA 94402   650-348-2764
    FAX: 650-358-9817

Sterling Speirn, President
Ellen Clear, VP, Community Programs

For more than 36 years, Peninsula Community Foundaiton has built involvement and investment in the community. We develop resources and imaginative programs that make it easy for Peninsula and Silicon Valley residents - from Daly City to San Jose, from the Pacific Ocean to the San Francisco Bay - to support the common good and connect with causes they care about.

3165 RC Baker Foundation

PO Box 6150
Orange, CA 92863   714-750-8987

Established in 1952, for general philanthropic purposes, and the bulk of assistance and support has been to religious, scientific, educational institutions and youth organizations.

3166 Ralph M. Parsons Foundation

1055 Wilshire Boulevard
Suite 1701
Los Angeles, CA 90017   213-482-3185
    FAX: 213-482-8878

Joseph Hurley, President

The Foundation is concerned with the encouragement and support of projects and programs deemed beneficial to mankind in several major areas of interest such as: Education; Social Impact; Civic and Cultural; Health and Special Products.

3167 Read Natural Childbirth Foundation

PO Box 150956
San Rafael, CA 94915   415-456-8462

Prepares expectant parents for childbirth. Also certifies birthing teachers.

3168 Richard F. Dwyer and Elanor W. Dwyer Fund for Excellence

321 Las Casas
Pacific Palisades, CA 90272

Allan Lasher, Vice President/ Secretary

3169 Robert Ellis Simon Foundation

152 South Lasky Drive
Beverly Hills, CA 90212   310-273-9190

Dr. Joan Willens

Mental health and visually impaired grants are the main concerns of this organization.

3170   San Diego Community Foundation

1420 Kather Boulevard
Suite 500
San Diego, CA   92101   619-263-7600

e-mail: info@sdcf.org
www.sdcf.org

Helen Monroe

Mentally retarded, physically disabled and vocational training grants are the top areas of funding for this organization.

3171   San Francisco Foundation

225 Bush Street
500
San Francisco, CA   94104   415-733-8500
FAX: 415-477-2783
www.sff.org

Robert Fisher

The Foundation's purpose is to improve life, promote greater equality of opportunity and assist those in need or at risk in the San Francisco Bay Area. The Foundation strives to protect and enhance the unique resources of the Bay Area, committed to equality of opportunity for all and the elimination of any injustice, seeks to enhance human dignity and seeks to establish mutual trust, respect and communication among the Foundation.

3172   Santa Barbara Foundation

15 East Carrillo Street
Santa Barbara, CA   93101   805-967-1234

Edward Spaulding

Giving is limited to Santa Barbara County, California with no support given to individuals or religious organizations.

3173   Sidney Stern Memorial Trust

PO Box 893
Pacific Palisades, CA   90272

Peter HoOffers peer counsel,, Chair
Marvin Hoffenberg, Advisor

A Southern California-based foundation providing grants to nonprofit organizations for various projects. The foundation gives priority to the following areas of interest: education, health and science, community service projects, youth, services to the mentally and emotionally disabled, the arts, organizations and activities serving California. The Board prefers to make contributions to organizations that use the funds directly in the furtherance of their charitable and public purposes.

3174   Sierra Health Foundation

2525 Natomas Park Drive
Suite 200
Sacramento, CA   95833   916-922-4755
FAX: 916-635-3362

Dorothy Beaumont, Vice President

The Foundation strives to establish a collaborative relationship with its grantees, and with other funders and foundations, through an open dialogue. The Foundation approaches each grant as a partnership, with opportunities for the grantee and grantor to work cooperatively to enhance the effectiveness of the grant project.

3175   Sonora Area Foundation

20100 Cedar Road, No. E
PO Box 577
Sonsora, CA   95370   209-533-2596
FAX: 209-533-2412
e-mail: acorn@sonora-area.org
www.sonora-area.org

Mick Grimes, Executive Director

3176   Stella B. Gross Charitable Trust

c/o Bank of the West
PO Box 1121
San Jose, CA   95108   408-998-6856

Lori C. Stetzenmyer, Trust Officer

3177   Teichert Foundation

3500 American River Drive
Sacramento, CA   95864   916-484-3255

Frederick A. Teichert, Executive Director

3178   Times Mirror Corporate Giving Foundation

Times Mirror Square
Los Angeles, CA   90053   213-237-3945

Bonnie G. Hill, President and C.E.O.

3179   WM Keck Foundation

550 South Hope Street
Suite 2500
Los Angeles, CA   90071   213-680-3833
FAX: 213-614-0934
www.wmkeck.org

Dr. Dorothy Fleisher, Program Director

Created to support accredited colleges and universities with particular emphasis on the sciences, engineering and medical research. The Foundation also maintains a Southern California Grant Program that provides support for non-profit organizations in the field of civic and community services, health care, precollegiate education and the arts.

3180   Willam G. Gilmore Foundation

120 Montgomery Street
San Francisco, CA   94101   415-546-1400
FAX: 415-391-8732

Faye Wilson, Secretary

Colorado

3181 Adolph Coors Foundation

3773 Cherry Creek North Drive
Suite 995
Denver, CO 80209   303-388-1636
FAX: 303-388-1684

Linda Tafoya

Applicant organizations must be classified as 501 and must operate within the United States. The areas covered by the Foundation are health, education, youth, community services, civic and cultural and public affairs.

3182 Anschutz Family Foundation

2400 Anaconda Tower
555 17th Street
Denver, CO 80202
                        FAX: 303-298-8881

Sue Anschutz Rodgers, President

The Foundation's interests are to support efforts helping the elderly, the young and the economically disadvantaged. The Foundation has supported over 600 public and private charities sharing in the concern for neighborhood strengthening and community cooperation.

3183 Arc of Colorado

777 Grant Street
Suite 203
Denver, CO 80203   303-864-9334

e-mail: info@thearcfco.org

3184 Bal F. and Hilda N. Swan Foundation

PO Box 5825
Denver, CO 80217

James Kimmett

Grants are given in the areas of rehabilitation, with emphasis on the physically disabled and visually impaired.

3185 Bonfils-Stanton Foundation

1601 Arapahoe Street
Suite 5
Denver, CO 80202   303-825-3774

www.users.uswest.net/~bstanto

Eileen Greenawalt, Executive Secretary

Grants limited to Colorado 501 (c) (3) organizations. Grants are for general, charitable philanthropic activities within the State. Major categories include education, scientific (including hospital and health services), civic and cultural, community and human services. Organizations should request foundation guidelines before submitting a proposal.

3186 Carl W. and Carrie Mae Joslyn Charitable Foundation

PO Box 1699
Colorado Springs, CO 80942

Physically disabled, visually impaired and education to resident children, elderly and handicapped in the Colorado area.

3187 Carl and Carrie Mae Joslyn Charitable Trust, c/o Bank One, Colorado Springs, N.A.

PO Box 71
Colorado Springs, CO 80942   719-471-5125

3188 Comprecare Foundation

1145 Bannock Street
Denver, CO 80204   303-629-8661

J.R. Gilsdorf, Executive Director

3189 Denver Foundation

455 Sherman Street
Suite 220
Denver, CO 80203   303-778-7587

Robert Lee, Director

Neighbors helping neighbors, that's what the foundation is for. As Denver's only community foundation we've been accepting charitable donations since 1925. Those funds have been given back to the community in ongoing grants to nonprofit organizations - organizations that touch nearly every meaningful artistic, cultural, civic, health and human services interest of metro Denver's citizens.

3190 El Pomar Foundation

10 Lake Circle
Colorado Springs, CO 80906   719-633-7733
                               800-554-7711
                          FAX: 719-577-5702
                             www.elpomar.org

William J. Hybl, Chairperson

3191 Gates Family Foundation

3200 Cherry Creek South Drive
Suite 630
Denver, CO 80209   303-722-1881
                          FAX: 303-698-9031
                    e-mail: Gatesfdn@aol.com

Charles Cannon, Executive Director

Purpose is to aid, encourage, initiate or carry on activities that will promote the health, well-being, security and education of all people. Because of a deep concern for and confidence in the future of Colorado, the foundation will invest primarily in institutions, projects and programs that will enhance the quality of life of those who live and work in the state, especially the Denver metropolitan area. Also finds ways to encourage greater cooperation between public and private sectors.

3192 Harry W. Rabb Foundation

4500 Prospect Drive
Littleton, CO 80123

Vincent A. Zarlengo, Secretary

3193 Helen K. and Arthur E. Johnson Foundation

1700 Broadway
Suite 2302
Denver, CO 80290   303-861-4127

Stan Kamprath, Executive Director
A nonprofit, grantmaking private foundation incorporated under the laws of the State of Colorado in 1948. The Foundation is a general purpose foundation whose grant program consists of a wide variety of creative efforts to solve problems and to enrich the quality of life. The areas of interest are: education, youth, health, community services, civic and culture and senior citizens. Grants limited to the state of Colorado.

3194 Herbert F. Parker Foundation

First Interstate Bank of Denver
PO Box 5825
Denver, CO 80217

Cancer research, care and education of mentally retarded children and promoting sporting programs for youths.

3195 Hill Foundation

First Interstate Bank of Denver
PO Box 5825
Denver, CO 80217

Robert Lorentz, Vice President
Offers grants primarily for higher education (private), health and human services, cultural projects.

3196 J.M. McDonald Foundation

PO Box 3219
Evergreen, CO 80437   303-674-9300
                    FAX: 303-674-9216

Donald R. McJunkin, President

3197 Kenneth Kendal King Foundation

900 Pennsylvania Street
Denver, CO 80203   303-832-3200
                    FAX: 303-832-4176

Robert F. Sweeny, President

3198 Kitzmiller-Bales Trust

PO Box 96
Wray, CO 80758   970-332-3484

Robert U. Hansen

3199 V. Hunter Trust

650 South Cherry Street
Suite 535
Denver, CO 80246   303-399-5450
                    FAX: 303-399-5499

Sharon Siddons, Secretary

Connecticut

3200 Aetna Foundation

151 Framington Avenue
Hartford, CT 06156   860-273-6382

www.aetna.com/foundation

Diana Kinosh, Consultant

3201 Arc of Connecticut

1030 New Britain Avenue
Suite 102-B
West Hartford, CT 06110   860-953-8335
                    e-mail: arcct@aol.com

3202 Bristol Association for Retarded Citizens

621 Jerome Avenue
PO Box 726
Bristol, CT 06011   860-582-9102
                    FAX: 860-582-8280
          e-mail: brstl.assoc.rtrddo1@snet.net
               www.geocities.com/bristolarc

Rosemarie Cassin, Executive Director
Marcia Lada, Program Coordinator

The Bristol Association for Retarded Citizens is a non-profit, nationally accredited, United Way organization which has provided services to men and women with disabilities for over forty five years. Bristol ARC is committed to helping adults with developmental disabilities achieve maximum independence by providing educational, vocational, residential, social and advocacy services that will allow inclusion into the community.

3203 Catherine and Henry J. Gaisman Foundation

44 North Stanwich Road
Greenwich, CT 06830

3204 Clipper Ship Foundation

Hartford Insurance Group
Hartford Plaza
Hartford, CT 06115   860-547-4945

Richard M. Madden, Director
The purpose of this Foundation is to offer financial help to federally, nonprofit operating organizations serving the poor and the sick of the greater Boston area in order to assist them in fulfilling their goals and broadening the scope of their activities. Priority will be given to organizations devoted to helping the homeless, destitute, handicapped, children and the aged, or supplying the special needs of minority, low-income families and individuals.

3205 Community Foundation of Southeastern Connecticut

1 Union Plaza
PO Box 769
New London, CT   06320   860-442-3572
                               FAX: 860-442-0582
                               e-mail: jenno@cfsect.org
                               www.cfsect.org

Alice F. Fitzpatrick, Executive Director

3206 Connecticut Association for Children with Learning Disabilities

25 Van Zant Street
Suite 15-5
Norwalk, CT   06855   203-743-3861
                               FAX: 203-866-6108
                               e-mail: cacld@juno.com
                               www.cacld.org.

Beryl Kaufman, Executive Director

The Connecticut Association for Children and Adults with Learning Disabilities is a regional, non-profit organization that supports individuals, families, and professionals by providing information, education, and consultation while promoting public awareness and understanding. CACLD's goal is to ensure access to the resources needed to help children and adults with learning disabilities and attention deficits achieve their full potential.

3207 Connecticut Mutual Life Foundation

140 Garden Street
Hartford, CT   06154   860-727-3000

Astrida Olds, Executive Director

Distinguished throughout its long history by unusual commitment to high principles of corporate purpose and business ethics. That commitment has been reflected not only in the firm belief that normal business functions must be carried out with a sense of responsibility beyond that required by the marketplace. Maintains an ongoing program of corporate contributions, a nationwide matching gifts plan for all employees on behalf of private and public education, skills training programs, and more.

3208 Cornelia de Lange Syndrome Foundation

302 West Main Street 100
Avon, CT   06001   860-693-0159
                               800-223-8355

Provides information about birth defects caused by Cornelia de Lange Syndrome.

3209 Fidelco Guide Dog Foundation

PO Box 142
Bloomfield, CT   06002   860-243-5200
                               FAX: 860-243-7215
                               www.fidelco.org

Roberta Kaman, Executive V.P.

Purpose is to breed, train and place Fidelco German shepherd guide dogs with persons who are visually impaired throughout the Northeast. Provides in community training services to persons receiving guide dogs, reviews performance of the guide dog teams to see that satisfactory level of achievement is maintained, utilizes genetic processes and clinical methods to improve and refine the breed and maintains an ongoing program for development and improvement of training methods.

3210 GE Foundation

3135 Easton Turnpike
Fairfield, CT   06431   203-373-2178
                               FAX: 203-373-3029

Joyce Hergenhan, President

Believes that our greatest national resource is the work force. If we are to successfully compete in the global arena, then we become involved in improving the education of all of our citizens. The Foundation sets examples for others to emulate helping people with their international grant program to higher education and to health care for children in developing countries.

3211 General Electric Foundation

3135 Easton Turnpike
Fairfield, CT   06431   203-373-3180
                               FAX: 203-373-2573
                               www.ge.com

Joyce Hergenhan, President

Blind, physically and mentally disabled and rehabilitation grants are among the priorities of the company.

3212 Hartford Foundation for Public Giving

85 Gillett Street
Hartford, CT   06105   860-246-5236

                               e-mail: hfpg2@ursa.hartnet.org
                               www.hartnet.org

R. Malcolm Salter

Developmentally disabled, housing, deaf, recreation and education grants.

3213 Hartford Insurance Group

Hartford Plaza
Hartford, CT   06115   860-547-5000

                               www.thehartford.com

Sandra Sharr

Giving is primarily in the Hartford, CT area and in communities where the company has a regional office. No support is available for political or religious purposes. Grants are given in the areas of education, health and United Way organizations.

3214 Henry Nias Foundation

2 Batterson Park Road
Milford, CT   06460   203-874-2787

Charles D. Fleischman, Vice President

3215   Heublein Foundation

PO Box 778
Hartford, CT   06142   860-702-4000

Moira E. Burke, Treasurer

The Foundation awards grants to class organizations
in communities where there is a high concentration of
employees, or in which the company has a major
operating facility. The areas of interest are charitable,
civic and health and social care.

**3216   Jane Coffin Childs Memorial Fund for Medical
Research**

Jane Coffin Childs Memorial Fund
333 Cedar Street
New Haven, CT   06510   203-785-4612
                                 FAX: 203-785-3301
                            e-mail: jccfund@yale.edu
                                   www.jccfund.org

Elizabeth M. Ford, Administrative Director

The Fund awards fellowships to suitably qualified
individuals for full time postdoctoral studies in the
medical and related sciences bearing on cancer.

**3217   John H. and Ethel G. Nobel Charitable Trust c/o
Bankers Trust Company, Limited**

I Fawcett Place
Greenwich, CT   06830   203-629-7120

Paul J. Bisset, Vice President

3218   Pauline E. Fitzpatric Charitable Trust

PO Box 411
Norwalk, CT   06852

John B. Devine

3219   Scheuer Associates Foundation

c/o Robert Scheuer
960 Lake Avenue
Greenwich, CT   06831   203-869-3644

3220   Swindells Charitable Foundation Trust

Shawmut Bank
777 Main Street
242
Hartford, CT   06115   860-728-4900
                                 FAX: 860-240-1210

Maggie Willard, Assistant V.P.
Joseph Giangreco, Personal Trust Assoc

Grants made to charitable organizations or societies
incorporated for the relief of sick and suffering poor
children and/or the relief of sick suffering and indigent aged men and women and/or the support of
public charitable hospitals. Geographic area includes
Hartford, CT area primarily. Application is required,
deadlines are Feb. 1 and Aug. 1.

3221   Vernal W. F;Orence H. Bates Foundation

PO Box 1302
New Haven, CT   06505

James O. Walsh

Delaware

3222   Arc of Delaware

1016 Centre Road
Suite 1
Wilmington, DE   19805   302-996-9400

3223   Chichester DuPont Foundation

3120 Kennett Pike
Wilmington, DE   19807

Gregory Fields

Grants are given in the areas of culture, education and
health.

3224   Laffey-Mchugh Foundation

1220 Market Boulevard
PO Box 2207
Wilmington, DE   19899   302-658-9141

Arthor G. Connolly, Jr., Junior President

3225   Longwood Foundation

100 West 10th Street
Suite 1109
Wilmington, DE   19801   302-654-2477

David D. Wakefield, Executive Secretary

Offers grants to the mentally and physically disabled
- capital, program, education and housing grants in
the state of Delaware.

District of Columbia

**3226   Albert L. and Elizabeth T. Tucker Foundation c/o
Jackson & Campbell**

1120 20th Street NW
Suite 300
Washington, DC   20036   202-457-1600

Nicholas S. McConnell

3227   Alexander and Margaret Stewart Trust

888 17th Street NW
Suite 210
Washington, DC   20006   202-785-9892
                                 FAX: 202-785-0918

Doris Lustine, Executive Secretary

Grants are given only to the Washington, DC area
organizations providing care or treatment to cancer
patients or those with childhood afflictions.

3228 American Association of People with Disabilities

1819 H Street NW
Suite 330
Washington, DC   20006   202-457-0046
                               800-840-8844
                          FAX: 202-457-0473
                      e-mail: aapd@aol.com
                           www.aapd-dc.org

Amelie Bush, author

The American Association of People with Disabilities (AAPD) is a non-profit non-partisan, cross-disability, national membership organization whose goals are unity, leadership and impact. AAPD's mission is to advance the economic and political power of all people with disabilities. AAPD Member Benefits include a mail order prescription service, legal services, life settlements, a quarterly newsletter, adaptive automobile insurance, online career center, online shopping marketplace.

3229 Appleby Foundation

Sun Trust Bank
1445 New York Avenue NW
Washington, DC   20005   202-879-6284
                               888-786-8787
                            www.suntrust.com

Funding for the blind and mental health.

3230 Change

1413 Park Road NW
Washington, DC   20010   202-387-3725
                          FAX: 202-387-3729

Andrea Dorsett, Executive Director

Offers counseling/assessment, emergency food and clothing referrals, rental assistance and job assistance to disabled persons in the District of Columbia area.

3231 Charles Delmar Foundation

1918 16th Street NW
Number 203
Washington, DC   20006   202-293-2494

Mareen D. Hughes, President

3232 District of Columbia Arc

900 Varnum Street NE
Washington, DC   20017   202-636-2950

3233 Dole Foundation

1819 H Street NW
Suite 340
Washington, DC   20006

Randy Davis, Program Officer

Project grants are made for the general purpose of promoting greater economic independence for people with disabilities through competitive employment. Areas of interest include: promoting access to job opportunities in the marketplace; application of entrepreneurial techniques to create new jobs; employment of minorities, women and older workers with disabilities, applications of assistive technologies in the workplace, programs targeting rural areas and innovative employment projects.

3234 Eugene and Agnes E. Meyer Foundation

1400 16th Street NW
Suite 360
Washington, DC   20036   202-483-8294
                          FAX: 202-328-6850
                       www.meyerfoundation.org

Julie Rogers, President

Awards grants to projects dealing with the learning disabled, blind, mental health and vocational training in the Washington metropolitan area.

3235 Federal Student Aid Information Center

US Department of Education
400 Maryland Avenue SW
Washington, DC   20202   202-260-2226
                               800-433-3243
              www.ed.gov/prog_info/SFA/StudentGuide

William J. Ryan, Acting Director

Answers questions about Federal student aid from students, parents and Members of Congress, as well as financial aid administrators.

3236 GEICO Philanthropic Foundation

One Geico Plaza
Washington, DC   20076   301-986-2911
                          TDY:800-833-8255

Hospitals, physically disabled and Special Olympics.

3237 Giant Food Foundation

PO Box 1804
Washington, DC   20013   202-449-7483

Israel Sohen, Chairman

Offers grants in the areas of mental health, recreation, community and cultural programs, art, and educational programs for the health and prosperity of the greater Washington area.

3238 Jacob and Charlotte Lehrman Foundation

1027 33rd Street NW
2nd Floor
Washington, DC   20007

Robert Lehrman, Persident

3239 John Edward Fowler Memorial Foundation

1725 K Street NW
Suite 1201
Washington, DC   20006   202-728-9080
                          FAX: 202-728-9082

Richard Lee

Although not a program priority, the foundation does offer grants to the physically disabled in the Washington, DC area only.

3240 Joseph P. Kennedy, Jr. Foundation

1325 G Street NW
Suite 500
Washington, DC   20005   202-393-1250
                                FAX: 202-824-0351
        e-mail: sbadeau@specialolympics.org
              www.familyvillage.wisc.edu/jpkf/

Eunice Shriver, Executive Vice President

Has two firm objectives: to seek the prevention of
mental retardation, and to improve the way society
deals with its citizens who are already mentally retarded. The Foundation uses its funds in areas where
a multiplier effect can be achieved through development of innovative models for the prevention and
amelioration of mental retardation, through provision
of seed money that encourages new researchers, and
thorough use of the Foundation's influence to promote public awareness.

3241 Kiplinger Foundation

1729 H Street NW
Washington, DC   20006   202-887-6400
                                FAX: 202-778-8976

Andrea Wilkes, Secretary

Limited to the greater Washington, DC area, the
grants focus primarily on education, social welfare,
cultural activities and community programs. Matching grants to eligible secondary or higher education
institutions are provided on behalf of employees and
retirees of Kiplinger Washington Editors, Inc. The
Foundation does not fund scholarships.

3242 Morris and Gwendolyn Cafritz Foundation

1825 K Street NW
14th Floor
Washington, DC   20006   202-223-3100

        www.cafritzfoundation.org

Anne Allen, Executive Director

3243 Paul and Annetta Himmelfarb Foundation

4545 42nd Street NW
Suite 203
Washington, DC   20016   202-966-3795

Lilian N. Khronstadt, Executive Director

3244 Public Welfare Foundation

1200 U Street NW
Washington, DC   20009   202-965-1800
                                800-275-7934
                                FAX: 202-265-8851
        e-mail: reviewcommittee@publicwelfare.org
              www.publicwelfare.org

The foundation's funding is specifically targeted
to economically disadvantaged populations. Proposals must fall within one of the following categories: criminal justice, disadvantaged elderly,
disadvantaged youth, environment, health and
population and reproductive health, human rights
and global security, and community economic developmental and participation. Proposals should
be addressed to the Review Committee.

3245 United States Department of Education

400 Maryland Avenue Southwest
Washington, DC   20202
                                800-872-5327

William J. Ryan, Acting Director

The National Institute of Disability and Rehabilitation Research within the Department of Education
awards over 15 grants to provide technical assistance
to those with rights and duties under The Americans
With Disabilities Act. This new program establishes:
10 regional disability and business accommodation
centers; 3 materials development projects; 2 national
training projects; and 1 national coordination contract.

Florida

3246 Able Trust

Florida Endowment Foundation for Vocational Rehab.
106 East College Avenue
Suite 820
Tallahassee, FL   32301   850-224-4493
                                 888-838-2253
                                 FAX: 850-224-4496
                          e-mail: info@abletrust.org
                                www.abletrust.org

Sharon Griffith, President & CEO
Kristen Knapp, Dir. of Public Relat./Marketing
Guenevere Crum, Grants Manager

Provides grant funds for small business start-up costs
for people with disabilities and employment-related
programs for non-profit agencies in Florida. Assists
families, individuals and agencies through an information and referral helpline, educational conferences, and youth training programs. Provides
businesses free resources for hiring people with disabilities.

3247 Arc of Florida

411 E College Avenue
Tallahassee, FL   32301   850-921-0460

                          e-mail: arcfl@supernet.net

3248 BCR Foundation

PO Box 13307
Pensacola, FL   32591   850-438-2509

Betty G. Rainwater, President

3249 Barnett Charities

100 North Laura Street
Jacksonville, FL   32202   904-633-2040

Beth Bollinger, Director

A non-profit, private foundation established in 1987 to provide a common source of funding for bank-wide civic and charitable sponsorships. Contributions from Barnett Charities, Inc. should provide identity for Barnett either through funding of specific programs or through the establishment of an endowment and have statewide impact in Florida and/or Georgia. The funding targets include: education, culture & the arts, fitness, health & human services, special sports and patriotic events.

3250   Baron de Hirsch Meyer Foundation

407 Lincon Road
Suite 6J
Miami Beach, FL   33139   305-672-0934

Colleen Steadman

3251   Barron Collier Jr. Foundation

2600 Golden Gate Parkway
Suite 200
Naples, FL   34105   941-262-2600
                            FAX: 941-262-1840

Giving to the Special Olympics is a top priority of the Foundation.

3252   Camiccia-Arnautou Charitable Foundation

c/o Bill T. Smith, Jr.
980 North Federal Highway
Suite 402
Boca Raton, FL   33432

3253   Chatlos Foundation

PO Box 915048
Longwood, FL   32791   407-862-5077

                            www.chatlos.org

William J. Chatlos, President
Joy D'Arata, Vice President

Funds nonprofit organizations in the USA and around the globe. Funding is provided in the following areas of giving: Bible Colleges/Seminaries, Religious Causes, Medical Concerns, Liberal Arts Colleges and Social Concerns. Category of placement is determined by the organizations overall mission rather than the project under consideration. The Foundation does not make scholarship grants directly to individuals but rather to educational institutions which in turn select recipients.

3254   Dade Community Foundation

200 South Biscayne Boulevard
Suite 2780
Miami, FL   33131   305-371-2711
                            FAX: 305-371-5342
                    e-mail: dadecomfdn@aol.com

Ruth Shack, President

3255   Dodson Family Foundation

c/o Robert Weiss
7383 Orangewood Lane
Suite 303
Boca Raton, FL   33433

3256   Dr. Jack Widrich Foundation

400 West Rivo Alto Drive
Miami Beach, FL   33139

3257   EIS Foundation

6931 Queenferry Circle
Boca Raton, FL   33496   561-852-6854
                            FAX: 561-852-6884

Maurice L. Schwarz, President

3258   Edyth Bush Charitable Foundation

199 East Welbourne Avenue
PO Box 1967
Winter Park, FL   32790   407-647-4322
                                 888-647-4322
                            FAX: 407-647-7716
                      e-mail: edyth@aol.com
                    fdncenter.org/grantmaker.bush

Deborah J. Hessler, Program Associtate

3259   FPL Group Foundation

700 Universe Boulevard
Juno Beach, FL   33408

John L. Kitchens

3260   Florida Rock Industries Foundation

155 East 21st Street
Jacksonville, FL   32206

H.B. Horner, Secretary

3261   Foundation for Toxic Free Dentistry

PO Box 608010
Orlando, FL   32860

Nonprofit groups to educate and make referrals to biological dentists.

3262   Frank Stanley Beveridge Foundation

301 Yamato Road
Suite 1130
Boca Raton, FL   33431

                                 800-600-3723
                            FAX: 561-241-8388
                e-mail: administrator@beveridge.org
                            www.beveridge.org

Philip Caswell, President

3263   Greenburg-May Foundation

PO Box 54-5816
Miami, FL   33154   305-864-8639

Isabel May, President

3264   Henry L. & Kathryn Mills Charitable Foundation

PO Box 822056
South Florida, FL   30082

Debra Anne Mills

3265 Jack Eckerd Corporation Foundation

PO Box 4689
Clearwater, FL 33758   727-395-6000
                              FAX: 727-395-7934

James M. Santo, Chairman

The foundation limits its giving to nonprofit, tax-exempt organizations located in Eckerd Drug Company's 13-state marketing area. The majority of our funds are committed to national health organizations, the United Way campaigns, and scholarship funding at various colleges of pharmacy.

3266 Janet and Stanley Kane Foundation

539 Norsota Way
Sarasota, FL 34242

3267 Jefferson Lee Ford III Memorial Foundation

9600 Collins Avenue
546487
Bal Harbour, FL 33154   305-885-5447
                               FAX: 305-868-2646

Herbert Kurras, Trustee
Suzanne Kingsbury, Trustee

Disabled children, hearing and speech center. Grants are only given to tax exempt organizations, no individual grants are offered.

3268 Jessie Ball duPont Fund

One Independent Drive
Suite 1400
Jacksonville, FL 32202   904-353-0890
                                800-252-3452
                          FAX: 904-353-3870
          e-mail: jessie@dupontfund.org
                   www.dupontfund.org

Sherry P. Mcgill, PhD, President
JoAnn P. Bennett, Director of Administration

Established in 1976 under the terms of the will of the late Jessie Ball duPont. The fund is a national foundation having a special though not exclusive interest in issues affecting the South. The Fund works with the approximately 325 individual institutions to which Mrs. duPont personally contributed during the five-year period, 1960 through 1964.

3269 Joe and Emily Lowe Foundation

249 Royal Palm Way
Palm Beach, FL 33480   561-659-1203
                              FAX: 561-655-7130

Bernard Sterm, President

Emphasis is on Jewish welfare funds, the arts, museums, higher education including medical education, hospitals, medical research, aid to the handicapped, underprivileged children's organizations and women's projects. The funding is limited to the New York Metropolitan Area including New Jersey and Palm Beach County, Florida. No grants are made to individuals.

3270 John E. and Nellie J. Bastien Memorial Foundation

440 East Sample Road
Suite 209
Pompano Beach, FL 33064   954-942-3203

3271 John S. and James L. Knight Foundation

1 Biscayne Tower
Suite 3800
Miami, FL 33131   305-908-2600

                         www.knightfdn.org

3272 KW Grader Foundation

1925 Hermosa Avenue
Bartow, FL 33830

Grants for the visually impaired and physically disabled are a top priority of the Foundation.

3273 Leonard and Sophie Davis Foundation

601 Clearwater Park Road
West Palm Beach, FL 33401   561-832-6466

Marilyn Hoadley, President

3274 Lost Tree Village Charitable Foundation

11555 Lost Tree Way
North Palm Beach, FL 33408   561-622-3780
                                    FAX: 561-622-7558
                           e-mail: itvcfi@aol.com

James Gillin, President

3275 NationsBank Community Foundation

1800 2nd Street
Suite 750
Sarasota, FL 34236   941-957-0442

Debra Jacobs, Administrator

3276 Publix Super Markets Charities

1936 George Jenkins Boulevard
Lakeland, FL 33815   941-688-1188

Barbara O. Hart, President

3277 Richard W. Higgins Charitable Foundation Trust

c/o Marshall & Ilsley Trust of Florida
800 Laurel Oak Drive
Suite 101
Naples, FL 34108

3278 Vic and Vicki Weinstein Family Foundation

17776 Buckingham Court
Boca Raton, FL 33496

3279 William G. Selby and Marie Selby Foundation

1800 2nd Street
Suite 750
Sarasota, FL 34236   941-379-3222

Debra Jacobs, President

Capital project funding for human services, the arts and education. Funding is limited to Sarasota and adjoining counties in Florida.

Georgia

3280 Arc of Georgia

1945 Cliff Valley Way
Suite 220
Atlanta, GA 30329   404-634-5512

e-mail: gaarcnetwork@earthlink.net

3281 Community Foundation for Greater Atlanta

Hurt Building
Suite 449
Atlanta, GA 30303   404-688-5525
FAX: 404-688-3060
www.atlcf.org

Jessie Bond, Senior Program Officer

3282 Equifax Foundation

PO Box 4472
Atlanta, GA 30302   404-885-8000

The contribution's program focuses on the communities where our employees live and work, educational institutions, and selected organizations dealing with company-wide or national issues. Equifax supports nonprofit organizations in the fields of education, health and welfare, culture and art and civic programs.

3283 Florence C. and Harry L. English Memorial Fund

c/o Sun Trust Bank
PO Box 4418-MC041
Atlanta, GA 30302   404-588-8246
FAX: 404-230-5550
e-mail: bill.bowdoin@suntrust.com
www.suntrustatlantafoundation.org

William R. Bowdoin, Jr., First Vice President
Renee Barnett, Administrative Assistant

Grants only made to Metro Atlanta non-profit organizations; no grants to churches or individuals.

3284 Georgia Power Company Contirbutions Program

241 Ralph McGill Boulevard NE
Bin 10230
Atlanta, GA 30308   404-506-6784

Linda Leathers, Manager

3285 Harriet McDaniel Marshall Trust in Memory of Sanders McDaniel

c/o SunTrust Bank Atlanta
PO Box 4418 MC 041
Atlanta, GA 30302   404-588-8246
FAX: 404-230-5550
www.suntrustatlantafoundation.org

William R. Bowdoin, Jr., Vice President
Renee Barnett, Administrative Assistant

Grants only made to Metro Atlanta non-profit organizations, no grants to churches or individuals.

3286 IBM Corporation

4111 Northside Parkway NW
Atlanta, GA 30327
FAX: 404-238-3409

Manages disability programs (which leverage IBM resources through partnerships) designed to train persons with disabilities and assist them in gaining employment. Also, disseminates information regarding products and resources for persons with disabilities with those of other companies and organizations.

3287 Ira C. Herbert Family Foundation

c/o Lila Herbert
3555 Ranier Drive
Atlanta, GA 30327

3288 John H. and Wilhelmina D. Harland Charitable Foundation

2 Piedmont Center
Suite 106
Atlanta, GA 30305   404-264-9912

e-mail: harland@randomc.com

John A. Conant, Secretary

3289 Lettie Pate Whitehead Foundation

50 Hurt Plaza
Suite 1200
Atlanta, GA 30303   404-522-7026
FAX: 404-522-7026
www.lpwhitehead.org

Charles H. McTier, President

3290 Marcus Foundation

2455 Paces Ferry Road
Building C 22nd Floor
Atlanta, GA 30338

Frederick Slagle, Secretary

3291 Patterson-Barclay Memorial Foundation

6487 Peachtree Industrial Boulevard
Suite A
Atlanta, GA 30360   770-458-9888

Hugh R. Powell, Jr., Secretary

3292 Perkins-Ponder Foundation

c/o Bank of America
PO Box 4007
Macon, GA 31213   912-744-6454

3293 Rich Foundation

11 Piedmont Center
Suite 204
Atlanta, GA 30305   404-262-2266

Anne Poland-Berg, Grant Consultant

3294 Savannah Widows Society
3025 Bull Street
Savannah, GA 31405   912-232-6312

Martha Peeples

3295 SunTrust Bank, Atlanta Foundation
c/o SunTrust Bank, Atlanta
PO Box 4418
Atlanta, GA   30302   404-588-8250
                             FAX: 404-230-5550

William R. Bowdoin, Jr., Secretary

Hawaii

3296 Arc of Hawaii
3989 Diamond Head Road
Honolulu, HI   96816   808-737-7995

e-mail: arc-hi@aloha.net

3297 Atherton Family Foundation
111 South King Street
Honolulu, HI   96813

Jane Smith

Supports educational projects, programs and institutions have the highest priority, with the enterprises of a religious nature and those concerned with health and social services given careful attention. The Foundation is one of the largest private resources in the State devoted exclusively to the support of activities of a charitable nature.

3298 Clarence T.C. Ching Foundation
PO Box 4107
Honolulu, HI   96812

Lawrence S.L Ching, Chairperson

3299 G.N. Wilcox Trust
c/o Pacific Century Trust
PO Box 3170
Honolulu, HI   96802   808-538-4540

3300 Hawaii Community Foundation
900 Fort Street Mall, Pioneer Plaza
Suite 1300
Honolulu, HI   96813   808-537-6333

e-mail: hcf@pixi.com
www.hcf-hawaii.org

Kevin Taketa, President

3301 McInerny Foundation
c/o Pacific Century Trust
130 Merchant Street
Honolulu, HI   96813   808-538-4944

Lois C. Loomis, Vice President

3302 Sophie Russell Testamentary Trust
PO Box 2390
Honolulu, HI   96804   808-524-4488
                             FAX: 808-523-2195

Lois Loomis, Secretary

Supports qualified tax-exempt charitable organizations, in the State of Hawaii only. Offers grants to the Humane Society and institutions giving nursing care and serving the physically and mentally handicapped.

Illinois

3303 Abbott Laboratories Fund
Contributions Committee
Abbott Park
N. Chicago, IL   60064

An Illinois, nonprofit, philanthropic organization that makes a significant contribution to human welfare through the development and worldwide distribution of technologically advanced health care products.

3304 Albert Goodstien Family Foundation
1534 Forrest Avenue
Highland Park, IL   60035

Marilyn Kushen, President

3305 Alfred Bersted Foundation
231 South Lasalle Street
Chicago, IL   60604   312-251-8850

M. Catherine Ryan

Grants are given to programs serving the mentally and physically disabled, organizations included in the broader focus of the foundation. Grants are restricted to organizations in four Illinois counties: DuPage, Kane, McHenry and DeKalb.

3306 Alzheimer's Association
c/o Medical and Scientific Affairs
919 North Michigan Avenue
Suite 1000
Chicago, IL   60611
                             800-272-3900
                             FAX: 312-335-4034
                             e-mail: nico.stanculescu@alz.org
                             www.alz.org

Timothy J. Morgan, Director of Financial Operations

3307 American Foundation for the Blind-Midwest
401 North Michigan Avenue
Suite 308
Chicago, IL   60611   312-245-9961

e-mail: chicago@afb.net
www.afb.org

Paul Schroeder, Director

3308 American National Bank and Trust Company

33 North LaSalle Street
Chicago, IL 60690 773-376-1400
FAX: 312-661-3562

Joan M. Klaus, Foundation Director

Supports the endeavors of organizations working to meet the critical needs of the city and its surrounding communities. Success is greatly affected by the well-being of the communities the company serves, thus the foundation seeks to fulfill the social obligations both through financial funding and human resources. The Foundation funding categories include organizations and programs involved in economic development, education, community and social services, healthcare and culture and the arts.

3309 Ameritech Corporation Contributions Program

30 South Wacker Drive
34th Floor
Chicago, IL 60606 312-750-5037
FAX: 216-822-5522
www.ameritech.com/community

Michael E. Kuhlin, Senior Director

3310 Amerock Corporation

4000 Auburn Street
PO Box 7018
Rockford, IL 61125 815-963-9631
FAX: 815-969-6029

Lawrence Gloyd

Grants are given to organizations promoting wellness, health and rehabilitation of the visually impaired and physically disabled.

3311 Arc of Illinois

1820 Ridge Road
#300
Homewood, IL 60430 708-206-1930

3312 Benjamin Benedict Green-Field Foundation

33 North Dearborn Street
Suite 1410
Chicago, IL 60602

Harriet Brady, Vice President

3313 Blowitz-Ridgeway Foundation

1 Northfield Plaza
Suite 230
Northfield, IL 60093

Tina M. Erickson, Administrator

Provides limited program, capital and research grants to organizations aiding the physically and mentally disabled, and agencies serving children and youth. Grants generally limited to Illinois.

3314 Burlington Northern Santa Fe Foundation

5601 West 26th Street
Cicero, IL 60804 708-222-4815
FAX: 708-222-4857

Dick Russack, President

3315 Chicago Community Trust and Affiliates

222 North LaSalle Street
Suite 1400
Chicago, IL 60601 312-372-3356

e-mail: sandy@cct.org
www.cct.org

Sandy Chears, Grants Manager

3316 Community Foundation of Champaign County

404 West Church Street
Champaign, IL 61820 217-359-0125
FAX: 217-352-6494

Jill Niles, Executive Director

3317 Dr. Scholl Foundation

11 South LaSalle Street
Suite 2100
Chicago, IL 60603 312-782-5210

Pamela Scholl, President

3318 Duchossois Foundation

845 North Larch Avenue
Elmhurst, IL 60126 630-279-3600
FAX: 630-993-6911

Kimberly Duchossois Lenczuk, President

Established in 1984, the foundation returns dollars to the communities supporting its facilities and employees. Within these following areas, organizations are carefully selected on the basis of community needs and the organization's value and performance. Areas aimed at include: medical research, children/youth programs and cultural institutions.

3319 Evenston Community Foundation

828 Davis Street
Suite 300
Evanston, IL 60201 847-475-2402
FAX: 847-475-2469

Thomas K. Jager, Administrator

3320 Field Foundation of Illinois

200 South Wacker Drive
Suite 3860
Chicago, IL 60606 312-831-0910

Handy Lindsey, Jr., Executive Director

The Foundation awards grants to institutions and agencies in the fields of health, welfare, education, cultural and conservation activities, and urban and community affairs, primarily serving the people of the Chicago metropolitan area.

3321 Francis Beidler Charitable Trust

53 West Jackson Boulevard
Suite 530
Chicago, IL 60604 312-922-3792

Thomas B. Dorris

3322 Fred J. Brunner Foundation

9300 King Street
Franklin Park, IL   60131   847-678-3232
                                 FAX: 847-678-0642

General disability grants.

3323 GJ Aigner Foundation

5617 Dempster Street
Morton Grove, IL   60053

General disability grants.

3324 Generations Fund

335 Sheridan Road
Winnetka, IL   60093

Robert Morris, President

3325 George M. Eisenberg Foundation for Charities

2340 South Arlington Heights Road
Suite 480
Arlington Heights, IL   60005   847-981-0545
                                 FAX: 847-941-0548

3326 George Zoltan Lefton Family Foundation

c/o George Zoltan Lefton Company
3622 South Morgan Street
Chicago, IL   60609   773-254-4344

Magda Lefton, Secretary

3327 Green Bay Foundation

Goldman, Sachs & Company
233 South Wacker Drive
Suite 4900
Chicago, IL   60606

General disability grants.

3328 Grover Hermann Foundation

Paul K. Rhoads
233 South Wacker Drive
Suite 7200
Chicago, IL   60606   312-876-1000

Paul Rhoads

Provides funds for educational, health, public policy,
community and religious organizations throughout
the United States. Its major interests are in higher
education and health.

3329 Harken Foundation

c/o Michael R. Friedberg
899 Skokie Boulevard
Suite 314
Northbrook, IL   60062   847-498-0150

Harold E. Foreman, Jr., President

3330 Harry F. and Elaine Chaddick Foundation

123 West Maddison Street
Suite 200
Chicago, IL   60602   312-704-4100

Elaine M. Chaddick

**3331 Harry and Saddie Lasky Foundation c/o Sandra
Siegal, Warady & Davis, L.L.P.**

108 Wilmont Road
Suite 500
Deerfield, IL   60015

Robert Handelsman, Secretary

3332 Helen Brach Foundation

55west Wacker Drive
Suite 701
Chicago, IL   60601   312-372-4417
                                 FAX: 312-372-0290

Raymond F. Simon, President

3333 John D. and Catherine T. MacArthur Foundation

140 Dearborn Street
Suite 100
Chicago, IL   60603   312-726-8000
                                 FAX: 312-920-6258
                          e-mail: 4answers@macfnd.org
                                 www.macfdn.org

Richard Kaplan, Director

3334 Kazma Family Foundation

c/o Gerald Kazma
4343 Commerce Court
Suite 621
Lisle, IL   60532

3335 LaSalle Chicago Community Trust

222 North Lasalle Street
Suite 1400
Chicago, IL   60601   312-372-3356
                                 FAX: 312-580-7411
                                 www.cct.org

Sandy Chears, Grants Manager

A community foundation established in 1915, which
receives gifts and bequests from individuals, families
or organizations interested in providing through the
community foundation, financial support for the
charitable agencies or institutions which serve the
residents of metropolitan Chicago.

**3336 Les Turne Amyotrophic Laterial Sclerosis
Foundation**

3325 Main Street
Skokie, IL   60076   847-679-3311
                                 FAX: 847-679-9103
                          e-mail: info@lturner-als.org

Harvey Gaffen, President
Wendy Abrams, Executive Director

Voluntary health organization dedicated to raising funds for ALS research, patient services and public awareness. Provides educational mateials for affected individuals and family members, health care professionals, and the general public. Program services include referrals and counseling; audio-visual aids and periodic newsletters. Offers support groups and patient networking to affected individuals, family members, and caregivers.

3337 Little City Foundation

1760 West Algonquin Road
Palatine, IL 60067   847-358-5510
                                   FAX: 847-358-3291
                                   www.littlecity.org

Alan Dachman, Executive Director
Rena Zaid, Associate Executive Director

Provides progressive community-based services and service coordination for children and adults with mental retardation or other developmental, emotional and behavioral challenges. Services include direct care with up to 24-hour per day support for children and adults, Foster Care, Families One, adoption opportunities, respite care, supported employment, studio and multidisciplinary fine arts, public education, and advocacy.

3338 Lucille S. Thompson Family Foundation

c/o The Northern Trust Company
50 South LaSalle Street
Chicago, IL 60675

Lila K. Pfleger, Foundation Manager

3339 Margaret O'Maller DeSelvester Charitable Foundation

10 South Wacker Drive
Number 4000
Chicago, IL 60606

Donald A. Gillies

3340 Mark Morton Memorial Fund

100 North Riverside Plaza
Chicago, IL 60606

3341 McDonald's Corporation Contributions Program

McDonalds Plaza
Oak Brook, IL 60521   630-623-7048

www.mcdonalds.com/community/index.html

Jackie Meara, Supervisor of Contributions

3342 Michael Reese Health Trust

20 North Wacker Drive
Suite 760
Chicago, IL 60606   312-726-1008
                                  FAX: 312-726-2797
                           e-mail: info@healthtrust.net
                        fdncenter.org/grantmaker.health

Dorothy H. Gardner, President

3343 Moen Foundation

c/o First National Bank of Chicago
1 South Northwest Highway
Park Ridge, IL 60068   847-518-7392

3344 Molner Foundation

c/o Marvin M. Siegel, CPA PC
3330 Old Glenview Road
Number7
Wilmette, IL 60091

Morton John Barnard

3345 National Eye Research Foundation (NERF)

910 Skokie Boulevard
Suite 207A
Northbrook, IL 60062   847-564-4652
                                  800-621-2258
                             FAX: 847-564-0807
                         e-mail: nerfl955@aol.com
                           www.eyemac.com/nerf

Dedicated to improving eye care for the public and meeting the professional nees of eye care practitioners; sponsors eye research projects on contact lens applications and eye care problems. Special study sections in such fields as orthokcrtology, primary eyecare, pediatrics, and through continuing education programs. Provides eye care information for the public and professionals. Educational materials including pamphlets. Program activities include education and referrals.

3346 National Headache Foundation

5252 North Western Avenue
Chicago, IL 60625
                                  800-843-2256

Headache physicians.

3347 OMRON Foundation

c/o OMRON Systems
1 East Commerce Drive
Schaumburg, IL 60173   847-843-7900
                             FAX: 847-240-5362

Nicholas Hahn, Director

3348 Oris B. Hastings Charitable Foundation

230 8th Street
PO Box 186
Cairo, IL 62914   618-734-2800

John G. Holland

3349 Peoria Area Community Foundation

124 Southwest Adams Street
Suite 1
Peoria, IL 61602
                             FAX: 309-674-8754
                      e-mail: PACF@worldnet.att.net

George H. Kreiss, Executive Director

3350 Polk Brothers Foundation

420 North Wabash Avenue
Number 204
Chicago, IL 60611   312-527-4684

Nikki W. Stein, Executive Director

3351 Retirement Research Foundation

8765 West Higgins Road
Suite 430
Chicago, IL 60631   773-714-8080
                             FAX: 773-714-8089

Marilyn Hennessey, President

A private philanthropy with primary interest in improving the quality of life of older persons in the United States.

3352 Rush Hayward Masonic Fund

14 Bel Air Court
Champaign, IL 61820

3353 Sara Lee Foundation

3 First National Plaza
Chicago, IL 60602   312-558-8448

www.saraleefoundation.org

Robyn S. Tryloff, Executive Director

3354 Sears-Roebuck Foundation

Sears Tower
Department 903
Chicago, IL 60684   847-286-2500

3355 Siragusa Foundation

919 North Michigan Avenue
Chicago, IL 60611   312-280-0833
                             FAX: 312-943-4489

Irene S. Phelps, Executive Director

3356 Square D Foundation

1415 South Roselle Road
Palatine, IL 60067

                             FAX: 847-397-8814

Makes donations for operating support, capital development needs, and special projects to nonprofit organizations that have been granted exemption from the Federal Income Tax. The Foundation has a strong commitment to the following areas: health and welfare, education, civic and community affairs, and culture and the arts. Support of higher education is also made for scholarships, endowments for facility and acquisition or expansion of equipment or facilities, through Matching Gift Program.

3357 United Parkinson Foundation

833 West Washington Boulevard
Chicago, IL 60607   312-733-1893
                             FAX: 312-733-1896
                             e-mail: upf_itf@msn.com

Harold L. Klawans, MD, President
Judy Rosner, Executive Director

International voluntary not-for-profit organization dedicated to patient services; education of affected individuals, family members, and healthcare professionals; and promotion and support of research for Parkinson's Disease and related disorders. Offers an extensive referral service to guide affected individuals to proper diagnosis and clinical care. Provides referrals to genetic counseling and support groups; promotes patient advocacy; and offers a variety of educational and support materials

3358 Vladimir A. Geringer Foundation

c/o The Norhtern Trust Company
50 South LeSalle Street
Chicago, IL 60675

3359 WP and HB White Foundation

540 West Frontage Road
Suite 332
Northfield, IL 60093   847-446-1441

Margaret Blandford, Executive Director

The Foundation's funds are allocated on a continuing basis within the metropolitan area of Chicago where our founder's business prospered. The Foundation helps organizations specializing in the visually impaired, mental health, youth and recreation.

3360 Washington Square Health Foundation

875 North Michigan Avenue
Suite 3516
Chicago, IL 60611   312-664-6488

                             e-mail: washington@wshf.org
                             www.wshf.org

Howard Nochumson, Executive Director

3361 Wheat Ridge Ministries

1 Pierce Place
Suite 250E
Itasca, IL 60143   630-766-9066
                             800-762-6748
                             FAX: 630-766-9622
                             e-mail: wrmin@aol.com
                             www.wheatridge.org

Indiana

3362 Arc of Indiana

22 E Washington
Suite 210
Indianapolis, IN 46204   317-977-2375

                             e-mail: arcin@in.net

John Dickerson, Executive Director

3363 Ball Brothers Foundation

222 South Mulberry Street
1408
Muncie, IN 47305

                             FAX: 765-741-5518

Douglas Bakken, Executive Director

Mentally and physically disabled, only serving Indiana area.

3364 Central Indiana Community Foundation

615 North Alabama Street
Suite 119
Indianapolis, IN 46204   317-634-2423
                            FAX: 317-684-0943
                    e-mail: program@cicf.org
                                www.cicf.org

Kenneth L. Gladish, PhD., Executive Director

3365 Community Foundation of Boone County

60 East Cedar Street
PO Box 92
Zionsville, IN 46077   317-873-0210
                            FAX: 317-873-0219
                    e-mail: cfbc@in-motion.net
          www.bccn.boone.in.us/cf/index.html

Lisa Latz John, Executive Director

3366 Crown Point Community Foundation

Courthouse Square, Suite 302
PO Box 522
Crown Point, IN 46307   219-662-7252

Linda Davis, Executive Director

3367 Eli Lilly and Company Corporate Contributions Program

Lilly Corporate Center
Indianapolis, IN 46285   317-276-3177

                    www.lilly.com/info/citizenship

Kendy S. Smith, Secretary

3368 English-Bonter-Mitchell Foundation

900 Ft. Wayne Natl. Bank Building
Fort Wayne, IN 46802

General disability grants.

3369 Frank L. and Laura L. Smock Foundation

PO Box 960
Fort Wayne, IN 46801   219-461-6000

Alice Kopfer, Vice President
This foundation is restricted to assisting needy, elderly, individuals who are of the Presbyterian faith and residents of the state of Indiana.

3370 Hazel Teegarden Foundation

c/o William Helmbrecht
500 Washington Street
Columbus, IN 47201

3371 Hook Drug Foundation

1180 East 38th Street
Indianapolis, IN 46205

Donna Galerman, Secretary

3372 Indianapolis Foundation

615 North Alabama Street
Room 119
Indianapolis, IN 46204   317-634-7497

                    www.cicf.org/about/fsetif.htm

Kenneth L. Gladish, PhD, Executive Director

3373 John W. Anderson Foundation

402 Wall Street
Valparaiso, IN 46383   219-462-4611

William N. Vinovich, Vice-Chairman
Physically and mentally disabled, recreation and youth agencies in Northwest Indiana area.

3374 Trabant North Knox

c/o Bank One, Trust Group
111 Monument Circle
Suite 1501
Indianapolis, IN 46277

3375 William H. Willennar Foundation

c/o Fort Wayne National Bank
PO Box 110
Fort Wayne, IN 46801

M.C. Haggarty, Secretary

Iowa

3376 Arc of Iowa

715 East Locust
Des Moines, IA 50309   515-283-2358

                    e-mail: arciowa@aol.com

3377 Hall-Perrine Foundation

115 3rd Street SE
Suite 803
Cedar Rapids, IA 52401   319-362-9079

Jack B. Evans, President

3378 Hawley Foundation

1530 Financial Center 666 Walnut
Des Moines, IA 50309

Amos Pearsall, Jr., Executive Director
Grants are considered only from Des Moines organizations. Each year the Trustees designate a high-priority area schedule. For 1994 these are: Affordable Housing, Youth at Risk and Substance Abuse.

3379 Homer G. Barr Trust

PO Box 370
Webster City, IA 50595   515-832-1133

3380 Kinney-Lindstrom Foundation

PO Box 520
Mason City, IA 50402

Lowell Hall

Offers grants only to the area of Iowa for projects to
help; Special Olympics, physically disabled and art
and cultural affairs.

3381 Mid-Iowa Health Foundation

553 39th Street
Suite 104
Des Moines, IA 50312   515-277-6411

Kathryn Bradley, Director

3382 Principal Financial Group Foundation

711 High Street
Des Moines, IA 50392   515-247-5091
FAX: 515-246-5475
e-mail: bassett.kendra@principal.con
www.principal.com/about/giving

Kendra Bassett, Contributions Assistant

3383 Siouxland Foundation

PO Box 2014
Sioux County, IA 51104   712-239-3303
FAX: 712-239-3303
e-mail: sxlfdn@aol.com

Debbie Hubbard, Executive Director

Kansas

3384 Arc of Kansas

3601 SW 29th Street
S-105
Topeka, KS 66614   785-271-8783

e-mail: thearcks@cjnetworks.com

3385 Cessna Foundation

PO Box 7706
Wichita, KS 67277   316-517-7810
FAX: 316-517-7812

Marilyn Richwine, Secretary Treasurer

Some grants are available to organizations which
meet the guidelines for serving the physically disabled. Grants are restricted to communities where
Cessna has manufacturing facilities.

3386 Hutchinson Commununity Foundation

PO Box 298
Hutchinson, KS 67601   785-625-8327

Joseph A. Hess

3387 Victor Murdock Foundation

c/o Bank of America
PO Box 1122
Wichita, KS 67201   316-261-4087

Richard B. Chambers, Assistant Vice President

Kentucky

3388 Arc of Kentucky

833 East Main Street
Frankfort, KY 40601   502-875-5225

e-mail: arcfky@aol.com

3389 Gheens Foundation

1 Riverfront Palza
Suite 705
Louisville, KY 40202   502-584-4650
FAX: 502-584-4652

James N. Davis, Executive Director

3390 Kentucky Social Welfare Foundation

c/o PNC Bank, N.A.
500 West Jefferson Street
Citizens Plaza
Louisville, KY 40296   502-581-2157

W. Michael Hanks, Vice President

3391 Mansbach Foundation

PO Box 1179
Ashland, KY 41105

3392 Omnicare Foundation

1717 Dixie Highway
Suite 800
Fort Wright, KY 41011

Cheryl D. Hodges, Secretary

Louisiana

3393 Arc of Louisiana

PO Box 65129
Baton Rouge, LA 70896   225-383-1033

3394 Baton Rouge Area Foundation

406 North 4th Street
Baton Rouge, LA 70802   225-387-6126
FAX: 225-387-6153

John G. Davies, President

3395 Booth-Bricker Fund

826 Union Street
Suite 300
New Orleans, LA   70112   504-581-2430

Gray S. Parker, Chairperson

3396 Community Foundation of Shrevport-Bossier

401 Edwards Street
1111 Louisiana Tower
Shrevport, LA   71101   318-221-0582

e-mail: cfsb@comfoundsb.org
www.comfoundsb.org

Dorothy Gwin, Executive Director

3397 Grayson Foundation

PO Box 206
Shreveport, LA   71162   318-222-3218

Sam B. Grayson, President

Maine

3398 Edith H. McCobb Trust

c/o Harmon, Jones, Sanford & Elliot
20 Merchant Street
Camden, ME   04843

3399 UNUM Charitable Foundation

2211 Congress Street
Portland, ME   04122   207-770-2211
                               FAX: 800-447-2498

Janine Manning, Manager

The Foundation encourages projects that: stimulate others in the private or public sector to participate in problem solving; advance innovative and cost-effective approaches for addressing defined, recognized needs; and demonstrate ability to obtain future project funding, if needed. The foundation generally limits its consideration of capital campaign requests to the Greater Portland, Maine area.

3400 UNUM Foundation

2211 Congress Street
P349
Portland, ME   04122   207-770-4378

Janine M. Manning, Secretary

3401 Wheeler Charitable Foundation

c/o Robert G. Gregory
PO Box 760
Damariscotta, ME   04543

Maryland

3402 American Health Assistance Foundation

15825 Shady Grove Road
Suite 140
Rockville, MD   20850

3403 American Occupational Therapy Foundation

4720 Montgomery Lane
PO Box 31220
Bethesda, MD   20824   301-656-3620
                              FAX: 301-656-7711
                              www.aotf.org

Martha Kirkland, Executive Director

3404 Arc of Maryland

49 Old Solomon's Island Road
Suite 205
Annapolis, MD   21401   410-571-9320

e-mail: info@thearcmd.org

3405 Baltimore Community Foundation

2 East Read Street
Latrobe Building, 9th Floor
Baltimore, MD   21202   410-332-4171
                              FAX: 410-837-4701

Timothy D. Armbruster, President

3406 Baltimore Gas and Electric Foundation

PO Box 1475
Baltimore, MD   21203   410-234-7480

Malinda B. Small

3407 Children's Fresh Air Society Fund

Baltimore Community Foundation
2 East Read Street
Baltimore, MD   21202   410-962-0848
                              FAX: 410-837-4701

Anne Khoeller, Grants Administrator
Martha Johnston, Program Officer

Makes grants to nonprofit camps to provide tuition for disadvantaged and disabled Maryland children to attend summer camp.

3408 Clark-Winchcole Foundation

3 Bethesda Metro Center
Suite 550
Bethesda, MD   20814   301-654-3607
                              FAX: 301-654-3140

Laura Phillips

Supported tax-exempt charitable organizations operating in the metropolitan area of Washington, DC in the following areas: deaf, higher education and physically disabled.

3409 Clark-Winchole Foundation

3 Bethesda Metro Center
Suite 550
Bethesda, MD   20814   301-654-3607

Laura E. Phillips, President

3410 Columbia Foundation

10221 Wincopin Circle
Columbia, MD   21044   410-730-7840
                              FAX: 410-715-3043

Barbara K. Lawson, Executive Director

3411 Cystic Fibrosis Foundation

6931 Arlington Road
Bethesda, MD   20814   301-654-4055
                              800-FIG-HTCF
                              FAX: 301-951-6378
                              e-mail: info@cff.org
                              www.cff.org/research.htm

Robert Dressing, President

3412 Foundation Fighting Blindness

11435 Cronhill Drive
Owings Mills, MD   21117   410-568-0150
                              800-683-5555
                              888-394-3937
                              FAX: 410-363-2393
                              www.blindness.org

Bob Gray, CEO

The urgent mission of The Foundation Blindness is to
fund the research with will discover the causes, treatments, preventive methods and cures for Retinitis
Pigmentosa, Macular Degeneration, Usher Syndrome, Stargart disease, and the entire spectrum of
retinal degenerative diseases.

3413 George Wasserman Family Foundation

c/o Grossberg Company
6707 Democracy Boulevard
Suite 300
Bethesda, MD   20817   305-524-0700

Janice W. Goldsten, President

3414 Harry and Jeanette Weinberg Foundation

7 Park Center
Owings Mills, MD   21117

Bernard Siegel, President

3415 John B. Parsons Foundation

PO Box 2916
Salisbury, MD   21802   410-742-3176

Ernest Cornbrooks, President

3416 Miracle-Ear Children's Foundation

PO Box 59261
Minneapolis, MD   55459   612-520-9550
                              800-234-5422
                              FAX: 612-520-9793
                              TDY:612-520-9791
                              www.miracle-ear.com

Jerry Krbec, President
Richard C. Brandt, Executive Director

Nonprofit organization that provides hearing aids to
children whose families to not qualify for public assistance. Provides hearing aid fittings and follow-up
care and services free of charge through Miracle-Ear
Hearing Centers. Provides information on alternative
communication. Offers educational materials and
brochures.

3417 Nathan & Suzanne Cohen Foundation

2 Wyndhurst Avenue
Baltimore, MD   21210   410-576-7805

Wilbert H. Sirota, Secretary

3418 National Federation of the Blind

1800 Johnson Street
Baltimore, MD   21230   410-659-9314
                              FAX: 410-685-5653
                              e-mail: nfb@access.digex.net
                              www.nfb.org

Marc Maurer, President

The largest consumer membership organization of the
blind, founded in 1940, it has 50,000 members nationwide in 52 affiliates and over 700 local chapters.
Provides public education about blindness, support
services to the newly blinded, scholarships, publications about blindness, adaptive equipment for the
blind, advocacy services, Newsline for the Blind,
assistive technology information and Job Opportunities for the Blind.

**3419 National Retinitis Pigmentosa Foundation
       Fighting Blindness**

11350 McCormick Road
800
Hunt Valley, MD   21031
                              800-683-5555
                              FAX: 410-659-4086

Robert Gray, Executive Director

The Foundation provides information and referral
services, support networks. The main focus of the
Foundation is to fund research on causes, cures and
prevention of RP and related retinal degenerations.
Volunteer affiliates throughout the United States are
offered to promote public awareness, raise funds and
provide opportunity for those who have RP to interact.

3420 Ryland Group Corporate Giving Program

11000 Broken Land Parkway
Columbia, MD   21044   410-715-7000

Maurice M. Simpkins, Vice President

Massachusetts

3421 Abbot and Dorothy H. Stevens Foundation
PO Box 111
North Andover, MA   01845   978-688-7211
                                         FAX: 978-686-1620
e-mail: 74722.637@compuserve.com

3422 Arc of Massachusetts
217 South Street
Waltham, MA   02154   617-891-6270

arcmass@gis.net

3423 Bank of Boston Corporation Charitable Foundation
100 Federal Street
Boston, MA   02110   617-434-2200

Giving primarily to New England.

3424 Boston Foundation
1 Boston Place
24th Floor
Boston, MA   02108   617-723-7415
                                    FAX: 617-723-7415
                                    e-mail: alk@tbf.ork
                                    www.tbf.org

Ann Kurk, Director of Public Relations

3425 Boston Globe Foundation
135 Morrissey Boulevard
PO Box 2378
Boston, MA   02107   617-929-2895
                                    FAX: 617-929-2041
                        e-mail: foundation@globe.com
                        www.bostonglobe.com/foundation

Seeks to empower low income families and children in the Boston area plus youth frequently excluded from equal participation in our society. The Foundation hopes their funding will have a special impact on children in communities of color. Focus areas are on: community services; education; culture; health care and environment.

3426 Bresky Foundation
200 Boylston Street
Chestnut Hill, MA   02167

3427 Bushrod H. Campbell and Ada F. Hall Charity Fund
Palmer & Dodge
1 Beacon Street
Boston, MA   02108   617-371-9500
                                    FAX: 617-227-4420

Helena Joyce, Legal Assistant
The fund's areas of interest include organizations and/or their projects supporting aid to the elderly, healthcare and population control. Medical research grants are administered through the Medical Foundation. No grants are awarded to individuals and the geographical area of support is limited to organizations located in Massachusetts within the area of Boston and Route 128.

3428 Clipper Ship Foundation
c/o Grants Management Associates
77 Summer Street
8th Floor
Boston, MA   02110   617-426-7172
                                    FAX: 617-426-5441
                        agmconnect.org/clipper1.html

Raymond C. Woodring, Foundation Assistant

3429 Community Foundation of Western Massachusetts
1500 Main Street, Suite 622
PO Box 15769
Springfield, MA   01115   413-733-8565
                                         FAX: 413-732-2858
e-mail: wmass@communityfoundation.org

Kent W. Faerber, President

3430 Frank R. and Elizabeth Simoni Foundation
434 Providence Highway
Norwood, MA   02062

Victor F. Coletti, Vice President

3431 Friendly Ice Cream Corporation Contributions Program
c/o Public Affairs Department
1855 Boston Road
Wilbraham, MA   01095   413-543-2400

Barbara Miller

3432 GenRad Foundation
PO Box 444
West Groton, MA   01472   978-448-8942

Linda B. Schuler

3433 Greater Boston Aid to the Blind
PO Box 218
West Roxbury, MA   02132   617-323-6413
                                         FAX: 617-323-6687
                        e-mail: eyeinfo@gbab.org

Elliot Feldman, Executive Director
Offers services for the totally blind, legally blind, visually impaired, mentally retarded blind and more with health, counseling, educational, recreational, rehabilitation, computer training and professional training services.

3434 Greater Worcester Community Foundation
44 Front Street
Suite 530
Worcester, MA   01608   508-755-0980
                                         FAX: 508-755-3406
                  e-mail: atlis@greaterworcester.org
                        www.greaterworcester.org

Ann T. Lisi, Executive Director

3435 Hyams Foundation

175 Federal Street
14th Floor
Boston, MA   02110   617-426-5600
                                    FAX: 617-426-5696
                         e-mail: info@hyamsfoundation.org
                              www.hyamsfoundation.org

Elizabeth B. Smith, Executive Director

3436 Nathaniel and Elizabeth P. Stevens Foundation

PO Box 111
Norht Andover, MA   01845   978-688-7211
                            FAX: 978-686-1620
            e-mail: 74722.2637@compuserve.com

Elizabeth A. Beland, Administrator

3437 Nehemias Gorin Foundation

1330 Beacon Street
Brookline, MA   02146   617-738-4319

Ida G. Leckart

3438 Phillips-Green Foundation

PO Box 654
Truro, MA   02666

Carol P. Green, President

3439 Raytheon Company Contributions Program

141 Spring Street
Lexington, MA   02173   781-862-6600

Janet C. Taylor, Manager

3440 Spero Charitable Foundation

c/o Shirley Spero
79 Florence
Suite 200
Chestnut Hill, MA   02167

3441 TJX Foundation

c/o TJX Companies
770 Cochiuate Road
Route 1E
Framingham, MA   01701   508-390-3199

Christine A. Strickland, Foundation Manager

3442 Vision Foundation

818 Mount Auburn Street
Watertown, MA   02172   781-926-4232
                                800-852-3029
                           FAX: 781-926-1412

Barbara Kibler, Executive Director

Offers counseling, support groups, seminars and
transportation for the blind providing 600 members.

Michigan

3443 Ann Arbor Area Community Foundation

201 Main Street
Suite 801
Ann Arbor, MI   48104   734-663-0401
                           FAX: 734-663-0401
                                www.aaacf.org

Terry Foster, President
Cheryl Elliott, Program Director

Interested in funding projects which will improve the
quality of life for citizens of the Ann Arbor Area.
Eligible projects generally fall within these categories: education, culture, social service, community
development, environmental awareness and health
and wellness. The Foundation aims to support creative approaches to community needs and problems by
making grants which will benefit the widest possible
range of people.

3444 Arc of Michigan

1325 South Washington Avenue
Lansing, MI   48910   517-487-5426

3445 Berrien Community Foundation

2900 South State Street
Suite 2E
St Joseph, MI   49085   616-983-3304
                           FAX: 616-983-4939
                           e-mail: bcf@gtm.net

3446 Blind Children's Fund

4740 Okemos Road
Okemos, MI   48864   517-347-1357
                           FAX: 517-347-1459
                   e-mail: blindchfnd@aol.com
                     www.blindchildrensfund.org

Karla B. Storrer, Executive Director

Provides parents and profesionsals informaion materials and resouces that help them scuccesfullly teach
and nurture blind, visually and multi-impanred infants and preschoolers.

3447 Bugas Fund

PO Box 1882
Jackson, MI   49204   517-787-1800

3448 Chrysler Motors Organization

Physically Challenged Assistance Program
PO Box 3124
Bloomfield Hills, MI   48302
                                800-255-9877

Mike Claya, Supervisor

Provides a cash reimbursement to assist in reducing
the cost of adaptive driving equipment and conversion aids installed on new model Chrysler Corporation vehicles. Up to a maximum of $1000 on full size
ram vans and up to $750 on all other vehicles.

3449 Clarence & Grace Chamberlin Foundation
600 Woodbridge Place
Detroit, MI 48226   313-567-1000
FAX: 313-567-1001
e-mail: jking@berrymoorman.com

John L. King, President

3450 Community Foudation of Monroe County
111 East 1st Street
PO Box 627
Monroe, MI 48161   734-242-1976
FAX: 734-242-1234

Claudette Goff, Office Administrator ·

3451 Cowan Slavin Foundation
7881 Dell Road
Saline, MI 48176   734-944-0469
FAX: 734-944-3529

Marjorie Bovee, Executive Director

3452 Elizabeth E. Kennedy Fund
110 Miller Avenue
No. 300
Ann Arbor, MI 48104

John S. Dobson, Secretary

3453 Frank S. and Mollie S. VanDervoort Memorial Foundation
4646 Okemos Road
Okemos, MI 48864   517-249-7232

Ann L. Gessert, Secretary

3454 Fremont Area Foundation
4424 West 48th Street
PO Box B
Fremont, MI 49412   231-924-5350
231-924-5391
e-mail: gzerlaut@tfaf.org
http://www.tfaf.org

Elizabeth Cherin, President and C.E.O.

3455 General Motors Foundation
11-134 General Motors Building
3044 West Grand Boulevard
Detroit, MI 48202   313-556-2057

Thomas E. Kimble, Vice-Chair.

3456 Grand Rapids Foundation
209-Cg Waters Building
161 Ottawa NW
Grand Rapids, MI 49503   616-454-1751
FAX: 616-454-6455
e-mail: grfound@grfoundation.org
http://www.grfoundation.org

Marcia Rapp, V.P. Progs.

3457 Granger Foundation
PO Box 22187
Lansing, MI 48909   517-393-1670

Alton L. Granger, Tr.

3458 Harvey Randall Wickes Foundation
4800 Fashion Square Boulevard
Plaza North, Suite 472
Saginaw, MI 48604   517-799-9850
FAX: 517-799-3327

James Finkbeiner
Grants for rehabilitation.

3459 Havirmill Foundation
3503 Greenleaf Boulevard
Suite 203
Kalamazoo, MI 49008   616-375-1800

Jerry L. Miller, President

3460 Kelly Services Foundation
999 W Big Beaver Road
Troy, MI 48084   248-813-3945

Lori Beirne-Kennedy, Director, Marketing

3461 Kresge Foundation
3215 W Big Beaver Road
Troy, MI 48084   248-643-9630
FAX: 248-643-0588
www.krege.org

John E. Marshall, III, President

This foundation offers challenge grants for capital projects, most often for construction or renovation of buildings, but also for the purchase of major equipment and real estate. As challenge grants, they are intended to stimulate new, private gifts in the midst of an organized fund raising effort. Offers special opportunities to build capacity, both in providing enhanced facilities in which to present programs and in generating private support. Only charitable organizations may apply.

3462 Lanting Foundation
c/o Arlyn Lanting
1575 South Shore Drive
Holland, MI 49423

3463 Metro Health Foundation
333 West Fort Street
Suite 1370
Detroit, MI 48226   313-965-4220
FAX: 313-965-3626
e-mail: ghpmhf@worldnet.att.net

Glenn F. Kossick, Executive Director

3464 Ransom Fidelity Company Foundation

702 Michigan National Tower
Lansing, MI 48933   517-482-1538
                                     FAX: 517-482-1539

Grants for the schools, Native Americans, minorities, environmnt, youth and physically disabled.

3465 Rollin M. Gerstacker Foundation

PO Box 1945
Midland, MI 48641   517-631-6097

E.N. Brandt, Vice President

3466 Steelcase Corporate Giving Program

c/o Corp Rels.
PO Box 1967, CH-4e
Grand Rapids, MI 49501

          e-mail: hsutton@steelcase.com

Howard Sutton, V.P. Corp. Rels.

3467 Steelcase Foundation

PO Box 1967, CH-4E
Grand Rapids, MI 49501   616-246-4695
                                 FAX: 616-475-2200
          e-mail: sbroman@steelcase.com

Susan Broman, Executive Director

3468 Young Woman's Home Association of Detroit

5039 Van Ness Drive
Bloomfield Hills, MI 48302   248-626-9610

Marianne Walsh, President

Minnesota

3469 Alex and Mollie Tankenoff Foundation

1314 Marquette Avenue
Suite 2801
Minneapolis, MN 55403

Joyce E. Malmon, Tr.

3470 Arc of Minnesota

770 Transfer Road
Suite 6
St Paul, MN 55114   651-523-0823

          e-mail: mail@arcminnesota.com

3471 Bush Foundation

E-900 First National Bank Building
332 Minnesota Street
Saint Paul, MN 55101   651-227-0891
                                FAX: 651-297-6485

Thomas E. Holloran, Chariman

A regional grantmaking foundation, with broad interests in education, human services, health, arts and culture and in the development of leadership. The foundation is interested in encouraging education at all levels, seeks to support projects which will help prevent or resolve social problems, seeks to encourage the delivery of good healthcare, supports the arts, develops leadership potential and promotes programs for minorities and programs of interest to women.

3472 Charlson Foundation

5780 Lincoln Drive
Suite 109
Edina, MN 55436   612-938-6968

3473 Dayton Hudson Foundation

Department Store Division c/o Dayton's
700 On The Mall
Minneapolis, MN 55402

                                800-272-2450

Dayton Hudson has invested five percent of its federally taxable income in the communities in which they operate. The effectiveness of this giving is strengthened by focusing 80 percent of the total giving into two areas: social action and the arts. The remaining 20 percent of giving responds to special community needs and opportunities.

3474 Deluxe Corporation Foundation

PO Box 64235
St. Paul, MN 55164   651-483-7842

Jennifer A. Anderson, Director, Fdns.

3475 Emma B. Howe Memorial Foundation

A200 Foshay Tower
Minneapolis, MN 55402   612-785-7882
                                FAX: 612-672-3846

Brian Malloy, Program Officer

This Foundation will only accept applications from organizations or groups which serve the following populations: (1) People who are poor or disadvantaged. (2) Children. (3) People who are disabled and those in need of rehabilitation. (4) Victims of discrimination.

3476 General Mills Foundation

PO Box 113
Minneapolis, MN 55440   612-540-7891
                                FAX: 612-540-4114
          e-mail: mills999@mail.genmills.com
       http://www.generalmills.com/explore/community

Reatha Clark King, President and Executive Director

3477 Hugh J. Andersen Foundation

PO Box 204
Bayport, MN 55003   651-439-1557
                                888-439-9508
                                FAX: 681-439-9480
                                www.sriver@mn.uswest.net

Sarah J. Andersen, President
Christine E. Andersen, Vice President
William H. Rubenstein, Secretary

Established in 1962, this fund is a nonprofit charitable corporation classified as a private foundation. The Foundation was established as a general charitable fund, but now identifies projects that build individual and community capacity to be a priority. Giving is focused primarily in the counties of Washington, Minnesota, & St, Croix, Polk and Pierce of Wl. Grants are given in the areas of human services, health, education, arts and culture, community services and the environment.

3478 James R. Thorpe Foundation

5201 Eden Circle
Suite 202
Minneapolis, MN   55436   612-929-1093

Edith D. Thorpe, President

3479 Jay and Rose Phillips Family Foundation

10 2nd Street NE
Suite 200
Minneapolis, MN   55413   612-623-1654
                              FAX: 612-623-1653
          e-mail: phillipsfnd@phillipsfnd.org

Patricia A. Cummings, Secretary and Executive Director

3480 Margaret Rivers Fund

c/o First National Bank
PO Box 197
Stillwater, MN   55082

David F. Pohl, President

3481 Minneapolis Foundation

A200 Foshay Tower
821 Marquette Avenue, South
Minneapolis, MN   55402   612-339-7343
                              FAX: 612-672-3870
          http://www.mplsfoundation.org

Emmett D. Carson, President

3482 Minnesota Mining and Manufacturing Foundation

3M Center
Saint Paul, MN   55144   612-733-1110

3483 Ordean Foundation

424 W Superior Street
Duluth, MN   55802   218-726-4785
                          FAX: 218-726-4848

Stephen A. Mangan, Executive Director

Grants are given for a variety of purposes including: treatment and rehabilitation for persons who are chronically or temporarily mentally ill, persons whose physical capacity is impaired by injury or illness, promotes mental and physical health of the elderly, provide for youth guidance programs designed to avoid delinquency, and provides relief, aid and charity to people with no or low incomes. Grants are only offered to certain cities and townships near and around St. Louis County/Duluth.

3484 Otter Tail Power Company Contributions Program

215 South Cascade Street
Fergus Falls, MN   56537

John C. MacFarlane, Chair, President and C.E.O.

3485 Otto Bremer Foundation

445 Minnesota Street
Suite 2000
St. Paul, MN   55101   651-227-8036
                          FAX: 651-227-2522
                      e-mail: obf@bfsi.com
          http://fdncenter.org/grantmaker/bremer

John Kostishack, Executive Director

3486 Rochester Area Foundation

21 First Street SW
Suite 350
Rochester, MN   55902   507-282-0203
                          FAX: 507-282-4938
                      e-mail: rafmn@aol.com

Steve Thornton, Executive Director

3487 Tozer Foundation

c/o US Bank Trust N.A.
332 Minnesota Street
St. Paul, MN   55101   651-244-0949

Penney Berger

Mississippi

3488 Arc of Mississippi

1900 North West Street
Suite C-100
Jackson, MS   39202   601-714-4830

                      e-mail: thearc@arcms.org

3489 Comm-Care Corporation

763 Avery Boulevard N
Ridgeland, MS   39157

Missouri

3490 Allen P. & Josephine B. Green Foundation

222 S Jefferson Street
PO Box 523
Mexico, MO   65265   573-581-5568
                          FAX: 573-581-1714

Walter G. Staley, Jr., Secretary/Treasurer

While the Foundation makes grants in a variety of fields, its major support has been in the field of medical research. During a 20-year period, 1951-71, it contributed over $900,000 to research in Parkinson's and related diseases of the nervous system; $600,000 for research in pediatric neurology and lesser amounts in other areas of medical research. Grants are limited to Missouri, and none are offered to individuals.

3491 Anheuser-Busch Foundation

1 Busch Place
Saint Louis, MO 63118   314-577-2453

Giving in areas of company operation.

3492 Greater Kansas City Community Foundation and Affiliated Trusts

1055 Broadway
Suite130
Kansas City, MO 64105   816-842-0944
                               FAX: 816-842-8079
                               http://www.fkccf.org

Janice C. Kreamer, President

3493 H&R Block Foundation

4410 Main Street
Kansas City, MO 64111   816-932-8453

Barbara Allmon, President

A charitable organization under the not-for-profit corporation law of the state of Missouri. Grants are made only to organizations which are tax exempt from Federal Income taxation and which are not classified as private foundations. Major emphasis is placed in the metropolitan areas of Kansas City, Missouri: and Columbus, Ohio. The goal is to provide proportionately significant support of relatively few activities, as opposed to minor support for a great many.

3494 Hall Family Foundations

PO Box 419580-6580
Kansas City, MO 64141   816-968-3000

Hall Family Foundations are private philanthropic organizations dedicated to enhancing the quality of individual and community life in the Kansas City area. The Foundations encourage programs which strive for local, regional or national excellence and try to be responsive to programs which are innovative yet seek to create permanent solutions to identified needs in Kansas City.

3495 Hallmark Corporate Foundation

PO Box 419580, M.D. 323
Kansas City, MO 64141   816-545-6906

Karen Bartz, V.P.

3496 James S. McDonnell Foundation

1034 South Brentwood Boulevard
Suite 1850
St. Louis, MO 63117   314-721-1532
                               FAX: 314-721-7421
                               http://www.jsmf.org

Dr. John T. Bruer, President

3497 Lutheran Charities Foundation of St. Louis

211 North Broadway
Suite 1290
St. Louis, MO 63102   314-231-2244
                               FAX: 314-231-0799
                               e-mail: lcfjan@tetranet.net

Fred A. Bleeke, President and C.E.O.

3498 Mary's Call

12400 Olive
Kansas City, MO 64146   816-942-9783

Ray Goffinet, President

3499 Oppenstein Brothers Foundation

PO Box 13095
Kansas City, MO 64199   816-234-8671

Sheila K. Rice, Prog. Off.

3500 R.A. Bloch Cancer Foundation

4400 Main Street
Kansas City, MO 64111   816-932-8453
                               800-433-0464
                               FAX: 816-931-7486
                               e-mail: hotline@hrblock.com
                               www.blochcancer.org

Vangie Rich, Assistant to Richard Bloch
Ann Hron, Co-Director Bloch Cancer Hotline

Provides a hotline that matches newly diagnosed cancer patients with someone who has survived the same kind of cancer. Offers free infomration, resources and support groups, and distributes lists of multidisciplinary second opinion centers. Also supplies three books at no charge: Fighting Cancer; Cancer... There's Hope; and A Guide for Cancer Supporters. All services and books are free of charge.

3501 RA Bloch Cancer Foundation

4435 Main Street
Suite 500
Kansas City, MO 64111   816-932-8453
                               800-433-0464
                               FAX: 816-931-7486
                               e-mail: hotline@hrblock.com
                               www.blochcancer.org

Richard & Annette Bloch, author
Vangie Rich, Asst. to Richard Bloch
Ann Hron, Coordinator, Cancer Hotline
Donna O'Connor, Coordinator, Cancer Hotline

Offers counseling through hotlines and for persons with cancer. Will match caller with survivor who has had same type of cancer. Also offers free books Fighting Cancer, Cancer...there's hope, and Guide for Cancer Supporters and other resource information. Interactive Web Site. Fighting Cancer available in Spanish.

3502 St. Louis Community Foundation

319 Noth 4th Street
Suite 501
St. Louis, MO 63102   314-588-8088
FAX: 314-588-8200
e-mail: foff@anet.stl.com

Tullia Hamilton, Exec.Dir.

3503 Stanley and Lucy Lopata Foundation

c/o Lopata, Hoffman, Flegal & Co.
500 Washington Avenue Suite 1204
St. Louis, MO 63101

Monte Lopata, Tr.

3504 Victor E. Speas Foundation

14 West 10th Street
PO Box 419119
Kansas City, MO 64141   816-979-7481

David P. Ross, Sr. V.P. Bank of America

Montana

3505 Arc of Montana

400 Echo Road
Big Fork, MT 59911   406-837-4652

Nebraska

3506 Arc of Nebraska

1672 Van Dorn
Lincoln, NE 68502   402-475-4407

e-mail: arcneb@inetnebr.com

3507 Bernard K. & Norma F. Heuermann

c/o Norwest Bank Nebraska, N.A.,
10010 Regency Circle, Suite 300
Omaha, NE 68114

John B. Atkins, Treas.

3508 Cooper Foundation

304 Cooper Plaza
Lincoln, NE 68508   402-476-7571
FAX: 402-476-2356

Elwood Thompson, President
Serves only Nebraska with the primary interest in education, arts and humanities and the human services area.

3509 Hazel R. Keene Trust

c/o Fremont National Bank & Trust
PO Box 169
Fremont, NE 68025   402-721-1050

Joe Twidwell

3510 Slosburg Family Charitable Trust

10040 Regency Circle
Suite 200
Omaha, NE 68114   402-391-7900

D. David Slosburg, Tr.

3511 Union Pacific Foundation

1416 Dodge Street
Room 802
Omaha, NE 68179   402-271-5600
FAX: 402-271-5477
e-mail: union_pacific_foundation@notes.up.com
http://www.up.com/found/index.htm

Darlynn Herweg, Director

3512 Woods Charitable Fund

PO Box 81309
Lincoln, NE 68501   402-436-5971
FAX: 402-436-4128
e-mail: pbaker@woodscharitable.org
www.woodscharitable.org

Pam Baker, Executive Director
The Fund makes grants to nonprofit organizations working to build a stronger community in Lincoln, Nebraska. Special interest areas include children, youth and families, education, arts and culture, human services and community development. Funding only in Lincoln, Nebraska.

Nevada

3513 Conrad N. Hilton Foundation

100 W Liberty Street
Suite 840
Reno, NV 89501   775-323-4221
FAX: 775-323-4150

Steven M. Hilton, President
Our grant-making style is to initiate and develop major long-term projects and then seek out the organizations to implement them. As a consequence of this proactive approach, the Foundation does not generally consider unsolicited proposals. Our major projects currently include: blindness prevention and treatment, support the work of the Catholic Sisters, drug abuse prevention among youth, support of the Conrad N. Hilton College of Hotel and Restaurant Management, and much more.

3514 E.L. Wiegand Foundation

165 West Liberty Street
Reno, NV 89501   775-333-0310

Kristen A. Avansino, President and Executive Director

3515 Hall Family Foundation

PO Box 1479
Mindin, NV 89423

Joanne Hall, Secy-Treas.

3516 Mark B. Wallner Foundation

5386 Hidden Valley Center
Reno, NV 89502

Kimberly England, President

3517 Nell J. Redfield Foundation

PO Box 61
1755 East Plumb Lane, Suite 212
Reno, NV 89502   775-323-1373

Gerald C. Smith, Director

3518 William N. and Myriam Pennington Foundation

441 West Plumb Lane
Reno, NV 89509   775-333-9100

Kent Green, Cont.

New Hampshire

3519 Agnes M. Lindsay Trust

660 Chestnut Street
Manchester, NH 03104   603-669-1366
FAX: 603-665-8114
e-mail: admin@lindsaytrust.org
www.lindsaytrust.org

Robert Chiesa, Managing Trustee
Susan Bouchero, Administrative Director

Funding for mental health, blind, deaf and cultural programs to organizations located in the New England states of Maine, Massachusetts, New Hampshire and Vermont. We highly recommend you visit our web site.

3520 Arc of New Hampshire

PO Box 1173
Concord, NH 03302   603-228-9092

3521 Foundation for Seacoast Health

100 Campus Drive
Suite 1
Portsmouth, NH 03801   603-422-8200
FAX: 603-422-8207
e-mail: ffsh@communitycampus.org
www.ffsh.org

Susan R. Bunting, EdD, President/CEO

Giving limited to Portsmouth, Rye, New Castle, Greenland, Newington, North Hampton, NH; and Kittery, Eliot, and York, ME.

New Jersey

3522 Acorn Alcinda Foundation

c/o Flackman, Goodman & Potter
PO Box 419
Ridgewood, NJ 07451

Robert J. Kennedy, President and Treas.

3523 Arc of New Jersey

985 Livingston Avenue
North Brunswick, NJ 08902   732-246-2525

e-mail: info@arcnj.org

3524 Arnold A. Schwartz Foundation

c/o Bivona, Cohen, Kunzman, et. al.
15 Mountain Boulevard
Warren, NJ 07059   908-757-7800

Edwin D. Kunzman, President

3525 Beer Foundation

131 Brayton Street
Englewood, NJ 07631

M.L. Beer, Tr.

3526 Campbell Soup Foundation

Campbell Place
Camden, NJ 08103   856-342-4800
FAX: 856-342-3878

John M. Coleman, Chairman
James J. Baldwin, Vice Chairman

Goal of this foundation is to match the company's assets with community needs in order to help forge solutions to community challenges. The Foundation believes that involvement at the community level can play a catalytic role in improving the quality of life. Giving is located in the areas of education, nutrition and health, cultural and youth related programs. The major focus of the foundation is on nutrition and health related matters, and places a high priority on Camden, New Jersey areas.

3527 Children's Hopes & Dreams Wish Fulfillment Foundation

280 Route 46
Dover, NJ 07801   973-361-7366
800-IDR-EAM2
FAX: 973-361-6627
e-mail: chdfdover@juno.com
www.childrenswishes.org

Victor Franklin, Jr., President
Mariann Oswald, Program Director

Provides continual support for children and their families through the International Pen-Pal Program and the Kid's Kare Packages program. All services are free. Fulfills the last dreams of children eith life threatening illnesses. Retreat home for parents of ill children.

3528 Community Foundation of New Jersey
PO Box 317
Morristown, NJ 07963   973-267-5533
                          FAX: 973-257-2903
                          www.cfnj.org

Giving limited to the state of New Jersey.

3529 Cowles Charitable Trust
PO Box 219
Rumson, NJ 07760   732-936-9826

Gardner Cowles III, President

3530 F. Mason Perkins Trust
c/o Summit Bank, Trust Dept.
210 Main Street
Hackensack, NJ 07601   201-646-5225
                          FAX: 201-646-9881

3531 F.M. Kirby Foundation
17 DeHart Street
PO Box 151
Morristown, NJ 07963   973-538-4800

F.M. Kirby, President

3532 Fannie E. Rippel Foundation
180 Mount Airy Road
Suite 200
Basking Ridge, NJ 07920   908-766-0404

e-mail: rippel@gti.net
http://fdncenter.org/grantmaker/rippel

Edward W. Probert, C.E.O. and Pres.

3533 Fox Foundation
PO Box 708
Newfield, NJ 08344   856-697-9226

Rex S. Fox, Tr.

3534 Fund for New Jersey
94 Church Street
Suite 303
New Brunswick, NJ 08901   732-220-8656

3535 Merck Company Foundation
1 Merck Drive
PO Box 100
Whitehouse Station, NJ 08889   908-423-2042
                                  FAX: 908-423-1987

John R. Taylor, Exec. Vice President

3536 Merrill Lynch & Company Foundation
100 Union Avenue
Cresskill, NJ 07626   201-871-0350

Eddy Bayardelle, Dir. Philanthropic Progs.

3537 Milton Schamach Foundation
810 Belmont Avenue
Noth Haledon, NJ 07508   973-423-9494

Andrew E.R. Frommelt Jr., Secy-Treas.

3538 Nabisco Foundation
Nabisco Plaza
7 Campus Drive
Parsippany, NJ 07054   973-682-7098

3539 Ostberg Foundation
277 Fountain Road
Englewood, NJ 07631

Charles Borhan

3540 Paragano Family Foundation
899 Mountain Avenue
Springfield, NJ 0781   973-376-1010

Nazario Paragano, Tr.

3541 Prudential Foundation
751 Broad Street
15th Floor
Newark, NJ 07102   973-802-4791
                      FAX: 973-802-3345
                      www.prudential.com

Donald Treloar

Gives priority to national programs that further our objectives and programs serving areas where The Prudential has a substantial employee presence. Places special emphasis on the home state of New Jersey and the headquarters city, Newark.

3542 Robert Wood Johnson Foundation
Route 1 and College Road E
PO Box 2316
Princeton, NJ 08543   609-452-8701

e-mail: mail@rwjf.org
http://www.rwjf.org

Richard J. Toth, Director Office Of Proposal Mgmt

3543 Victoria Foundation
40 South Fullerton Avenue
Montclair, NJ 07042   973-783-4450
                         FAX: 973-783-6664
                         e-mail: CMCFFarvic@aol.com

Catherine M. McFarland, Exec. Off.

3544 Walking Tomorrow
Christopher Reeve Paralysis Foundation
500 Morris Avenue
Springfield, NJ 07081
                      800-225-0292
                      FAX: 973-912-9433
                      e-mail: info@crpf.org
                      www.paralysis.org

Pam Gold, Director of Special Projects

3545 Whelan Foundation

18 Jersey Avenue
Spring Lake, NJ 07762

Thomas Whelan, President

New Mexico

3546 Arc of New Mexico

3655 Carlisle NE
Albuquerque, NM 87110 505-883-4630

e-mail: arcnm@abq.com

3547 Frost Foundation, Ltd.

511 Armijo Street
Suite A
Santa Fe, NM 87501 505-986-0208
FAX: 505-986-0430

Mary Whited-Howell, President

3548 McCune Charitable Foundation

345 E Alameda Street
Santa Fe, NM 87501 505-983-8300
FAX: 505-983-7887
e-mail: fsowers@trail.com
http://www.nmmccune.org

Frances R. Sowers, Associate Director

3549 Santa Fe Community Foundation

516 Alto Street
Santa Fe, NM 97501 505-988-9715

e-mail: foundation@santafecf.org
http://www.santafecf.org

Elizabeth Bremner, Executive Director

New York

3550 AT&T Foundation

32 Avenue of Americas
24th Floor
New York, NY 10013 212-387-4801
FAX: 212-387-5809
e-mail: rdabney@att.com
http://www.att.com/foundation

Ronald Dabney, Comm. Mgr.

3551 Achelis Foundation

Morris & McVeigh
767 3rd Avenue
New York, NY 10017 212-888-0347

Giving primarily in the New York area.

3552 Ala Vi Foundation of New York

500 5th Avenue
Floor 34
New York, NY 10110

3553 Alan & Peggy Tishman Foundation

55 East 59th Street
New York, NY 10022 212-326-4884

Alan V. Tishman, President

3554 Altman Foundation

220 E 42nd Street
Room 411
New York, NY 10017 212-907-1500

Karen L. Rosa, Executive Director
Jane B. O'Connell, President

Giving limited to New York, with emphasis on the boroughs of New York City. Four specific areas of interest are covered: Education; support for independent and non-public schools with an emphasis on access for historically disadvantaged youth; Health & Hospitals; Support of voluntary hospitals and health centers with an emphasis on access to care; Social Welfare; direct service programs which provide individuals with the means to achieve long-term self-sufficiency; & Arts & Cultural Development.

3555 Ambrose Monell Foundation

c/o Fulton Rowe, Hart & Coon
1 Rockefeller Plaza, Suite 301
New York, NY 10020 212-586-0700

http://www.monellvetlesen.org

George Rowe Jr., President

3556 American Chai Trust

c/o Perlman & Perlman
220 5th Avenue, 7th Floor
New York, NY 10001

Clifford Perlman, Tr.

3557 American Express Foundation

American Expressway
New York, NY 10285 212-640-2000

Giving primarily in Arizona, California, Colorado, Florida, Georgia, Illinois, Minnesota, North Carolina, Nebraska, New York, Texas, Utah, Massachusetts and Pennsylvania. Also include international committees.

3558 American Foundation for the Blind

11 Penn Plaza
Suite 300
New York, NY 10001 212-502-7600

e-mail: afbinfo@afb.org

Regina Genwright, Director of Information Center

3559 American Foundation for the Prevention of Venereal Disease

799 Broadway
Suite 638
New York, NY 10003 212-759-2069

Provides educational material and encourages responsible sexual relations.

3560 Arthur Ross Foundation
20 E 74th Street, 4-C
New York, NY   10021   212-737-7311

Arthur Ross, President

3561 Artists Fellowship
c/o Salmagundi Club
47 5th Avenue
New York, NY   10003

Richard Pionk, Tr.

3562 Atran Foundation
23-25 E 21st Street
3rd Floor
New York, NY   10010   212-505-9677

3563 Beatrice & Samuel A. Seaver Foundation
c/o Eisner & Lubin
444 Madison Avenue
New York, NY   10022

Hirschel E. Levine, Tr.

3564 BelCer Foundation
Belco Oil & Gas Corporation
767 5th Avenue
46th Floor
New York, NY   10153   212-756-4863

3565 Bell Atlantic Foundation
1095 Avenue of the Americas
Room 3200
New York, NY   10036
                              800-360-7955
                         FAX: 212-398-0951
          e-mail: suzanne_dubose@smtp.nynex.com
              http://www.bellatlanticfoundation.com

Suzanne A. Du Bose, President

3566 Bodman Foundation
767 3rd Avenue
4th Floor
New York, NY   10017   212-644-0322
                         FAX: 212-759-6510
          www.fdncenter.org/grantmaker/bodman

3567 Booth Ferris Foundation
60 Wall Street
46th Floor
New York, NY   10005   212-483-2323

Giving limited to the New York metropolitan area.

3568 Brooklyn Home for Aged Men
9701 Shore Road
Brooklyn, NY   11209   718-745-1638

Nancy K. Munson, President

3569 Cancer Care
1180 Avenue of the Americas
New York, NY   10036   212-221-3300
                            800-813-HOPE
                       FAX: 212-719-0263
           e-mail: info@cancercareinc.org
               http://www.cancercareinc.org

Diane Blum, Executive Director

3570 Capital Cities/ABC Foundation
77 W 66th Street
Room 16-15
New York, NY   10023   212-456-7777

Giving in the areas where company properties are located.

3571 Carles A. Dana Foundation
745 5th Avenue
Suite 700
New York, NY   10151   212-223-4040
                         FAX: 212-593-7623
            e-mail: danainfo@danany.dana.org
                http://www.dana.org

David Mahoney, Chair

3572 Charles J. & Burton S. August Family Foundation
c/o Monro Muffler Brake
200 Holleder Parkway
Rochester, NY   14615

Charles J. August, Tr.

3573 Clark Foundation
250 Park Avenue
Suite 900
New York, NY   10177   212-551-1100
                         FAX: 212-986-4558
Giving in New York and New York City.

3574 Commonwealth Fund
1 E 75th Street
New York, NY   10021   212-535-0400

                         e-mail: mm@cmwf.org
                              www.cmwf.org

3575 Community Foundation for Greater Buffalo
712 Main Street
Buffalo, NY   14202   716-852-2857
                        FAX: 716-852-2861
            e-mail: cfgb@buffnet.net
                http://www.cfgb.org

Jean M. Brun, Prog. Off.

3576 Community Foundation for the Capitol Region
Executive Park Drive
Albany, NY   12203   518-446-9638
                       FAX: 518-446-9638
            e-mail: info@cfcr.org
                http://www.cfcr.org

Judith Lyons, Executive Director

3577 Community Foundation of Herkimer & Oneida Counties

270 Genesse Street
Utica, NY 13502   315-735-8212
FAX: 315-735-9363
e-mail: commfdn@borg.com

Susan D. Smith, Sr. Prog. Off.

3578 Comsearch: Broad Topics

Foundation Center
79 Fifth Avenue
Department ZE
New York, NY 10003   212-421-0771
800-424-9836
FAX: 212-807-3677
www.fdncenter.org

Thomas Buckman, President

Subset publications of The Foundation Grants Index, are printouts of actual foundation grants, covering 26 key areas of grantmaking. This tool is designed for fundraisers who wish to examine grantmaking activities in a broad field of interest. $55.00

3579 D.E. French Foundation

120 Genesee Street
Room 503
Auburn, NY 13021   315-253-9321

J. Douglas Pedley, President

3580 David & Minnie Berk Foundation

1101 Stewart Avenue
Garden City, NY 11530

Ronald Berk, President

3581 David J. Green Foundation

599 Lexington Avenue, No. 12
New York, NY 10022   212-371-4200

Barbara A. McBride, Secy.

3582 Dextra Baldwin McGonagle Foundation

PO Box 58, Main Post Office
Purchase, NY 10577

Jonathan G. Spanier, President

3583 Easter Seals New York

845 Central Avenue
Albany, NY 12206   518-438-8785
800-727-8785
essofny@aol.com

Christine McMahon, Chief Operating Officer

3584 Edith M. Schweckendieck Trusts

c/o Citibank, N.A.
153 East 53rd Street, 25th Floor
New York, NY 10043

Michael Festa, Asst. V.P., Citibank, N.A.

3585 Edward John Noble Foundation

32 E 57th Street
New York, NY 10022   212-759-4212

3586 Epilepsy Foundation of Long Island

506 Stewart Avenue
Garden City, NY 11530   516-739-7733
e-mail: rdaly@epil.org
www.efli.org

Richard Delay, Executive Director

3587 Epilepsy Society of New York

305 7th Avenue
12th Floor
New York, NY 10001   212-633-2930
e-mail: epsocny@aol.com

George H. Smith, Executive Director

3588 Episcopal Charities

1047 Amsterdam Avenue
New York, NY 10025   212-316-7426
FAX: 212-316-7431
e-mail: EPCHARNY@aol.com

David P. Shover, M.S.W., M.Div., Exec. Dir.

3589 Esther A. & Joseph Klingenstein Fund

787 7th Avenue
6th Floor
New York, NY 10019   212-492-6181
FAX: 212-492-7007

John Klingenstein, President

3590 Faith Home Foundation

6 Flower Hill Lane
Bay Shore, NY 11706   631-665-3118

A. T. Pearson, Admin.

3591 Fay J. Lindner Foundation

1161 Meadowbrook Road
North Merrick, NY 11566

Robert M. Goldberg, President

3592 Florence V. Burden Foundation

630 5th Avenue
Suite 2900
New York, NY 10111   212-332-1100

Publishes an annual or periodic report.

3593 Ford Foundation

320 East 43rd Street
New York, NY 10017   212-573-5000
http://www.fordfound.org

Barron M. Tenny, Secy.

3594 Fortis Foundation

1 World Trade Center
Suite 5001
New York, NY 10048

FAX: 212-859-7058

Jacqueline A. Gentile, Director

Grants are offered in healthcare fields, especially in medical research ($500-$5,000). New York City social, educational organizations also receive funds ($250-$5,000).

3595 Foundation Center Library Services

Foundation Center
79 Fifth Avenue
Department ZE
New York, NY 10003

212-421-0771
800-424-9836
FAX: 212-807-3677
www.fdncenter.org

Thomas Buckman, President

The Center disseminates current information on foundation and corporate giving through our national collections in New York City and Washington D.C., our field offices in San Francisco and our network of over 180 cooperating libraries in all 50 states and abroad.

3596 Foundation for Advancement in Cancer Therapy

PO Box 1242
Old Chelsea Station, NY 10113   212-741-2790

www.fact-ltd.org

A clearinghouse for information regarding alternative cancer therapies, emphasizing nutritional and metabolic approaches.

3597 Foundation for the Advancement of Innovative Medicine

PO Box 338
Kinderbrook, NY 12106

Organization of professionals and lay persons advocating for holistic and alternative practices.

3598 GGM Trust

c/o Horace Michelson
70 East 10 Street Suite 6U
New York, NY 10003

3599 Gebbie Foundation

110 West 3rd Street
Suite 308
Jamestown, NY 14701   716-487-1062
FAX: 716-484-6401

Giving in Chautauqua County, and secondly, in neighboring areas of western New York. Giving is offered in other areas only when the project is consonant with program objectives that cannot be developed locally.

3600 Gladys Brooks Foundation

226 7th Street
Garden City, NY 11530   516-248-8660

Harman Hawkins, Chairman
James J. Daly, Board of Governors

The purpose of this Foundation is to provide for the intellectual, moral and physical welfare of the people of this country by establishing and supporting nonprofit libraries, educational institutions, hospitals and clinics. The Foundation will make grants only to private, publicly supported, nonprofit, tax-exempt organizations.

3601 Glickenhaus Foundation

6 East 43rd Street
New York, NY 10017   212-953-7867

Maddy Wehle

3602 Graphic Controls Corporate Giving Program

189 Van Rensselaer Street
PO Box 1271
Buffalo, NY 14240   716-853-7500

Phyllis Rudz

3603 Green Fund

c/o Jennifer Gee
1400 Broadway
New York, NY 10018

3604 Guide Dog Foundation for the Blind

371 E Jericho Turnpike
Smithtown, NY 11787   516-265-2121
800-548-4337
FAX: 516-361-5192
e-mail: guidedog@guidedog.org
www.guidedog.org

Wells B. Jones, CAE, CFRE, Executive Director
Catherine I. McDougall, Office Manager

Established in 1946, the Foundation provides rehabilitation for the blind by breeding and training guide dogs. A fully trained guide dog is given to blind applicants from all over the United States and some foreign countries. They train together as a team for 25 days on campus. All of these programs, including the cost of transportation and after-care programs, are given without cost to the blind recipients. Quarterly newsletter, video cassette, audio cassette.

3605 H. van Ameringen Foundation

509 Madison Avenue
New York, NY 10022

Henry P. van Ameringen

3606 Hagedorn Fund

c/o The Chase Manhattan Bank, N.A.
1211 Avenue of the Americas 38th Fl
New York, NY 10036

Robert Rosenthal, V.P., The Chase Manhattan Bank

3607 Hearst Foundation

888 7th Avenue
45th Floor
New York, NY 10106   212-586-5404

Robert M. Frehse Jr., V.P. and Executive Director

3608 Henry and Lucy Moses Fund

c/o Moses and Singer
1301 Avenue of the Americas
New York, NY 10019   212-554-7800

3609 Herman Goldman Foundation

61 Broadway, 18th Floor
New York, NY 10006   212-797-9090

Richard K. Baron, Exec. Director

3610 Horace W. Goldsmith Foundation

375 Park Avenue
Suite 1602
New York, NY 10152   212-319-8700

James C. Slaughter, C.E.O.

3611 International Paper Company Foundation

2 Manhattanville Road
Purchase, NY 10577   914-397-1500
                   FAX: 914-397-1500
                   www.internationalpaper.com

3612 JM Foundation

60 East 42nd Street
Room 1651
New York, NY 10165   212-687-7735
                   FAX: 212-697-5495

Chris K. Olander, Executive Director

3613 James E. & Jacob A. Barkey Memorial Fund u/w Jeanne E. Barkey

c/o Citibank, N.A. Tax Department
1 Court Square, 22nd Floor
Long Island City, NY 11120

M.A. Ingram, Trust Officer, Citibank, N.A.

3614 Jedra Charitable Foundation

110-11 Queens Boulevard
Apartment 208
Forest Hills, NY 11375   718-263-4956

David Shechet, President

3615 Joseph Alexander Foundation

400 Madison Avenue
Room 906
New York, NY 10017   212-980-0600

3616 Juliet Rosenthal Foundation

1370 Broadway
New York, NY 10018

3617 Kenneth & Evelyn Lipper Foundation

c/o Lipper & Company
101 Park Avenue, 6th Floor
New York, NY 10178   212-883-6333

Kenneth Lipper, Tr.

3618 Kim and Deborah Fennebresque Family Foundation

c/o Sontag Advisory
261 Madison Avenue
New York, NY 10016

Kim S. Fennebresque, Tr.

3619 Kramer Foundation

c/o Wald & Wald
1 Penn Plaza, Suite 4307
New York, NY 10119

Saul Kramer, President

3620 Leona and Harry B. Helmsley Foundation

240 Park Avenue
Suite 659
New York, NY 10169

3621 Litwin Foundation

1200 Union Turnpike
New Hyde Park, NY 11040

Leonard Litwin, President

3622 Liz Claiborne Foundation

1441 Broadway
New York, NY 10018   212-626-3211

Organizations are served that are engaged in work that advances the Foundation's program goals in the fields of social welfare, health, education, the environment or cultural advancement.

3623 Louis and Anne Abrons Foundation

First Manhattan Company
437 Madison Avenue
New York, NY 10022   212-756-3100
                   FAX: 212-832-6698

3624 Margaret L. Wendt Foundation

40 Fountain Plaza
Suite 277
Buffalo, NY 14202   716-855-2146

Robert J. Kresse, Secy.-Treas

3625 Marquis George MacDonald Foundation

c/o The Chase Manhattan Bank N.A.
270 Park Avenue
New York, NY 10017

Donna M. Bowers, Administrator

3626 Metropolitan Life Foundation

1 Madison Avenue
New York, NY   10010   212-578-6272
                             FAX: 212-685-1435
http://www.metlife.com/companyinfo/community/

A. Dennis White, V.P. Corp. Contribs.

3627 Metzger-Price Fund

230 Park Avenu
Suite 2300
New York, NY   10169   212-867-9500

Isaac A. Saufer, Secy.-Treas.

3628 Morgan Stanley Dean Witter Foundation

1221 Avenue of the Americas
27th Floor
New York, NY   10020   212-762-7848
                             FAX: 212-762-7790

Joan Steinberg, Dir. Community Affairs

3629 Morris P. Leibovitz Foundation

c/o Radin, Glass & Co, LLP
360 Lexington Avenue, 22nd Floor
New York, NY   10017

3630 Moses L. Parshelsky Foundation

26 Court Street
Room 904
Brooklyn, NY   11242

Tony B. Berk, Tr.

3631 NYSArc

393 Delaware Avenue
Delamr, NY   12054   518-439-8311

e-mail: nysarc@nysarc.org

3632 National Foundation for Facial Reconstruction

317 E 34th Street
Room 901
New York, NY   10016   212-263-6656
                             FAX: 212-263-7534
                             www.nffr.org
A nonprofit organization whose major purposes
are to provide facilities for the treatment and assistance of individuals who are unable to afford
private reconstructive surgical care, to train and
educate professionals in this surgery, to encourage
research in the field and to carry on public education.

3633 National Hemophilia Foundation

Soho Building
110 Greene Street
Suite 406
New York, NY   10012

3634 National Neurofibromatosis Foundation

95 Pine Street
16th Floor
New York, NY   10005   212-344-6633
                             800-323-7938
                             FAX: 212-747-0004
                             e-mail: nnff@nf.org
                             www.nf.org

Peter Bellermann, President
Jacqueline Medina, Director of Programs
A nonprofit 501 (c)(3) medical foundation, dedicated
to improving the health and well-being of individuals
and families affected by neurofibromatosis. The
Foundation sponsors medical research, clinical services, public education programs and patient support
services. It is the central source for up-to-date and
accurate information about NF. It also assists patients
and families with referrals to NF clinics and healthcare professionals specializing in NF. The goal is to
find a cure for NF.

3635 Neisloss Family Foundation

1737-7 Veterans Highway
Central Islip, NY   11722   631-234-1600

Stanley Neisloss, President

3636 New York Community Trust

2 Park Avenue
24th Floor
New York, NY   10016   212-686-0010
                             FAX: 212-532-8528
                             http://www.nycommunitytrust.org

Lorie A. Slutsky, President and Director

3637 New York Foundation

350 5th Avenue, No. 2901
New York, NY   10118   212-594-8009

                             http://www.nyf.org

Madeline Lee, Executive Director

3638 Northern New York Community Foundation

120 Washington Street
Watertown, NY   13601   315-782-7110

Alex C. Velto, Executive Director

3639 Parkinson's Disease Foundation

710 W 168th Street
New York, NY   10032   212-923-4700
                             800-457-6676
                             FAX: 212-923-4778
                             e-mail: info@pdf.org
                             www.pdf.org

Robin Elliott, Executive Director
Renay D. Crooms, Assistant Director

National not-for-profit organization dedicated to funding scientific research to investigate the cause and cure of Parkinson's disease and related disorders. The Foundation has a post-doctoral training program, Interntional Research Grant Program, and makes referrals to physicians who treat PD. Other services include supporting advocacy efforts, making referrals to self-help groups, conducting educational symposiums for patients and professionals.

3640 Reader's Digest Foundation

Reader's Digest Road
Pleasantville, NY 10570 914-238-1000
FAX: 914-238-4559
www.readersdigest.com

3641 Research to Prevent Blindness

645 Madison Avenue
21st Floor
New York, NY 10022 212-752-4333
800-621-0026
FAX: 212-688-6231
www.rpbusa.org

Diane S. Swift, President
Thomas Furlong, Director of Public Information

National voluntary health foundation supported by foundations, corporations, and voluntary gifts and bequests from individuals. Established to stimulate basic and applied research into the causes, prevention and treatment of blinding eye diseases.

3642 Rhodebeck Charitable Trust

c/o McLaughind Stern LLP
245 Park Avenue, 40th Floor
New York, NY 10167

Huyler C. Held, Tr.

3643 Rita J. and Stanley H. Kaplan Foundation

866 United Nations Plaza
Suite 306
New York, NY 10017 212-688-1047
FAX: 212-688-6907

Rita J. Kaplan, Director

3644 Robert Sterling Clark Foundation

135 East 64th Street
New York, NY 10021 212-288-8900
FAX: 212-288-1033

Margaret Ayers, Executive Director

Giving primarily in New York with emphasis on advocacy, research, and public education aimed at informing New York City of state policies.

3645 Samberg Family Charitable Foundation

159 Campfire Road
Chappaqua, NY 10514

3646 Samuel & Rae Eckman Charitable Foundation

c/o Baer, Marks& Upham
805 3rd Avenue
New York, NY 10022

Stephan F. Selig, President

3647 Sandra Atlas Bass and Edythe and Sol G. Atlas Fund

185 Great Neck Road
Great Neck, NY 11021 516-829-6182

Giving primarily in the New York metropolitan area.

3648 Sjogren's Syndrome Foundation

366 North Broadway
Suite PH/W2
Jericho, NY 11753 516-933-6365
800-475-6473
www.sjogrens.org

Alexis Stegemann, Executive Director

Provides patients practical information and coping strategies that minimize the effects of Sjogren's syndrome. In addition, the Foundation is the clearinghouse for medical information and is the recognized national advocate for Sjogren's syndrome. *$25.00*

Monthly

3649 Skadden Fellowship Foundation

919 3rd Avenue
New York, NY 10022 212-735-2956

http://www.sasmf.com/fellows/default.html

Susan Plum

3650 St. George's Society of New York

175 9th Avenue
New York, NY 10011 212-924-1434
FAX: 212-727-1566

John Shannon, Executive Director

3651 Stanley W. Metcalf Foundation

120 Genesse Street
Room 503
Auburn, NY 13021 315-253-9321

J. Douglas Pedley, President

3652 Stewart W. & Willma C. Hoyt Foundation

300 Security Mutual Building
80 Exchange Street
Binghamton, NY 13901 607-722-6706
FAX: 607-722-6752
e-mail: hoyt2jcp@aol.com

Judith C. Peckham, Executive Director

3653 Stonewall Community Foundation

119 West 24th Street
9th Floor
New York, NY 10011 212-367-1155
FAX: 212-367-1157
e-mail: STNWLCMFD@aol.com

William P. Epke, Executive Director

3654 Surdna Foundation

330 Madison Avenue
30th Floor
New York, NY 10017   212-557-0010
FAX: 212-557-0003
e-mail: request@surdna.org

3655 Sydney & Helen Jacoff Foundation

c/o Berlack, Israels & Liberman
120 West 45th Street
New York, NY 10036

3656 Tisch Foundation

655 Madison Avenue
8th Floor
New York, NY 10021   212-521-2930

Mark J. Krinsky, V.P.

3657 Universal Studios Foundation

PO Box 5023
New York, NY 10150

Helen Giambone, Admin.

3658 Van Ameringen Foundation

509 Madison Avenue
New York, NY 10022   212-758-6221

http://fdncenter.org/grantmaker/vanmeringen

Henry P. van Amerigen, President

3659 Western New York Foundation

Main Seneca Building Suite 1402
237 Main Street
Buffalo, NY 14203   716-847-6440

Welles V. Moot Jr., President

3660 William Second Betterment Fund

330 Madison Avenue
Room 3500
New York, NY 10017   212-687-8564

3661 William T. Grant Foundation

570 Lexington Avenue
18th Floor
New York, NY 10022   212-752-0071

e-mail: info@wtgrantfdn.org
http://fdncenter.org/grantmaker/wtgrant

3662 William and Jane Brachfield Foundation

4455 Douglas Avenue
Riverdale, NY 10471

3663 Yaron Foundation

201 East 37th Street
Lobby Suite
New York, NY 10016

Norman Horowitz, Executive Director

North Carolina

3664 Arc of North Carolina

16 E Rowan Street
Suite 204
Raleigh, NC 27609   919-782-4632

e-mail: arcfnc@arcnc.org

3665 Bob & Kay Timberlake Foundation

c/o Bob Timberlake
1660 East Center Street
Lexington, NC 27292

3666 Broyhill Family Foundation

PO Box 500
Lenoir, NC 28645   828-758-5505
FAX: 828-754-7335

3667 Duke Endowment

100 North Tryon Street
Suite 3500
Charlotte, NC 28202   704-376-0291
FAX: 704-376-9336
e-mail: info@tde.org
www.dukeendowment.org

3668 First Union Foundation

c/o First Union Corporation
301 South College Street
Charlotte, NC 28288   704-374-4689
FAX: 704-374-2484

Judy Allison, Director

3669 Foundation for the Carolinas

1043 East Morehead Street
Suite 100
Charlotte, NC 28204   704-376-9541
FAX: 704-376-1243
www.fftc.org

Giving primarily to organizations serving the citizens of North and South Carolina.

3670 John H. Wellons Foundation

PO Box 1254
Dunn, NC 28335   910-892-0436

John H. Wellons, Sr., Pres.

3671 Kate B. Reynolds Charitable Trust

128 Reynolda Village
Winston-Salem, NC 27106   316-723-1456
FAX: 336-723-7765

E. Ray Cope, President

3672 Kathleen Price Bryan Family Fund

220 South Eugene Street
Greensboro, NC 27401   336-273-0080
FAX: 336-273-9580
http://fdncenter.org/grantmaker/kpbryan

J.M. Bryan Taylor, Executive Director

3673 Kathleen Price and Joseph M. Bryan Family Foundation

220 S Eugene Street
Greensboro, NC 27401   336-273-0080
                                   FAX: 336-288-5458

Nancy H. Poteet, Interim Director
Joseph M. Bryan Jr., President

Only organizations or projects demonstrating direct benefits to North Carolina are eligible for consideration with emphasis on Greensboro and Guilford County and rural communities in North Carolina with financial need. The Foundation does not consider support for annual campaigns, conferences, video production, individuals, research, travel for band and sports teams. There are no discretionary or emergency funds.

3674 Mary Reynolds Babcock Foundation

102 Reynolda Village
Winston Salem, NC 27106
                                   FAX: 919-777-0095
                                   e-mail: info@mrbf.org

Gayle W. Dorman, Executive Director

For 1994, this foundation is committed to an extensive educational and planning process to better understand the Southeast and to articulate the role the foundation seeks to play in the region into the twenty-first century.

3675 Triangle Community Foundation

100 Park Offices, Suite 209
PO Box 12834
Research Triangle Park, NC 27709 919-549-9840
                                   FAX: 919-990-9066
                                   e-mail: polly@trianglecf.org
                                   http://www.trianglecf.org

Polly Guthrie, Prog. Dir.

North Dakota

3676 Alex Stern Family Foundation

Bill Stern Building, Suite 205
609 1/2 1st Avenue, N
Fargo, ND 58102   701-237-0170

E.G. Preston, Executive Director

3677 Arc of North Dakota

c/o Arc, Upper Valley
2500 DeMers Avenue, PO Box 12420
Grand Forks, ND 58208

3678 North Dakota Community Foundation

PO Box 387
Bismarck, ND 58502   701-222-8349

Kevin J. Dvorak, President

Ohio

3679 Akron Community Foundation

345 West Cedar Street
Akron, OH 44307   330-376-8522
                                   FAX: 330-376-0202
                                   e-mail: acf_fund@ix.netcom.com
                                   http://www.ohio.com/nonprofit/acf

Jody Bacon, Executive Director

3680 Albert G. and Olive H. Schlink Foundation

49 Benedict Avenue
Suite C
Norwalk, OH 44857   419-668-8211
                                   FAX: 419-668-2813

Robert A. Wiedemann, President

3681 American Foundation Corporation

720 Nat'l City Bank Building
Cleveland, OH 44114   216-241-6664

3682 Arc of Ohio

1335 Dublin Road
Suite 205-C
Columbus, OH 43215   614-487-4720

                                   e-mail: thearcohio@aol.com

3683 Britton Fund

c/o Advisory Services
1422 Euclid Avenue, 1010 Hanna Bldg
Cleveland, OH 44115   216-363-6489

Nick Valentino, Treas.

3684 Cleveland Foundation

1422 Euclid Avenue
Suite 1400
Cleveland, OH 44115   216-861-3810
                                   FAX: 216-861-1729
                   http://www.clevelandfoundation.org

Steven A. Minter, Executive Director

3685 Columbus Foundation and Affiliated Organizations

1234 East Broad Street
Columbus, OH 43206   614-251-4000
                                   FAX: 614-251-4009
                                   e-mail: info@columbusfoundation.com
                                   http://www.columbusfoundation.com

James I. Luck, President

3686 Eleanora C. U. Alms Trust

Fifth Third Bank
Dept 00864
9990 Montgomery Road
Cincinnati, OH 45263   513-793-2200

Giving limited to Cincinnati, OH.

3687 **Emma Leah and Laura Bell Bahmann Foundation**
8041 Hosbrook Road
Suite 210
Cincinnati, OH 45236   513-891-3799

John T. Gatch, Executive Director

3688 **Eva L. and Joseph M. Bruening Foundation**
627 Hanna Building
1422 Euclid Avenue
Cleveland, OH 44115   216-621-2632
    FAX: 216-621-8198

Janet E. Narten, Executive Director

3689 **Federated Dpeartment Stores Corporate Giving Program**
7 West 7th Street
Cincinnati, OH 45202

Dixie Barker, Mgr., Corp. Contribs.

3690 **Fred & Lillian Deeks Memorial Foundation**
c/o Star Bank, N.A.
PO Box 1118, ML 5145
Cincinnati, OH 45201

3691 **GAR Foundation**
50 South Main Street
PO Box 1500
Akron, OH 44309   330-643-0201

e-mail: rob_briggs@akron.BDBLaw.com

Robert W. Briggs, Executive Director

3692 **George Gund Foundation**
1845 Guildhall Building
45 Prospect Avenue West
Cleveland, OH 44115   216-241-3114
    FAX: 216-241-6560
    http://www.gundfdn.org

David Bergholz, Executive Director

3693 **Greater Cincinnati Foundation**
300 West 4th Street
Suite 200
Cincinnati, OH 45202   513-241-2880
    FAX: 513-852-6886
    http://www.greatercincinnatifdn.org

3694 **HCR Manor Care Foundation**
PO Box 10086
333 North Summit Street
Toledo, OH 43699
    FAX: 412-525-5521
    e-mail: jsteiner@hcr-manorcare.com
    http://www.hcr-manorcare.com

Jennifer Steiner, Executive Director

3695 **Harry C. Moores Foundation**
100 South 3rd Street
Columbus, OH 43215   614-227-8884

Mary B. Cummins

3696 **Helen Steiner Rice Foundation**
221 East 4th Street, Suite 2100
Atrium 2, PO Box 0236
Cincinnati, OH 45201   513-451-9241

Andrea Cornett, Grant Coord.

3697 **Herbert W. Hoover Foundation**
220 Market Avenue S
United Bank Plaza, Suite 40
Canton, OH 44701

3698 **John P. Murphy Foundation**
Tower City Center
924 Terminal Tower, 50 Public Sq.
Cleveland, OH 44113   216-623-4770
    FAX: 216-623-4773

Herbert E. Strawbridge, Pres. and Treas.

3699 **Nationwide Foundation**
1 Nationwide Plaza
Columbus, OH 4325   614-249-5095

http://www.nationwide.com/oys/company/com-minv

Stephan A. Rish, President

3700 **Nordson Corporate Giving Program**
28601 Clemens Road
Westlake, OH 44145   440-892-1580

Constance T. Haqq, Executive Director

3701 **Nordson Corporation Foundation**
28601 Clemens Road
Westlake, OH 44145   440-892-1580

Constance T. Haqq, Executive Director

3702 **Parker-Hannifin Foundation**
6035 Parkland Boulevard
Cleveland, OH 44124   216-896-3000
    FAX: 216-896-4057

3703 **Reinberger Foundation**
27600 Chagrin Boulevard
Cleveland, OH 44122   216-292-2790
    FAX: 216-292-4466

Robert N. Reinberger, Director

3704 **Richland Country Foundation**
24 West 3rd Street
Suite 100
Mansfield, OH 44902   419-525-3020
    FAX: 419-525-1590

Pamela H. Siegenthaler, President

3705 **Robert Campeau Family Foundation**
7 W 7th Street
Cincinnati, OH 45202   513-579-7000
    FAX: 513-579-7555

3706 Sisler McFawn Foundation

PO Box 149
Akron, OH   44309   330-849-8887
                                   FAX: 330-996-6215

Charlotte M. Stanley, Grants Mgr.

3707 Stark Community Foundation

The Saxton House
331 Market Avenue South
Canton, OH   44702   330-454-3426
                                   FAX: 330-454-5855
                        e-mail: starkcf@cannet.com

James A. Bower, President

3708 Stocker Foundation

559 Broadway Avenue
2nd Floor
Lorain, OH   44052   440-246-5719
                                   FAX: 440-246-5720
               e-mail: stocker-prob@centuryinter.net

Ellen Briemont, Executive Director

3709 Tipp City Foundation

c/o Star Bank N.A.
910 West Main Street
Troy, OH   45373

Thomas Kleptz, Trust Off., Star Bank N.A.

3710 Toledo Community Foundation

608 Madison Avenue
Suite1540
Toledo, OH   43604   419-241-5049
                                   FAX: 419-242-5549

Pam Howell-Beach, Director

3711 William J. and Dorothy K. O'Neill Foundation

30195 Chagrin Boulevard
Suite 310
Cleveland, OH   44124   216-831-9667
                                   FAX: 216-831-3779
                        e-mail: oneillfdn@aol.com
                        http://www.oneillfdn.org

Christine E. Henry, Director

3712 Youngstown Foundation

Dollar Savings & Trust Company
PO Box 450
Youngstown, OH   44501   330-744-0320
                                   FAX: 330-744-0344

Oklahoma

3713 Anne and Henry Zarrow Foundation

401 South Boston
Suite 900
Tulsa, OK   74103   918-285-8004

                        e-mail: ZFFound@aol.com

Jeanne Gillert, Grants Mgr.

3714 Arc of Oklahoma

7513 South 85th East Place
Tulsa, OK   74133

3715 International Bio-Oxidative Medicine Foundation (IBOM)

PO Box 13205
Oklahoma City, OK   73113   405-478-IBOM

Offers educational programs, referrals and a newsletter.

3716 Merkel Family Foundation

c/o Turner John B.
1256 East 28th Street
Tulsa, OK   74114

John B. Turner, Tr.

3717 Sarkeys Foundation

530 East Main
Suite 219
Norman, OK   73021   405-364-3703
                                   FAX: 405-364-8191
                                   sarkeys.org

Cheri D. Cartwright, Executive Director
Susan C. Frantz, Program Officer
Ann M. Way, Program Officer

Improves the quality of life in Oklahoma. Offers contributions in the areas of social services, arts and cultural programs, educational funding and health care and medical research. Funding only in agencies in the state of Oklahoma.

3718 William K. Warren Foundation

PO Box 470372
Tulsa, OK   74147   918-481-7900
                                   FAX: 918-481-7935

Oregon

3719 Arc of Oregon

1745 State Street
Salem, OR   97301   503-581-2726

                        e-mail: arcoforg@open.org

3720 Chiles Foundation

111 SW 5th Avenue
Suite 4050
Portland, OR   97204   503-222-2143

Giving in Oregon, with emphasis on Portland, and the Pacific Northwest.

3721 Jackson Foundation

PO Box 3168
Portland, OR   97208   503-275-6564

Robert H. Depew, V.P., U.S. Bank, N.A.

3722 Leslie G. Ehmann Trust

c/o US Bank Idaho, Trust Group
PO Box 3168
Portland, OR 97208   503-275-5929

Marilyn Norquist

3723 Marilyn Moyer Charitable Trust

1000 Broadway Avenue
Suite 910
Portland, OR 97205   503-241-1111

Thomas P. Moyer, Tr.

3724 Samuel S. Johnson Foundation

PO Box 356
Redmond, OR 97756   541-548-8104
                           FAX: 541-548-2014
                           e-mail: ssjohnson@empnet.com

Elizabeth H. Johnson, President

Pennsylvania

3725 Air Products Foundation

7201 Hamilton Boulevard
Allentown, PA 18195   610-481-4911

Giving primarily in areas of company operations
throughout the US.

3726 Arc of Pennsylvania

2001 N Front Street
Building #2, Suite 221
Harrisburg, PA 17102   717-234-2621

3727 Arcadia Foundation

105 East Logan Street
Norristown, PA 19401   610-275-8460

Marilyn L. Steinbright, President

3728 Brachial Plexus Palsy Foundation

210 Spring Haven Circle
Royersford, PA 19468   610-792-0974
                              FAX: 610-792-0974
                              e-mail: brachial@aol.com
                              www.membrane.com/bpp

Thomas J. Cirino, President
Michael F. Cirino, Executive Director

Nonprofit organization dedicated to raising funds for
support of families who hae children with brachial
plexus injuries. Supports medical facilities that research and treat such injuries, holds fund-raising
events to support further research, has support
groups, and produces educational materials including
a newsletter, Outreach, and brochures.

3729 Bright & Christella Erichson Charitable Trust

1735 Market Street
Suite 3800
Philadelphia, PA 19103

Harvey N. Shapiro, Tr.

3730 Claude Washington Benedum Foundation

1400 Benedum
Trees Building
Pittsburgh, PA 15222

Giving limited to West Virginia and southwestern
Pennsylvania.

**3731 Columbia Gas of Pennsylvania Columbia Gas of
Maryland, Corporate Giving**

650 Washington Road
Pittsburgh, PA 15228   412-572-7104
                             FAX: 412-572-7140
                             e-mail: mmarti@columbiaenergygroup.com
                             http://www.columbiagaspamd.com/html/

Rosemary Martinelli, Mgr. Corp

3732 Connelly Foundation

1 Tower Bridge
Suite 1450
West Conshohocken, PA 19428   610-834-3222
                               FAX: 610-834-0866
                               e-mail: info@connellyfdn.org
                               http://www.connellyfdn.org

3733 Dolfinger-McMahon Foundation

c/o Duane, Morris & Heckscher
1 Liberty Plaza
Philadelphia, PA 19103   215-979-1768

Marlene Valcich, Exec. Secy.

3734 Harry C. Trexler Trust

33 S 7th Street
Suite 205
Allentown, PA 18101   610-434-9645
                             FAX: 610-437-5721

Thomas Christman, Secretary Trustees
Giving limited to Lehigh County, Pennsylvania.

3735 Henry L. Hillman Foundation

2000 Grant Building
Pittsburg, PA 15219   412-338-3466
                             FAX: 412-338-3463
                             e-mail: foundation@hillmanfo.com

Ronald W. Wertz, Secy. and Executive Director

3736 Hillman Foundation

2000 Grant Building
Pittsburg, PA 15219   412-338-3466
                             FAX: 412-338-3463

Ronald W. Wertz, President

3737 **Horsehead Community Development Fund**
PO Box 351
Palmerton, PA 18071 610-826-4377

Charles H. Campton, Executive Consultant

3738 **Howard Heinz Endowment**
625 Liberty Avenue
Pittsburgh, PA 15222 412-227-1599

3739 **Hoxie Harrison Smith Foundation**
350 Pond View
Devon, PA 19333 610-688-0143

Bruce M. Brown, Secy.-Treas.

3740 **Jewish Healthcare Foundation of Pittsburgh**
Centre City Tower, Suite 2330
650 Smithfield Street
Pittsburgh, PA 15222 412-594-2550
FAX: 412-232-6240
e-mail: info@jhf.org
http://www.jhf.org

Karen W. Feinstein, Ph. D., Pres

3741 **Juliet L. Hillman Simonds Foundation**
2000 Grant Building
Pittsburgh, PA 15219 412-338-3466
FAX: 412-338-3463
e-mail: foundation@hillmanfo.com

Ronald W. Wertz, Secy.

3742 **Millard Foundation**
PO Box 572
Wayne, PA 19087

Marion M. Thompson, Secy.

3743 **Nineteen Hundred Fifty Seven Charity Trust**
c/o Mellon Bank, N.A.
PO Box 7236, AIM No. 193-0224
Philadelphia, PA 19101 610-828-8145

Judith L. Bardes, Mgr.

3744 **Oberkotter Foundation**
1600 Market Street
Suite 3600
Philadelphia, PA 19103 215-751-2601
FAX: 215-751-2678
e-mail: george_nofer@shsl.com

George H. Nofer, J.D., Executive Director

3745 **Ochiltree Foundation**
c/o Jennifer Lyons
1 Mellon Bank Center, Room 3810
Pittsburg, PA 15258

3746 **PECO Energy Company Contributions Program**
2301 Market Street
7th Floor
Philadelphia, PA 19103 215-841-4124
FAX: 215-841-4040

Anne Baker, Mgr.

3747 **PNC Bank Foundation**
1 PNC Plaza
249 5th Avenue
Pittsburgh, PA 15222 412-762-2000
FAX: 412-768-3779
www.pncbank.com

3748 **Philadelphia Foundation**
1234 Market Street
Suite 1900
Philadelphia, PA 19107 215-563-6417
FAX: 215-563-6882
e-mail: parkow@philafound.org
www.philafound.org

R. Andrew Swinney, President

3749 **Pittsburg Foundation**
1 PPG Place, 30th Floor
Pittsburgh, PA 15222 412-391-5122
FAX: 421-391-7259
e-mail: email@pghfdn.org
http://www.pittsburghfoundation.org

Alfred W. Wishart, Jr., President and C.E.O.

3750 **Shenango Valley Foundation**
41 Chestnut Street
Sharon, PA 16146 724-981-5882
FAX: 724-981-5480

Larry Haynes, Executive Director

3751 **Snee-Reinhardt Charitable Foundation**
2101 1 Mellon Bank Center
500 Grant Street
Pittsburgh, PA 15219 412-271-2944

Joan E. Szymanski, Fdn. Mgr.

3752 **Staunton Farm Foundation**
Center City Tower , Suite 210
650 Smithfield Street
Pittsburgh, PA 15222 412-281-8020
FAX: 412-232-3115
e-mail: info@stauntonfarm.org
http://www.stauntonfarm.org

Joni Schwager, Prog. Off. and Fdn. Mgr.

3753 **Stewart Huston Charitable Trust**
76 South 1st Avenue
Coatesville, PA 19320 610-384-2666
FAX: 610-384-3396
e-mail: admin@stewarthuston.org

Scott G. Huston, Prog. Dir.

3754 Teleflex Foundation
630 West Germantown Pike
Suite 461
Plymouth Meeting, PA 19462   610-834-6364

Thelma A. Fretz, Secy.

3755 USX Foundation
600 Grant Street
Suite 685
Pittsburgh, PA 15219   412-433-5237
FAX: 412-433-6847

C.D. Mallick, General Manager
Patricia Funaro, Program Manager
Giving primarily in areas of company operations located within the United States.

3756 W. W. Smith Charitable Trust
3515 West Chester Pike
Suite E
Newtown Square, PA 19073   610-359-1811
FAX: 610-359-9717

Frances R. Pemberton, Trust Admin.

3757 William B. Dietrich Foundation
PO Box 58177
Philadelphia, PA 19102   215-979-1919

William B. Dietrich, President

3758 William Talbott Hillman Foundation
2000 Grant Building
Pittsburg, PA 15219   412-338-3466
FAX: 412-338-3463
e-mail: foundation@hillmanfo.com

Ronald W. Wertz, Secy.

3759 William V. and Catherin A. McKinney Charitable Foundation
National City Center [25-154]
20 Stanwix Street
Pittsburgh, PA 15222   412-644-8332

William M. Schmidt, V.P. National City Bank Of Penn.

Rhode Island

3760 Champlin Foundations
300 Centerville Road
Suite 300S
Warwick, RI 02886

David King, Director
Giving in the Rhode Island area.

3761 Citizens Charitable Foundation
Citizens Bank
1 Citizens Plaza
Providence, RI 02903   401-456-7849

3762 Horace A. Kimball and S. Ella Kimball Foundation
c/o The Washington Trust Company
23 Broad Street
Westerly, RI 02891   401-364-3565
FAX: 401-364-7799

Thomas F. Black III, President

3763 Rhode Island Arc
99 Bald Hill Road
Cranston, RI 02920   401-463-9191

riarc@compuserve.com

3764 Rhode Island Foundation
1 Union Station
Providence, RI 02903   410-274-4564
FAX: 401-331-8085
http://www.rifoundation.org

Ronald D. Thorpe, V.P., Prog.

South Carolina

3765 Arc of South Carolina
PO Box 8707
Columbia, SC 29202   803-395-5266

e-mail: thearcssc@aol.com

3766 Center for Developmental Disabilities
University of South Carolina
8301 Farrow Road
School of Medicine, Education Bldg.
Columbia, SC 29208   803-935-5231
FAX: 803-935-5059
e-mail: scsis@dccisc.edu
www.scsis.org

Denise Rivers, Project Coordinator

A University Affiliated Program which develops model programs designed to serve persons with disabilities and to train students in fields related to disabilities.

3767 Colonial Life and Accident Insurance Company Contributions Program
1200 Colonial Life Boulevard
Columbia, SC 29202   803-798-7000

Edwina Carns, Public and Comm. Rels.

South Dakota

3768 Alpha & Omega Family Foundation

c/o NW Bank South Dakota N.A.
101 North Phillips Avenue
Sioux Falls, SD 57104

3769 Arc of South Dakota

208 W Capitol
PO Box 220
Pierre, SD 57501   605-224-8211

Tennessee

3770 Arc of Tennessee

1719 West End Avenue
Suite 300E, Midtown Plaza
Nashville, TN 37203   615-327-0294

e-mail: arctn@usit.net

3771 Benwood Foundation

736 Market Street
Chattanooga, TN 37402   423-757-3723

Giving primarily in the Chattanooga area.

3772 Community Foundation of Greater Chattanooga

1270 Market Street
Chattanooga, TN 37402   423-265-0586
FAX: 423-265-0586
e-mail: pcooper@cfgc.org
http://www.cfgc.org

Peter T. Cooper, Executive Director

3773 Education and Auditory Research Foundation

1817 Patterson Street
Nashville, TN 37203   615-329-7807
800-545-4327
FAX: 615-329-7935
TDY:615-329-7849
e-mail: tef@earfoundation.org
www.earfoundation.org

Sam Hook, Executive Director

Not-for-profit organization dedicated to integrating persons with hearing impairments into the mainstream of society through public awarness and medical education. Sponsors a variety of programs including a medical educatin program that offers continuing medical education courses to physicians, the young ears program which focuses on raising the level of hearing loss prevention in grades K-3rd. Minnie Pearl scholorship program for hearing impaired high school seniors.

3774 International Health Foundation

PO Box 3404
Jackson, TN 38303   901-427-8100

www.ihf.net

Focuses on hyperactivity and learning problems in children and the possible link of chronic ear infections and the repeated use of antibiotics; collects and disseminates information about these health problems in children and works to encourage further research.

3775 Jeniam Clarkson Foundation

270 Bremington Plaza
Memphis, TN   901-454-7080

Charlotte Giannini, Executive Director

3776 Joe C. Davis Foundation

28 White Bridge Road
Suite 210
Nashville, TN 37205   615-352-2080

Anne Fergerson, Admin.

3777 Rheumatoid Disease Foundation

5106 Old Harding Road
Franklin, TN 37064

Lists physicians who use one or more of the various recommendations for osteoarthritis, rheumatoid disease, and gout. Non-profit, charitable, tax-exempt.

Texas

3778 Abell-Hangar Foundation

303 W Wall
Suite 615
Midland, TX 79701   915-684-6655

Giving limited to Texas, preferably within the Permian Basin.

3779 Abell-Hanger Foundation

PO Box 430
Midland, TX 79702   915-684-6655
FAX: 915-684-4474
e-mail: AHF@abell-hanger.org

David L. Smith, Executive Director

3780 Abercrombie Foundation

5005 Riverway Drive
Suite 500
Houston, TX 77056   713-629-4777

3781 Albert & Bessie Mae Kronkosky Charitable Foundaiton

112 East Pecan
Suite 830
San Antonio, TX 78205   210-475-9000
FAX: 210-354-2204
e-mail: kronfdn@kronkosky.org
www.kronkosky.org

Palmer Moe, Executive Director

3782 American Foundation for the Blind- Southwest

260 Treadway Plaza
Exchange Park
Dallas, TX 75235   214-352-7222

e-mail: dallas@afb.net
www.afb.org

Mary Ann Siller, National Education Consultant

3783 Arc of Texas

1600 West 38th Street
Suite 200
Austin, TX 78731   512-454-6694

e-mail: secretary@thearcoftexas.org
www.thearcoftexas.com

Mike Bright, Executive Director

3784 Arch and Stella Rowan Foudation

307 West 7th Street
Number 1900
Fort Worth, TX 76102   817-336-2679
FAX: 817-336-2679

Alice B. Myatt, Secretary

3785 Arnold J. and Irene B. Kocurek Family Foundation

562 PR 2635
Rio Medina, TX 78066   830-751-2881

Arnold J. Kocurek

3786 B.A. and Elinor Steinhagen Benevoent Trust

c/o Chase Bank of Texas
PO Box 3928
Beaumont, TX 77704
FAX: 409-880-1437

Jean Monica, Vice President

3787 Brown Foundation

2217 Welch Street
Houston, TX 77019

Giving primarily in Texas, with emphasis on Houston.

3788 Burlington Northern Foundation

3800 Colonial Plaza
777 Main Street
Fort Worth, TX 76102   817-878-2000

Beverly Edwards, President
Becky Blankenship, Administrator

Giving primarily in the areas of company operations, included, but not limited to the areas of civic service, culture and the arts, education, federated, human service and youth.

3789 Burnett Foundation

801 Chrry Street
Suite 1400
Fort Worth, TX 76102   817-877-3344

Thomas F. Beech, Executive V.P.

3790 C.J. & Syble Fowlston Charitable Trust

PO Box 51259
Amarillo, TX 79124   806-355-7640

Joyce Perkins

3791 CH Foundation

PO Box 16458
Lubbock, TX 79490   806-792-0448
FAX: 806-792-7824

Nelda Thompson, Secretary

3792 Cockrell Foundation

1600 Smith Street
Suite 3900
Houston, TX 77002   713-209-7300

Jennifer Delaney, Assistant to the Board
M. Nancy Williams, Executive Vice President

Purpose is for giving for higher education at the University of Texas at Austin; support also for cultural programs, social services, youth services and health care. Limitations are giving in Houston, Texas and no grants are awarded to individuals.

3793 Communities Foundation of Texas

4605 Live Oak Street
Dallas, TX 75204   214-827-0955

Giving in the Dallas area.

3794 Community Foundation of the Metropolitan Tarrant County

306 West 7th Street, Suite 702
Fort Worth Club Building
Fort Worth, TX 76102   817-877-0702
FAX: 817-877-1215
e-mail: hdowd@cfmtc.com
www.cfmtc.com

Homer M. Dowd, President

3795 Cullen Foundation

601 Jefferson Street
40th Floor
Houston, TX 77002   713-659-7839
FAX: 713-651-2374

Alan M. Stewart, Executive Director

Grants are restricted to Texas-based organizations for programs in Texas, primarily in the Houston area.

3796 **Curtis & Doris K. Hankamer Foundation**
9039 Katy Freeway
Suite 530
Houston, TX   77024

Gregory A. Herbst

3797 **Dallas Foundation**
900 Jackson Street
Dallas, TX   75202   214-741-9848
                                     FAX: 214-741-9848
        e-mail: mjalonick@dallasfoundation.org
                www.dallasfoundation.org

Mary M. Jalonick, Executive Director

3798 **David D. & Nona S. Payne Foundation**
Hughes Building
Suite 436
Pampa, TX   79065   806-665-7281

Adelaide S. Colwell, Secretary

3799 **Early Foundation**
6319 Mimosa Lane
Dallas, TX   75230

Jeannette B. Early, President

3800 **El Paso Natural Gas Foundation**
PO Box 2511
Houston, TX   77252   713-420-3750

Karen King

3801 **Epilepsy Foundation of Greater North Texas**
2906 Swiss Avenue
Dallas, TX   75204   214-823-8809
                                          800-447-7778
            e-mail: postmaster@afgnt.org
                    www.efgnt.org

3802 **Epilepsy Foundation of Southeast Texas**
2650 Fountain View
Suite 316
Houston, TX   77057   713-789-6295
                                          888-548-9716
            e-mail: dstahlhut@efset.org
                    www.efset.org

Donna Stahlhut, Executive Director

3803 **Epilepsy Foundation, Central and South Texas**
10615 Perrin Beitel
Suite 602
San Antonio, TX   78217   210-653-5353
                                          888-606-5353
            e-mail: sindi@efcst.org
                    www.efcst.org

Sindy Rosales, Executive Director

3804 **Foresight Foundation**
2605 Pecan Drive
Temple, TX   76502

Alan C. Jones, M.D., President

3805 **Gil and Dody Weaver Foundation**
500 West 7th Street
Suite 1714
Fort Worth, TX   76102   817-877-1712

William R. Weaver

3806 **Harris and Eliza Kempner Fund**
2201 Market Street
Suite 601
Galveston, TX   77550   409-762-1603
                                     FAX: 409-762-5435

Elaine R. Perachio, Executive Director

3807 **Harry S. and Isabel C. Cameron Foundation**
c/o Bank of America
PO Box 2518
Houston, TX   77252

Diane Guiberteau

3808 **Henry & Tommy Lehmann Charitable Foudation**
PO Box 223
Giddings, TX   78942   409-542-3636

Jake Jacobson, Chairperson

3809 **Hesta Stuart Christian Charitable Trust**
c/o Bank One, Texas N.A
PO Box 2050
Fort Worth, TX   76113   817-884-4151

Robert Lansford, Trust Officer

3810 **Hillcrest Foundation**
c/o Bank of America
PO Box 830214
Dallas, TX   75283   214-209-1965

Daniel Kelly, Vice President

3811 **Hoblitzelle Foundation**
5956 Sherry Lane
Suite 901
Dallas, TX   75225   214-373-0462

                           home.att.net/~hoblitzelle

Paul W. Harris, Executive Vice President

3812 **Houston Endowment**
600 Travis Street
Suite 6400
Houston, TX   77002   713-238-8100
                                     FAX: 713-238-8810
                           www.houstonendowment.org

H. Joe Nelson, III, President

3813 John G. and Marie Stella Kennedy Memorial Foundation
1700 First City Tower II
Corpus Christi, TX 78478

3814 John S. Dunn Research Foundation
3355 West Alabama
Suite 702
Houston, TX 77098 713-626-0368

Lloyd J. Gregory Jr., M.D., Executive Vice President

3815 Kent Waldrep National Paralysis Foundation
16415 Addison Road
Suite 550
Addison, TX 75001 972-248-7100
877-SCI-CURE
FAX: 972-248-7313
e-mail: astokes@spinalvictory.org
www.spinalvictory.org

Allen Stokes, Personal Assistant to President

Not-for-profit organization dedicated to raising funds for research to find a cure for paralysis caused by brain injury, spinal cord injury, or stroke. Educational materials include brochures and a quarterly newsletter.

3816 Lola Wright Foundation
PO Box 1138
Georgetown, TX 78627 512-869-2574

Patrick H. O'Donnell, President

3817 Marcia & Otto Koehler Foundation
c/o Bank of America
PO Box 121
San Antonio, TX 78291 210-270-5371

Gregg Muenster, Senior Vice President

3818 Meadows Foundation
2922 Swiss Avenue
Dallas, TX 75204 214-821-3290
FAX: 214-827-7042
e-mail: grants@mfi.org
www.mfi.org

3819 Moody Foundation
704 Moody National Bank Building
Galveston, TX 7550 409-763-5333

Peter M. Moore, Director of Grants

3820 Paul and Mary Haas Foundation
PO Box 2928
Corpus Christi, TX 78403 361-887-6955
FAX: 361-883-5992
e-mail: haasfdn@aol.com

Karen L. Wesson, Executive Director

3821 Pearle Vision Foundation
2534 Royal Lane
Dallas, TX 75229 972-277-5993

Trina Parasiliti, Secretary

3822 Robert S. and Marilyn I. Silverthorn Foundation
c/o Trust Tax Compliance
PO Box 831041
Dallas, TX 75283

3823 Rockwell Foundation
1360 Post Oak Road
Suite 780
Houston, TX 77056 713-629-9022
FAX: 713-629-7702

R. Terry Bell, President

3824 San Antonio Area Foundation
PO Box 120366
San Antonio, TX 78212 210-225-2243
FAX: 210-225-1980
e-mail: saaf@dcci.com
www.saafdn.org

Marion T. Lee, Executive Director

3825 Shell Oil Company Foundation
One Shell Plaza, Suite 4137
PO Box 2099
Houston, TX 77252 713-241-3616
FAX: 713-241-3329
e-mail: socfoundation@shellus.com
www.countonshell.com

A.H. Myresty, Vice President
B.L. McHam, Executive Director

A not-for-profit foundation funded by donations from Shell Oil Company and other participating Shell companies and subsidiaries.

3826 South Texas Charitable Foundation
PO Box 2549
Victoria, TX 77902 512-573-4383

Rayford L. Keller, Secretary

3827 Sterling-Turner Foundation
811 Rusk
Suite 205
Houston, TX 77002 713-237-1117
FAX: 713-223-4638

Eyvonne Moser, Assistant Secretary

3828 Swalm Foundation
11511 Katy Freeway
Suite 430
Houston, TX 77079 281-497-5280
FAX: 281-497-7340

Miriam Minkoff, Secretary

3829 T.L.L. Temple Foundation
109 Temple Boulevard
Lufkin, TX 75901   409-639-5197

e-mail: tlltf@lcc.com

A. Wayne Corely, Executive Director

3830 Texas Commerce Bank Foundation
c/o Texas Commerce Bank-Houston, N.A.
712 Main Street
Houston, TX 77002

Jana Gunter

3831 Vale-Asche Foundation
1010 River Oaks Bank Building
2001 Kirby Drive
Houston, TX 77019   713-520-7334

Vale-Asche Russell, President

3832 William Stamps Farish Fund
1100 Louisiana Street
Suite 1250
Houston, TX 77002   713-227-0408

Primary giving in Texas.

Utah

3833 Arc of Utah
455 East 400 South
Suite 202
Salt Lake City, UT 94111   801-364-5060

e-mail: Arcutah@burgoyne.com

3834 Ben B. and Iris M. Margolis Foundation
c/o First Security Bank of Utah
PO Box 628
Salt Lake City, UT 84110   801-350-5583

Julie Webster

3835 Marriner S. Eccles Foundation
701 Deseret Building
79 South Main Street
Salt Lake City, UT 84111   801-246-5157

Shannon K. Toronto

3836 Questar Corporation Contributions Program
180 East 1st South Street
PO Box 45433
Salt Lake City, UT 84145   801-324-5435
                                   FAX: 801-324-5435

Janice Bates, Director of Community Affairs

Vermont

3837 Vermont Community Foundation
3 Court Street
PO Box 30
Middlebury, VT 05753   802-388-3355
                               FAX: 802-388-3398
                        e-mail: vcf@vermontcf.org
                              www.vermontcf.org

Judy Dunning

Virginia

3838 Arc of Virginia
6 North 6th Street
Suite 403-A
Richmond, VA 23219   804-649-8481

e-mail: arcva@richmond.infi.net

3839 Arlington Health Foundation
2425 Wilson Boulevard
Suite 230
Arlington, VA 22201   703-276-8700
                             FAX: 703-276-7566
                e-mail: info@arlingtonhealthfdn.org
                      www.arlingtonhealthfdn.org

James Cole, President and CEO

3840 Bell Atlantic Foundation
1310 N Ct House Road
Arlington, VA 22201   703-524-9761
                             FAX: 703-974-0131
                www.bellatlanticfoundation.com

James Cullen, President
Denise Bailey, Director

Concentrates efforts on programs that support its vision to produce more scientifically and technically literate population effecting measurable improvements in the way pre-collegiate science, math and technology education is delivered to and understood by students.

3841 Camp Foundation
PO Box 813
Franklin, VA 23851   757-562-3439

Bobby B. Worrell, Executive Director

3842 Candlelighters Childhood Cancer Foundation
3910 Warner Street
Kensington, MD 20895
                             800-366-2223
                e-mail: info@candlelighters.org
                      www.candlelighters.org

An international organization providing information and support, and advocacy to parents of children with cancer and survivors of childhood cancer.Health and Education professionals also welcome as members.Network of local support groups. Information on disabilities related to treatment of childhood cancer. Publications.

3843 Community Foundation Serving Richmond & Central Virginia

7325 Beaufont Springs Drive
Suite 210
Richmond, VA   23225   804-330-7400
                              FAX: 804-330-5992
                              www.tcfrichmond.org

Darcy S. Oman, President

3844 Gannett Foundation

1100 Wilson Boulevard
30th Floor
Arlington, VA   22234
                    FAX: 703-558-3819
          e-mail: isimpson@gcil.gannett.com
                    www.gannett.com

Irma Simpson, Manager

3845 Greater Lynchburg Community Trust

c/o Central Fidelity
National Bank Building, 19th Floor
PO Box 714
Lynchburg, VA   24505   804-845-6500
                              FAX: 804-845-6530
                    e-mail: glct.inmind.com
                    www.lychburgtrust.org

Stuart J. Turille, Executive Director

3846 John Randolph Foundation

106 Norht Main Street, Suite B
PO Box 1606
Hopewell, VA   23860   804-458-2239
                              FAX: 804-458-3754
                    e-mail: jrf@new-quest.net

3847 Norfolk Foundation

1410 Nations Bank Court
Norfolk, VA   23510   757-622-7951

Lee C. Kitchin, Executive Director

3848 Robey W. Estes Family Foundation

c/o Robey W. Estes. Jr.
PO Box 25612
Richmond, VA   23260   804-353-1900

3849 Virginia Beach Foundation

PO Box 4629
Virginia Beach, VA   23454   757-422-5249
                                   FAX: 757-422-1849
                    fdncenter.org/grantmaker/vbf

Ted Clarkson, Executive Director

3850 W Alton Jones Foundation

232 E High Street
Charlottesville, VA   22902   804-295-2134
                                    FAX: 804-295-1648
                                    www.whn.org

Washington

3851 Arc of Washington State

1703 East State Street
Olympia, WA   98506   206-357-5596

                    e-mail: thearc@nwrain.com

3852 Ben B. Cheney Foundation

1201 Pacific Avenue
Suite 1600
Tacoma, WA   98402   253-572-2442

William Rieke, M.D., Executive Director

3853 Burlington Resources Foundation

999 3rd Avenue
45th Floor
Seattle, WA   98104   206-447-8827

Giving in the areas of company operations.

3854 Foundation Northwest

555 Paulson Court
421 West Riverside Aveune
Spokane, WA   99201   509-624-2606
                            FAX: 509-624-2608

Peter A. Jackson, President

3855 Gerater Wenatchee Community Foundation

7 North Wenatchee Avenue, Suite 201
PO Box 3332
Wenatchee, WA   98807   809-663-7716
                              FAX: 509-664-9569

Raymond Taylor, President and CEO

3856 Glaser Foundation

PO Box 6548
Bellevue, WA   98008

3857 Greater Tacoma Community Foundation

PO Box 1995
Tacoma, WA   98401   253-383-5622
                            FAX: 253-272-8099
                    e-mail: margy@gtcf.org

Margy McGroarty

3858 International Foundation for Homeopathy

2366 Eastlake Avenue East
Suite 301
Seattle, WA   98102   206-324-8230

Provides educatonal courses and referrals to homeopathic professionals and the general public.

3859 Medina Foundation

801 2nd Avenue, 13th Floor
1300 Norton Building
Seattle, WA   98104   206-464-5231

                    ww.medinafoundation.org

Gregory P. Barlow, Executive Director

3860 Norcliffe Foundation

999 3rd Avenue, Suite 1006
1st Interstate Court
Seattle, WA   98104

Ann P. Wycoff, President

3861 Norman Archibald Charitable Foundation

c/o Wells Fargo Bank, MAC 6540-141
Wells Fargo Bank, 14th Floor
PO Box 21927
Seattle, WA   98111   206-343-8367

Stuart H. Prestud, Secretary

3862 Stewardship Foundation

Tacoma Financial Center, Ste. 1500
1145 Broadway
Tacoma, WA   98402   253-539-2969

Giving internationally, nationally,in Washington.

3863 Weyerhaeuser Company Foundation

Box CH1L32
Tacoma, WA   98477   253-924-6731
                            FAX: 253-924-3658

Karen Veitenhans, Finance Manager

Although the foundation does fund programs for disabled persons from time to time, it is not a specific priority for the foundation. Since it was formed in 1948, the foundation has given more than $81.1 million to nonprofit organizations and is one of the oldest funds for corporate philanthropy in the country. Nearly all of its contributions have been made within the communities where Weyerhaeuser employees live and work and awards approximately 600 grants annually.

West Virginia

3864 Bernard McDonough Foundation

1000 Grand Central Mall
PO Box 6130
Vienna, WV   26105   304-485-4494

James T. Wakley, President

Wisconsin

3865 Arc of Wisconsin

600 Wilhamson Street
Madison, WI   53703   608-251-9272

e-mail: arcw@itis.com

3866 Evjue Foundation

1901 Fish Hatchery Road
PO Box 8060
Madison, WI   53708   608-252-6401

Marrianne D. Pollard, Executive Director

3867 Faye McBeath Foundation

1020 North Broadway
Milwaukee, WI   53202   414-272-2626
                              FAX: 414-272-6235
                    e-mail: mcbeath@execpc.com

Sarah M. Dean, Executive Director

3868 Helen Bader Foundation

233 North Water Street
Milwaukee, WI   53202   414-244-6464
                              FAX: 414-244-1441
                        e-mail: info@hbf.org
                                www.hbf.org

Daniel J. Badger, President

3869 Johnson Controls Foundation

PO Box 591
Milwaukee, WI   53201   414-228-1200
                              800-333-2222
                              FAX: 414-228-3200

Denise Zutz, Secretary, Advisory
Valerie Adisek, Secretary, Admin.

Organized and directed to be operated for charitable purposes which include the distribution and application of financial support to soundly managed and operated organizations or causes which are fundamentally philanthropic.

3870 Lynde and Harry Bradley Foundation

PO Box 92848
Milwaukee, WI   53202
                              FAX: 414-291-9991
                              www.townhall.com

Dr. Hillel Fradkin, Vice President

The Foundation recognizes that responsible self-government depends on enlightened citizens and informed public opinion. The Foundation offers grants to areas of concern such as educational activities of Wisconsin's universities. Supports initiatives to improve the cultural and economic areas of the Metropolitan area.

3871 Milwaukee Foundation

1020 North Broadway
Milwaukee, WI   53202   414-272-5805
                              FAX: 414-272-6235
                  e-mail: milwfdn@execpc.com
                  www.milwaukeefoundation.org

Douglas M. Jansson, Executive Director

3872 NMC Projects

PO Box 6000
Stoughton, WI   53589

3873 Norhtwestern Mutual Life Foundation

720 East Wisconsin Avenue
Milwaukee, WI 53202   414-299-2200

Fredric H. Sweet, Executive Vice President

3874 Patrick and Anna M. Cudahy Fund

PO Box 11978
Milwaukee, WI 53211   414-271-6020

e-mail: jborcher@ix.netcom.com

Judith L. Borchers, Executive Director

3875 S.B. Waterman & E. Blade Charitable Foundation

c/o Marshall & Ilsley Trust Company
PO Box 2980
Milwaukee, WI 53201   414-287-7228

Thomas C. Boettcher

Wyoming

3876 Arc of Wyoming

PO Box 2161
Casper, WY 82602   307-237-9110

3877 George B. Storer Foundation

PO Box 1270
Saratoga, WY 82331

Peter Storer, President

Funding Directories

3878 AIDS Funding

Foundation Center
79 Fifth Avenue
Department ZE
New York, NY 10003   212-421-0771
800-424-9836
FAX: 212-807-3677
www.fdncenter.org

Thomas Buckman, President

Gives vital information on over 450 foundations, corporate giving programs, and public charities; more than twice the number of grantmakers appeared in the last edition. All the grantmakers listed have proven their commitment by funding projects such as direct relief, medical research, legal aid and other programs to empower AIDS victims and combat the disease. *$60.00*

ISBN 0-87954 -82-5

3879 Chronicle Guide to Grants

Chronicle Guide to Grants
1255 23rd Street NW
Washington, DC 20037   202-331-4267
800-287-6072
FAX: 202-659-2236

Edward R. Weidlein, Publisher

A computerized research tool, on floppy disks or a CD-ROM, for immediate use on any IBM compatible personal computer. Offers electronic listings of 10,000 grants from hundreds of foundations, with a subscription that offers 1,000 plus new listings every two months. Each listing offers grant information as well as names, addresses and phone numbers of the grant-making organizations. *$295.00*

3880 Community Health Funding Report

CD Publications
8204 Fenton Street
Silver Spring, MD 20910   301-588-6380
800-666-6380
FAX: 301-588-6385
e-mail: chf@cdpublications.com
www.cdpublications.com

Mike Gerecht, Publisher

Gives the widest range of funding information available anywhere, including public and private grant announcements, reports on successful health programs nationwide, interviews with grant officials, plus national news on health policy topics affecting various organizations. *$329.00*

18 pages BiWeekly

3881 Corporate Foundation Files

Foundation Center
79 Fifth Avenue
Department ZE
New York, NY 10003   212-421-0771
800-424-9836
FAX: 212-807-3677
www.fdncenter.org

Thomas Buckman, President

Provides an even more updated in-depth examination of over 250 of America's top corporate foundations, grantmakers with assets of $1 million plus or annual giving of $100,000 or more. This book supplements information presented on leading corporate foundations and provides 4-6 page reports with full background data on each Corporation and foundation structure plus a complete grants analysis and listing of sample grants awarded to nonprofit organizations. *$125.00*

ISBN 0-87954 -36-1

3882 Corporate Foundation Profiles

Foundation Center
79 Fifth Avenue
Department ZE
New York, NY 10003   212-421-0771
800-424-9836
FAX: 212-807-3677
www.fdncenter.org

Offers foundation portraits, grants analysis and grants list. *$135.00*

3883 Crime and Justice

Foundation Center
79 Fifth Avenue
Department ZE
New York, NY 10003   212-421-0771
800-424-9836
FAX: 212-807-3677
www.fdncenter.org

Thomas Buckman, President

This comprehensive work examines foundation funding for programs involved with crime prevention, juvenile justice, law enforcement, correction facilities, rehabilitation and victim assistance. This book looks at significant developments in the criminal justice field, changing public perceptions of crime and cuts in governmental expenditures. *$35.00*

ISBN 0-87954 -90-6

3884 Directory of Financial Aids for Minorities

Reference Service Press
1100 Industrial Road
Suite 9
San Carlos, CA 94070   510-841-2636
FAX: 650-594-0411
e-mail: findaid@aol.com

Gail Ann Schlachter, Author
R. David Weber, Author

A guide to millions of dollars set aside just for Black Americans, Hispanic Americans, Native Americans and Asian Americans. Contains more than 2,000 references to scholarships, fellowships, grants, loans and internships available to ethnic minorities. *$47.50*

600 pages Cloth

3885 Directory of Japanese Giving

Foundation Center
79 Fifth Avenue
Department ZE
New York, NY 10003   212-421-0771
800-424-9836
FAX: 212-807-3677
www.fdncenter.org

Offers crucial information on the fastest growing sector of corporate philanthropy. *$190.00*

3886 Directory of New and Emerging Foundations

Foundation Center
79 Fifth Avenue
Department ZE
New York, NY 10003   212-421-0771
800-424-9836
FAX: 212-807-3677
www.fdncenter.org

Provides information on over 3,000 foundations that have incorporated as grantmaking institutions in the United States. *$95.00*

3887 Disability Funding News

8204 Fenton Street
Silver Spring, MD 20910   301-588-6380
800-666-6380
FAX: 301-588-6385
e-mail: cdpubs@clark.net
www.cdpublications.com/cdpubs

Wayne Welch, Editor
Leonard Curry, Associate Publisher

Offers comprehensive listings on federal grants, detailed listings of foundations, legal news, grant-seeking techniques and more. *$249.00*

18 pages SemiWeekly
ISSN 1069-13 9

3888 Federal Funding to Fight AIDS

Government Information Services
4301 Fairfax Drive
Suite 875
Arlington, VA 22203   703-465-9100
800-876-0226
FAX: 800-926-2012

Describes all the federal government grants and financial aid programs to fight the AIDS epidemic. Includes agency-by-agency description of $1.9 billion in available grants, including the name, address and telephone number of the federal official responsible for each program. *$57.00*

74 pages Special Report

3889 Federal Grants & Contracts Weekly

Capitol Publications
1101 King Street
Suite 444
Alexandria, VA 22314   703-683-4100
800-655-5597
FAX: 703-736-6501

Pam Moore, Editor
Claudia Moran, Marketing Manager

The latest funding announcements of federal grants for project opportunities in research, training and services. Provides profiles of key programs, tips on seeking grants, updates on legislation and regulations, budget developments and early alerts to upcoming funding opportunities. *$369.00*

Weekly

3890 Financial Aid for African Americans

Reference Service Press
5000 Windplay Drive
Suite 4
El Dorado Hills, CA 95762   916-939-9620
FAX: 916-939-9626
e-mail: findaid@aol.com
www.rspfunding.com

Gail Ann Schlachter, Author
R David Weber, Author

Organized to easily identify funding opportunities not only by type, but by specific subject coverage, sponsoring organization, program title, residency requirements, where the money can be spent, and even deadline date; includes a detailed program descriptions. Program profiles indicate purpose, eligibility, financial data, duration, special features, limitations, number awarded, and application. Complete contact information is also provided including fax numbers, toll-free, and email/website. *$37.50*

508 pages Cloth 1999
ISBN 1-588410-01-3

3891 Financial Aid for Asian Americans 2001-2003

Reference Service Press
5000 Windplay Drive
Suite 4
El Dorado Hills, CA   95762   916-939-9620
FAX: 916-939-9626
e-mail: findaid@aol.com
www.rspfunding.com

Gail Ann Schlachter, Author
R David Weber, Author

Each program entry gives you everything you need to tell if a program is right for you: contact information (including fax numbers, toll-free numbers, e-mail addresses, and web site locations), purpose, eligibility, financial data, duration, special features, limitations, number awarded, and deadline data. Plus, there's an annotated bibliography of other important financial aid resources and a set of six indexes, program title, sponsoring organization, residency, tenability, subject coverage. *$35.00*

336 pages 1999

3892 Financial Aid for Hispanic Americans 1999-2001

Reference Service Press
5000 Windplay Drive
Suite 4
El Dorado Hills, CA   95762   916-939-9620
FAX: 916-939-9626
e-mail: findaid@aol.com
www.rspfunding.com

Gail Ann Schlachter, Author
R David Weber, Author

The programs listed here cover every major subject area, are sponsored by nearly 800 different private and public agencies and organizations, and are opten to Hispanic Americans at any level—from high school through post-doctorate and professional. These funds can be used by Hispanic Americans to support study, research, creative activities, past accomplishments, future projects, professional. These funds can be used by Hispanic Americans to support study, research, creative activities. *$ 35.00*

486 pages Cloth 1999
ISBN 0-918276-78-0

3893 Financial Aid for Native Americans 1999-2001

Reference Service Press
5000 Windplay Drive
Suite 4
El Dorado Hills, CA   95762   916-939-9620
FAX: 916-939-9626
e-mail: findaid@aol.com
www.rspfunding.com

Gail Ann Schlachter, Author
R David Weber, Author

The funding opportunities cover every major subject area, are sponsored by more than 800 different private and public agencies and organizations, and can be used to support study, research, creative activities, past future projects, professional development, and work experience. The following information is provided in each entry: purpose, eligibility, financial data, duration, special steatures, limitations, number awarded, and deadline date. Complete contact information is also supplied. *$37.50*

512 pages Cloth 1999
ISBN 0-918276-79-9

3894 Financial Aid for Veterans, Military Personnel and Their Dependents

Reference Service Press
1100 Industrial Road
Suite 9
San Carlos, CA   94070   510-841-2636
FAX: 650-594-0411
e-mail: findaid@aol.com
www.rspfunding.com
Gail Ann Schlachter and R. David Weber, author

Veterans, military personnel and their dependents, (spouses, children, grandchildren and dependent parents) make up more than one third of America's population today. This directory has been prepared to identify the scholarships, fellowships, loans, grants-in-aid, awards and internships designed for military-related personnel. Hardcover. Bi-Annually. *$40.00*

350 pages Cloth

3895 Financial Aid for the Disabled and Their Families

Reference Service Press
5000 Windplay Drive
Suite 4
El Dorado Hills, CA   95762   916-939-9620
FAX: 916-939-9626
e-mail: findaid@aol.com
www.rspfunding.com
Gail Ann Schlachter, author

A guide to about 1,000 funding programs available for America's largest minority. This funding is available to applicants at any level (high school through post doctorate/professional) for study, research, travel, training, career development, emergencies, assistive technology, specially-adapted housing, and many other purposes. Also listed are state sources of benefits, an annotated bibliography of 60 key directories and a set of indexes. *$40.00*

370 pages Cloth/Hardcover
ISBN 0-91827 -65-9

3896 Foundation & Corporate Grants Alert

Capitol Publications
1101 King Street
Suite 444
Alexandria, VA 22314   703-683-4100
     800-655-5597
FAX: 703-736-6501

Patricia Hagmann, Editor
Claudia Moran, Marketing Manager

A complete guide to foundation and corporate grant
opportunities for nonprofit organizations. Tracks developments and trends in funding and provides notification of changes in foundations' funding priorities.
$245.00

Monthly
ISSN 1062-46 6

3897 Foundation 1000

Foundation Center
79 Fifth Avenue
Department ZE
New York, NY 10003   212-421-0771
     800-424-9836
FAX: 212-807-3677
www.fdncenter.org

Full profiles of all 1,000 grantmakers across the
United States. *$195.00*

3898 Foundation Center's User-Friendly Guide

Foundation Center
79 Fifth Avenue
Department ZE
New York, NY 10003   212-421-0771
     800-424-9836
FAX: 212-807-3677
www.fdncenter.org

Judith Margolin, author
Thomas Buckman, President

This helpful book answers the most commonly asked
questions about fundraising in an upbeat, easy-to-
read style. Specifically designed for novice grantseekers, this publication will lead you through the
maze of unfamiliar jargon and the wide range of
research guides used successfully by professional
grantseekers everyday. *$9.95*

ISBN 0-87954 -42-6

3899 Foundation Directory

Foundation Center
79 Fifth Avenue
Department ZE
New York, NY 10003   212-421-0771
     800-424-9836
FAX: 212-807-3677
www.fdncenter.org

Thomas Buckman, President

An expanded, updated version of the fundraising research classic, offers a chance to bolster your prospect files with newly gathered data on these
influential funders: over 7,500 foundation entries and
over 1,100 foundations covered for the very first time
in a Foundation Directory. *$140.00*

ISBN 0-87954 -45-0

3900 Foundation Grants to Individuals

Foundation Center
79 Fifth Avenue
Department ZE
New York, NY 10003   212-421-0771
     800-424-9836
FAX: 212-807-3677
www.fdncenter.org

The only publication that provides extensive coverage of foundation funding prospects for individual grantseekers. *$40.00*

Biennially

3901 From the State Capitals: Public Health

Wakeman/Walworth
300 N Washington Street
Alexandria, VA 22314   703-768-9600
     800-876-2545
FAX: 703-768-9690
e-mail: newsletters@statecapitals.com
www.statecapitals.com

Keyes Walworth, Publisher
Christine Ryan, Circulation

Digest of state and municipal health care financing
and cost containment measures, includes medical legislation, disease control, etc. *$245.00*

6 pages

**3902 Guide to Federal Funding for Child Care and
Early Childhood Development**

Government Information Services
4301 Fairfax Drive
Suite 875
Arlington, VA 22203   703-465-9100
     800-225-5750
FAX: 703-528-6060

James J. Marshall, Publisher
Joel M. Drucker, Associate Publisher

Describes more than 60 federal grant, loan and tax
credit programs to assist child care and early childhood development programs. The guide describes
more than $25 billion in federal aid for traditional day
care, developmental programs such as Head Start and
school-based early childhood education programs
such as Even Start. *$169.00*

372 pages 3-Ring Binder

**3903 Guide to Federal Funding for Hospitals and
Health Centers**

Government Information Services
4301 Fairfax Drive
Suite 875
Arlington, VA 22203   703-465-9100
     800-225-5750
FAX: 703-528-6060

James J. Marshall, Publisher
Joel M. Drucker, Associate Publisher

Describes approximately 150 federal grant and loan
programs for hospitals, health centers, and other
agencies involved in administering health services.
$297.00

958 pages 3-Ring Binder

3904 Guide to Federal Funding for Volunteer Programs & Community Service

Government Information Services
4301 Fairfax Drive
Suite 875
Arlington, VA 22203   703-465-9100
800-225-5750
FAX: 703-528-6060

James J. Marshall, Publisher
Joel M. Drucker, Associate Publisher

Guide describes in detail roughly 60 federal programs that provide aid to establish and operate volunteer programs. *$85.00*

3-Ring Binder

3905 How to Find Out About Financial Aid and Funding

Reference Service Press
5000 Windplay Drive
Suite 4
El Dorado Hills, CA 95762   916-939-9620
FAX: 916-939-9626
e-mail: findaid@aol.com
www.rspfunding.com

Gail Ann Schlachter, author

A guide to over 600 directories listing scholarships, fellowships, loans, grants, awards and internships. Hardcover. *$37.50*

334 pages BiAnnual
ISBN 0-91827 -75-6

3906 International Encyclopedia of Foundations

Foundation Center
79 Fifth Avenue
Department ZE
New York, NY 10003   212-421-0771
800-424-9836
FAX: 212-807-3677
www.fdncenter.org

Joseph C. Kiger, author
Thomas Buckman, President

Compiled volume of useful and often hard-to-find information on the history and operation of major foundations located outside the U.S. One of the very few book-length accounts of international foundations in English, the book is made up of 146 historical sketches of the most significant foundations in 31 countries. *$75.00*

ISBN 0-31325 -83-6

3907 Japanese Corporate Connection: A Guide for Fundraisers

Foundation Center
79 Fifth Avenue
Department ZE
New York, NY 10003   212-421-0771
800-424-9836
FAX: 212-807-3677
www.fdncenter.org

Shows how certain U.S. nonprofits have successfully approached major Japanese philanthropics. *$90.00*

3908 National Data Book of Foundations

Foundation Center
79 Fifth Avenue
Department ZE
New York, NY 10003   212-421-0771
800-424-9836
FAX: 212-807-3677
www.fdncenter.org

Thomas Buckman, President

Gives fast access to vital information on 32,000 U.S. foundations, the most complete listing of grantmakers ever published. It reflects the broad scope of this important foundation locator. It can help you quickly develop a list of initial funding prospects from the largest national to the smallest local foundations. *$125.00*

ISBN 0-87954 -85-0

3909 National Directory of Corporate Giving

Foundation Center
79 Fifth Avenue
Department ZE
New York, NY 10003   212-421-0771
800-424-9836
FAX: 212-807-3677
www.fdncenter.org

Offers over 2,000 corporate funders, current giving reviews and profiles of sponsoring companies. *$195.00*

3910 National Guide to Funding Religion

Foundation Center
79 Fifth Avenue
Department ZE
New York, NY 10003   212-421-0771
800-424-9836
FAX: 212-807-3677
www.fdncenter.org

Thomas Buckman, President

This book gives access to a fundraising guide designed specifically for them. This new subject directory brings together a group of 2,800 foundations and corporate direct giving programs, all of which have a history of funding churches, religious welfare and religious education programs. *$125.00*

ISBN 0-87954 -80-9

3911 National Guide to Funding for Children, Youth & Families

Foundation Center
79 Fifth Avenue
Department ZE
New York, NY 10003   212-421-0771
800-424-9836
FAX: 212-807-3677
www.fdncenter.org

Thomas Buckman, President

Caters specifically to development professionals for organizations serving the needs of children, youth and families. With over 2,400 listings of funding sources, both foundations and direct giving programs and over 8,000 sample grants. *$125.00*

ISBN 0-87954 -91-5

3912   National Guide to Funding for Elementary & Secondary Education

Foundation Center
79 Fifth Avenue
Department ZE
New York, NY   10003   212-421-0771
                              800-424-9836
                         FAX: 212-807-3677
                         www.fdncenter.org

Thomas Buckman, President

This guide gathers together, in one convenient source, a list of grantmakers committed to improving pre-college education. This book provides full profiles for over 1,400 foundations and corporate direct giving programs. *$125.00*

ISBN 0-87954 -94-9

3913   National Guide to Funding for Libraries and Information Services

Foundation Center
79 Fifth Avenue
Department ZE
New York, NY   10003   212-421-0771
                              800-424-9836
                         FAX: 212-807-3677
                         www.fdncenter.org

Thomas Buckman, President

This guide features a long list of grantmakers that support facilities. This directory provides essential data on over 400 foundations and corporate direct giving programs. In addition, many of these grantmaker entries include grant lists. *$75.00*

ISBN 0-87954 -95-7

3914   National Guide to Funding for Women and Girls

Foundation Center
79 Fifth Avenue
Department ZE
New York, NY   10003   212-421-0771
                              800-424-9836
                         FAX: 212-807-3677
                         www.fdncenter.org

Thomas Buckman, President

Fundraisers who seek support for nonprofits that provide services and advocate women and girls can now turn to this new subject directory. This book offers grantseekers the benefit of over 700 foundations and corporate direct giving program entries. *$95.00*

ISBN 0-87954 -93-0

3915   National Guide to Funding in Aging

Foundation Center
79 Fifth Avenue
Department ZE
New York, NY   10003   212-421-0771
                              800-424-9836
                         FAX: 212-807-3677
                         www.fdncenter.org

Thomas Buckman, President

Professional fundraisers recognize this book as the premier source of information on the agencies and foundations that support aging projects. This volume covers federal and state programs as well as foundations and other voluntary organizations. *$75.00*

ISBN 0-87954 -33-7

3916   National Guide to Funding in Arts and Culture

Foundation Center
79 Fifth Avenue
Department ZE
New York, NY   10003   212-421-0771
                              800-424-9836
                         FAX: 212-807-3677
                         www.fdncenter.org

Thomas Buckman, President

Designed specifically to meet the needs of development professionals in the field of arts and culture, this guide thoroughly prepares you for an informed grant search. With over 3,300 listings of foundations and corporate direct giving programs, the volume offers fundraisers in the field an excellent opportunity to increase their funding base. *$125.00*

ISBN 0-87954 -48-9

3917   National Guide to Funding in Health

Foundation Center
79 Fifth Avenue
Department ZE
New York, NY   10003   212-421-0771
                              800-424-9836
                         FAX: 212-807-3677
                         www.fdncenter.org

Thomas Buckman, President

Contains essential facts on more than 2,500 foundations and corporate direct giving programs, each with a history of awarding grant dollars to hospitals, universities, research centers, community-based facilities, rural health-care projects and a range of other health-related programs and projects. *$125.00*

ISBN 0-87954 -79-5

3918   National Guide to Funding in Higher Education

Foundation Center
79 Fifth Avenue
Department ZE
New York, NY   10003   212-421-0771
                              800-424-9836
                         FAX: 212-807-3677
                         www.fdncenter.org

Thomas Buckman, President

Designed for those seeking foundation support for higher education, this National Guide allows researchers to immediately find information on top funders in the field. This directory covers nearly 3,000 foundations, all with a history of awarding grants to colleges, universities, graduate programs and research institutes. *$125.00*

ISBN 0-87954 -90-1

3919   New York State Foundations

Foundation Center
79 Fifth Avenue
Department ZE
New York, NY   10003   **212-421-0771**
                                  800-424-9836
                            FAX: 212-807-3677
                              www.fdncenter.org

Provides a complete list of every grantmaking foundation in the state. *$150.00*

3920   Report on Disability Programs

Business Publishers
8737 Colesville Road
Suite 1100
Silver Spring, MD   20910
                                  800-274-6737
                            FAX: 301-587-4530
                    e-mail: bpinews@bpinews.com
                              www.bpinews.com

Leonard A. Eiserer, Publisher
Bob Grupe, Editor
Melissa Rao, Marketing Manager

Follows all programs and funding sources in education, housing, job training, therapy, Social Security Supplemental Security Income, Medicare, Medicaid and more of importance to persons with disabilities. Also covers the latest on the Americans with Disabilities Act. Publishes a newsletter. *$327.00*

25x Year

3921   Source Book Profiles

Foundation Center
79 Fifth Avenue
Department ZE
New York, NY   10003   **212-421-0771**
                                  800-424-9836
                            FAX: 212-807-3677
                              www.fdncenter.org

Thomas Buckman, President

Now the fundraising resource that publishes comprehensive portraits of the country's most influential foundations over a two-year cycle offers even more for your research dollars. A database publication which means that it is now more flexible and efficient than ever before, an even more essential part of your philanthropic library. *$350.00*

ISBN 0-87954 -83-3

3922   Student Guide

US Department of Education
400 Maryland Avenue SW
Washington, DC   20202   **202-260-2226**
                                  800-USA-LEAR

William J. Ryan, Acting Director

Describes the major student aid programs the U.S. Department of Education administers and gives detailed information about program procedures.

74 pages Annual

3923   Substance Abuse Funding News

CD Publications
8204 Fenton Street
Silver Spring, MD   20910   **301-588-6380**
                                     800-666-6380
                              FAX: 301-588-6385
                        e-mail: cdpubs@clark.net
                           www.cdpublications.com

Carol Solomon, List Manager
Mike Blankenheim, Editor
Mike Gerecht, Publisher

Newsletter covers private and federal funding opportunities for alcohol, tobacco and drug abuse programs. Plus advice on grantseeking and proposal writing, tips from funding officials and reports on the latest federal and state initives to address substance abuse and related concerns.

18 pages 2x Month

Federal

3924   Administration on Developmental Disabilities

US Dept. of Health and Human Services
200 Independence Avenue SW
Washington, DC   20201   202-619-0257
                                877-696-6775
                                www.us.dhhs.gov

Deborah McFadden, Commissioner
Will Wolstein, Deputy Commissioner

Works with state governments, local communities
and the private sector to promote self sufficiency and
protect the rights of individuals with developmental
disabilities.

3925   Administration on the Aging

US Dept. of Health & Human Services
3330 Independence Avenue SW
Washington, DC   20201   202-401-4634

                                www.aoa.gov

Carol Fish, Commissioner

Administers the Older Americans Act of 1965 to assist states and local communities to develop programs
for older persons.

**3926   Clearinghouse on Disability Information Office of
Special Education & Rehab**

US Department of Education
330 C Street SW
Room 3132
Washington, DC   20202   202-205-8241
                           FAX: 202-401-2608
                    www.ed.gov/OFFICES/OSERS

Carolyn Corlett, Director

Provides information to people with disabilities, or
anyone requesting information, by doing research
and providing documents in response to inquiries.
The information provided includes areas of federal
funding for disability-related programs. Information
provided may be useful to disabled individuals and
their families, schools and universities, teacher's
and/or school administrators, and organizations who
have persons with disabilities as clients.

**3927   Client Assistance Program Office of Program
Operations**

U.S. Dept. of Education
Switzer Street
Building 330
Washington, DC   20202   202-205-8241

                                www.ed.gov

Programs in each state provide information and
assistance to individuals seeking or receiving services under the Rehabilitation Act of 1973.

**3928   Committee for Purchase from People Who Are
Blind or Severely Disabled**

1421 Jefferson Davis Highway
Suite 403
Arlington, VA   22202   703-603-7740
                           FAX: 703-603-0655
                      e-mail: info@jwod.gov
                                www.jwod.gov

Leon A. Wilson, Jr., Executive Director
Rita L. Wells, Deputy Executive Director
Robert M. Hartt, Program Analyst

A federal agency that administers the Javits-Wagner-
O'Day Program, directing federal agencies to purchase products and services from nonprofit agencies
that employ people who are blind or have other severe
disabilities. Provides a wide range of vocational options to individuals with severe disabilities.

3929   Developmental Disabilities Administration

U.S. Dept. of Health and Human Services
200 Independence Avenue SW
Washington, DC   20201   202-619-0257

                                www.us.dhhs.gov

Gathers, analyzes and distributes information
about mental retardation, autism, cerebral palsy
and other developmental disabilities which occur
before the individual reaches adulthood.

3930   Directory of Venture Capital Firms

Grey House Publishing
185 Millerton Road
PO Box 860
Millerton, NY   12546   518-789-8700
                                800-562-2139
                           FAX: 518-789-0545
                  e-mail: books@greyhouse.com
                            www.greyhouse.com

Leslie Mackenzie, Publisher
Richard Gottlieb, Editor

   Annual

3931   Equal Opportunity Employment Commission

1801 L Street NW
Washington, DC   20036   202-663-4900
                                800-669-4000

This agency is responsible for drafting and implementing the regulations of Title I of the ADA.

**3932   Eric Clearinghouse on Disabilities and Gifted
Education**

1920 Association Drive
Reston, VA   20191   703-264-9474
                                800-328-0272
                           FAX: 703-264-9494
                           TDY:703-264-9446
                   e-mail: service@cec.sped.org
                            www.cec.sped.org

Nancy Safer, Executive Director

Provides information on special and gifted education. Provides referrals, offers patient networking services, and provides information on current research programs. Focuses its efforts on prevention, identification, assessment, intervention, and enrichment both in special settings and within mainstream communities. Offers a variety of materials including brochures and Spanish language matereials.

3933 Federal Communications Commission

1919 M Street NW
Washington, DC 20554
202-418-0008
FAX: 202-632-6999
www.fcc.gov

Jennifer Simpson

Enforces ADA telecommunications provisions, which require that companies offering telephone service to the general public must offer telephone relay services to individuals who use text telephones or similar devices.

3934 Health Care Financing Administration

200 Independence Avenue SW
Washington, DC 20201
202-619-0257

William Roper, Administrator

Through the Social Security administration, it administers the Medicare program under Title XVIII of the Social Security Act. Administers grants to the states for Medicaid under Title XIX of the Social Security Act for individuals who are medically indigent.

3935 National Coalition of Federal Aviation Employees with Disabilities

Federal Aviation Administration
6500 South Mac Authur Street
AMP-400
Oklahoma City, OK 73169
405-954-7398
FAX: 405-954-4490
TDY:405-954-4587
www.faa.gov/acr/ncfaed.htm

Becky Pritchett, Tres., Special Advisor on ADA
Alan Jones, Aeronautical Ctr Chapter, Pres.

NCFAED is working on: 1) Improvement of work conditions for employees; 2) Expansion on National Coalition to serve all FAA employees; 3) Promote equal opportunity for people with disabilities in the FAA workplace; 4) Assist the FAA in its commitment to remove physical and attudinal barriers which inhibit opportunities for people with disabilities; 5) Align with internal and external organizations to attract future generations of people with disabilities to the FAA as employees.

3936 National Council on Disability

1331 F Street NW
Suite 1050
Washington, DC 20004
202-546-8000
FAX: 202-272-2022
www.ncd.gov

Mark Quigley, Public Affairs Specialist

Federal agency led by 15 members appointed by the President of the United States and confirmed by the United States Senate. The overall purpose of the National Council is to promote policies, programs, practices and procedures that guarantee equal opportunity for all people with disabilities, regardless of the nature of severity of the disability; and to empower people with disabilities to achieve economic self-sufficiency, independent living and integration into all aspects of society.

3937 National Division of the Blind and Visually Impaired

330 C Street NW
Washington, DC 20001
202-205-8520

Chester Avery, Director

Develops methods, standards and procedures to assist state agencies in the rehabilitation of blind persons. Administers the Randolph-Sheppard Act, which assures priority for blind persons in the operation of vending facilities on federal property and serves as a program manager for the Helen Keller National Center for Youth who are deaf-blind.

3938 National Institutes of Health - National Eye Institute

10 Center Drive, MSC 1860
Building 10/10N226
Bethesda, MD 20892
301-402-8714
FAX: 301-496-9970
e-mail: abg@b31.9ei.nih.gov
www.nei.nih.gov

Carl Kupfer, Director

Finances intramural and extramural research on eye diseases and vision disorders. Supports training of eye researchers.

3939 Office of Policy

Social Security Administration
2100 M Street NW
Washington, DC 20037
202-523-0412
800-772-1213
TDY:800-325-0778
www.ssa.gov/policy

Administers grants to the states for social services under Title XX of the Social Security Act to welfare recipients and others likely to become them.

3940 Office of Special Education Programs, Department of Education

330 C Street SW
Room 3086
Washington, DC 20202
202-482-2721
FAX: 202-205-9519
e-mail: gblumenthal@acs.dhhs.gov

Gary Baumantha, Director
Madeline Will, Asst. Secretary

Administers the Education of the Handicapped Act and related programs for the education of handicapped children, including grants to institutions of higher learning and fellowships to train educational personnel. Grants to states for the education of handicapped children, research and demonstration.

3941 President's Committee on Mental Retardation

330 Independence Avenue SW
Washington, DC 20547 202-619-0736
FAX: 202-205-9519
e-mail: info@pcepd.gov
www.pcepd.gov

Advises and assists the President and the Secretary of Health and Human Services on issues related to mental retardation. Evaluates national, state and local programs for individuals who are mentally retarded.

3942 Presidents Committee on Mental Retardation Admin. for Children & Families

330 C Street SW
Room 3086
Washington, DC 20201 202-619-3482
FAX: 202-205-9519
e-mail: gblumenthal@acf.dhhs.gov
www.acf.dhhs.gov/programs/pcmr

Gary Blumenthal, Executive Director
Olivia Golden, Asst. Sec. for Children/Families

Administers the Education of the Handicapped Act and related programs for the education of handicapped children, including grants to institutions of higher learning and fellowships to train educational personnel. Grants to states for the education of handicapped children, research and demonstration.

3943 Social Security Administration

6401 Security Boulevard
Baltimore, MD 21235

800-772-1213
www.ssa.gov

Martha McSteen, Acting Commissioner

Administers old age, survivors, and disability insurance programs under Title II of the Social Security Act. Also administers the federal income maintenance program under Title XVI of the Social Security Act. Maintains network of local/regional offices nationwide.

3944 Social Security Bulletin

US Social Security Administration
4301 Connecticut Avenue NW
Room 209
Washington, DC 20008

800-772-1213
FAX: 202-282-7219
www.ssa.gov/policy/pubs/SSB/index.html

Reports on results of research and analysis pertinent to the Social Security and SSI programs.
$16.00

Monthly

3945 US Department of Education Office of Civil Rights

300 C Street NW
Room 5414
Washington, DC 20202 202-205-5413
800-421-3481

Prohibits discrimination on the basis of disability in programs and activities funded by the Department of Education. Investigates complaints and provides technical assistance to individuals and entities with rights and responsibilities under Section 504.

3946 US Department of Education, Office of Civil Rights

400 Maryland Avenue SW
Washington, DC 20202 202-260-2226

Prohibits discrimination on the basis of disability in programs and activities funded by the Department of Education. Investigates complaints and provides technical assistance to individuals and entities with rights and responsibilities under Section 504.

3947 US Department of Justice

Civil Rights Division/Disability Rights Section
Washington, DC 202-307-2227

John L. Wodatch, Section Chief of DRS

Coordinates the implementation by federal agencies of section 504 of the Rehabilitation Act of 1973, as amended, which prohibits discrimination on the basis of handicap in federally assisted programs and in programs and activities conducted by federal executive agencies.

3948 US Department of Labor, Office of Federal Contract Programs

200 Constitution Avenue NW
Washington, DC 20210 202-401-2051

Prohibits discrimination on the basis of disability and requires federal contractors and sub-contractors with contracts of $2,500 or more to take affirmative action to employ and advance individuals with disabilities.

3949 US Department of Transportation

400 7th Street SW
Washington, DC 20590 202-366-2680
FAX: 202-366-9313
www.dot.gov

Rodney Slater, Director

Enforces ADA provisions that require nondiscrimination in public and private mass transportation systems and services.

3950 US Employment Service

601 D Street NW
Washington, DC 20213

Robert Schaereli, Director

Administers the federal-state employment service program. Has selective placement personnel in state employment service offices to serve handicapped individuals.

3951 US Office of Personnel Management

1900 E Street NW
Washington, DC 20415

Constance Horner, Director

Establishes policies for employment of the handi-capped within the federal service. Administers a merit system for the federal employment that includes recruiting, examining, training, and promoting people on the basis of knowledge and skills, regardless of sex, race, religion or other factors.

Alabama

3952 Alabama - Protection & Advocacy for Persons with Mental Illness

Box 870395
Tuscaloosa, AL   35487   205-348-4920
                                       800-826-1675
                            FAX: 205-348-3909
                            e-mail: adap@ban.ua.edu
                                       www.adap.net

Reuben W. Coor, Executive Director
Ann Marshall, Outreach and Training

3953 Alabama Department of Rehabilitation Services

2129 E S Boulevard
Montgomery, AL   36111   334-281-8780
                                       800-441-7607
                            FAX: 334-281-1388
                    e-mail: sshivers@rehab.state.al.us
                            www.rehab.state.al.us

Jim Harris, Assistant Commissioner
Steve Shivers, Commissioner

State agency which provides a continuum of services for infants, toddlers, children and adults with disabilities, from birth throughout a lifetime. ADRS annually assists more than 80,000 individuals with disabilities and their families with services such as clinical diagnosis, medical care, education, assistive technology, counseling, vocational training and job placement. Offices are located strategically throughout the state to serve residents in all 67 counties.

3954 Alabama Department of Public Health

PO Box 303017
Montgomery, AL   36130   334-264-2352

Claude Fox, State Health Officer

3955 Alabama Department of Rehabilitation Services

2129 E S Boulevard
Montgomery, AL   36116   334-288-0220
                                       800-441-7607
                            FAX: 334-281-1973
                    e-mail: llucas@rehab.state.al.us

Lamona H. Lucas, Commissioner
Dean Arkin, Asst. Commissioner

3956 Alabama Department of Senior Services

770 Washington Street
RSA Plaza, Suite 470
Montgomery, AL   36131   334-242-5743
                                       877-425-2243
                            FAX: 334-242-5594
                    e-mail: ageline@adss.state.al.us
                            www.adss.state.al.us

Melissa Mauser Galvin, Ph.D., Executive Director

3957 Alabama Developmental Disability Planning Council

RSA Union Building
PO Box 310410
Montgomery, AL   36130   334-242-3973
                                       800-232-2158
                            FAX: 334-242-0797

Sheryl R. Matney, Executive Director
Elizabeth Prince, Council Chairperson

Made up of adults with disabilities, parents of children with disabilities, and representatives of all service provider agencies that serve people with disabilities. The Council generates a state plan and identifies priority areas for service planning.

3958 Alabama Disabilities Advocacy Program

University of Alabama
Box 870395
Tuscaloosa, AL   35487   205-348-4928
                                       800-826-1675
                            FAX: 205-348-3909
                            TDY:205-348-9484
                    e-mail: adap@law.ua.edu
                            www.adap.net

Reuben W. Cook, Executive Director

The Alabama Disabilities Advocacy (ADAP) is the federally mandated, statewide, protection, and Advocacy system serving eligible individuals with disabilities in Alabama. ADAP has four programs components: Protection and Advocacy for persons with developmental disabilities (PADD), protection and advocacy for individuals with mental illness (PAIMT), Protection and Advocacy of individual rights (PAIR), and Protection and Advocacy for Assistive Technology (PAAT).

3959 Alabama Division of Rehabilitation and Crippled Children

2129 E S Boulevard
Montgomery, AL   36116   334-288-0220
                                       800-441-7607
                            FAX: 334-281-1973
                            www.rehab.state.al.us

Lamona Lucas, Director

3960 Alabama State Department of Human Resources

64 S Union Street
Montgomery, AL   36130   334-263-0364

3961 Alabama State Department of Mental Health

200 Interstate Park Drive
Montgomery, AL   36109   334-263-0364

Richard E. Hanan, Commissioner

3962 Client Assistance Program - Alabama

PO Box 11586
Montgomery, AL   36111   334-281-2276
                            FAX: 334-281-1973
                            www.rehab.state.al.us

Lamona Lucas, Director

3963 Disability Determination Service – Birmingham

PO Box 830300
Birmingham, AL 35283 205-870-1205
FAX: 256-773-2296

Tammy Warren, Director

3964 Governor's Committee on Employment of Persons with Disabilities

Division of Rehabilitation Service
PO Box 11586
Montgomery, AL 36111 334-242-9102
FAX: 334-613-3893

Lamona Lucas, Director

3965 Social Security – Mobile Disability Determination Services

PO Box 2371
Mobile, AL 36652

800-772-1213
www.ssa.gov

3966 Social Security – Montgomery Disability Determination Services

State Office Building
Montgomery, AL 36130

800-772-1213
www.ssa.gov

3967 Workers Compensation Board Alabama

Department of Industrial Relations
Industrial Relations Building
Montgomery, AL 35131 205-362-9040
FAX: 334-261-3143

Alaska

3968 Alaska – Governor's Committee on Employment and Rehab. of People with Disabilities

801 W 10th Avenue
Juneau, AK 99801 907-465-2814

3969 Alaska – Protection & Advocacy System

Disability Law Center of Alaska
615 E 82nd Avenue
Suite 101
Anchorage, AK 99518 907-344-1002
800-478-1234
FAX: 907-349-1002
e-mail: cklinger@dlcak.org
www.dlcak.org

3970 Alaska – Protection & Advocacy for Persons with Developmental Disabilities

Advocacy Services of Alaska
615 E 82nd Avenue
Suite 101
Anchorage, AK 99518
FAX: 907-349-1002
e-mail: rtessardore@dlcakelcak.org

Rick Tessardore, Director

3971 Alaska Department of Aging

Pouch C Mail Station 0209
Juneau, AK 99811 907-465-2500

Connie Sipe, Director

3972 Alaska Department of Handicapped Children

1231 Gambell Street
Room 314
Anchorage, AK 99501 907-269-3400

Rita Schmidt, Chief

3973 Alaska Division of Mental Health and Developmental Disabilities

350 Main Street
110620
Juneau, AK 99801 907-465-3562
FAX: 907-465-2668
www.state.ak.us

Julie Neyhart, Director
Mike Renfro, Program Director

The Division plans for and provides appropriate prevention, treatment and support for families impacted by mental disorders or developmental disabilities while maximizing self-determination. Community based services are provided by grantees. Inpatient services are provided in two division operated facilities.

3974 Alaska Division of Vocational Rehabilitation

801 W 10th Street
Suite A
Juneau, AK 99801 907-465-2814
FAX: 907-465-2856

Duane French, Director
David Quisenberry, Rehab. Services Chief

Provides comprehensive services to people with disabilities to assist in achieving an employment outcome.

3975 Alaska Welcomes You

PO Box 91333
Anchorage, AK 99509 907-349-6301
800-349-6301
FAX: 907-344-3259
e-mail: awy@customcpu.com
www.accessiblealaska.com

Paul Sandhofer, President

Corporation that researches, inspects, and assesses accommodations, restauraunts, parks, fishing, cruises, trails, trains, tours, and other Alaskan activities for travelers with disabilities. Additionally, they assess trails and design map for hikers with special needs.

3976 Assistive Technology of Alaska

2217 Tudor Road
Suite 4
Anchorage, AK   99501   907-563-2599
                              FAX: 907-563-0699

Statewide program to promote assistive technology devices and sources for persons of all ages with all disabilities. Referral and informational services offered about devices, where to obtain them and their cost.

3977 Client Assistance Program - Alaska

ASIST
2900 Boniface Parkway
Suite 100
Anchorage, AK   99504   907-333-2211
                              800-478-0047
                          FAX: 907-333-1186
                   e-mail: akcap@alaska.com
                   www.home.gci.net/~alaskacap

Pam Stratton, Director

We provide Informatory Referral to other programs in Alaska that are funded under the rehabilitation Act of 1973 as a amended; Individual Assistance or Advocacy, if an individual with disability has applied for or received services from an agency funded under the rehabilitation act and has concerns or questions we will work with them to help resolve their concerns with the agency.

3978 Developmental Disability Council

540 W International Airport Road
Anchorage, AK   99518   907-561-5335

3979 Social Security - Juneau Disability Determination Services

801 W 10th Street
Suite 200
Juneau, AK   99801

                              800-772-1213
                              www.ssa.gov

3980 Workers Compensation Board Alaska

Department of Labor
PO Box 25512
Juneau, AK   99802   907-465-2790
                          FAX: 907-465-2797
                          www.labor.state.ak.us

Paul Grossi, Director

Arizona

3981 Arizona - Protection & Advocacy for Persons with Disabilities

Arizona Center for Disability Law
3839 N 3rd Street
Suite 209
Phoenix, AZ   85012   602-274-6287
                              800-927-2260
                          FAX: 602-274-6779
                   e-mail: center@acdl.com

3982 Arizona Department of Aging

1789 West Jefferson
Phoenix, AZ   85007   602-542-4446
                          FAX: 602-542-6575
                   www.dr.az/links/aaa/page2.html

Henry Blanco, Program Administrator

3983 Arizona Department of Children's Rehabilitative Services

1740 W Adams Street
Room 205
Phoenix, AZ   85007   602-604-1801

W. Sundin Applegate

3984 Arizona Department of Economic Security

1717 W Jefferson Street
Phoenix, AZ   85007   602-604-1801

Linda J. Blessing, Director

The Department of Economic Security is a human service agency providing services in six areas: Aging and Community Services, Benefits and Medical Eligibility, Child Support Enforcement, Children and Family Services, Developmental Disabilities and Employment and Rehabilitation Services.

3985 Arizona Department of Family Health Services

1740 W Adams Street
Room 202
Phoenix, AZ   85007   602-604-1801

Rosilyn Ryals

3986 Arizona Department of Handicapped Children

1740 W Adams Street
Room 205
Phoenix, AZ   85007   602-604-1801
                          FAX: 602-542-2589

W. Sundin Applegate, Chief

3987 Arizona Rehabilitation State Services for the Blind and Visually Impaired

4620 N 16th Street
Suite 100
Phoenix, AZ   85016   602-439-4200

Kenneth House, State Manager

Offers clients a conservation program, eye examinations, treatments, counseling, social work, psychological testing and evaluation, professional training, computer training and more for the visually impaired. The staff includes 56 full time employees.

3988 Developmental Disability Council - Arizona

1717 W Jefferson Street
Phoenix, AZ   85007   602-542-4791
                          FAX: 602-547-5320

Bill Hixon, Director

3989 Governor's Council on Developmental Disabilities
1717 W Jefferson Street
Phoenix, AZ 85007   602-542-4791
FAX: 602-542-5320

Michael Ward, Director

The purpose of the Council is to advocate for and assure that individuals with developmental disabilities and their families participate in the design of and have access to culturally competent services, supports and provides opportunities to become integrated and included in the community.

3990 International Dyslexia Association of AZ Arizona Branch
PO Box 6284
Scottsdale, AZ 85261   480-941-0308
800-222-3123
e-mail: info@interdys.org
www.interdys.org

Judy Zola, President

Provides free information and referral services for diagnosis and tutoring for parents, educators, physicians, and individuals with dyslexia. The voice of our membership is heard in 48 countries. Membership includes yearly journal and quarterly newsletter. Call for conference dates.

3991 Social Security - Phoenix Disability Determination Services
PO Box 6123
Phoenix, AZ 85005
800-772-1213
www.ssa.gov

3992 Social Security - Tucson Disability Determination Services
PO Box 40060
Tucson, AZ 85717
800-772-1213
www.ssa.gov

3993 Workers Compensation Board Arizona
Industrial Commission
800 W Washington Street
Phoenix, AZ 85007   602-542-5141

Arkansas

3994 Arkansas - Developmental Disability Council
4815 W Markham Street
Little Rock, AR 72205   501-661-2262
FAX: 501-661-2399

Wilma Stewart, Director

3995 Arkansas - President's Committee on People with Disabilities
7th & Main Street
Little Rock, AR 72203

3996 Arkansas Assistive Technology Projects
Increasing Capabilities Access
2201 Brookwood Drive
Suite 117
Little Rock, AR 72202   501-666-8868
FAX: 501-666-5319

Sue Gaskin, Project Director

A consumer responsive statewide program promoting assistive technology devices and sources for persons of all ages with all disabilities. Referral and information services provide information about devices, where to obtain them and their cost.

3997 Arkansas Division of Aging & Adult Services
Department of Human Services
PO Box 1437, Slot 1412
Little Rock, AR 72203   501-682-2441
FAX: 501-682-8155
e-mail: ron.tatus@mail.state.ar.us
www.state.ar.us/dhs/aging

Herb Sanderson, Director
Suzanne Crisp, Assistant Director
Sandra Barrett, Assistant Director

The division provides services geared for adults and the elderly including supervised living, home delivered meals, adult day care, senior centers, personal care, household chores, and adult protective services.

3998 Arkansas Division of Developmental Disabilities Services
PO Box 1437
Little Rock, AR 72203   501-682-8654
FAX: 501-682-8380

Mike McCreight, Director

State agency to assist persons with developmental disabilities and their family in obtaining appropriate assistance and services.

3999 Arkansas Division of Services for the Blind
411 S Victory Street
3237
Little Rock, AR 72201   501-682-8654

James Hudson, Commissioner

State program which offers services in the areas of health, counseling, social work, self help and education for the visually and multihandicapped. The staff includes 4 full time and 13 part time members including mobility specialists and rehabilitation teachers.

4000 Baptist Rehabilitation Institute
9601 Interstate 630 Ext 7
Little Rock, AR 72205   501-202-7011
FAX: 501-202-7259
www.baptist-health.com

Doug Weeks, Senior V P/Administrator

Acute rehab facility serving patients with ortho, spinal cord injury, brain injury, CVA, arthritis, cardiac and generalized weakness; CARF accrecdited; 12 outpatient therapy centers throughout central Arkansas.

4001 Children's Medical Services

PO Box 1437, Slot 526
Little Rock, AR   72203   501-682-8224
                                 800-482-5850
                            FAX: 501-682-8247

Gilbert Buchanan, Medical Director
Nancy Church, Program Director
Inis Fehn, Nursing Director

4002 Social Security - Arkansas Disability Determination Services

701 S Pulaski Street
Little Rock, AR   72201

                                 800-772-1213
                            FAX: 501-682-7553
                                 www.ssa.gov

California

4003 California - Client Assistance Program

2000 Evergreen Street
Sacramento, CA   95815   916-263-7367
                                 800-952-5544
                            FAX: 916-263-7464
                  e-mail: smentkow@dor.ca.gov
                            www.rehab.ca.gov

Sheila Conlon Mentkowski, Chief

4004 California - Governor's Committee for Employment of the Disabled

PO Box 826880
Sacramento, CA   94280   916-654-9072

4005 California Department of Aging

1600 K Street
Sacramento, CA   95814   916-445-2417

Chris Arnold, Director

4006 California Department of Handicapped Children

714 P Street
Room 323
Sacramento, CA   95814   916-657-0582

Maridee Gregory

4007 California Department of Rehabilitation

830 K Street Mall
Sacramento, CA   95814   916-654-5326
                             TDY:916-445-3971
            e-mail: doroa.bpremo@hwl.cahwnet.gov

Brenda Premo, Director

Assists people with disabilities, particularly those with severe disabilities, in obtaining and retaining meaningful employment and living independently in their communities. The Department develops, purchases, provides and advocates for programs and services in vocational rehabilitation, habilitation and independent living with a priority on serving persons with all disabilities, especially those with the most severe disabilities.

4008 California Developmental Disability Council

2000 O Street
Suite 100
Sacramento, CA   95814   916-322-8481
                            FAX: 916-443-4957
                     e-mail: scdd@dss.ca.gov
                            www.scdd.ca.gov

Judy McDonald, Executive Director

4009 California Protection & Advocacy (PAI) A Non-Profit Organization

Protection and Advocacy (PAI)
100 Howe Avenue
Suite 185
Sacramento, CA   95825   916-488-9955
                                 800-776-5746
                            www.pai-ca.org

Working in partnership with people with disabilities - to protect, advocate for and advance their human, legal and service rights; striving toward a society that values all people and supports their rights to dignity, freedom, choice and quality of life.

4010 International Dyslexia Association of CA Central California Branch

4594 Michigan
Fresno, CA   93924   559-435-5402
                                 800-222-3123
                  e-mail: info@interdys.org
                            www.interdys.org

Joy Moody, President

Provides free information and referral services for diagnosis and tutoring for parents, educators, physicians, and individuals with dyslexia. The voice of our membership is heard in 48 countries. Membership includes yearly journal and quarterly newsletter. Call for conference dates. Other locations also available in California.

4011 Long Beach Department of Health and Human Services

2525 Grand Avenue
Long Beach, CA   90815   562-570-4000
                            FAX: 562-570-4049
         e-mail: info@ci.long-beach.ca.us/health
                  www.ci.long-beach.ca.us/health

4012 Los Angeles County Department of Health Services

313 North Figueroa Street
Los Angeles, CA   90012   310-940-8011

                  e-mail: webmaster@dhs.co.la.ca.us
                            www.ladhs.org

4013 Social Security - California Disability Determination Services

PO Box 60999
Los Angeles, CA   90060

                                 800-772-1213
                                 www.ssa.gov

4014 **Social Security - Fresno Disability Determination Services**

PO Box 1072
Fresno, CA   93714

800-772-1213
www.ssa.gov

4015 **Social Security - Los Angeles Disability Determination Services**

PO Box 3819
Los Angeles, CA   90051

800-772-1213
www.ssa.gov

4016 **Social Security - Oakland Disability Determination Services**

PO Box 24225
Oakland, CA   94623

800-772-1213
www.ssa.gov

4017 **Social Security - Sacramento Disability Determination Services**

8351 Fulton Boulevard
Sacramento, CA   95812

800-772-1213
www.ssa.gov

4018 **Social Security - San Diego Disability Determination Services**

PO Box 85326
San Diego, CA   92186

800-772-1213
www.ssa.gov

4019 **Windmills - California Governor's Committee for Disabled Employment**

PO Box 826880
Sacramento, CA   94280

916-654-8055
800-695-0350
FAX: 916-654-9821
www.disabilityemployiment.org

Provides sensitivity training kits designed to help participants examine their own attitudes, fears, and biases towards people with disabilities in the workplace.

Colorado

4020 **Colorado Department of Aging**

1575 Sherman Street
10th Floor
Denver, CO   80203

303-866-5994
FAX: 303-620-4191

Rita Barreras, Manager

4021 **Colorado Department of Handicapped Children**

4210 E 11th Avenue
Denver, CO   80220

303-912-7266

Sue Dunn

4022 **Colorado Developmental Disabilities Planning Council**

777 Grant Street
Suite 304, CO   80203

303-894-2345
FAX: 303-894-2880
e-mail: cddpc@aol.com

4023 **Colorado Division of Mental Health**

3520 W Oxford Avenue
Denver, CO   80236

303-866-7253
FAX: 303-762-4373

George Kawamura, Director

4024 **Eastern Colorado Services for the Disabled**

211 W Main Street
Sterling, CO   80751

970-842-2413
FAX: 970-522-7121

Charles W. Hayes, Executive Director
MaryLu Walton, Admin. Assistant

Case coordination, infant stimulation, family support, residential and vocational programs.

4025 **International Dyslexia Association of CO Rocky Mountain Branch (CO, UT, WY)**

508 South Pontiac Way
Denver, CO   80224

303-721-9425
800-222-3123
e-mail: info@interdys.org
www.interdys.org

Holly Graves, Vice-President

Provides free information and referral services for diagnosis and tutoring for parents, educators, physicians, and individuals with dyslexia. The voice of our membership is heard in 48 countries. Membership includes yearly journal and quarterly newsletter. Call for conference dates.

4026 **Legal Center**

455 Sherman Street
Suite 130
Denver, CO   80203

303-722-0300
800-288-1376
FAX: 303-722-0720
e-mail: tlcmail@thelegalcenter.org
www.thelegalcenter.org

Mary Anne Harvey, Executive Director

Uses the legal system to protect and promote the rights of people with disabilities and older people in Colorado through direct legal representation, advocacy, education and legislative analysis. The Legal Center is Colorado's Protection and Advocacy System. We are also the State Ombudsman for nursing homes and personal care boarding homes. Call for a free publications and products list.

4027 **Workers Compensation Board Colorado**

Division of Labor
1120 Lincoln Street
14th Floor
Denver, CO   80203

303-573-6666

Connecticut

4028 Bureau of Rehabilitation Services Disability Determination Services

10 Griffin Road North
Windsor, CT 06095 860-298-2216
800-537-2549
TDY:860-298-2231

Richard Carlson, Chief Division of Client Service

Provides vocational rehabilitation, independent living and social security disability determination services to persons with disabilities.

4029 Connecticut Board of Education and Service for the Blind

170 Ridge Road
Wethersfield, CT 06109 860-249-8525

George Precourt, Executive Director

Offers rehabilitative services and information for persons with legal blindness.

4030 Connecticut Department of Aging

175 Main Street
Hartford, CT 06106 860-527-0856

Mary Ellen Klinick, Commissioner

4031 Connecticut Department of Children and Youth Services

505 Hudson Street
Hartford, CT 06106 860-270-8131
FAX: 860-566-7947

Linda D'Amario Rossi, Commissioner

4032 Connecticut Developmental Disabilities Council

60 Weston Street
Suite B
Hartford, CT 06120 860-297-4310

4033 Connecticut Office of Protection and Advocacy for Persons with Disabilities

60 B Weston Street
Hartford, CT 06120 860-297-4300
800-842-7303
FAX: 860-566-8714
e-mail: ctopapd@connix.com
www.state.ct.us/opapd

Stan Kosloski, Assistant Director

Seeks to protect the rights of and to advocate for people with disabilities. The Consumer Information Section provides information, referral services and short-term advocacy assistance. The Case Services unit staff advocates and attorney's for individuals who have been discriminated against based on disability or who have been denied needed services to which they are entitled to under state or federal law. Offers training & technical assistance to individuals and groups to empower self-advocacy.

4034 Connecticut Protection & Advocacy for Persons with Disabilities

60 Weston Street
Hartford, CT 06120 860-727-3000
800-842-7303
FAX: 860-566-8714

Consumer information unit for persons with disabilities.

4035 Social Security - Hartford Area Office

PO Box 2363
Hartford, CT 06146

800-772-1213
www.ssa.gov

Delaware

4036 Delaware Assistive Technology Initiative

Univ. of Delaware/DuPont Hospital for Children
1600 Rockland Road
200 Research & Administration Bldg.
Wilmington, DE 19803
800-870-DATI
FAX: 302-651-6793
TDY:302-651-6794
e-mail: dati@asel.udel.edu
www.asel.udel.edu/dati

Beth Mineo Mollica, Project Director

As one of the projects funded under the Assistive Technology Act of 1998, the DATI focuses on improving public awareness, public access to information, training, technical assistance, and funding for assistive technology devices and services. The project maintains three resource centers that house assistive technology devices and materials that are available for demonstration and short-term loan.

4037 Delaware Client Assistance Program

United Cerebral Palsy
254 East Camden-Wyoming Avenue
Camden, DE 19934 302-698-9336
800-640-9336
FAX: 302-698-9338
e-mail: capdir@magpage.com

Melissa Shahan, Director

Provides advocacy services for persons involved with programs covered under the Rehabilitation Act of 1973 as amended, information and referrals on ADA, Title I.

4038 Delaware Department of Aging

1901 N Dupont Highway
New Castle, DE 19720 302-577-4760

Eleanor Cain, Director

4039 Delaware Department of Health and Social Services

Administration Building DHSS Campus
1901 N Dupont Highway
New Castle, DE 19720 302-577-4760

e-mail: dwallace@state.de.us

Debra Wallace, Director

4040 Delaware Department of Public Instructing

PO Box 1402
Dover, DE 19903   302-739-5471

Dr. Pascal D. Forgione, Jr., Superintendent

A publicly funded state agency that gives information about local facilities and administers supplemental funds for visually handicapped students in local schools. It also maintains special teachers of sight conservation and braille programs for both children and adults.

4041 Delaware Developmental Disability Council

PO Box 1401
Dover, DE 19903   302-739-2260

4042 Delaware Division for the Visually Impaired

305 W Eighth Street
Wilmington, DE 19801   302-652-7441

Debra A. Wallace, Division Director

State agency serving the visually impaired persons from birth, with or without other handicaps. Services offered include educational, computer training, employment and pre-vocational training.

4043 Delaware Division of Child Mental Health Services

Excelsior Building
Wilmington, DE 19801   302-652-7441
FAX: 302-633-2614

Julian Taplin, Executive Director

4044 Delaware Protection & Advocacy for Persons with Disabilities

144 E Market Street
Georgetown, DE 19947   302-856-6019
FAX: 305-856-6133

4045 Social Security - Wilmington Disability Determination

PO Box 8862
Wilmington, DE 19899

800-772-1213
www.ssa.gov

4046 Workers Compensation Board Delaware Workers Compensation Board

Industrial Accident Board
820 N French Street
Wilmington, DE 19801   302-577-3970

District of Columbia

4047 District of Columbia Department of Handicapped Children

DC General Hospital Building #10
19th & Massachusetts Avenue SE
Washington, DC 20003   202-675-5214
FAX: 202-675-7694

Jacqueline McMorris, Acting Chief

4048 District of Columbia Office on Aging

441 4th Street NW
9th Floor
Washington, DC 20001   202-638-5448
FAX: 202-724-4979

E Veronica Pace, Executive Director

Serves the District of Columbia residents 60 years of age and older. Contact the Information and Assistance Unit for more information about innovative programs and services offered by the Office.

4049 Information, Protection & Advocacy for Persons with Disabilities

IPACHI
4455 Connecticut Avenue NW
Suite B
Washington, DC 20008
FAX: 202-966-6313

Vivianne Hardy-Townes, Executive Director
Ronald Tyson, Info. & Referral

Offers services and support for persons with disabilities in the Washington, DC area.

4050 Information, Protection and Advocacy Center for Handicapped Individuals

4455 Connecticut Avenue NW
Suite B100
Washington, DC 20008   202-775-6932
FAX: 202-966-6313

Vivianne Hardy-Townes, Executive Director

Serves all persons with disabilities in the DC, Maryland and Virginia areas offering them legal representation and advocacy, information and referrals and several publications.

4051 International Dyslexia Association of D.C. D.C. Capital Area

5312 McKinley Street
Bethesda, MD 20814   703-827-9019
800-222-3123
e-mail: info@interdys.org
www.interdys.org

Julia Pascu, President
Ruth Tifford, Vice President

Provides free information and referral services for diagnosis and tutoring for parents, educators, physicians and individuals with dyslexia. The voice of our membership is heard in 48 countries. Membership includes yearly journal and quarterly newsletter. Call for conference dates.

4052 Wage and Hour Division of the Employment Standards Administration

US Department of Labor
200 Constitution Avenue NW
Washington, DC 20210   202-693-0519
FAX: 202-693-1406
www.dol.gov

Administers regulations governing the employment of individuals with disabilities in sheltered workshops and the disabled workers industries.

4053 Washington Hearing and Speech Society

5255 Loughboro Road NW
Washington, DC 20016 202-265-7335

Judyth Tinsley

Offers individuals with hearing or speech impairments, in the DC area, speech reading classes, audiological services and new aids.

4054 Well Mind Association of Greater Washington

18606 New Hampshire
Ashton, MD 20861 301-774-6617
FAX: 301-946-1402

Holistic mental health information and publications, public lectures in the Washington D.C. area, and nationwide referrals.

4055 Workers Compenation Board District of Columbia

1200 Upshur Street NW
Washington, DC 20011

Florida

4056 Advocacy Center for Persons with Disabilities

2671 W Executive Center Circle West
Tallahassee, FL 32301 850-222-5790
800-342-0823
FAX: 850-488-8640
e-mail: info@advocacy.org
www.advocacycenter.org

Gary Blumenthal, Executive Director

4057 Assistive Technology Educational Network of Florida

434 N Tampa Avenue
Orlando, FL 32805
800-328-3678
FAX: 407-317-3518
TDY:407-317-3508

Cathy George, Training Coordinator

Provides state-wide information, awareness, and training for students, family members, teachers and other professionals in the area of assisted technology; a quarterly newsletter and a network of specialists (Local Assistive Technology Specialists) trained by ATEN to provide support at the district level.

4058 Association for Retarded Citizens/Escambia

3916 N 10th Avenue
Pensacola, FL 32503 850-434-2638
FAX: 850-438-2180
e-mail: aresc@aol.com
www.arc-escambia.org

Donna Fassett, Executive Director

To secure for all people with mental retardation the opportunity to choose and realize their goals of where and how they learn, live, work and play. ARC/Escambia is committed to increasing the opportunities for all persons with, or at risk of, development disabilities, the opportunity to choose where, how and with whom they live, learn, work and play.

4059 Bureau of Education for Exceptional Children

Knott Building
Tallahassee, FL 32399 850-488-9250
FAX: 850-922-7088

Diane Gillespie, Bureau Chief

Provides consultative services for the establishment and operation of school programs for visually impaired students. Provides assistance for in-service teacher training through state or regional workshops or technical assistance to individual programs.

4060 Department of Health & Rehabilitative Services

1317 Winewood Boulevard
Tallahassee, FL 32399 850-488-8304

Offers counseling and referrals on rehabilitation facilities.

4061 Division of Workers Compensation

310 Hartman Building
2012 Capital Circle Southeast
Tallahassee, FL 32399 850-488-2514
FAX: 850-922-6779
www2.myflorida.com/les/wc/

4062 Florida Adult Services

1317 Winewood Boulevard
Suite 2
Tallahassee, FL 32399 850-488-2881
FAX: 850-922-4193

Nancy J. Fulton, Director

4063 Florida Client Assistance Program

2671 Executive Center West
Suite 100
Tallahassee, FL 32301

4064 Florida Department of Handicapped Children

1317 Winewood Boulevard
Building 5
Tallahassee, FL 32399 850-488-8304
FAX: 850-488-3813

W.W. Ausbon, Director

4065 Florida Department of Mental Health and Rehabilitative Services

1317 Winewood Boulevard
Tallahassee, FL 32399 850-488-8304
FAX: 850-487-2239

Dr. Ira Rose, Director

4066 Florida Developmental Disabilities Council

124 Marriott Drive
Suite 203
Tallahassee, FL 32301 850-488-4180
850-580-7801
FAX: 850-922-6702
e-mail: fddc@netally.com
www.fddc.org

K. Joseph Krieger, Director

4067 Florida Division of Vocational Rehabilitation

2002 Old St. Augustine Road
Building A
Tallahassee, FL 32301   850-488-6210
                            FAX: 850-921-7215
                            TDY:850-488-2867
                    e-mail: milleca@fdles.state.fl.us

Carl F. Miller, Jr., Director
Ken Baer, Assistant Director

State agency serving individuals with physical or
mental disabilities that interfere with them keeping or
maintaining employment.

**4068 International Dyslexia Association of FL Florida
Branch (FL, Puerto Rico)**

5005 Laurel
Suite 100
Tampa, FL 33607   813-281-2859
                               800-222-3123
                    e-mail: info@interdys.org
                           www.interdys.org

Barbara King, President

Provides free information and referral services for
diagnosis and tutoring for parents, educators, physicians, and individuals with dyslexia. The voice of our
membership is heard in 48 countries. Membership
includes yearly journal and quarterly newsletter. Call
for conference dates.

4069 Social Security - Miami Disability Determination

9495 Sunset Drive
Suite B100
Miami, FL 33173

                               800-772-1213
                               www.ssa.gov

4070 Social Security - Orlando Disability Determination

PO Box 144040
Orlando, FL 32814

                               800-772-1213
                               www.ssa.gov

4071 Social Security - Tampa Disability Determination

PO Box 15550
Tampa, FL 33684

                               800-772-1213
                               www.ssa.gov

4072 Social Security Administration

227 N Bronough Street
Suite 2070
Tallahassee, FL 32301

                               800-772-1213
                          FAX: 850-942-8980
                               www.ssa.gov

Mary Ann Phillips, Operations Supervisor
Verdine Spicer, Staff Assistant

Administers the Title II and Title XVII disability
programs. To be insured for Title II benefits, applicants must have worked in covered employment for
at least five of the last ten years prior to becoming
disabled. To be eligible for Title XVII disability
benefits, applicants must meet an income and resource test.

Georgia

4073 ADA Technical Assistance Program

Southeast Disability and Business Technical Center
490 Tenth Street
Atlanta, GA 30318   404-385-0636
                               800-949-4232
                          FAX: 404-385-0641
                 e-mail: se-dbtac@mindspring.com
                           www.sedbtac.org

Amy Oliveras, Administrative Asst.

One of ten regional centers funded by NIDRR, to
provide information and technical assistance to assist
in voluntary compliance with the Americans with
Disabilities Act.

**4074 Division of Birth Defects and Developmental
Disabilities**

4740 Buford Highway NE
Mailstop F-34
Atlanta, GA 30341   770-488-7150
                          FAX: 770-488-7156

4075 Georgia Advocacy Office

100 Crescent Centre Parkway
Suite 520
Tucker, GA 30084   770-493-4998
                               800-537-2329
                          FAX: 770-414-2948
                    e-mail: info@thegao.org
                           www.thegao.org

Protection and advocacy services for Georgians
with disabilities.

4076 Georgia Client Assistance Program

Division of Rehabilitation Services
2 Peachtree Street
Room 23-307
Atlanta, GA 30303   404-657-2410
                               800-822-9727

Helps eligible persons with complaints, appeals
and understanding available benefits under the
1992 Rehabilitation Act Amendments and Title I
of the Americans with Disabilities Act. CAP investigates complaints, mediates conflict, represents
complainants in appeals, provides legal services if
warranted, advocates for due process, identifies
and recommends solutions to system problems, advises of benefits available under the 1992 Rehab
Act Amendments and Americans with Disabilities
Act.

4077 Georgia Department of Aging

878 Peachtree Street NE
Apartment 318
Atlanta, GA 30309   404-657-2410
                          FAX: 404-730-7950

Fred McGinnis, Director

4078 Georgia Department of Handicapped Children

2600 Skyland Drive NE
Atlanta, GA 30319   404-679-4700

Linnette Jackson-Hunt, Manager

4079 Georgia Division of Mental Health, Mental Retardation and Substance Abuse

2 Peachtree Street
Suite 22-224
Atlanta, GA 30303   404-657-2252
                                 FAX: 404-657-1137

Jerry Lovrien, Director

4080 Georgia State Board of Workers' Compensation

270 Peachtree Street NW
Atlanta, GA 30303   404-656-3875
                                      800-533-0682
                                 FAX: 404-657-1767
                                 www.ganet.org/sbwc

Julie Y. John, Executive Director

4081 Governor's Council on Developmental Disabilities

Two Peachtree Street
Suite 3-210
Atlanta, GA 30303   404-657-2126
                                      888-275-4233
                                      888-275-4233
                                 FAX: 404-657-2132
                                 TDY:404-657-3000
                         e-mail: eejacobson@dhr.state.ga.us
                                 www.ga-ddcouncil.org

Eric E. Jacobson, Executive Director
Marcey Dolgoff, Program Director
Yau Seidu, Public Information Officer

Advocacy and support organization focusd on improving the lines of people with disabilities and their families.

4082 International Dyslexia Association of GA Georgia Branch

1951 Greystone Road
Atlanta, GA 30318   404-256-1232
                                      800-222-3123
                                 e-mail: info@interdys.org
                                 www.interdys.org

Laurie Spegener, President

Provides free information and referral services for diagnosis and tutoring for parents, educators, physicians, and individuals with dyslexia. The voice of our membership is heard in 48 countries. Membership includes yearly journal and quarterly newsletter. Call for conference dates.

4083 Social Security - Atlanta Disability Determination

878 Peachtree Street NE
Apartment 706
Atlanta, GA 30309
                                      800-772-1213
                                      www.ssa.gov

4084 Social Security - Decatur Disability Determination

PO Box 1187
Decatur, GA 30031
                                      800-772-1213
                                      www.ssa.gov

Hawaii

4085 Diabetes Network of East Hawaii

1221 Kilauea Avenue
Suite 70
Hilo, HI 96720   808-933-9718

Mary Glass, Executive Director

4086 Disability and Communication Access Board

919 Ala Moana Boulevard
Suite 101
Honolulu, HI 96814   808-586-8121
                                 FAX: 808-586-8129
                         e-mail: accesshi@aloha.net
                                 www.hawaii.gov/health/dcab

Francine Wai, Executive Director
Charlotte Townsend, Assistant Director

Clearinghouse of information related to disability issues, lead agency in the community for dissemination of ADA information, systems advocacy provided through the introduction and lobbying of bills at the State Legislation, review of blueprints for State and county renovation and new construction to make recommendations for physical accessibility; establishment of guidelines for communication access, including sign language interpreters and conducts state test to credential interpreters. Admini

4087 Hawaii Assistive Technology Training and Services

414 Kuwili Street
104
Honolulu, HI 96822   800-532-7110
                                      800-645-3007
                                 FAX: 808-532-7120
                                 e-mail: bflapixi.com
                                 www.hatts.org

Barbara Fischlowitz-Leong, Executive Director

Provides information and referral to anyone interested in assistive technology devices and services. Operates eight equipment loan banks. Provides training to consumer and professional groups including self-advocacy skills for consumers and family mcmbers. Works to ensure that schools, vocational rehabilitation agencies and health insurers provide assessments, funding and training in the use of assistive technology devices and services for their clients. Low-interest loan programs available.

4088 Hawaii Department for Handicapped Children

741A Sunset Avenue
Honolulu, HI 96816   808-733-9030

Alan Taniguchi, Chief

4089 Hawaii Department of Adult Mental Health

PO Box 3378
Honolulu, HI 96801   808-586-4258
                                 FAX: 208-334-0828

Dr. Nalene Andratti, Director

4090 Hawaii Department of Human Services

Services for the Blind Branch
1901 Bachelot Street
Honolulu, HI 96817   808-586-5282

Provides services to blind and visually impaired persons in Adjustment to Blindness, Vocational Rehabilitation, Low Vision evaluation and assistance. Work Evaluation, Work Activities Center, Vending training and operates the Ho'opono Workshop, a sheltered workshop program for the blind and visually impaired persons.

4091 Hawaii Disability Compensation Division Dept. Labor and Ind. Relations

830 Punchbowl Street
Room 211
Honolulu, HI 96813   808-586-9116
                                 FAX: 808-586-9219

Gary Hamada, Administrator
Clyde Imada, Workers Comp Chief

Administers Hawaii's Workers' Compensation Program.

4092 Hawaii Disability Rights Center

900 Ford Street
Suite 1040
Honolulu, HI 96813   808-949-2922
                                 FAX: 808-949-2928
                            e-mail: pahi@pixi.com
                               www.pixi.com/~pahi

Gary L. Smith, President

4093 Hawaii Executive Office on Aging

250 S Hotel Street
Suite 109
Honolulu, HI 96813   808-235-5466
                                 FAX: 808-586-0100
                    e-mail: mrseely@health.state.hi.us

Marilyn R Seely, Director

State unit on aging responsible for policy formulation, program development, planning, information dissemination, advocacy, and other activities, for persons age 60 and over.

4094 Hawaii State Planning Council on Developmental Disabilities

500 Ala Moana Boulevard
Honolulu, HI 96813   808-532-6900
                                 FAX: 808-586-7543
                            e-mail: hiddc@pixi.com

Diana Tizerd, Executive Director

4095 International Dyslexia Association of HI Hawaii Branch

PO Box 51510
Honolulu, HI 96839   808-538-7007
                                      800-222-3123
                                 FAX: 808-538-7007
                          e-mail: info@interdys.org
                               www.interdys.org

Sandra Keawe, Co-President
Ron Yashimoto, Co-President

Provides free information and referral services for diagnosis and tutoring for parents, educators, physicians, and individuals with dyslexia. The voice of our membership is heard in 48 countries. Membership includes yearly journal and quarterly newsletter. Call for conference dates.

4096 Social Security - Honolulu Disability Determination

PO Box 339
Honolulu, HI 96809   808-586-5355
                                      800-772-1213
                       e-mail: hivrsbd@kestrok.com
                                      www.ssa.gov

Neil Shim, Administrator

4097 State Council on Developmental Disabilities

919 Ala Moana Boulevard
#113
Honolulu, HI 96814   808-586-8100
                                 FAX: 808-586-7543
                           e-mail: hiddc@pixi.com

Diana Tizerd, Executive Director

4098 State Planning Council on Developmental Disabilities

919 Ala Moana Boulevard
Suite 113
Honolulu, HI 96814
                                 FAX: 808-586-8129
                  e-mail: tiza100w@wonder.cm.cdc.gov

Diana Tizard, Executive Director

Consists of 25 Hawaii residents appointed by the Governor. The council addresses the needs of the people with developmental disabilities: specifically, develops a state plan that sets the priorities for persons with developmental disabilities.

Idaho

4099 Idaho Commission of Aging

PO Box 83702
Boise, ID 83720   208-334-3833
                              FAX: 208-334-3033
                              www.idahoaging.com

Richard Juengling, Acting Director
Jacqueline Hooper, Administrative Assistant

4100 Idaho Commission on Aging

3380 Americana Terrace
Suite 120
Boise, ID 83706   208-334-3833
                                   877-471-2777
                              FAX: 208-334-3033
                    e-mail: senglesb@icoa.state.id.us
                              www.idahoaging.com

Richard Juenglinge, Director
Gioia M. Frahm, Planner/Statistician
Cathy Hart, State Ombudsman

4101 Idaho Council on Developmental Disablities

802 West Bannock Street, #308
Boise, ID 83702

800-544-2433
FAX: 208-334-3417
TDY:208-334-2179
e-mail: msword@icdd.state.id.us
www.state.id.us/icdd

Marilyn B. Sword, Executive Director

4102 Idaho Department of Handicapped Children

Statehouse
Boise, ID 83720   208-334-4200

Thomas Bruck, Chief

4103 Idaho Developmental Disability Council

802 West Bannock
Suite 308
Boise, ID 83702   208-334-2178
800-544-2433
FAX: 208-334-3417
e-mail: msword@icdd.state.id.us
www.state.id.us/icdd

Marilyn Sword, Director

4104 Idaho Disability Determinations Service

1505 McKinney Street
PO Box 21
Boise, ID 83707   208-327-7333
800-626-2681
FAX: 208-373-7287
www.accessidaho.org/dds.html

Barbara Bauer, Director

Under contract with the Social Security Administration, makes determinations of medical eligibility for disability benefits.

4105 Idaho Industrial Commission

317 Main Street
PO Box 83720
Boise, ID 83720   208-334-6000
800-950-2110
FAX: 208-334-2321
www2.state.id.us/iic

Free rehabilitation services to workers' who have suffered on the job injuries in Idaho. Field offices throughout the state.

4106 Idaho Mental Health Center

1720 Westgate Drive
Boise, ID 83704   208-334-0800
FAX: 208-334-0828

Dr. Gary Payne, Director

4107 Attorney General's Office Disability Rights Bureau

100 W Randolph Street
Chicago, IL 60601   312-814-2700
FAX: 312-814-1656
www.ag.state.il.us

Tracy Hartlieb, Chief

Information on Illinois' Comprehensive Health Insurance Plan and architectural accessibility. Enforcement of Illinois' access law and standards. Information on initiatives such as: Opening the Courthouse Doors to People with Disabilities; accessing effective communication in a medial setting and addressing the abuse, neglect or financial exploitation of people with disabilities. Other information and referrals.

4108 Client Assistance Program (CAP)

100 N 1st Street
1st Floor
Springfield, IL 62702   217-782-4876
800-641-3929
FAX: 217-524-1790

4109 Equip for Equality

11 E Adams Street
Suite 1200
Chicago, IL 60603   312-341-0022
800-537-2632
FAX: 312-341-0295
e-mail: contactus@equipforequality.org

Joanne Schwartz

Their mission is to advance the human and civil rights of individuals with physical and mental disabilities or who have a disability as defined by the American with Disabilities Act.

4110 Illinois Assistive Technology Project

1 West Old State Capitol Plaza
Springfield, IL 62701   217-522-7985
800-852-5110
FAX: 217-522-8067
TDY:217-522-9966
www.iltech.org

Sherry Edwards, Info. & Assistance
Sue Castles, Info & Assistance, Funding Advoc

Directed by and for people with disabilities and their family members. As a federally mandated program, IATP strives to break down barriers and change policies that make getting and using technology difficult. IATP offers solutions to help people find what is available in products and services that will best meet their needs, where to find it, and how to get it.

4111 Illinois Council on Developmental Disability

State of Illinois Center
100 W Randolph Street
Chicago, IL 60601   312-814-2700
FAX: 312-814-7441

Rene Leininger, Director

4112 Illinois Department of Mental Health and Developmental Disabilities

401 Stratton Office
Springfield, IL   62765   217-782-7820
                                 FAX: 217-524-0835

Jess McDonald, Director

4113 Illinois Department of Rehabilitation

622 E Washington Street
Springfield, IL   62701   217-782-7820
                                 FAX: 217-557-0142

Susan Suter, Director

4114 Illinois Department on Aging

421 E Capitol Avenue
100
Springfield, IL   62701   217-785-3356
                                 800-252-8966
                                 FAX: 217-785-4477
                      e-mail: ilsenior@age084r1.state.il.us
                                 www.state.il.us/aging

Margo E. Schreiber, Director
Janet S. Costello, Communications Director

4115 International Dyslexia Association of IL Illinois Branch (IL, E/MO)

751 Roosevelt Road
Building 7, Suite 301
Glen Ellyn, IL   60137   630-469-6900
                                 800-222-3123
                                 FAX: 808-538-7007
                      e-mail: slonghall@aol.com
                                 www.interdys.org

Susan Hall, President
Maria Leibold, Executive Director

Provides free information and referral services for diagnosis and tutoring for parents, educators, physicians, and individuals with dyslexia. The voice of our membership is heard in 48 countries. Membership includes yearly journal and quarterly newsletter. Call for conference dates.

4116 Social Security - Springfield Disability Determination

PO Box 19429
Springfield, IL   62794

                                 800-772-1213
                                 www.ssa.gov

4117 Workers Compensation Board Illinois

100 W Randolph Street
Suite 8-200
Chicago, IL   60601
                                 FAX: 312-814-6523

John Hallock, Jr., Director

Indiana

4118 Indiana Client Assistance Program

850 N Meridian Street
Suite 2C
Indianapolis, IN   46204   317-888-8366
                                 800-622-4845

4119 Indiana Developmental Disability Council

143 W Market Street
Suite 404
Indianapolis, IN   46204   317-231-7100

4120 Indiana Protection & Advocacy Services

4701 N Keystone Avenue
222
Indianapolis, IN   46205   317-722-5555
                                 800-622-4845
                                 FAX: 317-722-5564
                      e-mail: info@ipas.state.in.us
                                 www.state.in.us/ipas

Thomas Gallagher, Executive Director
Milo Gray, Client & Legal Services Director
Gary Richter, Support Services Director

An independent state agency established to protect, promote the rights of individuals with disabilities, through empowerment and advocacy.

4121 Indiana State Commission for the Handicapped

PO Box 1964
Indianapolis, IN   46206   317-233-1292

4122 International Dyslexia Association of IN Indiana Branch

1100 West 42nd Street
Suite 385
Indianapolis, IN   46208   317-926-1450
                                 800-222-3123
                                 FAX: 317-573-0146
                      e-mail: info@interdys.org
                                 www.interdys.org

Wayne L Lamade, President

Provides free information and referral services for diagnosis and tutoring for parents, educators, physicians, and individuals with dyslexia. The voice of our membership is heard in 48 countries. Membership includes yearly journal and quarterly newsletter. Call for conference dates.

Iowa

4123 International Dyslexia Association of IA Iowa Branch

1155 330th Street
Box 50A
Gowrie, IA   50543   515-352-3548
                                 800-222-3123
                      e-mail: info@interdys.org
                                 www.interdys.org

Marlin Geisler, President

Provides free information and referral services for diagnosis and tutoring for parents, educators, physicians, and individuals with dyslexia. The voice of our membership is heard in 48 countries. Membership includes yearly journal and quarterly newsletter. Call for conference dates.

4124 Iowa Child Health Specialty Clinics

Iowa Child Health Specialty Clinics
100 Hawkins Drive
Room 247
Iowa City, IA   52242   319-356-1469
                          FAX: 319-356-3715

Jeffrey Lobas, Director
Lucia Dhooge, Associate Director
Brian Wilkes, Health & Disease Manager

Child Health Specialty Clinics has a mission to improve the health, development, and well-being of Iowa's children and youth with special health care needs in partnership with families, service providers, and communities.

4125 Iowa Commission of Persons with Disabilities

Locust Street
Des Moines, IA   50309
                          FAX: 915-242-6111
                  e-mail: tmaktin@max.state.ia.us.

4126 Iowa Compass, Center for Development and Disabilities

Center for Development and Disabilities
100 Hawkins Drive
Iowa City, IA   52242
                          800-779-2001
                      FAX: 319-356-1343
                      TDY:877-686-0032
                e-mail: iowacompass@uiowa.edu
                www.medicine.uiowa.edu/iowacompass/index.html

Jane Gay, Project Director

A statewide program provides free information and referral about disability related services and resources: advocacy, assistive technology, community services, early intervention, education, financial support, healthcare, legal aid, residential services and transportation.

BiMonthly

4127 Iowa Department for the Blind

524 4th Street
Des Moines, IA   50309   515-281-1333
                          800-362-2587
                      FAX: 515-281-1263
                      TDY:515-281-1355
            e-mail: slayton.craig@blind.state.ia.us
                    www.blind.state.ia.us

Creig Slayton, Director

Offers services to blind, and visually impaired persons. Provides counseling, educational, recreational, rehabilitation, computer training and professional training services.

4128 Iowa Department of Aging

914 Grand Avenue
Des Moines, IA   50319   515-281-4461
                          FAX: 515-281-4036

Betty Grandquist, Executive Director

4129 Iowa Department of Elder Affairs

914 Grand Avenue
Des Moines, IA   50309   515-281-4461
                          FAX: 515-281-4036

Betty Grandquist, Executive Director

4130 Iowa Developmental Disability Council

Hoover
1st Floor
Des Moines, IA   50319   515-242-6892

4131 Iowa Division of MHDD - Department of Human Services

1305 East Walnut Street
Hoover State Office Building
Des Moines, IA   50319   515-281-5874
                          FAX: 515-281-8512
                  e-mail: lhinton@dhs.state.ia.us
                      www.dhs.state.ia.us/mhdd

Linda Hinton, Administrator

4132 Iowa Protection & Advocacy for the Disabled

3015 Merle Hay Road
Suite 6
Des Moines, IA   50310   515-278-2502
                          FAX: 515-278-0539
                  e-mail: hn5317@handsnet.org

Marvin Roth, Director

4133 Social Security - Des Moines Disability Determination

510 E 12th Street
Des Moines, IA   50309

                          800-532-1486
                      FAX: 515-281-3507
                      TDY:515-281-1333
                  e-mail: dmrb@edu.gte.net
                          www.ssa.gov

Marge Knudsen, Administrator

4134 Workers Compensation Board Iowa

1000 E Grand Avenue
Des Moines, IA   50319   515-281-6647

Kansas

4135 Beach Center on Families and Disability

University of Kansas
3111 Haworth Hall
Lawrence, KS   66044   785-864-7600
                          FAX: 785-864-7605
            e-mail: beach@dole.lsi.ukans.edu
                www.lsi.ukans.edu/beach/beachp.htm

A federally funded center that conducts research and training in the factors that contribute to the successful functioning of families with members who have disabilities.

4136 International Dyslexia Association of KS Kansas/W. Missouri Branch

2812 SW Osborn Road
Topeka, KS 66614   785-228-1717
                          FAX: 785-271-6453
                  e-mail: cwajr@compuserve.com
                          www.interdys.org

Wilson Anderson, President
Michele Bay, Ph.D., Vice President

Provides free information and referral services for diagnosis and tutoring for parents, educators, physicians, and individuals with dyslexia. The voice of our membership is heard in 48 countries. Membership includes yearly journal and quarterly newsletter. Call for conference dates.

4137 Kansas Advocacy and Protective Services

3745 SW Wanamaker
Topeka, KS 66610   785-776-1541
                          800-432-8476
                     FAX: 785-776-5783
                 e-mail: michelle@ksadv.org

James Germer, Executive Director
Tim Voth, Attorney
Michelle Rola, CFO

Protection and advocacy for persons with disabilities.

4138 Kansas Client Assistance Program

300 SW Oakley Avenue
Topeka, KS 66606   785-296-4454

4139 Kansas Commission on Disability Concerns

1430 SW Topeka Boulevard
Topeka, KS 66612   785-296-1722
                          800-295-5232
                     FAX: 785-296-0466
                     TDY:800-295-5232
                     www.hr.state.ks.us/dc

Martha Gabehart, Executive Director
Randy Fisher, Program Consultant

KCDC believes that all people with disabilities are entitled to be equal citizens and partners in Kansas society. The purpose is to involve all segments of the Kansas Community through legislative advocacy, education and resource networking to ensure full and equal citizenship for all Kansans with disabilities.

4140 Kansas Department on Aging

New England Building
503 South Kansas
Topeka, KS 66603   785-296-4986
                     FAX: 785-296-0256
                     www.k4s.org/kdoa

Wilda Davison, Customer Relations Director
Mike Hammond, Public Information Officer

4141 Kansas Developmental Disability Council

Docking State Office
Building # 141
Topeka, KS 66612

Kentucky

4142 Kentucky Department for Mental Health Mental Retardation Services

100 Fair Oaks Lane, 4E-B
Frankfort, KY 40621   502-564-4527
                            FAX: 502-564-5478

Margaret Pennington, Commissioner

The Department of Mental Health and Mental Retardation Services contracts with fourteen regional community mental health and mental retardation boards to provide an array of community based mental health services, operates four psychiatric hospitals and contracts with a fifth hospital for 100 adult beds.

4143 Kentucky Department for the Blind

209 St Clair Street
PO Box 757
Frankfort, KY 40601   502-695-6350
                            800-321-6661
                        TDY:502-564-2929
            e-mail: dbohannon@state.ky.us.dfblind
                    www.state.ky.us/agencies/wforce

Denise Placido, Commissioner (Acting)

Provides career services and assistance to adults with severe visual handicaps who want to become productive in the home or work force. Also provides the Client Assistance Program established to provide advice, assistance and information available from rehabilitation programs to persons with handicaps.

4144 Kentucky Developmental Disability Council

100 Fair Oakes Lane, 4EF
Frankfort, KY 40621   502-564-6631
                            800-928-6583

Patricia Seybold, Executive Director
Barbara Wright, Associate Coordinator

Implementation of Developmental Disabilities Planning Council responsible under P.L. 101-496.

4145 Kentucky Office of Aging Services

Cabinet for Health Services
275 E Main Street
5W-A
Frankfort, KY 40621   502-564-6663
                            FAX: 502-564-4595
              e-mail: sarah.watson@mail.state.ky.us

Sarah Watson, Human Services Manager

The Kentucky Office of Aging Services is the state agency directly responsible for programs and services for people with disabilities. Efforts are made to fully integrate the service response info and klutheric model that considers broad farmiliar implications.

4146 Kentucky Protection & Advocacy Division

100 Fair Oaks Lane
3rd Floor
Frankfort, KY 40601   502-564-2967
                          800-372-2988
                          FAX: 502-564-0848
e-mail: mfitzgerald@mail.pa.state.ky.us

Protecting the rights of persons with disabilities in Kentucky with a disability-related rights violation, providing information and referral, training, and technical assistance.

4147 Social Security - Frankfort Disability Determination

275 E Main Street
1st Floor
Frankfort, KY 40621
                          800-772-1213
                          www.ssa.gov

4148 Social Security - Louisville Disability Determination

PO Box 1061
Louisville, KY 40201
                          800-772-1213
                          www.ssa.gov

Louisiana

4149 International Dyslexia Association of LA Louisiana Branch

606 Walker Drive
Houma, LA 70364   504-876-0034
                          800-222-3123
                          FAX: 504-448-4423
                          e-mail: info@interdys.org
                          www.interdys.org

Carol Ronka, President

Provides free information and referral services for diagnosis and tutoring for parents, educators, physicians, and individuals with dyslexia. The voice of our membership is heard in 48 countries. Membership includes yearly journal and quarterly newsletter. Call for conference dates.

4150 Louisiana Assistive Technology Access Network

PO Box 3455
Baton Rouge, LA 70821   225-342-6804
                          800-922-3452
                          FAX: 225-342-8823

Jill Revers, Project Director

An information and training resource on Assistive Technology for the State of Louisiana. LATAN operates three regional centers to provide better access for consumers.

4151 Louisiana Client Assistance Program

225 Baronne Street
Suite 2112
New Orleans, LA 70112   504-566-1600
                          800-960-7705
                          FAX: 504-522-5507
                          e-mail: adce@advocacyla.org

Diane Mirvis, CAP Director

Assistance to persons seeking, receiving or who have been denied rehabilitation services from Louisiana Rehabilitaton Services (LRS) or other projects, programs or facilities funded under the Rehabilitation Act (such as Vocational Rehabilitation, Independent Living or Supported Living). Must be a Louisiana resident and have a physical or mental disability.

4152 Louisiana Department of Aging

Office of Elderly Affairs
4550 N Boulevard
2nd Floor
Baton Rouge, LA 70806   225-927-4583
                          FAX: 225-342-7100

Richard Collins, Director

4153 Louisiana Developmental Disability Council

PO Box 3455
Baton Rouge, LA 70821   225-342-6804
                          800-922-DIAL
                          FAX: 225-342-1970

Clarice Eichelberger, Executive Officer

4154 Louisiana Division of Mental Health

PO Box 4049
Baton Rouge, LA 70821   225-342-2540
                          FAX: 504-342-5066

Jerry Vincent, Director

4155 Louisiana Learning Resources System

2525 Wyandotte Street
Baton Rouge, LA 70805   225-355-6197

Dr. Charlene Bishop, Director

Provides consultation on educational services for local schools, offers psychological testing and evaluation, maintains resource rooms in district schools and more for the blind and handicapped throughout the state.

4156 Louisiana Protection & Advocacy for Persons with Developmental Disabilities

225 Baronne Street
Suite 2112
New Orleans, LA 70112   504-566-1600
                          800-960-7705
                          FAX: 504-522-5507
                          e-mail: adce@advocacyla.org

Lois Simpson, Executive Director

Legal and advocacy services and training to persons whose legal issue is directly related to their disablity and has been designated an AC priority issue. Provides legal representation, counseling, information and referral, outreach, technical assistance, special subject speakers, and staff/professional training.

4157 Protection & Advocacy of Individual Rights

Advocacy Center
225 Baronne Street
Suite 2112
New Orleans, LA 70112   504-522-2337
                          800-960-7705
                          FAX: 504-522-5507
                          e-mail: adce@advocacyla.org

Lois Simpson, Executive Director

Legal services and training to people whose legal issue is directly related to their disability and has been designated an AC priority issue. Provides legal representation, counseling, information and referral, outreach, technical assistance, special subject speakers, and staff/professional training.

4158 Social Security - Baton Rouge Disability Determination

PO Box 94065
Baton Rouge, LA 70804

800-772-1213
FAX: 225-342-4252
www.ssa.gov

4159 Workers Compensation Board Louisiana

PO Box 94040
Baton Rouge, LA 70804 225-342-7555
FAX: 504-342-655

Maine

4160 Maine Assistive Technology Projects

University of Maine at Augusta
University Heights
Augusta, ME 04330 207-621-3000
FAX: 207-772-1302

Kathleen Powers, Project Director

A statewide program promoting assistive technology devices and services for persons of all ages with all disabilities.

4161 Maine Bureau of Elder and Adult Services

11 State House Station
Augusta, ME 04333 207-287-2826
FAX: 207-624-5361
www.state.me.us/dhs/beas

Christine Gianopoulos, Director

4162 Maine Department of Mental Health & Mental Retardation & Substance Abuse Serv.

State House Station
40
Augusta, ME 04333 207-287-4223
FAX: 207-287-4268
e-mail: lynn.f.duby@state.me.us.web
www.state.me.us/dmhmrsa

Lynn F Duby, Commissioner

Provision of services to people with Mental Illness, Mental Retardation, Substance Abuse issues, Children with Special needs and people with developmental disabilities.

4163 Maine Developmental Disability Council

45 Memorial Circle
Suite 3
Augusta, ME 04330 207-622-6345
FAX: 207-622-6346
www.mdf.org

4164 Maine Division for the Blind and Visually Impaired

150 State House Station
Augusta, ME 04333 207-624-5120
FAX: 207-287-5166
TDY:800-698-4440
e-mail: harold.j.lewis@state.me.us

Harold Lewis, Director

Offers rehabilitative services for vocational rehabilitation. Independent living service and educational services for all blind and visually impaired person in Maine.

4165 Maine Workers' Compensation Board

27 State House Station
AMHI Complex-Deering Building
Augusta, ME 04333 207-287-3751
888-801-9087
FAX: 207-287-7198
www.state.me.us/wcb

4166 Social Security - Maine Disability Determination

32 Winthrop Street
Augusta, ME 04330

800-772-1213
www.ssa.gov

Maryland

4167 Augmentative and Alternative Communication 2nd Edition

Int'l Society/Argumentative/Alternative Comm.
Williams & Wilkins 428 E Preston
Baltimore, MD 21202

Scholarly journal publishing articles with direct application to the communication needs of persons with severe speech and language impairments. $35.00

4168 Health Resources & Services Administration - State Bureau of Health

5600 Fishers Lane
Rockville, MD 20857 301-443-2216
FAX: 301-443-2111

Thomas Hatch, Director

Through appropriated funds, supports education programs, credentialing analysis, and development of human resources needed to staff the U.S. health care system.

4169 International Dyslexia Association of MD Maryland Branch

PO Box 984
Sevema Park, MD 21146 410-825-2881
800-222-3123
e-mail: info@interdys.org
www.interdys.org

Jean-Fryer Schedler, President

Provides free information and referral services for diagnosis and tutoring for parents, educators, physicians, and individuals with dyslexia. The voice of our membership is heard in 48 countries. Membership includes yearly journal and quarterly newsletter. Call for conference dates.

4170 Maryland Assistive Technology Projects

Governor's Office for Handicapped Individuals
300 W Lexington Street
Suite 10
Baltimore, MD 21201

Jay Brill, Director

A statewide program promoting assistive technology devices and services for persons of all ages with all disabilities.

4171 Maryland Client Assistance Program Division of Rehabilitation Services

2301 Argonne Drive
Baltimore, MD 21218   410-554-9385
                                      800-638-6243
                              FAX: 410-554-9362
                              TDY:800-735-2258
              e-mail: dors@msde.state.md.us

Beth Lash, Program Director

Helps individuals with disabilities understand the rehabilitation process and receives appropriate and quality services from the Division of Rehabilitation Services and other programs and facilities providing services under the Rehabilitation Act of 1973.

4172 Maryland Department of Aging

State Office Building
301 W Preston Street
Suite 1004
Baltimore, MD 21201   410-225-1095

Rosalie Abrams, Director

4173 Maryland Department of Handicapped Children

201 W Preston Street
Unit 50
Baltimore, MD 21201   410-767-4055

Judson Force, Director

Children's Medical Services is a joint federal/state/local program which assists in obtaining specialized medical, surgical and related habilitative/rehabilitative evaluation and treatment services for children with special health care needs and their families. To be eligible for the program's services, an individual must be a resident of Maryland, younger than 22 years, have or be suspected of having an eligible medical condition and meet both medical and financial criteria.

4174 Maryland Developmental Disabilities Council

300 W Lexington Street
Box 10
Baltimore, MD 21201   410-333-3688
                                      800-305-6441
                              FAX: 410-333-3686
              e-mail: info@md-councl.org
                      www.md-council.org

4175 Maryland Division of Mental Health

2301 Argonne Drive
Baltimore, MD 21218   410-243-7495
                              FAX: 410-333-7482

4176 Maryland's Protection & Advocacy System for Persons with Disabilities

Maryland Disability Law Center
1800 N Charles Street
Suite 400
Baltimore, MD 21201   410-727-6352
                                      800-233-7201
                              FAX: 410-727-6389
                              TDY:410-727-6387
                      e-mail: MDLCBalto.org

Philip Fornaci, Executive Director

Legal assistance provided to Maryland residents with any mental and or physical disability and to their families for disability related problems. Due to limited resources, not all cases are accepted, no criminal, domestic or employment cases.

4177 Social Security - Baltimore Disability Determination

2301 Argonne Drive
Baltimore, MD 21218
                                      800-772-1213
                                      www.ssa.gov

4178 Workers Compensation Board Maryland

6 N Library Street
Baltimore, MD 21201   410-333-4700

Massachusetts

4179 Massachusetts Assistive Technology Partnership

MATP Center
1295 Boylston Street
Suite 310
Boston, MA 02215
                                      800-848-8867
                              FAX: 617-345-6345

Judy Brewer, Project Director

A statewide program promoting assistive technology devices and services for persons with all disabilities.

4180 Massachusetts Client Assistance Program

1 Ashburton Place
Room 1305
Boston, MA 02108   617-727-7440
                                      800-322-2020
                              FAX: 617-727-0965
              e-mail: barbara.lybarger@state.ma.us
                      www.state.ma.us/mod

Barbara Lybarger, Assistant Director

Provides advocacy and information services.

4181 Massachusetts Department of Handicapped Children

150 Tremont Street
Boston, MA 02111 617-864-2000
FAX: 617-864-7468

Gerald Tuttle, Director

4182 Massachusetts Department of Mental Health

25 Staniford Street
Boston, MA 02114 617-367-0944
FAX: 617-727-4350

Eileen Elias, Commissioner

4183 Massachusetts Developmental Disabilities Council

600 Washington Street
Room 670
Boston, MA 02111 617-727-6374
FAX: 617-727-1174

Group of citizens which analyzes needs of people with severe, lifelong disabilities and works to improve public policy. MDDC produces several publications and has committees and a grants program to study and advocate for changes in the service system.

4184 Massachusetts Protection & Advocacy for Disabled Persons

22 Green Street
Northampton, MA 01060 413-584-1644
FAX: 413-586-5711

4185 Social Security - Boston Disability Determination

27 Wormwood Street
43
Boston, MA 02210
800-772-1213
FAX: 617-727-1354
www.ssa.gov

4186 Workers Compensation Board Massachusetts

1 Ashburton Place
Room 211
Boston, MA 02108 617-727-2720
FAX: 617-727-3285
www.state.ma.us/dia

James J. Campbell, Director

Michigan

4187 Bureau of Workers' Disability Compensation

PO Box 30016
Lansing, MI 48909 888-396-5041
FAX: 517-322-1808
e-mail: bwdcinfo@cis.state.mi.us
www.cis.state.mi.us/wkrcomp

4188 Department of Blind Rehabilitation

Western Michigan University
3404 Sangren Hall
Kalamazoo, MI 49008 616-657-2223
FAX: 617-387-3567

Dr. William Wiener, Chairperson

4189 International Dyslexia Association of MI Michigan Branch

8548 Rivercrest Drive SW
Jenison, MI 49428 616-457-5892
800-222-3123
e-mail: info@interdys.org
www.interdys.org

Jim Grant, President

Provides free information and referral services for diagnosis and tutoring for parents, educators, physicians, and individuals with dyslexia. The voice of our membership is heard in 48 countries. Membership includes yearly journal and quarterly newsletter. Call for conference dates.

4190 Michigan Association for the Deaf, Hearing and Speech Services

2929 Covington Center
Suite 200
Lansing, MI 48912 517-364-8733
800-YOU-REAR
FAX: 517-487-2586
TDY:517-487-0202
e-mail: yourear@pilot.msu.edu
www.miserybay.com/madhs

Jody Smith, Executive Director
Pat Walton, Office Manager

Substance Abuse Prevention for the deaf and hard of hearing students (alcohol, marijuana, inhalents) acted in sign language, voicing, and captioning. AIV/AIDS Prevention and Information for the deaf and hard of hearing. Lending Library books, videos and audio tapes. Accessibility in Courts video and information. TTY distribution Program. TRACK-MAN-Youth Substance Abuse Video and Education Series.. *$150.00*

4191 Michigan Client Assistance Program

Michigan Protection and Advocacy Service
PO Box 30008
Lansing, MI 48909 517-373-3900
800-292-5896

Amy Maes, CAP Manager

4192 Michigan Coalition for Staff Development and School Improvement

530 West Ionia
Suite C
Lancing, MI 48933 734-513-9080
800-444-2014
FAX: 517-371-1170

4193 Michigan Commission for the Blind

201 N Washington Square
PO Box 30652
Lansing, MI 48933 517-373-2062
800-292-4200
FAX: 517-335-5140
TDY:517-373-4025
e-mail: kreinerc@state.mi.us

Patrick Cannon, Director

The Commission for the Blind serves as the vocational rehabilitation agency for the blind. The Commission also operates a residential training center in Kalamazoo, provides independent living services for Michigan's older blind population, low-vision services for the state's youth, a deaf/blind program, and entrepreneurial opportunities for blind persons through its Business Enterprise Program.

4194 Michigan Council of the Blind and Visually Impaired (MCBVI)

George Illingworth
1037 Winchester Avenue
Lincoln Park, MI 48146   313-381-7844
FAX: 313-381-7844

Neal Freeling, President

Advocate for blind and visually impaired people throughout the state of Michigan.

4195 Michigan Department of Community Health

Lewis Cass Building
320 South Walnut
Lansing, MI 48933   517-335-0196
FAX: 517-335-3090
www.mdch.state.mi.us

James K. Haveman, Jr., Director

4196 Michigan Department of Handicapped Children

3423 N Logan Street
Lansing, MI 48906   517-335-8873
FAX: 517-335-9222

Karen Schrock, Chief

4197 Michigan Developmental Disability Council

Lewis
6th Floor
Lansing, MI 48913   517-485-4126
FAX: 517-334-7353

4198 Michigan Office of Services to the Aging

PO Box 30026
Lansing, MI 48909   517-373-0219
FAX: 517-373-4092

Diane K. Braunstein, Director

State unit on aging; allocates and monitors state and federal funds for the Older American Act services: nutrition, community services, administers home and community based waiver, develops programs through Area Agencies on Aging, advocates on behalf of seniors with legislature, governor, state departments, federal government, responsible for state planning of aging services, develops formula for distribution of state and federal funds.

4199 Michigan Rehabilitation Services

PO Box 30010
Lansing, MI 48909   517-373-3390
800-605-6722
FAX: 517-373-0565
TDY: 517-373-4035
www.mrs.state.mi.us

A state and federally funded program that helps persons with disabilities prepare for and fund a job that matches their interests and abilities. Assistance is also available to workers with disabilities who are having difficulty keeping a job. A person is eligible for MRS services if he or she has a disability, is unemployed and needs vocational rehabilitation services to prepare for and find a job or independent living services.

4200 Social Security - Lansing Disability Determination

PO Box 30011
Lansing, MI 48909   517-373-7830
800-772-1213
TDY: 800-366-3404
www.ssa.gov

Linda Dorn, State Director

4201 State of Michigan/Bureau of Workers' Disability Compensation

PO Box 30016
Lansing, MI 48909   888-396-5014
FAX: 517-322-1808
www.cis.state.mi.us/wkrcomp

Minnesota

4202 International Dyslexia Association of MN

5021 Vernon Avenue
Minneapolis, MN 55436   651-450-7589
800-222-3123
e-mail: info@interdys.org
www.interdys.org

Hannah Toiles, President

Provides free information and referral services for diagnosis and tutoring for parents, educators, physicians, and individuals with dyslexia. The voice of our membership is heard in 48 countries. Membership includes yearly journal and quarterly newsletter. Call for conference dates.

4203 Minnesota Assistive Technology Project

STAR/Governor's Advisory Council on Technology for
360 Centennial Building
658 Cedar Street
St. Paul, MN 55155   651-296-2771
800-657-3862
FAX: 651-282-6671
e-mail: star.program@state.mn.us
www.admin.state.mn.us/assistivetechnology

Mary Brogdon, Executive Director
Tom Shaffer, Program Development Specialist
Ronna Linroth, Funding and Policy Specialist

A statewide program promoting assistive technology devices and services for persons of all ages with all disabilities.

4204 Minnesota Board on Aging

444 Lafayette Road North
Saint Paul, MN   55155   551-296-2770
                               800-882-6262
                          FAX: 651-297-7855
            e-mail: mba.dhs@state.mn.us
                        www.mnaging.org

Jim Varpness, Director

A state unit on aging for the state of Minnesota. Funds 14 area agencies on aging throughout the state that provide services at the local level. The mission is to keep older people in the homes or places of residence for as long as possible.

**4205 Minnesota Children with Special Needs,
        Minnesota Department of Health**

PO Box 9441
717 Delaware Street SE
Minneapolis, MN   55440   612-676-5274
                          FAX: 651-215-8953

Guidelines of care for children with special health needs: Down Syndrome, Cerebral Palsy, Cystic Fibrosis, Asthma, Diabetes, Hemophilia, Seizure Disorders, Congenital Heart Disease and Spina Bifida, and neurofibromatosis, Deaf & Hard of Hearing, Juvenile Rheumatoid Arthritis, Sickle Cell Disease Muscular Dystrophy, Pheneylketoneureal, Cleft Lip and Palate.

**4206 Minnesota Department of Labor & Industry
        Workers Compensation Division**

443 Lafayette Road North
Saint Paul, MN   55155   651-296-2464
                               800-342-5354
                          FAX: 651-296-9634
       e-mail: dli.workcomp@state.mn.us
                     www.doli.state.mn.us

To reduce the impact of work related injuries for employees and employers. Advice is given and questions answered on the toll-free number.

4207 Minnesota Disability Law Center

430 1st Avenue North
Suite 300
Minneapolis, MN   55401   612-332-1441
                          FAX: 612-334-5755
            www.mnlegalservices.org/mdlc

Lisa Cohen, Administrator
Pamela Hoopes, Legal Director

Provides free civil legal assistance to Minnesotans with disabilities on issues related to their disability.

**4208 Minnesota Governor's Council on Developmental
        Disabilities**

370 Centennial Building
658 Cedar Street
St. Paul, MN   55155   651-296-4018
                               877-348-0505
                          FAX: 651-297-7200
          e-mail: admin.dd@state.mn.us
                        www.mncdd.org

Colleen Wieck, Ph.D, Executive Director

4209 Minnesota Mental Health Division

Human Services Building
444 Lafayette Road North
Saint Paul, MN   55155   651-296-6117

Edwin Swenson, Director

Oversees the provision of services to people with mental illness in the state of Minnesota. Services are provided on the local level through a network of 87 county social service departments.

**4210 Minnesota Protection & Advocacy for Persons
        with Disabilities**

Minnesota Disability Law Center
430 1st Avenue North
Suite 300
Minneapolis, MN   55401   612-332-1441
                               800-292-4150
                          FAX: 612-334-5755
            www.mnlegalservices.org/mdlc

Lisa Cohen, Administrator
Pamela Hoopes, Legal Director

4211 Minnesota State Council on Disability

121 7th Place East
Suite 107
Saint Paul, MN   55101   651-296-6785
                               800-945-5913
                          FAX: 651-296-5935
          e-mail: cliff.miller@state.mn.us
                  www.disability.state.mn.us

Cliff Miller, Information Officer

To promote public policy leading to the independence, productivity and inclusion of people with disabilities in all aspects of society. This mission is accomplished through planning, evaluation, collaboration, education, research, earning and technical assistance.

8-12 pages Newsletter

4212 Minnesota State Services for the Blind

2200 University Avenue West
240
Saint Paul, MN   55114   651-642-0500
                               800-652-9000
                          FAX: 651-649-5927
                          TDY: 612-642-0506
         www.belsey.ngwmail.des.state.mn.us

Bonnie Elsey, Asst. Commissioner
Linda Lingen, Self-Sufficiency Unit
Chuk Hamilton, Business Services Unit

State agency serving blind and visually impaired persons with rehabilitation, information access, assistive technology, training, and job placement services. Extensive older blind program.

4213 Social Security - St. Paul Disability Determination

Metro Square Building
Suite 300
St. Paul, MN   55101

                               800-772-1213
                          FAX: 651-297-5167
                               www.ssa.gov

Noreen Hale, Director

Mississippi

4214 International Dyslexia Association of MS
Mississippi Branch

408 Megan Lane
Columbus, MS 39701   601-327-7539
800-222-3123
e-mail: info@interdys.org
www.interdys.org

Judy Robinson, President

Provides free information and referral services for diagnosis and tutoring for parents, educators, physicians, and individuals with dyslexia. The voice of our membership is heard in 48 countries. Membership includes yearly journal and quarterly newsletter. Call for conference dates.

4215 Mississippi Workers Compensation Board

PO Box 5300
Jackson, MS 39296   601-987-4200

www.mdcc.state.ms.us

Ray Minor, Director

4216 Mississippi Assistive Technology Projects

PO Box 1698
Jackson, MS 39215   601-853-5100
FAX: 601-853-5160
www.mdrs.state.ms.us

Pete Martin

A statewide program promoting assistive technology devices and services for persons of all ages with all disabilities.

4217 Mississippi Bureau of Mental Retardation

1101 Robert E Lee Building
Jackson, MS 39201   601-373-1019
FAX: 601-354-6945

Roger McMurtry, Chief

4218 Mississippi Client Assistance Program

3226 N State Street
Jackson, MS 39216   601-362-2585
FAX: 601-982-1951

Vocational training for rehabilitation clients.

4219 Mississippi Department of Aging

421 W Pascagoula Street
Jackson, MS 39203

800-948-3090

Billie Marshall, Director

4220 Mississippi Department of Mental Health

1101 Robert E Lee Building
Jackson, MS 39201   601-359-1288
FAX: 601-359-6295

Albert Hendrix, PhD., Executive Director

The Mississippi Department of Mental Health administers Mississippi's public programs of serving persons with mental illness, mental retardation, alcohol and substance abuse problems, and Alzheimer's Disease and related dementia.

4221 Mississippi State Department of Health

Children's Medical Program
PO Box 1700
Jackson, MS 39215   601-960-7963
800-844-0898
FAX: 601-987-5560

Mike Gallarno MSSW, LCSW, Director
Mary Marbury RN, State Nursing Coord.
Marilyn Graves MD, Medical Director

Financial assistance to families of children with physical handicaps. Rehabilitative in nature, and has as its goal the correction or reduction of physical handicaps. Eligibility determined by diagnosis, and provided to children from birth to age twenty-one. Financial eligibility is determined by factors of family income, family size, estimated cost of treatment and family liabilities. Categories include, but not limited to: orthopedic, congenital heart defects, cerebral palsy, etc.

4222 Mississippi: Workers Compensation Commission

1428 Lakeland Drive
Jackson, MS 39216   601-987-4200

Ray Minor, Director

Missouri

4223 Institute for Human Development

University of Missouri- Kansas
2220 Holmes Street
Health Sciences Building, 3rd Floor
Kansas City, MO 64108   816-235-1770
800-444-0821
FAX: 816-235-1762
e-mail: ellenbuschk@umkc.edu
www.ird.umkc.edu

Carl Calkins, Director

A statewide program promoting person-centered planning and services for persons of all ages with all disabilities.

4224 Missouri Department of Aging

615 Howerton Center
1337
Jefferson City, MO 65109   573-751-7961

Edwin Walker, Director

4225 Missouri Department of Mental Health

1706 E Elm
Jefferson City, MO 65101   573-751-7961
FAX: 573-526-7926
e-mail: royc.wilsonmd.web.www.state.mo.us/dmh

Keith Schafer, Director

4226 Missouri Division of Mental Retardation & Developmental Disabilities

Department of Mental Health
PO Box 687
Jefferson City, MO   65102   573-751-8611
                                    FAX: 573-751-9207
          e-mail: mzdeata@mail.amh.state.mo.us

Anne Deaton, Division Director

4227 Missouri Protection & Advocacy Services

925 South Country Club Drive
Jefferson City, MO   65109   573-893-3333
                                    800-392-8667
                                    FAX: 573-893-4231
              e-mail: mopasjc@socket.net
          members.socket.net/~mopasjc/mopla.htm

Shawn T. de Loyola, Executive Director
Linda Snider, Information Specialist
Connie Wright, Information Specialist

MO P&A provides protection of the rights of persons with disabilities in Missouri and assistance to clients who have disabilities through information, referral, advocacy, or legal counsel. Informational brochures, Alliance newsletter, Client Assistance Program (CAP) Manual available upon request.

4228 Missouri Protection and Advocacy Services

925 S Country Club Drive
Jefferson City, MO   65109   573-893-3333
                                    800-392-8667
                                    FAX: 573-893-4231
              e-mail: mopasjc@socknet.net
          www.members.socket.net/~mopasjc/

Missouri Protection and Advocacy Services protects the rights of persons with disabilities through information, education, advocacy, investigation, legal counsel, and litigation services for clients.

4229 Missouri Rehabilitation Services for the Blind

3418 Knipp Drive
PO Box 88
Jefferson City, MO   65103   573-751-4249
                                    800-592-6004
                                    FAX: 573-751-4984
          e-mail: mmerrick@mail.state.mo.us
          www.dss.state.mo.us/dfs/rehab/rehab.htm

Sally Howard, Director

Offers services for the totally blind, legally blind, visually impaired, including counseling, educational, recreational, rehabilitation, computer training and professional training services.

4230 Social Security - Jefferson City Disability Determination

2401 E McCarty Street
Jefferson City, MO   65101

                                    800-772-1213
                                    FAX: 573-751-1441
                                    www.ssa.gov

Dr. Don Gann, Director

4231 Workers Compensation Board Missouri

PO Box 58
Jefferson City, MO   65102   573-751-4231
                                    FAX: 573-751-2012
              www.dolir.state.mo.us

Montana

4232 Addictive & Mental Disorders Division

1400 Broadway, Room C118
PO Box 202951
Helena, MT   59620   406-444-3964
                                    FAX: 406-444-4435
                                    www.dphhs.state.mt.us

Dan Anderson, Administrator

4233 Montana Advocacy Program

PO Box 1680
Helena, MT   59624   406-449-3266
                                    800-245-4743
                                    FAX: 406-444-0261
                                    TDY:800-245-4743
                e-mail: advocate@mt.net
                www.mt.net/~advocate

Bernadette Franks-Ongoy, Executive Director

Protects and advocates the human and legal rights of Montanans with mental and physical disabilities while advancing dignity, equality, and self-determination. Designated federal P&A, with AT, CAP, PADD, PAIMI and PAIR programs. Advocacy and legal services for abuse, neglect, rights violations, access, discrimination in employment, accommodations and housing, and assistance with vocational rehabilitation/visual services.

4234 Montana Assistive Technology Projects

111 Sanders
Helena, MT   59604   406-443-4032

William Lamb, Program Officer
Peter Leech, Director

A statewide program promoting assistive devices and services for persons of all ages with all disabilities.

4235 Montana Department of Aging

Capitol Station
Room 219
Helena, MT   59620   406-225-4411
                                    FAX: 406-444-5529

Hank Hudson, Aging Coordinator

4236 Montana Department of Handicapped Children

Cogswell Building
Helena, MT   59620   406-225-4411
                                    FAX: 406-444-2606

Sidney Pratt, Bureau Chief

4237 Montana Department of Social and Rehabilitation Services

PO Box 4210
Helena, MT   59604   406-444-2618

James Good, President
Offers services for the disabled.

4238 Montana Developmental Disability Council

PO Box 526
Helena, MT 59624　　　　406-444-1334
　　　　　　　　　　FAX: 406-444-5999
　　　　　　e-mail: dswingley@state.mt.us

Deborah Swingley, Executive Director

4239 Montana Protection & Advocacy for Persons with Disabilities

1410 8th Avenue
Helena, MT 59601　　　　406-449-6177
　　　　　　　　　　　800-245-4743

4240 Social Security - Helena Disability Determination

PO Box 4210
Helena, MT 59604
　　　　　　　　　　800-772-1213
　　　　　　　　　　www.ssa.gov

4241 Workers Compensation Board Montana

5 S Last Chance Gulch Street
Helena, MT 59601　　　　406-444-7794
　　　　　　　　　　FAX: 406-444-5963

Dr. Carl Swanson, Director

Nebraska

4242 International Dyslexia Association of NE Nebraska Branch

PO Box 6302
Lincoln, NE 68506　　　　402-486-2506
　　　　　　　　　　　800-222-3123
　　　　　　e-mail: jeforbes@ucollege.edu
　　　　　　　　　　www.interdys.org

Jennifer Forbes, President

Provides free information and referral services for diagnosis and tutoring for parents, educators, physicians, and individuals with dyslexia. The voice of our membership is heard in 48 countries. Membership includes yearly journal and quarterly newsletter. Call for conference dates.

4243 Nebraska Advocacy Services

215 Centennial Mall South
Suite 522
Lincoln, NE 68508　　　　402-475-6282
　　　　　　　　　　FAX: 402-474-3274
　　　　　　　　　　TDY:402-474-3183
　　　　　　　e-mail: nas@navix.net

Timothy Shaw, Director

Offers protection and advocacy services to people with developmental disabilities or mental illness. Direct assistance provided if issue within broad case priorities. Sliding scale fee. Information and referral at no cost.

4244 Nebraska Client Assistance Program

301 Centennial Mall South
Lincoln, NE 68508

Victoria Rasmussen, Director

4245 Nebraska Commission for the Blind & Visually Impaired

4600 Valley Road
Suite 100
Lincoln, NE 68510　　　　402-471-2891
　　　　　　　　　　FAX: 402-471-3009
　　　　　　　　　　TDY:402-471-2891
　　　　　　e-mail: pvanz@ncbvi.state.ne.us
　　　　　　　　　www.ncbvi.state.ne.us

Pearl Van Zandt, Ph.D., Executive Director

Offers services for the totally blind, legally blind, visually impaired, mentally retarded blind and more with health, counseling, educational, recreational, rehabilitation, computer training and professional training services.

4246 Nebraska Department of Health and Human Services, Division of Aging Services

PO Box 95044
Lincoln, NE 68509　　　　402-471-2307
　　　　　　　　　　FAX: 402-471-4619
　　　　　　e-mail: pattie.flury@hhss.state.ne.us

Pattie Flury, Long Term Care Liason

4247 Nebraska Department of Mental Health

301 Centennial Mall South
Lincoln, NE 68508　　　　402-471-4997
　　　　　　　　　　FAX: 402-423-7045
　　　　　　　　　www.nmhc-clinics.com

4248 Nebraska Department of Social Services of Medically Handicapped Children's Programs

1555 Colsax Street
Blair, NE 68008　　　　402-426-4129
　　　　　　　　　　FAX: 402-426-8960

Jeanne Garvin, MD, Medical Director
Roger Hillman, Program Specialist
Rolanda Snuttjer, Program Manager

Maternal and child health, Title V, children with special health care needs. Community based, statewide programs to facilitate diagnoses and care of children with disabilities and chronic medical conditions.

4249 Nebraska Developmental Disability Council

PO Box 95007
Lincoln, NE 68509　　　　402-471-2871
　　　　　　　　　　FAX: 402-471-0180

Mary Gorden, Director

4250 Social Security - Lincoln Disability Determination

PO Box 94987
Lincoln, NE 68509　　　　402-471-3649
　　　　　　　　　　　800-772-1213
　　　　　　　　　　FAX: 471-362-6
　　　　　　　　　　TDY:402-471-3659
　　　　　　e-mail: flloyd@nde4.nde.state.ne.us
　　　　　　　　　　www.ssa.gov

Frank Lloyd, Assistant Commissioner

4251 Workers Compensation Board Nebraska

PO Box 98908
Lincoln, NE 68509   402-471-2568
FAX: 402-471-1823

Dr. Carl Thompson, Director

Nevada

4252 Assistive Technology Center at NCEP - Nevada Community Enrichment Program

2820 W Charleston Boulevard
D-37
Las Vegas, NV 89102   702-259-1903
FAX: 702-259-1907

Terry Sjoberg, OTR/L, Manager
Robert Hogan, Executive Director
Reggie Bennett, Independent Living Coordinator

Provides information, demonstration and training to adults and children with disabilities in the use of microcomputers and other assistive technology product systems and devices. ATC offers peer screening, pre-service financial and resource planning, low interest loan program, technology matching, rehabilitation engineering, outreach training, and maintains a product information database.

4253 Nevada Assistive Technology Projects

711 S Stewart Street
Carson City, NV 89701   775-687-4452
FAX: 775-687-3292
e-mail: nvreach@powernet.netdirec

Donny Loux

Serves all ages and all disabilities through partnerships with community organizations. The NATP provides training, advocacy, funding, information and referral services, a newsletter and weekly television show.

4254 Nevada Bureau of Services to the Blind and Visually Impaired

505 E King Street
Carson City, NV 89701   775-687-5943
FAX: 775-687-5980
e-mail: mbecker@govmail.state.nv.us

Michael A. Becker, Chief
Barbara Legier, Deputy Chief

Offers services for the totally blind, legally blind, visually impaired, mentally retarded blind and more with health, counseling, educational, recreational, rehabilitation, computer training and professional training services.

4255 Nevada Department of Mental Health - Neuro Clinic

1001 Mountain Street
Suite 1H
Carson City, NV 89703   775-883-5757
FAX: 775-684-5966

Pat Hardy, Director

4256 Nevada Developmental Disability Council

505 E King Street
Suite 502
Carson City, NV 89701   775-687-4440
FAX: 687-329-2

4257 Nevada Disability Advocacy and Law Center NDALC

1311 North McCarron Boulevard
Suite 106
Sparks, NV 89431   775-333-7878
800-992-5715
FAX: 775-788-7825
TDY:702-788-7825
e-mail: reno@ndalc.org
www.ndalc.org

Jack Mayes, Executive Director
Lois Johnson, Deputy Director

Nevada's protection and advocacy system for the human legal, and service rights of individuals with disabilities. NDALC has offices in Reno and Las Vegas, with services provided statewide.

4258 Nevada Division for Aging - Carson City

3416 Goni Road, Suite 132
Carson City, NV 87706   775-687-4210
FAX: 775-687-4264
e-mail: dascc@govmail.state.nv.us
www.nvaging.net

Mary Liveratti, Administrator
Terry Stricker, Ombudsman Supervisor, Las Vegas

Provides services for seniors in Nevada including community based care. advocacy, and volunteer programs. Call write or e-mail for more information.

4259 Nevada Division for Aging - Las Vegas

340 N 11th Street
203
Las Vegas, NV 89101   702-486-6455
FAX: 702-486-3572

Develops, coordinates and delivers a comprehensive support service system in order for Nevada' senior citizens to lead independent, meaningful and dignified lives.

4260 Social Security - Carson City Disability Determination

505 E King Street
Carson City, NV 89701

800-772-1213
FAX: 775-684-4010
www.ssa.gov

Dan Mooney, Director

4261 State of Nevada Client Assistance Program

2450 Wrondel Street
Suite E
Reno, NV 89502   775-688-1440
800-633-9879
FAX: 775-688-1627

4262 Workers Compensation Board Nevada

6515 E Musser Street
Carson City, NV 89714   775-687-6492
FAX: 775-687-5786

New Hampshire

4263 **International Dyslexia Association of New England (CT, ME, NH, RI, VT)**

6 Seabee Street
Bedford, NH   03110   603-669-3719
                             800-222-3123
                    e-mail: info@interdys.org
                             www.interdys.org

Caryl Patten, President

Provides free information and referral services for diagnosis and tutoring for parents, educators, physicians, and individuals with dyslexia. The voice of our membership is heard in 48 countries. Membership includes yearly journal and quarterly newsletter. Call for conference dates.

4264 **New Hampshire Workers Compensation Board**

46 Donovan Street
Concord, NH   03301   603-225-2841
                        FAX: 603-226-6903

4265 **New Hampshire Assistive Technology Projects**

Department of Education
State of New Hampshire
Concord, NH   03824   603-862-2260
                        FAX: 603-228-2468

Jan Nisbet

A statewide program promoting assistive technology devices and services for persons of all ages with all disabilities.

4266 **New Hampshire Client Assistance Program**

57 Regional Drive
Concord, NH   03301   603-226-0111
                        FAX: 603-271-2837

4267 **New Hampshire Commission for Human Rights**

2 Chenell Drive
Concord, NH   03301   603-271-2767
                        FAX: 603-271-6339
                e-mail: humanrights@state.nh.us
                             www.state.nh.us

Katharine A. Daly, Executive Director

Offers legal help and information for disabled persons who are discriminated against in the housing employment or public accomodations.

4268 **New Hampshire Department of Mental Health**

State Office Park South
Concord, NH   03301   603-226-0111
                        FAX: 603-271-5058

Donald Shumway, Director
Paul Garmon

4269 **New Hampshire Developmental Disabilities Council**

10 Concord Street
Concord, NH   03301   603-226-0111
                        FAX: 271-115-6

Al Robeshaw, Director

Offers information, referral and support services to disabled persons.

4270 **New Hampshire Division of Developmental Services**

105 Pleasant Street
Concord, NH   03301   603-271-5034
                        FAX: 603-271-5166
                e-mail: sfox@dhhs.state.nh.us
                             www.nhdds.org

Susan Fox, Director

Developmental Services promotes opportunities for normal life experiences for persons with developmental disabilities and aquired brain disorders in all areas of community life: employment, housing, recreation, social relationships, and community association. Services and supports are organized throught a central state office and twelve private non-profit community area agencies. Family support is provided to families of children with chronic health conditions or are developmentally disabled.

4271 **New Hampshire Division of Elderly and Adult Services**

DEAS Office Park South
129 Pleasant Street
Concord, NH   03301   603-271-4394
                             800-351-1888
                        FAX: 603-271-4643

Catherine Keane, Director
Mary Maggioncaida, Manager, Program Dev.

State agency on aging services; limited services to incapacitated adults, age 18 and older.

4272 **New Hampshire Governor's Commission on Disability**

57 Regional Drive
Concord, NH   03301   603-271-2773
                             800-852-3405
                        FAX: 603-271-2837
                e-mail: mjenkins@gov.state.nh.us

Michael Jenkins, Executive Director

4273 **New Hampshire Protection & Advocacy for Persons with Disabilities**

PO Box 3660
Concord, NH   03302   603-225-0432
                             800-834-1721
                        FAX: 603-225-2077
                e-mail: advocacy@drcnh.org

Donna Woodfin, Executive Director
Ron Lospennato, Legal Director

Legal services for individuals with disabilities; I & R.

4274 **Social Security - Concord Disability Determination**

78 Regional Drive
Building JB
Concord, NH   03301

                             800-772-1213
                             www.ssa.gov

4275 Workers Compensation Board New Hampshire

95 Pleasant Street
Concord, NH 03301   603-271-3483
                                       800-272-4353
                                FAX: 603-271-6149
e-mail: workerscomp@labor.state.nh.us
www.labor.state.nh.us

New Jersey

4276 Families Magazine

New Jersey Developmental Disabilities Council
20 W State Street
PO Box 700
Trenton, NJ 08625   609-292-3745
                                 FAX: 609-292-7114
                         e-mail: njddc@njddc.org
                                   www.njddc.org

Ethan Ellis, Executive Director/Editor
Norman Reim, Managing Editor

Quarterly magazine for people with disabilities, their
families and the public, features family profiles,
news, columns and the New Jersey Family support
councils newsletter.

Quarterly

**4277 International Dyslexia Association of NJ New
Jersey Branch**

Box 32
Long Valley, NJ 07853   908-879-0466
                                 FAX: 908-879-0466
                         e-mail: info@interdys.org
                                  www.interdys.org

David Katz, President

Provides free information and referral services for
diagnosis and tutoring for parents, educators, physicians, and individuals with dyslexia. The voice of our
membership is heard in 48 countries. Membership
includes yearly journal and quarterly newsletter. Call
for conference dates.

Quarterly

4278 New Jersey Client Assistance Program

210 South Broad Street
3rd Floor
Trenton, NJ 08608   609-292-9742
                                       800-922-7233
                                 FAX: 609-777-0187
                         e-mail: adudea@njpanda.org
                                  www.njpanda.org

Sarah Mitchell, Extecutive Director

The Client Assistance Program (CAP) assists persons
with disabilities who are seeking or receiving services from federally funded rehabilitation programs.
CAP provides legal and nonlegal individual and systems advocacy.

**4279 New Jersey Commission for the Blind and
Visually Impaired**

153 Halsey Street
6th Floor, PO Box 47017
Newark, NJ 07102   201-648-2324
                                 FAX: 973-648-7364
                                 TDY:201-648-4559
                      e-mail: jchilton@dhs.state.nj.us

Jamie C. Hilton, Executive Director
Pamela Gaston, Executive Assistant

Offers services for the totally blind, legally blind,
visually impaired, deaf blind and more with eye
health, counseling, educational, recreational, rehabilitation, computer training and vocational services.

4280 New Jersey Department of Aging

S Broad and Front Street
Trenton, NJ 08625   609-530-5200
                                 FAX: 609-633-6609

Ruth Leader, Director

**4281 New Jersey Department of Health/Special Child
Health Services**

50 E State Street
Trenton, NJ 08608   609-392-3000
                                 FAX: 609-292-3580
                      e-mail: 6k1@dohstate.nj.us

Barbara Kern, Director

4282 New Jersey Division of Mental Health Servi ces

50 East State Street
PO B727
Trenton, NJ 08625   609-777-0700
                                       800-382-6717
                                 FAX: 609-777-0662
                  e-mail: dmhsmail@dhs.state.nj.us
www.state.nj.us/humanservices/dhsmhl.htm

Alan G. Kaufman, Director

Oversees the public mental health system for the state
of New Jersey. Operates six regional and specialty
psychiatric hospitals, and contracts with over 125
not-for-profit agencies to provide a comprehensive
system of community mental health services throughout all counties in the state.

**4283 New Jersey Governor's Liaison to the Office of
Disability Employment Policy**

New Jersey Dept of Labor
John Fitch Plaza, PO Box 110
Trenton, NJ 08625   609-292-2323
                                 FAX: 609-633-9271
                  e-mail: cmycoff@dol.state.nj.us
                                www.state.nj.us/labor

Mark B. Boyd, Commisioner
Al Kirk, Assistant Director
Rick Shanberg, Program Assistant

The Division of Vocational Rehabilitation Services
providesa vocational rehabilitation services to prepare and place in employment eligilbe individuals
with disabilities who, because of their disabling conditions, would otherwise be unable to secure and/or
mantain employment

4284 New Jersey Protection & Advocacy for Persons with Disabilities

Trenton, NJ 08625   609-530-5200
FAX: 609-292-6610

Robert Nickolas, Director

4285 People with Disabilities Magazine

New Jersey Devlopmental Disabilities Council
20 PO Box 700
Trenton, NJ 08625   609-292-3745
FAX: 609-292-7114
e-mail: njddc@njddc.org
www.njddc.org

Ethan Ellis, Director/Editor
Susan Richmond, Assistant Director
Norman Reim, Communications

A free magazine for people with disabilities, their families and the public about disability topics such as personal assistance, deinstitutionalization, health care and community living. Published by the New Jersey Developmental Disabilities council, a federally funded advocacy and policy advisory body. The council has 30 members - 15 consumer/product volunteers and 15 professionals.

48 pages Quarterly

4286 Social Security Administration

50 E State Street
Trenton, NJ 08608
    800-772-1213
www.ssa.gov

Social Security disability is a social insurance program that workers and employers pay for with their Social Security taxes. Eligibility is based on your work history, and the amount of your benefit is based on your carnings. Social Security also has a disability program for people with limited income and resources- the Supplemental Security Income (SSI) program. For more information on these federal programs, please call our nationwide toll-free number.

New Mexico

4287 New Mexico Workers Compensation Board

PO Box 27198
Albuquerque, NM 87125   505-256-3529
FAX: 505-841-6840

Steven Kennedy, Director

4288 New Mexico Client Assistance Program

1720 Louisiana Boulevard NE
Suite 204
Albuquerque, NM 87110   505-260-4330
800-342-4687
FAX: 505-256-3184
e-mail: nmpanda@nmprotection-advocacy.com
www.nmprotection-advocacy.com

James Jackson, Director

4289 New Mexico Commission for the Blind

Pera Building
Room 553
Santa Fe, NM 87503   505-827-4479
888-513-7968
FAX: 505-827-4475
TDY:505-243-6427
e-mail: greg.trapp@state.nm.us
www.cftb.state.nm.us

Greg Trapp, Executive Director

Offers services for the totally blind, legally blind, visually impaired, mentally retarded blind and more with health, counseling, educational, recreational, rehabilitation, computer training and professional training services.

4290 New Mexico Department of Health - Children's Medical Services

1190 S Saint Francis Drive
Santa Fe, NM 87505   505-827-2548
FAX: 505-827-1697
e-mail: lchristiansen@doh.state.nm

Lynn Christiansen, Program Manager

Title V MCH Program for children with special health care needs from birth to age 21 years. Services provided include: diagnosis, medical intervention, clinics and service coordination.

4291 New Mexico Governor's Committee on Concern of the Handicapped

491 Old Santa Fe Trail
Santa Fe, NM 87501   505-471-5242
FAX: 505-827-6328

4292 New Mexico Protection & Advocacy for Persons with Disabilities

1720 Louisiana Boulevard NE
Suite 204
Albuquerque, NM 87110   505-256-3100
800-432-4687
FAX: 505-256-3184
e-mail: nmpanda@inmprotection-advocacy.com
www.nmprotection-advocacy.com

James Jackson, Director

4293 New Mexico State Agency on Aging

228 East Palace Avenue
La Villa Rivera Bldg., Ground Floor
Santa Fe, NM 87501   505-827-7640
800-432-6040
FAX: 505-827-7649
www.nmaging.state.nm

Michelle Lujan Grisham, Director
Ross Becker, Deputy Director

4294 New Mexico Technology

435 Saint Michaels Drive
Suite D
Santa Fe, NM 87505   505-754-2437

Andrew Winnegar, Director Program

A statewide program promoting assistive technology devices and services for persons of all ages with all disabilities.

4295 Social Security - Santa Fe Disability Determination

604 W San Mateo Road
Santa Fe, NM 87505

FAX: 505-827-3512
e-mail: terryb@oscar.state.nm.us

Terry Brigance, Director

4296 Southwest Branch of the International Dyslexia Association

PO Box 25891
Albuquerque, NM 87125 505-255-8234
FAX: 505-262-8547
e-mail: swida84@hotmail.com
www.interdys.org

Mary Gilroy, President

Provides free information and referral services for diagnosis and tutoring for parents, educators, physicians, and individuals with dyslexia. The voice of our membership is heard in 48 countries. Membership includes yearly journal and quarterly newsletter. Call for conference dates.

4297 Workers Compensation Board New Mexico

PO Box 27198
Albuquerque, NM 87125 505-841-6039
FAX: 841-606-0

Steven Kennedy, Director

New York

4298 International Dyslexia Association of NY Buffalo Branch

10348 Boston State Road
Springville, NY 14141 715-941-5285
800-222-3123
e-mail: info@interdys.org
www.interdys.org

Denise Lawton, Contact

Provides free information and referral services for diagnosis and tutoring for parents, educators, physicians, and individuals with dyslexia. The voice of our membership is heard in 48 countries. Membership includes yearly journal and quarterly newsletter. Call for conference dates. Other locations available in New York State.

4299 NYS Commission on Quality of Care for the Mentally Disabled

401 State Street
Schenectady, NY 12305 518-381-7000
FAX: 518-381-7079
www.cqc.state.ny.us

4300 NYS Office of Advocate for Persons with Disabilities

1 Empire Plaza
Suite 1001
Albany, NY 12223 518-474-5567
800-522-4369
e-mail: information@oapwd.state.ny.us
www.state.ny.us/disabledadvocate

Richard Warrender, State Advocate

4301 NYSARC

393 Delaware Avenue
Delmar, NY 12054 518-439-8311
800-724-2094
e-mail: brandtm@nysarc.org
www.nysarc.org

Marc Brandt, Executive Director

4302 National Alliance for the Mentally Ill of NY State

260 Washington Avenue
Albany, NY 12210 518-462-2000
800-950-3228
e-mail: naminys@knick.net
www.naminys.org

Michael Silverberg, President

4303 New York Client Assistance Program

99 Washington Avenue
Suite 1002
Albany, NY 12210 518-869-1543
FAX: 518-474-2652
www.cacstate.ny.us

4304 New York Department of Aging

New York State Plaza
2
Albany, NY 12223 212-442-1000

Jane Gould, Director

4305 New York Department of Handicapped Children

Department of Health
Tower Building
Room 780
Albany, NY 12237 518-474-0881

Thomas Blake, Acting Bureau Chief

4306 New York State Commission for the Blind

40 North Pearl Street
Albany, NY 12207 518-473-1801
FAX: 518-486-5819

Thomas Robertson, Associate Commissioner

Offers services for the totally blind, legally blind, visually impaired, mentally retarded blind and more with health, counseling, educational, recreational, rehabilitation, computer training and professional training services.

4307 New York State Commission on Quality of Care

401 State Street
Schenectady, NY 12305 518-381-7098
FAX: 518-381-7095
e-mail: marcelc@cqc.state.ny.us
www.cqc.state.ny.us

Marcel Chaine, Director of Advocacy Services

4308 New York State Congress of Parents and Teachers

One Way Square
Albany, NY 12205 518-452-8808

e-mail: office@nypta.com

Jane Bernhard, President

4309 New York State Office of Advocate for Persons with Disabilities

1 Empire State Plaza
Suite 1001
Albany, NY 12223 518-474-5567
800-522-4369
FAX: 518-473-6005
TDY:800-522-4369
e-mail: information@advoc4disabled.state.ny.us
www.advoc4disabled.state.ny.us

Rosemary Lamb, Associate Advocate
Gregory Jones, Esq., Counsel
Lisaard Rosano-Kaczkowski, TRAID Project Director

Provides information and referral services; administers NYS Tech Art Project; and promotes implementation of disability-related laws.

4310 New York State Office of Mental Health

44 Holland Avenue
Albany, NY 12229
800-597-8481
FAX: 518-474-1846
www.omh.state.ny.us

James L. Stone, MSW, CSW, Commissioner

4311 New York State TRAID Project

NYS One Empire State Plaza
Suite 1001
Albany, NY 12223 518-474-2825
800-522-4369
e-mail: traid@emi.com
www.advoc4disabled.state.ny.us

Deborah Buck, Project Director

4312 Parent to Parent of New York State

500 Balltown Road
Schenectady, NY 12304 518-381-4350
800-305-8817
e-mail: Parent2par@aol.com
www.parenttoparentnys.org

Carolyn Schimanski, Director

4313 Protection and Advocacy Agency of NY

401 State Street
Schenectady, NY 12305 518-381-7098

e-mail: marcelc@cqc.state.ny.us
www.cqc.state.ny.us

Marcel Chaine, Director Advocacy Bureau

4314 Regional ADA Technical Assistance Center

354 South Broad Street
Trenton, NY 08608 609-392-4004
800-949-4232
e-mail: BTACUPNJ@aol.com
www.disabilityyact.com

4315 Regional Early Childhood Director Center

Box 601
601 Elmwood Avenue
Rochester, NY 14642 716-275-2263
800-462-4344

Michael Reif, Director

4316 Resources for Children with Special Needs

200 Park Avenue South
Suite 816
New York, NY 10003 212-667-4650

e-mail: info@resourcesnyc.org
www.resourcesnyc.org

Karen Schlesinger, Director

4317 Rockland County Center for the Physically Handicapped

Jawonio Vocational Center
260 S Little Tor Road
New City, NY 10956 845-634-4648

Esther White

Offers vocational evaluation, training, counseling and job placement services.

4318 Singeria/Metropolitan Parent Center

15 West 65th Street
6th Floor
New York, NY 10023 212-496-1300

e-mail: Sinergia@panix.com
www.sinergiany.org

Donald Lash, Acting Executive Director

4319 Social Security - Albany Disability Determination

40 N Pearl Street
Albany, NY 12243 518-474-6812
800-772-1213
FAX: 518-473-9286
TDY:518-474-7501
www.ssa.gov

Thomas A. Robertson, Assistant Commissioner

4320 State Agency for the Blind and Visually Impaired

40 North Pearl Street
Albany, NY 12243 518-473-1801

www.dfa.state.ny.us/cbvh

Thomas Robertson, Associated Commissioner

4321 State Developmental Disabilities Planning Council

155 Washington Avenue
2nd Floor
Albany, NY 12210 518-486-7505
800-395-3372
e-mail: scarey@nycap.rr.com
www.ddpc.state.ny.us

Sheila Carey, Executive Director

4322 State Education Agency Rural Representative

Education Building Annex
Room 876
Albany, NY 12234 518-474-3936

e-mail: sspear@mail.nysed.gov
www.nysed.gov

Suzanne Spear, Supervisor

4323 State Mental Health Agency

44 Holland Avenue
Albany, NY 12229   518-474-4403

e-mail: cocojls@omh.state.ny.us

James Stone, Commissioner

4324 State Mental Health Representative for Children and Youth

44 Holland Avenue
Albany, NY 12229   518-473-6902

e-mail: cocompz@omh.state.ny.us

Michale Zuber, Associate Commissioner

4325 State Mental Retardation Program

44 Holland Avenue
Albany, NY 12229   518-473-1997

www.omr.state.ny.us

Thomas Maul, Commissioner

4326 State Vocational Rehabilitation Agency

1 Commerce Plaza
Room 1606
Albany, NY 12234   518-474-2714

www.nysed.gov

Lawrence Gloeckler, Deputy Commissioner

4327 TRAID, Project NYS Office of Adv, for Persons with Disabilities

1 Empire State Plaza
Suite 1001
Albany, NY 12223

800-522-4369
TDY:518-473-4231
e-mail: information@oapwdoswd.state.ny.us
www.advocadvoc4disabled.state.ny.us

Richard Warddner, State Advocate

Technology related assistance for individuals with all disabilities. Hoblo esponol.

4328 United We Stand of New York

312 S 3rd Street
Brooklyn, NY 11211   718-302-4313

e-mail: uwsofny@aol.com

Lourdes Rivera-Putz, Program Director

4329 Univ. Afiliated Program/Rose F. Kennedy Center

1410 Pelham Parkway South
Bronx, NY 10461   718-430-8522

hcohen@accom.yu.edu

Hebert J. Cohen, Director

4330 University of Rochester Medical Center

601 Elmwood Avenue
Box 671
Rochester, NY 14642   716-275-2986

e-mail: phil_davison@urmc.rochester.edu
www.urmc.rochester.edu/strong/scdd

Philp W. Davidson, Director

4331 VSA Arts of New York City

18-05 215 Street Bayside
Suite 15N
Bayside, NY 11360   718-225-6305

e-mail: Bbvsanyc@msn.com

Dr. Bebe Berenstein, Director

4332 WIHD/ University Affiliated Program

Weschester Medical Center
Valhalla, NY 10595   914-493-8204

e-mail: Ansley_Bacon@NYMC.edu
www.nymc.edu/wihd

Ansley Bacon, Director

4333 Workers Compensation Board New York

180 Livingston Street
Brooklyn, NY 11248   718-222-4302

North Carolina

4334 Developmental Disability Services Section

325 N Salisbury Street
Mail Service Center 3006
Raleigh, NC 27699   919-733-3654
FAX: 919-733-3604
e-mail: pat.porter@ncmail.net
www.dhhs.state.nc.us/mhddsas/dd

Patricia Porter, Chief
Stan Slawinski Ph.D., Assistant Chief

4335 International Dyslexia Association of NC North Carolina Branch

2005 Riverview Drive
Clayton, NC 27520   252-243-8843
800-222-3123
e-mail: info@interdys.org
www.interdys.org

Jean Rackley, President

Provides free information and referral services for diagnosis and tutoring for parents, educators, physicians, and individuals with dyslexia. The voice of our membership is heard in 48 countries. Membership includes yearly journal and quarterly newsletter. Call for conference dates.

4336 North Carolina Workers Compensation Board

430 N Salisbury Street
Raleigh, NC 27611   919-676-2288
FAX: 919-715-0282
www.comp.state.nc.us/

J Howard Bunn Jr., Director

4337 North Carolina Assistive Technology Projects

1110 Navaho Drive
Suite 101
Raleigh, NC   27609   919-676-2288
                            FAX: 919-850-2792
                  e-mail: ncatp@minespring.com
                      www.mindspring.com/~ncatp

Ricki Cook, Project Director
Annette Lauber, Funding Specialist
Jacquelyne Gordon, Consumer Resource Specialist

The North Carolina Assistive Technology Project exists to create a statewide, consumer-responsive system of assistive technology services for all North Carolinians with disabilities. The project's activities impact children and adults with disabilities across all aspects of their lives.

4338 North Carolina Children & Youth Branch

1928 Mail Service Center
Raleigh, NC   27699   919-733-7437
                            800-737-3028
                      FAX: 919-715-3187

Carol Tant, Head, Children & Youth Branch
Cheryl Walker, Unit Manager, Spec. Service
Dianne Tyson, Help Line Manager

4339 North Carolina Client Assistance Program

2801 Mail Service Center
Raleigh, NC   27699   919-733-6300
                      FAX: 919-715-2456
             e-mail: kathy.brack@ncmail.net

Kathy Brack, Director

4340 North Carolina Developmental Disabilities

1001 Navaho Drive
Suite GL-103
Raleigh, NC   27609   919-850-2833
                            800-357-6916
                      FAX: 919-850-2895
            e-mail: Holly.Riddle@ncmail.net
                      www.nc-ddc.org

Holly Riddle

A planning council established to assure that individuals with developmental disabilities and their families participate in the planning of and have access to culturally competent services, supports, and other assistance and opportunities that promote independence, productivity, and integration and inclusion into the community; and to promote, through systemic change, capacity building and advocacy activities, a consumer and family-centered comprehensive system.

4341 North Carolina Division of Aging

2101 Mail Service Center
Raleigh, NC   27699   919-733-3983
                      FAX: 919-733-0443
          www.dhhs.state.nc.us/aging/home.htm

Karen Gottovi, Director

4342 North Carolina Industrial Commission

430 N Salisbury Street
Raleigh, NC   27603   919-733-3484
                      FAX: 919-715-0282
                      www.comp.state.nc.us

J. Howard Bunn, Jr., Chairman

4343 Social Security - Raleigh Disability Determination

325 N Salisbury Street
Raleigh, NC   27603
                            800-772-1213
                            www.ssa.gov

North Dakota

4344 Division of Mental Health and Substance Abuse

600 South 2nd Street
Suite 1D & 1E
Bismark, ND   58504   701-328-8924
                            800-755-2745
                      FAX: 701-328-8969
                      TDY:701-328-8968
             e-mail: solark@state.nd.us
          www.discovernd.com/healthsafety

Karen Romiglarson, Director
Bonnie Selzler, Assistant Director,Mental Health
Don Wright, Ass't. Dir. for Substance Abuse

4345 North Dakota Workers Compensation Board

4007 N State Street
Bismarck, ND   58501   701-223-6372

4346 North Dakota Client Assistance Program

600 South 2nd Street
Suite 1B
Bismarck, ND   58504   701-328-8947
                            800-207-6122
                      FAX: 701-328-8969

4347 North Dakota Department of Aging

State Capitol Building
Bismarck, ND   58505   701-223-6372

Larry Brewster, Administrator

4348 North Dakota Department of Human Services

Children's Special Health Services
600 E Boulevard Avenue
Department 325
Bismarck, ND   58505   701-328-2436
                            800-755-2714
                      FAX: 701-328-2359
             e-mail: dhscshs@state.nd.us
          www.state.nd.us/humanservices/

Tamara Gallud-Millner, Deputy Director

Provides services for children special health care needs and their families. Provides services and diagnosis, treatment, clinics, information, referral and care coordinators.

4349 North Dakota Developmental Disability Council - Dacotah Foundation Bldg

600 S 2nd Street
Suite 1B
Bismarck, ND 58504   701-328-8953
                          FAX: 701-328-8969

4350 Protection & Advocacy Project

400 E Broadway Avenue
Suite 616
Bismarck, ND 58501   701-328-2950
                          800-472-2670
                      FAX: 701-328-3934
              e-mail: panda@state.nd.us
                      www.ndpanda.org

Teresa Larsen, Executive Director

The Protection and Advocacy is a state agency whose purpose is to advocate for, and protect the rights of people with disabilities. The Protection and Advocacy Project has programs to serve people with developmental disabilities, mental illnesses, and other types of disabilities. The projects programs and services are free to eligible individuals.

4351 Social Security - Bismarck Disability Determination

400 E Broadway Avenue
Suite 303
Bismarck, ND 58501

                          800-772-1213
                          www.ssa.gov

4352 Workers Compensation Board North Dakota

4007 State Street
Bismarck, ND 58501   701-224-3800

Ohio

**4353 Bureau for Children with Medical Handicaps
Ohio Department of Health**

PO Box 1603
Columbus, OH 43216   614-466-1549
                      FAX: 614-728-3616
          e-mail: bcmb@gw.odh.state.us
                  www.odh.state.oh.us

James Bryant, MD, Bureau Chief

Provides funding for the diagnosis, treatment and coordination of services for eligible Ohio children, under age 21, with medical handicaps; conducts quality assurance activities to establish standards of care and determine unmet needs of children with handicaps and their families; collaborates with public health nurses to increase access to care; and assists families to access and use third party resources. Conducts a separate program for adults with cystic fibrosis.

4354 Epilepsy Council of Greater Cincinnati

3 Centennial Plaza
895 Central Avenue
Cincinnati, OH 45202   513-721-2905

                  e-mail: www.ecgc.net
                      www.ecgc@fuse.net

Marge Frommeyer, Executive Director

4355 International Dyslexia Association of OH Central Ohio Branch

3545 Fishinger Boulevard
Columbus, OH 43026   614-899-5711
                          800-222-3123
              e-mail: info@interdys.org
                      www.interdys.org

Anita Gardner, Co-President
Karen Bradford, Co-President
Cameron Jones, President

Provides free information and referral services for diagnosis and tutoring for parents, educators, physicians, and individuals with dyslexia. The voice of our membership is heard in 48 countries. Membership includes yearly journal and quarterly newsletter. Call for conference dates. Other locations available in Ohio state.

4356 Ohio Client Assistance Program

30 E Broad Street
Room 120
Columbus, OH 43215   614-466-6920
                      FAX: 614-752-4197

4357 Ohio Department of Aging

50 West Broad Street
9th Floor
Columbus, OH 43215   614-466-5500
                          888-243-5678
                      FAX: 614-466-5741
    www.state.oh.us/age or www.ohio.gov/age/

Joan W Lawrence, Director
Steve Proctor, Communications Chief

The department serves & represents about 2 million Ohioans age 60 & older. They advocate for the needs of all older citizens with emphasis on improving the quality of life, helping senior citizens live active, healthy, & independent lives, & promoting positive attitudes toward aging & older people. Committed to helping the frail elderly who choose to remain at home by providing home & community based services, their goal is to promote the level of choice, independence & self-care.

4358 Ohio Department of Mental Health

30 E Broad Street
Suite 1180
Columbus, OH 43215   614-488-1294
                      FAX: 614-466-1571

Mike Hogan, Director

4359 Ohio Developmental Disability Council

8 East Long Street
12th Floor
Columbus, OH 43215   614-466-5205
                          800-766-7426
                      FAX: 614-466-0298
                      TDY:614-644-5530
      e-mail: david.zwyer@dmr.state.oh.us
                  www.state.oh.us/ddc

David Zwyer, Director

The Ohio Developmental Disabilities Council is one of 55 Councils found in all states and territories which provides funding for grant projects. The DD Council is a planning and advocacy agency that seeks to improve the lives of Ohioans with disabilities.

4360 Ohio Governor's Council on People with Disabilities

400 East Campus View Boulevard
Columbus, OH 43235 614-438-1255
FAX: 614-438-1274

Karla Lortz, Executive Secretary
Maureen Fitzgerald, Program Specialist
Marcella Eblin, Secretary

Advisory body to the governor and the legislature on issues that concern Ohioans with disabilities. State liaison to President's Committee on Employment of People with Disabilities and National Organization on Disability.

4361 Ohio Legal Rights Service

8 E Long Street
5th Floor
Columbus, OH 43215 614-466-7264
800-282-9181
FAX: 614-644-1888
www.state.oh.us/OLRS/

4362 Ohio Rehabilitation Services Commission

400 E Campus View Boulevard
Columbus, OH 43235 614-438-1200
FAX: 614-438-1257
www.state.oh.us/rsc

Robert Rabbe, Director

Offers rehabilitation information and referrals to the disabled individual.

4363 Ohio Worker's Compensation Board

246 N High Street
Columbus, OH 43266

4364 Social Security - Columbus Disability Determination

400 E Campus View Boulevard
Columbus, OH 43235
800-772-1213
FAX: 614-438-1251
www.ssa.gov

Robert Rabbe, Director

4365 Workers Compensation Board Ohio

246 N High Street
Columbus, OH 43215 614-466-4110

Oklahoma

4366 Oklahoma Workers Compensation Board

1915 N Stiles
Oklahoma City, OK 73105 405-670-3100

4367 Oklahoma Client Assistance Program

4300 N Lincoln Boulevard
Oklahoma City, OK 73105 405-424-8378
FAX: 405-943-7550

Helene Kutz, Director

4368 Oklahoma Department of Aging

PO Box 25352
Oklahoma City, OK 73125 504-702-6114
FAX: 405-521-2086

Roy Keen, Director

4369 Oklahoma Department of Children with Disabilities

4001 N Lincoln Boulevard
4th Floor
Oklahoma City, OK 73105 405-528-1500

Charles Brodt, Asst. Director

4370 Oklahoma Department of Human Services Aging Services Division

PO Box 25352
Oklahoma City, OK 73125 405-521-4358
FAX: 405-521-2086

Roy Keen, Division Administrator

4371 Oklahoma Department of Mental Health & Substance Abuse Services

1200 NE 13th Street
PO Box 53277
Oklahoma City, OK 73152 405-522-3908
FAX: 405-522-3650
www.odmhsas.org

Terry Cline, Ph.D., Commissioner

4372 Oklahoma Developmental Disability Council

PO Box 25352
Oklahoma City, OK 73125 405-521-4358

4373 Oklahoma Protection & Advocacy for Persons with Disabilities

9726 E 42nd Street
Tulsa, OK 74146 918-665-8084
FAX: 918-743-6220

4374 Oklahoma State Office of Rehabilitation Services, Visually Impaired

2409 North Kelly Street
Oklahoma City, OK 73126 405-843-5929

Offers services for the totally blind, legally blind, visually impaired, mentally retarded blind and more with health, counseling, educational, recreational, rehabilitation, computer training and professional training services.

4375 Social Security - Oklahoma City Disability Determination

PO Box 25352
Oklahoma City, OK 73125
800-772-1213
FAX: 405-521-6408
www.ssa.gov

George Miller, Director

4376 Workers Compensation Board Oklahoma

1915 N Stiles Avenue
Oklahoma City, OK 73105

Oregon

4377 International Dyslexia Association of OR Oregon Branch

PO Box 3677
Portland, OR 97208   503-774-9554
800-530-2234
e-mail: orbida@aracnet.com
www.interdys.org

Gary B Wright, President

Provides free information and referral services for diagnosis and tutoring for parents, educators, physicians, and individuals with dyslexia. The voice of our membership is heard in 48 countries. Membership includes yearly journal and quarterly newsletter. Call for conference dates.

4378 Oregon Advocacy Center

620 SW 5th Avenue
5th Floor
Portland, OR 97204   503-243-2081
FAX: 503-243-1738
e-mail: oradvocacy@aol.com

The protection and advocacy system for Oregon.

4379 Oregon Assistive Technology Projects

2045 Silverton Road NE
Salem, OR 97310   503-362-3645

Joy Rostson

A statewide program promoting assistive technology devices and services for persons of all ages with all disabilities.

4380 Oregon Client Assistance Program

620 South West 5th Avenue
Suite 500
Portland, OR 97204   503-243-2081
FAX: 503-243-1738
www.oradvocacy.org

4381 Oregon Commission for the Blind

535 SE 12th Avenue
Portland, OR 97214   503-731-3221
FAX: 503-731-3230
TDY:503-731-3224
www.cfb.state.or.us

Linda Mock, Administrator
Daeia Johnson, Director of Rehabilitation Servi

Offers vocational rehabilitation and independent living services for the totally blind, legally blind, visually impaired, mentally retarded blind and more with health, counseling, educational, recreational, rehabilitation, computer training and professional training services.

4382 Oregon Department of Aging

313 Public Service Building
Salem, OR 97310   503-304-3400
FAX: 503-304-3434

James Wilson, Administrator

4383 Oregon Department of Mental Health

2600 Center Street NE
Salem, OR 97310   503-945-9499
FAX: 503-945-2807

Stan Mazurhart, Director

4384 Oregon Developmental Disability Council on Developmental Disabilities

540 24th Place NE
Salem, OR 97301   503-945-9941
800-292-4154
FAX: 503-945-9947
e-mail: oddc@od.com
www.oddc.org

4385 Social Security - Salem Disability Determination

2045 Silverton Road NE
Salem, OR 97310   800-722-1213
www.ssa.gov

4386 Vocational Rehabilitation Division

Vocational Rehabilitation Division
500 Summer Street NE
Salem, OR 97310   503-945-5880
FAX: 503-947-5025
TDY:503-378-3933

Joil A. Southwell, Administrator
Lynnae Ruttledge, Asst. Administrator

The mission of the Division is to assist Oregonians with disabilities to achieve and maintain employment and independence.

Pennsylvania

4387 Disability Compliance Bulletin

LRP Publications
747 Dresher Road
PO Box 980
Horsham, PA 19044   215-784-0941
800-341-7874
FAX: 215-784-9639
e-mail: custserve@lrp.com
www.lrp.com

Thomas D'Agostino Esq., author
Honora McDowelll, Product Group Mgr.

This biweekly newsletter gives you timely coverage and insightful analyses of the latest developments in disability law. You'll learn the most recent case law dealing with the Americans with Disabilities Act, the Family and Medical Leave Act, and more. Disability Compliance Bulletin will help you understand the laws' obligations and show you emerging legal trends. *$165.00*

24 pages BiWeekly

4388 International Dyslexia Association Philadelphia Branch

PO Box 251
Bryn Mawr, PA   19010   610-527-1548
800-222-3123
FAX: 610-527-5011
e-mail: info@interdys.org
www.interdys.org

Jann Glider, Ph.D., President
Janet Hoopes, Ph.D., Office Manager

Provides free information and referral services for diagnosis and tutoring for parents, educators, physicians, and individuals with dyslexia. The voice of our membership is heard in 48 countries. Membership includes yearly journal and quarterly newsletter. Call for conference dates.

4389 Pennsylvania Workers Compensation Board

1171 S Cameron Street
Room 103
Harrisburg, PA   17104   717-939-9551
FAX: 717-772-0342

4390 Pennsylvania Bureau of Blindness

PO Box 2675
Harrisburg, PA   17105   717-787-6176
FAX: 717-787-3210
e-mail: jbirt@dpw.state.pa.us

Jay Birt, Interim Director

Offers services for the totally blind, legally blind, visually impaired, mentally retarded blind and more with health, counseling, educational, recreational, rehabilitation, computer training and professional training services.

4391 Pennsylvania Client Assistance Program

1650 Arch Street
Suite 2310
Philadelphia, PA   19103   215-988-4750
FAX: 215-555-7602

4392 Pennsylvania Department of Aging

400 Market Street
Harrisburg, PA   17101   717-238-9948
FAX: 717-783-6842

Richard Browed, Director
Linda Rhodes, Secretary

4393 Pennsylvania Department of Children with Disabilities

PO Box 90
Harrisburg, PA   17108   717-783-1289
FAX: 717-772-0323

Donna Wenger, Acting Director

4394 Pennsylvania Department of Mental Health

120 S Street
Harrisburg, PA   17101   717-697-8586
FAX: 717-787-5394

Susan Reider, Director

4395 Pennsylvania Developmental Disabilities Council

569 Forum Building
Harrisburg, PA   17120   717-939-9551
FAX: 717-772-0738
e-mail: paddpc@aol.com

Graham Mulholland, Executive Director

4396 Pennsylvania Protection & Advocacy for Persons with Disabilities

1414 North Cameron Street
Second Floor
Harrisburg, PA   17103   717-236-8110
800-692-7443
FAX: 717-236-0192
e-mail: ppa@ppainc.org
www.ppainc.org

Provide advocacy, information and referral for persons with disabilities and mental illness issues.

4397 Public Interest Law Center of Philadelphia

125 South 9th Street
Suite 700
Philadelphia, PA   19107   215-985-1113
FAX: 215-627-3183
e-mail: pobint@aol.com

Mike Churchill, Chief Counsel
Judith Gramd, Director

A non-profit, public interest law firm with a Disabilities Project specializing in class action suits brought by individuals and organizations.

4398 Social Security - Harrisburg Disability Determination

7th & Forster Street
Harrisburg, PA   17120   717-787-5244
800-442-6351
TDY:717-783-8917
e-mail: ovr@dli.state.pa.us
www.ssa.gov

Susan Aldrete, Executive Director

4399 Workers Compensation Board Pennsylvania

1171 S Cameron Street
Suite 103
Harrisburg, PA   17104   717-783-5421
FAX: 717-772-0342

Rhode Island

4400 Department of Mental Health, Retardation and Hospitals of Rhode Island

14 Harrington Road
Cranston, RI   02920   401-462-3201
FAX: 401-462-3204

A. Kathryn Power, Director

State department responsible for creating and administering systems of care for individuals with disabilities, specifically focused on mental health and mental illness; developmental disabilities, substance abuse and long term hospital care.

4401 Rhode Island Department of Aging

160 Pine Street
Providence, RI   02903   401-277-2894

Maureen Maigret, Director

**4402 Rhode Island Department of Handicapped
Children**

3 Capitol Hill
Providence, RI   02908   401-277-2401

Peter Simon

4403 Rhode Island Department of Mental Health

Cottage 405 Ct B
Cranston, RI   02920   401-467-9200
                              FAX: 401-464-2005

Reed Cosper, Director

4404 Rhode Island Developmental Disabilities Council

600 New London Avenue
Cranston, RI   02920   401-462-3588
                              FAX: 401-462-3570
                  e-mail: ac808.osfn.rhilinet@gov
                              www.riddc.org

Marie Citrone, Executive Director

The Rhode Island Developmental Disabilities Council works to make Rhode Island a better place for people with developmental disabilities to live, work, go to school, and be part of their community.

**4405 Rhode Island Governor's Committee on the
Disabled**

555 Valley Street
Building 51
Providence, RI   02908   401-621-6569
                              FAX: 401-222-2823

4406 Rhode Island Parent Information Network

175 Main Street
1st Floor
Pawtucket, RI   02860   401-727-4144
                              800-464-3399
                         FAX: 401-727-4040
                      e-mail: ripin@ripin.org
                              www.ripin.org

Elizabeth Priestley, Executive Director
Debra Spaziano, Intake Coordinator

A non-profit organization established by parents and concerned professionals providing culturally appropriate information, training and support for families and professionals designed to improve educational and life outcomes for all children with special emphasis on children with disabilities and those from disadvantaged backgrounds. Serving the state of Rhode Island.

**4407 Rhode Island Protection & Advocacy for Persons
with Disabilities**

Rhode Island Disability Law Center
349 Eddy Street
Providence, RI   02903   401-831-3150
                              FAX: 401-274-5568

Raymond Bandusky, Director

**4408 Rhode Island Services for the Blind and Visually
Impaired**

40 Fountain Street
Providence, RI   02903   401-277-2300
                              800-752-0888
                         FAX: 401-222-1328
                         TDY: 401-277-3010
                 e-mail: thompson@ors.state.ri.us

Jack Thompson, Deputy Administrator

Offers services for the totally blind, legally blind, visually impaired, mentally retarded blind and more with health, counseling, educational, recreational, rehabilitation, computer training and professional training services.

4409 Services for the Blind and Visually Impaired

40 Fountain Street
Providence, RI   02903   401-222-2300
                              FAX: 401-222-1322
                 e-mail: thompson@ors.state.ri.us
                              www.ors.state.ri.us

Jack Thompson, Deputy Administrator

Offers services for the blind and visually impaired.

**4410 Social Security - Providence Disability
Determination**

40 Fountain Street
3rd Floor
Providence, RI   02903
                              800-772-1213
                              www.ssa.gov

4411 Workers Compensation Board Rhode Island

1 Darrance Plaza
Providence, RI   02903   401-458-5000
                              FAX: 401-421-3123

South Carolina

**4412 International Dyslexia Association of SC South
Carolina Branch**

512 Guild Hall Drive
Columbia, SC   29212   803-772-8065
                              800-222-3123
                      e-mail: info@interdys.org
                              www.interdys.org

Linda Heyward, President

Provides free information and referral services for diagnosis and tutoring for parents, educators, physicians, and individuals with dyslexia. The voice of our membership is heard in 48 countries. Membership includes yearly journal and quarterly newsletter. Call for conference dates.

4413 Protection & Advocacy for People with Disabilities

3710 Landmark Drive
Suite 208
Columbia, SC   29204   803-782-0639
                              800-922-5225
                         FAX: 803-790-1946
           e-mail: info@protectionandadvocacy-sc.org

Anne Trice, Director of Administration

An Independent, non-profit organization responsible for safe guarding rights of South Carolinians with disabilities and other handicapped individuals without regard to age, income, severity of disability, sex, race, or religion.

4414 Social Security - West Columbia Disability Determination

PO Box 15
West Columbia, SC 29171

800-772-1213
www.ssa.gov

4415 South Carolina Assistive Technology Projects

PO Box 15
West Columbia, SC 29171   803-896-6333

P. Charles LaRosa

A statewide program promoting assistive technology devices and services for persons of all ages with all disabilities.

4416 South Carolina Client Assistance Program

Office of the Governor of South Carolina
1205 Pendleton Street
Room 306
Columbia, SC 29201   803-734-0285
803-868-0040
FAX: 803-734-0546
e-mail: lbarker@govpoepp.state.ce.us
www.govoepp.stat.sc.us

Larry Barker, Ph.D., Director

Provides information and advocacy to and for persons with disabilities in regards to vocational rehabilitation and independent living issues.

4417 South Carolina Commission for the Blind

1430 Confederate Avenue
Columbia, SC 29201   803-734-7522
800-922-2222
FAX: 803-734-7885
e-mail: dgist@sccd.state.sc.us

Donald Gist, Commissioner

Offers services for the totally blind, legally blind, visually impaired, mentally retarded blind and more with health, counseling, educational, recreational, rehabilitation, computer training and professional training services.

4418 South Carolina Department of Children with Disabilities

2600 Bull Street
Columbia, SC 29201   803-734-5000

Ann Lee, Director

4419 South Carolina Department of Mental Health and Mental Retardation

PO Box 485
Columbia, SC 29202   803-898-8581
FAX: 803-898-8316
www.state.sc.us/dmh

Maureen Donnelly, Director

4420 South Carolina Developmental Disability Council

1205 Pendleton Street
Columbia, SC 29201   803-734-0465
FAX: 803-734-0465

Charles Lang, Director

4421 South Carolina Services Information System

University of South Carolina
School of Medicine
Columbia, SC 29208   803-935-5300
FAX: 803-935-5342
e-mail: scsis@cdd.sc.edu
www.scsis.org

Denise Rivers, Program Director

SCSIS provides information on aging and disability services in the state of South Carolina. Also, has a used equipment referral exchange where buyers and sellers are matched.

4422 Workers Compensation Board South Carolina

1612 Marien Street
PO Box 1715
Columbia, SC 29202   803-737-5744
FAX: 803-737-5764
www.state.sc.us\wcc

South Dakota

4423 South Dakota Advocacy Services

221 S Central Avenue
Pierre, SD 57501   605-224-8294
FAX: 605-224-5125
e-mail: sdas@sdadvocacy.com

Robert J Kean, Executive Director

Designated protection and advocacy progam for South Dakota providing legal, administrative, mediation and other services to elgible persons with disabilities in the state.

4424 South Dakota Client Assistance Program

221 S Central Avenue
Pierre, SD 57501   605-224-8641
FAX: 605-224-5125
e-mail: sdas@iw.net

Nancy Schade, Program Director

4425 South Dakota Department of Aging

700 N Illinois Street
Pierre, SD 57501   605-224-8641
FAX: 605-773-6834

Gail Ferris, Executive Director

4426 South Dakota Department of Children's Special Health Services

615 East 4th Street
Pierre, SD 57501   605-773-3737
FAX: 605-773-5942

Nancy Hoyme, Program Director

4427 South Dakota Department of Mental Health

700 Governors Drive
Pierre, SD 57501   605-773-5991
                          FAX: 605-773-7076

Betty Oldenkamp, Division Director

4428 South Dakota Developmental Disability Council

700 Governors Drive
Pierre, SD 57501   605-773-3423
                          FAX: 605-773-5483

4429 South Dakota Division of Rehabilitation

700 Governors Drive
Pierre, SD 57501   605-773-3423
                          FAX: 605-773-5483

David Miller, Director

Offers diagnosis, evaluation and physical restoration services, counseling, social work, educational and professional training, employment and rehabilitation services for the disabled.

4430 Workers Compensation Board South Dakota

700 Governors Drive
Pierre, SD 57501   605-773-3423
                          FAX: 605-773-4211
                 e-mail: jamesmarsh@state.sd.us

James Marsh, Director

Tennessee

**4431 International Dyslexia Association of TN
Tennessee Branch**

190 Woodcliff Circle
Signal Mountain, TN 37377   877-836-6432
                                  800-222-3123
                 e-mail: info@interdys.org
                        www.interdys.org

Margaret Smith, President

Provides free information and referral services for diagnosis and tutoring for parents, educators, physicians, and individuals with dyslexia. The voice of our membership is heard in 48 countries. Membership includes yearly journal and quarterly newsletter. Call for conference dates.

**4432 Social Security - Nashville Disability
Determination**

400 Deaderick Street
Nashville, TN 37243

                                  800-772-1213
                                  www.ssa.gov

4433 Tennessee Assistive Technology Projects

Doctor's Building
300
Nashville, TN 37243   615-322-1210

E.H. Buddy White

A statewide program promoting assistive technology devices and services for persons of all ages with all disabilities.

4434 Tennessee Client Assistance Program

PO Box 121257
Nashville, TN 37212   615-298-1080
                          FAX: 615-298-2046

4435 Tennessee Commission on Aging

500 Deaderick Street
9th Floor
Nashville, TN 37243   615-741-2056
                          FAX: 615-741-3309

James Whaley, Executive Director

4436 Tennessee Council on Developmental Disabilities

425 5th Avenue North
Cordell Hull Building, 5th Floor
Nashville, TN 37243   615-532-6615
                          FAX: 615-532-6964
                 e-mail: cnddc@mail.state.tn.us

Wanda Willis, Executive Director

Provides leadership to ensure independence, productivity, integration and inclusion of individuals with disabilities in the community through promotion of systems change. The council works with members of the community, including public and private aencies, business, legislators and policymakers, to create a future in which: People with disabilities are full included in the community and experience no barriers related to attitudes about their disabilities as they persue their goals.

**4437 Tennessee Department of Children with
Disabilities**

436 6th Avenue North
Room 525
Nashville, TN 37243   615-532-5571

Judy Womack, Director

**4438 Tennessee Department of Mental Health and
Developmental Disabilities**

425 Fifth Avenue North
Cordell Hull Building 3rd Floor
Nashville, TN 37243   615-532-6500
                          FAX: 615-532-6514
                 e-mail: mrobinson@state.tn.us
                        www.state.tn.us/mental

Elisabeth Rukeyser, Commissioner

4439 Tennessee Division of Rehabilitation

400 Deaderick Street
Nashville, TN 37243   615-248-4996

Patsy Matthews, Commissioner

Offers rehabilitation, medical and therapeutic information and referrals to the disabled.

4440 Workers Compensation Board Tennessee

710 James Robertson Parkway
Andrew Johnson Tower, Floor 2
Nashville, TN 37243   615-741-2395
                          FAX: 615-532-5929
                 www.state.tn.us/labor-wsv/wcform.ls.html

Texas

4441 Disability Policy Cosortium

7800 Shoal Creek Bolevard
Suite 171-E
Austin, TX   78757   512-454-4816

e-mail: klandrum@advodcacyinc.org
www.dpctexas.org

4442 Division of Special Education

1701 North Congress Avenue
Austin, TX   78701   512-463-9414

e-mail: glenz@tmail.tea.state.tx.us
www.tea.state.tx.us/special.ed

Gene Lenz, Senior Director

4443 Easter Seal of Greater Dallas, TX

4443 N Josey Lane
Carrollton, TX   75010   972-394-8900
800-580-4718
e-mail: rrabinowitz@easterseals.com
www.easterseals.com

Rebecca Rabinowitz, President/CEO

4444 Easter Seals Greater Northwest TX

2100 Circle Drive
Ft Worth, TX   76119   817-536-8693
888-288-8324
e-mail: info@easterseals.fw.org

4445 El Valle Community Parent Resource Center

530 South Texas
Suite J
Weslaco, TX   78596   956-969-3611
800-680-0255
e-mail: texasfiestaedu.org
www.tfevalleycenter.org

Laura Reagan, Project Coordinator

4446 Grossroots Consortium

6202 Belmark
Houston, TX   77087   713-643-9576

Speckids@aol.com

Agnes A. Johnson, Director

4447 International Dyslexia Association of TX Austin Branch

PO Box 164195
Austin, TX   78716   512-452-7658
800-222-3123
e-mail: info@interdys.org
www.interdys.org

Dena Crook, President

Provides free information and referral services for diagnosis and tutoring for parents, educators, physicians, and individuals with dyslexia. The voice of our membership is heard in 48 countries. Membership includes yearly journal and quarterly newsletter. Call for conference dates. Other locations available in Texas state.

4448 NAMI Texas

3710 Cedar Street
Suite 229
Austin, TX   78705   512-374-9339
800-366-3760
e-mail: lynn@texami.org

4449 Parent Connection

1020 Reverwood Court
Conroe, TX   77304   936-756-8321

ParentCNCT@aol.com

4450 Parents Suppporting Parents Network

601 N Texas Boulevard
Weslaco, TX   78596   954-447-8408
888-857-8668
e-mail: weslaco@gte.net

4451 Partners Resource Network

1090 Longfellow Drive
Suite B
Beaumont, TX   77706   409-898-4684
800-866-4726
e-mail: txprn@pnx.com
www.partnerstx.org

4452 Social Security - Austin Disability Determination

118 E Riverside Drive
Austin, TX   78704

800-772-1213
www.ssa.gov

4453 Statewide Information at Texas School for the Deaf

1102 South Congress Avenue
PO Box 3538
Austin, TX   78764   512-462-5329

e-mail: ercod@tsd.state.tx.us
www.tsd.state.tx.us

4454 Texas Advocates Supporting Kids with Disabilities

PO Box 162685
Austin, TX   78716   512-336-0897

e-mail: ASKTASK@aol.com

4455 Texas Assistive Technology Partnership

SZB 252/D5100
Austin, TX   78712   512-471-7621
800-828-7839
e-mail: s.elrod@mail.utexas.edu
www.tatp.edb.utexas.edu

Susanne Elrod, Project Director

4456 Texas Commission for the Blind

PO Box 12866
Austin, TX   78711   512-459-2500
800-252-5204
FAX: 512-459-2685

Terrell I. Murphy, Executive Director

Offers services for the totally blind, legally blind, and visually impaired, with counseling, educational, recreational, rehabilitation, computer training and professional training services.

4457 Texas Commission for the Deaf and Hard of Hearing

PO Box 12904
Austin, TX 12904 512-407-3250

e-mail: david.mu\yers@tcdhh.state.tx.us
www.tcdhh.state.tx.us

David Myers, Executive Director

4458 Texas Department of Human Services

701 W 51st Street
Austin, TX 78751 512-438-3011
888-834-7406
e-mail: mail@dhs.tx.us
www.@dhs.state.tx.us

Eric M. McCain, Division Director

4459 Texas Department of Mental Health & Mental Retardation

PO Box 12668
Austin, TX 78711 512-454-3761
FAX: 512-206-4560
e-mail: karen.hale@mhmr.state.tx.us
www.mhmr.state.tx.us

Karen F. Hale, Commissioner
Offers information and referrals.

4460 Texas Department on Aging

4900 North Lamar
Suite 4301
Austin, TX 78751 512-424-6840
800-252-9240
FAX: 512-424-6890
e-mail: mail@tdoa.state.tx.us
www.tdoa.state.tx.us

Mary Sapp, Executive Director
John Willis, Director, Ombudsman

The state's visible advocate and steward for a full range of services and opportunities that allow older Texans to live healthy, dignified and independent lives.

4461 Texas Developmental Disability Council

4900 N Lamar Boulevard
Austin, TX 78751 512-424-4000

4462 Texas Educational Agency, Services for the Deaf

1701 North Congress Avenue
Austin, TX 78701 512-463-9424

www.tea.state.tx.us

Sha Cowan, Director

4463 Texas Federation of Families for Children's Mental Health

7701 North Lamar
Suite 500
Austin, TX 78752 512-451-3191
800-860-6057

Patti Derr, Director

4464 Texas Governor's Committee on People with Disabilities

1100 San Jacinto
Austin, TX 78701 512-463-5739
FAX: 513-463-5745
e-mail: ppound@governor.state.tx.us
www.governor.state.tx.us/disabilities

Pat Pound, Executive Director

4465 Texas PTA

408 West 11th Street
Austin, TX 78701 512-476-6769
800-825-5782
e-mail: txpta@txpat.org
www.txpta.org

Sylvia Ostos, President

4466 Texas Planning Council for Developmental Disabilities

4900 N Lamar Boulevard
Austin, TX 78751 512-424-4000

Roger Webb, Executive Director

4467 Texas Protection & Advocacy Services for Disabled Persons

Advocacy
7800 Shoal Creek Boulevard
Suite 171-E
Austin, TX 78757 512-371-0414
800-252-9108
FAX: 512-323-0902
e-mail: infoai@advocacyinc.org
www.advocacyinc.org

James Comstock-Galagan, Executive Director

A federally funded independent, non-profit agency that advocates for the legal, human and service rights of persons with disabilities. Publishes 'sSpecial Edition,' newsletter, at a small fee and 'It's a Good Idea!' a parent manual for $10, plus many other handouts free of charge.

4468 Texas Respite Resource Network

519 W Houston Street
San Antonio, TX 78207
FAX: 210-704-2797
e-mail: elizabethnewhouse@srhcc.org

Jennifer Cernoch, Director
Liz Newhouse, Assistant Director

A state clearinghouse and technical assistance network for respite in Texas. TRRN identifies, initiates and improves respite options for families caring for individuals with disabilities on the local, state and national levels. TRRN provides training/technical assistance to programs/groups wanting to establish respite services.

4469 Texas UAP for Developmental Disabilities

SZB 252/D5100
Austin, TX 78712 512-471-7621
800-828-7839
e-mail: pseay@mail.utexas.edu
www.uap.edb.utexas.edu

Penny Seay, Executive Director

4470 Texas Workers Compensation Commission

4000 S IH 35
Austin, TX   78704   512-448-7900
                                       FAX: 512-440-3547

4471 United Cerebral Palsy of Texas

5555 N Lamar
Suite L139
Austin, TX   78751   512-472-8696
                                            800-798-1492
                                     e-mail: ucptx@onr.com

Patty Anderson, Executive Director

Utah

**4472 Department of Human Services Utah Office of
Social Services**

120 N 200 West
Room 324
Salt Lake City, UT   84103   801-538-4222

Steve Wrigley, Director

Information and referrals offering many different office locations for various counties in the state of Utah.

**4473 Social Security - Salt Lake City Disability
Determination**

555 East 300 South
Box 144032
Salt Lake City, UT   84114   801-321-6500
                                        800-772-1213
                                   FAX: 801-321-6599
                                         www.ssa.gov

Dan Hooper, Director

4474 Utah Assistive Technology Projects

Utah State University
Developmental Center
Logan, UT   84322   435-797-0184

                             e-mail: garthe@coe.usu.edu

Marvin Fifield, Director

A statewide program promoting assistive technology devices and services for persons of all ages with all disabilities.

4475 Utah Client Assistance Program

455 East 400 South
Suite 410
Salt Lake City, UT   84111   801-363-1347
                                        800-662-9080
                                   FAX: 801-363-1437
                             www.disabilitylawcenter.org

Nancy Friel, Director

4476 Utah Department of Aging

120 N 200 W
Salt Lake City, UT   84103   801-538-3910
                                   FAX: 801-538-4395
                                         www.dhs.ut.us

Helan Geddard, Director

4477 Utah Department of Mental Health

2001 S State Street
Suite 2600
Salt Lake City, UT   84190   801-530-6628
                                   FAX: 801-530-6511

Dave Dangerfield, Director

4478 Utah Developmental Disabilities Council

350 E 5005 Avenue
Suite 201
Salt Lake City, UT   84111

                                   FAX: 801-533-5305

4479 Utah Division of Services for the Disabled

309 E 1st S
Salt Lake City, UT   84111   801-323-4343
                                        800-284-1823

William G. Gibson, Director

Offers services for the totally blind, legally blind, visually impaired, mentally retarded blind and more with health, counseling, educational, recreational, rehabilitation, computer training and professional training services.

**4480 Utah Protection & Advocacy Services for Persons
with Disabilities**

Disability Law Center
455 East 400 South
Suite 410
Salt Lake City, UT   84111   801-363-1347
                                        800-662-9080
                                   FAX: 801-363-1437
                   e-mail: jstuart@disabilitylawcenter.org
                             www.disabilitylawcenter.org

Fraser Nelson, Executive Director
Ron Gardner, Esq., Senior Counsel
Eric Dmitchell, Advocacy Director

4481 Workers Compensation Board Utah

160 E 3rd S
Salt Lake City, UT   84111   801-530-6701

Vermont

4482 Disability Law Project

57 North Main Street
Rutland, VT   05701   852-775-0021
                                        800-769-7459
                                   FAX: 802-775-0022
                           e-mail: nbreiden@vtlegalaid.org
                                         vtlegalaid.org

Nancy Breiden, Director

Legal services (protection and advocacy) for people with disabilities on legal issues arising from disability. Statewide. Adults and children. Employment, education, discrimination, housing, public benefits, health care.

4483 Social Security - Waterbury Disability Determination
103 S Main Street
Waterbury, VT 05676

800-772-1213
www.ssa.gov

4484 Vermont Assistive Technology Projects
103 S Main Street
Waterbury, VT 05676 802-241-2284

Jesse Broth, Project Director

A statewide program promoting assistive technology devices and services for persons of all ages with all disabilities.

4485 Vermont Client Assistance Program
PO Box 370
Waterbury, VT 05676 802-244-8134

4486 Vermont Department of Aging and Disabilities
Aging and Disabilities
103 S Main Street
Waterbury, VT 05671 802-241-2400
FAX: 802-241-2325
http://www.dad.state.vt.us

Patrick Flood, Commissioner

4487 Vermont Department of Developmental and Mental Health Services
103 S Main Street
Waterbury, VT 05671 802-241-2614
FAX: 802-241-1129

Susan Besio, Commissioner
Theresa Wood, Director Development Services
Paul Blake, Director Division Mental Healths

4488 Vermont Department of Health, Children with Special Health Needs
PO Box 70
Burlington, VT 05402 802-863-7338
FAX: 802-863-7635

Carol Hassler MD, Director

Multidisciplinary clinics and family support for children with chronic conditions, birth to age 21 years.

4489 Vermont Developmental Disabilities Council
103 S Main Street
Waterbury, VT 05671 802-241-2612
FAX: 802-241-2989

4490 Vermont Division for the Blind and Visually Impaired
103 South Main Street
Waterbury, VT 05671 802-241-2210
888-405-5005
FAX: 802-241-2128
e-mail: steve@dad.state.vt.us
www.dad.state.vt.us/dbvi

Steven R. Stone, Director
Scott Langley, Chief of Field Operations

Offers services for the totally blind, legally blind, visually impaired, mentally retarded blind and more with health, counseling, educational, recreational, rehabilitation, computer training and professional training services.

4491 Vermont Protection & Advocacy
141 Main Streetki Avenue
Suite 7
Montpelier, VT 05602 802-229-1355
800-834-7890
FAX: 802-229-1359
TDY:800-889-2047
e-mail: info@vtpa.org

Judy Rex, Director

Legal services for people with mental illness on legal issues arising, out of disabilities. Children and adults.

4492 Workers Compensation Board Vermont
State Office Building
Montpelier, VT 05602 802-828-2286

Virginia

4493 Department for Rights of Virginians with Disabilities
202 North 9th Street
9th Floor
Richmond, VA 23219 804-225-2042
800-552-3962
FAX: 804-225-3221
www.cns.state.va.us/drvd

Susan Ferguson, Director
Heidi Lawyer, Deputy Director

An executive branch agency that helps ensure that the rights of persons with disabiltiies in the Commonwealth are protected. The mission of DRVD is to provide zealous and effective advocacy and legal representation to protect and advance legal, human and civil rights of persons with disabilities, combat and prevent abuse, neglect and discrimination, and promote independence, choice and self-determination by persons with disabilities.

4494 Dept for Rights of Virginians with Disabilities
202 N Ninth Street
9th Floor
Richmond, VA 23219 804-225-2042
800-522-3962
FAX: 804-225-3221
www.cns.state.va.us/drvd

Sandy Ferguson, Director

4495 International Dyslexia Association of VA Virginia Branch
13637 Prince William Drive
Midlothian, VA 23113 800-998-8336
800-222-3123
e-mail: info@interdys.org
www.interdys.org

Sherrell Sherron, President

Provides free information and referral services for diagnosis and tutoring for parents, educators, physicians, and individuals with dyslexia. The voice of our membership is heard in 48 countries. Membership includes yearly journal and quarterly newsletter. Call for conference dates.

4496 US Department of Military Affairs

100 Emancipation Drive
Hampton, VA 23667   757-728-3128

Jenny Shafer Tankersley, Director Of Public Affairs
William G. Wright, Executive Vice President

Serving military veterans in the Tidewater area since 1870, the Hampton Veterans Affairs Medical Center has specialized services in medicine, surgery, psychiatry, with a 120 bed extended care & Rehabilitation center, a 240 bed domiciliary (residential treatment program), and a 64 bed Spinal cord injury unit. More than 1150 dedicated employees provide care to veterans on this 83.5 acre campus.

4497 Virginia Board for People with Disabilities

202 North 9th Street
Ninth Floor
Richmond, VA 23219   804-786-0016
                              800-846-4464
                         FAX: 804-786-1115
       e-mail: parsonbs@vbpd.state.va.us
                         www.vaboard.org

Barbara Ettner, Assistant Director Policy & Prog
Brian S. Parsons, Director

4498 Virginia Department for the Visually Impaired

397 Azalea Avenue
Richmond, VA 23227   804-371-3145
                         FAX: 804-371-3351
                         TDY:804-371-3140
       e-mail: grizzawr@dvhmail.state.va.us
                    www.cns.state.va.us/dvh

Dr. W. Roy Grizzard, Jr., Director

Offers services for the totally blind, legally blind, visually impaired, mentally retarded blind and more with health, counseling, educational, recreational, rehabilitation, computer training and professional training services.

4499 Virginia Department of Children with Disabilities

Madison Building
6th Floor
Richmond, VA 23219   804-786-3906
                         FAX: 804-371-6031

W.R. Ferguson, Director

4500 Virginia Department of Mental Health

1220 Bank Street
PO Box 1797
Richmond, VA 23218   804-692-1849
                         FAX: 804-786-3827

Joe Damico, Dir of Adminitrative Services

4501 Virginia Developmental Disability Council

101 N 14th Street
17th Floor
Richmond, VA 23219   804-225-3144
                         FAX: 804-225-3221

Sandra Reen, Director

4502 Virginia Protection & Advocacy for Persons with Disabilities

101 N 14th Street
17th Floor
Richmond, VA 23219   804-225-3144
                         FAX: 804-225-3221

Washington

4503 DSHS/Aging & Adult Services Administration

PO Box 45600
Woodland Square, Loop SE
Olympia, WA 98504   360-725-2300
                            800-422-3263
                       FAX: 360-407-0369
                       www.aasa.dshs.wa.gov

Kathy Leitch, Assistant Secretary

4504 International Dyslexia Association of WA
Washington State Branch (AK, ID, MT, WA)

PO Box 7192
Seattle, WA 23113   206-382-1020
                            800-222-3123
                     e-mail: info@interdys.org
                            www.interdys.org

Stacy Turner, President

Provides free information and referral services for diagnosis and tutoring for parents, educators, physicians, and individuals with dyslexia. The voice of our membership is heard in 48 countries. Membership includes yearly journal and quarterly newsletter. Call for conference dates.

4505 Social Security - Olympia Disability Determination

402 Yauger Way SW
Olympia, WA 98504
                            800-772-1213
                            www.ssa.gov

4506 WA Department of Services for the Blind

402 Legion Way
Olympia, WA 98501   360-352-3833
                            800-552-7103
                       FAX: 360-586-7627

Vocational rehabilitation for the blind.

4507 Washington Client Assistance Program

2531 Rainier Avenue South
Seattle, WA 98144   206-721-5999
                            800-544-2121
                       FAX: 206-721-5980
                  e-mail: capseattle@att.net

Jerry Johnsen, Director

Advocacy and information assistance for persons of disability seeking services through Vocational Rehabilitation or other program under the 1973 rehabilitation Act as commented. We provide counseling.

4508 Washington Department of Mental Health

PO Box 592
Olympia, WA   98507   888-713-6010
                             FAX: 360-902-7691

Dave Novseri, Director

4509 Washington Developmental Disability Council

906 Columbia Street SW
Olympia, WA   98504   360-753-3908
                             800-634-4473
                             e-mail: edh@cted.wa.gov
                             www.ddc.wa.gov

Ed Holen, Executive Director

4510 Washington Governor's Committee on Disability Issues & Employment

PO Box 9046
Olympia, WA   98507   360-753-6780
                             FAX: 360-438-3208

4511 Washington Office of Public Instruction

Old Capitol Building
Olympia, WA   98504   360-753-6738
                             FAX: 360-753-6712

Judy Schrag, Asst. Superintendent

Provides consultation on educational services for local schools, offers psychological testing and evaluation, maintains resource rooms in district schools and more for the blind and handicapped throughout the state.

4512 Washington Protection & Advocacy System

180 West Dayton
Suite 102
Edmonds, WA   98020   425-776-1199
                             800-562-2702
                             FAX: 425-776-0601
                             e-mail: wpas@wpas-rights.org

Laura Allen, Resource Advocate

WPAS is a private, non-profit right protection agency for persons with disabilities residin in Washington state. Our advocacy services include information referral, technical assistance, training, publications and systemic advocacy.

4513 Workers Compensation Board Washington

Highway Contract 01
Olympia, WA   98504

West Virginia

4514 Bureau of Employment Programs Division of Workers' Compensation

4700 MacCorkle Avenue
Charleston, WV   25304   304-926-5048

4515 Disability Determination Section

500 Quanier Street
Suite 500
Charleston, WV   25301   304-343-5055
                                FAX: 304-353-4212

4516 Social Security - Charleston Disability Determination

1800 Washington Street E
Charleston, WV   25305
                                800-772-1213
                                FAX: 304-353-4212
                                www.ssa.gov

4517 West Virginia Advocates

1207 Quarrier Street
4th Floor
Charleston, WV   25301   304-346-0847
                                800-950-5250
                                FAX: 304-346-0867
                                e-mail: wvadvocates@newwave.com

Intake Advocate

4518 West Virginia Client Assistance Program

West Virginia Advocates
1524 Kanawha Boulevard E
Charleston, WV   25311   304-755-5700
                                FAX: 304-346-0867

4519 West Virginia Department of Aging

Holly Grove State Capitol
Charleston, WV   25305   304-755-5700
                                FAX: 304-558-0004
                                e-mail: hollygrove@juno.com

Patricia Bedford, Director

4520 West Virginia Department of Children with Disabilities

1116 Quarrier Street
Charleston, WV   25301   304-755-5700

Pat Kent, Administrative Dir.

4521 West Virginia Department of Health

1900 Capital Complex
Building 3
Charleston, WV   25305   304-755-5700
                                FAX: 304-558-1008

Taunja Willis-Miller, Secretary

4522 West Virginia Developmental Disabilities Council

110 Stockton Street
Charleston, WV   25312   304-558-0416
                                FAX: 304-558-0941
                                e-mail: jchankins@wvdhhr.org
                                www.state.us.wv/ddpc

Jonathan Hankins, Office Manager

6-8 pages Quarterly Newsl

4523 West Virginia Division of Rehabilitation Services

1900 Washington Street E
Charleston, WV   25305   304-558-3428

Wisconsin

4524   International Dyslexia Association of WI Wisconsin Branch

437 South Yellowstone Drive
18
Madison, WI   53719

414-299-0551
800-222-3123
e-mail: info@interdys.org
www.interdys.org

Nira Scherz-Busch, Co-President
William Kitz, Co-President

Provides free information and referral services for diagnosis and tutoring for parents, educators, physicians, and individuals with dyslexia. The voice of our membership is heard in 48 countries. Membership includes yearly journal and quarterly newsletter. Call for conference dates.

4525   Social Security - Madison Disability Determination

1 W Wilson Street
Madison, WI   53702

800-772-1213
www.ssa.gov

4526   Wisconsin Assistive Technology Projects

State Grants Program
1 W Wilson Street
8th Floor
Madison, WI   53702

608-266-6463
FAX: 608-243-5680

Sue Kidder, Director

A statewide program promoting assistive technology devices and services for persons of all ages with all disabilities.

4527   Wisconsin Bureau for Exceptional Children

PO Box 7842
Madison, WI   53707   608-266-2381

Victor Contrucci, Asst. Superintendent

Provides consultation on educational services for local schools, offers psychological testing and evaluation, maintains resource rooms in district schools and more for the blind and handicapped throughout the state.

4528   Wisconsin Coalition for Advocacy

16 N Carroll Street
Suite 400
Madison, WI   53703

608-250-3442
800-928-8778
FAX: 608-267-0368

Kim Hogan, Intake Specialist
Mr. Lynn Breedolve, Director

The protection and advocacy agency for people with disabilities in Wisconsin. WCA provides guidance, advice, investigation, negotiation, and in some cases legal representation to people with disabilities and their families. Local and state level systems advocacy and training are also provided.

4529   Wisconsin Council on Developmental Disabilities (WCDD)

600 Williamson Street
PO Box 7851
Madison, WI   53707   608-266-7826

e-mail: wiswcdd@dhfs.state.wi.us
www.wcdd.org

Jennifer Ondrejka, Executive Director

Statewide systems advocacy group for people with developmental disabilities in Wisconsin.

4530   Wisconsin Department of Aging

217 S Hamilton Street
Suite 300
Madison, WI   53703

608-250-3442
FAX: 608-267-3203

Donna McDowell, Director

4531   Wisconsin Department of Health and Family Services

Program for Children w/Special Health Care Needs
1 West Wilson, Room 351
PO Box 2659
Madison, WI   53701

608-267-2945
800-441-4576
FAX: 608-267-3824
e-mail: helmqp@dhfs.state.wi.us
www.dhfs.state.wi.us/DPH-BFCH/FamilyHealth

Peggy Helm-Quest, Supervisor

The Department of Health and Family Services operates the federal Title V Maternal and Child Health Block Grant Program for Children with Special Health Care Needs. The program provides program monitoring, consultation and technical assistance to five regional CSHCN centers throughout Wisconsin; a Birth Defects Monitoring and Surveillance Program and a Universal Newborn Hearing Screening Program.

4532   Wisconsin Governor's Committee for People with Disabilities

PO Box 7852
Madison, WI   53707

608-250-3442
FAX: 608-267-0949

4533   Workers Compensation Board Wisconsin

PO Box 7901
Madison, WI   53707

FAX: 608-267-0394

Wyoming

4534   Social Security - Cheyenne Disability Determination

1100 Herschler
Cheyenne, WY   82002

800-772-1213
FAX: 800-972-2372
www.ssa.gov

Vicky Johnson, Director

4535 Workers Compensation Board Wyoming

122 W 25th Street
2nd Floor
Cheyenne, WY 82001   307-777-7960

4536 Wyoming Client Assistance Program

2424 Pioneer Avenue
Suite 101
Cheyenne, WY 82001   307-638-7668
                            FAX: 307-638-0815

Kristen Smith, Director

4537 Wyoming Department of Aging

Hathaway
Room 139
Cheyenne, WY 82002   307-777-4146

Morris Gardner, Administrator

4538 Wyoming Developmental Disability Council

122 W 25th Street
Cheyenne, WY 82001   307-777-7230
                            FAX: 307-777-5690

Lynn Achter, Director

4539 Wyoming Division of Mental Health

6101 Yellowstone Road
QWEST Building, Room 259 B
Cheyenne, WY 82002   307-777-7094
                            FAX: 307-777-5580
                            www.wdbh.state.wy.us

Dr. Pablo Hernandez, Administrator
Marilyn J. Patton, MSW, Deputy Administrator

State office responsible for purchase of service and
program development policy.

**4540 Wyoming Protection & Advocacy for Persons
with Disabilities**

320 West 25th Street
2nd Floor
Cheyenne, WY 82001   307-638-7668
                            FAX: 307-638-0815

Alabama

4541 Birdie Thornton Center
2309 Hine Street South
Athens, AL 35611 256-232-0366
FAX: 256-216-5681

Sharon Travis, Program Manager

4542 Independent Living Center
206 13th Street S
Birmingham, AL 35233 205-251-2223
FAX: 205-251-0605
www.myindependentliving.org

Linda Taylor, Director
Independent living center.

4543 Independent Living Center of Mobile
5304 Overlook Road
Mobile, AL 36618 251-460-0301
FAX: 251-341-1267
e-mail: ilc@zebra.net
www.ilcmobilc.org

Michael Davis, Contact

Alaska

4544 Access Alaska - Anchorage
121 West Fireweed Lane
Anchorage, AK 99503 907-248-4777
FAX: 907-248-0639
e-mail: access@alaska.net
www.alaska.net/~access

Serena Dowling, Info. & Referral Coordinator

4545 Access Alaska - Fairbanks
3550 Airport Way
Suite 3
Fairbanks, AK 99709 907-479-7940
FAX: 907-474-4052
e-mail: palacc@mosquitonet.com
www.fairnet.org/agencies/accessak

David Jacobson, Statewide Director

4546 Access Alaska-ADA Partners Project
AK
888-462-1444
FAX: 907-235-0159
e-mail: adaalaska@netscape.net
www.adapartners.org

Since the passage of the Americans with Disabilities Act (ADA), Access Alaska developed the ADA Partners Project as a means of providing information, training and technical assistance, statewide to businesses and surrounding communities in better understanding and complying with this very important civil rights legislation.

4547 Access Alaska-Anchorage
3901 Taft Drive
Suites A and B
Anchorage, AK 99517 907-248-4777
800-770-4488
FAX: 907-248-0639
e-mail: access@alaska.net

Serena Dowling, Information/Referral Coordinator
Provides independent living services to persons with significant disabilities. Mission is to encourage and promote the total integration of persons with disabilities into the community of their choice. Services include independent living skills training, information and referral, advocacy, peer support, case management services, care coordination, interim accessible transportation and at home modifications.

4548 Access Alaska-Fairbanks
3550 Airport Way
Suites 3
Fairbanks, AK 99709 907-479-7940
800-770-7940
FAX: 907-474-4052
e-mail: palace@mosquitonet.com
www.fairnet.org/agencies/accessak/index.html

Provides independent living services to persons with significant disabilities. Mission is to encourage and promote the total integration of persons with disabilities into the community of their choice. Services include independent living skills training, information and referral, advocacy, peer support, case management services, care coordination, interim accessible transportation and at home modifications.

4549 Access Alaska-Mat-Suvalley
901 Commercial Drive
Wasilla, AK 99687 907-357-2588
800-770-0228
FAX: 907-352-2547

Provides independent living services to persons with significant disabilities. Mission is to encourage and promote the total integration of persons with disabilities into the community of their choice. Services include independent living skills training, information and referral, advocacy, peer support, case management services, care coordination, interim accessible transportation and at home modifications.

4550 Artic Access
PO Box 930
Kotzebue, AK 99752 907-442-2393
FAX: 907-442-2393
e-mail: arcticac@ptialaska.net

Roger Wright

4551 Hope Cottages
540 W International Airport Road
Anchorage, AK 99518 907-561-5335

Stephen Lesko, Director
Independent living centers offer peer counseling, disability education and awareness, attendant care registry and other services to the community.

4552 Independent Living Center of Homer

PO Box 2474
Homer, AK   99603   907-235-7911
                            FAX: 907-235-6236
                            e-mail: llc@xyz.net

Joyanna Geisler, Director

Offers peer counseling, disability education and awareness, attendant care registry and information on accessible housing.

4553 Kenai Peninsula ILC - Juneau

8800 Glacier Highway
Suite 236
Juneau, AK   99801   907-789-9665

peninsulaailc.org

Joyanna Geisler, Executive Director

4554 Kenai Peninsula ILC - Seward

PO Box 3523
Seward, AK   99664   907-224-8711
                            FAX: 907-224-7793
                            e-mail: ilc@seward.net
                            peninsulaailc.org

Joyanna Geisler, Executive Director

4555 Kenai Peninsula ILC - Soldotna

PO Box 1907
Soldotna, AK   99669   907-262-6333
                            FAX: 907-260-4495
                            e-mail: solic@worldnet.att.net
                            peninsulaailc.org

Joyanna Geisler, Executive Director

4556 Kenai Peninsula Independent Living Center

PO Box 2474
Homer, AK   99603   907-235-7911
                            FAX: 907-235-6236
                            e-mail: ilc@xyz.net
                            peninsulaailc.org

Joyanna Geisler, Executive Director

4557 Kodiak Independent Learning Center

PO Box 8593
Kodiak, AK   99615   907-486-6522

e-mail: duch@qci.net
www.peninsulaailc.org

Karen Duchateaux, Contact

4558 Seward Independent Learning Center

PO Box 3523
Seward, AK   99664   907-224-7793
                            FAX: 907-224-8711
                            e-mail: ilc@seward.net
                            www.peninsulaailc.org

Jean Sether, Contact

4559 Southeast Alaska ILC - Ketchikan

1621 Tongass Avenue
Suite 205
Ketchikan, AK   99901   907-225-4735
                            FAX: 907-225-4753
                            TDY:907-225-4735
                            peninsulaailc.org

Joyanna Geisler, Executive Director

4560 Southeast Alaska Independent Learning Center (SAIL)

3225 Hospital Drive
Suite 300
Juneau, AK   99801   907-586-4920
                            800-478-7245
                            FAX: 907-586-4980

Joan Herbage-O'Keefe, Executive Director

4561 Southeast Alaska Independent Living-Sitka

210 Lake Street
Suite A
Sitka, AK   99835   907-747-6850
                            FAX: 907-747-6783
                            TDY:907-747-6859
                            peninsulaailc.org

Joyanna Geisler, Executive Director

Arizona

4562 Arizona Bridge to Independent Living

1229 E Washington Street
Phoenix, AZ   85034   602-256-2245
                            FAX: 602-254-6407
                            e-mail: azbridge@abil.org
                            www.abil.org

Sue Castle Webb, Executive Director

Services include personal assistant training and referral, independent living skills instruction, home modification, information and referral, social/recreation activities, employment readiness and job search assistance and Americans with Disabilities Act training and consulting.

4563 Community Outreach Program for the Deaf

268 W Adams Street
Tucson, AZ   85705   520-792-1906
                            FAX: 520-770-8514

Gail Lanham, Executive Director

Independent living centers offering peer counseling, disability education and awareness, advocacy and other services to the community.

4564 DIRECT Center for Independence

1023 North Tyndall Avenue
Tucson, AZ   85719   520-624-6452
                            800-342-1853
                            FAX: 520-792-1438
                            e-mail: directilc@earthlink.net

Ann Meyer, Executive Director

4565 Direct Center for Independence

1023 N Tyndall Avenue
Tucson, AZ 85719   520-624-6452
                          800-342-1853
e-mail: Direct@Azstarnet.com

Ann Meyer, Executive Director
Offers peer counseling, disability education, information and referral services.

4566 New Horizons Community Services

Dewey, AZ 86327

4567 New Horizons Independent Living Center

8085 East Manly Drive
Suite 1
Prescott Valley, AZ 86314   520-772-1266
                                800-406-2377
FAX: 520-772-3808
e-mail: nhilc@northlink.com
northlink.com/~nhilc

Ken Edwards, Executive Director
Mary Hesselschwerdt, Outreach Coordinator

4568 Services Maximizing Independent Living and Empowerment (SMILE)

1495 South 4th Avenue
Yuma, AZ 85364   520-329-6681
FAX: 520-329-6715
e-mail: smilele@mindspring.com
www.neiaw.com/smile/smileindex.html

Sandra Hayes, Executive Director
Independent Living Center

4569 Sterling Ranch - Residence for Special Women

Sterling Ranch
PO Box 36
Skull Valley, AZ 86338   520-442-3289
FAX: 520-442-9272
e-mail: sterlingranch@juno.com

Russell S. Dryer, Executive Director
A non-profit residence for mentally handicapped women which has been in operation since 1947. As a small facility (18 residents) the orientation is personal and family-like. Offers activities that range from gardening, quilting, academics, sign-language, crafts and a myriad of field trips and excursions. Private rooms and spacious living on 3 1/2 acres. *$900.00*

Arkansas

4570 Arkansas SILC

209 West Capitol
Suite 331
Little Rock, AR 72201   501-372-0607
FAX: 501-372-0598
TDY:501-372-0607
e-mail: 105344.1767@kcompuserve.com

4571 Delta Resource Center for Independent Living

400 S Main Street
Suite 118
Pine Bluff, AR 71601   870-535-2222
FAX: 870-534-8191
e-mail: deltar@seark.net

Billy Altom, Executive Director
Independent living center providing information and referrals, advocacy, peer counseling and independent living skills training to the Southeast region of Arkansas.

4572 Delta Resource Independent Living Center

Suite 118
Pine Bluff, AR 71601   870-535-2222
FAX: 870-535-8191
e-mail: deltar@seark.net

Billy Altom, Contact

4573 Mainstream

1818 S University Avenue
Little Rock, AR 72204   501-280-0012
FAX: 501-280-9267
TDY:501-280-9262
e-mail: mainstreamlr@earthlink.net
www.mainstreamilrc.com

Rita Byers, Director
Peer counseling, disability education and awareness, and advocacy services, information and referrals, independent living skills training and more.

4574 Our Way

10434 W 36th Street
Little Rock, AR 72204   501-225-5030
FAX: 501-225-5190

Greg Goodwin, Project Manager
Advocacy and information services. One bedroom apartments for mobility impaired and elderly 62 years or older persons.

Based on income

4575 Sources for Community IL Services

540 Appleby Road
Fayetteville, AR 72703   501-442-5600

4576 Sources for Community Independent Living

1918 North Birch Avenue
Fayetteville, AR 72703   501-442-5600
                               888-284-7521
FAX: 501-442-5192
e-mail: source@lynks.com

William Knight, Executive Director
Cheri McGowen, Administrative Assistant

Monthly

4577 Spa Area IL Services

600 Main
Hot Springs, AR 71913   501-624-7710

4578 Spa Area Independent Living Services

600 Main Street
Suite O
Hot Springs, AR   71913   501-624-7710
                               FAX: 501-624-7510
                  e-mail: sails@direclynx.net

Brenda Stinebuck, Contact

California

4579 Access Center of San Diego

1295 University Avenue
Suite 10
San Diego, CA   92103   619-293-3500
                               FAX: 619-293-3508
                               TDY:619-293-7757
                  e-mail: Accessctr@aol.com
                          www.accesscentersd.org

Bud Sayles, Director

Offers peer counseling, disability awareness, advocacy services, client assistance programs, employment counseling, information and referral, personal assistant services, housing referral, financial benefits advocacy, durable medical equipment sales and repair, and assistance in compliance with the ADA (Americans with Disabilities Act).

4580 Branc Office - Independent Living Resource Costa County

1545 Webster Street
Suite Dc
Fairfield, CA   94553   707-435-8174
                               FAX: 707-435-8177
                  e-mail: joanne@ilrccc.org

JoAnne Bell, Executive Director
Paul Demange, Program Director
Rich Broaddus, Branch Manager

4581 CAPH Independent Living Center

1617 East Saginaw Way
Suite 109
Fresno, CA   93704   209-222-2274

4582 CIL - Fresno

3475 West Shaw
Suite 101
Fresno, CA   93711   209-276-6777
                               FAX: 209-276-6778
                               TDY:209-276-6779
          e-mail: CILFMAILI@EATHLINK.NETprogram_dir@eathlink.ne

4583 CIL - Fresno (Visalia Branch)

Visalia Branch
121 East Main
Visalia, CA   93277   559-622-9276
                               FAX: 559-622-9638
                               TDY:559-622-9276

4584 California Foundation for Independent Living Centers

910 K Street
Suite 350
Sacramento, CA   95814   916-325-1690
                               FAX: 916-325-1699
                               TDY:916-325-1695
                  e-mail: cfile@cfilc.org

4585 California State Independent Living Council (SILC)

1600 K Street
Suite 100
Sacramento, CA   95814   916-445-0142
                               FAX: 916-445-5973
                               TDY:916-445-5627
          e-mail: casilc@calsilc.org.Michael C. Collins

4586 Center for Independence of the Disabled

875 Oneill Street
Belmont, CA   94002   408-733-5778
                               FAX: 407-895-5255

Kent Mickelson, Director

Counseling, disability education and awareness, attendant care registry, information on accessible housing and other services to the community.

4587 Center for Independent Living

2539 Telegraph Avenue
Berkeley, CA   94704   510-841-4776
                               FAX: 510-841-6168
                  e-mail: webmaster@cilberkeley.org
                          www.cilberkeley.org

Jacqueline Garrett, Executive Director
Gerald Baptiste, Deputy Director

4588 Center for Independent Living in Fresno

3475 West Shaw Avenue
Suite 101
Fresno, CA   93711   559-276-6779
                               FAX: 559-276-6778
                  e-mail: f_phillips@cuk-fresno.org
                          www.cil.fresno.org

Fran Phillips, Co-Executive Director
Robin Libbee, Co-Executive Director

4589 Center for Independent Living/California

2539 Telegraph Avenue
Berkeley, CA   94704   510-841-4776
                               FAX: 510-841-6168
                               TDY:510-848-3101
                  e-mail: cii@hooked.net
                          www.cilberkeley.org

Mike Donnelly, Executive Director
Gordon Harvey, Public Relations Specialist

The Center for Independent Living (CIL) is a national leader in helping people with disabilities live independently and becoming productive members of society. Founded in 1972, CIL is a pioneer for advocating more accessibility in communities, designing techniques in independent living, and providing direct services to people with disabilities. A partial list of services include Information and Referral, Personal Assistance Services, Independent Living Skills Training, Peer Counseling, & Job Dev

4590 Center for the Independence of the Disabled

875 Oneill Avenue
Belmont, CA 94002 650-595-0783
FAX: 650-595-0261
e-mail: cidbelmont@aol.com
www.cidbelmont.org

Kent Mickelson, Contact
Ray Pittsinger, Program Manager
Arsie Tuquero-Zacarigs, Administrative Assistant

4591 Center of Independent Living - South Valley

430 W Caldwell
Suite D
Visalia, CA 93277 559-622-9276
FAX: 559-622-9638

Michelle Christiansen, South Valley Office Manager

4592 Central Coast Center - Independent Living - Santa Cruz Office

1395 41st Avenue
Suite "B"
Capitola, CA 95010 408-462-8720
FAX: 408-462-8727

4593 Central Coast Center for IL - San Benito

San Benito Office
300 West Street
Hollister, CA 95023 408-638-1271
FAX: 408-638-1728

4594 Central Coast Center for Independent Living

234 Capitol Street
Suite A
Salinas, CA 93901 408-752-2968
FAX: 408-757-5549
TDY:408-752-2968
e-mail: info@progway.org

4595 Community Access Center

4960 Arlington Avenue
Suite C
Riverside, CA 92504 909-637-6900
FAX: 909-637-6906
TDY:909-637-6902
e-mail: lgwalls@aol.com

Lucille Walls, Contact
Paul Van Doren, Contact

4596 Community Access Center - Indio

Indio Office
83203 Indio Boulevard #5
Indio, CA 92201 760-347-4888
FAX: 760-347-2728

4597 Community Rehabilitation Services

4716 Cesar E Chavez Avenue
Los Angeles, CA 90022 323-266-0453
FAX: 323-266-7992
TDY:213-266-3016
e-mail: crsela@icnt.net

Juan Orantez, Info. And Ref./Stat. Coordinator
Yelanda Raminez, Care Services Program Dir.
Al Rivera, Executive Director

Community Rehabilitation Services, Inc. (CRS) is a private, non-profit agency established in 1974 to assist persons with disabilities within the East/North East areas of Los Angeles County to enhance their options for living independently. Any person who is 18 yrs of age or more with physical, sensory, mental/emotional or developmental disabilities can work with us to become more self-sufficient. Our intake procedures provide an orientation to the staff, facilities and services at CRS.

4598 Community Rehabilitation Services (CRS) Pasadena Office

980 North Fair Oaks Avenue
Room 16 & 17
Pasadena, CA 91103 626-794-9860
FAX: 626-794-9884

4599 Community Rehabilitation Services - Downtown Office

3325 Wilshire Boulevard
Suite 850
Los Angeles, CA 90010 323-427-9090
FAX: 323-427-0172
e-mail: watu@pacbell.net

4600 Community Rehabilitation Services for Independent Living

4716 Brooklyn Avenue
Los Angeles, CA 90022 323-266-0453
FAX: 323-266-7992
e-mail: crsela@pacbell.net

Al Rivera, Director

Offer people with disabilities transportation, housing assistance, advocacy, attendant referral, peer counseling and information services. New programs include job club and independent living skills training and deaf services.

4601 Community Rehabilitation Services- San Gabriel Office

1323 South San Gabriel Boulevard
Suite A
San Gabriel, CA 91775 626-307-2900
FAX: 626-307-1635
TDY:626-307-4188

4602 Community Resouirces for Independence Fort Bragg Office

310 East Redwood Lane
Fort Bragg, CA 95437 707-964-6714
FAX: 707-961-1761
e-mail: Crifortbragg@excite.com

4603 Community Resources for Independence

980 Hopper Avenue
Santa Rosa, CA 95403 707-528-2745
800-528-7703
FAX: 707-528-9477
e-mail: cri-santarosa@ap.net
www.cri-dove.org

Michael Humphrey, Director
Sandy Hobart, Assistant Director
Dominique Gaiton, Office Manager/Receptionist

Offers peer counseling, disability education and awareness, attendant care, advocacy, housing access modification, disability law clinic, housing I&R, and ASL classes. Serves Sonoma, Mendocino, Lake and Napa counties.

4604 Community Resources for Independence - Ukiah Office

1040 North State Street
"E"
Ukiah, CA 95482   707-463-8875

e-mail: cri_4@hotmail.com

4605 Community Resources for Independent Living - Hayward

439 A Street
Hayward, CA 94541   510-881-5743
                            FAX: 510-881-1593
                    e-mail: crilsvc4u@aol.com

4606 Community Resources for Independent Living

439 A Street
Hayward, CA 94541   510-881-5743
                            FAX: 510-881-1593
                    e-mail: cril@pacbell.net

Jack G. Chapman, Executive Director
Elizabeth Pazdral, Program Director

4607 Darrell McDaniel Independent Living Center

14354 Haynes Street
Van Nuys, CA 91401   818-988-9525
                            FAX: 818-785-0330

Norma Jean Vescovo, Executive Director

Offers barrier free residential services to the physically challenged with a staff on location for 24 hour a day needs.

4608 Dayle McIntosh Center for the Disabled

150 West Cerritos Avenue
Building 4
Anaheim, CA 92805   714-772-8285
                            FAX: 714-772-8292
                    e-mail: rdevylde@pacbell.net
                    www.daylemcintoshcenter.org

Liz Gonzalez, Information & Referrals
Margaret Drda, Assistant Director
Anita Adams, Community Events Coordinator

Offers advocacy, counseling, attendant registry, information and referral, independent living skills training, communications, commend (medical emergency network for the deaf and children's services), housing, assistive technology, and emergency services.

4609 Dayle McIntosh Center/South County

27782 El Lazo Road
Suite 100
Laguna Niguel, CA 92677   949-643-7275
                                FAX: 949-643-7284

Norma Vescovo, Contact
Kyle Minnis, Field Coordinator
Myvan Mguyen, Office Manager

4610 Disability Resource Agency for Independent Living - Stockton Office

San Joaquin ILC
4505 Precissi Lane Suite A
Stockton, CA 95207   209-477-8143

e-mail: draila1@earthlink.net

4611 Disability Resource Agency for IL Sonora Office - Mother Lode ILC

975 Morningstar
Suite A
Sonora, CA 95370   209-532-0963

e-mail: barrysmith_mllilc@yahoo.com

4612 Disability Resource Agency for Independent Living - Modesto

221 McHenry Avenue
Modesto, CA 95354   209-521-7260
                            FAX: 209-521-4763
                            TDY:209-521-1425
                    e-mail: dwight@netfeed.com

4613 Disabled Resources Center

2750 E Spring Street
Suite 100
Long Beach, CA 90806   562-426-0665
                              FAX: 562-427-2027
                        e-mail: info@drcinc.org
                              www.drcinc.org

Jeanette Nishikawa, Director
Dolores Nason, Associate Director

Offers peer counseling, disability awareness, information on accessible housing, attendant registry, benefits advocacy and other services.

4614 FREED Center for Independent Living

154 Hughes Road
Suite 1
Grass Valley, CA 95945   530-272-1732
                                FAX: 530-272-7793
                        e-mail: tony@freed.org
                              www.freed.org

Ann Guerra, Executive Director

Offers peer counseling, disability education and awareness, personal assistant care registry and information on accessible housing and assistive technology.

4615 First Step Independent Living

1174 Nevada Street
Redlands, CA 92374

                            800-362-0312
                    e-mail: cvsfs@deltanet.com

4616 ILC of Kern County

1927 Eye Street
Bakersfield, CA 93301   805-325-1063
                              FAX: 805-325-6702
                              TDY:805-325-3092
                    e-mail: ilckernl@eathlink.net

4617 Imperial Valley ILC

395 Broadway
Suite 10
El Centro, CA 92243

                            TDY:760-353-4191

4618 Independence Center
3640 South Sepulveda Boulevard
Suite 102
Los Angeles, CA 90034   310-202-7102
                         FAX: 310-202-7180
e-mail: judym@independencecenter.com
www.independencecenter.com

Judy Maizlish, Executive Director

A mainstreamed residential program teaching independent living to young adults (18-30+) with learning disabilities.

4619 Independent Learning Center of Kern County
1631 30th St
Bakersfield, CA 93301   661-325-4143
                         FAX: 661-325-6702
e-mail: ilckernl@ilcofkerncounty.org
www.ilcofkerncounty.org

David Bolin, Contact

4620 Independent Living Center of Southern California
356-B E Avenue K-4
Lancaster, CA 93535   661-945-6602
                         FAX: 661-945-5690
e-mail: ilcsclanc@aol.com

Norma Vescovo, Contact

4621 Independent Living Center of Southern California
14354 Haynes Street
103
Van Nuys, CA 91401   818-981-5000
                         FAX: 818-785-0330
                         TDY: 818-988-3533
e-mail: ilcscserv1@aol.com

Cynthia Tovar, Supervisor of Services

Housing, advocacy, benefits counseling and independent living skills.

4622 Independent Living Resource of Contra Costa County-Fairfield Office
1545 Webster Street "C"
Fairfield, CA 94533   707-435-8174

4623 Independent Living Resource Center
423 W Victoria Street
Santa Barbara, CA 93101   805-963-0595
                         FAX: 805-963-1350
e-mail: jblack3910@aol.com

Josephine Black, Executive Director
Kathleen Riel, Human Resources Director
Steven Wall, Peer Support

A private, nonprofit organization founded by and for persons with disabilities to assist individuals to achieve optimal levels of self-sufficiency. Services include personal assistant referrals, peer and benefits counseling, advocacy, sign language interpreter/communication services, independent living skills training, information and referrals, community education and systems advocacy, housing and employment assistance.

4624 Independent Living Resource Center - Santa Maria Office
327 E Plaza Drive # 3A
Santa Maria, CA 93454   805-925-0015
                         FAX: 805-349-2416
www.ilrc-trico.org

Madelena Nieto, Coordinator
Tina Horr, Benefits

4625 Independent Living Resource Center - Ventura Office
1802 Eastman Avenue
Suite 112
Ventura, CA 93003   805-925-0015
                         FAX: 805-650-9278

4626 Independent Living Resource Center of San Francisco
649 Mission Street
3rd Floor
San Francisco, CA 94105   415-543-6222
                         FAX: 415-543-6318
www.ilrcsf.org

Carol Bradley, Executive Director

4627 Independent Living Resource of Contra Costa County - Antioch Office
310 West 10th Street
Antioch, CA 94509   510-754-0539

4628 Independent Living Resource of Contra Costa County
3200 Clayton Road
Concord, CA 94519   925-363-7293
                         FAX: 925-363-7296
e-mail: joanne@ilrccc.org

JoAnne Bell, Executive Director
Paul Demange, Program Director
Rich Broaddus, Branch Manager

4629 Independent Living Service Northern California - Redding Office
1411 Yuba Street
Redding, CA 95001   530-242-8550
                         FAX: 530-241-1454
e-mail: ilsncrdg@maxinet.com

4630 Independent Living Services of Northern California
555 Rio Lindo Avenue
Chico, CA 95926   530-893-8527
                         FAX: 530-893-8574
e-mail: ilsnc@maxinet.com

4631 Independent Living Services of Northern California
1161 East Avenue
Chico, CA 95926   530-893-8527
                         FAX: 530-893-8574
e-mail: ilsnc@maxinet.com

Rocky Burks, Executive Director

Independent Living Services of Northern California is a consumer-run agency providing support services to help persons with disabilities maintain their optimal level of self-reliance and independence.

4632 Marin Center for Independent Living

1562 Cherokee Street
PO Box 151268
San Rafael, CA   94915   415-461-1440
                        FAX: 415-459-7047
           e-mail: mcilbob@marincil.org
                        www.marincil.org

Bob Roberts, Executive Director

Offers peer counseling, disability education and awareness, attendant care registry and information on accessible housing.

4633 Modesto Independent Living Center

221 McHenry Avenue
Modesto, CA   95354   209-521-7260
                        FAX: 209-521-4763
            e-mail: dwight@drail.org
                        www.drail.org

Dwight Bateman, Director
Fred J. Dickinson, Director of Services

Offers peer counseling, disability awareness and education, benefits advising, attendant care registry and other services to the community.

4634 Mother Lode Independent Living Center

67 Linoberg Street
Suite A
Sonora, CA   95370   209-532-0963
                        FAX: 209-532-1591
            e-mail: barry@drail.org
                        www.drail.org

Dwight Bateman, Executive Director
Barry Smith, Center Coordinator

Disability Resources Agency for Independent Living (DEAIL).

4635 Placer Independent Resource Services

11768 Atwood Road
Suite 29
Auburn, CA   95603   530-885-6100
                        FAX: 530-885-3032
                        TDY:530-885-0326
       e-mail: tmiller@pirs.puhsd.k12.ca.us

4636 Placer Indepndent Resource Services

11768 Atwood Road
Suite 29
Auburn, CA   95603   530-885-6100
                        FAX: 530-885-3032
            e-mail: tmiller@pirs.org
                        www.pirs.org

Susan Miller , Contact

4637 Resources for Independent Living

1211 H Street
Suite B
Sacramento, CA   95814   916-446-3074
                        FAX: 916-446-2443

Frances Gracechild, Contact

Independent living center serving Sacramento and Yolo counties.

4638 Rolling Start

570 W 4th Street
Suite 103
San Bernardino, CA   92401   909-884-2129
                        FAX: 909-386-7446
            e-mail: rolinstart@aol.com
        hometown.aol.com/rolinstart/home.html

Don Vigil, Contact

4639 San Gabriel/Pomona Valley Center for Indep

963 West Bardillo
PO Box 1296
Claremont, CA   91711   909-621-6722
                        FAX: 909-445-0727
        e-mail: scilclmt@tstonramp.com

Carol Lane, President & CEO
Leepi Shimklada, Operations Manager

4640 San Joaquin Independent Living Center

4555 Precissi Lane
Stockton, CA   95207   209-477-8143
                        FAX: 209-477-7730
            e-mail: richard@drail.org
                        www.drail.org

Richard Gross, Coordinator

4641 Service Center for Independent Living - Corvina Office

963 West Badillo Street
Covina, CA   626-967-0995
                        FAX: 626-967-3132
                        TDY:626-967-4401
        e-mail: scilcovn@stonramp.com

4642 Service Center for Independent Living

Claremont Office
109 South Spring Street
Claremont, CA   91711   909-621-6722
                        FAX: 909-445-0727
        e-mail: scilclmt@tstonramp.com

4643 Silicon Valley Independent Living Center - Gilroy Office

7415 Eigleberry Street
Suite C
Gilroy, CA   95020   408-847-1805
                        FAX: 408-847-5595
                        TDY:408-847-7845

4644 Silicon Valley Independent Living Center

1601 Civic Center Drive
Suite 100
Santa Clara, CA   95050   408-985-1243
                        FAX: 408-985-067
                        TDY:408-985-9243
            e-mail: vandanam@svilc.org

4645 Southeast Center for Independent Living

7830 Quill Drive
Suite D
Downey, CA   90242   562-862-6531
                              800-844-3089
                        FAX: 562-923-5274
                        TDY:562-869-0931
                        www.scnspwi.org

Mary Rios, Executive Director
Steve Bramdt, Program Director

Offers peer counseling, disability awareness, information on accessible housing and other services to the community.

4646 Southern California Rehabilitation Services

7830 Quill Drive
Suite D
Downey, CA 90242
562-862-6531
FAX: 562-923-5274
TDY:562-869-0931
e-mail: scrsenid@aol.com

4647 Through the Looking Glass

2198 Sixth Street
Suite 100
Berkeley, CA 94710
510-848-1112
800-644-2666
FAX: 510-848-4445

4648 Westside Center for Independent Living

11201 South La Cienega Boulevard
Los Angeles, CA 90045
310-568-0107
FAX: 310-568-1015
TDY:310-568-0756
e-mail: wcil@aol.com

Colorado

4649 Atlantic Community

201 S Cherokee St
Denver, CO 80223
303-733-9324
FAX: 303-733-6211
e-mail: adaptden@plinet.com

Michael W. Auberger, Contact

4650 CONNECTION for Independent Living

1024 9th Avenue
Suite E
Greeley, CO 80631
970-352-8682
FAX: 970-353-8058

Beth Danielson, Contact

4651 Center for Independence

1600 Ute Avenue
Suite 100
Grand Junction, CO 81501
970-241-0315
800-613-2271
e-mail: cfi@gj.net

4652 Center for Independent Living

16090 Ute Avenue
Suite 100
Grand Junction, CO 81501
970-241-0315
FAX: 970-245-3341
e-mail: cfi@gj.net
www.gj.net/~cfi

Mary Lynn McNutt, Contact

4653 Center for People with Disabilities

948 North Street
#7
Boulder, CO 80304
303-442-8662

e-mail: cpwd@bcn.boulder.co.us

Robert Trujillo, Contact

4654 Center on Deafness

1490 Lafayette Street
Suite 408
Denver, CO 80203
303-839-8022
FAX: 303-839-8027
TDY:3038398022
e-mail: cod@pcisys.net
www.centerondeafness.org

Danielle Jansen

Offers sign language and oral interpreting services, sign language classes (both public and private), client services, ADA technical assistance, community education and advocacy.

4655 Choices for Independent Living

1024 Ninth Avenue
Suite E
Greeley, CO 80631
303-352-8682

4656 Colorado Springs Independence Center

405 E Colorado Avenue
Colorado Springs, CO 80903
719-578-9947
FAX: 719-471-7829

Vicki Mitschler, Director

Offers peer counseling, disability education and awareness and information on accessible housing.

4657 Connections for Independent Living

1024 - 9th Avenue
Suite E
Greeley, CO 80631
970-330-2840
FAX: 970-353-8058
e-mail: connectionsil!viawest.net

Beth Danielson, Executive Director

Certified IL Center, I and R advocacy, peer support, skills training, sign language interpretations, reader services, housing. Cross-disability, all ages.

4658 Deaf Counseling Services at Mental Health Corporation of Denver

4353 East Colfax Avenue
Denver, CO 80220
303-504-1200
FAX: 303-320-4830
e-mail: kmallah@mhcd.com
www.mhcd.com

Kara Mallah, Ph.D., Program Manager

Provides conseling to deaf and hard of hearing persons who reside in Metro Denver. Our goal is to provide therapeutic service that respects the dignity, privacy, and unique needs of the person.

4659 Denver CIL

455 Sherman Street
Suite 140
Denver, CO   80203   303-698-1900

**4660 Disability Center for Independent Living -
Colorado**

CO

e-mail: laurahershey@compuserve.com

4661 Disability Center for Independent Living

5900 East 39th Avenue
Suite 4
Denver, CO   80207   303-320-1345
                            FAX: 303-320-1355

John Pipe, Executive Director
Carol Reynolds, Deputy Director

4662 Disabled Resource Services

424 Pine Street
Suite 101
Fort Collins, CO   80524   970-482-2700
                            FAX: 970-407-7072
                            e-mail: drs@jymis.com
                            www.drs@fortnet.org

Nancy Jackson, Executive Director

Offers peer counseling, loan closet, employment assistance, information and referral, case management, volunteer coordination, equipment loan closet, advocacy, financial assistance, housing assistance, newsletter publication, and independent living skills, training to persons with disabilities to help increase their independence and quality of life.

4663 Greeley Center for Independence

2780 28th Avenue
Greeley, CO   80634   970-339-2444
                            800-748-1012
                            FAX: 970-339-0033
                            e-mail: gciinc.gci.org
                            www.gci.org

Hope Cassidy , Executive Director

4664 Martin Luther Homes - Denver

2480 W 26th Avenue
Suite 120B
Denver, CO   80211   303-455-8006
                            FAX: 303-455-8106

Cecelia Camp, Administrator
Fred Naumann III, Communications

Providing a wide array of services to assist individuals and families in achieving positive life goals. Services to persons with disabilities and other special needs include community living options, training and employment options, spiritual growth and development options, training and counseling support.

4665 Martin Luther Homes - Fort Collins

109 Cameron Drive
Unit A
Fort Collins, CO   80525   970-223-1751
                            FAX: 970-223-1781

Sharon Jacksi, PhD, Administrator
Fred Naumann III, Communications

Providing a wide array of services to assist individuals and families in achieving positive life goals. Services to persons with disabilities and other special needs include community living options, training and employment options, spiritual growth and development options, training and counseling support.

4666 Pueblo Goodwill Center for Independent Living

250 S Santa Fe Avenue
Pueblo, CO   81003   719-543-4483
                            FAX: 719-545-5134

Bill Bolt, Director

Must be a client of DVR to be eligible for their program of independent living skills and work training skills.

4667 Sangre De Cristo Independent Living Center

803 W 4th Street
Suite Df
Pueblo, CO   81003   719-546-1271
                            FAX: 719-546-1374

Albert Martinez, Acting Director

4668 Sangre de Cristo Independent Living Center

131 South Union
Pueblo, CO   81004   719-546-1271

4669 Southwest Center for Independence

801 Florida Road
Unit 3
Durango, CO   81301   970-259-1572
                            FAX: 970-259-0947
                            e-mail: swcidur@frontier.net

Larry Wales, Executive Director
Offers peer counseling and disability education.

Connecticut

4670 Center for Disability Rights

764 A Campbell Avenue
West Haven, CT   06516   203-934-7077
                            FAX: 203-934-7078
                            e-mail: CDR7077@aol.com

Marc K. Gallurri, Executive Director
Carmen Conea, Info & Referral Specialist

4671 Chapel Haven

1040 Whalley Avenue
Westville, CT   06515   203-397-1714
                            FAX: 203-392-3698
                            www.chapelhaven.org

Judith Lefkowitz, Director of Admissions

Independent living skills program that provides residential and community support services to adults with cognitive disabilities in life skills, employment, education, and recreation.

4672 Co-Op Initiatives
999 Asylum Avenue
Suite 506
Hartford, CT 06105   860-724-4940
    FAX: 860-724-7102
    e-mail: BCrum@coopinit.org
    www.coopinit.org

Betsy Crum, Housing and Homelessness

4673 Connecticut Center's for Independent Living
Disabilities Network of Eastern Ct.
107 Route 32
North Franklin, CT 06254

    e-mail: dnec@snet.net

4674 Disabilities Network of Eastern Connecticut
107 Route 32
North Franklin, CT 06254   860-823-1898
    FAX: 860-886-2316
    e-mail: dnec@snet.net

Carolyn Newcombe, Contact

4675 Disability Resource Center of Fairfield County - Stratford Office
80 Ferry Boulevard
Suite 210
Stratford, CT 06497   203-378-6977
    FAX: 203-375-2748
    TDY: 203-378-3248
    e-mail: info@drcfc.org

4676 Independence Northwest
1183 New Haven Road
Suite 200
Naugatuck, CT 06770   203-397-1714
    FAX: 203-397-8004

Eileen Horndt, Contact

4677 Independence Northwest Center for Independent Living
1183 New Haven Road
Suite 200
Naugatuck, CT 06770   203-729-3299
    FAX: 203-729-2839
    e-mail: indnw@aol.com

Eileen Horndt, Director
Offers peer counseling, disability education and awareness.

4678 Independence Unlimited
151 New Park Avenue
Suite D
Hartford, CT 06106   860-523-5021
    FAX: 860-523-5603
    e-mail: indun@aol.com

Candace Low, Executive Director

4679 New Horizons
37 Bliss Road
Unionville, CT 06085   860-675-4711
    FAX: 860-675-4369

Michael Shaw, Contact

Delaware

4680 Easter Seal Independent Living Center
24 Reads Way
New Castle, DE 19720   302-324-4488
    FAX: 302-324-4481
    e-mail: rab@nc.esdel.org

Ray Brouillette, Contact

4681 Independent Living
1800 N Broom Street
Wilmington, DE 19802   302-888-5900
    FAX: 302-429-8034

Susan Cycyk, Director
Providing skilled support and caring guidance to adults with disabilities. Our case management services include: daily living skills training, medical coordination, transportation assistance, financial management, housing assistance, and vocational/educational planning.

Sliding Scale

4682 Independent Resources
52 Reads Way
New Castle, DE 19720   302-328-6704

4683 Martin Luther Homes of Delaware
822 Basin Road
Suite D
Newcastle, DE 19720   302-453-1933
    FAX: 302-328-4795

Terry Olson, Administrator
Fred Naumann III, Communications
Providing a wide array of services to assist individuals and families in achieving positive life goals. Services to persons with disabilities and other special needs include community living options, training and employment options, spiritual growth and development options, training and counseling support.

District of Columbia

4684 Centers for Independent Living Program Rehabilitation Services Department
Mary E. Switzer Building
330 C Street SW
Washington, DC 20201   202-619-3482

Approximately 400 Independent Living Centers, most funded by this program, provide local services and programs to enable individuals with severe disabilities to live and function independently.

4685 D.C. Center for Independent Living
1400 Florida Avenue NE
Suite 3
Washington, DC 20002
    FAX: 202-398-3018
    e-mail: dccil@aol.com

Richard A. Simms, Executive Director

4686 Disability Rights Center
2500 G Street NW
Washington, DC   20007   703-934-2020
                      FAX: 703-352-5762
                      e-mail: drc@patriot.net

Susan Ferris, Contact

4687 Human Resources Management
American Assn. of Children's Residential Centers
440 1st Street NW
3rd Floor
Washington, DC   20001   202-628-1816
                      FAX: 202-638-4004
                      e-mail: aacrc@dc.net
                      www.aacrc-dc.org

Richard Biolsi, ACSW, President
Elissa Malter Schwartz, Association Director

One-day seminar addresses the Management of Human Resources standards in the Comprehensive Accreditation Manuarll for Hospitals, Behavioral Health, Long Term Care, Ambulatory and Home Care, plus standards on orientation and education, staffing and managing staff requests. July 13, 2001. Four Points Sheraton Hotel in San Diego, California.

Florida

4688 Adult Day Training
Goodwill Industries-Suncoast
10596 Gandy Boulevard
PO Box 14456
St. Petersburg, FL   33733   727-523-1512
                      FAX: 727-577-2749
                      www.goodwill-suncoast.org

Joe Mc Cloe, Director of Resource Development

An innovative program which uses job skills to teach self-help, daliy living, communication, mobility, travel, decision-making, behavioral and social skills. This focus provides concrete, transferable experiences to help prepare individuals for greater community inclusion by achieving the highest possible degree of independence in their daily life, increasing their confidence and supporting their successful transitions to less structured, self-suffficient environments.

4689 Caring and Sharing Center for Independent Living
1130 94th Avenue N
Saint Petersburg, FL   33702   727-577-0065
                      FAX: 727-577-2932
                      e-mail: cascil@mindspring.com

Michael Cook, Contact

4690 Cathedral Center for Independent Living
3599 University Boulevard S
Jacksonville, FL   32216   904-399-4185

Susan Hughes, Administrator
Offers comprehensive rehabilitation.

4691 Center for Independent Living in Central Florida-Advocacy Living Skills Peer Support
720 North Denning Drive
Winter Park, FL   32789   407-623-1070
                      877-891-6448
                      FAX: 407-623-1390

Elizabeth Howe, Executive Director

Information and referral services, advocacy, living skills, peer support, employment.

4692 Center for Independent Living of North Florida
572-C Appleyard Drive
Tallahassee, FL   32304   850-575-9621
                      800-226-9621
                      FAX: 850-575-5740
                      TDY:8505765245
                      e-mail: cilnf@nettally.com
                      www.cilnf.org

Janet Kahn, Executive Director

CILNF is a non-profit organization whose mission is to empower persons with disabilities to live independently and participate actively in their community.

4693 Center for Independent Living of Broward
8857 W McNab Road
Tamarac, FL   33321   954-722-6400
                      FAX: 954-722-9801
                      e-mail: cilb@cilbroward.org

Karen Dickerdorf, Executive Director

4694 Center for Independent Living of North Central Florida
720 NW 23rd Avenue
Gainesville, FL   32606   352-378-7474
                      FAX: 352-378-5582
                      www.ilncf.org

4695 Center for Independent Living of Northwest Florida
1302 Dunmire Street
Pensacola, FL   32504   850-484-5444
                      FAX: 850-484-3900
                      e-mail: cilnwf@gulf.net
                      www.cilnwf.org

Frank Cherry, Contact

4696 Center for Independent Living of South Florida
501 NE 1st Avenue
Suite 102
Miami, FL   33132   305-379-6650
                      FAX: 305-379-6653
                      e-mail: soflacil@aol.com

Kelly Greene, Executive Director
Ubaldo Alvarez, Project Director

4697 Center for Independent Living of Southwest Florida
3626 Evans Avenue
Fort Myers, FL   33901   941-277-3964
                      FAX: 941-227-1647
                      e-mail: cilfl@mindspring.net
                      cilfl.org

Jim Zakas, Contact

4698 Center for Independent Technology and Education (C.I.T.E.)

215 E New Hampshire Street
Orlando, FL 32804   407-896-3177
                         888-898-2483
                    FAX: 407-895-5255
                    e-mail: comcite@aol.com

Carol Adams, Executive Director

4699 Coalition for Independent Living Option

6800 Forest Hill Boulevard
West Palm Beach, FL 33413   561-966-4288
                        FAX: 561-641-6619
              e-mail: cilpbc19@mail.idt.netxxxd693n

Shelly Gottsager, Executive Director

Independent living centers offer peer counseling, advocacy, information and referral and independent living skills development. CILO offers teen programs, an adaptive equipment loan closet, disability and accessibility studies.s.

4700 Freedom Villages and Heritage Oaks

Goodwill Industries-Suncoast
10596 Gandy Boulevard
PO Box 14456
St. Petersburg, FL 33733   727-523-1512
                         FAX: 727-577-2749
                    www.goodwill-suncoast.org

Joe Mc Cloe, Director of Resource Development

Provides a variety of affordable, barrier -free or accessibilty- enhanced housing to the low-income elderly and/or physically impaired. Eligibilty varies between properties. Amenities also vary, but typically include spacious, scenic grounds excellent for bird watching and strolling, patio, sunroom or deck, cookout areas, (covered) parking, access to Support Coordinators, recreational opportunities and computer labs. Transportation may be provided through Client Transportation Services.

4701 Independent Living Resource Center of Northeast Florida

2709 Art Museum Drive
Jacksonville, FL 32207   904-399-8484
                         888-427-4313
                    FAX: 904-396-0859
                    TDY:904-398-6322
                    e-mail: cilj@southeast.net
                    www.cilf.com

Marcia Randall, Executive Director
Pamela Williams, Office Manager
Andrea Williamson, Program Manager

Offers information/referral, advocacy, peer mentoring, independent living skills training, up to date ADA information, FIRI program, deaf consumer programs, interpreting services, and high school career choice. Serves Duval, Clay, Nassau, Flagler, St. Johns, Volusia, and Baker counties in Florida.

4702 Independent Living Resource Center of Northeast Florida

2709 Art Museum Drive
Jacksonville, FL 32207   904-399-8484
                         888-427-4313
                    FAX: 904-396-0859
                    TDY:904-398-6322
                    e-mail: cilj@southeast.net
                    www.cilf.com

Marcia Randall, Executive Director
Pamela Williams, Office Manager
Andrea Williamson, Program Manager

Offers information/referral, advocacy, peer mentoring, independent living skills training, up to date ADA information, FIRI program, deaf consumer programs, interpreting services, and high school career choice. Serves Duval, Clay, Nassau, Flagler, St. Johns, Volusia, and Baker counties in Florida.

4703 Independent Living for Adult Blind

101 W State Street
Jacksonville, FL 32202   904-633-8220
                        FAX: 904-632-5107
                    e-mail: bsimpson@fccj.org

Becky Simpson, Project Coordinator

Offers services for the totally blind, legally blind and visually impaired. Services include independent living skills, training and guidance toward rehabilitation. Also provides vocational training in computers. Supported by government grants and private donations.

4704 Miami-Dade County Disability Services and Independent Living (DSAIL)

1335 NW 14th Street
Miami, FL 33125   305-547-5444
                        FAX: 305-547-7355

Paul Prevost, Director

Offers information and referral services serving all types of disabilities with the goal of assisting the disabled acquiring independence and control over their lives. Teaches independent living skills, job readiness and placement, home health care, sensitivity training, training in ASL and Braille, counsel people with disabilities or wide range of problems.

4705 Northern Florida Center for Independent Living

572 Appleyard Drive
Suite C
Tallahassee, FL 32304   850-759-21
                        FAX: 850-575-5740
                    e-mail: janetkahn@nettally.com
                    www.cilnf.org

Janet Kahn, Contact

4706 Seacoast Center for Independent Living at Titusville

725 S Deleon Avenue
Titusville, FL 32780   321-268-2244
                        FAX: 321-383-5625

Gerri , Contact

4707 Self Reliance

11215 N Nebraska Avenue
Suite B#
Tampa, FL 33612 813-975-6560
FAX: 813-975-6559
e-mail: wbuckner@sprynet.com
www.self-reliance.org

Susan Stacy, Executive Director
Yvonne Epps, Administrative Assistant

4708 Self-Reliance Center for Independent Living

11215 N Nebraska Avenue
Suite B3
Tampa, FL 33612 813-975-6560
FAX: 813-975-6559
e-mail: self-reliance@slef-reliance.org

Susan Stacey, Executive Director
Yvonne Epps, Administrative Assistant

Offers peer counseling, disability education and awareness, advocacy and other services to the community.

4709 Space Coast Center for Independent Living

331 Ramp Road
Cocoa Beach, FL 32931 321-784-9008
FAX: 321-784-3702
e-mail: sccil@bellsouth.net

Barbara Allard, Executive Director

4710 Suncoast Center for Independent Living

330 S Pineapple Avenue
Suite 110
Sarasota, FL 34236 941-993-4142
FAX: 941-351-9545

William Knight, Executive Director

Offers information and referrals, advocacy, peer counseling, independent living skills training, equipment, loan and consultation on ADA laws.

**4711 Suncoast Residential Training Center/
Developmental Services Program**

Goodwill Industries-Suncoast
10596 Gandy Boulevard
PO Box 14456
St. Petersburg, FL 33733 727-523-1512
FAX: 727-577-2749
www.goodwill-suncoast.org

Joe Mc Cloe, Director of Resource Development

A large group home which serves individuals diagnosed as mentally retarded with a secondary diagnosed of psychiatric difficulties as evidenced by problem behavior. Providing residential, behavioral and instructional support and services that will promote the development of adaptive, socially appropriate behavior, each individual is assessed to determine strengths and needs in such skill areas as self-care, daily living, human growth and development, socialization, basic academics and recreation.

4712 Supported Living Program

Goodwill Industries-Suncoast
10596 Gandy Boulevard
PO Box 14456
St. Petersburg, FL 33733 727-523-1512
FAX: 727-577-2749
www.goodwill-suncoast.org

Joe Mc Cloe, Director of Resource Development

Provides comprehensive suports and individualized services to persons with developmental disabilities who demonstrate motivation to live in integrated settings in the community. Services include daily living skills training while living in the community and additional supports such as legal, safety procedures, self-medication, hygeine, household management, banking, meal preparation, nutrition, problem solving, interpersonal relationships, parent training and community resource utilization.

4713 Tampa Lighthouse for the Blind

1106 W Platt Street
Tampa, FL 33606 813-251-2407
FAX: 813-254-4305
e-mail: tpalight@gate.net
www.gate.net/tpalight

C.E. Olstrom, Executive Director

Our purpose is to maximize independence and provide employment opportunities for persons who are blind or visually impaired.

Georgia

4714 Access Center for Independent Living

PO Box 908484
Gainesville, GA 30501 770-534-6656
FAX: 770-534-6656
e-mail: stwells@bellsouth.net

Stephanie Wells, Contact

4715 Bain

1235 E Shotwell Street
Bainbridge, GA 31717 912-246-0150
FAX: 912-246-1715
e-mail: bain@surfsouth.com

Virginia Harris, Contact

4716 Disability LINK

755 Commerce Drive
Suite 415
Decatur, GA 30030 404-687-8890
FAX: 404-687-8298
www.disabilitylink.org

Rebecca Ramage-Tuttle, Executive Director

4717 District of Columbia Center for Independent Living

1400 Florida Avenue Northeast
Suite 3
Washington, DC 20002 202-388-0033
FAX: 202-398-3018
e-mail: dccil@aol.com

Richard A. Simms, Executive Director

4718 Division of Rehabilitation Services
410 Mall Boulevard
Suite B
Savannah, GA 31406
FAX: 912-691-6816

Allen Beall, Regional Director
Vocational rehabilitation services.

4719 Georgia Field Services Independent Living Program
3125 Presidential Parkway
Atlanta, GA 30340   770-452-9601

Pat Puckett, Director
Offers disability education, attendant care registry and information on housing.

4720 Living Independently for Everyone (LIFE)
17-21 East Travis Street
Savannah, GA 31406   912-920-2419
FAX: 912-920-0007
e-mail: hodgep@mindspring.com

Pamela Hodge, Contact

4721 Middle Georgia Center for Independent Living (Dba Disability Connections)
170 College Street
Macon, GA 31201   912-741-1425
FAX: 912-743-9806
e-mail: kilby8494@aol.com

Jerilyn Leverett, Executive Director
Tina Hopper, Information Coordinator

4722 North District Independent Living Program
311 Green Street NW
Suite 209
Gainesville, GA 30501

Sharon McCurry, Coordinator
Information and referral, advocacy, peer counseling, service coordination and ADA consultation.

4723 Roosevelt Warm Springs Institute for Rehabilitation
PO Box 1000
Warm Springs, GA 31830   706-655-5000
FAX: 706-655-5011
www.rooseveltrehab.org

Frank Ruzycki, Executive Director
Martin Harmon, Public Relations Director
Carolyn McKinley, Dir. of Organizational Develop.

Comprehensive medical rehabilitation is offered for brain injury, spinal cord injury, stroke, diabetic foot care, post-polio syndrom and rehab technology, as well as vocational rehabilitations.

4724 Southwest District Independent Living Program
PO Box 1606
Albany, GA 31702   912-430-4170
FAX: 912-430-4466

Bill Layton, Director

Offers peer counseling, disability education and awareness, attendant care registry, and information on accessible home for the disabled.

4725 Walton Option for Independent Living
PO Box 519
Augusta, GA 30903   407-623-1070
FAX: 407-623-1390
e-mail: cilorando@mpinet.net
www.cilorland.org

Tiffany Johnston, Contact

4726 Walton Options for Independent Living
PO Box 519
Augusta, GA 30903   706-724-6262
FAX: 706-724-6729
e-mail: tjohnson@waltonoptions.org
www.waltonoptions.org

Tiffany Johnston, Contact

Hawaii

4727 Center for Independent Living-East Hawaii
400 Hualani Street
Suite 16D
Hilo, HI 96720   808-935-3777
FAX: 808-961-6737
e-mail: cileh@interpac.net
www.hcil.org

Laura Tobosa, Branch Coordinator
Provides an array of support services for people with all types of disabilities of any age.

4728 East Hawaii Center for Independent Living
400 Hualani Street
Suite 16D
Hilo, HI 96720   808-935-3777
FAX: 808-961-6737
e-mail: cileh@interpac.net

Laura Tobosa, Contact

4729 Hawaii Centers for Independent Living
414 Kuwili Street
Suite 102
Honolulu, HI 96817   808-522-5400
FAX: 808-522-5427
e-mail: jimamura@diversabilities.org
www.hcil.org

Mark Obata, Contact

4730 Kailua Kona Center for Independent Living - West Hawaii
PO Box 2197
Kealakekua, HI 96750   808-323-2221
FAX: 808-323-4250

Morel Martin, Branch Office Dir.
A nonprofit organization run by and for persons with disabilities. Information on housing referrals, financial benefits, advocacy, personal care attendants, services for elderly blind, and independent living skills counseling. Services are free to all disabled persons.

4731   Kauai Center for Independent Living

PO Box 3529
Lihue, HI   96766   808-245-4034
                              FAX: 808-245-7218
                    e-mail: kcil@mail.aloha.net

Humberto Blanco, Administrator
Teri Yamashiro, IL Specialist
Gordon Dodd, ILF Counselor

Offers peer counseling, disability education and attendant care registry.

4732   Maui Center for Independent Living

1446-D Lower Main Street
Wailuku, HI   96793   808-242-4966
                              FAX: 808-244-6978
                    e-mail: mcilogg@qte.net

Ruth Hamilton, Administrator

Offers disability education and awareness, advocacy and counseling.

4733   West Hawaii Center for Independent Living

PO Box 2197
Kealakekua, HI   96750   808-323-2221
                              FAX: 808-323-2383
                    e-mail: cilwh@ilhawaii.net

Merle Martin, Contact

Idaho

4734   Access for Idaho

PO Box 4185
Pocatello, ID   83201   208-233-3115
                              FAX: 208-232-2753
                    e-mail: access@poky.srv.net

Robert Sikes, Executive Director

Provides peer counseling, disability education, attendant care registry and information and referral services to the disabled.

4735   American Falls Office - Living Independently for Everyone (LIFE)

223 Harrison Street
American Falls, ID   83211   208-226-2673

                    www2.state.id.us/silc/cils.htm

4736   Blackfoot Office - Living Independently for Everyone (LIFE)

PO Box 86
Blackfoot, ID   83221   208-785-9648
                              FAX: 208-785-9648
                    e-mail: bfoot@ida.net
                    www2.state.id.us/silc/life.htm

Dean Nielson, Contact
Sheila Jones, Independent Living Advisor

4737   Dawn Enterprises

PO Box 388
Blackfoot, ID   83221   208-785-5890
                              FAX: 208-785-3095
                    e-mail: dawnent2@if.rmci.net
                    www.orgsites.com/id/dawnent

Donna Butler, Executive Director

4738   Disability Action Center

1323 E Sherman Avenue
Street 5
Coeur D Alene, ID   83814   208-664-9896
                              FAX: 208-666-1362
                    e-mail: michelle71port@hotmail.com

Michelle Porter, Independent Living Specialist

4739   Disability Action Center NW

124 E 3rd Street
Moscow, ID   83843   208-883-0523
                              FAX: 208-883-0524
                    e-mail: kkramer@moscow.com

Mark Leeper, Director
Todd Devries, Satellite Offuce Coordinator

Information and referrals, accessibility consultant, advocacy, personal care attendant registry, peer support groups, counseling and recreation opportunities and skills training Satellite office at 601 Sherman ave, Coeur d' Alene, ID 83814. Also provides assistive technology services and information. *$45.00*

4740   Housing Southwest #2

SICHA
1102 W Finch Drive
4
Nampa, ID   83651

                              FAX: 208-463-1772

Jeanne S. Troutner, Director

Provides medical, therapeutic and counseling services - housing only.

Income-based

4741   Idaho Commission for the Blind

341 W Washington Street
PO Box 83720
Boise, ID   83720   208-334-3220
                                      800-542-8688
                              FAX: 208-334-2963
                    e-mail: mblackal@icbvi.state.id.us

Mike Blackaller, Director

Provides medical, counseling, education, training and other services needed to prepare for the working world and independent living.

4742   LINC-Satellite Office

1002 Shoshone Street E
Twin Falls, ID   83301   208-733-1712

Dennis McDermott, Director

Offers peer counseling, disability education and information on accessible housing.

4743 Life

PO Box 4185
Pocatello, ID 83205   208-232-2747
                    FAX: 208-232-2753
               e-mail: dean@poky.srv.net

Dean Nielson, Executive Director

Provides peer counseling, disability education, attendant care registry and information and referral services to the disabled.

4744 Living Independence Network Corporation

708 W Franklin Street
Boixe, ID 83702
                    FAX: 208-384-5037
               e-mail: lincinfo@aol.com
               www2.state.id.us

Rebecca Blackwell, Community Resource Coordinator

LINC, a non-profit organizaition, empowers people with disabilities to achieve their desired level of independence.

4745 Living Independently Network Corporation (LINC)

2500 Kootenai Street
Boise, ID 83705   208-336-3335
                    FAX: 208-384-5037
               e-mail: lincinfo@aol.com
               www2.state.id.us/silc/linc.htm

Kim McCulley, Contact

4746 Northwest Disability Action Center

124 E 3rd Street
Moscow, ID 83843   208-883-0523
                    FAX: 208-883-0524
                    e-mail: dacn.htm

Mark Leeper, Contact

4747 Pocatello Main Office - Living Independently for Everyone (LIFE)

PO Box 4185
Pocatello, ID 83205   208-232-2747
                         800-631-2747
                    FAX: 208-232-2753
               e-mail: dean@if.rmci.net
               www2.state.id.us/silc/life.htm

Dean Nielson, Contact

4748 Pocatello Main Office - Living Independent for Everyone (LIFE)

PO Box 4185
845 West Center
Pocatello, ID 83201   208-232-2747
                    FAX: 208-232-2753
               e-mail: dean@if.rmci.net
               www2.state.id.us/silc/cils.htm

4749 Southwestern Idaho Housing Authority

1108 W Finch Drive
Nampa, ID 83651   208-467-7461
                    FAX: 208-463-1772

Jeanne Troutner, Contact

4750 Access Living of Metro Chicago

310 S Peoria Street
Suite 201
Chicago, IL 60607   312-226-1687
                    FAX: 312-226-2030
               e-mail: generalinfo@accessliving.org

Marca Bristo, Contact

4751 Access Living of Metropolitan Chicago

310 S Peoria Street
Suite 210
Chicago, IL 60607
                    FAX: 312-226-2030

Jim Charlton, Executive Director

4752 Center for Comprehensive Service

PO Box 2825
Carbondale, IL 62902   618-529-3060
                    FAX: 618-457-5372

Mary Moore, Contact

4753 Center for Comprehensive Services

306 W Mill Street
Carbondale, IL 62901   618-453-7932
                    FAX: 618-457-5372
               e-mail: ccs@midwest.net

Mary Kay Moore, Executive Director

Offers peer counseling, disability education and advocacy services.

4754 Central Illinois Center for Independent Living

614 West Glen Avenue
Peoria, IL 61614   309-682-3500
                         877-501-9808
                    FAX: 309-682-3989
               e-mail: jmiller@cicil.org
                    www.cicil.org

John Miller, Executive Director
Heather Fischer, Development Director

Offers peer counseling, disability education, advocacy services, independent living skills training, interpreter referral program, TTY distribution program, deaf community services, personal assistant program, community reintegration program, transition resources program, and accessibility audits.

4755 Community Residential Alternative

Coleman Tri-County Services
100 W Walnut Street
Harrisburg, IL 62946   618-252-3204
                    FAX: 618-252-2389

Samantha Austin, Coordinator

Six bed group home that provides a residential alternative for the developmentally disabled adult. This program is designed to promote independence in daily living skills, economic self-sufficiency, and integration into the community.

4756 Cornerstone Services

777 Joyce Road
Joliet, IL 60436 815-727-6666
FAX: 815-723-1177
www.cornerstoneservices.org

James A. Hogan, President/CEO
Matthew Lansue, PR Coordinator

Cornerstone Services provides progressive, comprehensive services for people with disabilities, promoting choice, dignity, and the opportunity to live and work in the community. Established in 1969, the agency provides developmental, vocational, employment, and behavior health services.

4757 DuPage Center for Independent Living

739 Roosevelt Road, Suite 109
Building 8
Glen Ellyn, IL 60137 630-469-2300
FAX: 630-469-2606
e-mail: dcil@mcs.com
www.incil.org/dupagecil.html

Gregg Newberry, M.A., Executive Director

4758 Fox River Valley Center for Independent Living

730 West Chicago Street
Elgin, IL 60123 847-695-5818
FAX: 847-695-5892
e-mail: frvcil1@att.net
www.incil.org/frvcil.html

Cindy Ciancio-Wallace, CEO

Provides services to people with disabilities in Kane, Kendall and McHenry counties. Our non-residential agency provides independent living skills training, advocacy, information and referral, and housing services. Also provides technical assistance to businesses and agencies to work with people with disabilities.

4759 IMPACT Center for Independent Living

2735 E Broadway
Alton, IL 62002 618-462-1411
FAX: 618-474-5309
e-mail: staff@impactcil.org
www.impactcil.org

Dick Goodwin, Executive Director

4760 Illinois/Iowa Center for Independent Living

PO Box 6156
Rock Island, IL 61204 319-324-1460
FAX: 319-324-1036
e-mail: iicil@revealed.net
www.iicil.com

Elizabeth Sherwin, Contact

A non-residential service and advocacy program for people with disabilities.

4761 Impact Center for Independent Living

2735 E Broadway
Alton, IL 62002 618-462-1411
FAX: 618-474-5309

Dick Goodwin, Executive Director

Offers peer counseling, disability education and awareness.

4762 Independence Network Center

406 N 24th Street
Durst Building, Suite 3
Quincy, IL 62301 217-223-0400
FAX: 217-223-0479
e-mail: inc@rnet.com
www.incil.org/inccil.html

Madeline Bikus, Contact

4763 Jacksonville Area Center for Independent Living

60 East Central Park Plaza
Jacksonville, IL 62650 217-245-8371
888-317-3287
FAX: 217-245-1872
TDY:Two above #s
e-mail: info@jacil.org
www.jacil.org

Becky McGinnis, Executive Director

4764 LIFE Center for Independent Living

2201 Eastland Drive
Suite 1
Bloomington, IL 61704 309-663-5433
888-543-3245
FAX: 309-663-7024
TDY:309-663-0054
e-mail: lifecil@lifeol.org

Gale Kear, Executive Director

Disability advocacy, information & referral, independent living skills training, peer counseling, sign language interpreter referrals, braille & alternate formats, equipment loan. Services people with disabilities and their families and friends in DeWitt, Ford, Livingston, and McLean Counties in Illinois.

4765 LINC - Living Independently Now Center

120 E A Street
Belleville, IL 62220 618-235-9988
FAX: 618-235-9244
e-mail: linccil@apic.net
www.lincinc.org

John Laker, Executive Director

4766 Lake County Center for Independent Living

706 E Hawley Street
Mundelein, IL 60060 847-949-0060
FAX: 847-949-4445

Lorie Clark, Executive Director

Offers peer counseling, disability education and advocacy services.

4767 Living Independently Now Center

120 E A Street
Belleville, IL 62220 618-235-9988
FAX: 618-235-9244
e-mail: lifecil@lifecil.org
www.lifecil.org

4768 Martin Luther Homes of Illinois

223 1/2 N Mill
Pontiac, IL 61764 815-844-3159
FAX: 815-842-4053

Maurie Grafton, Administrator
Fred Naumann III, Communications

Providing a wide array of services to assist individuals and families in achieving positive life goals. Services to persons with disabilities and other special needs include community living options, training and employment options, spiritual growth and development options, training and counseling support.

4769   Northwestern Illinois Center for Independent Living

229 1st Avenue
Suite 2
Rock Falls, IL   61074   815-747-6894
                                      888-886-4245
                            FAX: 815-625-7876
                    e-mail: nicil@essex1.com
                    www.incil.org/nincil.html

Cilvia Rivera, Program Director
Kathy Fischer, Executive Director

Provides services to people with disabilities. Services provided include information and referral, skills training, peer counseling, site accessibility surveys, personal assistant referral interpreters, and support groups.

4770   Office of Rehabilitation Services

Department of Human Services
100 S Grand Avenue E
Springfield, IL   62762   217-782-2094
                                     800-843-6154
                           FAX: 217-558-4270
                   e-mail: ilvr@rehabnetwork.org
                   www.state.il.us/agency/dhs

Carl Suter, Associate Director

Provides medical, therapeutic and counseling services for the disabled, as well as employment services. TTY #: 800-447-6404

4771   Opportunities for Access, A Center for Independent Living

3300 W Broadway
Suite 5
Mt. Vernon, IL   62864   618-244-9212
                                     800-938-7400
                           FAX: 618-244-9310
                   e-mail: info@ofacil.org
                   www.ofacil.org

Michael Spud Egbert, Executive Director

Serves, trains, and provides information to persons with disabilities, family members and significant others, service providers and anyone who may increase one independent living. Services include: advocacy, information and referral, peer support, skills training, volunteer programs and other related services. Services are free. A cross disability community based, non-residential, not-for-profit organization serving Clinton, Jefferson, Marion, Washington and Wayne counties in southern IL.

4772   Options Center for Independent Living

22 Heritage Drive
Bourbonnais, IL   60914   815-936-0100
                           FAX: 815-936-0117
                   www.incil.org/ocil.org

Kathy Jackson, Contact

4773   PACE Center for Independent Living

1317 East Florida Avenue
Urbana, IL   61801   217-344-5433
                           FAX: 217-344-2414
                   e-mail: paceurbana@aol.com
                   www.incil.org/pacecil.html
Newsletter - At Your PACE, author
Nancy McClellen-Hickey, Executive Director
Barb Pritchard, Director of Programs

Services for people with disabilities, PACE supports efforts to achieve or maintain independence. *$10.00*

8-10 pages

4774   Progress Center for Independent Living

7521 Madison Street
Forest Park, IL   60130   708-209-1500
                           FAX: 708-209-1735
                   e-mail: progress@theramp.net

Diane Coleman, Executive Director
Nic Steehout, Program Director

Offers peer counseling, attendant registry, information and referral services, advocacy, independent living skills, paid internships, housing assistance, national headquarters of Not Dead Yet.

4775   RAMP Regional Access & Mobility project

202 Market Street
Rockford, IL   61107   815-968-7467
                           FAX: 815-968-7612
                   e-mail: rampcil@rampcil.org
                   www.rampcil.org

Julie Bosma, Executive Director
Lydia Grzywa, Marketing Coordinator

Provides services and advocacy for people with disabilities. Services include information and referral, personal assistant services, sign language interpreters, 24 hour emergency sign language service, bus training, peer counseling, independent living skills training, accessibility assessments and information on the Americans with Disabilities Act (ADA) serving Boone, DeKalb, Stephenson and Winnebago counties in north central Illinois.

4776   Southern Illinois Center for Independent Living

100 North Glenview
PO Box 617
Carbondale, IL   62903   618-457-3318
                           FAX: 618-549-0132
                   e-mail: sicilccc@aol.com

Bonnie Vaughn, Director

Services include: advocacy, skills training, peer counseling, information and referral, elderly blind, deaf services, personal attendant screening, community reintegration programs, limited transportation services, and supported employment services.

4777   Soyland Access to Independent Living (SAIL)

2545 Millikin Parkway
Suite 1305
Decatur, IL   62526   217-876-8888
                                     800-358-8080
                           FAX: 217-876-7245
                   www.incil.org/sailcil.html

Bill Rienzle, Executive Director

4778 Springfield Center for Independent Living

426 W Jefferson Street
Springfield, IL 62702   217-523-2587
FAX: 217-523-0427
www.incil.org/sprinfcil.html

Peter Robinson, Director
Pete Roberts, Contact

4779 Stone-Hayes Center for Independent Living

39 North Prairie Street
Galesburg, IL 61401   309-344-1306
888-347-4245
FAX: 309-344-1305
e-mail: stonehayes@gellatinriver.net
www.incil.org/s_hcil.org

Catherine Holland, Executive Director

4780 Will Grundy Center for Independent Living

2415A W Jefferson Street
Joliet, IL 60435   815-723-2928
FAX: 815-729-3697
e-mail: wil.grundy.c.i.l.juno.com

Pam Heavens, Director
Information and referral services.

Indiana

4781 ATTIC

CA Resource Center for Independent Living
2758 B East Pine Hill Drive
PO Box 2441
Vincennes, IN 47591   812-886-0575
800-962-8842
FAX: 812-886-1128
e-mail: inattic1@aol.com
www.theattic.org

Patricia Stewart, Executive Director
Ruth Kimberley, Assistant Director

4782 Damar Homes

PO Box 41
Camby, IN 46113   317-856-5201
FAX: 317-856-2333

Greg Johnson, Executive Director

Providers of residential services: developmental center, group homes and alternative family homes.

4783 Everybody Counts

9111 Broadway, Suite A
Broadfield Center
Merrillville, IN 46410   219-769-5055
888-769-3636
FAX: 219-769-5325
e-mail: ecount@netnitco.net

Teresa Torez, Executive Director
Emas Bennett, Assistant Director

4784 Four Rivers Resource Services

PO Box 249
Highway 59 South
Linton, IN 47441   812-847-2231
FAX: 812-847-8836
e-mail: fourrivers@frrs.org
www.frrs.org

Lyna Landis, Marketing Coordinator

4785 Indiana SILC Indiana Council on Independent Living (ICOIL)

402 W Washington Street, Room W453
PO Box 7083
Indianapolis, IN 46207   317-232-1303
800-545-7763
FAX: 317-232-6478
TDY:317-232-1427
e-mail: nyoung@fssa.state.in.us

Nancy Young, Program Director
Mark Bair, SILC Chairperson

4786 Indianapolis Resource Center for Independent Living

2110 North Capitol Avenue
Indianapolis, IN 46202   317-596-6440
FAX: 317-596-6446
e-mail: ircil@direct.net

Melissa Madill, Co-Executive Director
David Scott, Info & Referral
Emma Lewis Sullivan, Co-Executive Director

Offers advocacy, information and referral services, independent living skills training, peer counseling, supported employment services and information on the Americans with Disabilities Act.

4787 League for the Blind and Disabled

5800 Fairfield Avenue
Suite 210
Fort Wayne, IN 46807   219-745-5491
800-889-3443
FAX: 219-744-2202
e-mail: 1bdfw@ctlnet.com
www.the-league.org

David Nelson, President/CEO
John Guingrich, Program Director

Peer counseling, education, advocacy services training and support, independent living skills training, assistive equipment loaner program, youth services, orientation and mobility training, information and referral, disability awareness, Braille transcription, Center for Independent living, and public education.

4788 Martin Luther Homes of Indiana

PO Box 7057
Terre Haute, IN 47802   812-235-3399
FAX: 812-235-1590
e-mail: thaute@mlhs.com
www.mlhs.com

Anita Bean, Administrator

Providing a wide array of services to assist individuals and families in achieving positive life goals. Services to persons with disabilities and other special needs include community living options, training and employment options, spiritual growth and development options, training and counseling support.

4789 Southern Indiana Center for Independent Living

3300 West 16th Street
Stone City Mall
Bedford, IN 47421 812-277-9626
FAX: 812-277-9628
e-mail: sicil@tima.com

Albert Tolbert, Executive Director
Denise Mullis, Assistant Director

Iowa

4790 Black Hawk Center for Independent Living

312 Jefferson Street
Waterloo, IA 50701 319-291-7755
FAX: 319-291-7781
e-mail: bhcil@cedarnet.org
www.cedarnet.org/bhcil

Jane Nelson-Kuhn, Executive Director

4791 Central Iowa Center for Independent Living

1024 Walnut Street
Des Moines, IA 50309 515-243-1742
888-503-2287
FAX: 515-243-5385
e-mail: cicil@raccoon.com
www.raccoon.com/-cicil

Robert Jeppesen, Director
Frank Strong, Asst. Director for Programs

A non-residential, consumer controlled, community bases organization assisting people with disabilities who seek to live independently within the community. Provides independent living skills training, peer support, advocacy and self advocacy training and information and referral services. Publishes a quarterly newsletter and annual Disablity Awareness Guide.

4792 Evert Conner Rights and Resources Center for Independent Living

20 E Market Street
Iowa City, IA 52245 319-338-3870
FAX: 319-338-8385
e-mail: connerctr@aol.com

Ethel Madison, Contact

4793 Hope Haven

1800 19th Street
Rock Valley, IA 51247 712-476-2737
FAX: 712-476-2802
www.hopehaven.org

David VanNingen, Executive Director

Purpose is to assist persons with mental/physical/emotional disabilities to reach their potential based on Biblical convictions. Services group homes, supervised apartments, and vocational employment services.

4794 Independent Living - Iowa

20 E Market Street
Iowa City, IA 52245 319-337-3400
FAX: 319-338-8385
e-mail: connerctr@aol.com

Ethel Madison, Executive Director

An independent living center, non-profit, nonresidential, consumer run, community based. The center assists individuals with disabilities to maintain control over day to day activities and to advocate for themselves in order to achieve greater independence and full participation in an integrated society.

4795 League of Human Dignity

1417 1/2 W Broadway
Council Bluffs, IA 51501 712-323-6863
FAX: 712-323-6811
e-mail: lhd@mitec.net

Joan La Belle, Director

4796 Martin Luther Homes of Iowa

445 7th Avenue SE
Waukon, IA 52172 319-568-3992
FAX: 319-568-3992

Mary Lynn ReVoir, Administrator
Fred Naumann III, Communications

Providing a wide array of services to assist individuals and families in achieving positive life goals. Services to persons with disabilities and other special needs include community living options, training and employment options, spiritual growth and development options, training and counseling support.

4797 South Central Iowa Center for Independent Living

121 1/2 High Avenue E
Suite 301
Oskaloosa, IA 52577 641-672-1867
FAX: 641-672-1867
e-mail: scicil@kdsi.net
www.welcome.to/scicil

Nika Naylor, Contact

4798 Three Rivers Center for Independent Living

505 6th Street
Suite 504
Sioux City, IA 51101 712-258-2657
FAX: 712-255-1065
e-mail: bjdenny@aol.com

Brenda Denney, Contact

Kansas

4799 Coalition for Independence

3738 State Avenue
Kansas City, KS 66102 913-321-5140
FAX: 913-321-5182
TDY:913-321-5216
e-mail: mail@cfi-kc.org
www.cfi-kc.org

Editor: Jessica Childers Salas, author
Tom Lally, Executive Director
Jessica Childers Salas, Marketing Coordinator

Publishes monthly newsletter - "Keys to Independence."

6 pages

4800 Cowley County Developmental Services
Arkansas City, KS 67005   316-442-7777

Martha Crane, Director

Offers peer counseling, attendant care registry and other services to the community.

4801 Independence
2001 Haskell Avenue
Lawrence, KS 66046   785-841-0333
                             888-824-7277
                        FAX: 785-841-1094
e-mail: webmaster@indpendenceinc.org
        www.independenceinc.org

Susan Mikesic, Community Coordinator

Services include individual and systems advocacy, assistance obtaining benefits, technical assistance, housing, assistance with modifications for accessibility, counseling peer support, microcomputer training, transportation, community outreach and education, business management services for persons using attendants, a resource library, independent living skills training, assistive technology, information and referral, human diversity workshops and volunteer involvement.

4802 Independent Connection
1710 W Schilling Road
Salina, KS 67401   755-827-9383
                           800-526-9731
                      FAX: 785-823-2015

Sheila Nelson, Director

Offers peer counseling, disability education, independent living skills training advocacy, information and referrals, attendant care registry and information on accessible housing.

4803 Independent Living Center of Northeast Kansas
PO Box 292
Atchison, KS 66002   913-367-1830
                        FAX: 913-367-1430
              e-mail: ilcnek@journey.com
                          www.knek.org

Laura Young, Contact

4804 Independent Living Resource Center
3330 W Douglas Avenue
Wichita, KS 67203   316-942-6300
                       FAX: 316-942-2078
              e-mail: llrc@earthlink.org
hubris.net/ilarc.org/contact/wichita.htm

Judy Weigel, Executive Director

4805 Kansas Services for the Blind & Visually Impaired
2601 SW East Circle Drive N
Topeka, KS 66606   785-296-3311
                      FAX: 785-291-3138

Dianne Hemphill, Administrator

Offers peer counseling, advocacy and other services to the community.

4806 LINK
2401 E 13th Street
Hays, KS 67601   785-625-6942
                    FAX: 785-625-2334
        e-mail: mramey@eaglecom.net
                    www.odsys.netlink

Brian Atwell, Director

Offers personal care attendants, independent living skills instruction, adaptive equipment, community involvement and peer support, legal advocacy, interpreting services, recreation, transportation, HCBS services, and support groups.

4807 Osage City Resource Center for Independent Living
PO Box 257
Osage City, KS 66523   785-528-3105
                          FAX: 785-528-3665
              e-mail: mery@rcilinc.org
hubris.net/ilarc.org/contact/osage.html

Mary Holloway, Contact

4808 Prairie Independent Living Resource Center
17 South Main Street
Hutchinson, KS 67501   620-663-3989
                               888-715-6818
                          FAX: 620-663-4711
           e-mail: pilr@southwind.net
                    hubris.net/ilarc.org

Christine Owens, Director

4809 Southwest Kansas Center for Independent Living
111 North Grant Street
Garden City, KS 67846   316-276-1900
                           FAX: 316-271-0200
              e-mail: cilswks@gcnet.com
                          www.ilarc.org

Troy Horton, Contact

4810 Three Rivers Independent Living
408 Lincoln
PO Box 408
Wamego, KS 66547   785-456-9915
                           800-555-3994
                      FAX: 785-456-9923
   e-mail: reception@threeriversinc.org
              www.threeriversinc.org

Audrey Schremmer-Philip, Executive Director

Non-profit organization that assists people with all types of disabilities, of all income levels, to reach their personal goals and live as independently as possible.

4811 Three Rivers Independent Living Center
PO Box 33
Clay Center, KS 67432   785-632-6117
                           FAX: 785-632-3105
   www.angelfire.com/il/threeriversilrc

Audrey Schremmer-Philip, Contact

4812 Three Rivers Independent Living Resource Center

PO Box 408
Wamego, KS   66547   913-456-9915
                                  FAX: 913-456-9923
e-mail: egerte@mail.midusa.net
www.angelfire.com/il/threeriversilrc

Audrey Schremmer-Philip, Contact

4813 Three Rivers Independent Resource Center

136 W 3rd Street
Junction City, KS   66441   785-762-8826
                                  FAX: 785-762-8822
e-mail: paula@threerivers.org
www.threeriversinc.org

Audrey Schremmer-Philip, Contact

4814 Topeka Independent Living Resource Center

501 SW Jackson Street
Suite 100
Topeka, KS   66603   785-233-4572
                                       800-443-2207
                                  FAX: 785-233-5072

Michael Oxford, Executive Director

Offers peer counseling, attendant care registry and
disability education, independent living skills training, housing assistance, advocacy (individual and
system), interpreting services and legal services.

Kentucky

4815 Best Center for Independent Living

624A Eastwood Avenue
Bowling Green, KY   42103   270-796-5992
                                  FAX: 270-796-5992
e-mail: klesieur@aol.com

Karen Lesieur, Contact

4816 Center for Accessible Living

981 S 3rd Street
Suite 102
Louisville, KY   40203   502-589-6620
                                  FAX: 502-589-3980
e-mail: jday@calky.org
www.calky.org

Jan Day, Executive Director
Independent living center.

4817 Center for Accessible Living - Murray

1304 Chestnut Street # U
Murray, KY   42071   279-753-7676
                                  FAX: 270-753-7726
e-mail: jeannegal@kih.net
www.cfal.com

Jeanne Gallimore, Contact

**4818 Center for Independent Living Kentucky
Department for the Blind**

Independent Living Office
1210 Johnson Boulevard
Murray, KY   42071   270-759-9227
                                       800-334-6920
                                  FAX: 270-759-9227
e-mail: buel.stalls@mail.state.ky.us

Buel E. Stalls. Jr., Office Manager & IL Specialist
Offers peer counseling, attendant care registry and
other services to the community as they relate to the
blind community. The Murray office is an independent living regional office which covers 20 far
western counties of Kentucky.

4819 Community Alternatives

103 Bridge Street
Frankfort, KY   40601   502-223-1736
                                  FAX: 502-223-4404

Carol Filson, Executive Director
Offers peer counseling, education, advocacy, information and referral services.

4820 Disability Coalition of Northern Kentucky

36 West Pike Street
Covington, KY   41011   859-431-7668
                                  FAX: 859-431-7688
e-mail: ger@iglou.com

Gerry Rader, Contact

4821 Independence Place

153 Patchen Drive
Suite 33
Lexington, KY   40517   859-266-2807
                                  FAX: 859-335-0627
e-mail: cwesalb@aol.com

Wes Albright, Contact

4822 Pathfinders for Independent Living

109 E Mound Street
Harlan, KY   40831   606-573-5777
                                  FAX: 606-573-5739
e-mail: pathfinderil@kin.net

Sandra Goodwyn, Executive Director

We publish a newsletter called LifeLine 6-10 times a
year. Most articles are written by Sandra Goodwyn.
Editor is F.E. Goodwyn.

Louisiana

4823 Baton Rouge Resources for Independent Living

5700 Florida Boulevard
Baton Rouge, LA   70806   225-272-4102
                                  FAX: 225-216-3845

Emily Blackwell, Site Director
Shannon Breaux, Social Worker

Non-profit organization serving people with disabilites. Services include personal care attendants,
independent living training, peer counseling, disability awareness training, information and referrel.

4824 Independent Living Center

401 Veterans Memorial Boulevard
Suite 100
New Orleans, LA 70005   504-841-0591
          FAX: 504-841-0595

Joan Meunier, Contact

4825 New Horizons

6670 Saint Vincent Avenue
Shreveport, LA 71106   318-865-1000
        FAX: 318-865-1094
    e-mail: nhilc@nhilc.org
         www.nhilc.org

Helen Moses, Contact

4826 New Horizons - Louisiana

1261 Royal Avenue
Suite 101B
Monroe, LA 71201   318-323-4374
        FAX: 318-323-4374
    e-mail: horizon@bayou.com

Peggy Coleman, Independent Living Directory
advocacy, information and referral support groups.

4827 Resources for Independent Living

1555 Poydras Street
Suite 1500
New Orleans, LA 70112   504-522-1955
        FAX: 504-522-1954
    e-mail: noril@aol.com

Esther Boutte, Info. & Referral Program Manager
Non-profit agency that advocates for a fully accessible and integrated community and provides services for individuals with disabilities that enhance personal choice and promote social, vocational and economic opportunities. Programs include Personal Assistant Services, Independent Living Skills training, Advocacy, Peer Support, Supported Living, Deafblind services, Lending Library and Accessibility Surveys.

4828 Southwest Louisiana Independence Center

1605 W Common Street
A
Lake Charles, LA 70601   318-477-7194
        FAX: 318-477-7198
    e-mail: slic@deltech.net

Ray Coltrin, Executive Director
Offers information and referral services.

4829 Southwest Louisiana Independent Center

3505 Fifth Avenue
Suite A-2
Lake Charles, LA 70607   337-477-7194
        FAX: 337-477-7198
    e-mail: slic@usunwired.net

Mitch Granger, Contact

4830 Volunteers of America Supported Living Program

3939 Causeway Boulevard
Suite 3200
Metairie, LA 70002   504-835-3005
        FAX: 504-835-0409

Suzanne Howell, Program Director

Provides supported living services including pca, respite, skills traning, day, night, and behavior companion.

4831 Volunteers of America—Independent Living

3939 N Causeway Boulevard
Suite 200
Metairie, LA 70002   504-834-7015

Neil Grandstand, Contact

4832 W Troy Cole Independent Living Specialist New Horizons, I.L. Center

2000-A Tower Drive
Monroe, LA 71201
        FAX: 318-323-5445
    e-mail: horizons@bayou.com

W. Troy Cole, Independent Living Specialist

New Horizons provides the following four core services: Advocacy; Information & Referral; Peer Support; Independent Living Skills Training. Other services include: ADA Accessibility Site Surveys (for a fee); Cross disABILITY Independent Living support Groups; Housing Information; Assistive Driving Information; Personal Care Attendant Services; disABILITY Based Community Education; Medical Equipment Loan Closet; Quarterly News Letter; For other services available, please call.

Maine

4833 Alpha One

242 Western Avenue
Augusta, ME 04330   207-623-1115
        800-499-2357
        FAX: 207-623-1369
        www.alphaonenow.com

Steven Tremblay, Director

Works throughout the state of Maine. The Board of Directors, staff and a network of personal and professional connections assist people with disabilities to gain access to and achieve their own independent living goals. Wherever persons are in Maine, this network creates improved and increased opportunities for people with disabilities.

4834 Alpha One

127 Main Street
South Portland, ME 04106   207-767-2189
        800-640-7200
        FAX: 207-799-8346
    e-mail: steven_tremblay@alphaonenow.com
        www.alphaonenow.org

Steven Tremblay, Director
Ketra Crosson, Branch Manager

4835 Alpha One - Aroostook Branch

PO Box 560
Mapleton, ME 04757   207-764-6466
        800-974-6466
        FAX: 207-764-5396
    e-mail: alphaone@ainop.org
        www.alpha-one.org

Darlene Stewart, Branch Manager

Committed to being a leading enterprise providing the community with information, services and products that create opportunities for people with disabilities to live independently. Offers adaptive equipment loan program, independent skills instruction, adapted driver evaluation and training, information and referral services, peer support, advocacy, access design consultation, and more.

4836   Alpha One - Brewer Office

41 Acme Road
Brewer, ME   04412   207-989-4968
                                     800-300-6016
                      FAX: 207-989-7976

Kelley McTague, Branch Manager

Committed to being a leading enterprise providing the community with information, services and products that create opportunities for people with disabilities to live independently. Provides many services including adaptive and mobility equipment selection, peer support, advocacy, information and referral services, adapted drive evaluation and training, and consumer directed personal assistance.

4837   Alpha One - Main Office

127 Main Street
South Portland, ME   04106   207-767-2189
                                     800-640-7200
                      FAX: 207-799-8346
                      www.alpha-one.org

Steven Tremblay, Director
Ketra Crosson, Branch Manager

Alpha One, directed by people with disabilities, is committed to being a leading enterprise providing the community with information, services and products that create opportunities for people with disabilities to live independently. Offer a variety of services including access design consultation, information and referrals, attendant services, independent living skills instruction and more.

4838   Maine Independent Living Services

424 Western Avenue
Augusta, ME   04330
                                     800-499-5434
                      FAX: 207-622-6947

4839   Maine Mental Health Connections

150 Union Street
Bangor, ME   04401   207-941-2897
                      FAX: 207-941-2996
                      e-mail: together@mint.net
                      www.mmhcommunityconnection.org

Robert J Mathien, Executive Director
Shelley Smith, Community Connections Manager
Sharon Shepard, Employment Connections Manager

Offers a variety of social, recreational, residential, vocational and personal growth opportunities as well as peer support, education and advocacy services.

4840   Motivational Services

PO Box 229
Augusta, ME   04332   207-626-3465
                      FAX: 207-626-3469
                      e-mail: rweiss@mocomaine.com
                      www.mocomaine.com

Richard Weiss, Ph.D., Executive Director

Residential treatment, supervised apartment living, case management, supported employment, drop-in centers, and affirmative businesses.

4841   Shalom House

400 Congress Street, 3rd Floor
PO Box 560
Portland, ME   04112   207-874-1080
                      FAX: 207-874-1077
                      e-mail: shalomhs@gwi.net
                      www.gwi.net/shalomhouse

Joseph Brannigan, Executive Director

A non-profit agency providing a range of housing and community support services for adults recovering from serious mental illness. Service in the greater Portland, Maine area.

Maryland

4842   Broadmead

13801 York Road
Cockeysville, MD   21030   410-527-1900
                      FAX: 410-527-0259
                      e-mail: broadmead@erols.com
                      www.broadmead.org

Peggy Porter

A continuing care retirement community, near Baltimore, maryland, wich offers independent living, enriched living, assisted living and comprehensive care. Accredited by the American Association of Homes & Services for the Aging's Continuing Care Accrediation.

4843   Housing Unlimited

4928 Wyaconda Road
Suite 15
Rockville, MD   20852   301-230-2825
                      FAX: 301-230-2826
                      e-mail: hui97@erols.com
                      http:/handhousing.org/housingunlimited

Abe Schuchman

To address the housing crisis for adults with psychiatric disabilities who reside in Montgomery County, Maryland.

4844   Independence Now

6811 Kenilworth Avenue
Suite 504
Riverdale, MD   20737   301-277-2839
                      FAX: 301-588-3951
                      www.md-cils.org

Catherine Raggio, Contact

4845   MCIL Resources for Independent Living

5807 Harford Road
Baltimore, MD   21214   410-444-1400
                      FAX: 410-444-0825
                      e-mail: mcil@clark.net

Frank Pinter

People with disabilities help themselves to become as independent as possible.

4846 Making Choices for Independent Living

5807 Harford Road
Baltimore, MD   21214   410-444-1400
                          FAX: 410-444-0825
                          e-mail: mcil@mcil-md.org
                          www.mcil-md.org

Frank Pinter, Executive Director

4847 Resources for Independence Living

100 North Mechanic Street
Cumberland, MD   21502   301-784-1774
                          FAX: 301-784-1776
                          e-mail: phcil@hereintown.net
                          www.phcil.org

Lori Magruder, Executive Director

4848 Southern Maryland Center for LIFE

PO Box 657
Charlotte Hall, MD   20622   301-884-4498
                          FAX: 301-884-6099
                          e-mail: cflife@us.hsanet.net

Barbara Hayden, Contact

Massachusetts

4849 AD Lib Center for Independent Living

215 North Main Street
Pittsfield, MA   01201   413-442-7047
                          FAX: 413-443-4338

Bill Cavanaugh, Contact

4850 AD-LIB

221 N Street
Pittsfield, MA   01201
                          FAX: 413-443-4338

William Cavanaugh, Executive Director

Offers information and referral services, independent
living skills training, peer counseling, individual and
group advocacy services available to all people with
disabilities. Access consultation provided to businesses, agencies and institutions in accordance to the
Americans with Disabilities Act.

4851 American Red Cross of Cape Cod

286 South Street
Hyannis, MA   02601   508-775-1540
                          FAX: 508-771-2209
                          e-mail: capecod@cape.com
                          www.capecodredcross.org

Marlene Weir, Executive Director

Handicapped accessible motor service to Boston
Area Hospitals from Cape Cod with pick-up for Nan-
tucket residents.

4852 Boston Center for Independent Living

95 Berkeley Street
Suite 206
Boston, MA   02116   617-338-6665
                          FAX: 617-338-6661

James Tierney, Executive Director
Jimi Tierney, Acting Executive Director
Holly Vernon, Information Coordinator

Offers skills training, peer counseling, advocacy
training, and information services to help persons
with disabilities of all ages assume full control over
their own life choices. Works with youth in schools
to promote effective transition into adult independence. Empowers people with disabilities and
their friends and families by providing information in
all aspects of daily living, including the statewide
housing registry, personal care assistant program and
ongoing assistance.

**4853 Cape Organization for Rights of the Disabled
(CORD)**

1019 Iyannough Road #4
Hyannis, MA   02601   508-775-8300
                          FAX: 508-775-7022
                          e-mail: bhcord@cape.com
                          www.vse.com/~bhcord

Bill Henning, Contact

4854 Center for Living & Working

67 Millbrook Street
Worcester, MA   01608   508-363-1222
                          FAX: 508-363-1254
                          www.centerforlw.org

Bob Bailey, Director

Skills training, peer counseling, advocacy, information and referral services related to achieving and
maintaining independent living in the community for
people with disabilities.

4855 Center for Living and Working

67 Millbrook Street
Worcester, MA   01606   508-363-1226
                          FAX: 508-363-1254
                          e-mail: centerlw@ix.netcom.com
                          www.tiac.net.users.cflaw

4856 DEAF

215 Brighton Avenue
Allston, MA   02134   617-523-8928

Heidi Reed, Director

Multi-service agency operated by the community to
provide advocacy, training and access assistance.

4857 Il Center: Ad Lib

442 N Street
Pittsfield, MA   01201
                          FAX: 413-443-4338
                          TDY:413-442-7194

William Cavanaugh, Executive Director
Marilyn J. Fontana

4858 Il Center: Boston Center for Independent Living

95 Berkeley Street
Suite 206
Boston, MA   02116   617-338-6665
                             FAX: 617-338-6661
                             TDY:617-338-6662

Mary Wambach, Executive Director

4859 Il Center: Center for Living & Working

67 Millbrook Street
WBC, 1st Floor
Worcester, MA   01606   508-363-1226
                             FAX: 508-363-1254
                     e-mail: centerlw@ix.netcom.com
                             www.centerlw.org

Joe Bellil, Acting Executive Director

4860 Il Center: Independent Living Center of the North Shore & Cape Ann (ILNSCA)

27 Congress Street
Suite 107
Salem, MA   01970   978-741-0077
                             FAX: 978-741-1133
                       e-mail: ilcnsca@aol.com
                             www.ilcnsca.org

Mary M. Moore, Executive Director

ILNSCA is a service and advocacy center run by and for people with disabilities. Offered services include independent living skills training, peer counseling, information and referral, and advocacy; home modification, vehicle modifications and assistive equipment limited funding; ADA technical assistance.

4861 Il Center: Metrowest Center for Independent Living

63 Fountain Street
Framingham, MA   01702
                             FAX: 508-875-8359

Paul Spooner, Executive Director

Offers information & referral, peer counseling, advocacy, and independent living skills training.

4862 Il Center: Southeast Center for Independent Living

66 Troy Street
1st Floor
Fall River, MA   02720   508-679-9210
                             FAX: 508-677-2377
                       e-mail: scil@cntn.net
                             www.scil.org

Cheryl Finnerty, Executive Director

4863 Il Center: The Northeast Independent Living Program

20 Ballard Road
Lawrence, MA   01843   978-685-1518
                             800-845-6457
                             FAX: 978-689-4488

Charlie Carr, Executive Director

4864 Independence Associates

10 Oak Street
2nd Floor
Taunton, MA   02780   508-880-5325
                             FAX: 508-880-6311
                       e-mail: cgallant@iacil.org

Constance Gallant, Executive Director

We offer Advocacy Services, Information and referral, Independent living skills training, Peer counseling. Also personal care management training program.

4865 Independent Living Center - Massachusetts Community for the Blind

88 Kingston Street
Boston, MA   02111   617-727-5550
                             FAX: 617-727-5960
                   e-mail: chris.crawford@mcb:bbs.pm.com

Donald Johnson, Director

Offers peer counseling and disability education.

4866 Independent Living Center of the North Shore and Cape Ann

583 Chestnut Street
Lynn, MA   01904   781-596-8255
                             FAX: 781-741-1133
                       e-mail: ilcnsca@aol.com
                             www.ilcnsca.org

Lori Stewart, Executive Director
Shawn McDuff, Community Affairs

ILCNSCA works to address individual, community-wide and broad systemic issues that affect the ability of people with disabilities to live independently in the community. The staff provides peer counseling, independent living skills training, individual advocacy, information and referral to people with disabilities, and more. These services are offered to empower individuals with disabilities and assist them in gaining the control and skills needed to live independent lives.

4867 Metro West Center for Independent Living

63 Fountain Street
Framingham, MA   01702   508-879-3300
                             FAX: 508-875-8359

Paul Spooner, Director

Information and referral, peer counseling, independent living skills training and advocacy.

4868 MetroWest Center for Independent Living

63 Fountain Street
Suite 401
Framingham, MA   01702   508-875-7883
                             FAX: 508-875-8359
                             www.mcil.org

Paul Spooner, Executive Director

Advocacy organization serving individuals with disabilities.

4869   Northeast Independent Living Program

20 Ballard Road
Lawrence, MA   01843   978-687-4288
                              FAX: 978-689-4488
                         e-mail: nilp@ultranet.com

Charlie Carr, Executive Director

Provides advocacy and independent living services (i.e., information and referral, peer counseling, skills training) to people with disabilities, to empowering them to live and work as independently as possible.

4870   Renaissance Clubhouse

176 Walker Street
Lowell, MA   01854   978-454-7944
                              FAX: 978-937-7867
                      e-mail: renclub@channel1.com
                       www.channel1.com/~renclub

Elaine Walker, Director
Tammy Savoie, Assistant Director

Offers daily structure, assistance wtih jobs, retirement, and housing.

4871   Southeast Center for Independent Living

66 Troy Street
Suite 103
Fall River, MA   02720   508-679-9210
                              FAX: 508-677-2377

Cheryl Finnerty, Director

4872   Stavros Center for Independent Living

691 South East Street
Amherst, MA   01002   413-256-0473
                              800-804-1899
                              FAX: 413-256-0190
                              www.stavros.org

James Kruidenier, Executive Director

Offers peer counseling, advocacy, skills training, information and referral, disability education/awareness, personal assistance services, services to all disabilities and deaf and hard of hearing individuals, equipment loan, assistive technology education, and related issues.

4873   Student Independent Living Experience

3 Randolph Street
Canton, MA   02021   781-828-1519
                              FAX: 781-821-4086

Tom Bosco, Director

Transitional living program serving adolescents with disabilities teach independent living skills.

Michigan

4874   Ann Arbor Center for Independent Living

2568 Packard Street
Ann Arbor, MI   48104   734-971-0277
                              FAX: 734-971-0826
                              TDY:734-971-0310
                       e-mail: cilstaff@aacil.org

Sue Probert, Information & Referral Coord.

It is the mission of the Center for Independent Living in Ann Arbor to assure equality of opportunity, independent living and the economic self-sufficiency of people with disabilities.

4875   Arc Detroit

51 W Hancock Street
Detroit, MI   48201
                              FAX: 313-831-7974

Shirley Moordian, Director

Advocacy for people with developmental disabilities, clerical aide training, parent outreach, mental affairs, self advocacy, newsletter. Membership dues $20 per year. Includes state and national Arc membership.

4876   Association for Retarded Citizens of Muskegon County

1145 Wesley Avenue
Muskegon, MI   49442   616-773-5355
                              FAX: 616-777-3507

Margaret O'Toole, Director

Offers information and referral, advocacy services and peer counseling.

4877   Bay Area Coalition for Independent Living

935 Barlow
Traverse City, MI   49684   231-941-7150
                              FAX: 231-941-3421

Mary Jean Brick, Contact

4878   Blue Water Center for Independent Living

310 Water Street
Port Huron, MI   48060   810-987-9337
                              FAX: 810-987-9548
                      e-mail: bob925@hotmail.com

Rob Devary, Director

Offers disability education, peer counseling, advocacy, transpotation, employment, substance abuse counseling, support groups and information on accessible housing.

4879   Capital Area Center for Independent Living

3815 West Saint Joseph Street
Suite D
Lansing, MI   48917   517-334-7830
                              FAX: 517-334-7849
                         e-mail: cacil@cacil.org
                              www.cacil.org

Janet Del Valle, Contact

4880   Center for Independent Living of Mid-Michigan

114 Tuscola Road
Bajo City, MI   48706   989-835-4041
                              800-782-4160
                              FAX: 989-835-8121
                      e-mail: cilmm@concentric.net

Melissa Gleason, Associate Director
Melissa Davert, Executive Director
Bethaney Stevenson, Information & Referral

The Center for Independent Living of Mid-Michigan (CIL) is comprised of over 51 percent of people with disabilities, and advocates for the rights of people with disabilities in the Mid-Michigan area. Call for information on disability issues or for assistance in obtaining services, within your community..

4881 Center for Independent Living of Mid-Michigan
1206 James Savage
Midland, MI 48640 517-835-4041
FAX: 517-835-8121
e-mail: cilmm@concentric.net

Melissa Davert, Contact

4882 Cristo Rey Handicappers Program
1717 North High Street
Lansing, MI 48906 517-372-4700
FAX: 517-372-8499

Tony Bevavides, Director
Cindi Benavides, Program Coordinator
Social/recreational program, outreach, support and self sufficiency services, drop in area.

4883 Cristo Rey Hispanic Center for Independent Living
1717 N High Street
Lansing, MI 48906 517-372-4700
FAX: 517-372-8499

Tony Benavides, Director
Peer counseling, attendant care registry and referrals.

4884 Disability Network
3600 South Dort Highway
Suite 54
Flint, MI 48507 810-742-1800
FAX: 810-742-2400
e-mail: disnet@tir.com

Mike Zelley, Executive Director

4885 Disability Resource Center
517 East Crosstown Parkway
Kalamazoo, MI 49001 616-345-1516
FAX: 616-577-3805
e-mail: abilit2@ibm.net

Karen Duckworth, Contact

4886 Disability Resource Center of Southwestern Michigan
517 E Crosstown Parkway
Kalamazoo, MI 49001 616-345-1516
800-394-7450
FAX: 616-345-0229
TDY:616-345-1516
e-mail: dshortt@drccil.org
www.drccil.org

Joel Cooper, President/CEO
Debra Shortt, Info. & Referral Specialist

The DRC is a Center for Independent Living offering core services in the areas of advocacy, peer support, independent living skills training, and information and referral to persons with disabilities living in the following southwestern Michigan counties: Allegan, Barry, Berrien, Calhoun, Cass, Kalamazoo, St. Joseph and Van Buren. Specialized services available through the DRC include: occupational therapy assessments; accessibility assessments, driver evaluation and training.

4887 Family Resource Center
51 W Hancock
Detroit, MI 48201
FAX: 313-831-7974

Cheryl Meridian, Director
Information and referrals.

4888 Grand Rapids Center for Independent Living
3600 Camelot Drive SE
Grand Rapids, MI 49546 616-949-1100
FAX: 616-949-7865
e-mail: contact@grcil.org
www.grcil.org

David Bulkowski, Director
Anne E. Everitt, Resource Coordinator
Offers 4 core services: Information and Referral, Advocacy, Peer Support and Independent Living Skills training for people with disabilities. Specific programs and services include accessibility and occupational therapy assessments, transitions services, assistance with personal care attendant issues, interpreter referral and other services for hearing impaired persons.

4889 Grand Rapids Center for Independent Living
3600 Camelot Drive SE
Grand Rapids, MI 49546 616-949-1100
FAX: 616-949-7865
e-mail: contact@grcil.org
www.grcil.org

Dave Bulkowski, Executive Director

4890 Grand Traverse Area Community Living Center
935 Barlow Street
Traverse City, MI 49686 616-941-7150
FAX: 616-941-3421

Juanita Lyon, Program Director
Laura Tougas, Administrative Director
We are a training home for individuals with developmental disabilities over the age of 18

4891 Great Lakes Center for Independent Living
2995 East Grand Boulevard
Detroit, MI 48202 313-870-4580
FAX: 313-832-3850
e-mail: jmeece@glcil.org
www.glcil.org

Jeannie Meece, Executive Director
Independent living skills training, de-institutionalization and empowerment training for persons with disabilities.

4892 Great Lakes/Macomb Rehabilitation Group

4 East Alexandrine
Suite 104
Detroit, MI 48201   313-832-3371
FAX: 313-832-3850
e-mail: jlcil@home.msen.com

Jeannie Meece-Brooks, Contact

4893 Hope Network Independent Living Program

1550 E Beltline Avenue SE
Office 125
Grand Rapids, MI 49506   616-831-2000
FAX: 616-940-8151

Kathryn Mullarkey, F.S.E., Manager

Postacute rehabilitation program serving adults with physical disabilities, especially spinal cord injuries, blindness, MS, brain injuries and stroke. Home adaptation, independent living skills and vocational services are highlighted. Program focus is independent living and return to work.

4894 JARC - Jewish Association for Residential Care

28366 Franklin Road
Southfield, MI 48034   248-352-5272
FAX: 248-352-5279
e-mail: jarc@jarc.org
www.jarc.org

Joyce Keller, Executive Director
Randee Klein, Intake Social Worker

Non-profit organizations providing residential care and support services to adults with developmental disabilities. Operates 13 licensed homes and 5 unlicensed transition homes, and supports over 60 people who live on their own. JARC aldo offers an array of services to families of children with any disability, including respite care, life planning, educatinoal and social programming, outreach, and peer support.

4895 Lakeshore Center for Independent Living

426 Century Lane
Holland, MI 49423   616-850-9781
800-656-5245
FAX: 616-396-3220
e-mail: aimee@egl.net

Ruth Stegeman, Executive Director
Clare Clark, Office Manager
Lorette Evans, Support Staff

Promotes personal initiative and pride among those with disabilities, fostering an integrated community of people who remove barriers to full participation.

4896 Life Skills Services

1608 Lake Street
Kalamazoo, MI 49001

FAX: 616-344-0285

Don Vanderkooy, Director

Offers skill development and monitoring for children and supported living and respite services for adults with developmental disabilities and/or mental illnesses.

4897 Michigan Commission for the Blind Independent Living Rehabilitation Program

411 East Genesee Avenue
Saginaw, MI 48607   989-758-1765
FAX: 989-758-1405

Robert Utrup, Supervisor

Rehabilitation teaching, independent living skills for persons over 55 with severe vision loss.

4898 Oakland/Macomb Center for Independent Living

3765 East 15 Mile Road
Sterling Heights, MI 48310   810-268-4160
FAX: 810-268-4720
e-mail: ricks@omcil.org
www.omcil.org

Richard Sides, Contact

4899 Southeastern Michigan Center for Independent Living

1200 Sixth Avenue
15th Floor, South Tower
Detroit, MI 48226   313-256-1524
FAX: 313-256-1519

Charlene Edge, Contact

4900 Southeastern Michigan Commission for the Blind

1200 6th Street
3rd floor, N Tower
Detroit, MI 48226   313-256-1524
FAX: 313-256-1519
www.mfia.state.mi.us/mcb

Leamon Jones, Southeast Regional Supervisor

Vocational rehabilitation agency. Personal adjustment vocational assessment and training, job placement and follow-up services.

4901 Superior Alliance for Independent Living (SAIL)

129 West Baraga Avenue
Suite H
Marquette, MI 49855   906-228-5744
800-729-SAIL
FAX: 906-228-5573
e-mail: sail@up.net
www.sail.match.org

Amy Rosemergy, Contact

Minnesota

4902 Accessibility Home Fund

400 Sibley Street
Suite 300
Saint Paul, MN 55101   651-296-7613
FAX: 651-296-8292

Barb Collins, Program Manager

Offers peer counseling, education and referral services.

4903 Accessible Space

2550 University Avenue West
Suite 330N
Saint Paul, MN 55114   651-645-7271
800-466-7722
FAX: 651-645-0541
www.accessiblespace.org

Stephen Vander Schaaf, President/CEO

Provides accessible, affordable community-based housing with support services at residential apartment sites in other states. Support services offered in Minnesota, Montana, Nevada, North Dakota and Tennessee.

4904 Center for Independent Living

424 West Superior Street
Suite 400
Duluth, MN 55802   218-726-4896
FAX: 218-726-4897
e-mail: val@accessnorth.net
www.accessnorth.net

Valerie LePorte, Contact

4905 Center for Independent Living of Northeast Minnesota

Mesabi Mall
Suite 11
Hibbing, MN 55746   218-262-6675
FAX: 218-262-6677
e-mail: kim@accessnorth.net
www.accessnorth.net

Kimberly Breznik, Contact

4906 Courage Center

3915 Golden Valley Road
Minneapolis, MN 55422   612-588-0811
888-846-8253
FAX: 612-520-0577
www.courage.org

Tony Lebahn, Client Services Rep.

A comprehensive rehabilitation center serving both people with physical and sensory disabilities. Over 70 different services are available to children and adults with physical disabilities. Some services are physical, occupational and speech therapies, a young adult residential program, camping opportunities, driving evaluations, sports and recreation services, vocational services and much more.

4907 Freedom Resource Center for Independent Living

3505 Eight Street South
Suite 7
Moorhead, MN 56560   218-236-0459
800-450-0459
FAX: 218-236-0510
e-mail: freedom@moorheadcity.com
www.macil.org/freedom

Nate Aalgaard, Executive Director

Work toward equility and inclusion for people with disabilities throuogh programs of empowerment, community education and systems change. We serve eighteen counties, ten in North Dakota and eight in Minnesota. A quarterly newsletter, Freedom Focus, is published

4908 Independence Crossroads

8932 Old Cedar Avenue South
Bloomington, MN 55425   952-854-8004
FAX: 952-854-7842
e-mail: info@independencecrossroads.org
www.independencecrossroads.org

Donna Robb, Director

Offers free information and referral, advocacy, mental health, counseling services and public education.

4909 Independent Lifestyles A Center for Independent Living

709 West St. Germain
Suite 200
Saint Cloud, MN 56301   320-529-9000
FAX: 320-529-0747
e-mail: ilcilcara@aol.com
www.macil.org/cmcil

Cara Ruff, Executive Director

4910 Metropolitan Center for Independent Living

1600 University Avenue West
Suite 16
Saint Paul, MN 55104   651-646-8342
FAX: 651-603-2006
e-mail: mcil3@aol.com

David Hanscock, Director

Offers peer counseling, disability education and information on accessible housing.

4911 Metropolitan Center for Independent Living

1600 University Avenue West
Suite 16
Saint Paul, MN 55104   612-646-8342
FAX: 612-603-2006
e-mail: mcill@aol.com
www.macil.org/mcil

David Hancox, Contact

4912 New Horizons Home Care

600 25th Avenue South
Suite 111
Saint Cloud, MN 56301   320-255-1882
FAX: 320-255-5137

Courtney Salzl, Director of Nursing
Brenda Fuchs, Human Resources Intake

Offers skilled nursing services RN, LPN, TV Therapy, Pediatrics, Rehabilitation Services, PT, OT, ST, Paraprofessional staff, Home Health Aides, Homemakers, Personal Care Attendents, Companions, Live-ins, Sleep overs, Respite care, Extended hours.

4913 Options Interstate Resource Center for Independent Living

318 Third Street NW
East Grand Forks, MN 56721   218-773-6100
FAX: 218-773-7119
e-mail: options@rrv.net
www.macil.org/options

Jay Johnson, Contact

4914 Southeastern Minnesota Center for Independent Living

2720 North Broadway
Rochester, MN 55906   507-452-5490
FAX: 507-228-8070
www.semcid@sparc.isl.net

Dave Schwartzkoff, Executive Director
Laurie Brownell, Operations Manager

Offers peer counseling, disability education and referrals, support groups, independent living skills training, used equipment, information and referral, accessibility assistance and brain injury services.

4915 Southern Minnesota Independent Living Enterprises & Services

709 South Front Street
Mankato, MN 56001   507-345-8590
FAX: 507-345-8429
e-mail: aasmiles@mctcnet.net
www.macil.org/smiles

Alan Augustin, Director
Doug Miller, Operations Manager
Mary Mensing, Program Manager

A nonprofit organization committed to providing an array of services to assist individuals with disabilities to live independently, pursue meaningful goals, and have the same opportunities and choices as all persons. Offers direct services such as: individual and systems advocacy, peer counseling, independent living skills training, transition from school to community living, information and referral, semi-independent living services, assistive technology, ramp projects, and community education.

4916 Southwestern Center for Independent Living

109 South Fifth Street
Suite 700
Marshall, MN 56258   507-532-2221
FAX: 507-532-2222
e-mail: swcil@swcil.com
www.macil.org/swcil

Steven Thovson, Executive Director

4917 Vinland National Center

PO Box 308
Loretto, MN 55357   612-479-3555
FAX: 612-479-2605
e-mail: vinland@mtn.org

Sue Rivard, Director

Offers peer counseling, disability education and other services to the community.

Mississippi

4918 Alpha Home Royal Maid Association for the Blind

PO Box 30
Hazlehurst, MS 39083
FAX: 601-894-2993
e-mail: sigworks@teclink.net

Howard Becker, Director

Offers attendant care registry, information on accessible housing and referrals.

4919 Gulf Coast Independent Living Center

18 JM Tatum Industrial Drive
Hattiesburg, MS 39401   601-544-4860
FAX: 601-582-2544

Albert Holifield, Contact

4920 Jackson Independent Living Center

300 Capers Avenue
Jackson, MS 39203   601-969-3649
800-378-9156
FAX: 601-351-1484

Bridget James, Counselor III

Provides services to consumers with severe disabilities.

4921 LIFE of Central Mississippi

754 North President Street
Suite 2
Jackson, MS 39203   601-969-4009
FAX: 601-969-1662
e-mail: mslife@tsbbs02.tnet.com

Christy Gilliland, Contact

4922 LIFE of Southern Mississippi

710 Katie Avenue
Hattiesburg, MS 39401   601-583-2108
FAX: 601-583-1814
www.cdd-life.org

Elna Garner, Center Director

4923 Mississippi State Independent Living Center

PO Drawer 6321
Mississippi State, MS 39762   601-351-1525
FAX: 601-351-1484
www.mdrs.state.ms.us

Butch McMillian, Director

Offers peer counseling and disability education.

4924 Oxford Center for Independent Living

PO Box 1415
Oxford, MS 38655   601-234-6086

4925 Starkville Center for Independent Living

10 Montgomery Hall
PO Box 6321
Starkville, MS 39762   601-325-8511

Robin Copeland, Contact

Missouri

4926 Access II Independent Living Center

611 West Johnson Street
Gallatin, MO 64640   660-663-2423
FAX: 660-663-2517
e-mail: access@ccp.com
www.ccp.com/~access

Gary Maddox, Executive Director
Leslie Anderson, Program Manager

4927 Bootheel Area Independent Living Services

PO Box 326
Kennett, MO   63857   573-888-0002
                                  FAX: 573-888-0708
                         e-mail: bails@jrwent.com

Kelly Barfoot, Contact

4928 Council for Extended Care of Mentally Retarded Citizens

1600 S Hanley Road
Suite 100A
Saint Louis, MO   63144
                                  FAX: 314-781-3850

Cynthia Compton, Executive Director

Services are provided to individuals with mental retardation. Supported living arrangements are located in St. Louis. Group homes and camping services are located in Dittmer, MO.

4929 Delta Center for Independent Living

5933 Highway 94, South
Suite 107
Saint Charles, MO   63304   314-926-8761
                                  FAX: 314-447-0341
                         e-mail: delta@mail.win.org

Selena Korte, Contact

4930 Disability Resource Association

420-B South Truman Boulevard
Crystal City, MO   63019   636-931-7696
                                  FAX: 636-937-9019
                         e-mail: dra@jcn1.com

Craig Henning, Contact

4931 Disabled Citizens Alliance for Independence

PO Box 675
Viburnum, MO   65566   314-244-3315
                                  FAX: 314-244-5609
                         e-mail: dcitizen@misn.com

Juanita Hagemeier, Contact

4932 Independence Center

4380 W Pine Boulevard
Saint Louis, MO   63108   314-533-4380
                                  FAX: 314-531-7372

Robert Harvey, Executive Director

Provides psychiatric rehabilitation, housing, vocational rehabilitation and evening, weekend and holiday services to adults with serious and persistent mental illnesses.

4933 Independent Living Center

2650 East 32nd Street
Suite 102
Joplin, MO   64804   417-659-8086
                                  FAX: 417-659-8087
                         e-mail: ilcjoplin@lanics.com

Leatta Workman, Contact

4934 Independent Living Center of Southeast Missouri

809 West Pine Street
Poplar Bluff, MO   63901   573-686-2333
                                       888-890-2333
                                  FAX: 573-686-0733
                         e-mail: ilc@pbmo.net

James Venable Alexander, Executive Director
Bruce Lynch, IL Manager
Pam Houart, PAS Manager

4935 Independent Living Resource Center

3620 West Truman Boulevard
Suite D
Jefferson City, MO   65109   573-556-0400
                                  FAX: 573-556-0402
                         e-mail: fnease@ibm.net

Frank Nease, Contact

4936 LIFE Center for Independent Living

1109 Saint Genevieve Avenue
Farmington, MO   63640   573-756-4314
                                       800-596-7273
                                  FAX: 573-756-3507
                         e-mail: life_cen@swbell.net

Tim Azinger, Executive Director

4937 Life Skills Foundation

1158 Huntsman Drive
Saint Louis, MO   63137   314-567-7705
                                  FAX: 314-567-6539
                         e-mail: lifeskills@aol.com

4938 Midland Empire Resources (MERIL)

3715 Beck Road
Suite D-B
Saint Joseph, MO   64506   816-279-8558
                                       800-242-4326
                                  FAX: 816-279-1550
                         e-mail: meril@meril.org
                                  www.meril.org

Debbie Merritt, Executive Director

4939 Northeast Independent Living Services

109 Virginia
5th Floor, Suite 560
Hannibal, MO   63401   573-221-8282
                                  FAX: 573-221-9445
                         e-mail: neils@nemonet.com

Michelle Green, Executive Director

4940 On My Own

3102 Industrial Parkway
Nevada, MO   64772   417-667-7007
                                  FAX: 417-667-6262
                         e-mail: onmyown@ipa.net

Jack Brock, Executive Director
Susie Kimmell, PAS Director
Tina Overton, Program Director

4941 Ozark Independent Living

1598 Imperial Center
Suite 2011
West Plains, MO   65775   417-257-0038
                                 FAX: 417-257-2380
                    e-mail: ozark@townsqr.com
                    www.users.townsqr.com/ozark

Cynthia Moore, Contact

4942 Paraquad

311 North Lindbergh Boulevard
Saint Louis, MO   63141   314-567-1558
                                 FAX: 314-567-1559
                                 TDY:314-567-5552
                    e-mail: paraquad@paraquad.org
                    www.paraquad.org

Max Starkloff, President

4943 Places for People

4120 Lindell Boulevard
Saint Louis, MO   63108   314-535-5600
                                 FAX: 314-535-6037

Scott Bayliff, Associate Director
Francie Broderick, Executive Director

Places for People provides individualized, high quality, and cost effective servies to adults with serious and persistent mental disorders to assist them in living, working and socializing in environments of their choice. We accept a special responsibility to serve these individuals who rely on public funding.

4944 Rehabilitation Institute, Kansas City

3011 Baltimore Avenue
Kansas City, MO   64108   816-751-7700
                                 FAX: 816-751-7988

Ron Hendrick, President

The Rehabilitation Institute, is a licensed, non-profit medical and vocational facility, established for the sole purpose of serving children, youth and adults with disabilities. The Institute offers comprehensive inpatient and outpatient medical services for general rehabilitation, spinal cord injuries, head injuries and other disabling conditions. It is also one of the largest vocational rehabilitation centers in Missouri with extensive work evaluation, counseling and placement programs.

1947

4945 Services for Independent Living

1301 Vandiver Drive
Suite Q
Columbia, MO   65202   573-874-1646
                                 800-766-1968
                                 FAX: 573-874-3564
                    e-mail: sic@midamerica.net

Mark Stone, Executive Director
Tarzie Hart, Administrative Manager

A non-residential, community-based center for independent living. Provides individualized and group services to persons with severe disabilities in the Mid-Missouri area; works to help people with disabilities achieve their highest potential in independent living and community life.

4946 Southeastern Missouri Alliance for Independence (SEMO Alliance)

121 South Broadview Plaza
Suite 12
Cape Girardeau, MO   63703   573-651-6464
                                 FAX: 573-651-6565
                    e-mail: miki@mail.sadi.org

Maryann Gudermuth, Executive Director
Scarlett Seabaugh, Program Director

4947 Southwest Center for Independent Living

1856 East Cinderella
Springfield, MO   65804   417-886-1188
                                 800-676-7245
                                 FAX: 417-886-3619
                    e-mail: scil@mindspring.com

Ann Morris, Contact

4948 Southwest Center for Independent Living

1856 East Cinderella Road
Springfield, MO   65804   417-886-1188
                                 800-676-7245
                                 FAX: 417-886-3619
                    e-mail: scil@mindspring.com

Ann Morris, Director

Offers disability education, referrals, information and advocacy on all disability issues. Serves people with every disability at no charge.

4949 The Whole Person

301 E Armour Boulevard
Suite 430
Kansas City, MO   64111   816-561-0304
                                 FAX: 816-753-8163
                    e-mail: jlyle@thewholeperson.org
                    thewholeperson.org

David Robinson, Executive Director
Jonathan Lyle, Director, IL Programs

Offers peer counseling, education and advocacy services, information and referral, independent living skills training, interpreter referral service, community training, consumer training and deinstitutionalization

4950 Tri-County Center for Independent Living

1704 East Tenth Street
Suite D
Rolla, MO   65401   573-368-5933
                                 FAX: 573-368-5991
                    www.rollanet.org/~tricil2

Victoria Heitxler, Contact

4951 Warrenburg Independent Living Services

123 East Gay
Suite S-2
Warrensburg, MO   64093   660-422-7883
                                 FAX: 660-422-7895
                    e-mail: wils@iland.net
                    www.w-ils.org

Robert Honan, Contact

4952 Whole Person

301 East Armour Boulevard
Suite 430
Kansas City, MO   64111   816-561-0304
                          FAX: 816-753-8163
                          e-mail: dcrinkc@aol.com

David Robinson, Contact

Montana

4953 Billings Chapter - Living Independently for Today and Tomorrow (LIFTT)

929 Broadwater Square
Billings, MT   59101   406-256-5181
                          FAX: 409-259-5259
                          e-mail: pat@cw2.com

Pat Lockwood, Contact

4954 Living Independently for Today and Tomorrow

929 Broadwater Square
Billings, MT   59101   406-256-5404
                          800-669-6319
                          FAX: 406-259-5259
                          e-mail: lifh@cwz.com

Patricia Lockwood, Executive Director
Suzanne Harrison, Info. & Referral
Offers peer mentoring, disability education and referrals, information advocacy, domestic violence information and referral, ADA services community advocacy, accessibility, equipment loan, housing referral, independent living skills and accessment pass plans, ramp, service coordination transition and personal assistance services.

4955 Miles City Chapter - Living Independently for Today and Tomorrow (LIFTT)

2200 Box Elder
Suite 2
Miles City, MT   59301   406-232-2599
                          FAX: 406-365-4064
                          e-mail: liftt@midrivers.com

Pat Lockwood, Contact

4956 Montana Independent Living Project

PO Box 5415
1130 Bute Avenue
Helena, MT   59604   406-442-5755

James Meldrum, Executive Director

4957 North Central Independent Living Services

1120 25th Avenue NE
Black Eagle, MT   59414   406-452-9834
                          FAX: 406-453-3940

Tom Osborn, Director
Independent living center.

4958 North Central Independent Living Services

1120 25th Avenue NE
Black Eagle, MT   59414   406-452-9834
                          FAX: 406-453-3940

Tom Osborn, Executive Director

4959 Summit Independent Living Center

700 Southwest Higgins Avenue
Suite 101
Missoula, MT   59803   406-728-1630
                          800-398-9002
                          FAX: 406-829-3309
                          e-mail: summitil@montana.com
                          www.summitilc.com

Michael Mayer, Executive Director
Summit ILC helps its consumers continue to live independently in the community through a variety of individual and community services.

Nebraska

4960 Center for Independent Living of Central Nebraska

1804 S Eddy Street
Grand Island, NE   68801   308-382-9255
                          877-400-1004
                          FAX: 308-384-9231
                          e-mail: scook@cilnc.org

Sid Cook, Executive Director

Offers independent living skills training, peer sharing, information and referral, housing counseling and referral, accessibility and barrier removal consultation including ADA training and technical assistance, driver education and training, assistive technology services including demonstration and equipment loan, and a free lending library of adapted toys and ability switches for children with severe disabilities. Serves all diabilities and all ages.

4961 League of Human Dignity

1701 P Street
Lincoln, NE   68508   402-441-7871
                          FAX: 402-441-7650

Mike Schafer, Contact

4962 League of Human Dignity Center for Independent Living Center

5513 Center Street
Omaha, NE   68106   402-595-1256
                          FAX: 402-595-1410
                          e-mail: lhdomaha@navix.net
                          leagueofhumandignity.com

Mike Schafer, CEO
Peg Westfall, Director
Provides information and referral, independent living skills training, advocacy, case coordination, peer counseling, personal assistant services, barrier removal services, public education and awareness.

4963   Martin Luther Homes of Beatrice

722 S 12th Street
607
Beatrice, NE   68310   402-223-4066
                              FAX: 402-223-4951
                     e-mail: beatrice@mlhs.com
                                www.mlhs.com

Jerry Campbell, Administrator
Amky Bell, Clinical Director

Providing a wide array of services to assist individuals and families in achieving positive life goals. Services to persons with disabilities and other special needs include community living options, training and employment options, spiritual growth and development options, training and counseling support.

4964   Martin Luther Homes of Nebraska

220 W South 21st Street
York, NE   68467   402-362-2180
                              FAX: 402-362-2961
                     e-mail: mlyork@alltel.net
                                www.mlhs.com

Jessica Schoepf, Program Coordinator
Tim Summers, Program Director

Providing a wide array of services to assist individuals and families in achieving positive life goals. Services to persons with disabilities and other special needs include community living options, training and employment options, spiritual growth and development options, training and counseling support.

4965   Panhandle Independent Living Services

510 South Broadway
Suite 2, PO Box 2454
Scottsbluff, NE   69363   308-635-7901
                                    800-644-5352
                              FAX: 308-635-7676
                        e-mail: pils@bbc.net

Carolyn Foged, Executive Director

PILS Pathfinder - Quarterly newsletter that contains 8 pages. No charge to be added to our mailing list.

Nevada

4966   Carson City Center for Independent Living

1923 North Carson Street
Suite 102
Carson City, NV   89701   775-841-2580
                              FAX: 775-267-3969

Sandy Coyle, Contact

4967   Nevada Association for the Handicapped

6200 W Oakey Boulevard
Las Vegas, NV   89146   702-870-7050
                              FAX: 702-870-7649
                     e-mail: Handi77@aol.com
                                www.nah-ns.org

Vince Triggs, Executive Director

A community based agency providing training, advocacy, support to persons with disabilities, regardless of age or type or degree of disability.

4968   Northern Nevada Center for Independent Living

999 Pyramid Way
Sparks, NV   89431   775-353-3599
                                    800-552-5588
                              FAX: 775-353-3588
                e-mail: info@medtech-services.com
                        www.medtech-services.com

Joe Bohl, Contact

Community based, not for profit organizaiton providing quality support services that include: independent living skills training, information and referral, peer counseling, and aggressive advocacy for all people with disabilites and disability issues.

4969   Southern Nevada Center for Independent Living (SNCIL)

6039 Eldora
Suite F-6
Las Vegas, NV   89146   702-889-4216
                              FAX: 702-889-4574
                     e-mail: sncilnv@aol.com

Mary Evilsizer, Contact

New Hampshire

4970   Granite State Independent Living Foundation

21 Chenell Drive
Concord, NH   03302   603-228-9680
                              FAX: 603-225-3304
                                   www.gsil.org

Larry Robinson, Director

Offers attendant care registry, disability education and referrals.

4971   New Hampshire Technology Partnership Project, Institute on Disability

Concord Center
Concord, NH   03301   603-862-4320
                                    800-427-3338
                              FAX: 603-226-0389
                              TDY:603-224-0630
                e-mail: mcschuh@cisunix.unh.edu
                www.iod.unh.edu/projects/assist.htm

Jan Nisbet, Ph.D., Principal Investigator
Terese Wilkomm, Ph.D., Principal Investigator

Provides extensive training and network development focused on: (1)early intervention, (2) inclusive education, (3) supported living and employment, and (4) using alternative and augmentative communication to develop free expression and citizenship.

New Jersey

4972 A Center for Independent Living - Alliance for Disabled in Action

629 Emboy Avenue
Lower Level Suite
Edison, NJ   08837   732-738-4388
                       FAX: 732-738-4416
               e-mail: adacil@adacil.org
                           www.adacil.org

Deborah Bain, Executive Director

Serves Middlesex, Somerset and Union counties in NJ.

4973 Alliance for Disabled In Action

629 Amboy Avenue
Edison, NJ   08837   732-738-4388
                       FAX: 732-738-9644
                           www.adacil.org

Deborah Bain, Contact

4974 Camden City Independent Living Center

30 North Fifth Street
Suite 222-223
Camden, NJ   08102   609-966-0800
                       FAX: 609-966-0832
           e-mail: ccilc@bellatlantic.net

Lorraine Culbertson, Contact

4975 Center for Independent Living of South Jersey

1200 Delsea Drive
Plaza 47, Suite 6
Westville, NJ   08093   856-853-6490
                               800-413-3791
                           FAX: 856-853-1466
                           TDY:856-853-7602
                   e-mail: cilsj@aol.com

Hazel Lee, Executive Director
Danuta Debicki, Administrator
Edith Gray, Independent Living Specialist

The Center for Independent Living of South Jersey is dedicated to providing people with disabilities in Gloucester and Camden counties the opportunity to actively participate in society, to provide freedom of choice, to work, to own a home, raise a family and in general, to participate to the fullest extent in day-to-day activities. The center provides information and referrals, advocacy, peer support, and independent living skills training.

4976 Center for Independent Living of South New Jersey

1200 Delsea Drive
Plaza 47, Suite 6
Westville, NJ   08093   856-853-6490
                           FAX: 856-853-1466
                   e-mail: cilcj@aol.com

Hazel Lee, Contact

4977 Community Action for Independent Living

One Cornell Parkway
Springfield, NJ   07081   973-564-7557
                           FAX: 973-467-4255
                   e-mail: CAILnj@aol.com
http://community.nj.com/cc/communityaction

Dawn Caris, Contact

Private, non-profit, New Jersey based agency dedicated to providing quality services to individuals with developmental disabilities and mental health issues. Designed to maintain and improve the emotional well-being and quality of life of all individuals receiving services.

4978 DIAL — Disabled Information Awareness & Living

66 Mount Prospect Avenue
Building C
Clifton, NJ   07013   973-470-8090
                       FAX: 973-470-8171
                       TDY:973-470-2521
               e-mail: dial.inc@yahoo.com
                   community.nj.com/cc/dial

John Fedix, Jr., Executive Director

DIAL, Inc. is a non-profit center for Independent Living offering information and referral, peer support, independent living skills training, recreation and advocacy guidance to persons with disabilities in north New Jersey Passaic and Essex counties. *$25.00*

8 pages Annually

4979 Disabled Advocates Working for Northwest (DAWN)

400 South Main Street
Suite 3
Wharton, NJ   07885   973-361-5666
                       FAX: 973-361-7086
               e-mail: dawninc@nac.net

Carmela Slivinski, Executive Director
Roberta Schwartz, Specialist

4980 Disabled Information Awareness and Living (DIAL)

66 Mount Prospect Avenue
Building C
Clifton, NJ   07013   973-470-8090
                       FAX: 973-470-8171

4981 Family Resource Associates

35 Haddon Avenue
Shrewsbury, NJ   07702   732-530-9646
                           FAX: 732-747-1896

Susan Levine, Social Worker

A private, non-profit agency serving disabled and developmentally delayed children birth to 8 years old and their families. Education, therapy, parent training, counseling and support in a home-based setting is emphasized. Recreation programs and other resources are available for the community. Physical, Occupational, Speech and Developmental services Also the TECH CONNECTION provides technology access, resource information and training for all ages.Free to per hour cost depending on service.

4982 Heightened Independence & Progress

131 Main Street
Suite 120
Halkensack, NJ 07601   201-996-9100
FAX: 201-996-9422
TDY:201-966-9424
e-mail: ber@hipcil.org
www.hipcil.org

Eileen Goff, Executive Director

Provides a comprehensive variety of independent living services and activities for people with all disabilities which include: information and referral, advocacy, peer support, home modifications, adaptive equipment, recreation. Workshops on Americans with Disabilties Act and other informative issues. In addition, Multimedia Transcription Services is an agency project which converts print into braille and other accessible formats.

4983 Heightened Independence and Progress

131 Main Street
Suite 120
Hackensack, NJ 07601   201-996-9100
FAX: 201-996-9422
e-mail: ber@hipcil.org

Eileen Goff, Executive Director

4984 Jersey City Chapter - Heightened Independence and Progress

2815 Kennedy Boulevard
Suite 2G
Jersey City, NJ 07306   201-413-1200
FAX: 201-413-0520
e-mail: hud@hipcil.org

Kathleen Wood, Contact

4985 MOCEANS Center for Independent Living

279 Broadway
1st Floor
Long Branch, NJ 07740   732-571-4884
FAX: 732-571-4003
TDY:732-571-4878
e-mail: moceans@moceans.org

Patricia K. McShane, Education Director
Stanley Soden, IL Specialist

Offers peer counseling, disability education and attendant care registry. Serving Monmouth and Ocean Counties with information and referrals, adocacy, peer support and independent living instructions. In Monmouth county only disability awareness through education.

4986 New Jersey Technology Assistive Resource Program (TARP)

New Jersey Protection & Advocacy
210 South Broad Street, Third Floor
Trenton, NJ 08608   609-777-0945
800-342-5832
FAX: 609-341-3327
TDY:609-633-7106
e-mail: gblue@njpanda.org
www.njpanda.org/tarp

Ellen Lence, Project Director

Consumer-driven program whose mission is to increase awareness of and improve access to assistive technology for all people with disabilities in the state. Provides information and referral through its 800 telephone number and Web site regarding all aspects of assistive technology.Also provides advocacy saervices.

4987 Progressive Center for Independent Living

831 Parkway Avenue
Suite B-2
Ewing, NJ 08618   609-530-0006
FAX: 609-530-1166
e-mail: SPeins@aol.com

Suzanne Peins, Information/Referral Specialist

To foster the independence of peple with disabilities through information and referall services, advocacy, peer support and independent living skills training.

4988 Project Freedom

223 Hutchinson Road
Robbinsville, NJ 08691   609-448-2998
FAX: 609-448-5821
e-mail: projectfreedom@aol.com
www.projectfreedom.org

Norman Smith, Associate Executive Director

Provides services with the goal of empowering people with disabilities to live independently; Housing Development/Administration geared to develop and administer various barrier-free apartment complexes with support services.

4989 Resources for Independent Living

126 Franklin Street
Riverside, NJ 08075   856-764-2745
FAX: 856-764-5573
e-mail: preid@rilnj.com
rilnj.com

Pam Reid, Executive Director

4990 Total Living Center

402 A White Horse Pike
PO Box 342
Egg Harbor City, NJ 08215   609-965-3734
FAX: 609-965-1270
e-mail: totalctr@bellatlantic.net
www.total-living-center.org

Carolyn G. Silvestro, Executive Director

One of nine Independent Living Centers in New Jersey. TLC is a community-based, consumer-driven non-profit, working with cross disability population and offers information and referral, advocacy, peer counseling and life skills training. TLC works with the severely disabled population.

New Mexico

4991 Ability Center

424 North Downtown Mall
Suite 100
Las Cruces, NM 88001   505-526-5016
                              800-376-4372
                         FAX: 505-526-1202
        e-mail: ability_center@hotmail.com
                         www.snmcil.org

Bobbie J. Marquez, Executive Director

4992 CASA

PO Box 36916
Albuquerque, NM 87176

Francis Nye, Director

Offers peer counseling and information and referral services.

4993 CHOICES Center for Independent Living

400 North Pennsylvania
Suite 425
Roswell, NM 88201   505-627-6727
                       FAX: 505-627-6754
          e-mail: choicesed@zianet.com

Barbara Thomson, Executive Director

4994 Independent Living Resource Center

4401-B Lomas Boulevard NE
Albuquerque, NM 87110   505-266-5022
                               800-260-5022
                          FAX: 505-266-5150
             e-mail: ilrcabq@aol.com

Gil Yildiz, Executive Director
Kathy Petrella, Program Manager

Using a self-help peer approach model, ILRC staff provides services, such as, independent living skills training, peer counseling, individual and systems advocacy, information and referral and service coordination to more than 400 people with disabilities annually in the counties of Bernalillo, Valencia, Cibola, Sandoval, Torrance, Guadalupe and DeBaca. Also provides funding for home modifications, vehicle modifications, assistive technology, adaptive devices, and professional counseling.

4995 New Mexico Technology Assistance Program New Mexico State Department of Education

Division /Vocational Rehabilitation
435 Saint Michaels Drive, Bldg D
Santa Fe, NM 87505   505-954-8533
                            800-866-2253
                       FAX: 505-954-8562
                       TDY:800-659-4915
           e-mail: aklaus@state.nm.us
                    www.nmtap.com

Alan Klaus, Project Director
Caroll Cadena, Public Contact

Examines and works to eliminate barriers to obtaining assistive technology in New Mexico. Has established a statewide program for coordinating assistive technology services; is designed to assist people with disabilities to locate, secure, and maintain assistive technology.

4996 New Vistas

1205 Parkway Drive
Santa Fe, NM 87505   505-471-1001
                        FAX: 505-471-4427
          e-mail: rgarcia@newvistas.org

Ronald Garcia, Contact

4997 San Juan Center for Independence

504 North Main Street
Aztec, NM 87410   505-334-5805
                     FAX: 505-334-5528
          e-mail: sjciofisi.net
                    www.sjci.org

Sherry Watson, Contact

New York

4998 AIM Independent Living Center

271 E 1st Street
Corning, NY 14830   607-962-8225
                       FAX: 607-937-5125
          e-mail: aimilc@surftech.com

Maria Sweet, Director
Peter Maier, Executive Director

A non-residential resource center run by and for people with disabilities, works with individuals providing I & R, peer support, IL skills, development & advocacy. Works with the community to promote a barrier free inclusive environment.

4999 ARISE-Center for Independent Living

1065 James Street
Suite 110
Syracuse, NY 13203   315-472-3171
                        FAX: 315-472-9252

Melissa Weiss, Executive Director

Offers peer counseling, attendant care registry, referrals and advocacy services, computer recycling, supported employment, career ladders transition program, universal design center.

5000 Access to Independence and Mobility

271 East First Street
Corning, NY 14830   607-962-8225
                       FAX: 607-937-5125
          e-mail: caim@stny.lrun.com

Peter Maier, Contact

5001 Action Toward Independence

2927 Route 6
Slate Hill, NY 10973   845-355-2030
                          FAX: 845-355-2060
             e-mail: ati@warwick.net

Margaret Jeffries, Executive Director

Services for people with disabilities, including information and referral, peer support, independent living skills development, and advocacy.

5002 Alternatives for Reaching Independence Through Services and Engineering (ARISE)

1065 James Street
Suite 110
Syracuse, NY 13202   315-472-3171
                             FAX: 315-472-9252
                   e-mail: mweiss@ariseinc.org

Melissa Weiss, Contact

5003 Barrier Free Living

270 E 2nd Street
New York, NY 10009   212-223-3771
                             FAX: 212-539-1526
e-mail: pbfbflny@aol.com or cfbflnyc@aol.com
             www.barrierfreeliving.org

Paul Feuerstein, C.S.W., President
Adela Castillo, R.N., Shelter Director

Operates a transitional residence for homeless disabled people providing independent living training, case management, housing placement and care attendant services and a mental health clinic for the disabled New Yorkers. Residence: R.A./S.S.I Clinic: Medicaid or sliding scale; Mobile Outreach: Free; Domestic Violence Program for disabled victims and their children: sliding scale and Medicaid.

5004 Batavia Center for Independent Living

61 Swan Street
Batavia, NY 14020
                             FAX: 716-343-6656

Ann Bell, Director

Offers peer counseling, education, referrals and information on accessible housing.

5005 Bergeron Health Care

PO Box 0082
148 Spencer Road
Dolgeville, NY 13329   315-429-8407
                               866-529-8407
                             FAX: 315-429-8862
              e-mail: info@adaptivemall.com
                   www.adaptivemall.com

Jamie Bergeron, Customer Service
Katie Bergeron, Customer Service

Adaptive equipment on display, strollers, wheelchairs, walkers, gait trainers, car seats, seating, tricycles, and more.

5006 Bronx Independent Living Services

3525 Decatur Avenue
Bronx, NY 10467   718-515-2800
                         FAX: 718-515-2844

Barbara Linn, Contact

5007 Brooklyn Center for Independence of the Disabled

2044 Ocean Avenue
Suite B-3
Brooklyn, NY 11230   718-998-3000
                             FAX: 718-998-3743
              e-mail: advocate@bcid.org

Sharon Shapiro-Lacks, Contact

5008 Buffalo Independent Living Center

3108 Main Street
Buffalo, NY 14214   716-836-0822
                            FAX: 716-835-3967

Douglas Usiak

A nonprofit, cross-disability, consumer/citizen directed services and advocacy organization for persons with disabilities in Western New York. Its main purpose is to assist and educate persons with disabilities to take control of the events and processes that influence their daily lives. Services include: transportation, peer counseling, interpreters of the deaf, blind/deaf instruction, housing and architectural consultation.

5009 Capital District Center for Independence

845 Central Avenue
Albany, NY 12206   518-438-8785
                           FAX: 518-459-7847

Laura Hegen, Executive Director
An independent living center.

5010 Capitol District Center for Independence

855 Central Avenue
Suite 110
Albany, NY 12206   518-459-6422
                           FAX: 518-459-7847
                           www.ilusa/cdci.com

Laura Hagen, Contact

5011 Catskill Center for Independence

Route 23 Southside
PO Box 1247
Oneonta, NY 13820   607-432-8000
                            FAX: 607-432-6907
                   e-mail: ccfi@wpe.com
                   www.wpe.com/~ccfi

Chris Zachmeyer, Executive Director

One of 35 community-based independent living centers located throughout the state of New York. As an advocacy agency, we provide a vareity of services to people with disabilities, their friends and family members. In addition, we provide advocacy, training, and technical assistance to our community members, organizations, businesses and state and local governments in a variety of disability related areas. Serves Otsego, Delaware and Schoharie counties.

5012 Center for Independence of the Disabled of New York (CIDNY)

841 Broadway
Suite 205
New York, NY 10003   212-674-2300
                             FAX: 212-254-5953
                   e-mail: info@cidny.org
                         www.cidny.org

Susan Sheer, Executive Director
Sharon Shapiro-Lacks, Deputy Director
Charles Nolan, Training Education Coordinator

5013 Center for Independent Living Action Towards Independence

2927 Route 6
Slate Hill, NY   10973   845-355-2030
FAX: 845-355-2060
e-mail: ati@warwick.net

Nancy Horton, Co-Director
Margaret Jeffries, Co-Director

Information, referral, case management, transportation and system and individual advocacy, architectural barrier removal consultations, peer support, independent living skills development and parenting classes.

5014 DD Center/St.Lukes- Roosevelt Hospital Center

1000 10th Avenue
New York, NY   10019   212-523-6230

Dr. Steven Wolf, Director

5015 Directions in Independent Living

512 West State Street
Olean, NY   14760   716-373-4602
FAX: 716-373-4604
e-mail: oleanilc@yahoo.com

Leonard X. Liquori, Executive Director

5016 Finger Lakes Independence Center

609 W Clinton Street
Suite 112
Ithaca, NY   14850   607-272-2433
FAX: 607-272-0902
e-mail: flic@clarityconnect.com
www.fliconline.org

Lenore Schwager, Executive Director

Offers peer counseling, attendant care registry, information on accessible housing and referrals.

5017 Genesee Region Independent Living

61 Swan Street
Batavia, NY   14020   716-343-4524
FAX: 716-343-6656
e-mail: grilc@freenet.buffalo.edu
freenet.buffalo.edu/~grilc

Ann Bell, Contact

5018 Genesee Region Independent Living Center

61 Swan Street
Batavia, NY   14020   716-343-4524
FAX: 716-343-6656

Ann Bell, Executive Director

Offers: Advocacy, peer counseling, benefits advisement (information and assistance), support groups, loan closet, transportation (ten passenger lift equipped van), library - books, tapes and brochures on various aspects of disabilities, also closed circuit TV print enlarger, and a print scanner with synthesized speech, architectural barrier consultations, independent living skills instruction, community education and information and referral.

5019 Glens Falls Independent Living Center

71 Glenwood Avenue
Queensboro, NY   12804   518-792-3537
FAX: 518-792-0979
e-mail: cil@interpcs.net
www.loweradirondackik.com

Patrick Doyle, Executive Director

Offers standard ILC core services. Programs include Center for Assistive Computer Technology; Capital District Regional TRAID Center; and monthly consumer luncheons; Polly's House - Center for Therapeutic Arts.

5020 Harlem Independent Living Center

5-15 West 125th Street
New York, NY   10027   212-369-2371
800-673-2371
FAX: 212-369-9283
e-mail: harlemilc@aol.com
www.retrofit.net/hilc

Yonette Douglas, Contact

A non-profit agency that advocates for people with disabilities by assisting with the application process of housing, benefits, etc. Our services are free of charge.

5021 Herkimer Resource Center for Independent Living

401 East German Street
Steuben Center, 2nd Floor
Herkimer, NY   13350   315-866-7246
FAX: 315-866-7280
e-mail: dannym_13350@yahoo.com
www.rcil.com

Danny McLain, Advocacy Coordinator
Kathy Brown, Information Resource Coordinator
Ann Abramczyk, Coordinator, ADAC

RCIL's varied services are consumer-driected. With expertise in law and services assistance is available not only to persons with disabilities, but the community at large. Advocacy, independent living skills training, peer counseling information and referral, benefits advisement and a coalition of support services to persons with Alzheimer's disease and related dementias and to the families, caregivers and professionals involved with them.

5022 Independent Living

5 Washington Terrace
Newburgh, NY   12550   845-565-1162
FAX: 914-565-0567
e-mail: ilid@frontiernet.net

Doug Hovey, Contact

5023 Independent Living Center of Amsterdam

12 Chestnut Street
Amsterdam, NY   12010   518-373-5874
800-824-6071
FAX: 518-842-0905
TDY:518-842-3593
e-mail: ilca@superior.net

Richard Tyler, Executive Director
Agnes Rodd, Finance Director

Peer counseling, advocacy, independent living skills training, information and referral services, wheelchair accessible van transportation, agency sponsored family care, self-advocacy training, ADA consultation, home and community based services, community education, disability benefits, advisement, and more. All programs and services are available in English and Spanish.

5024   Independent Living Center of Western New York

3108 Main Street
Buffalo, NY   14214   716-836-0822
                             FAX: 716-835-3967
                 e-mail: djusiak@acsu.buffalo.edu

Douglas Usiak, Contact

5025   Independent Living Center of the Hudson Valley

Troy Atrium
Broadway & Fourth Street
Troy, NY   12180   518-274-0701
                             FAX: 518-274-7944
                     e-mail: dfigny@aol.com
                         www.ilusa.com/ilchv

Denise Figueroa, Contact

5026   Long Island Center for Independent Living

3601 Hempstead Turnpike
Suite 208
Levittown, NY   11756   516-731-7385
                             FAX: 516-796-0529
                             TDY:516-796-0135
                       e-mail: licil@aol.com
           www.members.aol.com/licil/prof/index.htm

Joan Lynch, Program Manager (CDPAP)
Therese Aprile, Director of Advocacy
Marc Miller, Resource Specialist

Offers peer counseling, information and referral services and other services to te community. Benefits, advisement, advocacy, counseling, attendant care referral, housing referral, equipment loan bank, transportation service, consumer directed personal assistant program (CDPAP).

5027   Long Island Center for Independent Living

3601 Hempstead Turnpike
Suite 312
Levittown, NY   11756   516-796-0144
                             FAX: 516-796-1529
                       e-mail: lincil@aol.com

Patricia Moore, Contact

5028   Massena Independent Living Center

156 Center Street
Massena, NY   13662   315-764-9442
                             FAX: 315-764-9464
                    e-mail: milc@northnet.org

Jeff Reifensnyder, Executive Director

Provides a variety of non-residential direct services as well as educating the public through community awareness campaigns. Also seeks to address the current appropriate unmet needs of persons experiencing a disability - primarily in St. Lawrence and Franklin Counties.

5029   Nassau County Office for the Physically Challenged

1550 Franklin Avenue
Mineola, NY   11501   516-571-3119
                             FAX: 516-571-6150

Don Dreyer, Director

This agency serves as the ADA compliance coordinating office for all Nassau County governmental facilities, programs and services. It also serves in an advisory capacity to regional and national policy-making organizations, planning committees and legislative bodies, and conducts advocacy as well as directprograms and services to enhance inclusion by people with disabilities to employment, consumerism, and transportation.

5030   Niagara Frontier Center for Independent Living

1522 Main Street
Niagara Falls, NY   14305   716-282-4730
                             FAX: 716-284-0829

Kathleen , Executive Director

Offers peer counseling, referrals and disability education.

5031   North Country Center for Independence

82 Washington Street
Suite 214
Poughkeepsie, NY   12601   845-452-3913
                             FAX: 914-485-3196
                       e-mail: tri@idsi.net
                     www.taconicresources.net

Cynthia Burchfield, Contact

5032   Northern Regional Center for Independent Living

165 Mechanic Street
Watertown, NY   13601   315-785-8704
                             800-585-8703
                             FAX: 315-785-8612
                     e-mail: nrcil@nrcil.org
                             www.ncil.org

Aileen Geiling, Contact

5033   Office for the Physically Challenged

1550 Franklin Avenue
Mineola, NY   11501   516-535-3147
                             FAX: 516-535-3108

Don Dreyer, Contact

5034   Options for Independence

75 Genesee Street
Auburn, NY   13021   315-255-3447
                             FAX: 315-255-0836
                 www.optionsforindependence.org

Guy Cosentino, Contact

5035 Options for Independence - Auburn

75 Genesee Street
Auburn, NY   13021   315-253-9786
                                       800-496-9148
                                    FAX: 315-255-0836
                              e-mail: opforind.@aol.com
                              www.optionsforindependence.org

Guy Thomas Cosentino, Executive Director
Crystal Purcell, Seneca County Coordinator
Rosemarie Homick, Peer Advocate

Offers peer counseling, disability education and information on accessible housing and information regarding the Americans with Disabilities Act.

5036 Options for Independence - Seneca Falls

55 Fall Street
Seneca Falls, NY   13148   315-568-2724
                                    FAX: 315-568-1844
                              e-mail: opforind.@aol.com
                              www.optionsforindependence.org

Guy Thomas Cosentino, Executive Director
Crystal Purcell, Seneca County Coordinator
Rosemarie Homick, Peer Advocate

Offers peer counseling, disability education and information on accessible housing and information regarding the Americans with Disabilities Act.

5037 Queens Independent Living Center

140-40 Queens Boulevard
Jamaica, NY   11435   718-658-2526
                                    FAX: 718-658-5295

Robin Shaikun, Contact

5038 Queens Independent Living Center

14040 Queens Boulevard
Jamaica, NY   11435   718-658-2526
                                    FAX: 718-658-5295

Robin S. Shaikun, Executive Director

Provides resources, individual advocacy and systems advocacy to ensure independence and the civil rights of people with disabilities through peer counseling, education and referrals.

5039 Regional Center for Independent Living

1641 East Avenue
Rochester, NY   14610   716-442-6470
                                    FAX: 716-271-8558
                              e-mail: rcil@rcil.org
                                    www.rcil.org

5040 Resource Center for Accessible Living

602 Albany Avenue
Kingston, NY   12401   845-331-0541
                                    FAX: 845-331-2076
                              e-mail: rcal@ulster.net
                                    www.rcalonline.org

Joan Gundersen, Executive Director

5041 Resource Center for Independent Living

401-409 Columbia Street
PO Box 210
Utica, NY   13503   315-797-4642
                                    FAX: 315-797-4747
                                    TDY:315-797-5837
                              e-mail: rcil@rcil.com

Burt Danovitz, Ph.D., Executive Director
Rose Marie Roberts, CRC, Associate Director
Wendy Gagliardo, Asso. Director of Administration

A nonresidential, nonprofit agency which administers a wide range of independent living and advocacy services for and with people with disabilities. As part of the Independent Living Movement, we believe that the basic right of contributing to and participating in society as a self-determining individual must extend to all citizens. All Center services are consumer directed and aimed to increase individual rights, options and achievements.

5042 Rockland Independent Living Center

238 North Main Street
Spring Valley, NY   10977   845-426-0707
                                    FAX: 914-426-0989
                              e-mail: rilc@aol.com

Lorraine Jackson-Ordia, Contact

5043 Saratoga County Options for Independent Living

8 Butler Place
Saratoga Springs, NY   12866   518-584-8202
                                    FAX: 518-584-1195

Teena Willard, Assistant Director

5044 Southern Tier Independence Center

24 Prospect Avenue
Binghamton, NY   13901   607-724-2111
                                    FAX: 607-722-5646
                              e-mail: stic@stic-cil.org
                                    www.stic-cil.org

Maria Dibble, Executive Director

Offers supported employment, consumer directed personel assistance, assistive technology services, sign language interpreters, ADA training/consultation, servive coordinator, peer counseling, advocacy.

5045 Southwestern Independent Living Center

843 N Main Street
Jamestown, NY   14701   716-661-3010
                                    FAX: 716-661-3011

Marie Carrubba, Executive Director

Offers disability education, attendant care registry and information on accessible housing.

5046 Staten Island Center for Independent Living

470 Castleton Avenue
Staten Island, NY   10301   718-720-9016
                                    FAX: 718-720-9664
                              e-mail: dorothy.doran@verizon.net
                                    community.silive.com/cc/sicil

Dorothy Doran, Executive Director

5047 Suffolk Independent Living Organization (SILO)

745 Waverly Avenue
Holtsville, NY   11742   631-654-8007
                          FAX: 631-654-8077
                          e-mail: suffolkilc1@aol.com

June Roberts, Executive Director

5048 Taconic Resources for Independence

82 Washington Street
Suite 214
Poughkeepsie, NY 12601   845-452-3913
                          FAX: 845-485-3196
                          TDY:845-485-8110
                          e-mail: triadvocates@worldnet.att.net
                          www.taconicresources.net

Cynthia Burchfield, Executive Director
Marguerite Loskowitz, Resource Advocate

A center for independent living, benefits advisement information, and referral, advocacy, independent living skills, peer counseling, parent advocacy, sign language interpreters.

5049 Utica Resource Center for Independent Living

PO Box 210
Utica, NY   13503   315-797-5846
                          FAX: 315-797-4747
                          e-mail: burt.danovitz@rcil.com
                          www.rcil.com

Burt Danovitz, Contact

5050 Visions/Services for the Blind & Visually Impaired

500 Greewich Street
Third Floor
New York, NY   10013   212-625-1616
                          FAX: 212-219-4078
                          e-mail: info@visionsvcb.org
                          www.visionsvcb.org

Nancy Miller, Executive Director

5051 Westchester County Independent Living Center

200 Hamilton Avenue
White Plains, NY   10601   914-328-0441
                          FAX: 914-682-8518

Joseph Bravo, Executive Director

Offers peer counseling, attendant care registry and referrals.

5052 Westchester Disabled on the Move

984 North Broadway
Suite L-01
Yonkers, NY   10701   914-968-4717
                          FAX: 914-968-6137
                          e-mail: info@wdom.org
                          wdom.org

Melvyn R. Tanzman, Executive Director
Scott Smith, Program Director

Full range of independent living services including housing search and acquisition assistance, ADA compliance, services to high school students with disabilities.

5053 Westchester Independent Living Center

200 Hamilton Avenue
White Plains, NY   10601   914-682-3926
                          FAX: 914-682-8518
                          e-mail: jbravo297@aol.com
                          www.wilc.org

Joe Bravo, Contact

5054 Wiswall Center for Independent Living

71 Glenwood Avenue
Queensbury, NY   12804   518-792-3537
                          FAX: 518-792-0979
                          e-mail: cil@interpcs.net

Patrick Doyle, Jr., Contact

North Carolina

5055 Advocacy Project for Persons with Disabilities

620 South Elm Street
Suite 309
Greensboro, NC   27406   336-272-0572
                          FAX: 336-272-0572

Aaron Shabazz, Contact

5056 Center for Accessible Housing

North Carolina State University
PO Box 8613
Raleigh, NC   27695   919-515-3015
                          FAX: 919-515-3023
                          e-mail: cahd@ncsu.edu

Established in 1989, the Center improves the quality and availability of housing for people with disabilities. The center provides assistance and information to individuals and industry through research, collaborative efforts with manufacturers, training and information services.

5057 Disability Awareness Network

609 Country Club Drive
Suite C
Greenville, NC   27834   252-355-5272

Marty Silverthorne, Contact

5058 Heritage Hills Mature Life

38 East Sylva Shopping Center
Sylva, NC   28779   828-631-0433
                          FAX: 828-586-1120
                          e-mail: mature@main.nc.us
                          www.main.nc.us/jackson/hhdir.htm

Al Bouchard, Contact

A Mature Life Campus to acquire property and build permanent facilities on the same grounds for the existing senior services, programs and activities now in older leased buildings in Jackson County, North Carolina.

5059 Live Independently Networking Center

PO Box 1135
Newton, NC   28658   704-464-0331
                      FAX: 704-464-7375
                      e-mail: linc@twave.net
                      www.conninc.com/linc

Donavon Kirby, Deputy Director....Li

Private, nonprofit, federally funded center for independent living located in Western North Carolina.

5060 Pathways for the Future

525 Mineral Springs Drive
Sylva, NC   28779   828-631-1167
                      FAX: 828-631-1169
                      e-mail: pathways@dnet.net
                      www.main.nc.us/pathways

Aimee Speers, Program Development Coordinator

Dedicated to increasing independence, changing attitudes, promoting equal access and building a peer support network in Western North Carolina through the use of community education, independent living services and advocacy. Quarterly newsletter is published. Call or write to Pathways to add your name to the mailing list for Pathfinder.

5061 Programs for Accessible Living

5701 Executive Center Drive
Suite 320
Charlotte, NC   28212   704-537-0550
                      FAX: 704-566-0507

Julia Sain, Executive Director

Offers information and referrals, peer counseling for people with disabilities, advocacy and independent living skills classes. PAL helps people with disabilities achieve and maintain their independence in the community.

North Dakota

5062 Dakota Center for Independent Living

3111 East Broadway Avenue
Bismarck, ND   58501   701-222-3636
                      FAX: 701-222-0511
                      e-mail: dcil@dcil.org

Robert Gomez, Contact

5063 Fraser

2902 S University Drive
Fargo, ND   58103   701-232-3301
                      FAX: 701-237-5775
                      e-mail: fraser@fraserltd.org
                      www.fraserltd.org

Sandra Leyland, Executive Director

5064 Freedom Research Center for Independent Living

PO Box 1795
Fargo, ND   58107

                      e-mail: frcilfg@mail.corpcomm.net

Nathan Algaard, Contact

5065 Independence

900 North Broadway
Minot, ND   58703   701-839-4724
                      FAX: 701-838-1677
                      e-mail: life@minot.ndak.net

Sandy Johnson, Contact

Ohio

5066 Ability Center of Greater Toledo

5605 Monroe
Sylvania, OH   43560   419-885-5733
                      FAX: 419-882-4813
                      e-mail: act@abilitycenter.org
                      www.abilitycenter.org

Timothy Harrington, Contact

5067 Access Center for Independent Living

35 South Jefferson
Dayton, OH   45402   937-341-5202
                      FAX: 937-394-5217
                      e-mail: roy@acils.com
                      www.acils.com

Roy Puston, Interim Executive Director

Offers peer counseling, disability education and other services to the community.

5068 Center for Independent Living Options

632 Vine Street
Suite 601
Cincinnati, OH   45202   330-762-0007

                      e-mail: cilo@fuse.net
                      www.home.fuse.net/cilo

Lin Laing, Contact

5069 HELP Six Chimneys

3622 Prospect Avenue
Cleveland, OH   44115   216-432-4810
                      FAX: 216-361-2608
                      e-mail: helpfoundation@worldnet.att.net

Walter Zborowsky, Help Foundation
Daniel Rice, Chief Operating Officer
Patricia Schwartz, Quality Resurance Director

Offers disability education and referrals as well as subsidized housing and independent living services at several locations. Program support services to adults with mental retardation and other developmental disabilities. Serving Northeast Ohio.

5070 Help Foundation

3622 Prospect Avenue E
Cleveland, OH   44115   216-432-4810
                      FAX: 216-361-2608
                      e-mail: helpfoundation@worldnet.att.net

Patricia Schwartz, Quality Assurance Manager
Walter Zborowsky, ACSW, LISW, Executive Director
Daniel Rice, MSW, LISW, Chief Operating Officer

A private, not-for-profit social agency providing subsidized housing, independent living and group home services to children and adults with mental retardation and other developmental disabilities in Cuyahoga Lake and Summit counties (northeast Ohio), as well as summer all day special education services to children with disabilities.

5071 Independent Living Center of Central Ohio

1 Marion Avenue
Suite 115C
Mansfield, OH 44903 419-526-6870
FAX: 419-526-6870

Jonnie Fisher, Contact

5072 Independent Living Options

632 Vine Street
Suite 601
Cincinnati, OH 45202 513-232-1777

Lisa Corbett, Director

Offers peer counseling, disability education and information on accessible housing.

5073 Linking Employment Ability Potential - Independent Living Center

2100 North Ridge Road
Elyria, OH 44035 440-324-3444
FAX: 440-324-2112
e-mail: leap@kellnet.com
www.kellnet.com/leapweb

Elsie Danevich, Contact

5074 Mid-Ohio Board for Independent Living Environment

690 South High Street
Columbus, OH 43206 614-443-5936
FAX: 614-443-5954
e-mail: bev@mobileonline.org
www.mobileinline.org

Beverly Rackett, Executive Director

5075 Mid-Ohio Board for an Independent Living Environment (MOBILE)

690 South High Street
Columbus, OH 43206 614-443-5936
FAX: 614-443-5954
TDY:614-443-5957
e-mail: bev@infinet.com
www.mobileonline.org

Beverly Rackett, Executive Director

Offers information and research, advocacy, independent living skills training, peer support, disability awareness training and accessibility design standards technical assistance.

5076 Rehabilitation Service of North Central Ohio

270 Sterkel Boulevard
Mansfield, OH 44907 419-756-1133
FAX: 419-756-6544
e-mail: rehabvp@richnet.net
www.therehabcenter.org

David Daugherty, President/CEO
Linda Williams, V P Medical Rehab Services
Linda Kafer, V P Behavioral Health Services

Private nonprofit organization providing coordinated, team-oriented comprehensive outpatient rehabilitation services to children and adults of all ages. Serves approximately 18 counties in N/C Ohio. Four umbrella areas of service include medical rehabilitation services, vocational rehabilitation services, behavioral health service, and drug and alcohol addiction services.

5077 Samuel W. Bell Home for the Sightless

1507 Elm Street
Cincinnati, OH 45210 513-241-0720
FAX: 513-241-2560

Louis Hoff, Director

Offers a residential home for the totally blind and legally blind adults, male and female.

5078 Services for Independent Living

25100 Euclid Avenue
Suite 105
Cleveland, OH 44117 216-731-1529
FAX: 216-731-3083
e-mail: sil@stratos.net

Lynn Hildebrand, Executive Director

Offers support, accessibility education, advocacy, transitional education services, independent living skills training, information and referrals.

5079 Society for Equal Access Independent Living Center

821 Anola Street
Suite B
Dover, OH 44663 330-343-3668
FAX: 330-343-3721
e-mail: ilc@tusco.net
www.tusco.net/ilc/home.html

Nanette Robertson, Contact

5080 Society for Equals Acces, Independent Living Center

821 Anola Avenue
Suite B
Dover, OH 44622 330-343-3668
888-213-4452
FAX: 330-343-3721
TDY:330-602-2557
e-mail: ilc@tusco.net
www.ilc.tusco.net

Julie A. Ronald, Executive Director
Ruthanne Fulmer, Advocate
Jerome Geisinger, Ind. Living Skills Specialist

The Society works with individuals to become more independent. Our agency assists with peer support, advocacy, information and referral, independent living skills and transportation. Our goal is to move those with challenges in the direction ofn independence.

5081 Tri-County Independent Living Center

680 East Market Street
Suite 205
Akron, OH 44304 330-762-0007
FAX: 330-762-7416
e-mail: rose@tcilc.tnet.com

Rose Juriga, Contact

5082 United Cerebral Palsy of Central Ohio

440 Industrial Mile Road
Columbus, OH 43228 614-279-0109
    800-670-9146
    FAX: 614-279-2527
    e-mail: ucp1@mindspring.com
    www.ucpofcentralohio.org

Marc Guthrie, Executive Director
Kathy Streblo, Assistant Executive Director
Meg Werner, Assistant Executive Director

5083 United Cerebral Palsy of Columbus and Franklin County

440 Industrial Mile Road
Columbus, OH 43228 614-279-0109
    FAX: 614-279-2527
    e-mail: uspoco@prodiax.net

Mark Guthry, Executive Director
Karen D. Osborne, Development Director

The mission of the organization is to encourage and facilitate growth of self-sufficient, productive and participating citizens who are differently-abled. Services are individually tailored to the consumer.

Oklahoma

5084 Ability Resources

823 South Detroit
Suite 110
Tulsa, OK 74120 918-592-1235
    FAX: 918-592-5651

Carla Lawson, Director

Offers disability education, peer counseling and referrals, assistive technology lending library, job readiness training, employment placement, nursing home outreach, literacy tutoring, ADA training and technical assistance.

5085 Green County Independent Living Resource Center

4100 SE Adams Road
Suite C106
Bartlesville, OK 74006 918-335-0567
    800-559-0567
    FAX: 918-333-1814
    e-mail: gcilrc@aol.com

Gary Donley, Executive Director
Judy Viles, Assistive Technology Specialist
Tammy Williams, Independent Skills Specialist

Independent skills training, living information and referrals, advocacy, a loan library of adaptive equipment and books. Services available to all individuals with disabilities and their family members who reside in Northeastern Oklahoma.

5086 Oklahomans for Independent Living

321 S 3rd
Suite 2
McAlester, OK 74501 918-426-6220
    FAX: 918-426-3245
    e-mail: mikew@icok.net
    www.icok.net

Mike Ward, Executive Director
Pam Pulchny, Associate Director

OIL is a resource center for people with disabilities. Its mission is to encourage individuals of all ages, with all type of disabilities, to increase their personal independence, empowerment, and self determination, and to achieve full integration and participation in their work, community and school.

5087 Progressive Independence

121 North Porter Avenue
Norman, OK 73071 405-321-3203
    800-801-3203
    FAX: 405-321-7601
    e-mail: progind@telepath.com
    www.progind.org

Jeff Hughes, Executive Director
Joseph S. Mecham, AT Program Manager
Debbie Fidler, IL Programs Manager

Preovides four cores services of Information & Referral, Individual& Systems Advocacy, Peer Counseling, and Skills Training; in addition, offers accessible computer lab, short term DME loans, ande benefits counseling for SSI/SSDI.

5088 Sandra Beasley Independent Living Center

705 South Oakwood
Enid, OK 73703 580-237-8508
    FAX: 580-233-6403
    e-mail: sbilcenter@pldi.net
    www.mebeaf.tripod.com/~lew_31

Lew Blockcolski, Contact

5089 Sandra Beasley Independent Living Center

705 S Oakwood Road
Suite B1
Enid, OK 73703 580-237-8508
    800-375-4358
    FAX: 580-233-6403
    e-mail: sbilcenter@pldi.net

Lew Blockcolski, Director
Carolyn Thompson, Associate Director
Cindy Keith, Service Coordinator

An independent living center which offers independent living skills training, peer counseling, attendant care registry, ADA consultation, advocacy services and an equipment Loan Closet.

Oregon

5090 Central Oregon Resources for Independent Living

PO Box 9425
Bend, OR 97708 541-388-8103
    FAX: 541-388-1226
    e-mail: donstew@bendnet.com

Don Stewart, Contact

5091 Columbia Gorge Center

2940 Thomsen Road
Hood River, OR 97031 541-386-2376
    FAX: 541-386-7788

William F. Uhlman, Director

Provides residential and vocational services for people with disabilities in the community.

5092 HASL Independent Abilities Center

1252 Redwood Avenue
Grants Pass, OR   97527   541-479-4275
                                 800-758-4275
                            FAX: 541-479-7261
                    e-mail: thaslinc@cdsnet.net

Don Drake, Chairman Board of Directors
Tina Snyro, Executive Director

To promote public awareness of the special needs and
legal rights of individuals with cross-disabilities; to
facilitate their integration into society and provide
support through advocacy, peer counseling, skills
training and information and referral to encourage
independence.

**5093 Handicapped Ability Support League
Independent Living Center**

1252 Redwood Avenue
Grants Pass, OR   97527   541-473-4275
                            FAX: 541-479-7261
                    e-mail: thaslinc@cdsnet.net

Don Drake, Contact

5094 Independent Living Resources

2410 SE 11th Avenue
Portland, OR   97214   503-232-7411
                            FAX: 503-232-7480
                      e-mail: ilr@teleport.com
                                www.irl.org

Suzanne Westwood, Contact

5095 Laurel Hill Center Independent Living Program

2145 Centennial Plaza
Eugene, OR   97401
                            FAX: 541-345-9218

Mary Alice Brown, PhD, Executive Director

Offers vocational evaluation, training and job placement services; socialization and independent living
skills training and support; serving adults with psychiatric and/or physical disabilities.

5096 Oregon Commission for the Blind

535 SE 12th Avenue
Portland, OR   97214   503-731-3221
                            FAX: 503-731-3230

Linda R. Mock, Administrator
Dacia Johnson, Dir of Rehabilitation Services

Provides medical, therapeutic, counseling, education,
training and other services needed to prepare for
work.

5097 SPOKES Unlimited

111 North Seventh Street
Klamath Falls, OR   97601   541-883-7547
                            FAX: 541-885-2469
                    e-mail: sustaff@cdsnet.net

Peggy McConnell, Services Coordinator

5098 Umpqua Valley Disabilities Network

PO Box 507
Roseburg, OR   97470   541-672-6336
                            FAX: 541-672-8606
                     e-mail: uvdn@jeffnet.org

Tricia Hoelscher, Contact

Pennsylvania

5099 Abilities in Motion

416 Blair Avenue
Reading, PA   19601   610-376-0010
                                 888-376-0120
                                 888-376-0120
                            FAX: 610-376-0021
                 e-mail: aimcil@netcarrier.com
                      www.abilitiesinmotion.org

Ralph Trainer, Executive Director

5100 Anthracite Region Center for Independent Living

44 West Broad Street
Hazleton, PA   18201   570-455-9800
                            FAX: 570-455-1731

Shirley Ray, Contact

5101 Brian's House

1300 S Concord Road
West Chester, PA   19382   610-873-3460
                            FAX: 610-399-1828

Lori Plunkett, Executive Director

Residential care in a variety of homes and apartments
for people with a range of development disabilities.
Cost varies with needs. Also year-round recreation
programs, vocational training and employment programs.

**5102 Center for Independent Living of Southcentral
Pennsylvania**

17th Street & 9th Avenue
Station Mall, Lot 30
Altoona, PA   16602

                                 800-237-9009
                            FAX: 814-949-1909
                     e-mail: cilscpa@penn.com
                              www.cilscpa.org

David Brown, Srvc Coordinator/Skills Trainer
Howard Ermin, Jr., Independent Living Specialist

The Center is a non-profit tax exempt community
based organization, non-residential in nature. Programs are consumer controlled, accessible to the public and focusing on the individual. CILSCPA stresses
the importance of utilizing community resources in
meeting independent living needs in South Central
PA. The Center provides services to people with disabilities and their families in Bedford, Blair, Cam-
bria, Fulton, Huntingdon, Indiana and Somerset
counties.

5103 Center for Independent Living of Central Pennsylvania

415 Fallowfield Road
Suite 101
Camp Hill, PA 17011   717-731-1900
800-323-6060
FAX: 717-731-8150
e-mail: office@cilcp.org
www.cilcp.org

Theotis Braddy, Director
Janetta Green, Assistant Director
Ann Neimer, IL Program Manager

Offers information and referral services, sign language, interpreter services, independent living skills, and advocacy.

5104 Center for Independent Living of North Central Pennsylvania

210 Market Street
Suite A
Williamsport, PA 17701   717-327-9070
FAX: 717-327-8610
e-mail: cilcp@aol.com

George Morton, Contact

5105 Citizens for Independence and Access

3450 Industrial Drive
York, PA 17402   717-840-9653
FAX: 717-840-9748
e-mail: cilo@yorkinternet.net

Vicki Cuscino, Executive Director
Matt Feeser, Associate Director

5106 Community Resources for Independence

2222 Filmore Avenue
Erie, PA 16506   814-838-7222
FAX: 814-838-8491
e-mail: cri@cri.org
www.crinet.org

Timothy Finegan, Contact

5107 Erie Independence House Center for Independent Living

2222 Filmore Avenue
Erie, PA 16506   814-833-6083
FAX: 814-838-8491

Tim Finegan, Director

Offers peer counseling, disability education and advocacy services.

5108 Freedom Valley Disability Enablement

3607 Chapel Road
Newtown Square, PA 19073   610-353-6640
800-423-4754
FAX: 610-353-6753

Ann Cope, Contact

5109 Lehigh Valley Center for Independent Living

919 S 9th Street
Allentown, PA 18103   610-770-9781
FAX: 610-770-9801

Amy C. Beck, Director

Advocacy services and information and referral services, peer support, independent living skills training, housing search assistance and computer network.

5110 Liberty Resources

1341 N Delaware Avenue
Suite 105
Philadelphia, PA 19125   215-634-2000
FAX: 215-634-6628

David J. Schultheis, Comptroller

Provides lists of accessible housing and attendants, courses in independent living, recreational programs, equipment referrals and loans. Recently a merger with Liberty Center for Independent Living, has enabled this center to offer a wider spectrum of services for the disabled throughout the northeastern and southeastern Pennsylvania.

5111 Life and Independence for Today

503 Arch Street Extension
St. Marys, PA 15857   814-781-3050
FAX: 814-781-1917
e-mail: lift@penn.com

Robert Mecca, Contact

5112 Northeastern Pennsylvania Center for Independent Living

431 Wyoming Avenue
Scranton, PA 18503   570-344-7211
FAX: 570-344-7218

John F. Boland, Director

Offers information and referral services.

5113 Pennsylvania's Iniative on Assistive Technology (PIAT), Temple University

1301 Cecil B. Moore Avenue
423 Ritter Annex
Philadelphia, PA 19122   215-204-5966
800-204-7428
FAX: 215-204-9371
TDY:215-204-1356
e-mail: piat@astro.ocis.temple.edu
www.temple.edu/inst_disabilities/PIAT

Amy S. Goldman, Public Contact

Focuses on the creation of a consumer responsive system, supported by combined public and private resources, through which Pennsylvanians with disabilities have access to the assistive technology services and supports.

5114 Three River Center for Independent Living

7110 Penn Avenue
Pittsburgh, PA 15208   412-371-7700
FAX: 412-371-9430
e-mail: cilswpa@aol.com

W.D. Chrisner, Contact

5115 Three Rivers Center for Independent Living

7110 Penn Avenue
Pittsburgh, PA 15208   412-371-7700
800-633-4583
FAX: 412-371-9430
htrfn.clpgh.org/trcil

W.D. Chrisner, III, President

Offers peer counseling, information and referral services, housing data and referral service, assistive technology program, deinstitutionalization program, consumer-controlled personal assistance program, independent living skills training, advocacy and accessibility consultants.

Sliding Fee

5116   Tri-County Partnership for Independent Living

69 E Beau Street
Washington, PA   15301   724-627-8826
FAX: 401-738-1083
e-mail: doug@tripil.com

Kathleen Kleinmann, Director

Offers peer counseling, disability education and information on accessible housing.

5117   Tri-County Patriots for Independent Living

69 East Beau Street
Washington, PA   15301   724-223-5115
FAX: 724-223-5119
e-mail: kleinman@tripil.com
www.tripil.com

Kathleen Kleinmann, Contact

5118   Voices for Independence

3711 West 12th Street
Suite 3
Erie, PA   16505   814-838-9890
FAX: 814-838-9779
e-mail: vfi@erie.net

Shona Eakin, Contact

Rhode Island

5119   Blackstone Valley Chapter RI Arc

115 Manton Street
Pawtucket, RI   02861   401-727-0150
FAX: 401-727-0153
e-mail: contact@bucriarc.org
www.bucriarc.org

Peter Holden, Executive Coordinator
Barbara Lindsay, Development Director

5120   Franklin Court Assisted Living

180 Franklin Street
Bristol, RI   02809   401-253-3679

www.seniorlivingresidences.com

Offers local seniors an affordable assisted living option with first-rate services and gracious accommodations.

5121   IN-SIGHT Independent Living

43 Jefferson Boulevard
Warwick, RI   02888   401-941-3322
FAX: 401-941-3356

Judith Smith, Contact

5122   Ocean State Center for Independent Living

59 W Shore Road
Warwick, RI   02889   401-738-1013

www.oscil.org

Lorna Ricci, Director

Information and referral services.

5123   Ocean State Center for Independent Living

59 West Shore Road
Warwick, RI   02889   401-738-1015
FAX: 401-738-1083
e-mail: oscil@rida.net
www.oscil.org

Lorna Ricci, Contact

5124   PARI Independent Living Center

500 Prospect Street
Suite 18
Pawtucket, RI   02860   401-725-1966
FAX: 401-725-2104
www.pari-ilc.org

Leo Canuel, M.A., Executive Director

Offers information and referral services, personal care attendant services, home modifications, advocacy services and peer counseling, independent living skills training, and recycled equipment.

5125   People Actively Reaching Independence (PARI) Independent Living Center

500 Prospect Street
Pawtucket, RI   02860   401-725-1966
FAX: 401-725-2104
www.pari-ilc.org

Leo Canuel, Contact

5126   Rhode Island Assistive Technology Access Partnership (ATAP),RI Department of Human Services

Office of Rehabilitation Services
40 Fountain Street
Providence, RI   02903   401-421-7005
800-752-8088
FAX: 401-421-9259
TDY:401-421-7016
e-mail: reginac@ors.state.ri.us
www.atap.state.ri.us

Regina Connor, Project Director

Statewide partnership of organizations, each with a targeted focus, working together with a consumer council to remove barriers and increase access to assistive technology for individuals with disabilities of all ages.

South Carolina

5127   Coastal Disability Access

1021 Third Avenue
Conway, SC   29526   843-488-1309
FAX: 843-488-0994
e-mail: iadvocate@aol.com

Steve Avinger, Contact

5128 Disability Action Center

3126 Beltline Boulevard
Columbia, SC   29204   803-779-5121
                              FAX: 803-779-5114
                   e-mail: dacdirect1@aol.com

Kathy Pelletier, Executive Director

**5129 South Carolina Assistive Technology Program
(SCATP)**

USC School Of Medicine
Center for Disability Resources
Columbia, SC   29208   803-935-5263
                              FAX: 803-935-5342
                   e-mail: jjendron@usit.net
              wwww.public.usit.net/jjendron

Evelyn Evans, Project Director

Catalyst for uniting assistive technology services
statewide into an easily accessible system that is responsive to the needs of all South Carolinians with
disabilities.

5130 South Carolina Independent Living Council

810 Dutch Square Boulevard
Suite 214
Columbia, SC   29210   803-731-1607
                                877-217-2331
                              FAX: 803-731-1439
                              TDY:803-731-1608
                   e-mail: scilc@usit.net

Maris Burton, Executive Director
DeeAnn Jones, Executive Assistant

The SC Independent Living Council's mission is to
jointly (with the DSUs) develop uses for Part B funding throughout the state. These monies can be used
to: develop Centers for Independent Living; outreach
to unserved and underserved populations; conduct
needs assessments and research; make recommenda-
tion to policy makers regarding the delivery of IL
services; and provide resources for direct services.

South Dakota

5131 Aberdeen Communication Service for the Deaf

315 South Wilson Avenue
Aberdeen, SD   57401   605-626-2668
                              FAX: 605-626-3089
                   e-mail: csdabr@iw.net
                              www.c-s-d.org

Nancy Schlichenmayer, Contact

5132 Adjustment Training Center

612 10th Avenue SE
Aberdeen, SD   57401   605-229-0263
                              FAX: 605-225-3455

Rob Wanous, Director

Offers peer counseling, attendant care registry and
referrals.

5133 Black Hills Workshop & Training Center

PO Box 2104
Rapid City, SD   57702   605-343-4550
                              FAX: 605-343-0879
                   e-mail: dennisp@bhws.com
                              www.bhws.com

Dennis Popp, CEO
Colleen Ronning, VP

Offers job placement, housing options, case coordination, supported employment and supported living
for all disability groups, as well as specialized services for head trauma victims.

5134 Communication Services for the Deaf

102 North Krohn Place
Sioux Falls, SD   57103   605-367-5760
                                800-642-6410
                              FAX: 605-367-5958
                              www.c-s-d.org

Ben Soukup, CEO

5135 Native American Advocacy Project

PO Box 527
Winner, SD   57580   605-842-3977
                              FAX: 605-842-3977
                              www.sdnaap.org

Marla Bull Bear, Contact

5136 Opportunities for Independent Living

421 S Main Street
1571
Aberdeen, SD   57401   605-626-2976
                              FAX: 605-229-3954

Jeff Kisecker, Director

Offers peer counseling, attendant care registry and
other services to the community.

5137 Prairie Freedom Center for Independent Living

301 South Garfield Avenue
Suite 8
Sioux Falls, SD   57104   605-367-5630
                                800-947-3770
                              FAX: 605-367-5639
                   e-mail: prairie@ideasign.com

Char Crisp, Director

Mission: To empower individuals with disabilities
who choose to live independently.

5138 Prairie Freedom Center for Independent Liv

301 South Garfield Avenue
Suite 8
Sioux Falls, SD   57104   605-367-5630
                              FAX: 605-397-5639
                   e-mail: prairie@ideasign.com

Char Crisp, Contact

5139 Quad Squad

Big Foot Trail
102 BIA Highway 2
Kyle, SD   57712   605-455-1170

5140   Rapid City Communication Service for the Deaf

150 Knollwood Drive
Rapid City, SD   57701   605-394-2544
                                FAX: 605-394-1933
                                e-mail: wrdi@dtgnet.com

Greta Greer, Contact

5141   South Dakota Assistive Technology Project

DakotaLink
21 South Central
Pierre, SD   57501   605-224-5336
                                800-244-5336
                                FAX: 605-224-8320
                                e-mail: dvogel@tie.net
                                http://dakotalink.tie.net

Dave Vogel, Public Contact

Works with consumers, state and private agencies, and organizations providing services to, or advocating for, people with disabilities to identify and eliminate barriers to individuals receiving assistive technology devices or services in a timely manner. Uses a mobile unit, outreach coordinators, rehabilitation technicians, and training programs.

5142   Western Resources for dis-ABLED Independence

36 E Chicago Street
Rapid City, SD   57701   605-394-1930
                                800-226-3938
                                FAX: 605-394-1933
                                e-mail: wrdi@dtgnet.com

Glade Jones, Executive Director

Offers peer counseling, disability education and advocacy services, independent living skills training, information and referral services, home modifications and adaptive devices.

5143   Western Resources for disABLED Independence

809 Rapid Street
Suite 303
Rapid City, SD   57701   605-394-1930
                                FAX: 605-394-1933
                                e-mail: wrdi@dtgnet.com

Glade Jones, Contact

5144   Yankton Communication Service for the Deaf

231 Broadway Street
Suite C6
Yankton, SD   57078   605-668-9759
                                FAX: 605-668-3712
                                e-mail: kmerril@iw.net

Kathy Merril, Contact

5145   Center for Independent Living of Middle Tennessee

480 Craighead Street
Suite 200
Nashville, TN   37204   615-292-5803
                                FAX: 615-383-1176
                                e-mail: cilmt@tndisability.org
                                www.cilmt.org

Tom Hopton, Contact
Floyd Stewart, Contact

5146   Disability Resource Center

900 East Hill Avenue
Suite 120
Knoxville, TN   37915   865-637-3666
                                FAX: 865-637-5616
                                e-mail: drc@korrnet.org
                                www.korrnet.org/drc

Cathy Randall, Contact

5147   Jackson Center for Independent Living

231 North Parkway
Jackson, TN   38305   901-668-2211
                                FAX: 901-668-0406
                                e-mail: jcil@usit.net

Glen Barr, Contact

5148   Memphis Center for Independent Living

163 North Angelus Street
Memphis, TN   38104   901-726-6404

                                e-mail: mcil@mcil.org
                                www.mcil.org

Deborah Cunningham, Executive Director

Offers peer counseling, disability education and information and referral services.

5149   Nashville Center for Independent Living

1617 16th Avenue South
Nashville, TN   37212   615-385-7214
                                FAX: 615-383-1176

5150   Tennessee Technology Access Project (TTAP)

Cordell Hull Building,5th Floor
425 5th Avenue North
Nashville, TN   37243   615-532-3122
                                800-732-5059
                                FAX: 615-532-4685
                                TDY:615-741-4566
                                e-mail: kwright@mail.state.tn.us
                                www.state.tn.us/mental/ttap.html

Kevin R. Wright, Project Director

Emphasizes the implementation and pursuit of systems change and advocacy activities by developing an information/communication network, working with state agency policy values and developing alternate funding mechanisms. Involves consumers, and facilitates interagency cooperation and interaction with the private sector.

5151   Tri-State Resource and Advocacy

5708 Uptain Road
Suite 350
Chattanooga, TN   37411   423-892-4774
                          FAX: 423-892-9866
                 e-mail: trac.jat@bellsouth.net

Dr. Chu , Contact

Texas

5152   A.B.L.E. Center for Independent Living

208 West 23rd Street
Odessa, TX   79761   915-580-3439
                          FAX: 915-580-0280
                 e-mail: jerik4able@aol.com
                          www.able-cil.org

Jeri Kounce, Executive Director

5153   Austin Resource Center for Independent Living

825 E Rundberg Lane
Suite A-1
Austin, TX   78753   512-832-6349
                          FAX: 512-832-1869
                 e-mail: arcil@arcil.com
                          www.arcil.com

Ronald Rocha, Executive Director

5154   Center for the Retarded Independent Living Program

PO Box 13403
Houston, TX   77218   281-579-8096

5155   Crockett Resource Center for Independent Living

1020 E Loop 304
Crockett, TX   75835   409-544-2811
                                 800-784-8710
                          FAX: 409-544-7315
                 e-mail: crcil@sat.net

Cynthia Cook, Executive Director

Provides independent living services to cross-disability groups to increase their personal self-determination and minimize dependence on others. Maintain comprehensive information on availability of resources and provides referrals to such resources. Provides instruction to assist people with disabilities to gain skills that would empower them to live independently. Peer counseling, advocacy - both individual and community by assisting to obtain support services to make changes in society.

5156   Houston Center for Independent Living

7000 Regency Square Boulevard
Suite 160
Houston, TX   77036   713-654-1864
                          FAX: 713-974-6927

Sandra Bookman, Director

Information on accessible housing, advocacy services and peer counseling.

5157   Independent Life Styles

1917 Augusta Drive
Apartment 2
Houston, TX   77057   713-861-4266

Peter Simmons, Director

Offers peer counseling, advocacy and other services to the community.

5158   Independent Living Research Utilization Project

Institute for Rehabilitation and Research
2323 S Shepherd Drive
Suite 1000
Houston, TX   77019   713-520-0232
                          FAX: 713-520-5785
                 e-mail: ilru@ilru.org
                          www.ilru.org

Lex Frieden, Director

ILRU is a national center for information, training, research and technical assistance in independent living. Its goal is to expand the body of knowledge in independent living and to improve utilization of results of research programs and demonstration projects in this field. ILRU is a program of The Institute for Rehabilitation and Research, a nationally recognized medical rehabilitation facility for persons with disabilities. TTY phone number: (713) 520-5136.

5159   LIFE Independent Living Center

3212 34th
Lubbock, TX   79410   806-795-5433
                          FAX: 806-781-5607

Rich Van Hersch, Contact

5160   LIFE/ Run Centers for Independent Living

1001 West Tenth Avenue
Amarillo, TX   79101   806-372-7556
                          FAX: 806-372-2045
                 e-mail: chinan3@aol.com

Nancy Penland, Coordinator

5161   Martin Luther Homes of Texas

324 S Loop 123 - Business
Seguin, TX   78155   830-372-2525
                          FAX: 830-372-3076

Barbara Hokum, Administrator
Fred Naumann III, Communications

Providing a wide array of services to assist individuals and families in achieving positive life goals. Services to persons with disabilities and other special needs include community living options, training and employment options, spiritual growth and development options, training and counseling support.

5162   Office for Students with Disabilities University of Texas at Arlington

PO Box 19355
Arlington, TX   76019   817-272-3364
                          FAX: 817-272-5221
                 e-mail: dianne@uta.edu
                          www.uta.edu/disability

Dianne Hengst, Director
Ron Venable, Assistant Director

Offers disability counseling and academic accomodation for UTA community.

5163 Palestine Resource Center
421 Avenue A
Palestine, TX   75801   903-729-7505
FAX: 903-729-7540
e-mail: prscil@risecom.net

Mary Killough, Contact

5164 Palestine Resource Center for Independent Living
421 Avenue A
Palestine, TX   75801   903-729-7505
888-326-5166
FAX: 903-729-7540
e-mail: prscil@risecom.net

Cheryl Bass, Executive Director
Provides independent living services to cross-disability groups to increase their personal self-determination and minimize dependence on others. Maintain comprehensive information on availability of resources and provides referrals to such resources. Provides instruction to assist people with disabilities to gain skills that would empower them to live independently. Peer counseling, advocacy - both individual and community by assisting to obtain support services to make changes in society.

5165 Panhandle Action Center for Independent Living Skills
3608 S Washington Street
Amarillo, TX   79110   806-374-1400
FAX: 806-374-4550

Leanne Wesley, Director
Offers peer counseling, attendant care registry and information on accessible housing.

5166 Panhandle Independent Living Center
1118 South Taylor Street
Amarillo, TX   79101   806-374-1400
FAX: 806-374-4550
e-mail: mpanilc@tcac.net

Carl McMillan, Contact

5167 REACH of Dallas Resource Center for Independent Living
8625 King George Drive
Suite 210
Dallas, TX   75235   214-630-4796
FAX: 214-630-6390
e-mail: reachdallas@reachcils.org
www.reachcils.org

Charlotte Stewart, Contact
Susie Reukenia, Assistant Director

Information and referral services, peer counseling, independent living skills training, loaner adaptive technology equipment, advocacy assistance, social recreational activities and ADA technical assistance.

5168 REACH of Denton Resource Center
405 South Elm
Suite 101
Denton, TX   76201   940-383-1062
FAX: 940-383-2742
e-mail: reachden@gte.net
www.reachcils.org

Charlotte Stewart, Contact
Becky Teal, Office Manager

5169 REACH of Fort Worth Resource Center for Independent Living
1205 Lake Street
Fort Worth, TX   76102   817-870-9082
FAX: 817-877-1622
e-mail: reachftw@reachcils.org
www.reachcils.org

Charlotte Stewart, Executive Director

5170 REACH/Resource Center on Independent Living
1205 Lake Street
Fort Worth, TX   76102   817-870-9082
FAX: 817-877-1622
e-mail: reachftw@reachcils.org
www.reachcils.org

Charlotte Stewart, Executive Director
Anne Ancy, Case Manager

Information and referral services, peer counseling, independent living skills training, loaner equipment, advocacy assistance, ADA technical assistance and social/recreational activities.

5171 SAILS
1028 South Alamo
San Antonio, TX   78210   210-281-1878
FAX: 210-281-1759

5172 Southeast Texas Living Indepence for Everyone (SETLIFE)
780 South Fourth Street
Beaumont, TX   77701   409-832-2599
FAX: 409-838-4499
e-mail: setlife@sat.net

Nancy Comeaux, Contact

5173 Texas Rehabilitation Commission Independent Living Services
4900 N Lamar Boulevard
Austin, TX   78751   512-424-4136
FAX: 512-424-4982
e-mail: terryshelden@rehab.state.tx.us

Terry Sheldon, Program Specialist
Provides technical assistance and other support services to the state's Independent Living Council, Independent Living Centers and Independent Living Counseling programs.

5174 VAIL
PO Box 5035
McAllen, TX   78502   956-781-7733
FAX: 956-781-7735
e-mail: available@acnet.net

Oscar Cardenas, Contact

5175 VOLAR, Center for Independent Living

8929 Viscount
Suite 101
El Paso, TX 79925   915-591-0800
                                 FAX: 915-591-3506
                                 e-mail: volar1whc.net

Luis Enrique Chew, Contact

5176 Valley Association for Independent Living

PO Box 5035
McAllen, TX 78502   956-781-7733
                                 FAX: 956-781-7735
                                 e-mail: valleyassociation@earthlink.net

Laura Sexton, Interim Executive Director
Doresdo Jay-Pang, Deputy Director

Utah

5177 Active Re-Entry

451 S Carbon Avenue
931
Price, UT 84501   435-637-4950
                                 FAX: 807-637-4952

Nancy Bentley, Director
Offers information and referral services.

5178 OPTIONS for Independence

Northern Utah Center for Independent Living
1095 N Main Street
Logan, UT 84341   435-753-5353
                                 800-753-2344
                                 FAX: 435-753-5390
                                 e-mail: jbiggs@optionind.org
                                 www.optionsind.org

Helen Roth, Executive Director
Craig Shaffer, IL Coordinator
Pat Haskell, IL Coordinator

Information and referral, systems change advocacy, individual advocacy, peer counseling, independent living skills training, PAS registry, assistive technology assessment and acquisition and recreation for people with disabilities.

5179 Red Rock Center for Independence

515 West 300 North
Suite A
St. George, UT 84770   435-673-7501
                                 FAX: 435-673-8808
                                 e-mail: gowens@rrci.org
                                 www.rrci.org

Garry Owens, Executive Director

5180 Utah Assistive Technology Program (UTAP) Utah State University

Center Persons with Disabilities
6588 Old Main Hill
Logan, UT 84322   435-797-3824
                                 FAX: 435-797-2355
                                 TDY: 435-797-7089
                                 e-mail: meblair@cc.usu.edu
                                 www.uatpat.org

Martin E. Blair, Program Director

Provides expertise, resources, and a structure to enhance and expand AT services provided by private and public agencies in Utah. Occurs through monitoring, coordination, information dissemination, empowering individuals, the identification and removal of barriers, and expanding state resources.

5181 Utah Independent Living Center

764 S 200 W
Salt Lake City, UT 84101   801-359-2444
                                 FAX: 801-466-2363

Debra Mair, Director
Offers information and referral services.

Vermont

5182 Vermont Assistive Technology Project Vermont Department of Aging & Disabilities

103 South Main Street
Weeks Building
Waterbury, VT 05671   502-241-2620
                                 800-750-6355
                                 FAX: 802-241-2174
                                 e-mail: lynnec@dad.state.vt.us
                                 www.dad.state.vt.us/atp

Lynne Cleveland, Project Director

Encompasses a state coordinating council for assistive technology issues, regional centers for demonstration, trial and technical support with computer and augmentative communication equipment; and regional seating and positioning centers.

5183 Vermont Center for Independent Living

11 E State Street
Montpelier, VT 05602   802-229-0501
                                 800-639-1522
                                 FAX: 802-229-0503
                                 e-mail: vcil@vcil.org

Deborah Lisi-Baker, Executive Director

Information and referral services, peer advocacy counseling, home modification funding, community advocacy and independent living services, and cibil rights advocacy.

Virginia

5184 Access Independence

403 B South Loudoun Street
Winchester, VA 22601   540-662-4452
                                 FAX: 540-662-4474
                                 e-mail: access@visuallink.com

Kim Schick, Executive Director
Joan Davis, Manager of Operations

Offers support services to persons with disabilities to assist in maintaining or increasing their independence and self-determination. Includes housing assistance, independent living skills training, information, referral services, assistance and representative payee, and advocacy.

5185 Appalachian Independence Center

230 Charwood Drive
Abingdon, VA   24210 540-628-2979
FAX: 540-628-4931

Greg Morrell, Executive Director
Charley Barry, Program Director
Lisa Domby, Director of Operations

A nonprofit center for independent living serving
people with disabilities in Southwestern Virginia.
Services include peer counseling, independent living
skills training, information and referrals, accessible
transportation, community education, technical assistance and individual and systems advocacy.

5186 Blue Ridge Independent Living Center

1502-D Williamson Road Northeast
Roanoke, VA   24012 540-342-1231
FAX: 540-342-9505
e-mail: kmichalski@brilc.org
www.brilc.org

Karen Michalski, Director

Offers independent living skills training, peer counseling, support groups, advocacy, information and
referral, technical assistance, community education
and housing assistance.

5187 Central Virginia Independent Living Center

2900 W Broad Street
Richmond, VA   23230 804-353-6503
FAX: 804-358-5606

Sandra Wagner, Director
Information and referral services.

5188 Central Virginia Independent Living Center

2900 West Broad Street
Richmond, VA   23230 804-353-6503
FAX: 804-353-5606
e-mail: cvilc1@aol.com

Sandra Wagener, Executive Director

5189 Clinch Independent Living Services

PO Box 2741
Grundy, VA   24614 540-935-6088
FAX: 540-935-6342
e-mail: cils@netscope.net

Betty Bevins, Executive Director
Barbara Crouse, Administrative Assistant

5190 DisAbility Resource Center

409 Progress Street
Fredricksburg, VA   22401 540-373-2559
800-644-6324
FAX: 540-373-8126
e-mail: yvonne@drc-fredericksburg.org
www.drc-fredericksburg.org

Robert J. Boyd, III, Executive Director
Yvonne Bosch, Community Outreach Coordinator

5191 Eastern Shore Center for Independent Living

4376 Lankford Highway
Suite 3
Exmore, VA   23350 757-414-0100
FAX: 757-414-0205

Althea Pittman, Exeutive Director

5192 Endependence Center

Interstate Corporated Center, Bldg #15
6320 Center Drive
Suite 100
Norfolk, VA   23502 757-461-8007
FAX: 757-455-8223
TDY: 757-461-7527
e-mail: ecinorth@whro.org

Steve Johnson

A private, nonprofit center for independent living
serving South Hampton Roads. The Center serves
people with disabilities who wish to make positive
life changes in self-direction, housing, education,
employment and community involvement. ECI serves
the community in creating an environment which is
accessible to all citizens.

5193 Endependence Center of Northern Virginia

3100 Clarendon Boulevard
Arlington, VA   22201 703-525-3268
FAX: 703-525-3585
e-mail: coopecnv@aol.com

Michael Cooper, Contact

5194 Independence Empowerment Center

9001 Digges Road
103
Manasses, VA   20110 703-257-5400
FAX: 703-257-5043
e-mail: iecinc@starpower.net
www.empower.org

Bill Ward, Executive Director
Lisa Fletcher, Community Services Program Coor.

5195 Independence Resource Center

201 W Main Street
Apartment 8
Charlottesville, VA   22902 804-981-7723
FAX: 804-971-8242
e-mail: irc1@comcilin.net

Tom Vandover, Director
Information and referral services.

**5196 Independent Living Center Network Department
of the Visually Handicap**

1809 Staples Mill Road
Richmond, VA   23230 804-355-7900

Bob Burton, Director
Information and referral services.

5197 Junction Center for Independent Living

247 West Morgan Avenue
Pennington Gap, VA 24277 540-546-5093
FAX: 540-546-3360
e-mail: jcil1@bellatlantic.net

Gwen Gillenwater, Executive Director
Sam Smith, Assistant Director

A private non-profit community-based, non-residential organization that is consumer directed and controlled. Services provided to people with disabilities include advocacy, peer counseling, independent living, skills training and information and referral. Our goal is total community inclusion for everyone - including people with diabilities.

5198 Lynchburg Area Center for Independent Living

500 Alleghany Avenue
Suite 520
Lynchburg, VA 24501 804-528-4971
FAX: 804-528-4976
e-mail: lacil@lacil.org
www.lacil.org

, Executive Director

5199 Peninsula Center for Independent Living

2021 A Cunningham Drive
Suite 2
Hampton, VA 23666 757-827-0275
FAX: 757-827-0655
e-mail: iepcil@aol.com
www.jepcic.com

Ralph Shelman, Contact

5200 Woodrow Wilson Independent Living Skills Training Program

PO Box 1500
Fishersville, VA 22939 540-332-7103
800-345-9972
FAX: 540-332-7330
e-mail: clemencb@wwrc.state.va.us

David Schwemer, Director

Information & referral services. Six week Virginia residential programs and evaluation services.

Washington

5201 Adventures in Independence Development

819 S Hatch Street
Spokane, WA 99202 509-468-2264

Missy Karyl

5202 Center for Independence

407 14th Avenue SE
Puyallup, WA 98372 253-858-1880

Jim Lindley, Director
Kimberly Rinehardt-Dodd, Independent Living Specialist

The Center For Independence is a resource organization dedicated to serving individuals with disabilities to more fully access and participate in the community through outreach, advocacy and skills development. We participate in community activities that address civil and equal rights issues, peer counseling and monitoring, individual advocacy, independent living skills development and information referral.

5203 Coalition of Responsible Disabled

612 North Maple Street
Spokane, WA 99201 509-326-6355
FAX: 509-327-2420
e-mail: elecord@cet.com
www.rip-cord.org

Linda Schappals- McClain, Executive Director

5204 Community Service Center for the Deaf and Hard of Hearing

1609 19th Avenue
Seattle, WA 98122 206-322-4996
FAX: 206-720-3251
TDY:206-568-1234
e-mail: cscdhh@cscdhh.org

Kenneth Puckett, Executive Director

Community information and referral services; interpreter referral services such as sign language interpreting, real time captioning, relay interpreting, oral interpreting; 9-1-1/TTY eduction program; communication access advocacy; and community education.

5205 Community Services for the Blind

9709 3rd Avenue NE
Suite 100
Seattle, WA 98115 206-525-5556
FAX: 206-525-0422
e-mail: csbps@csbps.com
www.csbps.com

June Mansfield, Director
Clarice Hutchinson, VP, Marketing and Communitcaiton

Gounded in 1965 as an independent nonprofit, CSBPS works to restore, maintain, and enhance the independence and well-being of people with impaired vision. Programs include professional counseling and support; safe travel and orientation training; instruction in independent living skills; low vision clinic and low vision rehavilitation; one-on-one volunteer services, education, information and referral, assistive technology center; and an adaptive aids retail site, online store and mail order cat

5206 Designs for Independent Living

819 South Hatch
Spokane, WA 99202 509-535-9696

Gloria Caryl, Contact

5207 DisAbility Resource Center

607 Southeast Everett Mall Way
Suite 17
Everett, WA 98208 425-347-5768
FAX: 425-710-0767
e-mail: ilsc@richpoor.com
www.wa-ilsc.org

Sarajane Siegfriedt, Executive Director

5208 Disability Resource Network

16315 North 87th Street
Suite B-5
Redmond, WA   98052   425-558-0993
                              800-216-3335
                         FAX: 425-558-4773
e-mail: shalernadnet@yahoo.com
                            www.wccd.org

Sherry Hillebrant, Manager
Karen Suyana, Information and Asst. Specialist

5209 Epilepsy Foundation of Washington

3800 Aurora Avenue N
Suite 370
Seattle, WA   98103   206-547-4551
                              800-752-3509
                         FAX: 206-547-4557
e-mail: mail@epilepsyfoundationwash.org
             www.epilepsyfoundationwash.org

Joel Neier, Executive Director

5210 Everett Coalition of People with Disabilities

1301 Hewitt Avenue
Everett, WA   98201   425-742-8533

5211 Greater Lakes Mental Health Care

9330 59th Avenue SW
Lakewood, WA   98499   253-581-5013
                         FAX: 253-620-5013

Joann Freimund, Contact

5212 Greater Lakes Mental Healthcare

9330 59th Avenue SW
Lakewood, WA   98499   253-581-7020
                         FAX: 254-620-5140
                            www.glmhc.org

Richard J Towell, President/CEO
Madelaine A Thompson, Director of Development
Jane-Ellen Delgado, Community Relations &
Marketing

Greater Lakes Mental Healthcare is a premier behavioral healthcare facility in the Pacific Northwest helping individuals develop solutions for successful living. Greater Lakes provides a wide range of confidential professional counseling services for all ages.

5213 Independent Lifestyles Services

422 North Pine Street
Ellensburg, WA   98926   509-962-9620
                         FAX: 509-962-9630
                    e-mail: ils@televar.com

Noelle Blazevich, Contact

5214 Independent Living Center of SW Washington

PO Box 2129
Vancouver, WA   98668
                         FAX: 253-848-0798

Morris Gielser, Director

Offers peer counseling, referral and advocacy services.

5215 Independent Living Resources of Southwest Washington

3305 Main Street
Suite 109
Vancouver, WA   98663   360-694-6790
                         FAX: 360-694-6910
e-mail: ilrswwa@netzero.net
                            www.ilr.org

Chuck Davisgher, Director Program & Services
Lyn Wilson, Specialist/ Peer Counselor

5216 Kitsap Community Action Program

1201 Park
Bremerton, WA   98337   360-377-0053

Larry Eyer, Contact

5217 Kitsap Community Resources

1201 Park Avenue
Bremerton, WA   98337   360-377-0053
                         FAX: 360-792-8708

Larry Eyer, Executive Director

KCR provides services to low-income residents of Kitsap County. These services include emergency housing, WIC nutrition and health, Head Start preschool, employment and training. Information and referral services.

5218 Lilac Blind Foundation

1212 N Howard Street
Spokane, WA   99201   509-328-6900
                              800-422-7893
                         FAX: 509-328-8965
e-mail: info@lilacblindfoundation.org
             www.lilacblindfoundation.org

Cherly L. Martin, Director

5219 Resource Center for the Handicapped

20150 45th Avenue NE
Seattle, WA   98155   206-364-8179
                         FAX: 425-271-1096
                            www.rch.prodigy

Jeff Sykes, Director
Information and referral services.

5220 Tacoma Area Coalition of Individuals with Disabilities

6315 S 19th Street
Tacoma, WA   98466   253-565-9000
                              877-538-2243
                         FAX: 253-565-5578
e-mail: tacid@tacid.org
                            www.tacid.org

Chris Ensor, Executive Director
Offers information and referral services.

5221 Vision & Independent Living Agency

2400 Queen Street
Bellingham, WA   98226

JoAnn Mancinelli, Director

Offers information and referral services, advocacy and peer counseling for the community.

5222 Washington Coalition for Citizens with Disabilities (WCCD)

4649 Sunnyside North
Suite 100
Seattle, WA 98103 206-545-7055
FAX: 206-545-7059
e-mail: wccd@premieer1.net

JoAnn Fritsche, Contact

West Virginia

5223 Appalachian Center for Independent Living

Elk Office Center
4710 Chimney Drive
Suite C
Charleston, WV 25302 304-965-0376
800-642-3003
FAX: 304-965-0377

Larry E. Paxton, Executive Director
Vicky L. Robinson, Executive Secretary

Provides services and formation to handicapped persons including professional and peer counseling, advocacy, referral, housing, transportation, support groups, build wheelchair ramps, mobility equipment loan, attendant care, older blind services and skills training.

5224 Appalachian Center for Independent Living

4710 Chimney Drive
Suite C
Charleston, WV 25302 304-965-0376
FAX: 304-965-0377

Larry Paxton, Contact

5225 Mountain State Center for Independent Living

914-1/2 Fifth Avenue
Huntington, WV 25701 304-525-3324
FAX: 304-525-3360

Anne Weeks

5226 Northern West Virginia Center for Independent Living

601-3 East Brockway Avenue
Suite A&B
Morgantown, WV 26505 304-296-6013
FAX: 301-292-5217
e-mail: nwvcil@labyrinth.net

Jan Desey, Executive Director
Madeline Miralles, Admin. Assistant

Independent living services to persons with disabilities including skills training, peer counseling, orientation and mobility training, advocacy and self-help training, community based systems advocacy, disability awareness training, ADA consultation, technical assistance and information and referrals are provided.

Wisconsin

5227 Access to Independence

2345 Atwood Avenue
Madison, WI 53704 608-242-8484
800-362-9877
FAX: 608-242-0383
TDY:608-242-8485
e-mail: ati@chorus.net

Wendy Hecht, Executive Director

An Independent Living Center serving people with disabilities. Services include: information and referral, housing counseling, advocacy, deaf services, assistive technology, peer support, independent living skills training, and volunteer opportunities, among others.

5228 Center for Independent Living

University of Wisconsin
Menomonie, WI 54751 715-232-2150

Karen Hodgson

5229 Center for Independent Living of Western Wisconsin

2920 Schneider Avenue East
Menomonie, WI 54751 715-233-1070
800-228-3287
FAX: 715-233-1083
e-mail: cilww@cilww.com
cilww.com

Tim Sheehan, Contact

5230 Great Rivers Independent Living Services

4328 Mormon Coulee Road
La Crosse, WI 54601 608-787-1148
FAX: 608-787-1148
e-mail: advocacy@greatrivers.org

Kathie Knoble-Iverson, Contact

5231 Independence FIRST

600 West Virginia Street
Suite 301
Milwaukee, WI 53204 414-291-7520
FAX: 414-291-7525
e-mail: lee@independencefirst.org
www.independencefirst.org

Lee Schulz, Contact

5232 Independence First

600 W Virginia Street
Suite 301
Milwaukee, WI 53204 414-291-7520
FAX: 414-291-7525
e-mail: info@independencefirst.org
www.independencefirst.org

Lee Schulz, Executive Director
Karen Avery, Associate Director

Serves individuals with disabilities in the metro-Milwaukee four county area. Services include advocacy, independent living skills training, information/referral, peer counseling, youth camp and personal assistance services.

5233 Inspiration Ministries
Corner Route 67/Cty F
PO Box 948
Walworth, WI 53184   262-275-6131
                              FAX: 262-275-3355
        e-mail: inspirationministries@elknet.net
                www.inspirationministries.org

David Rowland, President
Tim Schnake, V P Resident Services

Formerly known as Christian League for the Handicapped. The ministry is a caring Christian community who enable and encourage people with disabilities. We address physical, mental and spiritual needs through accessible residential accommodations, work opportunities and integration into the local community and its churches. 160 acre campus including residential apartments, a work center, a Christian bookstore and gift shop, and a retreat center/summer camp (Inspiration Center).

5234 Midstate Independent Living Center
PO Box 369
203 Schiek Plaza
Rhinelander, WI 54501   715-369-5040
                              800-331-5044
                         FAX: 715-369-5043
             e-mail: milc2@newnorth.net
                  www.Newnorth.net/milc

John Nousaine, Contact
Julie Bemis, Director

5235 North Country Independent Living
2231 Catlin Avenue
PO Box 1245
Superior, WI 54880   715-392-9118
                              800-924-1220
                         FAX: 715-392-4636

John Novsainc, Director

5236 Options for Independent Living
555 Country Club Road
PO Box 11967
Green Bay, WI 54807   920-490-0500
                              888-485-1515
                              888-465-1515
                         FAX: 920-490-0700

Thomas J. Diedrick, Director
Kathryn C. Barry, Assistant Director

Provides independent living core services including: peer counseling, information and referral, IL skills training, advocacy - individual and systems, and housing referrals. Rehabilitation technology services provided include: home evaluations, vehicle evaluations, computer evaluations, deaf/hard of hearing equipment evaluations and ADA Title III Technical Assistance and benefits counseling.

5237 Society's Assets
5200 Washington Avenue
Suite 225
Racine, WI 53406   262-637-9128
                         FAX: 262-637-8646
                e-mail: info@sai-inc.org

Bruce Nelsen, Executive Director
Karen Olufs, Director of Indepedent Living
Jean Rumachik, Director Of Home Care Services

Society's Assets assists people with disabilities to live as indpendently as possible. A non-profit human services agency, Society's Assets provides information and referal, independent living skills training, peer support, advocacy, and supportive home care. Home health care is provided by SAI Home Health Care. The agency serves 5 counties in southeastern Wisconsin and also provides information about interpreters, employment, benefits, home modifications, assistive equipment and accessibility.

Fees vary

Wyoming

5238 LifeQuest - Interdisciplinary Rehabilitation
339 W Loucks Street
Sheridan, WY 82801   307-674-4462
                              800-684-2289
                         FAX: 307-674-5117

Shannon Trierweiler, Manager

Multi-disciplines organization dedicated to the highest possible economic and social independence for persons with disabilities. Extensive referral service, specialized employment placement, occupational therapy, psychological services, evaluation services, and coordination of external services as needed to meet client plans and objectives.

5239 Rehabilitation Enterprises of North Eastern Wyoming
245 Broadway Street
Sheridan, WY 82801   307-672-7481
                         FAX: 307-674-5117

Larry W. Samson, President & CEO
Jeff Holsinger, Director of Operations

Committed to enhancing personal and community relationships, providing opportunities for growth, and helping people with varying abilities achieve their personal goals.

5240 Rehabilitation Enterprises of Northeastern Wyoming (RENEW)
245 Broadway
Sheridan, WY 82801   307-672-7481
                         FAX: 307-674-5117
                e-mail: renew@renew-wyo.com
                     www.renew-wyo.com

Larry Samson, Contact

5241 Western Wyoming Center for Independent Living
190 Custer Street
Lander, WY 82520   307-332-4889
                         FAX: 307-332-2491
                e-mail: wwcfil@rmisp.com

Carol Fontaine, Contact

5242 **Wyoming Independent Living Rehabilitation Center**
305 W 1st Street
Casper, WY 82601   307-473-1767
                    FAX: 307-266-6957
                    e-mail: dpotter@trib.com
                    w3.trib.com/~dpotter

Ken Hoff, Director
Creates opportunities for severely disabled individuals to live more independently, direct services, advocacy, home modifications and independent living skills.

5243 **Wyoming Independent Living Rehabilitation**
305 West First Street
Casper, WY 82601   307-266-6956
                    800-736-8322
                    FAX: 307-266-6959
                    e-mail: dpotter@trib.com
                    w3.trib.com/~dpotter

Ken Hoff, Director
Creates opportunities for severly disabled individuals to live more independently, direct services, advocacy, home modifications and independent living skills.

Associations & Referral Agencies

5244 AIDS Legal Council of Chicago

188 West Randolph
Suite 2400
Chicago, IL 60601   312-427-8990
FAX: 312-427-8419
e-mail: info@aidslegal.com
www.aidslegal.com

Justin Hayford, Case Manager

Legal advice and services for persons who are HIV positive or have AIDS, and their companions, families, etc., regarding HIV-related legal matters.

5245 AIDSLAW of Louisiana

Greater New Orleans Foundation
2515 Canal Street
New Orleans, LA 70119   504-581-6363
FAX: 504-821-8326

Gregory Ben Johnson

Second year of funding for new legal agency serving persons affected by HIV/AIDS.

5246 Center for Disability and Elder Law

710 North Lake Shore Drive
3
Chicago, IL 60611
FAX: 312-908-0866
TDY:312-908-8705

Jann Dragswich, Executive Director
Amy Peterson, Managing Attorney
Miriam Seitz, System Manager

Provides legal services at no cost to low income persons with disabilities in Cook County. LCD staff screen applicants to determine if they meet the financial, disability and geographical eligibility requirements for service.

5247 Chicago Lawyers' Committee for Civil Rights Under Law

100 North LaSalle Street
Suite 600
Chicago, IL 60604   312-630-9744
FAX: 312-630-1127
e-mail: clccrul@aol.com
www.clccrul.org

Provides legal services to individuals and groups with civil rights problems through class action and law reform cases. Also provides technical assistance to community groups. Spanish-speaking staff available. Individual cases and walk-ins are not accepted. Wheelchair accessible.

5248 DNA People's Legal Services

PO Box 306
Window Rock, AZ 86515   520-871-4151

Offers legal assistance to Native Americans.

5249 Disability Rights Education and Defense Fund

2212 6th Street
Berkeley, CA 94710   510-644-2555
800-466-4232
FAX: 510-841-8645
TDY:8004664232
e-mail: dredf@dredf.org
www.dredf.org

Marilyn Golden, Linda Kilb, Arlene Mayerson, author

Non-profit organization dedicated to advancing the civil rights of individuals with disabilities through legislation, litigation, informal and formal advocacy, and education and training of lawyers, advocates and clients with respect to disability issues. DREDF operates a Department of Justice funded national ADA information hotline for Titles II and III of the ADA. DREDF also provides training, advocacy, technical assistance and referrals for parents of disabled children.

5250 Disabled Americans Rally for Equality

4752 S Kilpatrick Avenue
Chicago, IL 60632   773-873-8703

Promotes awareness and lobbies for disabled persons rights.

5251 Equal Employment Advisory Council

1015 15th Street NW
Suite 1200
Washington, DC 20005   202-789-8600
FAX: 202-789-2291

A nonprofit association for the purpose of monitoring federal equal employment litigation and filing amicus curiae briefs in precedent-setting cases. Also file comments on equal opportunity employment and affirmative action regulatory proposals and monitors judicial developments.

5252 Guardianship Services Associates

41-A South Boulevard
Oak Park, IL 60302   708-386-5398
FAX: 708-386-5970
e-mail: GSAoakpark@aol.com

Robert R Wohlgemuth, Director

Information and counseling on guardianship issues. Can provide direct assistance in obtaining guardianship for disabled adults. Also provides information and direct assistance on durable powers of attorney. Can assume appointment as guardian in selected cases.

5253 Judge David L. Bazelon Center for Mental Health Law

1101 15th Street NW
Suite 1212
Washington, DC 20005   202-767-5730
FAX: 202-223-0409
e-mail: hn1660@handsnet.org
www.bazelon.org

Robert Bernstein, Executive Director

National litigation and technical assistance center for advocates for people with mental disabilities. Offers a website with advocacy resources and a variety of publications, handbooks, issue papers and manuals to help advocate for, implement, enforce and comply with federal laws and court orders on involuntary outpatient commitment, discrimination based on a label of mental disability, fair housing, criminalization, custody relinquishment for access to children's mental health care.

5254 Legal Action Center

236 Massachusetts Avenue NE
Suite 505
Washington, DC 20002   202-544-5478
                         FAX: 202-544-5712
                    e-mail: lacdc@lac-dc.org

Ellen Weber, Senior Vice President

Provides technical assistance and education programs on ADA issues related to individuals with drug and alcohol abuse and HIV disease and legal assistance to individuals who have faced discrimination on the basis of these disabilities.

5255 Legal Center

455 Sherman Street
Suite 130
Denver, CO 80203   303-722-0300
                              800-288-1376
                     FAX: 303-722-0720
      e-mail: tlcmail@thelegalcenter.org
              www.thelegalcenter.org

Mary Anne Harvey, Executive Director

The Legal center uses the legal system to protect & promote the rights of people with disabilities and older people in Colorado through direct legal representation, advocacy, education and legislative analysis. We are also the State Ombudsman for nursing homes and personal care boarding homes. Call for a free publications and products list.

5256 Legal Center for the Elderly and Disabled

2862 Arden Way
Sacramento, CA 95825   916-488-5298
                         FAX: 916-973-3199
           e-mail: jellison@california.net

Jon Ellison, Executive Director
Shannon Sutherland, Staff Attorney
Carol Pasch, Office Manager

Free civil legal services for low-income people over sixty and permanently disabled persons under sixty, specializing in social security, medical benefits, and housing in North Central California.

5257 Maryland Disabilities Law Office Southern Maryland Branch Office

1400 Mercantile Lane
Suite 242
Largo, MD 20774   301-925-9871
                              800-870-6362
                     FAX: 301-925-8618
                     TDY:301-925-9874

Legal representation for the disabled and non-disabled.

5258 National Center for State Courts

300 Newport Avenue
Williamsburg, VA 23185   804-253-2000
                         FAX: 978-474-8088

Art Williams

Develops a national clearinghouse and resource center for local and state courts to focus on requirements and methods of compliances with ADA.

5259 National Center for Youth Law

114 Sansome Street
Suite 900
San Francisco, CA 94104   415-543-3307
                         FAX: 415-956-9024
                   e-mail: ncyl@lanminds.com

Chris Palamountain, Skadden Fellows
Kristen Weber, Staff Attorney
John O'Toole, Director

Support services to legal services attorneys and child advocates on SSI (Supplemental Security Income) disability benefits for children.

5260 National Right to Work Legal Defense and Education Foundation

8001 Braddock Road
Suite 600
Springfield, VA 22160   703-321-9820
                              800-336-3600
                     FAX: 703-321-9613
                    e-mail: infoAnrtw.org
                              www.nrtw.org

Reed Larson, President
Stefan Gleason, Vice President

Provides free legal aid to employees whose human and civil rights are being violated by compulsory unionism abuses.

5261 REACH/Resource Center on Independent Living

617 7th Avenue
Suite 304
Fort Worth, TX 76104
                         FAX: 817-877-1622
              e-mail: reachdal@fiberramp.net
                   www.fiberramp.net/~reachdal

Charlotte Stewart, Director
Anne Ancy, Case Manager

Information and referral services, peer counseling, independent living skills training, loaner equipment, advocacy assistance, ADA technical assistance and social/recreational activities.

5262 Winifred Law Opportunity Center

106 E 2nd Avenue
Indianola, IA 50125   515-961-5341
                         FAX: 515-961-5002

Diane M. Griffith, M.S., Executive Director

Information Services

5263 AACD Legal Series

American Association for Counseling & Devel.
5999 Stevenson Avenue
Alexandria, VA 22304   703-823-9800
           800-347-6647

Offering three volumes: Preparing for Court Appearances; Documentation in Counseling Records; and The Counselor and The Law.

3 Volumes

5264 ADA Mandate for Social Change

Paul H. Brookes Publishing Company
PO Box 10624
Baltimore, MD 21285
           800-638-3775
         FAX: 410-337-8539
Paul Wehman, author

This timely book moves a large step beyond detailing the legislative requirements of the ADA by focusing on the changes the ADA is generating for persons with disabilities. *$32.00*

320 pages Paperback 1993
ISBN 1-557661-17-0

5265 Americans with Disabilities Act Manual

American Bar Association
1800 M Street NW
Suite 200
Washington, DC 20036   202-331-5556
         FAX: 202-662-1032

An in-depth analysis of the legal and practical implications of the ADA using non-technical language. *$20.00*

5266 Americans with Disabilities Act: Selected Resources for Deaf

Gallaudet University Bookstore
11030 S Langley Avenue
Chicago, IL 60628   202-651-5488
           800-621-2736
         FAX: 202-651-5489

This resource identifies programs and publications specific to the ADA and deafness and also lists ADA materials and programs for people with any disability. *$1.00*

5267 Approaching Equality

TJ Publishers
817 Silver Spring Avenue
Suite 206
Silver Spring, MD 20910   301-585-4440
           800-999-1168
         FAX: 301-585-5930
      e-mail: TJPubinc@aol.com
Frank Bowe, author
Angela K Thames, President
Jerald A Murphy, Vice President

Public education laws guarantee special education for all deaf children, but may find the special education system confusing, or are unsure of their rights under current laws. For anyone with an interest in education, advocacy and the deaf community, this book reviews dramatic developments in education of deaf children, youth and adults since COED's 1988 report, *Toward Equality*. *$12.95*

112 pages
ISBN 0-93266-39-6

5268 Assessment of the Feasibility of Contracting with a Nominee Agency

Rehab/Training Center on Blindness and Low-Vision
PO Box 6189
Mississippi State, MS 39762   601-325-2001
           800-675-7782
         FAX: 662-325-8989
    e-mail: rrtc@ra.msstate.edu
        www.blind.msstate.edu
J.E. Moore, B. Cavenaugh, J.M. Glesen & J.H. Maxon, author
Kelly Schaefer, Publications Manager

Only five State Licensing Agencies currently utilize nominee agreements. This study compared the Pennsylvania program with four states that utilize nominee agencies and four states that do not. Results and recommendations compared state and national data from Federal FY 1991-1993. *$20.00*

152 pages Paperback

5269 Bluebook: Explanation of the Contents of the ADA

Disability Rights Education and Defense Fund
2212 6th Street
Berkeley, CA 94710   510-644-2629
           800-466-4232
         FAX: 510-841-8645

Written in narrative form for both professionals and lay people, DREDF's bluebook offers detailed, thorough analysis of all of the law's provisions, encompassing ADA legislative history, the statute and regulations. Available in alternative formats. *$100.00*

214 pages

5270 Can America Afford to Grow Old?

Brookings Institution
1775 Massachusetts Avenue NW
Washington, DC 20036   202-797-6000

Henry J. Aaron, author
Social security laws and regulations. *$8.95*

144 pages Paperback

5271 Childcare and the ADA

Eastern Washington University
705 W 1st Avenue
Room 223
Spokane, WA 99201   509-623-4246
         FAX: 509-623-4230
    e-mail: susan.vanmeter@mail.ewu.edu

Susan VanMeter, Special Projects Manager

Provides information on how childcare providers must comply with the ADA. Eight videotapes plus an instructional manual with examples of situations and problems. *$85.00*

Set

5272   Complying with the Americans with Disabilities Act

Greenwood Publishing Group
88 Post Road West
 # 5007
Westport, CT   06880   203-226-3571
                                FAX: 203-222-1502
                                www.greenwood.com
Don Fersch, Peter Thomas, author

A guidebook for management and people with disabilities. Hardcover.

280 pages $52.95 - $57.95
ISBN 0-899307-14-0

5273   Convicting the Innocent

Brookline Books
PO Box 1047
Cambridge, MA   02238   617-868-0360
                                800-666-2665
                                FAX: 617-868-1772
                                e-mail: brooklinebks@delphi.com
                                www.brooklinebooks.com

Exposes the dirtiest secret of American Law Enforcement: the process of subjecting innocent citizens- often poor or mentally impaired- to inquisitions to elicit confessions which often result in wrongful convictions. These thoughtful and compassionate essays analyze scandals nationwide, spotlighting the Richard Lapointe case featured on 60 minutes. Contributes include Pulitzer Prize winners William Styron, Arthur Miller, and Richard Ofshe. *$16.95*

220 pages Paperback
ISBN 1-57129 -21-4

5274   Council for Disability Rights

205 West Randolph Street
Suite 1650
Chicago, IL   60606   312-444-9484
                                FAX: 312-444-1977
                                TDY:312-444-1967
                                e-mail: cdrights@interaccess.com
                                www.disabilityrights.org
Jo Holzer, author
Jo Holzer, Executive Director/Editor
Sharon Schaff, Associate Director

Promotes human rights of persons with disabilities and their families. Offers a job preparation and placement service, legal referrals, information services, education advocacy services, disability awareness training, and mediation services. *$15.00*

8 pages Newsletter
ISSN 1083-94 1

5275   Court-Related Needs of the Elderly and Persons with Disabilities

Mental Health Commission
2700 Martin Luther King Avenue SE
Washington, DC   20032   202-373-7595
                                FAX: 202-373-7982

This book features the ground-breaking recommendations from the national Conference on the Court-Related Needs of the Elderly and Persons with Disabilities, funded by the States Justice Institute and co-sponsored by the American Bar Association and National Judicial College. Accompanying the recommendations are detailed commentaries and extensive background research papers organized around issues. *$20.00*

276 pages

5276   Critical Issues in the Lives of People with Severe Disabilities

Paul H. Brookes Publishing Company
PO Box 10624
Baltimore, MD   21285
                                800-638-3775
                                FAX: 410-337-8539
Luanna H. Meyer, author

This comprehensive book explores the values, practices and empirical research that have guided legal and practical decisions concerning the lives of people with severe disabilities in the past. *$90.00*

704 pages Hardcover 1991
ISBN 1-557660-48-4

5277   Dealing with Mental Incapacity

Center for Public Representation
PO Box 260049
Madison, WI   53726   608-251-4008
                                800-369-0388
                                FAX: 606-251-1263
                                e-mail: cpr@lawmail.law.wisc.edu
                                www.law.wisc.edu/pal

This manual contains a comprehensive introduction to the problem of guardianship as well as chapters of financial and health care planning tools, guardianship under Wisconsin law, protective placement and Watts reviews. *$19.95*

5278   Dimensions of State Mental Health Policy

Greenwood Publishing Group
88 Post Road West
 # 5007
Westport, CT   06880   203-226-3571
                                FAX: 203-222-1502
                                www.greenwood.com
Christopher G. Hudson, and Arthur F. Cox, author

Introduces students to the emerging field of state mental health policy. Hardcover.

320 pages $59.95 - $65
ISBN 0-275932-52-4

5279 Directory of Lawyers Practicing Disability Law

ABA Commission on Mental & Physical Disability
Law
740 15th Street NW
9th Floor
Washington, DC   20055   202-662-1581
                                800-285-2221
                        FAX: 202-662-1032

This first-of-its-kind, state-by-state directory lists
practitioners and organizations working in the
disability law field. Compiled from information
collected by the American Bar Association, the
directory contains more than 3,000 listings. The
listings provide lawyers' names, addresses,
phone/fax/TTY numbers, and their specific areas
of disability law practice. A must-have resource
for referrals and networking. Seperate state listings available. 1998, PC 4410085 *$55.00*

5280 Disability Law in the United States

William Hein & Company
1285 Main Street
Buffalo, NY   14209   716-675-3555
                             800-828-7571
                        FAX: 716-883-8100
                   e-mail: mail@wshein.com
                             www.wshein.com

Customer Service Department

Offers thousands of pages of information on the laws
and legislation affecting the disabled in the United
States. Its purpose is to provide a clear and comprehensive mandate to end discrimination against individuals with disabilities and to bring disabled persons
into the economic and social midstream of American
Life. *$650.00*

5,300 pages

5281 Disability Rights Now

Disability Rights Education and Defense Fund
2212 6th Street
Berkeley, CA   94710   510-644-2629
                              800-466-7232
                        FAX: 510-841-8645

Free quarterly publication describing the activities of the Disability Rights Education and Defense
Fund, available in alternative formats.

Quarterly

5282 Disabled People as Second Class Citizens

Springer Publishing Company
536 Broadway
New York, NY   10012   212-431-4370
                        FAX: 212-941-7842
Myron G. Eisenberg, author
Disability and legal practice. *$26.95*

320 pages Hardcover
ISBN 0-82613 -20-0

**5283 Education of the Handicapped: Laws, Legislative
Histories and Administrative Documents**

William Hein & Company
1285 Main Street
Buffalo, NY   14209   800-828-7571
                        FAX: 716-883-8100
                   e-mail: mail@wshein.com
                             www.wshein.com
Bernard D. Reams, Jr., author

Focuses upon elementary and secondary Education
Act of 1965 and its amendment, Education For All
Handicapped Children Act of 1975 and its amendments and acts providing services for the blind, deaf,
mentally retarded, etc. Hardcover. *$2850.00*

55 Volume set
ISBN 0-899411-57-6

5284 Ethical and Legal Issues in School Counseling

American Association for Counseling & Development
5999 Stevenson Avenue
Alexandria, VA   22304   703-823-9800
                                800-347-6647

This comprehensive text is filled with answers to
many of the most controversial and challenging
questions faced by the professional every day. This
text helps avoid ethical violations and provides
thorough information on: confidentiality, privacy,
privileged communication, access to school records, using group techniques ethically, computerized record keeping and reporting unethical
practices. *$24.95*

341 pages
ISBN 1-55620 -55-2

**5285 Evaluation of the Association for Children with
Learning Disabilities**

National Center for State Courts
300 Newport Avenue
Williamsburg, VA   23185   804-253-2000

Final report on children with learning disabilities
training institute. *$6.96*

116 pages Manuscript

**5286 Families Forward: Health Care Resource Guide
for Children with Special Care Needs**

Center for Public Representation
PO Box 260049
Madison, WI   53726   608-251-4008
                             800-369-0388
                        FAX: 606-251-1263
              e-mail: cpr@lawmail.law.wisc.edu
                   www.law.wisc.edu/pal/famfrwd.htm
*Attorneys Benjamin Griffiths & Robert A. Peterson,
author*

Extensive resource material: health insurance,
HMOs, dealing with medical debt, services to keep
your child at home and more. *$10.00*

ISBN 0-932622-54-2

5287 Federal Laws of the Mentally Handicapped: Laws, Legislative Histories and Admin. Documents

William Hein & Company
1285 Main Street
Buffalo, NY 14209

800-828-7571
FAX: 716-883-8100
e-mail: mail@wshein.com
www.wshein.com

Bernard D. Reams, Jr., author

Chronological compilation of all relevant federal laws dealing with the mentally handicapped along with supporting documentation necessary to create a complete legislative history. *$2200.00*

42 Volume/Set
ISBN 0-899411-06-1

5288 Formed Families: Adoption on Children with Handicaps

Haworth Press
10 Alice Street
Binghamton, NY 13904

604-722-5857
800-429-6784
FAX: 607-722-6362
e-mail: getinfo@haworthpressinc.com
www.haworthpressinc.com

Laraine Masters Glidden, PhD, author
Jackie Blakeslee, Advertising

Provides broad coverage of the issues relating to the adoption of children with handicaps. Concerned professionals can find here all the answers about clinical programs, legal issues, estimates of frequency, and important factors related to positive and negative outcomes of these adoptions. *$54.95*

242 pages Hardcover 1990
ISBN 0-866569-14-6

5289 Free Appropriate Public Education

Love Publishing Company
9101 East Kenyon Avenue
Denver, CO 80222

303-221-7333
FAX: 303-221-7444
e-mail: lovepublishing@compuserve.com

H. Rutherford Turnbull III, author

Information on significant legislation regarding the handicapped. Laws are discussed with attention to their impact on the child, the parents, the public schools and higher education. *$44.95*

ISBN 0-89108 -11-5

5290 Health Care Quality Improvement Act of 1986

William Hein & Company
1285 Main Street
Buffalo, NY 14209

716-882-2600
800-828-7571
FAX: 716-883-8100
e-mail: mail@wshein.com
www.wshein.com

Bernard D Reams Jr, author

In order to encourage more stringent peer review by doctors and hospitals, and to protect reporting physicians and institutions from retaliatory lawsuits, Congress enacted The Health Care Quality Improvement Act. The Act was also intended to address the increasing incidence of medical malpractice and to prevent the ease with which incompetent practitioners moved from state to state. Hardcover. *$75.00*

730 pages
ISBN 0-899416-93-4

5291 Helping You to Understand SSDI and SSI

Accent Books & Products
PO Box 700
Bloomington, IL 61702

309-378-2961
800-787-8444
FAX: 309-378-4420
e-mail: acmtlvng@aol.com

Daniel Scarbourgh, author
Raymond C. Cheever, Publisher
Betty Garee, Editor

These articles have been so popular with ACCENT readers, we have put them all in one handy guide. This guide gives you valuable tips on getting the benefits to which you are entitled. *$3.25*

12 pages Paperback
ISBN 0-91570 -40-0

5292 Housing and Transportation of the Handicapped

William Hein & Company
1285 Main Street
Buffalo, NY 14209

716-882-2600
800-828-7571
FAX: 716-883-8100
e-mail: mail@wshein.com
www.wshein.com

Bernard D. Reams, Jr., author

National laws, recognizing the problems encountered by the handicapped in the areas of Housing and Transportation and providing assistance in an effort to surmount those problems. Hardcover or microfilm. *$1850.00*

250 documents
ISBN 0-899412-47-5

5293 How Libraries Must Comply with the Americans with Disabilities Act

ORYX Press
4041 N Central Avenue
Phoenix, AZ 85012

602-279-7999
800-279-ORYX
FAX: 800-279-4663
e-mail: info@oryxpress.com

Magon Kinzle, Directory, Editorial Systems

Designed for all in America's library system who need a clear and concise explanation of how the ADA affects them. *$29.95*

192 pages
ISBN 0-89774 -60-7

5294 Human Resource Management and the Americans with Disabilities Act

Greenwood Publishing Group
88 Post Road West
5007
Westport, CT   06880   203-226-3571
                              FAX: 203-222-1502
                              www.greenwood.com

John G. Veres, III, Editor
Ronald R. Sims, Editor .

Concrete advice for human resource professionals on how to cope with the vague, often obscure provisions of the Americans with Disabilities Act.

232 pages $59.95 - $62.95
ISBN 0-899308-57-0

5295 International Handbook on Mental Health Policy

Greenwood Publishing Group
88 Post Road West
5007
Westport, CT   06880   203-226-3571
                              FAX: 203-222-1502
                              www.greenwood.com

Donna R. Kemp, author

The first major reference book for academics and practitioners that provides a systematic survey and analysis of mental health policies in twenty representative countries.

512 pages $110 - $125
ISBN 0-313275-67-X

5296 Knowing Your Rights

AARP Fulfillment
601 E Street NW
Washington, DC 20049   202-434-2277
                              800-424-3410
                              FAX: 202-434-3443
                              e-mail: member@aarp.org
                              www.aarp.org

Describes how changes in Medicare's reimbursement policies are designed to reduce health care costs and suggests steps that Medicare beneficiaries, their families and friends can take to assure that they continue to receive quality care under the Prospective Payment System.

19 pages

5297 Law Center Newsletter

Public Interest Law Center of Philadelphia
125 S 9th Street
Philadelphia, PA   19107   215-922-6854

Information on mental health, foster care and public education. Provides all updates concerning the law in these areas.

5298 Legal Center

455 Sherman Street
Suite 130
Denver, CO   80203   303-722-0300
                              800-288-1376
                              FAX: 303-722-0720
                              e-mail: tlcmail@thelegalcenter.org
                              www.thelegalcenter.org

Mary Anne Harvey, Executive Director

The Legal center uses the legal system to protect & promote the rights of people with disabilities and older people in Colorado through direct legal representation, advocacy, education and legislative analysis. We are also the State Ombudsman for nursing homes and personal care boarding homes. Call for a free publications and products list.

5299 Legal Rights of Persons with Disabilities: An Analysis of Federal Law

LRP Publications
747 Dresher Road
PO Box 980
Horsham, PA   19044   215-784-0941
                              800-341-7874
                              FAX: 215-784-9639
                              e-mail: custserve@lrp.com
                              www.lrp.com

Bonnie P. Tucker And Bruce A. Goldstein, author
Gary Bagin, Director of Communications

A comprehensive analysis of the rights accorded individuals with disabilities under federal law covering such issues as: Definitions of individuals with disabilities, reasonable accomidations, architectural barriers, access to transportation and communication services, education, and newborns. *$185.00*

1536 pages
ISBN 0-934753-46-6

5300 Legislative Network for Nurses

Business Publishers
8737 Colesville Road
Suite 1100
Silver Spring, MD   20910
                              800-274-6737
                              FAX: 301-587-4530
                              e-mail: bpinews@bpinews.com
                              www.bpinews.com

Leonard A. Eiserer, Publisher
Sarah Spencer, Editor

Provides up-to-date information on the nursing shortage, nurse training programs, AIDS and Hepatitis B, unionization, registered care technologies, compensation, child care, home health care staffing and much more. *$286.00*

8 pages Newsl./BiMonth

5301 Madness in the Streets

Free Press
135 S Mount Zion Road
Lebanon, IN   46052
                              800-323-7445
                              FAX: 800-882-8583

Rael Jean Isaac, author

How psychiatry and the law abandoned the mentally ill. *$24.95*

436 pages
ISBN 0-02915 -80-8

5302 Making News: How to Get News Coverage of Disability Rights Issues

Advocado Press
PO Box 145
Louisville, KY 40201   502-894-9492
                          FAX: 502-899-9562
            e-mail: office@advocadopress.org
                www.advocadopress.org

Mary Johnson, Editor

This book gives examples and tips on how to fight back and get on the front pages, lead the newscasts and influence public debate. *$10.95*

    165 pages
    ISBN 0-96270 -43-4

5303 Medicare and Medicaid Patient and Program Protection Act of 1987

William Hein & Company
1285 Main Street
Buffalo, NY 14209   716-882-2600
                          800-828-7571
                 FAX: 716-883-8100
               e-mail: mail@wshein.com
                    www.wshein.com

Bernard D Reams Jr, author

This act enables the Department of Health and Human Services to protect Medicare and Medicaid patients and federal health care programs from censured practitioners. Hardcover. *$185.00*

    3 Volumes
    ISBN 0-899416-95-0

5304 Mental Disabilities and the Americans with Disabilities Act

Greenwood Publishing Group
88 Post Road West
5007
Westport, CT 06880   203-226-3571
                 FAX: 203-222-1502
                 www.greenwood.com

John F. Fielder, author

A clear, practical compliance guide, written by a psychologist, to help organizations conform to provisions on mental disabilities in the Americans with Disabilities Act. Hardcover.

    216 pages $45 - $49.95 1997
    ISBN 0-899308-26-0

5305 Mental Disabilities and the Americans with Disabilities Act

ABA Commission on Mental & Physical Disability Law
740 15th Street NW
9th Floor
Washington, DC 20055   202-662-1581
                          800-285-2221
                 FAX: 202-662-1032

Written for lawyers, advocates, teachers, consumers, employers, and employees, this ADA handbook examins the ADA from the legal and non-legal practitioner's point of view. In six parts, the handbook covers ADA Titles I, II, and III and provides new and updated case law summaries of ADA court decisions affecting individuals with mental disabilities- including mental illness, developmental disabilities, learning disabilities, substance abuse, and organic brain injuries; practical handbook. *$40.00*

5306 Mental Disability Law: A Primer

ABA Commission on Mental & Physical Disability Law
740 15th Street NW
9th Floor
Washington, DC 20055   202-662-1581
                          800-285-2221
                 FAX: 202-662-1032

The Primer is a valuable handbook for attorneys new to mental disability law practive, specialists in the field, other mental disability terms and definitions and offers tips for effective representation of clients; focuses on major commmunity issues as they relate to the ADA, including employment, housing, education, insurance, social security, and Medicaid; and explains such issues as institutional rights, deinstitutionalization, liability concerns, insanity defense, and confidentiality. *$15.00*

5307 Mental Health Law News

Interwood Publications
3 Interwood Place
20241
Cincinnati, OH 45220   513-221-375

Frank Bardack, Marketing Director/Editor

Mental health case law summaries — malpractice, patient rights, discrimination, alcoholism, guardianship, negligence, professional liability, commitment, drug dependency and conservatorship. *$99.00*

    6 pages Monthly Nwslttr
    ISSN 0889-01 0

5308 Mental Health Law Reporter

Business Publishers
8737 Colesville Road
Suite 1100
Silver Spring, MD 20910 301-587-6300
                          800-274-6737
                 FAX: 301-589-8493
            e-mail: custserv@bpinews.com
                    www.bpinews.com

Leonard A. Eiserer, Publisher
Bonnie Becker, Editor

Brings you the most timely, focused and thorough information on the legal issues that concern mental health practitioners in mental health litigation. Topics include: malpractice litigation, patient-therapist confidentiality, sexual victimization of patients, the insanity defense, social security administrative case law and much more. *$286.00*

8 pages Monthly

5309 Mental and Physical Disability Law Reporter

American Bar Association
1800 M Street NW
Suite 200
Washington, DC 20036   202-331-5556
                    FAX: 202-662-1032
www.abanet.org/disability/reporter/home.html

John W. Parry, Editor

Covers case law, legislative and regulatory developments that affect persons with mental or physical disabilities. *$194.00*

BiMonthly

5310 Mentally Disabled and the Law, 3rd Edition

William Hein & Company
1285 Main Street
Buffalo, NY 14209   716-882-2600
                    800-828-7571
              FAX: 716-883-8100
          e-mail: mail@wshein.com
                    www.wshein.com

Offers information on treatment rights, the provider-patient relationship, and the rights of the mentally disabled persons in the community. *$85.00*

867 pages
ISBN 0-910059-05-5

5311 NAD Broadcaster

National Association of the Deaf
814 Thayer Avenue
Silver Spring, MD 20910   301-587-1788
                    FAX: 301-587-1791
                    TDY:301-587-1789
          e-mail: nadinfo@nad.org
                    www.nad.org

Dawn Bradley, Editor

National newspaper published 11 times a year by the nation's largest organization safeguarding the accessibility and civil rights of 28 million deaf and hard of hearing Americans in education, employment, health care, and telecommunications. Membership: individual $30 per year. *$7.00*

5312 National Focus

PO Box 37485
Phoenix, AZ 85069   602-943-6044
                    FAX: 602-866-9206

Offers information on disabilities issues and legal information for the disabled.

5313 No Longer Disabled: The Federal Courts

Greenwood Publishing Group
88 Post Road West
5007
Westport, CT 06880   203-226-3571
                    FAX: 203-222-1502
                    www.greenwood.com

Susan Gluck Mezey, author

This book is a case study of judicial policy making. It focuses on the role of adjudication in the making and refining of federal policy.

208 pages $45 - $55
ISBN 0-313254-24-9

5314 Opening the Courthouse Door: An ADA Access Guide for State Courts

American Bar Association
1800 M Street NW
Suite 200
Washington, DC 20036   202-331-5556
                    FAX: 202-662-1032

Practical, step-by-step guide explains how to comply with the public access provisions of the ADA in the courthouse. The centerpiece of the guide is a series of action steps. *$12.00*

5315 Operation Help: A Mental Health Advocate's Guide to Medicaid

National Council of Community Mental Health
12300 Twinbrook Parkway
Suite 230
Rockville, MD 20852   301-670-6331
                    FAX: 301-881-7159
                    www.nccbh.org

This book explains the Medicaid entitlement program in easy-to-read language and focuses on the needs of your clients. *$17.00*

5316 PAL News

Parent Professional Advocacy League
95 Berkeley Street
Suite 104
Boston, MA 02116   617-482-2915
                    800-331-0688

Offers information on medical and technological updates in the area of research on birth defects, support groups and family resources for persons with disabled children.

Quarterly

5317 Power of Attorney for Health Care

Center for Public Representation
PO Box 260049
Madison, WI 53726   608-251-4008
                    800-369-0388
                    FAX: 606-251-1263

Helen Marks Dicks, author

Discusses Wisconsin law regarding medical decisions, the Cruzan case and ethical considerations in addition to legal implications and advantages of this document. Book tells how to create a personalized Power Of Attorney document, including language for the Special Provisions portion. *$49.95*

132 pages
ISBN 0-93262 -38-0

5318   Tax Options and Strategies for People with Disabilities

Demos Medical Publishing
386 Park Avenue South
Suite 201
New York, NY   10016   212-683-0072
                                    800-532-8663
                                    FAX: 212-683-0118
                                    e-mail: info@demospub.com
                                    www.demosmedpub.com
Steven B. Mendelsohn, J.D, author
Dr. Diana M Schneider, Ph.D., President

A guide for financial and tax planning for disabled people and their families. *$29.95*

288 pages Paperback
ISBN 0-93995 -85-X

5319   Toward Independence

National Council on Disability
1331 F Street NW
Suite 1050
Washington, DC   20004   202-546-8000
                                    FAX: 202-272-2022
                                    TDY:202-272-2074

A 1986 report to the U.S. Congress on the federal laws and programs serving people with disabilities, and recommendations for legislation.

5320   US Department of Health and Human Services Office for Civil Rights

200 Independence Avenue SW
Room 509F HHH Building
Washington, DC   20201
                                    800-368-1019
                                    FAX: 202-619-3818

Enforces the Rehabilitation Act of 1973, which prohibits discrimination against handicapped persons by recipients of federal funding.

5321   US Department of Labor

200 Constitution Avenue NW
Washington, DC   20210   202-693-5000
                                    FAX: 202-219-7312

Offers publications to assist employers in determining and achieving workplace accessibility.

5322   US Department of Labor Office of Federal Contract Compliance Programs

Regional Office
230 S Dearborn Street
Room 570
Chicago, IL   60604   312-353-8260

Investigates complaints brought under section 504 of the Rehabilitation Act of 1973 against federal contractors.

5323   Washington Watch

United Cerebral Palsy Associations
1660 L Street NW
Suite 700
Washington, DC   20036   202-269-1500
                                    800-USE-5UCP
                                    FAX: 202-776-0414
                                    TDY:202-973-7197

Susanna L. Gorton, Editor

Dependable, timely information on national legislative and regulatory issues affecting people with disabilities and their families. *$25.00*

4 pages BiWeekly

5324   William S. Hein & Company

1285 Main Street
Buffalo, NY   14209   716-675-3555
                                    800-828-7571
                                    FAX: 716-883-8100
                                    e-mail: mail@wshein.com
                                    www.wshein.com

Offers a catalog of periodicals, publications and reprints, microforms and government publications on medical, handicapped and health law.

5325   Word from Washington

United Cerebral Palsy Associations
1660 L Street NW
Suite 700
Washington, DC   20036   202-269-1500
                                    800-USA-5UCP
                                    FAX: 202-526-0519
                                    TDY:202-973-7197

Akua Kouyate

Provides information on national legislation and regulatory affairs, updates on disability and social service fields. *$25.00*

24-36 pages Quarterly

Alabama

5326 Alabama Institute for Deaf and Blind Library and Resource Center

705 S Street
PO Box 698
Talladega, AL   35160   256-761-3337
                          FAX: 256-761-3561
                e-mail: tlacy@aidb.state.al.us

Teresa Lacy, Librarian

Book collection includes discs, cassettes, braille and large print. Also closed-circuit T.V. and magnifiers.

5327 Alabama Radio Reading Service Network (ARR

650 11th Street S
Birmingham, AL   35233   205-934-6576
                          800-444-9246
                     FAX: 205-934-5075
                e-mail: philip@wbhm.org
                          www.wbhm.org

Philip Habesh, Director

Services and readings are broadcast over a subcarrier service of public radio WBHM. This is a statewide station devoted to Alabama's blind and handicapped community.

5328 Alabama Regional Library for the Blind and Physically Handicapped

Alabama Public Library Service
6030 Monticello Drive
Montgomery, AL   36130   334-213-3906
                          800-392-5671
                     FAX: 334-213-3993
                e-mail: fzaleski@apls.state.al.us
                          www.apls.state.al.us

Fara Zaleski, Regional Librarian

Recreational reading in special format for persons unable to use standard print. Reference materials offered include materials on blindness and other handicaps, films, local subjects and authors.

5329 Houston-Love Memorial Library

212 W Burdeshaw Street
PO Box 1369
Dothan, AL   36302   334-793-9767
                     FAX: 334-793-6645

Myrtis Merrow, Librarian

Offers magnifiers, summer reading programs and more for the blind and physically handicapped. Scanner, software, jaws for Windows.

5330 Huntsville Subregional Library for the Blind & Physically Handicapped

PO Box 443
915 Monroe Street
Huntsville, AL   35804   256-532-5980
                     FAX: 256-532-5994
                e-mail: bphdept@hpl.lib.al.us
                          www.hpl.lib.al.us/main.html

Joyce Smith, Librarian

Talking books for people who are blind or disabled offering reference materials on the blind and other disabilities, large-print photocopier, thermaform duplicator and more.

5331 Library for the Blind & Handicapped Public Library - Anniston/Calhoun Counties

PO Box 308
Anniston, AL   36202   256-237-8503
                     FAX: 256-238-0474
                e-mail: library@quicklink.net

Deenie Culver, Librarian

Reference materials on blindness, cassettes, large print books and discs.

5332 Multipurpose Arthritis & Musculoskeletal Diseases Center - UAB

Tinsley Harrison Tower
Birmingham, AL   35294   205-934-5306
                     FAX: 205-934-1564

Dr. Robert Kimberly, M.D., Director

Arthritis and related rheumatic disorders are studied.

5333 Research for Rett Foundation

PO Box 50347
Mobile, AL   36605   334-479-8293
                          800-422-7388
                     FAX: 334-479-8293

Patty Cofer, President
Anna Luce, Executive Director

National not-for-profit voluntary organization dedicated to raising funds for critical ongoing medical research into Rett Syndrome, hosting medical research symposia, and funding grant applications. Committed to expanding public awareness of and encouraging Rett Syndrome research within the National Institute of Child Health and Human Development. Provides a variety of educational mateials including brochures and fact sheets.

5334 Technology Assistance for Special Consumers

PO Box 443
Huntsville, AL   35804   205-532-5950
                     FAX: 256-532-5994
                     TDY:205-532-5996
                e-mail: tasc@traveller.com
                          tasc.ataccess.org

Pam Harnden, Contact

Offers reference materials on the blind and other disabilities, large-print photocopier, thermaform duplicator and more. Provides the Library of Congress talking book services for persons with disabilities. Braille transcribing of short materials (not books).

5335 Tuscaloosa Public Library

1801 Jack Warner Parkway
Tuscaloosa, AL   35401   205-345-5820
                     FAX: 205-752-8300
                          www.tuscaloosa-library.org

Barbara Jordan, Librarian

Reference materials on blindness and other handicaps, films, story hour, home visits and more.

**5336 Tuscaloosa Subregional Library for the Blind &
Physically Handicapped**

1801 River Road
Tuscaloosa, AL   35401   205-345-5820
                                      FAX: 205-752-8300

Barbara Jordan, Librarian

Provide talking books to patrons who are unable to
use standard print because of a visual or physical
limitation. Deliver playback equipment to qualified
patrons. Provides reference and referral service to
this special population also.

Alaska

5337 Alaska State Library Talking Book Center

344 W 3rd Avenue
Suite 125
Anchorage, AK   99501   907-269-6575
                                      FAX: 907-269-6580
                   e-mail: patmemuskox.alaska-edu
                   www.eed.state.ak.us/lam/library.html

Patricia Meek

Offers reference materials on blindness and other
handicaps, native language materials, local subjects
and authors.

5338 Alaska State Library, Talking Book Center

344 W 3rd Avenue
Suite 125
Anchorage, AK   99501   907-269-6575
                                          800-776-6566
                                      FAX: 907-269-6580
                   e-mail: pat_meek@eed.state.ak.us
                          www.library.state.ak.us

Pat Meek, Librarian

Discs, cassettes, large print books and braille are
offered.

5339 Alaska State Library/Talking Book Center

344 W 3rd Avenue
Suite 125
Anchorage, AK   99501   907-269-5528
                                      FAX: 907-272-8484

Mary Jennings, Librarian
Patricia Meek, Library Assistant

Discs, cassettes, large print books and braille are
offered.

Arizona

5340 Arizona Braille and Talking Book Library

1030 N 32nd Street
Phoenix, AZ   85008   602-255-5578
                                      FAX: 602-255-4312
                             e-mail: btbl@lib.az.us
                                www.lib.az.us/braille

Linda Montgomery, Director

Closed-circuit T.V., summer reading programs, volunteer-produced cassette books, braille writer, films,
large-print photocopier and more.

5341 Arizona State Braille and Talking Book Library

1030 N 32nd Street
Phoenix, AZ   85008   602-255-5578
                                      FAX: 602-255-4312
                       e-mail: btbl@dlapr.lib.az.us

Linda Montgomery, Librarian

Closed-circuit T.V., summer reading programs, volunteer-produced cassette books, braille writer, films,
large-print photocopier and more.

5342 Books for the Blind of Arizona

6120 E 5th Street
Unit A107
Tucson, AZ   85711

Betty Evans, Chairperson

Offers large print photocopier, textbooks, recreational, career, vocational, braille books, talking
books, cassettes, large print books and more for the
visually impaired K-12, college students and adults.

5343 Center for Neurodevelopmental Studies

8434 N 39th Avenue
Phoenix, AZ   85051   602-934-7166

Lorna Jean King, Director, Emeritus

Effective treatment methods for autism and developmental disabilities are subjects researched and studied at the Center.

5344 Flagstaff City-Coconino County Public Library

300 W Aspen Avenue
Flagstaff, AZ   86001   520-779-7670
                                      FAX: 520-774-9573
                      e-mail: colguin@ci.flagstaff.az.us

Christina Olgwin, Librarian

Reference materials on blindness and other handicaps, braille writer, magnifiers and large-print photocopier. Large-type books, closed captioned videos,
adapters and a sub-lending agency for talking books.

5345 Fountain Hills Lioness Braille Service

PO Box 18332
Fountain Hills, AZ   85268   602-837-1555

Jean Hauck, Chairperson

Braille and large print books on the subjects of recreation, career and vocations, religion, novels and
cookbooks for the visually impaired.

5346 Harrington Arthritis Research Center

1800 E Van Buren Street
Phoenix, AZ   85006   602-254-0377
                                      FAX: 602-253-4817
                             e-mail: info@harcaz.org
                                        www.harcaz.org

John Theobald, President/ CEO

Research into the various areas of arthritis, including assistive devices, joint repair and replacement, medical treatment and early detection and prevention.

5347 Prescott Public Library/Talking Book Center

215 East Goodwin Street
Prescott, AZ 86303   520-445-8110
     FAX: 520-445-1851
     www.prescottlib.lib.az.us

Katherine Kujawa, Adult Services Librarian

Assistive listening devices; large print, braille, and audio books; magnifiers; text to voice scanner; talking book machine exchange; toy library for children with special needs; special needs product catalogs; braille writers; home book delivery; reference collection on disabilities; TTY machine exchange; descriptive videos; 43 point PC monitor.

5348 Prescott Talking Book Library

215 East Goodwin Street
Prescott, AZ 86301   520-445-8110
     FAX: 520-771-5829
     www.prescottlib.lib.az.us

John Burton, Director

Home visits, book discussion groups, magnifiers, braille writers and reference materials on blindness and other handicaps.

5349 Special Needs Center/Phoenix Public Library

12 E McDowell Road
Phoenix, AZ 85004   602-495-7665

Mary Roatch, Supervisor

Offers talking books and records, braille books and magazines, large print books, video print enlarger, video magnifier and VersaBraille software with synthetic speech for the blind, visually handicapped, physically/mentally handicapped and speech and hearing impaired children and adults.

5350 WAHEC Medical Library Consortium

Bullhead Community Hospital
2735 Silver Creek Road
Bullhead City, AZ 86442   520-763-1505
     FAX: 520-704-6759

Kathleen Stanley, Medical Library Co.
Medical library management.

Arkansas

5351 Arkansas Regional Library for the Blind and Physically Handicapped

One Capitol Mall
Little Rock, AR 72201   501-682-1155
     FAX: 501-682-1529
     TDY:501-682-1002
     e-mail: jhall@asl.lib.ar.us

John D. Hall, Director

Public library books in recorded or braille format. Popular fiction and nonfiction books for all ages, books and players are on free loan, sent to patrons by mail and may be returned postage free. Anyone who cannot see well enough to read regular print with glasses on or who has a disability that makes it difficult to hold a book or turn the pages is eligible.

5352 Educational Services for the Visually Impaired

PO Box 668
Little Rock, AR 72203   501-663-4540

David Beavers, Director

Offers textbooks, braille books and more to the visually impaired grades K-12 in the Arizona area.

5353 Library for the Blind and Physically Handicapped SW Region of Arkansas

220 East Main Street
PO Box 668
Magnolia, AR 71753   870-234-0399
     866-234-8273
     FAX: 870-234-5077
     e-mail: lbph@hotmail.com

Susan Walker, Supervisor

A free library service that serves adults and children who meet the eligiblity requirements, offers free loan of cassette machine and recorded books, which meet the reading preferences of a highly diverse clientele.

5354 Northwest Ozarks Regional Library for the Blind and Handicapped

217 E Dickson S
Fayetteville, AR 72701   501-442-6243
     FAX: 501-442-6254
     www.vark.edu

Rachel Anne Ames, Librarian

Offers a summer reading program, closed-circuit TV, magnifiers, braille writers and large print books.

California

5355 Association of Visual Science Librarians

Berkeley, CA 94720   415-642-1020

Bette Anton, President

Promotes information services in ophthalmology and optometry. Conducts institutes, workshops, and training courses for professional personnel and provides legislative consultation.

5356 Autism Research Institute

4182 Adams Avenue
San Diego, CA 92116   619-281-7165
     FAX: 619-563-6840
     e-mail: autismresearchinstitute.com
     www.autismresearchinstitute.com

B. Rimland, PhD, Director

Conducts research on the causes, diagnosis, and treatment of autism and publishes a quarterly newsletter that reviews worldwide research. Literature on causes and treatment available. Refers patients and families to health care professionals and clinics. Request publication list and sample newsletter, Autism Research Review.

5357 Books Aloud

PO Box 5731
San Jose, CA   95150   408-277-4839
                               FAX: 408-277-4818
                       e-mail: booksaloud@juno.com
                               www.booksaloud.org

David Rich, Director

Loands books on tape at no fees to visually, physically, and learning impaired people of all ages. Over 4,500 titles available.

5358 Braille Institute Desert Center

70-251 Ramon Road
Rancho Mirage, CA   92270   760-321-2555

Dedicated to providing blind and visually impaired men, women and children with the training, programs and services they need to enjoy productive lives. Services offered include child development, youth programs, library services and adult education.

5359 Braille Institute Library

741 N Vermont Avenue
Los Angeles, CA   90029   323-663-1111
                                800-808-2555
                        FAX: 323-663-0867
                        e-mail: dls@brailib.org

Dr. Henry C. Chang, Librarian

Cassettes, braille, reference materials on blindness and other disabilities. Reading lab area with closed-circuit TV, Kurzweil Personal Reader (scanner), and typewriters. Field visits and interlibrary loans of books on cassettes, braille or other medium.

5360 Braille Institute Orange County Center

527 N Dale Avenue
Anaheim, CA   92801   714-821-5000

Offers services, publications, information and programs to blind and visually impaired persons.

5361 Braille Institute Santa Barbara Center

2031 De La Vina Street
Santa Barbara, CA   93105   805-682-6222

Offers programs, services and information for persons with visual impairments.

5362 Braille Institute Sight Center

741 N Vermont Avenue
Los Angeles, CA   90029   213-663-1111

                        e-mail: bils@brailib.org

Dr. Henry Chang, Librarian

Offers help, programs, services and information to the blind and visually impaired children and adults.

5363 Braille Institute Youth Center

3450 Cahuenga Boulevard West
Los Angeles, CA   90068   213-851-5695

Offers various youth programs and services for the blind and visually impaired youngster.

5364 Broadcast Services for the Blind

1155 Mission Street
San Francisco, CA   94103   415-431-1481

Randy Scott, Director

Offers radio broadcasting, braille books, cassettes, records, and more for the visually handicapped in the nine San Francisco Bay Area major cities.

5365 California State Library Braille and Talking Book Library

900 North Street
Sacramento, CA   95814   916-654-0640
                                800-952-5666
                        FAX: 916-654-1119
                        e-mail: btbl@library.ca.gov
                www.library.ca.gov/html/pubser05.html

Donine Hedrick, Program Manager

Regional library for braille, talking books and cassettes for the visually impaired.

5366 Clearinghouse for Specialized Media and Technology

California Department of Education
PO Box 944272
Sacramento, CA   94244   916-445-5103
                        FAX: 916-323-9732

Assists schools and students in the identification and acquisition of textbooks, reference books and study materials in aural media, braille, large print and electronic media access technology.

5367 Foundation for Glaucoma Research

490 Post Street
Suite 830
San Francisco, CA   94102   415-986-3162

Robert N. Shaffer, MD, Chairman

Clinical and laboratory studies of glaucoma.

5368 Fresno County Free Library Talking Book Library for the Blind

770 N San Pablo Avenue
Fresno, CA   93728   559-486-1770
                               800-742-1101
                        FAX: 559-488-1971
                        e-mail: weisenbecsjvls.lib.ca.us

Wendy Eisenberg, Librarian

Loans recorded books and magazines to residents of Fresno, Kings, Madera and Tulare counties

5369 Fresno County Free Library Blind and Handicapped Services

770 N San Pablo Avenue
Fresno, CA 93728   209-488-3217

Ms. Deborah Janzen, Librarian

Magnifiers, home visits, volunteer-produced cassette books, discs and cassettes.

5370 Fresno County Public Library Talking Book Library for the Blind

770 N San Pablo Avenue
Fresno, CA 93728   559-488-3217
                                    FAX: 559-488-1971
                    e-mail: djanzen@sjvls.lib.ca.us

5371 Herrick Health Sciences Library

Alta Bates Medical Center
2001 Dwight Way
Berkeley, CA 94704   510-848-9023
                                    FAX: 510-204-3521

Laurie Bagley, Librarian

Information on rehabilitation, psychiatry and psycho-analysis.

5372 Kuzell Institute for Arthritis and Infectious Diseases

Medical Research Institute of San Francisco
2200 Webster Street
R305
San Francisco, CA 94115   415-561-1734
                                    FAX: 415-441-8548

Lowell S. Young, Director

One of seven units comprising the Medical Research Institute of San Francisco that offers basic and applied research in arthritis and related diseases.

5373 Multipurpose Arthritis and Musculoskeletal Diseases Center

University of California, San Diego
9500 Gilman Drive
La Jolla, CA 92093   619-552-7439
                                    FAX: 619-534-5475

Dr. Dennis Carson, Co-Director

Causes and treatment of arthritis.

5374 New Beginnings - The Blind Children's Center

4120 Marathon Street
Los Angeles, CA 90029   323-664-2153
                                    800-222-3566
                                    FAX: 323-665-3228
                                    blindchildrenscenter.org

The purpose of the Center is to turn initial fears into hope. Helps children and their families become independent by creating a climate of safety and trust. Children learn to develop self confidence and to master a wide range of skills. Services include an infant stimulation program, educational preschool, interdisciplinary assessment services, family services, correspondence program, toll free national hotline and a publication and research service.

5375 Research & Training Center on Mental Health for Hard of Hearing Persons

California School of Professional Psychology
6215 Ferris Square
Suite 140
San Diego, CA 92121   619-282-4443
                                    800-HEA-R619
                                    FAX: 800-642-0266

Raymond J. Trybus, Ph.D., Director
Thomas J. Goulder, Ph.D., Associate Director

Funded by the National Institute on Disability and Rehabilitation Research, this training center aims to address issues of psychological relevance to persons who are hard of hearing or late deafened (as distinct from prelingually, culturally deaf persons). Also serves as information clearinghouse on this topic.

5376 Rosalind Russell Medical Research Center for Arthritis

350 Parnassus Avenue
Room 600
San Francisco, CA 94143   415-476-1141
                                    FAX: 415-476-3526
                                    www.ucsf.edu

Ephraim P. Engelman, MD, Director

Arthritis research and its probable causes.

5377 San Francisco Public Library for the Blind and Print Handicapped

100 Larkin Street
San Francisco, CA 94102   415-557-4293

                    e-mail: lbphmgr@sfpl.lib.ca.us

Martin Maqid, Librarian

Foreign-language books on cassette, children's books on cassettes and more.

5378 San Jose State University Library

One Washington Square
San Jose, CA 95192   408-924-2805
                                    FAX: 408-924-2701
                    e-mail: sliu@email.sisu.edu

Susana Liu, Reference Librarian

Information on physical disabilities, accessibility and learning disabilities.

5379 World Research Foundation

41 Bell Rock Plaza
Sedona, AZ 86351   520-284-3530

                                    e-mail: info@wrf.org
                                    www.wrf.org

Large research library of alternative medicine; offers a computer search and printout of specific health issues for a nominal fee.

Colorado

5380 AMC Cancer Research Center

1600 Pierce Street
Denver, CO   80214   303-233-7419
                              800-525-3777
                         FAX: 970-223-9562

Provides trained counselors who provide understanding and support for cancer patients; information and referral services; and screening
programs.

5381 Boulder Public Library

PO Box H
Boulder, CO   80306   303-441-3120

www.boulder.lib.co.us

Priscilla Simmons, Director

Offers braille books, cassettes, talking books, large
print photocopier, large print books and more for the
visually impaired.

**5382 Colorado Library for the Blind and Physically
Handicapped**

Colorado Centennial Building
1313 Sherman Street
Denver, CO   80203   303-863-5000
                             800-332-5852

Barbara Goral, Librarian

Offers reference materials on blindness and other
handicaps, children's print/braille books, discs, cassettes, large print books, radio reading services, home
visits and volunteer-produced cassette books and
magazines.

5383 Colorado Talking Book Library

180 Sheridan Boulevard
Denver, CO   80226   303-727-9277
                             800-685-2136
                        FAX: 303-727-9281
        e-mail: ctbl.info@cde.state.co.us
              www.cde.state.co.us/ctbl

Barbara Goral, Supervisor

Offers books on cassette, large print and a braille
readers service from Utah.

**5384 Colorodo Regional Library Colorado Talking
Book Library**

180 Sheridan Boulevard
Denver, CO   80226   303-727-9277
                        FAX: 303-727-9281
                 e-mail: ctbl@csn.net
                 www.cde.state.co.us

Barbara Goral

5385 National Jewish Medical & Research Center

1400 Jackson Street
Denver, CO   80206   303-388-4461
                             800-222-LUNG
              www.nationaljewish.org

The only medical center in the country whose research and patient care resources are dedicated to
respiratory and immunologic diseases.

Connecticut

**5386 Connecticut Assistive Technology Project
Connecticut Department of Social Services**

Bureau of Rehabilitation Services
25 Sigourney Street, 11th Floor
Hartford, CT   06106   860-424-4881
                             800-537-2549
                        FAX: 860-424-4850
                        TDY:860-424-4839
               e-mail: cttap@aol.com
               www.techact.uconn.edu

Judith Fein, NIDRR Officer

Single point of entry, advocacy, information and referral, peer counseling, and access to objective expert
advice and consultation for people with disabilities.

5387 Connecticut Braille Association

664 Oakwood Avenue
West Hartford, CT   06110   860-953-9692

Anne Murphy, Executive Secretary

Offers textbooks, cassettes, large print books, braille
books and more.

5388 Connecticut State Library

198 W Street
Rocky Hill, CT   06067   860-566-2151
                             800-842-4516
                        FAX: 860-566-6669
                e-mail: lbph@cslib.org

Carol Taylor, Librarian

Discs, cassettes, braille, reference materials on blindness and other handicaps, closed-circuit TV and
large-print photocopier.

5389 Prevent Blindness Connecticut

1275 Washington Street
Middletown, CT   06457   860-628-0347
                             800-850-2020
                        FAX: 860-347-0613

The mission of Prevent Blindness Connecticut is to
save sight and prevent blindness through eye
screenings, education, safety activities and research.

5390 Yale University, Vision Research Center

330 Cedar Street
New Haven, CT   06510   203-785-4640
                        FAX: 203-785-6123

Marvin Sears, Prin/ Investigator

Vision including studies on growth and development.

Delaware

5391 Delaware Assistive Technology Initiative Center for Applied Science and Engineering

University of Delaware
Alfred I. duPont Hospital
Wilmington, DE 19899
302-651-6790
800-870-DATI
FAX: 302-651-6793
TDY:302-651-6794
e-mail: dati@asel.udel.edu
www.asel.udel.edu/dati

Sonja Simowitz, Project Coordinator

Project has established county resource centers in each of Delaware's three counties. These centers serve as information and equipment resource sites, offering short-term equipment loans, training and demonstration workshops and regular informational mailings.

5392 Delaware Division of Libraries for the Blind and Physically Handicapped

43 South Dupont Highway
Dover, DE 19901
302-736-4748
800-282-8676
FAX: 302-736-6787
e-mail: blandon@lib.de.us

Beth Landon, Librarian

Braille readers receive service from Philadelphia and Pennsylvania, summer reading program, braille writer and cassettes.

5393 Rehabilitation Engineering Library

321 E 11th Street
Wilmington, DE 19801
302-657-5601
FAX: 302-654-5815

Robert Rodgers

Rehabilitation engineering and physical disabilities.

District of Columbia

5394 District of Columbia Public Library, Services to the Deaf Community

901 G Street NW
Room 215
Washington, DC 20001
202-393-5420
FAX: 202-727-1129
e-mail: lbphb_2000@yahoo.com
www.dclibrary.org

Janice Rosen, Librarian

Offers reference services through TTY, signers for library programs, sign language classes, information about deafness, print and non-print materials for persons who have hearing disabilities.

5395 District of Columbia Regional Library for the Blind and Physically Hanicapped

901 G Street NW
Room 215
Washington, DC 20001
202-727-2142
FAX: 202-727-1129
TDY:202-727-2145

Grace J. Lyons

5396 Georgetown University Child Development Center

2233 Wisconsin Avenue NW
215
Washington, DC 20007
202-944-2130

5397 Project Eyes and Ears

1844 T Street SE
Washington, DC 20020
202-889-7045
FAX: 202-889-6312

Janice Wellborn

Disseminates information about resources to families and service providers, provides transition services for pre-kindergarten children who are deaf-blind and integrates children into normalized settings.

5398 Senior Center for the Hearing Impaired

1510 9th Street NW
Washington, DC 20001
202-232-4288
FAX: 202-667-9781

Angela Jones, Director
Alma Beasley, Administrative Assistant

Offers daily programs, activities, counseling, noon meals, and transportation for deaf and hard of hearing seniors, 60 and older, living in the District of Columbia.

5399 University Legal Services AT Program

300 I Street NE
Suite 200
Washington, DC 20002
202-547-0198
FAX: 202-547-2662
TDY:202-547-2657
e-mail: atpdc@uls-dc.com
www.atpdc.org

Alicia C. Johns, Principal Investigator
Carol Cohen, NIDRR Officer

Designed to empower individuals with disabilities; to promote consumer involvement and advocacy, and provide information, referral and training as they relate to accessing assistive technology services and devices; and to identify and improve access to funding resources.

Florida

5400 Brevard County Library System Talking Books Library

308 Forrest Avenue
Cocoa, FL 32922
407-454-7265
FAX: 407-633-1838
TDY:407-633-1811
e-mail: kbriley@sunplus.brev.lib.fl.us

Kay Briley, Librarian

Offers reference materials on blindness and other handicaps. Subregional library for the blind and physically handicapped, assistive reading devices collection, reference materials on blindness and other handicaps; CCTV, phonic ear and reading edge and LOUD-R, assistive listening device, available..

5401 Brevard County Talking Books Library

308 Forrest Avenue
Cocoa, FL 32922   407-633-1792
     FAX: 407-633-1838
e-mail: kbritey@sunmail.brev.lib.fl.us

Kay Briley, Librarian

Offers reference materials on blindness and other handicaps; Subregional Library for the Talking Books program for the blind & physically handicapped.

5402 Broward County Talking Book Library

100 S Andrews Avenue
Ft. Lauderdale, FL 33301   954-357-7457

Barbara Kelly, Librarian

Reference materials on blindness and other handicaps, films, closed-circuit T.V., discs, cassettes and a book discussion group is offered.

5403 DREAMMS for Kids

273 Ringwood Road
Freeville, NY 13068   607-539-9981

An educational technology and parent service agency, founded in 1988 by parents of a Down Syndrome child. DREAMMS is committed to increasing the use of computers, assistive technologies, and quality instructional technology for special needs students in school and homes throughout the country.

5404 Dade County Talking Book Library

Miami-Dade Public Library System
150 NE 79th Street
Miami, FL 33138   305-751-8687
     800-451-9544
     FAX: 305-757-8401
e-mail: moyerb@seflin.lib.fl.us

Barbara Moyer, Librarian

Library services for people with disabilities.

5405 Florida Division of Blind Services

Regional Library
420 Platt Street
Daytona Beach, FL 32114   904-258-8692
     FAX: 850-239-6069
     TDY:800-226-6079
e-mail: weberd@mail.firn.edu

Donald John Weber, Librarian

Discs, cassettes, closed-circuit T.V., large-print photocopier, films, children's books on cassettes and more.

5406 Florida Instructional Materials Center for the Visually Handicapped

5002 N Lois Avenue
Tampa, FL 33614   813-872-5281

Suzanne Dalton, Supervisor

Operates a clearinghouse depository and production center for braille, large print and recorded texts. Provides assistance in assessment of materials and specialized apparatus, organizes volunteers for material production and more for the visually handicapped.

5407 Florida Ophthalmic Institute

7106 NW 11th Plaza
Gainesville, FL 32605   352-331-2020

Norman S. Levy, MD, Director

Nonprofit organization that understands and treats ocular diseases including glaucoma.

5408 Florida Subregional Libraries Talking Book Service

6081 26th Street W
Bradenton, FL 34207   941-484-5914
     FAX: 941-749-7189
     TDY:941-742-5951

Candace Conklin

5409 Hillsborough County Talking Book Library
Tampa-Hillsborough County Public Library

900 N Ashely Street
Tampa, FL 33602   813-264-3831
     FAX: 813-273-3641
     TDY:813-273-3610
e-mail: myersl@scfn.thpl.lib.fl.us
www.scfn.thpl.lib.us

Kurt Jasielonis

5410 Jacksonville Public Library

2809 Commonwealth Avenue
Jacksonville, FL 32205   904-388-6135

Gloria Zittrauer, Librarian

Discs, cassettes, reference materials on blindness and other handicaps and children's books on cassettes.

5411 Lee County Library System - Talking Books Library

13240 North Cleveland Avenue
5-6
North Fort Myers, FL 33903   941-995-2665
     800-854-8195
     FAX: 941-995-1681
     TDY:941-995-2665
lee-county.com/library/progserv/sscvs/tb.htm

Provides free books and magazines to Lee County residents of all ages who have any disability that prevents them from reading printed material. Books are played on special players provided free by the National Library Service. Circulates low tech assistive aids and devices for temporary loan to Lee County Library card holders. Directs people to assistive technology and disability related resources.

5412   Louis de la Parte Florida Mental Health Institute Research Library Univ. of South Florida

13301 Bruce B Downs Boulevard
Tampa, FL   33612   813-974-4471
                                FAX: 813-974-7242
                    e-mail: library@fmhi.usf.edu
                                www.fmhi.usf.edu

Information offered on mental illness, autism and pervasive development disabilities mental health research and archives management.

5413   Orange County Library System Audio-Visual Department

101 E Central Boulevard
Orlando, FL   32801   407-425-4694
                                FAX: 407-425-6779
                                TDY:407-425-5668

Sally Fry

5414   Pearlman Biomedical Research Institute

Mt. Sinani Medical Center
4300 Alton Road
Miami Beach, FL   33140   305-674-2121
                                FAX: 305-674-2198

Dr. William Abraham, Director
Pulmonary medicine, arthritis, sleep disorders and gynecology departments of research.

5415   Pinellas Talking Book Library for the Blind and Physically Handicapped

12345 Starkey Road
Suite L
Largo, FL   33773   727-441-9958
                                FAX: 813-538-8731
                                TDY:813-538-8949
                    e-mail: zonefive@scfn.thpl.lib.fl.us
                                www.tblc.org/ptbl

Greg Carlson

5416   Subregional Talking Book Library

Jacksonville Public Library
1755 Edgewood Avenue West
Suite 1
Jacksonville, FL   32208   904-765-5588
                                FAX: 904-768-7404
                                TDY:904-768-7822
                    e-mail: arthurs@mail.firn.edu

Laurie Baumgardner, Department Head
Nkoyo Ross, Librarian

Offers cassettes, reference materials on blindness and other handicaps, children's braille books, descriptive videos, and some assistive devices.

5417   Talking Book Service - Mantatee County Central Library

6081 26th Street West
Bradenton, FL   34207   941-742-5914
                                FAX: 941-751-7098

Patricia Schubert, Librarian
Offers children's books on disc and cassette and more reference materials for the blind and physically handicapped.

5418   Talking Books Library for the Blind and Physically Handicapped

Palm Beach County Library Annex
7950 Central Ind Drive
Suite 104
Riviera Beach, FL   33404   561-775-8274
                                FAX: 561-845-4640

Pat Mistretta, Librarian
Library services for people with disabilities.

5419   Talking Books for the Blind

Talking Book Library
1755 Edgewood Avenue West
Suite 1
Jacksonville, FL   32208   904-765-5588
                                FAX: 904-768-7404
                    e-mail: laurieb@coj.net

Laurie Baumgardner, Manager
Offers books on cassette for adults and children, reference materials on blindness and other handicaps, and descriptive videos.

5420   Talking Books/Homebound Services

Brevard County Library System
308 Forrest Avenue
Cocoa, FL   32922   407-454-7265
                                FAX: 407-633-1838
                                TDY:407-633-1811
                    e-mail: kbriley@sunplus.brev.lib.fl.us

Kay Briley, Librarian
Offers reference materials on blindness and other handicaps. Subregional library for the blind and physically handicapped, assistive reading devices collection, reference materials on blindness and other handicaps; CCTV, phonic ear and reading edge and LOUD-R, assistive listening device, available.

5421   University of Miami, Bascom Palmer Eye Institute

Department of Ophthalmalogy
1638 NW 10th Avenue
Miami, FL   33136   305-326-6031
                                FAX: 305-326-6306

John G. Clarkson, MD, Chairman
Clinical and basic research into blindness and visual impairments.

5422   University of Miami, Mailman Center For Child Development

PO Box 016820
Miami, FL   33101   305-585-2703
                                FAX: 305-547-6309

Dr. Robert Stempfel, Jr., Director
Focuses on birth defects and children's illnesses.

5423   West Florida Regional Library

200 W Gregory Street
Pensacola, FL   32501   850-435-1760
                                FAX: 850-432-9582

Martha Lazor, Librarian
Offers children's print/braille books.

Georgia

5424 Albany Talking Book Center

Dougherty County Public Library
300 Pine Avenue
Albany, GA   31701   912-420-3220
                                   FAX: 912-420-3240

Kathryn Sinquefield, Librarian

Offers discs, cassettes, reference materials on blindness and other handicaps, large-print photocopiers, summer reading programs, cassette books and more.

5425 Athens Regional Library Talking Book Center

2025 Baxter Street
Athens, GA   30606   706-613-3655
                                   FAX: 706-613-3660

Paige Burns, Manager

Discs, cassettes, large print books, reference materials on blindness, descriptive videos, films, closed-circuit T.V., magnifiers, braille writer, summer reading programs, cassette books and magazines and more.

5426 Augusta Talking Book Center

425 9th Street
Augusta, GA   30901   706-821-1155
                                   FAX: 706-724-5403
                            e-mail: gswint@csra,net

Gary Swint, Librarian

Discs, cassettes, braille writer, films, large print books, summer reading program, magnifiers and reference materials on blindness and other handicaps.

5427 Bainbridge Subregional Library for the Blind & Physically Handicapped

SW Georgia Regional Library
301 S Monroe Street
Bainbridge, GA   31717   229-248-2680
                                        800-795-2680
                                   FAX: 229-248-2670
                                        www.swgri.org

Susan Whittle, Librarian
Kathy Hutchins, Supervisor
Priscilla Southall, Library Assistant

Discs, cassettes, large print books, summer reading programs, closed-circuit T.V., magnifiers and more.

Monthly Newsltr

5428 CEL Regional Library

2002 Bull Street
Savannah, GA   31499   912-234-5127
                                   FAX: 912-652-3638
                    e-mail: lstokes@cel.co.chatman.ga.us

Linda Stokes, Librarian

Summer reading programs, braille writer, magnifiers, closed-circuit T.V., large-print photocopier, cassette books and magazines, children's books on cassette, home visits and other reference materials on blindness and other handicaps.

5429 Division of Birth Defects and Genetic Diseases

4770 Buford Highway
Chamblee, GA   30341   770-488-7150
                                   FAX: 770-488-7156

Muin J. Khoury, MD

5430 Emory Autism Resource Center

Emory University
718 Gatewood Road
Atlanta, GA   30322   404-727-3360
                                   FAX: 404-727-8350

Offers on-line bulletin boards which are relevant to autism.

5431 Emory University Laboratory for Ophthalmic Research

1327 Clifton Road NE
Room 37045
Atlanta, GA   30322   404-321-0111

Henry F. Edelhauser, Director

Various studies into the aspects of blindness.

5432 Georgia Library for the Blind and Physically Handicapped

1150 Murphy Avenue SW
Atlanta, GA   30310   404-756-4619
                                        800-248-6701
                                   FAX: 404-756-4618

Linda Stetson, Director

Discs, cassettes, braille, films, closed-circuit T.V., braille writer, large-print photocopier, cassette books and magazines.

5433 Georgia Regional Library

1150 Murphy Avenue SW
Atlanta, GA   30310   404-756-4619
                                   FAX: 404-756-4618

Lindaey Koldenhoven, Librarian

Discs, cassettes, braille, films, closed-circuit T.V., braille writer, large-print photocopier, cassette books and magazines.

5434 Hall County Library East Hall Branch and Special Needs Library

2434 Old Cornelia Highway
Gainesville, GA   30507   770-531-2500
                                   FAX: 770-532-2502
             e-mail: kevans@mail.hall.public.lib.ga.us
                            www.hall.public.lib.ga.us

Kathy Evans, Branch Manager

Summer reading programs, braille writer, magnifiers, scanners and readers, audio described videos, closed captioned videos, closed-circuit T.V., large-print photocopier, cassette books and magazines, large print books, children's books on cassette, home visits and other reference materials on blindness and other handicaps.

5435 Hall County Library System - Special Needs Library

E Hall Branch & Special Needs Lib.
2434 Old Cornelia Highway
Gainesville, GA 30507   770-531-2500
                               FAX: 770-531-2502
e-mail: kevans@mail.hall.public.lib.ga.us
                    www.hall.public.lib.ga.us

Kathy Evans, Manager

Magnifiers, closed-circuit T.V., cassette books and magazines, mail-a-book for homebound, home visits and other reference materials on blindness and other handicaps.

5436 La Fayette Subregional Library for the Blind and Physically Disabled

301 S Duke Street
La Fayette, GA 30728   706-638-2342
                               FAX: 706-638-4028

Charles Stubblefield, Librarian

Summer reading programs, braille writer, magnifiers, closed-circuit T.V., large-print photocopier, cassette books and magazines, children's books on cassette, home visits and other reference materials on blindness and other handicaps.

5437 Lafayette Subregional Library for the Blind and Physically Handicapped

305 S Duke Street
PO Box 707
La Fayette, GA 30728   706-638-1958
                               888-506-0509
                               FAX: 706-638-4028
e-mail: stubblec@yahoo.com
                    www.walker.public.lib.ga.us

Charles H. Stubblefield, Library Manager

Summer reading programs, magnifiers, closed-circuit T.V., large-print photocopier, cassette books and magazines, children's books on cassette, home visits and other reference materials on blindness and other handicaps.

5438 Macon Library for the Blind and Physically Handicapped

Washington Memorial Library
1180 Washington Avenue
Macon, GA 31201   912-743-3345
                               800-805-7613
                               FAX: 912-742-3161
e-mail: sherrilr@mail-bibb.public.lib.ga.us

Rebecca Sherrill, Librarian

Summer reading programs, braille writer, magnifiers, closed-circuit T.V., large-print photocopier, cassette books and magazines, children's books on cassette, home visits and other reference materials on blindness and other handicaps.

5439 Oconee Regional Library

Bellevue Avenue
PO Box 100
Dublin, GA 31040   912-275-5382
                               FAX: 912-272-0524

Betty Schild, Director
Linda Kight, Special Service Manager

Summer reading programs, braille writer, magnifiers, closed-circuit T.V., large-print photocopier, cassette books and magazines, children's books on cassette, home visits and other reference materials on blindness and other handicaps.

5440 Rome Subregional Library for the Blind and Physically Handicapped

205 Riverside Parkway NE
Rome, GA 30161   706-236-4600
                               FAX: 706-236-4631
e-mail: dianam@mail.floyd.public.lib

Diana Mills

5441 Sara Hightower Regional Library

205 Riverside Parkway
Rome, GA 30161   706-236-4618
                               FAX: 706-236-4631
                    www.floyd.public.lib.ga.us

Diana Mills, Librarian

Summer reading programs, braille writer, magnifiers, closed-circuit T.V., large-print photocopier, cassette books and magazines, children's books on cassette, home visits and other reference materials on blindness and other handicaps.

5442 South Georgia Regional Library

300 Woodrow Wilson Drive
Valdosta, GA 31602   912-896-3988
                               FAX: 912-333-7669
e-mail: sbernste@surfsouth.com

Sharon Bernstein, Librarian

Summer reading programs, braille writer, magnifiers, closed-circuit T.V., large-print photocopier, cassette books and magazines, children's books on cassette, home visits and other reference materials on blindness and other handicaps.

5443 South Georgia Regional Library for the Blind and Physically Handicapped

300 Woodrow Wilson Drive
Valdosta, GA 31602   912-333-5285
                               FAX: 912-245-6483

Sharon Bernstein

5444 Subregional Library for the Blind and Physically Handicapped

1120 Bradley Drive
Columbus, GA 31906   706-649-0780
                               FAX: 706-649-1259

Dorothy Bowen, Librarian

Braille writer, magnifiers, closed-circuit T.V., large-print photocopier, cassette books and magazines, children's books on cassette, home visits and other reference materials on blindness and other handicaps.

5445 Subregional Library of Blind & Physically Handicapped

1120 Bradley Drive
Columbus, GA 31906   706-649-0780
                               800-652-0782
                               FAX: 706-649-1914
e-mail: slbph@mail.muscogee.public.lib.ga.us.

Dorthy Bowen, Librarian

Summer reading programs, braille writer, magnifiers, large-print photocopier, cassette books and magazines, children's books on cassette, and other reference materials on blindness and other handicaps.

5446 Talking Book Center Brunswick-Glynn County Regional Library

606 O Street
Brunswick, GA 31523   912-267-1212

Betty Ransom, Librarian

Hawaii

5447 Assistive Technology Resource Centers of Hawaii (ATRC)

414 Kuwili Street
Suite 104
Honolulu, HI 96817   808-532-7110
                             800-645-3007
                        FAX: 808-532-7120
                        TDY:808-532-7110
                        e-mail: atrc@atrc.org
                        www.atrc.org

Provides information and training on assistive technology devices, services, and funding resources. Conducts presentations and demonstrations in the community to increase AT awareness and promote self-advocacy among people with disabilities.

5448 Hawaii State Library for the Blind and Physically Handicapped

402 Kapahulu Avenue
Hanolulu, HI 96815   808-733-8444
                             800-559-4096
                        FAX: 808-733-8449
                        TDY:808-733-8444
                        e-mail: olbcirc@state.lib.hi.us
                        www.hcc.hawaii.edu

Fusako Miyashiro

5449 Library for the Blind and Physically Handicapped of Hawaii

402 Kapahulu Avenue
Honolulu, HI 96815
                        FAX: 808-733-8449
                        e-mail: olbeire@state.lib.hi.us

Fusako Miyashiro, Librarian

Summer reading programs, braille writer, magnifiers, closed-circuit T.V., large-print photocopier, cassette books and magazines, children's books on cassette, home visits and other reference materials on blindness and other handicaps.

Idaho

5450 Idaho Assistive Technology Project

University of Idaho
129 West Third Street
Moscow, ID 83843   208-885-3559
                           800-432-8324
                      FAX: 208-885-3628
                      TDY:208-885-3559
                      e-mail: seile861@uidahol.edu
                      www.ets.uidaho.edu/iidatech

Susan House, Information Specialist

Project engages in systems change activities, training, materials development, information dissemination, and advocacy activities directed at increasing the availability of assistive devices and services to Idahoans who have disabilities.

5451 Idaho State Library, Talking Book Library

325 W State Street
Boise, ID 83702   208-334-2117
                          800-233-4931
                     FAX: 208-334-4016
                     e-mail: ksalmon@isl.state.id.us
                     www.lili.org/isl

Andrea R. Testi, Regional Librarian

Offers talking books and magazines, large print materials, braille, equipment and accessories. Available to all residents of Idaho who are visually impaired and/or have disabilities which disallows the use of print material.

Illinois

5452 Catholic Guild for the Blind

180 N Michigan Avenue
Chicago, IL 60601   312-236-8569

Offers books in braille and large print, cassettes and a lending library.

5453 Chicago Library Service for the Blind

1055 W Roosevelt Road
Chicago, IL 60608   773-738-9200

Carol Pellish, Librarian

Summer reading programs, braille writer, magnifiers, closed-circuit T.V., large-print photocopier, cassette books and magazines, children's books on cassette, home visits and other reference materials on blindness and other handicaps.

5454 Chicago Public Library Talking Book Center

400 S State Street 5 N
Chicago, IL 60605   312-747-4200
                            800-757-4654
                       FAX: 312-747-1609
                       e-mail: tbc@chipublib.org

Mamie Grady, Librarian

Summer reading programs, braille writer, closed-circuit T.V., large-print photocopier, cassette books and magazines, children's books on cassette, home visits and other reference materials on blindness and other handicaps.

5455 Department of Ophthalmology/Eye and Ear Infirmary

1855 W Taylor Street
Chicago, IL 60612 312-996-6582

Offers help, support, information and research for persons with vision problems, including Retinitis Pigmentosa.

5456 Harold Washington Library Talking Book Center

400 S State Street
Room 5N7
Carterville, IL 62918 618-985-8375
800-445-2665
FAX: 618-985-4211
TDY:618-985-8375
e-mail: kgordon@shawnet.shawls.lib.il.

Kristi Gordon

5457 Horizons for the Blind

7001 N Clark Street
Chicago, IL 60626 773-973-7600

Braille and large-print books offered at museums, zoos and theaters; also provides tactile pictures.

5458 Illinois Early Childhood Intervention Clearinghouse

830 S Spring Street
Springfield, IL 62704 217-544-5809
800-852-4302
FAX: 217-524-5339

Chet Brandt, Project Director
Patricia Taylor, Project Associate

Free lending library of materials related to early childhood and disability. Books, audiovisuals and articles available. Computerized database with more than 26,000 items available to Illinois residents. Provides funding for individuals with disabilities to attend conferances and workshops (Illinois residents only).

5459 Illinois Regional Library for the Blind and Physically Handicapped

1055 W Roosevelt Road
Chicago, IL 60608 312-746-9210
800-331-2351
FAX: 773-746-9192

Shawn Thomas, Reference Librarian
Barbara Perkins, Acting Director

Summer reading programs, braille writer, magnifiers, closed-circuit T.V., large-print photocopier, cassette books and magazines, descriptive videos, children's books on cassette, home visits and other reference materials on blindness and other handicaps.

5460 Mid - Illinois Talking Book Center

515 York Street
Quincy, IL 62301 217-224-5546
FAX: 217-224-9818
e-mail: eshepard@darkstar.rsa.lib.il

Eileen Sheppard, Librarian

Summer reading programs, braille writer, magnifiers, large-print photocopier, cassette books and magazines, children's books on cassette, home visits and other reference materials on blindness and other handicaps.

5461 Mid-Illinois Talking Book Center

515 York
Quincy, IL 62301 217-224-6619
800-537-1274
FAX: 217-224-9818
e-mail: emeyer@darkstar.rsa.lib.il.us
www.rsa.lib.il.us/~mitbc/heart.htm

Eileen Meyer, Director

Subregional library provides Talking book and Braille Book program to eligible persons unable to use standard print materials due to visual or physical disabilities. Includes cassette books and magazines; summer reading program.

5462 National Eye Research Foundation (NERF)

910 Skokie Boulevard
Suite 207A
Northbrook, IL 60062 847-564-4652
800-621-2258
FAX: 847-564-0807
e-mail: nerfl955@aol.com
www.eyemac.com/nerf

Dedicated to improving eye care for the public and meeting the professional nees of eye care practitioners; sponsors eye research projects on contact lens applications and eye care problems. Special study sections in such fields as orthokertology, primary eyecare, pediatrics, and through continuing education programs. Provides eye care information for the public and professionals. Educational materials including pamphlets. Program activities include education and referrals.

5463 National Lekotek Center

2100 Ridge Avenue
Evanston, IL 60201 847-328-0001
800-366-7529
FAX: 847-328-5514
e-mail: lekotek@lekotek.org
www.lekotek.org

Helen McCarthy, Executive Director

Toy library and play-centered programs for children with special needs and their families with branches in 17 states. Sliding fee scale. Lekotek also has a Toy Resource Helpline that provides individualized assistances in the selection of toys and play materials and general resources for families with children with disabilities.

5464 Northwestern University Asthma and Allergy Disease Center

303 E Chicago Avenue
Chicago, IL 60611   312-908-8171
                                 FAX: 312-908-0205
        e-mail: R-Patterson@northwestern.edu
                        www.northwestern.edu

Roy Patterson, MD, Head

5465 Northwestern University Multipurpose Arthritis & Musculoskeletal Center

303 E Chicago Avenue
Chicago, IL 60611   312-908-8171
                                 FAX: 312-503-0994

Dr. Richard Pope, Head
Conducts biomedical, educational and health services research into musculoskeletal diseases.

5466 Philip H. Cohen Institute for the Visually Handicapped

5200 S Hyde Park Boulevard
Chicago, IL 60615   773-752-2770

Braille and large-print books and taped transcriptions for the Jewish Braille Institute of America.

5467 Rehabilitation Institute of Chicago Learning Resource Center

345 E Superior Street
Chicago, IL 60611   312-908-6000
                                 FAX: 312-908-1369

Elizabeth DeLaHunt, Coordinator
Offers information on rehabilitation and physical disabilities.

5468 Shawnee Library System

607 Greenbriar Road
Carterville, IL 62918   618-985-3711
                                 FAX: 618-985-4211
        e-mail: kqurden@shawnet.shawls.lib.il

Kristi Gorden, Librarian
Summer reading programs, braille writer, magnifiers, closed-circuit T.V., large-print photocopier, cassette books and magazines, children's books on cassette, home visits and other reference materials on blindness and other handicaps.

5469 Skokie Accessible Library Services

Skokie Public Library
5215 Oakton Street
Skokie, IL 60077   847-673-7774
                                 FAX: 847-673-7797
        e-mail: tellus@skokie.lib.il.us
                        www.skokie.lib.il.us

Gary Gustin, Program Manager
Patricia Grobs, Coordinator of Community Service
Library services for people with disabilities, including electronic aids, materials in special formats, programs and special services, and access to the North Suburban Library System.

5470 Skokie Public Library

5215 Oakton Street
Skokie, IL 60077   847-673-7774
                                 FAX: 847-673-7797

Pat Groh, Librarian
Library services for people with disabilities.

5471 Southern Illinois Talking Book Center

607 S Greenbriar Road
Carterville, IL 62918   618-985-8375
                                 800-455-2665
                                 FAX: 618-985-4211
        e-mail: dbrawley@shawls.lib.il.us
                        www.shawls.lib.il.us

Diana Brawley- Sussman, Director
Free library service to those who are blind, visually impaired, physically disabled, or reading disabled. Our collection consists of all types of popular interest reading material from preschool through adult that have been recorded on cassette, flexible disc and translated into braille. Loan out small collection of descriptive videos.

5472 Statewide Library of Information for Caregivers of the Disabled

800 Governors Highway
Flossmoor, IL 60422   708-957-7100

Statewide reference service with special library collections for all Illinois public libraries and their patrons needing information about disabilities.

5473 Suburban Audio Visual Service

920 Barnsdale Road
La Grange Park, IL 60525   630-352-7671

Leon Drolet, Jr., Librarian
Summer reading programs, braille writer, magnifiers, closed-circuit T.V., large-print photocopier, cassette books and magazines, children's books on cassette, home visits and other reference materials on blindness and other handicaps.

5474 Talking Book Center of Northwest Illinois

PO Box 125
Coal Valley, IL 61240   309-799-3137
                                 800-747-3137
                                 FAX: 309-799-7916

Karen Odean, Librarian
Subregional library provides Talking Book and Braille Book program to eligible persons unable to use standard print materials due to visual or physical disabilities. Includes cassette books and magazines; summer reading program.

5475 University of Illinois at Chicago, Lions of Illinois Eye Research Institute

UIC Eye Center
1905 West Taylor Street
Chicago, IL 60612   312-996-8937
                                 FAX: 312-996-7770

Prf. Jose Pulrdo, Head

Visual impairments and blindness research, including glaucoma studies.

5476 Voices of Vision Talking Book Center @ DuPage Library System

127 S First Street
Geneva, IL 60134   630-208-0398
     800-227-0625
FAX: 630-208-0399
e-mail: vovtbc@dupagels.lib.il.us
www.dupagels.lib.il.us/pages/voices.html

Indiana

5477 Allen County Public Library

Box 2270
Fort Wayne, IN 46801   219-424-7241

Joyce Misner, Librarian

Summer reading programs, braille writer, magnifiers, closed-circuit T.V., large-print photocopier, cassette books and magazines, children's books on cassette, home visits and other reference materials on blindness and other handicaps.

5478 Bartholomew County Public Library

5th at Lafayette
Columbus, IN 47201   812-376-9253
FAX: 812-379-1275

Wilma Perry, Librarian

Summer reading programs, braille writer, magnifiers, closed-circuit T.V., large-print photocopier, cassette books and magazines, children's books on cassette, home visits and other reference materials on blindness and other handicaps.

5479 Elkhart Public Library

300 S Second
Elkhart, IN 46516   219-522-2665

Pat Ciancio, Librarian

Summer reading programs, braille writer, magnifiers, closed-circuit T.V., large-print photocopier, cassette books and magazines, children's books on cassette, home visits and other reference materials on blindness and other handicaps.

5480 Elkhart Public Library - Blind and Physically Handicapped Department

300 S 2nd Street
Elkhart, IN 46516   219-522-2665
FAX: 219-293-9213

Pat Ciancio, Department Supervisor

Hand-held magnifier, closed-circuit TV (V-Tex), cassette books and magazines, children's books on cassettes and reference materials on blindness and other handicaps.

5481 Evansville-Vanderburgh County Public Library

Allen County Public Library
PO Box 2270
Fort Wayne, IN 46802   219-424-7241

Joyce Misner

Offers books on disc and cassette.

5482 Indiana Resource Center for Autism

Inst. for the Study of Developmental Disabilities
2853 E Tenth Street
Bloomington, IN 47408   812-855-6508

5483 Indiana University, Multipurpose Arthritis Center

School of Medicine, Rheumatology Division
541 Clinical Drive
Room 492
Indianapolis, IN 46202   317-274-4225

Dr. Kenneth Brandt, Contact

Integral unit of the Division of Rheumatology, this department researches the causes and treatment of arthritis. Offers programs for health care providers and promotes cost-efficient care methods through community demonstration projects.

5484 Lake County Public Library Talking Books Service

1919 W 81st Avenue
Merrillville, IN 46410   219-769-7800
FAX: 219-769-0690
e-mail: tbooks@lakeco.lib.in.us

Renee Lewis

Large-print books, descriptive videos, braille writer, magnifiers, closed-circuit T.V., large-print photocopier, cassette books and magazines, children's books on cassette, and other reference materials on blindness and other handicaps.

5485 Northwest Indiana Subregional Library for Blind and Physically Handicapped

1919 W 81st Avenue
Merrillville, IN 46410   219-769-3541
FAX: 219-769-0690

Renee Lewis

Summer reading programs, braille writer, magnifiers, closed-circuit T.V., large-print photocopier, cassette books and magazines, children's books on cassette, home visits and other reference materials on blindness and other handicaps.

5486 Readers' Services Department Allen County Public Library

PO Box 2270
Fort Wayne, IN 46801   219-421-1200
FAX: 219-422-9688
www.acpl.lib.in.us

Summer reading programs, braille writer, magnifiers, closed-circuit T.V., large-print photocopier, cassette books and magazines, children's books on cassette, home visits and other reference materials on blindness and other handicaps.

5487 Special Services Division - Indiana State Library

140 North Senate Avenue
Indianapolis, IN   46204   317-232-3682
                                         800-622-4970
                         FAX: 317-232-3728
               e-mail: lbph@statelib.lib.in.us
                      www.statelib.lib.in.us

Lissa Shanahan, Librarian

Circulates a collection of braille, recorded, and large print books and magazines and the special equipment needed to play the recorded materials to anyone in Indiana who cannot read regular print due to a visual or physical disability.

5488 St. Joseph's Hospital Rehabilitation Center

700 Broadway
Fort Wayne, IN   46802   219-425-3740
                         FAX: 219-425-3741

Robert Archer, RN LSW, Case Manager
Information offered on rehabilitation.

5489 Talking Books Service Evansville Vanderburgh County Public Library

22 SE Fifth Street
Evansville, IN   47708   812-428-8235
                         FAX: 812-428-8215
               e-mail: tbs@evans.evcpl.lib.in.us

Barbara Shanks

Iowa

5490 Iowa Department for the Blind - Library

524 4th Street
Des Moines, IA   50309   515-281-1333
                         FAX: 515-281-1378
               e-mail: library@blind.state.ia.us
                      www.blind.state.ia.us

Karen Kenninger, Program Administrator

Summer reading programs, large print, disc, braille and cassette books and magazines, descriptive videos, home visits and reference materials on blindness and other handicaps.

5491 Library Commission for the Blind

524 Fourth Street
Des Moines, IA   50309   515-281-1333
                         FAX: 515-281-1378
               e-mail: iisad@blind.dtate.ia.us

Catherine Ford, Librarian

Summer reading programs, braille writer, magnifiers, closed-circuit T.V., large-print photocopier, cassette books and magazines, children's books on cassette, home visits and other reference materials on blindness and other handicaps.

5492 University of Iowa Birth Defects and Genetic Disorders Unit

2614 JCP
Iowa City, IA   52242   319-335-9901
                         FAX: 319-356-3347

Val Sheffield, MD

Kansas

5493 Braille Association of Kansas

PO Box 17032
Wichita, KS   67217

Mary Ann Oblinger

Supplies adults and children general interest, textbooks, professional and vocational books in print and braille. Also offers cassettes or open reel tape to people who need braille or tape reading materials.

5494 CKLS Headquarters

1409 Williams
Great Bend, KS   67530   316-792-2409
                         FAX: 316-793-7270
               e-mail: cenks@ink.org

Jerri Robinson, Librarian

Summer reading programs, braille writer, magnifiers, closed-circuit T.V., large-print photocopier, cassette books and magazines, children's books on cassette, home visits and other reference materials on blindness and other handicaps.

5495 Center for Applied Psychophysiology Menninger Clinic

PO Box 829
Topeka, KS   66601   913-273-7500

Research, treatment, and workshops in min/body medicine, including biofeedback and brainwave therapy.

5496 Center for the Improvement of Human Functioning

3100 North Hillside Avenue
Wichita, KS   67219   316-682-3100

Medical, research, and educational facility specializing in the treatment of chronic illness.

5497 Kansas State Library

ESU Memorial Union
1200 Commercial Street
Emporia, KS   66801
                         FAX: 316-343-7124
               e-mail: ksst16lb@ink.org

2aroline Lang, Librarian

Summer reading programs, braille writer, magnifiers, closed-circuit T.V., large-print photocopier, cassette books and magazines, children's books on cassette, home visits and other reference materials on blindness and other handicaps.

5498 Manhattan Public Library

629 Poyntz Avenue
Manhattan, KS   66502   785-776-4741
                         FAX: 785-776-1545
               e-mail: marionr@manhaHan.lib.ks.us
                      www.manhattan.lib.ks.us

Marion Rice, Librarian

Summer reading programs, braille writer, magnifiers, closed-circuit T.V., large-print photocopier, cassette books and magazines, children's books on cassette, home visits and other reference materials on blindness and other handicaps.

5499 Northwest Kansas Library System Talking Books

2 Washington Street
PO Box 446
Norton, KS 67654 785-877-5148
FAX: 785-877-5697
e-mail: tbook@ruraltel.net
www.skyways.lib.ks.us/nwkls/howard/bph.html

Clarice Howard, Librarian

Offers books on disc and cassette. Library of Congress talking book and program for qualified individuals. Also offers descriptive videos to eligible persons.

5500 South Central Kansas Library System

Talking Bookz/ S.C.K.L.S
901 N Main
Hutchinson, KS 67501 316-663-5441
800-234-0529
FAX: 316-663-1215
e-mail: ksocha@holsck.org
www.holsk.org/libraryservicesindex.htm

Karen Socha, Librarian

Summer reading programs, braille writer, magnifiers, closed-circuit T.V., large-print photocopier, cassette books and magazines, children's books on cassette, home visits and other reference materials on blindness and other handicaps.

5501 Topeka & Shawnee County Public Library Talking Book Service

1515 SW 10th Avenue
Topeka, KS 66604 785-231-0574
800-432-2925
FAX: 785-231-0579
e-mail: tbooks@tscpl.lib.ks.us
www.tscpl.org

Suzanne Bundy, Librarian

Summer reading programs, braille writer, magnifiers, closed-circuit T.V., large-print photocopier, cassette books and magazines, children's books on cassette, home visits and other reference materials on blindness and other handicaps.

5502 Wichita Public Library

223 S Main
Wichita, KS 67202 316-262-0611
FAX: 316-262-4540

Brad Reha, Librarian

Summer reading programs, braille writer, magnifiers, closed-circuit T.V., large-print photocopier, cassette books and magazines, children's books on cassette, home visits and other reference materials on blindness and other handicaps.

5503 Wichita Public Library/Talking Book Service

223 S Main Street
Wichita, KS 67202 316-264-8308
FAX: 316-262-4540

Brad Reha, Librarian

Furnish recorded reading material (books and magazines) for visually and physically challenged citizens.

Kentucky

5504 EnTech: Enabling Technologies of Kentuckiana

301 York Street
Louisville, KY 40203
800-890-1840
FAX: 502-574-1671
e-mail: entech@iglou.com
www.kde.state.ky.us/assistive/home.htm

Sherrill Williams, Program Director
Donna Jentes, Technology Spec.
April Kerr, Contact

Assistive technology resource and demonstration center, serving persons of all ages and disabilities in Western Kentucky and Southern Indiana. Services include: assistive technology information, demonstration, evaluation, training, technical support and short-term loan of equipment.

5505 Kentucky Library for the Blind and Physically Handicapped

300 Coffee Tree Road
PO Box 818
Frankfort, KY 40602 502-564-8300
800-372-2968
FAX: 502-564-5773
e-mail: rfeindel@ctr.kdla.state.ky.us
www.kdla.net/libserv/ktnl.htm

Richard Feindel, Librarian

Braille book and magazines, large-print photocopier, cassette books and magazines, children's books on cassette, and other reference materials on blindness and other handicaps.

5506 Louisville Free Public Library

301 York Street
Louisville, KY 40203 502-574-1625
FAX: 502-574-1657
e-mail: denning@lfpf.org

Tom Denning, Coord, Special Adult Services

Summer reading programs, braille writer, magnifiers, closed-circuit T.V., large-print photocopier, cassette books and magazines, children's books on cassette, home visits and other reference materials on blindness and other handicaps.

Louisiana

5507 Central Louisiana State Hospital Medical and Professional Library

PO Box 5031
Pineville, LA 71361 318-484-6200
FAX: 318-484-6284

Carol Benton McGee, Librarian

Information offered on psychiatry, psychology and mental health.

5508 Louisiana State Library
760 N Fouth Street
Baton Rouge, LA 70802　　225-342-4944
　　　　　　　　　　　　　　　800-543-4702
　　　　　　　　　　　　FAX: 225-342-6817
　　　e-mail: sbph@pelican.state.lib.la.us

Elizabhet H. Perkins, Regional Librarian
Leola H. Walker, Library Manager

Summer reading programs, braille writer, magnifiers, closed-circuit T.V., large-print photocopier, cassette books and magazines, children's books on cassette. Descriptive videoss and other reference materials on blindness and other handicaps.

5509 Louisiana State Library - Section for the Blind and Physically Handicapped
701 N 4th Street
Baton Rouge, LA 70802　　225-924-2484
　　　　　　　　　　　　　　　800-543-4702
　　　　　　　　　　　　FAX: 504-342-3547
Emma Schroth, author
Jennifer Anjier, Librarian

Summer reading programs, braille writer, magnifiers, closed-circuit T.V., large-print photocopier, cassette books and magazines, children's books on cassette and other reference materials on blindness and other handicaps. Louisiana Hotlines - quarterly newsletter.

5510 Louisiana State University Genetics Section of Pediatrics
1501 Kings Highway
Shreveport, LA 71130　　318-675-5681

T.F. Thurman, MD, Director

Maine

5511 Bangor Public Library
145 Harlow Street
Bangor, ME 04401　　207-947-8336

Judith Leighton, Librarian

Summer reading programs, braille writer, magnifiers, closed-circuit T.V., large-print photocopier, cassette books and magazines, children's books on cassette, home visits and other reference materials on blindness and other handicaps.

5512 Cary Library
107 Main Street
Houlton, ME 04730

Norma Watson, Librarian

Summer reading programs, braille writer, magnifiers, closed-circuit T.V., large-print photocopier, cassette books and magazines, children's books on cassette, home visits and other reference materials on blindness and other handicaps.

5513 Lewiston Public Library
105 Park Street
Lewiston, ME 04240　　207-784-7919

Muriel Landry, Librarian

Summer reading programs, braille writer, magnifiers, closed-circuit T.V., large-print photocopier, cassette books and magazines, children's books on cassette, home visits and other reference materials on blindness and other handicaps.

5514 Maine State Library
64 State House Station
Augusta, ME 04333　　207-287-5650
　　　　　　　　　　　　FAX: 207-287-5624
　　　e-mail: benitad@ursus3.ursus.maine.edu

Benita Davis, Cooridinator Special Services

Summer reading programs, cassette books and magazines, children's books on cassette, home visits and other reference materials on blindness and other handicaps.

　　　Newsl./BiAnnual

5515 New England Regional Genetics Group
PO Box 682
Gorham, ME 04038　　207-839-5324
　　　　　　　　　　　　FAX: 207-839-8637

Ms. A. Merrill Henderson, Coordinator

Human genetic services and educational planning pertaining to birth defects.

5516 Portland Public Library
5 Monument Square
Portland, ME 04101　　207-871-1700
　　　　　　　　　　　　FAX: 207-871-1703
　　　　　　　　　　www.portlandlibrary.com

Sheldon Kaye, Librarian

Summer reading programs, braille writer, magnifiers, closed-circuit T.V., large-print photocopier, cassette books and magazines, children's books on cassette, home visits and other reference materials on blindness and other handicaps.

5517 Voices for the Blind
PO Box 837
Bethel, ME 04217　　207-824-2920

Connie Hindman, Director

Tape library and depository for people with visual and learning disabilities. Recording services available by request.

5518 Waterville Public Library
73 Elm Street
Waterville, ME 04901　　207-873-4779
　　　　　　　　　　　　FAX: 207-873-4779

Meta Vigue, Librarian

Summer reading programs, braille writer, magnifiers, closed-circuit T.V., large-print photocopier, cassette books and magazines, children's books on cassette, home visits and other reference materials on blindness and other handicaps.

Maryland

5519 Friends of Libraries for Deaf Action

2930 Criaglawn Road
Silver Spring, MD   20904   301-572-5168
                                    FAX: 301-572-4134
                                    TDY:301-572-5168
                          e-mail: alhagemeyer@juno.com
                              www.librarydeaf.com

Alice L Hagemeyer, Founder

FOLDA is a subsidary of Library for Deaf Action. FOLDA has no membership dues. FOLDA encourages the deaf community to become involved in activities of their local public library and its friends. Some public libraries have FOLDA's copy of THE RED NOTEBOOK, an information service in the form of a regularly updated loose-leaf binder containing deaf fact sheets, library reprints, and announcements. Check website to keep up with library access for the public on hearing loss and ASL.

5520 Johns Hopkins University Dana Center for Preventive Ophthalmology

Wilmer Ophthalmology Institute
601 North Broadway
Baltimore, MD   21205   410-955-5080

Harry A. Quigley, Director

5521 Johns Hopkins University, Asthma and Allergy Center

5501 Hopkins Bayview Circle
Baltimore, MD   21224   410-550-2101
                                FAX: 410-550-2090

Dr. Lawrence Lichtenstein, Director

Studies of allergic diseases and individuals with allergic disease, pulmonary diseases and diseases involving inflammation and immunological processes.

5522 Maryland State Library for the Blind and Physically Handicapped

415 Park Avenue
Baltimore, MD   21201

                              800-964-9209
                          FAX: 410-333-2095
                          TDY:800-934-2541
                  e-mail: ms269@umail.umd.edu

Sharron McFarland, Librarian

Summer reading programs, braille writer, magnifiers, large-print photocopier, cassette books and magazines, children's books on cassette, and other reference materials on blindness and other handicaps.

5523 Montgomery County Department of Public Libraries/Special Needs Library

6400 Democracy Boulevard
Bethesda, MD   20817   301-897-2212

Charlette Stinnett, Head Librarian
Susan F. Cohen, Asst. Head Librarian

Serves the library information and reading needs of people with disabilities, family members, students and service providers. Some of its services include books, periodicals, and videos on disability issues, adaptive technology, community information; the National Library for the Blind and Physically Handicapped Talking Book program; large print books; and computer room with adaptive technology.

5524 National Epilepsy Library (NEL)

Epilepsy Foundation
4351 Garden City Drive
Landover, MD   20785   301-457-3700
                              800-332-4050
                          FAX: 301-577-4941
                      e-mail: postmaster@efa.org
                              www.efa.org

Cecille Jech, Manager, NEL Library

Contains information about epilepsy and seizure disorders and serves physicians and other health professionals. Provides in-house bibliographic database (ESDI), searches and documents delivery and interlibrary loans. Maintains the Albert and Ellen Grass Archives.

5525 National Rehabilitation Information Center NARIC

1010 Wayne Avenue
Suite 800
Silver Spring, MD   20910   301-562-2400
                                    800-346-2742
                              FAX: 301-562-2401
                              TDY:301-495-5626
                      e-mail: naricinfo@kra.com
                              www.naric.com

A national disability and rehabilitation library and information center that collects and disseminates the results of NIDRR-funded research projects. The collection, which also includes commercially published books, journals, articles and audiovisuals, grows at a rate of 300 documents a month. NARIC currently has more than 50,000 documents on all aspects of disability and rehabilitation. Searchable web page includes 5 databases and a calendar of events.

5526 Social Security Library

US Social Security Administration
PO Box 17330
Baltimore, MD   21235

                              800-772-1213
                              www.ssa.gov

Leo Hollenbeack, Reference Librarian

Information on social security and disability insurance.

5527 Virginia Prosthetics Research and Library

103 S Gay Street
Baltimore, MD 21202   410-962-3092

Helen Nowotarski, Technical Info. Spec

Audio visual programs, video and films on rehabilitation.

5528 Warren Grant Magnuson Clinical Center

Building 10-Room 1C255
9000 Rockville Pike
Bethesda, MD 20892   301-496-2563
                           FAX: 301-402-0664
                           www.cc.nih.gov

Established in 1953 as the research hospital of the National Institutes of Health. Designed so that patient care facilities are close to research laboratories so new findings of basic and clinical scientists can be quickly applied to the treatment of patients. Upon referral by physicians, patients are admitted to NIH clinical studies.

Massachusetts

5529 Affiliated Children's Arthritis Centers of New England

New England Medical Center
750 Washington Street
PO Box 286
Boston, MA 02111   617-636-5528
                          FAX: 617-350-8388

Jane G. Schaller, M.D., Coordinator

Research organization comprised of a network of 15 teritory pediatric centers throughout New England and based at the Floating Hospital of New England Medical Center.

5530 Berman-Gund Laboratory for the Study of Retinal Degenerations

Massachusetts Eye & Eye Infirmary
243 Charles Street
Boston, MA 02114   617-523-4545

5531 Boston University Arthritis Center

Conte Building
5th Floor
Boston, MA 02118   617-638-8000
                          FAX: 617-534-3573

Dr. Joseph Korn, M.D., Director

5532 Boston University Center for Human Genetics

80 E Concord Street
Boston, MA 02118   617-638-8000

Aubrey Milunsky, MD, Director

Offers research into genetic disorders and growth disorders.

5533 Boston University Robert Dawson Evans Memorial Dept. of Clinical Research

75 E Newton Street
Boston, MA 02118   617-638-7250
                          FAX: 617-638-7931

Dr. Joseph Loscalzo, Director

Integral unit of the University Hospital specializing in arthritis and connective tissue studies.

5534 Braile and Talking Book Library Perkins School for the Blind

175 N Beacon Street
Watertown, MA 02172   781-972-7240
                             800-852-3133
                        FAX: 781-972-7363
                        e-mail: perkins@bpl.org

Patricia Kirk

5535 Brigham and Women's Hospital, Asthma and Allergic Disease Research Center

75 Francis Street
Boston, MA 02115   617-732-5500
                          FAX: 617-432-0979

K. Frank Austen, MD, Director

Integral unit of the hospital focusing research attention on asthma and allergy related disorders.

5536 Brigham and Women's Hospital, Robert B. Brigham Multipurpose Arthritis Ctr.

75 Francis Street
Boston, MA 02115   617-732-5500

Dr. Matthew Liang, Director

Research studies into arthritis and rheumatic diseases.

5537 Caption Center

125 Western Avenue
Boston, MA 02134   617-492-9225
                          FAX: 617-562-0590

Lori Kay, Co-Director
Tom Apone, Co-Director

Provides closed captioning for videos, including training, safety, instructional and educational films. Maintains a consumer information service for overcoming communications barriers in the workplace.

5538 Center for Interdisciplinary Research on Immunologic Diseases

Children's Hospital Medical Center
300 Longwood Avenue
Boston, MA 02115   617-355-6000

Fred S. Rosen, MD, Prin. Investigator

Organizational research unit of the Children's Hospital that focuses on the causes, prevention and treatments of asthma, infections and allergies.

5539 Harvard University Howe Laboratory of Ophthalmology

Massachusetts Eye & Ear Infirmary
243 Charles Street
Boston, MA 02114   617-523-4545

Development ophthalmology and eye research.

5540 Laboure College Library

2120 Dorchester Avenue
Boston, MA 02124   617-296-8300

Maryann O'Toole, Director
Offers information on physical disabilities, independent living, peer counseling and advocacy.

5541 Massachusetts Rehabilitation Commission Library

27-43 Wormwood Street
Boston, MA 02210   617-727-2172
                         FAX: 617-727-1354
                         TDY: 617-727-9063

Elmer C. Bartels, Commissioner
Library and information science, rehabilitation and the handicapped.

5542 Talking Book Library at Worcester Public Library

3 Salem Square
Worcester, MA 01608   508-799-1730
                             800-762-0085
                         FAX: 508-799-1676
                         e-mail: jizatt@site.cwmars.org

James L. Izatt, Librarian
Summer reading programs, braille writer, magnifiers, closed-circuit T.V., large-print photocopier, cassette books and magazines, children's books on cassette, reference materials on blindness and other disabilities.

Michigan

5543 Burger School for the Autistic

30922 Beechwood Street
Garden City, MI 48135   734-425-5660

5544 Glaucoma Laser Trabeculoplasty Study

Sinai Hospital of Detroit
29275 Northwestern Highway
Southfield, MI 48034   248-493-5157

Hugh Beckman, Chairman
Examines the effectiveness and safety of the treatments of glaucoma.

5545 Grand Traverse Area Library for the Blind and Physically Handicapped

322 Sixth Street
Traverse City, MI 49684   616-935-6520
                             FAX: 616-922-0904
                             TDY: 616-922-0901

Evelyn Welty

5546 Kent County Library for the Blind

775 Ball Avenue NE
Grand Rapids, MI 49503   616-336-3250
                            FAX: 616-336-3256
                            e-mail: kdlem@lakeland.lib.mi.us

Claudya Muller, Librarian
Summer reading programs, braille writer, magnifiers, closed-circuit T.V., large-print photocopier, cassette books and magazines, children's books on cassette, home visits and other reference materials on blindness and other handicaps.

5547 Kent District Library for the Blind and Physically Handicapped

775 Ball Avenue NE
Grand Rapids, MI 49503   616-774-3250
                            FAX: 616-336-3256
                            e-mail: kdlsc@lakeland.lib.mi.us
                            www.kentlibrary.lib.mi.us

Claudya Muller, Director
Summer reading programs, braille writer, magnifiers, large-print photocopier, cassette books and magazines, children's books on cassette, and other reference materials on blindness and other handicaps.

5548 Library of Michigan Service for the Blind

PO Box 30007
Lansing, MI 48909   517-373-5614
                        FAX: 517-373-5865
                        e-mail: info@sbph.libomich.lib.mi.us

Maggie Bacon, Manager
Braille writer, magnifiers, closed-circuit T.V., large-print photocopier, cassette books and magazines, children's books on cassette, and other reference materials on blindness and other handicaps.

5549 Macomb Library for the Blind and Physically Handicapped

16480 Hall Road
Clinton Township, MI 48038   810-286-1580
                                FAX: 810-286-0634
                                e-mail: macbld@libcoop.net
                                www.libcoop.net/macspe

Beverlee Babcock, Librarian
Summer reading programs, braille writer, closed-circuit T.V., large-print books, cassette books and magazines, children's books on cassette, home visits and other reference materials on blindness and other handicaps, descriptive videos and bifokal kits.

5550 Michigan Capital Medical Center John W Chi Memorial Medical Library

2727 S Pennsylvania Avenue
Lansing, MI 48910   517-377-8332
                        FAX: 517-334-2939

Judith Barnes, Information Resources Coordinato
Extensive consumer health and patient education collection in books, videotapes, pamphlets. Open to the public.

5551 Michigan's Assistive Technology Resource

1023 S Us 27
St. Johns, MI   48879   517-224-0333
                                      800-274-7426
                              FAX: 517-224-0330
                    e-mail: matr@match.org
                              www.matr.org

Maryann Jones, Coordinator
R. Hunt Riegel, Ph.D., Interim Director

MATR provides a range of information, technical, and consultative services to ensure that chidren with disabilities receive services that will enable maximum performance in academic settings and daily living. A print shop on site provides Braille and large-print services. Also available are database searches for Braille, large-print and tape cassettes. We are a state-wide agency funded by the Michigan Department of Education and a member of the Alliance For Technology Access.

5552 Mideastern Michigan Library Co-op

G-4195 W Pasadena Avenue
Flint, MI   48504   810-232-7119
                              FAX: 810-732-1715
            e-mail: cnash@genesse.freeret.org
                      www.falcon.edu/libraries

Carolyn Nash, Librarian

Summer reading programs, braille writer, magnifiers, closed-circuit T.V., large-print photocopier, cassette books and magazines, children's books on cassette, home visits and other reference materials on blindness and other handicaps.

5553 Muskegon County Library for the Blind

97 East Apple Avenue
Muskegon, MI   49442   231-724-6257
                              FAX: 231-724-6675
                              TDY:231-722-4103
                      www.lakeland.lib.mi.us

Sheila Miller, Librarian

Braille typewriter, magnifiers, closed-circuit T.V., large-print photocopier, cassette books and magazines, children's books on cassette, home visits and other reference materials on blindness and other handicaps, The Reading Edge, and large print books.

5554 Northland Library Cooperative

316 E Chisholm
Alpena, MI   49707   517-356-1622
                              FAX: 517-354-3939
                    e-mail: nlc.lib.mi.us/lbph.htm

Catherine Glomski, Librarian

Summer reading programs, braille writer, magnifiers, closed-circuit T.V., large-print photocopier, cassette books and magazines, children's books on cassette, home visits and other reference materials on blindness and other handicaps.

5555 Oakland County Library for the Blind and Physically Handicapped

1200 N Telegraph Dept 482
Pontiac, MI   48341   248-673-4496
                              FAX: 248-452-9145
            e-mail: oakllbph@oakland.lib.mi.us
                www.oakland.lib.mi.us/oakllbph.htm

Betty Ramey

5556 St. Clair County Library Special Technologies Alternative Resources (S.T.A.R.)

210 McMorran Boulevard
Port Huron, MI   48060   810-987-3600
                                      800-272-8570
                              FAX: 810-987-7327
                  e-mail: star@gccl.lib.mi.us
                        sccl.lib.mi.us/star.html

Mary Jo Koch, Subregional Librarian

Offers library services to the blind, deaf and blind, visually disabled, phsyically disabled, and reading disabled.

5557 University of Michigan, Orthopaedic Research Laboratories

400 N Ingalls Building
Ann Arbor, MI   48109   734-763-6784
                              FAX: 734-747-0003

Dr. S.A. Goldstein, Director

Develops and studies the causes and treatments for arthritis including new devices and assistive aids.

5558 Upper Peninsula Library for the Blind

1615 Presque Isle Avenue
Marquette, MI   49855   906-228-7697
                                      800-562-8985
                              FAX: 906-228-5627
                  e-mail: rruff@uproc.lib.mi.us

Ruth Ruff, Librarian

Summer reading programs, braille writer, magnifiers, closed-circuit T.V., large-print photocopier, cassette books and magazines, children's books on cassette, home visits and other reference materials on blindness and other handicaps.

5559 Washtenaw County Library

PO Box 8645
Ann Arbor, MI   48107   734-971-6059
                              FAX: 734-971-3892
                    e-mail: wash@tln.lib.mi.us

Margoret Wolfe, Librarian

Summer reading programs, braille writer, magnifiers, closed-circuit T.V., large-print photocopier, cassette books and magazines, children's books on cassette, home visits and other reference materials on blindness and other handicaps.

5560 Washtenaw County Library for the Blind & Physically Handicapped

4133 Washtenaw Avenue
Ann Arbor, MI   48108   734-971-6059
                              FAX: 734-971-3892
        www.co.washtenaw.mi.us/depts/lib/liblbpd.html

Mary Udoji, Director

Michigan Subregional Library, Library of Congress National Library Service network. General library service for persons unable to use standard print materials for various physical reasons. Lends audio books and listening equipment, large type books, descriptive videos. Provides reference information and programs. Kurzweil scanner with components which convert standard print to Braille, large type or audio and closed circuit TV magnifier on site.

5561 Wayne County Regional Library for the Blind

30555 Michigian Avenue
Westland, MI 48186   734-727-7300
                                   888-968-2737
                              FAX: 734-727-7333
                              TDY:313-326-3008
e-mail: wcrlbph@wayneregional.lib.mi.us
wayneregional.lib.mi.us

Frederick R Howkins, Director

Summer reading programs, braille writer, magnifiers, closed-circuit T.V., large-print photocopier, cassette books and magazines, children's books on cassette, and other reference materials on blindness and other handicaps.

5562 Wayne State University, C.S. Mott Center for Human Genetics and Development

275 E Hancock Street
Detroit, MI 48201   313-577-4603
                              FAX: 313-577-8554

Dr. Ernest Abel, Director
Human growth and development disorders.

Minnesota

5563 Century College

3300 Century Avenue North
White Bear Lake, MN 55110   651-779-3300
                                   800-228-1978
                              FAX: 651-779-5779
                              www.centurycollege.net

Ed Haddon, Faculty
Jill Gebhardt, Public Relations

Programs of study - Orthotic Practitioner, Orthotic Technician, Prosethetic Practitioner, Prosthetic Technician. In addition, Century College offers more than 50 other programs in liberal arts, career and occupational programs.

5564 Communication Center/Minnesota State Services for the Blind

2200 University Avenue West
240
Saint Paul, MN 55114   651-642-0500
                                   800-652-9000
                              FAX: 651-649-5927
e-mail: chamilto@ssb.state.mn.us

Chuck Hamilton, Director

Special library service for the blind and physically handicapped providing tape and braille transcription of textbooks and vocational materials; Minnesota Radio Talking Book providing current newspaper, magazines, and best selling books; Dial-in-News, a touch tone phone accessed newspaper service; Library of Congress cassette and phonograph talking book equipment; repair services for special audio reading equipment, with most services free to Minnesota Residents.

5565 Duluth Public Library

520 W Superior Street
Duluth, MN 55802   218-723-3821

Randall Vogt, Coordinator

Adapted access to Apple computer, adapted toys and adapted library equipment.

5566 Minnesota Library for the Blind

Lighway 298
PO Box 68
Fairbault, MN 55021   507-332-3279
                              FAX: 507-332-3260

Nancy Walton, Librarian

Summer reading programs, braille writer, magnifiers, closed-circuit T.V., large-print photocopier, cassette books and magazines, children's books on cassette, home visits and other reference materials on blindness and other handicaps.

5567 Minnesota Library for the Blind and Physically Handicapped

Highway 298
PO Box 68
Faribault, MN 55021   507-332-3279
                                   800-722-0550
                              FAX: 507-332-3260
e-mail: libblnd@sate.mn.us

Nancy Walton, Program Director
Rene Perrance, Librarian

Provides books and magazines in Braille, large print, records, and cassettes to qualified residents of Minnesota who have a visual or physical impairment, including reading disabilities due to an organic cause certified by a Medical Doctor, that prevents residents from reading standard print or physically handling a book. Equipment for in-house use include magnifiers, braillers, listening equipment, and CCTV. Reference collection for in-house use only on visual impairment topics.

5568 National Resource Library on Youth with Disabilities

University of Minnesota
Box 721-UMHC
Minneapolis, MN 55455   612-625-5000

Offers comprehensive sources of information related to adolescents, disability and transition. The database contains bibliographic, programs, training/education and technical assistance files for the medical community, families, parents and children with chronic illnesses.

Mississippi

5569 Mississippi Library Commission

5455 Executive Plaza
Jackson, MS 39206   601-354-7208
                           FAX: 601-354-6077
                           TDY:601-354-6411
                           e-mail: tbbs@mls.lib.ms.us
                           www.mlc.lib.ms.us

Rahya Puckett, Librarian
Summer reading programs, braille writer, magnifiers, closed-circuit T.V., large-print photocopier, cassette books and magazines, children's books on cassette, home visits and other reference materials on blindness and other handicaps.

5570 Mississippi Library Commission\Talking Book and Braille Services

5455 Executive Plaza
Jackson, MS 39206   601-366-5112
                           800-446-0892
                           FAX: 601-731-3405
                           e-mail: tbbs@mlc.lib.ms.us
                           www.mlc.lib.ms.us

Rahye Puckett, Coordinator
Library service for the print handicapped braille, cassette and disc materials (books & periodicals) for children and adults. Large print RG production (copier & printer), braille embosser and other handicaps.

5571 Mississippi Project START (Success Through Assistive/Rehab Technology)

PO Box 1698
Jackson, MS 39215   601-987-4872
                           800-852-8328
                           FAX: 601-364-2349
                           TDY:601-987-4872
                           e-mail: xposdf@mdrs.state.ms.us

Eugenie Bradshaw, Public Contact
Multifaceted, collaborative effort which includes an advisory council, information clearinghouse, training program, model service-delivery system and an equipment loan program.

Missouri

5572 Assemblies of God National Center for the Blind, Adriene Resource Center for Blind Children

1445 Boonville Avenue
Springfield, MO 65802   417-862-2781
                           FAX: 417-862-5120
                           e-mail: blind@ag.org
                           www.ag.org

Paul Weingartner, National Director
Offers Braille and cassette lending library, Braille and cassette Sunday School materials for all ages, Braille and cassette periodicals, resource assistance, and resources for blind children and children of blind parents.

5573 Assembllies of God National Center for the Blind

1445 N Boonville Avenue
Springfield, MO 65802   417-862-2781
                           FAX: 417-863-7276

Paul Weingariner, Librarian
Offers braille and cassette lending library, braille and cassette Sunday school materials for all ages, braille and cassette periodicals and resource assistance.

5574 Church of the Nazarene

Nazarene Publishing House
Box 419527
Kansas City, MO 64141   816-931-1900

Offers braille and large print books. Also offers a lending library and cassettes for the blind.

5575 Judevine Center for Autism

9455 Rott Road
St. Louis, MO 63127   314-849-4440

5576 Lutheran Library for the Blind

Lutheran Church - Missouri Synod
1333 South Kirkwood Road
Saint Louis, MO 63122   314-965-9000
                           800-433-3954
                           FAX: 314-965-0959
                           e-mail: ic_borchele@icms.org
                           www.blindmission.org

Lynne Borchelt, Administrative Assistant
Offers Christian books in braille and large print books and cassettes for the blind and visually impaired, on loan, as well as Christian periodicals in braille, large print and cassette tape.

5577 University of Missouri, Columbia Arthritis Center

MA427 Health Sciences Center
1 Hospital Drive
Columbia, MO 65212   573-882-8738
                           FAX: 573-884-3996

Gordon C. Sharp, MD, Director
Research into arthritis and rheumatic diseases.

5578 Wolfner Library for the Blind

PO Box 387
Jefferson City, MO 65102   573-751-8720
                           800-392-2614
                           FAX: 573-526-2985
                           TDY:800-347-1379
                           e-mail: wolfner@mailsos.state.mo.us

Sara Parker, State Librarian
Free library service in alternate formats, braille, recorded, large print. For any Missouri resident who cannot read standard print, due to a physical disability. Summer reading programs, braille writer, magnifiers, closed-circuit T.V., large-print photocopier, cassette books and magazines, children's books on cassette, home visits and other reference materials on blindness and other handicaps.

Montana

5579 MonTECH University of Montana

Rural Institute on Disabilities
634 Eddy Avenue
Missoula, MT   59812   406-243-5676
                                            800-732-0323
                                       FAX: 406-243-4730
                                       TDY:406-243-5676
              e-mail: montech@selway.umt.edu
      http://ruralinstitute.umt.edu/HDC/montech.htm

Gail McGregor, Project Director

Develops a comprehensive statewide system of technology-related assistance to ensure that all Montanans with disabilites have equitable access to the
assistive technology devices and services they need.

**5580 Montana State Library/Montana Talking Book
Library**

1515 E Sixth Avenue
PO Box 201800
Helena, MT   59620   406-444-2064
                                            800-332-3400
                                       FAX: 406-444-0266
                                       TDY:406-444-5431
              e-mail: cbriggs@msl.state.mt.us
                    www.msl.state.mt.us/tbl

Christie Briggs, Supervisor

Over 50,000 titles on 4-track cassette, WebBraille,
Web0pac, WebBlud, summer reading programs,
braille writer, magnifiers, closed-circuit T.V., large-
print photocopier, cassette books and magazines,
children's books on cassette, home visits and other
reference materials on blindness and other handicaps.
Large print and Braille services to blind, low vision,
physically handicapped and reading disabled citizens
of Montana.

5581 Montana State Library\Talking Book Library

1515 E 6th Avenue
Helena, MT   59601   406-444-3115
                                            800-332-3400
                                       FAX: 406-444-5612
                                       www.msl.state.mt.us

Sandra Jarbie, Librarian

Summer reading programs, braille writer, magnifiers,
large-print photocopier, cassette books and magazines, children's books on cassette, and other reference materials on blindness and other handicaps.

Nebraska

5582 Martin Luther Home Society Resource Center

804 J Street
Suite 305
Lincoln, NE   68508
                                            800-443-4899
              e-mail: mlhs_MEINTS@compuserve.com

Alice Meints, Resource Center Dir.
Fred Naumann III, Communications Dir.

Provides materials and opportunities for consultation
with individuals and communities assisting persons
with special needs.

5583 Nebraska Assistive Technology Partnership
Nebraska Department of Education

5143 South 48th Street
Suite C
Lincoln, NE   68516   402-471-0734
                                            888-806-6287
                                       FAX: 402-471-6052
                                       TDY:402-471-0735
              e-mail: atp@atp.state.ne.us
                    www.nde.state.ne.us/ATP/

Mark Schultz, Project Director
Kathryn Kruse, Public Contact

Provides statewide assistive technology and home
modification services for Nebraskans of all ages and
disabilities.

**5584 Nebraska Library Commission, Talking Book and
Braille Service**

Talking Book and Braille Service
1200 North Street
Suite 120
Lincoln, NE   68508
                                            800-742-7691
                                       FAX: 402-471-6244
              e-mail: readadv@nlc.state.ne.us
                    www.nlc.state.ne.us/tbbs/tbbs2.html

Dave Oertli, Program Director

Summer reading programs, braille writer, magnifiers,
closed-circuit T.V., large-print photocopier, cassette
books and magazines, children's books on cassette,
home visits and other reference materials on blindness and other handicaps.

Nevada

5585 Las Vegas-Clark County Library District

1401 E Flamingo Road
Las Vegas, NV   89119   702-382-3493
                                       FAX: 702-733-1567

Mary Anne Morton, Librarian

Summer reading programs, braille writer, magnifiers,
closed-circuit T.V., large-print photocopier, cassette
books and magazines, children's books on cassette,
home visits and other reference materials on blindness and other handicaps.

5586 Nevada Assistive Technology Collaborative
Nevada Rehabilitation Division

Community-Based Services
711 South Stewart Street
Carson City, NV   89710   775-687-4452
                                            888-337-3839
                                       FAX: 775-687-3292
                                       TDY:775-687-3388

Paul Haugen, Public Contact

Accomplishing 15 major goals in systems change that
have been established in response to identified needs
in consultation with the state's consumer-directed
executive board.

5587 **Nevada State Library and Archives**
Capitol Complex
Carson City, NV 89710   775-687-5469
FAX: 702-687-8311
TDY:702-687-8338
e-mail: putnam@equinox.unr.edu

Kevin E. Putnam, Librarian
Summer reading programs, braille writer, magnifiers, closed-circuit T.V., large-print photocopier, cassette books and magazines, children's books on cassette, home visits and other reference materials on blindness and other handicaps.

New Hampshire

5588 **New Hampshire State Library**
117 Pleasant Street
Concord, NH 03301   603-226-2900

e-mail: talking@lilac.nhsh.lib.nh.us
www.state.nh.us

Eileen Keim, Librarian
Summer reading programs, braille writer, magnifiers, closed-circuit T.V., large-print photocopier, cassette books and magazines, children's books on cassette, home visits and other reference materials on blindness and other handicaps.

5589 **Voices for the Blind**
PO Box 781
Barrington, NH 03825

Connie Hindman, Director
Tape library and depository for people with visual and learning disabilities. Recording services available by request.

New Jersey

5590 **Children's Specialized Hospital Medical Library/ Parent Resource Center**
150 New Providence Road
Mountainside, NJ 07092   908-233-3720
FAX: 908-301-5576

Contains some 3,000 books, and journals specializing in nursing, pediatrics, child neurology, and rehabilitation. Also provides a Parent Resource Center, a special collection of books, videos and pamphlets designed to meet the information needs of parents and families, as well as the local community.

5591 **Eye Institute of New Jersey**
New Jersey Medical School
90 Bergen Street
Newark, NJ 07103   973-982-4812

Marshall S. Klein, Director
Ophthamology, including research into corenea, retina and neuro-ophthamalogy.

5592 **Mycoclonus Research Foundation**
200 Old Palisade Road
Suite 17D
Fort Lee, NJ 07024   201-585-0770
FAX: 201-585-0770

Supports clinical and basic research into the cause and treatment of myoclonus; four international workshops facilitated the sharing of information by physicians, scientists, and investigators active in the field, resulted in three publications; supports promising research projects, clinical neurological fellows, with special emphasis on posthypoxic myoclonus and encourages all who are interested in futhering the understanding, treatment, and cure of myoclonus.

5593 **New Jersey Center for Outreach and Services for the Autism Community (COSAC)**
1450 Parkside Avenue
Suite 22
Ewing, NJ 08638   609-883-8100
800-428-8476
FAX: 609-883-5509
e-mail: information@njcosac.org
www.njcosac.org

Paul A Potito, Executive Director
Purpose is to assist families, individuals and agencies concerned with the welfare and education of children and adults with autism and other pervasive development disorders.

5594 **New Jersey Library for the Blind and Handicapped**
2300 Stuyvesant Avenue
PO Box 501
Trenton, NJ 08625   609-530-6527
800-792-8322
FAX: 609-530-6384
TDY:877-882-5593
e-mail: njlbh@njstatelib.org
www.state.nj.us/statelibrary/njlbh.htm

Deborah Toomey-Rutledge, Director
Luz Sanchez, Outreach Services
Karen Messick, Children's Services
Summer reading programs, braille writer, magnifiers, closed-circuit T.V., large-print, cassette, braille books and magazines, children's books on cassette, and other reference materials on blindness and other handicaps. Provides reading material on audio, cassette, large print and Braille to eligible NJ residents.

New Mexico

5595 **Los Lunas Hospital and Training School**
PO Box 1269
Los Lunas, NM 87031   505-866-1405

Jeannie Stanfield, Director
Information on mental retardation and medical librarianship.

5596 New Mexico State Library for the Blind and Physically Handicapped

325 Don Gaspar Avenue
Santa Fe, NM 87501 505-754-2437
FAX: 505-827-3888
e-mail: jbrewstr@stlib.state.nm.us
www.stlib.state.nm.us

Glee Wenzel, Librarian

Summer reading programs, braille writer, magnifiers, closed-circuit T.V., large-print photocopier, cassette books and magazines, children's books on cassette, home visits and other reference materials on blindness and other handicaps.

New York

5597 Braille Book Bank

National Braille Association
3 Townline Circle
Rochester, NY 14623 716-427-8260

Contains over 1800 titles and braille music scores that are constantly being updated and enlarged by transcriptions from BTAS and RTR. Braille readers from the United States and several foreign countries order materials annually.

5598 Braille Textbook Assignment Service

National Braille Association
3 Townline Circle
Rochester, NY 14623 716-427-8260

Certified braillists provide readers with technical and nontechnical materials by transcribing for this service.

5599 Center on Human Policy

Syracuse University
805 S Crouse Avenue
Syracuse, NY 13244 315-443-3851
800-894-0826
FAX: 315-443-4338
e-mail: thechp@sued.syr.edu
soeweb.syr.edu/thechp/

Steve Taylor, Director
Rachael Zubal, Information Coordinator

The Center on Human Policy is a Syracuse University-based policy, research, and advocacy organization involved in the national movement to ensure the rights of people with disabilities.

5600 Eastern Paralyzed Veterans Association

75-20 Astoria Boulevard
Flushing, NY 11370 718-397-4181
800-444-0120
FAX: 718-803-0414
e-mail: info@epva.org
www.epva.org

Angela Wu, Library Director

Library offering information on physical disabilities, spinal cord injury and rehabilitation. Also provides literature searches on specific topics. Association news and free publications on architecture and barrier-free designs, legislation and other current events affecting Americans with Disabilities.

5601 Ehrman Medical Library

New York University Medical Center
550 1st Avenue
New York, NY 10016 212-263-5372
FAX: 212-263-6534

Barbara Schiffer, Librarian

Statistics, reports and evaluation.

5602 Foundation Center

79 Fifth Avenue
Department ZE
New York, NY 10003 212-421-0771
800-424-9836
FAX: 212-807-3677
www.fdncenter.org

Thomas Buckman, President

The Center disseminates current information on foundation and corporate giving through our national collections in New York City and Washington D.C., our field offices in San Francisco and our network of over 180 cooperating libraries in all 50 states and abroad.

5603 Helen Keller National Center

111 Middle Neck Road
Sands Point, NY 11050 516-944-8900
FAX: 516-944-7302

Provides diagnostic, evaluation, short term comprehensive rehabilitation and personal adjustment training. A technical assistance center is offered providing assistance to public and private agencies and to parent groups who work towards community integration and the enhancement of the quality of life. A national parent network is also provided that develops and shares information about advocacy, legislation, new services and achievements.

5604 Helen Keller Worldwide

90 Washington Street
New York, NY 10006 212-766-5266
FAX: 212-791-7590

Joh M. Palmer, Executive Director

Nonprofit organization for the blind.

5605 Institute for Basic Research in Developmental Disabilities

1050 Forest Hill Road
Staten Island, NY 10314 718-494-0600
FAX: 718-494-0837

Conducts research into neurodegenerative diseases, Alzheimer's disease, developmental disabilities, fragile X syndrome, Down's Syndrome, autism, epilepsy and basic science issues underlying all developmental disabilities.

5606 Institute for Visual Sciences
1 E 71st Street
New York, NY   10021   212-305-2919

Melissa Mount, Executive Director
Ophthalmology with emphasis on the development of
care for the eye.

5607 JGB Audio Library for the Blind
15 West 65th Street
New York, NY   10023   212-769-6771
                               800-284-4422
                          FAX: 212-769-6266

Peter Williamson
Ken Stanley
Books (best sellers) on tape. Also monthly audio
cassettes of top news stories from TIME & PEOPLE.

$25 Annual fee

5608 JGB Cassette Library International
15 W 65th Street
New York, NY   10023   212-769-6331

Bruce Massis
Summer reading programs, braille writer, magnifiers,
closed-circuit T.V., large-print photocopier, cassette
books and magazines, children's books on cassette,
home visits and other reference materials on blindness and other handicaps.

5609 Keren-Or
1133 Broadway
Suite 1227/1228
New York, NY   10010   212-255-1180

Paul Goldenberg, Executive Director
Maintains the Keren-Or Center for the Multiply
Handicapped Blind Child in Jerusalem for rehabilitation and training. Funds acquired through contributions, bequests and legacies.

5610 Medical Diagnostic Laboratory
3250 Westchester Avenue
Bronx, NY   10461   212-828-1500

Offers comprehensive parasitological testing.

5611 Monroe Developmental Center
620 Westfall Road
Rochester, NY   14620   716-461-8970
                          FAX: 716-473-1963
                e-mail: folwelbe@nysomr.emi.com

Steve Jarose, Staff Development
Information on mental retardation and developmental
disabilities.

5612 Nassau Library System
900 Jerusalem Avenue
Uniondale, NY   11553   516-292-8920
                          FAX: 516-481-4777
                     e-mail: nls@lilrc.org

Dorothy Pruyear, Librarian
Summer reading programs, braille writer, magnifiers,
closed-circuit T.V., large-print photocopier, cassette
books and magazines, children's books on cassette,
home visits and other reference materials on blindness and other handicaps.

**5613 New York Public Library: Andrew Heiskell
Library for the Blind and Physically Handicapped**
40 W 20th Street
New York, NY   10011   212-206-5400
                          FAX: 212-206-5418
                          TDY:212-206-5458
                e-mail: ablgph@nypl.org
                www.nypl.org/branch/lb/

Kathleen Rowan, Regional Librarian
By mail and on-site offers talking books and braille
books to eligible patrons in New York City and Long
Island. Additional on-site services include large-
print books, books on tape, descriptive videos, class
visits, programs, and assistive devices such as closed
circuit televisions and Karzweil Personal Readers

5614 New York State Talking Book & Braille Library
Empire State Plaza CEC
Albany, NY   12230   518-862-1090
                          FAX: 518-474-5786
                          TDY:518-474-7121
                e-mail: jane@unix2.nysed.gov
                www.suffolk.lib.ny.us

Jane Somers, Director
Books on audio cassette, cassette players, braille
books, summer reading programs, braille writer,
magnifiers, closed-circuit T.V., large-print photocopier, cassette books and magazines, children's
books on cassette, reference materials on blindness
and other handicaps.

5615 Postgraduate Center for Mental Health
124 E 28th Street
New York, NY   10016   212-689-7700
                          FAX: 212-696-1679

Leona Mackler, Director
Information on mental health.

5616 Reader-Transcriber Registry
National Braille Association
3 Townline Circle
Rochester, NY   14623   716-427-8260

Certified braillists fill requests for college textbooks and other technical works through this
service of the National Braille Association.

5617 Rehabilitation Research Library
Human Resources Center
Albertson, NY   11507   516-741-2010
                          FAX: 516-746-3298

Amnon Tishler, Research Librarian

Information on rehabilitation and occupational rehabilitation.

5618 State University of New York Health Sciences Center

450 Clarkson Avenue
PO Box 32
Brooklyn, NY 11203 718-778-5332
FAX: 718-778-5397

Adolf Christ, Director
Child psychiatry research programs.

5619 Suffolk Cooperative Library System

Somerset State Hospital
627 N Sunrise Service Road
Bellport, NY 11713 516-286-1600

Julie Klauber, Adjunct Professor
Talking books services.

5620 Suffolk Cooperative Library System - Talking Books Plus

627 N Sunrise Highway
Bellport, NY 11713 516-286-1600
FAX: 516-286-1647
e-mail: lbph@suffolk.lib.ny.us
www.suffolk.lib.ny.us/tbp

Julie Klauber, Librarian
Talking book services, assistive device center, disability reference, information and referral services for local libraries, organizations and residents.

5621 Wallace Memorial Library

Rochester Institute of Technology
1 Lomb Memorial Drive
Rochester, NY 14623 716-475-2562
FAX: 716-475-7007
TDY:716-475-2760
wally.rit.edu

Joan Naturale, Special Needs Ref. Librarian
Information on physical disabilities and deafness.

5622 Xavier Society for the Blind

154 E 23rd Street
New York, NY 10010 212-473-7800
800-637-9193

Alfred Cervana, Executive Director
Robert Nealon, Librarian

Provides spiritual and inspirational reading material to visually impaired persons in suitable format: braille, large print and cassette, throughout U.S. and Canada. Services are provided both by way of regular periodical publications sent through the mail and non-returnable; and by means of a lending library where books are returned. All services are provided free. Interested readers can write or phone using toll-free number 10am to noon; 1pm to 4pm EST, Mondays thru Fridays.

North Carolina

5623 Autism Society of North Carolina

Autism Society of North Carolina Bookstore
505 Oberlin Road
Suite 230
Raleigh, NC 27605 919-743-0204
800-442-2762
FAX: 919-743-0208
e-mail: ASNC@aol.com
www.autismsociety-nc.org

Offers a library that carries one of the largest selections of books about autism.

5624 Duke University Asthma and Allergic Disease Center

School of Medicine
Box 2898
Durham, NC 27710 919-684-2922

Rebecca H. Buckley, Director

5625 Great Smokies Diagnostic Laboratory

18A Regent Park Boulevard
Asheville, NC 28806
800-522-4762

Offers a comprehensive profile of tests.

5626 North Carolina Library for the Blind

1811 Capital Boulevard
Raleigh, NC 27635 919-733-4376
888-388-2460
FAX: 919-733-6910
TDY:919-733-1462
e-mail: nclbph@library.dcr.state.nc.us

Francine Martin, Librarian

Provides free loan of books in cassette tape, braille and large-print formats for North Carolinana who cannot read standard print due to a visual or physical disability.

5627 North Carolina Library for the Blind and Physically Handicapped

1811 Capital Boulevard
Raleigh, NC 27604 919-676-2288
800-662-7726
FAX: 919-733-6910
e-mail: ncleph@ncsl.dcr.state.nc.us

Francine Martin, Librarian

Free loan of large print, braille, and cassette tape books and magazines and specialized playback equipment to registered eligible North Carolinians. Call for an application form. Collection contains general fiction and nonfiction titles. Registered borrowers may subscribe to receive descriptive videos for a one time fee.

5628 Pediatric Rheumatoid Clinic

Duke Medical Center
Box 3212
Durham, NC 27710 919-684-6575
FAX: 919-681-8943

Dr. Deborah Kredich, Chairman

Clinical and laboratory pediatric rheumatoid studies.

5629 University of North Carolina at Chapel Hill, Brain Research Center
CB 7250
Chapel Hill, NC 27599   919-966-2405
                            FAX: 919-966-1844

Kunihiko Suzuki, MD, Director

North Dakota

5630 North Dakota State Library Talking Book Services
604 East Boulevard Avenue
Department 250
Bismarck, ND 58505   701-328-1408
                         800-843-9948
                         FAX: 701-328-2040
                         TDY:800-892-8622
                         e-mail: tbooks@state.nd.us.
                         ndsl.lib.state.nd.us

Terri Wilhelm, Talking Book Manager

5631 Services for the Visually Impaired - Department of Public Instruction
PO Box 8117
Grand Forks, ND 58202   701-777-2577

Betty Bender
Eligible readers of North Dakota receive library service from the regional library in Pierre, South Dakota.

Ohio

5632 American Council of Blind Parents
34400 Cedar Road
Apartment 108
University Heights, OH 44121   216-381-1822

Nola Webb, President
Members are sighted parents of blind or visually impaired children. Offers a forum for support and outreach, sharing of experiences in parent-child relationships, and educational and cultural information about child development. Monitors developments in technical and legislative arenas.

5633 Case Western Reserve University
25100 Euclid Avenue
Suite 105
Cleveland, OH 44117   216-731-3217
                          800-666-2353

Jeanne O'Malley Teeter, Manager
Research in electrical stimulation and rehabilitation technology.

5634 Case Western Reserve University Northeast Ohio Multipurpose Arthritis Center
University Hospitals of Cleveland
2074 Abington Road
Cleveland, OH 44106   216-844-7242
                          FAX: 216-844-5172

Dr. Roland Moskowitz, Director
Basic and clinical research into the causes, diagnosis and treatment of arthritis.

5635 Cleveland FES Center
11000 Cedar Avenue
Cleveland, OH 44106
                          800-666-2353
                          FAX: 216-231-3258
                          e-mail: clevefes@po.cwru.edu
                          feswww.fes.cwru.edu

Jeanne O'Malley Teeter, Communications Dir.
Research and development center on functional electrical stimulation. Houses the FES Information Center, a resource center with a library. Publications, newsletters and videotapes for persons with disabilities and others interested in electrical stimulation are offered.

5636 Cleveland Public Library
17121 Lake Shore Boulevard
Cleveland, OH 44110   216-623-2911
                          FAX: 330-623-7036
                          e-mail: lbphmgr1@library.cpl.org
                          www.lbph@cpi.org

Barbara Mates, Librarian
Summer reading programs, braille writer, magnifiers, closed-circuit T.V., large-print photocopier, cassette books and magazines, children's books on cassette, and other reference materials on blindness and other handicaps.

5637 Clovernook Center - Oportunities for the Blind
7000 Hamilton Avenue
Cincinnati, OH 45231   513-522-3860
                           888-234-7156
                           FAX: 513-728-3950
                           www.clovernook.org

Non-profit organization which offers various braille library services, rehabilitation, manufacturing employment opportunities and more for the visually impaired.

5638 Ohio Regional Library for the Blind and Physically Handicapped
800 Vine Street
Library Square
Cincinnati, OH 45202
                          800-582-0335
                          FAX: 513-369-3111
                          TDY:513-369-6072
                          e-mail: ifbaplch.lib.oh.us
                          plch.lib.oh.us

Donna Foust, Librarian
Summer reading programs, braille writer, magnifiers, closed-circuit T.V., large-print photocopier, cassette books and magazines, children's books on cassette, and other reference materials on blindness and other handicaps.

5639 State Library of Ohio - Talking Book Program

274 E 1st Avenue
Columbus, OH 43201   614-644-6895
FAX: 614-995-2186

Judith Bow
A machine-lending agency for the visually impaired.

5640 University Affiliated Cincinnati Center for Developmental Disabilities

Elland & Bethesda Avenues
Cincinnati, OH 45229   513-559-4626

Dr. Jack Rubinstein, Director

Oklahoma

5641 Oklahoma Library for the Blind & Physically Handicapped

300 NE 18th Street
Oklahoma City, OK 73105   405-521-3514
FAX: 405-521-4582
e-mail: olbph@altn.odl.state.ok.us
www.state.ok.us/~library

Geraldine Adams, Librarian
Braille writer, magnifiers, closed-circuit T.V., large-print photocopier, cassette books and magazines, children's books on cassette, home visits and other reference materials on blindness and other handicaps.

5642 Oklahoma Medical Research Foundation

825 NE 13th Street
Oklahoma City, OK 73104   405-271-6673
FAX: 405-271-3980

J. Donald Capra, M.D., President
Focuses on arthritis and muscoloskeletal disease research.

5643 Tulsa City-County Library System - Outreach Services

400 Civic Center
Tulsa, OK 74103   918-596-7922
FAX: 918-596-7941
e-mail: astephe@tulsalibrary.org
www.tulsalibrary.org

Amy Stephens, Librarian
Homebound delivery of library services for the physically disabled.

Oregon

5644 Oregon Health Sciences University, Elks' Children's Eye Clinic

Casey Eye Institute
3375 South West Terwilliger Boulevard
Portland, OR 97201   503-494-7672
FAX: 503-494-5347
e-mail: Roystere@ohsu.edu
www.ohsu.edu/cei/ecec.html

Earl A. Palmer, MD, Director
Eleen Reyster, Clinic Manager
The elks children's eye clinic is the major charitable project of the Oregon State Elks association. The clinic would not be possible without the organization's dedication and commitment to providing eye care for babies and children.

5645 Oregon Talking Book & Braille Services

250 Winter Street NE
Salem, OR 97301   541-737-6145
800-452-0292
FAX: 503-588-7119
TDY:503-378-4276
e-mail: carolynn.m.avery@state.or.us
www.osl.state.or.us/tbooks/tbooks.html

Carolynn Avery, Regional Librarian
We serve the blind and physically handicapped. Cassette books and magazines, Braille books-magazines, for children and adults. Descriptive videos. Audio-cassette machines are provided free of charge. Call us for an application.

5646 Talking Back & Braille Services Oregon State Library

State Library Building
Salem, OR 97310   503-378-3849
FAX: 503-588-7119
e-mail: tbabs@sparkie.osl.state.or.us
www.osl.state.or.us/tbabs/tbabs.html

Donna Bensen, Librarian
Braille writer, magnifiers, large-print photocopier, cassette books and magazines, children's books on cassette and braille books.

Pennsylvania

5647 Carnegie Library of Pittsburgh Library for the Blind & Physically Handicapped

Leonard C. Staisey Building
4724 Baum Boulevard
Pittsburgh, PA 15213   412-687-2440
800-242-0586
FAX: 412-687-2442
e-mail: clbph@clpgh.org
www.clpgh.org/clp/LBPH

Sue Murdock, Director
Kathleen Kappel, Assistant

Loans recorded books/magazines and playback equipmetn, large print books and described videos to western PA residents unable to use standard printed materials due to a visual, physical, or physically-based reading disability.

5648 Free Library of Philadelphia Library for the Blind and Physically Handicapped

919 Walnut Street
Philadelphia, PA 19107   215-683-3213
    800-222-1754
    FAX: 215-683-3211
e-mail: flpblind@library.phila.gov

Vickie Lange Collins, Administrator
Richard Riddell, Technical Services Manager
Reneee Snowten, Public Services Manager

Summer reading programs for children and teens. Closed-circuit T.V.for enlarging print for low vision; computers with screen readers and large print; cassette books and magazines; braille books and magazines; and descriptive videos for the blind and visually impaired.

5649 Hahnemann University, Orthopedic and Arthritis Center

221 N Broad Street
Philadelphia, PA 19107   215-854-8100

Dr. Arnold Berman, Director

Research activity at Hahnemann University into the areas of arthritis.

5650 Pennsylvania College of Optometry Eye Institute

1200 West Godfrey Avenue
Philadelphia, PA 19141   215-276-6000
    FAX: 215-276-1329

Mr. Eugene Wayne, Director

5651 Reading Rehabilitation Hospital

RR 1 Box 250
Reading, PA 19607   610-926-4017
    FAX: 610-796-6303

Margaret Hsieh, Librarian

Information on physical disabilities, stroke, head injuries, aging and spinal cord injuries.

5652 Recorded Periodicals

Associated Services for the Blind
919 Walnut Street
Philadelphia, PA 19107   215-629-2990
    FAX: 215-922-0692
e-mail: pjohnson@asb.org
www.asb.org

Patricia C. Johnson, Chief Executive Officer

A service of Associated Services for the Blind. 26 magazines are available on cassette through this subscription service. A magazine list can be sent, in both large print and on audio cassette. *$18.00*

Rhode Island

5653 Regional Library for the Blind and Physically Handicapped

Talking Books Plus
1 Capitol Hill
Providence, RI 02908   401-222-2080
    FAX: 401-277-4195
www.dsls.state.ri.us

Richard Leduc, Librarian

Offers talking book services for the blind and physically handicapped. Collection includes reference materials, braille printer, braille writer, large-print books, adaptive computer workstations and referrals to appropriate agencies/programs for other services.

5654 Rhode Island Department of State Library for the Blind and Physically Handicapped

One Capital Hill
Providence, RI 02908   401-277-2726
    FAX: 401-277-4195
e-mail: richard@dsl.rhilinet.gov

Richard Ledue, Librarian

Offers information and services for the visually impaired including reference materials, braille printers, braille writers, large-print books and more.

South Carolina

5655 Medical University of South Carolina Arthritis Clinical/Research Center

96 Jonathan Lucas Street
Box 250623
Charleston, SC 29425   843-792-1991
    FAX: 843-792-7121

Richard M. Silver, Director

Offers patient care services and basic and clinical research on various types of arthritis and connective tissue diseases.

5656 South Carolina State Library

301 Gervais Street
PO Box 821
Columbia, SC 29202   803-734-0470
    FAX: 803-737-9983
    TDY:803-734-7298
e-mail: guynell@leo.scsl.state.sc.us
www.state.sc.us./scsl.bph.html

Guynell Williams, Librarian

Summer reading programs, braille writer, magnifiers, closed-circuit T.V., large-print photocopier, cassette books and magazines, children's books on cassette, home visits and other reference materials on blindness and other handicaps.

South Dakota

5657 South Dakota State Library

800 Governors Drive
Pierre, SD 57501   605-224-8641
                          FAX: 605-773-4950
                          TDY:605-773-4950
                          e-mail: darn@stlib.state.sd.us

Daniel Boyd, Librarian

Summer reading programs, braille writer, magnifiers, closed-circuit T.V., large-print photocopier, cassette books and magazines, children's books on cassette, home visits and other reference materials on blindness and other handicaps.

Tennessee

5658 LRC for Students with Disabilities

MSU Library Reference Department
Memphis State University
Memphis, TN 38152   901-544-0237

Ross Johnson, Reference Librarian

Information on physical disabilities, blindness and visual impairments.

5659 Tennessee Library for the Blind and Physically Handicapped

403 Seventh Avenue North
Nashville, TN 37243   615-741-3915
                            800-342-3308
                       FAX: 615-532-8856
            e-mail: tlbph@mail.state.tn.us

Mary Lou Markham, Director

Offers free public library services to those unable to hold, read or turn the pages of ordinary books and magazines due to physical or visual impairment. Special library materials are provided by the Library of Congress, and free mailing priviledges for these materials is provided through the U.S. Post Office. Playback equipment is provided along with books on cassette, in braille and in large print.

Texas

5660 Baylor College of Medicine Birth Defects Center

6621 Fannin Street
Houston, TX 77030   713-770-3013
                       FAX: 713-770-4294

Frank Greenberg, M.D., Director

5661 Baylor College of Medicine, Cullen Eye Institute

6501 Fannin
Houston, TX 77030   713-798-3200
                       FAX: 713-798-4364

Dan B. Jones, MD, Chairman

Research activities focus on restoring vision and preventing blindness through a better understanding of the disease.

5662 Brown-Heatly Library

4900 N Lamar Boulevard
Austin, TX 78751   512-424-4240
                      FAX: 512-424-4245
            e-mail: library@rehab.state.tx.us

Geneva Davis, Librarian
Judy Reinhart, Assistant Librarian

Houses a collection of books, audio and video tapes and periodicals focusing on rehabilitation, disabilities, employment skills and practices and management for the Texas Rehabilitation Commission. Houses materials on developmental and other disabilities, assessment and evaluation for the Texas Interagency on Early Childhood Intervention.

5663 Center for Research on Women with Disabilities

3400 Richmond Avenue
Suite B
Houston, TX 77046   713-960-0505
                            800-442-7693
                       FAX: 713-961-3555
            e-mail: mnosek@bcm.tmc.edu
                    www.bcm.tmc.edu/crowd/

Margaret Nosek, PhD, Executive Director

Research organization dedicated to conducting research and promoting, developeing, and disseminating information to expand the life choices of women with disabilities. Conducts research and training activities on issues related to the health, independence and community integration of women and men with physical disabilities. The center has a database of psychosocial behaviors of women with disabilities.

5664 Christian Education for the Blind

PO Box 331388
Fort Worth, TX 76163   817-531-8824

Offers braille and large print books and cassettes for the visually impaired.

5665 Houston Public Library - Access Center

500 McKinney
Houston, TX 77002   713-224-2492
                       TDY:713-247-3546
            e-mail: kcurry@htp.lib.tx.us
                    www.hpl.lib.tx.us

Kemo Curry, Supervisor

The Access Center houses two open book reading machines, a closed circuit television with a color monitor, a computer with text magnification capabilities and connection to the Internet, braille typewriters, a collection of 9,000 large print titles and a reference collection with information on services and organizations pertaining to disabilities.

5666 Talking Book Program/Texas State Library

Talking Book Program
PO Box 12927
Austin, TX 78711   512-463-5460
                           800-252-9605
                      FAX: 612-463-5436
            e-mail: tbp.services@tsl.state.tx.us

Dale Propp, Director
Renulfo Ramirez, Admin. Services Lib.

Provides reading materials in special formats to Texas residents who cannot read conventional printed matter because of visual or physical limitations, whether permanent or temporary. The service is free and materials are sent through the mail free. Books and magazines are available in cassette, braille, recorded disk and large print formats. A Disabilities Reference Center can answer questions on topics related to disabilities.

5667 Texas State Library - Talking Book Program
PO Box 12927
Austin, TX 78711 512-463-5458
800-252-9605
FAX: 512-936-0685
e-mail: tbp.services@tsl.state.tx.us
www.tsl.state.tx.us/tbp

Provides free library service to Texans of all ages who are unable to read standard print material due to visual, physical, or reading disabilities, whether permanent or temporary. Books and magazines are avaialble in different formats, mainly on cassette, but also in braille and large print. All of the items are sent and returned through the mail free of charge.

5668 University of Texas Southwestern Medical Center/Allergy & Immunology
5323 Harry Hines Boulevard
Dallas, TX 75235 214-648-3004
FAX: 214-648-6377

Paul Bergstresser, M.D., Principal Investor

5669 University of Texas at Austin
PO Box P
Austin, TX 78713 512-495-4350

e-mail: www@lib.utexas.edu
www.lib.utexas.edu

Ann Neville, Coordinator
Services for library users with disabilities.

Utah

5670 Family Resource Library/Center for Persons with Disabilities
1780 N Research Parkway
Suite 112
North Logan, UT 84341 801-752-0238
FAX: 801-753-9750
TDY:801-753-9750
e-mail: cope@cc.usu.edu

Marilyn Thomas, President
Julia Burnham, Executive Director

Not-for-profit service organization dedicated to collecting materials containing practical information for families of persons with disabilities. Serves persons with disabilities and their famlies in Utah, Idaho, Wyoming and Nevada. Educational materials include books, booklets, videotapes and audiotapes.

5671 Utah State Library Division/Program for the Blind and Physically Handicapped
250 North 1950 West
Suite A
Salt Lake City, UT 84116 801-715-6789
FAX: 801-715-6767
e-mail: blind@state.lib.ut.us
www.state.lib.ut.us

Gerald Buttars, Librarian

Summer reading programs, braille embosser, cassette books and magazines, children's books on cassette and other reference materials on blindness and other handicaps, descriptive videos, braille books, large print books, and radio reading service.

Vermont

5672 Vermont Department of Libraries Special Services Unit
578 Paine Turnpike N
Berlin, VT 05602 802-828-3273
FAX: 802-828-2199
e-mail: ssu@dol.state.vt.us

S. Francis Woods, Librarian
Jennifer Hart, Assistant Librarian

Service consists of reading material in large print and in talking book formats. The book collection consists of cassettes and large print. Special collections include: childrens print/braille books, reference materials on blindness.

Virginia

5673 Alexandria Library Talking Book Service
826 Slaters Lane
Alexandria, VA 22314
FAX: 703-838-4614
TDY:703-838-4568
e-mail: emccaffr@lea.eda
www.alexandria.lib.va.us

Patricia Bates, Librarian

Summer reading programs, braille writer, magnifiers, closed-circuit T.V., large-print photocopier, cassette books and magazines, children's books on cassette, home visits and other reference materials on blindness and other handicaps.

5674 Arlington County Department of Libraries
1015 N Quincy Street
Arlington, VA 22201 703-358-6548
FAX: 703-358-5962
TDY:703-358-6320

Roxanne Barnes, Librarian

Summer reading programs, braille writer, magnifiers, closed-circuit T.V., large-print photocopier, cassette books and magazines, children's books on cassette, home visits and other reference materials on blindness and other handicaps.

5675 Braille Circulating Library for the Blind

2700 Stuart Avenue
Richmond, VA   23220   804-359-3743
                             FAX: 804-359-4777
              e-mail: brailleCL@aol.com

Robert Gordon, Executive Director

Offers library materials for the blind and visually impaired on a free-loan basis. Serves the entire USA and 41 foreign countries with cassette tapes, reel to reel tapes, braille books, large print books along with talking book records.

5676 Central Rappahannock Regional Library

1201 Caroline Street
Fredericksburg, VA   22401   540-372-1160
                                    FAX: 540-373-9411
                                    TDY:540-371-9165
               e-mail: nschiff@hq.crrl.org

Nancy Schiff, Librarian

Offers reference materials on blindness and other disabilities.

5677 Division for the Visually Handicapped

1920 Association Drive
Reston, VA   20191   703-620-3660
                           888-232-7232
                           www.cec.sped.org

Dr. Kay Ferrell, President

Members are teachers, college faculty members, administrators, supervisors and others concerned with the education and welfare of visually handicapped and blind children and youth. This is a division of the Council For Exceptional Children.

5678 Hampton Subregional Library for the Blind

4207 Victoria Boulevard
Hampton, VA   23669   757-727-1154
                             FAX: 757-717-1151
              e-mail: swoolard@leo.vsla.edu

Mary Sue Woolard, Librarian

Summer reading programs, braille writer, magnifiers, closed-circuit T.V., large-print photocopier, cassette books and magazines, children's books on cassette, home visits and other reference materials on blindness and other handicaps.

5679 James Branch Cabell Library

Virginia Commonwealth University
901 Park Avenue
Richmond, VA   23284   804-828-1103

Sally Jacobs, Reference Librarian
Library services for the visually disabled.

5680 James P. Mills Arthritis Resource Center

Virginia Chapter of the Arthritis Foundation
565 Southlake Boulevard
Richmond, VA   23236
                             800-456-4687

Provides free information, services and counseling to the public. Services include assistance in locating and accessing government and other health care programs for persons with arthritis, referral to doctors specializing in the treatment of arthritis, free literature about the different types of arthritis and counseling for people with arthritis and their families.

5681 Newport News Public Library System

112 Main Street
Newport News, VA   23601   757-591-7418
                                  FAX: 757-591-7425
               e-mail: shalswin@leo.vsla.edu

Sue Balswin, Librarian

Summer reading programs, braille writer, magnifiers, closed-circuit T.V., large-print photocopier, cassette books and magazines, children's books on cassette, home visits and other reference materials on blindness and other handicaps.

5682 Northern Virginia Resource Center for Deaf and Hard of Hearing Persons

10363 Democracy Lane
Fairfax, VA   22030   703-352-9055
                             FAX: 703-352-9058
              e-mail: nvrcinfo@aol.com
                           www.nvrc.org

Cheryl A. Heppner, Executive Director
Gay N. Nagy, Outreach Manager

Empowering deaf and hard-of-hearing individuals and their families through education, advocacy and community involvement.

5683 Roanoke City Public Library System

2607 Salem Turnpike NW
Roanoke, VA   24017   540-853-2621
                             FAX: 540-853-1030

Rebecca Cooper, Librarian

Summer reading programs, braille writer, magnifiers, closed-circuit T.V., large-print photocopier, cassette books and magazines, children's books on cassette, home visits and other reference materials on blindness and other handicaps.

5684 Special Services/Talking Books

2501 Sherwood Hall Lane
Alexandria, VA   22306   703-765-3645
                                FAX: 703-765-5893
              e-mail: sjapikse@leo.vsld.edu
              www.co.fairfax.va.us/library/homepage.ht

Jeanette Studley, Manager

Offers talking books, TDD access, assistive devices such as decoders for three-week loans, support groups for people who are visually impaired, library program interpreters available with four weeks advance notice, adapted computer work station with braille printer and assistive listening devices.

5685 Staunton Public Library Talking Book Center

One Churchville Avenue
Staunton, VA 24401   540-332-3902
     800-995-6215
FAX: 540-332-3906
e-mail: talkingbooks@ci.staunton.va.us

Oakley Pearson, Librarian

Offers free library service by circulating recorded books, magazines, and playback equipment to individuals unable to use standard print materials because of visual or physical impairment.

5686 University of Virginia General Clinical Research Center

School of Medicine
Box 410
Charlottesville, VA 22908   804-924-2394

Dr. Michael Thorner, Director

Focuses on asthmatic disorders.

5687 Virginia Autism Resource Center

PO Box 1300
Stephens City, VA 22655   540-869-3377

Carol Schall, Director
Brenda Whitlock, Administrative Specialist

Information on autism, mental retardation and developmental disabilities. Free consultation and lending library to anyone within Virginia.

5688 Virginia Beach Public Library Special Services Library

930 Independence Boulevard
Virginia Beach, VA 23455   757-464-9175
FAX: 757-460-7606

Susan Head, Librarian

A public library for people with visual and physical disabilities, braille writer, magnifiers, closed-circuit T.V., large-print photocopier, cassette books and magazines, children's books on cassette, and other reference materials on blindness and other disabilities.

5689 Virginia State Library for the Visually and Physically Handicapped

395 Azalea Avenue
Richmond, VA 23227   804-371-3661
FAX: 804-371-3508

Barbara McCarthy, Director

Summer reading programs, braille writer, magnifiers, closed-circuit T.V., large-print photocopier, cassette books and magazines, children's books on cassette, home visits and other reference materials on blindness and other handicaps.

Washington

5690 Ophthalmic Research Laboratory Eye Institute

Swedish Hospital Medical Center
747 Summit Avenue
Seattle, WA 98104   206-386-6000
FAX: 206-386-2625

Dr. Brian Godell, Director

Color vision physiology, vision disorders and blindness research.

5691 Washington Talking Book & Braille Library

2021-9th Avenue
Seattle, WA 98121   206-615-0400
FAX: 206-615-0437
e-mail: wtbbl@wtbbl.org
www.spl.lib.wa.us

Jan Ames, Librarian

The Library provides cassette and large print books and magazines, a local tape transcription service, a local braille transcription program, a radio reading service, a children's program that includes a summer reading program, limited reference service, and print reference materials on blindness and disabilities. The service is available only to individuals unable to read regular print.

5692 Washington Talking Book and Braille Library

2021 9th Avenue
Seattle, WA 98121   206-464-1011
FAX: 206-464-0247
TDY: 206-464-6930
e-mail: wtbbl@spl.lib.wa.us
www.spl.lib.wa.us/wtbbl/wtbbl.html

Jan Ames, Librarian

Summer reading programs, braille writer, magnifiers, closed-circuit T.V., large-print photocopier, cassette books and magazines, children's books, and other reference materials on blindness and other handicaps, online catalog, reference station with assistive devices and a radio reading service.

West Virginia

5693 Autism Services Center

605 9th Street
PO Box 507
Huntington, WV 25710   304-525-8014

Ruth Christ Sullivan, Director

Works to improve the processes by which appropriate and professional training, advocacy, consulting and information are provided by individuals responsible for the welfare and care of autistic individuals and others with developmental disabilities.

5694 Autism Training Center

Marshall University
400 Hal Greer Boulevard
Huntington, WV 25755   304-696-3640
     800-344-5115

5695 Cabell County Public Library

455 Ninth Street Plaza
Huntington, WV 25701 304-528-5700
FAX: 304-528-5701
e-mail: smarshall@cabell.lib.wv.us

Suzanne Marshall, Public Service Assistant

Summer reading programs, braille writer, magnifiers, closed-circuit T.V., large-print enlarger Arkenstone Reader, magazines, children's books on cassette, and other reference materials on blindness and other handicaps.

5696 Cabell County Public Library/Talking Book Department/Subregional Library for the Blind

455 Ninth Street Plaza
Huntington, WV 25701 304-528-5700
FAX: 304-528-5739
e-mail: tbooks@cabell.lib.wv.us
cabell.lib.wv.us

Suzanne Marshall, Coordinator

Summer reading programs, braille writer, magnifiers, closed-circuit T.V., cassette books and magazines, children's books on cassette reference materials on blindness and other handicaps, enlargers and Arkenstone Reader.

5697 Kanawha County Public Library

123 Capitol Street
Charleston, WV 25301 304-348-7770
FAX: 304-348-6530

Reference, Librarian

Summer reading programs, large print PC option, magnifiers, large type books, cassette books, and magazines, children's books on cassette, home visits and other reference materials on blindness and other handicaps

5698 Ohio County Public Library Services for the Blind and Physically Handicapped

52 16th Street
Whelling, WV 26033 304-232-0244
FAX: 304-232-6848

Lori Nicholson

5699 Talking Book Department, Parkersburg and o Wood County Public Library

3100 Emerson Avenue
Parkersburg, WV 26104 304-420-4587
800-642-8674
FAX: 304-420-4589
e-mail: hickman@hp9K.park.lib.wv.us

Michael Hickman, Coordinator of Services

Services for the bind and physically handicapped. Library of Congress Talking Book Program.

5700 West Virginia Library Commission

1900 Kanawha Boulevard E
Charleston, WV 25305 304-755-5700
FAX: 304-558-4061
e-mail: fesenmf@mars.wr1c.wvnet.edu
www.wv1c.wvnet.edu

Francis Fesenmainer, Librarian

Summer reading programs, braille writer, magnifiers, closed-circuit T.V., large-print photocopier, cassette books and magazines, children's books on cassette, home visits and other reference materials on blindness and other handicaps.

5701 West Virginia School for the Blind Library

301 E Main Street
Romney, WV 26757 304-822-3521
FAX: 304-822-4896
e-mail: cjohn@access.mountain.net

Cynthia Johnson, Librarian

Summer reading programs, braille writer, magnifiers, closed-circuit T.V., large-print photocopier, cassette books and magazines, children's books on cassette, home visits and other reference materials on blindness and other handicaps.

Wisconsin

5702 Brown County Library

515 Pine Street
Green Bay, WI 54301 920-448-4300

Angela Basten, Librarian

Summer reading programs, braille writer, magnifiers, closed-circuit T.V., large-print photocopier, cassette books and magazines, children's books on cassette, home visits and other reference materials on blindness and other handicaps.

5703 Medical College of Wisconsin Eye Institute

8700 W Wisconsin Avenue
Milwaukee, WI 53226 414-257-4565

Richard Schultz, MD, Director

Research vision loss including ophthalmology.

5704 Trace Center

University of Wisconsin-Madison
5901 Research Park Boulevard
Madison, WI 53719 608-263-5776
FAX: 608-262-8848
TDY:608-263-5408
e-mail: info@trace.wisc.edu
www.trace.wisc.edu

Nancy Gores, Public Information Coordinator

Research and development center at the University of Wisconsin-Madison that focuses on making off-the-shelf technologies and systems more usable for everyone. Trace is designated as the Rehabilitation Engineering Research Center (RERC) on information technology access and it also a partner with Gallaudet University in the RERC on universal telecommunications access and Trace's work is in great part funded throught the National Institute on Disability and Rehabilitaiton Research (NIDRR).

5705 University of Wisconsin Asthma and Allergic Disease Center

600 Highland Avenue
Madison, WI 53792 608-263-6180

5706 **Wisconsin Regional Library for the Blind &
Physically Handicapped**
813 West Wells Street
Milwaukee, WI 53233   414-286-3045
                                  800-242-8822
                             FAX: 414-286-3102
                             TDY:414-286-3548
                        e-mail: mvalne@mpl.org
            www.dpi.state.wi.us/dpi/dld/rll/libinfo

Marsha Valance, Regional Librarian
Constance Pirtle, Assistant Librarian
Circulates recorded materials, playback equipment
and braille materials to print-handicapped Wisconsin
residents.

Wyoming

5707 **Wyoming Services for the Visually Disabled**
State Department of Education
Hathaway Building
Room 144
Cheyenne, WY 82002   307-777-7363

Kent Jensen
Eligible readers of Wyoming receive library service
from the regional library in Salt Lake City, Utah.

5708 **Wyoming's New Options in Technology
(WYNOT), University of Wyoming**
Wyoming Institute for Disabilities
1465 North Fourth Street, Suite 111
Laramie, WY 82072   307-766-2051
                                 800-861-4312
                            FAX: 307-721-2084
                      e-mail: wynot.uw@uwyo.edu
          http://wind.uwyo.edu/wynot/wynot.htm

Kathy Laurin, Public Contact
Designed to develop and implement a consumer oriented statewide system of technology-related assistance for people with disabilities of all ages.

AIDS

5709 AIDS 2nd Edition

JB Lippincott
227 East Washington Square
Philadelphia, PA 19106

215-521-8300
800-777-2295
FAX: 215-824-7390

Vincent DeVita, Jr., author

Gives the latest information on AIDS covering basic science considerations, clinical aspects and public health issues. *$55.00*

474 pages

5710 AIDS Alert

American Health Consultants
PO Box 740056
Atlanta, GA 30374

404-262-7436
800-688-2421
www.ahcpub.com

Glen Harris, Managing Editor

Covers risks, hazards, costs and prevention of AIDS and related conditions. *$279.00*

12 pages Monthly
ISSN 0887-02 2

5711 AIDS Disease State Management Resource

PO Box 740056
Atlanta, GA 30374

404-262-7436
FAX: 800-284-3291
e-mail: customerservices@ahcpub.com
www.ahcpub.com

Skip Connett, author
Milo Falcon, Managing Editor

Provides staff and patient education materials on HIV/AIDS. *$299.00*

Paperback

5712 AIDS Fundraising in the 90's

Foundation Center
79 Fifth Avenue
Department ZE
New York, NY 10003

212-421-0771
800-424-9836
FAX: 212-807-3677
www.fdncenter.org

Michael Seltzer, author
Thomas Buckman, President

This guide helps nonprofit groups plan a strategy for raising money. Specifically designed for AIDS related projects and organizations, this book covers an array of money-generating initiatives, from membership drives to special events, direct mail, and grant applications. *$10.00*

ISBN 0-87954 -90-6

5713 AIDS War

Asklepios
26 Saint Marks Place
New York, NY 10003

John Lauritson, author

Contains the latest information regarding the dangers of using AZT to treat AIDS, as well as information on Peter Duesberg and the censure he recieved from the conventional medical establishment for his theory that HIV does not cause AIDS.

1993

5714 AIDS, What Does it Mean to You?

Walker Publishing Company
435 Hudson Street
New York, NY 10014

212-727-8300
800-289-2553
FAX: 212-727-0984
e-mail: orders@walkerbooks.com

Margaret Hyde, author

Researchers have been working frantically to solve the puzzle of AIDS - a disease that has taken the lives of thousands of men and women during the past ten years. *$13.95*

128 pages Cloth/Hardcover
ISBN 0-802782-02-7

5715 AIDS: The HIV Myth

St. Martin's Press
New York, NY

An exploration of Peter Duesberg's HIV hypothesis that debunks the theory that the virus causes AIDS.

5716 Healing AIDS Naturally

Healing Energy Press
Foster City, CA

Laurence Badgley, M.D., author

Outlines Dr. Badgley's protocol for treating AIDS using alternative medicine.

1987

5717 Poison by Prescription: The AZT Story

Asklepios
26 Saint Marks Place
New York, NY 10003

John Lauritson, author

An expose of the politics involved with AIDS research and how AZT, a known toxic substance, became the conventional medical establishment's drug of choice for dealing with AIDS and HIV.

1990

5718 Rethinking AIDS

Free Press
New York, NY

Robert Root-Berstein, author

A thorough investigation which indicates that HIV alone does not cause AIDS.

1993

5719 Surviving AIDS

HarperCollins
New York, NY

Michael Callen, author

Outlines the alternative medicine approach to health taken by the author, one of the longest survivors of AIDS.

5720 World Without AIDS

Thorsons Publishing Group
London, England,

Leon Chaitow, DO, ND, author

A convincing argument that conventional medicine approaches do not 'cure' disease, which outlines how AIDS can be treated using methods of naturopathic medicine. Also includes an appendix outlining 21 ways to strengthen the immune system.

Children & Young Adults

5721 ADHD with Comorbid Disorders: Clinical Assessment and Management

Guilford Press
72 Spring Street
New York, NY   10012   212-431-9800
                              800-365-7006
                         FAX: 212-966-6708
                              www.guilford.com

Steven R. Pliszka, Caryn L. Carlson, author
James M. Swanson, Author
$36.95

  Cloth
  ISBN 1-572304-78-2

5722 Adolescent in Family Therapy: Breaking the Cycle of Conflict and Control

Guilford Press
72 Spring Street
New York, NY   10012   212-431-9800
                              800-365-7006
                         FAX: 212-966-6708
                              www.guilford.com

Joseph A. Micucci, PhD, author

Presenting a developmentally grounded approach, Joseph Micucci shows how troubled teenagers and their parents can be helped to use family relationships as catalysts for growth and change. Filled with case examples and clinical advice, the book describes specific family intervention strategies for eating disorders, depression, underachievement, stress caused by psychotic symptoms and other conditions. Also in cloth at $35.00 (ISBN# 1-57230-389-1) *$19.95*

  336 pages Paper 1900
  ISBN 1-572305-88-6

5723 All About Asthma

Asthma and Allergy Foundation of America
1233 20th Street NW
Suite 402
Washington, DC   20036   202-466-7643
                                800-7AS-THMA
                           FAX: 202-466-8940
                         e-mail: info@aafa.org
                                www.aafa.org

William Ostrow & Vivian Ostrow, author

Premier patient organization dedicated to improving the quality of life for people with asthma and allergies through education, advocacy, and research. Serves the 50 million Americans with asthma and allergic diseases. Headquartered in Washington, D.C., AAFA has a full-time professional staff and a national network of 14 chapters and more than 140 educational support groups to provide community-based programs and raise funds for asthma care and research. *$5.00*

  39 pages Paperback

5724 Asthma Care Training for Kids

Asthma and Allergy Foundation of America
1125 15th Street NW
Suite 502
Washington, DC   20005   202-466-7643
                           FAX: 202-466-8940
                         e-mail: info@aafa.org
                                www.aafa.org

Designed to help children ages 7 to 12 and their parents take charge of their asthma. In a series of three action-filled sessions, children and their parents meet separately with their peers to learn about asthma management.

5725 Autism Research Review

Autism Research Institute
4182 Adams Avenue
San Diego, CA   92116   619-281-7165
                          FAX: 619-563-6840
                www.ausitmresearchinstitute.com

B. Rimland, PhD, Director
$18.00

  8 pages Quarterly

5726 Belonging

Dial Books
375 Hudson Street
New York, NY   10014   212-366-2000
                         FAX: 212-414-3394

Deborah Kent, author

Meg attended special schools for the blind until she was ready for high school. She decided that she wanted to go to a regular high school. She and her mother practiced her walks to school and studied the layout of the building prior to school starting, but Meg was unprepared for the trip when there were 1,500 students. She adjusted quickly to the crowds and the pace of the new school.

  200 pages Hardcover
  ISBN 0-80370 -30-1

5727 Best Toys, Books, Videos & Software for Kids

Exceptional Parent Library
PO Box 1807
Englewood Cliffs, NJ   10116
                              800-535-1910
                    e-mail: eplibrary@aol.com
                              www.eplibrary.com

J. Oppenheim and S. Oppenheim, author

Guide to over 1,000 kid-tested, classic and new products including software, audio and special-needs products. *$13.00*

5728 Burnish Me Bright

Pantheon Books
201 East 50th Street
New York, NY 10022   212-751-2600
    800-638-6460

Julia Cunningham, author

Hilaire, a famous mime, had retired to a small village to live out his life. He met frail Auguste, who was unable to speak, and immediately he saw the potential for this agile and physically expressive youth to become a mime.

80 pages Hardcover

5729 Bus Girl: Selected Poems

Brookline Books
PO Box 1047
Cambridge, MA 02238   617-868-0360
    800-666-2665
    FAX: 617-868-1772
    e-mail: brooklinebks@delphi.com
    www.brooklinebooks.com

Gretchen Josephson, author

Poems written over several decades by a young woman with Down Syndrome. *$14.95*

144 pages Paperback
ISBN 1-57129-41-9

5730 But I'm Ready to Go

Bradbury Press
866 3rd Avenue
New York, NY 10022   212-832-2101
    800-257-5755

Louise Albert, author

Judy always had a problem learning math and performing skills that required good motor control.

230 pages Hardcover
ISBN 0-87888-07-7

5731 Child Who Never Grew Up

Exceptional Parent Library
PO Box 1807
Englewood Cliffs, NJ 10116
    800-535-1910
    e-mail: eplibrary@aol.com
    www.eplibrary.com

P. Buck, author

Offers Pearl Buck's inspiring account of her struggle to help her daughter with mental retardation. *$14.95*

5732 Child and Adolescent Therapy: Cognitive-Behavioral Procedures, Second Edition

Guilford Press
72 Spring Street
New York, NY 10012   212-431-9800
    800-365-7006
    FAX: 212-966-6708
    www.guilford.com

Philip C. Kendall, PhD, ABPP, Editor, author

Incorporating significant developments in treatment procedures, theory and clinical research, new chapters in this second edition examine the current status of empirically supported interventions and developmental issues specific to work with adolescents. *$45.00*

432 pages Cloth 1900
ISBN 1-572305-56-8

5733 Child's Courage, A Doctor's Devotion - Triumph Over Head Trauma

Special Needs Project
3463 State Street
282
Santa Barbara, CA 93105
    800-333-6867

Frances Mahanes

Offers valuable information for the disabled. *$6.95*

164 pages

5734 Childhood Asthma, Learning To Manage

Asthma and Allergy Foundation of America
1125 15th Street NW
Suite 502
Washington, DC 20005   202-466-7643
    FAX: 202-466-8940
    e-mail: info@aafa.org
    www.aafa.org

Self-paced, entertaining activity books for home use featuring practical guidelines for managing childhood asthma with a focus on using peak flow meters.

5735 Childhood Ear Infections: What Every Parent Should Know

North Atlantic Books
Berkley, CA

Michael Schmidt, D.C., author

A guide to helping control and eliminate ear infections in children. Other topics include the use of antibiotics, the unnecessary removal of adenoids, and the implantation of tubes into the ear drums.

1992

5736 Children with Disabilities, Fourth Edition

Brookes Publishing
PO Box 10624
Baltimore, MD 21285   410-337-9580
    800-638-3775
    FAX: 410-337-8539
    e-mail: custserv@brookesopublishing.com
    www.brookespublishing.com

Mark L. Batshaw, M.D., Editor, author

Professionals, families, and students rely on this fully illustrated, comprehensive resource for all of their disability reference needs. *$58.00*

960 pages Hardcover 1997
ISBN 1-557662-93-2

5737 Clubhouse Kids Learn About Asthma

Asthma and Allergy Foundation of America
1125 15th Street NW
Suite 502
Washington, DC 20005   202-466-7643
    FAX: 202-466-8940
    e-mail: info@aafa.org
    www.aafa.org

Interactive CD-ROM helps children ages 4-12 learn about asthma at their own pace. Sound, animation and game-like features draw players into the life of Janie, who has just been diagnosed with asthma. *$60.00*

5738 Communication Coloring Book
Speech Bin
1965 25th Avenue
Vero Beach, FL 32960　　561-770-0007
　　　　　　　　　　　　　800-477-3324
　　　　　　　　　　　　FAX: 561-770-0006
　　　　　　　　　　　　www.speechbin.com
Denise Grigas, author
Jan J Binney, Vice President

Publisher and distributor of books and materials for professionals in rehabilitation, speech-language pathology, special education and related fields and persons interested in communication disorders and related disabilities. Major product lines include professional and children's books, computer software, diagnostic tests, instructional games and materials for children and adults and specialty items. *$14.95*

48 pages
ISBN 0-93785-53-0

5739 Complete IEP Guide: How to Advocate for Your Special Ed Child
NOLO
950 Parker Street
Berkeley, CA 94710　　510-549-1976
　　　　　　　　　　　　800-955-4775
　　　　　　　　　　　FAX: 510-548-5902
　　　　　　　　　　　　www.nolo.com
Attorney Lawrence M. Siegel, author
Maira Dizgalvis, Trade Customer Service Manager
Susan McConnell, Director of Sales
Natasha Kaluza, Sales Assistant

This book has all the plain-English suggestions, strategies, resources and forms to develop an effective IEP. *$24.95*

300 pages paperback
ISBN 0-873376-07-2

5740 Coping When a Parent Has Multiple Sclerosis
Rosen Publishing Group
29 East 21st Street
New York, NY 10010　　212-777-3017
　　　　　　　　　　　　800-237-9932
　　　　　　　　　　　FAX: 888-436-4643
　　　　　　e-mail: rosenpub@tribeca.ios.com
Barbara Cristall, author
Tricia Bauer, Director of Special Markets

Explains to young people how living with a parent who has Multiple Sclerosis will affect their lives. Hardcover. *$17.95*

128 pages
ISBN 0-823914-06-2

5741 Coping for Kids Who Stutter
Speech Bin
1965 25th Avenue
Vero Beach, FL 32960　　561-770-0007
　　　　　　　　　　　　800-477-3324
　　　　　　　　　　　　FAX: 561-770-0006
　　　　　　　　　　　　www.speechbin.com
John Weber, author
Jan J. Binney, Senior Editor

Informative book for children and adults about stuttering and how to manage it. *$15.95*

32 pages
ISBN 0-93785-43-2

5742 Coping with Being Physically Challenged
Rosen Publishing Group
29 East 21st Street
New York, NY 10010　　718-851-4859
　　　　　　　　　　　FAX: 888-436-4643
　　　　　　e-mail: rosenpub@tribeca.ios.com
Linda Lee Ratto, author

Ratto deals with strong emotions, such as general anger and depression, which affect these young adults and their families. The author shows them how to deal and cope on a day-to-day basis. *$15.95*

ISBN 0-82391-44-9

5743 Coping with Special Needs Classmates
Rosen Publishing Group
29 East 21st Street
New York, NY 10010　　212-777-3017
　　　　　　　　　　　　800-237-9932
　　　　　　　　　　　FAX: 888-436-4643
　　　　　　e-mail: rosenpub@tribeca.ios.com
Shrri McCarthy-Tucker, author
Tricia Bauer, Director of Special Markets

Special needs classmates include people who are physically different, disfigured or challenged, emotionally disturbed, or those who have learning disabilities. The author offers guidance on how to get past discomfort or fear of confrontation with someone who seems very different, but is, in reality, not so different after all. Hardcover. *$17.95*

128 pages
ISBN 0-823915-98-0

5744 Coping with a Learning Disability
Rosen Publishing Group
29 East 21st Street
New York, NY 10010　　212-777-3017
　　　　　　　　　　　　800-237-9932
　　　　　　　　　　　FAX: 888-436-4643
　　　　　　e-mail: rosenpub@tribeca.ios.com
Dr Lawrence Clayton and Jaydene Morrison, author
Tricia Bauer, Director of Special Markets

Being a teen with a learning disorder does not have to be a devastating experience. The authors discuss family, personal, and peer emotional reactions. Biographies of famous people with learning disorders provide positive role models and special education is discussed. Hardcover. *$17.95*

128 pages
ISBN 0-823928-87-X

5745 Coping with a Physically Challenged Brother or Sister
Rosen Publishing Group
29 East 21st Street
New York, NY 10010　　212-777-3017
　　　　　　　　　　　　800-237-9932
　　　　　　　　　　　FAX: 888-614-7389
　　　　　　e-mail: rosenpub@tribeca.ios.com
Linda Lee Ratto, author
Tricia Bauer, Director of Special Needs

Dealing with a relative who is born physically challenged or who suffers a personal tragedy is one of the biggest adjustments in life. This book shows step-by-step methods of coping with these emotions so the reader may learn how to have a happy life once again. Hardcover. *$17.95*

ISBN 0-823914-92-5

5746 Deenie

Bradbury Press
135 South Mount Zion Road
Lebanon, IN 46052

800-257-5755
FAX: 800-882-8583

Judy Blume, author

Deenie, a beautiful thirteen-year-old girl, had a mother who was pushing her to become a model. The agency representatives told Deenie she had the looks but walked differently. Deenie's main wish was to become a cheerleader. Her close friend, Janet, made the cheerleading squad but Deenie didn't make the final list. After this her gym teacher noticed her posture and called her family. After seeing therapists, the diagnosis of adolescent idiopathic scoliosis was made.

159 pages Hardcover
ISBN 0-02711 -20-6

5747 Determined to Win: Children Living with Allergies and Asthma

Gareth Stevens
1555 North Rivercenter Drive
Milwaukee, WI 53212

414-225-0333
800-542-2595
FAX: 414-225-0377
www.gsinc.com

Thomas Bengman, author
Claire Messier, Marketing Associate

Isabell, a six year old girl, has been living with allergies and asthma almost her entire life. With proper medical care and a determined attitude, she leads an active life. *$15.95*

48 pages
ISBN 0-83681 -75-9

5748 Don't Feel Sorry for Paul

JB Lippincott
East Washington Square
Philadelphia, PA 19105

FAX: 215-824-7390

Bernard Wolf, author

Paul is seven but was born with deformities of both hands and feet. Paul must wear a prosthesis on both feet so that he can walk. He has a third prosthesis for his right hand. The third prosthesis has a pair of hooks Paul uses as fingers.

94 pages Hardcover
ISBN 0-39731 -88-0

5749 Every Second Child

Keats Publishing
New Canaan, CT

203-966-8721
800-323-4900
www.keats.com

Dr. Archie Kalokerinos, author

A thorough investigation of the crucial role of nutrition in preventing infant crib death.

1981

5750 Family Therapy for ADHD: Treating Children , Adolescents and Adults

Guilford Press
72 Spring Street
New York, NY 10012

212-431-9800
800-365-7006
FAX: 212-966-6708
www.guilford.com

Craig A. Everett and Sandra Volgy Everett, author

$32.95

Cloth
ISBN 1-572304-38-3

5751 Feed Your Kids Right

McGraw-Hill
New York, NY

Lendon H. Smith, M.D., author

Covers most of the health problems associated with childhood and the more natural methods of treating them.

1978

5752 Follow My Leader

Viking Press
7000 Washington Avenue South
Eden Prairie, MN 55344

800-328-7327

James B. Garfield, author

Jimmy was an active eleven year old. One of his friends found a firecracker with a short fuse. Although the boys advised him not to light it, Mike set it off. When the fuse started to burn, Mike threw the firecracker even though Jimmy was near by. The explosion occurred in Jimmy's face, blinding him. At first he was very bitter toward Mike and his blindness, but he soon found that with the help of his tutor and his friends he could learn braille and use a cane.

191 pages Hardcover
ISBN 0-67032 -32-2

5753 Funology Fables: Stories for Phonology Learning

Speech Bin
1965 25th Avenue
Vero Beach, FL 32960

561-770-0007
800-477-3324
FAX: 561-770-0006
www.speechbin.com

Roberta Sunderbruch, author

Talking Tales develop children's language skills and enhance their phonological competence. *$45.00*

264 pages
ISBN 0-93785 -59-9

5754 Getting a Grip on ADD: A Kid's Guide to Understanding & Coping with ADD

Educational Media Corporation
4256 Central Avenue NE
Box 21311
Minneapolis, MN 55421   616-781-0088
    800-966-3382
    FAX: 616-781-7753

Kim T. Frank & Susan J. Smith, author
$9.95

64 pages Paperback
ISBN 0-932796-60-3

5755 Goldilocks and the Three Bears in Signed English

Gallaudet University Press
11030 S Langley Avenue
Chicago, IL 60628
    800-621-2736
    FAX: 800-621-8476
    TDY:800-621-9347
    gupress.gallaudet.edu

Harry Bornstein, Co-Author
Karen L. Saulnier, Co-Author
The classic story is told again but with a twist. Full color illustrations show the Bears, Goldilocks and the text. Includes line drawings that show the story in Signed English. *$15.95*

48 pages Hardcover

5756 Guide to ACA Accredited Camps

American Camping Association
5000 State Road 67 North
Martinsville, IN 46151   765-342-8456
    800-428-2267
    FAX: 765-342-2065
    e-mail: books@acacamps.org
    www.acacamps.org

American Camping Association, author
Melody Snider, Director of Bookstore
A national listing of accredited camping programs. Listed by: special clientele, specific disabilities, camp name, activities. *$14.95*

Yearly

5757 Handbook of Infant Mental Health

Guilford Press
72 Spring Street
New York, NY 10012   212-431-9800
    800-365-7006
    FAX: 212-966-6708
    www.guilford.com

Charles H. Zeanah, Jr., Editor, author
$60.00

Cloth
ISBN 1-572305-15-0

5758 Help for the Hyperactive Child: A Good Sense Guide for Parents

Professional Books
Jackson, TN

William G. Crook, M.D., author

A large-print, easy-to-read book for parents and children that simply describes options and approaches to dealing with what have come to be known as hyperactivity, attention deficit disorder, and other behavior and learning problems.

1991

5759 Helping Children Understand Disabilities

Brookline Books
PO Box 1046
Cambridge, MA 02238   617-868-0360
    800-666-2665
    FAX: 617-868-1772
    e-mail: brooklinebks@delphi.com
    www.brooklinebooks.com

John Quicke, author
Examines children's literature as a vehicle to help children, parents and teachers understand important issues relating to the effects of disability on children. Using the child as narrator, Quicke demonstrates how to use popular children's fiction to explore taboo areas and stimulate discussion by children and adults. $10.95

Hardcover
ISBN 0-91479 -09-3

5760 How to Raise a Healthy Child...In Spite of Your Doctor

Ballantine Books
New York, NY

Robert S. Mendelsohn, M.D., author
A practical and informative guide that demystifies medical treatment for children, helps parents determine what ailments require an office visit and which can be dealt with at home, and calms parents' fears with sound advice on childhood illnesses.

1987

5761 Howie Helps Himself

Exceptional Parent Library
PO Box 1807
Englewood Cliffs, NJ 10116
    800-535-1910
    e-mail: eplibrary@aol.com
    www.eplibrary.com

J. Fassler, author
Designed to help the child with a disability and the sibling identify with some of the joys, stresses and strains of a disability. *$13.95*

5762 I'm Tougher Than Asthma!

Albert Whitman & Company
6340 Oakton Street
Morton Grove, IL 60053   847-581-0033
    800-255-7675
    FAX: 847-581-0039
    e-mail: mail@awhitmanco.com
    www.albertwhitman.com

Siri M. Carter & Alden R. Carter, author
Joe Boyd, President
Joe Campbell, Customer Service

Eight-year-old Siri loves to sing. play baseball, and catch toads. She won't let her asthma stop her! In her own words (with a little help from Dad), she tells how she was first diagnosed with asthma at age three and how she is learning to understand and manage her disease. $ 6.95

32 pages Paperback
ISBN 0-807534-74-9

5763   I'm a Meter Reader

Allergy and Asthma Network/Mothers of Asthmatics
3554 Chain Bridge Road
Suite 200
Fairfax, VA   22030   703-385-4403
                                      800-878-4403
                               FAX: 703-352-4354

Nancy Sander, author

Provides expert advice on how a peak flow meter can help detect when an asthma attack can occur in an easy to understand format, also available in Spanish. $4.00

Ages 4-9

5764   I'm the Big Sister Now

Exceptional Parent Library
PO Box 1807
Englewood Cliffs, NJ   10116
                               800-535-1910
                        e-mail: eplibrary@aol.com
                               www.eplibrary.com

M. Emmert, author

A look at how the loving care of family and friends can influence and benefit the quality of life for children with mental retardation and/or physical disabilities. $13.95

5765   Ideas for Kids on the Go

Accent Books & Products
PO Box 700
Bloomington, IL   61702   309-378-2961
                                      800-787-8444
                               FAX: 309-378-4420
                        e-mail: acmtlvng@aol.com

Raymond C. Cheever, Publisher
Betty Garee, Editor

This guide shows kids with physical disabilities how to go for it! Lists products and where to get them, and includes tips from others for having fun and getting ahead. Ages 1-18. $6.95

69 pages Paperback
ISBN 0-91570 -17-5

5766   Infant & Toddler Health Sourcebook

Omnigraphics
615 Griswold Street
Detroit, MI   48226
                               800-234-1340
                               FAX: 800-875-1340
                               www.omnigraphics.com

Jenifer Swanson, author
Paul Rogers, Publicity Associate

Includes information on the mental and physical development of infants, including nutrition, and common pediatric disorders. $ 78.00

600 pages 1900

5767   It isn't Fair!: Siblings of Children with Disabilities

Greenwood Publishing Group
88 Post Road West
 # 5007
Westport, CT   06880   203-226-3571
                                  FAX: 203-222-1502
                                  www.greenwood.com

Stanley D. Klein, author

This book presents a wide range of perspectives on the relationship of siblings to children with disabilities. These perspectives are written in the first person by parents, young adult siblings, younger siblings, and professionals.

200 pages $39.95 - $45
ISBN 0-897893-32-8

5768   JRA and Me

American Juvenile Arthritis Organization
PO Box 19000
Atlanta, GA   30326
                                      800-283-7800

A workbook for school-aged children who have juvenile arthritis. This book offers a variety of educational games, puzzles and worksheets to teach children about their illness and how to take care of themselves. $7.85

57 pages

5769   Jason & Nordic Publishers

PO Box 441
Hollidaysburg, PA   16648   814-696-2920
                                  FAX: 814-696-4250
                            e-mail: turtlbks@nb.net
                               www.jasonandnordic.com

Richard S. McPhee, Director

Turtle Books for children with disabilities present heroes who look like them, have problems like theirs, have similar doubts and feelings in non-threatening, fun stories. They are motivational, bridge the gap and promote understanding among peers and siblings. 12 children's books (grades preK-3) plus Sensitivity and Awareness Guide containing lesson plans, activities, background information keyed to the series. Disabilities include: Down syndrome; cerebral palsy, blindness, deafness and more.

5770   Jazz Man

Atheneum
135 South Mount Zion Road
Lebanon, IN   46052
                                  FAX: 800-882-8583

Mary Hays Weik, author

Zeke and his family moved to Harlem from the South and lived in a walk-up tenement. He didn't go to school; instead, he watched out the window all day, especially at the yellow room. The yellow room came to be inhabited by the Jazz Man, who played all day and night to the whole family's delight.

42 pages Paperback

5771 Joey and Sam

Exceptional Parent Library
PO Box 1807
Englewood Cliffs, NJ 10116
800-535-1910
e-mail: eplibrary@aol.com
www.eplibrary.com

I. Katz and E. Ritvo, M.D., author

A heartwarming story about autism, a family and a brother's love. *$9.95*

5772 Josh: A Boy with Dyslexia

Waterfront Books
85 Crescent Road
Burlington, VT 05401
802-658-7477
800-639-6063

Caroline Janover, author

This is an adventure story for kids with a section in the back of facts about learning disabilities and a list of resources for parents and teachers. *$11.95*

100 pages Hardcover
ISBN 0-91452-18-2

5773 Jumpin' Johnny Get Back to Work! A Child's Guide To ADHD/Hyperactivity

C.A.C.L.D.
25 Van Zant Street
Suite 15-5
East Norwalk, CT 06855
203-838-5010
FAX: 203-866-6108
e-mail: CACLD@JUNO.com
www.CACLD.org

Michael Gordon, PhD, author

Written primarily for elementary age youngsters with ADHD to help them understand their disability. Also valuable as an educational tool for parents, siblings, friends, and classmates. Includes two pages on medication. Published by the Connecticut Association for Children & Adults with Learning Disabilities (CACLD). *$12.50*

24 pages

5774 Just One Friend

Charles Scribner & Sons
866 3rd Avenue
New York, NY 10022
212-832-2101
FAX: 212-319-1216

Lynne Hall, author

Dory, a learning disabled teenager, wanted pretty, smart Robin for her friend. Scared of being mainstreamed into the regular school, she decided that if Meredith were out of the way, Robin would take her to school and become her friend again.

118 pages Hardcover
ISBN 0-68418-71-0

5775 Keeping Childhood

Alliance for Parental Involvement in Education
PO Box 59
East Chatham, NY 12060
518-392-6900
FAX: 518-392-6900

Nancy Aldrich, author

Understanding the anthropological views of child development. *$12.00*

5776 Kid-Friendly Parenting with Deaf and Hard of Hearing Children: A Treasury of Fun Activities

Gallaudet University Press
11030 S Langley Avenue
Chicago, IL 60628
800-621-2736
FAX: 800-620-8476
TDY:800-621-9347
gupress.gallaudet.edu

Denise Chapman, Co-Author
Daria Medwid, Co-Author

Scores of activities, parenting techniques and insights by experts, both hearing and deaf, to help parents of deaf and hard of hearing children. Activities are designed to promote better behavior and educate. *$24.95*

382 pages Softcover

5777 Kitten Who Couldn't Purr

William Morrow & Company
1350 Avenue of the Americas
New York, NY 10019
212-261-6500
FAX: 212-261-6925
www.williammorrow.com

Eve Titus, author

Jonathan the kitten doesn't know how to purr to say thank you, so he sets off to find someone to teach him. *$12.95*

32 pages

5778 Language and the Developing Child

Orton Dyslexia Society
Chester Building
Suite 382
Baltimore, MD 21286
800-ABC-D123
FAX: 410-296-0232

Katrina De Hirsch, author

This collection of papers introduces a new generation of teachers, clinicians, and parents to the work of one of the key figures in the search for the causes and treatment of dyslexia. *$15.00*

5779 Let's Talk About Having Asthma

Rosen Publishing Group's PowerKids Press
29 E 21st Street
New York, NY 10010
212-777-3017
800-237-9932
FAX: 888-436-4643
e-mail: rosenpub@tribeca.ios.com

Elizabeth Weitzman, author

This book talks about the cause and treatments for asthma as well as the precautions sufferers should take. Recommended for grades K-4. *$13.95*

ISBN 0-823950-32-8

5780 Living with Asthma

Walker & Company
720 Fifth Avenue
New York, NY 10019
212-265-3632

Margaret O. Hyde & Elizabeth Forsythe, author

$14.95

112 pages

ISBN 0-802782-86-8

5781   Lollipop Lunch

Speech Bin
1965 25th Avenue
Vero Beach, FL   32960   **561-770-0007**
                                              800-477-3324
                                        FAX: 561-770-0006
                                      www.speechbin.com

Patricia Easterly Hoon, author

Cleverly illustrated stories and activities for phonological and language development. *$19.95*

128 pages

ISBN 0-93785 -54-8

5782   Loop the Loop

William Morrow & Company
1350 Avenue of the Americas
New York, NY   10019   **212-974-3100**
                                        FAX: 212-261-6595
                                     www.williammorrow.com

Anne has never met anyone like Mrs. Simpson. She travels in a wheelchair and performs fabulous yo-yo tricks. *$14.00*

32 pages

5783   Luke Has Asthma, Too

Waterfront Books
85 Crescent Road
Burlington, VT   05401   **802-658-7477**

Alison Rogers, author

This gentle book will make for good reading with children whether they have asthma or not. The story shows that asthma can be managed in a calm fashion. The child who has moderate asthma can now have a normal life, taking part in all sports and special activities. For the more than two million families who have children with asthma, this is an important message.

32 pages

ISBN 0-91452 -06-9

5784   Lynda Madaras Talks to Teens About Aids

Waterfront Books
85 Crescent Road
Burlington, VT   05401   **802-658-7477**

Lynda Madaras, author

An essential guide for parents, teachers and young people about the subject of AIDS. *$5.95*

106 pages

ISBN 1-55704 -09-5

5785   Mandy

William Morrow & Company
1350 Avenue of the Americas
New York, NY   10019   **212-974-3100**
                                        FAX: 212-261-6595
                                     www.williammorrow.com

Told from the point of view of a deaf child, this warm picture book is neither saccharine nor preachy. Mandy has never heard anyone speak or sing. It is from her close relationship with her grandmother that the small girl learns about the world through lip-reading, facial expression, gesture, touch and sign. *$14.95*

32 pages

5786   Me, Too

JB Lippincott
227 E Washington Square
Philadelphia, PA   19106   **215-238-4200**
                                              800-777-2295
                                        FAX: 215-824-7390

Vera Cleaver, author

Lydia and Lornie were twins. Lydia was a bright twelve year old who vowed to spend her summer vacation teaching her retarded sister, Lornie, how to be normal.

158 pages Hardcover

ISBN 0-39731 -85-X

5787   Mine for Keeps

Little, Brown & Company
3 Center Plaza
Boston, MA   02108
                                              800-343-9204

Jean Little, author

Sarah Jean Copeland was born with cerebral palsy. At four years of age she was placed in a school for handicapped children but made such good progress that she could return home. Coming home for Sarah meant a new school, and new adjustments to her parents, two sisters, and her brother. At first Sarah was scared and didn't think she could do all the things she needed to do, but she soon learned her fears were not well-founded.

186 pages Hardcover

5788   My Book for Kids with Cancer

Waterfront Books
85 Crescent Road
Burlington, VT   05401   **802-658-7477**

Jason Gaes, author

Frustrated because he couldn't find any books about kids who survived cancer, Jason decided to write his own. This book is a poignant, true story of courage and hope which describes his successful battle against the disease. *$12.95*

32 pages

5789   My Buddy

Exceptional Parent Library
PO Box 1807
Englewood Cliffs, NJ   10116
                                              800-535-1910
                                   e-mail: eplibrary@aol.com
                                         www.eplibrary.com

A. Osofsky, author

This book demonstrates the desire of people with disabilities to be independent. *$5.95*

5790 My Signing Book of Numbers

Gallaudet University Press
800 Florida Avenue NE
Washington, DC 20002   202-651-5000
                               800-621-2736
                               FAX: 202-651-5489
                               TDY:888-630-9347

Patricia Bellan Gillen, author
Dan Wallace, Marketing Manager

This full-color book helps children learn their numbers in sign language. Each two-page spread of this delightfully illustrated book has the appropriate number of things or creatures for the numbers 0 through 20. *$14.95*

56 pages Hardcover
ISBN 0-93032-37-8

5791 Natural Child Care: A Complete Guide to Safe Holistic Remedies for Infants and Children

Crown Publishing Group
New York, NY

Maribeth Riggs, author

Devoted to raising children by natural, drug-free methods, this comprehensive, easy-to-use guide includes charts showing the uses of sixty readily available medicinal herbs.

1988

5792 Nursery Rhymes from Mother Goose

Gallaudet University Press
800 Florida Avenue NE
Washington, DC 20002   202-651-5000
                               800-660-8476
                               FAX: 800-660-8476
                               TDY:888-630-8347

Harry Bernstein, author
Dan Wallace, Marketing Manager

Each complete nursery rhyme is presented in Signed English and delightfully illustrated in full color. *$14.95*

64 pages
ISBN 0-93032-99-8

5793 On Our Own Terms: Children Living with Physical Disabilities

Gareth Stevens
1555 N River Center Drive
Milwaukee, WI 53212   414-225-0333
                               800-542-2595
                               FAX: 414-225-0377

Thomas Bergman, author

Meet Kicki, a three-year-old with Spina Bifida, battling to walk for the first time. Meet Annelie, nine years old, learning to walk again after a bad car accident. Face the physical challenges with her. *$13.95*

48 pages
ISBN 1-555329-42-X

5794 One Day at a Time: Children Living with Leukemia

Gareth Stevens
1555 N Rivercenter Drive
Milwaukee, WI 53212   414-225-0333
                               800-542-2595
                               FAX: 414-225-0377
                               www.infoegsinc.com

Thomas Bergman, author
Claire Messier, Marketing Associate

Focus on Hanna, two years old, and 3 year old Frederick. Both diagnosed with Leukemia and follows them as they are treated for their illness. Includes such daily routines as eating breakfast, washing and playing. *$16.95*

56 pages Hardcover
ISBN 1-55532-13-6

5795 Out of the Corner of My Eye

American Foundation for the Blind/AFB Press
PO Box 1020
Sewickley, PA 15143   412-741-1142
                               800-232-3044
                               FAX: 412-741-0609
                               e-mail: afborders@abdintl.com
                               www.afb.org

Nicolette Ringgold, author

A personal account of students' vision loss and subsequent adjustment that is full of practical advice and cheerful encouragement, told by an 87 year old retired college teacher who has maintained her independence and zest for life. *$14.95*

ISBN 0-891281-93-2

5796 Pinballs

Harper & Row
10 E 53rd Street
New York, NY 10022   212-207-7000
                               800-242-7737

Betsy Byars, author

The story of three children who are placed in foster care: Harvey, whose two broken legs were crushed when his drunken father ran over him in a car; Thomas J., who was left at the door of an eighty-year-old couple as a toddler; and Carlie, a street-wise kid who caused trouble at home with her many step fathers. The children were defiant at first, than the fine Mason home began to take effect. The children first began to like each other and then faced their problems.

136 pages Hardcover
ISBN 0-06020-17-8

5797 Please Don't Say Hello

Human Sciences Press
233 Spring Street
New York, NY 10013   212-229-2859
                               800-221-9369
                               FAX: 212-463-0742

Phyllis-Terri Gold, author

Paul and his family moved into a new neighborhood. Paul's brother was autistic. The children thought that Eddie was retarded until they learned that there were skills that he could do better than they could. *$10.95*

47 pages Paperback
ISBN 0-89885-99-8

5798 Princess Pooh

Exceptional Parent Library
PO Box 1807
Englewood Cliffs, NJ   10116
800-535-1910
e-mail: eplibrary@aol.com
www.eplibrary.com

K.M. Muldoon, author

A sibling secretly doubts her sister Princess Pooh because she sits on her throne of wheels and gives orders. An honest look at some universal feelings. *$13.95*

5799 Quad City Deaf & Hard of Hearing Youth Group: Tomorrow's Leaders for our Community

Independent Living Research Utilization ILRU
2323 S Shepherd Drive
Suite 1000
Houston, TX   77019
713-520-0232
FAX: 713-520-5785
www.ilru.org

Susan Ann Sacco, author

IICIL staff see this program as a way to develop young leaders for themovement. Emphasis is given to providing oppportunities for memebers of the youth group to develop skills in planning and organizing activities.

10 pages

5800 Queens Services for Autistic Children Newsletter

120-55 Queens Boulevard
Room 209
Kew Gardens, NY   11424
718-793-7202
FAX: 718-268-1308

Offers information on books and resources, meetings and support groups, chapter information and more for parents and families affected by autism.

Monthly

5801 Raising a Child Who Has a Physical Disability

Exceptional Parent Library
PO Box 1807
Englewood Cliffs, NJ   10116
800-535-1910
e-mail: eplibrary@aol.com
www.eplibrary.com

D.G. Albrecht, author

This compassionate book will help the parent handle every facet of raising and loving your special child. *$12.95*

5802 Rajesh

Atheneum
135 S Mount Zion Road
Lebanon, IN   46052
FAX: 800-882-8583

Curt Kaufman, author

Rajesh, a student in a headstart program, was born without complete legs and must wear two prostheses to walk. When Rajesh first attended school he found that older children teased him. After he explained about his legs to the class, his classmates began to accept him.

32 pages Hardcover
ISBN 0-68931 -74-9

5803 Reading, Writing and Speech Problems in Children

Orton Dyslexia Society
Chester Building
Suite 382
Baltimore, MD   21286
800-ABC-D123
FAX: 410-296-0232

Samuel T. Orton, author

A tribute to the man who more than any other aroused the attention of the scientific community and who provided the sound educational principles on which much teaching of dyslexics today is based. *$27.00*

ISBN 0-89079 -79-1

5804 Reflections on Growing Up Disabled

Council for Exceptional Children
1920 Association Drive
Reston, VA   20191
703-620-3660
888-232-7733
FAX: 703-264-9494
TDY:703-264-9446
e-mail: service@cec.sped.org
www.cec.sped.org

Reginald L. Jones, author
Nancy Safer, Executive Director

Understand how it feels to be a disabled person in school by tuning in to the first-hand accounts of people who have disabilities. *$10.00*

112 pages
ISBN 0-86586 -34-X

5805 Ride the Red Cycle

Houghton Mifflin
1 Beacon Street
Boston, MA   02108
617-371-9500
800-225-3362

Harriette Robinet, author

Jerome Johnson is nine, but due to brain damage he can't walk and his speech is hard to understand. Jerome gets around in a wheelchair, but he knows that if he could get a tricycle he could go where and when he wanted. His parents not only agreed to buy him the cycle, but his dad built up the pedals and added a seat with a back and a seatbelt to hold Jerome.

34 pages Hardcover
ISBN 0-39529 -83-6

5806 Rose-Colored Glasses

Human Sciences Press
233 Spring Street
New York, NY   10013
212-229-2859
800-221-9369
FAX: 212-463-0742

Linda Leggett, author

After a vacation, Deborah was excited about going back to school. Renewing old friendships, she met a classmate who seemed stuck up. Deborah learned that Melanie was in a recent accident resulting in impaired vision. She did not wish to wear her glasses, which were rose-colored and very funny looking. With Deborah's help, Miss Davis, the teacher showed a blurry film and then had Melanie speak about her impaired vision. When Melanie began to participate in the class they accepted her. *$16.95*

30 pages Hardcover
ISBN 0-87705 -08-8

5807 Science Accessed for All Students

Center for Accessible Technology
2547 8th Street
Suite 12-A
Berkeley, CA   94710　　　510-841-3224
　　　　FAX: 510-841-7956
　　　e-mail: info@cfarat.org
　　　　　www.el.net/cat

Lisa Wahl, Director

A 10 minute video that demonstrates inclusive in elementary school science two peer support, adaptation of notifices, and assistance technology. *$15.00*

Video Casette

5808 Seeing-Children Living with Blindness

Gareth Stevens
1555 N RiverCenter Drive
Milwaukee, WI   53212　　414-225-0333
　　　　　800-341-3569
　　　FAX: 414-225-0377

Thomas Bergman, author

Go with Thomas to a special school for children who can't see, where you will meet Andrew, Kate, Jordan, Katherine, Peter and Kent. Read what they told Thomas about being blind, about daily life, their feelings, the funny things, and the sad. *$10.95*

ISBN 1-555329-15-2

5809 Self-Control Games & Workbook

Western Psychological Services
12031 Wilshire Boulevard
Los Angeles, CA   90025　　310-478-2061
　　　　　800-648-8857
　　　FAX: 310-478-7838
Berthold Berg, PhD, author

This game is designed to teach self-control in academic and social situations. Addresses a total of 24 impulsive, inattentive and hyperactive behaviors. The companion workbook reinforces the use of positive self-statements, and problem-solving techniques, instead of expressing anger. *$62.50*

Game TCGS

5810 Shot in the Dark

Avery Publishing Group
Garden City, NY

Harris Coulter, Ph.D. and Barbara Fisher, author

A comprehensive, well-referenced discussion of vaccinations, including an examination of the sometimes lethal effects of the pertussis (whooping cough) component of the DPT vaccine, a vaccine required by law for all children, written as a guide for concerned parents.

1991

5811 Sleeping Beauty

Gallaudet University Press
800 Florida Avenue NE
Washington, DC   20002　　202-651-5000
　　　　　800-621-2736
　　　FAX: 800-660-8476
　　　TDY:888-630-9347
Robert Newby, author
Dan Wallace, Marketing Manager

The popular fairytale of the princess put to sleep for a hundred years is presented with beautiful full color illustrations and selected sentences in American Sign Language. *$14.95*

64 pages
ISBN 0-93032 -97-1

5812 Solve Your Child's Sleep Problems

Simon & Schuster
New York, NY

Richard Ferber, M.D., author

An invaluable book on the common sleep problems of children, from babies to teens, that offers clear explantions and common sense solutions.

1985

5813 Solving the Puzzle of the Hyperactive Child

Professional Books
Jackson, TN

William G. Crook, M.D., author

An excellent book which summarizes the many things that can make children hard to raise and provides workable solutions.

1987

5814 Somebody Called Me a Retard Today...and My Heart Felt Sad

Walker Publishing Company
435 Hudson Street
New York, NY   10014　　212-727-8300
　　　　　800-289-2553
　　　e-mail: orders@walkerbooks.com
Ellen O'Shaughnessy, author

A simple, moving story that empowers mentally challenged children and sensitizes everyone to the need to celebrate the differences in all of us. *$14.85*

24 pages Cloth/Hardcover
ISBN 0-802781-97-7

5815 Son-Rise: The Miracle Continues

Option Institute and Fellowship
2080 S Undermountain Road
Sheffield, MA   01257   413-229-8737
                                    800-562-7171
                              FAX: 413-229-8737
                       e-mail: indigo@option.org
                            www.optionindigo.com

Barry Neil Kaufman, author
Kate Wilde

Part One is the astonishing record of Raun Kaufman's development from an autistic and retarded child into a brilliant youngster who shows no traces of his former condition. Part Two follows Raun's development after the age of four, teaching the limitless possibilities of the Son-Rise Program. Part Three shares moving accounts of five other ordinary families who became extraordinary when they used the Son-Rise Program to reach their own unreachable children. *$12.95*

343 pages
ISBN 0-915811-61-8

5816 Sorrow's Song

Atlantic-Little Brown
34 Beacon Street
Boston, MA   02108
                                    800-343-9204
                              FAX: 800-286-9471
                            www.twbookmark.com

Larry Callen, author

Sorrow never learned to talk. Her parents had taken her to all the specialists to find out why she couldn't talk, but no reason was ever found.

150 pages Hardcover
ISBN 0-31612-97-4

5817 Special Education Report

Aspen Publishers
7201 McKinney Circle
Frederick, MD   21704   301-417-7591
                                    800-638-8437
                              FAX: 301-695-7931
           e-mail: customer.service@aspenpubl.com
                         www.aspenpublishers.com

Published biweekly, Special Education Report is the independent news service on law, policy and funding of programs for disabled children. *$16.00*

8-12 pages Newsletter

5818 Students with Learning Disabilities

McGraw-Hill, School Publishing
220 East Danieldale Road
DeSoto, TX   75115   972-224-1111
                                    800-442-9685
                              FAX: 972-228-1982
                                  mhschool.com

A comprehensive text which introduces students to the entire field of learning disabilities.

512 pages

5819 Superkids

60 Clyde Street
Newton, MA   02160

Newsletter for families and friends of children with limb differences. It is published twice a year and is free to interested families and professionals. Offers timely information and support to those affected by limb differences.

5820 Talkable Tales

Speech Bin
1965 25th Avenue
Vero Beach, FL   32960   561-770-0007
                                    800-477-3324
                              FAX: 561-770-0006
                             www.speechbin.com

Lois Muehl, author
Jan J. Binney, Senior Editor

Read-a-rebus stories and pictures targeting most consonant phonemes for K-5 children. *$25.95*

128 pages
ISBN 0-93783-44-0

5821 Teen Mental Health Book

Omnigraphics
615 Griswold Street
Detroit, MI   48226
                                    800-234-1340
                              FAX: 800-875-1340
                      e-mail: info@omnigraphics.com
                            www.omnigraphics.com

Karen Bellenir, Editor, author

Health tips for teens about mental health and mental illness, including facts about depression, suicide, addictive disorders, eating disorders, obsessive-compulsive disorders, panic attacks, phobias, schizophrenia, aggression, violence and more. *$48.00*

250 pages Hardcover 1900
ISBN 0-780804-42-2

5822 Tempered Wind

Atheneum
135 S Mount Zion Road
Lebanon, IN   46052
                              FAX: 800-882-8583

Joanne Dixon, author

Gabrielle was a dwarf and was never out of her house until her parents died and she was sent from one aunt to the next. At age thirteen she was enrolled in school for the first time. The children teased her about being a dwarf, and although she excelled academically, she failed socially. After three years in school an illness forced her aunt to take Gabrielle to the doctor. The doctor's prognosis was grim and led Gabrielle's aunt to tell her that she would have to find a job.

210 pages Hardcover
ISBN 0-68931-39-X

5823 Thinking Big

William Morrow & Company
1350 Avenue of the Americas
New York, NY   10019   212-974-3100
                              FAX: 212-261-6595
                           www.williammorrow.com

Susan Kuklin, author

Eight-year-old Jaime's lively personality shines through in this perceptive photo essay which explains what being a dwarf means physically and then presents Jaime's world at home and at school from her viewpoint. *$15.95*

48 pages

5824 Trouble with Explosives

Bradbury Press
135 South Mount Zion Road
Lebanon, IN   46052

800-257-5755
FAX: 800-882-8583

Sally Kelley, author

Polly moved regularly with her family, changing schools almost every year. This was especially difficult as she couldn't pronounce her explosive name, Polly Banks, without stuttering.

117 pages Hardcover
ISBN 0-87888 -94-1

5825 Understanding Cub Scouts with Disabilities

Boy Scouts of America
1325 W Walnut Hill Lane
Irving, TX   75038

214-351-1010
800-323-0732

Boy Scouts of America, author

Manual on how to teach and understand boy scouts with handicaps.

10 pages

5826 Vegetarian Baby

McBooks Press
Ithaca, NY

Sharon K. Yntema, author

Gives information on the basics of a healthy diet, how to prepare vegetarian foods, and when to introduce different types of foods; includes recipes.

1984

5827 Views from Our Shore

Woodbine House
6510 Bells Mill Road
Bethesda, MD   20817

800-843-7323
www.woodbinehouse.com

Donald J. Meyer, author

Siblings share what it is like to have a brother or sister with a disability. *$14.95*

106 pages Paperback

5828 We Laugh, We Love, We Cry: Children Living with Mental Retardation

Gareth Stevens
1555 N River Center Drive
Milwaukee, WI   53212

414-225-0333
800-524-2595
FAX: 414-225-0377

Thomas Bergman, author

Two sisters, Asa and Anna Karin, are mentally retarded. They find it hard to understand things quickly, so learning to walk and talk has been slow work for them. With help from their parents, friends and teachers and their doctors, they are both learning to do the things that most of us are not lucky enough to learn easily. *$13.95*

48 pages
ISBN 1-555329-14-4

5829 What About Me? Growing Up with a Developmentally Disabled Sibling

Plenum Publishing Company
233 Spring Street
New York, NY   10013

212-229-2859
800-221-9369
e-mail: info@plenum.com

Bryna Siegel and Stuart Silverstein, author

An excellent guide for families and mental health professionals alike. The authors' new book provides the parents and siblings of a developmentally disabled child with the information and understanding needed to promote a better family life. *$24.95*

316 pages
ISBN 0-30644 -50-2

5830 What Happens Next?

Exceptional Parent Library
PO Box 1807
Englewood Cliffs, NJ   10116

800-535-1910
e-mail: eplibrary@aol.com
www.eplibrary.com

C. Christian and L. Dwight, author

Babies will love the colorful photographs and hidden surprises in this sturdy little book. *$4.95*

5831 What It's Like to be Me

Friendship Press
PO Box 37844
Cincinnati, OH   45222

513-948-8733
FAX: 513-761-3722
www.ncccusa.org

Helen Exley, author
Nancy Kennedy, Customer Service

This was written and illustrated entirely by children with handicapped conditions. These contributions invite the reader to set aside any pity or prejudices and listen. Black and white, and color drawings and photographs make this book visually appealing, enjoyable for all ages. *$10.95*

5832 What's a Virus, Anyway? The Kid's Book About AIDS

Waterfront Books
85 Crescent Road
Burlington, VT   05401

802-658-7477

David Fassler, M.D. and Kelly McQueen, M.D., author

A simple introduction to help adults talk with children about the subject of AIDS. Includes children's drawings and questions and provides basic information in a manner appropriate for 4-10 years old. *$8.95*

67 pages

5833 Wheels for Walking

Little, Brown & Company
3 Center Plaza
Boston, MA 02108
800-343-9204

Sandra Richmond, author

Sally tried to accept the rules and regulations set up by her family. As a teenager she didn't understand why her parents doubted her judgement. Sally rebelled and insisted on going on a trip with her boyfriend. Although the weekend was innocent, it ended in a car accident that left her a quadriplegic.

195 pages Hardcover
ISBN 0-87113-41-6

5834 Winning Over Asthma

Asthma and Allergy Foundation of America
1125 15th Street NW
Suite 502
Washington, DC 20005
202-466-7643
FAX: 202-466-8940
e-mail: info@aafa.org
www.aafa.org

Eileen Dolan Savage, author

Simple coloring book explains asthma through a story about five-year-old Graham. *$7.00*

30 pages Paperback

5835 You Can Control Asthma

Asthma and Allergy Foundation of America
1125 15th Street NW
Suite 502
Washington, DC 20005
202-466-7643
FAX: 202-466-8940
e-mail: info@aafa.org
www.aafa.org

A set of low-literacy asthma education books for children ages 6-12 and their families. Developed at Georgetown University and pre-tested with urban families to ensure comprehension and appropriateness. *$8.00*

5836 You Seem Like a Regular Kid to Me

American Foundation for the Blind/AFB Press
PO Box 1020
Sewickley, PA 15143
412-741-1142
800-232-3044
FAX: 412-741-0609
e-mail: afborders@abdintl.com
www.afb.org

Anne Corn, author

An interview with Jane, a blind child, tells other children what it's like to be blind. Jane explains how she gets around, takes care of herself, does her school work, spends her leisure time and even pays for things when she can't see money.

16 pages
ISBN 0-891289-21-6

Community

5837 Attending to America: Personal Assistance for Independent Living

World Institute on Disability
510-16th Street
Suite 100
Oakland, CA 94612
510-763-4100
FAX: 510-763-4109
TDY:510-208-9493
e-mail: wid@wid.org
www.wid.org

Nora Groce, author

This unique 1987 report explores the then-current publicly provided personal assistance system in the U.S. It contains policy recommendations and action steps, a definition of terms, a directory of attendant service programs in the U.S. and a bibliography. *$20.00*

190 pages Paperback

5838 Community Recreation and People with Disabilities: Strategies for Inclusion

Brookes Publishing
PO Box 10624
Baltimore, MD 21285
410-337-9580
800-638-3775
FAX: 410-337-8539
e-mail: custserv@brookespublishing.com
www.brookespublishing.com

Stuart J. Schleien, Ph.D., CTRS, CLP, author

Offers creative ideas and new techniques for including people with disabilities in community recreation programs. *$39.00*

368 pages Paperback 1997
ISBN 1-55766-59-2

5839 Crossing the River: Creating a Conceptual Revolution in Community & Disability

Brookline Books
PO Box 1047
Cambridge, MA 02238
617-868-0360
800-666-2665
FAX: 617-868-1772
e-mail: brooklinebks@delphi.com
www.brooklinebooks.com

David B. Schwartz, author

For persons with disabilities, a new conception of care is beginning to emerge—a conception seeking to embed these persons in a web of personal relationships, and to involve them in the dynamics of their community. Schwartz explores the promise, potential, and limits of this new direction. *$24.95*

238 pages Paperback
ISBN 0-91479-82-4

5840 Culture and the Restructuring of Community Mental Health

Greenwood Publishing Group
88 Post Road West
5007
Westport, CT 06880
203-226-3571
FAX: 203-222-1502
www.greenwood.com

William A. Vega and John W. Murphy, author

Examines treatment, organizational planning and research issues and offers a critique of the theoretical and programmatic aspects of providing mental health services to traditionally underserved populations. $45.00-$52.95.

168 pages Hardcover
ISBN 0-313268-87-8

5841　Disablement in the Community

Oxford University Press
2001 Evans Road
Cary, NC　27513　　　212-726-6000
　　　　　　　　　　　800-451-7556
　　　　　　　　FAX: 919-677-1303
　　　　　　　　　www.oup-usa.org

Donald L. Patrick, author

This book shows how the knowledge of the epidemiology of disablement can help planners, service providers, patients and voluntary organizations choose strategies for community care. *$39.95*

248 pages Illustrated

5842　Free and User Supported Software for the IBM PC: A Resource Guide

McFarland & Company
PO Box 611
Jefferson, NC　28640　　　336-246-4460
　　　　　　　　　　　800-253-2187

A guide for libraries and individuals which offers information on personal computers. Specific applications are included. Selected product (IBM and Apple) and vendor information with price, hardware requirements, and a description is also furnished. *$27.50*

224 pages
ISBN 0-89950-99-0

5843　Housing, Support, and Community

Brookes Publishing
PO Box 10624
Baltimore, MD　21285　　　410-337-9580
　　　　　　　　　　　800-638-3775
　　　　　　　　FAX: 410-337-8539
　　e-mail: custserv@brookespublishing.com
　　　　　www.brookespublishing.com

Choices and strategies for adults with disabilities. *$ 32.00*

416 pages Paperback
ISBN 1-55766-90-5

5844　Inclusive Child Care for Infants and Toddlers: Meeting Individual and Special Needs

Brookes Publishing
PO Box 10624
Baltimore, MD　21285　　　410-337-9580
　　　　　　　　　　　800-638-3775
　　　　　　　　FAX: 410-337-8539
　　e-mail: custserv@brookespublishing.com
　　　　　www.brookespublishing.com

Marion O'Brien, Ph.D., author

This book gives child care providers the practical guidance they need to serve infants and toddlers with and without disabilities in inclusive settings. It offers information and helpful advice on handling daily care tasks, teaching responsively, meeting individual needs, developing rapport with parents, understanding toddlers' behavior, working with IFSPs, and maintaining high standards of care. *$34.95*

400 pages Paperback 1997
ISBN 1-55766 -96-7

5845　Positive Behavioral Support: Including People with Difficult Behavior in the Community

Brookes Publishing
PO Box 10624
Baltimore, MD　21285　　　410-337-9580
　　　　　　　　　　　800-638-3775
　　　　　　　　FAX: 410-337-8539
　　e-mail: custserv@brookespublishing.com
　　　　　www.brookespublishing.com

This text demonstrates how people with challenging behavior can be fully included at home, at school, and in the community. Offers intervention techniques and explores the planning and assistance needed to implement nonaversive inclusion strategies. *$37.95*

528 pages Paperback
ISBN 1-55766 -28-2

5846　Prevention in Community Mental Health

Brookline Books
PO Box 1046
Cambridge, MA　02238　　　617-868-0360
　　　　　　　　　　　800-666-2665
　　　　　　　　FAX: 617-868-1772
　　e-mail: brooklinebks@delphi.com
　　　　　www.brooklinebooks.com

N.D. Reppucci, author

Describes prevention programs written through a collaborative effort between university researchers and community practitioners. The result is theoretical and practical perspectives in each chapter which provide explicit examples of how prevention focused community mental health networks operate and evaluate efforts. *$27.95*

ISBN 0-91479 -70-0

5847　Supporting Young Adults Who are Deaf-Blind in Their Communities

Brookes Publishing
PO Box 10624
Baltimore, MD　21285　　　410-337-9580
　　　　　　　　　　　800-638-3775
　　　　　　　　FAX: 410-337-8539
　　e-mail: custserv@brookespublishing.com
　　　　　www.brookespublishing.com

A Transition Planning Guide for Service Providers, Families, and Friends. This handbook stresses the importance of person-centered planning in helping individuals who are deaf-blind make the transition from school to adult life. *$39.95*

384 pages Paperback
ISBN 1-55766 -61-8

5848 Total Resource for the Wheelchair Community

Spinal Network Extra
PO Box 4162
Boulder, CO   80306

800-338-5412

A humorous satire for persons who have suffered spinal cord injuries. This book offers cartoons scattered throughout the book for wheelchair users and persons who spend time with people with wheelchairs. *$24.94*

372 pages

5849 Transitioning Exceptional Children and Youth Into the Community

Haworth Press
10 Alice Street
Binghamton, NY   13904

604-722-5857
800-429-6784
FAX: 607-722-6362
e-mail: getinfo@haworthpressinc.com
www.haworthpressinc.com
Ennio Cipani, PhD, author
Jackie Blakeslee, Advertising

Focusing on the dynamic process of mainstreaming exceptional children and youth into the community, experts examine some of the exciting technological advances made to accompany the social changes enacted over the years. *$69.95*

202 pages Hardcover
ISBN 0-866567-33-X

5850 Transitions to Adult Life

Books on Special Children
PO Box 305
Congers, NY   10920

845-638-1236
FAX: 845-638-0847
e-mail: irene@boscbooks.com
A.P. Turnbull, author

Transition programs that can help severely handicapped people become participating, contributing members of the community. *$ 37.00*

385 pages Softcover

Elderly

5851 Abstracts in Social Gerontology: Current Literature on Aging

National Council on the Aging
600 Maryland Avenue SW
Washington, DC   20024

202-554-5981
FAX: 202-479-0735

Detailed abstracts are provided for recent major journal articles, books, reports and other materials on many facets of aging, including: adult education, demography, family relations, institutional care and work attitudes.

5852 Activities in Action

Haworth Press
10 Alice Street
Binghamton, NY   13904

604-722-5857
800-429-6784
FAX: 607-722-6362
e-mail: getinfo@haworthpressinc.com
www.haworthpressinc.com
Phyllis Foster, ACC, author
Jackie Blakeslee, Advertising

An invaluable resource which serves as a catalyst for professional and personal growth and provides a national forum on geriatric and activity issues. *$69.95*

98 pages Hardcover
ISBN 1-560241-32-2

5853 Activities with Developmentally Disabled Elderly and Older Adults

Haworth Press
10 Alice Street
Binghamton, NY   13904

604-722-5857
800-429-6784
FAX: 607-722-6362
e-mail: getinfo@haworthpressinc.com
www.haworthpressinc.com
M. Jean Keller, EdD, CTRS, author
Jackie Blakeslee, Advertising

Learn how to effectively plan and deliver activities for a growing number of older people with developmental disabilities. It aims to stimulate interest and continued support for recreation program development and implementation among developmental disability and aging service systems. *$54.95*

156 pages Hardcover
ISBN 1-560240-92-X

5854 Aging & Vision News

Lighthouse Industries/Publications Department
370 Starke Road
Carlstadt, NJ   07072

201-896-1112
800-334-5497
FAX: 212-821-9706
e-mail: info@lighthouse.org
www.lighthouse.org

Intended for professionals engaged in research, education or service delivery in the field of vision and aging.

Quarterly

5855 Aging Eye and Low Vision

Lighthouse Industries/Publications Department
370 Starke Road
Carlstadt, NJ   07072

201-896-1112
800-334-5497
e-mail: info@lighthouse.org

A study guide for physicians on common age-related vision disorders.

5856 Aging News Alert

CD Publications
8204 Fenton Street
Silver Spring, MD   20910

301-588-2280
800-666-6380
FAX: 301-588-6385
e-mail: cdpubs@clark.net
www.cdpublications.com/seniors/ana.htm
Alan Cohen, Editor, author

Publishes short articles on legislation and other federal action affecting elderly people. *$237.00*

16-18 pages Weekly
ISSN 1050-31 8

5857   Aging Process: Therapeutic Implications

Lippincott, Williams & Wilkins
227 E Washington Square
Philadelphia, PA   19106   215-238-4200
                                      800-777-2295
                                      FAX: 301-824-7390
                                      www.lpub.com

Robert Butler, author

Experts examine the physiological and biological aspects of aging that impinge upon drug disposition and medical therapeutics.

352 pages

5858   Aging Research & Training News

Business Publishers
8737 Colesville Road
Suite 1100
Silver Spring, MD   20910
                                      800-274-6737
                                      FAX: 301-587-4530
                                      e-mail: bpinews@bpinews.com
                                      www.bpinews.com

Leonard A. Eiserer, Publisher
Nancy Aldrich, Editor
Katie Johnson, Marketing Manager

Compilation of studies of aging populations; reports on innovative programs with aging community; federal funding and laws. *$ 267.00*

8 pages Monthly

5859   Aging and Family Therapy: Practitioner Perspectives on Golden Pond

Haworth Press
10 Alice Street
Binghamton, NY   13904   604-722-5857
                                      800-429-6784
                                      FAX: 607-722-6362
                                      e-mail: getinfo@haworthpressinc.com
                                      www.haworthpressinc.com

George A. Hughston, author
Jackie Blakeslee, Advertising

Here are creative strategies for use in therapy with older adults and their families. This significant new book provides practitioners with information, insight, reference tools, and other sources that will contribute to more effective intervention with the elderly and their families. *$69.95*

244 pages Hardcover
ISBN 0-866567-78-X

5860   Aging and Our Families

Human Sciences Press
233 Spring Street
New York, NY   10013   212-229-2859
                                      800-221-9369
                                      FAX: 212-463-0742

Donna P. Couper, author

Handbook for family caregivers. *$18.95*

132 pages Paperback
ISBN 0-89885 -41-5

5861   Aging and Vision News

National Center for Vision and Aging
The Lighthouse-800 Second Avenue
New York, NY   10017   212-808-0077
                                      800-334-5497

3x Year

5862   Aging in the Designed Environment

Haworth Press
10 Alice Street
Binghamton, NY   13904   604-722-5857
                                      800-429-6784
                                      FAX: 607-722-6362
                                      e-mail: getinfo@haworthpressinc.com
                                      www.haworthpressinc.com

Margaret Christenson, author
Jackie Blakeslee, Advertising

The key sourcebook for physical and occupational therapists developing and implementing environmental designs for the aging. *$ 69.95*

133 pages
ISBN 1-560240-31-8

5863   Aging with a Disability

Special Needs Project
3463 Stat Street
 # 282
Santa Barbara, CA   93105
                                      800-333-6867

This unique and recent book discusses the role of family, financial resources and the American health care system in the life of aging adults with developmental disabilities. $32.95

5864   Beat the Nursing Home Trap: A Consumer's Guide to Assisted Living and Long Term Care

NOLO
950 Parker Street
Berkeley, CA   94710   510-549-1976
                                      800-955-4775
                                      FAX: 510-548-5902
                                      www.nolo.com

Joseph L. Matthews with Dorothy Matthews Berman, author
Maira Dizgalvis, Trade Customer Service Manager
Susan McConnell, Director of Sales
Natasha Kaluza, Sales Assistant

Don't guess. Use this book to figure out how to choose a nursing home, or find a viable alternative. Covers how to get the most out of Medicare and other benefit programs. *$21.95*

336 pages paperback
ISBN 0-873375-15-7

5865   California Financial Power of Attorney

NOLO
950 Parker Street
Berkeley, CA   94710   510-549-1976
                                      800-955-4775
                                      FAX: 510-548-5902
                                      www.nolo.com

Maira Dizgalvis, Trade Customer Service Manager
Susan McConnell, Director of Sales
Natasha Kaluza, Sales Assistant

A plain-English book packed with forms and instructions to give a trusted person the legal authority to handle your financial affairs.

paperback

5866 Caring for Alzheimer's Patients

Plenum Publishing Company
233 Spring Street
New York, NY 10013   212-229-2859
                              800-221-9369
                    e-mail: info@plenum.com

Gary D. Miner, author

This handbook is designed for families, friends, and health-care professionals coping with the myriad of problems encountered by those afflicted with Alzheimer's disease. *$22.95*

308 pages Cloth
ISBN 3-06431-98-

5867 Caring for Those You Love - A Guide to Compassionate Care for the Aged

Horizon Publishers
50 S 500 W
Bountiful, UT 84010   801-295-9451

This book is a practical guide to coping with special problems of the aged and infirm, and examines the many challenges of caring for the elderly on a personal and family level. *$12.98*

ISBN 0-88290-70-9

5868 Caring for the Disabled Elderly

Brookings Institution
1775 Massachusetts Avenue NW
Washington, DC 20036   202-797-6000

Alice M. Rivlin, author
Financial information for the elderly. *$31.95*

318 pages Cloth

5869 Chronically Disabled Elderly in Society

Greenwood Publishing Group
88 Post Road West
5007
Westport, CT 06880   203-226-3571
                    FAX: 203-222-1502
                    www.greenwood.com

Merna F. Alpert, author

This timely work increases awareness of and knowledge about problems of societal living among the chronically disabled elderly, with implications for policy makers, educational institutions, advocacy groups, families and individuals. Hardcover.

160 pages $52.95 - $55
ISBN 0-313291-09-8

5870 Communication Disorders in Aging

Gallaudet University Press
800 Florida Avenue NE
Washington, DC 20002   202-651-5000
                              800-451-1073
                    FAX: 202-651-5489

H. Gustav Mueller, author

This text presents contemporary practices in the medical and clinical assessment of the aged, reviews clinical evaluation techniques, and provides a comprehensive discussion of neurological imaging techniques. *$39.95*

528 pages Hardcover

5871 Consumer Health Information-Spanish Edition

ORYX Press
4041 N Central Avenue
Suite 700
Phoenix, AZ 85012   602-265-2651
                              800-279-6799
                    FAX: 800-279-4663
                    e-mail: info@oryxpress.com
                    www.oryxpress.com

Alan Rees, Author
Irene Affranchino-Miniello, Author

For the first time, consumer health information entirely in Spanish and directed at the Hispanic population of the United States has been brought together in one convenient volume. this collection contains the full text in Spanish of over 150 articles available from the National Cancer Institute, the Food and Drug Administration, Leukemia Society of America, and other federal and private authoritative agencies. A list of Spanish-language health publications is also included. *$74.95*

ISBN 1-57356-66-5

5872 Consumer Health USA, Volume 2

ORYX Press
4041 N Central Avenue
Suite 700
Phoenix, AZ 85012   602-265-2651
                              800-279-6799
                    FAX: 800-279-4663
                    e-mail: info@oryxpress.com
                    www.oryxpress.com

Alan M. Rees, author

This highly regarded reference source features the full text of nearly 150 articles available from the National Cancer Institute, the Food and Drug Administration, the National institute on Aging,the Leukemia Society of America, the National Parkinson's Foundation, and the Alzheimer's Association. Chapters on stroke and musculoskeletal and connective tissue diseases are also included. The reference gives a helpful list of national toll-free numbers for readers who need additional information. *$65.00*

608 pages
ISBN 1-57356-68-5

5873 Coping and Caring: Living with Alzheimer's Disease

AARP Fulfillment
601 E Street NW
Washington, DC 20049   202-434-2277
                              800-424-3410
                    FAX: 202-434-3443
                    e-mail: member@aarp.org
                    www.aarp.org

Addresses the questions: What is Alzheimer's? How does the disease progress? How long does it last? How can families cope?.

24 pages

5874 Destination Southern California

ORYX Press
4041 N Central Avenue
Suite 700
Phoenix, AZ 85012   602-265-2651
800-279-6799
FAX: 800-279-4663
e-mail: info@oryxpress.com

Michael Meyer, author

Here are 91 recommended facilities for active seniors looking to vacation or retire in Southern California. This book identifies the type of housing available at each planned community, number of sites or units, restrictions or requirements, and fees. *$14.50*

232 pages
ISBN 0-89774 -46-5

5875 Destination Southwest

ORYX Press
4041 N Central Avenue
Suite 700
Phoenix, AZ 85012   602-265-2651
800-279-6799
FAX: 800-279-4663
e-mail: info@oryxpress.com

Active seniors spend millions of dollars retiring or vacationing in the Southwest. This book identifies housing in that area. *$14.50*

240 pages
ISBN 0-89774 -07-4

5876 Directory of Nursing Homes

ORYX Press
4041 N Central Avenue
Suite 700
Phoenix, AZ 85012   602-265-2651
800-279-6799
FAX: 800-279-4663
e-mail: info@oryxpress.com

Sam Mongeau, author

The most complete directory in print is now annually updated and expanded and includes even more in-depth facility profiles. In addition to facility name, address and telephone number, each new or updated listing identifies contact names, admission requirements and more. *$225.00*

1,512 pages
ISBN 0-89774 -65-1

5877 Directory of Self-Help/Mutual Aid Support Groups for Older People

Lighthouse Industries/Publications Department
370 Starke Road
Carlstadt, NJ 07072   201-896-1112
800-334-5497
e-mail: info@lighthouse.org

State-by-state listings of over 650 support groups for older people with impaired vision, plus listings of state commissions for the blind, self-help clearinghouses, vision rehabilitation agencies, and national resource organizations. *$10.00*

5878 Domestic Mistreatment of the Elderly: Towards Prevention

AARP Fulfillment
601 East Street NW
Washington, DC 20049   202-434-2277
800-424-3410
FAX: 202-434-3443
e-mail: member@aarp.org
www.aarp.org

This comprehensive publication addresses the problem of mistreatment or neglect in the home.

39 pages

5879 Early Story of Alzheimer's Disease

Lippincott, Williams & Wilkins
227 East Washington Square
Philadelphia, PA 19106   215-238-4200
800-777-2295
FAX: 301-824-7390
www.lpub.com

Katherine Bick, author

Translation of the historical papers by Alos Alzheimer. *$58.50*

160 pages Illustrated
ISBN 0-88167 -68-4

5880 Elder Abuse

Human Sciences Press
233 Spring Street
New York, NY 10013   212-229-2859
800-221-9369
FAX: 212-463-0742

Rachel Filinson, author

Practice, policy and laws for abuse on the aging.

232 pages Cloth
ISBN 0-89885 -15-6

5881 Elder Care

Center for Public Representation
PO Box 260049
Madison, WI 53726   608-251-4008
800-369-0388
FAX: 606-251-1263
www.law.misc.edu/pal

Joseph Matthews, author

A compendium of alternatives for providing and financing long-term care. This practical guide provides the most comprehensive and comforting information to help navigate a number of consumer mine fields. *$16.95*

224 pages
ISBN 0-87337 -13-5

5882 Elder Services

ORYX Press
4041 North Central Avenue
Suite 700
Phoenix, AZ   85012   602-265-2651
                                                 800-279-6799
                                 FAX: 800-279-4663
                        e-mail: info@oryxpress.com

Lists home health services, information and referral agencies, support groups, home delivered meals and organizations for the elderly. *$22.50*

360 pages
ISBN 0-89774-63-5

5883 Exercise and the Older Adult

Kendall/Hunt Publishing Company
1900 Association Drive
Reston, VA   20191   703-476-3400
                                                 800-213-7193
                                 FAX: 703-476-9527
                        e-mail: aaalf@aahperd.org
                                 www.aahperd.org
Wayne Osness, Editor, author
Jan A. Seaman, MBA, P.E.D., Executive Director

The latest information on physical activity for the older adults is in this textbook. Biomechanics, exercise physiology, health issues, sensory-motor function and measurement are covered by leading experts in the field. Other topics addressed include low-impact aerobics, strength development, exercise and activities for the frail elderly. *$35.00*

202 pages
ISBN 0-787210-04-8

5884 Falling in Old Age

Springer Publishing Company
536 Broadway
New York, NY   10012   212-431-4370
                                 FAX: 212-941-7842
Rein Tideiksaar, author

Presented are practical techniques for the prevention of falls and for determining and correcting the causes.

5885 Family Carebook

CAREsource Program Development
505 Seattle Tower
Seattle, WA   98101   206-625-9128
                                                 800-448-5213
                                 FAX: 206-682-2901
                        e-mail: service@caresource.com
                                 www.caresource.com
CareSource, author

Guide to aging, the special needs of older adults, and the demands of providing care and support. Experts explain potential conflicts, planning opportunities and strategies for success. Six guides. *$49.95*

475 pages Paperback
ISBN 1-87886-12-5

5886 Functional Fitness Assessment for Adults

American Alliance for Health, Phys. Ed. & Dance
1900 Association Drive
Reston, VA   20191   703-476-3400

                        e-mail: aaalf@aahperd.org
ARAPCA Council on Aging and Adult Development, author

This field test assesses the functional fitness of adults over 60 years of age. It is designed to serve the larger population through field based measurement techniques that can be used in a facility where older persons live and can be conducted by personnel not necessarily trained for clinical responsibilities. *$7.50*

24 pages
ISBN 0-88314-47-6

5887 Handbook of Assistive Devices for the Handicapped Elderly

Haworth Press
10 Alice Street
Binghamton, NY   13904   604-722-5857
                                                 800-429-6784
                                 FAX: 607-722-6362
                        e-mail: getinfo@haworthpressinc.com
                                 www.haworthpressinc.com
Joseph M. Breuer, MA, RPT, author
Jackie Blakeslee, Advertising

Concise yet comprehensive reference of the latest and most assistive devices for handicapped elders. *$29.95*

77 pages Hardcover
ISBN 0-866561-52-8

5888 Handbook on Ethnicity, Aging and Mental Health

Greenwood Publishing Group
88 Post Road West
5007
Westport, CT   06880   203-226-3571
                                 FAX: 203-222-1502
                                 www.greenwood.com
Deborah K. Padgett, Editor, author

State-of-the-art reference by leading experts and first book-length appraisal of research, practices and policies concerning mental health needs of the ethnic elderly in America. $95-$99.50.

376 pages Hardcover
ISBN 0-313282-04-8

5889 Health Care of the Aged

Haworth Press
10 Alice Street
Binghamton, NY   13904   604-722-5857
                                                 800-429-6784
                                 FAX: 607-722-6362
                        e-mail: getinfo@haworthpressinc.com
                                 www.haworthpressinc.com
Abraham Monk, PhD., author
Jackie Blakeslee, Advertising

Focusing on the need for developing new service delivery models for the aged, this book examines fiscal, political, and social criteria influencing this challenge of the 1990's. The aged are caught in the sweeping changes currently occurring in the financing, organizing and delivery of human health care services. *$69.95*

183 pages Hardcover
ISBN 1-560240-65-2

5890 Health Promotion and Disease Prevention

Lippincott, Williams & Wilkins
227 E Washington Square
Philadelphia, PA   19106   215-238-4200
                                  800-777-2295
                           FAX: 301-824-7390
                                  www.lpub.com

Ronni Chernoff, author

Professional directory offering information on health care and rehabilitation for the elderly. *$87.00*

> *218 pages*
> *ISBN 0-88167-90-0*

5891 International Health Guide for Senior Citizen Travelers

Pilot Books
PO Box 2102
Greenport, NY   11944   516-477-1094
                        FAX: 516-661-4379

W. Robert Lange, author

Covers essential pre-departure health planning; advice on specific health concerns; disease prevention and more. *$4.95*

5892 Managing Aging and Human Services Agencies

Springer Publishing Company
536 Broadway
New York, NY   10012   212-431-4370
                        FAX: 212-941-7842

Edward Morgan, Jr., author

Offers specialized information for the human resources professional who works with the elderly. *$27.95*

> *160 pages*

5893 Mastering the Medicare Maze

Center for Public Representation
PO Box 260049
Madison, WI   53726   608-251-4008
                             800-369-0388
                        FAX: 606-251-1263

Betsy Abramson, author

This book provides simple explanations of how to appeal denied Medicare claims. Less than 3% of Medicare claims are ever appealed. But of those that are, over 60% are successful in returning dollars to beneficiaries. With simple instructions, this book tells you how to do it and includes all the necessary forms. *$9.95*

> *128 pages*
> *ISBN 0-93262-40-2*

5894 Medicare Maximization

Center for Public Representation
PO Box 260049
Madison, WI   53726   608-251-4008
                             800-369-0388
                        FAX: 606-251-1263
          e-mail: cpr@lawmail.law.wisc.edu
                    www.law.wisc.edu/pal

Jeffrey Spitzer-Resnick, author

This manual for nursing homes provides information on Medicare billing procedures, Medicare coverage guidelines - Part A and Part B as well as Medicare Bed Certification for nursing homes. Chapters with examples and exercises give you the knowledge to maximize Medicare reimbursements. *$39.95*

> *150 pages*
> *ISBN 0-93262-34-8*

5895 Mentally Impaired Elderly: Strategies and Interventions to Maintain Function

Haworth Press
10 Alice Street
Binghamton, NY   13904   604-722-5857
                                800-429-6784
                           FAX: 607-722-6362
     e-mail: getinfo@haworthpressinc.com
                  www.haworthpressinc.com

Ellen Taira, OTR/L, MPH, author
Jackie Blakeslee, Advertising

Provides effective support and sensitive care for the most vulnerable segment of the elderly population, those with mental impairment. *$69.95*

> *171 pages Hardcover*
> *ISBN 1-560241-68-3*

5896 Mirrored Lives: Aging Children and Elderly Parents

Greenwood Publishing Group
88 Post Road West
5007
Westport, CT   06880   203-226-3571
                         FAX: 203-222-1502
                           www.greenwood.com

Tom Koch, author

Discusses geriatric decline connected to nonterminal illness in old age. Koch takes a sensitive but thorough look at the declining years of his father. $19.95-$21.95.

> *240 pages Hardcover*
> *ISBN 0-275936-71-6*

5897 National Directory of Retirement

ORYX Press
4041 N Central Avenue
Suite 700
Phoenix, AZ   85012   602-265-2651
                             800-279-6799
                        FAX: 800-279-4663
          e-mail: info@oryxpress.com

This award-winning reference source lists more than 22,000 facilities nationwide. Entries identify and describe facilities that are assisted living, congregate care, independent living and continuing care. *$195.00*

> *1,208 pages*
> *ISBN 0-89774-67-8*

5898 Now Where Did I Put My Keys?

AARP Fulfillment
601 E Street NW
Washington, DC   20049   202-434-2277
                              800-424-3410
                         FAX: 202-434-3443
                 e-mail: member@aarp.org
                              www.aarp.org

Your copies of this brochure won't last long on your information counter.

5899 Older & Wiser: A Workbook for Coping with Aging

New Harbinger Publications
5674 Shattuck Avenue
Oakland, CA   94609   510-652-0215
                              800-748-6273

This compassion guide teaches the practical skills and elicits personal insight necessary to meet the demands of aging in our society. *$12.95*

300 pages
ISBN 1-87923 -10-5

5900 On Your Behalf

CAREsource Program Development
505 Seattle Tower
Seattle, WA   98101   206-625-9128
                              800-448-5213
                         FAX: 206-682-2901
              e-mail: service@caresource.com
                          www.caresource.com

CareSource, author

This book takes the mystery out of very important sets of legal options. It gives lay people as well as advisors, service providers, and caregivers the information they need to understand their options and the importance of individual choice.

16 pages Books & Video
ISBN 1-87886 -14-1

5901 Operation Help: A Mental Health Advocate Guide to Medicaid

National Council of Community Mental Health Center
12300 Twinbrook Parkway
Suite 320
Rockville, MD   20852   301-670-6331

Explains the Medicaid entitlement program in easy-to-understand language and focuses on the needs of adults with serious mental illness, children with serious emotional disturbance and elderly persons who need mental health care. *$17.00*

5902 Perspective on Aging

National Council on the Aging
600 Maryland Avenue SW
Washington, DC   20024   202-554-5981
                         FAX: 202-479-0735

Explores significant developments in the field of aging, including disabilities, through opinion articles, profiles and book reviews. *$4.00*

5903 Perspectives on Prevention and Treatment of Cancer in the Elderly

Lippincott, Williams & Wilkins
227 E Washington Square
Philadelphia, PA   19106   215-238-4200
                              800-777-2295
                         FAX: 301-824-7390
                              www.lpub.com

Rosemary Yancik, author

This book presents an exchange of ideas and information on the complexities of cancer and aging. Clinicians and investigators from a wide range of pertinent disciplines highlight the issues unique to the elderly patient in cancer prevention, diagnosis and treatment. *$113.00*

360 pages

5904 Prescriptions for Independence

American Foundation for the Blind/AFB Press
PO Box 1020
Sewickley, PA   15143   412-741-1142
                              800-232-3044
                         FAX: 412-741-0609
              e-mail: afborders@abdintl.com
                              www.afb.org

Nora Griffin-Shirley, Gerda Groff, author

Easy-to-read manual on how older visually impaired persons can pursue their interests and activities in community residences, senior centers, long-term care facilities and other community settings. Paperback. *$29.95*

ISBN 0-891282-44-0

5905 Rehabilitation in the Aging

Lippincott, Williams & Wilkins
227 E Washington Square
Philadelphia, PA   19106   215-238-4200
                              800-777-2295
                         FAX: 301-824-7390
                              www.lpub.com

Franklin Williams, author

This volume provides the physician with a comprehensive approach to the medical and rehabilitative management of geriatric patients. *$82.50*

390 pages

5906 Respiratory Health Association

223 N Van Dien Avenue
Ridgewood, NJ   07450   201-445-1173

Elaine DeMicco, Community Relations

Offers eight-day cruises for people with respiratory conditions to Bermuda and Alaska at least twice a year.

5907 Senior Citizens and the Law

Center for Public Representation
PO Box 260049
Madison, WI   53726   608-251-4008
                              800-369-0388
                         FAX: 606-251-1263
          e-mail: cpr@lawmail.law.wisc.edu
                          www.law.wisc.edu

Betsy Abramson, author

An introduction to legal problems facing the elderly in Wisconsin. This edition discusses legal problems associated with Social Security, Medicare, SSI, guardianship and its alternatives, community-based services, probate, taxes, private health insurance and consumer protection. *$5.00*

ISBN 0-936226-15-1

5908 Sharing Solutions: A Newsletter for Support Groups

Lighthouse Industries/Publications Department
370 Starke Road
Carlstadt, NJ 07072   201-896-1112
                                  800-334-5497
                       FAX: 212-821-9707
             e-mail: info@lighthouse.org
                      www.lighthouse.org

A newsletter for members and leaders of support groups for older adults with impaired vision. The letter provides a forum for support groups members to network and share information, printed in a very large type format.

5909 So Many of My Friends Have Moved Away or Died

AARP Fulfillment
601 E Street NW
Washington, DC 20049   202-434-2277
                                  800-424-3410
                       FAX: 202-434-3443
             e-mail: member@aarp.org
                      www.aarp.org

A typical problem faced by older persons, discussion focuses on coping with the loss of old friends and finding new ones.

5910 Social Security, Medicare, and Pensions

NOLO
950 Parker Street
Berkeley, CA 94710   510-549-1976
                                 800-955-4775
                      FAX: 510-548-5902
                      www.nolo.com
Joseph L. Matthews with Dorothy Matthews Berman, author
Maira Dizgalvis, Trade Customer Service Manager
Susan McConnell, Director of Sales
Natasha Kaluza, Sales Assistant

A plain-speaking guide explaining the ins and outs of the Social Security system; retirement, disability and benefits for dependents and survivors. *$24.95*

320 pages paperback
ISBN 0-873374-87-8

5911 Statistical Handbook on Aging Americans

ORYX Press
4041 N Central Avenue
Suite 700
Phoenix, AZ 85012   602-265-2651
                                800-279-6799
                     FAX: 800-279-4663
            e-mail: info@oryxpress.com
                     www.oryxpress.com
Frank L. Schick, author

A resource for economic, demographic, social, health, employment and financial statistics. More than 300 tables and illustrative charts are accompanied by concise and expert commentary. *$54.50*

360 pages
ISBN 0-89774 -21-6

5912 Successful Models of Community Long Term Care Services for the Elderly

Haworth Press
10 Alice Street
Binghamton, NY 13904   604-722-5857
                                  800-429-6784
                       FAX: 607-722-6362
      e-mail: getinfo@haworthpressinc.com
                    www.haworthpressinc.com
Eloise Killeffer, EdM, author
Jackie Blakeslee, Advertising

Experienced practitioners provide examples of successful community-based long term care service programs for the elderly. *$ 69.95*

174 pages
ISBN 0-866569-87-1

5913 Therapeutic Interventions in Alzheimer

Aspen Publishers
200 Orchard Ridge Drive
Gaithersburg, MD 20878   301-698-7100
                                    800-234-1660
                         FAX: 301-695-7931
                      www.aspenpublishers.com
Glickstein, author

A program of functional skills for activities of daily living. Hardcover. *$65.00*

256 pages
ISBN 0-834209-30-6

5914 Topics in Geriatric Rehabilitation

Aspen Publishers
200 Orchard Ridge Road
Gaithersburg, MD 20878   301-698-7100
                                    800-638-8437
                         FAX: 301-695-7931
                      www.aspenpublishers.com

Peer-review journal presenting clinical, basic and applied research as well as theoretical information. Published quarterly. *$ 86.00*

90 pages

5915 Trager Mentastics: Movement as a Way to Agelessness

Station Hill Press

Milton Trager & Cathy Guadagno, author
1987

5916 US SERVAS

11 John Street
Room 505
New York, NY 10038   212-267-0252
FAX: 212-267-0292
e-mail: info@usservas.org
www.usservas.org

Lara Fisher, Administrator
Shoshie Iteu, Assistant Administrator
Carole Wagner

International network that links travelers with hosts in 130+ countries with the hope of building world peace through understanding and friendship.

Quarterly

5917 Unloving Care

Harper Collins Publishers/Basic Books
10 E 53rd Street
New York, NY 10022   212-207-7000
800-242-7737
FAX: 212-207-7203

Bruce C. Vladeck, author

A leading public health expert gives a definitive account of what nursing homes are really like. *$9.95*

305 pages
ISBN 0-46508-81-3

5918 Vision and Aging: Issues in Social Work Practice

Haworth Press
10 Alice Street
Binghamton, NY 13904   604-722-5857
800-429-6784
FAX: 607-722-6362
e-mail: getinfo@haworthpressinc.com
www.haworthpressinc.com
Nancy Weber, MSW, author
Jackie Blakeslee, Advertising

Responds to the needs of the growing population of blind or severely disabled elderly. *$69.95*

196 pages Hardcover
ISBN 1-560241-99-3

5919 Visually Impaired Seniors as Senior Companions: A Reference Guide

American Foundation for the Blind/AFB Press
PO Box 1020
Sewickley, PA 15143   412-741-1142
800-232-3044
FAX: 412-741-0609
e-mail: afborders@abdintl.com
www.afb.org

This useful guide describes the Senior Companion Program that is intended to broaden opportunities for older persons with disabilities. Appendix includes training materials, evaluation forms, recruitment and public relations information. *$15.00*

108 pages Paperback
ISBN 0-891282-38-6

5920 Work, Health and Income Among the Elderly

Brookings Institution
1775 Massachusetts Avenue NW
Washington, DC 20036   202-797-6000

Gary Burtless, author

Employment, health and financial information for the elderly. *$26.95*

276 pages Cloth

Employment

5921 ANCOR Wage and Hour Handbook

ANCOR
4200 Evergreen Lane
Suite 315
Annandale, VA 22003   703-642-6614
FAX: 703-642-0497
e-mail: joniancor@radix.net OR
suellenancor@radix.net
www.ancor.org

Joni Fritz, Executive Director
Suellen R. Galbraith, Director for Public Policy
Jerri McCandless, Mgr Comm. & Conference Planning

This useful publication contains the latest rules and interpretations from the U.S. Department of Labor relative to employment in residential support services for people with disabilities, including copies of enforcement policies and letters of interpretation. It outlines in detail when exemptions from miniimum wage and overtime rules can be applied,a nd when and how employees may be paid on a salary basis. Sample staffing patterns are provided.

121 pages

5922 Career Education for Handicapped Individuals

McGraw-Hill, School Publishing
220 East Danieldale Road
DeSoto, TX 75115   972-224-1111
800-442-9685
FAX: 972-228-1982
mhschool.com

Based on a life-centered career education program that goes beyond elementary school level to include handicapped people of all ages.

454 pages

5923 Earning a Living

Accent Books & Products
PO Box 700
Bloomington, IL 61702   309-378-2961
800-787-8444
FAX: 309-378-4420
e-mail: acmtlvng@aol.com
Lynn Winston, author
Raymond C. Cheever, Publisher
Betty Garee, Editor

Discusses how to prepare a person for a career, what to say in an interview, and gives examples of both home businesses and jobs away from home. Tells how to modify a worksite and how to be successful on the job. *$9.50*

88 pages Paperback
ISBN 0-91570-23-0

5924 Employee Complaint Handling: Tested Techniques for Human Resource Mgrs.

Greenwood Publishing Group
88 Post Road West
5007
Westport, CT 06880   203-226-3571
                             FAX: 203-222-1502
                             www.greenwood.com
Keith D. Denton and Charles Boyd, author

Examines issues of human relations and communications as well as those of legal and ethical concerns. *$59.95*

208 pages Hardcover
ISBN 0-899304-33-8

5925 Employment in the Mainstream

Mainstream
3 Bethesda Metro Center
Suite 830
Bethesda, MD 20814   301-891-8777
                             800-247-1380
                             FAX: 301-891-8778
                    e-mail: info@mainstreaminc.org
                             www.mainstreaminc.org

David Pichette, Executive Director
Fritz Rumpel, Editor

Reports on issues, ideas, problems and solutions in employing persons with any kind of physical or mental disability. Quarterly magazine. *$25.00*

32 pages

5926 Good Employee Is Capable, Conscientious, Productive

American Foundation for the Blind/AFB Press
PO Box 1020
Sewickley, PA 15143   412-741-1142
                              800-232-3044
                              FAX: 412-741-0609
                    e-mail: afborders@abdintl.com
                              www.afb.org
Gerald Miller, author

Answers employers' questions about the blind and visually handicapped and provides assurance to employees with visual impairments can get to work, perform their jobs safely and require little in the way of special training.

ISBN 0-891289-19-4

5927 Guide to Successful Employment for Individuals with Autism

Brookes Publishing
PO Box 10624
Baltimore, MD 21285   410-337-9585
                              800-638-3775
                              FAX: 410-337-8539
                    e-mail: custserv@brookespublishing.com
                              www.brookespublishing.com
Marcia Datlow Smith, Ph.D., Ronald Belcher, Ph.D, author

Describing all aspects of job placement, this book details strategies for assessing workers, networking for job opportunities, and tailoring job supports to each individual. Also illustrates how to help individuals with autism become productive workers, and with detailed descriptions of specific jobs help provide ideas for employment. *$ 32.95*

336 pages Paperback
ISBN 1-55766-71-5

5928 Handbook of Career Planning for Special Needs Students

Pro-Ed Publications
8700 Shoal Creek Boulevard
Austin, TX 78757   512-451-3426
                           800-879-3202
                           FAX: 512-451-8542
                    e-mail: info@proedinc.com
                           www.proedinc.com
Thomas F. Harrington, author

The practitioner's guide will show you how to help special needs adolescents and young adults overcome barriers to employment by identifying goals and problems, assessing interests and aptitudes, involving client families and developing communication skills. *$37.00*

358 pages Hardcover 1982
ISBN 0-890792-43-7

5929 JIST, The Job Search People

8902 Otis Avenue
Indianapolis, IN 46216   817-613-4200
                                 800-648-5478
                                 FAX: 800-547-8329
                          e-mail: info@jist.com
                                 www.jist.com
Tom Abeel, Editor, author
Thomas Abeel, V.P. Marketing

FREE catalog! Foster self-directed attitudes and behaviors with products focused on career planning, job search, career development, job retention, and life skills. Includes career assessments, occupational references, interactive workbooks, instructional videos, multimedia software, intructor's guides, and training. $4.95-$995.

160 pages Yearly

5930 Job Hunting Tips for the So-Called Handicapped

Special Needs Project
3463 Stat Street
282
Santa Barbara, CA 93105
                                 800-333-6867

Richard Bolles

This nifty booklet from the guru of job hunting himself is sincere, useful and careful brief. *$4.95*

5931 Job Opportunities and Benefits

17292 Eucalyptus Street
Hesperia, CA 92345

Janice Harbaugh
Provides remunerative work.

5932 Keys to the Workplace: Skills and Supports for People with with Disabilities

Brookes Publishing
PO Box 10624
Baltimore, MD 21285 410-337-9585
    800-638-3775
   FAX: 410-337-8539
e-mail: custserv@brookespublishing.com
www.brookespublishing.com
Michael Callahan, M.Ed., and J. Bradley Garner, Ph, author

This manual gives employment professionals step-by-step instructions for helping people with developmental disabilities find appropriate and fulfilling employment. Introduced here is the Seven-Phase Sequence, which fosters the natural supports that are vital to long-term job satisfaction and success. $26.95

304 pages Paperback 1997
ISBN 1-55766-76-2

5933 Let Community Employment be the Goal for Individuals with Autism

Autism Society of North Carolina Bookstore
505 Oberlin Road
Suite 230
Raleigh, NC 27605 919-743-0204
    800-442-2762
   FAX: 919-743-0208
e-mail: ASNC@aol.com
www.autismsociety-nc.org
Joanne Suomi, author

A guide designed for people who are responsible for preparing individuals with autism to enter the work force. $7.00

5934 Making the Workplace Accessible: Guidelines, Costs & Resources

Mainstream
3 Bethesda Metro Center
Suite 830
Bethesda, MD 20814 301-891-8777
    800-247-1380
   FAX: 301-891-8778
e-mail: info@mainstreaminc.org
www.mainstreaminc.org
Fritz Rumpel, author
Lillie Harrison, Info. Programs Clerk

A 20-page reference guide on how to provide physical access to persons with disabilities in a cost-effective manner. $4.95

20 pages Paperback

5935 Marketing Your Abilities: A Guide for the Disabled Job-Seeker

Mainstream
3 Bethesda Metro Center
Suite 830
Bethesda, MD 20814 301-951-6122

e-mail: info@mainstreaminc.org

A publication designed to assist the individual with a disability in conducting a successful job search. Major topics include how to write an effective resume and how to give a good interview. $ 4.95

24 pages

5936 Meeting the Needs of Employees with Disabilities

Resources for Rehabilitation
33 Bedford Street
Suite 19A
Lexington, MA 02420 781-862-6455
   FAX: 781-861-7517

Susan Greenblatt

Provides information to help people with disabilities retain or obtain employment. Information on government programs and laws, supported employment, training programs, environmental adaptations and the transition from school to work are included. Chapters on mobility impairment, vision impairment and hearing and speech impairments. $ 47.95

167 pages Biennial
ISBN 0-92971-13-5

5937 Mental Health in the Workplace: An Employer's & Manager's Guide

Greenwood Publishing Group
88 Post Road West
5007
Westport, CT 06880 203-226-3571
   FAX: 203-222-1502
   www.greenwood.com
Donna R. Kemp, author

A guide to the impact of mental health issues on the workplace, with special attention to complying with provisions of the Americas with Disabilities Act. $59.95

296 pages $59.95 - $67.95
ISBN 0-899307-03-5

5938 Model Program Operation Manual: Business Enterprise Program Supervisors

Rehab/Training Center on Blindness and Low-Vision
PO Box 6189
Mississippi State, MS 39762 601-325-2001
    800-675-7782
   FAX: 662-325-8989
   TDY:601-325-8693
e-mail: rrtc@ra.msstate.edu
www.msstate.edu
J. Elton Moore, Ed.D., CRC and Angula Tucker, author
Kelly Schaefer, Publications Manager

This monograph serves as a Model Program Operation Manual for Business Enterprise Program Supervisors who administer Randolph-Sheppard vending facilities under the Randolph-Sheppard Act. A wide variety of topics are covered including the role of the State Committee of Blind Venders, the role and responsibilities of the Vending Facility Operator, model qualification, for potential Facility Managers, guidelines for location of vending facilities and policies for closing vending facilities. $20.00

199 pages Paperback

5939 More Than a Job: Securing Satisfying Careers for People with Disabilities

Brookes Publishing
PO Box 10624
Baltimore, MD 21285   410-337-9585
                              800-638-3775
                    FAX: 410-337-8539
e-mail: custserv@brookespublishing.com
www.brookespublishing.com

This text shows employment professionals how to transform job placement into career counseling for people with physical and developmental disabilities. Issues such as transition from school to adult life, transportation, social relationships, and community access are also discussed. *$34.95*

368 pages Paperback 1998
ISBN 1-55766 -28-9

5940 Paraplegics and Quadriplegics

Mainstream
3 Bethesda Metro Center
Suite 830
Bethesda, MD 20814   301-951-6122
                              800-247-1380
           e-mail: info@mainstreaminc.org
Mainstream, Inc., author

Mainstreaming paraplegics and quadriplegics into the workplace. *$2.50*

12 pages

5941 People with Hearing Loss and the Workplace Guide for Employers/ADA Compliances

Self Help for Hard of Hearing People
7910 Woodmont Avenue
Suite 1200
Bethesda, MD 20814
                    FAX: 301-913-9413
           e-mail: national@shhh.org

Nancy Macklin, Business Manager

A guide for both people with hearing loss and their employers to learn about accommodations under the law. Includes employment guidelines, resource list of manufacturers and case studies. *$15.00*

40 pages Paperback

5942 Planning Reasonable Accommodations: A Cost-Effective Guide

Mainstream
3 Bethesda Metro Center
Suite 830
Bethesda, MD 20814   301-891-8777
                              800-247-1380
                    FAX: 301-891-8778
           e-mail: info@mainstreaminc.org
www.mainstreaminc.org
Fritz Rumpel, author
Lillie Harrison, Info. Programs Clerk

A reference guide on the reasonable accommodation process under the Americans with Disabilities Act. It includes how to determine essential functions through performing a job analysis. *$4.95*

24 pages

5943 Project LINK Guidebook

Mainstream
3 Bethesda Metro Center
Suite 830
Bethesda, MD 20814   301-951-6122
                              800-247-1380
           e-mail: info@mainstreaminc.org

A manual for operating an employment services program for persons with disabilities. *$49.95*

78 pages

5944 Providing Employment Support for People with Long-Term Mental Illness

Brookes Publishing
PO Box 10624
Baltimore, MD 21285   410-337-9585
                              800-638-3775
                    FAX: 410-337-8539
e-mail: custserv@brookespublishing.com
www.brookespublishing.com
Laurie Howton Ford, M.S., author

Choices, resources, and practical strategies. Topics covered include natural supports, behavior management, Social Security issues, vocational barriers to productive employment, and workers' rights under the Americans with Disabilities Act. Also includes detailed discussions of specific psychiatric diagnoses vocational assessment and career development, crisis intervention, interdisciplinary support models, and more. *$30.95*

352 pages Paperback
ISBN 1-55766 -90-1

5945 Supported Employment for Disabled People

Human Sciences Press
233 Spring Street
New York, NY 10013   212-229-2859
                              800-221-9369
                    FAX: 212-463-0742
Paul Wehman, author

Highlights the major features of supported employment. Contributions offer service providers in social work, education and mental health much-needed information. *$38.95*

288 pages Cloth
ISBN 0-89885 -46-6

5946 Survey of Direct Labor Workers Who Are Blind & Employed by NIB

Rehab/Training Center on Blindness and Low-Vision
PO Box 6189
Mississippi State, MS 39762   601-325-2001
                                      800-675-7782
                    FAX: 662-325-8989
           e-mail: rrtc@ra.msstate.edu
www.blind.msstate.edu
Moore, Crudden & Giesen, author
Kelly Schaefer, Publications Manager

This report is a follow-up to surveys by National Industries for the Blind in 1983 and 1987 and summarizes the results of a national survey of approximately 500 legally blind direct labor workers. *$10.00*

101 pages Paperback

5947 Understanding and Accommodating Physical Disabilities: Desk Reference

Greenwood Publishing Group
88 Post Road West
5007
Westport, CT 06880   203-226-3571
                         FAX: 203-222-1502
                         www.greenwood.com
Dorothy Stonely Shrout, author

Medical conditions that qualify as disabilities under the American's with Disabilities Act are explained in non-medical terminology. Hardcover.

200 pages $52.95 - $55
ISBN 0-899308-14-7

5948 Vocational Counseling for Special Populations

Charles C. Thomas, Publisher
2600 S 1st Street
Springfield, IL 62704   217-789-8980
                            800-258-8980
             e-mail: books@ccthomas.com
Chrisann Schiro-Geist, author

$34.95

172 pages Paperback
ISBN 0-398056-50-1

5949 Vocational Training and Employment of the Autistic Adolescent

Charles C. Thomas, Publisher
2600 South 1st Street
Springfield, IL 62704   217-789-8980
                            800-258-8980
                       FAX: 217-789-9130
             e-mail: books@ccthomas.com
Elva Duran, author

Professionals and parents are now advocating, demanding and arranging that persons receive vocational training and equal rights for the disabled. Also available in paper edition for $27.95 (ISBN# 0398061017) *$41.95*

182 pages Cloth
ISBN 0-398058-01-6

5950 WORK

330 State Street
Suite A
Santa Barbara, CA 93101   805-963-5831
                              FAX: 805-965-2912

Robert Hand
Work adjustment and remunerative work programs.

5951 Working Together: Workplace Culture, Employment and Disabilities

Brookline Books
PO Box 1046
Cambridge, MA 02238   617-868-0360
                          800-666-2665
                     FAX: 617-868-1772
          e-mail: brooklinebks@delphi.com
               www.brooklinebooks.com
David Hagner and Dale Dileo, author

Presents a new approach to assisting individuals with significant disabilities achieve meaningful careers, the book stresses partnerships between work, service providers and natural support systems to achieve positive employment outcomes. *$27.95*

Paperback
ISBN 0-91479 -88-3

General

5952 A Commitment to Inclusion: Outreach to Unserved/Underserved Populations

Independent Living Research Utilization ILRU
2323 S Shepherd Drive
Suite 1000
Houston, TX 77019   713-520-0232
                        FAX: 713-520-5785
                        www.ilru.org
Carol Bradley, author

Carol Bradley describes Independent Living Resource Center San francisco's community organizing/outreach approach to serving under-represented consumers. This organization successfully reaches persons with pychiatric disabilities, environmental illness/multiple chemical sensitivities, chronic fatigue immune deficiency syndrome, learning disabilities, institutionalized persons, Chinese, Latinos, deaf/hard of hearing, and lesbian/bisexual populations.

10 pages

5953 ACLD Newsbriefs

Learning Disabilities Association of America
4156 Library Road
Pittsburgh, PA 15234   412-653-5330

Jean Petersen, Nat'l Executive Dir.

Articles of interest to all persons concerned with learning disabilities.

BiMonthly

5954 AFB News

American Foundation for the Blind/AFB Press
PO Box 1020
Sewickley, PA 15143   412-741-1142
                          800-232-3044
                     FAX: 412-741-0609
          e-mail: afborders@abdintl.com
                   www.afb.org

Liz Greco, Vice President, Communications

Contains articles about AFB activities, programs, and people.

8 pages BiAnnually

5955 AID Bulletin

Project AID Resource Center
PO Box 5190
Kent, OH 44242   330-672-2672
                     FAX: 330-672-4724

Alex Boros, PhD, Director of AID
J. Sue Adams, Senior Counselor

Has the latest news on upcoming conferences, literature, developments in programs and/or services for disabled persons who are substance abusers. Offers articles on their experiences, ideas and questions of others in this field which includes providers and consumers. *$7.50*

5956   AJAO Newsletter

American Juvenile Arthritis Organization
1330 W Peachtree Street
Atlanta, GA   30309   404-872-7100

Janet Austin, MEd., Editor

Offers information and updates about the organization's activities and events. Legislative information, medical updates, camp information and more for children living with arthritis.

Quarterly

5957   APLA Update

AIDS Project Los Angeles
550 N Larchmount
Suite 202
Los Angeles, CA   90004   323-962-1600
FAX: 323-962-9536

Presents news about AIDS and programs of AIDS Project Los Angeles to people affected by the disease.

20 pages

5958   ARC's Government Report

Association for Retarded Citizens
1730 K Street NW
Suite 1212
Washington, DC   20006   202-636-2950
FAX: 202-636-2996
www.thearc.org/governmental_affairs.htm

Reports on government activities related to individuals with disabilities with a focus on persons with mental retardation. *$ 50.00*

5959   ARCA Newsletter

ARCA - Dakota County Technical College
1300 145th Street E
Rosemount, MN   55068   612-423-2281

Offers information on support groups, conventions, books, manuscripts and programs for the rehabilitation professional and the disabled.

Monthly

5960   Ability

George J. DePontis
PO Box 370788
Miami, FL   33137

Features articles on living, working, playing and entertainment for the disabled. *$12.00*

5961   Ability Magazine

Jobs Information Business Service
1682 Langley Avenue
Irvine, CA   92614   949-622-1040
800-453-JOBS

Provides an electronic classified system which allows employers to recruit qualified individuals with disabilities, and people with disabilities to locate employment opportunities.

5962   Accent on Living Magazine

Cheever Publishing
PO Box 700
Bloomington, IL   61702   309-378-2961
800-787-8444
FAX: 309-378-4420

Julie Cheever, Marketing Manager

A magazine published for forty four years, serves physically disabled people, general interest, includes, travel , home modification etc. *$12.00*

112 pages Quarterly

5963   Access Design Services: CILs as Experts

Independent Living Research Utilization ILRU
2323 S Shepherd Drive
Suite 1000
Houston, TX   77019   713-520-0232
FAX: 713-520-5785
www.ilru.org

Ketra S. Crosson, author

Featuring the Access Design Services of Alpha One in Maine, this month's Readings is another of the winners of the recent competition for innovative CIL programs.

10 pages

5964   Access Info

Access to Independence
2345 Atwood Avenue
Madison, WI   53704   608-242-8484
TDY:608-242-8485

Frank Martin, Editor

Covers news, features and resources for people with disabilities living in the Madison, Wisconsin area.

16-20 pages Quarterly

5965   Accessible Gardening for People with Physical Disabilities

Woodbine House
6510 Bells Mill Road
Bethesda, MD   20817
800-843-7323
www.woodbinehouse.com

Janeen Adil, author

Presents all the information and practical know-how necessary for designing, planting, and maintaining a garden that suits the special needs of young and older gardeners. Dozens of mail-order sources are provided for the many tools, seeds, plants, and other materials discussed. From measuring for planter boxes to selecting suitable tools and plants, the author thoroughly describes how to garden in a variety of situations. *$16.95*

300 pages Paperback

5966 Achieving Diversity at Independence

Independent Living Research Utilization ILRU
2323 S Shepherd Drive
Suite 1000
Houston, TX 77019 713-520-0232
FAX: 713-520-5785
www.ilru.org

Susan Mikesic, author

10 pages

5967 Acu-Yoga: The Acupressure Stress Managemen Management Book

Japan Publications

Michael R. Gach, author

Handbook describing the origin, practice and benefits of acupression and yoga.

1981

5968 Acupressure's Potent Points

Bantam Books

Michael R. Gach, author

How to utilize acupressure with easy-to-follow line drawings.

1990

5969 Acupuncture: Is it for You?

Harper & Row
10 E 53rd Street
New York, NY 10022 212-207-7000
800-242-7737

J.R. Worsley, author

1973

5970 Ad Lib Drop-In Center: Consumer Management, Ownership and Empowerment

Independent Living Research Utilization ILRU
2323 S Shepherd Drive
Suite 1000
Houston, TX 77019 713-520-0232
FAX: 713-520-5785
www.ilru.org

Joe Castellani, author

Joe describes how Ad Lib ensured consumer control in their Drop-In Center: the DIC came about because of consumer input, and consumers are involved in planning the program; members can choose to become volunteers or paid staff members. All of the staff at the DIC are consumers; and active consumer advisory board helps develop policies and programs and provides input to the Ad Lib board.

10 pages

5971 Advance

Asthma and Allergy Foundation of America
1125 15th Street NW
Suite 502
Washington, DC 20005 202-466-7643
FAX: 202-466-8940
e-mail: info@aafa.org
www.aafa.org

Newsletter for members will increase the patients understanding and ability to control asthma and allergies. Topics include food allergies, exercising and asthma, ragweed and allergies and asthma and pregnancy. Also keeps parents up to date with the key facts for keeping their asthmatic child as healthy as possible and live a full life.

BiMonthly

5972 Advocacy-Oriented Peer Support — Part Two : Moving from Talk to Action

Independent Living Research Utilization ILRU
2323 S Shepherd Drive
Suite 1000
Houston, TX 77019 713-520-0232
FAX: 713-520-5785
www.ilru.org

Steve Brown, author

This month's Readings examines how staff at centers for independent living can identify and support potential leaders who will move beyond talking about their problems to making changes in their communities.

10 pages

5973 Ageless Body, Timeless Mind

Harmony Books
231 Broad Street
Nevada City, CA 95959 530-265-9564

www.harmonybookstore.com

Deepak Chopra, M.D., author

1993

5974 Alcoholism Sourcebook

Omnigraphics
605 Griswold Street
Detroit, MI 48226
800-234-1340
FAX: 800-875-1340
www.omnigraphics.com

Karen Bellenir, Editor

Provides information on the disorders which may result from alcohol abuse. *$78.00*

650 pages 1900
ISBN 0-780803-25-6

5975 Alerter

San Diego Area Chapter of the Arthritis Foundation
9089 Clairemont Mesa Boulevard
300
San Diego, CA 92123 619-492-1090
800-422-8885
FAX: 619-492-9248

Offers chapter updates, information on activities and events, resources and medical research for members.

5976 Alexander Technique
St. Martin's Press
175 Fifth Avenue
New York, NY 10010   212-674-5151
                                 800-221-7945
                            FAX: 212-420-9314

John Gray, author
Guide that shows the correct and incorrect positions
to use for exercises.

1991

5977 Allergies Sourcebook, 2nd Edition
Omnigraphics
615 Griswold Street
Detroit, MI 48226
                                 800-234-1340
                            FAX: 800-875-1340
                            www.omnigraphics.com

Annmarie S. Muth, Editor
Includes information on the causes of allergies, identification, treatments, and statistics *$78.00*

650 pages 1900
ISBN 0-780803-76-0

5978 American Herb Association Newsletter
PO Box 353
Rescue, CA 96672

Discusses a wide variety of herbal issues and internal developments.

5979 Americans with Disabilities Department of Justice
Consumer Information Center
Department 577A
Pueblo, CO 81009   719-948-3334
                            FAX: 734-326-2610
                            e-mail: catalog.pueblo@gsa.gov

Michael Clark, Public Affairs
Explains how civil rights of persons with disabilities
are protected at work and in public places.

5980 Americans with Disabilities Act: Questions and Answers
Federal Consumer Information Center
Department 513H
Pueblo, CO 81009
                                 888-878-3256
                            FAX: 719-948-9724
                            e-mail: catalog.pueblo@gsa.gov
                            www.pueblo.gsa.gov

Judi Mahoney, Public Affairs
Explains how the Civil Rights of Persons with dis-
abilities are protected at work and in public places.
Free.

5981 Annual Community Awards Booklet
National Organization on Disability
910 16th Street NW
Suite 600
Washington, DC 20006   202-965-9850
                            FAX: 202-293-7999
                            TDY:202-293-5968
                            e-mail: ability@nod.org
                            www.nod.org

Mary Dolan, author
Alan Reich, President
Information on disability programs in communities
across the nation.

Quarterly

5982 Aromatherapy Book: Applications and Inhalations
North Atlantic Books

Jeanne Rose, author
Considered a bible for those interested in aromatherapy.

1992

5983 Aromatherapy Workbook
Healing Arts Press

Marcel Lavabre, author
Practical guide to essential oils of aromatherapy.

1990

5984 Aromatherapy for Common Ailments
Simon & Schuster
1230 Avenue of the Americas
New York, NY 10020   212-698-7000
                                 800-223-2348

Shirley Price, author
Explains aromatherapy with emphasis on medicinal
uses.

1991

5985 Aromatherapy, to Heal and Tend the Body
Lotus Light Press

Robert Tisserand, author
Explains the history of aromatherapy.

1988

5986 Art of Aromatherapy
Destiny Books

Robert B. Tisserand, author
Reference book on essential oils.

1987

5987 Arthritis Accent

Arthritis Foundation Southern N.E. Chapter
35 Cold Spring Road
Suite 411
Rocky Hill, CT   06067   860-563-1177
                               800-541-8350
                         FAX: 860-563-6018
                e-mail: inpubne@arthritis.org
                         www.arthritis.org

Susan Nesci, Program Director - CT

Offers information on chapter events and activities.

Quarterly

5988 Arthritis Foundation

Greater Southwest Chapter - Arthritis Foundation
1313 East Osborn Road
Suite 200
Phoenix, AZ   85014   602-264-7679
                             800-477-7679
                       FAX: 602-264-0563
           e-mail: info.caz@arthritis.org
                       www.arthritis.org

Michele Gama, Director of Public Relations

Provides information, programs and services for people affected by arthritis.

Quarterly

5989 Arthritis Foundation of Illinois News

111 E Wacker Drive
Suite 1928
Chicago, IL   60601   312-616-3470

Marilynn J. Cason, Chairman

A publication offering information about the activities of the chapter. Program news, legislative information, workshops and resources are also included.

Quarterly

5990 Arthritis News

Wisconsin Chapter of the Arthritis Foundation
8556 W National Avenue
West Allis, WI   53227   414-321-3933
                          FAX: 414-321-0365
            e-mail: info@wi@arthritis.org
                        www.arthritis.org

Dana Motley, Public Relations Coordinator

Offers information on activities, events, medical research, information and referrals to persons living in the Wisconsin area that are afflicted with arthritis.

8 pages Quarterly

5991 Arthritis Observer

Rocky Mountain Chapter of the Arthritis Foundation
2280 S Albion
Denver, CO   80222

                               800-475-6647

Offers chapter information and updates on fundraising events and activities, resources and publications and medical updates for the arthritis community.

Quarterly

5992 Arthritis Reporter

New York Chapter of the Arthritis Foundation
122 E 42nd Street
18th Floor
New York, NY   10168   212-984-8700

Chapter newsletter offering information on upcoming events, activities and groups for the arthritis community.

Quarterly

5993 Arthritis Today

Arthritis Foundation
1330 West Peachtree Street
Atlanta, GA   30309   770-253-1300
                       FAX: 404-872-9559
                        www.arthritis.org

Magazine for patients, physicians, public authorities and others with an interest in the field of arthritis. (Price noted paid for yearly subscription) *$20.00*

5994 Asthma & Allergy ADVOCATE Newsletter

American Academy of Allergy, Asthma and Immunology
611 E Wells Street
Milwaukee, WI   53202   414-272-6071
                               800-822-2762
                         FAX: 414-272-6070
                 e-mail: info@aaaai.org
                         www.aaaai.org

Offers tips and medical information on allergies and asthmatic conditions including the newest treatments and public awareness news. *$6.00*

4 pages Quarterly

5995 Attention

Children & Adults with Attention Deficit Disorder
499 NW 70th Avenue
Suite 101
Plantation, FL   33317   954-587-3700
                                800-233-4050
                          FAX: 954-587-4599

Quarterly

5996 Attitudes Toward Persons with Disabilities

Springer Publishing Company
536 Broadway
New York, NY   10012   212-431-4370
                          FAX: 212-941-7842
Harold E. Yuker, author

This volume examines what is known of people's complex and multifaceted attitudes toward persons with disabilities. Divided into five areas of concern: theory, origin of attitudes, attitude measurement, attitudes of specific groups and attitude change. *$38.95*

352 pages Hardcover
ISBN 0-82616 -90-1

5997 Augmentative and Alternative Communication

Brookes Publishing
PO Box 10624
Baltimore, MD   21285   410-337-9580
                                        800-638-3775
                              FAX: 410-337-8539
e-mail: custserv@brookespublishing.com
www.brookespublishing.com
*David R. Beukelman, Ph.D., and Pat Mirenda,
Ph.D., author*

Management of Severe Communication Disorders in
Children and Adults, 2nd edition. This textbook contains the most recent information available on implementing augmentative and alternative
communication (AAC), explaining principles and
procedures of AAC assessment and offering intervention techniques. *$59.95*

592 pages Hardcover 1998
ISBN 1-55766 -33-5

**5998 Authoritative Guide to Self- Help Resource in
Mental Health**

Guilford Press
72 Spring Street
New York, NY   10012   212-431-9800
                                        800-365-7006
                              FAX: 212-966-6708
www.guilford.com
*John C. Norcross, PhD, John W. Santrock, PhD,
author*
Linda F. Campbell, PhD, Author
Thomas P. Smith, PsyD, Author
Robert Sommer, PhD, Author

Reviews and rates 600+ self-help books, autobiogra-
phies, and popular films, and evaluates hundreds of
Internet sites. Addresses 28 of the most prevalent
clinical disorders and life challenges- from ADHD,
Alzheimer's, and anxiety disorders, to marital problems, mood disorders and weight management. Also
in cloth at $39.95 (ISBN# 1-57230-506-1) *$23.95*

377 pages Paperback 1900
ISBN 1-572305-80-0

5999 Autism Research Institute

4182 Adams Avenue
San Diego, CA   92116   619-281-7165
                              FAX: 619-563-6840
www.autism.com/ari

Bernard Rimland, PhD, Director

Offers information and conducts research on autism
and related disorders. Please write for info. *$18.00*

8 pages Qtrly. nwsltr.

**6000 Awareness through Movement: Health Exercises
for Personal Growth**

Harper & Row
10 East 53rd Street
New York, NY   10022   212-207-7000
                                        800-242-7737

Moshe Feldenkrais, author

Self-help guide to improved posture.

1972

6001 Bach Flower Therapy

Inner Traditions
1 Park Street
Rochester, VT   05767   802-767-3174

Mechthild Scheffer, author

Contains a list of symptoms with a complete remedies
guide.

**6002 Be Sick Well - A Healthy Approach to Chronic
Illness**

New Harbinger Publications
5674 Shattuck Avenue
Oakland, CA   94609   510-652-0215
                                        800-748-6273

This new book makes the crucial distinction between disease - what is objective and measurable
- and illness, the subjective, unmeasurable experience of being sick. *$11.95*

188 pages

6003 Beating the Odds

Contemporary Books
Chicago, IL

Albert Marchetti, M.D., author

An overview of alternative cancer treatments that
have proven successful in treating cancer.

1988

6004 Behavior Problems

Research Press
PO Box 9177
Champaign, IL   61826   217-352-3273
                                        800-519-2707
                              FAX: 217-352-1221
e-mail: rp@researchpress.com
www.researchpress.com
Dr. Bruce Baker, et al., author
Russell Pence, V P Marketing

A practical book that provides effective techniques
for solving behavior problems that are characteristic
of children with developmental disabilities. Numerous charts and examples accompanied by helpful illustrations make this book an invaluable resource for
parents, special education teachers and residential
staff. *$12.95*

80 pages Paperback
ISBN 0-878221-70-0

6005 Beleifs: Pathways to Health and Well Being

Metamorphous Press

Robert Dilts, author

Introduction to neurolinguistic programming and
how it can change your life.

6006 Beliefs, Values, and Principles of Self Advocacy

Brookline Books
PO Box 1047
Cambridge, MA   02238   617-868-0360
                                 800-666-2665
                        FAX: 617-868-1772
                e-mail: brooklinebks@delphi.com
                www.brooklinebooks.com

Written by self-advocates around the world, they tell about the beliefs, values, and principles important to them, and the empowerment and personal growth they experience through self-advocacy. $7.00

48 pages Paperback
ISBN 0-57129-22-2

6007 Bell

National Mental Health Association
1021 Prince Street
Alexandria, VA   22314   703-684-7722
                                 800-969-NMHA
                        FAX: 703-684-5968
                        TDY:800-433-5959
                e-mail: nmhainfo@aol.com
                        www.nmha.org
National Mental Health Association, author
Sandy Alexander, Publications Manager
Patrick Cody, Sr. Director of Media Relations

Targets public and private mental health organizations as well as interested corporations, agencies and individuals. The Bell contains information about a variety of issues pertaining to mental health, including: the effects of managed care on mental health care; the implications of Congressional decisions for mental health; prevention efforts on the local, state and national levels; national anti-stigma efforts and national public education campaigns. $24.00

Monthly

6008 Between Heaven and Earth: A Guide to Chinese Medicine

Ballantine Books
201 East 50th Street
New York, NY   10022   212-751-2600
                        FAX: 212-782-8438
Harriet Beinfield & Efrem Korngold, author

Researches areas of Chinese medicine.

1991

6009 Beyond Antibiotics: Healthier Options for Families

North Atlantic Books
Berkley, CA

Michael Schmidt, D.C., author

An overview of ways to boost immunity and avoid antibiotics. Provides a range of alternative health measures, including vitamins and herbal medicines.

1992

6010 Beyond Gentle Teaching

Autism Society of North Carolina Bookstore
505 Oberlin Road
Suite 230
Raleigh, NC   27605   919-743-0204
                                 800-442-2762
                        FAX: 919-743-0208
                e-mail: ASNC@aol.com
                www.autismsociety-nc.org
John J. McGee & Frank J. Manolascino, author

A nonaversive approach to helping those in need, caregivers. $35.00

6011 Birth Defect News

Birth Defects Research for Children
930 Woodcock Road
Suite 225
Orlando, FL   32803   407-895-0802
                        FAX: 407-895-0824
                e-mail: abdc@birthdefects.org
                www.birthdefects.org

Betty Mekdeci, Executive Director

Offers updated information on the association activities, events and updates regarding birth defects and environmental exposures.

Monthly

6012 Body Awareness in Action

Schocken Books
201 East 50th Street
New York, NY   10019   212-261-6500

Frank P. Jones, author

1976

6013 Body Electric: Electromagnetism and the Foundation of Life

William Morrow and Company
1350 Avenue of the Americas
New York, NY   10019   212-261-6500

Robert O. Becker and Gary Selden, author

6014 Body Reflexology: Healing at Your Fingertips

Parker Publishing Company
1501 Broadway
2605
New York, NY   10036   212-719-9777

Mildred Carter, author

Safe and easy-to-use methods to relieve pain and discomfort.

1986

6015 Body Silent

Special Needs Project
3463 Stat Street
282
Santa Barbara, CA   93105

                        800-333-6867

Robert Murphy

This book is a narrative of an adult with progressive and terminal loss of muscle function caused by a spinal tumor. $9.95

242 pages

6016 Body of Knowledge/Hellerwork

406 Berry Street
Mt. Shasta, CA 96067   916-926-2500

Information, referral directory, training and certification.

6017 Body/Mind Purification Program

Simon and Schuster/Gaia
1230 Avenue of the Americas
New York, NY 10020   212-698-7000

Leon Chaitow, author

Author guides reader through detoxification and a clean healthy diet.

6018 Book of Massage

Fireside
1230 Avenue of the Americas
New York, NY 10020   212-698-7313

Lucinda Lidell, author

Step-by-step instructional guide.

1984

6019 Brain Allergies: The Psychonutrient Connection

Keats Publishing
New Canaan, CT   203-966-8721
                        800-323-4900

D.K. Kalita Ph.D. and William Philpott M.D., author

6020 Breaking New Ground

Purdue University
1146 Agricultural & Biological Bldg
West Lafayette, IN 47907   765-494-2038
                                   800-825-4264
                    e-mail: bng@ecn.purdue.edu
     abe.www.ecn.purdue.edu/ABE/Extension/BNG

Barry Delks, Coordinator
Rita Smith, Public Awareness Coordinator

News, practical ideas and success stories of and for farmers with physical disabilities.

12-16 pages Quarterly

6021 Breaking New Ground Resource Center

Purdue University
1146 ABE
West Lafayette, IN 47907   765-494-5088
                                   800-825-4264
                             FAX: 765-496-1356
                    e-mail: bng@ecn.purdue.edu
                         www.agrability.org

William Field, Director
Paul Jones, Information Specialist

A resource center devoted to helping farmers and ranchers with physical disabilities. Several resource materials and a free newsletter are available to anyone.

6022 Breathe Free

Lotus Press
Wilmot, WI

Daniel Gagnon and Amadea Morningstart, author

A nutritional and herbal medicine self-help guide to treating a full range of respiratory conditions, including colds and flu.

1990

6023 Brown University Long Term Care Advisor

Manisses Communications Group
208 Governor Street
Providence, RI 02906   401-831-6020
                               800-333-7771
                          FAX: 401-861-6370
           e-mail: manisses@manisses.com
                    www.manisses.com

Vincent Mor, Ph.D, author
Fraser Lang, Publisher

Contains practical reports for health care professionals working in long-term care facilities. Published monthly. *$329.00*

8 pages Newsletter
ISSN 1088-92 8

6024 Building Bridges: Including People with Disabilities in International Programs

Mobility International USA
PO Box 10767
Eugene, OR 97440   541-343-1284
                      FAX: 541-343-6812
                      TDY:541-343-1284
            e-mail: info@miusa.org
                    www.miusa.org

Julie Ann Cheshire, author
Susan Sygall, Executive Director
Rhonda Neuhaus, Public Relations Coordinator

Features more than 200 pages of suggestions and creative ideas for including, recruiting and accommodating people with disabilities in international programs. This third edition contains expanded and updated information, as well as new chapters on cross-cultural issues in disability, volunteer service programs and legal issues for international advisors. Available in alternative formats. *$20.00*

1998
ISBN 1-880034-36-0

6025 Bulletin of the Association on the Handicapped

Assoc. on Handicapped Student Service Program
PO Box 21192
Columbus, OH 43221   614-365-5216
                        FAX: 614-365-6718

Membership journal including Association news, articles and sections such as Literature in Review and Speak Out. *$16.00*

6026 CAPSule

Children of Aging Parents
1609 Woodbourne Road
Suite 302A
Levittown, PA 19057   215-945-6999
                              800-227-7294
                         FAX: 215-945-8720
           e-mail: CAPS4caregivers@aol.com
                    www.CAPS4caregivers.com

Lorraine Sailor, Operations Coordinator

Provides practical information for family caregivers. CAPS is a non-profit organization serving the family caregivers of the elderly with information and referrals, a network of support groups, and public information and a newsletter bimonthly. *$20.00*

12 pages BiMonthly

6027 California Community Care News

PO Box 163270
Sacramento, CA   95816   916-455-0723
                                FAX: 916-455-7201

Charles W. Skoien, Jr., Editor & Publisher

Forum for the exchange of ideas, information, and opinions among clients, families and service providers. Information regarding services and assisted living programs for the elderly, mentally ill and disabled. *$45.00*

24 pages Monthly

6028 California Financial Power of Attorney

NOLO
950 Parker Street
Berkeley, CA   94710   510-549-1976
                              800-955-4775
                              FAX: 510-548-5902
                              www.nolo.com

Maira Dizgalvis, Trade Customer Service Manager
Susan McConnell, Director of Sales
Natasha Kaluza, Sales Assistant

A plain-English book packed with forms and instructions to give a trusted person the legal authority to handle your financial affairs.

paperback

6029 Cancer Industry

Paragon House
New York, NY

Ralph Moss, Ph.D., author

A thorough exploration of the political and economical forces behind the suppression of alternative treatments for cancer.

1989

6030 Career Development Quarterly

American Counseling Association
5999 Stevenson Avenue
Alexandria, VA   22304   703-823-9800

Mark L. Savickas, Editor
$35.00

Quarterly

6031 Caring Concepts

469 7th Rue-14th Place
New York, NY   10018   212-244-1193
                              800-321-2856
                              FAX: 800-433-1407
                              e-mail: caringconcepts@usanet

Jeff Kaplan, Vice President
Fred Cordiano, Sales Mgr.

The nations leading designer and manufacturer of assistive clothing for men and women. Free 56 page catalog available by calling 800-500-0260. 100% guarantee on all products.

6032 Caring for Children with Chronic Illness

Springer Publishing Company
536 Broadway
New York, NY   10012   212-431-4370
                              FAX: 212-941-7842

Ruth E. Stein, author

A critical look at the current medical, social, and psychological framework for providing care to children with chronic illnesses. Emphasizing the need to create integrated, interdisciplinary approaches, it discusses issues such as the roles of families, professionals, and institutions in providing health care, the impact of a child's illness on various family structures, financing care, the special problems of chronically ill children as they become adolescents and more. *$36.95*

320 pages Hardcover
ISBN 0-82615 -00-1

6033 Case Management in the Vocational Rehabilitation of Disabled Persons

Berkeley Planning Associates
440 Grand Avenue
Suite 500
Oakland, CA   94610   510-465-7884
                             FAX: 510-465-7885

Linda Toms Barker

Journal examining the effectiveness of case management services in the context of vocational rehabilitation for persons with psychiatric disabilities.

6034 Center for Libraries and Educational Improvement

400 Maryland Avenue SW
Washington, DC   20202   202-260-2226

Malcolm Davis, Acting Director

Administers the Library Services Construction Act, which authorizes grants to the states for library services to the physically handicapped.

6035 Centers for Disease Control Public Health Service

US Department of Health and Human Services
MS C09 1600 Clifton Road NE
Atlanta, GA   30333   404-639-3311

Publishes an annually updated list of infectious and communicable diseases transmitted through the handling of food in accordance with Section 103 of Title I.

6036 Chadder

Children & Adults with Attention Deficit Disorder
499 NW 70th Avenue
Suite 101
Plantation, FL   33317   954-587-3700
                                800-233-4050
                                FAX: 954-587-4599

Quarterly

6037 Children Who Vary from the Normal Type: Special Education in Boston, 1838-1930

Gallaudet University Press
11030 S Langley Avenue
Chicago, IL   60628

800-621-2736
FAX: 800-621-8476
TDY:800-621-9347
gupress.gallaudet.edu

Robert L. Osgood, author

Identifies Boston as both typical of and a national leader in Special Education programs, tracing its history with an eye towards the future. *$49.95*

220 pages Hardcover

6038 Chinese Herbal Medicine

Shambhala Publications
PO Box 308
Boston, MA   02117   617-424-0030

Daniel P. Reid, author

Gives an in-depth look into herbal medicine.

6039 Closing the Gap

PO Box 68
Henderson, MN   56044   507-248-3294
FAX: 507-248-3810
e-mail: info@closingthegap.com
www.closingthegap.com

Bud Hagen

Explores use of microcomputers as personal and educational tools for persons with disabilities. *$29.00*

36+ pages BiMonthly
ISSN 0886-19 5

6040 Color Therapy

Aurora Press

Reuben B. Amber, author

Guide to daily uses.

6041 Common Cold and Common Sense

Fireside Books
New York, NY

Dale Alexander, author

A practical approach to treating colds and flu based on diet and nutrition.

1981

6042 Communicating at the End oF the Twentieth Century: Innovative Computer Programs

Independent Living Research Utilization ILRU
2323 S Shepherd Drive
Suite 1000
Houston, TX   77019   713-520-0232
FAX: 713-520-5785
www.ilru.org

Steve Brown, author

This month's readings features two more of the winners in last year's Innovative CIL competitions. Steve brown of the Institute on Disability culture has combined the submissions of MetroWest Center for Independent Living and Pathways for the future, Inc. into an article that looks at how centers can use their independence.

10 pages

6043 Communication Outlook

Artificial Language Laboratory
405 Computer Center
Michigan State University
East Lansing, MI   48824   517-353-0870
FAX: 517-353-4766
e-mail: artling@msu.edu
www.msu.edu/~artlang

Caroline Watt, Editor
Katie Smith, Editor

Communication Outlook (CO) is an international quarterly magazine, which focuses on the techniques and technology of augmentative and alternative communication. CO provides information on technological developments for persons experiencing communication handicaps due to neurological, sensory or neuromuscular conditions. *$18.00*

32 pages Quarterly

6044 Complete & Easy Guide to Social Security and Medicare

EMCRSON-ADAMS PRISS
1259 SW 14 Street
Boca Raton, FL   33486   561-391-0964
800-234-8781
FAX: 800-304-7224

Faustin Jehle, Author
Fred Murphy, Publisher

A reference manual offering considerable information about social security programs of interest to those with disabilities. (Disability insurance, SSI, social security, retirement and Medicare). *$16.95*

176 pages Hardcover
ISBN 0-93004 -14-9

6045 Complete Aromatherapy Handbook: Essential Oils for Radiant Health

Sterling Press
420 West 1700 South
Salt Lake City, UT   84115   801-486-4641
FAX: 801-467-2221

Suzanne Fisher-Rizzi, author

Describes the history of aromatherapy.

1991

6046 Complete Guide to Health and Nutrition

Delacorte Press

Gary Null, author

Explores the nurtitional field.

6047 Concentration Cockpit: Explaining Attention Deficits

Educators Publishing Service
31 Smith Place
Cambridge, MA   02138   617-367-2700
                               800-225-5750
                               FAX: 617-547-0412
                               www.epsbooks.com

Dr. Mel Levine, author

This eight-page pamphlet explains the administration of The Concentration Cockpit, a newly revised poster that helps children with attention deficits gain insight into their problems and monitor their progress in grappling with these problems. *$64.50*

ISBN 0-838820-59-X

6048 Consumer Buyer's Guide for Independent Living

American Occupational Therapy Association (AOTA)
4720 Montgomery Lane
Bethesda, MD   20814   301-654-7655
                              800-OHE-LP4U
                              FAX: 301-652-7711

Cheryl Hager, Marketing Director

A buyer's directory of products and publications for the general public listing suppliers' names, addresses and telephone numbers. This directory lists AOTA publications on numerous topics (back pain, Alzheimers, Carpal Tunnel Syndrome, etc.) and suppliers of equipment to assist in activities of daily living for individuals with disabilities.

60 pages Annual

6049 Consumer Information Catalog

Consumer Information Center
Pueblo, CO   81009
                              888-878-8256
                              FAX: 719-948-9724
                              e-mail: catalog.pueblo@gsa.gov
                              www.pueblo.gsa.gov

Judi Mahaney, Media Specialist

The Consumer Information Center publishes the free, quarterly Consumer Information Catalog. The catalog lists over 200 selected booklets of consumer interest published by more than 40 agencies of the federal government. Topics covered includes employment and education, children, cars, small business, housing, health, nutrition, money management, federal programs and more. Nearly half of the publications listed are available for free; the remainder are moderately priced.

6050 Coping with Your Allergies

Simon and Schuster
New York, NY

Natalie Golos and Francis Golbita, author

6051 Coping+Plus: Dimensions of Disability

Greenwood Publishing Group
88 Post Road West
5007
Westport, CT   06880   203-226-3571
                              FAX: 203-222-1502
                              www.greenwood.com

Frank M. Robinson, Jr., author

Everyone can learn new or more effective coping skills and strategies to deal with times of loss, crisis and disability. $55-$59.95

280 pages Hardcover
ISBN 0-275945-44-8

6052 Creating Wholeness: Self-Healing Workbook Using Dynamic Relaxation, Images and Thoughts

Plenum

Erik Peper, author

6053 Creative Care Package Catalog

Centering Corporation
1531 N Saddle Creek Road
Omaha, NE   68104   402-553-1200
                              FAX: 402-533-0507
                              e-mail: j1200@aol.com
                              www.centering.org

Janet Sieff, Editor

A full catalog of all our available bereavement resources. We are a small, non-profit organization providing help to families in crisis situations.

32 pages BiAnnually

6054 Cross Currents

Jeremy P. Tarcher

Robert O. Becker, author

Describes electromagmetism and how it is used in medicine.

6055 DAV Magazine

DAV Magazine
807 Maine Avenue SW
Washington, DC   20024   202-554-3501
                              FAX: 202-554-3581
                              e-mail: davcomms@erols.com
                              www.dav.com

Charles Joeckel, Jr., National Adjutant
David Gorman, Executive Director

Reports the news, activities and programs of the organization and its members.

6056 Demand Response Transportation Through a Rural ILC

Independent Living Research Utilization ILRU
2323 S Shepherd Drive
Suite 1000
Houston, TX   77019   713-520-0232
                              FAX: 713-520-5785
                              www.ilru.org

Mike Ward, author

Oklahomans for Independent Living's transportation program was selected as exemplary becuase they marketed it by emphasizing people with disabilities as economic constituency.

10 pages

6057 Detecting Your Hidden Allergies
Professional Books/Future Health

William G. Crook M.D., author

6058 Developing Organized Coalitions and w Strategic Plans
Independent Living Research Utilization ILRU
2323 S Shepherd Drive
Suite 1000
Houston, TX   77019   713-520-0232
                                FAX: 713-520-5785
                                www.ilru.org
Bobby Silverstein, author

   10 pages

6059 Dictionary of Developmental Disabilities Terminology
Brookes Publishing
PO Box 10624
Baltimore, MD   21285   410-337-9580
                                800-638-3775
                        FAX: 410-337-8539
e-mail: custserv@brookesopublishing.com
            www.brookespublishing.com
Pasquale J. Accardo, M.D. Editor, author
Barbara Y. Whitman, M.S.W., PhD, Editor
Carla Laszewski, M.S.W.

With more than 3,000 easy-to-understand entries, this dictionary provides thorough explanations of terms associated with developmental disabilities and disorders. *$55.95*

   368 pages Hardcover 1996
   ISBN 1-557662-45-2

6060 Directions
Families of Spinal Muscular Dystrophy
PO Box 196
Libertyville, IL   60048   847-367-7620
                                800-886-1762
                        FAX: 847-367-7623
                        e-mail: sma@fsma.org
                                www.fsma.org

Audrey Lewis, Executive Director
Colleen McCarthy

   60-70 pages Quarterly

6061 Directory of College Facilities and Services for People with Disabilities
ORYX Press
4041 N Central Avenue
Suite 700
Phoenix, AZ   85012   602-265-2651
                                800-279-6799
                        FAX: 800-279-4663
            e-mail: info@oryxpress.com
Ruth A. Velleman, author

This in-depth examination of the needs of the physically or mentally disabled, blind and deaf is completely revised and updated. It reveals how librarians and other professionals can meet those needs, covering current information services and more. *$37.95*

   288 pages
   ISBN 0-89774-21-3

6062 Directory of Financial Aids for Women
Reference Service Press
5000 Windplay Drive
Suite 4
El Dorado Hills, CA   95762   916-939-9620
                                FAX: 916-939-9626
                        e-mail: findaid@aol.com
                                www.rspfunding.com

Gail Ann Schlachter, Author

The funding programs listed in the directory support study, research, travel, training, career development, or innovative effort at any level (from high school seniors to study engineering or chemistry); descriptions of more than 1,700 funding programs—representing billions of dollars in financial aid set aside specifically for women; also, an annotated bibliography of 60 key directories that identify even more financial aid opportunities and a set of indexes that let you search the directory. *$45.00*

   578 pages Cloth 1999
   ISBN 0-918276-80-2

6063 Directory of Members
ANCOR
4200 Evergreen Lane
Suite 315
Annandale, VA   22003   703-642-6614
                                FAX: 703-642-0497
            e-mail: joniancor@radix.net OR
                    suellenancor@radix.net
                                www.ancor.org

Joni Fritz, Executive Director
Suellen R. Galbraith, Director for Public Policy
Jerri McCandless, Mgr Comm. & Conference Planning

The Directory lists over 600 agencies that provide residential services and supports in 48 states and the District of Columbia. The listings include the name of the Executive Directors, the name, address, and phone number of the agency, describe the types of services that are provided and how many individuals receive services from that agency. *$25.00*

   189 pages

6064 Disability Bookshop Catalog
PO Box 129
Vancouver, WA   98666   360-694-2462
                                800-637-2256
        e-mail: 73743.263u@comuserve.com

Offers more than 400 hard-to-find titles covering a wide range of health topics for the general public, and matters of interest to people with disabilities. Catalog. *$4.00*

   40 pages

6065 Disability Rights Movement
Children's Press
Sherman Turnpike
Danbury, CT   06813
                                800-621-1115
                        FAX: 800-374-4329
Deborah Kent, author
Elena Rockman, Marketing Manager

Author Deborah Kent illuminates both the history of the National Disability Rights Movement and the inspiring personal stories of individuals with various disabilities. *$18.00*

32 pages Hardcover
ISBN 0-53106 -32-3

6066 Disabled Outdoors Magazine

HC 80 Box 395
Grand Marais, MN 55604   218-387-2559

John Kopchik, Publisher
Carolyn Dohme, Editor

A quarterly publication that covers all types of outdoor recreation including hunting, fishing, boating, mountaineering, skydiving, scuba diving, snow and water skiing for people of all ages with all types of disabilities. Also acts as a clearinghouse for information on adaptive products and service providers across the United States and Canada. *$ 10.00*

32-40 pages Quarterly
ISSN 1067-09 0

6067 Disabled People's International's Fifth World Assembly As Reported by Two U.S. Participant

Independent Living Research Utilization ILRU
2323 S Shepherd Drive
Suite 1000
Houston, TX   77019   713-520-0232
                              FAX: 713-520-5785
                              www.ilru.org

Kaye Beneke, author

This report describes the international conference on independent living held in Mexico City in December 1998 as experienced by staff members from two U.S. centers. Kaye Beneke interviewed Luis Chew and Marco Antonio Coronado for htis edition of Readings in Independent Living.

10 pages

6068 Disabled Poeple's International's Fifth World Assembly As Reported By Two US Participants

Culture
2323 S Shepherd Drive
Suite 1000
Houston, TX   77019   713-520-0232
                              FAX: 713-520-5785
                              www.ilru.org

Kaye Beneke, author

This report describes the international confrence on independent living held in Mexico city in December 1998 as experienced by staff members from two U.S. centers. Kaye Beneke interviewed Luis Chew & Marco Antonio Coronado forthis edition of Readings in Independent Living.

10 pages

6069 Disabled We Stand

Brookline Books
PO Box 1046
Cambridge, MA   02238   617-868-0360
                              800-666-2665
                              FAX: 617-868-1772
                              e-mail: brooklinebks@delphi.com
                              www.brooklinebooks.com

Allan T. Sutherland, author

This book is impassioned, often angry, but also hopeful and practical, suggesting a series of actions that will lead to constructive change. It is imbued with spirit and energy of disabled people who are determined to take their lives into their own hands. *$10.95*

Paperback
ISBN 0-25331 -80-0

6070 Disabled, the Media, and the Information Age

Greenwood Publishing Group
88 Post Road West
 # 5007
Westport, CT   06880   203-226-3571
                              FAX: 203-222-1502
                              www.greenwood.com

Jack A. Nelson, Editor, author

A short and easy-to-read overview of how disabled Americans have been portrayed by the media and how images and the role of the handicapped are changing. *$55.00*

264 pages Hardcover
ISBN 0-313284-72-5

6071 Diverse Abilities: An Outcome of Organizational Collab. & Oper. Integration

Independent Living Research Utilization ILRU
2323 S Shepherd Drive
Suite 1000
Houston, TX   77019   713-520-0232
                              FAX: 713-520-5785
                              www.ilru.org

Mark T. obatake, author

Hawaii Centers for independent Living collaborated with other non-profit agencies to reduce costs and expand services. Although the resulting platform organization, DiverseAbilities, is still in its infancy, Mark Obatake, executive director of HCIL and one of this months authors, believes that the processthey went through in developing the collaboration has value for centers and SILCs.

10 pages

6072 E P Resource Guide

Exceptional Parent Library
PO Box 1807
Englewood Cliffs, NJ   10116
                              800-535-1910
                              e-mail: eplibrary@aol.com
                              www.eplibrary.com

Lists directories of national organizations, associations, products and services. *$9.95*

6073 Easy Things to Make Things Simple: Do It Yourself Modifications for Disabled Persons

Brookline Books
PO Box 1047
Cambridge, MA   02238   617-495-3682
                              800-666-2665
                              FAX: 617-868-1772
                              e-mail: brooklinebks@delphi.com
                              www.brooklinebooks.com

Doreen Greensein, author

This book aims at older adults and others with physical limitations who require adaptations for safer and easier living in the kitchen, bathroom, bedroom, yard, and garden. The adaptations can be done inexpensively, from common materials. Large print format and detailed diagrams, plus special sections with advice caregivers . *$15.95*

160 pages Paperback
ISBN 1-571290-24-9

6074   Eating Out: Your Guide to More Enjoyable Dining

RA Rapaport Publishing
150 West 22nd Street
New York, NY   10011   212-691-7676

Hope Warshaw, author

In this book, a nationally recognized expert on diabetes nutrition, shows you how eating out can be fun, without fear of weight gain or an uncontrolled rise in blood sugar. *$4.95*

56 pages Paperback
ISBN 0-96317 -12-

6075   Eating Right for a Bad Gut

Plume Books
New York, NY

James Scala, author

A guide to proper diet and nutrition for the treatment of gastrointestinal disorders.

1992

6076   Educational Care

Educators Publishing Service
31 Smith Place
Cambridge, MA   02138   617-367-2700
617-367-2700
800-225-5750
FAX: 617-547-0412
www.epsbooks.com

Dr. Mel Levine, author

This book, written for both parents and teachers, is based on the view that education should be a system of care that is able to look after the specific needs of individual students. Using case studies, it analyzes various types of learning disorders and then suggests ways to help students with these problems. *$31.50*

325 pages
ISBN 0-838819-87-7

6077   Effective Strategies for Interacting with Policy-Makers

Independent Living Research Utilization ILRU
2323 S Shepherd Drive
Suite 1000
Houston, TX   77019   713-520-0232
FAX: 713-520-5785
www.ilru.org

Bobby Silverstein, author

10 pages

6078   Empowering Youth

Independent Living Research Utilization ILRU
2323 S Shepherd Drive
Suite 1000
Houston, TX   77019   713-520-0232
FAX: 713-520-5785
www.ilru.org

Heather Leigh Harrison & Carolyn Newcombe, author

The Disabilities Network of Eastern Connecticut recognized that in order for young people to take on leadership roles and bring about change in their communities, they needed support in establishing their own identities. DNEC's innovative program demonstrates how they combined peer support and hands-on advocacy projects to empower teens to become leaders.

10 pages

6079   Encyclopedia of Natural Medicine

Prima Publishing
Rocklin, CA

Michael Murray, N.D. and Joseph Pizzorno, N.D., author

An authoritative guide to naturapathic medicine outlining the basic principles of health and how they can be used to treat over sixty health conditions, including candidiasis. Includes self-help approaches using diet, nutrition, and herbal medicine.

1991

6080   EpilepsyUSA

Epilepsy Foundation
4351 Garden City Drive
Landover, MD   20785   301-457-3700
800-332-1000
FAX: 301-577-2684
e-mail: postmaster@efa.org
www.efa.org

Judith O'Toole, Editor

Newspaper reporting on issues of interest to people with epilepsy and their families. *$20.00*

24 pages BiMonthly

6081   Ethical Conflicts in Management of Home Care

Springer Publishing Company
536 Broadway
New York, NY   10012   212-431-4370
FAX: 212-941-7842

Rosalie Kane, author

Offers answers to the questions what is case management and why does it raise ethical issues. *$29.95*

288 pages

6082   EveryBody's Different: Understanding and Changing Our Reactions to Disabilities

Brookes Publishing
PO Box 10624
Baltimore, MD   21285   410-337-9580
800-638-3775
FAX: 410-337-8539
e-mail: custserv@brookespublishing.com
www.brookespublishing.com

Nancy B. Miller, Ph.D., M.S.W., author

This book discusses the emotions, questions, fears, and stereotypes that people without disabilities sometimes experience when they interact with people who do have disabilities. The author teaches readers to become more at ease with the concept of disability and to communicate more effectively with each other. Features activities and exercises that encourage self-examination, helping people to create more enriching personal relationships and work toward a fully inclusive society.

Paperback 1998
ISBN 1-55766 -59-9

6083   Everybody's Guide to Homeopathic Medicines
Jeremy P. Tarcher

Dana Ullman and Stephen Cummings M.P.H., author

Covers alternative treatments in homeopathic medicines.

6084   Everyday Social Interaction: A Program for People with Disabilities, 2nd Edition
Brookes Publishing
PO Box 10624
Baltimore, MD   21285   410-337-9580
                                                    800-638-3775
                               FAX: 410-337-8539
        e-mail: custserv@brookespublishing.com
                     www.brookespublishing.com
Vivienne C. Riches, B.A. Dip. Ed., M.A., M.A.P.s.S, author

This source guides teachers and human services professionals in helping people with disabilities acquire social interaction skills and develop satisfying relationships. Included is a checklist and task analyses that shows how complex skills can be broken down into major components for easy performance monitoring accompanied by tips on social courtesies, rewards, praise, and criticism. *$41.95*

342 pages Paperback
ISBN 1-55766 -58-4

6085   Exclusively Female: A Nutrition Guide for Better Menstrual Health
Borgo Press
San Bernadino, CA

Linda Ojeda, author

This book pioneered the nutritional approach to menstrual self-care; gives comprehensive guidelines on the use of diet and supplementation to alleviate menstrual problems.

1985

6086   Farmington Valley ARC
10 Tower Lane
Avon, CT   06001   860-678-0313
                               FAX: 860-676-0275

Lynn Flerri, President
Tom Thompson, Executive Director

The official newsletter containing information, new ideas, progress and more on the Farmington Valley Association for Retarded and Handicapped Citizens.

6087   Fertility Awareness Handbook
Hunter House Publishers
Alameda, CA

Barbara Kass-Assese, R.N. C.N.P. & Hal Danzer M.D., author

Provides noninvasive and side-effect free natural family planning methods that teach you how to be more in touch with your body, more secure in your lovemaking, and more in control of your health and sexual well-being.

1992

6088   Fertility: A Comprehensive Guide to Natural Family Planning
David and Charles
Ponfret, UT

Elizabeth Clubb and Jone N. Knight, author

Clear accessible information for couples who want to take control of their own family planning without using chemicals or technology.

1989

6089   Focus
Arthritis Foundation
Central Ohio Chapter
3740 Ridge Mill Drive
Hilliard, OH   43026   614-876-8200
                                                    888-382-4673
                               FAX: 614-876-8363
                                 www.arthritis.org

Offers updated information on arthritis as well as news of the services and activities of the Chapter.

Quarterly

6090   For Siblings Only
Family Resource Associates
35 Haddon Avenue
Shrewsbury, NJ   07702   732-747-5310
                               FAX: 732-747-1896

Mary Allan, Social Worker

A newsletter for brothers and sisters, aged 4 through 10, whose sibling has a disablilty. Includes stories, library resources, activities and discussion of feelings. $12/year for families, $20/year for professionals. *$12.00*

12 pages Quarterly

6091   Forever Young: A Practical Guide to Youth Extension
Witkower Press
West Hartford, CT

Michael E. Molnar, author
Describes what cell therapy is.

6092   Fosters Botanical and Herb Reviews
B & H Reviews
PO Box 106
Eureka Springs, AK   72632

                               FAX: 501-253-7442

6093   Four-Ingredient Cookbook

Laurel Designs
5 Laurel Avenue
Belvedere, CA   94920

FAX: 415-435-1451
e-mail: laureld@ncal.verio.com

Janet Sawyer, Owner
Lynn Montoya, Owner

Simple, easy to follow recipes, each containing four ingredients. Particularly suited to persons with limited physical ability. Includes 400 recipes, appetizers to desserts. *$9.00*

6094   Free Yourself From Pain

Bresler Center
115 South Topanga Canyon Boulevard
Suite 158
Topanga, CA   90290   310-455-3634

David E. Bresler, author

This self-help book for managing chronic pain and depression includes several chapters illustrating the use of imagery for pain control.

1992

6095   Freedom from Headaches

Fireside Books
New York, NY

Joel Saper, author

Covers the causes, treatments, and different varieties of headaches.

6096   Freedom of Movement: IL History and Philosophy

Independent Living Research Utilization ILRU
2323 S Shepherd Drive
Suite 1000
Houston, TX   77019   713-520-0232
FAX: 713-520-5785
www.ilru.org

Steve Brown, author

10 pages

6097   Frequently Asked Questions About Multiple Chemical Sensitivity

Independent Living Research Utilization ILRU
2323 S Shepherd Drive
Suite 1000
Houston, TX   77019   713-520-0232
FAX: 713-520-5785
www.ilru.org

Bob Michaels, author

This FAQ covers important information about multiple chemical sensitivity and environmental illness. The FAQ describes the conditions, recommends strategies for improving access, and lists resources for CILs and other organizations. As the fact sheet states, centers must set an example in assuring that all people can enter their offices.

10 pages

6098   Front Row Advisor

3109 Grand Avenue
Coconut Grove, FL   33133   305-774-6040
FAX: 305-774-6070

Matthew J. Bennett, Publisher

Newsletter dedicated to business and First Class Air Travel and the alluring world of free upgrades.

Monthly

6099   Functional Electrical Stimulation for Ambulation by Paraplegics

Krieger Publishing Company
PO Box 9542
Melbourne, FL   32902   407-724-9542
800-724-0025
FAX: 407-951-3671
e-mail: info@krieger-pub.com
www.krieger-publishing.com

Daniel Graupe and Kath H. Kohn, author

FES is employed to enable spinal cord injury patients who are complete paraplegics to stand and ambulate without bracing. The text covers 12 years of amulation experience. Also available in hardcover, ISBN #0-89464-845-4, selling for $39.50. *$19.95*

210 pages Softcover
ISBN 1-576240-28-9

6100   Gastrointestinal Health

Harper Perennial
New York, NY

Steven Perkins, M.D., author

Comprehensive self-help guide for treating a full range of gastrointestinal disorders using diet and nutrition.

1992

6101   General Guidelines for Disability Policy Change Agents

Independent Living Research Utilization ILRU
2323 S Shepherd Drive
Suite 1000
Houston, TX   77019   713-520-0232
FAX: 713-520-5785
www.ilru.org

Bobby Silverstein, author

10 pages

6102   Genetic Disorders Sourcebook

Omigraphics
615 Griswold Street
Detroit, MI   48226

800-234-1340
FAX: 800-875-1340
www.omnigraphics.com

Kathy Massimini, Editor

Provides information on hereditary diseases and disorders. *$7800.00*

650 pages 1900
ISBN 0-789892-41-1

6103 Getting the Most Out of Consultation Services

Independent Living Research Utilization ILRU
2323 S Shepherd Drive
Suite 1000
Houston, TX   77019   713-520-0232
                                FAX: 713-520-5785
                                www.ilru.org
*Patricia Yaeger, Laurel Richards & Laurie G.
Redd, author*

A practical, nuts-and-bolts approach to help make working with a consultant a positive, helpful experience for independent living centers.

10 pages

6104 Grief-What it is and What You Can Do

Centering Corporation
1531 N Saddle Creek Road
Omaha, NE   68104   402-553-1200
                                FAX: 402-533-0507
                                e-mail: j1200@aol.com
                                www.centering.org
Joy Johnson, author

General grief information for all grief issues. *$3.50*

32 pages Paperback

6105 Guide to Polarity Therapy: The Gentle Art of Hands-on Healing

Elan Press

Maruti Seidman, author

Explains the theory of polarity therapy and basic techniques.

1991

6106 Guidelines on Disability

US Dept. of Housing & Urban Development
Washington, DC   20410   202-708-1112

Contains information on housing and accessibility for persons with disabilities.

6107 Hand and Foot Reflexology: A Self-Help Guide

Simon & Schuster
1230 Avenue of the Americas
New York, NY   10020   212-698-7000
                                800-223-2348
Kevin & Barbara Kunz, author

Comprehensive encyclopedia of personal reflexology.

1987

6108 Handbook of Mental and Mental Disorder Among Black Americans

Greenwood Publishing Group
88 Post Road West
5007
Westport, CT   06880   203-226-3571
                                FAX: 203-222-1502
                                www.greenwood.com
Dorothy S. Ruiz, Editor, author

In addition to providing a wealth of new data on the mental health status of black communities, this handbook presents analyses of specific social, structural, and cultural conditions that affect the lives of individual Black Americans. $55-$65.

352 pages Hardcover
ISBN 0-313263-30-2

6109 Handbook of Services for the Handicapped

Greenwood Publishing Group
88 Post Road West
5007
Westport, CT   06880   203-226-3571
                                FAX: 203-222-1502
                                www.greenwood.com
Alfred H. Katz and Knute Martin, author

A handy reference book offering information and services for disabled individuals. $59.95-$65.00.

291 pages Hardcover
ISBN 0-313213-85-2

6110 Handbook on Mental Health Policy in the United States

Greenwood Publishing Group
88 Post Road West
5007
Westport, CT   06880   203-226-3571
                                FAX: 203-222-1502
                                www.greenwood.com
David A. Rochefort, author

Covers the historical, policy and administrative aspects of public mental health care. *$95.00*

563 pages $95 - $99.50
ISBN 0-313250-09-0

6111 Harris Communications

15159 Technology Drive
Eden Prairie, MN   55344   612-906-1180
                                800-825-6758
                                FAX: 612-906-1099
                                e-mail: mail@harriscomm.com
                                www.harriscomm.com

Robert I. Harris, Owner

A national distributor of assistive devices for the Deaf and hard of hearing with many manufacturers represented. Catalog includes a wide range of assistive devices as well as a variety of books and videotapes related to deaf and hard of hearing issues. Products available for children, teachers, hearing professionals, interpreters, and anyone interested in deaf culture, hearing loss, and sign language. Published bi-annually.

200 pages Catalog

6112 Haubrichs Archival Handicap Directory Handicapped Disabled Services

University of Karachi, Pakistan D. Haubrich
24 Woodland Avenue
Franklinville, NJ   08322   609- -
                                FAX: 180-081-0001

Dr. Masood Answer, Professor of Theology
Edward Elias Elias, Asst. Publisher
Daniel Haubrich, Founder, Philanthropist

A publication edited and designed to aid and assist the disabled and handicapped, especially facilitized children, even those with noncureable viruses. Patented new technological hieroglyphic symbols and other formulated inventions for the blind (versus braille), by world renowned English scientists in the Middle East.

6113 Head First: The Biology of Hope

Thorndike Press
Depot Street
Unity, ME 04988 207-948-2962

Norman Cousins, author

Helps the patients to see the positive sides of all situations.

6114 Healing Herbs

Rodale Press
33 East Minor Street
Emmaus, PA 18098 610-967-5171

Michael Castleman, author

Covers everything from growing the herbs to home remedies.

6115 Healing Yourself: a Step-by-Step Program for Better Health Through Imagery

Pocket Books
1230 Avenue of the Americans
New York, NY 10020 212-698-7000

Martin L. Rossman, author

6116 Healing and the Mind

Doubleday
1540 Broadway
New York, NY 10036 212-782-9000

Bill Moyers, author

Authors personal approach to illness.

6117 Health Affairs

Project HOPE
Millwood, VA 22646 540-837-2100

Multidisciplinary journal of health-care policy with articles on health-care cost, practices, innovations and new data. *$ 45.00*

6118 Heart of the Mind

Real People Press

Andreas Connierae and Steve Moab, author

Provides common NLP problems and several new techniques.

6119 Help for the Hyperactive Child

Professional Books

William G. Crook M.D., author

6120 Herbs for the Mind: What Science Tells Us about Nature's Remedies for Depression, Stress...

Guilford Press
72 Spring Street
New York, NY 10012 212-431-9800
800-365-7006
FAX: 212-966-6708
e-mail: info@guilford.com
www.guilford.com

Jonathan R.T. Davidson, MD, Kathryn M. Conner, MD, author

Translates hard data into the accessible answers consumers need to make informed decisions on taking St. John's wort for depression, kava for stress or anxiety, valerian for insomnia or ginko for memory loss. *$14.95*

278 pages Paperback 1900
ISBN 1-572304-76-6

6121 Home and Community Care for Chronically Ill Children

Oxford University Press
2001 Evans Road
Cary, NC 27513 212-726-6000
800-451-7556
FAX: 919-677-1303
www.oup-usa.org

James Perrin, author

This book lays common ground for all who have reason and responsibility to enhance the capability of families to care for their ill children over the long term at home. *$32.95*

192 pages

6122 Homeopathic Medicines at Home: Natural Remedies for Everyday Ailments and Minor Injuries

Jeremy P. Tarcher

Jane Heimlich and Maesimund B. Panos M.D., author

Guide for common ailments and their cures.

6123 Hormone Replacement Therapy, Yes or No: How to Make an Informed Decision

Nutrition Encounter
Novato, CA

Betty Kamen, Ph.D., author

Safe, non-toxic and medically valid alternatives to conventional hormone replacement treatment for menopausal symptoms and osteoporosis.

1993

6124 Hospice Alternative

Harper Collins Publishers/Basic Books
10 E 53rd Street
New York, NY 10022 212-207-7000
800-242-7737
FAX: 212-207-7203

Anne Munley, author

An account of the hospice experience. An innovative and humane way of caring for the terminally ill. $8.95

256 pages
ISBN 0-46503 -61-0

6125 Housing and Independence: How Innovative CILs are Assisting Housing for Disabled People

Independent Living Research Utilization ILRU
2323 S Shepherd Drive
Suite 1000
Houston, TX 77019 713-520-0232
FAX: 713-520-5785
www.ilru.org

Kaye Beneke, author

This month's Readings is the first of many publications which will feature the winners of the Innovative CILs competition. This article is a compilation of the four winning essays as well as telephone interviews with the key staff members at each of the centers.

10 pages

6126 How to Live Longer with a Disability

Accent Books & Products
PO Box 700
Bloomington, IL 61702 309-378-2961
800-787-8444
FAX: 309-378-4420
e-mail: acmtlvng@aol.com

Elle Friedman Becker, MA and Robert Mauro, author
Raymond C. Cheever, Publisher
Betty Garee, Editor

Eleven chapters to help you enjoy every aspect of your life, and live easier and happier. Includes sexuality and disability, getting more from the medical community and benefit programs. Co-authored by Robert Mauro, sociologist and Elle Becker, counselor and psychologist, both disabled. *$11.50*

266 pages Paperback
ISBN 0-19570 -38-8

6127 How to Select and Use Manual Wheelchairs

Rehabilitation Press
PO Box 380
Topping, VA 23169

e-mail: abennett@crosslimb.net
A.Bennett Wilson, Jr, author
A. Bennett Wilson Jr, Owner

The only publication written specifically for users and potential users of manual wheelchairs to provide them with comprehensive, unbiased information about wheelchairs. *$12.50*

67 pages
ISBN 1-88090 -04-4

6128 IAL News

International Association of Laryngectomees
1599 Clifton Road NE
Atlanta, GA 30329 404-329-7942

Focuses on rehabilitation and well-being of persons who have had laryngectomy surgery.

6129 If I Only Knew What to Say or Do

AARP Fulfillment
601 E Street NW
Washington, DC 20049 202-434-2277
800-424-3410
FAX: 202-434-3443
e-mail: member@aarp.org
www.aarp.org

Provides a concise discussion of how to help a friend in crisis. Learn what to say and what not to say.

6130 If it Weren't for the Honor - I'd Rather Have Walked

Accent Books & Products
PO Box 700
Bloomington, IL 61702 309-378-2961
800-787-8444
FAX: 309-378-4420
e-mail: acmtlvng@aol.com

Jan Little, author
Raymond C. Cheever, Publisher
Betty Garee, Editor

Revealing, often humorous, highly interesting and important reading. This book offers an account told by the author who was on the scene and actually saw and participated in many events that paved the way for progress for all those with disabilities. *$14.50*

262 pages Paperback
ISBN 0-91570 -41-8

6131 Imagery in Healing Shamanism and Modern Medicine

Shambalab Publications

Jeanee Achterberg, author

Patients use self imagery to fight sickness and pain throughout their lives.

6132 Impacts of Creative Self-Expression in the Arts on Special Problems

National Institute of Art and Disablities
551 23rd Street
Richmond, CA 94804

A report from the American Psychological Association convention on August 12, 1994, summarizing discussions by practitioners and researchers from psychology, art, education, psychoanalysis, and related fields who have worked with special populations in various art media (visual arts, dance, per forming arts, etc.).

6133 Independence & Transition to Community Living: The Role of Independent Living Centers

Independent Living Research Utilization ILRU
2323 S Shepherd Drive
Suite 1000
Houston, TX 77019 713-520-0232
FAX: 713-520-5785
www.ilru.org

Bonnie O'Day, author

This publication covers important information on why we all should make assistance to people living in nursing homes a priority. Just as important, this is an excellent summary of all the facts - quality of life, health, and costs - which support deinstitutionalization.

10 pages

6134   Independent Living Centers and Managed Care: Results of an ILRU Study on Involvement

Independent Living Research Utilization ILRU
2323 S Shepherd Drive
Suite 1000
Houston, TX   77019   713-520-0232
                          FAX: 713-520-5785
                          www.ilru.org
Drew Batavia, author

This month's Readings presents findings from an ILRU study of roles centers are taking vis-a-vis managed care. Initiated in spring 1998, we asked Drew Batavia to take the lead in conducting this study for us. We were interested in collecting data on frequency with which centers are contacted by consumers with managed care problems. This is a study that will need to be repeated periodically as our experiences with managed care evolves. Meanwhile, here are the initial findings.

10 pages

6135   Independent Living Challenges the Blues

Independent Living Research Utilization ILRU
2323 S Shepherd Drive
Suite 1000
Houston, TX   77019   713-520-0232
                          FAX: 713-520-5785
                          www.ilru.org
Patricia L. Puckett, author

Patricia's article highlights the Georgia SILC's health care advocacy efforts: the Georgia legislature passed a bill enabling Georgia Bleu to convert to for-profit status without a distribution of assets to similar nonprofit corporations; the Georgia SILC joined other health care advocates in filing a class action law suit to challenge the legality of the conversion; the Georgia SILC continues advocacy efforts to involve people with disabilities in developing and monitoring health care policy.

10 pages

6136   Independent Living Office

Department of Housing & Urban Development (HUD)
451 7th Street SW
Washington, DC   20410   202-708-1422

This office within HUD is charged with encouraging the construction of housing that is accessible to handicapped persons. The Office of Independent Living encourages modifications of apartments and other dwellings so that handicapped persons can enter without assistance.

6137   Infertility and Birth Defects - Is Mercury from Silver Dental Fillings a Hidden Cause?
Bio-Probe

Sam and Michael Ziff, author

Explains the facts about mercury and lead.

1987

6138   Information Services for People with Developmental Disabilities

Greenwood Publishing Group
88 Post Road West
 # 5007
Westport, CT   06880   203-226-3571
                          FAX: 203-222-1502
                          www.greenwood.com
Linda Lucas Walling and Marilyn M. Irwin, Editor, author
Linda Lucas Walling, Editor
Marilyn M. Irwin, Editor

Overviews the information needs of people with developmental disabilities and tells librarians how to meet them. $65.oo-$75.00.

368 pages Hardcover
ISBN 0-313287-80-5

6139   Innovative Programs: An Example of How CILs Can Put Their Work in the Context of

Culture
2323 S Shepherd Drive
Suite 1000
Houston, TX   77019   713-520-0232
                          FAX: 713-520-5785
                          www.ilru.org
Steve Brown, author

Another winner in the innovative CIL competition-Steve Brown describes the Talking Books Program of Southeast Alaska Independent Living, discussing their efforts to record the oral history and life experiances of people with disabilities in the larger context of disability culture.

10 pages

6140   Inside MS

National Multiple Sclerosis Society
733 3rd Avenue
New York, NY   10017   212-450-1702
                          800-FIG-HTMS

News and information on research progress, medical treatments, patient services, therapeutic claims and activities.

6141   International Ventilator Users Network

Gazette International Networking Institute
4207 Lindell Boulevard
 # 110
Saint Louis, MO   63108   314-534-0475
                          FAX: 314-534-5070
                          e-mail: gini_intl@msn.com
                          www.post-polio.org/ivun.html
Judith R. Fischer, Editor, author
Joan L. Headley, Executive Director

IVUN is a worldwide network of ventilator users and health professionals experienced in and committed to home care and long term mechanical ventilation. IVUN News, a quarterly newsletter, offers articles on family adjustments, equipment, techniques, travel, ethical issues, medical topics, and resources. Also publishes the annual iVUN resource directory, listing ventilator users, health professionals, equipment manufacturers and vendors, as well as other related organizations. *$ 17.00*

8 pages Quarterly

591

6142 Introducing Neuro-Linguistic Programming: The New Psychology of Personnel Excellance

HarperCollins Publishers

J. Seymour and J. O'Connor, author

6143 Irritable Bowel Syndrome and Diverticulosis

Thorson's/HarperCollins Publishers
London, England,

Shirley Trickett, author

A comprehensive self-help approach for treating irritable bowel syndrome, divertculosis, and other gastrointestinal tract conditions using diet, nutrition, bodywork, homeopathy, and exercise.

1992

6144 Is This Your Child?: Discovering and Treating Unrecognized Allergies

William Morrow and Company

Doris Rapp M.D., author

6145 It Feels Good to be in Control

Accent Books & Products
PO Box 700
Bloomington, IL   61702   309-378-2961
                                800-787-8444
                        FAX: 309-378-4420
                    e-mail: acmtlvng@aol.com
Robert P. Bennett, author
Raymond C. Cheever, Publisher
Betty Garee, Editor

Understanding yourself can make almost anything work better, your health, your personal relationships, your happiness, you name it. This small book could be the best medicine and the most inexpensive a person could ever have. *$4.50*

18 pages Paperback
ISBN 0-91570 -39-6

6146 Just Like Everyone Else

World Institute on Disability
510 16th Street
Suite 100
Oakland, CA   94612   510-763-4100
                        FAX: 510-763-4109
                    e-mail: wid@wid.org

The oversize-format publication, intended for general audiences, provides perspective, inspiration and information about the Independent Living Movement and the Americans with Disabilities Act. *$5.00*

16 pages

6147 KEEP THE PROMISE - Managed Care and People with Disabilities

ANCOR
4200 Evergreen Lane
Suite 315
Annandale, VA   22003   703-642-6614
                        FAX: 703-642-0497
            e-mail: joniancor@radix.net OR
                    suellenancor@radix.net
                            www.ancor.org

Joni Fritz, Executive Director
Suellen R. Galbraith, Director for Public Policy
Jerri McCandless, Mgr Comm. & Conference Planning

This publication presents a detailed review of the process and the lessons learned. Details a way for all stake holders to work together for a state or local system.

119 pages $18 - $22

6148 Kaleidoscope: Exploring the Experience of Disability Through Literature & the Fine Arts

United Disability Services
701 S Main Street
Akron, OH   44311   330-762-9755
                        FAX: 330-762-0912
                        TDY:330-379-3349
            e-mail: mshiplett@udsakron.org
                        www.udsakron.org
Darshan Perusek, Ph.D, Editor-in-Chief, author
Mildred Shiplett, Editorial Coordinator
Gail Willmott, Senior Editor
Phyllis Boerner, Publication Director

This magazine explores the experiences of disability through the lens of creative arts. Unlike rehabilitation, advocacy or independent living journals, this journal challenges and transcends stereotypical, patronizing and sentimental attitudes about disability. Offers a variety of articles, fiction, art and poetry relating to issues of disability, literature and the fine arts. *$10.00*

64 pages BiAnnually

6149 Killing Pain Without Prescription

Harper Perennial
New York, NY

Harold Gelb, D.M.D., author

An outline of treatments to deal with chronic pain, including diet, nutrition, applied kinesiology, osteopathy, and bodywork. Also includes a resource guide of organizations offering help nationwide.

1982

6150 Laugh with Accent, #3

Accent Books & Products
PO Box 700
Bloomington, IL   61702   309-378-2961
                                800-787-8444
                        FAX: 309-378-4420
                    e-mail: acmtlvng@aol.com

Raymond C. Cheever, Publisher
Betty Garee, Editor

These special cartoons prove laughter is the best medicine of all. It's when the laughter stops that we become truly disabled, say readers. *$3.50*

89 pages Paperback
ISBN 0-91570 -16-7

6151 Learning to Listen: Positive Approaches & People with Difficult Behavior

Brookes Publishing
PO Box 10624
Baltimore, MD   21285   **410-337-9580**
                                              800-638-3775
                                    FAX: 410-337-8539
    e-mail: custserv@brookespublishing.com
          www.brookespublishing.com
Herbert Lovett, Ph.D., author

This book describes how the interactive process of learning to listen provides practical alternatives to overly controlling behavior modification techniques. Includes compelling and detailed case studies that illustrate possible positive approaches and reveal how people with disabilities can take control of their lives. *$27.00*

288 pages Paperback
ISBN 1-55766 -64-2

6152 Life After Trauma: A Workbook for Healing

Guilford Press
72 Spring Street
New York, NY   10012   **212-431-9800**
                                              800-365-7006
                                    FAX: 212-966-6708
                          www.guilford.com
Dena Rosenbloom, PhD, Mary Beth Wiliams,PhD LCSW, author

$18.95

352 pages Paperback 1999
ISBN 1-572302-39-9

6153 Life Planning Workbook

Exceptional Parent Library
PO Box 1807
Englewood Cliffs, NJ   10116
                                              800-535-1910
                          e-mail: eplibrary@aol.com
                              www.eplibrary.com
L.M. Russell, et al., author

A hands-on guide to help parents provide for the future security and happiness of their child with a disability after their death. *$24.95*

6154 LifeLines

Disabled & Alone/Life Services for the Handicapped
352 Park Avenue South
Room 703
New York, NY   10010   **212-532-6740**
                                              800-995-0066
                                    FAX: 212-532-6740
          e-mail: disabledandalone@aol.com
                    www.disabledandalone.org
Leslie D. Park, author
Roslyn Brilliant, Executive Director
Leslie D. Park, Chairman

Newsletter providing current and valuable information about lifetime care and planning for persons with disabilities and their families and the organizations serving them. Free upon request.

4-10 pages BiAnnual

6155 Lifelong Leisure Skills and Lifestyles for Persons with Developmental Disabilities

Brookes Publishing
PO Box 10624
Baltimore, MD   21285   **410-337-9580**
                                              800-638-3775
                                    FAX: 410-337-8539
    e-mail: custserv@brookespublishing.com
          www.brookespublishing.com
Stuart J. Schleien, Ph.D., CTRS,, author

This instructional manual offers ideas and detailed examples that describe how to guide individuals of all ages through popular activities using adaptations that foster skill acquisition and inclusion. Some of the concepts explored are home-school-community collaboration, choice making and the dignity of risk, and leisure skill acquisition for the life span. *$35.00*

352 pages Paperback
ISBN 1-55766 -47-2

6156 Living in a State of Stuck

Brookline Books
PO Box 1046
Cambridge, MA   02238   **617-868-0360**
                                              800-666-2665
                                    FAX: 617-868-1772
          e-mail: brooklinebks@delphi.com
                    www.brooklinebooks.com
Marcia J. Scherer, author

Offers explanations on how adaptive technologies affect the lives of people with disabilities. *$24.95*

3rd ed., paper
ISBN 1-571290-27-3

6157 Living in the Community

Independent Living Research Utilization ILRU
2323 S Shepherd Drive
Suite 1000
Houston, TX   77019   **713-520-0232**
                                    FAX: 713-520-5785
                              www.ilru.org
James Strudivant, Lori Baskette, & Jamey George, author

James, Lori, and Jamey describe the elements of their successful program to move people out of nursing homes and into the community: providing funding for deposits, first month's rent and other neccessities, including assistive technology; providing training and the other core services before and after consumers leave the nursing home; developing relationships with housing and other service providers.

10 pages

6158 Living the Therapeutic Touch: Healing as Lifestyle

Quest Books

Dolores Krieger, author
How to do Therapeutic Touch.

1988

6159   Loud, Proud and Passionate

Mobility International USA
PO Box 10767
Eugene, OR   97440   541-343-1284
                                    FAX: 541-343-6812
                                    TDY:541-343-1284
                                    e-mail: info@miusa.org
                                    www.miusa.org

Cindy Lewis, Susan Sygall, author
Susan Sygall, Executive Director
Rhonda Neuhaus, Public Relations Coordinator

Aims to educate development and women's organizations about the importance of including women with disabilities in community development projects. This resource book features examples of profects organized by women with disabilities, recommendations from women with disabilities who have organized from grassroots, national and international levels, practical strategies for outreach, inclusion and support of women with disabilities, resource materials and supportive organizations. *$25.00*

1998

6160   Love - Where to Find It, How to Keep It

Accent Books & Products
PO Box 700
Bloomington, IL   61702   309-378-2961
                                         800-787-8444
                                    FAX: 309-378-4420
                                    e-mail: acmtlvng@aol.com

Raymond C. Cheever, Publisher
Betty Garee, Editor

Offers ideas such as how to meet other single people, avoid the wrong type; communications skills and much more for the disabled person wanting to date. *$6.95*

104 pages Paperback
ISBN 0-91570 -31-0

6161   MOOSE: A Very Special Person

Brookline Books
PO Box 1046
Cambridge, MA   02238   617-868-0360
                                         800-666-2665
                                    FAX: 617-868-1772
                                    e-mail: brooklinebks@delphi.com
                                    www.brooklinebooks.com

W. Scott MacDonald and Chester W. Oden, Jr.,
author

Moose, which in very human terms, teaches us that each of us is different and that we have our own unique capacity for loving, sharing, enjoying and learning. *$10.95*

Paperback
ISBN 0-91479 -73-5

6162   Mainstream Magazine

2973 Beech Street
San Diego, CA   92102   619-234-3138
                                    FAX: 619-234-3155
                                    e-mail: editor@mainstream.mag.com
                                    www.mainstream-mag.com

Cyndi Jones, Publisher

The authoritative, national voice of people with disabilities, publishes in-depth reports on employment, education, new products and technology, legislation and disability rights advocacy, recreation and travel, disability arts and culture, plus personality profiles and challenging commentary. *$24.00*

Monthly

6163   Making Changes: Family Voices on Living Disabilities

Brookline Books
PO Box 1047
Cambridge, MA
                                         800-666-2665
                                    FAX: 617-868-1772
                                    e-mail: brooklinebks@delphi.com
                                    www.brooklinebooks.com

Jan A. Spiegle and Richard Van Den Pol, author

What are the day to day impacts on the family when a disabled child is born? Or when a child who grows up without a disability becomes disabled through accident or disease? This provocative set of reports illuminates the conditions of those peoples lives, and the way they and those around them adjust to the disabilities. *$16.95*

216 pages Paperback
ISBN 0-91479 -93-

6164   Making Informed Medical Decisions: Where to Look and How to Use What You Find

Patient-Centered Guides
101 Morris Street
Sebastopol, CA   95472   707-829-0515
                                         800-998-9938
                                    FAX: 707-829-0104
                                    www.patientcenters.com

Nancy Oster, Lucy Thomas, & Darol Joseff, MD,
author

You are involved in healthcare decisions-whether you want to be or not. Making Informed Medical Decisions acts like a friendly reference librarian, explaining: tips for researching for someone else; medical journal articles; statistics and risk; standard treatment options; clinical trial; making an ally of your doctor; and determining your own best course. Authors Oster, Thomas, and Joseff-a pateint advocate, medical librarian, and medical doctor-also share examples and stories. *$17.95*

280 pages Paperback
ISBN 1-565924-59-2

6165   Making Wise Decisions for Long-Term Care

AARP Fulfillment
601 E Street NW
Washington, DC   20049   202-434-2277
                                         800-424-3410
                                    FAX: 202-434-3443
                                    e-mail: member@aarp.org
                                    www.aarp.org

Here's a comprehensive consumer education effort in the area of long-term care.

28 pages

6166 Management of Chronic Disease and Disability
Demos Medical Publishing
386 Park Avenue S
Suite 201
New York, NY 10016   212-683-0072
                            800-532-8663
                       FAX: 212-683-0118
                 e-mail: indo@demospub.com
Ross Hays, M.D., author
Mary L. Paskewicz, Customer Service

Over 10% of the American population is disabled from chronic disease, with a vast majority from disorders of the cardiovascular and neuromuscular systems. This important volume is a basic introduction to the management of chronic illness. *$24.95*

> *280 pages Paperback*
> *ISBN 0-939957-46-9*

6167 Managing Pain before it Manages You
Guilford Press
72 Spring Street
New York, NY 10012   212-431-9800
                            800-365-7006
                       FAX: 212-966-6708
                        www.guilford.com
Margaret A. Caudill, MD, PhD, author
$19.95

> *224 pages Paperback 1994*
> *ISBN 0-898622-24-7*

6168 Marriage & Disability
Accent Books & Products
PO Box 700
Bloomington, IL 61702   309-378-2961
                            800-787-8444
                       FAX: 309-378-4420
                 e-mail: acmtlvng@aol.com

Raymond C. Cheever, Publisher
Betty Garee, Editor

This guide can help you make the right decision and it can help smooth the way to a happier life. *$7.95*

> *Paperback*
> *ISBN 0-91570 -34-5*

6169 Massage Book
Random House
201 E 50th Street
New York, NY 10022   212-751-2600
                            800-726-0600
George Downing, author
Hailed as the 'classic book' on massage.

> *1972*

6170 Massage Magazine
NOAH Publishing Company
PO Box 1500
Davis, CA 95617   916-757-6033

Covers the art and science of massage, bodywork and related healing arts.

> *BiMonthly*

6171 Massage for Common Ailments
Fireside

Sara Thomas, author
Step-by-step guide on how to alleviate everyday health problems.

> *1989*

6172 Matrix and Matrix Regulation Basis for an Holistic Theory in Medicine
Karl Haug International

Alfred Pischinger M.D., author

6173 Medical Herbalism
Bergner Communications
PO Box 33080
Portland, OR 97233

Newsletter written by physicians and is published six times a year.

6174 Meditative Mind
Jeremy P. Tarcher

Daniel Goleman, author
Describes how various differant religous organizations use meditation.

6175 Meeting the Needs of People with Disabilities
ORYX Press
4041 N Central Avenue
Suite 700
Phoenix, AZ 85012   602-265-2651
                            800-279-6799
                       FAX: 800-279-4663
                 e-mail: info@oryxpress.com
Ruth A. Velleman, author

This in-depth examination of the needs of the physically or mentally disabled, blind and deaf is completely revised and updated. It reveals how librarians and other professionals can meet those needs, covering current information services and more. *$37.95*

> *288 pages*
> *ISBN 0-89774 -21-3*

6176 Mending the Body, Mending the Mind
Bantam
Reading, MA

Joan Borysenko, author

6177 Menopausal Years
Ash Tree Publishing
New York, NY

Susan S. Weed, author

This book focuses on various aspects of women's health including osteoporosis, and reviews a wide range of remedies from massage and energy work to supplements and medication.

> *1992*

6178 Menopause Naturally (Updated): Preparing for the Second Half of Life

Volcano Press
Volcano, CA

Sadja Greenwood, M.D., author

Addresses questions women have about using post-menopausal hormones. New information includes screening tests for osteoporosis, and nonhormonal treatments, new ways to deal with hot flashes, what natural progesterone in, testosterone therapy, exercise, diet, and maintaining postmenopausal health.

1992

6179 Menopause Self-Help Book

Celestial Arts
Berkley, CA

Susan M. Lark, M.D., author

An easy-to-understand workbook on how to approach menopause; explains what menopause is and explores the many natural treatments available and gives the pros and cons of estrogen replacement therapy. Resources are listed.

1990

6180 Menopause Without Medicine (Second Edition)

Hunter Hous
Alameda, CA

Linda Ojeda, Ph.D., author

Research on nutrition, exercise, and osteoporosis, including good news about the body's ability to rebuild bone later in life; describes how women can best prepare their minds and bodies for the transition of menopause, and explains how women can prevent osteoporosis and control the disturbing symptoms of hot flashes, insomnia, fatigue, and weight gain.

1992

6181 Menopause: A Second Spring

Blue Poppy Press
Boulder, CO

Honora Lee Wolfe, author

The first book-length decription of the traditional Chinese medical view of menopause, menopausal syndrome, and postmenopausal disorders. Extensive sections on self-help, preventative therapies, and remedial treatment of specific problems, as well as a complete TCM explanation of menopausal symptoms.

1992

6182 Mental Retardation

Allyn & Bacon
160 Gould Street
Needham Heights, MA   02194

800-852-8024

Stanley J. Vitello, author

Examines mental retardation within a larger social context. Provides an understanding of how social and legal events have shaped the lives of mentally retarded people.

224 pages Paper 1986
ISBN 0-135765-21-8

6183 Mental Retardation, Third Edition

McGraw-Hill, School Publishing
220 East Danieldale Road
DeSoto, TX   75115   972-224-1111
                           800-442-9685
                    FAX: 972-228-1982
                        mhschool.com

Combines significant findings from the most current research, focusing on a unique relationship between the special educator and the learner with mental retardation.

656 pages Casebound

6184 Mental Retardation: A Life-Cycle Approach

McGraw-Hill, School Publishing
220 East Danieldale Road
DeSoto, TX   75115   972-224-1111
                           800-442-9685
                    FAX: 972-228-1982
                        mhschool.com

This text considers the needs of the retarded individual at every stage of life.

512 pages

6185 Mental and Physical Disability Law Reporter

ABA Commission on Mental & Physical Disability Law
740 15th Street NW
9th Floor
Washington, DC   20005   202-662-1581
                         FAX: 202-662-1032

Provides the most comprehensive coverage of disability law issues and developments at the most affordavle rates. Each issue gives you hundreds of case summaries of the most important disability law decisions, updates on the latest state and federal legislation, and special feature articles by leading disability law experts, all fully indexed and cross-referenced for easy use. Annually digests more than 2,000 cases; highlight most important laws/trends, and original articles by national experts.

6186 Mercury Poisining from Dental Amalgam - A Hazard to Human Brain

Bio-Probe

Patrick Stortebecker, M.D., author

1986

6187 Midtown Sweep: Grassroots Advocacy at its Best

Independent Living Research Utilization ILRU
2323 S Shepherd Drive
Suite 1000
Houston, TX   77019   713-520-0232
                         FAX: 713-520-5785
                            www.ilru.org

Josie Byzek, Janetta Green, & Linda Reigel, author

Josie, Janetta, and Linda describe the steps their center's advocacy group have taken to ensure enforcement of the ADA: target one neighborhood; survey and collect information on businesses that are inaccessible; send letters offering to work with the businesses to help them become accessible and providing information on tax incentives; file lawsuits against businesses that do not respond; involve the media.

10 pages

6188 Migraine and the Allergy Connection

Healing Arts Press
Rochester, NY

John Mansfield, MD, author

Discusses the connection between food, environmental allergies, and migraine headaches.

1990

6189 Migraine: Beating the Odds

Addison Wesley
Reading, MA

Richard Lipton, MD and Lawrence Newman, MD, author

Discusses how diet, nutrition, and medicine affect migraine headaches.

1992

6190 Miles Away and Still Caring - A Guide for Long Distance Caregivers

AARP Fulfillment
601 E Street NW
Washington, DC   20049   202-434-2277
                                    800-424-3410
                              FAX: 202-434-3443
                    e-mail: member@aarp.org
                              www.aarp.org

This is one of the most helpful and frequently requested publications. Helps people who must coordinate the care of a loved one from a long distance.

18 pages

6191 Mind Over Mood: Change How You Feel By Changing the Way You Think

Guilford Press
72 Spring Street
New York, NY   10012   212-431-9800
                                   800-365-7006
                             FAX: 212-966-6708
                             www.guilford.com
Dennis Greenberger, PhD, Christine A. Padesky, PhD, author

$21.00

243 pages Paperback 1995
ISBN 0-898621-28-3

6192 Missing Diagnosis

Missing Diagnosis
PO Box 26508
Birmingham, AL   26508

C. Orian Truss, M.D., author

A comprehensive overview of candidiasis and how to treat it by a pioneer in the field.

1985

6193 Moisture Seekers

Sjogren's Syndrome Foundation
366 North Broadway
Suite PH/W2
Jericho, NY   11753   516-933-6365
                                  800-475-6473
                             www.sjogrens.org

Alexis Stegemann, Executive Director

Newsletter of the organization for lay people and professionals interested in Sjogren's Syndrome. Contains medical news, current research, and essential tips for daily living. *$25.00*

Monthly

6194 Most Frequently Asked Questions About Lobbying and CILs (Revised 3/98)

Independent Living Research Utilization ILRU
2323 S Shepherd Drive
Suite 1000
Houston, TX   77019   713-520-0232
                             FAX: 713-520-5785
                                  www.ilru.org
Bob Michaels, author

This FAQ was written to provide an overview of the federal laws and regulations about lobbying which apply to non-profit organizations. It also covers what constitutes advocacy and what distinguishes it from lobbying. This FAQ is not intended to be a substitute for sound guidance from your organization's attorney and accountant. Consult them before engaging in these activities.

10 pages

6195 Myotherapy

Ballantine Books
201 E 50th Street
New York, NY   10022   212-751-2600
                             FAX: 212-572-4912
Bonnie Prudden, author

Myotherapy explained as a technique.

1985

6196 NCD Bulletin

National Council on Disability
1331 F Street NW
Suite 1050
Washington, DC   20004   202-546-8000
                             FAX: 202-272-2022
                                    www.ncd.gov

Mark S. Quigley, Editor

Reports on the latest issues and news affecting people with disabilities.

2 pages Monthly

6197   NHIF Newsletter

National Head Injury Foundation
1776 Massachusetts Avenue NW
Washington, DC   20036   202-452-1999
                                800-444-6443
                          FAX: 202-466-4265
                             www.biausa.org

George Zitnay, President

Contains news and articles for families and professionals concerned with head injury. *$25.00*

6198   NORD Resource Guide

National Organization for Rare Disorders (NORD)
100 Route 37
PO Box 8923
New Fairfield, CT   06812   203-746-6518
                                800-999-NORD
                          FAX: 203-746-6481
                          TDY:203-746-6927
          e-mail: orphan@rarediseases.org
                  www.rarediseases.org

Mary Dunkle, Senior Director/Communications

Book providing information on more than 1,200 organizations, support groups and government agencies offering help to people with rare diseases.

6199   National Hookup

ISC
16 Liberty Street
Larkspur, CA   94939   415-924-3549
                          FAX: 415-927-9556
          e-mail: russab@earthlink.net
Meredith Schwartz, author
Russ Bohlke, Executive Secretary

Newsletter published by ISC, a national organization of people with physical disabilities. *$6.00*

12 pages 6x Year

6200   National Networker

National Network of Learning Disabled Adults
PO Box 32611
Phoenix, AZ   85064   602-277-0999

Bill Butler, Vice President

Offers general information, software, articles and products for the learning disabled. *$7.00*

Quarterly

6201   National Registry of Community Mental Health Services

National Council/Community Mental Health Centers
12300 Twinbrook Parkway
Suite 320
Rockville, MD   20852   301-670-6331

Lists more than 1,900 agencies in all 50 states giving names, addresses and phones. *$59.00*

6202   Natural Health Bulletin

Princeton Educational Publishers
117 Cuttermill Road
Great Neck, NY   11021   516-482-3800

Carlson Wade, Editor

Diet and nutrition, physical fitness lifestyle, attitude, developments in natural and preventive medicine.

4 pages Monthly

6203   Natural Menopause: Guide to a Woman's Most Misunderstood Passage

Addison-Wesley
New York, NY

Susan Perry and Katherine O'Hanlan, M.D., author

Natural Menopause dispels the common myths about menopause—the horror stories about raging hormones, violent mood swings, and the loss of femininity—by explaining to women what to expect during a time that, if approached as a natural phase rather than a crisis, can be a positive experience.

1992

6204   Negotiating the Disability Maze

Charles C. Thomas, Publisher
2600 S 1st Street
Springfield, IL   62704   217-789-8980
                                800-258-8980
                          FAX: 217-789-9130
          e-mail: books@ccthomas.com
Les Sternberg, Ronald Taylor and Steven Russell, author

This book has been designed and written to furnish people from diverse backgrounds with important information regarding education of children with disabilities. The authors are as thorough as they are explicit. They analyze the concepts, translate the jargon, and outline the characteristics of various disabilities. Also avalable in cloth edition for $51.95 (ISBN# 0-398-06663-9) *$36.95*

206 pages Paperback
ISBN 0-398066-64-7

6205   Neurophysiology of Enlightenment

Neuroscene Press

Robert Wallace, author

Provides an in-depth look at transcendental meditation.

6206   New Directions

Nat'l Assoc. of State Directors of DD Services
113 Oronoco Street
Alexandria, VA   22314   703-683-4202

Features articles on new funding sources, changes in national and state policies, publications, policy trends, pending lawsuits and emerging program activities. It also contains an annual review of state legislation relevant to people with disabilities. *$55.00*

Monthly

6207 New Horizons in Sexuality

Accent Books & Products
PO Box 700
Bloomington, IL   61702

309-378-2961
800-787-8444
FAX: 309-378-4420
e-mail: acmtlvng@aol.com

Pamela J. Bielunis, MHS, PTII, author
Raymond C. Cheever, Publisher
Betty Garee, Editor

This manual helps both males and females progress toward a satisfying post-injury relationship. *$7.95*

50 pages Paperback
ISBN 0-91570 -42-6

6208 New Mobility

23815 Stuart Ranch Road
Malibu, CA   90265

310-317-4522
800-543-4116
FAX: 310-317-9644
www.newmobility.com

Sam Maddox, Publisher
Barry Corbet, Editor

The full-service, full-color lifestyle magazine for the disability community. The award-winning magazine is contemporary, witty and candid. Produced by professional journalists and visual artists, the magazine's voice is uncompromising and unsentimental, yet practical, knowing and friendly. The magazine covers issues that matter to readers: medical news, and cure research; jobs, benefits and civil rights; sports, recreation and travel; product news, technology and innovation.

ISSN 1065-21 4

6209 New No Pill, No Risk Birth Control Guide

McMillan
New York, NY

Nona Aguilar, author

The latest in natural family planning and contraception without drugs, chemicals, IUDs or barrier devices.

1985

6210 New Our Bodies, Ourselves

Simon and Schuster
New York, NY

Boston Women's Health Collective, author

Provides factual information about women's health care combined with women's own personal experiences and perspectives. Encourages women to challenge the medical establishment and take control of their own health.

1992

6211 New Voices: Self Advocacy By People with Disabilities

Brookline Books
PO Box 1047
Cambridge, MA   02238

617-868-0360
800-666-2665
FAX: 617-868-1772
e-mail: brooklinebks@delphi.com
www.brooklinebooks.com

Gunnar Dybwad & Hank Bersani, author

A collection of original papers many by self advocates themselves that vividly illustrate the dynamic, ever-growing self-advocacy movement (persons with disabilities speaking out and seeking better non-institutional living situations, social and political equality and decent jobs at reasonable pay. *$29.95*

274 pages Paperback
ISBN 1-57129 -04-4

6212 NewsLine

Federation for Children with Special Needs
95 Berkeley Street
Boston, MA   02116

617-482-2915
800-331-0688
FAX: 617-572-2094
e-mail: scsinfo@fcns.org

Carolyn Romano, Editor

Offers information for parents and families on resources, medical updates, activities, fund-raising events and association news for their disabled children.

Quarterly

6213 No One to Play with - The Social Side of Learning Disabilities

Special Needs Project
3463 Stat Street
282
Santa Barbara, CA   93105

800-333-6867

Betty Osman

Your child suffers from a learning disability, and you have read reams on how to improve his or her academic skills and now want to address his or her social needs. *$10.00*

188 pages

6214 Nolo's Guide to Social Security Disability

NOLO
950 Parker Street
Berkeley, CA   94710

510-549-1976
800-955-4775
FAX: 510-548-5902
www.nolo.com

David A. Morton III, MD, author
Maira Dizgalvis, Trade Customer Service Manager
Susan McConnell, Director of Sales
Natasha Kaluza, Sales Assistant

Not many bureaucratic programs are as large- and as confusing- as Social Security disability. This book shows you the ins and outs of the system. *$29.95*

350 pages paperback
ISBN 0-873375-74-2

6215 Nutritional Action Health Letter: Center for Science in the Public Interest

1875 Connecticut Avenue NW
Washington, DC   20009   202-332-9111

6216 Nutritional Desk Reference

Keats Publishing
New Canaan, CT   203-966-8721
                        800-323-4900

Robert Garrison Jr., M.D. & Elizabeth Somer, M.D., author

6217 Nutritional Influences on Illness 2nd Edition

Third Line Press

Melvyn A. Werbach, author

6218 OT Practice

American Occupational Therapy Association
164 Rollins Avenue
Suite 301
Rockville, MD   20852   301-951-9070
                               800-877-1383
                          FAX: 301-652-7711

Jeanette Bair, Executive Director

Offers information on conferences, books, resources, materials and information and referral services for persons with disabilities.

6219 Obesity Sourcebook

Omnigraphics
615 Griswold Street
Detroit, MI   48226
                        800-234-1340
                   FAX: 800-875-1340
                   www.omnigraphics.com

Wilma Caldwell, Editor

Discusses diseases and other problems associated with obesity. *$48.00*

400 pages 1900
ISBN 0-780803-33-7

6220 Occupational Therapy Strategies and Adaptations for Independent Daily Living

Haworth Press
10 Alice Street
Binghamton, NY   13904   604-722-5857
                                800-429-6784
                           FAX: 607-722-6362
e-mail: getinfo@haworthpressinc.com
            www.haworthpressinc.com
Florence S. Cromwell, MA, OTR, FAOTA, author
Jackie Blakeslee, Advertising

This contains clinical expertise of some fourteen authors or author teams addressing the issue of occupational therapy to assist in independent daily living. Also available as hardcover. *$69.95*

186 pages Hardcover
ISBN 0-866563-50-4

6221 Occupational Therapy in Health Care

Haworth Press
10 Alice Street
Binghamton, NY   13904   604-722-5857
                                800-429-6784
                           FAX: 607-722-6362
e-mail: getinfo@haworthpressinc.com
            www.haworthpressinc.com
Susan Kaplan And Anne E. Dickerson, author
Jackie Blakeslee, Advertising

Each issue focuses on significant practices and concerns involving occupational therapy and therapists.

$50 - $150

6222 Older Adults with Developmental Disabilities: Optimizing Choice and Change

Brookes Publishing
PO Box 10624
Baltimore, MD   21285   410-337-9580
                               800-638-3775
                          FAX: 410-337-8539
e-mail: custserv@brookespublishing.com
            www.brookespublishing.com

$37.00

416 pages Paperback
ISBN 1-55766 -20-0

6223 One Hundred Fifty Most-Asked Questions About Menopause

Hearst Books
New York, NY

Ruth S. Jacobwitz, author

This book provides the plain facts on a host of topics including: the pros and cons of hormone replacement therapy; choosing the right doctor; how to de-stress your life; and twelve tips to make the most of a physician visit.

1993

6224 Organ Transplants: Making the Most of Your Gift of Life

Patient-Centered Guides
101 Morris Street
Sebastopol, CA   95472   707-829-0515
                                800-998-9938
                           FAX: 707-829-0104
                   www.patientcenters.com
Robert Finn, author
Linda Lamb, Editor
Shawnde Paull, Marketing

Over 64,000 people in the US are awaiting an organ transplant. Although transplant surgeries are now fairly routine and can give their recipients the gift of new life, the road to getting a transplant can be long and harrowing. Living with immunosuppressive drugs and strong emotional responses can also be more challenging than families imagine. Medical journalist Robert Finn answers the concerns of these families, with the latest facts about transplantation - as well as the stories behind them. *$19.95*

326 pages Paperback
ISBN 1-565926-34-X

6225 Orthotics and Prosthetics Almanac

Orthotics and Prosthetics National Office
1650 King Street
Suite 500
Alexandria, VA   22314   703-836-7114
                                FAX: 703-836-0838
                         e-mail: opalmanac@aol.com
                                www.aopanet.org

Stacey L. Bell, Editor-in-Chief

Features articles covering current professional, patient care, government, business and National Office activities affecting the orthotics and prosthetics profession and industry. $40.00

80 pages Monthly
ISSN 1061-46 1

6226 Osteoporosis Sourcebook

Omnigraphics
615 Griswold Street
Detroit, MI   48226

                                800-234-1340
                                FAX: 800-875-1340
                                www.omnigraphics.com

Allan R. Cook, Editor

Discusses causes, risk factors, treatments, and traditional and non-traditional pain management issues concerning osteoporosis. $ 78.00

600 pages 1900
ISBN 0-780802-39-X

6227 Overcoming Binge Eating

Guilford Press
72 Spring Street
New York, NY   10012   212-431-9800
                                800-365-7006
                                FAX: 212-966-6708
                                www.guilford.com
Dr. Christopher G. Fairburn, author
    $15.95

247 pages Paperback 1995
ISBN 0-898621-79-8

6228 Oxygen Therapies

Energy Publications

Ed McCabe, author

Covers the effects of having low oxygen in the enviroment.

6229 Pacing Yourself

Accent Books & Products
PO Box 700
Bloomington, IL   61702   309-378-2961
                                800-787-8444
                                FAX: 309-378-4420
                         e-mail: acmtlvng@aol.com
Diane Christy, M.S. and Carol A. Sarafronn, author
Raymond C. Cheever, Publisher
Betty Garee, Editor

A guide loaded with ideas and tips on starting the day, housekeeping, meal preparation, parenting and socializing. Also includes information on how to group errands and manage household chores, improve posture to make movement easier, and much more. $10.95

141 pages Paperback
ISBN 0-91570 -31-0

6230 Parent Centers and Independent Living Centers: Collectively We're Stronger

Independent Living Research Utilization ILRU
2323 S Shepherd Drive
Suite 1000
Houston, TX   77019   713-520-0232
                                FAX: 713-520-5785
                                www.ilru.org
Beth Wright, author

This article describes several examples of effective working relationships of PTIs and CILs. The examples highlight how parent and consumer organizations have identified complimentary strengths and formed partnerships to better support children with disabilities and their families. These partnerships can also be a very important way of involving youth in the disability movement so they may become leaders of tomorrow.

10 pages

6231 Part Two: A Preview of Independence and Transition to Community Living

Independent Living Research Utilization ILRU
2323 S Shepherd Drive
Suite 1000
Houston, TX   77019   713-520-0232
                                FAX: 713-520-5785
                                www.ilru.org
Bonnie O'Day, author

This publication covers important strategies for helping people leave nursing homes. It includes several important recommendations which CIL leaders and staffs will find useful in organizing transition activities.

10 pages

6232 Partnering with Publi Health: Funding & Advocacy Opportunities for CILs and SILCs

Independent Living Research Utilization ILRU
2323 S Shepherd Drive
Suite 1000
Houston, TX   77019   713-520-0232
                                FAX: 713-520-5785
                                www.ilru.org
Laura Rauscher, author

Laura Rauscher discusses how CILs and SCILs can use funding from the Centers for Disease Control and partnerships with public health agencies to provide innovative programs promoting the health of people with disabilities.

10 pages

6233 Partners in Everyday Communicative Exchanges

Brookes Publishing
PO Box 10624
Baltimore, MD 21285 410-337-9580
800-638-3775
FAX: 410-337-8539
e-mail: custserv@brookespublishing.com
www.brookespublishing.com

Nancy Butterfield, Grad Dip Ed St, author

A Guide to Promoting Intervention Involving people with Severe Intellectual Disability. This book helps improve communication with people with severe disabilities using practical forms, numerous examples, and illustrative case studies. *$43.00*

192 pages Paperback
ISBN 1-55766 -41-X

6234 Pause: Positive Approaches to Menopause

Dutton
New York, NY

Lonnie Barbach, Ph.D., author

Gives a symptom-by-symptom breakdown of the physical changes that women experience as well as advice on how to choose the right treatment and make the right lifestyle adjustments. Barbach also offers the most up-to-date and pratical ways to make the 'third third' of a woman's life healthier and more productive.

1993

6235 Peer Counseling: Advocacy-Oriented Peer Support —Part One

Independent Living Research Utilization ILRU
2323 S Shepherd Drive
Suite 1000
Houston, TX 77019 713-520-0232
FAX: 713-520-5785
www.ilru.org

Steve Brown, author

This month's Readings examines how peer support from the point of view of how in talking to each other and sharing life experiences, we help to form groups that are making changes around the world.

10 pages

6236 Peer Counseling: Roles, Functions, Bounderies

Independent Living Research Utilization ILRU
2323 S Shepherd Drive
Suite 1000
Houston, TX 77019 713-520-0232
FAX: 713-520-5785
www.ilru.org

Thomas D. Carter, Jr., Ed.D, author

In this article, the following points were discussed: Describing peer support as counseling suggests safeguards and expectations which cannot be provided by nonprofessionals; the ppurpose of peer counseling is to promote the independent living philosophy and encourage consumers to embrace it; peer counseling cannot and is not intended to help individuals deal with intense emotional stress, whether it is related to their disability or to something else.

10 pages

6237 Peer Mentor Volunteers: Empowering People for Change

Independent Living Research Utilization ILRU
2323 S Shepherd Drive
Suite 1000
Houston, TX 77019 713-520-0232
FAX: 713-520-5785
www.ilru.org

Donna Redford & Pam Whitaker-Lee, author

Arizona Bridge to Independent Living (ABIL) in phoenix, featured inthis issue, is another winner in the innovative CIL program competition.

10 pages

6238 People with Disabilities & Abuse: Implications for Center for Independent Living

Independent Living Research Utilization ILRU
2323 S Shepherd Drive
Suite 1000
Houston, TX 77019 713-520-0232
FAX: 713-520-5785
www.ilru.org

Leslie Myers, author

10 pages

6239 People with Disabilities Who Challenge the System

Brookes Publishing
PO Box 10624
Baltimore, MD 21285
800-638-3775
FAX: 410-337-8539
e-mail: custserv@brookespublishing.com
www.brookespublishing.com

Helpful forms, tables, and case studies plus an emphasis on self-determination point the way to the development of supports so that people who are deaf-blind, have severe to profound physical and cognitive disabilities, or have serious behavior problems can be fully included in the classroom, workplace, and community. *$34.00*

464 pages Paperback
ISBN 1-55766 -29-0

6240 Peoplenet

PO Box 897
Levittown, NY 11756

e-mail: mauro@idt.net
www.idt.net/~mauro

Robert Mauro, Editor/Publisher

News by and for persons with disabilities on relationships and sexuality. Includes personal ads, short stories, poems and articles on relationships for disabled singles. Free.

6241 Persecution and Trial of Gaston Naessens

H.J. Kramer
Tiburon, CA

Christopher Bird, author

Highlights the work of Gaston Naessens in the field of cancer and other illnesses, including 714X, and the trial he faced because of his discoveries.

1991

6242 Personal Perspectives on Personal Assistance Services

World Institute on Disability
510 16th Street
Suite 100
Oakland, CA 94612   510-763-4100
FAX: 510-763-4109
TDY:510-208-9493
e-mail: wid@wid.org
www.wid.org

Julie Weissman, Jae Kennedy and Simi Litvak, author

This collection of personal essays explores a wide range of perspectives on Personal Assistance Services. Family issues and PAS concerns for people with various different disabilities, of different ages and as members of minority groups are addressed. *$5.00*

80 pages Paperback

6243 Perspectives on Disability

Health Markets Research
851 Moana Center
Palo Alto, CA 94306   650-948-1960

e-mail: hmrpub@aol.com

Mark Nagler, author

A collection of articles about attitudes, social interactions, the family, education and medical and legal issues related to disability. *$60.00*

Softcover

6244 Phoenix Project

PO Box 84151
Seattle, WA 98124   206-655-2121
FAX: 206-623-4251
e-mail: brain@headinjury.com
www.headinjury.com

Constance Miller And Kay Campbell, author
Constance Miller

Disseminates head injury information and provides referrals to facilitate adjustment to life following head injury. Organizes seminars for professionals, head injury survivors, and their families. *$20.00*

121 pages Paperback

6245 Place to Live

Accent Books & Products
PO Box 700
Bloomington, IL 61702   309-378-2961
800-787-8444
FAX: 309-378-4420
e-mail: acmtlvng@aol.com

Raymond C. Cheever, Publisher
Betty Garee, Editor

Many disabled people have found that group housing or accessible apartments are the best alternative to living in a nursing home. These articles tell about some of the alternatives people have found so they can live independently. Just one idea might be the answer for better living for you. *$4.95*

64 pages Paperback
ISBN 0-91570 -30-2

6246 Planning for the Future

American Publishing Company
PO Box 988
Evanston, IL 60204   847-869-0588
800-247-6553

L.M. Russell, et al., author
L. Mark Russell, Attorney

A highly acclaimed new book that offers information on how to prepare a Life Plan, a Letter of Intent, a Special Needs Trust, and basically how to provide a meaningful life for a child with a disability after your death. *$24.95*

440 pages Paperback
ISBN 0-96357 -00-6

6247 Polarity Therapy: The Complete and Collected Works

CRCS Publications

Randolph Stone, author

Energy-balancing principles and therapeutic techniques.

1987

6248 Polio Network News

Gazette International Networking Institute
4207 Lindell Boulevard
110
Saint Louis, MO 63108   314-534-0475
FAX: 314-534-5070
e-mail: gini_intl@msn.com
www.post-polio.org

International newsletter for polio survivors, support groups and health professionals concerned about the late effects of polio. *$20.00*

12 pages Quarterly

6249 Potent Self: A Guide to Spontaneity

Harper & Row
10 E 53rd Street
New York, NY 10022   212-207-7000
800-242-7737

Moshe Feldenkrais & M. Kimmey, author

Explanation of the revolutionary theory behind the Feldenkrais method.

1992

6250 Practice of Aromatherapy

Inner Traditions
One Park Street
Rochester, VT 05767   802-767-3174
800-246-8648
www.gotoit.com

Jean Valnet, author

1990

6251 Premenstrual Syndrome Self-Help Book

Celestial Arts
Berkley, CA

Susan Lark, M.D., author

Every month, 10 to 15 million women experience symptoms such as irritability, anxiety, mood swings, depression, weight gain, breast tenderness, bloating, and more. Dr. Lark gives a complete step-by-step plan to help women cope with, and overcome PMS.

1993

6252 Prescription for Nutritional Healing: a Practical A-Z Referance to Drug-Free Remedies

Avery Publishing

James Balch M.D. and Phyllis Balch R.N., author

Prescription for Nutritional Healing: a Practical A-Z Refrance to Drug-Free Remedies Using Vitamins, Minerals, Herbs, and Food Supplements.

6253 Proceedings

AHEAD
PO Box 21192
Columbus, OH   43221   **614-488-4972**
                              FAX: 740-448-1174
          e-mail: aagad@postbox.acs.ohio-state.edu
                              www.ahead.org

National conferences, innovative programs, research, evaluation services, auxiliary aids, career information and other vital information.

6254 Progress in Research

Christopher Reeve Paralysis Foundation
500 Morris Avenue
Springfield, NJ   07081   **973-379-6299**
                              800-225-0292
                              FAX: 973-912-9433
                              e-mail: paralysis@aol.com
                              www.paralysis.org

Summarizes research on paralysis and spinal cord injury, emphasizing neural regeneration.

6255 Psyching Out Diabetes: A Positive Approach to Your Negative Emotions

Lowell House
Los Angeles, CA

Richard Rubin, author

Offers realistic strategies for dealing with the emotional issues associated with diabetes. Diabetics can learn to integrate diabetes into their lives, rather than segregating it.

1992

6256 Psychology and Health

Springer Publishing Company
536 Broadway
New York, NY   10012   **212-431-4370**
                              FAX: 212-941-7842
Donald Bakal, author

Content of this book spans a wide range of clinical conditions, including somatization disorders, chronic pain, migraine, anxiety and cancer. *$29.95*

256 pages

6257 Psychology of Disability

Springer Publishing Company
536 Broadway
New York, NY   10012   **212-431-4370**
                              FAX: 212-941-7842

Carolyn L. Vash, author

Reactions to the disabled. *$27.95*

288 pages
ISBN 0-82613 -40-1

6258 Psychopathology in Persons with Mental Retardation

Research Press
PO Box 9177
Champaign, IL   61826   **217-352-3273**
                              800-519-2707
                              FAX: 217-352-1221
                              e-mail: rp@researchpress.com
                              www.researchpress.com
Dr. Christine M. Nezu, author
Russell Pence, V P Marketing

In this volume, the authors apply their practical decision-making model to clinical work with a frequently underserved population of dually diagnosed individuals with both mental illness and mental retardation. *$24.95*

342 pages Paperback
ISBN 0-878223-28-2

6259 Public Policy Report

National Council of Community Mental Health Center
12300 Twinbrook Parkway
Suite 320
Rockville, MD   20852   **301-670-6331**
                              FAX: 301-881-7159
                              www.nccbh.org

Information on promoting advocacy, action and association for people with mental disabilities.

Monthly

6260 Public Technology

US Department of Transportation
Urban Mass Transportation Admin
Washington, DC   20016   **202-366-9191**

One of a series of reports concerned with improving transportation for elderly and disabled persons.

28 pages

6261 Pure Facts

Feingold Association of the United States
127 East Main Street
 # 106
Riverhead, NY   11901   **631-369-9340**
                              800-321-3287
                              www.feingold.org

Jane Hersey, Editor

Relationship between foods, food additives and behavior/learning problems, including Attention Deficit Disorder (ADD) and hyperactivity. *$38.00*

8 pages 10x Year

6262 Qigong Magazine
Pacific Rim Publishers
PO Box 31578
San Francisco, CA 94131
800-824-2433

Quarterly magazine.

6263 Qigong for Health: Chinese Traditional Exercise for Cure and Prevention
Japan Publications
New York, NY

Stephen Brown and Masaru Takahashi, author

6264 Quality of Life for Persons with Disabilities
Brookline Books
PO Box 1046
Cambridge, MA 02238
617-868-0360
800-666-2665
FAX: 617-868-1772
e-mail: brooklinebks@delphi.com
www.brooklinebooks.com

Quality of life generally refers to a person's subjective experience of his or her life and focuses attention on how the individual with a disabling condition experiences the world. This book presents a comprehensive and international view of this concept as applied to a broad range of settings in which persons with disabilities live, work and play. *$35.00*

Paperback
ISBN 0-91479-92-1

6265 Quantum Healing
Bantam Books
201 E 50th Street
New York, NY 10022
212-751-2600
FAX: 212-940-7868
www.randomhouse.com

Deepak Chopra, M.D., author
$14.95

1990
ISBN 0-553348-69-8

6266 RTC Connection
Research and Training Center
University of Wisconsin - Stout
Menomonie, WI 54751
715-232-2236
FAX: 715-232-2251
TDY: 715-232-5025
e-mail: menz@uwstout.edu
www.rtc.uwstout.edu

Julie Larson, Program Assistant
Bi-annual reports on disability and rehabilitation research and policy topics.

Newsletter

6267 Radiation Protection Manual
Grassroots Network

Lita Lee Ph.D., author

6268 Ragged Edge: The Disability Experience
Advocado Press
PO Box 145
Louisville, KY 40201
502-894-9492
FAX: 502-899-9562
e-mail: editor@ragged-edge-mag.com
www.ragged-edge-mag.com

Barrett Shaw, Editor
Anthology of writing from the pages of the first 15 years of The Disability Rag. *$18.95*

245 pages
ISBN 0-96270-45-0

6269 Reclamation
Reclamation
2502 Waterford Drive
San Antonio, TX 78217

Don Culwell, Director
Serves as a voice for mental health and other patients in consumer, social and political affairs. Helps members to live outside a hospital setting by providing assistance in the areas of resocialization, employment, and housing. *$12.00*

8 pages

6270 Reflexology for Good Health: Mirror for the Body
Wilshire Book Company

Anna Kaye & Don Matchan, author
Answers the most commonly asked questions on reflexology.

1980

6271 Rehab Update
New England Medical Center
750 Washington Street
75 K-R
Boston, MA 02111
617-499-6951
FAX: 617-350-8388

Vincent Licenziato, Training Coordinator
Reports on causes and consequences of injuries among children and adolescents. Focus on rehabilitation research, family adjustment, special education, and violence prevention. Special attention on brain injury among youth. Yearly newsletter.

8 pages BiAnnual

6272 Rehabilitation Gazette
Gazette International Networking Institute
4207 Lindell Boulevard
110
Saint Louis, MO 63108
314-534-0475
FAX: 314-534-5070
e-mail: gini_intl@msn.com
www.post-polio.org

International journal of independent living for people with disabilities. *$12.00*

4 pages BiAnnually

6273 Relaxation Manual for Adults and Children with Special Needs

Research Press
2612 N Mattis Avenue
Champagne, IL 61821   217-325-3273
800-519-2707
FAX: 217-352-1221
e-mail: rp@researchpress.com
www.researchpress.com

Dr. Joseph Cautala and Dr. June Groden, author

This unique contribution to the field of relaxation training presents: self relaxation techniques designed for adults, methods for teaching relaxation to adults and older children, and procedures for teaching relaxation to young children and children with developmental disabilities. The clear, concise text is supplemented by over 100 helpful illustrations. $14.95

108 pages Paperback
ISBN 0-878221-86-7

6274 Relaxation Response
Outlet Books

Herbert Benson, author

Covers the ability to releave stress and relax the body through alternative means.

6275 Resources for People with Disabilities and Chronic Conditions

Resources for Rehabilitation
33 Bedford Street
Suite 19A
Lexington, MA 02420   781-890-6371
FAX: 781-861-7517

Susan Greenblatt

A comprehensive resource directory that helps people with disabilities and chronic conditions achieve their maximum level of independence. Chapters on spinal cord injuries, low back pain, diabetes, hearing and speech impairments, epilepsy, multiple sclerosis. Describes organizations, products and publications. $49.95

215 pages Biennial
ISBN 0-92971 -12-7

6276 Role Portrayal and Stereotyping on Television

Greenwood Publishing Group
88 Post Road West
5007
Westport, CT 06880   203-226-3571
FAX: 203-222-1502
www.greenwood.com

nanct Signorielli, Author

An annotated bibliography of studies relating to women, minorities, aging, health and handicaps.

214 pages $55 - $59.95
ISBN 0-313248-55-9

6277 Rolfing: The Intergration of Human Structures

Harper & Row
10 E 53rd Street
New York, NY 10022   212-207-7000
800-242-7737

Ida P. Rolfe, author

1977

6278 Screening in Chronic Disease

Oxford University Press
2001 Evans Road
Cary, NC 27513   212-726-6000
800-451-7556
FAX: 919-677-1303
www.oup-usa.org

Alan Morrison, author

Early detection, or screening, is a common strategy for controlling chronic disease, but little information has been available to help determine which screening procedures are worthwhile, until this textbook. $42.50

256 pages

6279 Self-Applied Health Enhancement Methods

Health Action Books
Santa Barbara, CA

Roger Jahnke, author

6280 Serving Adults with Cognitive Disabilities

Independent Living Research Utilization ILRU
2323 S Shepherd Drive
Suite 1000
Houston, TX 77019   713-520-0232
FAX: 713-520-5785
www.ilru.org

Darrel Christenson, Tyrone Harrington & Susan Webb, author

Darrel, Tyrone and Susan of Arizona Bridge to Independent Living (ABIL) describe the success of their Community Living Options Program for adults with developmental disabilities in this months readings.

10 pages

6281 Seven Weeks to a Healthy Stomach

Pocket Books
New York, NY

Ronald Hoffman, M.D., author

A seven-week program to restore the gastrointestinal tract to optimal health, using diet, nutrition, and herbal medicine.

1990

6282 Sexual Adjustment

Accent Books & Products
PO Box 700
Bloomington, IL 61702   309-378-2961
800-787-8444
FAX: 309-378-4420
e-mail: acmtlvng@aol.com

Martha Ferguson Gregory, author
Raymond C. Cheever, Publisher
Betty Garee, Editor

Essential information concerning sexual adjustment for the paraplegic male. *$4.95*

73 pages Paperback
ISBN 0-19570 -00-0

6283 Sexuality and Disabilities: A Guide for Human Service Practitioners

Haworth Press
10 Alice Street
Binghamton, NY   13904   604-722-5857
                                     800-429-6784
                              FAX: 607-722-6362
          e-mail: getinfo@haworthpressinc.com
                   www.haworthpressinc.com
Romel W. Mackelprang, DSW and Deborah Valentine, P, author
Jackie Blakeslee, Advertising

This book addresses persons with physical, sensory, intellectual and cognitive disabilities and their concerns in the areas of intimacy, family issues, sexuality and sexual functioning. *$69.95*

159 pages Hardcover
ISBN 1-560243-75-9

6284 Sibling Forum

Family Resource Associates
35 Haddon Avenue
Shrewsbury, NJ   07702   732-747-5310
                              FAX: 732-747-1896

Mary Allan, Social Worker

A newsletter for brothers and sisters, aged 10 through teen, whose sibling has a disablilty. Includes input from readers, library resources and discussion of feelings. $12/year for families, $20/year for professionals. *$12.00*

10 pages Quarterly

6285 Silver Dental Fillings - The Toxic Time Bomb

Aurora Press
PO Box 573
Santa Fe, NM   87504   207-363-4393

Sam Ziff, author
1986

6286 Simon Foundation for Continence

PO Box 815
Wilmette, IL   60091   847-864-3913
                             800-23S-IMON
                        FAX: 847-864-9758
                   www.simonfoundation.org

Cheryle B. Gartley, President

Publishes items of interest to people with bladder or bowel incontinence, including medical articles, helpful devices, publications and a pen pal list.

6287 Sinus Survival

Jeremy P. Tarcher
Los Angeles, CA

Robert Ivker, MD, author

Self-help manual for sufferers of bronchitis, sinusitis, allergies, and colds.

6288 Sixty Days of Low-Fat, Low-Cost Meals in Minutes

Chronimed Publishing
13911 Ridgedale Drive
Minnetonka, MN   55305   612-916-2500
                                    800-848-2793
                             FAX: 612-513-6170
M.J. Smith, author
Leigh Anne Godfreg, Sales Coordinator

A great way to get patients on the road to healthy eating. It contains 150 recipes complete with facts on lowering calories, fat, salt and cholesterol. It contains complete menu plans for 60 days and recipes that use ingredients you can find anywhere. *$12.95*

294 pages Paperback
ISBN 1-56561 -10-5

6289 Social Perceptions of People with Disabilities in History

Charles C. Thomas, Publisher
2600 S 1st Street
Springfield, IL   62704   217-789-8980
                                     800-258-8980
                              FAX: 217-789-9130
                    e-mail: books@ccthomas.com
Herbert C. Covey, author

This book helps to develop a social history on disabilities by providing a multidisciplinary overview of images of people with disabilities in Western history; promotion the exchange of cross-disciplinary information on disabled people from art, literature, original data, and historical works. With the growing interest in people with disabilities and the recent passage of the American Disability Act, this book will be of interest to special educators, humanities students, and social scientists. *$49.95*

324 pages Paperback 1998
ISBN 0-398068-38-0

6290 Socialization Games for Persons with Disabilities

Charles C. Thomas, Publisher
2600 S 1st Street
Springfield, IL   62704   217-789-8980
                                     800-258-8980
                              FAX: 217-789-9130
                    e-mail: books@ccthomas.com
Nevalyn Nevil, Marna Beatty, and David Moxley, author

This book is a compilation of practical suggestions and games with easy-to-follow guide lines that provide a solid foundation for the encouragement of positive social behavior. Clothbound edition $62.95 (ISBN# 0-398-06749-X *$32.95*

176 pages Paperback 1997
ISBN 0-398067-46-5

6291 Solving the Puzzle of Chronic Fatigue

Life Sciences Press
Tacoma, WA

Micael Rosenbaum, M.D. and Murray Susser, M.D., author

Although primarily a book about CFS, this comprehensive study also provides a detailed overview of candidiasis, including its causes and best approaches for treatment.

1992

6292 **Sometimes You Just Want to Feel Like a Human Being**

Brookes Publishing
PO Box 10624
Baltimore, MD   21285   410-337-9580
                              800-638-3775
                       FAX: 410-337-8539
e-mail: custserv@brookespublishing.com
          www.brookespublishing.com
Mary Ann Blotzer, L.C.S.W.-C., and Richard Ruth, P, author

Case studies of empowering psychotherapy with people with disabilities. This text reveals how counseling can be beneficial to individuals with disabilities of all kinds, including autism, mental retardation, sensory impairment, cerebral palsy, or HIV infection. *$ 26.95*

272 pages Paperback
ISBN 1-55766 -96-0

6293 **Son-Rise: The Miracle Continues**

Option Institute and Fellowship
2080 S Undermountain Road
Sheffield, MA   01257   413-229-8737
                              800-562-7171
                       FAX: 413-229-8737
          e-mail: indigo@option.org
               www.optionindigo.com
Barry Neil Kaufman, author
Kate Wilde

Part One is the astonishing record of Raun Kaufman's development from an autistic and retarded child into a loving, brilliant youngster who shows no traces of his former condition. Part Two tells of Raun's development after the age of four and teaches us much about love and limitless possibilities. Part Three shares moving accounts of five other ordinary families who became extraordinary when they used the Son-Rise program to reach their own unreachable children. *$12.95*

343 pages Paperback
ISBN 0-915811-61-8

6294 **Sound Connections for the Adolescent**

Speech Bin
1965 25th Avenue
Vero Beach, FL   32960   561-770-0007
                               800-477-3324
                        FAX: 561-770-0006
                        www.speechbin.com
Jane C Webb, author

A resource to help older elementary and secondary students understand their sound systems an how it functions. It targets skills critical for academic achievement: phonological awareness, phonemic relationships, phonemic processing, listening and memory and teaches linguistic rules they need to succeed. *$19.95*

Paperback

6295 **Source of Help and Hope Newsletter**

Arthritis Foundation
Central Pennsylvania Chapter
PO Box 668
Camp Hill, PA   17001   717-763-0900
                              800-776-0746
                       FAX: 717-763-0903
                       www.arthritis.org

Offers information on activities and events of the Chapter.

3x Year

6296 **Special Care in Dentistry**

Academy of Dentistry for Persons with Disabilities
211 East Chicago Avenue
5th Floor
Chicago, IL   60611   312-440-2661
                      FAX: 312-440-2824
e-mail: fosccdzz@worldnet.att.net
          www.specialdentistry.org
Ronald L. Ettinger, author
$125.00

48 pages BiMonthly

6297 **Special Edge**

Resources in Special Education
J Street
Sacramento, CA   95814   916-568-7058
                               800-869-4337
                        FAX: 916-492-9995
                 e-mail: rise@wested.org

Provides education news, collaborative programs, amendments to the laws, tools for accommodations, resource information, a calendar of events, and more.

BiMonthly

6298 **Special Format Books for Children and Youth Ages 3-19. Serving Upstate New York**

New York State Library
Cultural Education Center
Albany, NY   12230   518-474-5935
                           800-342-3688
                  www.nysl.nysed.gov/talk

Jane Somers, Director

6299 **Special Format Books for Children and Youth: Ages 3-19.Serving New York City/Long Island**

Ney York Public Library
476 5th Avenue
New York, NY   10018   212-206-5400

e-mail: pleclerc@nypl.org
          www.nypl.org

Paul LeClerc, President

6300 Spinal Cord Injury Life

National Spinal Cord Injury Association
8701 Georgia Avenue
500
Silver Spring, MD   20910   617-469-0004
                                   800-962-9629
                              FAX: 301-588-9414
                         e-mail: nscia2@aol.com
                             www.spinalcord.org

Thomas H. Countee, Jr., Executive Director

Includes sections such as Legislative Action, Information Resources and Research Notes. *$30.00*

45-60 pages Quarterly

6301 Spine

JB Lippincott
E Washington Square
Philadelphia, PA   19105
                              FAX: 215-824-7390

Publishes original papers on theoretical issues and research concerning the spine and spinal cord injuries. *$9.00*

Monthly

6302 Startling New Facts About Osteoporosis: Why Calcium Alone Does Not Prevent Bone Disease

Nutrition Encounter
Novato, CA

Betty Kamen, Ph.D., author

Presents the latest medical evidence about calcium and other supplements in relation to osteoporosis. Dr. Kamen tell what women can do to prevent, control, and even reverse this debilitating and lethal disease. This booklet raises a multitutde of fascinating new questions about osteoprosis, and answers them with validating medical research.

1990

6303 Statistical Handbook on Disability

ORYX Press
4041 N Central
Phoenix, AZ   85012   602-265-2651
                             800-279-ORYX
                        FAX: 800-279-4663
                   e-mail: info@oryxpress.com

A single, reliable and current source of statistical information on disability, including the related concepts of impairment and handicap. *$64.50*

352 pages 1993
ISBN 0-897747-11-9

6304 Staying Healthy with Nutrition

Celestial Arts

Elson Haas, author

Guide to nutrition, proper dieting, and the mind and body.

6305 Sterilization of People with Mental Disabilities

Greenwood Publishing Group
88 Post Road West
5007
Westport, CT   06880   203-226-3571
                         FAX: 203-222-1502
                            www.greenwood.com

Ellen Brantlinger, author

An examination of the medical and legal trends in sterilization with an emphasis on people with disabilities. Hardcover.

280 pages $59.95 - $65
ISBN 0-865692-25-4

6306 Straight Talk About Psychiatric Medications for Kids

Guilford Press
72 Spring Street
New York, NY   10012   212-431-9800
                              800-365-7006
                         FAX: 212-966-6708
                            www.guilford.com

Timothy E. Wilens, author

Also in cloth at $29.95 (ISBN# 1-57230-404-9
$15.95

280 pages Paperback 1998
ISBN 1-572302-04-6

6307 Straight Talk with Your Gynecologist: How to Get Answers that Will Save Your Life

Beyond Words Publishing
Hillsborough, OR

Eddie C. Sollie, M.D., author

Gives women the information and skills to form an equal partnership with their gynecologist. Provides frank talk on sexually transmitted diseases in simple language. Prevention and health maintenance recieve in-depth coverage throughout the book.

1993

6308 Strategies for Teaching Learners with Special Needs

McGraw-Hill, School Publishing
220 East Danieldale Road
DeSoto, TX   75115   972-224-1111
                            800-442-9685
                       FAX: 972-228-1982
                          mhschool.com

This is a text that helps special educators develop the full range of teaching competencies needed to be effective.

560 pages

6309 Strengthening the Roles of Independent Living Centers Through Implementing Legal Services

Independent Living Research Utilization ILRU
2323 S Shepherd Drive
Suite 1000
Houston, TX   77019   713-520-0232
                        FAX: 713-520-5785
                            www.ilru.org

Adam Brown, author

Featuring the Disability Law Clinic at Community Resources for Independence (CRI) in Northern California.

10 pages

6310 Stroke Connection

American Heart Association
7272 Greenville Avenue
Dallas, TX 75231 972-735-8501
800-553-6321
FAX: 214-696-5211

A forum for stroke survivors and their families to share information about coping with stroke. Provides information and referral and carriers stroke related books, videos and literature available for purchase. *$76.00*

BiMonthly

6311 Substance Abuse and Physical Disability

Haworth Press
10 Alice Street
Binghamton, NY 13904 604-722-5857
800-429-6784
FAX: 607-722-6362
e-mail: getinfo@haworthpressinc.com
www.haworthpressinc.com
Allen Heinemann, PhD, author
Jackie Blakeslee, Advertising

This book offers information on alcohol and drug abuse being a contributing factor in traumatic and disabling injuries. *$ 69.95*

289 pages Hardcover
ISBN 1-560242-89-2

6312 Tao of Nutrition

SevenStar Communication
Santa Monica, CA

Maoshing Ni, D.O.M., Ph.D., author

Defines Chinese nutrition as 'the science that deals with the healing properties of foods to correct disharmonies within the body.' Here Dr. Ni breaks down various food by their healing nature, includes preparation methods and lists remedies for common health conditions.

1993

6313 Tao: The Subtle Universal Law and the Integral Way of Life

Seven Star Communications
Santa Monica, CA

Hua-Ching Ni, author

6314 Taoist Ways to Transform Stress

Healing Tao Books
Huntington, NY

Mantak Chia, author

6315 Teaching Adults with Learning Disabilities

Krieger Publishing Company
PO Box 9542
Melbourne, FL 32902 407-724-9542
800-724-0025
FAX: 407-951-3671
e-mail: info@krieger-pub.com
www.krieger-publishing.com
Dale R. Jordan, author

This book is designed to teach literacy providers and classroom instructors how to recognize specific learning disability (LD) patterns and block reading, spelling, writing, and arithmetic skills in students of all ages. One of the major problems faced by literary providers is keeping low-skill adults involved in basic education programs long enough to increase their literacy skills to the level of success. This book will show instructors in adult education how to modify teaching strategies *$21.50*

160 pages Hardcover
ISBN 0-894649-10-8

6316 Teaching Dressing Skills: Buttons, Bows and More

Therapro
225 Arlington Street
Framingham, MA 01702 508-872-9494
800-257-5376
FAX: 508-875-2062
e-mail: info@theraproducts.com
www.theraproducts.com
Mary Coppelman Goldsmith, OTR, BCP, author

Finally there is a book that teaches us how to teach children and adults of varying abilities how to tie shoes, button buttons, use zippers and put on/remove clothing. Developed by an experienced occupational therapist, these methods have been successfully used with many children. Each task is broken down with each step clearly illustrated and specific verbal directions given to avoidconfusion and to eliminate verbalization that can distract the learner. *$8.95*

5 pages Pamphlets

6317 Third Opinion

Avery Publishing Group
Garden City Park, NJ

John M. Fink, author

An international directory of alternative therapy centers for the treatment and prevention of cancer.

1988

6318 To Live with Grace and Dignity

World Institute on Disability
510-16th Street
Suite 100
Oakland, CA 94612 510-763-4100
FAX: 510-763-4109
TDY:510-208-9493
e-mail: wid@wid.org
www.wid.org

Lydia Gans, author

This unique book combines photographs and essays to allow the reader to enter some of the real day to day relationships that develop between individuals with disabilities and their personal assistants. Looking at and listening to what these relationships are all about is what motivated and inspired this book, says author Lydia Gans. The individuals included in this book represent a wide range of ages, disabilities, and cultural backgrounds. *$26.00*

72 pages Paperback

6319   Today's Health Alternative

America West Publishers

Raquel Martin, author

Short history about the history, and many anecdotes on emotional disorders.

6320   Touch/Ability Connects People with Disabilities & Alternative Health Care Pract.

Independent Living Research Utilization ILRU
2323 S Shepherd Drive
Suite 1000
Houston, TX   77019   **713-520-0232**
                                        FAX: 713-520-5785
                                        www.ilru.org

Tracy Williams, author

The people at DIRECT center for Independence and Touch/Ability in Tuscon, Arizona, have collaborated to develop a wellness program that makes alternative health care choices available to people with disabilities. The Touch/Ability Wellness program was selected as one of last year's winners in the Innovative CILs competition because of this outcome of increased options open to people with disabilities.

10 pages

6321   Treatment for Chronic Depression

Guilford Press
72 Spring Street
New York, NY   10012   **212-431-9800**
                                        800-365-7006
                                        FAX: 212-966-6708
                                        www.guilford.com

James P. McCullough, Jr., author
$35.00

Cloth
ISBN 1-572305-27-4

6322   Tsubo: Vital Points for Oriental Therapy

Japan Publications

Toru Serizawa, author

Textook showing how to locate vital points.

1992

6323   Turning the Tide

ADD/ADHD Education & Resource Associaton
PO Box 8167
Shawnee Mission, KS   66208   **913-362-6108**

e-mail: seg2@aol.com
Karen Kirk Richards and John B Lester M.D., author

A complete, single-source guide to all aspects of identifying, teaching and managing ADD/ADHD children. An essential tool for parents and educators giving classroom consultant intervention techniques. Includes a discussion of symptoms, treatment, medication, social skills competency, current laws and sources of help. Paperback. *$8.95*

96 pages
ISBN 0-93964 -88-6

6324   US Government TTY Directory

Consumer Information Center
Department 627F
Pueblo, CO   81009

e-mail: catalog.pueblo@gsa.gov

Judi Mahoney, Public Affairs

Gives details on how to use the Federal Relay Service and which agencies and congressional offices have text telephone devices.

6325   US Role in International Disability Activities: A History

World Institute on Disability
510 16th Street
Suite 100
Oakland, CA   94612   **510-763-4100**
                                        FAX: 510-763-4109
                                        TDY:510-208-9493
                                        e-mail: wid@wid.org
                                        www.wid.org

Nora Groce, author

This study, commissioned by WID, the World Rehabilitation Fund and Rehabilitation International, was undertaken to present an initial introduction to U.S. involvement in the field of international rehabilitation and disability. *$12.00*

169 pages Paperback

6326   Understanding and Managing Learning Disabilities in Adults

Krieger Publishing Company
PO Box 9542
Melbourne, FL   32902   **407-724-9542**
                                        800-724-0025
                                        FAX: 407-951-3671
                                        e-mail: info@krieger-pub.com
                                        www.krieger-publishing.com

Dale R. Jordan, author

This book first explains how the brain functions in learning and remembering throughout one's life span. Individual chapters then describe the types of learning disabilities (LD) that exist throughout adulthood: dyslexia, attention deficit disorders, Scotopic Sensitivity syndrome, Nonverbal LD, Social-Emotional LD, and mental health factors that frequently accompany learning disabilities. The discussion is two-fold. First each type of LD is described and explained, then management strategies *$22.50*

150 pages Hardcover
ISBN 1-575241-08-0

6327 Vaccinations: Mothering Special Edition

Mothering Magazine
Santa Fe, NM

Articles and commentary on the pros and cons of vaccinations.

1989

6328 Vaccines: Are They Really Safe and Effective?

New Atlantean Press
Santa Fe, NM

Neil Z. Miller, author

Evaluates 'mandated' and many newer vaccines to determine their safety and both short- and long-term effects.

1992

6329 Vibrational Medicine

Bear & Company

Richard Gerber, author

6330 Vision, Values & Vitality: Bringing IL Principles to Mental Health Peer Support

Independent Living Research Utilization ILRU
2323 S Shepherd Drive
Suite 1000
Houston, TX   77019   713-520-0232
                        FAX: 713-520-5785
                            www.ilru.org

Frederick Moe
Cindy Perkins
Pat Spiller

Frederick, Cindy, and Pat describe the technical assistance GSIL provides to drop-in centers to enable them to become consumer-controlled peer support centers.

10 pages

6331 Vitamin C: Who Needs It?

Arlington Press
Birmingham, AL

Emmanuel Cheraskin, M.D., author

An informational book on the nutritional benefits of vitamin C.

1993

6332 VoRtechs

Center for Rehabilitation Technology
1410-C Boston Avenue
15
West Columbia, SC   29170
                  FAX: 803-822-4301
           e-mail: rerc-br@scsn.net
           www.scsn.net/users/crts

Neil Lown, Technical Services

Rehabilitation technology and assistive device newsletter. Available in alternate formats.

8 pages Quarterly

6333 Vocal Rehabilitation: A Practice Book for Voice Improvement, 3rd Edition

Pro-Ed
8700 Shoal Creek Boulevard
Austin, TX   78757
                      FAX: 512-451-8542
              e-mail: proed1@aol.com
Virginia L. Agnello & Cindy Garcia, author

A complete program that clinicians can use to help clients eliminate vocal misuses or abuse and gain a healthy, proficient voice. *$49.00*

6334 Volunteer Voice

Kentucky Chapter of the Arthritis Foundation
410 W Chestnut Street
Suite 750
Louisville, KY   40207   502-893-9771
                            800-633-5335

Newsletter offering information and updates on chapter activities, events, camps, juvenile programs and government/legislative information.

6335 WA & NEWS

Wheelchair Access
PO Box 12
Glenmoore, PA   19343   610-942-3266
                      FAX: 610-942-0282
              e-mail: info@waccess.org
                    www.waccess.org

Frank Gomez, Publisher

Features wheelchair accessible houses and apartments for rent or for sale. Currently the newsletter includes ads from all states. Ads received from any State will be accepted free of charge. Featured also are ads of wheelchairs, vans, equipment, etc., for sale. Complete ad information and more is listed in the Web site. A free copy of WA & NEWS sent upon request. *$12.00*

20 pages Monthly

6336 Walking Tomorrow

Christopher Reeve Paralysis Foundation
500 Morris Avenue
Springfield, NJ   07081   973-379-6299
                            800-252-0292
                      FAX: 973-912-9433
              e-mail: paralysis@aol.com
                    www.paralysis.com

A newsletter offering medical and technological updates for people with physical disabilities, including paralysis.

Quarterly

6337 We Can Speak for Ourselves: Self Advocacy By Mentally Handicapped People

Brookline Books
PO Box 1047
Cambridge, MA   02238   617-868-0360
                            800-666-2665
                      FAX: 617-868-1772
           e-mail: brooklinebks@delphi.com
                    www.brooklinebooks.com
Paul Williams & Bonnie Shoultz, author

Practical advice and support for parents, group resident workers, and others interested in fostering self-advocacy for people with developmental disabilities. $10.00

246 pages Paperback
ISBN 0-25336 -65-9

6338   Web That Has No Weaver: Understanding Chinese Medicine
Contemporary Books
Chicago, IL

Ted Kaptchuk, author

6339   Web that has No Weaver: Understanding Chinese Medicine
Congond and Weed

Ted Kaptchuk, author
1992

6340   Weiner's Herbal
Quantum Books

Michael Weiner Ph.D., author
A-Z index covering all aspects of herbs.

6341   Well Pregnancy Book
Fireside Books

Mike Samuels, author
Information on exercise, nutrition, drugs, sex, and all physical and emotional stages of pregnancy.

1986

6342   What Your Doctors Won't Tell You
Harper Perennial
New York, NY

Jane Heimlich, author
A look at the world of alternative medicine, with a comprehensive chapter on constipation, and the illnesses it can contribute to. Also provides a treatment program based diet, nutritional supplements, herbal medicine, and colonic irrigation.

1990

6343   What's Line
Alabama Public Library Service
6030 Monticello Drive
Montgomery, AL   36130   334-213-3906
                                    800-392-5671
                              FAX: 334-213-3993
              e-mail: fzaleski@apls.state.al.us
                            www.apls.state.al.us

Fara Zaleski, Regional Librarian
4 pages Quarterly

6344   What's Wrong with my Hormones?
Desmond Ford Publications
Newcastle, CA

Gillian Ford, author
Discusses PMS, postpartum depression, premenopause and menopause, and associated hypothyroidism; describes the consequences of taking the pill, or having a tubal sterilization, ovarian surgery, or a hysterectomy; shows the connection between endometriosis and hormonal dysfunction; covers treatment, including information on both natural and hormonal remedies.

1992

6345   Who Needs Headaches
Literary Visions Publishing
Cedar Rapids, IA

Cass Ingram, DO, author
Discusses the causes, treatments, and varieties of headaches.

6346   Why Me? Harnessing the Healing Power of the Human Spirit
Stilpoint International

Garrett Porter and Patricia Norris, author

6347   Wizard Within: The Krasner Method of Clinical Hypnotherapy
American Board of Hypnotherapy Press

A.M. Krasner Ph.D., author
Includes a look into the history and induction techniques.

6348   Women with Physical Disabilities: Achieving & Maintaining Health & Well-Being
Brookes Publishing
PO Box 10624
Baltimore, MD   21285   410-337-9580
                                    800-638-3775
                              FAX: 410-337-8539
      e-mail: custserv@brookespublishing.com
                  www.brookespublishing.com

Examined here is sexuality and reproduction, love, marriage, and relationships, bowel and bladder management, stress, and physical fitness of women with physical disabilities. $42.95

512 pages Paperback
ISBN 1-55766 -34-7

6349   Women's Health Alert
Addison-Wesley Publishing Company
Reading, MA

Sidney M. Wolfe, M.D. and Rhoda Donkin Jones, author

This book provides up-to-date information on the practice of female medicine with data and statistics that can help a woman make wise decisions about her health. Information on hormone-replacement therapy and osteoporosis are detailed.

1991

6350 Women's Health Forum

6113 Abbey Road
Aptos, CA 95003

An interdisciplinary newsletter for physicians and medical students.

6351 Work in the Context of Disability Culture

Independent Living Research Utilization ILRU
2323 S Shepherd Drive
Suite 1000
Houston, TX 77019   **713-520-0232**
                              FAX: 713-520-5785
                              www.ilru.org
Steve Brown, author

Another winner in the innovative CIL competition-Steve Brown describes the Talking Books Program of Southeast Alaska Independent Living, discussing their efforts to record the oral history and life experiences of people with disabilities in the larger context of the disability culture.

10 pages

6352 Working with Your Doctor: Getting the Healthcare You Deserve

Patient-Centered Guides - O'Reilly
101 Morris Street
Sebastopol, CA 95472   **707-829-0515**
                               800-998-9938
                               FAX: 707-829-0104
                               e-mail: health@oreilly.com
                               www.patientcenters.com
Nancy Keene, author
Linda Lamb, Editor
Shawnde Paull, Marketing
Kerri Bonasch, Sales & Marketing Manager

Working with Your Doctor shows how to form a satisfying partnership with your doctor in a rapidly changing healthcare environment. It contains in-depth and practical information on how to find the right doctor, communicate clearly, ask about tests and treatments, seek opinions, take action when wronged, and deal effectively with managed care. This book is a great primer for patient empowerment. *$15.95*

377 pages Paperback
ISBN 1-565922-73-5

6353 World Awaits You

Mobility International USA
PO Box 10767
Eugene, OR 97440   **541-343-1284**
                               FAX: 541-343-6812
                               TDY:541-343-1284
                               e-mail: info@miusa.org
                               www.miusa.org
Michelle Scheib, author
Susan Sygall, Executive Director
Rhonda Neuhaus, Public Relations Coordinator

A journal of success in international exchange for people with disabilities. Includes personal experience stores, accommodation information and opportunities for people with disabilities. Bi-annual. Free.

6354 World of Options

Mobility International USA
PO Box 10767
Eugene, OR 97440   **541-343-1284**

e-mail: info@miusa.org

Susann Sygall, Executive Director
Rhonda Neuhaus, Public Relations Coordinator

A guide to international, educational exchange, community service and travel for persons with disabilities. *$16.00*

338 pages
ISBN 1-88003 -01-8

6355 World of Options: A Guide to International Educational Exchange

Mobility International USA
PO Box 10767
Eugene, OR 97440   **541-343-1284**
                               FAX: 541-343-6812
                               TDY:541-343-1284
                               e-mail: info@miusa.org
                               www.miusa.org
Christa Bucks, author
Susan Sygall, Executive Director
Rhonda Neuhaus, Public Relations Coordinator

'A Guide to International Educational Exchange, Community Service, and Travel for People with Disabilities' includes information travel and international programs, as well as personal experience stories from people with disabilities who have had successful internaitonal experiences. *$45.00*

600 pages 1997
ISBN 1-880034-24-7

6356 Your Fertility Signals

Smooth Stone Press
St. Louis, MO

Merryl Winstein, author

Naturally, cooperatively, and effectively achieve or prevent pregnancy, reduce or eliminate contraceptive use, enhance intimacy in your relationship, and possibly choose your baby's sex.

1991

6357 Your Healing Hands: The Polarity Experience

Wingbow Press

Richard Gordon, author

Hands-on approach to learning therapeutic touch.

1978

6358 Your Inner Physician and You: CranioSacral Therapy SomatoEmotional Release

North Atlantic Books
Berkley, CA

John E. Upledger D.O., author

Hearing Impaired

6359 ASHA Magazine; ASHA Leader

American Speech-Language-Hearing Association
10801 Rockville Pike
Rockville, MD 20852   301-897-5700
    800-498-2071
FAX: 301-571-0457
e-mail: actioncenter@asha.org
professional.asha.org
Ellen Offen, Marat Moore, author
Joanne K. Jessen; ASHA Leader, Managing Editor
In Chief

Association publication containing news, notices of events and activities and information for members on issues facing the profession of audiology and speech-language pathology. *$60.00*

    16 pages Newsletter
    ISSN 1085-9586

6360 Adult Bible Lessons for the Deaf

LifeWay Christian Resources Southern Baptist Conv.
127 9th Avenue North
Nashville, TN 37234   615-251-2000
    800-458-2772
e-mail: specialed@lifeway.com
www.lifeway.com

Omar Fernandez, Manager

Bible study lessons for every three months written by and for persons who are deaf. Based on the Family Bible Series (International Sunday School Lessons).

    Quarterly

6361 Advanced Sign Language Vocabulary

Charles C. Thomas, Publisher
2600 S 1st Street
Springfield, IL 62704   217-789-8980
    800-258-8980
FAX: 217-789-9130
e-mail: books@ccthomas.com
Janet R. Coleman, author

A resource text for educators, interpreters, parents and sign language instructors. *$46.95*

    202 pages Paperback
    ISBN 0-398057-22-2

6362 American Sign Language Handshape Dictionary

Gallaudet University Press
11030 S Langley Avenue
Chicago, IL 60628
    800-621-2736
FAX: 800-621-8476
TDY:800-621-9347
gupress.gallaudet.edu

Richard A. Tennant, Co-Author
Marianne Gluszak Brown, Co-Author

More than 1,600 sign illustrations arranged by handshape for easy identification. Allows readers to look up signs they have seen without needing to know their English meaning beforehand, complemented by a complete English index cross-referenced to every sign. *$35.00*

    408 pages Hardcover

6363 American Sign Language Phrase Book

TJ Publishers (Distributors)
817 Silver Spring Avenue
Suite 206
Silver Spring, MD 20910   301-585-4440
    800-999-1168
FAX: 301-585-5930
e-mail: TJPubinc@aol.com
Lou Fant, author
Angela K Thames, President
Jerald A Murphy, Vice President

The author provides interesting, realistic and meaningful situations. Sign language is learned through novel remarks cleverly organized around everyday topics. *$18.95*

    362 pages Softcover
    ISBN 0-80923 -00-5

6364 American Sign Language: A Look at Its Structure & Community

TJ Publishers
817 Silver Spring Avenue
Suite 206
Silver Spring, MD 20910   301-585-4440
    800-999-1168
FAX: 301-585-5930
e-mail: TJPubinc@aol.com
Charlotte Baker-Shenk and Carol Padden, author
Angela K Thames, President
Jerald A Murphy, Vice President

Answers basic questions about American Sign Language. What is it? What is its history? Who uses it? What is the deaf community? *$3.95*

    22 pages Softcover
    ISBN 0-93266 -01-9

6365 Anna's Silent World

JB Lippincott
227 E Washington Square
Philadelphia, PA 19106   215-238-4200
    800-777-2295
FAX: 215-824-7390
Bernard Wolf, author

Anna was a hearing impaired child who lived in New York City with her family. The text followed Anna through a hearing evaluation, speech therapy, and her participation in a class for hearing impaired children.

    48 pages Hardcover
    ISBN 0-39731 -39-5

6366 At Home Among Strangers

TJ Publishers (Distributors)
817 Silver Spring Avenue
Suite 206
Silver Spring, MD 20910   301-585-4440
    800-999-1168
FAX: 301-585-5930
e-mail: TJPubinc@aol.com
Jerome D. Schein, author
Angela K Thames, President
Jerald A Murphy, Executive Assistant

Discusses deaf culture and its uniqueness in two sections: the first describes the deaf community - its development, structure and culture; the second explains Schein's theory of deaf community development. $24.95

254 pages Hardcover
ISBN 0-930323-51-3

6367 Aural Habilitation

Alexander Graham Bell Association of the Deaf
3417 Volta Place NW
Washington, DC 20007
FAX: 202-337-8314
e-mail: lquigley@agbell.org
www.agbell.org
Daniel Ling, author

This classic text for proffesionals educators and parents discusses verbal learning and aural habilitation of young children with hearing losses to ensure that each child is educated in the best setting. It discusses communication, normal development of spoken language, speech audiologic assessment, hearing aids and use of residual hearing, and program designs for individualized needs, including the assessment and planning of IEPs. $26.95

324 pages

6368 Basic Course in Manual Communication

Gallaudet University Bookstore
11030 S Langley Avenue
Chicago, IL 60628
202-651-5488
800-621-2736
FAX: 202-651-5489
Terrence J. O'Rourke, author

Teach your students manual communication - that living, changing, growing language of signs. $11.95

158 pages Softcover

6369 Basic Vocabulary: ASL for Parents and Children

TJ Publishers
817 Silver Spring Avenue
Suite 206
Silver Spring, MD 20910
301-585-4440
800-999-1168
FAX: 301-585-5930
e-mail: TJPubinc@aol.com
Terrence J. O'Rourke, author
Angela K Thames, President
Jerald A Murphy, Vice President

Carefully selected words and signs include those that children use every day. Alphabetically organized vocabulary incorporates developmental lists helpful to both deaf and hearing children and over 1000 clear sign language illustrations. $8.95

240 pages Softcover
ISBN 0-93266 -00-0

6370 Ben's Story: A Deaf Child's Right to Sign

TJ Publishers (Distributors)
817 Silver Spring Avenue
Suite 206
Silver Spring, MD 20910
301-585-4440
800-999-1168
FAX: 301-585-5930
e-mail: TJPubinc@aol.com
Lorraine Fletcher, author
Angela K Thames, President
Jerald A Murphy, Executive Assistant

This is a mother's story of how she responded to the diagnosis of her son's deafness and how she struggled to have her son educated using sign language. $7.95

267 pages Softcover
ISBN 0-930323-47-5

6371 Between Friends

Beltone Electronics Corporation
4201 W Victoria Street
Chicago, IL 60646
FAX: 773-583-4681
Renee Rockoff, Editor

For hearing aid wearers: quizzes, jokes, health, recipes and financial items.

6 pages

6372 Book of Name Signs

Gallaudet University Bookstore
11030 S Langley Avenue
Chicago, IL 60628
202-651-5488
800-621-2736
FAX: 202-651-5489
Samuel Supalla, author

Discusses the rules for American Sign Language name sign formation and their appropriate use. $12.95

112 pages

6373 Bridges Beyond Sound

Brookes Publishing
PO Box 10624
Baltimore, MD 21285
410-337-9580
800-638-3775
FAX: 410-337-8539
e-mail: custserv@brookespublishing.com
www.brookespublishing.com
Corinne K. Jensema, Ph.D., author

An instructional workbook on understanding and including students with a hearing loss. Supplement to the Bridges Beyond Sound videotape. Besides the videotape script, background information on hearing loss, discussion questions, activities, and reproducible worksheets are included. $33.00

176 pages Spiral-bound
ISBN 1-55766 -26-6

6374 Changing the Rules

TJ Publishers
817 Silver Spring Avenue
Suite 206
Silver Spring, MD 20910
301-585-4440
800-999-1168
FAX: 301-585-5930
e-mail: TJPubinc@aol.com
Frank Bowe, author
Angela K Thames, President
Jerald A Murphy, Vice President

Like many deaf adults, Frank Bowe was main-streamed in the small Pennsylvania town where he was raised. This is a humorous and poignant account of the obstacles that shaped this leading disability rights activist. Bowe's account of coming of age and personal growth, the discovery of signed language and an insider's view of the equal rights movement is a compelling record of one man's struggle with the challenges of profound deafness. *$8.95*

204 pages Hardcover
ISBN 0-93266 -31-0

6375 Chelsea: The Story of a Signal Dog

Gallaudet University Bookstore
800 Florida Avenue NE
Washington, DC 20002   202-651-5000
                                   800-451-1073
                              FAX: 202-651-5489

Paul Ogden, author

This is a story of a young deaf couple and their Belgian sheepdog, who acts as their ears. It explains how these dogs are trained and paired with their new owners. *$18.95*

169 pages

6376 Children of a Lesser God

Gallaudet University Bookstore
11030 S Langley Avenue
Chicago, IL 60628   202-651-5488
                                800-621-2736
                           FAX: 202-651-5489

Mark Medoff, author

The play that won the hearts of thousands. This is a story of a deaf woman who refuses to succumb to the hearing people's image of what a deaf person should be. *$4.50*

91 pages Softcover

6377 Choices in Deafness

Woodbine House
6510 Bells Mill Road
Bethesda, MD 20817
                                 800-843-7323
                            www.woodbinehouse.com

Sue Schwartz, Ph. D., author

A useful aid in choosing the appropriate communication option for a child with a hearing loss. Experts present the following communication options: Auditory-Verbal Approach, Bilingual-Bicultural Approach, Cued Speech, Oral Approach, and Total Communication. This new edition explains medical causes of hearing loss, the diagnostic process, audiological assessment, and cochlear implants. Children and parents also offer their personal experiences. *$16.95*

275 pages Paperback
ISBN 0-933149-85-9

6378 Clerc: The Story of His Early Years

TJ Publishers (Distributors)
817 Silver Spring Avenue
Suite 206
Silver Spring, MD 20910   301-585-4440
                                       800-999-1168
                                  FAX: 301-585-5930
                           e-mail: TJPubinc@aol.com

Cathryn Carroll, author
Angela K Thames, President
Jerald A Murphy, Vice President

This imaginative tale recounts the youthful history of Laurent Clerc, the deaf teacher who helped Thomas Gallaudet establish schools for the deaf in the 19th century. Early experiences influenced the teaching methods Clerc developed in later life, and young adults will relish identifying with the hero of this entertaining story. *$9.95*

208 pages Softcover
ISBN 0-93032 -23-8

6379 Client Assistance Program - Arizona

3839 N 3rd Street
Suite 209
Phoenix, AZ 85012
                              FAX: 602-274-6779

John Guiterrez, Director

6380 Cochlear Implants and Children

A.G. Bell Association of the Deaf/Hard of Hearing
2000 M Street
Washington, DC 20036   202-337-5220
                              FAX: 202-337-8314
                              TDY:202-337-5220
                         e-mail: agbell2@aol.com
                                  www.agbell.org

Nancy Tye-Murray, PhD, author
Elizabeth Quigley, Director of Publications

Designed to educate readers about cochlear implants, including surgery, the importance of rehabilitation, and the significance of parents' and professionals' roles. *$42.95*

189 pages Paperback

6381 Cochlear Implants for Kids

Alexander Graham Bell Association of the Deaf
3417 Volta Place NW
Washington, DC 20007   202-337-5220
                              FAX: 202-337-8314
                              TDY:202-337-5220
                        e-mail: lquigley@agbell.org
                                  www.agbell.org

Warren Estabrooks, Editor, author
Elizabeth Quigley, Director of Publication Sales

Designed to educate readers about cochlear implants, including surgery, the importance of rehabilitation, and significance fo parensts' and professionals' rules. *$42.95*

404 pages Paperback
ISBN 0-88200 -08-0

6382 Cognition, Education and Deafness

Gallaudet University Press
800 Florida Avenue NE
Washington, DC 20002   202-651-5000
                                   800-451-1073
                              FAX: 202-651-5489

David S. Martin, author

The work of 54 authors is gathered in this definitive collection of current research on deafness and cognition. The articles are grouped into seven sections: cognition, problem solving, thinking processes, language development, reading methodologies, measurement of potential, and intervention programs. *$21.95*

260 pages Hardcover

6383 College and Career Programs for the Deaf

Gallaudet University Bookstore
11030 S Langley Avenue
Chicago, IL 60628   202-651-5488
                                          800-621-2736
                                     FAX: 202-651-5489
National Institute for the Deaf, author

Which college is the right one for you? This is a guide to colleges in the United States and Canada that offer special programs for deaf students. *$12.95*

108 pages Softcover

6384 Come Sign with Us: Sign Language Activities for Children

TJ Publishers (Distributors)
817 Silver Spring Avenue
Suite 206
Silver Spring, MD 20910   301-585-4440
                                          800-999-1168
                                     FAX: 301-585-5930
                          e-mail: TJPubinc@aol.com
Jan Hafer & Robert Wilson, author
Angela K Thames, President
Jerald A Murphy, Vice President

Illustrated activities manual contains more than 300 line drawings of adults and children signing familiar words, phrases, and sentences using ASL in English word order. *$29.95*

144 pages Softcover
ISBN 0-930321-56-3

6385 Communicating with Deaf People: An Introduction

Gallaudet University Bookstore
800 Florida Avenue NE
Washington, DC 20002   202-651-5000
                                          800-451-1073
                                     FAX: 202-651-5489

This illustrated publication introduces the various ways deaf people can communicate, including gesture and facial expression, speech-reading, fingerspelling and other manual communication systems. *$2.00*

20 pages

6386 Comprehensive Reference Manual for Signers and Interpreters 4th Edition

Charles C. Thomas, Publisher
2600 S 1st Street
Springfield, IL 62704   217-789-8980
                                          800-258-8980
                                     FAX: 217-789-9130
                     e-mail: books@ccthomas.com
Cheryl M. Hoffman, author
Manual for signers. *$47.95*

314 pages/Paperback
ISBN 0-398059-19-5

6387 Comprehensive Signed English Dictionary

Gallaudet University Press
11030 S Langley Avenue
Chicago, IL 60628
                                          800-621-2736
                                     FAX: 800-621-8476
                                     TDY:800-621-9347
                               gupress.gallaudet.edu

Harry Bornstein, Co-Author
Karen L. Saulnier, Co-Author
Lillian B. Hamilton, Co-Author

This complete dictionary has over 3,100 signs, including signs reflecting lively and contemporary vocabulary. *$35.00*

464 pages Hardcover

6388 Comprehensive Signed English Dictionary

Harris Communications
15159 Technology Drive
Eden Prairie, MN 55344   612-906-1180
                                          800-825-6758
                                     FAX: 612-906-1099
                       e-mail: mail@harriscomm.com
                               www.harriscomm.com
Harry Bornstein, author
Karen L Saulnier, Author
Lillian B Hamilton, Author
Bill Williams, National Sales Manager

Complete dictionary offers 3,100 signs, including signs reflecting contemporary vocabulary. *$35.00*

457 pages Hardcover
ISBN 0-913580-81-3

6389 Connect

Hearing, Speech & Deafness Center
1620 18th Avenue
Seattle, WA 98122   206-323-5770
                                     FAX: 206-328-6871
                          e-mail: hsdc@hsdc.org
                               www.hsdc.org

David Stoner, Editor

The Center's mission to enrich the lives of all adults and childrenwho experience hearing loss, speech and language impairments, or who are Deaf, by providing professional services and technology and by promoting community awareness and accessibility. A not-for-profit United Way Agency since 1937. Call V/TTY.

8 pages Quarterly

6390 Conscious Ear
Staton Hill Books

Alfred Tomatis, author

Autobiography of physician Alfred Tomatis and his accomplishments in the world of medicine.

6391 Conversational Sign Language II

Harris Communications
15159 Technology Drive
Eden Prairie, MN   55344   612-906-1180
                                       800-825-6758
                                    FAX: 612-906-1099
                            e-mail: mail@harriscomm.com
                                    www.harriscomm.com

Willard J Madsen, author
Bill Williams, National Sales Manager

This book presents English words and their American Sign Language equivalents. *$12.95*

218 pages Paperback
ISBN 0-913580-00-7

6392 Coping with the Multi-Handicapped Hearing Impaired: A Practical Approach

Charles C. Thomas, Publisher
2600 S 1st Street
Springfield, IL   62704   217-789-8980
                                       800-258-8980
                                    FAX: 217-789-9130
                            e-mail: books@ccthomas.com

Hugh T. Prickett, author

Professional text offers suggestions on how to deal with the multi-handicapped deaf person. Also available in cloth for $30.95 (ISBN# 0-398-05912-6)

90 pages $20.95
ISBN 0-398063-33-8

6393 Deaf Empowerment: Emergence, Struggle and Rhetoric

Gallaudet University Press
11030 S Langley Avenue
Chicago, IL   60628

                                       800-621-2736
                                    FAX: 800-621-8476
                                    TDY:800-621-9347
                            gupress.gallaudet.edu

Katherine A. Janowski, author

The story of the Deaf social movement, from its beginnings in the mid 1800s through its growth and strengthening in the late 20th century, much of it due to rhetoric and tactics adopted from other social movements. *$34.95*

192 pages Hardcover

6394 Deaf Heritage: A Narrative History

Gallaudet University Bookstore
11030 S Langley Avenue
Chicago, IL   60628   202-651-5488
                                   800-621-2736
                                FAX: 202-651-5489

Jack R. Gannon, author

This in-depth history of deaf America contains pictures, illustrations, vignettes, and biographical profiles. *$21.95*

500 pages Paperback

6395 Deaf History Unveiled: Interpretations from the New Scholarship

Gallaudet University Press
11030 S Langley Avenue
Chicago, IL   60628
                                       800-621-2736
                                    FAX: 800-621-8476
                                    TDY:800-621-9347
                            gupress.gallaudet.edu

John Vickrey Van Cleve, Editor

An all-star cast of historians explores the new themes driving Deaf History, including comparisons with other minority cultures and the social paternalism that affects deaf communities around the globe. *$27.50*

316 pages Softcover

6396 Deaf Like Me

Gallaudet University Press
800 Florida Avenue NE
Washington, DC   20002   202-651-5000
                                   800-451-1073
                                FAX: 202-651-5489

Thomas S. Spradley, author

Written by the uncle and father of a deaf girl, this is an account of parents coming to terms with deafness. This paperback edition contains a special epilogue by Lynn Spradley, grown and in her twenties, as she reflects on her growing-up years with the advantage of hindsight. *$10.95*

292 pages Softcover

6397 Deaf in America: Voices from a Culture

TJ Publishers (Distributors)
817 Silver Spring Avenue
Suite 206
Silver Spring, MD   20910   301-585-4440
                                   800-999-1168
                                FAX: 301-585-5930
                            e-mail: TJPubinc@aol.com

Carol Padden and Tom Humphries, author
Angela K Thames, President
Jerald A Murphy, Vice President

Now available in paperback, this book opens deaf culture to outsiders, inviting readers to imagine and understand a world of silence. This book shares the joy and satisfaction many people have with their lives and shows that deafness may not be the handicap most hearing people think. *$12.95*

134 pages Softcover
ISBN 0-67419-24-1

6398 Deafness: A Personal Account

Faber & Faber
53 Shore Road
Winchester, MA   01890   781-721-1427
                                   800-666-2211

David Wright, author
Liz Wolfson, Sales Manager
Anna Lowi, Marketing Director

Poet, critic and translator David Wright's enduring memoir (now with a substantial new introduction by the author) describes with humor and insight his early life, his development as a poet, and little-known history of deaf education. *$8.95*

202 pages Paperback
ISBN 0-57114-95-1

6399 Discovering Sign Language

Gallaudet University Press
800 Florida Avenue NE
Washington, DC 20002   202-651-5000
800-451-1073
FAX: 202-651-5489

Laura Greene, author

Here is a book of information about deaf people and sign communication. *$6.95*

104 pages Softcover

6400 Ear Gear

Kendall/Hunt Publications
4050 Westmark Drive
Dubuque, IA 52002   319-589-1000
800-338-5578
FAX: 800-772-9165
e-mail: webmaster@kendallhunt.com
www.kendallhunt.com

Carole Bugosh Simko, author

A workbook for hearing impaired students. It uses the rebus approach to teach about hearing loss and hearing aids.

128 pages Paperback
ISBN 0-93032 -15-7

6401 Effectiveness of Cochlear Implants and Tactile Aids for Deaf Children

3417 Volta Place NW
Washington, DC 20007   202-337-5220
FAX: 202-337-8314
TDY:202-337-5220
e-mail: agbell2@aol.com

Ann E. Geers, Ph.D., and Jean S. Moog, Editors, author
Elizabeth Quigley, Director Of Mem/Mht

This monograph presents a fascinating study to evaluate differences in the rate of change in speech perception, speech production and spoken language skills among children using the Nucleus 22-channel cochlear implant, tactile aids and conventional hearing aids. This monograph also offers teaching strategies in perception, lipreading, and spoken language. *$13.95*

232 pages Paperback

6402 Encyclopedia of Deafness and Hearing Disorders

Gallaudet University Bookstore
800 Florida Avenue NE
Washington, DC 20002   202-651-5000
800-451-1073
FAX: 202-651-5489

Carol Turkington and Allen E. Sussman, author

Presents the most current information on deafness and hearing disorders in an authoritative A-to-Z compendium. *$45.00*

278 pages

6403 Expressive and Receptive Fingerspelling

Gallaudet University Bookstore
800 Florida Avenue NE
Washington, DC 20002   202-651-5000
800-451-1073
FAX: 202-651-5489

LaVera M. Guillory, author

Here is a new and meaningful way for adults to increase their comfort with fingerspelling. The system is based on the principles of phonetics rather than letters of the English alphabet. *$2.50*

42 pages Softcover

6404 Flute Song Magic

TJ Publishers (Distributors)
817 Silver Spring Avenue
Suite 206
Silver Spring, MD 20910   301-585-4440
800-999-1168
FAX: 301-585-5930
e-mail: TJPubinc@aol.com

Andrea Shettle, author
Angela K Thames, President
Jerald A Murphy, Executive Assistant

Gallaudet student Andrea Shettle created a memorable fantasy world, Nevlin, where it is forbidden to talk with people below one's class. An improbable friendship leads the High Noble Flutir to discover that friendship and individuality defy class limitations. *$ 2.95*

218 pages Softcover
ISBN 0-380762-25-0

6405 For Hearing People Only

Harris Communications
15159 Technology Drive
Eden Prairie, MN 55344   612-906-1180
800-825-6758
FAX: 612-906-1099
e-mail: mail@harriscomm.com
www.harriscomm.com

Matthew Moore, author
Bill Williams, National Sales Manager

A book that answers some of the questions hearing people ask about deaf culture. Also availible in hardcover. *$19.95*

336 pages Paperback
ISBN 0-963401-61-0

6406 From Gesture to Language in Hearing and Deaf Children

Gallaudet University Press
11030 S Langley Avenue
Chicago, IL 60628
800-621-2736
FAX: 800-621-8476
TDY:800-621-9347
gupress.gallaudet.edu

Virginia Volterra, Editor
Carol J. Erting, Editor

In 21 essays on communicative gesturing in the first two years of life, this vital collection demonstrates the importance of gesture in a child's transition to a linguistic system. *$34.95*

358 pages Softcover

6407 GA and SK Etiquette

Gallaudet University Bookstore
800 Florida Avenue NE
Washington, DC 20002   202-651-5000
800-451-1073
FAX: 202-651-5489

Sharon T. Cagle And Keith M. Cagle, author

This booklet presents guidelines for proper usage of the TDD. It includes everything you wanted to know about sending and receiving TDD calls. *$8.95*

53 pages

6408 Gallaudet Survival Guide to Signing

Harris Communications
15159 Technology Drive
Eden Prairie, MN   55344   **612-906-1180**
                                     800-825-6758
                          FAX: 612-906-1099
              e-mail: mail@harriscomm.com
                     www.harriscomm.com
Leonard Lane, author
Bill Williams, National Sales Manager
Features 500 of the most frequently used signs, with clear illustrations and descriptions for each one. *$6.95*

203 pages Paperback
ISBN 0-930323-67-

6409 Growing Together: Information for Parents of Deaf Children

Gallaudet University Bookstore
800 Florida Avenue NE
Washington, DC   20002   **202-651-5000**
                                    800-451-1073
                          FAX: 202-651-5489
This publication answers questions often asked by parents of children with a hearing loss. *$8.00*

92 pages

6410 Handi-Cabs of the Pacific

PO Box 22428
Honolulu, HI   96823   **808-524-3866**

Craig Kimura, General Manager
Handi-Cabs of the Pacific, Inc. since 1973 has been offering the handicapped traveler an easy and convenient means of touring Oahu. Our radio dispatched, air conditioned vehicles are specially equipped with ramps and wheelchair lock downs. The customer is simply rolled into the vehicle then the wheelchair is locked in place and the tour begins. Our drivers are expertly trained and have the sensitivity and understanding to deal with your wheelchair customer.

6411 Handtalk Zoo

MacMillan Publishing Company
135 S Mount Zion Road
Lebanon, IN   46052
                                    800-257-5755
                          FAX: 800-882-8583
George Ancona, author
Wonderful photographs are used to show children at the zoo communicating with sign language.

28 pages Hardcover
ISBN 0-02700 -01-0

6412 Hearing Impaired Employee

G. Fritz, author

An invaluable aid for both large and small firms for employment agencies and counselors and for all firms, schools and associations providing equipment or services for the hearing impaired.

140 pages Paper

6413 Hearing Loss: The Journal of Self Help for Hard of Hearing People

Self Help for Hard of Hearing People (SHHH)
7910 Woodmont Avenue
Suite 1200
Bethesda, MD   20814   **301-657-2248**
                          FAX: 301-913-9413
                          TDY:301-657-2249
              e-mail: national@shhh.org
                     www.shhh.org

Bonnie Sporren, Business Manager
SHHH, a non-profit, educational organization is dedicated to the well-being of people of all ages and communication styles who do not hear well. SHHH is the largest international consumer organization of its kind. SHHH offers a nationwide support network of chapters and groups, a bi-monthly magazine, discounted publications and resource materials for members, an annual convention, state and regional conferences and more.

40 pages BiMonthly

6414 Hearing, Speech & Deafness Center

1620 18th Avenue
Seattle, WA   98122   **206-323-5770**
                          FAX: 206-328-6871
              e-mail: development@hsdc.org
                     www.hsdc.org

Susie Burdick, Dir of Development & Marketing
Bi-annual agency newsletter and clinical material for membership and community. Also available on website.

8 pages

6415 Hearing-Impaired Children and Youth with Developmental Disabilities

Gallaudet University Bookstore
800 Florida Avenue NE
Washington, DC   20002   **202-651-5000**
                                    800-451-1073
                          FAX: 202-651-5489
Evelyn Cherow, author
The insights of 24 experts help clarify relationships between hearing impairment and developmental difficulties and propose interdisciplinary cooperation as an approach to the problems created. *$29.95*

416 pages

6416 Hollywood Speaks

Gallaudet University Bookstore
800 Florida Avenue NE
Washington, DC   20002   **202-651-5000**
                                    800-451-1073
                          FAX: 202-651-5489
John Schuchman, author

How deafness has been treated in movies and how it provides yet another window onto social history in addition to a fresh angle from which to view Hollywood. *$24.95*

167 pages Hardcover

6417 How You Gonna Get to Heaven if You Can't Talk with Jesus?

TJ Publishers
817 Silver Spring Avenue
Suite 206
Silver Spring, MD   20910   301-585-4440
                                    800-999-1168
                          FAX: 301-585-5930
                  e-mail: TJPubinc@aol.com
James Woodward, author
Angela K Thames, President
Jerald A Murphy, Vice President

This collection of articles examines deaf culture and its relationship, profiling sociolinguistic and anthropological perspectives in research on American deaf society and culture. *$4.50*

78 pages Softcover
ISBN 0-93266 -15-9

6418 I Have a Sister, My Sister is Deaf

TJ Publishers (Distributors)
817 Silver Spring Avenue
Suite 206
Silver Spring, MD   20910   301-585-4440
                                    800-999-1168
                          FAX: 301-585-5930
                  e-mail: TJPubinc@aol.com
Jeanne Whitehouse Peterson, author
Angela K Thames, President
Jerald A Murphy, Vice President

An emphatic, affirmative look at the relationship between siblings, as a young deaf child is affectionately described by her older sister. This Coretta Scott King Honor Award winner helps young children develop an understanding that deaf children share the same interests as hearing children. *$5.95*

32 pages Softcover
ISBN 0-06443 -59-6

6419 I Was #87: A Deaf Woman's Ordeal of Misdiagnosis, Institutionalization and Abuse

Gallaudet University Press
11030 S Langley Avenue
Chicago, IL   60628
                                  800-621-2736
                          FAX: 800-621-8476
                          TDY:800-621-9347
                          gupress.gallaudet.edu
Anne M. Bolander, Co-Author
Adair N. Renning, Co-Author

Misdiagnosed as mentally retarded, a deaf woman emerges from six torturous years at an institution for unwanted children and a lifetime of abuse and neglect to tell her remarkable, sobering story. *$24.95*

232 pages Hardcover

6420 In This Sign

Gallaudet University Bookstore
800 Florida Avenue NE
Washington, DC   20002   202-651-5000
                                800-451-1073
                          FAX: 202-651-5489
Joanne Greenberg, author

This modern classic follows a family of deaf parents and their hearing child through several decades of growth and pain, tragedy and triumph. *$10.95*

275 pages Softcover

6421 Innovative Practices for Teaching Sign Language Interpreters

Gallaudet University Press
11030 S Langley Avenue
Chicago, IL   60628
                                  800-621-2736
                          FAX: 800-621-8476
                          TDY:800-621-9347
                          gupress.gallaudet.edu
Cynthia B. Roy, Editor

Six experts draw upon the new understanding of sign language interpreting as a discourse between two languages and cultures. Develops bold, original techniques for training interpreters. *$34.95*

200 pages Hardcover

6422 Intermediate Conversational Sign Language

TJ Publishers (Distributors)
817 Silver Spring Avenue
Suite 206
Silver Spring, MD   20910   301-585-4440
                                    800-999-1168
                          FAX: 301-585-5930
                  e-mail: TJPubinc@aol.com
Willard J. Madsen, author
Angela K Thames, President
Jerald A Murphy, Vice President

Unique approach to using American Sign Language and English in a bilingual setting. Each of the 25 lessons includes an introductory paragraph, glossed vocabulary review, translation exercises, grammatical notes, substitution drills and activities. *$21.95*

400 pages Softcover
ISBN 7-91358 -79-1

6423 International Directory of Periodicals Related to Deafness

Gallaudet University Bookstore
800 Florida Avenue NE
Washington, DC   20002   202-651-5000
                                800-451-1073
                          FAX: 202-651-5489
Steven A. Frank, author

This one-of-a-kind directory has useful information on more than 500 magazines and journals related to deafness. The entries come from all over the world. *$10.00*

150 pages

6424 International Telephone Directory

Gallaudet University Bookstore
800 Florida Avenue NE
Washington, DC 20002   202-651-5000
                            800-451-1073
                    FAX: 202-651-5489

Telecommunications for the Deaf, Inc., author

Almost 12,000 TDD numbers for Telecommunications for the Deaf, members and organizations serving deaf people. *$20.00*

190 pages Softcover

6425 Interpretation: A Sociolinguistic Model

Gallaudet University Bookstore
800 Florida Avenue NE
Washington, DC 20002   202-651-5000
                            800-451-1073
                    FAX: 202-651-5489

Dennis Cokely, author

This text presents a sociolinguistically sensitive model of the interpretation process. The model applies to interpretation in any two languages although this one focuses on ASL and English. *$16.95*

199 pages

6426 Interpreting: An Introduction, Revised Edition

TJ Publishers (Distributors)
817 Silver Spring Avenue
Suite 206
Silver Spring, MD 20910   301-585-4440
                                800-999-1168
                        FAX: 301-585-5930
                    e-mail: TJPubinc@aol.com

Nancy Frishberg, author
Angela K Thames, President
Jerald A Murphy, Vice President

This text is written by a practicing interpreter and includes information on history, terminology, research, competence, setting and a comprehensive bibliography. *$22.50*

244 pages Softcover
ISBN 0-91688-01-9

6427 Journal of Speech and Hearing Disorders

American Speech-Language-Hearing Association
10801 Rockville Pike
Rockville, MD 20852   301-897-5700

                    e-mail: irc@asha.org

Articles cover case histories, clinical techniques, position papers and literature surveys. *$68.00*

6428 Journal of the Academy of Rehabilitation Audiology

Academy of Rehabilitative Audiology
VA Medical Ctr Audiology (126A)
Temple, TX 76504   254-547-1375

Robert J. Dunlop, Ph.D., JARA Circulation Mgr

Professional journal providing a forum for the exchange of ideas on, knowledge of and experience with habilitative and rehabilitative aspects of audiology. *$30.00*

ISSN 0149-88 6

6429 Journal of the American Deafness and Rehabilitation Association

JADARA
6212 Ferris Square
San Diego, CA 92121   619-558-7444

Articles of interest to professionals providing services to deaf people, with special emphasis on research-practice interactions and on mental health issues. *$46.00*

6430 Joy of Signing

Gallaudet University Bookstore
800 Florida Avenue NE
Washington, DC 20002   202-651-5000
                            800-451-1073
                    FAX: 202-651-5489

Lottie L. Riekehof, author

This manual on signing includes illustrations, information on sign origins, practice sentences, and step-by-step descriptions of hand positions and movements. *$16.95*

336 pages Hardcover

6431 Joy of Signing Puzzle Book

Harris Communications
15159 Technology Drive
Eden Prairie, MN 55344   612-906-1180
                                800-825-6758
                        FAX: 612-906-1099
                e-mail: mail@harriscomm.com
                        www.harriscomm.com

Linda Lascelle Hillebrand, author
Bill Williams, National Sales Manager

Whether you are learning sign language to communicate with a family member, co-worker, student or friend, this puzzle book makes the learning fun and interesting. *$3.95*

57 pages Paperback
ISBN 0-882435-38-8

6432 Keys to Raising a Deaf Child

Barron's Educational Series
250 Wireless Boulevard
Hauppauge, NY 11788   516-434-3311
                            800-645-3476
                    FAX: 516-434-3723
            e-mail: info@barronseduc.com
                    www.barronseduc.com

Virginia Frazier-Maiwald and Lenore M Williams MA, author Lonny Stein , Director of Marketing

Two educators offer positive advice and encouragement on helping children adapt to deafness. They show how problems related to deafness can be overcome so that the child interacts as a social and intellectual equal with children who can hear. The authors recommend bimodal communication - having the child, parents and other non-deaf family members combine sign language and speech as a first step in normal communication. *$6.95*

208 pages Paperback
ISBN 0-764107-23-2

6433 Language, Speech and Hearing Services in School

American Speech-Language-Hearing Association
10801 Rockville Pike
Rockville, MD 20852 301-897-5700
FAX: 301-571-0457
e-mail: irc@asha.org
www.asha.org/asha

Professional journal for clinicians, audiologists and speech-language pathologists. *$30.00*

6434 Legal Right: The Guide for Deaf and Hard of Hearing People

Gallaudet University Press
11030 S Langley Avenue
Chicago, IL 60628
800-621-2736
FAX: 800-621-8476
TDY:800-621-9347
gupress.gallaudet.edu

The National Association of the Deaf, author

This revised fifth edition is in easy-to-understand language, offering the latest state and federal statues and administrative procedures that prohibit discrimination against the deaf, hard of hearing and other physically challenged people. *$24.95*

264 pages Softcover

6435 Life Without Pain

Addison-Wesley Publishing Company
Reading, MA

Richard Linchitz, M.D., author

A self-help approach for eliminationg chronic pain, including back pain, using diet, nutrition, exercise, and mind/body techniques.

1987

6436 Linguistics of ASL: An Introduction

Gallaudet University Press
11030 S Langley Avenue
Chicago, IL 60628
800-621-2736
FAX: 800-621-8476
TDY:800-621-9347
gupress.gallaudet.edu

Clayton Valli, Co-Author
Ceil Lucas, Co-Author

An introduction to the struture of American Sign Language, featuring all the linguistic disciplines plus practice exercises. *$ 60.00*

460 pages Hardcover

6437 Linguistics of American Sign Language

McFarland & Company
PO Box 611
Jefferson, NC 28640 336-246-4460
800-253-2187

John O. Isenhath, author

How signers communicate thoughts, ideas and feelings through a gesturing/seeing medium instead of a speaking/hearing process. Also explored in this book is the grammatical structure and technical aspects of the language. *$45.00*

268 pages
ISBN 0-89950 -93-0

6438 Lisa and Her Soundless World

Human Sciences Press
233 Spring Street
New York, NY 10013 212-229-2859
800-221-9369
FAX: 212-463-0742

Edna S. Levine, author

Describes the impact deafness has on communication and functioning in a hearing world. Lisa, born with a severe hearing loss, was not diagnosed as hearing impaired until her parents were worried about her lack of speech and other children had rejected her. *$18.95*

30 pages Hardcover
ISBN 0-87705 -04-6

6439 Listen to Me

Alexander Graham Bell Association of the Deaf
3417 Volta Place NW
Washington, DC 20007 202-337-5220
FAX: 202-337-8314
e-mail: lquigley@agbell.org
www.agbell.org

Mary Wood Whitehurst, author
Elizabeth Quigley, Director of Publications

Entertaining wookbook contains exercises that help adults who are hard of hearing learn to listen and concentrate. *$9.95*

65 pages Paperback

6440 Listening and Talking

Alexander Graham Bell Association of the Deaf
3417 Volta Place NW
Washington, DC 20007 202-337-5220
FAX: 202-337-8314
TDY:202-337-5220
e-mail: lquigley@agbell.org
www.agbell.org

Elizabeth Cole, Ed. D, author
Elizabeth Quigley, Director of Publications

This research-based text for professionals promotes communication by developing language, audition and speech in early intervention programs for young children with hearing loss. *$25.95*

191 pages Paperback

6441 Literature Journal

Gallaudet University Bookstore
800 Florida Avenue NE
Washington, DC 20002 202-651-5000
800-451-1073
FAX: 202-651-5489

Pre-College Outreach, author

This book includes extensive examples of student and teacher entries taken from actual journals of deaf high school students. *$7.95*

44 pages

6442 Loss for Words

Gallaudet University Bookstore
11030 S Langley Avenue
Chicago, IL 60628 202-651-5488
800-621-2736
FAX: 202-651-5489

Lou Ann Walker, author

She was an interpreter for her parents at four, a virtual head of household at eight, teacher and helper for her little sisters, buffer between her family and the world. Here is a daughter's account of growing up with loving parents, both of whom are deaf. *$11.00*

208 pages Paperback

6443 Mask of Benevolence: Disabling the Deaf Community

Gallaudet University Bookstore
800 Florida Avenue NE
Washington, DC   20002   **202-651-5000**
800-451-1073
FAX: 202-651-5489

Harlan Lane, author

Dr. Harlan Lane does not view deafness as a handicap but rather a different state from hearing. Deaf people are a societal minority and should be treasured, not eradicated. *$23.00*

310 pages

6444 Matthew Pinkowski's Special Summer

TJ Publishers (Distributors)
817 Silver Spring Avenue
Suite 206
Silver Spring, MD   20910   **301-585-4440**
800-999-1168
FAX: 301-585-5930
e-mail: TJPubinc@aol.com

Patrick Quinn, author
Angela K Thames, President
Jerald A Murphy, Executive Assistant

Matthew Pinkowski meets an unlikely crew of friends - Sandy, the acrobat, Tommy, her brother who moves and learns slowly, and Laura, a deaf girl visiting an overprotective aunt and uncle. In solving a mystery together, the friends learn to expect the best of people. Funny, genuine story about a memorable summer. *$5.95*

150 pages Softcover
ISBN 0-930323-82-3

6445 Mind Over Back Pain

Berkley Books
New York, NY

John Sarno, M.D., author

An exploration of the role mind/body medicine can play in alleviating back pain caused by excess mental stress and tension.

1986

6446 My First Book of Sign

TJ Publishers (Distributors)
817 Silver Spring Avenue
Suite 206
Silver Spring, MD   20910   **301-585-4440**
800-999-1168
FAX: 301-585-5930
e-mail: TJPubinc@aol.com

Pamela J. Baker, author
Angela K Thames, President
Jerald A Murphy, Vice President

Full-color book gives alphabetically grouped signs for 150 words most frequently used by young children. *$14.95*

76 pages Hardcover
ISBN 0-93032 -20-3

6447 National Association of the Deaf

814 Thayer Avenue
Silver Spring, MD   20910   **301-587-1788**
FAX: 301-587-1791
TDY:Y)3015871789
e-mail: nadinfo@nud.org
www.nad.org

Nation's largest organization safeguarding the accessibilty and civil rights of 28 million deaf and hard of hearing Americans in education, employment, health care, and telecommunications. Focuses on grassroots advocacy and empowerment, captioned media, deafness-related information and publications, legal assistance, policy development and research, public awareness, and youth leadership development. *$20.00*

6448 Newsletter of American Hearing Research Foundation

American Hearing Research Foundation
55 E Washington Street
Suite 2022
Chicago, IL   60602   **312-226-5880**
FAX: 312-726-9695

William Lederer, Editor

Concerned with hearing research and education. Only if one can afford to pay, a suggested appropriate donation of $15 for cover postage and printing.

6-8 pages TriAnnual

6449 Northwest Limousine Service

9950 West Lawrence Avenue
Schiller Park, IL   60176   **847-671-5444**
800-376-5466
FAX: 847-671-5482

Kathleen Maloney, Manager
Ann Walsh, Office Reservations

Offers wheelchair accessible mini vans, sedans, stretch and super stretch limousines for hourly or daily rental.

6450 Outsiders in a Hearing World

Gallaudet University Bookstore
800 Florida Avenue NE
Washington, DC   20002   **202-651-5000**
800-451-1073
FAX: 202-651-5489

Paul C. Higgins, author

An introduction to the social world of deaf people. The author gives a sociologists view of what it's like to be deaf. *$19.95*

240 pages Softcover

6451 Perigee Visual Dictionary of Signing

Harris Communications
15159 Technology Drive
Eden Prairie, MN 55344   612-906-1180
                                 800-825-6758
                            FAX: 612-906-1099
                    e-mail: mail@harriscomm.com
                            www.harriscomm.com
Rod Butterworth, author
Bill Williams, National Sales Manager

An A-to-Z guide to American Sign Language vocabulary. *$15.95*

        450 pages Paperback
        ISBN 0-399519-52-1

6452 Perspective: Parent-Child Folio

Gallaudet University Bookstore
800 Florida Avenue NE
Washington, DC 20002   202-651-5000
                               800-451-1073
                          FAX: 202-651-5489
Pre-College Outreach, author

Ranging from table conversation to bedtime reading, the seven articles collected here emphasize family communications while providing important information for parents about deafness and deaf culture. *$5.95*

        29 pages

6453 Perspectives: Whole Language Folio

Gallaudet University Bookstore
800 Florida Avenue NE
Washington, DC 20002   202-651-5000
                               800-451-1073
                          FAX: 202-651-5489
Pre-College Outreach, author

The 19 articles in this collection offer practical help to teachers seeking to emphasize whole language strategies in their classroom. *$9.95*

        64 pages

6454 Phone of Our Own: The Deaf Insurrection Against Ma Bell

Gallaudet University Press
11030 S Langley Avenue
Chicago, IL 60628   202-651-5488
                               800-621-2736
                          FAX: 202-651-5489
                          TDY:800-621-9347
                          gupress.gallaudet.edu
Harry G. Lang, author

A recount of the history of the teletypewriter, from the three deaf engineers who developed the acoustic coupler that made mass communication on TTY's feasible, through the deaf community's twenty-year struggle against the government and AT&T to have TTY's produced and distributed. *$29.95*

        304 pages Hardcover

6455 Place of Their Own: Creating the Deaf Community in America

TJ Publishers (Distributors)
817 Silver Spring Avenue
Suite 206
Silver Spring, MD 20910   301-585-4440
                                  800-999-1168
                             FAX: 301-585-5930
                        e-mail: TJPubinc@aol.com
John Van Cleve and Barry Crouch, author
Angela K Thames, President
Jerald A Murphy, Vice President

Traces development of American deaf society to show how deaf people developed a common language and sense of community. Views deafness as the distinguishing characteristic of a distinct culture. *$16.95*

        212 pages Paperback
        ISBN 0-930324-91-

6456 PreReading Strategies

Gallaudet University Bookstore
800 Florida Avenue NE
Washington, DC 20002   202-651-5000
                               800-451-1073
                          FAX: 202-651-5489
David Schleper, author

Here is a wealth of good advice for preparing students to understand what they read, building comprehension and enjoyment. *$8.95*

        65 pages

6457 Psychology of Deafness

Longman Publishing Group
10 Bank Street
White Plains, NY 10606   914-993-5000
                            FAX: 914-993-0112
McCay Vernon, author

Portrays hearing impairments as a psychological variable causing life experiences of the deaf to consistently differ from those of the non-deaf. Covers all levels of hearing loss, from prelingual and profound deafness to partial and mild hearing loss. It demonstrates how and why a hearing loss creates psychological stress no matter what its degree.

        292 pages Hardcover
        ISBN 0-801303-22-2

6458 Registry of Interpreters for the Deaf

8630 Fenton Street
Suite 324
Silver Spring, MD 20910   301-608-0050
                             FAX: 301-608-0508
                          e-mail: pr@rid.org
                              www.rid.org

Membership association for sign language interpreters; promoting national certification, professional development and training, and quality assurance through ethical practices system.

        Monthly

6459 Religious Signing: A Comprehensive Guide for All Faiths

TJ Publishers (Distributors)
817 Silver Spring Avenue
Suite 206
Silver Spring, MD 20910 301-585-4440
800-999-1168
FAX: 301-585-5930
e-mail: TJPubinc@aol.com
www.agbell.org

Elaine Costello, author
Angela K Thames, President
Jerald A Murphy, Vice President

Contains over 500 religious signs for all denominations and their meanings illustrated by clear upper torso illustrations that show movements of hand, body and face. Includes a section on signing favorite verses, prayers and blessings. *$17.95*

219 pages Paperback
ISBN 0-553344-44-

6460 Seeing Voices: A Journey into the World of the Deaf

TJ Publishers (Distributors)
817 Silver Spring Avenue
Suite 206
Silver Spring, MD 20910 301-585-4440
800-999-1168
FAX: 301-585-5930
e-mail: TJPubinc@aol.com

Oliver Sacks, author
Angela K Thames, President
Jerald A Murphy, Vice President

Well known for his exploration of how people respond to neurological impairments, Dr. Sacks explores the world of the deaf and discovers how deaf people respond to their loss of hearing and how they develop language. A highly readable introduction to deaf people, deaf culture and American Sign Language. *$11.00*

186 pages Softcover
ISBN 0-06097 -47-1

6461 Sign Language Coloring Books

Gallaudet University Bookstore
800 Florida Avenue NE
Washington, DC 20002 202-651-5000
800-451-1073
FAX: 202-651-5489

Ralph Miller, author

A mischievous mouse and a spinning top, a doll on the sofa, a hobo clown with this friend the elephant: these coloring books are a FUNtastic way for children to learn to sign, fingerspell, read and write. *$4.50*

6462 Sign Language Feelings

Gallaudet University Bookstore
800 Florida Avenue NE
Washington, DC 20002 202-651-5000
800-451-1073
FAX: 202-651-5489

Worksheets teach signs for happy, sad and all of the feelings in between. *$4.50*

6463 Sign Language Interpreters and Interpreting

Gallaudet University Bookstore
800 Florida Avenue NE
Washington, DC 20002 202-651-5000
800-451-1073
FAX: 202-651-5489

Dennis Cokely, author

This monograph presents articles about personal characteristics and abilities of interpreters, the effects of lag time on interpreter errors, and the interpretation of register. *$15.95*

161 pages

6464 Sign with Me Books

Gallaudet University Bookstore
11030 S Langley Avenue
Chicago, IL 60628 202-651-5488
800-621-2736
FAX: 202-651-5489

Susan P. Shroyer, author

Bold, colorful pictures and accurate diagrams make it fun for beginners to learn everyday signs. Titles in this series include ABC Sign With Me; Colors Sign With Me; Weather Sign With Me; and 1,2,3 Sign With Me. *$3.95*

Per Title

6465 Signed English Starter

Harris Communications
15159 Technology Drive
Eden Prairie, MN 55344 612-906-1180
800-825-6758
FAX: 612-906-1099
e-mail: mail@harriscomm.com
www.harriscomm.com

Harry Bornstein, author
Bill Williams, National Sales Manager

The first book to use when learning Signed English. *$13.95*

208 pages Paperback
ISBN 0-913580-82-1

6466 Signing for Reading Success

Gallaudet University Bookstore
800 Florida Avenue NE
Washington, DC 20002 202-651-5000
800-451-1073
FAX: 202-651-5489

Jan C. Hafer, author

This booklet provides summaries of four research students on the usefulness of signing for reading achievement. *$3.95*

24 pages Softcover

6467 Signing: How to Speak with Your Hands

TJ Publishers (Distributors)
817 Silver Spring Avenue
Suite 206
Silver Spring, MD 20910 301-585-4440
800-999-1168
FAX: 301-585-5930
e-mail: TJPubinc@aol.com

Elaine Costello, author
Angela K Thames, President
Jerald A Murphy, Vice President

Presents 1,200 basic signs with clear illustrations in logical topical groupings. Linguistic principles are described at the beginning of each chapter, giving insight into the rules which govern American Sign Language. *$17.95*

248 pages Paperback
ISBN 0-553375-39-3

6468 Signs Across America

TJ Publishers (Distributors)
817 Silver Spring Avenue
Suite 206
Silver Spring, MD   20910   **301-585-4440**
                                        800-999-1168
                                  FAX: 301-585-5930
                      e-mail: TJPubinc@aol.com
Edgar H. Shroyer and Susan P. Shroyer, author
Angela K Thames, President
Jerald A Murphy, Vice President

A look at regional variations in ASL. Signs for selected words collected from 25 different states. More than 1,200 signs illustrated in the text. *$19.95*

285 pages Paperback
ISBN 0-913589-61-

6469 Signs Everywhere

Harris Communications
15159 Technology Drive
Eden Prairie, MN   55344   **612-906-1180**
                                        800-825-6758
                                  FAX: 612-906-1099
                  e-mail: mail@harriscomm.com
                          www.harriscomm.com
Nancy Kelly-Jones, author
Bill Williams, National Sales Manager

This books includes signs for towns, cities, states and provinces. *$14.95*

254 pages Paperback
ISBN 0-916708-05-5

6470 Signs for Computing Terminology

Gallaudet University Bookstore
11030 S Langley Avenue
Chicago, IL   60628   **202-651-5488**
                                  800-621-2736
                            FAX: 202-651-5489
Steven L. Jamison, author

This sign reference will facilitate communication among deaf persons involved with computers by providing a significant vocabulary base for the computing field of today and tomorrow. *$12.95*

182 pages Softcover

6471 Signs for Me: Basic Sign Vocabulary for Children, Parents & Teachers

TJ Publishers (Distributors)
817 Silver Spring Avenue
Suite 206
Silver Spring, MD   20910   **301-585-4440**
                                        800-999-1168
                                  FAX: 301-585-5930
                      e-mail: TJPubinc@aol.com
Ben Bahan and Joe Dannis, author
Angela K Thames, President
Jerald A Murphy, Vice President

Sign language vocabulary for preschool and elementary school children introduces household items, animals, family members, actions, emotions, safety concerns and other concepts. *$12.95*

112 pages Softcover
ISBN 0-91503 -27-8

6472 Signs for Sexuality: A Resource Manual

Gallaudet University Bookstore
800 Florida Avenue NE
Washington, DC   20002   **202-651-5000**
                                      800-451-1073
                                FAX: 202-651-5489
Susan Doughten, author

An important book for those who want to listen to and talk with other people about feelings, loving and caring. *$24.95*

122 pages Softcover

6473 Signs of the Times

Gallaudet University Press
11030 S Langley Avenue
Chicago, IL   60628
                                      800-621-2736
                                FAX: 800-621-8476
                                TDY:800-621-9347
                          gupress.gallaudet.edu
Edgar H. Shroyer, author

An excellent beginner's contact signing book that fills the gap between sign language dictionaries and American Sign Language text. Designed for use as a classroom text. *$24.95*

448 pages Softcover

6474 Simultaneous Communication, ASL, and Other Communication Modes

Gallaudet University Bookstore
800 Florida Avenue NE
Washington, DC   20002   **202-651-5000**
                                      800-451-1073
                                FAX: 202-651-5489
William Stokoe, author

This monograph presents four major articles that examine issues surrounding communications in an educational environment. *$ 15.95*

236 pages

6475 Sing Praise Hymnal

Broadman and Holman
127 9th Avenue South
Nashville, TN   37203   **615-251-2000**
                                      800-458-2772
                                  www.bssb.com
The Sunday School Board, author
A song book for the deaf. *$6.95*

6476 Spring Dell Center

6040 Radio Station Road
La Plata, MD   20646   **301-934-4561**
                                  FAX: 301-870-2439

Melissa Tyner, Transportation Director

Since 1967, Spring Dell center has been, bridging the gap to enhance the lives of developmentally disabled people. Spring Dell's goal is to empower people in every aspect of their lives through the implementation of two programs, employment/vocational services and residential services including transportation. Spring Dell offers transportation door-to-door for persons with developmental disabilities, including day care programs, supportive environment, residential and any other transportation

6477   Teaching Social Skills to Hearing-Impaired Students

2200 M Street
Washington, DC   20007   202-337-5220

e-mail: agbell2@aol.com
www.agbell.org

This book provides teachers and parents with a comprehensive, clearly presented hands-on program to develop social skills in children and young adults who are deaf or hard of hearing. *$21.95*

203 pages

6478   Telephone Communication and Hearing Impaired

Taylor & Francis
47 Runway Drive
G
Levittown, PA   19057
                                FAX: 215-785-5515
N.P. Erber, author

This is a practical book containing valuable information for audiologists, teachers and others concerned with rehabilitation of the hearing impaired.

200 pages Illustrated
ISBN 0-85066 -18-3

6479   Theoretical Issues in Sign Language Research (Vol. I & II)

Gallaudet University Bookstore
11030 S Langley Avenue
Chicago, IL   60628   202-651-5488
                                800-621-2736
                            FAX: 202-651-5489
Susan Fischer, author

These volumes are an outgrowth of a conference held at the University of Rochester in 1986, dealing with the four traditional core areas of phonology, morphology, syntax and semantics. *$29.95*

338 pages

6480   They Grow in Silence

Taylor & Francis
47 Runway Drive
G
Levittown, PA   19057
                                FAX: 215-785-5515
Eugene D. Mindel, author

Gives a comprehensive picture of the deaf child in society, not only looking at the individual but also, at the related problems for the family, community and the professional. Only by the examination of such a broad perspective can questions on the position and circumstances of the deaf child be fully considered.

223 pages Paper
ISBN 0-85066 -54-6

6481   Tinnitus Today

American Tinnitus Association (ATA)
PO Box 5
Portland, OR   97207   503-248-9985
                                800-634-8978
                            FAX: 503-248-0024
                    e-mail: tinnitus@ata.org
                                www.alta.com
Barbara Sanders, author

Information, hearing service providers, support group contacts, and a bibliography service are available as well as this quarterly magazine. *$25.00*

26 pages Quarterly

6482   Understanding Deafness Socially

Charles C. Thomas, Publisher
2600 S 1st Street
Springfield, IL   62704   217-789-8980
                                800-258-8980
                            FAX: 217-789-9130
                e-mail: books@ccthomas.com
Paul C. Higgins and Jeffrey E. Nash, author

A look at the social difficulties of being hearing impaired in a hearing society. Also available in cloth edition for $45.95 (ISBN# 0-398-06569-1) *$29.95*

168 pages Softcover
ISBN 0-398065-70-5

6483   Very Special Friend

TJ Publishers (Distributors)
817 Silver Spring Avenue
Suite 206
Silver Spring, MD   20910   301-585-4440
                                800-999-1168
                            FAX: 301-585-5930
                e-mail: TJPubinc@aol.com
Dorothy Levi, author
Angela K Thames, President
Jerald A Murphy, Vice President

Six-year-old Frannie finds a very special friend who talks in sign language. She learns to sign and the two become best friends. *$9.95*

32 pages Hardcover
ISBN 0-93032 -55-6

6484   Vision

National Catholic Office for the Deaf
7202 Buchanan Street
Landover Hills, MD   20784   301-577-1684
                            FAX: 301-577-1690
                    e-mail: ncod@erols.com

Arvilla Rank, Executive Director/Editor

Published as a pastoral service for the deaf and hard of hearing. Provides information to members and others working in ministry. Prepares an annual gathering called Pastoral Week meeting in January. Price: $15.00 per year, $25 for 2 years; Foreign: $17 per year; $27 for 2 years.

16 pages TriAnnual

6485 Volta Review

Alexander Graham Bell Association of the Deaf
3417 Volta Place NW
Washington, DC 20007   202-337-5220
                                  FAX: 202-337-8314
                                  TDY:202-337-5220
                           e-mail: lquigley@agbell.org
                                      www.agbell.org

Michelle Vanderhoff, Managing Editor

Professionally refereed journal that publishes articles and research on education, rehabilitation and communicative development of people who have hearing impairments. Also includes subscription to Valta Voices, up-to-date magazine, bimonthly. *$62.00*

Quarterly

6486 Volta Voices

Alexander Graham Bell Association of the Deaf
3417 Volta Place NW
Washington, DC 20007   202-337-5220
                                  FAX: 202-337-8314
                           e-mail: lquigley@agbell.org
                                      www.agbell.org

Michelle Vanderhoff, Managing Editor

Contains Association news and educates readers on the abilities and needs of children and adults who are deaf or hard of hearing. Includes subscription to The Valta Review, published four times a year. *$62.00*

6487 We CAN Hear and Speak

Alexander Graham Bell Association of the Deaf
3417 Volta Place NW
Washington, DC 20007   202-337-5220
                                  FAX: 202-337-8314
                                  TDY:202-337-5220
                           e-mail: lquigley@agbell.org
                                      www.agbell.org
Parents of Natural Communication, Inc., author
Carol Flexer, Ph.D, Contributing Writer
Catherine Richards, M.A., Contributing Writer
Elizabeth Quigley, Director, Publications Sales

Written by parents for families of children who are deaf or hard of hearing, this work describes auditory-verbal terminology and approaches and contains personal narratives written by parents and their children who are deaf or hard of hearing. *$24.95*

171 pages Paperback
ISBN 0-88200 -09-0

6488 Week the World Heard Gallaudet

Gallaudet University Press
800 Florida Avenue NE
Washington, DC 20002   202-651-5000
                                         800-451-1073
Jack R. Gannon, author

This day-to-day description of the events surrounding the Deaf President Now movement at Gallaudet University includes full color and black and white photographs and interviews with people involved in the events of that week.

192 pages

6489 Wheelers Accessible Van Rentals

6614 W Sweetwater Avenue
Glendale, AZ 85304   623-776-8830
                                         800-456-1371
                                  FAX: 623-412-9920
                           e-mail: wheeler2@quest.net

Tammy Smith, Manager

Offers customized van rentals to the disabled persons allowing them freedom and independence in their travel.

6490 When the Mind Hears

Gallaudet University Bookstore
800 Florida Avenue NE
Washington, DC 20002   202-651-5000
                                         800-451-1073
                                  FAX: 202-651-5489
Harlan Lane, author

Comprehensive history of the deaf and their relationship with hearing academic communities. *$19.95*

414 pages Paperback

6491 You and Your Hearing Impaired Child: A Self-Instructional Parents Guide

TJ Publishers (Distributors)
817 Silver Spring Avenue
Suite 206
Silver Spring, MD 20910   301-585-4440
                                         800-999-1168
                                  FAX: 301-585-5930
                           e-mail: TJPubinc@aol.com
John W. Adams, author
Angela K Thames, President
Jerald A Murphy, Vice President

Designed specifically for parents who have children newly diagnosed as hearing impaired. Provides vital information on hearing impairment, setting limits, behavior management, nonverbal behavior and much more. *$17.95*

142 pages Softcover
ISBN 0-93032 -40-8

Music

6492 Braille Book Bank, Music Catalog

National Braille Association
3 Townline Circle
Rochester, NY 14623   716-427-8260

Offers hundreds of musical titles in print form, braille and on cassette.

62 pages

6493 Clinically Adapted Instruments for the Multiply Handicapped

MMB Music
3526 Washington Avenue
Saint Louis, MO 63103   314-531-9635
                                         800-543-3771
                           e-mail: mmbmusic@mmbmusic.com

A very unique book containing one hundred adapted and original instrument designs, descriptions and results of extensive practical applications. *$14.50*

6494 Creative Therapy and General Music Education Catalog-MMB Music

MMB Music
3526 Washington Avenue
Saint Louis, MO   63103   314-531-9635
800-343-3771
FAX: 314-531-8384
e-mail: sharonpemmbmusic.com
www.mmbmusic.com

Sharon Pirrone, Education/Therapy Director

Publisher and distributor of creative arts therapy materials in the areas of music, dance, art, drama, and poetry. Free catalog contains hundreds of books, recordings, and videos.

6495 Guide to the Selection of Musical Instruments

MMB Music
3526 Washington Avenue
Saint Louis, MO   63103   314-531-9635
800-543-3771
e-mail: mmbmusic@mmbmusic.com

A marvelous resource book to aid therapists teaching disabled to play musical instruments. *$7.75*

6496 MUSIC

409 30 1/4 Road
Grand Junction, CO   81504

Jeanine Linster

Jeanine dictates printed sheet music onto cassette. Pops, showtunes, religious, classics. Easy to advanced. Individualized lessons also available. $15 for 60 minute cassette; $23 for 90 minute cassette.

6497 Mainstreaming Exceptional Learners in Music

Pearson Education
One Lake Street
Upper Saddle River, NJ   07458   201-236-7000

Betty W. Atterbury, author

This complete introduction provides present and future music educators and therapists with the information necessary to understand the individual differences of the variety of students designated exceptional.

224 pages

6498 Music Therapy for the Developmentally Disabled

Pro-Ed Publications
8700 Shoal Creek Boulevard
Austin, TX   78757   512-451-3426
800-879-3202
FAX: 512-451-8542
e-mail: info@proedinc.com
www.proedinc.com

Edith Hillman Boxill, author

Included are practical guidelines, case samples and step-by-step instructions that enable a music therapist to bring about dramatic improvements in developmentally disabled adults and children. *$36.00*

269 pages Hardcover
ISBN 0-89079 -90-2

6499 Music for the Hearing Impaired

MMB Music
3526 Washington Avenue
Saint Louis, MO   63103   314-531-9635
800-543-3771
e-mail: mmbmusic@mmbmusic.com

A resource manual and curriculum guide. It is the product of a four-year developmental music program, placing emphasis on the needs of those with severe and profound losses. *$29.95*

6500 Music: Physician for Times to Come

Quest Books
Wheaton, IL

Don Campbell, author

A resource guide for various types of music and their theraputic oputcome.

6501 Teaching Basic Guitar Skills to Special Learners

MMB Music
3526 Washington Avenue
Saint Louis, MO   63103   314-531-9635
800-543-3771
e-mail: mmbmusic@mmbmusic.com

The first-of-its-kind guitar book for use with persons who have difficulty learning to play via traditional methods. *$16.00*

6502 Uncommon Fathers

Exceptional Parent Library
PO Box 1807
Englewood Cliffs, NJ   10116
800-535-1910
e-mail: eplibrary@aol.com
www.eplibrary.com

D.J. Meyer, Editor, author

A compelling collection of essays by fathers who were asked to reflect and write about the life-altering experiences of having a child with a disability. *$14.95*

Parenting: General

6503 A Miracle to Believe In

Option Institute and Fellowship
2080 S Undermountain Road
Sheffield, MA   01257   413-229-8737
800-562-7171
FAX: 413-229-8737
e-mail: happiness@option.org
www.option.org

Barry Neil Kaufman, author

A group of people from all walks of life come together and are transformed as they reach out, under the direction of the Kaufmans, to help a little boy the medical world has given up as hopeless. This heart-warming journey of loving a child back to life will inspire and presents a compelling new way to deal with life's traumas and difficulties. *$7.99*

379 pages Paperback
ISBN 0-44920 -08-2

6504 **AEPS Family Report: For Children Ages Three to Six**

Brookes Publishing
PO Box 10624
Baltimore, MD 21285   410-337-9580
    800-638-3775
FAX: 410-337-8539
e-mail: custserv@brookespublishing.com
www.brookespublishing.com

This is a 64-item questionnaire that asks parents to rank their child's abilities on specific skills. In packages of 10 paperback. *$23.00*

28 pages Saddle-stiched
ISBN 1-557662-50-9

6505 **After the Tears**

Centering Corporation
1531 N Saddle Creek Road
Omaha, NE 68104   402-553-1200
FAX: 402-533-0507
e-mail: j1200@aol.com
www.centering.org

Dan Rothermel, author

Offers talk, articles on raising a child with a disability. This one book combines feelings and emotions of parents on the subject of raising their disabled child. *$11.00*

87 pages Paperback
ISBN 0-15602 -00-6

6506 **Alexander Technique**

Alfred A. Knopf
New York, NY

Wilfred Barlow, author

The founder of the Alexander Institute shows how to reduce mental stress and muscular tension by becoming more aware of balance, posture, and movement in everyday activities.

1973

6507 **An Alternative Approach to Allergies**

Harper Perennial
New York, NY

Theron Randolph, M.D. and Ralph Moss, Ph.D., author

A comprehensive guide to staying well and allergy-free by a pioneer in the field of environmental medicine.

6508 **Arthritis Helpbook**

Addison-Wesley Publishing Company
Reading, MA

Kale Lorrig and James Fries, author

A self-care program for coping with arthritis that includes diet, nutrition, exercise, and mind/body techniques such as guided imagery and meditation.

6509 **Arthritis Relief at Your Fingertips**

Warner Books
New York, NY

Michael Reed Gach, PhD, author

A self-help guide for relieving arthritis pain through exercise and acupressure massage by a leader in the field.

6510 **Attention Deficit Disorder: Children**

Aquarius Health Care Videos
5 Powderhouse Lane
PO Box 1159
Sherborn, MA 01770   508-651-2963
    888-440-2963
FAX: 508-650-4216
e-mail: aqvideos@tiac.net
www.aquariusproductions.com

Leslie Kussmann, President/Producer

Everyone has been impulsive or easily distracted for different periods of time, so these symptoms that are hallmarks of Attention Deficit Disorder (ADD) have also led to criticism that too many people are being diagnosed with this biochemical brain disorder. This program examines who is being diagnosed, and what treatments are working. An innovative private school specializing in alternative education is profiled, and tips on structuring the school and home environment are included. *$149.00*

Video

6511 **Awareness Through Movement**

Harper and Row
New York, NY

Moshe Feldenkrais, author

A genuine self-help guide to improved posture, flexibility, breathing, health, and functioning through twelve easy-to-follow Awareness through Movement lessons.

1977

6512 **Baby Book for the Developmentally Challenged Child**

Exceptional Parent Library
PO Box 1807
Englewood Cliffs, NJ 10116
    800-535-1910
e-mail: eplibrary@aol.com
www.eplibrary.com

Rene Metthews and Christina Haberman RN, author

This baby book is for parents to write milestones for their developmentally challenged child. It incorporates the usual baby book features with very special sections covering any special needs child. *$25.00*

48 pages Hardcover

6513 **Back Care Basics: A Doctor's Gentle Yoga Program for Back and Neck Pain Relief**

Rodmell Press
Berkley, CA

Mary Pullig Schatz, M.D., author

Offers a gentle and effective approach to back rehabilitation without drugs or surgery. Uses the therapeutic techniques of Iyengar-style yoga.

1992

6514 Backyards and Butterflies

Brookline Books
PO Box 1047
Cambridge, MA   02238   617-868-0360
                                800-666-2665
                        FAX: 617-868-1772
                e-mail: brooklinebks@delphi.com
                        www.brooklinebooks.com
Doreen Greenstein, author

Backyards And Butterflies: Ways to Include Children with Disabilities In Out Door Activites is a wonderful illustrated book with dozens of imaginative ways parents can include children with physical disabilities in outdoor activities. Offers clear concise, how-to directions for constructing homemaode toys, utensils, and other items that can be enjoyed outside safely and comfortably *$14.95*

72 pages Paperback
ISBN 1-57129 -11-7

6515 Beating Alzheimer's

Avery Park Publishing Group
Garden City, NY

Tom Warren, author

The author's experience with, and recovery from, Alzheimer's, including diagnosis and treatment of food allergies, toxic amalgram 'silver' dental fillings, and mineral and vitamin deficiencies. Includes documented research.

6516 Before and After Zachariah

Special Needs Project
3463 Stat Street
282
Santa Barbara, CA   93105
                                800-333-6867

This intimate chronicle of one family's life with a severely brain damaged child is recently back in print. *$7.95*

241 pages

6517 Books on Special Children

BOSC
PO Box 305
Congers, NY   10920   845-638-1236
                        FAX: 845-638-0847
                e-mail: irene@boscbooks.com
                        www.boscbooks.com

Irene Slovak, Owner

Distributes books by mail to professionals and parents of handicapped children. The BOSC Directory contains facilities for people with learning disabilities (all disabilities, published annually)

300+ pages Hardcover
ISBN O-G61386-08-8

6518 Brain Allergies: The Psychonutrient

Keats Publishing
New Canaan, CT   203-966-8721
                        800-323-4900
William H. Philpott, M.D. and Dwight Kalita, Ph.D., author

A comprehensive look at the role nutrition and ortho-molecular medicine can play in treating brain allergies, including a self-help protocol and a special appendix for physicians.

6519 Brothers, Sisters, and Special Needs

Brookes Publishing
PO Box 10624
Baltimore, MD   21285   410-337-9580
                                800-638-3775
                        FAX: 410-337-8539
                e-mail: custserv@brookespublishing.com
                        www.brookespublishing.com
Debra H, Lobato, Ph.D., author

Information and activities for helping young siblings of children with chronic illnesses and developmental disabilities. *$30.00*

224 pages Paperback
ISBN 1-55766 -43-3

6520 Building the Healing Partnership: Parents, Professionals and Children

Brookline Books
PO Box 1046
Cambridge, MA   02238   617-868-0360
                                800-666-2665
                        FAX: 617-868-1772
                e-mail: brooklinebks@delphi.com
                        www.brooklinebooks.com
Patricia T. Leff & Elaine H. Walizer, author

Successful programs understand that the disabled child's needs must be considered in the context of a family. This book was specifically written for practitioner's who must work with families but who have insufficient training in family systems assessment and intervention. It is a valuable blend of theory and practice with pointers for applying the principles. *$24.95*

Paperback
ISBN 0-91479 -63-8

6521 Case Manager

Mosby
Professional Media Group
PO Box 189
Pitman, NJ   08071   856-589-5454
                        FAX: 856-582-7611
                e-mail: ppalmer@wmccausland.com
                        www.mosby.com/casemgr.

Tom Strickland, Editor-in-Chief
Nathania Sawyer, Managing Editor
Catherine Mullahy, Editor

$48.00

BiMonthly

6522 Children with Disabilities, 4th Edition

Brookes Publishing
PO Box 10624
Baltimore, MD 21285
410-337-9580
800-638-3775
FAX: 410-337-8539
e-mail: custserv@brookespublishing.com
www.brookespublishing.com

Extensive coverage of genetics, heredity, pre- and postnatal development, specific disabilities, family roles, and intervention. Features chapters on substance abuse, HIV and AIDS, Down syndrome, fragile X syndrome, behavior management, transitions to adulthood, and health care in the 21st century. Also reveals the causes of many conditions that can lead to developmental disabilities. $58.00

960 pages Hardcover 1997
ISBN 1-55766-93-2

6523 Children with Facial Difference

Woodbine House
6510 Bells Mill Road
Bethesda, MD 20817
800-843-7323
www.woodbinehouse.com
Hope Charkins, M.S.W., author

The first guide for parents about their child's congenital craniofacial anomaly - a condition that affects the appearance and function of the head and face. This accessible book discusses conditions such as cleft lip, cleft palate, and Teacher Collins, Apert, and Crouzon syndromes, and more. Parents learn about the diagnostic process, interdisciplinary treatment approach, education, speech and language issues, and how to help their child and family adjust emotionally. $ 16.95

361 pages Paperback
ISBN 0-933149-61-1

6524 Children with Mental Retardation

Woodbine House
6510 Bells Mill Road
Bethesda, MD 20817
800-843-7323
www.woodbinehouse.com
Romayne Smith, M.A., CCC-SLP, author

A book for parents of children with mild to moderate mental retardation, whether or not they have a diagnosed syndrome or condition. It provides a complete and compassionate introduction to their child's medical, therapeutic, and educational needs, and discusses the emotional impact on the family. New parents can rely on Children with Mental Retardation to provide that solid foundation and confidence they need to help their child reach his or her highest potential. $14.95

437 pages Paperback
ISBN 0-933149-39-5

6525 Conditional Love: Parents' Attitudes Toward Handicapped Children

Greenwood Publishing Group
88 Post Road West
5007
Westport, CT 06880
203-226-3571
www.greenwood.com

Offers parents information on understanding disabled children and mainstreaming them into their normal family life. $49.95

312 pages
ISBN 0-89789-24-7

6526 Coordinacion De Servicios Centrado En La Familia

Brookline Books
PO Box 1047
Cambridge, MA 02238
617-868-0360
800-666-2665
FAX: 617-868-1772
e-mail: brooklinebks@delphi.com
www.brooklinebooks.com
Iren Zipper, C Hinton, M. Weil, K. Rounds, author

This book, translated into Spanish from the English original, is designed to orient and educate parents about issues of service coordination, to assist families in caring for an infant or toddler with developmental delays or disabilities. $7.00

34 pages Paperback
ISBN 0-91479-90-5

6527 Counselling Parents of Children with Chronic Illness or Disability

Brookes Publishing
PO Box 10624
Baltimore, MD 21285
410-337-9580
800-638-3775
FAX: 410-337-8539
e-mail: custserv@brookespublishing.com
www.brookespublishing.com
Hilton Davis, Ph.D., author
$23.00

144 pages Paperback
ISBN 1-85433-91-8

6528 Creative Play Activities for Children with Disabilities

Human Kinetics
PO Box 5076
Champaign, IL 61825
800-747-4457
FAX: 217-351-2674
e-mail: orders@hkusa.com
www.humankinetics.com
Lisa Rappaport Morris MS and Linda Schultz, MS, Ed, author

Contains 250 games and activities designed to help children with all types of disabilities grow through play. Each chapter focuses on a particular world or activity theme. Themes include exploring the world of the senses, active games, building and creating, imaginative outdoor fun and water play, and group games and activities. $16.95

232 pages
ISBN 0-873229-33-9

6529 Deciphering the System: a Guide for Familes of Young Disabled Children

Brookline Books
PO Box 1047
Cambridge, MA   02238   617-868-0360
                               800-666-2665
                          FAX: 617-868-1772
          e-mail: brooklinebks@delphi.com
                  www.brooklinebooks.com

Paula J. Beckman and Gayla Beckman Boyes, author

This book helps parents of children with disabilities to understand the system that provides services to their child. Co-written by a professional and a parent, this book includes a glossary with professional jargons and an extensive list of resources. *$14.95*

208 pages Paperback
ISBN 0-91479 -87-5

6530 Delicate Threads

Woodbine House
6510 Bells Mill Road
Bethesda, MD   20817
                               800-843-7323
                  www.woodbinehouse.com

Debbie Staub, author

How do friendships between children with and without disabilities develop? How do they compare to friendships between typically developing children? What happens to these friendships over time? In Delicate Threads, author Debbie staub helps to answer these questions through careful observations of friendships between seven pairs of children - each including a child with a moderate to severe disability - who are classmates in an inclusive Pacific Northwest elementary school. *$16.95*

250 pages Paperback
ISBN 0-933149-90-5

6531 Detecting Your Hidden Allergies

Professional Books; Future Health
Jackson, TN

William G. Crook, M.D., author

Gives specific instructions on how to use an elimination diet to determine food allergies.

6532 Developing Personal Safety Skills in Children with Disabilities

Brookes Publishing
PO Box 10624
Baltimore, MD   21285   410-337-9580
                               800-638-3775
                          FAX: 410-337-8539
          e-mail: custserv@brookespublishing.com
                  www.brookespublishing.com

Freda Briggs, M.A., author

A guide for teachers, parents, and caregivers, this volume explores the issue of personal safety for children with disabilities and offers strategies for empowering and protecting them at home and in school. Recognizing that children with disabilities are vulnerable to abuse, this work explores why children with disabilities need personal safety skills, offers, curriculum ideas and exercises, and advocates the development of self-esteem and assertiveness so that children can protect themselves. *$34.00*

220 pages Paperback
ISBN 1-557661-84-7

6533 Developmental Disabilities in Infancy and Childhood, 2nd Edition

Brookes Publishing
PO Box 10624
Baltimore, MD   21285   410-337-9580
                               800-638-3775
                          FAX: 410-337-8539
          e-mail: custserv@brookespublishing.com
                  www.brookespublishing.com

This two volume set explores advances in assessment and treatment, retains a clinical focus, and incorporates recent developments in research and theory. Can be purchased individually or as a set (Vol. 1: Neurodevelopmental Diagnosis and Treatment Vol. 2: The Spectrum of Developmental Disabilities). *$210.00*

Hardcover
ISBN 1-55766O-CA-P

6534 Dictionary of Developmental Disabilities Terminology

Brookes Publishing
PO Box 10624
Baltimore, MD   21285   410-337-9580
                               800-638-3775
                          FAX: 410-337-8539
          e-mail: custserv@brookespublishing.com
                  www.brookespublishing.com

Pasquale J. Accardo, M.D., author

Answers thousands of questions for medical or human services professionals, parents or advocates of children with disabilities, or students preparing for their careers. Provides thorough explanations of the most common terms associated with disabilities. *$55.95*

368 pages Hardcover
ISBN 1-557662-45-2

6535 Dr. Braly's Food Allergy and Nutrition Revolution

Keats Publishing
New Canaan, CT   203-966-8721
                               800-323-4900

James Braly, author

Research on food allergies, testing methods, and a detailed treatment method based upon diet and nutrition; includes treatment protocols for some forty illnesses linked to food allergies.

6536 Dying and Disabled Children: Dealing with Loss and Grief

Haworth Press
10 Alice Street
Binghamton, NY   13904   604-722-5857
                              800-429-6784
                         FAX: 607-722-6362
e-mail: getinfo@haworthpressinc.com
              www.haworthpressinc.com
Harold M. Dick, M.D., author
Jackie Blakeslee, Advertising

In this sensitive and compassionate look at terminally ill and disabled children, professionals from the medical community examine the stresses faced by their parents and siblings. They address the crucial element of communication in dealing with a child's serious illness. Ethical decision making, learning to recognize the child's suffering, and talking to children about death are honestly and clearly discussed. $ 54.95

153 pages Hardcover
ISBN 0-866567-59-3

6537 Everday Social Interaction

Brookes Publishing
PO Box 10624
Baltimore, MD   21285   410-337-9580
                             800-638-3775
                        FAX: 410-337-8539
e-mail: custserv@brookespublishing.com
             www.brookespublishing.com
Vivienne Riches, B.A. Dip.Ed., M.A., M.A.P.s.S., author

Useful strategies for assessing needs and setting objectives, along with helpful teaching techniques, are accompanied by tips on social courtesies, rewards, praise, and criticism. Checklists and task analyses that show how complex skills can be broken down into major components for easy performance monitoring are also included. $41.95

342 pages Paperback
ISBN 1-55766 -58-4

6538 Exceptional Children

Council for Exceptional Children
1920 Association Drive
Reston, VA   20191   703-620-3660
                            888-232-7733
                       FAX: 703-264-9494
                       TDY:703-264-9446
e-mail: service@cec.sped.org
             www.cec.sped.org

Nancy Safer, Executive Director
Articles include research, literature surveys and position papers concerning exceptional children, special education and mainstreaming. $58.00

96 pages BiMonthly

6539 Exceptional Parent Magazine

Psy-Ed Corp
555 Kinderkamack Road
Oradell, NJ   07649   201-634-6550
                            800-EPA-RENT
                       FAX: 201-634-6599
e-mail: epedit@aol.com
             www.eparent.com

Rick Rader, MD, author
Bridget Lyne, Managing Editor

Addresses concerns of raising, treating or teaching children or young adults with disabilities, for parents and professionals. $39.95

100 pages Monthly
ISSN 0046-91 7

6540 Face of Inclusion

Exceptional Parent Library
PO Box 1807
Englewood Cliffs, NJ   10116
                            800-535-1910
                e-mail: eplibrary@aol.com
                    www.eplibrary.com
J. & R. Vargo, author

A unique and moving parents' perspective of inclusion for administrators, teachers, and parents of children with disabilities. $99.00

6541 Failure to Thrive and Pediatric Undernutrition: A Transdisciplinary Approach

Brookes Publishing
PO Box 10624
Baltimore, MD   21285   410-337-9580
                             800-638-3775
                        FAX: 410-337-8539
e-mail: custserv@brookespublishing.com
             www.brookespublishing.com

Offers comprehensive coverage of pediatric undernutrition complete with assessment and intervention techniques. Theoretical as well as practical concerns such as epidemiology, nutrition, medical issues, feeding, families, history, research, and community programs are addressed. A family-centered approach shows practitioners how to enhance treatment by capitalizing on family strengths and acknowledging the impact of larger issues such as culture, social environment, and public policy. $62.95

592 pages Hardcover 1998
ISBN 1-55766 -48-3

6542 Families in Recovery

Brookes Publishing
PO Box 10624
Baltimore, MD   21285   410-337-9580
                             800-638-3775
                        FAX: 410-337-8539
e-mail: custserv@brookespublishing.com
             www.brookespublishing.com
Carolyn Seval Brooks, R.N., author

This book teaches professionals how to use each families strengths to promote recovery. The authors demonstrate effective, family-focused intervention techniques developed in their combined 35 years of practice. Motivational techniques and stress reducers for counselors are also provided. $34.00

352 pages Paperback 1997
ISBN 1-55766 -64-9

6543 Family Interventions Throughout Disability

Springer Publishing Company
536 Broadway
New York, NY   10012   212-431-4370
                       FAX: 212-941-7842

Paul W. Power, author

Family attitudes throughout chronic illness and disability. *$31.95*

320 pages
ISBN 0-82615 -80-4

6544   Family-Centered Service Coordination: A Manual for Parents

Brookline Books
PO Box 1047
Cambridge, MA   02238   617-868-0360
800-666-2665
FAX: 617-868-1772
e-mail: brooklinebks@delphi.com
www.brooklinebooks.com

Irene Zipper, C. Hinton, M. Weil, & K. Rounds, author

A manual designed to orient and educate parents about issues of service coordination, to assist families in caring for an infant or toddler with developmental delays or disabilities. *$7.00*

34 pages Paperback
ISBN 0-91479 -90-5

6545   Focus

American Academy of Biological Dentistry
PO Box 856
Carmel Valley, CA   93924   408-659-5385

Promotes biological dental medicine, which uses non-toxic diagnostic and therapeutic approaches in the field of clinical dentistry.

Quarterly

6546   Free Yourself From Pain

Bresler Center
115 South Topanga Canyon Boulevard
Suite 158
Topanga, CA   90290   310-455-3634

David E. Bresler, author

This self help book for managing chronic pain and depression includes several chapters illustrating the use of guided imagery for pain control.

1992

6547   From the Heart

Exceptional Parent Library
PO Box 1807
Englewood Cliffs, NJ   10116
800-535-1910
e-mail: eplibrary@aol.com
www.eplibrary.com

J.D.B. Marsh, author

Eye-opening narratives based on their parent support process, nine mothers explore the intense, sometimes painful terrain of raising a child with special needs. *$14.95*

6548   Getting Our Heads Together

Thoms Rehabilitation Hospital
68 Sweeten Creek Road
Asheville, NC   28803   828-274-2400
FAX: 828-274-9452

Kathi Petersen, Dir. of Planning & Communication
Edgardo Diez, MD, Medical Director Of Brain Injury
Kathy Price, Director of Admissions

A handbook for families of head injured patients - available in Spanish as well as English. *$4.00*

40 pages Paperback

6549   Giant Steps

Option Institute and Fellowship
2080 S Undermountain Road
Sheffield, MA   01257   413-229-8737
800-562-7171
FAX: 413-229-8737
e-mail: indigo@option.org
www.optionindigo.com

Barry Neil Kaufman, author
Kate Wilde

This book illustrates the powerful, life-changing Option Process Dialogue in action. Barry takes us on a very intimate journey presenting ten uplifting, in-depth portraits of young people engaged in transformative dialogues with him. The reader witnesses moments of extreme crisis involving rape, questions of sexuality, a dying parent, divorce, the prison of drugs as these people learn to break through their pain and triumph in the face of challenge and crisis. *$5.99*

351 pages Paperback
ISBN 0-449215-69-5

6550   God's Special Children

Horizon Publishers
PO Box 490
Bountiful, UT   84011   801-295-9451

K.J. Karren, author

The book is divided into three sections. First: handicapped individuals share their own stories, second: parents give useful insights, third: professional guidance is offered concerning true challenges and encouragements of those individuals. *$14.98*

220 pages Hardbound
ISBN 0-88290 -86-2

6551   Growing Up Gifted

McGraw-Hill, School Publishing
220 East Danieldale Road
DeSoto, TX   75115   972-224-1111
800-442-9685
FAX: 972-228-1982
mhschool.com

A book that develops the potential of children at home and at school.

512 pages

6552 Handbook About Care in the Home

AARP Fulfillment
601 E Street NW
Washington, DC   20049   202-434-2277
800-424-3410
FAX: 202-434-3443
e-mail: member@aarp.org
www.aarp.org

Offers valuable information for the disabled.

24 pages

6553 Happiness is a Choice

Ballantine Books
2080 South Undermountain Road
Sheffield, MA   01257   413-229-8737
800-562-7171
FAX: 413-229-8737
e-mail: indigo@option.org
www.optionindigo.com
Barry Neil Kaufman, author
Kate Wilde

Happiness is a Choice represents the cutting edge of Barry Neil Kaufman's evolving teaching, focusing on empowering our moment of change, the moment in which we can make self-acceptance, inner peace, joy and love immediately tangible with these easy-to-use tools. This book takes us step by step on a journey to increase personal power. A book to cherish and to share, a book that will ignite the healing process. $10.95

284 pages Paperback
ISBN 0-449907-99-6

6554 How to Deal with Back Pain and Rheumatoid Joint Pain

Global Health Solutions
Falls Church, VA

Fereydoon Batmanghelidj, M.D., author

The physiology of pain production and its direct relationship to chronic regional dehydration of some joint spaces is explained: Special movements that would create vacuum in the disc spaces and draw water and the displaced discs into the vertebral joints are demonstrated.

6555 Hug Just Isn't Enough

Gallaudet University Bookstore
11030 South Langley Avenue
Chicago, IL   60628   202-651-5488
800-621-2736
FAX: 202-651-5489
Caren Ferris, author

Offers valuable information for the disabled. *$15.95*

94 pages Hardcover

6556 Human Kinetics

1607 North Market Street
PO Box 5076
Champaign, IL   61825   217-351-5076
FAX: 217-351-2674
www.humankinetics.com

6557 I Wish . . .

Exceptional Parent Library
PO Box 1807
Englewood Cliffs, NJ   10116
800-535-1910
e-mail: eplibrary@aol.com
www.eplibrary.com
K.D. McAnaney, author

A book about conflict, courage and creative solutions. *$8.95*

6558 In Time and with Love: Caring for the Special Needs Infant and Toddler, Second Edition

Newmarket Press
18 E 48th Street
New York, NY   10017   212-832-3575
FAX: 212-832-3629
e-mail: sales@newmarketpress.com
www.newmarketpress.com
Marilyn Segal, Ph.D., author
Ellen Simon, Director of Sales

For families and caregivers of preteen and handicapped children in their first three years - more than one hundred tips for adjusting and coping. *$15.95*

208 pages
ISBN 1-557044-45-7

6559 Infant Development and Risk

Brookes Publishing
PO Box 10624
Baltimore, MD   21285   410-337-9585
800-638-3775
FAX: 410-337-8539
e-mail: custserv@brookespublishing.com
www.brookespublishing.com
Anne H. Widerstrom, Ph.D., Barbara A. Mowder, Ph.D, author

Provides a comprehensive overview of typical & atypical development while explaining key assessment issues and intervention programs. Deals head-on with complex and sensitive subjects such as eligibility for services and NICU ethics. *$44.00*

384 pages Paperback 1997
ISBN 1-55766 -69-X

6560 It's All in Your Head

Life Sciences Press
Tacoma, WA

Hal A. Huggins and Sharon A. Huggins, author

Dr. Higgins's critique of the use of mercury, a toxic element and environmental hazard, in dentistry. For those suffering mercury poisoning, the book examines a number of conventional and alternative treatments.

6561 Keys to Parenting a Child with a Learning Disability

Barron's Educational Series
250 Wireless Boulevard
Hauppauge, NY   11788   516-434-3311
800-645-3476
FAX: 516-434-3723
e-mail: info@barronseduc.com
www.barronseduc.com
Barry E. McNamara, Ed.D. and Francine J. McNamara, author
Lonny Stein, Director of Marketing

The authors discuss the diagnosis and treatment of learning disabilities. They provide a practical course of action for parents who suspect a learning disability is present in their child. They also describe methods of special education, dealing with learning disabled children at home, and integrating them into community activities. *$ 6.95*

208 pages Paperback
ISBN 0-812016-79-3

6562 Kids to the Rescue

Alliance for Parental Involvement in Education
PO Box 59
East Chatham, NY   12060   518-392-6900
                                    FAX: 518-392-6900

Lory Freeman, author

Parents and children should read this book together. The author offers children the information they need for fourteen emergency situations. *$7.95*

6563 LifeLines

352 Park Avenue South
Suite 703
New York, NY   10010   212-532-6740
                                  800-995-0066
                             FAX: 212-532-6740
              e-mail: disabledandalone@aol.com
                      www.disabledandalone.org

Life services is a national not-for-profit organization founded in 1988 whose sole purpose is to assure the well being of disabled individuals, particularly those whose families wish to plan for the time when they will no longer be able to provide care.

6564 Little Children, Big Needs

Exceptional Parent Library
PO Box 1807
Englewood Cliffs, NJ   10116
                                    800-535-1910
                     e-mail: eplibrary@aol.com
                               www.eplibrary.com
D. Weinhouse, Ph.D. and M. Weinhouse, M.A., author

Contains candid interviews with fifty families of children with a wide variety of disabilities. *$12.95*

6565 Loving & Letting Go

Centering Corporation
1531 N Saddle Creek Road
Omaha, NE   68104   402-553-1200
                             FAX: 402-533-0507
                          e-mail: j1200@aol.com
                                www.centering.org

Dr. Deborah Davis, author

For parents who decide to turn away from aggressive medical intervention for their critically ill newborn. *$5.95*

48 pages Paperback

6566 Magic Feather

Alliance for Parental Involvement in Education
PO Box 59
East Chatham, NY   12060   518-392-6900
                                    FAX: 519-392-6900

Lori Granger, author

The Grangers were the victims of the special education system. Their son was mistested, mislabeled and more, but their story has a happy ending. *$9.95*

6567 Misunderstood Child

Gallery Bookshop
PO Box 270
Mendocino, CA   95460   707-937-2665

Larry B. Silver, author

A guide for parents with learning disabled children. *$ 8.95*

224 pages Paperback
ISBN 0-07057 -89-5

6568 Mobility Training for People with Disabilities

Charles C. Thomas, Publisher
2600 S 1st Street
Springfield, IL   62704   217-789-8980
                                  800-258-8980
                             FAX: 217-789-9130
                  e-mail: books@ccthomas.com
William Goodman, author

Children and adults with mental, visual, physical and hearing impairments can learn to travel. Also available in cloth for $40.95 (ISBN# 0-398-05572-6) *$28.95*

144 pages Paper
ISBN 0-398063-56-7

6569 Mother to Be: A Guide to Pregnancy and Birth for Women with Disabilities

Demos Medical Publishing
386 Park Avenue South
Suite 201
New York, NY   10016   212-683-0072
                                  800-532-8663
                             FAX: 212-683-0118
                   e-mail: info@demospub.com
Judith Rogers and Molleen Matsumura, author
Dr. Diana M. Schneider, Publisher
Janis Bentley, Customer Service Manager

Provides an in-depth look at every aspect of pregnancy from the disabled woman's perspective, including how to find the best medical care, exercise, nutrition, body changes, fetal development and more. *$29.95*

457 pages Paperback
ISBN 0-93995 -29-9

6570 Mothers Talk About Learning Disabilities

Gallery Bookshop
PO Box 270
Mendocino, CA   95460   707-937-2665

Elizabeth Weiss, author

In this work, the mother of two learning disabled boys seeks to give mothers in similar circumstances encouragement, support and everyday advice. *$17.95*

157 pages
ISBN 0-13502 -70-1

6571 New Language of Toys

Exceptional Parent Library
PO Box 1807
Englewood Cliffs, NJ 07632   201-947-6000
800-535-1910
FAX: 201-947-9376
e-mail: eplibrary@aol.com
www.eplibrary.com
S. Schwartz, Ph.D. & J.E. Heller Miller, M.Ed., author
Ron Richards, Director

An updated and expanded how-to guide for using everyday toys to develop communication skills in children with disabilities and make playtime a fun educational experience. Paperback *$16.95*

6572 No More Allergies

Villiard Books
New York, NY

Gary Null, PhD, author

A detailed investigation into the causes of allergies related both to food and the environment, as well as their link to other illnesses, such as asthma, arthritis, chrinic fatigue syndrome, and diabetes. Also outlines testing methods, treatments, and a diet plan to restore immune function.

6573 No Time for Jello: One Family's Experience

Brookline Books
PO Box 1046
Cambridge, MA 02238   617-868-0360
800-666-2665
FAX: 617-868-1772
e-mail: brooklinebks@delphi.com
www.brooklinebooks.com
Berneen Bratt, author

One family's story of their attempts to remediate and cure the effects of a cerebral palsied condition the oldest son was born with. The Bratts traveled traditional routes, through distinguished medical centers in Boston, and nontraditional routes in a search for treatments that would help their son. *$17.95*

Softcover
ISBN 0-91479 -56-5

6574 Nobody's Perfect: Living and Growing with Children Who Have Special Needs

Brookes Publishing
PO Box 10624
Baltimore, MD 21285   410-337-9580
800-638-3775
FAX: 410-337-8539
e-mail: custserv@brookespublishing.com
www.brookespublishing.com
Nancy B. Miller, Ph.D., M.S.W., author

This book offers parents who have children with special needs a new and positive perspective on the challenges of family life. This book guides parents through the process of adaptation, describing specific strategies for success in balancing one's own life, developing a parenting partnership, and interacting with children, friends, relatives, professionals, and others. *$21.00*

352 pages Paperback
ISBN 1-55766 -43-X

6575 Nutritional Influences on Mental Illness

Third Line Press
Encino, CA

Melvyn Werbach, M.D., author

A comprehensive, professional guide to the current medical research on nutrition and mental illness.

1991

6576 On the Road to Autonomy: Promoting Self-Competence in Children & Youth with Disabilities

Brookes Publishing
PO Box 10624
Baltimore, MD 21285   410-337-9580
800-638-3775
FAX: 410-337-8539
e-mail: custserv@brookespublishing.com
www.brookespublishing.com

This book provides detailed conceptual, practical, and personal information regarding the promotion of self-esteem, self-determination, and coping skills among children and youth with and without disabilities. *$48.00*

432 pages Paperback
ISBN 1-55766 -35-5

6577 One-Two-Three Magic - Effective Discipline for Children 2-12

Child Management
800 Roosevelt Road
Glen Ellyn, IL 60137   630-469-0484
800-442-4453
FAX: 630-469-4571
Thomas W. Phelan, Ph.D., author
Nancy Roe, Office Manager

Time tested program provides easy-to-follow steps for disciplining children ages 2-12 without arguing, yelling or spanking. Excellent for parents, grandparents and teachers. Available on video ($39.95) audio ($24.95), and book ($12.95) *$12.95*

180 pages Paperback
ISBN 0-96338 -61-9

6578 Our Own Road

Aquarius Health Care Videos
5 Powderhouse Lane
PO Box 1159
Sherborn, MA 01770   508-651-2963
FAX: 508-650-4216
e-mail: aqvideos@tiac.net
www.aquariusproductions.com

Leslie Kussmonn, President

This heartwarming video was filmed in Mexico and portrays "The importance of community based rehabilitation". This video shows the disabled helping other people who are disabled and portrays their sense of pride they get from helping others. This multiculture program features many different healing techniques, including "honey and sugar" for wounds. This video teaches about the importance of helping those who are disabled become independent and productive. *$99.00*

6579 Pain Erasure

M. Evans and Company
New York, NY

Bonnie Prudden, author

This book explains Bonnie Prudden's method for pain relief using myotherapy, a method hailed by doctors and patients.

1980

6580 Parent Survival Manual

Exceptional Parent Library
PO Box 1807
Englewood Cliffs, NJ 10116
800-535-1910
e-mail: eplibrary@aol.com
www.eplibrary.com

E. Schopler, Ed., author

A guide to crises resolution in autism and related developmental disorders. *$39.95*

6581 Parent-Child Interaction and Developmental Disabilities

Greenwood Publishing Group
88 Post Road West
5007
Westport, CT 06880
203-226-3571
FAX: 203-222-1502
www.greenwood.com

Kofi Marfo, Editor, author

This volume brings together the original papers by international scholars and practitioners on the question of the effects of parent interaction with developmentally disabled children. $65.00-$69.50.

395 pages Hardcover
ISBN 0-275928-35-7

6582 Parenting

Accent Books & Products
PO Box 700
Bloomington, IL 61702
309-378-2961
800-787-8444
FAX: 309-378-4420
e-mail: acmtlvng@aol.com

Raymond C. Cheever, Publisher
Betty Garee, Editor

Experienced parents (who are disabled) discuss: raising children from infant to teens, balancing career and motherhood, discipline methods and more when both parents are disabled. *$7.95*

83 pages
ISBN 0-91570-26-4

6583 Parents and Young Mentally Handicapped Children

Brookline Books
PO Box 1046
Cambridge, MA 02238
617-868-0360
800-666-2665
FAX: 617-868-1772
e-mail: brooklinebks@delphi.com
www.brooklinebooks.com

Helen McConachie, author

Critically reviews and analyzes the effects of having a developmentally delayed child on the daily life of the family. Examined are the parents' crucial role in their child's development, the part played by other extended family members, parents' attitudes and parents' styles of interaction with their disabled and non-disabled child. *$ 29.95*

Hardcover
ISBN 0-91479-28-X

6584 Perspectives on a Parent Movement

Brookline Books
PO Box 1046
Cambridge, MA 02238
617-868-0360
800-666-2665
FAX: 617-868-1772
e-mail: brooklinebks@delphi.com
www.brooklinebooks.com

Rosemary F. Dybwad, author

This book captures Rosemary Dybwad's truly innovative wisdom and pioneering for people with intellectual limitations in these previously unpublished essays and speeches. *$17.95*

Paperback
ISBN 0-91479-74-3

6585 Power Dialogues

Option Institute and Fellowship
2080 S Undermountain Road
Sheffield, MA 01257
413-229-8737
800-562-7171
FAX: 413-229-8737
e-mail: indigo@option.org
www.optionindigo.com

Barry Neil Kaufman, author
Kate Wilde

Learn our core system for helping others. This key program teaches participants the simple, yet profound principles and practical skills involved in using the Option Process Dialogue. This process consists of a system of nonjudgmental, non-directive questions that enables people to uncover the beliefs that underlie their feelings and behaviors. *$49.95*

301 pages Paperback
ISBN 1-88725-06-4

6586 Promoting Communication in Infants and Young Children: 500 Ways to Succeed

Speech Bin
1965 25th Avenue
Vero Beach, FL 32960
561-770-0007
800-477-3324
FAX: 561-770-0006
www.speechbin.com

Jennifer Quick and Alexandra O'Neal, author

This practical reference for parents, caregivers and professional service providers how to promote communication development in infants and yourn children. Gives down-to-earth information and activities to help your youngest children succeed. It provides step-by-step suggestions for stimulationg children's speech and language skills. Paperback. *$14.95*

6587 Raising Your Child to be Gifted

Brookline Books
PO Box 1047
Cambridge, MA   02238   617-868-0360
                             800-666-2665
                          FAX: 617-868-1772
              e-mail: brooklinebks@delphi.com
                       www.brooklinebooks.com

James R. Campbell, author

Dr. Campbell studied more than 10,000 gifted children in four countries, and found that what they shared most was not IQ, but parents who nurtured their ability and supported their efforts in school. This book explains the underlying principles and strategies these parents used in nurturing their childrens' abilities. *$15.95*

196 pages Paperback
ISBN 1-57129 -00-1

6588 Risk, Resilience, & Prevention: Promoting the Well-Being of All Children

Brookes Publishing
PO Box 10624
Baltimore, MD   21285   410-337-9580
                             800-638-3775
                          FAX: 410-337-8539
          e-mail: custserv@brookespublishing.com
                   www.brookespublishing.com

This book investigates the implications of a primary prevention agenda for policy, practice, and research. Provides an in-depth examination of the increase in teenage pregnancy, school dropout, neglect and abuse, unintentional injury, depression and mental illness, behavior disorders, sexually transmitted disease, and illiteracy. An essential for health care professionals, educators, and administrators, psychologists, school counselors, policy makers, and child services providers. *$34.00*

384 pages Paperback
ISBN 1-55766 -66-9

6589 Rolfing: The Integration of Human Structures

Harper and Row
New York, NY

Ida Rolf, author

The mother of Rolfing explains how, 'once free of the muscular rigidity imposed by past experience, the body structure can be put back into natural alignment with the forces of gravity, a process necessary for physical well-being.

1977

6590 Sexuality and the Developmentally Handicapped

Edwin Mellen Press
PO Box 450
Lewiston, NY   14092

                          FAX: 716-754-4056
                   e-mail: mellen@wzrd.com

Presents the knowledge, attitudes, and skills pertinent to responding to the sexual problems of developmentally handicapped persons, their families and communities. Details fully documented cases, issues concerning the law, and resource materials available. *$89.95*

245 pages Hardcover
ISBN 0-88946 -32-5

6591 Shattered Dreams - Lonely Choices: Birth Parents of Babies with Disabilities

Greenwood Publishing Group
88 Post Road West
5007
Westport, CT   06880   203-226-3571
                          FAX: 203-222-1502
                       www.greenwood.com

Joanne Finnegan, author

Written by a mother who, without warning, gave birth to a boy with Down Syndrome, this book is meant to help parents through the initial shock and the realization that they are not able to care for their child. $29.95-$35.00. *$29.95*

208 pages Hardcover
ISBN 0-897892-86-0

6592 Sibshops: Workshops for Siblings of Children with Special Needs

Brookes Publishing
PO Box 10624
Baltimore, MD   21285   410-337-9580
                             800-638-3775
                          FAX: 410-337-8539
          e-mail: custserv@brookespublishing.com
                   www.brookespublishing.com

Donald Meyer, M.Ed., and Patricia Vadasy, M.P.H., author

Sibshops is a program that brings together 8-to 13-year-old brothers and sisters of children with special needs. The siblings receive support and information in a recreational setting, so they have fun while they learn. *$32.00*

256 pages Paperback
ISBN 1-55766 -69-3

6593 Since Owen, A Parent-to-Parent Guide for Care of the Disabled Child

Special Needs Project
3463 Stat Street
282
Santa Barbara, CA   93105

                          800-333-6867

Charles Callahan, Editor

Against the background of his experience as the parent of a severely disabled young man, Callahan writes conscientiously to other parents. *$16.95*

486 pages

6594 Sleep Better! A Guide to Improving Sleep for Children with Special Needs

Brookes Publishing
PO Box 10624
Baltimore, MD   21285   410-337-9580
                             800-638-3775
                          FAX: 410-337-8539
          e-mail: custserv@brookespublishing.com
                   www.brookespublishing.com

V. Mark Durand, Ph.D., author

This book offers step-by-step, how to instructions for helping children with disabilities get the rest they need. For problems ranging from bedtime tantrums to night waking, parents and caregivers will find a variety of widely tested and easy-to-implement techniques that have already helped hundreds of children with special needs. *$21.95*

288 pages Paperback 1997
ISBN 1-55766 -15-7

6595   Slow Motion/Sea Legs

Aquarius Health Care Videos
5 Powderhouse Lane
PO Box 1159
Sherborn, MA   01770   508-651-2963
                                FAX: 508-650-4216
                    e-mail: aqvideos@tiac.net
                    www.aquariusproductions.com

Leslie Kussmonn, President

Probably the last place you would expect to find a disabled person is flying down a mountain in a bucket...attached to a board. Mario Solis and Carla toll introduce a community where physical limitations need no longer stand in the way of strenuous physical performance... the community of disabled snow skiing *$79.00*

6596   Something's Wrong with My Child!

Charles C. Thomas, Publisher
2600 S 1st Street
Springfield, IL   62704   217-789-8980
                                800-258-8980
                        FAX: 217-789-9130
                e-mail: books@ccthomas.com
Harriet Wallace Rose, author

A straight forward presentation to help professionals and parents to better understand themselves in dealing with the emotionally charged subject of disabled children. Also available in cloth for $46.95 (ISBN# 0-398-06898-4) *$26.95*

210 pages Paperback
ISBN 0-398068-99-2

6597   Sometimes I Get All Scribbly

Exceptional Parent Library
PO Box 1807
Englewood Cliffs, NJ   10116
                            800-535-1910
                e-mail: eplibrary@aol.com
                    www.eplibrary.com
Maurren Bissen Neuville, author

Clinical, educational and emotional information from the point of view of a parent. *$16.00*

6598   Special Kind of Parenting

La Leche League International
PO Box 4079
Schaumburg, IL   60168   847-519-7730
                        FAX: 847-519-0035
                e-mail: JTorgus@llli.org
                    www.lalecheleague.org

Julia Darnell Good, author
Schielany Bautista, Marketing Assistant
Judy Torgus, Publications Director

Disabled children have special needs which challenge their parents' emotional and physical resources. This book guides parents through the problems and helps them discover their disabled child as an individual. The author covers both facts and feelings about handicaps, parents' reactions to the initial diagnosis, the grieving process, and effects on the marriage and the rest of the family. They also provide suggestions for choosing the programs and professionals best suited. *$7.50*

172 pages Softcover
ISBN 0-912500-27-1

6599   Special Parent, Special Child

Exceptional Parent Library
PO Box 1807
Englewood Cliffs, NJ   10116
                            800-535-1910
                e-mail: eplibrary@aol.com
                    www.eplibrary.com
T. Sullivan, author

Offers information for facing the challenges of being a special parent. *$21.95*

Hardcover

6600   Spoiling Childhood: How Well-Meaning Paren ts Are Giving Children Too Much...

Guilford Press
72 Spring Street
New York, NY   10012   212-431-9800
                                800-365-7006
                        FAX: 212-966-6708
                            www.guilford.com

Diane Ehrensaft, PhD, author
$14.95

263 pages Paperback 1999
ISBN 1-572304-50-2

6601   Steps to Independence

Brookes Publishing
PO Box 10624
Baltimore, MD   21285   410-337-9580
                                800-638-3775
                        FAX: 410-337-8539
            e-mail: custserv@brookespublishing.com
                    www.brookespublishing.com
Bruce Baker, author

A resource guide for teaching independent living. Includes sample activities, self-help sources and case examples. *$24.00*

6602 Strategies for Working with Families of Young Children with Disabilities

Brookes Publishing
PO Box 10624
Baltimore, MD 21285   410-337-9580
800-638-3775
FAX: 410-337-8539
e-mail: custserv@brookespublishing.com
www.brookespublishing.com

This text offers useful techniques for collaborating with and supporting families whose youngest members either have a disability or are at risk for developing a disability. The authors address specific issues such as cultural diversity, transitions to new programs, and disagreements between families and professionals. *$33.00*

272 pages Paperback
ISBN 1-55766 -57-6

6603 Strategies for Working with families of Young Children with Disabilities

Brookes Publishing
PO Box 10624
Baltimore, MD 21285   410-337-9580
800-638-3775
FAX: 410-337-8539
e-mail: custserv@brookespublishing.com
www.brookespublishing.com
Paula J. Beckman, PhD, author

Offers useful techniques for collaborating with and supporting families whose youngest members either have disabilities or are at risk for developing disabilities. *$33.00*

272 pages Paperback 1996
ISBN 1-557662-57-6

6604 Taking Care of Arthritis

Harper Perennial
New York, NY

Fred Kantrowicz, M.D., author

A comprehensive overview of the types of arthritis, the factors which them them, and the best methods of treatment.

6605 Talk with Me

2000 M Street
Washington, DC 20007   202-337-5220
FAX: 202-337-8314
e-mail: agbell2@aol.com
www.agbell.org

Ellyn Altman, PhD, author
Donna L Sorken, Executive Director
Elizabeth Quigley, Director of Membership

This book addresses the urgent need to enlighten parents and professionals responsible for the crucial early decisions that affect the speech, language, social, emotional and intellectual development of children who are deaf and hard of hearing. *$22.95*

222 pages Paperback

6606 That's My Child

Exceptional Parent Library
PO Box 1807
Englewood Cliffs, NJ 10116
800-535-1910
e-mail: eplibrary@aol.com
www.eplibrary.com
L. Capper, author

Offers information to help parent successfully navigate the maze of resources and services available for children with special needs. *$12.95*

6607 Tips for Teaching Infants & Toddlers The How-T Behind the Theory of Early Intervention

Speech Bin
1965 25th Avenue
Vero Beach, FL 32960   561-770-0007
800-477-3324
FAX: 561-770-0006
www.speechbin.com
C Weil, E D'Amato, D Benson and F Cagan, author

A pratical multisensory approach to Early Intervention including a whole year's worth of weekly thematic lessons which give children abundant opportunities to see, hear, feel, manipulate, smell and taste. Lessons cover: early concepts, prespeech and language, body image, directionality, fine and gross motor, categories, early acitons, activities just for fun and attributes. Paperback. *$39.95*

6608 To a Different Drumbeat

Alliance for Parental Involvement in Education
PO Box 59
East Chatham, NY 12060   518-392-6900
FAX: 518-392-6900
P. Clarke, author

Parents of special needs children contributed to this book. *$16.95*

6609 Uncommon Fathers

Woodbine House
6510 Bells Mill Road
Bethesda, MD 20817
800-843-7323
www.woodbinehouse.com
Donald V.Meyer, author

Nineteen fathers talk about the life-altering experience of having a child with special needs and offer a welcome, seldom-heard perspective on raising kids with disabilities, including autism, cerebral palsy, and Down syndrome. Uncommon Fathers is the first book for fathers by fathers, but it is also helpful to partners, family, friends, and service providers. *$14.95*

206 pages Paperback
ISBN 0-933149-68-9

6610 Vaccination Social Violence and Criminality: Medical Assault on the American Brain

North Atlantic Books
Berkley, CA

Harris L. Coulter, author

The author argues that vaccination has produced a generation of neurologic defectives and changed the tone and atmosphere of modern society.

1990

6611 **What Works in Children's Mental Health Services? Uncovering Answers to Critical Questions**

Brookes Publishing
PO Box 10624
Baltimore, MD   21285   410-337-9580
                               800-638-3775
                          FAX: 410-337-8539
e-mail: custserv@brookespublishing.com
www.brookespublishing.com

Krista Kutash, Ph.D., and Vestena Robbins Rivera,, author

Provides a comprehensive overview of research on the effectiveness of eight mental health service components in systems of care for children with emotional and behavioral disabilities. *$30.00*

256 pages Paperback
ISBN 1-55766 -54-1

6612 **Why Can't My Child Behave?**

Feingold Association
PO Box 6550
Alexandria, VA   22306   703-768-3287

www.feingold.org

Jane Hersey, author
$22.00

400 pages

6613 **Why Mine?**

Centering Corporation
1531 N Saddle Creek Road
Omaha, NE   68104   402-553-1200
                          FAX: 402-533-0507
                    e-mail: j1200@aol.com
                         www.centering.org

Joy Johnson, author

Offers quotes from parents all across the country on their fears, feelings, marriage, the ill child and other children. *$3.25*

32 pages Paperback

6614 **Without Reason, A Family Copes with Autism**

Books on Special Children
PO Box 305
Congers, NY   10920   845-638-1236
                          FAX: 845-638-0847
                    e-mail: irene@boscbooks.com

Charles Hart, author

The author discovers his son has autism. He delves into problems of the autistic person and explains reasons for their actions. *$20.95*

292 pages Hardcover

6615 **Worst Loss**

Exceptional Parent Library
PO Box 1807
Englewood Cliffs, NJ   10116
                               800-535-1910
                    e-mail: eplibrary@aol.com
                         www.eplibrary.com

Barbra D. Rosof, author

Offers information that can help families heal from the death of a child. *$25.00*

6616 **Yeast Connection**

Professional Books
Jackson, TN

William G. Crook, M.D., author

One of the first and best book giving practicle advice regarding what has come to be known as the candida or yeast problem.

6617 **Your Body's Many Cries for Water**

Global Health Solutions
Falls Church, VA

Fereydoon Batmanghelidj, M.D., author

A fascinating discussion about the importance of water in the body, and how simply increasing the amount of water consumed per day can significantly improve arthritic and other pain conditions.

6618 **Your Child Has a Disability: A Complete Sourcebook of Daily and Medical Care**

Brookes Publishing
PO Box 10624
Baltimore, MD   21285   410-337-9580
                               800-638-3775
                          FAX: 410-337-8539
e-mail: custserv@brookesopublishing.com
www.brookespublishing.com

Mark L. Batshaw, M.D., author

Offers expert advice on a wide range of issues-from finding the right doctor and investigating the medical aspects of a child's condition to learning care techniques and fulfilling education requirements. *$24.95*

368 pages Paperback 1998
ISBN 1-557663-74-2

6619 **Your Child and Health Care**

Exceptional Parent Library
PO Box 1807
Englewood Cliffs, NJ   10116
                               800-535-1910
                    e-mail: eplibrary@aol.com
                         www.eplibrary.com

L.R. Rosenfeld, L.C.S., Ph.D., author

Helps parents negotiate the maze of financial assistance programs, organizations and government services. *$29.00*

6620 **Your Defiant Child: Eight Steps to Better Behavior**

Guilford Press
72 Spring Street
New York, NY   10012   212-431-9800
                               800-365-7006
                          FAX: 212-966-6708
                         www.guilford.com

Russell A. Barkley, PhD, Christine M. Benton, author

Also in cloth at $29.95 (ISBN# 1-57230-405-7) *$14.95*

239 pages Paperback 1998
ISBN 1-572303-21-2

Parenting: Specific Disabilities

6621 Attention-Deficit/Hyperactivity Disorder, What Every Parent Wants to Know

Brookes Publishing
PO Box 10624
Baltimore, MD   21285   410-337-9580
                              800-638-3775
                         FAX: 410-337-8539
         e-mail: custserv@brookespublishing.com
              www.brookespublishing.com
David L. Wodrich, Ph.D., author

New easy-to-understand, non-technical edition helps teachers and parents get accessible answers to their ADHD. *$21.95*

304 pages Paperback 1900
ISBN 1-557663-98-X

6622 Bipolar Disorders: A Guide to Helping Children & Adolescents

Patient-Centered Guides
101 Morris Street
Sebastopol, CA   95472   707-829-0515
                               800-998-9938
                          FAX: 800-997-9901
              e-mail: order@oreilly.com
                 www.patientcenters.com
Mitzi Waltz, author
Linda Lamb, Editor
Shawnde Paull, Marketing

A million children and adolescents in the U.S. may have childhood-onset bipolar disorder, including an estimated 23 percent of those currently diagnosed with ADHD. Bipolar Disorders helps parents and professionals recognize, treat, and cope with bipolar disorders in children and adolescents. It covers diagnosis, family life, medications, talk therapies, other interventions (improving sleep patterns, diet, preventing seasonal mood swings), insurance, and school. *$24.95*

458 pages Paperback
ISBN 1-565926-56-0

6623 Can't Your Child See? A Guide for Parents of Visually Impaired Children

Pro-Ed
8700 Shoal Creek Boulevard
Austin, TX   78757
                          FAX: 512-451-8542
                     e-mail: proed1@aol.com
Eileen Scott, James Jan, Roger Freeman, author

This second edition offers parents optimistic, practical guidelines for helping visually impaired children reach their full potential. *$26.00*

279 pages Paperback
ISBN 0-89079-04-1

6624 Cancer Clinical Trials: Experimental Treatments and How They Can Help You

Patient-Centered Guides
101 Morris Street
Sebastopol, CA   95472   707-829-0515
                               800-998-9938
                          FAX: 707-829-0104
                    www.patientcenters.com
Robert Finn, author
Linda Lamb, Editor
Shawnde Paull, Marketing

Most cancer patients face treatment options that are less than ideal, whether because of a risk of recurrence or side effects. Finally, however, basic research on cell biology is leading to promising new treatments. If you are not evaluating potential experimental treatments alongside the standard treatment protocols, you aren't considering all the facts you need. Cancer Clinical Trials guide you through understanding your options and finding and considering experimental treatments. *$14.95*

222 pages Paperback
ISBN 1-565925-66-1

6625 Caring for Children with Cerebral Palsy: A Team Approach

Brookes Publishing
PO Box 10624
Baltimore, MD   21285   410-337-9580
                              800-638-3775
                         FAX: 410-337-8539
         e-mail: custserv@brookespublishing.com
              www.brookespublishing.com

A guide to the interdisciplinary care of children with cerebral palsy. Delivers detailed information on a multitude of issues relevant to treatment and supports. *$38.95*

496 pages Paperback 1998
ISBN 1-55766-22-X

6626 Childhood Cancer Survivors: A Practical Guide to Your Future

Patient-Centered Guides
101 Morris Street
Sebastopol, CA   95472   707-829-0515
                               800-998-9938
                          FAX: 707-829-0104
                    www.patientcenters.com
Nancy Keene, Wendy Hobbie & Kathy Ruccione, author
Linda Lamb, Editor
Shawnde Paull, Marketing

More than 250,000 people have survived childhood cancer - a cause for celebration. Authors Keene, Hobbie, and Ruccione chart the territory of long-term survivorship: relationships; overcoming employment or insurance discrimination; maximizing health; follow-up schedules; medical late effects. The stories of over sixty survivors - their challenges and triumphs - are told. Includes medical history record-keeper. *$27.95*

510 pages Paperback
ISBN 1-565924-60-6

6627 Childhood Cancer: A Parent's Guide to Solid Tumor Cancers

Patient-Centered Guides
101 Morris Street
Sebastopol, CA   95472   707-829-0515
                                    800-998-9938
                                    FAX: 707-829-0104
                                    www.patientcenters.com
Honna Janes-Hodder & Nancy Keene, author
Linda Lamb, Editor
Shawnde Paull, Marketing

Childhood Cancer: A Parent's Guide to Solid Tumor Cancers features a wealth of resources for parents of children with solid tumor cancers, plus many stories of veteran parents. Parents will encounter medical facts simply explained, practical advice to ease their daily lives, and tools to be strong advocates for their child. Includes a passport to record patient's medical history. *$24.95*

> *537 pages Paperback*
> *ISBN 1-565925-31-9*

6628 Childhood Leukemia: A Guide for Families, Friends & Caregivers

Patient-Centered Guides
101 Morris Street
Sebastopol, CA   95472   707-829-0515
                                    800-998-9938
                                    FAX: 707-829-0104
                                    www.patientcenters.com
Nancy Keene, author
Linda Lamb, Editor
Shawnde Paull, Marketing

The second edition of this comprehensive guide offers detailed and precise medical information for parents that includes day-to-day practical advice on how to cope with procedures, hospitalization, family and friends, school, and social, emotional, and financial issues. It features a wealth of tools for prents and contains significant updates on treatments and procedures. *$24.95*

> *513 pages Paperback*
> *ISBN 1-565926-32-3*

6629 Children with Autism

Woodbine House
6510 Bells Mill Road
Bethesda, MD   20817
                                    800-843-7323
                                    www.woodbinehouse.com
Michael D. Powers, author

Recommended as the first book parents should read, this volume offers information and a complete introduction to autism, while easing the family's fears and concerns as they adjust and cope with their child's disorder. *$17.95*

> *368 pages Paperback*
> *ISBN 0-933149-16-6*

6630 Choosing a Wheelchair: A Guide for Optimal Independence

Patient-Centered Guides
101 Morris Street
Sebastopol, CA   95472   707-829-0515
                                    800-294-4747
                                    FAX: 800-997-9901
                                    e-mail: order@oreilly.com
                                    www.patientcenters.com
Gary Karp, author
Linda Lamb, Editor
Shawnde Paull, Marketing

With the right wheelchair, quality of life increases dramatically and even people with severe disabilities can have a considerable degree of independence and activity. Choosing the wrong chair can indeed the tantamount to confinement. This book describes technology, options, and the selection process to help you identify the chair than can provide you with optimal independence. *$9.95*

> *186 pages Paperback*
> *ISBN 1-565924-11-8*

6631 Educational Rights for Children with Arthritis: A Parents Manual

AJAO
1314 Spring Street NW
Atlanta, GA   30309   404-872-7100

A self-instructional manual helping parents to identify and obtain school services needed by their child with arthritis. Covers laws and special services, explores strategies for working with school personnel and stresses good communication and advocacy techniques. *$ 10.00*

6632 Helping Your Hyperactive - Attention Deficit Child

Prima Publishing
Box 1260
Rocklin, CA   95677   916-624-5718

John F. Taylor, author
$19.95

> *ISBN 1-559584-23-8*

6633 If Your Child Has Diabetes: An Answer Book for Parents

Putnam Publishing Group
200 Madison Avenue
New York, NY   10016   212-889-6330

Joanne Elliott, author

Provides information and recommendations for parents of children with diabetes on subjects such as school, recreation, medical and life insurance and employment as well as general information about diabetes. *$9.95*

6634 If Your Child Stutters: A Guide for Parents

Stuttering Foundation of America
PO Box 11749
Memphis, TN 38111   901-452-7343
     800-992-9392
e-mail: stuttersfa@aol.com
www.stuttersfa.org

A guide that enables parents to provide appropriate help to children who stutter. *$1.00*

6635 Keys to Parenting a Child with Attention Deficit Disorder

Barron's Educational Series
250 Wireless Boulevard
Hauppauge, NY 11788   516-434-3311
     800-645-3476
FAX: 516-434-3723
e-mail: info@barronsedu.com
www.barronseduc.com

Barry E. and Francine J. McNamara, authorLonny Stein , Director of Marketing

This book shows how to work with the child's school, effectively manage the child's behavior and act as the child's advocate. *$6.95*

160 pages Paperback
ISBN 0-812014-59-6

6636 Keys to Parenting a Child with Autism

Barron's Educational Series
250 Wireless Boulevard
Hauppauge, NY 11788   516-434-3311
     800-645-3476
FAX: 516-434-3723
e-mail: barrons@barronsedu.com
www.barronseduc.com

Marlene Targ Brill, author

Parents of children with autism will find a solid balance between home and practical information in this book. It explains what autism is and how it is diagnosed, then advises parents on how to adjust to their child and give the best care. *$6.95*

208 pages Paperback
ISBN 0-812016-79-3

6637 Keys to Parenting a Child with Cerebral Palsy

Barron's Educational Series
250 Wireless Boulevard
Hauppauge, NY 11788   516-434-3311
     800-645-3476
FAX: 516-434-3723
e-mail: info@barronsedu.com
www.barronseduc.com

Jane F. Leonard, Sheri L. Cadenhead, author
Margaret E Myers, Author

This volume helps parents adjust to the challenge of having a child with cerebral palsy. It stresses the child's potential and encourages independence. Facets of the child's total well-being are discussed, including common health problems, physical, mental and social development, therapy, and new trends in medical management. *$6.95*

Paperback
ISBN 0-764100-91-2

6638 Keys to Parenting a Child with Down's Syndrome

Barron's Educational Series
250 Wireless Boulevard
Hauppauge, NY 11788   516-434-3311
     800-645-3476
FAX: 516-434-3723
e-mail: info@barronsedu.com
www.barronseduc.com

Marlene Targ Brill, author
Lonny Stein, Director of Marketing

Down Syndrome poses many challenges for children and their families. This book prepares parents and guardians to raise a child with Down Syndrome by discussing adjustment, advocacy, health and behavior, education and planning for greater independence. *$5.95*

160 pages Paperback
ISBN 0-812014-58-8

6639 Keys to Parenting the Child with Autism

Autism Society of North Carolina Bookstore
505 Oberlin Road
Suite 230
Raleigh, NC 27605   919-743-0204
     800-442-2762
FAX: 919-743-0208
e-mail: ASNC@aol.com
www.autismsociety-nc.org

Marlene Targ Brill, author

This book explains what autism is and how it is diagnosed. *$6.95*

6640 Legislative Handbook for Parents

NAPVI
PO Box 317
Watertown, MA 02272
     800-562-6265

E.E. Castillo, author

Written by parents for parents in dealing with Legislative Processes that ultimately affect their children's lives. *$5.50*

24 pages Paperback

6641 Life on Wheels: For the Active Wheelchair User

Patient-Centered Guides
101 Morris Street
Sebastopol, CA 95472   707-829-0515
     800-294-4747
FAX: 800-997-9901
e-mail: order@oreilly.com
www.patientcenters.com

Gary Karp, author
Linda Lamb, Editor
Shawnde Paull, Marketing

For 1.5 million Americans, life includes a wheelchair for mobility. Life on Wheels is for people who want to take charge of their life experience. Author Gary Karp describes medical issues (paralysis, circulation, rehab, cure research); day-to-day living (exercise, skin, bowel and bladder, sexuality, home access, maintaining a wheelchair); and social issues (self-image, adjustment, friends, family, cultural attitudes, activism). *$24.95*

573 pages Paperback
ISBN 1-565922-53-0

6642 Non-Hodgkin's Lymphomas: Making Sense of Diagnosis, Treatment & Options

O'Reilly
101 Morris Street
Sebastopol, CA 95472 707-829-0515
800-294-4747
FAX: 800-997-9901
e-mail: order@oreilly.com
www.patientcenters.com

Lorraine Johnston, author

$24.95

580 pages Paperback
ISBN 1-565924-44-4

6643 Not Deaf Enough: Raising a Child Who is Hard of Hearing

3417 Volta Place NW
Washington, DC 20007 202-337-5220
FAX: 202-337-8314
TDY:202-337-5220
e-mail: agbell2@aol.com

Patricia Ann Morgan Candlish, author
Elizabeth Quigley, Director Mem/Mht

This sensitive book portrays a family's struggle to identify accept, and support their youngest child through his diagnosis of mild to moderate hearing loss. This book provides a much needed overview of this under-diagnosed and under-served disability. *$24.95*

242 pages Paperback

6644 Obsessive-Compulsive Disorder: Help for Children and Adolescents

Patient-Centered Guides
101 Morris Street
Sebastopol, CA 95472 707-829-0515
800-998-9938
FAX: 707-829-0104
www.patientcenters.com

Mitzi Waltz, author
Linda Lamb, Editor
Shawnde Paull, Marketing

Obsessive-compulsive disorders (OCD) is one of the most common psychiatric problems faced by children. Childhood OCD can be a truly debilitating disability, not just a minor problem or personality quirk. The good news is that it is very treatable. Obsessive-Compulsive Disorder helps parents secure a diagnosis, manage family life, understand medical interventions, explore therapeutic interventions, get care within their existing healthcare plan, and navigate the special education system. *$24.95*

400 pages Paperback
ISBN 1-565927-58-3

6645 Parent's Guide to Allergies and Asthma

National Allergy and Asthma Network
3554 Chain Bridge Road
Suite 200
Fairfax, VA 22030 703-385-4403
FAX: 703-352-4354

Marion Steinmann, author

A up-to-date, easy-to-read resource offering essential information on asthma and allergies.

6646 Parent's Guide to Autism

Autism Society of North Carolina Bookstore
505 Oberlin Road
Suite 230
Raleigh, NC 27605 919-743-0204
800-442-2762
FAX: 919-743-0208
e-mail: ASNC@aol.com
www.autismsociety-nc.org

Charles A. Hart, author

An essential handbook for anyone facing autism. *$14.00*

6647 Parent's Guide to Down Syndrome: Toward a Brighter Future: 2nd Edition

Brookes Publishing
PO Box 10624
Baltimore, MD 21285 410-337-9580
800-638-3775
FAX: 410-337-8539
e-mail: custserv@brookespublishing.com
www.brookespublishing.com

Siegfried M. Pueschel, M.D., Ph.D., M.P.H., author

Highlights developmental stages and shows the advances that improve a child's quality of life. Includes discussions on easing the transition from home to school and choosing integration and curricular priorities, as well as guidelines for confronting adolescent and adult issues such as social and sexual needs and independent living and vocational options. *$22.95*

336 pages Paperback
ISBN 1-55766 -60-3

6648 Parents Helping Parents: A Directory of Support Groups for ADD

Novartis Pharmaceuticals Division
Customer Response Literature Dept.
59 Route 10
East Hanover, NJ 07936
800-742-2422

6649 Pervasive Developmental Disorders; Finding a Diagnosis and Getting Help

Patient-Centered Guides
101 Morris Street
Sebastopol, CA 95472 707-829-0515
800-998-9938
FAX: 707-829-0104
www.patientcenters.com

Mitzi Waltz, author
Linda Lamb, Editor
Shawnde Paull, Marketing

This unique book encompasses both the practical aspects as well as ther personal stories and emotional facets of living with PDD-NOS, the most common pervasive developmental disorder. Parents of an undiagnosed child may suspect many things, from autism to servere allergies. Pervasive Developmental Disorders is for parents (or newly diagnosed adults) who struggle with this neurological condition that profoundly impacts the life of child and family. *$24.95*

580 pages Paperback
ISBN 1-565925-30-0

6650 Preschool Learning Activities for the Visually Impaired Child

NAPVI
PO Box 317
Watertown, MA   02272

800-562-6265

Illinois Department Of Education, author

This guide for parents offers games and activities to keep visually impaired children active during the pre-school years. *$9.50*

91 pages Paperback

6651 Reaching the Autistic Child, 2nd Edition A Parent Training Program

Brookline Books/Lumen Editions
PO Box 1047
Cambridge, MA   02238   617-868-0360
                                800-666-2665
                         FAX: 617-868-1772
            e-mail: brooklinebks@delphi.com

Martin Kozloff, author

Detailed case studies of social and behavioral change in autistic children and their families show parents how to implement the principles for improved socialization and behavior. *$15.95*

Softcover
ISBN 1-571290-56-7

6652 Retarded Isn't Stupid, Mom! Revised Edition

Brookes Publishing
PO Box 10624
Baltimore, MD   21285   410-337-9580
                                800-638-3775
                         FAX: 410-337-8539
      e-mail: custserv@brookespublishing.com
             www.brookepublishing.com

Sandra Z. Kaufman, author

Sandra Kaufman reveals the feelings of denial, guilt, frustration and eventual acceptance that resulted in a determination to help her daughter, Nicole, live an independent life. This edition, revised on the 10th anniversary of the book's original publication, adds a "progress report" that updates readers on Nicole's adult years and reflects on the revolutionary changes in society's attitudes toward people with disabilities since Nicole's birth. *$22.95*

272 pages Paperback 1999
ISBN 1-557663-78-5

6653 Show Me How: A Manual for Parents of Preschool Blind Children

American Foundation for the Blind/AFB Press
PO Box 1020
Sewickley, PA   15143   412-741-1142
                                800-232-3044
                         FAX: 412-741-0609
          e-mail: afborders@abdintl.com
                        www.afb.org

Mary Brennan, author

A practical guide for parents, teachers and others who help preschool children attain age-related goals. Covers issues on playing precautions, appropriate toys and facilitating relationships with playmates. Paperback. *$12.95*

56 pages
ISBN 0-891281-13-4

6654 Signing Family: What Every Parent Should Know About Sign Communication

Gallaudet University Press
11030 S Langley Avenue
Chicago, IL   60628

800-621-2736
FAX: 800-621-8476
TDY:800-621-9347
gupress.gallaudet.edu

David A. Stewart, Co-Author
Barbara Luetke-Stahlman, Co-Author

This reader-friendly book shows parents how to create a set of goals around the communication needs of their deaf child. Describes in even-handed terms the major signing options available, from American Sign Language to Signed English. *$24.95*

192 pages Softcover

6655 Special Child

Brookes Publishing
PO Box 10624
Baltimore, MD   21285   410-337-9580
                                800-638-3775
                         FAX: 410-337-8539
      e-mail: custserv@brookesopublishing.com
             www.brookespublishing.com

Siegfried M. Pueschel, M.D., PhD, M.P.H., author
Patricia S. Scola, M.D., M.P.H., Author
E. Weidenman, PhD, Author
James C. Bernier, A.C.S.W, Author

Includes specifics on the detection, prognosis and treatment of various conditions as well as detailed information on education, intervention, advocacy, financial planning and technological advances that may affect the lives of children with special needs. *$29.95*

464 pages Paperback 1995
ISBN 1-557661-67-7

6656 Taking Charge of ADHD

Guilford Press
72 Spring Street
New York, NY   10012   212-431-9800
                                800-365-7006
                         FAX: 212-966-6708
                         www.guilford.com

Russell A. Barkley, PhD, author

Revised and updated to incorporate the most current information on ADHD and its treatment. Provides parents with the knowledge, guidance and confidence they need to ensure that their child receives the best care possible. Also in cloth at $37.95 (ISBN# 1-57230-600-9 *$18.95*

311 pages Paperback 1900
ISBN 1-572305-60-6

6657 Teaching Your Child with Motor Delays

Exceptional Parent Library
PO Box 1807
Englewood Cliffs, NJ   10116

800-535-1910
e-mail: eplibrary@aol.com
www.eplibrary.com

M. Hanson and S. Harris, author

Provides information to parents on how motor development influences other areas of development. *$29.00*

6658 **We Can: A Guide for Parents of Children with Arthritis**

AJAO
1330 W Peachtree Street
Atlanta, GA 30309   404-872-7100

Offers parents tips for daily living and practical points for helping their child toward independent adulthood. *$4.58*

6659 **You and Your ADD Child**

Nelson Publications
One Gateway Plaza
Port Chester, NY 10573   914-937-8400

Paul Warren & Judy Capehart, author

$12.99

252 pages Paperback
ISBN 0-785278-95-8

6660 **You and Your Deaf Child: A Self-Help Guide for Parents of Deaf and Hard of Hearing Children**

Gallaudet University Press
11030 S Langley Avenue
Chicago, IL 60628

                        800-621-2736
                   FAX: 800-621-8476
                   TDY:800-621-9347
                   gupress.gallaudet.edu
John Adams, author

The classic self-instructional guide has been completely written with more information dealing with feelings, communication and other issues. Includes worksheets and practice exercises. *$19.95*

224 pages Softcover

6661 **Your Child in the Hospital: A Practical Guide for Parents**

Patient-Centered Guides
101 Morris Street
Sebastopol, CA 95472   707-829-0515
                               800-998-9938
                        FAX: 707-829-0104
                   www.patientcenters.com
Nancy Keene & Rachel Prentice, author
Linda Lamb, Editor
Shawnde Paull, Marketing

This book offers advice from dozens of veteran parents on how to cope with a child's hospitalization, relieving anxious parents so they can help dispel their child's fears and concerns. Parents will find easy-to-read tips on preparing their child, handling procedures without trauma, and preventing insurance snafus. The second edition features a journal to help open communication and give the child a measure of control over the experience. *$11.95*

166 pages Paperback
ISBN 1-565925-73-4

Parenting: School

6662 **ADHD in Schools: Assessment and Intervention Strategies**

Guilford Publications
72 Spring Street
New York, NY 10012   212-431-9800
                             800-365-7006
                        FAX: 212-966-6708
                   e-mail: info@guilford.com
George J. DuPaul and Gary Stoner, author

This landmark volume emphasizes the need for a team effort among parents, community-based professionals, and educators. Provides practical information for educators that is based on empirical findings. Chapters focus on: how to identify and assess students who might have ADHD; the relationship between ADHD and learning disabilities; how to develop and implement classroom-based programs; communication strategies to assist physicians; and the need for community-based treatments. *$30.00*

269 pages Hardcover
ISBN 0-898622-45-0

6663 **Adapted Physical Education for Students with Autism**

Charles C. Thomas, Publisher
2600 South 1st Street
Springfield, IL 62704   217-789-8980
                                800-258-8980
                        FAX: 217-789-9130
                   e-mail: books@ccthomas.com
Kimberly Davis, author

Focuses on the physical education, needs and curriculum for autistic children. Available in cloth, paperback and hardcover. Also available in cloth for $36.95 (ISBN# 0-398-05688-9) *$23.95*

142 pages Paper
ISBN 0-398060-85-1

6664 **Adapting Instruction for the Mainstream: A Sequential Approach to Teaching**

McGraw-Hill, School Publishing
220 East Danieldale Road
DeSoto, TX 75115   972-224-1111
                           800-442-9685
                    FAX: 972-228-1982
                    mhschool.com

This text gives both regular and special education teachers everything they need to help mildly handicapped students succeed in the mainstream.

226 pages

6665 **Attention Deficit Disorders: Assessment & Teaching**

Brooks/Cole Publishing Company
511 Forest Lodge
Pacific Grove, CA 93950   408-373-0728
                            FAX: 408-375-6414
                   e-mail: bc-info@brookscole.com
                   www.brookscole.com

Janet W. Lerner, et al., author

A handy resource that offers teachers, school psychologists, councelors, social workers, administrators, and parents practical advice for working with children who have attention deficit disorders. *$18.95*

258 pages Paperback
ISBN 0-534250-44-0

6666 Carolina Curriculum for Infants and Toddlers with Special Needs, 2nd Edition

Brookes Publishing
PO Box 10624
Baltimore, MD 21285   410-337-9580
                             800-638-3775
                        FAX: 410-337-8539
e-mail: custserv@brookespublishing.com
www.brookespublishing.com
Nancy M. Johnson-Martin, Ph.D., author

This book includes detailed assessment and intervention sequences, daily routine integration strategies, sensorimotor adaptations, and a sample 24-page Assessment Log that shows readers how to chart a child's individual progress. *$41.95*

384 pages Spiral-bound
ISBN 1-557660-74-3

6667 Carolina Curriculum for Preschoolers with Special Needs

Brookes Publishing
PO Box 10624
Baltimore, MD 21285   410-337-9580
                             800-638-3775
                        FAX: 410-337-8539
e-mail: custserv@brookespublishing.com
www.brookespublishing.com
Nancy M. Johnson-Martin, Ph.D., author

This curriculum provides detailed teaching and assessment techniques, plus a sample 28-page Assessment Log that shows readers how to chart a child's individual progress. This guide is for children between 2 and 5 in their developmental stages who are considered at risk for developmental delay or who exhibit special needs. *$35.95*

352 pages Spiral-bound
ISBN 1-557660-32-8

6668 Children and Youth Assisted by Medical Technology in Educational Settings: 2nd Edition

Brookes Publishing
PO Box 10624
Baltimore, MD 21285   410-337-9580
                             800-638-3775
                        FAX: 410-337-8539
e-mail: custserv@brookespublishing.com
www.brookespublishing.com

Guidelines for Care, 2nd Edition. Contains detailed daily care guidelines and emergency-response techniques, including information on working with a range of students who have the HIV infection, that rely on ventilators, that utilize tube feeding, or require catheterization. Also covers every aspect of planning for inclusive classrooms, including information on personnel training, entrance planning and transition, legal requirements, and transportation issues. *$52.00*

432 pages Spiral-bound 1997
ISBN 1-55766 -36-3

6669 Children, Problems and Guidelines

Slosson Educational Publications
PO Box 280
East Aurora, NY 14052   716-625-0930
                               888-756-7766
                          FAX: 800-655-3840
e-mail: slosson@slosson.com
www.slosson.com
LaDeane Casey, author

Dr. Casey's book is a professional and responsible resource book which addresses many of the most common problems involving children and their homes or schools. Student achievement is very sensitive to home environments, family structure, emotional state, drugs and alcohol usage, and pressures from a great number of sources. Information relevant to answering questions or concerns is provided for dozens of common but devastating problems such as dicipline, study skills, and school behavior. *$39.00*

6670 Choosing Outcomes and Accommodations for Children (COACH) 2nd Edition

Brookes Publishing
PO Box 10624
Baltimore, MD 21285   410-337-9580
                             800-638-3775
                        FAX: 410-337-8539
e-mail: custserv@brookespublishing.com
www.brookespublishing.com
Michael F. Giangreco, Ph.D., author

A guide to educational planning for students with disabilities, second edition. Focuses on life outcomes such as social relationships and participation in typical home, school, and community activities. *$37.95*

400 pages Spiral bound 1997
ISBN 1-55766 -23-8

6671 Cognitive Strategy Instruction That Really Improves Children's Academic Skills

Brookline Books
PO Box 1046
Cambridge, MA 02238   617-868-0360
                             800-666-2665
                        FAX: 617-868-1772
e-mail: brooklinebks@delphi.com
www.brooklinebooks.com

Michael Pressley, Series Editor

A concise and focused work that summarily presents the few procedures for teaching strategies that aid academic subject matter learning: decoding reading comprehension, vocabulary, math, spelling and writing. Learning unrelated facts and science. Completely revised in 1995. *$27.95*

Paperback
ISBN 1-571290-07-9

6672 College Admissions: A Guide for Homeschoolers

Alliance for Parental Involvement in Education
PO Box 59
East Chatham, NY 12060   518-392-6900
                           FAX: 518-392-6900
Judy Gelner, author

The author's son was educated at home through junior and senior high school without much imposed structure. *$7.50*

6673 Complete IEP Guide: How to Advocate for Your Special Ed Child

NOLO
950 Parker Street
Berkeley, CA 94710   510-549-1976
800-955-4775
FAX: 510-548-5902
www.nolo.com

Attorney Lawrence M. Siegel, author
Maira Dizgalvis, Trade Customer Service Manager
Susan McConnell, Director of Sales
Natasha Kaluza, Sales Assistant

This book has all the plain-English suggestions, strategies, resources and forms to develop an effective IEP. *$24.95*

300 pages paperback
ISBN 0-873376-07-2

6674 Directory of College Facilities and Services for People with Disabilities

ORYX Press
4041 N Central Avenue
Suite 700
Phoenix, AZ 85012   602-265-2651
800-279-6799
FAX: 800-279-4663
e-mail: info@oryxpress.com
www.oryxpress.com

William E. Burgess, author

Each profile in this guide reveals a complete picture of each campus facility, including the accessibility of classrooms, labs studios, dorms, dining facilities, gyms, student unions, libraries, and other buildings. Clearly noted are the levels of degree(s) granted, the number of students with disabilities enrolled, and the disability category represented. *$125.00*

Paperback
ISBN 0-89774 -94-8

6675 Exceptional Children in Focus

McGraw-Hill, School Publishing
220 East Danieldale Road
DeSoto, TX 75115   972-224-1111
800-442-9685
FAX: 972-228-1982
mhschool.com

Combines a light, personal look at the problems of special educators experiences with the basic facts of exceptionality.

288 pages

6676 Exceptional Student in the Regular Classroom

McGraw-Hill, School Publishing
220 East Danieldale Road
DeSoto, TX 75115   972-224-1111
800-442-9685
FAX: 972-228-1982
mhschool.com

Offers good, solid information through a practical understandable presentation unencumbered by specialized jargon. Covers topics associated with special learners.

480 pages

6677 Families Writing

Alliance for Parental Involvement in Education
PO Box 59
East Chatham, NY 12060   518-392-6900
FAX: 518-392-6900

Peter Stillman, author

This book is full of writing activities and examples of ways writing can be encouraged and enjoyed in the home. *$14.99*

6678 Family Math

Alliance for Parental Involvement in Education
PO Box 59
East Chatham, NY 12060   518-392-6900
FAX: 518-392-6900

Stenmark, author

Here are dozens of interesting activities to share with your children. *$18.00*

6679 Getting the Best Bite of the Apple

Alliance for Parental Involvement in Education
PO Box 59
East Chatham, NY 12060   518-392-6900
FAX: 518-392-6900

Linwood Laughy, author

This book takes a hard critical look at public school. The author is a parent who is also a former public school classroom teacher, school psychologist and principal. *$11.95*

6680 Home Education Resource Packet for New York State

Longview Publishing
R9 Kinderhook Street
Chatham, NY 12037   518-392-6900
FAX: 518-392-6900

Katharine Houk, author

For those considering home education in New York State, a packet containing the complete NYS Home Instruction Regulation, the laws referred to in the regulation, how to comply, resource listings, curriculum providers, support groups and more. *$8.00*

Paperback

6681 Homeschooling for Excellence

Alliance for Parental Involvement in Education
PO Box 59
East Chatham, NY 12060   518-392-6900
FAX: 518-392-6900

Micki Colfax, author

Children will learn if we recognize and respect their different interests and abilities and give them a chance to develop them. *$11.99*

6682 In Their Own Way

Alliance for Parental Involvement in Education
PO Box 59
East Chatham, NY 12060   518-392-6900
FAX: 518-392-6900

Thomas Armstrong, author

For the parents whose children are not thriving in school, Armstrong offers insight into individual learning styles. *$11.95*

6683 Inclusive & Heterogeneous Schooling: Assessment, Curriculum, and Instruction

Brookes Publishing
PO Box 10624
Baltimore, MD 21285   410-337-9580
800-638-3775
FAX: 410-337-8539
e-mail: custserv@brookespublishing.com
www.brookespublishing.com

Presents methods for successfully restructuring classrooms to enable all students, particularly those with disabilities, to flourish. Provides specific strategies for assessment, collaboration, classroom management, and age-specific instruction. *$34.95*

448 pages Paperback
ISBN 1-557662-02-9

6684 Information Access and Adaptive Technology

ORYX Press
4041 N Central Avenue
Suite 700
Phoenix, AZ 85012   602-265-2651
800-279-6799
FAX: 800-279-4663
e-mail: info@oryxpress.com
Carmela Cunningham and Norman Coombs, author

This book covers computer access issues, as well as the use of computer-based compensatory tools-special adaptive technology designed to enable students with disabilities to participate more fully in the academic environment. *$34.95*

216 pages 1997
ISBN 0-89774-92-8

6685 LD Child and the ADHD Child: Ways Parents & Professionals Can Help

John F. Blair, Publisher
1406 Plaza Drive
Winston Salem, NC 27103
800-222-9796
FAX: 336-768-9194
e-mail: blairpub@aol.com
www.blairpub.com
Suzanne H. Stevens, author
Carolyn Sakowski, President

Book about learning disabilities available to parents. Stevens cuts through the jargon and complex theories which usually characterize books on the subject to present effective and practical techniques that parents can employ to help their child succeed at home and at school. New edition adds information about ADHD children. *$12.95*

201 pages Paperback
ISBN 0-895871-42-4

6686 Learning All the Time

Alliance for Parental Involvement in Education
PO Box 59
East Chatham, NY 12060   518-392-6900
FAX: 518-392-6900
John Holt, author

Writes about how to aid young children in learning and how to allow them to figure things out for themselves, with the same insight and love of children that was apparent in his book. *$12.00*

6687 Mainstreaming: A Practical Approach for Teachers

McGraw-Hill, School Publishing
220 East Danieldale Road
DeSoto, TX 75115   972-224-1111
800-442-9685
FAX: 972-228-1982
mhschool.com

Provides teachers, administrators and school psychologists with the background, techniques and strategies they need to offer appropriate services for mildly handicapped students in the mainstream classroom.

6688 Making the Writing Process Work

Brookline Books
PO Box 1047
Cambridge, MA 02238   617-868-0360
800-666-2665
FAX: 617-868-1772
e-mail: brooklinebks@delphi.com
www.brooklinebooks.com
Karen Harris and Steve Graham, author

Making the Writing Process Work: Strategies for Composition and Self-Regulation is geared toward students who have difficulty organizing their thoughts and developing their writing. The specific strategies teach students how to approach, organize, and produce a final written product. *$24.95*

240 pages Paperback
ISBN 1-57129-10-9

6689 Nurturing Independent Learners Brookline Press

PO Box 1047
Cambridge, MA 02238   617-868-0360
800-666-2665
FAX: 617-868-1772
e-mail: brooklinebks@delphi.com
www.brooklinebooks.com
Donald Meichenbaum and Andrew Biemiller, author

Presents programs that effectively improve students' independence—the ability to manage their own learning—and explain how to implement them in the classroom. *$24.95*

256 pages Paperback
ISBN 1-57129-47-8

6690 One School at a Time: School Based Management

Alliance for Parental Involvement in Education
PO Box 59
East Chatham, NY 12060   518-392-6900
FAX: 518-392-6900
Carl L. Marburger, author

School based management is a school-by-school approach to educational reform. Parents, students and other community members work with the principal, teachers and other members of the school staff to shape the schools the community wants. *$8.95*

6691 Parent's Guide to the Montessori Classroom

Alliance for Parental Involvement in Education
PO Box 59
East Chatham, NY 12060   518-392-6900
FAX: 518-392-6900
Aline D. Wolf, author

This guide gives a concise explanation of the meaning of Montessori. It describes in detail the Montessori program for children between the ages of three to six. *$5.95*

6692 Rethinking Attention Deficit Disorder

Brookline Books
PO Box 1047
Cambridge, MA   02238   617-868-0360
**   800-666-2665**
**   FAX: 617-868-1772**
**   e-mail: brooklinebks@delphi.com**
**   www.brooklinebooks.com**
Miriam Checkes-Julkowski, Susan Sharp, Stolzenberg, author

In contrast to the common focus on behavioral symptoms of attention disorders, this book emphasizes internal factors that make attention regulation difficult. In-depth discussions of social, emotional, and academic consequences and appropriate interventions are provided. *$27.95*

250 pages Paperback
ISBN 1-57129 -37-0

6693 School Information Packet

Allergy and Asthma Network/Mothers of Asthmatics
3554 Chain Bridge Road
Suite 200
Fairfax, VA   22030
**   800-878-4403**
**   FAX: 703-352-4354**

Practical, medical, and legal information for school administrators and parents of students with asthma. *$7.00*

6694 Scoffolding Student Learning

Brookline Books
PO Box 1047
Cambridge, MA   02238   617-495-3682
**   800-666-2665**
**   FAX: 617-868-1772**
**   e-mail: brooklinebks@delphi.com**
**   www.brooklinebooks.com**

Collection of papers on the theory and practice of scoffolding—an interactive style of instructions that helps students develop more powerful thinking tools.. *$21.95*

180 pages Paperback
ISBN 1-571290-36-2

6695 Sharing Nature with Children

Alliance for Parental Involvement in Education
PO Box 59
East Chatham, NY   12060   518-392-6900
**   FAX: 518-392-6900**
Joseph Cornell, author

A book of wonderful games for exploring nature in a natural, comfortable way. *$7.95*

6696 So Your Child Has a Learning Problem?

CPPC
605 3rd Avenue
New York, NY   10158
**   212-476-9000**
**   800-433-8234**

Fred H. Wallbrown, author

Designed for parents of children who are encountering learning problems in the classroom. *$19.95*

160 pages

6697 Study Power: Study Skills to Improve Your Learning and Your Grades: A Workbook

Brookline Books
PO Box 1047
Cambridge, MA   02238   617-868-0360
**   800-666-2665**
**   FAX: 617-868-1772**
**   e-mail: brooklinebks@delphi.com**
**   www.brooklinebooks.com**
William R. Luckie & Wood Smethurst, author

The techniques in the easy-to-use, self-teaching manual have yielded remarkable success for students from elementary to medical school, at all levels of intelligence and achievement. Key skills covered include: listening, note taking, concentration, summarizing, reading comprehension, memorization, test taking, preparing papers and reports, time management, and more. These abilities are vital to success throughout every stage of learning; the benefits will last a lifetime. 1999.ISBN 157129067X *$15.95*

Paperback 1998
ISBN 1-57129 -46-X

6698 Symptoms and Treatment of Child's Learning

Health Publishing Company
PO Box 3805
San Francisco, CA   94119   415-282-8585
**   FAX: 415-750-6550**
Morrison F. Gardner, author

Handbook for parents who need to know the symptoms and treatments of a child's learning and academic disorders. *$4.95*

6699 Symtoms and Treatment of a Child's Learning and Academic Disorders

Psychological & Educational Publications
PO Box 520
Hydesville, CA   95547   707-768-1807
**   800-523-5775**
Morrison Gardner, author

A handbook for parents who need to know the symptoms and treatment of a child's academic and learning disorders. *$4.95*

ISBN 0-93142 -62-4

6700 Taking Charge Through Homeschooling

Alliance for Parental Involvement in Education
PO Box 59
East Chatham, NY   12060   518-392-6900
**   FAX: 518-392-6900**
Susan Kaseman, author

While this book offers solid information and suggestions for educating children without school, it also offers concrete suggestions on ways home schoolers can unite to protect their rights and freedoms. *$12.95*

6701 Teaching Children Self-Discipline

Alliance for Parental Involvement in Education
PO Box 59
East Chatham, NY   12060   518-392-6900
**   FAX: 518-392-6900**
Thomas Gordon, author

Mr. Gordon draws on research findings and his experience helping parents and teachers. *$17.95*

6702 Teaching Students with Learning Problems

McGraw-Hill, School Publishing
220 East Danieldale Road
DeSoto, TX   75115   972-224-1111
                           800-442-9685
                           FAX: 972-228-1982
                           mhschool.com

Expanded coverage of learning strategies, generalization training, self-monitoring techniques, and techniques for increasing the time students spend on academic tasks.

608 pages

6703 Teaching Young Children to Read Brookline Books

PO Box 1047
Cambridge, MA   02238   617-868-0360
                              800-666-2665
                         FAX: 617-868-1772
            e-mail: brooklinebks@delphi.com
                 www.brooklinebooks.com

Wood Smethurst, author

Detailed instructions on teaching reading to preschoolers. Gradually develops full fluency. *$16.95*

192 pages Paperback
ISBN 0-57129 -48-6

6704 Vermont Interdependent Services Team Approach (VISTA)

Brookes Publishing
PO Box 10624
Baltimore, MD   21285   410-337-9580
                               800-638-3775
                          FAX: 410-337-8539
      e-mail: custserv@brookespublishing.com
              www.brookespublishing.com

Michael F. Giangreco, Ph.D., author

A guide to coordinating educational support services. This manual enables IEP team members to fulfill the related services provisions of IDEA as they make effective support services decisions using a collaborative team approach. *$27.95*

176 pages Spiral bound
ISBN 1-55766 -30-4

6705 You are Your Child's First Teacher

Alliance for Parental Involvement in Education
PO Box 59
East Chatham, NY   12060   518-392-6900
                          FAX: 518-392-6900

Rahima Baldwin, author

Presents principles of Waldorf early education in the home from birth to age six. *$12.95*

6706 You, Your Child, and "Special" Education: A Guide to Making the System Work

Brookes Publishing
PO Box 10624
Baltimore, MD   21285   410-337-9580
                               800-638-3775
                          FAX: 410-337-8539
      e-mail: custserv@brookespublishing.com
              www.brookespublishing.com

Barbara Coyne Cutler, Ed.D., author

This book shows parents how to obtain the educational services their children rightfully deserve. It examines the internal workings of the education system, reveals the challenges that await, lists the services that are available, and discusses the rights that are federally guaranteed. Comes with a resource list, directions for filing a complaint, and explanations of relevant legislation and regulations. *$24.00*

272 pages Paperback
ISBN 1-55766 -15-4

Parenting: Spiritual

6707 AFB Directory of Services for Blind and Visually Impaired Persons in the U.S. and Canada

American Foundation for the Blind/AFB Press
PO Box 1020
Sewickley, PA   15143   412-741-1142
                               800-232-3044
                          FAX: 412-741-0609
            e-mail: afborders@abdintl.com
                           www.afb.org

Stephanie Biagioli, Marketing Coordinator

Comprehensive CD-ROM and print resource containing more that 2,500 local, state, regional, and national services throughout the U.S. and Canada for persons who are blind or visually impaired. *$74.95*

624 pages Hardcover/CDROM
ISBN 0-89128 -00-5

6708 Bethy and the Mouse: A Father Remembers His Children with Disabilities

Brookline Books
PO Box 1047
Cambridge, MA   02238   617-868-0360
                               800-666-2665
                          FAX: 617-868-1772
            e-mail: brooklinebks@delphi.com
                 www.brooklinebooks.com

Donald C. Bakely, author

A moving collection of poetry, photographs, and prose following a father's experiences with two disabled children—one with Down Syndrome and one with an underdeveloped brain. *$16.95*

184 pages Paperback
ISBN 0-57129 -35-4

6709 Communication Skills for Visually Impaired Learners, 2nd Edition

Charles C. Thomas, Publisher
2600 S 1st Street
Springfield, IL   62704   217-789-8980
                               800-258-8980
                          FAX: 217-789-9130
             e-mail: books@ccthomas.com

Randall Harley, Mila Truan and LaRhea Sanford, author

Contents of this publication include historical perspectives, reading readiness, approaches to readiness instruction, building word identification skills, assessment of reading skills factors to consider in assessment, identifying visually impaired students with learning problems, teaching techniques for students with learning problems and more. Also available in cloth for $ 69.95 (ISBN# 0-398-06692-2) *$ 49.95*

322 pages Softcover
ISBN 0-398066-93-0

6710 Dimensions: Visually Impaired Persons with Multiple Disabilities

American Foundation for the Blind/AFB Press
PO Box 1020
Sewickley, PA   15143　　　　**412-741-1142**
　　　　　　　　　　　　　　　　800-232-3044
　　　　　　　　　　　　　FAX: 412-741-0609
　　　　　　　　e-mail: afborders@abdintl.com
　　　　　　　　　　　　　　　www.afb.org

Stephanie Biagioli, Marketing Coordinator

Twenty-one articles from the Journal of Visual Impairment and Blindness, present a wide range of approaches for working with persons with multiple disabilities. *$24.95*

116 pages Paperback
ISBN 0-89128 -63-0

6711 Disabled God: Toward a Liberatory Theology of Disability

Abingdon Press
201 Eighth Avenue South
S. Nashville, TN   37202　　　　**615-749-6000**
　　　　　　　　　　　　　　　　800-251-3320
　　　　　　　　　　　　　FAX: 800-836-7802
　　　　　　　　　　　　　www.abingdon.org

Nancy L. Eiesland, author
Dr. Rex Matthews, Senior Editor

Draws on themes of the disability rights movement to identify people with disabilities as members of a socially disadvantaged minority group rather than as individuals who need to adjust. Highlights the history of people with disabilities in the church and society. *$ 13.95*

27 pages Paperback
ISBN 0-68710 -01-2

6712 Eye-Centered: A Study of Spirituality of Deaf People

NCOD
7202 Buchanan Street
Landover Hills, MD   20784　　　**301-577-8057**
　　　　　　　　　　　　　FAX: 301-577-1690
　　　　　　　　　　e-mail: ncod@erols.com

The findings of the five-year De Sales Project conducted by The National Catholic Office for the Deaf. *$12.00*

167 pages

6713 Family Bible Series: Adults

LifeWay Christian Resources Southern Baptist Conv.
127 9th Avenue North
Nashville, TN   37234　　　　**615-251-2000**
　　　　　　　　　　　　　　　　800-458-2772
　　　　　　e-mail: specialed@lifeway.com
　　　　　　　　　　　　www.lifeway.com

Woody Parker, Editor

Features Sunday school lessons recorded on audiocassette as printed in Family Bible series: Adults (international sunday school lessons). Three cassettes quarterly. *$12.00*

Quarterly

6714 From Barriers to Bridges

Exceptional Parent Library
PO Box 1807
Englewood Cliffs, NJ   10116
　　　　　　　　　　　　　　800-535-1910
　　　　　　　e-mail: eplibrary@aol.com
　　　　　　　　　　　www.eplibrary.com

Designed to foster dialogue between people with disabilities, their family members, religious leadership and the larger community. *$10.00*

6715 How to Thrive, Not Just Survive

American Foundation for the Blind/AFB Press
PO Box 1020
Sewickley, PA   15143　　　　**412-741-1142**
　　　　　　　　　　　　　　　　800-232-3044
　　　　　　　　　　　　FAX: 412-741-0609
　　　　　　　e-mail: afborders@abdintl.com
　　　　　　　　　　　　　　www.afb.org

Rose-Marie Swallow and Kathleen Mary Huebner, author
Stephanie Biagioli, Marketing Coordinator

Practical, hands-on guide for parents, teachers, and everyone involved in helping children develop the skills necessary for socialization, orientations and mobility, and leisure and recreational activities. Some of the subjects covered are eating, dressing, personal hygiene, self-esteem and etiquette. *$24.95*

104 pages Paperback
ISBN 0-89128 -48-7

6716 Independence Without Sight or Sound

American Foundation for the Blind/AFB Press
PO Box 1020
Sewickley, PA   15143　　　　**412-741-1142**
　　　　　　　　　　　　　　　　800-232-3044
　　　　　　　　　　　　FAX: 412-741-0609
　　　　　　　e-mail: afborders@abdintl.com
　　　　　　　　　　　　　　www.afb.org

Dona Sauerburger, author
Stephanie Biagioli, Marketing Coordinator

Written in a personal and informal style, this practical guidebook covers the essential aspects of communicating and working with deaf-blind adults. *$39.95*

193 pages Paperback
ISBN 0-89128 -46-7

6717 Loving Justice

Exceptional Parent Library
PO Box 1807
Englewood Cliffs, NJ 10116
800-535-1910
e-mail: eplibrary@aol.com
www.eplibrary.com

How the Americans with Disabilities Act affects religious institutions, including congregations, hospitals, nursing homes, seminaries, universities and more. *$10.00*

6718 My Left Foot: The Story of Christy Brown

Faber & Faber
53 Shore Road
Winchester, MA 01890
781-721-1427
800-666-2211

Shane Connaughton, author
Liz Wolfson, Sales Manager
Anna Lowi, Marketing Director

This is the screenplay of the brilliant film that tells the true story of the remarkable Christy Brown. Born into a poverty-stricken Dublin family in 1932, the tenth of 22 children, Brown was severely handicapped with cerebral palsy. Through the faith and the encouragement of his mother and his own strength of will, Christy Brown managed to demonstrate that his crippled body concealed a fierce intelligence which he was able to channel through his left foot. *$8.95*

96 pages

6719 Pastoral Care of the Mentally Disabled:
Advancing Care of the Whole Person

Haworth Press
10 Alice Street
Binghamton, NY 13904
604-722-5857
800-429-6784
FAX: 607-722-6362
e-mail: getinfo@haworthpressinc.com
www.haworthpressinc.com

Sally Severino, M.D. and Rev. Richard Liew, PhD., author
Jackie Blakeslee, Advertising

The beginning step to encourage a partnership for treating and evaluating patients with mental illness. It addresses the perceived roles of clergy and physicians for hearing the whole person which best occurs when medicine and ministry are linked. *$54.95*

116 pages Hardcover
ISBN 1-560246-65-0

6720 Place for Everyone: A Guide for Special
Education Bible Teaching

Baptist Sunday School Board
127 Ninth Avenue North
Nashville, TN 37234
800-458-2772
FAX: 615-251-5933
www.bssb.com

Athalene McNay, author
Ron Brown, Team Leader
Doug Merritt, Manager

Begin a ministry for exceptional people in your church or strengthen an existing ministry. This resource helps pastors, ministers of education, and Sunday School directors understand educational and developmental issues in meeting special education needs. It will train leaders to minister in specific ways, emphasizing the need to reach disabled persons for Christ and for church membership through life-changing Bible study. *$19.95*

ISBN 0-767318-98-6

6721 Place for Everyone: Guide for Special Ed Bible
Teaching-Reaching Ministry

LifeWay Christian Resources Southern Baptist Conv.
127 9th Avenue N
Nashville, TN 37234
615-251-2000
800-458-2772
e-mail: specialed@lifeway.com
www.lifeway.com

Athalene McNay, author
Ellen Beene, Editor

Begin a ministry for exceptional people in your church or strengthen an existing ministry. This resource helps pastors, ministers of education, and Sunday School directors understand educational and developmental issues in meeting special education needs. It will train leaders to minister in specific ways, emphasizing the need to reach disabled persons for Christ and for church membership through life-changing Bible study. *$19.95*

128 pages Paperback
ISBN 0-76731 -98-6

6722 Sound Truths: Life and Work Bible Studies On
Tape

LifeWay Christian Resources Southern Baptist Conv.
127 9th Avenue North
Nashville, TN 37234
615-251-2000
800-458-2772
e-mail: specialed@lifeway.com
www.lifeway.com

Bev Sullivan, Editor

Insights, commentary, and application for each Sunday's lesson recorded on audiocassette by Calvin Miller. Approximately 15 minutes in length for each lesson. *$12.00*

Quarterly

6723 Special Education Bible Study

LifeWay Christian Resources Southern Baptist Conv.
127 9th Avenue N
Nashville, TN 37234
615-251-2000
800-458-2772
e-mail: SpecialEd@lifeway.com
www.lifeway.com

Ellen Beene, Editor

Easy to use Bible study helps for mentally handicapped adults and youth. Features full-color pictures plus an emphasis on applying biblical truth to real-life situations. *$1.50*

48 pages Quarterly

6724 Special Education Teacher Packet

LifeWay Christian Resources Southern Baptist Conv.
127 9th Avenue North
Nashville, TN 37234   615-251-2000
                                   800-458-2772
          e-mail: SpecialEd@lifeway.com
                  www.lifeway.com

Ellen Beene, author
Ellen Beene, Editor

Resources to help teachers who lead Sunday School
classes for adults and older youth with mental retardation. Includes teaching plans, posters, and one copy
of Special Education Bible Study. *$10.00*

Quarterly

6725 That All May Worship

Exceptional Parent Library
PO Box 1807
Englewood Cliffs, NJ 10116
                                   800-535-1910
          e-mail: eplibrary@aol.com
                  www.eplibrary.com

An interfaith handbook to assist congregations in
welcoming people with disabilities to promote acceptance and full participation. *$10.00*

**6726 Two Hundred Fifty Tips for Making Life with
Arthritis Easier**

Arthritis Foundation Distribution Center
PO Box 6996
Alpharetta, GA 30009
                                   800-207-8633
                            FAX: 770-442-9742
                                www.arthritis.com

What do aerosol cooking spray and snow-shovel-
ing have in common? Learn the answer to this
question, and other clever and handy tips to make
your life with-or without-arthritis easier. Plus
learn about helpful serviced you didn't know were
available through you bank, post office, phone
company, grocery store, and other businesses you
frequent. *$9.95*

88 pages

Professional

6727 ADHD Report

Guilford Publications
72 Spring Street
New York, NY 10012   212-431-9800
                                   800-365-7006
                            FAX: 212-966-6708
                       e-mail: info@guilford.com

Presents the most up-to-date information on the
evaluation, diagnosis and management of ADHD
in children, adolescents and adults. This important newsletter is an invaluable resource for all
professionals interested in ADHD. *$49.95*

BiMonthly
ISSN 1065-8025

**6728 American Association of Spinal Cord Injury
Nurses**

American Assoc. of Spinal Cord Injury Nurses
75-20 Astoria Boulevard
Jackson Heights, NY 11370   718-397-4181
                            FAX: 718-803-0414
                                www.aascin.org

SCI Nursing Journal, author
Sara Lerman, MPH, Program Manager

Disseminates information to nurses and others caring
for spinal cord injured individuals. Membership in
AASCIN represents registered and licensed practical
and vocational nurses in the US and Canada who
practice in the diverse SCI settings such as intensive
care, acute care and long-term care; rehabilitation;
home care; and outpatient care. There is a Nursing
Research Program which funds research in the area
of spinal cord impairment. Annual educational conference.

6729 American Forensic Association Journal

American Forensic Association
University of Wisconsin-River Falls
River Falls, WI 54022   715-262-3605
                            FAX: 715-425-9533
                  e-mail: james.wpratt@uwrf.edu

Communication disorders newsletter. *$25.00*

6730 American Journal of Art Therapy

Vermont College of Norwich University
Montpelier, VT 05602   802-828-8540
                            FAX: 802-828-8585
                    e-mail: mzimmerm@norwich.edu

Gladys Agell PhD ATR-BC HLM, Editor

Discusses the graphic and plastic arts as they contribute to human understanding, psycotherapy, rahabili-
tation and education. *$ 32.00*

35-40 pages Quarterly
ISSN 0007-47 4

6731 American Journal of Orthopsychiatry

American Orthopsychiatric Association
330 7th Avenue
18th Floor
New York, NY 10001   212-564-5930
                            FAX: 212-564-6180
                      e-mail: amerortho@aol.com

Joan Adler, Managing Editor
Ellen L. Bassuk, Editor

Mental health issues from multidisciplinary and in-
terprofessionals perspectives: clinical, research and
expository approaches. *$45.00*

160 pages Quarterly

6732 American Journal of Physical Medicine

Lippincott, Williams & Wilkins
PO Box 1551
Hagerstown, MD 21741
                                   800-638-3030
                            FAX: 301-824-7390
                                    www.lww.com

Journal of the Association of Academic Psychiatrists. Articles covering research and clinical studies and applications of new equipment, procedures
and therapeutic advances. *$45.00*

6733 American Journal of Psychiatry

American Psychiatric Association
1400 K Street NW
Washington, DC 20005   202-326-7759

Professional papers on topics in psychiatry.
$56.00

Monthly

6734 American Journal of Public Health

American Public Health Association
1015 15th Street NW
Washington, DC 20005   202-777-2742
                               FAX: 202-777-2534
              e-mail: comments@msmail.apha.org
                               www.apna.org

Dr. Mervyn Susser, Editor

Association journal containing professional articles
and sections such as Notes from the Field and Association News. Single copies are $15.00. $50.00 per
year for special consumer membership.

Monthly
ISSN 0090-00 6

6735 American Journal on Mental Retardation

American Association on Mental Retardation
444 N Capitol Street NW
Washington, DC 20001   202-387-1968
                               800-424-3688
                               FAX: 202-387-2193
              e-mail: aamr@access.digex.net
                               www.aamr.org

Donald Routh, Editor, author
Bruce Appelgen, Director of Publications

Articles cover biological, behavioral, and educational research: theory papers; and reviews of research literature on specific aspects of mental
retardation. *$142.00*

112 pages BiMonthly

6736 American Rehabilitation

Rehabilitation Services Administration
330 C Street SW
3033 Mes
Washington, DC 20202   202-205-8296
                               FAX: 202-205-9874
              e-mail: frank.romano@ed.gov
              www.ed.gov/pubs/americanrehab

Frank Romano, Editor

Covers medical, social and employment aspects of
vocational rehabilitation. *$10.00*

40 pages Quarterly

6737 Annals of Otology, Rhinology and Larynology

Annals Publishing Company
4507 Laclede Avenue
Saint Louis, MO 63108   314-367-4987
                               FAX: 314-367-4988
              e-mail: manager@annals.com
                               www.annals.com

Brian F. McCabe, M.D., author
Kenneth A Cooper, Jr, Business Manager

Original, peer-reviewed articles in the fields of oto-
laryngology - head and neck medicine and surgery,
broncho-esophagology, audiology, speech, pathology, allery, and maxillofacial surgery. Official journal of the American Laryngological Association and
the American Broncho-Esophagological Association.
Published monthly. *$170.00*

112 pages Monthly

6738 Archives of Neurology

American Medical Association
515 North State Street
Chicago, IL 60610   312-464-5000
                            FAX: 312-464-2580
                            e-mail: ama-assn.org

Roger Rosenberg, M.D., Editor
Peter Payerli, Publisher, Interim Vice Pres.

Articles range from reports of original research to
case studies. *$225.00*

Monthly

6739 Art Therapy

American Art Therapy Association
1202 Allanson Road
Mundelein, IL 60060   847-837-1190
                              FAX: 312-566-4580

Nancy Stygar

Publishes articles on the uses of art in the education,
enrichment, development and treatment of disabled
people. *$10.00*

76+ pages Quarterly
ISSN 0742-16 6

6740 Cancer Therapy

Paragon House
New York, NY

Ralph Moss, Ph.D., author

Reviews alternative medicine therapies for cancer.

1992

6741 Cancer and Nutrition

Avery Publishing Group
Garden City Park, NJ

Charles B. Simone, author

A ten point plan for the prevention and treatment of
cancer using nutrition; includes a discussion of the
various risk factors which contribute to cancer.

1992

6742 Careers & the Disabled

Equal Opportunities Publications
445 Broad Hollow Road
Suite 425
Melville, NY 11747   631-421-9421
                             FAX: 631-421-0359
              e-mail: jschneider@eop.com
                             www.eop.com

James Schneider, author
John R. Miller, III, President/Publisher
James Schneider, Editorial Director

A career magazine for professional career seekers who have disabilities. Profiles disabled people who have achieved successful careers. Features a career section in Braille, career guidance, career news, affirmative action news and free resume service. Career opportunities in industries businesses, schools, hospitals, service utilities and government. *$10.00*

64 pages 5X

6743 Clinician's Practical Guide to Attention-Deficit/Hyperactivity Disorder

Brookes Publishing
PO Box 10624
Baltimore, MD 21285

800-638-3775
FAX: 410-337-8539
www.brookespublishing.com

Mercugliano, Power, Blum, author

Quick reference volume with comprehensive data on psychoeducational and neuropsychological assessment, related symptoms, drug and counseling therapies and critical issues. *$39.95*

368 pages 1999
ISBN 1-557663-58-0

6744 Colon Health: Key to a Vibrant Life

Norwalk Press
Prescott, AZ

Norman Walker, author

Includes complete glossary of terms and index of referrals.

6745 Colon Irrigation: A Forgotten Key to Health

Mark Baker
St. Louis, MO

Mark Baker, author

Helpful booklet about autointoxification.

6746 Complete Guide to Cancer Prevention

Harper and Row
New York, NY

Henry Dreher, author

A comprehensive guide to preventing cancer using nutrition in combination with preventative environmental and psychological measures.

1988

6747 Connections Newsletter

Kessler Institute for Rehabilitation
1199 Pleasant Valley Way
West Orange, NJ 07052

973-731-3600
888-KES-SLER
FAX: 973-243-6992

Maura Bergen, Editor/Public Relations Coordin.
Maria Anan, Editor/N. NJSCI System Coordin.
Karen Hwang, Editor

Quarterly newsletter for individuals with a spinal cord injury. Funded by the Northern New Jersey Spinal Cord Injury System.

Quarterly-Free

6748 Conquest of Cancer

Franklin Watts
New York, NY

Virginia Livingston-Wheeler, M.D., author

An outline of Livingston Therapy as it applies to treating cancer. Includes the role of diet and the use of the Livingston vaccine.

1984

6749 Controlling Asthma

American Lung Association
1740 Broadway
New York, NY 10017

212-315-8700

For parents of children with asthma, this newsmagazine tells how parents can help their child deal with the many problems presented by asthma.

16 pages

6750 Diabetes Self-Management

RA Rapaport Publishing
150 W 22nd Street
New York, NY 10011

212-989-0200
FAX: 212-989-4786

James Hazlett, Editor

Publishes practical how-to information, focusing on the day-to-day and long-term aspects of diabetes in a positive and upbeat style. Gives subscribers up-to-date news, facts and advice to help them maintain their wellness and make informed decisions regarding their health. *$18.00*

BiMonthly

6751 Disability Analyst

American Board of Disability Analysts
345 24th Avenue North
Suite 200
Nashville, TN 37203

615-327-2984
FAX: 615-327-9235
e-mail: americanbd@aol.com

Alex Horwitz, MD, Executive Officer

Official newsletter of the American Board of Disability Analysts; features Healthnews Headlines, Meeting Calendar, Application Packet, and much more. Free to members; $20 per year for non-members.

8-12 pages BiAnnually

6752 Educating Children with Disabilities A Transdisciplinary Approach, Third Edition

Brookes Publishing
PO Box 10624
Baltimore, MD 21285

800-638-3775
FAX: 410-337-8539
www.brookespublishing.com

Orelove & Sobsey, author

Widely respected textbook presents you with the strategies you need for developing an inclusive curriculum, integrating health care and educational programs and addressing needs and concerns. *$38.00*

512 pages 1996
ISBN 1-557662-46-0

6753 Education and Training in Mental Retardation and Dev. Disabilities

Council for Exceptional Children
1920 Association Drive
Reston, VA   20191   703-620-3660
                           888-232-7733
                    FAX: 703-264-9494
            e-mail: sercice@cec.sped.org
                    www.cec.sped.org

A medium for continuing education for teachers and practitioners by providing timely information about the direction, management and accountability of special education programs for individuals with mental retardation and developmental disabilities. Individual, $30; Institution, $75.

Quarterly

6754 Family and Community Health

Aspen Publishers
7201 McKinney Circle
Frederick, MD   21704   301-698-7100
                              800-234-1660
                       FAX: 301-695-7931
                  www.aspenpublishers.com

Peer-view journal addressing the information needs of health-care practitioners. *$124.00*

Quarterly

6755 Health Care Management Review

Aspen Publishers
7201 McKinney Circle
Frederick, MD   21704   301-698-7100
                              800-234-1660
                       FAX: 301-695-7931
                  www.aspenpublishers.com

Provides health care administrators with useful information on health care management. *$145.00*

6756 Health Technology Trends

Emergency Care Research Institute (ECRI)
5200 Butler Pike
Plymouth Meeting, PA   19462   610-825-6000
                           FAX: 610-834-1275
                       e-mail: info@ecri.org
                              www.ecri.org

Damian Carlson, Associate Editor

Provides analysis and information about health care technology to administrators and health care providers. *$275.00*

12 pages Monthly

6757 Home Health Care Services Quarterly

Haworth Press
10 Alice Street
Binghamton, NY   13904   604-722-5857
                               800-429-6784
                        FAX: 607-722-6362
      e-mail: getinfo@haworthpressinc.com
                  www.haworthpressinc.com
W. June Simmons, Editor, author
Jackie Blakeslee, Advertising
Roger Hall, Senior Vice President

Professional journal in book format. *$60.00*

Quarterly

6758 Immune Deficiency Foundation Newsletter

Immune Deficiency Foundation
40 W Chesapeake Avenue
Suite 308
Towson, MD   21204   410-321-6647
                           800-296-4433
                    FAX: 410-321-9165
         e-mail: idf@primaryimmune.org
                 www.primaryimmune.org

Thomas L. Moran, President
Tracy Namie, Office Manager

Offers information on immune deficiencies. How to treat them, what they are, and more.

4-6 pages

6759 Including Students with Severe and Multiple Disabilities in Typical Classrooms

Brookes Publishing
PO Box 10624
Baltimore, MD   21285   410-337-9580
                              800-638-3775
                       FAX: 410-337-8539
      e-mail: custserv@brookespublishing.com
                 www.brookespublishing.com
June E. Downing, Ph.D., author

Straightforward resource gives you the guidance you need to educate learners who have one or more sensory impairments in addition to cognitive and physical disabilities. Offers numerous ideas for modifying the general education curriculum. *$35.00*

244 pages Paperback 1996
ISBN 1-557662-39-8

6760 Informer

Simon Foundation
PO Box 835
Wilmette, IL   60091   847-864-3913
                              800-237-4666
                       FAX: 847-864-9758
                  www.simonfoundation.org

Cheryle B Gartley, President

Publishes items of interest to people with bladder or bowel incontinence, including medical articles, helpful devices, publications and a pen pal list. Quarterly newsletter.

6761 Issues in Law and Medicine

National Legal Center for the Medically Dependent
3 S Sixth Street
Terre Haute, IN   47807   812-232-0103
                          FAX: 812-232-0103

James Bopp, Jr., Editor-in-Chief
Larry Ligget, Subscriptions

A peer-reviewed journal providing technical and informational assistance to attorneys, health care professionals, educators, and administrators concerned with severely disabled persons of all ages who may be subjected to discrimination in the delivery of medical care. *$89.00*

124 pages 3x Year
ISSN 8756-81 0

6762 JAMA: The Journal of the American Medical Association

American Medical Association
515 North State Street
Chicago, IL 60610   312-464-5000
                          FAX: 312-464-2580
                          e-mail: ama.jama
                          jama.ama-assn.org

Roger Rosenberg, M.D., Editor
Peter Payerli, Publisher, Interim Vice Pres.

Articles cover all aspects of medical research and clinical medicine. *$66.00*

6763 Journal of Addictions and Offender Counseling

American Counseling Association
5999 Stevenson Avenue
Alexandria, VA 22304   703-823-9800

Bob Shearer, Editor

$14.00

2x Year

6764 Journal of Adolescent Health Care

655 Avenue of the Americas
New York, NY 10010   212-989-5800
                            FAX: 212-633-3990
                            www.elsewee.com

Micheal Targwwsk, Advertising Rep.

Peer-reviewed publication for the multidisciplinary study of adolescent medicine and health care. *$7.00*

6765 Journal of Applied Rehabilitation Counseling

National Rehabilitation Counseling Association
8807 Sudley Road
Suite 102
Manassas, VA 20110   703-361-2077
                            FAX: 703-361-2489
                            e-mail: nrcaoffice@aol.com

Debra Harley, Editor
Ellen Fabian, Associate Editor
Hal Cain, Book and Media Review Editor

Articles on counseling history, research and practice of interest in rehabilitation. $20.00 for individuals, $35.00 institutional. *$20.00*

Quarterly

6766 Journal of Children's Communication Development

CEC Div for Childrens' Communication Development
1920 Association Drive
Reston, VA 20191   703-620-3660

Alexander Brice, Editor

Contains scholarly articles pertaining to the many aspects of communication disorders in children, encompassing speech, language, hearing and learning disabilities. *$16.00*

2x Year

6767 Journal of Cognitive Rehabilitation

Neuroscience Publishers
6555 Carrollton Avenue
Indianapolis, IN 46220   317-257-9672
                                FAX: 317-257-9674
                                e-mail: obracy@inetdirect.net
                                www.neuroscience.cnter.com

Odie L. Bracy III, Ph.D., Editor, author
Sandra Reichle, Production Manager

Publication for therapists, family and patient, designed to provide information relevant to the rehabilitation of impairment resulting from brain injury. U.S individual, $40; U.S. insitution, $80. *$35.00*

32 pages BiMonthly

6768 Journal of Employment Counseling

American Counseling Association
5999 Stevenson Avenue
Alexandria, VA 22304   703-823-9800
                              FAX: 703-823-0252

Robert Drummond, Editor

$20.00

Quarterly

6769 Journal of Head Trauma Rehabilitation

Aspen Publishers
200 Orchard Ridge Drive
Gaithersburg, MD 20878   301-698-7100
                                800-234-1660
                                FAX: 301-695-7931
                                www.aspenpublishers.com

Scholarly journal designed to provide information on clinical management and rehabilitation of the head-injured for the practicing professional. Published bimonthly. *$119.00*

128 pages

6770 Journal of Humanistic Education and Development

American Counseling Association
5999 Stevenson Avenue
Alexandria, VA 22304   703-823-9800
                              FAX: 703-823-0252

Richard J. Hazler, Editor

$12.00

Quarterly

6771 Journal of Multicultural Counseling and Development

American Counseling Association
5999 Stevenson Avenue
Alexandria, VA 22304   703-823-9800
                              FAX: 703-823-0252

Frederick D. Harper, Editor

$14.00

Quarterly

6772 Journal of Rehabilitation

National Rehabilitation Association
633 S Washington Street
Alexandria, VA 22314   703-836-0850

e-mail: info@nationalrehab.org

Paul Leung, Editor

Sponsored by the National Rehabilitation Association, this journal offers information on rehabilitation services and programs for the disabled and the professional. *$12.50*

100 pages Quarterly

6773 Journal of Rehabilitation & Development

Rehabilitation Research & Development Center
103 S Gay Street
Baltimore, MD 21202   410-962-3092

Presents scientific papers, special articles and technical notes in areas of rehabilitation research and engineering.

6774 Journal of Religion, Disability & Health

Haworth Press
10 Alice Street
Binghamton, NY 13904   604-722-5857
    800-429-6784
FAX: 607-722-6362
e-mail: getinfo@haworthpressinc.com
www.haworthpressinc.com

Wiliam Gaventa, M.D., Co-Editor
David Coulter, M.D., Co-Editor
Jackie Blakeslee, Advertising/Journal Liaison

This journal aims to inform religious professionals about developments in the field of disability and rehabilitation in order to facilitate greater contributions on the part of pastors, religious educators and pastoral counselors. *$60.00*

Quarterly

6775 Journal of Vision Rehabilitation

Media Productions & Marketing
2440 O Street
Suite 202
Lincoln, NE 68510   402-474-2676

Multidisciplinary journal containing articles and papers dealing with low vision, its evaluation, instrumentation and rehabilitation. *$45.00*

6776 Just in Case

OptionCare
100 Corporate North
Suite 212
Bannockburn, IL 60015

    800-999-4363

Offers current case management information designed to inform, educate and sometimes amuse the reader. The newsletter is filled with articles of interest to case managers offering clinical updates, general interest items, and even tips to help make the job easier and more effective.

Quarterly

6777 Kenny Foundation

21700 Northwestern Highway
Suite 730
Southfield, MI 48075   248-552-0202
    800-237-3422
FAX: 248-552-0275
e-mail: kennyFdn@aol.com
www.comnet.org/kenny

Russell Derry, Executive Director

Provides education advocacy and direct services to people with mobility impairmants throughout Michigan. Services include Equipment Connection, a database, available online, that connects buyers and sellers of used adaptive equipment. Attitudes, a disability awareness program for first and second graders, and information and referral services.

6778 MS Quarterly Report

Demos Medical Publishing
386 Park Avenue South
Suite 201
New York, NY 10016   212-683-0072
    800-532-8663
FAX: 212-683-0118
e-mail: info@demospub.com

Janis Bentltey, Customer Service

Review articles on a wide range of topics concerning multiple sclerosis, reports of current research and book reviews. *$ 19.50*

12-16 pages Quarterly

6779 Manual for Below-Knee (Trans-Tibial) Amputees

Rehabilitation Press
PO Box 380
Topping, VA 23169   804-758-0850

e-mail: abennett@crosslimb.net
Alvin Miulenburg and A. Bennett Wilson Jr, author

Provides information useful to the below-knee amputee in helping with his or her rehabilitation. *$3.00*

18 pages Paperback

6780 Modern Healthcare

Crain Communications
740 N Rush Street
Chicago, IL 60611   312-649-5200

Business news magazine for healthcare professionals. *$ 7.00*

Weekly

6781 National Clearinghouse of Rehabilitation Training Materials

5202 North Richmond Hill Drive
Stillwater, OK 74078   405-624-7650
    800-223-5219
FAX: 405-624-0695
www.nchrtm.okstate.edu

David Brooks, Director

Newsletter produced quarterly to provide information and opportunities to learn more about related fields.

6782   Neurolorehabilitation and Neural Repair
Demos Medical Publishing
386 Park Avenue South
Suite 201
New York, NY   10016   212-863-0072
                                     800-532-8663
                              FAX: 212-683-0118
                        e-mail: info@demospub.com
Michael E. Selzer, M.D., Ph.D., Editor-in-Chief,
author
Janis Bentley, Customer Service

The premier source of information for all clinicians
who comprehensively manage the rehabilitation of
neurologically impaired patients. Rates: $120 indi-
viduals, $160 institutional, US and Canada; $140 individual, $185 institution, elsewhere. *$95.00*

Quarterly

**6783   Newsletter of Medical Rehabilitation
Administrators**
Assn. of Medical Rehabilitation Administrators
1733 Forest Hills Drive
Vienna, WV   26105

Millie City, Editor

Items relating to individual members as well as rehabilitation administration, management and rehabilitation trends.

6784   Occupational Therapy in Mental Health
Haworth Press
10 Alice Street
Binghamton, NY   13904   604-722-5857
                                      800-429-6784
                               FAX: 607-722-6362
                  e-mail: getinfo@haworthpressinc.com
                        www.haworthpressinc.com

Marie Louise Blount, AM, BS, Co-Editor
Mary Donohue, Co-Editor
Jackie Blakeslee, Advertising/Journal Liaison

An essential journal for all OT's in mental health
fields. Provides professionals with a forum in which
to discuss challenges. *$ 50.00*

Quarterly

6785   Options: The Alternative Cancer Therapy Book
Avery Publishing Group
Garden City Park, NJ

Richard Walters, author

Overviews available alternative cancer therapies, including an explanation of how they work and guidelines for selecting an appropriate treatment.   Also
includes a comprehensive resource guide.

1993

6786   Parkinsons Report
National Parkinson Foundation
1501 NW 9th Avenue
Miami, FL   33136   305-547-6666
                                      900-327-4545

Julian Pearson, Administrator

Articles, reports and news on Parkinson's disease and
the activities of the National Parkinson Foundation.

32 pages Qarterly

6787   Part B News
United Communications Group
11300 Rockville Pike
Rockville, MD   20852   301-816-8950
                               FAX: 301-816-8945
                                      www.ucg.com

Washington news practical strategies for maximizing Medicare Part B.

6788   Physical Therapy
American Physical Therapy Association
1111 N Fairfax Street
Alexandria, VA   22314   703-684-2782

Contains articles on clinical and testing procedures. *$45.00*

Monthly

6789   Professional Report
National Rehabilitation Association
3 S Washington Street
Alexandria, VA   22314   703-548-1502

                        e-mail: info@nationalrehab.org

Association newsletter containing news, programs
and information of interest to the Association and
its members.

6790   Provider Magazine
American Health Care Association
1201 L Street NW
Washington, DC   20005   202-842-4444
                                      800-321-0343

Magazine for long-term healthcare professionals.
$48.00

72 pages Monthly
ISSN 0888-03 2

6791   Psychiatric Rehabilitation Journal
940 Commonwealth Avenue W
Boston, MA   02215   617-731-5599
                               FAX: 617-353-9209
                              e-mail: iepoys@tu.edu
                                     www.bu.edu/cpr

LeRoy Spaniol, Ph.D., Executive Publisher

Discusses issues, programs and research on psychiatric rehabilitation. Magazine for $50 for individual,
$105 for organizations, $10 mailing to Canada, $20
mailing to other countries. Published quarterly.

Quarterly Magaz
ISSN 0147-56 2

6792   Public Health Reports
Public Health Reports
13 Parklawn
26
Rockville, MD   20857

Marian P. Tebben, Executive Editor

Scholarly articles on pertinent medical problems that relate to public health and the healthcare system. *$13.00*

> *BiMonthly*

6793 Public Health/State Capitals

Wakeman/Walworth
300 N Washington Street
Alexandria, VA 22314   **703-549-8606**
                                    800-876-2545
                          FAX: 703-549-1372
          e-mail: newsletters@statecapitals.com
                      www.statecapitals.com

Christine Ryan, author
Keyes Walworth, Publisher
Christine Ryan, Editor

Digest of state and municipal health care financing and legislation, including disease control, medicaid, AIDS, abortion, substance abuse programs, cancer prevention such as smoking restrictions, mental health and disability programs, regulation of hospitals, & nursing homes, food safety, medical policies, health insurance for children, home regulation, managerial care, public health issues, pest control, and water quality. Issued weekly-52 issues/year. *$245.00*

> *10 pages*
> *ISSN 0734-11 6*

6794 Ragged Edge Magazine

Advocado Press
PO Box 145
Louisville, KY 40201   **502-894-9492**
                          FAX: 502-899-9562
      e-mail: circulation@raggededgemagazine.com
                  www.raggededgemagazine.com

Mary Johnson, Editor

Ragged Edge magazine is the successor to The Disability Rag, and covers disability in America today: rights, culture, ideas and controversy. Here you'll find new voices speaking out about disability culture and lives; you'll get the newest cutting-edge thinking on headlines in the news today on genetic discrimination, assisted suicide, healthcare policy. *$17.50*

> *40 pages BiMonthly*
> *ISSN 0749-95 6*

6795 Rehabilitation Counseling Bulletin

American Association for Counseling & Development
5999 Stevenson Avenue
Alexandria, VA 22304   **703-823-9800**

Randall M. Parker, Editor

A research journal for professionals in rehabilitation counseling. *$18.00*

> *64 pages Quarterly*

6796 Rehabilitation Psychology

Springer Publishing Company
536 Broadway
New York, NY 10012   **212-431-4370**

Publishes articles addressing psychological and behavioral aspects of rehabilitation. *$28.00*

6797 Reversing Diabetes

Warner Books
New York, NY

Julian M. Whitaker, author

Dr. Whitaker argues that conventional treatments are unnecessary, or even dangerous, and shows how diabetics can naturally control their condition through diet and exercise.

> *1987*

6798 Sexuality and Disability

Human Sciences Press
233 Spring Street
New York, NY 10013   **212-620-8000**
                                    800-221-9369
                          FAX: 212-463-0742
                              www.wkap.com

Stanley H. Ducharme, author

A journal devoted to the psychological and medical aspects of sexuality in rehabilitation and community settings. The journal features original scholarly articles that address the psychological and medical aspects of sexuality in the field of rehabilitation, case studies, clinical practice reports, and guidelines for clinical practice. Plenum Publishers is now part of Kluner Academic Publishers. Journal fulfillment in the NYC office as before for HSP and Plenum Journals. *$160.00*

> *64 pages Quarterly*
> *ISSN 0146-10 4*

6799 Simon Foundation for Continence

PO Box 835
Wilmette, IL 60091
                                    800-237-4666

Information on incontinence.

6800 Spinal Network

Spinal Network Extra
PO Box 4162
Boulder, CO 80306
                                    800-338-5412

Kathleen Carrigan, Advertising Manager

Offers information and articles on assistive devices and more for spinal injury persons. *$5.00*

6801 St. Anthony's Healthcare Resources Alert

St. Anthony Publishing
11410 Isaac Newton Square
Reston,, VA 20190   **703-708-1515**
                                    800-632-0123
                          FAX: 703-707-5700

Suzanne Vel, Jr. Product Manager

News, resources and services for practicing healthcare professionals.

6802 Strategic Health Care Marketing

Health Care Communications
11 Heritage Lane
Rye, NY 10580   **914-666-0158**

Michele Von Dambrowski, Editor

Marketing strategies for hospitals, medical group practices, home health services, urgent care centers.

12 pages Monthly

6803 TeamRehab Report

PO Box 3640
Culver City, CA 90231

800-543-4116
FAX: 310-337-1041

Andria Segedy, Publisher
Kim Pfaff, Managing Editor

A magazine for rehab professionals who prescribe, purchase or recommend assistive technology and related services for clients who are permanently disabled. *$24.00*

48 pages Monthly

6804 VA Practitioner

Cahners Publishing Company
275 Washington Street
Newton, MA 02458

Nina Tobier, author

The magazine for health care professionals of the Department of Veterans Affairs.

Monthly

6805 Victory Over Diabetes

Keats Publishing
New Canaan, CT

203-966-8721
800-323-4900

W.H. Philpott, M.D. and D.K. Kalita, Ph.D., author

A guide for lifestyle and nutritional changes with the potential of healing diabetics' disordered metabolism; includes a nutritional protocol.

1992

Specific Disabilities

6806 ADD Challenge: A Practical Guide for Teachers

Research Press
2612 N Mattis
Champaign, IL 61821

217-352-3275

e-mail: rp@researchpress.com
Steven B. Gordon & Michael J. Asher, author
$15.95

196 pages
ISBN 0-878223-45-2

6807 ADD: Helping Your Child

Warner Books
3 Center Plaza
Boston, MA 02108

212-522-7200

Warren Umansky & Barbara S. Smalley, author
$12.95

224 pages Paperback
ISBN 0-446670-13-8

6808 ADHD in the Schools: Assessment and Intervention Strategies

Guilford Press
72 Spring Street
New York, NY 10012

212-431-9800
800-365-7006
FAX: 212-966-6708
e-mail: info@guilford.com
www.guilford.com

George J. DuPaul & Gary Stoner, author
$30.00

269 pages Paperback
ISBN 0-898622-45-0

6809 ADHD: Handbook for Diagnosis & Treatment

Western Psychological Services
12031 Wilshire Boulevard
Los Angeles, CA 90025

310-478-2061
800-648-8857
FAX: 310-478-7838

Russell A. Barkley, PhD, author

This second edition helps clinicians diagnose and treat Attention Deficit Hyperactivity Disorder. Written by an internationally recognized authority in the field, it covers the history of ADHD, its primary symptoms, associated conditions, developmental course and outcome, and family context. A workbook companion manual is also available. *$ 68.00*

700 pages

6810 Activities for Developing Pre-Skill Concepts In Children with Autism

Autism Society of North Carolina Bookstore
505 Oberlin Road
Suite 230
Raleigh, NC 27605

919-743-0204
800-442-2762
FAX: 919-743-0208
e-mail: ASNC@aol.com
www.autismsociety-nc.org

Toni Flowers, author

Chapters include auditory development, concept development, social development and visual-motor integration. *$36.00*

6811 Adolescents with Down Syndrome: Toward a More Fulfilling Life

Brookes Publishing
PO Box 10624
Baltimore, MD 21285

410-337-9580
800-638-3775
FAX: 410-337-8539
e-mail: custserv@brookespublishing.com
www.brookespublishing.com

Written for health care professionals, psychologists, other developmental disabilities practitioners, educators, and parents, it covers biomedical concerns; behavioral, psychological, and psychiatric challenges; and education, employment, recreation, community, and legal concerns. *$35.95*

416 pages Paperback 1997
ISBN 1-55766 -81-9

6812 Adult Leukemia: A Comprehensive Guide for Patients and Families

Patiented-Centered Guides
101 Morris Street
Sebastopol, CA 95472　　　707-829-0515
　　　　　　　　　　　　　800-998-9938
　　　　　　　　　FAX: 707-829-0104
　　　　　　　　www.patientcenters.com
Barb Lackritz, author
Linda Lamb, Editor
Shawnde Paull, Marketing

For the tens of thousands of Americans with adult leukemia, Adult Leukemia: A Comprehensive Guide for Patients and Families addresses diagnosis, medical tests, finding a good oncologist, treatments, side effects, getting emotional and other support, resources for further study, and much more. The book includes real-life stories from those who have battled leukemia themselves. *$29.95*

536 pages Paperback
ISBN 0-596500-01-7

6813 Advanced Breast Cancer: A Guide to Living with Metastic Disease

Patiented-Centered Guides
101 Morris Street
Sebastopol, CA 95472　　　707-829-0515
　　　　　　　　　　　　　800-998-9938
　　　　　　　　　FAX: 707-829-0104
　　　　　　　　www.patientcenters.com
Musa Mayer, author
Linda Lamb, Editor
Shawnde Paull, Marketing

This is the only book on breast cancer that deals honestly with the realities of living with metastic disease, yet offers hope and comfort. All aspects of facing the disease are covered, including: coping with the shock of recurrence, seeking information and making treatment decisions, communicating effectively with medical personnel finding support, and handling disease progression and end-of-life issues. A comprehensive guide, it also provides updated resources and treatment developments. *$24.95*

532 pages Paperback
ISBN 1-565925-22-X

6814 Alphabet Soup: A Recipe for Understanding & Treating ADD

Minerva Books, Ltd.
137 W 14th Street
New York, NY 10011　　　212-929-2833
　　　　　　　　　　　　　800-345-5946
James Javorsky, author
$6.95

50 pages Paperback
ISBN 0-934695-00-8

6815 American Heart Association Guide to Stroke Treatment, Recovery & Prevention

Random House
400 Hahn Road
Westminster, MD 21157
　　　　　　　　　　　　　800-726-0600
Louis Caplan, author

From the nation's premier authority on heart disease and stroke, the definitive book on stroke prevention, treatment and recovery. *$29.00*

304 pages

6816 Annals of Dyslexia

Orton Dyslexia Society
Chester Building
Suite 382
Baltimore, MD 21286
　　　　　　　　　　　　800-ABC-D123
　　　　　　　　　FAX: 410-296-0232

Offers information on auditory discrimination, dyslexia, attitudes, advocacy and more on people with learning disabilities. *$15.00*

Paper

6817 Aphasia: What is It?

Speech Bin
1965 25th Avenue
Vero Beach, FL 32960　　　561-770-0007
　　　　　　　　　　　　　800-477-3324
　　　　　　　　　FAX: 561-770-0006
　　　　　　　　　www.speechbin.com
Barbara J. LeComte, author

Brochures for families and caregivers of persons who have suffered aphasic language disorders secondary to strokes. Set of ten copies. *$14.95*

16 pages Package of 10
ISBN 0-93785 -56-4

6818 Arthritic's Cookbook

Zebra Books
475 Park Avenue S
New York, NY 10016　　　212-889-2299

Collin H. Doug, author
$8.95

Paperback
ISBN 0-821748-83-1

6819 Arthritis 101: Questions You Have - Answers You Need

Longstreet Press
Atlanta, GA　　　　　　　770-980-1488

A thorough guide to basic information, this book answers possible questions you may have about arthritis or related conditions. *$11.95*

160 pages

6820 Arthritis 101: Questions You Have. Answer You Need.

Arthritis Foundation Distribution Center
PO Box 6996
Alpharetta, GA 30009
　　　　　　　　　　　　　800-207-8633
　　　　　　　　　FAX: 770-442-9742
　　　　　　　　　www.arthritis.com

Expert reviewers answer questions about basic arthritis facts, treatments, research, surgery and more. Also, specific information about six common conditions: rheumatoid arthritis, osteoarthritis, osteoporosis, fibromyalgia, lupus and gout. *$11.95*

144 pages

6821 Arthritis Helpbook: A Tested Self-Management Program for Coping

Addison-Wesley
Route 128
Reading, MA   01867   781-944-3700
                            800-238-9682
                     FAX: 781-944-9338

Kate Lorig & James F. Fries, author

$13.50

288 pages 4th Edition
ISBN 0-201409-63-1

6822 Arthritis Self Help Products

Aids for Arthritis
3 Little Knoll Center
Medford, NJ   08055   609-654-6918

Offers lists of arthritis self-help devices.

6823 Arthritis Self-Help Book

Addison-Wesley
Route 128
Reading, MA   01867   781-944-3700
                            800-238-9682
                     FAX: 781-944-9338

Kate Lorig, RN, author

A useful and informative book used in conjunction with the Arthritis Foundation's Self-Help Course. *$12.00*

6824 Arthritis Sourcebook: Everything You Need to Know

Lowell House
2029 Century Park East
Los Angeles, CA   90067   310-556-2715
                     FAX: 310-552-7555

Earl J. Brewer, Jr. and Kathy C. Angel, author

$21.95

252 pages
ISBN 1-565650-36-0

6825 Arthritis: A Comprehensive Guide

Addison-Wesley
Route 128
Reading, MA   01867   781-944-3700
                            800-238-9682
                     FAX: 781-944-9338

James F. Fries, M.D., author

Reviews types of arthritis, different aspects of treatment including exercise, medications, surgery, the role of diet and an extensive section on challenges of daily living. *$12.00*

6826 Arthritis: Stop Suffering, Start Moving

Walker & Company
720 Fifth Avenue
New York, NY   10019   212-265-3632

Darlene Cohen, author

$22.95

160 pages
ISBN 0-802713-08-4

6827 Arthritis: Taking Care of Yourself Health Guide for Understanding Your Arthritis

Addison-Wesley
Route 128
Reading, MA   01867   781-944-3700
                     FAX: 781-944-9338

James F. Fries, author

$13.50

4th Edition
ISBN 0-201409-17-8

6828 Arthritis: What Exercises Work

St. Martin's Press
175 Fifth Avenue
New York, NY   10010   212-674-5151
                            800-221-7945
                     FAX: 212-420-9314

Dava Sobel & Arthur C. Klein, author

$19.95

160 pages
ISBN 0-312097-43-3

6829 Arthritis: Your Complete Exercise Guide

Human Kinetics Press
PO Box 5076
Champaign, IL   61825   217-351-5076
                     FAX: 217-351-2674
                e-mail: orders@hkusa.com
                www.humankinetics.com

Neil F. Gordon, M.D., PhD., MPH, author

The Cooper Clinic and Research Institute Fitness Series provides an exercise rehabilitation alternative for people with chronic meidcal conditions. *$13.95*

152 pages Paperback
ISBN 0-873223-92-6

6830 Ask the Doctor: Asthma

Andrews McMeel Publishing
PO Box 419150
Kansas City, MO   64141   816-932-6700
                            800-826-4216
                     FAX: 660-859-6559

Vincent Frieldewald, M.D, author

$8.95

128 pages Soft Cover
ISBN 0-836270-23-1

6831 Asthma Challenge

Asthma and Allergy Foundation of America
1125 15th Street NW
Suite 502
Washington, DC   20005   202-466-7643
                     FAX: 202-466-8940
                e-mail: info@aafa.org
                www.aafa.org

An exciting new team game for large or small groups. Custom-designed, full color, stand-up board and two sets of pre-tested question cards. Teens and adults win AAFA Bucks as they test their knowledge in categories like Sneezes and Wheezes and Asthma Nuts and Bolts. *$75.00*

6832 Asthma Resource Directory

National Allergy and Asthma Network
3554 Chain Bridge Road
Suite 200
Fairfax, VA 22030   703-385-4403
                            FAX: 703-352-4354
Carol Rudoff, author

Valuable reference tool with over 2,500 listings of resources and products nationwide including suppliers, camps, research centers and support groups.

6833 Asthma Self Help Book

Allergy Control Products
96 Danbury Road
PO Box 793
Ridgefield, CT 06877   203-438-9580
                               800-422-3878
                          FAX: 203-431-8963
                          www.allergycontrol.com
Paul J. Hannaway, M.D., author

A comprehensive manual on the management of asthma for parents of asthmatic children, adult asthmatics, and for health professionals. *$13.95*

Softcover

6834 Asthma Self-Help Book

Asthma and Allergy Foundation of America
1125 15th Street NW
Suite 502
Washington, DC 20005   202-466-7643
                          FAX: 202-466-8940
                          e-mail: info@aafa.org
                          www.aafa.org
Paul J. Hannaway, M.D., author

A thorough, practical look at asthma that includes information from the National Heart, Lung and Blood Institute's 1991 Asthma Guidelines. *$13.00*

271 pages Paperback

6835 Asthma Sourcebook

Omnigraphics
615 Griswold Street
Detroit, MI 48226

                          800-234-1340
                          FAX: 800-875-1340
                          www.omnigraphics.com

Annemarie S. Muth, Editor

Provides information about asthma, including symptoms, remedies and research updates. *$78.00*

650 pages 1900
ISBN 0-780803-81-7

6836 Asthma and Exercise

Henry Holt and Company
3554 Chain Bridge Road
Suite 200
Fairfax, VA 22030   703-385-4403
                          FAX: 703-352-4354
Nancy Hogshead and Gerald S. Couzens, author

This book offers clear and detailed advice on how adults and children with asthma can participate in exercise and sports activities. *$10.00*

6837 Asthma in the School: Improving Control with Peak Flow Monitoring

National Allergy and Asthma Network
3554 Chain Bridge Road
Suite 200
Fairfax, VA 22030   703-385-4403
                          FAX: 703-352-4354
Guillermo Mendoza, M.D., author

Comprehensive and practical guide to help the school nurse monitor and assist students with asthma. *$7.00*

6838 Asthma in the Workplace

John H. Dekker & Sons
2941 Clydon Street SW
Grand Rapids, MI 49509   616-538-5160
                            FAX: 616-538-0720
Bernstein, et al., author

$199.00

664 pages
ISBN 0-824787-99-4

6839 Asthma: The Complete Guide

Asthma and Allergy Foundation of America
1125 15th Street NW
Suite 502
Washington, DC 20005   202-466-7643
                          FAX: 202-466-8940
                          e-mail: info@aafa.org
                          www.aafa.org
Allan M. Weinstein, M.D., author

An excellent self-management guide for asthma and allergy patients and their families. *$6.00*

357 pages Paperback

6840 Attention Deficit Disorder & Learning Disabilities

Doubleday
666 Fifth Avenue
New York, NY 10103   212-782-8200
                          FAX: 212-492-9700
Barbara D. Ingersoll & Sam Goldstein, author

$12.95

ISBN 0-385469-31-4

6841 Attention Deficit Disorder and Learning Disabilities

Books on Special Children
PO Box 305
Congers, NY 10920   845-638-1236
                          FAX: 845-638-0847
                          e-mail: irene@boscbooks.com
B.D. Ingersoll and S. Goldstein, author

Introduces ADD and learning disabilities. This is an easy reading book. Gives definitions and discusses some effective and controverial medication, dietary, biofeedback, cognitive therapy, and many more issues. *$15.95*

246 pages Softcover
ISBN 0-385469-31-4

6842 Attention Deficit Disorder in Adults Workbook

Taylor Publishing
1550 W Mockingbird
Dallas, TX   75235   214-637-2800

Lynn Weiss, author
$17.99

192 pages Paperback
ISBN 0-878338-50-0

6843 Attention Deficit Disorder in Children and Adolescents

Charles C. Thomas Publisher
2600 S First Street
Springfield, IL   62794
                    FAX: 217-789-9130
                    e-mail: books@ccthomas.com
                    www.ccthomas.com
Jack L. Fadely and Virginia N. Hosler, author

Presents an analysis of case studies of children and adolescents with attentional deficits and hyperactivity, demonstrating causal factors in these disorders and suggesting treatment strategies both in psychological and medical practice. Written as a review and summary of twenty years of private practice. *$35.95*

292 pages Paper
ISBN 0-398061-12-2

6844 Attention Deficit Disorder: A Different Perception

Underwood-Miller
708 Westover Drive
Lancaster, PA   17601   717-285-2255

Thomas Hartmann, author
$9.95

180 pages Paperback
ISBN 0-887331-56-4

6845 Attention Deficit Hyperactivity Disorder: What Every Parent Wants To Know

Paul H. Brookes & Company
Box 10624
Baltimore, MD   21285   410-337-9580

David L. Woodrich, author
$19.95

320 pages Paperback
ISBN 1-557661-41-3

6846 Attention Deficit/Hyperactivity Disorder

David Fulton Publishers
2 Barbon Close Great Ormond Street
London,   WCIN   171-405-5606
                    FAX: 171-831-4840
Paul Cooper and Katherine Ideus, author

Resource material for teachers of children aged between five and sixteen, particularly of interest to those in the SEN field and those concerned with EBD in schools. Addresses many of the key questions that teachers raise about AD/HD, and deals with them in a clear and concise manner. Major emphasis on practical guidance for classroom practice. Also helps teachers deal with parents' questions and helps them in their work with professionals.

112 pages Paperback
ISBN 1-853464-31-7

6847 Attention-Deficit Hyperactivity Disorder

Guilford Publications
72 Spring Street
New York, NY   10012   212-431-9800
                    800-365-7006
                    FAX: 212-966-6708
                    e-mail: info@guilford.com
Russell A. Barkley, author

A second edition that is the handbook on the diagnosis and treatment of ADHD in the 1990s. A companion workbook is also available with forms that may be photocopied. *$55.00*

747 pages Hardcover
ISBN 0-898624-43-6

6848 Attention-Deficit Hyperactivity Disorder: Symptoms and Suggestons for Treatment

Slosson Educational Publications
PO Box 280
East Aurora, NY   14052   716-625-0930
                    FAX: 800-655-3840
                    e-mail: slosson@slosson.com
                    www.slosson.com
Sue Larson and Teresa Frields, author

An exhaustive review of current research and decades of experience as practicing school-based professionals, as well as being a parent of an ADHD child, have culminated in this brief, to-the-point, and yet informed ADHD package which has recieved tremendous reviews. Well-grounded answers and suggestions which would facillitate behavior, learning, social-emotional functioning, and other factors in preschool and adolesence are discussed. Answers most commonly asked questions about ADHD/ADD. *$52.00*

6849 Augmenting Basic Communcation in Natural Contexts

Brookes Publishing
PO Box 10624
Baltimore, MD   21285   410-337-9580
                    800-638-3775
                    FAX: 410-337-8539
                    e-mail: custserv@brookespublishing.com
                    www.brookespublishing.com
Jeanne M. Johnson, Ph.D., Diane Baumgart, Ph.D., author

Here you will find the techniques needed to establish a basic communication system for people of all ages with cognitive disabilities or motor sensory impairments. *$41.95*

304 pages Paperback
ISBN 1-55766 -43-6

6850 Autism

Autism Society of North Carolina Bookstore
505 Oberlin Road
Suite 230
Raleigh, NC 27605   919-743-0204
                           800-442-2762
                        FAX: 919-743-0208
                      e-mail: ASNC@aol.com
                      www.autismsociety-nc.org

Laura Schreibman, author

Everything there is to know about autism research book. *$17.95*

6851 Autism Handbook: Understanding & Treating Autism & Prevention Development

Oxford University Press
2001 Evans Road
Cary, NC 27513   212-726-6000
                         800-451-7556
                      FAX: 919-677-1303
                      www.oup-usa.org

Bryne Siegal, author

$25.00

320 pages
ISBN 0-195076-67-2

6852 Autism Treatment Guide

Autism Society of North Carolina Bookstore
505 Oberlin Road
Suite 230
Raleigh, NC 27605   919-743-0204
                           800-442-2762
                        FAX: 919-743-0208
                      e-mail: ASNC@aol.com
                      www.autismsociety-nc.org

Elizabeth K. Gerlach, author

A comprehensive book covering treatments and methods used to help individuals with autism. *$12.95*

6853 Autism and Asperger Syndrome

Autism Society of North Carolina Bookstore
505 Oberlin Road
Suite 230
Raleigh, NC 27605   919-743-0204
                           800-442-2762
                        FAX: 919-743-0208
                      e-mail: ASNC@aol.com
                      www.autismsociety-nc.org

Uta Frith, author

Chapters include topics such as the relationship of autism and asperger syndrome, living with the syndrome and asperger syndrome in adulthood. *$23.95*

6854 Autism and Learning

David Fulton Publishers
2 Barbon Close Great Ormond Street
London, WCIN   171-405-5606
                    FAX: 171-831-4840

Ed. Stuart Powell and Rita Jordan, author

This book is about how a cognitive perception on the way in which individuals with autism think and learn may be applied to particular curriculum areas.

160 pages Paperback
ISBN 1-853464-21-X

6855 Autism in Adolescents and Adults

Plenum Press
233 Spring Street
New York, NY 10013   212-620-8000
                          FAX: 212-463-0742
                       e-mail: info@plenum.com

$63.00

456 pages
ISBN 0-306410-57-5

6856 Autism...Nature, Diagnosis and Treatment

Autism Society of North Carolina Bookstore
505 Oberlin Road
Suite 230
Raleigh, NC 27605   919-743-0204
                           800-442-2762
                        FAX: 919-743-0208
                      e-mail: ASNC@aol.com
                      www.autismsociety-nc.org

Geraldine Dawson, author

Covers perspectives, issues, neurobiological issues and new directions in diagnosis and treatment. *$49.00*

6857 Autism: A Strange, Silent World

Filmakers Library
124 E 40th Street
New York, NY 10016   212-808-4980
                          FAX: 212-808-4983
                       e-mail: info@filmakers.com

British educators and medical personnel offer insight into autism's characteristics and treatment approaches through the cameos of three children.

6858 Autism: Explaining the Enigma

Autism Society of North Carolina Bookstore
505 Oberlin Road
Suite 230
Raleigh, NC 27605   919-743-0204
                           800-442-2762
                        FAX: 919-743-0208
                      e-mail: ASNC@aol.com
                      www.autismsociety-nc.org

Uta Firth, author

Explains the nature of autism. *$27.95*

6859 Autism: From Tragedy to Triumph

Branden Publishing Company
17 Station Street
PO Box 843
Brookline Village, MA 02147   617-734-2045
                             FAX: 617-734-2046
                          e-mail: branden@branden.com
                             www.branden.com

Carol Johnson & Julia Crowder, author

A new book that deals with the Lovaas method and includes a foreward by Dr. Ivar Lovaas. The book is broken down into two parts — the long road to diagnosis and then treatment. *$12.95*

6860 Autism: Identification, Education and Treatment

Autism Society of North Carolina Bookstore
505 Oberlin Road
Suite 230
Raleigh, NC   27605

919-743-0204
800-442-2762
FAX: 919-743-0208
e-mail: ASNC@aol.com
www.autismsociety-nc.org

Dianne Berkell, author

Chapters include medical treatments, early intervention and communication development in autism. *$36.00*

6861 Autism: The Facts

Oxford University Press
2001 Evans Road
Cary, NC   27513

212-726-6000
800-451-7556
FAX: 919-677-1303
www.oup-usa.org

Simon Baron-Cohen, author

$19.95

128 pages
ISBN 0-192623-28-1

6862 Autistic Adults at Bittersweet Farms

Haworth Press
10 Alice Street
Binghamton, NY   13904

604-722-5857
800-429-6784
FAX: 607-722-6362
e-mail: getinfo@haworthpressinc.com
www.haworthpressinc.com

Norman Giddan, author

A touching view of an inspirational residential care program for autistic adolescents and adults. *$89.95*

Hardcover
ISBN 1-560240-42-3

6863 Away with Arthritis

Vantage Press
516 W 34th Street
New York, NY   10001

212-736-1767
FAX: 212-736-2273

Rex E. Newhnam, author

$12.50

ISBN 0-533108-14-4

6864 BOSC - Directory Facilities for People with Learning Disabilities

Books on Special Children
PO Box 305
Congers, NY   10920

845-638-1236
FAX: 845-638-0847
e-mail: irene@boscbooks.com
www.boscbooks.com

Irene Slovak, author
Irene Slovak, Owner
Dr. Julius Kliener, Marketing Director

Directory of schools, independent living programs, clinics and centers, colleges and vocational programs, agencies and commercial products. Five sections in special post binder that can be updated annually. Hardcover. *$70.00*

300+ pages Yearly
ISSN 0961-3888

6865 Beyond the Rainbow: A Guide for Parents of a Child with Dyslexia

Educational Interventions Publishing
2810 E Cedar Bayou
Baytown, TX   77522

713-943-2331

Dr. Patricia Dodds

This book was written because a parent found answers to questions about her child's difficulties in school. She wanted other parents to gain the same understanding about their child. *$12.95*

123 pages

6866 Biology of the Autistic Syndromes, 2nd Edition

Autism Society of North Carolina Bookstore
505 Oberlin Road
Suite 230
Raleigh, NC   27605

919-743-0204
800-442-2762
FAX: 919-743-0208
e-mail: ASNC@aol.com
www.autismsociety-nc.org

Christopher Gillberg & Mary Coleman, author

A revision of the original, classic text in the light of new developments and current knowledge. This book covers the epidemiological, genetic, biochemical, immunological and neuropsychological literature on autism. *$74.95*

6867 Biomedical Concerns in Persons with Down Syndrome

Brookes Publishing
PO Box 10624
Baltimore, MD   21285

410-337-9580
800-638-3775
FAX: 410-337-8539
e-mail: custserv@brookespublishing.com
www.brookespublishing.com

$48.00

336 pages Paperback
ISBN 1-55766 -89-1

6868 Blooming Where You're Planted

Meeting Life's Challenges, LLC
9042 Aspen Grove Lane
Madison, WI   53717

608-824-0402
FAX: 608-824-0403
e-mail: help@MeetingLifesChallenges.com
www.MeetingLifesChallenges.com

Shelley Peterman Schwarz, author

Author Shelley Peterman Schwarz takes you on her journey of self-discovery and change following her diagnosis of multiple sclerosis in 1979. Her personal stories are warm and humorous, and insightful. This 138-page book will motivate and inspire you to rise above life's challenges and live life to its fullest. *$12.95*

138 pages
ISBN 0-891854-01-1

6869 Bone Up on Arthritis

Arthritis Foundation
PO Box 6996
Alpharetta, GA   30009
                          800-207-8633
                    FAX: 770-442-9742
                    www.arthritis.com
A self-help education packet designed for home-study use, this program can improve your pain and function levels by teaching proven self-help techniques. *$19.50*

w/Audio Tapes

6870 Bowel Cancer

Oxford University Press
2001 Evans Road
Cary, NC   27513
                          212-726-6000
                          800-451-7556
                    FAX: 919-677-1303
                      www.oup-usa.org
John Northover, author
Offers information and public awareness on the disease of bowel cancer. *$18.95*

152 pages

6871 Bowel Management: A Manual of Ideas and Techniques

Accent Books & Products
PO Box 700
Bloomington, IL   61702
                          309-378-2961
                          800-787-8444
                    FAX: 309-378-4420
                e-mail: acmtlvng@aol.com

Raymond C. Cheever, Publisher
Betty Garee, Editor

Paras and quads can gain much greater freedom. Includes considerations as frequency, timing, water intake, exercise and successful programs from three rehab centers. *$3.50*

25 pages Paperback
ISBN 0-91570 -02-7

6872 Breaking the Speech Barrier: Language Develpment Through Augmented Means

Brookes Publishing
PO Box 10624
Baltimore, MD   21285
                          410-337-9580
                          800-638-3775
                    FAX: 410-337-8539
          e-mail: custserv@brookespublishing.com
                www.brookespublishing.com
Mary Ann Romski, Ph.D., and Rose A. Sevcik, Ph.D., author

This resource describes the creation of the System for Augmenting Language (SAL) for school-age youth with mental retardation and offers important insights into the language development of children who are not learning to communicate typically. *$37.00*

224 pages Paperback
ISBN 1-557663-90-4

6873 Breast Cancer Sourcebook

Omnigraphics
615 Griswold Street
Detroit, MI   48226
                          800-234-1340
                    FAX: 800-875-1340
                    www.omnigraphics.com

Edward J. Prucha, Editor
Provides information on the prevention of Breast Cancer, self care, treatment options, alternative therapies, and diagnostic methods. *$78.00*

600 pages 1900
ISBN 0-780802-44-6

6874 Breathing Disorders: Your Complete Exercise Guide

Human Kinetics
PO Box 5076
Champaign, IL   61825   **217-351-5076**
                          800-747-4457
                    FAX: 217-351-1549
                  e-mail: orders@hkusa.com
                    www.humankinetics.com
Neil F. Gordon, M.D., PhD, MPH, author
$11.95

144 pages Paperback
ISBN 0-873224-26-4

6875 Bronchial Asthma: Principles of Diagnosis and Treatment

Humana Press
Crescent Manor
Clifton, NJ   07015   **973-773-4389**
                    FAX: 973-773-5235
Eric M. Gershwin & Georges Halpern, author
$125.00

784 pages
ISBN 0-896032-53-1

6876 Building Communicative Competence with Indiv. Who Use Augmentative & Alternative Commun.

Brookes Publishing
PO Box 10624
Baltimore, MD   21285
                          410-337-9580
                          800-638-3775
                    FAX: 410-337-8539
          e-mail: custserv@brookespublishing.com
                www.brookespublishing.com
Janice Light, Ph.D. and Cathy Binger, M.S., CCC-SL, author

This is a hands-on instructional program offering goal-setting, teaching, and coaching methods for improving the communicative skills of people who depend on AAC systems. Appropriate for children, adolescents, and adults at any state of communicative development. *$36.95*

336 pages Spiral-bound 1997
ISBN 1-55766 -24-6

6877 Cancer Sourcebook for Women, 2nd Edition

Omnigraphics
615 Griswold Street
Detroit, MI 48226
800-234-1340
FAX: 800-875-1340
www.omnigraphics.com

Edward J. Prucha, Editor
Provides information on the specific forms of cancer that affect women. *$78.00*

600 pages 1900
ISBN 0-780802-26-8

6878 Cancer Sourcebook, 3rd Edition

Omnigraphics
615 Griswold Street
Detroit, MI 48226
800-234-1340
FAX: 800-875-1340
www.omnigraphics.com

Edward J. Prucha, Editor
Includes information on the major forms and stages of cancer. *$78.00*

1100 pages 1900
ISBN 0-780802-27-6

6879 Charting: The Systematic Approach to Achieving Control

RA Rapaport Publishing
150 W 22nd Street
New York, NY 10011
212-691-7676
FAX: 212-989-4787

Janice Roth, author
One of America's leading diabetes educators shows you, in this book, how to analyze your body's responses to diet, exercises and medication, and how to create a personalized systematic program for total diabetes control. *$3.95*

38 pages Paperback
ISBN 0-96317 -10-

6880 Child Care and the ADA: A Handbook for Inclusive Programs

Brookes Publishing
PO Box 10624
Baltimore, MD 21285
410-337-9580
800-638-3775
FAX: 410-337-8539
e-mail: custserv@brookespublishing.com
www.brookespublishing.com
Victoria Youcha Rab, Ed.D., author

This book is designed for educators and administrators in child care settings. It offers a straightforward discussion of the Americans with Disabilities Act including children with disabilities in community programs. *$25.95*

240 pages Paperback
ISBN 1-55766 -85-5

6881 Childen with Cerebral Palsy

Woodbine House
6510 Bells Mill Road
Bethesda, MD 20817
800-843-7323
www.woodbinehouse.com

Children with Cerebral Palsy, considered by many to be the first book that families should read, is newly revised and updated. As one of Woodbine House's Parents' Guides, it provides a complete spectrum of information and compassionate advice about cerebral palsy and its effect on their child's development and education. Covers these areas: diagnosis, medical issues, family life, legal rights, early intervention, coping, therapies, treatment, development, advocacy, special ed., and daily care. *$16.95*

470 pages Paperback
ISBN 0-933149-82-4

6882 Children with Acquired Brain Injury: Educating and Supporting Families

Brookes Publishing
PO Box 10624
Baltimore, MD 21285
410-337-9580
800-638-3775
FAX: 410-337-8539
e-mail: custserv@brookespublishing.com
www.brookespublishing.com

This guide provides practical strategies for helping children with acquired brain injury and their families move through the rehabilitation and recovery process. It addresses the medical, educational, psychosocial, and prevocational supports needed and explains how coping supports can be created to meet the individual needs of each family. *$28.95*

288 pages Paperback
ISBN 1-55766 -33-9

6883 Children with Acquired Brain Injury:2 Education and Supporting Families

Brookes Publishing
PO Box 10624
Baltimore, MD 21285
410-337-9580
800-638-3775
FAX: 410-337-8539
e-mail: custserv@brookespublishing.com
www.brookespublishing.com
George H.S. Singer, PhD, Editor, author
Ann Glang, PhD, Editor
Janet M. Williams, MSW, Editor

$28.95

288 pages Paperback 1996
ISBN 1-557662-33-9

6884 Children with Asthma: A Manual for Parents

Allergy Control Products
96 Danbury Road
PO Box 793
Ridgefield, CT 06877
203-438-9580
800-422-3878
FAX: 203-431-8963
www.allergycontrol.com

Thomas E. Plaut, M.D., author

Known as the asthma bible, this second edition is sprinkled with anecdotes by patients and their parents. *$10.00*

296 pages Paperback

6885 Children with Tourette Syndrome

Exceptional Parent Library
PO Box 1807
Englewood Cliffs, NJ 10116
800-535-1910
e-mail: eplibrary@aol.com
www.eplibrary.com

T. Haerle, author

Written by a team of professionals and parents, this book covers medical, educational, legal, family life, daily care, and emotional issues. *$14.95*

6886 Children with Visual Impairments

Woodbine House
6510 Bells Mill Road
Bethesda, MD 20817
800-843-7323
www.woodbinehouse.com

Cay Holbrook, PhD, author

For families of children with visual impairments ranging from low vision to total blind, this book offers aythoritative and empathetic parental insight on diagnosis and treatment, family adjustment, orientation and mobility, literacy, legal issues, and more. *$16.95*

395 pages Paperback
ISBN 0-933149-36-0

6887 Clinical Care in the Rheumatic Disease

Arthritis Foundation Distribution Center
PO Box 6996
Alpharetta, GA 30009
800-207-8633
FAX: 770-442-9742
www.arthritis.com

This book was written for all health professionals caring for people with rheumatic diseases and for students in these disciplines. *$35.00*

224 pages

6888 Colon & Rectal Cancer: A Comprehensive Guide for Patients & Families

Patient-Centered Guides
101 Morris Street
Sebastopol, CA 95472
707-829-0515
800-998-9938
FAX: 707-829-0104
www.patientcenters.com

Lorraine Johnston, author
Linda Lamb, Editor
Shawnde Paull, Marketing

The fourth most common cancer, colon and rectal cancer is diagnosed in 130,000 new cases in the United States each year. Patients and families need uo-to-date and in-depth information to participate wisely in treatment decisions (e.g., knowing what sexual and fertility issues to discuss with the doctor before surgery). This book covers coping with tests and treatment side effects, caring for ostomies, finding supportt, and other practical issues. *$24.95*

544 pages Paperback
ISBN 1-565926-33-1

6889 Come Sign with Us

Gallaudet University Press
11030 S Langley Avenue
Chicago, IL 60628
800-621-2736
FAX: 800-621-8476
TDY:800-621-9347
gupress.gallaudet.edu

Jan C. Hafer, Co-Author
Robert M. Wilson, Co-Author

This fun guide for parents and educators on teaching hearing children how to sign has been thoroughly revised with completely new activities that provide contexts for practice. *$29.95*

160 pages Softcover

6890 Communication Development and Disorders in African American Children

Brookes Publishing
PO Box 10624
Baltimore, MD 21285
410-337-9580
800-638-3775
FAX: 410-337-8539
e-mail: custserv@brookespublishing.com
www.brookespublishing.com

Research, Assessment, and Intervention. This text presents research on communication disorders and language development in African American children. Also addresses multicultural aspects of service delivery and intervention and discusses issues in assessing, diagnosing, and treating communication disorders. *$39.00*

400 pages Paperback
ISBN 1-55766 -53-3

6891 Communication Development in Children with Down Syndrome

Brookes Publishing
PO Box 10624
Baltimore, MD 21285
410-337-9580
800-638-3775
FAX: 410-337-8539
e-mail: custserv@brookespublishing.com
www.brookespublishing.com

This book offers an extensive, detailed explanation of communication development in children with Down syndrome relative to their advancing cognitive skills. It introduces a critical framework for assessing and treating hearing, speech, and language problems and provides explicit intervention methods and tested clinical protocols.

Paperback 1998
ISBN 1-55766 -50-5

6892 Communication-Based Intervention for Problem Behavior

Brookes Publishing
PO Box 10624
Baltimore, MD 21285   410-337-9580
800-638-3775
FAX: 410-337-8539
e-mail: custserv@brookespublishing.com
www.brookespublishing.com

Len Levin, MA, Duane Kemp, Ph.D., Jane Carlson, MA, author

A user's guide for producing positive change. This manual details methods for conducting functional assessments, communication-based intervention strategies, procedures for facilitating generalization and maintenance, and crisis management tactics. Useful for handling intense behavior problems. Also included are case studies and checklists of things to do to ensure success. *$38.00*

288 pages Paperback
ISBN 1-557662-46-0

6893 Compendiums of Educational Resources on Spinal Cord/Traumatic Brain Injury

Institute for Rehabilitation & Research
1333 Moursund Street
Houston, TX 77030   713-799-7011

e-mail: ilru@tsbbs0z.tnet.com

Linda Herson, Coordinator/Material

Two directories of information about videotapes and non-published resources, one for spinal cord injury and another for traumatic brain injury. Information has been categorized by major subject headings and includes name of vendors, address, phone number, short description, year of production, cost and target audience. Resources have been developed primarily from rehabilitation centers and other medical facilities throughout the U.S. Available for purchase for $50.00 for each compendium.

6894 Comprehensive Guide to ADD in Adults: Research, Diagnosis & Treatment

Taylor & Francis Publishers
7625 Empire Drive
Florence, KY 41042
800-634-7064
FAX: 800-248-4724

Kathleen G. Nadeau, author
$50.95

426 pages
ISBN 0-876307-60-8

6895 Conquering Asthma: An Illustrated Guide To Understanding & Care for Adults

Login Publishers Consortium
1436 W Randolph Street
Chicago, IL 60607   312-733-8228
FAX: 312-666-2680

Michael T. Newhouse & Peter J. Barnes, author

This text shows asthmatics how to live a healthier and happier life hardly aware that they have asthma. *$12.95*

124 pages Paperback
ISBN 0-969517-11-4

6896 Coping with ADD/ADHD

Rosen Publishing Group
29 E 21st Street
New York, NY 10010   212-777-3017
800-237-9932
FAX: 888-436-4643
e-mail: rosenpub@tribeca.ios.com

Jaydene Morrison, MS, author

At least 3.5 million American youngsters suffer from attention deficit disorder. This book defines the syndrome and provides specific information about treatment and counseling. *$16.95*

ISBN 0-823920-70-4

6897 Coping with Asthma

Rosen Publishing Group
29 E 21st Street
New York, NY 10010   212-777-3017
800-237-9932
FAX: 888-436-4643
e-mail: rosenpub@tribeca.ios.com

Carolyn Simpson, author

This book prepares students by explaining to them the dangers of asthma, a condition which, when properly treated, is completely manageable. *$16.95*

ISBN 0-823920-69-0

6898 Coping with Cerebral Palsy

Pro-Ed
8700 Shoal Creek Boulevard
Austin, TX 78757
FAX: 512-451-8542
e-mail: proed1@aol.com

This second edition book provides parents of children and adults with cerebral palsy the answers to more than 300 questions that have been carefully researched. It represents 40 years of experience by the author and is presented in a highly readable, jargon-free manner. *$26.00*

252 pages
ISBN 0-89079 -76-2

6899 Counseling for Heart Disease

Brookes Publishing
PO Box 10624
Baltimore, MD 21285   410-337-9580
800-638-3775
FAX: 410-337-8539
e-mail: custserv@brookespublishing.com
www.brookespublishing.com

Paul Bennett, S.R.N., R.M.N., Ph.D., author
$25.00

144 pages Paperback
ISBN 1-85433 -96-9

6900 Counseling in Terminal Care & Bereavement

Brookes Publishing
PO Box 10624
Baltimore, MD 21285   410-337-9580
800-638-3775
FAX: 410-337-8539
e-mail: custserv@brookespublishing.com
www.brookespublishing.com

Colin Murray Parkes, M.D., D.P.M, FRCPsych, author

Provides practical suggestions for addressing the needs of patients and family members who are anticipating or currently dealing with grief and bereavement, such as hospice care, hospitals, or at home care. *$34.00*

210 pages Paperback
ISBN 1-85433 -78-7

6901   Counselling People with Diabetes

Brookes Publishing
PO Box 10624
Baltimore, MD   21285   410-337-9580
800-638-3775
FAX: 410-337-8539
e-mail: custserv@brookespublishing.com
www.brookespublishing.com
Richard Shillitoe, Ph.D., author

$29.00

158 pages Paperback
ISBN 1-85433 -36-1

6902   Count Us In

Exceptional Parent Library
PO Box 1807
Englewood Cliffs, NJ   10116
800-535-1910
e-mail: eplibrary@aol.com
www.eplibrary.com
J. Kingsley & M. Levitz, author

Offers information on growing up with Downs Syndrome. *$9.95*

6903   Diabetes 101

Chronimed Publishing
13911 Ridgedale Drive
Minnetonka, MN   55305   612-916-2500
800-848-2793
FAX: 612-513-6170
Betty Page Brackenridge, M.S., RD, CDE, author
Sandra A. Hintz, Marketing Coord.

A pure and simple guide for people who use insulin. *$ 10.95*

208 pages Paperback
ISBN 1-56561 -24-5

6904   Diagnosis and Treatment of Autism

Autism Society of North Carolina Bookstore
505 Oberlin Road
Suite 230
Raleigh, NC   27605   919-743-0204
800-442-2762
FAX: 919-743-0208
e-mail: ASNC@aol.com
www.autismsociety-nc.org
Christopher Gillberg, Et Al., author

Various chapters written by professionals working with autistic children and adults. *$150.00*

6905   Dictionary of Congenital Malformations & Disorders

Parthenon Publishing Group
120 Mill Road
Park Ridge, NJ   07656   201-391-6796

Olivers Potparic & John Gibson, author

$55.00

193 pages
ISBN 0-850705-77-1

6906   Disorders of Motor Speech: Assessment, Treatment, and Clinical Characterization

Brookes Publishing
PO Box 10624
Baltimore, MD   21285   410-337-9580
800-638-3775
FAX: 410-337-8539
e-mail: custserv@brookespublishing.com
www.brookespublishing.com

This book provides a probing examination of normal, dysarthric, and apraxic speech. Great for speech-language pathologists, neurologists, physical or occupational therapists, and physiatrists. *$47.00*

400 pages Hardcover
ISBN 1-55766 -23-1

6907   Dressing Tips and Clothing Resources for Making Life Easier

Attainment Company
PO Box 930160
Verona, WI   53593
800-327-4269
e-mail: help@MeetingLifesChallenges.com
www.MeetingLifesChallenges.com
Shelley Peterman Schwarz, author
Don Bastian, President

Learn hundreds of simple tips and techniques to make dressing easier. Learn how to adapt/modify ready-to-wear garments to accommodate your special dressing needs. Find out how to locate more than 100 resources offering specially designed or easy-on/easy-off clothing for men, women, children and/or wheelchair users. You'll find everything you need to look your best. An invaluable resource for people with special dressing needs, people with disabilities, caregivers and healthcare professionals. *$19.00*

144 pages 2000
ISBN 1-578611-19-9

6908   Driven to Distraction

National Alliance for the Mentally Ill
PO Box 753
Waldorf, MD   20604   703-524-7600

Edward Hallowell and John Ratey, author

A practical book discussing adult as well as child attention deficit disorder (ADD). Non-technical, realistic and optimistic, it is an informative how-to manual for parents and consumers. *$23.00*

6909   Dyslexia over the Lifespan

Educators Publishing Service
31 Smith Place
Cambridge, MA   02138   617-367-2700
800-225-5750
FAX: 617-547-0412
www.epsbooks.com
Margaret B. Rawson, author

Discusses the educational and career development of 56 dyslexic boys from a private school that was one of the first to have a program to detect and treat developmental language disabilities. $ 18.00

224 pages
ISBN 0-838816-70-3

6910   Eating Disorders Sourcebook

Omnigraphics
615 Griswold Street
Detroit, MI   48226

800-234-1340
FAX: 800-875-1340
www.omnigraphics.com

Dawn D. Mattews, Editor

Provides general imformation, causes, and treatments of eating disorders. *$78.00*

600 pages 1900
ISBN 0-780803-35-3

6911   Effective Teaching Methods for Autistic Children

Charles C. Thomas Publisher, Ltd.
2600 South First Street
Springfield, IL   62704

217-789-8980
800-258-8980
FAX: 217-789-9130
e-mail: books@ccthomas.com
www.ccthomas.com

Rosalind C. Oppenheim, author

$20.95

124 pages Paper
ISBN 0-398063-09-5

6912   Encounters with Autistic States

Jason Aronson
400 Keystone Industrial Park
Dunmore, PA   18512

800-782-0015
FAX: 201-840-7242
www.aronson.com

Theodore Mitrani and Judith Mitrani, author

$50.00

Hardcover
ISBN 0-765700-62-

6913   Environmental Birth Defect Digest

930 Woodcock Road
Suite 225
Orlando, FL   32803

407-245-7035
800-313-ABCD
www.birthdefects.org

Compendium of research briefs from the world medical literature, plus original articles covering birth defects associated with medications, radiation, chemicals, toxic sites, dioxin, pesticides, lead, mercury, Bendectin, aspartame and more. *$15.00*

42 pages

6914   Family Health Guide: Arthritis & Rheumatism

Sterling Publications
387 Park Avenue South
5th Floor
New York, NY   10016

212-532-7160

Lee Rodwell, author

$9.95

80 pages Paperback
ISBN 0-706372-57-3

6915   Fetal Alcohol Syndrome

Brookes Publishing
PO Box 10624
Baltimore, MD   21285

410-337-9580
800-638-3775
FAX: 410-337-8539
e-mail: custserv@brookespublishing.com
www.brookespublishing.com

Ann Streissguth, Ph.D., author

This text conveys urgent information about medical and social issues surrounding fetal alcohol syndrome (FAS). Explains how to identify the disorder, how to work with children (and adults) who have it, how to talk to parents about it, and how to prevent its occurrence through sensitive education of prospective mothers and society at large. *$ 22.95*

336 pages Paperback 1997
ISBN 1-55766 -83-5

6916   Fighting for Darla: Challenges for Family Care & Professional Responsibility

Baker & Taylor, Int'l
1200 US Highway 22 E
Bridgewater, NJ   08807

908-429-4074
FAX: 908-429-4037
e-mail: intsale@bakertaylor.com

Ellen Brantlinger, author

Follows the story of Darla, a pregnant adolescent with autism. *$18.95*

176 pages
ISBN 0-807733-56-3

6917   Focus Your Energy: Succeeding in Business with ADD

PB Consulting Services
Box 7
New York, NY   10024

212-799-3854

Thom Hartmann, author

$10.00

Paperback
ISBN 0-671516-89-2

6918   Fragile Success - Nine Autistic Children, Childhood to Adulthood

Autism Society of North Carolina Bookstore
505 Oberlin Road
Suite 230
Raleigh, NC   27605

919-743-0204
800-442-2762
FAX: 919-743-0208
e-mail: ASNC@aol.com
www.autismsociety-nc.org

Virginia Walker Sperry, author

A book about the lives of autistic children, whom the author has followed from their early years at the Elizabeth Ives School in New Haven, CT, through to adulthood. *$27.50*

6919 Frames of Reference for the Assessment of Learning Disabilities

Brookes Publishing
PO Box 10624
Baltimore, MD 21285   410-337-9580
                             800-638-3775
                        FAX: 410-337-8539
e-mail: custserv@brookespublishing.com
www.brookespublishing.com

New views on measurement issues. Here you'll find an in=depth look at the fundamental concerns facing those who work with children with learning disabilities - assessment and identification. *$55.00*

672 pages Hardcover
ISBN 1-55766-38-3

6920 Freedom From Arthritis Through Nutrition & Help for Allergies Sixth Edition

Tree of Life Publications
PO Box 126
Joshua Tree, CA 92252   760-366-3695
                           FAX: 760-366-3596
Philip J. Welsh & Bianca Leonardo, author
$14.95

256 pages Paperback
ISBN 0-930852-15-X

6921 Going Places, Children Living with Cerebral Palsy

Gareth Stevens
1555 N River Center Drive
Milwaukee, WI 53212   414-225-0333
                             800-542-2595
                        FAX: 414-225-0377
Thomas Bergman, author

Mathias is a charming six-year-old with cerebral palsy. He needs special exercises to help him learn to control his muscles. He is also almost completely deaf. But with the love and encouragement of his family, Mathias is developing an interesting and busy life. Every morning finds him eager to start the day's activities. *$13.95*

48 pages
ISBN 0-836801-99-7

6922 Handbook of Autism and Pervasive Developmental Disorders

Autism Society of North Carolina Bookstore
505 Oberlin Road
Suite 230
Raleigh, NC 27605   919-743-0204
                           800-442-2762
                      FAX: 919-743-0208
e-mail: ASNC@aol.com
www.autismsociety-nc.org
Donald J. Cohen, author

A list of contributors address such topics as characteristics of autistic syndromes and interventions. *$125.00*

6923 Heart Disease in Persons with Down Syndrome

Brookes Publishing
PO Box 10624
Baltimore, MD 21285   410-337-9580
                             800-638-3775
                        FAX: 410-337-8539
e-mail: custserv@brookespublishing.com
www.brookespublishing.com

Offers access to findings from state-of-the-art research on congenital heart disease in children and adults with Down syndrome. Information on cardiac malformations and anomalies, heart and lung pathology, hemodynamic evaluations, and surgical intervention. *$62.00*

240 pages Hardcover
ISBN 1-55766-24-X

6924 Help Yourself Cookbook

Arthritis Foundation
PO Box 6996
Alpharetta, GA 30009
                             800-207-0633
                        FAX: 770-442-9742
www.arthritis.com
$12.95

158 pages

6925 Help for the Learning Disabled Child: Symptoms and Solutions- Revised

Slosson Educational Publications
PO Box 280
East Aurora, NY 14052   716-652-0930
                               800-756-7766
                          FAX: 800-655-3840
e-mail: slosson@slosson.com
www.slosson.com
Lou Stewart, author

This easy-to-read text describes observable behaviors, offers remediation techniques, materials, and specific tests to assist teachers in further diagnosis. This revision has been updated to include specific information and techniques to use with children who appear to have attention deficit disorders. Teachers and parents gain a better understanding of their child's difficulties in school and at home. *$ 31.00*

6926 Helping People with Autism Manage Their Behavior

Autism Society of North Carolina Bookstore
505 Oberlin Road
Suite 230
Raleigh, NC 27605   919-743-0204
                           800-442-2762
                      FAX: 919-743-0208
e-mail: ASNC@aol.com
www.autismsociety-nc.org
Nancy J. Dalrymple, author

Covers the broad topic of helping people with autism manage their behavior. *$7.00*

6927 Hidden Child: The Linwood Method for Reaching the Autistic Child

Woodbine House
6510 Bells Mill Road
Bethesda, MD 20817
                             800-843-7323
www.woodbinehouse.com
Heanne Simons, author

Chronicle of the Linwood Children's Center's successful treatment program for autistic children. *$17.95*

286 pages Paperback
ISBN 0-933149-06-9

6928   Honey are You Listening?

Nelson Publications
One Gateway Plaza
Port Chester, NY   10573   **914-937-8400**

Rick & Jerilyn Fowler, author
  $12.99

  Paperback
  ISBN 0-840777-10-8

6929   How to Live with a Spinal Cord Injury

Accent Books & Products
PO Box 700
Bloomington, IL   61702   **309-378-2961**
                                     800-787-8444
                           FAX: 309-378-4420
            e-mail: acmtlvng@aol.com
Elle Becker, M.A., author
Raymond C. Cheever, Publisher
Betty Guree, Editor

A guide packed with realistic information about how this disability affects your life and what you can do about it. Answers lots of questions and gives you positive information providing hope and plenty of encouragement. *$6.95*

58 pages Paperback
ISBN 0-91570 -27-2

6930   How to Teach Autistic & Severely Handicapped Children

Autism Society of North Carolina Bookstore
505 Oberlin Road
Suite 230
Raleigh, NC   27605   **919-743-0204**
                                 800-442-2762
                       FAX: 919-743-0208
            e-mail: ASNC@aol.com
        www.autismsociety-nc.org
Robert L. Koegel, author

Book provides procedures for effectively assessing and teaching autistic and other severely handicapped children. *$8.00*

6931   Hydrocephalus: A Guide fpr Patients, Families & Friends

Patient-Centered Guides
101 Morris Street
Sebastopol, CA   95472   **707-829-0515**
                                    800-998-9938
                          FAX: 707-829-0104
          www.patientcenters.com
Chuck Toporek & Kellie Robinson, author
Linda Lamb, Editor
Shawnde Paull, Marketing

Hydrocephalus is a life-threatening condition often referred to as, water on the brain, that is treated by surgical placement of a shunt system. Hydrocephalus: A Guide for Patients, Families and Friends educates families so they can select a skilled neurosurgeon, understand treatments, participate in care, know what symptoms need attention, discover where to turn for support, keep records needed for follow-up treatments, and make wise lifestyle choices. *$19.95*

379 pages Paperback
ISBN 1-565924-10-X

6932   Hyperactive Child, Adolescent, and Adult: ADD Through the Lifespan

C.A.C.L.D.
25 Van Zant Street
Suite 15-5
East Norwalk, CT   06855   **203-838-5010**
                           FAX: 203-866-6108
            e-mail: CACLD@JUNO.com
                www.CACLD.org
Paul Wender, M.D., author

Comprehensive general review. Update on previous research by the author, offering a basic text. Published by Ccnnecticut Association for Children & Adults with Learning Disabilities (CACLD). *$8.75*

162 pages

6933   In Control

Arthritis Foundation
1330 W Peachtree Street
Atlanta, GA   30309   **404-872-7100**
                                 800-283-7800
                       FAX: 404-872-0457

An excellent at-home program which includes video, audio cassettes and the Arthritis Helpbook. Provides tools to help meet the challenges of arthritis.

6934   Increasing Behaviors of Persons with Severe Retardation and Autism

Research Press
2612 N Mattis Avenue
Champaign, IL   61821   **217-352-3273**
                                   800-519-2707
                         FAX: 217-352-1221
          e-mail: rp@researchpress.com
              www.researchpress.com
Richard M. Foxx, Author, author
Russell Pence, V P Marketing

Shows how to increase desirable behaviors by using techniques such as shaping, prompting, fading, modeling, backward chaining, and graduated guidance. Includes exercises, review questions, and numerous examples. *$15.95*

230 pages Paperback
ISBN 0-878222-63-4

6935   Individuals with Arthritis

Mainstream
3 Bethesda Metro Center
Suite 830
Bethesda, MD   20814   **301-951-6122**
                                  800-247-1380
          e-mail: info@mainstreaminc.org
Mainstream, Inc., author

Mainstreaming individuals with arthritis into the workplace. *$2.50*

12 pages

6936 Individuals with Cerebral Palsy

Mainstream
3 Bethesda Metro Center
Suite 830
Bethesda, MD   20814   301-951-6122
                                    800-247-1380
        e-mail: info@mainstreaminc.org
Mainstream, Inc., author

Mainstreaming individuals with cerebral palsy into the workplace. *$2.50*

12 pages

6937 Injured Mind, Shattered Dreams: Brian's Survival from a Severe Head Injury

Brookline Books
PO Box 1046
Cambridge, MA   02238   617-868-0360
                                  800-666-2665
                             FAX: 617-868-1772
        e-mail: brooklinebks@delphi.com
                www.brooklinebooks.com
Janet Miller Rife, author

Brian, headed for normal adulthood, crashes his car and suffers a severe head injury. This book speaks to the issues in his recovery and the victory a family can achieve through caring advocacy and faith. *$17.95*

Paperback
ISBN 0-91479 -95-6

6938 Interdisciplinary Clinical Assessment of Young Children with Developmental Disabilities

Brookes Publishing
PO Box 10624
Baltimore, MD   21285   410-337-9580
                                  800-638-3775
                             FAX: 410-337-8539
    e-mail: custserv@brookespublishing.com
            www.brookespublishing.com
Michael J. Guralnick, PhD, author

Offers insight from veteran team members on interdisciplinary team assessments. Professionals organizing a team as well as students preparing for practice will find advice on how practitioners gather information, approach assessment, make decisions, and face the challenges of their individual fields. Includes case studies and appendix of photocopiable questionnaires for clinicians and parents. *$42.00*

432 pages Hardcover 1900
ISBN 1-557664-50-1

6939 Is the Child Really Stuttering? Questions & Answers About Disfluency

Speech Bin
1965 25th Avenue
Vero Beach, FL   32960   561-770-0007
                                  800-477-3324
                             FAX: 561-770-0006
                             www.speechbin.com
Julie A Blonigen, author

In a question and answer format concisely shows differences between normal developmental and abnorlam disfluency and motivates adult listeners to deal with problems speech behaviors in a positive way. Set of ten brochures. *$9.95*

6940 Joslin Guide to Diabetes

Joslin Diabetes Center
1 Joslin Place
Boston, MA   02215   617-732-2400

Discusses the causes of diabetes, the role of diet and exercise, meal planning and complications. Also provide information on drawing blood, mixing and injecting insulin, special challenges, living with diabetes. *$20.00*

352 pages

6941 Journeys on Dialysis

65 E India Row
Apartment 22G
Boston, MA   02110
                                  800-622-0446
                             FAX: 617-523-7970

Linda Byers McGrath, President

Organization provides help for persons who depend on dialysis but still want to enjoy cruises to many destinations around the world.

6942 Labeling the Mentally Retarded

University of California Press
2120 Berkeley Way
Berkeley, CA   94720   510-643-7154
                             FAX: 510-643-7127
                             www.ucpress.edu
Jane R. Mercer, author

Clinical and social system perspectives on mental retardation. *$12.95*

333 pages Paper

6943 Language Disabilities in Children and Adolescents

McGraw-Hill, School Publishing
220 East Danieldale Road
DeSoto, TX   75115   972-224-1111
                                  800-442-9685
                             FAX: 972-228-1982
                             mhschool.com

A comprehensive review of research in language disabilities.

6944 Language-Related Learning Disabilities: Their Nature and Treatment

Brookes Publishing
PO Box 10624
Baltimore, MD   21285   410-337-9580
                                  800-638-3775
                             FAX: 410-337-8539
    e-mail: custserv@brookespublishing.com
            www.brookespublishing.com
Adele Gerber, M.A., CCC-SLP, author

$47.00

464 pages Paperback
ISBN 1-55766 -53-0

6945 Lead Poisoning in Childhood
Brookes Publishing
PO Box 10624
Baltimore, MD 21285   410-337-9580
                               800-638-3775
                        FAX: 410-337-8539
e-mail: custserv@brookespublishing.com
        www.brookespublishing.com

This book examines the epidemiology, etiology, and pathophysiology of lead poisoning - the most prevalent preventable childhood health problem today. Also provides practical prevention strategies that are cost-effective and easy to implement. *$31.95*

256 pages Paperback
ISBN 1-55766-32-0

6946 Learning Disabilities, Literacy, and Adult Education
Brookes Publishing
PO Box 10624
Baltimore, MD 21285   410-337-9580
                               800-638-3775
                        FAX: 410-337-8539
e-mail: custserv@brookespublishing.com
        www.brookespublishing.com

This book focuses on adults with severe learning disabilities and the educators who work with them. Described are the characteristics, demographics, and educational and employment status of adults with LD and the laws that protect them in the workplace and in educational settings.

450 pages Paperback 1998
ISBN 1-55766-47-5

6947 Learning Disabilities: Lifelong Issues
Brookes Publishing
PO Box 10624
Baltimore, MD 21285   410-337-9580
                               800-638-3775
                        FAX: 410-337-8539
e-mail: custserv@brookespublishing.com
        www.brookespublishing.com

Sections of this book are devoted to education, labor, justice, and health and human services offering an overview of research and a critical appraisal of the status of learning disability practices. This book sets forth an agenda for improving the educational and ultimately, the social and economic futures of people with learning disabilities. *$36.00*

352 pages Paperback
ISBN 1-55766-40-1

6948 Living Well with Asthma
Guilford Press
72 Spring Street
New York, NY 10012   212-431-9800
                               800-365-7006
                        FAX: 212-966-6708
www.guilford.com
Michael R. Freedman, PhD, Samuel J. Roseberg, PhD, author
Cynthia L. Divino, PhD, Author

$15.95

213 pages Paperback 1998
ISBN 1-572300-51-5

6949 Living with Rheumatoid Arthritis
John's Hopkins University Press
2715 North Charles Street
Baltimore, MD 21218   410-516-6900
                               800-537-5487
                        FAX: 410-516-6998
www.jhupbooks.com
Tammi Shlotzhauer, M.D., author

This book offers practical and usable answers to the questions of everyday life. The authors provide clear explanations of the causes, diagnosis, and treatment of the disease, and why medication, joint protection, physical activity, and good nutrition are essential components of care. *$16.95*

280 pages Paperback
ISBN 0-801851-85-8

6950 Lung Cancer: Making Sense of Diagnosis, Treatment, & Option
Patient-Centered Guides
101 Morris Street
Sebastopol, CA 95472   707-829-0515
                               800-998-9938
                        FAX: 707-829-0104
www.patientcenters.com
Lorraine Johnston, author
Linda Lamb, Editor
Shawnde Paull, Marketing

Straightforward language and the words of patients and their families are the hallmarks of this book on the number one cancer killer in the US. Written by a widely respected author and patient advocate, Lung Cancer: Making Sense of Diagnosis, Treatment, & Options has been meticulously reviewed by top medical experts and physicians. Readers will find medical facts simply explained, advice to ease their daily life, and tools to be strong advocates for themselves or a family member. *$ 27.95*

530 pages Paperback
ISBN 0-596500-02-5

6951 Management of Autistic Behavior
Pro-Ed
8700 Shoal Creek Boulevard
Austin, TX 78758   512-451-3246
                        FAX: 512-451-8542
                e-mail: proed1@aol.com
Richard Simpson, author

Comprehensive and practical book that tells what works best with specific problems. *$41.00*

450 pages Paperback
ISBN 0-890791-96-1

6952 Managing Attention Disorders in Children: A Guide for Practitioners
Books on Special Children
PO Box 305
Congers, NY 10920   845-638-1236
                        FAX: 845-638-0847
                e-mail: irene@boscbooks.com
Sam Goldstein, Ph.D., author

Offers information about human personality, structure and dynamics, assessment and adjustment. *$27.50*

214 pages

6953 Medications for Attention Disorders and Related Medical Problems

Specialty Press
Plantation, FL
800-233-9273

Edna D. Copeland, PhD, author

A comprehensive handbook covering the history, characteristics, and causes of ADHD. The equal importance of appropriate academic programming, counseling, and medication are stressed throughout. $40.00

415 pages Hardcover

6954 Motor Speech Disorders

WB Saunders Company
Independence Square West
Philadelphia, PA 19106
215-238-7800

www.wbsaunders.com

Frederic L. Darley, author

Professional text on rehabilitation techniques for motor speech disorders. $74.00

304 pages
ISBN 0-72162-78-8

6955 Motor Speech Disorders: Advances in Assessment and Treatment

Brookes Publishing
PO Box 10624
Baltimore, MD 21285
410-337-9580
800-638-3775
FAX: 410-337-8539
e-mail: custserv@brookespublishing.com
www.brookespublishing.com

$38.00

288 pages Paperback
ISBN 1-55766-37-5

6956 Multiple Sclerosis: A Guide for Patients and Their Families

Lippincott, Williams & Wilkins
227 E Washington Square
Philadelphia, PA 19106
215-238-4200
800-777-2295
FAX: 301-824-7390
www.lpub.com

Labe Scheinberg, author

$16.00

288 pages

6957 Muscular Dystrophy and Other Neuromuscular Diseases

Haworth Press
10 Alice Street
Binghamton, NY 13904
604-722-5857
800-429-6784
FAX: 607-722-6362
e-mail: getinfo@haworthpressinc.com
www.haworthpressinc.com

Leon I. Charash, author
Jackie Blakeslee, Advertising

A thoughtful new book from professionals who assist persons afflicted with neuromuscular disorders to help them and their families adapt to lifestyle changes accompanying the onset of these disorders. $69.95

250 pages Hardcover
ISBN 1-560240-77-6

6958 National Association for the Visually Handicapped

22 W 21st Street
New York, NY 10010
212-889-3141
FAX: 212-727-2931
e-mail: staff@navh.org
www.navh.org

Eva Cohen, Asst. to Director

24 pages

6959 Neurobiology of Autism

Johns Hopkins University Press
2715 N Charles Street
Baltimore, MD 21218
410-516-6936
FAX: 410-516-6998

Margaret L. Bauman, M.D. & Thomas L. Kemper, M.D., author

This book discusses recent advances in scientific research that point to a neurobiological basis for autism and examines the clinical implications of this research. $28.00

272 pages
ISBN 0-801856-80-9

6960 Neuromotor Speech Disorders: Nature, Assessment, and Management

Brookes Publishing
PO Box 10624
Baltimore, MD 21285
410-337-9580
800-638-3775
FAX: 410-337-8539
e-mail: custserv@brookespublishing.com
www.brookespublishing.com

Topics included in this book are: motor-speech imaging, anatomical structure and function in dysarthria, physiological and acoustic analyses of dysarthria intelligibility, dysphonia, and linguistic considerations in apraxia of speech. $44.95

320 pages Hardcover 1998
ISBN 1-55766-26-2

6961 One Minute Asthma...What You Need to Know

Asthma and Allergy Foundation of America
1125 15th Street NW
Suite 502
Washington, DC 20005
202-466-7643
FAX: 202-466-8940
e-mail: info@aafa.org
www.aafa.org

Thomas F. Plaut, M.D., author

A concise booklet covers the basics of childhood asthma, including medications. $3.00

40 pages Paperback

6962 Otitos Media in Young Children: Medical, Developmental, & Educational Considerations

Brookes Publishing
PO Box 10624
Baltimore, MD 21285   410-337-9580
                              800-638-3775
                         FAX: 410-337-8539
e-mail: custserv@brookespublishing.com
www.brookespublishing.com

Joanne E. Roberts, PhD, Editor, author
Ina F. Wallace, PhD, Editor
Frederick W. Henderson, Editor

This book reviews the current literature on the epidemiology, diagnosis, and medical management of otitis media; its secondary audiologic and communicative effects; and its impact on children and families. *$48.95*

352 pages Hardcover 1997
ISBN 1-557662-78-9

6963 PDF Newsletter

Parkinson's Disease Foundation
710 W 168th Street
New York, NY 10032   212-923-4700
                              800-457-6676
                         FAX: 212-923-4778
e-mail: info@pdf.org
www.pdf.org

Robin Elliott, Executive Director
Renay D. Crooms, Assistant Director

12-16 pages Quarterly

6964 Parenting Preschoolers: Suggestions for Raising Young Blind Children

American Foundation for the Blind/AFB Press
PO Box 1020
Sewickley, PA 15143   412-741-1142
                               800-232-3044
                          FAX: 412-741-0609
e-mail: afborders@abdintl.com
www.afb.org

Kay Alicyn Ferrell, author

Provides practical answers to questions most frequently asked by parents and gives advice on what to expect, how to adapt to a child's situation and what to look for in early education programs. $50.00/pack of 25.

28 pages
ISBN 0-891289-98-4

6965 Partial Seizure Disorders: Help for Patients and Families

Patient-Centered Guides
101 Morris Street
Sebastopol, CA 95472   707-829-0515
                                800-998-9938
                           FAX: 707-829-0104
www.patientcenters.com

Mitzi Waltz, author
Linda Lamb, Editor
Shawnde Paull, Marketing

Partial Seizure Disorders helps patients and families get an accurate diagnosis of this condition, understand medications and their side effects, and learn coping skills and other adjuncts to medication. It walks readers through developmental and school issues for young children; adult issues such as employment and driving; working with an existing health plan; and getting further help through advocacy and support organizations, articles, and online resources. *$19.95*

288 pages Paperback
ISBN 0-596500-03-3

6966 Personal Guide to Living Well with Fibromyalgia

Arthritis Foundation Distribution Center
PO Box 6996
Alpharetta, GA 30009
                              800-207-8633
                         FAX: 770-442-9742
www.arthritis.com

With this guide you'll learn the latest information about fibromyalgia, what researchers have uncovered about its causes, and an overview of the best treatment options available. Helpful worksheets and tables allow you to manage your condition and document your progress. *$14.95*

224 pages

6967 Post Polio

Accent Books & Products
PO Box 700
Bloomington, IL 61702   309-378-2961
                                 800-787-8444
                            FAX: 309-378-4420
e-mail: acmtlvng@aol.com

Raymond C. Cheever, Publisher
Betty Garee, Editor

What does post-polio syndrome mean? What can make a difference in a persons future mobility? These questions and more are answered in this great guide. *$3.95*

47 pages Paperback
ISBN 0-91570 -21-3

6968 Pressure Sores

Accent Books & Products
PO Box 700
Bloomington, IL 61702   309-378-2961
                                 800-787-8444
                            FAX: 309-378-4420
e-mail: acmtlvng@aol.com

Raymond C. Cheever, Publisher
Betty Garee, Editor

All it takes is one to put a stop to all of your activities. This book offers ways to be able to be comfortable and worry-free by knowing how to treat, recognize and prevent pressure sores. *$3.50*

29 pages Paperback
ISBN 0-91570 -20-5

6969 Preventable Brain Damage

Springer Publishing Company
536 Broadway
New York, NY 10012   212-431-4370
                         FAX: 212-941-7842

Donald Templer, author

Offers information on brain injuries from motor vehicle accidents, contact sports and injuries of children. *$35.95*

256 pages

6970 Primer on the Rheumatic Diseases

Arthritis Foundation
PO Box 6996
Alpharetta, GA 30009

800-207-8633
FAX: 404-872-0457
www.arthritis.com

Written to educate medical students and family physicians, this is the authoritative guide on the rheumatic diseases. *$39.95*

513 pages

6971 Reality of Dyslexia

Brookline Books
PO Box 1047
Cambridge, MA 02238

617-868-0360
800-666-2665
FAX: 617-868-1772
e-mail: brooklinebks@delphi.com
www.brooklinebooks.com

John Osmond, author

An informative and sensitive study of living with dyslexia which affects one in 25. He introduces the reader to the subject by sharing the difficulties of his dyslexic son. He then uses the personal accounts of other children and adult dyslexics, even entire dyslexic families, to illuminate the problems they encounter. *$14.95*

150 pages Paperback
ISBN 1-57129-17-6

6972 Record Book for Individuals with Autism

Autism Society of North Carolina Bookstore
505 Oberlin Road
Suite 230
Raleigh, NC 27605

919-743-0204
800-442-2762
FAX: 919-743-0208
e-mail: ASNC@aol.com
www.autismsociety-nc.org

Nancy Dalrymple, author

Developed with parent input to provide one place to keep information about an autistic child. *$7.00*

6973 Riddle of Autism: A Psychological Analysis

Jason Aronson
400 Keystone Industrial Park
Dunmore, PA 18512

800-782-0015
FAX: 201-840-7242
www.aronson.com

George Victor, author

Dr. Victor examines the myths that cloud an understanding of this disorder and describes the meanings of its specific behavioral symptoms. *$30.00*

356 pages Softcover
ISBN 1-568215-73-8

6974 Self-Therapy for the Stutterer

Stuttering Foundation of America
PO Box 11749
Memphis, TN 38111

901-452-7343
800-992-9392
e-mail: stuttersfa@aol.com
www.stuttersfa.org

Malcolm Fraser, author

A guide to help adults who stutter overcome the problem on their own. *$3.00*

191 pages Paperback
ISBN 0-933388-32-2

6975 Sexuality After Spinal Cord Injury: Answers to Your Questions

Brookes Publishing
PO Box 10624
Baltimore, MD 21285

410-337-9580
800-638-3775
FAX: 410-337-8539
e-mail: custserv@brookespublishing.com
www.brookespublishing.com

Stanley Ducharme, Ph.D., and Kathleen Gill, Ph.D., author

Anatomy, fertility, sexually transmitted diseases, self-esteem, sexual satisfaction, and parenting are among the many physical and emotional issues discussed in this guide. Question-and-answer format. *$24.95*

272 pages Paperback 1997
ISBN 1-557662-65-7

6976 Shoebox Tasks: Work Activities

Autism Society of North Carolina Bookstore
505 Oberlin Road
Suite 230
Raleigh, NC 27605

919-743-0204
800-442-2762
FAX: 919-743-0208
e-mail: ASNC@aol.com
www.autismsociety-nc.org

Ron and Linda Larsen, author

$250.00

6977 Single-Handed: A Book for Persons with the Use of Only One Hand

Accent Books & Products
PO Box 700
Bloomington, IL 61702

309-378-2961
800-787-8444
FAX: 309-378-4420
e-mail: acmtlvng@aol.com

Raymond C. Cheever, Publisher
Betty Garee, Editor

Includes information on devices and aids; special techniques; tips on how-to; illustrations; other helpful publications and more. *$4.25*

25 pages Paperback
ISBN 0-91570-06-0

6978 Soon Will Come the Light

Autism Society of North Carolina Bookstore
505 Oberlin Road
Suite 230
Raleigh, NC 27605   919-743-0204
                              800-442-2762
                         FAX: 919-743-0208
                    e-mail: ASNC@aol.com
                    www.autismsociety-nc.org
Thomas S. McKean, author

Offers new perspectives on the perplexing disability of autism. *$19.95*

6979 Spinal Cord Injury Home Care Manual

Santa Clara Valley Medical Center
751 S Bascom Avenue
San Jose, CA 95128   408-297-0467

Provides people with spinal cord injury, their families and professionals with information about physical care, independent living, psychosocial issues, attendant care and supplies. *$50.00*

6980 Students with Acquired Brain Injury: The School's Response

Brookes Publishing
PO Box 10624
Baltimore, MD 21285   410-337-9580
                                800-638-3775
                           FAX: 410-337-8539
          e-mail: custserv@brookespublishing.com
                    www.brookespublishing.com

This book is designed for school professionals and describes a range of issues that this population faces and presents proven means of addressing them in ways that benefit all students. Included topics are hospital-to-school transitions, effective assessment strategies, model programs in public schools, interventions to assist classroom teachers, and ways to involve family members in the educational program. *$29.95*

424 pages Paperback 1997
ISBN 1-557662-85-1

6981 Stuttering: Hope Through Research

Federal Government
31 Center Drive MSC2320
Bethesda, MD 20892
                                800-241-1044
                           FAX: 301-402-0018
              e-mail: nidcdinfo@nidcd.nih.gov
                    www.nidcd.nih.gov

Marin P. Allen, Ph. D., Chief, OHCPL

Describes how speech is produced, treatments for stuttering and research supported by the federal government.

6982 Teach and Reach Students with Attention Deficit Disorders

MultiGrowth Resources
12345 Jones Road
 # 101
Houston, TX 77070   281-890-5334

Nancy L. Eisenberg & Pamela H. Esser, author

Handbook adn resource guide for parents and educators of ADD students. *$19.95*

200 pages
ISBN 0-963084-70-4

6983 Teaching Children with Autism - Strategies to Enhance Communication

Autism Society of North Carolina Bookstore
505 Oberlin Road
Suite 230
Raleigh, NC 27605   919-743-0204
                              800-442-2762
                         FAX: 919-743-0208
                    e-mail: ASNC@aol.com
                    www.autismsociety-nc.org
Kathleen Ann Quill, EdD, author

This valuable new book describes teaching strategies and instructional adaptations which promote communication and socialization in children with autism. *$38.95*

6984 Teaching and Mainstreaming Autistic Children

Love Publishing Company
1777 S Bellaire Street
Denver, CO 80222   303-221-7333
                         FAX: 303-221-7444
          e-mail: lovepublishing@compuserve.com
Peter Knoblock, author

Dr. Knoblock advocates a highly organized, structured environment for autistic children, with teachers and parents working together. His premise is that the learning and social needs of autistic children must be analyzed and a daily program be designed with interventions that respond to this functional analysis of their behavior. *$24.95*

ISBN 0-891081-11-9

6985 Techniques for Aphasia Rehab: (TARGET) Generating Effective Treatment

Speech Bin
1965 25th Avenue
Vero Beach, FL 32960   561-770-0007
                                800-477-3324
                           FAX: 561-770-0006
                    www.speechbin.com
Mary Jo Santo Pietro and Robert Goldfarb, author

Practical treatment manual for use by aphasia clinicians. *$45.00*

384 pages
ISBN 0-93785 -50-5

6986 Teenagers with ADD

Woodbine House
6510 Bells Mill Road
Bethesda, MD 20817
                                800-843-7323
                    www.woodbinehouse.com
Chris A. Zeigler Dendy, M.S., author

This best selling guide to understanding and coping with teenagers with attention deficit disorder (ADD) provides complete coverage of the special issues and challenges faced by these teens. Based on current diagnostic criteria and the latest literature and research in the field, the book discusses diagnosis, medical treatment, family and school life, intervention, advocacy, legal rights, and options after high school. Parents find strategies for dealing with their teen's difficult behaviors. *$18.95*

370 pages Paperback
ISBN 0-933149-69-7

6987   Three Hundred Tips for Making Life with Multiple Sclerosis Easier

Demos Medical Publishing
386 Park Avenue South
Suite 201
New Yorok, NY   10016   212-683-0072
800-532-8663
FAX: 212-683-0118
e-mail: help@MeetingLifesChallenges.com
www.MeetingLifesChallenges.com
Shelley Peterman Schwarz, author
Diana Schneider, Ph.D., President

This latest book in the Making Life Easier series features tip, techniques and shortcuts for conserving time and energy so you can do more of the things you want to do. These tips should help increase the number of good days you have while encouraging you to develop your own techniques for making life easier. *$16.95*

112 pages 1999
ISBN 1-888799-23-4

6988   Tourette's Syndrome: Finding Answers and Getting Help

Patient-Centered Guides
101 Morris Street
Sebastopol, CA   95472   707-829-0515
800-998-9938
FAX: 707-829-0104
www.patientcenters.com
Mitzi Waltz, author
Linda Lamb, Editor
Shawnde Paull, Marketing

Tourette's Syndrome is a neurological disorder usually diagnosed in childhood and characterized by tics, physical jerks, and involuntary vocalizations. Tourette's can be a devastating disability. The good news is that it's very treatable. Tourette's Syndrome helps you secure a diagnosis, understand medical interventions, get healthcare coverage, and manage Tourette's in family life, school, community, and workplace. *$24.95*

356 pages Paperback
ISBN 0-596500-07-6

6989   Toward Healthy Living - A Wellness Journal

Arthritis Foundation Distribution Center
PO Box 6996
Alpharetta, GA   30009
800-207-8633
FAX: 770-442-9742
www.arthritis.com

This spiral-bound journal has ample pages where you can unleach you thoughts, plus scales to monitor your mook and pain. Throught the book you will also find wisdom from a variety of famous and ordinary people - those who live with chronic illness, and those whose life lessons can help you gain a more positive outlook on daily living. *$9.95*

144 pages

6990   Two Hundred Fifty Tips for Making Life with Arthritis Easier

Longstreet Press
2140 Newmarket Parkway
Suite 122
Marietta, GA   30067   770-690-1035

e-mail: help@MeetingLifesChallenges.com
www.MeetingLifesChallenges.com
Shelley Peterman Schwarz, author
Thomas Cogburn, Distribution Director

Is it difficult for you to handle everyday chores because of pregnancy, back problems, or the general effects of aging? If so, you'll find tremendous help in the 250 tips in this book. Discover ways to do everything from adapting your home to completing chores and organizing household activities. Even if your limitations are only minimal, you'll find an abundance of suggestions to help you work smarker, faster and more efficiently. *$9.95*

88 pages 1997
ISBN 1-563523-81-7

6991   Ultimate Stranger, The Autistic Child

Academic Therapy Publications
20 Commercial Boulevard
Novato, CA   94949
800-442-7249
FAX: 415-883-3720
www.atpub.com
Carl Delacato, author
Anna M. Arena, President

Clinical background and theories of rehabilitation for the autistic child. *$15.00*

240 pages Paperback
ISBN 0-878794-46-8

6992   Understanding Asthma: The Blueprint for Breathing

National Allergy and Asthma Network
3554 Chain Bridge Road
Suite 200
Fairfax, VA   22030   703-385-4403
FAX: 703-352-4354

A layman's guide to asthma facts based on a presentation from the first national asthma patient conference.

6993 Understanding Down Syndrome: An Introduction for Parents

Brookline Books
PO Box 1046
Cambridge, MA 02238 617-868-0360
800-666-2665
FAX: 617-868-1772
e-mail: brooklinebks@delphi.com
www.brooklinebooks.com
Cliff Cunningham, author

Using positive and readable language, this book helps parents understand Down Syndrome. Medical details are explained in lay terms, and advice is given on working with professionals, obtaining services, and treatment techniques that help the child. Cunningham alerts families to potential problems, the prospects for the child in schooling and the passage to adulthood. Revised 1996. *$14.95*

Softcover
ISBN 1-57129-09-5

6994 Understanding Juvenile Rheumatoid Arthritis

American Juvenile Arthritis Organization
PO Box 19000
Atlanta, GA 30326
800-283-7800

A manual for health professionals to use in teaching children with JRA and their families about disease management and self-care. *$61.20*

372 pages

6995 Understanding Multiple Sclerosis

MacMillan Publishing Company
135 S Mount Zion Road
Lebanon, IN 46052
FAX: 800-882-8583
Robert Shuman, author

Two psychologists discuss their roles with a member who has multiple sclerosis. Includes chapters on adolescents with multiple sclerosis, employment, and research.

6996 Understanding the Nature of Autism

Autism Society of North Carolina Bookstore
505 Oberlin Road
Suite 230
Raleigh, NC 27605 919-743-0204
800-442-2762
FAX: 919-743-0208
e-mail: ASNC@aol.com
www.autismsociety-nc.org
Jan Janzen, M.S. Ph.D. and Lorelei Dake, B.A., author

$54.00

6997 Until Tomorrow: A Family Lives with Autism

Autism Society of North Carolina Bookstore
505 Oberlin Road
Suite 230
Raleigh, NC 27605 919-743-0204
800-442-2762
FAX: 919-743-0208
e-mail: ASNC@aol.com
www.autismsociety-nc.org
Dorothy Zietz, author

The central theme of this book is an effort to show what it is like to live with a child who cannot communicate. *$10.00*

6998 Victims of Dementia: Services, Support and Care

Haworth Press
10 Alice Street
Binghamton, NY 13904 604-722-5857
800-429-6784
FAX: 607-722-6362
e-mail: getinfo@haworthpressinc.com
www.haworthpressinc.com
William Michael Clemmer, PhD., author
Jackie Blakeslee, Advertising

Provides an in-depth look at the concept, construction and operation of Wesley Hall, a special living area at the Chelsea United Methodist retirement home in Michigan. *$69.95*

155 pages Hardcover
ISBN 1-560242-64-7

6999 Visually Structured Tasks

Autism Society of North Carolina Bookstore
505 Oberlin Road
Suite 230
Raleigh, NC 27605 919-743-0204
800-442-2762
FAX: 919-743-0208
e-mail: ASNC@aol.com
www.autismsociety-nc.org

Independent activites for students with autism and other visual learners. *$24.95*

7000 Voice of the Diabetic

Diabetes Action Network of the NFB
811 Cherry Street
Suite 309
Columbia, MO 65201 573-875-8911
FAX: 573-875-8902
www.nfb.org/voice.htm

Ed Bryant, Editor

Newsletters containing personal stories and practical guidelines by blind diabetics and medical professionals, medical news, resource column and a recipe corner. We are a support and information network for all diabetics.

28 pages Quarterly

7001 What is Vocal Hoarseness?

Speech Bin
1965 25th Avenue
Vero Beach, FL 32960 561-770-0007
800-477-3324
FAX: 561-770-0006
www.speechbin.com
Julie A. Blonigen, author

Brochures to teach parents, teachers and individuals with voice disorders about chronic hoarseness and what to do about it. Set of ten copies. *$16.95*

24 pages Package of 10
ISBN 0-93785-55-6

7002 What's This Thing Called Dyslexia?

Ray Ham Company
6417 Ponderosa Lane
Colleyville, TX 76034

Ray Ham, M.Ed., author
Ray Ham, Editor

This booklet is for all public or private school students who are struggling with a learning disability. An interested adult can read this booklet aloud to students and encourage discussion. Students are offered an understanding of dyslexia, some methods for compensating and a message of encouragement. The booklet is illustrated by three students and one adult with dyslexia. *$2.95*

29 pages

7003 Winter Blues: Seasonal Affective Disorder: What It Is and How To Overcome It

Guilford Press
72 Spring Street
New York, NY   10012   212-431-9800
                                  800-365-7006
                          FAX: 212-966-6708
                              www.guilford.com
Norman E. Rosenthal, MD, author
$15.95

355 pages Paperback 1998
ISBN 1-572303-95-6

7004 You Mean I'm Not Lazy, Stupid or Crazy?

Tyrell & Jerem Press
PO Box 20089
Cincinnati, OH   45220
                                  800-622-6611
Peggy Ramundo & Kate Kelly, author

A new self-help book is the first written by ADD adults for ADD adults. This comprehensive guide provides accurate information, practical how-to's and moral support. *$24.95*

Visually Impaired

7005 ABC Sign with Me

TJ Publishers
817 Silver Spring Avenue
Suite 206
Silver Spring, MD   20910   301-585-4440
                                  800-999-1168
                          FAX: 301-585-5930
                      e-mail: TJPubinc@aol.com
Sugar Sign Press, author
Angela K Thames, President
Jerald A Murphy, Vice President

Offers bright pictures of familiar objects, lower case alphabet and corresponding manual alphabet hand shapes. *$3.95*

32 pages Softcover
ISBN 0-93984 -00-3

7006 AFB News

American Foundation for the Blind/AFB Press
11 Penn Plaza
Suite 300
New York, NY   10001   212-502-7614
                                  800-232-3044
                          FAX: 212-502-7777
                  e-mail: afborders@abdintl.com
                              www.afb.org

National newsletter for general readership about blindness and visual impairments featuring people, programs, services and activities.

12 pages Quarterly

7007 APH Catalog of Accessible Books for People Who Are Visually Impaired

American Printing House for the Blind
1839 Frankfort Avenue
Louisville, KY   40206   502-895-2405
                                  800-223-1839
                          FAX: 502-895-1509
                        e-mail: info@aph.org

Offers thousands of selections and publishers of large type and braille books for persons with visual impairments.

7008 Access to Art: A Museum Directory for Blind and Visually Impaired People

American Foundation for the Blind/AFB Press
PO Box 1020
Sewickley, PA   15143   412-741-1142
                                  800-232-3044
                          FAX: 412-741-0609
                  e-mail: afborders@abdintl.com
                              www.afb.org

Details the access facilities of over 300 museums, galleries and exhibits in the United States. Also included are organizations offering art-related resources such as, art classes, competitions and traveling exhibits. *$19.95*

144 pages Large Print
ISBN 0-891281-56-8

7009 Age-Related Macular Degeneration

National Association for Visually Handicapped
22 W 21st Street
6th Floor
New York, NY   10010   212-889-3141
                          FAX: 212-727-2931
                        e-mail: staff@navh.org
                              www.navh.org

A large booklet offering information, with illustrations and up-to-date research, on Macular Degeneration. Also available in Russian. Revised in 1999.

7010 Aging and Vision: Declarations of Independence

American Foundation for the Blind/AFB Press
PO Box 1020
Sewickley, PA 15143
412-741-1142
800-232-3044
FAX: 412-741-0609
e-mail: afborders@abdintl.com
www.afb.org

A very personal look at five older people who have successfully coped with visual impairment and continue to lead active, satisfying lives. Their stories are not only inspirational, but also provide practical, down-to-earth suggestions for adapting to vision loss later in life. 18 minute video tape. Also available in PAL, $52.95, 0-89128-276-9. *$42.95*

VHS
ISBN 0-891282-20-3

7011 American Heritage Large Type Dictionary

Science Products
Box 888
Southeastern, PA 19399
610-296-2111
800-888-7400

35,000 easy to read entries. *$8.95*

7012 American Printing House for the Blind

1839 Frankfort Avenue
6085
Louisville, KY 40206
502-895-2405
800-223-1839
FAX: 502-899-2274
e-mail: info@aph.org
www.aph.org

Fred Gissoni, Customer Support

The world's largest company devoted solely to producing products for people who are visually impaired. We manufacture books and magazines in braille, large type and recorded form from over 200 vendors across the U.S. We also make a wide range of educational and daily living aids, such as braille paper and styluses, talking book equipment, and synthetic speech computer products. APH also offers LOUIS, an electronic database that lists accessible books in all formats.

7013 An Orientation and Mobility Primer for Families and Young Children

American Foundation for the Blind/AFB Press
PO Box 1020
Sewickley, PA 15143
412-741-1142
800-232-3044
FAX: 412-741-0609
e-mail: afborders@abdintl.com
www.afb.org

Bonnie Dodson-Burk, Everett W Hill, author

Practical information for helping a child learn about his or her environment right from the start. Covers sensory training, concept development and orientation skills. Paperback. *$14.95*

48 pages
ISBN 0-891281-57-6

7014 Annual Report/Newsletter

National Accreditation Council for Agencies/Blind
15 E 40th Street
Room 1004
New York, NY 10016
FAX: 212-683-4475

Ruth Westman, Executive Director

Provides standards and a program of accreditation for schools and organizations which serve children and adults who are blind or vision impaired.

7015 Art and Science of Teaching Orientation and Mobility to Persons with Visual Impairments

American Foundation for the Blind/AFB Press
PO Box 1020
Sewickley, PA 15143
412-741-1142
800-232-3044
FAX: 412-741-0609
e-mail: afborders@abdintl.com
www.afb.org

William H. Jacobson, author

Comprehensive decription of the techniques of teaching orientation and mobility, presented along with considerations and strategies for sensitive and effective teaching. Hardcover. Paperback also available. *$48.00*

200 pages
ISBN 0-891282-45-9

7016 Awareness

NAPVI
PO Box 317
Watertown, MA 02272
800-562-6265

Newsletter offering regional news, sports and activities, conferences, camps, legislative updates, book reviews, audio reviews, professional question and answer column and more for the visually impaired and their families.

Quarterly

7017 Basic Course in American Sign Language

TJ Publishers
817 Silver Spring Avenue
Suite 206
Silver Spring, MD 20910
301-585-4440
800-999-1168
FAX: 301-585-5930
TDY:301-585-4440
e-mail: TJPubinc@aol.com

Angela K Thames, President
Jerald A Murphy, Vice President

Accompanying videotapes and textbooks include voice translations. Hearing students can analyze sound for initial instruction, or opt to turn off the sound to sharpen visual acuity. Package includes the Basic Course in American Sign Language text, Student Study Guide, the original four 1-hour videotapes plus the ABCASI Vocabulary videotape. *$139.95*

280 pages Video Cassette

7018 Behavioral Vision Approaches for Persons with Physical Disabilities

Optometric Extension Program Foundation
2912 S Daimler Street
Santa Ana, CA   92705   949-250-0846

William Padula, author

A discussion of the behavioral vision/neuro-motor approach to providing directions for prescriptive and therapeutic services for the visually handicapped child or adult. *$49.50*

197 pages

7019 Berthold Lowenfeld on Blindness and Blind People

American Foundation for the Blind/AFB Press
PO Box 1020
Sewickley, PA   15143   412-741-1142
                              800-232-3044
                         FAX: 412-741-0609
         e-mail: afborders@abdintl.com
                              www.afb.org

Berthold Lowenfeld, author

These writings of the pioneering educator, author and advocate range over a forty-year period include various ground-breaking papers for the blind educator, a rememberance of Helen Keller and other essays on education, sociology and history. *$21.95*

254 pages Paperback
ISBN 0-891281-01-0

7020 Blind Educator

National Federation of the Blind
1800 Johnson Street
Baltimore, MD   21230   410-659-9314
                         FAX: 410-685-5653
            e-mail: nfb@iamdigex.net
                              www.nfb.org

Magazine specifically for blind educators.

7021 Blind and Vision-Impaired Individuals

Mainstream
3 Bethesda Metro Center
Suite 830
Bethesda, MD   20814   301-951-6122
                              800-247-1380
         e-mail: info@mainstreaminc.org

Mainstream, Inc., author

Mainstreaming blind individuals into the workplace. *$ 2.50*

12 pages

7022 Blindness and Early Childhood Development Second Edition

American Foundation for the Blind/AFB Press
PO Box 1020
Sewickley, PA   15143   412-741-1142
                              800-232-3044
                         FAX: 412-741-0609
         e-mail: afborders@abdintl.com
                              www.afb.org

David H. Warren, author

A review of current knowledge on motor and locomotor development, perceptual development, language and cognitive processes, and social, emotional and personality development. Paperback. *$34.95*

384 pages
ISBN 0-891281-23-1

7023 Blindness, A Family Matter

American Foundation for the Blind/AFB Press
PO Box 1020
Sewickley, PA   15143   412-741-1142
                              800-232-3044
                         FAX: 412-741-0609
         e-mail: afborders@abdintl.com
                              www.afb.org

A frank exploration of the effects of an individual's visual impairment on other members of the family and how those family members can play a positive role in the rehabilitation process. Features interviews with thr ee families whose 'success stories' provide advice and encouragement, as well as interviews with newly blinded adults currently involved in a rehabilitation program. 23 minute video tape. Also available in PAL, $49.95, 0-89128-271-8. *$43.95*

VHS 1986
ISBN 0-891282-22-X

7024 Blindness: What it is, What it Does and How to Live with it

American Foundation for the Blind/AFB Press
PO Box 1020
Sewickley, PA   15143   412-741-1142
                              800-232-3044
                         FAX: 412-741-0609
         e-mail: afborders@abdintl.com
                              www.afb.org

Rev. Thomas J. Carroll, author

A classic work on how blindness affects self-perception and social interaction and what can be done to restore basic skills, mobility, daily living and an appreciation of life's pleasures. *$15.95*

396 pages Paperback
ISBN 0-891282-05-

7025 Braille Book Review

National Library Service for the Blind
1291 Taylor Street NW
Washington, DC   20542   202-707-5100
                         FAX: 202-707-0712
                              www.loc.gov/nls

Robert Fistick, Head, Publications/Media Section

New braille books and product news.

30 pages BiMonthly

7026 Braille Documents

Metrolina Sight Services
704 Louise Avenue
Charlotte, NC   28204   704-372-3870

This production shop creates Braille and large-print documents.

7027 Braille Forum

American Council of the Blind
1155 15th Street NW
Suite 1004
Washington, DC   20005

202-467-5081
800-424-8666
FAX: 202-467-5085
e-mail: slovering@acb.org
www.acb.org

Penny Reeder, Editor

Offered in print, braille, cassette, IBM computer disk, and e-mail. $25 per format per year for companes and non-U.S. residents.

48 pages Magazine 1912

7028 Braille Monitor

National Federation of the Blind
1800 Johnson Street
Baltimore, MD   21230

410-837-6763
FAX: 410-685-5653
e-mail: nfb@iamdigex.net

The leading publication in the blindness field, with a circulation of 30,000, this publication addresses issues of concern to the blind and the philosophy and activities of the National Federation of the Blind.

Monthly

7029 Building Blocks: Foundations for Learning for Young Blind and Visually Impaired Children

American Foundation for the Blind/AFB Press
PO Box 1020
Sewickley, PA   15143

412-741-1142
800-232-3044
FAX: 412-741-0609
e-mail: afborders@abdintl.com
www.afb.org

Presents the essential components of a successful early intervnetion program, including collaboration with family members, positive relationships between parents and professionals, public education, and attention to important programming components such as space exploration, braille readiness, orientation and mobility, play, cooking and music. Includes interviews with parents. Available in English or Spanish. 10 minute video tape. Also available in PAL, $33.95, 0-89128-268-8. *$26.95*

VHS
ISBN 0-891282-14-9

7030 Bulletin

National Association for Visually Handicapped
22 W 21st Street
New York, NY   10010

212-889-3141

e-mail: staff@navh.org

Annual report offering information on Association activities and events, conferences, vision aids and resources for the visually impaired.

7031 Burns Braille Transcription Dictionary

American Foundation for the Blind/AFB Press
PO Box 1020
Sewickley, PA   15143

412-741-1142
800-232-3044
FAX: 412-741-0609
e-mail: afborders@abdintl.com
www.afb.org

Mary F. Burns, author

A handy, portable guide that is a quick reference for anyone who needs to check print-to-braille and braille-to-print meanings and symbols. Paperback. *$19.95*

96 pages
ISBN 0-891292-32-7

7032 Career Perspectives: Interviews with Blind and Visually Impaired Professionals

American Foundation for the Blind/AFB Press
PO Box 1020
Sewickley, PA   15143

412-741-1142
800-232-3044
FAX: 412-741-0609
e-mail: afborders@abdintl.com
www.afb.org

Marie Attmore, author

Profiles of 20 successful archivers who describe in their own words what it takes to pursue and attain professional success in a sighted world. Available in large print, cassette and braille. *$16.95*

96 pages Large Print
ISBN 0-891281-70-3

7033 Cataracts

National Association for Visually Handicapped
22 W 21st Street
6th Floor
New York, NY   10010

212-889-3141
FAX: 212-727-2931
e-mail: staff@navh.org
www.navh.org

A booklet offering information about Cataracts, diagnosis and treatment of this common condition. *$2.50*

7034 Characteristics, Services, & Outcomes of Rehab. Consumers who are Blind/Visually Impaired

Mississippi State University
PO Box 6189
Mississippi State, MS   39762

601-325-2001
800-675-7782
FAX: 662-325-8989
TDY:601-325-8693
e-mail: rrtc@ra.state.edu
www.blind.msstate.edu

Brenda Cavenaugh, Principal Investigatorst
Steven J. Pierce, Graduate Research Assistant
Kelly Schaefer, Dissemination Specialist

Issues regarding the efficacy of separate state agencies providing specialized vocational rehabilitation (VR) services to consumers who are blind have generated spirited discussions within the rehabilitation community throughout the history of the state-federal program. In this monograph, RRTC researches report results of their investigation of services provided to blind consumers in separate and general (combined) rehabilitation agencies. *$20.00*

45 pages Paperback

7035 Childhood Glaucoma - A Reference Guide for Families

NAPVI
PO Box 317
Watertown, MA   02272

800-562-6265

7036 Children with Visual Impairments Wodbine House

American Foundation for the Blind/AFB Press
11 Penn Plaza
Suite 300
New York, NY   10001   212-502-7600
800-232-3044
FAX: 212-502-7774
e-mail: afborder@abdintl.com
www.afb.org

Written by parents and professional, this book presents a comprehensive overview of the issues that are crucial to the healthy development of children with mild to severe visual impaiments. It also offers insight from parents about coping with the emotional aspects of raising a child with special needs. *$16.95*

416 pages
ISBN 0-933149-36-0

7037 Choice Magazine Listening

85 Channel Drive
Department 17
Port Washington, NY   11050   516-883-8280
FAX: 516-944-6849
e-mail: choicemag@aol.com

Lois Miller, Office Manager

A free audio anthology is available bi-monthly to visually impaired/physically disabled persons nationwide. Playable on the special free 4-track cassette playback equipment which is provided by the Library of Congress through the National Library Service. Each issue features eight hours of unabridged magazine articles, short stories, poetry and media selections from over 100 sources. College level and older. Published bimonthly.

Audio Cassette

7038 Communication Skills for Visually Impaired Learners

Charles C. Thomas, Publisher
2600 S 1st Street
Springfield, IL   62704   217-789-8980
800-258-8980
FAX: 217-789-9130
e-mail: books@ccthomas.com
Randal Harley, Mila Truan & LaRhea Sanford, author

This book has been designed to provide a foundation for a better understanding of teaching reading, writing, and listening skills to students with visual impairments from preschool age through adult levels. The plan of the book incorporates the latest research findings with the practical experiences learned in the classroom. *$49.95*

322 pages Paperback 1997
ISBN 0-39806 -93-0

7039 Comprehensive Examination of Barriers to Employment Among Persons who are Blind or Impaired

Mississippi State University
PO Box 6189
Mississippi State, MS   39762   601-325-2001
800-675-7782
FAX: 662-325-8989
TDY:601-325-8693
e-mail: rrtc@ra.state.edu
www.blind.msstate.edu
Adele Crudden, Lynn McBroom, Amy Skinner, author
J. Elton Moore, Author
Kelly Shaefer, Dissemination Specialist

A multi-phase research project designed to: identify barriers to employment; identify and develop innovative successful strategies to overcome these barriers; develop methods for others to utilize these strategies; disseminate this information to rehabilitation providers; replicate the use of selected strategies in other settings. *$20.00*

90 pages Paperback

7040 Concept Development for Visually Handicapped Children: A Resource Guide

American Foundation for the Blind/AFB Press
PO Box 1020
Sewickley, PA   15143   412-741-1142
800-232-3044
FAX: 412-741-0609
e-mail: afborders@abdintl.com
www.afb.org
William T Lydon, Loretta McGraw, author

A program for integrating such concepts as body imagery, gross motor movement, posture and tactile discrimination into the curriculum from kindergarten on. Paperback. *$16.95*

80 pages
ISBN 0-891280-18-9

7041 Contrasting Characteristics of Blind and Visually Impaired Clients

Rehab/Training Center on Blindness and Low-Vision
PO Box 6189
Mississippi State, MS   39762   601-325-2001
800-675-7782
FAX: 662-325-8989
e-mail: rrtc@ra.msstate.edu
www.blind.msstate.edu
G.K. Herndon, author
Kelly Schaefer, Publications Manager

This report examines cases in the National Blindness and Low Vision Employment Database to identify and profile environmental and personal characteristics of clients who are blind or visually impaired and who were achieving successful and unsuccessful retention of competitive jobs. A total of 787 cases were analyzed. *$15.00*

44 pages Paperback

7042   DVH Quarterly

University of Arkansas at Little Rock
2801 S University Avenue
Little Rock, AR   72204

Bob Brasher, Editor

Offers information on upcoming events, conferences and workshops on and for visual disabilities. Book reviews, information on the newest resources and technology, educational programs, want ads and more.

Quarterly

7043   Data on Blindness and Visual Impairment in the US: A Resource Manual

American Foundation for the Blind/AFB Press
PO Box 1020
Sewickley, PA   15143   412-741-1142
                                                    800-232-3044
                                    FAX: 412-741-0609
                    e-mail: afborders@abdintl.com
                                            www.afb.org

Corine Kirchner, author

Provides facts and figures for long-range planning, preparing grant proposals and legislative services. Paperback. *$47.00*

412 pages
ISBN 0-891281-52-5

7044   Development of Social Skills by Blind and Visually Impaired Students

American Foundation for the Blind/AFB Press
PO Box 1020
Sewickley, PA   15143   412-741-1142
                                                    800-232-3044
                                    FAX: 412-741-0609
                    e-mail: afborders@abdintl.com
                                            www.afb.org

Sharon Sacks, Linda Kekelis, Robert J Gaylord-Ross, author

Offers an examination of the social interactions of blind and visually impaired children in mainstreamed settings and the community that highlights the need to teach social interaction skills to children and provide them with support. Paperback. *$39.95*

232 pages
ISBN 0-891282-17-3

7045   Diabetic Retinopathy

National Association for Visually Handicapped
22 W 21st Street
6th Floor
New York, NY   10010   212-889-3141
                                        FAX: 212-727-2931
                            e-mail: staff@navh.org
                                        www.navh.org

A booklet offering information about Diabetic Retinopathy.

7046   Dialogue Magazine

Blindskills
PO Box 5181
Salem, OR   97304
                                                    800-860-4224
                                        FAX: 503-581-0178
                    e-mail: blindskl@teleport.com
                                    www.blindskills.com

Carol M. McCarl, Editor, Publisher, Exec. Dir.

Publishes quarterly magazine in braille, large-type, cassette and disk of news items, fiction and articles of special interest to visually impaired youth and adults. $40.00 for not blind/legally blind. *$28.00*

Quarterly

7047   Directory of Camps for Blind and Visually Impaired Children & Adults

American Foundation for the Blind/AFB Press
PO Box 1020
Sewickley, PA   15143   412-741-1142
                                                    800-232-3044
                                    FAX: 412-741-0609
                    e-mail: afborders@abdintl.com
                                            www.afb.org

A guide to 200 sleepaway camps and day camps in the United States. Descriptions cover types of campers, age ranges, special activities offered, length of seasons and contact names. *$15.95*

34 pages Papberack
ISBN 0-891281-59-2

7048   Early Focus: Working with Young Blind and Visually Impaired Children

American Foundation for the Blind/AFB Press
PO Box 1020
Sewickley, PA   15143   412-741-1142
                                                    800-232-3044
                                    FAX: 412-741-0609
                    e-mail: afborders@abdintl.com
                                            www.afb.org

Rona L Pogrund, Diane L Fazzi, Jessica S Lampert, author

Describes early intervention techniques used with blind and visually impaired children and stresses the benefits of family involvement and transdisciplinary teamwork. Paperback. *$32.95*

176 pages
ISBN 0-891282-15-7

7049 Encyclopedia of Blindness and Vision Impairment

Facts on File
132 West 31 Street
17th Floor
New York, NY 10001   212-907-8800
800-322-8755
FAX: 212-967-9196
www.factsonfile.com

Jill Sardegna and Otis Paul, M.D., author
James Chamber, Editor in Chief

Designed to provide both laymen and professionals with concise, practical information on the second most common disability in the U.S. *$65.00*

340 pages Hardbound
ISBN 6-810021-53-8

7050 Equals in Partnership: Basic Rights for Families of Children with Blindness

NAPVI
PO Box 317
Watertown, MA 02272
800-562-6265

$18.00

7051 Eye and Your Vision

National Association for Visually Handicapped
22 West 21st Street
6th Floor
New York, NY 10010   212-889-3141
FAX: 212-727-2931
e-mail: staff@navh.org
www.navh.org

A large booklet offering information, with illustrations, on the eye. Includes information on protection of eyesight, how the eye works and vision disorders. Available in Russian and Spanish also. *$ 2.75*

7052 Fighting Blindness News

RP Foundation Fighting Blindness
1401 Mt Royal Avenue
4th Floor
Baltimore, MD 21217   410-225-9400
800-683-5555
TDY:410-225-9409

Offers information on medical updates, donor programs, assistive devices, resources and clinical trial information for persons with visual impairments, blindness and retinal degenerative diseases.

2x Year

7053 First Steps

Blind Children's Center
4120 Marathon Street
Los Angeles, CA 90029
800-222-3566
FAX: 323-665-3828
e-mail: info@blindchildrenscenter.com
www.blindcntr.org

A handbook for teaching young children who are visually impaired. Designed to assist students, professionals and parents working with children who are visually impaired. *$35.00*

203 pages

7054 Focus

Visually Impaired Center
725 Mason Street
Flint, MI 48503   313-235-2544

Laurie MacArthur, Executive Director

Newsletter offering information for the visually impaired person in the forms of legislative and law updates, ADA information, support groups, hotlines, and articles on the newest technology in the field.

Quarterly

7055 Foundations of Orientation and Mobility

American Foundation for the Blind/AFB Press
PO Box 1020
Sewickley, PA 15143   412-741-1142
800-232-3044
FAX: 412-741-0609
e-mail: afborders@abdintl.com
www.afb.org

This text has been updated and revised and includes current research from a variety of disciplines, an international perspective, and expanded contents on low vision, aging, multiple disabilities, accessibility, program design and adaptive technology from more that 30 eminent subject experts. *$68.95*

775 pages
ISBN 0-891289-46-1

7056 Foundations of Rehabilitation Counseling with Persons Who Are Blind

American Foundation for the Blind/AFB Press
PO Box 1020
Sewickley, PA 15143   412-741-1142
800-232-3044
FAX: 412-741-0609
e-mail: afborders@abdintl.com
www.afb.org

J Elton Moore, William Graves, Jeanne B Patterson, author

Rehabilitation professionals have long recognized that the needs of people who are blind or visually impaired are unique and requie a special knowledge and expertise to provide and corrdinate rehabilitation services. *$59.95*

477 pages
ISBN 0-891289-45-3

7057 Future Reflections

National Federation of the Blind
1800 Johnson Street
Baltimore, MD 21230   410-837-6763
FAX: 410-685-5653
e-mail: nfb@iamdigex.net

National magazine written specifically for parents and educators of blind children. Each issue addresses various topics important to blind children, their families and to school personnel.

Quarterly

7058 Get a Wiggle On

American Alliance for Health, Phys. Ed. & Dance
1900 Association Drive
Reston, VA   20191   703-476-3400

e-mail: aaalf@aahperd.org

Sherry Reynor, author

Gives teachers and parents practical suggestions for helping blind and visually impaired infants grow and learn like other children. *$5.00*

80 pages
ISBN 0-88314-77-2

7059 Gleams Newsletter

Foundation for Glaucoma Research
200 Pine Street
San Francisco, CA   94129   415-986-3162
                                  800-826-6693
                                  www.glaucoma.orge

Offers updated and medical information on vision loss and glaucoma. Included are legislative information, professional articles and book reviews.

7060 Guide to Independence for the Visually Impaired and Their Families

Demos Vermande
386 Park Avenue South
Suite 201
New York, NY   10016   212-683-0072
                                  800-532-8663
                         FAX: 212-683-0118

Vivian Younger & Jill Sardegna, author

This first comprehensive, hands-on book for the newly visually impaired and their families presents detailed instructions to deal with emotional reactions and fioght depression; contact organizations and get information; obtain federal and other types of financial aid; use the other senses more effectively; adapt their homes and do household chores; handle paperwork and become socially active. *$29.95*

248 pages Paperback
ISBN 0-939957-61-2

7061 Guidelines and Games for Teaching Efficient Braille Reading

American Foundation for the Blind/AFB Press
PO Box 1020
Sewickley, PA   15143   412-741-1142
                                  800-232-3044
                         FAX: 412-741-0609
              e-mail: afborders@abdintl.com
                                  www.afb.org

Myrna R. Olson, Sally S Mangold, author

Based on research in the areas of rapid reading and precision teaching, these guidelines represent a unique adaptation of a general reading program to the needs of braille readers. Paperback. *$ 24.95*

116 pages
ISBN 0-891281-05-3

7062 Guideway

Guide Dog Foundation for the Blind
371 E Jericho Turnpike
Smithtown, NY   11787   516-265-2121
                                  800-548-4337
                         FAX: 516-361-5192

Offers updates and information on the foundation's activities and guide dog programs. In print form but is also available on cassette.

Monthly

7063 Hammond Large Type World Atlas

Science Products
Box A
Southeastern, PA   19399   610-296-2111
                                  800-888-7400

Mary Ann Case, Marketing Director

Hardcover book listing 100 maps with a 2,000 entry index. *$29.95*

7064 Handbook for Itinerant and Resource Teachers of Blind Students

National Federation of the Blind
1800 Johnson Street
Baltimore, MD   21230   410-659-9314

e-mail: nfb@iamdigex.net

Doris M. Willoughby & Sharon L.M. Duffy, NFB, author

The Handbook provides help to teachers, school administrators or other school personnel that have experience with blind or visually impaired students. The Handbook devotes 45 pages to Braille and how to teach Braille for parents and teachers. There are other chapters offering information on the law, physical education, fitting in socially, testing and evaluation, home economics, daily living skills and more. *$23.00*

533 pages Softcover
ISBN 0-962412-20-1

7065 Hearsay

Association of Radio Reading Services
PO Box 3663
Pittsburgh, PA   15230   412-434-6023

Newsletter for persons interested in radio reading services. *$7.00*

Quarterly

7066 Helen and Teacher The Story of Helen Keller & Anne Sullivan Macy

American Foundation for the Blind/AFB Press
PO Box 1020
Sewickley, PA   15143   412-741-1142
                                  800-232-3044
                         FAX: 412-741-0609
              e-mail: afborders@abdintl.com
                                  www.afb.org

Joseph P. Lash, author
Stephanie Biagioli, Marketing Coordinator

A pictorial biography emphasizing Hellen Keller's accomplishments in public life over a period of more than 60 years. Traces Anne Sullivan's early years and her meeting with Helen Keller, and goes on to recount the joint events of their lives. A definitive biography. $29.95.

Paperback
ISBN 0-891282-89-0

7067   Helping the Visually Impaired Child with Developmental Problems

Teachers College Press
Columbia University
New York, NY   10027

800-575-6566
FAX: 212-678-4149

Sally M. Rogow, author

This book aims to explore the human consequences of severe visual problems combined with other handicaps. The application of child development research to educational interventions, the need for educational and rehabilitative services that serve the human and the special needs of children and their families and the promise of technology in helping to expand communicative possibilities are also discussed. *$18.95*

216 pages Paperback
ISBN 0-807729-02-7

7068   Hub

SPOKES Unlimited
PO Box 7896
Klamath Falls, OR   97602

541-883-7547

Meg Graf, Resource Librarian

Newsletter on rehabilitation, peer counseling, blindness, visual impairments, information and referral.

7069   If Blindness Comes

National Federation of the Blind
1800 Johnson Street
Baltimore, MD   21230

410-659-9314
FAX: 410-685-5653
e-mail: nfb@iamdigex.net
www.nfb.org

An introduction to issues relating to vision loss and provides a positive, supportive philosophy about blindness. It is a general information book which includes answers to many common questions about blindness, information about services and programs for the blind and resource listings. Contact the Materials Center.

7070   If Blindness Strikes; Don't Strike Out

Charles C. Thomas, Publisher
2600 S 1st Street
Springfield, IL   62704

217-789-8980
800-258-8980
FAX: 217-789-9130
e-mail: books@ccthomas.com

Margaret M. Smith, author

This book is a storehouse of information on daily life for the visually impaired and those around them. From opticons and laser canes to housekeeping to travel, the author describes how to successfully cope with the problems posed by visual impairment and blindness. Also available in cloth for $51.95 (ISBN# 0-398-04937-8) *$36.95*

316 pages Paperback
ISBN 0-398064-34-2

7071   InSight

National Society to Prevent Blindness
500 East Remington Road
Schaumburg, IL   60173

847-843-2020
800-331-2020
FAX: 847-843-8458
e-mail: info@preventblindness.org
www.preventblindness.org

Quarterly

7072   Increasing Literacy Levels: Final Report

Mississippi State University
PO Box 6189
Mississippi State, MS   39762

601-325-2001
800-675-7782
FAX: 662-325-8989
TDY:601-325-8693
e-mail: rrtc@ra.state.edu
www.blind.msstate.edu

Pennsylvania College of Optometry, author
Kelly Schaefer, Dissemination Specialist

This study is composed of three research projects to identify and analyze the appropriate use of and instruction in Braille, optical devices, and other technologies as they relate to literacy and employment of individuals who are blind or visually impaired. *$20.00*

148 pages Paperback

7073   Independence Without Sight and Sound: Suggestions for Practitioners

American Foundation for the Blind/AFB Press
PO Box 1020
Sewickley, PA   15143

412-741-1142
800-232-3044
FAX: 412-741-0609
e-mail: afborders@abdintl.com
www.afb.org

Dona Sauerburger, author

This practical guidebook covers the essential aspects of communicating and working with deaf-blind persons. Includes useful information on how to talk with deaf-blind people, adapt orientation and mobility techniques for deaf-blind travelers. Paperback. *$39.95*

193 pages
ISBN 0-891282-46-7

7074   Information Access Project

National Federation of the Blind
1800 Johnson Street
Baltimore, MD   21230

410-837-6763
FAX: 410-685-5653
e-mail: nfb@iamdigex.net
www.nfb.org

Marc Maurer, President

Assists entities covered by the ADA in finding methods for converting visually displayed information, such as flyers, brochures and pamphlets, to formats accessible to individuals who are visually impaired.

7075 International Directory of Libraries for the Disabled

KG Saur/ A Division of R.R. Bowker
121 Chanlon Road
New Providence, NJ 07974   212-337-6900
                                       800-521-8110
                                       FAX: 908-665-6688

Hiroshi Kawamura, author

An essential resource for improving the quality and quantity of materials available to the print-handicapped audience. Featuring talking books, braille books, large print books as well as production centers for these materials. *$46.00*

257 pages
ISBN 3-59821-81-1

7076 Intervention Practices in the Retention of Competitive Employment Among Indiv. who are Blind

Mississippi State University
PO Box 6189
Mississippi State, MS 39762   601-325-2001
                                          800-675-7782
                                   FAX: 662-325-8989
                                   TDY:601-325-8693
                             e-mail: rrtc@ra.state.edu
                             www.blind.msstate.edu

Anjoo Sikka and Barry C. Stephens, author
Kelly Schaefer, Dissemination Specialist

This study investigated the methods by which an individual can retain competitive employment after the onset of a significant vision loss. Interviews were conducted with 89 rehabilitation counselors across the U.S. Strategies that contribute to successful job retention were identified as well as best rehabilitation practices in job retention. *$15.00*

60 pages Paperback

7077 Jewish Heritage for the Blind

1655 E 24th Street
Brooklyn, NY 11229   718-338-8200

Offers large print traditional prayer books for the High Holy days, festivals, fast days and daily rituals for those finding it difficult or impossible to read small print.

7078 Journal of Visual Impairment and Blindness

Sheridan Press, c/o FB
PO Box 465
Hanover, PA 17331   717-632-3535
                               800-352-2210
                          FAX: 717-633-8929
                e-mail: pubsvc@tsp.sheridan.com
                www.sheridanreprints.com

Sharon Shively, Managing Editor
Jane Erin, Editor-in-Chief

Published in braille, regular print and on ASC II disk and cassette, this journal contains a wide variety of subjects including rehabilitation, psychology, education, legislation, medicine, technology, employment, sensory aids and childhood development as they relate to visual impairments. $90 Annual individual subscription, $125 Annual institutional subscription.

64 pages
ISSN 0145-48 x

7079 Kernal Book Series

National Federation of the Blind
1800 Johnson Street
Baltimore, MD 21230   410-659-9314
                            FAX: 410-685-5653
                      e-mail: nfb@iamdigex.net
                      www.nfb.org

A series of books written by the blind themselves. Each book is a collection of articles and stories about the real life experiences of blind persons. These books help educate the blind and the sighted alike about a positive philosophy regarding blindness. Contact the Materials Center.

$5 - $10 each

7080 King James Bible, Large Print

Science Products
Box A
Southeastern, PA 19399   610-296-2111
                                    800-888-7400

Mary Ann Case, Marketing Director

A hardcover book with 24 point type easily seen with 20/200 acuity. Makes bible reading for children easier too. New Testament ($39.95: Old Testament $119.95).

7081 Knotholes are for Seeing - Therapy Through Poetry, Prose & Other Writings

Business of Living Publications
PO Box 8388
Corpus Christi, TX 78468   512-852-8515

Dorothy H. Stiefel, author
$12.95

ISBN 1-879518-08-2

7082 Large Print Loan Library

National Association for Visually Handicapped
22 W 21st Street
New York, NY 10010   212-889-3141

                           e-mail: staff@navh.org

A huge large print catalog of all the publications, fiction and non-fiction, cassette tapes, books-on-tape and videos available for the visually impaired from the loan library of the National Association for the Visually Handicapped.

100 pages

7083 Library Resources for the Blind and Physically Handicapped

National Library Service for the Blind
1291 Taylor Street NW
Washington, DC 20542   202-707-5100
                              FAX: 202-707-0712
                              TDY:202-707-0744
                              e-mail: nls@loc.gov
                              www.loc.gov/nls

NLS administers a national library service that provides braille and recorded books and magazines on free loan to anyone who cannot read standard print because of visual or physical disabilities who are eligible residents of the United States or American citizens living abroad. The directory describes the cooperating libaries. Online at www.loc.gov/reference/directories.html.

83 pages

7084 Library Services for the Blind

South Carolina State University Library
301 Gervais Street
821
Columbia, SC 29201   803-771-0520
                             800-922-7818

News and information on developments in library services for readers who are blind and physically disabled.

7085 Lifestyles of Employed Legally Blind People: A Study of Exp and Time Use

Rehab Research & Training Center on Blindness
PO Box 6189
Mississippi State, MS 39762   601-325-2001
                                  800-675-7782
                             FAX: 662-325-8989
                             TDY:601-325-8693
                             e-mail: rrtc@ra.state.edudu
                             www.blind.msstate.edu
Kirchner, McBroom, Nelson, and Graves, author
Lynn W. McBroom, Ph.D., Senior Research Scientist

Results from a telephone survey show that visually impaired respondents are involved in a wide variety of activities with little restrictions on their range of activities. Sighted respondents tended to spend more time in child care, obtaining goods and services, attending to self-care activities, and engaging in social activities, while visually impaired respondents spent more time in education and passive activities. This report is a study of expenditures and time use. *$10.00*

193 pages Paperback

7086 Lion

Lion's Clubs International
300 22nd Street
Oak Brook, IL 60521   312-571-5466

Publication for the blind.

7087 Long Cane News

American Foundation for the Blind/AFB Press
PO Box 1020
Sewickley, PA 15143   412-741-1142
                              800-232-3044
                         FAX: 412-741-0609
                         e-mail: afborders@abdintl.com
                              www.afb.org

Liz Greco

SemiAnnual

7088 Low Vision Questions and Answers: Definitions, Devices, Services

American Foundation for the Blind/AFB Press
PO Box 1020
Sewickley, PA 15143   412-741-1142
                              800-232-3044
                         FAX: 412-741-0609
                         e-mail: afborders@abdintl.com
                              www.afb.org

What does low vision mean? What do low vision services cost? What diseases cause low vision? Answers to these and other questions are presented in a comprehensive format with accompanying photographs. $50.00/pack of 25.

21 pages
ISBN 0-891281-96-7

7089 Low Vision: Reflections of the Past, Issues for the Future

American Foundation for the Blind/AFB Press
PO Box 1020
Sewickley, PA 15143   412-741-1142
                              800-232-3044
                         FAX: 412-741-0609
                         e-mail: afborders@abdintl.com
                              www.afb.org
Virginia Bishop, Jane Elih, Anne L Corn, author

Background papers and a strategies section are used to identify the shifting needs of visually impaired persons and the resources that may be needed to address them. Paperback. *$29.95*

ISBN 0-891282-18-1

7090 Madness of Usher's - Coping with Vision & Hearing Loss

Business of Living Publications
PO Box 8388
Corpus Christi, TX 78468   512-852-8515

Dorothy H. Stiefel, Author
$7.50

Paperback
ISBN 1-879518-06-6

7091 Mainstreaming and the American Dream

American Foundation for the Blind/AFB Press
PO Box 1020
Sewickley, PA 15143   412-741-1142
                              800-232-3044
                         FAX: 412-741-0609
                         e-mail: afborders@abdintl.com
                              www.afb.org

Howard L. Nixon II, author

Based on in-depth interviews with parents and professionals, this research monograph presents information on the needs and aspirations of parents of blind and visually impaired children. Paperback. *$34.95*

256 pages
ISBN 0-891281-91-6

7092 Mainstreaming the Visually Impaired Child

NAPVI
PO Box 317
Watertown, MA   02272
                                          800-562-6265

Michael D. Orlansky, author

A unique, informative guide for teachers and educational professionals that work with the visually impaired. *$10.00*

121 pages Paper

7093 Making Life More Livable

American Foundation for the Blind/AFB Press
11 Penn Plaza
Suite 300
New York, NY   10001   **212-502-7600**
                                        800-232-5463
                              FAX: 212-502-7774
        e-mail: afbordcr@abdintl.com
                                   www.afb.org

Shows how simple adaptations in the home and environment can make a big difference in the lives of blind and visually impaired older persons. The suggestions offered are numerous and specific, ranging from how to mark food cans for greater visibility to how to get out of the shower safley. Large print. *$19.95*

96 pages
ISBN 0-891281-15-0

7094 Meeting the Needs of People with Vision Loss: Multidisciplinary Perspective

Resources for Rehabilitation
33 Bedford Street
Suite 19A
Lexington, MA   02420   **781-890-6371**
                              FAX: 781-867-7517

Susan Greenblatt

Written by rehabilitation professionals, physicians, and a sociologist, this book discusses how to provide appropriate information and how to serve special populations. Chapters on the role of the family, diabetes and vision loss, special needs of children and adolescents, adults with hearing and vision loss. *$29.95*

ISBN 0-92971 -07-0

7095 More Alike Than Different: Blind and Visually Impaired Children

American Foundation for the Blind/AFB Press
PO Box 1020
Sewickley, PA   15143   **412-741-1142**
                                        800-232-3044
                              FAX: 412-741-0609
        e-mail: afborders@abdintl.com
                                   www.afb.org

Offers photographs of blind and visually impaired children around the world learning to read and write, travel independently and performing basic living skills. Covers the most recent technological advances and demonstrates the universality of educational needs and goals. Paperback. $100.00/pack of 25.

ISBN 0-891281-69-0

7096 Musical Mainstream

National Library Service for the Blind
1291 Taylor Street NW
Washington, DC   20542   **202-707-5100**
                              FAX: 202-707-0712

Articles selected from print music magazines.

Quarterly

7097 NLS News

National Library Service for the Blind
1291 Taylor Street NW
Washington, DC   20542   **202-707-5100**
                              FAX: 202-707-0712

Newsletter on current program developments.

Quarterly

7098 NLS Update

National Library Service for the Blind
1291 Taylor Street NW
Washington, DC   20542   **202-707-5100**
                              FAX: 202-707-0712

Newsletter on the services volunteer activities.

Quarterly

7099 Nat'l Study of Participation Levels of African Amer. in the Profession of Blindness Svc.

Mississippi State University
PO Box 6189
Mississippi State, MS   39762   **601-325-2001**
                                        800-675-7782
                              FAX: 662-325-8989
                              TDY:601-325-8693
        e-mail: rrtc@ra.state.edu
                              www.blind.msstate.edu

Giesen et al., author
Kelly Schaefer, Dissemination Specialist

This study investigated the level of participation by African Americans in vocational rehab. (VR) services to persons who are visually impaired. Using surveys & interviews with all state VR directors, national Census data, and national RSA data, it was found nationally that African Americans are substantially under-represented in the service provider ranks, yet over-represented as clients. *$20.00*

61 pages Paperback

7100 Newsline for the Blind

National Federation of the Blind
1800 Johnson Street
Baltimore, MD   21230   410-659-9314
                   FAX: 410-685-5653
                   e-mail: nfb@iamdigex.net
                   www.nfb.org

Peggy Chong, Contact

Nation's only digital talking newspaper service for the blind. Allows the blind to read the full text of leading national and local newspapers by using a touch-tone telephone. Service is free of charge and available 24 hours a day, 7 days per week.

7101 Not Without Sight

American Foundation for the Blind/AFB Press
PO Box 1020
Sewickley, PA   15143   412-741-1142
                   800-232-3044
                   FAX: 412-741-0609
                   e-mail: afborders@abdintl.com
                   www.afb.org

This video describes the major types of visual impairment and their causes and effects on vision, while camera simulations approximate what people with each impairmant actually see. Also demonstrates how people with low vision make the best use of the vision they have. 20 minute video tape. Also available in PAL, $52.95, 0-89128-272-6. *$42.95*

VHS 1975
ISBN 0-891282-27-0

7102 One Two Three Sign with Me

TJ Publishers (Distributors)
817 Silver Spring Avenue
Suite 206
Silver Spring, MD   20910   301-585-4440
                   800-999-1168
                   FAX: 301-585-5930
                   e-mail: TJPubinc@aol.com

Sugar Sign Press, author
Angela K Thames, President
Jerald A Murphy, Vice President

Charming full color illustrations include basic shapes, circle, square, triangle and rectangle, for additional counting practice. *$3.95*

24 pages Softcover
ISBN 0-93984 -01-1

7103 Open Windows, Audiocassette

LifeWay Christian Resources Southern Baptist Conv.
127 9th Avenue North
Nashville, TN   37234   615-251-2000
                   800-458-2772
                   e-mail: specialed@lifeway.com
                   www.lifeway.com

Rhoda Royce, author
Judy Wooldridge, Product Development Specialist

Guide for personal devotions on audiocassette tape, using Bible references, devotional readings, and prayer calendar of popular Open Windows devotional guide. Available quarterly on three cassette tapes. *$10.70*

Quarterly

7104 Opportunity

National Industries for the Blind
524 Hamburg Turnpike CN 969
Wayne, NJ   07474   973-595-9200

George J. Mertz, President & CEO

Offers information and articles on the newest technology, equipment, services and programs for blind and visually impaired persons.

Quarterly

7105 Out of Left Field

American Foundation for the Blind/AFB Press
PO Box 1020
Sewickley, PA   15143   412-741-1142
                   800-232-3044
                   FAX: 412-741-0609
                   e-mail: afborders@abdintl.com
                   www.afb.org

Illustrates how youngsters who are blind or visually impaired integrated with their sighted peers in a variety of recreational and athletic activities. 17 minute video tape. Also available in PAL, $33.95, 0-89128-270-X. *$26.95*

VHS 1975
ISBN 0-891282-28-9

7106 Out of the Corner of My Eye Living with Vision Loss in Later Life

American Foundation for the Blind/AFB Press
PO Box 1020
Sewickley, PA   15143   412-741-1142
                   800-232-3044
                   FAX: 412-741-0609
                   e-mail: afborders@abdintl.com
                   www.afb.org

Nicolette Ringgold, author
Stephanie Biagioli, Marketing Coordinator

A personal account of student's vision loss and subsequent adjustment that is full of practical advice and cheerful encouragement, told by an 87 year old retired college teacher who has maintained her independence and zest for life. Available in paperback or on audio cassette. *$23.95*

120 pages
ISBN 0-891281-82-1

7107 Perkins Activity and Resource Guide: A Handbook for Teachers

Perkins School for the Blind, Publications
175 N Beacon Street
Watertown, MA   02172

This is a comprehensive, two volume guide with over 1,000 pages of activities, resources and instructional strategies for teachers and parents of students with visual and multiple disabilities. *$65.00*

7108 Personal Reader Update

Personal Reader Department
9 Centennial Drive
Peabody, MA   01960   978-977-2000
                                       800-343-0311
                          FAX: 978-977-2437

Offers information on new services, assistive devices and technology for the blind.

7109 Picture is Worth a Thousand Words for Blind and Visually Impaired Persons Too!

American Foundation for the Blind/AFB Press
PO Box 1020
Sewickley, PA   15143   412-741-1142
                                       800-232-3044
                          FAX: 412-741-0609
               e-mail: afborders@abdintl.com
                                       www.afb.org

Audiodescription - the art of describing in words for visually impaired viewers the visual aspects seen in television, film, etc. - is highlighted in this book for the blind and visually impaired person. *$7.95*

32 pages Large Print
ISBN 0-891282-12-2

7110 Popular Activities and Games for Blind, Visually Impaired & Disabled People

American Foundation for the Blind/AFB Press
PO Box 1020
Sewickley, PA   15143   412-741-1142
                                       800-232-3044
                          FAX: 412-741-0609
               e-mail: afborders@abdintl.com
                                       www.afb.org

Peter Rickards, author

A manual of easy-to-follow instructions for more than 50 games and activities for blind and visually impaired persons of all ages, their families, recreation leaders and health care professionals. Large print. *$19.95*

64 pages
ISBN 0-959974-78-4

7111 Prevent Blindness News

National Society to Prevent Blindness
500 East Remington Road
Schaumburg, IL   60173   847-843-2020

               e-mail: info@preventblindness.org
                        www.preventblindness.org

Patricia Dahlberg, Editor

Offers information and articles on eye safety, programs and services of the Society, conferences and seminars on safety in the workplace, sports eye safety information and more.

Quarterly

7112 Providing Services for People with Vision Loss: Multidisciplinary Perspective

Resources for Rehabilitation
33 Bedford Street
Suite 19A
Lexington, MA   02173   781-862-6455
                          FAX: 781-861-7517
                                       www.nfr.org

A collection of articles by ophthalmologists and rehabilitation professionals, including chapters on operating a low vision service, starting self-help programs, mental health services, aids and techniques that help people with vision loss. *$19.95*

136 pages
ISBN 0-929718-02-0

7113 Psychoeducational Assessment of Visually Impaired and Blind Students

Pro-Ed
8700 Shoal Creek Boulevard
Austin, TX   78758   512-451-3246
                          FAX: 512-451-8542
                    e-mail: proed1@aol.com

Sharon Johnson, author

Professional reference book that addresses the problems specific to assessment of visually impaired and blind children. Of particular value to the practitioner are the extensive reviews of available tests, including ways to adapt those not designed for use with the visually handicapped. *$29.00*

140 pages Paperback
ISBN 0-890791-08-2

7114 Quarterly Update

National Association for Visually Handicapped
22 W 21st Street
6th Floor
New York, NY   10010   212-889-3141
                          FAX: 212-727-2931
                    e-mail: staff@navh.org
                                       www.navh.org

Quarterly newsletter offering information on new products for the visually impaired, advances in medical treatments, new books available in the NAVH large print loan library and any new/updated booklets. Free. *$2.25*

7115 RP Messenger

Texas Association of Retinitis Pigmentosa
PO Box 8388
Corpus Christi, TX   78468   512-852-8515

A bi-annual newsletter offering information on Retinitis Pigmentosa. *$15.00*

BiAnnual

7116 Raised Dot Computing Newsletter

Raised Dot Computing
408 S Baldwin Street
Madison, WI   53703   608-257-9595

               e-mail: info@rdcbraille.com

Discusses braille computer techniques and devices for blind persons. *$7.00*

7117 Recording for the Blind News

Recording for the Blind
20 Rosel Road
Princeton, NJ 08540   609-452-0606
      800-221-4792
      FAX: 609-987-8116

A non-profit organization that provides recorded books free of charge to blind and print-handicapped individuals.

3x Year

7118 Resources for Family Centered Intervention for Infants, Toddlers, and Preschoolers

Hope
1856 North 1200 East
Logan, UT 84341   435-245-2888
      FAX: 435-245-2888
      e-mail: hope@hopepubl.com
      www.hopepubl.com

Susan Watkins, Owner

Describes children with vision impairment in terms of characteristics, needs, and parent concerns. $98.00

Two volumes

7119 SCENE

Braille Institute
527 North Dale Avenue
Anaheim, CA 92801   714-821-5000
      800-808-2555
      FAX: 714-527-7621

Paul J. Porelli, Managing Editor

Offers information on the organization, question and answer column, articles on the newest technology and more for visually impaired persons.

7120 Seeing Eye Guide

Seeing Eye
Washington Valley Road
PO Box 375
Morristown, NJ 07963   973-539-4425
      FAX: 973-539-0922

Quarterly

7121 Smith Kettlewell Rehabilitation Engineering Research Center

Smith-Kettlewell Eye Research Institute
2318 Fillmore Street
San Francisco, CA 94115   615-345-2000
      FAX: 615-345-8655
      e-mail: rerc@ski.org
      www.ski.org

Reports on technology and devices for persons with visual impairments. $7.00

7122 Social Maturity Scale for Blind Preschool Children: A Guide to Its Use

American Foundation for the Blind/AFB Press
PO Box 1020
Sewickley, PA 15143   412-741-1142
      800-232-3044
      FAX: 412-741-0609
      e-mail: afborders@abdintl.com
      www.afb.org

Kathryn E. Maxfield and Sandra Bucholz, author

An adaptation of the Vineland Social Maturity Scale for use with children from infancy to 6 years of age. $9.95

57 pages Paperback
ISBN 0-891280-59-6

7123 Specifications for Selecting a Vocabulary and Teaching Method/Braille Readers

American Foundation for the Blind/AFB Press
PO Box 1020
Sewickley, PA 15143   412-741-1142
      800-232-3044
      FAX: 412-741-0609
      e-mail: afborders@abdintl.com
      www.afb.org

Hilda Caton, author

Specifications for a reading series developing braille developed at the American Printing House For The Blind. Paperback. $ 12.95

84 pages
ISBN 0-891280-69-3

7124 Starting Points

Blind Children's Center
4120 Marathon Street
Los Angeles, CA 90029
      800-222-3566
      FAX: 323-665-3828
      e-mail: info@blindchildrenscenter.org

Basic information for the clasroom teacher of 3 to 8 year olds whose multiple disabilities include visual impairment. $35.00

160 pages

7125 Step-By-Step Guide to Personal Management for Blind Persons

American Foundation for the Blind/AFB Press
PO Box 1020
Sewickley, PA 15143   412-741-1142
      800-232-3044
      FAX: 412-741-0609
      e-mail: afborders@abdintl.com
      www.afb.org

A manual of techniques in the areas of hygiene, grooming, clothing, shopping and child care. $19.95

136 pages Spiralbound
ISBN 0-891280-61-8

7126 Student Advocate

National Alliance of Blind Students
1010 Vermont Avenue NW
Suite 1100
Washington, DC 20005   202-393-3666
      800-424-8666

A communication forum covering issues of concern to postsecondary students who are blind.

7127 Student Perception of Careers in Blindness Rehab. Svcs. at Historically White Universities

Mississippi State University
PO Box 6189
Mississippi State, MS 39762   601-325-2001
    800-675-7782
    FAX: 662-325-8989
    TDY:601-325-8693
    e-mail: rrtc@ra.state.edu
    www.blind.msstate.edu

McBroom et al., author
Kelly Schaefer, Dissemination Specialist

In a follow-up study in a series examining the substantial under-representation of African Americans as professionals in blindness services, researchers questioned college students about their knowledge, opinions, and interests in blindness services. *$15.00*

54 pages Paperback

7128 Student Teaching Guide for Blind and Visually Impaired College Students

American Foundation for the Blind/AFB Press
PO Box 1020
Sewickley, PA 15143   412-741-1142
    800-232-3044
    FAX: 412-741-0609
    e-mail: afborders@abdintl.com
    www.afb.org

Lou Alonso, author

A comprehensive resource designed to enable the student to enter the classroom of a university or college with confidence. Large print. *$14.95*

52 pages
ISBN 0-891281-42-8

7129 Talking Book Topics

National Library Services for the Blind
1291 Taylor Street NW
Washington, DC 20542   202-707-5100
    FAX: 202-707-0712

Offers hundreds of listings of books, fiction and nonfiction, for adults and children on cassette. Also offers listings on foreign language books on cassette, talking magazines and reviews.

BiMonthly

7130 Teaching Visually Impaired Children

Charles C. Thomas, Publisher
2600 S 1st Street
Springfield, IL 62704   217-789-8980
    800-258-8980
    FAX: 217-789-9130
    e-mail: books@ccthomas.com

Virginia E. Bishop, author

A comprehensive resource for the classroom teacher who is working with a visually impaired child for the first time, as well as a systematic overview of education for the specialist in visual disabilities. It approaches instructional challenges with clear explanations and practical suggestions, and it addresses common concerns of teachers in a reassuring and positive manner. Also available in cloth for $51.95 (ISBN# 0-398-06595-0) *$35.95*

274 pages Paperback
ISBN 0-398065-96-9

7131 Telephone Pioneer

Telephone Pioneers of America
930 15th Street
12th Floor
Denver, CO 80202   303-571-1200
    FAX: 303-571-9292
    www.telephonepioneers.org

Quarterly

7132 Textbook Catalog

National Braille Association
3 Townline Circle
Rochester, NY 14623   716-427-8260

Lists hundreds of scholarly, college and professional textbooks offered in large print, braille or on cassette for visually impaired readers.

80 pages

7133 To Love this Life: Quotations by Helen Keller

American Foundation for the Blind/AFB Press
11 Penn Plaza
Suite 300
New York, NY 10001   212-502-7600
    800-232-5463
    FAX: 212-502-7774
    e-mail: afborder@abdintl.com
    www.afb.org

Inspirational work that offers the penetrating observations of Helen Keller, the beloved deaf-blind champion of the rights of people with disabilities. Also available on cassette at $21.95 (ISBN# 0-89128-348-X) *$21.95*

144 pages Hardcover 1900
ISBN 0-891283-47-1

7134 Touch the Baby: Blind & Visually Impaired Children As Patients

American Foundation for the Blind/AFB Press
PO Box 1020
Sewickley, PA 15143   412-741-1142
    800-232-3044
    FAX: 412-741-0609
    e-mail: afborders@abdintl.com
    www.afb.org

Lois Harrell, author

A how-to manual for health care professionals working in hospitals, clinics and doctors' offices. Teaches the special communication and touch-related techniques needed to prevent blind and visually impaired patients from withdrawing from the healthcare workers and the outside world. $25.00/pack of 25.

13 pages
ISBN 0-891281-97-5

7135 Transition Activity Calendar for Students with Visual Impairments

Mississippi State University
PO Box 6189
Mississippi State, MS 39762   601-325-2001
    800-675-7782
    FAX: 662-325-8989
    TDY:601-325-8693
    e-mail: rrtc@ra.state.edu
    www.blind.msstate.edu

Lynn W. McBroom, author
Kelly Schaefer, Dissemination Specialist

The Transition Activity Calendar guides the student with a visual disability through the maze of college preparation. Beginning in junior high school, clearly written steps are listed for each grade level. Students planning to enter college after high school graduation can check-off their accomplishments each step of the way. The calendar helps students focus on their goals, while providing reminders of tasks yet to be completed. It can be used in a self-directed manner or in a group format. *$4.25*

16 pages Paperback

7136 Transition to College for Students with Visual Impairments - Report

Rehab Research & Training Center on Blindness
PO Box 6189
Mississippi State, MS   39762   601-325-2001
                                              800-675-7782
                                              FAX: 662-325-8989
                                              TDY:601-325-8693
                                              e-mail: rrtc@ra.state.eduu
                                              www.blind.msstate.edu
McBroom, L.W., Sikka, A., Jones.L.B.(1994), author
Lynn McBroom, PhD, Sr. Research Scientist

A report offering results from telephone interviews of college students with visual impairments and mail surveys of college officials which examines the transition experience of successful college students. General domains in the study include demographics, educational history, computers, specialized and adaptive equipment,resources, college preparation, problems adjusting to college, and O&M skills. A literature review covers preparing for college, task timelines, and classroom, lab and tests. *$20.00*

151 pages Paperback

7137   USABA Newsletter

United States Association for Blind Athletes
33 N Institute Brown Hall
Colorado Springs, CO   80903   719-333-4195
                                              FAX: 719-630-0616
                                              e-mail: media@usaba.org
                                              www.usaba.org

Covers news, announcements and activities of the Association.

20 pages Quarterly

7138   Unseen Minority: A Social History of Blindness in the United States

American Foundation for the Blind/AFB Press
PO Box 1020
Sewickley, PA   15143   412-741-1142
                                     800-232-3044
                                     FAX: 412-741-0609
                                     e-mail: afborders@abdintl.com
                                     www.afb.org
Frances A. Koestler, author

A lively narrative, peppered with anecdotes, recounts how the blind overcame discrimination to gain full participation in the social, educational, economic and legislative spheres. Hardcover. *$ 40.00*

573 pages
ISBN 0-679505-39-3

7139   Visual Aids and Informational Material

National Association for Visually Handicapped
22 W 21st Street
6th Floor
New York, NY   10010   212-889-3141
                                     FAX: 212-727-2931
                                     e-mail: staff@navh.org
                                     www.navh.org

A complete listing of the visual aids NAVH carries such as magnifiers, talking clocks, large print playing cards, etc. *$2.50*

65 pages

7140   Visual Handicaps and Learning

Pro-Ed
8700 Shoal Creek Boulevard
Austin, TX   78758   512-451-3246
                                  FAX: 512-451-8542
                                  e-mail: proed1@aol.com
Natalie Barraga, author

This text covers a range of topics associated with visual impairment, from past practices to up-to-date research, and from legal responsibilities to personal beliefs, without losing sight of the individual child. *$28.00*

180 pages
ISBN 0-890791-56-2

7141   Visual Handicaps and Learning, Third Edition

Pro-Ed
8700 Shoal Creek Boulevard
Austin, TX   78757
                                  FAX: 512-451-8542
                                  e-mail: proed1@aol.com
Natalie C. Barraga and Kane N. Erin, author

The major focus of this new third edition is to present a new way of thinking about individuals with visual impairment so that they are viewed as participating members of a seeing world despite their reduced visual functioning. *$28.00*

213 pages
ISBN 0-89079 -15-0

7142   Visual Impairment: An Overview

American Foundation for the Blind/AFB Press
PO Box 1020
Sewickley, PA   15143   412-741-1142
                                     800-232-3044
                                     FAX: 412-741-0609
                                     e-mail: afborders@abdintl.com
                                     www.afb.org
Ian L Bailey, Amanda Hall, author

An overall look at the most common forms of vision loss and their impact on the individual. Includes drawings as well as photographs that stimulate how people with vision loss see. Paperback. *$19.95*

56 pages
ISBN 0-891281-74-6

7143   Visually Handicapped Child in Your Class

Paul H. Brookes Publishing Company
PO Box 10624
Baltimore, MD   21285
                                              800-638-3134
Elizabeth K. Chapman, author

This book considers the theory and issues relating to the movement to integrate visually handicapped children into ordinary schools and offers practical suggestions to teachers to help such children participate fully in school life. *$21.50*

192 pages Paper
ISBN 0-304314-00-5

7144   Viva Vital News
5016 Silk Oak Drive
Sarasota, FL   34232

Membership service organization offering information for veterans and is an affiliate of the American Council of the Blind.

7145   Voice of Vision
GW Micro
310 Racquet Drive
Fort Wayne, IN   46825   **219-483-3625**

e-mail: sales@gwnicro.com

Offers product reviews, product announcements, tips for making systems or applications more accessible, or explanations of concepts of interest to any computer user or would-be computer user. This association newsletter is available in braille, in large print, on audio cassette and on 3.5 or 5.25 IBM format diskette.

Quarterly

7146   Walking Alone and Marching Together
National Federation of the Blind
1800 Johnson Street
Baltimore, MD   21230   **410-659-9314**
                                   FAX: 410-685-5653
                          e-mail: nfb@iamdigex.net
                                   www.nfb.org

The history of the organized blind movement, this book spans more than 50 years of civil rights, social issues, attitudes and experiences of the blind. Published in 1990, it has been read by thousands of blind and sighted persons and is used in colleges, libraries and programs across the country as an important tool in understanding blindness and it's impact on both personal lives and the society at large. Braille $130, 2 track or 4 track cassette $40, Print $33.00. Contact Materials Center.

7147   We Can Do it Together!
American Foundation for the Blind/AFB Press
PO Box 1020
Sewickley, PA   15143   **412-741-1142**
                                   800-232-3044
                          FAX: 412-741-0609
                  e-mail: afborders@abdintl.com
                                   www.afb.org

This video illustrates a transdisciplinaty team orientation and mobility program for students with severe visual and multiple impairments, covering both adapted communication systems used to teach mobility skills and basic indoor mobility in the school. For mobility instructors, administrators, teachers of the visually and severely handicapped, occupational, physical and speech therapists and parents. Discussion guide included. 10 minute video tape. Also available in PAL, $33.95, 0-89128-267-X. *$26.95*

VHS
ISBN 0-891282-13-0

7148   Webster Large Print Thesaurus/Dictionary
Science Products
Box A
Southeastern, PA   19399   **610-296-2111**
                                      800-888-7400

Mary Ann Case, Marketing Director

10 point type, more than 57,000 word entries and illustrations, 14 pt. body copy, 16 pt. heads and 20 pt. page headings. *$39.95*

7149   What Museum Guides Need to Know: Access for the Blind and Visually Impaired
American Foundation for the Blind/AFB Press
PO Box 1020
Sewickley, PA   15143   **412-741-1142**
                                   800-232-3044
                          FAX: 412-741-0609
                  e-mail: afborders@abdintl.com
                                   www.afb.org

Gerda Groff and Laura Gardner, author

Explains how blind and visually impaired museumgoers experience art and offers pointers on greeting people, asking if help is needed and teaching about a specific work of art. Contains information on access laws, resources, training guides and guidelines for preparing large print, cassette and braille materials. *$14.95*

64 pages Paperback
ISBN 0-891281-58-4

7150   Witch's Daughter
JB Lippincott
227 E Washington Square
Philadelphia, PA   19106   **215-238-4200**
                                      800-777-2295
                             FAX: 215-824-7390

Nina Bawden, author

Perdeta had been scorned by her peers on the small Scottish island where she lived. The island children believed her to be a witch and spent their time chasing and teasing her. When Tim and his blind sister Janey arrived for a vacation, Perdeta had her first opportunity to make friends. Janey and Perdeta enjoyed each other's company immediately, while Tim eventually accepted their new friend.

181 pages Hardcover

7151 You Seem Like a Regular Kid to Me

American Foundation for the Blind/AFB Press
PO Box 1020
Sewickley, PA 15143
412-741-1142
800-232-3044
FAX: 412-741-0609
e-mail: afborders@abdintl.com
www.afb.org
Anne L Corn, Chris M Cowan, Elaine Moses, author

An interview with Jane, a blind child, tells other children what it's like to be blind. Jane explains how she gets around, takes care of herself, does her schoolwork, spends her leisure time and even pays for things when she can't see money. Paperback and pamphlet. $25.00/pack of 25. *$25.00*

16 pages Pack of 25
ISBN 0-89128-21-6

Vocations

7152 ABC's of Starting a Private School

Alliance for Parental Involvement in Education
PO Box 59
East Chatham, NY 12060
518-392-6900
FAX: 518-392-6900
Bonnie Schreiter, author

Job placement programs, remunerative work services and work adjustment training programs. *$17.95*

7153 Cambridge Career Products Catalog

Cambridge Educational
PO Box 931
Monmouth Junction, NJ 08852
304-744-9323
800-468-4227
FAX: 304-744-9351
e-mail: lisa.schmuclei@films.com
www.cambridgeeducational.com
Lisa Schmuclei, author
Lisa Schmuclei, Marketing Director

A full color catalog featuring hundreds of products designed to aid people in career exploration, selecting specific occupations and obtaining these jobs through resume and interview preparation.

64 pages BiAnnual

7154 Closer Look: The English Program at the Model Secondary School for the Deaf

Gallaudet University Bookstore
800 Florida Avenue NE
Washington, DC 20002
202-651-5000
800-451-1073
FAX: 202-651-5489
Pre-College Outreach, author

Job placement programs, remunerative work services and work adjustment training programs incorporating the whole language philosophy into classroom routines. *$8.50*

67 pages

7155 College Guide for Students with Learning Disablities

Riverside Publishing/Wintergreen Orchard House
425 Spring Lake Drive
Itasca, IL 60143
630-232-7047
800-323-9540
FAX: 630-467-6194
Tina Tripoli, Marketing/Acct.Mgr.

There is a role to play whether you are a teacher, counselor, administrator or parent and this guide explains them all. *$26.95*

372 pages

7156 Economic Opportunity Report

Business Publishers
8737 Colesville Road
Suite 1100
Silver Spring, MD 20910
800-274-6737
FAX: 301-587-4530
e-mail: bpinews@bpinews.com
www.bpinews.com
Leonard A. Eiserer, Publisher
Lan Wilhelm, Editor

Reports the latest on key poverty programs such as homelessness, housing, welfare reform, job training, early childhood education, health care, adult literacy, and more. *$417.00*

10 pages Newsletter Wkly

7157 Economics, Industry and Disability

Paul H. Brookes Publishing Company
PO Box 10624
Baltimore, MD 21285
800-638-3775
FAX: 410-337-8539
William E. Kiernan, author

An analysis of the movement toward nonsheltered employment, this book addresses the expanding opportunities, future challenges and economic changes surrounding efforts to ensure the development of positive and constructive employment for persons with disabilities. *$42.00*

Hardcover

7158 Employment Standards Administration Department of Labor

200 Constitution Avenue NW
Washington, DC 20210
202-219-6666
Corlis Sellers, Branch Chief

Monitors compliance with sub-minimum wage requirements for handicapped workers in sheltered workshops, competitive industry and hospitals and institutions under Section 14 of the Fair Labor Standards Act of 1938.

7159 Guide to Developing Language Competence in Handicapped Preschool Children

Charles C. Thomas, Publisher
2600 S First Street
Springfield, IL 62794   217-789-8980
                              800-258-8980
                         FAX: 217-789-9130
                    e-mail: books@ccthomas.com

Ennio Cipani

Job placement programs, remunerative work services and work adjustment training programs handicaps: teachers, administrators and parents. *$54.95*

268 pages Cloth 1991
ISBN 0-398057-48-6

7160 Handbook for Counseling the Gifted and Talented

American Association for Counseling & Development
5999 Stevenson Avenue
Alexandria, VA 22304   703-823-9800
                              800-347-6647

Barbara A. Kerr, Editor

Tells how to identify, inspire and nurture gifted and talented students. Effective techniques for making a qualitative and quantitative differentiation of gifted students, conducting a successful search for gifted students, nurturing underachievers and helping multipotential students make career choices. *$32.95*

218 pages
ISBN 1-55620-79-1

7161 Mentally Retarded Individuals

Mainstream
3 Bethesda Metro Center
Suite 830
Bethesda, MD 20814   301-951-6122
                            800-247-1380
                e-mail: info@mainstreaminc.org
Mainstream, Inc., author

Mainstreaming mentally retarded individuals into the workplace. *$2.50*

12 pages

7162 Occupational Outlook Quarterly

US Department of Labor/Bureau of Labor Stats
2 Massachusetts Avenue NE
Washington, DC 20212   202-606-6312
                         FAX: 202-606-5745

Kathleen Green, Managing Editor

Information on new educational and training opportunities, emerging jobs, prospects for change in the work world, and occupational projections. *$9.50*

40 pages Quarterly

7163 Preparation and Employment of Students

Paul H. Brookes Publishing Company
PO Box 10624
Baltimore, MD 21285
                              800-638-3775
                         FAX: 410-337-8539

Jo-Ann Sowers, author

A practical guide on vocational training and employment issues for persons with severe multiple and physical disabilities. *$ 213.00*

224 pages Paper

7164 Principles and a Philosophy for Vocational Education

Center on Education and Training for Employment
Ohio State
1900 Kenny Road
Columbus, OH 43210   614-292-4277
                              800-848-4815
                         FAX: 614-292-1260

Att:, Publications Office

Identifies and analyzes underlying principles of vocational education and uses them as a basis for coherent philosophical position for vocational education that reflects human and economic needs, a contemporary knowledge base, and the values inherent in our society. *$15.50*

250 pages

7165 Retaining At-Risk Students: The Role of Career and Vocational Education

Center on Education and Training for Employment
Ohio State - 1900 Kenny Road
Columbus, OH 43210   614-292-1102
                              800-848-4815
                         FAX: 614-292-1260

Reviews the causes of at-risk students and their implications for the U.S. Labor force. *$6.00*

48 pages

7166 Social Competence for Workers with Developmental Disabilities

Paul H. Brookes Publishing Company
PO Box 10624
Baltimore, MD 21285
                              800-638-3775
                         FAX: 410-337-8539

Carl F. Calkins, author

A guide to enhancing employment outcomes in integrated settings. *$35.00*

128 pages Paper 1990

7167 Successful Job Accommodation Strategies

LRP Publications
747 Dresher Road
PO Box 980
Horsham, PA 19044   215-784-0941
                              800-341-7874
                         FAX: 215-784-9639
                    e-mail: custserve@lrp.com
                              www.lrp.com

Linda Segall, author
Honora McDowell, Product Group Mgr.

This monthly newsletter provides you with quick tips, new accommodation ideas and innovative workplace solutions. You learn the outcomes of the latest cases involving workplace accommodations. *$ 140.00*

12 pages Monthly

7168 Transition From School to Work for Persons with Disabilities

Longman Publishing Group
95 Church Street
White Plains, NY 10601   914-993-5000

Diane E. Berkell, author

This collection examines the multidimensional process needed to effectively prepare persons with disabilities for life after school and addresses the key issues in the transition process.

251 pages Paper 1989
ISBN 0-801302-28-5

7169 Transition from School to Work

Paul H. Brookes Publishing Company
PO Box 10624
Baltimore, MD 21285

800-638-3775
FAX: 410-337-8539

Paul Wehman, author

A hands-on guide to planning and implementing successful transition programs for adolescents with disabilities. *$25.00*

336 pages Paper 1988

7170 Vocal Rehabilitation: A Practice Book for Voice Improvement, Third Edition

Pro-Ed
8700 Shoal Creek Boulevard
Austin, TX 78757   512-451-3246
FAX: 512-451-8542
e-mail: proed1@aol.com
Virginia L. Agnello & Cindy Garcia, author

A complete program that clinicians can use to help clients eliminate vocal misuses or abuse and gain a healthy, proficient voice. *$49.00*

7171 Vocational Assessment and Curriculum Guide

Exceptional Education
PO Box 15308
Seattle, WA 98115   206-542-3971
FAX: 475-486-4510

J E Stewart, Owner

Use this guide to develop a plan for your client leading directly to competitive employment. The Inventory addresses expectations for light industrial and service occupations based on two surveys involving 108 employers. The Summary Profile graphically prioritizes and shows progress toward competitive employment. The Curriculum Guide lists training goals for each assessment item. *$12.00*

16 pages Complete Set
ISBN 1-87786 -24-5

7172 Vocational Education for Multihandicapped Youth

Paul H. Brookes Publishing Company
PO Box 10624
Baltimore, MD 21285

800-638-3775
FAX: 410-337-8539

Paul Wehman, author

The first book with specific vocational teaching strategies, adaptations and rehabilitation guidelines for preteens and young adults with cerebral palsy. *$25.00*

320 pages Paper 1988

7173 Vocational Evaluation Systems and Software

Rehabilitation Resource
University of Wisconsin-Stout
Menomonie, WI 54751   715-232-1478
FAX: 715-232-2356

Ronald R. Fry, Manager
Darlene Botterbusch, Program Assistant

This guide describes and reviews eighteen commercially available vocational assessment and evaluation systems and nine job search software packages. The primary purpose of the guide is to help administrators, vocational evaluation and assessment personnel, personnel directors and teachers to understand the products so that they can make the best possible purchase decision. *$24.00*

185 pages Softcover

7174 Vocational Evaluation and Traumatic Brain Injury: A Procedural Manual

Stout Vocational Rehab Institute
University of Wisconsin-Stout
Menomonie, WI 5413G

FAX: 715-232-2356

Ronald R. Fry, Manager
Darlene Botterbusch, Program Assistant

This is a written guide for rehabilitation professionals interested in effectively developing new or modifying existing evaluation/assessment services for persons with traumatic brain injury. A practical manual for identifying local support services; creating specific processes, tools and techniques; and formulating meaningful outcome information to facilitate the provision or goal-directed services *$ 14.75*

61 pages Softcover

7175 Vocational Rehabilitation and Employment

Books on Special Children
PO Box 305
Congers, NY 10920   845-638-1236
FAX: 845-638-0847
e-mail: irene@boscbooks.com
M.S. Moon, author

Defines kinds of work, expectations, goals and programs. Contributions in general issues of supported employment, training and management and community based programs. *$47.00*

372 pages Hardcover

7176 Vocational Rehabilitation and Supported Employment

Paul H. Brookes Publishing Company
PO Box 10624
Baltimore, MD 21285

800-638-3775
FAX: 410-337-8539

Paul Wehman, author

A timely, comprehensive resource on how vocational rehabilitation can play a major role in facilitating and implementing supported employment programs. *$43.00*

384 pages Paper 1988

Pamphlets

7177 ABDC Newsletter Volume Reprints

Birth Defect Research for Children
930 Woodcock Road, Suite 225
Suite 270
Orlando, FL   32803   407-895-0802
                                          FAX: 407-895-0824
                                  e-mail: abdc@birthdefects.org
                                          www.birthdefects.org

Betty Mekdeci, Executive Director
Offers a variety of reprints from the ABCD newsletter on birth defects.

monthly

7178 ADHD

Learning Disabilities Association of America
4156 Library Road
Pittsburgh, PA   15234   412-341-1515

Larry B. Silver, M.D., author
A booklet for parents offering information on Attention Deficit-Hyperactivity Disorders and learning disabilities. *$3.00*

7179 ADHD in the Classroom

Guilford Publications
72 Spring Street
New York, NY   10012   212-431-9800
                                            800-365-7006
                                       FAX: 212-966-6708
                                 e-mail: info@guilford.com
Russell A. Barkley, author

Designed specifically to help teachers with their ADHD students, thereby providing a better learning environment for the entire class. *$95.00*

7180 About Asthma

American Lung Association
1740 Broadway
New York, NY   10017   212-315-8700

A popular style pamphlet explaining symptoms, treatment and more for persons with asthma.

16 pages

7181 About Attention Disorder

C.A.C.L.D.
25 Van Zant Street
Suite 15-5
East Norwalk, CT   06855   203-838-5010
                                       FAX: 203-866-6108
                                  e-mail: CACLD@JUNO.com
                                          www.CACLD.org

C.L. Bete Co., author

Introduction to ADHD for the child with the disorder, parents, professionals, family, and friends. Brief description as well as causes, challenges involved, treatment options, ways for parents and teachers to help, and how children can help themselves. Published by Connecticut Association for Children & Adults with Learning Disabilities (CACLD). *$2.00*

14 pages

7182 About Children's Eyes

National Association for Visually Handicapped
22 W 21st Street
6th Floor
New York, NY   10010   212-889-3141
                                       FAX: 212-727-2931
                                  e-mail: staff@navh.org
                                          www.navh.org

How to identify the child with a visual problem.

7183 About Children's Vision: A Guide for Parents

National Association for Visually Handicapped
22 W 21st Street
6th Floor
New York, NY   10010   212-889-3141
                                       FAX: 212-727-2931
                                  e-mail: staff@navh.org
                                          www.navh.org

Offers a better understanding of the normal and possible abnormal development of a child's eyesight. *$.50*

7184 Ankylosing Spondylitis

Arthritis Foundation
PO Box 7669
Atlanta, GA   30357   404-872-7100
                                            800-283-7800
                                       FAX: 404-872-0457

7185 Around the Clock

Guilford Publications
72 Spring Street
New York, NY   10012   212-431-9800
                                            800-365-7006
                                       FAX: 212-966-6708
                                 e-mail: info@guilford.com
Joan F. Goodman and Susan Hoban, author

This videotape provides both professionals and parents a helpful look at how the difficulties facing parents of ADHD children can be handled. *$150.00*

7186 Arthritis Answers: Basic Information About Arthritis

Arthritis Foundation
PO Box 7669
Atlanta, GA   30357   404-872-7100
                                            800-283-7800
                                       FAX: 404-872-0457

7187 Arthritis Foundation Services

Arthritis Foundation
PO Box 7669
Atlanta, GA   30357   404-872-7100
                                            800-283-7800
                                       FAX: 404-872-0457

7188 Arthritis Information: Children

Arthritis Foundation
PO Box 7669
Atlanta, GA   30357   404-872-7100
                                       800-283-7800
                               FAX: 404-872-0457

List of materials for children with arthritis, their families and the health professionals who care for them.

7189 Arthritis and Diet

NAMSIC, National Institutes of Health
1 AMS Circle
Bethesda, MD   20892   301-495-4484
                               FAX: 301-587-4352
                               www.nih.gov/niams

Offers information on nutrition and diet pertaining to the arthritis community. *$2.00*

16 pages

7190 Arthritis and Employment: You Can Get the Job You Want

Arthritis Foundation
PO Box 7669
Atlanta, GA   30357   404-872-7100
                                       800-283-7800
                               FAX: 404-872-0457

7191 Arthritis and Pregnancy

Arthritis Foundation
PO Box 7669
Atlanta, GA   30357   404-872-7100
                                       800-283-7800
                               FAX: 404-872-0457

How arthritis affects pregnancy, managing pregnancy and a new baby.

7192 Arthritis in Children

NAMSIC, National Institutes of Health
1 AMS Circle
Bethesda, MD   20892   301-495-4484
                               FAX: 301-587-4352
                               www.nih.gov/niams

7193 Arthritis in Children and La Artritis Infantojuvenil

American Juvenile Arthritis Organization
PO Box 19000
Atlanta, GA   30326
                                       800-283-7800

A medical information booklet about juvenile rheumatoid arthritis. This booklet is written for parents or other adults and includes details about different forms of JRA, medications, therapies and coping issues.

7194 Arthritis in Children: Resources for Children, Parents and Teachers

National Arthritis and Skin Diseases Clearinghouse
9000 Rockville Pike
Bethesda, MD   20892   301-495-4484

A resource offering information on juvenile arthritis, causes, treatments and prevention.

38 pages

7195 Arthritis on the Job: You Can Work with It

Arthritis Foundation
PO Box 7669
Atlanta, GA   30357   404-872-7100
                                       800-283-7800
                               FAX: 404-872-0457

7196 Arthritis, Rheumatic Diseases and Related Disorders

Nat'l Arthritis/Skin Diseases Info. Clearinghouse
9000 Rockville Pike
Bethesda, MD   20892   301-495-4484

This pamphlet offers information, technical articles and research on arthritis and related disorders. Also included are referral organizations to help patients uncover more information.

7197 Arthritis: Do You Know?

Arthritis Foundation
PO Box 7669
Atlanta, GA   30357   404-872-7100
                                       800-283-7800
                               FAX: 404-872-0457

A brief overview of arthritis and the services of the Arthritis Foundation.

7198 Asthma & Allergy Medications

American Academy of Allergy, Asthma and Immunology
611 E Wells Street
Milwaukee, WI   53202   414-272-6071
                                       800-822-2762
                               FAX: 414-272-6070
                               e-mail: info@aaaai.org
                               www.aaaai.org

$.50

4 pages

7199 Asthma Alert

American Lung Association
1740 Broadway
New York, NY   10017   212-315-8700

Quick reference folders with information on asthma, the symptoms and what to do in an emergency.

7200 Asthma Handbook

American Lung Association
1740 Broadway
New York, NY   10017   212-315-8700

Explains asthma, gives self-care methods for handling it and helps patients work more effectively with their doctor.

28 pages

7201 Asthma Lifelines

American Lung Association
1740 Broadway
New York, NY 10017   212-315-8700

Promotional brochure providing descriptions of ALA asthma education materials.

12 pages

7202 Asthma and Pregnancy

American Academy of Allergy, Asthma and Immunology
611 E Wells Street
Milwaukee, WI 53202   414-272-6071
                              800-822-2762
                         FAX: 414-272-6070
                     e-mail: info@aaaai.org
                              www.aaaai.org

$.50

7203 Attention Deficit Disorders and Hyperactivity

ERIC Clearinghouse on Disabled and Gifted Children
1920 Association Drive
Reston, VA 20191   703-620-3660
                            888-232-7232

7204 Attention Deficit-Hyperactivity Disorder: Is It a Learning Disability?

Georgetown University, School of Medicine
3800 Reservoir Road NW
Washington, DC 20007   202-687-2000

Larry Silver, M.D., author

Offers information on learning disabilities and related disorders.

7205 Avoiding Unfortunate Situations

Autism Society of North Carolina Bookstore
505 Oberlin Road
Suite 230
Raleigh, NC 27605   919-743-0204
                             800-442-2762
                        FAX: 919-743-0208
                   e-mail: ASNC@aol.com
                   www.autismsociety-nc.org

Dennis Debbaudt, author

A collection of tips and information from and about people with autism and other developmental disabilities. *$5.00*

7206 BVA Bulletin

Blinded Veterans Association
477 H Street NW
Washington, DC 20001   202-371-8880
                             800-669-7079
                        FAX: 202-371-8258
                     e-mail: bva@bva.org
                              www.bva.org

Thomas H. Miller, Executive Director
John K. Williams, Administrative Director
George E. Brummell, Nat'l Dir, Field Service Program

BiMonthly

7207 Being Close

National Jewish Center for Immunology
1400 Jackson Street
Denver, CO 80206   303-388-4461

A booklet offering information to patients suffering from a respiratory disorder such as emphysema, asthma or tuberculosis, that discusses sexual problems and feelings.

7208 Blind and Vision-Impaired Individuals

Mainstream
1030 5th Street NW
Washington, DC 20005   202-898-1400

                    e-mail: info@mainstreaminc.org
Mainstream, Inc., author

Mainstreaming blind individuals into the workplace. *$ 2.50*

12 pages

7209 Books are Fun for Everyone

National Library Service for the Blind
1291 Taylor Street NW
Washington, DC 20542   202-707-5100
                        FAX: 202-707-0712

7210 Braille: An Extraordinary Volunteer Opportunity

National Library Service for the Blind
1291 Taylor Street NW
Washington, DC 20542   202-707-5100
                        FAX: 202-707-0712

7211 Bursitis, Tendonitis and Other Soft Tissue Rheumatic Syndromes

Arthritis Foundation
PO Box 7669
Atlanta, GA 30357   404-872-7100
                             800-283-7800
                        FAX: 404-872-0457

7212 COGREHAB

Life Science Associates
1 Fenimore Road
Bayport, NY 11705   516-472-2111

Divided into six groups for diagnosis and treatment of attention, memory and perceptual disorders to be used by and under the guidance of a professional. $95.-$1,950

7213 Carpal Tunnel Syndrome

Arthritis Foundation
PO Box 7669
Atlanta, GA 30357   404-872-7100
                             800-283-7800
                        FAX: 404-872-0457

Offers an introduction to Carpal Tunnel, causes, symptoms, diagnosis and resources.

7214 Cataracts

National Eye Institute, Information Office
Building 31
Room 6A32
Bethesda, MD 20892   301-496-5248

Provides information about this common condition and its treatment.

7215 Childhood Asthma

American Academy of Allergy, Asthma and Immunology
611 E Wells Street
Milwaukee, WI 53202   414-272-6071
                            800-822-2762
                            FAX: 414-272-6070
                            e-mail: info@aaaai.org
                            www.aaaai.org

$.50

4 pages

7216 Childhood Asthma: A Guide for Parents

Asthma and Allergy Foundation of America
1125 15th Street NW
Suite 502
Washington, DC 20005   202-466-7643
                             FAX: 202-466-8940
                             e-mail: info@aafa.org
                             www.aafa.org

P.A. Eggleston, M.D., author

This colorful booklet helps parents learn all about asthma in children. *$2.00*

32 pages

7217 Childhood Asthma: A Matter of Control

American Lung Association
1740 Broadway
New York, NY 10017   212-315-8700

A guide for parents of children with asthma, this booklet covers topics such as identifying asthma signs and symptoms as well as controlling the condition.

28 pages

7218 Children with ADD: A Shared Responsibility

Council for Exceptional Children
1920 Association Drive
Reston, VA 20191   703-620-3660
                         888-232-7232
                         FAX: 703-264-9494
                         e-mail: service@cec.sped.org
                         www.cec.sped.org

Cathy Mack, Production Manager

This book represents a consensus of what professionals and parents believe ADD is all about and how children with ADD may best be served. Reviews the evaluation process under IDEA and 504 and presents effective classroom strategies.

35 pages
ISBN 0-865862-33-8

7219 Classification of Impaired Vision

National Association for Visually Handicapped
22 W 21st Street
6th Floor
New York, NY 10010   212-889-3141
                            FAX: 212-727-2931
                            e-mail: staff@navh.org
                            www.navh.org

Describes various degrees of impaired vision.

7220 Club Foot & Other Foot Deformities Fact Sheet

March of Dimes
1275 Mamaroneck Avenue
White Plains, NY 10605
                            888-663-4637
                            888-663-4637
                            FAX: 914-997-4763
                            e-mail: resourcecenter@modimes.org
                            www.modimes.org

Cathy Church-Balin, Director, Education Services

Provides information about pregnancy, birth defects, genetics, drug use, environmental hazzards and related topics. The Resource Center's health information specialists provide acccurate and up-to-date information via a toll free telephone line, fax, e-mail, and Web site. One copy of this fact sheet can be obtained free of charge by calling 888-MODIMES.

$5.00/pkg. 50

7221 Communicating with People Who Have Trouble Hearing & Seeing: A Primer

National Association for Visually Handicapped
22 W 21st Street
6th Floor
New York, NY 10010   212-889-3141
                            FAX: 212-727-2931
                            e-mail: staff@navh.org
                            www.navh.org

Line drawings that depict problems for those with both deficiencies. *$2.00*

7222 Connect Information Service

150 S Progress Avenue
Harrisburg, PA 17109   717-657-1798
                             800-692-7288

Pamphlet offering information on child development, special education programs, resources for parents and local contact persons.

7223 Developing a Functional and Longitudinal Plan

Autism Society of North Carolina Bookstore
505 Oberlin Road
Suite 230
Raleigh, NC 27605   919-743-0204
                          800-442-2762
                          FAX: 919-743-0208
                          e-mail: ASNC@aol.com
                          www.autismsociety-nc.org

Nancy Dalrymple, author

This booklet examines the importance of planning, and possible goals in self-care. *$4.00*

7224 Diet and Arthritis

Arthritis Foundation
PO Box 7669
Atlanta, GA 30357   404-872-7100
                           800-283-7800
                      FAX: 404-872-0457

7225 Dog Sponsorship Program

Guide Dog Foundation for the Blind
371 E Jericho Turnpike
Smithtown, NY 11787   516-265-2121
                           800-548-4337
                      FAX: 516-361-5192

Offers information to an individual or an organization that wishes to sponsor a guide dog.

7226 Don't Lose Sight of Cataracts

National Eye Institute, Information Office
Building 31
Room 6A32
Bethesda, MD 20892   301-496-5248

7227 Don't Lose Sight of Glaucoma

National Eye Institute, Information Office
Building 31
Room 6A32
Bethesda, MD 20892   301-496-5248

7228 Easy Access Housing

Easter Seals
230 W Monroe Street
Suite 1800
Chicago, IL 60606   312-726-6200
                      FAX: 312-726-1494

Janet D. Jamieson, Communications Mgr.

A 12-page booklet with a checklist for finding homes that are already accessible or structurally adaptable to accommodate changes in physical abilities and needs. Includes suggestions for solving common accessibility problems such as narrow doors, high thresholds and round knob fixtures.

7229 Efficacy of Asthma Education, Selected Abstracts

American Lung Association
1740 Broadway
New York, NY 10017   212-315-8700

Abstracts documenting the efficacy of asthma education programs for physicians and other health professionals.

7230 Enhancing Communication in Individuals with Autism Through Pictures/Words

Autism Society of North Carolina Bookstore
505 Oberlin Road
Suite 230
Raleigh, NC 27605   919-743-0204
                           800-442-2762
                      FAX: 919-743-0208
                    e-mail: ASNC@aol.com
                    www.autismsociety-nc.org

Michelle G. Winner, author

Booklet addressing the description and implementation of visually aided communication. *$4.00*

7231 Exercise and Your Arthritis

Arthritis Foundation
PO Box 7669
Atlanta, GA 30309   404-872-7100
                           800-283-7800
                      FAX: 404-872-0457

Types of exercise for people with arthritis and how to do them.

7232 Exercise-Induced Asthma

American Academy of Allergy, Asthma and Immunology
611 E Wells Street
Milwaukee, WI 53202   414-272-6071
                           800-822-2762
                      FAX: 414-272-6070
                   e-mail: info@aaaai.org
                         www.aaaai.org

This brochure covers testing, treatment, and other advice on how to deal with exercise-induced asthma. *$.50*

7233 Eye-Q Test

National Association for Visually Handicapped
22 W 21st Street
6th Floor
New York, NY 10010   212-889-3141
                      FAX: 212-727-2931
                   e-mail: staff@navh.org
                         www.navh.org

Five questions and answers to assist in knowing more about vision. Also available in Spanish and Russian.

7234 Fact Sheet - Attention Deficit-Hyperactivity Disorder

Learning Disabilities Association of America
4156 Library Road
Pittsburgh, PA 15234   412-341-1515

A pamphlet offering factual information on ADHD.

7235 Fact Sheet: Autism

Autism Society of America
7910 Woodmont Avenue
Suite 300
Bethesda, MD 20814   301-657-0881
                           800-3AU-TISM
                      FAX: 301-657-0869
                    www.autism-society.org

Offers information on autism. What it is, symptoms, causes, diagnosis, treatments and research.

7236 Facts About Asthma

American Lung Association
1740 Broadway
New York, NY 10017   212-315-8700

Primary public information leaflet on asthma.

12 pages

7237 Facts: Books for Blind and Physically Handicapped Individuals

National Library Service for the Blind
1291 Taylor Street NW
Washington, DC 20542   202-707-5100

Annual

7238 Facts: Music for Blind and Physically Handicapped Individuals

National Library Service for the Blind
1291 Taylor Street NW
Washington, DC 20542   202-707-5100

Annual

7239 Family Guide - Growth & Development of The Partially Seeing Child

National Association for Visually Handicapped
22 W 21st Street
6th Floor
New York, NY 10010   212-889-3141
                            FAX: 212-727-2931
                            e-mail: staff@navh.org
                            www.navh.org

Offers information for parents and guidelines in raising a partially seeing child. *$.60*

7240 Family Guide to Vision Care

American Optometric Association
243 N Lindbergh Boulevard
St. Louis, MO 63141   314-991-4100

Offers information on the early developmental years of your vision, finding a family optometrist and how to take care of your eyesight through the learning years, the working years and the mature years.

7241 Free Information/Membership Kit

National Association for Visually Handicapped
22 W 21st Street
New York, NY 10010   212-255-4224
                            FAX: 212-727-2931
                            e-mail: staff@navh.org
                            www.navh.org

Eva M. Cohen, CEO Assistant
Lorraine H. Marchi, Founder/CEO

A free packet describing brochures, pamphlets, and flyers available addressing the needs of the partially seeing, their families, friends and professionals who serve them: large print, visual aids, self-help, referrals. Includes information regarding vision dysfunction and coping with vision loss.

Quarterly

7242 General Facts and Figures on Blindness

National Society to Prevent Blindness
500 E Remington Road
Schaumberg, IL 60173

                            800-331-2020

7243 General Interest Catalog

National Braille Association
3 Townline Circle
Rochester, NY 14623   716-427-8260

Lists hundreds of titles of fiction and non-fiction books offered in large print, braille or on cassette to visually impaired readers.

19 pages

7244 Gift of Sight

RP Foundation Fighting Blindness
1401 Mt Royal Avenue
Baltimore, MD 21217   410-225-9409
                            800-683-5555

A pamphlet offering information on the Retina Donor Program, which studies diseased, human retinal tissue in their search for a cure of retinal degenerative diseases.

7245 Glaucoma

Foundation for Glaucoma Research
200 Pine Street
San Francisco, CA 94129   415-986-3162
                                800-826-6693
                                www.glaucoma.orge

Offers information on what glaucoma is, the causes, treatments, types of glaucoma, eye exams and prevention.

7246 Glaucoma - The Sneak Thief of Sight

National Association for Visually Handicapped
22 W 21st Street
6th Floor
New York, NY 10010   212-889-3141
                            FAX: 212-727-2931
                            e-mail: staff@navh.org
                            www.navh.org

A pamphlet describing the disease, treatment and medications. Also available in Russian and Spanish. Revised in 1999. *$3.50*

7247 Guide Dog Foundation Flyer

Guide Dog Foundation for the Blind
371 E Jericho Turnpike
Smithtown, NY 11787   516-265-2121
                            800-548-4337
                            FAX: 516-361-5192

Offers information on the programs and services provided by the Foundation.

7248 Guidelines for Comprehensive Low Vision Care

National Association for Visually Handicapped
22 W 21st Street
6th Floor
New York, NY 10010   212-889-3141
                            FAX: 212-727-2931
                            e-mail: staff@navh.org
                            www.navh.org

A description of the proper method to conduct a low vision evaluation. *$.50*

7249 **Guidelines for Helping Deaf-Blind Persons**

Helen Keller National Center
111 Middle Neck Road
Sands Point, NY 11050   516-944-8900

Pamphlet offering information on how persons should interact with deaf-blind individuals. Includes drawings of the one hand manual alphabet.

7250 **Healthy Breathing**

National Jewish Center for Immunology
1400 Jackson Street
Denver, CO 80206   303-388-4461

Offers patients with lung or respiratory disorders information on exercise and healthy breathing.

7251 **Heart to Heart**

Blind Children's Center
4120 Marathon Street
Los Angeles, CA 90029

                              800-222-3566
                         FAX: 323-665-3828
          e-mail: info@blindchildrenscenter.org
                         www.blindcntr.org
Parents of blind and partially sighted children talk about their feelings. *$10.00*

          12 pages

7252 **Heartbreak of Being "A Little Bit Blind"**

National Association for Visually Handicapped
22 W 21st Street
6th Floor
New York, NY 10010   212-889-3141
                         FAX: 212-727-2931
                 e-mail: staff@navh.org
                         www.navh.org

Summary of what it means to have impaired vision with illustrations.

7253 **Helping Others Breathe Easier**

National Allergy and Asthma Network
3554 Chain Bridge Road
Suite 200
Fairfax, VA 22030   703-385-4403
                         FAX: 703-352-4354

Offers information on educational resources, support groups and the Network for persons afflicted with asthma or allergic disorders.

7254 **Helping Your Child with Attention-Deficit Hyperactivity Disorder**

Learning Disabilities Association of America
4156 Library Road
Pittsburgh, PA 15234   412-341-1515

7255 **History and Use of Braille**

American Council of the Blind
1155 15th Street NW
Suite 1004
Washington, DC 20005   202-467-5081
                              800-424-8666
                         FAX: 202-467-5085

7256 **Home Control of Allergies and Asthma**

American Lung Association
1740 Broadway
New York, NY 10017   212-315-8700

Discusses substances in the home that may trigger asthma and allergy problems and offers suggestions for controlling them.

          12 pages

7257 **How Does a Blind Person Get Around?**

American Foundation for the Blind/AFB Press
PO Box 1020
Sewickley, PA 15143   412-741-1142
                              800-232-3044
                         FAX: 412-741-0609
              e-mail: afborders@abdintl.com
                         www.afb.org

Offers information on daily living as a blind person.

7258 **How to Choose an Air Ambulance**

National Air Ambulance
PO Box 22460
Fort Lauderdale, FL 33335   954-359-9900
                              800-327-3710
                         FAX: 954-359-9500
              e-mail: inquiry@nationaljets.com
                 www.nationalairambulance.com

Alan Altman, MD, Medical Director
Thomas E. Boy, President
George Martinez, Operations Manager

This booklet was prepared to help inform persons about air ambulance operations and to assist if the need for air ambulance transportation should arise.

          15 pages

7259 **How to Find More About Your Child's Birth Defect Or Disability**

Birth Defect Research for Children
930 Woodcock Road
Suite 225
Orlando, FL 32803   407-895-0802
                         FAX: 407-895-0824
              e-mail: abdc@birthdefects.org
                 www.birthdefects.org

Betty Mekdeci, Executive Director

An informational fact sheet that encourages parents who have a child with a birth defect or disability to become the expert on the child's disability with some suggestions on how to educate themselves.

7260 **How to Own and Operate an Attention Deficit Disorder**

Learning Disabilities Association of America
4156 Library Road
Pittsburgh, PA 15234   412-341-1515

Clear, informative and sensitive introduction to ADHD. Packed with practical things to do at home and school, from a professional and mother of a son with ADHD. *$8.95*

          43 pages

7261 Hyperactivity, Attention Deficits, and School Failure: Better Ways

Learning Disabilities Association of America
4156 Library Road
Pittsburgh, PA   15234   412-341-1515

7262 Individuals with Arthritis

Mainstream
1030 5th Street NW
Washington, DC   20005   202-898-1400

e-mail: info@mainstreaminc.org
Mainstream, Inc., author
Mainstreaming individuals with arthritis into the workplace. *$2.50*

12 pages

7263 Indoor Allergens

American Academy of Allergy, Asthma and Immunology
611 E Wells Street
Milwaukee, WI   53202   414-272-6071
                                    800-822-2762
                          FAX: 414-272-6070
                          e-mail: info@aaaai.org
                          www.aaaai.org

This brochure covers some good ideas on how to reduce dust in the home. *$.50*

4 pages

7264 Information on Glaucoma

Foundation for Glaucoma Research
200 Pine Street
San Francisco, CA   94129   415-986-3162
                                    800-826-6693
                          www.glaucoma.orge

7265 Inhaled Medications for Asthma

American Academy of Allergy, Asthma and Immunology
611 E Wells Street
Milwaukee, WI   53202   414-272-6071
                                    800-822-2762
                          FAX: 414-272-6070
                          e-mail: info@aaaai.org
                          www.aaaai.org

This brochure gives helpful information on classes of inhaled medication, types of inhalation devices, spacers and holding chambers, how proper training is necessary. *$.50*

4 pages

7266 Issues in Independent Living

Independent Living Research Utilization
2323 S Shepherd
Suite 1000
Houston, TX   77019   713-520-0232
                          FAX: 713-520-5785

Lex Frieden, Program Director
This booklet is a report of the National Study Group on the Implications of Health Care Reform for Americans with Disabilities and Chronic Health Conditions.

30 pages

7267 It's All Right to be Angry

National Association for Visually Handicapped
22 W 21st Street
6th Floor
New York, NY   10010   212-889-3141
                          FAX: 212-727-2931
                          e-mail: staff@navh.org
                          www.navh.org

A helpful pamphlet describing reactions to learning to live with vision impairment. Also available in Russian. *$2.25*

7268 Know Your Eye

American Council of the Blind
1155 15th Street NW
Suite 1004
Washington, DC   20005   202-467-5081
                                    800-424-8666
                          FAX: 202-467-5085

7269 Large Print Loan Library Caralog

National Association for Visually Handicapped
22 W 21st Street
6th Floor
New York, NY   10010   212-889-3141
                          FAX: 212-727-2931
                          e-mail: staff@navh.org
                          www.navh.org

Listing of over 7,000 commercially published and NAVH large print books avaiable through NAVH on a loan basis. Includes a limited selection of titles available for purchase. *$5.00*

7270 Learning to Play

Blind Children's Center
4120 Marathon Street
Los Angeles, CA   90029
                                    800-222-3566
                          FAX: 323-665-3828
                          e-mail: info@blindchildrenscenter.org

Discusses how to present play activities to the visually impaired preschool child. *$10.00*

12 pages

7271 Ledger

Mental Health Risk Retention Group
PO Box 206
Cedar Grove, NJ   07009   973-239-9107

Information on the Mental Health Risk Retention Group, a liability insurance company.

7272 Mama - Your Guide to a Healthy Pregnancy

March of Dimes
1275 Mamaroneck Avenue
White Plains, NY   10605
                                    888-663-4637
                          FAX: 914-997-4763
                          www.modimes.org

Cathy Church-Balin, Director, Education Services

The March of Dimes Resource Center provides information about pregnancy, birth defects, genetics, drug use, environmental hazzards and related ttopics. The Resource Center's health information specialists provide accurate, up-to-date information via a toll free telephone line, fax, e-mail, and Web site. One free copy of this magazine can be obtained by calling 888-MODIMES.

$5.00/pkg. 50

7273   Management of Children and Adolescents with AD-HD

Learning Disabilities Association of America
4156 Library Road
Pittsburgh, PA   15234   412-341-1515

Friedman/Royal, author

7274   Managing Your Activities

Arthritis Foundation
PO Box 7669
Atlanta, GA   30357   404-872-7100
                                        800-283-7800
                        FAX: 404-872-0457

7275   Managing Your Fatigue

Arthritis Foundation
PO Box 7669
Atlanta, GA   30357   404-872-7100
                                        800-283-7800
                        FAX: 404-872-0457

7276   Managing Your Health Care

Arthritis Foundation
PO Box 7669
Atlanta, GA   30357   404-872-7100
                                        800-283-7800
                        FAX: 404-872-0457

7277   Managing Your Pain

Arthritis Foundation
PO Box 7669
Atlanta, GA   30357   404-872-7100
                                        800-283-7800
                        FAX: 404-872-0457

7278   Many Faces of Asthma

American Lung Association
1740 Broadway
New York, NY   10017   212-315-8700

Provides an overview of asthma as a major public health problem, describes what happens during asthma attacks and explains how asthma is treated and managed.

12 pages

7279   Marfan Syndrome Fact Sheet

March of Dimes
1275 Mamaroneck Avenue
White Plains, NY   10605
                                        888-663-4637
                                        888-663-4637
                        FAX: 914-997-4763
                        www.modimes.org

Cathy Church-Balin, Director-Education Services

1 page fact sheet. $5.00 pk of 50

1 pages $5.00/pkg. 50

7280   Mealey's Viagra Watch

Mealey Publications
217 W Church Road
PO Box 62090
King of Prussia, PA   19406   610-768-7800
                                        800-MEA-LEYS
                        FAX: 610-768-0880
                        e-mail: news@mealeys.com
                        www.mealeys.com

Michael Mealey, President
Tom Hagy, Publisher

The report covers the controversy and claims surrounding the impotency drug Viagra. The report tracks lawsuits, class action complaints, insurance coverage disputes, reports of alleged health risks, medical studies, regulatory developments, sales and marketing disputes and manufacturer finances. *$295.00*

10-25 pages Monthly 1998

7281   Mental Health Resource Guide

1 Renaissance Boulevard
Oakbrook Terrace, IL   60181   630-792-5000

A small pamphlet listing education programs and publications for community mental health centers, child/adolescent services, adult mental health services and MR/DD services.

7282   Move with Me

Blind Children's Center
4120 Marathon Street
Los Angeles, CA   90029
                                        800-222-3566
                        FAX: 323-665-3828
                        e-mail: info@blindchildrenscenter.org

A parent's guide to movement development for visually impaired babies. *$10.00*

12 pages

7283   Myositis

Arthritis Foundation
PO Box 7669
Atlanta, GA   30357   404-872-7100
                                        800-283-7800
                        FAX: 404-872-0457

7284   National Institute of Mental Health: Decade of the Brain

6001 Executive Boulevard
Room 8184 MSC 9663
Bethesda, MD   20892   301-443-4513

A consumer's pamphlet to services for persons with mental illness or retardation.

7285   Nocturnal Asthma

National Jewish Center for Immunology
1400 Jackson Street
Denver, CO   80206   303-388-4461

Offers information to patients about how to understand and manage asthma at night.

7286 Occupational Asthma

American Academy of Allergy, Asthma and Immunology
611 E Wells Street
Milwaukee, WI   53202   414-272-6071
                                         800-822-2762
                                    FAX: 414-272-6070
                                e-mail: info@aaaai.org
                                         www.aaaai.org

This brochure also contains a list of most common agents theat cause occupational asthma and who is at risk. *$.50*

4 pages

7287 Occupational Asthma: Lung Hazards on the Job

American Lung Association
1740 Broadway
New York, NY   10017   212-315-8700

Discusses occupational asthma, a form of asthma in which airways overreact to various irritants in the workplace.

7288 Oral/Facial Clefts Fact Sheet

March of Dimes
1275 Mamaroneck Avenue
White Plains, NY   10605
                                         888-663-4637
                                         888-663-4637
                                    FAX: 914-997-4763
                                         www.modimes.org

Cathy Church-Balin, Director, Education Services

The March of Dimes Resource Center provides information about pregnancy, drug use, environmental hazzards and other related topics. The Resource Center's health information specialists provide accurate and up-to-date information via a toll free telephone line, fax, e-mail and Web site. One fact sheet may be obtained free of charge be calling 888-MODIMES.

$5.00/pkg. 50

7289 Osteoarthritis

Arthritis Foundation
PO Box 7669
Atlanta, GA   30357   404-872-7100
                                         800-283-7800
                                    FAX: 404-872-0457

Offers introductions, examples, explanations and research pertaining to this type of arthritis.

7290 Out of Darkness

Connecticut Association for Children and Adults with Learning Disabilities
25 Van Zant Street, Suite 15-5
East Norwalk, CT   06855   203-838-5010
                                    FAX: 203-866-6108
                                e-mail: CACLD@JUNO.com
                                         www.CACLD.org

Article by an adult who discovers at age 30 that he has ADD. *$1.00*

4 pages

7291 Overcoming Rheumatoid Arthritis

Michigan Chapter of the Arthritis Foundation
23999 Northwestern Highway
201
Southfield, MI   48075   313-350-3030
                                         800-968-3030

Provides extensive information about the disease and treatment, with an emphasis on what you can do for yourself. *$5.00*

7292 Parenting Attention Deficit Disordered Teens

C.A.C.L.D.
25 Van Zant Street
Suite 15-5
East Norwalk, CT   06855   203-838-5010
                                    FAX: 203-866-6108
                                e-mail: CACLD@JUNO.com
                                         www.CACLD.org

Patricia C. Landi, LCSW, author

Detailed outline of the various problems of adolescents with ADHD. Published by Connecticut Association for Children & Adults with Learning Disabilities (CACLD). *$3.25*

14 pages

7293 Patient's Guide to Visual Aids and Illumination

National Association for Visually Handicapped
22 W 21st Street
New York, NY   10010   212-889-3141

                                e-mail: staff@navh.org

A reference booklet offering information on aids for the visually impaired.

7294 Peak Flow Meter-A Thermometer for Asthma

American Academy of Allergy, Asthma and Immunology
611 E Wells Street
Milwaukee, WI   53202   414-272-6071
                                         800-822-2762
                                    FAX: 414-272-6070
                                e-mail: info@aaaai.org
                                         www.aaaai.org

$.50

4 pages

7295 Polymyalgia Rheumatica and Giant Cell Arthritis

Arthritis Foundation
PO Box 7669
Atlanta, GA   30357   404-872-7100
                                         800-283-7800
                                    FAX: 404-872-0457

7296 Psoriatic Arthritis

NAMSIC, National Institutes of Health
1 AMS Circle
Bethesda, MD   20892   301-495-4484
                                    FAX: 301-587-4352
                                         www.nih.gov/niams/

7297 Raynaud's Phenomenon

Arthritis Foundation
PO Box 7669
Atlanta, GA   30357   404-872-7100
                                         800-283-7800
                                    FAX: 404-872-0457

7298 **Reaching, Crawling, Walking - Let's Get Moving**

Blind Children's Center
4120 Marathon Street
Los Angeles, CA   90029

800-222-3566
FAX: 323-665-3828
e-mail: info@blindchildrenscenter.org

Orientation and mobility for visually impaired preschool children. *$10.00*

24 pages

7299 **Reading Is for Everyone**

National Library Service for the Blind
1291 Taylor Street NW
Washington, DC   20542   202-707-5100
FAX: 202-707-0712

7300 **Reading with Low Vision**

National Library Service for the Blind
1291 Taylor Street NW
Washington, DC   20542   202-707-5100
FAX: 202-707-0712

7301 **Reference and Information Services From NLS**

National Library Service for the Blind
1291 Taylor Street NW
Washington, DC   20542   202-707-5100
FAX: 202-707-0712
TDY:202-707-0744
e-mail: nls@loc.gov
www.loc.gov/nls

7302 **Referring Blind and Low Vision Patients for Rehabilitation Services**

American Foundation for the Blind/AFB Press
PO Box 1020
Sewickley, PA   15143   412-741-1142
800-232-3044
FAX: 412-741-0609
e-mail: afborders@abdintl.com
www.afb.org

Clear information on such basic topics as the objectives of low vision services, what's covered in the examinations, what rehabilitation services do and how to locate these services. Available in purchase of bulk quantity only.

ISBN 0-891289-13-5

7303 **Reiter's Syndrome**

Arthritis Foundation
PO Box 7669
Atlanta, GA   30357   404-872-7100
800-283-7800
FAX: 404-872-0457

7304 **Resource List for Persons with Low Vision**

American Council of the Blind
1155 15th Street NW
Suite 1004
Washington, DC   20005   202-467-5081
800-424-8666
FAX: 202-467-5085

7305 **Rheumatoid Arthritis**

NAMSIC, National Institutes of Health
1 AMS Circle
Bethesda, MD   20892   301-495-4484
FAX: 301-587-4352
www.nih.gov/niams/

Offers an introduction and definition of Rheumatoid Arthritis, treatments, causes, objectives, daily living, resources and medical information.

7306 **School Based Assessment of Attention Deficit Disorders**

National Clearinghouse of Rehabilitation Materials
5202 N Richmond Hill Drive
Stillwater, OK   74078   405-624-7650
800-223-5219
FAX: 405-624-0695

The 1992 OSEP ruling, placing more responsibility on schools for the assessment of students who may have attention deficit disorders, has raised questions concerning the assessment process. This guide was developed to help states formulate new policies. The paper seeks to: present an overview of current thoughts concerning ADD from an educational perspective, contrast traditional assessment strategies with an alternative model, and describe phases of evaluation.Paperback *$ 6.10*

61 pages

7307 **Selecting a Program**

Blind Children's Center
4120 Marathon Street
Los Angeles, CA   90029

800-222-3566
FAX: 323-665-3828
e-mail: info@blindchildrenscenter.org

A guide for parents of infants and preschoolers with visual impairments. *$10.00*

28 pages

7308 **Sex Education: Issues for the Person with Autism**

Autism Society of North Carolina Bookstore
505 Oberlin Road
Suite 230
Raleigh, NC   27605   919-743-0204
800-442-2762
FAX: 919-743-0208
e-mail: ASNC@aol.com
www.autismsociety-nc.org

Nancy Dalrymple, author

Discusses issues of sexuality and provides methods of instruction for people with autism. *$4.00*

7309 **Standards for the Diagnosis and Care of Patients with Asthma**

American Lung Association
1740 Broadway
New York, NY   10017   212-315-8700

Standards developed by the American Thoracic Society, the medical section of the ALA. For physicians.

24 pages

7310 Standing on My Own Two Feet

Blind Children's Center
4120 Marathon Street
Los Angeles, CA 90029

800-222-3566
FAX: 323-665-3828
e-mail: info@blindchildrenscenter.org

A step-by-step guide to designing and constructing simple, individually tailored adaptive mobility devices for preschool-age children who are visually impaired. *$10.00*

36 pages

7311 Student Asthma Action Card

Asthma and Allergy Foundation of America
1125 15th Street
Suite 502
Washington, DC 20005

202-466-7643
FAX: 202-466-8940
e-mail: info@aafa.org
www.aafa.org

Indispensable tool for familiarizing school personnel with asthma triggers, daily medications and emergency directions for each of their students with asthma.

7312 Surgery: Information to Consider

Arthritis Foundation
PO Box 7669
Atlanta, GA 30357

404-872-7100
800-283-7800
FAX: 404-872-0457

7313 Talk to Me

Blind Children's Center
4120 Marathon Street
Los Angeles, CA 90029

800-222-3566
FAX: 323-665-3828
e-mail: info@blindchildrenscenter.org

A language guide for parents of deaf children. *$10.00*

11 pages

7314 Talk to Me II

Blind Children's Center
4120 Marathon Street
Los Angeles, CA 90029

800-222-3566
FAX: 323-665-3828
e-mail: info@blindchildrenscenter.org

A sequel to Talk To Me, available in English and Spanish. *$10.00*

15 pages

7315 Teaching Social Skills to Youngsters with Disabilities

Federation for Children with Special Needs
95 Berkeley Street
Boston, MA 02116

617-482-2915
800-331-0688

Explains the importance of instruction and training to learn appropriate social behavior.

7316 There are Solutions for the Student with Asthma

American Lung Association
1740 Broadway
New York, NY 10017

212-315-8700

Leaflet telling how parents and school personnel can work together to make life easier for children with asthma.

4 pages

7317 Thinking About Tomorrow: A Career Guide for Teens with Arthritis

Arthritis Foundation
PO Box 7669
Atlanta, GA 30357

404-872-7100
800-283-7800
FAX: 404-872-0457

7318 Tips to Remember

American Academy of Allergy & Immunology
611 E Wells Street
Milwaukee, WI 53202

414-272-6071

A set of 23 tip sheets offering information on various topics including allergy and asthma treatments, pregnancy and asthma, animal allergies, sinusitis and more.

7319 Triggers Management of Asthma

American Academy of Allergy, Asthma and Immunology
611 E Wells Street
Milwaukee, WI 53202

414-272-6071
800-822-2762
FAX: 414-272-6070
e-mail: info@aaaai.org
www.aaaai.org

This brochure gives helpful information on what will cause an asthma attack. *$.50*

7320 Understanding

Easter Seals
230 West Monroe Street
Suite 1800
Chicago, IL 60606

312-726-6200
FAX: 312-726-1494

Janet D. Jamieson, Communications Mgr.

A brochure series for use in patient, family and public education programs and in career recruitment and counseling.

10 Brochures

7321 Understanding Asthma

National Jewish Center for Immunology
1400 astackson Street
Denver, CO 80206

303-388-4461

Offers a brief introduction to asthma and then goes into the physiology of asthma, the triggers of asthma, and diagnosis and monitoring of asthma.

27 pages

7322 Understanding Learning Disabilities: A Guide for Faculty

C.A.C.L.D.
25 Van Zant Street
Suite 15-5
East Norwalk, CT   06855   203-838-5010
FAX: 203-866-6108
e-mail: CACLD@JUNO.com
www.CACLD.org

Georgetown University, Office of Student Affairs, author

Written for the faculty at Georgetown to help them identify, understand, teach, and advise students in their classes who have learning disabilities. Ideal for any college offering special services to the learning disabled as well as high school guidance counselors and propective college students with LD and their parents. Published by Connecticut Association for Children & Adults with Learning Disabilities (CACLD). *$10.00*

36 pages

7323 What Do You Do When You See a Blind Person - and What Don't You Do?

American Foundation for the Blind/AFB Press
PO Box 1020
Sewickley, PA   15143   412-741-1142
800-232-3044
FAX: 412-741-0609
e-mail: afborders@abdintl.com
www.afb.org

Examples of real-life situations that teach sighted persons how to interact effectively with blind persons. Topics covered include how to help someone across the street, how not to distract a guide dog and how to take leave of a blind person.

8 pages
ISBN 0-891281-95-9

7324 What Every Parent Should Know About Learning Diabilities

C.A.C.L.D.
25 Van Zant Street
Suite 15-5
East Norwalk, CT   06855   203-838-5010
FAX: 203-866-6108
e-mail: CACLD@JUNO.com
www.CACLD.org

C.L. Bete Co., author

Published by Connecticut Association for Children & Adults with Learning Disabilities (CACLD). *$2.00*

7325 What Everyone Needs to Know About Asthma

National Allergy and Asthma Network
3554 Chain Bridge Road
Suite 200
Fairfax, VA   22030   703-385-4403
FAX: 703-352-4354

Offers information and facts on gaining control of asthma, asthma triggers and monitoring asthma disorders.

7326 What is Auditory Processing?

Speech Bin
1965 25th Avenue
Vero Beach, FL   32960   561-770-0007
800-477-3324
FAX: 561-770-0006
www.speechbin.com

Jan J. Binney, Senior Editor

Booklet for parents and teachers explaining children's difficulties in listening and auditory skills. Set of ten copies. *$14.95*

16 pages
ISBN 0-93785-45-9

7327 What to Do When a Friend is Depressed: Guide for Students

National Institute of Mental Health
5600 Fishers Lane
Government Printing Office
Rockville, MD   20857   202-512-1800

National Institute of Mental Health, author

This pamphlet provides students with valuable information about depression: how to overcome it and how to help others.

7328 When Your Student Has Arthritis: A Guide for Teachers

Arthritis Foundation
PO Box 7669
Atlanta, GA   30357   404-872-7100
800-283-7800
FAX: 404-872-0457

A medical information booklet written for teachers or other adults who have arthritis. The booklet describes different forms of juvenile arthritis, how arthritis might affect the child at school, and how to help the child work around these problems.

7329 Wings for the Future

American Printing House for the Blind
1839 Frankfort Avenue
Louisville, KY   40206   502-895-2405
800-223-1839
FAX: 502-895-1509
e-mail: info@ahp.org

This booklet offers an introduction to the American Printing House For The Blind's programs, services, tools, aids and more.

13 pages

7330 Without Sight and Sound

Helen Keller National Center
111 Middle Neck Road
Sands Point, NY   11050   516-944-8900

Pamphlet offering facts, causes, types and descriptions of deaf-blindness.

7331 Your Child and Asthma

National Jewish Center for Immunology
1400 Jackson Street
Denver, CO   80206   303-388-4461

A booklet offerring information to parents and family about their child with asthma. Offers information on diagnosis, treatments, triggers and family concerns.

Audio/Visual

7332   A.D.D. From A To Z

CACLD
25 Zant Street
Suite 5-15
East Norwalk, CT   08855   203-838-5010
                                 FAX: 203-866-6108
                                    www.CACLD.org

Edward Halkwell, M.D., author

Understanding the diagnosis and treatment of attention deficit disorder in children and adults. Topics include: symptoms to look for, how to tell if it is not A.D.D., 20 steps to diagnosis, methods of treatment and the ritalin controversy.

7333   ADD, Stepping Out of the Dark

ADD Videos
PO Box 622
New Paltz, NY   12561   845-255-3612
                                 FAX: 845-883-6452

Lenae Madonna, Producer

A powerful, effective video, ideal for health professionals, educators and parents providing a visual montage designed to promote an understanding and awareness of attention deficit disorder. Based on actual accounts of those who have ADD, including a neurologist, an office worker, and parents of children with ADD. The video allows the viewer to feel the frustration and lack of attention that ADD brings to many. *$52.95*

Video

7334   ADHD in Adults

Guilford Publications
72 Spring Street
New York, NY   10012   212-431-9800
                                 800-365-7006
                                 FAX: 212-966-6708
                           e-mail: info@guilford.com

Russell A. Barkley, author

This program integrates information on ADHD with the actual experiences of four adults who suffer from the disorder. Representing a range of professions, from a lawyer to a mother working at home, each candidly discusses the impact of ADHD on his or her daily life. These interviews are augmented by comments from family members and other clinicians who treat adults with ADHD. *$95.00*

Video

7335   ADHD: What Can We Do?

Guilford Publications
72 Spring Street
New York, NY   10012   212-431-9800
                                 800-365-7006
                                 FAX: 212-966-6708
                           e-mail: info@guilford.com

R.A. Barkley, author

A video program that introduces teachers and parents to a variety of the most effective technologies for managing ADHD in the classroom, at home, and on family outings. *$95.00*

Video

7336   ADHD: What Do We Know?

Guilford Publications
72 Spring Street
New York, NY   10012   212-431-9800
                                 800-365-7006
                                 FAX: 212-966-6708
                           e-mail: info@guilford.com

R.A. Barkley, author

An introduction for teachers and special education practitioners, school psychologists and parents of ADHD children. Topics outlined in this video include the causes and prevalence of ADHD, ways children with ADHD behave, other conditions that may accompany ADHD and long-term prospects for children with ADHD. *$95.00*

Video

7337   AFB Press

American Foundation for the Blind/AFB Press
PO Box 1020
Sewickley, PA   15143   .   412-741-1142
                                 800-232-3044
                                 FAX: 412-741-0609
                       e-mail: afborders@abdintl.com
                                    www.afb.org

Develops, publishes, and sells a wide variety of informative books, pamphlets, periodicals, and videos for students, professionals, and researchers in the blindess and visual impairment fields, for people professionally involved in making the mainstream community accessible, and for blind and visually impaired people and their families; publication and video orders.

7338   Able to Laugh

Fanlight Productions
4196 Washington Street
Suite 2
Boston, MA   02131   617-469-4999
                                 800-937-4113
                                 FAX: 617-469-3379
                       e-mail: fanlight@fanlight.com
                                 www.fanlight.com

Sandy St. Louis, Marketing Director

An exploration of the world of disability as interpreted by six professional comedians who happen to be disabled. It is also about the awkward ways disabled and able-bodied people relate to one another. *$ 195.00*

ISBN 1-572951-05-2

7339   Access for All: Integrating Deaf, Hard of Hearing and Hearing Preschoolers

Gallaudet University Bookstore
800 Florida Avenue NE
Washington, DC   20002   202-651-5000
                                 800-451-1073
                                 FAX: 202-651-5489

Pre-College Outreach, author

This exciting new 90 minute videotape and manual describes a model program for integrating deaf and hard of hearing children in early education. *$24.95*

150 pages

7340 Activity-Based Intervention: 2nd Edition

Brookes Publishing
PO Box 10624
Baltimore, MD 21285 410-337-9580
800-638-3775
FAX: 410-337-8539
e-mail: custserv@brookespublishing.com
www.brookespublishing.com

This video illustrates how activity-based intervention can be used to turn everyday events and natural interactions into opportunities to promote learning in young children who are considered at risk for developmental delays or who have mild to significant disabilities. *$39.00*

14-min. VHS
ISBN 1-55766 -86-3

7341 All About Attention Deficit Disorders, Revised

Child Management
800 Roosevelt Road
Suite 309
Glen Ellyn, IL 60137 630-469-0484
FAX: 630-469-4571
www.thomasphelan.com
Thomas W. Phelan, PhD, author
Nancy Roe, Office Manager

A psychologist and expert on ADD outlines the symptoms, diagnosis and treatment of this neurological disorder. Also available on video ($49.95 - 2 parts) and audio ($24.95) cassette. *$12.95*

248 pages Paperback
ISBN 1-889140-11-2

7342 All of Us: Talking Together, Sex Education for People with Developmental Disabilities

Aquarius Health Care Videos
5 Powderhouse Lane
PO Box 1159
Sherborn, MA 01770 508-651-2963
888-440-2963
FAX: 508-650-4216
e-mail: aqvideos@tiac.net
www.aquariusproductions.com

Leslie Kussmann, President/Producer

For parents, caregivers and young people with developmental disabilities often feel isolated and unsure when approaching sex education with their children. In this video, parents of children with developmental disabilities share their difficulties in talking to their children about the social/sexual arena. Real life conversations between parents and their children demonstrate their discomfort, concerns, thoughts and hopes. *$195.00*

Video cassette

7343 All the Way Up There

Britannica Film Company
345 4th Street
San Francisco, CA 94107 415-777-9876

Valhalla Film Production, author

This is the story of Bruce Burgess who has Cerebral Palsy but wants to climb a mountain. Bruce makes his dreams come true with the help of Grame Dingle, a New Zealand mountain climber.

Films

7344 Allergic Rhinitis

American Academy of Allergy, Asthma and Immunology
611 E Wells Street
Milwaukee, WI 53202 414-272-6071
800-822-2762
FAX: 414-272-6070
e-mail: info@aaaai.org
www.aaaai.org

Allergic rhinitis, often called hay fever, affects the quality of life of millions of Americans. This video covers the causes and symptoms of seasonal and chronic allergic rhinitis, as well as controls and treatments. *$25.00*

10-13 Minutes

7345 Allergies: Medicine for the Public

National Allergy and Asthma Network
3554 Chain Bridge Road
Suite 200
Fairfax, VA 22030 703-385-4403
FAX: 703-352-4354

An informative video and booklet produced by the National Institutes of Health which describes the causes of allergic and asthmatic reactions, diagnosis and treatment. *$15.00*

7346 Anaphylaxis

American Academy of Allergy, Asthma and Immunology
611 E Wells Street
Milwaukee, WI 53202 414-272-6071
800-822-2762
FAX: 414-272-6070
e-mail: info@aaaai.org
www.aaaai.org

For a few people, allergic reactions can be extremely serios-even life-threatening. This video provides vital information on the symptoms, causes and treatment of those anaphylactic reactions, and how your allergist can help you take precautions to ensure your safety. *$25.00*

10-13 Minutes

7347 As I Am

Fanlight Productions
4196 Washington Street
Suite 2
Boston, MA 02131 617-469-4999
800-937-4113
FAX: 617-469-3379
e-mail: fanlight@fanlight.com
www.fanlight.com

Sandy St. Louis, Marketing Director

Three young people with developmental disabilities speak for themselves about their lives, the problems they face and their hopes and expectations for the future. *$99.00*

ISBN 1-572950-58-7

7348 Asthma Handbook Slides

American Lung Association
1740 Broadway
New York, NY 10017   212-315-8700

Slides and script based on The Asthma Handbook for asthma patients and others.

Film

7349 Asthma Management

American Academy of Allergy, Asthma and Immunology
611 E Wells Street
Milwaukee, WI 53202   414-272-6071
                              800-822-2762
                         FAX: 414-272-6070
                    e-mail: info@aaaai.org
                              www.aaaai.org

Although there is currently no cure for asthma, attacks can be controlled by appropriate asthma management. This video describes what happens during an asthma attack, how your allergists diagnoses asthma, and ways your allergist can help you to manage your condition. *$25.00*

10-13 Minutes

7350 Asthma Triggers

American Academy of Allergy, Asthma and Immunology
611 E Wells Street
Milwaukee, WI 53202   414-272-6071
                              800-822-2762
                         FAX: 414-272-6070
                    e-mail: info@aaaai.org
                              www.aaaai.org

In the U.S. alone, over 50 million people suffer from asthma, and the incidence is rising. This video relates how patients with asthma can reduce their risk of an attack by avoiding triggers and practicing appropriate asthma management. *$25.00*

10-13 Minutes

7351 Asthma and the Athlete

American Academy of Allergy, Asthma and Immunology
611 E Wells Street
Milwaukee, WI 53202   414-272-6071
                              800-822-2762
                         FAX: 414-272-6070
                    e-mail: info@aaaai.org
                              www.aaaai.org

In the past, people with asthma were sometimes discouraged from exercising. Today we know that everyone, including asthmatics, can benefit from physical actilvity. This video details which exercises are best for those with asthma, and how an allergist can help asthmatic athletes to properly manage and treat their disease. *$25.00*

10-13 Minutes

7352 Attention Deficit Disorder

Pro-Ed
8700 Shoal Creek Boulevard
Austin, TX 78758   512-451-3246
                      FAX: 512-451-8542
                   e-mail: proed1@aol.com

D.R. Jordan, author

A book providing helpful suggestions for both home and classroom management of students with attention deficit disorder. *$ 19.00*

7353 Attention Deficit Disorder: Adults

Aquarius Health Care Videos
5 Powderhouse Lane
PO Box 1159
Sherborn, MA 01770
                         FAX: 508-650-4216
                 e-mail: aqvideos@tiac.net
              www.aquariusproductions.com

Adults with ADD talk about how the disorder that went undiagnosed for so many years has affected their choice of spouses and work, and what they have found to help them. Biofeedback, which is growing as a treatment, is explained and demonstrated by its founder, Dr. Joel Lubar. Medical treatments like antidepressants and stimulants are also discussed, along with behavioral changes that can help the person with ADD and his or her spouse and family. *$149.00*

Video

7354 Autism

Aquarius Health Care Videos
5 Powderhouse Lane
PO Box 1159
Sherborn, MA 01770
                         FAX: 508-650-4216
                 e-mail: aqvideos@tiac.net
              www.aquariusproductions.com

This video takes you into the lives of autistic people and their families to understand more about autism. What defines autism and how can we help those living with the disability? Children, teens, and adults are also profiled and we begin to see the varying levels of development and new technology to help these people communicate. Preview Available. *$149.00*

Video

7355 Autism: A World Apart

Fanlight Productions
4196 Washington Street
Suite 2
Boston, MA 02131   617-469-4999
                              800-937-4113
                         FAX: 617-469-3379
                 e-mail: fanlight@fanlight.com
                              www.fanlight.com

Karen McMillen, Marketing Director

Autism's cause is unknown. There is no cure, and it strikes each victim differently. In this documentary, three families show us what the textbooks and studies cannot - what it is like to live with autism day after day - to love and raise children who may be withdrawn and violent, and unable to make personal connections with their families. *$195.00*

7356 Awareness Training (4-Part Series)

Landmark Media
3450 Slade Run Drive
Falls Church, VA 22042   703-241-2030
800-342-4336
FAX: 703-536-9540
e-mail: landmarkmed@aol.com
www.landmarkmedia.com

M.L. Hartogs

Covers disabilities of various types — vision, hearing, speech disorders, loss of limbs, loss of mobility, or mental/emotional limitations and how to integrate such individuals into various business and educational settings. It is a 4-part series designed to identify and enable others to interact effectively with those suffering such disabilities. *$495.00*

Set of 4

7357 Basic Course in American Sign Language Videotapes

Harris Communications
15159 Technology Drive
Eden Prairie, MN 55344   612-906-1180
800-825-6758
FAX: 612-906-1099
e-mail: mail@harriscomm.com
www.harriscomm.com

Bill Williams, National Sales Manager

This series of four one-hour tapes is designed to illustrate the various exercises and dialogues in the text. *$39.95*

Video cassette

7358 Beginning ASL Video Course

Harris Communications
15159 Technology Drive
Eden Prairie, MN 55344   612-906-1180
800-825-6758
FAX: 612-906-1099
e-mail: mail@harriscomm.com
www.harriscomm.com

Bill Williams, National Sales Manager

You'll watch a family teach you to learn American Sign Language during funny and touching family situations. A total of 15 tapes in the course. *$49.95*

Video

7359 Beginning Reading and Sign Language

Harris Communications
15159 Technology Drive
Eden Prairie, MN 55344   612-906-1180
800-825-6758
FAX: 612-906-1099
e-mail: mail@harriscomm.com
www.harriscomm.com

Bill Williams, National Sales Manager

Features deaf performers' signing more than 120 words while standing in front of the object she is signing. Appropriate for children eighteen months to eight years. *$21.95*

Video

7360 Beyond the Barriers

Aquarius Health Care Videos
5 Powderhouse Lane
PO Box 1159
Sherborn, MA 01770   508-651-2963
888-440-2963
FAX: 508-650-4216
e-mail: aqvideos@tiac.net
www.aquariusproductions.com

Leslie Kussmann, Presdient

For too many years, paraplegics, amputees, quadraplegics and the blind have felt trapped by their disabilities. No more! Mark Wellman and other disabled adventurers, rock climb the deser towers of Utah, sail in British Columbia, body-board the big waves of Pipeline and Waimea Bay, scuba dive with sea lions in Mexico and hand glide the California coast. This film delivers the simple message: Don't give up, and never give in. If you can't ever lose, then you can't ever win. Preview option. *$90.00*

Video cassette

7361 Biology Concepts Through Discovery

Educational Activities
PO Box 392
Freeport, NY 11520   516-223-4666
800-645-3739
FAX: 516-623-9282
e-mail: learn@edact.com
www.edact.com

Harvey D. Goodman, author
Alan Stern, Vice President

These videos, available in English and Spanish versions, encourage learning by presenting interactive problem solving in an effective VISUAL/AUDITORY style. *$89.00*

Video cassette

7362 Blindness

Landmark Media
3450 Slade Run Drive
Falls Church, VA 22042   703-241-2030
800-342-4336
FAX: 703-536-9540

M.L. Hartogs

Cataracts are the most common cause of blindness in the 42 million people worldwide defined as blind. 90% live in developing countries. Cataracts are the most common cause but now can be treated cheaply and safely. *$250.00*

Video

7363 Braille Documents

Metrolina Sight Services
704 Louise Avenue
Charlotte, NC   704-372-3870

This production shop creates Braille and large-print documents.

7364 Breakthroughs: How to Reach Students with Autism

Aquarius Health Care Videos
5 Powderhouse Lane
PO Box 1159
Sherborn, MA   01770   508-651-2963
                             FAX: 508-650-4216
                      e-mail: aqvideos@tiac.net
                      www.aquariusproductions.com

A hands-on, how-to program for reaching students with autism, featuring Karen Sewell, Autism Society of America's teacher of the year. Here Sewell demonstrates the successful techniques she's developed over a 20-year career. A separate 250 page manual ($59) is also available which covers math, reading, fine motor, self help, social adaptive, vocational and self help skills as well as providing numerous plan reproducibles and an exhaustive listing of equipment and materials resources. Video. *$99.00*

Preview option

7365 Breathe Easy Young People's Guide to Asthma

Magination Press
3554 Chain Bridge Road
Suite 200
Fairfax, VA   22030   703-385-4403
                             800-878-4403
                      FAX: 703-352-4354
Jonathan H. Weiss, PhD, author

Practical, personal guide for those up to age 13 with asthma. They will learn how to control their asthma with techniques that will bring increased self-confidence. *$9.95*

Video

7366 Breathing Lessons: The Life and Work of Mark O'Brien

Fanlight Productions
4196 Washington Street
Suite 2
Boston, MA   02131   617-469-4999
                             800-937-4113
                      FAX: 617-469-3379
                      e-mail: fanlight@fanlight.com
                      www.fanlight.com

A new documentary which focuses on poet-journalist Mark O'Brien. Crippled by polio in childhood, and later forced to rely on an iron lung as a result of post-polio syndrome, for more than forty years he has fought against illness and bureaucracy in his determination to lead an independent life. According to Mark O'Brien, the two mythologies of disabled people break down to one: we can't do anything or two; we can do everything. But the truth is we're just human. *$195.00*

35 Minutes

7367 Bridging the Gap: A Nat'l Directory of Svs for Women & Girls with Disabilities, 2nd Edition

Educational Equity Concepts
114 E 32nd Street
New York, NY   10016   212-686-2531
                       FAX: 212-725-0947
                       TDY:212-725-1803
                e-mail: infomration@edequity.org
                       www.edequity.org
Ellen Rubin, Merle Froschl, author
Ellen Rubin, Coordinator, Disability Programs
Merle Froschl, Editor

Contains a resource section of publications and videos geared specifically to women and girls with disabilities. Available in print, on cassette, and also in braille. *$24.95*

ISBN 0-931629-16-0

7368 Bringing Out the Best

Research Press
PO Box 9177
Champaign, IL   61826   217-352-3273
                               800-519-2707
                        FAX: 217-352-1221
                  e-mail: rp@researchpress.com
                        www.researchpress.com
Elizabeth Cooley, author
Russell Pence, V P Marketing

This video training program introduces teachers, staff and parents to a variety of techniques for teaching expressive communication skills to children with multiple handicaps. The video illustrates how to assess a child's current levels of expressive ability, build on that ability, then gradually work toward more advanced communication. It shows how to use everyday situations to help children move beyond passive understanding to more active, intentional communication. *$150.00*

Video

7369 Business Enterprise Service: Marketing the Randolph-Sheppard Program

Rehab/Training Center on Blindness and Low-Vision
PO Box 6189
Mississippi State, MS   39762   601-325-2001
                                       800-675-7782
                                FAX: 662-325-8989
                         e-mail: rrtc@ra.msstate.edu
                                www.blind.msstate.edu

Kelly Schaefer, Publications Manager

This 10-minute videotape and Marketing Information Kit are for use by State Licensing Agencies throughout the country. They are designed for use in promoting the BEP with building managers, plant managers, building superintendents, and others who might be interested in utilizing the services provided under the Randolph-Sheppard Act. *$ 30.00*

Tape & Kit

7370 Business as Usual

Fanlight Productions
4196 Washington Street
Suite 2
Boston, MA   02131   617-469-4999
                             800-917-4113
                      FAX: 617-469-3379
                      e-mail: fanlight@fanlight.com
                      www.fanlight.com

Karen McMillen, Marketing Director

An enlightening new documentary, brings a unique international perspective to this struggle. This film examines five innovative programs which create opportunities for people with mental and physical disabilities to own and operate their own businesses. *$145.00*

7371 Buying Time: The Media Role in Health Care

Fanlight Productions
4196 Washington Street
Suite 2
Boston, MA 02131 617-469-4999
800-937-4113
FAX: 617-469-3379
e-mail: fanlight@fanlight.com
www.fanlight.com

Karen McMillen, Marketing Director

This video program is a thoughtful and disturbing examination in the role of the media in determining the allocation of health care resources. This program is a powerful tool on ethics, policy, journalism, sociology, medicine and nursing as well as for professional workshops, and continuing education programs. *$99.00*

7372 Caring for People with Developmental Disabilities

Research Press
PO Box 9177
Champaign, IL 61826 217-352-3273
FAX: 217-352-1221
e-mail: rp@researchpress.com
www.researchpress.com

Dr. Nancy A. Neef, author
Russell Pence, V P Marketing

Respite care is emerging as one of the most frequently requested and rapidly growing services offered to parents of children and young adults with developmental disabilities. Agencies are continually pressed to meet the demand for trained care providers. This video series has been developed to address this critical need. *$495.00*

Video

7373 Caring for Persons with Developmental Disabilities

Research Press
2612 N Mattis Avenue
Champaign, IL 61821 217-352-3273
800-519-2707
FAX: 217-352-1221
e-mail: rp@researchpress.com
www.researchpress.com

Dr. Nancy A. Neef, Author, author
Russell Pence, V P Marketing

A competency-baced video traning program that teaches the skills needed to care for individuals with a wide range of psysical and mental disabilities. Consists of six videotapes that feature demonstrations of respite care procedures. Provides quizzes in which viewers are asked to respond to on-screen situations. *$495.00*

Video

7374 Center for Health Research, Eastern Washington University

Eastern Washington University
MS-10 Hargreaves 217
Cheney, WA 99004 509-235-5799
800-221-9369
e-mail: susan.vanmeter@mail.ewu.edu

Produces eight videotapes, accompanying printed materials, and a videotaped public services announcement to serve as training and resource materials for use by daycare centers.

7375 Children's Classics Videotape Sets

Gallaudet University Bookstore
11030 S Langley Avenue
Chicago, IL 60628 202-651-5488
800-621-2736
FAX: 202-651-5489

Tells fairytales from the Grimm Brothers and Hans Christian Anderson in American Sign Language. Includes The Little Mermaid, Emperor's New Clothes, Fisherman & His Wife, Hansel and Gretal and The Musician's of Bromon. *$29.95*

Per Tape

7376 Christmas Stories

Gallaudet University Bookstore
11030 S Langley Avenue
Chicago, IL 60628 202-651-5488
800-621-2736
FAX: 202-651-5489

Bobby Giles and Doris Wilding, author

The unique talents of Bobby Giles and Doris Wilding present these great stories in American Sign Language. *$29.95*

Video

7377 Clinicians View

6007 Osuna Road NE
Albuquerque, NM 87109 505-880-0058
FAX: 505-880-0059

Gary J. Magrun, President
W. Michael Magrun, V.P.

A video and book publishing catalog dedicated to bringing clinicians (PTs; OTs; SLPs) and parents of children with special needs, the best educational and instructional information available. Paperback and videocassette.

7378 Clockworks

Learning Corporation of America
6493 Kaiser Drive
Fremont, CA 94555 510-490-7311

Points East, author

Scotty, who has Down Syndrome, is fascinated by clocks. This film follows him on his adventures of employment in the clock shop.

Films

7379 Close Encounters of the Disabling Kind

Mainstream
6930 Carroll Avenue
204
Takoma Park, MD 20912 301-891-8777
FAX: 301-891-8778
e-mail: info@mainstreaminc.org
www.mainstreaminc.org

Lillie Harrison, Info. Programs Clerk
Fritz Rumpel, Editor

A training video that provides a hiring manager with information on how to learn the basics of disability etiquette and, by the end of the video, seems much better prepared and willing to interview qualified individuals with disabilities. Includes trainer and trainee guides. *$99.95*

Video cassette

7380 **Come Back Jack: The Revealing Story of a Child Diagnosed with Autism**

Aquarius Health Care Videos
5 Powderhouse Lane
PO Box 1159
Sherborn, MA 01770   508-651-2963
                             FAX: 508-650-4216
                  e-mail: aqvideos@tiac.net
                  www.aquariusproductions.com

He celebrated his first birthday, not long after, Jack began to slowly slip away from his family. Persistent ear infections, medically misguided over-treatment with antibiotics, and other mysterious physiological factors sent Jack's mind spinning. By the time Jack reached the age of two, his intellectual and emothional development had come to a schreeching halt. Terrified by the prospect of losing their youngest son, Jack's parents began searching for answers. Chronicles the ups and downs. *$99.00*

Preview option

7381 **Concentration Video**

Learning disAbilities Resources
PO Box 716
Bryn Mawr, PA 19010   610-525-8336
                               800-869-8336
                          FAX: 610-525-8337

An instructional video which provides a perspective about attention problems, possible causes and solutions. *$19.95*

Video

7382 **Dancing From the Inside Out**

Fanlight Productions
4196 Washington Street
Suite 2
Boston, MA 02131   617-469-4999
                           800-937-4113
                      FAX: 617-469-3379
              e-mail: fanlight@fanlight.com
              www.fanlight.com

Karen McMillen, Marketing Director

This eloquent new video looks at the lives and work of three talented dancers who dance professionally with the acclaimed AXIS Dance Troupe, which includes both disabled and non-disabled dancers. They discuss the process they went through in adapting to their disability and how they came to re-discover physical expression through dance. *$ 195.00*

7383 **Deaf Children Signers**

Harris Communications
15159 Technology Drive
Eden Prairie, MN 55344   612-906-1180
                                  800-825-6758
                             FAX: 612-906-1099
                  e-mail: mail@harriscomm.com
                  www.harriscomm.com

Bill Williams, National Sales Manager

This three-part collection of children signers is great for children, teachers, parents and interpreters. *$39.95*

Video

7384 **Deaf Culture Series**

Harris Communications
15159 Technology Drive
Eden Prairie, MN 55344   612-906-1180
                                  800-825-6758
                             FAX: 612-906-1099
                  e-mail: mail@harriscomm.com
                  www.harriscomm.com

Bill Williams, National Sales Manager

Each video in this five-part series features a topic dealing with the unique culture of deaf people. It is an excellent resource for deaf studies programs, Interpreter Preparation programs and Sign Language programs. *$59.95*

Video

7385 **Deaf Mosaic Series**

Harris Communications
15159 Technology Drive
Eden Prairie, MN 55344   612-906-1180
                                  800-825-6758
                             FAX: 612-906-1099
                  e-mail: mail@harriscomm.com
                  www.harriscomm.com

Bill Williams, National Sales Manager

A national magazine show produced monthly by Gallaudet University, this show has been awarded nine Emmys. As the only nation-wide program about the deaf community, these videotapes are the best of the best from the shows programs. *$29.95*

Video

7386 **Descriptive Video Service**

WGBH Educational Foundation
125 Western Avenue
Boston, MA 02134   617-492-2777
                           800-333-1203
                      FAX: 617-300-1011
              e-mail: ncam@wgbh.org
              www.wgbh.org

Sharon King, Outreach Director
Mary Ann Pack, Assistant Director

A national service that makes PBS television programs, Hollywood movies on video and other visual media accessible to people who are blind or visually impaired. DVS provides narrated descriptions of the key visual elements without interfering with the audio or dialogue of a program or movie. The narration describes visual elements such as actions, settings, body language and graphics.

7387 **Different Heart**

Fanlight Productions
4196 Washington Street
Suite 2
Boston, MA 02131   617-469-4999
                           800-937-4113
                      FAX: 617-469-3379
              e-mail: fanlight@fanlight.com

Karen McMillen, Marketing Director

Though hundreds of children are born each year with potentially fatal heart disease, their parents may feel isolated from those facing similar crises. This sensitive video profiles three such families. *$99.00*

7388 Do You Hear That?

Alexander Graham Bell Association of the Deaf
3417 Volta Place NW
Washington, DC 20007   202-337-5220
                              FAX: 202-337-8314
                    e-mail: lquigley@agbell.org
                              www.agbell.org

Elizabeth Quigley, Director of Publications

This video shows auditory-verbal therapy sessions of a therapist working individually with 11 children who range in age from 7 months to 7 years old and have hearing aids or cochlear implants. $125.00

Video Cassette

7389 Doing Things Together

Britannica Film Company
345 4th Street
San Francisco, CA 94107   415-777-9876

Alan P. Sloan, author

Steve went with his parents to an amusement park. He met another boy named Martin who at first was shocked by Steve's prosthetic hand.

Films

7390 Down Syndrome

Aquarius Health Care Videos
5 Powderhouse Lane
PO Box 1159
Sherborn, MA 01770
                              FAX: 508-650-4216
                    e-mail: aqvideos@tiac.net
                    www.aquariusproductions.com

This is an excellent video for families who have just had a baby with Down Syndrome as well as professionals in the field of genetics and nursing. Through honest and open discussion, parents of children with Down Syndrome express the feelings and concerns they had during the early years of their child's life. Preview option available. $150.00

Video

7391 Dream Catchers

University of New Hampshire/Disability Institute
312 Morrill Hall
Durham, NC 03824   603-862-4320

This video tells the stories of three young people with disabilities, and how they each pulled together a network of people called the circle of support.

7392 Educating Inattentive Children

Western Psychological Services
12031 Wilshire Boulevard
Los Angeles, CA 90025
                              800-648-8857
                         FAX: 310-478-7838
Samuel Goldstein, Ph.D., & Michael Goldstein, M.D., author

An excellent resources for teachers who encounter inattention and hyperactivity in the classroom. It helps teachers distinguish deliberate misbehavior from the incompetent, nonpurposeful behavior of the inattentive child. *$120.00*

Video

7393 Effective Behavioral Programming

Research Press
PO Box 9177
Champaign, IL 61826   217-352-3273
                              800-519-2707
                         FAX: 217-352-1221
                    e-mail: rp@researchpress.com
                              www.researchpress.com
Dr Richard M Foxx, author
Russell Pence, V P Marketing

A comprehensive video-based training program for educators and residential staff who work with people with developmental disabilities. It is presented in clear, nontechnical language and does not require an extensive background in the use of behavioral procedures. The program includes eight instructional videotapes, a leader's guide and a set of five participant's manuals. It is suitable for group training or individual study and has no rigid time line. *$895.00*

Video

7394 Effective Intervention for Self-Feeding Success

Exceptional Parent Library
PO Box 1807
Englewood Cliffs, NJ 10116
                              800-535-1910
                    e-mail: eplibrary@aol.com
                              www.eplibrary.com
C.A. Nelson, Ph.D., OTR, author

An effective and easy to follow video program for parents, which provides the tools needed to be successful in moving your child toward independent self-feeding. *$39.95*

7395 Einstein and Me: Talking About Learning Disabilities

Fanlight Productions
4196 Washington Street
Suite 2
Boston, MA 02131   617-469-4999
                              800-937-4113
                         FAX: 617-469-3379
                    e-mail: fanlight@fanlight.com
                              www.fanlight.com

Karen McMillen, Marketing Director

In this straightforward and engaging video, panels of teens and younger students speak candidly with Schultz, a Clinical Psychologist, about how they found out about their learning disabilities, the policies and people who have made life difficult, the programs which have helped them cope, their strengths and talents, and their futures. *$99.00*

7396 Emerging Leaders

Mobility International USA
PO Box 10767
Eugene, OR 97440   541-343-1284

                    e-mail: info@miusa.org

Susan Sygall, Executive Director
Rhonda Neuhaus, Public Relations Coordinator

Looks at the emergence of people with disabilities as leaders in the world community this video discusses the value of internation exchange programs in fostering leadership skills. Available in English, Spanish and Russian. *$49.00*

Video

7397 Emotional Intelligence, Lessons in Conflict and Anger

Aquarius Health Care Videos
5 Powderhouse Lane
PO Box 1159
Sherborn, MA   01770   508-651-2963
                              FAX: 508-650-4216
                      e-mail: aqvideos@tiac.net
                      www.aquariusproductions.com

Up until recently, most of us expected to learn those kinds of skills, like listening, sharing, being kind, at home, and not find them in any organized class at school. Buth that is changing because of reserach shoing that school age children stay healthier, and learn better, when they know how to handle the ups and downs of growing up. this video profiles classes and programs in the New Have, Conneticut school system and in Highland Park, New Jersey. — Videocassette. *$149.00*

Preview option

7398 Endurance & Body Sculpting Exercise Programs

Seat-A-Robics
PO Box 1253
Jamestown, NC   27282
                              FAX: 336-454-4615
                      e-mail: seatarobics@hotmail.com
                      www.seat-a-robics.com

Clarice Burns, President

Safe, affordable and medically approved exercisc videos developed by a health advisory board in conjunction with a licensed aerobics instructor and paraplegic. These videos are aimed at persons with temporary injuries, permanent disabilities, health professionals and educators. Both programs are available on one tape. *$36.95*

56 min video

7399 Environmental Control Measures

American Academy of Allergy, Asthma and Immunology
611 E Wells Street
Milwaukee, WI   53202   414-272-6071
                              800-822-2762
                      FAX: 414-272-6070
                      e-mail: info@aaaai.org
                      www.aaaai.org

By conrtolling your environment, you can reduce your exposure to substances called allergens that trigger your allergic symptoms. This program depicts common outdoor and indoor allergens, methods an allergist uses to diagnose which substances you're allergic to, and how to reduce your exposure to allergic triggers. *$25.00*

10-13 Minutes

7400 Explore the Bible: Adult Audiocassette

LifeWay Christian Resources Southern Baptist Conv.
127 9th Avenue North
Nashville, TN   37234   615-251-2000
                              800-458-2772
                      e-mail: specialed@lifeway.com
                      www.lifeway.com

Ben Garner, Editor

Full-length recorded bible study lessons as printed in Explore the Bible: Adults. *$12.00*

Quarterly

7401 Face First

Fanlight Productions
4196 Washington Street
Suite 2
Boston, MA   02131   617-469-4999
                              800-937-4113
                      FAX: 617-469-3379
                      e-mail: fanlight@fanlight.com
                      www.fanlight.com

Karen McMillen, Marketing Director
Cynthia Conti, Publicity Coordinator
Mike Grundmann, Producer

In this documentary, the stories told reflect the reality faced by all those who are seen as different. Despite their difficult experiences, the survival of the profiled individuals affords comic relief &, by adulthood, they possess unusual strengths that shape their careers in pediatrics, disability care, public speaking, and journalism. *$ 195.00*

7402 Fairy Tales & Christmas Stories

Harris Communications
15159 Technology Drive
Eden Prairie, MN   55344   612-906-1180
                              800-825-6758
                      FAX: 612-906-1099
                      e-mail: mail@harriscomm.com
                      www.harriscomm.com

Bill Williams, National Sales Manager

A collection of videotapes featuring classic fairytales and Christmas stories signed by deaf storytellers. *$29.95*

Video

7403 Family Challenges: Parenting with a Disability

Aquarius Health Care Videos
5 Powderhouse Lane
PO Box 1159
Sherborn, MA   01770   508-651-2963
                              888-440-2963
                      FAX: 508-650-4216
                      e-mail: aqvideos@tiac.net
                      www.aquariusproductions.com

Leslie Kussmann, President/Producer

When a parent has a disability, everyone in the family is affected. For children, these experiences may profoundly influence their lives and views of the world. In this sensitive film, you will hear about different roles that all the family members take on at varying times. *$195.00*

Preview option

7404 Family-Guided Activity-Based Intervention for Toddlers & Infants

Brookes Publishing
PO Box 10624
Baltimore, MD   21285   410-337-9580
                              800-638-3775
                         FAX: 410-337-8539
e-mail: custserv@brookespublishing.com
       www.brookespublishing.com

Early childhood professionals will be able to teach parents and other caregivers how to use daily routines and activities to help young children with special needs gain vital skills. Included on the video are activity-based teaching methods that enhance children's development, accommodate families' daily schedules, address children's IFSP goals, and promote family interactions. *$37.00*

20-min VHS
ISBN 1-55766 -19-3

7405 Fanlight Productions

4196 Washington Street
Suite 2
Boston, MA   02131   617-469-4999
                             800-937-4113
                        FAX: 617-469-3379
e-mail: fanlight@fanlight.com
       www.fanlight.com

Sandy St. Louis, Marketing Director
Distributor of videos on a wide array of health-related topics. *$195.00*

Videocassette

7406 Fantastic Series

Harris Communications
15159 Technology Drive
Eden Prairie, MN   55344   612-906-1180
                             800-825-6758
                        FAX: 612-906-1099
e-mail: mail@harriscomm.com
       www.harriscomm.com
Gallaudet University Dept. of TV, Film & Photo., author
Bill Williams, National Sales Manager
These videotapes offer a blend of entertainment and information to both deaf and hearing children ages 6-10. A total of eight tapes in the series. *$29.95*

Per Tape Fee

7407 Fibromyalgia Interval Training

Arthritis Foundation Distribution Center
PO Box 6996
Alpharetta, GA   30009
                             800-207-8633
                        FAX: 770-442-9742
                        www.arthritis.com

This video was designed for people with fibromyalgia. The video features warm water exercises in shallow and deep water, including warmup, stretching, upper and lower body exercises, aerobics, strengthing, cool-down and relaxation. Designed to help you manage the pain, stiffness and fatigue of fibromyalgia. *$29.99*

7408 Filmakers Library

124 E 40th Street
New York, NY   10016   212-808-4980
                        FAX: 212-808-4983
e-mail: info@filmakers.com
       www.filmakers.com

Sue Oscar, Co-President
A distributor of educational, award-winning videotapes and films on issues relating to disabilities for educators, counsellors and organizations. The films and tapes are available for rental or sale to institutions, schools, hospitals and organizations. Among the topics covered in the videotapes are autism, schizophrenia, and physical disabilties.

$100 - $300

7409 Films & Videos on Aging and Sensory Change

Lighthouse Industries/Publications Department
370 Starke Road
Carlstadt, NJ   07072   201-896-1112
                             800-334-5497
                        e-mail: info@lighthouse.org

An annotated list of over 80 films and videos dealing with age-related sensory change, divided into sections on vision impairment, hearing impairment, and multiple sensory impairments. *$5.00*

7410 Fingerspelling: Expressive and Receptive Fluency

Gallaudet University Bookstore
11030 S Langley Avenue
Chicago, IL   60628   202-651-5488
                             800-621-2736
                        FAX: 202-651-5489
Joyce Linden Groode, author
Improve your fingerspelling with this new video guide. A 24-page instructional booklet is included with fingerspelling practice suggestions. *$39.95*

120 minutes

7411 Foundation Fundamentals for Nonprofit Organizations

Foundation Center
79 Fifth Avenue
Department ZE
New York, NY   10003   212-421-0771
                             800-424-9836
                        FAX: 212-807-3677
                        www.fdncenter.org

Thomas Buckman, President
This video is designed to give fundraisers a general overview of the foundation funding process and to introduce them to the many resources available through our libraries and cooperating collections. The video gives clear, step-by-step instructions on how to build a fundraising program. *$24.00*

Video

7412   Foundations: The People and the Money

Foundation Center
79 Fifth Avenue
Department ZE
New York, NY   10003   212-421-0771
                                          800-424-9836
                                    FAX: 212-807-3677
                                    www.fdncenter.org

Thomas Buckman, President

This award-winning documentary film, introduced by Robert MacNeil, provides a fascinating introduction to the world of American philanthropic foundations. Through interviews with both grant-makers and grantees, this book offers a vivid and human perspective on the work of foundations today. *$5.00*

Video

7413   Fred's Story

Aquarius Health Care Videos
5 Powderhouse Lane
PO Box 1159
Sherborn, MA   01770
                                    FAX: 508-650-4216
                              e-mail: aqvideos@tiac.net
                              www.aquariusproductions.com

Fred tells about the 40 years he spent inside Mansfield Training School, a Connecticut institution closed in 1990 by the Department of Mental Retardation. The film cuts between Fred's telling of the reality of the institution and black-and-white newsreel footage of state officials describing their visions of and goals for the institution in which Fred lived. Fred's indomitable, lyrical spirit shines throughout. Golden Chris Award, Columbus International Film Festival. Preview option available. *$90.00*

Video

7414   Free to Breathe

Allergy and Asthma Network/Mothers of Asthmatics
3554 Chain Bridge Road
Suite 200
Fairfax, VA   22030
                                          800-878-4403
                                    FAX: 703-352-4354

Characters rap, joke, and learn different ways to use inhalers. Kids are encouraged to talk to their parents and doctor about their choices. 8 minutes. *$10.00*

Video

7415   From Mime to Sign Package

TJ Publishers
817 Silver Spring Avenue
Suite 206
Silver Spring, MD   20910   301-585-4440
                                          800-999-1168
                                    FAX: 301-585-5930
                              e-mail: TJPubinc@aol.com

Gilbert C. Eastman, author
Angela K Thames, President
Jerald A Murphy, Vice President

As a drama professor, television personality, performer and storyteller, multiple Emmy winner Gil Eastman has developed a unique presentation style. Now, he shares his expressive communication approach in a highly illustrated American Sign Language text and videotape series. A text and three videotapes. *$139.95*

183 pages Text & Videos
ISBN 0-93266 -34-5

7416   Fundamentals of Reading Success

Educators Publishing Service
31 Smith Place
Cambridge, MA   02138   617-367-2700
                                          800-225-5750
                                    FAX: 617-547-0412
                                    www.epsbooks.com

Arlene W. Sonday, author

This video series is designed to help teachers learn a phonics or code-emphasis approach to teaching reading, spelling and handwriting. There is one set for teaching children and one for teaching adults. *$480.00*

Complete Set
ISBN 0-838872-52-2

7417   Getting Started with Facilitated Communication

Syracuse University, Institute on Communication
805 S Krouse
Syracuse, NY   13244   315-443-2693

Describes in detail how to help individuals with autism and/or severe communication difficulties to get started with facilitated communication.

Videotape

7418   Getting Together: A Head Start/School District Collaboration

Brookes Publishing
PO Box 10624
Baltimore, MD   21285   410-337-9580
                                          800-638-3775
                                    FAX: 410-337-8539
                        e-mail: custserv@brookespublishing.com
                              www.brookespublishing.com

This video describes how to include children with disabilities in the Head Start classrooms. Addresses such issues as leadership, staff support, and policy development. Comes with a 24-page saddle-stitched booklet. *$34.95*

25min. VHS
ISBN 1-55766 -97-5

7419   Getting in Touch

Research Press
PO Box 9177
Champaign, IL   61826   217-352-3273
                                          800-519-2707
                                    FAX: 217-352-1221
                              e-mail: rp@researchpress.com
                              www.researchpress.com

Elizabeth Cooley, author
Russell Pence, V P Marketing

When communicating with a child who is deaf/blind, there are certain basic procedures that can be used to help the child understand. This video introduces these procedures to teachers, staff, parents and others who work with children who have sensory impairments. The video demonstrates techniques that involve the use of two types of tactile cues - Touch Cues (signals made by actually touching the child) and Object Cues (signals made by presenting an object to the child). *$150.00*

19min pages Video

7420 Going to School with Facilitated Communication

Syracuse University, School of Education
Educational Resource Center
230 Huntington Hall
Syracuse, NY   13244   **315-443-4751**

D. Biklen, author

A video in which students with autism and/or severe disabilities illustrate the use of facilitated communication focusing on basic principles fostering facilitated communication.

Videotape

7421 Good Weather or Not

Nat'l Council of Community Mental Health Center
12300 Twinbrook Parkway
Suite 320
Rockville, MD   20852

One of the few resources of its kind, this set will help clinicians present material about parents' mental illness that is generated to young children's levels of thinking. *$290.00*

7422 Granny Good's Signs of Christmas

Gallaudet University Bookstore
11030 S Langley Avenue
Chicago, IL   60628   **202-651-5488**
                                        800-621-2736
                                   FAX: 202-651-5489

Kaye M. Good, author

Come join the folks at Granny's cottage where Hans Signer, from the silent forest, interprets his favorite story, Twas The Night Before Christmas. *$29.95*

Video

7423 Harry

Research Press
PO Box 9177
Champaign, IL   61826   **217-352-3273**
                                         800-519-2707
                                    FAX: 217-352-1221
                           e-mail: rp@researchpress.com
                               www.researchpress.com

Dr Richard M Foxx, author
Russell Pence, V P Marketing

Harry is one of the most unforgettable documentaries ever produced. It is honest, dramatic, touching and REAL. None of the scenes were staged, actual treatment sessions, conducted by Dr. Richard M. Foxx, were videotaped through a one-way mirror. Harry is the subject of the remarkably successful treatment program. At the time of this taping he was 24 years old and had spent most of his life in institutions wearing various types of physical restraints. 38 minutes. $495.00.

Video

7424 Hear to Listen & Learn: A Language Approach for Children with Ear Infections

Brookes Publishing
PO Box 10624
Baltimore, MD   21285   **410-337-9580**
                                         800-638-3775
                                    FAX: 410-337-8539
                   e-mail: custserv@brookespublishing.com
                           www.brookespublishing.com

This video describes the behavioral characteristics that signal when middle ear fluid is causing problems for a child. Also provides professionals with ideas for modifying classrooms and incorporating teaching practices that promote learning opportunities and language acquisition for children with middle ear fluid and associated hearing loss. *$42.00*

20-min VHS
ISBN 1-55766 -99-5

7425 Hearing Impaired Infants: Support in the First Eighteen Months

Brookes Publishing
PO Box 10624
Baltimore, MD   21285   **410-337-9580**
                                         800-638-3775
                                    FAX: 410-337-8539
                   e-mail: custserv@brookespublishing.com
                           www.brookespublishing.com

Jacqueline Stokes, Editor, author

Parents and professionals will discover the important role each plays in providing infants with hearing loss the help they need to acquire critical communicative skills. Parents learn what influences professionals' decisions while professionals learn what it's like to care for an infant with atypical hearing. *$38.00*

246 pages Paperback 1999
ISBN 1-861561-06-7

7426 Heart to Heart

Blind Children's Center
4120 Marathon Street
Los Angeles, CA   90029

                                         800-222-3566
                                    FAX: 323-665-3828
                   e-mail: info@blindchildrenscenter.org

Parents of blind and partially sighted children talk about their feelings. *$35.00*

Video

7427   Helping Hands

Fanlight Productions
4196 Washington Street
Suite 2
Boston, MA   02131   617-469-4999
                                        800-937-4113
                                        FAX: 617-469-3379
                                        e-mail: fanlight@fanlight.com
                                        www.fanlight.com

The ADA mandates equal access and opportunity for the 43 million people with disabilities in the United States. These individuals may have limited speech, sight or mobility; a developmental disability; or a medical condition which limits some life activities. Many, however, are ready, willing and very able to join the workforce. This video demonstrates that many modifications or adaptations can be made simply by using ingenuity or common sense — such as keeping the aisles clear, etc. *$145.00*

37 Minutes

7428   Home is in the Heart: Accommodating People with Disabilities in the Homestay Experience

Mobility International USA
PO Box 10767
Eugene, OR   97440   541-343-1284
                                        FAX: 541-343-6812
                                        TDY:541-343-1284
                                        e-mail: info@miusa.org
                                        www.miusa.org

Susan Sygall, Executive Director
Rhonda Neuhaus, Public Relations Coordinator

Provides information and ideas for exchange organizations. Discusses how to recruit homestay families, meet accessibility needs and accommodate international participants with disabilities. *$49.00*

Video

7429   How Difficult Can This Be ?

CACLD
25 Van Street
Suite 15-5
East Norwalk, CT   06855   203-838-5010
                                        FAX: 203-866-6108
                                        www.CACLD.org

This informative and entertaining video allows the viewer to see the world through the eyes of a learning disabled child. It features a unique workshop attended by teacher, psychologists, social workers, parents, siblings and a student with L.D. They participate in a series of classroom activiteis which cause frustration, anxiety and tension; emotions all too familiar to a student with a learning disability.

7430   How We Play

Fanlight Productions
4196 Washington Street
Suite 2
Boston, MA   02131   617-469-4999
                                        800-937-4113
                                        FAX: 617-469-3379
                                        e-mail: fanlight@fanlight.com
                                        www.fanlight.com

Karen McMillen, Marketing Director

Though most of the people in this new, short documentary are in wheelchairs, and one is blind, they are anything but handicapped. Playing tennis, snorkeling, whitewater canoeing, practicing karate - they are living proof that a disability can be a challenge, not an obstacle. *$99.00*

7431   I Can Do It

Britannica Film Company
345 4th Street
San Francisco, CA   94107   415-777-9876

Alan P. Sloan, author

Tommy's parents took him shopping. Although he had trouble moving around with his braces he wanted to go shopping alone. In the pet shop he had some trouble moving around, but he was able to solve his problems and even help other customers. A teacher's guide is available with this video.

Films

7432   I Want My Little Boy Back

A Britsh Broadcasting Corporation Documentary
2080 South Undermountain Road
Sheffield, MA   01257   413-229-2100
                                        800-714-2779
                                        FAX: 413-229-8931
                                        e-mail: happiness@option.org
                                        www.option.org

A great video for parents and professionals caring for children with special needs. Join one British family and their autistic son before, during and after their journey to America to attend The Son-Rise Program at The Autism Treatment Center of America. This informative, inspirational and deeply moving story not only captures the joy, tears, challenges and triumps of this amazing little boy and his family, but also serves as a powerful introduction to the attitude and principles of the program. *$25.00*

7433   I'm Not Disabled

Landmark Media
3450 Slade Run Drive
Falls Church, VA   22042   703-241-2030
                                        800-342-4336
                                        FAX: 703-536-9540

M.L. Hartogs

Young people talk about their disabilities and the importance of sports in their lives. The afflictions range from blindness and missing limbs to paralysis. Through physical education and therapy they enjoy freedom of movement and participate in sports such as tennis, basketball, kayaking, skiing, and swimming. *$195.00*

Video

7434 If I Can't Do It

Fanlight Productions
4196 Washington Street
Suite 2
Boston, MA   02131   617-469-4999
                           800-937-4113
                      FAX: 617-469-3379
          e-mail: fanlight@fanlight.com
                      www.fanlight.com

Karen McMillen, Marketing Director
Cynthia Conti, Publicity Coordinator
Walter Brock, Producer

Arthur Campbell, Jr. doesn't want your sympathy, he just wants what most people want: a living wage, a meaningful social life, a few good laughs and the means to get around. This outstanding documentary is an unflinching portrait of one cantankerous and courageous disabled man. *$245.00*

7435 Imagery Procedures for People with Special Needs

Research Press
PO Box 9177
Champaign, IL   61826   217-352-3273
                              800-519-2707
                         FAX: 217-352-1221
          e-mail: rp@researchpress.com
                      www.researchpress.com
Dr June Groden and Joseph Cautela, author
Russell Pence, V P Marketing

This video features numerous training sessions in which clinicians are shown leading individuals through imagery scenes that focus on controlling specific behaviors. *$195.00*

32min pages Video

7436 In the Middle

Fanlight Productions
4196 Washington Street
Suite 2
Boston, MA   02131   617-469-4999
                           800-937-4113
                      FAX: 617-469-3379
          e-mail: fanlight@fanlight.com
                      www.fanlight.com

Karen McMillen, Marketing Director

Documents the problems and joys shared by Ryanna, who has Spina Bifida, and her parents, teachers and classmates during her first year of being mainstreamed in a Head Start Program. *$99.00*

7437 In the Mind of the Beholder.... a Video About Newly Blind Adults

Aquarius Health Care Videos
5 Powderhouse Lane
PO Box 1159
Sherborn, MA   01770   508-651-2963
                         FAX: 508-650-4216
          e-mail: aqvideos@tiac.net

Newly blind adults making the transition to using their non-visual senses. In a society in which most people are terrified of losing their vision- and yet know virtually nothing about vision loss- the blind are wrongly viewed as mysterious, pitiful or courageous. Produced by Karen Brown Davison, this film puts a human face and voice to blindness. By sharing the experience of losing their eyesight and relearning skills they once took for granted, the people in this film: nonvisual clues. *$195.00*

Preview option

7438 Include Us

Exceptional Parent Library
PO Box 1807
Englewood Cliffs, NJ   10116
                              800-535-1910
          e-mail: eplibrary@aol.com
                      www.eplibrary.com

First children's video to feature a proportionate number of children with disabilities. Inclusion works via eight songs. *$19.95*

7439 Intensive Early Intervention and Beyond School-Based Inclusion Program

Research Press
2612 N Mattis Avenue
Champaign, IL   61821   217-352-3273
                              800-519-2707
                         FAX: 217-352-2707
          e-mail: rp@researchpress.com
                      www.researchpress.com
June Groden, Richard Spratt and Patricia Fiske, author
Russell Pence, V P Marketing

Shows the successful application of a school-based inclusion program. The video focuses on the lives of young children with autism who have shown remarkable progress in personal, social, and academic skills. 22 minutes. *$195.00*

Video Cassette

7440 Interpretations

Fanlight Productions
4196 Washington Street
Suite 2
Boston, MA   02131   617-469-4999
                           800-937-4113
                      FAX: 617-469-3379
          e-mail: fanlight@fanlight.com
                      www.fanlight.com

Karen McMillen, Marketing Director

This new film uses humor and drama to explore the interaction between the deaf and hearing communities. Janice, a freelance photographer who is deaf, has been given her first assignment by an advertising agency. She hires her hearing friend Maureen to interpret for her. When conflicts arise between Janice and the client, Maureen changes Janice words. The film looks at the interplay of dependence and responsibility in the relationship of communicator and interpreter. $145.00.

7441 Invisible Children

Learning Corporation of America
6493 Kaiser Drive
Fremont, CA 94555   510-490-7311

Renaldo was blind, Mandy was deaf, and Mark had Cerebral Palsy and used a wheelchair. These child-size puppet characters interacted with non-handicapped puppets.

Films

7442 It's Just Attention Disorder

Western Psychological Services
12031 Wilshire Boulevard
Los Angeles, CA 90025   310-478-2061
                                   800-648-8857
                              FAX: 310-478-7838
Samuel Goldstein, Ph.D., & Michael Goldstein, M.D., author

This ground-breaking videotape takes the critical first steps in treating attention-deficit disorder: it enlists the inattentive or hyperactive child as an active participant in his or her treatment. *$99.50*

Video NL-3

7443 Journey

Landmark Media
3450 Slade Run Drive
Falls Church, VA 22042   703-241-2030
                                    800-342-4336
                               FAX: 703-536-9540

M.L. Hartogs

A moving portrayal of the extraordinary journey to Japan of 74-year-old Billie Sinclair, who is deaf, blind and mute. He funds his travels by weaving and selling baskets. In Japan he rides a roller coaster, tries judo and visits a deaf and blind acupuncturist. He demonstrates how it is possible to communicate by touch alone. *$195.00*

Video

7444 Juggler

Beacon Press
25 Beacon Street
Boston, MA 02108   617-742-2100
                         FAX: 617-743-3097
Black Sea Productions, author

Andre was the young son of a wealthy, early Quebec fur trader. Because he was almost totally blind, he was overly protected by his family, and his movement outside his home was very limited.

Films

7445 Just 4 Kids

Seat-A-Robics
PO Box 1253
Jamestown, BC 27282   336-454-4615
                            FAX: 336-454-4615
                 e-mail: seatarobics@hotmail.com
                         www.seat-a-robics.com

Clarice Burns, President

Kid tested, parent/teacher approved! Seated aerobic exercise program incorporates animation, props and musical themes that children five through adolescent can relate to. Adaptive instruction and safety tips are provided while demonstrating proper form. The warm-up and marching band sections include eight kid instructors as participants. Recommended for ages five through adolescents. *$39.95*

Ages 5-14
ISBN 1-887479-03-1

7446 Keeping the Balance

Fanlight Productions
4196 Washington Street
Suite 2
Boston, MA 02131   617-469-4999
                              800-937-4113
                         FAX: 617-469-3379
              e-mail: fanlight@fanlight.com
                      www.fanlight.com

Karen McMillen, Marketing Director

Brothers and sisters of children with serious lung diseases share their experiences of being the normal child. Insightful and articulate, they explore the frequent conflict between their feelings of love and concern, and their resentment over the attention denied to them because of the sibling's illness. *$99.00*

7447 Kenny Foundation

21700 Northwestern Highway
Suite 730
Southfield, MI 48075   248-552-0202
                                  800-237-3422
                             FAX: 248-552-0275
                          www.comnet.org/kenny

Susan Burstein, Executive Director

Provides education, advocacy & direct services to people with mobility impairments throughout Michigan. Services include Equipment Connection, a database, available online, that connects buyers & sellers of used adaptive equipment; Attitudes is a disability awareness program for 1st & 2nd graders; Information & Referral services; and Accessbility, a program that uses volunteer labor and donated materials to buid ramps for people who can't afford them.

7448 Key Changes: A Portrait of Lisa Thorson

Fanlight Productions
4196 Washington Street
Suite 2
Boston, MA 02131   617-469-4999
                              800-937-4113
                         FAX: 617-469-3379
              e-mail: fanlight@fanlight.com
                      www.fanlight.com

Karen McMillen, Marketing Director

A documentary profiling Lisa Thorson, a gifted vocalist who uses a wheelchair. Ms. Thorson defines herself as a performer first, a person with a disability second, and this thoughtful portrait respects that distinction. Her work as a jazz singer is at the heart of the film, reflecting her philosophy that the biggest contribution that she can make to the struggle for the rights of people with disabilities is doing her art the best way she can. *$145.00*

7449 Know Your Diabetes, Know Yourself

Joslin Diabetes Center
1 Joslin Plaza
Boston, MA 02215   **617-732-2400**

An hour-long videotape in which Joslin patients talk about daily issues of diabetes management - meal planning, exercise, monitoring, injections, foot and eye care, and managing the disease when sick or traveling. *$3.00*

7450 Landmark Media

3450 Slade Run Drive
Falls Church, VA 22042   **703-241-2030**
800-342-4336
FAX: 703-536-9540
e-mail: landmrkmed@aol.com
Supplier and distributor of educational videocassettes and CD's. $79-$280.00.

7451 Learning Center

MN Governor's Council Developmental Disabilities
370 Centennial Office Building
658 Cedar Street
St. Paul, MN 55155   **651-296-4018**
877-348-0505
FAX: 651-297-7200
e-mail: admin.dd@state.mn.us
www.mncdd.org

Colleen Wieck, Ph.D., Executive Director

The Learning Center is a collection of more than 10,000 pages of documents including State Plans, policy papers, studies, reports, curriculum modules, publications and briefing booklets produced by the Council during its twenty-five year history. This CD-ROM contains a search component, and many documents are in an editable text version which allows for both viewing and editing in a word processing program

7452 Learning Disabilities and Discipline

CACLD
25 Van Street
Suite 15-5
East Norwalk, CT 06855   **203-838-5010**
FAX: 203-866-6108
www.CACLD.org

This video comes with a 16 page Program Guide containing information about specific aspects of the learing disabilities profile that can cause misbehavior. Some basic concepts which can be valuable as you develop your own behavior management plans are discussed. Included are dozens of field test techniques and strategies that can be used to monitor, evaluate and manage childrens behavior; and more.

7453 Learning Disabilities and Self Esteem

CACLD
25 Van Street
Suite 15-5
East Norwalk, C 06855   **203-838-5010**
FAX: 203-866-6108
www.CACLD.org

The 60 minute Teacher video contains program material for building self-esteem in the classroom. The 60 minute parent video contains program material for building self esteem in the home. A 16 page Program Guide accompanies each video.

7454 Learning Disabilities and Social Skills

CACLD
25 Van Street
East Norwalk, CT 06855   **203-838-5010**
FAX: 203-866-6108
e-mail: www.CACLD.org
www.CACLD

Noting that L.D. children do not have the cognitive skills to simply "pick up" socially correct behavior by watching their parents, like most children do, nationally recognized expert on learning disabilities, Richard Lavoie, gives parents and teachers examples on how to help their L.D. children succeed in everyday situations where they might normally fail. The program includes an explanation of "social autopsies" and the techniques Lavoie uses to correct them.

7455 Let's be Friends

Britannica Film Company
345 4th Street
San Francisco, CA 94107   **415-777-9876**

Alan P. Sloan, author

The teacher left the room and asked Shelly, a hearing impaired child to be the mother. Margaret, an emotionally disturbed child, became frightened and verbally attacked Shelly. The teacher worked to get them to become friends and understand each other's problems.

Films

7456 Living with Spinal Cord Injury

Fanlight Productions
4196 Washington Street
Suite 2
Boston, MA 02131   **617-469-4999**
800-937-4113
FAX: 617-469-3379
e-mail: fanlight@fanlight.com
www.fanlight.com

Barry Corbett, author
Karen McMillen, Marketing Director

A series of three videos produced by an individual who has experienced spinal cord injury himself. Changes; is about the consequences of spinal cord injury and the process of rehabilitation. Outside; emphasizes the life-long aspect of rehabilitation for people with spinal cord injury. Survivors; interviews 23 men and women who have lived at least 24 years with spinal cord injury. *$200.00*

7457 Look Out for Annie

Lighthouse Industries/Publications Department
370 Starke Road
Carlstadt, NJ 07072　　　201-896-1112
　　　　　　　　　　　　800-334-5497
e-mail: info@lighthouse.org

Depicts an older woman coping with her vision loss. It focuses on the emotional issues surrounding vision loss and conveys the idea that both the person with the vision disorder and their family and friends will need to make adjustments. *$25.00*

Video

7458 Look Who's Laughing

Aquarius Health Care Videos
5 Powderhouse Lane
PO Box 1159
Sherborn, MA 01770
　　　　　　　　FAX: 508-650-4216
　　　　　　e-mail: aqvideos@tiac.net
　　　　　　www.aquariusproductions.com

This video is packed with laugh-out-loud comedic moments, but is also full of intelligent and inspiring messages. Look Who's Laughing introduces viewers to some of today's funniest comedians - who just happen to be physically disabled. We hear them talk openly and honestly about their limitations as well as their abilities and talents. Helpful for those who work with the disabled and motivational to both the disabled and able-bodied. Preview option available. *$95.00*

Video

7459 Loud, Proud and Passionate States

Mobility International USA
PO Box 10767
Eugene, OR 97440　　　541-343-1284
　　　　　　　　FAX: 541-343-6812
　　　　　　　TDY:541-343-1284
　　　　　　e-mail: info@miusa.org
　　　　　　　　www.miusa.org

Susan Sygall, Executive Director
Rhonda Neuhaus, Public Relations Coordinator

Documents MIUSA's Women's Institute on Leadership and Disability. Interviews with participants highlight the vision, determination, challanges and recommendations of women with disabilities who are grassroots leaders in over 25 countries. MIUSA's unique model of international leadership training is illustrated as women with mobility, visual and hearing disabilities are shown in training workshop and team-building activities. Available in English, Spanish and Russian. *$49.00*

Video

7460 Making a Difference - A Wise Approach

Easter Seals
230 W Monroe Street
Chicago, IL 60606　　　312-726-6200
　　　　　　　　FAX: 312-726-1494

Janet D. Jamieson, Communication Mgr.

The town of Wise, Virginia, and its leading citizen, Virgil Craft, personify what Making a Difference is all about when a community supports implementing the provisions of the Americans with Disabilities Act. Craft, a person with a disability, has spent his life giving back to the community. The community, in turn, has supported Craft's efforts to improve the environment, education, healthcare and access for disabled persons. A must buy for companies of all sizes, clubs and organizations. *$50.00*

7461 Managed Mental Healthcare Video

National Council of Community Mental Health Center
12300 Twinbrook Parkway
Rockville, MD 20852　　　301-670-6331

Get an overview of the managed healthcare climate with this premier strategic planning and training tool.

7462 Managing Asthma in School: An Action Plan

Asthma and Allergy Foundation of America
1125 15th Street
Washington, DC 20005　　　202-466-7643
　　　　　　　　FAX: 202-466-8940
　　　　　　e-mail: info@aafa.org
　　　　　　　　www.aafa.org

Gives the basics of asthma and a plan for school nurses, parents and physicians to work together. *$15.00*

14 minutes

7463 Manic Depression: Voices of an Illness

Fanlight Productions
4196 Washington Street
Suite 2
Boston, MA 02131　　　617-469-4999
　　　　　　　　800-937-4113
　　　　　　　FAX: 617-469-3379
　　　　e-mail: fanlight@fanlight.com

Karen McMillen, Marketing Director

This audio cassette focuses on the lives of nine people and their families who are living with the pervasive illness. *$29.00*

Audiotape

7464 Martin Luther Home Society

650 J Street
Suite 305
Lincoln, NE 68508
　　　　　　　　800-727-8317
　　　　　　　FAX: 402-434-3253
　　　　　　e-mail: info@mlhs.com
　　　　　　　　www.mlhs.com

Faye Colburn, Communications Specialist
David Frye, Communications Director

Video production: public education and public relations programs. Staff training materials. Public Service announcements and script writing services.

7465 More Than Just a Job

Institution on Disability
University of New Hampshire
Morrill Hall, Room 312
Durham, NH 03824

Narrative case studies and interviews with persons with disabilities, their employers, families and experts in the field. *$ 20.00*

7466 My Body is Not Who I Am

Aquarius Health Care Videos
5 Powderhouse Lane
PO Box 1159
Sherborn, MA 01770   508-651-2963
                            888-440-2963
                  FAX: 508-650-4216
            e-mail: aqvideos@tiac.net
            www.aquariusproductions.com

Leslie Kussman, President

This thought-provoking video introduces viewers to people who openly discuss the struggles and triumphs they have experienced living in a body that is physically disabled. They talk honestly about the social stigma of their disability and the problems they face in terms of mobility, health care and family relationships, as well as the challenges of emotional and sexual intimacy. Preview option available. *$195.00*

Video

7467 My Country

Aquarius Health Care Videos
5 Powderhouse Lane
PO Box 1159
Sherborn, MA 01770   508-651-2963
                            888-440-2963
                  FAX: 508-650-4216
            e-mail: aqvideos@tiac.net
            www.aquariusproductions.com

Leslie Kussmann, President

By telling the stories of three people with disabilities and their struggle for equal rights under the law, this film draws a powerful parallel between the efforts of disability rights activists and the civil rights struggle of the 1960s. Great for disability awareness programs, and for discussions of disability rights issues. Should be part of every college curriculum on disabilities. Awarded Best of Show Superfest 98. Preview option available. *$195.00*

Video

7468 Nancy's Special Workout for the Physically Challenged

Laurel Designs
5 Laurel Avenue
Belvedere, CA 94920

                  FAX: 415-435-1451
            e-mail: laureld@ncal.verio.com

Janet Sawyer, Owner
Lynn Montoya, Owner

45-minute aerobic exercise video with syncopated music for seated people with disabilities from minimal to severe. *$42.00*

7469 Narcolepsy

Fanlight Productions
4196 Washington Street
Suite 2
Boston, MA 02131   617-469-4999
                  FAX: 617-469-3379
            e-mail: fanlight@fanlight.com
                  www.fanlight.com

Jason Margolis, author

25-minute video that presents the experiences of three individuals who lives and relationships have been disrupted by narcolepsy. Rental $50/day. *$195.00*

7470 No Barriers

Aquarius Health Care Videos
5 Powderhouse Lane
PO Box 1159
Sherborn, MA 01770

                  FAX: 508-650-4216
            e-mail: aqvideos@tiac.net
            www.aquariusproductions.com

Brookes Publishing, author

Everyone faces the world with different abilities and disabilities. But everyone has at least one goal in common...to break through their own barriers says Mark Wellman. Mark, a paraplegic, knows this well. No Barriers takes us into Mark's world where he defies the odds for most able bodied individuals by climbing Yosemite's Half Dome and El Capitan. This video is more than inspiring and fun to watch...it helps one make that paradigm shift from can't do to can do! Preview option available *$90.00*

Video

7471 NoBody's Perfect....Educating Children about Disabilities

Aquarius Health Care Videos
5 Powderhouse Lane
PO Box 1159
Sherborn, MA 01770   508-651-2963
                  FAX: 508-650-4216
            e-mail: aqvideos@tiac.net

An upbeat, inclusion-friendly program for kids that profiles three children with disabilties. Viewers discover that accepting differences is an essential part of growing up. We learn how the kids cope and, in the process, are introduced to signing, prosthetics, and assistive technology and Braille. Videocassette, preview option is available. *$ 99.00*

7472 Nobody is Burning Wheelchairs

Easter Seals
230 W Monroe Street
Chicago, IL 60606   312-726-6200
                  FAX: 312-726-1494

Janet D. Jamieson, Communications Mgr.

Explains the employment, public accommodations, transportation and telecommunications provisions of the Americans with Disabilities Act and what this law means to people with disabilities and business and industry. The video can be used for training and information seminars, awareness training and for groups interested in learning more about people with disabilities. *$35.00*

7473 Observing Kassandra

Brookes Publishing
PO Box 10624
Baltimore, MD 21285   410-337-9580
     800-638-3775
     FAX: 410-337-8539
e-mail: custserv@brookespublishing.com
www.brookespublishing.com

This video provides professionals with a firsthand opportunity to practice taking notes during a TPBA. Comes with summary forms that can be completed for additional guidance in learning how to use TPBA. Also included is a 28-page saddle-stitched booklet. *$169.00*

50-min VHS
ISBN 1-55766 -66-5

7474 Once Upon a Time...Children's Classics Retold in American Sign Language

Harris Communications
6541 City W Parkway
Eden Prairie, MN 55344   612-906-1180
     800-825-6758
     FAX: 612-906-1099
     TDY:612-946-0922
     e-mail: mail@harriscomm.com

Children's classics come alive on videotapes. Six tapes are available, each telling a favorite fairy tale. *$29.95*

Per Tape Fee

7475 One to Grow On

National Council of Community Mental Health Center
12300 Twinbrook Parkway
Rockville, MD 20852   301-670-6331

Provides an important service to clinicians. This video will allow therapists to make in-depth observations of clients' treatment needs and reduce therapist-client mismatches. *$595.00*

7476 Open for Business

Disability Rights Education and Defense Fund
2212 6th Street
Berkeley, CA 94710   510-644-2629
     800-466-4232
     FAX: 510-841-8645

An award-winning film that depicts the disability and business communities working together in one small town to remove architectural barriers, when readily achievable, as required by the Americans with Disabilities Act. Package includes 15 and 30 minute closed-captioned versions and 15 to 30 m-inute versions with audio description. *$179.00*

7477 Open to the Public

Aquarius Health Care Videos
5 Powderhouse Lane
PO Box 1159
Sherborn, MA 01770   FAX: 508-650-4216
     e-mail: aqvideos@tiac.net
     www.aquariusproductions.com

Provides an overview of the Americans with Disabilities Act as it applies to state and local governments. The ADA doesn't provide recommendations for solving common problems, but this film could provide enough information for governments to solve some common problems without turning to high-priced consultants. Preview option available. *$125.00*

Video

7478 PACE II

Arthritis Foundation
PO Box 6996
Alpharetta, GA 30009
     800-207-8633
     FAX: 770-442-9742
     www.arthritis.com

$19.50

7479 Pariallels in Time

MN Governor''s Council on Development Disabilities
370 Centennial Office Building
658 Cedar Street
St. Paul, MN 55155   651-296-4018
     877-348-0505
     FAX: 651-297-7200
     e-mail: admin.dd@state.mn.us
     www.mncdd.org

Colleen Wieck, Ph.D., Executive Director

Parallels in Time traces present attitudes and the treatment of people with disabilities, and supplements the first weekend seesion of Partners in Policymaking. This CD-ROM includes the History of the Parent Movement and the History of the Independent Living Movement, as well as personal stories of self advocates, leaders in the self advocacy movement.

7480 Part of the Team

Easter Seals
230 West Monroe Street
Suite 1800
Chicago, IL 60606   312-726-6200
     FAX: 312-726-1494

Janet D. Jamieson, Communications Mgr.

Designed for employers of all sizes, rehabilitation organizations and all others concerned with the employment of people with disabilities. It addresses managers' concerns and questions about supervising persons with disabilities and can be used as a discussion/team-building tool for employees with and without disabilities. The video recognizes people with disabilities as strong contenders for almost any job. *$15.00*

7481 Passion for Justice

Fanlight Productions
4196 Washington Street
Suite 2
Boston, MA 02131   617-469-4999
    800-937-4113
FAX: 617-469-3379
e-mail: fanlight@fanlight.com
www.fanlight.com

An engaging portrait of Bob Perske, the author of Unequal Justice and a crusader for the rights of people with developmental disabilities. The tape focuses on cases in which people with developmental disabilities have been convicted of crimes they didn't commit. The tape asks challenging questions about society's responsibility to this population, and about ways to protect their rights to equality and justice. *$99.00*

29 Minutes

7482 Pathways to Better Living

Arthritis Foundation
PO Box 6996
Alpharetta, GA 30009

    800-207-8633
FAX: 770-442-9742
www.arthritis.com

$29.95

7483 Paul

Miriam Perrone
440 Park Avenue
Saint Simons Island, GA 31522

How a determined mother carved a semi-independent life for her now-grown Down Syndrome child. *$63.20*

7484 Pharmacologic Therapy of Pediatric Asthma

American Lung Association
1740 Broadway
New York, NY 10017   212-315-8700

A Learning Resource Program developed by a joint committee of the American Thoracic Society and the ALA.

Film

7485 Place for Me

Educational Productions
9000 SW Gemini Drive
Beaverton, OR 97008   503-644-7000
    800-950-4949
FAX: 503-350-7000
e-mail: custserve@edpro.com
www.edpro.com

Linda Freedman, President/Co-Owner
Daylene Crudo, Director of Marketing
Molly Krumm, Marketing Assistant

In this video, parents discuss the issues they face in planning for their child's future. This program is designed to stimulate discussion of these issues and help increase awareness of the options available in your local community.

7486 Pool Exercise Program

Arthritis Foundation Distribution Center
PO Box 6996
Alpharetta, GA 30009

    800-207-8633
FAX: 770-442-9742
www.arthritis.com

This video features water exercises that will help you increase and maintain joint flexibility, strengthen and tone muscles, and increase endurance. All exercises are performed in water at chest level. No swimming skills are necessary. *$19.50*

7487 Positioning for Infants and Young Children

Love Publishing Company
4925 E Pacific Place
22353
Denver, CO 80222   303-221-7333
FAX: 303-221-7444
e-mail: lovepublishing@compuserve.com

This video unit is a resource for daily caregivers of children with motor problems. Nurses, physical therapists, and occupational therapists will find the tape extremely valuable for procedures to reinforce therapy sessions. *$198.00*

7488 Potty Learning for Children who Experience Delay

Exceptional Parent Library
PO Box 1807
Englewood Cliffs, NJ 10116
    800-535-1910
e-mail: eplibrary@aol.com
www.eplibrary.com
S.R. Hays, M.S., R.N., C.R.R.N., author

This video presents a unique developmental approach to supporting the child in learning independence in the management of bathroom skills. *$39.95*

7489 Raising Kids with Special Needs

Aquarius Health Care Videos
5 Powderhouse Lane
PO Box 1159
Sherborn, MA 01770   508-651-2963
FAX: 508-650-4216
e-mail: aqvideos@tiac.net
www.aquariusproductions.com

An intimate look into the lives of parents of three kids with very different disabilities. The objective of this video is an understanding of paprenting a child with special nees. THis outstanding program looks at safety concerns, issues of anger and grief, the importance of a support network and other important issues. Ultimately, this is a narrative about raising and educating a child with disabilities. Preview option is available. *$89.00*

Video cassette

7490 Reasonable Accommodations of the Enabling Kind

Mainstream
3 Bethesda Metro Center
830
Bethesda, MD 20814   301-654-2400

e-mail: info@mainstreaminc.org
Fritz Rumpel, author
Lillie Harrison, Info. Programs Clerk

In this training video a hiring manager demonstrates the basics of doing a job analysis and is shown using the information in interview sessions to determine the reasonable accommodation needs of three individuals with disabilities. Includes trainer and trainee guide. *$59.95*

7491 Recognizing Children with Special Needs

Aquarius Health Care Videos
5 Powderhouse Lane
PO Box 1159
Sherborn, MA 01770
FAX: 508-650-4216
e-mail: aqvideos@tiac.net
www.aquariusproductions.com

A great overview for caregivers of children on how to recognize special needs. Often-times it is the little things children do everyday to compensate for, or express, a disability that can be observed by their caregiver. All types of disabilities are addressed: emotional, physical, psychological, and chronic illness. A wonderful tool for teachers, childcare staff, and students on how to play a vital role in our children's development. Preview option available. *$125.00*

Video

7492 Regular Kid

American Lung Association
1740 Broadway
New York, NY 10017
212-315-8700

This film shows how families and children cope with asthma problems. Proven asthma management strategies are presented through the experiences of four children with asthma, ranging in age from toddler to teenager.

Film

7493 Relaxation Techniques for People with Special Needs

Research Press
PO Box 9177
Champaign, IL 61826
217-352-3273
800-519-2707
FAX: 217-352-1221
e-mail: rp@researchpress.com
www.researchpress.com
Dr June Groden, Joseph Cautela and Gerald Groden, author
Russell Pence, V P Marketing

The developers discuss and demonstrate how to use special relaxation procedures with children and adolescents who have developmental disabilities. They emphasize the need for students to learn relaxation as a means of coping with stress and developing self-control. During the scenes of Dr. June Groden conducting relaxation training, viewers will see how to correctly use the training procedures, how to use reinforcement during training and how to use guided imagery. 23 minutes. *$195.00*

Video

7494 Right at Home

Aquarius Health Care Videos
5 Powderhouse Lane
PO Box 1159
Sherborn, MA 01770
508-651-2963
FAX: 508-650-4216
e-mail: aqvideos@tiac.net
www.aquariusproductions.com

Shows simple solutions for complying with the Fair Hoiusing Act amendments. Emphasizes low-cost, practical solutions, and working with people with disabilities to find the best applicable solution. Ideal for people with disabilities and their families, as well as housing providers, university courses, and disability awareness organizations. Preview option is available. *$99.00*

Video Cassette

7495 Say it with Sign Videotape

Harris Communications
15159 Technology Drive
Eden Prairie, MN 55344
612-906-1180
800-825-6758
FAX: 612-906-1099
e-mail: mail@harriscomm.com
www.harriscomm.com

Bill Williams, National Sales Manager

Contains both the serious and fun side of signing and provides the basic signs that might be needed in an emergency situation. *$39.95*

Video

7496 See What I Feel

Britannica Film Company
345 Fourth Street
San Francisco, CA 94107
415-777-9876

Alan P. Sloan, author

A blind child tells her friends about her trip to the zoo. Each experience was explained as a blind child would experience it. A teacher's guide comes with this video.

Films

7497 See What I'm Saying

Fanlight Productions
4196 Washington Street
Suite 2
Boston, MA 02131
617-469-4999
800-937-4113
FAX: 617-469-3379
e-mail: fanlight@fanlight.com
www.fanlight.com

Karen McMillen, Marketing Director

This program illustrates how the acquisition of communication skill, particularly sign language, enhances a child's self esteem and family and peer relationship. The documentary follows Patricia, who is deaf and from a Spanish-speaking family, through her first year at the Kendall Demonstration Elementary School of Gallaudet University. *$195.00*

7498 See for Yourself

Lighthouse Industries/Publications Department
370 Starke Road
Carlstadt, NJ   07072   201-896-1112
                                     800-334-5497
                       e-mail: info@lighthouse.org

This video features older adults with impaired vision who have been helped by vision rehabilitation. *$50.00*

7499 Shape Up 'n Sign

Gallaudet University Bookstore
11030 S Langley Avenue
Chicago, IL   60628   202-651-5488
                                     800-621-2736
                              FAX: 202-651-5489
Gina Olivia and Linda Crider, author

An aerobic exercise tape introducing the basic sign language for deaf and hearing children ages six to ten. *$22.95*

30 minutes

7500 Shining Bright: Head Start Inclusion

Brookes Publishing
PO Box 10624
Baltimore, MD   21285   410-337-9580
                                     800-638-3775
                              FAX: 410-337-8539
          e-mail: custserv@brookespublishing.com
                    www.brookespublishing.com
David P. Lindeman, Ph.D., & Tracy Adams, M.A., author

This documentary depicts the collaborative efforts of a Head Start and a local education agency to include children with severe disabilities in a Head Start program. This video addresses issues such as support for children with severe health impairments, benefits of participating in Head Start, ability of teachers with a general education background to serve children with severe disabilities, and staff relations. Includes a 28-page saddle-stitched booklet. *$45.00*

240 pages 23-min VHS
ISBN 1-55766-95-9

7501 Sight by Touch

Landmark Media
3450 Slade Run Drive
Falls Church, VA   22042   703-241-2030
                                     800-342-4336
                              FAX: 703-536-9540

M.L. Hartogs

This video features the life and importance of Louis Braille. Vision-impaired performers and teachers demonstrate how Braille has benefitted their lives, and how improvements are constantly being made. *$195.00*

Video

7502 Sign of the Times

Fanlight Productions
4196 Washington Street
Suite 2
Boston, MA   02131   617-469-4999
                                     800-937-4113
                              FAX: 617-469-3379
               e-mail: fanlight@fanlight.com
                        www.fanlight.com

Karen McMillen, Marketing Director

A Sign of the Times profiles a public school in the heart of Los Angeles - an American microcosm where over 300 languages are spoken, and where cultures and races collide. Fairfax High, publicized as the site of gang activity and murder, has long been a focus for bad press. But something very right is going on in this school. A Sign of the Times offers a positive example of how the American Dream and American education are still alive *$154.00*

7503 Sleeping Beauty Videotape

Gallaudet University Bookstore
11030 S Langley Avenue
Chicago, IL   60628   202-651-5488
                                     800-621-2736
                              FAX: 202-651-5489

This 30-minute tape presents the entire story of Sleeping Beauty told in American Sign Language. Includes voice over. *$29.95*

30 minutes

7504 Small Differences

Aquarius Health Care Videos
5 Powderhouse Lane
PO Box 1159
Sherborn, MA   01770
                              FAX: 508-650-4216
                 e-mail: aqvideos@tiac.net
              www.aquariusproductions.com

What happens when you give children with and without disabilities a camera and ask them to produce a video about disabilities? The result is an uplifting, award-winning disability video that both children and adults can relate to. The kids interviewed adults and children with physical and sensory disabilities. A top-quality production that increases understanding and awareness. Winner, Columbus International Film & Video Festival. Winner, National Education Media Network. Preview option availabe *$110.00*

Video

7505 Social Skills on the Job

AGS
Publishers Building
PO Box 99
Circle Pines, MN   55014
                                     800-328-2560
                              FAX: 612-786-9007
                                 www.agsnet.com

Macro Systems, Inc., author
Robert Zaske, Market Manager

Gives students a realistic picture of what's expected of them at work and models appropriate behavior on the job through a variety of videos and software. *$259.95*

7506 Someday's Child

Educational Productions
9000 SW Gemini Drive
Beaverton, OR 97008   503-644-7000
                                            800-950-4949
                                   FAX: 503-350-7000
                        e-mail: custserv@edpro.com
                               www.edpro.com

Linda Freeman, President/Co-Owner
Daylene Crudo, Director of Marketing
Crystal Crowder, Marketing Assistant

This video focuses on three families' search for help
and information for their children with disabilities.
$250.00

7507 Something Magical

Educational Productions
9000 SW Gemini Drive
Beaverton, OR 97008   503-644-7000
                                   800-950-4949
                          FAX: 503-350-7000
                e-mail: custserve@edpro.com
                       www.edpro.com

Linda Freedman, President/Co-Owner
Daylene Crudo, Director of Marketing
Crystal Crowder, Marketing Assistant

In 1984 two teachers and one music therapist decided
that a collaboration between their two schools would
be mutually beneficial. The result is recorded in this
heart-warming documentary.

7508 Sound & Fury

Aquarius Health Care Videos
5 Powderhouse Lane
PO Box 1159
Sherborn, MA 01770   508-651-2296
                                   888-440-2963
                          FAX: 508-650-4216
                e-mail: aqvideos@tiac.net
                www.aquariusproductions.com

Leslie Kussmann, President/Producer

This film takes viewers inside the seldom seen world
of the deaf to witness a painful family struggle over
a controversial medical technology called the cochlear implant. Some of the family members celebrate the implant as a long overdue cure for deafness
while others fear it will destroy their language and
way of life. This documentary explores this seem-
ingly irreconcilable conflict as it illuminates the ongoing struggle for identity among deaf people today.
$195.00

Video

7509 Sound and Fury

Aquarius Health Care Videos
5 Powderhouse Lane
PO Box 1159
Sherborn, MA 01770   508-651-2963
                          FAX: 508-650-4216
                e-mail: aqvideos@tiac.net
                www.aquariusproductions.com

Leslie Kussmonn, President

This film takes viewers inside the seldom seen world
of the deaf to witness a painful family struggle over
a controversial medical technology called the cochlear implant. Some of the family members celebrate the implant as a long overdue cure for deafness,
while others fear it will destroy their language and
way of life. This documentary explores this seem-
ingly irreconcilable conflict as it illuminates the ongoing struggle for the identity among deaf people
today. Preview option available. *$195.00*

7510 Special Children/Special Solutions

Option Institute and Fellowship
2080 S Undermountain Road
Sheffield, MA 01257   413-229-8727
                                   800-562-7171
                          FAX: 413-229-8727
                e-mail: indigo@option.org
                       www.optionindigo.com

Samahria (Suzi) Lyte Kaufman, author
Kate Wilde

This four-tape audio series presents concrete, down-
to-earth, no-nonsense alternatives which are full of
love and acceptance for the special child while being
wholly supportive of parents, professionals and helpers who want to reach out. The accepting (nonjudgmental) attitude presented is the basis of all
Samahria's work and is the foundation for the nurturing teaching process that has encouraged and helped
parents, children and others to accomplish more than
most would have believed. *$55.00*

Audio tapes

7511 Special Education Cassette Recording

LifeWay Christian Resources Southern Baptist
Conv.
127 9th Avenue North
Nashville, TN 37234   615-251-2000
                                   800-458-2772
                e-mail: specialed@lifeway.com
                       www.lifeway.com

Ellen Beene, Editor

This annual audiocassette features the 12 unit songs
suggested for a special education Sunday school curriculum. *$15.00*

Yearly

7512 Stay Tuned

Fanlight Productions
4196 Washington Street
Suite 2
Boston, MA 02131   617-469-4999
                                 800-937-4113
                        FAX: 617-469-3379
                e-mail: fanlight@fanlight.com
                       www.fanlight.com

Karen McMillen, Marketing Director

This program looks at ways of coping with hearing
loss. The program introduces us to one woman who,
after suffering a mid-life hearing loss, confronts her
situation and regains her ability to function and enjoy
her life through taking advantage of hearing aids,
speech reading instruction, assistive listening devices and the support of other hearing impaired people. *$99.00*

7513 Stuttering & Your Child: A Videotape for Parents

Stuttering Foundation of America
3100 Walnut Grove Road, Suite 603
PO Box 11749
Memphis, TN 38111   901-452-7343
                              800-992-9392
                         FAX: 901-452-3931
                    e-mail: stutter@vantek.net
                         www.stuttersfa.org

Anne Edwards, Coordinator
  $10.00

7514 TERI

3225 Roymar Road
Oceanside, CA 92054

A private, nonprofit corporation which has been developing and operating programs for individuals with developmental disabilities since 1980. Offers staff training videos, staff training tools and technique manuals.

7515 Teaching People with Developmental Disabilities

Research Press
PO Box 9177
Champaign, IL 61826   217-352-3273
                               800-519-2707
                          FAX: 217-352-1221
                e-mail: rp@researchpress.com
                        www.researchpress.com

Russell Pence, V P Marketing
Hands-on video training series designed to help teachers, staff, volunteers, or family members master four behavioral techniques vital to teaching functional living skills. The videotapes which provide clear and simple teaching demonstrations, are designed to be stopped and started frequently to allow time for viewer response. Each tape includes numerous scenes of training sessions in which teachers and staff are shown working with individual students. *$595.00*

  Video

7516 Technology for the Disabled

Landmark Media
3450 Slade Run Drive
Falls Church, VA 22042   703-241-2030
                                  800-342-4336
                             FAX: 703-536-9540

M.L. Hartogs
Physically disabled people cope with the frustrations of a body they cannot control. The computer age has made many disabled more self-reliant; armless feed themselves, the blind read newspapers and the voiceless speak through marvelous technological breakthroughs. *$195.00*

  Video

7517 Telling Stories

Harris Communications
15159 Technology Drive
Eden Prairie, MN 55344   612-906-1180
                                  800-825-6758
                             FAX: 612-906-1099
                   e-mail: mail@harriscomm.com
                           www.harriscomm.com
William Moses, author
Bill Williams, National Sales Manager

This international, award winning play, now on video, uses the symbols and myths drawn from the struggles between the world of the deaf and the world of the hearing. *$59.95*

  Video

7518 Theatre Without Limits

VSA arts of Maine
PO Box 4002
Portland, ME 04101   207-761-3861
                         FAX: 207-761-4740

David C. Webster, Executive Director

This video demonstrates how to make theatrical performances accessible to people who are blind, deaf, or who have other disabilities.

7519 They Don't Come with Manuals

Fanlight Productions
4196 Washington Street
Suite 2
Boston, MA 02131   617-469-4999
                            800-937-4113
                       FAX: 617-469-3379
               e-mail: fanlight@fanlight.com
                       www.fanlight.com

Karen McMillen, Marketing Director

The parents and adoptive parents in this video speak candidly of their day to day experiences caring for children with physical and mental disabilities. *$145.00*

7520 They're Just Kids

Aquarius Health Care Videos
5 Powderhouse Lane
PO Box 1159
Sherborn, MA 01770   508-651-2963
                              888-440-2963
                         FAX: 508-650-4216
                   e-mail: aqvideos@tiac.net
                   www.aquariusproductions.com

Leslie Kussmann, President/Producer

The importance and value of inclusion, excellent for anyone working with kids with disabilities. The documentary explores the advantages of the inclusion of disabled children in the classroom, cub scouts and other extracurricular activities. *$99.00*

  Video cassette

7521 Three R's for Special Education: Rights, Resources, Results

Brookes Publishing
PO Box 10624
Baltimore, MD 21285   410-337-9580
                            800-638-3775
                       FAX: 410-337-8539
e-mail: custserv@brookespublishing.com
www.brookespublishing.com

This is a guide for parents, and a tool for educators. Through this video parents learn how to work through the steps of the special education system and work toward securing the best education and services for their children. Reviews the laws to protect children with disabilities in easy to understand language. Also provides a list of national organizations that can offer resources, information and advice to parents. *$49.95*

50-min. VHS
ISBN 0-96461-80-7

7522 Tools for Students

Aquarius Health Care Videos
5 Powderhouse Lane
PO Box 1159
Sherborn, MA 01770   508-651-2963
                       FAX: 508-650-4216
e-mail: aqvideos@tiac.net
www.aquariusproductions.com

Provides a series of 26 fun occupational therapy sensory processing activities. Designed as an in-home, in-workshop, and in-class exercise leader with students. Activities include: Strenghten the muscles necessary for normal activities, provide the muscles necessary to enhance alertness and concentration, increase the ability to use good posture, help social skills and fitting in and increase coordination; concludes with emphasis on team collaboration between the student, teacher, and parents. *$99.00*

Video Cassette

7523 Tools for Teachers: Practical Strategies f or Students with ADD, Learning Disabilties or Aut

Aquarius Health Care Videos
5 Powderhouse Lane
PO Box 1159
Sherborn, MA 01770   508-651-2963
                       FAX: 508-650-4216
e-mail: aqvideos@tiac.net
www.aquariusproductions.com

Designed to provide a beneficial overview, Tools for Teachers is ideal for in-service programs, parent education, teacher familiarization, and group discussion. Useful for an adult audience, it explains why students rock in their chairs, why a student may have so much difficulty coordinating hand movements, why untreated sensory integration deficits can bring all kinds of problems in the classroom, how inclusion can be successful, and how OT techniques can help build successful education. *$99.00*

Video Cassette

7524 Trackman: Y-Saves (Youth Substance Abuse Video Educational Series)

Michigan Association for Deaf, Hearing and Speech
2929 Covington Center
Lansing, MI 48912   517-487-0066
                           800-YOU-HEAR

Katherine Draper, Executive Director
Jody Smith, Program Director

A three part substance abuse educational video program created by the Michigan Association for Deaf, Hearing and Speech services. The program provides a stimulating format for educating youth about drugs and alcohol. This video was written and produced especially for deaf middle and high school students, but is appropriate for all youth as it includes signing, open captioning and voice overs. An extensive guide provides guidance and plenty of ideas for activities and exercises.

7525 Twitch and Shout

Fanlight Productions
4196 Washington Street
Suite 2
Boston, MA 02131   617-469-4999
                          800-937-4113
                     FAX: 617-469-3379
e-mail: fanlight@fanlight.com
www.fanlight.com

Karen McMillen, Marketing Director
Cynthia Conti, Publicity Coordinator
Laurel Chiten, Producer

This documentary provides an intimate journey into the startling world of Tourette Syndrome (TS), a genetic disorder that can cause a bizarre range of involuntary movements, vocalizations, and compulsions. Through the eyes of a photojournalist with TS, the film introduces viewers to others who have this puzzling disorder. This is an emotionally absorbing, sometimes, unsettling, and finally uplifting program about people who must contend with a society that often sees them as crazy or bad. *$275.00*

7526 Understanding ADHD

Aquarius Health Care Videos
5 Powderhouse Lane
PO Box 1159
Sherborn, MA 01770
                       FAX: 508-650-4216
e-mail: aqvideos@tiac.net
www.aquariusproductions.com

A look at some of the controversies surrounding Attention Deficit Hyperactivity Disorder. This video shows how the disorder is diagnosed and presents strategies for living with a child with the disorder. Diverse and candid opinions from teachers, social workers, a behavior specialist, a pediatrician and a parent with ADHD twins. Recommended for child development students, social workers, and caregivers. Preview option available. *$120.00*

Video

7527 Understanding Allergic Reactions

American Academy of Allergy, Asthma and Immunology
611 E Wells Street
Milwaukee, WI 53202   414-272-6071
800-822-2762
FAX: 414-272-6070
e-mail: info@aaaai.org
www.aaaai.org

During an allergic reaction, your body responds to a substance generally considered harmless to most people. This video portrays what happens in you body's immune system during an allergic reaction, how to avoid allergic substances, and methods your allergist uses to treat your allergies. *$25.00*

10-13 Minutes

7528 Understanding Attention Deficit Disorder

C.A.C.L.D.
25 Van Zant Street
Suite 15-5
East Norwalk, CT 06855   203-838-5010
FAX: 203-866-6108
e-mail: CACLD@JUNO.com
www.CACLD.org

Simsom Epstein,MD, author

A video in an interview format for parents and professionals providing the history, symptoms, methods of diagnosis and three approaches used to ease the effects of attention deficit disorder. Published by Connecticut Association for Children & Adults with Learning Disabilities (CACLD). *$20.00*

45 minutes

7529 Understanding Autism

Fanlight Productions
4196 Washington Street
Suite 2
Boston, MA 02131   617-469-4999
800-937-4113
FAX: 617-469-3379
e-mail: fanlight@fanlight.com
www.fanlight.com

Karen McMillen, Marketing Director

This program explores some basic components of a behavioral analysis approach to educating individuals with autism. After giving an introduction to the disability, the program goes on to illustrate the principles of reinforcement, teaching methods and data collection and analysis, as well as outlining the philosophy behind using behavior modification techniques with children with autism. *$195.00*

7530 Understanding Learning Disabilities

Aquarius Health Care Videos
5 Powderhouse Lane
PO Box 1159
Sherborn, MA 01770

FAX: 508-650-4216
e-mail: aqvideos@tiac.net
www.aquariusproductions.com

This video explains various learning disabilities that may effect many areas - language, reading, math skills, and behavior. Attention Deficit Disorder is gaining a lot of press these days and here we see the link between it and other disorders. Teaching children new ways to overcome their disability is shown in a how-to method. Preview option available. *$125.00*

Video

7531 Video Guide to Disability Awareness

Aquarius Health Care Videos
5 Powderhouse Lane
PO Box 1159
Sherborn, MA 01770

FAX: 508-650-4216
e-mail: aqvideos@tiac.net
www.aquariusproductions.com

President Clinton opens and concludes this informative video about disability awareness. A series of candid interviews with people who have a wide range of disabilities provide personal insights into the issues surrounding visual, hearing, physical and mental disabilities. Video comes with written reference guide and is also available with open or closed captioning. Preview option available. *$195.00*

Video

7532 Video Intensive Parenting

Systems Unlimited/LIFE Skills
1556 S 1st Avenue
Iowa City, IA 52240   319-338-9212

Ginny Kirschling, Public Info. Spec.
Geoffrey Lauer, Program Director

Parents who have children with special needs share their reactions to their child's diagnosis and how they have learned to cope with their feelings. *$69.95*

7533 Video Services - Captioning and Audio Description

Access-USA
PO Box 160
Clayton, NY 13624

800-263-2750
e-mail: info@access-usa.com
www.access-usa.com

Deborah Haight

Video services inclide open and/or closed captioning, subtitling, and audio descrption. Language versioning available. Accommodate all international and tape formats.

7534   Vital Signs: Crip Culture Talks Back

Fanlight Productions
4196 Washington Street
Suite 2
Boston, MA   02131   617-469-4999
                                   800-937-4113
                         FAX: 617-469-3379
              e-mail: fanlight@fanlight.com
                      www.fanlight.com

Karen McMillen, Markrting Director
Cynthia Conti, Publicity Coordinator

This edgy, raw video documentary explores the politics of disability through the performances, debates and late-night conversations of artists at a recent national conference of disabilities and the art's. Vital Signs conveys the intensity, variety and vitality of disability culture today. *$225.00*

Video cassette

7535   We're Not Stupid

Aquarius Health Care Videos
5 Powderhouse Lane
PO Box 1159
Sherborn, MA   01770
                         FAX: 508-650-4216
              e-mail: aqvideos@tiac.net
              www.aquariusproductions.com

The U.S. Department of Education has estimated that up to five percent of students have problems in school because of attention deficit disorders. These kids often are impulsive and angry. They hear throughout their schooling what not to do, but not what to do. I know because I was diagnosed in high school with mild dyslexia and ADD. This film is about people discussing what their lives were like having learning problems. $125.00

Video

7536   What About Me?

Educational Productions
9000 SW Gemini Drive
Beaverton, OR   97008   503-644-7000
                                   800-950-4949
                         FAX: 503-350-7000
              e-mail: custserve@edpro.com
                      www.edpro.om

Linda Freedman, President/Co-Owner
Daylene Crudo, Director of Marketing
Crystal Crowder, Marketing Assistant

This video focuses on two siblings of children with disabilities. The siblings (Brian and Julie) share their perspectives, their worries, concerns and victories about living with a sibling with a disability.

7537   What Can Baby Hear?: Auditory Tests and Interventions for Infants with Multiple Disabilities

Brookes Publishing
PO Box 10624
Baltimore, MD   21285   410-337-9580
                                   800-638-3775
                         FAX: 410-337-8539
         e-mail: custserv@brookespublishing.com
                  www.brookespublishing.com
Deborah Chen, Ph.D., author

This video and accompanying booklet explain the principles and methods of various auditory tests designed for early detection and teach viewers how to assess infants' auditory needs to begin appropriate intervention. *$45.00*

30-min VHS 1997
ISBN 1-557662-88-6

7538   What School Personnel Should Know About Asthma

American Lung Association
1740 Broadway
New York, NY   10017   212-315-8700

Professionally produced videotape discussing the triggers, symptoms and management of childhood asthma.

Videotape

7539   When Billy Broke His Head...and Other Tales of Wonder

Fanlight Productions
4196 Washington Street
Suite 2
Boston, MA   02131   617-524-0980
                                   800-937-4113
              e-mail: fanlight@fanlight.com
                      www.fanlight.com

Elena Cambio

When Billy Golfus, an award-winning journalist, became brain damaged as the result of a motor scooter accident, he joined the ranks of the 43 million Americans with disabilities, this country's largest and most invisible minority. He helped create this video, which blends humor with politics and individual experience with a chorus of voices, to explain what it is really like to live with a disability in America. #136 *$195.00*

ISBN 1-57295 -36-2

7540   When I Grow Up

Britannica Film Company
345 4th Street
San Francisco, CA   94107   415-777-9876

Alan P. Sloan, author

At a costume party each child was to come as what they wanted to be when they grew up. Some of the children had handicaps, and they talked about why their handicaps would not prevent them from fulfilling their desires.

Films

7541   When Parents Can't Fix It

Fanlight Productions
4196 Washington Street
Suite 2
Boston, MA   02131   617-469-4999
                                   800-937-4113
                         FAX: 617-469-3379
              e-mail: fanlight@fanlight.com
                      www.fanlight.com

Sharon Thomson & Dr. Virginia Cruz - Producers, author
Karen McMillen, Marketing Director
Cynthia Conti, Publicity Coordinator

This documentary looks at the lives of five families who are raising children with disabilities - the problems they face, how they have learned to cope, & the rewards & stresses of adapting to their child's condition. It explores the medical complexities & financial pressures families encounter, the emotional & physical toll on parents & siblings, & the dangers of child abuse in this population. It offers a very realistic look at different family strengths and coping styles. *$245.00*

7542 When the Brain Goes Wrong

Fanlight Productions
4196 Washington Street
Suite 2
Boston, MA 02131   **617-524-0980**
                              800-937-4113
        e-mail: fanlight@fanlight.com
                www.fanlight.com

Elena Cambio, Contact

An extraordinary and provocative series of seven short films which profile individuals with a range of brian dysfunctions. The seven brief segments focus on schizophrenia, manic depression, epilepsy, head injury, headaches and addiction. In addition to the personal stories, the segments include interviews with physicians who speak briefly about what is known about the disorders and treatment. #131 *$245.00*

ISBN 1-572951-31-1

7543 Why My Child

                              800-313-ABDC
                        www.birthdefects.org

A 9 1/2 minute video that explores the feelings every parent has when their child is born with a birth defect. Emmy-award-winning producer, Karen Dorsett, has created a compelling video that begins with the parents' question, why my child? Follows through to concerns about links between birth defects and environmental exposures to drugs, pesticides, dioxin, radiation, hazardous wastes, etc. *$25.00*

7544 Why Won't My Child Pay Attention?

Western Psychological Services
12031 Wilshire Boulevard
Los Angeles, CA 90025   **310-478-2061**
                                  800-648-8857
                            FAX: 310-478-7838

Samuel Goldstein, PhD, author

Practical and reassuring videotape, noted child psychologist tells parents about two of the most common and complex problems of childhood: inattention and hyperactivity. *$49.50*

Video

7545 Without Pity

Aquarius Health Care Videos
5 Powderhouse Lane
PO Box 1159
Sherborn, MA 01770   **508-651-2963**
                          FAX: 508-650-4216
              e-mail: aqvideos@tiac.net
            www.aquariusproductions.com

This HBO documentary, narratd by Christopher Reeve, celebrates the eggorts of the disabled to live full, productive lives. We meet a cross section of Americans. A young woman with cerebral palsy cares for her baby, while a man with cerebral palsy lives successfully on his own after forty years in an institution. We go to tschool with a remarkable 6-year-old without arms or legs, visit the workplace of a blind computer expert and meet a professor with polio. Preview option is available. *$129.00*

Video cassette

7546 Withstanding Ovation

Aquarius Health Care Videos
5 Powderhouse Lane
PO Box 1159
Sherborn, MA 01770   **508-651-2963**
                          FAX: 508-650-4216
              e-mail: aqvideos@tiac.net
            www.aquariusproductions.com

Profiles two dynamic young people, Peaches and Daniel, who were born with severe congenital lim deformities; spent much of their time as children in hospitals learning to use mechanical prostheses to aid them in their daily activities. Despite the training however, both shed the devices and mastered active and creative lives with only a minimal reliance on their prostheses. Encourages health care providers to view their occupational therapy and rehabilitation patients as people with abilities. *$195.00*

Video cassette

7547 Work Sight

Lighthouse Industries/Publications Department
370 Starke Road
Carlstadt, NJ 07072   **201-896-1112**
                                800-334-5497
              e-mail: info@lighthouse.org

Intended for employers and employees who have concerns about vision loss and job performance. *$25.00*

7548 World Through Their Eyes

Lighthouse Industries/Publications Department
370 Starke Road
Carlstadt, NJ 07072   **201-896-1112**
                                800-334-5497
              e-mail: info@lighthouse.org

Intended to help nursing home staff understand how residents with impaired vision perceive the world. Concrete suggestions help staff provide better care to visually impaired residents. *$25.00*

7549 You're in Charge: Teens with Asthma

Asthma and Allergy Foundation of America
1125 15th Street NW
Suite 502
Washington, DC 20005 202-466-7643
FAX: 202-466-8940
e-mail: info@aafa.org
www.aafa.org

Designed for young adults dealing with the daily challenges of asthma management. Teens share their experiences and use of peak flow meters and prescribed medications. *$20.00*

10 minutes

Web Sites

7550 Abledata

800-227-0216
disabilities.about.com/health/disabili

Premier source for information on assistive technology.

7551 Ablewear Aids for Daily Living

www.ableware.com

Quality products to achieve independence in performing daily living activities.

7552 Academy for Educational Development

www.aed.org

Committed to addressing human development needs in the United States and throughout the world.

7553 Access Unlimited

e-mail: webmaster@accessunlimited.com
accessunlimited.com

Adaptive transportation and mobility equipment for people with disabilities.

7554 Ai Squared

www.aisquared.com

Leaders in low vision software.

7555 Alternatives in Education for the Hearing Impaired (AEHI)

www.aehi.org

AEHI fosters literacy and empowers people with hearing impairments to achieve their full potential through unique educational options.

7556 American Academy of Audiology

www.audiology.org/conshome.htm

7557 American Association of People with Disabilities

www.aapd.com

Non-profit, non-partisan, cross-disability, national membership organization whose goals are unity, leadership and impact. AAPD's mission is to advance the economic and political power of all people with disabilities.

7558 American Botanical Councial

512-331-8868

www.herbalgram.org

Conducts research and provides education on the safe, responsible and scientific uses of medicine herbs to the public, healthcare professionals, government, industry, and the media.

7559 American College of Rheumatology Research and Education Foundation

1800 Century Place
Suite 250
Atlanta, GA 30345 404-633-3777
FAX: 404-633-1870
e-mail: ref@rheumatology.org
www.rheumatology.org

Arthritis afflictsone in every seven Americans. Your gift supports research, investigates the causes, improves treatment and works toward the prevention and cure of arthritis.

7560 American Liver Foundation

75 Maiden Lane
Suite 603
New York, NY 10038 973-256-2550
800-465-4837
www.liverfoundation.org

Is the only national voluntary health organization dedicated to preventing, treating, and curing hepatitis and other liver and gall bladder diseases through research and education.

7561 American Mobility Personal Mobility Solutions

e-mail: info@americanmobility.com
www.americanmobility.com

Source of Pride Scooters, Jazzy Power Chairs, personal mobility vehicles, and lift and recline chairs.

7562 American Speech-Language and Hearing Association

www.asha.org

7563 Americans with Disabilities Act ADA Home Page

www.usdoj.gov

Provides facts on the Americans with Disabilities Act and other information relating to disability rights.

7564 Appliance 411

appliance411.com

A guide to remodeling and appliances for people with disabilities.

7565 Arc of the United States

1010 Wayne Avenue
Suite 650
Silver Spring, MD   20910   301-565-3842
                                  FAX: 301-565-5342
                                  e-mail: info@thearc.org
                                  www.http://thearc.org

National organization of and for people with mental retardation anad thier families.

7566 Assist.com

www.assist.com

Assistive technology web resource.

7567 Assistive Technology Disabilities

www.netins.net

Provides information on assistive technology.

7568 Association for the Cure of Cancer of the Prostate
                                  310-458-2873

e-mail: hsoule@capcure.org
www.capcure.org.il

CURE is a nonprofit public charity that is dedicated to supporting prostate cancer research and hastening the conversion of research into cures or controls.

7569 Asthma and Allergy Foundation of America
                                  202-466-7643

www.aafa.org

Supports research to cure asthma and allergies and helps sufferers through patient education, practical advice, and a nationwide chapter and support group network.

7570 Audiology Foundation of America

www.audfound.org

Commited to fostering the education and training of audiologists to meet the needs of the public, especially those with impaired hearing.

7571 Auditory-Verbal International

www.auditory-verbal.org

7572 Beebe Center

www.beebecenter.org

At the Beebe center our mission is to help hearing-impaired children to listen and talk.

7573 Cancer Biotherapy Research Group
                                  888-791-6393

www.cbrg.org

Cancer patients receive promising treatments in their communities through a nationwide research network of physicians and hospitals. All contributions are used to fund clinical research.

7574 Cancer Immunology Research Foundation

8383 Wilshire Boulevard
Suite 337
Beverly Hills, CA   90211   310-724-5333
                                  800-867-2279
                                  FAX: 310-858-1474
                                  e-mail: concern@cwix.com
                                  www.cancer-research.org

Immunology research will discover why the immune system fails and cancer develops. Herein lies the cure for cancer, AIDS, and other autoimmune diseases.

7575 Cancer Immunotherapy and Gene Therapy Institute
                                  619-450-5990

www.skcc.org

Researches effective, non-toxic therapies for cancer. Accelerates taking promising discoveries from the laboratories to clinics to treat people victimized by cancer. Treatments given at no charge.

7576 Cancer Research Fund of Damon Runyon - Walter Winchell Foundation

675 Third Avenue
New York, NY   10017   877-7CA-NCER

e-mail: crfinfo@cancerresearchfund.org
www.cancerresearchfund.org

Goal is to cure cancer. 100% of your gift funds research. With 49 Runyon-Winchell scientists who have won Nobel Prizes, chances are good.

7577 Disability Information and Resources

www.eskimo.com

7578 Disability Mall

www.disabilityproducts.com

Online directory committed to featuring information on disability and medical products, resources and services, with over 2,500 links including over 400 companies for one-stop shopping convenence.

7579 Disability Net

www.disabilitynet.co.uk

The internet resource for disabled people that offers the latest news and events.

7580 Disability Rights Activist

www.disrights.org

Provides information to enable anyone intersted in the rights of disabled people to work for those rights.

7581 DisabilityResources.org

www.disabilityresources.org

Provides information on disability-related material on the Web.

7582 Discover Technology

discovertechnology.com

Provides links to websites that are specifically geared toward persons with disabilities who have special interest in adaptive technology.

7583 Dynamic Living

888-940-0605
www.dynamic-living.com

Kitchen products, bathroom helpers, and unique daily living products that provide a convienient, comfortable, and safe environment for people with disabilities.

7584 Federal Resource Center for Special Education

www.dss.org

7585 Foundation Fighting Blindness

888-394-3937

www.blindness.org

Largest voluntary, non-government sponsor to cure retinitis pigmentosa (RP), macular degeneration and related inherited disorders—leading causes of blindness and deaf-blindness.

7586 Freedom Scientific

www.hj.com

Assistive technology for blind and visually impaired computer users.

7587 Gallaudet University Press

www.gallaudet.edu

Kendall Green

Source for titles on deafness and deaf related subjects.

7588 Glaucoma Research Foundation

415-986-3162

www.glaucoma.org

Protecting both sight and independence for those with glaucoma, by providing improved treatments and education today and by leading research towards a cure for tomarrow.

7589 Herb Research Foundation

1007 Pearl Street
Suite 200
Boulder, CO   80302   303-449-2265
                                   800-748-2617
                              FAX: 303-449-7849
                           e-mail: info@herbs.org
                                   www.herbs.org

Research and public education on the health benefits of medicinal plants. Dedicated to world health through the informed use of herbs.

7590 Hypokalemic Periodic Paralysis Resource Page

e-mail: editor@calexplorer.com
www.calexplorer.com/ushkpp.html

Provides understandable information on HKPP, dynamia linkage to several additional sources of helpful information on the Internet, and offers several online networking opportunities.

7591 Innovation Management Group

22311 Ventura Boulevard
Suite 104
Woodland Hills, CA   91364   818-346-3581
                                   800-889-0987
                              FAX: 877-464-7763
                        e-mail: info@imgpresents.com
                                   www.imgpresents.com

Jerry Hussong, VP Sales

US and international onscreen keyboards, Word Prediction, Switch Scanning, Hover and Dwell, Joystick emulation, and Magnification software programs.

7592 Interstitial Cystitis Association

51 Monroe Street
Suite 1402
Rockville, MD   91364   301-610-5300
800-435-7422
FAX: 301-610-5308
e-mail: icamail@ichelp.org
www.ichelp.com

Providing information, support and assistance to the patients of Interstitial Cystitis, a highly debilitating bladder disease. We'll find a cure by funding and encouraging research.

7593 LDOnLine

www.ldonline.org

The interactive guide to learning disabilities for parents, teachers, and children.

7594 Learning Disabilities Association of America (LDA)

e-mail: ldanatl@usaor.net
www.ldanatl.org

Our purpose is to advance the education and general welfare of children and adults of normal or potentially normal intelligence who manifest disabilities of a perceptual, conceptual, or coordinative nature.

7595 Lyme Disease Foundation

One Financial Plaza
18th Floor
Hartford, CT   06103   860-525-2000
800-886-5963
FAX: 860-525-8425
e-mail: lymefnd@aol.com
www.lyme.org

Provides critical information about tick-borne disease prevention, improves healthcare and funds research for solutions. 500,000 children, adults, and professionals assisted 25 countries.

7596 Mainstream Online Magazine of the Able-Disabled
619-234-3138

e-mail: webmaster@mainstream-mag.com
www.mainstream-mag.com

The leading news, advocacy and lifestyle magazine for people with disabilities.

7597 Med-Sell

medsell.com

Helps people buy and sell new and previously owned medical equipment and find accessible housing.

7598 Medem Network Societies American Academy of Opthamology

www.medem.com

Physician web site service empowered by the leading medical specialty societies.

7599 Microsoft Accessibility Technology for Everyone

eumicrosoft.com

Information about accessibility features and options included in Microsoft products.

7600 MossRehab ResourceNet

www.mossresourcenet.org

Accessible travel, disability fact sheets, ADA, newsgroups, search tools.

7601 Multiple Sclerosis National Research Institute

3550 General Atomics Court
San Diego, CA   92121   858-455-3712
FAX: 858-455-3804
e-mail: ms-research@ms-national-research.org
www.ms-national-research.org

Conducts research for development of a vaccine to halt progression of mutiple sclerosis. Initial patient trials show promising results. Help us find a cure soon.

7602 National Alliance of the Disabled (NAOTD)

www.naotd.org

Premier source for information on assistive technology.

7603 National Association for Visually Handicapped

www.navh.org

Works with millions of people worldwide in dealing with the difficulties of vision impairment.

7604 National Brain Tumor Foundation

414 Thirteenth Street
Suite 700
Oakland, CA   94612   510-839-9777
800-934-2873
FAX: 510-839-9799
e-mail: nbtf@braintumor.org
www.braintumor.org

Brain tumors strike children and adults in the prime of life. Your support gives help and gives hope by funding research and patient support services.

7605 National Business & Disability Council

www.business-disability.com

Works toward furthering the intersts of business and people with disabilities.

7606 National Organization on Disability

www.nod.org

7607 National Rehabilitation Center

www.naric.com

Serves both professionals and the general public intersted in disability and rehabilitation.

7608 National Women's Health Information Center

800-994-WOMA
www.4women.gov

Provides information for women with disabilities, health professionals, researchers, and caretakers.

7609 NeuroControl Corporation

www.neurocontrol.com

Helps people with spinal cord injuries lead more independent lives.

7610 Osteogenesis Imperfecta (Brittle Bone) Foundation

804 West Diamond Avenue
Suite 210
Gaithersburg, MD 20878   301-947-0083
800-981-2663
FAX: 301-947-0456
e-mail: bonelink@oif.org
www.oif.org

Strives to improve the quality of life for indivduals with this brittle bone disorder through research, education, awareness, and mutual support.

7611 Quantum Technology

www.quantech.com

Provides access to information and tools for independence to serve the visually impaired and those with a learning disability.

7612 Research!America

908 King Street
Suite 400 East
Alexandria, VA 22314   703-739-2577
800-366-2873
e-mail: info@researchamerica.org
www.researchamerica.org

Builds active public support for more government and private-industry research to find treatments and cures for both physical and mental disorders.

7613 Skin and Dental Dysfunction Foundation

618-566-2020

www.nfed.org

Children left toothless from Ectodermal Dysplasia are provided dentures, support services and education. Established by National Foundation for Ectodermal Dysplasias which searches for a cure.

7614 Social Security Online

www.ssa.gov

Official website of the Social Secuirity Administration.

7615 Special Clothes for Special Children

508-896-7939

www.special-clothes.com

A catalog of adaptive clothing for children with disabilities - helping boys and girls with special needs meet the world with pride and confidence since 1987.

7616 V Foundation for Cancer Research

1201 Walnut Street
Suite 202
Cary, NC   27511   919-380-9505
800-454-6698
FAX: 919-380-0025
e-mail: info@jimmyv.org
www.jimmyv.org

Named for basketball coach and broadcaster, Jim Valvano. The V Foundation funds critical stage research conducted by young researchers at NCI approved cancer research facilities.

7617 ValueOptions

e-mail: info@valueoptions.com
www.valueoptions.com

Serves over 22 million people in behavioral healthcare through publicaly funded, federal, and commercial contracts.

7618 Wardrobe Wagon The Special Needs Clothing Store

800-WWC-ARES
e-mail: info@wardrobewagon.com
www.wardrobewagon.com

Wearing apparel for individuals with special clothing needs.

7619 We Magazine

wemagazine.com

Lifestyle magazine for people with disabilities.

7620 We Media

www.wemedia.com
Online network for people with disabilities.

7621 WebABLE

www.webable.com
Provides disability-related internet resources.

7622 WheelchairNet

www.wheelchairnet.com

7623 World Association of Persons with Disabilities

www.wapd.org
Dedicated to improving the quality of life for those with disabilities.

Alabama

7624 Lakeshore Rehabilitation Hospital
3800 Ridgeway Drive
Birmingham, AL   35209   205-868-2000
                        FAX: 205-868-2007

**7625 Mobile Infirmary Medical Center - Rotary
Rehabilitation Division**
5 Mobile Infirmary Drive
Mobile, AL   36617   334-435-3414
                   FAX: 334-435-3403
                          mimc.com

7626 Montgomery Rehabilitation Hospital
4465 Narrow Lane
Montgomery, AL   36116   334-262-5945
                        FAX: 334-288-3789

7627 North Alabama Rehabilitation Hospital
107 Governors Drive SW
Huntsville, AL   35801   256-539-2800
                        FAX: 256-535-2402

7628 UAB Spain Rehabilitation Center
1717 6th Avenue South
Birmingham, AL   35233   205-934-3360
                          800-UAB-8816
                   FAX: 205-934-5584

Sonia A. Arledge, Marketing Director

Spain offers a comprehensive approach to healing for persons challenged by stroke, spinal cord injury, arthritis, head injury, chronic pain or other disabilities resulting from illness or accident. In addition to a model facility, dedicated physicians and staff, and efficient programs tailored to meet the diverse needs of the physically challenged Spain has a wealth of resources found at the UAB Hospital, the number three health care facility in the United States.

Arizona

7629 Barrow Neurological Institute Rehab Center
350 W Thomas Road
Phoenix, AZ   85013   602-406-3000
                        FAX: 602-406-4104

Irwin Altman

7630 Health South Rehab Institute of Tucson
2650 N Wyatt Drive
Tucson, AZ   85712   520-325-1300
                          800-333-8628
                   FAX: 520-327-4045

Lora Williams, Admissions

7631 HealthSouth Rehabilitation Center
1151 S La Canada # 100
Green Valley, AZ   85614   520-625-4625
                        FAX: 520-648-5272

*Shaunna Schelin, Administrator
Greta Bame, OTR/L, Director of Marketing
Carol Altschuler, Front Office Group Coordinator*

Outpatient rehabilitation services, focus on orthopedic, sports and hand rehabilitation. Heavy industrial rehab focus. Accept all major insurances except Cigna and Pacfica.

7632 HealthSouth Rehabilitation Center of Tucson
75 N Wilmot Road
Tucson, AZ   85711   520-790-0900
                          800-476-2036
                   FAX: 520-745-0974

*Shaunna Schelin, Administrator
Greta Bame, OTR/L, Director of Marketing
Carol Altschuler, Front Office Group Coordinator*

Outpatient rehabilitation services, focus on orthopedic, sports and hand rehabilitation. Heavy industrial rehab focus. Accept all major insurances except Cigna and Pacfica.

7633 HealthSouth Rehabilitation Centers of Tuscon
7400 N Oracle
Suite 142
Tucson, AZ   85704   520-742-4822
                   FAX: 520-742-6711

*Shaunna Schelin, Administrator
Greta Bame, OTR/L, Director of Marketing
Carol Altschuler, Front Office Group Coordinator*

Outpatient rehabilitation services, focus on orthopedic, sports and hand rehabilitation. Heavy industrial rehab focus. Accept all major insurances except Cigna and Pacfica.

7634 HealthSouth Sports Medicine Center
7900 E Florentine
Prescott Valley, AZ   86314   520-772-6227
                        FAX: 520-772-1276
e-mail: chamine@wiley@healthsouth.com
                   www.healthsouth.com

Chamine Wiley, Administrator

7635 Meridian Point Rehabilitation Hospital
11250 N 92nd Street
Scottsdale, AZ   85260   602-860-0671
                        FAX: 602-860-0318

Kathleen Cahill, Admissions

7636 St. Joseph's Hospital and Medical Center

Home Care Services
2700 N Central Avenue
Suite 600
Phoenix, AZ 85004

800-279-7007

Rehabilitation programs offered by the clinic assists clients with rehabilitation health needs in the comfort of their own home. The home care rehabilitation team of professionals focuses on correcting deficiencies in self-care, mobility skills and communication. Services offered include physical therapy, occupational therapy, speech pathology, rehabilitative nursing and restorative nursing assistants.

Arkansas

7637 Central Arkansas Rehab Hospital

2201 Wildwood Avenue
Sherwood, AR 72120

501-834-6636
FAX: 501-834-2227

Randy Harris, Admissions

7638 HealthSouth Rehabilitation Hospital

1401 South J Street
Fort Smith, AR 72901

501-785-3300
FAX: 501-785-5203

Raymond Lenz, Administrator

7639 HealthSouth Rehabilitation Hospital of Jonesboro

1201 Fleming Avenue
Jonesboro, AR 72401

870-932-0440
FAX: 870-933-5157

Brenda Antwine, Administrator

Comprehensive physical rehabilitation hospital. Services include inpatient and outpatient services in Jonesboro, Newport, Paragould, Blytheville, and Pocahontas. Programs include stroke, amputee, brain injury, multiple trauma, joint replacement, spinal injury, arthritis, aquatic, pediatric, sports medicine, incontinence and balance.

7640 Northwest Arkansas Rehabilitation Hospital

153 E Monte Painter Drive
Fayetteville, AR 72703

501-444-2207
FAX: 501-444-2390

7641 Rebsamen Rehabilitation Center

1400 Braden Street
Jacksonville, AR 72076

501-982-9515
FAX: 501-985-7384

7642 St. Michael Hospital - RehabCare Unit

6th & Hazel Street
Texarkana, AR 75502

903-792-7380
FAX: 903-614-4060

California

7643 Bakersfield Regional Rehabilitation Hospital

5001 Commerce Drive
Bakersfield, CA 93309

805-323-5500
800-288-9829
FAX: 805-323-5521

Susan Golino, Admissions

7644 Brotman Medical Center - RehabCare Unit

3828 Delmas Terrace
Culver City, CA 90232

310-836-7000
FAX: 310-202-4105

Ellen Graham, Program Manager

7645 Casa Colinas Hospital for Rehabilitation Medicine

255 E Bonita Avenue
Pomona, CA 91767

909-596-5110
FAX: 714-562-0356

Sandra Chester, Administrator

7646 Cedars-Sinai Medical Center and Inpatient Rehabilitation Center

8700 Beverly Boulevard
Los Angeles, CA 90048

310-657-3360
FAX: 310-659-0235
e-mail: jurt.vaillancourt@cshs.com
www.csmc.edu

Kurt Vaillancourt MA, Intake Coordinator

A comprehensive team approach with the primary goal of helping patients achieve optimal physical functioning in their daily activities. The Center also strives to educate both the patient and the patient's family and to help them adjust emotionally and socially. The Center offers various inpatient and outpatient programs including brain injury, spinal cord injury, stroke, orthopedic and a chronic pain management program.

7647 Daniel Freeman Hospitals - Center for Diagnostic and Rehab Medicine

333 N Prairie Avenue
Inglewood, CA 90301

310-674-7050
FAX: 310-419-8365

Provides a full spectrum of rehabilitation services from sub-acute, skilled nursing, acute rehabilitation, post-acute day program for brain injury, comprehensive outpatient, home health and home/community services. Also offer pediatric rehabilitation and accept ventilator patients. The facility is CARF and JCAHO accredited and have specialized teams for each program such as brain injury, spinal cord injury, stroke/neuro and pain management. Specialized support groups are also offered.

7648 Garfield Medical Center

525 N Garfield Avenue
Monterey Park, CA 91754

626-573-2222
FAX: 626-307-2077

Shelly Hansen, Referrals

7649 Grossmont Hospital Rehabilition Center

PO Box 158
La Mesa, CA   91944   619-644-4100
                                     FAX: 619-644-4159

Clair Jonesn, Contact

7650 Holy Cross Comprehensive Rehabilitation Center

15031 Rinaldi Street N
Mission Hills, CA   91345   818-898-1628
                                     FAX: 818-898-4472

Craig Johnson, Case Manager

7651 Kentfield Rehabilitation Hospital

1125 Sir Francis Drake Boulevard
Kentfield, CA   94904   415-485-3541
                                     FAX: 415-485-3613

Susan Jensen, Liaison

7652 Laurel Grove Hospital - Rehab Care Unit

19933 Lake Chabot Road
Castro Valley, CA   94546   510-727-2755
                                     FAX: 510-727-2778

Judith Mather, Program Manager

7653 Lodi Memorial Hospital West

800 S Lower Sacramento Road
Lodi, CA   95242   209-333-3100
                                     FAX: 209-368-3745

Gary Sadler, Rehab Services

7654 Long Beach Memorial Medical Center Memorial Rehabilitation Hospital

2801 Atlantic Avenue
Long Beach, CA   90806   562-933-9000

Trish Baeseman, Administrator

The hospital offers rehabilitation after catastrophic injury of disabling disease to give patients the opportunity for maximum recovery. The Hospital offers many of the area's finest rehabilitation specialists and most advanced technology, making it one of Southern California's most respected rehabilitation centers.

7655 Los Gatos Rehabilitation Hospital

815 Pollard Road
Los Gatos, CA   95030   408-377-8000
                                     FAX: 408-866-4077

Janet Jabri, Program Admissions

7656 Meadowbrook Neurologic Center

340 Northlake Drive
San Jose, CA   95117   408-249-0344
                                     800-826-9152
                                     FAX: 408-249-5275

Mary Ligetti, Marketing

7657 Mercy American River Hospital

4747 Engle Road
Carmichael, CA   95608   916-484-2222
                                     FAX: 916-482-4203

Christine Shipman, Rehab Director

7658 North Coast Rehabilitation Center

151 Sotoyome Street
Santa Rosa, CA   95405   707-433-9600
                                     FAX: 707-525-8413

Joyce Cavagnaro, Admissions

7659 North Valley Rehabilitation Hospital

340 W E Avenue
Chico, CA   95926   530-345-9592
                                     FAX: 530-894-4139

Karen Geissinger, Admissions

7660 Northridge Hospital Medical Center

18300 Roscoe Boulevard
Northridge, CA   91328   818-885-8500
                                     FAX: 818-885-5435

Niamh Doyle, Rehab Coordinator

7661 PEERS Program

8912 W Olympic Boulevard
Beverly Hills, CA   90211   310-553-9322
                                     FAX: 310-858-8008

Dr. Paul Berns, Medical Director

Offers a new approach for wheelchair users. PEERS uses a combination of modern physical therapy, the DOUGLAS Reciprocating Gait System and when necessary, functional electrical stimulation to assist selected individuals to walk with recently patented specially made lightweight braces.

7662 Pacifica Nursing and Rehab Center

385 Esplanade
Pacifica, CA   94044   650-993-5576
                                     FAX: 650-359-9388

Bill Connell, Administrator
Lana Ronin, Director Of Admissions

68 beds offering skilled nursing and complete rehabilitation services, PT, OT, Speech and respiratory therapy, social services, nutritional services, and restorative nursing care.

7663 Providence Holy Cross Medical Center

15031 Rinaldi Street
Mission Hills, CA   91345   818-898-4561
                                     FAX: 818-898-4472

Betsy Jansen, Case Manager

7664 Queen of Angels/Hollywood Presbyterian Medical Center

1300 Vermont Avenue
Los Angeles, CA   90027   213-413-3000
                                     FAX: 323-660-0446
                  e-mail: maurine.cate@tenethealth.com
                                     www.qahpmc.com

Lu Hallam, Program Manager

7665 Queen of the Valley Hospital

1000 North Trancas Street
Napa, CA   94558   707-252-4411

                                     www.thequeen.org/

Jane Muir, Director

7666   Rancho Los Amigos National Rehabilitation Center

7601 Imperial Highway
Downey, CA   90242   562-401-7022
                               888-RAN-CHO
                               FAX: 562-803-0056
                               www.rancho.org

Consuelo C Diaz, CEO
Leslie Lynch, RN, Director of Admissions
Ann Potter, Marketing Director

Specialty programs: APR, AMP, CIR, COR, DYS, HI, MT, NPT, OT, ORT, PED, PT, RN, SS, SLP, ST, TR, VR. Credentials include: JCAHO, CARF, SCI/BI/CARF approved. Prices vary, please call for information.

7667   Rehabilitation Center at Community Hospital of Los Gatos

730 Magnolia Street
Los Gatos, CA   95032   408-866-3888
                               FAX: 408-866-4077

Modestine Fain, Program Director

7668   San Diego Rehabilitation Institute

6645 Alvarado Road
San Diego, CA   92120   619-286-7374
                               FAX: 619-229-4590
                               www.alvaradohospital.com

Provides acute and subacute level physical rehab programs specializing in brain injuries, spinal cord injuries and pulmonary/ventilator management. Outpatient programs include brain injury day treatment, pain management, visual rehabilitation and work reconditioning.

7669   San Joaquin Valley Rehabilitation Hospital

7173 North Sharon Avenue
Fresno, CA   93720   559-436-3600
                               FAX: 559-436-3688

James A. Page, Director of Marketing

Complete comprehensive rehabilitation services from acute rehab, outpatient and community fitness services.

7670   San Ramon Rehabilitation Hospital

7777 Norris Canyon Road
San Ramon, CA   94583   925-830-2943
                               FAX: 925-275-0686

Connie Lambein, Human Resource Manager

A free-standing, 80-bed physical rehabilitation facility offering acute physical rehabilitation and skilled nursing facility services. Shares a conveniently located hilltop campus with San Ramon Regional Medical Center which overlooks the city of San Ramon. San Ramon is designed to help patients achieve maximum independence and resume a rewarding life at home, work, school and in the community, or in another care giving facility. Strives to enhance each patient's quality of life.

7671   Santa Clara Valley Medical Center

751 South Bascom Avenue
San Jose, CA   95128   408-885-5000

7672   Scripps Memorial Hospital

354 Santa Fe Drive
Encinitas, CA   92024   760-753-6501
                               FAX: 760-633-7348
                               www.scrippshealth.org

7673   Scripps Memorial Hospital at La Jolla

9888 Genessee Avenue
La Jolla, CA   92037   858-457-4123
                               800-727-4777
                               FAX: 858-626-6122
                               www.scrippshealth.org

7674   Sierra Vista Regional Medical Center Rehab Unit

1010 Murray Street
San Luis Obispo, CA   93405   805-546-7782
                               FAX: 805-546-7871
                               e-mail: 388@rehabcare.com

Liz Johnston, LCSW, Social Worker
Patricia Odum, RN, Director

Acute impatient rehabilitation center. Sponsors community stroke support group. Family education and support group for families of patients with stroke, head injury or other disabilities.

7675   St. Joseph Rehabilitation Center

2200 Harrison Avenue
Eureka, CA   95501   707-445-5111
                               FAX: 707-441-4429

Sam Fallon, Admissions Liaison Nurse

Comprehensive inpatient and outpatient rehabilitation services.

7676   St. Jude Brain Injury Network

251 East Imperial Highway #440
Fullerton, CA   92835   714-449-4848
                               866-785-8332
                               FAX: 714-447-0987
                               e-mail: jgable@sif.stjoe.org

Jana Gable, Program Coordinator
David Bogdan, Service Coordinator

Provides comprehensive planning, program referral, assists with funding possibilities, and interagency coordination of services. Areas of emphasis include day treatment, vocational and housing options, and the requirements are adults who have suffered a brain injury from an external force.

7677   St. Jude Medical Center

101 E Valencia Mesa Drive
Fullerton, CA   92835   714-871-3280

                               www.stjudemc.com

A 331 bed full-service regional medical center that serves as a major referral hospital attracting rehabilitation patients throughout southern California for over twenty years.

7678 St. Mary Medical Center

1050 Linden Avenue
Long Beach, CA   90813   562-491-9000
                        FAX: 562-436-6378
                            www.smmc.com

A 556-bed hospital owned by the Sisters of Charity of the Incarnate World Healthcare Systems, one of the nation's largest Catholic healthcare networks. Services include a trauma unit, a comprehensive Cancer Care Center, complete older adult services, a Low Vision Center, a Rehabilitation Institute, an outpatient Surgi/Center and the only kidney transplant program in Long Beach. St. Mary's is a teaching hospital affiliated with the UCLA School of Medicine.

7679 St. Mary's Hospital and Medical Center Acute Rehab

450 Stanyan Street
San Francisco, CA   94117   415-750-5715
                        FAX: 415-750-4843

7680 Sunnyside Nursing Center

22617 S Vermont Avenue
Torrance, CA   90502   310-320-4130
                        FAX: 310-320-8602

John MacArthur

7681 Tustin Rehabilitation Hospital

14851 Yorba Street
Tustin, CA   92780   714-832-9200
                        FAX: 714-508-4550

Linda McCaskill, CEO

7682 UCLA Medical Center - Department of Anesthesiology, Acute Pain Services

200 Medical Plaza
Suite 660
Los Angeles, CA   90095   310-794-1841
                        FAX: 310-794-1511

Teresa Zaroda, Clinical Director

7683 White Memorial Medical Center Rehabilitation

1720 Cesar Chavez Avenue
Los Angeles, CA   90033   323-260-5841
                               800-995-4389
                        FAX: 323-260-5786

Ann Smith, Gerontologist

Strokes/neurological disorders, brain injury, musculoskeletal injuries, pulmonary disorders, developmental disorders (arthritis, cardiac rehabilitation), cleft palate, fractures, amputations, joint replacement, burns, swallowing disorders, pain and more.

Colorado

7684 Children's Hospital Rehabilitation Center

1056 E 19th Avenue
Denver, CO   80218
                        FAX: 303-861-6066

Dennis Matthews, Medical Director

7685 Hilltop Rehabilitation Hospital

1331 Hermosa Avenue
Grand Jct, CO   81506   970-243-8238
                        FAX: 970-244-6035

7686 Mapleton Center

Boulder Community Hospital
311 Mapleton Avenue
Boulder, CO   80304   303-546-6100
                               800-634-7167
                        FAX: 303-441-0484

Pat Gaddis, RN, CRRN, Rehab. Client Svcs.

Comprehensive inpatient and outpatient rehabilitation services for all age groups. Treatment provided by interdisciplinary teams and staff physicians. A warm water therapy pool, low ropes challenge course, Easy Street environment, and on-campus cottages are available. CARF accredited in brain injury rehabilitation, pediatric rehabilitation, pain management, work hardening and inpatient rehabilitation.

7687 Mediplex Rehab - Denver

8451 Pearl Street
Thornton, CO   80229   303-288-3000
                        FAX: 303-286-1253

7688 Rehabilitation Hospital of Colorado Springs

325 Parkside Drive
Colorado Springs, CO   80910   719-630-2313
                        FAX: 719-636-3772

7689 Spalding Rehabilitation Hospital

900 Potomac Street
Aurora, CO   80011   303-367-1166
                        FAX: 303-360-8208
e-mail: melissa.francis@heaalthonecares.com
                        www.spaldingrehab.com

Melissa Francis, Director Of Marketing/Volunteers

Connecitcut

7690 Mariner Health Care - Connecticut

125 Eugene Oneill Drive
New London, CT   06320   860-701-2000

District of Columbia

7691 National Rehabilitation Hospital

102 Irving Street NW
Washington, DC   20010   202-877-1152
                        FAX: 202-722-4432

Douglas Shepherd, Administrator

A private facility dedicated solely to medical rehabilitation. The hospital offers intensive inpatient programs and full-service outpatient programs.

Florida

7692 Brooks Health System

3599 University Boulevard S
Jacksonville, FL 32216   904-858-7208
800-487-7342
FAX: 904-858-7610
e-mail: rehab@brookshealth.org
www.brookshealth.org

Charles Schauer PhD, COO

A 127 bed rehabilitation hospital focused on treatment of brain and spinal cord injuries, orthopedic and neurological impairment. Treating adults and pediatrics in our hospital and outpatient networks.

7693 Florida Hospital Rehabilitation Center

601 E Rollins Street
Orlando, FL 32803   407-893-8055
FAX: 407-893-9459

Diane Lowder, Admissions Director

7694 HealthSouth Regional Rehab Center/Florida

20601 Old Cutler Road
Miami, FL 33189   305-251-3800
FAX: 305-251-0498

7695 HealthSouth Rehab Hospital - Largo

901 Clearwater Largo Road North
Largo, FL 33770   727-586-2999
FAX: 727-588-3404

Lisa Pervin, Marketing Coordinator

Inpatient Physical Rhabilitation 60 beds.

7696 HealthSouth Sports Medicine and Rehabilitation Center

2141 ALT A1A South
300
Jupiter, FL 33477   561-625-3666
FAX: 561-840-8637

Curtis Becker, PT, Administrator

Outpatient orthopedic and sports medicine/physical therapy.

7697 HealthSouth Sunrise Rehabilitation Hospital

4399 N Nob Hill Road
Fort Lauderdale, FL 33351   954-746-1501
800-648-9111
FAX: 954-746-1300

Fran Warm Hundley, RN, CEO
Dave Rafter, PR Representative

A 108-bed, JCAHO-accredited, comprehensive medical rehabilitation hospital treating patients from throughout South Florida, the Caribbean and Latin America. HEALTHSOUTH Sunrise Rehabilitation Hospital is known for its CARF-accredited specialty programs, including brain injury, spinal cord, pain management, traumatic burns, and pediatrics. Services available on inpatient and outpatient basis.

7698 HealthSouth Treasure Coast Rehabilitation Hospital

1600 37th Street
Vero Beach, FL 32960   561-778-2100
FAX: 561-567-7041

Meg McNally, Director, Business Development
Barbara Harvey, Case Management Coordinator

HSTCRH is a 90-bed inpatient comprehensive rehabilitation hospital serving Indian River, St. Lucie, Martin, and Okeechobee counties. Outpatient services are available at the hospital including physical, occupational, speech and recreational therapies as well as psychology services.

7699 Infusion Therapies

7901 SW 36th Street
Suite 206
Davie, FL 33328
800-342-3777
FAX: 954-452-4262

Specializes in fully managed enteral and parenteral therapies. Offers pharmaceuticals, supplies, pumps, equipment and delivery. Infusion cares for pediatrics to geriatrics, patients at home, in extended care facilities, clinics, physician offices, adult congregate living facilities are on site. Provides IV hydration, chemotherapy, gastric/tube feedings, lab/blood work and medical equipment and supplies.

7700 Mediplex Rehab - Bradenton

5627 9th Street E
Bradenton, FL 34203   941-753-8941
FAX: 941-756-7563

Kris Hendrix, Admissions Director

Inpatient and outpatient rehabilitation services specializing in subacute, brain injury, neurological and work reconditioning. CARF and JCAHO accredited.

7701 Miami Rehabilitation Institute

3280 Ponce De Leon Boulevard
Coral Gables, FL 33134   305-444-0909
FAX: 305-444-5760

7702 Perry Health Facility

207 Forest Drive
Perry, FL 32347   850-584-6334
FAX: 850-838-2370

Jo Ann Gnewuch, Facility Administrator
Michael Brust, Director of Rehabilitation

Full rehabilitation team available, Physiatrist, DOR, Psychiatrist, Psychologist, RD, Geriatric Nursing, PT/OT/ST/RT, Orthotiet/Prosthetist. Provider for PPO's & HMO's as well as medicare, private insurance and medicare/medicaid.

7703 Pinecrest Rehabilitation Hospital

5360 Linton Boulevard
Delray Beach, FL 33484   561-488-0050
FAX: 561-495-3082

7704 Rehabilitation Institute of Sarasota

3251 Proctor Road
Sarasota, FL 34231   941-923-4625
FAX: 941-922-6228

7705 Sea Pines Rehabilitation Hospital

101 E Florida Avenue
Melbourne, FL 32901

FAX: 407-727-7440

7706 Shriners Hospitals for Children

Shriners International Headquarters
2900 North Rocky Point Drive
Tampa, FL 33607

813-281-0300
800-237-5055
FAX: 813-281-8496
www.shrinershq.org

Michael C. Andrews, P.R. Director
Michelle Fox, Projects Manager
Sonja Monsen, Corporate Website Manager

Provide specialized acute and reconstructive burn care, orthopaedic care and spinal cord injury rehabilitation to children under 18 at absolutely no cost to the child or family. No insurance monies or government funds are sought or received. Call for application or visit our website.

7707 Shriners Hospitals for Children - Tampa

12502 Pine Drive
Tampa, FL 33612

813-972-2250
FAX: 813-975-7125

Alice Lanford, Administrator
Pediatric orthopedic.

7708 Shriners Hospitals for Children, Erie

1645 West 8th Street
Erie, PA 16505

814-875-8700
FAX: 814-875-8756
www.shrinershq.org/shc/erie/index.html

Richard W. Bruzuz, Administrator
James O. Sander, MD, Chief of Staff
Bridge Hines, Applications/Admissions Coord.

The Shriners Hospitals for Children, Erie, is a 30-bed pediatric orthopaedic hospital providing comprehensive orthopaedic care to children at no charge. The hospital is one of 22 Shriners Hospitals throughout North America. The Erie Hospital accepts and treats children with routine and complex orthopaedic and neuromuscular problems, utilizing the latest treatments and technology available in pediatric orthopaedices, resulting in early ambulation and reduced length of stay.

7709 South Miami Hospital

6200 SW 73rd Street
Miami, FL 33143

305-661-4611
FAX: 305-662-5302
www.baptisthealth.net

D. Wayne Brackin, CEO

7710 Tampa General Rehabilitation Center

PO Box 1289
Tampa, FL 33601

813-251-7000
FAX: 813-253-4283

Michael Daniels, Director
Norma Fowler, Admission Nurse
Sandra Taylor, Admission Nurse

Offers a full range of inpatient and outpatient programs all aimed at helping patients achieve their full potentials. JCAHO and CARF accredited and V.R. designated center. A wide range of inpatient and outpatient programs are available such as Brain and Spinal Cord Injury Programs, Comprehensive Medical Rehabilitation, Pain Management, Cardiac Rehab, Pediatric Therapy Service, Sleep Disorders, Epilepsy, and Wheelchair Seating.Hosts the Florida Alliance for Assistive Services and Technolgy.

7711 University of Miami - Jackson Memorial Rehabilitation Center

1611 NW 12th Avenue
Miami, FL 33136

305-325-5588
FAX: 305-585-6092

7712 West Gables Rehabilitation Hospital and Healthcare Center

2525 SW 75th Avenue
Miami, FL 33155

305-262-6800
FAX: 305-264-9031

Offers case management services, patient services, a neurological rehabilitation program, cancer rehabilitation, spinal cord injury rehabilitation, orthopedic program, functional restoration and pain management programs, as well as outpatient programs.

Georgia

7713 Bowdon Area Hospital

501 Mitchell Avenue
Bowdon, GA 30108

770-258-7207
FAX: 770-258-9627

Kathy Gunter, Program Director

7714 Candler General Hospital - Rehabilitation Unit

5353 Reynolds Street
Savannah, GA 31405

912-354-9211
FAX: 912-692-2039

Virginia Donaldson, Admissions Director

7715 Children's Healthcare of Atlanta at Egleston

1405 Clifton Road NE
Atlanta, GA 30322

404-325-6646
FAX: 404-315-2158

Tricia Easley, OTR/L, Satellite Manager

Rehabilitation Center at Egleston accepts children from birth to age 18 with acute or chronic problems. The length of rehab stay varies for each child according to the determined program of care. The center offers inpatient, outpatient & day rehab programs for comprehensive evaluation & treatment. The program emphasizes the development of the child's abilities & concentrates on helping the family & child compensate for any long-term disabilities. Short term stays require one or two weeks.

7716 Emory University Center for Rehabilitation Medicine

1441 Clifton Road NE
Atlanta, GA 30322 404-712-7593
FAX: 404-712-4746
www.emoryhealthcare.org

Sheryl Hope, Manager/Admissions & Referrals
Sara Swanson, Intake Nurse Coordinator
Karen Howard, Manager, Outpatient Services

Dedicated to restoring wholeness to a patient after experiencing a stroke, brain injury, spinal cord injury or other disabling injury or illness. Offers an entire interdisciplinary team who work with patients to help them regain or compensate for lost abilities and to adapt to the many changes in their lives. Services provide a continuum of care by offering a wide variety of inpatient/outpatient programs.

7717 Health South Central Georgia Rehabilitation Hospital

3351 Northside Drive
Macon, GA 31210 478-471-3500
FAX: 478-474-6601

Veronica L. Moseley, Director Business Development

7718 RehabCare Unit - Cobb Hospital and Medical Center

Rehab Unit - Promina/Cobb Hospital
3950 Austell Road
Austell, GA 30106 770-732-4000

7719 Shepherd Center

Shepherd Center
2020 Peachtree Street NW
Atlanta, GA 30309 404-352-2020
FAX: 404-350-7773

Gary R. Ulicny, Ph.D., President/CEO
James Shepherd, Chairman

A private hospital specializing in treatment of people with spinal cord and acquired brain injury, multiple sclerosis and other neuromuscular diseases, and urological diseases. Houses the largest model spinal cord injury program in the country and the Southeastern Multiple Sclerosis Center, designated by the National Multiple Sclerosis Society. Serving the Southeast since 1975, the 100-bed specialty hospital offers a continuum of services from intensive care through rehabilitation.

Hawaii

7720 Shriners Hospital for Crippled Children - Honolulu Unit

1310 Punahou Street
Honolulu, HI 96826

FAX: 808-951-3708

Idaho

7721 Eastern Idaho Regional Medical Center Rehabilitation Program

3100 Channing Way
Idaho Falls, ID 83404 208-529-6132
800-575-8426
FAX: 208-529-7075

CARF certified rehabilitation program in Eastern Idaho, providing acute medical rehabilitation services to patients recovering from strokes, spinal cord injury, head trauma, amputation, fractures, arthritis, multiple trauma, neurological disorders, burns, congenital deformity, generalized deconditioning, etc. The rehabilitation team consists of three psychiatrists, physical therapists, occupational therapists, speech pathologists, etc.

7722 Pocatello Regional Medical Center

777 Hospital Way
Pocatello, ID 83201 208-236-6920
FAX: 208-239-3719

Illinois

7723 Builders of Skills

9021 N Clifton Avenue
Niles, IL 60714 847-296-6783

Residential setting for hearing-impaired, developmentally disabled adults who are assisted with daily living skills.

7724 Center for Learning

National-Louis University
2840 Sheridan Road
Evanston, IL 60201

Psychoeducational evaluations for children, adolescents, and adults.

7725 Clearbrook

2800 Central Road
Rolling Meadows, IL 60008 847-870-7711
FAX: 847-870-7741
e-mail: tmartin@clearbrook.org
www.clearbrook.org

Carl M. La Mell, President
Tracy Martin, Admissions Director

Offers educational, employment and residential services to the developmentally disabled.

7726 Copley Memorial Hospital - Rehab Physical Unit

2000 Ojden Avenue
Aurora, IL 60504 630-978-6230
FAX: 630-978-6846

Mary Bailey, Director Physical Rehabilitation
Lisa Hancock, Manager, Physical Rehabilitation

7727 Illinois Center for Rehabilitation and Education (ICRE-Wood)

1151 S Wood Street
Chicago, IL 60612 312-996-1508
FAX: 312-633-3575

Residential rehabilitation center for adults who are blind or visually impaired.

7728 Institute of Physical Medicine and Rehabilitation

6501 North Sheridan Road
Peoria, IL 61614 309-692-8100
800-957-4767
FAX: 309-692-8673
www.ipmr.org

Richard Erickson, President

7729 LaRabida Children's Hospital and Research Center

E 65th and Lake Michigan
Chicago, IL 60649
FAX: 773-363-9554

Counseling, educational services, medical and nursing services for children through age 18.

7730 Marianjoy Rehabilitation Hospital and Clinics

26 W 171 Roosevelt Road
Wheaton, IL 60189 630-462-4000
FAX: 630-462-4440
www.marianjoy.org

Kathleen Yosko, President and CEO

7731 RehabLink, Affiliated with Marianjoy

26W171 Roosevelt Road
Wheaton, IL 60187 630-268-6002
FAX: 630-462-4526

LaVonne St. Amand, Sr. V.P., Business Development

7732 Rehabilitation Institute of Chicago

345 E Superior Street
Chicago, IL 60611 312-908-6000
800-354-REHA
FAX: 847-981-6854
TDY:312-908-8523

Each year more than 14,000 children and adults benefit from the full range of inpatient, outpatient, day treatment and subacute services offered by the Rehabilitation Institute of Chicago (RIC) at its 18 sites of care. Specialized treatment programs include: amputee, arthritis, brain injury, burn, general rehab, pain management and more. RIC is an academic affiliate of Northwestern University Medical School and houses the nation's largest residency program in physical medicine.

7733 Shriners Hospitals for Children

2211 N Oak Park Avenue
Chicago, IL 60707 773-622-5400
FAX: 773-385-5453
e-mail: vlwalter@earthlink.net
www.shrinerschicago.org

A. James Spang, Administrator
Paul Canham, Admissions Coordinator
Vickie Walter, Director of Public Relations

A leading Midwest children's hospital providing high quality orthopedic treatments, plastic and reconstructive surgery, and spinal chord injury care with innovative education and research, the hospital is one of 22 oporated by the Shrine fraternity, the only health care system in the U.S. funded totally through philanthropy. Any child under 18 is eligable for treatment, as long as there is a reasonable possibility that there will benefit the child.

7734 Wood River Township Hospital - RehabCare Unit

Edwardsville Road
Wood River, IL 62095 618-254-3134
FAX: 618-251-4307

Jo Anne Baker, Clinical Coordinator

Indiana

7735 Assistive Technology Through Action in Indiana

2346 S Lynhurst Drive
Suite 507
Indianapolis, IN 46241 317-486-8808
800-528-8246
FAX: 317-486-8809
e-mail: attain@attaininc.org
www.attaininc.org

Cris Fulford, Project Director

7736 Clark Memorial Hospital - RehabCare Unit

1220 Missouri Avenue
Jeffersonville, IN 47130 812-282-6631
FAX: 812-283-2656

Jan Goldhammer, Program Manager

7737 Developmental Disabilities Planning Council

143 West Market Street
Suite 404
Indianapolis, IN 46204 317-232-7770

e-mail: gpcpd@gpcpd.org
www.state.in.us/gpcpd

Suelle Jackson-Boner, Director

7738 Down Syndrome Association of North East Indiana

PO Box 80141
Fort Wayne, IN 46898 219-497-9927
877-713-7264
www.dsani.org

7739 Easter Seals Wayne/Union Counties

5632 US Highway 40 East
PO Box 86
Centerville, IN 47330 765-855-2482

e-mail: easterseals@juno.com

Pat Bowers, Executive Director

7740 IN Speechllanguage-Hearing Association

233 McCrea Street
Suite 200
Indianapolis, IN   46225   317-955-1063

e-mail: isha@in-motion.org
www.isha.org

Michael Flahive, President

7741 IN-SOURCE

809 Nosth Michigan Street
South Bend, IN   46601   219-234-7101
                                800-332-4433
e-mail: insource@insource.org
www.insource.org

Richard Burden, Executive Director

7742 Indiana Congress of Parent and Teachers

2525 N Shadeland Avenue
D-4
Indianapolis, IN   46219   317-357-5881

e-mail: www.indianapta.org
in_office@pta.org

Mary Williams, President

7743 Indiana Institute on Disability and Community

2853 East Tenth Street
Bloomington, IN   47408   812-855-6508

e-mail: uap@indiana.edu
www.iidc.indiana.edu

David M. Mank, Director

7744 Indiana Parent Information Association

4755 Kingsway Drive
Suite 105-A
Indianapolis, IN   46205   317-257-8683

e-mail: FamilyNetw@aol.com
www.ai.org/ipin

Donna Gore Olsen, Executive Director

7745 Kokomo Rehabilitation Hospital

829 N Dixon Road
Kokomo, IN   46901

FAX: 765-868-8108

Brenda Harry, Admissions Director

7746 Learning Disabilities Association of IN

PO Box 20584
Indianapolis, IN   46220

800-284-2519
e-mail: dlytle@netusal.net

Dawn Lytle, IN State President

7747 Memorial Regional Rehabilitation Center

615 North Michigan Street
South Bend, IN   46601   219-284-7903
                                FAX: 219-284-3195

Julie Fanner, Unit Director

30-bed CARF accredited inpatient rehabilitation, out-patient orthopedic clinic and work performance program, head injury clinic. Outpatient neuro rehab and TBI Day treatment program, rehab technology center and a driver education and training program are provided.

7748 Mental Health Association in Indiana

55 Monumental Circle
Suite 455
Indianapolis, IN   46204   317-638-3501
                                  800-555-6424
e-mail: mhai@indy.net
www.al.com/mhai

Stephen McCaffrey, President

7749 Methodist Hospital Rehabilitation Institute

8701 Broadway
Merrillville, IN   46410   219-738-5500
                                FAX: 219-738-6636

7750 NAMI Indiana

PO Box 22697
Indianapolis, IN   46222   317-925-9399
                                  800-677-6442
e-mail: nami-in@nami.org
www.namiindiana.org

7751 Office of State Coordinator of Vocational Education for Students with Disability

10 N Senate Avenue
Room 212
Indianapolis, IN   46207   317-232-1829

e-mail: tfields@dwd.state.in.us
www.state.in.us/dwd/techd

7752 Parkview Regional Rehabilitation Center

2200 Randallia Drive
Fort Wayne, IN   46805   219-484-6636

Elizabeth Williamson, Admissions Coord.

7753 Programs for Children with Disabilities: Ades 3 Through 5

Division of Special Education
State House, Room 229
Indianapolis, IN   46204   317-232-0567

e-mail: cochra@speed.doe.state.in.us
http://web.instate.edu/soe/iseas/dse.html

Sheron Cochran, Preschool Coordinator

7754 Programs for Children with Special Healthcare Needs

2 N Meridian Street
Section 7-B
Indianapolis, IN   46204   317-233-5578

e-mail: wgettelf@isdh.state.in.us

Wendy Gettelfinger, Director

7755 Programs for Infants and Toddlers with Disabilities: Ages Birth Through 2

402 West Washington Street
Room W-386
Indianapolis, IN 46204   317-233-9292

e-mail: mgreer@fssa.state.in.us

7756 Protection and Advocacy Agency of Indiana

4701 N Keystone Avenue
Suite 222
Indianapolis, IN 46205   317-722-5555
                                 800-838-1131
e-mail: info@ipas.state.in.us
www.state.in.us

Thomas Gallagher, Executive Director

7757 Regional ADA Technical Assitance Agency

1640 West Roosevelt Road
Chicago, IL 60608   312-413-1407
                                 800-949-4232
e-mail: gldbtac@uic.edu
www.adagreatlakes.org

Robin Jones, Project Director

7758 Riley Child Development Center

702 Barnhill Drive
Room 5837
Indianapolis, IN 46202   317-274-8167

e-mail: jdrau@child-dev.com

7759 Saint Vincent Children's Specialty Hospital

1707 West 86th Street
PO Box 40407
Indianapolis, IN 46240   317-415-5500
                            FAX: 317-415-5595

Debbie Johnson, Clinical Liaison
Diane Reeder, Case Manager

A free-standing pediatric facility providing children with the opportunity to grow physically and emotionally. SVCSA offers specialty programs in burn treatment, Cerebral Palsy, feeding disorders, juvenile rheumatoid arthritis, neuromuscular disorders, orthopedic conditions, spinal cord injuries, traumatic brain injuries, and children who require pulmonary rehab. Patients are involved with a professional interdisciplinary team, nurses, respiratory therapists, social workers and others.

7760 Spina Bifida Association of Northern IN

PO Box 1935
South Bend, IN 46634   219-234-6260

Carla Beres, Director

7761 St. Anthony Hospital - Indiana RehabCare Unit

301 W Homer Street
Michigan City, IN 46360   219-877-1586
                            FAX: 219-877-1838

Ruth Dodson, Program Manager

7762 State Blind and Visually Impaired Services Agency

402 West Washington Street
Room W-453, PO Box 7083
Indianapolis, IN 46207   317-232-1143
                                 800-962-8408
e-mail: lquarles@fssa.state.in.us
www.state.in.us/fssa/servidisabl/deaf/

Linda Quarles, Interim Deputy Director

7763 State Developmental Disability Agency

PO Box 7083
Indianapolis, IN 46207   317-323-7842

Steven C. Cook, Director

7764 State Division of Vocational Rehabilitation

402 W Washington Street, Room W453
PO Box 7083
Indianapolis, IN 46207   317-232-1319
                                 800-545-7763
e-mail: martin@fssa.state.in.us
www.state.in.us/fssa

Rita Martin, Deputy Director

7765 State Mental Health Agency

402 West Washington Street
Room W353
Indianapolis, IN 46204   317-232-7845

e-mail: jcorson@fssa.state.in.us
www.IN.gov/fssa

7766 State Mental Health Representative for Children

402 West Washington Street
Room W353
Indianapolis, IN 46204   317-232-7934

e-mail: JPhillips3@fssa.state.in.us

Jim Phillips, Chief

7767 VSA Arts of Indiana

Harrison Centre for the Arts
1505 N Delaware Avenue
Indianapolis, IN 46202   317-974-4123
                            FAX: 317-974-4124
e-mail: jnulty@vsai.org
www.vsai.org

Jim Nulty, President

7768 Wabash Valley Spina Bifida Support Group

PO Box 21
Farmersburg, IN 47850   812-696-2288

e-mail: sbawareness@hoymail.com
www.homestead.com/planetzachary/main.html

Kim Zink, Coordinator

Iowa

7769 Younker Rehabilitation Center of Iowa Methodist Medical Center

1200 Pleasant Street
Des Moines, IA 50309   515-241-6201
FAX: 515-241-5872

Fran Wendling, Admissions Coord.

Kansas

7770 Kansas Rehabilitation Hospital

1504 SW 8th Avenue
Topeka, KS 66606   785-235-6600
FAX: 785-232-8556

Julie DeJean, Administrator

7771 Mid-America Rehabilitation Hospital

5701 W 110th Street
Overland Park, KS 66211   913-491-5697
FAX: 913-491-1097

Steven Simon, MD, Medical Director

Kentucky

7772 Cardinal Hill Rehabilitation Hospital

2050 Versailles Road
Lexington, KY 40504   606-254-5701
800-888-5377
FAX: 606-255-9303
e-mail: sws@cardinalhill.org
www.cardinalhill.org

Sandy Shill, CRRN, Mgr., Referral Rel.
Beth A. Monarch, COO

CARF-accredited rehab center provides comprehensive inpatient and outpatient services in two locations to people with physical and cognitive disabilities. We provide diagnosis-specific programs to 100 inpatients, outpatient clinics, outpatient therapies, pain management and therapeutic pool services. The Pediatric Center serves children from birth to age 18 years of age.

7773 HealthSouth Rehabilitation of Louisville

1227 Goss Avenue
Louisville, KY 40217

FAX: 502-636-0351

Diane Phelps, Marketing Representative

7774 Humana Hospital - Lake Cumberland Rehab Unit

305 Langdon Street
Somerset, KY 42503   606-679-5488
FAX: 606-679-5739

Chris Lovelace, Program Manager

7775 Lakeview Rehabilitation Hospital

134 Heartland Drive
Elizabethtown, KY 42701   502-769-3100
FAX: 502-769-6870

Diane Stephens, Asst. Dir. Of Mktg.
40-beds, comprehensive physical rehabilitation.

7776 Shriners Hospitals for Children, Lexington

1900 Richmond Road
Lexington, KY 40502   606-266-2101
800-444-8314
FAX: 606-268-5636
www.shrinershq.org

Joan Snowden, Director, Family & Community Ser
A 50-bed, pediatric orthopedic hospital providing FREE, expert orthopedic medical care to children and adolescents in Kentucky, Tennessee, West Virginia, Ohio, and Indiana.

7777 Shriners Hospitals, Lexington Unit, for Crippled Children

1900 Richmond Road
Lexington, KY 40502   606-266-2101
FAX: 606-268-5636

Glenda Ross, Administrator

Louisiana

7778 HealthSouth North Louisiana Rehabilitation

1401 Ezelle Street
Ruston, LA 71270   318-251-3126
800-548-9157
FAX: 318-251-5491

7779 Our Lady of Lourdes Rehabilitation Center

611 Saint Landry Street
Lafayette, LA 70506   318-684-5732
FAX: 318-289-2681

7780 Regional Rehabilitation Center - Thibodaux Hospital

602 N Acadia Road
Thibodaux, LA 70301   504-447-5500

7781 Rehabilitation Center of Lake Charles Memorial Hospital

1701 Oak Park Boulevard
Lake Charles, LA 70601   318-494-3253
FAX: 318-494-2656

Rehabilitation center offering intensive physical, occupational, speech, neuropsychology, recreational therapies along with rehabilitation nursing.

7782 Rehabilitation Institute of New Orleans at F. Edward Herbert Hospital

1 Sanctuary Drive
New Orleans, LA 70114   504-363-2291
FAX: 504-362-7233

7783 Shriners Hospital, Shreveport Unit, for Crippled Children

3100 Samford Avenue
Shreveport, LA 71103 318-222-5704
FAX: 318-424-7610

7784 South Louisiana Rehabilitation Hospital

4040 N Boulevard
Baton Rouge, LA 70806 225-926-2549
FAX: 504-383-8021

Sharon Black, Administrator
Jan A. Moppert, Director of Planning

7785 St. Frances Cabrini Hospital - Rehab Unit

3330 Masonic Drive
Alexandria, LA 71301 318-487-1122
FAX: 318-448-6822

Judith Rozier, Program Manager

7786 St. Patrick Hospital - Rehab Unit

524 Ryan Street
Lake Charles, LA 70601 318-491-7730
FAX: 318-491-7157

Maine

7787 Head Injury Treatment Program at Brewer

74 S Road
Brewer, ME 04412

Mary Goyoi, Program Rep

7788 New England Rehabilitation Hospital of Portland

335 Brighton Avenue
Portland, ME 04102 207-775-4000
FAX: 207-879-8168

Amy Weinschenk, Referrals

Maryland

7789 Mt. Washington Pediatric Hospital

1708 W Rogers Avenue
Baltimore, MD 21209 419-578-8600
FAX: 410-542-8717

Winne Sherman, RN, Admissions Center Manager
Violet Ebbesen, RN, Admissions Nurse

7790 Sinai Rehabilitation Center

2401 West Belvedere Avenues
Baltimore, MD 21215 410-601-5631
FAX: 410-601-8284

Bonnie Hartley, Senior Field Service Nurse

Provides comprehensive inpatient and outpatient medical rehabilitation services to individuals disabled by head injury, stroke, musculoskeletal/orthopedic disorders, neurologic conditions and other medical diagnoses that impact on their functional capacity. Recognizing that many individuals have special needs, SRC has developed the following specialty programs: driver evaluation and training, electrodiagnostics, oncology, prosthetic/orthotic services, acute and post-acute brain injury services.

Massachusetts

7791 Braintree Hospital

250 Pond Street
Braintree, MA 02184 781-848-7740
800-99R-EHAB
FAX: 781-849-9949

Elizabeth Glenn, RN, BSN, CRRN, Patient Access

Since Braintree Hospital's founding in 1975, we have gained recognition as a world class health care provider. Today the Braintree Rehabilitation Network serves as the flagship hospital of Horizon Health Care, the largest independent provider of comprehensive medical rehabilitation in the world. The network consists of a growing number of rehabilitation facilities which provide both inpatient and outpatient services Programs include: amputee, general rehab, neuro rehab and stroke.

7792 Greenery Extended Care Center

59 Acton Street
Worcester, MA 01604 508-791-3147
FAX: 508-757-0423

Tom Johnsrud, Admissions

7793 Greenery Rehab Center Massachusetts

99 Chestnut Hill Avenue
Boston, MA 02135 617-787-3390
FAX: 617-787-9169

William Garvin, Medical Director

7794 Mediplex Rehabilitation Hospital

4499 Acushnet Avenue
New Bedford, MA 02745 508-588-8294
FAX: 508-998-8131

7795 New England Home for the Deaf

154 Walter Street
Danvers, MA 01923 978-774-0445
FAX: 781-337-6742

Eddy Laird, Executive Director

Offers services for the deaf, totally blind, legally blind, visually impaired, mentally retarded blind and more with health, counseling, educational, recreational, rehabilitation, computer training and professional training services.

7796 New England Rehabilitation Hospital - Massachusetts

2 Rehabilitation Way
Woburn, MA 01801 781-935-5050
FAX: 781-932-8152
www.healthsouth.com

Dianne Landy, Marketing Coordinator

7797 Shriners Burns Hospital - Boston Unit

51 Blossom Street
Boston, MA 02114 617-722-3000
FAX: 617-523-1684
www.shrinershq.org

Robert F. Bories, Jr., FACHE, Administrator
Richard W. Burgess, P.R. Director

Provides treatment for children to their 18th birthday with acute, fresh burns, plastic reconstructive surgery for patients with healed burns, severe scarring and facial deformity. Some non-burn conditions such as Scalded Skin Syndrome, Cleft Lip, Cleft Palate and purpura fulminians are also treated. Call the Institute for information. All medical treatment is without cost to the patient, parents, or any third party.

7798 Shriners Hospital - Springfield Unit - for Crippled Children

516 Carew Street
Springfield, MA 01104 413-787-2000
FAX: 413-735-1226

Michigan

7799 Community Rehabilitation Center

Community Hospital
400 Medical Park Drive
Watervliet, MI 49098 616-463-5754
800-463-1164
FAX: 616-463-6729

Sandra L. Dugal, Community Relations Coordinator
Linda Beushausen, Program Administrator

Comprehensive medical rehabilitation program in a community hospital setting, providing inpatient and outpatient services to individuals who have become physically challenged by stroke, spinal cord injuries, traumatic brain injuries, major multiple trauma, orthopedic conditions, neurologic disorders, amputation, arthritis conditions and other diagnoses.

7800 Covenant Healthcare Rehabilitation Program

515 N Michigan Avenue
Saginaw, MI 48602 989-583-2817
FAX: 989-583-2843

Marcia Fuhshop, Program Manager

7801 Farmington Health Care Center

34225 Grand River Avenue
Farmington, MI 48335 248-477-7373
FAX: 248-477-2888

7802 Flint Osteopathic Hospital - RehabCare Unit

3921 Beecher Road
Flint, MI 48532 810-762-4682

Susan Malone, Program Manager

7803 Integrated Health Services of Michigan at Clarkston

4800 Clintonville Road
Clarkston, MI 48346 248-674-0903
FAX: 248-674-3359

Carol Doll, Admissions Director
Maggy Canny, Administrator
Rose Berg, Admission

7804 Mecosta County General Hospital Rehabilitation Center

Mecosta County General Hospital
405 Winter Avenue
Big Rapids, MI 49307 616-592-4444
FAX: 616-592-4429

Beth Ann Daugherty, Program Director

Comprehensive medical rehabilitation program in a hospital setting, providing inpatient and outpatient services to individuals who have become physically challenged by stroke, spinal cord injuries, brain injuries, traumatic multiple traumas, arthritis conditions and other diagnoses.

7805 Rehabilitation Institute of Michigan

261 Mack Boulevard
Detroit, MI 48201 313-745-1203
FAX: 313-745-1175
e-mail: cangelel@dmc.org
www.RIMrehab.org

Terry Reiley, President
Cheryl Angelelli, Marketing & Public Relations

Rehabilitation Institute of Michigan is a national leader in the delivery of physical medicine and rehabilitation, and one of the country's largest freestanding rehabilitation hospitals. A comprehensive spectrum of both inpatient and outpatient services and programs are available for spinal cord injuries, brain injuries, stroke, cerebral palsy, musculoskeletal disorders, low back problems, amputations, sports injuries, work-related injuries and other medical conditions requiring physical rehab.

7806 St. John Hospital - North Shore

26755 Ballard Street
Harrison Township, MI 48045 810-465-5501

Susan Looney Smith, Intake Coordinator

7807 Three Rivers Rehabilitation Pavilion

Three Rivers Area Hospital
1111 W Broadway Street
Three Rivers, MI 49093 616-279-5224
FAX: 616-279-7375

Christine M. Strom, RN, CRRN, Program Director
Sandra L. Cooper, Community Relations

Comprehensive medical rehabilitation program in a community hospital setting, providing inpatient and outpatient services to individuals who have become physically challenged by stroke, spinal cord injuries, traumatic brain injuries, major multiple trauma, orthopedic conditions, neurologic disorders, amputation, arthritis conditions and other diagnoses.

Minnesota

7808 North Memorial Medical Center - North Rehabilitation Center

3300 Oakdale Avenue North
Minneapolis, MN 55422   612-379-4937
                                FAX: 612-520-1772
                                www.northmemorial.com

Pete Pytlak, Director
Susan Keeney, R.N.-Eval.

Inpatient unit primarily serves adults and young adults that have a physical disability as a result of TBI, SCI, CVA, multiple trauma, spinal cord dysfunction or tumors, and amputation. The interdisciplinary team approach includes the patient and family, as well as representatives from all rehab related disciplines. The program is CARF and JCAHO accredited, consisting of 24 beds.

7809 Sister Kenny Institute

800 E 28th Street
Minneapolis, MN 55407   612-863-4495
                                FAX: 612-863-8942

Helen Kettner, Nurse- Liaison

Missouri

7810 Columbia Regional Hospital - RehabCare Unit

404 Keene Street
Columbia, MO 65201   573-875-9520
                             FAX: 573-875-4417

George Gumbert, Program Manager

7811 Jewish Hospital of St. Louis - Department of Rehabilitation

216 N Kings Highway
Saint Louis, MO 63108   314-454-7390
                                FAX: 314-454-5277

Mary Mitchell, Admitting Clerk

7812 PremierCare Neurohabilitation Program of Bethesda General Hospital

3655 Vista Avenue
Saint Louis, MO 63110   314-772-9200
                                FAX: 314-772-1819

Tim Imhoff, Program Director

7813 Rusk Rehabilitation Center

315 Business Loop 70 West
Columbia, MO 65203   573-817-2703
                             FAX: 573-817-4690

Tracy Rimki, Marketing Coordinator
Patrick Lee, Hospital Administrator

A 60-bed comprehensive rehabilitation hospital. This CARF-accredited facility utilizes a multidisciplinary approach to provide inpatient and outpatient services with specialized programming in head injury, spinal cord injury and chronic pain.

7814 St. Mary's Regional Rehabilitation Center

201 W R D Mize Road
Blue Springs, MO 64014
                                FAX: 816-655-5525

Susan Bottmker, RN, Assessment Coord.

A 17-bed inpatient physical rehabilitation unit offering PT, OT, ST, recreational therapy, psychiatry and all other ancillary services of a full-service hospital. Specialize in orthopedic and neurologic disabilities.

7815 Three Rivers Health Care

2620 North Westwood Boulevard
Poplar Bluff, MO 63902   573-785-1657

Montana

7816 St. Vincent Hospital and Health Center

1233 N 30th Street
Billings, MT 59101   406-657-8778
                             FAX: 406-657-8817

John Brewer, Admission

Nebraska

7817 Madonna Rehabilitation Hospital

5401 S Street
Lincoln, NE 68506   402-489-7102
                            800-676-5448
                            FAX: 402-483-9494
                            e-mail: feedback@madonna.org
                            www.madonna.org

Kent Eichelberger, Admissions Manager
Carol Jess, Marketing/Public Relations Mgr

Nebraska's premier rehabilitation facility for children and adults, Madonna offers many services and programs. It is a place where comfort and support are offered to every patient, resident, family member and friend.

Nevada

7818 University Medical Center

1800 W Charleston Boulevard
Las Vegas, NV 89102
                                FAX: 702-383-2536

Debbie Gulo, Rehab Evaluator

New Hampshire

7819 Head Injury Treatment Program at Dover
307 Plaza Drive
Dover, NH   03820   603-742-2676
FAX: 603-749-5375

Sue Mills, Program Rep

7820 Lakeview NeuroRehabilitation Center
101 Highwatch Road
Effingham Falls, NH   03814   603-539-7451
800-4RE-HAB1
FAX: 603-539-8888
www.lakeviewsystem.com

Susan Bartlett MSW, CRC, Director of Admissions
Tina Trudel, Ph.D., VP of Clinical Services
Edward C. Morton, Jr., Executive Director
Residential treatment center serving individuals with neurologic/behavioral disorders. Lakeview serves both children and adults in functionally based program environment. Transistional programs in various group homes also available to clients as they progress in their treatment.

7821 Northeast Rehabilitation Hospital
70 Butler Street
Salem, NH   03079   603-893-2900
FAX: 603-893-1628

Ellyn Dempsey, Intake Coordinator

7822 St. Joseph New England Rehabilitation Center
172 Kinsley Street
Nashua, NH   03060   603-595-3032
FAX: 603-595-3192

Mary Beth Harney, Program Director
A 24-bed acute rehabilitation unit offering general and specialized programs. Located within St. Joseph acute care hospital and affiliated with Advantage Health Corporation.

New Jersey

7823 Betty Bacharach Rehabilitation Hospital
Jim Leeds Road
Pomona, NJ   08240   609-652-9057
FAX: 609-748-3586

Virginia Wells, Admissions

7824 Children's Specialized Hospital
150 New Providence Road
Mountainside, NJ   07092   908-233-3720
FAX: 908-233-4176

Jeannie Brooke, RN, Pre-Admission Coord.
New Jersey's only comprehensive pediatric rehabilitation hospital, treats children and adolescents from birth through 21 years of age. Programs include spinal dysfunction, brain injury, respiratory, burn, Day Hospital, early intervention, preschool, and cognitive rehabilitation.

7825 Garden State Rehabilitation Hospital
14 Hospital Drive
Toms River, NJ   08755   732-244-3100
FAX: 732-244-2542

Dave Coluzzie, Intake Coordinator

7826 JFK Johnson Rehab Institute
65 James Street
Edison, NJ   08820   732-321-7056
FAX: 732-321-0994

Patricia Dulin, Client Services

7827 Kessler Institute for Rehabilitation, Welkind Facility
Pleasant Hill Road
Chester, NJ   07930   973-584-7500
FAX: 973-252-6343

Joyce Kment, Admissions Director
Carol Waggner, Exec Secretary to Administration
Inpatient and outpatient acute rehabilitation hospital serving 72 inpatients for general rehab, head injury program and pain management program

7828 Mediplex Rehab - Camden
2 Cooper Plaza
Camden, NJ   08103   609-342-7600
FAX: 609-342-7979

Beth Crawford, Admissions

7829 Summit Ridge Center Genesis Eldercare
20 Summit Street
West Orange, NJ   07052   973-736-2000
FAX: 973-731-4582
www.ghv.com

Charlene Harn, Admissions & Marketing Director

New Mexico

7830 HealthSouth Rehabilitation Center - New Mexico
7000 Jefferson Street NE
Albuquerque, NM   87109   505-342-1992
FAX: 505-344-2851

7831 St. Joseph Rehabilitation Hospital and Outpatient Center
505 Elm Street NE
Albuquerque, NM   87102   505-727-4700
FAX: 505-727-4793
www.sjhs.org

Sherri Milone, Exective Director
A member of the four hospital, St. Joseph healthcare system, this facility provides inpatient and outpatient care for those requiring physical medicine and rehabilitation. Specialty programs include brain injury, stroke, spinal cord, orthopedics, occupational and physical therapies, clinical psychology, speech/language pathology, hand clinic and functional capacity evaluations. The only facility in New Mexico accredited in four areas by the commission on accreditation of rehab facilities.

New York

7832 Burke Rehabilitation Hospital

785 Mamaroneck Avenue
White Plains, NY 10605 914-597-2500
888-99B-URKE
FAX: 914-597-2787
e-mail: burke@burke.org
www.burke.org

Ann Herring, Marketing

A 150 bed rehabilitation hospital providing both in and out patient physical rehabilitation to people with stroke, spinal cord injury, head injury, pulmonary, cardiac, amputee, orthopedic arthritis and other related diagnoses.

7833 Rusk Institute of Rehabilitation Medicine

400 East 34th Street
New York, NY 10016 212-263-6034
FAX: 212-263-8510
www.rusknyu.org

North Carolina

7834 Cypress Point Rehabilitation and Health Care Center

2006 S 16th Street
Wilmington, NC 28401 910-763-6271
FAX: 910-763-3878
e-mail: APM-7794vencor/nc

Anita Mistrough, Program Director

7835 Horizon Rehabilitation Center

3100 Erwin Road
Durham, NC 27705 919-383-1546
800-541-7750
FAX: 919-382-0156

Maureen O'Neal, Administrator

A 125-bed rehabilitation, subacute and long term care facility. HRC is JCAHO and CARF accredited with a physician-directed rehabilitation program, internal case management and a therapy department composed of physical, occupational, speech, recreational and respiratory therapists - pulmonary rehabilitation/ventilator unit.

7836 Integrated Health Services of Durham- N

3100 Erwin Road
Durham, NC 27705 919-383-1546
FAX: 919-383-0862

Lenon McDaver, Marketing Director/ Admissions

7837 Learning Services Corporation

707 Morehead Avenue
Durham, NC 27707 919-419-9955
800-765-5327
FAX: 603-425-2176

Randall W. Evans, Ph.D., President & CEO

A licensed postacute rehabilitation program for adults who have an acquired brain injury. Individuals who are enrolled in the program participate in active, intensive rehabilitation carried out by a team of neuropsychology, speech/language therapy, physical therapy, occupational therapy, vocational services, family services and life skills training. Services include residential rehabilitation, home based treatment, day treatment, subacute rehabilitation and supported living.

Ohio

7838 Arbor Health Care Company

1100 Shawnee Road
804
Lima, OH 45805 414-271-9696
FAX: 419-227-8319

Offers various subacute facilities in Ohio, Florida, Delaware, West Virginia and Indiana.

7839 Arbors at Columbus

44 S Souder Avenue
Columbus, OH 43222 614-228-5900
FAX: 614-228-3989

Postacute rehabilitation program.

7840 Franciscan Rehabilitation Center

1 Franciscan Way
Dayton, OH 45408 937-229-6079
800-272-8042
FAX: 937-229-6074

Linda Didas, RN, CRRN, CCM, Case Manager

Acute, inpatient rehabilitation, 77 beds. Twenty-plus years serving the Dayton community. Vocational and assistive technology services are available. Extensive outpatient services include: hand therapy, back school, drivers' training. Accredited by JCAHO and CARF. Liaison with community support groups: SCI, BI, stroke, amputee, ALS, chronic pain. On-site clinics: SCI, MDA, amputee and wheelchair/seating.

7841 Great Lakes Regional Rehabilitation Center

3700 Kolbe Road
Lorain, OH 44053 440-960-3950
FAX: 440-960-4636

Roberta Yehman, Admissions Director

7842 HCR Health Care Services

1 Seagate
Toledo, OH 43604 419-321-5470
800-736-4427
FAX: 419-252-5543

Specialty transitional care and intensive rehabilitation services. Specialized services are focused on patients with catastrophic conditions or whose length of stay at an acute care or rehabilitation hospital can be dramatically reduced by transferring to a subacute level of care.

7843   Heather Hill Rehabilitation Hospital

Heather Hill
12340 Bass Lake Road
Chardon, OH   44024   440-285-9151
                             800-423-2972

Individualized treatment programs for adults and adolescents can participate in and benefit from three-plus hours a day of active therapy.

7844   Holzer Medical Center - RehabCare Center

100 Jackson Pike
Gallipolis, OH   45631   740-446-5000
                        FAX: 740-446-5904

Sharon Stout, Patient Care Manager

7845   Parma Community General Hospital RehabCare Unit

7007 Powers Boulevard
Parma, OH   44129   440-743-3000
                        FAX: 440-743-4036

Donna Courtwright, Program Director

The mission of this CARF accredited unit is to provide the most comprehensive, cost-effective, acute rehabilitation program possible in order for every patient and family to adjust to his/her disability and to achieve the maximum potential of independent functioning when returning to community living.

7846   Rehabilitation Hospital at Heather Hill

12340 Bass Lake Road
Chardon, OH   44024   440-285-9151
                        FAX: 440-285-0946
                        www.heatherhill.org

Sheila LaRosa, Admissions Coordinator

250-bed, non-profit, multi-level care facility serving the frail elderly and physiclaly disabled.

7847   Rehabilitation Institute of Ohio at Miami Valley Hospital

1 Wyoming Street
Dayton, OH   45409   937-208-2063
                        FAX: 937-208-4534

Cass Swank, RN, Rehab Coordinator

Provides inpatient rehab (39 beds), acute inpatient and outpatient physical therapy, occupational therapy and speech pathology services, comprehensive outpatient rehabilitation program, work hardening, head injury return to work, pain center, disabled driving programs, hand therapy and ADA services.

7848   Shriners Burn Institute - Cincinnati Unit

3229 Burnet Avenue
Cincinnati, OH   45229   513-872-6000
                        FAX: 513-872-6999

Ronald Hitzler, Administrator

7849   St. Francis Health Care Centre

401 N Broadway Street
Green Springs, OH   44836   419-639-2626
                             800-248-2552
                        FAX: 419-639-6222
                        e-mail: jholmer@sfhcc.org
                        www.sfhcc.org

Greg Raubenolt, Director of Marketing
Jane Holmer, Admissions Coordinator
Joy Kinnear, CRRN, Dir Admissions/Care Coordinator

7850   St. Rita's Medical Center Rehabilitation Services

730 W Market Street
Lima, OH   45801
                        FAX: 419-226-9705

Kelly Recker, Administrative of Physical Med

7851   University of Cincinnati Hospital

234 Goodman Street
Cincinnati, OH   45219   513-584-1000
                        FAX: 513-584-7712

Brook Vargason, Administrator

7852   Upper Valley Medical/Rehab Services

3130 N Dixie Highway
Troy, OH   45373   937-440-4000
                        FAX: 937-440-7337
                        www.uvmc.com

Pam Cornett, Director of Rehab Services

Oklahoma

7853   HealthSouth Rehab Center - Oklahoma

700 Northwest 7th Street
Oklahoma City, OK   73102   405-236-3131
                        FAX: 405-553-1042
                        www.healthsouth.com

Jennifer Pickard, M.S.W., Admissions Coordinator

7854   Hilcrest Medical Center - Kaiser Rehab Center

1125 S Trenton Avenue
Tulsa, OK   74120   918-579-7100
                        FAX: 918-584-6304

7855   Jane Phillips Episcopal Memorial Medical Center - RehabCare Unit

3500 E Frank Phillips Boulevard
Bartlesville, OK   74006   918-335-6655
                        FAX: 918-331-1360

7856   Jim Thorpe Rehabilitation Center at Southwest Medical Center

RehabCare Unit
4401 S Western Avenue
Oklahoma City, OK   73109   405-636-7700
                             800-677-1238
                        FAX: 405-636-7501

Gary Zook, Unit Director
Denise Uvino, Marketing Director

Provides inpatient rehabilitation for people with head injuries, spinal cord injuries, orthopedic conditions, pain management, neurological diseases, strokes and a variety of diagnoses that stop individuals from being able to take care of themselves independently. Services available include medical direction, physical therapy, social work, occupational therapy, speech therapy, recreational therapy, and aftercare follow-up.

7857 Mercy Memorial Health Center RehabCare Unit

1011 14th Avenue NW
Ardmore, OK   73401   580-223-5400
                                   FAX: 580-220-6681

7858 St. Anthony Hospital - RehabCare Unit

1000 North Lee Street
Oklahoma City, OK   73102   405-272-7386
                                   FAX: 405-270-7563

7859 St. Mary's Hospitals - RehabCare Unit

305 S 5th Street
Enid, OK   73701
                                   FAX: 405-270-7563

Oregon

7860 Shriners Hospitals for Children - Portland

3101 SW Sam Jackson Park Road
Portland, OR   97201
                                   FAX: 503-241-5090
                                   www.shrinershq.org

Barbara Flaherty, New Patient Coordinator
Larry Soule, Rehabilation Services Manager
Elon Shlosberg, Care Coordination Manager

Pediatric orthopedic and plastic surgery; inpatient and outpatient services. No charge for any services provided at the Hospital. Diagnosis, rehabilitation, surgery, sports and recreation for ages 0-18 for people with physical disabilities involving bones, muscles or joints or in need of plastic surgery for burn scars or cleft lip/palate.

Pennsylvania

7861 Allied Services John Heinz Institute of Re habilitation Medicine

150 Mundy Street
Wilkes Barre, PA   18702   570-823-3300
                                    888-JHR-EHAB
                                   FAX: 570-826-3840

A 112-bed hospital offering comprehensive inpatient and outpatient rehabilitation services. The Institute specializes in rehabilitation programs in the areas of head trauma, injured worker recovery and pediatrics.

7862 Allied Services Rehabilitation Hospital

475 Morgan Highway
Scranton, PA   18508   570-348-1300
                                   FAX: 570-348-1281
                           e-mail: alliedcom@aol.com

Donna Esken, Admissions

7863 Brighten Place

131 North Main Street
Chalfont, PA   18914   215-997-7746
                                   FAX: 215-997-0403
                          e-mail: brightenplace@enter.net
                               members.aol.com/vmoc3

Suzann Ditzel, Program Director

A residential brain injury program with the mission to encourage growth and foster independence on an individual level for each resident. We are CARF accredited and provide additional services which include a day program and respite care.

7864 Chestnut Hill Rehabilitation Hospital

8601 Stenton Avenue
Wyndmoor, PA   19038   215-233-9700
                                   FAX: 215-233-6879

Leslie Gilman, Administrator

7865 Doylestown Hospital Rehabilitation Center

595 W State Street
Doylestown, PA   18901   215-345-6412
                                   FAX: 215-345-2007
                              e-mail: dseife@dh.org
                         www.dh.org and www.rehabl.net

Donna Seif, RN, Outpatient Rehab Case Manager
Gloria Peterson, Inpatient Rehab Services

7866 Health Care Solutions

701 Chester Pike
Sharon Hill, PA   19079   610-583-3500
                                    800-451-1671
                                   FAX: 610-583-3550

Donna Sewlin, Regional Sales Manager

Develops unique containment programs, offers equipment set-up, patient instruction, patient assessment and equipment usage. Offers clinical services that include oxygen systems, ventilators, aerosol therapy, suction equipment, T.E.N.S. programs, compression pumps, custom orthotics, enteral feeding.

7867 HealthSouth

143 E 2nd Street
Erie, PA   16507   814-878-1200
                                   FAX: 814-878-1448
                                   www.healthsouth.com

Kathy Lamb, Admissions

7868 HealthSouth Harmarville Rehabilitation Hospital

Guys Run Road
Pittsburgh, PA   15238   412-828-1300
                                    800-624-4673
                                   FAX: 412-828-0748

Sharon Noro, CEO

A 202-bed facility providing inpatient and outpatient physical medicine and rehabilitation to adults and adolescents in Pennsylvania, West Virginia, Ohio and Maryland.

7869 HealthSouth Nittany Valley Rehabilitation Hospital

550 West College Avenue
Pleasant Gap, PA 16823   814-359-3421
    800-842-6026
    FAX: 814-359-5898
    www.healthsouth.com

Jodi Drummond, MS, PT, Program Dir, Neurology/Oncology
Robert Drummond, MPT, Program Dir, Orthopedics

Comprehensive inpatient and outpatient facilities. Treatment for symptoms relating to: stroke, head injury, pulmonary disease, orthopedic conditions, neurological disorders, cardiac illnesses and spinal cord injuries. Healthsouth Nittany Valley Rehabilitation Hospital is a part of Healthsouth's national network of more than 2,000 facilities in 50 states.

7870 HealthSouth Rehabilitation Hospital of Altoona

2005 Valley View Boulevard
Altoona, PA 16602   814-944-3535
    FAX: 814-944-6160

Scott Fuler, Administrator/CEO

7871 Healthsouth Rehabilitation Hospital of Mechanicsburg

175 Lancaster Boulevard
Mechanicsburg, PA 17055   717-691-3700
    FAX: 717-697-6524

Roberta Weaver, Director od Admissions

7872 Healthsouth Rehabilitation Hospital of York

1850 Normandie Drive
York, PA 17404   717-767-6941
    800-752-9675
    FAX: 717-764-1341

Cheryl Fleming, Chief Exec. Officer
Marion Houser, Business Development
Mike Felice, Controller

An 90-bed rehabilitation hospital dedicated to providing advanced, comprehensive services to patients who have suffered head injury, spinal cord injury, stroke, burns, amputation, chronic pain and other neurological and musculoskeletal disorders. HRH of York provides outpatient services in three locations, including a freestanding CARF accredited work hardening center. Healthsouth is located in York, Pennsylvania, approximately 50 miles north of Baltimore and 25 miles south of Harrisburg.

7873 Healthsouth Rehabilitation Hospital of2 Greater Pittsburgh

2380 McGinley Road
Monroeville, PA 15146   412-856-2400
    FAX: 412-856-2437

7874 Lake Erie Institute of Rehabilitation

137 W 2nd Street
Erie, PA 16507   814-878-2233
    FAX: 814-878-1448

Jeff Ondrey, Program Director

7875 Magee Rehabilitation Hospital

6 Franklin Plaza
Philadelphia, PA 19102   215-587-3000
    FAX: 215-568-1409

Chuck Hepser, Admissions

7876 Moss Rehabilitation Hospital

1200 W Tabor Road
Philadelphia, PA 19141   215-329-5715
    FAX: 215-456-9646

Pat Wieckowski, Intake Coordinator

The Philadelphia region's major resource for medical rehabilitation since 1959. This 152 bed facility offers comprehensive care to people with broad ranges of conditions, diagnostic laboratories and a multidisciplinary team of rehabilitation professionals.

7877 Shriners Hospital for Children

1645 W 8th Street
Erie, PA 16505   814-875-8700
    FAX: 814-875-8778

7878 Shriners Hospitals for Children, Philadelphia

3551 N Broad Street
Philadelphia, PA 19140   215-430-4000
    800-281-4051
    www.shrinershg.org

Sharon Rajnic, Administrator

The Shriners Hospital in Philadelphia is a 59-bed pediatric orthopaedic hospital providing a complete range of specialized medical and rehabilitation services at no charge to children with orthopaedic problems or spinal injuries. The hospital is one of 22 Shriners Hospitals for Children throughout North america. In addition to treating children with routine and complex orthopaedic problems, the Philadelphia Hospital provides a comprehensive and individualized rehabilitation program.

7879 Shriners Hospitals, Philadelphia Unit, for Crippled Children

3551 North Broad Street
Philadelphia, PA 19152   215-430-4000
    FAX: 215-430-4126
    www.shrinershp.org

South Carolina

7880 Colleton Regional Hospital - RehabCare Unit

501 Robertson Boulevard
Walterboro, SC 29488

Johnnie Benson, Program Manager

7881 HealthSouth Rehab Hospital - South Carolina

2935 Colonial Drive
Columbia, SC 29203   803-254-7777
    FAX: 803-779-8307

7882 Rebound Head Injury Recovery Services of the Carolinas

800 W Meeting Street
Lancaster, SC   29720   803-286-1418
                                FAX: 803-286-1824

7883 Shriners Hospitals for Children, Greenville

950 W Faris Road
Greenville, SC   29605   864-271-3444
                                     800-591-7564
                                FAX: 864-271-4471
                                www.shrinershp.org

Aenne Doughty, Executive Assistant

Tennessee

7884 Health South Cane Creek Rehabilitation Center

180 Mount Pelia Road
Martin, TN   38237   901-587-4231
                                FAX: 901-587-6716

Dayle Unger, RN, NHN, Administrator
Martha Stephenson, RN, Rehab Liaison
Ray Ann Dudley, LPN, Rehab Liaison

7885 HealthSouth Chattanooga Rehabilitation Hospital

2412 McCallie Avenue
Chattanooga, TN   37404   423-698-0221
                                     800-763-5189
                                FAX: 423-697-9124

Donna L. Bourdon, Administrator/CEO
Scooter Brunson, Marketing Coordinator

Offers orthopaedic rehabilitation, stroke rehabilitation, amputee rehabilitation, brain injury program, pain management, ventilator weaning, carpal tunnel screening, low intensity program, oncology program, aquatic therapy, day treatment, burn program and outpatient services.

7886 HealthSouth Rehabilitation Cntr/Tennessee

6100 Primacy Parkway
Suite 115
Memphis, TN   38119   901-682-3730
                                FAX: 901-685-1968

7887 Healthsouth Rehabilitation at Sumner

555 Hartsville Pike
Gallatin, TN   37066   615-230-3900
                                FAX: 615-230-3903

Andrea Sanders, Program Director
Doug Danforth, Director of Nurses

Inpatient general rehabilitation programs for orthopedic injury, joint replacements, head injury, arthritis, general weakness and cardio/pulmonary diseases.

7888 Humana Hospital - Morristown RehabCare Unit

726 McFarland Street
Morristown, TN   37814   423-586-2930
                                FAX: 423-581-6988

7889 Nashville Rehabilitation Hospital

610 Gallatin Road
Nashville, TN   37206   615-226-4330
                                     800-227-3108
                                FAX: 615-650-2562

Anne Jacobs, RN, Director CM/UR
Sherry Lawlwer, LCSW, Social Services

A free-standing physical rehabilitation facility offering services to patients on an inpatient and outpatient basis. Programs include CVA, orthopedic, neuromuscular, traumatic brain injury, spinal cord injury, general rehabilitation and Bridges - geriatric psychiatric unit. Intra-disciplinary team approach is utilized to assist patients in obtaining their maximum fuctional level.

7890 Northeast Tennessee Rehabilitation Hospital

3511 Wesley Street
Johnson City, TN   37601   423-434-5150
                                     800-235-1994
                                FAX: 423-283-0153

Dennis Falck, CEO
Jim Perkins, Marketing Director

A 60-bed, freestanding comprehensive medical rehabilitation hospital. Full range of outpatient and day treatment, 14-bed traumatic brain injury unit, in ground therapeutic pool, transitional living apartment, outdoor ambulation course. All inpatient and outpatient programs utilize an interdisciplinary team approach designed to improve a patient's physical and cognitive functioning.

7891 Patricia Neal Rehab Center - Ft. Sanders Regional Medical Center

1901 W Clinch Avenue
Knoxville, TN   37916   423-541-1167
                                FAX: 865-541-3977

7892 Rebound Comprehensive Rehabilitation Center at Cane Creek

180 Mt Pelia Road
Martin, TN   38237
                                FAX: 901-587-6716

7893 Rehabilitation Center Baptist Hospital

137 Blount Avenue
Knoxville, TN   37920   865-632-5360

                                www.baptist.org

7894 Rehabilitation Center at McFarland Hospital

University Medical Center
500 Park Avenue
Lebanon, TN   37087   615-449-0500
                                FAX: 615-444-7901

Johnny Harrison, M.S., Director

7895 St. Mary's Medical Center - RehabCare Center

Oak Hill Avenue
Knoxville, TN   37917   865-545-8000
                                FAX: 865-545-8133

Texas

7896   Bayshore Medical Center - Rehab

4000 Spencer Highway
Pasadena, TX   77504   713-944-6666
                              FAX: 713-359-1121

Bill Brady, Program Manager

7897   Brown Schools Rehabilitation Center

1106 W Dittmar Road
Austin, TX   78745   512-444-4835
                            800-252-5151
                     FAX: 512-462-6636
          e-mail: nbond@brownschools.com
          www.brownschools.com/rehabcenter

Carol Freeman, Admissions Department

One of the nation's leading providers in brain injury/neuropsychiatric treatment for children, adolescents and adults with complex physical and/or behavioral problems. Medical rehabilitation; neurobehavioral; neuropsychiatry and community reentry programs combine traditional therapies with educational; vocational; substance abuse; and outpatient services.

7898   Brown Schools Rehabilitation Center - A Brain Injury Hospital

1106 W Dittmar Road
Austin, TX   78745   512-444-4835
                            800-252-5151
                     FAX: 512-462-6636
          e-mail: bcollier@brownschools.com
          www.brownschools.com/rehabcenter

Admissions Department, Contact

Internationally recognized provider in brain injury/neurobehavioral treatment for children, adolescents, and adults with complex medical, physical and/or behavioral issues. Medical rehabilitation, neurobehavioral, and transitional living programs combine traditional therapies with education, vocational, substance abuse, and outpatient services.

7899   Cecil R. Bomhr Rehabilitation Center of Nacogdoches Memorial Hospital

1204 N Mound Street
Nacogdoches, TX   75961   409-568-8547
                                 FAX: 409-569-4616

Bette M. Guzman, Director of Rehabilitation Serv.

The only JCAHO and CARF, ASHA/PSB certified acute inpatient physical rehab center in East Texas.

7900   Clear Lake Rehabilitation Hospital

655 E Medical Center Boulevard
Webster, TX   77598   281-286-8783
                             FAX: 281-286-3569

Nancy Dungan

7901   Dallas Rehabilitation Institute

9713 Harry Hines Boulevard
Dallas, TX   75220
                             FAX: 214-904-6119

Judi McCann, Intake Coordinator

A 126-bed facility offering comprehensive and outpatient programs for brain injury, spinal cord injury, chronic pain, amputation, orthopedic and work-related injuries. Houses a full-service ICU and two surgical suites, a 14,000 square foot physical therapy gym, hydrotherapy pool and an on-site orthotics and prosthetics lab. The Institute is also accredited by CARF, JCAHO and Texas Rehabilitation Commission; certified by Medicare and is an affiliate of the University of Texas Medical School.

7902   Del Oro Institute for Rehabilitation

8081 Greenbriar Street
Houston, TX   77054
                              800-388-1HCA

Cece Matthews, Admissions

Del Oro offers an interdisciplinary team approach to care, meeting the needs of rehabilitation patients with a wide spectrum of services, including immediate access to surgery, intensive care or other medical treatment which may be required in an emergency.

7903   Ft. Worth Rehabilitation Hospital

6701 Oakmont Boulevard
Fort Worth, TX   76132   817-370-4727
                                FAX: 817-370-4977

Gala Lewis, Admissions

7904   Gonzales Warm Springs Rehabilitation Hospital

PO Box 58
Gonzales, TX   78629   830-672-6592
                              FAX: 830-672-8102

7905   Good Shepherd Medical Center - RehabCare Unit

621 N 5th Street
Longview, TX   75601   903-236-3937
                              FAX: 903-236-2497

Retta Crim, Program Manager

7906   HealthSouth Rehabilitation Center of Humble Texas

18903 S Memorial Drive
Humble, TX   77338   409-760-3443
                            FAX: 281-446-8022

7907   Heights Hospital - RehabCare Unit

1917 Ashland Street
Houston, TX   77008   713-861-6161
                             FAX: 713-802-8657

Peggy Kelso, Program Director

7908   Hillcrest Baptist Medical Center - Rehab Care Unit

3000 Herring Avenue
Waco, TX   76708   254-202-4262
                          FAX: 254-202-8975

7909   IHS Hospital at Dallas

7955 Harry Hines
Dallas, TX   75235

                             800-366-4736
                             FAX: 214-637-6512

Richard G. Allison, Admissions

7910 Institute for Rehab and Research

1333 Moursund Street
Houston, TX   77030   713-799-7011
                                    FAX: 713-797-5988

7911 Mabee Rehabilitation Center

1301 Pennsylvania Avenue
Fort Worth, TX   76104   817-882-2364
                                    FAX: 813-882-2753

7912 Memorial Hospital Nacogdoches - RehabCare Unit

1204 Mound Street
Nacogdoches, TX   75961   409-275-3446
                                    FAX: 409-569-4616

7913 Memorial Hospital and Medical Center

821 Jessee Drive
Drawer H
Midland, TX   79701   915-586-5864

7914 Navarro Regional Hospital - RehabCare Unit

3201 W Highway 22
Corsicana, TX   75110   903-654-6800
                                    FAX: 903-872-4627

7915 Neurobehavioral Institute of Houston

4100 Wellman Road
Conroe, TX   77384   409-788-7742
                                    FAX: 281-367-5610

7916 Plano Rehabilitation Hospital

2800 W 15th Street
Plano, TX   75075   972-612-9118
                                    FAX: 972-423-4293

7917 Rebound - San Antonio

12412 Judson Road
San Antonio, TX   78233   210-650-4949

7918 Rehabilitation Hospital of Austin

1215 Red River Street
Austin, TX   78701   512-479-8900
                                    FAX: 512-474-2720

7919 Rehabilitation Hospital of North Texas

3200 Matlock Road
Arlington, TX   76015   817-419-0866
                                    FAX: 817-468-3055

7920 Rehabilitation Hospital of South Texas

6226 Saratoga Boulevard
Corpus Christi, TX   78414
                                    FAX: 512-994-8998

7921 Rehabilitation Institute - Methodist Hospital

3615 19th Street
Lubbock, TX   79410   806-793-4251
                                    FAX: 806-793-4037

7922 Rehabilitation Institute of San Antonio Healthsouth

9119 Cinnamon Hill
San Antonio, TX   78240   210-691-0737
                                    FAX: 210-558-1297
                                    www.healthsouth.com

Diane B. Lampe, CEO
Larry Spriggs, Chief Financial Officer

7923 Rio Vista Rehabilitation Hospital

1740 Curie Drive
El Paso, TX   79902   915-544-3399
                                    800-999-8392
                                    FAX: 915-544-4838

7924 San Antonio Warm Springs Rehabilitation Hospital

5101 Medical Drive
San Antonio, TX   78229   210-616-0100
                                    FAX: 210-592-5452
                                    www.warmsprings.org

7925 Shannon Medical Center - RehabCare Unit

120 E Harris Avenue
San Angelo, TX   76903   915-657-5227
                                    FAX: 915-657-8261

7926 Shriners Burn Institute - Galveston Unit

815 Market Street
Galveston, TX   77550
                                    FAX: 409-770-6749

7927 Shriners Hospitals for Children, Houston

6977 Main Street
Houston, TX   77030   713-797-1616
                                    800-853-1240
                                    FAX: 713-793-3770
                                    e-mail: shriners@argolink.net

Steven Reiter, Administrator

Shriners Hospitals provides at no charge quality pediatric orthopedic serivces to children ages newborn to 18 years old. These services include both outpatient and inpatient needs. Specialties include cerebral palsy, spina bifida, scoliosis, hand, hip and feet problems. An application is required and may be completed by phone.

7928 South Arlington Medical Center - RehabCare Unit

3301 Matlock Road
Arlington, TX   76015   817-472-4900
                                    FAX: 817-472-4963

7929 Southeast Texas Rehabilitation Hospital

3340 Plaza 10 Drive
Beaumont, TX   77707   409-835-0835
                                    FAX: 409-835-0649

7930 St. David's Rehabilitation Center

919 E 32nd Street
Austin, TX   78705   512-867-5100
                                    FAX: 512-370-4439

7931 Valley Regional Medical Center - RehabCare Unit

100 Alton Glore Boulevard
Brownsville, TX   78520   956-350-7790
                                    FAX: 956-350-7796

Utah

7932 LDS Hospital Rehabilitation Center

Eighth Avenue & C Street
Salt Lake City, UT   84143   801-321-1415
                                    888-301-3880
                              FAX: 801-321-5610

Jeanette Kucharski, CRRN, Rehab Liaison

Located within a Trauma I Center, this facility provides comprehensive inpatient and outpatient rehabilitation to people with physical disabilities. CARF/JCAHO accredited. Low cost family housing is available and Medicaid/Medicare is accepted.

7933 Pocatello Rehabilitation Center

777 Hospital Way
Pocatello, ID   83201   208-239-3600
                            FAX: 208-239-3795
                                 www.ihc.com

R. Eric Goodwin, Director of Rehab

Provides the full spectrum of medical rehabilitation services including acute inpatient rehab, subacute rehab, home health and comprehensive outpatient services. Accredited by CARF and JCAHO.

7934 Primary Children's Medical Center

100 N Medical Drive
Salt Lake City, UT   84113   801-588-2000
                              FAX: 801-588-2318

7935 Rehabilitation Services

University of Utah Hospitals and Clinics
50 N Medical Drive
Salt Lake City, UT   84132   801-581-2267
                              FAX: 801-585-3778

Sunny Vance-Lauritzen, Director
Trish Jensen, Program Coordinator

Provides quality, comprehensive, rehabilitation services to persons with complex rehabilitation needs, including spinal cord injuries, head trauma, stroke, and other disabling conditions. Rehabilitation Services has been serving physicians, their patients, and the community since 1965. Rehabilitation Services has been an established leader in comprehensive inpatient, outpatient and home/community rehabilitation programs. Accredited by CARF and JCAHO.

7936 Shriners Hospitals for Children - Intermountain

Fairfax Avenue at Virginia Street
Salt Lake City, UT   84103
                                  800-841-0204
                            FAX: 801-536-3621

Dr. James Roach, Chief of Staff
Linda Raccuia, Applications Coord.

One of nineteen hospitals in North America specializing in pediatric orthopedics (plus four hospitals providing pediatric burn treatment). This hospital serves the Intermountain region. All services provided in the hospital are at no cost to family, insurance company, nor state/federal agency regardless of ability to pay.

7937 Stewart Rehabilitation Center - McKay Dee Hospital

4335 South Harrison Boulevard
Suite D
Ogden, UT   84403   801-398-2080
                              FAX: 801-398-6610

Bob Martin, Nurse Coordinator

7938 Western Rehabilitation Institute

8074 S 1300 East
Sandy, UT   84094   801-565-6500
                              FAX: 801-565-6576

Vauna Allison, Admissions

Vermont

7939 Vermont Achievement Center

88 Park Street
Rutland, VT   05701   802-775-1360
                              FAX: 802-773-9656

Virginia

7940 Inova Mt. Vernon Hospital Inpatient Rehabilitation Program

Inova Rehabilitation Center
2501 Parkers Lane
Alexandria, VA   22306   703-664-7592
                              FAX: 703-664-7128

Toni Jones, Rehab Admissions
Mary Beth Ireland, Inpatient Program Director
Ann Vennell, Outpatient Program Director

7941 Kluge Children's Rehabilitation Center

2270 Ivy Road
Charlottesville, VA   22903   804-924-5161
                              FAX: 804-924-5559

7942 Portsmouth General Hospital - RehabCare Unit

850 Crawford Parkway
Portsmouth, VA   23704   757-465-7772

Anne Fisher, Program Manager

Washington

7943 Good Samaritan Hospital and Rehab Center

407 14th Avenue SE
PO Box 190
Puyallup, WA   98371   253-848-6661
                              FAX: 253-770-5188
          e-mail: (can be accessed from web page)
                         www.goodsamhealth.org

7944 Northwest Hospital Center for Medical Rehabilitation

1550 N 115th Street
Seattle, WA   98133   206-706-7600
                              FAX: 206-368-1399

7945 Providence Medical Center
500 17th Avenue
Seattle, WA 98122   206-320-2098
      FAX: 206-320-3387

7946 Providence Rehabilitation Services
Providence Rehabilitation Services
Pacific and Nassau
Everett, WA 98206   425-316-5020

Elaine Thayer, PT, Clinical Director

Continuum of care available: Acute Care, Inpatient Rehabilitation Unit, Transitional Care, Outpatient therapies, and In-home services.

7947 Shriners Hospitals for Children - Spokane
PO Box 2472
Spokane, WA 99210   509-455-7844
      FAX: 509-623-0474
      www.shrinershq.org

Chuck Young, Administrator
Cheri Hollenback, Director of Nursing
Ron L. Ferguson, M.D., Chief of Staff

Provides pediatric orthopedic services plus burn scar revision to children birth to 18. All services at no charge to the family.

West Virginia

7948 MountainView Regional Rehabilitation Hospital
1160 Van Voorhis Road
Morgantown, WV 26505   304-292-8006
      800-388-2451
      FAX: 304-598-1103

Carla Stadelman, Asst. Administrator

An 80-bed freestanding rehabilitation hospital serving central WV, southwestern PA, western MD and northwestern VA. Offers specialized programs to serve the patient population. Brain injury, spinal cord injury, stroke, neuromuscular, pulmonary disorders, pediatrics, ventilator dependence, orthopedics, amputee, case management and pain management.

7949 Western Hills Rehabilitation Hospital
3 Western Hills Drive
Parkersburg, WV 26102   304-420-1300
      FAX: 304-420-1374

Wisconsin

7950 Midwest Neurological Rehabilitation Center
1701 Sharp Road
Waterford, WI 53185
      800-697-5380
      FAX: 414-534-8505

A comprehensive, integrated neurological rehabilitation center located only 25 minutes from Milwaukee. The Center provides seven comprehensive programs: acute hospital rehabilitation, pediatric acute rehabilitation, pediatric postacute rehabilitation, rehabilitation and skilled nursing, community-based rehabilitation and vocational rehabilitation.

7951 St. Catherine's Hospital
3556 7th Avenue
Kenosha, WI 53140
      FAX: 414-656-3590

Rick Schultz, Program Manager

7952 St. Joseph's Hospital
611 Saint Joseph Avenue
Marshfield, WI 54449
      FAX: 715-389-3900

Cindy Bokath, Head Nurse

Wyoming

7953 Spalding Rehabilitation Hospital at Memorial Hospital of Laramie
300 E 23rd Street
Cheyenne, WY 82001   307-633-7770

Alabama

7954 Alabama Department of Rehabilitation Services

2129 E S Boulevard
Montgomery, AL 36116   334-288-0220
800-441-7607

7955 Alabama Goodwill Industries

2350 Green Springs Highway South
Birmingham, AL 35205   205-323-6331
FAX: 205-324-9059

Don Smith, Director
Work adjustment and remunerative work programs.

7956 Alabama Veterans Facility

809 Green Spring Highway
Homewood, AL 35209   205-916-2700

Veterans medical clinic offering disabled veterans medical treatments.

7957 American Rehab Center Neuro Care Unit Mobile Infirmary

5 Mobile Infirmary Circle
Mobile, AL 36607   334-431-5559

Robert Berg, President
Postacute rehabilitation program.

7958 Arc of Jefferson County

215 21st Avenue South
Birmingham, AL 35205   205-323-6383
FAX: 205-323-0085

William F. Hoeble, II, PhD, Executive Director
The Arc of Jefferson County serves children and adults with mental retardation and/or other developmental disabilities. Services are provided through the following programs: the HOPE (Helping Others through Parent Education) Early Intervention Program; Adult Day Services; Residential Services; and Arc-Way Industries, a sheltered and supported employment program.

7959 Association for Retarded Citizens of Jefferson County (The Arc)

215 21st Avenue South
Birmingham, AL 35205   205-323-6383
FAX: 205-323-0085

William F. Hoehle, II, PhD, Executive Director
The ARC has four primary components. The HOPE Program provides early intervention therapy services to developmentally delayed infants and toddlers up to the age of three years. The ARC also provides services to adults ages 21 and over with mental retardation. Adult services provides education, pre-vocational screening, and socialization skills training. Employment services provides vocational training, a sheltered workshop, off-site job skills training, job coach services and more. Residential s

7960 Briarcliff Nursing Center

850 9th Street NW
Alabaster, AL 35007   205-663-3859
FAX: 205-663-9791

Jenny Long, Case Manager
Postacute rehabilitation program.

7961 Butler Adult Training Center

680 Hardscramble Road
Greenville, AL 36037   334-382-2353

Sheila Martin, Director
Clients 21 years of age and older who are mentally retarded. School age clients are also served at the center and must also be mentally retarded. Clients receive training in Independent Living Skills, Self-Care, Language Skills, Learning, Self Direction and Economic Self-Sufficiency. The clients also participate in Special Olympics activities.

7962 Cheaha Mental Health

1623 Old Birmingham Highway
Sylacauga, AL 35150   256-245-1340
FAX: 256-245-1343

Larry Morris, Executive Director
Offers mental health rehabilitation, respite care, residential facilities and more for the mentally disabled.

7963 Children's Rehabilitation Service

2121 E S Boulevard
Montgomery, AL 36116
FAX: 334-281-1388

7964 Chilton-Shelby Mental Health Center/ The Mitchell Center

PO Box 679
Calera, AL 35040   205-668-1327
FAX: 205-668-2443

Ronald Kendall, Executive Director
Offers mental health rehabilitation services and more for the recovery of mentally disabled adults.

7965 EL Darden Rehabilitation Center

1001 E Broad Street
Gadsden, AL 35999
FAX: 256-547-5761

Tom Strother
Work hardening and disciplinary programs.

7966 Easter Seals Central Alabama

2125 E S Boulevard
Montgomery, AL 36116   334-288-0240
FAX: 334-288-7171
e-mail: easterseals@worldnet.att.net

J. Larry Johnson, Administrator
Dr. Susan McKim, Director Of Rehab

A private, nonprofit organization offering services audiology, physical, occupational, lymphedema and speech therapy, psychological counseling, vocational evaluation and assessment, person, social and work adjustment training, GED preparation, computer service training, job placement and follow-up, and special learning disabilities service and supported employment service.

7967 Easter Seals West Alabama

1110 6th Avenue East
Tuscaloosa, AL 35401   205-759-1211
                               800-726-1216
                          FAX: 205-349-1162
             e-mail: eswa@dbtech.net

Loie Sears Robinson, Administrator

Leading organization in helping children and adults with disabilities to live with equality, dignity and independence. Rehabilitation services are provided in two divisions: outpatient rehabilitation division (physical therapy, occupational therapy, speech therapy, hearing evaluation, sell and service hearind aids) and vocational division (vocational evaualtion and vocational development). Services are rendered regardless of age, race, sex, color, creed, national origin, veteran's status.

7968 Gadsden Rehabilitation Center

2013 Rainbow Drive
Gadsden, AL 35901   256-546-9000
                          FAX: 256-546-9085

Steve Winkler

Work hardening and disciplinary programs.

7969 Geer Adult Training Center

PO Box 419
Carrollton, AL 35447   205-367-8032
                          FAX: 205-367-8032

Yvonne Williams, Program Coordinator

7970 Goodwill Easter Seals of the Gulf Coast

2448 Gordon Smith Drive
Mobile, AL 36617   334-471-1581
                               800-411-0068
                          FAX: 334-476-4303
             e-mail: frank@gwimobile.org
             www.goodwill-easterseals.org

Frank Harkins, President/CEO

Vocational, medical, pre-school education, day care, recreation, and other support services.

7971 Indian Rivers

1915 6th Street
2190
Tuscaloosa, AL 35401   205-345-1600
                          FAX: 205-391-0106

Laurie Prentice-Dunn, Director

Services are available to adults who have serious mental illness resulting in personal, family or work-related problems. Counseling may take place in either individual or group settings, identification, evaluation and treatment services are available to persons who experience problems related to alcohol and drug abuse and counseling services are available for children and adolescents who have a severe emotional disturbance causing discipline problems at home and school.

7972 Lighthouse

PO Box 218
Brent, AL 35034   205-926-4681
                          FAX: 205-926-6016

Gwen Langley, Program Coordinator

7973 Low Vision Clinic/UAB School of Optometry

1716 University Boulevard
Birmingham, AL 35294   205-934-2625
                          FAX: 205-934-0911

Dr. R.W. Nowakowski, Chief of Staff
Dr. D.K. DeCarlo, Chief, Low Vision Patient Care
Brenda Watkins, Optometric Assistant

Multidisciplinary clinic in a major medical center which provides a comprehensive vision evaluation and prescription of low vision aids for those who are visually impaired. Fees are charged for all examination procedures, special diagnostic tests and materials with most insurance plans accepted. Cost depends on services rendered.

7974 MARC Enterprises

759 Congress Street
Mobile, AL 36603   334-470-0821
                          FAX: 334-470-0824

Andrew Acklin, Division Director

Serving the mentally retarded of Mobile County both locally and through its state and national affiliations. Their united efforts through this voluntary association assure the availability of services and provide the opportunity for achievement.

7975 North Central Alabama Mental Retardation Authority

1621 Wolverine Drive SE
597
Decatur, AL 35601   256-355-7315
                          FAX: 256-355-7317

Earl E. Brightwell, Director

NCA, MRA, Inc. functions as an entrance to the service delivery system for the Alabama Department of Mental Health and Mental Retardation and is responsible for planning, development, implementation of programs, sanction, monitoring, referral, and case management for persons with mental retardation/developmental disabilities in Morgan, Lawrence and Limestone Counties.

7976 Rehabilitation Center - Northwest Alabama Easter Seal

1450 Avalon Avenue
Muscle Shoals, AL 35661
                          FAX: 256-381-1110

Robert H. Nelson, Administrator
Sheila Phillips, Admin. Asst.

7977 Southeastern Blind Rehabilitation Center

Department of Veterans Affairs Medical Center
700 19th Street South
Birmingham, AL   35233　　　205-933-8101
　　　　　　　　　　　　　　FAX: 205-933-4484

Mark Voorhies, Director
George Sands, Assistant Director

The Center is a 32-bed inpatient blind rehabilitation program which serves the southeastern region. The majority of client services are for basic adjustment and management to sight loss. Basic services include: low vision, orientation and mobility, manual skills, ADL and communications. Training on electronic mobility aids and adapted computers is also available on a restricted basis. The program maintains graduate education affiliations and an active applied research program.

7978 Tennessee Valley Rehabilitation

PO Box 1926
Decatur, AL   35602　　　　256-350-2041
　　　　　　　　　　　　　　FAX: 256-350-2806

Charles Harvell

Work hardening and disciplinary programs.

7979 Vaughn-Blumberg Center

2715 Flynn Road
Dothan, AL   36303　　　　334-793-3102
　　　　　　　　　　　　　　FAX: 334-793-7740

H. David Johnston, Director

7980 West Central Alabama Easter Seals Rehabilitation Center

2906 Citizens Parkway
PO Box 750
Selma, AL   36702　　　　334-872-8421
　　　　　　　　　　　　　　800-801-4776
　　　　　　　　　　　　　　FAX: 334-872-3907
　　　　　　　　e-mail: wcarcdw@tomnet.com
　　　　　　　　www.al.easter-seals.org/selma

Larry F. Lewis, Administrator
David White, Program Coordinator

Vocational evaluation, job development, employment development, job coaching, counseling, medical services, audiology, pre-school development programs.

Alaska

7981 Alaska Center for the Visually Impaired

3903 Taft Drive
Anchorage, AK   99517　　　907-248-7770
　　　　　　　　　　　　　　FAX: 907-248-7517
　　　　　　　　e-mail: info@alaskablind.com
　　　　　　　　www.alaskablind.com

Jim King, Executive Director

Services to help the adult residential or community-based student become independent and self-sufficient by offering independent travel, braille reading, writing, use of talking computers and calculators, manual skills, activities and projects and personal, as well as home management.

7982 Alaska Veterans Facility

4201 Tudor Centre Drive
Suite 115
Anchorage, AK   99508　　　907-277-3224

Veterans medical clinic offering disabled veterans medical treatments.

Arizona

7983 Arizona Center for the Blind and Visually Impaired

3100 E Roosevelt Street
Phoenix, AZ   85008　　　602-273-7411
　　　　　　　　　　　　　FAX: 602-273-7410
　　　　　　　　e-mail: sgibbs@acbvi.org
　　　　　　　　www.acbvi.org

James LeMay, Executive Director
Sharon Gibbs, Info & Referral Specialist
Diana Miladin, Communication & Development Coor

A private, nonprofit organization that provides comprehensive rehabilitation services and more for the blind and visually handicapped. The staff includes 20 instructional and adminstrative professionals.

7984 Arizona Industries for the Blind

3013 W Lincoln Street
Phoenix, AZ   85009　　　602-269-5131
　　　　　　　　　　　　　FAX: 602-269-5797
　　　　　　　　www.azrsa.org/aib

D.H. Peterson, General Manager

Offers rehabilitation services, vocational/pre-vocational evaluation and training, work adjustment, job development and employment and training opportunties for individuals who are blind.

7985 Beacon Foundation for the Mentally Retarded

25 East Drachman Street
Tucson, AZ   85705　　　520-624-3454
　　　　　　　　　　　　　FAX: 520-623-3494

Paul Wagler, Chief Executive Director

Committed to effectively assisting adults with disabilities to maximize their personal, social, vocational and educational skills in order to attain a successful and meaningful independence within the Tucson community.

7986 Carondelet Brain Injury Programs and Services

350 North Wilmot Road
Tucson, AZ   85711　　　520-873-3881
　　　　　　　　　　　　　FAX: 520-873-3743
　　　　　　　　e-mail: kspredling@carondelet.org

Kary Spredling, Rehab Coordinator

Comprehensive outpatient rehabiltation program.

7987 Carondelet Rehabilitation Services St Joseph's Hospital

350 North Wilmot Road
Tucson, AZ 85711   520-872-4386
                        FAX: 520-872-6279
                        www.carondelet.org

Kristy Mills, Supervisor

Provides comprehensive care from diagnosis to rehabilitation for the person with the simplest to most omplex neurological problem. Specialized programs and clinics offer services that are supported by a large variety of professional specialties thus ensuring both continuity and quality care within a single setting.

7988 Carondelet St. Mary's

1601 West Saint Marys Road
Tucson, AZ 85745   520-740-6275
                        FAX: 520-740-6279
                        e-mail: rpeel@carondelet.org

Staffed by physicians board certified in neurology, psychiatry and by a comprehensive team of allied health professionals trained in physical therapy, vocational rehabilitation, rehabilitation nursing and occupational therapy.

7989 Casa Grande Rehabilitation Programs

208 W Main Street
Casa Grande, AZ 85222   602-254-0754
                              FAX: 520-426-9471

James Musick, Executive Director

7990 Community Rehabilitation Services - Tucson

1789 West Jefferson
2nd Floor NW
Phoenix, AZ 85007   602-542-3332
                          TDY:602-542-6049

Skip Bingham, Administration
Postacute rehabilitation program.

7991 Desert Life Health Care Center

1919 W Medical Street
Tucson, AZ 85704
                          FAX: 520-544-0930

Postacute rehabilitation program.

7992 Freestone Rehabilitation Center

10617 E Oasis Drive
Apache Junction, AZ 85220   602-986-1531
                                  FAX: 480-986-1538

Randy Gray, Executive Director

7993 Institute for Human Development

PO Box 5630
Flagstaff, AZ 86011   520-523-7319
                            FAX: 520-523-9127

Richard Carroll, Director

7994 John C. Lincoln Hospital North Mountain

250 E Dunlap Avenue
Phoenix, AZ 85020   602-943-2381
                          FAX: 602-944-8062
                          www.jcl.com

Dan Coleman, President

7995 La Frontera Center

502 W 29th Street
Tucson, AZ 85713   520-884-9920

Dr. Floyd Martinez
Provides remunerative work.

7996 Manor Care Nursing and Rehab Center Tucson

3705 N Swan Road
Tucson, AZ 85718
                          FAX: 520-529-0038

Mark Bedinger, Administrator
Sheila Powell, Director, Admissions & Marketing
Postacute rehabilitation program.

7997 Nova Care

2539 N 35th Avenue
Suite 10
Phoenix, AZ 85009   602-417-3939
                          FAX: 602-484-7773

Elaine Ralls
Work hardening and disciplinary programs.

7998 Perry Rehabilitation Center

3146 E Windsor Avenue
Phoenix, AZ 85008   602-958-0400
                          FAX: 602-957-7610
                          e-mail: perrycenteratuswest.com

Robin Ratcliff, Director

Provides services for people with disabilities, cognitive disabilities including residential services, day treatment, job training and job placement.

7999 Phoenix Veterans Center

141 E Palm Lane
Suite 100
Phoenix, AZ 85004   602-379-4769
                          FAX: 602-379-4130

Veterans medical clinic offering disabled veterans medical treatments.

8000 Progress Valley - Phoenix

4430 N 23rd Avenue
Phoenix, AZ 85015   602-274-5424
                          888-241-1117
                          FAX: 602-274-5473

Phoebe Muto, Program Director

Provides appropriate primary care to persons who have had harmful involvement with mood altering chemicals. Addresses both alcoholism and other drug dependency rehabilitation needs.

8001 Samaritan Rehabilitation Institute

1111 E McDowell Road
Phoenix, AZ 85006   602-239-2635
                          FAX: 602-239-5868

Ronald Herrick, Assoc. Administrator

8002 Scottsdale Memorial Hospital Rehabilitation Services

7400 E Osborn Road
Scottsdale, AZ 85251   602-314-2100
                          FAX: 480-675-4478

Peter Frick, President

8003 Toyei Industries

HC-58 Box 55
Ganado, AZ 86505   520-736-2418
                          FAX: 520-736-2495
                          e-mail: toyindi@aol.com

Russell Morgan, Interim Executive Director
Anita Hildreth, Social Services Manager

Serves the needs of developmentally disabled and the severely mentally impaired adult citizens of the Navajo Nation and other Indian Nations. Staff of 40+ serves the needs of all the Navajo adults. Services include day treatment programs, and home community-based services.

8004 Tucson Association for the Blind and Visually Imparied

3767 E Grant Road
Tucson, AZ 85716   520-795-1331
                          FAX: 520-795-1336
                          e-mail: gluini@tabvi.org

Gene Luini, Executive Director

Offers health services, counseling, social work, home and personal management, computer training, low vision aids and more for the visually handicapped 18 years or older.

8005 Valley of the Sun Rehabilitation Hospital

13460 N 67th Avenue
Glendale, AZ 85304   602-214-2256
                          FAX: 602-878-5254

Ken Manders, Chief Exec. Officer

8006 Yuma Center for the Visually Impaired

2770 South Avenue B
Yuma, AZ 85364   928-726-1310
                          FAX: 928-783-3261

Calvin Roberts, Director

A private, nonprofit agency offering services for totally blind and legally blind children and adults in the Arizona area.

Arkansas

8007 Arkansas Lighthouse for the Blind

PO Box 192666
Little Rock, AR 72219   501-562-2222
                          FAX: 501-568-5275
                          e-mail: ALB49799@aol.com

Sue Walker, Executive V.P.

Offers educational industrial evaluation and training to the legally blind and multihandicapped. Funded by workshop sales and contributions, the staff includes ten full time employees

8008 Arkansas Veterans Facility

201 W Broadway Street
Suite A
North Little Rock, AR 72114   501-354-3451

Veterans medical clinic offering disabled veterans medical treatments.

8009 Beverly Enterprises Network

1200 S Waldron Road
Fort Smith, AR 72903   501-452-0469
                          800-666-9996
                          FAX: 501-452-5131

Offers a progressive approach to subacute care. The goal of this organization is to assist injured and disabled individuals regain the level of independence to which they have been accustomed. Provides support and training programs, patient and family services and specialty programs for patients.

8010 Easter Seals of Arkansas

3920 Woodland Heights Road
Little Rock, AR 72212   501-227-3600
                          FAX: 501-227-3658
                          e-mail: smoonejochum@ar.easter-seals.org
                          www.arkeasterseals.org

Sharon Moone-Jochus, President & CEO

8011 HEALTHSOUTH Rehabilitation Hospital Fort Smith

1401 S J Street
Fort Smith, AR 72901   501-785-3300
                          FAX: 501-785-8599
                          www.healthsouth.com

Holli Baker, Director of Business Development

A free-standing 80-bed comprehensive physical medicine and rehabilitation hospital offering inpatient and outpatient services. Provides specialized medical and therapy services, designed to assist physically challenged persons to reach their highest level of independent function.

8012 Lions World Services for the Blind

2811 Fair Park Boulevard
Little Rock, AR 72204   501-664-7100
                          800-248-0754
                          FAX: 501-664-2743
                          e-mail: training@lwsb.org
                          www.lwsb.org

Ramona Sangalli, Executive Director

Offers services in the areas of health, education, recreation, rehabilitation, counseling, social work, employment, computer training and more for all legally blind residents of the U.S. The staff includes 56 full time employees.

8013 New Medico Rehabilitation Center at Timber Ridge Ranch

PO Box 90
Benton, AR 72018   501-594-5211

Dr. Jack Robertson, Executive Director

California

8014 ACCENTCARE

800 S Broadway
Suite 309
Walnut Creek, CA 94596   925-944-5800
FAX: 925-944-5840
www.accentcare.com

Kristy Cosentino, Care Center Manager
Joan Anderson, Care Manager

Postacute rehabilitation program: home care aides follow through with rehabilitation instructions given by physical, occupational and speech therapists. Other home care services are available, serving special needs for Alzheimer's, blind, brain injury, MS, ostomies, parkinsonism, spinal injury and stroke.

8015 ARC - VC Ventura

2647 N Ventura Avenue
Ventura, CA 93001   805-652-0541
FAX: 805-652-0542

Tom Wright, Executive Associate

8016 ARC Mid-Cities

108 W Victoria Street
Carson, CA 90248   310-329-9272
FAX: 310-323-3839
e-mail: betsog@hotmail.com
www.arcmid-cities.com.org

Betsog Jueo, Program Manager

ARC Mid-Cities provides a system for individuals who may require on-going support in order to ba a contributing member of society. The programs offered enhance the independence, self-sufficiency, and productivity of the persons served.

8017 ARC-VC Magic Muffin Cafe

1661 Pacific Avenue
Oxnard, CA 93033   805-483-0341
FAX: 805-483-2594

Shirley Dove

Provides remunerative work.

8018 American Rehab Centers Neuro Care Unit

2776 Pacific Avenue
Long Beach, CA 90806   562-426-4561
FAX: 562-427-0149

Postacute rehabilitation program.

8019 Arrow Center

3035 G Street
San Diego, CA 92102   619-233-8855
FAX: 619-233-4932

Dorothy Cummings

Work hardening and disciplinary programs.

8020 Assistance League of Santa Clara County

169 State Street
Los Altos Hills, CA 94022   650-941-2610
FAX: 650-917-9420

Nancy Griffith, President

Offers educational services, supplements mainstreamed K-12 students in public school systems, teaches communication, mobility, daily living skills, recreational field trips and more for the blind and physically handicapped.

8021 Association for Retarded Citizens-Alameda County

575 Independent Road
Oakland, CA 94621   510-639-4680
FAX: 510-639-4684

Offers the Right Track program in which selected workers are grouped together on a contract basis to maximize work productivity. Provides a full benefit package, as well as a permanent supervisor. A worker is matched to a job of at least 20 hours per week and then trained by the staff of The Right Track.

8022 Azure Acres Chemical Dependency Recovery Center

2264 Green Hill Road
Sebastopol, CA 95472   707-823-3385
FAX: 707-823-8972

Uwe Gunnersen, President

Offers rehabilitation services and residential care for the person with an alcohol or drug abuse related problems.

8023 Back in the Saddle

14371 Crow Road
Apple Valley, CA 92307   760-240-3217
FAX: 760-946-3412

Richard Smith, Ph.D., Co-Director
Erika Reed, Co-Director

A long term community residential facility for head injured adults. House parents live on-site; and oversee a variety of programs which are individually designed and might include classes in community college, placement in a workshop or on a workstation, volunteer positions and home skills assignments. Recreational outing range from horseback riding to weekend camping. Apartment programs available as set-up. Price: $2800-$3000 per month.

8024 Ballard Rehabilitation Hospital

1760 West 16th Street
San Bernardino, CA 92411   909-473-1200
                                  FAX: 909-473-1276
                                  www.ballardrehab.org

Robert Herrick, CEO
Mary Hunt, COO
Patty Meinhardt, Director of Marketing/Admissions

Ballard Rehab Hospital is a free standing specialty hospital and provides the complete continuum of acute, subacute and outpatient rehabilitation, dedicated to providing rehab seminars to adults and children. The following inpatient and outpatient programs are available: CNA (Stroke) Rehab; Spinal Cord Injury Rehab; Brain Injury Rehab; Pain Management Rehab; Injured Worker Programs; and Post Amputation Rehab:

8025 Bayview Nursing and Rehabilitation

516 Willow Street
Alameda, CA 94501   510-521-5600
                                 FAX: 510-865-6441

Postacute rehabilitation program.

8026 Belden Center

606 Humboldt Street
Santa Rosa, CA 95404   707-579-2735
                                 FAX: 707-579-4145

Wes Killian, Program Director
Postacute rehabilitation program.

8027 Build Rehabilitation Industries

1323 Truman Street
San Fernando, CA 91340   818-898-0020
                                 FAX: 818-898-1949

Matthew Lynch, President/CEO
Michele A. Utley, Vice President

Comprehensive C.A.R.F. Accredited vocational rehabilitation services for adults with disabilities or other barriers to employment. Programs include: Sheltered Workshops, Work Evaluation, Work Hardening and Adjustment, Supported Employment, Job Placement, Independent Living Skills, Behavior Management, Adult Development Center, On-the-Job Training, and One-Stop Workforce Development Career Center.

8028 California Elwyn

18325 Mount Baldy Circle
Fountain Valley, CA 92708   714-557-6313
                                 FAX: 714-963-2961
                                 e-mail: hmichaels@ogelwyn.org
                                 www.elwyn.org

Henry Michales, Program Manager
Joan McKinney, Executive Director

Provides opportunities for people challenged by physical and mental disabilities who are 18 or older. California Elwyn develops an Individual Rehabilitation Plan for all consumers. Contract work, shrink-wrap, janitorial are just some of the types of jobs done. Supported Employment Services are available and over 100 consumers currently are employed. Funded by the State Department of Rehabilitation and Vocational Rehabilitation.

8029 California Eye Institute

1360 E Turdan Avenue
Fresno, CA 93720   559-225-2737
                                 FAX: 559-499-5090

Virgil Snow, M.D.

A private, nonprofit agency offering services such as health, educational, recreational, rehabilitation and employment counseling to the totally blind, legally blind and visually impaired. The staff includes two full time workers.

8030 California Veterans Center

859 S Harbor Boulevard
Anaheim, CA 92805   714-776-0161

Veterans medical clinic offering disabled veterans medical treatments.

8031 Camp Recovery Centers

Camp
3192 Glen Canyon Road
Scotts Valley, CA 95066   831-438-1868
                                 800-924-2879
                                 FAX: 831-438-5833
                                 www.camprecovery.com

Melissa Preshaw, Marketing Manager

A free-standing social model recovery center for chemical dependency located on 25 wooded acres in the Santa Cruz Mountains. The services include: medical detoxification, complete medical evaluation, psychiatric evaluation and counseling, psychological testing, individual counseling and more. Helps the recovery from chemical dependency in a easier, warm and caring environment.

8032 Campobello Chemical Dependency Recovery Center

3400 Guerneville Road
Santa Rosa, CA 95401   707-579-4066
                                 FAX: 707-579-1603
                                 e-mail: campocdrc@aol.com

Kathy Willis, NCAC, CEAP, Executive Director

8033 Casa Colina Centers for Rehabilitation

255 East Bonita Avenue
PO Box 6001
Pomona, CA 91769   909-596-7733
                                 800-926-5462
                                 FAX: 909-596-7306
                                 e-mail: rehab@casacolina.org
                                 www.casacolina.org

Fred Arrow, Public Relations

Casa Colina, has pioneered effective programs to create opportunity for health, productivity and self-esteem for persons with disability since 1936. Through medical rehabilitation, transitional living, return to work, residential, community, and prevention and wellness programs. Casa Colina serves more than 6,000 persons annually. Casa Colina, a non-profit organization, offers a unique spectrum of opportunities, achievement and results to patients and their families.

8034 Casa Colina Paova Village
PO Box 6001
Pomona, CA 91769   909-596-7733
    800-926-5462
    FAX: 909-593-0153
    e-mail: rehab@casacolina.org
    www.casacolina.org

Michelle Stoddard, Director, Residential Services
Fred Arotuan, Director, Public Relations

Long term residential services for adults with developmental disability. Residences include Malmquist House, Woodbend House, and Hillsdale House, all located in Claremont, California.

8035 Casa Colina Peninsula Rehabilitation Center
26303 Western Avenue
Lomita, CA 90717   310-325-3202
    FAX: 310-534-2782

Postacute rehabilitation program.

8036 Casa Colina Residential Services - Rancho Pino Verde
11981 Midway Avenue
Lucerne Valley, CA 92356
    FAX: 619-248-2245

Postacute rehabilitation program.

8037 Casa Colina Residential Services- Rancho Pino Verde
11981 Midway
Lucerne Valley, CA 92356   760-248-6245
    FAX: 760-248-2245
    e-mail: rehab@casacolina.org
    www.casacolina.org

Long term redidential servicse in rural environment for adults with brain injury.

8038 Casa Colina Transitional Living Center
255 East Bonita Avenue
Pomonana, CA 91767   909-593-7611
    FAX: 909-593-7541
    www.casacolina.org

Postacute rehabilitation program.

8039 Casa Colina Transitional Living Center - Pomona
2850 N Garey Avenue
6001
Pomona, CA 91767   909-596-7733
    800-926-5462
    FAX: 909-596-7306
    e-mail: ccrehabe@lightside.com
    www.casacolina.org

Fred Aronow, Director, Public Relations

Post acute short term residential program for persons with brain injury. In a home-like setting, therapy promotes successful re-entry to home and community living.

8040 Cedars of Marin
Bolinas Avenue & Upper Road
Ross, CA 94957
    FAX: 415-454-0573

Brenda McIvor, Executive Director

Provides residential and day programs for adults with developmental disabilities.

8041 Center for Neuro Skills
2658 Mount Vernon Avenue
Bakersfield, CA 93306   805-323-4199
    800-843-2943
    FAX: 805-872-5150
    e-mail: cns@neuroskills.com
    www.neuroskills.com/~cns

John Schultz, Vice President
Steve Katomski, Admissions

A comprehensive, post-acute, community based head-injury rehabilitation program serving over 100 clients per year. Since 1980, CNS has effectively treated the entire spectrum of head-injured clients, including those with severe behavioral disorders, cognitive/perceptual impairments, speech/language problems, physical disabilities and post-concussion syndrome.

8042 Center for the Partially Sighted
12301 Wilshire
Suite 600
Los Angeles, CA 90025   310-458-3501
    800-481-EYES
    FAX: 310-458-8179
    e-mail: info@low-vision.org
    www.low-vision.org

LaDonna Ringering PhD, Executive Director
Pat Jordan, Public Information Manager
Phyllis Amarai Ph.D, Clinical Director

Services for partially sighted and legally blind people includes low vision evaluations, the design and prescription of low vision devices and adaptive technology, as well as counseling and rehabilitation training (independent living skills and orientation and mobility training). Special programs include children's program, diabetes and vision loss program, HIV and vision loss program. Store carries low vision aids. Catalog available.

8043 Center of Excellence on Mobility
3801 Miranda Avenue MS153
Palo Alto, CA 94304

    e-mail: info@roses.stanford.edu
    guide.stanford.edu

Develops new ways to assist disabled veterans.

8044 Central Coast Neurobehavioral Center OPTIONS
PO Box 877
800 Quintana # 2-C
Morro Bay, CA 93442   805-772-6066
    FAX: 805-772-6067
    www.options.ccnbc.org

Mike Mamot, CEO
De Von Frausing- Borch

Serves individuals head injured or neurologically impaired. CCNBC operates two transitional living centers (one for adults, one for children); a rehabilitation agency, and a supported work program. Services offered include: neuropsychology, physical therapy, occupational therapy, speech therapy, counseling, behavioral intervention, independent living and life skills training.

8045 Children's Hospital Los Angeles Rehabilitation Program

4650 W Sunset Boulevard
6
Los Angeles, CA 90027   323-669-2231
FAX: 323-665-4118

Maureen McMorrow, Medical Director

A comprehensive program specializing in the treatment of patients with brain injury.

8046 Children's Therapy Center

770 Paseo Camarillo
Suite 120
Camarillo, CA 93010   805-383-1501
FAX: 805-383-1504
e-mail: ctcinc@paragon,net
www.ctcinc@paragon.net

Jo Murphy Hyland, Administrative Director

Provides individual occupational therapy, speech/language therapy, family/child consulting, education services and physical therapy consultation for children. Evaluations and treatment are on an individual basis and special emphasis is placed on a multidisciplinary approach with information sharing, and often team treatment.

8047 Clausen House

88 Vernon Street
Oakland, CA 94610   510-839-0050
FAX: 510-839-0518

Nan Butterworth, Executive Director
Dale Tedeschi, Director

A private, nonprofit organization which emphasizes greater independence for developmentally disabled adults. Programs encompass residential, educational, recreational, vocational and independent living skills training.

8048 Coastline Enterprises

700 Northcrest Drive
Suite D4
Crescent City, CA 95531   707-464-8338
FAX: 707-465-1029

Nancy L. Boage, Director

Services people with special needs, and their families.

8049 Community Access Program - Hilltop

2800 Hilltop Mall Road
Suite 1250
Richmond, CA 94806   510-374-3994
FAX: 510-222-8290
e-mail: cmccrary@earthlink.net

Carol Anne McCrary, Director

A private, nonprofit membership-based organization dedicated to enhancing the quality of life of individuals with mental retardation and other developmental disabilities.

8050 Community Hospital and Rehabilitation Center of Los Gatos-Saratoga

815 Pollard Road
Los Gatos, CA 95032   408-866-3888
FAX: 408-866-4077

David Heartman, Rehab Program Dir.

Offers rehabilitation services, inpatient and outpatient care, physical therapy, occupational therapy and more for the physically challenged adult.

8051 Coronado Hospital

250 Prospect Place
Coronado, CA 92118   619-435-6250
FAX: 619-522-3782

Postacute rehabilitation program.

8052 Critical Air Medicine

Montgomery Field
4141 Kearny Villa Road
San Diego, CA 92123   619-514-6060
800-247-8326
FAX: 619-571-0835

Offers emergency medical care by air medical transport carriers. These carriers are fully equipped with medical equipment and supplies for cardiovascular emergencies, respiratory supplies, orthopedic supplies and medications.

8053 Crutcher's Serenity House

50 Hillcrest Drive
PO Box D
Deer Park, CA 94576
877-274-4968
FAX: 707-963-2309
www.crutcherssh.com

Robert Crutcher, CEO/ Owner
Lu Crutcher, Executive Director

A privately owned and operated facility that introduces to residents a new lifestyle free of all chemicals, and a new awareness of their total being. The length of the program is four weeks and is within five minutes of an acute care hospital. The Center is licensed for 19 beds, male and female located in a home-like setting with an emphasis on maintaining a family atmosphere.

8054 Daniel Freeman Rehabilitaion Centers

333 N Prairie Avenue
Inglewood, CA 90301   310-674-7050
FAX: 310-419-8232

Louis Ceppi, Assoc. Administrator

Comprehensive rehabilitation services which address needs and issues of the physically diabled and their families. We offer accute input rehabilitation, outpatient and short term skilled nursing rehabilitaion. Specialty areas include: brain injury, stroke, spinal chord injury, chronic pain, arthritis.

8055 Delano Regional Medical Center

1401 Garces Highway
Delano, CA 93215   661-725-4800
FAX: 661-721-5211

Postacute rehabilitation program.

8056   Devereux Santa Barbara
PO Box 1079
Santa Barbara, CA   93102   805-968-2525
                                   800-359-7979
                          FAX: 805-968-3247
                 e-mail: ca1kmco@devereux.org
                          www.devereux.org

Kelly McCool, Director of Admissions
Anna Martinez, Admissions Coordinator
Janis Johnson, Public Relations Coordinator

Serves ages 8-88, who have developmental disabilities, emotional disturbances, neurological impairments, brain injuries, schizophrenia, autism, and dual diagnosis. The Center has a licensed capacity of 188 served in a continuum of services including residential, vocational, educational and more.

8057   Division of Physical Medicine and Rehabilitation
San Joaquin General Hospital
500 W Hospital Road
French Camp, CA   95231   209-468-6280
                          FAX: 209-468-6281
                 www.sjphysicalmedicine.com

Carolyn Genschmer, Rehabilitation Coordinator

Offers rehabilitation services, inpatient and outpatient care, speech therapy, physical therapy, occupational therapy and more for the physically challenged individual.

8058   Doctors Medical Center Rehabilitation Services
1441 Florida Avenue
Modesto, CA   95350   209-578-1211
                          FAX: 209-576-3902

J. Douglas Dent, Chief Exec. Officer

Offers rehabilitation services, outpatient and inpatient care, respite care and more for the physically challenged individual.

8059   Dr. Karen H. Chao Developmental Optometry
Karen H. Chao. O.D.
121 South Del Mar Avenue
Suite A
San Gabriel, CA   91776   626-287-0401
                          FAX: 626-287-1457
                 e-mail: drkhchao@yahoo.com
                          www.BeacoNet.com/Dr.Chao

James Young, Practice Manager

Developmental optometrist specializing in the testing and treatment of vision problems and the enhancement of visual performance. Performs visual perceptual testing and training for children and adults. Undetected vision problems interfere with the ability to achieve and are highly correlated with learning difficulties and developmental problems. Provides the opportunity to overcome vision and visual-perceptual dysfunctions.

8060   Early Childhood Services
216 North Gold Canyon
Ridgecrest, CA   93555   760-384-4963
                          FAX: 760-375-1288
                 e-mail: Pam Lord DART_ecs1@ridgenet.net

Pam Lord, Director

8061   East County Training Center
1855/1865 John Towers Avenue
El Cajon, CA   92020   619-590-9324
                          FAX: 619-449-7853

Val Swan

Work adjustment and remunerative work programs.

8062   East Los Angeles Doctors Hospital
4060 Whittier Boulevard
Los Angeles, CA   90023   323-881-1112
                          FAX: 323-980-9824

Postacute rehabilitation program.

8063   Easter Seals Bay Area
2757 Telegraph Avenue
Oakland, CA   94612   510-835-2131
                          FAX: 510-444-2470
                          www.esba.org

Mike Pelfini, Exec. Vice President & CEO
Johnny Jones, Vice President

8064   Easter Seals Superior California
Sacramento Center & Regional Offices
3205 Hurley Way
Sacramento, CA   95864   916-485-6711
                          FAX: 916-485-2653
                 e-mail: info@eastersealsca.com
                          www.eastersealsca.com

Gary Kasai, President/CEO
Terry Colborn, V P of Programs & Gov't Affairs
Jessica Cone, Director of Marketing/Developmen

Provide outpatient rehabilitation services including day training programs for adults with disabilities and traumatic brain injuries, warm water therapy, non-public agency services to children including pediatric OT and PT services, work training/employment services, medical equipment loans, early intervention services for infants and toddlers. Serving the counties of Alpine, Calaveras, El Dorado, Sacramento, San Joaquin, Sutter, Tuolumne, Yolo, Yuba and others.

8065   El Mirador Rehabilitation Center at Desert Hospital
1180 North Indian Canyon Drive
Suite W214
Palm Springs, CA   92262   760-416-4550
                          FAX: 760-416-4555

Offers occupational, physical and speech therapy.

8066   Exceed: A Division of Valley Resource Cent er
3519 North Perris Boulevard
Perris, CA   92571   909-657-0609
                          FAX: 909-657-2277

Kathy Coke, Program Coordinator

8067   Eye Medical Clinic of Fresno
1122 S Street
Fresno, CA   93721   559-486-5000
                          FAX: 559-439-7854

Virgil Snow, M.D.

A private, nonprofit agency offering services such as health, educational, recreational, rehabilitation, employment and counseling to the totally blind, legally blind and visually impaired. The staff includes hundreds of full time workers.

8068 Fontana Rehabilitation Workshop
Industrial Support Systems
130 N Lilac Avenue
Rialto, CA   92376   909-820-0230

Carole Holt, Executive Director

8069 Foothill Vocational Opportunities
789 N Fair Oaks Avenue
Pasadena, CA   91103   626-449-0218
                                 FAX: 626-449-4802

James Hall, Executive Director

8070 Fred Finch Youth Center
3800 Coolidge Avenue
Oakland, CA   94602   510-482-2244
                                 FAX: 510-488-1860
e-mail: adamchase@fredfinch.org
www.fredfinch.org

John Steinfirst, MSW, Executive Director
Adame Chase, Admissions Director

A structured, psychiatric (JCAH accredited) residential treatment center for emotionally disturbed girls and boys between the ages of 12 and 18. Our treatment incorporates an on-site, non-public, special education school, an extensive activities and recreational program, a strong professional psychotherapy component (providing individual, group, and family therapy) and a parent support group. We provide 24-hour awake staff.

8071 Friendship Center for the Blind
2032 Kern Street
Fresno, CA   93721   559-266-9496
                                 FAX: 559-266-6879

Phillip Kimble, Director
Vicki Zehrung, Rehab. Social Worker III
Roben Asher, Specialist

A private, nonprofit organization that offers educational, health, recreational and professional training services to the totally blind, legally blind or severely visually impaired. Staff numbers one full- time and four part- time employees.

8072 Gateway Center of Monterey County
850 Congress Avenue
Pacific Grove, CA   93950   831-372-8002
                                 FAX: 831-372-2411
wwww.gateway-center.org

John Wecker, Chief Executive Officer

Provides residential and day programs for developmentally disabled adults.

8073 Gateway Industries - Castroville
1663 Catalina Street
Sand City, CA   93955   831-393-1575

Mike Sweeney, Executive Director

8074 Gilroy Workshop
8855 Murray Avenue
Gilroy, CA   95020   408-842-0334
                                 FAX: 408-842-6770

Cathy Andrade

Work adjustment and remunerative work programs.

8075 Glendale Memorial Hospital and Health Center Rehabilitation Unit
1420 S Central Avenue
Glendale, CA   91204   818-551-0045
                                 FAX: 818-409-7688

William Parente, President

Offers rehabilitation services, occupational therapy, physical therapy, residential services and more for the disabled.

8076 Goleta Valley Cottage Hospital
351 S Patterson Avenue
Santa Barbara, CA   93111   805-967-3411
                                      800-782-2288
                                 FAX: 805-681-6437

Postacute rehabilitation program.

8077 Goose Hill
PO Box 1101
Santa Ynez, CA   93460

Else Wolff, Owner/Operator

A small facility licensed for three developmentally disabled children. Provides residential services for the children currently residing there. The Center is located in a small Danish community of Solvang 45 miles north of Santa Barbara.

8078 Greenery Rehabilitation Center - Pacifica
385 Esplanade
Pacifica, CA   94044
                                      800-356-5959
                                 FAX: 650-359-9388

68 beds offering active/acute rehabilitation, brain injury day treatment, complex care and short-term evaluation.

8079 Hacienda La Puente Adult Education
333 Newquist Avenue
City Of Industry, CA   91745   626-333-7884
                                 FAX: 626-855-3169

Debra Zirkle-Fleischman, Supervisor

8080 Hi-Desert Continuing Care Center
6722 White Feather Road
Joshua Tree, CA   92252   760-366-2281
                                      800-782-2288

Postacute rehabilitation program.

8081 Hillhaven Extended Care
1115 Capitola Road
Santa Cruz, CA   95062
                                 FAX: 831-462-9812

Postacute rehabilitation program.

8082 Hillhaven San Francisco at Nobhill
1359 Pine Street
San Francisco, CA 94109   415-673-8405
                                  FAX: 415-563-2174

Postacute rehabilitation program.

8083 Home of the Guiding Hands
1100 N Magnolia Avenue
Suite O
El Cajon, CA 92020   530-579-2501
                                  FAX: 619-448-7208

Eleanor Lassiter
Work hardening and disciplinary programs.

**8084 Hospital of the Good Samaritan Acute
Rehabilitation Unit**
616 Witmer Street
Los Angeles, CA 90017   213-977-2358
                                  FAX: 213-482-2770

Andrew B. Leeks, President & CEO
David N. Shaw, MD, Medical Dir. of Acute Rehab.

Physicians, researchers and staff are united by a common mission: to foster growth into one of the most comprehensive medical centers in the West. Services offered include: cardiology and cardiovascular services, neurosciences, movement disorders and Parkinsons disorder, wound care center and transfusion-medicine and surgery center.

8085 Industrial Therapy Center
St. John's Regional Medical Center
295 Hueneme Road
Port Hueneme, CA 93041   805-986-3069
                                  FAX: 805-986-3535

Mark Witman, PT, Manager
A non-profit health care facility offering multi-disciplinary programs for pain management and work hardening, as well as physical and occupational therapy.

8086 Janus of Santa Cruz
200 7th Avenue
Suite 150
Santa Cruz, CA 95062   831-462-1060
                                  FAX: 831-462-4970
                                  www.janussc.org

Jan Tice, Executive Director

**8087 John Muir Medical Center Rehabilitation
Services, Therapy Center**
1601 Ygnacio Valley Road
Walnut Creek, CA 94598   925-947-5300
                                  FAX: 925-947-3262

Sandra Reese, Vice President

8088 Kelso Activity Center
404 S Hughes Avenue
Fresno, CA 93706   559-237-5101
                                  FAX: 559-237-5326

Tami Grinstead
Heather Harrison
Serves DTAC and ADP consumers.

8089 King's View Work Experience Center
100 Airpark Road
Atwater, CA 95301
                                  FAX: 209-357-0398

Samuel Kalember, Executive Director

8090 King-Drew Medical Center
12021 S Wilmington Avenue
Los Angeles, CA 90059   310-668-4321
                                  FAX: 310-632-6965

A private, nonprofit agency offering services such as health, educational, recreational, rehabilitation, employment and counseling to the totally blind, legally blind and visually impaired. The staff includes many full time workers.

8091 LaPalma Intercommunity Hospital
7901 Walker Street
La Palma, CA 90623   714-670-7400
                                  FAX: 714-670-6004

Steven Dickson, President

8092 Lawrence L. Frank Center Workshop
201 S Kinneloa Avenue
Pasadena, CA 91107   626-449-5661

Provides remunerative work.

8093 Lawrence L. Frank Rehabilitation Workshop
3812 S Grand Avenue
Los Angeles, CA 90037   213-748-7309
                                  FAX: 213-748-7248

Marilyn Graves, Executive Director

8094 Learning Services - Gilroy
10855 De Bruin Way
Gilroy, CA 95020   408-848-4379
                                  FAX: 408-848-6509

Mike Howard PhD, Program Director
Flexible sub and post acute rehabilitation for persons with acquired brain injury. Services include subacute long term care and rehab, residential post acute rehab, day treatment, outpatient and home-based rehab.

8095 Learning Services - Los Gatos
2005 Hamilton Avenue
Suite 130
San Jose, CA 95125
                                  FAX: 408-848-6509

Ann Kent, Marketing Manager
Graduates several hundred individuals each year from its community-integrated rehabilitation programs. These people accomplish renewed productivity in meeting the challenge of their disabling injury, and are more likely to avoid economic and human costs of unnecessary dependency.

8096 Learning Services - South Valley Ranch
10855 De Bruin Way
Gilroy, CA 95020   408-848-4379
                                  FAX: 408-848-6509

8097 Learning Services - Supported Living Programs

10855 De Bruin Way
Gilroy, CA 95020   408-848-4379
                                         800-466-4379
                                    FAX: 408-848-6509

Carol Hughes, Admissions Director
Steven P. Johnson, PhD, Program Director

Long term living programs provided in normalized community settings. Programs include campus-based living for person in need of high levels of support and/or 24 hour nursing; supervised apartment living and assisted apartment living programs for persons with acquired brain injuries.

8098 Leon S. Peters Rehabilitation Center

Fresno & R Street
PO Box 1232
Fresno, CA 93715   559-459-3957
                                         800-628-9099
                                    FAX: 559-498-0261

Jeff DiMarco, RN, Manager
Jenny Lau, RTC, CTRS, Community Liaision, Rehab Serv.

8099 Lion's Blind Center

Lions Blind Center
101 N Bascom Avenue
San Jose, CA 95128   408-295-4016
                                    FAX: 408-295-1308
                             e-mail: LBCSCV@AOL.Com

Ed Thomas, Executive Director

The Santa Clara Valley BlindCenter, Inc. DBA The Lions Blind Center is a social/recreational training facility for any blind or sight impaired person in Santa Clara County over the age of 12. It provides an hospitable atmosphere that utilizes interactive socialization methods and classes to assist the blind and sight-impaired cope with their disability. Staff includes 2 sighted individuals in management positions.

8100 Lion's Blind Center of Diablo Valley

175 Alvarado Avenue
Pittsburg, CA 94565

Phil Sitzman, Director

A private, nonprofit agency offering services such as health, educational, recreational, rehabilitation, employment and counseling to the totally blind, legally blind and visually impaired. The staff includes two full time workers.

8101 Lion's Blind Center, Oakland

3834 Opal Street
Oakland, CA 94609   510-450-1580
                                    FAX: 510-654-3603

Charles Boyer, Executive Director

A private, nonprofit organization offering services for the totally blind, legally blind, deaf-blind and multihandicapped blind. Services include: professional training, rehabilitation, educational, counseling, social work, self help and more. The staff includes 17 full time and two part time workers.

8102 Lions Center for the Blind of Oakland

3834 Opal Street
Oakland, CA 94609   510-450-1580
                                    FAX: 510-654-3603

Job placement service orientation and mobility services for cane users. Computer training for the blind or visually impaired. Work activity program for the developmentally disabled and the visually impaired. Life enrichment program.

8103 Living Skills Center for the Visually Impaired

2430 Road 20
Apartment B112
San Pablo, CA 94806   510-234-4984
                                    FAX: 510-234-4986
                          e-mail: skillscr@flash.net
                     www.livingskillscenter.locality.com

Patricia Williams, Director

A private, nonprofit agency offering services such as independent living skills training, recreational, employment and accessible technology training to the totally blind, legally blind and visually impaired. The staff includes six full time teachers.

8104 Loma Linda University Medical Center, Rehabilitation Institute

11234 Anderson Street
Loma Linda, CA 92354   909-558-4213
                                    FAX: 909-558-4133

Mara McCarville, Marketing Director

Offers a full range of clinical programs for both inpatients and outpatient. The specific diagnosis leading to patient admission includes stroke, spinal cord injury, traumatic or anoxic brain damage, amputation, post neurosurgery, chronic neurological disease, Guillain-Barre syndrome, arthritis, multiple trauma or other complex orthopedic problems. The facilities and professional services are comprehensive and ensure that the best care is provided to pediatric and adult patients.

8105 Manor Care Nursing - Citrus Heights

7807 Uplands Way
Citrus Heights, CA 95610   916-967-2929
                                    FAX: 916-965-8439

Postacute rehabilitation program.

8106 Manor Care Nursing - Fountain Valley

11680 Warner Avenue
Fountain Valley, CA 92708   714-241-9800
                                    FAX: 714-966-1654

Postacute rehabilitation program.

8107 Manor Care Nursing - Hemet

1717 W Stetson Avenue
Hemet, CA 92545   909-925-9171
                                    FAX: 909-925-8186

Postacute rehabilitation program.

8108 Manor Care Nursing - Palm Desert

74350 Country Club Drive
Palm Desert, CA 92260   760-341-0261
                                    FAX: 760-779-1564

Postacute rehabilitation program.

8109 Manor Care Nursing - Sunnyvale

1150 Tilton Drive
Sunnyvale, CA 94087
408-735-7200
FAX: 408-736-8619

Postacute rehabilitation program.

8110 Manor Care Nursing - Walnut Creek

1226 Rossmoor Parkway
Walnut Creek, CA 94595
925-975-5000
FAX: 925-947-2149

Postacute rehabilitation program.

8111 Maynard's Chemical Dependency Recovery Centers

19325 Cherokee Road
Tuolumne, CA 95379
408-279-0136
FAX: 209-928-1152

Don Blount, President

8112 Maynard's Ranch for Men

19325 Cherokee Road
Tuolumne, CA 95379
408-279-0136
FAX: 209-928-1152

Robert Maynord, President

Provides treatment for chemical dependency problems to men. The treatment addresses their recovery through a comprehensive plan created for their individual needs. Also offers a program for women called the Meadows.

8113 Meadowbrook Los Angeles - Community Re-Entry Services

4600 Woodley Avenue
Encino, CA 91436
818-994-4634

Postacute rehabilitation program.

8114 Meadows

16185 Tuolumne Road
Sonora, CA 95370

Don Blount, Director

Provides treatment designed for women that is directed at every important facet of their lives - mentally, physically and spiritually. Clients receive a variety of treatment approaches to facilitate their recovery and a comprehensive treatment plan is created for their individual needs. Issues relating to the cause of addictions are addressed in lectures, one-on-one counseling sessions, group therapy and re entry groups. Also offers a male treatment programs called Maynord's Ranch.

8115 Medical Center of La Mirada

14900 Imperial Highway
La Mirada, CA 90638
562-944-1900

John Edwards, Executive Director

8116 Memorial Hospital of Gardenia

1145 W Redondo Beach Boulevard
Gardena, CA 90247
310-532-4200
800-782-2288

Postacute rehabilitation program.

8117 Mercy Outpatient Rehab Center for NeuroRet raining

406-1/2 Sunrise Avenue
Suite 300
Roseville, CA 95661
916-486-2145
FAX: 916-780-5770
e-mail: leaton@chw.edu

Lynda Eaton, PT, Client Services Liaison

Postacute rehabilitation program for traumatic brain injury survivors.

8118 Napa County Mental Health

2344 Old Sonoma Road
Napa, CA 94559
707-253-4728
FAX: 707-253-4155

Work hardening and disciplinary programs.

8119 Napa Valley Support Systems

650 Imperial Way
Suite 202
Napa, CA 94559
707-253-7466
FAX: 707-253-0115

Isabel Harris

Work hardening and disciplinary programs.

8120 North County Center - Cerebral Palsy

205 W Mission
Suite 6
Escondido, CA 92025
760-743-1050
FAX: 760-746-0172

Gill Hennessey, Director

Provides remunerative work.

8121 North Valley Services #2

RR 5 Box 5475
Orland, CA 95963
530-846-2081
FAX: 530-865-4633

Robert Thomas, Assistant Director

8122 NorthRidge Hospital Medical Center for Rehabilitative Medicine

18300 Roscoe Boulevard
North Ridge, CA 91328
818-885-5330
FAX: 818-701-7367
northridgehospital.com

Debra Flaherty, Director, Rehabilitation Service

8123 Old Adobe Developmental Services

235 Casa Grande Road
Petaluma, CA 94954
707-763-0646
FAX: 707-763-7708
e-mail: nickbobo@aol.com

Dennis Orner, Executive Director

Provides remunerative work.

8124 PRIDE Industries

10030 Foothills Boulevard
Suite 200A
Roseville, CA   95747   916-783-8234
                              800-550-6005
                         FAX: 916-783-8234
                         www.prideindustries.com

Michael Ziegler, President
Samuel K. Seaton, Vice President

To provide opportunities through employment, training, evaluation and education, and to maximize community integration, independence and overall quality of life for people with barriers to employment.

8125 Pain Center

9888 Genesee Avenue
La Jolla, CA   92037   858-626-6952
                         FAX: 858-626-7213

Corinna Nyquist, Outreach Coord.

Offers both inpatient and outpatient programs including: physical activity management, individual pain management, group therapy, medication adjustment, pain control classes, occupational therapy, biofeedback training, family counseling, vocational and leisure counseling and recreational therapy.

8126 Parents and Friends

350 Cypress Street
Fort Bragg, CA   95437   707-964-4916

George Griffith, Executive Director

8127 Peninsula Center for the Blind

2470 El Camino Real
Suite 107
Palo Alto, CA   94306   650-858-0202
                              800-660-2009
                         FAX: 650-858-0857

Pam Brandin, Executive Director

Private, nonprofit agency that serves the visually impaired in the San Mateo and Santa Clara counties. Offers services in health, counseling, social work, self help and education. The staff includes nine full time employees and five part time.

8128 Peninsula ReCare

1764 Marco Polo Way
Burlingame, CA   94010   650-259-8500
                         FAX: 650-697-5010

Kirk F. Cunningham, President/CEO

Vocational, health and recreational services for individuals with disabilities.

8129 Penn Rehabilitation Center

12360 Penn Street
Whittier, CA   90602   562-698-7514

Linda Argyle, Director
Provides remunerative work.

8130 People Services

4195 Lakeshore Boulevard
Lakeport, CA   95453   707-263-3810
                         FAX: 707-263-0552
              e-mail: peopleservices@mindspring.com
                         www.peopleservices.org

F. Ilene Dumont, Executive Director
Martin Diesman, Director of Community Services

Providing an array of services for adults with developmental disabilities and other people with disabilities. Services include supported employment, work services, supported living, personal, social and community training, transportation, specialized individual services and much more.

8131 Petaluma Recycling Center

315 2nd Street
Petaluma, CA   94952   707-763-4761
                         FAX: 707-763-4921

David Donati, Executive Director

8132 Pomerado Rehabilitation Outpatient Service

15708 Pomerado Road
Suite N102
Poway, CA   92064   858-613-4636
                         FAX: 858-613-4248

Sheila Brown, Dir. Rehab Services

A modern outpatient rehabilitation facility featuring state-of-the-art therapies, techniques and equipment in the areas of physical therapy, occupational therapy and speech/language pathology.

8133 Pride Industries

10030 Foothills Boulevard
Roseville, CA   95747   916-788-2100
                              800-550-6005
                         FAX: 916-788-2560
              e-mail: sseaton@prideindustries.com
                         www.prideindustries.com

Sam Seaton, Director of Rehabilitation
Rosemary Elston, Rehabilitation Services Manager

Vocational rehabilitation and employment services creating jobs for people with disabilites; services include career counseling, vocational assessment, work adjustment, work services, job seeking skills, job development, job placement, on-the-job support (coaching), mentoring, independent living skills, transition services, and case management.

8134 Pride Industries - Grass Valley

12451 Loma Rica Drive
Grass Valley, CA   95945   530-477-1832
                         FAX: 530-477-8038

Kimberly Jonesad, Site Manager
Lisa Bowers, Counselor
Craig Hays, Adult Day Program Coordinator

Work adjustment and remunerative work programs. We offer an adult day program as well.

8135 Project Headway

8640 Corbin Avenue
Northridge, CA 91324   818-772-1419
                              FAX: 818-344-3340
e-mail: project_headway@netzero.net

Lena Reinhold, Director
Pat Digre, Administrator

A life long residential care for persons with acquired brain injuries. Personal care assistance, supportive services in small group homes, community based. Accepts all types of funding, licensed by the state of California.

Sliding Fee

8136 Rancho Adult Day Care Center

Rancho Los Amigos Medical Center
7600 Consuelo Street
Downey, CA 90242   562-940-7981

Provides personal care, social services and a therapeutic program to older adults in order to improve their quality of life. Offers a Clinical Gerontology Service, an Alzheimer's Disease Diagnostic and Treatment Center and a Geriatric Assessment and Rehabilitation Unit.

8137 Redlands Psychological and Psychiatric Group

Maxine McGowan Smith
440 Cajon Street
Redlands, CA 92373   909-793-4475

Marjorie Smith, Director

8138 Redwoods United

45 Ericson Court
Arcata, CA 95521   707-822-2352
                          FAX: 707-822-7075

Rochelle Parkinson, Executive Director

8139 Regional Center for Rehabilitation

2288 Auburn Boulevard
Sacramento, CA 95821   916-421-4167
                              FAX: 916-925-1586

Postacute rehabilitation program.

8140 Regional Infant Center

3010 W Harvard Street
Santa Ana, CA 92704

Joan Hess, Public Health Nurse

8141 RehabCare Unit - Brotman Medical Center

3828 Delmas Terrace
Culver City, CA 90232   310-836-7000
                                800-677-1238
                          FAX: 310-202-4105

Ellen Graham, Program Manager
Kevin McAninch, Dir. Provider

Culver City is centrally located within the city of Los Angeles. These are two programs offering inpatient rehabilitation. The acute rehab program is designed for patients who need physical rehabilitation due to injury or medical disability. This program requires patients to participate in 3 hours therapy per day. The sub-acute program is designed especially for patients who need rehab but cannot tolerate the intensity of the acute rehab program.

8142 Rehabilitation Center at Corona Community Hospital

800 S Main Street
Corona, CA 91720   909-737-4343

Michael Schultz, President

Offers inpatient and outpatient rehabilitation services. The Center consists of an acute rehab unit, a subacute rehab unit containing modules for long-term ventilator care, respiratory rehab, coma intervention and orthopedics. In addition to inpatient therapies, the Center's outpatient programs include sports and industrial medicine.

8143 Rehabilitation Institute Glendale Adventist Medical Center

1509 Wilson Terrace
Glendale, CA 91206   818-409-8071
                            FAX: 818-546-5609

Melanie Meners, Admission Coordinator

8144 Rehabilitation Institute of Santa Barbara

427 Camino Del Remedio
Santa Barbara, CA 93110   805-683-3788
                                FAX: 805-683-0381

Rusty Pollock, President/CEO
Rosemary Resch, R.N. Admissions Manager

A regional rehabilitation system with an acute care hospital at the center, the Institute provides specialized inpatient and outpatient programs for brain injury, spinal cord injury, stroke, work-related injury, chronic pain, orthopedic problems and more. Offers a 46-bed acute-care rehabilitation hospital, a free-standing outpatient center, the brain injury continuum, chronic pain program.

8145 Rehabilitation Institute of Southern California

1800 E La Veta Avenue
Orange, CA 92866   714-633-7400
                          FAX: 714-633-4586
e-mail: rhayes@rio.rehab
www.rio-rehab.com

Raylene Hays, Director of Programs

Outpatient rehabilitation serving physically and disabled children and adults. Child development programs, adult day care for disabled seniors, child care for disabled and non-disabled children, outpatient therapy, aquatics, adult day healthcare, independent living, vocational services, social services, and housing.

8146 Rehabilitation Research and Development Center

Dept. of Veterans Affairs, Palo Alto Health Care S
3801 Miranda Avenue MS-153
Palo Alto, CA 94304   650-493-5000
                    FAX: 650-493-4919
        e-mail: jaffe@roses.stanford.edu
                    guide.stanford.edu

David L. Jaffe, MS, Research Biomedical Engineer

The VA Center of Excellence on Moblity in Palo Alto is dedicated to developing innovative clinical treatments and assistive devices for veterans with physical disabilities to increase independence and improve quality of life. The clinical emphasis is to improve mobility, either ambulation or manipulation, in individuals with neurologic impairments or orthopaedic impairments. The center targets four conditions that cause significant loss of mobility: stroke, spinal cord inury, arthritis and osteo

8147 Rehabilitation Unit Northridge Hospital Medical Center

18300 Roscoe Boulevard
Northridge, CA 91325   818-885-5330
                    FAX: 818-701-7367

Debra Flaherty, Director of Rehabilitation

8148 Rex Industries

9575 Aero Drive
San Diego, CA 92123   760-471-0250
                    FAX: 858-715-3788

Gary Luce, Operations Manager

Offers many different programs including: North County Parent/Infant Program which is an educational program for children, birth to three years who are showing delays in development or who are at risk for developmental delays. The Adult Development Center is a program for adults, eighteen and over, with a developmental disability in the severe to profound range. The program focuses on self-help, communication, daily living and pre-vocational skills. Other programs are available.

8149 Rohnert Park Services (Behavioral)

6920 Commerce Boulevard
Suite 114
Rohnert Park, CA 94928   707-585-6700
                    FAX: 707-664-8057

Patricia Vreeland, Program Director
Judith Clover, Asst. Program Dir.

The program services are designed to assist individuals who demonstrate basic work skills, to develop social skills and work habits necessary to succeed in supported or competitive employment. Most often individual program services involve working with the client to replace those behavioral excesses that have been a barrier to vocational placement.

8150 Rubicon Programs

2500 Bissell Avenue
Richmond, CA 94804   510-235-1516
                    FAX: 510-235-2025
                    www.rubiconpgms.org

Richard Aubry, Director
Provides remunerative work, placement and training.

8151 San Bernadino Valley Lighthouse for the Blind

762 North Sierra Way
San Bernardino, CA 92410   909-884-3121
                    FAX: 909-884-2964

Robert McBay, Executive Director
Sandra Wood, Administrative Assistant

Provides training in independent living skills - cooking, mobility and orientation, sewing, braille and typing. Also, we have classes in macrame, ceramics, basket weaving. Weekly support group and bible study.

8152 San Diego Center

3821-C Calle Fortunada
San Diego, CA 92123   619-263-7600
                    FAX: 619-571-0919

Nancy Oro
Provides remunerative work.

8153 San Gabriel Valley Training Center and Workshop for the Handicapped

400 S Covina Boulevard
La Puente, CA 91746   626-285-6407
                    FAX: 626-330-5966

Randall Hyatt, Executive Director

8154 Shriners Hospitals for Children - Los Angeles

3160 Geneva Street
Los Angeles, CA 90020   213-388-3151
                    888-486-5437
                    FAX: 213-387-7528
        e-mail: edefilipplo@shrinenet.org
                    www.shrinershq.org

Elizabeth DeFilippo, Director of Public Relations
Faviola Ramirez, Applications Coordinator

Treats children under the age of 18 with burn scars and orthopedic conditions. All medical care is provided completely free of charge for patients and their families. Conditions commonly treated include scoliosis, club feet, leg length discrepancies, arthrogryposis, orthopedic problems related to cerebral palsy and spina bifida. Treats amputation or limb deficiency. Also treated are deformities due to burns, scar revision and reconstructive surgery.

8155 Shriners Hospitals, San Francisco Unit, for Crippled Children

2425 Stockton Boulevard
Sacramento, CA 95817   916-451-7025
                    FAX: 415-661-3615

8156 Society for the Blind

2750 24th Street
Sacramento, CA 95818   916-452-8271
                    FAX: 916-452-2622
                    www.societyfortheblind.org

Bryan Bashin, Executive Director

A private, local nonprofit organization providing blind and visually impaired people with the training supplies and support they need to live independent, productive and fulfilled lives with limited vision. Services include the Low Vision Clinic, Braille classes, computer training, support groups, living skills instruction, mobility training and the Products for Independence Store.

8157 Solutions at Santa Barbara - Transitional Living Center

1135 N Patterson Avenue
Santa Barbara, CA 93111   805-683-1995
FAX: 805-683-4793
e-mail: 5011135@aol.com

Susan Hannigan, OTR, CCM, Director
Susan Farber, MA, Case Manager

Postacute rehabilitation program. Short-term transitional living program for individuals with traumatic brain injury, stroke, aneurysm and other neurological disorders.

8158 South Bay Rehabilitation Center at Paradise Valley Hospital

2400 E 4th Street
National City, CA 91950   619-470-4239
FAX: 619-470-4126

Fred Harder, President

8159 Southeast Industries

9501 Washburn Road
Downey, CA 90242   562-803-4606
FAX: 562-803-4080

Howard Buswell

Work hardening and disciplinary programs.

8160 St. John's Pleasant Valley Hospital Neuro Care Unit

2309 Antonio Avenue
Camarillo, CA 93010   805-389-5846
FAX: 805-389-5968

Rosa Vasquez, Director

Subacute rehabilitation program; ventilator dependent.

8161 Starlight Center

1280 Nolan Avenue
Chula Vista, CA 91911   619-427-7524
FAX: 619-427-4657

Laura Orcutt

Provides remunerative work.

8162 Sub-Acute Saratoga Hospital

18611 Sousa Lane
Saratoga, CA 95070   408-378-1382
FAX: 408-866-8144

Postacute rehabilitation program.

8163 Synergos Neurological Center - Hayward

27200 Calaroga Avenue
Hayward, CA 94545   510-264-4000

Postacute rehabilitation program.

8164 Synergos Neurological Center - Mission Hills

15031 Rinaldi Street
Mission Hills, CA 91345   818-898-4412

Postacute rehabilitation program.

8165 Tehama County Opportunity Center

13315 Baker Road
Red Bluff, CA 96080   530-527-0407
FAX: 530-527-7091

Delbert Brownfield, Executive Director

8166 Temple Community Hospital

235 North Hoover Street
Los Angeles, CA 90004   213-382-7252
FAX: 213-389-4559

Postacute rehabilitation program.

8167 Ukiah Valley Association for Habilitation

564 South Dora Street
Suite D
Ukiah, CA 95482   707-468-8824
FAX: 707-468-9149
e-mail: roy@uvah.org
www.uvah.org

Roy Smith, Executive Director
Elaine Thaler, Mayacama Industries Director

Work adjustment and remunerative work programs.

8168 Valley Center

546 Brunken Avenue
Salinas, CA 93901   831-754-5509
FAX: 831-758-0250

Ruth Grigsby, Executive Director

8169 Valley Children's Hospital Rehabilitation Center

9300 Valley Children's Place
Madiera, CA 93638   559-353-8030
FAX: 559-353-8650
www.valleychildrens.org

Robin Gomez, RN, Manager

We provide rehabilitation services for those birth through 21 years in both inpatient and outpatient settings.

8170 Valley Rehabilitation Industries

806 E Flora Street
Stockton, CA 95202   209-948-2065
FAX: 209-463-1511
e-mail: arcsj@gotnet.net

Ronald Tognoli, Executive Director
Sandra Monroe, Director

Vocational training, supported employment and job placement for persons with mental retardation and other developmental disabilities. Valley Rehabilitation Industries is a program of the Association for Retarded Citizens-San Joaquin.

8171 Variety Club Blind Babies Foundation

1200 Gough Street
San Francisco, CA 94109   415-771-9035
FAX: 415-771-9026

Dr. Phillip Hatlen, Executive Director

A private, nonprofit agency offering services in the areas of health, counseling, social work, self help and education to blind and visually impaired infants. The educated staff includes 8 full time and 3 part time employees.

8172 Villa Esperanza Services

2116 East Villa Street
Pasadena, CA 91107   626-449-2919
                        FAX: 626-449-3141
              www.villaesperanzaservices.org

Dottie Cebula Nelson, CEO

Serving developmentally disabled infants to seniors
in a school, adult day program, adult work program
and residences, and adult day health care program and
care management program.

8173 Village Square Nursing Center

1586 W San Marcos Boulevard
San Marcos, CA 92069   760-471-2986
                        FAX: 760-471-5176

Postacute rehabilitation program.

8174 Walker Institute

881 Alma Real Drive
Pacific Palisades, CA 90272   213-989-0544

Postacute rehabilitation program.

8175 Western Neuro Care Center

165 N Myrtle Avenue
Tustin, CA 92780   714-832-9200
                        FAX: 714-508-4550

John Fenton, Chief Exec. Officer

8176 Winways

20682 E Santiago Canyon Road
Orange, CA 92869   714-771-5276
                        FAX: 714-771-1452
       e-mail: helpdesk@winwaysrehab.com
                www.winwaysrehab.com

Nancy R Silver, MACCM, Director of Admissions
Postacute rehabilitation program

Colorado

8177 Capron Rehabilitation

Penrose/St. Francis Healthcare System
2215 N Cascade Avenue
Colorado Springs, CO 80907
                        FAX: 719-776-2534

Gary A. Morse, Director
Southern Colorado's most complete inpatient and
outpatient rehabilitation center.

8178 Cherry Hills Health Care Center

3575 South Washington Street
Englewood, CO 80110   303-789-2265
                        FAX: 303-781-8808

Jody Porupski, Administrator
Postacute rehabilitation program.

8179 Community Hospital Back and Conditioning Clinic

1060 Orchard Avenue
Grand Junction, CO 81501   970-243-3400
                              800-621-0926
                        FAX: 970-856-6510

Amy Hibberd, Executive Director

8180 Developmental Preschool

1720 Brookside Avenue
Canon City, CO 81212   719-275-0550

Paulette Bolton, Deputy Director

8181 Heritage Rehabilitation Center

1500 Hooker Street
Denver, CO 80204   303-534-5968
                        FAX: 303-534-0930

Postacute rehabilitation program.

8182 Laradon Hall Society for Exceptional Children and Adults

5100 Lincoln Street
Denver, CO 80216   303-296-2400
                        FAX: 303-296-0737

Timothy C. Hall, Executive Director
Laradon provides educational, vocational and residential services to children and adults with developmental disabilities and other special needs. Laradon
was founded in 1948. It is among the largest and most
comprehensive service providers in Colorado.

8183 Learning Services - Bear Creek

7201 West Hampden Avenue
Lakewood, CO 80227   303-989-6660
                        FAX: 303-989-2830

Supported living program for persons with acquired brain injury.

8184 Manor Care Nursing - Denver

290 S Monaco Parkway
Denver, CO 80224   303-355-2525
                        FAX: 303-355-6960

Nancy Schwalm, Administrator
Rose Reinhardt, Admissions Director
Postacute rehabilitation program.

8185 Manor Care Nursing and Rehabilitation Center - Boulder

2800 Palo Parkway
Boulder, CO 80301   303-440-9100
                        FAX: 303-440-9251

Sherry Howell Ph.D. ,Ccc-Slp, Rehab. Director
Postacute rehabilitation program. Inpatient and Outpatient programs.

8186 Mapleton Center for Rehabilitation

311 Mapleton Avenue
Boulder, CO 80304
                        FAX: 303-441-0484

David Gehant, President

8187 Martin Luther Homes - Colorado Springs

3707 Parkmoor Village Drive
101
Colorado Spgs, CO 80917

FAX: 719-531-0582

Coleen Abeyta, Administrator
Fred Naumann III, Communications

Providing a wide array of services to assist individuals and families in achieving positive life goals. Services to persons with disabilities and other special needs include community living options, training and employment options, spiritual growth and development options, training and counseling support.

8188 Mediplex of Colorado

8451 Pearl Street
Thornton, CO 80229

303-288-3000
FAX: 303-286-1253

Peggy DiTommaso, Marketing Director

Our programs and services help each patient along the road to recovery toward our ultimate aim; the greatest possible restoration of the individual's self-esteem, ability to set goals, and self-sufficiency. Also offer specialized acute inpatient rehabilitative services, including special programs in Trauma Rehabilitation.

8189 Platte River Industries

490 Bryant Street
Denver, CO 80204

303-825-0041
FAX: 303-825-0564

Robert Smith, Executive Director

8190 Pueblo Diversified Industries

2828 Granada Boulevard
Pueblo, CO 81005

FAX: 719-564-3407

Karen Lillie, President
Will Dell, Director of Operations

8191 SHALOM Denver

1212 Delaware Street
Denver, CO 80204

303-623-0251
FAX: 303-620-9584

Arnold Kover

Work hardening and disciplinary programs.

8192 Schaefer Rehabilitation Center

500 26th Street
Greeley, CO 80631

FAX: 970-353-2779

Richard Kuhn

Work hardening and disciplinary programs.

8193 Spalding Rehab Hospital West Unit

150 Spring Street
Morrison, CO 80465

303-697-4334
FAX: 303-697-0570

Postacute rehabilitation program.

8194 United Cerebral Palsy of Colorado

2200 South Jasmine Street
Denver, CO 80222

303-691-9339
FAX: 303-691-0846
e-mail: info@ucpco.org
www.ucpco.org

Robin Bolduc, Statewide Services

Provides services for children 0-5 years, employment services for adults, information and referral, and donation pickup.

Connecticut

8195 ACES/ACCESS Inclusion Program

333 State Street
North Haven, CT 06473

203-248-8869

Susan Huntley, Director

Provides a person centered planning approach for integrated employment, volunteer community based opportunities for adults who have developmental disabilities.

8196 APT Residential Services Division

Mile Hill Road
Newtown, CT 06470

FAX: 203-781-4792

Sharon Sokolowski, Executive Director

8197 Apria Health Care

141 S Street
Suite D
W. Hartford, CT 06110

860-666-6199
800-732-0035
FAX: 860-632-9675

Provides a broad range of high quality and cost effective specialty infusion therapies and related services to patients in their homes throughout the Northeastern United States. Offer home infusion antibiotic therapy, quality pharmacy services, skilled nursing services and related support services.

8198 Central Connecticut Association for Retarded Citizens

1 Hartford Square
New Britain, CT 06052

860-224-6993

James McCann, Executive Director

8199 Connecticut Subacute Corporation

955 S Main Street
Middletown, CT 06457

860-347-6300
800-257-6300
FAX: 860-347-2446

Evan K. Lyle, Managed Care Dir.
Cheri Kauset, Corporate Rep.

Specializes in subacute medical and rehabilitation programming. The strength of our system is in its' ability to service a broad range of clinical and psychosocial needs which enable each individual to attain his/her optimal potential. Programming includes neurological and orthopedic rehabilitation, post-surgical and wound care management, intravenous therapy, pulmonary rehabilitation including ventilator services, and long term care.

8200 Datahr Rehabilitation Institute

135 Old State Road
Brookfield, CT 06804   203-775-2418
                              888-8DA-TAHR
                    FAX: 203-740-7129
                    www.datahr.org

Thomas Fanning, President

Providers of comprehensive rehabilitation services with a history of nearly 5 decades of service. This institute is recognized as a leading resource in meeting the needs of those disabled by illness, injury or developmental disorders in Connecticut and New York. A team of rehabilitation and health care professionals offering career development, residential services, supported employment, volunteer services, occupational therapy, day activities and more.

8201 Eastern Blind Rehabilitation Center

West Spring Street
West Haven, CT 06516   203-932-5711
                    FAX: 203-937-3806

Penny Schuckers, Director, Chief Eastern Blind

Provides residential rehabilitation services to eligible legally blind veterans in the Northeast and Middle Atlantic portions of the country. Referral applications by Veterans Administration Medical Centers and Outpatient Clinics in the geographical area served by the Blind Rehabilitation Center.

8202 FAVRAH

Avon Park North
Building 23
Avon, CT 06001

                    FAX: 860-676-0275
Provides remunerative work.

8203 Farmington Valley Arc

10 Tower Lane
Avon, CT 06001   860-678-0313
                    FAX: 860-676-0275

Tom Thompson

Serving over 300 mentally retarded adults through a comprehensive program of residential and support services. These include three group homes, three apartments, competitive and supported employment options, a day program for mentally retarded seniors, community experience day services for severe and profoundly disabled adults, recreation and leisure services, advocacy, transportation, case management, in-home respite and other support services.

8204 Gaylord Hospital

PO Box 400
Wallingford, CT 06492   203-284-2800
                              800-64R-EHAB
                    FAX: 203-284-2894
          e-mail: pjohnson@gaylord.org
                    www.gaylord.org

Paul Johnson, President

Works to restore ability and build courage. Offers rehabilitation care with one goal in mind: to help patients return to their homes, communities and jobs.

8205 Hockenum Greenhouse

Route 44A And Bone Mill Road
Mansfield, CT 06251   860-429-6697

Sarah Beardsley, Program Director

8206 Kuhn Employment Oppurtunities

165 Pratt Street
Meriden, CT 06480   203-235-2583
                    FAX: 203-235-0827

Dennis Plante, Executive Director

8207 Lake Grove at Durham

Christopher Ezzo
459R Wallingford Road
Durham, CT 06422   203-265-0413
                    FAX: 860-349-1382

8208 Litchfield County Association for Retarded Citizens

84-R Main Street
Torrington, CT 06790   860-567-9401
                    FAX: 860-489-2492

Lawrence Cassella, Executive Director

A private, nonprofit organization whose mission is to improve the quality of life for individuals with mental retardation or associated disabilities and their families through its vocational, residential and community services departments. The vocational component of LARC, provides adults with vocational opportunities with supports in mobile work crews, enclaves, and individual placements.

8209 Meriden-Wallingford Society

224 Cook Avenue
226
Meriden, CT 06451   203-272-8911
                    FAX: 203-639-0946

Peter McManus, Executive Director

Provides remunerative work, supported employment and job placement.

8210 Rehabilitation Associates

60 Katona Drive
Fairfield, CT 06430   203-384-8681
                    FAX: 203-384-0722

Carol Landsman, Director
Myra Watnick, Director

A comprehensive outpatient rehabilitation facility offering physical therapy, occupational therapy, speech-language pathology, clinical social work services and nutritional services to all age groups. Facility locations in Fairfield, Stratford, Milford and Shelton. All facilities are CARF accredited.

8211 Rehabilitation Center of Fairfield County

226 Mill Hill Avenue
Bridgeport, CT   06610   203-378-0092
                               FAX: 203-336-5465

Sally Gammon, President

Medical services are provided by physicians who are specialists in physical medicine and rehabilitation. The physical therapy department provides a variety of services and utilizes sophisticated modalities to restore and reinforce physical abilities.

8212 Reliance House

40 Broadway
Norwich, CT   06360   860-887-6536
                             FAX: 860-885-1970

David Burnett, Executive Director

A residential vocational and recreational support network. An active and productive clubhouse where people with mental illness can gain skills, strength and self-esteem.

8213 Section of Physical Medicine and Rehabilitation

Norwalk Hospital 24 Stevens Street
Norwalk, CT   06856
                             FAX: 203-852-2027

Dr. Claudio Petrillo, Director

8214 South Church Activity Program

99 Main Street
New Britain, CT   06051   860-224-9480
                                 FAX: 860-827-8681

Margaret Stowell, Supervisor

Delaware

8215 Alfred I. DuPont Hospital for Children

Division of Rehabilitation
1600 Rockland Road
Wilmington, DE   19803   302-651-5600
                                FAX: 302-651-5612
                                www.nemours.org

Thomas Ferry, Administrator
Offers rehabilitative services for the physically challenged individual.

8216 Community Systems

3204 Drummond Plaza
Newark, DE   19711   302-322-5066
                            FAX: 302-456-5733

George Baer, Executive Director

8217 Delaware Association for the Blind

800 West Street
Wilmington, DE   19801   302-655-2111
                                888-777-3925
                                FAX: 302-655-1442
                                www.dabdel.org

Linda Lauria, Executive Director

A private, nonprofit organization that offers adjustment to blindness counseling, recreation activities, summer camps and financial assistance for the legally blind. The staff includes five full time, nine part time and twelve seasonal. Operates a store selling items for the blind.

8218 Delaware Elwyn

321 E 11th Street
Wilmington, DE   19801   302-657-5601
                                FAX: 302-654-5815

Lewis C. Monges, Executive Director

8219 Delaware Veterans Center

1601 Kirkwood Highway
Wilmington, DE   19805   302-764-0848
                                FAX: 302-633-5250

Veterans medical clinic offering disabled veterans medical treatments.

8220 Easter Seal Rehabilitation Center - New Castle County

61 Corporate Circle
New Castle Common
New Castle, DE   19720   302-324-4488
                                FAX: 302-324-4481

Bill Adami, Executive Director

8221 Edgemoor Day Program

500 Duncan Road
Office A
Wilmington, DE   19809   302-762-1391
                                FAX: 302-762-2416

Betty Brown, Executive Director

8222 First State Senior Center

291A N Rehoboth Boulevard
Milford, DE   19963   302-422-1510
                             FAX: 302-422-1354

Marcella Wilson, Supervisor

8223 Georgetown Day Program

5 Academy Street
Georgetown, DE   19947   302-856-5366
                                FAX: 302-856-5360

Joyce Oliver, Supervisor

8224 Salvation Army Developmental Service

210 N Race Street
Georgetown, DE   19947   302-856-7145

Michael Paoli, Executive Director

8225 Woodside Day Program

941 Walnut Shade Road
Dover, DE 19901 302-739-4494
FAX: 302-697-4490

Connie Grace, Supervisor

District of Columbia

8226 Audiology Clinic (Children)

Audiology/HSCSN, Building 10
19th & Massachusetts Avenue SE
Washington, DC 20003 202-675-5000
800-675-7694
FAX: 202-675-7694

Margot Timke, M.Ed., CCCA&SLP, Audiologist

Offers diagnostic and treatment services for children
with suspected or actual disorders of communication.

8227 Barbara Chambers Children's Center

1470 Irving Street NW
Washington, DC 20010 202-387-6755
FAX: 202-319-9066

Francisca Torres

Offers special education, play and speech therapy
services to children 2-5 years of age with developmental delays.

**8228 District of Columbia General Hospital Physical
Medicine & Rehab Services**

19th and Mass Avenue
Room 1358
Washington, DC 20003 202-529-6211
FAX: 202-675-7819

Dr. Maribel Bieberach, Chairperson, PM&R
Dr. Raman Kapur, Staff Physiatrist

Offers comprehensive physical medicine and rehabilitation services including in and outpatient consultations and electrodiagnostic testing; in and
outpatient physical and occupational therapy; inpatient recreational therapy, and a multidisciplinary
prosthetic clinic which meets once a month.

8229 George Washington University Medical Center

2150 Pennsylvania Avenue NW
Washington, DC 20037 202-994-0825
FAX: 202-994-4005

Offers an Ambulatory Physical Therapy/Sports
Medicine Center, a Medical Center Prosthet-
ics/Orthotics Clinic and a Speech and Hearing
Center to persons in the District of Columbia, Virginia and Maryland.

8230 Hospital for Sick Children

1731 Bunker Hill Road NE
Washington, DC 20017 202-832-4400
FAX: 202-529-1646

Vernell P. DeWitty, Executive Officer

Offers chronically ill, severely disabled or respira-
tory-impaired children integrated rehabilitation and
habilitative care.

8231 Howard University Child Development Center

525 Bryant Street NW
Washington, DC 20089 202-806-4750
FAX: 202-806-7940

Marceline Dahl

Offers children with developmental problems diagnosis, treatment, evaluation and follow along visits.

8232 Psychiatric Institute of Washington

4228 Wisconsin Avenue NW
Washington, DC 20016 202-885-5600
FAX: 202-966-7374

Psychiatric intensive care, crisis intervention,
adult day treatment, drug treatment and other
services to children and adults who have psychiatric and chemical dependency problems.

8233 Spina Bifida Program of D.C. Children's Hospital

Department of Physical Medicine and Rehabilitation
111 Michigan Avenue NW
Washington, DC 20010 202-884-3092
FAX: 202-884-3422
e-mail: edonovan@cnmc.org,
pshilouya@cnmc.org
www.cnmc.org

*Eileen Donovan M.D., Medical Director, Spina Bi-
fida*
Peter Shilouya, Clinical Director, Spina Bifida

Offers neurosurgery, orthopedics, physical medicine,
social work, urology and nursing.

Florida

8234 Back Technology of Miami

545 San Esteban Avenue
Miami, FL 33146

Jerry Fogel
Provides remunerative work.

8235 Bayfront Rehabilitation Center

Bayfront Medical Center
701 6th Street South
Saint Petersburg, FL 33701 727-893-6702
FAX: 727-893-6779

Nute C. Meeker, Jr., Director

Inpatient and outpatient services provide progressive,
comprehensive one-on-one treatment. Specialized
care in physical and occupational therapy, speech and
recreational therapy, patient/family services and psychology is tailored to each patient from admission to
re-entry into the community.

8236 Bon Secours Hospital

1050 NE 125th Street
North Miami, FL 33161 305-893-0068

Julie Rog, Exec. Vice President

Offers rehabilitation services, occupational therapy, physical therapy, inpatient and outpatient care and more for the physically challenged.

8237 Brain Injury Rehabilitation Center Sand Lake Hospital

9400 Turkey Lake Road
Orlando, FL 32819   407-351-8500
      FAX: 407-351-8584

Tina Whatley, BIRC Admissions

Dedicated to restoring brain injured patients with rehabilitation potential to their highest level of functioning. This is accomplished through an interdisciplinary team demonstrating personal responsibility to the patient, their family and each other.

8238 Center for Pain Control and Rehabilitation

2780 Cleveland Avenue
Suite 607
Fort Myers, FL 33901   941-337-4332

Dr. Harris Bonnette, Medical Director

8239 Central Florida Sheltered Workshop

1600 Aaron Avenue
Orlando, FL 32811   407-295-4640
      FAX: 407-299-6050

Gerald Peaden, Executive Director
Joan Harris, Rehab Director

A multi-faceted, vocational rehabilitation facility. Programs offered are vocational evaluation and assessment, work adjustment, placement, supported employment, developmental training, long-term sheltered care and residential treatment.

8240 Comprehensive Rehabilitation Center at Lee Memorial Hospital

2776 Cleveland Avenue
Fort Myers, FL 33901   941-334-5200

Palma Fuson, Director

Offers rehabilitation services, occupational therapy, physical therapy, respite services and more for the physically challenged individual.

8241 Comprehensive Rehabilitation Center of Naples Community Hospital

350 7th Street North
Naples, FL 34102   941-436-5324
      FAX: 941-436-5250

William Crone, President
Heather Baker, Administrative Director
Ken Schields, Marketing Coordinator

Offers rehabilitation services, inpatient and outpatient care at 5 locations in the county and more for the benefit of the disabled.

8242 Conklin Center for the Blind

405 White Street
Daytona Beach, FL 32114   904-258-3441
      FAX: 904-258-1155
      e-mail: robert@conklincenter.org
      www.conklincenter.org

Robert Kelly, Executive Director

Offers services for the totally blind, legally blind, visually impaired, mentally retarded blind and more with health, counseling, educational, recreational, rehabilitation, through computer training and professional training services.

8243 Davis Center for Rehabilitation Baptist Hospital of Miami

8900 N Kendall Drive
Miami, FL 33176   305-596-6520
      FAX: 305-270-3640

Elizabeth Matalon, Administrative Dir.

A full-service, nonprofit community hospital providing a full range of inpatient and outpatient rehabilitation services. The overall commitment to excellence has extended to this specialized field. Access to medical expertise and services ensures that the best in medical resources are available should an unforeseen medical problem arise.

8244 Division of Blind Services

2551 W Executive Center Circle
Lafayette Building, Suite 200
Tallahassee, FL 32399   850-488-1330
      800-342-1828
      FAX: 850-487-1804
      e-mail: randy_touchton@fdles.state.fl.us

Randy Touchton, Director

Serves the totally blind, legally blind, visually impaired, deaf-blind, learning disabled, mentally retarded and other multiply handicapped by offering health, counseling, educational, recreational and computer training services.

8245 Easter Seal Society of Broward County

6951 West Sunrise Boulevard
Plantation, FL 33313   954-792-8772
      FAX: 954-791-8275
      e-mail: esdevel@laker.net

Jane Bauman, President

A nonprofit health agency dedicated to helping individuals of all ages with temporary and long-term physical disabilities become as self-reliant as possible. Coordinates and guides each client through the therapy process. All treatment is done by licensed and supervised therapists.

8246 Easter Seal Society of Dade County

1475 Northwest 14th Avenue
Miami, FL 33125   305-325-0470

Joan L. Bornstein, PhD., Acting President
Lillianne Camargo, MSW, Admissions Soc. Wkr.

8247 Easter Seals, Volusia and Flagler Counties FL

1219 Dunn Avenue
Daytona Beach, FL   32120   904-255-4568
                                   877-255-4568
                          FAX: 904-258-7677
                  e-mail: LSinnott@seals.org

Lynn Sinnott, President

Provides early intervention services: center based
pre-school, OT, PT, ST and parenting programs,
equipment loan closet, assistive technology information and referral. Residential summer camp and counseling programs

8248 Easter Seals/MARC

350 Braden Avenue
Sarasota, FL   34243   941-355-7637
                                  800-221-6827
                          FAX: 941-351-4997
                  e-mail: esociety@aol.com

Mary Hitchcock, Interim President & CEO

8249 F.I.R.E.

1286 Cedar Center Drive
Tallahassee, FL   32301   850-942-3658
                          FAX: 850-942-4518
                  e-mail: blind@noblestar.net

Skip Koch, Executive Director

Provides independent living and vocational rehabilitation services to Florida residents who are legally
blind. Services include instruction in orientation and
mobility, accessible technology, daily living skills
and employability skills. Information, referral and
counseling services are also offered. Operates a
store, which specializes in products specifically designed for persons who are blind. All services are
provided without charge.

8250 Florida Association of Workers for the Blind

601 SW 8th Avenue
Miami, FL   33130   305-856-2288
                          FAX: 305-285-6967
                  e-mail: mialight@gate.net
                  www.miamilighthouse.com

Vernon Metcalf, Executive Director

Offers services for the totally blind, legally blind,
visually impaired, mentally retarded blind and more
with health, counseling, educational, recreational, rehabilitation, computer training and professional
training services.

$150 per day

8251 Florida C.O.R.F.

2701 S Ridgewood Avenue
Suite A-8
S Daytona, FL   32119   904-761-7999
                          FAX: 904-947-4504

John Feore, Executive V.P.

Offers Medicare authorized therapy programs for
seniors, disabled and others who need rehabilitation.
CORF can provide coordinated and extended services
in the home after a hospital stay, or when physical
status changes. Patients who are treated at CORF,
include amputations, arthritis, chronic/acute pain, de-
pression/anxiety, nerve injury, sports injury, stroke
and swallowing problems.

8252 Florida Community College at Jacksonville/ Disabled Student Services

4501 Capper Road
Jacksonville, FL   32218   904-766-6500

Jeffrey Oliver, Assistant Dean

8253 Florida Veterans Centers

713 NE 3rd Avenue
Fort Lauderdale, FL   33304   954-356-7926
                          FAX: 954-356-7609

Veterans medical clinic offering disabled veterans
medical treatments.

8254 Goodwill Industries, Suncoast

10596 Gandy Boulevard North
14456
Saint Petersburg, FL   33702   727-523-5354
                          FAX: 727-577-2749

Deborah A. Passerini, V.P. Human Services

A nonprofit, community-based organization whose
purpose is to improve the quality of life for people
who are handicapped, disabled and/or disadvantaged
or aged. This mission is accomplished through providing independent living skills, affordable housing,
training and placement in useful employment. Annually, the facility serves over 1,000 people who are
handicapped, disabled or disadvantaged in various
components within the Human Services Department.
Staff consists of 120+ full-time employees.

8255 Halifax Hospital Medical Center Eye Clinic Professional Center

306 N Clyde Morris Boulevard
Daytona Beach, FL   32114   904-322-4700
                          FAX: 904-274-5889

James Clower, M.D.

Offers services for the totally blind, legally blind,
visually impaired, mentally retarded blind and more
with health, counseling, educational, recreational, rehabilitation, computer training and professional
training services.

8256 HealthQuest Subacute and Rehabilitation Programs

Regenta Park
7130 Southside Boulevard
Jacksonville, FL   32256
                          FAX: 904-641-7896

HealthQuest offers four centers within the state of
Florida offering exceptional staff, comfortable
surroundings and individually designed, closely
monitored programs dedicated to enabling patients to achieve their goals. Each location offers a
progressive and cost effective alternative to in-
hospital subacute and rehabilitative care. Centers
are offered in Jacksonville, Winter Park, Sarasota
and Sunrise.

8257 HealthSouth Regional Rehabilitation Center

20601 Old Cutler Road
Miami, FL   33189   305-251-3800
                          FAX: 305-251-5978

Les Alt, Administrator

A comprehensive source of medical rehabilitation services for Pinellas County, Florida area residents, their families and their physicians. Offers the people of Florida all the clinical, technical and professional resources of the nation's leading provider of comprehensive rehabilitation care.

8258 HealthSouth Rehabilitation Hospital of Tallahassee

1675 Riggins Road
Tallahassee, FL 32308   850-656-4800
FAX: 850-656-4809

Michael Carney, Administrator
Gini West RN, Director Business Development
Paula Adams PT, Director Clinical Services

North Florida's sole acute rehabilitation hospital between Jacksonville \, Panama City, and Gainesville. With 250 employees providing a full continuum of care form its 70 bed facility, the hospital is accredited by JCAHO, CARF and state designated and certified by Vocational Rehabilitation for traumatic brain injury, as well as a wide variety of other diagnoses. With the addition of our outpatients, the facility has served the greater community by touching the lives of over 50,000 patients.

8259 HealthSouth Rehabilitation Hospital of Sarasota

3251 Proctor Road
Sarasota, FL 34231   941-921-8600
800-873-4222
FAX: 941-925-7526

Laurie Boggus, Administrator

8260 HealthSouth Sports Medicine & Rehabilitation Center/Worksite Program

1710 Lisenby Avenue
Panama City, FL 32405   850-784-4878
FAX: 850-769-7566

Jim MsGonley, MPT/ATC, Director of Clinical Services

Outpatient sports medicine and rehabilitation center providing physical therapy, occupational therapy, industrial rehab, work hardening/work simulation, worksite and ergonomic analysis, FCE's, work assessment and pre-employment goals of returning the clients back to work, and returning to all recreational, sports and functional activities safely.

8261 Holy Cross Hospital

4725 North Federal Highway
Fort Lauderdale, FL 33308   954-771-8000
FAX: 954-351-5994

Barbara Dale, Director

8262 Lee Memorial Hospital

PO Box 2218
Fort Myers, FL 33902   941-332-1111

Mary Kalina, Marketing Director

Offers a complete inpatient program of intensive rehabilitation designed to restore a patient to a more independent level of functioning. The comprehensive care includes medical rehabilitation and training for spinal cord injury, brain injury, stroke and neurological disorders.

8263 Lehrman Back Center

1680 Michigan Avenue
Suite 1104
Miami Beach, FL 33139
FAX: 305-674-1094

David Lehrman, President

Testing for employee placement to determine potential for back injuries. Also sell portable back support pillows and back exercise videotapes.

8264 Lighthouse for the Blind of Palm Beach

7810 South Dixie Highway
West Palm Beach, FL 33405   561-586-5600
FAX: 561-586-5630

William S. Thompson, President & CEO
Sandra L. Lamb, VP of Admin. & Human Resources
Dawn M. Clemons, VP of Development & Services

A private, non-profit rehabilitation and education agency in its 55th year of service. Offers programs to assist persons who areblind or visually impaired, an on-site Industrial Center, a technology training center, an Aids and appliances Store, special equipment grant programs, outreach services for children and adults, Early Intervention and Preschool Services, and a variety of support groups. These programs provide services and education for blind children and their parents.

8265 Lighthouse for the Visually Impaired and Blind

8610 Galen Wilson Boulevard
Port Richey, FL 34668   727-815-0303
FAX: 727-815-0203
e-mail: ccaprera@lighthouse-pasco.org
lighthousepasco-hernando.org

Roxann Mayros, Executive Director
Cherie Caprera, Director of Client Services

The Lighthouse offers services for visually impaired or blind adults and children ages 0-5 years old. Counseling, educational, recreational, rehabilitation, computer training, support groups and job training and placement services are provided.

8266 MacDonald Training Center

5420 West Cypress Street
Tampa, FL 33607
FAX: 813-872-6010
TDY:813-873-7631

Jim Freyvogel, President
Mara Brad, V.P., Consumer Aff.

A private, non-profit, community-based human services organization serving adults with disabilities (since 1953). Persons are provided the opportunity to achieve their highest potential through the Center's various programs that include day training, employment, community living and various support services.

8267 Medical Rehabilitation Center of Jacksonville

836 Prudential Drive
Jacksonville, FL 32216   904-202-1611
FAX: 904-202-3147

Mark Kosier, Executive Director

8268 Medicenter of Tampa
4411 N Habana Avenue
Tampa, FL 33614   813-872-2271

Robert Westhoff, Administrator
Postacute rehabilitation program.

8269 Memorial Hospital Rehabilitation Center
3599 University Boulevard
Jacksonville, FL 32216   904-858-7600
                                   FAX: 904-858-7610

Dr. Charles Schauer, President
An entire care facility featuring five day inpatient
evaluation, pre-operative evaluation programs, five
week pain management program, referral criteria and
treatment goals, therapy services, psychological services and more to the physically challenged.

8270 Mount Sinai Medical Center Rehabilitation Unit
4300 Alton Road
Miami Beach, FL 33140   305-674-9662
                                   FAX: 305-674-2923

Charles Tirrell, Administrator

8271 Neuropsychiatric Pain Rehabilitation Clinic
5330 George Street
New Port Richey, FL 34652   727-849-2005
                                   FAX: 727-849-2087

Charlene Evina, Administrative Asst.
Vickie Penick, Administrator
A multidisciplinary outpatient program for the evaluation and treatment of chronic pain. Consultation
services for hospitalized patients are also provided
upon request.

8272 New Medico Rehabilitation Center of Florida
1962 Bandola Road
Wauchula, FL 33873   941-773-2857
                                   FAX: 803-773-0867
                                   www.finr.net

Gary Toche, Chief Executive Off.
A residential rehabilitation facility providing a therapeutic environment in which children, adolescents
and adults who have survived head-injury can develop the independence and skills necessary to re-enter the community.

8273 North Broward Rehab Unit
North Broward Medical Center
201 E Sample Road
Pompano Beach, FL 33064   954-786-6405
                                   FAX: 954-786-6476

Wendy Burkholder, Regional Manager
CARF accredited, 30-bed inpatient rehabilitation unit
treating adults with brain injuries, spinal cord injuries, stroke, orthopedic and neurologic injuries.

8274 Northwest Medical Center
5901 Colonial Drive
Margate, FL 33063   954-974-0400
                                   FAX: 954-984-1463

8275 Pain Institute of Tampa
4178 N Armenia Avenue
Tampa, FL 33607   813-875-5913
                                   FAX: 813-872-6215

Dave Braughton
Pain management.

8276 Pain Treatment Center, Baptist Hospital of Miami
8900 N Kendall Drive
Miami, FL 33176   305-596-6525
                                   FAX: 305-273-2406

Brian Keeley, President

8277 Pine Castle
4911 Spring Park Road
Jacksonville, FL 32207   904-733-2650
                                   FAX: 904-733-2681
                                   e-mail: pcastle@ilnk.com
                                   www.jvm.com/pinecastle

Jonathan May, Executive Director
Provides remunerative work, training, community
employment and community living options for adults
with developmental disabilities.

8278 Polk County Association for Handicapped Citizens
1038 Sunshine Drive E
Lakeland, FL 33801   941-665-3846
                                   FAX: 941-665-2330

Shirley Balogh
Work adjustment and remunerative work programs.

8279 Rebound Head Injury Rehabilitation Center
1300 New US Highway 441 E
Mt. Dora, FL 32757

Linda Pappas, Marketing Coordin.
Providers of comprehensive rehabilitation services
for survivors of severe head injuries. Rebound has
achieved national recognition for their unique and
cost-effective approach to rehabilitation. Offer superior medical care, nursing, physical therapy, occupational therapy, speech and language therapy and
psychological services. They also offer innovative,
effective therapies based on music, recreation, computers, exercise, art and dance movement.

8280 Rehab of Melbourne
Sea Pines Rehabilitation Hospital
101 E Florida Avenue
Melbourne, FL 32901
                                   FAX: 407-952-6532

Mark Tellier, Administrator

8281 Rehabilitation Center for Children and Adults
300 Royal Palm Way
Palm Beach, FL 33480   561-655-7266
                                   FAX: 561-655-3269
                                   e-mail: info@rcca.org
                                   www.rcca.org

Pamela Henderson, Executive Director

A private, nonprofit organization whose purpose is to improve physical function, independence and communication of people with physical disabilities. Any child or adult with a physical or speech disability is eligible for services.

8282 Renaissance Center

PO Box 17067
Jacksonville, FL 32245   904-354-1305
FAX: 904-353-3804

David Panken, President

8283 Sandybrook Center of Rebound

1300 US Highway 441
Mt. Dora, FL 32757   352-383-6007

Linda Pappas, Marketing Director

Exclusively dedicated to the rehabilitation of the brain injured client ages 18 or older. The complete program offers personal adjustment, family support, self care, health maintenance, leisure lifestyle management, vocational preparation, community access, financial management and more.

8284 Sarasota Memorial Hospital/Comprehensive Rehabilitation Unit

1700 S Timiami Trail
Sarasota, FL 34239   941-952-2535

Phillip Beauchamp, President

8285 South Dade Nursing Home, Ltd.

2525 SW 75th Avenue
Miami, FL 33155   305-262-6800

Frank Jimenez, Executive Director

8286 Strive Physical Therapy

2620 SE Maricamp Road
Ocala, FL 34471   352-351-8883
FAX: 352-351-4219

Kyle Schaneville, MPT, Clinical Director

8287 Sunbridge Care and Rehabilitation

5627 9th Street East
Bradenton, FL 34203   941-753-8941
FAX: 941-739-4409

Anita Faulmann, Administrator

A comprehensive medical rehabilitation facility that is committed to helping individuals with disabilities improve their quality of life. This is a 120-bed facility offering a full range of acute and sub-acute inpatient programs as well as community-based outpatient programs.

8288 Tampa Bay Academy

12012 Boyette Road
Riverview, FL 33569   813-677-6999
FAX: 813-671-3145

Malcolm Harriman

A psychiatric residential treatment center and partial hospitalization program for ages 7 to 17.

8289 Tampa General Rehabilitation Center

PO Box 1289
Tampa, FL 33601   813-251-7000
FAX: 813-253-4283

Cindy Leistner, Development Director

Offers a full range of programs all aimed at helping patients achieve their full potentials. It is one of three centers in the state that provides Driver Training and Evaluation Programs for persons with disabilities, and also an Assisted Reproduction Program for neurologically impaired males. A Community Re-entry Day Treatment Program is available for individuals who have recovered from a brain injury. A wide variety of inpatient and outpatient programs are available.

8290 Tampa Lighthouse for the Blind

1106 W Platt Street
Tampa, FL 33606   813-251-2407
FAX: 813-254-4305

C.E. Olstrom, Executive Director

Offers services for the totally blind, legally blind, visually impaired, mentally retarded blind and more with health, counseling, educational, recreational, rehabilitation, computer training and professional training services.

8291 University of Miami Comprehensive Pain and Rehabilitation Center

600 Alton Road
Miami Beach, FL 33139   305-532-7246
FAX: 309-534-3974

Renee Stelle-Rosomoff, Programs Director

8292 UpReach Pavilion

8900 NW 39th Avenue
Gainesville, FL 32606

Cindy Toth, Administrator

8293 Upper Pinellas Association for Retarded Citizens

1501 N Belcher Road
Clearwater, FL 33765   727-726-2029
FAX: 727-799-4632
e-mail: uparc@aol.com
www.members.aol.com/uparc/index.htm

Thomas J. Buckley, Ed. D., Executive Director

Offers services to more than 500 persons with mental retardation and other developmental disabilities. Services include two early intervention pre-schools, physical, speech and occupational therapies, homebound education and family support for children, birth to five years and transitional, vocational, habilitation, employment and placement services for adolescents and adults. UPARC operates 31 group homes, a 22 unit apartment complex, and Supported Living options to provide for residential need

8294 **Visually Impaired Persons of Southwest Florida**

35 West Mariana Avenue
Fort Myers, FL 33903 941-997-7797
FAX: 941-997-8462
e-mail: sdanko@olsusa.com
www.vip.org

Sherry Danko, Executive Director
William Goldsmith, Social Worker

Provides training in independent living skills, orientation and mobility, counseling, computer and other communication skills, family support groups, peer counseling, socialization and a low vision clinic.

8295 **West Florida Hospital - The Rehabilitation Institute**

8391 N Davis Highway
Pensacola, FL 32514 850-494-6000
FAX: 850-494-4881

Jerald F. Mitchell, President/CEO
Carol Saxton, VP Rehabilitation Services

A 58-bed comprehensive rehabilitation facility offering inpatient and outpatient services. JCAHO and CARF accredited and a State designed head and spinal cord injury center. CARF accredited programs include: comprehensive inpatient rehab, spinal cord injury, brain injury and work hardening.

8296 **Willough at Naples**

9001 Tamiami Trail East
Naples, FL 34113 941-775-4500
800-722-0100
FAX: 941-775-0534

A licensed psychiatric hospital in Southwest Florida which provides quality management and treatment for eating disorders and chemical dependency in adults.

Georgia

8297 **Annandale at Suwanee**

3500 Annandale Lane
Suwanee, GA 30024 770-945-8381
FAX: 770-945-8693
www.annandale.org

Patricia M. Brown, Executive Director

Private non-profit residential facility for adults with developmental disabilities. Located on 136 acres just north of Atlanta. Annandale provides full program and 24 hour residential services.

8298 **Atlanta Institute of Medicine and Rehabilitation**

2915 Piedmont Road
Suite A
Atlanta, GA 30305 404-365-0160
FAX: 404-365-0754

8299 **Bobby Dodd Center**

1440 Dutch Valley Plaza
Suite A
Atlanta, GA 30324 404-231-0580
FAX: 404-872-6540

Norman Meyers, Executive Director

8300 **Cave Spring Rehabilitation Center**

Georgia Avenue
Cave Spring, GA 30124 706-777-3382

Loring Kirk, Executive Director

8301 **Center for Assistive Technology & Environmental Access**

490 10th Street
Georgia Tech
Atlanta, GA 30332 404-874-1414
800-726-9116
FAX: 404-894-9320
www.arch.gatech.edu/crt/crthome.htm

Zena Rubin, MS, CRC, Rehab Counselor

A nonprofit research center with a focus on disseminating information on assistive technology, telecommunications, the ADA and environmental accessibility. Techknowledge is a clearinghouse providing this information to consumers, rehabilitation professionals, employers, educators and other interested parties.

8302 **Center for the Visually Impaired**

763 Peachtree Street NE
Atlanta, GA 30308 404-875-9011
FAX: 404-607-0062

Susan B. Green, Executive Director
Joan Stuart, CFRE, Director of Development
Kell Hicklin, Marketing Manager

Offers services to people of all ages who are blind or visually impaired with training in orientation and mobility, computer technology, activities of daily living, communication skills and employment readiness. The Center also offers two children's programs, a community-based rehabilitation program for senior citizens, and a low vision clinic.

8303 **Devereux Georgia Treatment Network**

1291 Stanley Road NW
PO Box 1688
Kennesaw, GA 30144 770-427-0147
800-342-3357
FAX: 770-427-4030
e-mail: ga1jzden@devereux.org
www.devereux.org

John Zdencanovic, Director of Admissions

Serves ages 11 to 17, males and females, with a capacity for up to 125. Serves moderate to severe emotional, behavioral, and/or learning disabilities. A specialized psychiatric hospital/intensive residential treatment program for low average to superior intelligence.

8304 **Easter Seals East Georgia**

1500 Wrightsboro Road
PO Box 2441
Augusta, GA 30903 706-667-9695
FAX: 706-667-8831
e-mail: sthomas@esega.org
www.ga-ea.easter-seals.org

Sheila H. Thomas, President/CEO

8305 Georgia Industries for the Blind

PO Box 218
Bainbridge, GA 31718 912-248-2666
FAX: 912-248-2669

Jim Hughes, Executive Director

Offers services for the totally blind, legally blind, visually impaired, mentally retarded blind and more with health, counseling, educational, recreational, rehabilitation, computer training and professional training services.

8306 Head Injury Treatment Program at Marietta

26 Tower Road
Marietta, GA 30060 770-422-8913
800-526-5782

Karen Erlinger, Program Director

Postacute rehabilitation program.

8307 Hillhaven Rehabilitation

26 Tower Road
Marietta, GA 30060 770-422-8913
800-526-5782
FAX: 770-425-2085

Leslie Ann Marie Parrish, Case Manager

Routine skilled and subacute medical and rehabilitation care including physical therapy, occupational therapy, speech pathology and therapeutic recreation. Programs include stroke and head injury rehab; orthopedic rehab; complex IV therapy; woundcare; cancer; total parental nutrition and dialysis.

8308 In-Home Medical Care

CareMaster Medical Services
1428 US 41 Bi-Pass South
PO Box 278
Griffin, GA 30224
800-542-8889
FAX: 770-412-0014
e-mail: caremaster@accesunited.com
www.caremastermedical.com

Nancy Frederick, Vice President

Offers the devoted attention of a professional nurse, the use of I.V. therapies, pain management and provision of medical equipment and supplies right where the patient wants to be.

8309 Learning Services - Peachtree

337 W Pike Street
Suite B
Lawrenceville, GA 30045 770-962-4828
FAX: 770-995-1253
www.learningservices.com

Greg Lang, Admissions

Postacute rehabilitation program.

8310 Meadowbrook Atlanta/Community Re-Entry

1946 Clairmont Road
200
Decatur, GA 30033 404-248-1667
FAX: 404-248-9833

Becky Waide, Marketing Director

Postacute rehabilitation program.

8311 Pain Control & Rehabilitation Institute of Georgia

2786 North Decatur Road
Suite 220
Decatur, GA 30033 404-897-1400
FAX: 404-297-1427

Dr. Shulim Spektor, CEO
Anna Britman, Office Manager

Provides pain management for chronic and acute pain resulted from injuries, diseases of muscles and nerve, Reflex Sympathetic Dystrophy, perform disabilities and impairment ratings.

8312 Savannah Association for the Blind

214 Drayton Street
Savannah, GA 31401 912-236-4473
FAX: 912-234-4156

W. Chandler Simmons, Executive Director

Offers services for the totally blind, legally blind, visually impaired, mentally retarded blind and more with health, counseling, educational, recreational, rehabilitation, computer training and professional training services.

8313 Shepherd Center for Treatment of Spinal Injuries

2020 Peachtree Road NW
Atlanta, GA 30309 404-352-2020
FAX: 404-350-7479

James Collins, Administrator

Dedicated exclusively to the care of patients with spinal cord injuries and other paralyzing spinal disorders. It serves predominately residents of Georgia and neighboring states as one of the only 14 hospitals designated by the U.S. Department of Education as a Model Spinal Cord Injury System Program.

8314 Transitional Hospitals Corporation

7000 Central Parkway NE
Suite 1000
Atlanta, GA 30328 404-378-8353
800-683-6868
FAX: 770-913-0015

A national network of intensive care hospitals providing care for patients who suffer from a chronic illness and/or catastrophic accident. The mission is founded on providing quality health care to patients who require highly skilled nursing care and access to technologically advanced therapies.

8315 Vince Dooley Easter Seal Center

3035 N Druid Hills Road NE
Atlanta, GA 30329 404-325-1470
FAX: 404-633-2740

Donna Davidson, President/CEO

Easter Seals is and will continue to be the leading organization in helping chioldren and adults with disabilities to live with equality, dignity, and independence.

8316 Walton Rehabilitation Hospital

1355 Independence Drive
Augusta, GA   30901   706-823-8511
                                   866-492-5866
                         FAX: 706-724-5752
                e-mail: postmaster@wrh.org
                              www.wrh.org

Dennis Skelley, President
Frank Lewis, Chief Operating Officer
Mike Warrell, Chief Financial Officer

A 58-bed comprehensive physical rehabilitation hospital offering inpatient and outpatient services. Services offered include: stroke recovery, orthopedic injury, pediatrics, head injury, pain management for chronic pain syndrome, TMJ/Craniofacial pain and chronic headache disorders, spinal cord injury, driving instruction, work re-entry, independent living, assistive technology and ADA consulting.

Hawaii

8317 Rehabilitation Hospital of the Pacific

226 N Kuakini Street
Honolulu, HI   96817   808-531-3511
                                   800-973-4226
                         FAX: 808-544-3335
                      www.rehabhospital.org

William D. O'Connor, President and CEO

Idaho

8318 Ashton Memorial Nursing Home and Chemical Dependency Center

801 Main
Ashton, ID   83420   208-652-7461
                         FAX: 208-652-7252

Sheila King, Executive Director

8319 Easter Seal Society

1465 Vinnell Way
Boise, ID   83709   208-378-9924
                                   800-374-1910
                         FAX: 208-378-9965

Donna Grummer, Vice President

8320 Idaho Elks Rehabilitation Hospital

PO Box 1100
Boise, ID   83701   208-343-2583
                         FAX: 208-489-4005

A nonprofit hospital serving Idaho and the Pacific Northwest. All inpatient and outpatient programs and services are supervised by the hospital's full-time medical directors whose specialty is psychiatry, the profession of physical rehabilitative medicine. Services include: occupational therapy, rehabilitative nursing, social skills, head injury program, physical therapy, speech pathology, audiology and cardiac rehabilitation.

8321 Intermountain Rehabilitation Center

777 Hospital Way
Pocatello, ID   83201   208-239-2660

Terri Ross, Director

Illinois

8322 Albany Park Community Center

3401 W Ainslie Street
Chicago, IL   60625   312-583-5111
                         FAX: 773-539-3916

Advocacy, case coordination, case management for mentally ill adults, educational publications and seminars for the mentally ill.

8323 Alexian Brothers Medical Center

800 Biesterfield Road
Elk Grove Village, IL   60007   847-437-5500

A threefold mission: Works toward maximizing physical function, enhance independent social skills and optimize communication skills consistent with an individual's ability. The Center helps those disabled by accident or illness achieve a new personal best.

8324 Anixter Center

6610 N Clark
Chicago, IL   60660   773-973-7900
                         FAX: 773-973-5268
            e-mail: AskAnixter@Anixter.org
                           www.anixter.org

Stuart Ferst, President & CEO

Anixter Center's mission is to assist people with disabilities to live and work successfully in the community. Anixter Center is a leading provider of quality, vacational, residential, educational option, substance abuse prevention, health care, advocacy for the rights of people with disabilities to be full and equal members of the community.

8325 Austin Center for Development

515 W N Avenue
Chicago, IL   60610   773-287-2020
                         FAX: 773-854-8300

Provides an educational program designed to enhance academic, behavioral and social performance of children 4-14 years of age experiencing emotional disorders that result in exclusion from the public school setting.

8326 Back in the Saddle Hippotherapy Program

Corcoran Physical Therapy
4200 W Peterson Avenue
Suite 114
Chicago, IL   60646   312-697-4430
                         FAX: 773-286-4399

Julie Naughton, Program Coordinator
Maureen Corcoran, Physical Therapist

A direct medical treatment used by licensed physical therapists who have a strong treatment background in posture and movement, neuromotor function and sensory processing. The benefits of Hippotherapy are available to individuals with just about any disability. Two locations: Glen Grove, IL and Morton Grove, IL. Accepts all insurance.

8327 Barbara Olson Center of Hope

3206 North Central Avenue
Rockford, IL 61101   815-964-9275
                            FAX: 815-964-9607
                            www.b-olsoncenterofhope.org

Carm Kilker, Executive Director
Jackie Neil Boss, Director of Administrative Serv.
Susan Nagy, Accoutant

We provide vocational employment, educational and social opportunities for adults with developmental disabilities.

8328 Baxter Healthcare Corporation

1 Baxter Parkway
Deerfield, IL 60015   847-948-2000

Ed Dobryzkowski, Executive Director

8329 Beacon Therapeutic Diagnostic and Treatment Center

10650 S Longwood Drive
Chicago, IL 60643   773-881-1005
                          FAX: 773-881-1164

Offers community day treatment, education, diagnostic services, family counseling, learning disabled, speech and hearing and psychiatric services.

8330 Blind Service Association

22 W Monroe Street
11th Floor
Chicago, IL 60603   312-236-0808
                          FAX: 312-236-8679

Debbie Grossman, Executive Director

Offers services for the totally blind, legally blind and visually impaired with reading and recording low vision network, social services, referrals and support groups.

8331 Brandecker Rehabilitation Center

9455 S Hoyne Avenue
Chicago, IL 60620   773-239-2191
                          FAX: 773-239-6229

Mary Howell, Ph.D, Executive Director

We offer early intervention services for infants and toddlers with developmental delays and disabilities. Our outpatient Medical Rehabilitation Program offers direct therapy services for children from age birth-16.

8332 Brentwood Nursing & Rehabilitation Center

5400 West 87th Street
Burbank, IL 60459   708-423-1200
                          FAX: 708-423-1590

Linda Schumann, Case Manager

Postacute rehabilitation program.

8333 Caremark Healthcare Services

2211 Sanders Road
Northbrook, IL 60062   847-559-4700
                              800-423-1411

An 80-service-center network providing services anywhere in the U.S. Offers 24 hour access to nursing and pharmacy services, case management resource centers, HIV/AIDS services, women's health services, transplant care services, nutrition support services, infectious disease management and other therapies and programs.

8334 Center for Comprehensive Services

306 W Mill
Carbondale, IL 62902   618-453-7932
                              FAX: 618-457-5372

Dr. Kathleen Fralish

Specifically designed to meet the needs of children and adults with neurologic impairments in the Carbondale area and surrounding region. Those who would benefit include persons who have experienced brain injury, a stroke or those with other neurologic problems.

8335 Center for Neuro Rehabilitation and Re-Entry

307 E Grand Avenue
Chicago, IL 60611   312-908-7532
                          FAX: 312-321-9134

Gloria Tarvin, Administrator
Postacute rehabilitation program.

8336 Center for Rehabilitation at Rush Presbyterian

17 South Palina Road
Chicago, IL 60612   312-946-6336

Timothy Flesch, Admissions Director
Postacute rehabilitation program.

8337 Center for Spine, Sports & Occupational Rehabilitation

1030 North Clark Street
Suite 500
Chicago, IL 60610   312-238-7767
                          FAX: 312-238-7709
                          www.rehabchicago.org

Offers evaluation and treatment of patients with acute and subacute musculoskeletal and sports injuries.

8338 Children's Home and Aid Society of Illinois

125 South Wacker Drive
Suite 14
Chicago, IL 60606 312-424-0200

www.chasisystems.org

Private state-wide. Multi-service, racially integrated staff and client populations. Provides educational, placement and community services for children-at-risk and their families. Advocacy, consultation and follow-up services provided according to our philosophy of continuum of care. No one, child or adult, is denied service because of disabilities, if the program services meet their needs. Higher quality in-service training for staff as well as parenting figures.

8339 Christ Hospital and Medical Center

4440 W 95th Street
Oak Lawn, IL 60453 708-346-3144
FAX: 708-346-2072

Ronald Struxness, Executive Director

8340 Clinton County Rehabilitation Center d/b/a CCRC Community Link

1665 North Fourth Street
PO Box 157
Breese, IL 62230 618-526-2252
FAX: 618-526-2021
e-mail: John@commlink.org
www.commlink.org

John Sedivy, Executive Director

8341 Continucare, A Service of the Rehab Institute of Chicago

West Suburban Hospital Medical Center
Erie at Austin
Oak Park, IL 60302 708-383-6200
800-354-7342
FAX: 312-908-1369

Offers inpatient subacute rehabilitation program.

8342 Delta Center

1400 Commercial Avenue
Cairo, IL 62914 618-734-3626
FAX: 618-734-1999

Frederica Garnett, Executive Director

8343 Division of Rehabilitation-Education Services, University of Illinois

1207 S Oak Street
Champaign, IL 61820 217-333-4600
FAX: 217-333-0248

Brad Hedrick, Director

Offers services for the totally blind, legally blind, visually impaired, mentally retarded blind and more with health, counseling, educational, recreational, rehabilitation, computer training and professional training services.

8344 Easter Seal Rehabilitation Center

1230 N Highland Avenue
Aurora, IL 60506 FAX: 630-896-6257

Beverly Brownel, Program Services
Richard N. Merz, Executive Director

Provides comprehensive outpatient rehabilitation services for physical, developmental and speech/language disabilities. Serves all ages. Also operates short-term residential camp for children with disabilities. Charges bases on third party coverage and family ability to pay. Private, non-profit organization.

8345 Easter Seal Rehabilitation Center of Will Grundy Counties

212 Barney Drive
Joliet, IL 60435 815-725-2194
FAX: 815-725-5150

Debra Condotti, Executive Director

8346 Easter Seals DuPage Dold Center for Children

830 S Addison Avenue
Villa Park, IL 60181 630-620-4433
FAX: 630-620-1148

James A. Johnson, Executive Director
Linda Matheson, Program Services

Maximizes independence for infants, children and adults with disabilities by providing physical, occupational and speech therapy, audiology, social work, early intervention, assistive technology, toy lending, equipment loan and special needs day care.

8347 El Valor Corporation

Early Intervention Program
1951 W 19th Street
Chicago, IL 60608 312-997-2021
FAX: 312-432-9849

Catalina Ariza, Director

Mission is to challenge people with disabilities. It is a center for people with disabilities and their families and serves Chicago and surrounding areas, providing services in English and Spanish to individuals whose lives would be drastically impoverished without them.

8348 Elgin Rehabilitation Center

1485 Davis Road
Elgin, IL 60123 847-888-5540

Robert Borchert, Vice President

8349 Family Counseling Center

Washington & Market Street
Golconda, IL 62938 618-683-2461
FAX: 618-683-2066
e-mail: fccgolconda@shawneelink.com

Larry Mizell, Executive Director
Beci Gates, Behavioral Health Division Dir.
Donna Perez, Housing Coordinator

Provides counseling, developmental training, evaluations, assisted living services, referrals, psychosocial rehabilitation, and a variety of work services.

8350 **Five Star Industries**
PO Box 60
Du Quoin, IL 62832   618-542-5421
                                       FAX: 618-542-5556

Thomas Hamlin, Executive Director
Incorporated as a private, non-profit corporation under the laws of the State of Illinois, is an equal opportunity employer and provides equal opportunity in compliance with the Civil Rights Act of 1964 and all other appropriate laws, rules and regulations referring to civil rights.

8351 **Gilchrist-Marchman Rehabilitation Center**
2345 W N Avenue
Chicago, IL 60647
                                       FAX: 773-276-5653

Therese O'Shea, Executive Director

8352 **Hardin County Center**
Main Street
Elizabethtown, IL 62931   618-287-2171
                                       FAX: 618-287-2017

W. Theo Wells, Executive Director

8353 **Henry County Clinic**
117 S E Street
Cambridge, IL 61238   309-937-5391
                                       FAX: 309-937-2023

Individual, group, marital and family therapy, psychological testing and evaluation services offered.

8354 **Hyde Park-Woodlawn**
950 E 61st Street
Chicago, IL 60637   773-702-0660
                                       FAX: 773-493-2397

William Cinwell, Executive Director

8355 **ILC Enterprises**
6415 Stanley Avenue
Berwyn, IL 60402   708-789-0511
                                       FAX: 708-788-0831

Cindy Holbrook, Program Director
A nonprofit tax exempt private social service agency serving suburban Chicago offering day treatment and vocational counseling to individuals who encountered a pattern of job loss due to emotional problems.

8356 **Illinois Center for Autism**
548 S Ruby Lane
Fairview Heights, IL 62208   618-398-7500
                                       FAX: 618-397-9869

A community-based mental health/educational treatment center dedicated to serving autistic clients.

8357 **Illinois Masonic Medical Center**
836 W Wellington Avenue
Chicago, IL 60657   773-975-1600

Consultation, education, family counseling, parent training in behavior modification techniques offered to developmentally disabled adults.

8358 **Infant Program**
409 W New Indian Trail
Aurora, IL 60506   630-879-9119

E. Duane Thompson, Executive Director

8359 **Jayne Shover Easter Seal Rehabilitation Center**
799 S McLean Boulevard
Elgin, IL 60123   847-742-3264
                                       FAX: 847-742-9436
                                       e-mail: jeastersea@aol.com
                                       www.jayneshover.org

Peggy Muetterties, President
A free-standing, comprehensive outpatient rehabilitation center serving children and adults with physical and developmental disabilities.

8360 **Julius and Betty Levinson Center**
332 Harrison Street
Oak Park, IL 60304   708-383-8887
                                       FAX: 708-383-9025
                                       e-mail: soneill@ucp.net.org

Houses one of its three adult developmental training programs for substantially physically disabled men and women.

8361 **Little Friends**
140 North Wright Street
Naperville, IL 60540   630-355-6533
                                       FAX: 630-355-3176
                                       www.littlefriendsinc.com

Jack Ryan, President/CEO
Tom Foley, Vice President

8362 **MAP Training Center**
7th and McKinley Street
Karnak, IL 62956   618-634-9401
                                       FAX: 618-634-9090

Larry Earnhart, Executive Director
Training, employment, residential and support services, targeted for adults with developmental disabilities.

8363 **Macon Resources**
PO Box 2760
Decatur, IL 62524   217-875-1910
                                       FAX: 217-875-8899
                                       TDY: 217-875-8898

Kay Scrogin, Executive Director
Shirley Paceley, Associate Director

The purpose is to provide a comprehensive array of habilitative/rehabilitative training programs and support services to assist individuals and/or family units of an individual with a developmental disability, mental illness, or other handicapping condition to live, attend school or day program, and/or work in the least restrictive, most normalized environment possible.

8364 Marianjoy Rehablink

26 W 171 Roosevelt Road
Wheaton, IL 60187   630-462-4000
                              FAX: 630-462-4440
                              www.maranjoy.org

Kathleen C. Yosko, President and CEO

Marinjoy Rehabilitation Hospital is a 120-bed hospital in Wheaton, Illinois that is dedicated to the delivery of rehabilitative medicine. Founded in 1972 by the Wheaton Franciscan Sisters, the hospital is a division of   Marianjoy provides comprehensive inpatient and outpatient rehabilitation   services, including programs that assist patients with re-entry, such as driver rehabilitation and return-to-work programs.

8365 Mary Bryant Home for the Blind

2960 Stanton Avenue
Springfield, IL 62703   217-529-1611
                              FAX: 217-529-6975
                  e-mail: MBHA@springnet1.com

Jerry Curry, Administrator

Offers services for the blind, legally blind, visually impaired, with health, counseling, educational, recreational, rehabilitation, computer training and professional training services.

8366 Nanon Wood Center for Children

ARC Community Support Systems
2502 S Veterans Drive
Effingham, IL 62401   217-347-5118
                              FAX: 217-347-5119

Debbie Einhorn, Dir., Family Support

Family support programs for families with children who have disabilities from the ages of birth through age 20. Services include: Early termination (Birth-3), Parent support and training, school advocacy, home visits, informaiton and referral, parent-to-parent networking, and special education rights workshops.

8367 Northern Illinois Medical Center

4201 W Medical Center Drive
McHenry, IL 60050   815-363-1220
                                       800-734-7342
                              FAX: 815-759-8062

Kathryn Murauskas, Inpatient Rehabilitation Unit
Nora Connors, Director Rehabilitation Network
Lisa Forino, Marketing Coordinator

Providing rehabilitation services in Lake and McHenry Counties, the Rehabilitation Unit is a complete living environment for up to 15 patients after a debilitating illness of trauma. Various locations offering a multitude of services: PT, OT, speech, HT, RT aquatics, work hardening, FCE's, vocational counseling, rehab nursing, physiatry, neuropsychology, case management. Comprehensive Inpatient Rehabilitation Unit, and many more services.

8368 Northern Illinois Special Recreation Association

10 W Terra Cotta Avenue
Crystal Lake, IL 60014   815-455-5515
                              FAX: 815-455-6011

Leisure and recreation services to those who are unable to participate successfully in park district and city recreation programs.

8369 Oak Forest Hospital of Cook County

15900 Cicero Avenue
Oak Forest, IL 60452   708-687-7200
                              FAX: 708-687-7979

Cyntjia T. Henderson, Interim Hospital Director
Joe Turner, Public Information

A 654 bed health care center devoted to the diagnosis, rehabilitation and long-term care of adults suffering from chronic illnesses, diseases and physical impairments.

8370 Peoria Association for Retarded Citizens

PO Box 3418
Peoria, IL 61612   309-691-3800
                              FAX: 309-689-3613
                  e-mail: peoriainc@yahoo.com
                              www.peoriainc.org

Ron Wisecarver, President/CEO
Roy Ricketts, V.P./COO

Serves all ages that are diagnosed with mental retardation and other developmental disabilities. Programs include early intervention, family support, respite care, vocational training and residential services. Serves 1,000 clients with 425 staff members.

8371 Peoria Blind People's Center

2905 W Garden Street
Peoria, IL 61605   309-637-3693

Mabel VanDeusen, Executive Director

Offers services for the totally blind, legally blind, visually impaired, mentally retarded blind and more with health, counseling, educational, recreational, rehabilitation, computer training and professional training services.

8372 Phoenix I

3075 Grand Avenue
Galesburg, IL 61401   309-343-6126
                              FAX: 309-344-1754
                  e-mail: kccdd@galesburg.net

Ned Hippensteel, Executive Director

8373 Pioneer Center of McHenry County

4001 W Dayton Street
McHenry, IL 60050   815-344-1230
                              FAX: 815-344-3815

Jeff A. Epstein, Ph.D., Executive Director
Lorraine Kopczynski, Associate Director

Early intervention, sheltered employment, developmental training, employment services, residential services, mental health services and respite care.

8374 Prosthetics and Orthotics Center in Blue Island

12255 Western Avenue
Blue Island, IL   60406   708-489-1899
                                        800-354-7342
                                   FAX: 800-908-1932

Provides orthotic and prosthetic fittings and follow-up services to adults and children in the south suburbs of Chicago.

8375 RB King Counseling Center

2300 N Edward Street
Decatur, IL   62526   217-877-8121
                                   FAX: 217-875-0966

Offers outpatient, individual, group, divorce and meditation, family and re-adjustment counseling.

8376 REACH Rehabilitation Program - Americana Healthcare

9401 S Kostner Avenue
Oak Lawn, IL   60453

Postacute rehabilitation program.

8377 REHAB Products and Services

3715 N Vermilion Street
Danville, IL   61832   217-446-1146
                                   FAX: 217-446-1191

Larry McConkey, President/CEO

8378 RIC Northshore

345 East Superior Street
Chicago, IL   60611
                                        800-354-7342
               e-mail: webmaster@rehabchicago.org
                         www.rehabchicago.org

Provides rehabilitation for sports-related injuries, musculoskeletal conditions, neurological conditions, stroke, arthritis, amputation, burns, and general deconditioning.

8379 RIC Prosthetics and Orthotics Center

12255 South Western Avenue
Blue Island, IL   60406   312-238-2810

               e-mail: webmaster@rehabchicago.org
                         www.rehabchicago.org

Offers almost all the prosthetics and orthotics services provided at RIC's main hospital in downtown Chicago, including consultations, fittings and training.

8380 RIC Windermere House

5548 South Hyde Park Boulevard
Chicago, IL   60637   312-908-9554
                                        800-354-7342
                                   FAX: 773-256-5060
                         www.rehabchicago.org

Evaluation, therapeutic services and patient education are offered in the areas of arthritis, multiple sclerosis, musculoskeletal conditions, orthopedics, stroke, spinal cord injury, brain injury and sports medicine.

8381 RIC and Swedish Covenant Hospital Rehabilitation Services

5145 North California Avenue
Chicago, IL   60625   773-989-3990
                                   FAX: 773-256-5060
                         www.rehabchicago.org

Provides acute rehabilitation services, subacute care and outpatient services for many types of disabling injuries and conditions, including amputation, arthritis, brain injury, general deconditioning, multiple sclerosis, musculoskeletal injuries, stroke, and joint replacements.

8382 Ray Graham Association for People with Disabilities

340 W Butterfield Road
Suite 3C
Elmhurst, IL   60126   630-993-0155
                                   FAX: 630-832-7337

William Murphy, President
John Voit, Vice President

Provides developmental services at 15 sites to infants, children and adults with disabilities. Services range from 1 hr/wk respite to full-time residential.

8383 Rehabilitation Achievement Center

5150 Capitol Drive
Wheeling, IL   60090   847-215-9977
                                   FAX: 847-215-9376

Richard Green, Program Director
Mary Helen Ekstam, Dir. Of Clinial Rel.

A post-acute head injury program designed specifically to help survivors and their families meet the challenge of community re-entry after discharge from acute care settings. RAC uses an integrated team approach to develop and implement a realistic program to suit each person's individual needs.

8384 Rehabilitation Institute of Chicago - Alexian Brothers Medical Center

800 Biesterfield Road
Elk Grove Village, IL   60007   847-981-3694
                                        800-354-7342
                                   FAX: 312-908-9561

A 32-bed rehabilitation unit under the medical direction and supervision of the Rehabilitation Institute of Chicago.

8385 Riverside Medical Center

Mental Health Unit
350 N Wall
Kankakee, IL   60901
                                   FAX: 815-935-7485

Offers recreation, parenting therapy, emergency services, psychological testing and inpatient treatment programs.

8386 Robert Young Mental Health Center Division of Trinity Regional Haelth System

2701 17th Street
Rock Island, IL   61201   309-779-2031
FAX: 309-779-2027

Services include comprehensive inpatient rehabilitation, chronic pain management programs, outpatient medical rehabilitation, work hardening programs, vocational evaluation, alcohol and other drug dependency rehabilitation programs, Burn Center, and mental health services for inpatient, partial hospitalization, residential treatment, case management, emergency/crisis intervention and outpatient therapy. Licensed for 443 beds, it is the largest health care institution in the Iowa/Illinois area.

8387 Sampson-Katz Center

2020 W Devon Avenue
Chicago, IL   60659

                                 FAX: 773-764-3131

Jim Balark, Executive Director

8388 Shelby County Community Services

1810 W S 3rd Street
Shelbyville, IL   62565   217-774-3911
FAX: 217-774-5120

Richard Gloede, Executive Director

8389 St. Elizabeth Hospital Physical Rehabilitation Unit In-Patient/CARFT Certified

211 South 3rd Street
Belleville, IL   62220   618-234-2120
FAX: 618-234-8741

Lucy Beaver, Rehab Services Director
Patricia Parsaghian, Rehab Nurse Manager
Tom Dibadj, Rehab Therapy Manager

Comprehensive inpatient and outpatient physical rehab services that include the services of a psychiatrist, rehab nursing, OT, PT, Speech, RT, social service, neuro psychologist and other resource and support personnel that support the rehab program.

8390 Streator Unlimited

305 N Sterling Street
Streator, IL   61364   815-675-5574
FAX: 815-673-1714

Jeffrey Dean, Executive Director
Beth Lawless, Director of Rehabilitation

Vocational and personal skills training, residential services, client and family support, CARF accredited.

8391 TCRC Sight Center TCRC

119 E Washington Street
East Peoria, IL   61611   309-698-4001
FAX: 309-698-9227

Linda Haas, RN, VP, Visual & Medical Services

Offers services for persons who are totally blind, legally blind, partially sighted or visually impaired along with other disabilities. Have support group, rehabilitation classes, orientation and mobility services, counseling services, low vision clinic, braille transcription services, technology services, and specialized aids and appliances for sale.

8392 Tazewell County Resource Center

RR 1 Box 12
Tremont, IL   61568   309-477-2272
FAX: 309-925-4241

Gus Van Den Brink, Executive Director

A private, nonprofit agency providing programs for the special needs of infants, adults, children and their families residing in Tazewell County. Services offered include: birth-three infant/parent program, adult day care services, family support, residential, vocational services, sheltered work and activity services programs.

8393 Thresholds AMISS

12145 Western Avenue
Blue Island, IL   60406   708-597-8073
FAX: 708-597-8053

Natalie Marsh, Program Director
Malissa Landis, Assistant Program Director
Camille Rucks, Team Leader

Services offered include psychosocial, vocational and residential programs for ages 18 or older with a primary diagnosis of mental illness. Facility is wheelchair accessible.

8394 Thresholds Bridge Deaf North

4814 North California Avenue
Chicago, IL   60625   773-989-8991
FAX: 773-989-1075
TDY:773-989-1875
ww.thresholds.org

Herminio Cardona Jr., Program Director

A private, nonprofit psychosocial rehabilitation center that serves the hearing impaired mental health consumers at the highest risk of hospitalization, those with serious and persistent mental illness. The program provides residential and assertive treatment case management services focused on rehabilitation.

8395 Tri-County Rehabilitation Center

1650 S Kanner Highway
Stuart, FL   34994   561-221-4050
FAX: 561-286-4364

Suzanne Hutcheson, President & CEO

8396 Trumbull Park

10530 S Oglesby Avenue
Chicago, IL   60617   773-375-7022
FAX: 773-375-5528

Gregory Terry, Director
Diana Moore, Site Supervisor

Offers consultation, education, general counseling, recreation, self-help and social services for children and adults.

8397 University of Illinois Medical Center

1855 W Taylor Street
Chicago, IL   60612   312-355-0746
FAX: 312-996-7770

Timothy McMahon, Chief

Offers services for the totally blind, legally blind, visually impaired, mentally retarded blind and more with health, counseling, educational, recreational, rehabilitation, computer training and professional training services.

8398 VanMatre Rehabilitation Center

2400 N Rockton Avenue
Rockford, IL   61103   815-971-3737
                                         800-752-9907
                           FAX: 815-969-5797

Vicki McDonnough, Administrative Services

A CARF-accredited comprehensive rehabilitation center based within the Rockford Memorial Hospital providing inpatient and outpatient services for physically and cognitively challenged persons with debilitating illness and injuries.

8399 Warren Achievement Center

1220 E 2nd Avenue
Monmouth, IL   61462   309-734-3131
                           FAX: 309-734-7114
                    e-mail: jmae@maplecity.com

Mrs. J. McVey, President

For developmentally disabled children and adults. Parent-infant education programs are for parents of infants with disabilities or developmental delays; Children's Group Homes which serve children on a fulltime basis and can serve additional children on a respite basis; Vocational training and residential programs assist the handicapped adult and developmental training for adults; adult residential community living; manufacturing, capabilities in workshop includes packaging, and assembly.

8400 Waukegan Outpatient Mental Health Services

3012 Grand Avenue
Waukegan, IL   60085   847-360-6725
                           FAX: 847-336-1517
                              www.co.lake.il.us

Includes counseling, crisis intervention, emergency management, psychotherapy and chemotherapy management for individuals and families.

Indiana

8401 Ball Memorial Hospital

2401 W University Avenue
Muncie, IN   47303   765-285-8431
                           FAX: 765-747-3313

Robert Brodhead, President

Offers rehabilitation services, occupational therapy, physical therapy and more for the physically challenged child or adult.

8402 Center for Neuropsychological Rehabilitation

8945 N Meridian Street
Suite 100
Indianapolis, IN   46260   317-865-6240
                           FAX: 317-844-3152

Carole Cheshire, Admissions Director
Postacute rehabilitation program.

8403 Community Hospitals, Indianapolis

1500 N Ritter Avenue
Indianapolis, IN   46219   317-633-8210
                           FAX: 317-351-7723

Barbara Gebhardt, Executive Director

8404 Crossroads Industrial Services

4740 Kingsway Drive
Indianapolis, IN   46205   317-254-0228
                           FAX: 317-897-9763

Jack Costello, Executive Director

8405 Department of Veterans Affairs Vet Center #418

311 North Weinbach Avenue
Evansville, IN   47711   812-473-5993
                           FAX: 812-473-4028
                    e-mail: vcen418@evansvilla.net

Jack Weber, LCSW, MPA, Team Leader

Provides readjustment counseling to combat veterans of all eras. Onsite assistance for employment problems and Department of Veteran Affairs, Vocational Rehabilitation, and Sexual Trauma Counsel.

8406 Evansville Association for the Blind

EAB Industries
500 N 2nd Avenue
PO Box 6445
Evansville, IN   47719   812-422-1181
                           FAX: 812-424-3154
                    e-mail: eabcdc@evansville.net
                    www.2evansville.edu/ebaweb/

Frank E. Kern, Executive Director
Kathy Patton, Personnel Mgr.

Services are offered to individuals with a physical or mental handicap and their families in the form of educational and vocational counseling, rehabilitation assistance, useful and profitable employment, vocational skills training in office occupations, computer adaptive technology, low vision support groups and professional in-service training.

8407 Frasier Rehabilitation Center Division of Clark Memorial Hospital

2201 Greentree North
Clarksville, IN   47129   812-282-4257
                           FAX: 812-288-1161

Designed to help patients in their adjustment to a physically limiting condition, both psychologically and physically, by helping to maximize each patient's abilities so he or she can function as independently as possible. The program treats patients whose functional impairment may range from temporary to permanent, from partial to total disability.

8408 HealthSouth Tri-State Regional Rehabilitation Hospital

4100 Covert Avenue
Evansville, IN   47714
                                         800-677-3422
                           FAX: 812-476-4270
                              www.healthsouth.com

Barb Butler, CEO
Myra Wetzel, Marketing Coordinator
Dick Ondrey, Director of Clinical Services

An 80-bed JCAHO accredited freestanding hospital specializing in comprehensive medical rehabilitation for Brain Injury, Spinal Cord Injury, Orthopedic, Pulmonary, Cardiac, Oncology and disabilities and general disabilities.

8409 Healthwin Specialized Care

20531 Darden Road
South Bend, IN 46637   219-272-0100
                           FAX: 219-277-3233

Patrock Pingel, Administrator

Postacute rehabilitation program.

8410 Memorial Regional Rehabilitation Center

221 W Wayne Street
South Bend, IN 46601   219-232-4861
                           FAX: 219-282-4692

Margaret Sak, OTR, Manager, ILC

CARF accredited outpatient medical rehabilitation and post acute brain injury program. Serves neurologically impaired adults and young adults.

8411 Saint Joseph's Medical Center

PO Box 1935
South Bend, IN 46634   219-237-7111
                           FAX: 219-239-6070

Kathleen A. Kish, MSN, CRRN, Information Dir.
Krista Samide Barnes, MS/CRCC, Outpatient Case Manager
Phyllis Syers, MSN, CRRN, Dir., Rehabilitation Center

Continuum of rehabilitation services offered. Included are: acute rehabilitation, a 26 bed CARF accredited comprehensive inpatient unit, a CARF certified inpatient brain injury program, a CARF outpatient day treatment brain injury program, comprehensive outpatient services, with available case management, and Driver's Training Program, a 30 bed state of the art subacute rehab unit, CARF accredited Industrial Rehabilitation Programs, and CARF accredited Pain and Complimentary Medicine Program.

Iowa

8412 Adults Incorporated

3420 University Avenue
Waterloo, IA 50701   319-236-0901
                              888-879-1365
                         FAX: 319-236-3701
                 e-mail: ainc@cedarnet.org
                  www.cedarnet.org/ainc

Mark Witmer, Executive Director
Denise Hinders, Director of Rehabilitation
Donna Davis, Dir. of Development & Pub. Rel.

Provides adult day care, employment services, and supported community living so people with disabilities can live and work in the community. Populations served include, but are not limited to: senior adults with age-related disabilities, youth with disabilities (age 15+), adults with disabilities, including those with mental and physical disabilities. CARF accredited. Serves northeast and central Iowa. Head Injury Program serves the whole state.

8413 Crossroads of Western Iowa

One Crossroads Place
Missouri Valley, IA 51555   712-642-4114
                           FAX: 712-642-4115

David Lovell, CEO

8414 Crossroads of Western Iowa

301 10th Street
Onawa, IA 51040   712-423-1477
                           FAX: 712-423-1480

David Lovell, CEO

8415 Easter Seals Iowa

PO Box 4002
Des Moines, IA 50333   515-289-1933
                           FAX: 515-289-1281
                  e-mail: essia@netins.net
                  www.eastersalesia.org

Martha H. Wittkowski, President/CEO

Easter Seals is a leading nonprofit provider of services to Iowans with disabilities. Services include vocational and employment training, camping recreation and respite services, craft training and sales, home and farm adaptations, transportation, scholarships and a club for stroke survivors and their families.

8416 Genesis Regional Rehabilitation Center

2720 West Locust
Suite 2B
Davenport, IA 52804   319-421-3495
                           FAX: 319-421-3499

Janet King, Executive Director

Serves persons of all ages experiencing a disability, whether acquired at birth or following a serious interdisciplinary service. Rehabilitation programs include acute rehabilitation; adult rehabilitation, pediatric rehabilitation, outpatient orthopaedics. LIFT, a community based, a nontraditional approach to the treatment of adolescents and adults with brain injuries is also offered at Genesis. It is designed to facilitate re-entry into the community or return to appropriate employment.

8417 Homelink

Van G. Miller & Associates
PO Box 2817
Waterloo, IA 50704   319-235-7100
                              800-482-1993
                           FAX: 319-235-7822

A national network of home medical equipment, respiratory therapy, rehabilitation and infusion therapy service providers with over 2,500 locations serving all fifty states.

8418 Iowa Central Industries

127 Avenue M
Fort Dodge, IA 50501   515-576-2126
                           FAX: 515-576-2251

Quentin Weidner, Director

Services include evaluation and training in pre-vocational and vocational skills, personal behavior management, cognitive skills, communication skills, self-care skills and social skills. Services arranged include: independent living training, medical services, psychological services, therapeutic services and social services.

8419 Iowa Veterans Centers

2600 Harding Road
Des Moines, IA 50310   515-285-6701
FAX: 515-284-4901

Veterans medical clinic offering disabled veterans medical treatments.

8420 Life Skills Laundry Division

1510 Industrial Road SW
Le Mars, IA 51031   712-546-4786
FAX: 712-546-4985

Cindi Kruse, Executive Director

8421 MIW

909 S 14th Avenue
Marshalltown, IA 50158
FAX: 515-752-1614
e-mail: jstegmamann@miwi.org

Janet Stegmann, Services Manager

Vocational services for adults with disabilities. Includes organizational employment services, supported employment, job placement.

8422 Mercy Pain Center

400 University Avenue
Des Moines, IA 50314
FAX: 515-248-8867

Dianne Alber Ed.D, Administrative Director

An outpatient program dedicated to helping people with chronic pain live more productive, satisfying lives. The program is not designed for conditions that are surgically curable, but rather approaches the problem using a comprehensive, holistic treatment.

8423 Mercy Physical Rehabilitation Unit

Mercy Drive
Dubuque, IA 52001
FAX: 319-589-8162

Joan Hentges, Director

Provides services which open the door to improved communication, offering the opportunity to enrich the quality of life. Mercy offers many other branches of services including, rehabilitation services for children, pulmonary rehabilitation program, services for the head-injured patient, back to school, and the disabled driver program.

8424 Nishna Productions

902 Day Street
PO Box 70
Shenandoah, IA 51601   712-246-1242
FAX: 712-246-1243

Sherri Clark, Executive Director

Shelter, workshop and job training for the disabled.

8425 Options of Linn County

1019 7th Street SE
Cedar Rapids, IA 52401   319-892-5800
FAX: 319-892-5849
www.linncounty.org/dhrm/options

Vivian Davis, Director
Reggie Ancelet, Associate Director
Todd Hoyer, Associate Director

Provides employment services to adults with disabilities. Options serves over 300 people annually in community based and facility based services.

8426 RISE, Ltd.

107 Gunder Road
Elkader, IA 52043   319-245-1868
FAX: 319-245-2859

Edward Josten, Executive Director

8427 Ragtime Industries

116 N 2nd Street
Albia, IA 52531   641-932-7813
FAX: 641-932-7814

Diana Shehan, Executive Director

A work-oriented rehabilitation organization which provides training for mentally and physically disabled adults in Monroe County. A variety of programs which help to develop each person's individual potential are offered so that the person may live as normal a life as possible.

8428 Sunshine Workers

PO Box 75
Spencer, IA 51301   712-262-7805
FAX: 712-262-8369

Dan Penkert, Executive Director

8429 Tenco Industries

710 Gateway Drive
1287
Ottumwa, IA 52501   515-682-8114
FAX: 515-684-4223

Robert L Dvorak, Executive Director

To advocate and provide opportunities for people with disabilities, or conditions taht limit their abilities, to develop and maintain the skills necessary for personal dignity and independence in all areas of life. Provide a wide array of services to individuals with disabilties. By looking at each person as individuals, we are able to work with them to maximize their skills. Residentials services, including HCBS and CSALA, are also provided in all communities.

8430 Vision Rehabilitation Institute

Genesis Vision Rehabilitation
1351 W Central Park Avenue
Suite 3700
Davenport, IA 52804
800-383-1298
FAX: 319-421-1595

Mark Wilkinson, OD, Optometric Director

Offers comprehensive vision rehabilitation for the legally blind, visually impaired, mentally retarded blind and more with counseling, educational rehabilitation, and professional training services.

Kansas

8431 Arrowhead West

1100 E Wyatt Earp Boulevard
PO Box 1417
Dodge City, KS   67801   316-227-8803
                                FAX: 316-227-8812
                                www.arrowhead.org

Lori Pendergast, President
Janet Heit, Admission Coordinator
Julie Nelson, Public Relations Coordinator

Services and programs offered include: developmental and therapy services for children birth to age 3. Adult center-based work services and community integrated employment options; adult life skills and retirement programs; adult residential services including supervised living, supported living and independent living services. Staff includes over 200 employees. Services are provided over a 14 county area with service centers in Dodge City, Kinsley, Pratt, Medicine Lodge and Wichita.

8432 Bethany Rehabilitation Center

51 N 12th Street
Kansas City, KS   66102   913-281-8400
                                 FAX: 913-281-7696

Wayne Kutz, Vice President

Offers rehabilitation services, inpatient and outpatient care, respite programs, psychiatric evaluations and more.

8433 Big Lakes Developmental Center

1416 Hayes Drive
Manhattan, KS   66502   785-776-9201
                               FAX: 785-776-9830
                   e-mail: biglakes@networkpius.net
                               www.biglakes.org

James Shaver, President/CEO

Work services, community employment and residential services. Serving adults with developmental disabilities. Family support services also available.

8434 Developmental Services of Northwest Kansas

2703 Hall Street
Hays, KS   67601   785-625-5678
                          FAX: 785-625-8204
               e-mail: jim_blume@notes1.dsnwk.org
                          www.dsnwk.org

James W. Blume, President

A private, not-for-profit organization serving both children and adults with disabilities. Offers services to children ages birth to three years, youth and adults through a network of community-based and outreach programs and inter-agency agreements with other service providers in the eighteen counties of Northwest Kansas.

8435 ENVISION

2301 South Water
Wichita, KS   67213   316-267-2244
                             FAX: 316-267-4312
                 e-mail: envision@envisionus.com
                             www.envisionus.com

Sandy Evans, Community Relations Coordinator

Provides jobs, job training and rehavilitation services to people who are blind or low vision, deaf blind and/or developmentally disabled.

8436 Heartspring

8700 East 29th Street North
Wichita, KS   67226   316-634-8700
                             800-835-1043
                             FAX: 316-634-0555
                             www.heartspring.org

Charles Wolford, Admissions Director
Jennifer Wolthaa, P.R. Director
Charlene Kuzma Lmsw,Clp, Life Care Planner

Private, not-for-profit residential school for children from across the country ages five to twenty-one with multiple disabilities. Heartspring students are diagnosed with mental retardation and one or more of the following: autism, cerebral palsy, maladaptive behaviors, seizures, or other disabilities. Services are provided by an interdisciplinary team of specialists. Assessments and therapies are provided in the areas of speech/language, physical, occupational and hearing development.

8437 Indian Creek Nursing Center

6515 W 103rd Street
Overland Park, KS   66212   913-648-5093
                                   FAX: 913-642-3982

Linnea Brandt, Administrator

Postacute rehabilitation program.

8438 Johnson County Developmental Supports

10501 Lackman Road
Lenexa, KS   66219   913-492-6161
                            FAX: 913-492-5171

Mark Elmore, Executive Director
Shelly Toft, Executive Assistant

8439 Kansas Vocational Rehabilitation Center

3140 Centennial Road
Salina, KS   67401   785-827-9356

Michael Ahlers, Supervisor

Provides care for Kansans with disabilities to help achieve and sustain independence, primarily through employment by providing a supportive environment that encourages active participation in self-management planning. Working with a counselor to develop an Individual Evaluation Program, job seeking skills, assessment, rehabilitation engineer evaluation, physical functioning assessment, physical therapy evaluation and more services are offered.

8440 Ketch Industries

201 Ida Street
Wichita, KS   67211

Kaye Herman, Executive Director

8441 Lakemary Center

100 Lakemary Drive
Paola, KS   66071   913-557-4000
                           FAX: 913-294-4361

William R. Craig, Ph.D., President

A private, not-for-profit day and residential training facility which provides for the assessment, education, training, therapy and social development of children and adults, moderate and severe mental retardation. The Center is based 28 miles southwest of Kansas City in Paola, Kansas.

8442 Northview Developmental Services

700 E 14th Street
Newton, KS   67114   316-283-5170
                            FAX: 316-283-5196
                            e-mail: nds@northviewdsi.com

Stan Zienkewicz, President

Kentucky

8443 Cardinal Hill Outpatient Center

3050 Harrodsburg Road
Lexington, KY   40503   606-367-6000
                            800-428-7755
                            FAX: 606-224-2081

Karen J. Miller, Mgr., Referral Rel.
Elizabeth A. Monarch, V.P., Patient Services

Provides occupational health services, therapy services and urgent medical treatment of injured workers.

8444 Frazier Institute

220 Abraham Flexner Way
Louisville, KY   40202   502-582-7400
                            FAX: 502-582-7477
                            www.jewishhospital.org

Joanne Berryman, Senior Vice President
Barth Weinberg, Vice President, Inpatient Rehab
Jean Russell, Vice President, Rehab Operations

Frazier Rehab Institute is a regional healthcare system dedicated entirely to rehabilitation. Through an expansive network of inpatient and outpatient facilites in Kentucky and southern Indiana, Frazier offers a wide array of services based on one common goal - helping people with disabilities reach their full potential.

8445 HealthSouth Northern Kentucky Rehabilitation Hospital

201 Medical Village Drive
Edgewood, KY   41017   606-341-2044
                            800-860-6004
                            FAX: 606-341-2813

Jean Davis, CEO/Administrator

Offers all types of rehabilitation services such as occupational therapy, physical therapy, speech therapy, inpatient and outpatient care and more for the disabled.

8446 King's Daughter's Medical Center's Rehab Unit/Work Hardening Program

2201 Lexington Avenue
Ashland, KY   41101

                            800-633-6388
                            FAX: 606-327-7542
                            www.komc.com

Harry Bell, Medical Director
Sue Strehle, Service Line Manager

Offers a 27-bed, inpatient rehabilitation services unit treating physical disabilities related to accident or illness. The program provides an interdisciplinary inpatient program designed to restore the individual to the highest level of independence. It is the goal of the staff to provide rehabilitative services that will enable the disabled or injured person to return home and re-enter the community at the maximum level of efficiency.

8447 LifeSkills Industries

2420 Russellville Road
Bowling Green, KY   42101   502-842-8813
                            FAX: 502-782-0058

Joe Miller, Executive Director

8448 Low Vision Services of Kentucky

120 N Eagle Creek Drive
Suite 501
Lexington, KY   40509
                            800-627-2020
                            FAX: 859-263-3757

William Wood, M.D., Clinical Director
Jeanne Vanarsdall, Low Vision Specialist
Helen T. Wade, Administratr

Offers services for the totally blind, legally blind, visually impaired, mentally retarded blind and more with health, counseling, educational, recreational, rehabilitation, computer training and professional training services.

8449 Muehlenberg County Opportunity Center

Opportunity Way
Greenville, KY   42345   502-338-5970
                            FAX: 502-338-0301

Michael Morgan, Executive Director

8450 New Vision Enterprises

1900 Brownsboro Road
Louisville, KY   40206   502-893-0211
                            800-405-9135
                            FAX: 502-893-3885

Robert Jarboe, CEO

Offers employment training and services for the blind and legally blind.

8451 Northfield Manor Healthcare Facility

6000 Hunting Road
Louisville, KY   40222
                            FAX: 502-426-1401

Mark Malone, Administrator

Postacute rehabilitation program.

8452 Park DuValle Community Health Center

1817 S 34th Street
Louisville, KY   40211   502-774-4401
                            FAX: 502-775-6195
                            www.access.gov

Richard Jones, Executive Director

Offers services for the totally blind, legally blind, visually impaired, mentally retarded blind and more with health, counseling, educational, recreational, rehabilitation, computer training and professional training services.

Louisiana

8453 Alliance House

2902 Florida Boulevard
Baton Rouge, LA 70802   225-343-5393
                              FAX: 225-346-0857

A non-residential facility serving male and female chronically mentally ill. Services include: social service, vocational evaluation, pre-vocational training and job placement.

8454 Assumption Activity Center

4201 Highway 1
Napoleonville, LA 70390   504-369-2907
                                FAX: 504-369-2657

Teal Stroud, On-Site Supervisor
James Owens, Community Services

A community work center providing prevocational training and extended employment for adults with disabilities. Services include: social services, work activities, specialized training and supported employment.

8455 Caddo-Bossier Association for Retarded Citizens
Vivian Work Center

1012 S Pine Street
Vivian, LA 71082

                                FAX: 318-221-4262

A community operated workshop for male and female mentally retarded individuals. It provides work evaluation and transitional and extended employment.

8456 Deaf Action Center of GNO

1231 Prytania Street
New Orleans, LA 70130   504-525-0700

Kathy Treubig, Administrator
Shari Bernius, Interpreter Coord.

This community service and resource center serves deaf, deaf-blind, hard of hearing and speech-impaired persons in the greater New Orleans area regardless of age, religion, race or secondary disability. DAC provides interpreting services, equipment distribution, sign language classes, case management and advocacy.

8457 Donaldsville Association for Retarded Citizens

1030 Clay Street
Donaldsonville, LA 70346

A private, nonprofit sheltered work program working with the mentally retarded and developmentally disabled adults.

8458 East Jefferson General Hospital Rehab Center

3601 Houma Boulevard
Metairie, LA 70006   504-885-4677
                          FAX: 504-456-7381

Yolanda Cameron, Program Manager
Postacute rehabilitation program.

8459 Family Service Society

2515 Canal Street
Suite 201
New Orleans, LA 70119

                          FAX: 504-822-0831

Robert Quintana, Executive Director

Offers services for the totally blind, legally blind, visually impaired, mentally retarded blind and more with health, counseling, educational, recreational, rehabilitation, computer training and professional training services.

8460 Foundation Industries

9995 Highway 64
Zachary, LA 70791   225-654-6283
                          FAX: 225-654-3988

A private, nonprofit sheltered workshop providing extended employment and work activities for the mentally retarded and developmentally disabled clients.

8461 Handi-Works Productions

2700 Lee Street
Alexandria, LA 71301   318-442-3377
                              FAX: 318-473-0858

This is a nonprofit workshop for male and female clients who have vocational handicapping conditions. All types of handicapped persons are served in this non-residential workshop.

8462 Iberville Association for Retarded Citizens

PO Box 201
Plaquemine, LA 70765   225-687-4062
                              FAX: 225-687-3272
                              e-mail: arci@eatel.net

A private sheltered work program operating out of one facility and providing transitional, extended employment and work activities for mentally and developmentally ill adults.

8463 Lighthouse for the Blind in New Orleans

123 State Street
New Orleans, LA 70118   504-899-4501
                              FAX: 504-895-4162

R.G. Harmer, Executive Director

Offers services for the totally blind, legally blind, visually impaired, mentally retarded blind and more with health, counseling, educational, recreational, rehabilitation, computer training and professional training services.

8464 Louisiana Center for the Blind

101 S Trenton Street
Ruston, LA 71270   318-255-6277
                                     800-234-4166
                                 FAX: 318-251-0109
                   e-mail: wilsonj@lcb-ruston.com
                               www.lcb-ruston.com

Joanne Wilson, Director

A new kind of orientation and training center for blind persons. The center is privately operated and provides quality instruction in the skills of blindness. Offers employment assistance, computer literacy training, summer training and employment project, special seminars, outreach and referral services.

8465 Louisiana State University Eye Center

2020 Gravier Street
New Orleans, LA 70112   504-412-1200
                                 FAX: 504-412-1315

8466 New Orleans Speech and Hearing Center

1639 Toledano Street
New Orleans, LA 70115   504-524-9631
                                 FAX: 504-891-6048

Lesley Jernigan, Executive Director
Patty Connolly, Coordinator Clinical Services

This non-residential facility serves male and female clients for purposes of evaluating speech and hearing problems and providing speech therapy, hearing aids and other assistive technology for speech and hearing.

8467 Port City Enterprises

PO Box 113
Port Allen, LA 70767   225-344-1142
                                 FAX: 225-344-1192

Christine Dunlevy, Executive Director

Offers supported employment, sheltered work and supervised programs for the mentally retarded, ages 22 and over.

8468 Rehabilitation Center at Thibodeaux Regional

RehabCare
602 N Acadia Road
Thibodaux, LA 70301   985-493-4435
                                 FAX: 985-493-4436

Jan Torres, Program Manager
Rose Pipes, Clinical Coordinator

Designed to help patients in their adjustment to a physically limiting condition, both physically and psychologically, by helping to maximize each patients abilities so he or she can function as independently as possible.

8469 Rehabilitation Hospital of Baton Rouge

8595 United Plaza Boulevard
Baton Rouge, LA 70809   225-927-0567
                                     800-264-0567
                                 FAX: 504-926-2357

Jill Root, Admissions Director
Amy Searles, Community Relations

Dedicated to one field of medicine - physical rehabilitation medicine - and are committed to one goal, helping patients achieve the highest level of functioning possible after a debilitating injury or illness.

8470 Rehabilitation Living Centers

3434 Canal Street
New Orleans, LA 70119   504-482-3075
                                 FAX: 504-483-2135

Dr. Robert Voogt, Owner

Postacute rehabilitation program.

8471 St. Patrick RehabCare Unit

RehabCare
524 S Ryan Street
Lake Charles, LA 70601   318-491-7789
                                 FAX: 318-491-7194

Annette Harlow, Program Manager
Ruth Thornton, Admissions

Provides inpatient rehabilitation services in acute-care and sub-acute facilities. Treatment is provided for neurological and degenerative disorders.

8472 Touro Rehabilitation Center

1401 Foucher Street
New Orleans, LA 70115   504-897-8524
                                 FAX: 504-897-8393

Dr. Gary Glynn, Medical Director

This center works to help every challenged individual live more freely and more independently. They've created an exceptional care and support system, the best people, the best facilities and more to help the patients achieve all of their potential for independent living. Services include: physical therapy, occupational therapy, therapeutic recreation, rehabilitation counseling, rehabilitation nursing, vocational services, driving assessment and rehabilitation, swallowing program and more.

8473 Training, Resource & Assistive-Technology

University of New Orleans
Lakefront Campus
New Orleans, LA 70148   504-280-5700
                                 FAX: 504-280-5707

Kenneth Zangca, Program Director

This facility provides a curriculum utilizing innovative technology for people with disabilities, emphasizing microcomputer training, assessments, self-employment, disability awareness, education and international exchange.

8474 University of New Orleans Training and Resource Center for the Blind

Metro Campus Lakefront Campus
New Orleans, LA 70148   504-280-6603
                                 FAX: 225-286-7294

This center offers a range of computer courses for the blind and visually impaired; maintains a resource lab with adaptive technology; conducts vocational evaluations for persons with disabilities; and provides information on the ADA.

Maine

8475 Charlotte White Center

572 Route 15
PO Box 380
Dover Foxcroft, ME   04426   207-564-2499
                                    888-440-4158
                              FAX: 207-564-2404

Richard Brown, Executive Director
Anthony Zambrono, Director of Operations

8476 Iris Network for the Blind

189 Park Avenue
Portland, ME   04102   207-774-6273
                        FAX: 207-774-0679
                        e-mail: sobremski@theiris.org
                              www.theiris.org

Steven Obremski, President/CEO

Offers services to persons who are blind, visually impaired or multi-disabled blind with rehabilitation, counseling, educational, recreational, computer training and professional training services.

8477 Limerick Adult Day Program

Foss Road
Limerick, ME   04048

Carol Snyder, Executive Director

8478 Roger Randall Center

50 Green Street
Houlton, ME   04730   207-532-9196
                        FAX: 207-532-9494

Dawn Ledger, Director of Day Programs

The Roger Randall Cneter is one of five Day Habilitation Programs adminsitered by Community Living Association, a private, non-profit agency. These programs may provide a supportive environment that allows the individual to achieve their maximum growth potential. Individualized services address but are not limtied to the following areas: fine/gross motor skills, communication, community awareness and involvement, appropriate social skills, and independent living skills.

8479 Sebasticook Farms

PO Box 65
Saint Albans, ME   04971   207-938-4615
                            FAX: 207-938-5670

Tom Davis, Executive Director

Provides residential, educational and vocational services to adults who are developmentally disabled in order to maximize independent living and to provide assistance in obtaining an earned income.

8480 Social Learning Center

984 Sabattus Street
Lewiston, ME   04240   207-783-4672
                        FAX: 207-783-4673

Deborah Beam, Unit Manager

Maryland

8481 Blind Industries and Services of Maryland

2901 Strickland Street
Baltimore, MD   21223   410-233-4567
                               888-322-4567
                         FAX: 410-233-0544
                              www.bism.com

Rosemary Lerdahl, Rehab Director

Offers a comprehensive residential rehabilitation training program for people who are blind. Areas of instruction: braille, cane travel, independent living, computer, adjustment and blindness seminars.

8482 Center for Neuro-Rehabilitation

222 Severn Avenue
Annapolis, MD   21403   410-267-5963
                               800-405-3737
                         FAX: 410-263-2344
                         e-mail: cnrnhq@erols.com

Karen Sanders, VP Marketing & Development

Provide community-based inpatient and outpatient acute rehabilitation, vocational services and long-term care. Specializing in treating complex neurological conditions including spinal cord injuries, multiple sclerosis, strokes, and other brain injuries resulting from trauma, anoxia, tumors, genetic malformations and other related conditions. Locations in Annapolis, Bethesda, Frederick, Towson, MD and Fairfax, Va. CNR is licensed, a Medicare provider and CARF accredited.

8483 Child Find/Early Childhood Disabilities

850 Hungerford Drive
Room 208
Rockville, MD   20850   301-279-3421
                         FAX: 301-279-8479

Patricia Keough

Offers free developmental screening for children ages 2 years 9 months through 4 years, evaluation and placement services.

8484 Greater Baltimore Medical Center Richard E. Hoover Rehabilitation Services

6569 N Chales Street
Baltimore, MD   21204   410-828-2658
                               800-597-9142
                         FAX: 410-828-3167

Kim Ridgon, Certified Low Vision Therapist
Linda Wolinski, Director of Hoover Services

Offers services for the visually impaired and blind with low vision exams. Rehabilitation teaching and orientation and mobility in the home or workplace. Also offers a bimonthly newsletter for $12/yr for Hoover patients and monthly share group.

8485 Greenery Extended Care Center - Baltimore

1300 S Ellwood Avenue
Baltimore, MD   21224   410-342-6644
                         FAX: 301-327-3949

150 beds offering complex care treatment, extended rehabilitation and neurological restorative care.

8486 James Lawrence Kerman Hospital
2200 N Forest Park Avenue
Baltimore, MD 21207 410-285-6566
FAX: 410-448-6854

Dennis Grote, Executive Director

8487 Levindale Hebrew Geriatric Center
2434 W Belevedere Avenue
Baltimore, MD 21215 410-664-4566
FAX: 410-367-9066

Stanford Aliker, Executive Director

8488 Maryland Rehabilitation Center Workforce Technology
2301 Argonne Drive
Baltimore, MD 21218 410-554-9439
888-200-7117
FAX: 410-554-9112
www.dors.state.md.us

Susan Schaffer, Program Director

One of nine state operated comprehensive rehabilitation facilities in the country which provides a wide range of services to individuals with disabilities. The Center is an integral part of the Maryland Div. of Rehab. Services. Available services include vocational evaluation, medical functional evaluation, career training, mobility training, placement assistance, career assessment, rehab. technology assessments, driver's education and independent living skills training.

8489 Meridian Subacute
Corporate Offices
515 Fairmount Avenue
Towson, MD 21286 410-494-1397
FAX: 410-337-7233

Patients receive around-the-clock professional nursing care; physical and occupational, speech and respiratory therapists also assist patients. Each patient's individualized plan of care is reviewed and updated as patient needs change. Careful discharge planning prepares patients and their families for success at home by teaching them how to avoid complications that might lead to rehospitalization.

8490 Rehabilitation Opportunities
5100 Philadelphia Way
Suite A
Lanham Seabrook, MD 20706 301-731-4242
FAX: 301-322-5891

Rory Brett, Executive Director

Organization offering day programs, evaluation, work adjustments and sheltered workshops for persons who are mentally retarded or developmentally disabled.

8491 Rosewood Center
200 Rosewood Lane
Owings Mills
Baltimore County, MD 21117 410-951-5301
FAX: 410-581-6157

Michael G. Edukat, Facility Director
James Anzalone, Deputy Director

Offers a full range of habilitation services.

8492 Treatment and Learning Centers
9975 Medical Center Drive
Rockville, MD 20850 301-424-5200
FAX: 301-424-8063
www.ttlc.org

Patricia A. Ritter, PhD, Asst. Executive Dir.

Provides audiological evaluations, testing and hearing aids, physical and occupational therapy and evaluation; speech-language evaluation and therapy, psycho-educational testing and tutoring services for learning disabled students, head injury services and infant and early childhood services including child care, summer therapeutic camp and a preschool speech-language program, a special education preschool-8th grade.

Massachusetts

8493 Baroco Corporation
PO Box 574
Williamstown, MA 01096 413-584-9978
FAX: 413-585-9010

Ellen Hedlund, Center Director

Provides training and therapeutic support for its recipients with developmental disabilities in order to aid them in securing and maintaining placement in a less-restrictive setting.

8494 Berkshire Meadows
249 N Plain Road
Housatonic, MA 01236 413-528-2523
FAX: 413-528-0293
e-mail: bmeadows@bcn.net

Gail Charpenter, Executive Director

Private, non profit school for children, adolescents, young adults who are severely, developmentally disabled. approved special education learning center, work site program and foster care. Physical therapy, speech and language development, behavioral programming, occupational therapy, aquatic therapy, round-the-clock nursing. Also included is our state of the art equipment. *$8200.00*

8495 Blueberry Hill Healthcare
75 Brimbal Avenue
Beverly, MA 01915 781-598-2107
FAX: 978-922-4643

Phil Sher, Administrator

Postacute rehabilitation program.

8496 Boston University Hospital Vision Rehabilitation Services
720 Harrison Avenue
Boston, MA 02118 617-638-8340
FAX: 617-638-8321

Offers services for the totally blind, legally blind, visually impaired, mentally retarded blind and more with health, counseling, educational, recreational, rehabilitation, computer training and professional training services.

8497 Burbank Rehabilitation Center

275 Nichols Road
Fitchburg, MA   01420   978-343-5660
FAX: 978-343-5342

Diane O'Brien, Program Director

The largest community hospital and regional referral center in the area. Offers the most extensive high quality, cost-effective healthcare services in the region. The hospital provides outstanding hospital-based services such as case management of high risk elderly and the region's only comprehensive geriatric evaluation service. Also offers patients access to a complete continuum of healthcare, skilled nursing homes, and adult day care. This range of services affords patients prompt care.

8498 CPB/WGBH National Center for Access Media

WGBH Educational Foundation
125 Western Avenue
Boston, MA   02134   617-300-3400
FAX: 617-300-1035
TDY:617-492-9258
e-mail: ncam@wgbh.org
www.wgbh.org/ncam

Larry Goldberg, Director

A division within the WGBH Educational Foundation that works to make media accessible to under-served populations, such as disabled persons, minority language users, and people with low literacy skills. NCAM researches and develops new technologies that create access to public mass media (TV, radio, movies, newspapers, etc.), investigates how existing access technologies may benefit other populations, and conducts community outreach to educate people about media access issues.

8499 Carroll Center for the Blind

770 Centre Street
Newton, MA   02158   617-969-6200
800-852-3131
FAX: 617-969-6204
e-mail: rrosenbaum@carroll.org
www.carroll.org

Rachel Rosenbaum, Executive Director, President
Arthur O'Neill, Public Relations Director

Offers services for the totally blind, legally blind, visually impaired, mentally retarded blind and more with health, counseling, educational, recreational, rehabilitation, computer training and professional training services.

8500 Center for Neurobehavioral Rehabilitation at Middlesex

Greenery Rehabilitation Groups
Middlesex County Hospital
Waltham, MA   02254

800-722-4744
FAX: 724-746-8780

The first facility in Massachusetts to offer an intensive behavioral program for clients with brain injury requiring a closed unit. The unit serves those whose personality and behavioral changes may be so significant that they require unique treatment modalities offered only within a closed unit.

8501 Center for Psychiatric Rehabilitation

Boston University
730 Commonwealth Avenue
Boston, MA   02215   617-734-5855
FAX: 617-353-7700

William A. Anthony, PhD, Executive Director

The mission of the Center is to increase knowledge, to train treatment personnel, to develop effective rehabilitation programs and to assist in organizing both personnel and programs into efficient and coordinated service delivery systems for people with mental illness.

8502 Clark House of Fox Hill Village

30 Longwood Drive
Westwood, MA   02090   781-326-5652
FAX: 781-326-4034

Jim Brusstar, Administrator

Postacute rehabilitation program.

8503 College Internship Program at the Berkshire Center

18 Park Street
160
Lee, MA   01238   413-243-2576
FAX: 413-243-3351
e-mail: bcenter@bcn.net
www.berkshirecenter.org

Gary Shaw, Admissions Director

A highly individualized postsecondary program for learning disabled young adults 18-30. Provides job placement services and follow-ups; college support; money management and social skills. Residential students share an apartment and have their own room. They learn independent living skills and leisure skills. Clinically, each student has individual and group therapy. Psychiatric consultation is available as well as medication supervision if necessary.

8504 Eagle Pond

One Love Lane
South Dennis, MA   02660   508-385-6034
FAX: 508-385-7064
e-mail: health@eaglepond.com
eaglepond.com

Scott Stone, Administrator

Postacute rehabilitation program. Alzheimer's disorder and related dementia long-term care.

8505 FOR Community Services

75 Litwin Lane
Chicopee, MA   01020   413-592-6142
FAX: 413-598-0478

Gina M. Golash, Executive Director

8506 Fairlawn Rehabilitation Hospital

189 May Street
Worcester, MA   01602   508-791-6351
FAX: 508-753-2087

Ellen Ferrante, President

Offers comprehensive rehabilitation on both an inpatient and outpatient basis. Specialty programs include: head injury, spinal cord injury, young/senior stroke, oncology, geriatrics and orthopedics.

8507 Greenery Extended Care Center - Worcester

59 Acton Street
Worcester, MA 01604   508-791-3147
                             800-633-0887
                        FAX: 508-753-6267

173 beds offering complex care, extended rehabilitation and neurobehavioral intervention.

8508 Greenery Rehabilitation Center - Boston

99 Chestnut Hill Avenue
Boston, MA 02135   617-787-3390
                     FAX: 617-787-9169

201 beds offering programs of active/acute rehabilitation, cognitive rehabilitation, respiratory care and short-term evaluations.

8509 Harrington House

160 Main Street
Walpole, MA 02081   508-660-3080
                       FAX: 508-660-1634

William McGinley, Administrator

Postacute rehabilitation program, sub-acute medical services and respiratory therapy program. Subacute accreditation by JCAHO.

8510 Holiday Inn Boxborough Woods

242 Adams Plaza
Boxborough, MA 01719   978-263-8701
                          FAX: 978-263-0518
              e-mail: box_sales@fine-hotels.com
              www.holiday-inn.com/boxboroughma

Kathleen Kelly, Director of Sales

Located on 35 acres of wooded countryside just off I-495 at exit #28. Minutes from the Mass Turnpike, Route 2, 290 and 9. Conference center located on main level with 30,000 square feet of meeting space. Guest rooms feature two-line telephones, voice mail and dataports, irons and ironing boards, hair dryers and coffemakers. $129-$159.

$129 - $159

8511 Kolburne School

Southfield Road
New Marlborough, MA 01230   413-229-8787
                          FAX: 413-229-7708

Peter Weinstein, Executive Director

A family owned residential treatment center offering psychiatric services, clinical services, special education programs, vocational programs and occupational therapy.

8512 Lifeworks Employment Services

588 Pleasant Street
Norwood, MA 02062   781-769-1212
                       FAX: 781-551-0045

Ruth Antonucci, Director

8513 Mariner Health Care - Massachusetts

53 Parker Hill Avenue
Boston, MA 02120   617-232-9370
                          800-348-7676
                     FAX: 617-277-1530

Postacute rehabilitation program.

8514 Massachusetts Eye and Ear Infirmary & Vision Rehabilitation Center

243 Charles Street
Boston, MA 02114   617-573-4177
                     FAX: 617-573-4177
                     www.meei.harvard.edu

Joel Kraut, MD, FACS, Medical Director
Pat McCabe, MPH, Director
Paulette Denero Turco, Associate Director

Visual rehabilitation encompasses a low vision rehabilitation evaluation, occupational therapy evaluation (with home visit if necessary), and social service evaluation.

8515 New England Center for Children

33 Turnpike Road
Southborough, MA 01772   508-481-1015
                            FAX: 508-485-3421
                      e-mail: cwelch@necc.org
                               www.necc.org

Catherine Welch, Director of Admissions

A comprehensive year-round program for students who require a highly specialized educational and behavior management program. Students are from all over the country and receive intensive, positive, behavioral counseling and social skills training free of aversive treatment and excessive medication.

8516 New England Medical Center

Vision Rehabilitation Service
750 Washington Street
Boston, MA 02111
                               800-231-3316
                          FAX: 617-636-4867
              e-mail: eli@vision.eri.harvard.edu

Eli Peli, O.D., Dir., Vision Rehab.
Maria Mercuri, O.D., Optometrist

Offers services for the legally blind, visually impaired, mentally retarded blind and more with health, counseling, educational, recreational, rehabilitation, computer training and professional training services.

8517 New Medico Rehabilitation and Skilled Nursing Center at Lewis Bay

89 Lewis Bay Road
Hyannis, MA 02601   508-775-7601
                       FAX: 508-790-4239

Edmund Steinle, Executive Director

8518 Protestant Guild

411 Waverly Oaks Road
Waltham, MA 02452   781-899-0222
                       FAX: 781-893-1171

Edmund Hagerty, Executive Director

Offers services for the diagnostically disabled adolescents with health, counseling, educational, recreational, rehabilitation, computer training and professional training services.

8519 Rehabilitation Hospital of Western New England

14 Chestnut Plaza
Ludlow, MA   01056   413-547-9063
                    FAX: 413-547-6530

Bonnie Breit, Outpatient Services
Postacute rehabilitation program.

8520 Shaughnessy-Kaplan Rehabilitation Hospital

Dove Avenue
Salem, MA   01970   978-745-9000
                    FAX: 978-741-1967

Anthony Sciola, Executive Director
Rehabilitation for disabled.

8521 Son-Rise Program

The Autism Treatment Center of America
2080 South Undermountain Road
Sheffield, MA   01257   413-229-2100
                    800-714-2779
                    FAX: 413-229-8931
               e-mail: sonrise@option.org
                    www.son-rise.org

Suzanne Son-Rise Family Couns.

Since 1983, The Son-Rise Program at the Autism Treatment Center of America has provided innovative training programs for parents and professionals and caring for children challenged by Autism, Autism Spectrum Disorders, PDD and other developmental difficulties. The Son-Rise Program teached a specific yet comprehensive system of treatment and education designed to help families and caregivers enable their children to dramatically improve in all areas of learning, development, and communication.

8522 Southern Worcester County Rehabilitation Center

44 Morris Street
Webster, MA   01570   508-943-0700
                    FAX: 508-949-6129
               e-mail: swcrc@swcrc.inc.org

J. Thomas Amick, Executive Director

Provides day habilitation services, residential services, evaluation and personal adjustment training, sheltered employment, supported employment services, supported work services for individuals with mental health problems. Serves the physically disabled, developmentally disabled, mental health and mental retardation. Vocational services and job placement programs are available as well.

8523 Vinfen Corporation

950 Cambridge Street
Cambridge, MA   02141   617-441-1800
                    877-284-6336
                    FAX: 617-441-1858

Gary W Lamson, President & CEO

A private, nonprofit company, Vinfen Corporation is the largest human services provider in Massachusetts. Vinfen offers clinical, educational, residential and support services to individuals of all ages with mental illness and or mental retardation, who also may have another disability (e.g. substance abuse, homelessness, AIDS). The company also trains professionals in the mental health field and helps consumers to learn to live in community-based settings at the highest levels.

8524 Visiting Nurse Association of North Shore

5 Federal Street
Danvers, MA   01923   978-777-6100
                    800-457-8999
                    FAX: 978-777-6517

Susan Comparone, President

Home health services including nurses, physical, occupational and speech therapy, home health aides and more. Special programs include nutrition counseling, IV care, pediatric therapy, HIV/AIDS services and wound management. Provides services 7 days a week, 365 days a year and we accept Medicare, Medicaid and most HMO's and health insurers.

8525 Weldon Center for Rehabilitation

233 Carew Street
Springfield, MA   01104   413-748-6800
                    FAX: 413-748-6806

Dr. James. Lomastro, Vice President

8526 Westridge Healthcare Center

121 Northboro Road
Marlborough, MA   01752
                    FAX: 508-481-5585

Ivan Howard, Administrator
Postacute rehabilitation program.

8527 Youville Hospital & Rehab Center

1575 Cambridge Street
Cambridge, MA   02138
                    FAX: 617-547-5501

T. Richard Quigley, President

Meets the long and short term health care and rehabilitation needs of patients who are physically disabled and chronically ill. Strives to develop and maintain health as a human right on physical, social, vocational and spiritual levels. The ultimate goal of the hospital is to treat and assist each individual patient in reaching his or her optimal level of living. Services include: stroke, brain injury, spinal cord trauma, orthopedic disabilities and more.

Michigan

8528 Botsford General Hospital Inpatient Hospitalization Unit

28050 Grand River Avenue
Farmington Hills, MI   48336   248-471-8000
                    FAX: 313-471-8773

Gina Massengill, ACSW

A 20 bed inpatient physical rehabilitation unit, servicing individuals who have experienced a stroke, amputation, orthopedic fracture, or other neurological impairment.

8529   Chelsea Community Hospital Rehabilitation Unit

775 S Main Street
Chelsea, MI   48118   734-475-4138
                                  FAX: 734-475-4102
                                        www.cch.org

Sally Flack, Coordinator IP Services
Diane Fenske, Coordinator of Services

A private, non-profit, acute care facility that combines the best of small town values with national standards of healthcare excellence. The hospital has a 19-bed acute care inpatient rehabilitation unit with comprehensive outpatient programs, including a coordinated brain injury program.

8530   Clare Branch

790 Industrial Drive
Clare, MI   48617   517-386-7707
                                  FAX: 517-386-2199

Sherrie Johnson, Executive Director

8531   Eight CAP

904 Oak Drive Turk
Greenville, MI   48838   616-754-9315
                                  FAX: 616-754-9310

Ralph Loeschner, Executive Director

8532   Greenery Healthcare Center - Clarkston

4800 Clintonville Road
Clarkston, MI   48346   248-674-0903
                                        800-837-1913
                                  FAX: 313-674-3431

120 beds offering active/acute rehabilitation, complex care, day treatment, extended rehabilitation, neurobehavioral intervention and short-term evaluation.

8533   Haggerty Center for Neurorehabilitation

42005 W 12 Mile Road
Novi, MI   48377   248-305-7575
                                  FAX: 248-347-4578

Helene Rimer, Intake Coordinator
Postacute rehabilitation program.

8534   Lakeland Center

26900 Franklin Road
Southfield, MI   48034   248-350-8070
                                  FAX: 248-350-8078
                                  www.thelakelandcenter.net

Adrienne Shepperd, Marketing Director
Subacute rehabilitation program directed toward those with severe neurologic diagnoses, ie: TBI, cerebral aneurysm, anoxic encephalopathy, CVA and cerebral hemorrhage and spinal cord injury. Subacute rehabilitation is provided for those who recover slowly and require individualized treatment plans.

8535   Mary Free Bed Hospital and Rehabilitation Center

235 Wealthy Street SE
Grand Rapids, MI   49503   616-242-0300
                                        800-528-8989
                                  FAX: 616-454-3939
                             e-mail: mderrer@mfbrc.com
                                        www.mfbrc.com

William Blessing, President
Meg Derrer, Marketing Director/Web Master

8536   Men-O-Mee Activity Center

W5522 First Street
Hermansville, MI   49847
                                  FAX: 906-498-7606

Thomas Warren, Executive Director

8537   Michigan Commission for the Blind Training Center

1541 Oakland Drive
Kalamazoo, MI   49008   616-337-3848
                                  FAX: 616-337-3872

Melody Lindsey, Director
Residential facility that provides instruction to legally blind adults in Braille, computers, handwriting, keyboarding, mobility, adaptive kitchen skills, daily living, industrial arts, and crafts. Clients may also learn to use a variety of adaptive devices such as raised dot timers and watches, hand tools, talking calculators, tape recorders, reading machines and computers. Special training is also offered in vending stand operation, college preparation and job seeking skills.

8538   Mid-Michigan Industries

2426 Parkway Drive
Mt Pleasant, MI   48858   517-773-6918
                                        888-773-7664
                                  FAX: 517-773-1317
                           e-mail: mail@mmionline.com
                                        www.mmionline.com

M. Judith Garland, President
Andrea Christopher, Director of Admissions
Providing training program for persons with barriers to employment. Services include vocational evaluation, job placement, supported employment, work services, prevocational training and case management

8539   New Medico Community Re-Entry Service

216 Saint Marys Lake Road
Battle Creek, MI   49017
                                  FAX: 616-962-2241

James Rekshan, Executive Director

8540   Rehabilitation Services

Hope Network
1490 E Beltline Avenue SE
Grand Rapids, MI   49506   616-940-0040
                                  FAX: 616-940-8151

Tom Stranz, M.A., Director of Rehab
Elizabeth Lock, Admissions Manager

A department of Hope Network, one of the largest, private, nonprofit organizations of its kind in Michigan. The purpose is to assist people with brain injuries and/or physical disabilities in achieving an optimal level of self-determination, dignity, and independence as they develop and attain goals to overcome environmental barriers and mobilize adaptive skills.

8541 Sanilac County Community Mental Health

217 East Sanilac
Suite 1
Sandusky, MI 48471   810-648-0330
                                   888-225-4447
                          FAX: 810-648-0319

Dr. Roger Dean, Executive Director

8542 Special Tree Rehabilitation System

1640 Axtell Road
Troy, MI 48084   248-649-0101
                                   800-649-5011
                          FAX: 248-649-5445

Michael Malley, Communications
Postacute rehabilitation program.

8543 State Technical Institute and Rehabilitation Center

Alber Drive
Plainwell, MI 49080   616-664-9257
                          FAX: 616-664-5850

Leonard Lee, Executive Director

8544 Thumb Industries

1263 Sand Beach Road
Bad Axe, MI 48413   517-269-9229
                          FAX: 517-269-9229

Teresa Rabideau, Executive Director
Provides job training and employment for disabled persons.

8545 Upshaw Institute for the Blind

16625 Grand River Avenue
Detroit, MI 48227   313-272-3900
                          FAX: 313-272-6893
                          www.upshawinst.org

Carroll L. Jackson, Executive Director
Gail L. McEntee, Dir. of Develop. & Communication

Offers services for seniors 60 and over who are legally blind, and provide eye health information, counseling, education, and rehabilitation services.

8546 Visually Impaired Center

725 Mason Street
Flint, MI 48503   810-235-2544
                          FAX: 810-235-2597

Sharon Reigle, Executive Director
Criss Kellog, Social Worker

Sharing skills and resources for an independent life with vision loss for residents of Genesee, Shiawassee, and Lapeer counties, Michigan. Services include: information and referral, assessments of needs, peer support groups, independent living skills training by a Rehabilitation Teacher of the Blind, safe travel skills training by an Orientation and Mobility Specialist, Summer Youth Program, Vocatioinal Exploration.

8547 Welcome Home to the Blind

1953 Monroe Avenue NW
Grand Rapids, MI 49505   616-363-9088
                          FAX: 616-363-3099

Mrs. Johnson, Administrator
Offers services for the totally blind, legally blind, visually impaired, mentally retarded blind and more with health, counseling, educational, recreational, rehabilitation, computer training and professional training services.

8548 William H. Honor Rehabilitation Center Henry Ford Wyanclotte Hospital

2333 Biddle Street
Wyandotte, MI 48192   734-284-2400
                          FAX: 734-246-6926

Denise Dailing, Admin. Leader/Rehabiliation Svcs

Minnesota

8549 Brown-Nichollet Industries

21st N Street & Broadway
New Ulm, MN 56073
                          FAX: 507-345-4507

Arne Berg, Executive Director

8550 Industries

500 Walnut Street South
Mora, MN 55051   320-679-2354
                          FAX: 320-679-2355

Nonprofit organization that does vocational assessment and training for people with disabilities.

8551 Shriners Hospitals for Children - Twin Cities

2025 E River Parkway
Minneapolis, MN 55414   612-596-6100
                                   888-293-2832
                          FAX: 612-339-5954
                          www.shrinershq.org

Erin Enright, Community Outreach/Volunteer Crd

Shriners Hospital for Children-Twin Cities offers quality orthopedic medical care at no cost. Shriners Hospitals provide inpatient and outpatient services, surgery, casts, braces, artificial limbs, X-rays, and physical and occupational therapy to any child under 18 who may benefit from treatment. To obtain an application, call toll free at (888)293-2832.

8552 **Vision Loss Resources**

1936 Lyndale Avenue South
Minneapolis, MN 55403 612-871-2222
FAX: 612-872-0189
www.visionlossresources.org

Steve Fischer, Executive Director

Private non-profit United Way affiliated organization. Provides rehabilitation services, support, information and referral for individuals who are blind or visually impaired.

8553 **Vision Loss Resources**

216 Wabasha Street South
Saint Paul, MN 55107 651-224-7662
FAX: 651-224-9526

Steven Fischer, Executive Director

Offers services for the totally blind, legally blind, visually impaired, and more with health, counseling, educational, recreational, rehabilitation, computer training and professional training services.

Mississippi

8554 **Addie McBryde Rehabilitation Center for the Blind**

2550 Peachtree Street
PO Box 5314
Jackson, MS 39296 601-364-2700
FAX: 601-364-2677
e-mail: cponder@mdrs.state.ms.us

Carrie Ponder, Director
Karen Wallace, Assistant Director
Rosie Gibson, Assistant Director

Offers services for the totally blind, legally blind, visually impaired, mentally retarded blind and more with health, counseling, educational, recreational, rehabilitation, computer training services and orientation and mobility.

8555 **Mississippi Methodist Rehabilitation Center**

1350 E Woodrow Wilson Avenue
Jackson, MS 39216 601-364-3481
800-981-2611
FAX: 601-364-3465

Rebuild lives that have been broken by disabilities and impairments from serious illness or severe injury. The challenge is to help patients regain abilities, restore function and movement, and renew emotionally. It features personal rehabilitation treatment plans administered by specialized teams of health care professionals through a variety of outpatient programs, treatments and other services.

Missouri

8556 **Alpine North Nursing and Rehabilitation Center**

4700 NW Cliff View Drive
Kansas City, MO 64150
FAX: 816-746-1301

Sharon Garcia, Clinical Director

Postacute rehabilitation program.

8557 **Christian Hospital Northeast**

11133 Dunn Road
Saint Louis, MO 63136 314-653-5000
FAX: 314-653-4174

Nancy Bartmess, Executive Director

8558 **Harry S. Truman Children's Neurological Center**

15600 Woods Chapel Road
Kansas City, MO 64139 816-373-5060
FAX: 660-373-5878

Richard Lade, Executive Director

A licensed habilitation center established for the purpose of assisting severely developmentally disabled children and adults to achieve the optimum level of development in all phases of their life through the services of residential and adult developmental habilitative training programs. There are 72 beds. The minimum age is 5, and there is no age limit.

8559 **Integrated Health Services of St. Louis at Gravois**

10954 Kennerly Road
Saint Louis, MO 63128 314-843-4242
FAX: 314-843-5370

Cathy Deffendall, Administrator
Fran Jackson, Marketing Director

Subacute, skilled and intermediate care; ventilator/tracheostomy management program; wound management program and complex rehabilitation program.

8560 **Joplin House Healthcare**

2502 S Moffet Avenue
Joplin, MO 64804
FAX: 417-623-0880

Jan Zacny, Administrator

Postacute rehabilitation program.

8561 **Metropolitan Employment & Rehabilitation Service**

1727 Locust Street
Saint Louis, MO 63103 314-241-3464
FAX: 314-241-9348
www.mers.org

Dr. Lewis C. Chartock, President
Zip Rzeppa, Vice President Public Affairs

Vocational rehabilitation, primarily with the disabled, skills training and placement services.

8562 **Missouri Easter Seal Society - Southeast Region**

1912 Broadway
Cape Girardeau, MO 63701 573-335-3377
FAX: 573-335-3389

Charles R. Martin, Executive Director
Suzanne Holland, Director/Child Svcs.

The mission of the Easter Seal Society is to work with individuals, their families and the community to enhance the independence and quality of life for persons with disabilities.

8563 Poplar Bluff RehabCare Program

Lucy Lee Hospital
PO Box 88
Poplar Bluff, MO   63902   573-686-7320
FAX: 573-686-7307

Jim Martin, Program Manager
Chris Murray, Care Coordinator
Darlene Hill, Care Admissions Coordinator

Provides physical medicine and rehabilitation to individuals with a physically limiting condition. The
program is designed to help individuals function as
independently as possible by maximizing their
strength and abilities.

**8564 Psycho-Social Rehabilitation Center Places for
People**

4120 Lindell Boulevard
Saint Louis, MO   63108   314-535-5600
FAX: 314-535-6037

Francine Broderick, Executive Director
Therapy for disabled persoms.

8565 Service Club for the Blind

3719 Watson Road
Saint Louis, MO   63109   314-647-3306
FAX: 314-647-3306

Fred Keller, President
Joann Hall, Office Assistant
Kathleen Demsky, Office Assistant

Offers services for the totally blind, legally blind,
visually impaired, mentally retarded blind and more
with health, counseling, educational, recreational, rehabilitation, computer training and professional
training services.

8566 Shriners Hospitals for Children St. Louis

2001 S Lindbergh Boulevard
Saint Louis, MO   63131   314-432-3600
FAX: 314-432-2930

Carolyn P. Golden, Administrator
Bob Davidson, Dir. Community Relations

Medical care is provided free of charge for children
18 and under with orthopaedic conditions.

**8567 St. Louis Society for the Blind and Visually
Impaired**

8770 Manchester Road
Saint Louis, MO   63144   314-968-9000
FAX: 314-968-9003
e-mail: info@slsbvi.org
www.slsbvi.org

David C. Ekin, Executive Director
Doris Westfall, Director of Programs & Services

Offers vision rehabilitation services for the totally
blind, legally blind, visually impaired, including
counseling, educational, recreational, rehabilitation,
computer training and professional training services.
Low vision aids and appliance available through low
vision clinic by appointment.

8568 Visual Independence Program

Eye Foundation of Kansas City
2300 Holmes Street
Kansas City, MO   64108   816-881-6157
FAX: 816-881-6246

Camille Matta, M.D., Medical Director
Brendan Smith, OTR, Program Director

Program offers in home rehabilitation services to
older adults with visual impairments including training in use of magnifying devices for reading and other
activities of daily living. Specialized rehabilitation
program for persons with visual impairment secondary to stroke or head trauma.

Montana

8569 Adult and Child Study Center

3021 6th Avenue North
Billings, MT   59101   406-245-9284
FAX: 406-252-5463

Stan Gardner, MD, Medical Director

Offers medical services, psychological counseling
and educational diagnostic testing for attention hyperactivity and learning problems at all ages.

8570 Benefis Healthcare

1101 26th Street South
Great Falls, MT   59405   406-761-1200
FAX: 406-455-2110

Lloyd Smith, President/CEO

8571 Department of Social and Rehabilitation Services

PO Box 4210
Helena, MT   59604   406-444-2618
FAX: 406-444-1970

Janice Frisch

Information on developmental disabilities and automated systems.

8572 Disability Services Division

PO Box 4210
Helena, MT   59604   406-444-2590
877-296-1197
FAX: 406-444-3632
TDY:406-444-2590
www.dphhs.state.mt.us/dsd

Joe A. Mathews, Administrator

Responsible for coordinating, developing and implementing comprehensive programs to assist Montanans with disabilities with activities of daily living,
community base services, and coordinated programs
of habilitation, rehabilitation and independent living.

Nebraska

8573 Career Achievement Center - 48th Street
822 S 48th Street
Lincoln, NE 68510
FAX: 402-483-1127

Susie Feistner, Executive Director

Nevada

8574 Las Vegas Convalescent Center
2832 S Maryland Parkway
Las Vegas, NV 89109   702-796-3855
FAX: 702-735-6218

Postacute rehabilitation program.

8575 Sierra Pain Institute
265 Golden Lane
Reno, NV 89502   775-323-7092
FAX: 775-323-5259

The program consists of a medically supervised outpatient program managed by an interdisciplinary team with input from specialties of Pain Medicine, Physical Therapy and Occupational Science. The format insures that each patient receives the full range of behavioral techniques in a well-integrated, individually tailored therapeutic regimen.

New Hampshire

8576 Adroscoggin Valley Mental Health Center
Page Hill Road
Berlin, NH 03570
FAX: 603-752-5194

Arthur Froburg, Executive Director

8577 Crotched Mountain Adult Brain Injury Center
Crotched Mountain Rehabilitation Center
1 Verney Drive
Greenfield, NH 03047   603-547-3311
FAX: 603-547-3232
e-mail: admissions@cmf.org
www.info@cmf.org

Brant A. 'Bud' Elkind MS CI, Director, Brain Injury Services
Rita Phinney, Director Of Admissions
John Young, Associate Director, Admissions

Adult Brain Injury Unit provides sub-acute rehabilitative services and individualized care to survivors of acquired (including traumatic) brain injury. Ambulatory and non-ambulatory adults are served. Ages range from 18-59, the staff to client ratio is 4:1 and services are provided by experienced interdisciplinary clinical and therapeutic teams. Crotched Mountain is a licensed Special Hospital providing 24 hour medical coverage and skilled nursing. Clients reside in semi-private rooms w/supervis

8578 Department of Physical Medicine and Rehabilitation
Exeter Hospital
10 Buzell Avenue
Exeter, NH 03833   603-778-7311
FAX: 603-778-6671

Robert Haskins, Administrator

Offers patient treatment, committed to enhancing the lives of individuals with short and long term physically disabling conditions.

8579 Farnum Rehabilitation Center
580 Court Street
Keene, NH 03431   603-357-3018
FAX: 603-355-2078

Susan Loughrey, Program Director

Offers rehabilitation services, occupational therapy, physical therapy and more for the physically challenged individual.

8580 Hackett Hill Nursing Center and Integrated Care
191 Hackett Hill Road
Manchester, NH 03102   603-668-8161
FAX: 603-622-2584

Claudia Gallo, Case Manager

Postacute rehabilitation program.

8581 New Hampshire Rehabilitation and Sports Medicine
Catholic Medical Center
769 S Main Street
Suite 201
Manchester, NH 03102   603-663-5863
800-437-9666
FAX: 603-668-5348

Heidi George, Director

A specialized facility for comprehensive rehabilitation for individuals who have been injured or have a disability.

8582 New Medico, Highwatch Rehabilitation Center
Highwatch Road
Effingham Falls, NH 03814
FAX: 603-539-8888

Dr. William Burke, Executive Director

8583 Northern New Hampshire Mental Health and Developmental Services
87 Washington Street
Conway, NH 03818   603-430-2101
FAX: 603-447-8893

Stanley Marsden, Director

Provides mental health and developmental services to northern New Hampshire, including early intervention, elderly services, residential program, outpatient services, employee assistance programs, inpatient services, etc.

New Jersey

8584 All Garden State Physical Therapy
750 Broadway
Paterson, NJ 07514   973-345-1312
          FAX: 973-742-0669

Evelyn Perez, General Manager
Postacute rehabilitation program.

8585 Atlantic Coast Rehabilitation and Health Care Center
485 River Avenue
Lakewood, NJ 08701   732-364-7100
          FAX: 732-364-2442

Adult subacute programs including intensive respiratory care including mechanical ventilators, complex care, traumatic brain injury, cerebral vascular accident, wound care, pain management, and oncology care are provided in specialty units in suburban locations in Pennsylvania, New Jersey and Massachusetts.

8586 Bancroft NeuroHealth
PO Box 20
Haddonfield, NJ 08033   609-429-5637
          FAX: 609-429-1613
          e-mail: inquiry@bancroft.org
          www.bancroft.org

Dr. George Niemann, President/CEO
Jim Powers, Vice President, Marketing Pub Af
Michelle Stewart, Director of Communciations

Private, not-for-profit organization serving people with disabilities since 1883. Based in Haddonfield, New Jersey, help more than 1000 children and adults with autism, developmental disabilities, brain injuries, and other neurological impairments. Operates more than 140 sites throughout the U.S. and abroad.

8587 Cerebral Palsy of Monmouth & Ocean Counties
Schroth School & Technical Education Center
1701 Kneeley Boulevard
Asbury Park, NJ 07712   732-493-5900
          FAX: 732-493-5980

K. David Holmes, Executive Director
Patti Carbone, Executive Director

Provides an array of services and programs specifically for children and adults with developmental and physical disabilities. Services include approved Department of Education school programs; adult education and training; vocational training, personal care assistance services, in-home and Saturday respite; child care programs, housing opportunities, and more.

8588 Daughters of Miriam Center for the Aged
155 Hazel Street
Clifton, NJ 07011   973-772-3700
          FAX: 973-772-7117

Harvey Adelsburg, Executive Director

8589 Devereux Center in New Jersey
230 Pottersville Road
520
Chester, NJ 07930
          FAX: 908-879-6370

Kristy Hartman, Admissions Director
Lynn Jones, Executive Director
Carol Poirier, Admissions Assistant

Serves emotionally disturbed females, ages 5-21, who have affective disorders, bi-polar disorders, adjustment reactions, behavioral disorders, specific developmental disorders, identity disorders, attention deficit disorders, schizoid disorders, anxiety disorders, enuresis, runaway behavior, substance abuse, in remission and personality disturbances. The center offers 95-100 full-time staff including, teachers, administrators, counselors, therapists, recreation staff and support services.

8590 Integrated Health Services of New Jersey at Somerset Valley
1621 Route 22 West
Bound Brook, NJ 08805   732-469-2000
          FAX: 732-469-8917

Carolyn Allen, Executive Director
Janine Vyzas, Social Work/Admissions Director
Postacute rehabilitation program.

8591 Lourdes Regional Rehabilitation Center
1600 Haddon Avenue
Camden, NJ 08103   609-757-3840
          FAX: 609-968-2522

Tammy Feuer, Admin., Rehab & Post Acute Serv.

8592 Matheny School and Hospital
PO Box 339
Peapack, NJ 07977   908-234-0011
          FAX: 908-719-2137
          e-mail: info@matheny.org
          www.matheny.org

Steven Proctor, President
Gabor Barabas, M.D., Medical Director

A residential and outpatient facility for persons with physical disabilities such as Cerebral Palsy, Spina Bifida, Muscular Dystrophy and Lesch-Nyhan disease aged 3 to 40. Matheny offers medical, occupational and physical therapy, augmentative communication, and other allied health services as well as education, respite care and adult medical day care.

8593 Mt. Carmel Guild
494 Broad Street
Newark, NJ 07105   973-639-9534

Edda Stewart, Coordinator

Offers services for the totally blind, legally blind, visually impaired, mentally retarded blind and more with health, counseling, educational, recreational, rehabilitation, computer training and professional training services.

8594 Pediatric Rehabilitation Department, JFK Medical Center

2050 Oak Tree Road
Edison, NJ 08820   732-548-7610
                          FAX: 732-548-7751

Dr. Patricia Munday, Dir. Pediatric Rehab

Comprehensive interdisciplinary, family focused outpatient pediatric rehabilitation services including evaluation and individual and group treatment programs for children birth-21.

8595 REACH Rehabilitation Program - Leader Nursing and Rehabilitation Center

550 Jessup Road
Paulsboro, NJ 08066   609-848-9551

Karen Fattore, Case Manager

Postacute rehabilitation program.

8596 REACH Rehabilitation and Catastrophic Long-Term Care

1180 Route 22
Mountainside, NJ 07092   908-654-0020

Linda Sweeney, Program Director

Postacute rehabilitation program.

8597 Rehabilitation Specialists

33 Sicomac Road
North Haledon, NJ 07508   973-636-9366
                                  800-441-7488
                          FAX: 973-427-1463

Doug Cerminaro, Admissions Coordinator

Rehabilitation Specialists, founded in 1983, is a quality, cost effective community re-entry center treating individuals with acquired brain injury. A non clinical environment based in the community is utilized that offers professional services enabling participants to learn skills they need to return to a productive life. Both our Day and Residential programming emphases focus on Functional Life Skills, Work Skills and Learning Skills. Each participant's program is tailored to meet their needs.

8598 Summit Ridge Center

20 Summit Street
West Orange, NJ 27052   973-736-2000
                          FAX: 973-731-4582
                          www.ghv.com

Charlene Harn, Admissions & Marketing Director

Offers rehabilitation services, occupational therapy, physical therapy and more for the physically challenged.

New Mexico

8599 Lifecourse Rehabilitation Services

525 S Schwartz Avenue
Farmington, NM 87401   505-325-6645
                          FAX: 505-327-6562

Bobi Logsdon, RN, CRRN, Case Manager

Uses a team of professionals to provide a comprehensive rehabilitation program. Accomplishing the best possible physical and cognitive improvement is the aim of the following treatment members: nurses, physical therapists, physicians, speech and occupational therapists, therapeutic recreation specialist. Providing inpatient and out patient services.

8600 Southwest Communication Resource

PO Box 788
Bernalillo, NM 87004   505-867-3396
                          FAX: 505-867-3398

Norman Segel, Executive Director

New York

8601 Bronx Continuing Treatment Day Program

1527 Southern Boulevard
Bronx, NY 10460   718-893-1414
                          FAX: 718-893-0707

Ellen Stoller, Executive Director

8602 Brooklyn Bureau of Community Service

285 Schermerhorn Street
Brooklyn, NY 11217   718-885-5600
                          FAX: 718-855-1517

Leslie Klein, Director of Adult Rehabilitation
Maryclare Scerbo, Director of Volunteer Services

Offers independent living skills, counseling, work readiness, vocational trianing, job placement and job follow-up services to individuals with disabilities (to include individuals with psychiatric, physical, and developmental disabilities). Special programs to move disabled welfare recipients from welfare to work. Publishes a bi-annual newsletter.

8603 Buffalo Hearing and Speech Center

50 E N Street
Buffalo, NY 14203   716-885-8318
                          FAX: 716-885-4229

Janet Maher, President

Assists individuals with speech, language and/or hearing impairments to achieve maximum communication potential.

8604 Consolidated Industries of Greater Syracuse

100 W Court Street
Syracuse, NY 13204   315-424-8260
                          FAX: 315-425-0461

George Mango, Executive Director

8605   Cora Hoffman Center

2324 Forest Avenue
Staten Island, NY   10303   718-447-8205
                                    FAX: 718-815-2182

Kevin Kenney, Executive Director

8606   Elmhurst Hospital Center

7901 Broadway
Elmhurst, NY   11373   718-334-2600
                              FAX: 718-334-2623

Offers rehabilitation services, occupational therapy, physical therapy and more for the physically
challenged individual.

8607   F-E-G-S

315 Hudson Street
New York, NY   10013   212-366-8400
                              FAX: 212-366-8441
                    e-mail: execoffice@fegs.org
                                www.fegs.org

Jill Colon-Regus, Day Habilitation Services
Loel Tayler, Continuing Day Treatment Prgms
Rena Moore, Intensive Psychiatric Rehab Prgm

8608   Flushing Hospital

4500 Parsons Boulevard
Flushing, NY   11355   718-670-3134
                              FAX: 718-670-3082

David Karan, MD, Director, Clinic

Offers services for the totally blind, legally blind,
visually impaired, mentally retarded blind and more
with health, counseling, educational, recreational, rehabilitation, computer training and professional
training services.

8609   Gateway New Palz

137 N Chestnut Street
New Paltz, NY   12561   845-255-6700
                               FAX: 845-255-6706

Mark Hildebrandt, Executive Director

**8610   Henkind Eye Institute Division of Montefiore
         Hospital**

3400 Bainbridge Avenue
Bronx, NY   10467   718-920-6244
                           FAX: 718-920-6244

Lanny M. Binstock, O.D.

Offers services for the totally blind, legally blind,
visually impaired, mentally retarded blind and more
with health, counseling, educational, recreational, rehabilitation, computer training and professional
training services. Low vision services offered.

8611   Industries for the Blind of New York State

230 Washington Avenue
Albany, NY   12210   518-456-8671
                            FAX: 518-456-3587

Steven M. Ennis, President

Offers services for the totally blind, legally blind,
visually impaired, mentally retarded blind and more
with health, counseling, educational, recreational, rehabilitation, computer training and professional
training services.

8612   Inpatient Pain Rehabilitation Program

301 E 17th Street
New York, NY   10003   212-598-6606
                              FAX: 212-598-6468
                 e-mail: isaac.pinter@med.nyu.edu
                    www.hjd.edu/html/pain_ctr.html

Isaac Pinter Ph.D, Administrative Director

The Inpatient Rehabilitation Program, established in
1983 specializes in the treatment of chronic pain. Our
inpatient program is one of the oldest ans well established pain programs in the country. It is the only
interdisciplinary inpatient pain program in the tri-
state area, and one of only 20 pain programs in the
entire United States to have C.A.R.F. accreditation.
Upon completion of an extensive evaluation, patients
are admitted for an 18-day inpatient stay.

8613   Koicheff Clinic

2324 Forest Avenue
Staten Island, NY   10303   718-447-0200

8614   Marcus Pain Institute

30 E 40th Street
New York, NY   10016   212-532-7999
                              FAX: 212-532-5957
                      e-mail: njm@nmpi.com
                             www.nmpi.com

Norman Marcus, M.D., Medical Director

We focus on muscles as the cause of most common
pains, i.e. back, neck, shoulders, and headaches. We
make specific muscle diagnoses and have specific
treatments that in many cases will eliminate the need
for surgery or relieve the pain. Patients diagnosed
with herniated disc, spinal stenosis, rotator cuff tear,
impingement syndrome, sciatica, fibromyalgia and
headache will generally find relief.

8615   Pain Alleviation Center

125 S Service Road
Jericho, NY   11753   718-258-9222
                             FAX: 516-997-7281

Dr. Richard Linchitz, Medical Director

One of the first pain clinics to gain national accreditation from the Commission on Accreditation of Rehabilitation Facilities. This is due largely to a
patient-centered program based on the latest research.

8616   Pathfinder Village

3 Chenango Road
Edmeston, NY   13335   607-965-8377
                              FAX: 607-965-8655
                 e-mail: info@pathfindervillage.org
                        www.pathfindervillage.org

Marian Mullet, President & CEO

A community that serves all ages of people who have
Down Sydrome. These indivuals are experiancing
things thought impossible, getting higher education,
a sense of independence as well as living in an enviroment that nurtures and celebrates the values and
abilities of each individual. Provides housing, education, work and strength through a vibrant community.

8617 Pilot Industries - Ellenville
48 Canal Street
Ellenville, NY 12428   845-647-7711
                         FAX: 845-647-7711

Peter Pierri, Executive Director

8618 Presbyterian Hospital in the City of New York
622 W 168th Street
New York, NY 10032   212-874-6633
                         FAX: 212-305-1017

Michael Bradley, Executive Director

8619 Skills Unlimited
405 Locust Avenue
Oakdale, NY 11769   516-567-3320
                       FAX: 516-567-3285

Richard Kassnove, Executive Director

8620 United Cerebral Palsy of Western New York
7 Community Drive
Buffalo, NY 14225   716-894-0130
                       FAX: 716-894-8257

Virginia C. Purcell, Executive Director

Provides comprehensive services, to individuals with disabilities from infancy through adulthood. Also serves people with all types of developmental disabilities as well as providing clinical services to persons with other types of disabilities such as: spinal cord injury, multiple sclerosis, head trauma and others. The center employs over 750 people.

North Carolina

8621 Center for Vision Rehabilitation
Academy Eye Associations, OD, PLLC
3115 Academy Road
Durham, NC 27707   919-493-7456
                        800-942-1499
                   FAX: 919-493-1718
           e-mail: hgeyesomindspring.com
                     www.academyeye.com

Henry A. Greene, O.D., President

Vision rehabilitation and low-vision care for the visually impaired, post-stroke, head trauma and for neuro-oncology vision complications.

8622 Diversified Opportunities
610 N Pender Street
Wilson, NC 27893   252-291-0378
                      FAX: 252-291-1402

Mike Petty, Executive Director

8623 Hillhaven Convalescent Center
616 Wade Avenue
Raleigh, NC 27605
                      FAX: 919-828-3294

Dennis Redmond, Administrator
Postacute rehabilitation program.

8624 Industries of the Blind
920 West Lee Street
Greensboro, NC 27403   336-274-1591
                         FAX: 336-274-9207

Anette Klinard, Personnel/Safety Administrator

Offers services for the totally blind, legally blind, visually impaired, mentally retarded blind and more with health, counseling, educational, recreational, rehabilitation, computer training and professional training services.

8625 John C. Whitaker Regional Rehabilitation
3333 Silas Creek Parkway
Winston Salem, NC 27103   336-718-5780
                            FAX: 336-718-9272
                   www.forsythmedical.org/services

Mary Jo Weavil, Executive Director

8626 Johnston County Industries
912 Bright Leaf Boulevard
Smithfield, NC 27577   919-934-0677

Vicki Shore, Executive Director

8627 Learning Services - Carolina
707 Morehead Avenue
Durham, NC 27707   919-419-9955
                      FAX: 919-687-0530

Gary Ulciny, Admission
Postacute rehabilitation program.

8628 LifeSpan
940 Beaumont Avenue
High Point, NC 27260   336-884-7937
                         FAX: 336-884-6983

Patti Huggins, Program Director
Community rehabilitation program.

8629 Lions Club Industries for the Blind
1810 E Main Street
Durham, NC 27703
                      FAX: 919-598-1179

William Hudson, Executive Director

Offers services for the totally blind, legally blind, visually impaired, mentally retarded blind and more with health, counseling, educational, recreational, rehabilitation, computer training and professional training services.

8630 Lions Services
4600 N Tryon Street
A
Charlotte, NC 28213   704-921-1527
                         FAX: 704-921-1577

Charles Lamb, Adminstrator

Offers services for the totally blind, legally blind, visually impaired, mentally retarded blind and more with health, counseling, educational, recreational, rehabilitation, computer training and professional training services.

8631 McLeod Center West

Old Highway 70
Black Mountain, NC   28711

FAX: 828-669-4164

Steve Lee, Executive Director

**8632 Regional Rehabilitation Center Pitt County
Memorial Hospital**

2100 Stantonsburg Road
Greenville, NC   27834

252-816-4715
FAX: 252-816-7552
e-mail: mdixon@pcmh.com

Martha M. Dixon, Vice President General Services

8633 Rehab Home Care

2660 Yonkers Road
Raleigh, NC   27604

800-447-8692
FAX: 919-831-2211

Alan Silver, Chief Executive Officer
Janis Hansen, Chief Operating Officer

A Medicare/Medicaid certified, state-licensed home
health agency with emphasis on rehabilitation.

8634 Rehab Therapy

9825 Chapel Hill Road
C
Morrisville, NC   27560

FAX: 919-231-9407

Alan Silver, Chief Executive Officer
Janis Hansen, Chief Operating Officer

Outpatient medical rehabilitation service serving
Wake and surrounding counties since 1953. A private, nonprofit United Way agency providing physical, occupational and speech therapy services with an
emphasis on services to children. Offices in Raleigh
and Cary.

8635 Thoms Rehabilitation Hospital

Thoms Rehabilitation Hospital
68 Sweeten Creek Road
Asheville, NC   28803

828-274-6179
FAX: 828-274-9452

Kathi Petersen, Dir. of Planning & Communication
Edgardo Diez, MD, Medical Dir. of Brain Injury
Kathy Price, Dir. of Admissions

Freestanding physical rehabilitation hospital,
founded 1938 - 100 beds, including 90 acute and 10
transitional - JCAHO accredited.

8636 Winston-Salem Industries for the Blind

7730 N Point Drive
Winston Salem, NC   27106

336-759-0551
FAX: 336-759-0990

Daniel Boucher, President

Offers services for the totally blind, legally blind,
visually impaired, mentally retarded blind and more
with health, counseling, educational, recreational, rehabilitation, computer training and professional
training services.

Ohio

8637 Bellefaire Jewish Children's Bureau

22001 Fairmount Boulevard
Shaker Heights, OH   44118

216-932-2800
800-879-2522
FAX: 216-932-8520
e-mail: yulishj@bellefairejcb.org
www.bellefairejcb.org

Jill Yulish, Intake Coordinator

Residential treatment for ages 12 to 17 1/2 at time of
admission offering individualized psychotherapy,
special education, and group living for severaly emotionally disturbed children and adolescents. Also offers a variety of other programs including specialized
and therapuetic foster care, partial hospitilization,
outpatient counseling, home-based intensive counseling and adoption services.

8638 Christ Hospital Rehabilitation Unit

2139 Auburn Avenue
Cincinnati, OH   45219

513-585-2205
FAX: 513-585-3300

Richard Seim, Senior Vice President

8639 Cleveland Society for the Blind

Cleveland Sight Center
1909 E 101st Street
PO Box 1988
Cleveland, OH   44106

216-791-8118
FAX: 216-791-1101
e-mail: jkozak@clevelandsightcenter.org
www.clevelandsightcenter.org

Josephine R Kozak, Dir. Public Education
Michael E Grady, Executive Director

Social, rehabilitation, education and support services
for blind and visually impaired children and adults,
early intervention program for children birth to age
6, low vision clinic, aid and appliance shop, braille
and taping transcription, training for rehabilitation,
orientation, mobility and computer access, employment services and job placement, recreation program,
resident camping, talking books, radio reading services, food service training and snack bar employment.
Free screening.

8640 Columbus Speech and Hearing Center

510 East North Broadway
Columbus, OH   43214

614-263-5151
FAX: 614-263-5365
www.columbusspeech.org

Roy Smoot, President/CEO
Joanne Shannon, Director, Vocational Services

Serves persons who have speech-language, and hearing challenges. Provides vocational rehabilitation
services for individuals who are deaf, hard-of-hearing or deaf-blind. Covers the geographic regions of
central Ohio and Ohio.

**8641 CommuniCare of Clifton Nursing and
Rehabilitation Center**

625 Probasco Street
Cincinnati, OH   45220

513-281-2464
FAX: 513-281-2559

Lisa Renaker, Director of Nursing

A long term care facility which specializes in rehabilitation. Offers a full range of rehabilitative services including physical therapy, occupational therapy and speech therapy.

8642 Doctors Hospital

5100 West Broad Street
Columbus, OH 43228 614-297-5639
FAX: 614-870-9639

Janet Hymiak, Executive Director

8643 Dodd Hall at the Ohio State University Hospitals

480 W 9th Street
Columbus, OH 43215 614-293-3300

Sue Arnold, Admissions Coord.
Dr. William Pease, Medical Director

Dodd Hall is a full service medical rehabilitation hospital offering comprehensive inpatient and outpatient rehabilitation.

8644 Easter Seal Society of Mahoning

299 Edwards Street
Youngstown, OH 44502 330-743-1168
FAX: 330-743-1616

Ken Sklenar, Executive Director

8645 Fairfield Regional Vision Rehabilitation Center

784 East Main
Suite D
Lancaster, OH 43130 740-687-4785
800-969-3490
FAX: 740-689-9753
e-mail: frvrc@thevisioncenter.org
www.thevisioncenter.org

John Sterba, Director
Bonnie Conight, Administrative Assistant

Offers services for the blind and visually impaired to include functional low vision evaluations, community rehabilitation trading, counseling, educational, recreational, rehabilitation, computer training and professional training services.

8646 Four Oaks School

623 Dayton Xenia Road
Xenia, OH 45385 937-222-7474

Judith Pierce, School Administrator

Starts children on the road to discovery by providing a learning environment rich in opportunities and encouragement. The program was designed to give children with delays or disabilities, or those at-risk the extra help needed to develop fully. Any child under the age of six who exhibits developmental delays, handicapping conditions, or is considered at risk may qualify to participate.

8647 George A. Martin Center

3603 Washington Avenue
Cincinnati, OH 45229 513-961-0144

William Poole, Administrator

Offers services for the totally blind, legally blind, visually impaired, mentally retarded blind and more with health, counseling, educational, recreational, rehabilitation, computer training and professional training services.

8648 Good Genesis Healthcare System

Rehabilitation Center
800 Forest Avenue
Zanesville, OH 43701 740-454-5000
800-322-4762
FAX: 740-455-7527
e-mail: sparker@genesishes.org
www.genesishes.org

Sharon Parker, Director Of Rehabilitation
Lisa Lynn, Inpatient Services Manager

A CARF accredited 20-bed rehabilitation facility located within Genesis Healthcare System Good Samaritan Campus, a 732 bed, non-profit hospital system, located in Zanesville, Ohio. Freestanding outpatient services, including work hardening and pain management programs.

8649 Grady Memorial Hospital

561 W Central Avenue
Delaware, OH 43015 740-369-8711
FAX: 740-363-3175

Everett Weber, Executive Director

8650 Hamilton Center

3400 Symmes Road
Hamilton, OH 45015 513-867-5970
FAX: 513-874-2977

Donald Musnuff, Executive Director

8651 Holzer Clinic

385 Jackson Pike
Gallipolis, OH 45631 740-286-6417
FAX: 740-446-5448

Robert Daniel, Executive Director

8652 Holzer Medical Center RehabCare

100 Jackson Pike
Gallipolis, OH 45631 740-446-5000
FAX: 740-446-5904

Carol Wellman, Program Manager
Kaye Rutherford, Nurse Manager

Offers an individualized quality comprehensive rehabilitation program for people with disabilities by an interdisciplinary team including physical therapy, occupational, speech, nursing and social services to restore the patient to the highest degree of rehab outcomes attainable.

8653 Human Resource Consultants

1946 N 13th Street
Toledo, OH 43624

8654 IKRON Institute for Rehabilitative and Psychological Services

2347 Vine Street
Cincinnati, OH 45219   513-621-1117
FAX: 513-621-2350

Randy E. Strunk, Executive Director
Chris Etter, Fiscal Officer
Ann Webb, Program Director

An accredited mental health facility and a certified rehabilitation center. Through a variety of creative treatment and rehabilitation services, IKRON assists adults with mental health and/or substance abuse problems to attain greater independence, to lead lives of sobriety, to obtain competitive work and live more satisfying lives. IKRON places a strong emphasis on respect and support for persons with problems of adjustment. Special contracts to persons desiring job placement.

8655 Integrated Health Services at Waterford Commons

955 Garden Lake Parkway
Toledo, OH 43614   419-382-2200
FAX: 419-381-0188

Mary E. McConnell, Provider Relations

A subacute and rehabilitation program specializing in ventilator weaning and management, I.V. therapeutics and pain management, wound management and subacute rehabilitation.

8656 Lake County Society for Rehabilitation

9521 Lake Shore Boulevard
Mentor, OH 44060   440-255-8835
FAX: 330-652-6632

Ahby Mansour, Executive Director

8657 Lester H. Higgins Adult Center

2950 Whipple Avenue NW
Canton, OH 44708   330-484-4814

Dr. Joseph James, Superintendent

8658 Live Oaks Career Development Campus

5956 Buckwheat Road
Milford, OH 45150   513-575-1900
FAX: 513-771-6575

Dr. Harold Carr, Superintendent

8659 MERIT Industries

300 Phillips Avenue
Toledo, OH 43612   419-269-0772
FAX: 419-470-5985

Nancy Rawson, Executive Director

8660 Metro Health - St. Luke's Medical Center Pain Management Program

11311 Shalar Boulevard
Cleveland, OH 44104   216-778-7800
FAX: 216-368-7140

CARF accredited comprehensive multidisciplinary pain management program.

8661 MetroHealth Medical Center

3395 Scranton Road
Cleveland, OH 44109   216-459-5192
FAX: 216-778-8376

Henry Manning, Executive Director

8662 Middletown Regional Hospital - Inpatient Rehabilitation Unit

105 McKnight Drive
Middletown, OH 45044   513-423-9265
FAX: 513-420-5718

Bob Gauder, Program Manager

8663 Newark Healthcare Center

75 McMillen Drive
85
Newark, OH 43055   FAX: 740-344-8615

Joanne Whiteman, Administrator
Subacute rehabilitation program.

8664 Parma Community General Hospital RehabCare Unit

7007 Powers Boulevard
Parma, OH 44129   440-743-3000
FAX: 440-743-4036

Donna Courtwright, Program Director

The mission of this CARF accredited unit is to provide the most comprehensive, cost-effective, acute rehabilitation program possible in order for every patient and family to adjust to his/her disability and to achieve the maximum potential of independent functioning when returning to community living.

8665 Peter A. Towne Physical Therapy Center

447 Nilles Road
Fairfield, OH 45014   513-779-8666
FAX: 513-829-7726

Peter Towne, Executive Director

8666 Philomatheon Society of the Blind

2810 Tuscarawas Street W
Canton, OH 44708   330-453-9157

Gerald Deffecker, President

Offers services for the totally blind, legally blind, visually impaired, mentally retarded blind and more with health, counseling, educational, recreational, rehabilitation, computer training and professional training services.

8667 Providence Hospital Work

2270 Banning Road
Cincinnati, OH 45239   513-853-5261
FAX: 513-853-5910

Christopher West, Executive Director

8668 SCI - Six County
2927 Bell Street
Zanesville, OH 43701 740-452-9953
FAX: 740-455-4134

David O. Wesner, Ph.D., Program Research

8669 St. Francis Rehabilitation Hospital
401 N Broadway Street
Green Springs, OH 44836 419-639-6218
FAX: 419-639-6222

Martha Stevens, Marketing Coord.

Program offers specialized treatment for patients who have suffered a head injury, spinal cord injury, or stroke, or who have an orthopedic injury. The Head Injury Program provides a continuum of care from coma stimulation through transitional living. Their physicians, nurses, counselors and therapists are dedicated to helping our patients develop the motivation, strength and skills needed to overcome or adapt to their disability.

8670 TAC I
110 W Leffel Lane
Springfield, OH 45506
FAX: 937-325-4623

William Hoke, Executive Director

8671 TAC II
110 W Leffel Lane
Springfield, OH 45506
FAX: 937-325-4623

William Kent Hoke, Executive Director

8672 Therapy Services Dept. of Orthopedic and Rehabilitation Center
Hershey Medical Center at Penn State University
PO Box 850
Hershey, PA 17033 717-531-8070
FAX: 717-531-4558

Oklahoma

8673 Dean A. McGee Eye Institute
608 Stanton L Young Boulevard
Oklahoma City, OK 73104 405-271-1092

Dr. Amelia Miranda, Director

Offers services for the totally blind, legally blind, visually impaired, mentally retarded blind and more with health, counseling, educational, recreational, rehabilitation, computer training and professional training services.

8674 Jane Phillips Rehab Services
RehabCare
3500 E Frank Phillips Boulevard
Bartlesville, OK 74006 918-335-6655
FAX: 918-333-7801

Scott Smith, Program Manager
Kathy Potts, Social Worker

Comprehensive inpatient rehabilitation services are provided to patients with orthopedic, neurologic, and other medical conditions of recent onset or regression, who have experienced a loss of function in activities of daily living, mobility, cognition and communication.

8675 McAlester Regional Health Center RehabCare Unit
1 Clark Bass Boulevard
McAlester, OK 74501 918-421-8063
FAX: 918-426-1016

A 19-bed inpatient physical rehabilitation unit serving the Southeast Oklahoma area. Offers physical therapy, occupational therapy, social work, speech and psychological services in an interdisciplinary framework.

8676 Oklahoma League for the Blind
PO Box 24020
Oklahoma City, OK 73124 405-232-4644
FAX: 405-236-5438

LeRoy Saunders, Executive Director

Offers services for the totally blind, legally blind, visually impaired, mentally retarded blind and more with health, counseling, educational, recreational, rehabilitation, computer training and professional training services.

8677 St. Anthony Hospital Rehabilitation Center
1000 N Lee
PO Box 205
Oklahoma City, OK 73003
FAX: 405-231-8759

Ginger Castleberry, Director of Rehabilitation

24 bed inpatient rehabilitation unit. General rehab with stroke and orthopedic program specialties. Community re-entry, support groups, pet therapy and aquatic therapy programs are some possibilities.

8678 Valley View Regional Hospital RehabCare Unit
430 N Monte Vista Street
Ada, OK 74820 580-332-2323
FAX: 580-421-1395

Rita Baumgartner, Program Manager

Comprehensive physical medicine and rehabilitation services designed to help patients in their adjustment to a physically limiting condition.

Oregon

8679 Emanuel Rehabilitation Center
3025 North Vancouver
Portland, OR 97227 503-335-2000
FAX: 503-413-1501

Gary Guidetta, Executive Director

8680 Garten Services

3334 Industrial Way NE
Salem, OR   97303   503-581-4472
                              FAX: 503-581-4497
                        e-mail: garten@garten.org

Emil Graziani, Executive Director

8681 Oakcrest Care Center

2933 Center Street NE
Salem, OR   97301
                              FAX: 503-588-5251

Postacute rehabilitation program.

8682 Oakhill-Senior Program

1190 Oakhill Avenue SE
Salem, OR   97302   503-364-9086
                              FAX: 503-365-2879

Jan Dillon, Senior Services Manager

Garten Senior Services provides an adult day service program to seniors with and without developmental disabilities. The program will provide community opportunities, college classes and a wide variety of leisure activities in group and individual settings.

8683 Pacific Spine and Pain Center

1801 Highway 99 N
Ashland, OR   97520   541-482-5515
                              FAX: 541-482-2433

Linda Dunn, Executive Director

8684 Vision Northwest

621 SW Alder
Portland, OR   97205   503-221-0705
                              FAX: 503-243-2537

Evelyn Maizels, Executive Director

Offers services for the totally blind, legally blind, visually impaired, mentally retarded blind and more with health, counseling, educational, recreational, rehabilitation, computer training and professional training services.

8685 Willamette Valley Rehabilitation Center

4390 S Santiam Highway
Lebanon, OR   97355   541-258-8121
                              FAX: 541-451-1762

Pennsylvania

8686 Alcohol and Drug Abuse Services

2 Main Street
Bradford, PA   16701   814-362-6517
                              FAX: 814-362-3202

Carma Horner, Supervisor

Offers rehabilitation services to individuals with an alcohol or drug related problem.

8687 Alpine Nursing and Rehabilitation Center of Hershey

820 Rhue Haus Lane
Hershey, PA   17033
                              FAX: 717-533-8698

Abe Locker, Executive Director

Postacute rehabilitation program.

8688 Alpine Ridge and Brandywood

Devereux Foundation
600 Boot Road
Downingtown, PA   19335   610-942-5915
                                     800-345-1292
                              FAX: 610-873-4961

Offers a continuum of services for residents requiring services ranging from minimal care and supervision to total physical and medical care.

8689 Amity Lodge

Devereux Foundation
600 Boot Road
Downingtown, PA   19335   610-942-5915
                                     800-345-1292
                              FAX: 215-873-4961

Offers residents a continuum of services ranging from minimal care and supervision to total physical and medical care.

8690 Beechwood Rehabilitation Services A Community Integrated Brain Injury Program

469 East Maple Avenue
Langhorne, PA   19047   215-750-4299
                                     800-782-3299
                              FAX: 215-750-4327
                        e-mail: dcerra-tyl@wood.org
                        www.beechwoodrehab.com

Deborah Cerra-Tyl, Dir of Program Development

Services include residential, day treatment and community based support services. Beechwood has programs in both Pennsylvania and New Jersey. Individuals with an acquired brain injury are served.

8691 Bryn Mawr Rehabilitation Hospital

414 Paoli Pike
PO Box 3007
Malvern, PA   19355   610-251-5400
                              FAX: 610-647-3648
                        www.mainlinehealth.org

Patricia M. Ryan, Senior Vice President
Helen Carmine, Assistant VP of Clinical Oper.

8692 Clara Burke Nursing Home

251 Stenton Avenue
Plymouth Meeting, PA   19462   610-828-2272
                              FAX: 610-828-2519

Terri Herd, Admissions
Postacute rehabilitation program.

8693 Concord Training Center

I-95 Industrial Park
Chester Township, PA   19014

Scott Selkowitz, Executive Director

8694 Daman Villa

Devereux Foundation
889 Boot Road
Downingtown, PA 19335
610-942-5915
800-345-1292
FAX: 215-873-4961

Offers residents a continuum of services ranging from minimal care and supervision to total physical and medical care.

8695 Devereux

444 Devereux Drive
Villanova, PA 19085
800-345-1292
FAX: 610-542-3100
e-mail: knash@devereux.org
www.devereux.org

Kimberleigh Nash, Dir. of Corporate Communications
Michele Petti, Director of Client Services

Nationwide network of residential, day, and community-based services for children and adults who have special emotional and/or developmental needs.

8696 Devereux Foundation Health Services Center

600 Boot Road
Downingtown, PA 19335
610-942-5915
800-345-1292
FAX: 610-971-4600
www.devereux.org

Provides a continuum of residential services for adults with developmental disabilities. active treatment is offered in a safe and therapeutic environment which allows on-going assessment and individual growth that will enhance the quality of life for each of its residents. Candidates could have needs that range from minimal care and supervision to those requiring medical and behavioral assistance with an intensive support system. $145-$161.00 per day.

8697 Devereux's Kanner Center

950 E Haverford Road
200
Bryn Mawr, PA 19010
610-431-8100
800-345-1292
FAX: 610-430-0567

Michelle Petti, Referral Services

Devereux is a private, not for profit nationwide network of treatment services for individuals of all ages with emotional and/or developmental disabilities. Located in twelve states and the District of Columbia, Devereux's continuum includes inpatient and partial hospitalization, residential treatment, community based programs and outpatient services.

8698 Fox Subacute Center

2644 Bristol Road
Warrington, PA 18976
215-491-1191
FAX: 215-343-8023

Gerry Nevilln, Admissions
Postacute rehabilitation program.

8699 Greater Pittsburgh Guild for the Blind

311 Station Street
Bridgeville, PA 15017
724-224-8700
FAX: 412-257-8573

Leroy Bectwy, Director

Offers services for the totally blind, legally blind, visually impaired, mentally retarded blind and more with health, counseling, educational, recreational, rehabilitation, computer training and professional training services.

8700 IHS of Greater Pittsburgh

890 Weatherwood Lane
Greensburg, PA 15601
724-837-8076
FAX: 724-837-7456

Eileen Plundo, RN, Case Manager
Laurie Tamay, Director of Admissions

Subacate care, ventilator and pulmonary managment, comprehensive rehabilitation.

8701 Pediatric Center at Plymouth Meeting Integrated Health Services

900 E Germantown Pike
Norristown, PA 19401
610-265-9290
800-220-PEDS
FAX: 610-265-2772

Lori Dildine, Program Director

Subacute programs such as intensive respiratory care, stressing ventilator dependent children, pre and post transplant care, total parenteral nutrition, IV therapy, intensive/behavioral oral feeding programs. Provides extensive discharge planning including teaching or review for all the above programs with an emphasis on development and accessing community resources.

8702 Pennsylvania Pain Rehabilitation Center

252 West Swamp Road
Bailiwick #2, PO Box 1802
Doylestown, PA 18901
215-348-5104
FAX: 215-348-5106

Dr. Reza Azar, Executive Director

8703 Robert L. Miller Rehab Center

Good Samaritan Hospital
PO Box 1281
Lebanon, PA 17042
717-270-7500
FAX: 717-270-7840

Joanne Ebert, Rehab Coordinator
Stuart Hartman, Medical Director

Comprehensive inpatient rehab unit for adults regarding general physical rehabilitation. Specific programs include orthopedic, neurological, stroke, amputee, etc.

8704 Willis Eye Hospital

Nonth & Walnut Street
Philadelphia, PA 19107
FAX: 215-238-0804

John Jeffers, M.D.

Offers services for the totally blind, legally blind, visually impaired, mentally retarded blind and more with health, counseling, educational, recreational, rehabilitation, computer training and professional training services.

Rhode Island

8705 **In-Sight**

43 Jefferson Boulevard
Warwick, RI   02888   401-941-3322
FAX: 401-941-3356

Judith Smith, Executive Director

Offers services for the totally blind, legally blind, visually impaired, mentally retarded blind and more with health, counseling, educational, recreational, rehabilitation, computer training and professional training services.

8706 **Vanderbilt Rehabilitation Center**

Friendship Street
Newport, RI   02840   401-783-9718
FAX: 401-845-1087

Robert Healey, Executive Director

South Carolina

8707 **Association for the Blind**

2209 Mechanic Street
Charleston, SC   29405   843-723-6915
FAX: 843-577-4312

Bettye Dorn, Director of Programs & Planning

Offers services for people who are blind, or are visually impaired with health, counseling, educational, recreational, rehabilitation, computer training and professional training services.

8708 **Healthsouth Central Carolinas Rehabilitation Complex**

134 E Rebound Road
Lancaster, SC   29720   803-286-1470
FAX: 803-286-4497

Jan Edwards, Marketing Coordinator
Mark Stepanik, Administrator
Jeanie Beasley, Director of Business Development

Subacute rehabilitation program. Comprehensive physical therapy, occupational therapy and speech therapy programs for stroke, orthopaedic, spinal cord, neurologic, brain injury, and general rehab patients. Outpatient therapy provided for all the above in addition to work-related injuries. Healthsouth has over 2,000 national contracts with insurers, employers, and managed care organizations.

8709 **Hitchcock Rehabilitation Center**

690 Medical Park Drive
Aiken, SC   29801   803-648-8344
800-207-6924
FAX: 803-649-4639
e-mail: dhillman@hitchcockrehab.com
www.hitchcockrehab.com

Pat Samuel, Executive Director
Dan Hillman, Case Manager
Carrie Morgan, Finance Director

Comprehensive outpatient rehabilitation for adults, children, geriatrics, pediatric therapy, special needs preschool, sports medicine, home health and hospice.

8710 **Mentor of South Carolina**

3200 Devine Street
Columbia, SC   29205   803-799-9025
FAX: 803-931-8959

Lynny Morton-Epps, State Director

Mentor provides a full network of individually tailored services for people with development disabilities and their families. Individuals may be served in their homes, shared living home, or in a host home.

Tennessee

8711 **Humana Hospital Morristown - RehabCare**

726 McFarland Street
Morristown, TN   37814   423-586-2930
FAX: 423-581-6988

Nickie Tabor, Program Director
Chuck Olson, Clinical Director

Designed to help patients in their adjustment to a physically limiting condition by helping to maximize each patient's abilities so he or she can function as independently as possible.

8712 **Patrick Rehab Wellness**

Lincoln County Health System
1001 Huntsville Highway
Fayetteville, TN   37334   931-433-0273
FAX: 931-438-0378

Laura Clark, Director of Rehab
Gloria Meadows, Administrator

Provides rehabilitation services of physical, occupational, and speech therapy. Also, wellness memberships are available to the public.

8713 **PharmaThera**

Corporate Offices, Suite 107
1785 Nonconnah Boulevard
Memphis, TN   38132   901-754-5485
800-767-6714
FAX: 901-348-8270

Offers 10 locations serving patients throughout the southern United States, each with an in-house, expertly trained staff. All locations use the latest technologies and techniques in infusion care to provide a broad range of individualized home infusion therapies.

8714 Siskin Rehabilitation Hospital

3 Siskin Plaza
Chattanooga, TN 37403   423-634-1700

Debby Barker, VP of Development

8715 St. Mary's RehabCare Center

Oak Hill Avenue
Knoxville, TN 37917
                                FAX: 423-545-8133

Debbie Keeton, Director

Provides comprehensive rehabilitation services for
patients experiencing CVA, head trauma, orthopedic
conditions, spinal cord injury or neurological impairment.

8716 Volunteer Blind Industries

758 W Morris Boulevard
Morristown, TN 37815   423-586-3922
                                FAX: 423-586-1479

Fred Overbay, Executive Director

Offers services for the totally blind, legally blind,
visually impaired, mentally retarded blind and more
with health, counseling, educational, recreational, rehabilitation, computer training and professional
training services.

Texas

8717 Baylor Institute for Rehabilitation

3505 Gaston Avenue
Dallas, TX 75246   214-826-7030
                              888-7BA-YLOR
                              FAX: 214-841-2679

Alice Douden, Admissions Manager

A 92-bed specialty hospital offering comprehensive
rehabilitation services for persons with spinal cord
injury, traumatic brain injury, stroke, amputation,
and other orthopedic and neurological disorders.

8718 Brown-Karhan Health Care

PO Box 419
Dripping Springs, TX 78620   512-894-0801
                                FAX: 512-858-4627
e-mail: info@brown-karhan.com
www.brown-karhan.com

Dr. Jim Misko, Clinical Director/Vice President

Postacute rehabilitation program, long-term neuropsychiatric program, apartment living and full compliment of therapies, including cognitive rehabilitation.
$225-$800/day.

8719 Center for Neuro Skills

3501 N Macarthur Boulevard
Suite 200
Irving, TX 75062   972-597-7715
                              FAX: 972-255-3162

Rocky Brogdon, Admissions
Postacute rehabilitation program.

8720 Center for Neuro Skills - Texas

3501 N Macarthur Boulevard
Suite 200
Irving, TX 75062   972-597-7715
                              FAX: 972-255-3162
e-mail: cns@neuroskills.com
www.neuroskills.com/~cns

David Krych, Executive Director
Peter O'Neill, Admissions
Rocky Brogdon, Admissions

A comprehensive, post-acute, community based
head-injury rehabilitation program serving over 100
clients per year. Since 1985, CNS has effectively
treated the entire spectrum of head-injured clients,
including those with severe behavioral disorders,
cognitive/perceptual impairments, speech/language
problems, physical disabilities and post-concussion
syndrome.

8721 Comprehensive Rehabilitation

Hillcrest Baptist Medical Center
3000 Herring Avenue
Waco, TX 76708   254-202-5100
                              FAX: 254-202-5674

Carl Lutz, MSW, Program Director
Ann Gammel, Nurse Manager

Designed to assist patients in adjustment to a physically limiting condition, utilizing interdisciplinary
strategies to maximize each patient's ability and capability.

8722 Dallas Services for Visually Impaired Children

4242 Office Parkway
Dallas, TX 75204   214-828-9900
                              FAX: 214-828-9901

Robert Berger, Executive Director

Offers services for the totally blind, legally blind,
visually impaired, mentally retarded blind and more
with health, counseling, educational, recreational, rehabilitation, computer training and professional
training services.

8723 Devereux Texas Treatment Network Adult Community

120 David Wade Drive
PO Box 2666
Victoria, TX 77902   361-575-8271
                              800-383-5000
                              FAX: 361-575-6520

Ric Tinney, Adult Services Administrator
Shirley Heron, Case Coordinator
Ward Starrak, Case Coordinator

Provides a permanent home for individual's with
chronic psychiatric and/or developmental disabilities
who require long term or lifelong care, support or a
transitional home for individuals who progress to a
less structured setting. Located on a beautiful 400+
acre campus in sunny south Texas, the primary focus
is to offer, in keeping with the philosophies of least
restrictive alternatives and normalization, active
treatment which will facilitate growth.

8724 El Paso Lighthouse for the Blind

200 Washington Street
El Paso, TX   79905   915-542-1969
                            FAX: 915-532-6338
                    e-mail: tomdyles@whc.net

Tom Doyle, Executive Director

Enables people of all ages to embody blindness and vision impairment through training, rehabilitation, employment opportunity, advocacy and research. Provides access to opportunities and quality of life so that the blind and visually impaired can reach their fullest potential for self-sufficiency and independence.

8725 Harris Methodist Fort Worth/Mabee Rehabilitation Center

1301 Pennsylvania Avenue
Fort Worth, TX   76104   817-882-2364
                            FAX: 817-882-2753

Michelle Wilson, Speciality Program Manager
Peggyo Ehrlich, Rehab Manager

A hospital based inpatient rehab program and outpatient day programs in chronic pain management, work hardening and brain injury transitional services.

8726 Heights Hospital Rehab Unit

1917 Ashland Street
Houston, TX   77008   713-861-6161
                            FAX: 713-802-8537

Leticia Bravo, Program Manager
Kim Willis, Admissions

This program is designed to assist patients with physical disabilities achieve their maximum functional abilities.

8727 Houston Rehabilitation Institute

17506 Red Oak Drive
Houston, TX   77090   713-223-5971
                            FAX: 281-580-6714

Jerome Lengel, Executive Officer

Offers an individualized approach to the process of rehabilitation for severely injured or disabled individuals. The process begins with a pre-admissions assessment of each referred patient. The Center combines state-of-the-art technology and equipment with multi-disciplinary therapy and education in a cheerful, secure environment.

8728 IHS Hospital at Dallas

7955 Harry Hines
Dallas, TX   75235

                            800-366-4736
                    FAX: 214-637-6512

Richard G. Allison, Admissions

66 beds offering active/acute rehabilitation, brain injury day treatment, cognitive rehabilitation, complex care, extended rehabilitation, pediatric brain injury rehabilitation and short-term evaluation.

8729 Institute for Rehabilitation & Research

1333 Moursund Street
Houston, TX   77030   713-799-7011
                            FAX: 713-797-5289

Karen Hart, V.P. For Education

A national center for information, training, research, and technical assistance in independent living. The goal is to extend the body of knowledge in independent living and to improve the utilization of results of research programs and demonstration projects in this field. It has developed a variety of strategies for collecting, synthesizing, and disseminating information related to the field of independent living.

8730 Integrated Health Services of Amarillo

5601 Plum Creek Drive
Amarillo, TX   79124   806-351-1000
                            FAX: 806-355-9650

Jackie Forbis, Case Manager
Neal Duncan, Executive Director
Paula Washington, Administrator

Postacute rehabilitation program including ventilator weening, complex wound program and interdisciplinary team case management.

8731 Lighthouse of Houston

3602 West Dallas Street
Houston, TX   77019   713-527-9561
                            FAX: 713-284-8451
        e-mail: gduterroil@houstonlighthouse.org
                www.thelighthouseofhouston.org

Gibson M. DuTerroil, President
Shelagh Moran, VP, Programs & Services
Tracy Cardinell, Director, Public Relations

Serves the blind, visually impaired, deaf-blind, and multihandicapped blind. Provides workshops, vocational training and placement, low vision clinic, orientation and mobility, housing, braille, volunteer services, senior center, visual aid sales, counseling and support, diabetic education and day health activity services and day summer camp, Summer Transition for Youth.

8732 Mainland Center Hospital RehabCare Unit

Highway 1764
Texas City, TX   77592   281-534-3522
                            FAX: 409-938-5501

David Roberts, Program Manager

The RehabCare program is designed and staffed to assist functionally impaired patients improve to their maximum potential. The opportunities for improvement and adjustments are provided in a pleasant, supportive inpatient environment by therapists from the occupational, physical, recreational and speech therapy disciplines.

8733 North Texas Rehabilitation Center

1005 Midwestern Parkway
Wichita Falls, TX   76302   940-322-0771
                            FAX: 940-766-4943

Lesa Enlow, Director of Programs

Provides outpatient rehabilitation services to maximize independence or promote development to children and adults with disabilities. Programs include: physical, occupational, speech therapy, closed head injury, back to work, learning remediation, infant/child development, support groups, aquatics and wellness program.

8734 South Texas Lighthouse for the Blind

PO Box 9697
Corpus Christi, TX 78469   512-883-6553
FAX: 512-883-1041

Barbara Russell, Executive Director

Offers services for the totally blind, legally blind, visually impaired, mentally retarded blind and more with health, counseling, educational, recreational, rehabilitation, computer training and professional training services.

8735 Transitional Learning Center at Galveston

1528 Postoffice Street
Galveston, TX 77550   409-762-6661
800-TLC-GROW
FAX: 409-763-3930

Lee Kinard, Managed Care & Account Manager
Jim McCurdy, Director of Business Development

The Transitional Learning Center at Galveston has specialized in post-acute brain injury since 1982. TLC is a leader who offers comprehensive therapies in a residential setting, 24-hour monitoring, outcome focused pathways, superior staff credentials - including physician and nursing staff on-site to address medical issues, innovative clinical research integrated into treatment plans, discharge lifecare planning, and long-term living at Tideway Lodge.

8736 Treemont

5550 Harvest Hill Road
Dallas, TX 75230   972-404-0833
FAX: 972-715-5550

Donna Snyder, Administrator
Postacute rehabilitation program.

8737 West Texas Lighthouse for the Blind

2001 Austin Street
San Angelo, TX 76903   915-653-4231
FAX: 915-657-9367
e-mail: wtlb@wee.net
www.lighthousefortheblind.org

Robert Porter, Executive Director
Ron Beard, Operations Manager
Margene Hale, Office Manager

Offers services for the totally blind, legally blind, visually impaired, mentally retarded blind and more with health, counseling, educational, recreational, rehabilitation, computer training and professional training services.

Utah

8738 Quincy Rehabilitation Institute of Holy Cross Hospital

1050 E S Temple
Salt Lake City, UT 84102   801-350-8140
FAX: 801-350-4483

Postacute rehabilitation program.

8739 Wasatch Villa

2200 E 3300 S
Salt Lake City, UT 84109   801-328-2020
FAX: 801-486-0105

Postacute rehabilitation program.

Vermont

8740 Rutland Mental Health Services

78 S Main Street
Rutland, VT 05701
FAX: 802-747-7699

Mark G Monson, President & CEO

A private, non-profit comprehensive community mental health center. It provides services to individuals and families for mental health and substance abuse related problems and also to persons who are mentally retarded.

Virginia

8741 Bay Pine-Virginia Beach

1148 First Colonial Road
Virginia Beach, VA 23454   757-481-3321
FAX: 757-481-4413

Willie Alston, Jr., Administrator
Postacute rehabilitation program.

8742 Carilion Rehabilitation - New River Valley

2900 Tyler Road
PO Box 5
Radford, VA 24141   540-731-2992
FAX: 540-731-2011
e-mail: jsmith@carilion.com

Jennie Smith, Clinical Team Leader
Rhonda Fanning, Department Secretary/Referrals
Robin Sutphin, Rehabilitation Assistant

CARF-accredited pain management program, work hardening program and comprehensive outpatient therapy clinic, massage therapy, outpatient programs and more. Program emphasis is on interdisiplinary behavioral rehab based pain management and functional restoration in conjunction with medical treatment. Work hardening is a transdisciplinary work simulation program taylored to the individual. Comprehensive outpatient program is multi-disciplinary with emphasis on manual treatment.

8743 Faith Mission Home

3540 Mission Home Lane
Free Union, VA 22940   804-985-2294
                              FAX: 804-985-7633

Merle Miller, Administrator
Reubem Yoder, Director

A Christian residential center that serves 60 mentally
retarded children, including individuals with Down
Syndrome, Cerebral palsy, and other similar conditions. Children may be admitted from the time they
are ambulatory until they reach 15 years of age. He
or she may stay as long as it is in the child's best
interests. The training program stresses the following
areas: self-care, social, academic, vocational, crafts,
speech and physical development.

8744 Pines Residential Treatment Center

825 Crawford Parkway
Portsmouth, VA 23704   757-391-6602
                              FAX: 757-393-1029

Dr. Lenard Lexier, M.D., Medical Director
Judy Kemp, Admissions Director

A 310-bed residential treatment center in Portsmouth
Virginia, providing a therapeutic environment for severely emotionally disturbed children and youth. Five
unique programs meet behavioral, educational and
emotional needs of males and females, five to twenty-
two years of age. Multi-disciplinary teams devise
individual service plans to enhance strengths and reverse self-defeating behavior. A highly effective
positive reinforcement program with a proven track
record.

8745 REACH Rehabilitation Program - Manor Care

550 S Carlin Springs Road
Arlington, VA 22204   703-379-7200
                              FAX: 703-820-2535

Barb Feege, Program Director
Ruth Gurinsky, RN, Referral & Marketing

Postacute rehabilitation program.

8746 Resurrection Children's Center

2280 N Beauregard Street
Alexandria, VA 22311   703-578-1314

Charlie Armstrong, Administrative Dir.
Kim Messinger, Program Director

Offers children ages 2-5 with varying disabilities academic education, parent education, opportunities including classes, workshops, support groups and
individual counseling.

8747 Roanoke Memorial Hospital

PO Box 13367
Roanoke, VA 24033   540-981-8215
                           FAX: 540-981-8233

Kathy Robertson, Director

8748 Scandia Centrum for Rehab Medicine

2205 Fontaine Avenue
Suite 302
Charlottesvle, VA 22903
                           FAX: 804-984-3000

Jill Pehlke, Office Manager

Postacute rehabilitation program.

8749 Southside Virginia Training Center

PO Box 4110
Petersburg, VA 23803   804-520-2275
                              FAX: 804-524-7228

Richard Buckley

Offers residential, vocational, occupational, physical, and speech therapies.

8750 Woodrow Wilson Rehabilitation Center

Box 37
Fishersville, VA 22939   540-332-7000
                                 800-345-9972
                              FAX: 540-332-7132
                              TDY:800-811-7893
          e-mail: coleman1@wwrc.state.va.us
                              www.wwrc.net

Barbie Ostrander, Admissions Director
Wendell L Coleman, Public Service Director

Comprehensive, residential rehabilitation center offering complete medical and vocational rehabilitation
services including: vocation evaluation, vocational
training, transition from school to work, occupational
therapy, physical therapy, speech, language and audiology, assistive technology, rehabilitation engineering, counseling/case management, behavioral health
services, nursing and physician services, etc.

Washington

8751 Arden Nursing Home

16357 Aurora Avenue North
Seattle, WA 98133
                              FAX: 206-546-5480

Postacute rehabilitation program.

8752 Ballard Convalescent Center

820 NW 95th Street
Seattle, WA 98117   206-782-0100
                           FAX: 206-781-1448

Postacute rehabilitation program.

8753 Bellingham Care Center

1200 Birchwood Avenue
Bellingham, WA 98225   360-734-9295
                              FAX: 360-671-4368

Postacute rehabilitation program.

**8754 Division of Vocational Rehabilitation Department
of Social and Health Services**

PO Box 45340
Olympia, WA 98504   360-438-8000
                           800-637-5627
                           FAX: 360-438-8007
          e-mail: krulik@dshs.wa.gov
                   www.wa.gov/dshs/dvr

Jeanne Munro, Director

Information on computers, supported employment,
marketing rehabilitation facilities and transition.

8755 First Hill Care Center

1334 Terry Avenue
Seattle, WA 98101   206-624-1484
                                  FAX: 206-624-3090

Postacute rehabilitation program.

8756 Harborview Medical Center, Low Vision Aid Clinic

325 9th Avenue
Seattle, WA 98104   206-521-1600

Thomas Gillette, Director

Offers services for the totally blind, legally blind, visually impaired, mentally retarded blind and more with health, counseling, educational, recreational, rehabilitation, computer training and professional training services.

8757 Hillhaven Rehabilitation and Health Services Center

400 E 33rd Street
Vancouver, WA 98663
                                  FAX: 360-750-0665

Postacute rehabilitation program.

8758 Integrated Health Services of Seattle

820 NW 95th Street
Seattle, WA 98117   206-782-0100
                                  FAX: 206-781-1448

Jerry Harvey, Administrator
Marlette Basada, Director of Nursing
Flavia Lagrange, Director of Admissions

Postacute rehabilitation program. IHS provides 24 hour subacute and long-term care. We can handle vent/trach/hemo andritoneal dialysis and provide a full scope of rehabilitation services.

8759 Lakeside Recovery Centers

535 E Dock Street
Tacoma, WA 98402   253-573-0250
                                  FAX: 253-272-0171

Hugh Long, Administrator

8760 Lakewood Health Care Center

11411 Bridgeport Way SW
Tacoma, WA 98499   253-581-9002
                                  FAX: 253-581-7016

Janice Olson, Admissions Coordinator
Patty Wood, Administrator
Linda Doll, Social Services

Postacute rehabilitation program.

8761 Manor Care Nursing - Tacoma

5601 S Orchard Street
Tacoma, WA 98409
                                  FAX: 253-474-8172

Postacute rehabilitation program.

8762 ManorCare Health Services

3701 188th Street SW
Lynnwood, WA 98037   425-775-9222
                                  FAX: 425-744-1602

Renee Johnson, Admissions Director
Postacute rehabilitation program.

8763 ManorCare Health Services - Spokane

6025 N Assembly Street
Spokane, WA 99205
                                  FAX: 509-326-4790

Susan Cooper, Admissions Director
Postacute rehabilitation program.

8764 Northwest Continuum Care Center

128 Beacon Hill Drive
Longview, WA 98632   360-423-4060
                                  FAX: 360-636-0958

Postacute rehabilitation program.

8765 Park Manor Convalescent Center

1710 Plaza Way
Walla Walla, WA 99362   509-529-4218
                                  FAX: 509-522-1729

Postacute rehabilitation program.

8766 Queen Anne Health Care

Queen Anne Health Care
2717 Dexter Avenue North
Seattle, WA 98109   206-284-3936
                                  FAX: 206-283-3936

Postacute rehabilitation program.

8767 Rainier Vista Care Center

920 12th Avenue SE
Puyallup, WA 98372   253-875-9999
                                  FAX: 253-848-3937

Postacute rehabilitation program.

8768 Rehabilitation Enterprises of Washington

2626 12th Center SW
Suite 6
Olympia, WA 98502   360-943-7654
                                  FAX: 360-943-7680
                                  e-mail: phaney@cco.net

Penny Jo Hanley, Business Manager

REW is the professional trade association representing community rehabilitation programs before government and other publics. These organizations provide a wide array of employment and training services for people with disabilities. The goal is to assist member organizations to provide the highest quality rehabilitative and employment services to their customers.

8769 Seattle Medical and Rehabilitation Center

Evergreen Healthcare
555 16th Avenue
Seattle, WA   98122   206-362-6998
                                   800-877-3422
                              FAX: 206-324-4345

Donna Stromski, Executive Director
Christine Lafrenz, Director of Nursing
Matt Murray, Director of Admissions

103 beds offering subacute rehabilitation, complex care, subacute treatment and short-term evaluation. Pulmonary unit offering long and short term care for ventilator dependent patients.

8770 Slingerland Institute for Literacy

Educators Publishing Service
411 108th Avenue
Suite 2060
Bellevue, WA   98004   425-453-1190
                           FAX: 425-635-7762
                  e-mail: SlingInst@aol.com
                       www.slingerland.org

Madeline P Beery, Executive Director
Annette Calvagno, Program Support
Sue Heinz, Dean

A nonprofit public corporation founded in 1977 to carry on the work of Beth H. Slingerland in providing classroom teachers with the techniques, knowledge and understanding necessary for identifying and teaching children with Specific Language Disability. The main objective is to educate teachers in successful methods of identifying, diagnosing and instructing children and adults with SLD and to promote literacy through reading, writing and oral expression.

8771 Synergos NeuroMedical Rehab Unit - Seattle

Highline Community Hospital
12844 Military Road South
Seattle, WA   98168   206-248-4552
                           FAX: 206-248-4663

Graciella Cuevas, RN, Case Mgr/Referral Coordinator
Matt Crockett, Director of Rehab Services

Sub-acute rehabilitation program specializing in brain injuries.

8772 Timberland Opportunities Association

T00 W Curtis Street
Aberdeen, WA   98520   360-533-5823
                           FAX: 360-533-5848

Jim Eddy, Executive Director

Provides training and employment for disabled people.

West Virginia

8773 West Virginia Rehabilitation Center

Barron Drive
Institute, WV   25112   304-766-4696
                           FAX: 304-766-4989
                                www.wvdrs.org

Michael Meadows, Assistant Director, Client
Bill Tanzey, Manager, Center Services
Robin Wilson, Manager, Public Affairs

The West Virinia Rehabilitation Center has been called West Virginia's best kept secret. Set on a 33-acre campus near Charleston, WV, the Center complex houses a school with 13 training areas, dormitories, a full-service rehabilitation hospital, a recreation program, a state-of-the-art assistive technology program and extension services statewide.

Wisconsin

8774 Christian League for the Handicapped

PO Box 948
Walworth, WI   53184   414-275-6131
                           FAX: 414-275-3355

Steven Jensen, Executive Director
Tim Schnake, Dir./Resident Srvcs.

Multifaceted ministry including independent living apartments, assisted living housing, employment, camping, retreats, employment counseling, and more. 103 people with physical disabilities live and work on 160 acre campus. The League generally serves those over 18.

8775 Colonial Manor of Wausau - Extended Rehab Services

1010 E Wausau Avenue
Wausau, WI   54403   715-842-2028
                           FAX: 715-848-0510

Jean Burgener, Administrator

Postacute rehabilitation program.

8776 Waushers Industries

210 E Townline Road
Wautoma, WI   54982

                           FAX: 920-787-4698

Richard King, Executive Director

8777 Woodstock/Kenosha Health Center

3415 Sheridan Road
Kenosha, WI   53140

                           FAX: 414-657-5756

Mary Petersen, Administrator

Postacute rehabilitation program.

Associations

8778 Access to Sailing
19744 Beach Boulevard
Suite 340
Huntington Beach, CA 92648

Sports association.

8779 Achilles Track Club
42 West 38th Street
4th Floor
New York, NY 10018 212-354-0300
FAX: 212-354-3978
e-mail: achillestc@aol.com

Leslie Winter, Executive Director
Organization whose goal is to guide disabled athletes
into the able-bodied community. Also has affiliate
chapters in various cities overseas.

8780 Adaptive Sports Center
PO Box 1639
Crested Butte, CO 81224 970-349-2296
FAX: 970-349-4950
e-mail: info@adaptivesports.org
www.adaptivesports.org

Christopher Hensley, Director
Year round adaptive, adventure recreation program
located at the base of Crested Butte Mountain Resort,
Crested Butte ,CO. The Adaptive Sports Centers provides adaptive downhill and cross country ski lessons, ski rentals and snowboarding lessons in the
winter. Also offers a variety of wilderness based programs in the summer including multi-day trips into
the back country.

8781 American Blind Bowling Association
411 Sheriff Street
Mercer, PA 16137 724-652-8411

Alice Hoover, Secretary
Legally blind men and women competing in organized tenpin bowling.

8782 American Blind Skiing Association
610 South William Street
Mount Prospect, IL 60056 847-255-1739

Sam Skobel, Executive Director
Blind skiers training and trainers.

8783 American Hearing Impaired Hockey Association
1143 West Lake Street
Chicago, IL 60607 312-829-2250
FAX: 312-829-2098
e-mail: ahiha2@aol.com
Hockey for hearing-impaired youths.

8784 American Wheelchair Bowling Association
6264 North Andrews Avenue
Fort Lauderdale, FL 33309 954-491-2886
FAX: 954-491-2886

Sports association.

8785 Blind Outdoor Leisure Development
533 E Main Street
Aspen, CO 81611 303-923-3811

Francis Campione, Director
Bill Dunaway, President
Outdoor recreation for the blind. Winter program of
skiing with guides plus numerous summer programs
for the visually impaired.

8786 Chesapeake Region Accessible Boating
1525 Grooms Lane
Woodstock, MD 27163 410-461-8652
FAX: 410-461-9151
e-mail: crabsailin@aol.com

Michael D Story, Executive Director
CRAB provides opportunities for the disabled and
their friends to sail the Chesapeake Bay. Day sails,
lessons, organized races. Call for charter information. Sail for free on the fourth Sunday of each month,
May through October.

8787 Conquerors Gym and Swim Program
Leaning Tower YMCA
600 W Touhy
Niles, IL 60648

8788 Disabled Watersports Program (Mission Bay Aquatic Center)
1001 Santa Clara Plaza
San Diego, CA 92109 619-488-1036
FAX: 619-488-9625

Peter K. Ballantyne, Program Manager
Marci Honstead, Program Coordinator
A cooperative, collegiate waterfront facility which is
intended and designed to provide water-oriented programs and equipment and to be a resource center for
water oriented sports and activities of all types, instructional and recreational. Since 1980, the center
has offered aquatic activities for disabled individuals. This program serves hundreds of people yearly
throughout the southwest United States and particularly San Diego, and serves as a model for similar
programs.

8789 FORE! Future Opportunity for Recreation and Employment for the Handicapped
Southern California Golfing Association
3740 Cahuenga Boulevard
North Hollywood, CA 91604 818-980-3630

Golfing association for the physically handicapped.

8790 Handicapped Scuba Association International

Handicapped Scuba Association
1104 Prado
San Clemente, CA 92672   949-498-4540
                            FAX: 949-498-6128
                    e-mail: hsa@hsascuba.com
                            www.hsascuba.com

Jim Gatacre, President
Julie Perez, Travel Coordinator

A nonprofit volunteer organization dedicated to improving the physical and social well being of those with special needs through the exhilarating sport of scuba diving. An educational program for able bodied scuba instructors to learn to teach and certify people with special needs. Accessible travel opportunities. Publishes quarterly newsletter.

8 pages BiAnnually

8791 ISC: National Organization of People with Physical Disabilities

16 Liberty Street
Larkspur, CA 94939   415-924-3549
                        FAX: 415-927-9556
                e-mail: russab@earthlink.net

Russ Bohlke, Executive Secretary

Providing opportunities for the handicapped to participate in accessible community activities is the objective of this service organization which has regional chapters in many states.

8792 Lakeshore Foundation

3800 Ridgeway Drive
Birmingham, AL 35209   205-868-2303
                          FAX: 205-868-2069
                  e-mail: jremick@ikshore.org
                          www.lakeshore.org

Offers fitness, recreation and competitive sports programs for persons with physical disabilities.

8793 National Skeet Shooting Association

5931 Roft Road
San Antonio, TX 78253   210-688-3371
                           800-877-5338
                           FAX: 210-688-3014
                           www.nssa-nsca.com

Offers information on sporting clay targets for the disabled hunter.

8794 National Sports Center for the Disabled

PO Box 1290
Winter Park, CO 80482   970-726-1540
                           FAX: 970-726-4112
                   e-mail: info@nscd.org
                           www.nscd.org

Gigi Glass Domingy, Operations Manager

Innovative non-profit organization that provides year-round recreation for children and adults with disabilities. The world's largest adaptive ski program, teaching 25,000 lessons per winter at Winter Park Resort, Colorado. Also snowboarding, ski racing, snowshoeing, cross-country skiing. Summer sports: rafting, sailing, camping, hiking, hand cycling, mountain biking, tandem biking, in-line skating, horseback riding, fishing, rock climbing. Sports symposium and clinics.

8795 Quickie Sports Camps

Quickie Designs
2842 N Business Park Avenue
Fresno, CA 93727   559-292-2171
                      800-456-8168

Tennis and basketball camps for the wheelchair bound.

8796 Rehabilitation Institute of Chicago's Virginia Wadsworth Sports Program

710 N Lake Shore Drive
Chicago, IL 60611   312-908-6000
                       FAX: 312-908-1051
           e-mail: jjones02@rehabchicago.org
                       www.richealthfit.org

Jeff Jones, Director
Tom Richey, Sports Coordinator
Mitch Carr, Fitness Coordinator

RIC's Center for Health and Fitness is a full service fitness center for individuals with disabilities and the administrative offices for RIC's Wirtz Sports Program. Eighteen different sport and recreation programs are offered free of charge. The facility is adjacent to RIC's main building and also is the location of a branch of The National Center for Physical Activity and Disability (NCPAD), a joint project operated by the University of Illinois-Chigcago.

8797 Seat-A-Robics

PO Box 630064
Little Neck, NY 11363
                       800-484-7046
                       FAX: EXT- 11-30

Daria Alinovi, President

Offers a variety of safe, affordable and medically approved video exercise programs that are listed in our video chapter. In addition the company offers two resources. The first Healthy Eating & Facts For Kids is geared specifically to health professionals and educators that work with disabled children ($39.95). The second is a recreational resource guide that stimulates children to be creative and get involved. It keeps them actively engaged while having fun and getting fit ($29.95).

8798 Special Olympics

1325 G Street NW
Suite 500
Washington, DC 20005   202-628-3630
                          FAX: 202-824-0200
                  e-mail: soimail@aol.com
                          www.specialolympics.org

Timothy Shriver, President/CEO
Kim Elliott, COO
J. Drake Turrentine, General Counsel

A year-round worldwide program that promotes physical fitness, sports training and athletic competition for children and adults with mental retardation.

8799 Special Recreation

362 Koser Avenue
Iowa City, IA 52246   319-337-7578

bailiwick.lib.uiowa.edu

John Nesbitt, Ed.D., President & CEO

Non-profit voluntary national information service organization serving the recreation needs, rights, interests and aspirations of people with disabilities. Information and referrals provided on activities, employment, grants, programs and services. Publications include; Access to Recreation for the Disabled; International Compendium of Programs & Services; and reprints from the Special Education Digest.

8800 US Hang Gliding Association

PO Box 1330
Colorado Springs, CO   80903   719-632-8300
FAX: 719-632-6417
e-mail: ushga@ushga.org
www.ushga.org

Jayne Defanfilis, CEO

Offers information for the disabled about how they may learn to hang glide or paraglide or try the sports just once with a tandem flight.

8801 USA Deaf Sports Federation

3607 Washington Boulevard
4
Ogden, UT   84403
FAX: 801-393-2263
www.usadsf.org

Muriel Strassler, author
Bobbie Beth Scoggins, President
Valerie G. Kinney, Administrative Assistant

Governing body for all deaf sports and recreation in the United States. Sixteen different sports organizations and 20 member clubs are affiliates of USADSF.

ISSN 1059-30 3

8802 Wheelchair Motorcycle Association

101 Torrey Street
Brockton, MA   02301   508-583-8614

Founded in 1975, after Scott Factor sustained injury resulting in paraplegia, this association offers information on all types of off-road vehicles for use by people with disabilities, also offers a newsletter.

Books

8803 Adapted Physical Education National Standards

Human Kinetics
PO Box 5076
Champaign, IL   61825
800-747-4457
FAX: 217-351-2674
e-mail: orders@hkusa.com
www.humankinetics.com

The book presents fifteen broad standards based on the responsibilities and perceived professional needs of practicing physical educators. Each standard is broken down into levels that include content that physical educators who work with individuals with disabilities should know, additional content for adapted physical educators, and sample applications that adapted physical educators should be able to demonstrate. *$28.00*

224 pages Paperback
ISBN 0-873229-62-2

8804 Adapted Physical Education and Sport, 2nd Edition

Human Kinetics
PO Box 5076
Champaign, IL   61825
800-747-4457
FAX: 217-351-2674
e-mail: orders@hkusa.com
www.humankinetics.com
Joseph P. Winnick, Ed.D., author

Designed as a resource for both present and future physical education leaders, this book is an exceptional book for teaching exceptional children. It emphasizes the physical education of young people with disabilities. *$47.00*

472 pages
ISBN 0-873225-78-1

8805 Conditioning with Physical Disabilities

Human Kinetics
PO Box 5076
Champaign, IL   61825
800-747-4457
FAX: 217-351-2674
e-mail: orders@hkusa.com
www.humankinetics.com
Kevin F. Lockette PT, CSCS & Ann M. Keyes PT CSCS, author

The first practical, authoritative exercise guide for people with all classifications and levels of physical disabilities. The authors share the successful strength and conditioning program they created at the highly regarded Rehabilitation Institute of Chicago - a pioneering program that is now the leading exercise approach for people with physical disabilities. *$22.95*

288 pages
ISBN 0-873226-14-3

8806 Disability and Sport

Human Kinetics
PO Box 5076
Champaign, IL   61825

800-747-4457
FAX: 217-351-2674
e-mail: orders@hkusa.com
www.humankinetics.com

Karen DePauw, PhD, Editor, author

This new book, written by leading experts in adapted physical education and disability sport, is intended to serve as a comprehensive reference about the disability sport world. Topics include adapted equipment, event management, women and disability sport, medical management of disabled athletes and research highlights. This book should serve as a valuable reference for disabled individuals and their families interested in sport, physical educators and medical personnel who work with disabled. *$40.00*

312 pages
ISBN 0-873228-48-0

8807 Exercise Activities for the Elderly

Springer Publishing Company
536 Broadway
New York, NY   10012
212-431-4370
FAX: 212-941-7842

Kay Flatten, author

A variety of exercises geared to clients with such conditions as arthritis, diabetes and Parkinson's disease, and others which are designed to build up muscular strength and maintain flexibility. *$23.95*

240 pages Softcover
ISBN 0-82615 -10-9

8808 Fitness Programming for Physical Disabilities

Human Kinetics
PO Box 5076
Champaign, IL   61825

800-747-4457
FAX: 217-351-2674
e-mail: orders@hkusa.com
www.humankinetics.com

Patricia D. Miller, MA, Editor, author

A book offering information for developing and conducting exercise programs for groups that included people with physical disabilities. A dozen authorities in exercise science and adapted exercise programming explain how to effectively and safely modify existing programs for individuals with physical disabilities. *$32.00*

208 pages
ISBN 0-873224-34-5

8809 Guide to Wheelchair Sports and Recreation

Paralyzed Veterans of America
801 18th Street NW
Washington, DC   20006
202-872-1300
888-860-7244
FAX: 301-843-0159

PVA's new booklet has been produced in part through a generous grant from Everest & Jennings, Inc., to serve individuals as a resource guide to sports and recreation activities and equipment suppliers.

28 pages

8810 Inclusive Games

Human Kinetics
PO Box 5076
Champaign, IL   61825

800-747-4457
FAX: 217-351-2674
e-mail: orders@hkusa.com
www.humankinetics.com

Susan L. Kasser, author

Features more than 50 games, helpful illustrations, and hundreds of game variations. The book shows how to adapt games so that children of every ability level can practice, play and improve their movement skills together. The game finder makes it easy to locate an appropriate game according to its name, approximate grade level, difficulty within the grade level, skills required/developed, and number of players. *$14.95*

120 pages Paperback
ISBN 0-873226-39-9

8811 Physical Activity for Individuals with Mental Retardation

Human Kinetics
PO Box 5076
Champaign, IL   61825

800-747-4457
FAX: 217-351-2674
e-mail: orders@hkusa.com
www.humankinetics.com

Carl E. Eischtaedt, PhD & Barry W. Lavay, PhD, author

The first movement-oriented text to cover the life span of people with mental retardation. Readers will discover the characteristics and unique needs of individuals with mental retardation. They will also become familiar with methodologies for facilitating fitness and movement competencies. *$33.00*

480 pages
ISBN 0-873223-61-6

8812 Physical Fitness Testing of the Disabled

Human Kinetics
PO Box 5076
Champaign, IL   61825

800-747-4457
FAX: 217-351-2674
e-mail: orders@hkusa.com
www.humankinetics.com

Joseph P. Winnick, Ed.D. & Francis X. Short, PED, author

A physical fitness testing manual for selected disabled groups thanks to the research and professional teamwork of the authors. In this manual, they offer practitioners norm-referenced tests of physical fitness for youngsters with cerebral palsy, visual and auditory impairments, and spinoneuro-muscular conditions. *$25.00*

184 pages Spiral bound
ISBN 0-931250-45-7

8813 Recreation & Sports

Accent Books & Products
PO Box 700
Bloomington, IL 61702   309-378-2961
                               800-787-8444
                          FAX: 309-378-4420
                    e-mail: acmtlvng@aol.com

Lynn Winston, author
Raymond C. Cheever, Publisher
Betty Garee, Editor

A guide to fun, excitement and travel offering options for disabled persons. Includes photos and sources of some special products. *$4.95*

65 pages Paperback
ISBN 0-91570-18-3

8814 Sport Science Review, Vol. 5 #1 - Adapted Physical Activity

Human Kinetics
PO Box 5076
Champaign, IL 61825
                               800-747-4457
                          FAX: 217-351-2674
                  e-mail: orders@hkusa.com
                        www.humankinetics.com

Gundrun Doll-Tepper, Editor, author

This special issue addresses disability and sport. Researchers from diverse academic backgrounds and parts of the world review the issues and controversies surrounding inclusion in physical education and sport. The papers explore inclusion in school settings, the history of disability sport, psychological and sociological aspects of adapted physical activity, and the need to identify reliable classification systems. *$15.00*

96 pages
ISBN 0-736029-88-5

8815 Sports & Recreation for the Disabled

Exceptional Parent Library
PO Box 1807
Englewood Cliffs, NJ 10116
                               800-535-1910
                  e-mail: eplibrary@aol.com
                        www.eplibrary.com

M.J. Paciorek and J.A. Jones, author

A book designed to make dreams come true. *$32.00*

8816 Sports and Exercise for Children with Chronic Health Conditions

Human Kinetics
PO Box 5076
Champaign, IL 61825
                               800-747-4457
                          FAX: 217-351-2674
                  e-mail: orders@hkusa.com
                        www.humankinetics.com

Barry Goldberg, M.D., Editor, author

Written by leading pediatric authorities, the practical guidelines in Sports and Exercise for Children with Chronic Health Conditions address these twenty common medical conditions: spina bifida, epilepsy, childhood progressive neuromuscular disease, cerebral palsy, childhood arthritis, asthma, cystic fibrosis, AIDS, hepatitis, hypertension, congenital heart disease-shunt lesions, congenital obstructive valvular heart disease, carditis, anemia, hemophilia and more. *$49.00*

392 pages Hardcover

8817 Sports for the Handicapped

Walker and Company
435 Hudson Street
New York, NY 10014   212-727-8300

Anne Allen, author

This text outlines six sports that handicapped individuals may be able to participate in. Skiing, basketball, swimming, track and field, football and horseback riding are each presented. Each of the sports requirements are told by an athlete who is handicapped and who has excelled at the sport. At the end of the text is a good resource/reference guide for organizations that serve handicapped sports enthusiasts.

80 pages Hardcover
ISBN 0-80276-36-3

8818 Wheelchair Workout

3418 SW 31st Street
Des Moines, IA 50321

Offers information for the physically challenged on sports and recreation. *$16.75*

Exercise Devices

8819 Abilitations by Sportime International

1 Sportime Way
Atlanta, GA 30340   770-449-5700
                           800-850-8603
                      FAX: 800-845-1535
               e-mail: orders@sportime.com

Ilana Danneman, Marketing Director

Catalog provides products to patients, therapists and parents to assist in maximizing functional levels through movement, cognition, recreation and positioning.

240 pages Quarterly

8820 CC-M Productions

8512 Cedar Street
Silver Spring, MD 20910
                               800-453-6280
                          FAX: 301-585-2321
                    e-mail: cc-m@cc-m.com
                        www.cc-m.com

Jon Abel, Marketing

Armchair Fitness video series. 4 cassettes: Armchair Fitness Aerobic, Armchair Fitness Gentle, Armchair Fitness Strength and Armchair Fitness Yoga. $29.95-$39.95.

$29.95 - $39.95

8821 Equalizer 1000 Series

Helm Distributing
911 Kings Point Road
Polson, MT 59860

Pruett B. Helm, President/Owner

Weight training equipment designed with the wheelchair user in mind. *$7050.00*

8822 Equalizer 5000 Home Gym

Helm Distributing
911 Kings Point Road
Polson, MT 59860

Pruett B. Helm, President/Owner

Exercise machine for the able-bodied and the disabled, but specifically designed with a wheelchair user in mind. *$4250.00*

8823 Equalizer Exercise Machines

Helm Distributing
911 Kings Point Road
Polson, MT 59860

Offers exercise and gym equipment for the disabled.

8824 Freedom Ryder Handcycles

Brike International
20589 SW Elk Horn Center
Tualatin, OR 97062   503-692-1029
                               800-800-5828

Mike Lofgren, President
Brian Stewart, Vice President

The finest handcycle in the world. The cycles incorporate body, lean steering and the finest bicycle components to make this a three-wheeled vehicle without equal. Suitable for both recreation and competition. *$1995.00*

8825 Freedom's Wings International

1832 Lake Avenue
Scotch Plains, NJ 07076

Raymond Temchus, Jr., President

A therapeutic recreational program utilizing aircraft. *$75.00*

Membership Fee

8826 Modular QuadDesk

GPK
535 Floyd Smith Drive
El Cajon, CA 92020

                               800-468-8679
                               FAX: 619-593-7514
                               e-mail: rajesh@gpk.com
                               www.gpk.com -or- www.quadriplegia.com

Rajesh Kanwar, President

Worktable specially dsigned for people in wheelchairs who lack grip strength, or cannot learn or reach. Small or medium.

8827 Pedal-in-Place Exerciser

Thoele Manufacturing
475 County Road 100 North
Montrose, IL 62445   217-924-4553

A great in-home exerciser that can benefit quadraplegics, paraplegics, stroke patients or anyone with limited use of their arms and legs.

8828 Quad Commander

GPK
535 Floyd Smith Drive
El Cajon, CA 92020

                               800-468-8679
                               FAX: 619-593-7514
                               e-mail: rajesh@gpk.com
                               www.gpk.com -or- www.quadriplegia.com

Rajesh Kanwar, President

Joystick for people with quadriplegia.

8829 Uppertone

GPK
535 Floyd Smith Drive
El Cajon, CA 92020

                               800-468-8679
                               FAX: 619-593-7514
                               e-mail: rajesh@gpk.com
                               www.gpk.com -or- www.quadriplegia.com

Rajesh Kanwar, President

Unassisted muscle strengthening and conditioning system for quads. *$2495.00*

8830 Versatrainer

PRO-MAX/Division of Bow-Flex of America
2200 NE 65th Avenue
 # C
Vancouver, WA 98661

One exercise system for the disabled person that does everything. Incorporates full body strength, muscle development, cardiovascular conditioning, gives full muscle movement and balanced muscle development.

Periodicals

8831 Access to Recreation

Access to Recreation
8 Sandra Center
Newbury Park, CA   91320   805-498-7535
                                  800-634-4351
                         FAX: 805-498-8186
                  e-mail: dkrebs@gte.net
                       www.accesstr.com

Donald A. Krebs, President
The Access to Recreation catalog is full of recreation and exercise equipment. One can find items such as electric fishing reels and other fishing and hunting equipment for the disabled sportsman. There are also adapted golf clubs, swimming pool lifts, wheelchair gloves and cuffs, and bowling. There are devices to help with embroidery, knitting and card playing, videos, books, and practical aides such as wheelchair ramps and book holders.

44 pages BiAnnual

8832 Adapted Aquatics: Swimming for Persons with Physical or Mental Impairments

American Red Cross
17th and D Street
Washington, DC   20006   202-942-2512

Magazine for disabled swimmers.

8833 Information on Whitewater Kayaking for the Handicapped

209 Columbus Avenue
Port Angeles, WA   98362   360-373-1621

Information on outdoor tours and river expeditions for the disabled.

8834 Nationals

Sawyer & Finn
PO Box 370788
Miami, FL   33137

Offers information on the national handicapped ski championships.

8835 Outrigger

National Sports Center for the Disabled
PO Box 1290
Winter Park, CO   80482   970-726-1540
                         FAX: 970-726-4112
                  e-mail: info@nscd.org
                       www.nscd.org

Gigi Doming, Operations Manager
Free newsletter with information and tips for adaptive skiing and other mountain sports for people with disabilities.

6-8 pages Quarterly

8836 PALAESTRA: Forum of Sport/P.E./Recreation for Those with Disabilities

Challenge Publications, Ltd.
PO Box 508
Macomb, IL   61455   309-833-1902
                   FAX: 309-833-1902
          e-mail: challpub@macomb.com
               www.palaestra.com

David P. Beaver, Editor-in-Chief, author
Dr. Julian Stein, Associate Editor

The most comprehensive resource on sport, physical education and recreation for individuals with disabilities, their parents, and professionals in the field of adapted phyical activity. PALAESTRA is published in cooperation with the USOC's Committee on Sports for the Disabled and AAHPERD's Adapted Physical Activity Council. PALAESTRA is informative yet entertaining and delivers valuable insights for consumers, families and professionals in the field. Published quarterly *$19.00*

64 pages Magazine

8837 Special Recreation Digest

362 Koser Avenue
Iowa City, IA   52246   319-337-7578

                  bailiwick.lib.uiowa.edu

John Nesbitt, Ed.D., President & CEO
Presents information on programs, services, publications, meetings, organizations, materials and special recreation needs of people with disabilities. *$10.00*

48 pages Quarterly

8838 Wheelchair Basketball World

23 Farm Drive
East Hartford, CT   06108

Jay Kennedy, Publisher
Offers information services to all interested parties in the sport of basketball. *$15.00*

30 pages Quarterly

Skiing

8839 Bold Tracks - Skiing for the Disabled

Johnson Books - A Cordillera Press Guide
1880 57th Center S
Boulder, CO   80301
                                  800-258-5830
                         FAX: 303-443-1106
                  e-mail: books@jpcolorado.com

Hal O'Leary, author
Richard Croog, Sales & Promotion

The first complete teaching and learning guide to skiing for the disabled. The guide is essential for instructor and student alike. Beginning with the basic American Teaching System and continuing through three-track and four-track methods, the manual covers skiing for the visually and hearing impaired as well as the physically and developmentally disabled. It includes glossaries of skiing and medical terms and tips for skin program development. *$24.95*

160 pages Paperback
ISBN 1-555661-14-9

8840 Disabled Sports USA, Far West

Tahoe Adaptive Ski School
PO Box 9780
Truckee, CA 96162   530-581-4161
                    FAX: 530-581-3127
               e-mail: dsusatahoe@truckee.net
                    www.dsusafw.org

Katherine Rodriguez, Program Director
Haakon Lang-Ree, Assistant Director
Cindy Smith, Office Manager

Snow ski and snowboard lessons for people with
disabilities. December through April. Two and a half
hour lesson, adaptive equipment, and beginner lift
ticket: $45 midweek, $55 weekend & holidays. Summer programs include: Water Skiing, Whitewater
Rafting, Cycling, 4WD Backcountry Access, and Tahoe Adaptive Adventures.

8841 National Sports Center for the Disabled

PO Box 1290
Winter Park, CO 80482   970-726-1540
                    FAX: 970-726-4112
                 e-mail: info@nscd.org
                    www.nscd.org

Innovative non-profit organization that provides
year-round recreation for children and adults
with disabilities. The world's largest adaptive ski
program, teaching 25,000 lessons per winter at
Winter Park Resort, Colorado. Also snowboarding, ski racing, showshoeing, cross-country skiing.
Summer sports: rafting, sailing, camping, hiking,
hand cycling, mountain biking, tandem biking, in-
line skating, horseback riding, fishing, rock climbing. Sports symposium and clinics.

Tennis

8842 Special Olympics Tennis Sports Skills

United States Tennis Association
707 Alexander Road
Princeton, NJ 08540   609-419-4418

Establishes coaching criteria and guidelines for
the Special Olympics coach. It contains coaching
tips for conditioning drills, basic racket skills,
stroking techniques and match-playing concepts.
$5.00

64 pages Illustrated

8843 Tennis in a Wheelchair

United States Tennis Association
707 Alexander Road
Princeton, NJ 08540   609-419-4418
                    FAX: 504-641-2267
Brad Parks, author

A practical manual of tennis playing techniques for
the wheelchair athlete. Included are sections on basic
strokes from a wheelchair, wheelchair mobility, singles and doubles strategy, and more. Readers will
discover how enjoyable and challenging the game of
wheelchair tennis can be. $3.75

40 pages Illustrated

Products & Programs

8844 Ability Flex

8 Sandra Court
Newbury Park, CA 91320   800-634-4351
               www.accesstr.com/exercisers4.cfm

The Ability Flex workout variations include three
keys to personal fitness- strengthening, stretching
and aerobics.

8845 Adaptive Gold Car Model 4850

Fairway Golf Cars
W220 N507 Springfield Road
Waukesha, WI 53186   414-521-2151
                    888-320-4850
                    FAX: 414-542-4258

John Perez, Director of Sales & Marketing

The Fairway 4850 is designed to allow access to all
aspects of the game of golf- even greens and tee. The
Fairway 4850 features a 48 volt electronic system to
provide unsurpassed power, range and speed. Couple
the drive system performance with ergonomic features like an adjustable seat with flip ap arm rests, 360
degree swivel and an adjustable tilter position.

8846 Aerospace Compadre

Aerospace America Incorporated
900 Truman Parkway
189
Bay City, MI 48706   517-684-2121
                    800-843-6168
                    FAX: 517-684-4173

Murray Sutherland, President

Fully customized golf cart type vehicle for the physically impaired person. Fully equipped with hand controls, wheelchair rack, storage racks, head and tail
lights and full safety belts. *$2500.00*

8847 Basketball: Beeping Foam

Maxi Aids
42 Executive Boulevard
Farmingdale, NY 11735   516-752-0521
                    800-522-6294
                    FAX: 516-752-0689
                    TDY:516-752-0738
                 e-mail: sales@max.aids.com
                    www.maxiaids.com

Customer Service

This sound making basketball enables the visually
impaired to play basketball or other games. *$29.95*

8848 Bounce Back

8 Sandra Court
Newbury Park, CA 91320
                    800-634-4351
               www.accesstr.com/excercisers7.cfm

8849 Bowling: Ball Ramp

Cleo of New York
S Buckout Street
Trent Building
Irvington, NY   10533

800-321-0595

Bowling devices for wheelchair occupants.
$109.00

8850 Center for Health and Fitness

710 N Lake Shore Drive
Chicago, IL   60671

312-908-7532
FAX: 312-908-1051
e-mail: mcsport@megsinet.net

Jeff Jones, Director
Tom Rishey, Sports Coordinator

Provides free sports and programs to individuals with
physical disabilities in the greater Chicago area. Programs in 16 different sports including center for
health and fitness which provides exercise opportunities seven days a week.

8851 Challenge Golf

Motivation Media
1245 Milwaukee Avenue
Glenview, IL   60025

847-808-0717
FAX: 847-297-6829

Dorothy Bauer, Coordinator

A plain-language video, Challenge Golf is packed
with information for beginners or veterans. Peter
Longo covers 5 handicaps (one-arm, one-leg, in a
seated position, blind, and arthritis) clearly and concisely, on how to play golf with a physical disability.
In color, complete with special effects, graphs and
real handicapped golfers at play. *$38.95*

Home Edition

8852 EasyStand 6000 Glider

8 Sandra Court
Newbury Park, CA   91320

800-634-4351
www.accesstr.com/excercisers.cfm

The EasySatnd Glider provides dynamic leg motion for individuals who are unable to santd upright or walk on their own.

8853 Golf Xpress

eMotorsports
4275 County Line Road #214
Chalfont, PA   18914

215-997-9555
877-494-6532
FAX: 215-997-9560
e-mail: info@golfxpress.com
www.golfxpress.com

Don Labowsky, President

Patented single-rider adaptive golf cart allows you to
play golf seated or supported. Hit woods, irons, and
putt from the car. Drives onto tees and greens and into
traps without damaging the course. Golf Xpress is in
44 states and 7 foreign countries, making it the leader
in adaptive golf carts. Fun, safe, and affordable.
Don't let age, injuries, or illness keep you away from
this great game... Golf Xpress keeps you playing!

8854 High Adventure Hang Gliding

4231 Sepulveda Avenue
San Bernardino, CA   92404

909-883-8488
FAX: 909-883-8488
e-mail: robndi@flytandem.com

Rob McKenzie, Tandem Instructor
Tandem adventures.

8855 Rickshaw Exerciser

8 Sandra Court
Newbury Park, CA   91320

800-634-4351
www.accesstr.com/excercisera5.cfm

This Excerciser develops the muscle used most by
those in wheelchairs. It develops the strength you
need to lift yourself for pressure relief, doing
transfers, and pushing your wheelchair.

8856 Sailing Fascination

4010 Park Newport
Apartment 224
Newport Beach, CA   92660

949-640-1678
FAX: 949-760-8650
e-mail: bbg2506@webtv.net

Jack W. Hester, President
Tom Tolbert, Vice President

Sailing Fascination provides sailing programs for
anyone who is disabled. A non profit educational and
charitable California State Corp. with an all volunteer
staff, officers, and directors. Year round sailing
classes are held on a 24 foot sailboat that is equipped
to be accessible to the disabled student sailor.

8857 Score Card Set

American Printing House for the Blind
1839 Frankfort Avenue
6085
Louisville, KY   40206

502-895-2405
800-223-1839
FAX: 502-899-2274
e-mail: info@aph.org
www.aph.org

This handy card is made of durable plastic, has
twenty buttons in two rows of ten and may be
pushed up and down hundreds of times without
wearing out. Can be used to keep count of the
number of points scored by a sports team, or to
count how many questions have been asked during
20 Question.

8858 Wheelchair Roller

8 Sandra Park
Newbury Park, CA   91320

800-634-4351
www.accesstr.com/excercisers6.cfm

The McClain Wheelchair Roller allows you to
build strength and stamina in the comfort of your
own home.

General

8859 AAN's Toll-Free Hotline

National Allergy and Asthma Network
3554 Chain Bridge Road
Suite 200
Fairfax, VA 22030

800-878-4403

Offers answers to questions regarding allergies and asthma, provides referrals and support to assist the patient and his or her family.

8860 Aarskog Syndrome Parent Support Group

c/o Shannon Caranci
62 Robin Hill Lane
Levittown, PA 19055

Offers newsletter, informational materials, networking and matching, and a research registry.

8861 Advocate for People with Disabilities

106 Packard Street
Apartment 109
Ann Arbor, MI 48104

734-930-0343

William Nee, Advocate
Volunteer advocate for people with disabilities in Michigan, Wisconsin, Alaska and Illinois.

8862 American SIDS Institute

6065 Roswell Road NE
Suite 876
Atlanta, GA 30328

706-692-1050
800-232-SIDS
FAX: 404-843-0577
www.sids.org

Betty McEntire, PhD, Executive Director
Hotline for information on Sudden Infant Death Syndrome. Offers research, clinical services, education and family support/counseling.

8863 American Speech and Hearing Association

10801 Rockville Pike
Rockville, MD 20852

800-637-TALK
e-mail: ilc@esha.org
www.esha.org

Hotline for the speech and hearing impaired.

8864 Anchor Houses

1212 Monroe Street NW
Washington, DC 20010

202-832-5555
FAX: 202-832-8216

Francis Palilkarambi
Offers support groups and services such as: counseling, case management, advocacy for financial entitlements and more for individuals and families dealing with mental illness.

8865 Arthritis Foundation Information Hotline

PO Box 19000
Atlanta, GA 30357

800-283-7800

Offers information and referrals, counseling, physicians information and more to persons living with arthritis.

8866 Aurora of Central New York

518 James Street
Syracuse, NY 13203

315-422-7263
FAX: 315-422-9746
TDY:315-422-4792
e-mail: auroracny@aol.com

Professional counseling services to assist individuals and their families deal with the trauma of hearing or vision loss.

8867 Autism Society of America

7910 Woodmont Avenue
Suite 650
Bethesda, MD 20814

301-657-0881
800-3AU-TISM
FAX: 301-657-0869

Provides support groups nationwide for persons with autism and their families.

8868 Braille Institute

527 North Dale Avenue
Anaheim, CA 92801

714-821-5000
800-272-4553
FAX: 714-527-7621

A toll free information and referral service where callers can obtain information about community programs and referrals to organizations serving the blind in their local areas.

8869 Cancer Information Service

National Cancer Institute
9000 Rockville Pike
Building 31
Bethesda, MD 20892

301-907-0035
800-4CA-NCER

A nationwide network of 19 regional field offices supported by the National Cancer Institute which provides accurate, up-to-date information on cancer to patients and their families, health professionals and the general public. The CIS can provide specific information in understandable language about particular types of cancer, as well as information on second opinions and the availability of clinical trials.

8870 Center for Information Technology Accomodation (CITA)

US General Services Administration
18th &F NW Street NW
Room 1234
Washington, DC 20405

202-501-8252
FAX: 202-501-6269
TDY:202-501-2010
www.gsa.gov/coca

Susan A Brummel, Director, CITA
Marilyn Estep, Computer Specialist

Has information available concerning computer accommodations for all disabilities; its primary focus is assistance to federal agencies. Distributes handbook on Managing Information Resources for Accessibility.

8871 Clearinghouse on Disability Information

Office of Special Educaiton & Rehabilitative Svcs.
330 C Street SW
Room 3132
Washington, DC 20202   202-205-8241
FAX: 202-401-2608
www.ed.gov/OFFICE/OSERS

Carolyn Corlett

The Clearinghouse provides information to people with disabilities, or anyone requesting information, by doing research and providing documents in response to inquiries. The information provided includes areas of federal funding for disability-related programs. Clearinghouse staff is trained to serve as experts in referring requests to other sources of disability-related information, if necessary.

8872 Community Connections

801 Pennsylvania Avenue SE
201
Washington, DC 20003   202-726-2756
FAX: 202-544-5365

Offers support groups and support systems for adults with mental and emotional disabilities.

8873 Community Support Center

13301 Bruce B Downs Boulevard
Tampa, FL 33612   813-974-4615

Cecil Woodside, CSC Division Dir.

Provides an alternative to institutionalization for persons 18 years to 55 years of age, with a mental disability. There are approximately 60 staff members and daily census for clients is about 600.

8874 Community and Support Services

33-R Water Street
Guilford, CT 06437   860-347-4465

Roberta Hurley, Manager

Operate 15 programs at various sites. The services offer development of programs to meet individual needs and to engage in all types of activities which shall promote and foster more normal and independent lives for persons with disabilities.

8875 Compassionate Friends

PO Box 3696
Oak Brook, IL 60522   630-990-0010
877-969-0010
FAX: 630-990-0246
e-mail: nationaloffice@compassionatefriends.org
www.compassionatefriends.org
Mary Clark, author
Patricia Loder, Executive Director

Peer support for bereaved parents, grandparents and siblings, offering 600 chapters in the United States. The organization also offers a quarterly magazine, We Need Not Wake Alone, and TCF resources of booklets, tapes and brochures for the bereaved parent, grandparent and sibling. *$5.00*

Quarterly

8876 Cornerstone Services

777 Joyce Road
Joliet, IL 60436   815-741-7602
FAX: 815-723-1177

James A. Hogan, President/CEO
Susan Murphy, PR Coordinator

Cornerstone Services provides progressive, comprehensive services for people with disabilities, promoting choice, dignity, and the opportunity to live and work in the community. Established in 1969, the agency provides developmental, vocational, employment, residential and mental health services at various community-based locations. The nonprofit social service agency helps approximately 750 people each day.

8877 Department of Ophthalmology Information Line

Eye & Ear Infirmary
1855 W Taylor Street
Chicago, IL 60612   773-ITR-AUMA

Offers eye clinic and physician referrals to persons suffering from vision disorders as well as offers emergency information.

8878 Dial-a-Hearing Screening Test

PO Box 1880
Media, PA 19063   610-544-7700
800-222-EARS
FAX: 610-543-2802
e-mail: dahst@aol.com

George Biddle, Executive Director

Hearing help information center. Provides local phone number for accurate telephone hearing screening test. Provides referral to audiologist or ear, nose and throat doctor. All services are free.

8879 Disability Network

3600 S Dort Highway
Suite 54
Flint, MI 48507   810-742-1800
FAX: 810-742-2400
TDY:810-742-7647
e-mail: disnet@tir.com

Mike Zelley, Executive Director

The Disability Network offers the opportunity for everyone in the community to come together as a part of a working and growing system of support for persons with disabilities. This includes Peer Support, Information and Referral of Resources, Advocacy, Planning for Independent Living, and Americans with Disabilities Act Consultations.

8880 Disability and Health, National Center for Birth Defects and Developmental Disabilities

4770 Buford Highway NE
F-35
Atlanta, GA 30341 770-488-7080
FAX: 770-488-7075
TDY:770-488-7083
e-mail: ncehinfo@cdc.gov
www.cdc.gov/nceh/cddh/schome.html

Larry Burt, Program Manager
Lisa Sinclair, Health Science Analyst

Located within the new CDC, National Center for Birth Defects and Developmental Disabilities, the Disability and Health section, operates a ralatively small program that primarily supports: data collection on the prevalence of people with disabilities & their health status and risk factors for poor health and well-being; research on measures of disabily, funtioning and health; health promotion intervention studies; and diddemination of health information.

8881 Easter Seals

230 W Monroe Street
Suite 1800
Chicago, IL 60606 312-726-6200
800-221-6827
FAX: 312-726-1494
TDY:312-726-4258
e-mail: info@easter-seals.org
www.easter-seals.org

James E Williams Jr, President/CEO

Easter Seals' mission is to create solutions that change lives for childrena nd adults with disabilities, their families, and their communities. We work to identify the needs of people with disabilities and to provide appropriate developmental and rehabilitation services. 407 sites provide services to children and adults with disabilities and their families. All sites provide different services.

8882 Epilepsy Foundation for the National Capitol Area

1331 H Street NW
Suite 307
Washington, DC 20005 202-561-6114
FAX: 202-293-0814

Sandra Coshner Weinstein

Offers information and referrals, support groups for dually diagnosed persons.

8883 Family Support Project for the Developmentally Disabled

North Central Bronx Hospital
3424 Kossuth Avenue, Room 15A10
Bronx, NY 10467 718-519-4797

Monica Sanabria, Project Coordinator

8884 Green Door

1623 16th Street NW
Washington, DC 20009 202-462-4092
FAX: 202-462-7562
e-mail: g1admin@aol.com

Judith Johnson, Executive Director
Brenda Randall, Program Director

Green Door is a community program which prepares people with a severe and persistent mental illness to live and work independently. Since 1976, Green Door has provided comprehensive services to mentally ill people-members, including housing, job training, job placement, education, homeless outreach, case management, support for people with substance abuse problems, family support,and specialized help for people who have had repeated hospitalizations.

8885 Head Injury Hotline

PO Box 84151
Seattle, WA 98124 206-329-1371
FAX: 206-624-4961
e-mail: brain@headinjury.com
www.headinjury.com

Constance Miller and Kay Campbell, author

Disseminates head injury information and provides referrals to facilitate adjustment to life following head injury. Organizes seminars for professionals, head injury survivors, and their families. *$20.00*

121 pages Paperback

8886 Headlines Support Group

Center for Community Re-entry
313 N Main Street
Rockford, IL 61101 815-964-9555
FAX: 815-962-6113

Pamela Solberg, Office Manageror

A local support group reaching northern Illinois and southern Wisconsin, for survivors and families of brain injury. The group helps survivors and families cope with awareness difficulties, social adjustment, and leisure awareness. The group shares information regarding head injuries and provides updates from the state and national associations. Headlines continually searches for new ideas, information and services which can help survivors fulfill their maximum potential.

8887 Human Policy Press

University Station
PO Box 35127
Syracuse, NY 13235 315-443-3851
800-894-0826
FAX: 315-443-4338
e-mail: thechp@sued.syr.edu
soeweb.syr.edu/thechp/HumanPolicyPress/

Rachael Zubal, Information Coordinator

Independent press started by the Center on Human Policy in 1974, to promote positive attitudes towards people with disabilities.

8888 Inter-Church Fellowship of the Blind

PO Box 163
Denver, CO 80201 303-666-1476

8889 International Braille and Technology Center for the Blind

National Federation of the Blind
1800 Johnson Street
Baltimore, MD 21230 410-659-9314
FAX: 410-685-5653
e-mail: nfb@iamdigex.net
www.nfb.org

Richard Ring, Director

World's largest and most complete evaluation and demonstration center of all assistive technology used by the blind from around the world. Includes all Braille, synthetic speech, print-to-speech scanning, internet and portable devices and programs. Available for tours by appointment to blind persons, employers, technology manufacturers, teachers, parents and those working in the assistive technology field.

8890   Job Opportunities for the Blind

National Federation of the Blind
1800 Johnson Street
Baltimore, MD   21230   410-659-9314
                                                   FAX: 410-685-5653
                                             e-mail: nfb@iamdigex.net
                                                       www.nfb.org

Anthony Cobb, Director
A specialized service that provides free support, resources and information to blind persons seeking employment and to employers interested in hiring the blind. A partnership program with the U.S. Department of Labor, this is the most successful program of it's kind in helping blind persons find competitive work.

8891   KALEIDOSCOPE Network

1777 NE Loop 410
Suite 300
San Antonio, TX   78217   210-436-2611
                                                   FAX: 210-829-1388
                                                   www.kALIVE.com

Phyllis Nichols, Chief Operating Officer
Ron Dixon, President Programming,Production
KALEIDOSCOPE Network, inc. (KNI) is a broadband, multimedia health and lifestyle company which produces and distributes television and on-line programming and content emphasizing health and wellness. KNI airs its programming on PAX Television with a reach to 73% of the country or 74 million households. KNI's interactive Web site provides authoritative health content, with links to its more than 240 health and disability-related National Advisory Board organizations.

8892   Kids on the Block Arthritis Programs

Arthritis Foundation
PO Box 19000
Atlanta, GA   30357   404-872-7100
                                                   800-283-7800
                                                   FAX: 404-872-0457

State and local programs that use puppetry to help children understand what it is like for children and adults who have arthritis.

8893   Lighthouse International Information and Resource Service

111 E 59th Street
New York, NY   10022   212-821-9200
                                                   800-829-0500
                                                   FAX: 212-821-9705
                                             e-mail: info@lighthouse.org
                                                   www.lighthouse.org

Provides information about eye diseases, low vision, age-related vision loss, adaptive technology, optical devices, large print and braille publishers, helps people find low vision services, vision rehabilitation services, and support groups across the U.S.; offers large selection of consumer products.

8894   Lung Line Information Service

National Jewish Center for Immunology
1400 Jackson Street
Denver, CO   80206   303-697-5095
                                                   800-222-LUNG
                                                   www.nationaljewish.org

Lynn Taussig, President
A free information service answering questions, sending literature and giving advice to patients with immunologic or respiratory illnesses. The Line is an educational service and not a substitute for medical care. Diagnosis or suggested treatment will not be provided for a caller's specific condition.

8895   Medic Alert

PO Box 1009
Turlock, CA   95381   209-668-3333
                                                   800-825-3785
                                                   FAX: 209-669-2495

Tanya Glazebrook, C.E.O./President
Emergency equipment, medallions and bracelets containing emergency medical information and 24-hour emergency information telephone services.

8896   Medicaid Information

7500 Security Boulevard
Baltimore, MD   21244   410-786-9911

Information about eligibility and benefits for needy citizens who require health care is available by contacting the Health Care Financing administration or by contacting the local public welfare office.

8897   Medicare Information

200 Independence Avenue SW
Washington, DC   20201   202-619-0257

Eligibility and benefits for the health care of the older american is available by contacting the health care financing office.

8898   National AIDS Hotline

US Department of Health & Human Services
Public Health Service
Washington, DC   20210
                                                   800-342-2437
                                                   www.cdcnac.org

Offers free confidential information and publications on HIV infection and AIDS.

8899   National Association for Home Care

Val J. Halomandaris
228 7th Street SE
Washington, DC   20003   202-547-7424
                                                   FAX: 202-547-3540
                                             e-mail: subscription@nahc.org
                                                       www.nahc.org

This is a non-profit trade association representing various home care, hospice and health aid organizations. Website contains a section with information on how to choose a home care provider and a zip code driven locator for hotcare and hospice. *$49.00*

50-60 pages Monthly pub.

8900 National Association for Parents of Children with Visual Impairments (NAPVI)

National Office
PO Box 317
Watertown, MA 02472   617-972-7441
                              800-562-6265
                         FAX: 781-972-7444

Susan LaVenture, Executive Director
Mary Zabelski, President
Lars Anderson, Vice President

A partnership organization with the National Eye Health Education Program and the National Agenda for the Education of Children and Youths with Visual Impairments including those with multiple disabilities. Information and support network for parents of children with visual impairments.

8901 National Association for Parents of the Visually Impaired

2180 Linway Drive
Beloit, WI 53511

                              800-562-6265

8902 National Autism Hotline - Autism Services Center

PO Box 507
Huntington, WV 25710   304-525-8014
                         FAX: 304-525-8026

Ruth C. Sullivan, Ph.D., Director

Service agency for individuals with autism and developmental disabilities, and their families. Assists families and agencies attempting to meet the needs of individuals with autism and other developmental disabilities. Makes available technical assistance in designing treatment programs and more. The hotline provides informational packets to callers and assists via telephone when possible.

8903 National Center for Sight

National Society To Prevent Blindness
500 E Remington Road
Schaumburg, IL 60173   847-843-8458
                              800-331-2020
                         FAX: 847-843-2020

A toll-free line offering information on a broad range of vision, eye health and safety topics including sports eye safety, lazy eye, diabetic retinopathy, glaucoma, cataracts, children's eye disorders, and more.

8904 National Child Safety Council

PO Box 1368
Jackson, MI 49204   517-764-6070
                              800-222-1464
                         FAX: 517-764-3069
Hotline.

8905 National Depressive and Manic Depressive Association

730 North Franklin Street
Suite 501
Chicago, IL 60610   312-642-0049
                              800-826-3632
                         FAX: 312-642-7243
                              www.ndmda.org

Lydia Lewis, Executive Director
April Robinson, Program Manager

Mission is to educate patients, families, professionals and the public concerning the nature of depressive and manic-depressive illnesses as treatable medical diseases; to foster self-help for patients and families; to eliminate discrimination and stigma; to improve access to care; and to advocate for research toward the elimination of these illnesses; to improve access to care; and to advocate for research toward the elimination of these illnesses.

8906 National Eye Health Education Program Department of Opthamology

University of Illinois
1855 W Taylor Street
Chicago, IL 60612   312-996-4356

Offers information and support for persons with vision disorders, including retinitis pigmentosa.

8907 National Health Information Center

PO Box 1133
Washington, DC 20013   301-529-7770
                              800-336-4797
                              301-468-7394
                    e-mail: nhicinfo@health.org
                www.ada.org/consumer/faq/prevent.html

Ramona Arnett, Project Director
Alison Telesford, Information Specialist

Identifies health information resources, channels requests for information to these resources and develops publications available for small handling fees.

8908 National Information Center for Health Related Services

University of South Carolina
First Benson
Columbia, SC 29208   803-434-4300
                              800-922-9236
                    e-mail: scsis@dccisc.edu
Hotline.

8909 National Institute of Child Health and Human Development

Building 31
Room 232
Bethesda, MD 20892   301-402-8714
                         FAX: 301-496-7101
Hotline.

8910 National Service Dog Center

Delta society
289 Perimeter Road E
Renton, WA 98055   425-226-7357
                         FAX: 425-235-1076
                e-mail: info@deltasociety.org.com
                         www.deltasociety.org

Linda M. Hines, President/ CEO
Tamara Whitehall, Program Manager

A service of the Delta Society, provides information about the selection, training, stewardship, and roles of service dogs; referral to service dog training programs and related resources; education to businesses and health care professionals regarding service dog issues; research assistance through a resource library and network of professional experts and advocacy on behalf of people with service dogs.

8911   PALS Support Groups
Parent Professional Advocacy League
95 Berkeley Street
Suite 104
Boston, MA   02116   617-482-2915
                              800-331-0688

Offers emotional support to parents and families of disabled children.

8912   PXE International
23 Mountain Street
Sharon, MA   02067   781-784-3817

Offers vital services to those with pseudoxanthoma elasticum, a connective tissue disorder causing calcification of connective tissue in various places throughout the body, often affecting the membrane behind the eye.

8913   Parent Assistance Network
Good Samaritan Hospital Foundation
PO Box 1810
Kearney, NE   68848   308-865-2700
                              FAX: 308-865-2933
                    e-mail: pan_safecom@kearney.net

Sheila Meyer, Parent Assistance
Lesley Bollwitt, Director Of Grants

Provides information and emotional support to parents of children with disabilities in the central Nebraska area. Ongoing activities include parent support group meetings, parent-to-parent networking and referrals and Respite Care provider trainings.

8914   Parent Group for the Retarded
PO Box 764
Mattoon, IL   61938   217-895-2341
                              FAX: 217-895-3658

Don H. McDowell, Camp Director
Terri Taylor, Director's Assistant

Offers advocacy services, social and recreational services and a summer camp for the disabled.

8915   Parent Support Network
Independence Square
500 Prospect Street
Pawtucket, RI   02860   401-728-7800
                              FAX: 401-727-2810
                       e-mail: mmhra@aol.com

Laure Turn, Director

Offers support groups for parents of children and adolescents with emotional/behavioral disabilities.

8916   Physician Referral and Information Line
American Academy of Allergy, Asthma and Immunology
611 E Wells Street
Milwaukee, WI   53202
                              800-822-2762
                              FAX: 414-272-6070
                       e-mail: info@aaaai.org
                              www.aaaai.org

Referral line offering information on allergy and asthma, referral to an allergy/immunology specialist.

8917   Post-Polio Support Group
Hinsdale Hospital
120 N Oak Street
Hinsdale, IL   60521   630-856-7525
                              FAX: 630-856-7524
                              ahsmidwest.org

Information and support for polio patients and their families; meets the fourth Wednesday of each month.

8918   Prevent Child Abuse of Metropolitan Washington
PO Box 57194
Washington, DC   20037   202-223-0020
                              FAX: 202-296-4046
                       e-mail: pcamw@juno.com

Leila Smith, Executive Director

Offers telephone crisis intervention, information and referrals to anyone in need in the DC area through Crisis and Family Stress Hotline (202-223-2255). PhoneFriend (202-223-2244) is a telephone supportline for children who are at home without adult supervision. Also publishes The Comprehensive Referral Directory of Free and Low Cost Services. *$43.00*

600 pages BiAnnual

8919   RET Project - (Rehabilitation Engineering Technology San Francisco State University
1600 Holloway Avenue
San Francisco, CA   94132   415-338-1333
                              FAX: 415-338-1501
                       e-mail: rgrott@sfsu.edu

Ray Grott, Director

This program provides graduate-level training in the field of assistive technology for people with disabilities. Assistive technology consultation, assessments, and custom fabrication are also offered.

8920   Recorded Periodicals
Associated Services for the Blind
919 Walnut Street
Philadelphia, PA   19107   215-627-0600
                              FAX: 215-922-0692

John Corrigan, Manager

A subscription service of Associated Services for the Blind, these periodicals provide 21 magazines through this subscription service. A magazine list can be sent, in both large print and on audio cassette. *$18.00*

8921 Son-Rise Program

2080 S Undermountain Road
Sheffield, MA 01257   413-229-2100
                             800-714-2779
                        FAX: 413-229-8931
             e-mail: sonrise@option.org
                        www.son-rise.org

Internationally renowned and highly effective method for working with children challenged by autism, autism spectrum disorders, PDD and all other developmental difficulties. The program teaches parents, relatives, volunteers and professionals how to design and implement a child-centered, home-based educational program. Modality comprises an innovative and comprehensive system for learning and growth with specific impact in areas including eye contact, speech and communication, and more.

8922 Special Children

1306 Wabash Avenue
Belleville, IL 62220   618-234-6876
                          FAX: 618-234-6150
         e-mail: kcwllan@peaknet.net
                www.specialchildren.net

A not-for-profit agency serving children with developmental disabilities ages birth to 21 years old.

8923 Special Education Action Commette

PO Box 161274
Mobile, AL 36616   334-478-1208
                              800-222-7322
                         FAX: 334-473-7877
        e-mail: seacofmobile@zebra.net
                www.hiwaay.net/~seachsv/

Carol R. Blades, Director

8924 Stuttering Foundation of America

PO Box 11749
Memphis, TN 38111   901-452-7343
                              800-992-9392
                         FAX: 901-452-3931
           e-mail: stutter@vantek.net
                     www.stuttersfa.org

Jane Fraser, President
Anne Edwards, Coordinator

Toll-free hotline, brochures, books and videotapes on stuttering.

8925 Support for Asthmatic Youth (SAY)

Asthma and Allergy Foundation of America
1080 Glen Cove Avenue
Glen Head, NY 11545   516-625-5735
                         FAX: 516-625-2976
          e-mail: reneetheo1@aol.com
                          www.aafa.org

Renee Theodorakis, M.A., Director of Adolescent Services

A network of educational/support groups for adolescents between the ages of 9 and 17. All meetings are free and feature guest speakers, informational programs, games and other fun activities.

8926 Support for Asthmatic Youth Pals

Asthma and Allergy Foundation of America
1080 Glen Cove Avenue
Glen Head, NY 11545   516-625-5735
                         FAX: 516-625-2976
                 e-mail: info@aafa.org

Renee Theodorakis, M.A., Adolescent Services

A pen pal program that matches adolescents ages 9 to 17 who share similar interests and also happen to have asthma and/or allergies.

8927 SupportWorks

1018 E Boulevard
Suite 5
Charlotte, NC 28203   704-331-9500

                     www.supportworks.org

SupportWorks helps people find and form support groups. It's 8 page publication Power Tools clearly walks new group leaders through steps of putting together a healthy self-help group; it costs $3.00. SupportWorks also has a telephone conference program which allows people with similar diseases or other nonprofit issues to meet by phone conference for free or at very low cost.

8928 Teratogen and Birth Defects Information Project

University of South Dakota
414 East Clark
Vermillion, SD 57069   605-677-5623
                         FAX: 605-677-5778

For South Dakota residents only.

8929 Toll-Free Information Line

Asthma and Allergy Foundation of America
1125 15th Street
Suite 502
Washington, DC 20005   202-466-7643
                              800-7AS-THMA
                         FAX: 202-466-8940
                 e-mail: info@aafa.org
                          www.aafa.org

Referral line for questions about asthma and allergies and how to get involved in your local chapter and support groups.

8930 VUE - Vision Use in Employment

Carroll Center for the Blind
770 Centre Street
Newton, MA 02158   617-969-6200
                              800-852-3131
                         FAX: 617-969-6204

Dina Rosenbaum, Vice President of Marketing
Robert McGilliuray, Low Vision Administration

Provides engineering solutions plus training to help people keep jobs despite their vision loss.

8931   **Visiting Nurse Association of America**

3801 E Florida Avenue
Suite 9003
Denver, CO   80210   303-753-0218
                                          800-426-2547

This agency represents independent VNA units across the United States. Each VNA unit may vary in their services, but most provide skilled nursing, physical therapy, occupational therapy, speech therapy, and home health aid services.

8932   **Washington Connection**

American Council of the Blind
1155 15th Street NW
Suite 1004
Washington, DC   20005   202-467-5081
                                          800-424-8666
                                   FAX: 202-467-5085

Coverage of issues affecting blind people via legislative information, participates in law-making, legislative training seminars and networking of support resources across the U.S.

General

8933 Age Appropriate Puzzles
7756 Winding Way
Fair Oaks, CA 95628 916-961-3507
FAX: 916-961-0765
e-mail: miltcher@aol.com

Cheryl Meyers, President

These unique puzzles teach numerous concepts: picture, name, color and shape recognition. Each of the four themes (food, animals, holidays, and clothing) comes with self-adhesive stickers that name each picture in English, Hmong, Russian, Spanish and Vietnamese. A notch at each puzzle piece makes grasping and lifting the pieces easy to use., They are designed for children from 18 months and up. *$9.95*

8934 All-Turn-It Spinner
AbleNet
1081 10th Avenue SE
Minneapolis, MN 55414

800-322-0956
FAX: 612-379-9143
e-mail: customerservice@ablenetinc.com
www.ablenetinc.com

The All-Turn-It Spinner is a random spinner that comes with a dice overlay allowing user's to participate in any commercially-available game that require dice. Activate the spinner with its built-in switch or connect an external switch. Overlays are interchangeable with AbleNet designed spinner games or create your own overlay. A great inclusion tool!. *$89.00*

8935 Alphabet Circus
DLM Teaching Resources
3578 Powder Mill Road
Beltsville, MD 20705 301-937-3884
800-527-5030

This six game software program provides language drill and practice with color graphics; letters are introduced by displaying a picture for each.

8936 Anthony Brothers Manufacturing
1945 S Rancho Santa Fe Road
San Marcos, CA 92069 760-744-8299
FAX: 760-744-2994
e-mail: kids@kidtrikes.com
www.kidtrikes.com

Tom Anthony, President
Sue Coffin, Vice President
Nairne Farner, Executive Vice President

Manufacture wheeled toys and goods for disabled children.

8937 Automatic Card Shuffler
Maxi Aids
42 Executive Boulevard
3209
Farmingdale, NY 11735 516-752-0521
800-522-6294
FAX: 516-752-0689
e-mail: sales@maxiaids.com
www.maxiaids.com

Simple to use, the cards are physically challenging for the player with limited hand dexterity. *$14.95*

8938 Backgammon Set: Deluxe
Maxi Aids
42 Executive Boulevard
3209
Farmingdale, NY 11735 516-752-0521
800-522-6294
FAX: 516-752-0689
e-mail: sales@maxiaids.com
www.maxiaids.com

Completely factual with a felt board, raised white dividers and white braille dice for the blind and visually impaired. *$29.95*

8939 Board Games: Snakes and Ladders
Maxi Aids
42 Executive Boulevard
3209
Farmingdale, NY 11735 516-752-0521
800-522-6294
FAX: 516-752-0689
e-mail: sales@maxiaids.com
www.maxiaids.com

A dice game for 2 to 6 players. This children's game is also fun for the whole family. Offers recreation, competition and eye/hand coordination skills. *$34.95*

8940 Board Games: Solitaire
Maxi Aids
42 Executive Boulevard
3209
Farmingdale, NY 11735 516-752-0521
800-522-6294
FAX: 516-752-0689
e-mail: sales@maxiaids.com
www.maxiaids.com

This popular solo board game lends itself to a number of less well-known variations. The board is accompanied by brightly colored pieces that are reversible for the visually impaired player. *$30.95*

8941 Braille Playing Cards: Pinochle
Maxi Aids
42 Executive Boulevard
3209
Farmingdale, NY 11735 516-752-0521
800-522-6294
FAX: 516-752-0689
e-mail: sales@maxiaids.com
www.maxiaids.com

Cards offer regular print as well as braille on each plastic card for the blind or visually impaired player. *$9.95*

8942   Braille Playing Cards: Plastic

Maxi Aids
42 Executive Boulevard
3209
Farmingdale, NY   11735   516-752-0521
                                 800-522-6294
                          FAX: 516-752-0689
                 e-mail: sales@maxiaids.com
                         www.maxiaids.com

Playing cards that offer regular print and braille on plastic cards for the blind or visually impaired player. *$9.95*

8943   Braille: Bingo Cards, Boards and Call Numbers

Maxi Aids
42 Executive Boulevard
3209
Farmingdale, NY   11735   516-752-0521
                                 800-522-6294
                          FAX: 516-752-0689
                 e-mail: sales@maxiaids.com
                         www.maxiaids.com

Bingo products for the visually impaired. Cards, boards and call numbers offer regular print and braille. *$4.99*

8944   Braille: Rook Cards

Maxi Aids
42 Executive Boulevard
3209
Farmingdale, NY   11735   516-752-0521
                                 800-522-6294
                          FAX: 516-752-0689
                 e-mail: sales@maxiaids.com
                         www.maxiaids.com

This set of cards for Rook, the popular bidding card game with 23 variations, has regular size print and braille print for the blind/visually impaired player. *$13.75*

8945   Card Holder Deluxe

Maxi Aids
42 Executive Boulevard
3209
Farmingdale, NY   11735

                                 800-522-6294
                          FAX: 516-752-0689
                 e-mail: sales@maxiaids.com
                         www.maxiaids.com

A handsome-looking card holder takes the struggle out of holding playing cards in weak or arthritic hands. The two clear plastic tiers hold up to 18 cards. The wooden base has a non-skid bottom to prevent slipping, and is also great for holding recipe cards. *$19.75*

8946   Cards: Musical

Sense-Sations
919 Walnut Street
Philadelphia, PA   19107   215-629-2990
                                  800-876-5456

These cards, for all occasions, play music when they are opened, for the visually impaired and blind persons. *$2.50*

8947   Cards: UNO

Maxi Aids
42 Executive Boulevard
3209
Farmingdale, NY   11735   516-752-0521
                                 800-522-6294
                          FAX: 516-752-0689
                 e-mail: sales@maxiaids.com
                         www.maxiaids.com

Traditional card game in Braille for the blind player recreation. *$10.95*

8948   Checker Set: Deluxe

Maxi Aids
42 Executive Boulevard
3209
Farmingdale, NY   11735   516-752-0521
                                 800-522-6294
                          FAX: 516-752-0689
                 e-mail: sales@maxiaids.com
                         www.maxiaids.com

A wooden board with sunken playing squares. The squares have drilled holes for inserting the checker, offering help with eye/hand coordination for the physically challenged. *$25.95*

8949   Chess Set: Deluxe

Maxi Aids
42 Executive Boulevard
3209
Farmingdale, NY   11735   516-752-0521
                                 800-522-6294
                          FAX: 516-752-0689
                 e-mail: sales@maxiaids.com
                         www.maxiaids.com

Made out of wood material. Boards have raised dark squares and all squares have drilled holes for inserting pegged chessmen, for the physically challenged player with poor eye/hand coordination. *$43.95*

8950   Dice - Jumbo Size

New Vision Store
919 Walnut Street
Philadelphia, PA   19107   215-629-2990

The large white and black dice are over-sized and have grooved dots to indicate the numbers, for easy reading for the visually handicapped. *$4.95*

8951   Hands-Free Controller

Nintendo
PO Box 97032
Redmond, WA   98073

                                  800-255-3700

Nintendo controller for the physically disabled.

8952   One Hundred Board and Pegs

Maxi Aids
42 Executive Boulevard
3209
Farmingdale, NY   11735   516-752-0521
                                 800-522-6294
                          FAX: 516-752-0689
                 e-mail: sales@maxiaids.com
                         www.maxiaids.com

Cognitive skills and motor stimulation. *$34.95*

8953 PI Bear

PI Bear Company
PO Box 248
Hays, KS 67601   785-625-0088
800-467-BEAR

Marvin Malcom, President
Sara Engel, Secretary

A unique tool/toy. Through P.I. (Physically Inconvenienced) BEAR's three illustrated storybooks (included in his chair backpack) about his own accident, struggles and triumphs he can help a disabled child understand his or her own feelings of fear and uncertainty. And when his beary special friendship is needed, P.I. BEAR will be there to hug. P.I. and his wheelchair are approximately 14 inches tall and also comes with a club membership certificate and a one-year warranty. *$99.95*

8954 Puzzle Games - Cooking, Eating, Community and Grooming

Programming Concepts
PO Box 12428
San Antonio, TX 78212
800-594-4263
FAX: 218-248-055

Janie Haugen, Program Director
Jeff McLane, President/CEO

Each game has 63 pieces which are 2 inches in size. The completed full color puzzle is 19 inch x 15 inch. Step 1 - Work the puzzle. Step 2 - Match picture or Word cards to the correct space on the puzzle. These puzzles teach basic life skills. *$19.95*

8955 Single Switch Latch and Timer

AbleNet
1081 10th Avenue SE
Minneapolis, MN 55414
800-322-0956
FAX: 612-379-9143
e-mail: customerservice@ablenetinc.com
www.ablenetinc.com

A Single Switch Latch and Timer allows a user to activate a battery-operated toy or appliance in the latch, timed seconds and timed minutes modes of control. Choose for one user and one device at a time. *$63.00*

8956 Socialization Games for Persons with Disabilities

Charles C. Thomas, Publisher
2600 S 1st Street
Springfield, IL 62704   217-789-8980
800-257-8980
FAX: 217-789-9130
e-mail: books@ccthomas.com
Donna Irons-Reavis, author

This text will assist those who want to teach severely multiple disabled students by providing information on: general principles of intervention and classroom organization; managing the behavior of students; physically managing students and using adaptive equipment; teaching eating skills; teaching toileting, dressing , and hygiene skills; teaching cognition, communication, and socialization skills; teaching independent living skills; and teaching infants and preschool students. *$24.95*

140 pages Paperback
ISBN 0-39806 -73-4

8957 Stacking the Deck

Research Press
PO Box 9177
Champaign, IL 61826   217-352-3273
800-519-2707
FAX: 217-352-1221
e-mail: rp@researchpress.com
www.researchpress.com

Dr. Richard Foxx, author
Russell Pence, V P Marketing

A unique training program designed for use with any table game that involves progressive movement around a game board to home. During the game, players are required to draw cards and react to specific social situations. Training focuses on three areas: general social skills; social/vocational skills; and social/sexual skills. The training package contains 144 situation cards, detailed instructions and reproducible forms for scoring, recording and evaluating progress. *$19.95*

Game

8958 Take a Chance

Speech Bin
1965 25th Avenue
Vero Beach, FL 32960   561-770-0007
800-477-3324
FAX: 561-770-0006
www.speechbin.com

Gary J. Cooper, author
Jan J. Binney, Senior Editor

Card game for practice of commonly misarticulated speech sounds. *$18.75*

16 pages Book & Cards
ISBN 0-93785 -46-7

8959 Tic Tac Toe Plus

Maxi Aids
42 Executive Boulevard
3209
Farmingdale, NY 11735   516-752-0521
800-522-6294
FAX: 516-752-0689
e-mail: sales@maxiaids.com
www.maxiaids.com

Offers the traditional tic-tac-toe game but with pieces that are 3/4 inch in diameter and 1/4 inch high in black and green, for the visually impaired player. *$5.95*

8960 Toys for Special Children/Enabling Devices

385 Warburton Avenue
Hastings On Hudson, NY 10706   914-478-0960
800-832-8697
FAX: 914-479-1369
e-mail: customer_support@enablingdevices.com
www.enablingdevices.com

Rachel Duclos, Marketing Director
Karen O'Connor, VP of Operations

A manufacturer and distributor of all types of assistive products such as activity centers, adapted toys, specialty switches, training devices and augmentative communication devices.

8961   Trikes

PCA Industries
5642 Natural Bridge Avenue
Saint Louis, MO   63120

800-787-8180

Heavy-duty institutional trikes for children.

8962   Turnabout Game

Maxi Aids
42 Executive Boulevard
3209
Farmingdale, NY   11735   516-752-0521
                                          800-522-6294
                             FAX: 516-752-0689
                    e-mail: sales@maxiaids.com
                            www.maxiaids.com

A game of strategy for two, with large playing
pieces and a bright gameboard for the visually
impaired player. *$7.70*

Newsletters & Books

8963 Access Travel: Airports

Consumer Information Center
Department 575A
Pueblo, CO   81009   719-948-3334

e-mail: catalog.pueblo@gsa.gov

Michael Clark, Public Affairs

Tips and suggestions for easier travel for persons
with disabilities and the elderly. Lists designs, facilities, and services at 553 airport terminals worldwide.

8964 Architectural Barriers Action League

PO Box 57088
Tucson, AZ   85732   520-628-8118

Offers guides to accessible hotels and motels
across the country.

8965 Directory for Disabled Travelers

Travelin' Talk
PO Box 3534
Clarksville, TN   37043

Rick Crowder, President

Lists all resources a traveler with a disability should
ever need to plan their trips and find help should any
emergencies arise. *$35.00*

550 pages

8966 Directory of Accessible Van Rentals

Disability Bookshop
PO Box 129
Vancouver, WA   98666   360-694-2462

Designed to help people with disabilities locate
rental vans that are accessible throughout the U.S.
$9.95

30+ pages
ISBN 0-93326 -09-9

8967 Directory of Travel Agencies for the Disabled

Twin Peaks Press
PO Box 129
Vancouver, WA   98666   360-694-2462

Directory lists more than 360 travel agents specializing in arrangements for people with disabilities.
Handbook provides information about accessibility. *$19.95*

40 pages Paperback
ISBN 0-93326 -04-8

8968 Elderly Guide to Budget Travel/Europe

Pilot Books
PO Box 2102
Greenport, NY   11944   516-477-1094
                                 FAX: 516-661-4379

Paige Palmer, author

Includes a list of over 250 inexpensive hotels in prime
tourist areas. Covers special needs of senior citizens
including inexpensive accommodations and fares.
$3.95

8969 Ideas for Easy Travel

Accent Books & Products
PO Box 700
Bloomington, IL   61702   309-378-2961
                                    800-787-8444
                               FAX: 309-378-4420
                         e-mail: acmtlvng@aol.com

Heidi Johnson-Wright and Steve Wright, author
Raymond C. Cheever, Publisher
Betty Garee, Editor

Ideal for helping the new traveler get started having
fun. Points out favorite accessible high-spots as re-
ported by two travel experts (one is disabled), and
offers basic ideas to help wherever you go. *$3.25*

55 pages Paperback
ISBN 0-91570 -36-1

8970 Travel Information Center

Moss Rehabilitation Hospital
12th And Tabor Road
Philadelphia, PA   19141   215-329-5715

Supplies travel information about three different
locations worldwide. *$5.00*

8971 Travel Information Service/Moss Rehab Hospital

Moss Rehabilitation Hospital
1200 W Tabor Road
Philadelphia, PA   19141   215-329-5715

Joan Appel, Manager

Offers information and resources, to telephone callers only, for persons with special traveling/accessi-
bility needs.

**8972 United States Department of the Interior National
Park Service**

Superintendent of Documents
1100 Ohio Drive SW
Washington, DC   20024   202-619-7222
                               FAX: 202-619-7302

James Ridenour, Director

Offers an informational packet containing books,
guides and tours for the disabled and elderly.

8973 Wheelchair Traveler

123 Ball Hill Road
Milford, NH   03055   603-673-4539

Douglas R. Annand, author

Travel directory that lists hotels, motels, restaurants
and sightseeing attractions that are wheelchair accessible. *$15.00*

240 pages Paperback
ISBN 9-990546-73-8

8974 Wheelin' Around

Wheelers Accessible Van Rentals
710 N 55th Avenue
Glendale, AZ   85301

800-456-1371
FAX: 602-435-9989
e-mail: wheelens@primenet.com
www.wheelerz.com

Tammy Smith, President

A newsletter for persons with physical disabilities by Wheelers Accessible Van Rentals offering information on automotive assistive devices, van conversions and travel tips for the disabled.

Quarterly

8975 Where to Stay U.S.A.

Council on International Educational Exchange
633 3rd Avenue
New York, NY   10017

212-822-2600
888-COU-NCIL
FAX: 212-822-2649

Priscilla Tovey, Information Services

A guide to low-cost lodging throughout the United States including information on whether the establishment is accessible. *$ 15.95*

250 pages
ISBN 0-67179 -49-5

Organizations

8976 Access America

Northern Cartographic
4050 Williston Road
Suite 131
South Burlington, VT   05403   802-860-2886

Offers information on 36 national parks, providing detailed information on accessibility.

8977 Access Wheels

710 N 55th Avenue
Glendale, AZ   85301

800-631-5791
FAX: 602-435-1518
e-mail: wheelens@primenet.com
www.wheelerz.com

Tammy Smith, President

Nations largest operator of lowered floor mini-vans. Technically advanced engineering features bring a world of independence to the user. Lowered floor modification provided on all GM and Chrysler front wheel drive mini-vans.

Quarterly

8978 Access Yosemite National Park

Special Needs Project
3463 Stat Street
 # 282
Santa Barbara, CA   93105

800-333-6867

Represents unprecedented combinations of intensive information survey data with high quality cartography. *$7.95*

31 pages

8979 America West Airlines

4000 E Sky Harbor Boulevard
Phoenix, AZ   85034

602-693-0800
800-526-8077

Diana Lawson

This airline trains employees to make sure that passengers with disabilities enjoy convenient, safe and comfortable travel.

8980 American Hotel and Lodging Association

1201 New York Avenue
Washington, DC   20005

202-289-3100
FAX: 202-289-3199
e-mail: comments@ahlaonline.org
www.ahlaonline.org

William Fisher, President/CEO

Will disseminate information, develop and conduct a series of seminars for the hotel and motel industry at state-level association conferences, and develop and distribute an ADA Compliance handbook for use by the lodging industry.

8981 Amtrak

60 Massachusetts Avenue NE
Washington, DC   20002

202-906-2121
800-USA-RAIL
TDY:800-523-6590
e-mail: access@w0.amtrak.com
www.amtrak.com

Amtrak is committed to making travel for passengers with disabilities more accessible. Anyone interested should contact Amtrak's Special Services Desk at 1-800-USA-RAIL at least 24 hours in advance to arrange for special assistance. The type of equipment and accessibility vary from train to train and station to station.

8982 Disabled Outdoors Foundation

320 Lake Street
Oak Park, IL   60302

Outdoor activities for persons with disabilities.

8983 Easter Seals Project ACTION

700 13th Street NW
Suite 200
Washington, DC   20005

202-347-3066
800-659-6428
FAX: 202-737-7914
TDY:202-347-7385
e-mail: project_action@opa.easter-seals.org
www.projectaction.org

Bryna Helfer, Director
Sharon Ransome Smith, Newsletter Editor

A national technical assistance program designed to improve access to transportation services for people with disabilities and assist transit providers in implementing the Americans with Disabilities Act. Publishes quarterly newsletter.

8984 Easy Access to National Parks: The Sierra Club Guide for the Disabled

Sierra Club Books
85 Second Street
2nd Floor
San Francisco, CA 94105   415-977-5500

Includes practical information on planning safe trips to 50 national parks that are designated as best visits for their accessibility. *$16.00*

> *432 pages*
> *ISBN 0-87156 -20-6*

8985 Front Row Advisor

3109 Grand Avenue
Coconut Grove, FL 33133   305-723-3805
                    FAX: 954-774-6070

Matthew J. Bennett, Publisher

Newsletter dedicated to business and First Class Air Travel & the alluring world of free upgrades.

> *Monthly*

8986 General Motors Mobility Program for Persons with Disabilities

GM Mobility Program
PO Box 9011
Detroit, MI 48202

                    800-323-9935

Mary Anne Meade, Manager, GM Mobility

GM Mobility Program provides up to $1000 reimbursement toward mobility adaptations for drivers or passengers and/or vehicle alerting devices for drivers who are deaf or hard of hearing. Provided on eligible new Chevrolet, Pontiac, Oldsmobile, Buick, Cadillac, and GMC vehicles. Complete GMC financing available. GM Mobility also offers free resource information, including list of area adaptive equipment installers, plus free resource video.

8987 Melwood Access Adventures

9035 Ironsides Road
Nanjemoy, MD 20662   301-870-3226
                    FAX: 301-870-2620
        e-mail: accessadventures@erols.com

Heidi Aldous, Director
Ann Davis, Office Manager

A year round recreation facility that serves mentally and physically disabled individuals, offers a variety of vacations, outdoor recreation, travel and respite care.

8988 Nantahala Outdoor Center

13077 Highway 19 W
Bryson City, NC 28713   828-488-2175
                    800-232-7238
                    FAX: 828-488-2498
                    e-mail: rafting@noc.com
                    www.noc.com

Jennifer Petos, Advertising Coordinator

Nantahala Outdoor Center, the leader in outdoor recreation and education for over 30 years, strongly encourages and supports participants with disabilities. We offer whitewater rafting adventures on six rivers in the Southeast for all skill and thrill levels, also kayak and canoe adaptive instruction. NOC will tailor a whitewater program to your skill and ability level, modify the gear, and pace instruction for you. We also offer a Ropes Challenge Course and team building programs.

8989 New Hope Guest House Ministry

115 Thunder Road
Hawkinsville, GA 31036

Sam Vines
Christine Vines

A renovated country guest house located in Georgia just 10 min. from I-75. This home is designed for anyone with a physical disability. Includes a full kitchen, living area, two bedrooms, & a large bathroom featuring a whirlpool tub & a wheelchair accessible shower. No charge - run by donations only. This is a private ministry with many people in mind: members of the local community who'd enjoy a night out, military families relocating, missionary families, tourists passing through, etc.

8990 Paralysis Society of America

801 18th Street NW
Washington, DC 20006   202-872-1300
                    800-772-1711
                    FAX: 202-973-8421
                    e-mail: info@psa.org
                    www.psa.org

Michelle Mearham, Communications Coordinator

A national organization whose members are people with spinal cord injury or disease, their family members and caregivers, health-care professionals, and others with an interest in the disciplines of spinal cord medicine and paralsis. One year membership includes NewsWheels, a quarterly newsletter. *$10.00*

8991 Professional Respite Care

Act for Health
1385 S Colorado Boulevard
Denver, CO 80222   303-757-4808
                    FAX: 303-757-3821

Pamela Erickson, RN

Offers travel accompaniment services for disabled persons or senior citizens.

8992 Rodeway Inns Airport
124 S 24th Street
Phoenix, AZ 85034 602-220-0044
FAX: 602-244-0174
e-mail: jimp124@juno.com

Jaeques Pichardie, General Manager
Rita Reyes, Assistant Manager

This organization has a limited number of rooms for the handicapped with extra wide doors and special bathroom assist bars.

8993 Shilo Inns & Resorts
11600 SW Shilo Lane
Portland, OR 97225 503-641-6565
800-222-2244
FAX: 503-644-0868

Daria Sharer

Offers handicapped-assist rooms including larger bathrooms equipped with assistance railings and wheelchair access. Please call for property specifics.

8994 Special Assistance Services (S.A.S.)
3 High Street
Helmetta, NJ 08828
FAX: 732-521-9333

James J. Muzikowski, President
Steve Rosenel, Asst. Travel Coord.

The mission of this organization is to empower the quest to travel. They supply this by offering flexible plans and personal assistance. S.A.S. is dedicated to providing various types of assistance to persons with disabilities. The organization serves guests with a variety of special needs, including but not limited to persons with visual and hearing impairments, physical and development disabilities, and the mentally challenged.

8995 Ticket Counter
6900 Wisconsin Avenue
Suite 706
Chevy Chase, MD 20815 301-986-0790
FAX: 301-913-0166

Tracey Bullan Rattner

Offers airlines, train, vacation and honeymoon packages, leisure and business, cruises, skiing, horseback riding and other interest tickets to persons with or without disabilities.

8996 Travelers Aid Society
1612 K Street NW
Washington, DC 20006 202-546-1127
FAX: 202-546-1625

Pauline Dunn

Provides crisis intervention and casework services, limited financial assistance, protective travel assistance and information and referrals for travelers, transients and newcomers.

8997 Westin Hotels and Resorts
PO Box 141609
Austin, TX 78714
FAX: 512-835-4417
www.westin.com

Westin Hotels include special parking stalls, wheelchair ramps, wide doors, wheelchairs, braille elevator buttons, recreational facilities for people with disabilities, restaurants and restrooms.

8998 Wilderness Inquiry
1313 5th Street SE
Minneapolis, MN 55414 612-379-3854
800-728-0179
FAX: 612-379-5972

Greg Lais, Executive Director
Tracy Fredin, Outreach Director

Allows people of all ages and abilities to share the adventure of wilderness travel. This nonprofit organization was formed in 1978 and conducts tours to some of the most beautiful and remote parts of the world.

Tours

8999 Accessible Journeys
35 W Sellers Avenue
Ridley Park, PA 19078 610-521-0339
800-846-4537
FAX: 610-521-6959
e-mail: sales@disabilitytravel.com
www.disabilitytravel.com

Howard Mccoy III, Director
Deborah Richards, Associate Director

Tour operator for slow walker and wheelchair travelers their families and their friends offering tours to culturally intriguing destinations like Africa, China, Brazil, Alaska and Hawaii. Also offers a quarterly newsletter.

9000 Anglo California Travel Service
4250 Williams Road
San Jose, CA 95129 408-257-2257
FAX: 408-257-2664

Helen Jones

Plans for one and two week accessible tours.

9001 Bill Dvorak, Kayak and Rafting Expeditions
17921 US Highway 285
Nathrop, CO 81236 719-539-6851
800-824-3795
FAX: 719-539-3378
e-mail: dvorakex@amigo.net
www.dvorakexpeditions.com

Bill Dvorak, President
Jaci Dvorak, Vice President

This organization does river trips for people who are deaf, visually impaired, physically or mentally disabled. Rafting trips with groups and families and whitewater instruction.

$38 - $2500

9002 Canwee Travel Agency

553 Broadway
Massapequa, NY 11758   516-795-6000

Joanne Gering, Director
Arranges individual trips for people with disabilities.

9003 Cunard Line

6100 Blue Lagoon Drive
Miami, FL 33126   305-463-3000
                         800-528-6273
                         FAX: 305-463-3010
                         www.cunardline.com

Cunard Line, one of the world's most recognized brand names with a classic British heritage, operated by Cunard Line Limited, has provided the ultimate in deluxe ocean travel experience for the past 158 years. The fleet consists of famed liner Queen Elizabeth 2 and the Caronia, a classic ship formerly identified as Vistafjord. The Cunard Line brand, the epitome of British essence, focuses on recalling the golden age of sea travel for those who missed the first.

9004 Dell Rapids Sportsmen's Club

714 E 9th Street
Dell Rapids, SD 57022   605-428-5494

A club offering education and experience in planning, designing or using accessible shooting or gun club.

9005 Diabetic Cruise Desk

Hartford Holiday Travel
PO Box 536
Williston Park, NY 11596   516-746-6670
                                   800-645-2120

Offers a seven-day cruise to Alaska for people with diabetes. Includes seminars on diabetes, self management, planning, special guidance for exercise classes and individual dietary advice.

9006 Dialysis at Sea Cruises

107 13th Avenue
218
Indian Rocks Beach, FL 33785   727-518-7311
                                       800-544-7604
                                       FAX: 727-518-7332
                                       e-mail: dasc@dialysis-at-sea.com
                                       dialysisatsea.com

Andrew Carrabus, President
Been in the business of providing travel opportunities for persons on hemodialysis and CAPD since 1977. Handle all aspects of their travel and medical requirements. Not Sold Through Travel Agents! Make all reservations and coordinates the total set-up and operation of an onboard ship mobile dialysis clinic. Cruises run from seven days to three weeks and have departures from cities around the world on a variety of cruise lines.

9007 Directions Unlimited Acccessible Tours

123 Green Lane
Bedford Hills, NY 10507   914-241-4477
                                  800-533-5343
                                  FAX: 914-241-0243

Lois Bonanni, Director
Arrange vacations throughout the world for all disabilities including accessible cruises, African safari, rafting and scuba diving, European and Caribbean vacations.

9008 Environmental Traveling Companions

Fort Mason Center Building
San Francisco, CA 94110   415-544-0452

Diane Poslosky
Aids travelers regardless of physical or financial limitations to experience the beauty and challenge of the wilderness.

9009 Flying Wheels Travel

143 W Bridge Street
PO Box 382
Owatonna, MN 55060   507-451-5005
                             800-535-6790
                             FAX: 507-451-1685
                             e-mail: thq@ll.net
                             www.flyingwheelstravel.com

Barbara Jacobson, President
Arranges escorted group and individual cruise trips to the Caribbean, Panama Canal and Europe. Tours are offered in Europe, Israel, Egypt, and more. People traveling in wheelchairs will need to be able to push themselves and take care of personal needs or bring along an attendant.

9010 Golden Eagle Passport

US Dept. of the Interior, National Park Service
PO Box 37127
Washington, DC 20013   202-208-4747

                               www.nps.gov

A free lifetime passport to federally operated parks, monuments, historic sites, recreation areas and wildlife refuges for persons who are blind or permanently disabled.

9011 Guide Service of Washington

733 15th Street NW
Washington, DC 20005   202-628-2842
                               FAX: 202-638-2812

Renee Price, Resident
A guide service offering tours of Washington DC and vicinity.

9012 Guided Tour for Persons 17 & Over Over with Developmental and Physical Challenges

7900 Old York Road
Suite 114B
Elkins Park, PA 19027   215-782-1370
                                FAX: 215-635-2637

Irv Segal MSW, ACSW, Director
Ari Segal MSW, ACSW, Assistant Director

Offers unique travel and vacation programs for individuals with mild to moderate developmental disabilities. We publish a free "Rates & Dates" brochure.

8 pages BiAnnually

9013 Hostelling North America Hostelling International - American Youth Hostels

733 15th Street NW
Suite 840
Washington, DC 20005   **202-783-6161**
                                 FAX: 202-783-6171
                      e-mail: hiayhserv@hiayh.org
                                    www.hiayh.org
Hostelling International - American Youth Hostels, author
Ms. Toby Pyle, PR Manager

Hostels are very inexpensive accommodations for travelers of all ages. They provide dorm-style sleeping rooms with separate quarters for males and females, fully equipped self-service kitchens, dining areas and common rooms for relaxing and socializing. HI-AYH has hostels in major cities, in national and state parks, near beaches and in the mountains. Send for a copy of Hostelling North America, a directory of hostels in U.S. and Canada, which lists hostels that are handicap accessible. *$ 3.00*

400 pages Yearly

9014 New Courier Travel

532 Duane Street
Glen Ellyn, IL 60137   **630-469-7349**
                               FAX: 630-469-7390

Janice Perkins, Travel Consultant

Offers specialized assistance for independent travel or tours for persons with disabilities including cruises and travel in the USA and abroad. Fee charged for out-of-state clients, long-distance calls and clients who have free air.

9015 New Directions

5276 Hollister Avenue
Suite 207
Santa Barbara, CA 93111   **805-967-2841**
                                     888-967-2841
                               FAX: 805-964-7344
                      www.newdirectionstravel.com

Dee Duncan, Executive Director

New Directions is a 501 (c) non-profit organization providing vacation travel and special educational exchange programs for people with developmental disabilities. The purpose of the program is to promote understanding, acceptance, and appreciation of people with disabilities as important and contributing members of society.

9016 Norwegian Cruise Line

7665 NW 19th Street
Miami, FL 33126   **305-436-4652**
                             800-327-7030
                        FAX: 305-436-4117
                             www.ncl.com

Has accessible cabins but urges mobility impaired passengers to travel in the same cabin with a person who is not mobility impaired. Cruise fares vary.

9017 People and Places

3909 Genesee Street
Cheektowaga, NY 14225   **716-631-8223**

Joie Budington, Director
Patty Brown Schieder, Assistant Director

Nonprofit organization that provides escorted small group vacation opportunities and outdoor experiences throughout the world for persons with developmental disabilities. Brochure available.

9018 River Odysseys West (Row)

PO Box 579-DI
Coeur D'Alene, ID 83814   **208-667-1835**
                                     800-451-6034
                               FAX: 208-667-6506
                         e-mail: info@rowinc.com
                                  www.rowinc.com

Offers one to six day rafting trips to physically disadvantaged people. Designs custom itineraries, or trips with a special focus for small groups. For those with special dietary needs, they prepare special meals. So come ride the rapids and enjoy life. They also offer canoe trips aboard 34' voyager canoes along the trail of Lewis and Clark on Montana's upper Missouri River. Free brochure upon request.

9019 Search Beyond Adventures

400 Cedar Lake Road South
Minneapolis, MN 55405   **612-374-4845**
                               FAX: 612-374-1670

Operates a wide variety of tours for adults with mental retardation. Programs vary from 2 to 16 days throughout North America, Caribbean and Europe. Offices in Minneapolis, Chicago, Denver, Boston and Phoenix areas. Camping and accommodation tours are also offered. Catalog of over 135 tours are available.

9020 Sundial Special Vacations

Sundial Tours
2609 Hiway 101 North
Seaside, OR 97138   **503-738-9491**
                               800-547-9198
                          FAX: 503-738-3369
                      e-mail: sundial@aone.com

Jill Conner Ross, Tour Operations Dir./Owner
Patsy Conner, Owner
Nancy Wyse, Tour Leader

Provides special vacations for developmentally disabled persons. Provides quality vacations for persons with developmental disabilities. Ratio is 1 for 7 or 1 for 5 depending on tour. Only two people to a room. Exciting destinations. 3 to 4 star properties. Great fun.

9021 Wheelchair Express

PO Box 700637
Saint Cloud, FL 34770

                               FAX: 407-957-2043

Robert Mann, President

Transports individuals, families or groups, with disabilities in Central Florida. All attractions, plus a Florida tour.

9022 Wheelchair Getaways

PO Box 605
Versailles, KY 40383
800-642-2042
www.wheelchair-getaways.com

Accessible van rentals featuring wheelchair lift or ramp, raised roof or lowered floor, securement system for wheelchairs or scooters.

Vehicle Rentals

9023 ABC Union, ACE, ANLV, Vegas Western Cab

5010 South Valley View Boulevard
Las Vegas, NV 89118
702-643-1041
FAX: 702-736-8813

Art McGill, Manager

Taxi service in Las Vegas that uses vans with wheelchair lifts at regular taxi rates.

9024 Associated Leasing: Handicappable Vans

12117 Riverwood Drive
Burnsville, MN 55337
612-441-6449

Luxury wheelchair conversion vans equipped with fully automatic lifts with tie-downs; no hand controls. Daily, weekly or monthly rentals.

9025 Avis Rent A Car

900 Old Country Road
Garden City, NY 11530
516-222-3000
800-331-1212
FAX: 918-621-4819
e-mail: custserv@avis.com
www.avis.com

James A Keyes, VP Human Resourses
Richard A Fuller, VP Media Relations

Requires 24-hour notice for hand control vehicles, available in any location across the US.

9026 CEH

4457 63rd Circle
Pinellas Park, FL 33781
727-522-0364
800-677-0364
FAX: 727-522-9024

Phillip G. Faas, President

New vans, used vans, rental vans; specializing in quad conversions, all types of handicap equipment. Celebrating 28 years in business.

9027 Mobile Care, Ltd.

6201 Riverdale Road
Suite 101
Riverdale, MD 20737
301-649-0564
FAX: 301-699-1865
e-mail: jaklimo@aol.com

Jeffery A. Koch, President

Specializing in non-emergency wheelchair service for the elderly and physically challenged.

9028 National Car Rental System

200 South Andrews Avenue
Fort Lauderdale, FL 33301
800-CAR-RENT
www.nationalcar.com

Accommodates special requests subject to availability. Offers hand controls, bench seats, extra mirrors and vans with lifts at many major locations.

9029 Over the Rainbow Disabled Travel Services & Wheelers' Accessible Van Rentals

186 Mehani Circle
Kihei, HI 96753
808-879-5521
FAX: 808-871-7533

David McKown, VP & Director

Offers the disabled traveler Hawaii airport arrangements and ticketing accessible accommodations, hotels and condos including roll-in showers, Wheelers' Accessible Van Rentals on Maui and Honolulu or cars with hand controls, personal care attendants, medical or recreational equipment rentals and activities such as: helicopter rides, luau's, whalewatching, boating and more. Airfare varies from departure points and time of the year. Hotels $90-$425; Condos $85-$150; Van Rentals $495 per week.

9030 Rehabiliation Engineering Center for Personal Licensed Transportation

University of Virginia School of Engineering
PO Box 9003
Charlottesville, VA 22906
804-924-0311

9031 Wheelchair Getaways Wheelchair/Scooter Accessible Van Rentals

PO Box 605
Versailles, KY 40383
606-873-4973
800-642-2042
FAX: 606-873-8039
e-mail: sgatewood@aol.com
www.wheelchair-getaways.com

Rents wheelchair/scooter accessible vans by the day, week, month or longer and offers delivery to major airports and other conbenient locatioins in more than 200 cities in 42 states and Puerto Rico. Also offers full size and mini vans with automatic lifts and ramps. Some vans are equipped with hand controls, six-way power seats and remote controls for powered door operation and lifts.

9032 Wheelers

7101 N 55th Avenue
Glendale, AZ 85301
800-456-1371
FAX: 602-435-9989

Offers delivery to airports in 29 states and Washington, D.C. In about 40 cities, Wheelers works directly with Avis Rent-a-Car. Wheelers offers a variety of van configurations with capacity for up to three wheelchairs, automatic ramps or lifts and nylon tie-downs, hand controls or other modifications.

9033 Wheelers Accessible Van Rentals
7101 N 55th Avenue
Glendale, AZ   85301   602-931-7474
                                          800-456-1371
                               FAX: 602-435-1518

Tammy Smith, President

National Administrations

9034 DAV National Service Headquarters

807 Maine Avenue SW
Washington, DC 20024   202-554-3501
FAX: 202-554-3581
e-mail: feedback@davmail.org
www.dav.org

Arthur H. Wilson, National Adjutant
David W. Gorman, Executive Director

Serves America's disabled veterans and their families. Direct services include legislative advocacy; professional counseling about compensation, pension, educational and job training programs and VA health care; and assistance in applying for those entitlements.

9035 Department of Medicine and Surgery Veterans Administration

810 Vermont Avenue NW
Washington, DC 20420   202-273-8504
FAX: 202-273-9108

Gerald McDonald, M.D., Senior Consultant

Provides hospital and outpatient treatment as well as nursing home care for eligible veterans in Veterans Administration facilities. Services elsewhere provided on a contract basis in the United States and its territories. Provides non-vocational inpatient residential rehabilitation services to eligible legally blinded veterans of the armed forces of the United States.

9036 Department of Veterans Affairs Regional Office - Vocational Rehab Division

380 Westminster Street
Providence, RI 02903   401-528-4580
800-827-1000
FAX: 401-528-4894

Gerald E. Allen, Counseling Officer

Vocational rehabilitation is a program of services administered by the Department of Veterans Affairs for service members and veterans with service-connected physical or mental disabilities. If persons are compensibly disabled and are found in need of rehabilitation services because they have an employment handicap, this program can prepare them for a suitable job; get and keep that job; assist persons to become fully productive and independent.

9037 Department of Veterans Benefits

810 Vermont Avenue NW
Washington, DC 20420

800-827-1000

Raymond Vogel, Chief Benefits

Furnishes compensation and pensions for disability and death to veterans and their dependents. Provides vocational rehabilitation services, including counseling, training, assistance and more towards employment, to blinded veterans disabled as a result of service in the armed forces during World War II, Korea and the Vietnam era; also provides rehabilitation services to certain peace-time veterans.

9038 Disabled American Veterans

PO Box 14301
Cincinnati, OH 45250   606-441-7300
FAX: 859-441-1416
www.dav.org

Advises veterans of their rights and employers of their obligations, under the Rehabilitation Act, the Americans with Disabilities Act, and legislation governing the employment and training of Vietnam era veterans with disabilities.

9039 Federal Benefits for Veterans and Dependents

Government Printing Office
Washington, DC 20402   202-512-1067
800-827-1000

Offers information on benefits for veterans and their families.

93 pages
ISBN 0-16048 -58-

9040 Hospitalized Veterans Writing Project

5920 Nall Avenue
Suite 105
Mission, KS 66202   913-432-1214

Charlotte Black, Secretary

Individuals and organizations united to encourage hospitalized veterans to write for pleasure and rehabilitation during the hospital stay. Maintains speakers' bureau and audio tape version for the blind. Bestows numerous monetary awards in six areas: article; book review; cartoon and drawing; light verse; poetry and short story. *$ 15.00*

64 pages Magazine
ISSN 0504-07 9

9041 U.S. Department of Veterans Affairs National Headquarters

1120 Vermont Avenue NW
Washington, DC 20420   202-273-5400
800-827-1000
e-mail: washingtondc.query@vba.va.gov
www.va.gov

Togo D. West, Jr., Secretary of Veterans Affairs
Hershel W. Gober, Deputy Secretary of Vet. Affairs

Administers the laws providing benefits and other services to veterans, their dependents, and their beneficiaries. Acts as their principal advocate in ensuring that they recieve medical care, benefits, social support, and lasting memorials promoting the health, welfare, and dignity of all veterans in recognition of their service to this nation. As the DVA heads into the 21st century, they will strive to meet the needs of the Nation's veterans today and tomorrow.

9042 US Veteran's Administration

810 Vermont Avenue NW
Washington, DC 20420   202-273-5400

Provides a wide range of services for those who have been in the military and their dependents, as well as offering information on driver assessment and education programs.

Alabama

9043 Alabama VA Regional Office

Veterans Benefits Administration, US Dept. of V.A.
345 Perry Hill Road
Montgomery, AL   36109
800-827-1000
e-mail: montgomery.query@vba.va.gov
www.va.gov

9044 Birmingham VA Medical Center

Veterans Health Administration, US Dept. of V.A.
700 South 19th Street
Birmingham, AL   35233   205-933-8101
800-827-1000
e-mail: g.vhacss@forum.va.gov
www.va.gov

9045 Central Alabama Veterans Health Care

Veterans Health Administration, US Dept. of V.A.
2400 Hospital Road
Tuskegee, AL   36083   334-727-0550
800-827-1000
e-mail: g.vhacss@forum.va.gov
www.va.gov

9046 Central Alabama Veterans Healthcare System

Veterans Health Administration, US Dept. of V.A.
West Campus
215 Perry Hill Road
Montgomery, AL   36109   334-272-4670
800-827-1000
e-mail: g.vhacss@forum.va.gov
www.va.gov

9047 Tuscaloosa VA Medical Center

Veterans Health Administration, US Dept. of V.A.
3701 Loop Road, East
Tuscaloosa, AL   35404   205-554-2000
FAX: 205-554-2845
www.va.gov

Donna Channell, Director Public Affairs

Alaska

9048 Anchorage Regional Office

Veterans Benefits Administration, US Dept. of V.A.
2925 DeBarr Road
Anchorage, AK   99508
800-827-1000
e-mail: anchorage.query@vba.va.gov
www.va.gov

9049 Department of Alaska, DAV Department of Alaska

2352 Broadmoor Avenue
Fairbanks, AK   99709   907-479-4008
FAX: 907-479-4007
e-mail: WebVet

Anne M. Ruppert, Adjutant/Treasurer

Arizona

9050 Carl T. Hayden VA Medical Center

Veterans Health Administration, US Dept. of V.A.
650 East Indian School Road
Phoenix, AZ   85012
800-827-1000
e-mail: g.vhacss@forum.va.gov
www.va.gov

Carl Hayden

9051 Northern Arizona VA Health Center

Veterans Health Administration, US Dept. of V.A.
500 North Highway 89
Prescott, AZ   86313   520-445-4860
800-827-1000
e-mail: g.vhacss@forum.va.gov
www.va.gov

9052 Phoenix Regional Office

Veterans Benefits Administration, US Dept. of V.A.
3225 North Central Avenue
Phoenix, AZ   85012
800-827-1000
e-mail: phoenix.query@vba.va.gov
www.va.gov

9053 Southern Arizona VA Healthcare System

Veterans Health Administration, US Dept. of V.A.
3601 South 6th Avenue
Tucson, AZ   85723   520-792-1450
800-827-1000
e-mail: g.vhacss@forum.va.gov
www.va.gov

Arkansas

9054 Eugene J. Towbin Healthcare Center

Veterans Health Administration, US Dept. of V.A.
2200 Fort Roots Drive
North Little Rock, AR   72114   501-396-4444
800-827-1000
e-mail: g.vhacss@forum.va.gov
www.va.gov

9055 Fayetteville VA Medical Center

Veterans Health Administration, US Dept. of V.A.
1100 North College Avenue
Fayetteville, AR   72703   501-444-4301
800-827-1000
e-mail: g.vhacss@forum.va.gov
www.va.gov

9056 John L. McClellan Memorial Hospital

Veterans Health Administration, US Dept. of V.A.
4300 West 7th Street
Little Rock, AR   72205   501-257-1000
800-827-1000
e-mail: g.vhacss@forum.va.gov
www.va.gov

9057 North Little Rock Regional Office

Veterans Benefits Administration, US Dept. of V.A.
Building 65, Fort Roots
PO Box 1280
Little Rock   ,, AR 72115
               800-827-1000
e-mail: littlerock.query@vba.va.gov
www.va.gov

California

9058 Jerry L. Pettis Memorial VA Medical Center

Veterans Health Administration, US Dept. of V.A.
11201 Benton Street
Loma Linda, CA 92357   909-825-7084
               800-827-1000
e-mail: g.vhacss@forum.va.gov
www.va.gov

9059 Long Beach VA Medical Center

Veterans Health Administration, US Dept. of V.A.
5901 East 7th Street
Long Beach, CA 90822   562-597-3592
               800-827-1000
e-mail: g.vhacss@forum.va.gov
www.va.gov

9060 Los Angeles Regional Office

Veterans Benefits Administration, US Dept. of V.A.
Federal Building
11000 Wilshire Boulevard
Los Angeles, CA 90024
               800-827-1000
e-mail: losangeles.query@vba.va.gov
www.va.gov

9061 Martinez Center for Rehab & Extended Care

Veterans Health Administration, US Dept. of V.A.
150 Muir Road
Martinez, CA 94553   925-372-2665
               800-827-1000
e-mail: g.vhacss@forum.va.gov
www.va.gov

9062 Oakland VA Regional Office

Veterans Benefits Administration, US Dept. of V.A.
1301 Clay Street
Suite 1300N
Oakland, CA 94612
               800-827-1000
e-mail: oakland.query@vba.va.gov
www.va.gov

9063 Sacramento Medical Center

Veterans Health Administration, US Dept. of V.A.
10535 Hospital Way
Sacramento, CA 95655   916-366-5470
               800-827-1000
e-mail: g.vhacss@forum.va.gov
www.va.gov

9064 San Diego VA Regional Office

Veterans Benefits Administration, US Dept. of V.A.
8810 Rio San Diego Drive
San Diego, CA 92108
               800-827-1000
e-mail: oakland.query@vba.va.gov
www.va.gov

9065 San Francisco VA Medical Center

Veterans Health Administration, US Dept. of V.A.
4150 Clement Street
San Francisco, CA 94121   415-750-4810
               800-827-1000
          FAX: 415-750-2185
e-mail: g.vhacss@forum.va.gov
www.va.gov

9066 VA Central California Health Care Syste

Veterans Health Administration, US Dept. of V.A.
2615 East Clinton Avenue
Fresno, CA 93703   559-225-6100
          FAX: 559-268-6911
e-mail: g.vhacss@forum.va.gov
www.va.gov

9067 VA Greater Los Angeles Healthcare System

Veterans Health Administration, US Dept. of V.A.
11301 Willchire Boulevard
Los Angeles, CA 90073   310-478-3711
               800-827-1000
          FAX: 310-268-4848
e-mail: g.vhacss@forum.va.gov
www.va.gov

9068 VA Northern California Healthcare System

Veterans Health Administration, US Dept. of V.A.
150 Muir Road
Martinez, CA 94553   925-372-2179
               800-827-1000
          FAX: 925-372-2020
e-mail: g.vhacss@forum.va.gov
www.va.gov

9069 VA Palo Alto Healthcare System

Veterans Health Administration, US Dept. of V.A.
3801 Miranda Avenue
Palo Alto, CA 94304   650-493-5000
               800-827-1000
          FAX: 650-852-3228
e-mail: g.vhacss@forum.va.gov
www.palo-alto.med.va.gov

Elizabeth Joyce Freeman, Director

9070 VA Palo Alto Rehabilitation Research and Development Center

Department of Veterans Affairs
3801 Miranda Avenue MS153
Palo Alto, CA 94304   650-493-5000
          FAX: 650-493-4919
e-mail: info@roses.stanford.edu

Dennis R Carter PhD, Director
Charles G Burgar MD, Medical Director

Dedicated to developing innovative clinical treatments and assistive devices for physically disabled veterans; to improve mobility-ambulation and manipulation- in persons with neurologic or orthopaedic impairments, specifically targets four conditions that cuase significant loss of mobility to veterans as well as non-veterans: strok, spinal cord injury, arthritis and osteoporosis. Research includes basic experimental and theoretical investigations of tissue properties and muscular coordination.

9071 VA San Diego Healthcare System

Veterans Health Administration, US Dept. of V.A.
3350 La Jolla Village Drive
San Diego, CA   92161   858-552-8585
                               800-827-1000
e-mail: g.vhacss@forum.va.gov
www.va.gov

Colorado

9072 Boulder Vet Center

2336 Canyon Boulevard
Suite 103
Boulder, CO   80302   303-440-7306
FAX: 303-449-3907

Stew Brown, Ph.D., Team Leader

Offers trauma and readjustment from military and civilian life counseling and assistance with disability claims, military benefits and employment are provided.

9073 Colorado/Wyoming VA Medical Center

Veterans Benefits Administration, US Dept. of V.A.
155 Van Gordon Street
Lakewood, CO   80228
800-827-1000
e-mail: denver.query@vba.va.gov
www.va.gov

9074 Denver VA Medical Center

Veterans Health Administration, US Dept. of V.A.
1055 Clermont Street
Denver, CO   80220   303-399-8020
                               800-827-1000
e-mail: g.vhacss@forum.va.gov
www.va.gov

9075 Grand Junction VA Medical Center

Veterans Health Administration, US Dept. of V.A.
2121 North Avenue
Grand Junction, CO   81501   970-242-0731
                               800-827-1000
FAX: 970-244-1300
e-mail: g.vhacss@forum.va.gov
www.va.gov

9076 National Veterans Training Institute

University of Colorado at Denver
1100 Stout Street
Suite 300
Denver, CO   80204   303-871-2000
                               800-331-0562
FAX: 303-825-0977

Training for specialists who serve veterans with disabilities.

9077 Southern Colorado Healthcare System System

Veterans Health Administration, US Dept. of V.A.
1339 South Pueblo Boulevard
Pueblo, CO   81005   719-566-6193
                               888-544-6724
FAX: 719-560-1806
e-mail: g.vhacss@forum.va.gov
www.va.gov

Connecticut

9078 Disabled American Veterans - Connecticut

35 Cold Spring Road
Suite 315
Rocky Hill, CT   06067   203-639-8387

www.davct.org/pages/youcanhelp.html

9079 Hartford Regional Office

Veterans Benefits Administration, US Dept. of V.A.
450 Main Street
Hartford, CT   06103
800-827-1000
e-mail: hartford.query@vba.va.gov
www.va.gov

9080 VA Connecticut Healthcare System, Newington Division

Veterans Health Administration, US Dept. of V.A.
555 Willard Avenue
Newington, CT   06111   860-666-6951
                               800-827-1000
FAX: 860-667-6764
e-mail: g.vhacss@forum.va.gov
www.va.gov

The mission of VA Connecticut Healthcare Systems is to fulfill a nation's commitment to its veterans by providing quality healthcare, promoting health through prevention and maintaining excellence in teaching and research. Provides primary, secondary and tertiary care in medicine, geriatrics, neurology, psychiatry and surgery with an operating capacity of 211 hospital beds.

9081 VA Connecticut Healthcare System, West Haven

Veterans Health Administration, US Dept. of V.A.
950 Campbell Avenue
West Haven, CT   06516   203-934-5711
                               800-827-1000
FAX: 203-937-3878
e-mail: g.vhacss@forum.va.gov
www.va.gov

Delaware

9082 Delaware Commission of Veterans Affairs

Robbins Building
802 Silver Lake Boulevard,Suite 100
Kdover, DE   19904   302-739-2792
                               800-344-9900
FAX: 302-739-2794
e-mail: adavila@state.de.us
www.state.de.us/veteran/index.htm

Antonio Davila, Executive Director

9083 Delaware VA Regional Office

Veterans Benefits Administration, US Dept. of V.A.
1601 Kirkwood Highway
Wilmington, DE   19805
800-827-1000
e-mail: wilmington.query@vba.va.gov
www.va.gov

9084 Wilmington VA Medical

Veterans Health Administration, US Dept. of V.A.
1601 Kirkwood Highway
Wilmington, DE   19805   302-994-2511
800-827-1000
FAX: 302-633-5516
e-mail: g.vhacss@forum.va.gov
www.va.gov

District of Columbia

9085 Disabled American Veterans, National Service & Legislative Headquarters

807 Maine Avenue SW
Washington, DC   20024   202-554-3501

www.dav.org/about/contact_dav.html

9086 VA Medical Center, Washington D.C.

50 Irving Street NW
Washington, DC   20422   202-273-5400
888-553-0242
www.washington.med.va.gov

Acute general and specialized services in medicine, surgery, neurology, and psychiatry.

9087 Washington D.C. VA Medical Center

Veterans Health Administration, US Dept. of V.A.
50 Irving Street NW
Washington, DC   20422   202-745-8000
800-827-1000
FAX: 202-754-8530
e-mail: g.vhacss@forum.va.gov
www.va.gov

Florida

9088 Bay Pines VA Medical Center

Veterans Health Administration, US Dept. of V.A.
10000 Bay Pines Boulevard
Bay Pines, FL   33744   727-398-6661
800-827-1000
e-mail: g.vhacss@forum.va.gov
www.va.gov

9089 Gainesville Division, North Florida/South Georgia Veterans Healthcare System

Veterans Health Administration, US Dept. of V.A.
1601 Southwest Archer Road
Room 165A
Gainesville, FL   32608   352-376-1611
800-827-1000
FAX: 352-374-6113
e-mail: g.vhacss@forum.va.gov
www.va.gov

Richard Blount, Disabled Veterans Service Office

9090 James A. Haley VA Medical Center

Veterans Health Administration, US Dept. of V.A.
13000 Bruce B. Downs Boulevard
Tampa, FL   33612   813-972-2000
800-827-1000
e-mail: g.vhacss@forum.va.gov
www.va.gov

9091 Lake City Division, North Florida/South Georgia Veterans Healthcare System

Veterans Health Administration, US Dept. of V.A.
801 South Marion Street
Lake City, FL   32025   904-755-3016
800-827-1000
FAX: 904-758-3209
e-mail: g.vhacss@forum.va.gov
www.va.gov

9092 Miami VA Medical Center

Veterans Health Administration, US Dept. of V.A.
1201 Northwest 16th Street
Miami, FL   33125   305-324-4455
800-827-1000
e-mail: g.vhacss@forum.va.gov
www.va.gov

9093 St. Petersburg Regional Office

Veterans Benefits Administration, US Dept. of V.A.
9500 Ba Pines Boulevard
St. Petersburg, FL   33744
800-827-1000
e-mail: stpete.query@vba.va.gov
www.va.gov

9094 West Palm Beach VA Medical Center

Veterans Health Administration, US Dept. of V.A.
7305 North Military Trail
West Palm Beach, FL   33410   561-882-8262
800-827-1000
FAX: 561-882-6707
e-mail: g.vhacss@forum.va.gov
www.va.gov

Georgia

9095 Atlanta Regional Office

Veterans Benefits Administration, US Dept. of V.A.
730 Peachtree Street NE
Atlanta, GA   30365
800-827-1000
e-mail: atlanta.query@vba.va.gov
www.va.gov

9096 Atlanta VA Medical Center

Veterans Health Administration, US Dept. of V.A.
1670 Clairmont Road
Decatur, GA   30033   404-321-6111
800-827-1000
FAX: 404-728-7734
e-mail: g.vhacss@forum.va.gov
www.va.gov

9097 Augusta VA Medical Center

Veterans Health Administration, US Dept. of V.A.
One Freedom Way
Augusta, GA   30904   706-733-0188
800-827-1000
FAX: 706-823-3934
e-mail: g.vhacss@forum.va.gov
www.va.gov

9098   Carl Vinson VA Medical Center

Veterans Health Administration, US Dept. of V.A.
1826 Veteran's Boulevard
Dublin, GA   31021   912-272-1210
                                          800-827-1000
                             FAX: 912-277-2717
                    e-mail: g.vhacss@forum.va.gov
                                          www.va.gov

9099   Georgia Veterans Centers

922 W Peachtree Street NW
Atlanta, GA   30309
                             FAX: 404-347-7274

Veterans medical clinic offering disabled veterans
medical treatments.

Hawaii

9100   Hawaii Veterans Centers

Keewe Street
Suite 201
Hilo, HI   96720   808-969-3833
                             FAX: 808-969-2025

Veterans medical clinic offering disabled veterans
medical treatments.

9101   Honolulu VBA Regional Office

Veterans Benefits Administration, US Dept. of V.A.
300 Ala Moana Boulevard
Room 1004
Honolulu, HI   96850   808-541-2570
                                          800-827-1000
                e-mail: honolulu.query@vba.va.gov
                                          www.va.gov

9102   Spark M. Matsunaga VA Medical Center &
           Regional Office

Veterans Health Administration, US Dept. of V.A.
459 Patterson Road
Honolulu, HI   96819   808-433-1000
                                          800-827-1000
                             FAX: 808-433-0390
                    e-mail: g.vhacss@forum.va.gov
                                          www.va.gov

Idaho

9103   Boise Regional Office

Veterans Benefits Administration, US Dept. of V.A.
805 West Franklin Street
Boise, ID   83702
                                          800-827-1000
                    e-mail: boise.query@vba.va.gov
                                          www.va.gov

9104   Boise VA Medical Center

Veterans Health Administration, US Dept. of V.A.
500 West Fort Street
Boise, ID   83702   208-422-1000
                                          800-827-1000
                             FAX: 208-422-1326
                    e-mail: g.vhacss@forum.va.gov
                                          www.va.gov

9105   Idaho Division of Veterans' Affairs

320 Collins Road
Boise, ID   83702   208-334-3513
                             FAX: 208-334-2627
                    www.nasdva.com/idaho.html

Gary Bermeosolo, Administrator

Illinois

9106   Chicago-Lakeside VA Medical Center

Veterans Health Administration, US Dept. of V.A.
333 East Huron Street
Chicago, IL   60611   312-943-6600
                                          800-827-1000
                             FAX: 312-640-2248
                    e-mail: g.vhacss@forum.va.gov
                    norden1.com/~monty/visniz/535.htm

9107   Chicago-West Side VA Medical Center

Veterans Health Administration, US Dept. of V.A.
820 South Damen Avenue
Chicago, IL   60612   312-666-6500
                                          800-827-1000
                    e-mail: g.vhacss@forum.va.gov
                                          www.va.gov

Thomas Stelmack, OD, Director

Interdisciplinary team of optometry, ophthalmology,
low vision training specialists, psychology, social
work and audiology provide comprehensive low vision rehabilitation services for the partially sighted.

9108   Edward Hines Jr. Hospital

Veterans Health Administration, US Dept. of V.A.
Fifth Avenue & Roosevelt Road
Hines, IL   60141   708-202-8387
                                          800-827-1000
                             FAX: 708-202-2506
                    e-mail: g.vhacss@forum.va.gov
                    www.va.gov/sta/guide/facility.asp?ID=58

9109   Edward Hines, Jr. VA Hospital

5th Avenue & Roosevelt Road
Hines, IL   60141   708-202-8387

9110   Illinois VA Regional Office Center

Veterans Benefits Administration, US Dept. of V.A.
536 South Clark Street
Chicago, IL   60605
                                          800-827-1000
                    e-mail: chicago.query@vba.va.gov
                                          www.va.gov

9111   Marion VA Medical Center

Veterans Health Administration, US Dept. of V.A.
2401 West Main Street
Marion, IL   62959   618-997-5311
                                          800-827-1000
                    e-mail: g.vhacss@forum.va.gov
                                          www.va.gov

9112 North Chicago VA Medical Center

Veterans Health Administration, US Dept. of V.A.
3001 Green Bay Road
North Chicago, IL   60064   847-688-1900
                                            800-827-1000
e-mail: g.vhacss@forum.va.gov
www.va.gov

9113 VA Illiana Health Care System

Veterans Health Administration, US Dept. of V.A.
1900 East Main Street
Danville, IL   61832   217-442-8000
                                         800-827-1000
FAX: 217-554-4552
e-mail: g.vhacss@forum.va.gov
www.va.gov

Indiana

9114 Indianapolis Regional Office

Veterans Benefits Administration, US Dept. of V.A.
575 North Pennsylvania Street
Indianapolis, IN   46204   317-226-7860
                                            800-827-1000
e-mail: indianapolis.query@vba.va.gov
www.va.gov

9115 Richard L. Roudebush VA Medical Center

Veterans Health Administration, US Dept. of V.A.
1481 West 10th Street
Indianapolis, IN   46202   317-554-0000
                                            800-827-1000
FAX: 317-554-0127
e-mail: g.vhacss@forum.va.gov
www.va.gov

**9116 VA North Indiana Health Care System - Marion
Campus**

Veterans Health Administration, US Dept. of V.A.
1700 East 38th Street
Marion, IN   46953   765-674-3321
                                         800-827-1000
e-mail: g.vhacss@forum.va.gov
www.va.gov

**9117 VA North Indiana Health Care System - Fort
Wayne Campus**

Veterans Health Administration, US Dept. of V.A.
2121 Lake Avenue
Fort Wayne, IN   46805   219-426-5431
                                         800-827-1000
FAX: 219-460-1336
e-mail: g.vhacss@forum.va.gov
www.va.gov

Iowa

9118 Des Moines VA Medical Center

Veterans Health Administration, US Dept. of V.A.
3600 30th Street
Des Moines, IA   50310   515-699-5850
                                         800-827-1000
FAX: 515-699-5862
e-mail: g.vhacss@forum.va.gov
www.va.gov

9119 Des Moines VA Regional Office

Veterans Benefits Administration, US Dept. of V.A.
210 Walnut Street
Des Moines, IA   50309
                                         800-827-1000
e-mail: desmoines.query@vba.va.gov
www.va.gov

9120 Iowa City VA Medical Center

Veterans Health Administration, US Dept. of V.A.
Highway 6 West
Iowa City, IA   52246   319-338-0581
                                         800-827-1000
e-mail: g.vhacss@forum.va.gov
www.va.gov

Kirt A Sickels, Public Affairs Officer

Tertiary care facility, affiliated teaching hospital, and
research center seving an aging veteran populatiaon
in eastern Iowa and western Illinois. Satellite clinics
are located in Bettendord, Dubuque, and Waterloo,
Iowa and in Quincy and Galesburg, Illinois.

9121 Knoxville VA Medical Center

Veterans Health Administration, US Dept. of V.A.
1515 Pleasant Street
Knoxville, IA   50138   515-828-5000
                                         800-827-1000
FAX: 515-828-5124
e-mail: g.vhacss@forum.va.gov
www.va.gov

9122 VA Central Iowa Health Care System

3600 30th Street
Des Moines, IA   50130   515-699-5999
                                         FAX: 515-699-5214

Elaine Brewster, EEO Program Manager

Fulfilling the promise is our primary mission.

Kansas

9123 Colmery-O'Neil VA Medical Center

Veterans Health Administration, US Dept. of V.A.
2200 Gage Boulevard
Topeka, KS   66622   785-350-3111
                                         800-827-1000
e-mail: g.vhacss@forum.va.gov
www.va.gov

9124 Dwight D. Eisenhower VA Medical Center

Veterans Health Administration, US Dept. of V.A.
4101 South 4th Street
Leavenworth, KS   66048   913-682-2000
                                         800-827-1000
e-mail: g.vhacss@forum.va.gov
www.va.gov

9125 Kansas VA Regional Office

Veterans Benefits Administration, US Dept. of V.A.
5500 East Kellogg
Wichita, KS   67218
                                         800-827-1000
e-mail: wichita.query@vba.va.gov
www.va.gov

9126 Wichita VA Medical Center

Veterans Health Administration, US Dept. of V.A.
5500 East Kellogg Drive
Wichita, KS 67218   316-685-2221
                                  800-827-1000
          e-mail: g.vhacss@forum.va.gov
                                  www.va.gov

Kentucky

9127 Lexington VA Medical Center

Veterans Health Administration, US Dept. of V.A.
Lexington, KY 40511   606-233-4511
                                  800-352-4000
          e-mail: g.vhacss@forum.va.gov
      www.va.gov/sta/guide/facility.asp?ID=72

9128 Louisville VA Medical Center

Veterans Health Administration, US Dept. of V.A.
800 Zorn Avenue
Louisville, KY 40206   502-895-3401
                                  800-827-1000
          e-mail: g.vhacss@forum.va.gov
                                  www.va.gov

9129 Louisville VA Regional Office

Veterans Benefits Administration, US Dept. of V.A.
545 South 3rd Street
Louisville, KY 40202
                                  800-827-1000
       e-mail: louisville.query@vba.va.gov
                                  www.va.gov

Louisiana

9130 Alexandria VA Medical Center

Veterans Health Administration, US Dept. of V.A.
2495 Highway 71 North
Alexandria, LA 71301   318-473-0010
                                  800-827-1000
                            FAX: 318-483-5029
          e-mail: g.vhacss@forum.va.gov
                                  www.va.gov

9131 New Orleans VA Medical Center

Veterans Health Administration, US Dept. of V.A.
1601 Perdido Street
New Orleans, LA 70112   504-568-0811
                                  800-827-1000
                            FAX: 504-589-5210
          e-mail: g.vhacss@forum.va.gov
                                  www.va.gov

9132 New Orleans VA Regional Office

Veterans Benefits Administration, US Dept. of V.A.
701 Loyola Avenue
New Orleans, LA 70113
                                  800-827-1000
      e-mail: neworleans.query@vba.va.gov
                                  www.va.gov

9133 Shreveport VA Medical Center

Veterans Health Administration, US Dept. of V.A.
510 East Stoner Avenue
Shreveport, LA 71101   318-221-8411
                                  800-827-1000
                            FAX: 318-424-6156
          e-mail: g.vhacss@forum.va.gov
                                  www.va.gov

Maine

9134 Chapter 15 Disabled American Veterans

PO Box 544
Brunswick, ME 04011   207-677-6033

          e-mail: re.nee@verizon.net

Cliff Workman, Commander

9135 Disabled American Veterans - Maine

PO Box 3151
Togus, ME 04330   207-623-5725

              e-mail: dav@mint.net
                    www.mint.net/DAV/

9136 Maine VA Regional Office

Veterans Benefits Administration, US Dept. of V.A.
One VA Center
Togus, ME 04330
                                  800-827-1000
          e-mail: togus.query@vba.va.gov
                                  www.va.gov

9137 Togus VA Medical Center

Veterans Health Administration, US Dept. of V.A.
1 VA Center
Togus, ME 04330   207-623-8411
                                  800-827-1000
          e-mail: g.vhacss@forum.va.gov
                                  www.va.gov

Maryland

9138 Baltimore Regional Office

Veterans Benefits Administration, US Dept. of V.A.
31 Hopkins Plaza Federal Building
Baltimore, MD 21201
                                  800-827-1000
       e-mail: baltimore.query@vba.va.gov
                                  www.va.gov

9139 Baltimore VA Medical Center

Veterans Health Administration, US Dept. of V.A.
10 North Greene Street
Baltimore, MD 21201   410-605-7000
                                  800-463-6295
          e-mail: g.vhacss@forum.va.gov
     www.vamhcs.med.va.gov/balto/baltimor.htm

9140   Fort Howard VA Medical Center

Veterans Health Administration, US Dept. of V.A.
9600 North Point Road
Fort Howard, MD   21052   410-477-1800
                                 800-827-1000
          e-mail: g.vhacss@forum.va.gov
                                 www.va.gov

9141   Maryland Veterans Centers

6666 Security Boulevard
Suite 2
Gwynn Oak, MD   21207   410-277-3600
                            FAX: 410-277-3605

Veterans medical clinic offering disabled veterans
medical treatments.

9142   Perry Point VA Medical Center

Veterans Health Administration, US Dept. of V.A.
Perry Point, MD   21902   410-642-2411
                                 800-827-1000
          e-mail: g.vhacss@forum.va.gov
                                 www.va.gov

9143   VA Maryland Health Care System

10 N Greene Street
Baltimore, MD   21201   410-605-7000
                                 800-827-1000
                            FAX: 410-605-7900
          www.vamhcs.med.va.gov

R Daved Edwards, Chief, Public & Comm. Relations
Monica A Smith, Public Affairs Specialist

A dynamic and exciting health care organization that
is dedicated to providing quality, compassionate and
accessible care and service to Maryland's veterans.
As a part of one of the largest health care systems in
the United States, the VAMHCS has a reputation as
a leader in veterans' health care, reserch and education. Provides comprehensive service to veterans including medical, surgical, rehabilitative, nurological
and mental health care on both an inpatient and outpatient basis.

Massachusetts

9144   Boston VA Regional Office

Veterans Benefits Administration, US Dept. of V.A.
JFK Federal Building
Government Center
Boston, MA   02114
                                 800-827-1000
          e-mail: boston.query@vba.va.gov
                                 www.va.gov

9145   Edith Nourse Rogers Memorial Veterans Hospital

Veterans Health Administration, US Dept. of V.A.
200 Springs Road
Bedford, MA   01730
                                 800-827-1000
          e-mail: g.vhacss@forum.va.gov
                                 www.va.gov

9146   Northampton VA Medical Center

Veterans Health Administration, US Dept. of V.A.
421 North Main Street
Leeds, MA   01053   413-584-4040
                                 800-827-1000
                            FAX: 413-582-3121
          e-mail: g.vhacss@forum.va.gov
                                 www.va.gov

9147   VA Boston Healthcare System, Brockton Division

Veterans Health Administration, US Dept. of V.A.
940 Belmont Street
Brockton, MA   02310   508-583-4500
                                 800-827-1000
                            FAX: 617-323-7700
          e-mail: g.vhacss@forum.va.gov
                                 www.va.gov

9148   VA Boston Healthcare System, Jamaica Plain Campus

Veterans Health Administration, US Dept. of V.A.
150 South Huntington Avenue
Boston, MA   02130   617-232-9500
                                 800-827-1000
                            FAX: 617-278-4549
          e-mail: g.vhacss@forum.va.gov
                                 www.va.gov

9149   VA Boston Healthcare System, West Roxbury Division

Veterans Health Administration, US Dept. of V.A.
1400 VFW Parkway
West Roxbury, MA   02132   413-584-4040
                                 800-827-1000
                            FAX: 413-582-3121
          e-mail: g.vhacss@forum.va.gov
                                 www.va.gov

Michigan

9150   Aleda E. Lutz VA Medical Center

Veterans Health Administration, US Dept. of V.A.
1500 Weiss Street
Saginaw, MI   48602   517-793-2340
                                 800-827-1000
                            FAX: 517-791-2217
          e-mail: g.vhacss@forum.va.gov
                                 www.va.gov

9151   Ann Arbor VA Medical Center

Veterans Health Administration, US Dept. of V.A.
2215 Fuller Road
Ann Arbor, MI   48105   734-769-7100
                                 800-827-1000
                            FAX: 734-761-5398
          e-mail: g.vhacss@forum.va.gov
                                 www.va.gov

9152   Battle Creek VA Medical Center

Veterans Health Administration, US Dept. of V.A.
5500 Armstrong Road
Battle Creek, MI   49016   616-966-5600
                                 800-827-1000
                            FAX: 616-966-5483
          e-mail: g.vhacss@forum.va.gov
                                 www.va.gov

9153   Iron Mountain VA Medical Center

Veterans Health Administration, US Dept. of V.A.
325 East H Street
Iron Mountain, MI   49801   906-774-3300
       800-827-1000
       FAX: 906-779-3114
       e-mail: g.vhacss@forum.va.gov
       www.va.gov

9154   John D. Dingell VA Medical Center

Veterans Health Administration, US Dept. of V.A.
4646 John R.
Detroit, MI   48201   313-576-1000
       800-827-1000
       FAX: 313-576-1025
       e-mail: g.vhacss@forum.va.gov
       www.va.gov

9155   Michigan VA Regional Office

Veterans Benefits Administration, US Dept. of V.A.
Patrick V McNamara Federal Building
477 Michigan Avenue, Room 1400
Detroit, MI   48226
       800-827-1000
       e-mail: detroit.query@vba.va.gov
       www.va.gov

9156   Michigan Veterans Centers

1940 Eastern Avenue SE
Grand Rapids, MI   49507   616-243-0385
       FAX: 616-243-5390

Veterans medical clinic offering disabled veterans
medical treatments.

Minnesota

9157   Minneapolis VA Medical Center

Veterans Health Administration, US Dept. of V.A.
One Veterans Drive
Minneapolis, MN   55417   612-725-2000
       800-827-1000
       FAX: 612-725-2049
       e-mail: g.vhacss@forum.va.gov
       www.va.gov

9158   St. Cloud VA Medical Center

Veterans Health Administration, US Dept. of V.A.
4801 8th Street North
St. Cloud, MN   56303   320-252-1670
       800-827-1000
       FAX: 320-255-6494
       e-mail: g.vhacss@forum.va.gov
       www.va.gov

9159   St. Paul Regional Office

Veterans Benefits Administration, US Dept. of V.A.
One Federal Drive
Fort Snelling
St. Paul, MN   55111
       800-827-1000
       e-mail: stpaul.query@vba.va.gov
       www.va.gov

Mississippi

9160   Biloxi/Gulfport VA Medical Center

Veterans Health Administration, US Dept. of V.A.
400 Veterans Avenue
Biloxi, MS   39531   228-523-5000
       800-827-1000
       e-mail: g.vhacss@forum.va.gov
       www.va.gov

9161   Jackson Regional Office

Veterans Benefits Administration, US Dept. of V.A.
1600 East Woodrow Wilson Avenue
Jackson, MS   39216
       800-827-1000
       e-mail: jackson.query@vba.va.gov
       www.va.gov

9162   Jackson VA Medical Center

Veterans Health Administration, US Dept. of V.A.
1500 East Woodrow Wilson Drive
Jackson, MS   39216   601-362-4471
       800-827-1000
       FAX: 601-364-1359
       e-mail: g.vhacss@forum.va.gov
       www.va.gov

Missouri

9163   Harry S. Truman Memorial

Veterans Health Administration, US Dept. of V.A.
800 Hospital Drive
Columbia, MO   65201   573-443-2511
       800-827-1000
       FAX: 573-814-6600
       e-mail: g.vhacss@forum.va.gov
       www.va.gov

9164   John J. Pershing VA Medical Center

Veterans Health Administration, US Dept. of V.A.
1500 North Westwood Boulevard
Poplar Bluff, MO   63901   573-686-4151
       800-827-1000
       e-mail: g.vhacss@forum.va.gov
       www.va.gov

9165   Kansas City VA Medical Center

Veterans Health Administration, US Dept. of V.A.
4801 Linwood Boulevard
Kansas City, MO   64128   816-861-4700
       800-827-1000
       e-mail: g.vhacss@forum.va.gov
       www.va.gov

Juliette Leach, EEO Manager
Thirza Thompson, SEPM Manager

The Kansas City VA Medical Center is a modern,
well-equipped teriary care inpatient and outpatient
center. As the third largest teaching hospital in the
metropolitan area, it maintains educational affiliations with the University of Kansas School of Medicine.

9166 Missouri Veterans Centers

3931 Main Street
Kansas City, MO   64111　　　816-753-1866
　　　　　　　　　　　　　FAX: 816-753-2328

Veterans medical clinic offering disabled veterans medical treatments.

9167 St. Louis Regional Office

Veterans Benefits Administration, US Dept. of V.A.
Federal Building
400 South, 18th Street
St. Louis, MO   63103

　　　　　　　　　　800-827-1000
　　　e-mail: stlouis.query@vba.va.gov
　　　　　　　　　　www.va.gov

9168 St. Louis VA Medical Center

Veterans Health Administration, US Dept. of V.A.
Jefferson Barracks Division #1
Jefferson Barracks Drive
St. Louis, MO   63125　　　314-652-4100
　　　　　　　　　　　　800-827-1000
　　　e-mail: g.vhacss@forum.va.gov
　　　　　　　　　　www.va.gov

9169 Vet Center

405 E Superior Street
Duluth, MN   55802　　　218-722-8654
　　　　　　　　　FAX: 218-723-8212

*Michael J. Muller, PhD, Psychologist & Team
Leader*
Cynthia Macaulay, M. Ed., Counselor
Rob Evanson, Counselor

Counseling, social services and benefits assistance for combat veterans and those sexually traumatized in the military.

Montana

9170 Montana VA Regional Office

Veterans Benefits Administration, US Dept. of V.A.
Williams Street
Fort Harrison, MT   59636

　　　　　　　　　　800-827-1000
　　　e-mail: ftharrison.query@vba.va.gov
　　　　　　　　　　www.va.gov

9171 VA Montana Healthcare System

Veterans Health Administration, US Dept. of V.A.
William Street
Fort Harrison, MT   59636　　406-442-6410
　　　　　　　　　　　　800-827-1000
　　　　　　　　　　FAX: 406-447-7965
　　　e-mail: g.vhacss@forum.va.gov
　　　　　　　　　　www.va.gov

9172 Vet Center

1234 Avenue C
Billings, MT   59102　　　406-657-6071
　　　　　　　　　FAX: 406-657-6603

Bob Phillips, MSW, Team Leader
Luanne Oakland, MS, Office Manager
Barry Osgard, MS, Counselor

Readjustment counseling service for counseling veterans who are having difficulty adjusting from military service especially those diagnosed with PTSD.

Nebraska

9173 Grand Island VA Medical System

Veterans Health Administration, US Dept. of V.A.
2201 North Brodwell Avenue
Grand Island, NE   68803　　　308-382-3660
　　　　　　　　　　　　　　800-827-1000
　　　e-mail: g.vhacss@forum.va.gov
　　　　　　　　　　www.va.gov

9174 Lincoln Regional Office

Veterans Benefits Administration, US Dept. of V.A.
5631 South 48th Street
Lincoln, NE   68516
　　　　　　　　　　　800-827-1000
　　　e-mail: lincoln.query@vba.va.gov
　　　　　　　　　　www.va.gov

9175 Lincoln VA Medical Center

Veterans Health Administration, US Dept. of V.A.
600 South 70th Street
Lincoln, NE   68510　　　402-489-3802
　　　　　　　　　　　　800-827-1000
　　　　　　　　　　FAX: 402-486-7840
　　　e-mail: g.vhacss@forum.va.gov
　　　　　　　　　　www.va.gov

9176 Omaha VA Medical Center

Veterans Health Administration, US Dept. of V.A.
4101 Woolworth Avenue
Omaha, NE   68105　　　402-346-8800
　　　　　　　　　　　800-827-1000
　　　　　　　　　FAX: 402-449-0684
　　　e-mail: g.vhacss@forum.va.gov
　　　　　　　　　　www.va.gov

Nevada

9177 Las Vegas Veterans Center

1040 E Sahara Avenue
Suite 102
Las Vegas, NV   89104　　　702-388-6369
　　　　　　　　　　　FAX: 702-388-6664

Gerald Eusf, Clinical Coordinator, LCSW
Daryl Harding, Resident Counselor, LCSW
Matt Watson, Team Leader, MSW

Veterans clinical counseling center for veterans and their dependent individual and group counseling, marital and family counseling, alcohol and drug assessment referral or treatment. Community education and consultation, employment counseling.

9178 Reno Regional Office

Veterans Benefits Administration, US Dept. of V.A.
1201 Terminal Way
Reno, NV   89520

　　　　　　　　　　800-827-1000
　　　e-mail: reno.query@vba.va.gov
　　　　　　　　　　www.va.gov

9179 VA Sierra Nevada Healthcare System

Veterans Health Administration, US Dept. of V.A.
1000 Locust Street
Reno, NV 89520   775-786-7200
                                   800-827-1000
                              FAX: 775-328-1464
                                   www.va.gov

Lisa Howard, Office of the Director

9180 VA Southern Nevada Healthcare System

Veterans Health Administration, US Dept. of V.A.
1700 Vegas Drive
Las Vegas, NV 89106   702-636-3000
                                   800-827-1000
                              FAX: 707-636-4000
e-mail: g.vhacss@forum.va.gov
                                   www.va.gov

New Hampshire

9181 Manchester Regional Office

Veterans Benefits Administration, US Dept. of V.A.
Norris Cotton Federal Building
275 Chestnut Street
Manchester, NH 03101
                                   800-827-1000
e-mail: manchester.query@vba.va.gov
                                   www.va.gov

9182 Manchester VA Medical Center

Veterans Health Administration, US Dept. of V.A.
718 Smyth Road
Manchester, NH 03104   603-624-4366
                                   800-827-1000
e-mail: g.vhacss@forum.va.gov
                                   www.va.gov

9183 New Hampshire Veterans Centers

103 Liberty Street
Manchester, NH 03104   603-668-7060
                              FAX: 603-666-7404

Caryl Ahern, MSW, Team Leader
Paulette Landry, Office Manager
Veterans clinic offering combat veterans outpatient
counseling

New Jersey

**9184 Disabled American Veterans - Ocean County
Memorial Chapter #24**

PO Box 1806
Toms River, NJ 08754   732-929-0907

e-mail: bvenga@thecore.com
http://community.nj.com/cc/dav24

Mary Bencivenga, Contact

**9185 Disabled American Veterans, New Jersey
Northern Valley Chapter 32**

PO Box 505
8 Veterans Plaza
Bergenfield, NJ 07621   201-384-0001

e-mail: DAV32GIN@aol.com
www.njdavchapter32.big
step.com/homepage.html

Virginia McAleer-Hujber, Adjutant

**9186 East Orange Campus of the VA New Jersey
Healthcare System**

Veterans Health Administration, US Dept. of V.A.
385 Tremont Avenue
East Orange, NJ 07018   973-676-1000
                                   800-827-1000
                              FAX: 973-676-4226
e-mail: g.vhacss@forum.va.gov
                                   www.va.gov

**9187 Lyons Campus of the VA New Jersey Healthcare
System**

Veterans Health Administration, US Dept. of V.A.
151 Knollcroft Road
Lyons, NJ 07939   908-647-0180
                                   800-827-1000
                              FAX: 908-647-3452
e-mail: g.vhacss@forum.va.gov
                                   www.va.gov

9188 Newark Regional Office

Veterans Benefits Administration, US Dept. of V.A.
20 Washington Place
Newark, NJ 07102
                                   800-827-1000
e-mail: newark.query@vba.va.gov
                                   www.va.gov

New Mexico

9189 Albuquerque Regional Office

Veterans Benefits Administration, US Dept. of V.A.
Danis Chevez Federal Building
500 Gold Avenue, Southwest
Albuquerque, NM 87102
                                   800-827-1000
e-mail: albuquerque.query@vba.va.gov
                                   www.va.gov

9190 New Mexico VA Healthcare System

Veterans Health Administration, US Dept. of V.A.
1501 San Pedro Drive SE
Albuquerque, NM 87108   505-265-1711
                                   800-827-1000
                              FAX: 505-256-2855
e-mail: g.vhacss@forum.va.gov
                                   www.va.gov

9191 New Mexico Veterans Centers

PO Box 927
TRC, NM 87901   505-894-4200

Veterans medical clinic offering disabled veterans
medical treatments.

New York

9192 Albany VA Medical Center: Samuel S. Stratton

Veterans Health Administration, US Dept. of V.A.
113 Holland Avenue
Albany, NY   12208
518-462-3311
800-827-1000
FAX: 518-462-0528
e-mail: g.vhacss@forum.va.gov
www.va.gov

Linda Blumenstock, Director, Marketing

9193 Albany Vet Center

875 Central Avenue
Albany, NY   12206
518-438-2505
FAX: 518-458-8613

James C. Garrett, Ph.D., Team Leader
Provides readjustment counseling for combat veterans, benefits and job counseling.

9194 Bath VA Medical Center

Veterans Health Administration, US Dept. of V.A.
76 Veterans Medical Center
Bath, NY   14810
607-664-4000
800-827-1000
FAX: 607-664-4000
e-mail: g.vhacss@forum.va.gov
www.va.gov

9195 Bronx VA Medical Center

Veterans Health Administration, US Dept. of V.A.
130 West Kingsbridge Road
Bronx, NY   10468
718-584-9000
800-827-1000
e-mail: g.vhacss@forum.va.gov
www.va.gov

9196 Brooklyn Campus of the VA NY Harbor Healthcare System

Veterans Health Administration, US Dept. of V.A.
800 Poly Place
Brooklyn, NY   11209
718-836-6600
800-827-1000
e-mail: g.vhacss@forum.va.gov
www.va.gov

9197 Buffalo Regional Office

Veterans Benefits Administration, US Dept. of V.A.
Federal Building
111 West Huron Street
Buffalo, NY   14202
800-827-1000
e-mail: buffalo.query@vba.va.gov
www.va.gov

9198 Canandiagua VA Medical Center

Veterans Health Administration, US Dept. of V.A.
400 Fort Hill Avenue
Canandaigua, NY   14424
716-394-2000
800-827-1000
e-mail: g.vhacss@forum.va.gov
www.va.gov

9199 Castle Point Campus of the VA Hudson Valley Healthcare System

Veterans Health Administration, US Dept. of V.A.
Castle Point, NY   12511
914-831-2000
800-827-1000
e-mail: g.vhacss@forum.va.gov
www.va.gov

9200 New York City Campus of the VA NY Harbor Healthcare System

Veterans Health Administration, US Dept. of V.A.
423 East 23rd Street
New York, NY   10010
212-686-7500
800-827-1000
FAX: 212-951-3487
e-mail: g.vhacss@forum.va.gov
www.va.gov

9201 New York Regional Office

Veterans Benefits Administration, US Dept. of V.A.
245 West Houston Street
New York, NY   10014
800-827-1000
e-mail: newyork.query@vba.va.gov
www.va.gov

9202 Northport VA Medical Center

Veterans Health Administration, US Dept. of V.A.
79 Middlevale Road
Northport, NY   11768
516-261-4400
800-827-1000
e-mail: g.vhacss@forum.va.gov
www.va.gov

9203 Syracuse VA Medical Center

Veterans Health Administration, US Dept. of V.A.
800 Irving Avenue
Syracuse, NY   13210
315-476-7461
800-827-1000
e-mail: g.vhacss@forum.va.gov
www.va.gov

9204 Torah Alliance of Families of Kids with Disabilities

TAFKID
1433 Coney Island Avenue
Brooklyn, NY   11230
718-252-2236
FAX: 718-252-2216
e-mail: tafkid@idt.net

Juby Shapiro, President & Programs Director
Serves over 900 families whose children have a variety of disabilities and special needs. Many of these families are large families in the low socioeconomic level. Offers monthly meetings, guest lectures, parent matching, information of new developments in software, technology and techniques, sibling support groups, pen pal lists, audio and video library, alternative medicine and nutrition information and education on legal awareness and rights of disabled citizens.

9205 VA Hudson Valley Health Care System

PO Box 100
Montrose, NY   10548
845-737-4400
FAX: 845-788-4244

9206 VA Western NY Healthcare System, Batavia

Veterans Health Administration, US Dept. of V.A.
222 Richmond Avenue
Batavia, NY 14020   716-343-7500
                                      800-827-1000
                     e-mail: g.vhacss@forum.va.gov
                                      www.va.gov

9207 VA Western NY Healthcare System, Buffalo

Veterans Health Administration, US Dept. of V.A.
3495 Bailey Avenue
Buffalo, NY 14215   716-834-9200
                                      800-827-1000
                     e-mail: g.vhacss@forum.va.gov
                                      www.va.gov

North Carolina

9208 Asheville VA Medical Center

Veterans Health Administration, US Dept. of V.A.
1100 Tunnel Road
Asheville, NC 28805   828-298-7911
                                      800-827-1000
                                 FAX: 828-299-2502
                     e-mail: g.vhacss@forum.va.gov
                                      www.va.gov

9209 Charlotte Vet Center

223 S Brevard Street
Suite 103
Charlotte, NC 28202   704-333-6107
                                 FAX: 704-344-6470

Loretta Deaton, Team Leader

Preadjustment Counseling for Combat Veterans with
Post Traumatic Stress Disorder (PTSD).

9210 Durham VA Medical Center

Veterans Health Administration, US Dept. of V.A.
508 Fulton Street
Durham, NC 27705   919-286-0411
                                      800-827-1000
                                 FAX: 919-286-6825
                     e-mail: g.vhacss@forum.va.gov
                                      www.va.gov

9211 Fayetteville VA Medical Center

Veterans Health Administration, US Dept. of V.A.
2300 Ramsey Street
Fayetteville, NC 28301   910-488-2120
                                      800-827-1000
                                 FAX: 910-822-7927
                     e-mail: g.vhacss@forum.va.gov
                                      www.va.gov

**9212 Franklin Delano Roosevelt Campus of the VA
Hudson Valley Healthcare System**

Veterans Health Administration, US Dept. of V.A.
Route 9A, 622 Albany Post Road
PO Box 100
Montrose, NC 10548   914-737-4400
                                      800-887-2001
                                 FAX: 800-997-2817
                     e-mail: g.vhacss@forum.va.gov
                                      www.va.gov

9213 W.G. Hefner VA Medical Center

Veterans Health Administration, US Dept. of V.A.
1601 Brenner Avenue
Salisbury, NC 28301   704-638-9000
                                      800-827-1000
                                 FAX: 704-638-3395
                     e-mail: g.vhacss@forum.va.gov
                                      www.va.gov

9214 Winston-Salem Regional Office

Veterans Benefits Administration, US Dept. of V.A.
Federal Building
251 North Main Street
Winston-Salem, NC 27155
                                      800-827-1000
                     e-mail: winsalem.query@vba.va.gov
                                      www.va.gov

North Dakota

9215 Fargo VA Medical Center

Veterans Health Administration, US Dept. of V.A.
2101 Elm Street
Fargo, ND 58102
                                      800-827-1000
                     e-mail: g.vhacss@forum.va.gov
                                      www.va.gov

9216 North Dakota Department of Veterans' Affairs

PO Box 9003
1411 32nd Street South
Fargo, ND 58106   701-239-7165
                                 FAX: 701-239-7166
                     www.nasdva.com/northdakota.html

Ray Harkema, Commissioner

9217 North Dakota VA Regional Office

Veterans Benefits Administration, US Dept. of V.A.
2101 Elm Street
Fargo, ND 58102
                                      800-827-1000
                     e-mail: fargo.query@vba.va.gov
                                      www.va.gov

Ohio

9218 Chillicothe VA Medical Center

Veterans Health Administration, US Dept. of V.A.
17273 State Route 104
Chillicothe, OH 45601   740-773-1141
                                      800-827-1000
                                 FAX: 740-772-7023
                     e-mail: g.vhacss@forum.va.gov
                                      www.va.gov

9219 Cincinnati VA Medical Center

Veterans Health Administration, US Dept. of V.A.
3200 Vine Street
Cincinnati, OH 45220   513-861-3100
                                      800-827-1000
                                 FAX: 513-475-6500
                     e-mail: g.vhacss@forum.va.gov
                                      www.va.gov

9220 Cincinnati Veterans Centers

801B W 8th Street
Suite 126
Cincinnati, OH   45203   513-741-5600
                                 FAX: 513-763-3505

Veterans medical clinic offering disabled veterans
medical treatments.

9221 Cleveland Regional Office

Veterans Benefits Administration, US Dept. of V.A.
A.J. Celebrezze Federal Building
1240 East 9th Street
Cleveland, OH   44199

                                 800-827-1000
         e-mail: cleveland.query@vba.va.gov
                                 www.va.gov

9222 Dayton VA Medical Center

Veterans Health Administration, US Dept. of V.A.
4100 West 3rd Street
Dayton, OH   45428   937-268-6511
                                 800-827-1000
                    FAX: 937-262-2179
             e-mail: g.vhacss@forum.va.gov
                                 www.va.gov

9223 Louis Stokes VA Medical Center

Veterans Health Administration, US Dept. of V.A.
10701 East Boulevard
Cleveland, OH   44106   440-526-3030
                                 800-827-1000
                    FAX: 440-838-6017
             e-mail: g.vhacss@forum.va.gov
                                 www.va.gov

Oklahoma

9224 Muskogee VA Medical Center

Veterans Benefits Administration, US Dept. of V.A.
1011 Honor Heights Drive
Muskogee, OK   74401   918-683-3261
                                 800-827-1000
         e-mail: muskogee.query@vba.va.gov
                                 www.va.gov

9225 Oklahoma Veterans Centers Vet Center

3033 N Walnut Avenue
Suite W101
Oklahoma City, OK   73105   405-528-5583
                                 FAX: 405-270-5125

Peter Sharp, Team Leader
PTSP Counseling for all combat Veterans and victims
of sexual trauma/sexual harassment.

9226 Oklahome City VA Medical Center

Veterans Health Administration, US Dept. of V.A.
921 Northeast 13th Street
Oklahoma City, OK   73104   405-270-0501
                                 800-827-1000
                    FAX: 405-270-1560
             e-mail: g.vhacss@forum.va.gov
                                 www.va.gov

Steven J. Gentling, Director
Barbara C. Watkins, Associate Director
D. Robert McCaffree, Chief of Staff

Oregon

9227 Oregon Health Sciences University

3181 SW Sam Jackson Park Road
Portland, OR   97201   503-418-4016

Thomas Talboe, M.D.
Offers services for the totally blind, legally blind,
visually impaired, mentally retarded blind and more
with health, counseling, educational, recreational, rehabilitation, computer training and professional
training services.

9228 Portland Regional Office

Veterans Benefits Administration, US Dept. of V.A.
1220 Southwest 3rd Avenue
Portland, OR   97204

                                 800-827-1000
          e-mail: portland.query@vba.va.gov
                                 www.va.gov

9229 Portland VA Medical Center

Veterans Health Administration, US Dept. of V.A.
3710 SW US Veterans Hospital Road
PO Box 1034
Portland, OR   97201   503-220-8262
                                 800-827-1000
                    FAX: 503-273-5319
             e-mail: g.vhacss@forum.va.gov
                                 www.va.gov

9230 Roseburg VA Medical Center

Veterans Health Administration, US Dept. of V.A.
913 NW Garden Valley Boulevard
Roseburg, OR   97470   541-440-1000
                                 800-827-1000
                    FAX: 541-440-1225
             e-mail: g.vhacss@forum.va.gov
                                 www.va.gov

9231 White City VA Domiciliary

Veterans Health Administration, US Dept. of V.A.
8495 Crater Lake Highway
White City, OR   97503   541-826-2111
                                 800-827-1000
             e-mail: g.vhacss@forum.va.gov
                                 www.va.gov

Pennsylvania

9232 Butler VA Medical Center

Veterans Health Administration, US Dept. of V.A.
325 New Castle Road
Butler, PA   16001   724-287-4781
                                 800-827-1000
                    FAX: 724-282-4408
             e-mail: g.vhacss@forum.va.gov
                                 www.va.gov

9233 Coatesville VA Medical Center

Veterans Health Administration, US Dept. of V.A.
1400 Black Horse Hill Road
Coatesville, PA   19320   610-384-7711
                                 800-827-1000
             e-mail: g.vhacss@forum.va.gov
                                 www.va.gov

9234 Department of Veterans Affairs Medical Center -
Altoona
Altoona, PA 16602

9235 Erie VA Medical Center

Veterans Health Administration, US Dept. of V.A.
135 East 38th Street
Erie, PA 16504 814-868-8661
800-827-1000
e-mail: g.vhacss@forum.va.gov
www.va.gov

9236 James E. Van Zandt VA Medical Center

Veterans Health Administration, US Dept. of V.A.
2907 Pleasant Valley Boulevard
Altoona, PA 16602 814-943-8164
800-827-1000
FAX: 814-940-7898
e-mail: g.vhacss@forum.va.gov
www.va.gov

9237 Lebabon VA Medical Center

Veterans Health Administration, US Dept. of V.A.
1700 South Lincoln Avenue
Lebanon, PA 17042
800-827-1000
FAX: 717-228-6045
e-mail: g.vhacss@forum.va.gov
www.va.gov

9238 Pennsylvania Veterans Centers

G Daniel Baldwin Building
1000 State Street
Suite 2
Erie, PA 16501
FAX: 814-456-5464

Veterans medical clinic offering disabled veterans
medical treatments.

9239 Philadelphia Regional Office and Insurance
Center

Veterans Benefits Administration, US Dept. of V.A.
5000 Wissahickon Avenue
Philadelphia, PA 19101
800-827-1000
e-mail: phillyro.query@vba.va.gov
www.va.gov

9240 Philadelphia VA Medical Center

Veterans Health Administration, US Dept. of V.A.
University and Woodland Avenues
Philadelphia, PA 19104 215-823-5800
800-827-1000
e-mail: g.vhacss@forum.va.gov
www.va.gov

9241 Pittsburgh Regional Office

Veterans Benefits Administration, US Dept. of V.A.
1000 Liberty Avenue
Pittsburgh, PA 15222
800-827-1000
e-mail: pittsburgh.query@vba.va.gov
www.va.gov

9242 VA Pittsburgh Healthcare System, University
Drive Division

Veterans Health Administration, US Dept. of V.A.
University Drive
Pittsburgh, PA 15240 412-688-6901
800-827-1000
FAX: 412-688-6000
e-mail: g.vhacss@forum.va.gov
www.va.gov

9243 VA Pittsburgh Healthcare System, Highland
Drive Division

Veterans Health Administration, US Dept. of V.A.
7180 Highland Drive
Pittsburgh, PA 15206 412-365-4900
800-827-1000
e-mail: g.vhacss@forum.va.gov
www.va.gov

9244 Wilkes-Barre VA Medical Center

Veterans Health Administration, US Dept. of V.A.
1111 East End Boulevard
Wilkes-Barre, PA 18711 570-824-3521
800-827-1000
e-mail: g.vhacss@forum.va.gov
www.va.gov

Rhode Island

9245 Providence Regional Office

Veterans Benefits Administration, US Dept. of V.A.
380 Westminister Hall
Providence, RI 02903
800-827-1000
e-mail: providence.query@vba.va.gov
www.va.gov

9246 Providence VA Medical Center

Veterans Health Administration, US Dept. of V.A.
830 Chalkstone Avenue
Providence, RI 02908 401-273-7100
800-827-1000
FAX: 401-457-3370
e-mail: g.vhacss@forum.va.gov
www.va.gov

Alan Kordlenko, Human Resources Mgmt Service
Benson Werthan, EED Manager

9247 Rhode Island Veterans Center

789 Park Avenue
Cranston, RI 02910 401-467-2046
FAX: 401-467-7945

Veterans medical clinic offering disabled veterans
medical treatments.

South Carolina

9248 Columbia Regional Office

Veterans Benefits Administration, US Dept. of V.A.
1801 Assembly Street
Columbia, SC 29201 803-734-0200
800-827-1000
e-mail: columbia.query@vba.va.gov
www.va.gov

9249 Ralph H. Johnson VA Medical Center

Veterans Health Administration, US Dept. of V.A.
109 Bee Street
Charleston, SC 29401   843-937-5011
                             800-827-1000
                    FAX: 843-937-6100
          e-mail: g.vhacss@forum.va.gov
                             www.va.gov

9250 William Jennings Bryan Dorn VA Medical Center

Veterans Health Administration, US Dept. of V.A.
6439 Garners Ferry Road
Columbia, SC 29209   803-776-4000
                             800-827-1000
                    FAX: 803-695-6739
          e-mail: g.vhacss@forum.va.gov
                             www.va.gov

South Dakota

9251 Sioux Falls VA Medical Center

Veterans Health Administration, US Dept. of V.A.
2501 West 22nd Street
PO Box 5046
Sioux Falls, SD 57117   605-336-3230
                             800-827-1000
                    FAX: 605-333-6878
          e-mail: g.vhacss@forum.va.gov
                             www.va.gov

9252 South Dakota VA Regional Office

Veterans Benefits Administration, US Dept. of V.A.
PO Box 5046
Sioux Falls, SD 57117
                             800-827-1000
          e-mail: siouxfalls.query@vba.va.gov
                             www.va.gov

9253 South Dakota Veterans Centers

610 Kansas City Street
Rapid City, SD 57701   605-348-0077
                    FAX: 605-348-0878

Veterans medical clinic offering disabled veterans
medical treatments.

9254 VA Black Hills Healthcare System

Veterans Health Administration, US Dept. of V.A.
113 Comanche Road
Fort Meade, SD 57741   605-347-2511
                             800-827-1000
                    FAX: 605-347-7171
          e-mail: g.vhacss@forum.va.gov
                             www.va.gov

Tennessee

9255 Alvin C. York VA Medical Center

Veterans Health Administration, US Dept. of V.A.
3400 Lebanon Road
Murfreesboro, TN 37129   615-893-1360
                             800-827-1000
                    FAX: 615-898-4872
          e-mail: g.vhacss@forum.va.gov
                             www.va.gov

9256 Memphis VA Medical Center

Veterans Health Administration, US Dept. of V.A.
1030 Jefferson Avenue
Memphis, TN 38104   901-523-8990
                             800-827-1000
          e-mail: g.vhacss@forum.va.gov
                             www.va.gov

9257 Mountain Home VA Medical Center

Veterans Health Administration, US Dept. of V.A.
Mountain Home, TN 37684   423-926-1171
                             800-827-1000
          e-mail: g.vhacss@forum.va.gov
                             www.va.gov

9258 Nasheville Regional Office

Veterans Benefits Administration, US Dept. of V.A.
110 9th Avenue South
Nashville, TN 37203
                             800-827-1000
          e-mail: nashville.query@vba.va.gov
                             www.va.gov

9259 Nashville VA Medical Center

Veterans Health Administration, US Dept. of V.A.
1310 24th Avenue South
Nashville, TN 37212   615-327-4751
                             800-827-1000
                    FAX: 615-321-6350
          e-mail: g.vhacss@forum.va.gov
                             www.va.gov

Texas

9260 Amarillo VA Healthcare System

Veterans Health Administration, US Dept. of V.A.
Amarillo, TX 79106   806-355-9703
                             800-827-1000
                    FAX: 806-354-7869
          e-mail: g.vhacss@forum.va.gov
                             www.va.gov

9261 Amarillo Vet Center

Department of Veterans Affairs
3414 Olsen Boulevard
Suite E
Amarillo, TX 79109   806-354-9779
                    FAX: 806-354-9837
          e-mail: info@roses.stanford.edu

Pedro Garcia, Jr., Team Leader
Mary J. Williams, Program Assistant

Provides individual, group and family counseling to
veterans who served in combat theaters of World War
II and Korea, Veterans of the Vietnam Era, and veterans of conflicts zones in Lebanon, Grenada, Panama, the Persian Guld and Somalia.

9262 El Paso VA Healthcare Center

Veterans Health Administration, US Dept. of V.A.
5001 North Piedras Street
El Paso, TX 79930   915-564-6100
                             800-827-1000
                    FAX: 915-564-7920
          e-mail: g.vhacss@forum.va.gov
                             www.va.gov

9263 Houston Regional Office

Veterans Benefits Administration, US Dept. of V.A.
6900 Almeda Road
Houston, TX 77030
713-791-1414
800-827-1000
e-mail: houston.query@vba.va.gov
www.va.gov

9264 Houston VA Medical Center

Veterans Health Administration, US Dept. of V.A.
2002 Holcombe Boulevard
Houston, TX 77030
713-791-1414
800-827-1000
e-mail: g.vhacss@forum.va.gov
www.va.gov

9265 South Texas Veterans Healthcare System

Veterans Health Administration, US Dept. of V.A.
7400 Merton Minter Boulevard
San Antonio, TX 78284
210-617-5300
800-827-1000
e-mail: g.vhacss@forum.va.gov
www.va.gov

9266 VA North Texas Health Care System: Sam Rayburn Memorial Veterans Center

Veterans Health Administration, US Dept. of V.A.
1201 East 9th Street
Bonham, TX 75418
800-827-1000
FAX: 903-583-6688
e-mail: g.vhacss@forum.va.gov
www.va.gov

9267 VA North Texas HealthCare System: Dallas VA Medical Center

Veterans Health Administration, US Dept. of V.A.
4500 South Lancaster Road
Dallas, TX 75216
214-742-8387
800-849-3597
FAX: 214-857-1171
www.va.gov

Alan G Harper, Director
William E Cox, Associate Director
Daniel K Heers, Assistant Director

Health care system which serves veterans with medical care and rehabilitation services. For VA benefit inquiries contact 1-800-827-1000. This system has locations in Bonham, Dallas, and Fort Worth.

9268 Waco Regional Office

Veterans Benefits Administration, US Dept. of V.A.
1 Veterans Plaza
701 Clay Avenue
Waco, TX 76799
800-827-1000
e-mail: waco.query@vba.va.gov
www.va.gov

9269 West Texas VA Healthcare System

Veterans Health Administration, US Dept. of V.A.
3000 Veterans Boulevard
Big Spring, TX 79720
915-263-7361
800-728-7000
FAX: 800-728-7878
e-mail: g.vhacss@forum.va.gov
www.va.gov

Utah

9270 Disabled American Veterans Department of Utah

272 East 800 South
Salt Lake City, UT 84111
801-359-8168
FAX: 801-328-3442
e-mail: utdav.juno.com
www.utdav.org/

9271 Salt Lake City Regional Office

Veterans Benefits Administration, US Dept. of V.A.
125 South State Street
Salt Lake City, UT 84147
800-827-1000
e-mail: saltlake.query@vba.va.gov
www.va.gov

9272 VA Salt Lake City Healthcare System

Veterans Health Administration, US Dept. of V.A.
500 Foothill Drive
Salt Lake City, UT 84148
801-582-1565
800-827-1000
FAX: 801-584-1289
e-mail: g.vhacss@forum.va.gov
www.va.gov

Vermont

9273 Vermont VA Regional Office Center

Veterans Benefits Administration, US Dept. of V.A.
215 North Main Street
White River Junction, VT 05009
800-827-1000
e-mail: whiteriver.query@vba.va.gov
www.va.gov

9274 Vermont Veterans Centers

359 Dorset Street
South Burlington, VT 05403
802-862-1806

Veterans medical clinic offering disabled veterans medical treatments.

9275 White River Junction VA Medical

Veterans Health Administration, US Dept. of V.A.
215 North Main Street
White River Junction, VT 05009
802-295-9363
800-827-1000
e-mail: g.vhacss@forum.va.gov
www.va.gov

Virginia

9276 Hampton VA Medical Center

Veterans Health Administration, US Dept. of V.A.
100 Emancipation Drive
Hampton, VA 23667
757-722-9961
800-827-1000
FAX: 757-723-6620
e-mail: mike.eisenberg@med.va.gov
http://152.128.127.205/

Jenny Tankersly, Public Affairs Officer
Mike Eisenberg, Ph.D., Chief, Psychology Services

9277 Hunter Holmes McGuire VA Medical Center

Veterans Health Administration, US Dept. of V.A.
1201 Broad Rock Boulevard
Richmond, VA 23249   804-675-5000
                             800-827-1000
                     FAX: 804-675-5585
         e-mail: g.vhacss@forum.va.gov
                            www.va.gov

9278 Roanoke Regional Office

Veterans Benefits Administration, US Dept. of V.A.
210 Franklin Road, Southwest
Roanoke, VA 24011   540-857-7104
                             800-827-1000
         e-mail: roanoke.query@vba.va.gov
                            www.va.gov

9279 Salem VA Medical Center

Veterans Health Administration, US Dept. of V.A.
1970 Roanoke Boulevard
Salem, VA 24153   540-982-2463
                             800-827-1000
                     FAX: 540-983-1096
         e-mail: g.vhacss@forum.va.gov
                            www.va.gov

Washington

**9280 Jonathan M. Wainwright Memorial VA Medical
Center**

Veterans Health Administration, US Dept. of V.A.
77 Wainwright Drive
Walla Walla, WA 99362   509-525-5200
                             800-827-1000
                     FAX: 509-527-3452
         e-mail: g.vhacss@forum.va.gov
                            www.va.gov

Bruce E. Stewart, Chief Operating Officer

9281 Seattle Regional Office

Veterans Benefits Administration, US Dept. of V.A.
Federal Building
915 2nd Avenue
Seattle, WA 98174

                             800-827-1000
         e-mail: seattle.query@vba.va.gov
                            www.va.gov

9282 Spokane VA Medical Center

Veterans Health Administration, US Dept. of V.A.
4815 North Assembly
Spokane, WA 99205   509-328-4521
                             800-827-1000
                     FAX: 509-327-0222
         e-mail: g.vhacss@forum.va.gov
                            www.va.gov

9283 VA Puget Sound Health Care System

Veterans Health Administration, US Dept. of V.A.
1660 South Columbian Way
Seattle, WA 98108   206-762-1010
                             800-827-1000
         e-mail: g.vhacss@forum.va.gov
                            www.va.gov

West Virginia

9284 Beckley VA Medical Center

Veterans Health Administration, US Dept. of V.A.
200 Veterans Avenue
Clarksburg, WV 25801   304-255-2121
                             800-827-1000
                     FAX: 304-255-2431
         e-mail: g.vhacss@forum.va.gov
                            www.va.gov

9285 Huntington Regional Office

Veterans Benefits Administration, US Dept. of V.A.
640 Fourth Avenue
Huntington, WV 25701
                             800-827-1000
         e-mail: huntington.query@vba.va.gov
                            www.va.gov

9286 Huntington VA Medical Center

Veterans Health Administration, US Dept. of V.A.
1540 Spring Valley Drive
Huntington, WV 25704   304-623-3461
                             800-827-1000
         e-mail: g.vhacss@forum.va.gov
                            www.va.gov

9287 Louis A. Johnson VA Medical Center

Veterans Health Administration, US Dept. of V.A.
One Medical Center Drive
Clarksburg, WV 26301   304-623-3461
                             800-827-1000
         e-mail: g.vhacss@forum.va.gov
                            www.va.gov

9288 Martinsburg VA Medical Center

Veterans Health Administration, US Dept. of V.A.
Route 9
Martinsburg, WV 25401   304-263-0811
                             800-827-1000
                     FAX: 304-262-7433
         e-mail: g.vhacss@forum.va.gov
                            www.va.gov

Marilyn La Freniere, Sci Coordinator

**9289 U.S. Department Veterans Affairs Beckley Vet
Center**

101 Ellison Avenue
Beckley, WV 25801   304-252-8220
                     FAX: 304-256-5475

Vet Center services includes individual and group
readjustment counseling, referral for benefits assistance, liason with community agencies, marital
and family counseling, substance abuse counseling, job counseling and referral, sexual trauma
counseling, and community education.

Wisconsin

9290   Clement J. Zablocki VA Medical Center

Veterans Health Administration, US Dept. of V.A.
5000 West National Avenue
Milwaukee, WI   53295   414-384-2000
                                        800-827-1000
                              FAX: 414-382-5319
              e-mail: g.vhacss@forum.va.gov
                                    www.va.gov

9291   Tomah VA Medical Center

Veterans Health Administration, US Dept. of V.A.
500 East Veterans Street
Tomah, WI   54660   608-372-3971
                                        800-827-1000
              e-mail: g.vhacss@forum.va.gov
                                    www.va.gov

9292   William S. Middleton Memorial VA Medical Center

Veterans Health Administration, US Dept. of V.A.
2500 Overlook Terrace
Madison, WI   53705   608-256-1901
                                        800-827-1000
              e-mail: g.vhacss@forum.va.gov
                                    www.va.gov

9293   Wisconsin VA Regional Office

Veterans Benefits Administration, US Dept. of V.A.
5000 West National Avenue
Building 6
Milwaukee, WI   53295
                                        800-827-1000
              e-mail: milwaukee.query@vba.va.gov
                                    www.va.gov

Wyoming

9294   Cheyenne VA Medical Center

Veterans Health Administration, US Dept. of V.A.
2360 East Pershing Boulevard
Cheyenne, WY   82001
                                        800-827-1000
              e-mail: g.vhacss@forum.va.gov
                                    www.va.gov

9295   Sheridan VA Medical Center

Veterans Health Administration, US Dept. of V.A.
1898 Fort Road
Sheridan, WY   82801   307-672-1639
                                        800-827-1000
                              FAX: 307-672-1675
              e-mail: g.vhacss@forum.va.gov
                                    www.va.gov

9296   Wyoming Veterans Centers

111 S Jefferson Street
Casper, WY   82601   307-266-3633
                              FAX: 307-261-5439

Veterans medical clinic offering disabled veterans
medical treatments.

9297   Wyoming/Colorado VA Regional Office

Veterans Benefits Administration, US Dept. of V.A.
155 Van Gordon Street
Lakewood, CO   80228
                                        800-827-1000
              e-mail: denver.query@vba.va.gov
                                    www.va.gov

Alabama

9298 Achievement Center - Easter Seal

510 West Thomason Circle
Opelika, AL 36801   334-745-3501
FAX: 334-749-5808

Willie Huff, CEO
Elizabeth Griffin, Administratives Services

Job placement programs, remunerative work services and work adjustment training programs. Clients must be at least 16 years old.

9299 Alabama Department of Rehabilitation Services

2129 E S Boulevard
Montgomery, AL 36116   334-288-0220
800-441-7607

Dean Akin, Director

9300 Coffee County Training Center

801 Aviation Boulevard
PO Box 311343
Enterprise, AL 36330   334-347-1732
FAX: 334-347-0252

Vickie Florence, Director

Clients 21 years and up receive training in Independent Living Skills, Self-Care, Language Skills, Learning, Self-Direction and Economic Self-Sufficiency. Transportation is also provided to clients of the center.

9301 Employment Service Division - Alabama

Department of Industrial Relations
649 Monroe Street
Room 2813
Montgomery, AL 36131   334-242-8003
FAX: 334-242-8012
e-mail: shorton@dir.state.al.us
www.dir.state.al.us/es

Stephen A Horton, ES Programs Manager

9302 Fort Payne-Dekalb Rehab Center

311 Gault Avenue North
Fort Payne, AL 35967   256-845-9367
FAX: 256-547-5761

Kenny Maness, Work Adjustment

Offers work adjustment, evaluation and job readiness skills for people with disabilities.

9303 Montezuma Training Center

Academy Drive
Andalusia, AL 36420   334-222-2525

Lillian Dixon, Director

Individuals served in this program must be at least 21 years of age and have a primary diagnosis of mental retardation. Clients receive training in Independent Living Skills, Learning, Self-Direction and Economic Self-Sufficiency. Special Olympic activities are also emphasized.

9304 Opportunity Center - Easter Seal

PO Box 2247
Anniston, AL 36202   256-237-0381

Mike Almaroad

Work adjustment and remunerative work programs.

9305 Wiregrass Rehabilitation Center

805 Ross Clark Circle
Dothan, AL 36303   334-792-0022

Dorothy Morris, Administrator

Provides remunerative work.

9306 Workshops

4244 3rd Avenue South
Birmingham, AL 35222   205-592-9683
FAX: 205-592-9687
e-mail: mail@workshopsinc.com
www.workshopsinc.com

J.E. Crim, Executive Director
Shan Glenn, Director of Client Services

Provides vocational training, sheltered employment and other support services to people with disabilities in central Alabama.

Alaska

9307 Anchorage Job Training Center

235 E 8th Avenue
Anchorage, AK 99501   907-343-6560
FAX: 907-343-6584
www.ci.anchorage.ak.us

9308 Employment Service - Alaska

Alaska Department of Labor
PO Box 25509
Juneau, AK 99802   907-465-2723

9309 Fair Employment Practice Agency

Alaska State Commission for Human Rights
800 A Street
Anchorage, AK 99501   907-276-6563

9310 Vocational Rehabilitation Agency - Alaska

801 W 10th Street
Suite 200
Juneau, AK 99801   907-465-2814
800-478-2815
TDY:907-465-2814
e-mail: dfrench@educ.state.ak.us

Duane French, Director

Arizona

9311 Downtown Neighborhood Learning Center

1001 West Jefferson Street
Phoenix, AZ   85007   602-256-0784
                              800-869-8521
                         FAX: 602-256-2524
        e-mail: marcian@first.inter.net
                    www.swlink.net/~dnlc

Marcia R. Newman, Executive Director
Mattie Johnson, Receptionist
Peg Osinski, El Mirage Learning Lab

Adult education agency providing basic skills, GED, ESOL, life skills, computer skills, resume assistance and career testing.

9312 Employment Service - Arizona

Department of Economic Security
PO Box 6160
Phoenix, AZ   85005   602-254-7213
                         FAX: 602-271-4128
                    www.utilitytraderaz.com

Bill Hernandez, Assistant Director

9313 Fair Employment Practice Agency - Arizona

Arizona Civil Rights Division
1275 W Washington Street
Phoenix, AZ   85007   602-542-5263

9314 JOBS Administration Job Opportunities & Basic Skills

1717 W Jefferson Street
Phoenix, AZ   85007   602-542-9596
                         FAX: 602-542-5171

Gretchen Evans, Program Administrator

Assist applicants and recipients of temporary assistance to needy families to obtain job training and employment that will lead to economic independence.

9315 Job Training Program Liaison - Arizona

Department of Economic Security
PO Box 6160
Phoenix, AZ   85005   602-254-7213
                         FAX: 602-271-4128
                    www.utilitytraderaz.com

Gretchen Evans, Program Administrator

The Job Opportunities and Basic Skills Administration assists applicants and recipients of Temporary Assistance to needy families to obtain training and employment.

9316 TETRA Corporation

308 W Glenn Street
Tucson, AZ   85705   520-622-4874

Steven King

Work hardening and disciplinary programs.

9317 Vocational Rehabilitation Agency - Arizona

1789 W Jefferson Street
Phoenix, AZ   85007   602-542-3981

9318 Vocational Rehabilitation Program Rehabilitation Services Administrations

Division of Employment & Rehabilitation Services
Department of Economic Security
1789 W Jefferson Street
Phoenix, AZ   85007   602-542-3332
                              800-563-1221
                         FAX: 602-542-3778
                         TDY: 6025426049
        e-mail: azrsa@rehabnet.org
                    www.azrsa.org

Jozef de Groot, Manager, Program Services
Skip Bingham, Administrator

This program serves individuals seeking jobs and job training.

9319 Yavapal Rehabilitation Center

436 N Washington Avenue
Prescott, AZ   86301   520-445-0991

Bradley Newman

Provides remunerative work.

Arkansas

9320 Arkansas - Vocational Rehabilitation Agency

PO Box 3781
1616 Brookwood Drive
Little Rock, AR   72203   501-296-1616

        e-mail: daturrentine@ars.state.ar.us

Dale Turrentine, Special Program Adminstrator

9321 Arkansas Employment Service Agency and Job Training Program

Arkansas Employment Security Department
PO Box 2981
Little Rock, AR   72203   501-682-2121

9322 Easter Seal Work Center

11801 Fairview Road
Little Rock, AR   72212   501-223-8077

Renee Hubbard

Work hardening and disciplinary programs.

9323 VCT/A Job Retention Skill Training Program

Hot Springs Rehabilitation Center
PO Box 1358
Hot Springs, AR   71902   501-624-4411
                              FAX: 501-624-3515

A training program designed for use in rehabilitation and educational settings. Using a social skill training strategy, VCT helps participants learn how to solve on-the-job problems and cope with common supervisory demands.

9324 Vocational Rehabilitation Agency for Persons Who Are Visually Impaired
Arkansas Department of Human Services
PO Box 3237
Little Rock, AR   72203   501-682-5463
                                 800-960-9270
                                 TDY:501-324-9271
                                 e-mail: arkblind@edu.gte.net

James C. Hudson, Director

California

9325 ARC-Adult Vocational Program
657 Harrison Street
San Francisco, CA   94107   415-626-5710

Patricia Kemerling
Job placement programs, remunerative work services and work adjustment training programs.

9326 Ability First
3770 E Willow Street
Long Beach, CA   90815   562-426-6161
                                FAX: 562-426-6148

Michael Lande
Job placement programs, remunerative work services and work adjustment training programs.

9327 Bakersfield Association for Retarded Citizens
BARC
2240 S Union Avenue
Bakersfield, CA   93307   805-834-2272
                                 FAX: 805-834-9813
                                 e-mail: barc@lightspeed.net

Skip Covell, Executive Director
Employment training & placement.

9328 CRY-ROP - Colton-Redlands-Yucaipa ROP
1214 Indiana Center
Redlands, CA   92374   909-793-3115
                              FAX: 909-793-6901

Stephanie Houston, Manager Adult Programs & Service
Provides quality hands-on training programs in over 40 high demand career fields to assist high school students and adults in acquiring marketable job skills. Works in cooperation with local high schools, adult education colleges, and employees providing a collaborative team of academic and ROP occupational teachers who integrate academic and vocational competencies to provide sequenced paths within career majors. Support services are provided, career guidance and services for the disabled.

9329 California - Employment Service
Employment Development Department
PO Box 826880
Sacramento, CA   94280   916-654-9072

9330 California - Job Training Program Liaison
Employment Development Department
800 Capitol Mall MIC83
Sacramento, CA   95814   916-654-9072

9331 California Department of Fair Employment & Housing
2014 T Street
Suite 210
Sacramento, CA   95814   916-227-2873
                                FAX: 916-227-2870
                                www.dfeh.ca.gov

Dia S. Poole, Deputy Director, Public Affairs

9332 Career Connection KAP-Transition Program
Whittier High School District
9401 Painter Avenue
Whittier, CA   90605   562-698-8121
                              FAX: 562-693-4136
            e-mail: Richard.Rosenberg@wuhsd.k12.co.us
                              www.wehsd.k12.co.us

Richard L. Rosenberg, Ph.D., Vocational Coordinator
Job placement programs, remunerative work services and work adjustment training programs.

9333 Career Development Program (CDP)
260 W Grand Avenue
Escondido, CA   92025   760-738-0277
                               FAX: 760-741-9452

Dr. Richard Brady
Wendy Hope, Supported Employment
Jill Hennessy, Independent Living
Work hardening and disciplinary programs.

9334 Center for Rehabilitation Engineering and Appropriate Technology Education
1600 Holloway Avenue
San Francisco, CA   94132   415-338-1001

Offers federally funded education programs leading to a master's degree in several areas.

9335 Community Outpatient Rehabilitation Center
1925 E Dakota Avenue
Suite 120A
Fresno, CA   93726   559-459-1842
                            FAX: 559-459-1004

Tracie Rawson, Case Manager
Jan Erik Paris, Service Coordinator
Physical occupation and speech Therapy, Neuropsychology services available for orthopedic and neurological diagnosis. Lymphedema program.

9336 Desert Haven Training Center
PO Box 2119
Lancaster, CA   93539   805-948-8402

Roy Williams
Work adjustment and remunerative work programs.

9337 Do-It-Leisure - Work Training Center

621 1/2 Mangrove Avenue
Chico, CA 95926   530-343-6055
                        FAX: 530-343-4619
                        e-mail: doitl@ewrc.org

Ken Steidley, Program Manager
Carl Ochsner, Executive Director

Therapeutic recreation programs providing a wide variety of services designed to meet individual needs with specialized, transitional or integrated activities.

9338 ESS Work Center

858 Stanton Road
Burlingame, CA 94010   650-692-3377

Jerry Martin, Executive Director

9339 Feather River Industries

1811 Kusel Road
Oroville, CA 95966   530-534-4112
                           FAX: 530-534-3137

Amy Brown, Rehabilitation Coordinator

Vocational training for persons with developmental disabilities provided through wood products fabrication and assembly tasks. Instructor to trainer rating ranging from 1 to 12, 1 to 8, 1 to 6, and 1 to 4 depending on individual needs and complexity of tasks.

9340 Fit to Work

3581 Palmer Drive
Suite 401
Cameron Park, CA 95682   530-676-7485
                                FAX: 530-676-9114

Jennifer Roach

Provides remunerative work.

9341 Fresno City College Enabler Program

1101 E University Avenue
Fresno, CA 93741   559-442-8297

Brice W. Harris, President

This program offers students with severe disabilities who are educated and guided in vocational exploration and preparation, the ability to intern in various on-campus, job-sites.

9342 Heartland Opportunity Center

323 N E Street
Madera, CA 93638   559-674-8828
                         FAX: 559-674-8857

Robert J. Hand, Director

Job placement programs, remunerative work services and work adjustment training programs.

9343 Hollister Workshop

Hope Rehabilitation Services
2300 Technology Parkway
Suite 7
Hollister, CA 95023   831-637-8283
                            FAX: 831-637-8726

Work adjustment and remunerative work programs.

9344 Humboldt Access Project

235 Fourth Street
Eureka, CA 95501   707-445-8404
                         FAX: 707-445-9751
                         e-mail: hap@northcoast.com

To provide programs, services and information for people with disabilities in an effort to allow choices for individuals to optimize their independence.

9345 King's Rehabilitation Center

490 E Hanford Armona Road
Hanford, CA 93230   559-582-9234
                          FAX: 559-582-1182

Donald Larson

Work adjustment and remunerative work programs.

9346 Konocti Industries - People Services

4195 Lakeshore Boulevard
Lakeport, CA 95453   707-263-3811
                           FAX: 707-263-0552

Hank Montgomery

Work hardening and disciplinary programs.

9347 Morongo Basin Work Activity Center

74325 Joe Davis Drive
Twentynine Palms, CA 92277   760-366-8474

Sheree Fraser

Job placement programs, remunerative work services and work adjustment training programs.

9348 Mother Lode Rehabilitation Enterprises

399 Placerville Drive
Placerville, CA 95667   530-622-4848

Jerry Demarest

Job placement programs, remunerative work services and work adjustment training programs.

9349 NCI Affiliates

1434 Chestnut Street
Paso Robles, CA 93446   805-238-6630

Laura Simpson, Executive Director
Judy Jacobson, Services Director

Provides independent living skills and vocational training to people with disabilities.

9350 **Napa Valley P.S.I.**
651 Trabajo Lane
PO Box 600
Napa, CA 94559 707-255-0177
FAX: 707-255-0802

Jeanne Fauquet, Executive Director
Work adjustment, work training and educational
services for developmentally disabled adults. Emphasis is on manufacture of quality wood products, primarily wooden office furniture.

9351 **New Opportunity Workshops**
PO Box 91476
Pasadena, CA 91109

Ron Johnston, Rehabilitation Mgr.
Offers a work services program, vocational rehabilitation, work activity programs and supported employment programs.

9352 **Oakland Work Activity Area**
6315 San Leandro Street
Oakland, CA 94621 510-639-9350

Greg Whalley
Job placement programs, remunerative work services
and work adjustment training programs.

9353 **Opportunities for the Handicapped**
3340 Marysville Boulevard
Sacramento, CA 95838 916-925-3522

Kathy Dodd
Work adjustment and remunerative work programs.

9354 **Orange County ARC**
225 W Carl Karcher Way
Anaheim, CA 92801 714-444-5301
FAX: 714-744-5312

Joyce Hearn, Chief Executive Officer
Provides remunerative work through both site and
community placements.

9355 **Pomona Valley Workshop**
4650 Brooks Street
Montclair, CA 91763 909-624-3555
FAX: 909-624-5675
e-mail: pvwkaren@juno.com

Karen Jones, Executive Director
Assisting adults with disabilities reach their potential
in vocational and socialization skills in order that
they may achieve their highest level of employment
and comminity integration in Work Program, Supported Employment Services, Adult Dev. Center and
Senior Services.

9356 **Porterville Sheltered Workshop**
187 W Olive Avenue
Porterville, CA 93257 559-784-1399
FAX: 559-781-5651

Nick Brown
Work adjustment and remunerative work programs.

9357 **Project Independence Supported Employment**
3505 Cadillac P 101
Costa Mesa, CA 92626 714-549-3464
FAX: 714-549-3559
P-I.org

Andrea Erickson
Provides remunerative work.

9358 **Ramona Training Center**
2138 San Vicente Road
Ramona, CA 92065 760-789-6018

Charlene Wutthe
Job placement programs, remunerative work services
and work adjustment training programs.

9359 **Sacramento Vocational Services**
6950 21st Avenue
Sacramento, CA 95820 916-484-0550

Diane De Rodeff, Director
Work hardening and disciplinary programs.

9360 **Salinas Valley Training Center**
PO Box 453
Salinas, CA 93902 831-758-8270

Rosemary Anderson, Day Activity Manager

9361 **San Francisco Vocational Services**
814 Mission Street
Suite 600
San Francisco, CA 94103 415-512-9500
FAX: 415-512-9507
www.sfvocationalservices.org

Craig King, Executive Director
Jeffrey Faircloth, Manager, Case Management
Comprehensive vocational rehabilitation center offering vocational evaluation, rehabilitative counseling, business office training, work experience, and
job placement.

9362 **Shasta County Opportunity Center**
1265 Redwood Boulevard
Redding, CA 96003 530-225-5000

Carol Keating, Executive Director

9363 Social Vocational Services
350 S Crenshaw
Suite A104
Torrance, CA   90503   310-787-4740

Dr. Dale Dutton, Executive Director

9364 South Bay Vocational Center
1526 240th Street
Harbor City, CA   90710   310-784-2032
                                   FAX: 310-539-6342
                                   www.sbvcl.com

Corey Sylve, President & CEO
Clare Grey, Director of Programs

9365 South Bay Vocational Center Retarded
1526 240th Street
Harbor City, CA   90710   310-784-2032
                                   FAX: 310-539-6342

Max Gorski, Executive Director
Job placement programs, remunerative work services
and work adjustment training programs.

9366 Tulare County Training Center Able Industries
2525 S K Street
Tulare, CA   93274   559-686-8506

Robert Stephenson
Provides remunerative work.

9367 Tulare Workcenter Able Industries
2325 S K Street
Tulare, CA   93274

Gary Horton, Executive Director

9368 Unyeway
2330 Main Street
Suite E
Ramona, CA   92065

Hank Newman, Director
Job placement programs, remunerative work services
and work adjustment training programs.

9369 V-Bar Enterprises
720 Gordon Circle
Suisun City, CA   94585   707-864-1334

Lu Brunet
Job placement programs, remunerative work services
and work adjustment training programs.

9370 Valley Light Industries
822 N Grand Avenue
Covina, CA   91724   626-331-9966

Gary Miller
Provides remunerative work.

9371 Visalia Workshop
2544 E Valley Oaks Drive
Visalia, CA   93292   559-734-1964

Hortensia Venegas
Work hardening and disciplinary programs.

9372 Vocational Vision
26041 Pala
Mission Viejo, CA   92691   949-588-5898
                                   FAX: 949-859-9962

Kathryn Hebel, Director
Work hardening and disciplinary programs.

9373 Westside Opportunity Workshop
9503 Jefferson Boulevard
Culver City, CA   90232   310-838-0521

Edward Oritz
Job placement programs, remunerative work services
and work adjustment training programs.

9374 Work Training Center
2255 Fair Street
Chicago, CA   95928   530-343-7994
                                   FAX: 530-343-4616
                                   e-mail: info@wtcinc.org
                                   www.wtcinc.org

Lee Laney, Commercial Services Manager
Program for persons with developmental disabilities.
We provide vocational services, community integration services, recreation and leisure services and self-
care services.

9375 Work Training Center for the Handicapped
2255 Fair Street
Chico, CA   95928   530-343-3107

Barrie Dyer
Work hardening and disciplinary programs.

9376 Work Training Programs
20931 Nordhoff Street
Chatsworth, CA   91311   818-773-9000

Stephen Miller
Work hardening and disciplinary programs.

Colorado

9377 Cheyenne Village
6275 Lehman Drive
Colorado Springs, CO   80918   719-592-0200
                                   FAX: 719-548-9947

Linda Bloom, Executive Director
Residential and employment programs for adults
with developmental disabilities.

9378 Colorado Employment Service

Department of Labor and Employment
600 Grant Street
Suite 900
Denver, CO 80203   303-676-7461

9379 Colorado Fair Employment Practice Agency

Colorado Civil Rights Division
1560 Broadway
Suite 1050
Denver, CO 80202   303-894-2997
                           800-514-0301
                    FAX: 303-894-7830

9380 Colorado Vocational Rehabilition Agency
Department of Social Services

1575 Sherman Street
4th Floor
Denver, CO 80203   303-866-5994

9381 Developmental Disabilities Center

1400 Dixon Avenue
Lafayette, CO 80026   303-665-7789
                       FAX: 303-665-2648
         e-mail: caroline@ddcboulder.com
                     www.ddcboulder.com

John Taylor, Executive Director
Caroline Siegfried, Executive Assistant
Provides services for people with developmental disabilities so that they can live fulfilling lives in their communities.

9382 Developmental Training Services

1401 Oak Creek Grade Road
Canon City, CO 81212   719-275-4504

Roger Jensen, President

9383 Dynamic Dimensions

1778 Martin Avenue
Burlington, CO 80807   719-346-5367
                         FAX: 719-346-6010

Cheryl Reese, Executive Director
Vocational, evaluation and assessment, training and placement for most disabilities.

9384 Gray Street Workcenter

5685 Gray Street
Arvada, CO 80002   303-422-1305
                     FAX: 303-467-2793

Shelley Richardson, Executive Director

9385 Hope Center

3400 Elizabeth Street
Denver, CO 80205   303-388-4801
                     FAX: 303-388-0249

George Brantley
Work adjustment and remunerative work programs.

9386 Las Animas County Rehabilitation Center

1205 Congress Drive
Trinidad, CO 81082   719-846-3388
                       FAX: 719-846-4543

Duane Roy
Job placement programs, remunerative work services and work adjustment training programs.

9387 NORESCO Workshop

903 E Burlington Avenue
Fort Morgan, CO 80701

Robert Duffield
Provides remunerative work.

9388 Regional Assessment and Training Center

3520 W Oxford Avenue
Denver, CO 80236   303-866-7253

Russell Porter, Executive Director

9389 Sedgwick County Workshop

113 Elm Street
Julesburg, CO 80737   970-474-3504

Robert Christiansen
Provides remunerative work.

9390 Valley Industries

330 State Avenue
Alamosa, CO 81101

Tim Johnson
Provides remunerative work.

9391 Yuma County Workshop

710 E 2nd Avenue
Yuma, CO 80759   970-848-3011

Robert Stephens
Provides remunerative work.

Connecticut

9392 Area Cooperative Educational Services

250 State Street
North Haven, CT 06473   203-498-6800
                          FAX: 203-498-6890
            e-mail: acesinfo@acesk12.ct.us
                        www.acesk12.ct.us

Dr. Cheryl S Saloom, Deputy Executive Director

9393 CCARC

1 Hartford Square
New Britain, CT 06052   860-224-6993

Julie Erickson, Day Service Director

Supported employment, work services, habilitation services, advocacy, recreation and residential services.

9394 Cheshire Occupational and Career Center

615 W Johnson Avenue
Suite 3
Cheshire, CT   06410   203-272-5607
                             FAX: 203-272-4284

Peter Mason

Work adjustment and remunerative work programs.

9395 Community Enterprises

41 Mechanic Street
PO Box 176
Windsor, CT   06095   860-688-7918
                             FAX: 860-688-5599
                             e-mail: cehftd@aol.com
                             www.communityenterprises.com

Susan Cauley, Vice President, CT Operation

Provide supported Education services in a community college setting; supported employment including job training, placement and follow-up; transitional services from group homes and other settings to supported living within the community.

9396 Connecticut Fair Employment Practice Agency

90 Washington Street
Hartford, CT   06106   860-727-3000

9397 Connecticut Governor's Committee on Employment of Disabled Persons

200 Folly Brook Boulevard
Wethersfield, CT   06109   860-566-5505

9398 Constructive Workshops

24 Willow Street
East Hartford, CT   06118   860-549-1410
                                  FAX: 860-895-1168

Sandie Lavoy, Coordinator

9399 Fotheringhay Farms

84 Waterhole Road
Colchester, CT   06415   860-267-4463
                               FAX: 860-267-7628

Dr. Wesley Martins

Job placement programs, remunerative work services and work adjustment training programs.

9400 George Hegyi Industrial Training Center

5 Coon Hollow Road
Derby, CT   06418   203-735-8727

Joan Bucci

Work adjustment and remunerative work programs.

9401 Greater Enfield Association of Retarded Citizens

3 Pearson Way
Enfield, CT   06082   860-763-0192

Dean Wem

Work hardening and disciplinary programs.

9402 Hartford Vet Center

30 Jordan Lane
Wethersfield, CT   06109   860-240-3543
                                 FAX: 860-240-3415

Donna Dube Hryb, CSW, Team Leader

A U.S. Department of Veterans Affairs counseling center offering counseling to Vietnam era and combat veterans. Sexual trauma/harassment counseling, medical screening and benefit referral is available to all veterans.

9403 Kennedy Center

2440 Reservoir Avenue
Trumbull, CT   06611   203-365-8522
                             FAX: 203-365-8533
                             e-mail: kctrum@aol.com
                             www.thekennedycenterinc.org

Martin Schwartz, President/CEO

Provides vocational rehabilitation, job training and job placement services to 1,000 adults with disabilities including mental retardation, traumatic brain injury, psychiatric disabilities and more. Residential services, well integrated within the community, serve 97 individuals on a daily basis. Children's programs provide support to 85 children age birth to three, in addition to after hours and recreation programs to appromxately 100 school age children. Staff size is presently 400 employees.

9404 Quaezar

2480 Black Rock Turnpike
Suite 8
Fairfield, CT   06432   203-339-3476
                              FAX: 203-377-6144

William J. Sedarweck, President

Agency for adult mentally retarded/autistic people providing residential care in a group home or apartment setting. Also provides placement in community employment.

9405 Services for the Blind, State of Connectic

184 Windsor Avenue
Windsor, CT   06095   860-602-4000
                             800-842-4570
                             FAX: 860-602-4020
                             www.besb.state.ct.us

Dr. Donna Balaski, Executive Director
Carole Donagher, Director, Finance and Business O

9406 TEAM Vocational Program

227 Elm Street
West Haven, CT   06516   203-934-5221

Peter Schwartz, Executive Director
Hannah Carlson, DD Director

Provides remunerative work, vocational training, supported employment, and supportive services. Residential program including group living and supervised apartment, social club.

9407 Valley Memorial Health Center

435 E Main Street
Ansonia, CT 06401

Marilyn Cormack, Director
Provides remunerative work.

Delaware

9408 Delaware Division of Vocational Rehabilitation-Department of Labor

4425 N Market Street
PO Box 9969
Wilmington, DE 19809   302-761-8275
                                    FAX: 302-761-6611
                                    www.state.de.us/labor

Andrea Guest, Director

Provides opportunities and resources to eligible individuals with disabilities leading to success in employment and independent living.

9409 Delaware Fair Employment Practice Agency

Delaware Department of Labor
820 N French Street
6th Floor
Wilmington, DE 19801   302-577-3970

9410 Delaware Job Training Program Liaison

Division of Employment & Training
PO Box 9828
Wilmington, DE 19809   302-761-8127

9411 Opportunity Center

3030 Bowers Street
Wilmington, DE 19802   302-762-0300
                                    FAX: 302-762-8797
                                    e-mail: blennon@oppctr.com
                                    www.oppctr.com

Bob Lennon, VP Community Development
Cindy Sterling, VP Employment Services
Cathie Field Lloyd, President & CEO

Work adjustment and remunerative work programs. Also offers career guidance, supported employment, work readiness, job placement, and remunerative work programs.

9412 Wilmington Vet Center

1601 Kirkwood Highway
Wilmington, DE 19805   302-998-9448
                                    FAX: 302-633-5250

Mark A. Kaufki, Ed.D., Team Leader

Veterans counseling program offering individual counseling services, advocacy services, and group counseling. The focus is the counseling of all veterans coping with the aftermath of war, sexual abuse/harassment in the military, and all veterans of the Vietnam era. The center also has an active outreach program to seek veterans needing services. Hours of operation are between 8:00 a.m. - 4:30 p.m., Monday - Friday and other times by appointment only.

No Fees

District of Columbia

9413 Davis Memorial Goodwill Industries

2200 South Dakota Avenue NE
Washington, DC 20018   202-636-4225
                                    FAX: 256-526-3994

David Becker, President

Offers vocational training, job training, sheltered employment and work experience.

9414 District of Columbia Department of Employment Services

500 C Street NW
Room 600
Washington, DC 20001   877-319-7346
                                         877-319-7346
                                    FAX: 202-724-7112
                                    e-mail: des15@erols.com
                                    does.ci.washington.dc.us

Diana C. Johnson, Public Information Officer
Marianna Lourenco, Specialist/ADA Coordinator

To foster economic development and growth in the District of Columbia by providing workforce training, bringing together job seekers and employers, compensating unemployed and injured workers and promoting safe and healthy workplaces.

9415 District of Columbia Dept. of Employment Services, Office of Workforce Development

500 C Street NW
Washington, DC 20001   877-319-7346
                                         877-319-7346
                                    FAX: 202-724-7112
                                    e-mail: des15@erols.com
                                    does.ci.washington.dc.us

Diana C. Johnson, Public Information Officer
Marianna Lourenco, Specialist/ADA Coordinator

To foster economic development and growth in the District of Columbia by providing workforce training, bringing together job seekers and employers, compensating unemployed and injured workers and promoting safe and healthy workplaces.

9416 District of Columbia Fair Employment Practice Agencies

DC Office of Human Rights
2000 14th Street NW
Suite 3
Washington, DC 20009   202-727-3071

9417 Green Door

1623 16th Street NW
Washington, DC 20009   202-462-4092
FAX: 202-462-7562
e-mail: gdiadmin@aol.com

Judith Johnson, Director

Green Door is a community program which prepares people with a severe and persistent mental illness to live and work independently. Since 1976, Green Door has provided comprehensive services to mentally ill people, including housing, job training, job placement, education, homeless outreach, case management, support for people with substance abuse problems, family support,and specialized help for people who have had repeated hospitalizations.

9418 Operation Job Match

2021 K Street NW
Suite 715
Washington, DC 20006   202-887-0136
FAX: 202-296-3425

Diane Afes, Program Director
Steve Nissen, Program Supervisor

Job readiness program for individuals with adult-onset physical disabilities.

9419 President's Committee on Employment of People with Disabilities

1331 F Street NW
Washington, DC 20004   202-376-6200
FAX: 202-376-6219
e-mail: info@pcepd.gov
www.pcepd.gov

An independent federal agency whose mission is to facilitate the communication, coordination and promotion of public and private efforts to enhance the employment of people with disabilities. The Committee provides information, training and technical assistance to America's business leaders, organized labor, rehabilitation and service providers, advocacy organizations, families and individuals with disabilities.

9420 WAVE Work, Achievement, Value, & Education

525 School Street SW
Suite 500
Washington, DC 20024   202-484-0103
800-274-2005
FAX: 202-488-7595
e-mail: wave4kids@aol.com
www.waveinc.org

Job placement programs, remunerative work services and work adjustment training programs for 18 and 21 years of age in many cities across the country including Drop-Out Recovery Programs and Drop-Out Prevention Programs. Programs also available for youth ages 12-18. Youth Professionals Development and Training and key aspects of WAVE services, as well.

Florida

9421 Abilities Division of Lockheed Martin IMS Workforce Services

2735 Whitney Road
Clearwater, FL 33760   727-538-7370
FAX: 727-538-7387

Alyse B. Stone, Director, Voc. Rehab Programs

Provides a full range of employment services including work evaulation, training, job coaching, job placement, advocacy and education. Also provides housing assistance and specialized to adults with cystic fibrosis.

9422 Adult Day Training

Goodwill Industries-Suncoast
10596 Gandy Boulevard
PO Box 14456
St. Petersburg, FL 33733   727-523-1512
FAX: 727-577-2749
www.goodwill-suncoast.org

Joe Mc Cloe, Director of Resource Development

An innovative program which uses job skills to teach self-help, daliy living, communication, mobility, travel, decision-making, behavioral and social skills. This focus provides concrete, transferable experiences to help prepare individuals for greater community inclusion by achieving the highest possible degree of independence in their daily life, increasing their confidence and supporting their successful transitions to less structured, self-suffficient environments.

9423 Career Assessment & Planning Services

Goodwill Industries-Suncoast
10596 Gandy Boulevard
PO Box 14456
St. Petersburg, FL 33733   727-523-1512
FAX: 727-577-2749
www.goodwill-suncoast.org

Joe Mc Cloe, Director of Resource Development

Provides comprehensive assessment, which can predict current and future employment and potential adjustment factors for physically, emotionally or developmentally disabled persons who may be unemployed or underemployed. Assessment evaluate interests, aptitudes, academic acheivements, and physical abilities through coordinated testing, interviewing and behavioral observations.

9424 Center for Independence, Training and Education

215 E New Hampshire Street
Orlando, FL 32804   407-896-3177
FAX: 407-895-5255

Mara Schlosser, Program Director

Offers services for the totally blind, legally blind, visually impaired, mentally retarded blind and more with health, counseling, educational, recreational, rehabilitation, computer training and professional training services.

9425 Choices for Work Program

Goodwill Industries-Suncoast
10596 Gandy Boulevard
PO Box 14456
St. Petersburg, FL 33733 727-523-1512
FAX: 727-577-2749
www.goodwill-suncoast.org

Joe Mc Cloe, Director of Resource Development

Assisting individuals currently eligible for Workman's Compensation, this program allows those recovering from injury on the job to prepare to return to independent employment, either through increasing ability and confidence in using adaptive behaviors and/or equipment to return to related employment, or adjusting to a more compatible employment environment.

9426 Div. of Vocational Rehabilitation Services Florida Department of Education

2002 Old Saint Augustin Road
Tallahassee, FL 32399 850-488-6925
FAX: 850-921-7216

9427 Florida Division of Vocational Rehabilitation

4221 N Himes Avenue
Tampa, FL 33607 813-871-7300
FAX: 813-873-4773

Renee Dominic, Librarian

Rehabilitation services are important when a physical or mental handicap interferes with your ability to work. Our purpose is to help prepare for, and return to, gainful employment.

9428 Florida Fair Employment Practice Agency

Florida Commission on Human Relations
325 John Knox Road
Building F
Tallahassee, FL 32303 850-297-1386

9429 Florida Vocational Rehabilitation for Persons Who Are Visually Impaired

2540 W Executive Center Circle
Tallahassee, FL 32399

9430 Florida's Governor's Alliance of Citizens with Disabilities

106 E College Avenue
Suite 820
Tallahassee, FL 32301 850-224-4493
888-838-2253
FAX: 850-224-4496
e-mail: info@abletrust.org
www.abletrust.org

Sharon Griffith, President/CEO
Kristen Knapp, VP, Of Public Relations
Guenevere Crum, Grants Director

Provides grant funds for small business start-up costs for people with disabilities and employment-related programs for nonprofit agencies in Florida. Assists families, individuals and agencies through educational conferences, and youth training programs. Provides businesses free resources for hiring people with disabilities.

9431 Goodwill Temporary Services

Goodwill Industries-Suncoast
10596 Gandy Boulevard
PO Box 14456
St. Petersburg, FL 33733 727-523-1512
FAX: 727-577-2749
www.goodwill-suncoast.org

Joe Mc Cloe, Director of Resource Development

Provides employment links from potential employees, both disabled and non-disabled alike to employers with immediate employment opportunities seeking qualified candidates. Pre-screening on all applicants include: Employment history, personal references, law enforcement background checks and substance screening.

9432 IMPACT - Ocala Vocational Services

Goodwill Industries-Suncoast
10596 Gandy Boulevard
PO Box 14456
St. Petersburg, FL 33733 727-523-1512
FAX: 727-577-2749
www.goodwill-suncoast.org

Joe Mc Cloe, Director of Resource Development

Designed to enable individuals with disabilities to work in integrated settings in the community, receiving wages and benefits matching those of non-handicapped workers.

9433 Job Works NISH Food Service

Goodwill Industries-Suncoast
10596 Gandy Boulevard
PO Box 14456
St. Petersburg, FL 33733 727-523-1512
FAX: 727-577-2749
www.goodwill-suncoast.org

Joe Mc Cloe, Director of Resource Development

An enclave style (or group) supported employment program designed to give consumers additional supports that allow and encourage increasingly independent employment opportunities within a food services environment.

9434 Job Works NISH Postal Service

Goodwill Industries-Suncoast
10596 Gandy Boulevard
PO Box 14456
St. Petersburg, FL 33733 727-523-1512
FAX: 727-577-2749
www.goodwill-suncoast.org

Joe Mc Cloe, Director of Resource Development

An enclave style (or group) supported employment program designed to give consumers additional supports that allow and encourage increasingly independent employment opportunities within a mailroom environment.

9435 MAClown Vocational Rehabilitation Workshop

6390 NE 2nd Avenue
Miami, FL 33138 305-754-5015

Pat Chavis
Provides remunerative work.

9436 One-Stop Service

Goodwill Industries-Suncoast
10596 Gandy Boulevard
PO Box 14456
St. Petersburg, FL   33733   727-523-1512
                            FAX: 727-577-2749
www.goodwill-suncoast.org

Joe Mc Cloe, Director of Resource Development

Provides universal job search and placement related services are available to any person entering the service center. Each One-Stop Services Center provides on-site representation from a variety of employment-related service providers. All One-Stops host and/or facilitate local employment fairs, and provides access to computerized job-postings.

9437 Palm Beach Habilitation Center

4522 S Congress Avenue
Lake Worth, FL   33461   561-965-8500

Tina Philips, President/CEO

Providing work evaluation, work adjustment, job placement, employment, residential and retirement services for mentally, emotionally and physically disabled adults.

9438 Primrose Supported Employment Programs

2733 S Ferncreek Avenue
Orlando, FL   32806   407-898-7201

Terry Provancha

Provides remunerative work.

9439 SCARC

213 W McCollum Avenue
Bushnell, FL   33513   352-793-5156

Marsha Woodard Perkins, Executive Director

Training and employment program for adults with disabilities. SCARC offers vocational evaluation, training, work services, transportation, supported independent living and community based training.

9440 Seagull Industries for the Disabled

3879 West Industrial Way
Riviera Beach, FL   33404   561-842-5814
                            FAX: 561-881-3554
e-mail: main@seagull.org
www.seagull.org

Alfred Elsinger, Executive Director

Dedicated to improving the quality of life of mentally, physically, and emotionally challenged adults in Palm Beach County, Florida through advocacy and the provision of a variety of social service and training programs designed to encourage self reliance and independence.

9441 Supported Employment Program

Goodwill Industries-Suncoast
10596 Gandy Boulevard
PO Box 14456
St. Petersburg, FL   33733   727-523-1512
                            FAX: 727-577-2749
www.goodwill-suncoast.org

Joe Mc Cloe, Director of Resource Development

Provides an employment option that enables individuals with severe disabilities to work in integrated settings in the community, receiving wages and benefits matching those of their non-disabled counterparts. The individual is provided with intensive, on-the-job training at job sites that have been carefully analyzed to be suitable for each individual.

9442 Work Exploration Center

3000 Northwest 83rd Street I40
Gainesville, FL   32606   352-395-5619
                            FAX: 352-395-5271

Alvaro Ortiz, Program Coordinator
Karla Wouten, Comm. Employment & Development
Julie McCullough-Patrick, Voc. Evaluator Team Leader

The Work Exploration Center embraces a holistic approach to comprehensive vocational evaluation services, employee development services and community employment services for the student, encouraging individual understanding, hope and growth for a productive and fulfilling future.

Georgia

9443 Employment and Training Division, Region B

Goodwill Industries of North Georgia
PO Box 447
Ellijay, GA   30540   706-276-4722
                            888-514-8112
                      FAX: 706-276-4732
e-mail: vti@ellijay.com

Linda Rau, Director of Programs & Services

Employment training, assessment and job placement for people who have disabilities and/or are disadvantaged. Serving 15 counties in Northern Georgia.

9444 Fair Housing and Fair Employment

Georgia Commission on Equal Opportunity
229 Peachtree Street NE
710 Int Tower
Atlanta, GA   30303   404-656-1736
                            FAX: 404-656-4399
e-mail: gceo@gceo.state.ga.us
www.gceo.state.ga.us

Mark Cicero, Fair Housing Manager
Stephanie Randolph, Intake Coordinator/Housing
Lisa Burroughs, Equal Employment Manager

9445 Griffin Area Resource Center Griffin Community Workshop Division

511 Hamilton Boulevard
847
Griffin, GA 30223 770-228-3766
FAX: 770-228-3448
e-mail: griffincomwrkshp@aol.com

Lynn H. Leaptrot, Workshop Director
Charles Cary Grubbs, GARC, Executive Director

A CARF (The Rehabilitation Accreditation Commission) accredited Employment and Community Support organization providing daily services to participants with disabilities from 16 years of age and up in a 5 county area.

9446 Kelley Diversified

PO Box 967
Athens, GA 30603 706-549-4398
FAX: 706-549-4479

Mary Patton, Executive Director
Sherry Burns, Rehabilitation Services Director
Jenny Taylor, Business Operations Manager

Work adjustment and remunerative work programs.

9447 New Ventures

304 Fort Drive
LaGrange, GA 30240 706-882-7723

Dave Miller, Executive Director

A rehabilitation and work training facility for individuals with barriers to employability. The program utilizes community based industrial work of varying levels of difficulty. A return to work conditioning program for the industrially injured is offered which features: first-day contact, workers compensation rehabilitation team management, and light-duty work conditioning. A training stipend is paid to defray costs associated with training.

Hawaii

9448 ASSETS School

1 Ohana Nui Way
Honolulu, HI 96818 808-423-1356
FAX: 808-422-1920
e-mail: info@assets-school.net
assets-school.net

Lou Salza, Head of School
Ron Yoshmoto, Principal
Patti Jenks, Dean of Students

ASSETS is an independent school for gifted and or dyslexic children which provides an individualized, integrated learning enviroment. ASSETS' enviroment empowers these children to maximize their potential and to find their place as lifelong learners in school and society.

9449 Hawaii Fair Employment Practice Agency

888 Mililani Street Ph 2
Honolulu, HI 96813 808-599-5449
800-586-8800

9450 Hawaii Vocational Rehabilitation Division

601 Kamokila Boulevard
Room 515
Kapolei, HI 96707 808-692-7715
FAX: 808-692-7727

9451 Lanakila Rehabilitation Center

1809 Bachelot Street
Honolulu, HI 96817 808-531-0555
FAX: 808-533-7264
e-mail: lrc@pixi.com

James Wakafuji, President
Clarita Ayson, Rehab Services Director

A private, nonprofit corporation that provides prevocational and vocational evaluation, job placement and follow up and employment for person with disabilities.

9452 Wahiawa Family

330 Walker Avenue
Wahiawa, HI 96786 808-621-7407

Leslie Chinna

Work adjustment and remunerative work programs.

Idaho

9453 High Reachers Employment and Training

245 E 6th S
Mountain Home, ID 83647 208-587-5804

Joe McNeal, Executive Director

9454 Idaho Commission for the Blind and Visually Impaired

341 W Washington Street
Boise, ID 83702 208-334-3220
800-542-8688
FAX: 208-334-2963
www.icbvi.state.id.us

Cheryl Tapp, Special Programs Coordinator

Vocational rehabilitation, independent living training, medical intervention, adaptive technology and devices and employer advocacy.

9455 Idaho Division of Vocational Rehabilitation

650 W State Street
Room 150
Boise, ID 83720
800-856-2720
TDY:208-334-3390

George Pelletier, Jr., Administrator

Offers services for the totally blind, legally blind, visually impaired, mentally retarded blind and more with health, counseling, educational, recreational, rehabilitation, computer training and professional training services.

9456 Idaho Employment Service and Job Training Program Liaison

Idaho Department of Employment
317 Main Street
Boise, ID 83735   208-334-4200

9457 Idaho Fair Employment Practice Agency

Idaho Human Rights Commission
450 W State Street
Boise, ID 83702   208-334-5747

9458 Idaho Governor's Committee on Employment of People with Disabilities

317 Main Street
Boise, ID 83735

9459 Idaho Vocational Rehabilitation Agency

650 W State Street
Boise, ID 83702

Illinois

9460 Ada S. McKinley Vocational Services

1863 S Wabesh Avenue
Chicago, IL 60616   312-554-0600
FAX: 312-554-0292
TDY:312-697-9794
www.adasmckinley.org

Aberra Zewdie, Division Director
Kent Smith, Chief Development Officer

9461 Anixter Center

6610 N Clark Street
Chicago, IL 60626   773-973-7900

Stuart G. Ferst, President

A Chicago-based human services agency that assists people with disabilities to live and work successfully in the community. Anixter Center provides vocational training, employment services, residences, special education, prevention programs, community services and health care. In addition, Anixter Center offers Illinois' only substance abuse treatment programs specifically for people with disabilities including Addiction Recovery of the Deaf.

9462 C-4 Work Center

5710 North Broadway
Chicago, IL 60660   773-728-1000
FAX: 773-728-6517

Gino Balbuena, Production Manager
Anthony A. Kopera, Chief Executive Officer
Mark T. Hicks, Program Director

Aftercare, case finding, information and referrals, vocational training and work activities offered to mentally ill persons.

9463 Cornerstone Services

777 Joyce Road
Joliet, IL 60436   815-741-7602
FAX: 815-723-1177

James A. Hogan, President/CEO
Susan Murphy, PR Coordinator

Cornerstone Services provides progressive, comprehensive services for people with disabilities, promoting choice, dignity, and the opportunity to live and work in the community. Established in 1969, the agency provides developmental, vocational, employment, residential and mental health services at various community-based locations. The nonprofit social service agency helps approximately 750 people each day.

9464 Crystal Lake Vocational Rehabilitation Center

Pioneer Center
3941 W Dayton Street
McHenry, IL 60050   815-344-1230

Thomas Gollan, Executive Director

9465 Fulton County Rehab Center

500 N Main Street
Canton, IL 61520   309-649-1000
FAX: 309-649-1047

Rex Lewis

Work adjustment and remunerative work programs.

9466 Glenkirk

3504 Commercial Avenue
Northbrook, IL 60062   847-272-5111
FAX: 847-272-7350

Alan Spector, Executive Director

Helps infants, children and adults with developmental disabilities reach higher levels of independence. A non-profit organization serving people in north and northwest Chicago suburbs. Glenkirk's residential, vocational, educational and support programs include services which provide individual evaluation, therapeutic treatment and training.

9467 Illinois - President's Committee on Employment of the Disabled

623 E Adams Street
Springfield, IL 62701   217-785-0218
800-ASK-DORI
TDY:217-782-5734

Audrey McCrimon, Director

9468 Illinois Employment Service

Department of Employment Security
401 S State Street
Room 615
Chicago, IL 60605   312-353-5133

9469 Illinois Vocational Rehabilitation Agency

PO Box 14929
Springfield, IL 62794   217-529-0181

9470 Jewish Vocational Services

1 S Franklin Street
Chicago, IL 60606   312-357-4500
    FAX: 312-855-3282

Occupational training and job placement for handicapped persons of all religions.

9471 JoDavies Workshop

706 S W Street
Galena, IL 61036

Intake and referral, early intervention for children only, vocational evaluation and work adjustment training services offered.

9472 Kennedy Job Training Center

7361 S Meade
Bedford Park, IL 60638   708-594-7155
    FAX: 708-594-7156

Robin Mertes, Placement Manager
Kandy Stamer, QMRP/Intake Coordinator

Offers vocational evaluation, vocational training work adjustment training, and job placement services for developmentally disabled and hearing impaired persons.

9473 Knox County Council for Developmental Disabilities

2015 Windish Drive
Galesburg, IL 61401   309-344-2600
    FAX: 309-344-1754
    e-mail: kccdd@galesburg.net

Ned Hippensteel, Executive Director

Developmental training, vocational evaluation, work adjustment training, extended training, placement, supported employment, and CILA.

9474 Kreider Services

500 Anchor Road
Dixon, IL 61021   815-453-2074
    FAX: 815-288-1636

Arlan McClain, Executive Director

Offers day service programs, vocational training programs, job placement, supported employment, respite care, residential and family support for ages birth to three years.

9475 Lambs Farm

PO Box 520
Libertyville, IL 60048   847-362-4636
    FAX: 847-362-0742
    e-mail: jmc@lambsfarm.org
    www.lambsfarm.org

Jackie Cohen, Director of Program Services

Lambs Farm is a goal-oriented, comprehensive program of residential, vocational and social support services for adults with developmental disabilities.

9476 Lambs Vocational Work Center

PO Box 520
Libertyville, IL 60048   847-362-4636
    FAX: 847-362-0742
    e-mail: angelaf@lambsfarm.org
    www.lambsfarm.org

James Lundstrom, Executive Director
Jackie Cohen, Director of Program Services
Craig Lindley, Director of Vocational Services

Goal-oriented, comprehensive program of residnetial, vocational and social support service to adults with developmental disabilities.

9477 Land of Lincoln Goodwill Industries

800 N 10th Street
PO Box 8528
Springfield, IL 62703   217-789-0400
    FAX: 217-789-0540

Larry Hupp, Executive Director

Offers a developmental training and community employment programs for persons with disabilities.

9478 Orchard Association for the Retarded

7670 Marmora Avenue
Skokie, IL 60077   847-967-1800

Vocational program and counseling, respite services and community living facility for the retarded.

9479 Owens Vocational Training Center

2639 N Kildare Avenue
Chicago, IL 60639

Janie Nelson, Executive Director

9480 Sertoma Centre

4343 W 123rd Street
Alsip, IL 60803   708-371-9700

Gus van den Brink, Executive Director

Offers vocational services to promote independence and community integration; day training and residential services provided to individuals. Programs include: vocational evaluation, work adjustment training, janitorial training, job placement, sheltered work, supported employment, developmental training, respite care, residential services.

9481 Shore Training Center

8035 Austin Avenue
Morton Grove, IL 60053   847-581-0200

Mark Robinson
Provides remunerative work.

9482 Skills

1122 5th Avenue
Moline, IL 61265   309-797-3586
    FAX: 309-794-4914

Stuart Olson, President
William Taylor, Transitional Service

Accredited through the Commission on Accreditation of Rehabilitation Facilities; offers job training partnership act and vocational evaluation services offered.

9483 Thresholds AMISS
12145 Western Avenue
Blue Island, IL 60406 708-597-7997
FAX: 708-597-8073

Julia Rupp, Executive Director
Camille Rucks, Team Leader
Services offered include psychosocial, vocational and residential programs for ages 18 or older with a primary diagnosis of mental illness. Facility is wheelchair accessible.

9484 Washington County Vocational Workshop
PO Box 273
Nashville, IL 62263 618-327-4461

Keith Currin, Executive Director

9485 Westside Parents Work Activity Center
3765 W Odgen Avenue
Chicago, IL 60623 773-522-1200

Offers developmental training programs providing basic skills in self care for multiply and physically handicapped persons.

Indiana

9486 ADEC Resources for Independence
19607 State Road 120
Boonville, IN 46507 219-293-9597

Matt Leachman, Contact
Serves Elkhart County and surrounding area.

9487 ARC of Allen County
2542 Thompson Avenue
Fort Wayne, IN 46807 219-456-4534
FAX: 219-745-5200

Dan Winkle, Contact

9488 Anthony Wayne Rehabilitation Center for the Handicapped and Blind
2628 South Calhoun Street
Fort Wayne, IN 46807 219-774-6145
FAX: 219-744-0006

Bill Smith, Contact

9489 BI-Couinty Services
425 East Harrison Road
Bluffton, IN 46714 219-824-1253
FAX: 219-824-1892

Joice Bussard, Contact
Serves Wells and Adam Counties.

9490 Balance Centers of America
521 East 86th Avenue
Suite H
Merrillville, IN 46410 219-736-2930

Jane Labar, Contact

9491 Bridgepointe Goodwill Industries and Easter Seal Society
1329 Applegate Lane
PO Box 2117
Clarksville, IN 47129 812-283-7908
FAX: 812-283-6248

Terry Richards, Contact

9492 Carey Services
2724 South Carey Street
Marion, IN 46795 317-668-8961
FAX: 317-668-6747

Grant Black, Contact

9493 Division of Disability, Aging and Rehabilitative Services
402 W Washington Street, Room 451
PO Box 7083
Indianapolis, IN 46207 317-232-1147
FAX: 317-232-1240

Jeff Hendrickson, Contact

9494 EAB Industries
500 Second Avenuke
PO Box 6445
Evansville, IN 47719 812-422-1181
FAX: 812-424-3154

Margie Shank, Contact

9495 Four Rivers Resource Services
PO Box 249
Linton, IN 47441 812-847-2231
FAX: 812-847-8836
e-mail: fourrivers@frrs.org
www.frrs.org

Stephen Sacksteder, CEO
Lyna Landis, Marketing Coordinator
Employment, community living, connections, follow-along, early intervention, preschool, healthy families, child care resource and referral and child care voucher program, impact, and transpotation services.

9496 Gateway Services/JCARC
PO Box 216
Franklin, IN 46131 317-738-5500
FAX: 317-738-5522

Beth Hurst, Contact

9497 Goodwill Industries of Central Indiana
1635 West Michigan Street
Indianapolis, IN 46222 317-264-1313
FAX: 317-264-1336

Irene McClesky, Contact

9498 Indiana Employment Services and Job Training Program Liaison

10 N Senate Avenue
Indianapolis, IN 46204   317-232-6702
                                FAX: 317-233-5499

9499 Indiana Fair Employment Practice Agency

32 E Washington Street
Suite 900
Indianapolis, IN 46204   317-872-9991

9500 LCAR

2650 West 35th Street
Gary, IN 46408   219-884-1138

Brian Davis, Contact

9501 LaPorte County Sheltered Workshop

4315 E Michigan Boulevard
Michigan City, IN 46360   219-874-4288
                                FAX: 219-879-2139

Vocational training center for persons 16 and older with disabilities.

9502 New Hope Services

725 Wall Street
Jeffersonville, IN 47130   812-288-8248
                                FAX: 812-228-1206

Lynn Snow, Contact

9503 New Horizons Rehabilitation

237 Six Pine Ranch Road
PO Box 98
Batesville, IN 47006   812-934-4528

Greg Tow, Contact

Serves Ripley, Franklin, Ohio, Switzerland Dearborn, and Decatur.

9504 Noble Centers

2400 North Tibbs Avenue
Indianapolis, IN 46222   317-264-1510
                                FAX: 317-264-5300

Tom Cain, Contact

9505 Putnam Countyi Comprehensive Services

630 Tennessee Street
Greencastle, IN 46135   765-653-9753
                                FAX: 765-653-7646

Tammy Amore

9506 Southern Indiana Resource Solutions

1579 South Folsomville Road
Boonville, IN 47601   812-897-4840
                                FAX: 812-897-0123

9507 Sycamore Rehabilitation Services

1001 Sycamore Lane
Danville, IN 46122   317-745-4715
                                FAX: 317-745-8271

Patrick Cockrum, Contact

9508 Wabash/Employability Center

SC6395 Earl Avenue
Suite 2
Lafayette, IN 47903   765-447-0300
                                FAX: 765-447-6456

Bill Carmichael, Contact
Serves Tippecanoe County.

Iowa

9509 ACT Assessment Test Preparation Reference Manual

American College Testing Program
2201 Dodge
168
Iowa City, IA 52243   319-337-1000

This reference manual was developed as a resource for high school teachers and counselors in assisting students with test preparation.

9510 ACT Asset Technical Manual

American College Testing Program
2201 Dodge
168
Iowa City, IA 52243   319-337-1000

Provides a technical description of the ASSET program to guide users in working with the program and interpreting test results.

9511 Franklin County Work Activity Center

20 5th Street NW
Hampton, IA 50441   515-456-5293

Steven Paul Woods, Executive Director

Nonprofit organization providing residential and vocational services in Franklin and Hardin counties in the state of Iowa. Residential Services include RCF/MR services, Supported Community Living Services and Community Supervised Apartment Living Arrangement Services. Vocational Services include Work Services and Supported Employment Services. Accredited by the Commission on Accreditation of rehabilitation Facilities since 1984, and serves individuals with a wide range of needs.

9512 Innovative Industries

405 E Madison Street
Winterset, IA 50273   515-462-2926
                                FAX: 515-462-2870
                        e-mail: winnind@iowalink.com

Donna Dodson, Program Manager
Connie Bailey, Client Services Coordinator

9513 Iowa Civil Rights Commission

211 E Maple Street
2nd Floor
Des Moines, IA 50309   515-281-4121
                                FAX: 515-242-5840
                        www.state.ia.us/government/crc

9514   Iowa Employment Service
1000 E Grand Avenue
Des Moines, IA   50319   515-281-6647

9515   Iowa Job Training Program Liaison
Iowa Department of Economic Development
200 E Grand Avenue
Des Moines, IA   50309   515-242-4827

9516   Iowa State Vocational Rehabilitation Facility
510 E 12th Street
Des Moines, IA   50309   515-281-4311
                                 FAX: 515-281-7643

John Larson, Assistant Chief

9517   Iowa Valley Community College
3702 S Center Street
Marshalltown, IA   50158   515-752-4643
                                 FAX: 515-752-5909

Bill Martin, Career Development

Offers two levels of specialized vocational preparatory programming for adults with disabilities. The Career Development Center serves dependent adults. The goal of the program is to maintain or improve skills to enable persons served to enter sheltered or supported employment. The IRP/CBVT programs are non-credit specialized vocational programs for independent adults served by Vocational Rehabilitation and our programs. The goals are for competitive placements in jobs. CARF accredited.

9518   Iowa Vocational Rehabilitation Agency
510 E 12th Street
Des Moines, IA   50309   515-281-4311
                                 FAX: 515-281-7643

9519   New Focus
102 W Washington
Centerville, IA   52544   515-437-1722

Keith Lindley, Executive Director
Peggy Oden, Director of Rehabilitation

Provides vocational services for adults with disabilities. Includes work activity, supported employment and supported community living.

9520   Second Time Around
110 W Jackson Street
Centerville, IA   52544   515-437-7355

Keith Lindley, Executive Director
Debbie Steen, Store Supervisor

Work training site for adults with disabilities.

Kansas

9521   Clay Center Adult Training Center
701 4th Street
Clay Center, KS   67432   785-632-5357
                                 FAX: 785-632-5371

Lillian Bosch, Executive Director

9522   Kansas Fair Employment Practice Agency
900 SW Jackson Street
Topeka, KS   66612   785-296-1500

9523   Kansas Vocational Rehabilitation Agency
300 SW Oakley Avenue
Biddle Building, 1st Floor
Topeka, KS   66606   913-296-3911
                                 TDY:913-296-7029
e-mail: jac@srkspo.wpo.state.ks.us

Joyce Cussimanio, Director

Kentucky

9524   Kentucky Committee on Employment of People with Disabilities
600 W Cedar Street
Louisville, KY   40202   502-595-4165

9525   Kentucky Department for Employment Service and Job Training Program Liaison
275 E Main Street 2-W
Frankfort, KY   40621   502-564-2367
                                 FAX: 502-564-7799
www.kentuckyhomepage.com

9526   Kentucky Department for the Blind
Kentucky Department for the Blind
209 St. Clair Street
PO Box 757
Frankfort, KY   40602   502-564-4754
                                 877-592-5463
                                 FAX: 502-564-2951
                                 TDY:502-564-6742
e-mail: Denise.Placido@mail.state.ky.us
                                 kyblind.state.ky.us

Denise Placido, Commissioner

The Kentucky Department for the Blind provides a wide range of services including: medical evaluation and assistance; personel counseling and independent living skills development; vocational evaluation, training and job placement; job retention services; and technical equipment and visual devices. Although the services provided vary depending upon individual needs, all of the department's efforts share one common goal: To help provide blind or visually impaired individuals with opportunities.

9527   Kentucky Vocational Rehabilitation Agency
500 Mero Street
Frankfort, KY   40601   502-564-4896

9528 Pioneer Vocational/Industrial Services

590 Stanford Road
Danville, KY 40422

Jack Goodbey, Executive Director

9529 Work Enhancement Center of Western Kentucky

803 Poplar Street
Murray, KY 42071   502-762-1100
FAX: 502-767-3600

Steve Passmore, Director

The center has been established in order to service industry in the three state area surrounding Kentucky. This service includes job/skill evaluation, job design consultation, pre-employment employee evaluations and economic evaluation.

Louisiana

9530 Community Opportunities of East Ascension

1122 E Ascension Complex Boulevard
Gonzales, LA 70737   225-621-2000
FAX: 225-621-2022

Mark Thomas, Director

Committed to affording individuals the opportunities that reflect and support choices, dignity, individuality, self-determination, community, coherency and commen sense. Programs incloude Respite, Personal Care Attendant, Support Living, Support Environment, Adult Day Training, and Elderly/Adult Waiver Services.

9531 Louisiana Employment Service and Job Training Program Liaison

PO Box 94094
Baton Rouge, LA 70804   225-342-3111
FAX: 225-342-3030

9532 Louisiana Vocational Rehabilitation Agency

4051 Veterans Boulevard
Suite 408
Metairieuge, LA 70002   504-838-5180
FAX: 504-838-5413

9533 St. James Association for Retarded Citizens

29150 Health Unit Street
Vacherie, LA 70090   225-265-7910

A private sheltered work program for mentally retarded and developmentally disabled adults.

9534 Westbank Sheltered Workshop

1728 Hermosa Street
New Orleans, LA 70114   504-362-1311

A private non-residential facility serving severely disabled individuals referred through Louisiana Rehabilitation Services.

Maine

9535 Addison Point Specialized Services

PO Box 207
Addison, ME 04606   207-483-2817
FAX: 207-483-2817

Paula Chartrand, Executive Officer

Provides services to individuals who are deaf/blind, mentally retarded, autistic, behaviorally challenged and/or dual diagnosed. Training services to place these individuals in community employment.

9536 Bangor Veteran Center - Veterans Outreach Center

352 Harlow Street
Bangor, ME 04401   207-947-3391
FAX: 207-941-8195

Joseph A. DeGrasse, Team Leader
Robert L. Daisey, MSW, Clinical Coordinator

Readjustment counseling services for veterans of Vietnam, Vietnam Era, Persian Gulf, Panama, Grenada, Lebanon, Somalia, WWII and Korean conflicts.

9537 Creative Work Systems

443 Congress Street
Portland, ME 04101   207-879-1140
FAX: 207-879-1146
e-mail: cws@gwi.net
www.creativesystems.com

Susan Percy, Executive Director

Provides residential, day habilitation and supported emploment in Central and Southern Maine.

9538 Maine Employment Service

20 Union Street
Augusta, ME 04330   207-287-3788

9539 Maine Fair Employment Practice Agency

Maine Human Rights Commission
51 State House Station
Augusta, ME 04333   207-624-6050
FAX: 207-624-6063
TDY: 207-624-6064
www.state.me.us/mhrc

State agency with the responsibility of enforcing Maine's anti-discrimination laws. The commission investigates complaints of unlawful discrimination in employment, housing, education, access to public accommodations, extension of credit, and offensive names.

9540 Maine Governor's Committee on Employment of the Disabled

35 Anthony Avenue
Augusta, ME 04330   207-624-5335

9541 Maine Vocational Rehabilitation Agency

35 Anthony Avenue
Augusta, ME 04330   207-624-5300
       800-332-1003
       TDY:207-624-5322
       e-mail: harold.j.lewis@state.me.us

Harold Lewis, Director

9542 Northeast Occupational Exchange

248 Center Street
Bangor, ME 04401   207-942-3816

Dr. Charles Tingley, Executive Director

Maryland

9543 Ardmore Developmental Center

3000 Lottsford Vista Road
Bowie, MD 20721
       FAX: 301-731-4551

Donalda Lovelace, Chief Executive Officer

Offers supported employment programs and vocational education for persons who are mentally retarded as well as residential services and Emergency Respite Care.

9544 Job Opportunities for the Blind

National Federation of the Blind
1800 Johnson Street
Baltimore, MD 21230   410-837-6763
       FAX: 410-685-5653
       e-mail: nfb@iamdigex.net
       www.nfb.org
James Geshel, Director of Governmental Affairs
Anthony Cobb, Director Job Opportinities for

This free service allows individuals touch-tone telephone access to the thousands of jobs listed in America's Job Bank, and internet service run by the Department of Labor. Any person registered with either a state rehabilitation agency or a state employment service can search across the country for jobs by either type of work or location.

9545 Mainstream

3 Bethesda Metro Center
Suite 830
Bethesda, MD 20814   301-891-8777
       FAX: 301-891-8778
       e-mail: mainstrm@aol.com

Patricia M. Jackson, Executive Director

Nonprofit organization dedicated to improving competitive employment opportunities for persons with disabilities. Provides specialized services and acts as a bridge that links service providers, employers and persons with disablties. Provides training, educational publications, and videos on disablityemployment issues. Educationa materials include a magazine, brochures, and audio-visual aids.

9546 Maryland Employment Services and Job Training Program Liaison

1100 N Eutaw Street
Room 600
Baltimore, MD 21201   410-767-2173

9547 Maryland Fair Employment Practice Agency

400 Washington Avenue
Room 124
Towson, MD 21204   410-887-5557
       FAX: 410-769-8914

9548 Maryland State Department of Education

Division of Rehabilitation Services (DIRS)
2301 Argonne Drive
Baltimore, MD 21218   410-554-9385

Robert Burns, Asst. State Super.

The Vocational Rehabilitation Program delivers to eligible individuals with physical and/or mental disabilities to enable them to become employed. The Independent Living Program's goal is to assist people in remaining in their homes and communities. The Division operates the Maryland Rehabilitation Center, a comprehensive evaluation and training center that has dormitory space. There are field offices located statewide with counselors to advise and manage the provision of services offered.

9549 PWI Profile

Projects W/Industry, Goodwill Industries of Amer.
9200 Wisconsin Avenue
Bethesda, MD 20814

Newsletter on employment of persons with disabilities.

9550 Project LINK

Mainstream
3 Bethesda Metro Center
Suite 830
Bethesda, MD 20814   301-891-8777
       800-247-1380
       FAX: 301-891-8778
       e-mail: info@mainstreaminc.org
       www.mainstreaminc.org

Provides job development and placement in services to dislocated workers with disabilities in the Washington, DC and Dallas, TX areas.

9551 TLC - The Treatment and Learning Centers

9975 Medical Center Drive
Rockville, MD 20850   301-738-1415

Richard Pavlin, Executive Director

Helps parents, children and teachers understand and overcome educational difficulties. They offer interdisciplinary diagnostic testing individually tailored to pinpoint the specific strengths and needs of students who may have learning disabilities, Dyslexia or other learning problems.

Massachusetts

9552 Division of Employment & Training
State of Massachusetts
19 Staniford Street
3rd Floor
Boston, MA 02114   617-626-6560

9553 Gateway Crafts: Crafts Store and Gallery
Vinfen Corporation
62 Harvard Street
Brookline, MA 02445   617-734-1577
FAX: 617-734-3199
e-mail: gateway@vinfen.org

Rae T. Edelson, Program Director
Ted Lampe, Asst. Program Dir.
Mona Thaler, Marketing Director

An arts based vocational service for adults with developmental and other disabilities including mental illness, autism and head injury who can pursue paid work in fine art and crafts with the aid of professional artists/teachers, a professional marketer, and a crafts store and gallery. *$53.98*

9554 Massachusetts Fair Employment Practice Agency
1 Ashburton Place
Room 601
Boston, MA 02108   617-727-8900

9555 Massachusetts Governor's Commission on Employment of Disabled Persons
19 Standiford Street
3rd Floor
Boston, MA 02114   617-864-2000

9556 Massachusetts Vocational Rehab for the Blind and Visually Impaired
88 Kingston Street
Boston, MA 02111   617-727-5550
800-392-6556
TDY:800-392-6556
e-mail: ccrawford@state.ma.us

Charles Crawford, Commissioner

9557 Massachusetts Vocational Rehabilitation Agency
27-43 Wormwood Street
Boston, MA 02119   617-727-2183
FAX: 617-727-1354

9558 Work
3 Arlington Street
North Quincy, MA 02171   617-328-0300

Dr. William Wolk, Executive Director

Michigan

9559 Disability Community Small Business Development Center
Ann Arbor Center for Independent Living
2568 Packard
Ann Arbor, MI 48104   734-484-5310
FAX: 734-971-0826

Roseanne Herzog, Director

Offers small business counseling and training to individuals with disabilities in the state of Michigan.

9560 Lamplighter's Work Center
1320 W State Street
Cheboygan, MI 49721   906-274-5456

Robert Spinella, Executive Director

9561 Michigan Employment Service
7310 Woodward Avenue
Detroit, MI 48202   313-876-5217

9562 Michigan Fair Employment Practice Agency
1200 Sixth Avenue, North Tower
6th Floor
Detroit, MI 48226   313-256-2202
FAX: 313-256-2167

9563 Michigan Vocational Rehab for Persons Who Are Blind & Visually Impaired
201 N Washington Square
Lansing, MI 48933   517-372-1380

9564 Michigan Vocational Rehabilitation Agency
PO Box 30010
Lansing, MI 48909   517-335-1343

Minnesota

9565 Jewish Vocational Service of Jewish Family and Children's Services
1500 Lilac Drive South
Suite 311
Minneapolis, MN 55416   612-546-0616
FAX: 612-593-1778

Jeremy Waldman, Executive Director

9566 Minnesota Department of Jobs and Training
390 Robert Street North
Saint Paul, MN 55101   651-296-3683

9567 Minnesota Employment Practice Agency
Laura Sengil, Dept. of Human Rights
190 E 5th Street
Suite 700
St. Paul, MN 55101   651-296-9044

9568 Minnesota Vocational Rehabilitation Agency
390 Robert Street North
5th Floor
Saint Paul, MN   55101   612-296-3900
                                800-328-9095
                        TDY:612-296-3900
        e-mail: mick.coleman@state.mn.us

Michael Coleman, Assistant Commissioner

9569 PWI Forum
Multi Resource Centers
1900 Chicago Avenue
Minneapolis, MN   55404   612-871-2402

Newsletter for business, community and government leaders. Focuses on employment of persons with disabilities.

Mississippi

9570 Allied Enterprises of Tupelo
613 Pegram Drive
Tupelo, MS   38801   662-287-1461
                      FAX: 662-287-1463

J. Barry Bray, Facility Manager
Vocational evaluation, work adjustment and job placement of disabled persons in a rehabilitation workshop.

9571 Mississippi Employment Secutity Commission
PO Box 1669
Jackson, MS   39215   601-961-7501
                      FAX: 601-961-7405
                      www.mesc.state.ms.us

9572 Mississippi Vocational Rehabilitation
PO Box 1698
Jackson, MS   39215   601-853-5100
                             800-443-1000
                      FAX: 601-853-5158
                      TDY:800-443-1000

Offers low vision aids and appliances, counseling, social work, educational and professional training, residential services, recreational services, computer training and employment opportunities for the handicapped.

9573 Worksight
Mississippi State University
PO Box 6189
Mississippi State, MS   39762   601-325-2001
                                       800-675-7782
                                FAX: 662-325-8989
                        e-mail: rrtc@ra.state.edu
                        www.blind.msstate.edu

Discusses news, activities, research projects and training programs of the Center.

Missouri

9574 Missouri Employment Services
PO Box 59
Jefferson City, MO   65102   573-751-4091

                        www.dolir.state.mo.us

Renell Wynn, Director

9575 Missouri Fair Employment Practice Agency
3315 W Truman Boulevard
Jefferson City, MO   65102   573-751-4091

                        www.dolir.state.mo.us

Renell Wynn, Director

9576 Missouri Governor's Council on Disability
PO Box 1668
Jefferson City, MO   65102   573-751-2600
                                    800-877-8249
                               FAX: 573-526-4109
                               TDY:573-751-2600
                e-mail: gcd@dolir.state.mo.us
                www.dolir.state.mo.us/gcd

Advocate training, civil rights, community education services, community resource referral, conferences, consumer education, disability awareness program, educational information and resources, information and education services, information and referral, newsletter, policy issues and services, publications, resource directory, seminars, technical assistance, training and seminars.

9577 Missouri Job Training Program Liaison
221 Metro Drive
Jefferson City, MO   65109   573-634-2321

9578 Missouri Vocational Rehabilitation Agency
3024 West Truman Boulevard
Jefferson Cty, MO   65109   573-751-3251
                             FAX: 573-741-1441
                             TDY:573-751-3251

Don Glann, Assistant Commissioner

9579 WX: Work Capacities
17331 E 40th Highway
Suite 103
Independence, MO   64055

Carol Lett, Executive Director

Montana

9580 Montana Employment Services and Job Training Programs Liaison
PO Box 1728
Helena, MT   59624   406-444-3697

9581 Montana Fair Employment Practice Agency

PO Box 1728
Helena, MT 59624   406-444-3697
    800-542-0807

9582 Montana Governor's Committee on Employment of Disabled People

Mitchell Building
Room 130
Helena, MT 59620

9583 Montana Vocational Rehabilitation for Persons Who Are Visually Impaired

PO Box 4210
Helena, MT 59604   406-444-2618

Nebraska

9584 Nebraska Employment Services

Department of Labor
550 S 16th Street
Lincoln, NE 68508   816-426-5481

9585 Nebraska Fair Employment Practice Agency

301 Centennial Mall S
Lincoln, NE 68508   402-471-4997

9586 Nebraska Governor's Committee on the Employment of the Handicapped

550 S 16th Street
Lincoln, NE 68508   402-472-1415

9587 Nebraska Vocational Rehabilitation Agency

301 Centennial Mall South
Lincoln, NE 68509   402-471-3644
    877-637-3422
    FAX: 402-471-0788
e-mail: vr_stateoffice@vocrehab.state.ne.us

Services for individuals with disabilities who want to become employed. Services are free to those who qualify.

9588 Nebraska Work Force Development

550 South 16th Street
Lincoln, NE 68509   402-471-9792
    FAX: 402-471-2318

Fernando Lecuona III, Commissioner

Nevada

9589 Nevada Fair Employment Practice Agency

1515 E Tropicana Avenue
Suite 590
Las Vegas, NV 89119

9590 Nevada Governor's Committee on Employment of Persons with Disabilities

3100 Mill Street
Suite 115
Reno, NV 89502

9591 Nevada Job Training Program Liaison

400 Capitol
Carson City, NV 89710

9592 Nevada Vocational Rehabilitation Agency

505 E King Street
5th Floor
Carson City, NV 89701   775-684-4070
    TDY:702-687-4440

Elizabeth Breshears, Administrator

9593 State of Nevada Rehabilitation Division, Administrative Office

Dept. of Employment, Training, and Rehabilitation
505 E King Street
Carson City, NV 89701   775-684-4040
    FAX: 775-684-3705
    www.detrjoblink.org

Maynard Yasmer, Administrator
Peter Singleton, Rehab. Program Supervisor
Bob Nichols, Rehabilitation Manager

The Rehabilitation Division is comprised of four bureaus and the community-based services unit to address prevention, assessment, training, treatment and job placement for Nevadans with functional disabilities. The division places primary emphasis on providing necessary services to help clients work and live independently and substance-free. The division administrator, based in Carson City, oversees programs offered in offices throughout the state.

New Hampshire

9594 Fit for Work at Exeter Hospital

10 Buzell Avenue
Exeter, NH 03833   603-778-7311
    FAX: 603-778-6671

Staffed by a team of allied health professionals, our outpatient rehabilitation program offers functional restoration, work therapy, diagnostic testing and physical therapy.

9595 New Hampshire Division of Vocational Rehabilitation

78 Regional Drive
Concord, NH 03301   603-271-3471
    TDY:603-271-3471
e-mail: pleather@ed.state.nh.us

Paul Leather, Director

Offers services for the totally blind, legally blind, visually impaired, mentally retarded blind and more with health, counseling, educational, recreational, rehabilitation, computer training and professional training services.

9596 New Hampshire Employment Security

32 South Main Street
Concord, NH 03301　　　603-224-3311
　　　　　　　　　　　　800-852-3400
　　　　　　　　　FAX: 603-228-4145
　　　　　　　　　TDY:800-735-2964
　　　　　　　　　www.nhes.state.nh.us

Sandy Smith Dupree, Public Info. Officer

Operates a free public employment service and provides assisted and self directed employment and career related services and labor market information for employers and the general public.

9597 New Hampshire Fair Employment Practice Agency

2 Chanelle Drive
Concord, NH 03301　　　603-225-3699
　　　　　　　　　FAX: 603-271-6339

9598 New Hampshire Job Training Program Liaison

64 Old Suncook Road
Concord, NH 03301　　　603-228-3349

New Jersey

9599 ARC of Bergen and Passaic Counties

223 Moore Street
Hackensack, NJ 07601　　　201-343-0322
　　　　　　　　　FAX: 201-343-0401
　　　　　　　e-mail: arcbp@aol.com
　　　　　　　www.arcbergenpassaic.org

Alice Siegel, Dir Community Presidential Serv.
Kathy Walsh, Senior VP Program Services
Anne Gallucci, Director, Vocational Services

serving persons with Mental Retardation and developmental disabilities in Bergen and Passaic Counties, NJ.

9600 ARC of Hunterdon County - New Jersey

1322 State Route 31
Suite 5
Annandale, NJ 08801　　　980-730-7827
　　　　　　　　　FAX: 980-730-7726

Barbara Gustassen, Contact
Serves Hunterdon County.

9601 ARC/Gloucester County

1555 Gateway Boulevard
Woodbury, NJ 08096　　　856-848-8648
　　　　　　　　　FAX: 856-848-7753

Mike Carlin, Contact

9602 ARC/Mercer County

180 Ewingville Road
Ewing, NJ 08638　　　609-406-0181
　　　　　　　　　FAX: 609-406-9258
　　　　　　　　　www.arcmercer.org

Joseph Gousie, Executive Director

9603 Abilities Center of New Jersey

790 North Delsea Drive
Westville, NJ 08093　　　856-848-1025
　　　　　　　　　FAX: 856-848-4229

Susan Buchaman, Contact

9604 Abilities of Northwest Jersey

264 Route 31 North
Washington, NJ 07882

　　　　　　　　　www.abilities-nw.com

Program designated for individuals with disabilities who may need more time to complete their goal of competitive employment and for those individuals who may work best in a more structured work environment.

9605 Abilities of Northwest New Jersey

264 Route 31 North
PO Box 251
Washington, NJ 07882　　　908-689-1118
　　　　　　　　　FAX: 908-689-6363

Denny Senke, Contact
Serves northwestern New Jersey.

9606 Alliance for Disabled in Action New Jersey

629 Ambuy Avenue
LL Suite
Edison, NJ 08837　　　732-738-4388

Debbie Bain, Contact
Serves Summerset, Union and Middlesex Counties.

9607 Alternatives for Growth - New Jersey

16-00 208 South
Fair Lawn, NJ 07410　　　201-797-8330
　　　　　　　　　FAX: 201-797-3586

Donna Flannery, Contact
Serves all New Jersey.

9608 Arc Monmouth County

1158 Wayside Road
Tinton Falls, NJ 07712　　　732-493-1919
　　　　　　　　　FAX: 732-493-3604
　　　　　　e-mail: arcmon@superlink.net
　　　　　　　www.arcofmonmouth.org

Jacqueline Moskowitz, Contact

9609 Career Opportunity Development, New Jersey

901 Atlantic Avenue
Egg Harbor, NJ 08215　　　732-756-5575

Jenine Emil, Contact
Serves Bergen and Passaic Counties.

9610 Center for Educational Advancement New Jersey

11 Minneakoning Road
Flemington, NJ 08822　　　908-782-1480
　　　　　　　　　FAX: 908-782-5370

Jill Zawbowski, Contact

Serves Summerset and Mercer Counties.

9611   Cerebral Palsy Association of Middlesex County
Roosevelt Park
Oak Drive
Edison, NJ   08837   201-549-5580
                                    FAX: 201-603-0284

Dominic Ursino, Contact
Serves Central New Jersey.

9612   Commission for the Blind & Visually Impaired -
New Jersey
153 Halsey Street, 6th Floor
PO Box 47017
Newark, NJ   07101   973-648-3333
                                    FAX: 973-648-7364
              e-mail: jhilton@dhs.state.nj.us

Jamie C. Hilton, Executive Director
State agency that provides services to people with
vision loss.

9613   Easter Seal Hackensack
171 Atlantic Street
Hackensack, NJ   07601   201-342-5739
                                    FAX: 201-342-4480

Denise Sredeen, Contact
Serves Hackensack.

9614   Easter Seal Society of New Jersey Highlands
Workshop
133 Main Street
Franklin, NJ   07416   973-827-9066
                                    FAX: 973-827-3828

Dave Shickle, Contact
Serves all New Jersey.

9615   Easter Seal of Ocean County
150 Oberlin Avenue
Lakewood, NJ   08701   732-363-6621
                                    FAX: 732-363-7540

Greg Makely, Contact

9616   Easter Seals New Jersey
1 Kimberly Road
East Brunswick, NJ   08815   732-257-6662

Wilma Rosa, Contact
Serves all New Jersey.

9617   Eden WERCS
1 Eden Way
Princeton, NJ   08540   609-987-0099
                                    FAX: 609-734-0069

Peter Gerhardt, Contact

9618   Edison Sheltered Workshop
328 Plainfield Avenue
Edison, NJ   08817   732-985-3844
                                    FAX: 732-985-2216

Ann Marie Stone, Vocational Rehab. Counselor
Serves Middlesex County. Vocational training and
job placement services.

9619   First Occupational Center of New Jersey
391 Lakeside Avenue
Orange, NJ   07050
                                    800-894-6232
                                    FAX: 973-672-0065
                                    e-mail: ocnj@idt.net
                                    www.focnj.com

Rocco J. Meola, President/CEO
Tanya Edghill, Dir of Rehabilitation Services
A private, not-for-profit multi-service community rehabilitation program. Services are offered to the developmentally disabled, visually impaired, hearing
impaired and welfare recipients. Services include vocational evaluation and training, respite care, basic
and remedial education and job placement and community support services.

9620   Goodwill Industries of Southern New Jersey
2835 Route 735
Maple Shades, NJ   08052   856-665-7270

Dan Hanson, Contact

9621   Hausmann Industries
130 Unikon Street
Northvale, NJ   07647   201-767-0255
                                    FAX: 201-767-1369
Jim
Serves all New Jersey.

9622   Jersey Cape Diagnostic Training & Opportunity
Center
152 Crest Haven Road
Cape May Court House, NJ   08210 609-465-4117
                                    FAX: 609-465-3899

George Plewa, Contact
Serves Cape May County.

9623   Medical Economics
Five Paragon Drive
Montvale, NJ   07645   201-358-7203

Pam Bilash, Contact

9624   New Jersey Employment Service and Job
Training Program Services
Department of Labor
Trenton, NJ   08625   609-292-1040

9625 New Jersey Vocational Rehabilitation Agency

135 E State Street CN398
Trenton, NJ 08625   609-292-5987
                              FAX: 609-292-8347
                              TDY:609-292-2919
               e-mail: dirnjdvr@concentric.net

Thomas G. Jennings, Director

9626 Occupational Center of Hudson County

780 Montgomery Street
Jersey City, NJ 07306   201-432-5959
                              FAX: 201-432-6227

Christine Romier, Contact
Serves Hudson County.

9627 Occupational Center of Union County

301 Cox Street
Roselle, NJ 08540   908-241-7200
                              FAX: 908-241-2025

Michele Ford, Contact

9628 Occupational Training Center of Burlington County

130 Hancock Lane
Mount Holly, NJ 08060   609-267-6677
                              FAX: 609-265-8418

Karen Elliott, Contact

9629 Occupational Training Center of Camden County - New Jersey

215 West White Horse Pike
Berlin, NJ 08009   856-768-0845
                              FAX: 856-768-1378

Peggy Engelburt, Contact
Serves Camden County.

9630 Pathway To Independence

450 Schuyler Avenue
Kearny, NJ 07306   201-997-6155
                              FAX: 201-997-7070

Lisa Johnson, Contact
Serves Hudson and Bergen Counties.

9631 Somerset Training and Employment Program

36 4th Street
Somerville, NJ 08876   732-846-2734

Laurie Falka, Executive Director

9632 St. John of God Community Services Vocational Rehabilitation

1145 Delsea Drive
Westville Grove, NJ 08093   856-848-4700
                              FAX: 856-848-1512

Carol Stark, Contact
Serves Gloucester and Camden Counties.

9633 United Cerebral Palsy Associations of New Jersey

354 South Broad Street
Trenton, NJ 08608   609-392-4004
                              FAX: 609-392-3505

Jacqueline Stroman, Contact

9634 West Essex Rehab Center

83 Walnut Street
Montclair, NJ 07042   201-744-7733
                              FAX: 201-744-3744

Ben Viearisi, Contact
Shannon Williams, Contact

New Mexico

9635 Adelante Development Center

4906-A Jefferson, Northeast
Albuquerque, NM 88310   505-341-2000

Reina Chavez, Contact
Serves Albuquerque and Belin.

9636 Commission for the Blind - New Mexico

PERA Building
Room 553
Santa Fe, NM 87503   505-827-4479

9637 Goodwill Industries of New Mexico

500 San Mateo Boulevard, Northeast
Albuquerque, NM 87109   505-881-6401
                              FAX: 505-884-3157

Charles Lynn, Contact
Serves all New Mexico.

9638 New Mexico Employment Services and Job Training Liaison

PO Box 1928
Albuquerque, NM 87103   505-827-6827
                              FAX: 505-827-6860
                  e-mail: djones2@state.nm.us

9639 Opportunity Center - New Mexico

873 Wright Avenue
Alamogordo, NM 88310   505-437-0919
                              FAX: 505-437-1135

Larry Weber, Contact
Serves Alamogorda area.

9640 RCI

1023 Stanford Drive NE
Albuquerque, NM 87106   505-255-5501
                              FAX: 505-255-9971

Elizabeth Domzalski, Contact
Serves Bernalillo County.

9641 State Department of Education New Mexico Division of Vocational Rehabilitation

435 St. Michael Drive
Building D
Santa Fe, NM 87505   505-954-8500

www.business-disability.com

9642 Tohatchi Area of Opportunity & Services

PO Box 49
Tohatchi, NM 87325   505-733-2200
                            FAX: 505-733-2678

Patrick Keptner, Executive Director
Marcella Franklin, Program Director
Daric Kalleco, Community Living Coordinator

Serves McKinley County, San Jose County and the Havanjo Nation.

New York

9643 JOBS V and SAGE

PESCO International
21 Paulding Street
Pleasantville, NY 10570   914-769-4266
                                800-431-2016
                           FAX: 914-769-2970
                       e-mail: pesco@pesco.org
                              www.pesco.org

Charles Kass, Vice President

A micro computer matching system matching people to occupations, training, local jobs, local employers and giving job outlooks for the year 2005. Sage 2001 is online computerized testing with the ability for system to read all questions, and job descriptions. Sage is a hands on-computer scored test battery with various adaptation. Braille, large print, bi-lingual and special devices.

9644 Just One Break (JOBS)

120 Wall Street
Floor 20
New York, NY 10005   212-785-7300
                           FAX: 212-785-4513
               e-mail: justonebreak@interactive.net
                        www.justonebreak.com

9645 New York State Department of Labor

State Office Campus
Building 12
Albany, NY 12240   518-432-9000

e-mail: nysdol@labor.state.ny.us
www.labor.state.ny.us

James J. McGowan, Commissioner
Fredda Peritz, Employment Servic. Div. Dir.
Thomas Malone, Unemployment Insur. Div. Dir.

The missin of the New York State Department of Labor is to help New York work by preparing individuals for the jobs of today and tomorrow. Provides direct job search and counseling services to job seekers, and can refer people who have disabilities for training opportunities. Provides unemployment insurance for those out of work through no fault of their own.

9646 New York Vocational Rehabilitation Agency

1 Commerce Plaza
Room 1606
Albany, NY 12210   518-486-4032
                          FAX: 518-486-4154

9647 Rational Effectiveness Training Systems

IRET Corporate Services Division
45 E 65th Street
New York, NY 10021   212-570-2868

Dr. Dominic DiMattie, Director

Offers advanced training for employee assistance professionals, full service outpatient counseling, consulting services and on-site workshops for the disabled.

North Carolina

9648 Division of Employment & Training

4111 N Harrington Street
Raliegh, NC 27603   919-715-6500

9649 Iredell Vocational Workshop

PO Box 8
Troutman, NC 28166   704-873-5646
                            FAX: 704-871-9881

Ben Garrison, Director

9650 North Carolina Division of Services for the Blind

2601 Mail Service Center
Raleigh, NC 27699   919-733-9822
                          FAX: 919-733-9769
                          TDY:919-733-9700
                  e-mail: john.deluca@ncmail.net
                       www.dhhs.state.nc.us/dsb

John Deluca, Director

9651 North Carolina Employment Services

PO Box 25903
Raleigh, NC 27611   919-733-2790
                          FAX: 919-733-0981

9652 North Carolina Vocational Rehabilitation

PO Box 26053
Raleigh, NC 27611   919-733-3364
                          FAX: 919-733-7968
                          TDY:919-733-5924
                e-mail: bphilbeck@dhr.state.nc.us

Bob Philbeck, Director

Offers services for the totally blind, legally blind, visually impaired, mentally retarded blind and more with health, counseling, educational, recreational, rehabilitation, computer training and professional training services.

9653 Rowan County Vocational Workshop

2728 Old Concord Road
Salisbury, NC 28146   704-633-6223
                            FAX: 704-633-6224

Terry Osborne, Executive Director

Offers vocational assessment and training, adult developmental activities.

9654 Rutherford Vocational Workshop

200 Fairground Road
Spindale, NC 28160 828-287-9302

Judith Toney, Executive Director

9655 Transylvania Vocational Services

PO Box 1115
Brevard, NC 28712 828-884-3195
FAX: 828-884-3102

Nancy Stricker, Executive Director

9656 Webster Enterprises of Jackson County

PO Box 220
Webster, NC 28788 828-586-8981
FAX: 828-586-8125

Arlene C. Stewart, Executive Director
Eileen Wheeldon, Controller

A community based employment and training program for people with disabilities. A full service program which includes a youth transitional program for life beyond high school, job coaching, vocational assessment and job placement.

9657 Western Regional Vocational Rehabilitation Facility Clifford File, Jr.

PO Box 1443
Morganton, NC 28680

Clifford File, Jr., Executive Director

Vocational Evaluation, Work Adjustment, Job Placement, On-site Work Services Program. Serves most disability groups including CMI, DD, Deaf and Physically impaired.

North Dakota

9658 North Dakota Department of Labor, Equal Employment Opportunity Division

600 East Boulevard Avenue
Dept 406
Bismarck, ND 58505 701-328-2660
800-582-8032
FAX: 701-328-2031
e-mail: labor@state.nd.us
www.state.nd.us/labor

Through a work-sharing agreement with the Equal Employment Opportunity Commission (EEOC), the North Dakota Department of Labor enforces the Americans with Disabilities Act (ADA) as related to employment discrimination.

9659 North Dakota Employment Service and Job Training Program Liaison

Job Service North Dakota
PO Box 1537
Bismarck, ND 58502 701-258-6353

9660 North Dakota Governor's Committee on Employment of Disabled Persons

600 S 2nd Street
Suite 1B
Bismarck, ND 58501 701-328-8953
FAX: 701-328-8969

9661 North Dakota Rehabilitation

Dacotah Foundation Building
600 S 2nd Street, Suite 1B
Bismarck, ND 50504 701-328-8950
888-755-2745
FAX: 701-328-8969

Gene Hysjulien, Director

Offers services for the totally blind, legally blind, visually impaired, mentally retarded blind and more with health, counseling, educational, recreational, rehabilitation, computer training and professional training services.

9662 North Dakota Vocational Rehabilitation Agency

400 E Broadway Avenue
Suite 303
Bismarck, ND 58501 701-223-6372

Ohio

9663 Cornucopia

18120 Sloane Avenue
Lakewood, OH 44107 216-521-4600
FAX: 216-521-9460
www.naturesbin.com

Chris Yurick, Program Manager

Provides work adjustment training for people with and developmental disabilities in a unique community based setting; Nature's Bin, a natural fresh foods market. Consumers learn through participation in retail operations in produce, grocery, bakery, deli, maintenance and customer service areas. Retail revenues help offset the cost of the program. Job search skills training and placement assistance available to program graduates.

9664 Great Oaks Joint Vocational School

3254 E Kemper Road
Cincinnati, OH 45241 513-772-4603

Dr. Harold Carr, Executive Director

9665 Hearth Day Treatment and Vocational Services

8301 Detroit Avenue
Cleveland, OH 44102 216-281-2660

Ralph Fee, Executive Director

9666 Highland Unlimited Business Enterprises of CRI

1322 East McMillan Street
Cincinnati, OH 45206   513-569-4730
     FAX: 513-751-2938
     e-mail: ddutton@cricincy.com
     www.cricincy.com

*Debbie Dutton Lambert, Director of Employment
Programs*

9667 Ohio Civil Rights Commission

1111 E Broad Street
301
Columbus, OH 43205   614-466-5928
     FAX: 614-644-8776

9668 Ohio Employment Services and Job Training

145 S Front Street
Columbus, OH 43215   614-466-4000
     FAX: 614-752-9049

9669 Ohio Vocational Rehabilitation Agency

400 E Campus View Boulevard
Columbus, OH 43235   614-438-1255
     FAX: 614-438-1257

Oklahoma

9670 Oklahoma Employment Services and Job
Training Program Liaison

2401 N Lincoln Boulevard
Oklahoma City, OK 73105   405-557-7211
     FAX: 405-557-5368

9671 Oklahoma Governor's Committee on
Employment of People with Disabilities

2712 Villa Prom
Oklahoma City, OK 73107   405-424-8378
     FAX: 405-943-7550

9672 Oklahoma Vocational Rehabilitation Agency

2409 N Kelley Avenue
Oklahoma City, OK 73111   405-424-6006

Orgon

9673 Bend Work Activity Center

275 NE 2nd
Bend, OR 97701   541-389-0129
     FAX: 541-389-2084

Bob Weeber, Executive Director

9674 Oregon Fair Employment Practice Agency

Oregon Bureau of Labor & Industry
PO Box 800
Portland, OR 97207   503-229-6601

9675 Oregon Vocational Rehabilitation Agency

1550 Dewey Avenue
Suite 253B
Baker City, OR 97814   541-524-1800
     FAX: 541-524-1803

Paige Grooms, VRC
Brian Stauff, Branch Manager

Pennsylvania

9676 AC-ACLD/An Association for Children and
Adults with Learning Disabilities

4900 Girard Road
Pittsburgh, PA 15227   412-881-2253
     FAX: 412-881-2263
     e-mail: info@acldnline.org

Thomas Fogarty, President

Offers services to children, adolescents and adults
with specific learning disabilities.

9677 Office of Vocational Rehabilitation

7th and Forster Street
Harrisburg, PA 17120   717-787-4746
     FAX: 717-783-5221

Barry Brandt, Rehab. Specialist

Information in vocational counseling and the governor's committee on Employment of People with Disabilities. Also serves persons with disabilities that
present a substantial handicap to employment and
independence. Services are provided when there is a
reasonable expectation that employment is possible
as a result of those services.

9678 Pennsylvania Employment Services and Job
Training

Labor & Industry Building
Room 1708
Harrisburg, PA 17120   717-787-5279
     FAX: 717-787-8826

9679 Pennsylvania Governor's Committee on
Employment of Disabled Persons

7th and Forster Street
Harrisburg, PA 17120   717-787-4746

9680 Pennsylvania Human Relations Commission
Agency

301 Chestnut Street
Suite 300
Harrisburg, PA 17101   717-787-4410
     FAX: 717-787-0420
     www.phrc.state.pa.us

9681 Pennsylvania Vocational Rehabilitation Agency

7th and Forster Street
Harrisburg, PA 17120   717-787-4746

9682 U.S. Healthworks

1114 Commons Boulevard
Reading, PA   19605   611-926-0960
                            FAX: 610-926-6225

Helps injured workers overcome injuries or disabilities and return to their jobs.

Rhode Island

9683 Association for Retarded

Citizens-Blackstone Valley Chapter
115 Manton Street
Pawtucket, RI   02861   401-727-0150
                            FAX: 401-727-0153

Peter Holden, Executive Director

9684 Groden Center

86 Mt. Hope Avenue
Providence, RI   02906   401-274-6310

Michael Smith, Administration

9685 Newport County Chapter of Retarded Citizens

PO Box 4390
Middletown, RI   02842   401-846-0340
                            FAX: 401-847-9459

John Mahler, Executive Director

9686 Rhode Island Department of Vocational Rehabilitation

40 Fountain Street
Suite 703
Providence, RI   02903   401-467-9200

Their goal is to help individuals with physical and mental disabilities prepare for and obtain appropriate employment.

9687 Rhode Island Employment Services and Job Training

101 Friendship Street
Providence, RI   02903   401-222-3732
                            FAX: 401-462-8798

9688 Vocational Resources

100 Houghton Street
Providence, RI   02904   401-861-2080
                            FAX: 401-454-0889

Paul Pickes, Director

South Carolina

9689 South Carolina Employment Services and Job Training Services

PO Box 995
700 Taylor Street
Columbia, SC   29202   803-737-9935
                            FAX: 803-737-0202

9690 South Carolina Governor's Committee on Employment of the Handicapped

1330 Boston Avenue
West Columbia, SC   29171   803-896-6333
                            FAX: 803-896-6373

9691 South Carolina Vocational Rehabilitation Department

PO Box 15
West Columbia, SC   29171   803-896-6504
                            FAX: 803-896-6525
                            TDY:803-896-6635
                    e-mail: scvrpi@infoave.net
                            www.scvrd.net

P. Charles LaRosa, Jr., Commissioner

The SCVRD's mission is to enable eligible South Carolinians with disabilities to prepare for, achieve and maintain competitive employment.

South Dakota

9692 South Dakota Governor's Advisory Committee on Employment of the Disabled

700 Governors Drive
Pierre, SD   57501   605-773-3423
                            FAX: 605-773-4236

9693 South Dakota Vocational Rehabilitation Agency

700 Governors Drive
Pierre, SD   57501   605-773-3423
                            FAX: 605-773-4236

9694 South Dakota Workforce Investment Act Training Programs

700 Governors Drive
Pierre, SD   57501   605-773-5017
                            FAX: 605-773-4211
                            www.sdjobs.org

Tennessee

9695 Tennessee Committee for Employment of Persons with Disabilities

400 Deaderick Street
Room 1100
Nashville, TN   37243   615-248-4996

9696 Tennessee Department of Labor - Job Training Program Liaison

501 Union Street
Nashville, TN   37219   615-741-6642

9697 Tennessee Fair Employment Practice Agency

Human Rights Commission
226 Capitol Boulevard
Suite 602
Nashville, TN   37219   615-741-5825

Texas

9698 Center for Computer Assistance to the Disabled - Texas

Infomart, Suite 2019
1950 Stemmons Freeway
Dallas, TX 75207   214-800-2223
                          FAX: 214-800-2224
                   e-mail: ccad@onramp.net
                          www.c-cad.org

9699 Handbook of Career Planning for Students with Special Needs

Pro-Ed
8700 Shoal Creek Boulevard
Austin, TX 78757
                          FAX: 512-451-8542
                   e-mail: proed1@aol.com
Thomas F. Harrington, author

The practitioner's guide will show you how to help special needs adolescents and young adults overcome barriers to employment by identifying goals and problems, assessing interests and aptitudes, involving client families and developing communication skills. *$42.00*

358 pages
ISBN 0-89079 -06-4

9700 Texas Commission for the Blind Blind

Texas Commission for the Blind
4800 N Lamar Boulevard
Austin, TX 78756   512-377-0500
                          FAX: 512-377-0685
          e-mail: donnagray@tcb.state.tx.us
                          www.tcb.state.tx.us

Tereli I. Murphy, Executive Director

9701 Texas Employment Services and Job Training Program Liaison

Texas Workforce Commission
101 E 15th Street
Austin, TX 78778   512-467-7774
                          800-735-2988
                   TDY:700-735-2989
                   www.two.state.tx.us

Utah

9702 Utah Employment Services

720 South 200 East
Salt Lake City, UT 84111   801-536-7401
                          FAX: 801-536-7011

9703 Utah Governor's Committee on Employment of the Handicapped

PO Box 45500
Salt Lake City, UT]4145   801-538-4222
                          FAX: 801-538-4446

9704 Utah Labor and Anti-Discrimination Division

160 E 300 South
Salt Lake City, UT 84111   801-530-6801
                          FAX: 801-530-7609

9705 Utah Veterans Centers

750 N 200 West
Suite 105
Provo, UT 84601   801-377-1117
                          800-246-1197
                   FAX: 801-377-0227

Ray Ross, LCSW, Team Leader
Readjustment counseling services to veterans.

9706 Utah Vocational Rehabilitation Agency

Utah State Office of Rehabilitation
250 East 5th South
Salt Lake City, UT 84111   801-538-7530
                          800-473-7530
                   FAX: 801-538-7522
          e-mail: bpeterse@usor.state.ut.us

Blaine Petersen, Executive Director
Don Uchida, Director

Vocational Rehabilitation Services for individuals with disabilities.

Vermont

9707 Vermont Division of Vocational Rehabilitation

103 S Main Street
Waterbury, VT 05671   802-241-2186
                          800-361-1239
                   FAX: 802-241-3359
                   TDY:802-241-2186
          e-mail: diane@dad.state.vt.us

Diane Dalmasse, Director

9708 Vermont Employment Services and Job Training

PO Box 488
Montpelier, VT 05601

9709 Vermont Governor's Committee on Employment of People with Disabilities

103 S Main Street
Waterbury, VT 05671   802-241-2186
                          800-361-1239
                   FAX: 802-241-3359

Virginia

9710 Achievement Center

615 N Jefferson Street
Roanoke, VA 24016
                          FAX: 540-982-3629
                   e-mail: tacenter@rev.net
                   www.achievementcenter.org

Barbara Ann Whitwell, Director

Private day school for children with diagnosed learning disabilities and attention deficit disorders aged 5-13; counseling and speech services are available at optional charge. Tuition: $8,431; $46.00 per hour counseling services, $44.00 per 1/2 hour speech services.

9711 Alexandria Community Y Head Start

418 S Washington Street
Alexandria, VA   22314   703-329-2050
FAX: 703-998-5707

Yvonne Walker

Offers social services, on-the-job-training for parents, play therapy, physical therapy, speech therapy and any other specialized services.

9712 Association for Persons in Supported Employment

5001 W Broad Street
Suite 34
Richmond, VA   23230   804-282-3655
FAX: 804-282-5055

Wendy Wood, Executive Director

Created to improve and expand integrated employment opportunities and services for persons with severe disabilities.

9713 Didlake

8621 Breeden Avenue
Manassas, VA   20110   703-631-9184
FAX: 703-369-7141

Rexford Parr, Jr., President/CEO
John S. Craig, Director, Rehabilitation Services

Offers situational assessments, work training, employment and job placement services to people with disabilities.

9714 Job Placement Digest

National Rehabilitation Association
613 S Washington Street
Alexandria, VA   22314   703-548-1502

e-mail: info@nationalrehab.org

Newsletter discussing employment options for persons with disabilities.

9715 Learning Services - Shenandoah

9524 Fairview Avenue
Manassas, VA   20110   703-335-9771
FAX: 703-338-1064

Peter Patrick, Administrator

Postacute rehabilitation program.

9716 NISH

2235 Cedar Lane
Vienna, VA   22182   703-560-6800
FAX: 703-560-9345
www.nish.org

E. Robert Chamberlin, President/CEO
Mary Jane Williamson

A nonprofit agency desigated by the Committee for Purchase from People Who Are Blind or Severely Disabled to provide technical assistance to rehabilitation programs interested in obtaining federal contracts under Public Law 92-28, the Javits-Wagner-O'Day Act. NISH's primary objective is to assist community rehabilitation programs in providing jobs for people with severe disabilities.

9717 Richmond Research Training Center

1314 West Main Street
PO Box 842011
Richmond, VA   23284   804-828-1222

Dr. Paul Wehman, Director

Research and training center report on the supported employment of persons with developmental and other disabilities.

9718 ServiceSource

6295 Edsall Road
Suite 175
Alexandria, VA   22312   703-461-6000
800-244-0817
FAX: 703-461-3906
www.ourpeoplework.org

Janet Samuelson

Provides training, job placement and employment services in private sector and government contract employment.

9719 Sheltered Occupational Center of Virginia

750 23rd Street South
Arlington, VA   22202
FAX: 703-521-3443

Charles Richman

Employs disabled adults in Northern Virginia.

9720 Virginia Vocational Rehabilitation Agency

397 Azalea Avenue
Richmond, VA   23227   804-371-3145

Washington

9721 Career Connections National Business & Disability Council

421 North Mullan Road
Spokane, WA   99206   509-928-0423
FAX: 509-928-0441

Bill Stout, Contact

9722 Department of Services for the Blind National Business & Disability Council

521 East Legion Way
MS:FD-11
Olympia, WA   98504   206-586-1224

9723 Department of Social & Health Services National Business & Disability Council

Dddd612 Woodland Square, Loop, SE
PO Box 45340
Lacey, WA   98504   425-902-8400

9724 **Department of Vocational Rehabilitation**

PO Box 45340
Olympia, WA 98504

800-637-5627
FAX: 360-438-8007

Provides information about job training and retraining for disabled persons.

9725 **Emil Fries Piano Hospital and Training Center**

Emil Fries School of Piano Tuning & Technology
2510 E Evergreen Boulevard
Vancouver, WA 98661 360-693-1511
FAX: 360-693-6891
e-mail: pianohospital@pianotuningschool.org
www.pianotuningschool.org

Kenneth Serviss, President, Manager
Donald Mitchell, Director of Instruction
Diane Hadley, Secretary, Treasurer/Registrar

Teaches piano tuning, repairing and rebuilding to blind, visually impaired and sighted men and women, leading to employment and/or self-employment in the piano service industry. Instruction also given in music appreciation and small business operation, including computer record keeping. Licensed by Washington State and nationally accredited by the Accrediting Commission of Career Schools and Colleges of Technology (ACCSCT). 20-month course. $525.00

9726 **S.L. Stuart and Associates**

25 West Nora Avenue
Spokane, WA 99205 509-328-2740

e-mail: raywhite@sistart.com

Ray White, Contact

West Virginia

9727 **West Virginia Employment Services and Job Training Programs Liaison**

112 California Avenue
Charleston, WV 25305 304-558-0342

9728 **West Virginia Vocational Rehabilitation Agency**

State Capitol Complex
Charleston, WV 25305 304-342-9952

9729 **West Virginia of Vocational Rehabilitation**

PO Box 1004
Institute, WV 25112 304-342-9952

Earl Wolfe, Director

Offers services for the totally blind, legally blind, visually impaired, mentally retarded blind and more with health, counseling, educational, recreational, rehabilitation, computer training and professional training services.

Wisconsin

9730 **Wisconsin Division of Vocational Rehabilitation**

2917 International Lane
Madison, WI 53704 608-243-5600
FAX: 608-243-5635

John Conway, Program Specialist

Offers services for the totally blind, legally blind, visually impaired, mentally retarded blind and more with health, counseling, educational, recreational, rehabilitation, computer training and professional training services.

9731 **Wisconsin Employment Services and Job Training Programs Liaison**

Department of Industry, Labor & Human Relations
201 E Washington Avenue
Madison, WI 53702 608-257-4971

9732 **Wisconsin Vocational Rehabilitation Agency**

PO Box 7852
2917 International Lane, 3rd Floor
Madison, WI 53707 608-243-5600
TDY:608-243-5601
e-mail: normaju@mail.state.wi.us

Judy R. Norman-Nunnery, Administrator

Wyoming

9733 **Division of Vocational Rehabilitation of Wyoming**

2300 Capitol Avenue
Cheyenne, WY 82001 307-777-5800

Robert Dingwall, Administrator

Offers services for the totally blind, legally blind, visually impaired, mentally retarded blind and more with health, counseling, educational, recreational, rehabilitation, computer training and professional training services.

9734 **Wyoming Employment Services and Job Training Programs**

PO Box 2760
Casper, WY 82602 307-235-3200
FAX: 307-255-3278

9735 **Wyoming Governor's Committee on Employment of the Handicapped**

Herschler
Room 1102
Cheyenne, WY 82002 307-777-7230
FAX: 307-777-5690

9736 **Wyoming Vocational Rehabilitation Agency**

1 East Herschler Building
Cheyenne, WY 82002 307-777-7385
TDY:307-777-7389
e-mail: gchild@missc.state.wy.us

Gary W. Child, Administrator

Alternative Therapies

League for the Hard of Hearing, 1113
Life Without Pain, 6435
Lifecycles for Women, 966
Living an Idea: Empowerment and the Evolution of an Alternative School, 2374
Living the Therapeutic Touch: Healing as Lifestyle, 6158
Long Beach Department of Health and Human Services, 4011
Los Angeles County Department of Health Services, 4012
Lotus Light, 968
Maharishi Ayur-Veda Medical Center, 1183
Massage Book, 6169
Massage Magazine, 6170
Massage for Common Ailments, 6171
Matrix and Matrix Regulation Basis for an Holistic Theory in Medicine, 6172
Medical Diagnostic Laboratory, 5610
Medical Herbalism, 6173
Meditative Mind, 6174
Medizone International, 971
Mending the Body, Mending the Mind, 6176
Menopausal Years, 6177
Menopause Naturally (Updated): Preparing for the Second Half of Life, 6178
Menopause Self-Help Book, 6179
Menopause Without Medicine (Second Edition), 6180
Menopause: A Second Spring, 6181
Meridan Valley Clinical Laboratory, 974
MetaMatrix Medical Laboratory, 975
Migraine and the Allergy Connection, 6188
Migraine: Beating the Odds, 6189
Mind Over Back Pain, 6445
Mind-Body Clinic Harvard Medical School, 976
Mind/Body Health Services, 977
Missing Diagnosis, 6192
Music: Physician for Times to Come, 6500
Myotherapy, 6195
NLP Comprehensive, 980
National Association for Holistic Aromatherapy, 981
National Association of Music Therapy, 983
National Association to Aid Fat Americans, 986
National Center for Accessible Media, 1121
National Center for Homeopathy, 2466
National College of Naturepathic Medicine, 991
National Cued Speech Association, 1123
National Guild of Hypnotists, 997
National Headache Foundation, 3346
National Information Clearinghouse for Children and Youth with Disabilities, 1127
National Rehabilitation Information Center, 1130
National Vaccine Information Center, 1009
National Voluntary Organizations for Independent Living for the Aging, 819
National Women's Health Network, 1010
Natural Child Care: A Complete Guide to Safe Holistic Remedies for Infants and Children, 5791
Natural Health Bulletin, 6202
Neurophysiology of Enlightenment, 6205
New No Pill, No Risk Birth Control Guide, 6209
New Our Bodies, Ourselves, 6210
North American Society of Teachers of the Alexander Technique, 1198

North Carolina Bio-Oxidative Health Center, 1013
Northwest Naturopathic Clinic, 1014
Nutritional Action Health Letter: Center for Science in the Public Interest, 6215
Nutritional Desk Reference, 6216
Nutritional Influences on Illness 2nd Edition, 6217
Nutritional Influences on Mental Illness, 6575
Occupational and Enviromental Unit Tri-Cities Hospital, 1016
One Hundred Fifty Most-Asked Questions About Menopause, 6223
Optometric Extension Program Foundation, 3161
Orcas Island Foundation, 1017
Oxygen Therapies, 6228
PACER Center, 1316
Pacific Institute of Aromatherapy, 1020
Pacific Toxicology, 1021
Pain Erasure, 6579
Pause: Positive Approaches to Menopause, 6234
Physicians for Social Responsibility, 1026
Polarity Therapy: The Complete and Collected Works, 6247
Portland Naturopathic Clinic NCNM National Health Centers Eastside Clinic, 1028
Potent Self: A Guide to Spontaneity, 6249
Practice of Aromatherapy, 6250
Presbyterian Health, Education and Welfare Association, 1029
Prescription for Nutritional Healing: a Practical A-Z Referance to Drug-Free Remedies, 6252
Pumpkin Hollow Farm, 1030
Qigong Magazine, 6262
Qigong for Health: Chinese Traditional Exercise for Cure and Prevention, 6263
Quan Yin Healing Arts Center, 1031
Radiation Protection Manual, 6267
Read Natural Childbirth Foundation, 3167
Reflexology for Good Health: Mirror for the Body, 6270
Rehabilitation Engineering Research Center on Hearing Enhancement and Assistive Devices, 1136
Relaxation Response, 6274
Rolf Institute, 1203
Rolfing: The Integration of Human Structures, 6589
Self-Applied Health Enhancement Methods, 6279
Seven Weeks to a Healthy Stomach, 6281
Sharp Institute for Human Potential and Mind/Body Medicine, 1039
Shot in the Dark, 5810
Sitike Counseling Center, 1040
Small Wonder, 2408
Society for Light Treatment and Biological Rythems, 1041
Solve Your Child's Sleep Problems, 5812
Solving the Puzzle of Chronic Fatigue, 6291
Solving the Puzzle of the Hyperactive Child, 5813
Sound, Listening, and Learning Center, 1141
Startling New Facts About Osteoporosis: Why Calcium Alone Does Not Prevent Bone Disease, 6302
Staying Healthy with Nutrition, 6304
Straight Talk with Your Gynecologist: How to Get Answers that Will Save Your Life, 6307

Stress Reduction Clinic University of Massachusetts Medical Center, 1046
Tao of Nutrition, 6312
Tao: The Subtle Universal Law and the Integral Way of Life, 6313
Taoist Ways to Transform Stress, 6314
Tele-Consumer Hotline, 1142
Today's Health Alternative, 6319
Tsubo: Vital Points for Oriental Therapy, 6322
Upledger Institute, 1053
Vaccination Social Violence and Criminality: Medical Assault on the American Brain, 6610
Vaccinations: Mothering Special Edition, 6327
Vaccines: Are They Really Safe and Effective?, 6328
Vegetarian Baby, 5826
Vestibular Disorders Association, 1146
Vibrational Medicine, 6329
Visiting Nurse Association of America, 8931
Vitamin C: Who Needs It?, 6331
Web That Has No Weaver: Understanding Chinese Medicine, 6338
Web that has No Weaver: Understanding Chinese Medicine, 6339
Weiner's Herbal, 6340
Well Pregnancy Book, 6341
Western States Training Associates, 1055
What Your Doctors Won't Tell You, 6342
Who Needs Headaches, 6345
Why Me? Harnessing the Healing Power of the Human Spirit, 6346
Wizard Within: The Krasner Method of Clinical Hypnotherapy, 6347
Women to Women, 1057
Women's Health Alert, 6349
Women's Health Forum, 6350
Wood Hygienic Institute, 1338
World Chiropractic Alliance, 1209
World Research Foundation, 5379
Yeast Connection, 6616
Your Body's Many Cries for Water, 6617
Your Fertility Signals, 6356
Your Healing Hands: The Polarity Experience, 6357
Your Inner Physician and You: CranioSacral Therapy SomatoEmotional Release, 6358

Amputation

Adjustable Amputee Stool, 225
American Amputee Foundation, 1216
Breaking New Ground Resource Center, 6021
Manual for Below-Knee (Trans-Tibial) Amputees, 6779
National Amputation Foundation, 1294

Amythrophic Lateral Sclerosis

Amytrophic Lateral Sclerosis Association, 1236
Link, 2616

Attention Deficit Disorder

Autism

New Jersey Center for Outreach and Services for the Autism Community (COSAC), 5593
Parent Survival Manual, 6580
Parent's Guide to Autism, 6646
Pervasive Developmental Disorders; Finding a Diagnosis and Getting Help, 6649
Please Don't Say Hello, 5797
Queens Services for Autistic Children Newsletter, 5800
Reaching the Autistic Child, 2nd Edition A Parent Training Program, 6651
Record Book for Individuals with Autism, 6972
Riddle of Autism: A Psychological Analysis, 6973
Sex Education: Issues for the Person with Autism, 7308
Shoebox Tasks: Work Activities, 6976
Son-Rise Program, 8921
Son-Rise: The Miracle Continues, 5815
Son-Rise: The Miracle Continues, 6293
Soon Will Come the Light, 6978
Summer Experience, 1671
TEACCH, 1047
Teaching Children with Autism - Strategies to Enhance Communication, 6983
Teaching Children with Autism: Strategies for Initiating Positive Interactions, 2914
Teaching and Mainstreaming Autistic Children, 2931
Teaching and Mainstreaming Autistic Children, 6984
Treating Disordered Speech Motor Control, 2942
Ultimate Stranger, The Autistic Child, 6991
Uncommon Fathers, 6609
Understanding Autism, 7529
Understanding the Nature of Autism, 6996
Until Tomorrow: A Family Lives with Autism, 6997
Visually Structured Tasks, 6999
Without Reason, A Family Copes with Autism, 6614

Behavioral Disorders

Alternative Teaching Strategies, 2642
American Academy of Child and Adolescent Psychiatry, 1215
American Association of Children's Residential Centers, 1160
Behavior Analysis in Education: Focus on Measurably Superior Instruction, 2665
Behavior Modification, 2666
Behavior Problems, 6004
Behavior Service Consultants, 2303
Behavior Skills - Learning How People Should Act, 2026
Behavior Therapy and Research Society, 1175
Behavioral Disorders, 2668
Center for Neuro Skills, 8041
Center for Neuro Skills - Texas, 8720
Childhood Behavior Disorders: Applied Research & Educational Practice, 2684
Communication-Based Intervention for Problem Behavior, 6892
Creating Positive Classroom Environments: Strategies for Behavior Management, 2707
Devereux Center in New Jersey, 8589

Effective Behavioral Programming, 7393
Emotional Intelligence, Lessons in Conflict and Anger, 7397
Journal of Emotional and Behavioral Disorders, 2565
Journal of Motor Behavior, 2567
Journal of Vocational Behavior, 2573
Lakeview NeuroRehabilitation Center, 7820
Learning to Listen: Positive Approaches & People with Difficult Behavior, 6151
National Council for Community Behavioral Healthcare, 1299
Positive Behavioral Support: Including People with Difficult Behavior in the Community, 5845
Progress Without Punishment: Approaches for Learners with Behavior Problems, 2856
Pure Facts, 6261
Self-Control Games & Workbook, 5809
Steps to Independence: Teaching Everyday Skills to Children with Special Needs, 3rd Edition, 2895
Teaching Students with Learning and Behavior Problems, 2926
Touch of Nature Environmental Center, 1498
ValueOptions, 7617
Why Can't My Child Behave?, 6612
Working Bibliography on Behavioral and Emotional Disorders, 2951
Your Defiant Child: Eight Steps to Better Behavior, 6620

Birth Defects

ABDC Newsletter Volume Reprints, 7177
Association of Birth Defect Children, 886
Baylor College of Medicine Birth Defects Center, 5660
Birth Defect News, 6011
Birth Defect Research for Children, 893
Cherub - Association of Families and Friends of Children with Limb Disorders, 1256
Club Foot & Other Foot Deformities Fact Sheet, 7220
Cornelia de Lange Syndrome Foundation, 3208
Dictionary of Congenital Malformations & Disorders, 6905
Different Heart, 7387
Division of Birth Defects and Developmental Disabilities, 4074
Division of Birth Defects and Genetic Diseases, 5429
Don't Feel Sorry for Paul, 5748
Environmental Birth Defect Digest, 6913
How to Find More About Your Child's Birth Defect Or Disability, 7259
Infertility and Birth Defects - Is Mercury from Silver Dental Fillings a Hidden Cause?, 6137
Informed Birth and Parenting, 949
Mama - Your Guide to a Healthy Pregnancy, 7272
March of Dimes Birth Defects Foundation, 1286
Marfan Syndrome Fact Sheet, 7279
New England Regional Genetics Group, 5515
Oral/Facial Clefts Fact Sheet, 7288
Rajesh, 5802
Teratogen and Birth Defects Information Project, 8928

University of Iowa Birth Defects and Genetic Disorders Unit, 5492
University of Miami, Mailman Center For Child Development, 5422
Why My Child, 7543
Withstanding Ovation, 7546

Brain Injuries

About the Tomatis Method, 2628
Before and After Zachariah, 6516
Brain Injury Association of New York State, 1250
Brain Injury Association of Texas, 1251
Brain Train, 2028
Children with Acquired Brain Injury: Educating and Supporting Families, 6882
Cranial Academy, 1263
Easter Seals Superior California, 8064
Educational Dimensions of Acquired Brain Injury, 2745
Genesis Regional Rehabilitation Center, 8416
Getting Our Heads Together, 6548
Headlines Support Group, 8886
Learning Services - Supported Living Programs, 8097
Measure of Cognitive-Linguistic Abilities (MCLA), 2984
NHIF Newsletter, 6197
Phoenix Project, 6244
Preventable Brain Damage, 6969
Project Headway, 8135
Quality Living, 1201
Rehabilitation Services, 8540
Res-Care Premier, 1202
Ride the Red Cycle, 5805
Students with Acquired Brain Injury: The School's Response, 2897
Students with Acquired Brain Injury: The School's Response, 6980
Synergos NeuroMedical Rehab Unit - Seattle, 8771
Traumatic Brain Injury: Mechanisms of Damage, Assessment & Internvention, 2940
Vocational Evaluation and Traumatic Brain Injury: A Procedural Manual, 7174
When Billy Broke His Head...and Other Tales of Wonder, 7539

Cancer

AMC Cancer Research Center, 5380
Adult Leukemia: A Comprehensive Guide for Patients and Families, 6812
Advanced Breast Cancer: A Guide to Living with Metastic Disease, 6813
Alexander and Margaret Stewart Trust, 3227
American Cancer Society, 1222
Arlin J. Brown Information Center, 1173
Association for the Cure of Cancer of the Prostate, 7568
Beating the Odds, 6003
Bowel Cancer, 6870
Breast Cancer Action, 1252
Breast Cancer Sourcebook, 6873
Camp Catch-A-Rainbow, 1555
Cancer Biotherapy Research Group, 7573
Cancer Care National Office, 1254

Cancer Care, 3569

Cancer Clinical Trials: Experimental Treatments and How They Can Help You, 6624

Cancer Control Society, 1255

Cancer Immunology Research Foundation, 7574

Cancer Immunotherapy and Gene Therapy Institute, 7575

Cancer Industry, 6029

Cancer Information Service, 8869

Cancer Research Fund of Damon Runyon - Walter Winchell Foundation, 7576

Cancer Sourcebook for Women, 2nd Edition, 6877

Cancer Sourcebook, 3rd Edition, 6878

Cancer Therapy, 6740

Cancer and Nutrition, 6741

Candlelighters Childhood Cancer Foundation, 3842

Childhood Cancer Survivors: A Practical Guide to Your Future, 6626

Childhood Cancer: A Parent's Guide to Solid Tumor Cancers, 6627

Colon & Rectal Cancer: A Comprehensive Guide for Patients & Families, 6888

Complete Guide to Cancer Prevention, 6746

Conquest of Cancer, 6748

Cure Cancer Now, 1264

Exceptional Cancer Patients, 1268

Foundation for Advancement in Cancer Therapy, 3596

International Association for Cancer Victors and Friends, 1277

Jane Coffin Childs Memorial Fund for Medical Research, 3216

Leukemia & Lymphoma Society, 1284

My Book for Kids with Cancer, 5788

Non-Hodgkin's Lymphomas: Making Sense of Diagnosis, Treatment & Options, 6642

One Day at a Time: Children Living with Leukemia, 5794

Options: The Alternative Cancer Therapy Book, 6785

People Against Cancer, 1319

Persecution and Trial of Gaston Naessens, 6241

Perspectives on Prevention and Treatment of Cancer in the Elderly, 5903

Psychology and Health, 6256

R.A. Bloch Cancer Foundation, 3500

RA Bloch Cancer Foundation, 3501

Sharks Don't Get Cancer, 2883

Simonton Cancer Center, 1327

Third Opinion, 6317

V Foundation for Cancer Research, 7616

Cerebral Palsy

All the Way Up There, 7343

American Academy for Cerebral Palsy and Developmental Medicine, 1213

Caring for Children with Cerebral Palsy: A Team Approach, 6625

Childen with Cerebral Palsy, 6881

Coping with Cerebral Palsy, 6898

Individuals with Cerebral Palsy, 6936

Keys to Parenting a Child with Cerebral Palsy, 6637

Mine for Keeps, 5787

My Left Foot: The Story of Christy Brown, 6718

No Time for Jello: One Family's Experience, 6573

Treating Cerebral Palsy for Clinicians by Clinicians, 2941

United Cerebral Palsy Association, 1335

United Cerebral Palsy Association of New York State, 1336

United Cerebral Palsy Research and Educational Foundation, 2475

Chronic Disabilities

Access to Health Care, Number 1 & 2, 2631

Access to Health Care, Number 3 & 4, 2632

Be Sick Well - A Healthy Approach to Chronic Illness, 6002

Brothers, Sisters, and Special Needs, 6519

Caring for Children with Chronic Illness, 2678

Caring for Children with Chronic Illness, 6032

Counselling Parents of Children with Chronic Illness or Disability, 6527

Developing Cross-Cultural Competence:Guide to Working with Young Children & Their Families, 2714

Family Interventions Throughout Disability, 6543

Home and Community Care for Chronically Ill Children, 6121

Screening in Chronic Disease, 2879

Screening in Chronic Disease, 6278

Cleft Palate

American Cleft Palate/Craniofacial Association, 1224

Children with Facial Difference, 6523

Cleft Palate Foundation, 1260

White Memorial Medical Center Rehabilitation, 7683

Cognitive Disorders

ABLEDATA, 1869

Evaluation and Treatment of the Psychogeriatric Patient, 2755

Technology Access Center of Tucson, 1929

Dementia

Eagle Pond, 8504

Herkimer Resource Center for Independent Living, 5021

Victims of Dementia: Services, Support and Care, 6998

Dental Issues

American Academy of Biological Dentistry, 1154

Dental Amalgam Syndrome (DAMS), 1266

Environmental Dental Association, 1178

International Academy of Oral Medicine and Toxicology, 954

International Medical and Dental Hypnotherapy Association, 959

Standard Search: Oral Health Care for People with Developmental Disabilities, 1045

Depression

Adolescent in Family Therapy: Breaking the Cycle of Conflict and Control, 5722

Coping with Being Physically Challenged, 5742

DAYS: Depression and Anxiety in Youth Scale, 2971

Free Yourself From Pain, 6094

Free Yourself From Pain, 6546

Herbs for the Mind: What Science Tells Us about Nature's Remedies for Depression, Stress..., 6120

Manic Depression: Voices of an Illness, 7463

National Depressive and Manic Depressive Association, 8905

Phenomenology of Depressive Illness, 2844

Premenstrual Syndrome Self-Help Book, 6251

Risk, Resilience, & Prevention: Promoting the Well-Being of All Children, 6588

Treatment for Chronic Depression, 6321

What to Do When a Friend is Depressed: Guide for Students, 7327

What's Wrong with my Hormones?, 6344

Developmental Disabilities

Administration on Developmental Disabilities, 3924

American Assoc. of University Affiliated Programs for Persons with Developmental Disability, 861

As I Am, 7347

Attainment Company/IEP Resources, 2021

Baby Book for the Developmentally Challenged Child, 6512

Building and Evaluating Family Support Initiatives, 2675

Caring for People with Developmental Disabilities, 7372

Caring for Persons with Developmental Disabilities, 7373

Catalog for Teaching Life Skills to Persons with Development Disability, 2327

Center for Developmental Disabilities, 904

Cheyenne Village, 9377

Child and Adolescent Therapy: Cognitive-Behavioral Procedures, Second Edition, 5732

Communication Development and Disorders in African American Children, 6890

Community Alternatives Unlimited, 2305

Community Opportunities of East Ascension, 9530

DOCS: Developmental Observation Checklist System, 2972

Developmental Disabilities Council, 1890

Developmental Disabilities in Infancy and Childhood, 2nd Edition, 6533

Developmental Disabilities: A Handbook for Interdisciplinary Practice, 2723

Developmental Services Center, 2974

Dictionary of Developmental Disabilities Terminology, 6059

Dictionary of Developmental Disabilities Terminology, 6534

Directory for Exceptional Children 2001 - 2002, 2480

East Brunswick Adult and Community Education Program, Adult Life Skills, 2453

Enhancing Children's Communication: Research & Foundations, 2484

Family Support Project for the Developmentally Disabled, 8883

Family-Centered Service Coordination: A Manual for Parents, 6544

Glenkirk, 9466

Handbook of Developmental Education, 2769

Information Services for People with Developmental Disabilities, 6138

Journal of Counseling & Development, 2563

Keeping Childhood, 5775

Keys to the Workplace: Skills and Supports for People with with Disabilities, 5932

Knox County Council for Developmental Disabilities, 9473

Lambs Farm, 9475

Lambs Vocational Work Center, 9476

Language, Learning & Living, 176

Life-Span Approach to Nursing Care for Individuals with Developmental Disabilities, 2812

Lifelong Leisure Skills and Lifestyles for Persons with Developmental Disabilities, 6155

Measurement and Evaluation in Counseling and Development, 2574

National Association of Developmental Disabilities Councils, 982

National Association of Protection and Advocacy Systems, 1188

Pariallels in Time, 7479

Professional Fit Clothing, 1758

Relaxation Techniques for People with Special Needs, 7493

Richmond Research Training Center, 9717

SIBPAGE, 2621

Sexuality and the Developmentally Handicapped, 6590

Social Competence for Workers with Developmental Disabilities, 7166

TERI, 7514

Teaching People with Developmental Disabilities, 7515

Vocational Rehabilitation Center, 1054

Work Training Center, 9374

Young Children with Special Needs: A Developmentally Appropriate Approach, 3022

Diabetes

American Diabetes Association, 1616

American Diabetes Association Annual Conference, 2231

American Diabetes Summer Camp, 1435

Camp Discovery American Diabetes Association - Kansas Area Office, 1517

Camp Joslin, 1539

Camp de los Ninos - Diabetes Society, 1452

Center for the Partially Sighted, 8042

Charting: The Systematic Approach to Achieving Control, 6879

Clara Barton Camp, 1544

Counselling People with Diabetes, 6901

Des Moines YMCA Camp, 1513

Diabetes 101, 6903

Diabetes Network of East Hawaii, 4085

Diabetes Self-Management, 6750

Diabetes: Caring for Your Emotions as Well as Your Health, 2478

Diabetic Cruise Desk, 9005

EDI, 1584

Eating Out: Your Guide to More Enjoyable Dining, 6074

Florida Camp for Children and Youth, 1481

Hickory Hill, 1585

If Your Child Has Diabetes: An Answer Book for Parents, 6633

John Warvel, 1506

Joslin Guide to Diabetes, 6940

Juvenile Diabetes Foundation International, 1283

Know Your Diabetes, Know Yourself, 7449

Lions Clubs International, 3041

Makemie Woods Camp Conference Retreat, 1697

Meeting the Needs of People with Vision Loss: Multidisciplinary Perspective, 7094

National Diabetes Action Network for the Blind, 1401

National Diabetes Information Clearinghouse, 1301

Nejeda, 1608

No More Allergies, 6572

Psyching Out Diabetes: A Positive Approach to Your Negative Emotions, 6255

Reversing Diabetes, 6797

Sweeney, 1684

Utada Camp, 1688

Victory Over Diabetes, 6805

Voice of the Diabetic, 7000

World's Best Books from the Diabetes Experts, Publications Catalog, 1339

Down Syndrome

Adolescents with Down Syndrome: Toward a More Fulfilling Life, 6811

Association for Children with Down Syndrome, 1239

Biomedical Concerns in Persons with Down Syndrome, 6867

Biomedical Concerns in Persons with Down's Syndrome, 2673

Bus Girl: Selected Poems, 5729

Clockworks, 7378

Communication Development in Children with Down Syndrome, 6891

Communication Skills in Children with Down Syndrome, 2700

Down Syndrome, 7390

Down Syndrome Association of North East Indiana, 7738

Keys to Parenting a Child with Down's Syndrome, 6638

National Association for Down Syndrome, 1296

National Down Syndrome Society, 1303

Parent's Guide to Down Syndrome: Toward a Brighter Future: 2nd Edition, 6647

Parents of Down Syndrome Children, 1318

Paul, 7483

Teaching Reading to Children with Down Syndrome, 2922

Understanding Down Syndrome: An Introduction for Parents, 6993

Dyslexia

ASSETS School, 9448

Beyond the Rainbow: A Guide for Parents of a Child with Dyslexia, 6865

DISCOVERY, 2123

Dyslexia, 2735

Dyslexia Centers, 1611

Dyslexia Screening Survey, 2975

Dyslexia Training Program, 2338

Dyslexia over the Lifespan, 6909

International Dyslexia Association, 1279

International Dyslexia Association Philadelphia Branch, 4388

International Dyslexia Association of AZ Arizona Branch, 3990

International Dyslexia Association of CA Central California Branch, 4010

International Dyslexia Association of CO Rocky Mountain Branch (CO, UT, WY), 4025

International Dyslexia Association of D.C. D.C. Capital Area, 4051

International Dyslexia Association of FL Florida Branch (FL, Puerto Rico), 4068

International Dyslexia Association of GA Georgia Branch, 4082

International Dyslexia Association of HI Hawaii Branch, 4095

International Dyslexia Association of IA Iowa Branch, 4123

International Dyslexia Association of IL Illinois Branch (IL, E/MO), 4115

International Dyslexia Association of IN Indiana Branch, 4122

International Dyslexia Association of KS Kansas/W. Missouri Branch, 4136

International Dyslexia Association of LA Louisiana Branch, 4149

International Dyslexia Association of MD Maryland Branch, 4169

International Dyslexia Association of MI Michigan Branch, 4189

International Dyslexia Association of MN, 4202

International Dyslexia Association of MS Mississippi Branch, 4214

International Dyslexia Association of NC North Carolina Branch, 4335

International Dyslexia Association of NE Nebraska Branch, 4242

International Dyslexia Association of NJ New Jersey Branch, 4277

International Dyslexia Association of NY Buffalo Branch, 4298

International Dyslexia Association of New England (CT, ME, NH, RI, VT), 4263

International Dyslexia Association of OH Central Ohio Branch, 4355

International Dyslexia Association of OR Oregon Branch, 4377

International Dyslexia Association of SC South Carolina Branch, 4412

Epilepsy

Head & Neck Injuries

Hearing Impairments

Understanding Deafness Socially, 6482
Very Special Friend, 6483
Vibrotactile Personal Alerting System, 219
Video Services - Captioning and Audio Description, 7533
Vision, 6484
Visual Alerting Guest Room Kit, 672
Volta Review, 6485
Volta Voices, 6486
WCI/Weitbrecht Communications, 503
Wallace Memorial Library, 5621
We CAN Hear and Speak, 6487
Week the World Heard Gallaudet, 6488
Welcoming Students who are Deaf-Blind into Typical Classrooms, 3020
When the Mind Hears, 6490
Whisper 2000, 224
Without Sight and Sound, 7330
World Recreation Association of the Deaf, 1149
You and Your Deaf Child: A Self-Help Guide for Parents of Deaf and Hard of Hearing Children, 6660
You and Your Hearing Impaired Child: A Self-Instructional Parents Guide, 6491
Youth Leadership Camp, 1538

Human Interaction Disabilities

Beach Center on Families and Disability, 891
Taking Part: Introducing Social Skills to Young Children, 3008
Teaching Resources & Assessment of Critical Skills, 3009

Immune Deficiencies

Allergic Rhinitis, 7344
Anaphylaxis, 7346
Environmental Control Measures, 7399
Immune Deficiency Foundation Newsletter, 6758
Immuno Labs, 1275
Indoor Allergens, 7263
Understanding Allergic Reactions, 7527

Incontinence

Adaptive Clothing - Adults, 450
Adaptive Clothing - Adults, 1735
Adult Absorbent Briefs, 1796
Basic Wheelchair, 717
Care Electronics, 515
Fashion Ease Division of MRR Health Care Apparel Company, 1748
Hygienics Direct Company, 480
Information on Incontinence, 1276
Informer, 6760
Priva, 134
Safe and Dry - Feel and Sure - Toddler Dry, 1808
Simon Foundation for Continence, 6286
Simon Foundation for Continence, 6799
Specialty Care Shoppe, 1763

Waterproof Sheet-Topper Mattress and Chair Pad, 137

Language Disorders

American Speech-Language-Hearing Association, 1070
Discriptive Language Arts Development, 2101
Funology Fables: Stories for Phonology Learning, 5753
Language Arts: Detecting Special Needs, 2801
Language Disabilities in Children and Adolescents, 2802
Language and Communication Disorders in Children, 2804
OWLS: Oral and Written Language Scales LC/OE & WE, 2986
PAT-3: Photo Articulation Test, Third Edition, 2987
Peabody Early Experiences Kit - PEEK, 2988
Peabody Language Development Kits-PLDK, 2990
Receptive-Expressive Emergent-REEL-2 Language Test, Second Edition, 2999
Specific Language Disability Test, 3003
Spotting Language Problems, 2894
Test of Language Development- Primary, Third Edition, 3013
Test of Phonological Awareness, 3016
Topics in Language Disorders, 2583

Laryngectomies

Annals of Otology, Rhinology and Laryngology, 6737
Health and Rehabilitation Products, 476
IAL News, 6128

Learning Disabilities

A Commitment to Inclusion: Outreach to Unserved/Underserved Populations, 5952
AC-ACLD/An Association for Children and Adults with Learning Disabilities, 9676
ACLD Newsbriefs, 5953
ADHD, 7178
ADHD in Schools: Assessment and Intervention Strategies, 6662
AEPS Child Progress Record: For Children Ages Three to Six, 2310
AEPS Child Progress Report: For Children Ages Birth to Three, 2955
AEPS Curriculum for Birth to Three Years (Volume 2), 2627
AEPS Curriculum for Three to Six Years, 2311
AEPS Data Recording Forms: For Children Ages Three to Six, 2312
AEPS Data Recording Forms: For Children Ages Birth to Three, 2956
AEPS Family Interest Survey, 2313
AEPS Family Report: For Children Ages Birth to Three, 2314
AEPS Measurement for Birth to Three Years (Volume 1), 2957

AEPS Measurement for Three to Six Years, 2958
AIR: Assessment of Interpersonal Relations, 2959
AVKO Dyslexia Research Foundation, 2438
Academic Skill Builders in Language Arts, 2629
Academic Skills Problems, 2961
Academy of Learning and Developmental Disorders, 1153
Accentuate the Positive - Expressive Arts for Children with Disabilities, 1
Achievement Center, 9710
Adaptive Education Strategies Building on Diversity, 2634
Adaptive Mainstreaming, 2962
Advanced Language Tool Kit, 2315
Affix & Root Cards, 2316
Ages & Stages Questionnaires: 2nd Edition, 2963
All Kinds of Minds, 2317
Alphabetic Phonics Curriculum, 2640
Alternative Educational Delivery Systems, 2641
American Chemical Society Committee on Chemists with Disabilities, 1223
American College Testing Program, 2442
American School Counselor Association, 2586
An Activity-Based Approach to Early Intervention: Second Edition, 2644
Annals of Dyslexia, 6816
Arizona Department of Education, 2510
Arkansas Department of Special Education, 2511
Art for All the Children: Approaches to Art Therapy for Children with Disabilities, 7
Assessing Bilingual Exceptional Children, 2653
Assessing Students with Special Needs, 2964
Assessing Young Children, 2965
Assessing and Screening Preschoolers, 2966
Assessment Log & Developmental Progress Charts for the CCPSN, 2967
Assessment of Learners with Special Needs, 2968
Assessment: The Special Educator's Role, 2662
Assistive Technology, 162
Association for Individually Guided Education, 2445
Association on Higher Education and Disability, 2446
Attention Deficit Disorder and Learning Disabilities, 6841
Attention Deficit-Hyperactivity Disorder: Is It a Learning Disability?, 7204
BOSC - Directory Facilities for People with Learning Disabilities, 6864
Beginning Reasoning and Reading, 2321
Behavioral Objectives for Learning Disabilities, 2322
Behind Special Education, 2669
Benchmark Measures, 2969
Best Toys, Books, Videos & Software for Kids, 5727
Bilingualism and Learning Disabilities, 2672
Board Games for Play and Say, 2323
Book of Possibilities: Elementary Edition, 2324
Book of Possibilities: Secondary Edition, 2325
Books on Special Children, 6517
But I'm Ready to Go, 5730

Lowe's Syndrome

Lung Disorders

Mental Health Disorders

Mental Retardation

Multiple Disabilities

Multiple Sclerosis

Muscular Dysthrophy

Neurological Impairments

Obsessive Compulsive Disorders

Orthopedical Disabilities

Orthopsychiatry

Parkinson Disease

Pediatric Disorders

Phenylketonuria

Physical Disabilities

Polio

Prader-Willi Syndrome

Rare Disabilities

Respiratory Disorders

Advances in Cardiac and Pulmonary
    Rehabilitation, 2636
Breathing Disorders: Your Complete
    Exercise Guide, 6874
International Ventilator Users Network, 6141
Sinus Survival, 6287

Severe Disabilites

Assessment of Individuals with Severe
    Disabilities, 2660
Association for Persons in Supported
    Employment, 9712
Collaborative Teams for Students with
    Severe Disabilities: Second Edition, 2696
Curriculum Decision Making for Students
    with Severe Handicaps, 2710
Developmental Diagnosis, Treatment, 2719
Including Students with Severe and Multiple
    Disabilites in Typical Classrooms, 2785
Including Students with Severe and Multiple
    Disabilities in Typical Classrooms, 6759
Instruction of Persons with Severe
    Handicaps, 2354
JASH: The Journal of the Association for
    Persons with Severe Handicaps, 2560
Partners in Everyday Communicative
    Exchanges, 6233
Preparation and Employment of Students,
    7163
TASH: The Association for Persons with
    Severe Handicaps, 2473
Transitions to Adult Life, 5850
Wyoming Independent Living
    Rehabilitation, 5243

Sexual Abuse

Shining Bright: Head Start Inclusion, 7500
Wilmington Vet Center, 9412

Sjogren's Syndrome

Moisture Seekers, 6193
Sjogren's Syndrome Foundation, 3648

Speech Disorders

American Speech-Language-Hearing
    Association, 2234
AniVox Computer Speech Systems, 1962
Assessment Log & Developmental Progress
    Charts for the Carolina
    Curriculum-CCITSN & CCPSN, 2656
Assessment and Remediation of Articulatory
    and Phonological Disorders, 2657
Audapter Speech System, 1964
Awareness Training (4-Part Series), 7356
Computerized Speech Lab, 2036
Davis Center for Hearing, Speech and
    Learning: Hearing Therapy, 1085
Electronic Speech Assistance Devices, 1967

Journal of Speech and Hearing Disorders,
    6427
Keys to Parenting a Child with Attention
    Deficit Disorder, 6635
Language Parts Catalog, 2364
Language Tool Kit, 2365
Language, Speech and Hearing Services in
    School, 6433
Motor Speech Disorders, 6954
Motor Speech Disorders: Advances in
    Assessment and Treatment, 6955
Neuromotor Speech Disorders: Nature,
    Assessment, and Management, 6960
PEPPER, 2109
Porta-Voice Speech System, 1977
Stickybear Parts of Speech, 2169
Talkable Tales, 5820

Spina Bifida

In the Middle, 7436
Mountaineer Spina Bifida Camp, 1703
On Our Own Terms: Children Living with
    Physical Disabilities, 5793
Shriners Hospitals for Children - Los
    Angeles, 8154
Shriners Hospitals for Children, Houston,
    7927
Spina Bifida Association of America, 1329
Spina Bifida Association of Northern IN,
    7760
Spina Bifida Program of D.C. Children's
    Hospital, 8233
Sports and Exercise for Children with
    Chronic Health Conditions, 8816
Wabash Valley Spina Bifida Support Group,
    7768

Spinal Cord Disorders

American Association of Spinal Cord Injury
    Nurses, 1218
American Association of Spinal Cord Injury
    Psychologists & Social Workers, 1219
American Association of Spinal Cord Injury
    Nurses, 6728
American Paraplegia Society, 1232
American Spinal Injury Association, 1234
Baptist Rehabilitation Institute, 4000
Brooks Health System, 7692
Compendiums of Educational Resources on
    Spinal Cord/Traumatic Brain Injury, 6893
Connections Newsletter, 6747
Crotched Mountain School and
    Rehabilitation Center, 1596
Dallas Rehabilitation Institute, 7901
Directions, 6060
Eastern Paralyzed Veterans Association, 5600
Families of Spinal Muscular Dystrophy, 1270
Functional Electrical Stimulation for
    Ambulation by Paraplegics, 6099
HealthSouth Rehabilitation Center, 7631
HealthSouth Rehabilitation Center of
    Tucson, 7632
HealthSouth Rehabilitation Centers of
    Tuscon, 7633
HealthSouth Sunrise Rehabilitation Hospital,
    7697

HealthSouth Tri-State Regional
    Rehabilitation Hospital, 8408
How to Live with a Spinal Cord Injury, 6929
Lakeland Center, 8534
Liaison Computer Work Station, 577
Living with Spinal Cord Injury, 7456
Nashville Rehabilitation Hospital, 7889
National Council on Spinal Cord Injury, 1300
NeuroControl Corporation, 7609
North Memorial Medical Center - North
    Rehabilitation Center, 7808
Opportunities Unlimited and Brain Injury
    Services of Village Northwest, 1199
Paralysis Society of America, 8990
Paralyzed Veterans of America, 1317
Progress in Research, 6254
Rehabilitation Institute, Kansas City, 4944
Resources for People with Disabilities and
    Chronic Conditions, 6275
Rusk Rehabilitation Center, 7813
SCI Psychosocial Process, 1324
Saint Vincent Children's Specialty Hospital,
    7759
San Diego Rehabilitation Institute, 7668
Sexuality After Spinal Cord Injury: Answers
    to Your Questions, 6975
Shake-A-Leg, 1326
Shepherd Center, 7719
Shepherd Center for Treatment of Spinal
    Injuries, 8313
Shriners Hospitals for Children, 7706
Spinal Cord Dysfunction, 2893
Spinal Cord Injury Home Care Manual, 6979
Spinal Cord Injury Life, 6300
Spinal Cord Society (SCS), 1330
Spine, 6301
St. Anthony's Healthcare Resources Alert,
    6801
St. Mary's RehabCare Center, 8715
Total Resource for the Wheelchair
    Community, 5848
United Cerebral Palsy of Western New York,
    8620
VA Palo Alto Rehabilitation Research and
    Development Center, 9070
Walking Tomorrow, 6336
West Florida Hospital - The Rehabilitation
    Institute, 8295
West Gables Rehabilitation Hospital and
    Healthcare Center, 7712

Stroke

ACCENTCARE, 8014
American Heart Association Guide to Stroke
    Treatment, Recovery & Prevention, 6815
American Heart Association: National
    Center, 1226
American Stroke Association, 1235
Aphasia: What is It?, 6817
Atlanta Institute of Medicine and
    Rehabilitation, 8298
Baylor Institute for Rehabilitation, 8717
Botsford General Hospital Inpatient
    Hospitalization Unit, 8528
Braintree Hospital, 7791
Burke Rehabilitation Hospital, 7832
Cedars-Sinai Medical Center and Inpatient
    Rehabilitation Center, 7646
Center for Comprehensive Services, 8334
Center for Neuro-Rehabilitation, 8482

Christopher Reeve Paralysis Foundation, 1259
Co:Writer, 2034
Community Rehabilitation Center, 7799
Consumer Health USA, Volume 2, 5872
Daniel Freeman Hospitals - Center for Diagnostic and Rehab Medicine, 7647
Daniel Freeman Rehabilitaion Centers, 8054
Dreamer, 2194
Easter Seals Iowa, 8415
Eastern Idaho Regional Medical Center Rehabilitation Program, 7721
Emory University Center for Rehabilitation Medicine, 7716
Fairlawn Rehabilitation Hospital, 8506
Florida C.O.R.F., 8251
Franciscan Rehabilitation Center, 7840
HealthSouth Chattanooga Rehabilitation Hospital, 7885
HealthSouth Nittany Valley Rehabilitation Hospital, 7869
HealthSouth Rehabilitation Hospital of Jonesboro, 7639
Healthsouth Central Carolinas Rehabilitation Complex, 8708
Healthsouth Rehabilitation Hospital of York, 7872
Hillhaven Rehabilitation, 8307
Hope Network Independent Living Program, 4893
Jim Thorpe Rehabilitation Center at Southwest Medical Center, 7856
Kent Waldrep National Paralysis Foundation, 3815
Kessler Institute for Rehabilitation, 963
Lee Memorial Hospital, 8262
Loma Linda University Medical Center, Rehabilitation Institute, 8104
Magic Crayon, 2073
Marianjoy Rehablink, 8364
Mecosta County General Hospital Rehabilitation Center, 7804
MountainView Regional Rehabilitation Hospital, 7948
National Stroke Association, 1315
North Broward Rehab Unit, 8273
PSS CogRehab software, 2110
Pedal-in-Place Exerciser, 8827
Productivity Plus (Basic Education), 2079
RIC Northshore, 8378
RIC Windermere House, 8380
RIC and Swedish Covenant Hospital Rehabilitation Services, 8381
Reading Rehabilitation Hospital, 5651
Rehabilitation Institute of Michigan, 7805
Rehabilitation Institute of Santa Barbara, 8144
Rehabilitation Research and Development Center, 8146
Rehabilitation Services, 7935
Robert L. Miller Rehab Center, 8703
Roosevelt Warm Springs Institute for Rehabilitation, 4723
SS-ACCESS Single Switch Interface for PC's with MS-DOS, 1845
Sierra Vista Regional Medical Center Rehab Unit, 7674
Sinai Rehabilitation Center, 7790
Solutions at Santa Barbara - Transitional Living Center, 8157
St. Anthony Hospital Rehabilitation Center, 8677
St. Francis Rehabilitation Hospital, 8669

St. Joseph Rehabilitation Hospital and Outpatient Center, 7831
Step on It! Computer Control Pedals, 1944
Stroke Connection, 6310
SuperKey, 2217
Symbi-Key Computer Switch Interface, 1850
Tennis in a Wheelchair, 8843
Three Rivers Rehabilitation Pavilion, 7807
UAB Spain Rehabilitation Center, 7628
Universal Institute , Rebah & Fitness Center, 1206
Visual Independence Program, 8568
Walton Rehabilitation Hospital, 8316
Youville Hospital & Rehab Center, 8527

Tinnitus

American Tinnitus Association, 1071
American Tinnitus Association/ Tinnitus Today, 1072
Tinnitus Today, 6481

Tourette Syndrome

Children with Tourette Syndrome, 6885
Tourette Syndrome Association, 1334
Tourette Syndrome Association of CT Camp, 1475
Tourette Syndrome Association of IL Camp, 1499
Twitch and Shout, 7525

Visual Impairments

ACB Government Employees, 1150
ACB Radio Amateurs, 1341
ACB Social Service Providers, 1151
AFB Directory of Services for Blind and Visually Impaired Persons in the U.S. and Canada, 6707
AFB News, 7006
AFB Press, 7337
APH Catalog of Accessible Books for People Who Are Visually Impaired, 7007
Abacuses, 649
About Children's Eyes, 7182
About Children's Vision: A Guide for Parents, 7183
Access Systems International Ltd., 1857
Access to Art: A Museum Directory for Blind and Visually Impaired People, 7008
Achromatopsia Network, 1342
Adaptek Systems, 151
Addie McBryde Rehabilitation Center for the Blind, 8554
Age-Related Macular Degeneration, 7009
Ai Squared, 2017
Ai Squared, 7554
Aicom Corporation, 1961
Alabama Radio Reading Service Network (ARR, 5327
Alaska Center for the Visually Impaired, 7981
Aluminum Adjustable Support Canes for the Blind, 650
American Academy of Ophthalmology, 1343

American Action Fund for Blind Children and Adults, 1344
American Blind Bowling Association, 8781
American Blind Skiing Association, 8782
American Council of Blind Lions, 1346
American Council of Blind Parents, 5632
American Council of the Blind, 1347
American Foundation for the Blind, 1348
American Hearing Impaired Hockey Association, 8783
American Heritage Large Type Dictionary, 7011
American Optometric Association, 1349
American Printing House for the Blind, 584
American Printing House for the Blind, 1350
American Printing House for the Blind, 7012
Amerock Corporation, 3310
An Orientation and Mobility Primer for Families and Young Children, 7013
Analog Clock Model, 651
Annual Report/Newsletter, 7014
Arizona Rehabilitation State Services for the Blind and Visually Impaired, 3987
Art and Science of Teaching Orientation and Mobility to Persons with Visual Impairments, 7015
Artic Business Vision (for DOS) and Artic WinVision (for Windows 95), 1963
Artificial Language Laboratory, 8
Associated Blind, 1351
Associated Services for the Blind, 1352
Association for Education & Rehabilitation of the Blind & Visually Impaired, 1353
Association for Macular Diseases, 1354
Association for the Blind, 8707
Association of Radio Reading Services, 1355
Association of Visual Science Librarians, 1356
Aud-A-Mometer, 302
Audio Book Contractors, 652
Awareness, 7016
BESTspeech, 163
BVA Bulletin, 7206
Backgammon Set: Deluxe, 8938
Bal F. and Hilda N. Swan Foundation, 3184
Basketball: Beeping Foam, 8847
Behavior Therapy for Developmentally Disabled, 2667
Berthold Lowenfeld on Blindness and Blind People, 7019
Beyond Sight, 653
Big Bold Timer Low Vision, 335
Big Number Pocket Sized Calculator, 654
Big Print Address Book, 633
Bill Dvorak, Kayak and Rafting Expeditions, 9001
Blind Babies Foundation, 3097
Blind Children's Center, 1357
Blind Children's Fund, 3446
Blind Educator, 7020
Blind Industries and Services of Maryland, 8481
Blind Outdoor Leisure Development, 8785
Blind Service Association, 8330
Blind and Vision-Impaired Individuals, 7021
Blind and Vision-Impaired Individuals, 7208
Blinded Veterans Association, 1358
Blindness, 7362
Blindness and Early Childhood Development Second Edition, 7022
Blindness: What it is, What it Does and How to Live with it, 7024
Board Games: Solitaire, 8940

Anna's Silent World, 6365
Annals Publishing Company, 6737
Annals of Dyslexia, 6816
Annals of Otology, Rhinology and
  Larynology, 6737
Annandale at Suwanee, 8297
Anne and Henry Zarrow Foundation, 3713
Annual Community Awards Booklet, 5981
Annual Report/Newsletter, 7014
Annual Santa Barbara Sports Festival, 2235
Annuziata Sanguinetti Foundation, 3083
Anschutz Family Foundation, 3182
Answerall 100, 160
Antecedent Control: Innovative Approaches
  to Behavioral Support, 2649
Anthony Brothers Manufacturing, 8936
Anthony Wayne Rehabilitation Center for
  the Handicapped and Blind, 9488
Anthracite Region Center for Independent
  Living, 5100
Antioch College, 3027
Aphasia: What is It?, 6817
Appalachian Center for Independent Living,
  5223
Appalachian Center for Independent Living,
  5224
Appalachian Independence Center, 5185
Apple Computer, 3084
Appleby Foundation, 3229
Appliance 411, 7564
Applied Kinesiology: Muscle Response in
  Diagnosis, Therapy and Preventive
  Medicine, 2650
Applied Rehabilitation Counseling, 2651
Approaching Equality, 5267
Apria Health Care, 8197
Apria Healthcare, 455
Aquarius Health Care Videos, 6510, 6578,
  6595, 7342, 7353, 7354, 7360, 7364, 7380,
  7390, 7397, 7403, 7413, 7437, 7458, 7466,
  7467, 7470, 7471, 7477, 7489, 7491, 7494,
  7504, 7508, 7509, 7520, 7522, 7523, 7526,
  7530, 7535, 7545, 7546
Aquatic Access, 409, 416, 417
Arbor Health Care Company, 7838
Arbors at Columbus, 7839
Arc Detroit, 4875
Arc Monmouth County, 9608
Arc of Alabama, 3062
Arc of Alaska, 3065
Arc of Arizona, 3067
Arc of Arkansas, 3075
Arc of California, 3085
Arc of Colorado, 3183
Arc of Connecticut, 3201
Arc of Delaware, 3222
Arc of Florida, 3247
Arc of Georgia, 3280
Arc of Hawaii, 3296
Arc of Illinois, 3311
Arc of Indiana, 3362
Arc of Iowa, 3376
Arc of Jefferson County, 7958
Arc of Kansas, 3384
Arc of Kentucky, 3388
Arc of Louisiana, 3393
Arc of Maryland, 3404
Arc of Massachusetts, 3422
Arc of Michigan, 3444
Arc of Minnesota, 3470
Arc of Mississippi, 3488
Arc of Montana, 3505
Arc of Nebraska, 3506

Arc of New Hampshire, 3520
Arc of New Jersey, 3523
Arc of New Mexico, 3546
Arc of North Carolina, 3664
Arc of North Dakota, 3677
Arc of Ohio, 3682
Arc of Oklahoma, 3714
Arc of Oregon, 3719
Arc of Pennsylvania, 3726
Arc of South Carolina, 3765
Arc of South Dakota, 3769
Arc of Tennessee, 3770
Arc of Texas, 3783
Arc of Utah, 3833
Arc of Virginia, 3838
Arc of Washington State, 3851
Arc of Wisconsin, 3865
Arc of Wyoming, 3876
Arc of the United States, 7565
Arcadia Foundation, 3727
Arch and Stella Rowan Foudation, 3784
Architectural Barriers Action League, 8964
Archives of Neurology, 6738
Arcola Bus Sales, 65
Arcola Mobility, 25
Arden Nursing Home, 8751
Ardmore Developmental Center, 9543
Area Access, 376
Area Cooperative Educational Services, 9392
Arena Stage, 5
Argyros Foundation, 3086
Arista Surgical Supply Company, 88, 96,
  115, 674, 678, 687, 754
Arizona - Protection & Advocacy for
  Persons with Disabilities, 3981
Arizona Association of Homes and Housing
  for the Aging, 792
Arizona Braille and Talking Book Library,
  5340
Arizona Bridge to Independent Living, 4562
Arizona Center for Disability Law, 3981
Arizona Center for the Blind and Visually
  Impaired, 7983
Arizona Civil Rights Division, 9313
Arizona Commnity Foundation, 3068
Arizona Department of Aging, 3982
Arizona Department of Children's
  Rehabilitative Services, 3983
Arizona Department of Economic Security,
  3984
Arizona Department of Education, 2510
Arizona Department of Family Health
  Services, 3985
Arizona Department of Handicapped
  Children, 3986
Arizona Industries for the Blind, 7984
Arizona Rehabilitation State Services for the
  Blind and Visually Impaired, 3987
Arizona State Braille and Talking Book
  Library, 5341
Arjo, 411
Arkansas - Developmental Disability
  Council, 3994
Arkansas - President's Committee on People
  with Disabilities, 3995
Arkansas - Vocational Rehabilitation
  Agency, 9320
Arkansas Assistive Technology Projects,
  3996
Arkansas Department of Human Services,
  9324
Arkansas Department of Special Education,
  2511

Arkansas Division of Aging & Adult
  Services, 3997
Arkansas Division of Developmental
  Disabilities Services, 3998
Arkansas Division of Services for the Blind,
  3999
Arkansas Employment Security Department,
  9321
Arkansas Employment Service Agency and
  Job Training Program, 9321
Arkansas Lighthouse for the Blind, 8007
Arkansas Regional Library for the Blind and
  Physically Handicapped, 5351
Arkansas Rehabilitation Research and
  Training Center for the Deaf and Hard of
  Hearing, 1073
Arkansas SILC, 4570
Arkansas Veterans Facility, 8008
Arkenstone, 1816, 2115
Arlin J. Brown Information Center, 1173
Arlington County Department of Libraries,
  5674
Arlington Health Foundation, 3839
Arlington Press, 6331
Armstrong Medical, 456
Army and Air Force Exchange Services, 3028
Arnold A. Schwartz Foundation, 3524
Arnold J. and Irene B. Kocurek Family
  Foundation, 3785
Aromatherapy Book: Applications and
  Inhalations, 5982
Aromatherapy Seminars, 882
Aromatherapy Workbook, 5983
Aromatherapy for Common Ailments, 5984
Aromatherapy, to Heal and Tend the Body,
  5985
Around the Clock, 7185
Arrow Center, 8019
Arrow Walker, 676
Arrowhead West, 8431
Art Therapy, 6739
Art and Disabilities, 6
Art and Science of Teaching Orientation and
  Mobility to Persons with Visual
  Impairments, 7015
Art for All the Children: Approaches to Art
  Therapy for Children with Disabilities, 7
Art of Aromatherapy, 5986
Art-Centered Education and Therapy for
  Children with Disabilities, 2652
Artec, 755
Arthritic's Cookbook, 6818
Arthritis 101: Questions You Have -
  Answers You Need, 6819
Arthritis 101: Questions You Have. Answer
  You Need., 6820
Arthritis Accent, 5987
Arthritis Answers: Basic Information About
  Arthritis, 7186
Arthritis Consulting Services, 1237
Arthritis Foundation, 1238, 5988, 1227,
  5993, 6089, 6295, 6869, 6924, 6933, 6970,
  7184, 7186, 7187, 7188, 7190, 7191, 7195,
  7197, 7211, 7213, 7224, 7231, 7274, 7275,
  7276, 7277, 7283, 7289, 7295, 7297, 7303,
  7317, 7328, 7478, 7482, 8892
Arthritis Foundation Distribution Center,
  6726, 6820, 6887, 6966, 6989, 7407, 7486
Arthritis Foundation Information Hotline,
  8865
Arthritis Foundation Services, 7187
Arthritis Foundation Southern N.E. Chapter,
  5987
Arthritis Foundation of Illinois News, 5989

Attending to America: Personal Assistance for Independent Living, 5837

Attention, 5995

Attention Deficit Disorder, 7352

Attention Deficit Disorder & Learning Disabilities, 6840

Attention Deficit Disorder Association, 1242

Attention Deficit Disorder Association- Southern Region, 1243

Attention Deficit Disorder and Learning Disabilities, 6841

Attention Deficit Disorder in Adults Workbook, 6842

Attention Deficit Disorder in Children and Adolescents, 2664

Attention Deficit Disorder in Children and Adolescents, 6843

Attention Deficit Disorder: A Different Perception, 6844

Attention Deficit Disorder: Adults, 7353

Attention Deficit Disorder: Children, 6510

Attention Deficit Disorders and Hyperactivity, 7203

Attention Deficit Disorders: Assessment & Teaching, 6665

Attention Deficit Hyperactivity Disorder: What Every Parent Wants To Know, 6845

Attention Deficit Information Network, 1244

Attention Deficit-Hyperactivity Disorder: Is It a Learning Disability?, 7204

Attention Deficit/Hyperactivity Disorder, 6846

Attention-Deficit Hyperactivity Disorder, 6847

Attention-Deficit Hyperactivity Disorder: Symptoms and Suggestons for Treatment, 6848

Attention-Deficit/Hyperactivity Disorder, What Every Parent Wants to Know, 6621

Attitudes Toward Persons with Disabilities, 5996

Attorney General's Office Disability Rights Bureau, 4107

Aud-A-Mometer, 302

Audapter Speech System, 1964

Audio Book Contractors, 652

Audio Recordings, 632

Audiogram/Clinical Records Manager, 1873

Audiology Clinic (Children), 8226

Audiology Foundation of America, 7570

Audiology/HSCSN, Building 10, 8226

Auditech - Audioport Personal Amplifier, 561

Auditech - Classroom Amplification Sy Focus CFM802, 562

Auditech - DirectEar Transmitter and H, 563

Auditech - Personal FM Educational System, 564

Auditech - Personal PA Value Pack System, 565

Auditech - Pocketalker Pro, 566

Auditory Learning Center, 1075

Auditory-Verbal International, 1076, 7571

Auditory-Verbal Therapy for Parents and Professionals, 2319

Auen-Berger Foundation, 3088

Augmentative Communiation Systems (AAC), 1818

Augmentative Communication Consultants, 2302

Augmentative and Alternative Communication, 4167, 5997

Augmenting Basic Communciation in Natural Contexts, 6849

Augusta Talking Book Center, 5426

Augusta VA Medical Center, 9097

Aural Habilitation, 6367

Aurora Press, 6040, 6285

Aurora of Central New York, 8866

Austin Center for Development, 8325

Austin Resource Center for Independent Living, 5153

Authoritative Guide to Self- Help Resource in Mental Health, 5998

Autism, 6850, 7354

Autism Handbook: Understanding & Treating Autism & Prevention Development, 6851

Autism Research Institute, 5356, 5999, 5725

Autism Research Review, 5725

Autism Services Center, 1245, 5693

Autism Society of America, 1246, 8867, 7235

Autism Society of North Carolina, 5623

Autism Society of North Carolina Bookstore, 5623, 5933, 6010, 6639, 6646, 6810, 6850, 6852, 6853, 6856, 6858, 6860, 6866, 6904, 6918, 6922, 6926, 6930, 6972, 6976, 6978, 6983, 6996, 6997, 6999, 7205, 7223, 7230, 7308

Autism Training Center, 5694

Autism Treatment Guide, 6852

Autism and Asperger Syndrome, 6853

Autism and Learning, 6854

Autism in Adolescents and Adults, 6855

Autism...Nature, Diagnosis and Treatment, 6856

Autism: A Strange, Silent World, 6857

Autism: A World Apart, 7355

Autism: Explaining the Enigma, 6858

Autism: From Tragedy to Triumph, 6859

Autism: Identification, Education and Treatment, 6860

Autism: The Facts, 6861

Autistic Adults at Bittersweet Farms, 1618, 6862

Automated Functions, 1973

Automatic Card Shuffler, 8937

Automatic Test Author, 2022

Automobile Lifts for Scooters, Wheelchairs and Powerchairs, 26

Automotion Mobility Division of Handicapped Mobility, 27

Autry Foundation, 3089

Avant Walker, 587

Avery Park Publishing Group, 6515

Avery Publishing, 6252

Avery Publishing Group, 2883, 5810, 6317, 6741, 6785

Avis Rent A Car, 9025

Avoid Eye Strain, Feel it T-Shirt, 1779

Avoiding Unfortunate Situations, 7205

Awareness, 7016

Awareness Through Movement, 6511

Awareness Training (4-Part Series), 7356

Awareness through Movement: Health Exercises for Personal Growth, 6000

Away We Ride, 2023

Away with Arthritis, 6863

Ayer Company Publishers, 2848

Ayurvedic Institute, 2447

Azure Acres Chemical Dependency Recovery Center, 8022

B

B & H Reviews, 6092

B.A. and Elinor Steinhagen Benevoent Trust, 3786

BARC, 9327

BCR Foundation, 3248

BESTspeech, 163

BG Industries, 133

BI-Couinty Services, 9489

BIGmack Communication Aid, 1819

BILBO Innovations, 1944

BIPAP S/T Ventilatory Support System, 303

BIT Talking Scale Bathroom Scale, 91

BOSC, 6517

BOSC - Directory Facilities for People with Learning Disabilities, 6864

BVA Bulletin, 7206

Baby Book for the Developmentally Challenged Child, 6512

Baby Jogger Company, 247

Bach Flower Therapy, 6001

Back Care Basics: A Doctor's Gentle Yoga Program for Back and Neck Pain Relief, 6513

Back Machine, 253

Back Technology of Miami, 8234

Back in the Saddle, 8023

Back in the Saddle Hippotherapy Program, 8326

Back-Huggar Pillow, 254

BackSaver Posture Chair, 231

BackSaver Products Company, 231

Backgammon Set: Deluxe, 8938

Backyards and Butterflies, 6514

Bagel Holder, 334

Bailey, 459

Bailey Manufacturing Company, 226, 227, 228, 230, 242, 244, 252, 374, 442, 516, 517, 518, 527, 528, 533, 545, 703

Bailey's Book House, 2024

Bain, 4715

Bainbridge Subregional Library for the Blind & Physically Handicapped, 5427

Baker & Taylor, Int'l, 6916

Baker Commodities Corporate Giving Program, 3090

Bakersfield Association for Retarded Citizens, 9327

Bakersfield Regional Rehabilitation Hospital, 7643

Bal F. and Hilda N. Swan Foundation, 3184

Balance Centers of America, 9490

Ball Bearing Spinner, 28

Ball Brothers Foundation, 3363

Ball Memorial Hospital, 8401

Ballantine Books, 5760, 6008, 6195, 6553

Ballard Convalescent Center, 8752

Ballard Rehabilitation Hospital, 8024

Baltimore Community Foundation, 3405, 3407

Baltimore Gas and Electric Foundation, 3406

Baltimore Regional Office, 9138

Baltimore VA Medical Center, 9139

Bancroft Camp, 1527

Bancroft NeuroHealth, 1598, 8586

Bangor Public Library, 5511

Bangor Veteran Center - Veterans Outreach Center, 9536

Bank Street Writer III, 2116

Bank of Boston Corporation Charitable Foundation, 3423

Bank of Santa Clara Foundation, 3091

BankAmerica Foundation, 3092

Bantam, 6176

Bantam Books, 5968, 6265

C

College Internship Program at the Berkshire Center, 8503
College and Career Programs for the Deaf, 6383
College and University, 2554
College of Maharishi Ayur-Veda Health Center, 911
College of Optometrists in Vision Development, 1176
College of Syntonic Optometry, 1261
Colleton Regional Hospital - RehabCare Unit, 7880
Collier County Public Library, 1366
Colmery-O'Neil VA Medical Center, 9123
Colon & Rectal Cancer: A Comprehensive Guide for Patients & Families, 6888
Colon Health: Key to a Vibrant Life, 6744
Colon Irrigation: A Forgotten Key to Health, 6745
Colonial Life and Accident Insurance Company Contributions Program, 3767
Colonial Manor of Wausau - Extended Rehab Services, 8775
Color Therapy, 6040
Colorado Association of Homes and Services for the Aging, 799
Colorado Centennial Building, 5382
Colorado Civil Rights Division, 9379
Colorado Department of Aging, 4020
Colorado Department of Education, 2514
Colorado Department of Handicapped Children, 4021
Colorado Developmental Disabilities Planning Council, 4022
Colorado Division of Mental Health, 4023
Colorado Easter Seal Society, 2080
Colorado Employment Service, 9378
Colorado Fair Employment Practice Agency, 9379
Colorado Library for the Blind and Physically Handicapped, 5382
Colorado Lions Camp, 1464
Colorado Springs Independence Center, 4656
Colorado Talking Book Library, 5383
Colorado Vocational Rehabilition Agency Department of Social Services, 9380
Colorado/Wyoming VA Medical Center, 9073
Colorodo Regional Library Colorado Talking Book Library, 5384
Columbia Foundation, 3410
Columbia Gas of Pennsylvania Columbia Gas of Maryland, Corporate Giving, 3731
Columbia Gorge Center, 5091
Columbia Lighthouse for the Blind, 1367
Columbia Medical Manufacturing Corporation, 98
Columbia Regional Hospital - RehabCare Unit, 7810
Columbia Regional Office, 9248
Columbus Foundation and Affiliated Organizations, 3685
Columbus McKinnon Corporation, 382
Columbus Speech and Hearing Center, 8640
Comanche Pants, 1789
Comb-O-Cycle, 589
Combination File/Reference Carousel, 567
Come Back Jack: The Revealing Story of a Child Diagnosed with Autism, 7380
Come Sign with Us, 6889
Come Sign with Us: Sign Language Activities for Children, 6384
Comm-Care Corporation, 3489

Command Corporation, 1969
Commission for the Blind & Visually Impaired - New Jersey, 9612
Commission for the Blind - New Mexico, 9636
Committee for Purchase from People Who Are Blind or Severely Disabled, 3928
Committee for a Barrier Free Environment, 2268
Commode, 99
Common Cold and Common Sense, 6041
Commonwealth Fund, 3574
CommuniCare of Clifton Nursing and Rehabilitation Center, 8641
Communicating at the End oF the Twentieth Century: Innovative Computer Programs, 6042
Communicating with Deaf People: An Introduction, 6385
Communicating with Parents of Exceptional Children, 2697
Communicating with People Who Have Trouble Hearing & Seeing: A Primer, 7221
Communication & Language Acquisition: Discoveries from Atypical Development, 2698
Communication Aids for Children and Adults, 464
Communication Center/Minnesota State Services for the Blind, 5564
Communication Coloring Book, 5738
Communication Development and Disorders in African American Children, 6890
Communication Development in Children with Down Syndrome, 6891
Communication Disorders in Aging, 5870
Communication Outlook, 6043
Communication Services for the Deaf, 5134
Communication Skills for Visually Impaired Learners, 6709, 7038
Communication Skills for Working with Elders, 2699
Communication Skills in Children with Down Syndrome, 2700
Communication Unbound, 2701
Communication-Based Intervention for Problem Behavior, 6892
Communities Foundation of Texas, 3793
Community Access Center, 4595
Community Access Center - Indio, 4596
Community Access Program - Hilltop, 8049
Community Action for Independent Living, 4977
Community Alternatives, 4819
Community Alternatives Unlimited, 2305
Community Connections, 8872
Community Enterprises, 1177, 9395
Community Exploration, 2120
Community Foudation of Monroe County, 3450
Community Foundation Serving Richmond & Central Virginia, 3843
Community Foundation for Greater Buffalo, 3575
Community Foundation for Greater Atlanta, 3281
Community Foundation for Monterey County, 3107
Community Foundation for the Capitol Region, 3576
Community Foundation of Boone County, 3365
Community Foundation of Champaign County, 3316

Community Foundation of Greater Chattanooga, 3772
Community Foundation of Herkimer & Oneida Counties, 3577
Community Foundation of New Jersey, 3528
Community Foundation of Santa Clara County, 3108
Community Foundation of Shrevport-Bossier, 3396
Community Foundation of Southeastern Connecticut, 3205
Community Foundation of Western Massachusetts, 3429
Community Foundation of the Metropolitan Tarrant County, 3794
Community Health Funding Report, 3880
Community Hospital, 7799
Community Hospital Back and Conditioning Clinic, 8179
Community Hospital and Rehabilitation Center of Los Gatos-Saratoga, 8050
Community Hospitals, Indianapolis, 8403
Community Opportunities of East Ascension, 9530
Community Outpatient Rehabilitation Center, 9335
Community Outreach Program for the Deaf, 4563
Community Recreation and People with Disabilities: Strategies for Inclusion, 5838
Community Rehabilitation Center, 7799
Community Rehabilitation Services, 4597
Community Rehabilitation Services (CRS) Pasadena Office, 4598
Community Rehabilitation Services - Downtown Office, 4599
Community Rehabilitation Services - Tucson, 7990
Community Rehabilitation Services for Independent Living, 4600
Community Rehabilitation Services- San Gabriel Office, 4601
Community Residential Alternative, 4755
Community Resouirces for Independence Fort Bragg Office, 4602
Community Resources for Independence, 4603, 5106
Community Resources for Independence - Ukiah Office, 4604
Community Resources for Independent Living - Hayward, 4605
Community Resources for Independent Living, 4606
Community Service Center for the Deaf and Hard of Hearing, 5204
Community Services for Autititic Adults and Children, 1262
Community Services for the Blind, 5205
Community Services for the Blind and Partially Sighted Store: Sight Connection, 2331
Community Services for the Deaf, 1082
Community Signs, 2332
Community Skills - Learning to Function in Your Neighborhood, 2035
Community Support Center, 8873
Community Systems, 8216
Community and Support Services, 8874
Commuter & Kid's Commuter, 759
Compassionate Friends, 8875
Compeer, 1977
Compendiums of Educational Resources on Spinal Cord/Traumatic Brain Injury, 6893

E

J

K

L

M

N

O

P

V

W

X

Y

Z

Alabama

Achievement Center - Easter Seal, 9298
Adventure Program, 1423
Alabama Association of Homes and Services for the Aging, 790
Alabama Department of Rehabilitation Services, 7954
Alabama Department of Rehabilitation Services, 9299
Alabama Goodwill Industries, 7955
Alabama Institute for Deaf and Blind Library and Resource Center, 5326
Alabama Power Foundation, 3060
Alabama Radio Reading Service Network (ARR, 5327
Alabama Regional Library for the Blind and Physically Handicapped, 5328
Alabama VA Regional Office, 9043
Alabama Veterans Facility, 7956
American Rehab Center Neuro Care Unit Mobile Infirmary, 7957
Andalusia Health Services, 3061
Arc of Alabama, 3062
Arc of Jefferson County, 7958
Association for Retarded Citizens of Jefferson County (The Arc), 7959
Basketball School, 1424
Birdie Thornton Center, 4541
Birmingham VA Medical Center, 9044
Blount Foundation, 3063
Briarcliff Nursing Center, 7960
Butler Adult Training Center, 7961
Camp ASCCA, 1425
Camp ASCCA/Easter Seals, 1426
Camp Alamisco, 1427
Camp Candlelight, 1428
Camp M-A-S-H, 1429
Camp Newsong, 1430
Camp Smile-A-Mile, 1431
Camp Sugar Falls, 1432
Central Alabama Veterans Health Care, 9045
Central Alabama Veterans Healthcare System, 9046
Cheaha Mental Health, 7962
Children's Rehabilitation Service, 7963
Chill Out '98, 1433
Chilton-Shelby Mental Health Center/ The Mitchell Center, 7964
Coffee County Training Center, 9300
EL Darden Rehabilitation Center, 7965
Easter Seals Central Alabama, 7966
Easter Seals West Alabama, 7967
Employment Service Division - Alabama, 9301
Fort Payne-Dekalb Rehab Center, 9302
Gadsden Rehabilitation Center, 7968
Geer Adult Training Center, 7969
Goodwill Easter Seals of the Gulf Coast, 7970
Houston-Love Memorial Library, 5329
Huntsville Subregional Library for the Blind & Physically Handicapped, 5330
Independent Living Center, 4542
Independent Living Center of Mobile, 4543
Indian Rivers, 7971
Lakeshore Rehabilitation Hospital, 7624
Library for the Blind & Handicapped Public Library - Anniston/Calhoun Counties, 5331
Lighthouse, 7972
Low Vision Clinic/UAB School of Optometry, 7973

MARC Enterprises, 7974
Mobile Association for the Blind, 1391
Mobile Infirmary Medical Center - Rotary Rehabilitation Division, 7625
Montezuma Training Center, 9303
Montgomery Rehabilitation Hospital, 7626
Multipurpose Arthritis & Musculoskeletal Diseases Center - UAB, 5332
North Alabama Rehabilitation Hospital, 7627
North Central Alabama Mental Retardation Authority, 7975
Opportunity Center - Easter Seal, 9304
Rehabilitation Center - Northwest Alabama Easter Seal, 7976
Research for Rett Foundation, 5333
Southeastern Blind Rehabilitation Center, 7977
Special Education Action Commette, 8923
Summer Camp for Children with Muscular Dystrophy, 1434
Technology Assistance for Special Consumers, 5334
Tennessee Valley Rehabilitation, 7978
Tuscaloosa Public Library, 5335
Tuscaloosa Subregional Library for the Blind & Physically Handicapped, 5336
Tuscaloosa VA Medical Center, 9047
UAB Spain Rehabilitation Center, 7628
Vaughn-Blumberg Center, 7979
West Central Alabama Easter Seals Rehabilitation Center, 7980
William H. and Kate Stockham Foundation, 3064
Wiregrass Rehabilitation Center, 9305
Workshops, 9306

Alaska

Access Alaska - Anchorage, 4544
Access Alaska - Fairbanks, 4545
Access Alaska-ADA Partners Project, 4546
Access Alaska-Anchorage, 4547
Access Alaska-Fairbanks, 4548
Access Alaska-Mat-Suvalley, 4549
Alaska Center for the Visually Impaired, 7981
Alaska State Library Talking Book Center, 5337
Alaska State Library, Talking Book Center, 5338
Alaska State Library/Talking Book Center, 5339
Alaska Veterans Facility, 7982
American Diabetes Summer Camp, 1435
Anchorage Job Training Center, 9307
Anchorage Regional Office, 9048
Arc of Alaska, 3065
Artic Access, 4550
Camp Alpine, 1436
Camp Wheeze Away, 1437
Champ Camp, 1438
Department of Alaska, DAV Department of Alaska, 9049
Employment Service - Alaska, 9308
Fair Employment Practice Agency, 9309
Hope Cottages, 4551
Independent Living Center of Homer, 4552
Kenai Peninsula ILC - Juneau, 4553
Kenai Peninsula ILC - Seward, 4554
Kenai Peninsula ILC - Soldotna, 4555

Kenai Peninsula Independent Living Center, 4556
Kodiak Independent Learning Center, 4557
Muscular Dystrophy Assocation Free Camp, 1439
Outdoor Recreation and Community Accesss, 1440
Rasmuson Foundation, 3066
Seward Independent Learning Center, 4558
Southeast Alaska ILC - Ketchikan, 4559
Southeast Alaska Independent Learning Center (SAIL), 4560
Southeast Alaska Independent Living-Sitka, 4561
Vocational Rehabilitation Agency - Alaska, 9310

Arizona

Arc of Arizona, 3067
Arizona Association of Homes and Housing for the Aging, 792
Arizona Braille and Talking Book Library, 5340
Arizona Bridge to Independent Living, 4562
Arizona Center for the Blind and Visually Impaired, 7983
Arizona Commnity Foundation, 3068
Arizona Industries for the Blind, 7984
Arizona State Braille and Talking Book Library, 5341
Barrow Neurological Institute Rehab Center, 7629
Beacon Foundation for the Mentally Retarded, 7985
Bonnie Pruden Pain Erasure, 894
Books for the Blind of Arizona, 5342
CARF The Rehabilitation Accrediation Commission, 897
Camp Civitan, 1441
Carl T. Hayden VA Medical Center, 9050
Carondelet Brain Injury Programs and Services, 7986
Carondelet Rehabilitation Services St Joseph's Hospital, 7987
Carondelet St. Mary's, 7988
Casa Grande Rehabilitation Programs, 7989
Center for Neurodevelopmental Studies, 5343
Community Outreach Program for the Deaf, 4563
Community Rehabilitation Services - Tucson, 7990
DIRECT Center for Independence, 4564
Desert Life Health Care Center, 7991
Direct Center for Independence, 4565
Downtown Neighborhood Learning Center, 9311
Easter Seals Arizona, 1442
Employment Service - Arizona, 9312
Fair Employment Practice Agency - Arizona, 9313
Flagstaff City-Coconino County Public Library, 5344
Fountain Hills Lioness Braille Service, 5345
Frances Moynihan Huger Foundation, 3069
Freestone Rehabilitation Center, 7992
Harrington Arthritis Research Center, 5346
Health South Rehab Institute of Tucson, 7630
HealthSouth Rehabilitation Center, 7631
HealthSouth Rehabilitation Center of Tucson, 7632

HealthSouth Rehabilitation Centers of Tuscon, 7633
HealthSouth Sports Medicine Center, 7634
Hermundslie Foundation, 3070
Institute for Human Development, 7993
JOBS Administration Job Opportunities & Basic Skills, 9314
JW Kieckhefer Foundation, 3071
Job Training Program Liaison - Arizona, 9315
John C. Lincoln Hospital North Mountain, 7994
La Frontera Center, 7995
Life Development Institute, 846
Manor Care Nursing and Rehab Center Tucson, 7996
Margaret T. Morris Foundation, 3072
Meridian Point Rehabilitation Hospital, 7635
Muscular Dystrophy Association, 1289
New Horizons Community Services, 4566
New Horizons Independent Living Center, 4567
Northern Arizona VA Health Center, 9051
Nova Care, 7997
Perry Rehabilitation Center, 7998
Phoenix Regional Office, 9052
Phoenix Veterans Center, 7999
Prescott Public Library/Talking Book Center, 5347
Prescott Talking Book Library, 5348
Progress Valley - Phoenix, 8000
R. & M. Clark Family Foundation, 3073
Samaritan Rehabilitation Institute, 8001
Scottsdale Memorial Hospital Rehabilitation Services, 8002
Services Maximizing Independent Living and Empowerment (SMILE), 4568
Sound, Listening, and Learning Center, 1141
Southern Arizona VA Healthcare System, 9053
Special Needs Center/Phoenix Public Library, 5349
St. Joseph's Hospital and Medical Center, 7636
Sterling Ranch - Residence for Special Women, 4569
Subacute Rehabilitation Conference, 2258
TETRA Corporation, 9316
Toyei Industries, 8003
Tucson Association for the Blind and Visually Imparied, 8004
Tucson Community Foundation, 3074
Valley of the Sun Rehabilitation Hospital, 8005
Vocational Rehabilitation Agency - Arizona, 9317
Vocational Rehabilitation Program Rehabilitation Services Administrations, 9318
WAHEC Medical Library Consortium, 5350
Wheelers, 9032
Wheelers Accessible Van Rentals, 9033
World Chiropractic Alliance, 1209
World Research Foundation, 5379
Yavapal Rehabilitation Center, 9319
Yuma Center for the Visually Impaired, 8006

Arkansas

American Amputee Foundation, 1216

American Association for Rehabilitation Therapy, 862
Arc of Arkansas, 3075
Arkansas - Vocational Rehabilitation Agency, 9320
Arkansas Employment Service Agency and Job Training Program, 9321
Arkansas Lighthouse for the Blind, 8007
Arkansas Regional Library for the Blind and Physically Handicapped, 5351
Arkansas Rehabilitation Research and Training Center for the Deaf and Hard of Hearing, 1073
Arkansas SILC, 4570
Arkansas Veterans Facility, 8008
Beverly Enterprises Network, 8009
Camp Aldersgate, 1443
Central Arkansas Rehab Hospital, 7637
Charles M. and Joan R. Taylor Foundation, 3076
Delta Resource Center for Independent Living, 4571
Delta Resource Independent Living Center, 4572
Easter Seal Work Center, 9322
Easter Seals of Arkansas, 8010
Educational Services for the Visually Impaired, 5352
Eugene J. Towbin Healthcare Center, 9054
Fayetteville VA Medical Center, 9055
HEALTHSOUTH Rehabilitation Hospital Fort Smith, 8011
HealthSouth Rehabilitation Hospital, 7638
HealthSouth Rehabilitation Hospital of Jonesboro, 7639
John L. McClellan Memorial Hospital, 9056
Library for the Blind and Physically Handicapped SW Region of Arkansas, 5353
Lions World Services for the Blind, 8012
Mainstream, 4573
New Medico Rehabilitation Center at Timber Ridge Ranch, 8013
North Little Rock Regional Office, 9057
Northwest Arkansas Rehabilitation Hospital, 7640
Northwest Ozarks Regional Library for the Blind and Handicapped, 5354
Our Way, 4574
Rebsamen Rehabilitation Center, 7641
Roy and Christine Sturgis Charitable Trust, 3077
Sources for Community IL Services, 4575
Sources for Community Independent Living, 4576
Spa Area IL Services, 4577
Spa Area Independent Living Services, 4578
St. Michael Hospital - RehabCare Unit, 7642
VCT/A Job Retention Skill Training Program, 9323
Vocational Rehabilitation Agency for Persons Who Are Visually Impaired, 9324
WalMart Foundation, 3078
Winthrop Rockefeller Foundation, 3079

California

ACCENTCARE, 8014
ARC - VC Ventura, 8015
ARC Mid-Cities, 8016
ARC-Adult Vocational Program, 9325

ARC-VC Magic Muffin Cafe, 8017
Ability First, 1444
Ability First, 9326
Ability First, Camp Paivika, 1445
Access Center of San Diego, 4579
Achromatopsia Network, 1342
Acupressure Institute, 853
Ahmanson Foundation, 3080
Alice Tweed Touhy Foundation, 3081
All Nations Camp, 1446
Alliance for Technology Access, 858
Amateur Athletic Foundation of Los Angeles, 3082
American Academy of Biological Dentistry, 1154
American Academy of Ophthalmology, 1343
American Action Fund for Blind Children and Adults, 1344
American Back Society Advanced Diagnosis and Treatment for Neck and Back, 1220
American College of Advancement in Medicine, 1162
American Foundation for Pain Research, 871
American Foundation of Traditional Chineses Medicine, 873
American Herbalists Guild, 874
American Institute of Hypnotherapy, 875
American Rehab Centers Neuro Care Unit, 8018
American Society for Deaf Children, 1068
Amytrophic Lateral Sclerosis Association, 1236
Anglo California Travel Service, 9000
Annual Santa Barbara Sports Festival, 2235
Annuziata Sanguinetti Foundation, 3083
Apple Computer, 3084
Arc of California, 3085
Argyros Foundation, 3086
Aromatherapy Seminars, 882
Arrow Center, 8019
Assistance League of Santa Clara County, 8020
Association for Retarded Citizens-Alameda County, 8021
Association of Visual Science Librarians, 1356
Association of Visual Science Librarians, 5355
Atkinson Foundation, 3087
Auen-Berger Foundation, 3088
Autism Research Institute, 5356
Autry Foundation, 3089
Azure Acres Chemical Dependency Recovery Center, 8022
Back in the Saddle, 8023
Baker Commodities Corporate Giving Program, 3090
Bakersfield Association for Retarded Citizens, 9327
Bakersfield Regional Rehabilitation Hospital, 7643
Ballard Rehabilitation Hospital, 8024
Bank of Santa Clara Foundation, 3091
BankAmerica Foundation, 3092
Bayview Nursing and Rehabilitation, 8025
Belden Center, 8026
Bergen Brunswig Corporation Contributions Program, 3093
Bertha Russ Foundation, 3094
Bertha Russ Lytel Foundation, 3095
Bireley Foundation, 3096
Blind Babies Foundation, 3097
Blind Children's Center, 1357

Fireman's Fund Foundation, 3118
First Step Independent Living, 4615
Fit to Work, 9340
Florence Nelson Foundation, 3119
Fontana Rehabilitation Workshop, 8068
Foothill Vocational Opportunities, 8069
Foundation for Glaucoma Research, 3120
Foundation for Glaucoma Research, 5367
Foundation for New Options, 3121
Foundation for the Advancement of the Blind, 3122
Foundation for the Junior Blind, 3123
Foundation on Employment and Disability, 3124
Frances Schermer Charitable Trust, 3125
Fred Finch Youth Center, 8070
Fred Geldert Family Foundation, 3126
Fred Gellert Foundation, 3127
Freeman E. Fairfield Foundation, 3128
Fresno City College Enabler Program, 9341
Fresno County Free Library Blind and Handicapped Services, 5369
Fresno County Free Library Talking Book Library for the Blind, 5368
Fresno County Public Library Talking Book Library for the Blind, 5370
Friendship Center for the Blind, 8071
Gallo Foundation, 3129
Garfield Medical Center, 7648
Gateway Center of Monterey County, 8072
Gateway Industries - Castroville, 8073
Georges & Germaine Fusenot Charity Foundation, 3130
Gilroy Workshop, 8074
Glaucoma Research Foundation, 3131
Glendale Memorial Hospital and Health Center Rehabilitation Unit, 8075
Gloriana Opera Company, 1458
Goleta Valley Cottage Hospital, 8076
Goose Hill, 8077
Greenery Rehabilitation Center - Pacifica, 8078
Grossmont Hospital Rehabilitation Center, 7649
Guide Dogs for the Blind, 1378
H.N. and Frances C. Berger Foundation, 3132
HEAR Center, 1099
Hacienda La Puente Adult Education, 8079
Harden Foundation, 3133
Harry and Grace Steele Foundation, 3134
Health Action, 940
Health Associates, 941
Hearing Education and Awareness for Rockers, 1103
Heartland Opportunity Center, 9342
Henry J. Kaiser Family Foundation, 3135
Henry W. Bull Foundation, 3136
Herbst Foundation, 3137
Herrick Health Sciences Library, 5371
Hi-Desert Continuing Care Center, 8080
Hillhaven Extended Care, 8081
Hillhaven San Francisco at Nobhill, 8082
Hollister Workshop, 9343
Holy Cross Comprehensive Rehabilitation Center, 7650
Home of the Guiding Hands, 8083
Homeopathic Educational Services, 944
Hospital Case Management Summit CMSA & American Health Consultants, 2242
Hospital of the Good Samaritan Acute Rehabilitation Unit, 8084
House Ear Institute, 1105

How to Find Out About Financial Aid and Funding, 3905
Humboldt Access Project, 9344
ILC of Kern County, 4616
Imperial Valley ILC, 4617
Independence Center, 4618
Independent Learning Center of Kern County, 4619
Independent Living Center of Southern California, 4620
Independent Living Center of Southern California, 4621
Independent Living Resource Center, 4623
Independent Living Resource Center - Santa Maria Office, 4624
Independent Living Resource Center - Ventura Office, 4625
Independent Living Resource Center of San Francisco, 4626
Independent Living Resource of Contra Costa County, 4628
Independent Living Resource of Contra Costa County - Antioch Office, 4627
Independent Living Resource of Contra Costa County-Fairfield Office, 4622
Independent Living Service Northern California - Redding Office, 4629
Independent Living Services of Northern California, 4630
Independent Living Services of Northern California, 4631
Industrial Therapy Center, 8085
Institute for Families of Blind Children, 1383
Institute of Transpersonal Psychology, 953
International Association for Cancer Victors and Friends, 1277
International Association for Colon Therapy, 1278
International Association of Yoga Therapists, 1181
International Foundation for Alternating Hemiplegia of Childhood, 3138
Irvine Health Foundation, 3139
James S. Copley Foundation, 3140
Janus of Santa Cruz, 8086
Jerry L. Pettis Memorial VA Medical Center, 9058
Jewish Deaf Congress, 1110
John & Geraldine Cusenza Family Foundaiton, 3141
John Muir Medical Center Rehabilitation Services, Therapy Center, 8087
John Tracy Clinic, 1111
Joni and Friends, 1282
Joseph Drown Foundation, 3142
Junior Wheelchair Sports Camp, 1459
Karl Kirchgessner Foundation, 3143
Kelso Activity Center, 8088
Kenneth T. and Eileen L. Norris Foundation, 3144
Kentfield Rehabilitation Hospital, 7651
King's Rehabilitation Center, 9345
King's View Work Experience Center, 8089
King-Drew Medical Center, 8090
Kings Daughter's Home Foundation, 3145
Konocti Industries - People Services, 9346
Koret Foundation, 3146
Krem Camps, 1460
Kuzell Institute for Arthritis and Infectious Diseases, 5372
LJ Skaggs and Mary C. Skaggs Foundation, 3147
LK Whittier Foundation, 3148

LaPalma Intercommunity Hospital, 8091
Lauralie Irving Foundation, 3149
Laurel Grove Hospital - Rehab Care Unit, 7652
Lawrence L. Frank Center Workshop, 8092
Lawrence L. Frank Rehabilitation Workshop, 8093
Lawrence Welk Foundation, 3150
Learning Services - Gilroy, 8094
Learning Services - Los Gatos, 8095
Learning Services - South Valley Ranch, 8096
Learning Services - Supported Living Programs, 8097
Legler Benbough Foundation, 3151
Leon S. Peters Rehabilitation Center, 8098
Levi Strauss Foundation, 3152
Lion's Blind Center, 8099
Lion's Blind Center of Diablo Valley, 8100
Lion's Blind Center, Oakland, 8101
Lions Center for the Blind of Oakland, 8102
Living Skills Center for the Visually Impaired, 8103
Lodi Memorial Hospital West, 7653
Loma Linda University Medical Center, Rehabilitation Institute, 8104
Long Beach Memorial Medical Center Memorial Rehabilitation Hospital, 7654
Long Beach VA Medical Center, 9059
Los Angeles Regional Office, 9060
Los Gatos Rehabilitation Hospital, 7655
Louis R. Lurie Foundation, 3153
Luke B. Hancock Foundation, 3154
Manor Care Nursing - Citrus Heights, 8105
Manor Care Nursing - Fountain Valley, 8106
Manor Care Nursing - Hemet, 8107
Manor Care Nursing - Palm Desert, 8108
Manor Care Nursing - Sunnyvale, 8109
Manor Care Nursing - Walnut Creek, 8110
Marin Center for Independent Living, 4632
Marin Community Foundation, 3155
Martinez Center for Rehab & Extended Care, 9061
Mary A. Crocker Trust, 3156
Maxx Factor Family Foundation, 3157
May and Stanley Smith Trust, 3158
Maynard's Chemical Dependency Recovery Centers, 8111
Maynard's Ranch for Men, 8112
Meadowbrook Los Angeles - Community Re-Entry Services, 8113
Meadowbrook Neurologic Center, 7656
Meadows, 8114
Medic Alert, 8895
Medical Center of La Mirada, 8115
Memorial Hospital of Gardenia, 8116
Mercy American River Hospital, 7657
Mercy Outpatient Rehab Center for NeuroRet raining, 8117
Modesto Independent Living Center, 4633
Morongo Basin Work Activity Center, 9347
Morris Stulsaft Foundation, 3159
Mother Lode Independent Living Center, 4634
Mother Lode Rehabilitation Enterprises, 9348
Multipurpose Arthritis and Musculoskeletal Diseases Center, 5373
NCI Affiliates, 9349
Napa County Mental Health, 8118
Napa Valley P.S.I., 9350
Napa Valley Support Systems, 8119
National Association to Aid Fat Americans, 986

Vocational Vision, 9372
WM Keck Foundation, 3179
Walker Institute, 8174
Western Neuro Care Center, 8175
Westside Center for Independent Living, 4648
Westside Opportunity Workshop, 9373
White Memorial Medical Center Rehabilitation, 7683
Willam G. Gilmore Foundation, 3180
Winways, 8176
Work Training Center, 9374
Work Training Center for the Handicapped, 9375
Work Training Programs, 9376
World Experience, 3057
World Institute on Disability, 1058
World Recreation Association of the Deaf, 1149

Colorado

AMC Cancer Research Center, 5380
Adolph Coors Foundation, 3181
American Academy of Environmental Medicine, 1155
American Society of Bariatric Physicians, 1170
American Universities International Programs, 3025
Anschutz Family Foundation, 3182
Arc of Colorado, 3183
Association for Applied Psychophysiology and Biofeedback, 883
Association for Network Chiropractic Spinal Analysis, 884
Atlantic Community, 4649
Bal F. and Hilda N. Swan Foundation, 3184
Bill Dvorak, Kayak and Rafting Expeditions, 9001
Bonfils-Stanton Foundation, 3185
Boulder Public Library, 5381
Boulder Vet Center, 9072
Breckenridge Outdoor Education Center, 1462
CONNECTION for Independent Living, 4650
Capron Rehabilitation, 8177
Carl W. and Carrie Mae Joslyn Charitable Foundation, 3186
Carl and Carrie Mae Joslyn Charitable Trust, c/o Bank One, Colorado Springs, N.A., 3187
Center for Independence, 4651
Center for Independent Living, 4652
Center for People with Disabilities, 4653
Center on Deafness, 4654
Challenge Aspen, 1463
Cherry Hills Health Care Center, 8178
Cheyenne Village, 9377
Children's Hospital Rehabilitation Center, 7684
Choices for Independent Living, 4655
Colarado Association of Homes and Services for the Aging, 798
Colorado Association of Homes and Services for the Aging, 799
Colorado Employment Service, 9378
Colorado Fair Employment Practice Agency, 9379

Colorado Library for the Blind and Physically Handicapped, 5382
Colorado Lions Camp, 1464
Colorado Springs Independence Center, 4656
Colorado Talking Book Library, 5383
Colorado Vocational Rehabilitation Agency Department of Social Services, 9380
Colorado/Wyoming VA Medical Center, 9073
Colorodo Regional Library Colorado Talking Book Library, 5384
Community Hospital Back and Conditioning Clinic, 8179
Comprecare Foundation, 3188
Connections for Independent Living, 4657
Deaf Counseling Services at Mental Health Corporation of Denver, 4658
Denver CIL, 4659
Denver Foundation, 3189
Denver VA Medical Center, 9074
Developmental Disabilities Center, 9381
Developmental Preschool, 8180
Developmental Training Services, 9382
Disability Center for Independent Living, 4661
Disability Center for Independent Living - Colorado, 4660
Disabled Resource Services, 4662
Dynamic Dimensions, 9383
El Pomar Foundation, 3190
Estate Planning for the Disabled, 929
Gates Family Foundation, 3191
Grand Junction VA Medical Center, 9075
Gray Street Workcenter, 9384
Greeley Center for Independence, 4663
Harry W. Rabb Foundation, 3192
Hear Now, 1102
Helen K. and Arthur E. Johnson Foundation, 3193
Herbert F. Parker Foundation, 3194
Heritage Rehabilitation Center, 8181
Hill Foundation, 3195
Hilltop Rehabilitation Hospital, 7685
Hope Center, 9385
Huggins Diagnostic Center, 945
Institute for Music, Health, and Education, 951
Inter-Church Fellowship of the Blind, 8888
International Hearing Dog, 1107
J.M. McDonald Foundation, 3196
Kenneth Kendal King Foundation, 3197
Kitzmiller-Bales Trust, 3198
Laradon Hall Society for Exceptional Children and Adults, 8182
Las Animas County Rehabilitation Center, 9386
Learning Services - Bear Creek, 8183
Lung Line Information Service, 8894
Magic of Music and Dance, 1465
Manor Care Nursing - Denver, 8184
Manor Care Nursing and Rehabilitation Center - Boulder, 8185
Mapleton Center, 7686
Mapleton Center for Rehabilitation, 8186
Martin Luther Homes - Colorado Springs, 8187
Martin Luther Homes - Denver, 4664
Martin Luther Homes - Fort Collins, 4665
Mediplex Rehab - Denver, 7687
Mediplex of Colorado, 8188
Mind/Body Health Services, 977
NLP Comprehensive, 980
NORESCO Workshop, 9387

National Association for Holistic Aromatherapy, 981
National Jewish Medical & Research Center, 5385
National Stroke Association, 1315
National Veterans Training Institute, 9076
North America Riding for the Handicapped Association, 1012
Platte River Industries, 8189
Pueblo Diversified Industries, 8190
Pueblo Goodwill Center for Independent Living, 4666
Regional Assessment and Training Center, 9388
Rehabilitation Hospital of Colorado Springs, 7688
Rocky Mountain Resource & Training Institute (RMRTI), 1036
Rocky Mountain Village, 1466
Rolf Institute, 1203
SHALOM Denver, 8191
Sangre De Cristo Independent Living Center, 4667
Sangre de Cristo Independent Living Center, 4668
Schaefer Rehabilitation Center, 8192
Sedgwick County Workshop, 9389
Sky Ranch Lutheran Camp, 1467
Southern Colorado Healthcare System System, 9077
Southwest Center for Independence, 4669
Spalding Rehab Hospital West Unit, 8193
Spalding Rehabilitation Hospital, 7689
United Cerebral Palsy of Colorado, 8194
United States Association for Blind Athletes, 1416
V. Hunter Trust, 3199
Valley Industries, 9390
Visiting Nurse Association of America, 8931
Wyoming/Colorado VA Regional Office, 9297
Yuma County Workshop, 9391

Connecticut

ACES/ACCESS Inclusion Program, 8195
APT Residential Services Division, 8196
Abilities Expo, 2225
Aetna Foundation, 3200
American Institute for Foreign Study, 3024
Apria Health Care, 8197
Arc of Connecticut, 3201
Area Cooperative Educational Services, 9392
Bristol Association for Retarded Citizens, 3202
CCARC, 9393
Camp Harkness, 1468
Catherine and Henry J. Gaisman Foundation, 3203
Center for Disability Rights, 4670
Center for Understanding Aging, 796
Central Connecticut Association for Retarded Citizens, 8198
Chapel Haven, 4671
Cheshire Occupational and Career Center, 9394
Clipper Ship Foundation, 3204
Co-Op Initiatives, 4672
Community Enterprises, 1177
Community Enterprises, 9395

Community Foundation of Southeastern
Connecticut, 3205
Community and Support Services, 8874
Connecticut Assistive Technology Project
Connecticut Department of Social
Services, 5386
Connecticut Association for Children with
Learning Disabilities, 3206
Connecticut Association of Not-for-Profit
Providers for the Aging, 800
Connecticut Braille Association, 5387
Connecticut Center's for Independent Living,
4673
Connecticut Fair Employment Practice
Agency, 9396
Connecticut Governor's Committee on
Employment of Disabled Persons, 9397
Connecticut Mutual Life Foundation, 3207
Connecticut State Library, 5388
Connecticut Subacute Corporation, 8199
Constructive Workshops, 9398
Cornelia de Lange Syndrome Foundation,
3208
Datahr Rehabilitation Institute, 8200
Disabilities Network of Eastern Connecticut,
4674
Disability Resource Center of Fairfield
County - Stratford Office, 4675
Disabled American Veterans - Connecticut,
9078
Eastern Blind Rehabilitation Center, 8201
Exceptional Cancer Patients, 1268
FAVRAH, 8202
Farmington Valley Arc, 8203
Favarh, 932
Fidelco Guide Dog Foundation, 1375
Fidelco Guide Dog Foundation, 3209
Fotheringhay Farms, 9399
GE Foundation, 3210
Gaylord Hospital, 8204
General Electric Foundation, 3211
George Hegyi Industrial Training Center,
9400
Georgiana Organization, 1274
Greater Enfield Association of Retarded
Citizens, 9401
Hartford Foundation for Public Giving, 3212
Hartford Insurance Group, 3213
Hartford Regional Office, 9079
Hartford Vet Center, 9402
Hemlocks Easter Seals Recreation, 1469
Henry Nias Foundation, 3214
Heublein Foundation, 3215
Hockenum Greenhouse, 8205
Independence Northwest, 4676
Independence Northwest Center for
Independent Living, 4677
Independence Unlimited, 4678
International Ozone Association, 960
Isola Bella, 1470
Jane Coffin Childs Memorial Fund for
Medical Research, 3216
John H. and Ethel G. Nobel Charitable Trust
c/o Bankers Trust Company, Limited, 3217
Kennedy Center, 9403
Kuhn Employment Oppurtunities, 8206
Lake Grove at Durham, 8207
Litchfield County Association for Retarded
Citizens, 8208
Mansfield's Holiday Hill, 1471
Mariner Health Care - Connecticut, 7690
Marvelwood Summer, 1472
Meriden-Wallingford Society, 8209

National Organization for Rare Disorders,
1312
National Theatre of the Deaf, 1132
New Horizons, 4679
Pauline E. Fitzpatric Charitable Trust, 3218
Prevent Blindness Connecticut, 5389
Quaezar, 9404
Rehabilitation Associates, 8210
Rehabilitation Center of Fairfield County,
8211
Reliance House, 8212
Scheuer Associates Foundation, 3219
Section of Physical Medicine and
Rehabilitation, 8213
Services for the Blind, State of Connectic,
9405
Shadybrook Learning Center, 1473
South Church Activity Program, 8214
Swindells Charitable Foundation Trust, 3220
TEAM Vocational Program, 9406
The Hole in the Wall Gang Camp, 1474
Tourette Syndrome Association of CT Camp,
1475
VA Connecticut Healthcare System,
Newington Division, 9080
VA Connecticut Healthcare System, West
Haven, 9081
Valley Memorial Health Center, 9407
Vernal W. F;Orence H. Bates Foundation,
3221
Yale University, Vision Research Center,
5390

Delaware

Alfred I. DuPont Hospital for Children, 8215
Arc of Delaware, 3222
Chichester DuPont Foundation, 3223
Children's Beach House, 1476
Community Systems, 8216
Delaware Assistive Technology Initiative
Center for Applied Science and
Engineering, 5391
Delaware Association for the Blind, 8217
Delaware Association of Nonprofit Homes
for the Aging, 801
Delaware Commission of Veterans Affairs,
9082
Delaware Division of Libraries for the Blind
and Physically Handicapped, 5392
Delaware Division of Vocational
Rehabilitation- Department of Labor, 9408
Delaware Elwyn, 8218
Delaware Fair Employment Practice Agency,
9409
Delaware Job Training Program Liaison,
9410
Delaware VA Regional Office, 9083
Delaware Veterans Center, 8219
Easter Seal Independent Living Center, 4680
Easter Seal Rehabilitation Center - New
Castle County, 8220
Edgemoor Day Program, 8221
First State Senior Center, 8222
Georgetown Day Program, 8223
Independent Living, 4681
Independent Resources, 4682
Laffey-Mchugh Foundation, 3224
Longwood Foundation, 3225
Martin Luther Homes of Delaware, 4683
Opportunity Center, 9411

Rehabilitation Engineering Library, 5393
Salvation Army Developmental Service, 8224
Wilmington VA Medical, 9084
Wilmington Vet Center, 9412
Woodside Day Program, 8225

District of Columbia

ACB Government Employees, 1150
ACB Radio Amateurs, 1341
ACB Social Service Providers, 1151
Advocates for Hearing Impaired Youth, 1061
Albert L. and Elizabeth T. Tucker
Foundation c/o Jackson & Campbell, 3226
Alexander Graham Bell Association for the
Deaf, 1062
Alexander Graham Bell Association for the
Deaf Annual Conference, 2226
Alexander and Margaret Stewart Trust, 3227
American Academy of Child and Adolescent
Psychiatry, 1215
American Association for the Advancement
of Science, 863
American Association of Homes and
Services for the Aging, 791
American Association of People with
Disabilities, 3228
American Association on Mental Retardation
AAMR Annual Meeting, 2228
American Camping Association Project on
Science, Technology and Disability, 867
American Chemical Society Committee on
Chemists with Disabilities, 1223
American College of Nurse Midwives, 1163
American Council of Blind Lions, 1346
American Council of the Blind, 1347
American Council of the Blind Annual
Convention, 2230
American Psychiatric Association, 1168
Anchor Houses, 8864
Appleby Foundation, 3229
Asthma and Allergy Foundation of America,
1240
Audiology Clinic (Children), 8226
Barbara Chambers Children's Center, 8227
Bazelon Center for Mental Health Law, 1248
Bazelton Center for Mental Health Law, 890
Blinded Veterans Association, 1358
Books for Blind and Physically Handicapped
Individuals, 1359
Braille Revival League, 1361
Center for Information Technology
Accomodation (CITA), 8870
Center for Mind/Body Studies, 905
Centers for Independent Living Program
Rehabilitation Services Department, 4684
Change, 3230
Charles Delmar Foundation, 3231
Children's National Medical Center, 908
Chronicle Guide to Grants, 3879
Clearinghouse on Disability Information,
8871
Clearinghouse on Disability Information
Office of Special Education, 910
Columbia Lighthouse for the Blind, 1367
Community Connections, 8872
Contemporary Issues in Behavioral Health
Care, 2239
Council of Families with Visual
Impairments, 1368
D.C. Center for Independent Living, 4685

DAV National Service Headquarters, 9034
Davis Memorial Goodwill Industries, 9413
Deaf REACH, 1088
Deafness and Communicative Disorders
Branch of Rehab Services Administration
Office, 1091
Department of Medicine and Surgery
Veterans Administration, 9035
Department of Veterans Benefits, 9037
Disability Rights Center, 4686
Disabled American Veterans, National
Service & Legislative Headquarters, 9085
Distance Education and Training Council,
914
District of Columbia Arc, 3232
District of Columbia Association Nonprofit
Services for the Aging, 802
District of Columbia Center for Independent
Living, 4717
District of Columbia Department of
Employment Services, 9414
District of Columbia Dept. of Employment
Services, Office of Workforce
Development, 9415
District of Columbia Fair Employment
Practice Agencies, 9416
District of Columbia General Hospital
Physical Medicine & Rehab Services, 8228
District of Columbia Public Library, Services
to the Deaf Community, 5394
District of Columbia Regional Library for
the Blind and Physically Hanicapped, 5395
Dole Foundation, 3233
Epilepsy Foundation for the National Capitol
Area, 8882
Eugene and Agnes E. Meyer Foundation,
3234
Eye Bank Association of America, 1374
Federal Benefits for Veterans and
Dependents, 9039
Federal Student Aid Information Center, 3235
GEICO Philanthropic Foundation, 3236
Gallaudet University, 1097
Gallaudet University, 1180
Gallaudet University Alumni Association,
1098
George Washington University Medical
Center, 8229
Georgetown University Child Development
Center, 5396
Giant Food Foundation, 3237
Golden Eagle Passport, 9010
Green Door, 8884
Green Door, 9417
Guide Dog Users, 1377
Guide Service of Washington, 9011
HEATH Resource Center, 939
Health Resource Center, 1101
Hospital for Sick Children, 8230
Hostelling North America Hostelling
International - American Youth Hostels,
9013
Howard University Child Development
Center, 8231
Human Resources Management, 4687
Independent Visually Impaired Enterprisers,
841
Jacob and Charlotte Lehrman Foundation,
3238
John Edward Fowler Memorial Foundation,
3239
Joseph P. Kennedy, Jr. Foundation, 3240
Kiplinger Foundation, 3241
Lab School of Washington, 1477

Library Users of America, 1387
Medicare Information, 8897
Morris and Gwendolyn Cafritz Foundation,
3242
NIH Osteoporosis and Related Bone
Diseases National Resource Center, 979
National AIDS Fund, 1291
National AIDS Hotline, 8898
National Alliance of Blind Students NABS
Liaison, 1392
National Association for Home Care, 8899
National Association of Blind Teachers, 1187
National Association of Developmental
Disabilities Councils, 982
National Association of Protection and
Advocacy Systems, 1188
National Council on Disability, 992
National Council on the Aging Conference,
2248
National Deaf Education Network and
Clearinghouse, 1124
National Deaf Education Network and
Clearinghouse, 1191
National Endowment for the Arts, Office for
AccessAbility, 996
National Health Information Center, 8907
National Information Center for Children and
Youth with Disabilities (NICHCY), 998
National Information Clearinghouse for
Children and Youth with Disabilities, 1127
National Institute on Disability and
Rehabilitation Research, 1000
National Organization on Disability, 1003
National Organization on Disability, 1313
National Parent Network on Disabilities,
1004
National Rehabilitation Hospital, 7691
National Voluntary Organizations for
Independent Living for the Aging, 819
National Women's Health Network, 1010
Operation Job Match, 9418
PVA Sports and Recreation Program, 2253
Paralyzed Veterans of America, 1317
Paul and Annetta Himmelfarb Foundation,
3243
People-to-People Committee for the
Handicapped, 1024
Physicians for Social Responsibility, 1026
Polio Society, 1321
President's Committee on Employment of
People with Disabilities, 9419
Prevent Child Abuse of Metropolitan
Washington, 8918
Project Eyes and Ears, 5397
Psychiatric Institute of Washington, 8232
Public Welfare Foundation, 3244
Rehabilitation Services Administration of the
District of Columbia, 1101
Scottish Rite Center for Childhood Language
Disorders, 1139
Senior Center for the Hearing Impaired, 5398
Sister Cities International, 3049
Spina Bifida Association of America, 1329
Spina Bifida Program of D.C. Children's
Hospital, 8233
Student Guide, 3922
SubAcute Care: American SubAcute Care
Association Annual Convention/Expo,
2257
Teacher Preparation and Special Education,
1048
Tele-Consumer Hotline, 1142
Toll-Free Information Line, 8929

U.S. Department of Veterans Affairs
National Headquarters, 9041
US Veteran's Administration, 9042
United Cerebral Palsy Association, 1335
United States Department of Education, 3245
University Legal Services AT Program, 5399
VA Medical Center, Washington D.C., 9086
Visually Impaired Data Processors, 1208
Visually Impaired Veterans of America, 1421
WAVE Work, Achievement, Value, &
Education, 9420
Washington Connection, 8932
Washington D.C. VA Medical Center, 9087
Youth for Understanding International
Exchange, 3059

Florida

Abilities Division of Lockheed Martin IMS
Workforce Services, 9421
Able Trust, 3246
Adult Day Training, 4688
Adult Day Training, 9422
Advocacy Center for Persons with
Disabilities, 855
American Academy of Orthomolecular
Medicine, 1156
American College of Addictionality and
Compulsive Disorders, 1225
American College of Hyperbaric Medicine
Ocean Medical Center, 869
American Society of Deaf Social Workers,
1069
Arc of Florida, 3247
Arthritis Consulting Services, 1237
Association of Birth Defect Children, 886
Ataxia-Telangiectasia Children's Project,
1241
BCR Foundation, 3248
Back Technology of Miami, 8234
Barnett Charities, 3249
Baron de Hirsch Meyer Foundation, 3250
Barron Collier Jr. Foundation, 3251
Bay Pines VA Medical Center, 9088
Bayfront Rehabilitation Center, 8235
Birth Defect Research for Children, 893
Bon Secours Hospital, 8236
Brain Injury Rehabilitation Center Sand Lake
Hospital, 8237
Brevard County Library System Talking
Books Library, 5400
Brevard County Talking Books Library, 5401
Brooks Health System, 7692
Broward County Talking Book Library, 5402
CEH, 9026
Camiccia-Arnautou Charitable Foundation,
3252
Camp Thunderbird, 1478
Career Assessment & Planning Services,
9423
Caring and Sharing Center for Independent
Living, 4689
Cathedral Center for Independent Living,
4690
Center Academy & Center Family, 900
Center for Independence, Training and
Education, 9424
Center for Independent Living in Central
Florida-Advocacy Living Skills Peer
Support, 4691

Sandybrook Center of Rebound, 8283
Sarasota Memorial Hospital/Comprehensive Rehabilitation Unit, 8284
Sea Pines Rehabilitation Hospital, 7705
Seacoast Center for Independent Living at Titusville, 4706
Seagull Industries for the Disabled, 9440
Self Reliance, 4707
Self-Reliance Center for Independent Living, 4708
Shriners Hospitals for Children, 7706
Shriners Hospitals for Children - Tampa, 7707
South Dade Nursing Home, Ltd., 8285
South Miami Hospital, 7709
Space Coast Center for Independent Living, 4709
St. Petersburg Regional Office, 9093
Strive Physical Therapy, 8286
Subregional Talking Book Library, 5416
Sunbridge Care and Rehabilitation, 8287
Suncoast Center for Independent Living, 4710
Suncoast Residential Training Center/ Developmental Services Program, 4711
Supported Employment Program, 9441
Supported Living Program, 4712
Talking Book Service - Mantatee County Central Library, 5417
Talking Books Library for the Blind and Physically Handicapped, 5418
Talking Books for the Blind, 5419
Talking Books/Homebound Services, 5420
Tampa A New Horizon for the 21st Century, 2260
Tampa Bay Academy, 8288
Tampa General Rehabilitation Center, 7710
Tampa General Rehabilitation Center, 8289
Tampa Lighthouse for the Blind, 4713
Tampa Lighthouse for the Blind, 8290
Tri-County Rehabilitation Center, 8395
University of Miami - Jackson Memorial Rehabilitation Center, 7711
University of Miami Comprehensive Pain and Rehabilitation Center, 8291
University of Miami, Bascom Palmer Eye Institute, 5421
University of Miami, Mailman Center For Child Development, 5422
UpReach Pavilion, 8292
Upledger Institute, 1053
Upper Pinellas Association for Retarded Citizens, 8293
VACC camp, 1483
Vic and Vicki Weinstein Family Foundation, 3278
Visually Impaired Persons of Southwest Florida, 8294
West Florida Hospital - The Rehabilitation Institute, 8295
West Florida Regional Library, 5423
West Gables Rehabilitation Hospital and Healthcare Center, 7712
West Palm Beach VA Medical Center, 9094
Wheelchair Express, 9021
William G. Selby and Marie Selby Foundation, 3279
Willough at Naples, 8296
Windmoor Healthcare of Clearwater, 1147
Windmoor Healthcare of Miami, 1148
Wood Hygienic Institute, 1338
Work Exploration Center, 9442

Georgia

Access Center for Independent Living, 4714
Albany Talking Book Center, 5424
American Cancer Society, 1222
American Juvenile Arthritis Organization (AJAO), 1227
American SIDS Institute, 8862
Annandale at Suwanee, 8297
Arc of Georgia, 3280
Arthritis Foundation, 1238
Arthritis Foundation Information Hotline, 8865
Athens Regional Library Talking Book Center, 5425
Atlanta Institute of Medicine and Rehabilitation, 8298
Atlanta Regional Office, 9095
Atlanta VA Medical Center, 9096
Augusta Talking Book Center, 5426
Augusta VA Medical Center, 9097
Bain, 4715
Bainbridge Subregional Library for the Blind & Physically Handicapped, 5427
Bobby Dodd Center, 8299
Bowdon Area Hospital, 7713
Bunker-Hill Military Summer Camp, 1484
CEL Regional Library, 5428
Camp Independence, 1485
Camp Lookout, 1486
Candler General Hospital - Rehabilitation Unit, 7714
Carl Vinson VA Medical Center, 9098
Cave Spring Rehabilitation Center, 8300
Center for Assistive Technology & Environmental Access, 8301
Center for the Visually Impaired, 8302
Children's Healthcare of Atlanta at Egleston, 7715
Community Foundation for Greater Atlanta, 3281
Devereux Georgia Treatment Network, 8303
Disability LINK, 4716
Disability and Health, National Center for Birth Defects and Developmental Disabilities, 8880
Division of Birth Defects and Genetic Diseases, 5429
Division of Rehabilitation Services, 4718
Easter Seals East Georgia, 8304
Emory Autism Resource Center, 5430
Emory University Center for Rehabilitation Medicine, 7716
Emory University Laboratory for Ophthalmic Research, 5431
Employment and Training Division, Region B, 9443
Equifax Foundation, 3282
Fair Housing and Fair Employment, 9444
Florence C. and Harry L. English Memorial Fund, 3283
Friends of Disabled Adults and Children, 935
Georgia Association of Homes and Services for the Aging, 804
Georgia Field Services Independent Living Program, 4719
Georgia Industries for the Blind, 8305
Georgia Library for the Blind and Physically Handicapped, 5432
Georgia Power Company Contirbutions Program, 3284
Georgia Regional Library, 5433

Georgia Veterans Centers, 9099
Griffin Area Resource Center Griffin Community Workshop Division, 9445
Hall County Library East Hall Branch and Special Needs Library, 5434
Hall County Library System - Special Needs Library, 5435
Harriet McDaniel Marshall Trust in Memory of Sanders McDaniel, 3285
Head Injury Treatment Program at Marietta, 8306
Health South Central Georgia Rehabilitation Hospital, 7717
Hillhaven Rehabilitation, 8307
Human Ecology Action League, 946
IBM Corporation, 3286
In-Home Medical Care, 8308
Ira C. Herbert Family Foundation, 3287
John H. and Wilhelmina D. Harland Charitable Foundation, 3288
Kelley Diversified, 9446
Kids on the Block Arthritis Programs, 8892
La Fayette Subregional Library for the Blind and Physically Disabled, 5436
Lafayette Subregional Library for the Blind and Physically Handicapped, 5437
Learning Services - Peachtree, 8309
Lettie Pate Whitehead Foundation, 3289
Living Independently for Everyone (LIFE), 4720
Macon Library for the Blind and Physically Handicapped, 5438
Marcus Foundation, 3290
Meadowbrook Atlanta/Community Re-Entry, 8310
MedTrade/Comtrade, FutureShow, 2247
MetaMatrix Medical Laboratory, 975
Middle Georgia Center for Independent Living (Dba Disability Connections), 4721
National Parent to Parent Support and Information Systems, 1005
New Ventures, 9447
North District Independent Living Program, 4722
Oconee Regional Library, 5439
Pain Control & Rehabilitation Institute of Georgia, 8311
Patterson-Barclay Memorial Foundation, 3291
Perkins-Ponder Foundation, 3292
RehabCare Unit - Cobb Hospital and Medical Center, 7718
Rich Foundation, 3293
Rome Subregional Library for the Blind and Physically Handicapped, 5440
Roosevelt Warm Springs Institute for Rehabilitation, 4723
Sara Hightower Regional Library, 5441
Savannah Association for the Blind, 8312
Savannah Widows Society, 3294
Shepherd Center, 7719
Shepherd Center for Treatment of Spinal Injuries, 8313
South Georgia Regional Library, 5442
South Georgia Regional Library for the Blind and Physically Handicapped, 5443
Southwest District Independent Living Program, 4724
Squirrel Hollow, 1487
Subregional Library for the Blind and Physically Handicapped, 5444
Subregional Library of Blind & Physically Handicapped, 5445
SunTrust Bank, Atlanta Foundation, 3295

Delta Center, 8342

Department of Ophthalmology Information Line, 8877

Department of Ophthalmology/Eye and Ear Infirmary, 5455

Division of Rehabilitation-Education Services, University of Illinois, 8343

Doctor's Data, 917

Dr. Scholl Foundation, 3317

DuPage Center for Independent Living, 4757

Duchossois Foundation, 3318

Easter Seal Rehabilitation Center, 8344

Easter Seal Rehabilitation Center of Will Grundy Counties, 8345

Easter Seal-Timber Pointe Outdoor Center, 1489

Easter Seals, 8881

Easter Seals Camp-Illinois, 1490

Easter Seals DuPage Dold Center for Children, 8346

Edward Hines Jr. Hospital, 9108

Edward Hines, Jr. VA Hospital, 9109

El Valor Corporation, 8347

Elgin Rehabilitation Center, 8348

Employment Resource Program, 924

Evenston Community Foundation, 3319

Families of Spinal Muscular Dystrophy, 1270

Family Counseling Center, 8349

Family Resource Center on Disabilities, 930

Field Foundation of Illinois, 3320

Five Star Industries, 8350

Fox River Valley Center for Independent Living, 4758

Francis Beidler Charitable Trust, 3321

Fred J. Brunner Foundation, 3322

Fulton County Rehab Center, 9465

GJ Aigner Foundation, 3323

Generations Fund, 3324

George M. Eisenberg Foundation for Charities, 3325

George Zoltan Lefton Family Foundation, 3326

Gilchrist-Marchman Rehabilitation Center, 8351

Glenkirk, 9466

Great Lakes Association of Clinical Medicine, 937

Green Bay Foundation, 3327

Grover Hermann Foundation, 3328

Hands Organization, 1100

Hardin County Center, 8352

Harken Foundation, 3329

Harold Washington Library Talking Book Center, 5456

Harry F. and Elaine Chaddick Foundation, 3330

Harry and Saddie Lasky Foundation c/o Sandra Siegal, Warady & Davis, L.L.P., 3331

Headlines Support Group, 8886

Health Resource Center for Women with Disabilities, 942

Helen Brach Foundation, 3332

Henry County Clinic, 8353

Horizons for the Blind, 1381

Horizons for the Blind, 5457

Hyde Park-Woodlawn, 8354

ILC Enterprises, 8355

IMPACT Center for Independent Living, 4759

Illinois - President's Committee on Employment of the Disabled, 9467

Illinois Center for Autism, 8356

Illinois Center for Rehabilitation and Education (ICRE-Wood), 7727

Illinois Early Childhood Intervention Clearinghouse, 5458

Illinois Employment Service, 9468

Illinois Masonic Medical Center, 8357

Illinois Regional Library for the Blind and Physically Handicapped, 5459

Illinois VA Regional Office Center, 9110

Illinois Vocational Rehabilitation Agency, 9469

Illinois/Iowa Center for Independent Living, 4760

Impact Center for Independent Living, 4761

Independence Network Center, 4762

Infant Program, 8358

Institute of Physical Medicine and Rehabilitation, 7728

International Catholic Deaf Association, 1106

Jacksonville Area Center for Independent Living, 4763

Jayne Shover Easter Seal Rehabilitation Center, 8359

Jewish Council for Youth Services, 1491

Jewish Vocational Services, 9470

JoDavies Workshop, 9471

John D. and Catherine T. MacArthur Foundation, 3333

Julius and Betty Levinson Center, 8360

Kazma Family Foundation, 3334

Kennedy Job Training Center, 9472

Knox County Council for Developmental Disabilities, 9473

Kreider Services, 9474

LIFE Center for Independent Living, 4764

LINC - Living Independently Now Center, 4765

LaRabida Children's Hospital and Research Center, 7729

LaSalle Chicago Community Trust, 3335

Lake County Center for Independent Living, 4766

Lambs Farm, 9475

Lambs Vocational Work Center, 9476

Land of Lincoln Goodwill Industries, 9477

Les Turne Amyotrophic Laterial Sclerosis Foundation, 3336

Life Service Network of Illinois- Springfield, 810

Life Services Network of Illinois, 811

Life Services Network of Illinois-Springfield, 812

Lions Clubs International, 3041

Lions World Services for the Blind, 1390

Little City Foundation, 3337

Little Friends, 8361

Living Independently Now Center, 4767

Lucille S. Thompson Family Foundation, 3338

MAP Training Center, 8362

Macon Resources, 8363

Margaret O'Maller DeSelvester Charitable Foundation, 3339

Marianjoy Rehabilitation Hospital and Clinics, 7730

Marianjoy Rehablink, 8364

Marion VA Medical Center, 9111

Mark Morton Memorial Fund, 3340

Martin Luther Homes of Illinois, 4768

Mary Bryant Home for the Blind, 8365

McDonald's Corporation Contributions Program, 3341

Michael Reese Health Trust, 3342

Mid - Illinois Talking Book Center, 5460

Mid-Illinois Talking Book Center, 5461

Moen Foundation, 3343

Molner Foundation, 3344

Nanon Wood Center for Children, 8366

National Association for Down Syndrome, 1296

National Center for Sight, 8903

National Depressive and Manic Depressive Association, 8905

National Easter Seal Society, 995

National Eye Health Education Program Department of Opthamology, 8906

National Eye Research Foundation (NERF), 3345

National Eye Research Foundation (NERF), 5462

National Fraternal Society of the Deaf, 1126

National Headache Foundation, 3346

National Lekotek Center, 5463

New Courier Travel, 9014

North American Society of Teachers of the Alexander Technique, 1198

North Chicago VA Medical Center, 9112

Northern Illinois Medical Center, 8367

Northern Illinois Special Recreation Association, 8368

Northwestern Illinois Center for Independent Living, 4769

Northwestern University Asthma and Allergy Disease Center, 5464

Northwestern University Multipurpose Arthritis & Musculoskeletal Center, 5465

OMRON Foundation, 3347

Oak Forest Hospital of Cook County, 8369

Office of Rehabilitation Services, 4770

Olympia, 1492

Opportunities for Access, A Center for Independent Living, 4771

Options Center for Independent Living, 4772

Orchard Association for the Retarded, 9478

Oris B. Hastings Charitable Foundation, 3348

Owens Vocational Training Center, 9479

PACE Center for Independent Living, 4773

Parent Group for the Retarded, 1493

Parent Group for the Retarded, 8914

Peacock Camp, 1494

Peoria Area Community Foundation, 3349

Peoria Association for Retarded Citizens, 8370

Peoria Blind People's Center, 8371

Philip H. Cohen Institute for the Visually Handicapped, 5466

Phoenix I, 8372

Pioneer Center of McHenry County, 8373

Polk Brothers Foundation, 3350

Post-Polio Support Group, 8917

Prevent Blindness America, 1411

Progress Center for Independent Living, 4774

Prosthetics and Orthotics Center in Blue Island, 8374

RAMP Regional Access & Mobility project, 4775

RB King Counseling Center, 8375

REACH Rehabilitation Program - Americana Healthcare, 8376

REHAB Products and Services, 8377

RIC Northshore, 8378

RIC Prosthetics and Orthotics Center, 8379

RIC Windermere House, 8380

RIC and Swedish Covenant Hospital Rehabilitation Services, 8381

Ray Graham Association for People with Disabilities, 8382

Regional ADA Technical Assitance Agency, 7757

Rehab Assist, 2308

RehabLink, Affiliated with Marianjoy, 7731

Rehabilitation Achievement Center, 8383

Rehabilitation Institute of Chicago, 7732

Rehabilitation Institute of Chicago - Alexian Brothers Medical Center, 8384

Rehabilitation Institute of Chicago Learning Resource Center, 5467

Retirement Research Foundation, 3351

Rimland Services for Autistic Citizens, 1495

Riverside Medical Center, 8385

Robert Young Mental Health Center Division of Trinity Regional Haelth System, 8386

Ronald McDonald House, 1037

Rotary Youth Exchange, 3047

Rush Hayward Masonic Fund, 3352

Sampson-Katz Center, 8387

Sara Lee Foundation, 3353

Sears-Roebuck Foundation, 3354

Sertoma Centre, 9480

Shady Oaks, 1496

Shawnee Library System, 5468

Shelby County Community Services, 8388

Shore Training Center, 9481

Shriners Hospitals for Children, 7733

Siragusa Foundation, 3355

Skills, 9482

Skokie Accessible Library Services, 5469

Skokie Public Library, 5470

Southern Illinois Center for Independent Living, 4776

Southern Illinois Talking Book Center, 5471

Southern Illinois University at Carbondale, 3050

Soyland Access to Independent Living (SAIL), 4777

Special Children, 8922

Springfield Center for Independent Living, 4778

Square D Foundation, 3356

St. Elizabeth Hospital Physical Rehabilitation Unit In-Patient/CARFT Certified, 8389

Statewide Library of Information for Caregivers of the Disabled, 5472

Stone-Hayes Center for Independent Living, 4779

Streator Unlimited, 8390

Suburban Audio Visual Service, 5473

Summer Wheelchair Sports Camp, 1497

TCRC Sight Center TCRC, 8391

Talking Book Center of Northwest Illinois, 5474

Tazewell County Resource Center, 8392

Thresholds AMISS, 8393

Thresholds AMISS, 9483

Thresholds Bridge Deaf North, 8394

Thresholds Psychiatric Rehabilitation Centers, 1050

Touch of Nature Environmental Center, 1498

Tourette Syndrome Association of IL Camp, 1499

Trumbull Park, 8396

United Parkinson Foundation, 3357

University of Illinois Medical Center, 8397

University of Illinois at Chicago, Lions of Illinois Eye Research Institute, 5475

VA Illiana Health Care System, 9113

VanMatre Rehabilitation Center, 8398

Vladimir A. Geringer Foundation, 3358

Voices of Vision Talking Book Center @ DuPage Library System, 5476

WP and HB White Foundation, 3359

Warren Achievement Center, 8399

Washington County Vocational Workshop, 9484

Washington Square Health Foundation, 3360

Waukegan Outpatient Mental Health Services, 8400

Westside Parents Work Activity Center, 9485

Wheat Ridge Ministries, 3361

Will Grundy Center for Independent Living, 4780

Wood River Township Hospital - RehabCare Unit, 7734

Indiana

ADEC Resources for Independence, 9486

ARC of Allen County, 9487

ATTIC, 4781

Allen County Public Library, 5477

American Academy of Osteopathy, 1157

Anthony Wayne Rehabilitation Center for the Handicapped and Blind, 9488

Arc of Indiana, 3362

Assistive Technology Through Action in Indiana, 7735

BI-Couinty Services, 9489

Balance Centers of America, 9490

Ball Brothers Foundation, 3363

Ball Memorial Hospital, 8401

Bartholomew County Public Library, 5478

Bradford Woods Outdoor Education Center, 1500

Bridgepointe Goodwill Industries and Easter Seal Society, 9491

Camp Isanogel, 1501

Camp Millhouse, 1502

Carey Services, 9492

Center for Neuropsychological Rehabilitation, 8402

Central Indiana Community Foundation, 3364

Clark Memorial Hospital - RehabCare Unit, 7736

Community Foundation of Boone County, 3365

Community Hospitals, Indianapolis, 8403

Cranial Academy, 1263

Crossroads Industrial Services, 8404

Crown Point Community Foundation, 3366

Damar Homes, 4782

Department of Veterans Affairs Vet Center #418, 8405

Developmental Disabilities Planning Council, 7737

Division of Disability, Aging and Rehabilitative Services, 9493

Down Syndrome Association of North East Indiana, 7738

EAB Industries, 9494

Easter Seal Society, 1503

Easter Seals Wayne/Union Counties, 7739

Eli Lilly and Company Corporate Contributions Program, 3367

Elkhart Public Library, 5479

Elkhart Public Library - Blind and Physically Handicapped Department, 5480

English-Bonter-Mitchell Foundation, 3368

Evansville Association for the Blind, 8406

Evansville-Vanderburgh County Public Library, 5481

Everybody Counts, 4783

Four Rivers Resource Services, 4784

Four Rivers Resource Services, 9495

Frank L. and Laura L. Smock Foundation, 3369

Frasier Rehabilitation Center Division of Clark Memorial Hospital, 8407

Gateway Services/JCARC, 9496

Goodwill Industries of Central Indiana, 9497

Happiness Bag Incorporated, 1504

Happy Hollow Children's Camp, 1505

Hazel Teegarden Foundation, 3370

HealthSouth Tri-State Regional Rehabilitation Hospital, 8408

Healthwin Specialized Care, 8409

Hook Drug Foundation, 3371

IN Speechllanguage-Hearing Association, 7740

IN-SOURCE, 7741

Indiana Association of Homes for the Aging, 806

Indiana Congress of Parent and Teachers, 7742

Indiana Employment Services and Job Training Program Liaison, 9498

Indiana Fair Employment Practice Agency, 9499

Indiana Institute on Disability and Community, 7743

Indiana Parent Information Association, 7744

Indiana Resource Center for Autism, 5482

Indiana SILC Indiana Council on Independent Living (ICOIL), 4785

Indiana University, Multipurpose Arthritis Center, 5483

Indianapolis Foundation, 3372

Indianapolis Regional Office, 9114

Indianapolis Resource Center for Independent Living, 4786

John W. Anderson Foundation, 3373

John Warvel, 1506

Kiwanis Twin Lakes Camp, 1507

Kokomo Rehabilitation Hospital, 7745

LCAR, 9500

LaPorte County Sheltered Workshop, 9501

Lake County Public Library Talking Books Service, 5484

Lake Luther Bible Camp, 1508

League for the Blind and Disabled, 4787

Learning Disabilities Association of IN, 7746

Lowe's Syndrome Association, 2246

Martin Luther Homes of Indiana, 4788

Memorial Regional Rehabilitation Center, 7747

Memorial Regional Rehabilitation Center, 8410

Mental Health Association in Indiana, 7748

Methodist Hospital Rehabilitation Institute, 7749

NAMI Indiana, 7750

New Directions for People with Disabilities, 3045

New Hope Services, 9502

New Horizons Rehabilitation, 9503

Noble Centers, 9504

Northwest Indiana Subregional Library for Blind and Physically Handicapped, 5485

Office of State Coordinator of Vocational Education for Students with Disability, 7751

Parkview Regional Rehabilitation Center, 7752

Programs for Children with Disabilities: Ades 3 Through 5, 7753

Programs for Children with Special Healthcare Needs, 7754

Programs for Infants and Toddlers with Disabilities: Ages Birth Through 2, 7755

Protection and Advocacy Agency of Indiana, 7756

Putnam Countyi Comprehensive Services, 9505

Readers' Services Department Allen County Public Library, 5486

Richard L. Roudebush VA Medical Center, 9115

Riley Child Development Center, 7758

Saint Joseph's Medical Center, 8411

Saint Vincent Children's Specialty Hospital, 7759

Southern Indiana Center for Independent Living, 4789

Southern Indiana Resource Solutions, 9506

Special Services Division - Indiana State Library, 5487

Spina Bifida Association of Northern IN, 7760

St. Anthony Hospital - Indiana RehabCare Unit, 7761

St. Joseph's Hospital Rehabilitation Center, 5488

State Blind and Visually Impaired Services Agency, 7762

State Developmental Disability Agency, 7763

State Division of Vocational Rehabilitation, 7764

State Mental Health Agency, 7765

State Mental Health Representative for Children, 7766

Sycamore Rehabilitation Services, 9507

Talking Books Service Evansville Vanderburgh County Public Library, 5489

Trabant North Knox, 3374

United Cerebral Palsy Association of Greater Indiana, 1052

VA North Indiana Health Care System - Fort Wayne Campus, 9117

VA North Indiana Health Care System - Marion Campus, 9116

VSA Arts of Indiana, 7767

Vision World Wide, 1419

Wabash Valley Spina Bifida Support Group, 7768

Wabash/Employability Center, 9508

William H. Willennar Foundation, 3375

Worthmore Academy, 1509

Iowa

ACT Assessment Test Preparation Reference Manual, 9509

ACT Asset Technical Manual, 9510

ADA Camp Hertko Hollow, 1510

Adults Incorporated, 8412

Arc of Iowa, 3376

Black Hawk Center for Independent Living, 4790

Camp Courageous of Iowa, 1511

Camp Tanager, 1512

Central Iowa Center for Independent Living, 4791

College of Maharishi Ayur-Veda Health Center, 911

Crossroads of Western Iowa, 8413

Crossroads of Western Iowa, 8414

Des Moines VA Medical Center, 9118

Des Moines VA Regional Office, 9119

Des Moines YMCA Camp, 1513

Easter Seals Camp Sunnyside, 1514

Easter Seals Iowa, 8415

Evert Conner Rights and Resources Center for Independent Living, 4792

Franklin County Work Activity Center, 9511

Genesis Regional Rehabilitation Center, 8416

Hall-Perrine Foundation, 3377

Hawley Foundation, 3378

Homelink, 8417

Homer G. Barr Trust, 3379

Hope Haven, 4793

Independent Living - Iowa, 4794

Innovative Industries, 9512

Iowa Association of Homes and Services for the Aging, 807

Iowa Central Industries, 8418

Iowa City VA Medical Center, 9120

Iowa Civil Rights Commission, 9513

Iowa Department for the Blind - Library, 5490

Iowa Employment Service, 9514

Iowa Job Training Program Liaison, 9515

Iowa State Vocational Rehabilitation Facility, 9516

Iowa Valley Community College, 9517

Iowa Veterans Centers, 8419

Iowa Vocational Rehabilitation Agency, 9518

Kinney-Lindstrom Foundation, 3380

Knoxville VA Medical Center, 9121

League of Human Dignity, 4795

Library Commission for the Blind, 5491

Life Skills Laundry Division, 8420

MIW, 8421

Maharishi Ayur-Veda Medical Center, 1183

Martin Luther Homes of Iowa, 4796

Mercy Pain Center, 8422

Mercy Physical Rehabilitation Unit, 8423

Mid-Iowa Health Foundation, 3381

New Focus, 9519

Nishna Productions, 8424

Opportunities Unlimited and Brain Injury Services of Village Northwest, 1199

Options of Linn County, 8425

People Against Cancer, 1319

Principal Financial Group Foundation, 3382

RISE, Ltd., 8426

Ragtime Industries, 8427

Res-Care Premier, 1202

Riverside Lutheran Bible Camp, 1515

Second Time Around, 9520

Siouxland Foundation, 3383

South Central Iowa Center for Independent Living, 4797

Sunshine Workers, 8428

Tenco Industries, 8429

Three Rivers Center for Independent Living, 4798

Universal Pediatric Services, 1207

University of Iowa - Wendell Johnson Speech and Hearing Clinic, 1516

University of Iowa Birth Defects and Genetic Disorders Unit, 5492

VA Central Iowa Health Care System, 9122

Vision Rehabilitation Institute, 8430

Younker Rehabilitation Center of Iowa Methodist Medical Center, 7769

Kansas

American Academy of Environmental Medicine, 1063

Arc of Kansas, 3384

Arrowhead West, 8431

Beach Center on Families and Disability, 891

Bethany Rehabilitation Center, 8432

Big Lakes Developmental Center, 8433

Braille Association of Kansas, 5493

CKLS Headquarters, 5494

Camp Discovery American Diabetes Association - Kansas Area Office, 1517

Center for Applied Psychophysiology Menninger Clinic, 5495

Center for the Improvement of Human Functioning, 5496

Cessna Foundation, 3385

Clay Center Adult Training Center, 9521

Coalition for Independence, 4799

Colmery-O'Neil VA Medical Center, 9123

Cowley County Developmental Services, 4800

Developmental Services of Northwest Kansas, 8434

Dwight D. Eisenhower VA Medical Center, 9124

ENVISION, 8435

Heartspring, 8436

Hospitalized Veterans Writing Project, 9040

Hutchinson Commununity Foundation, 3386

Independence, 4801

Independent Connection, 4802

Independent Living Center of Northeast Kansas, 4803

Independent Living Resource Center, 4804

Indian Creek Nursing Center, 8437

International Association of Machinists, 843

International College of Applied Kinesiology, 957

Johnson County Developmental Supports, 8438

Kansas Association of Homes for the Aging, 808

Kansas Fair Employment Practice Agency, 9522

Kansas Jaycees' Cerebral Palsy Ranch, 1518

Kansas Rehabilitation Hospital, 7770

Kansas Services for the Blind & Visually Impaired, 4805

Kansas State Library, 5497

Kansas VA Regional Office, 9125

Kansas Vocational Rehabilitation Agency, 9523

Kansas Vocational Rehabilitation Center, 8439

Ketch Industries, 8440

LINK, 4806

Lakemary Center, 8441

Manhattan Public Library, 5498

Mid-America Rehabilitation Hospital, 7771

Northview Developmental Services, 8442

Northwest Kansas Library System Talking Books, 5499

Osage City Resource Center for Independent Living, 4807

Kentucky

Louisiana

Maine

Cary Library, 5512

Chapter 15 Disabled American Veterans, 9134

Charlotte White Center, 8475

Creative Work Systems, 9537

Disabled American Veterans - Maine, 9135

Edith H. McCobb Trust, 3398

Head Injury Treatment Program at Brewer, 7787

Iris Network for the Blind, 8476

Lewiston Public Library, 5513

Limerick Adult Day Program, 8477

Maine Employment Service, 9538

Maine Fair Employment Practice Agency, 9539

Maine Governor's Committee on Employment of the Disabled, 9540

Maine Independent Living Services, 4838

Maine Mental Health Connections, 4839

Maine State Library, 5514

Maine VA Regional Office, 9136

Maine Vocational Rehabilitation Agency, 9541

Motivational Services, 4840

New England Regional Genetics Group, 5515

New England Rehabilitation Hospital of Portland, 7788

Northeast Occupational Exchange, 9542

Pine Tree Camp Children - Adults, 1531

Portland Public Library, 5516

Roger Randall Center, 8478

Sebasticook Farms, 8479

Shalom House, 4841

Social Learning Center, 8480

St. John Valley Associates, 1044

Togus VA Medical Center, 9137

UNUM Charitable Foundation, 3399

UNUM Foundation, 3400

Voices for the Blind, 5517

Waterville Public Library, 5518

Wheeler Charitable Foundation, 3401

Women to Women, 1057

Maryland

Alzheimer's Disease Education and Referral (ADEAR) Center, 1212

American Assoc. of University Affiliated Programs for Persons with Developmental Disability, 861

American Association of Children's Residential Centers, 1160

American Association of the Deaf-Blind, 1066

American Association of the Deaf-Blind, 1345

American Foundation for Urologic Disease, 872

American Health Assistance Foundation, 3402

American Occupational Therapy Association, 1167

American Occupational Therapy Foundation, 3403

American Speech and Hearing Association, 8863

American Speech-Language-Hearing Association, 1070

American Speech-Language-Hearing Association, 2234

American Venereal Disease Association, 1172

Arc of Maryland, 3404

Ardmore Developmental Center, 9543

Association for International Practical Training, 3029

Autism Society of America, 1246

Autism Society of America, 8867

Baltimore Community Foundation, 3405

Baltimore Gas and Electric Foundation, 3406

Baltimore Regional Office, 9138

Baltimore VA Medical Center, 9139

Behavior Service Consultants, 2303

Blind Industries and Services of Maryland, 8481

Broadmead, 4842

Camp Greentop, 1532

Cancer Information Service, 8869

Candlelighters Childhood Cancer Foundation, 3842

Center for Neuro-Rehabilitation, 8482

Child Find/Early Childhood Disabilities, 8483

Children and Adults with Attention Deficit Disorders (CHADD), 1258

Children's Fresh Air Society Fund, 3407

Clark-Winchcole Foundation, 3408

Clark-Winchole Foundation, 3409

Columbia Foundation, 3410

Community Health Funding Report, 3880

Community Services for Autitistic Adults and Children, 1262

Cystic Fibrosis Foundation, 3411

Deaf and Hard of Hearing Entrepreneurs Council, 1089

Deaf-Blind Division of the National Federation of the Blind, 1371

Disability Funding News, 3887

Easter Seals Camp Fairlee Manor, 1533

Epilepsy Foundation, 1267

Eye Associates, 1373

Fort Howard VA Medical Center, 9140

Foundation Fighting Blindness, 3412

Friends of Libraries for Deaf Action, 5519

George Wasserman Family Foundation, 3413

Goodwill Industries International, 936

Greater Baltimore Medical Center Richard E. Hoover Rehabilitation Services, 8484

Greenery Extended Care Center - Baltimore, 8485

Harry and Jeanette Weinberg Foundation, 3414

Health and Housing Association Mid-Atlantic Non-Profit, 805

Housing Unlimited, 4843

Independence Now, 4844

Information Access Project: National Federation of the Blind, 1382

International Agency for the Prevention of Blindness, 1384

International Braille and Technology Center for the Blind, 8889

International Dyslexia Association, 1279

International Rett Syndrome Association, 1281

James Lawrence Kerman Hospital, 8486

Job Opportunities for the Blind, 8890

Job Opportunities for the Blind, 9544

John B. Parsons Foundation, 3415

Johns Hopkins University Dana Center for Preventive Ophthalmology, 5520

Johns Hopkins University, Asthma and Allergy Center, 5521

Junior National Association of the Deaf, 1112

Kamp-A-Kom-Plish, 1534

Levindale Hebrew Geriatric Center, 8487

Lions Camp for the Deaf, 1535

MCIL Resources for Independent Living, 4845

Mainstream, 969

Mainstream, 9545

Making Choices for Independent Living, 4846

Maryland Employment Services and Job Training Program Liaison, 9546

Maryland Fair Employment Practice Agency, 9547

Maryland National Capital Park and Planning Commission, 1536

Maryland Rehabilitation Center Workforce Technology, 8488

Maryland State Department of Education, 9548

Maryland State Library for the Blind and Physically Handicapped, 5522

Maryland Veterans Centers, 9141

Medicaid Information, 8896

Meridian Subacute, 8489

Miracle-Ear Children's Foundation, 3416

Mobile Care, Ltd., 9027

Montgomery County Department of Public Libraries/Special Needs Library, 5523

Mt. Washington Pediatric Hospital, 7789

Nathan & Suzanne Cohen Foundation, 3417

National 4-H Council, 3043

National Arthritis and Musculoskeletal and Skin Diseases Info. Clearinghouse, 1295

National Association of Blind Educators, 1184

National Association of Blind Lawyers, 1185

National Association of Blind Secretaries and Transcribers, 1186

National Association of Blind Students, 1395

National Association of Guide Dog Users, 1396

National Association of Music Therapy, 983

National Association of the Deaf, 1117

National Association to Promote the Use of Braille, 1397

National Catholic Office of the Deaf, 1120

National Center for Family-Centered Care, 988

National Chronic Pain Outreach Association, 989

National Council for Community Behavioral Healthcare, 1299

National Diabetes Action Network for the Blind, 1401

National Diabetes Information Clearinghouse, 1301

National Digestive Diseases Information Clearinghouse, 1302

National Epilepsy Library (NEL), 5524

National Eye Institute, 1402

National Federation of the Blind, 1403

National Federation of the Blind, 3418

National Federation of the Blind - Human Services Division, 1404

National Federation of the Blind - Masonic Square Club, 1405

National Federation of the Blind - Music Division, 1406

National Federation of the Blind - Public Employees Division, 1193

National Federation of the Blind - Science and Engineering Division, 1194

National Federation of the Blind - Writers Division, 1195

National Federation of the Blind -Blind Industrial Workers of America, 1192

National Federation of the Blind in Computer Science, 1196

National Federation of the Blind- Merchants Division, 1197

National Information Clearinghouse, 999

National Institute of Arthritis and Musculoskeletal and Skin Diseases, 1306

National Institute of Child Health and Human Development, 8909

National Institute of Neurological Disorders and Stroke, 1307

National Institute on Deafness and Other Communication Disorders (NIDCD), 1129

National Kidney and Urologic Diseases Information Clearinghouse, 1308

National Organization of Parents of Blind Children, 1408

National Organization of the Senior Blind, 1409

National Rehabilitation Information Center, 1007

National Rehabilitation Information Center, 1130

National Rehabilitation Information Center NARIC, 5525

National Retinitis Pigmentosa Foundation Fighting Blindness, 3419

Orton Dyslexia Society Annual Conference, 2252

PWI Profile, 9549

Parents of Down Syndrome Children, 1318

Perry Point VA Medical Center, 9142

Project LINK, 9550

Rasmussen's Syndrom and Hemispherectomy Support Network, 1323

Raven Rock Lutheran Camp, 1537

Registry of Interpreters for the Deaf, 1135

RehabTech Associates, 2309

Rehabilitation Opportunities, 8490

Report on Disability Programs, 3920

Resources for Independence Living, 4847

Rosewood Center, 8491

Ryland Group Corporate Giving Program, 3420

Self Help for Hard of Hearing People, 1140

Services for the Visually Impaired, 1325

Sinai Rehabilitation Center, 7790

Social Security Library, 5526

Society for Progressive Supranuclear Palsy (SPSP), 1328

Southern Maryland Center for LIFE, 4848

Standard Search: Oral Health Care for People with Developmental Disabilities, 1045

Substance Abuse Funding News, 3923

TASH, 2259

TLC - The Treatment and Learning Centers, 9551

Telecommunications for the Deaf (TDI), 1143

Treatment and Learning Centers, 8492

VA Maryland Health Care System, 9143

Virginia Prosthetics Research and Library, 5527

Warren Grant Magnuson Clinical Center, 5528

Washington Ear, 1422

Youth Leadership Camp, 1538

Massachusetts

AD Lib Center for Independent Living, 4849

AD-LIB, 4850

Abbot and Dorothy H. Stevens Foundation, 3421

Affiliated Children's Arthritis Centers of New England, 5529

American Red Cross of Cape Cod, 4851

American Society of Teachers of the Alexander Technique, 881

Arc of Massachusetts, 3422

Assistive Technology, 2236

Association of Massachusetts Homes and Services for the Aging, 793

Attention Deficit Information Network, 1244

Bank of Boston Corporation Charitable Foundation, 3423

Baroco Corporation, 8493

Berkshire Meadows, 8494

Berman-Gund Laboratory for the Study of Retinal Degenerations, 5530

Blueberry Hill Healthcare, 8495

Boston Center for Independent Living, 4852

Boston Foundation, 3424

Boston Globe Foundation, 3425

Boston University Arthritis Center, 5531

Boston University Center for Human Genetics, 5532

Boston University Hospital Vision Rehabilitation Services, 8496

Boston University Robert Dawson Evans Memorial Dept. of Clinical Research, 5533

Boston VA Regional Office, 9144

Braile and Talking Book Library Perkins School for the Blind, 5534

Braintree Hospital, 7791

Bresky Foundation, 3426

Brigham and Women's Hospital, Asthma and Allergic Disease Research Center, 5535

Brigham and Women's Hospital, Robert B. Brigham Multipurpose Arthritis Ctr., 5536

Burbank Rehabilitation Center, 8497

Bushrod H. Campbell and Ada F. Hall Charity Fund, 3427

CAPP National Parent Resource Center, 896

CPB/WGBH National Center for Access Media, 8498

Camp Joslin, 1539

Camp Paul for Exceptional Children, 1540

Camp Ramah in New England (Summer), 1541

Camp Ramah in New England (Winter), 1542

Cape Organization for Rights of the Disabled (CORD), 4853

Caption Center, 1079

Caption Center, 1363

Caption Center, 5537

Carroll Center for the Blind, 8499

Carroll School Summer Programs, 1543

Center for Interdisciplinary Research on Immunologic Diseases, 5538

Center for Living & Working, 4854

Center for Living and Working, 4855

Center for Neurobehavioral Rehabilitation at Middlesex, 8500

Center for Psychiatric Rehabilitation, 8501

Clara Barton Camp, 1544

Clark House of Fox Hill Village, 8502

Clipper Ship Foundation, 3428

College Internship Program at the Berkshire Center, 8503

College of Syntonic Optometry, 1261

Community Foundation of Western Massachusetts, 3429

DEAF, 4856

Division of Employment & Training, 9552

Eagle Hill School - Summer Program, 1545

Eagle Pond, 8504

Easter Seals Society-Agassiz Village, 1546

Edith Nourse Rogers Memorial Veterans Hospital, 9145

FOR Community Services, 8505

Fairlawn Rehabilitation Hospital, 8506

Federation for Children with Special Needs, 933

Frank R. and Elizabeth Simoni Foundation, 3430

Friendly Ice Cream Corporation Contributions Program, 3431

Gateway Crafts: Crafts Store and Gallery, 9553

GenRad Foundation, 3432

Greater Boston Aid to the Blind, 3433

Greater Worcester Community Foundation, 3434

Greenery Extended Care Center, 7792

Greenery Extended Care Center - Worcester, 8507

Greenery Rehab Center Massachusetts, 7793

Greenery Rehabilitation Center - Boston, 8508

Handi-Kids/King Solomon Foundation, 1547

Harrington House, 8509

Harvard University Howe Laboratory of Ophthalmology, 5539

Holiday Inn Boxborough Woods, 8510

Hyams Foundation, 3435

Il Center: Ad Lib, 4857

Il Center: Boston Center for Independent Living, 4858

Il Center: Cape Organization for Rights of the Disabled, 948

Il Center: Center for Living & Working, 4859

Il Center: Independent Living Center of the North Shore & Cape Ann (ILNSCA), 4860

Il Center: Metrowest Center for Independent Living, 4861

Il Center: Southeast Center for Independent Living, 4862

Il Center: The Northeast Independent Living Program, 4863

Independence Associates, 4864

Independent Living Center - Massachusetts Community for the Blind, 4865

Independent Living Center of the North Shore and Cape Ann, 4866

Institute for Scientific Research, 952

Invincible Athletics, 962

Kolburne School, 8511

Kolburne School Camp, 1548

Laboure College Library, 5540

Lifeworks Employment Services, 8512

Mariner Health Care - Massachusetts, 8513

Massachusetts Easter Seals Camping Program, 1549

Massachusetts Eye and Ear Infirmary & Vision Rehabilitation Center, 8514

Massachusetts Fair Employment Practice Agency, 9554

Massachusetts Governor's Commission on Employment of Disabled Persons, 9555

Massachusetts Rehabilitation Commission Library, 5541

Massachusetts Vocational Rehab for the Blind and Visually Impaired, 9556

Massachusetts Vocational Rehabilitation Agency, 9557

Mediplex Rehabilitation Hospital, 7794

Metro West Center for Independent Living, 4867

MetroWest Center for Independent Living, 4868

Mind-Body Clinic Harvard Medical School, 976

Nathaniel and Elizabeth P. Stevens Foundation, 3436

National Association for Parents of Children with Visual Impairments (NAPVI), 1393

National Association for Parents of Children with Visual Impairments (NAPVI), 8900

National Braille Press, 1399

National Center for Accessible Media, 1121

National Council on Spinal Cord Injury, 1300

National Managed Health Care Congress, 2249

Nehemias Gorin Foundation, 3437

Network Conference, 2250

New England Center for Children, 8515

New England Experience, 1550

New England Home for the Deaf, 7795

New England Medical Center, 8516

New England Rehabilitation Hospital - Massachusetts, 7796

New Medico Rehabilitation and Skilled Nursing Center at Lewis Bay, 8517

Northampton VA Medical Center, 9146

Northeast Independent Living Program, 4869

PALS Support Groups, 8911

PXE International, 8912

Parent Professional Advocacy League, 1022

Phillips-Green Foundation, 3438

Protestant Guild, 8518

Raytheon Company Contributions Program, 3439

Rehabilitation Hospital of Western New England, 8519

Renaissance Clubhouse, 4870

Scandinavian Seminar, 3048

Schepens Eye Research Institute, 1413

Shaughnessy-Kaplan Rehabilitation Hospital, 8520

Shriners Burns Hospital - Boston Unit, 7797

Shriners Hospital - Springfield Unit - for Crippled Children, 7798

Son-Rise Program, 8521

Son-Rise Program, 8921

Southeast Center for Independent Living, 4871

Southern Worcester County Rehabilitation Center, 8522

Spero Charitable Foundation, 3440

Stavros Center for Independent Living, 4872

Stress Reduction Clinic University of Massachusetts Medical Center, 1046

Student Independent Living Experience, 4873

TJX Foundation, 3441

Talking Book Library at Worcester Public Library, 5542

Tower Program at Regis College, 1551

VA Boston Healthcare System, Brockton Division, 9147

VA Boston Healthcare System, Jamaica Plain Campus, 9148

VA Boston Healthcare System, West Roxbury Division, 9149

VUE - Vision Use in Employment, 8930

Vinfen Corporation, 8523

Vision Foundation, 1418

Vision Foundation, 3442

Visiting Nurse Association of North Shore, 8524

Weldon Center for Rehabilitation, 8525

Westridge Healthcare Center, 8526

Work, 9558

Youville Hospital & Rehab Center, 8527

Michigan

Academy of Rehabilitative Audiology, 1060

Advocate for People with Disabilities, 8861

Aleda E. Lutz VA Medical Center, 9150

Anchor Point Camp, 1552

Ann Arbor Area Community Foundation, 3443

Ann Arbor Center for Independent Living, 4874

Ann Arbor VA Medical Center, 9151

Arc Detroit, 4875

Arc of Michigan, 3444

Association for Retarded Citizens of Muskegon County, 4876

Battle Creek VA Medical Center, 9152

Bay Area Coalition for Independent Living, 4877

Berrien Community Foundation, 3445

Big Crystal Camp, 1553

Blind Children's Fund, 3446

Blue Water Center for Independent Living, 4878

Botsford General Hospital Inpatient Hospitalization Unit, 8528

Bugas Fund, 3447

Burger School for the Autistic, 5543

Camp Barakel, 1554

Camp Catch-A-Rainbow, 1555

Camp Fish Tales, 1556

Camp Niobe, 1557

Capital Area Center for Independent Living, 4879

Center for Independent Living of Mid-Michigan, 4880

Center for Independent Living of Mid-Michigan, 4881

Central Michigan University Summer Clinics, 1558

Chelsea Community Hospital Rehabilitation Unit, 8529

Chrysler Motors Organization, 3448

Clare Branch, 8530

Clarence & Grace Chamberlin Foundation, 3449

Community Foudation of Monroe County, 3450

Community Rehabilitation Center, 7799

Covenant Healthcare Rehabilitation Program, 7800

Cowan Slavin Foundation, 3451

Cristo Rey Handicappers Program, 4882

Cristo Rey Hispanic Center for Independent Living, 4883

Disability Community Small Business Development Center, 839

Disability Community Small Business Development Center, 9559

Disability Network, 4884

Disability Network, 8879

Disability Resource Center, 4885

Disability Resource Center of Southwestern Michigan, 4886

Discovery Center of Michigan, 1559

Eagle Village, 1560

Eden Acres Organic Network, 920

Educational Accessibility Services, 921

Eight CAP, 8531

Elizabeth E. Kennedy Fund, 3452

Family Resource Center, 4887

Farmington Health Care Center, 7801

Flint Osteopathic Hospital - RehabCare Unit, 7802

Fowler Center, 1561

Frank S. and Mollie S. VanDervoort Memorial Foundation, 3453

Fremont Area Foundation, 3454

General Motors Foundation, 3455

Glaucoma Laser Trabeculoplasty Study, 5544

Grand Rapids Center for Independent Living, 4888

Grand Rapids Center for Independent Living, 4889

Grand Rapids Foundation, 3456

Grand Traverse Area Community Living Center, 4890

Grand Traverse Area Library for the Blind and Physically Handicapped, 5545

Granger Foundation, 3457

Great Lakes Center for Independent Living, 4891

Great Lakes/Macomb Rehabilitation Group, 4892

Greenery Healthcare Center - Clarkston, 8532

Haggerty Center for Neurorehabilitation, 8533

Harvey Randall Wickes Foundation, 3458

Havirmill Foundation, 3459

Hope Network Independent Living Program, 4893

ICBR North American Information Office, 947

Indian Trails Camp, 1562

Informed Birth and Parenting, 949

Integrated Health Services of Michigan at Clarkston, 7803

International Hearing Society, 1108

International Medical and Dental Hypnotherapy Association, 959

Iron Mountain VA Medical Center, 9153

JARC - Jewish Association for Residential Care, 4894

John D. Dingell VA Medical Center, 9154

Kelly Services Foundation, 3460

Kent County Library for the Blind, 5546

Kent District Library for the Blind and Physically Handicapped, 5547

Kresge Foundation, 3461

Lakeland Center, 8534

Lakeshore Center for Independent Living, 4895

Lamplighter's Work Center, 9560

Lanting Foundation, 3462

Library of Michigan Service for the Blind, 5548

Life Skills Services, 4896

Macomb Library for the Blind and Physically Handicapped, 5549

Mary Free Bed Hospital and Rehabilitation Center, 8535

Mecosta County General Hospital Rehabilitation Center, 7804

Men-O-Mee Activity Center, 8536

Metro Health Foundation, 3463

Michigan Association for Deaf, Hearing and Speech Services, 1115

Michigan Association of Homes and Services for the Aging, 814

Michigan Capital Medical Center John W Chi Memorial Medical Library, 5550

Michigan Commission for the Blind Independent Living Rehabilitation Program, 4897

Michigan Commission for the Blind Training Center, 8537

Michigan Employment Service, 9561

Michigan Fair Employment Practice Agency, 9562

Michigan VA Regional Office, 9155

Michigan Veterans Centers, 9156

Michigan Vocational Rehab for Persons Who Are Blind & Visually Impaired, 9563

Michigan Vocational Rehabilitation Agency, 9564

Michigan's Assistive Technology Resource, 5551

Mid-Michigan Industries, 8538

Mideastern Michigan Library Co-op, 5552

Midicha, 1563

Muskegon County Library for the Blind, 5553

National Child Safety Council, 8904

New Medico Community Re-Entry Service, 8539

Northland Library Cooperative, 5554

O'Fair Winds Camp, 1564

Oakland County Library for the Blind and Physically Handicapped, 5555

Oakland/Macomb Center for Independent Living, 4898

Ransom Fidelity Company Foundation, 3464

Rehabilitation Institute of Michigan, 7805

Rehabilitation Services, 8540

Roger, 1565

Rollin M. Gerstacker Foundation, 3465

Sanilac County Community Mental Health, 8541

Southeastern Michigan Center for Independent Living, 4899

Southeastern Michigan Commission for the Blind, 4900

Special Technologies Alternative Resources (STAR), 1043

Special Tree Rehabilitation System, 8542

St. Clair County Library Special Technologies Alternative Resources (S.T.A.R.), 5556

St. John Hospital - North Shore, 7806

State Technical Institute and Rehabilitation Center, 8543

Steelcase Corporate Giving Program, 3466

Steelcase Foundation, 3467

Superior Alliance for Independent Living (SAIL), 4901

Three Rivers Rehabilitation Pavilion, 7807

Thumb Industries, 8544

University of Michigan, Orthopaedic Research Laboratories, 5557

Upper Peninsula Library for the Blind, 5558

Upshaw Institute for the Blind, 8545

Visually Impaired Center, 8546

Washtenaw County Library, 5559

Washtenaw County Library for the Blind & Physically Handicapped, 5560

Wayne County Regional Library for the Blind, 5561

Wayne State University, C.S. Mott Center for Human Genetics and Development, 5562

Welcome Home to the Blind, 8547

William D. Nee - Advocate for People with Disabilities, 847

William H. Honor Rehabilitation Center Henry Ford Wyanclotte Hospital, 8548

Young Woman's Home Association of Detroit, 3468

Minnesota

Accessibility Home Fund, 4902

Accessible Space, 4903

Alex and Mollie Tankenoff Foundation, 3469

American Sleep Disorders Association, 1233

Arc of Minnesota, 3470

Associated Leasing: Handicappable Vans, 9024

Brown-Nichollet Industries, 8549

Bush Foundation, 3471

Camp Buckskin, 1566

Camp Courage, 1567

Camp Friendship, 1568

Camp New Hope, 1569

Camp Winnebago, 1570

Center for Children with Chronic Illness and Disability, 903

Center for Independent Living, 4904

Center for Independent Living of Northeast Minnesota, 4905

Century College, 5563

Charlson Foundation, 3472

Closing the Gap's Annual Conference, 2238

Communication Center/Minnesota State Services for the Blind, 5564

Courage Camps, 1571

Courage Center, 4906

Courage North, 1572

Dayton Hudson Foundation, 3473

Deluxe Corporation Foundation, 3474

Duluth Public Library, 5565

Eden Wood Center, 1573

Emma B. Howe Memorial Foundation, 3475

Flying Wheels Travel, 9009

Freedom Resource Center for Independent Living, 4907

General Mills Foundation, 3476

Groves Learning Center, 1574

Higher Education Consortium for Urban Affairs (HECUA), 3034

Hugh J. Andersen Foundation, 3477

Independence Crossroads, 4908

Independent Lifestyles A Center for Independent Living, 4909

Industries, 8550

Institute for Health and Disability, 950

James R. Thorpe Foundation, 3478

Jay and Rose Phillips Family Foundation, 3479

Jewish Vocational Service of Jewish Family and Children's Services, 9565

Knutson, 1575

Margaret Rivers Fund, 3480

Metropolitan Center for Independent Living, 4910

Metropolitan Center for Independent Living, 4911

Minneapolis Foundation, 3481

Minneapolis VA Medical Center, 9157

Minnesota Department of Jobs and Training, 9566

Minnesota Employment Practice Agency, 9567

Minnesota Health and Housing Alliance, 815

Minnesota Library for the Blind, 5566

Minnesota Library for the Blind and Physically Handicapped, 5567

Minnesota Mining and Manufacturing Foundation, 3482

Minnesota Vocational Rehabilitation Agency, 9568

National Ataxia Foundation, 1297

National Resource Library on Youth with Disabilities, 5568

New Horizons Home Care, 4912

North Memorial Medical Center - North Rehabilitation Center, 7808

Options Interstate Resource Center for Independent Living, 4913

Ordean Foundation, 3483

Otter Tail Power Company Contributions Program, 3484

Otto Bremer Foundation, 3485

PACER Center, 1316

PDP Products, 1576

PWI Forum, 9569

Professional Development Programs, 1577

Rochester Area Foundation, 3486

Search Beyond Adventures, 1578

Search Beyond Adventures, 9019

Shriners Hospitals for Children - Twin Cities, 8551

Sister Kenny Institute, 7809

Southeastern Minnesota Center for Independent Living, 4914

Southern Minnesota Independent Living Enterprises & Services, 4915

Southwestern Center for Independent Living, 4916

Spinal Cord Society (SCS), 1330

St. Cloud VA Medical Center, 9158

St. Paul Academy and Summit School, 1579

St. Paul Regional Office, 9159

Tozer Foundation, 3487

University of Minnesota at Crookston, 3053

Vet Center, 9169

Vinland National Center, 4917

Vision Loss Resources, 8552

Vision Loss Resources, 8553

Mississippi

Addie McBryde Rehabilitation Center for the Blind, 8554

Allied Enterprises of Tupelo, 9570

Alpha Home Royal Maid Association for the Blind, 4918

Arc of Mississippi, 3488

Biloxi/Gulfport VA Medical Center, 9160

Comm-Care Corporation, 3489

Gulf Coast Independent Living Center, 4919

Jackson Independent Living Center, 4920

Jackson Regional Office, 9161

Jackson VA Medical Center, 9162

LIFE of Central Mississippi, 4921

LIFE of Southern Mississippi, 4922

Mississippi Association of Homes and Services for the Aging, 816

Mississippi Employment Secutity
Commission, 9571
Mississippi Library Commission, 5569
Mississippi Library Commission\Talking
Book and Braille Services, 5570
Mississippi Methodist Rehabilitation Center,
8555
Mississippi Project START (Success
Through Assistive/Rehab Technology),
5571
Mississippi State Independent Living Center,
4923
Mississippi Vocational Rehabilitation, 9572
Oxford Center for Independent Living, 4924
Starkville Center for Independent Living,
4925
Tik-A-Witha, 1580
Worksight, 9573

Missouri

Access II Independent Living Center, 4926
Allen P. & Josephine B. Green Foundation,
3490
Alpine North Nursing and Rehabilitation
Center, 8556
American Optometric Association, 1349
Anheuser-Busch Foundation, 3491
Assemblies of God National Center for the
Blind, Adriene Resource Center for Blind
Children, 5572
Assembllies of God National Center for the
Blind, 5573
Bootheel Area Independent Living Services,
4927
Camp Black Hawk, 1581
Camp Wee-Y, 1582
Christian Hospital Northeast, 8557
Church of the Nazarene, 5574
Columbia Regional Hospital - RehabCare
Unit, 7810
Council for Extended Care of Mentally
Retarded Citizens, 1583
Council for Extended Care of Mentally
Retarded Citizens, 4928
Delta Center for Independent Living, 4929
Disability Resource Association, 4930
Disabled Citizens Alliance for Independence,
4931
EDI, 1584
Gazette International Networking Institute,
1273
Greater Kansas City Community Foundation
and Affiliated Trusts, 3492
H&R Block Foundation, 3493
Hall Family Foundations, 3494
Hallmark Corporate Foundation, 3495
Harry S. Truman Children's Neurological
Center, 8558
Harry S. Truman Memorial, 9163
Hickory Hill, 1585
Independence Center, 4932
Independent Living Center, 4933
Independent Living Center of Southeast
Missouri, 4934
Independent Living Resource Center, 4935
Integrated Health Services of St. Louis at
Gravois, 8559
International Lutheran Deaf Association,
1109
International Polio Network, 1280

James S. McDonnell Foundation, 3496
Jewish Hospital of St. Louis - Department of
Rehabilitation, 7811
John J. Pershing VA Medical Center, 9164
Joplin House Healthcare, 8560
Judevine Center for Autism, 5575
Kansas City VA Medical Center, 9165
LIFE Center for Independent Living, 4936
Life Skills Foundation, 4937
Lions Den Outdoor Learning Center, 1586
Lutheran Charities Foundation of St. Louis,
3497
Lutheran Library for the Blind, 5576
Mary's Call, 3498
Metropolitan Employment & Rehabilitation
Service, 8561
Midland Empire Resources (MERIL), 4938
Missouri Association of Homes for the
Aging, 817
Missouri Easter Seal Society - Southeast
Region, 8562
Missouri Employment Services, 9574
Missouri Fair Employment Practice Agency,
9575
Missouri Governor's Council on Disability,
9576
Missouri Job Training Program Liaison, 9577
Missouri Veterans Centers, 9166
Missouri Vocational Rehabilitation Agency,
9578
Northeast Independent Living Services, 4939
On My Own, 4940
Oppenstein Brothers Foundation, 3499
Ozark Independent Living, 4941
Paraquad, 4942
People to People International, 3046
People-to-People International, Committee
for the Handicapped, 1025
Places for People, 4943
Poplar Bluff RehabCare Program, 8563
PremierCare Neurohabilitation Program of
Bethesda General Hospital, 7812
Psycho-Social Rehabilitation Center Places
for People, 8564
R.A. Bloch Cancer Foundation, 3500
RA Bloch Cancer Foundation, 3501
Rehabilitation Institute, Kansas City, 4944
Rusk Rehabilitation Center, 7813
Service Club for the Blind, 8565
Services for Independent Living, 4945
Shriners Hospitals for Children St. Louis,
8566
Sidney R. Baer Day Camp, 1587
Southeastern Missouri Alliance for
Independence (SEMO Alliance), 4946
Southwest Center for Independent Living,
4947
Southwest Center for Independent Living,
4948
St. Louis Community Foundation, 3502
St. Louis Regional Office, 9167
St. Louis Society for the Blind and Visually
Impaired, 8567
St. Louis VA Medical Center, 9168
St. Mary's Regional Rehabilitation Center,
7814
Stanley and Lucy Lopata Foundation, 3503
Sunnyhill, 1588
The Whole Person, 4949
Three Rivers Health Care, 7815
Tri-County Center for Independent Living,
4950

University of Missouri, Columbia Arthritis
Center, 5577
Victor E. Speas Foundation, 3504
Visual Independence Program, 8568
WX: Work Capacities, 9579
Warrenburg Independent Living Services,
4951
Whole Person, 4952
Wolfner Library for the Blind, 5578

Montana

Adult and Child Study Center, 8569
Arc of Montana, 3505
Benefis Healthcare, 8570
Billings Chapter - Living Independently for
Today and Tomorrow (LIFTT), 4953
Department of Social and Rehabilitation
Services, 8571
Disability Services Division, 8572
Living Independently for Today and
Tomorrow, 4954
Miles City Chapter - Living Independently
for Today and Tomorrow (LIFTT), 4955
MonTECH University of Montanta, 5579
Montana Employment Services and Job
Training Programs Liaison, 9580
Montana Fair Employment Practice Agency,
9581
Montana Governor's Committee on
Employment of Disabled People, 9582
Montana Independent Living Project, 4956
Montana State Library/Montana Talking
Book Library, 5580
Montana State Library\Talking Book
Library, 5581
Montana VA Regional Office, 9170
Montana Vocational Rehabilitation for
Persons Who Are Visually Impaired, 9583
North Central Independent Living Services,
4957
North Central Independent Living Services,
4958
St. Vincent Hospital and Health Center, 7816
Summit Independent Living Center, 4959
VA Montana Healthcare System, 9171
Vet Center, 9172

Nebraska

Arc of Nebraska, 3506
Bernard K. & Norma F. Heuermann, 3507
Boys Town National Research Hospital, 1078
Camp Easter Seals, 1589
Career Achievement Center - 48th Street,
8573
Center for Independent Living of Central
Nebraska, 4960
Christian Record Services, 1365
Cooper Foundation, 3508
Eastern Nebraska 4-H Center, 1590
Floyd Rogers, 1591
Grand Island VA Medical System, 9173
Hazel R. Keene Trust, 3509
League of Human Dignity, 4961
League of Human Dignity Center for
Independent Living Center, 4962
Lincoln Regional Office, 9174
Lincoln VA Medical Center, 9175

Easter Seal Society of New Jersey Highlands Workshop, 9614
Easter Seal of Ocean County, 9615
Easter Seals Camp Merry Heart, 1606
Easter Seals New Jersey, 9616
Eden WERCS, 9617
Edison Sheltered Workshop, 9618
Eye Institute of New Jersey, 5591
F. Mason Perkins Trust, 3530
F.M. Kirby Foundation, 3531
Family Resource Associates, 4981
Fannie E. Rippel Foundation, 3532
First Occupational Center of New Jersey, 9619
Fox Foundation, 3533
Fund for New Jersey, 3534
Garden State Rehabilitation Hospital, 7825
Goodwill Industries of Southern New Jersey, 9620
Handi-Camp-NJ, 1607
Hausmann Industries, 9621
Heightened Independence & Progress, 4982
Heightened Independence and Progress, 4983
Integrated Health Services of New Jersey at Somerset Valley, 8590
JFK Johnson Rehab Institute, 7826
Jersey Cape Diagnostic Training & Opportunity Center, 9622
Jersey City Chapter - Heightened Independence and Progress, 4984
Kessler Institute for Rehabilitation, 963
Kessler Institute for Rehabilitation, Welkind Facility, 7827
Lourdes Regional Rehabilitation Center, 8591
Lyons Campus of the VA New Jersey Healthcare System, 9187
MOCEANS Center for Independent Living, 4985
Matheny School and Hospital, 8592
Medical Economics, 9623
Mediplex Rehab - Camden, 7828
Merck Company Foundation, 3535
Merrill Lynch & Company Foundation, 3536
Milton Schamach Foundation, 3537
Mt. Carmel Guild, 8593
Mycoclonus Research Foundation, 5592
Nabisco Foundation, 3538
National Association of Retired Volunteer Program Directors, 984
National Industries for the Blind, 1407
Nejeda, 1608
New Eyes for the Needy, 1410
New Jersey Association of Non-Profit Homes for the Aging, 821
New Jersey Camp Jaycee, 1609
New Jersey Center for Outreach and Services for the Autism Community (COSAC), 5593
New Jersey Employment Service and Job Training Program Services, 9624
New Jersey Library for the Blind and Handicapped, 5594
New Jersey Technology Assistive Resource Program (TARP), 4986
New Jersey Vocational Rehabilitation Agency, 9625
Newark Regional Office, 9188
Occupational Center of Hudson County, 9626
Occupational Center of Union County, 9627
Occupational Training Center of Burlington County, 9628
Occuptational Training Center of Camden County - New Jersey, 9629

Ostberg Foundation, 3539
Paragano Family Foundation, 3540
Pathway To Independence, 9630
Pediatric Rehabilitation Department, JFK Medical Center, 8594
Progressive Center for Independent Living, 4987
Project Freedom, 4988
Prudential Foundation, 3541
REACH Rehabilitation Program - Leader Nursing and Rehabilitation Center, 8595
REACH Rehabilitation and Catastrophic Long-Term Care, 8596
Recording for the Blind & Dyslexic, 1412
Rehabilitation Specialists, 8597
Resources for Independent Living, 4989
Robert Wood Johnson Foundation, 3542
Round Lake Camp, 1610
Seeing Eye, 1414
Somerset Training and Employment Program, 9631
St. John of God Community Services Vocational Rehabilitation, 9632
Summit Ridge Center, 8598
Summit Ridge Center Genesis Eldercare, 7829
Total Living Center, 4990
United Cerebral Palsy Associations of New Jersey, 9633
Universal Institute , Rebah & Fitness Center, 1206
Victoria Foundation, 3543
Walking Tomorrow, 3544
West Essex Rehab Center, 9634
Whelan Foundation, 3545

New Mexico

Ability Center, 4991
Adelante Development Center, 9635
Albuquerque Regional Office, 9189
American Academy of Neural Therapy, 859
Arc of New Mexico, 3546
CASA, 4992
CHOICES Center for Independent Living, 4993
Commission for the Blind - New Mexico, 9636
Dental Amalgam Syndrome (DAMS), 1266
Dyslexia Centers, 1611
Easter Seal Camping Center Kamp Kiwanis, 1612
Family Voices, 931
Frost Foundation, Ltd., 3547
Goodwill Industries of New Mexico, 9637
HealthSouth Rehabilitation Center - New Mexico, 7830
Independent Living Resource Center, 4994
Lifecourse Rehabilitation Services, 8599
Los Lunas Hospital and Training School, 5595
McCune Charitable Foundation, 3548
Native American Protection and Advocacy Project, 1011
New Mexico Employment Services and Job Training Liaison, 9638
New Mexico State Library for the Blind and Physically Handicapped, 5596
New Mexico Technology Assistance Program New Mexico State Department of Education, 4995

New Mexico VA Healthcare System, 9190
New Mexico Veterans Centers, 9191
New Vistas, 4996
Opportunity Center - New Mexico, 9639
Overeaters Anonymous World Services Office, 1018
RCI, 9640
San Juan Center for Independence, 4997
Santa Fe Community Foundation, 3549
Santa Fe Mountain Center, 1613
Southwest Communication Resource, 8600
St. Joseph Rehabilitation Hospital and Outpatient Center, 7831
State Department of Education New Mexico Division of Vocational Rehabilitation, 9641
Tohatchi Area of Opportunity & Services, 9642

New York

AIDS Funding, 3878
AIM Independent Living Center, 4998
ARISE-Center for Independent Living, 4999
AT&T Foundation, 3550
Able to Work National Business & Disability Council, 2299
Academic Year Abroad, 3023
Access Unlimited, 851
Access to Independence and Mobility, 5000
Achelis Foundation, 3551
Action Toward Independence, 5001
Advocacy Center, 1614
Advocates for Children of New York, 1615
After We're Gone - A Program for the Lifetime Care of Persons with Disabilities, 856
Aging in America, 789
Ala Vi Foundation of New York, 3552
Alan & Peggy Tishman Foundation, 3553
Albany VA Medical Center: Samuel S. Stratton, 9192
Albany Vet Center, 9193
Alternatives for Reaching Independence Through Services and Engineering (ARISE), 5002
Altman Foundation, 3554
Ambrose Monell Foundation, 3555
American Association of Spinal Cord Injury Nurses, 1218
American Association of Spinal Cord Injury Psychologists & Social Workers, 1219
American Chai Trust, 3556
American Diabetes Association, 1616
American Express Foundation, 3557
American Foundation for the Blind, 1348
American Foundation for the Blind, 3558
American Foundation for the Prevention of Venereal Disease, 3559
American Group Psychotherapy Association, 1165
American Lung Association, 1228
American Oriental Bodywork Association, 877
American Paraplegia Society, 1232
American-Scandinavian Foundation, 3026
Arthur Ross Foundation, 3560
Artists Fellowship, 3561
Associated Blind, 1351
Association for Children with Down Syndrome, 1239

Cincinnati Veterans Centers, 9220
Cleveland FES Center, 5635
Cleveland Foundation, 3684
Cleveland Public Library, 5636
Cleveland Regional Office, 9221
Cleveland Society for the Blind, 8639
Clovernook Center - Oportunities for the Blind, 5637
Columbus Foundation and Affiliated Organizations, 3685
Columbus Speech and Hearing Center, 8640
CommuniCare of Clifton Nursing and Rehabilitation Center, 8641
Cornucopia, 9663
Dayton VA Medical Center, 9222
Disabled American Veterans, 9038
Doctors Hospital, 8642
Dodd Hall at the Ohio State University Hospitals, 8643
Easter Seal Society of Mahoning, 8644
Eleanora C. U. Alms Trust, 3686
Emanuel-Day, 1649
Emma Leah and Laura Bell Bahmann Foundation, 3687
Eva L. and Joseph M. Bruening Foundation, 3688
Fairfield Regional Vision Rehabilitation Center, 8645
Federated Dpeartment Stores Corporate Giving Program, 3689
Four Oaks School, 8646
Franciscan Rehabilitation Center, 7840
Fred & Lillian Deeks Memorial Foundation, 3690
Friedman, Domiano & Smith Company, L.P.A., 2306
GAR Foundation, 3691
George A. Martin Center, 8647
George Gund Foundation, 3692
Good Genesis Healthcare System, 8648
Grady Memorial Hospital, 8649
Great Lakes Regional Rehabilitation Center, 7841
Great Oaks Joint Vocational School, 9664
Greater Cincinnati Foundation, 3693
HCR Health Care Services, 7842
HCR Manor Care Foundation, 3694
HELP Six Chimneys, 5069
Hamilton Center, 8650
Handicapped Student Program Postsecondary Education Association, 2241
Happiness at St. Augustine Academy, 1650
Harry C. Moores Foundation, 3695
Hearth Day Treatment and Vocational Services, 9665
Heather Hill Rehabilitation Hospital, 7843
Helen Steiner Rice Foundation, 3696
Help Foundation, 5070
Herbert W. Hoover Foundation, 3697
Highbrook Lodge Camp, 1651
Highland Unlimited Business Enterprises of CRI, 9666
Holzer Clinic, 8651
Holzer Medical Center - RehabCare Center, 7844
Holzer Medical Center RehabCare, 8652
Human Resource Consultants, 8653
IKRON Institute for Rehabilitative and Psychological Services, 8654
Independent Living Center of Central Ohio, 5071
Independent Living Options, 5072

Integrated Health Services at Waterford Commons, 8655
John P. Murphy Foundation, 3698
Lake County Society for Rehabilitation, 8656
Lake Erie College, 3038
Lester H. Higgins Adult Center, 8657
Linking Employment Ability Potential - Independent Living Center, 5073
Live Oaks Career Development Campus, 8658
Louis Stokes VA Medical Center, 9223
MERIT Industries, 8659
Metro Health - St. Luke's Medical Center Pain Management Program, 8660
MetroHealth Medical Center, 8661
Mid-Ohio Board for Independent Living Environment, 5074
Mid-Ohio Board for an Independent Living Environment (MOBILE), 5075
Middletown Regional Hospital - Inpatient Rehabilitation Unit, 8662
Moving Forward, 1287
National Association of the Physically Handicapped, 985
National Cued Speech Association, 1123
Nationwide Foundation, 3699
Newark Healthcare Center, 8663
Nordson Corporate Giving Program, 3700
Nordson Corporation Foundation, 3701
Ohio Civil Rights Commission, 9667
Ohio Employment Services and Job Training, 9668
Ohio Regional Library for the Blind and Physically Handicapped, 5638
Ohio Vocational Rehabilitation Agency, 9669
Parker-Hannifin Foundation, 3702
Parma Community General Hospital RehabCare Unit, 7845
Parma Community General Hospital RehabCare Unit, 8664
Peter A. Towne Physical Therapy Center, 8665
Philomatheon Society of the Blind, 8666
Providence Hospital Work, 8667
Quest International, 1032
Rehabilitation Hospital at Heather Hill, 7846
Rehabilitation Institute of Ohio at Miami Valley Hospital, 7847
Rehabilitation Service of North Central Ohio, 5076
Reinberger Foundation, 3703
Richland Country Foundation, 3704
Robert Campeau Family Foundation, 3705
SCI - Six County, 8668
Samuel W. Bell Home for the Sightless, 5077
Services for Independent Living, 5078
Shriners Burn Institute - Cincinnati Unit, 7848
Sisler McFawn Foundation, 3706
Society for Equal Access Independent Living Center, 5079
Society for Equals Acces, Independent Living Center, 5080
St. Francis Health Care Centre, 7849
St. Francis Rehabilitation Hospital, 8669
St. Rita's Medical Center Rehabilitation Services, 7850
Stark Community Foundation, 3707
State Library of Ohio - Talking Book Program, 5639
Stepping Stone, 1652
Stocker Foundation, 3708
TAC I, 8670

TAC II, 8671
Tipp City Foundation, 3709
Toledo Community Foundation, 3710
Tri-County Independent Living Center, 5081
United Cerebral Palsy of Central Ohio, 5082
United Cerebral Palsy of Columbus and Franklin County, 5083
University Affiliated Cincinnati Center for Developmental Disabilities, 5640
University of Cincinnati Hospital, 7851
Upper Valley Medical/Rehab Services, 7852
William J. and Dorothy K. O'Neill Foundation, 3711
Youngstown Foundation, 3712

Oklahoma

Ability Resources, 5084
Anne and Henry Zarrow Foundation, 3713
Arc of Oklahoma, 3714
Dean A. McGee Eye Institute, 8673
Easter Seals Oklahoma, 1653
Enviro-Tech Products, 925
Green County Independent Living Resource Center, 5085
HealthSouth Rehab Center - Oklahoma, 7853
Hilcrest Medical Center - Kaiser Rehab Center, 7854
International Bio-Oxidative Medicine Foundation (IBOM), 3715
Jane Phillips Episcopal Memorial Medical Center - RehabCare Unit, 7855
Jane Phillips Rehab Services, 8674
Jim Thorpe Rehabilitation Center at Southwest Medical Center, 7856
McAlester Regional Health Center RehabCare Unit, 8675
Mercy Memorial Health Center RehabCare Unit, 7857
Merkel Family Foundation, 3716
Muskogee VA Medical Center, 9224
National Clearinghouse of Rehabilitation Training Materials, 1190
Oklahoma Association of Homes and Services for the Aging, 825
Oklahoma Employment Services and Job Training Program Liaison, 9670
Oklahoma Governor's Committee on Employment of People with Disabilities, 9671
Oklahoma League for the Blind, 8676
Oklahoma Library for the Blind & Physically Handicapped, 5641
Oklahoma Medical Research Foundation, 5642
Oklahoma Veterans Centers Vet Center, 9225
Oklahoma Vocational Rehabilitation Agency, 9672
Oklahomans for Independent Living, 5086
Oklahome City VA Medical Center, 9226
Progressive Independence, 5087
Sandra Beasley Independent Living Center, 5088
Sandra Beasley Independent Living Center, 5089
Sarkeys Foundation, 3717
St. Anthony Hospital - RehabCare Unit, 7858
St. Anthony Hospital Rehabilitation Center, 8677
St. Mary's Hospitals - RehabCare Unit, 7859

Lehigh Valley Center for Independent Living, 5109
Liberty Resources, 5110
Life and Independence for Today, 5111
Magee Rehabilitation Hospital, 7875
Make-a-Friend, 1667
MedEscort International, 970
Millard Foundation, 3742
Moss Rehabilitation Hospital, 7876
National Mental Health Consumer's Self-Help Clearinghouse, 1310
Nineteen Hundred Fifty Seven Charity Trust, 3743
Northeastern Pennsylvania Center for Independent Living, 5112
Oberkotter Foundation, 3744
Ochiltree Foundation, 3745
Office of Vocational Rehabilitation, 9677
PECO Energy Company Contributions Program, 3746
PNC Bank Foundation, 3747
Pediatric Center at Plymouth Meeting Integrated Health Services, 8701
Pennsylvania Association of Non-Profit Homes for the Aging, 827
Pennsylvania College of Optometry Eye Institute, 5650
Pennsylvania Employment Services and Job Training, 9678
Pennsylvania Governor's Committee on Employment of Disabled Persons, 9679
Pennsylvania Human Relations Commission Agency, 9680
Pennsylvania Pain Rehabilitation Center, 8702
Pennsylvania Veterans Centers, 9238
Pennsylvania Vocational Rehabilitation Agency, 9681
Pennsylvania's Iniative on Assistive Technology (PIAT), Temple University, 5113
Phelps School Summer School, 1668
Philadelphia Foundation, 3748
Philadelphia Regional Office and Insurance Center, 9239
Philadelphia VA Medical Center, 9240
Pittsburg Foundation, 3749
Pittsburgh Regional Office, 9241
Reading Rehabilitation Hospital, 5651
Recorded Periodicals, 5652
Recorded Periodicals, 8920
Robert L. Miller Rehab Center, 8703
Samuel Thompson Scout Camp, 1669
Shenango Valley Foundation, 3750
Shriners Hospital for Children, 7877
Shriners Hospitals for Children, Erie, 7708
Shriners Hospitals for Children, Philadelphia, 7878
Shriners Hospitals, Philadelphia Unit, for Crippled Children, 7879
Snee-Reinhardt Charitable Foundation, 3751
Souderton Special Needs Day Camp, 1670
Staunton Farm Foundation, 3752
Stewart Huston Charitable Trust, 3753
Summer Experience, 1671
Teleflex Foundation, 3754
Therapy Services Dept. of Orthopedic and Rehabilitation Center, 8672
Three River Center for Independent Living, 5114
Three Rivers Center for Independent Living, 5115

Tri-County Partnership for Independent Living, 5116
Tri-County Patriots for Independent Living, 5117
U.S. Healthworks, 9682
USX Foundation, 3755
VA Pittsburgh Healthcare System, Highland Drive Division, 9243
VA Pittsburgh Healthcare System, University Drive Division, 9242
Variety Club Camp & Development Center, 1672
Vocational Rehabilitation Center, 1054
Voices for Independence, 5118
W. W. Smith Charitable Trust, 3756
Wesley Woods, 1673
Wheelchair Access, 1056
Wilkes-Barre VA Medical Center, 9244
William B. Dietrich Foundation, 3757
William Talbott Hillman Foundation, 3758
William V. and Catherin A. McKinney Charitable Foundation, 3759
Willis Eye Hospital, 8704
Yomeca, 1674

Rhode Island

Association for Retarded, 9683
Blackstone Valley Chapter RI Arc, 5119
Champlin Foundations, 3760
Citizens Charitable Foundation, 3761
Department of Veterans Affairs Regional Office - Vocational Rehab Division, 9036
Franklin Court Assisted Living, 5120
Groden Center, 9684
Horace A. Kimball and S. Ella Kimball Foundation, 3762
IN-SIGHT Independent Living, 5121
In-Sight, 8705
Newport County Chapter of Retarded Citizens, 9685
Ocean State Center for Independent Living, 5122
Ocean State Center for Independent Living, 5123
PARI Independent Living Center, 5124
Parent Support Network, 8915
People Actively Reaching Independence (PARI) Independent Living Center, 5125
Providence Regional Office, 9245
Providence VA Medical Center, 9246
Regional Library for the Blind and Physically Handicapped, 5653
Rhode Island Arc, 3763
Rhode Island Assistive Technology Access Partnership (ATAP),RI Department of Human Services, 5126
Rhode Island Association of Facilities for the Aging, 829
Rhode Island Department of State Library for the Blind and Physically Handicapped, 5654
Rhode Island Department of Vocational Rehabilitation, 9686
Rhode Island Employment Services and Job Training, 9687
Rhode Island Foundation, 3764
Rhode Island Veterans Center, 9247
Shake-A-Leg, 1326
Vanderbilt Rehabilitation Center, 8706
Vocational Resources, 9688

South Carolina

Academy of Dispensing Audiologists, 1059
Arc of South Carolina, 3765
Association for the Blind, 8707
Burnt Gin Camp, 1675
Camp Gravatt, 1676
Captioned Media Program, 1080
Center for Developmental Disabilities, 904
Center for Developmental Disabilities, 3766
Coastal Disability Access, 5127
Colleton Regional Hospital - RehabCare Unit, 7880
Colonial Life and Accident Insurance Company Contributions Program, 3767
Columbia Regional Office, 9248
Disability Action Center, 5128
HealthSouth Rehab Hospital - South Carolina, 7881
Healthsouth Central Carolinas Rehabilitation Complex, 8708
Hitchcock Rehabilitation Center, 8709
Information on Incontinence, 1276
Medical University of South Carolina Arthritis Clinical/Research Center, 5655
Mentor of South Carolina, 8710
National Information Center for Health Related Services, 8908
Ralph H. Johnson VA Medical Center, 9249
Rebound Head Injury Recovery Services of the Carolinas, 7882
Shriners Hospitals for Children, Greenville, 7883
South Carolina Assistive Technology Program (SCATP), 5129
South Carolina Association of Nonprofit Homes for the Aging, 830
South Carolina Employment Services and Job Training Services, 9689
South Carolina Governor's Committee on Employment of the Handicapped, 9690
South Carolina Independent Living Council, 5130
South Carolina State Library, 5656
South Carolina Vocational Rehabilitation Department, 9691
William Jennings Bryan Dorn VA Medical Center, 9250

South Dakota

Aberdeen Communication Service for the Deaf, 5131
Adjustment Training Center, 5132
Alpha & Omega Family Foundation, 3768
Arc of South Dakota, 3769
Black Hills Workshop & Training Center, 5133
Communication Services for the Deaf, 5134
Community Services for the Deaf, 1082
Dell Rapids Sportsmen's Club, 9004
Native American Advocacy Project, 5135
Opportunities for Independent Living, 5136
Prairie Freedom Center for Independent Liv, 5138
Prairie Freedom Center for Independent Living, 5137
Quad Squad, 5139
Rapid City Communication Service for the Deaf, 5140

Harris Methodist Fort Worth/Mabee Rehabilitation Center, 8725

Harris and Eliza Kempner Fund, 3806

Harry S. and Isabel C. Cameron Foundation, 3807

HealthSouth Rehabilitation Center of Humble Texas, 7906

Heights Hospital - RehabCare Unit, 7907

Heights Hospital Rehab Unit, 8726

Henry & Tommy Lehmann Charitable Foudation, 3808

Hesta Stuart Christian Charitable Trust, 3809

Hill School of Fort Worth, 1682

Hillcrest Baptist Medical Center - Rehab Care Unit, 7908

Hillcrest Foundation, 3810

Hoblitzelle Foundation, 3811

Houston Center for Independent Living, 5156

Houston Endowment, 3812

Houston Public Library - Access Center, 5665

Houston Regional Office, 9263

Houston Rehabilitation Institute, 8727

Houston VA Medical Center, 9264

Hughen Center, 1683

IHS Hospital at Dallas, 7909

IHS Hospital at Dallas, 8728

Independent Life Styles, 5157

Independent Living Research Utilization Project, 5158

Institute for Rehab and Research, 7910

Institute for Rehabilitation & Research, 8729

Integrated Health Services of Amarillo, 8730

John G. and Marie Stella Kennedy Memorial Foundation, 3813

John S. Dunn Research Foundation, 3814

KALEIDOSCOPE Network, 8891

Kent Waldrep National Paralysis Foundation, 3815

LIFE Independent Living Center, 5159

LIFE/ Run Centers for Independent Living, 5160

Learning Disabilities Association of TX, 965

Lighthouse of Houston, 8731

Lisle, 3042

Little People of America, 1285

Lola Wright Foundation, 3816

Mabee Rehabilitation Center, 7911

Mainland Center Hospital RehabCare Unit, 8732

Marcia & Otto Koehler Foundation, 3817

Martin Luther Homes of Texas, 5161

Meadows Foundation, 3818

Memorial Hospital Nacogdoches - RehabCare Unit, 7912

Memorial Hospital and Medical Center, 7913

Mental Health Association in Texas, 972

Moody Foundation, 3819

Navarro Regional Hospital - RehabCare Unit, 7914

Neurobehavioral Institute of Houston, 7915

North Texas Rehabilitation Center, 8733

Occupational and Enviromental Unit Tri-Cities Hospital, 1016

Office for Students with Disabilities University of Texas at Arlington, 5162

Palestine Resource Center, 5163

Palestine Resource Center for Independent Living, 5164

Panhandle Action Center for Independent Living Skills, 5165

Panhandle Independent Living Center, 5166

Paul and Mary Haas Foundation, 3820

Pearle Vision Foundation, 3821

Plano Rehabilitation Hospital, 7916

REACH of Dallas Resource Center for Independent Living, 5167

REACH of Denton Resource Center, 5168

REACH of Fort Worth Resource Center for Independent Living, 5169

REACH/Resource Center on Independent Living, 5170

Rebound - San Antonio, 7917

Rehabilitation Hospital of Austin, 7918

Rehabilitation Hospital of North Texas, 7919

Rehabilitation Hospital of South Texas, 7920

Rehabilitation Institute - Methodist Hospital, 7921

Rehabilitation Institute of San Antonio Healthsouth, 7922

Rio Vista Rehabilitation Hospital, 7923

Robert S. and Marilyn I. Silverthorn Foundation, 3822

Rockwell Foundation, 3823

SAILS, 5171

San Antonio Area Foundation, 3824

San Antonio Warm Springs Rehabilitation Hospital, 7924

Shannon Medical Center - RehabCare Unit, 7925

Shell Oil Company Foundation, 3825

Shriners Burn Institute - Galveston Unit, 7926

Shriners Hospitals for Children, Houston, 7927

South Arlington Medical Center - RehabCare Unit, 7928

South Texas Charitable Foundation, 3826

South Texas Lighthouse for the Blind, 8734

South Texas Veterans Healthcare System, 9265

Southeast Texas Living Indepence for Everyone (SETLIFE), 5172

Southeast Texas Rehabilitation Hospital, 7929

St. David's Rehabilitation Center, 7930

Sterling-Turner Foundation, 3827

Swalm Foundation, 3828

Sweeney, 1684

T.L.L. Temple Foundation, 3829

TX Speech-Lenguage-Hearing Association, 1333

Talking Book Program/Texas State Library, 5666

Taping for the Blind, 1415

Texas 4-H Center, 1685

Texas Association of Homes and Services for the Aging, 833

Texas Commerce Bank Foundation, 3830

Texas Commission for the Blind Blind, 9700

Texas Employment Services and Job Training Program Liaison, 9701

Texas Lions Camp, 1686

Texas Rehabilitation Commission Independent Living Services, 5173

Texas State Library - Talking Book Program, 5667

Transitional Learning Center at Galveston, 8735

Treemont, 8736

University of Texas Southwestern Medical Center/Allergy & Immunology, 5668

University of Texas at Austin, 5669

VA North Texas Health Care System: Sam Rayburn Memorial Veterans Center, 9266

VA North Texas HealthCare System: Dallas VA Medical Center, 9267

VAIL, 5174

VOLAR, Center for Independent Living, 5175

Vale-Asche Foundation, 3831

Valley Association for Independent Living, 5176

Valley Regional Medical Center - RehabCare Unit, 7931

Waco Regional Office, 9268

West Texas Lighthouse for the Blind, 8737

West Texas VA Healthcare System, 9269

William Stamps Farish Fund, 3832

Utah

Active Re-Entry, 5177

Arc of Utah, 3833

Ben B. and Iris M. Margolis Foundation, 3834

Camp Kostopulos, 1687

Disabled American Veterans Department of Utah, 9270

Family Resource Library/Center for Persons with Disabilities, 5670

LDS Hospital Rehabilitation Center, 7932

Marriner S. Eccles Foundation, 3835

OPTIONS for Independence, 5178

Primary Children's Medical Center, 7934

Questar Corporation Contributions Program, 3836

Quincy Rehabilitation Institute of Holy Cross Hospital, 8738

Red Rock Center for Independence, 5179

Rehabilitation Services, 7935

Salt Lake City Regional Office, 9271

Shriners Hospitals for Children - Intermountain, 7936

Stewart Rehabilitation Center - McKay Dee Hospital, 7937

USA Deaf Sports Federation, 1145

Utada Camp, 1688

Utah Assistive Technology Program (UTAP) Utah State University, 5180

Utah Employment Services, 9702

Utah Governor's Committee on Employment of the Handicapped, 9703

Utah Independent Living Center, 5181

Utah Labor and Anti-Discrimination Division, 9704

Utah State Library Division/Program for the Blind and Physically Handicapped, 5671

Utah Veterans Centers, 9705

Utah Vocational Rehabilitation Agency, 9706

VA Salt Lake City Healthcare System, 9272

Wasatch Villa, 8739

Western Rehabilitation Institute, 7938

Western States Training Associates, 1055

Vermont

Bennington School, 1689

Farm and Wilderness Camps, 1690

Rutland Mental Health Services, 8740

Silver Towers Camp, 1691

Thorpe Camp, 1692

Vermont Achievement Center, 7939

Virginia Beach Foundation, 3849
Virginia Beach Public Library Special Services Library, 5688
Virginia State Library for the Visually and Physically Handicapped, 5689
Virginia Vocational Rehabilitation Agency, 9720
W Alton Jones Foundation, 3850
Wingaroo, 1700
Woodrow Wilson Independent Living Skills Training Program, 5200
Woodrow Wilson Rehabilitation Center, 8750
World's Best Books from the Diabetes Experts, Publications Catalog, 1339

Washington

Adventures in Independence Development, 5201
Alliance for Alternative Medicine, 857
American Association of Naturopathic Physicians, 1161
American Association of Naturopathic Physicians, 1217
American School of Ayurvedic Sciences, 1169
Arc of Washington State, 3851
Arden Nursing Home, 8751
Ballard Convalescent Center, 8752
Bastyr University Natural Health Clinic, 889
Bellingham Care Center, 8753
Ben B. Cheney Foundation, 3852
Burlington Resources Foundation, 3853
Camp Easter Seal West, 1701
Career Connections National Business & Disability Council, 9721
Center for Independence, 5202
Coalition of Responsible Disabled, 5203
Community Service Center for the Deaf and Hard of Hearing, 5204
Community Services for the Blind, 5205
Department of Services for the Blind National Business & Disability Council, 9722
Department of Social & Health Services National Business & Disability Council, 9723
Department of Vocational Rehabilitation, 9724
Designs for Independent Living, 5206
DisAbility Resource Center, 5207
Disability Resource Network, 5208
Division of Vocational Rehabilitation Department of Social and Health Services, 8754
Emil Fries Piano Hospital and Training Center, 9725
Epilepsy Foundation of Washington, 5209
Everett Coalition of People with Disabilities, 5210
First Hill Care Center, 8755
Foundation Northwest, 3854
Gerater Wenatchee Community Foundation, 3855
Glaser Foundation, 3856
Good Samaritan Hospital and Rehab Center, 7943
Greater Lakes Mental Health Care, 5211
Greater Lakes Mental Healthcare, 5212
Greater Tacoma Community Foundation, 3857

Harborview Medical Center, Low Vision Aid Clinic, 8756
Head Injury Hotline, 8885
Hillhaven Rehabilitation and Health Services Center, 8757
Independent Lifestyles Services, 5213
Independent Living Center of SW Washington, 5214
Independent Living Resources of Southwest Washington, 5215
Integrated Health Services of Seattle, 8758
International Foundation for Homeopathy, 3858
Jonathan M. Wainwright Memorial VA Medical Center, 9280
Kitsap Community Action Program, 5216
Kitsap Community Resources, 5217
Lakeside Recovery Centers, 8759
Lakewood Health Care Center, 8760
Lifecycles for Women, 966
Lilac Blind Foundation, 5218
Manor Care Nursing - Tacoma, 8761
ManorCare Health Services, 8762
ManorCare Health Services - Spokane, 8763
Medina Foundation, 3859
Meridan Valley Clinical Laboratory, 974
National Service Dog Center, 8910
Norcliffe Foundation, 3860
Norman Archibald Charitable Foundation, 3861
Northwest Continuum Care Center, 8764
Northwest Hospital Center for Medical Rehabilitation, 7944
Ophthalmic Research Laboratory Eye Institute, 5690
Orcas Island Foundation, 1017
Park Manor Convalescent Center, 8765
Providence Medical Center, 7945
Providence Rehabilitation Services, 7946
Queen Anne Health Care, 8766
Rainier Vista Care Center, 8767
Rehabilitation Enterprises of Washington, 8768
Resource Center for the Handicapped, 5219
S.L. Stuart and Associates, 9726
Safe Water Coalition, 1038
Seattle Medical and Rehabilitation Center, 8769
Seattle Regional Office, 9281
Shriners Hospitals for Children - Spokane, 7947
Slingerland Institute for Literacy, 8770
Spokane VA Medical Center, 9282
Stewardship Foundation, 3862
Synergos NeuroMedical Rehab Unit - Seattle, 8771
Tacoma Area Coalition of Individuals with Disabilities, 5220
Timberland Opportunities Association, 8772
VA Puget Sound Health Care System, 9283
Vision & Independent Living Agency, 5221
Washington Association of Homes for the Aging, 835
Washington Coalition for Citizens with Disabilities (WCCD), 5222
Washington Talking Book & Braille Library, 5691
Washington Talking Book and Braille Library, 5692
Western Washington University, 3056
Weyerhaeuser Company Foundation, 3863

West Virginia

Appalachian Center for Independent Living, 5223
Appalachian Center for Independent Living, 5224
Autism Services Center, 1245
Autism Services Center, 5693
Autism Training Center, 5694
Beckley VA Medical Center, 9284
Bernard McDonough Foundation, 3864
Cabell County Public Library, 5695
Cabell County Public Library/Talking Book Department/Subregional Library for the Blind, 5696
Huntington Regional Office, 9285
Huntington VA Medical Center, 9286
Job Accommodation Network, 844
Job Accommodation Network, 1182
Kanawha County Public Library, 5697
Louis A. Johnson VA Medical Center, 9287
Martinsburg VA Medical Center, 9288
Mountain Milestones Stepping Stones, 1702
Mountain State Center for Independent Living, 5225
MountainView Regional Rehabilitation Hospital, 7948
Mountaineer Spina Bifida Camp, 1703
National Autism Hotline - Autism Services Center, 8902
Northern West Virginia Center for Independent Living, 5226
Oak Leaf Camp, 1704
Ohio County Public Library Services for the Blind and Physically Handicapped, 5698
Rehabilitation Technology Association, 2255
Talking Book Department, Parkersburg and o Wood County Public Library, 5699
U.S. Department Veterans Affairs Beckley Vet Center, 9289
West Virginia Employment Services and Job Training Programs Liaison, 9727
West Virginia Hospital Association, 836
West Virginia Library Commission, 5700
West Virginia Rehabilitation Center, 8773
West Virginia School for the Blind Library, 5701
West Virginia Vocational Rehabilitation Agency, 9728
West Virginia of Vocational Rehabilitation, 9729
Western Hills Rehabilitation Hospital, 7949

Wisconsin

Access to Independence, 5227
American Academy of Allergy, Asthma and Immunology, 1214
Arc of Wisconsin, 3865
Brachia Plexus Injury Erb's Palsy Support & Information Network, 1249
Brown County Library, 5702
Center for Independent Living, 5228
Center for Independent Living of Western Wisconsin, 5229
Christian League for the Handicapped, 8774
Clement J. Zablocki VA Medical Center, 9290
Colonial Manor of Wausau - Extended Rehab Services, 8775

Wyoming

ONLINE DATABASES

Sedgwick Press is proud to announce that our Health and Education directories will be available in Online Databases by Fall 2001. Subscribers can access their subscription to our comprehensive databases via the Internet and do customized searches that instantly locate needed resources of information. It's never been faster or easier to locate just the right resource. Visit www.greyhouse.com and explore the subscription site free of charge or call (800) 562-2139 for more information.

MAILING LIST INFORMATION

This directory is available in mailing list form on mailing labels or diskettes. Please call 800-562-2139 to place an order or inquire about counts. There are a number of ways we can segment the database to meet your mailing list requirements.

---

www.greyhouse.com

Clicking on www.greyhouse.com takes you through our complete line of directories providing business, statistics, demographics, health and education information. The site is fully illustrated and provides comprehensive descriptions of each book along with easy ordering capability.

To preview any of our Directories for 30 days, please call toll-free (800) 562-2139 or fax to (518) 789-0556

an imprint of Grey House Publishing

Sedgwick Press Health & Education Directories

The HMO/PPO Directory, 2002

The HMO/PPO Directory is a comprehensive source that provides detailed information about Health Maintenance Organizations and Preferred Provider Organizations nationwide, including key contacts. This 2002 Edition details more information about more managed healthcare organizations than ever before. Over 1,700 HMOs, PPOs and affiliated companies are listed, arranged alphabetically by state. You'll find important, detailed information, including Key Contact Information, Prescription Drug Benefits Offered, Current Enrollment, Geographical Areas served, Number of Affiliated Physicians and Hospitals, Federal Qualifications, Nonprofit or For Profit Status, Year Founded, Type of HMO or PPO (Staff, Independent Practice, Affiliation, Group, Network), Managed Care Partners, Employer References with contact information, Monthly Subscriber Fees, Annual Subscriber Deductibles, Subscriber Co-payments, Maximum Home Health/Nursing Home Coverage, Physician and Hospital Qualifications, Average Claim Compensations for Physical and Hospital Fees. Plus, five years of historical information is included related to revenues, net income, medical loss ratio details, membership enrollment and number of patient complaints. Five easy-to-use, cross-referenced indexes will put this vast array of information at your fingertips: HMO Alphabetical Index, PPO Alphabetical Index; Other Providers Alphabetical Index, Personnel Index and Membership Enrollment Index. This is the only source that provides you with all the facts on more than 1,700 Health Maintenance Organizations, Preferred Provider Organizations and Affiliated companies.

500 pages; Softcover ISBN 1-930956-31-2, $250.00 • Hardcover ISBN 1-930956-32-0, $275.00

WinHMO/PPO Directory, 2002 - CD-ROM

An interactive CD-ROM (for Windows) with powerful search and retrieval software that takes seconds to access detailed information about Managed Care Companies and their key contacts. With *WinHMO/PPO 2002*, you get all the information from the print edition of the HMO/PPO Directory in a quick to search CD-ROM. You can search this comprehensive database by Organization, Personnel, City and State, plus advanced multiple combination criteria. Using *WinHMO/PPO 2002*, you can print our HMO/PPO profiles, create custom mailing lists – there's even space to add your own notes!

CD-ROM only (Windows) *ISBN 1-930956-57-6, $399.00* • HMO/PPO Directory and CD-ROM *ISBN 1-930956-58-4, $499.00*

The Directory of Hospital Personnel, 2002

The Directory of Hospital Personnel, 2002 is the best resource you can have at your fingertips when marketing a product or service to the hospital market. A "Who's Who" of the hospital universe, *The Directory of Hospital Personnel, 2002* puts you in touch with over 200,000 key decision-makers. With 100% verification of data, you can rest assured that you will reach the right person with just one call. Whether you're trying to find a group of hospitals fitting your profile or trying to find one individual, the answers you need are in this directory. This comprehensive directory lists every hospital in the U.S. arranged alphabetically by city within state. Plus three easy-to-use cross-referenced indexes put the facts at your fingertips faster and more easily than any other directory. *The Directory of Hospital Personnel, 2002* is the only complete source for key hospital decision-makers by name. Whether you want to define or restructure sales territories…locate hospitals with the purchasing power to accept your proposals… keep track of important contacts and colleagues… or find information on which insurance plans are accepted, *The Directory of Hospital Personnel, 2002* gives you the information you need – easily, efficiently, effectively and accurately.

2,400 pages; Softcover ISBN 1-930956-27-4, $275.00 • Hardcover ISBN 1-930956-28-2, $300.00

The Directory of Healthcare Group Purchasing Organizations, 2002

This comprehensive directory provides the important data you need to get in touch with over 600 Group Purchasing Organizations. By providing in-depth information on this growing market and its members, *The Directory of Healthcare Group Purchasing Organizations* fills a major need for the most accurate and comprehensive information on over 600 GPOs – Mailing Address, Phone & Fax Numbers, E-mail Addresses, Key Contacts, Purchasing Agents, Group Descriptions, Terms & Conditions, Membership Categorization, Standard Vendor Proposal Requirements, Membership Fees & Terms, Expanded Services, Total Member Beds represented, Total Outpatient Visits represented and more. Five Indexes provide a number of ways to locate the right GPO: Alphabetical Index, Expanded Services Index, Organization Type Index, Geographic Index and Member Institution Index. With its comprehensive and detailed information on each purchasing organization, *The Directory of Healthcare Group Purchasing Organizations, 2002* is the go-to source for anyone looking to target this market.

600 pages; Softcover ISBN 1-930956-08-8, $325.00 Hardcover ISBN 1-930956-09-6, $350.00

To preview any of our Directories for 30 days, please call toll-free
(800) 562-2139 or fax to (518) 789-0556

Sedgwick Press Health & Education Directories

The Complete Learning Disabilities Directory, 2002

The 2002 *Complete Learning Disabilities Directory* is the most comprehensive database of Programs, Services, Curriculum Materials, Professional Meetings and Resources, Camps, Newsletters and Support Groups for teachers, students and families concerned with learning disabilities. This information-packed directory includes information about Associations and Organizations, Schools, Colleges and Testing Materials, Government Agencies, Legal Resources and much more. For quick, easy access to information, this directory contains four indexes: Entry Name Index, Subject Index, Geographic Index and Web Sites Index.

"This is a valuable resource for professionals and consumers because of its comprehensiveness." – Choice

800 pages; Softcover ISBN 1-930956-36-3, $145.00 • Hardcover ISBN 1-930956-37-1, $170.00

The Complete Mental Health Directory, 2001

This is the most comprehensive resource covering the field of behavioral health, with critical information for both the layman and the mental health professional. For the layman, this directory offers understandable descriptions of 25 Mental Health disorders as well as detailed information on Associations, Media, Support Groups and Mental Health Facilities. For the professional, *The Complete Mental Health Directory* offers critical and comprehensive information on Managed Care Organizations, Information Systems, Government Agencies and Provider Organizations. This comprehensive volume of needed information will be widely used in any reference collection.

"... the strength of this directory is that it consolidates widely dispersed information into a single volume." – Booklist

"Valuable for any hospital, academic or public library." – Choice

695 pages, Softcover ISBN 1-891482-28-9, $165.00 • Hardcover ISBN 1-891482-40-8, $190.00

Older Americans Information Directory, 2000/01

Completely updated for 2000/01, this Third Edition has been completely revised and now contains over 1,000 new listings, over 8,000 updates to existing listings and over 3,000 brand new e-mail addresses and web sites. You'll find important resources for Older Americans including National, Regional, State and Local Organizations, Government Agencies, Research Centers, Libraries and Information Centers, Legal Resources, Discount Travel Information, Continuing Education Programs, Disability Aids and Assistive Devices, Health, Print Media and Electronic Media. Three indexes: Entry Index, Subject Index and Geographic Index, make it easy to find just the right resource. This comprehensive guide to resources for Older Americans will be a welcome addition to any reference collection.

"Highly recommended for academic, public, health science and consumer libraries serving seniors or offering programs for them." – Choice

999 pages; Softcover ISBN 1-891482-26-2, $165.00 • Hardcover ISBN 1-891482-27-0, $190.00

The Complete Directory for People with Rare Disorders, 1998/99

This outstanding reference is produced in conjunction with the National Organization for Rare Disorders. It provides comprehensive and needed access to important information on over 1,000 rare disorders, including Cancers, Muscular, Genetic and Blood Disorders and more. Each description is followed by information on Organizations, Publications and Government Agencies involved with the disorder. For quick, easy access to information, this directory contains two indexes: Entry Name Index and Acronym/Keyword Index.

"Quick access to information... public libraries and hospital patient libraries will find this a useful resource in directing users to support groups or agencies dealing with a rare disorder." – Booklist

"A worthy addition to health collections." – Library Journal

726 pages; Softcover ISBN 0-939300-98-2, $165.00 • Hardcover ISBN 1-891482-03-3, $190.00

To preview any of our Directories for 30 days, please call toll-free (800) 562-2139 or fax to (518) 789-0556

The Complete Directory for People with Chronic Illness, 2001/02

Thousands of hours of research have gone into this completely updated 2001/02 edition – chronic illness chapters for Sleep Apnea, Gulf War Syndrome, Raynaud's Disease and Carpal Tunnel Syndrome have been added along with thousands of new entries and enhancements to existing entries. This widely hailed directory is structured around the 84 most prevalent chronic illnesses – from Asthma to Cancer to Wilson's Disease – and provides a comprehensive overview of the support services and information resources available for people diagnosed with a chronic illness. Each chronic illness has its own chapter and contains a brief description in layman's language followed by important resources for National & Local Organizations, State Agencies, Newsletters, Books & Periodicals, Libraries & Research Centers, Support Groups & Hotlines, Web Sites and much more. This directory is an important resource for health care professionals, the collection of hospital and health care libraries, as well as an invaluable tool for people with a chronic illness and their support network.

"A must purchase for all hospital and health care libraries and is strongly recommended for all public library reference departments." – ARBA

1,152 pages; Softcover ISBN 1-891482-63-7, $165.00 • Hardcover ISBN 1-891482-64-5, $190.00

The Complete Directory for Pediatric Disorders

At last, a directory that provides parents and caregivers with information about Pediatric Conditions, Disorders, Diseases and Disabilities including Blood Disorders, Bone and Spinal Disorders, Brain Defects and Abnormalities, Chromosomal Disorders, Congenital Heart Defects, Movement Disorders, Neuromuscular Disorders, and Pediatric Tumors and Cancers. This carefully written directory offers: understandable Descriptions of 15 major bodily systems; Descriptions of more than 200 disorders; and a Resources Section, detailing National Agencies and Associations, State Associations, Online Services, Libraries and Resource Centers, Research Centers, Support Groups and Hotlines, Camps, Books and Periodicals. This resource will provide immediate access to information crucial to families and caregivers when coping with children's illnesses.

"Recommended for public and consumer health libraries." – Library Journal

993 pages; Softcover ISBN 1-891482-60-2, $165.00 • Hardcover ISBN 1-891482-61-0, $190.00

Educators Resource Directory, 2001/02

At last, a comprehensive directory that provides the educational professional with thousands of resources for professional development. This directory saves hours of research time by providing immediate access to Associations and Organizations, Conferences and Trade Shows, Educational Research Centers, Employment Opportunities and Teaching Abroad, School Library Services, Scholarships, Financial Resources and much more. New features to this Fourth Edition include new chapters on Professional Consultants and Computer Software & Testing Resources. Plus, this edition includes a brand new section on Statistics and Rankings with over 100 tables, including Average Teacher Salaries, SAT/ACT Scores, Revenues & Expenditures and much more. These important statistics will allow the user to see how their school rates among others, make relocation decisions and so much more. *Educators Resource Directory* will be a well-used addition to the reference collection of any school district, education department or public library.

"Recommended for all collections that serve elementary and secondary school professionals." – Choice

800 pages; Softcover ISBN 1-930956-48-7, $145.00 • Hardcover ISBN 1-930956-49-5, $170.00

The Comparative Guide to American Elementary & Secondary Schools

This comprehensive volume offers a snapshot profile of every public school district in the United States serving 2,500 or more students. You'll find important contact information on each school district (name, address, phone number and web site) plus Grades Served, the Numbers of Students and Teachers and the Number of Regular, Special Education, Alternative and Vocational Schools in the district. Also, *The Comparative Guide to American Elementary & Secondary Schools* provides statistics to help evaluate educational programs, including Student/Classroom Teacher Ratios, Number of Librarians, Number of Guidance Counselors and District Expenditures per student and a National Socioeconomic Indicator for the District. A useful City Index lists all districts which operate schools in the city. These important comparative statistics are necessary for anyone considering relocating and would be a perfect acquisition to any public library.

"This straightforward guide is an easy way to find general information... Valuable for academic and large public library collections." –ARBA

744 pages; Softcover ISBN 1-884925-63-4, $85.00

To preview any of our Directories for 30 days, please call toll-free
(800) 562-2139 or fax to (518) 789-0556